UNIVERSITY CASEBOOK SERIES®

# GELLHORN AND BYSE'S

# ADMINISTRATIVE LAW

## CASES AND COMMENTS

**THIRTEENTH EDITION**

TODD D. RAKOFF
Byrne Professor of Administrative Law,
Harvard University

GILLIAN E. METZGER
Harlan Fiske Stone Professor of Constitutional Law,
Columbia University

DAVID J. BARRON
Circuit Judge, U.S. Court of Appeals, First Circuit
Louis D. Brandeis Visiting Professor of Law,
Harvard University

ANNE JOSEPH O'CONNELL
Adelbert H. Sweet Professor of Law,
Stanford University

ELOISE PASACHOFF
Professor of Law & Anne Fleming Research Professor,
Georgetown University

FOUNDATION
PRESS

860 Blue Gentian Road, Suite 350
Eagan, MN 55121
1-877-888-1330

Printed in the United States of America

**ISBN:** 978-1-63659-464-4

# PREFACE

This is primarily a book about administrative law—the body of general rules and principles governing federal administrative agencies—how they operate and their connections to the President, the Congress, and the courts. Perhaps at no time since the New Deal has administrative law been as vibrant a subject as it has been in recent years. Conservative critics of President Obama and his Administration loudly claimed that he was using agencies to override Congress's laws and create executive authoritarianism. Liberal critics of President Trump forcefully made much the same claim about his Administration. And now, it seems that every major action of the Biden Administration is met by a lawsuit claiming that what it proposes to do is beyond what it legitimately can do. As shown in these pages, sometimes the courts agree with these claims, and sometimes not. For some time now it has been impossible even to follow the daily news intelligently without running into Executive Orders, administrative hearings, rulemaking proceedings, judicial review of agency actions, and indeed almost everything put before you in this volume.

In the midst of this clamor, are there rules governing the use of power by government that can be broadly accepted no matter who is in or out of power? Rules that provide for regularity in government and equality in its actions? Rules that provide for widespread participation in governance but also shield the rights of individuals and private entities? Rules that enable power to be used but also protect those who lack power? We hope so. Rules like these are a large part of what we mean when we say our society believes in the rule of law.

But what the content of these rules of proceeding should be is, without a doubt, a contested issue. In this book, we have tried to develop what the law is, as it stands, without claiming that it is the best possible set of rules. Indeed, we have gone out of our way to highlight controversies and present alternative points of view. The possibility of change pervades our subject—change coming perhaps from new decisions of the Supreme Court, perhaps from new statutes passed by Congress, or perhaps from new patterns of action undertaken by the executive branch itself. We think this possibility, and with it our subject as a whole, is exciting, even if it is at times also a little scary.

This book is very much up to date. It also has a long history. Walter Gellhorn first published "Administrative Law: Cases and Comments" in 1940. He was joined for the Third Edition, in 1954, by Clark Byse. Together they produced the book throughout the rest of the 'fifties, all of the 'sixties, and almost all of the 'seventies, such that the book became known as "Gellhorn and Byse," a title we retain. In 1979, Peter Strauss joined them for the Seventh Edition, becoming the senior editor with the Ninth Edition, in 1995. Now he, too, has retired from direct participation in preparing the book, but his influence still appears throughout—in his insistence on meticulous accuracy, his embrace of alternative viewpoints, and his interest in relating legal doctrine to the actual workings of administrative agencies—to name just a few matters. This book is much better for his presence, even if his name is no longer on its cover.

We hope that when you delve into this book you, too, will find administrative law to be both of great importance and of great interest.

TODD D. RAKOFF
GILLIAN E. METZGER
DAVID J. BARRON
ANNE JOSEPH O'CONNELL
ELOISE PASACHOFF

December 1, 2022

P.S.: A note about usage: As in earlier editions, we have omitted without indication many citations, footnotes, and internal quotation marks when we have reproduced opinions and other writings. The original call numbers have been used for the footnotes that we have retained. In quoted text, footnotes are quotations unless preceded by "[Ed.]." And while we have indicated omissions of text by ellipses (. . .), we have ordinarily given only one such signal; the omitted material may comprise words, phrases, sentences, or paragraphs.

# ACKNOWLEDGMENTS

*Excerpts from the following are reprinted with permission:*

Frank Ackerman & Lisa Heinzerling, Pricing the Priceless: Cost-Benefit Analysis Of Environmental Protection, 150 U. Pa. L. Rev. 1553 (2002).

Kate Andrias, The President's Enforcement Power, 88 N.Y.U. L. Rev. 1031 (2013).

Nicholas Bagley, Remedial Restraint in Administrative Law, 117 Colum. L. Rev. 253 (2017).

Nicholas Bagley, The Puzzling Presumption of Reviewability, 127 Harv. L. Rev. 1285 (2014).

Kenneth A. Bamberger, Normative Canons in the Review of Administrative Policymaking, 118 Yale L.J. 64 (2008).

Eugene Bardach & Robert A. Kagan, Going By the Book: The Problem of Regulatory Unreasonableness (New York: The Twentieth Century Fund, 1982).

David J. Barron & Elena Kagan, Chevron's Nondelegation Doctrine, The Supreme Court Review 201 (2001).

Sam Batkins, It is Premature to Label a Regulatory Budget Unconstitutional, Reg. Rev. (June 26, 2017).

Evan D. Bernick, Envisioning Administrative Procedure Act Originalism, 70 Admin. L. Rev. 807 (2018).

Nikolas Bowie & Daphna Renan, The Separation of Powers Counterrevolution, 131 Yale L.J. 2020 (2022).

Samuel L. Bray, Multiple Chancellors: Reforming the National Injunction, 131 Harv. L. Rev. 417 (2017).

Lisa Schultz Bressman, Disciplining Delegation After Whitman v. American Trucking Ass'ns, 87 Cornell L. Rev. 452 (2002).

Lisa Schultz Bressman & Kevin M. Stack, Chevron Is a Phoenix, 74 Vand. L. Rev. 465 (2021).

Lisa Schultz Bressman & Michael P. Vandenbergh, Inside the Administrative State: A Critical Look at the Practice of Presidential Control, 105 Mich. L. Rev. 47 (2006).

Stephen Breyer, Making Our Democracy Work: A Judge's View (Alfred A. Knopf 2010).

Rebecca L. Brown, Separated Powers and Ordered Liberty, 139 U. Pa. L. Rev. 1513 (1991).

Jessica Bulman-Pozen, Executive Federalism Comes to America, 102 Va. L. Rev. 953 (2016).

William W. Buzbee, Preemption, Hard Look Review, Regulatory Interaction, and the Quest for Stewardship and Intergenerational Equity, 77 Geo. Wash. L. Rev. 1521 (2009).

Cristina Isabel Ceballos, David Freeman Engstrom, & Daniel E. Ho, Disparate Limbo: How Administrative Law Erased Antidiscrimination, 131 Yale L.J. 370 (2021).

Cary Coglianese, Heather Kilmartin, & Evan Mendelson, Transparency and Public Participation in the Federal Rulemaking Process: Recommendations for the New Administration, 77 Geo. Wash. L. Rev 924 (2009).

Steven R. Croley, White House Review of Agency Rulemaking: An Empirical Investigation, 70 U. Chi. L. Rev. 821 (2003).

Christopher DeMuth, Sr. & Michael S. Greve, Agency Finance in the Age of Executive Government, 24 Geo. Mason L. Rev. 555 (2017).

John D. Donahue, The Transformation of Government Work, in Government by Contract (ed. Freeman & Minow, Harvard University Press, 2009).

John F. Duffy, Administrative Common Law in Judicial Review, 77 Tex. L. Rev. 113 (1998).

Christopher F. Edley, Jr., Administrative Law: Rethinking Judicial Control of Bureaucracy (Yale University Press 1990).

Harry T. Edwards, The Judicial Function and the Elusive Goal of Principled Decisionmaking, 1991 Wisconsin L. Rev. 837.

Harry T. Edwards & Michael A. Livermore, Pitfalls of Empirical Studies that Attempt to Understand the Factors Affecting Appellate Decisionmaking, 58 Duke L.J. 1895 (2009).

E. Donald Elliott, Chevron Matters: How the Chevron Doctrine Redefined the Roles of Congress, Courts, and Agencies in Environmental Law, 16 Vill. Envtl. L.J. 1 (2005).

Daniel R. Ernst, Tocqueville's Nightmare: The Administrative State Emerges in America, 1900–1940 (Oxford University Press 2014).

William N. Eskridge Jr., The New Textualism, 37 U.C.L.A. L. Rev. 621 (1990).

Dan Farber, Courts Should Kill Trump's Pricey "2-for-1" Deregulation Order, The Hill Blog (Feb. 9, 2017).

Daniel A. Farber & Anne Joseph O'Connell, Agencies as Adversaries, 105 Cal L. Rev. 1375 (2017).

Daniel A. Farber & Anne Joseph O'Connell, The Lost World of Administrative Law, 92 Tex. L. Rev. 1137 (2014).

Cynthia R. Farina, Conceiving Due Process, 3 Yale J.L. & Feminism 189 (1991).

Cynthia R. Farina, Statutory Interpretation and the Balance of Power in the Administrative State, 89 Colum. L. Rev. 452 (1989).

Cynthia R. Farina, The Consent of the Governed: Against Simple Rules for a Complex World, 72 U. Chi.-Kent L. Rev. 987 (1997).

Jody Freeman & Adrian Vermeule, Massachusetts v. EPA: From Politics to Expertise, 2007 Sup. Ct. Rev. 51 (2007).

Jody Freeman & Martha Minow, Reframing the Outsourcing Debates, in Government by Contract (ed. Freeman & Minow, Harvard University Press, 2009).

Jody Freeman & Sharon Jacobs, Structural Deregulation, 135 Harv. L. Rev. 585 (2021).

William Funk, A Primer on Nonlegislative Rules, 53 Admin. L. Rev. 1321 (2001).

William Funk, Requiring Formal Rulemaking is a Thinly Veiled Attempt to Halt Regulation, Reg. Rev. (May 18, 2017).

Ernest Gellhorn & Glen O. Robinson, Rulemaking "Due Process": An Inconclusive Dialogue, 48 U. Chi. L. Rev. 201 (1981).

Daniel J. Gifford, The Morgan Cases: A Retrospective View, 30 Admin. L. Rev. 237 (1978).

Abbe R. Gluck, Imperfect Statutes, Imperfect Courts: Understanding Congress' Plan in the Era of Unorthodox Lawmaking, 129 Harv. L. Rev. 62 (2015).

Abbe R. Gluck & Lisa Schultz Bressman, Statutory Interpretation from the Inside—An Empirical Study of Congressional Drafting, Delegation, and the Canons: Part 1, 65 Stan. L. Rev. 901 (2013).

Philip Hamburger, Is Administrative Law Unlawful? (University of Chicago Press 2014).

John C. Harrison, Remand Without Vacatur and the Ab Initio Invalidity of Unlawful Regulations in Administrative Law, 48 BYU L. Rev. (forthcoming).

John Harrison, Section 706 of the Administrative Procedure Act Does Not Call for Universal Injunctions or Other Universal Remedies, 37 Yale J. on Reg. Bull. 37 (2020).

Lisa Heinzerling, Cost-Benefit Jumps the Shark, Georgetown Law Faculty Blog (June 13, 2012).

Kristin E. Hickman, Did Little Sisters of the Poor Just Gut APA Rulemaking Procedures?, Notice & Comment Blog (July 9, 2020).

Kristin E. Hickman, The Three Phases of Mead, 83 Fordham L. Rev. 527 (2014).

Aziz Huq, The President and the Detainees, 165 U. Pa. L. Rev. 499 (2017).

M. Ernita Joaquin & Thomas M. Greitens, American Administrative Capacity: Decline, Decay, and Resilience (Springer Publications 2021).

Elena Kagan, Presidential Administration, 114 Harv. L. Rev. 2245 (2001).

Orin S. Kerr, Shedding Light on Chevron: An Empirical Study of the Chevron Doctrine in the U.S. Courts of Appeals, 15 Yale J. on Reg. 1 (1998).

Donald F. Kettl, The Transformation of Governance: Public Administration for the Twenty-First Century (Johns Hopkins University Press 2015).

Kathryn E. Kovacs, Superstatute Theory and Administrative Common Law, 90 Indiana L.J. 1207 (2015).

James M. Landis, The Administrative Process (Yale University Press 1938).

Gary Lawson, The Rise and Rise of the Administrative State, 107 Harv. L. Rev. 1231 (1994).

Gary Lawson, Katherine Ferguson, & Guillermo Montero, "Oh Lord, Please Don't Let Me Be Misunderstood!": Rediscovering the Mathews v. Eldridge and Penn Central Frameworks, 81 Notre Dame L. Rev. 1 (2005).

Lawrence Lessig & Cass R. Sunstein, The President and the Administration, 94 Colum. L. Rev. 6 (1994).

Jason A. MacDonald, Limitation Riders and Congressional Influence over Bureaucratic Policy Decisions, 104 Am. Pol. Sci. Rev. 766 (2010).

M. Elizabeth Magill, Agency Choice of Policymaking Form, 71 U. Chi. L. Rev. 1383 (2004).

John F. Manning, Separation of Powers as Ordinary Interpretation, 124 Harv. L. Rev. 1939 (2011).

John F. Manning, Textualism as a Nondelegation Doctrine, 97 Colum. L. Rev. 673 (1997).

Jerry L. Mashaw, Creating the Administrative Constitution: The Lost One Hundred Years of American Administrative Law (Yale University Press 2012).

Jerry L. Mashaw, Greed, Chaos and Governance: Using Public Choice to Improve Public Law (Yale University Press 1997).

Thomas O. McGarity, Deregulatory Riders Redux, 1 Mich. J. Envtl. & Admin. L. 33 (2012).

Nina Mendelson, The Permissibility of Acting Officials: May The President Work Around Senate Confirmation?, 72 Admin. L. Rev. 4 (2020).

Thomas W. Merrill, Textualism and the Future of the Chevron Doctrine, 72 Wash. U. L. Q. 351 (1994).

Gillian E. Metzger, Administrative Law as the New Federalism, 57 Duke L.J. 2023 (2008).

Gillian E. Metzger, Embracing Administrative Common Law, 80 Geo. Wash. L. Rev. 1293 (2012).

Gillian E. Metzger, Ordinary Administrative Law as Constitutional Common Law, 110 Colum. L. Rev. 479 (2010).

Gillian E. Metzger, The Constitutional Duty to Supervise, 124 Yale L.J. 1836 (2015).

Gillian E. Metzger, The Supreme Court 2016 Term—Foreword: 1930s Redux: The Administrative State Under Siege, 131 Harv. L. Rev. 1 (2017).

Gillian E. Metzger & Kevin M. Stack, Internal Administrative Law, 115 Mich. L. Rev. 1239 (2017).

Jonathan T. Molot, The Judicial Perspective in the Administrative State: Reconciling Modern Doctrines of Deference with the Judiciary's Structural Role, 53 Stanford L. Rev. 1 (2000).

Alan B. Morrison, The Administrative Procedure Act: A Living and Responsive Law, 72 Va. L. Rev. 258 (1986).

Julian Davis Mortenson & Nicholas Bagley, Delegation at the Founding, 121 Colum. L. Rev. 277 (2021).

Aaron L. Nielson, In Defense of Formal Rulemaking, 75 Ohio St. L.J. 237 (2014).

Jennifer Nou, Civil Service Disobedience, 94 Chi.-Kent L. Rev. 349 (2019).

Jennifer Nou, Subdelegating Powers, 117 Colum. L. Rev. 473 (2017).

Anne Joseph O'Connell, Actings, 120 Colum. L. Rev. 613 (2020).

Anne Joseph O'Connell, Bureaucracy at the Boundary, 162 U. Pa. L. Rev. 841 (2014).

Nicholas R. Parrillo, Against the Profit Motive: The Salary Revolution in American Government, 1780–1940 (Yale University Press 2013).

Eloise Pasachoff, The President's Budget as a Source of Agency Policy Control, 125 Yale L.J. 2182 (2016).

Richard J. Pierce, Jr., How Agencies Should Give Meaning to the Statutes They Administer: A Response to Mashaw and Strauss, 59 Admin. L. Rev. 197 (2007).

Richard J. Pierce, Jr., Making Sense of Procedural Injury, 62 Admin. L. Rev. 1 (2010).

David E. Pozen, Freedom of Information Beyond the Freedom of Information Act, 165 U. Pa. L. Rev. 1097 (2017).

David E. Pozen, The Leaky Leviathan: Why the Government Condemns and Condones Unlawful Disclosures of Information, 127 Harv. L. Rev. 512 (2013).

Jeremy Rabkin, The Origins of the APA: Misremembered and Forgotten Views, 28 Geo. Mason L. Rev. 547 (2021).

Todd D. Rakoff, Brock v. Roadway Express, Inc. and the New Law of Regulatory Due Process, 1987 Sup. Ct. Rev. 157.

Richard L. Revesz & Michael A. Livermore, Retaking Rationality: How Cost-Benefit Analysis Can Better Protect the Environment and Our Health (Oxford University Press 2008).

Alasdair Roberts, Strategies for Governing: Reinventing Public Administration for a Dangerous Century (Cornell University Press 2019).

Antonin Scalia, The Doctrine of Standing as an Essential Element of the Separation of Powers, 17 Suffolk U.L. Rev. 881 (1983).

Antonin Scalia, Vermont Yankee: The APA, the D.C. Circuit, and the Supreme Court, 1978 Sup. Ct. Rev. 345.

Peter H. Schuck, Delegation and Democracy: Comments on David Schoenbrod, 20 Cardozo L. Rev. 775 (1999).

Mark Seidenfeld, Demystifying Deossification: Rethinking Recent Proposals to Modify Judicial Review of Notice and Comment Rulemaking, 75 Tex. L. Rev. 483 (1997).

Peter M. Shane, The Bureaucratic Due Process of Government Watch Lists, 75 Geo. Wash. L. Rev. 804 (2007).

Sidney A. Shapiro & Richard Murphy, Eight Things Americans Can't Figure Out About Controlling Administrative Power, 61 Admin. L. Rev. 5 (2009).

Jonathan David Shaub, The Executive's Privilege, 70 Duke L.J. 1 (2020).

George B. Shepherd, Fierce Compromise: The Administrative Procedure Act Emerges from New Deal Politics, 90 Nw. U. L. Rev. 1557 (1996).

Mila Sohoni, The Lost History of the "Universal Injunction," 133 Harv. L. Rev. 920 (2020).

Kevin M. Stack & Michael Vandenbergh, Oversight Riders, 97 Notre Dame L. Rev. 127 (2021).

Richard B. Stewart, The Reformation of American Administrative Law, 88 Harv. L. Rev. 1669 (1975).

Peter L. Strauss, Changing Times: The APA at Fifty, 63 U. Chi. L. Rev. 1389 (1996).

Peter L. Strauss, Revisiting Overton Park: Political and Judicial Controls Over Administrative Actions Affecting the Community, 39 U.C.L.A. L. Rev. 1251 (1992).

Peter L. Strauss, The Place of Agencies in Government: Separation of Powers and the Fourth Branch, 84 Colum. L. Rev. 573 (1984).

Cass R. Sunstein, Law and Administration After Chevron, 90 Colum. L. Rev. 2071 (1990).

Cass R. Sunstein, The Cost-Benefit State: The Future of Regulatory Protection (American Bar Association 2002).

Cass Sunstein, There Are Two "Major Questions" Doctrines, 73 Admin. L. Rev. 475 (2021).

Cass R. Sunstein & Thomas J. Miles, Depoliticizing Administrative Law, 58 Duke L.J. 2193 (2009).

Karen M. Tani, States of Dependency: Welfare, Rights, and American Governance, 1935–1972 (Cambridge University Press 2016).

Kathryn A. Watts, Controlling Presidential Control, 114 Mich. L. Rev. 683 (2016).

Kathryn A. Watts, Proposing a Place for Politics in Arbitrary and Capricious Review, 119 Yale L.J. 2 (2009).

# SUMMARY OF CONTENTS



## PART 1. OVERVIEW



## PART 2. UNDERSTANDING STATUTES

## PART 3. THE AGENCY AT WORK

## PART 5. JUDGING THE WORK OF AGENCIES

# TABLE OF CONTENTS

# TABLE OF CASES

The principal cases are in bold type.

# TABLE OF STATUTES

# TABLE OF REGULATIONS AND RULES

# TABLE OF URLs

# TABLE OF AUTHORITIES

UNIVERSITY CASEBOOK SERIES®

# GELLHORN AND BYSE'S

# ADMINISTRATIVE LAW

## CASES AND COMMENTS

### THIRTEENTH EDITION

# PART 1

# OVERVIEW

# CHAPTER I

# AN INTRODUCTION TO ADMINISTRATIVE LAW



## SECTION 1. AN INTRODUCTORY EXAMPLE



What follows is a real problem: the legal materials are genuine, and the facts are true. It is a real problem in another sense, too; its pieces are complex and open to multiple solutions. Of course, if you are reading this at the beginning of your study of administrative law, you do not know much of what you would need to answer the questions posed, as an experienced lawyer or policymaker would. (Some of the questions are not so easy even if you do know what there is to know!) So, the purpose of the problem is twofold: first, to show you the kinds of questions administrative law tries to answer, and second, to invite you to use your imagination, along with the information given, to think about some of the complexities of the issues. To be sure, airplane tarmac delays are not one of the more consequential matters that federal agencies handle, but they do bring real-life costs.

### The Problem of Airplane Tarmac Delays

Most of you have taken an airplane to travel to a destination. Consider some descriptive questions: What has been the longest delay of a flight that you have experienced? Were you stuck in the airplane at the gate, on the tarmac, or even on the runway for some of that time? What has been the longest amount of time that you have remained on the airplane after boarding but before taking off? Think, too, about some normative questions: How long do you think passengers should be forced to stay on a grounded airplane before having access to food or water? Before having the opportunity to get off?

In the eight months between December 2006 and July 2007, hundreds of thousands of passengers boarded airplanes that then remained grounded on airport tarmacs for more than three hours, typically because of weather and its interactions with airline operations. In December 2006, passengers sat on an American Airlines plane, diverted in flight to the airport in Austin, Texas, for almost ten hours. During a February 2007 snowstorm, ten Jet Blue flights, full of passengers, kept their wheels down at New York City's John F. Kennedy International Airport. One plane scheduled to travel to Aruba remained on the ground for almost eleven hours. Another to Cancún stayed for almost nine hours before the flight was canceled. Because the airplanes were not at the gates in these situations, passengers could not get off—to walk around the airport, to use bigger bathrooms, or to eat or drink in airport restaurants.

Airline passengers were hopping mad. The airlines, though apologetic, argued that returning to the gate was not always possible and, even if possible, might have resulted in even longer delays.

*Assuming it were a completely open question, where in the legal universe should we put the law of airline passenger service? Should it be a matter of tort, requiring an airline to take "reasonable care"? Should it be a matter of contract, so that passengers get what they, individually or collectively, bargain for? Should we pass statutes, state or federal, specifying things like the length of time airplanes can sit on the tarmac and when food and drink have to be provided, and stipulating civil and possibly criminal penalties? Should we give the matter over to a state or federal administrative agency to consider and regulate? Or should we simply have no law on the subject and leave the issue to the forces of reputation and social norms?*

Let's consider the solution of just relying on courts first. *Should passengers stuck on a grounded flight for hours be able to sue the airline under tort or contract law?* If such suits were permissible and plausible, plaintiffs themselves could seek compensation (unlike with regulatory fines, which typically go, in major part, to the government).

One passenger on that December 2006 American Airlines flight, Catherine Ray, tried the courts. She filed a five-count class action suit in Arkansas state court (the case was later removed to federal court by the carrier) that alleged false imprisonment, intentional infliction of emotional distress, negligence, breach of contract, and deceit/fraud. These allegations come from the fact section of her complaint:

> 9. While confined on the ground in Austin, the toilets became full and would not flush and the stench of human excrement and body odor filled the plane.
>
> 10. While confined, in the aircraft, plaintiff and other passengers were unable to wash their hands due to the aircraft running out of water and not being re-supplied by AA.
>
> 11. Plaintiff and other passengers were provided only two soft drinks and only a few granola bars for food.

> 12. Plaintiff and other passengers were also deprived of access to medications, nutritional supplements and needs, and hydration especially needed by [the] infirm, elderly and children. . . .
>
> 18. Defendant had ample advanced warning of weather conditions at Dallas and knew or should have known that it was not able to land aircraft at Dallas (DFW) airport at the capacity it had scheduled on December 29th, 2006, due to transient thunder storms and could have cancelled or delayed from departing many of the flights that it diverted and stranded, thereby preventing the diversions and confinements.
>
> 19. With the exception of a few passengers whose destination was the Austin[,] Texas area, AA refused to permit passengers to exit the aircraft even though buses and available gates at the terminal were available to AA.

Complaint, Ray v. Am. Airlines, Inc., Civil Case No. 08–5025 (W.D. Ark. 2008) (removed from state court).

Some of Ray's claims were preempted by the Airline Deregulation Act, 47 U.S.C. § 41713(b)(1), and some others were dismissed for failing to state a claim. But her false imprisonment, intentional infliction of emotional distress, and negligence claims made it to the summary judgment stage. The district court granted summary judgment to the airline, however, holding that Ray did not revoke her consent to be on the plane (and therefore was not falsely imprisoned) and that the airline "had no duty to provide Plaintiff with a stress-free flight environment" (and therefore lacked a key element for the other tort claims). Ray v. Am. Airlines, Inc., 2009 WL 921124 (W.D. Ark. 2009), affirmed, 609 F.3d 917 (8th Cir. 2010). Courts in other cases have held that such claims were preempted, instead of assessing the elements of any tort claims. See, e.g., Biscone v. JetBlue Corp., 103 A.D.3d 158 (N.Y. App. Div. 2012). Litigation thus seems an unlikely avenue for changing airline practices, unless Congress enacts federal statutes that permit such suits (barring preemption defenses) or force airlines to put more guarantees in their contracts of carriage with passengers (making contract claims plausible). *Would you favor such changes?*

As noted above, an alternative to litigation is new legislation. Senators Barbara Boxer (D-CA) and Olympia Snowe (R-ME) introduced S. 678, the Airline Passenger Bill of Rights Act of 2007, in the Senate. In main part, the proposed bill would have amended Chapter 417 of Title 49 of the United States Code to add:

SEC. 41781. AIRLINE CUSTOMER SERVICE REQUIREMENTS.

> (a) IN GENERAL.—Not later than 60 days after the date of the enactment of the Airline Passenger Bill of Rights Act of 2007, each air carrier shall institute the following practices:

(1) PROVISION OF FOOD AND WATER.—In any case in which departure of a flight of an air carrier is delayed, such air carrier shall provide—

(A) adequate food and potable water to passengers on such flight during such delay; and

(B) adequate restroom facilities to passengers on such flight during such delay.

(2) RIGHT TO DEPLANE.—

(A) IN GENERAL.—Except as provided in subparagraph (B), if more than 3 hours after passengers have boarded an air carrier and the air carrier doors are closed, the air carrier has not departed, the air carrier shall provide passengers with the option to deplane safely before the departure of such air carrier. Such option shall be provided to passengers not less often than once during each 3-hour period that the plane remains on the ground.

(B) EXCEPTIONS.—Subparagraph (A) shall not apply—

(i) if the pilot of such flight reasonably determines that such flight will depart not later than 30 minutes after the 3 hour delay; or

(ii) if the pilot of such flight reasonably determines that permitting a passenger to deplane would jeopardize passenger safety or security.

(b) AIR CARRIER.—In this section the term "air carrier" means an air carrier holding a certificate issued under section 41102 that conducts scheduled passenger air transportation.

The proposed legislation also instructed the Secretary of Transportation to "promulgate such regulations as the Secretary determines necessary to carry out the amendments made by this Act" and imposed a tight deadline of 60 days after the Act's enactment for these regulations. Similar legislation was introduced in the House.

A passenger on one of the grounded flights formed a new group, the Coalition for Airline Passengers Bill of Rights, to lobby for this legislation.[1] The Consumer Federation of America, Consumers Union, and Public Citizen, among other groups, also supported the bill. The Business Travel Coalition, which represents "the managed travel community," announced its opposition. And the airlines, as expected, voiced their alarm, with the CEO of Virgin America worrying in a USA Today report: "We had a situation about a month ago at (New York's JFK), where we had a plane sit out on the taxiway for four hours and 10 minutes. . . . Well, if we had had a four-hour law in place, that plane

[1] This specific group no longer exists and has been replaced by FlyersRights.

would have gone back to the terminal and then would have been 35th or 40th in line to take off. As it was, they got in the air 10 minutes later."

To become law under the Constitution, a bill must pass both the House of Representatives and the Senate and receive the President's signature—or else repass each chamber with a two-thirds majority to overcome a presidential veto. Congress presents additional obstacles: bills must be voted out of committees (sometimes multiple) in the House and Senate and often require 60 Senate votes because of the filibuster. In this case, the relevant Senate committee was the Committee on Commerce, Science, and Transportation, which held a hearing on the proposed law on April 11, 2007. After the November 2006 elections, Democrats held majorities in both chambers of Congress. After the Senate hearing, neither the House nor the Senate advanced the legislation in that congressional session.

*Would you vote for this legislation? What were the legislation's chances of success in 2007? How much does party affiliation matter for this issue? What advantages does Congress have over the courts in addressing policy issues? Disadvantages?*

An alternative to both the courts and new legislation (almost always creating tasks for the bureaucracy) is agency regulation based on existing laws. The Federal Aviation Administration and the Department of Transportation are two of the primary entities that regulate airlines. The FAA is an agency within the Department of Transportation, which is one of fifteen current cabinet departments. The FAA has some independent authority but often must get approval from the Department for action. Both agencies are led by individuals nominated by the President and confirmed by the Senate. By statute, the Administrator of the FAA must "(1) be a citizen of the United States; (2) be a civilian; and (3) have experience in a field directly related to aviation," and serves (since 1994) a five-year term. 49 U.S.C. §§ 106(b)–(c). The Secretary of Transportation has no statutory term or qualifications. *Can you figure out who served as FAA Administrator and Secretary of Transportation in 2007 (and who serves in those positions now)? Why do you think they were chosen for those jobs? Should there be expertise requirements for either position? Why shouldn't a military officer be allowed to run the FAA?*

We include below the organizational charts for both these agencies from their websites (with names of officeholders removed) so you can get a sense of the institutional complexity.[2]

---

[2] In addition to the FAA and Department of Transportation, the National Transportation Safety Board, an independent establishment, also oversees airlines. It investigates airlines when their planes crash or get into other accidents and issues safety recommendations. The NTSB is not located within the Transportation Department. Unlike the other two agencies, it is run by five members, all of whom are appointed by the President and confirmed by the Senate to five-year terms; they can be removed only for "inefficiency, neglect of duty, or malfeasance in office." Like many independent regulatory commissions and boards, the NTSB has both party-balancing (no more than three of the five members can be from the same political party) and expertise mandates ("[a]t least 3 members shall be appointed on the basis of technical qualification, professional standing, and demonstrated knowledge in accident reconstruction, safety engineering, human factors, transportation safety, or transportation regulation"). 49 U.S.C. §§ 1111(b)–(c). *Should the leaders of an agency investigating airplane crashes have*

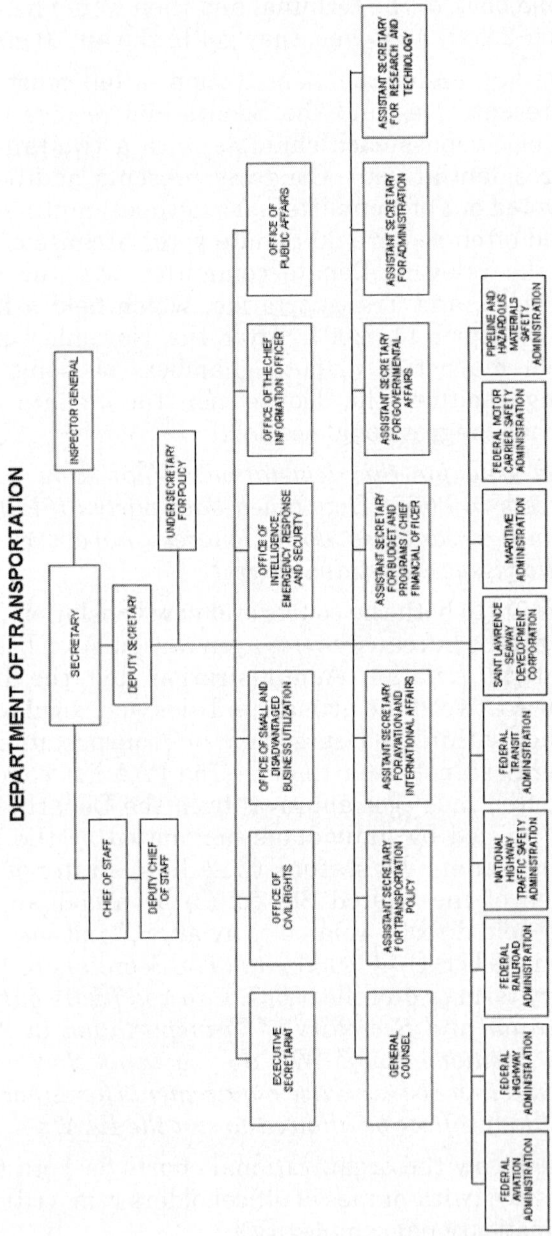


---

*protection from being fired? When should an agency be headed by one person (as opposed to a group, where a majority is needed to act)?*

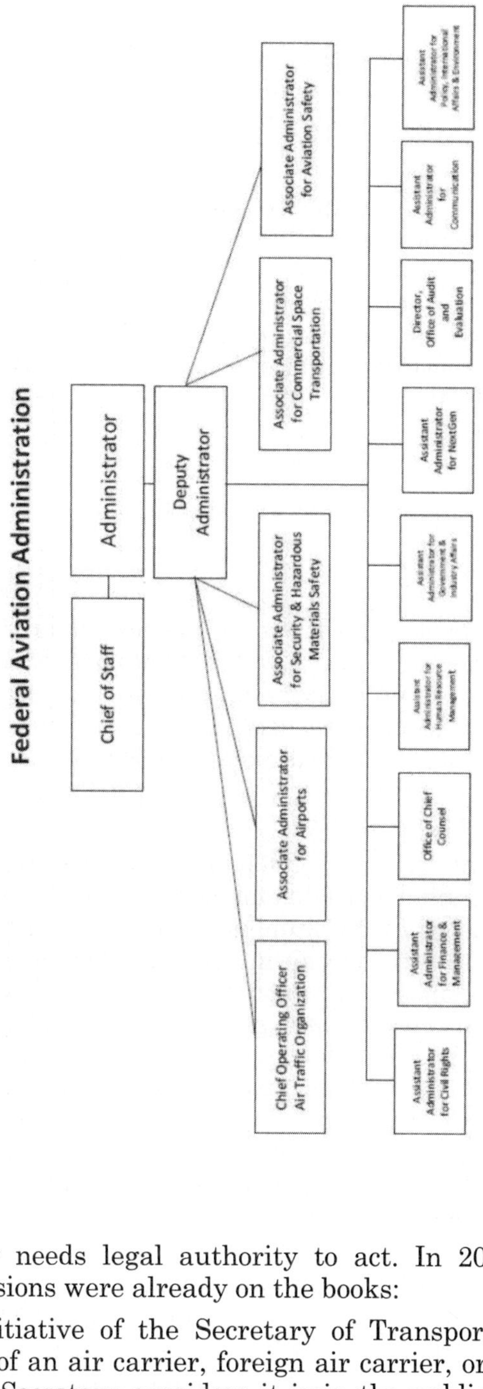


An agency needs legal authority to act. In 2007, the following statutory provisions were already on the books:

> On the initiative of the Secretary of Transportation or the complaint of an air carrier, foreign air carrier, or ticket agent, and if the Secretary considers it is in the public interest, the Secretary may investigate and decide whether an air carrier, foreign air carrier, or ticket agent has been or is engaged in an unfair or deceptive practice or an unfair method of competition

> in air transportation or the sale of air transportation. If the Secretary, after notice and an opportunity for a hearing, finds that an air carrier, foreign air carrier, or ticket agent is engaged in an unfair or deceptive practice or unfair method of competition, the Secretary shall order the air carrier, foreign air carrier, or ticket agent to stop the practice or method.

49 U.S.C. § 41712(a).

> . . . the Secretary of Transportation shall consider the following matters, among others, as being in the public interest and consistent with public convenience and necessity: . . . (4) the availability of a variety of adequate, economic, efficient, and low-priced services without unreasonable discrimination or unfair or deceptive practices. . . . (9) preventing unfair, deceptive, predatory, or anticompetitive practices in air transportation.

49 U.S.C. §§ 40101(a)(4), (9).

> An air carrier shall provide safe and adequate interstate air transportation.

49 U.S.C. § 41702.

*Under these provisions, what could the Secretary of Transportation do to address tarmac delays, if anything? What parts of the provisions are important to your reasoning? What might be some competing policy issues the Secretary of Transportation could choose to focus on, under these provisions? And given that there are additional provisions (beyond these) delegating authority to the agency, how should the Secretary prioritize potential policymaking?*

Those unhappy with a given decision by the Secretary of Transportation can "fil[e] a petition for review in the United States Court of Appeals for the District of Columbia Circuit or in the court of appeals of the United States for the circuit in which the person resides or has its principal place of business" within 60 days of any final "order" or "action" by the Secretary. *Why might Congress want to allow challengers to agency action to skip filing first in a district court? If the Secretary decides not to address tarmac delays, and consumer groups sue to force action, what should a court do?* The statutory provisions substantively promise consumers nondeceptive, adequate air travel. On the process side, they provide considerable discretion to the agency. *What is the role of the judiciary in a situation like this?*

The Secretary of Transportation is a member of the President's Cabinet. The President may well be involved whenever framing proper regulations implicates high-level political judgment. *Is this such an issue?* The Secretary hardly has time to determine how many airplanes sat on tarmacs for how long during specific periods. Most of the work, then, is done by offices or administrations within the Department, such as the FAA and the Office of Aviation Enforcement in the General Counsel's Office. In fiscal year 2008, the Department was allotted 55,150 full-time equivalent positions, of which only 23 were slots for Senate-confirmed presidential appointees, 41 were excepted Schedule C (political) positions, and 31 were noncareer Senior Executive Service (also political) jobs. Its FY 2008 budget exceeded $63.4 billion.[3] *How much should the Secretary of Transportation rely on political appointees? On career employees?*

*How would the Secretary (and subordinates) go about enacting a new policy?* The Administrative Procedure Act, which you will learn about in this casebook, briefly details procedures for notice-and-comment rulemaking: "After notice . . . , the agency shall give interested persons an opportunity to participate in the rule making through submission of written data, views, or arguments with or without opportunity for oral presentation. After consideration of the relevant matter presented, the agency shall incorporate in the rules adopted a concise general statement of their basis and purpose." 5 U.S.C. § 553. To simplify, this translates to a notice of proposed rulemaking (often called an NPRM), a comment period, and a final rule.

Rulemaking in practice is often far more complicated. In November 2007, the Department of Transportation issued an *Advance* NPRM (ANPRM, think of it as a prior notice to the notice), not discussed in the APA, asking for comment on the following seven possible measures:

1. Require contingency plans for lengthy tarmac delays and incorporate them in their contracts of carriage[4] [which would be tied, according to the ANPRM, to a four-hour delay]
2. Require carriers to respond to consumer problems
3. Declare the operation of flights that remain chronically delayed to be an unfair and deceptive practice and an unfair method of competition
4. Require carriers to publish delay data on their web sites
5. Require carriers to publish complaint data on their web sites
6. Require carriers to report on-time performance of international flights
7. Require carriers to audit their adherence to their customer service plans

Department of Transportation, Enhancing Airline Passenger Protections, 72 Fed. Reg. 65233, 65234–36 (Nov. 20, 2007) (cleaned up).

*How would you classify each of the seven items? How many rely on disclosure of information to regulate? How many impose duties other than*

---

[3] In FY 2022, the Department "employ[ed] almost 55,000 people" (with 18 Senate-confirmed slots, including the inspector general; 2 positions requiring presidential appointment, with no Senate role; 61 excepted Schedule C positions; and 41 noncareer Senior Executive Service jobs according to the 2020 Plum Book), and its budget exceeded $143 billion (in large part because of the 2021 Infrastructure Investment and Jobs Act).

[4] "With the contingency plan incorporated in the contract of carriage, passengers would be able to sue in court for damages if a carrier failed to adhere to its plan." Department of Transportation, Enhancing Airline Passenger Protections, 72 Fed. Reg. 65233, 65234 (Nov. 20, 2007).

*information disclosure? What are the advantages and disadvantages of specifying a particular time period for tarmac delays?*

The ANPRM also listed a series of questions for commenters to answer, including for the first measure:

> What costs would it impose on the carriers? Would it have any negative consequences? Is it likely to succeed in protecting passengers from the conditions described above? If not, why not? What additional or different measures should we consider adopting? Would incorporation of the contingency plan in the contract of carriage give consumers adequate notice of what might happen in the event of a long delay on the tarmac? When prolonged delays occur, would these measures succeed in reducing the resultant uncertainty and discomfort for passengers? Should the types of carriers covered by the regulation be expanded or limited? What would be the cost or benefit of narrowing or expanding coverage? Should the requirement of coordinating the plan with airport authorities apply to all primary airports (i.e., commercial service airports that enplane more than 10,000 passengers annually) rather than only to medium hub airports (primary airports that enplane between 0.25 and 1 percent of total U.S. passengers) and large hub airports (primary airports that enplane at least 1 percent of total U.S. passengers)?

Id. at 65235.

*How many comments do you think the Department received, and from whom, on its ANPRM?*

Surprisingly, fewer than 10 percent (of the approximately 200 comments) came from the airline industry. Only four airlines—Delta Air Lines, Virgin Atlantic Airways, Jet Airways (India), and China Eastern Airlines—submitted comments. Five carrier associations also provided their views. On the consumer side, 131 members of the Coalition for an Airline Passengers Bill of Rights "filed identical or nearly identical comments." Five consumer associations—the Aviation Consumer Action Project, National Business Travel Association, Federation of State Public Interest Groups, Public Citizen, and National Consumers League—and 34 other individuals also sent in reactions. The Department summarized the views as follows:

> In general, the consumers and consumer associations maintained that the Department's proposals do not go far enough, while the carriers and carrier associations attributed the current problems mostly to factors beyond their control such as weather and the air traffic control system and tended to characterize the proposals as unnecessary and unduly burdensome. The travel agency associations expressed support for consumer protections but not at their members' expense.

Department of Transportation, Enhancing Airline Passenger Protections, 73 Fed. Reg. 74586, 74587 (Dec. 8, 2008).

Between the November 2008 election and January 2009 inauguration, which changed party control of the White House from Republican George W. Bush to Democrat Barack Obama, the Department of Transportation published an NPRM, seeking comments before February 6, 2009 (a 60-day comment period). *Should then-Secretary of Transportation Mary Peters, who knew she would no longer be in her job in January 2009, have continued to engage in policymaking?* (President Obama chose Republican Ray LaHood, a former member of Congress, to head the Department of Transportation initially.) The NPRM continued with a subset of the ANPRM's issues. The proposed regulation would:

> (1) Require air carriers to adopt contingency plans for lengthy tarmac delays and to incorporate these plans in their contracts of carriage, (2) require air carriers to respond to consumer problems, (3) declare the operation of flights that remain chronically delayed to be an unfair and deceptive practice and an unfair method of competition, (4) require air carriers to publish delay data on their Web sites, and (5) require air carriers to adopt customer service plans, incorporate these in their contracts of carriage, and audit their adherence to their plans.

Id. at 74587.

Because it was a significant regulation under Executive Order 12866, the NPRM required the approval of the Office of Information and Regulatory Affairs, within the Office of Management and Budget in the Executive Office of the President, before it was published. The Order, issued by President Bill Clinton and continued by each of his successors, Republican and Democrat, requires OIRA to sign off on significant proposed and final rules by executive agencies and departments like the FAA and DOT.[5] One of OIRA's duties is to ensure that a rule's benefits exceed its costs and that an agency's action maximizes net benefits unless a statute prohibits decisions to be made on such cost-benefit analyses. (The APA makes no mention of these mandates.) The Executive Order thus directed the Transportation Department to complete a detailed evaluation of the proposed rule's benefits and costs.

In the NPRM, the agency stated:

> On the cost side, many of the measures suggested in this NPRM would impose costs for both implementation and operation on the entities that its proposed requirements would cover. The benefits we seek to achieve entail relieving consumers of the burdens they now face due to lengthy ground delays, chronically delayed flights, and other problems discussed in the NPRM. The benefits would be achieved by affording consumers significantly more information than they have now about delayed and cancelled flights and about how carriers will respond to their needs in the event of lengthy ground delays. Making this

[5] Independent agencies such as the NTSB do not need OIRA approval.

> information accessible should not only alleviate consumers' difficulties during long delays but also enable them to make better-informed choices when booking flights. The Regulatory Evaluation has concluded that the benefits of the proposal appear to exceed its costs. A copy of the Regulatory Evaluation has been placed in the docket.

Id. at 74600.

Interestingly, in May 2008, then-White House Chief of Staff Joshua Bolten told executive agencies and departments that "regulations to be finalized in this Administration should be proposed no later than June 1, 2008, and final regulations should be issued no later than November 1, 2008." The timing of this NPRM strongly suggested that the Transportation Department was not trying to finish the rulemaking by the time President George W. Bush left office. *Why did the agency not attempt to finish it before the change of Administration?*

Despite the problems recently experienced by hundreds of thousands of passengers, only 21 comments—split nearly equally between industry on one side and consumers and consumer associations on the other—came in during the 90-day comment period for the NPRM (the agency extended the original 60-day period). *Does the low number surprise you?* You can find information online about many rulemakings at www.regulations.gov. You can even file comments on many agencies' open rulemakings there. *How easy is it to navigate that website, compared to other online resources and services you use?*

Industry commenters supported some of the proposals but noted concerns about the regulatory evaluations (i.e., the cost-benefit analyses) and pushed for alternatives that "address[ed] weather-related and air traffic control related issues." As with the ANPRM, consumer comments indicated that "the Department's proposals do not go far enough and contend that additional regulatory measures are needed to better protect consumers." Department of Transportation, Enhancing Airline Passenger Protections, 74 Fed. Reg. 68983, 68983–84 (Dec. 30, 2009).

US Airways was one of two carriers to comment, on March 9, 2009, on the NPRM (it had not commented on the ANPRM):

> Although the Department is well-intentioned, this NPRM is overreaching and attempts to regulate air carriers for situations beyond their control. US Airways already has in place many of the elements that the Department is proposing to require in this NPRM. Nevertheless, US Airways opposes other provisions of the NPRM that would impose substantial new burdens on air carriers. In these comments, US Airways will highlight two particular areas of concern—the overall rationale for the NPRM and two needed revisions to any contingency plan requirement: (a) exclusion of international operations; and (b) enhanced regulatory accountability for airports. The Company also fully supports the comments of the Air Transport Association ("ATA") filed today in this docket. . . .

> As an initial proposition, the notion that air carriers want to delay or inconvenience passengers should be forever stricken as a credible argument. There is no air carrier that would ever knowingly want to put passengers on an airplane for extended periods of time. Unfortunately, there are times where gridlock occurs that causes schedule delay and passenger inconvenience. These excessive delays extending well beyond scheduled departure/arrival times usually result from extreme weather conditions beyond the control of the air carrier. . . .
>
> When facing extended delays, air carrier management makes decisions based on the based [sic] available data at the time, but weather forecasts do not always cooperate, and passengers, unfortunately, can experience long delays. . . .
>
> US Airways understands that it is tempting to want to regulate to give passengers some relief from the rare case of lengthy on-board delays. Even with continued improvements by all air carriers in on-time performance, passengers are still occasionally delayed. For delays that are within the control of the air carrier, the Department's effort to identify chronically delayed flights and remind air carriers of their disclosure obligations is a good example of government and industry working constructively to address a problem for the benefit of consumers. As the Department knows, US Airways worked aggressively in reviewing all of the flights that were identified as chronically delayed and has reduced the number of US Airways flights appearing on DOT Tables 5 and 6 to a very small number, if any. . . .
>
> US Airways understands the Department's interest in imposing an inflexible return-to-gate standard to attempt to avoid lengthy tarmac delays. As described above, however, US Airways already has a contingency plan in place to deal with lengthy onboard delays. . . .
>
> US Airways' existing contingency plan is substantially similar to the contingency plan that the Department proposes, except that it leaves to the carrier's expertise the decision about when the aircraft should return to the gate. We oppose any enforceable provision that the air carrier return to the gate at a fixed time. Not only will returning to the gate at a specific time result in the possibility of additional cancellations, but it could also trigger a spillover effect to the next day. Air carriers do not have unlimited resources to recover from these types of situations. . . .

Comment of US Airways, Inc. in Docket OST–2007–0022.[6]

*What do you find persuasive in US Airways' comment? Less persuasive?* The carrier filed its comment on the last possible day yet

[6] https://www.regulations.gov/document?D=DOT-OST-2007-0022-0246.

knew what another industry commenter, ATA, was going to say despite ATA filing at the same time. Consumer groups would not have had time to respond to either US Airways' or ATA's comment. *Is this sharing of information between US Airways and ATA, or the lack of time to respond, a problem?* As noted below, the rule was adopted. An academic study published five years after the rule took effect found the regulation "has been highly effective in reducing the frequency of occurrence of long tarmac times." On the other hand, the study also found that "another significant effect of the rule has been the rise in flight cancellation rates [and subsequent rebooking and delays to destination]." Overall, the study found "a significant increase in passenger delays, especially for passengers scheduled to travel on the flights which are at risk of long tarmac delays." Chiwei Yan, Vikrant Vaze, Allison Vanderboll, & Cynthia Barnhart, Tarmac Delay Policies: A Passenger-Centric Analysis, 83 Transp. Rsch. Part A: Pol'y and Prac. 42, 42 (2016). *Does this change your reaction to US Airways' comment?*

Some proposed rules that are not finalized before a change in administration are withdrawn under new leadership. That was not the case here. The Department of Transportation issued a final rule in December 2009, after clearing it with OIRA (then headed by administrative law scholar extraordinaire, Cass Sunstein), to take effect in April 2010 [hereinafter 2010 rule]. In short, according to the agency:

> We have decided to adopt a final rule along the lines set forth in the NPRM, with one important exception: We are strengthening the protections for consumers from those initially proposed by setting time limits (1) for carriers to provide food and water to passengers; and (2) to deplane passengers when lengthy tarmac delays occur on domestic flights. In adopting this approach, we have carefully considered all the comments in this proceeding and believe that our action strikes the proper balance between permitting carriers the freedom to make marketplace-based decisions while ensuring consumers can count on receiving the protections they deserve in the unlikely event of an extended tarmac delay.
>
> The final rule requires that each plan include, at a minimum, the following: (1) An assurance that, for domestic flights, the air carrier will not permit an aircraft to remain on the tarmac for more than three hours unless the pilot-in-command determines there is a safety-related or security-related impediment to deplaning passengers (e.g., . . . weather, air traffic control, a directive from an appropriate government agency, etc.), or Air Traffic Control advises the pilot-in-command that returning to the gate or permitting passengers to disembark elsewhere would significantly disrupt airport operations . . . .

Department of Transportation, Enhancing Airline Passenger Protections, 74 Fed. Reg. 68983, 68987 (Dec. 30, 2009). The final rule was weaker than the NPRM in some respects. Notably, the Department did not mandate that carriers incorporate their contingency plans in their contracts of carriage—which may have permitted breach of contract suits—after receiving comments that it lacked the legal authority to force such a change. Instead, the final rule "strongly encourages carriers to incorporate the terms of their contingency plans in their contracts of carriage, as most major carriers have done voluntarily with respect to their customer service plans." Id. at 68989.[7]

Had the final rule required a change to contracts of carriage, airlines could have sued the Transportation Department on substantive grounds, though they might not have succeeded. Theoretically, airlines could have argued that the enacted 3-hour time limit exceeded the agency's statutory authority. *Look back to the statutory provisions. Would you agree with such an argument? Are those provisions ambiguous? If so, should courts defer to the Department's interpretation of those provisions?* In other rulemakings, substantive objections may derive not only from relevant statutes but also from the U.S. Constitution.

Here, the Department of Transportation engaged in considerable process before issuing its final rule: an ANPRM with a comment period and an NPRM with a comment period. Those who were unhappy with the rule would not have had a plausible argument that the agency should have provided more opportunity to comment (though perhaps there would have been a plausible claim if the agency had denied the request for a 30-day extension of the NPRM's comment period and there were other extenuating circumstances making the original 60-day period insufficient). But there are other potential process objections to a rulemaking. For instance, a challenger might allege that the agency did not provide sufficient information with the NPRM to permit meaningful comment. In addition, if the final rule is not identical to the proposed rule, a challenger could claim that the final rule is not a "logical outgrowth" of the proposed rule, as is required. Overall, the final rule was largely stronger than the proposed rule. *Should that be permissible?* As with substantive challenges, statutes (particularly the APA) and the Constitution can come into play for procedural objections.

In fact, as with much significant agency regulation, this major rulemaking faced no legal challenges. It is a myth—largely held by commentators, even those who work in administrative law—that most rules result in legal challenges in federal courts.

The Department's final rule was followed by legislation. In 2012, Congress enacted, with support from both parties, a modified version of the proposed legislation discussed above—notably without the time limits on how long a plane can remain on the tarmac before giving passengers the opportunity to deplane. The FAA Modernization and Safety Improvement Act of 2012, a major reauthorization bill covering many issues, codified some of the earlier adopted regulatory structure. Section 415 mandates that carriers and airport operators of a certain size

7 Here is how the Department of Transportation currently explains the 2010 rule to consumers: https://www.transportation.gov/individuals/aviation-consumer-protection/tarmac-delays.

submit (for the Secretary of Transportation's approval) emergency contingency plans for how they will:

> (A) provide adequate food, potable water, restroom facilities, comfortable cabin temperatures, and access to medical treatment for passengers onboard an aircraft at the airport when the departure of a flight is delayed or the disembarkation of passengers is delayed; (B) share facilities and make gates available at the airport in an emergency; and (C) allow passengers to deplane following an excessive tarmac delay in accordance with [another section].

Although the legislation did not adopt the three-hour cut-off mandate that appears in the Department's final rule, it also did not repeal the regulation. Section 415 also requires the Secretary to "establish a consumer complaints toll-free hotline telephone number for the use of passengers in air transportation and shall take actions to notify the public of—(1) that telephone number; and (2) the Internet Web site of the Aviation Consumer Protection Division of the Department of Transportation." It also mandates covered carriers to provide information on the telephone hotline and the Aviation Consumer Protection Division, among other items. Pub. L. No. 112–95, 126 Stat. 11 (2012), § 415. *What have other countries done in this area? Check out the European Union's approach (specifically, EU Regulation 261).*

Having a regulation in place, of course, is not the end of the story. It may not be followed. *Should the agency that has authority to regulate also have authority to enforce? Or should another agency be in charge of enforcement? What kind of enforcement regime would you desire? For instance, should the agency be able to issue penalties itself or should the agency have to take the matter to a federal court? Should an enforcement agency go after every violation? Could it, as a practical matter, do so?*

By statute, the "Secretary of Transportation may impose a civil penalty for . . . [certain] violations [including of the 2010 rule] only after notice and an opportunity for a hearing." 49 U.S.C. § 46301. The Department learns of violations from carriers themselves (the rule has reporting mandates) and from consumer complaints.[8]

The Department's Office of Aviation Enforcement and Proceedings came after American Airlines for violating the 2010 rule, among other provisions. The parties settled in 2016. The agreement began:

> This consent order concerns violations by American Airlines, Inc. (American Airlines) of 14 CFR 259.4 (the Department's tarmac delay rule), 49 U.S.C. § 41712 (prohibition against unfair and deceptive practices), and 49 U.S.C. § 42301 (requirement to adhere to a carrier's tarmac delay contingency plan). American Airlines failed to adhere to the assurances in its contingency plan for lengthy tarmac delays for twenty domestic flights at Charlotte International Airport (CLT) on

[8] https://www.transportation.gov/airconsumer/file-consumer-complaint.

> February 16, 2013, six domestic flights at Dallas/Fort Worth International Airport (DFW) on February 27, 2015, and one domestic flight at Shreveport Regional Airport (SHV) on October 22, 2015. Specifically, the carrier permitted the flights to remain on the tarmac for more than three hours without providing passengers an opportunity to deplane. This order directs American Airlines to cease and desist from future similar violations of Part 259 and sections 41712 and 42301 and assesses American Airlines $1.6 million in civil penalties.

Department of Transportation, Consent Order with American Airlines, at 1 (Dec. 14, 2016).[9]

The fine was nontrivial. But unlike successful contract or tort litigation where any damages would go entirely to the plaintiff (and her attorneys), $602,000 of the fine got "credited to American Airlines for compensation provided to passengers on the affected flights," while $303,000 also went back to the carrier for part of "the carrier's expended costs of acquiring, operating and maintaining a surface management and surveillance system at CLT and DFW to monitor the location of each aircraft on the airfield." Id. at 15. *Does the fine, as structured, strike you as appropriate?* In September 2021, the Department fined United Airlines $1.9 million "for lengthy tarmac delays for 20 domestic flights and 5 international flights," the largest penalty of its kind at the time.

The 2010 rule and 2012 legislation, of course, did not make air travel trouble free. In April 2016, President Obama issued an Executive Order, Steps to Increase Competition and Better Inform Consumers and Workers to Support Continued Growth of the American Economy. In part, it directed executive departments and agencies "with authorities that could be used to enhance competition" to, "where consistent with other laws, use those authorities to promote competition, arm consumers and workers with the information they need to make informed choices, and eliminate regulations that restrict competition without corresponding benefits to the American public." Exec. Order No. 13,725, 81 Fed. Reg. 23417 (Apr. 20, 2016). *Should the President be able to order agencies to undertake particular rulemakings in this manner?*

Following the White House's directive, the Department of Transportation finalized rules requiring airlines to disclose more information and barring "cherry picking" of data for certain performance metrics. It also issued an ANPRM mandating that airlines refund baggage fees when the baggage is "substantially delayed." The White House touted both actions in a released fact sheet titled "Obama Administration Announces New Actions to Spur Competition in the Airline Industry, Give Consumers the Information They Need to Make Informed Choices." *What are the benefits and costs of having such coordination between the White House and a cabinet department on agency regulation?*

---

[9] https://www.transportation.gov/sites/dot.gov/files/docs/eo-2016-12-10.pdf.

In the first few months of President Trump's Administration, overbooking of airplane flights and poor customer service generated considerable media attention (and You Tube hits). For instance, David Dao was dragged off a United Airlines flight (operated by a regional carrier) in April 2017 after refusing to deplane so that airline crew (being relocated for a later flight) could take his seat. He obtained an attorney but settled with the airline before filing an actual suit. Some people called for additional legislation, and others for more regulation. The House Transportation and Infrastructure Committee and the Senate Subcommittee on Aviation (of the Transportation Committee) held hearings in May 2017.

Airlines for America, a lobbying organization for the aviation industry, sought to modify the 2010 rule "so that the time period for measuring a delay stops when a pilot requests authority to return to the gate," among other desired changes. Kari Paul, Delta Passengers Were Trapped on Plane for 12 Hours—But Did They Get Compensation?, MarketWatch (Feb. 26, 2018). And so, the circle of potential policymaking continued. *If you were advising President Trump and knew that one of the President's programs was to eliminate two regulations for every new regulation, would you have advised him to pressure the Transportation Department to get rid of the 2010 tarmac rule?*

Flight difficulties continue, of course. The summer of 2022 brought many flight delays and cancellations (*did you experience any?*) and subsequent pleas for federal action. In August 2022, the Department of Transportation issued a proposed rule (and sought public comments) "to codify its longstanding interpretation that it is an unfair business practice for a U.S. air carrier, a foreign air carrier, or a ticket agent to refuse to provide requested refunds to consumers when a carrier has cancelled or made a significant change to a scheduled flight."[10]

## SECTION 2. THE BASICS

***Frequently Asked Questions***

If you were to log on to a hypothetical website—say, www.adminlaw.gov—to find some fundamental background for understanding administrative law in general (or the preceding problem, in particular) you might find something like the following list. The responses to these FAQs are only initial entry points for more sophisticated questions and answers that will arise throughout this book.

---

[10] The docket is here: https://www.regulations.gov/document/DOT-OST-2022-0089-0004. *Take a look at some of the comments: what are your reactions?*

## Frequently Asked Questions

- What is administrative law?
- What entities are administrative agencies?
- Is everything the federal government does considered agency action?
- Is administrative law important?
- Is administrative law just politics by another name?
- How are administrative agencies organized?
- How do administrative agencies do their work?
- How do administrative agencies make regulations?
- How do administrative agencies decide cases?
- How do courts review the work of administrative agencies?
- How do the White House and Congress oversee the actions of administrative agencies?
- Is the administrative state legitimate?
- How does administrative law contribute to social welfare?
- How does administrative law contribute to freedom?
- How does administrative law contribute to social justice?

### What is administrative law?

Administrative law, as covered in this casebook (and website), comprises the body of general rules and principles governing federal administrative agencies—both how they do their own work and how the results of that work will be viewed, or reviewed, by the President, Congress, and the federal courts. It exists in every country and at all levels of government—federal, state, and local—in our system, and there are some emerging principles of international (sometimes called global) administrative law, too. Federal administrative law can be found in many sources: the Constitution, federal statutes, executive orders, and decisions of the federal courts—as well as in the decisions and rules of all sorts made by the agencies themselves.

Administrative law, as a body of general principles, needs to be distinguished from the particular substantive law implemented by each individual agency—distinguished, that is, from the tax law practiced by the Internal Revenue Service or the labor law of the National Labor Relations Board. Administrative law takes place on a more general, and more process-oriented, plane. The distinction is somewhat analogous to that between civil procedure and torts or contracts. Every torts or contracts case, because it came from a judicial proceeding, has a civil procedure matrix, even if the principal topic of dispute concerns a substantive torts or contracts doctrine. Similarly, administrative law addresses general questions like the process by which agency regulations must be made, rather than the more particular questions regarding labor or tax policy.

### What entities are administrative agencies?

Administrative agencies are all of the authorities and operating units of the federal government except for the constitutionally established entities in the first three Articles: Congress, the President and Vice President, and the Supreme Court (and the lower federal courts established by statute). They are sometimes called "agencies," sometimes "departments," sometimes "boards," sometimes "commissions"—they are all still agencies. Just as agents, in the ordinary sense of the term, carry out tasks for their principals, so, too, do agencies carry out the instructions of, and are responsible to, the three constitutionally established, institutional "principals." Because the Constitution barely mentions and doesn't establish any administrative agencies, they must be created by statute or, in some cases, by presidential order. ("Agency" sometimes has a more technical definition, such as for the Freedom of Information Act, see Chapter VI.)

There are five major categories of executive branch agencies. First, there are White House agencies, such as the Office of Management and Budget (which houses OIRA, described in the example above), which sit within the Executive Office of the President. Second, there are fifteen cabinet departments, including the most recent addition, the Department of Homeland Security, which started operations in 2003. Their leaders, along with the Vice President, make up the President's Cabinet. Third, executive agencies are sometimes housed within cabinet departments, like the FAA, discussed above. Other executive agencies in this category are freestanding, like the Environmental Protection Agency. Several of their leaders (along with some leaders of the White House agencies) are often considered "cabinet-level," at the discretion of the President. Fourth, independent regulatory commissions and boards, like the NTSB (another transportation agency, described briefly in footnote 2 on p. 7), are run by multi-member leadership and excluded from some administrative procedures imposed by the White House. As with cabinet departments and executive agencies, bodies in this category address a wide range of policy areas. Finally, there are agencies that are only partly federal in nature, including public-private entities like government corporations, federal-state organizations like those established under the Compact Clause, and federal-foreign institutions like those created by treaties.

Sometimes, agencies change type. The Postal Service, one of the country's oldest agencies (predating even the country's founding), started as a freestanding executive agency, with its leader considered cabinet-level for decades. Since 1971, it has functioned as a quasi-government corporation. It is the largest employer of nonmilitary government employees and the third largest employer of civilians in the United States, after Walmart and Amazon.

## Is everything the federal government does considered agency action?

Almost. When Congress passes a statute, that is not agency action, nor when a federal court makes a decision, nor when the President gives a speech or issues a pardon. But when the Internal Revenue Service collects taxes, the Bureau of Land Management leases public lands, the National Labor Relations Board supervises a workplace election, the Centers for Disease Control and Prevention collect epidemiological data, Immigration and Customs Enforcement deports an undocumented immigrant, the Environmental Protection Agency sets a new air quality standard, or the Social Security Administration pays disability benefits—these all are agency action.

However, some agency action is so dependent on officials' discretion that it almost disappears from the ken of administrative law. The decisions of the Air Force as to what jets to order, a federal prosecutor as to whether to press charges, or the State Department as to foreign policy in the Middle East are all agency action in some sense, but they are unlikely to raise issues subject to traditional forms of administrative law control covered in this casebook. Some raise unique issues of law, such as government contracting, with disputes over awards heard in front of the Government Accountability Office or the Court of Federal Claims, for example. And sometimes the extent of agency discretion, in the large sense of the term "discretion," is uncertain, as, for example, in the degree to which Congress intended to give individual agencies the complete freedom to decide what priorities they should establish in carrying out their general mandates.

## Is administrative law important?

Indeed! Given what has already been said, it is almost impossible to be a lawyer for the federal government (except perhaps for those who prosecute certain crimes) without some knowledge of administrative law. And the same is true for most practitioners with private clients who must comply with government regulation. Most transactions these days have a regulatory aspect to them, and understanding any regulatory framework requires knowledge not merely of the substantive policies but also of the types of processes and materials involved—knowledge, in short, of administrative law. A recent survey by the National Council of Bar Examiners found that over 20 percent of new law school graduates listed administrative law as a primary practice area (and over 70 percent did some work in the field).

Some might say that it is hard even to follow the news knowledgeably without some understanding of administrative law. Consider the fallout of the tragic events of September 11, 2001: the implications of requiring a federal agency to handle airport security, the proper distribution of emergency funds to airlines in need of bailout and to the families of those killed, the powers and limits of a new Department of Homeland Security—these were all deeply affected by the doctrines of administrative law. The same could be said of the responses to the "Great

Recession" (the financial crisis of 2007–2009): the administration of the Troubled Assets Relief Program and other bailout funds, the augmentation of the powers of the Federal Reserve Board and the Securities and Exchange Commission, and the establishment of a new agency, the Consumer Financial Protection Bureau. During the COVID-19 pandemic, federal agencies issued guidance (and sometimes regulations) for transportation, schools, hospitals, and businesses. Given the growth of federal regulation over the last century or so, administrative law is one of the best places to see how law works in the modern world. (One member of the current Supreme Court—Justice Kagan—used to be a professor of administrative law; another, Justice Barrett, taught statutory interpretation, which, as you will learn, overlaps substantially with administrative law. Justice Breyer, who recently retired, and the late Justice Scalia also taught administrative law before joining the bench.)

**Is administrative law just politics by another name?**

Some say so. Because administrative agencies wield the government's power, they are, of course, intimately connected with many issues that are the subject of political debate. They are subject to frequent oversight by the President and Congress at the federal level and by states and localities beneath. But because administrative law deals with the proper legal structure for that use of power and that process of oversight, it also brings to bear the values of the law: values such as regularity, consistency, evenhandedness, and participation. This tension—or if you like, this persistent problem of how to encapsulate political will in legal terms—bedevils administrative law. But this simultaneous closeness to and separation from politics also helps make the subject both interesting and important.

**How are administrative agencies organized?**

The Constitution provides few details on the federal government's structure, so each agency is basically organized by the statute (or sometimes, presidential directive) that creates it and tells it what its basic tasks are—this is often called the agency's "organic" statute (or founding memorandum). (Many times, but not always, the statute and the agency are eponyms: for example, the National Labor Relations Act established the National Labor Relations Board.) Nevertheless, and not surprisingly, there are many commonalities among most administrative agencies. There is a head of the agency, with a small cadre of advisers immediately responsible to that office. But the great bulk of agency personnel serve in "administrations," "services," "offices," or the like—subordinate units each with its own particular responsibilities and hierarchical organization. Thus, for example, the problem of controlling the gypsy moth is the immediate responsibility of a group of specialists in the Animal and Plant Health Inspection Service, headed by an Administrator and itself one of several bureaus under the authority of the Under Secretary for Marketing and Regulatory Programs, who is one of several undersecretaries under the authority of the Secretary of Agriculture. Legal staffs within agencies are typically segregated into special law offices. In any agency with substantial adjudicatory responsibilities, the administrative law judges (or other first-level adjudicators) and any appellate tribunal are separated from both the staff and the legal counsel of the agency. Descriptions of the various federal departments and agencies, and organizational charts of their various units, can be found in the U.S. Government Manual.[1]

At the top of most agencies are Senate-confirmed presidential appointees. There are, however, two different general patterns for these leadership structures. As described above, some agencies are regulatory commissions or boards, almost always headed by multi-member bodies, whose members can be removed from office by the President only for "cause," and accordingly are sometimes called "independent" agencies. The NTSB is such an example. Other entities—White House agencies, cabinet departments, and executive agencies—are typically headed by a single administrator who serves at the President's pleasure without any term specified at the start. There are agencies with unusual leadership arrangements. The CFPB, for example, was originally headed by an administrator appointed to a five-year term, who could be fired only for cause. In June 2020, in Seila Law LLC v. CFPB (p. 988), the Supreme Court held that separation of powers principles did not permit the agency's structure. A year later, the Court determined that the 2008 Housing and Economic Recovery Act's "for-cause restriction on the President's removal authority [over the head of the Federal Housing Finance Agency] violates the separation of powers." It noted that its "decision last Term in Seila Law is all but dispositive." (See p. 1007.) The single heads of the IRS and FAA have fixed terms (but no explicit removal protection). All but two members of the Postal Service's Board of Governors are appointed by the President and confirmed by the Senate; that Board (and not the President) then chooses the Postmaster General (and then the Board and Postmaster General select the Deputy Postmaster General) for the remaining two spots.

To determine who has what specific substantive responsibilities within an agency, one must rely on statutes that delegate authority as well as presidential directives and agency rules that redelegate it. Some of the procedural requirements of administrative law also vary with an agency's structure—for example, the Government in the Sunshine Act applies to agencies headed by multi-member boards but not to those headed by single administrators, and the Federal Vacancies Reform Act of 1998 largely permits acting officials only in agencies that are not run by multi-member boards. But the overwhelming majority of administrative law requirements do not turn on the particularities of each agency's organization. Rather, they are responsibilities placed on all federal agencies simply because they are agencies.

### How do administrative agencies do their work?

Agencies act in many ways. The Chairman of the Federal Reserve Board may well influence the course of the economy—or at least the

---

1 https://www.usgovernmentmanual.gov/.

financial markets—simply by giving a speech. The Department of Defense takes a more direct route to the same end—it spends a lot of money. According to a relatively new government website (www.usaspending.gov) that shows all government spending for the first time in one place, the federal government spent $10.1 trillion in FY 2021 (about 37 percent of that went to Social Security, Medicare, and national defense). Even spending actions have a legal structure, depending, as they do, on delegated authority, not to mention appropriations.

But agencies also do things that look more "law" like, and those are the things that mostly come to mind when one speaks of administrative law. Agencies make regulations. A quick look at the Code of Federal Regulations (available in hard copy or online at www.ecfr.gov) will show that agencies make a great many regulations. According to Federal Register tables, between 1976 and 2021, agencies published between 2,964 (in 2019) and 7,745 (in 1980) final rules per year. In addition, according to the Government Accountability Office's database, in the period of 1997 to 2021, "major rules," which are rules expected to have an annual economic impact of at least $100 million or other significant economic effects, ranged between an annual low of 49 (in 2017) and a high of 140 (in 2020). To compare, looking at two-year Congresses between 1977 and 2020, enacted laws ranged from 284 (for 2011 and 2012 together) to 804 (for 1977 and 1978).

Agencies also adjudicate more than the federal courts. In fiscal year 2019, the Social Security Administration received over 2 million initial claims for disability benefits (and presided over nearly 794,000 hearings). In 2021, the Veterans Administration processed over 1.4 million initial disability and pension claims for benefits, and immigration courts, under the Department of Justice, completed over 115,000 cases. All of these agencies have considerable backlogs of claims. To compare, in 2021, the federal appellate courts saw nearly 44,000 filings, and district courts received over 421,000 filings for both civil and criminal matters. Many of these matters, particularly at the district court level, are settled out of court.

Agencies license activities or individuals, too. One cannot just decide to be a pilot and start carrying passengers for hire! And agencies enforce their statutes and regulations—by sending out inspectors, revoking licenses, levying penalties, or bringing actions in court. Any particular agency can do only the things that its governing statutes authorize it to do, but the typical agency will have many of these powers. In other words, individual agencies can set priorities, administer budgets, make rules, decide cases, and pursue enforcement actions, and, in doing so, exercise legislative, executive, and judicial powers that, at the constitutional level, would be split among Congress, the President, and the federal courts.

Finally, although administrative law often assumes only one agency is acting in a particular issue area, there are considerable overlaps in regulatory authority across agencies. Sometimes, agencies work together in joint action; other times, they fight with each other over turf and policy outcomes.

### How do administrative agencies make regulations?

This is, in some respects, a technical question that can only be answered after considerable study. In general, administrative rulemaking begins as you might expect—with a decision on the part of an agency to do something to carry out one of its statutory responsibilities. Because agencies usually are empowered to do more than they have time or money for, this is not necessarily an easy decision to make. Thus, setting priorities, although usually thought of as a purely executive task, has important legal consequences. Once agencies decide to act, they must also decide how. Here, most commonly, a team within the agency—often with technical and legal expertise—will develop a more-or-less worked-out proposal. The archetypal procedure is then to conduct a "notice-and-comment" rulemaking—that is, to give notice that a rule is in the offing and to allow for those outside the agency to comment on the proposal. Staff then review that rulemaking record before making any rule final. The White House is often involved in big rulemakings by cabinet departments and executive agencies from the very start (in terms of prompting action) through to the very end (reviewing proposed and final rules). Assuming that the proper procedures have been followed, and the rule is within the agency's statutory authority, final administrative rules have full legislative force, binding courts, agencies, and private persons (and entities) alike to their terms.

### How do administrative agencies decide cases?

If by "cases" you mean the application of statutes or rules to individual circumstances, administrative agencies decide cases informally, and by the millions, all the time. If, for example, you have been away from the United States and, on returning, turned in a customs form (now often electronic) and passed through customs without paying duty, you have successfully "won" an administrative adjudication. If by "cases" you instead mean the relatively formal proceedings that lead to final determinations of contested matters and may form precedents for future agency action, then you will not be mistaken if you think of them as trial-type proceedings—with some differences. The most formal agency cases are heard in the first instance before administrative law judges, officials who are not judges as understood in Article III of the Constitution but currently have substantial removal protections to help them maintain their independence. Often there is an intermediate level of review before a reasonably sheltered appeals panel. But if the case is important, or has significant contested issues, the ultimate decision may be made by the head of the agency (the head may be a single person or a multi-member board or commission). These officials also have political and policy responsibilities; they are not the same as appellate judges. But they are empowered to decide the issues in the adjudication. In short, there is often a closer connection between overt policy authority and case decision in administrative adjudication than in courtroom adjudication. This might be viewed as the genius of administrative adjudication, or as its fatal flaw. Sometimes, Congress has shied away from this standard arrangement and separated adjudicatory matters from the rest of an agency's responsibilities. The Occupational Safety and Health Act, for example, created both a regulatory and an enforcement agency, the well-known Occupational Safety and Health Administration, and a separate case-hearing agency, the lesser-known Occupational Safety and Health Review Commission.

### How do courts review the work of administrative agencies?

Almost every statute that creates an administrative agency and delegates authority to it also provides for the major final decisions of the agency—the rules it makes and the cases it decides—to be reviewed by a federal court. Occasionally this review is de novo, for example, when a court reviews an agency's decision to withhold information that has been requested by someone under the Freedom of Information Act. And sometimes the matter on review can raise an issue, such as a constitutional issue, on which a court will ignore completely the agency's views. But on most factual and policy matters, the fact that the agency has decided one way or another has some weight before the court; to put the point another way, the court will to some extent defer to the agency's judgment. In part, this is a straightforward reflection of the reality that, in both rulemaking and adjudication, review most often takes place on the record the agency has built, which necessarily reflects how the agency framed the issue. (Indeed, Congress often provides for agency decisions to be reviewed for the first time in a federal court of appeals, that is, in a court that hears argument but doesn't take new evidence.) But deference to the agency is also grounded in the belief that, on many matters, the agency may have made a better decision than the judges would if they substituted their own judgment. This might be because the agency understands the factual context better because of its close involvement with the problem at hand, because the agency gets more political input on a matter that turns on a value-laden choice among possible policies, because the agency has a set of experts who understand the science or economics of the problem better than generalist judges, or perhaps some other reason. What the grounds of deference are, and how far they go, are a matter of considerable debate among scholars, judges, and politicians. Chevron, U.S.A., Inc. v. Natural Resources Defense Council, Inc., 467 U.S. 837—the Chevron case, decided in 1984, which you will hear much about—held that judges should even defer to an agency's interpretation of Congress's statutory language if the language is ambiguous and the agency's view, if delegated to act under the statute, is reasonable. It is both the most cited case in modern administrative law and one of the most controversial. The Supreme Court has not relied on Chevron deference since 2016, though lower courts continue to do so.

### How do the White House and Congress oversee the actions of administrative agencies?

Most agency actions are not reviewed by a court, though agencies, like private parties, act in the "shadow of the law." But agencies face considerable nonjudicial oversight, within and outside the federal government. A fair number of pages in these materials deal with this oversight. At the front end, top agency leaders are selected by the President and confirmed by the Senate. Congress orders agencies to perform tasks, and at times even imposes deadlines on them; notably, its appropriations of operating funds may not suffice for agencies to perform these tasks. The White House also "directs" certain agencies to undertake particular programs. In the middle, OIRA reviews significant regulations by cabinet departments and executive agencies before they are issued. The President (and any other agency leader for that matter) can also ask an agency—of any type—to consider her views in a particular policy area. Congress can withhold funding for particular agency programs through appropriations riders and can hold hearings to question agency officials on their plans.

At the back end, the President can fire almost all political officials not located in independent regulatory commissions and boards for any reason. In addition, the President can express her displeasure, short of doing so via firing, in public or private forums. Congress, too, can attack agency decisions at the back end: it can repeal certain important agency regulations under the Congressional Review Act, which then prevents an agency from issuing a rule in the future in "substantially the same form." Before 2017, only one regulation had been overturned through the CRA. Then, in 2017, with unified Republican government, Congress repealed 14 rules issued by agencies during President Obama's Administration (and one rule issued by the CFPB, which was still led by a President Obama appointee after President Trump took office) under the CRA's fast track procedures. (There was another repeal in 2018.)

In President Biden's first six months in office, with a unified Democratic government, members of Congress introduced six CRA resolutions. Three passed both chambers of Congress and were signed by the President, bringing the total number of enacted resolutions to 20 and marking the first time the CRA had successfully been used by Democrats. In addition to CRA use, Congress can also launch formal investigations, hold hearings, and engage in less formal oversight mechanisms.

How much force the White House's views should carry is a matter of considerable dispute, depending on agency type and other factors. (There is also conflict, although less, about congressional pressure). These tensions generally do not play out in court.

### Is the administrative state legitimate?

There has been considerable criticism of the modern administrative state's legitimacy from its advent in the New Deal. This criticism has waxed and waned in the ensuing decades, but it has become especially fierce in recent years, with commentators, members of Congress, a President, and judges both on and off the Supreme Court casting doubt on its legitimacy. For instance, a top staffer in President Trump's White House called for the "deconstruction of the administrative state." The Trump Administration attempted to carry out that goal (at least in part) through a series of deregulatory measures, including requiring two regulations to be repealed for every new one implemented. Justice Gorsuch (and some of his colleagues) have attacked broad delegations to federal agencies, positing that the "Constitution promises that only the people's elected representatives may adopt new federal laws restricting liberty."[2] While the Supreme Court has not broadly invalidated agency action on these constitutional concerns, some lower courts have. A Fifth Circuit panel recently determined that the Securities and Exchange Commission's in-house enforcement proceedings, conducted by administrative law judges with removal protection, violated the Seventh Amendment, Article I's Vesting Clause (nondelegation doctrine), and Article II's Take Care Clause. Administrative law and the ability to ensure that agency actions comply with applicable legal constraints is one of the key pillars supporting the legitimacy of administrative action.

**How does administrative law contribute to social welfare?**

The programs run by administrative agencies have considerable effects on our economy and on other aspects of our welfare as a society. The Federal Reserve Board sets interest rates; the Securities and Exchange Commission tries to keep securities markets free of fraud; the Environmental Protection Agency establishes and enforces pollution standards; and the National Park Service maintains many of our greatest natural treasures. Administrative law, as the law of the process by which these things happen, contributes to social welfare insofar as it improves the performance of these functions—insofar as it contributes to agency decisions being better thought-through and more reflective of varied interests, being better communicated to those affected, being more attentive to human dignity, being more rationally enforced, *and* by not creating enormous burdens such as making things costlier, more cumbersome, or slower. The cost-benefit analysis required by OIRA for significant rulemakings by many agencies appears, at first blush, to guarantee an improvement in social welfare. But the regulatory analysis is overseen by a White House agency, with close ties to presidential priorities, and it is only one component of what the agency considers in signing off on major rulemakings. Whether administrative law improves social welfare—or, perhaps better put, what the doctrines of

---

[2] Gundy v. United States, 139 S.Ct. 2116, 2131 (2019) (Gorsuch, J., dissenting). With regard to Chevron deference, then-Judge Gorsuch wrote that it "permit[s] executive bureaucracies to swallow huge amounts of core judicial and legislative power and concentrate federal power in a way that seems more than a little difficult to square with the Constitution of the framers' design." Gutierrez-Brizuela v. Lynch, 834 F.3d 1142, 1149 (10th Cir. 2016) (Gorsuch, J., concurring). More recently, Justice Gorsuch posited that Chevron deference "pose[s] a serious threat to some of our most fundamental commitments as judges and courts. . . . We place a finger on the scales of justice in favor of the most powerful of litigants, the federal government, and against everyone else. . . . Rather than provide individuals with the best understanding of their rights and duties under law a neutral magistrate can muster, we outsource our interpretive responsibilities. Rather than say what the law is, we tell those who come before us to go ask a bureaucrat." Buffington v. McDonough, No. 21–972, 2022 WL 16726027, *8–*9 (2022) (Gorsuch, J., dissenting from the denial of certiorari).

administrative law should be so it will have this beneficial effect—is one of the persistent problems of the subject.

### How does administrative law contribute to freedom?

Many administrative agencies regulate private activity. Libertarians argue that regulation inherently reduces the freedom of those regulated compared to what they would have had if only common law rules applied. Others disagree and posit that regulation can increase freedom—of regulatory beneficiaries (including the larger public) and even of regulated entities that receive permission to undertake particular actions. Whether any particular regulatory regime increases or decreases individual freedom overall is thus a program-by-program question. But freedom is not just an individual matter; it also is a matter of the working of our governmental institutions. Administrative law serves to increase this social or political freedom when it makes the workings of the government more transparent to citizens (and other residents) and when it provides increased opportunities for them to participate in governmental affairs. Whether American administrative law adequately does this or whether it overdoes this are persistent questions. But it is at least worth noting that many foreign legal scholars and law reformers consider some of the doctrines of American administrative law—for instance, the wide comment possibilities available during much rulemaking and the Freedom of Information Act—to be considerably better in this regard than their own existing arrangements.

### How does administrative law contribute to social justice?

The programs run by administrative agencies also have tremendous consequences for how benefits and burdens are distributed throughout the society—benefits as disparate as disability pensions, minimum wages, cleanups of toxic wastes, and admission to the United States itself, and burdens as disparate as filing forms, reengineering production processes, and, of course, paying taxes. The very disciplining of these activities to the regularity of the law—the reduction in arbitrariness of the distribution of either benefits or burdens—might be considered a considerable contribution to social justice. That administrative law doctrines make some real contribution of this sort is hard to deny. More difficult is the question whether administrative law conduces toward or away from social equality, or if not equality, then toward or away from the fair distribution of society's benefits. Seemingly technical doctrines can have distributive effects. Indeed, those effects have fueled some of the major disputes in the history of administrative law. As to what the overall balance is, perhaps all that can be said with safety is that the issue is contentious.

## SECTION 3. RACE (AND OTHER IDENTITIES) AND ADMINISTRATIVE LAW

Like the law in general, administrative law is usually stated in terms that are not directly tied to the race, gender, economic class, or other personal characteristics of the participants involved. Contract law, as set forth in the Restatement of Contracts, appears as the interaction of "A" and "B"; administrative law, as set forth in the Administrative Procedure Act, likewise appears as the interaction of "Persons," "Parties," and "Agencies." How these abstract categories relate to our actual society—where there is no "A" nor "Person" who lacks race, gender, economic class, or other characteristics—is a longstanding jurisprudential problem. Much of the work that needs to be done, at least with respect to administrative law, has not yet been done—namely exploring how identity shapes and is shaped by the field, though attention is increasing. We offer here some initial thoughts on relevant issues:

Rulemaking (Chapter IV): Courts and scholars largely extol the benefits of public participation in rulemaking. But commenters to a proposed rulemaking (and participants in ex parte meetings with agency officials) often do not reflect "the public." Agencies, with court permission, typically ignore brief, identical comments generated through group campaigns. Many individuals, however, lack the requisite expertise to draft a unique comment to which an agency must respond. *Should agencies have to consider the views of unrepresented, affected groups in rulemaking, and, if so, how should they solicit those views?* For more on how marginalized groups can use notice-and-comment rulemaking, see Matthew Cortland & Karen Tani, Reclaiming Notice and Comment, LPE Blog (July 31, 2019).[1] For a history of how the Federal Communications Commission and Federal Power Commission responded, with contrasting attention, to pressure to use state action doctrine to enact and enforce equal employment through rulemaking, see Sophia Z. Lee, Race, Sex, and Rulemaking: Administrative Constitutionalism and the Workplace, 1960 to the Present, 96 Va. L. Rev. 799 (2010).

Adjudication (Chapter V): The procedural due process revolution of the 1960s and 1970s (perhaps best exemplified by Goldberg v. Kelly, 397 U.S. 254 (1970)) helped provide protections to marginalized individuals who face government deprivations (see the excerpt from Karen Tani, p. 41, who wrote about earlier efforts to provide protections in federal agencies). The courts then pulled back from these protections. *Does current due process doctrine sufficiently protect individuals?* The government conducts large numbers of adjudications involving veterans, individuals with disabilities, and immigrants. *How do agency proceedings treat these individuals? For instance, how do race, and other aspects of identity (some of which intersect with race), shape credibility*

[1] https://lpeblog.org/2019/07/31/reclaiming-notice-and-comment/.

*determinations made by adjudicators tasked with evaluating claims of those seeking the government's assistance? And what changes should be made?* At present, it is very hard to disqualify an adjudicator (and even harder to disqualify a rulemaker) for bias. Historically, statutes established agency adjudicatory systems that perpetuated systemic racism. For instance, the Chinese Exclusion Act of 1882 created an anti-immigrant bureaucracy to figure out which Chinese individuals in the United States should be removed from the country. For more on that statute and the administrative law it created, see Lucy E. Salyer, Laws Harsh as Tigers (1995); Jonathan Weinberg, The Racial Roots of the Federal Administrative State, Notice & Comment Blog (July 20, 2020).[2]

Presidential Directives (Chapters IV and VII): Presidential directives to federal agencies can focus on underrepresented groups. For example, President Truman's Executive Order 9981 established the President's Committee on Equality of Treatment and Opportunity in the Armed Services, which committed the government to integrating the armed forces. President Clinton issued Executive Order 12898 (Federal Actions to Address Environmental Justice in Minority Populations and Low-Income Populations), which mandated that agencies "identif[y] and addres[s], as appropriate, disproportionately high and adverse human health or environmental effects of [their] programs, policies, and activities on minority populations and low-income populations." President Obama promulgated Executive Order 13583 (Establishing a Coordinated Government-wide Initiative to Promote Diversity and Inclusion in the Federal Workforce), which required a government-wide diversity and inclusion plan.

Of course, presidential directives focusing on underrepresented groups have also targeted those groups for discriminatory treatment. President Roosevelt's Executive Order 9066 authorized the incarceration of over 120,000 Japanese Americans in "relocation centers." The Supreme Court upheld this order in its infamous decision, Korematsu v. United States, 323 U.S. 214 (1944). Seventy-five years after Roosevelt's directive, in the beginning of his presidency, President Trump enacted the so-called "Muslim ban" through a series of Executive Orders: 13769, 13780, and Presidential Proclamation 9645.

On his first day in office, President Biden signed Executive Order 13985 (Advancing Racial Equity and Support for Underserved Communities Through the Federal Government): "Affirmatively advancing equity, civil rights, racial justice, and equal opportunity is the responsibility of the whole of our Government. Because advancing equity requires a systematic approach to embedding fairness in decision-making processes, executive departments and agencies . . . must recognize and work to redress inequities in their policies and programs that serve as barriers to equal opportunity." Among other items, the President called for OMB to study methods for assessing equity and to work with agencies to "allocate[e] federal resources to advance fairness and opportunity,"

---

[2] https://www.yalejreg.com/nc/the-racial-roots-of-the-federal-administrative-state-by-jonathan-weinberg/.

and for agencies to conduct an "equity assessment" of particular programs and to "promot[e] equitable delivery of government benefits and equitable opportunities." OMB issued its report on methods to assess equity in July 2021.[3] Many agencies released their first equity plans.[4]

In administrative law, considerable attention is given to presidential directives on regulatory review and the role of cost-benefit analysis in that process. Executive Order 12866 includes two brief references to "distributive impacts" and "equity" as part of what might count as a regulatory benefit. The Order states: "Further, in choosing among alternative regulatory approaches, agencies should select those approaches that maximize net benefits (including potential economic, environmental, public health and safety, and other advantages; distributive impacts; and equity)." On his first day, President Biden signed a memorandum, Modernizing Regulatory Review. Among other items, the memorandum sought recommendations from OMB, in consultation with federal agencies, on "procedures that take into account the distributional consequences of regulations, including as part of any quantitative or qualitative analysis of the costs and benefits of regulations, to ensure that regulatory initiatives appropriately benefit and do not inappropriately burden disadvantaged, vulnerable, or marginalized communities." *Should agencies have to prepare an equity analysis to issue significant rules?*

<u>Appointees and Career Workers (Chapter VII)</u>: Federal agency leaders do not look like the American public. The Obama Administration made concerted efforts to diversify top agency officials, but leadership did not come close to matching the diversity of the country's population.[5] Recent research by Chris Brummer found that, as of September 2020, only 10 of 327 leaders of financial regulatory agencies (for example, the Federal Reserve) have been Black.[6] Until President Biden took office, there had never been a woman or person of color heading the Treasury or Defense Departments (Janet Yellen became the first female Secretary of the Treasury and Lloyd Austin became the first Black Secretary of Defense in January 2021).

Career employees are somewhat more representative than political leaders in federal agencies. According to Rachel Potter's 2019 book, Bending the Rules: Procedural Politicking in the Bureaucracy, "federal employees tend to be older, whiter, more educated, and more likely to be male than the average U.S. resident," but compared to members of Congress and political appointees, "the bureaucracy ranks among the most diverse." For example, the Postal Service has employed many Black workers, contributing to the Black middle class. On the other hand, William Resh submitted written testimony to Congress in February 2021

[3] https://www.whitehouse.gov/wp-content/uploads/2021/08/OMB-Report-on-E013985-Implementation_508-Compliant-Secure-v1.1.pdf.

[4] https://www.whitehouse.gov/equity/#equity-plan-snapshots.

[5] For more information, see https://www.washingtonpost.com/politics/obama-ups-diversity-in-appointees/2015/09/20/5b042aac-5ffb-11e5-8e9e-dce8a2a2a679_graphic.html.

[6] https://www.brookings.edu/wp-content/uploads/2020/09/ES-09.02.20-Brummer.pdf.

showing "vast decreases of employees of color in some key agencies" from FY 2015 to FY 2019. According to the Partnership for Public Service, "[t]he Coast Guard, Farm Credit Administration, Government Accountability Office and Intelligence Community are including diversity, equity and inclusion into their strategic plans, and paying attention to issues ranging from how they recruit diverse groups of employees to how they retain and develop them."

Women and people of color make up a disproportionately small percentage of senior-level positions. According to PPS: "As of June 2018 women held only 34 percent of the government's more than 7,100 Senior Executive Service positions, according to the Office of Personnel Management. . . . Percentage-wise, women fared better in the overall federal workforce, making up 43 percent of the roughly 2 million federal government employees. However, they mostly fill positions at the lower end of the pay scale."[7] Similarly, from a different PPS report, "[a]s of March 2021, people of color represent 47% of all full-time, entry-level employees but only 33% of senior-level positions. And within the Senior Executive Service—the elite corps of experienced civil servants responsible for leading the federal workforce—the disparity is even wider. Only 23% of all career SES members are people of color." It also notes that "Black and other employees of color make up 53% of clerical positions but only 32% of the professional workforce . . . ." There are additional disparities amongst agencies. For example, "white people make up 76% of the Office of Management and Budget, a federal agency that has significant impact on policy and the nation's financial resources, while people of color are the majority at the Equal Employment Opportunity Commission, an important organization but one with significantly less influence."[8] *What changes should be made to the government work force?* Currently, the federal government places restrictions on hiring noncitizens to work as government employees or contractors. *How might this policy impact the federal government's ability to craft an appropriately representative workforce?*

Judicial Review (Chapter VIII): *If agencies were to consider (or fail to consider) impacts on underrepresented groups, how would courts review such action (or inaction)?* A recent lawsuit alleged that the Department of Agriculture's new Supplemental Nutrition Assistance Program rule, which limits waivers of work requirements for SNAP benefits, failed to address the disparate impact it would have on women and persons of color. (A district court issued a nationwide preliminary injunction against the rule, which the Trump Administration appealed in December 2020. The Biden Administration dismissed that appeal in March and formally rescinded the rule in June 2021.) Under arbitrary and capricious review, courts will not permit agencies to consider factors, such as the effects of their actions on women and persons of color, not

---

[7] For the full report, see: https://ourpublicservice.org/blog/governments-lack-of-diversity-in-leadership-positions/.

[8] For the complete report, see: https://ourpublicservice.org/blog/a-revealing-look-at-racial-diversity-in-the-federal-government/.

included in their statutory delegation of authority. (See the excerpt from Cristina Ceballos, David Freeman Engstrom, and Daniel E. Ho, p. 52.) When do statutes permit (and even require) such analysis? See, e.g., Prometheus Radio Project v. Federal Communications Commission, 939 F.3d 567, 584 (3d Cir. 2019) (finding "that the Commission did not adequately consider the effect its new rules would have on ownership of broadcast media by women and racial minorities"), rev'd, 141 S.Ct. 1150, 1160 (2021) ("The Commission further explained that its best estimate, based on the sparse record evidence, was that repealing or modifying the three rules at issue here was not likely to harm minority and female ownership. The APA requires no more.") (see p. 1144 for more on this case). *Should judicial review doctrines change?*

Reviewability (Chapter IX): Justiciability and jurisdictional barriers have limited the ability of regulatory beneficiaries, among others, to access the courts. These barriers also make it difficult to challenge systemic racism. For instance, in Allen v. Wright, 468 U.S. 737 (1984), the Supreme Court held that parents of children of color did not have standing to challenge the IRS's failure to enforce its policy of denying charitable tax-exempt status to racially discriminatory schools. On the other hand, in Massachusetts v. EPA, 549 U.S. 497 (2007), the Supreme Court arguably made it easier for states to get into court to challenge federal action, although more recent decisions and changes to the Court's composition have undermined that decision. *How do states protect (or, conversely, undermine) the interests of their most vulnerable residents?* (States and localities also play special roles in the construction and implementation of many federal programs.) *Should agency decisions be easier to challenge? What doctrines would you change (for instance, finality or reviewability under the APA, standing, etc.)?*

In the summer of 2020, the Notice & Comment Blog ran an online symposium, Racism in Administrative Law, with a range of thought-provoking essays that you may wish to consult.[9] The essays take a range of viewpoints on administrative law issues (for example, Melissa Luttrell and Jorge Roman-Romero critique cost-benefit analysis requirements, in part, because they "promot[e] weak health, safety, and environmental standards, a bias that—in the context of risk regulation—helps to prop up a status quo where racial disparities abound." By contrast, Philip Hamburger calls for *less* agency authority, which he sees as "systematically discriminatory," and for more legislative power, which he sees as "representativ[e] of a diverse people."). The University of Pennsylvania hosted a major lecture series, Race and Regulation, in the 2021–2022 academic year.[10]

[9] https://www.yalejreg.com/topic/racism-in-administrative-law-symposium/.

[10] For the lectures and related podcasts, see https://pennreg.org/race-and-regulation/.

## SECTION 4. THE TASKS OF ADMINISTRATIVE LAW



Administrative law begins with the statutes that establish and empower administrative agencies—decisions made by the political branches of government that define the scope of each agency's authority and mandate the modes through which that authority is to be exercised. *Have Congress and the President acted wisely?* Given the ubiquity of agencies in the modern world, these decisions are probably best evaluated not in absolute terms (administrative agencies are "good" or "bad") but in comparative terms (they are "better" or "worse").

Better or worse than what? When a new agency is being considered—such as the controversial Consumer Financial Protection Bureau—political rhetoric usually frames the choice in terms of action, inaction, or reverse action: administrative agencies are equated with "regulation" and contrasted with the choices of "doing nothing" or "deregulation." From the standpoint of legal analysis, however, this is insufficient. The difficulty can be seen most clearly if we ask: what in the legal universe does Congress's "doing nothing" equate with? It doesn't equate with "no law," if only because there are very few things on which there is ever "no law." There may be state statutes, state regulations, or common law requirements that govern, for example. Indeed, "doing nothing" from the political point of view might well leave in place a highly articulated and demanding set of legal norms.

In the American legal system, there are three likely alternatives to the establishment of administrative agencies. First, there are common law regimes, created and implemented through the courts. Products liability law is, by and large, an example of a common-law legal regime. Second, there are statutory law regimes, in which legislatures establish rules that are directly enforceable in court. The law of sales under the Uniform Commercial Code is an example of this type of legal regime. Third, there are privatization regimes, where legislatures or agencies contract with private entities to provide goods or services that the government could have dispensed. The use of private prisons and detention facilities to confine inmates and immigrants without proper documentation, respectively, is an example of the third regime. It is also important to keep in mind that agencies exist at the federal, state, and local levels, and that one alternative to federal regulation is state or local regulation. This casebook focuses on federal agencies, but many of the lessons also apply, at least in part, to nonfederal agencies.

To decide the value of establishing an administrative law regime to handle a particular topic, it is thus necessary to compare the advantages or disadvantages of it to each of these other possibilities. These pluses and minuses are of two general varieties. One is institutional: what are the advantages or disadvantages of creating special-purpose agencies staffed by appointed and career personnel rather than relying on general-purpose legislatures and courts or, alternatively, on a specialized private organization? The other is in terms of conferred powers: legislatures generally make rules, while courts usually decide cases; agencies can be given both these powers within their jurisdictions *and* the powers to conduct inspections, grant licenses, broadcast information, undertake research, and do other things as well. One might then ask whether the probable use of a panoply of powers by a specialized organ of government resting on delegated powers is likely to be better or worse overall, in addressing the matter at hand, than having the legislature itself establish a set of directly legally effective rules or than leaving the whole matter to the courts to work out as cases arise. In addition, one might query what decisions should be governmental decisions as opposed to private decisions with some or no governmental oversight. These are complex questions. In addition, administrative agencies are not static. Their design, authority, and oversight can change through time. Below we present some scholars' takes on some of the issues. We begin with some brief histories of the federal administrative state, presented in chronological order of the periods they describe. We then turn to some fundamental legal perspectives on the tasks and legitimacy of the administrative state, listed in chronological order of publication. Finally, we conclude with contemporary views of the modern federal bureaucracy, also provided in publication order.

## a. Historical Perspectives on the Administrative State

(1) NICHOLAS R. PARRILLO, AGAINST THE PROFIT MOTIVE: THE SALARY REVOLUTION IN AMERICAN GOVERNMENT, 1780–1940, at 1–4 (2013): "In America today, the lawful income of a public official consists of a salary. However, in the eighteenth century and often far into the nineteenth and early twentieth centuries, American law authorized a wider variety of ways for officials to make money. Judges charged fees for transactions in the cases they heard. District attorneys won a fee for each criminal they convicted. Tax investigators received a percentage of the evasions they discovered. Naval officers were awarded a percentage of the value of the ships they captured, plus bounties for the enemy sailors on board ships they sank. Militiamen enjoyed rewards for capturing Indians or taking their scalps. Policemen were allowed rewards for recovering stolen property or arresting suspects. Jailors collected fees from inmates for permitting them various privileges, and the managers of penitentiaries had a share of the product of inmates' labor. Clerks deciding immigrants' applications for citizenship took a fee for every application. Government doctors deciding veterans' applications for benefits did the same, as did federal land officers deciding settlers' applications for

homesteads. Even diplomats could lawfully accept a 'gift' from a foreign government upon finalizing a treaty.

"What these arrangements had in common was that the officers' incomes depended, immediately and objectively, on the delivery of services and the achievement of outputs. By a gradual yet profound transformation extending from the late eighteenth century through the early twentieth century, American lawmakers abolished all these forms of income and replaced them with the fixed salaries that we now take for granted in government service, thus attenuating the relationship of officials' income to their conduct. In so doing, they made the absence of the profit motive a defining feature of government.

"The key to comprehending this transformation is to understand the nonsalary forms of pay that initially predominated. There were two basic types, which I term *facilitative payments* and *bounties*. A facilitative payment was a sum that an officer received for performing a service that the affected person wanted or needed, such as processing an application or issuing a permit. A bounty was a sum that an officer received for performing a task that the affected person did not want and might resist, such as arresting a suspect, discovering tax delinquencies, or forcing an inmate to do hard labor.

"The two forms of payment tended to give rise to two very different social relationships between officials and the people with whom they dealt. The facilitative payment tended to promote reciprocal exchange between the officer and the recipient of the service, working to the benefit of both. It fostered mutual accommodation. . . . In contrast, the bounty tended to promote adversarialism. The officer gained by the affected person's loss—by taking state-mandated action that the affected person wanted left undone. . . .

"The two different social dynamics generated by facilitative payments and bounties inspired, respectively, two different arguments for why officials' profitseeking was incompatible with the needs and values of a liberal-democratic republic and therefore had to be abolished. The critique of facilitative payments was essentially that customer-seller accommodation no longer had a rightful place in government. . . . The critique of bounties was quite different. . . . The officer's monetary incentive to impose sanctions on laypersons placed him in such an adversarial posture toward them as to vitiate their trust in government and elicit from them a mirror-image adversarial response. In addition, officers' profit motive discouraged them from making the kind of subjective and discretionary decisions not to enforce the law that were (and are) necessary to sand off the hard edges of modern state power so it can win acceptance by the population. As lawmakers vested officials with more power and charged them with more ambitious missions, selflessness and forbearance became necessary to vest the officialdom with legitimacy and to foster the essential minimum of lay cooperation that makes the modem state workable."

(2) DANIEL R. ERNST, TOCQUEVILLE'S NIGHTMARE: THE ADMINISTRATIVE STATE EMERGES IN AMERICA, 1900–1940, at 1–3, 7–8 (2014): "When the

French aristocrat Alexis de Tocqueville visited America in the 1830s, he discovered that although the United States had 'centralized government,' it had little in the way of 'centralized administration,' bureaucracies through which federal officials could impose their will on a dispersed and factious people. This seeming shortcoming, Tocqueville decided, was a very good thing. . . .

"By 1940, America was still not Europe, but it had acquired a great deal of centralized administration. Teams of administrators resolved disputes; regulated agriculture and industry; collected taxes; and distributed grants, loans, and other benefits. . . . Something about the 'machinery of government' that Americans had built for themselves had confounded Tocqueville's expectations.

"That something was the rule of law. . . .

"Americans' belief that courts might deliver them from Tocqueville's nightmare gave a distinctly legalistic cast to the administrative state they created after 1900. Although courts accorded administrators great freedom when acting within their legislative and constitutional limits, they insisted on retaining the power to call wayward administrators to account, much as they would farmers who let their cattle forage on the land of others. Further, the agencies themselves usually acted by deciding individual cases rather than making rules and regulations, their most controversial activity today. Even when engaged in the 'legislative' act of prospectively setting rates for public utilities, administrators proceeded case by case. Judges readily assumed that norms of due process that had been worked out in the courts ought also to govern the 'quasi-adjudication' of administrative agencies, and they condemned administrators who violated these norms. In particular, they expected administrators to maintain a judicial aloofness from subordinates presenting the government's case against a respondent. To do otherwise would violate the ancient maxim that no man should be the judge in his own cause. It would also mix powers that, as Montesquieu and John Adams had insisted, must be kept separate if a government were to be one 'of laws and not of men.'

"The courts' influence went beyond the structure of an agency; it reached deep into the thought processes of administrators and taught them to justify their actions in a peculiarly legalistic way. . . .

"The story of how Americans faced down Tocqueville's nightmare still matters, but not because the solution they settled on by the end of the 1930s can or should be ours today. New forms of governance have emerged since 1940, in response, in part, to problems, such as expense, delay, and the 'capture' of regulators, that resulted after the rule of law became a rule of lawyers. Even so, the story told here answers a complaint that has gained in popularity since the eruption of the Tea Party movement in 2009: the statebuilders of the early twentieth century abandoned an American tradition of individualism in what amounted to 'the decisive wrong turn in the nation's history.' This claim overlooks a crucial fact: the reformers who supposedly sent the Constitution into exile, actually designed the principles of individual rights, limited government, and due process into the administrative state."

(3) KAREN M. TANI, STATES OF DEPENDENCY: WELFARE, RIGHTS, AND AMERICAN GOVERNANCE, 1935–1972, at 9–10 (2016): "Most scholars associate the concept of welfare rights with the second half of the 1960s: with the broadening of the modern civil rights movement, the establishment of the War on Poverty's Legal Services Program, the flourishing of grassroots welfare rights organizations, and a series of bold pronouncements from the Supreme Court about the constitutional rights of poor citizens. . . . In fact, however, the idea of welfare as a right—and the related but distinct idea of welfare recipients as rights holders—has a longer history, one that both helps us understand why rights language appealed to poor Americans and their allies in the 1960s and why rights claims met such fierce resistance from other parts of the polity.

"This longer history has been obscured from view by a construct that continues to dominate our understanding of U.S. social welfare provision: the 'two-track welfare state.' Historically, national-level insurance-based programs—constituting what scholars call the upper track—have been more generous, better administered, and more secure. Old Age Insurance ('Social Security') is the classic example. Payments from these programs have generally been framed as earned rights or entitlements, and white men and their dependents have benefited disproportionately. 'Means-tested' programs, in contrast, such as Aid to Dependent Children (ADC) (now Temporary Aid to Needy Families), have historically been less generous and secure, more vulnerable to maladministration, and more stigmatizing. This lower track has disproportionately served women and racial minorities, and its benefits, according to the two-track account, are decidedly not rights. . . .

"Peering underneath the hood of this two-track welfare state, [this book] reveals that well before the War on Poverty or the modern welfare rights movement some government officials eagerly introduced rights concepts into the world of welfare. The Social Security Act, we tend to forget, was not just about Social Security; it also authorized matching grants to states for programs of need-based income support. These 'welfare' programs encompassed large categories of the poor: dependent (i.e., fatherless) children, the aged, and the blind. Desperate for funds and overwhelmed by their citizens' needs, nearly all states applied for grants—and thereby enabled the federal government to claim an ongoing role in the administration of a jealously guarded local function. . . . The task facing New Deal administrators was to reform and supplant what they self-servingly referred to as the 'old poor law,' a localized, nonuniform system of poor relief with very deep roots. Rights language appeared to be a useful tool for reaching uncomprehending and at times uncooperative state and local officials. The old poor law, federal administrators explained in speeches, guidance documents, and training sessions, understood relief as charity or a gratuity; that is why poor relief could at one time be administered by nonexperts, in a highly discretionary fashion, with little regard for the individual in need. The benefits of the new public assistance programs, in contrast, came to recipients as a matter of right, and therefore had to be administered in a more systematic and professional way, with due regard for the recipient's other rights—to fair and equal treatment, to autonomy in his or her spending choices, and to some degree of privacy."

## b. Legal Perspectives on the Administrative State over Time

(1) FELIX FRANKFURTER, THE TASK OF ADMINISTRATIVE LAW, 75 U. Pa. L. Rev. 614, 614–15 (1927): "The widening area of what in effect is law-making authority, exercised by officials whose actions are not subject to ordinary court review, constitutes perhaps the most striking contemporary tendency of the Anglo-American legal order. . . . The formulation and publication of executive orders and rules and regulations are in this country still in a primitive stage, which only serves to render more portentous the operation of these forms of law. But the range of control conferred by Congress and the State legislatures upon subsidiary law-making bodies, variously denominated as heads of departments, commissions and boards, penetrates in the United States, as in Great Britain and the Dominions, the whole gamut of human affairs. Hardly a measure passes Congress the effective execution of which is not conditioned upon rules and regulations emanating from the enforcing authorities. These administrative complements are euphemistically called 'filling in the details' of a policy set forth in statutes. But the 'details' are of the essence; they give meaning and content to vague contours. The control of banking, insurance, public utilities, finance, industry, the professions, health and morals, in sum, the manifold response of government to the forces and needs of modern society, is building up a body of laws not written by legislatures, and of adjudications not made by courts and not subject to their revision. These powers are lodged in a vast congeries of agencies. . . . A systematic scrutiny of these issues and a conscious effort towards their wise solution are the concerns of administrative law. The broad boundaries and far-reaching implications of these problems may be indicated by saying that administrative law deals with the field of legal control exercised by law-administering agencies other than courts, and the field of control exercised by courts over such agencies."

(2) JAMES M. LANDIS, THE ADMINISTRATIVE PROCESS 7, 30–31, 33–34, 46 (1938): "Two tendencies in the expanding civilization of the late nineteenth century seem to me to foreshadow the need for methods of government different in kind from those that had prevailed in the past. These are the rise of industrialism and the rise of democracy. . . . A world that scarcely a hundred years ago could listen to Wordsworth's denunciation of railroads because their building despoiled the beauty of his northern landscapes is different, very different, from one that in 1938 has to determine lanes and flight levels for air traffic. . . .

"[T]he reasons which prompted a resort to the administrative process . . . would seem to be reasonably clear. In large measure these reasons sprang from a distrust of the ability of the judicial process to make the necessary adjustments in the development of both law and regulatory methods as they related to particular industrial problems.

"Admittedly, the judicial process suffers from several basic and more or less unchangeable characteristics. One of these is its inability to maintain a longtime, uninterrupted interest in a relatively narrow and carefully defined area of economic and social activity. . . . A general jurisdiction leaves the resolution of an infinite variety of matters within the hands of courts. In the disposition of these claims judges are uninhibited in their discretion except for legislative rules of guidance or such other rules as they themselves may distill out of that vast reserve of materials that we call the common law. This breadth of jurisdiction and freedom of disposition tends somewhat to make judges jacks-of-all-trades and masters of none. . . .

"To these considerations must be added two others. The first is the recognition that there are certain fields where the making of law springs less from generalizations and principles drawn from the majestic authority of textbooks and cases, than from a 'practical' judgment which is based upon all the available considerations and which has in mind the most desirable and pragmatic method of solving that particular problem. . . . The second consideration is, perhaps, even more important. It is the fact that the common-law system left too much in the way of the enforcement of claims and interests to private initiative. . . .

"The administrative process is, in essence, our generation's answer to the inadequacy of the judicial and the legislative processes. It represents our effort to find an answer to those inadequacies by some other method than merely increasing executive power. If the doctrine of the separation of power implies division, it also implies balance, and balance calls for equality. The creation of administrative power may be the means for the preservation of that balance, so that paradoxically enough, though it may seem in theoretic violation of the doctrine of the separation of power, it may in matter of fact be the means for the preservation of the content of that doctrine."

(3) RICHARD B. STEWART, THE REFORMATION OF AMERICAN ADMINISTRATIVE LAW, 88 Harv. L. Rev. 1669, 1683–85, 1760–62 (1975): "Today, the exercise of agency discretion is inevitably seen as the essentially legislative process of adjusting the competing claims of various private interests affected by agency policy. The unravelling of the notion of an objective goal for administration is reflected in statements by judges and legal commentators that the 'public interest is a texture of multiple strands,' that it 'is not a monolith,' and 'involves a balance of many interests.' Courts have asserted that agencies must consider all of the various interests affected by their decisions as an essential predicate to 'balancing all elements essential to a just determination of the public interest.' . . .

"The sense of uneasiness aroused by this resurgence of discretion is heightened by perceived biases in the results of the agency balancing process as it is currently carried on. Critics have repeatedly asserted, with a dogmatic tone that reflects settled opinion, that in carrying out broad legislative directives, agencies unduly favor organized interests, especially the interests of regulated or client business firms and other organized groups at the expense of diffuse, comparatively unorganized interests such as consumers, environmentalists, and the poor. In the midst of a 'growing sense of disillusion with the role which regulatory agencies play,' many legislators, judges, and legal and economic commentators have accepted the thesis of persistent bias in agency policies. At its crudest, this thesis is based on the 'capture' scenario, in which administrations are systematically controlled, sometimes corruptly, by the business firms within their orbit of responsibility. . . .

"The expansion of the traditional model to afford participation rights in the process of agency decision and judicial review to a wide variety of affected interests must ultimately rest on the premise that such procedural changes will be an effective and workable means of assuring improved agency decisions. Advocates of extended access believe that an enlarged system of formal proceedings can, by securing adequate consideration of the interests of all affected persons, yield outcomes that better serve society as a whole. The credibility of this belief must now be considered.

"Although the courts have displayed caution in expanding and reworking administrative law doctrine to ensure the representation of all affected interests, the thrust of decisions over the past decade supports the assessment of the Court of Appeals for the District of Columbia Circuit that: 'In recent years, the concept that public participation in decisions which involve the public interest is not only valuable but indispensable has gained increasing support.' . . . Such participation, it is claimed, will not only improve the quality of agency decisions and make them more responsive to the needs of the various participating interests, but is valuable in itself because it gives citizens a sense of involvement in the process of government, and increases confidence in the fairness of government decisions. Indeed, litigation on behalf of widely-shared 'public' interests is explicitly defended as a substitute political process that enables the 'citizen to cast a different kind of vote, [which] informs the court that . . . a particular point of view is being ignored or underestimated' by the agency. Its ultimate aim is seen as 'a basic reordering of governmental institutions so that access and influence may be had by all.' . . .

"The time has come for a critical assessment of this prescription for asserted biases and inadequacies in agency decisions. The judges' incipient transformation of administrative law into a scheme of interest representation is responding to powerful needs that have been neglected by other branches of government. There are serious perceived inadequacies in agency performance, and this perception must be addressed if attitudes towards government are not to degenerate into cynicism or despair. Moreover, the realities of agency performance may often indeed be far short of what is desirable or even tolerable. But whether a judicially implemented system of interest representation is an adequate or workable response to these needs is a question deserving the most careful consideration."

(4) CHRISTOPHER F. EDLEY, JR., ADMINISTRATIVE LAW: RETHINKING JUDICIAL CONTROL OF BUREAUCRACY 4–7 (1990): "Historically, the separation of powers bulwarks were intended to minimize the risk of arbitrary government. Beginning in the late nineteenth century, however, and culminating with the Supreme Court's acquiescence in the New Deal's suggestion of administrative hegemony, courts and commentators increasingly recognized that a less rigid design was necessary to

accommodate modern exigencies. In response, a variety of modern judicial doctrines and attitudes developed. The elements of this new approach to constraining bureaucratic discretion were the regularization of administrative processes, the presumptive availability of judicial review, and judicial deference to administrative expertise—expertise being itself a rational and professional constraint against arbitrariness. These elements were eventually reflected in the Administrative Procedure Act of 1946 (APA). . . .

"The 'administrative' state is now inevitable because of the ever-lengthening agenda of complex public policy problems and the institutional limitations of legislatures. The broad delegations of power to those agencies—make the workplace 'reasonably' safe, assist the disabled who cannot engage in 'substantial gainful activity,' award licenses and allocate scarce resources in accordance with the 'public interest, convenience and necessity,' and similar formulas—create administrative discretion far more sweeping in scope and pervasiveness than the familiar and inherent ministerial discretion of the executive.

"As if to codify sweeping discretion, many statutes include a catchall delegation of substantive rule making authority to the agency, instructing the administrator to make any rules 'necessary' or 'appropriate' to accomplish the purposes of the statute. The sense that this discretion must be controlled continues to animate administrative law. As the bureaucracy's role has grown, so have the risks and benefits associated with official action. The stakes involved in judicial intervention to check malfeasance and misfeasance have also grown, so that familiar postures of judicial review now assume unfamiliar dimensions. In a way, discontent with judicial activism and the powerful social role of unelected judges is only a derivative problem, the principal one being awesome agency power.

"The Rule of Law approach to constraining discretion, which achieved maturity with the enactment of the APA, entails a strong role for subconstitutional judicial review. Such oversight by the unelected branch, however, is itself problematic in terms of those same values that cause us to fear official abuses in the first place. Thus, the continuing dilemma for administrative law has been that the effort to impose Rule of Law constraints on agencies must contend with the critique that judicial review simply replaces the *objectionable discretion of the administrator* with the *objectionable discretion of the judge*.

"There is a hopeful response to that critique. We have a continuing project of constructing and reforming a matrix of legal doctrines and attitudes intended to discipline the judges. That project reflects our powerful commitment to legal formality. If it is successful, the discipline judges themselves impose on administrators will not be simply another form of arbitrariness. But that is a rather large 'if.' "

(5) CYNTHIA R. FARINA, THE CONSENT OF THE GOVERNED: AGAINST SIMPLE RULES FOR A COMPLEX WORLD, 72 U. Chi.-Kent L. Rev. 987, 987–89 (1997): "The 1980s saw the emergence of a rich separation of powers jurisprudence that has been channeled, in this decade, into more focused attention on

strengthening the hand of the President. . . . The ideological sources drawn upon are diverse—original intent, civic republicanism, public choice theory—but the central argument is consistent: The President, and the President alone, represents the entire citizenry. The President, uniquely, is situated to infuse into regulatory policymaking the will of the whole people.

"I argue here that this latest effort at making peace between regulatory government and representative democracy is fatally flawed. Despite the ingenuity and intensity with which strong presidentialism is advanced, it is premised upon a fundamentally untenable conception of the consent of the governed. The 'will of the people,' as invoked in that effort, is artificially bounded in time, homogenized, shorn of ambiguities—in short, fabricated. It obscures complex problems (recognized elsewhere in administrative law scholarship) of information, prediction, and risk perception. It slides over vexed questions (recognized elsewhere in scholarly literature about democracy) of when leaders should lead rather than follow and of how the act of governing becomes a process in which the collective will is formed, rather than merely implemented.

"My counter-proposition is a broad, and perhaps uncomfortably indeterminate one: No single mode of democratic legitimation can serve to mediate between the conflicted, protean, often inchoate will of the people and the modern regulatory enterprise. No single institution or practice is capable of performing the multiple tasks of registering, interpreting, educating, adapting, affording participation, facilitating deliberation, brokering accommodation, and umpiring conflict that are (or at least ought to be) entailed in shaping the public policy of a post-industrialized democracy with an activist regulatory government. There are no simple rules for this complex world. Rather, we must necessarily look to a plurality of institutions and practices as contributors to an ongoing process of legitimizing the regulatory state. Each of those institutions and practices will be partial and, of itself, insufficient. Each imposes its own kind of costs on the regulatory process. Each is capable, if overemphasized, of introducing its own kind of distortion.

"In sum, I am suggesting that the reconciliatory effort must abandon its yearning for a neat solution to the legitimacy problem and, instead, come to terms with 'the ugliness of democracy.' "

(6) PHILIP HAMBURGER, IS ADMINISTRATIVE LAW UNLAWFUL? 3–5 (2014): "Traditionally, under the U.S. Constitution, the government could bind its subjects only through its legislative and judicial powers. And because the Constitution granted these powers, respectively, to Congress and the courts, only the acts of these institutions could impose legally obligatory constraints on persons who were subject to the laws. In contrast, the executive's acts could not create this binding effect. Although the executive could implement the confining obligation of acts of Congress or the courts, it itself could not bind, but at most could impose force, whether by bringing matters to the courts or, ultimately, by physically carrying out their binding acts. Lawful executive power thus was very different from the two types of binding power authorized by the Constitution, and when the executive makes binding edicts and thereby strays into legislative and judicial power, it is exercising what, from a historical perspective, this book understands as administrative law.

"What exactly were the binding acts that the executive traditionally could not adopt? The secretary of the treasury, for example, could authorize the distribution of government largess, and could make regulations that instructed treasury officers, but he could not promulgate regulations altering tax rates. Although the Post Office could refuse a request to mail a letter, it could not issue regulations requiring subjects to avoid private carriers; and although the Interior Department could deny access to confidential government information, it could not issue an order compelling a business to supply information.

"Of course, the executive decisions granting or denying government money, services, information, and other benefits were very important. Yet they could be executive decisions precisely because they did not bind Americans.

"Nowadays, however, the executive enjoys binding legislative and judicial power. First, its agencies make legislative rules dictating what Americans can grow, manufacture, transport, smoke, eat, and drink. Second, the agencies make binding adjudications—initially demanding information about violations of the rules, and then reaching conclusions about guilt and imposing fines. Only then, third, does the executive exercise its own power—that of coercion—to enforce its legislation and adjudication. . . .

"And this points to the danger. The power to bind is a power to constrain liberty. Although only Congress and the courts have the power to bind and thereby confine liberty, this is exactly what executive and other administrative bodies claim to do through administrative law."

(7) GILLIAN E. METZGER, FOREWORD: 1930S REDUX: THE ADMINISTRATIVE STATE UNDER SIEGE, 131 Harv. L. Rev. 1, 7 (2017): "Anti-administrativists paint the administrative state as fundamentally at odds with the Constitution's separation of powers system, combining together in agencies the legislative, executive, and judicial authorities that the Constitution vests in different branches and producing unaccountable and aggrandized power in the process. In fact, however, the administrative state is essential for actualizing constitutional separation of powers today, serving both to constrain executive power and to mitigate the dangers of presidential unilateralism while also enabling effective governance. Far from being constitutionally suspect, the administrative state thus yields important constitutional benefits. Anti-administrativists fail to recognize that the key administrative state features that they condemn, such as bureaucracy with its internal oversight mechanisms and expert civil service, are essential for the accountable, constrained, and effective exercise of executive power.

"Even further, the administrative state today is constitutionally obligatory, given the broad delegations of authority to the executive branch that represent the central reality of contemporary national government. Those delegations are necessary given the economic, social, scientific, and technological realities of our day. Not surprisingly, therefore, very few anti-administrativists are willing to call such delegation of power into serious constitutional question. But they fail to realize that delegation comes with substantial constitutional strings attached. In particular, many of the administrative state's features that anti-administrativists decry follow as necessary consequences of delegation.

"By refusing to recognize the administrative state's essential place in our constitutional order, contemporary anti-administrativism forestalls development of a separation of powers analysis better tailored to the reality of current government. Rather than laying siege to the administrative state, such an analysis would seek to maximize the constitutional benefits that the administrative state has to offer. And it would reorient constitutional analysis to considering not just constitutional constraints on government but also constitutional obligations to govern."

## c. Contemporary Perspectives on the Administrative State

(1) ELENA KAGAN, PRESIDENTIAL ADMINISTRATION, 114 Harv. L. Rev. 2245, 2246–49 (2001): "The history of the American administrative state is the history of competition among different entities for control of its policies. All three branches of government—the President, Congress, and Judiciary—have participated in this competition; so too have the external constituencies and internal staff of the agencies. Because of the stakes of the contest and the strength of the claims and weapons possessed by the contestants, no single entity has emerged finally triumphant, or is ever likely to do so. But at different times, one or another has come to the fore and asserted at least a comparative primacy in setting the direction and influencing the outcome of administrative process. In this time, that institution is the Presidency. We live today in an era of presidential administration. . . .

"For administrative law scholars, the claim of presidential administration may seem puzzling. . . . These scholars—concerned as they are with the actual practices of administrative control, as carried out in executive branch as well as independent agencies—may well have viewed the claim as arguable, though perhaps premature, if made ten or fifteen years ago, when President Reagan or Bush was in office. In the first month of his tenure, Reagan issued an executive order creating a mechanism by which the Office of Management and Budget (OMB), an entity within the Executive Office of the President (EOP), would review all major regulations of executive branch agencies. As Reagan's and then Bush's terms proceeded, and the antiregulatory effects of this system of review became increasingly evident, administrative law scholars took part in a sharp debate about its propriety. With the advent of the Clinton Administration, however, this debate receded. Although President Clinton issued his own executive order providing for OMB review of regulations, the terms of this order struck most observers as moderating the aggressive approach to oversight of administration taken in the Reagan and Bush Presidencies. Perhaps as important, the Clinton OMB chose to implement the order in a way generally sympathetic to regulatory efforts. Because objections to OMB review in the Reagan and Bush era arose in large part from its deregulatory tendencies, this reversal of substantive direction contributed to the waning of interest in, and even recognition of, the involvement of the President and his EOP staff in administration.

"In fact, as this Article will show, presidential control of administration, in critical respects, expanded dramatically during the Clinton years, making the regulatory activity of the executive branch agencies more and more an extension of the President's own policy and political agenda. Faced for most of his time in office with a hostile Congress but eager to show progress on domestic issues, Clinton and his White House staff turned to the bureaucracy to achieve, to the extent it could, the full panoply of his domestic policy goals. Whether the subject was health care, welfare reform, tobacco, or guns, a self-conscious and central object of the White House was to devise, direct, and/or finally announce administrative actions—regulations, guidance, enforcement strategies, and reports—to showcase and advance presidential policies. In executing this strategy, the White House in large measure set the administrative agenda for key agencies, heavily influencing what they would (or would not) spend time on and what they would (or would not) generate as regulatory product.

"The resulting policy orientation diverged substantially from that of the Reagan and Bush years, disproving the assumption some scholars have made, primarily on the basis of that earlier experience, that presidential supervision of administration inherently cuts in a deregulatory direction. Where once presidential supervision had worked to dilute or delay regulatory initiatives, it served in the Clinton years as part of a distinctly activist and pro-regulatory governing agenda. Where once presidential supervision had tended to favor politically conservative positions, it generally operated during the Clinton Presidency as a mechanism to achieve progressive goals. Or expressed in the terms most sympathetic to all these Presidents (and therefore most contestable), if Reagan and Bush showed that presidential supervision could thwart regulators intent on regulating no matter what the cost, Clinton showed that presidential supervision could jolt into action bureaucrats suffering from bureaucratic inertia in the face of unmet needs and challenges."

(2) JODY FREEMAN & MARTHA MINOW, REFRAMING THE OUTSOURCING DEBATES IN GOVERNMENT BY CONTRACT 7–9, 15, 20 (Jody Freeman & Martha Minow eds., 2009): "Government in the nineteenth and twentieth centuries did purchase goods—including armaments—from private companies. In areas like human services, local governments also regularly arranged contracts to provide counseling, foster care, and sanitation. But toward the end of the twentieth century and the start of the twenty-first, federal and state governments have relied heavily on ongoing contracts with private providers for a much broader range of government functions, making contract the primary mechanism of government action, and arguably government's most important means of control over the provision of public services. This development makes the contracting process—from negotiation to oversight to remedies for breach—a key accountability mechanism in modern government. It also exposes the critical need for capacity *within* the government to develop and monitor such contracts. In this sense, outsourcing does not lessen government's burden; it changes it and may even increase it.

"Present-day outsourcing cannot be understood, however, without locating it as a reaction to an intervening period—beginning with the Progressive Era and lasting through the New Deal. After the Great Depression, widespread disillusionment with the private sector led to popular support for entrusting public institutions with greater responsibilities, and the government grew dramatically. By the late 1970s, however, the pendulum had swung in the other direction: there was newfound enthusiasm for private markets and competitive practices. . . .

"This account suggests how far contemporary expectations of government have evolved since the Progressive Era and the New Deal. In the United States today, government is just one among alternative forms of organization. Private for-profit, private not-for-profit, and hybrid state-sponsored enterprises each deliver services to the public. The government is not indispensable—even for functions we might think of as 'inherently governmental.' There is also a perceptible and relatively new understanding of the citizen as customer: someone who pays taxes and expects value in return, and who cares less about the identity of the provider than about the timely and affordable provision of the good or service. It is hard to know whether this shift in public attitudes helped fuel the demand for smaller government and more outsourcing, or vice versa. Likely it is both. . . .

"With contractual governance here to stay, the real question is not whether to outsource at all, but to what ends, using which strategies, and under what constraints. New energy must be devoted to determining which essential functions must remain not only formally directed by the government in theory, but actually performed by the government in fact. The 'inherently governmental' designation used for this purpose for over half a century has proven woefully inadequate, both conceptually and in practice. . . .

"Our current government contracting system does not work. It is largely invisible and unresponsive to the public in whose name it is undertaken. The existing rules and procedures fail to guard adequately against inefficiency, conflict of interest, and abuse. And much of the power being exercised through contracting is largely unaccountable to *any* regime of oversight—market, legal, or political. Yet government by contract has arrived, and it is here to stay. This fact should prompt serious and sustained public dialogue about the short- and long-term implications of outsourcing for American democracy."

(3) DANIEL A. FARBER & ANNE JOSEPH O'CONNELL, THE LOST WORLD OF ADMINISTRATIVE LAW, 92 Tex. L. Rev. 1137, 1137, 1188–89 (2014): "The reality of the modern administrative state diverges considerably from the series of assumptions underlying the Administrative Procedure Act (APA) and classic judicial decisions that followed the APA reviewing agency actions. Those assumptions call for statutory directives to be implemented by one agency led by Senate-confirmed presidential appointees with decision-making authority. The implementation (in the form of a discrete action) is presumed to be through statutorily mandated procedures and criteria, with judicial review to determine whether the reasons given by the agency at the time of its action match the delegated directions. This is the lost world of

administrative law, though it is what students largely still learn. Today, there are often statutory and executive directives to be implemented by multiple agencies often missing confirmed leaders, where ultimate decision-making authority may rest outside of those agencies. The process of implementation is also through mandates in both statutes and executive orders, where the final result faces limited, if any, oversight by the courts. . . .

"The lost world of the APA and administrative law and the real world of modern administrative practice do share the same overall focus: the exercise of discretion. The cleavages, some rather deep, turn on the sources, the wielders, and the reviewers of that discretion.

"Almost forty years ago, Richard Stewart posited that interest groups might become the basis of a 'fully-articulated model' of administrative discretion. In his view, if a wide range of interests could be captured in the administrative state, 'policy choices would presumably reflect an appropriate consideration of all affected interests and the pluralist solution to the problem of agency discretion might prove both workable and convincing.' Today, pluralism or some wider form of democratic legitimacy is just one goal of not only administrative law but administrative practice as well. These goals include agency efficiency and effectiveness, democratic legitimacy, and the rule of law. With such complex ends, it should not be surprising that the sources, exercise, and review of discretion are not simple, either as a descriptive or as a normative matter. We not only need to acknowledge the increasingly fictional yet deeply engrained account of administrative law, but also need to think seriously about how that account can better reflect current practices while still retaining its tractability and original objectives."

(4) JESSICA BULMAN-POZEN, EXECUTIVE FEDERALISM COMES TO AMERICA, 102 Va. L. Rev. 953, 954–56 (2016): "Executive federalism—'processes of intergovernmental negotiation that are dominated by the executives of the different governments within the federal system'—is pervasive in parliamentary federations, such as Canada, Australia, and the European Union. Given the American separation of powers arrangement, executive federalism has been thought absent, even 'impossible,' in the United States. But the partisan dynamics that have gridlocked Congress and empowered both federal and state executives have generated a distinctive American variant.

"Viewing American law and politics through the lens of executive federalism brings four key features into focus. First, executives have become dominant actors at both the state and federal levels. They formulate policy and manage intergovernmental relations. Although executive negotiations have shaped American federalism at least since the New Deal, Congress once superintended them. Today, from healthcare to marijuana to climate change, federal and state executives negotiate without Congress. Second, there is a substantial degree of mutuality among these executives, much more than is suggested by the federal government's legal supremacy. Federal and state actors turn to state law as well as federal law to further their agendas; sometimes this amplifies conflict, but it also enables officials to find paths to compromise. Third, national policy frequently comes to look different across the states as a result of executive negotiations. Some states more strongly press a position shared by the federal executive, while others offer competing views. Finally, horizontal relationships among the states are critical in setting national policy, as the federal executive builds on interstate agreements and reshapes them in turn. . . .

"The practice enhances the federal executive's capacity to act amid congressional dysfunction, but so too does it entail the multiplicity and pushback endemic to state-federal relations. Perhaps most notably, it facilitates a form of governance suited to polarization: state-differentiated national policy. . . . Executive federalism also offers a needed forum for bipartisan compromise. Rather than require a grand deal that satisfies an aggregate national body, executive federalism unfolds through many negotiations among disaggregated political actors. These discrete conversations facilitate intraparty difference at the same time as the process of implementation further complicates, and may attenuate, partisan commitments. . . .

"Any approach to national policymaking that leaves Congress on the sidelines has a clear strike against it as a matter of democratic representation, and the deficiencies of executive federalism in this respect are apparent. Yet, as recent work in political theory shows, representation is a more complicated process than the law's standard delegate models suggest. . . . If executive federalism is a potentially valuable practice, so too is it vulnerable. Challenges raising a host of doctrinal objections are already flooding the courts, and more can be expected."

(5) CRISTINA ISABEL CEBALLOS, DAVID FREEMAN ENGSTROM, & DANIEL E. HO, DISPARATE LIMBO: HOW ADMINISTRATIVE LAW ERASED ANTIDISCRIMINATION, 131 Yale L.J. 370, 374–76, 460–61 (2021): "If you are a local broadcaster and a new broadcasting policy will force you to buy expensive 'bleeping' equipment you cannot afford, you can ask the courts to protect you from the differential impacts of the federal agency's policy. If you are a kayaker in a federally-managed recreation area, and the agency's new management plan will introduce noisy and disruptive jetboaters, you can ask the courts to reconsider the plan's impacts on your subgroup of 'non-motorized' watercraft users. And if you are a Hawaiian dolphin in a small pod, rather than a large pod, you can rest assured that the courts will consider harms from sonar to your subpopulation, rather than lumping you in with all the other dolphin pods. In cases like these, courts will entertain claims under the Administrative Procedure Act (APA) by subgroups that were potentially negatively impacted by an agency's facially neutral rule or policy.

"Not so if you are a member of a racial, ethnic, or gender group. . . .

"How did we get here? How did we arrive at a place where the APA will consider claims from subgroups like kayakers and small dolphin pods, but not subgroups like Black farmers or Latinx schoolchildren? The answer requires a deep excavation of the history of the Civil Rights Act of 1964 and judicial interpretation of the relationship between civil rights and the APA, particularly § 704's ouster of claims when there is already an 'adequate remedy.' . . .

"If correct, our origin story can explain how the erasure of race constructed modern administrative law. Doctrinal developments that sit at the field's core—most notably the emergence of 'hard look' review and a more intrusive judicial role in administrative governance—may only have been feasible because courts excised differential impact by race from administrative law's domain. And this erasure allowed courts to harden their review, while simultaneously steering clear of increasingly divisive civil rights questions that imperiled courts' growing institutional power and their efforts to cabin and contain the modern administrative state. Our account thus places race—and the scrubbing of antidiscrimination from the APA—at the center of the construction of modern administrative law's empire. . . .

"Core to our argument is a bracing conjecture: modern administrative law's empire—the steady judicialization of agency action from the 1960s onwards—may have been constructed by erasing race. More specifically, had administrative law not erased race, and if arbitrary-and-capricious review had applied equally to questions of differential racial impact, courts might have re-evaluated the virtues of a more muscular approach to judicial review of agency action."

## SECTION 5. TEACHING AND STUDYING ADMINISTRATIVE LAW FROM THIS CASEBOOK

Administrative law is a big subject, and this is a big book. It would take a very big course of many semester hours to cover everything contained in the following chapters. None of your editors has ever taught so extensive a course. We expect our users to be selective among the topics addressed, as we are. We have edited the casebook to facilitate this selectivity. Some instructors will use it for a first-year introductory course to legislation and regulation. Others will use it for a more traditional, basic administrative law course in law schools that do not offer an introductory "leg-reg" class. And some will turn to it for an advanced administrative law class.

We have also edited this casebook to allow different users to take up its topics in varying sequences. Many administrative law topics are interrelated to a degree you may not have encountered in other courses. "What are the standards to be applied on judicial review?" interacts with "When is judicial review available?" and with "What agency procedures are required in developing agency rules?" It is unreasonable to attempt to present the issues all at once, and different instructors will select the most appropriate path through them. We have tried to edit the materials of this casebook to focus on the particular questions at hand, but also, in various ways, to signal or briefly anticipate the related issues you may not yet have dealt with in detail. By the end of the course, we trust the interrelationships will emerge, and your review of the course will bring fresh understanding of your course's earliest topics.

In sum, we have tried to treat most topics in this casebook thoroughly and with intellectual rigor. We have done so in the belief that what is not directly covered in your course might still prove helpful to you in gaining fuller understanding of what *is* covered and in the hope that, after you have finished your course, our casebook will remain useful as a reference.

PART 2

# UNDERSTANDING STATUTES

II. STATUTORY INTERPRETATION

# CHAPTER II

# STATUTORY INTERPRETATION

| | |
|---|---|
| *Sec. 1.* | ***How Statutes Are Made*** |
| *Sec. 2.* | ***Theories of Statutory Interpretation*** |
| *Sec. 3.* | ***Tools of Statutory Interpretation*** |

Federal agencies are, first and foremost, creatures of congressional statutes. Their powers and procedures are defined both by the statutes that create them, and pertain especially to them, and by other statutes that generally regulate their behavior, such as the Administrative Procedure Act. Statutory interpretation, then, is the bread and butter task of lawyers who work within the agencies or who represent clients that interact with and are affected by agencies, and of courts that resolve disputes over what agencies have done or may do. Indeed, because, as the scholar William Eskridge has put it, we live in a republic of statutes, statutory interpretation is central to all law practice today. And, as you may know, it is the subject of considerable dispute among lawyers and judges. For this reason, it is critical to understand not just the details of the particular statutes that govern federal agencies and that those agencies administer and enforce. It is also critical to understand how one goes about interpreting those statutes. And to understand that, one must understand how to interpret statutes generally—an endeavor known as statutory interpretation. The materials of this Chapter address statutory interpretation generally, leaving to Chapter VIII the special considerations that may arise when agencies themselves interpret statutes and when courts encounter statutory interpretations that agencies advance.

## SECTION 1. HOW STATUTES ARE MADE[1]

| | |
|---|---|
| *a.* | ***The Legislative Process*** |
| *b.* | ***Other Participants in the Legislative Process*** |

To understand how to interpret the federal statutes that govern federal administrative agencies, it is important first to understand the process for enacting federal statutes generally. That process is complex—at times, byzantine. It is the product of many detailed rules. The

[1] Much of the information in this Section is drawn from Chapters 15 and 16 of CQ PRESS, GUIDE TO CONGRESS (2008). Another brief summary appears in the opening pages of Robert Katzmann, Interpreting Statutes (2015)—a short, thorough, and balanced exploration of contemporary issues of statutory interpretation written by the late Chief Judge of the United States Court of Appeals for the Second Circuit.

Constitution mandates some of them. The House and Senate establish the rest.

These rules govern every step of the legislative process, from the introduction of a bill to its enactment into law. Along the way, at least if the usual rules are followed (which by no means always happens), hearings are held, reports are produced, bills are proposed, floor debates take place, amendments are proposed, and, after bills are passed by each chamber, differing versions are reconciled until a final bill is sent to the President to be either signed into law or vetoed. And, if the latter occurs, the chambers may vote again to override the veto and thereby enact the bill into law.

While you read the following material, think about why the American legislative process is so complicated. What do we gain from making it difficult to turn a bill into law? What are the downsides of this complicated process? Consider also how the process might affect statutory interpretation. What should we make of the dozens of reports and other congressional and executive statements that may be generated by a bill? What do we make of the fact that actors other than Senators and Representatives play key roles in the process of creating legislative text? Does the fact that some legislation is not actually drafted by elected officials or their aides change how you view the text of a statute? Does knowledge of the process change how we should read the text or understand the purpose of a statute? In particular, does the fact that this process is so complex suggest that judges should view themselves as partners in trying to ensure the legislation at issue results in sensible outcomes? Or does that fact instead indicate that judges should interpret statutes in a manner most likely to require drafters to be precise going forward?

## a. The Legislative Process

Article I, Section 7 of the Constitution sets out the basic legislative process:

> Every bill which shall have passed the House of Representatives and the Senate, shall, before it become a law, be presented to the President of the United States; if he approve he shall sign it, but if not he shall return it, with his objections to that House in which it shall have originated . . . .
>
> Every order, resolution, or vote to which the concurrence of the Senate and House of Representatives may be necessary (except on a question of adjournment) shall be presented to the President of the United States; and before the same shall take effect, shall be approved by him, or being disapproved by him, shall be repassed by two thirds of the Senate and House of Representatives, according to the rules and limitations prescribed in the case of a bill.

U.S. Const. Art. I, § 7, cls. 2–3. A bill, then, must reach the end of a daunting path in order to be enacted. It must first be passed by each chamber of Congress, the United States' bicameral legislature: the House and the Senate. Next, the bill is presented to the President. The President may either sign the bill, turning it into law, or veto the bill. If vetoed, Congress can override the President by a two-thirds supermajority in each chamber.

Although Section 7 of Article I articulates a broad outline of the legislative process, notice how little it says about congressional structure and process; the congressional committees, for example, are nowhere mentioned. Just as the Constitution leaves it to Congress to create the American government by statute, Article I, § 5, cl. 2 leaves it to each chamber to "determine the rules of its proceedings." The total body of congressional procedures and rules is vast, and it governs the legislative process's nuts-and-bolts: introduction of a bill and referral to committee, amendment and debate during committee consideration, debate on the floor of the chambers, or reconciliation between competing versions of a bill passed by the two chambers. Even a glance at some of the more important rules highlights just how involved the legislative process really is.

For a bill to go anywhere, it must first be introduced. A bill may be introduced by any member of either chamber and may have one or more "sponsors." Many bills are not actually drafted by elected legislators; much actual drafting occurs in professional offices maintained by each chamber, and members of Congress also can introduce bills written by lobbyists, special interest groups, or the White House. Once introduced, a bill is referred to a congressional committee for further consideration. Each chamber has its own committees, and each committee—such as Armed Services, Commerce, or Foreign Relations (among many, many others)—has jurisdiction over a discrete subject matter. Sometimes it is obvious which committee has jurisdiction. More often, a bill could justifiably be considered by a number of committees. The final referral decision rests with the leadership of each chamber—the Senate Majority Leader or the Speaker of the House.

Once a bill has been referred to a committee, that committee takes control and begins to consider the bill. Usually, the bill will be referred to a specialized subcommittee for initial consideration. While in subcommittee or, later, the full committee, a bill may be rewritten, amended, rejected, or reported to the full chamber for consideration. Typically, one of the first steps taken is to conduct hearings. These hearings, the transcripts of which may or may not be published, are used to take testimony from experts and interested parties (and sometimes even other legislators) and gather evidence about the bill. Hearings are followed by "mark-up" sessions, where the bill is revised, amended, and prepared to be sent from subcommittee to committee, or from the full committee to the chamber. The last step in committee is the final committee vote. If approved, the committee reports the bill to the chamber, and a detailed House or Senate report describing the bill and some of the committee's deliberations accompanies the bill. Minority views are often attached.

Next, a bill must be scheduled for floor consideration. The majority party in each chamber handles the scheduling for such consideration in that chamber. It may be days or weeks before a bill is actually sent to the floor. (Notably, the House and Senate have very different procedures for scheduling, as well as for floor discussion, bill amendments, and voting.) In the House, these matters are tightly controlled by a unique committee, the Rules Committee, that sets their terms. In the less numerous Senate, debate is not controlled in this way, and that opens the possibility that opponents will "filibuster"—that is, engage in continuous debate that can be ended only by a supermajority vote.

After a bill makes it to the floor and passes in the chamber in which it was introduced, the bill is sent to the other chamber, where—again—the process begins with referral to committee. Even if a bill then emerges from committee for floor consideration, the committee will often have modified the bill, or modification may happen in debate. And to become law, both chambers must agree on identical language.

Once adopted by the second chamber, if the bill does vary from the initial bill that passed the first, it will be returned to that chamber, where the simplest outcome is for the first chamber to accept the bill in the form the second has adopted. But if this does not happen, in order to reconcile the two versions of the bill and to send a unified bill to the President, each chamber designates members for a "conference committee" with the responsibility of creating a unified bill. The conference committee is made up of members of both the House and the Senate, and the conferees debate the two competing versions of the bill and make revisions until a majority of the conference committee reach an agreement on a revised bill. This revised version is then sent to each chamber for final approval with a conference report describing the bill and any compromises that have been made.

The legislative process has been complicated further by an increase in the use of "omnibus" bills since the 1970s. Omnibus bills are massive pieces of legislation combining many smaller bills. Often, these smaller bills are drafted by different committees (sometimes without any contact among the various committees) and then joined together before moving to the floor. These omnibus bills may contain provisions that—on their own—would attract far greater attention. For example, an omnibus appropriations bill contained a provision that quietly rolled back a provision of the Dodd-Frank financial reform legislation. See Abbe Gluck, Anne Joseph O'Connell, & Rosa Po, Unorthodox Lawmaking, Unorthodox Rulemaking, 115 Colum. L. Rev. 1789, 1805 (2015).

One particularly common type of omnibus legislation, the budget reconciliation bill, involves a unique and complex process. Each year, when adopting its annual budget resolution, Congress has the option of including "reconciliation instructions." These instructions trigger reconciliation procedures that allow Congress to more quickly craft and approve budget legislation. For instance, reconciliation limits the number and type of amendments that may be added to the budget legislation, restricts floor debate in the Senate to twenty hours, and prohibits filibustering the legislation. See Megan S. Lynch & James V. Saturno, Cong. Rsch. Serv., R44058, The Budget Reconciliation Process: Stages of Consideration 6–9 (Jan. 25, 2021). The use of the reconciliation process often courts controversy. In a high-profile recent example, in 2010, some key portions of the Affordable Care Act were enacted through budget reconciliation. See Abbe R. Gluck, Imperfect Statutes, Imperfect Courts: Understanding Congress's Plan in the Era of Unorthodox Lawmaking, 129 Harv. L. Rev. 62, 69–70, 78–79 (2015).

But even aside from omnibus bills, there are all kinds of exceptions to the standard process for passing a bill out of the House and the Senate. A recent study found, for example, that "in the first year of the 112th Congress, fewer than 10% of enacted laws proceeded through the 'textbook' legislative process (first passing through committees on each side, then moving to debate and vote in each chamber, followed by conference between the chambers, and concluding with a final vote by both chambers before passage). More than 40% of enacted statutes did not go through the committee process in either chamber, but proceeded directly from the floor or were shepherded through by party leadership or the White House." Gluck, O'Connell, & Po, supra, at 1800. And it appears this trend is on an upward trajectory. Id.

Once a bill passes out of the House and Senate (whether in textbook fashion or not), it goes to the President. If the President signs a bill, it becomes law. If the President vetoes a bill, it becomes law only if Congress can override the President's veto with a two-thirds majority of each chamber.

Sometimes, upon signing a bill, the President issues a signing statement. Such statements may do nothing more than sing the praises of the legislation. They may also offer the President's view of the purpose of the legislation. In some instances, the statement may offer an interpretive gloss on key provisions of the law. In still others, the statement may even announce the President's view that a particular provision is unconstitutional. See Symposium: The Last Word? The Constitutional Implications of Presidential Signing Statements, 16 Wm. & Mary Bill Rts. J. 1 (2007); Curtis A. Bradley & Eric A. Posner, Presidential Signing Statements and Executive Power, 23 Const. Comment. 307, 312 (2006).

## b. Other Participants in the Legislative Process

Although not often considered when discussing statutory interpretation, many institutional actors besides Congress and the President routinely interact with fledgling laws and play a significant role in the legislative process. One of the most important of these actors is the nonpartisan Congressional Budget Office. The CBO produces "formal cost estimate[s] for nearly every bill that is approved by a full committee of either the House or the Senate." Cong. Budget Office, Processes, https://www.cbo.gov/about/processes. These cost estimates, or "CBO scores," have a powerful influence on legislators—as well as on the ability of a bill to make it out of committee and survive a full-chamber vote—and legislators often draft bills with the CBO score firmly in mind. Indeed, given the importance of CBO calculations, some scholars have gone so far as to propose that courts adopt a new principle of interpretation: construe statutes consistently with their CBO scores. See Lisa Schultz Bressman & Abbe R. Gluck, Statutory Interpretation from the Inside—An Empirical Study of Congressional Drafting, Delegation, and the Canons: Part II, 66 Stan. L. Rev. 725, 782 (2014). In their view, this principle "could help courts reflect congressional expectations in resolving disputes that implicate the score." Id.

Other budgetary and oversight entities are also heavily involved in the legislative process. For example, the Government Accountability Office prepares reports on the desirability of enacting a bill into law, usually at the request of a committee. And the Office of Management and Budget, an executive agency, reviews legislation that agencies wish to propose to Congress to ensure that the legislation is consistent with the President's priorities. In addition, OMB makes sure that agencies have a chance to comment on a bill before the President signs it.

Perhaps most crucial to the day-to-day work of the House and Senate are the Offices of Legislative Counsel. These offices provide nonpartisan, confidential legislative drafting services to the two chambers. They assist legislators in drafting new bills, amending bills during committee or conference, and preparing motions to use on the floor of the House or Senate. See Office of the Legislative Counsel, U.S. House of Representatives, Our Services, https://legcounsel.house.gov/about/our-services. A recent survey of legislative staffers revealed that much—maybe even a majority—of legislative drafting is done by these two offices. According to the survey, the staffers give Legislative Counsel "rough outlines of statutory text, which Legislative Counsel then turns into legislative language." Bressman & Gluck, supra, at 740. The results of the survey suggest that there may often be a real disconnect, then, between legislators (and their staffers) and the statutory text. Id.

Finally, consider the Office of the Law Revision Counsel, charged with keeping the U.S. Code—the body of "codified" law to which courts often refer in interpreting statutes. After Congress passes a statute, OLRC edits and reorganizes its provisions. OLRC then presents its work to Congress in "codification bills," which Congress then approves. Congress has directed OLRC to try to discern the intended meaning of its words in this interpretive endeavor. See Jesse M. Cross & Abbe R. Gluck, The Congressional Bureaucracy, 168 U. Pa. L. Rev. 1541, 1653, 1681–82 (2020). Is law enacted this way an expression of congressional purpose? Or does the requirement for ultimate enactment by Congress express something about the unique value of statutory text?

## SECTION 2. THEORIES OF STATUTORY INTERPRETATION



Once a bill becomes law, questions inevitably arise about how the resulting statute should be interpreted. Here is a problem to spark your appreciation of the kinds of issues that can arise:

### The Case of the Negligently Placed Mail

**Here's the statutory pattern:**

(a) Under the Postal Reorganization Act, the Federal Tort Claims Act "shall apply to tort claims arising out of the activities of the Postal Service."

(b) A sovereign like the United States is immune from suit in its own courts unless it waives "sovereign immunity." The FTCA provides that the United States waives sovereign immunity, and confers jurisdiction on the federal courts, for

> claims against the United States, for money damages, accruing on and after January 1, 1945, for injury or loss of property, or personal injury or death caused by the negligent or wrongful act or omission of any employee of the Government while acting within the scope of his office or employment, under circumstances where the United States, if a private person, would be liable to the claimant in accordance with the law of the place where the act or omission occurred.

As to these claims, the FTCA provides:

> The United States shall be liable . . . in the same manner and to the same extent as a private individual under like circumstances, but shall not be liable for interest prior to judgment or for punitive damages.

However,

> The provisions of this [waiver] shall not apply to—[thirteen items including] . . .
>
> Any claim arising out of the loss, miscarriage, or negligent transmission of letters or postal matter.

**Here are the facts:**

A plaintiff has brought suit under the FTCA against the Postal Service. According to her complaint, she was injured when she tripped on a package that was placed by a postman on her steps where she would not see it. The Postal Service concedes that the postman's actions were negligent, which would create tort liability for a private party under state law. It nonetheless moves to dismiss the suit on the ground that the claim does not arise out of the "transmission" of postal matter. On this theory, the United States has not waived its sovereign immunity in the FTCA for this case, rendering the court without jurisdiction to hear the case. The United States' case thus hinges on whether its proposed interpretation of the word "transmission" is correct in the portion of the provision of the FTCA waiving sovereign immunity that specifies when that waiver of immunity shall not apply.

Does the Postal Service prevail in its motion? Why? How sure are you of the result?

**And here are some additional points:**

Are the following points, individually or cumulatively, relevant to deciding the case? Do they, individually or cumulatively, change your mind one way or the other as to the outcome, or as to the certainty with which you espouse it?

(a) In an earlier case, the Supreme Court had ruled that the postal service was not immune—that is, sovereign immunity had been waived by the FTCA—in regard to the negligent handling of postal motor vehicles.

(b) A dictionary defines "transmission" as "an act, process, or instance of transmitting" and "transmit" as "to cause to go or be conveyed to another person or place."

(c) The other items on the FTCA's list of thirteen sovereign immunity "shall not apply" situations include "any claim arising from the activities of the Tennessee Valley Authority," "any claim arising out of the combatant activities of the military forces during time of war," and "any claim arising in a foreign country."

(d) Each day the Postal Service delivers 660 million pieces of mail to 142 million delivery points.

(e) At a hearing held before a Senate subcommittee considering the FTCA, a Special Assistant to the Attorney General had testified: "Every person who sends a piece of postal matter can protect himself by registering it, as provided by the postal laws and regulations. It would be intolerable, of course, if in any case of loss or delay the Government could be sued for damages. Consequently, this provision was inserted."

Problem over. If you want to see what judges have said, you can look at Raila v. United States, 355 F.3d 118 (2d Cir. 2004) (cause of action survived); Dolan v. United States Postal Service, 377 F.3d 285 (3d Cir. 2004) (cause of action dismissed); Dolan v. United States Postal Service,

546 U.S. 481 (2006) (cause of action revived). For commentary, see Robert Katzmann, Judging Statutes 58 (2014).

Various theories of statutory interpretation have developed over time to structure thinking about how to resolve problems like this. Should the focus be on resolving the issue in the way that is most faithful to the text of the statutory provision being interpreted? That is most faithful to Congress's purpose when it passed the measure? That best addresses pragmatic concerns about what would make the most sense from a policy perspective? That reflects what Congress would have done if it had known how society would look at the time the interpretive dispute actually arises?

Theories of statutory interpretation aim to explain why a court might give one answer rather than another to such questions. And these theories can matter in practice. Two judges interpreting the same statute could decide a case regarding a dispute over the meaning of a statutory provision differently, for example, simply based on whether they place more emphasis on the ordinary meaning of the plain text of the statute or on the legislature's purpose in enacting the statute. Thus, a theoretical argument for opting for one approach rather than another can have very real practical consequences.

In reading the following materials on the leading theories of statutory interpretation—textualism, purposivism, pragmatism, and dynamic statutory interpretation—think about how each theory relates to what you have learned about the legislative process. Consider also the role that judges are assuming when applying each of the theories. Should judges be faithful to the text of the statute alone? Does the legislative purpose matter? The practical consequences? And how should we consider older statutes when they are applied in new contexts?

Here is one caution before you begin. The modes of statutory interpretation that are described below are approaches rather than doctrines; to put the point in another way, these modes of statutory interpretation are not mandated or forbidden by binding precedents. It is accepted that the Supreme Court—and lower courts, too—can decide a case on one day using approach A, and on the next day using approach B. Usually such a change happens because different justices have different approaches, and they write as they see fit (subject of course to being able to gain the assent of the rest of the majority). So one cannot expect to learn a mode of interpretation that as a matter of precedent must be followed. One can instead expect to learn a variety of modes of interpretation that will be met, again and again, in the practice of the law.

## a. Textualism

*WEST VIRGINIA UNIVERSITY HOSPITALS, INC. v. CASEY*
*TENNESSEE VALLEY AUTHORITY v. HILL*
*WOODEN v. UNITED STATES*
*Notes on Textualism*

Quite obviously, a statute's text matters. Less obvious is why the text matters and whether it is all that matters. In recent decades, a school of statutory interpretation known as "textualism" has emerged and had great influence. Defining "textualism" is not so easy. But while "textualism does not admit of a simple definition, . . . in practice [it] is associated with the basic proposition that judges must seek and abide by the public meaning of the enacted text, understood in context (as all texts must be)." John F. Manning, Textualism and Legislative Intent, 91 Va. L. Rev. 419 (2005).

Textualism's leading modern champion was the late Justice Scalia. But, as the materials below reveal, judges of all stripes have at times sung the praises of faithful adherence to the legislative text, consequences be damned. A key question such praise raises, however, is why the text should matter. Is it because only a theory of interpretation that privileges the text in some very strong manner is likely to constrain judges and thus preserve the role of the respective political branches in enacting and interpreting statutes? Is it because the legislators who enact laws actually intend that the text—and the text alone—express their intentions? Is it because laws have no intentions, only words that comprise them, and so any search for the legislature's intention in drafting the measure is a hopeless one?

As you read the three cases that follow, consider why strict adherence to the statutory language might make sense and why it might not. How does textualism relate to the legislative process and the statute produced? Should a judge confine her decision to the statutory language when a legislative purpose may be discerned that conflicts with the text? Is that last question one that even makes sense?

The first case considers the import of language added to a provision in the United States Code—42 U.S.C. § 1988—by the Civil Rights Attorney's Fees Award Act of 1976. The Act provided that "[i]n any action or proceeding to enforce" various identified civil rights statutes, "the court, in its discretion, may allow the prevailing party, other than the United States, a reasonable attorney's fee as part of the costs." The question presented is cleanly stated in the very first sentence of the opinion.

## WEST VIRGINIA UNIVERSITY HOSPITALS, INC. v. CASEY

Supreme Court of the United States (1991).
499 U.S. 83.

■ JUSTICE SCALIA delivered the opinion of the Court.

This case presents the question whether fees for services rendered by experts in civil rights litigation may be shifted to the losing party pursuant to 42 U.S.C. § 1988, which permits the award of "a reasonable attorney's fee."

I

Petitioner West Virginia University Hospitals, Inc. (WVUH), operates a hospital in Morgantown, W. Va., near the Pennsylvania border. The hospital is often used by Medicaid recipients living in southwestern Pennsylvania. In January 1986, Pennsylvania's Department of Public Welfare notified WVUH of new Medicaid reimbursement schedules for services provided to Pennsylvania residents by the Morgantown hospital. In administrative proceedings, WVUH unsuccessfully objected to the new reimbursement rates on both federal statutory and federal constitutional grounds. After exhausting administrative remedies, WVUH filed suit in Federal District Court. . . .

. . . Counsel for WVUH employed Coopers & Lybrand, a national accounting firm, and three doctors specializing in hospital finance to assist in the preparation of the lawsuit and to testify at trial. WVUH prevailed at trial in May 1988. The District Court subsequently awarded fees pursuant to 42 U.S.C. § 1988, including over $100,000 in fees attributable to expert services. The District Court found these services to have been "essential" to presentation of the case—a finding not disputed by respondents.

Respondents appealed both the judgment on the merits and the fee award. The Court of Appeals for the Third Circuit affirmed as to the former, but reversed as to the expert fees, disallowing them except to the extent that they fell within the $ 30-per-day fees for witnesses prescribed by 28 U.S.C. § 1821. . . .

II

. . . In Crawford Fitting Co. v. J. T. Gibbons, Inc., 482 U.S. 437 (1987), we held that [the general "costs" and "witness fees" statutes, not covering the claimed expert fees] define the full extent of a federal court's power to shift litigation costs absent express statutory authority to go further. The question before us, then, is—with regard to both testimonial and nontestimonial expert fees—whether the term "attorney's fee" in § 1988 provides the "explicit statutory authority" required by Crawford Fitting.

III

The record of statutory usage demonstrates convincingly that attorney's fees and expert fees are regarded as separate elements of litigation cost. While some fee-shifting provisions, like § 1988, refer only to "attorney's fees," see, e.g., Civil Rights Act of 1964, 42 U.S.C. § 2000e–5(k), many others explicitly shift expert witness fees *as well as* attorney's fees. In 1976, just over a week prior to the enactment of § 1988, Congress passed those provisions of the Toxic Substances Control Act, 15 U.S.C. §§ 2618(d), 2619(c)(2), which provide that a prevailing party may recover "the costs of suit and reasonable fees for attorneys *and expert witnesses.*" (Emphasis added.) Also in 1976, Congress amended the Consumer Product Safety Act, 15 U.S.C. §§ 2060(c), 2072(a), 2073, which as originally enacted in 1972 shifted to the losing party "costs of suit, including a reasonable attorney's fee," see 86 Stat. 1226. In the 1976 amendment, Congress altered the fee-shifting provisions to their present form by adding a phrase shifting expert witness fees *in addition to* attorney's fees. See Pub. L. 94–284, § 10, 90 Stat. 506, 507. Two other significant Acts passed in 1976 contain similar phrasing: the Resource Conservation and Recovery Act of 1976, 42 U.S.C. § 6972(e) ("costs of litigation (including reasonable attorney and expert witness fees)"), and the Natural Gas Pipeline Safety Act Amendments of 1976, 49 U.S.C. App. § 1686(e) ("costs of suit, including reasonable attorney's fees and reasonable expert witnesses fees").

Congress enacted similarly phrased fee-shifting provisions in numerous statutes both before 1976, . . . and afterwards, . . . These statutes encompass diverse categories of legislation . . . . At least 34 statutes in 10 different titles of the U.S. Code explicitly shift attorney's fees *and* expert witness fees.

The laws that refer to fees for nontestimonial expert services are less common, but they establish a similar usage both before and after 1976: Such fees are referred to *in addition to* attorney's fees when a shift is intended. . . .

. . . We think this statutory usage shows beyond question that attorney's fees and expert fees are distinct items of expense. If, as WVUH argues, the one includes the other, dozens of statutes referring to the two separately become an inexplicable exercise in redundancy. . . .

IV

[Extended discussion of pre-1976 cases omitted.] In sum, we conclude that at the time this provision was enacted neither statutory nor judicial usage regarded the phrase "attorney's fees" as embracing fees for experts' services.

V

. . . WVUH further argues that the congressional purpose in enacting § 1988 must prevail over the ordinary meaning of the statutory terms. It quotes, for example, the House Committee Report to the effect that "the judicial remedy [must be] full and complete," H.R. Rep. No. 94–1558, p. 1 (1976), and the Senate Committee Report to the effect that "citizens must have the opportunity to recover what it costs them to vindicate [civil] rights in court," S. Rep. No. 94–1011, supra, at 2. As we have observed before, however, the purpose of a statute includes not only what it sets out to change, but also what it resolves to leave alone. The best evidence of that purpose is the statutory text adopted by both Houses of Congress and submitted to the President. Where that contains a phrase that is unambiguous—that has a clearly accepted meaning in both legislative and judicial practice—we do not permit it to be expanded or contracted by the statements of individual legislators or committees during the course of the enactment process. Congress could easily have shifted "attorney's fees and expert witness fees," or "reasonable litigation expenses," as it did in contemporaneous statutes; it chose instead to enact more restrictive language, and we are bound by that restriction.

... [WVUH also contends] that, even if Congress plainly did not include expert fees in the fee-shifting provisions of § 1988, it would have done so had it thought about it. Most of the pre-§ 1988 statutes that explicitly shifted expert fees dealt with environmental litigation, where the necessity of expert advice was readily apparent; and when Congress later enacted the EAJA, the federal counterpart of § 1988, it explicitly included expert fees. Thus, the argument runs, the 94th Congress simply forgot; it is our duty to ask how they would have decided had they actually considered the question.

This argument profoundly mistakes our role. Where a statutory term presented to us for the first time is ambiguous, we construe it to contain that permissible meaning which fits most logically and comfortably into the body of both previously and subsequently enacted law. We do so not because that precise accommodative meaning is what the lawmakers must have had in mind (how could an earlier Congress know what a later Congress would enact?), but because it is our role to make sense rather than nonsense out of the corpus juris. But where, as here, the meaning of the term prevents such accommodation, it is not our function to eliminate clearly expressed inconsistency of policy and to treat alike subjects that different Congresses have chosen to treat differently. The facile attribution of congressional "forgetfulness" cannot justify such a usurpation. Where what is at issue is not a contradictory disposition within the same enactment, but merely a difference between the more parsimonious policy of an earlier enactment and the more generous policy of a later one, there is no more basis for saying that the earlier Congress forgot than for saying that the earlier Congress felt differently. In such circumstances, the attribution of forgetfulness rests in reality upon the judge's assessment that the later statute contains the *better* disposition. But that is not for judges to prescribe. We thus reject this last argument for the same reason that Justice Brandeis, writing for the Court, once rejected a similar (though less explicit) argument by the United States:

> "[The statute's] language is plain and unambiguous. What the Government asks is not a construction of a statute, but, in effect, an enlargement of it by the court, so that what was omitted, presumably by inadvertence, may be included within its scope. To supply omissions transcends the judicial function." Iselin v. United States, 270 U.S. 245, 250–251 (1926). . . .

The judgment of the Court of Appeals is affirmed.

■ JUSTICE MARSHALL, dissenting.

As Justice Stevens demonstrates, the Court uses the implements of literalism to wound, rather than to minister to, congressional intent in this case. That is a dangerous usurpation of congressional power when any statute is involved. It is troubling for special reasons, however, when the statute at issue is clearly designed to give access to the federal courts to persons and groups attempting to vindicate vital civil rights. . . .

■ JUSTICE STEVENS, with whom JUSTICE MARSHALL and JUSTICE BLACKMUN join, dissenting.

. . . In the early 1970's, Congress began to focus on the importance of public interest litigation, and since that time, it has enacted numerous fee-shifting statutes. In many of these statutes, which the majority cites at length, Congress has expressly authorized the recovery of expert witness fees as part of the costs of litigation. The question in this case is whether, notwithstanding the omission of such an express authorization in 42 U.S.C. § 1988, Congress intended to authorize such recovery when it provided for "a reasonable attorney's fee as part of the costs." In my view, just as the omission of express authorization in a will does not preclude compensation to an estate's attorney, the omission of express authorization for expert witness fees in a fee-shifting provision should not preclude the award of expert witness fees. We should look at the way in which the Court has interpreted the text of this statute in the past, as well as this statute's legislative history, to resolve the question before us, rather than looking at the text of the many other statutes that the majority cites in which Congress expressly recognized the need for compensating expert witnesses. . . .

. . . On those occasions . . . when the Court has put on its thick grammarian's spectacles and ignored the available evidence of congressional purpose and the teaching of prior cases construing a statute, the congressional response has been [dramatic, citing six prominent examples]. . . . In the domain of statutory interpretation, Congress is the master. It obviously has the power to correct our mistakes, but we do the country a disservice when we needlessly ignore persuasive evidence of Congress' actual purpose and require it "to take the time to revisit the matter" and to restate its purpose in more precise English whenever its work product suffers from an omission or inadvertent error. As Judge Learned Hand explained, statutes are likely to be imprecise.

> "All [legislators] have done is to write down certain words which they mean to apply generally to situations of that kind. To apply these literally may either pervert what was plainly their general meaning, or leave undisposed of what there is every reason to suppose they meant to provide for. Thus it is not enough for the judge just to use a dictionary. If he should do no more, he might come out with a result which every sensible man would recognize to be quite the opposite of what was really intended;

which would contradict or leave unfulfilled its plain purpose." L. Hand, How Far Is a Judge Free in Rendering a Decision?, in The Spirit of Liberty 103, 106 (I. Dilliard ed. 1952).

The Court concludes its opinion with the suggestion that disagreement with its textual analysis could only be based on the dissenters' preference for a "better" statute. It overlooks the possibility that a different view may be more faithful to Congress' command. The fact that Congress has consistently provided for the inclusion of expert witness fees in fee-shifting statutes when it considered the matter is a weak reed on which to rest the conclusion that the omission of such a provision represents a deliberate decision to forbid such awards. Only time will tell whether the Court, with its literal reading of § 1988, has correctly interpreted the will of Congress with respect to the issue it has resolved today. . . .

## NOTES

(1) ***What Is the Background of This Case?*** That Congress had passed a slew of statutes concerning attorney's fees in 1976 was not just an accident of history. Congress was reacting to ALYESKA PIPELINE SERVICE CO. v. WILDERNESS SOCIETY, 421 U.S. 240 (1975). There, several environmental organizations had successfully sought an injunction directing the Department of the Interior to perform legally required environmental analyses, and properly to apply federal land use laws, in connection with oil companies' application for permission to construct the Alaska Pipeline connecting the newly discovered oil fields of Alaska's North Slope to the port of Valdez. Because the plaintiffs had acted to vindicate "important rights of all citizens" by bringing an action to ensure that the government system functioned properly, the D.C. Circuit found them entitled to reimbursement for "the reasonable value of their services." Alaska Wilderness Soc. v. Morton, 495 F.2d 1026, 1032 (D.C. Cir. 1974) (en banc). Otherwise, the court reasoned, the cost of such litigation—especially against well-financed parties such as Alyeska—might deter private parties from seeking to have environmental statutes properly enforced. Statutorily precluded from entering such an award against the United States, the court held that the pipeline company Alyeska, an intervenor supporting the government's (wrongful) approval of its pipeline, was responsible for half of those costs. But, JUSTICE WHITE, writing for a majority, reversed the D.C. Circuit, emphasizing the need for legislative action given Congress's longstanding general endorsement of the American rule, in which, unlike under the British Rule, the loser does not pay the winner's attorney's fees:

> In the United States, the prevailing litigant is ordinarily not entitled to collect a reasonable attorneys' fee from the loser. We are asked to fashion a far-reaching exception to this "American Rule"; but having considered its origin and development, we are convinced that it would be inappropriate for the Judiciary, without legislative guidance, to reallocate the burdens of litigation in the manner and to the extent urged by respondents and approved by the Court of Appeals. . . .

> We do not purport to assess the merits or demerits of the "American Rule" with respect to the allowance of attorneys' fees. . . . It is deeply rooted in our history and in congressional policy; and it is not for us to invade the legislature's province by redistributing litigation costs in the manner suggested by respondents and followed by the Court of Appeals.

421 U.S. at 247, 263–4, 270–1. Justices Marshall and Brennan dissented.

The Civil Rights Attorney's Fees Award Act, at stake in the West Virginia University Hospitals case, like the other attorney's fees acts of 1976, was a response to this decision.

(2) ***And What Happened After This Case?*** Congress responded strongly to West Virginia University Hospitals. The Civil Rights Act Amendments of 1990 broadly authorized reimbursement of expert witness fees in a civil rights context. And when President George H.W. Bush vetoed that legislation, Congress then enacted the Civil Rights Act Amendments of 1991, which he signed into law. Its new subsection, § 1988(c), explicitly provided reimbursement for expert witness expenses "as part of the attorney's fee" for successful litigation under *some, but not all*, of the statutes mentioned in the amended provision, a pattern that has continued. Does this history of congressional responses to Supreme Court decisions show the virtues of textualism, in the sense that Congress is perfectly capable of making itself clear and that when in these instances it did make itself clear, it did not take an absolutist view one way or the other? Or does this history show the gap between text and legislative intent and thus the ways in which textualism may result in outcomes Congress never had in mind? After all, because Congress is the master, no matter which way the Court decides a case like West Virginia University Hospitals, Congress can "correct" the ruling. So, does the possibility of "correction" support the majority's approach more than the dissent's?

## TENNESSEE VALLEY AUTHORITY v. HILL

Supreme Court of the United States (1978).
437 U.S. 153.

■ CHIEF JUSTICE BURGER delivered the opinion of the Court.

I

. . . In this area of the Little Tennessee River the Tennessee Valley Authority [TVA], a wholly owned public corporation of the United States, began constructing the Tellico Dam and Reservoir Project in 1967, shortly after Congress appropriated initial funds for its development. Tellico is a multipurpose regional development project designed principally to stimulate shoreline development, generate sufficient electric current to heat 20,000 homes, and provide flatwater recreation and flood control, as well as improve economic conditions in "an area characterized by underutilization of human resources and outmigration of young people." Of particular relevance to this case is one aspect of the project, a dam. . . .

The Tellico Dam has never opened, however, despite the fact that construction has been virtually completed and the dam is essentially ready for operation. Although Congress has appropriated monies for Tellico every year since 1967, progress was delayed, and ultimately stopped, by a tangle of lawsuits and administrative proceedings. After unsuccessfully urging TVA to consider alternatives to damming the Little Tennessee, local citizens and national conservation groups brought suit in the District Court, claiming that the project did not conform to the requirements of the National Environmental Policy Act of 1969 (NEPA). . . .

A few months prior to the District Court's decision dissolving the NEPA injunction, a discovery was made in the waters of the Little Tennessee which would profoundly affect the Tellico Project. Exploring the area around Coytee Springs, which is about seven miles from the mouth of the river, a University of Tennessee ichthyologist, Dr. David A. Etnier, found a previously unknown species of perch, the snail darter, or *Percina (Imostoma) tanasi*. This three-inch, tannish-colored fish, whose numbers are estimated to be in the range of 10,000 to 15,000, would soon engage the attention of environmentalists, the TVA, the Department of the Interior, the Congress of the United States, and ultimately the federal courts, as a new and additional basis to halt construction of the dam.

Until recently the finding of a new species of animal life would hardly generate a cause célèbre. This is particularly so in the case of darters, of which there are approximately 130 known species, 8 to 10 of these having been identified only in the last five years. The moving force behind the snail darter's sudden fame came some four months after its discovery, when the Congress passed the Endangered Species Act of 1973 (Act), 87 Stat. 884, 16 U.S.C. § 1531 et seq. (1976 ed.). This legislation, among other things, authorizes the Secretary of the Interior to declare species of animal life "endangered" and to identify the "critical habitat" of these creatures. When a species or its habitat is so listed, the following portion of the Act—relevant here—becomes effective:

"The Secretary [of the Interior] shall review other programs administered by him and utilize such programs in furtherance of the purposes of this chapter. All other Federal departments and agencies shall, in consultation with and with the assistance of the Secretary, utilize their authorities in furtherance of the purposes of this chapter by carrying out programs for the conservation of endangered species and threatened species listed pursuant to section 1533 of this title and by taking such action necessary to insure that actions authorized, funded, or carried out by them do not jeopardize the continued existence of such endangered species and threatened species or result in the destruction or modification of habitat of such species which is determined by the Secretary, after consultation as appropriate with the affected States, to be critical."

In January 1975, the respondents in this case and others petitioned the Secretary of the Interior to list the snail darter as an endangered species. After receiving comments from various interested parties, including TVA and the State of Tennessee, the Secretary formally listed the snail darter as an endangered species on October 8, 1975. . . . [T]he Secretary determined that the snail darter apparently lives only in that portion of the Little Tennessee River which would be completely inundated by the reservoir created as a consequence of the Tellico Dam's completion. The Secretary went on to explain the significance of the dam to the habitat of the snail darter: . . . "The proposed impoundment of water behind the proposed Tellico Dam would result in total destruction of the snail darter's habitat."

Subsequent to this determination, the Secretary declared the area of the Little Tennessee which would be affected by the Tellico Dam to be the "critical habitat" of the snail darter. Using these determinations as a predicate, and notwithstanding the near completion of the dam, the Secretary declared that pursuant to § 7 of the Act, "all Federal agencies must take such action as is necessary to insure that actions authorized, funded, or carried out by them do not result in the destruction or modification of this critical habitat area." This notice, of course, was pointedly directed at TVA and clearly aimed at halting completion or operation of the dam. . . .

. . . Meanwhile, Congress had also become involved in the fate of the snail darter. Appearing before a Subcommittee of the House Committee on Appropriations in April 1975—some seven months before the snail darter was listed as endangered—TVA representatives described the discovery of the fish and the relevance of the Endangered Species Act to the Tellico Project. . . . At that time TVA presented a position which it would advance in successive forums thereafter, namely, that the Act did not prohibit the completion of a project authorized, funded, and substantially constructed before the Act was passed. TVA also described its efforts to transplant the snail darter, but contended that the dam should be finished regardless of the experiment's success. Thereafter, the House Committee on Appropriations, in its June 20, 1975, Report, stated the following in the course of recommending that an additional $29 million be appropriated for Tellico:

"The *Committee* directs that the project, for which an environmental impact statement has been completed and provided the Committee, should be completed as promptly as possible . . . ." H.R. Rep. No. 94–319, p. 76 (1975). (Emphasis added.)

Congress then approved the TVA general budget, which contained funds for continued construction of the Tellico Project. In December 1975, one month after the snail darter was declared an endangered species, the President signed the bill into law. . . .

In February 1976, pursuant to § 11(g) of the Endangered Species Act, 87 Stat. 900, 16 U.S.C. § 1540(g) (1976 ed.), respondents filed the case now under review, seeking to enjoin completion of the dam and impoundment of the reservoir on the ground that those actions would violate the Act by directly causing the extinction of the species. . . .

II

. . . It may seem curious to some that the survival of a relatively small number of three-inch fish among all the countless millions of species extant would require the permanent halting of a virtually completed dam for which Congress has expended more than $100 million. The paradox is not minimized by the fact that Congress continued to appropriate large sums of public money for the project, even after congressional Appropriations Committees were apprised of its apparent impact upon the survival of the snail darter. We conclude, however, that the explicit provisions of the Endangered Species Act require precisely that result.

One would be hard pressed to find a statutory provision whose terms were any plainer than those in § 7 of the Endangered Species Act. Its very words affirmatively command all federal agencies "to *insure* that actions *authorized, funded,* or *carried out* by them do not *jeopardize* the continued existence" of an endangered species or "*result* in the destruction or modification of habitat of such species . . . ." 16 U.S.C. § 1536 (1976 ed.). (Emphasis added.) This language admits of no exception. Nonetheless, petitioner urges, as do the dissenters, that the Act cannot reasonably be interpreted as applying to a federal project which was well under way when Congress passed the Endangered Species Act of 1973. To sustain that position, however, we would be forced to ignore the ordinary meaning of plain language. It has not been shown, for example, how TVA can close the gates of the Tellico Dam without "carrying out" an action that has been "authorized" and "funded" by a federal agency. Nor can we understand how such action will "*insure*" that the snail darter's habitat is not disrupted. Accepting the Secretary's determinations, as we must, it is clear that TVA's proposed operation of the dam will have precisely the opposite effect, namely the *eradication* of an endangered species.

Concededly, this view of the Act will produce results requiring the sacrifice of the anticipated benefits of the project and of many millions of dollars in public funds. But examination of the language, history, and structure of the legislation under review here indicates beyond doubt that Congress intended endangered species to be afforded the highest of priorities. . . .

By 1973, when Congress held hearings on what would later become the Endangered Species Act of 1973, it was informed that species were still being lost at the rate of about one per year. . .

As it was finally passed, the Endangered Species Act of 1973 represented the most comprehensive legislation for the preservation of endangered species ever enacted by any nation. Its stated purposes were "to provide a means whereby the ecosystems upon which endangered species and threatened species depend may be conserved," and "to provide a program for the conservation of such . . . species . . . ." In furtherance of these goals, Congress expressly stated in § 2(c) that "all Federal departments and agencies shall seek to conserve endangered species and threatened species . . . ." Lest there be any ambiguity as to the meaning of this statutory directive, the Act specifically defined "conserve" as meaning "to use and the use of all methods and procedures which are necessary to bring any endangered species or threatened species to the point at which the measures provided pursuant to this chapter are no longer necessary." . . .

Section 7 of the Act, which of course is relied upon by respondents in this case, provides a particularly good gauge of congressional intent. . . . Explaining the idea behind this language, an administration spokesman told Congress that it "would further signal to all . . . agencies of the Government that this is the first priority, consistent with their primary objectives." 1973 House Hearings 213 (statement of Deputy Assistant Secretary of the Interior). . . .

It is against this legislative background that we must measure TVA's claim that the Act was not intended to stop operation of a project which, like Tellico Dam, was near completion when an endangered species was discovered in its path. While there is no discussion in the legislative history of precisely this problem, the totality of congressional action makes it abundantly clear that the result we reach today is wholly in accord with both the words of the statute and the intent of Congress. The plain intent of Congress in enacting this statute was to halt and reverse the trend toward species extinction, whatever the cost. This is reflected not only in the stated policies of the Act, but in literally every section of the statute. All persons, including federal agencies, are specifically instructed not to "take" endangered species, meaning that no one is "to harass, harm, pursue, hunt, shoot, wound, kill, trap, capture, or collect" such life forms. Agencies in particular are directed by §§ 2 (c) and 3 (2) of the Act to "use . . . *all methods* and procedures which are necessary" to preserve endangered species. In addition, the legislative history undergirding § 7 reveals an explicit congressional decision to require agencies to afford first priority to the declared national policy of saving endangered species. The pointed omission of the type of qualifying language previously included in endangered species legislation reveals a conscious decision by Congress to give endangered species priority over the "primary missions" of federal agencies.

It is not for us to speculate, much less act, on whether Congress would have altered its stance had the specific events of this case been anticipated. In any event, we discern no hint in the deliberations of Congress relating to the 1973 Act that would compel a different result than we reach here. Indeed, the repeated expressions of congressional concern over what it saw as the potentially enormous danger presented by the eradication of *any* endangered species suggest how the balance would have been struck had the issue been presented to Congress in 1973. . . .

[N]either the Endangered Species Act nor Art. III of the Constitution provides federal courts with authority to make such fine utilitarian calculations. On the contrary, the plain language of the Act, buttressed by its legislative history, shows clearly that Congress viewed the value of endangered species as "incalculable." Quite obviously, it would be difficult for a court to balance the loss of a sum certain—even $100 million—against a congressionally declared "incalculable" value, even assuming we had the power to engage in such a weighing process, which we emphatically do not. . . .

Notwithstanding Congress' expression of intent in 1973, we are urged to find that the continuing appropriations for Tellico Dam constitute an implied repeal of the 1973 Act, at least insofar as it applies to the Tellico Project. In support of this view, TVA points to the statements found in various House and Senate Appropriations Committees' Reports; those Reports generally reflected the attitude of the *Committees* either that the Act did not apply to Tellico or that the dam should be completed regardless of the provisions of the Act. Since we are unwilling to assume that these latter Committee statements constituted advice to ignore the provisions of a duly enacted law, we assume that these Committees believed that the Act simply was not applicable in this situation. But even under this interpretation of the Committees' actions, we are unable to conclude that the Act has been in any respect amended or repealed.

Perhaps mindful of the fact that it is "swimming upstream" against a strong current of well-established precedent, TVA argues for an exception to the rule against implied repealers in a circumstance where, as here, Appropriations Committees have expressly stated their "understanding" that the earlier legislation would not prohibit the proposed expenditure. We cannot accept such a proposition. Expressions of committees dealing with requests for appropriations cannot be equated with statutes enacted by Congress, particularly not in the circumstances presented by this case. . . .

Second, there is no indication that Congress as a whole was aware of TVA's position, although the Appropriations Committees apparently agreed with petitioner's views.

(B)

. . . Here we are urged to view the Endangered Species Act "reasonably," and hence shape a remedy "that accords with some modicum of common sense and the public weal." Post, at 196. But is that our function? . . .

Our individual appraisal of the wisdom or unwisdom of a particular course consciously selected by the Congress is to be put aside in the process of interpreting a statute. Once the meaning of an enactment is discerned and its constitutionality determined, the judicial process comes to an end. We do not sit as a committee of review, nor are we vested with the power of veto. The lines ascribed to Sir Thomas More by Robert Bolt are not without relevance here:

"The law, Roper, the law. I know what's legal, not what's right. And I'll stick to what's legal. . . . I'm *not* God. The currents and eddies right and wrong, which you find such plain-sailing, I can't navigate, I'm no voyager. But in the thickets of the law, oh there I'm a forester. . . . What would you do? Cut a great road through the law to get after the Devil? . . . And when the last law was down, and the Devil turned round on you—where would you hide, Roper, the laws all being flat? . . . This country's planted thick with laws from coast to coast—Man's laws, not God's—and if you cut them down . . . d'you really think you could stand upright in the winds that would blow then? . . . Yes, I'd give the Devil benefit of law, for my own safety's sake." R. Bolt, A Man for All Seasons, Act I, p. 147 (Three Plays, Heinemann ed. 1967). . . .

[The Court of Appeals' injunction against building the dam is affirmed.]

■ JUSTICE POWELL, with whom JUSTICE BLACKMUN joins, dissenting.

. . . This decision casts a long shadow over the operation of even the most important projects, serving vital needs of society and national defense, whenever it is determined that continued operation would threaten extinction of an endangered species or its habitat. This result is said to be required by the "plain intent of Congress" as well as by the language of the statute.

In my view § 7 cannot reasonably be interpreted as applying to a project that is completed or substantially completed when its threat to an endangered species is discovered. Nor can I believe that Congress could have intended this Act to produce the "absurd result"—in the words of the District Court—of this case. If it were clear from the language of the Act and its legislative history that Congress intended to authorize this result, this Court would be compelled to enforce it. It is not our province to rectify policy or political judgments by the Legislative Branch, however egregiously they may disserve the public interest. But where the statutory language and legislative history, as in this case, need not be construed to reach such a result, I view it as the duty of this Court to adopt a permissible construction that accords with some modicum of common sense and the public weal.

[Justice Rehnquist's dissent is omitted.]

## NOTE

Partly as a response to the Court's opinion, Congress in 1978 created the Endangered Species Committee, a high-level group authorized under certain circumstances to grant exemptions from the operation of the Endangered Species Act. However, when this Committee reviewed the Tellico Dam project, it did not grant an exemption because it determined that the project was uneconomic in any case. Not to be deterred, Congress in 1979 passed a rider to an appropriations bill directing TVA to complete construction, which was done. Meanwhile, some other populations of the snail darter were found elsewhere in the river, so completion did not in fact annihilate the species.

## WOODEN v. UNITED STATES

Supreme Court of the United States (2022).
142 S.Ct. 1063.

■ JUSTICE KAGAN delivered the opinion of the Court.

In the course of one evening, William Dale Wooden burglarized ten units in a single storage facility. He later pleaded guilty, for that night's work, to ten counts of burglary—one for each storage unit he had entered. Some two decades later, the courts below concluded that those convictions were enough to subject Wooden to enhanced criminal penalties under the Armed Career Criminal Act (ACCA). That statute mandates a 15-year minimum sentence for unlawful gun possession when the offender has three or more prior convictions for violent felonies like burglary "committed on occasions different from one another." 18 U.S.C. § 924(e)(1). The question presented is whether Wooden's prior convictions were for offenses occurring on different occasions, as the lower courts held, because the burglary of each unit happened at a distinct point in time, rather than simultaneously. The answer is no. Convictions arising from a single criminal episode, in the way Wooden's did, can count only once under ACCA.

I

Begin in 1997, when Wooden and three confederates unlawfully entered a one-building storage facility . . . . The men stole items from, all told, ten different storage units. So Georgia prosecutors charged them with ten counts of burglary—though, as state law prescribes, in a single indictment. . . . Wooden pleaded guilty to all counts. The judge sentenced him to eight years' imprisonment for each conviction, with the ten terms to run concurrently.

Fast forward now to a cold November morning in 2014, when Wooden responded to a police officer's knock on his door. The officer asked to speak with Wooden's wife. And noting the chill in the air, the officer asked if he could step inside, to stay warm. Wooden agreed. But his good deed did not go unpunished. Once admitted to the house, the officer spotted several guns. Knowing that Wooden was a felon, the officer placed him under arrest. A jury later convicted him for being a felon in possession of a firearm, in violation of 18 U.S.C. § 922(g).

The penalty for that crime varies significantly depending on whether ACCA applies. Putting ACCA aside, the maximum sentence for violating § 922(g) is ten years in prison. See § 924(a)(2). But ACCA mandates a minimum sentence of fifteen years if the § 922(g) offender has three prior convictions for "violent felon[ies]" (like burglary) or "serious drug offense[s]" that were "committed on occasions different from one another." § 924(e)(1). In Wooden's own case, the record reveals the discrepancy as especially stark. Before the Government decided to seek an ACCA enhancement, its Probation Office recommended a sentence of 21 to 27 months. See App. 38–39, 42. The ACCA minimum sentence is about 13 years longer.

The District Court's sentencing hearing focused on whether Wooden's ten convictions for breaking into the storage facility sufficed to trigger ACCA. Wooden said they did not because he had burglarized the ten storage units on a single occasion, rather than "on occasions different from one another." § 924(e)(1). The burglaries, he explained, happened "during the same criminal episode," "at the same business location, under the same roof." App. 50. And given those facts, he continued, the burglaries were "charged in a single indictment." Ibid. But the District Court accepted the Government's view that every time Wooden busted into another storage unit, he commenced a new "occasion" of criminal activity. The court reasoned, relying on Circuit precedent, that the entry into "[e]ach separate [unit] provides a discrete point at which the first offense was completed and the second began and so on." Id., at 59. Based on the ACCA enhancement, the court sentenced Wooden to 188 months (almost 16 years) in prison for unlawfully possessing a gun.

The Court of Appeals for the Sixth Circuit affirmed the sentence, on the same reasoning. "[I]t is possible," the court stated, "to discern the point at which Wooden's first offense" was "completed and the subsequent point at which his second offense began." 945 F.3d 498, 505 (2019). After all, "Wooden could not be in two (let alone ten) of [the storage units] at once." Ibid. In the court's view, the sequential nature of Wooden's crimes—his progression from one unit in the storage facility to the next to the next—meant that the crimes were "committed on occasions different from one another." And so, the court concluded, Wooden qualified as a career offender under ACCA. . . .

II

Framed in terms of this case, the disputed question is whether Wooden committed his crimes on a single occasion or on ten separate ones.

The Government answers ten, relying on a legally fancified version of the Sixth Circuit's timing test. In the ACCA context, the Government argues, an "occasion" happens "at a particular point in time"—the moment "when [an offense's] elements are established." Brief for United States 9. So offenses "occur on different 'occasions' when the criminal conduct necessary to satisfy the offense elements occurs at different times." Id., at 13. Applying that elements-based, "temporal-distinctness test" to this case, the Government explains that Wooden's burglaries were "quintessentially sequential, rather than simultaneous." Id., at 10, 20. After all, a person can satisfy the elements of burglary only by entering (or remaining in) a structure with criminal intent. See, e.g., Ga. Code Ann. § 16–7–1(a). And it would have been "physically impossible" for Wooden to have entered (or remained in) multiple storage units "at once." Brief for United States 12. Each of Wooden's ten entries thus counts (so says the Government) as another "occasion," triggering ACCA's stringent penalties more than three times over.

We think not. The ordinary meaning of the word "occasion"—essentially an episode or event—refutes the Government's single-minded focus on whether a crime's elements were established at a discrete moment in time. And ACCA's history and purpose do so too: The origin of the "occasions" clause confirms that multiple crimes may occur on one occasion even if not at the same moment. . . .

A

Consider first how an ordinary person (a reporter; a police officer; yes, even a lawyer) might describe Wooden's ten burglaries—and how she would not. The observer might say: "On one occasion, Wooden burglarized ten units in a storage facility." By contrast, she would never say: "On ten occasions, Wooden burglarized a unit in the facility." Nor would she say anything like: "On one occasion, Wooden burglarized a storage unit; on a second occasion, he burglarized another unit; on a third occasion, he burglarized yet another; and so on." She would, using language in its normal way, group his entries into the storage units, even though not simultaneous, all together—as happening on a single occasion, rather than on ten "occasions different from one another." § 924(e)(1).

That usage fits the ordinary meaning of "occasion." The word commonly refers to an event, occurrence, happening, or episode. See, e.g., American Heritage Dictionary 908 (1981); Webster's Third New International Dictionary 1560 (3d ed. 1986). And such an event, occurrence, happening, or episode—which is simply to say, such an occasion—may itself encompass multiple, temporally distinct activities. The occasion of a wedding, for example, often includes a ceremony, cocktail hour, dinner, and dancing. Those doings are proximate in time and place, and have a shared theme (celebrating the happy couple); their connections are, indeed, what makes them part of a single event. But they do not occur at the same moment: The newlyweds would surely take offense if a guest organized a conga line in the middle of their vows. That is because an occasion may—and the hypothesized one does—encompass a number of non-simultaneous activities; it need not be confined to a single one.

The same is true (to shift gears from the felicitous to the felonious) when it comes to crime. In that sphere too, an "occasion" means an event or episode—which may, in common usage, include temporally discrete offenses. Consider a couple of descriptions from this Court's cases. "On one occasion," we noted, "Bryant hit his live-in girlfriend on the head with a beer bottle and attempted to strangle her." United States v. Bryant, 579 U.S. 140, 151 (2016). "On one occasion"—regardless whether those acts occurred at once (as the Government would require) or instead succeeded one another. Ibid. Likewise, we said: "[T]he State has stipulated that the robbery and murder arose out of 'the same set of facts, circumstances, and the same occasion.'" Turner v. Arkansas, 407 U.S. 366, 368–369 (1972) (per curiam). "[T]he same occasion"—irrespective whether the murder took place during (as the Government insists on) or instead just after the robbery. Ibid. Or take a hypothetical suggested by oral argument here: A barroom brawl breaks out, and a patron hits first one, then another, and then a third of his fellow drinkers. The

Government maintains those are not just three offenses (assaults) but also three "occasions" because they happened seriatim. See Tr. of Oral Arg. 52–53, 61–62. But in making the leap from three offenses to three occasions, based on a split-second separation between punches, the Government leaves ordinary language behind. The occasion in the hypothetical is the barroom brawl, not each individual fisticuff.

By treating each temporally distinct offense as its own occasion, the Government goes far toward collapsing two separate statutory conditions. Recall that ACCA kicks in only if (1) a § 922(g) offender has previously been convicted of three violent felonies, and (2) those three felonies were committed on "occasions different from one another." § 924(e)(1). In other words, the statute contains both a three-offense requirement and a three-occasion requirement. But under the Government's view, the two will generally boil down to the same thing: When an offender's criminal history meets the three-offense demand, it will also meet the three-occasion one. That is because people seldom commit—indeed, seldom can commit—multiple ACCA offenses at the exact same time. Take burglary. It is, just as the Government argues, "physically impossible" for an offender to enter different structures simultaneously. Brief for United States 16–17. Or consider crimes defined by the use of physical force, such as assault or murder. Except in unusual cases (like a bombing), multiple offenses of that kind happen one by one by one, even if all occur in a short spell. The Government's reading, to be sure, does not render the occasions clause wholly superfluous; in select circumstances, a criminal may satisfy the elements of multiple offenses in a single instant. But for the most part, the Government's hyper-technical focus on the precise timing of elements—which can make someone a career criminal in the space of a minute—gives ACCA's three-occasions requirement no work to do.

The inquiry that requirement entails, given what "occasion" ordinarily means, is more multi-factored in nature. . . . In many cases, a single factor—especially of time or place—can decisively differentiate occasions. Courts, for instance, have nearly always treated offenses as occurring on separate occasions if a person committed them a day or more apart, or at a "significant distance." United States v. Rideout, 3 F.3d 32, 35 (CA2 1993); see, e.g., United States v. Riddle, 47 F.3d 460, 462 (CA1 1995) (per curiam). In other cases, the inquiry just as readily shows a single occasion, because all the factors cut that way. That is true, for example, in our barroom-brawl hypothetical, where the offender has engaged in a continuous stream of closely related criminal acts at one location. Of course, there will be some hard cases in between, as under almost any legal test. When that is so, assessing the relevant circumstances may also involve keeping an eye on ACCA's history and purpose, which we next discuss. But in law as in life, it is usually not so difficult to identify an "occasion": Given that the term in ACCA has just its ordinary meaning, most cases should involve no extra-ordinary work.

. . . Here, every relevant consideration shows that Wooden burglarized ten storage units on a single occasion, even though his criminal activity resulted in double-digit convictions. Wooden committed his burglaries on a single night, in a single uninterrupted course of conduct. The crimes all took place at one location, a one-building storage facility with one address. Each offense was essentially identical, and all were intertwined with the others. The burglaries were part and parcel of the same scheme, actuated by the same motive, and accomplished by the same means. Indeed, each burglary in some sense facilitated the next, as Wooden moved from unit to unit to unit, all in a row. And reflecting all these facts, Georgia law treated the burglaries as integrally connected. Because they "ar[ose] from the same conduct," the prosecutor had to charge all ten in a single indictment. The indictment thus confirms what all the circumstances suggest: One criminal occasion notwithstanding ten crimes.

B

Statutory history and purpose confirm our view of the occasions clause's meaning, as well as our conclusion that Wooden is not a career offender. . . .

III

For the reasons stated, Wooden's ten burglary convictions were for offenses committed on a single occasion. They therefore count only once under ACCA. . . .

It is so ordered.

[Concurring opinions of Justices Sotomayor and Kavanaugh, opinion of Justice Barrett concurring in part and concurring in the judgment, and opinion of Justice Gorsuch concurring in the judgment are omitted.]

## NOTES ON TEXTUALISM

(1) ***Consider the Cases.*** West Virginia University Hospital, TVA v. Hill, and Wooden are textualist in the sense that the majority opinion in each relies on the particular wording of the statute involved to reach a decision. But that does not mean that the method used in each of the cases is exactly alike. Textualism should perhaps be seen as a family of approaches, perhaps closely related, rather than as a single methodology. Before going on, consider these questions: How does each of the opinions treat the relationship between statutory text and common language? Between statutory text and the text of other statutes? Between statutory text and the intent of Congress? Between statutory text and the rest of the legal system?

(2) ***What Distinguishes Textualism?*** JOHN F. MANNING, TEXTUALISM AND LEGISLATIVE INTENT, 91 Va. L. Rev. 419 (2005): "[C]lassical intentionalists emphasize that meaning depends on what the speaker actually intends to convey. In that sense, classical intentionalists treat Congress much as they would treat an individual speaker: If an individual uses a term that has multiple potential meanings, the true meaning of that term as used on a particular occasion depends on the meaning intended by the speaker. So when the words of a statute leave a residue of ambiguity, intentionalists find it appropriate to examine the bill's internal legislative history for further

evidence of what members of Congress "intended." More important, because people often speak loosely, listeners must adjust their understanding when circumstances suggest that an individual has poorly expressed his or her intentions. By the same token, intentionalists insist that judges enforce the spirit rather than the letter of the law when the enacted words fail to capture the legislature's apparent purposes, as revealed by the tenor of the legislation as a whole, the mischiefs giving rise to its enactment, the policy expressed in similar statutes, and whatever other circumstances may shed light on the policy of the enactment. Classical intentionalism thus presupposes that interpreters should try to ascertain how the legislative majority would have handled a problem that the fair import of the enacted text either does not resolve or resolves in a manner that does not adequately reflect the legislature's apparent aims.

"Like classical intentionalists, textualists work within the faithful agent framework; they believe that in our system of government, federal judges have a duty to ascertain and implement as accurately as possible the instructions set down by Congress (within constitutional bounds). . . . But textualists deny that a legislature has any shared intention that lies behind but differs from the reasonable import of the words adopted; that is, they think it impossible to tell how the body as a whole actually intended (or, more accurately, would have intended) to resolve a policy question not clearly or satisfactorily settled by the text. Building upon the realist tradition, textualists do not believe that the premises governing an individual's intended meaning translate well to a complex, multi-member legislative process. As one author has put it, Congress is a 'they,' not an 'it,' and legislative policies are reduced to law only through a cumbersome and highly intricate lawmaking process. . . .

"So . . . textualists reject perhaps the most important premise of classical intentionalism: the idea that behind most legislation lies some sort of policy judgment that is meaningfully identifiable, shared by a legislative majority, and yet imprecisely expressed in the public meaning of the text that has made its way through Congress's many filters. Textualists focus on the end product of the legislative process, as reflected in the way a reasonable person conversant with applicable conventions would read the enacted words in context. Because of the fractured, tortuous, and often concealed nature of legislative bargaining, textualists believe that such a construct is the best that interpreters can do—that objectified intent provides the most, if not the only, plausible way for a faithful agent to show fidelity to his principal."

(3) ***Justifications for Textualism.*** FRANK H. EASTERBROOK, TEXT, HISTORY, AND STRUCTURE IN STATUTORY INTERPRETATION, 17 Harv. J.L. & Pub. Pol'y 61, 63–64 (1994): "One thing we wish the legal system to do is to give understandable commands, consistently interpreted. This calls for empty-headed simplicity. Facilitate planning; facilitate settlement in litigation; avoid search for factors that will impress judges if only you can find them in a warehouse of documents.

"Another thing political society wishes to do is to confine judges. We are supposed to be faithful agents, not independent principals. Having a wide field to play—not only the statute but also the debates, not only the rules but also the values they advance, and so on—liberates judges. This is objectionable on grounds of democratic theory as well as on grounds of predictability.

"A third thing we wish to do is to empower Congress. Let it make rules. This means using whatever approach Congress picks, adhering rather than shifting. A shift from rules to standards frustrates compromises, undermines even the ability to choose. . . .

"A fourth thing we wish to do is to constrain Congress. Yes, I know this is exactly the opposite of the third objective. Yet it too is an important part of the design. Congress must act bicamerally. It needs presidential approval. The laws must be published. These requirements serve important values—they cut down on the amount of legislation and drive bargains into the open where they may be scrutinized. Enacting a vaporous statute and winking, or putting some stuff in the reports, avoids these constraints—which judges can resist by insisting that words in laws be taken seriously.

"A fifth thing we wish to do is to make the law sensible, to improve the substance of rules. But this goal, I submit, is entirely subordinate to the first four, and usually incompatible with them. It can be accomplished only by the strategy of defining ends and seeking them, a strategy that costs us dearly in ability to achieve the principal objectives. Making the law work is a proper goal for judges only at the retail level; substance is in the main for the political branches. 'Getting things right' may be a principal goal of law without its being a principal or even a particularly important goal of legal interpretation."

(4) ***Textualism and the Rule of Law.*** ANTONIN SCALIA, A MATTER OF INTERPRETATION 13, 23, 25 (1997): "[T]hough I have no quarrel with the common law and its process, I do question whether the *attitude* of the common-law judge—the mind-set that asks, 'What is the most desirable resolution of this case, and how can any impediments to the achievement of that result be evaded?'—is appropriate for most of the work that I do, and much of the work that state judges do. We live in an age of legislation, and most new law is statutory law. As [Lawrence M. Friedman] has put it, in modern times 'the main business of government, and therefore of law, [is] legislative and executive. . . . Even private law, so-called, [has been] turning statutory. The lion's share of the norms and rules that actually govern[ ] the country [come] out of Congress and the legislatures. . . . The rules of the countless administrative agencies [are] themselves an important, even crucial, source of law.' This is particularly true in the federal courts, where, with a qualification so small it does not bear mentioning, there is no such thing as common law. Every issue of law resolved by a federal judge involves interpretation of text—the text of a regulation, or of a statute, or of the Constitution. . . .

". . . To be a textualist in good standing, one need not be too dull to perceive the broader social purposes that a statute is designed, or could be designed to serve; or too hidebound to realize that new times require new laws. One need only hold the belief that judges have no authority to pursue those broader purposes or write those new laws. . . .

"Of all the criticisms leveled against textualism, the most mindless is that it is 'formalistic.' The answer to that is, *of course it's formalistic*! The rule of law is *about* form. If, for example, a citizen performs an act—let us say the sale of certain technology to a foreign country—which is prohibited by a widely publicized bill proposed by the administration and passed by both houses of Congress, *but not yet signed by the President*, that sale is lawful. It is of no consequence that everyone knows both houses of Congress and the President wish to prevent that sale. Before the wish becomes binding law, it must be embodied in a bill that passes both houses and is signed by the President. Is that not formalism? A murderer has been caught with blood on his hands, bending over the body of his victim; a neighbor with a video camera has filmed the crime; and the murderer has confessed in writing and on videotape. We nonetheless insist that before the state can punish this miscreant, it must conduct a full-dress criminal trial that results in a verdict of guilty. Is that not formalism? Long live formalism. It is what makes a government a government of laws and not of men."

(5) ***Another View?*** STEPHEN D. SMITH, LAW WITHOUT MIND, 88 Mich. L. Rev. 104, 112, 117–18 (1989): ". . . If the statute is understood not as the expression of a collective decision by the established political authority but rather as a kind of thing-in-itself, a free-floating text, then why is its right to command any greater than that of, say, the political treatise or the science fiction novel? . . .

". . . The result comes close to achieving, at least in aspiration, a law that is in the most literal sense 'mindless.' Of course, the law would still be the product of mental processes, just as decisions based on interpreting astrological configurations or on reading palms or tea leaves are the result of (perhaps very intricate) mental processes. But such decisions are not, at least not in the most important sense, based on 'mind.' Similarly, when statutes are understood as 'texts' but not as the expression of actual, conscious, temporally situated decisions, the connection to 'mind' is cut; the statute becomes a kind of Rorschach blot; it constrains—there are thousands of things that an observer just can't see in a Rorshach blot [sic]—but its constraints are fortuitous, not the product of conscious deliberation. And the critical question, more vexing now than in its earlier appearances, is not whether such a statute *can* guide judges, but whether there is any conceivable reason why it *should*. A person might search for answers to vital personal questions in a Rorschach blot; he might even *find* answers there. But who wants to turn his life over to a Rorschach blot?"

(6) ***Textualists v. Textualists.*** In a number of recent cases, whether concerning Title VII (Bostock v. Clayton County, 140 S.Ct. 1731 (2020)), criminal law (Van Buren v. United States, 141 S.Ct. 1648 (2021)), or immigration law (Niz-Chavez v. Garland, 141 S.Ct. 1474 (2021)), the debate between the majority and the dissent has been less about whether to follow the text where it goes than about where the text is taking us. The result has been sharply divided opinions in which each side claims that the text clearly compels the result it reaches. Such disagreements raise a question that might trouble defenders of textualism, who often, as you've just read, advance objectivity as a principal justification for the method. Can it be that

the plain meaning of the text is really plain if, say, four skilled readers of it find it plainly to mean the opposite of what five other skilled readers understand it plainly to mean? And if that can be true in a particular case, or even in a few of them that reach the Court, does the persistence of intratextualist disputes about how to read the text show the robustness of the method or the need to deploy something beyond the method?

(7) ***Which Textualism? Part I.*** Within the intra-textualist debates, one scholar has argued in favor of "formalistic textualism." In her view, formalism helps provide "a relatively rule-bound method that promises to better constrain judicial discretion and thus a judge's proclivity to rule in favor of the wishes of the political faction that propelled her into power." Emphasizing "semantic context, rather than social or policy context," helps a judge to "insulate herself from external influences" like politics. Tara Leigh Grove, Which Textualism?, 134 Harv. L. Rev. 265, 269 (2020). Do the basic principles of fairness, which require treating like cases alike, require judges to insulate themselves in this way? Or is that conclusion premised on a value judgment that the benefits of formalism outweigh the costs of that kind of inflexibility?

And what fills in the "semantic context" of speech in the first place? Does "ordinary meaning" exhaust the inquiry? Recall Wooden's analysis of the "ordinary meaning of the word 'occasion.' " (Did you find the Supreme Court's analysis of the congressional enactment persuasive? Should the answer to such a question turn on how you use English day-to-day?) Does vernacular usage necessarily provide the proper semantic context? Could interpretation of a criminal statute, where notice is paramount, call instead for precise technical meaning? In the context of the Civil Rights Act, consider the argument that "an ordinary reader would read Title VII like the kind of text that it is—a piece of legislation, not a transcript of a conversation between friends about a particular incident." Benjamin Eidelson, Dimensional Disparate Treatment, 95 S. Cal. L. Rev. (forthcoming). These might seem to be the kinds of questions about "social or policy context" that shape *any* act of interpretation. If so, is drawing a meaningful distinction between "semantic context" and "social or policy context" even possible?

(8) ***Which Textualism? Part II.*** In Niz-Chavez, Justice Kavanaugh accused the majority of relying on "literal" meaning rather than "ordinary" meaning in construing the word "a." A similar divergence cropped up in Bostock, discussed further below (pp. 128–141). Is the difference between how a word is described in a dictionary (literal meaning) and how it is expected to be applied by most people regardless of what a dictionary might say (ordinary meaning)? If so, is there much reason to privilege a dictionary-based meaning over the meaning that most people expect a word to carry? Yet, conversely, if we don't go by the dictionary, how do we know what most people expect? See Kevin P. Tobia, Testing Ordinary Meaning, 134 Harv. L. Rev. 726 (2020).

(9) ***Context and Appropriations?*** For another way of thinking about the import of context in applying textualism, consider the TVA Court's analysis of whether "continuing appropriations for Tellico Dam constitute[d] an implied repeal of the" Endangered Species Act. Recall that in West Virginia

University Hospitals, the Court began its textualist analysis not with the dictionary but with a review of how Congress had addressed a similar issue about paying for experts in other statutes. If we assume that Congress at least intends for courts to attend to how it generally operates (unless, that is, that assumption itself violates textualist principles), should courts also attend to the type of legislation that it deploys? That is the question raised in TVA with respect to the fact that Congress kept making appropriations to complete the dam. The majority addressed that issue this way:

"There is nothing in the appropriations measures, as passed, which states that the Tellico Project was to be completed irrespective of the requirements of the Endangered Species Act. These appropriations, in fact, represented relatively minor components of the lump-sum amounts for the entire TVA budget. To find a repeal of the Endangered Species Act under these circumstances would surely do violence to the ' "cardinal rule. . . that repeals by implication are not favored." ' . . .

"The doctrine disfavoring repeals by implication . . . applies with even greater force when the claimed repeal rests solely on an Appropriations Act. We recognize that both substantive enactments and appropriations measures are 'Acts of Congress,' but the latter have the limited and specific purpose of providing funds for authorized programs. When voting on appropriations measures, legislators are entitled to operate under the assumption that the funds will be devoted to purposes which are lawful and not for any purpose forbidden. Without such an assurance, every appropriations measure would be pregnant with prospects of altering substantive legislation. . . . Not only would this lead to the absurd result of requiring Members to review exhaustively the background of every authorization before voting on an appropriation, but it would flout the very rules the Congress carefully adopted to avoid this need.

"Perhaps mindful of the fact that it is 'swimming upstream' against a strong current of well-established precedent, TVA argues for an exception to the rule against implied repealers in a circumstance where, as here, Appropriations Committees have expressly stated their 'understanding' that the earlier legislation would not prohibit the proposed expenditure. We cannot accept such a proposition. Expressions of committees dealing with requests for appropriations cannot be equated with statutes enacted by Congress, particularly not in the circumstances presented by this case. First, the Appropriations Committees had no jurisdiction over the subject of endangered species, much less did they conduct the type of extensive hearings which preceded passage of the earlier Endangered Species Acts, especially the 1973 Act. We venture to suggest that the House Committee on Merchant Marine and Fisheries and the Senate Committee on Commerce would be somewhat surprised to learn that their careful work on the substantive legislation had been undone by the simple—and brief—insertion of some inconsistent language in Appropriations Committees' Reports.

"Second, there is no indication that Congress as a whole was aware of TVA's position, although the Appropriations Committees apparently agreed with petitioner's views. . . ." 437 U.S. 153, 189–92 (1978).

Increasing polarization has enhanced the relevance of appropriations measures as a mechanism for policy decisions. Gillian E. Metzger, Taking Appropriations Seriously, 121 Colum. L. Rev. 1075, 1086 (2021). Does applying the lens of TVA v. Hill, and its subordination of appropriations to "substantive legislation," render the policy decisions of an earlier, less polarized era frozen in time? Would that mean that governing by means of appropriations bills has been stymied, or that there is effectively a consensus not to disturb the status quo? Of course, a statute that specifically says, "no money shall be spent to do x . . ." is a different, more focused creature.

## b. Purposivism

***CHURCH OF THE HOLY TRINITY v. UNITED STATES***

***UNITED STEELWORKERS v. WEBER***

***Notes on Purposivism***

The leading counter-theory to textualism is purposivism. The purposivist approach need not ignore the legislative text. But this theory does necessarily encourage judges to ask about the legislature's purpose or reason for enacting the statute. A key question concerns just how strongly they should be encouraged to do so. Only when the text is unclear? Always?

As with textualism, there are defenders and critics of purposivism. And, as with textualism, there are deep questions about why legislative purpose should matter. After all, if that purpose has not been made manifest in the text, how is that purpose entitled to be given legal effect? On the other hand, statutory texts are rarely if ever perfectly clear in all respects. When an ambiguity arises, what is a judge to do if not search for the purpose underlying the statute? Moreover, why should the judge start with the text rather than the purpose? If the purpose of the statute is clear, but the text does not appear to reflect it, why should one assume that the text means what it seems to say?

As you read the materials on purposivism that follow, consider how a judge should determine the legislature's purpose. What if the statute has more than one purpose? Should the court be more concerned with the specific or general intent of those who drafted a statute? And, most fundamentally, is the purpose relevant only when the text is unclear or is the text relevant only insofar as it tracks the clear legislative purpose?

To sharpen your mind, consider (before reading the Court's opinion) the statute, quite old, involved in the next case, 23 Stat. 332, ch. 164 (Feb. 26, 1885):

> *Be it enacted by the Senate and House of Representatives of the United States of America in Congress assembled*, That from and after the passage of this act it shall be unlawful for any person, company, partnership, or corporation, in any manner whatsoever, to prepay the transportation, or in any way assist

> or encourage the importation or migration of any alien or aliens, any foreigner or foreigners, into the United States, its Territories, or the District of Columbia, under contract or agreement, parol or special, express or implied, made previous to the importation or migration of such alien or aliens, foreigner or foreigners, to perform labor or service of any kind in the United States, its Territories, or the District of Columbia.
>
> SEC. 2. That all contracts or agreements, express or implied, parol, or special, which may hereafter be made by and between any person, company, partnership, or corporation, and any foreigner or foreigners, alien or aliens, to perform labor or service or having reference to the performance of labor or service by any person in the United States, its Territories, or the District of Columbia previous to the migration or importation of the person or persons whose labor or service is contracted for into the United States, shall be utterly void and of no effect,
>
> SEC. 3. That for every violation of any of the provisions of section one of this act the person, partnership, company, or corporation violating the same, by knowingly assisting, encouraging or soliciting the migration or importation of any alien or aliens, foreigner or foreigners, into the United States, its Territories, or the District of Columbia, to perform labor or service of any kind under contract or agreement, express or implied, parol or special, with such alien or aliens, foreigner or foreigners, previous to becoming residents or citizens of the United States, shall forfeit and pay for every such offence the sum of one thousand dollars. . .
>
> SEC. 4. That the master of any vessel who shall knowingly bring within the United States on any such vessel, and land, or permit to be landed, from any foreign port or place, any alien laborer, mechanic, or artisan who, previous to embarkation on such vessel, had entered into contract or agreement, parol or special, express or implied, to perform labor or service in the United States, shall be deemed guilty of a misdemeanor. . .
>
> SEC. 5. That nothing in this act shall be so construed. . .to prevent any person, or persons, partnership, or corporation from engaging, under contract or agreement, skilled workmen in foreign countries to perform labor in the United States in or upon any new industry not at present established in the United States: *Provided*, That skilled labor for that purpose cannot be otherwise obtained; nor shall the provisions of this act apply to professional actors, artists, lecturers, or singers, nor to persons employed strictly as personal or domestic servants. . .

The question of the case is whether a church that contracts with a pastor from abroad to come to the United States and serve violates the statute.

## CHURCH OF THE HOLY TRINITY v. UNITED STATES

Supreme Court of the United States (1892).
143 U.S. 457.

■ JUSTICE BREWER delivered the opinion of the court.

Plaintiff in error is a corporation, duly organized and incorporated as a religious society under the laws of the State of New York. E. Walpole Warren was, prior to September, 1887, an alien residing in England. In that month the plaintiff in error made a contract with him, by which he was to remove to the city of New York and enter into its service as rector and pastor; and in pursuance of such contract, Warren did so remove and enter upon such service. It is claimed by the United States that this contract on the part of the plaintiff in error was forbidden by the act of February 26, 1885, 23 Stat. 332, c. 164, and an action was commenced to recover the penalty prescribed by that act. The Circuit Court held that the contract was within the prohibition of the statute, and rendered judgment accordingly, and the single question presented for our determination is whether it erred in that conclusion.

The first section describes the act forbidden, and is in these words:

"Be it enacted by the Senate and House of Representatives of the United States of America in Congress assembled, That from and after the passage of this act it shall be unlawful for any person, company, partnership, or corporation, in any manner whatsoever, to prepay the transportation, or in any way assist or encourage the importation or migration of any alien or aliens, any foreigner or foreigners, into the United States, its Territories, or the District of Columbia, under contract or agreement, parol or special, express or implied, made previous to the importation or migration of such alien or aliens, foreigner or foreigners, to perform labor or service of any kind in the United States, its Territories, or the District of Columbia."

Text of Statute

It must be conceded that the act of the corporation is within the letter of this section, for the relation of rector to his church is one of service, and implies labor on the one side with compensation on the other. Not only are the general words labor and service both used, but also, as it were to guard against any narrow interpretation and emphasize a breadth of meaning, to them is added "of any kind;" and, further, as noticed by the Circuit Judge in his opinion, the fifth section, which makes specific exceptions, among them professional actors, artists, lecturers, singers and domestic servants, strengthens the idea that every other kind of labor and service was intended to be reached by the first section. While there is great force to this reasoning, we cannot think Congress intended to denounce with penalties a transaction like that in the present case. It is a familiar rule, that a thing may be within the letter of the statute and yet not within the statute, because not within its spirit, nor within the intention of its makers. This has been often asserted, and the reports are full of cases illustrating its application. This is not the substitution of the will of the judge for that of the legislator, for frequently words of general meaning are used in a statute, words broad enough to include an act in question, and yet a consideration of the whole legislation, or of the circumstances surrounding its enactment, or of the absurd results which follow from giving such broad meaning to the words, makes it unreasonable to believe that the legislator intended to include the particular act. . . .

In [United States v. Kirby, 74 U.S. 482 (1868)] the court says: "All laws should receive a sensible construction. General terms should be so limited in their application as not to lead to injustice, oppression or an absurd consequence. It will always, therefore, be presumed that the legislature intended exceptions to its language which would avoid results of this character. The reason of the law in such cases should prevail over its letter. The common sense of man approves the judgment mentioned by Puffendorf, that the Bolognian law which enacted 'that whoever drew blood in the streets should be punished with the utmost severity,' did not extend to the surgeon who opened the vein of a person that fell down in the street in a fit. The same common sense accepts the ruling, cited by Plowden, that the statute of 1st Edw. II., which enacts that a prisoner who breaks prison shall be guilty of felony, does not extend to a prisoner who breaks out when the prison is on fire, 'for he is not to be hanged because he would not stay to be burnt.' And we think that a like common sense will sanction the ruling we make . . . ."

. . . Now, the title of this act is, "An act to prohibit the importation and migration of foreigners and aliens under contract or agreement to perform labor in the United States, its Territories and the District of Columbia." Obviously the thought expressed in this reaches only to the work of the manual laborer, as distinguished from that of the professional man. No one reading such a title would suppose that Congress had in its mind any purpose of staying the coming into this country of ministers of the gospel, or, indeed, of any class whose toil is that of the brain. The common understanding of the terms labor and laborers does not include preaching and preachers; and it is to be assumed that words and phrases are used in their ordinary meaning. So whatever of light is thrown upon the statute by the language of the title indicates an exclusion from its penal provisions of all contracts for the employment of ministers, rectors and pastors.

Again, another guide to the meaning of a statute is found in the evil which it is designed to remedy; and for this the court properly looks at contemporaneous events, the situation as it existed, and as it was pressed upon the attention of the legislative body. The situation which called for this statute was briefly but fully stated by Justice Brown when, as District Judge, he decided the case of U.S. v. Craig, 28 Fed. Rep. 795, 798 [(1886)]: "The motives and history of the act are matters of common knowledge. It had become the practice for large capitalists in this country to contract with their agents abroad for the shipment of great numbers of an ignorant and servile class of foreign laborers, under contracts, by which the employer agreed, upon the one hand, to prepay their passage, while, upon the other hand, the laborers agreed to work after their arrival for a certain time at a low rate of wages. The effect of this was to break down the labor market, and to reduce other laborers engaged in like occupations to the level of the assisted immigrant. The evil finally became so flagrant that an appeal was made to Congress for relief by the passage of the act in question, the design of which was to raise the standard of foreign immigrants, and to discountenance the migration of those who had not sufficient means in their own hands, or those of their friends, to pay their passage."

It appears, also, from the petitions, and in the testimony presented before the committees of Congress, that it was this cheap unskilled labor which was making the trouble, and the influx of which Congress sought to prevent. It was never suggested that we had in this country a surplus of brain toilers, and, least of all, that the market for the services of Christian ministers was depressed by foreign competition. Those were matters to which the attention of Congress, or of the people, was not directed. So far, then, as the evil which was sought to be remedied interprets the statute, it also guides to an exclusion of this contract from the penalties of the act.

A singular circumstance, throwing light upon the intent of Congress, is found in this extract from the report of the Senate Committee on Education and Labor, recommending the passage of the bill: "The general facts and considerations which induce the committee to recommend the passage of this bill are set forth in the Report of the Committee of the House. The committee report the bill back without amendment, although there are certain features thereof which might well be changed or modified, in the hope that the bill may not fail of passage during the present session. Especially would the committee have otherwise recommended amendments, substituting for the expression 'labor and service,' whenever it occurs in the body of the bill, the words 'manual labor' or 'manual service,' as sufficiently broad to accomplish the purposes of the bill, and that such amendments would remove objections which a sharp and perhaps unfriendly criticism may urge to the proposed legislation. The committee, however, believing that the bill in its present form will be construed as including only those whose labor or service is manual in character, and being very desirous that the bill become a law before the adjournment, have reported the bill without change." Page 6059, Congressional Record, 48th Cong. And, referring back to the report of the Committee of the House, there appears this language: "It seeks to restrain and prohibit the immigration or importation of laborers who would have never seen our shores but for the inducements and allurements of men whose only object is to obtain labor at the lowest possible rate, regardless of the social and material well-being of our own citizens and regardless of the evil consequences which result to American laborers from such immigration. This class of immigrants care nothing about our institutions, and in many instances never even heard of them; they are men whose passage is paid by the importers; they come here under contract to labor for a certain number of years; they are ignorant of our social condition, and that they may remain so they are isolated and prevented from coming into contact with Americans. They are generally from the lowest social stratum, and live upon the coarsest food and in hovels of a character before unknown to American workmen. They, as a rule, do not become citizens, and are certainly not a desirable acquisition to the body politic. The inevitable tendency of their presence among us is to degrade American labor, and to reduce it to the level of the imported pauper labor." Page 5359, Congressional Record, 48th Cong. . . .

Suppose in the Congress that passed this act some member had offered a bill which in terms declared that, if any Roman Catholic church in this country should contract with Cardinal Manning to come to this country and enter into its service as pastor and priest; or any Episcopal church should enter into a like contract with Canon Farrar; or any Baptist church should make similar arrangements with Rev. Mr. Spurgeon; or any Jewish synagogue with some eminent Rabbi, such contract should be adjudged unlawful and void, and the church making it be subject to prosecution and punishment, can it be believed that it would have received a minute of approving thought or a single vote? Yet it is contended that such was in effect the meaning of this statute. The construction invoked cannot be accepted as correct. It is a case where there was presented a definite evil, in view of which the legislature used general terms with the purpose of reaching all phases of that evil, and thereafter, unexpectedly, it is developed that the general language thus employed is broad enough to reach cases and acts which the whole history and life of the country affirm could not have been intentionally legislated against. It is the duty of the courts, under those circumstances, to say that, however broad the language of the statute may be, the act, although within the letter, is not within the intention of the legislature, and therefore cannot be within the statute.

The judgment will be reversed, and the case remanded for further proceedings in accordance with this opinion.

## UNITED STEELWORKERS v. WEBER

Supreme Court of the United States (1979).
443 U.S. 193.

■ JUSTICE BRENNAN delivered the opinion of the Court.

Challenged here is the legality of an affirmative action plan—collectively bargained by an employer and a union—that reserves for black employees 50% of the openings in an in-plant craft-training program until the percentage of black craftworkers in the plant is commensurate with the percentage of blacks in the local labor force. The question for decision is whether Congress, in Title VII of the Civil Rights Act of 1964, 78 Stat. 253, as amended, 42 U.S.C. § 2000e et seq., left employers and unions in the private sector free to take such race-conscious steps to eliminate manifest racial imbalances in traditionally segregated job categories. We hold that Title VII does not prohibit such race-conscious affirmative action plans.

I

In 1974, petitioner United Steelworkers of America (USWA) and petitioner Kaiser Aluminum & Chemical Corp. (Kaiser) entered into a master collective-bargaining agreement covering terms and conditions of employment at 15 Kaiser plants. The agreement contained, inter alia, an affirmative action plan designed to eliminate conspicuous racial imbalances in Kaiser's then almost exclusively white craftwork forces. Black craft-hiring goals were set for each Kaiser plant equal to the percentage of blacks in the respective local labor forces. To enable plants to meet these goals, on-the-job training programs were established to teach unskilled production workers—black and white—the skills necessary to become craftworkers. The plan reserved for black employees 50% of the openings in these newly created in-plant training programs.

This case arose from the operation of the plan at Kaiser's plant in Gramercy, La. Until 1974, Kaiser hired as craftworkers for that plant only persons who had had prior craft experience. Because blacks had long been excluded from craft unions, few were able to present such credentials. As a consequence, prior to 1974 only 1.83% (5 out of 273) of the skilled craftworkers at the Gramercy plant were black, even though the work force in the Gramercy area was approximately 39% black.

Pursuant to the national agreement Kaiser altered its craft-hiring practice in the Gramercy plant. Rather than hiring already trained outsiders, Kaiser established a training program to train its production workers to fill craft openings. Selection of craft trainees was made on the basis of seniority, with the proviso that at least 50% of the new trainees were to be black until the percentage of black skilled craftworkers in the Gramercy plant approximated the percentage of blacks in the local labor force.

During 1974, the first year of the operation of the Kaiser-USWA affirmative action plan, 13 craft trainees were selected from Gramercy's production work force. Of these, seven were black and six white. The most senior black selected into the program had less seniority than several white production workers whose bids for admission were rejected. Thereafter one of those white production workers, respondent Brian Weber (hereafter respondent), instituted this class action in the United States District Court for the Eastern District of Louisiana.

The complaint alleged that the filling of craft trainee positions at the Gramercy plant pursuant to the affirmative action program had resulted in junior black employees' receiving training in preference to senior white employees, thus discriminating against respondent and other similarly situated white employees in violation of §§ 703(a) and (d) of Title VII. . . .

II

. . . The only question before us is the narrow statutory issue of whether Title VII *forbids* private employers and unions from voluntarily agreeing upon bona fide affirmative action plans that accord racial preferences in the manner and for the purpose provided in the Kaiser-USWA plan. . . . ISSUE

Respondent argues that Congress intended in Title VII to prohibit all race-conscious affirmative action plans. Respondent's argument rests upon a literal interpretation of §§ 703(a) and (d) of the Act. Those sections make it unlawful to "discriminate . . . because of . . . race" in hiring and in the selection of apprentices for training programs. Since, the argument runs, McDonald v. Santa Fe Trail Transp. Co. settled that Title VII forbids discrimination against whites as well as blacks, and since the Kaiser-USWA affirmative action plan operates to discriminate against white employees solely because they are white, it follows that the Kaiser-USWA plan violates Title VII.

Respondent's argument is not without force. But it overlooks the significance of the fact that the Kaiser-USWA plan is an affirmative action plan voluntarily adopted by private parties to eliminate traditional patterns of racial segregation. In this context respondent's reliance upon a literal construction of §§ 703(a) and (d) and upon McDonald is misplaced. . . . It is a "familiar rule, that a thing may be within the letter of the statute and yet not within the statute, because not within its spirit, nor within the intention of its makers." Holy Trinity Church v. United States, 143 U.S. 457, 459 (1892). The prohibition against racial discrimination in §§ 703(a) and (d) of Title VII must therefore be read against the background of the legislative history of Title VII and the historical context from which the Act arose. Examination of those sources makes clear that an interpretation of the sections that forbade all race-conscious affirmative action would "bring about an end completely at variance with the purpose of the statute" and must be rejected.

Congress' primary concern in enacting the prohibition against racial discrimination in Title VII of the Civil Rights Act of 1964 was with "the plight of the Negro in our economy." 110 Cong. Rec. 6548 (1964) (remarks of Sen. Humphrey). Before 1964, blacks were largely relegated to "unskilled and semi-skilled jobs." Because of automation the number of such jobs was rapidly decreasing. As a consequence, "the relative position of the Negro worker [was] steadily worsening. In 1947 the nonwhite unemployment rate was only 64 percent higher than the white rate; in 1962 it was 124 percent higher." Id., at 6547 (remarks of Sen. Humphrey). . . .

Congress feared that the goals of the Civil Rights Act—the integration of blacks into the mainstream of American society—could not be achieved unless this trend were reversed. And Congress recognized that that would not be possible unless blacks were able to secure jobs "which have a future." Id., at 7204 (remarks of Sen. Clark). . . .

It plainly appears from the House Report accompanying the Civil Rights Act that Congress did not intend wholly to prohibit private and voluntary affirmative action efforts as one method of solving this problem. The Report provides:

"No bill can or should lay claim to eliminating all of the causes and consequences of racial and other types of discrimination against minorities. There is reason to believe, however, that national leadership provided by the enactment of Federal legislation dealing with the most troublesome problems *will create an atmosphere conducive to voluntary or local resolution of other forms of discrimination.*" H.R. Rep. No. 914, 88th Cong., 1st Sess., pt. 1, p. 18 (1963).

Given this legislative history, we cannot agree with respondent that Congress intended to prohibit the private sector from taking effective steps to accomplish the goal that Congress designed Title VII to achieve. The very statutory words intended as a spur or catalyst to cause "employers and unions to self-examine and to self-evaluate their employment practices and to endeavor to eliminate, so far as possible, the last vestiges of an unfortunate and ignominious page in this country's history," Albemarle Paper Co. v. Moody, 422 U.S. 405, 418 (1975), cannot be interpreted as an absolute prohibition against all private, voluntary, race-conscious affirmative action efforts to hasten the elimination of such vestiges. It would be ironic indeed if a law triggered by a Nation's concern over centuries of racial injustice and intended to improve the lot of those who had "been excluded from the American dream for so long," 110 Cong. Rec. 6552 (1964) (remarks of Sen. Humphrey), constituted the first legislative prohibition of all voluntary, private, race-conscious efforts to abolish traditional patterns of racial segregation and hierarchy.

Our conclusion is further reinforced by examination of the language and legislative history of § 703(j) of Title VII. Opponents of Title VII raised two related arguments against the bill. First, they argued that the Act would be interpreted to *require* employers with racially imbalanced work forces to grant preferential treatment to racial minorities in order to integrate. Second, they argued that employers with racially imbalanced work forces would grant preferential treatment to racial minorities, even if not required to do so by the Act. Had Congress meant to prohibit all race-conscious affirmative action, as respondent urges, it easily could have answered both objections by providing that Title VII would not require or *permit* racially preferential integration efforts. But Congress did not choose such a course. Rather, Congress added § 703(j) which addresses only the first objection. The section provides that nothing contained in Title VII "shall be interpreted to *require* any employer . . . to grant preferential treatment . . . to any group because of the race . . . of such . . . group on account of" a de facto racial imbalance in the employer's work force. The section does *not* state that "nothing in Title VII shall be interpreted to *permit*" voluntary affirmative efforts to correct racial imbalances. The natural inference is that Congress chose not to forbid all voluntary race-conscious affirmative action.

The reasons for this choice are evident from the legislative record. Title VII could not have been enacted into law without substantial support from legislators in both Houses who traditionally resisted federal regulation of private business. Those legislators demanded as a price for their support that "management prerogatives, and union freedoms . . . be left undisturbed to the greatest extent possible." H.R. Rep. No. 914, 88th Cong., 1st Sess., pt. 2, p. 29 (1963). Section 703(j) was proposed by

Senator Dirksen to allay any fears that the Act might be interpreted in such a way as to upset this compromise. The section was designed to prevent § 703 of Title VII from being interpreted in such a way as to lead to undue "Federal Government interference with private businesses because of some Federal employee's ideas about racial balance or racial imbalance." 110 Cong. Rec. 14314 (1964) (remarks of Sen. Miller). Clearly, a prohibition against all voluntary, race-conscious, affirmative action efforts would disserve these ends. Such a prohibition would augment the powers of the Federal Government and diminish traditional management prerogatives while at the same time impeding attainment of the ultimate statutory goals. In view of this legislative history and in view of Congress' desire to avoid undue federal regulation of private businesses, use of the word "require" rather than the phrase "require or permit" in § 703(j) fortifies the conclusion that Congress did not intend to limit traditional business freedom to such a degree as to prohibit all voluntary, race-conscious affirmative action. . . .

We conclude, therefore, that the adoption of the Kaiser-USWA plan for the Gramercy plant falls within the area of discretion left by Title VII to the private sector voluntarily to adopt affirmative action plans designed to eliminate conspicuous racial imbalance in traditionally segregated job categories. . . .

■ JUSTICE POWELL and JUSTICE STEVENS took no part in the consideration or decision of these cases.

■ CHIEF JUSTICE BURGER, dissenting.

. . . Often we have difficulty interpreting statutes either because of imprecise drafting or because legislative compromises have produced genuine ambiguities. But here there is no lack of clarity, no ambiguity. The quota embodied in the collective-bargaining agreement between Kaiser and the Steelworkers unquestionably discriminates on the basis of race against individual employees seeking admission to on-the-job training programs. And, under the plain language of § 703(d), that is "an *unlawful* employment practice." . . .

Arguably, Congress may not have gone far enough in correcting the effects of past discrimination when it enacted Title VII. The gross discrimination against minorities to which the Court adverts—particularly against Negroes in the building trades and craft unions—is one of the dark chapters in the otherwise great history of the American labor movement. And, I do not question the importance of encouraging voluntary compliance with the purposes and policies of Title VII. But that statute was conceived and enacted to make discrimination against *any* individual illegal, and I fail to see how "voluntary compliance" with the no-discrimination principle that is the heart and soul of Title VII as currently written will be achieved by permitting employers to discriminate against some individuals to give preferential treatment to others. . . .

It is often observed that hard cases make bad law. I suspect there is some truth to that adage, for the "hard" cases always tempt judges to exceed the limits of their authority, as the Court does today by totally rewriting a crucial part of Title VII to reach a "desirable" result. . . .

■ JUSTICE REHNQUIST, with whom THE CHIEF JUSTICE joins, dissenting.

. . .

The operative sections of Title VII prohibit racial discrimination in employment *simpliciter*. Taken in its normal meaning, and as understood by all Members of Congress who spoke to the issue during the legislative debates, this language prohibits a covered employer from considering race when making an employment decision, whether the race be black or white. Several years ago, however, a United States District Court held that "the dismissal of white employees charged with misappropriating company property while not dismissing a similarly charged Negro employee does not raise a claim upon which Title VII relief may be granted." McDonald v. Santa Fe Trail Transp. Co., 427 U.S. 273, 278 (1976). This Court unanimously reversed, concluding from the "uncontradicted legislative history" that "Title VII prohibits racial discrimination against the white petitioners in this case upon the same standards as would be applicable were they Negroes . . . ."

We have never wavered in our understanding that Title VII "prohibits *all* racial discrimination in employment, without exception for any group of particular employees." In Griggs v. Duke Power Co., 401 U.S. 424, 431 (1971), our first occasion to interpret Title VII, a unanimous Court observed that "[discriminatory] preference, for any group, minority or majority, is precisely and only what Congress has proscribed." And in our most recent discussion of the issue, we uttered words seemingly dispositive of this case: "It is clear beyond cavil that the obligation imposed by Title VII is to provide an equal opportunity for *each* applicant regardless of race, without regard to whether members of the applicant's race are already proportionately represented in the work force." Furnco Construction Corp. v. Waters, 438 U.S. 567, 579 (1978).

. . . [Here,] without even a break in syntax, the Court rejects "a literal construction of § 703(a)" in favor of newly discovered "legislative history," which leads it to a conclusion directly contrary to that compelled by the "uncontradicted legislative history" unearthed in McDonald and our other prior decisions. Now we are told that the legislative history of Title VII shows that employers are free to discriminate on the basis of race: an employer may, in the Court's words, "trammel the interests of the white employees" in favor of black employees in order to eliminate "racial imbalance." Our earlier interpretations of Title VII . . . were all wrong.

As if this were not enough to make a reasonable observer question this Court's adherence to the oft-stated principle that our duty is to construe rather than rewrite legislation, the Court also seizes upon § 703(j) of Title VII as an independent, or at least partially independent, basis for its holding. Totally ignoring the wording of that section, which is obviously addressed to those charged with the responsibility of interpreting the law rather than those who are subject to its proscriptions, and totally ignoring the months of legislative debates preceding the section's introduction and passage, which demonstrate clearly that it was enacted to prevent precisely what occurred in this case, the Court infers from § 703(j) that "Congress chose not to forbid all voluntary race-conscious affirmative action."

Thus, by a tour de force reminiscent not of jurists such as Hale, Holmes, and Hughes, but of escape artists such as Houdini, the Court eludes clear statutory language, "uncontradicted" legislative history, and uniform precedent in concluding that employers are, after all, permitted to consider race in making employment decisions. It may be that one or more of the principal sponsors of Title VII would have preferred to see a provision allowing preferential treatment of minorities written into the bill. Such a provision, however, would have to have been expressly or impliedly excepted from Title VII's explicit prohibition on all racial discrimination in employment. There is no such exception in the Act. And a reading of the legislative debates concerning Title VII, in which proponents and opponents alike uniformly denounced discrimination in favor of, as well as discrimination against, Negroes, demonstrates clearly that any legislator harboring an unspoken desire for such a provision could not possibly have succeeded in enacting it into law. . . .

[In the intervening sections of his opinion, Justice Rehnquist reviews the facts of this case and, at length, the legislative history of the statute.]

IV

Reading the language of Title VII, as the Court purports to do, "against the background of [its] legislative history . . . and the historical context from which the Act arose," one is led inescapably to the conclusion that Congress fully understood what it was saying and meant precisely what it said. Opponents of the civil rights bill did not argue that employers would be permitted under Title VII voluntarily to grant preferential treatment to minorities to correct racial imbalance. The plain language of the statute too clearly prohibited such racial discrimination to admit of any doubt. They argued, tirelessly, that Title VII would be interpreted by federal agencies and their agents to require unwilling employers to racially balance their work forces by granting preferential treatment to minorities. Supporters of H.R. 7152 responded, equally tirelessly, that the Act would not be so interpreted because not only does it not require preferential treatment of minorities, it also does not *permit* preferential treatment of any race for any reason. It cannot be doubted that the proponents of Title VII understood the meaning of their words, for "[seldom] has similar legislation been debated with greater consciousness of the need for 'legislative history,' or with greater care in the making thereof, to guide the courts in interpreting and applying the law."

To put an end to the dispute, supporters of the civil rights bill drafted and introduced § 703(j). Specifically addressed to the opposition's charge, § 703(j) simply enjoins federal agencies and courts from interpreting Title VII to require an employer to prefer certain racial groups to correct imbalances in his work force. The section says nothing about voluntary preferential treatment of minorities because such racial discrimination is plainly proscribed by §§ 703(a) and (d). Indeed, had Congress intended to except voluntary, race-conscious preferential treatment from the blanket prohibition of racial discrimination in §§ 703(a) and (d), it surely could have drafted language better suited to the task than § 703(j). It knew how. Section 703(i) provides:

"Nothing contained in [Title VII] shall apply to any business or enterprise on or near an Indian reservation with respect to any publicly announced employment practice of such business or enterprise under which a preferential treatment is given to any individual because he is an Indian living on or near a reservation."

V

Our task in this case, like any other case involving the construction of a statute, is to give effect to the intent of Congress. To divine that intent, we traditionally look first to the words of the statute and, if they are unclear, then to the statute's legislative history. Finding the desired result hopelessly foreclosed by these conventional sources, the Court turns to a third source—the "spirit" of the Act. But close examination of what the Court proffers as the spirit of the Act reveals it as the spirit animating the present majority, not the 88th Congress. For if the spirit of the Act eludes the cold words of the statute itself, it rings out with unmistakable clarity in the words of the elected representatives who made the Act law. It is *equality*. . . .

There is perhaps no device more destructive to the notion of equality than the *numerus clausus*—the quota. Whether described as "benign discrimination" or "affirmative action," the racial quota is nonetheless a creator of castes, a two-edged sword that must demean one in order to prefer another. In passing Title VII, Congress outlawed *all* racial discrimination, recognizing that no discrimination based on race is benign, that no action disadvantaging a person because of his color is affirmative. With today's holding, the Court introduces into Title VII a tolerance for the very evil that the law was intended to eradicate, without offering even a clue as to what the limits on that tolerance may be. We are told simply that Kaiser's racially discriminatory admission quota "falls on the permissible side of the line." By going not merely *beyond*, but directly *against* Title VII's language and legislative history, the Court has sown the wind. Later courts will face the impossible task of reaping the whirlwind.

## NOTES ON PURPOSIVISM

(1) ***Consider the Cases.*** As with textualism, there are many varieties of "purposivism." The preceding cases—Holy Trinity Church and Weber—might be arranged along several different dimensions. How do they differ in the level of generality or specificity of the "purpose" they are trying to locate? How do they differ as to the evidence they use to establish the "purpose" they find? How do they use that "purpose" in relation to the text they also construe? Is there a form of "purposivism" that is attractive, and a form that

is not? Are either of the cases truly purposivist or are they both rooted in the text enough to make each of them just a case about reading the text in context? It is perhaps worth noting that each of the cases has, among serious scholars, both its defenders and its detractors.

(2) ***A Classic Statement.*** HENRY M. HART & ALBERT M. SACKS, THE LEGAL PROCESS: BASIC PROBLEMS IN THE MAKING AND APPLICATION OF LAW 1374–80 (William N. Eskridge, Jr., & Phillip P. Frickey eds., 1994) (1958):

"In interpreting a statute a court should:

1. Decide what purpose ought to be attributed to the statute and to any subordinate provision of it which may be involved; and then

2. Interpret the words of the statute immediately in question so as to carry out the purpose as best it can, making sure, however, that it does not give the words either—

(a) a meaning they will not bear, or

(b) a meaning which would violate any established policy of clear statement. . . .

". . . The words of a statute, taken in their context, serve both as guides in the attribution of general purpose and as factors limiting the particular meanings that can properly be attributed. . . . A formally enacted statement of purpose in a statute should be accepted by the court if it appears to have been designed to serve as a guide to interpretation, is consistent with the words and context of the statute, and is relevant to the question of meaning at issue. . . .

". . . In drawing such inferences [about purpose] the court needs to be aware that the concept of purpose is not simple.

(a) Purposes may be shaped with differing degrees of definiteness.

The definiteness may be such that resolution of a doubt about purpose resolves, without more, a question of specific application. . . . Or a purpose may be deliberately formulated with great generality, openly contemplating the exercise of further judgment by the interpreter even after he has fully grasped the legislature's thought. . . .

(b) Purposes, moreover, may exist in hierarchies or constellations. E.g. (to give a very simple illustration), to do *this* only so far as possible without doing *that*.

(c) One form of such a constellation or relationship is invariable in the law and of immense importance. The purpose of a statute must always be treated as including not only an immediate purpose or group of related purposes but a larger and subtler purpose as to how the particular statute is to be fitted into the legal system as a whole. . . .

". . . In determining the more immediate purpose which ought to be attributed to a statute, and to any subordinate provision of it which may be involved, a court should try to put itself in imagination in the position of the legislature which enacted the measure. The court, however, should not do this in the mood of a cynical political observer, taking account of all the short-run currents of political expedience that swirl around any legislative session. It should assume, unless the contrary unmistakably appears, that the legislature was made up of reasonable persons pursuing reasonable purposes reasonably. It should presume conclusively that these persons, whether or not entertaining concepts of reasonableness shared by the court, were trying responsibly and in good faith to discharge their constitutional powers and duties. . . .

". . . The degree of definiteness to be attributed to the legislative purpose in the enactment of the statute is decisive of the nature of the task of interpretation which remains after the purpose has been grasped. . . . [An agency charged with applying the statute] should give sympathetic attention to indications in the legislative history of the lines of contemplated growth, if the history is available. It should give weight to popular construction of self-operating elements of the statute, if that is uniform. Primarily, it should strive to develop a coherent and reasoned pattern of applications intelligibly related to the general purpose."

(3) ***A Modern Statement.*** STEPHEN BREYER, MAKING OUR DEMOCRACY WORK 94–98 (2010): "I believe a purpose-oriented approach is better than a purely text-oriented approach. Three sets of considerations, taken together, explain why I believe the Court is obliged to follow a purpose-oriented approach.

"First, judicial consideration of a statute's purposes helps to further the Constitution's democratic goals. In a representative democracy, legislators must ultimately act in ways that voters find acceptable. But voters are unaware of the detailed language that legislators write. They can do no more than consider whether a legislator's work corresponds roughly to their own views, typically expressed in terms of general objectives, say peace, prosperity, healthy environment, and economizing.

"A legislator whose statute furthers a popular objective will seek credit at election time—at least if the statute works reasonably well. But suppose the statute does not work well. Then whom should the voters blame? If courts have interpreted the statute in accordance with the legislator's purposes, there is no one to blame but the legislator. But if courts disregard the statute's purposes, it is much harder for the voter to know who is responsible when results go awry. . . .

"No single court decision will make a difference. But over time, where vast numbers of statutory provisions are at issue, the following generalizations seem fair. The more the Court relies on text-based methods alone to interpret statutes, the easier it will be for legislators to avoid responsibility for a badly written statute simply by saying that the Court reached results they did not favor. The more the Court seeks realistically to ascertain the purposes of a statute and interprets its provisions in ways that further those purposes, the harder it will be for the legislator to escape responsibility for the statute's objectives, and the easier it will be for voters to hold their legislators responsible for their legislative decisions, including the consequences of the statutes for which they vote.

"Second, a purpose-oriented approach helps individual statutes work better for those whom Congress intended to help. . . .

"Third, and most important, by emphasizing purpose the Court will help Congress better accomplish its own legislative work. Congress does not, cannot, and need not write statutes that precisely and exhaustively explain where and how each of the statute's provisions will apply. For one thing, doing so would require too many words. Who wants statutory encyclopedias that spell out in excruciating detail all potential applications in all potential circumstances? Who could read them?

"For another thing, linguistic imprecision, vagueness, and ambiguity are often useful, even necessary, statutory instruments. Congress may not know just how its statute should apply in future circumstances where it can see that future only dimly, and new situations will always emerge. Congress may want to consider only one aspect of a complex, detailed subject, an aspect that warrants a few general words that simply point a court in the right direction. Congress may want to use a general standard, such as "restraint of trade," while intending courts to develop more specific content on a case-by-case common-law basis. Or, the English language may lack words that succinctly express, say, the necessary quantitative measurement, as, for example, when Congress seeks to punish more severely those who commit "serious" or "violent" crimes.

"In these circumstances, congressional drafting staffs may well use general or imprecise words while relying on committee reports, statements of members delivered on the floor of Congress, legislative hearings, and similar materials to convey intended purposes, hence meaning, scope, and reference. Congress can use that drafting system if, and only if, it can count on the courts to consider legislative purposes when interpreting statutes and look at the associated legislative materials to help determine legislative purpose. When courts do so, drafters, legislators, and judges can work together. They act in tandem with Congress, carrying out the legislators' objectives in even the most complex statutes, such as those dealing with bankruptcy, transit system mergers, or pension benefit guarantees.

"Without such teamwork, legislators and their staffs would face a drafting task that is daunting and even impractical. . . .

"In saying all this, I recognize that the political complexion of Congress can change. By looking at the purposes of those who once enacted a statute as I would do, the Court might produce an interpretation that a more recent Congress would disapprove. But in doing so, the Court emphasizes the need for *legislation* to depart from an earlier statute, and it thereby also assures the present Congress that their own intentions will be honored later when the Court considers the meaning of a statute that they have passed."

(4) ***Another View.*** ANTONIN SCALIA, A MATTER OF INTERPRETATION 17–18 (1997): "[I]t is simply incompatible with democratic government, or indeed, even with fair government, to have the meaning of a law determined by what the lawgiver meant, rather than by what the lawgiver promulgated. That

seems to me one step worse than the trick the emperor Nero was said to engage in: posting edicts high up on the pillars, so that they could not easily be read. Government by unexpressed intent is similarly tyrannical. It is the *law* that governs, not the intent of the lawgiver. That seems to me the essence of the famous American ideal set forth in the Massachusetts constitution: A government of laws, not of men. Men may intend what they will; but it is only the laws that they enact which bind us.

"In reality, however, if one accepts the principle that the object of judicial interpretation is to determine the intent of the legislature, being bound by genuine but unexpressed legislative intent rather than the law is only the *theoretical* threat. The *practical* threat is that, under the guise or even the self-delusion of pursuing unexpressed legislative intents, common-law judges will in fact pursue their own objectives and desires, extending their lawmaking proclivities from the common law to the statutory field. When you are told to decide, not on the basis of what the legislature said, but on the basis of what it *meant*, and are assured that there is no necessary connection between the two, your best shot at figuring out what the legislature meant is to ask yourself what a wise and intelligent person *should* have meant; and that will surely bring you to the conclusion that the law means what you think it *ought* to mean—which is precisely how judges decide things under the common law."

(5) ***What Informs Our Understanding of Purpose?*** Legislative history—as reflected in legislative reports, congressional testimony and the like—is an obvious source of knowledge about legislative purpose. But courts do not always confine themselves to such materials in trying to divine the purpose underlying a statute. For example, historical events that gave rise to the need for the legislation might be thought to provide a strong indication of what a statute must have been intended to accomplish. Consider BRNOVICH V. DEMOCRATIC NATIONAL COMMITTEE, 141 S.Ct. 2321 (2021), in which the Supreme Court addressed the meaning of § 2 of the Voting Rights Act of 1965. The provision reads:

> (a) No voting qualification or prerequisite to voting or standard, practice, or procedure shall be imposed on, or applied by any State or political subdivision in a manner which results in a denial or abridgment of the right of any citizen of the United States to vote on account of race or color, or in contravention of the guarantees set forth in [§] 10303(f)(2) of this title, as provided in subsection (b).
>
> (b) A violation of subsection (a) is established if, based on the totality of the circumstances, it is shown that the political processes leading to nomination or election in the State or political subdivision are not equally open to participation by members of a class of citizens protected by subsection (a) in that its members have less opportunity than other members of the electorate to participate in the political process and to elect representatives of their choice. The extent to which new members of a protected class have been elected to office in the State or political subdivision is one of the circumstances which may be considered: *Provided*, That nothing in this section establishes a right to have members of a

protected class elected in numbers equal to their proportion in the population.

The case involved a challenge to two Arizona state laws that, respectively, prohibited a vote from counting if not cast in the precinct in which the voter was assigned and made it a crime for anyone other than a postal worker, election official, or a voter's caregiver, family member, or household member to knowingly collect an early ballot. The Democratic National Committee and some of its affiliates sued, contending that the measures violated § 2 because they had an adverse and disparate impact on American Indian, Hispanic, and Black citizens in the state.

The majority, in an opinion by JUSTICE ALITO, held that neither Arizona provision violated § 2. In explaining why, Justice Alito focused in particular on the phrase "totality of the circumstances." He then set forth a nonexhaustive list of circumstances to consider that appears to have been derived less from an understanding of the ordinary meaning of the specific words in the statute than from an understanding of Congress's objective. Moreover, the understanding of that objective appears to have been derived less from formal legislative materials than from an understanding of the events that brought about that measure's passage. In this regard, Justice Alito gave a relatively detailed account of what led to the 1982 amendment to the Voting Rights Act that resulted in § 2(b) and then explained:

"[T]he degree to which a voting rule departs from what was standard practice when § 2 was amended in 1982 is a relevant consideration. Because every voting rule imposes a burden of some sort, it is useful to have benchmarks with which the burden imposed by a challenged rule can be compared. The burdens associated with the rules in widespread use when § 2 was adopted are therefore useful in gauging whether the burdens imposed by a challenged rule are sufficient to prevent voting from being equally 'open' or furnishing an equal 'opportunity' to vote in the sense meant in § 2. Therefore, it is relevant that in 1982 States typically required nearly all voters to cast their ballots in person on election day and allowed only narrow and tightly defined categories of voters to cast absentee ballots. . . . We doubt that Congress intended to uproot facially neutral time, place, and manner regulations that have a long pedigree or are in widespread use in the United States. We have no need to decide whether adherence to, or a return to, a 1982 framework is necessarily lawful under § 2, but the degree to which a challenged rule has a long pedigree or is in widespread use in the United States is a circumstance that must be taken into account."

He further explained in the same vein: "[W]e think it inappropriate to read § 2 to impose a strict 'necessity requirement' that would force States to demonstrate that their legitimate interests can be accomplished only by means of the voting regulations in question . . . . Demanding such a tight fit would have the effect of invalidating a great many neutral voting requirements with long pedigrees that are reasonable means of pursuing legitimate interests. It would also transfer much of the authority to regulate election procedures from the States to the federal courts."

JUSTICE KAGAN, for the three dissenters, offered a different understanding of what Congress aimed to achieve, in part by starting the clock well before 1982:

"The Voting Rights Act is ambitious, in both goal and scope. When President Lyndon Johnson sent the bill to Congress, ten days after John Lewis led marchers across the Edmund Pettus Bridge, he explained that it was 'carefully drafted to meet its objective—the end of discrimination in voting in America.' He was right about how the Act's drafting reflected its aim. 'The end of discrimination in voting' is a far-reaching goal. And the Voting Rights Act's text is just as far-reaching. A later amendment, adding the provision at issue here, became necessary when this Court construed the statute too narrowly. And in the last decade, the Court assailed the Act again, undoing its vital Section 5. See Shelby County v. Holder, 570 U.S. 529 (2013). But Section 2 of the Act remains, as written, expansive as ever—demanding that every citizen of this country possesses a right at once grand and obvious: the right to an equal opportunity to vote.

"Today, the Court undermines Section 2 and the right it provides. The majority fears that the statute Congress wrote is too 'radical'—that it will invalidate too many state voting laws. . . . So the majority writes its own set of rules, limiting Section 2 from multiple directions. . . . Wherever it can, the majority gives a cramped reading to broad language. And then it uses that reading to uphold two election laws from Arizona that discriminate against minority voters. I could say—and will in the following pages—that this is not how the Court is supposed to interpret and apply statutes. But that ordinary critique woefully undersells the problem. What is tragic here is that the Court has (yet again) rewritten—in order to weaken—a statute that stands as a monument to America's greatness, and protects against its basest impulses. What is tragic is that the Court has damaged a statute designed to bring about 'the end of discrimination in voting.' "

In response, Justice Alito had this to say about the dissent's historical framing of the interpretive issue: "The dissent provides historical background that all Americans should remember . . . but that background does not tell us how to decide these cases . . . . Only after this extended effort at misdirection is the dissent's aim finally unveiled: to undo as much as possible the compromise that was reached between the House and Senate when § 2 was amended in 1982. Recall that the version originally passed by the House did not contain § 2(b) and was thought to prohibit any voting practice that had 'discriminatory effects,' loosely defined. . . . That is the freewheeling disparate impact regime the dissent wants to impose on the States. But the version enacted into law is § 2(b), and that subsection directs us to consider 'the totality of the circumstances.' Not, as the dissent, would have it, the totality of just one circumstance."

Justice Alito also returned to the notion that the world as it existed in 1982 had to be considered: "The dissent objects to consideration of the 1982 landscape because even rules that were prevalent at that time are invalid under § 2 if they, well, violate § 2. We of course agree with that tautology. But the question is what it *means* to provide equal opportunity, and given that every voting rule imposes some amount of burden, rules that were and are commonplace are useful comparators when considering the totality of the circumstances. Unlike the dissent, Congress did not set its sights on every facially neutral, time, place, or manner voting rule in existence."

## c. The (Uncertain?) Line Between Textualism and Purposivism

*KING v. BURWELL*
*CONCEPCION v. UNITED STATES*
*Notes on the (Uncertain?) Line Between Textualism and Purposivism*

## KING v. BURWELL

Supreme Court of the United States (2015).
576 U.S. 473.

■ CHIEF JUSTICE ROBERTS delivered the opinion of the Court.

The Patient Protection and Affordable Care Act adopts a series of interlocking reforms designed to expand coverage in the individual health insurance market. First, the Act bars insurers from taking a person's health into account when deciding whether to sell health insurance or how much to charge. Second, the Act generally requires each person to maintain insurance coverage or make a payment to the Internal Revenue Service. And third, the Act gives tax credits to certain people to make insurance more affordable.

In addition to those reforms, the Act requires the creation of an "Exchange" in each State—basically, a marketplace that allows people to compare and purchase insurance plans. The Act gives each State the opportunity to establish its own Exchange, but provides that the Federal Government will establish the Exchange if the State does not.

This case is about whether the Act's interlocking reforms apply equally in each State no matter who establishes the State's Exchange. Specifically, the question presented is whether the Act's tax credits are available in States that have a Federal Exchange.

I

A

In the 1990s, several States began experimenting with ways to expand people's access to coverage. One common approach was to impose a pair of insurance market regulations—a "guaranteed issue" requirement, which barred insurers from denying coverage to any person because of his health, and a "community rating" requirement, which barred insurers from charging a person higher premiums for the same reason. Together, those requirements were designed to ensure that anyone who wanted to buy health insurance could do so.

The guaranteed issue and community rating requirements achieved that goal, but they had an unintended consequence: They encouraged people to wait until they got sick to buy insurance. Why buy insurance coverage when you are healthy, if you can buy the same coverage for the same price when you become ill? This consequence—known as "adverse selection"—led to a second: Insurers were forced to increase premiums to account for the fact that, more and more, it was the sick rather than the healthy who were buying insurance. And that consequence fed back into the first: As the cost of insurance rose, even more people waited until they became ill to buy it.

This led to an economic "death spiral." As premiums rose higher and higher, and the number of people buying insurance sank lower and lower, insurers began to leave the market entirely. As a result, the number of people without insurance increased dramatically. . . .

B

The Affordable Care Act adopts . . . guaranteed issue and community rating requirements. The Act provides that "each health insurance issuer that offers health insurance coverage in the individual . . . market in a State must accept every . . . individual in the State that applies for such coverage." The Act also bars insurers from charging higher premiums on the basis of a person's health.

Second, the Act generally requires individuals to maintain health insurance coverage or make a payment to the IRS. Congress recognized that, without an incentive, "many individuals would wait to purchase health insurance until they needed care." So Congress adopted a coverage requirement to "minimize this adverse selection and broaden the health insurance risk pool to include healthy individuals, which will lower health insurance premiums." In Congress's view, that coverage requirement was "essential to creating effective health insurance markets." Congress also provided an exemption from the coverage requirement for anyone who has to spend more than eight percent of his income on health insurance.

Third, the Act seeks to make insurance more affordable by giving refundable tax credits to individuals with household incomes between 100 percent and 400 percent of the federal poverty line. Individuals who meet the Act's requirements may purchase insurance with the tax credits, which are provided in advance directly to the individual's insurer.

These three reforms are closely intertwined. As noted, Congress found that the guaranteed issue and community rating requirements would not work without the coverage requirement. And the coverage requirement would not work without the tax credits. The reason is that, without the tax credits, the cost of buying insurance would exceed eight percent of income for a large number of individuals, which would exempt them from the coverage requirement. Given the relationship between these three reforms, the Act provided that they should take effect on the same day—January 1, 2014.

C

In addition to those three reforms, the Act requires the creation of an "Exchange" in each State where people can shop for insurance, usually online. An Exchange may be created in one of two ways. First, the Act provides that "[e]ach State shall . . . establish an American Health Benefit Exchange . . . for the State." Second, if a State nonetheless chooses not to establish its own Exchange, the Act provides that the Secretary of Health and Human Services "shall . . . establish and operate such Exchange within the State."

The issue in this case is whether the Act's tax credits are available in States that have a Federal Exchange rather than a State Exchange. The Act initially provides that tax credits "shall be allowed" for any "applicable taxpayer." The Act then provides that the amount of the tax credit depends in part on whether the taxpayer has enrolled in an insurance plan through "an Exchange *established by the State* under section 1311 of the Patient Protection and Affordable Care Act."

The IRS addressed the availability of tax credits by promulgating a rule that made them available on both State and Federal Exchanges. As relevant here, the IRS Rule provides that a taxpayer is eligible for a tax credit if he enrolled in an insurance plan through "an Exchange," which is defined as "an Exchange serving the individual market . . . regardless of whether the Exchange is established and operated by a State . . . or by HHS." At this point, 16 States and the District of Columbia have established their own Exchanges; the other 34 States have elected to have HHS do so. . . .

II

The Affordable Care Act addresses tax credits in what is now Section 36B of the Internal Revenue Code. . . . The parties dispute whether Section 36B authorizes tax credits for individuals who enroll in an insurance plan through a Federal Exchange. Petitioners argue that a Federal Exchange is not "an Exchange established by the State under [42 U.S.C. § 18031]," and that the IRS Rule therefore contradicts Section 36B. The Government responds that the IRS Rule is lawful because the phrase "an Exchange established by the State under [42 U.S.C. § 18031]" should be read to include Federal Exchanges. . . .

A

We begin with the text of Section 36B. As relevant here, Section 36B allows an individual to receive tax credits only if the individual enrolls in an insurance plan through "an Exchange established by the State under [42 U.S.C. § 18031]." In other words, three things must be true: First, the individual must enroll in an insurance plan through "an Exchange." Second, that Exchange must be "established by the State." And third, that Exchange must be established "under [42 U.S.C. § 18031]." We address each requirement in turn.

First, all parties agree that a Federal Exchange qualifies as "an Exchange" for purposes of Section 36B. . . .

Second, we must determine whether a Federal Exchange is "established by the State" for purposes of Section 36B. At the outset, it might seem that a Federal Exchange cannot fulfill this requirement. After all, the Act defines "State" to mean "each of the 50 States and the District of Columbia"—a definition that does not include the Federal Government. 42 U.S.C. § 18024(d). But when read in context, "with a view to [its] place in the overall statutory scheme," the meaning of the phrase "established by the State" is not so clear.

After telling each State to establish an Exchange, Section 18031 provides that all Exchanges "shall make available qualified health plans to qualified individuals." 42 U.S.C. § 18031(d)(2)(A). Section 18032 then defines the term "qualified individual" in part as an individual who "resides in the State that established the Exchange." § 18032(f)(1)(A). And that's a problem: If we give the phrase "the State that established the Exchange" its most natural meaning, there would be *no* "qualified individuals" on Federal Exchanges. But the Act clearly contemplates that there will be qualified individuals on *every* Exchange. As we just mentioned, the Act requires all Exchanges to "make available qualified health plans to qualified individuals"—something an Exchange could not do if there were no such individuals. § 18031(d)(2)(A). And the Act tells the Exchange, in deciding which health plans to offer, to consider "the interests of qualified individuals . . . in the State or States in which such Exchange operates"—again, something the Exchange could not do if qualified individuals did not exist. § 18031(e)(1)(B). This problem arises repeatedly throughout the Act. . . .

These provisions suggest that the Act may not always use the phrase "established by the State" in its most natural sense. Thus, the meaning of that phrase may not be as clear as it appears when read out of context.

Third, we must determine whether a Federal Exchange is established "under [42 U.S.C. § 18031]." This too might seem a requirement that a Federal Exchange cannot fulfill, because it is Section 18041 that tells the Secretary when to "establish and operate such Exchange." But here again, the way different provisions in the statute interact suggests otherwise.

The Act defines the term "Exchange" to mean "an American Health Benefit Exchange established under section 18031." § 300gg–91(d)(21). If we import that definition into Section 18041, the Act tells the Secretary to "establish and operate such 'American Health Benefit Exchange established under section 18031.'" That suggests that Section 18041 authorizes the Secretary to establish an Exchange under Section 18031, not (or not only) under Section 18041. Otherwise, the Federal Exchange, by definition, would not be an "Exchange" at all.

This interpretation of "under [42 U.S.C. § 18031]" fits best with the statutory context. All of the requirements that an Exchange must meet are in Section 18031, so it is sensible to regard all Exchanges as established under that provision. In addition, every time the Act uses the word "Exchange," the definitional provision requires that we substitute the phrase "Exchange established under section 18031." If Federal Exchanges were not established under Section 18031, therefore, literally none of the Act's requirements would apply to them. Finally, the Act repeatedly uses the phrase "established under [42 U.S.C. § 18031]" in situations where it would make no sense to distinguish between State and Federal Exchanges. . . .

The upshot of all this is that the phrase "an Exchange established by the State under [42 U.S.C. § 18031]" is properly viewed as ambiguous. The phrase may be limited in its reach to State Exchanges. But it is also possible that the phrase refers to *all* Exchanges—both State and Federal—at least for purposes of the tax credits. If a State chooses not to follow the directive in Section 18031 that it establish an Exchange, the Act tells the Secretary to establish "such Exchange." § 18041. And by using the words "such Exchange," the Act indicates that State and Federal Exchanges should be the same. But State and Federal Exchanges would differ in a fundamental way if tax credits were available only on State Exchanges—one type of Exchange would help make insurance more affordable by providing billions of dollars to the States' citizens; the other type of Exchange would not.

The conclusion that Section 36B is ambiguous is further supported by several provisions that assume tax credits will be available on both State and Federal Exchanges. . . .

Petitioners and the dissent respond that the words "established by the State" would be unnecessary if Congress meant to extend tax credits to both State and Federal Exchanges. But "our preference for avoiding surplusage constructions is not absolute." Lamie v. United States Trustee, 540 U.S. 526, 536 (2004). And specifically with respect to this Act, rigorous application of the canon does not seem a particularly useful guide to a fair construction of the statute.

The Affordable Care Act contains more than a few examples of inartful drafting. (To cite just one, the Act creates three separate Section 1563s. See 124 Stat. 270, 911, 912.) Several features of the Act's passage contributed to that unfortunate reality. Congress wrote key parts of the Act behind closed doors, rather than through "the traditional legislative process." And Congress passed much of the Act using a complicated budgetary procedure known as "reconciliation," which limited opportunities for debate and amendment, and bypassed the Senate's normal 60-vote filibuster requirement. As a result, the Act does not reflect the type of care and deliberation that one might expect of such significant legislation.

Anyway, we "must do our best, bearing in mind the fundamental canon of statutory construction that the words of a statute must be read in their context and with a view to their place in the overall statutory scheme." Utility Air Regulatory Group, 573 U.S. [302, 320 (2014).] After reading Section 36B along with other related provisions in the Act, we cannot conclude that the phrase "an Exchange established by the State under [Section 18031]" is unambiguous.

B

Given that the text is ambiguous, we must turn to the broader structure of the Act to determine the meaning of Section 36B. "A provision that may seem ambiguous in isolation is often clarified by the remainder of the statutory scheme . . . because only one of the permissible meanings produces a substantive effect that is compatible with the rest of the law." Here, the statutory scheme compels us to reject petitioners' interpretation because it would destabilize the individual insurance market in any State with a Federal Exchange, and likely create the very "death spirals" that Congress designed the Act to avoid. See New York State Dept. of Social Servs. v. Dublino, 413 U.S. 405, 419–420 (1973) ("We cannot interpret federal statutes to negate their own stated purposes.").

As discussed above, Congress based the Affordable Care Act on three major reforms: first, the guaranteed issue and community rating requirements; second, a requirement that individuals maintain health insurance coverage or make a payment to the IRS; and third, the tax credits for individuals with household incomes between 100 percent and 400 percent of the federal poverty line. In a State that establishes its own Exchange, these three reforms work together to expand insurance coverage. The guaranteed issue and community rating requirements ensure that anyone can buy insurance; the coverage requirement creates an incentive for people to do so before they get sick; and the tax credits—it is hoped—make insurance more affordable. Together, those reforms "minimize . . . adverse selection and broaden the health insurance risk pool to include healthy individuals, which will lower health insurance premiums."

Under petitioners' reading, however, the Act would operate quite differently in a State with a Federal Exchange. As they see it, one of the Act's three major reforms—the tax credits—would not apply. And a second major reform—the coverage requirement—would not apply in a meaningful way. As explained earlier, the coverage requirement applies only when the cost of buying health insurance (minus the amount of the tax credits) is less than eight percent of an individual's income. So without the tax credits, the coverage requirement would apply to fewer individuals. And it would be a *lot* fewer. In 2014, approximately 87 percent of people who bought insurance on a Federal Exchange did so with tax credits, and virtually all of those people would become exempt. If petitioners are right, therefore, only one of the Act's three major reforms would apply in States with a Federal Exchange.

The combination of no tax credits and an ineffective coverage requirement could well push a State's individual insurance market into a death spiral. . . .

It is implausible that Congress meant the Act to operate in this manner. Congress made the guaranteed issue and community rating requirements applicable in every State in the Nation. But those requirements only work when combined with the coverage requirement and the tax credits. So it stands to reason that Congress meant for those provisions to apply in every State as well. . . .

C

Finally, the structure of Section 36B itself suggests that tax credits are not limited to State Exchanges . . .

D

. . . Reliance on context and structure in statutory interpretation is a "subtle business, calling for great wariness lest what professes to be mere rendering becomes creation and attempted interpretation of legislation becomes legislation itself." Palmer v. Massachusetts, 308 U.S. 79, 83 (1939). For the reasons we have given, however, such reliance is appropriate in this case, and leads us to conclude that Section 36B allows tax credits for insurance purchased on any Exchange created under the Act. Those credits are necessary for the Federal Exchanges to function like their State Exchange counterparts, and to avoid the type of calamitous result that Congress plainly meant to avoid.

* * *

In a democracy, the power to make the law rests with those chosen by the people. Our role is more confined—"to say what the law is." Marbury v. Madison, 1 Cranch 137, 177 (1803). That is easier in some cases than in others. But in every case we must respect the role of the Legislature, and take care not to undo what it has done. A fair reading of legislation demands a fair understanding of the legislative plan.

Congress passed the Affordable Care Act to improve health insurance markets, not to destroy them. If at all possible, we must interpret the Act in a way that is consistent with the former, and avoids the latter. Section 36B can fairly be read consistent with what we see as Congress's plan, and that is the reading we adopt. . . .

[The judgment of the Fourth Circuit, upholding the Act, is affirmed.]

■ JUSTICE SCALIA, with whom JUSTICE THOMAS and JUSTICE ALITO join, dissenting.

The Court holds that when the Patient Protection and Affordable Care Act says "Exchange established by the State" it means "Exchange established by the State or the Federal Government." That is of course quite absurd, and the Court's 21 pages of explanation make it no less so.

I

. . . This case requires us to decide whether someone who buys insurance on an Exchange established by the Secretary gets tax credits. You would think the answer would be obvious—so obvious there would hardly be a need for the Supreme Court to hear a case about it. In order to receive any money under § 36B, an individual must enroll in an insurance plan through an "Exchange established by the State." The Secretary of Health and Human Services is not a State. So an Exchange established by the Secretary is not an Exchange established by the

State—which means people who buy health insurance through such an Exchange get no money under § 36B.

Words no longer have meaning if an Exchange that is *not* established by a State is "established by the State." It is hard to come up with a clearer way to limit tax credits to state Exchanges than to use the words "established by the State." And it is hard to come up with a reason to include the words "by the State" other than the purpose of limiting credits to state Exchanges. . . . Under all the usual rules of interpretation, in short, the Government should lose this case. But normal rules of interpretation seem always to yield to the overriding principle of the present Court: The Affordable Care Act must be saved. . . .

III

. . . Statutory design and purpose matter only to the extent they help clarify an otherwise ambiguous provision. Could anyone maintain with a straight face that § 36B is unclear? To mention just the highlights, the Court's interpretation clashes with a statutory definition, renders words inoperative in at least seven separate provisions of the Act, overlooks the contrast between provisions that say "Exchange" and those that say "Exchange established by the State," gives the same phrase one meaning for purposes of tax credits but an entirely different meaning for other purposes, and (let us not forget) contradicts the ordinary meaning of the words Congress used. On the other side of the ledger, the Court has come up with nothing more than a general provision that turns out to be controlled by a specific one, a handful of clauses that are consistent with either understanding of establishment by the State, and a resemblance between the tax-credit provision and the rest of the Tax Code. If that is all it takes to make something ambiguous, everything is ambiguous.

Having gone wrong in consulting statutory purpose at all, the Court goes wrong again in analyzing it. The purposes of a law must be "collected chiefly from its words," not "from extrinsic circumstances." Only by concentrating on the law's terms can a judge hope to uncover the scheme *of the statute,* rather than some other scheme that the judge thinks desirable. Like it or not, the express terms of the Affordable Care Act make only two of the three reforms mentioned by the Court applicable in States that do not establish Exchanges. It is perfectly possible for them to operate independently of tax credits. The guaranteed-issue and community-rating requirements continue to ensure that insurance companies treat all customers the same no matter their health, and the individual mandate continues to encourage people to maintain coverage, lest they be "taxed."

The Court protests that without the tax credits, the number of people covered by the individual mandate shrinks, and without a broadly applicable individual mandate the guaranteed-issue and community-rating requirements "would destabilize the individual insurance market." If true, these projections would show only that the statutory scheme contains a flaw; they would not show that the statute means the opposite of what it says. . . .

Compounding its errors, the Court forgets that it is no more appropriate to consider one of a statute's purposes in isolation than it is to consider one of its words that way. No law pursues just one purpose at all costs, and no statutory scheme encompasses just one element. Most relevant here, the Affordable Care Act displays a congressional preference for state participation in the establishment of Exchanges: Each State gets the first opportunity to set up its Exchange, 42 U.S.C. § 18031(b); States that take up the opportunity receive federal funding for "activities . . . related to establishing" an Exchange, § 18031(a)(3); and the Secretary may establish an Exchange in a State only as a fallback, § 18041(c). But setting up and running an Exchange involve significant burdens—meeting strict deadlines, § 18041(b), implementing requirements related to the offering of insurance plans, § 18031(d)(4), setting up outreach programs, § 18031(i), and ensuring that the Exchange is self-sustaining by 2015, § 18031(d)(5)(A). A State would have much less reason to take on these burdens if its citizens could receive tax credits no matter who establishes its Exchange. (Now that the Internal Revenue Service has interpreted § 36B to authorize tax credits everywhere, by the way, 34 States have failed to set up their own Exchanges.) So even if making credits available on all Exchanges advances the goal of improving healthcare markets, it frustrates the goal of encouraging state involvement in the implementation of the Act. *This* is what justifies going out of our way to read "established by the State" to mean "established by the State or not established by the State"? . . . All in all, the Court's arguments about the law's purpose and design are no more convincing than its arguments about context. . . .

## CONCEPCION v. UNITED STATES

Supreme Court of the United States (2022).
142 S.Ct. 2389.

■ JUSTICE SOTOMAYOR delivered the opinion of the Court.

There is a longstanding tradition in American law, dating back to the dawn of the Republic, that a judge at sentencing considers the whole person before him or her "as an individual." Koon v. United States, 518 U.S. 81, 113 (1996). In line with this history, federal courts today generally "exercise a wide discretion in the sources and types of evidence used" to craft appropriate sentences. Williams v. New York, 337 U.S. 241, 246 (1949). When a defendant appears for sentencing, the sentencing court considers the defendant on that day, not on the date of his offense or the date of his conviction. Pepper v. United States, 562 U.S. 476, 492 (2011). Similarly, when a defendant's sentence is set aside on appeal, the district court at resentencing can (and in many cases, must) consider the defendant's conduct and changes in the Federal Sentencing Guidelines since the original sentencing. Ibid.

Congress enacted the First Step Act of 2018 against that backdrop. The First Step Act authorizes district courts to reduce the prison sentences of defendants convicted of certain offenses involving crack cocaine. The Act allows a district court to impose a reduced sentence "as if" the revised penalties for crack cocaine enacted in the Fair Sentencing Act of 2010 were in effect at the time the offense was committed. The question in this case is whether a district court adjudicating a motion under the First Step Act may consider other intervening changes of law (such as changes to the Sentencing Guidelines) or changes of fact (such as behavior in prison) in adjudicating a First Step Act motion.

The Court holds that they may. It is only when Congress or the Constitution limits the scope of information that a district court may consider in deciding whether, and to what extent, to modify a sentence, that a district court's discretion to consider information is restrained. Nothing in the First Step Act contains such a limitation. . . .

I

A

In 2007, [Carlos] Concepcion pleaded guilty to one count of distributing five or more grams of crack cocaine . . . , and he was sentenced in 2009 to 19 years (228 months) in prison. Two features of his sentencing are relevant here. First, Concepcion was sentenced under a scheme that created a 100-to-1 disparity between crack-cocaine and powder-cocaine offenders. At the time Concepcion was sentenced, an offense involving five or more grams of crack cocaine resulted in a statutory sentencing range of 5 to 40 years' imprisonment; it required 100 times as much powder cocaine to trigger the same penalties. Second, when Concepcion was initially sentenced, he qualified as a "career offender." The career offender provision, together with other enhancements, increased Concepcion's Guidelines range from 57 to 71 months to 262 to 327 months.

. . . Just one year after Concepcion was sentenced, Congress passed the Fair Sentencing Act of 2010 to correct the harsh disparities between crack and powder cocaine sentencing. Section 2 of that Act increased the amount of crack cocaine needed to trigger the 5-to-40-year sentencing range from 5 grams to 28 grams. § 2(a)(2), 124 Stat. 2372. The Sentencing Commission then retroactively amended the Sentencing Guidelines to lower the Guidelines range for crack-cocaine offenses, but that amendment did not benefit all prisoners serving sentences handed down during the 100-to-1 regime. See United States Sentencing Commission, Guidelines Manual App. C, Amdt. 750 (Supp. Nov. 2011) (USSG). Concepcion was not eligible for retroactive relief under that 2011 Sentencing Commission's amendment because he was sentenced under the career offender enhancement, but he became eligible to have his sentence reduced in 2018, when Congress passed the First Step Act. The First Step Act authorized district courts to "impose a reduced sentence" for qualifying movants "as if sections 2 and 3 of the Fair Sentencing Act . . . were in effect at the time the covered offense was committed." Pub. L. 115–391, § 404(b), 132 Stat. 5222.

B

Concepcion filed a pro se motion under the First Step Act in 2019. He argued that he was serving a sentence for a "covered offense" because § 2 of the Fair Sentencing Act "modified" the statutory penalties for his conviction under 21 U.S.C. § 841(a)(1). Concepcion contended that retroactive application of the Fair Sentencing Act lowered his Guidelines range from 262 to 327 months to 188 to 235 months. The Government conceded Concepcion's eligibility for relief and his calculation of the Guidelines but opposed the motion, emphasizing that Concepcion's original sentence of 228 months fell within the new Guidelines range of 188 to 235 months. While recognizing Concepcion's participation in various programs in prison, the Government detailed "troubling behaviors such as '[f]ighting (12/19/2017); Interfering with Staff (11/15/2012); and Possession of a Weapon'" in Concepcion's prison records that, in the Government's view, counseled against a sentence reduction. Electronic Case Filing in No. 1:07–cr–10197 (Mass.) (ECF), Doc. 78, pp. 4–5, n. 4.

In his reply brief, represented by counsel, Concepcion made two primary arguments in support of a reduced sentence. First, he argued that he would no longer be considered a career offender under the amended Guidelines, because one of his prior convictions had been vacated and his remaining convictions would no longer be considered crimes of violence that trigger the enhancement. . . . Second, Concepcion pointed to postsentencing evidence of rehabilitation. . . .

The District Court denied Concepcion's motion. It adopted the Government's argument that if the Court "considered only the changes in law that the Fair Sentencing Act enacted, [Concepcion's] sentence would be the same." App. to Pet. for Cert. 71a. The court declined to consider that Concepcion would no longer qualify as a career offender on the ground that the First Step Act "does not authorize such relief." Id., at 72a. In doing so, the District Court adopted the reasoning of the Fifth Circuit, which understood the First Step Act to require a district court to " 'plac[e] itself in the time frame of the original sentencing, altering the relevant legal landscape only by the changes mandated by the 2010 Fair Sentencing Act.' " Id., at 74a (quoting United States v. Hegwood, 934 F.3d 414, 418 (C.A.5 2019)). The District Court did not address Concepcion's evidence of rehabilitation or the Government's countervailing evidence of Concepcion's disciplinary record.

The Court of Appeals affirmed in a divided opinion. The court interpreted the First Step Act as requiring a "two-step inquiry." 991 F.3d 279, 289 (C.A.1 2021). At the first step of that inquiry, a district court decides whether a movant should be resentenced at all, considering only the changes wrought by the Fair Sentencing Act. Ibid. If the district court answers in the affirmative at the first step, it may then, in its discretion, consider new factual or legal developments in determining how to resentence the movant. Id., at 289–290. Judge Barron dissented, rejecting the panel's bifurcated approach. In his view, the First Step Act requires only one step of analysis, at which district courts have "substantial discretion" to consider evidence of rehabilitation and Guidelines changes. Id., at 293, 309–310.

The Court of Appeals opinion added to the disagreement among the Circuits as to whether a district court deciding a First Step Act motion must, may, or may not consider intervening changes of law or fact. This Court granted certiorari to resolve this disagreement. . . .

II

. . .

A

There is a "long" and "durable" tradition that sentencing judges "enjo[y] discretion in the sort of information they may consider" at an initial sentencing proceeding. Dean v. United States, 581 U.S. 62, 66 (2017). This history dates back to before the founding: "[B]oth before and since the American colonies became a nation, courts in this country and in England practiced a policy under which a sentencing judge could exercise a wide discretion in the sources and types of evidence used to assist him in determining the kind and extent of punishment to be imposed within limits fixed by law." Williams, 337 U.S., at 246. Early state and English courts broadly recognized this discretion. . . .

That unbroken tradition characterizes federal sentencing history as well. . . . Accordingly, a federal judge in deciding to impose a sentence "may appropriately conduct an inquiry broad in scope, largely unlimited either as to the kind of information he may consider, or the source from which it may come." United States v. Tucker, 404 U.S. 443, 446 (1972).

B

The discretion federal judges hold at initial sentencings also characterizes sentencing modification hearings. Relying on Williams and Koon, the Court in Pepper found it "clear that when a defendant's sentence has been set aside on appeal and his case remanded for resentencing, a district court may consider evidence of a defendant's rehabilitation since his prior sentencing." 562 U.S., at 490. Pepper reached that conclusion in light of the "federal sentencing framework" that allows sentencing judges to consider the " 'fullest information possible concerning the defendant's life and characteristics.' " Id., at 488, 490.

Accordingly, federal courts resentencing individuals whose sentences were vacated on appeal regularly consider evidence of rehabilitation developed after the initial sentencing. . . . Similarly, district courts in resentencing proceedings frequently consider evidence of violence and rule breaking in prison. . . .

Where district courts must calculate new Guidelines ranges as part of resentencing proceedings, courts have also considered unrelated Guidelines changes in their discretion. In many cases, a district court is prohibited from recalculating a Guidelines range in light of nonretroactive Guidelines amendments, but the court may find those amendments to be germane when deciding whether to modify a sentence at all, and if so, to what extent.

C

The only limitations on a court's discretion to consider any relevant materials at an initial sentencing or in modifying that sentence are those set forth by Congress in a statute or by the Constitution. . . . .

Congress is not shy about placing such limits where it deems them appropriate. At an initial sentencing, Congress has provided generally that "[n]o limitation shall be placed on the information concerning the background, character, and conduct of a person convicted of an offense" when deciding what sentence to impose. 18 U.S.C. § 3661. Congress has, however, expressly prohibited a district court in crafting an initial sentence from considering a defendant's need for rehabilitation in support of a prison sentence. See § 3582(a); Tapia v. United States, 564 U.S. 319, 328 (2011).

In other aspects of sentencing, Congress also has expressly limited district courts to considering only certain factors. For example, in determining whether to include a term of supervised release, and the length of any such term, Congress has expressly precluded district courts from considering the need for retribution. See § 3583(c); [Tapia, 564 U.S.], at 326.

Congress has further imposed express statutory limitations on one type of sentencing modification proceeding. Section 3582(c)(2) provides that

> "in the case of a defendant who has been sentenced to a term of imprisonment based on a sentencing range that has subsequently been lowered by the Sentencing Commission . . . the court may reduce the term of imprisonment, after considering the factors set forth in section 3553(a) to the extent that they are applicable, if such a reduction is consistent with applicable policy statements issued by the Sentencing Commission."

For those proceedings, Congress expressly cabined district courts' discretion by requiring courts to abide by the Sentencing Commission's policy statements. See also § 3582(c)(1)(A) (permitting district courts to grant compassionate release in certain circumstances if "such a reduction is consistent with applicable policy statements issued by the Sentencing Commission").

III

A

Congress in the First Step Act simply did not contravene this well-established sentencing practice. Nothing in the text and structure of the First Step Act expressly, or even implicitly, overcomes the established tradition of district courts' sentencing discretion.

The first section of the First Step Act, § 404(a), sets out who is eligible for relief:

"In this section, the term 'covered offense' means a violation of a Federal criminal statute, the statutory penalties for which were modified by section 2 or 3 of the Fair Sentencing Act of 2010 . . . that was committed before August 3, 2010." 132 Stat. 5222.

The second section, § 404(b), describes what relief is available for the parties who meet § 404(a)'s criteria:

"A court that imposed a sentence for a covered offense may, on motion of the defendant, the Director of the Bureau of Prisons, the attorney for the Government, or the court, impose a reduced sentence as if sections 2 and 3 of the Fair Sentencing Act of 2010 . . . were in effect at the time the covered offense was committed." 132 Stat. 5222.

The third section, § 404(c), places two explicit limitations on available relief:

"No court shall entertain a motion made under this section to reduce a sentence if the sentence was previously imposed or previously reduced in accordance with the amendments made by sections 2 and 3 of the Fair Sentencing Act of 2010 . . . or if a previous motion made under this section to reduce the sentence was, after the date of enactment of this Act, denied after a complete review of the motion on the merits. Nothing in this section shall be construed to require a court to reduce any sentence pursuant to this section." 132 Stat. 5222.

The text of the First Step Act does not so much as hint that district courts are prohibited from considering evidence of rehabilitation, disciplinary infractions, or unrelated Guidelines changes. The only two limitations on district courts' discretion appear in § 404(c): A district court may not consider a First Step Act motion if the movant's sentence was already reduced under the Fair Sentencing Act or if the court considered and rejected a motion under the First Step Act. Neither of those limitations applies here. By its terms, § 404(c) does not prohibit district courts from considering any arguments in favor of, or against, sentence modification. In fact, § 404(c) only underscores that a district court is not required to modify a sentence for any reason. "Drawing meaning from silence is particularly inappropriate" in the sentencing context, "for Congress has shown that it knows how to direct sentencing practices in express terms." Kimbrough v. United States, 552 U.S. 85, 103 (2007).

Nor did Congress hide any limitations on district courts' discretion outside of § 404(c). Section 404(b) does not erect any additional such limitations. The term "as if" simply enacts the First Step Act's central goal: to make retroactive the changes in the Fair Sentencing Act. That language is necessary to overcome 1 U.S.C. § 109, which creates a presumption that Congress does not repeal federal criminal penalties unless it says so "expressly." To defeat the presumption established by this statute, Congress needed to make clear that the Fair Sentencing Act applied retroactively. Notably, the "as if" clause requires a district court to apply the Fair Sentencing Act as if it applied at the time of the commission of the offense, not at the time of the original sentencing. Had Congress intended to constrain district courts to consider only the record as it existed at the time of the original sentencing, Congress would have written the "as if" clause to refer to that sentencing, not the commission of the offense. Thus, the language Congress enacted in the First Step Act specifically requires district courts to apply the legal changes in the Fair Sentencing Act when calculating the Guidelines if they chose to modify a sentence. The "as if" clause does not, however, limit the information a district court may use to inform its decision whether and how much to reduce a sentence.

B

Consistent with this text and structure, district courts deciding First Step Act motions regularly have considered evidence of postsentencing rehabilitation and unrelated Guidelines amendments when raised by the parties. . . .

Likewise, when deciding whether to grant First Step Act motions and in deciding how much to reduce sentences, courts have looked to postsentencing evidence of violence or prison infractions as probative. . . .

Moreover, when raised by the parties, district courts have considered nonretroactive Guidelines amendments to help inform whether to reduce sentences at all, and if so, by how much. Nothing express or implicit in the First Step Act suggests that these courts misinterpreted the Act in considering such relevant and probative information.

C

The Court therefore holds that the First Step Act allows district courts to consider intervening changes of law or fact in exercising their discretion to reduce a sentence pursuant to the First Step Act.

. . . The contrary judgment of the Court of Appeals for the First Circuit is reversed, and the case is remanded for further proceedings consistent with this opinion.

■ JUSTICE KAVANAUGH, with whom CHIEF JUSTICE ROBERTS, JUSTICE ALITO, and JUSTICE BARRETT join, dissenting.

Beginning in the mid-1980s, Congress prescribed higher criminal sentences for crack-cocaine offenses than for powder-cocaine offenses involving the same amounts of cocaine. In 2010, Congress enacted the Fair Sentencing Act to narrow that crack/powder disparity by lowering the sentencing ranges for certain crack-cocaine offenses. But the Act lowered those crack-cocaine sentencing ranges only *prospectively*—that is, for crack-cocaine offenders who were sentenced on or after the Act's effective date of August 3, 2010.

The First Step Act of 2018 changed that. It provided that the 2010 Fair Sentencing Act's lower crack-cocaine sentencing ranges would also apply *retroactively* to offenders who were sentenced before August 3, 2010. But how to implement that change? Congress did not mandate a specific across-the-board reduction to all pre-August 3, 2010, crack-cocaine sentences. Instead, the First Step Act authorized district courts, on motion, to "impose a reduced sentence as if" the lower sentencing ranges for crack-cocaine offenses "were in effect at the time the covered offense was committed." § 404(b), 132 Stat. 5222.

The straightforward question in this case is whether district courts in First Step Act sentence-modification proceedings may reduce sentences based not only on the changes to the crack-cocaine sentencing ranges, but also on other *unrelated* legal or factual changes that have occurred since the original sentencing. For many crack-cocaine offenders who were sentenced before August 3, 2010, the most significant such change is a *non-retroactive* 2016 Sentencing Guidelines amendment that substantially altered the career-offender guideline and would significantly lower many of those offenders' Guidelines ranges. See United States Sentencing Commission, Guidelines Manual, App. C, Amdt. 798 (Nov. 2021).

The Court today concludes that district courts in First Step Act sentence-modification proceedings may reduce sentences based not only on the changes to the crack-cocaine sentencing ranges, but also on other unrelated legal or factual changes that have occurred since the original sentencing.

I respectfully disagree. The text of the First Step Act authorizes district courts to reduce sentences based only on changes to the crack-cocaine sentencing ranges, not based on other unrelated changes that have occurred since the original sentencing. In other words, the First Step Act directs district courts to answer one fundamental question: What would the offender's sentence have been if the lower crack-cocaine sentencing ranges had been in effect back at the time of the original sentencing?

The Court sidesteps the text of the Act and equates sentence-modification proceedings with plenary sentencing proceedings. But as this Court has recognized, there are "fundamental differences between sentencing and sentence-modification proceedings." Dillon v. United States, 560 U.S. 817, 830 (2010). The finality of criminal judgments is essential to the operation of the criminal justice system. Once a federal sentence becomes final, a court may alter that sentence "only in very limited circumstances." Pepper v. United States, 562 U.S. 476, 501–502, n. 14 (2011). As relevant here, Congress has made clear that courts may reduce "an imposed term of imprisonment to the extent" such a reduction is "*expressly permitted by statute*." 18 U.S.C. § 3582(c)(1)(B) (emphasis added).

The First Step Act states that the district court "may . . . impose a reduced sentence as if" the lower sentencing ranges for crack-cocaine offenses "were in effect at the time the covered offense was committed." § 404(b), 132 Stat. 5222. By its terms, the First Step Act authorizes consideration only of the lower sentencing ranges for crack-cocaine offenses. The First Step Act does not authorize consideration of unrelated intervening legal or factual changes. Indeed, the relevant provision of the First Step Act does not mention changes other than the lower sentencing ranges for crack-cocaine offenses. Therefore, the First Step Act does not "expressly permi[t]" reductions based on those unrelated intervening changes. 18 U.S.C. § 3582(c)(1)(B).

In support of its conclusion that district courts in First Step Act sentence-modification proceedings may consider other unrelated changes, the Court cites Pepper and similar decisions. But those decisions involved resentencings, not sentence-modification proceedings. Those cases therefore do not support the Court's approach here. To reiterate, for sentence-modification proceedings, Congress has declared that courts may reduce a sentence only as "expressly permitted by statute." 18 U.S.C. § 3582(c)(1)(B). And the First Step Act does not authorize consideration of unrelated intervening legal or factual changes since the original sentencing. . . .

The Court's disregard of the text of the First Step Act is especially audacious because the Act was a heavily negotiated and vigorously debated piece of legislation. The Act reflects a compromise among competing interests. Not for the first time in a sentencing case, the Court's decision today unravels the legislative compromise reflected in the statutory text. The Court in effect green-lights district courts, if they wish, to make the 2016 amendment to the career-offender guideline retroactive in First Step Act proceedings—even though neither Congress nor the Sentencing Commission has made that amendment retroactive. Perhaps the Court's decision represents better sentencing policy. Perhaps not. But under the Constitution's separation of powers, this Court may not simply rewrite the First Step Act as the Court thinks best.

In sum, I would conclude that the First Step Act authorizes district courts to reduce a sentence based on changes to the crack-cocaine sentencing ranges, but not based on other unrelated legal or factual changes since the original sentencing. The Court holds otherwise. Therefore, I respectfully dissent.

## NOTES ON THE (UNCERTAIN?) LINE BETWEEN TEXTUALISM AND PURPOSIVISM

(1) ***Backdoor Purposivism?*** Courts frequently justify a particular interpretation of a statutory provision by noting that an alternative interpretation would be in tension with other provisions located elsewhere in the statute. Although such an approach can be characterized as textualist, does it make any sense without some background notion of legislative intent? See Anita S. Krishnakumar, Backdoor Purposivism, 69 Duke L.J. 1275, 1317 (2020). Is a purely textualist approach to structure just purposivism in disguise (though unaided by some critical means of divining purpose, such as legislative history)? Might the same be said of a justification for a particular statutory interpretation that relies not on the ordinary meaning of words in the statutory text but instead on background understandings derived from past practices that Congress legislated against?

(2) ***King, Concepcion, and Backdoor Purposivism.*** Is King a case of backdoor purposivism? ABBE R. GLUCK, IMPERFECT STATUTES, IMPERFECT COURTS: UNDERSTANDING CONGRESS'S PLAN IN THE ERA OF UNORTHODOX LAWMAKING, 129 Harv. L. Rev. 62 (2015): "Whereas the Court's recent statutory interpretation jurisprudence has been marked by a targeted focus on a few contested words, King responds by looking at the full picture, at Congress's 'plan'—a term that itself sends a strong message about Congress's rationality and the inherent purposiveness and functionality of legislation. . . .

"Justice Scalia's dissent decries these moves as an activist departure from 'the normal rules of interpretation.' But imposing perfection on an imperfect statute, as the canons would have, would itself have been a kind of aggressive judicial legislation. Nor does King's emphasis on the 'plan' mean a resort to legislative history or other subjective factors maligned by textualists. The opinion derives its understanding of the ACA's scheme from its text, structure, and the statute's own, codified 'stated purposes' (not legislative history). . . . One way to understand King is that the Chief Justice chooses the holistic side of textualism, one that has always shared with purposivism the assumption that Congress legislates rationally, with means to an end. . . .

"The King challenge was . . . grounded in a particular view of the Court's inability, or unwillingness, to deal with legislative complexity. The challengers' vision of how the Court should see Congress, adopted by Justice Scalia in dissent, embraces a profound tension at the heart of modern statutory interpretation doctrine: Congress is assumed to be both irrational and perfect at once. Congress can never be understood, but when courts interpret statutes, they should hold Congress to standards of omniscience, precision, perfection, and simplicity. Textualism has deeply influenced this vision, but it is important to recognize that it has now come to be adopted by most judges, because it is embodied in the canons of interpretation that most judges (and all of the Justices) now deploy in virtually every statutory case. . . .

"Instead, the King majority responds with a different vision of both Congress's and the Court's capacities. Congress is imperfect, but it has a 'plan'—the most important word in the opinion, because it signals that Congress is nevertheless rational, that its work product is comprehensible, and that a laser focus on a few words is not the right perspective. Plans, as Professor Scott Shapiro has noted, are meant to be read by someone; they form the basis of relationships between those who write the plans and those who implement them. Plans also provide the whole story, all the pieces of the big picture. The King majority elevates the Court by putting the Court (and not the agency) on the receiving end of the plan; tells us that Congress can trust the Court to understand it; takes a macro, functionalist, view of how all the pieces of the ACA work together; and concludes that the Court has a duty not to 'undo what [Congress] has done.'

"Many courtwatchers saw these moves and cried 'purposivism!' Labels matter because the term 'purposivism' today means something different, as a term of art, from the mere use of purpose in interpretation. The term is a loaded one—a textualist foil—and tends to be coupled with charges of legislative-history use, atextual interpretation, and judicial activism. Indeed, critics have accused the majority of 'legislative gap-filling' for ignoring the 'usual rules of interpretation.' But what has escaped attention is that the kind of objectified, text-derived purpose the Court utilizes has textualist foundations, along with Legal Process ones. So does the concept of a comprehensive legislative plan. That concept has appeared in more than 100 cases in the U.S. Reports—it is a particular kind of purpose that derives from statutory text and structure, and so is different from the concept of 'purposivism' as we have come to know it. . . .

"King seems to be invoking a third way. It does not seem a coincidence that the King majority reaches back to 1973 for a citation on the value of a statute's "stated purposes." It also cites many other pretextualist era decisions—decisions not commonly cited by the Court in statutory cases—to support its interpretive choices. The Court seems to be looking to entrenched, earlier ways of using text and purposiveness together—and choosing a different term (the 'plan') to signal that it is doing something different—rather than aligning its view with one side or the other in the modern textualism-purposivism debates."

How about Concepcion? Is it a case of backdoor purposivism in that the Court reads the text in light of the sentencing discretion Congress had permitted in other contexts as if that history provides reason to "know" that Congress intended to preserve that discretion absent some relatively clear indication that it did not? What could lead us to "know" such a thing if a text does not itself inform us of it?

(3) ***Theory Versus Practice.*** Perhaps textualism is the appropriate theory in some circumstances and a purpose-driven approach is more appropriate in others—and King and Concepcion arguably sit in between these ends of the spectrum. Consider the following finding from interviews of forty-two judges on the federal appellate courts: "Several major themes emerge from the responses. First, what divides judges is not what academics and judges think divides judges. *None* of the judges is a 'textualist' in the extreme sense of that word, or even in the version of textualism that was practiced by Justice Scalia. Very few judges told us they read the entire statute, or even begin their analysis of statutory cases with the text of the statute. All of the judges use legislative history. Dictionaries are mostly disfavored. Even when asked to provide one word to describe their interpretive approaches, not one judge was willing to self-describe as 'textualist' without qualification. Even the text-centric judges described themselves in such terms as 'textualist-pragmatist' or 'textualist-contextualist.' Our findings reveal the academic *cliché de mode*—'we are all textualists now'—to be an overstatement.

"At the other end of the spectrum, however, there were no extreme purposivists either, in the sense of the purposivism that has been textualism's foil. No judge stated that purpose was a more important tool than statutory text, and only one judge claimed to begin analysis of a statutory case with the statute's purpose. Even those judges who emphasized the importance of purpose as an interpretive tool made clear they still would not use purpose to push a statute's interpretation beyond the limits of its text." ABBE R. GLUCK & RICHARD A. POSNER, STATUTORY INTERPRETATION ON THE BENCH: A SURVEY OF FORTY-TWO JUDGES ON THE FEDERAL COURTS OF APPEALS, 131 Harv. L. Rev. 1298, 1310–11 (2018).

If these theories are not as absolute as they appear, what should guide their application? One answer—pragmatism—is the subject of the following Section.

## d. Pragmatic and Dynamic Statutory Interpretation

***BOSTOCK v. CLAYTON COUNTY***
***HIVELY v. IVY TECH COMMUNITY COLLEGE***
***Notes on Dynamic Statutory Interpretation***

As we have seen, textualism focuses on the words of the statute and purposivism focuses on the purpose underlying those words. A different theory of statutory interpretation focuses on the practical consequences that would follow from an interpretation that is based on the statute's text or its seeming purpose (perhaps as divined from the applicable legislative history). Such an approach is often described as pragmatic statutory interpretation. Judge Richard A. Posner describes legal pragmatism as reflecting "a heightened concern with consequences" and "a disposition to ground policy judgments on facts and consequences rather than on conceptualisms, generalities, pieties, and slogans."

This approach has achieved special recognition as applied to the problem of statutes passed many years ago. Statutory interpretation, says William Eskridge, Jr., should respond to changes in the "societal, political, and legal context"; judges should implement the general goals of old statutes by adapting their meaning to new social contexts. He called this approach "dynamic statutory interpretation."

The excerpted cases that follow, Bostock v. Clayton County and Hively v. Ivy Tech Community College, directly engage with the questions Posner and Eskridge raise. In both cases, the statute at stake is a core provision of the 1964 Civil Rights Act, 42 U.S.C. § 2000e–2(a), otherwise known as Title VII:

> It shall be an unlawful employment practice for an employer—
>
> (1) to fail or refuse to hire or to discharge any individual, or otherwise to discriminate against any individual with respect to his compensation, terms, conditions, or privileges of employment, because of such individual's race, color, religion, sex, or national origin. . . .

Here's the question that faced the Seventh Circuit in Hively, which was decided before the Supreme Court decided Bostock: Does this statute outlaw discrimination by an employer on the basis of sexual orientation?

Hively held that Title VII did outlaw discrimination in employment on the basis of sexual orientation. The Supreme Court then took up that same question in Bostock, as well as the related question of whether Title VII also outlawed discrimination in employment on the basis of gender identity. The Court ruled that Title VII outlawed both, though it did so by relying on an analysis that was distinct from the one that the Seventh Circuit relied on in Hively in some key respects.

The different pathways the Seventh Circuit and the Supreme Court traveled to reach a similar result do reflect different methods of statutory interpretation. We thus do something we normally don't: we present you extended excerpts from both the lower court decision and the Supreme Court decision that superseded it.

If you think the result in each is right, do you prefer the mode of reasoning in Judge Wood's opinion in Hively or the mode of reasoning in Justice Gorsuch's in Bostock? Do you actually prefer Judge Posner's over both, because he would frankly embrace pragmatism—what Eskridge calls dynamic statutory interpretation? Assuming you think the result in each is wrong, why? Is it because only dynamic statutory interpretation could justify the result and such an interpretive method is problematic? If so, what is wrong with it?

## BOSTOCK v. CLAYTON COUNTY

Supreme Court of the United States (2020).
140 S.Ct. 1731.

■ JUSTICE GORSUCH delivered the opinion of the Court.[1]

Sometimes small gestures can have unexpected consequences. Major initiatives practically guarantee them. In our time, few pieces of federal legislation rank in significance with the Civil Rights Act of 1964. There, in Title VII, Congress outlawed discrimination in the workplace on the basis of race, color, religion, sex, or national origin. Today, we must decide whether an employer can fire someone simply for being homosexual or transgender. The answer is clear. An employer who fires an individual for being homosexual or transgender fires that person for traits or actions it would not have questioned in members of a different sex. Sex plays a necessary and undisguisable role in the decision, exactly what Title VII forbids.

Those who adopted the Civil Rights Act might not have anticipated their work would lead to this particular result. Likely, they weren't thinking about many of the Act's consequences that have become apparent over the years, including its prohibition against discrimination on the basis of motherhood or its ban on the sexual harassment of male

1 [Ed.] The Court uses the term "homosexual". Among other sources, GLAAD and major media guides caution against using that term. For more information, see: https://www.glaad.org/reference/.

employees. But the limits of the drafters' imagination supply no reason to ignore the law's demands. When the express terms of a statute give us one answer and extratextual considerations suggest another, it's no contest. Only the written word is the law, and all persons are entitled to its benefit.

I

Few facts are needed to appreciate the legal question we face. . . . Gerald Bostock worked for Clayton County, Georgia, as a child welfare advocate. Under his leadership, the county won national awards for its work. After a decade with the county, Mr. Bostock began participating in a gay recreational softball league. Not long after that, influential members of the community allegedly made disparaging comments about Mr. Bostock's sexual orientation and participation in the league. Soon, he was fired for conduct "unbecoming" a county employee.

Donald Zarda worked as a skydiving instructor at Altitude Express in New York. After several seasons with the company, Mr. Zarda mentioned that he was gay and, days later, he was fired.

Aimee Stephens worked [at a funeral home in Michigan]. When she got the job, she presented as a male. But two years into her service with the company, she began treatment for despair and loneliness. Ultimately, clinicians diagnosed her with gender dysphoria and recommended that she begin living as a woman. In her sixth year with the company, Ms. Stephens wrote a letter to her employer explaining that she planned to "live and work full-time as a woman" after she returned from an upcoming vacation. The funeral home fired her before she left, telling her "this is not going to work out."

II

This Court normally interprets a statute in accord with the ordinary public meaning of its terms at the time of its enactment. After all, only the words on the page constitute the law adopted by Congress and approved by the President. If judges could add to, remodel, update, or detract from old statutory terms inspired only by extratextual sources and our own imaginations, we would risk amending statutes outside the legislative process reserved for the people's representatives. And we would deny the people the right to continue relying on the original meaning of the law they have counted on to settle their rights and obligations.

With this in mind, our task is clear. We must determine the ordinary public meaning of Title VII's command that it is "unlawful . . . for an employer to fail or refuse to hire or to discharge any individual, or otherwise to discriminate against any individual with respect to his compensation, terms, conditions, or privileges of employment, because of such individual's race, color, religion, sex, or national origin." § 2000e–2(a)(1). To do so, we orient ourselves to the time of the statute's adoption, here 1964, and begin by examining the key statutory terms in turn before assessing their impact on the cases at hand and then confirming our work against this Court's precedents.

The only statutorily protected characteristic at issue in today's cases is "sex"—and that is also the primary term in Title VII whose meaning the parties dispute. Appealing to roughly contemporaneous dictionaries, the employers say that, as used here, the term "sex" in 1964 referred to "status as either male or female [as] determined by reproductive biology." The employees counter by submitting that, even in 1964, the term bore a broader scope, capturing more than anatomy and reaching at least some norms concerning gender identity and sexual orientation. But because nothing in our approach to these cases turns on the outcome of the parties' debate, and because the employees concede the point for argument's sake, we proceed on the assumption that "sex" signified what the employers suggest, referring only to biological distinctions between male and female.

Still, that's just a starting point. The question isn't just what "sex" meant, but what Title VII says about it. Most notably, the statute prohibits employers from taking certain actions "because of" sex. And, as this Court has previously explained, "the ordinary meaning of 'because of' is 'by reason of' or 'on account of.' " In the language of law, this means that Title VII's "because of" test incorporates the "simple" and "traditional" standard of but-for causation. . . .

This can be a sweeping standard. Often, events have multiple but-for causes. . . . When it comes to Title VII, the adoption of the traditional but-for causation standard means a defendant cannot avoid liability just by citing some *other* factor that contributed to its challenged employment decision. So long as the plaintiffs' sex was one but-for cause of that decision, that is enough to trigger the law. . . .

As sweeping as even the but-for causation standard can be, Title VII does not concern itself with everything that happens "because of" sex. The statute imposes liability on employers only when they "fail or refuse to hire," "discharge," "or otherwise . . . discriminate against" someone because of a statutorily protected characteristic, like sex. . . .

What did "discriminate" mean in 1964? As it turns out, it meant then roughly what it means today[.] . . . To "discriminate against" a person, then, would seem to mean treating that individual worse than others who are similarly situated. . . .

At first glance, another interpretation might seem possible. Discrimination sometimes involves "the act, practice, or an instance of discriminating categorically rather than individually." Webster's New Collegiate Dictionary 326 (1975). . . . On that understanding, the statute would require us to consider the employer's treatment of groups rather than individuals, to see how a policy affects one sex as a whole versus the other as a whole. That idea holds some intuitive appeal. Maybe the law concerns itself simply with ensuring that employers don't treat women generally less favorably than they do men. So how can we tell which sense, individual or group, "discriminate" carries in Title VII?

The statute answers that question directly. It tells us three times . . . that our focus should be on individuals not groups[.] . . .

The consequences of the law's focus on individuals rather than groups is anything but academic. Suppose an employer fires a woman for refusing his sexual advances. It's no defense for the employer to note that, while he treated that individual woman worse than he would have treated a man, he gives preferential treatment to women overall. . . . Nor is it a defense for an employer to say it discriminates against both men and women because of sex. . . . So an employer who fires a woman, Hannah, because she is insufficiently feminine and also fires a man, Bob, for being insufficiently masculine may treat men and women as groups more or less equally. But in *both* cases the employer fires an individual in part, because of sex.

B

From the ordinary public meaning of the statute's language at the time of the law's adoption, a straightforward rule emerges: An employer violates Title VII when it intentionally fires an individual employee based in part on sex. It doesn't matter if other factors besides the plaintiff's sex contributed to the decision. And it doesn't matter if the employer treated women as a group the same when compared to men as a group. If the employer intentionally relies in part on an individual employee's sex when deciding to discharge the employee—put differently, if changing the employee's sex would have yielded a different choice by the employer—a statutory violation has occurred. Title VII's message is "simple but momentous": An individual employee's sex is "not relevant to the selection, evaluation, or compensation of employees."

The statute's message for our cases is equally simple and momentous: An individual's homosexuality or transgender status is not relevant to employment decisions. That's because it is impossible to discriminate against a person for being homosexual or transgender without discriminating against that individual based on sex. Consider, for example, an employer with two employees, both of whom are attracted to men. The two individuals are, to the employer's mind, materially identical in all respects, except that one is a man and the other a woman. If the employer fires the male employee for no reason other than the fact he is attracted to men, the employer discriminates against him for traits or actions it tolerates in his female colleague. . . . Or take an employer who fires a transgender person who was identified as male at birth but who now identifies as a female. If the employer retains an otherwise identical employee who was identified as female at birth, the employer intentionally penalizes a person identified as male at birth for traits or actions that it tolerates in an employee identified as female at birth. The individual employee's sex plays an unmistakable and impermissible role in the discharge decision.

That distinguishes these cases from countless others where Title VII has nothing to say. Take an employer who fires a female employee for tardiness or incompetence or simply supporting the wrong sports team. Assuming the employer would not have tolerated the same trait in a man, Title VII stands silent. But unlike any of these other traits or actions, homosexuality and transgender status are inextricably bound up with sex. Not because homosexuality or transgender status are related to sex in some vague sense or because discrimination on these bases has some disparate impact on one sex or another, but because to discriminate on these grounds requires an employer to intentionally treat individuals differently because of their sex. . . .

Reframing the additional causes in today's cases as additional intentions can do no more to insulate the employers from liability. . . . There is simply no escaping the role intent plays here: Just as sex is necessarily a but-for *cause* when an employer discriminates against homosexual or transgender employees, an employer who discriminates on these grounds inescapably *intends* to rely on sex in its decisionmaking. Imagine an employer who has a policy of firing any employee known to be homosexual. The employer hosts an office holiday party and invites employees to bring their spouses. A model employee arrives and introduces a manager to Susan, the employee's wife. Will that employee be fired? If the policy works as the employer intends, the answer depends entirely on whether the model employee is a man or a woman. To be sure, that employer's ultimate goal might be to discriminate on the basis of sexual orientation. But to achieve that purpose the employer must, along the way, intentionally treat an employee worse based in part on that individual's sex.

An employer musters no better a defense by responding that it is equally happy to fire male and female employees who are homosexual or transgender. Title VII liability is not limited to employers, who, through the sum of all their employment actions, treat the class of men differently from the class of women. . . .

At bottom, [this case involves] no more than the straightforward application of legal terms with plain and settled meanings. For an employer to discriminate against employees for being homosexual or transgender, the employer must intentionally discriminate against individual men and women in part because of sex. That has always been prohibited by Title VII's plain terms—and that "should be the end of the analysis."

III

[The employers] contend that few in 1964 would have expected Title VII to apply to discrimination against homosexual and transgender persons. And whatever the text and our precedent indicate, they say, shouldn't this fact cause us to pause before recognizing liability?

It might be tempting to reject this argument out of hand. This Court has explained many times over many years that, when the meaning of the statute's terms is plain, our job is at an end. The people are entitled to rely on the law as written, without fearing that courts might disregard its plain terms based on some extratextual consideration. Of course, some Members of this Court have consulted legislative history when interpreting *ambiguous* statutory language. But that has no bearing here. "Legislative history, for those who take it into account, is meant to clear up ambiguity, not create it." And as we have seen, no ambiguity exists about how Title VII's terms apply to the facts before us. To be sure, the statute's application in these cases reaches "beyond the principal evil" legislators may have intended or expected to address. But " 'the fact that [a statute] has been applied in situations not expressly anticipated by Congress' " does not demonstrate ambiguity; instead, it simply " 'demonstrates [the] breadth' " of a legislative command. And "it is ultimately the provisions of" those legislative commands "rather than the principal concerns of our legislators by which we are governed."

Still, while legislative history can never defeat unambiguous statutory text, historical sources can be useful for a different purpose: Because the law's ordinary meaning at the time of enactment usually governs, we must be sensitive to the possibility a statutory term that means one thing today or in one context might have meant something else at the time of its adoption or might mean something different in another context. And we must be attuned to the possibility that a statutory phrase ordinarily bears a different meaning than the terms do when viewed individually or literally. To ferret out such shifts in linguistic usage or subtle distinctions between literal and ordinary meaning, this Court has sometimes consulted the understandings of the law's drafters as some (not always conclusive) evidence. . . .

The employers, however, advocate nothing like that here. . . . [T]he employers *agree* with our understanding of all the statutory language—"discriminate against any individual . . . because of such individual's. . . sex." Nor do the competing dissents offer an alternative account about what these terms mean either when viewed individually or in the aggregate. Rather than suggesting that the statutory language bears some other *meaning*, the employers and dissents merely suggest that, because few in 1964 expected today's *result*, we should not dare to admit that it follows ineluctably from the statutory text. When a new application emerges that is both unexpected and important, they would seemingly have us merely point out the question, refer the subject back to Congress, and decline to enforce the plain terms of the law in the meantime.

That is exactly the sort of reasoning this Court has long rejected. Admittedly, the employers take pains to couch their argument in terms of seeking to honor the statute's "expected applications" rather than vindicate its "legislative intent." But the concepts are closely related. One could easily contend that legislators only intended expected applications or that a statute's purpose is limited to achieving applications foreseen at the time of enactment. However framed, the employer's logic impermissibly seeks to displace the plain meaning of the law in favor of something lying beyond it.

If anything, the employers' new framing may only add new problems. The employers assert that "no one" in 1964 or for some time after would have anticipated today's result. But is that really true? Not long after the law's passage, gay and transgender employees began filing Title VII complaints, so at least *some* people foresaw this potential application. And less than a decade after Title VII's passage, during debates over the

Equal Rights Amendment, others counseled that its language—which was strikingly similar to Title VII's—might also protect homosexuals from discrimination.

Why isn't that enough to demonstrate that today's result isn't totally unexpected? How many people have to foresee the application for it to qualify as "expected"? Do we look only at the moment the statute was enacted, or do we allow some time for the implications of a new statute to be worked out? Should we consider the expectations of those who had no reason to give a particular application any thought or only those with reason to think about the question? How do we account for those who change their minds over time, after learning new facts or hearing a new argument? How specifically or generally should we frame the "application" at issue? None of these questions have obvious answers, and the employers don't propose any.

One could also reasonably fear that objections about unexpected applications will not be deployed neutrally. Often lurking just behind such objections resides a cynicism that Congress could not *possibly* have meant to protect a disfavored group. . . . Applying protective laws to groups that were politically unpopular at the time of the law's passage—whether prisoners in the 1990s or homosexual and transgender employees in the 1960s—often may be seen as unexpected. But to refuse enforcement just because of that, because the parties before us happened to be unpopular at the time of the law's passage, would not only require us to abandon our role as interpreters of statutes; it would tilt the scales of justice in favor of the strong or popular and neglect the promise that all persons are entitled to the benefit of the law's terms.

*

Some of those who supported adding language to Title VII to ban sex discrimination may have hoped it would derail the entire Civil Rights Act. Yet, contrary to those intentions, the bill became law. Since then, Title VII's effects have unfolded with far-reaching consequences, some likely beyond what many in Congress or elsewhere expected.

But none of this helps decide today's case[ ]. Ours is a society of written laws. Judges are not free to overlook plain statutory commands on the strength of nothing more than suppositions about intentions or guesswork about expectations. In Title VII, Congress adopted broad language making it illegal for an employer to rely on an employee's sex when deciding to fire that employee. We do not hesitate to recognize today a necessary consequence of that legislative choice: An employer who fires an individual merely for being gay or transgender defies the law.

■ JUSTICE ALITO, with whom JUSTICE THOMAS joins, dissenting.

There is only one word for what the Court has done today: legislation. The document that the Court releases is in the form of a judicial opinion interpreting a statute, but that is deceptive.

Title VII of the Civil Rights Act of 1964 prohibits employment discrimination on any of five specified grounds: "race, color, religion, sex,

[and] national origin." 42 U.S.C. § 2000e–2(a)(1). Neither "sexual orientation" nor "gender identity" appears on that list. For the past 45 years, bills have been introduced in Congress to add "sexual orientation" to the list, and in recent years, bills have included "gender identity" as well. But to date, none has passed both Houses. . . .

Because no such amendment of Title VII has been enacted in accordance with the requirements in the Constitution (passage in both Houses and presentment to the President, Art. I, § 7, cl. 2), Title VII's prohibition of discrimination because of "sex" still means what it has always meant. But the Court is not deterred by these constitutional niceties. . . .

The Court tries to convince readers that it is merely enforcing the terms of the statute, but that is preposterous. Even as understood today, the concept of discrimination because of "sex" is different from discrimination because of "sexual orientation" or "gender identity." And in any event, our duty is to interpret statutory terms to "mean what they conveyed to reasonable people *at the time they were written*." If every single living American had been surveyed in 1964, it would have been hard to find any who thought that discrimination because of sex meant discrimination because of sexual orientation—not to mention gender identity, a concept that was essentially unknown at the time.

The Court attempts to pass off its decision as the inevitable product of the textualist school of statutory interpretation championed by our late colleague Justice Scalia, but no one should be fooled. The Court's opinion is like a pirate ship. It sails under a textualist flag, but what it actually represents is a theory of statutory interpretation that Justice Scalia excoriated—the theory that courts should "update" old statutes so that they better reflect the current values of society. If the Court finds it appropriate to adopt this theory, it should own up to what it is doing.[5]

Many will applaud today's decision because they agree on policy grounds with the Court's updating of Title VII. But the question in these cases is not whether discrimination because of sexual orientation or gender identity *should be* outlawed. The question is *whether Congress did that in 1964.*

It indisputably did not.

I

Title VII, as noted, prohibits discrimination "because of . . . sex," § 2000e–2(a)(1), and in 1964, it was as clear as clear could be that this meant discrimination because of the genetic and anatomical characteristics that men and women have at the time of birth.

[5] That is what Judge Posner did in the Seventh Circuit case holding that Title VII prohibits discrimination because of sexual orientation. *See* Hively v. Ivy Tech Community College of Ind., 853 F.3d 339 (2017) (en banc). Judge Posner agreed with that result but wrote:

*"I would prefer to see us acknowledge openly that today we, who are judges rather than members of Congress, are imposing on a half-century old statute a meaning of 'sex discrimination' that the Congress that enacted it would not have accepted."* Id. at 357 (concurring opinion) (emphasis added).

Determined searching has not found a single dictionary from that time that defined "sex" to mean sexual orientation, gender identity, or "transgender status."

In all those dictionaries, the primary definition of "sex" was essentially the same as that in the then-most recent edition of Webster's New International Dictionary (2d ed. 1953): "[o]ne of the two divisions of organisms formed on the distinction of male and female."

The Court does not dispute that this is what "sex" means in Title VII, although it coyly suggests that there is at least some support for a different and potentially relevant definition. But the Court declines to stand on that ground and instead "proceed[s] on the assumption that 'sex' . . . . refer[s] only to biological distinctions between male and female."

If that is so, it should be perfectly clear that Title VII does not reach discrimination because of sexual orientation or gender identity. If "sex" in Title VII means biologically male or female, then discrimination because of sex means discrimination because the person in question is biologically male or biologically female, not because that person is sexually attracted to members of the same sex or identifies as a member of a particular gender. . . .

If an employer takes an employment action solely because of the sexual orientation or gender identity of an employee or applicant, has that employer necessarily discriminated because of biological sex?

The [answer to this question] must be no, unless discrimination because of sexual orientation or gender identity inherently constitutes discrimination because of sex. The Court attempts to prove that point, and it argues, not merely that the terms of Title VII *can* be interpreted that way but that they *cannot reasonably be interpreted any other way*. According to the Court, the text is unambiguous.

The arrogance of this argument is breathtaking. . . . [T]here is not a shred of evidence that any Member of Congress interpreted the statutory text that way when Title VII was enacted. But the Court apparently thinks that this was because the Members were not "smart enough to realize" what its language means. Hively v. Ivy Tech Community College of Ind., 853 F.3d 339, 357 (7th Cir. 2017) (Posner, J., concurring). . . .

Contrary to the Court's contention, discrimination because of sexual orientation or gender identity does not in and of itself entail discrimination because of sex. . . .

At oral argument, the attorney representing the employees, a prominent law professor of constitutional law, was asked if there would be discrimination because of sex if an employer with a blanket policy against hiring gays, lesbians, and transgender individuals implemented that policy without knowing the biological sex of any job applicants. Her candid answer was that this would "not" be sex discrimination. . . . And she was right.

Trying to escape the consequences of the attorney's concession, the Court offers its own hypothetical [in which the employer's application form "offered a single box to check if the applicant is either black or Catholic" and the employer refuses to hire anyone who checked that box but "studiously avoids learning any particular applicant's race or religion"].

How this hypothetical proves the Court's point is a mystery. A person who checked that box would presumably be black, Catholic, or both, and refusing to hire an applicant because of race or religion is prohibited by Title VII. Rejecting applicants who checked a box indicating that they are homosexual is entirely different because it is impossible to tell from that answer whether an applicant is male or female. . . .

The Court proclaims that "[a]n individual's homosexuality or transgender status is not relevant to employment decisions." That is the policy view of many people in 2020, and perhaps Congress would have amended Title VII to implement it if this Court had not intervened. But that is not the policy embodied in Title VII in its current form. Title VII prohibits discrimination based on five specified grounds, and neither sexual orientation nor gender identity is on the list. As long as an employer does not discriminate based on one of the listed grounds, the employer is free to decide for itself which characteristics are "relevant to [its] employment decisions." By proclaiming that sexual orientation and gender identity are "not relevant to employment decisions," the Court updates Title VII to reflect what it regards as 2020 values. . . .

The Court's textual arguments fail on their own terms. The Court tries to prove that "it is impossible to discriminate against a person for being homosexual or transgender without discriminating against that individual based on sex," but . . . it is entirely possible for an employer to do just that. "[H]omosexuality and transgender status are distinct concepts from sex," and discrimination because of sexual orientation or transgender status does not inherently or necessarily constitute discrimination because of sex. The Court's arguments are squarely contrary to the statutory text.

II

A

Textualists do not read statutes as if they were messages picked up by a powerful radio telescope from a distant and utterly unknown civilization. Statutes consist of communications between members of a particular linguistic community, one that existed in a particular place and at a particular time, and these communications must therefore be interpreted as they were understood by that community at that time.

For this reason, it is imperative to consider how Americans in 1964 would have understood Title VII's prohibition of discrimination because of sex. To get a picture of this, we may imagine this scene. Suppose that, while Title VII was under consideration in Congress, a group of average Americans decided to read the text of the bill with the aim of writing or calling their representatives in Congress and conveying their approval or disapproval. What would these ordinary citizens have taken "discrimination because of sex" to mean? Would they have thought that this language prohibited discrimination because of sexual orientation or gender identity?

B

The answer could not be clearer. In 1964, ordinary Americans reading the text of Title VII would not have dreamed that discrimination because of sex meant discrimination because of sexual orientation, much less gender identity. The *ordinary meaning* of discrimination because of "sex" was discrimination because of a person's biological sex, not sexual orientation or gender identity. The possibility that discrimination on either of these grounds might fit within some exotic understanding of sex discrimination would not have crossed their minds.

C

While Americans in 1964 would have been shocked to learn that Congress had enacted a law prohibiting sexual orientation discrimination, they would have been bewildered to hear that this law also forbids discrimination on the basis of "transgender status" or "gender identity," terms that would have left people at the time scratching their heads. The term "transgender" is said to have been coined " 'in the early 1970s,' " and the term "gender identity," now understood to mean "[a]n internal sense of being male, female or something else," apparently first appeared in an academic article in 1964. Certainly, neither term was in common parlance; indeed, dictionaries of the time still primarily defined the word "gender" by reference to grammatical classifications. . . .

It defies belief to suggest that the public meaning of discrimination because of sex in 1964 encompassed discrimination on the basis of a concept that was essentially unknown to the public at that time.

D

The Court's main excuse for entirely ignoring the social context in which Title VII was enacted is that the meaning of Title VII's prohibition of discrimination because of sex is clear, and therefore it simply does not matter whether people in 1964 were "smart enough to realize" what its language means. Hively, 853 F.3d, at 357 (Posner, J., concurring). According to the Court, an argument that looks to the societal norms of those times represents an impermissible attempt to displace the statutory language.

The Court's argument rests on a false premise. As already explained at length, the text of Title VII does not prohibit discrimination because of sexual orientation or gender identity. And what the public thought about those issues in 1964 is relevant and important, not because it provides a ground for departing from the statutory text, but because it helps to explain what the text was understood to mean when adopted.

* * *

The updating desire to which the Court succumbs no doubt arises from humane and generous impulses. Today, many Americans know individuals who are gay, lesbian, or transgender and want them to be treated with the dignity, consideration, and fairness that everyone deserves. But the authority of this Court is limited to saying what the law is.

The Court itself recognizes this:

"The place to make new legislation . . . lies in Congress. When it comes to statutory interpretation, our role is limited to applying the law's demands as faithfully as we can in the cases that come before us."

It is easy to utter such words. If only the Court would live by them.

I respectfully dissent.

■ JUSTICE KAVANAUGH, dissenting.

I

. . .

In the face of the unsuccessful legislative efforts (so far) to prohibit sexual orientation discrimination, judges may not rewrite the law simply because of their own policy views. Judges may not update the law merely because they think that Congress does not have the votes or the fortitude. Judges may not predictively amend the law just because they believe that Congress is likely to do it soon anyway. . . .

But in the last few years, a new theory has emerged. To end-run the bedrock separation-of-powers principle that courts may not unilaterally rewrite statutes, the plaintiffs here . . . have advanced a novel and creative argument. They contend that discrimination "because of sexual orientation" and discrimination "because of sex" are actually not separate categories of discrimination after all. Instead, the theory goes, discrimination because of sexual orientation always qualifies as discrimination because of sex: When a gay man is fired because he is gay, he is fired because he is attracted to men, even though a similarly situated woman would not be fired just because she is attracted to men. According to this theory, it follows that the man has been fired, at least as a literal matter, because of his sex.

Under this literalist approach, sexual orientation discrimination automatically qualifies as sex discrimination, and Title VII's prohibition against sex discrimination therefore also prohibits sexual orientation discrimination—and actually has done so since 1964, unbeknownst to everyone. Surprisingly, the Court today buys into this approach. . . .

As to common parlance, few in 1964 (or today) would describe a firing because of sexual orientation as a firing because of sex. As commonly understood, sexual orientation discrimination is distinct from, and not a form of, sex discrimination. . . .

Consider the employer who has four employees but must fire two of them for financial reasons. Suppose the four employees are a straight man, a straight woman, a gay man, and a lesbian. The employer with animosity against women (animosity based on sex) will fire the two women. The employer with animosity against gays (animosity based on sexual orientation) will fire the gay man and the lesbian. Those are two distinct harms caused by two distinct biases that have two different outcomes. To treat one as a form of the other—as the majority opinion does—misapprehends common language, human psychology, and real life. See Hively v. Ivy Tech Community College of Ind., 853 F.3d 339, 363 (7th Cir. 2017) (Sykes, J., dissenting).

It also rewrites history. Seneca Falls was not Stonewall. The women's rights movement was not (and is not) the gay rights movement, although many people obviously support or participate in both. So to think that sexual orientation discrimination is just a form of sex discrimination is not just a mistake of language and psychology, but also a mistake of history and sociology.

Importantly, an overwhelming body of federal law reflects and reinforces the ordinary meaning and demonstrates that sexual orientation discrimination is distinct from, and not a form of, sex discrimination. . . .

Congress knows how to prohibit sexual orientation discrimination. So courts should not read that specific concept into the general words "discriminate because of sex." We cannot close our eyes to the indisputable fact that Congress—for several decades in a large number of statutes—has identified sex discrimination and sexual orientation discrimination as two distinct categories. . . .

II

Title VII is not a general grant of authority for judges to fashion an evolving common law of equal treatment in the workplace. Rather, Title VII identifies certain specific categories of prohibited discrimination. And under the separation of powers, Congress—not the courts—possesses the authority to amend or update the law, as Congress has done with age discrimination and disability discrimination, for example.

So what changed from the situation only a few years ago when 30 out of 30 federal judges had agreed on this question? Not the text of Title VII. The law has not changed. Rather, the judges' decisions have evolved. . . .

The majority opinion insists that it is not rewriting or updating Title VII, but instead is just humbly reading the text of the statute as written. But that assertion is tough to accept. Most everyone familiar with the use of the English language in America understands that the ordinary meaning of sexual orientation discrimination is distinct from the ordinary meaning of sex discrimination. Federal law distinguishes the two. State law distinguishes the two. This Court's cases distinguish the two. Statistics on discrimination distinguish the two. History distinguishes the two. Psychology distinguishes the two. Sociology distinguishes the two. Human resources departments all over America distinguish the two. Sports leagues distinguish the two. Political groups distinguish the two. Advocacy groups distinguish the two. Common parlance distinguishes the two. Common sense distinguishes the two.

As a result, many Americans will not buy the novel interpretation unearthed and advanced by the Court today. Many will no doubt believe that the Court has unilaterally rewritten American vocabulary and American law—a "statutory amendment courtesy of unelected judges." Hively, 853 F.3d, at 360 (Sykes, J., dissenting). Some will surmise that the Court succumbed to "the natural desire that beguiles judges along with other human beings into imposing their own views of goodness, truth, and justice upon others."

I have the greatest, and unyielding, respect for my colleagues and for their good faith. But when this Court usurps the role of Congress, as it does today, the public understandably becomes confused about who the policymakers really are in our system of separated powers, and inevitably becomes cynical about the oft-repeated aspiration that judges base their decisions on law rather than on personal preference. The best way for judges to demonstrate that we are deciding cases based on the ordinary meaning of the law is to walk the walk, even in the hard cases when we might prefer a different policy outcome.

* * *

It is true that meaningful legislative action takes time—often too much time, especially in the unwieldy morass on Capitol Hill. But the Constitution does not put the Legislative Branch in the "position of a television quiz show contestant so that when a given period of time has elapsed and a problem remains unsolved by them, the federal judiciary may press a buzzer and take its turn at fashioning a solution." The proper role of the Judiciary in statutory interpretation cases is "to apply, not amend, the work of the People's representatives," even when the judges might think that "Congress should reenter the field and alter the judgments it made in the past."

## HIVELY v. IVY TECH COMMUNITY COLLEGE

United States Court of Appeals for the Seventh Circuit, en banc (2017).
853 F.3d 339.

■ JUDGE WOOD, CIRCUIT JUDGE.

. . .

I

[Kimberly] Hively is openly lesbian. She began teaching as a part-time, adjunct professor at Ivy Tech Community College's South Bend campus in 2000. Hoping to improve her lot, she applied for at least six full-time positions between 2009 and 2014. These efforts were unsuccessful; worse yet, in July 2014 her part-time contract was not renewed. . . .

II

A

. . .

B

. . . Hively alleges that if she had been a man married to a woman (or living with a woman, or dating a woman) and everything else had stayed the same, Ivy Tech would not have refused to promote her and would not have fired her. . . . This describes paradigmatic sex discrimination. . . . Ivy Tech is disadvantaging her *because she is a woman.* Nothing in the complaint hints that Ivy Tech has an anti-marriage policy that extends to heterosexual relationships, or for that matter even an anti-partnership policy that is gender-neutral.

Viewed through the lens of the gender nonconformity line of cases, Hively represents the ultimate case of failure to conform to the female stereotype (at least as understood in a place such as modern America, which views heterosexuality as the norm and other forms of sexuality as exceptional): she is not heterosexual. . . . Hively's claim is no different from the claims brought by women who were rejected for jobs in traditionally male workplaces, such as fire departments, construction, and policing. The employers in those cases were policing the boundaries of what jobs or behaviors they found acceptable for a woman (or in some cases, for a man).

The virtue of looking at comparators and paying heed to gender non-conformity is that this process sheds light on the interpretive question raised by Hively's case: is sexual-orientation discrimination a form of sex discrimination, given the way in which the Supreme Court has interpreted the word "sex" in the statute? The dissent criticizes us for not trying to *rule out* sexual-orientation discrimination by controlling for it in our comparator example and for not placing any weight on the fact that if someone had asked Ivy Tech what its reasons were at the time of the discriminatory conduct, it probably would have said "sexual orientation," not "sex." We assume that this is true, but this thought experiment does not answer the question before us—instead, it begs that question. It commits the logical fallacy of assuming the conclusion it sets out to prove. . . .

Hively also has argued that action based on sexual orientation is sex discrimination under the associational theory. It is now accepted that a person who is discriminated against because of the protected characteristic of one with whom she associates is actually being disadvantaged because of her own traits. This line of cases began with Loving, in which the Supreme Court held that "restricting the freedom to marry solely because of racial classifications violates the central meaning of the Equal Protection Clause." The Court rejected the argument that miscegenation statutes do not violate equal protection because they "punish equally both the white and the Negro participants in an interracial marriage." When dealing with a statute containing racial classifications, it wrote, "the fact of equal application does not immunize the statute from the very heavy burden of justification" required by the Fourteenth Amendment for lines drawn by race. . . .

The fact that we now accept this analysis tells us nothing, however, about the world in 1967, when Loving reached the Supreme Court. The dissent implies that we are adopting an anachronistic view of Title VII, enacted just three years before Loving, but it is the dissent's understanding of Loving and the miscegenation laws that is an anachronism. Thanks to Loving and [additional cases discussed] society understands now that such laws are (and always were) inherently racist. But as of 1967 (and thus as of 1964), Virginia and 15 other states had anti-miscegenation laws on the books. Loving, 388 U.S. at 6. These laws were long defended and understood as non-discriminatory because the legal obstacle affected *both* partners. The Court in Loving recognized that equal application of a law that prohibited conduct only between members of different races did not save it. Changing the race of one partner made a difference in determining the legality of the conduct, and so the law rested on "distinctions drawn according to race," which were unjustifiable and racially discriminatory. Loving, 388 U.S. at 11. So too, here. If we were to change the sex of one partner in a lesbian relationship, the outcome would be different. This reveals that the discrimination rests on distinctions drawn according to sex.

III

Today's decision must be understood against the backdrop of the Supreme Court's decisions, not only in the field of employment discrimination, but also in the area of broader discrimination on the basis of sexual orientation. . . .

The logic of the Supreme Court's decisions, as well as the common-sense reality that it is actually impossible to discriminate on the basis of sexual orientation without discriminating on the basis of sex, persuade us that the time has come to overrule our previous cases that have endeavored to find and observe that line. . . .

We hold only that a person who alleges that she experienced employment discrimination on the basis of her sexual orientation has put forth a case of sex discrimination for Title VII purposes. It was therefore wrong to dismiss Hively's complaint for failure to state a claim. The judgment of the district court is reversed and the case is remanded for further proceedings.

holding

■ JUDGE POSNER, concurring.

It is helpful to note at the outset that the interpretation of statutes comes in three flavors. The first and most conventional is the extraction of the original meaning of the statute—the meaning intended by the legislators—and corresponds to interpretation in ordinary discourse. Knowing English I can usually determine swiftly and straightforwardly the meaning of a statement, oral or written, made to me in English (not always, because the statement may be garbled, grammatically intricate or inaccurate, obtuse, or complex beyond my ability to understand).

The second form of interpretation, illustrated by the commonplace local ordinance which commands "no vehicles in the park," is interpretation by unexpressed intent, whereby we understand that although an ambulance is a vehicle, the ordinance was not intended to include ambulances among the "vehicles" forbidden to enter the park. This mode of interpretation received its definitive statement in Blackstone's analysis of the medieval law of Bologna which stated that "whoever drew blood in the streets should be punished with the utmost severity." William Blackstone, Commentaries on the Laws of England *60 (1765). Blackstone asked whether the law should have been interpreted to make punishable a surgeon "who opened the vein of a person that fell down in the street with a fit." (Bleeding a sick or injured person was a common form of medical treatment in those days.) Blackstone thought not, remarking that as to "the effects and consequence, or the spirit and reason of the law . . . the rule is, where words bear either none, or a very absurd signification, if literally understood, we must a little deviate from the received sense of them." The law didn't mention surgeons, but Blackstone thought it obvious that the legislators, who must have known something about the medical activities of surgeons, had not intended the law to apply to them. And so it is with ambulances in parks that prohibit vehicles.

Finally and most controversially, interpretation can mean giving a fresh meaning to a statement (which can be a statement found in a constitutional or statutory text)—a meaning that infuses the statement with vitality and significance today. An example of this last form of interpretation—the form that in my mind is most clearly applicable to the present case—is the Sherman Antitrust Act, enacted in 1890, long before there was a sophisticated understanding of the economics of monopoly and competition. Times have changed; and for more than thirty years the Act has been interpreted in conformity to the modern, not the nineteenth-century, understanding of the relevant economics. The Act has thus been updated by, or in the name of, judicial interpretation—the form of interpretation that consists of making old law satisfy modern needs and understandings. And a common form of interpretation it is, despite its flouting "original meaning." Statutes and constitutional provisions frequently are interpreted on the basis of present need and present understanding rather than original meaning—constitutional provisions even more frequently, because most of them are older than most statutes.

Title VII of the Civil Rights Act of 1964, now more than half a century old, invites an interpretation that will update it to the present, a present that differs markedly from the era in which the Act was enacted. But I need to emphasize that this third form of interpretation—call it judicial interpretive updating—presupposes a lengthy interval between enactment and (re)interpretation. A statute when passed has an understood meaning; it takes years, often many years, for a shift in the political and cultural environment to change the understanding of the statute. . . .

It is well-nigh certain that homosexuality, male or female, did not figure in the minds of the legislators who enacted Title VII. I had graduated from law school two years before the law was enacted. Had I been asked then whether I had ever met a male homosexual, I would have answered: probably not; had I been asked whether I had ever met a lesbian I would have answered "only in the pages of *À la recherche du temps perdu*." Homosexuality was almost invisible in the 1960s. It became visible in the 1980s as a consequence of the AIDS epidemic; today it is regarded by a large swathe of the American population as normal. But what is certain is that the word "sex" in Title VII had no immediate reference to homosexuality; many years would elapse before it could be understood to include homosexuality.

A diehard "originalist" would argue that what was believed in 1964 defines the scope of the statute for as long as the statutory text remains unchanged, and therefore until changed by Congress's amending or replacing the statute. But . . . statutory and constitutional provisions frequently are interpreted on the basis of present need and understanding rather than original meaning.

The majority opinion states that Congress in 1964 "may not have realized or understood the full scope of the words it chose." This could be understood to imply that the statute forbade discrimination against homosexuals but the framers and ratifiers of the statute were not smart enough to realize that. I would prefer to say that theirs was the then-current understanding of the key word—sex. "Sex" in 1964 meant gender, not sexual orientation. What the framers and ratifiers understandably didn't understand was how attitudes toward homosexuals would change in the following half century. They shouldn't be blamed for that failure of foresight. *We* understand the words of Title VII differently not because we're smarter than the statute's framers and ratifiers but because we live in a different era, a different culture. Congress in the 1960s did not foresee the sexual revolution of the 2000s. . . .

I would prefer to see us acknowledge openly that today we, who are judges rather than members of Congress, are imposing on a half-century-old statute a meaning of "sex discrimination" that the Congress that enacted it would not have accepted. This is something courts do fairly frequently to avoid statutory obsolescence and concomitantly to avoid placing the entire burden of updating old statutes on the legislative branch. We should not leave the impression that we are merely the obedient servants of the 88th Congress (1963–1965), carrying out their wishes. We are not. We are taking advantage of what the last half century has taught.

■ JUDGE FLAUM, with whom JUDGE RIPPLE, joins, concurring.

. . . I find the issue before us is simply whether discriminating against an employee for being homosexual violates Title VII's prohibition against discriminating against that employee because of their sex. In my view, the answer is yes, and the statute's text commands as much. . . . Ivy Tech allegedly refused to promote Professor Hively because she was homosexual—or (A) a woman who is (B) sexually attracted to women. Thus, the College allegedly discriminated against Professor Hively, at least in part, because of her sex. I conclude that Title VII, as its text provides, does not allow this.

■ JUDGE SYKES, with whom JUDGE BAUER and JUDGE KANNE, join, dissenting.

. . . The majority deploys a judge-empowering, common-law decision method that leaves a great deal of room for judicial discretion. So does Judge Posner in his concurrence. Neither is faithful to the statutory text, read fairly, as a reasonable person would have understood it when it was adopted. The result is a statutory amendment courtesy of unelected judges. Judge Posner admits this; he embraces and argues for this conception of judicial power. The majority does not, preferring instead to smuggle in the statutory amendment under cover of an aggressive reading of loosely related Supreme Court precedents. Either way, the result is the same: the circumvention of the legislative process by which the people govern themselves.

Respect for the constraints imposed on the judiciary by a system of written law must begin with fidelity to the traditional first principle of statutory interpretation: When a statute supplies the rule of decision, our role is to give effect to the enacted text, interpreting the statutory language as a reasonable person would have understood it at the time of enactment. We are not authorized to infuse the text with a new or unconventional meaning or to update it to respond to changed social, economic, or political conditions.

In a handful of statutory contexts, Congress has vested the federal courts with authority to consider and make new rules of law in the common-law way. The Sherman Act is the archetype of the so-called "common-law statutes," but there are very few of these and Title VII is not one of them. So our role is interpretive only; we lack the discretion to ascribe to Title VII a meaning it did not bear at its inception. . . .

Judicial statutory updating, whether overt or covert, cannot be reconciled with the constitutional design. The Constitution establishes a procedure for enacting and amending statutes: bicameralism and presentment. See U.S. Const. art. I, § 7. Needless to say, statutory amendments brought to you by the judiciary do not pass through this process. That is why a textualist decision method matters: When we assume the power to alter the original public meaning of a statute through the process of interpretation, we assume a power that is not ours. The Constitution assigns the power to make and amend statutory law to the elected representatives of the people. However welcome today's decision might be as a policy matter, it comes at a great cost to representative self-government.

I

. . . Sexual orientation is not on the list of forbidden categories of employment discrimination, and we have long and consistently held that employment decisions based on a person's sexual orientation do not classify people on the basis of sex and thus are not covered by Title VII's prohibition of discrimination "because of sex."...

Today the court jettisons the prevailing interpretation and installs the polar opposite. Suddenly sexual-orientation discrimination *is* sex discrimination and thus is actionable under Title VII. What justification is offered for this radical change in a well-established, uniform interpretation of an important—indeed, transformational—statute? My colleagues take note of the Supreme Court's "absence from the debate." What debate? There is no debate, at least not in the relevant sense....

Of course there *is* a robust debate on this subject in our culture, media, and politics. Attitudes about gay rights have dramatically shifted in the 53 years since the Civil Rights Act was adopted. Lambda Legal's proposed new reading of Title VII—offered on behalf of plaintiff Kimberly Hively at the appellate stage of this litigation—has a strong foothold in current popular opinion.

This striking cultural change informs a case for legislative change and might eventually persuade the people's representatives to amend the statute to implement a new public policy. But it does not bear on the sole inquiry properly before the en banc court: Is the prevailing interpretation of Title VII—that discrimination on the basis of sexual orientation is different in kind and not a form of sex discrimination—*wrong as an original matter*?

A

... To be clear, I agree with my colleagues that the proposed new interpretation is not necessarily incorrect simply because no one in the 1964 Congress that adopted Title VII intended or anticipated its application to sexual-orientation discrimination. The subjective intentions of the legislators do not matter. Statutory interpretation is an objective inquiry that looks for the meaning the statutory language conveyed to a reasonable person at the time of enactment. The objective meaning of the text is not delimited by what individual lawmakers specifically had in mind when they voted for the statute....

B

That is where our agreement ends....

Is it even remotely plausible that in 1964, when Title VII was adopted, a reasonable person competent in the English language would have understood that a law banning employment discrimination "because of sex" also banned discrimination because of sexual orientation? The answer is no, of course not....

Title VII does not define discrimination "because of sex." In common, ordinary usage in 1964—and now, for that matter—the word "sex" means biologically *male* or *female*; it does not also refer to sexual orientation. See, e.g., *Sex*, THE AMERICAN HERITAGE DICTIONARY OF THE ENGLISH LANGUAGE (1st ed. 1969) (defining "sex" as "[t]he property or quality by which organisms are classified according to their reproductive functions[;] [e]ither of two divisions, designated *male* and *female*, of this classification"); *Sex*, NEW OXFORD AMERICAN DICTIONARY (3d ed. 2010) (defining "sex" as "either of the two main categories (male and female) into which humans and many other living things are divided on the basis of their reproductive functions"); *Sex*, THE AMERICAN HERITAGE DESK DICTIONARY (5th ed. 2013) (defining "sex" as "[e]ither of the two divisions, female and male, by which most organisms are classified on the basis of their reproductive organs and functions[;] [t]he condition or character of being female or male").

To a fluent speaker of the English language—then and now—the ordinary meaning of the word "sex" does not fairly include the concept of "sexual orientation." The two terms are never used interchangeably, and the latter is not subsumed within the former; there is no overlap in meaning. . . . Classifying people by sexual orientation is different than classifying them by sex. The two traits are categorically distinct and widely recognized as such. There is no ambiguity or vagueness here. . . .

C

This commonsense understanding is confirmed by the language Congress uses when it *does* legislate against sexual-orientation discrimination. For example, the Violence Against Women Act prohibits funded programs and activities from discriminating "on the basis of actual or perceived race, color, religion, national origin, *sex*, gender identity, . . . *sexual orientation*, or disability." 42 U.S.C. § 13925(b)(13)(A) (emphases added). If sex discrimination is commonly understood to encompass sexual-orientation discrimination, then listing the two categories separately, as this statute does, is needless surplusage. . . .

II

. . . An employer who refuses to hire homosexuals is not drawing a line based on the job applicant's sex. He is not excluding gay men because they are men and lesbians because they are women. His discriminatory motivation is independent of and unrelated to the applicant's sex. Sexism (misandry and misogyny) and homophobia are separate kinds of prejudice that classify people in distinct ways based on different immutable characteristics. Simply put, sexual-orientation discrimination doesn't classify people by sex; it doesn't draw male/female distinctions but instead targets homosexual men and women for harsher treatment than heterosexual men and women. . . .

III

. . . Finally, drawing especially on Obergefell, my colleagues worry that adhering to the long-settled interpretation of Title VII "creates 'a paradoxical legal landscape in which a person can be married on Saturday and then fired on Monday for just that act.' " The concern is understandable, but my colleagues conflate the distinction between state action, which is subject to constitutional limits, and private action, which is regulated by statute. The Due Process and Equal Protection Clauses are constitutional restraints on government. Title VII is a statutory restraint on employers. The legal regimes differ accordingly. Any discrepancy is a matter for legislative, not judicial, correction.

* * *

If Kimberly Hively was denied a job because of her sexual orientation, she was treated unjustly. But Title VII does not provide a remedy for this kind of discrimination. The argument that it *should* must be addressed to Congress. . . .

## NOTES ON DYNAMIC STATUTORY INTERPRETATION

(1) ***In This Corner.*** WILLIAM N. ESKRIDGE, JR., DYNAMIC STATUTORY INTERPRETATION, 135 U. Pa. L. Rev. 1479, 1479, 1483, 1496 (1987): "Federal judges interpreting the Constitution typically consider not only the constitutional text and its historical background, but also its subsequent interpretational history, related constitutional developments, and current societal facts. Similarly, judges interpreting common law precedents normally consider not only the text of the precedents and their historical context, but also their subsequent history, related legal developments, and current societal context. In light of this, it is odd that many judges and commentators believe judges should consider only the text and historical context when interpreting statutes, the third main source of law. Statutes, however, should—like the Constitution and the common law—be interpreted 'dynamically,' that is, in light of their present societal, political, and legal context. . . .

". . . The dialectic of statutory interpretation is the process of understanding a text created in the past and applying it to a present problem. This process cannot be described simply as the recreation of past events and past expectations, for the 'best' interpretation of a statute is typically the one that is most consonant with our current 'web of beliefs' and policies surrounding the statute. That is, statutory interpretation involves the present-day interpreter's understanding and reconciliation of three different perspectives, no one of which will always control. These three perspectives relate to (1) the statutory text, which is the formal focus of interpretation and a constraint on the range of interpretive options available (textual perspective); (2) the original legislative expectations surrounding the statute's creation, including compromises reached (historical perspective); and (3) the subsequent evolution of the statute and its present context, especially the ways in which the societal and legal environment of the statute has materially changed over time (evolutive perspective). . . .

". . . The three perspectives implicated in dynamic interpretation . . . suggest a continuum. In many cases, the text of the statute will provide determinate answers, though we should trust our reading of the text primarily when the statute is recent and the context of enactment represents considered legislative deliberation and decision on the interpretive issue. This is one end of the continuum: the text controls. At the opposite end of the continuum are those cases where neither the text nor the historical context of the statute clearly resolves the interpretive question, and the societal and legal context of the statute has changed materially. In those cases, the evolutive context controls. In general, the more detailed the text is, the greater weight the interpreter will give to textual considerations; the more recent the statute and the clearer the legislative expectations, the greater weight the interpreter will give to historical considerations; the more striking the changes in circumstances (changes in public values count more than factual changes in society), the greater weight the interpreter will give to evolutive considerations."

(2) ***And in the Other Corner.*** MARTIN H. REDISH & THEODORE CHUNG, DEMOCRATIC THEORY AND THE LEGISLATIVE PROCESS: MOURNING THE DEATH OF ORIGINALISM IN STATUTORY INTERPRETATION, 68 Tul. L. Rev. 803, 807–08 (1994): "Despite its claim that it carves out only a minor exception to the general rule of judicial deference to the legislature in the realm of statutory interpretation, dynamic statutory interpretation effectively represents a dramatic and pernicious reordering of our democratic form of government. In short, dynamic statutory interpretation would establish the judiciary as a largely unaccountable ruling elite, the virtual equivalent of philosopher kings. Robert Dahl has labeled judges operating under such a model 'guardians,' empowered to pass judgment not merely on the constitutionality of legislative enactments but on their wisdom and morality as well.

"The judiciary that dynamic scholars envision for purposes of statutory interpretation bears little resemblance to the judiciary posited by either new textualist or originalist commentators. Instead of deciphering and implementing the decisions of a coordinate branch, the judiciary, from the dynamist perspective, acts as an adjunct in the legislative process or, more precisely, a super legislature.

"Underlying dynamic statutory interpretation, then, is an ominously antidemocratic conception of our system of government. Notions of separation of powers that typify traditional interpretive models are, in the eyes of dynamic scholars, impediments to good government. Indeed, dynamic scholars insist, the citizenry cannot afford to entrust its well-being to a Congress beholden to special interests. Because the federal judiciary remains insulated from special-interest and constituent pressures, dynamists further contend that it is the branch best suited to ascertain and protect the common good. However, by conferring on judges wide-ranging discretion to ignore what would otherwise be discernible legislative directives in favor of interpretations more consistent with their own notions of the common good, dynamic interpretation runs afoul of the normative political premise of self-determination that undergirds our representative democracy."

(3) ***Is Bostock Textualist Just Like It Claims to Be?*** BENJAMIN EIDELSON argues that a truly textualist reading of Title VII required extending Bostock's "implicit logic" "to prohibit making decisions based on *any* facts about what a person is like *in the named dimensions*":

"On this understanding, the fact of a person's *being Black* is a prohibited ground of decision-making, but so, too, is the fact of their *being of a different race than their spouse*, or the fact of their *being of the same race as most existing employees*. A decision made on any of these grounds is made on account of the person's race in the requisite sense: it is made based on a fact about what they are like "race-wise," or in respect of race. And that, in essence, is why Bostock was rightly decided: not because Gerald Bostock would have been treated better if his sex had been *female*, as the Court insisted, but because he would have been treated better if his sex had been *different than the sex of his desired romantic partners*—full stop. In short, disparate-treatment prohibitions make it unlawful to disfavor people because of properties—including relational properties—that they possess partly in virtue of how they stand in the dimensions enumerated in the statute." DIMENSIONAL DISPARATE TREATMENT, 95 S. Cal. L. Rev. (forthcoming).

Eidelson argues that this reading is the proper textualist reading "[b]ecause an ordinary reader would read Title VII like the kind of text that it is—a piece of legislation, not a transcript of a conversation between friends about a particular incident." And he contends that, given the role legislation plays in regulating conduct, the reading he proposes is the one that is proper. "Understanding that the ordinary purpose of legislative communication is to subject a class of conduct to general norms, the reader would seek an interpretation or analysis of 'because of such individual's X'; they would not understand the intended meaning of that phrase to align with their own linguistic intuitions about each conceivable scenario or individual characteristic considered in isolation from all others. . . . [T]hey would naturally treat that phrase as its own module or unit of statutory content, with a unitary meaning that does not depend on the particular characteristic (or, for that matter, employment action) that is at issue in a given case. And, . . . they ought to accept the dimensional account, . . . as capturing the standard meaning of that phrase."

But, does this textualist defense of Bostock beg the question about how "a piece of legislation" is to be read? What about reading a statute in light of an inferred legislative purpose—or in light of evidence from legislative history, like the social context of Title VII's enactment in 1964? Or what about reading a statute like Justice Kagan urged her readers to read the statute in Wooden, in which she asked them to interpret the key word there, "occasion", as they would interpret that word if it were used in an ordinary conversation, as it might be in talking about a wedding? And, if those are all possibilities, then what about reading a statute dynamically, on the understanding that Congress would not want a major civil rights statute to be read otherwise?

(4) ***Reactions to Bostock.*** An essay published shortly after the Court decided Bostock criticized the "mindlessness" of the decision:

"It is basic civics that the Constitution allocates different kinds of authority to the different branches of the national government. Legislative authority is assigned to Congress. Of course, it is also common knowledge that at least since the New Deal, the actual operations of government have a tenuous relation at best to the constitutional allocation of powers. But underlying both the classical model and the revisionist realities lies a more elementary and shared assumption: law should be the product of mindful decision-making *by someone*. . . .

"The Court admits that the Congress that enacted Title VII never intended that the law would contain any such prohibition [against sexual orientation discrimination]. . . . Whether federal law should prohibit sexual orientation discrimination has been a much-debated issue in our society. Now we have such a prohibition. But not because Congress deliberated and then decided to adopt it. And not (at least according to Gorsuch) because the Justices deliberated and decided to adopt it. What we have, it seems, is a highly consequential and controversial prohibition that is not the expression of a mindful decision by *anyone*."

STEVEN D. SMITH, ESSAY, THE MINDLESSNESS OF BOSTOCK, Law & Liberty (July 9, 2020).[2]

Others, like KATIE EYER, quickly noted the significance of a conservative Justice relying on textualism to recognize historic equality rights:

"Although textualism has often been viewed as a tool of conservative legal advocacy, it need not and ought not be viewed that way. . . . [T]extualism is not an inherently ideological methodology, only serving conservative aims. Rather, there are many reasons for progressives, like conservatives, to celebrate a methodology that places limits on the ability of biases and individual beliefs to infect judicial decision-making. Indeed, as the Bostock opinion notes, textualism properly understood can serve as a bulwark against the exclusion of politically unpopular groups from the law's protections. . . .

"[A]s Bostock demonstrates, progressives have the ability and the opportunity to reclaim the other side of the debate. As Justice Elena Kagan famously put it in describing Scalia's influence, "[w]e're all textualists now." That pronouncement ought not signal a defeat for progressive approaches to statutory interpretation. Rather, the rise of textualism offers powerful opportunities for progressive lawyers, scholars and judges to think about the relationship of text to law and the ways that text safeguards the most vulnerable among us."

KATIE EYER, SYMPOSIUM: PROGRESSIVE TEXTUALISM AND LGBTQ RIGHTS, SCOTUSblog (June 16, 2020).[3]

Still, some urged caution. JEANNIE SUK GERSEN, for example, noted that Bostock contains "some potential land mines" for liberals. In particular, Gersen wrote that:

"The extreme formalism of its vision of what it is to discriminate 'because of sex' means that a person's gender, sexual orientation, or transgender status should be irrelevant to institutional decisions. On this theory, heterosexual and cisgender people, too, may have valid Title VII claims if they are not hired or promoted because of their sexual orientation or gender identity, say, by an organization that preferred to hire or promote gay or transgender individuals to work with the communities it serves.

---

[2] https://lawliberty.org/bostock-mindlessness/.

[3] https://www.scotusblog.com/2020/06/symposium-progressive-textualism-and-lgbtq-rights/.

"And Bostock surely stands to affect other categories that Title VII addresses, most importantly race . . . [I]n Bostock, the echo we hear[ ] is of Chief Justice Roberts in Parents Involved in Community Schools v. Seattle, which found that race-based school assignments undertaken to produce racially diverse schools violated the equal-protection clause of the Constitution. In a famously hyper-formalist statement, Roberts wrote, 'The way to stop discrimination on the basis of race is to stop discriminating on the basis of race.'

"With the Court expected to hear affirmative-action cases within two years—including ongoing lawsuits against Harvard and the University of North Carolina at Chapel Hill—there is reason to think that Bostock's formalist articulations on discrimination will bolster a conservative decision to dismantle race-conscious admissions policies."

JEANNIE SUK GERSEN, COULD THE SUPREME COURT'S LANDMARK L.G.B.T.-RIGHTS DECISION HELP LEAD TO THE DISMANTLING OF AFFIRMATIVE ACTION?, The New Yorker (June 27, 2020).[4]

(5) ***Post-Bostock Developments.*** A key question is whether Bostock's construction of Title VII also applies to other statutes that prohibit discrimination in contexts other than employment and in settings beyond the workplace. Does a school district discriminate "because of sex" under Title IX when it prohibits students to use the bathroom that accords with their gender identity? In Adams v. Sch. Bd. of St. Johns Cnty., 968 F.3d 1286 (11th Cir. 2020), the court rejected the defendant's contention that the plaintiff, due to the sex he was assigned at birth, was a girl and so was treated the same as all girls at the school. Instead, it made the relevant baseline nontransgender male students. The plaintiff thus was denied the ability to use the boys' restroom solely because of his transgender status. Applying Bostock, the Eleventh Circuit found the plaintiff was discriminated against because of sex, given that discrimination on the basis of transgender status is discrimination because of sex.

The dissent in that case argued that "sex" refers to a person's reproductive function and has never meant gender identity. Thus, the School Board did not violate Title IX when it prohibited the student from using the boys' bathroom. Rather, it treated him the same as all other persons of the same biological sex.

In Grimm v. Gloucester County School Board, 972 F.3d 586 (4th Cir. 2020), the Fourth Circuit found a similar school bathroom policy was discrimination in violation of Title IX. The Grimm case affirmatively cited the Adams case as authority. But on July 14, 2021, an Eleventh Circuit panel vacated the opinion in the Adams case and substituted a new one. Adams v. Sch. Bd. of St. Johns Cnty., 3 F.4th 1299 (11th Cir. 2021). The new opinion did not interpret Title IX and did not rely on Bostock. But it, too, ruled in favor of the student, saying that the way the School District implemented its policy "targets some transgender students for bathroom restrictions but not others. In this way, the policy is arbitrary" and contrary to the Fourteenth

---

4 https://www.newyorker.com/news/our-columnists/could-the-supreme-courts-landmark-lgbt-rights-decision-help-lead-to-the-dismantling-of-affirmative-action.

Amendment. The court was frank to say that it changed the form and basis of its opinion "in an effort to get broader support among our colleagues."

On August 23, 2021, the Eleventh Circuit vacated the panel and granted rehearing en banc. 9 F.4th 1369 (11th Cir. 2021). Oral arguments occurred in February 2022. As of September 2022, there was no decision. The Supreme Court has yet to speak further.

(6) ***Can Congress Intend Dynamically Updated Statutes?*** Consider Bostock in light of NEW PRIME, INC. V. OLIVEIRA, 139 S.Ct. 532 (2019). There, the Court held that the phrase "contracts of employment" in a section of the Federal Arbitration Act encompassed not only contracts between employers and employees but also contracts with independent contractors. JUSTICE GORSUCH reasoned for the majority: "[W]e bear an important caution in mind. '[I]t's a "fundamental canon of statutory construction" that words generally should be "interpreted as taking their ordinary . . . meaning . . . at the time Congress enacted the statute." ' Wisconsin Central Ltd. v. United States, 138 S.Ct. 2067, 2070 (2018) (quoting Perrin v. United States, 444 U.S. 37, 42 (1979)); . . . After all, if judges could freely invest old statutory terms with new meanings, we would risk amending legislation outside the 'single, finely wrought and exhaustively considered, procedure' the Constitution commands. INS v. Chadha, 462 U.S. 919, 951 (1983). We would risk, too, upsetting reliance interests in the settled meaning of a statute. Cf. 2B N. Singer & J. Singer, Sutherland on Statutes and Statutory Construction § 56A:3 (rev. 7th ed. 2012). Of course, statutes may sometimes refer to an external source of law and fairly warn readers that they must abide that external source of law, later amendments and modifications included. Id., § 51:8 (discussing the reference canon). But nothing like that exists here. Nor has anyone suggested any other appropriate reason that might allow us to depart from the original meaning of the statute at hand."

With that marker in place, Justice Gorsuch then explained: "To many lawyerly ears today, the term 'contracts of employment' might call to mind only agreements between employers and employees (or what the common law sometimes called masters and servants). Suggestively, at least one recently published law dictionary defines the word 'employment' to mean 'the relationship between master and servant.' Black's Law Dictionary 641 (10th ed. 2014). But this modern intuition isn't easily squared with evidence of the term's meaning at the time of the Act's adoption in 1925. At that time, a 'contract of employment' usually meant nothing more than an agreement to perform work. As a result, most people then would have understood § 1 to exclude not only agreements between employers and employees but also agreements that require independent contractors to perform work."

JUSTICE GINSBURG responded in a concurring opinion that she agreed that "[l]ooking to the period of enactment to gauge statutory meaning ordinarily fosters fidelity to the 'regime . . . Congress established.' MCI Telecommunications Corp. v. American Telephone & Telegraph Co., 512 U.S. 218, 234 (1994)." But, she added, Congress "may design legislation to govern changing times and circumstances. See, e.g., Kimble v. Marvel Entertainment, LLC, 576 U.S. 446, 461 (2015) ('Congress . . . intended [the Sherman Antitrust Act's] reference to "restraint of trade" to have "changing content," and authorized courts to oversee the term's "dynamic potential." '); SEC v. Zandford, 535 U.S. 813, 819 (2002) ('In enacting the Securities Exchange Act, "Congress sought to substitute a philosophy of full disclosure for the philosophy of caveat emptor. . . . Consequently . . . the statute should be construed not technically and restrictively, but flexibly to effectuate its remedial purposes." '); H.J. Inc. v. Northwestern Bell Telephone Co., 492 U.S. 229, 243 (1989) ('The limits of the relationship and continuity concepts that combine to define a [Racketeer Influenced and Corrupt Organizations] pattern . . . cannot be fixed in advance with such clarity that it will always be apparent whether in a particular case a "pattern of racketeering activity" exists. The development of these concepts must await future cases . . . .'). As these illustrations suggest, sometimes, '[w]ords in statutes can enlarge or contract their scope as other changes, in law or in the world, require their application to new instances or make old applications anachronistic.' West v. Gibson, 527 U.S. 212, 218 (1999)."

Is Bostock consistent with the method deployed in New Prime or irreconcilable with it because "most people" in 1964 would not have understood "because of sex" to refer to discrimination based on either sexual orientation or gender identity? Does Justice Ginsburg's approach in New Prime offer a better explanation of how the result in Bostock could be right when compared to Bostock itself?

(7) ***Dynamic Statutory Interpretation and the APA.*** The APA has received many interpretations that would have been surprising to its drafters. What are the implications for them of Justice Gorsuch's opinions in New Prime and Bostock about whether meaning can change over time? What is the possible bearing on them of Justice Ginsburg's concurrence, as well as the opinion in Bostock and its view of whether meaning can change over time? Consider, too, whether certain statutes might be more properly interpreted dynamically than others. The Civil Rights Act of 1964 is no ordinary statute. Perhaps the same is true of the APA. Are such statutes enough like the Constitution in terms of the foundational role that they play in our legal order that it is appropriate to construe them as if they are "living" in the way that some argue that it is appropriate to construe the Constitution itself? For a discussion of originalism in interpreting the APA, see Chapter III (pp. 245–252).

# SECTION 3. TOOLS OF STATUTORY INTERPRETATION



Theories of statutory interpretation are helpful in structuring thinking about how to approach an interpretive issue raised by a statute. But one still needs to know how, in practice, to resolve the interpretive issue at hand. And that requires one to be aware of the relevant tools that may be deployed in the course of applying an interpretive theory, including, in particular, dictionaries, custom and usage, canons of construction, both linguistic and substantive, and legislative history.

As you read the following excerpts, consider the affinity between the major theories of statutory interpretation and the characteristic tools that may be associated with each of those theories—for instance, the relationship between textualism and the plain meaning rule, linguistic canons, and dictionaries; between purposivism and legislative history; between pragmatic and dynamic approaches and some of the substantive canons. Consider, too, the hazards presented by the deployment of some of these tools. Does it make sense to assume the drafters of the legislation understood that the tool being deployed would be deployed? If so, is that because the assumption accurately reflects the understandings of the drafters? Or is it because the assumption is legitimate even if it is not based on the reality of the drafting process? Why would such an assumption then be legitimate?

## a. Dictionaries

*TANIGUCHI v. KAN PACIFIC SAIPAN, LTD.*

An intuitive and obvious means of discerning a word's ordinary meaning is to look it up in a dictionary. This trend has increased in recent years. But are dictionaries useful? Judge Learned Hand famously cautioned that "it is one of the surest indexes of a mature and developed jurisprudence not to make a fortress out of the dictionary." Cabell v. Markham, 148 F.2d 737, 739 (2d Cir. 1945). As you think about the following problem and case, consider Hand's caution and consider whether a general definition of a word in a dictionary can (or should) really lend much insight into how to construe the federal statute at issue.

### WHAT DOES IT MEAN TO BE AN "INTERPRETER"?

Consider the following problem. The plaintiff in a tort action was visiting from Japan when he allegedly was injured by the negligence of the defendant. During pretrial discovery proceedings, and in response to the defendant's proper demand, the plaintiff supplied the defendant with a number of documents written in Japanese, which the defendant then had translated. The defendant prevailed at trial and so sought to recover its "costs" as defined by 28 U.S.C. § 1920, including the substantial costs of these documentary translations.

Until 1978, Section 1920 contained no provision that would have supported recovery of translation costs. In that year, the Court Interpreters Act added subsection (6) to Section 1920:

> A judge or clerk of any court of the United States may tax as costs the following: . . .
>
> (6) Compensation of court appointed experts, compensation of interpreters, and salaries, fees, expenses, and costs of special interpretation services under section 1828 of this title [concerning criminal actions and in civil actions initiated by the United States (including petitions for writs of habeas corpus initiated in the name of the United States by relators) in a United States district court].
>
> A bill of costs shall be filed in the case and, upon allowance, included in the judgment or decree.

Are the defendants entitled to recover their translation costs?

## TANIGUCHI v. KAN PACIFIC SAIPAN, LTD.

Supreme Court of the United States (2012).
566 U.S. 560.

■ JUSTICE ALITO delivered the opinion of the Court.

The costs that may be awarded to prevailing parties in lawsuits brought in federal court are set forth in 28 U.S.C. § 1920. The Court Interpreters Act amended that statute to include "compensation of interpreters." § 1920(6). The question presented in this case is whether "compensation of interpreters" covers the cost of translating documents. Because the ordinary meaning of the word "interpreter" is a person who translates orally from one language to another, we hold that "compensation of interpreters" is limited to the cost of oral translation and does not include the cost of document translation.

I

. . . Petitioner was injured when his leg broke through a wooden deck during a tour of respondent's resort property. Initially, petitioner said that he needed no medical attention, but two weeks later, he informed respondent that he had suffered cuts, bruises, and torn ligaments from the accident. Due to these alleged injuries, he claimed damages for medical expenses and for lost income from contracts he was unable to honor. [Defendants, here respondents, successfully moved for summary judgment] on the ground that petitioner offered no evidence that respondent knew of the defective deck or otherwise failed to exercise reasonable care.

In preparing its defense, respondent paid to have various documents translated from Japanese to English . . . [and] submitted a bill for those costs. Over petitioner's objection, the District Court awarded the costs to respondent as "compensation of interpreters" under § 1920(6). . . . The United States Court of Appeals for the Ninth Circuit affirmed both the District Court's grant of summary judgment and its award of costs. . . .

II

A

. . . Not until 1853 did Congress enact legislation specifying the costs allowable in federal court . . . which we have described as a "far-reaching Act specifying in detail the nature and amount of the taxable items of cost in the federal courts." Alyeska Pipeline Service Co. v. Wilderness Society, 421 U.S. 240 (1975), at 251–252. . . .

Federal Rule of Civil Procedure 54(d) gives courts the discretion to award costs to prevailing parties. . . . We have held that "§ 1920 defines the term 'costs' as used in Rule 54(d)." Crawford Fitting, 482 U.S.437 (1987), at 441. In so doing, we rejected the view that "the discretion granted by Rule 54(d) is a separate source of power to tax as costs expenses not enumerated in § 1920." Ibid.

As originally configured, § 1920 contained five categories of taxable costs . . . In 1978, Congress enacted the Court Interpreters Act, which amended § 1920 to add a sixth category: "Compensation of court appointed experts, compensation of interpreters, and salaries, fees, expenses, and costs of special interpretation services under section 1828 of this title." 28 U.S.C. § 1920(6); see also § 7, 92 Stat. 2044. We are concerned here with this sixth category, specifically the item of taxable costs identified as "compensation of interpreters."

B

. . . "[I]nterpreter" . . . is not defined in the Court Interpreters Act or in any other relevant statutory provision. When a term goes undefined in a statute, we give the term its ordinary meaning.

Many dictionaries in use when Congress enacted the Court Interpreters Act in 1978 defined "interpreter" as one who translates spoken, as opposed to written, language. The American Heritage Dictionary, for instance, defined the term as "[o]ne who translates orally from one language into another." American Heritage Dictionary 685 (1978). The Scribner-Bantam English Dictionary defined the related word "interpret" as "to translate orally." Scribner-Bantam English Dictionary 476 (1977). Similarly, the Random House Dictionary defined the intransitive form of "interpret" as "to translate what is *said* in a foreign language." Random House Dictionary of the English Language 744 (1973) (emphasis added). And, notably, the Oxford English Dictionary defined "interpreter" as "[o]ne who translates languages," but then divided that definition into two senses: "a. [a] translator of books or writings," which it designated as obsolete, and "b. [o]ne who translates the communications of persons speaking different languages; *spec.* one whose office it is to do so orally in the presence of the persons; a dragoman." 5 Oxford English Dictionary 416 (1933); see also Concise Oxford Dictionary of Current English 566 (6th ed. 1976) ("One who interprets; one whose office it is to translate the words of persons speaking different languages, esp. orally in their presence"); Chambers Twentieth Century Dictionary 686 (1973) ("one who translates orally for the benefit of two or more parties speaking different languages: . . . a translator (obs.)").

Pre-1978 legal dictionaries also generally defined the words "interpreter" and "interpret" in terms of oral translation. The then-current edition of Black's Law Dictionary, for example, defined "interpreter" as "[a] person sworn at a trial to interpret the evidence of a foreigner . . .to the court," and it defined "interpret" in relevant part as "to translate orally from one tongue to another." Black's Law Dictionary 954, 953 (rev. 4th ed. 1968); see also W. Anderson, A Dictionary of Law 565 (1888) ("One who translates the testimony of witnesses speaking a foreign tongue, for the benefit of the court and jury"); 1 B. Abbott, Dictionary of Terms and Phrases Used in American or English Jurisprudence 639 (1878) ("one who restates the testimony of a witness testifying in a foreign tongue, to the court and jury, in their language"). But see Ballentine's Law Dictionary 655, 654 (3d ed. 1969) (defining "interpreter" as "[o]ne who interprets, particularly one who interprets words written or spoken in a foreign language," and "interpret" as "to translate from a foreign language").

Against these authorities, respondent relies almost exclusively on Webster's Third New International Dictionary (hereinafter Webster's Third). The version of that dictionary in print when Congress enacted the Court Interpreters Act defined "interpreter" as "one that translates; *esp*: a person who translates orally for parties conversing in different tongues." Webster's Third 1182 (1976). The sense divider *esp* (for especially) indicates that the most common meaning of the term is one "who translates orally," but that meaning is subsumed within the more general definition "one that translates." . . . For respondent, the general definition suffices to establish that the term "interpreter" ordinarily includes persons who translate the written word. . . . We disagree.

That a definition is broad enough to encompass one sense of a word does not establish that the word is *ordinarily* understood in that sense. . . . It is telling that all the dictionaries cited above defined "interpreter" at the time of the statute's enactment as including persons who translate orally, but only a handful defined the word broadly enough to encompass translators of written material. Although the Oxford English Dictionary, one of the most authoritative on the English language, recognized that "interpreter" *can* mean one who translates writings, it expressly designated that meaning as obsolete. . . .

To be sure, the word "interpreter" can encompass persons who translate documents, but because that is not the ordinary meaning of the word, it does not control unless the context in which the word appears indicates that it does. . . . If anything, the statutory context suggests the opposite: that the word "interpreter" applies only to those who translate orally. As previously mentioned, Congress enacted § 1920(6) as part of the Court Interpreters Act. The main provision of that Act is § 2(a), codified in 28 U.S.C. §§ 1827 and 1828. See 92 Stat. 2040–2042. Particularly relevant here is § 1827. As it now reads, that statute provides for the establishment of "a program to facilitate the use of certified and otherwise qualified interpreters in judicial proceedings instituted by the United States." § 1827(a). Subsection (d) directs courts to use an interpreter in any criminal or civil action instituted by the United States if a party or witness "speaks only or primarily a language other than the English language" or "suffers from a hearing impairment" "so as to inhibit such party's comprehension of the proceedings or communication with counsel or the presiding judicial officer, or so as to inhibit such witness' comprehension of questions and the presentation of such testimony." § 1827(d)(1). As originally enacted, subsection (k) mandated that the "interpretation provided by certified interpreters . . . shall be in the consecutive mode except that the presiding judicial officer . . . may authorize a simultaneous or summary interpretation." § 1827(k) (1976 ed., Supp. II); see also 92 Stat. 2042. In its current form, subsection (k) provides that interpretation "shall be in the simultaneous mode for any party . . . and in the consecutive mode for witnesses," unless the court directs otherwise. The simultaneous, consecutive, and summary modes are all methods of oral interpretation and have nothing to do with the translation of writings. Taken together, these provisions are a strong contextual clue that Congress was dealing only with oral translation in the Court Interpreters Act and that it intended to use the term "interpreter" throughout the Act in its ordinary sense as someone who translates the spoken word. . . .

The references to technical terminology in the Court Interpreters Act further suggest that Congress used "interpreter" in a technical sense, and it is therefore significant that relevant professional literature draws a line between "interpreters," who "are used for oral conversations," and "translators," who "are used for written communications." [citations omitted] That Congress specified "interpreters" but not "translators" is yet another signal that it intended to limit § 1920(6) to the costs of oral, instead of written, translation.[6] . . .

C

No other rule of construction compels us to depart from the ordinary meaning of "interpreter.". . . Our decision is in keeping with the narrow scope of taxable costs. "Although 'costs' has an everyday meaning synonymous with 'expenses,' the concept of taxable costs under Rule 54(d) is more limited and represents those expenses, including, for example, court fees, that a court will assess against a litigant." 10 C.

---

[6] Some provisions within the United States Code use both "interpreter" and "translator" together, thus implying that Congress understands the terms to have the distinct meanings described above. See, e.g., 8 U.S.C. § 1555(b) (providing that appropriations for the Immigration and Naturalization Service "shall be available for payment of . . . interpreters and translators who are not citizens of the United States"); 28 U.S.C. § 530C(b)(1)(I) (providing that Department of Justice funds may be used for "[p]ayment of interpreters and translators who are not citizens of the United States").

Wright, A. Miller, & M. Kane, Federal Practice and Procedure § 2666, pp. 202–203 (3d ed. 1998).... Because taxable costs are limited by statute and are modest in scope, we see no compelling reason to stretch the ordinary meaning of the cost items Congress authorized in § 1920.

As for respondent's extratextual arguments, they are more properly directed at Congress....

* * *

Because the ordinary meaning of "interpreter" is someone who translates orally from one language to another, we hold that the category "compensation of interpreters" in § 1920(6) does not include costs for document translation. We therefore vacate the judgment of the United States Court of Appeals for the Ninth Circuit and remand the case for further proceedings consistent with this opinion.

It is so ordered.

■ JUSTICE GINSBURG, with whom JUSTICE BREYER and JUSTICE SOTOMAYOR join, dissenting.

To be comprehended by the parties, the witnesses, and the court, expression in foreign languages must be translated into English. Congress therefore provided, in 28 U.S.C. § 1920(6), that the prevailing party may recoup compensation paid to "interpreters." The word "interpreters," the Court emphasizes, commonly refers to translators of oral speech. But as the Court acknowledges, "interpreters" is more than occasionally used to encompass those who translate written speech as well.... In short, employing the word "interpreters" to include translators of written as well as oral speech, if not "the most common usage," is at least an "acceptable" usage. Moreover, the word "interpret" is generally understood to mean "to explain or tell the meaning of: translate into intelligible or familiar language or terms," while "translate" commonly means "to turn into one's own or another language." Webster's 1182, 2429....

Most federal courts of appeals confronted with the question have held that costs may be awarded under § 1920(6) for the translation of documents necessary to, or in preparation for, litigation. [citing cases].

In practice, federal trial courts have awarded document translation costs in cases spanning several decades. Before the Court Interpreters Act added § 1920(6) to the taxation of costs statute in 1978, district courts awarded costs for document translation under § 1920(4), which allowed taxation of "[f]ees for exemplification and copies of papers," 28 U.S.C. § 1920(4) (1976 ed.), or under § 1920's predecessor, 28 U.S.C. § 830 (1925 ed.). Pre-1978, district courts also awarded costs for oral translation of witness testimony. Nothing in the Court Interpreters Act, a measure intended to expand access to interpretation services, indicates a design to eliminate the availability of costs awards for document translation. Post-1978, rulings awarding document translation costs under § 1920(6) indicate the courts' understanding both that the term "interpreter" can readily encompass oral and written translation, and that Congress did not otherwise instruct.[2] I agree that context should guide the determination whether § 1920(6) is most sensibly read to encompass persons who translate documents. But the context key for me is the practice of federal courts both before and after § 1920(6)'s enactment.

The purpose of translation, after all, is to make relevant foreign-language communication accessible to the litigants and the court. See S. Rep., at 1 (The Court Interpreters Act is intended "to insure that all participants in our Federal courts can meaningfully take part."). Documentary evidence in a foreign language, no less than oral statements, must be translated to equip the parties to present their case clearly and the court to decide the merits intelligently.[3] And it is not extraordinary that what documents say, more than what witnesses testify, may make or break a case.

Distinguishing written from oral translation for cost-award purposes, moreover, is an endeavor all the more dubious, for, as the Court acknowledges, some translation tasks do not fall neatly into one category or the other. An interpreter, for example, may be called upon to "sight translate" a written document, i.e., to convey a written foreign-language document's content orally in English. . . . Similarly hard to categorize is the common court-interpreter task of listening to a recording in a foreign language, transcribing it, then translating it into English. . . . [And c]urrent practice in awarding translation costs . . . has shown that district judges are up to the task of confining awards to translation services necessary to present or defeat a claim. [citing cases]

In short, § 1920(6)'s prescription on "interpreters" is not so clear as to leave no room for interpretation. Given the purpose served by translation and the practice prevailing in district courts, there is no good reason to exclude from taxable costs payments for placing written words within the grasp of parties, jurors, and judges. . . .

## NOTE

LOOKING IT UP: DICTIONARIES AND STATUTORY INTERPRETATION, NOTE, 107 Harv. L. Rev. 1437 (1994): "Over the past decade, the Supreme Court's use of dictionaries in its published opinions has increased dramatically. Although the Court has consulted dictionaries almost since its inception, it rarely did so more than a handful of times per Term before the 1980s. In the quarter-century between 1958 and 1983, the Court cited dictionaries only 125 times—an average of five times per Term. Prior to 1980, in fact, the word "dictionary" never appeared more than fifteen times in a single volume of the Supreme Court Reporter.

---

[2] Currently, some federal district courts make the practice of allowing fees for translation of documents explicit in their local rules. [providing numerous examples]

[3] Noteworthy, other paragraphs Congress placed in § 1920 cover written documents. *See* 28 U.S.C. § 1920(2) (2006 ed., Supp. IV) ("Fees for printed or electronically recorded transcripts"); § 1920(3) (2006 ed.) ("Fees and disbursements for printing and witnesses"); § 1920(4) ("Fees for exemplification and the costs of making copies of any [necessary] materials"). Nothing indicates that Congress intended paragraph (6), unlike paragraphs (2)–(4), to apply exclusively to oral communications.

"By contrast, in the six Terms between 1987 and 1992, the Court never cited dictionaries fewer than fifteen times, with a high point of thirty-two references during the 1992 Term. Dictionary definitions appeared in twenty-eight percent of the 107 Supreme Court cases decided by published opinion in the 1992 Term—a fourteen-fold increase over the 1981 Term. . . .

"The Court's growing faith in dictionaries is tied to a broader methodological shift toward textualism in statutory interpretation. . . . Adherents to the plain meaning approach have long assumed that dictionaries are the best source of the common understanding of words. . . .

"The Court has rarely paused to consider the wisdom or the implications of relying on dictionaries in statutory interpretation. Of the opinions that do make explicit arguments about the practice, most are dissents that criticize the majority for its excessive reliance on dictionaries. Even when . . . the Justices acknowledge the limitations of their interpretive method, the assumption that dictionaries reveal ordinary meaning is usually left unquestioned. For some members of the Court, the dictionary has become a sort of default source, presumptively decisive unless there is specific evidence to the contrary. Yet dictionaries are neither as neutral nor as reductive as the Court supposes them to be, and they do not provide the sort of meaning the Court seeks to determine. . . .

"Individual judges must make subjective decisions about which dictionary and which definition to use. The same arguments about manipulability and arbitrariness that textualists use to attack the examination of legislative history can therefore be applied to dictionaries. The fiction that the particular definitions cited by the Court accurately capture statutory meaning is as tenuous as the assumption that scraps of legislative history reveal the intent of legislatures. Subjectivity may be an ineradicable component of the interpretive process; the point is that the use of dictionaries cannot eliminate this element, and may even exacerbate it. An opinion based on a dictionary must justify not only its chosen meaning for statutory terms, but also the choice of a particular dictionary definition to reach that conclusion."

## b. Custom and Usage

*NIX v. HEDDEN*

### NIX v. HEDDEN

Supreme Court of the United States (1893).
149 U.S. 304.

This was an action brought February 4, 1887, against the collector of the port of New York to recover back duties paid under protest on tomatoes imported by the plaintiff from the West Indies in the spring of 1886, which the collector assessed under 'Schedule G.-Provisions,' of the tariff act of March 3, 1883, (chapter 121,) imposing a duty on 'vegetables in their natural state, or in salt or brine, not specially enumerated or provided for in this act, ten per centum ad valorem;' and which the plaintiffs contended came within the clause in the free list of the same act, 'Fruits, green, ripe, or dried, not specially enumerated or provided for in this act.' 22 Stat. 504, 519.

At the trial the plaintiff's counsel, after reading in evidence definitions of the words 'fruit' and 'vegetables' from Webster's Dictionary, Worcester's Dictionary, and the Imperial Dictionary, called two witnesses, who had been for 30 years in the business of selling fruit and vegetables, and asked them, after hearing these definitions, to say whether these words had 'any special meaning in trade or commerce, different from those read.'

One of the witnesses answered as follows: 'Well, it does not classify all things there, but they are correct as far as they go. It does not take all kinds of fruit or vegetables; it takes a portion of them. I think the words 'fruit' and 'vegetable' have the same meaning in trade to-day that they had on March 1, 1883. I understand that the term 'fruit' is applied in trade only to such plants or parts of plants as contain the seeds. There are more vegetables than those in the enumeration given in Webster's Dictionary under the term 'vegetable,' as 'cabbage, cauliflower, turnips, potatoes, peas, beans, and the like,' probably covered by the words 'and the like.''

The other witness testified: 'I don't think the term 'fruit' or the term 'vegetables' had, in March, 1883, and prior thereto, any special meaning in trade and commerce in this country different from that which I have read here from the dictionaries.'

The plaintiff's counsel then read in evidence from the same dictionaries the definitions of the word 'tomato.'

The defendant's counsel then read in evidence from Webster's Dictionary the definitions of the words 'pea,' 'egg plant,' 'cucumber,' 'squash,' and 'pepper.'

The plaintiff then read in evidence from Webster's and Worcester's dictionaries the definitions of 'potato,' 'turnip,' 'parsnip,' 'cauliflower,' 'cabbage,' 'carrot,' and 'bean.'

No other evidence was offered by either party. The court, upon the defendant's motion, directed a verdict for him, which was returned, and judgment rendered thereon. The plaintiffs duly excepted to the instruction, and sued out this writ of error.

■ JUSTICE GRAY, after stating the facts in the foregoing language, delivered the opinion of the Court.

The single question in this case is whether tomatoes, considered as provisions, are to be classed as 'vegetables' or as 'fruit,' within the meaning of the tariff act of 1883.

The only witnesses called at the trial testified that neither 'vegetables' nor 'fruit' had any special meaning in trade or commerce different from that given in the dictionaries, and that they had the same meaning in trade to-day that they had in March, 1883.

The passages cited from the dictionaries define the word 'fruit' as the seed of plants, or that part of plants which contains the seed, and especially the juicy, pulpy products of certain plants, covering and containing the seed. These definitions have no tendency to show that tomatoes are 'fruit,' as distinguished from 'vegetables,' in common speech, or within the meaning of the tariff act.

There being no evidence that the words 'fruit' and 'vegetables' have acquired any special meaning in trade or commerce, they must receive their ordinary meaning. Of that meaning the court is bound to take judicial notice, as it does in regard to all words in our own tongue; and upon such a question dictionaries are admitted, not as evidence, but only as aids to the memory and understanding of the court.

Botanically speaking, tomatoes are the fruit of a vine, just as are cucumbers, squashes, beans, and peas. But in the common language of the people, whether sellers or consumers of provisions, all these are vegetables which are grown in kitchen gardens, and which, whether eaten cooked or raw, are, like potatoes, carrots, parsnips, turnips, beets, cauliflower, cabbage, celery, and lettuce, usually served at dinner in, with, or after the soup, fish, or meats which constitute the principal part of the repast, and not, like fruits generally, as dessert.

The attempt to class tomatoes as fruit is not unlike a recent attempt to class beans as seeds, of which Justice Bradley, speaking for this court, said: 'We do not see why they should be classified as seeds, any more than walnuts should be so classified. Both are seeds, in the language of botany or natural history, but not in commerce nor in common parlance. On the other hand in speaking generally of provisions, beans may well be included under the term 'vegetables.' As an article of food on our tables, whether baked or boiled, or forming the basis of soup, they are used as a vegetable, as well when ripe as when green. This is the principal use to which they are put. Beyond the common knowledge which we have on this subject, very little evidence is necessary, or can be produced.' Robertson v. Salomon, 130 U.S. 412, 414.

Judgment affirmed.

## NOTES

(1) ***Specific Customs, Too.*** Interpretation of statutory terms by reference to usages is not limited to general customs. If a statute, for instance, regulates a particular trade or trade practice, its terms can be understood by reference to the meaning of those terms within the trade. See, e.g., Corning Glass Works v. Brennan, 417 U.S. 188 (1974) (interpreting "working conditions" "in the language of industrial relations.")

(2) ***Subjective Versus Objective Readings?*** TODD D. RAKOFF, STATUTORY INTERPRETATION AS A MULTIFARIOUS ENTERPRISE, 104 Nw. U. L. Rev. 1559, 1572–75 (2010): "[M]ost statutory interpretation is not done by judges. Judges necessarily act after the fact—after the interpretive work done by ordinary citizens trying to comply with the law, by private lawyers advising clients, by public prosecutors deciding what charges (if any) to bring, by

administrative agencies enforcing statutes or making rules, and so on. In most instances, these nonjudicial determinations will have a determinative effect, either as a matter of law under a principle of deference or nonreviewability, or as a matter of practice because the determination will never be tested in court. . . .

"Because issues of statutory interpretation do not arise unless a statute has been passed, we are tempted to look at any statute from the point of view of the enactors of the legislation. Because of our predisposition to favor fully enacted statutes, we tend to try to see how the enactors might have resolved the particular ambiguity or uncertainty that has arisen. This approach has always been subject to the criticism that the point of view of those subject to the legislation—its readers—ought to count for something. To put the matter in language more commonly applied to private documents, there has long been a dispute between the "subjective" and the "objective" readings of statutory language. But we need now to recognize that in addition to enactors and readers, there is another legitimate category: the active users of statutes who have both the need and the authority, delegated or recognized, to interpret statutes within some significant leeway. These users are highly variegated, ranging from administrative agencies to organized trade groups, to more loosely constructed foci of expertise, on to ordinary people creating ordinary customs.

"Indeed, one could go further to argue that among the desirable design criteria for the legal system as a whole we should include keeping statutory law close to social practices, rather than distantly formal (recognizing that, at times, closeness implies changing common practice, too). Much can be said for the proposition that legal systems in which customs, social norms, and legislatively specified rules flow together are the most successful. Certainly the judge-made common law has traditionally taken a similar point of view."

## c. Canons of Construction

*(1) Linguistic Canons*
*(2) Substantive Canons*
*(3) The Absurdity Doctrine*

Courts have identified various rules of thumb for decoding statutory language—the so-called "canons of construction." These canons come in two types—linguistic canons and substantive canons. We present them, then separately consider what might be thought of as a substantive canon (sometimes treated as a separate doctrine), which counsels interpreters to avoid attributing to Congress a meaning that would yield an absurd result.

## (1) Linguistic Canons

*YATES v. UNITED STATES*
*LOCKHART v. UNITED STATES*
***Notes on Linguistic Canons***

Linguistic canons are said to merely reflect linguistic conventions about how the English language is generally used and understood. For that reason, one might think that these canons must be deployed to determine a statute's plain meaning, for without them the words in a given statute cannot be understood at all. Such words have meaning only because they are read in light of the ordinary way we understand any collection of words to be used in relation to one another. Alternatively, one might question whether linguistic canons might in fact be too rigid. Perhaps people sometimes use words in ways that do not track how the canons assume they will be used. If so, does it make sense for judges to insist that the words in a statute always were intended to be used in the manner that the canons suggest they were intended to be used?

There are literally dozens of rules that have been asserted as "canons." Here are some of the most common ones:

**Expressio unius est exclusio alterius.** Expression of one thing implies the exclusion of others.

**Noscitur a sociis.** A term is known by its associates.

**Ejusdem generis.** A general term is interpreted to include things of the same type as the more specific listed examples.

**Presumption against superfluity.** Provisions are construed so that others are not rendered superfluous or redundant.

**Presumption of consistency.** The same word used at different places in the statute is presumed to have the same meaning.

**Whole act rule.** The statute should be read as a coherent whole.

Does this list set forth rules that you consistently adhere to in your own use of words? If this list does not, does it still make sense to assume that Congress follows these rules, whether Congress does or not? Some of these canons, as well as other linguistic ones, are deployed by both the majority and dissenting opinions in the following cases. As you read them, consider whether these canons can be used to constrain judges from interpreting statutes to conform to the judges' preferred substantive outcome. Even if they can be used for that purpose, does that mean these canons are good guides to legislative intention? Moreover, are the canons so numerous, and so susceptible of interpretation in their own right, that they are too indeterminate to provide meaningful constraints on judges or guidance as to what Congress meant?

## YATES v. UNITED STATES

Supreme Court of the United States (2015).
574 U.S. 528.

■ JUSTICE GINSBURG announced the judgment of the Court and delivered an opinion, in which THE CHIEF JUSTICE, JUSTICE BREYER, and JUSTICE SOTOMAYOR join.

John Yates, a commercial fisherman, caught undersized red grouper in federal waters in the Gulf of Mexico. To prevent federal authorities from confirming that he had harvested undersized fish, Yates ordered a crew member to toss the suspect catch into the sea. For this offense, he was charged with, and convicted of, violating 18 U.S.C. § 1519, which provides:

> "Whoever knowingly alters, destroys, mutilates, conceals, covers up, falsifies, or makes a false entry in any record, document, or tangible object with the intent to impede, obstruct, or influence the investigation or proper administration of any matter within the jurisdiction of any department or agency of the United States or any case filed under title 11, or in relation to or contemplation of any such matter or case, shall be fined under this title, imprisoned not more than 20 years, or both."

Yates . . . maintains that fish are not trapped within the term "tangible object," as that term is used in § 1519.

Section 1519 was enacted as part of the Sarbanes-Oxley Act of 2002, legislation designed to protect investors and restore trust in financial markets following the collapse of Enron Corporation. A fish is no doubt an object that is tangible; fish can be seen, caught, and handled, and a catch, as this case illustrates, is vulnerable to destruction. But it would cut § 1519 loose from its financial-fraud mooring to hold that it encompasses any and all objects, whatever their size or significance, destroyed with obstructive intent. Mindful that in Sarbanes-Oxley, Congress trained its attention on corporate and accounting deception and cover-ups, we conclude that a matching construction of § 1519 is in order: A tangible object captured by § 1519, we hold, must be one used to record or preserve information. . . .

II

. . .

A

The ordinary meaning of an "object" that is "tangible," as stated in dictionary definitions, is "a discrete . . . thing," Webster's Third New International Dictionary 1555 (2002), that "possess[es] physical form," Black's Law Dictionary 1683 (10th ed. 2014). From this premise, the Government concludes that "tangible object," as that term appears in § 1519, covers the waterfront, including fish from the sea.

Whether a statutory term is unambiguous, however, does not turn solely on dictionary definitions of its component words. Rather, "[t]he plainness or ambiguity of statutory language is determined [not only] by reference to the language itself, [but as well by] the specific context in which that language is used, and the broader context of the statute as a whole." Robinson v. Shell Oil Co., 519 U.S. 337, 341 (1997). Ordinarily, a word's usage accords with its dictionary definition. In law as in life, however, the same words, placed in different contexts, sometimes mean different things. . . .

In short, although dictionary definitions of the words "tangible" and "object" bear consideration, they are not dispositive of the meaning of "tangible object" in § 1519. . . .

B

Familiar interpretive guides aid our construction of the words "tangible object" as they appear in § 1519. . . .

The words immediately surrounding "tangible object" in § 1519—"falsifies, or makes a false entry in any record [or] document"—. . . cabin the contextual meaning of that term. As explained in Gustafson v. Alloyd Co., 513 U.S. 561, 575 (1995), we rely on the principle of *noscitur a sociis*—a word is known by the company it keeps—to "avoid ascribing to one word a meaning so broad that it is inconsistent with its accompanying words, thus giving unintended breadth to the Acts of Congress." (internal quotation marks omitted). In Gustafson, we interpreted the word "communication" in § 2(10) of the Securities Act of 1933 to refer to a public communication, rather than any communication, because the word appeared in a list with other words, notably "notice, circular, [and] advertisement," making it "apparent that the list refer[red] to documents of wide dissemination." And we did so even though the list began with the word "any."

The *noscitur a sociis* canon operates in a similar manner here. "Tangible object" is the last in a list of terms that begins "any record [or] document." The term is therefore appropriately read to refer, not to any tangible object, but specifically to the subset of tangible objects involving records and documents, i.e., objects used to record or preserve information.

This moderate interpretation of "tangible object" accords with the list of actions § 1519 proscribes. The section applies to anyone who "alters, destroys, mutilates, conceals, covers up, *falsifies,* or *makes a false entry in* any record, document, or tangible object" with the requisite obstructive intent. (Emphasis added.) The last two verbs, "falsif[y]" and "mak[e] a false entry in," typically take as grammatical objects records, documents, or things used to record or preserve information, such as logbooks or hard drives. See, e.g., Black's Law Dictionary 720 (10th ed. 2014) (defining "falsify" as "[t]o make deceptive; to counterfeit, forge, or misrepresent; esp., to tamper with (a document, record, etc.)"). It would be unnatural, for example, to describe a killer's act of wiping his fingerprints from a gun as "falsifying" the murder weapon. But it would not be strange to refer to "falsifying" data stored on a hard drive as simply "falsifying" a hard drive. . . .

A canon related to *noscitur a sociis, ejusdem generis,* counsels: "Where general words follow specific words in a statutory enumeration, the general words are [usually] construed to embrace only objects similar in nature to those objects enumerated by the preceding specific words." In Begay v. United States, 553 U.S. 137, 142–143 (2008), for example, we relied on this principle to determine what crimes were covered by the statutory phrase "any crime . . . that . . . is burglary, arson, or extortion, involves use of explosives, or otherwise involves conduct that presents a serious potential risk of physical injury to another," 18 U.S.C. § 924(e)(2)(B)(ii). The enumeration of specific crimes, we explained, indicates that the "otherwise involves" provision covers "only *similar* crimes, rather than *every* crime that 'presents a serious potential risk of physical injury to another.' " 553 U.S., at 142. Had Congress intended the latter "all encompassing" meaning, we observed, "it is hard to see why it would have needed to include the examples at all." Just so here. Had Congress intended "tangible object" in § 1519 to be interpreted so generically as to capture physical objects as dissimilar as documents and fish, Congress would have had no reason to refer specifically to "record" or "document." The Government's unbounded reading of "tangible object" would render those words misleading surplusage.

Having used traditional tools of statutory interpretation to examine markers of congressional intent within the Sarbanes-Oxley Act and § 1519 itself, we are persuaded that an aggressive interpretation of "tangible object" must be rejected. It is highly improbable that Congress would have buried a general spoliation statute covering objects of any and every kind in a provision targeting fraud in financial record-keeping. . . .

[The Court reversed the judgment of the Eleventh Circuit, which had upheld the trial court's conviction.]

■ JUSTICE ALITO, concurring in the judgment.

This case can and should be resolved on narrow grounds. And though the question is close, traditional tools of statutory construction confirm that John Yates has the better of the argument. . . .

Section 1519 refers to "any record, document, or tangible object." The *noscitur a sociis* canon instructs that when a statute contains a list, each word in that list presumptively has a "similar" meaning. A related canon, *ejusdem generis* teaches that general words following a list of specific words should usually be read in light of those specific words to mean something "similar." Applying these canons to § 1519's list of nouns, the term "tangible object" should refer to something similar to records or documents. A fish does not spring to mind—nor does an antelope, a colonial farmhouse, a hydrofoil, or an oil derrick. All are "objects" that are "tangible." But who wouldn't raise an eyebrow if a neighbor, when asked to identify something similar to a "record" or "document," said "crocodile"? . . .

■ JUSTICE KAGAN, with whom JUSTICE SCALIA, JUSTICE KENNEDY, and JUSTICE THOMAS join, dissenting.

. . . I would begin with § 1519's text. When Congress has not supplied a definition, we generally give a statutory term its ordinary meaning. As the plurality must acknowledge, the ordinary meaning of "tangible object" is "a discrete thing that possesses physical form." A fish is, of course, a discrete thing that possesses physical form. See generally Dr. Seuss, One Fish Two Fish Red Fish Blue Fish (1960). So the ordinary meaning of the term "tangible object" in § 1519, as no one here disputes, covers fish (including too-small red grouper). . . .

That is not necessarily the end of the matter; I agree with the plurality (really, who does not?) that context matters in interpreting statutes. [But] here the text and its context point the same way. Stepping back from the words "tangible object" provides only further evidence that Congress said what it meant and meant what it said.

Begin with the way the surrounding words in § 1519 reinforce the breadth of the term at issue. Section 1519 refers to "any" tangible object, thus indicating (in line with *that* word's plain meaning) a tangible object "of whatever kind." This Court has time and again recognized that "any" has "an expansive meaning," bringing within a statute's reach *all* types of the item (here, "tangible object") to which the law refers. And the adjacent laundry list of verbs in § 1519 ("alters, destroys, mutilates, conceals, covers up, falsifies, or makes a false entry") further shows that Congress wrote a statute with a wide scope. Those words are supposed to ensure—just as "tangible object" is meant to—that § 1519 covers the whole world of evidence-tampering, in all its prodigious variety. . . .

II

A

The plurality searches far and wide for anything—*anything*—to support its interpretation of § 1519. But its fishing expedition comes up empty.

. . . [T]he plurality [hopes] that *noscitur a sociis* and *ejusdem generis* will save it. The first of those related canons advises that words grouped in a list be given similar meanings. The second counsels that a general term following specific words embraces only things of a similar kind. According to the plurality, those Latin maxims change the English meaning of "tangible object" to only things, like records and documents, "used to record or preserve information." But understood as this Court always has, the canons have no such transformative effect on the workaday language Congress chose.

[A]ssigning "tangible object" its ordinary meaning comports with *noscitur a sociis* and *ejusdem generis* when applied, as they should be, with attention to § 1519's subject and purpose. Those canons require identifying a common trait that links all the words in a statutory phrase. In responding to that demand, the plurality characterizes records and documents as things that preserve information—and so they are. But just as much, they are things that provide information, and thus potentially serve as evidence relevant to matters under review. And in a statute pertaining to obstruction of federal investigations, that evidentiary function comes to the fore. The destruction of records and documents prevents law enforcement agents from gathering facts relevant to official inquiries. And so too does the destruction of tangible objects—of whatever kind. Whether the item is a fisherman's ledger or an undersized fish, throwing it overboard has the identical effect on the administration of justice. For purposes of § 1519, records, documents, and (all) tangible objects are therefore alike. . . .

And the plurality's invocation of § 1519's verbs does nothing to buttress its canon-based argument. The plurality observes that § 1519 prohibits "falsif[ying]" or "mak[ing] a false entry in" a tangible object, and no one can do those things to, say, a murder weapon (or a fish). But of course someone can alter, destroy, mutilate, conceal, or cover up such a tangible object, and § 1519 prohibits those actions too. The Court has never before suggested that all the verbs in a statute need to match up with all the nouns. And for good reason. It is exactly when Congress sets out to draft a statute broadly—to include every imaginable variation on a theme—that such mismatches will arise. To respond by narrowing the law, as the plurality does, is thus to flout both what Congress wrote and what Congress wanted. . . .

## LOCKHART v. UNITED STATES

Supreme Court of the United States (2016).
577 U.S. 347.

■ JUSTICE SOTOMAYOR delivered the opinion of the Court.

Defendants convicted of possessing child pornography in violation of 18 U.S.C. § 2252(a)(4) are subject to a 10-year mandatory minimum sentence and an increased maximum sentence if they have "a prior conviction . . . under the laws of any State relating to aggravated sexual abuse, sexual abuse, or abusive sexual conduct involving a minor or ward." § 2252(b)(2). [The defendant had prior convictions for sexual abuse involving an adult.]

The question before us is whether the phrase "involving a minor or ward" modifies all items in the list of predicate crimes ("aggravated sexual abuse," "sexual abuse," and "abusive sexual conduct") or only the one item that immediately precedes it ("abusive sexual conduct"). . . . We affirm the Second Circuit's holding that the phrase "involving a minor or ward" in § 2252(b)(2) modifies only "abusive sexual conduct." . . .

### I

[The Court reviewed the proceeding below that resulted in Lockhart's being sentenced to the enhanced mandatory minimum.]

II

Section 2252(b)(2) reads in full:

> "Whoever violates, or attempts or conspires to violate [18 U.S.C. § 2252(a)(4)] shall be fined under this title or imprisoned not more than 10 years, or both, but . . . if such person has a prior conviction . . . under the laws of any State relating to aggravated sexual abuse, sexual abuse, or abusive sexual conduct involving a minor or ward, . . . such person shall be fined under this title and imprisoned for not less than 10 years nor more than 20 years."

. . . The issue before us is whether the limiting phrase that appears at the end of that list—"involving a minor or ward"—applies to all three predicate crimes preceding it in the list or only the final predicate crime. We hold that "involving a minor or ward" modifies only "abusive sexual conduct," the antecedent immediately preceding it. . . .

A

Consider the text. When this Court has interpreted statutes that include a list of terms or phrases followed by a limiting clause, we have typically applied an interpretive strategy called the "rule of the last antecedent." The rule provides that "a limiting clause or phrase . . . should ordinarily be read as modifying only the noun or phrase that it immediately follows."

. . . The rule reflects the basic intuition that when a modifier appears at the end of a list, it is easier to apply that modifier only to the item directly before it. That is particularly true where it takes more than a little mental energy to process the individual entries in the list, making it a heavy lift to carry the modifier across them all. For example, imagine you are the general manager of the Yankees and you are rounding out your 2016 roster. You tell your scouts to find a defensive catcher, a quick-footed shortstop, or a pitcher from last year's World Champion Kansas City Royals. It would be natural for your scouts to confine their search for a pitcher to last year's championship team, but to look more broadly for catchers and shortstops.

Applied here, the last antecedent principle suggests that the phrase "involving a minor or ward" modifies only the phrase that it immediately follows: "abusive sexual conduct." As a corollary, it also suggests that the phrases "aggravated sexual abuse" and "sexual abuse" are not so constrained.

Of course, as with any canon of statutory interpretation, the rule of the last antecedent "is not an absolute and can assuredly be overcome by other indicia of meaning." Barnhart, 540 U.S., at 26. For instance, take " 'the laws, the treaties, and the constitution of the United States.' " Post (Kagan, J., dissenting). A reader intuitively applies "of the United States" to "the laws," "the treaties" and "the constitution" because (among other things) laws, treaties, and the constitution are often cited together, because readers are used to seeing "of the United States" modify each of them, and because the listed items are simple and parallel without unexpected internal modifiers or structure. Section 2252(b)(2), by contrast, does not contain items that readers are used to seeing listed together or a concluding modifier that readers are accustomed to applying to each of them. And the varied syntax of each item in the list makes it hard for the reader to carry the final modifying clause across all three.

More importantly, here the interpretation urged by the rule of the last antecedent is not overcome by other indicia of meaning. To the contrary, § 2252(b)(2)'s context fortifies the meaning that principle commands.

B

Among the chapters of the Federal Criminal Code that can trigger § 2252(b)(2)'s recidivist enhancement are crimes "under . . . chapter 109A." Chapter 109A . . . places those . . . crimes under headings that use language nearly identical to . . . § 2252(b)(2) . . . . The first section in Chapter 109A is titled "Aggravated sexual abuse." 18 U.S.C. § 2241. The second is titled "Sexual abuse." § 2242. And the third is titled "Sexual abuse of a minor or ward." § 2243. . . .

This similarity appears to be more than a coincidence. We cannot state with certainty that Congress used Chapter 109A as a template for the list of state predicates set out in § 2252(b)(2), but we cannot ignore the parallel, particularly because the headings in Chapter 109A were in place when Congress amended the statute to add § 2252(b)(2)'s state sexual-abuse predicates.

If Congress had intended to limit each of the state predicates to conduct "involving a minor or ward," we doubt it would have followed, or thought it needed to follow, so closely the structure and language of Chapter 109A. . . .

III

A

Lockhart argues, to the contrary, that the phrase "involving a minor or ward" should be interpreted to modify all three state sexual-abuse predicates. He first contends, as does our dissenting colleague, that the so-called series-qualifier principle supports his reading. This principle, Lockhart says, requires a modifier to apply to all items in a series when such an application would represent a natural construction.

This Court has long acknowledged that structural or contextual evidence may "rebut the last antecedent inference." . . . But in none of those cases did the Court describe, much less apply, a countervailing grammatical mandate that could bear the weight that either Lockhart or the dissent places on the series qualifier principle. Instead, the Court simply observed that sometimes context weighs against the application of the rule of the last antecedent. Whether a modifier is "applicable as much to the first . . . as to the last" words in a list, whether a set of items form a "single, integrated list," and whether the application of the rule would require acceptance of an "unlikely premise" are fundamentally contextual questions.

Lockhart attempts to identify contextual indicia that he says rebut the rule of the last antecedent, but those indicia hurt rather than help his prospects. He points out that the final two state predicates, "sexual abuse" and "abusive sexual conduct," are "nearly synonymous as a matter of everyday speech." And, of course, anyone who commits "aggravated sexual abuse" has also necessarily committed "sexual abuse." So, he posits, the items in the list are sufficiently similar that a limiting phrase could apply equally to all three of them.

But Lockhart's effort to demonstrate some similarity among the items in the list of state predicates reveals far too much similarity. The three state predicate crimes are not just related on Lockhart's reading; they are hopelessly redundant. Any conduct that would qualify as "aggravated sexual abuse . . . involving a minor or ward" or "sexual abuse . . . involving a minor or ward" would also qualify as "abusive sexual conduct involving a minor or ward." We take no position today on the meaning of the terms "aggravated sexual abuse," "sexual abuse," and "abusive sexual conduct," including their similarities and differences. But it is clear that applying the limiting phrase to all three items would risk running headlong into the rule against superfluity by transforming a list of separate predicates into a set of synonyms describing the same predicate.

Applying the limiting phrase "involving a minor or ward" more sparingly, by contrast, preserves some distinction between the categories of state predicates by limiting only the third category to conduct "involving a minor or ward." We recognize that this interpretation does not eliminate all superfluity between "aggravated sexual abuse" and "sexual abuse." But there is a ready explanation for the redundancy that remains: It follows the categories in Chapter 109A's federal template. We see no similar explanation for Lockhart's complete collapse of the list.

The dissent offers a suggestion rooted in its impressions about how people ordinarily speak and write. The problem is that, as even the dissent acknowledges, § 2252(b)(2)'s list of state predicates is hardly intuitive. No one would mistake its odd repetition and inelegant phrasing for a reflection of the accumulated wisdom of everyday speech patterns. It would be as if a friend asked you to get her tart lemons, sour lemons, or sour fruit from Mexico. If you brought back lemons from California, but your friend insisted that she was using customary speech and obviously asked for Mexican fruit only, you would be forgiven for disagreeing on both counts.

Faced with § 2252(b)(2)'s inartful drafting, then, do we interpret the provision by viewing it as a clear, commonsense list best construed as if conversational English? Or do we look around to see if there might be some provenance to its peculiarity? With Chapter 109A so readily at hand, we are unpersuaded by our dissenting colleague's invocation of basic examples from day-to-day life. Whatever the validity of the dissent's broader point, this simply is not a case in which colloquial practice is of much use. Section 2252(b)(2)'s list is hardly the way an average person, or even an average lawyer, would set about to describe the relevant conduct if they had started from scratch. . . .

We conclude that the text and structure of § 2252(b)(2) confirm that the provision applies to prior state convictions for "sexual abuse" and "aggravated sexual abuse," whether or not the convictions involved a minor or ward. We therefore hold that Lockhart's prior conviction for sexual abuse of an adult is encompassed by § 2252(b)(2). The judgment of the Court of Appeals, accordingly, is affirmed.

■ JUSTICE KAGAN, with whom JUSTICE BREYER joins, dissenting.

Imagine a friend told you that she hoped to meet "an actor, director, or producer involved with the new Star Wars movie." You would know immediately that she wanted to meet an actor from the Star Wars cast—not an actor in, for example, the latest Zoolander. Suppose a real estate agent promised to find a client "a house, condo, or apartment in New York." Wouldn't the potential buyer be annoyed if the agent sent him information about condos in Maryland or California? And consider a law imposing a penalty for the "violation of any statute, rule, or regulation relating to insider trading." Surely a person would have cause to protest if punished under that provision for violating a traffic statute. The reason in all three cases is the same: Everyone understands that the modifying phrase—"involved with the new Star Wars movie," "in New York," "relating to insider trading"—applies to each term in the preceding list, not just the last.

That ordinary understanding of how English works, in speech and writing alike, should decide this case. Avondale Lockhart is subject to a 10-year mandatory minimum sentence for possessing child pornography if, but only if, he has a prior state-law conviction for "aggravated sexual abuse, sexual abuse, or abusive sexual conduct involving a minor or ward." 18 U.S.C. § 2252(b)(2). The Court today, relying on what is called the "rule of the last antecedent," reads the phrase "involving a minor or ward" as modifying only the final term in that three-item list. But properly read, the modifier applies to each of the terms—just as in the examples above. . . . And if any doubt remained, the rule of lenity would command the same result: Lockhart's prior conviction for sexual abuse *of an adult* does not trigger § 2252(b)(2)'s mandatory minimum penalty. I respectfully dissent.

## I

Begin where the majority does—with the rule of the last antecedent. This Court most fully discussed that principle in Barnhart v. Thomas, 540 U.S. 20 (2003), which considered a statute providing that an individual qualifies as disabled if "he is not only unable to do his previous work but cannot, considering his age, education, and work experience, engage in any other kind of substantial gainful work *which exists in the national economy*." The Court held, invoking the last-antecedent rule, that the italicized phrase modifies only the term "substantial gainful work," and not the term "previous work" occurring earlier in the sentence. Two points are of especial note. First, Barnhart contained a significant caveat: The last-antecedent rule "can assuredly be overcome by other indicia of meaning." Second, the grammatical structure of the provision in Barnhart is nothing like that of the statute in this case: The modifying phrase does not, as here, immediately follow a list of multiple, parallel terms. That is true as well in the other instances in which this Court has followed the rule.

Indeed, this Court has made clear that the last-antecedent rule does not generally apply to the grammatical construction present here: when "[t]he modifying clause appear[s] . . . at the end of a single, integrated list." Then, the exact opposite is usually true: As in the examples beginning this opinion, the modifying phrase refers alike to each of the list's terms. A leading treatise puts the point as follows: "When there is a straightforward, parallel construction that involves all nouns or verbs in a series," a modifier at the end of the list "normally applies to the entire series." A. Scalia & B. Garner, Reading Law: The Interpretation of Legal Texts 147 (2012). That interpretive practice of applying the modifier to the whole list boasts a fancy name—the "series-qualifier canon"—but, as my opening examples show, it reflects the completely ordinary way that people speak and listen, write and read.

Even the exception to the series-qualifier principle is intuitive, emphasizing both its common-sensical basis and its customary usage. When the nouns in a list are so disparate that the modifying clause does not make sense when applied to them all, then the last-antecedent rule takes over. Suppose your friend told you not that she wants to meet "an actor, director, or producer involved with Star Wars," but instead that she hopes someday to meet "a President, Supreme Court Justice, or actor involved with Star Wars." Presumably, you would know that she wants to meet a President or Justice even if that person has no connection to the famed film franchise. But so long as the modifying clause "is applicable as much to the first and other words as to the last," this Court has stated, "the natural construction of the language demands that the clause be read as applicable to all." In other words, the modifier then qualifies not just the last antecedent but the whole series.

. . . The relevant language—"aggravated sexual abuse, sexual abuse, or abusive sexual conduct involving a minor or ward"—contains a "single, integrated list" of parallel terms (i.e., sex crimes) followed by a modifying clause. Given the close relation among the terms in the series, the modifier makes sense "as much to the first and other words as to the last." In other words, the reference to a minor or ward applies as well to sexual abuse and aggravated sexual abuse as to abusive sexual conduct. (The case would be different if, for example, the statute established a mandatory minimum for any person previously convicted of "arson, receipt of stolen property, or abusive sexual conduct involving a minor or ward.") So interpreting the modifier "as applicable to all" the preceding terms is what "the natural construction of the language" requires.

The majority responds to all this by claiming that the "inelegant phrasing" of § 2252(b)(2) renders it somehow exempt from a grammatical rule reflecting "how people ordinarily" use the English language. But to begin with, the majority is wrong to suggest that the series-qualifier canon is only about "colloquial" or "conversational" English. In fact, it applies to both speech and writing, in both their informal and their formal varieties. Here is a way to test my point: Pick up a journal, or a book, or for that matter a Supreme Court opinion—most of which keep "everyday" colloquialisms at a far distance. You'll come across many sentences having the structure of the statutory provision at issue here: a few nouns followed by a modifying clause. And you'll discover, again and yet again, that the clause modifies every noun in the series, not just the last—in other words, that even (especially?) in formal writing, the series-qualifier principle works.[2] And the majority is wrong too in suggesting that the "odd repetition" in § 2252(b)(2)'s list of state predicates causes the series-qualifier principle to lose its force. Ibid. The majority's own made-up sentence proves that much. If a friend asked you "to get her tart lemons, sour lemons, or sour fruit from Mexico," you might well think her list of terms perplexing: You might puzzle over the difference between tart and sour lemons, and wonder why she had specifically mentioned lemons when she apparently would be happy with sour fruit of any kind. But of one thing, you would have no doubt: Your friend wants some produce *from Mexico*; it would not do to get her, say, sour lemons from Vietnam. However weird the way she listed fruits—or the way § 2252(b)(2) lists offenses—the modifying clause still refers to them all.

The majority as well seeks refuge in the idea that applying the series-qualifier canon to § 2252(b)(2) would violate the rule against superfluity. Says the majority: "Any conduct that would qualify as 'aggravated sexual abuse . . . involving a minor or ward' or 'sexual abuse . . . involving a minor or ward' would also qualify as 'abusive sexual conduct involving a minor or ward.' " But that rejoinder doesn't work. "[T]he canon against superfluity," this Court has often stated, "assists only where a competing interpretation gives effect to every clause and word of a statute." And the majority's approach (as it admits) produces superfluity too—and in equal measure. Now (to rearrange the majority's sentence) any conduct that would qualify as "abusive sexual conduct involving a minor or ward" or "aggravated sexual abuse" would also

---

[2] Too busy to carry out this homework assignment? Consider some examples (there are many more) from just the last few months of this Court's work. In OBB Personenverkehr AG v. Sachs, this Court described a lawsuit as alleging "wrongful arrest, imprisonment, and torture *by Saudi police*." In James v. Boise, this Court affirmed that state courts must follow its interpretations of "the laws, the treaties, and the constitution *of the United States*." In Musacchio v. United States, this Court noted that in interpreting statutes it looks to the "text, context, and relevant historical treatment *of the provision at issue*." In FERC v. Electric Power Supply Assn., this Court applied a statute addressing "any rule, regulation, practice, or contract *affecting [a wholesale] rate [or] charge*." And in Montanile v. Board of Trustees of Nat. Elevator Industry Health Benefit Plan, this Court interpreted an employee benefits plan requiring reimbursement "for attorneys' fees, costs, expenses or damages *claimed by the covered person*." In each case, of course, the italicized modifying clause refers to every item in the preceding list. That is because the series-qualifier rule reflects how all of us use language, in writing and in speech, in formal and informal contexts, all the time.

qualify as "sexual abuse." In other words, on the majority's reading as well, two listed crimes become subsets of a third, so that the three could have been written as one. And indeed, the majority's superfluity has an especially odd quality, because it relates to the modifying clause itself: The majority, that is, makes the term "involving a minor or ward" wholly unnecessary. Remember the old adage about the pot and the kettle? That is why the rule against superfluity cannot excuse the majority from reading § 2252(b)(2)'s modifier, as ordinary usage demands, to pertain to all the terms in the preceding series. . . .

IV

Suppose, for a moment, that this case is not as clear as I've suggested. Assume there is no way to know whether to apply the last-antecedent or the series-qualifier rule. Imagine, too, that the legislative history is not quite so compelling and the majority's "template" argument not quite so strained. Who, then, should prevail?

This Court has a rule for how to resolve genuine ambiguity in criminal statutes: in favor of the criminal defendant. As the majority puts the point, the rule of lenity insists that courts side with the defendant "when the ordinary canons of statutory construction have revealed no satisfactory construction." At the very least, that principle should tip the scales in Lockhart's favor, because nothing the majority has said shows that the modifying clause in § 2252(b)(2) *unambiguously* applies to only the last term in the preceding series.

But in fact, Lockhart's case is stronger. Consider the following sentence, summarizing various points made above: "The series-qualifier principle, the legislative history, and the rule of lenity discussed in this opinion all point in the same direction." Now answer the following question: Has only the rule of lenity been discussed in this opinion, or have the series-qualifier principle and the legislative history been discussed as well? Even had you not read the preceding 16-plus pages, you would know the right answer—because of the ordinary way all of us use language. That, in the end, is why Lockhart should win.

## NOTES ON LINGUISTIC CANONS

(1) ***Opposing Canons.*** KARL N. LLEWELLYN, REMARKS ON THE THEORY OF APPELLATE DECISION AND THE RULES OR CANONS ABOUT HOW STATUTES ARE TO BE CONSTRUED, 3 Vand. L. Rev. 395, 401 (1950): "When it comes to presenting a proposed construction in court, there is an accepted conventional vocabulary. As in argument over points of case-law, the accepted convention still, unhappily requires discussion as if only one single correct meaning could exist. Hence there are two opposing canons on almost every point. . . .Every lawyer must be familiar with them all: they are still needed tools of argument. . . . Plainly, to make any canon take hold in a particular instance, the construction contended for must be sold, essentially, by means other than the use of the canon: The good sense of the situation and a simple construction of the available language to achieve that sense, by tenable means, out of the statutory language."

Sometimes Llewellyn's insight is framed as the idea that "for every canon there is a counter-canon." E.g., William N. Eskridge, Jr., Quasi-Constitutional Law: Clear Statement Rules As Constitutional Lawmaking, 45 Vand. L. Rev. 593, 595 (1992). In a portion of Yates not excerpted in this casebook, the majority applies the "canon against surplusage," stating that a broad reading of 18 U.S.C. § 1519 would "render superfluous an entire provision passed in proximity as part of the same Act." Yates v. United States, 574 U.S. 528, 543 (2015). That provision, 18 U.S.C. § 1512(c)(1), applies to some destruction (among other things) of "a record, document, or other object." The dissent responds that any overlap of § 1519 ("tangible object") and § 1512(c) ("other object") may instead have merely "reflected belt-and-suspenders caution: If § 1519 contained some flaw, § 1512(c)(1) would serve as a backstop." Yates, 574 U.S. at 562 (Kagan, J., dissenting). Who has it right? Is the question an empirical one about what Congress actually meant? If not, what work are the canons doing, if any?

(2) ***The Interpretive Value of Code Placement.*** Congress isn't the only one to apply "belt-and-suspenders caution." Consider the following moves in the Yates majority opinion in addition to *ejusdem generis*, *noscitur a sociis*, and the canon against surplusage mentioned in Note 1:

"Familiar interpretive guides aid our construction of the words 'tangible object' as they appear in § 1519.

"We note first § 1519's caption: 'Destruction, alteration, or falsification of records in Federal investigations and bankruptcy.' That heading conveys no suggestion that the section prohibits spoliation of any and all physical evidence, however remote from records. Neither does the title of the section of the Sarbanes-Oxley Act in which § 1519 was placed, § 802: 'Criminal penalties for altering documents.' . . . While these headings are not commanding, they supply cues that Congress did not intend 'tangible object' in § 1519 to sweep within its reach physical objects of every kind, including things no one would describe as records, documents, or devices closely associated with them. See Almendarez-Torres v. United States, 523 U.S. 224, 234 (1998) ('[T]he title of a statute and the heading of a section are tools available for the resolution of a doubt about the meaning of a statute.' (internal quotation marks omitted)). . . .

"Section 1519's position within Chapter 73 of Title 18 further signals that § 1519 was not intended to serve as a cross-the-board ban on the destruction of physical evidence of every kind. Congress placed § 1519 (and its companion provision § 1520) at the end of the chapter, following immediately after the pre-existing § 1516, § 1517, and § 1518, each of them prohibiting obstructive acts in specific contexts. See § 1516 (audits of recipients of federal funds); § 1517 (federal examinations of financial institutions); § 1518 (criminal investigations of federal health care offenses). . . .

"But Congress did not direct codification of the Sarbanes-Oxley Act's other additions to Chapter 73 adjacent to these specialized provisions. Instead, Congress directed placement of those additions within or alongside retained provisions that address obstructive acts relating broadly to official proceedings and criminal trials: . . . . This placement accords with the view that Congress' conception of § 1519's coverage was considerably more limited than the Government's." Yates, 574 U.S. at 539–41.

Is this evidence compelling? In light of what you now know about the Office of the Law Revision Counsel (p. 62), under what circumstances would you infer statutory meaning from the structure of the U.S. Code?

(3) ***The Canons in Congress.*** What is the actual relationship between canons of construction and the way statutes are drafted? In STATUTORY INTERPRETATION FROM THE INSIDE—AN EMPIRICAL STUDY OF CONGRESSIONAL DRAFTING, DELEGATION, AND THE CANONS: PART I, 65 Stan. L. Rev. 901, 930–36 (2013), ABBE GLUCK & LISA SCHULTZ BRESSMAN interviewed 137 congressional counsels—staff members responsible for drafting—to try to answer this question. Here's a part of what they found:

"[O]ur respondents displayed a high degree of familiarity with the concepts underlying the textual canons, but much less familiarity with their formal names. Our respondents also appeared to regularly use several of these canons in the drafting process. But, of particular note, the concepts that our respondents indicated they used most often—for example, the concept underlying the *expressio unius* canon—are among the least consistently utilized textual canons by the courts, and they have come under criticism (even from textualist judges) about the extent to which they reflect drafting reality. In contrast, the canons most commonly employed by courts, including the rule against superfluities, the whole act rule, and the use of dictionaries, appear to be used the least often by our drafters—despite our respondents' awareness that the courts use them—due to a host of political or institutional factors that courts rarely take into account."

As to those canons drafters did use:

*"Concepts in use:* expressio, noscitur, *and* ejusdem

"Approximately 33% of our respondents told us that the assumption underlying the *expressio unius* canon—that the inclusion of specific terms signifies the exclusion of terms not mentioned—always or often applies. Five percent more agreed that the default rule is always exclusivity unless language indicates otherwise, and most of the remaining respondents likewise validated the assumption by explaining that they 'signaled' whether they wished a list to be something other than exclusive, usually through the use of the word 'including' or a catch-all term. Only 10% of respondents indicated that the presumption typically goes in the other direction, toward inclusivity.

*"Expressio* was also one of the most recognized textual canons by name (along with the rule against superfluities). But when asked about the rule by name, most of our respondents told us that they did not employ it (several respondents made statements such as 'we don't know any Latin'), even though, when asked about the concept, they already had substantiated their use of the assumptions underlying it. A number of respondents (18%) got at this disconnect by describing the ideas embraced by the textual canons as 'intuitive.' As one stated: 'We consider them not expressly but intuitively: how does this legislation interact with existing code? Is it inclusive,

exclusive, are like things treated alike—those values are thought about here.'

"With respect to the general concept underlying both the *noscitur* and *ejusdem* rules, 71% of respondents (ninety-seven) said that terms in a statutory list always or often relate to one another, and only two respondents said they rarely or never did. The vast majority of respondents, however, did not know those rules when asked by name (85% did not know *noscitur* and 65% did not know *ejusdem).*"

And why were some canons that were known still not used? Here's one example:

*"Superfluities: redundancy to satisfy political stakeholders*

"For instance, even though 62% of our respondents knew the rule against superfluities by name, 18% of respondents told us it rarely applies, and 45% more told us it only sometimes does. Eighteen percent also explained the relative weakness of this rule's application by reference to two recurring reasons, one practical and one political. From a practical perspective, our respondents focused on the need to ensure that the statute covers the intended terrain. They told us that drafters intentionally err on the side of redundancy to 'capture the universe' or 'because you just want to be sure you hit it.'

"These respondents also pointed out that the *political interests* of the audience often demand redundancy. They told us, for example, that 'sometimes politically for compromise they must include certain words in the statute—that senator, that constituent, that lobbyist wants to see that word'; similarly, they said that 'sometimes the lists are in there to satisfy groups, certain phrases are needed to satisfy political interests and they might overlap' or that 'sometimes you have it in there because someone had to see their phrase in the bill to get it passed.' One example provided was a statute drafted to cover 'medical service providers' that had to be amended to include a specific (and redundant) reference to 'hospitals' to satisfy stakeholders.

"We were not surprised to see pragmatic considerations trumping application of the rule against superfluities. Common sense tells us that, despite the popularity of this rule with judges, there is likely to be redundancy, especially in exceedingly long statutes. (We have seen no evidence, however, that judges take the length of statutes into account when applying the rule.) But what respondents told us was different from that common-sense assumption: namely, terms are often *purposefully redundant to satisfy audiences other than courts*.

"This is an argument that has been made in other contexts. Scholars have argued that the audience for legislative language or legislative history is much broader than judges, or even agencies, and that these statutory materials are sometimes expressly directed at noninterpreters, such as lobbyists and other stakeholders. Whether this 'audience' issue should have an effect on how courts interpret statutes is a different matter—after all, how will courts be able to discern when drafters are talking to them as opposed to other audiences? A fictitious interpretive rule may be required precisely *because* investigating the intended audience would be too difficult.

But that has not been the main judicial justification for the rule against superfluities.

"Our findings certainly call into question what has been the rule's primary justification: namely that, because it reflects how Congress drafts and also because Congress is aware of it, the rule helps faithful-agent judges effectuate congressional intent. We note also that, in several recent cases, the Court has divided over application of the rule—with the majority relying on the rule to decide the case over the objection of dissenters who have argued, like some of our respondents, that Congress is often intentionally redundant to be certain that it has made its point. We have seen no case, however, in which the Court acknowledged the political considerations, like satisfying stakeholders, that some of our respondents also mentioned. Our findings suggest that those considerations likewise may mean that judicial application of the rule does precisely the opposite of effectuating drafter intent."

(4) ***Here We Go Again.*** In FACEBOOK, INC. V. DUGUID, 141 S.Ct. 1163 (2021), the Supreme Court confronted the same debate over the competing canons that figured in Lockhart—the series qualifier canon and the last antecedent canon. The case concerned the Telephone Consumer Protection Act of 1991, which prohibits abusive telemarketing practices in part by restricting certain communications made with an autodialer, defined as equipment able both "to store or produce telephone numbers to be called, using a random or sequential number generator," and to dial those numbers. At issue was whether the clause "using a random or sequential number generator" modifies both of the verbs before it ("store" and "produce") or only the closest one ("produce"). The Court agreed with Facebook that the clause modifies both verbs. JUSTICE SOTOMAYOR authored the opinion, but this time she concluded that the series qualifier canon dominated the last antecedent canon. Even if the latter canon were relevant, she explained, it supported the Court's interpretation: "The last antecedent before 'using a random or sequential number generator' is not 'produce' . . . but rather 'telephone numbers to be called.' " JUSTICE ALITO wrote a concurring opinion in which he threw some shade at the series qualifier canon: "The Court refers to [the series qualifier] canon as a 'rul[e] of grammar.' Yet . . . interpretive canons 'are not "rules" of interpretation in any strict sense but presumptions about what an intelligently produced text conveys'. . . . Canons of interpretation can help in figuring out the meaning of troublesome statutory language, but if they are treated like rigid rules, they can lead us astray. When this Court describes canons as rules or quotes canons while omitting their caveats and limitations, we only encourage the lower courts to relegate statutory interpretation to a series of if-then computations. No reasonable reader interprets texts that way."

(5) ***Rewriting the Provision in Lockhart.*** Recall that the provision at issue in Lockhart applied to convictions "under the laws of any State relating to aggravated sexual abuse, sexual abuse, or abusive sexual conduct involving a minor or ward." How would you write this list to avoid triggering the last antecedent canon? Do you think Congress had such considerations in mind as it drafted 18 U.S.C. § 2252(b)(2)? Should it have? Is it

antidemocratic for courts to burden legislatures with such interpretive bookkeeping, or is it required by the Constitution or the rule of law? Should courts force Congress to be particularly careful with its words in the criminal context, as the dissent suggests in its discussion of the rule of lenity? On this last point, see Note 4 below (p. 192).

## (2) Substantive Canons

***BOND v. UNITED STATES***
***Notes on Substantive Canons***

Unlike the semantic canons, which purport to reflect neutral principles about everyday language use, the substantive canons of construction are different. These canons take the form of rules that require the legislature to clearly indicate its intent before courts will interpret a statute to conflict with a policy, whether rooted in a constitutional value like federalism or a longstanding legal principle like respect for tribal sovereignty. Some substantive canons serve as tie-breakers in the face of ambiguity; others, often referred to as clear-statement rules, require Congress to be unusually clear to accomplish a certain result, with the consequence that language that on its own might not be considered ambiguous is treated as insufficiently express to permit the reading that would appear to be the right one. Sometimes it is clear from the caselaw whether a substantive canon is of the tie-breaking sort or the clear-statement sort. But sometimes there is room for debate over whether a substantive canon is of the former or latter kind.

Are substantive canons (whether of the tie-breaking or the clear-statement variety) best understood as means of ensuring that statutes are construed in a manner faithful to the intentions of their drafters, on the theory that the drafters would not want the statute to be construed in a manner that would infringe upon the substantive policy reflected in the canon? Or are such canons best understood as constraints on legislative drafters that, for reasons of policy, ensure that drafters enact statutes that trench on certain policies only when they do so clearly? Is one understanding of the role that such canons play more defensible as a matter of constitutional structure than another?

One well-known substantive canon is the canon of constitutional avoidance. This canon instructs that statutes should be construed, though only when unclear, to avoid giving rise to serious constitutional questions. But there are many others—from canons favoring the rights of Native Americans to the rule of lenity (which aims to protect the notice rights of criminal defendants). Consider the following case:

## BOND v. UNITED STATES

Supreme Court of the United States (2014).
572 U.S. 844.

■ CHIEF JUSTICE ROBERTS delivered the opinion of the Court.

. . .

I

A

. . . In 1997, the President of the United States, upon the advice and consent of the Senate, ratified the Convention on the Prohibition of the Development, Production, Stockpiling, and Use of Chemical Weapons and on Their Destruction. . . . The Convention was conceived as an effort to update the Geneva Protocol's protections and to expand the prohibition on chemical weapons beyond state actors in wartime. The Convention aimed to achieve that objective by prohibiting the development, stockpiling, or use of chemical weapons by any State Party or person within a State Party's jurisdiction. . . .

Congress gave the Convention domestic effect in 1998 when it passed the Chemical Weapons Convention Implementation Act. The Act . . . forbids any person knowingly "to develop, produce, otherwise acquire, transfer directly or indirectly, receive, stockpile, retain, own, possess, or use, or threaten to use, any chemical weapon." 18 U.S.C. § 229(a)(1). It defines "chemical weapon" in relevant part as "[a] toxic chemical and its precursors, except where intended for a purpose not prohibited under this chapter as long as the type and quantity is consistent with such a purpose." § 229F(1)(A). "Toxic chemical," in turn, is defined in general as "any chemical which through its chemical action on life processes can cause death, temporary incapacitation or permanent harm to humans or animals." . . .

B

Petitioner Carol Anne Bond is a microbiologist from Lansdale, Pennsylvania. In 2006, Bond's closest friend, Myrlinda Haynes, announced that she was pregnant. When Bond discovered that her husband was the child's father, she sought revenge against Haynes. Bond stole a quantity of 10–chloro–10H–phenoxarsine (an arsenic-based compound) from her employer, a chemical manufacturer. She also ordered a vial of potassium dichromate (a chemical commonly used in printing photographs or cleaning laboratory equipment) on Amazon.com. Both chemicals are toxic to humans and, in high enough doses, potentially lethal. It is undisputed, however, that Bond did not intend to kill Haynes. She instead hoped that Haynes would touch the chemicals and develop an uncomfortable rash.

Between November 2006 and June 2007, Bond went to Haynes's home on at least 24 occasions and spread the chemicals on her car door, mailbox, and door knob. These attempted assaults were almost entirely unsuccessful. . . . Haynes repeatedly called the local police to report the suspicious substances . . . . [P]ostal inspectors placed surveillance cameras around her home. The cameras caught Bond opening Haynes's mailbox, stealing an envelope, and stuffing potassium dichromate inside the muffler of Haynes's car.

Federal prosecutors naturally charged Bond with two counts of mail theft, in violation of 18 U.S.C. § 1708. More surprising, they also charged her with two counts of possessing and using a chemical weapon, in violation of section 229(a). Bond moved to dismiss the chemical weapon counts on the ground that section 229 exceeded Congress's enumerated powers and invaded powers reserved to the States by the Tenth Amendment. . . .

II

. . . [I]t is "a well-established principle governing the prudent exercise of this Court's jurisdiction that normally the Court will not decide a constitutional question if there is some other ground upon which to dispose of the case." Bond argues that section 229 does not cover her conduct. So we consider that argument first.

III

. . .

A

. . . In the Government's view, the conclusion that Bond "knowingly" "use[d]" a "chemical weapon" in violation of section 229(a) is simple: The chemicals that Bond placed on Haynes's home and car are "toxic chemical[s]" as defined by the statute, and Bond's attempt to assault Haynes was not a "peaceful purpose." §§ 229F(1), (8), (7) . The problem with this interpretation is that it would "dramatically intrude[ ] upon traditional state criminal jurisdiction," and we avoid reading statutes to have such reach in the absence of a clear indication that they do.

Part of a fair reading of statutory text is recognizing that "Congress legislates against the backdrop" of certain unexpressed presumptions. As Justice Frankfurter put it in his famous essay on statutory interpretation, correctly reading a statute "demands awareness of certain presuppositions." . . .

Among the background principles of construction that our cases have recognized are those grounded in the relationship between the Federal Government and the States under our Constitution. . . . [One of] these is the well-established principle that " 'it is incumbent upon the federal courts to be certain of Congress' intent before finding that federal law overrides' " the "usual constitutional balance of federal and state powers." Gregory v. Ashcroft, 501 U.S. 452, 460 (1991). . . .

We have applied this background principle when construing federal statutes that touched on several areas of traditional state responsibility. Perhaps the clearest example of traditional state authority is the punishment of local criminal activity. Thus, "we will not be quick to assume that Congress has meant to effect a significant change in the sensitive relation between federal and state criminal jurisdiction." . . .

These precedents make clear that it is appropriate to refer to basic principles of federalism embodied in the Constitution to resolve ambiguity in a federal statute. In this case, the ambiguity derives from the improbably broad reach of the key statutory definition given the term—"chemical weapon"—being defined; the deeply serious consequences of adopting such a boundless reading; and the lack of any apparent need to do so in light of the context from which the statute arose—a treaty about chemical warfare and terrorism. We conclude that, in this curious case, we can insist on a clear indication that Congress meant to reach purely local crimes, before interpreting the statute's expansive language in a way that intrudes on the police power of the States.

B

We do not find any such clear indication in section 229. "Chemical weapon" is the key term that defines the statute's reach, and it is defined extremely broadly. But that general definition does not constitute a clear statement that Congress meant the statute to reach local criminal conduct. . . .

The Government would have us . . . adopt a reading of section 229 that would sweep in everything from the detergent under the kitchen sink to the stain remover in the laundry room. Yet no one would ordinarily describe those substances as "chemical weapons." The Government responds that because Bond used "specialized, highly toxic" (though legal) chemicals, "this case presents no occasion to address whether Congress intended [section 229] to apply to common household substances." That the statute *would* apply so broadly, however, is the inescapable conclusion of the Government's position: Any parent would be guilty of a serious federal offense—possession of a chemical weapon—when, exasperated by the children's repeated failure to clean the goldfish tank, he considers poisoning the fish with a few drops of vinegar. We are reluctant to ignore the ordinary meaning of "chemical weapon" when doing so would transform a statute passed to implement the international Convention on Chemical Weapons into one that also makes it a federal offense to poison goldfish. That would not be a "realistic assessment [ ] of congressional intent."

In light of all of this, it is fully appropriate to apply the background assumption that Congress normally preserves "the constitutional balance between the National Government and the States." That assumption is grounded in the very structure of the Constitution. And as we explained when this case was first before us, maintaining that constitutional balance is not merely an end unto itself. Rather, "[b]y denying any one government complete jurisdiction over all the concerns of public life, federalism protects the liberty of the individual from arbitrary power."

The Government's reading of section 229 would " 'alter sensitive federal-state relationships,' " convert an astonishing amount of "traditionally local criminal conduct" into "a matter for federal enforcement," and "involve a substantial extension of federal police resources." It would transform the statute from one whose core concerns are acts of war, assassination, and terrorism into a massive federal anti-poisoning regime that reaches the simplest of assaults. As the Government reads section 229, "hardly" a poisoning "in the land would fall outside the federal statute's domain." Of course Bond's conduct is serious and unacceptable—and against the laws of Pennsylvania. But the background principle that Congress does not normally intrude upon the police power of the States is critically important. In light of that principle, we are reluctant to conclude that Congress meant to punish Bond's crime with a federal prosecution for a chemical weapons attack. . . .

The judgment of the Court of Appeals [sustaining her conviction] is reversed, and the case is remanded for further proceedings consistent with this opinion.

■ JUSTICE SCALIA, with whom JUSTICE THOMAS joins, and with whom JUSTICE ALITO joins as to Part I, concurring in the judgment.

Somewhere in Norristown, Pennsylvania, a husband's paramour suffered a minor thumb burn at the hands of a betrayed wife. The United States Congress—"every where extending the sphere of its activity, and drawing all power into its impetuous vortex"—has made a federal case out of it. What are we to do?

It is the responsibility of "the legislature, not the Court, . . . to define a crime, and ordain its punishment." Today, the Court shirks its job and performs Congress's. As sweeping and unsettling as the Chemical Weapons Convention Implementation Act of 1998 may be, it is clear beyond doubt that it covers what Bond did; and we have no authority to amend it. . . .

The meaning of the Act is plain. No person may knowingly "develop, produce, otherwise acquire, transfer directly or indirectly, receive, stockpile, retain, own, possess, or use, or threaten to use, any chemical weapon." 18 U.S.C. § 229(a)(1). A "chemical weapon" is "[a] toxic chemical and its precursors, except where intended for a purpose not prohibited under this chapter as long as the type and quantity is consistent with such a purpose." § 229F(1)(A). A "toxic chemical" is "any chemical which through its chemical action on life processes can cause death, temporary incapacitation or permanent harm to humans or animals. The term includes all such chemicals, regardless of their origin or of their method of production, and regardless of whether they are produced in facilities, in munitions or elsewhere." § 229F(8)(A). A "purpose not prohibited" is "[a]ny peaceful purpose related to an industrial, agricultural, research, medical, or pharmaceutical activity or other activity." § 229F(7)(A).

Applying those provisions to this case is hardly complicated. Bond possessed and used "chemical[s] which through [their] chemical action on life processes can cause death, temporary incapacitation or permanent harm." Thus, she possessed "toxic chemicals." And, because they were not possessed or used only for a "purpose not prohibited," § 229F(1)(A), they were "chemical weapons." Ergo, Bond violated the Act. End of statutory analysis, I would have thought.

The Court does not think the interpretive exercise so simple. But that is only because its result-driven antitextualism befogs what is evident.

[The Court] *starts* with the federalism-related consequences of the statute's meaning and reasons backwards, holding that, if the statute has what the Court considers a disruptive effect on the "federal-state balance" of criminal jurisdiction, that effect causes the text, even if clear on its face, to be ambiguous. Just ponder what the Court says: "[The Act's] ambiguity *derives* from the improbably broad reach of the key statutory definition . . . the deeply serious consequences of adopting such a boundless reading; and the lack of any apparent need to do so. . . ." Ibid. (emphasis added). Imagine what future courts can do with that judge-empowering principle: Whatever has improbably broad, deeply serious, and apparently unnecessary consequences . . . *is ambiguous*! . . .

In this case, . . . the ordinary meaning of the term being defined is irrelevant, because the statute's own definition—however expansive—is utterly clear: any "chemical which through its chemical action on life processes can cause death, temporary incapacitation or permanent harm to humans or animals," § 229F(8)(A), unless the chemical is possessed or used for a "peaceful purpose," § 229F(1)(A), (7)(A). The statute parses itself. There is no opinion of ours, and none written by any court or put forward by any commentator since Aristotle, which says, or even suggests, that "dissonance" between ordinary meaning and the unambiguous words of a definition is to be resolved in favor of ordinary meaning. If that were the case, there would hardly be any use in providing a definition. No, the true rule is entirely clear: "When a statute includes an explicit definition, we must follow that definition, *even if it varies from that term's ordinary meaning*." Stenberg v. Carhart, 530 U.S. 914, 942 (2000) (emphasis added). Once again, contemplate the judge-empowering consequences of the new interpretive rule the Court today announces: When there is "dissonance" between the statutory definition and the ordinary meaning of the defined word, the latter may prevail.

But even text clear on its face, the Court suggests, must be read against the backdrop of established interpretive presumptions. Thus, we presume "that a criminal statute derived from the common law carries with it the requirement of a culpable mental state—even if no such limitation appears in the text." And we presume that "federal statutes do not apply outside the United States." Both of those are, indeed, established interpretive presumptions that are (1) based upon realistic assessments of congressional intent, and (2) well known to Congress—thus furthering rather than subverting genuine legislative intent. To apply these presumptions, then, is not to rewrite clear text; it is to interpret words fairly, in light of their statutory context. But there is nothing either (1) realistic or (2) well known about the presumption the Court shoves down the throat of a resisting statute today. Who in the world would have thought that a definition is inoperative if it contradicts ordinary meaning? When this statute was enacted, there was not yet a "Bond presumption" to that effect—though presumably Congress will have to take account of the Bond presumption in the future, perhaps by adding at the end of all its definitions that depart from ordinary connotation "and we really mean it.". . .

[Justice Scalia went on to say that even though the statute applied to the defendant's behavior, it was unconstitutional for entirely other reasons; thus, he concurred in the judgment.]

[Justice Thomas's concurrence is omitted.]

[Justice Alito's concurrence is omitted.]

## NOTES ON SUBSTANTIVE CANONS

(1) ***Clear Statement Rules as Opposed to Presumptions.*** WILLIAM N. ESKRIDGE, JR. & PHILIP P. FRICKEY, QUASI-CONSTITUTIONAL LAW: CLEAR STATEMENT RULES AS CONSTITUTIONAL LAWMAKING, 45 Vand. L. Rev. 593, 597 (1992): "[T]he current Court emphasizes a different array of clear statement rules than did the Court in the 1970s. The current Court is less inclined to protect individual rights through cautious statutory interpretation than the Court was a decade ago, and more inclined to protect constitutional structures through cautious interpretation. Moreover, consistent with its interest in textualism as its dominant interpretive methodology, the current Court emphasizes clear statement rules much more than presumptions. Indeed, the most striking innovation of the recent Court has been its creation of a series of new 'super-strong clear statement rules' protecting constitutional structures, especially structures associated with federalism.

"These super-strong clear statement rules are remarkable. On the one hand, they require a clearer, more explicit statement from Congress in the text of the statute, without reference to legislative history, than prior clear statement rules have required. This would suggest that such rules are protecting particularly important constitutional values. But, on the other hand, the super-strong clear statement rules the Court has actually adopted protect constitutional values that are virtually never enforced through constitutional interpretation. That is, the Court in the 1980s has tended to create the strongest clear statement rules to confine Congress's power in areas in which Congress has the constitutional power to do virtually anything. What the Court is doing is creating a domain of 'quasi-constitutional law' in certain areas: Judicial review does not prevent Congress from legislating, but judicial interpretation of the resulting legislation requires an extraordinarily specific statement on the face of the statute for Congress to limit the states or the executive department.

"That the Court's super-strong clear statement rules are new does not mean they are undesirable, of course. In fact, a good case can be made for such quasi-constitutional law: structural constitutional protections, especially those of federalism, are underenforced constitutional norms. They are essentially unenforceable by the Court as a direct limitation upon Congress's power, and are best left to the political process. But the Court may have a legitimate role in forcing the political process to pay attention to the constitutional values at stake, and super-strong clear statement rules are a practical way for the Court to focus legislative attention on these values."

(2) ***An Analogy to Contract Law.*** CASS R. SUNSTEIN, INTERPRETING STATUTES IN THE REGULATORY STATE, 103 Harv. L. Rev. 405, 452–54 (1989): "The canons of construction continue to be a prominent feature in the federal and state courts. The use of general guides to construction—in the form of 'clear-statement' principles and background understandings—can be found in every area of modern law.

"An analogy may be helpful here. The law of contracts is pervaded by—indeed, it consists largely of—a set of principles filling contractual gaps when the parties have been silent, or when the meaning of their words is unclear. Imagine, for example, that the parties have been silent on the time of performance, damages in the event of breach, or the consequences of dramatically changed circumstances and partial default. The use of implied terms, or 'off-the-rack' provisions, is a familiar part of the law of contract; and it would be most peculiar to say that they are an illegitimate incursion into the usual process of 'interpreting' the parties' intent. Without implied terms of some sort, contracts simply would not be susceptible to construction. Implied terms also provide the background against which people enter into agreements.

"To a large degree, interpretive principles—including the traditional 'canons'—serve the same function in public law. They too help judges to construe both statements and silences; they too should not be seen as the intrusion of controversial judgments into 'ordinary' interpretation. There are, however, differences as well as similarities. In the law of contracts, it is often said that implied terms should attempt to 'mimic the market' by doing what the parties would do if they had made provision on the subject. In this respect, contract law is pervaded by a background norm in favor of party autonomy and the market. In statutory construction, by contrast, the notion of 'mimicking the market' is unavailable, and the idea that one should do what Congress would have done is far from a complete guide. As we have seen, how Congress would have resolved the question is sometimes unclear; sometimes the resolution of the enacting Congress would produce difficulties as a result of changed circumstances; sometimes courts properly call into play principles—many of them constitutionally inspired—that push statutes in directions that diverge from the conclusion that Congress would have reached if it had resolved the matter. Despite these differences, the critical point is that, as in contract law, the interpretation of a text requires courts to refer to background norms in interpreting terms."

(3) ***Some Common Substantive Canons.*** Of the various substantive canons invoked by the Supreme Court, one of the most important is the canon of constitutional avoidance. It purports to function, as we noted above, more as a presumption than a clear-statement rule. Rust v. Sullivan, 500 U.S. 173, 190–91 (1991), stated the principle as follows: " '[A]s between two possible interpretations of a statute, by one of which it would be unconstitutional and by the other valid, our plain duty is to adopt that which will save the

Act.' . . . This principle is based at least in part on the fact that a decision to declare an Act of Congress unconstitutional 'is the gravest and most delicate duty that this Court is called on to perform.' [Cases have also] developed the corollary doctrine that '[a] statute must be construed, if fairly possible, so as to avoid not only the conclusion that it is unconstitutional but also grave doubts upon that score.' This canon is followed out of respect for Congress, which we assume legislates in the light of constitutional limitations. . . ." Rust thus narrowly read restrictions on funding for family-planning programs concerning abortion to avoid challenges under the First Amendment and the Fifth Amendment as defined by Roe v. Wade.

A closely related canon to constitutional avoidance is the requirement that abrogation or waiver of state sovereign immunity be clear and unequivocal. See Atascadero State Hosp. v. Scanlon, 473 U.S. 234, 242 (1985). But notice that this substantive canon purports to function more as a clear-statement rule than a presumption. It thus applies even when the statute in question might not be considered ambiguous enough to trigger a mere tie-breaking presumption, such as the constitutional avoidance canon. Rather, the sovereign immunity substantive canon requires a statute to be unusually clear to effect the abrogation or waiver of the immunity.

Still other substantive canons are rooted in protection of structural constitutional values, such as federalism. See Gregory v. Ashcroft, 501 U.S. 452, 464 (1991). Indeed, Bond purports to be applying this substantive canon. Do you think it is operating there as a tie-breaking presumption or as a clear-statement rule? Do you think it is serving as a means of capturing legislative intent or of constraining the legislature's ability to infringe on our federalism? Is there a difference between those two formulations, or do they inevitably collapse into one another depending on what one presumes about Congress's view of a constitutional value like federalism?

The major questions doctrine, to which we turn next, can be interpreted along these same structural constitutional lines, as protecting the separation of powers by avoiding interpretations that could pose issues under the nondelegation doctrine. But it might also be thought of as just a means of capturing Congress's likely intentions about what it anticipates agencies will do with the power give to them.

(4) ***Major Questions Doctrine.*** The most recent and consequential formulation of this doctrine is that clear statutory authorization is required when "agencies assert[ ] highly consequential power beyond what Congress could reasonably be understood to have granted." West Virginia v. EPA, 142 S.Ct. 2587, 2609 (2022). (Does that formulation assume the conclusion?) We discuss West Virginia and the major questions doctrine in greater depth in Chapter VIII (pp. 1341–1370).

The major questions doctrine, indeed, raises some major questions. For one, the provenance of the rule is murky. Is the doctrine rooted in enforcing a constitutional limitation on delegation of legislative power? Or is it rooted in a premise about congressional intent, independent of any concerns about delegation? See West Virginia, 142 S.Ct. at 2609 ("[I]n certain extraordinary cases, *both separation of powers principles and a practical understanding of legislative intent* make us 'reluctant to read into ambiguous statutory text' the delegation claimed to be lurking there." (emphasis added)). For another, the trigger for the doctrine is murky, as it is not entirely clear what makes a question "major." Finally, does the major questions doctrine articulate a tie-breaking presumption to be used in case of ambiguity, or is it a clear-statement rule that applies even when the text is not so ambiguous that an ordinary substantive canon would apply? Answering that question can be hard because there is arguably a recursive quality to the doctrine: the statute might be thought to be unclear about what it authorizes only to the extent that it is claimed to authorize the agency to tackle a major question.

(5) ***Whither the Rule of Lenity?*** The rule of lenity, discussed by Justice Kagan in the Lockhart case, applies chiefly to criminal statutes, including to those that concern sentencing. The canon serves to protect the notice rights of those subject to criminal punishment and to ensure that the line between the legislative role of defining a crime or criminal penalty and interpreting one is respected. Muscarello v. United States, 524 U.S. 125, 150 (1998) (Ginsburg, J., dissenting). In the standard formulation, the canon requires a criminal statute to be construed narrowly when it contains a "grievous ambiguity" in the relevant respect. See Ocasio v. United States, 578 U.S. 282, 295 n.8 (2016). But what is that kind of ambiguity compared to normal ambiguity?

In addition to issues about how the rule of lenity applies, there is increasingly a question as to whether the Court is willing to recognize the kind of ambiguity that could give rise to the canon's application. For example, in Borden v. United States, 141 S.Ct. 1817 (2021), the Court held, without resorting to the rule of lenity, that the Armed Career Criminal Act did not encompass offenses that only had a mens rea of recklessness. The Court explained that the statute clearly required that result, thereby rendering the rule of lenity inapplicable. Yet, while the Court found the statute to be clear in compelling that criminal-defendant-friendly result, the four dissenting justices thought that the ACCA compelled precisely the opposite conclusion, and the five justices in the majority did not agree on the reasons for reaching the interpretive result that they did. In addition, the lower courts had divided on the question before the Court. What, then, explains the Court's reliance on clarity rather than lenity to resolve the question raised in Borden, especially when, in an earlier case, the Court had applied the rule of lenity to resolve a very similar question? See Leocal v. Ashcroft, 543 U.S. 1, 9–11 (2004).

Similarly, in Van Buren v. United States, 141 S.Ct. 1648 (2021), which concerned the Computer Fraud and Abuse Act, the Court again divided 5–4 on the meaning of the criminal statute, with each side setting forth a distinct account of why the statute was in fact clear. Yet, there, too, the Court did not invoke the rule of lenity.

If the rule of lenity is not relevant to the resolution of interpretive questions such as those the Court faced in Borden or Van Buren, when would it be relevant?

(6) ***Are Substantive Canons Legitimate?*** Consider the following exchange at oral argument between Justice Kagan and an attorney for the United States as amicus curiae:

> JUSTICE KAGAN: I'm about to take you outside the scope of this case, so I apologize beforehand. But Justice Alito raised what to me is an interesting question that I've been thinking about a good deal about what these substantive canons of interpretation are and when they exist and when they don't exist. They're all over the place, of course. It's not just the Indian canon. Next week, we're going to be thinking about the supposed major questions canon. There are other canons. I mean, if you go through Justice Scalia's book, you'll find a wealth of canons of this kind, these sort of substantive canons. Some of them help the government. Some of them hurt the government. Is there any way that the government has of coming in and saying, like, how do we reconcile our views of all these different kinds of canons? Maybe we should just toss them all out, you know.
>
> MR. YANG: Well—
>
> JUSTICE KAGAN: I mean, I think kind of we should, honestly. Like, what are we doing here? But is there—do you have a view of, like, when these canons are the kind that you're going to talk about in your briefs and when these canons are not the kind that you're going to talk about in your briefs?
>
> MR. YANG: Well, I think our briefs generally grapple first with the text, right, as we've done here. And canons, I think, can play an important role in certain contexts. I think, for instance, Bryan recognized that in the Indian tribal sovereignty context, there is a very important principle that kind of underlays the body of the law there. You do not want to read statutes to grant state regulatory authority on tribal lands without kind of a clear expression of that. And I think that those types of principles reflect a background body of law that one brings when reading statutes.

Transcript of Oral Argument at 59–61, Ysleta Del Sur Pueblo v. Texas, 142 S.Ct. 1929 (2022) (No. 20–493).[1]

(7) ***Are Substantive Canons Necessary?*** In MCGIRT V. OKLAHOMA, 140 S.Ct. 2452 (2020), the Supreme Court held that much of eastern Oklahoma, reserved for the Creek Nation since the 1850s, remained "Indian country," a specific legal and jurisdictional designation within the field of Federal Indian Law. Writing for the majority, JUSTICE GORSUCH wrote that a federal reservation, once established, could be "disestablished" only if Congress, by statute, disestablished it. But how would one know whether it had done so? The answer: "If Congress wishes to break the promise of a reservation," wrote Justice Gorsuch, "it must say so." Id. at 2462. Some scholars have suggested that, in concluding that Congress had not said so, McGirt applied a "clear statement rule." See Michael C. Dorf, Will Liberal Justices Pay A Price For

---

[1] https://www.supremecourt.gov/oral_arguments/argument_transcripts/2021/20-493_7m48.pdf.

Signing Onto Justice Gorsuch's Textualist Opinions?, Dorf on Law (July 22, 2020). On this view, the Court may be requiring Congress to make its intent unmistakably clear if it wishes judges to interpret federal law in a manner that disestablishes a reservation. That viewpoint might be said to resemble traditional canons of construction favoring the interests of Native American tribes in the context of treaty interpretation. On the other hand, one might also read Justice Gorsuch's opinion to embrace textualist logic and thus to eschew a clear statement rule rooted in a substantive policy. The Seventh Circuit recently suggested that McGirt had applied the ordinary rules of statutory interpretation, placing "a greater focus on statutory text" in answering disestablishment questions. Oneida Nation v. Village of Hobart, 968 F.3d 664, 668 (7th Cir. 2020). What might seem like a clear statement rule could just be straightforward textualism. If so, though, what might that mean for whether a substantively-based presumption or clear statement rule should be applied not only in this context but in others as well?

(8) ***Substantive Canons in Disguise.*** Another possibility is that substantive canons are alive and well, even if they are not formally invoked. In Niz-Chavez v. Garland, 141 S.Ct. 1474 (2021), the question concerned the meaning of the phrase "a notice to appear" in the Illegal Immigration Reform and Immigrant Responsibility Act of 1996. The Court concluded that the phrase must be read to refer to a single document rather than, as JUSTICE GORSUCH put it in writing for the majority, notice by installment. (Not all notice requirements had been met by the government until a second notice was issued.) The majority relied heavily on the statute's use of the word "a" in the phrase at issue to explain the result. In dissent, JUSTICE KAVANAUGH disputed that line of analysis, noting that the statute itself defined "a notice to appear" as "written notice," thus dropping the "a." He further drew on the distinction between what he called literal meaning and ordinary meaning in explaining why the word "a" did not have to be referring to a single document.

JUSTICE GORSUCH disputed each of these points, but he also concluded his opinion with the following final paragraph, which might be read to reflect the application of a substantive canon in favor of narrow construction in the immigration realm. Its final turn of phrase is nearly identical to one that had been recently used in review of a different agency action concerning immigration (see Dep't of Homeland Sec. v. Regents, p. 1139):

"At one level, today's dispute may seem semantic, focused on a single word, a small one at that. But words are how the law constrains power. In this case, the law's terms ensure that, when the federal government seeks a procedural advantage against an individual, it will at least supply him with a single and reasonably comprehensive statement of the nature of the proceedings against him. If men must turn square corners when they deal with the government, it cannot be too much to expect the government to turn square corners when it deals with them."

## (3) The Absurdity Doctrine

> *PUBLIC CITIZEN v. U.S. DEP'T OF JUSTICE*
> *Notes on the Absurdity Doctrine*

We close our consideration of canons by considering an unusually powerful and controversial rule of thumb: the absurdity doctrine, which directs courts not to read statutes so as to produce absurd results. From one vantage point, this would seem to be uncontroversial. Why would one construe a statute to create an absurdity? From another vantage point, though, this doctrine is itself absurd because it invites interpreters to ignore what the text actually says. The same can be said of an analogous doctrine telling judges to ignore typos: the scrivener's error doctrine. These doctrines test textualism. Must a textualist reject the scrivener's error and the absurdity doctrines? Or, rather, are these the doctrines that save textualism from itself being deemed absurd? Relatedly, are the scrivener's error and absurdity doctrines just the natural consequence of a commitment to purposivism? Or are they instead an indication of the illegitimacy of purposivism? After all, isn't there a risk that an error or an absurdity is in the eye of the beholder?

## PUBLIC CITIZEN v. U.S. DEP'T OF JUSTICE

Supreme Court of the United States (1989).
491 U.S. 440.

■ JUSTICE BRENNAN delivered the opinion of the Court.

. . . Since 1952 the President, through the Department of Justice, has requested advice from the American Bar Association's Standing Committee on Federal Judiciary (ABA Committee) in making [judicial] nominations.

The American Bar Association is a private voluntary professional association of approximately 343,000 attorneys. It has several working committees, among them the advisory body whose work is at issue here. The ABA Committee consists of 14 persons belonging to, and chosen by, the American Bar Association. Each of the 12 federal judicial Circuits (not including the Federal Circuit) has one representative on the ABA Committee, except for the Ninth Circuit, which has two; in addition, one member is chosen at large. The ABA Committee receives no federal funds. It does not recommend persons for appointment to the federal bench of its own initiative.

Prior to announcing the names of nominees for judgeships on the courts of appeals, the district courts, or the Court of International Trade, the President, acting through the Department of Justice, routinely requests a potential nominee to complete a questionnaire drawn up by the ABA Committee and to submit it to the Assistant Attorney General for the Office of Legal Policy, to the chair of the ABA Committee, and to the committee member (usually the representative of the relevant judicial Circuit) charged with investigating the nominee. . . .

B

[The Federal Advisory Committee Act] was born of a desire to assess the need for the "numerous committees, boards, commissions, councils, and similar groups which have been established to advise officers and agencies in the executive branch of the Federal Government." Its purpose was to ensure that new advisory committees be established only when essential and that their number be minimized; that they be terminated when they have outlived their usefulness; that their creation, operation, and duration be subject to uniform standards and procedures; that Congress and the public remain apprised of their existence, activities, and cost; and that their work be exclusively advisory in nature.

. . . FACA requires that each advisory committee file a charter, § 9(c), and keep detailed minutes of its meetings. Those meetings must be chaired or attended by an officer or employee of the Federal Government who is authorized to adjourn any meeting when he or she deems its adjournment in the public interest. FACA also requires advisory committees to provide advance notice of their meetings and to open them to the public, unless the President or the agency head to which an advisory committee reports determines that it may be closed to the public in accordance with the Government in the Sunshine Act. In addition, FACA stipulates that advisory committee minutes, records, and reports be made available to the public, provided they do not fall within one of the Freedom of Information Act's exemptions, and the Government does not choose to withhold them. Advisory committees established by legislation or created by the President or other federal officials must also be "fairly balanced in terms of the points of view represented and the functions" they perform. Their existence is limited to two years, unless specifically exempted by the entity establishing them.

C

In October 1986, appellant Washington Legal Foundation (WLF) brought suit against the Department of Justice after the ABA Committee refused WLF's request for the names of potential judicial nominees it was considering and for the ABA Committee's reports and minutes of its meetings. WLF asked the District Court for the District of Columbia to declare the ABA Committee an "advisory committee" as FACA defines that term. WLF further sought an injunction ordering the Justice Department to cease utilizing the ABA Committee as an advisory committee until it complied with FACA. . . .

III

Section 3(2) of FACA, defines "advisory committee" as follows: . . .

> "(2) The term 'advisory committee' means any committee, board, commission, council, conference, panel, task force, or other similar group, or any subcommittee or other subgroup thereof (hereafter in this paragraph referred to as 'committee'), which is—. . .

(B) established or utilized by the President, . . ."

. . . Whether the ABA Committee constitutes an "advisory committee" for purposes of FACA therefore depends upon whether it is "utilized" by the President or the Justice Department as Congress intended that term to be understood.

A

There is no doubt that the Executive makes use of the ABA Committee, and thus "utilizes" it in one common sense of the term. As the District Court recognized, however, "reliance on the plain language of FACA alone is not entirely satisfactory." "Utilize" is a woolly verb, its contours left undefined by the statute itself. Read unqualifiedly, it would extend FACA's requirements to any group of two or more persons, or at least any formal organization, from which the President or an Executive agency seeks advice. We are convinced that Congress did not intend that result. A nodding acquaintance with FACA's purposes, as manifested by its legislative history and as recited in § 2 of the Act, reveals that it cannot have been Congress' intention, for example, to require the filing of a charter, the presence of a controlling federal official, and detailed minutes any time the President seeks the views of the National Association for the Advancement of Colored People (NAACP) before nominating Commissioners to the Equal Employment Opportunity Commission, or asks the leaders of an American Legion Post he is visiting for the organization's opinion on some aspect of military policy.

Nor can Congress have meant—as a straightforward reading of "utilize" would appear to require—that all of FACA's restrictions apply if a President consults with his own political party before picking his Cabinet. It was unmistakably *not* Congress' intention to intrude on a political party's freedom to conduct its affairs as it chooses, or its ability to advise elected officials who belong to that party, by placing a federal employee in charge of each advisory group meeting and making its minutes public property. FACA was enacted to cure specific ills, above all the wasteful expenditure of public funds for worthless committee meetings and biased proposals; although its reach is extensive, we cannot believe that it was intended to cover every formal and informal consultation between the President or an Executive agency and a group rendering advice. As we said in Church of the Holy Trinity v. United States: "[F]requently words of general meaning are used in a statute, words broad enough to include an act in question, and yet a consideration of the whole legislation, or of the circumstances surrounding its enactment, or of the absurd results which follow from giving such broad meaning to the words, makes it unreasonable to believe that the legislator intended to include the particular act."

Where the literal reading of a statutory term would "compel an odd result," we must search for other evidence of congressional intent to lend the term its proper scope. "The circumstances of the enactment of particular legislation," for example, "may persuade a court that Congress did not intend words of common meaning to have their literal effect."

Even though, as Judge Learned Hand said, "the words used, even in their literal sense, are the primary, and ordinarily the most reliable, source of interpreting the meaning of any writing," nevertheless "it is one of the surest indexes of a mature and developed jurisprudence not to make a fortress out of the dictionary; but to remember that statutes always have some purpose or object to accomplish, whose sympathetic and imaginative discovery is the surest guide to their meaning." Cabell v. Markham, 148 F.2d 737, 739 (CA2), aff'd, 326 U.S. 404 (1945). Looking beyond the naked text for guidance is perfectly proper when the result it apparently decrees is difficult to fathom or where it seems inconsistent with Congress' intention ....

B

[A] literalistic reading of § 3(2) would bring the Justice Department's advisory relationship with the ABA Committee within FACA's terms, particularly given FACA's objective of opening many advisory relationships to public scrutiny except in certain narrowly defined situations. A literalistic reading, however, would catch far more groups and consulting arrangements than Congress could conceivably have intended. And the careful review which this interpretive difficulty warrants of earlier efforts to regulate federal advisory committees and the circumstances surrounding FACA's adoption strongly suggests that FACA's definition of "advisory committee" was not meant to encompass the ABA Committee's relationship with the Justice Department. That relationship seems not to have been within the contemplation of Executive Order No. 11007. And FACA's legislative history does not display an intent to widen the Order's application to encircle it. Weighing the deliberately inclusive statutory language against other evidence of congressional intent, it seems to us a close question whether FACA should be construed to apply to the ABA Committee, although on the whole we are fairly confident it should not. ...

■ JUSTICE SCALIA took no part in the consideration or decision of these cases.

■ JUSTICE KENNEDY, with whom THE CHIEF JUSTICE and JUSTICE O'CONNOR join, concurring in the judgment.

... I cannot join the Court's conclusion that the Federal Advisory Committee Act (FACA), does not cover the activities of the American Bar Association's Standing Committee on Federal Judiciary in advising the Department of Justice regarding potential nominees for federal judgeships. The result seems sensible in the abstract; but I cannot accept the method by which the Court arrives at its interpretation of FACA, which does not accord proper respect to the finality and binding effect of legislative enactments.... [The concurrence would have decided a separation of powers question not reached by the Court to find FACA unconstitutional as applied.]

I

... Although I believe the Court's result is quite sensible, I cannot go along with the unhealthy process of amending the statute by judicial interpretation. Where the language of a statute is clear in its application, the normal rule is that we are bound by it. There is, of course, a legitimate exception to this rule, which the Court invokes, and with which I have no quarrel. Where the plain language of the statute would lead to "patently absurd consequences," United States v. Brown, 333 U.S. 18, 27 (1948), that "Congress could not *possibly* have intended," FBI v. Abramson, 456 U.S. 615, 640 (1982) (O'Connor, J., dissenting) (emphasis added), we need not apply the language in such a fashion. When used in a proper manner, this narrow exception to our normal rule of statutory construction does not intrude upon the lawmaking powers of Congress, but rather demonstrates a respect for the coequal Legislative Branch, which we assume would not act in an absurd way.

This exception remains a legitimate tool of the Judiciary, however, only as long as the Court acts with self-discipline by limiting the exception to situations where the result of applying the plain language would be, in a genuine sense, absurd, i.e., where it is quite impossible that Congress could have intended the result, and where the alleged absurdity is so clear as to be obvious to most anyone. . . . In today's opinion, however, the Court disregards the plain language of the statute not because its application would be patently absurd, but rather because, on the basis of its view of the legislative history, the Court is "fairly confident" that "FACA should [not] be construed to apply to the ABA Committee." I believe the Court's loose invocation of the "absurd result" canon of statutory construction creates too great a risk that the Court is exercising its own "WILL instead of JUDGMENT," with the consequence of "substituti[ng] [its own] pleasure to that of the legislative body." The Federalist No. 78 (A. Hamilton).

The Court makes only a passing effort to show that it would be absurd to apply the term "utilize" to the ABA Committee according to its commonsense meaning. It offers three examples that we can assume are meant to demonstrate this point: the application of FACA to an American Legion Post should the President visit that organization and happen to ask its opinion on some aspect of military policy; the application of FACA to the meetings of the National Association for the Advancement of Colored People (NAACP) should the President seek its views in nominating Commissioners to the Equal Employment Opportunity Commission; and the application of FACA to the national committee of the President's political party should he consult it for advice and recommendations before picking his Cabinet.

None of these examples demonstrate the kind of absurd consequences that would justify departure from the plain language of the statute. A commonsense interpretation of the term "utilize" would not necessarily reach the kind of ad hoc contact with a private group that is contemplated by the Court's American Legion hypothetical. . . . As for the more regular use contemplated by the Court's examples concerning the NAACP and the national committee of the President's political party, it would not be at all absurd to say that, under the Court's hypothetical, these groups would be "utilized" by the President to obtain "advice or recommendations" on appointments, and therefore would fall within the coverage of the statute. Rather, what is troublesome about these examples is that they raise the very same serious constitutional questions that confront us here (and perhaps others as well). The Court confuses the two points. The fact that a particular application of the clear terms of a statute might be unconstitutional does not, in and of itself, render a straightforward application of the language absurd, so as to allow us to conclude that the statute does not apply. . . .

## NOTES ON THE ABSURDITY DOCTRINE

(1) ***Textualism and the Absurdity Doctrine.*** JOHN F. MANNING, THE ABSURDITY DOCTRINE, 116 Harv. L. Rev. 2387, 2389–91 (2003): "The standard justification for the absurdity doctrine is straightforward. In a system marked by legislative supremacy (within constitutional boundaries), federal courts act as faithful agents of Congress. For that reason, legislative intent is widely assumed to be the touchstone of statutory interpretation. While the enacted text is generally considered the best evidence of such intent, Congress does not always accurately reduce its intentions to words because legislators necessarily draft statutes within the constraints of bounded foresight, limited resources, and imperfect language. The absurdity doctrine builds on that idea: If a given statutory application sharply contradicts commonly held social values, then the Supreme Court presumes that this absurd result reflects imprecise drafting that Congress could and would have corrected had the issue come up during the enactment process. Accordingly, standard interpretive doctrine (perhaps tautologically) defines an 'absurd result' as an outcome so contrary to perceived social values that Congress could not have 'intended' it. So understood, the absurdity doctrine is merely a version of strong intentionalism, which permits a court to adjust a clear statute in the rare case in which the court finds that the statutory text diverges from the legislature's true intent, as derived from sources such as the legislative history or the purpose of the statute as a whole.

"Despite the absurdity doctrine's deep roots, recent intellectual and judicial developments have undermined the doctrine's strong intentionalist foundations. Modern textualism, which emerged in the late twentieth century, maintains that, contrary to the tenets of strong intentionalism, respect for the legislative process requires judges to adhere to the precise terms of statutory texts. In particular, textualists argue that the (often unseen) complexities of the legislative process make it meaningless to speak of 'legislative intent' as distinct from the meaning conveyed by a clearly expressed statutory command. . . .

"Notwithstanding these considerations, even the staunchest modern textualists still embrace and apply, even if rarely, at least some version of the absurdity doctrine. The Supreme Court, at least until recently, has followed suit. One can readily understand why. No one, of course, is for absurd results. And the examples most frequently cited to justify the absurdity doctrine seem to reflect a compelling, if imprecise, intuition. The currently dominant version of textualism seems relatively attractive precisely because the absurdity doctrine provides an all-purpose backstop to the principle that judges must follow a clear text wherever it takes them. But this version of textualism is, I believe, wrong. If textualists object to strong intentionalism in general, the absurdity doctrine is particularly problematic because it permits judges to alter clear statutory language based on vaguely defined social values, rather than sources (such as legislative history) that are more immediately linked to the legislative process. And if one accepts the previously discussed inferences from the constitutional structure, then one cannot simply re-rationalize the absurdity doctrine as an inherent attribute of judicial power."

(2) ***What's Old Is New Again?*** Speaking generally, when administrative agencies interpret their statutory ambit, courts sometimes defer to that interpretation under the rule of Chevron v. NRDC (p. 1206). But when the agency interpretation would result in an extraordinarily broad or novel grant of authority, the major questions doctrine (Note 4 above at p. 192) may counsel against such deference. Consider the relatively recent development of the major questions doctrine in light of the long history of the absurdity canon discussed in Note 1. Does the doctrine merely reflect the application of the absurdity canon?

(3) ***A Problem to Consider: The Case of the Very Last Day.*** For a very long time, mining has been permitted on federal public lands. In order to keep track of the various mining claims, in 1976 Congress enacted the Federal Land Policy and Management Act. This Act established a recording system that required the claimant to file a notice each year of his intention to continue to hold the claim. The notice had to be filed, said Congress, "prior to December 31 of each year." Nothing in the Act or its legislative history explains why this language was chosen. The Act also provided that failure to file on time "shall be deemed conclusively to constitute an abandonment of the mining claim . . . by the owner." In the event, a miner filed his notice on December 31. Did he forfeit his claim? To find the authoritative answer, see United States v. Locke, 471 U.S. 84 (1985).

## d. Legislative History

***BABBITT v. SWEET HOME CHAPTER OF COMMUNITIES FOR A GREAT OREGON***

***Notes on Legislative History***

One of the biggest bones of contention between textualists and those who subscribe to other interpretive philosophies is the use of legislative history. Legislative history is a broad category that includes records of congressional debates, committee reports, and any other documents generated during the legislative process. (It should not be confused with the history of a piece of legislation in the broader sense of the social problem Congress meant to address or the events in the public arena that made the problem salient—matters to which judges of all stripes often refer.) Textualists (or at least the most diehard ones) shun the use of legislative history, while adherents to some other philosophies find it a useful tool for understanding the words of a statute. Consider the following materials.

## BABBITT v. SWEET HOME CHAPTER OF COMMUNITIES FOR A GREAT OREGON

Supreme Court of the United States (1995).
515 U.S. 687.

■ JUSTICE STEVENS delivered the opinion of the Court.

The Endangered Species Act of 1973 (ESA or Act) contains a variety of protections designed to save from extinction species that the Secretary of the Interior designates as endangered or threatened. Section 9 of the Act makes it unlawful for any person to "take" any endangered or threatened species. The Secretary has promulgated a regulation that defines the statute's prohibition on takings to include "significant habitat modification or degradation where it actually kills or injures wildlife." This case presents the question whether the Secretary exceeded his authority under the Act by promulgating that regulation.

I

Section 9(a)(1) of the Act provides the following protection for endangered species:

> Except as provided in sections 1535(g)(2) and 1539 of this title, with respect to any endangered species of fish or wildlife listed pursuant to section 1533 of this title it is unlawful for any person subject to the jurisdiction of the United States to—. . .
>
> (B) take any such species within the United States or the territorial sea of the United States. 16 U.S.C. § 1538(a)(1).

Section 3(19) of the Act defines the statutory term "take":

> The term 'take' means to harass, harm, pursue, hunt, shoot, wound, kill, trap, capture, or collect, or to attempt to engage in any such conduct. 16 U.S.C. § 1532(19).

The Act does not further define the terms it uses to define "take." The Interior Department regulations that implement the statute, however, define the statutory term "harm":

> Harm in the definition of 'take' in the Act means an act which actually kills or injures wildlife. Such act may include significant habitat modification or degradation where it actually kills or injures wildlife by significantly impairing essential behavioral patterns, including breeding, feeding, or sheltering. 50 CFR § 17.3 (1994).

This regulation has been in place since 1975.

A limitation on the § 9 "take" prohibition appears in § 10(a)(1)(B) of the Act, which Congress added by amendment in 1982. That section authorizes the Secretary to grant a permit for any taking otherwise prohibited by § 9(a)(1)(B) "if such taking is incidental to, and not the purpose of, the carrying out of an otherwise lawful activity."

In addition to the prohibition on takings, the Act provides several other protections for endangered species. Section 4 commands the Secretary to identify species of fish or wildlife that are in danger of extinction and to publish from time to time lists of all species he determines to be endangered or threatened. Section 5 authorizes the Secretary, in cooperation with the States, to acquire land to aid in preserving such species. Section 7 requires federal agencies to ensure that none of their activities, including the granting of licenses and permits, will jeopardize the continued existence of endangered species "or result in the destruction or adverse modification of habitat of such species which is determined by the Secretary . . . to be critical."

Respondents in this action are small landowners, logging companies, and families dependent on the forest products industries in the Pacific Northwest and in the Southeast, and organizations that represent their interests. They brought this declaratory judgment action against petitioners, the Secretary of the Interior and the Director of the Fish and Wildlife Service, in the United States District Court for the District of Columbia to challenge the statutory validity of the Secretary's regulation defining "harm," particularly the inclusion of habitat modification and degradation in the definition. Respondents challenged the regulation on its face. Their complaint alleged that application of the "harm" regulation to the red-cockaded woodpecker, an endangered species, and the northern spotted owl, a threatened species, had injured them economically. . . .

II

. . . The text of the Act provides three reasons for concluding that the Secretary's interpretation is reasonable. First, an ordinary understanding of the word "harm" supports it. The dictionary definition of the verb form of "harm" is "to cause hurt or damage to: injure." Webster's Third New International Dictionary 1034 (1966). In the context of the ESA, that definition naturally encompasses habitat modification that results in actual injury or death to members of an endangered or threatened species. . . .

Second, the broad purpose of the ESA supports the Secretary's decision to extend protection against activities that cause the precise harms Congress enacted the statute to avoid. . . .

Third, the fact that Congress in 1982 authorized the Secretary to issue permits for takings that § 9(a)(1)(B) would otherwise prohibit, "if such taking is incidental to, and not the purpose of, the carrying out of an otherwise lawful activity," strongly suggests that Congress understood § 9(a)(1)(B) to prohibit indirect as well as deliberate takings. . . .

III

Our conclusion that the Secretary's definition of "harm" rests on a permissible construction of the ESA gains further support from the legislative history of the statute. The Committee Reports accompanying the bills that became the ESA do not specifically discuss the meaning of "harm," but they make clear that Congress intended "take" to apply broadly to cover indirect as well as purposeful actions. The Senate Report stressed that " '[t]ake' is defined . . . in the broadest possible manner to include every conceivable way in which a person can 'take' or attempt to 'take' any fish or wildlife." S. Rep. No. 93–307, p. 7 (1973). U.S. Code Cong. & Admin. News 1973, pp. 2989, 2995. The House Report stated that "the broadest possible terms" were used to define restrictions on takings. H.R. Rep. No. 93–412, p. 15 (1973). The House Report underscored the breadth of the "take" definition by noting that it included "harassment, whether intentional or not." Id. at 11 (emphasis added). The Report explained that the definition "would allow, for example, the Secretary to regulate or prohibit the activities of birdwatchers where the effect of those activities might disturb the birds and make it difficult for them to hatch or raise their young." Ibid. These comments, ignored in the dissent's welcome but selective foray into legislative history, support the Secretary's interpretation that the term "take" in § 9 reached far more than the deliberate actions of hunters and trappers.

Two endangered species bills, S. 1592 and S. 1983, were introduced in the Senate and referred to the Commerce Committee. Neither bill included the word "harm" in its definition of "take," although the definitions otherwise closely resembled the one that appeared in the bill as ultimately enacted. See Hearings on S. 1592 and S. 1983 before the Subcommittee on Environment of the Senate Committee on Commerce, 93d Cong., 1st Sess., pp. 7, 27 (1973) (hereinafter Hearings). Senator Tunney, the floor manager of the bill in the Senate, subsequently introduced a floor amendment that added "harm" to the definition, noting that this and accompanying amendments would "help to achieve the purposes of the bill." 119 Cong. Rec. 25683 (1973). Respondents argue that the lack of debate about the amendment that added "harm" counsels in favor of a narrow interpretation. We disagree. An obviously broad word that the Senate went out of its way to add to an important statutory definition is precisely the sort of provision that deserves a respectful reading.

The definition of "take" that originally appeared in S. 1983 differed from the definition as ultimately enacted in one other significant respect: It included "the destruction, modification, or curtailment of [the] habitat or range" of fish and wildlife. Hearings, at 27. Respondents make much of the fact that the Commerce Committee removed this phrase from the "take" definition before S. 1983 went to the floor. See 119 Cong. Rec. 25663 (1973). We do not find that fact especially significant. The legislative materials contain no indication why the habitat protection provision was deleted. That provision differed greatly from the regulation at issue today. Most notably, the habitat protection provision in S. 1983 would have applied far more broadly than the regulation does because it made adverse habitat modification a categorical violation of the "take" prohibition, unbounded by the regulation's limitation to habitat modifications that actually kill or injure wildlife. The S. 1983 language also failed to qualify "modification" with the regulation's limiting adjective "significant." We do not believe the Senate's unelaborated disavowal of the provision in S. 1983 undermines the reasonableness of the more moderate habitat protection in the Secretary's "harm" regulation.[2]

The history of the 1982 amendment that gave the Secretary authority to grant permits for "incidental" takings provides further support for his reading of the Act. The House Report expressly states that "[b]y use of the word 'incidental' the Committee intends to cover situations in which it is known that a taking will occur if the other activity is engaged in but such taking is incidental to, and not the purpose of, the activity." H.R. Rep. No. 97–567, p. 31 (1982). U.S. Code Cong. & Admin. News 1982, pp. 2807, 2831. This reference to the foreseeability of incidental takings undermines respondents' argument that the 1982 amendment covered only accidental killings of endangered and threatened animals that might occur in the course of hunting or trapping other animals. Indeed, Congress had habitat modification directly in mind: Both the Senate Report and the House Conference Report identified as the model for the permit process a cooperative state-federal response to a case in California where a development project threatened incidental harm to a species of endangered butterfly by modification of its habitat. See S. Rep. No. 97–418, p. 10 (1982); H.R. Conf. Rep. No. 97–835, pp. 30–32 (1982). Thus, Congress in 1982 focused squarely on the aspect of the "harm" regulation at issue in this litigation. Congress' implementation of a permit program is consistent with the Secretary's interpretation of the term "harm." . . . .

[The judgment of the Court of Appeals, favoring the landowners, is reversed.]

■ JUSTICE SCALIA, with whom THE CHIEF JUSTICE and JUSTICE THOMAS join, dissenting.

. . . [T]he Court maintains that the legislative history of the 1973 Act supports the Secretary's definition. Even if legislative history were a legitimate and reliable tool of interpretation (which I shall assume in order to rebut the Court's claim); and even if it could appropriately be resorted to when the enacted text is as clear as this, here it shows quite the opposite of what the Court says. I shall not pause to discuss the Court's reliance on such statements in the Committee Reports as "[t]ake' is defined . . . in the broadest possible manner to include every conceivable way in which a person can 'take' or attempt to 'take' any fish or wildlife." S. Rep. No. 93–307, p. 7 (1973) U.S. Code Cong. & Admin. News 1973, pg. 2995. This sort of empty flourish—to the effect that "this

---

[2] [Ed.] In the footnote following this sentence, the Court discussed floor statements by Senator Tunney and Representative Sullivan relied upon by respondents, stating that these "merely explained features of the bills" eventually enacted as the ESA rather than supporting respondents' argument by inference.

statute means what it means all the way"—counts for little even when enacted into the law itself.

Much of the Court's discussion of legislative history is devoted to two items: first, the Senate floor manager's introduction of an amendment that added the word "harm" to the definition of "take," with the observation that (along with other amendments) it would "help to achieve the purposes of the bill"; second, the relevant Committee's removal from the definition of a provision stating that "take" includes "the destruction, modification or curtailment of [the] habitat or range" of fish and wildlife. The Court inflates the first and belittles the second, even though the second is on its face far more pertinent. But this elaborate inference from various pre-enactment actions and inactions is quite unnecessary, since we have direct evidence of what those who brought the legislation to the floor thought it meant—evidence as solid as any ever to be found in legislative history, but which the Court banishes to a footnote.

Both the Senate and House floor managers of the bill explained it in terms which leave no doubt that the problem of habitat destruction on private lands was to be solved principally by the land acquisition program of § 1534, while § 1538 solved a different problem altogether—the problem of takings. Senator Tunney stated:

> *Through [the] land acquisition provisions, we will be able to conserve habitats necessary to protect fish and wildlife from further destruction.*
>
> Although most endangered species are threatened primarily by the destruction of their natural habitats, a significant portion of these animals are subject to *predation by man for commercial, sport, consumption, or other purposes.* The provisions of [the bill] would prohibit the commerce in or the importation, exportation, or taking of endangered species. . . .
>
> 119 Cong. Rec. 25669 (1973) (emphasis added).

The House floor manager, Representative Sullivan, put the same thought in this way:

> [T]he principal threat to animals stems from destruction of their habitat. . . . *[The bill] will meet this problem by providing funds for acquisition of critical habitat. . . .* It will also enable the Department of Agriculture to cooperate with willing landowners who desire to assist in the protection of endangered species, *but who are understandably unwilling to do so at excessive cost to themselves.*
>
> Another hazard to endangered species arises from those who would *capture or kill them for pleasure or profit.* There is no way that the Congress can make it less pleasurable for a person to take an animal, but we can certainly make it less profitable for them to do so.
>
> Id. at 30162 (emphasis added).

Habitat modification and takings, in other words, were viewed as different problems, addressed by different provisions of the Act. The Court really has no explanation for these statements. All it can say is that "[n]either statement even suggested that [the habitat acquisition funding provision in § 1534] would be the Act's exclusive remedy for habitat modification by private landowners or that habitat modification by private landowners stood outside the ambit of [§ 1538]." That is to say, the statements are not as bad as they might have been. Little in life is. They are, however, quite bad enough to destroy the Court's legislative-history case, since they display the clear understanding (1) that habitat modification is separate from "taking," and (2) that habitat destruction on private lands is to be remedied by public acquisition, and not by making particular unlucky landowners incur "excessive cost to themselves." The Court points out triumphantly that they do not display the understanding (3) that the land acquisition program is "the [Act's] only response to habitat modification." Of course not, since that is not so (all public lands are subject to habitat-modification restrictions); but (1) and (2) are quite enough to exclude the Court's interpretation. They identify the land acquisition program as the Act's only response to habitat modification by private landowners, and thus do not in the least "contradic[t]," the fact that § 1536 prohibits habitat modification by federal agencies.

. . . [T]he Court seeks support from a provision that was added to the Act in 1982, the year after the Secretary promulgated the current regulation. The provision states:

> [T]he Secretary may permit, under such terms and conditions as he shall prescribe—. . .
>
> any taking otherwise prohibited by section 1538(a)(1)(B) . . . if such taking is incidental to, and not the purpose of, the carrying out of an otherwise lawful activity.
>
> 16 U.S.C. § 1539(a)(1)(B).

This provision does not, of course, implicate our doctrine that reenactment of a statutory provision ratifies an extant judicial or administrative interpretation, for neither the taking prohibition in § 1538(a)(1)(B) nor the definition in § 1532(19) was reenacted. The Court claims, however, that the provision "strongly suggests that Congress understood [§ 1538(a)(1)(B)] to prohibit indirect as well as deliberate takings." That would be a valid inference if habitat modification were the only substantial "otherwise lawful activity" that might incidentally and nonpurposefully cause a prohibited "taking." Of course it is not. This provision applies to the many otherwise lawful takings that incidentally take a protected species—as when fishing for unprotected salmon also takes an endangered species of salmon. . . .

This is enough to show, in my view, that the 1982 permit provision does not support the regulation. I must acknowledge that the Senate Committee Report on this provision, and the House Conference Committee Report, clearly contemplate that it will enable the Secretary to permit environmental modification. See S. Rep. No. 97–418, p. 10 (1982); H.R. Conf. Rep. No. 97–835, pp. 30–32 (1982). But the text of the amendment cannot possibly bear that asserted meaning, when placed within the context of an Act that must be interpreted (as we have seen) not to prohibit private environmental modification. The neutral language of the amendment cannot possibly alter that interpretation, nor can its legislative history be summoned forth to contradict, rather than clarify, what is in its totality an unambiguous statutory text. There is little fear, of course, that giving no effect to the relevant portions of the Committee Reports will frustrate the real-life expectations of a majority of the Members of Congress. If they read and relied on such tedious detail on such an obscure point (it was not, after all, presented as a revision of the statute's prohibitory scope, but as a discretionary-waiver provision) the Republic would be in grave peril. . . .

## NOTES ON LEGISLATIVE HISTORY

(1) ***What Counts?*** WILLIAM N. ESKRIDGE, JR., THE NEW TEXTUALISM, 37 UCLA L. Rev. 621, 636–40 (1990): "[T]he Court has worked out a rough hierarchy of evidence to resolve conflicts [between portions of the legislative history of a statute]. The hierarchy is based upon the comparative reliability of each source: How likely does this source reflect the views or assumptions of the enacting Congress? Is there a danger of strategic manipulation by individual Members or biased groups seeking to 'pack' the legislative history? How well-informed is the source? The figure below, which Professor Frickey and I have developed in teaching Legislation at the University of Minnesota School of Law and at the Georgetown University Law Center (respectively), reflects this hierarchy.

**HIERARCHY OF LEGISLATIVE HISTORY SOURCES (THE FRICKEY & ESKRIDGE MINI-FUNNEL)**

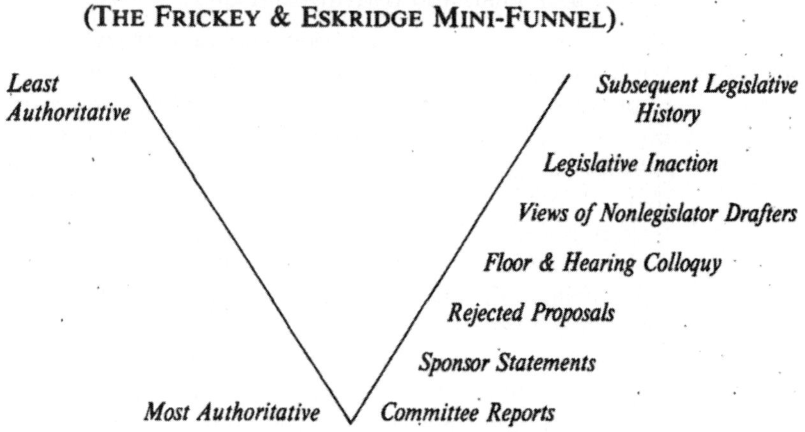


1. Committee Reports

". . . Committee reports are the most frequently cited and relied-upon sources of legislative history, and in the Court's traditional view the most authoritative source. 'A committee report represents the considered and collective understanding of those Congressmen involved in drafting and studying proposed legislation. Floor debates reflect at best the understanding of individual Congressmen. It would take extensive and thoughtful debate to detract from the plain thrust of a committee report . . . .' Committee reports are often the best evidence of bicameral agreement, either because the House and Senate reports are identical, or because a conference report explicates the chambers' resolution of differences.

2. Sponsor Statements

". . . Next only to committee reports in reliability are statements by sponsors and/or floor managers, and the Court relies on their statements routinely. '[R]emarks . . . of the sponsor of the language ultimately enacted, are an authoritative guide to the statute's construction,' because the sponsors are the Members of Congress most likely to know what the proposed legislation is all about, and other Members can be expected to pay special heed to their characterizations of the legislation. 'While the views of a sponsor of legislation are by no means conclusive, they are entitled to considerable weight, particularly in the absence of a committee report.'

3. Rejected Proposals

". . . 'Few principles of statutory construction are more compelling than the proposition that Congress does not intend sub silentio to enact statutory language that it has earlier discarded in favor of other language.' . . . This is a slight overstatement of the Court's practice. Oftentimes, the rejection of proposed language by the committee, on the floor of the House or Senate, or in conference is quite probative, since it is direct evidence that Congress considered an issue and agreed not to adopt a specified policy. But other times it is unclear that the rejection was truly a referendum on the issue later before the Court. The Court usually does not rely on evidence concerning rejected proposals as its primary legislative history.

4. Floor and Hearing Colloquy

" 'In construing laws [the Court has] been extremely wary of testimony before committee hearings and of debates on the floor of Congress save for precise analyses of statutory phrases by the sponsors of the proposed laws.' Thus, statements by legislators at hearings or on the floor are not as authoritative as those of sponsors and floor managers, unless the speakers can be identified as 'players' on that particular bill. According to the conventional wisdom, nonplayers are less likely to know what the consensus view is on the bill, and are more likely to behave strategically (engaging in the famed 'planned colloquy'). Further, the views of those unsupportive of the proposed legislation 'are no authoritative guide to the construction of legislation. It is the sponsors that we look to when the meaning of the statutory words is in doubt.' This conventional wisdom has been relaxed somewhat in the last twenty years, for the Court frequently looks to legislative colloquy, especially to discern the general assumptions made at the time a law was enacted. Moreover, where the sponsor's statements are either too general or suspicious, the Court will rely on more specific colloquy instead. Even the views of opponents have sometimes been considered.

5. Nonlegislative Drafters and Sponsors

"In [two Supreme Court cases], the testimony of nonlegislative supporters of the legislation (executive officials, law professors, environmental groups) was counted as relevant but not critical. Such use is typical of this evidence. The Court will usually invoke these statements as further evidence in support of conclusions gleaned from the statutory text, committee reports, and sponsors' statements. Nonlegislator evidence will be most important in cases where it is clear that the statute was a careful compromise reached outside the legislative process and merely ratified by the legislature, and sometimes in cases where there is virtually no other evidence.

6. Legislative Silence and Subsequent History

"For the reasons developed above, evidence of legislative silence and subsequent history is usually too ambiguous to count as legislative history, but in some contexts the sources are considered by the Court. '[W]hile the views of subsequent Congresses cannot override the unmistakable intent of the enacting one, such views are entitled to significant weight, and particularly so when the precise intent of the enacting Congress is obscure.' Much the same can be said of the dog that doesn't bark argument: Legislative silence will usually be supporting evidence of legislative intent and will be the main evidence only when there is virtually no other evidence of legislative intent."

(2) ***A Bad Idea.*** JOHN F. MANNING, TEXTUALISM AS A NONDELEGATION DOCTRINE, 97 Colum. L. Rev. 673 (1997): "In contrast with an old Supreme Court case that contains the common law meaning of a term of legal art, legislative history is endogenous to the legislative process; as an exercise of delegated law elaboration authority, it violates an important prophylactic safeguard of bicameralism and presentment—the constitutional choice to deny Congress authority to construe its own laws, except through the enactment of further law. When Congress enacts a statute containing an externally defined term of art, it takes the details of the art as it finds them. When, however, the Court gives authoritative weight to a committee's subjective understanding of statutory meaning (announced outside the statutory text), it empowers Congress to specify statutory details—without the structurally-mandated cost of getting two Houses of Congress and the President to approve them. Although neither a pre-enactment Supreme Court case nor a committee report formally goes through bicameralism and presentment, crediting a legislatively created source of meaning offers Congress a more substantial temptation to shift the specification of detail outside the cumbersome legislative process.

"To appreciate the importance of adopting interpretive rules designed to preserve the integrity of the constitutionally prescribed legislative process, it is helpful to recall the context that gave rise to the inclusion of bicameralism and presentment in the Constitution. Adopted in an era when many had lost confidence in the capacity of (unchecked) legislatures to safeguard liberty and respect law, the constitutional checks of bicameralism and presentment, codified in Article I, Section 7, comprised a key element of the Constitution's scheme to preserve individual liberty. Those requirements serve evident and well-understood purposes, which require only brief mention here. First, by dividing the legislative power between two chambers, bicameralism and presentment make it more difficult for factions to usurp legislative authority, ensuring a diffusion of governmental power and preserving the liberty and security of the governed. In this regard, the division of legislative power into distinct parts effectively operates 'to balance interest against interest, ambition against ambition, the combinations and spirit of dominion of one body against the like combinations and spirit of another.' Second, the requirements of Article I, Section 7 promote caution and deliberation; by mandating that each piece of legislation clear an intricate process involving distinct constitutional actors, bicameralism and presentment reduce the incidence of hasty and ill-considered legislation. Third, by relying on multiple, potentially antagonistic constitutional decisionmakers, the legislative process prescribed by Article I often produces conflict and friction, enhancing the prospects for a full and open discussion of matters of public import.

"These protections come at considerable expense. By design, they raise the decision costs associated with lawmaking, safeguarding liberty through a deliberate sacrifice of governmental efficiency. The Federalists recognized as much. They acknowledged that 'this complicated check on legislation may in some instances be injurious as well as beneficial,' and that 'the power of preventing bad laws includes that of preventing good ones.' However, they saw the risks of ill-advised governmental action as far greater than the risks of inaction. Madison thus contended that 'the facility and excess of law-making,' and not the converse, 'seem to be the diseases to which our governments are most liable.' Hamilton similarly contended that '[t]he injury which may possibly be done by defeating a few good laws will be amply compensated by the advantage of preventing a number of bad ones.' This trade-off, manifest in the constitutional structure, did not go unnoticed in the debate over the Constitution and was in fact expressly conceded by its strongest defenders. . . .

"Textualism's simple ambition is to require legislators to accept responsibility for their legislative acts. The authoritative use of legislative history undermines this objective; as things now stand, no legislator ever has to vote for any piece of legislative history. No legislator (other than a member of the relevant committee) is responsible for the understandings expressed in a committee report. No legislator, other than the sponsor, is responsible for the contents of a sponsor's explanation of a bill. Yet these documents may prove decisive in interpretation . . ."

(3) ***A Good Idea.*** STEPHEN BREYER, ON THE USES OF LEGISLATIVE HISTORY IN INTERPRETING STATUTES, 65 S. Cal. L. Rev. 845 (1992): "[One constitutional argument against the use of legislative history] concerns the Constitution's requirements for enacting a law. A bill must pass both houses of Congress and obtain the President's signature or a veto override. The result, says the Constitution, is a statute; and that statute, not a floor speech or committee report or testimony or presidential message or congressional 'intent,' is the law. The use of legislative history, according to this argument,

tends to make these other matters—report language and floor speeches—the 'law' even though they had received neither a majority vote nor a presidential signature. . . .

"The 'statute-is-the-only-law' argument misses the point. No one claims that legislative history is a statute, or even that, in any strong sense, it is 'law.' Rather, legislative history is helpful in trying to understand the meaning of the words that do make up the statute or the 'law.' A judge cannot interpret the words of an ambiguous statute without looking beyond its words for the words have simply ceased to provide univocal guidance to decide the case at hand. Can the judge, for example, ignore a dictionary or the historical interpretive practice of the agency that customarily applies some words? Is a dictionary or an historic agency interpretive practice 'law?' It is 'law' only in a weak sense that does not claim the status of a statute, and in a sense that violates neither the letter nor the spirit of the Constitution. . . ."

(4) ***Legislative History as a Check on Discretion.*** ROBERT A. KATZMANN, JUDGING STATUTES 48 (2014): "As to constraining judicial preferences, it seems to me that excluding legislative history when interpreting ambiguous statutes is just as likely to expand a judge's discretion as reduce it. When a statute is unambiguous, resorting to legislative history is generally not necessary; in that circumstance, the inquiry ordinarily ends. But when a statute is ambiguous, barring legislative history leaves a judge only with words that could be interpreted in a variety of ways without contextual guidance as to what legislators may have thought. Lacking such guidance increases the probability that a judge will construe a law in a manner that the legislators did not intend. It is seemingly inconsistent that textualists, who look to such extratextual materials as the records of the Constitutional Convention and The Federalist in interpreting the Constitution, would look askance at the use of legislative history sources when interpreting legislation."

(5) ***A Recent Skirmish.*** A recent version of the ongoing debate over the use of legislative history played out in DIGITAL REALTY TRUST, INC. V. SOMERS, 138 S.Ct. 767 (2018). The majority, in an opinion by JUSTICE GINSBURG, relied on a committee report to support its interpretation of a provision of the Dodd-Frank Wall Street Reform and Consumer Protection Act. JUSTICE THOMAS, joined by Justices Alito and Gorsuch, responded in a concurring opinion that it was not proper to rely on legislative history because "we are a government of laws, not of men, and are governed by what Congress enacted rather than by what it intended." Id. at 783 (quoting Lawson v. FMR LLC, 571 U.S. 429, 459–60 (2014) (Scalia, J., concurring in part and concurring in judgment)). JUSTICE SOTOMAYOR, joined by Justice Breyer, responded to that concurring opinion in a concurrence of her own, which she ended this way: "I do not think it wise for judges to close their eyes to reliable legislative history—and the realities of how Members of Congress create and enact laws—when it is available."

These issues flared up again in Gundy v. United States, 139 S.Ct. 2116 (2019), which you may read in Chapter VII (p. 837). There, JUSTICE KAGAN invoked, but did not premise her analysis on, legislative history, in finding that the Sex Offender Registration and Notification Act set forth a "feasibility" requirement to guide the discretion of the Attorney General in administering that statute and thus an intelligible principle sufficient to satisfy the requirements of the constitutional nondelegation doctrine. JUSTICE GORSUCH, in dissent, dismissed the invocation of legislative history in part on the ground that, as he put it, it was not "the law."

## PART 3

# THE AGENCY AT WORK

# CHAPTER III

# PROCEDURAL FRAMEWORKS FOR ADMINISTRATIVE ACTION



At the core of administrative law is the agency. A creature of statute and executive branch action, it stands in a complex relationship to the named constitutional branches of the federal government—Congress, the President, and the Supreme Court. Parts 4 and 5 of this casebook explore these relationships. This Part, by contrast, over the next few Chapters is devoted to exploring the agency itself, how it operates, and the legal constraints that govern its procedures.

Section 1 of this Chapter introduces the legal foundation for agencies, some basic forms of agency structure, and the two core procedures of administrative action, rulemaking and adjudication. Section 2 opens by identifying the constitutional distinction between rulemaking and adjudication. It then describes how the rulemaking/adjudication divide factors into the Administrative Procedure Act (APA), and provides an overview of the APA's adoption and interpretation over the years. It closes with a brief look at other sources of procedural constraint outside the APA. Section 3 addresses the principles that may constrain agency ability to use rulemaking or adjudication. It also introduces a key principle of administrative law: that courts will uphold or reject agency action only on the grounds invoked by the agency. Section 4 puts rulemaking and adjudication into a larger context, introducing the field of public administration and the connections between that field and administrative law.

## SECTION 1. INTRODUCTION

As Chapter I notes, the U.S. Constitution says very little about the structure of the federal government beyond occasional references to

"Departments," "Heads of Departments," and principal and inferior Officers. The agencies that dominate modern federal government—the Departments of Homeland Security, Treasury, and Health and Human Services, for instance, or the Federal Communications Commission and the Securities and Exchange Commission—owe their creation and powers to Congress rather than to the Constitution. Congress has broad authority to structure agencies as it sees fit, subject to constitutional limitations discussed in Chapter VII. And Congress has developed a number of different agency structures and forms. The most common form for executive agencies and departments—whether a cabinet department like the DHS, a stand-alone executive agency like the Environmental Protection Agency, or a unit of a larger agency, like the Federal Aviation Administration in the Department of Transportation—is to have a single agency head who is nominated by the President with Senate consent and is removable by the President at will. Another common form is an agency like the FCC, often termed an "independent regulatory commission," that is headed by a multi-member body, whose members are presidentially nominated with Senate confirmation for staggered, fixed terms, and who are removable only for cause.

These two categories hardly exhaust the different agency structures you will find in the federal government. Sometimes independent commissions are located within executive agencies. An example of this is the Federal Energy Regulatory Commission, a body located in the Department of Energy and charged with regulating the interstate transmission of electricity, gas, and oil. It is ostensibly subject to oversight by the Secretary of Energy, but its five members have term appointments and removal protection, denoting "independence." Congress has also at times created "private" corporations to serve its policy goals, such as the Federal Deposit Insurance Corporation, the Tennessee Valley Authority, and Amtrak. Further, many federal programs are implemented by state agencies subject to federal administrative oversight—Social Security Disability Insurance and Medicaid are two prime examples—with the result that much of these programs' front-line administration is not undertaken by federal agencies at all.

Congress generally assigns agencies a wide array of roles and responsibilities. Agencies provide benefits, generate information, issue licenses, promulgate rules that govern private conduct, enforce federal law, adjudicate disputes, develop and operate infrastructure, award grants and contracts, manage their internal administration, and much more. You can readily see this by exploring any agency's website—for example, that of the Occupational Safety and Health Administration (OSHA).[1] There you will find links for filing complaints or required reports, voluntary programs, statistical data, enforcement guidance, and more—a wide range of matters beyond the regulations whose generation is a principal emphasis of this casebook. Any lawyer working with workplace health and safety matters would, of necessity, become

---

1 https://www.osha.gov.

intimately familiar with much of OSHA's work. But agency-specific information is not the subject of this casebook, which stresses problems and principles applicable to most agencies. You will learn more about the subject matter specific to each agency when you take courses relevant to that agency's field, such as environmental law and the EPA, securities law and the SEC, or health law and HHS.

This casebook focuses on agency action through rulemaking and agency adjudication. These are the two categories of action at the heart of the federal Administrative Procedure Act, for executive and independent agencies alike. Since rulemaking results in a statute-like governing text, it is easy to analogize to a legislature's enactment of general policy; since much agency adjudication involves an arbiter resolving disputed questions after a hearing between parties, it is easy to analogize to the processes of judicial trial. Yet as the materials that follow suggest, the reality is much more complicated, and the line between these two procedural forms is not always clear. Adopting a rule specifying some parameters necessary to assure the safety of a nuclear reactor will turn on questions of scientific fact, dispute about which might also arise in litigation; agencies sometimes use adjudication as courts sometimes use common-law decisionmaking to set general policy that will affect a large number of individuals.

In the particular case of OSHA, Congress has chosen to place the responsibility for administrative adjudication of possible violations of federal occupational safety and health statutes and rules in a separate agency, the Occupational Safety and Health Review Commission. OSHA itself promulgates regulations and brings enforcement actions before OSHRC. For most federal agencies, however, the combination of rulemaking, executing, *and* adjudicating functions is a key feature of their responsibilities. Operating under what are frequently broad authorizations, agencies like the EPA simultaneously develop and promulgate binding regulatory standards, investigate and prosecute violations of those standards, and adjudicate the resultant disputes. It is a basic precept of administrative law that agencies can only exercise the powers they have been delegated, but Congress frequently entrusts agencies with extensive policy-setting powers, subject only to broad limitations, such as that they must regulate "in the public interest" or set emission standards "requisite to protect the public health."

These combinations of functions and broad delegations may be necessary to meet the needs of contemporary governance, yet they create enduring tensions between the constitutional framework and modern administrative government. Those tensions are explored in detail in Part 4 but surface as well, if less overtly, in the following materials on agency procedure. For example, judicial assessment of whether agencies have violated governing procedural requirements occurs against a background of anxiety about the tremendous power that agencies wield and the profound impact their regulations can have on our nation's society and economy. In reading the materials in this Part, keep in mind these larger constitutional tensions and how they may be influencing the development of what appears on the surface to be nonconstitutional or ordinary administrative law.

## SECTION 2. THE FUNDAMENTAL PROCEDURAL CATEGORIES OF ADMINISTRATIVE ACTION: RULEMAKING AND ADJUDICATION



### a. The Constitution



We begin with two foundational cases that distinguish rulemaking and adjudication from a constitutional perspective. While the cases both consider factual circumstances that appear to be far afield from the work of federal agencies—what protections must state and local tax authorities provide to individual property holders affected by their decisions?—the conclusions the Supreme Court reaches in each case are directly relevant. This is because the state-focused Due Process Clause of the Fourteenth Amendment on which the Court relies ("nor shall any State deprive any person of life, liberty, or property, without due process of law") has a federal analogue in the Fifth Amendment ("No person shall . . . be deprived of life, liberty, or property, without due process of law"). The distinction the Court develops in these cases is thus key to understanding the design of the modern federal administrative process.

## LONDONER v. DENVER

Supreme Court of the United States (1908).
210 U.S. 373.

■ JUSTICE MOODY delivered the opinion of the Court.

The plaintiffs in error began this proceeding in a state court of Colorado to relieve lands owned by them from an assessment of a tax for the cost of paving a street upon which the lands abutted. The relief sought was granted by the trial court, but its action was reversed by the Supreme Court of the State. . . . The [Colorado] Supreme Court held that the tax was assessed in conformity with the constitution and laws of the State, and its decision on that question is conclusive. . . .

The tax complained of was assessed under the provisions of the charter of the city of Denver, which confers upon the city the power to make local improvements and to assess the cost upon property specially benefited. . . . It appears from the charter that, in the execution of the power to make local improvements and assess the cost upon the property specially benefited, the main steps to be taken by the city authorities are plainly marked and separated:

> 1. The board of public works must transmit to the city council a resolution ordering the work to be done and the form of an ordinance authorizing it and creating an assessment district. This it can do only upon certain conditions, one of which is that there shall first be filed a petition asking the improvement, signed by the owners of the majority of the frontage to be assessed.
>
> 2. The passage of that ordinance by the city council, which is given authority to determine conclusively whether the action of the board was duly taken.
>
> 3. The assessment of the cost upon the landowners after due notice and opportunity for hearing.

In the case before us the board took the first step by transmitting to the council the resolution to do the work and the form of an ordinance authorizing it. It is contended, however, that there was wanting an essential condition of the jurisdiction of the board, namely, such a petition from the owners as the law requires. The trial court found this contention to be true. But, as has been seen, the charter gave the city council the authority to determine conclusively that the improvements were duly ordered by the board after due notice and a proper petition. In the exercise of this authority the city council, in the ordinance directing the improvement to be made, adjudged, in effect, that a proper petition had been filed. . . . The state Supreme Court held that the determination of the city council was conclusive that a proper petition was filed, and that decision must be accepted by us as the law of the State. The only question for this court is whether the charter provision authorizing such a finding, without notice to the landowners, denies to them due process of law. We think it does not. The proceedings, from the beginning up to and including the passage of the ordinance authorizing the work did not include any assessment or necessitate any assessment, although they laid the foundation for an assessment, which might or might not subsequently be made. Clearly all this might validly be done without hearing to the landowners, provided a hearing upon the assessment itself is afforded. The legislature might have authorized the making of improvements by the city council without any petition. If it chose to exact a petition as a security for wise and just action it could, so far as the Federal Constitution is concerned, accompany that condition with a provision that the council, with or without notice, should determine finally whether it had been performed. This disposes of the first assignment of error, which is overruled. . . .

The fifth assignment, though general, vague and obscure, fairly raises, we think, the question whether the assessment was made without notice and opportunity for hearing to those affected by it, thereby denying to them due process of law. The trial court found as a fact that no opportunity for hearing was afforded, and the Supreme Court did not disturb this finding. The record discloses what was actually done, and there seems to be no dispute about it. After the improvement was completed the board of public works, in compliance with § 29 of the charter, certified to the city clerk a statement of the cost, and an apportionment of it to the lots of land to be assessed. Thereupon the city clerk, in compliance with § 30, published a notice stating, inter alia, that the written complaints or objections of the owners, if filed within thirty days, would be "heard and determined by the city council before the passage of any ordinance assessing the cost." Those interested, therefore, were informed that if they reduced their complaints and objections to writing, and filed them within thirty days, those complaints and objections would be heard, and would be heard before any assessment was made. . . . Resting upon the assurance that they would be heard, the plaintiffs in error filed within the thirty days the following paper:

> "Denver, Colorado, January 13, 1900.
>
> "To the Honorable Board of Public Works and the Honorable Mayor and City Council of the City of Denver:
>
> "The undersigned, by Joshua Grozier, their attorney, do hereby most earnestly and strenuously protest and object to the passage of the contemplated or any assessing ordinance against the property in Eighth Avenue Paving District No. 1, so called, for each of the following reasons, to wit:
>
> "1st. That said assessment and all and each of the proceedings leading up to the same were and are illegal, voidable and void, and the attempted assessment if made will be void and uncollectible.
>
> "2nd. That said assessment and the cost of said pretended improvement should be collected, if at all, as a general tax against the city at large and not as a special assessment.
>
> "3rd. That property in said city not assessed is benefited by the said pretended improvement and certain property assessed is not benefited by said pretended improvement and other property assessed is not benefited by said pretended improvement to the extent of the assessment; that the individual pieces of property in said district are not benefited to the extent assessed against them and each of them respectively; that the assessment is arbitrary and property assessed in an equal amount is not benefited equally; that the boundaries of said pretended district were arbitrarily created without regard

to the benefits or any other method of assessment known to law; that said assessment is outrageously large. . . .

"8th. Because the city had no jurisdiction in the premises. No petition subscribed by the owners of a majority of the frontage in the district to be assessed for said improvements was ever obtained or presented. . . .

"Wherefore, because of the foregoing and numerous other good and sufficient reasons, the undersigned object and protest against the passage of the said proposed assessing ordinance."

This certainly was a complaint against and objection to the proposed assessment. Instead of affording the plaintiffs in error an opportunity to be heard upon its allegations, the city council, without notice to them, met as a board of equalization, not in a stated but in a specially called session, and, without any hearing, adopted the following resolution:

"Whereas, complaints have been filed by the various persons and firms as the owners of real estate included within the Eighth Avenue Paving District No. 1, of the city of Denver against the proposed assessments on said property for the cost of said paving, . . . and Whereas, no complaint or objection has been filed or made against the apportionment of said assessment made by the board of public works of the city of Denver, but the complaints and objections filed deny wholly the right of the city to assess any district or portion of the assessable property of the city of Denver; therefore, be it

"Resolved, by the city council of the city of Denver, sitting as a board of equalization, that the apportionments of said assessment made by said board of public works be, and the same are hereby, confirmed and approved."

Subsequently, without further notice or hearing, the city council enacted the ordinance of assessment whose validity is to be determined in this case. The facts out of which the question on this assignment arises may be compressed into small compass. The first step in the assessment proceedings was by the certificate of the board of public works of the cost of the improvement and a preliminary apportionment of it. The last step was the enactment of the assessment ordinance. From beginning to end of the proceedings the landowners, although allowed to formulate and file complaints and objections, were not afforded an opportunity to be heard upon them. Upon these facts was there a denial by the State of the due process of law guaranteed by the Fourteenth Amendment to the Constitution of the United States?

In the assessment, apportionment and collection of taxes upon property within their jurisdiction the Constitution of the United States imposes few restrictions upon the states. In the enforcement of such restrictions as the Constitution does impose this court has regarded substance and not form. But where the legislature of a state, instead of fixing the tax itself, commits to some subordinate body the duty of determining whether, in what amount, and upon whom it shall be levied, and of making its assessment and apportionment, due process of law requires that at some stage of the proceedings before the tax becomes irrevocably fixed, the taxpayer shall have an opportunity to be heard, of which he must have notice, either personal, by publication, or by a law fixing the time and place of the hearing. It must be remembered that the law of Colorado denies the landowner the right to object in the courts to the assessment, upon the ground that the objections are cognizable only by the board of equalization.

If it is enough that, under such circumstances, an opportunity is given to submit in writing all objections to and complaints of the tax to the board, then there was a hearing afforded in the case at bar. But we think that something more than that, even in proceedings for taxation, is required by due process of law. Many requirements essential in strictly judicial proceedings may be dispensed with in proceedings of this nature. But even here a hearing in its very essence demands that he who is entitled to it shall have the right to support his allegations by argument however brief, and, if need be, by proof, however informal. It is apparent that such a hearing was denied to the plaintiffs in error. The denial was by the city council, which, while acting as a board of equalization, represents the state. The assessment was therefore void, and the plaintiffs in error were entitled to a decree discharging their lands from a lien on account of it. . . .

Judgment reversed.

■ THE CHIEF JUSTICE and JUSTICE HOLMES dissent.

## BI-METALLIC INVESTMENT CO. v. STATE BD. OF EQUALIZATION OF COLORADO

Supreme Court of the United States (1915).
239 U.S. 441.

■ JUSTICE HOLMES delivered the opinion of the Court.

This is a suit to enjoin the State Board of Equalization and the Colorado Tax Commission from putting in force, and the defendant Pitcher as assessor of Denver from obeying, an order of the boards increasing the valuation of all taxable property in Denver forty per cent. The order was sustained and the suit directed to be dismissed by the Supreme Court of the State. The plaintiff is the owner of real estate in Denver and brings the case here on the ground that it was given no opportunity to be heard and that therefore its property will be taken without due process of law, contrary to the Fourteenth Amendment of the Constitution of the United States. That is the only question with which we have to deal. . . .

For the purposes of decision we assume that the constitutional question is presented in the baldest way—that neither the plaintiff nor the assessor of Denver, who presents a brief on the plaintiff's side, nor any representative of the city and county, was given an opportunity to be heard, other than such as they may have had by reason of the fact that the time of meeting of the boards is fixed by law. On this assumption it is obvious that injustice may be suffered if some property in the county already has been valued at its full worth. But if certain property has been valued at a rate different from that generally prevailing in the county the owner has had his opportunity to protest and appeal as usual in our system of taxation, so that it must be assumed that the property owners in the county all stand alike. The question then is whether all individuals have a constitutional right to be heard before a matter can be decided in which all are equally concerned—here, for instance, before a superior board decides that the local taxing officers have adopted a system of undervaluation throughout a county, as notoriously often has been the case. The answer of this court in the State Railroad Tax Cases, 92 U.S. 575 [(1875)], at least as to any further notice, was that it was hard to believe that the proposition was seriously made.

Where a rule of conduct applies to more than a few people it is impracticable that every one should have a direct voice in its adoption. The Constitution does not require all public acts to be done in town meeting or an assembly of the whole. General statutes within the state power are passed that affect the person or property of individuals, sometimes to the point of ruin, without giving them a chance to be heard. Their rights are protected in the only way that they can be in a complex society, by their power, immediate or remote, over those who make the rule. If the result in this case had been reached as it might have been by the state's doubling the rate of taxation, no one would suggest that the Fourteenth Amendment was violated unless every person affected had been allowed an opportunity to raise his voice against it before the body entrusted by the state constitution with the power. In considering this case in this court we must assume that the proper state machinery has been used, and the question is whether, if the state constitution had declared that Denver had been undervalued as compared with the rest of the state and had decreed that for the current year the valuation should be forty per cent higher, the objection now urged could prevail. It appears to us that to put the question is to answer it. There must be a limit to individual argument in such matters if government is to go on. In Londoner v. Denver, 210 U.S. 373, 385 [(1908)], a local board had to determine "whether, in what amount, and upon whom" a tax for paving a street should be levied for special benefits. A relatively small number of persons was concerned, who were exceptionally affected, in each case upon individual grounds, and it was held that they had a right to a hearing. But that decision is far from reaching a general determination dealing only with the principle upon which all the assessments in a county had been laid.

Judgment affirmed.

## NOTES ON THE LONDONER/BI-METALLIC DISTINCTION

(1) ***Just What Is the Nature of the Londoner/Bi-Metallic Distinction?*** Suppose that, to address a growing problem of alcoholism and public drinking in certain neighborhoods, a city passed a statute authorizing its

Liquor Commission to impose limits on alcohol sales in areas with high rates of public drinking and public disturbance. (This problem is based on Decatur Liquors v. District of Columbia, noted at p. 230 below.) The Commission can impose a variety of limits, ranging from restrictions on the quantity and timing of alcohol sales to flat bans on sales of certain beverages or by particular liquor establishments.

At what point in the following series of actions, if any, do you think due process would obligate the Commission to provide notice and some opportunity to be heard to liquor stores affected by its actions?

- The Commission designates an area as having a high rate of public drinking and public disturbance.
- The Commission determines that sales of single-serving beer bottles and flasks, or single-serving bottles of other alcoholic beverages, are particularly likely to lead to public drinking.
- The Commission enacts a ban on sales of single-serving bottles of alcoholic beverages (single-serving beer bottles or flasks) by those stores in a designated area whose sales of this nature produce more than 10% of their gross income.
- The Commission concludes that sales by a particular store in the area bring it under this ban.

In determining if or when the Londoner hearing right applies in each of the preceding scenarios, would it matter if there were only a few stores affected by the Commission's actions or instead the number was in the hundreds? Would it matter if single alcohol sales represented such a significant part of one liquor store's business that the ban forced it to close?

The answer to these questions depends on how we read Justice Holmes's description of Londoner as a case where "[a] relatively small number of persons was concerned, who were exceptionally affected, in each case upon individual grounds." If we conclude that "a relatively small number" is key, then the Londoner right would seem not to apply if a large number of liquor stores are affected. But is it plausible to think Londoner would have been decided differently if the street to be paved had been many miles in length and the affected plots had numbered in the thousands? How could a court determine when the number affected is large enough to extinguish the due process hearing right?

An alternative reading would put more emphasis on Holmes's observation that, however many persons were concerned, they were persons "who were exceptionally affected, in each case upon individual grounds." Recall that Londoner confined the right to a hearing to those facts bearing on the appropriate assessment for each particular lot. This reading would suggest that the hearing right is independent of the numbers involved but would obtain only when the Commission makes factual determinations with respect to a particular liquor store's sales volume.

Note that characterization of a matter as requiring "facts" to be decided is not, in itself, sufficient to determine whether an action is legislative or adjudicative. Agencies are often called upon to decide scientific or general facts that are independent of particular parties—for example, in the hypothetical above, the Commission's determination that single alcohol sales are likely to lead to public drinking. An agency may need to determine whether a certain chemical is a human carcinogen; if so, how much cancer is likely to be caused at what concentrations, and what would be the feasibility and/or cost of controlling exposure to a given level in different types of industrial settings. Facts like these are neither party-specific (the sort of fact frequently styled "adjudicative") nor so general as the kind of proposition often styled as "legislative fact"—whether, for example, smoking is hazardous to human health. Particularly as applied to these expert matters, the adjudicative-legislative fact distinction is imperfect. While one might conclude that not all factfinding requires a Londoner "hearing," calling a given kind of fact "legislative" hardly suggests that its determination by a legislature's political vote rather than trial techniques would be ideal.

Yet a third reading might understand "in each case upon individual grounds" as signaling the inadequacy of political avenues for relief. "When . . . government singles out an individual for adverse action, the political process provides little protection. Individuals singled out for adverse action can be protected only by forcing the government to use a decisionmaking process that ensures fairness to the individual. That is the purpose of the Due Process Clause." Kristen E. Hickman & Richard J. Pierce, Jr., Administrative Law Treatise § 7.2 (6th ed. 2018); see also John Hart Ely, Democracy and Distrust 87 (1980). Indeed, political intervention and influence on individual decisions seems inappropriate in many contexts. See INS v. Chadha, 462 U.S. 919, 959 (1983) (Powell, J., concurring in the judgment) (p. 886). On this view, the political process provides adequate protection against abuse of governmental power when broader policy is at stake and large numbers of people are concerned. But will political processes prove adequate when the policy being set will particularly affect a relatively small or politically disadvantaged group of people? Should additional procedural protections then be required?

On this point, consider PETER L. STRAUSS, REVISITING OVERTON PARK: POLITICAL AND JUDICIAL CONTROLS OVER ADMINISTRATIVE ACTIONS AFFECTING THE COMMUNITY, 39 UCLA L. Rev. 1251, 1256–57 (1992): "A . . . prominent distinction between the worlds of politics and law appears in Justice Holmes' opinion for the Court in the still influential Bi-Metallic Investment Co. v. State Board of Equalization. . . . Although Holmes' conclusion was procedural—at issue was the application of the Due Process Clause of the Constitution to require quasi-adjudicatory process—the contrast he drew was grounded in conventional notions regarding the relative strengths and weaknesses of legal and political process. Politicians, not judges, should be responsible for setting the dimensions of social policy that may involve trades among the interests of broad groupings of citizens; judges' strengths lie in resolving discrete controversies between individuals, in which one wins, another loses, and broad social adjustments are secondary to the outcome of their concrete dispute. That contrast was given later, influential expression by Professor Lon Fuller, who noted the difference between the 'bi-polar' disputes characterizing typical judicial action and the 'polycentric' controversies that characterize legislatures and the policy-making side of administrative action. The give-and-take resolutions typical of the latter are more readily achieved by meliorative than winner-take-all procedures and are less easily justified in terms of a system structured as rational analysis than one grounded in accommodation."

(2) ***How Has the Distinction Fared in the Courts?***

(a) JUSTICE O'CONNOR, speaking for the Court in MINNESOTA STATE BOARD FOR COMMUNITY COLLEGES v. KNIGHT, 465 U.S. 271, 283–287 (1984): "The Constitution does not grant to members of the public generally a right to be heard by public bodies making decisions of policy. . . . Policymaking organs in our system of government have never operated under a constitutional constraint requiring them to afford every interested member of the public an opportunity to present testimony before any policy is adopted. Legislatures throughout the nation, including Congress, frequently enact bills on which no hearings have been held or on which testimony has been received from only a select group. Executive agencies likewise make policy decisions of widespread application without permitting unrestricted public testimony. Public officials at all levels of government daily make policy decisions based only on the advice they decide they need and choose to hear. To recognize a constitutional right to participate directly in government policymaking would work a revolution in existing government practices.

"Not least among the reasons for refusing to recognize such a right is the impossibility of its judicial definition and enforcement. Both federalism and separation-of-powers concerns would be implicated in the massive intrusion into state and federal policymaking that recognition of the claimed right would entail. Moreover, the pragmatic considerations identified by Justice Holmes in Bi-Metallic Investment Co. v. State Board of Equalization are as weighty today as they were in 1915. Government makes so many policy decisions affecting so many people that it would likely grind to a halt were policymaking constrained by constitutional requirements on whose voices must be heard. 'There must be a limit to individual argument in such matters if government is to go on.' Absent statutory restrictions, the state must be free to consult or not to consult whomever it pleases.

"However wise or practicable various levels of public participation in various kinds of policy decisions may be, this Court has never held, and nothing in the Constitution suggests it should hold, that government must provide for such participation. In Bi-Metallic the Court rejected due process as a source of an obligation to listen. Nothing in the First Amendment or in this Court's case law interpreting it suggests that the rights to speak, associate, and petition require government policymakers to listen or respond to individuals' communications on public issues. . . . No other constitutional provision has been advanced as a source of such a requirement. Nor, finally, can the structure of government established and approved by the Constitution provide the source. It is inherent in a republican form of government that direct public participation in government policymaking is limited. See The Federalist No. 10 (Madison). Disagreement with public policy and disapproval of officials' responsiveness, as Justice Holmes suggested in Bi-Metallic, is to be registered principally at the polls."

(b) In JONES V. GOVERNOR OF FLORIDA, 975 F.3d 1016 (11th Cir. 2020) (en banc), a voter initiative successfully amended the state constitution to provide that "any disqualification from voting arising from a felony conviction shall terminate and voting rights shall be restored upon completion of all terms of sentence including parole or probation." The Florida legislature's implementing statute defined "completion of all terms of sentence" to include all financial obligations associated with the criminal sentence, including fines, fees, costs, and restitution. The statute further provided procedures for challenging the state's removal of a person from the voter rolls for not having completed all the terms of a felony sentence.

A class action challenged the requirement to satisfy all of a sentence's financial obligations on several grounds, including as a due process violation. The Eleventh Circuit acting en banc disagreed, citing the distinction "between legislative and adjudicative action" set forth in Bi-Metallic: "The felons were deprived of the right to vote through legislative action, not adjudicative action. Under its Constitution, Florida deprives all felons of the right to vote upon conviction. This constitutional provision is a law 'of general applicability' that plainly qualifies as legislative action. And even if we accept the argument that [the voter initiative and implementing statute] deprive felons of the right to vote by conditioning reenfranchisement on the completion of all terms of sentence, those laws also qualify as legislative acts. The legislative and constitutional-amendment processes gave the felons all the process they were due before Florida deprived them of the right to vote and conditioned the restoration of that right on completion of their sentences."

Dissenting judges offered a competing view of the matter: "[T]he majority is mistaken in its framing of the due process question as one concerning a legislative, rather than adjudicative, action. The Plaintiffs do not say that [the constitutional amendment or implementing statute] were enacted without due process of law. This alone makes the majority's reliance on Bi-Metallic [ ] misguided. . . . People are deprived of a protected due process interest when they cannot register to vote because they lack reliable information about their outstanding balances. . . . Because the [Division of Elections'] determinations [of voter eligibility based on those balances] are necessarily individualized and fact-specific, Florida's voter reenfranchisement scheme is one for which 'persons [are] . . . exceptionally affected, in each case upon individual grounds' and entitled to due process."

(c) In ONYX PROPS. LLC V. BD. OF CNTY. COMM'RS, 838 F.3d 1039 (10th Cir. 2016), the Board of County Commissioners of Elbert County, Colorado, discovered that the County zoning map had been lost and created a new one without following the procedures required by state law for doing so. That violation of state procedural requirements was not, however, a violation of the federal due process rights of property owners who had been required to comply with the new map in seeking a rezoning that would permit them to subdivide their properties. "Early in the last century the Supreme Court held that constitutional procedural due process does not govern the enactment of legislation. In Bi-Metallic the . . . Court held that a hearing was not constitutionally required for each affected landowner before the adoption of a generally applicable tax increase. It explained that such a requirement would be too burdensome, and the public had other means of influencing legislative decisions. . . . As the Supreme Court wrote decades after Bi-Metallic:

> In altering substantive rights through enactment of rules of general applicability, a legislature generally provides constitutionally adequate process simply by enacting the statute, publishing it, and, to the extent the statute regulates private conduct, affording those within the statute's reach a reasonable opportunity both to familiarize themselves with the general requirements imposed and to comply with those requirements.

United States v. Locke, 471 U.S. 84, 108 (1985). We recognize that not all actions by municipal boards are legislative. When the action has a limited focus (only a few people or properties are affected) and is based on grounds that are individually assessed, it may be more adjudicative than legislative and therefore subject to traditional procedural requirements of notice and hearing. . . . In such circumstances the need for additional procedural protections is greater because political remedies are often unattainable by individuals or small groups and the grant of procedural safeguards to a few does not impose as great a burden on government.

"Bi-Metallic controls here because . . . the adoption of a comprehensive zoning ordinance is a legislative act. A zoning plan is based on community-wide development goals, not on the particular facts of individual situations. It involves the discretionary implementation of prospective policies rather than the application of an existing policy to a specific landowner."

(d) In DECATUR LIQUORS, INC. V. DISTRICT OF COLUMBIA, 478 F.3d 360 (D.C. Cir. 2007), holders of liquor licenses sued the District of Columbia, claiming, among other things, that an amendment to the liquor code declaring a moratorium on off-premises single-unit sales of beer, malt liquor, and ale in a specified geographic area violated the U.S. Constitution. The court held that the District of Columbia did not violate license holders' due process rights by denying the affected licensees individualized notice and an opportunity to be heard. "Here, the moratorium zone covered all 73 liquor stores in Ward 4. This is the classic Bi-Metallic scenario—the statute prohibits the same conduct by all 73 licensees. Not only would individualized hearings be impractical, they would be unnecessary, as the only disputable issue would be the link between the forbidden sales and the District's legislative goal. Although there might be situations where the Due Process Clause entitled a party to a hearing on whether the relevant legislative purposes called for inclusion of the party's property within a special geographic zone, this is not such a case; the purpose of the moratorium zone was clear, and there is no dispute that encompassing all Ward 4 licensees matched the legislative goal."

(3) ***The Elements of the Distinction.*** The distinction between making a rule and adjudicating a case is one of the most basic in all of jurisprudence.

The APA's definitions of rule and adjudication, 5 U.S.C. §§ 551(4)–(7) (p. 236), quite fudge the issue. The definitions include in "rule" a statement of "particular applicability" and give "adjudication" a catchall meaning for any final disposition "other than rulemaking but including licensing"—but to grant a license is to make a statement of "particular applicability and future effect." Here are some materials that bear on the question of how the distinction is, as a general matter, to be drawn, and on the difficulties in doing so. Consider three different elements: (a) prospectivity, (b) generality, and (c) the rule of law.

(a) The element of prospectivity:

(i) 5 U.S.C. § 551(4) (emphasis added): " '[R]ule' means the whole or a part of an agency statement of general or particular applicability *and future effect* designed to implement, interpret, or prescribe law or policy or describing the organization, procedure, or practice requirements of an agency and includes the approval or prescription for the future of rates, wages, corporate or financial structures or reorganizations thereof, prices, facilities, appliances, services or allowances therefor or of valuations, costs, or accounting, or practices bearing on any of the foregoing."

(ii) JUSTICE HOLMES, in PRENTIS V. ATLANTIC COAST LINE CO., 211 U.S. 210, 226 (1908): "A judicial inquiry investigates, declares and enforces liabilities as they stand on present or past facts and under laws supposed already to exist. That is its purpose and end. Legislation on the other hand looks to the future and changes existing conditions by making a new rule to be applied thereafter to all or some part of those subject to its power. The establishment of a rate is the making of a rule for the future, and therefore is an act legislative not judicial in kind."

(iii) THOMAS M. COOLEY, A TREATISE ON THE CONSTITUTIONAL LIMITATIONS WHICH REST UPON THE LEGISLATIVE POWER OF THE STATES OF THE AMERICAN UNION 132 (7th ed. 1903 (Victor H. Lane, ed.)): "[I]t is said that that which distinguishes a judicial from a legislative act is, that the one is a determination of what the existing law is in relation to some existing thing already done or happened, while the other is a predetermination of what the law shall be for the regulation of all future cases falling under its provisions."

(iv) FREDERICK SCHAUER, A BRIEF NOTE ON THE LOGIC OF RULES, WITH SPECIAL REFERENCE TO BOWEN V. GEORGETOWN UNIVERSITY HOSPITAL, 42 Admin. L. Rev. 447, 454 (1990): "[N]othing . . . [in the distinction between whether a decision speaks forward or not] suggests one answer or another to the question of when 'the future' starts. Some decisions will pertain to a certain narrow temporal time frame, and these will be the 'orders,' and others will pertain to an open-ended time frame, and these are the 'rules,' but *that* distinction has nothing to do with when that time frame is or starts and nothing to do with the relationship between the time frame and the time of the making of the decision. To put the same point differently (and perhaps slightly more clearly), we are now able to appreciate that the creation of an open-ended rule and the designation of the starting time for the open-ended period encompassed by that rule are two distinct issues."

(b) The element of generality:

(i) RALPH F. FUCHS, PROCEDURE IN ADMINISTRATIVE RULE-MAKING, 52 Harv. L. Rev. 259, 263–64 (1938): "The most obvious definition of rule-making and the one most often employed in the literature of administrative law asserts simply that it is the function of laying down general regulations as distinguished from orders that apply to named persons or to specific situations. Most acts of legislatures, although by no means all, establish rights and duties with respect either to people generally or to classes of people or situations that are defined but not enumerated. Conversely, the judgments of courts usually are addressed to particular individuals or to situations that are definitely specified. Similarly, administrative action can be classified into general regulations, including determinations whose effect is to bring general regulations into operation, and orders or acts of specific application. . . .

"[I]t is feasible to distinguish a general regulation from an order of specific application on the basis of the manner in which the parties subject to it are designated. If they are named, or if they are in effect identified by their relation to a piece of property or transaction or institution which is specified, the order is one of specific application. If they are not named, but the order applies to a designated class of persons or situations, the order is a general regulation or a rule."

(ii) JOHN DICKINSON, ADMINISTRATIVE JUSTICE AND THE SUPREMACY OF LAW 17–20 (1927): "Our constitutional distinction between 'legislative,' 'executive' and 'judicial' powers draws the courts frequently into discussions in which the 'legislative' or 'executive' aspect of an administrative act is generally emphasized at the expense of the 'judicial.' Thus, for example, the act of a public-utilities commission in fixing a rate has been held to be 'legislative' for constitutional purposes.

"From one aspect of juristic analysis, legislative it no doubt is—that is, from the aspect of its future operation and its applicability to a whole class of cases. But the writ of mandamus is future in its operation, and yet is not for that reason regarded as legislative; and if we examine rate-fixing from the standpoint of the general applicability of the resulting rate to an indefinite number of future cases as a class, we observe the significant peculiarity that, while the rate applies indifferently, indeed, as against all future shippers, it applies only to the particular carrier or carriers who were parties to the hearing and other proceedings before the commission, and for whom, as the outcome of those proceedings, the rate is prescribed. From the standpoint of shippers, therefore, the rate may no doubt be regarded as legislation, but from the standpoint of the carriers it seems quite as truly adjudication. Even with respect to the shippers, however, it may be likened to the procedure whereby an injunction is obtained against a group of persons designated by a class-description and not named personally in the bill. If the latter procedure is judicial, there is certainly an element of adjudication in administrative rate-fixing; and that is all I wish to insist on here. There is no intention to deny that rate-fixing involves as one of its elements the exercise of a function which may as well as not be called 'legislative.' The whole discussion should go to demonstrate the futility of trying to classify a particular exercise of administrative power as either wholly legislative or wholly judicial. The tendency of the administrative procedure is to foreshorten both functions into a continuous governmental act."

(iii) RONALD M. LEVIN, THE CASE FOR (FINALLY) FIXING THE APA'S DEFINITION OF "RULE," 56 Admin. L. Rev. 1077, 1080 (2004): "[T]he ordinary understanding of a 'rule' is a governmental pronouncement that takes the form of a statute—a 'quasi-legislative' act that has 'general applicability.' Indeed, the due process foundations of the distinction between rules and adjudicative orders, reflected in a tradition that dates back to the venerable case of Bi-Metallic Investment Co. v. State Board of Equalization, are rooted in the distinction between generalized and particularized action. The classic doctrine holds that a regulated person has little if any constitutional right to a hearing in rulemaking, as opposed to adjudication, because of the impracticability of giving a hearing to numerous affected persons, and because 'legislative' rather than 'adjudicative' facts are likely to be involved. These rationales relate to generality, not prospectivity."

(c) The element of "the rule of law":

(i) FRIEDRICH A. HAYEK, THE CONSTITUTION OF LIBERTY 153–54 (1960): "The conception of freedom under the law . . . rests on the contention that when we obey laws, in the sense of general abstract rules laid down irrespective of their application to us, we are not subject to another man's will and are therefore free. It is because the lawgiver does not know the particular cases to which his rules will apply, and it is because the judge who applies them has no choice in drawing the conclusions that follow from the existing body of rules and the particular facts of the case, that it can be said that laws and not men rule. Because the rule is laid down in ignorance of the particular case and no man's will decides the coercion used to enforce it, the law is not arbitrary. This, however, is true only if by 'law' we mean the general rules that apply equally to everybody. This generality is probably the most important aspect of that attribute of law which we have called its 'abstractness.' As a true law should not name any particulars, so it should especially not single out any specific persons or group of persons."

(ii) KATIE R. EYER, ADMINISTRATIVE ADJUDICATION AND THE RULE OF LAW, 60 Admin. L. Rev. 647, 651 (2008): "[A]djudicative lawmaking theoretically has the potential to further a number of important rule-of-law goals. . . [including] the capacity to increase consistency in the legal standards applied to individual cases, promote predictability through rule creation, and restrain otherwise arbitrary discretion. . . . [T]he historically tepid academic view of adjudicative lawmaking by administrative agencies . . . is unwarranted—and is, in fact, dangerous—in cases where a decline in adjudicative lawmaking is unlikely to be accompanied by the creation of a legislative lawmaking program of comparable scope and vigor. Where such comparable substitutes are unlikely to be forthcoming, a reduction in an agency's use of adjudicative lawmaking is likely to have substantial negative effects, which should be cause for concern. . . .

"[C]ritiques of adjudicative lawmaking from a prospectivity perspective . . . may be of less importance than many authors have previously suggested. . . . [A]djudicative lawmaking—while it does create some prospectivity concerns in the short term and, in particular, as applied to the individual parties involved in the dispute—does not create a major deviation from the prospectivity norm over the long term. Most individuals will be subject to preexisting rules, and even those parties subject to ostensibly "new" rules created through adjudication will rarely be without forewarning that the new rule was forthcoming."

(iii) ROBERTO M. UNGER, KNOWLEDGE AND POLITICS 89–90 (1975): "To understand the nature of adjudication one must distinguish two different ways of ordering human relations. One way is to establish rules to govern general categories of acts and persons, and then to decide particular disputes among persons on the basis of the established rules. This is legal justice. The other way is to determine goals and then, quite independently of rules, to decide particular cases by a judgment of what decision is most likely to contribute to the predetermined goals, a judgment of instrumental rationality. This is substantive justice.

"In the situation of legal justice, the laws are made against the background of the ends they are designed to promote, even if the sole permissible end is liberty itself. Only after the rules have been formulated do decisions 'under the rules' become possible. Hence, the possibility of some sort of distinction between legislation and adjudication is precisely what defines legal justice. The main task of the theory of adjudication is to say when a decision can truly be said to stand 'under a rule,' if the rule we have in mind is the law of the state, applied by a judge. Only decisions 'under a rule' are consistent with freedom; others constitute arbitrary exercises of judicial power. . . .

"The distinctive feature of substantive justice is the nonexistence of any line between legislation and adjudication. In the pure case of substantive justice, there is neither rulemaking nor rule applying, because rather than prescriptive rules there are only choices as to what should be accomplished and judgments of instrumental rationality about how to get it done."

(4) ***Should Legislative Action Be Subject to Procedural Due Process Constraints?*** PETER M. SHANE, BACK TO THE FUTURE OF THE AMERICAN STATE: OVERRULING BUCKLEY V. VALEO AND OTHER MADISONIAN STEPS, 57 U. Pitt. L. Rev. 443, 455 (1996): "Under the current state of due process law, the Due Process Clauses exercise no procedural leverage over legislative deliberations. Under the relevant precedents, it is black-letter judicial interpretation that procedural due process attaches only to the government's adjudicatory processes and not to legislative-style decision making, even when conducted by an administrative agency. . . . But such a reading of the Due Process Clauses seems facially wrong. A proper analysis should begin with the proposition that limiting the reach of procedural due process to adjudication does not accord with the Constitution's text. The point seems

self-evident because the Due Process Clauses are routinely applied to the legislature in substantive due process cases. The question then ought to be posed whether legislative decisions that affect the rights and responsibilities of persons outside Congress deny liberty arbitrarily if such decisions are made under conditions in which no attention is given to the rudiments of sound decision-making procedure."

Shane's argument echoes one earlier made in Hans A. Linde, Due Process of Lawmaking, 55 Neb. L. Rev. 197 (1976). More recently, MAGGIE BLACKHAWK, in EQUITY OUTSIDE THE COURTS, 120 Colum. L. Rev. 2037, 2118 (2020), has argued "for an equivalence between the right protected by the Petition Clause" of the First Amendment ("the right of the people peaceably . . . to petition the Government for a redress of grievances") and "the right of procedural due process—a right that would mandate courts intervene in the lawmaking process sufficient to set a constitutional floor such that Congress must provide equal, transparent, and formal public access to the lawmaking process." On this view, "the courts would best protect due process by setting a minimum standard for process due to the public during the lawmaking process writ large. Rather than setting this process explicitly, however, it should force lawmaking institutions to establish a particular minimum level of process and to implement that process by the legislature's own terms. This is essentially the approach the Court took in Londoner when the city failed to follow its own procedures to provide notice and an opportunity to petition."

What about the possibility of applying procedural due process requirements to administrative rulemaking, notwithstanding the holding of Bi-Metallic? GILLIAN E. METZGER, in ORDINARY ADMINISTRATIVE LAW AS CONSTITUTIONAL COMMON LAW, 110 Colum. L. Rev. 479, 489–90 (2010), observes: "The Court periodically insists that procedural due process imposes no significant constraints on general policymaking. In doing so, however, it relies on precedents going back to the beginning of the twentieth century, before the advent of the modern administrative state, in which rulemaking is pervasive and agencies exercise broad discretion in devising requirements that can have a substantial impact on identified groups. The Court has not had to address the question of whether procedural due process requires some minimal level of notice and opportunity to be heard with respect to regulatory rulemaking in its modern form because the APA already mandates such procedures." That is, as Edward Rubin explains in It's Time to Make the Administrative Procedure Act Administrative, 89 Cornell L. Rev. 95, 111 (2003), "[t]he APA's requirements of notice, comments, and a statement of basis and purpose reiterate, in a diluted and adapted form, the due process requirements of notice, a hearing, and an impartial decision maker for adjudicatory decisions." Does it matter whether these statutory requirements (discussed at more length in Chapter IV) are constitutionally required, constitutionally inspired, or simply good governance practices? See generally Metzger, supra; Evan J. Criddle, When Delegation Begets Domination: Due Process of Administrative Lawmaking, 46 Georgia L. Rev. 117 (2011).

## b. The Fundamental Statute



This Section introduces the Administrative Procedure Act of 1946. The APA's core distinctions between the two fundamental categories of administrative action—rulemaking and adjudication—may feel familiar against the backdrop of the Londoner/Bi-Metallic distinction introduced in the previous Section. The first set of materials in this Section discusses the APA's definitions relevant to these two categories. The rest of the Section discusses the APA more generally, introducing background on its history and debates about the way the statute should be interpreted. These broader materials encompass not just the rulemaking/adjudication divide but also the statute's provisions on judicial review of agency action and litigants' access to courts to contest agency action. While subsequent chapters work through the APA's separate topics in more detail, this introductory material is generally relevant to thinking about the statute as a whole.

## ADMINISTRATIVE PROCEDURE ACT OF 1946[1]

5 U.S.C. § 551. Definitions. . .

(4) "rule" means the whole or a part of an agency statement of general or particular applicability and future effect designed to implement, interpret, or prescribe law or policy or describing the organization, procedure, or practice requirements of an agency and includes the approval or prescription for the future of rates, wages, corporate or financial structures or reorganization thereof, prices, facilities, appliances, services or allowances therefor or of valuations, costs, or accounting, or practices bearing on any of the foregoing;

(5) "rule making" means agency process for formulating, amending, or repealing a rule;

(6) "order" means the whole or a part of a final disposition, whether affirmative, negative, injunctive, or declaratory in form, of an agency in a matter other than rule making but including licensing;

(7) "adjudication" means agency process for the formulation of an order.

### NOTES ON THE APA DEFINITIONS

(1) ***Either a Rule or an Order.*** Note that the APA's definitions render *every* agency "final disposition, whether affirmative, negative, injunctive, or

---

[1] The full text of the APA appears in the Appendix, p. 1589.

declaratory in form" *either* a rule *or* an order. The latter—i.e., the products of "adjudication"—is the residual category. Sometimes application of these categories is quite obvious. Consider, for example, the Department of Transportation's tarmac delay rule discussed in Chapter I (p. 16): in setting standards governing airlines' treatment of passengers subject to lengthy delays on the runway, the agency was clearly "prescrib[ing] law or policy" with "general . . . applicability and future effect." Similarly, when DOT fines a particular airline for a violation of this rule (p. 18), it sets forth its findings and decision in a "final disposition" that is clearly an order.

Sometimes, however, the application of the categories is a little less clear. Chapter IV explores the difficulties presented by the definition of "rule." Here, observe that the definition sections give two concrete examples of their application: The definition of an "order" includes "licensing," and the definition of a "rule" includes "the approval or prescription for the future of rates, wages, corporate or financial structures or reorganization thereof, prices, facilities, appliances, services or allowances therefor or of valuations, costs, or accounting, or practices." Both licensing and ratemaking are somewhat ambiguous in Londoner/Bi-Metallic terms; each typically involves particular applicants for rate approvals or licenses whose individual facts will be central to a decision, on one side, and broadly diverse community interests and more general issues of fact on the other. Moreover, APA licensing procedures are more lenient in important ways than the ordinary APA procedures for on-the-record adjudication, and APA ratemaking procedures are more formal than the notice-and-comment procedures typically used to develop a typical rule. Even though licensing is explicitly mentioned in the general definition of adjudication, various portions of the provisions governing adjudication—§§ 554(d), 556(d), and 557(b)—make special provisions for initial licensing (the application process). So does § 558 of the Act, which governs not only the application process but also the suspension, revocation, and expiration of licenses. Similarly, ratemaking gets special treatment as a type of formal rulemaking, and is even mentioned in § 554(d), a provision about adjudication. These procedural variations are roughly equivalent and create a formal procedure of somewhat lesser intensity than ordinary on-the-record adjudication for both the kind of adjudication that is action on an initial license application and the kind of rulemaking that is ratemaking. In this concrete way, the Act's provisions accommodate the ambiguities of both the definitional sections and the constitutional test.

(2) ***Formal and Informal Agency Proceedings.*** The APA distinguishes between formal and informal versions of both rulemaking and adjudication. This is done not by means of additional definitions, but rather by making those sections of the Act which define formal hearings (§§ 556 and 557) applicable only to certain proceedings: those required to be "on the record." Thus, we find within § 553, "Rule making," that an informal procedure is defined in § 553(c), but that the subsection ends by saying: "When rules are required by statute to be made on the record after opportunity for an agency hearing, sections 556 and 557 of this title apply instead of this subsection." In turn, § 554, "Adjudications," opens by saying that it applies "in every case

of adjudication required by statute to be determined on the record after opportunity for an agency hearing"; § 554(c)(2) subsequently indicates that such adjudications shall provide the opportunity for "hearing and decision on notice and in accordance with sections 556 and 557 of this title." There is no general APA provision governing informal adjudication—that is, those adjudications that are *not* "required by statute to be determined on the record after opportunity for an agency hearing"—but isolated provisions of § 555, "Ancillary matters," provide some requirements, including prompt notice of denials of requests, "accompanied by a brief statement of the grounds for denial" unless the denial is self-explanatory or in affirmation of a previous denial. See § 555(e). Chapters IV and V work through these definitions and requirements in more depth.

## NOTES ON THE HISTORY OF THE APA

(1) ***The Background of the APA.*** The Court's early views of the APA were showcased in WONG YANG SUNG V. MCGRATH, 339 U.S. 33 (1950). Wong Yang Sung, a citizen of China, was arrested and charged with being unlawfully in the United States through overstaying his shore leave as a member of a shipping crew. After an administrative hearing, an immigration inspector recommended deportation; the acting Commissioner approved and the Board of Immigration Appeals affirmed. Wong Yang Sung then filed a habeas corpus proceeding in District Court for the District of Columbia, claiming that the administrative hearing was not conducted in conformity with provisions of the APA addressing what we now call Administrative Law Judges. Those provisions provide, inter alia, that officers presiding at formal hearings under the APA shall be independent of officers engaged in prosecution or investigation and shall have protection against dismissal. Although the government admitted that the hearing did not comply with the APA, it asserted that the Act did not apply to deportation hearings. In holding that the APA did apply, the Supreme Court in an opinion by JUSTICE JACKSON discussed in detail the history and purposes of the Act:

"Multiplication of federal administrative agencies and expansion of their functions to include adjudications which have serious impact on private rights has been one of the dramatic legal developments of the past half-century. Partly from restriction by statute, partly from judicial self-restraint, and partly by necessity—from the nature of their multitudinous and semi-legislative or executive tasks—the decisions of administrative tribunals were accorded considerable finality, and especially with respect to fact finding. The conviction developed, particularly within the legal profession, that this power was not sufficiently safeguarded and sometimes was put to arbitrary and biased use.

"Concern over administrative impartiality and response to growing discontent was reflected in Congress as early as 1929, when Senator Norris introduced a bill to create a separate administrative court. . . . The Executive Branch of the Federal Government also became concerned as to whether the structure and procedure of these bodies was conducive to fairness in the administrative process. . . . The President early in 1939 . . . directed the Attorney General to name 'a committee of eminent lawyers, jurists, scholars, and administrators to review the entire administrative process in the various departments of the executive Government and to recommend improvements, including the suggestion of any needed legislation.' ... So strong was the demand for reform, however, that Congress did not await the Committee's report but passed what was known as the Walter-Logan bill, a comprehensive and rigid prescription of standardized procedures for administrative agencies. This bill was vetoed by President Roosevelt December 18, 1940, and the veto was sustained by the House. But the President's veto message made no denial of the need for reform. Rather it pointed out that the task of the Committee, whose objective was 'to suggest improvements to make the process more workable and just,' had proved 'unexpectedly complex.' The President said, 'I should desire to await their report and recommendations before approving any measure in this complicated field.' ...

"The McCarran-Sumners bill, which evolved into the present Act, was introduced in 1945. Its consideration and hearing, especially of agency interests, was painstaking. ... It passed both Houses without opposition and was signed by President Truman June 11, 1946. ... The Act thus represents a long period of study and strife; it settles long-continued and hard-fought contentions, and enacts a formula upon which opposing social and political forces have come to rest. It contains many compromises and generalities and, no doubt, some ambiguities. Experience may reveal defects. But it would be a disservice to our form of government and to the administrative process itself if the courts should fail, so far as the terms of the Act warrant, to give effect to its remedial purposes where the evils it was aimed at appear. ...

"Of the several administrative evils sought to be cured or minimized, only two are particularly relevant to issues before us today. One purpose was to introduce greater uniformity of procedure and standardization of administrative practice among the diverse agencies whose customs had departed widely from each other. We pursue this no further than to note that any exception we may find to its applicability would tend to defeat this purpose.

"More fundamental, however, was the purpose to curtail and change the practice of embodying in one person or agency the duties of prosecutor and judge. ... [T]he Attorney General's Committee on Administrative Procedure, which divided as to the appropriate remedy, was unanimous that this evil existed. Its Final Report said: 'These types of commingling of functions of investigation or advocacy with the function of deciding are thus plainly undesirable. But they are also avoidable and should be avoided by appropriate internal division of labor. For the disqualifications produced by investigation or advocacy are personal psychological ones which result from engaging in those types of activity; and the problem is simply one of isolating those who engage in the activity.' Rep. Atty. Gen. Comm. Ad. Proc. 56 (1941), S. Doc. No. 8, 77th Cong., 1st Sess. 56 (1941). ...

"Turning now to the case before us, we find the administrative hearing a perfect exemplification of the practices so unanimously condemned. ... This hearing, which followed the uniform practice of the Immigration Service, was before an immigrant inspector, who, for purposes of the hearing, is called the 'presiding inspector.' Except with consent of the alien, the presiding inspector may not be the one who investigated the case. But the inspector's duties include investigation of like cases; and while he is today hearing cases investigated by a colleague, tomorrow his investigation of a case may be heard before the [examining] inspector whose case he passes on today. . . . The presiding inspector, when no examining inspector is present, is required to 'conduct the interrogation of the alien and the witnesses in behalf of the Government and shall cross-examine the alien's witnesses and present such evidence as is necessary to support the charges in the warrant of arrest.' 8 C.F.R. 150.6(b). . . .

"The Administrative Procedure Act did not go so far as to require a complete separation of investigating and prosecuting functions from adjudicating functions. But that the safeguards it did set up were intended to ameliorate the evils from the commingling of functions as exemplified here is beyond doubt. And this commingling, if objectionable anywhere, would seem to be particularly so in the deportation proceeding, where we frequently meet with a voteless class of litigants who not only lack the influence of citizens, but who are strangers to the laws and customs in which they find themselves involved and who often do not even understand the tongue in which they are accused. Nothing in the nature of the parties or proceedings suggests that we should strain to exempt deportation proceedings from reforms in administrative procedure applicable generally to federal agencies.

"Nor can we accord any weight to the argument that to apply the Act to such hearings will cause inconvenience and added expense to the Immigration Service. Of course it will, as it will to nearly every agency to which it is applied. But the power of the purse belongs to Congress, and Congress has determined that the price for greater fairness is not too high. The agencies, unlike the aliens, have ready and persuasive access to the legislative ear and if error is made by including them, relief from Congress is a simple matter. . . .

"[T]he difficulty with . . . [the government's] argument . . . that the deportation statute does not require a hearing is that, without such hearing, there would be no constitutional authority for deportation. . . . When the Constitution requires a hearing, it requires a fair one, one before a tribunal which meets at least currently prevailing standards of impartiality. A deportation hearing involves issues basic to human liberty and happiness and, in the present upheavals in lands to which aliens may be returned, perhaps to life itself. It might be difficult to justify as measuring up to constitutional standards of impartiality a hearing tribunal for deportation proceedings the like of which has been condemned by Congress as unfair even where less vital matters of property rights are at stake."

The Court's confidence about Congress's purposes was apparently misplaced, for the specific holding of Wong Yang Sung that § 554 of the APA applies to deportation proceedings was promptly reversed by legislation, and that reversal was subsequently upheld against constitutional challenge. See Marcello v. Bonds, 349 U.S. 302 (1955). Courts continue to cite Wong Yang Sung for the general proposition that noncitizens have due process rights in deportation hearings, but they no longer reason that the APA embodies

Congress's assessment of the procedures the Constitution requires. Chapter V explores the reasoning courts now use in giving concrete content to the requirements of due process in different kinds of hearings.

(2) ***On the APA's Adoption.*** Unanimously passed in both House and Senate in 1946, the APA emerged after a lengthy period of debate and development. Justice Jackson, President Roosevelt's Attorney General from 1940 to 1941, participated in the development of the APA at an early stage. Thus, his opinion in Wong Yang Sung reflects the knowledge possessed by the generation of its framers. As the excerpts from that opinion note, it emerged from a long political back and forth in reaction to the New Deal that, in 1939, led President Roosevelt to direct the Attorney General to form a committee to study administrative reform and propose legislation. The director of the Attorney General's Committee on Administrative Procedure was Walter Gellhorn, the first editor of this casebook; the Committee's final report, Sen. Doc. 8, 77th Cong. 1st Sess. (1941), has long been regarded as an exemplar of empirical study of government functioning. World War II then intervened, and the Act was passed after hearings and negotiations that began as that war drew to a close.

Subsequent scholarly accounts have offered additional views on the political context of the APA's adoption. Here are four excerpts:

(a) GEORGE B. SHEPHERD, FIERCE COMPROMISE: THE ADMINISTRATIVE PROCEDURE ACT EMERGES FROM NEW DEAL POLITICS, 90 Nw. U. L. Rev. 1557, 1560, 1680–82 (1996): "The APA's development was not primarily a search for administrative truth and efficiency. Nor was it a theoretically centered debate on appropriate roles for government and governed. Instead, the fight over the APA was a pitched political battle for the life of the New Deal. . . .

"In the debate and negotiations that led to the APA, scientific improvement of the administrative process was only a secondary concern. The APA was the armistice of a fierce political battle over administrative reform. The forces in the battle fought over the degree to which Congress would permit Roosevelt, through his agencies, to implement the New Deal. The political combatants used code words to describe their objectives. The administration, including Gellhorn as the Attorney General's Committee's director, sought agency 'efficiency.' Efficiency meant agencies' ability to implement New Deal programs quickly, without interference from either cumbersome procedural requirements or intrusive judicial review. In contrast, conservatives sought 'individual rights,' which were individuals' and businesses' rights to prevent an agency from implementing New Deal programs unless the agency both jumped through numerous procedural hoops and received the blessing of a conservative federal judge—until late in the Roosevelt administration, most federal judges were conservatives who would often strike down New Deal programs. Strong individual rights would hinder implementation of New Deal programs because of both administrative and judicial procedural delay and because of judicial rejection of the programs. To conservatives, agency efficiency was irrelevant. Indeed, conservatives opposed efficiency. An agency that inefficient procedures hamstrung was an agency that could not implement liberal New Deal programs.

"The degree to which Congress would permit Roosevelt to implement New Deal programs was an issue that scientific investigation of optimum agency practice could not resolve. The issue was political. Liberals and conservatives resolved the issue politically by means of the partisan battles and negotiations that produced the APA. It is no coincidence that the groups that favored and opposed strong administrative procedural reform were exactly the same groups that opposed and favored New Deal programs.

"Conservatives agreed to the APA not because they had come to approve of agency power, but because they had no choice; the administration would veto any stronger bill. As conservatives grudgingly voted for the bill, they indicated their preference for far stronger limits on agencies. Similarly, conservatives unanimously agreed to a bill that confirmed many existing agency practices not because conservatives had begun to recognize the practices' merits. Instead, the bill's weakness displeased conservatives. As their comments during debates directly before the APA's passage show, they would have preferred much stronger legislation. Nonetheless, they had no choice but to vote for the bill unanimously. To conservatives, small reform was better than no reform. But small reform was all that conservatives could hope to achieve. The administration could block stricter reform.

"Only after political warfare and negotiation had determined the fundamental balance between efficiency and individual rights could scientific investigation into the administrative process play a role. Experts on the administrative process could then suggest the soundest means for implementing the combatants' agreement. However, the scientific tweaking could have only modest impact. Politics had already determined the important issues. . . .

(b) In "A 'Bill of Rights' for the American State," the second chapter of THE UNWIELDY AMERICAN STATE: ADMINISTRATIVE POLITICS SINCE THE NEW DEAL 59–108 (2012), JOANNA L. GRISINGER gives a historical account that is less of fierce political struggles than of progressive moderation of perspectives from the American Bar Association resulting in accommodations, and in a "bill of rights for the administrative process . . . more complicated than that hopeful language suggested. Comparing the rhetoric that surrounded the APA with its practical effects suggests that the act did more to change opinions about the administrative process than to change the inner workings of the agencies. The act protected existing informal procedures, thus allowing cooperative relationships between regulated parties and agency officials to continue. At the same time, it made sure that those same parties had formal tools to challenge administrative action they opposed. . . . [T]he APA did not resolve questions about how to separate functions in the agencies and commissions. Nor did it end questions over who should be included in the hearing examiner corps or the appropriate level of judicial review for administrative action.

"Triumphalist language surrounding the APA did serve to insulate subsequent administrative activity and administrative reform from attack. As Kenneth Culp Davis famously argued in 1951, 'The battle over fundamentals had ceased. The federal administrative process was secure.' . . ."

(c) MATHEW MCCUBBINS, ROGER NOLL, & BARRY WEINGAST (collectively MCNOLLGAST), THE POLITICAL ORIGINS OF THE ADMINISTRATIVE PROCEDURE ACT, 15 J.L. Econ. & Org. 180, 182–83 (1999): "[T]he passage and structure of the APA presents many puzzles. . . . For example, why did New Deal Democrats change their position on procedural due process and agree to pass procedural limitations on agencies in 1946? Furthermore, why did the parties in Congress form a 'grand coalition' in favor of the APA? Why did it take until 1946 to codify procedural due process, given that much of the APA had been proposed a decade before? Why did Congress enact some proposals regarding procedural due process but not others? . . .

"Two profound partisan changes that took place in the 1940s provide answers to many of these questions. First, New Deal Democrats realized that their prospects for retaining the presidency were growing increasingly dim after Roosevelt's death in 1945. The New Dealers could no longer count on an executive administration that was sympathetic to New Deal policies and that would continue to implement its policies more or less in the ways that New Dealers preferred. This fear provided New Deal supporters with the incentive to consolidate the gains of the New Deal thus far. Second, following 13 years of unbroken Democratic control of the presidency, the character of the judiciary had changed substantially from the high point of conflict between 1932 and 1937. As a result, the New Dealers no longer feared a combative relationship with the courts if they delegated to them the responsibility to enforce the procedural due process requirements. In sum, by 1946, the New Dealers in Congress had an interest in consolidating their policy gains against the possible antipathy of a Republican presidency, and they could finally count on the courts to favor New Deal programs in adjudicating procedural provisions.

"The importance of this argument, if true, is that it demonstrates that more was at stake in the establishment of administrative procedure than fairness, equity, concern for individual liberties, and administrative efficiency. Because the very future of the New Deal was at stake, political preferences over economic outcomes as well as prosaic political strategizing and coalition building played major roles in shaping the foundations for the present administrative state. Liberal Democrats accepted legislative formalization of procedural due process and a greater role for judicial review only when it appeared to be advantageous to their interests and when combined in a logroll that consolidated the gains of the New Deal and empowered Congress vis-à-vis the executive."

(d) In THE ORIGINS OF THE APA: MISREMEMBERED AND FORGOTTEN VIEWS, 28 Geo. Mason L. Rev. 547, 567–69, 572 (2021), JEREMY RABKIN offers a competing view: "It is not persuasive to depict the APA as emerging from a 'pitched political battle for the life of the New Deal' in which '[c]onservatives sought to use administrative reform as a means to stop the New Deal,' as political scientists have contended. . . . Republican majorities gained control of both houses of Congress only a few months after enactment of the APA. They did impose new controls on the National Labor Relations Board, [but] [t]hey did not seek to alter the terms of the APA. Nor did they seek to do so after the 1952 elections, when renewed Republican congressional majorities could rely on a Republican president not to threaten a veto on wider measures. A dozen years later, Democrats won commanding majorities in both houses of Congress, while a Democratic president supported legislation to establish new regulatory agencies and programs. No one seems to have thought it would be logical to protect or enhance these programs by rewriting the APA.

"This subsequent history undermines the notion that the APA was, at the time, a painful compromise between supporters and opponents of the New Deal. Another, related reason for doubting such claims is that liberals and conservatives—or regulatory enthusiasts and regulatory skeptics—have changed sides on many fundamental elements of regulatory control. New Dealers preached trust in agency expertise, while liberals of the 1970s and 1980s, welcoming challenges from public interest legal advocates, urged courts to challenge administrative torpor and ensure that agencies take a 'hard look' at policy alternatives. Conservatives saw courts as essential guarantors for the rule of law in the 1930s; by the 1980s, as courts took up claims from environmental and consumer advocacy groups, conservatives preached judicial restraint and deference to agency expertise. Conservatives had distrusted presidential authority under FDR in the 1930s but under Republican presidents in the 1970s and 1980s embraced it with enthusiasm. Particular institutional arrangements do not have settled political valence. The institutional loyalties of parties and constituencies will vary as the surrounding political context changes. That lesson of subsequent history would no doubt have occurred to members of Congress even in 1946. . . .

"The APA sought to settle no more than seemed necessary at the time. That has probably helped explain its durability. It codified what its drafters could agree upon at the time as a guide to sound or fair procedure. For all the limitations in what they set down, they were not simply negotiating a partisan truce in a set of partisan disputes about contending policy priorities. They recognized that debate would continue on many issues but did not dismiss such debate as mere partisan posturing."

(3) ***Amending the APA?*** The APA is the foundational document governing the administrative state. And yet, with the notable exception of the 1966 Freedom of Information Act, which the APA incorporates and which you may study in Chapter VI, the APA has been little amended in the more than 75 years since its enactment. This lack of amendment is particularly striking in light of changes elsewhere in the legal environment that have made notice-and-comment rulemaking rather than ratemaking and formal adjudication the dominant procedures of concern. Congress has considered legislative proposals to reform the regulatory process with regularity during the first two decades of the twenty-first century, but none has become law.

How should we understand the lack of change to the APA's core requirements for rulemaking? Does it reflect the longlasting value of those statutory requirements? Is it instead due to political dynamics that limit plausible paths forward for reform? Is legislative reform unnecessary in light of reforms stemming from doctrine and the development of presidential control? Is it a sign that the APA is less relevant than it once was for administrative practice? For consideration of these and related questions, see Stuart Shapiro, The Impossibility of Legislative Regulatory Reform and the Futility of Executive Regulatory Reform, 28 Geo. Mason L. Rev. 717 (2021); Christopher J. Walker, The Lost World of the Administrative Procedure Act: A Literature Review, 28 Geo. Mason L. Rev. 733 (2021); Edward Rubin, It's Time to Make the Administrative Procedure Act Administrative, 89 Cornell L. Rev. 95 (2003).

Numerous other writings identify important omissions in or underdeveloped aspects of the APA. For example, the APA does little to govern the vast array of adjudications that take place under statutes that do not require formal adjudication. Michael Asimow, Federal Administrative Adjudication Outside the Administrative Procedure Act (2019); Emily S. Bremer, The Exceptionalism Norm in Administrative Adjudication, 2019 Wisc. L. Rev. 1351. Especially as implemented by the courts, the APA does little to protect or foster "internal administrative law," defined as "the internal directives, guidance, and organizational forms through which agencies structure the discretion of their employees and presidents control the workings of the executive branch." Gillian E. Metzger & Kevin M. Stack, Internal Administrative Law, 115 Mich. L. Rev. 1239, 1239 (2017). The APA does not address the role of the White House in the operation of the administrative state. Daniel A. Farber & Anne Joseph O'Connell, The Lost World of Administrative Law, 92 Tex. L. Rev. 1137 (2014); Elena Kagan, Presidential Administration, 114 Harv. L. Rev. 2245 (2001). And while administrative law can be a tool either to remedy or entrench racial subordination, the APA itself has provisions "that courts have used to scrub antidiscrimination from American administrative law." Cristina Isabel Ceballos, David Freeman Engstrom, & Daniel Ho, Disparate Limbo: How Administrative Law Erased Antidiscrimination, 131 Yale L.J. 370, 381 (2021). The savvy administrative lawyer must not only master the APA but also be aware of other sources of governing law, some of which are discussed at pp. 252–253 below. Should the APA be updated to account for these gaps?

## NOTES ON INTERPRETING THE APA

(1) ***The Supreme Court's Changing Approaches.*** Describing the Court's approach to interpreting the APA over the Act's first 50 years, PETER L. STRAUSS, in CHANGING TIMES: THE APA AT FIFTY, 63 U. Chi. L. Rev. 1389, 1392–93 (1996), identified "roughly . . . three phases. [The APA] was produced against a backdrop of empirical study and political contention; it used broad strokes, in the language of those who had participated in the studies and struggles, to address practical problems. In its first years, the lawyers and judges who litigated and decided issues about its meaning had been, to a greater or lesser extent, witnesses to its creation, and they evidently expected their experiences to contribute to the statute's interpretation; . . . the habits of using legislative materials to illuminate statutory text were firmly in place.

"In the middle period, represented here by the procedural ferment and paradigm shifts of the seventies, lawyers' arguments were less likely to draw upon the debates of the forties, and the Court proved willing to reinterpret the text to fit contemporary developments. The apparent exception to that trend, Vermont Yankee Nuclear Power Corp. v. NRDC [p. 312], might be thought to have involved a lower court's effort to give the statute meaning outside any reasonable possibility offered by the text, rather than a more general refusal to accommodate that text to contemporary understandings.

"Most recently, in the third phase, the Court has turned to formalism in matters of textual interpretation. Rejecting partnership assumptions about its relation with Congress that have characterized thinking about statutes since early in this century, it takes text as both time-bound and limiting. For the APA, that makes decisions turn on what its words would have been understood to mean as a matter of standard usage in 1946—usage independent of the political context and debates."

According to GILLIAN E. METZGER, THE ROBERTS COURT AND ADMINISTRATIVE LAW, 2019 Sup. Ct. Rev. 1, 55–57 (2019), this third phase has continued during the Roberts Court, but not entirely consistently: "[T]he Roberts Court has equivocated between textualist and common law approaches to major administrative law statutes. . . . [T]he Justices' views on textualist versus common law interpretations of administrative law statutes do not track their ideological divisions or overall stance on administrative government. Instead, many individual Justices oscillate between administrative law textualism and a more common law stance, as does the Court as a whole. To some extent, this oscillation may reflect the specific administrative law measures at issue. For example, FOIA's text is far more detailed and more recently amended than the APA . . . [while] not only are the APA's procedural requirements more detailed and specific than its judicial review provisions, but the Court has allowed courts more leeway to develop the latter. Significantly, however, such oscillation between APA textualism and administrative common law is not a new phenomenon. For many decades, the Court has periodically rejected administrative common law as being at odds with the APA while simultaneously developing new administrative common law doctrines. Despite this oscillation, the common law approach to the APA has dominated, especially in the area of judicial review."

(2) ***Evaluating the Approaches: APA Textualism, APA Originalism, and Administrative Common Law.*** While scholars generally agree as a descriptive matter that the Court's approaches to APA interpretation are changing, they disagree as a normative matter on what courts should be doing. Consider these excerpts:

(a) JOHN F. DUFFY, ADMINISTRATIVE COMMON LAW IN JUDICIAL REVIEW, 77 Tex. L. Rev. 113, 115–17, 141–44 (1998): "Anglo-American courts traditionally follow one of two methods to decide a case. Under the common-law method, a court decides a case without guidance from any textual codification of law and policy. . . . A second method—one that has become increasingly important in this age of statutes—turns on the interpretation of an authoritative, extra-judicial text. . . . One might expect that administrative law would be a most unlikely place to find an enormous body of judicially developed common law. Administrative agencies, after all, blossomed in the late nineteenth and early twentieth centuries as an alternative to regulation by common-law courts; their creation signaled a rejection of the common-law system. Enthusiasm for new expert agencies was coupled with pessimism about the ability of generalist courts to develop law consonant with changing modern conditions. Moreover, the substantive law applied by federal agencies was—and still is—statutory law. And, of course, ever since 1946 there has been the APA. . . . [But] judicial review of agency action remains dominated today by judge-made law. . . .

"Part of the thesis of this article is descriptive—that these anachronistic doctrines are, in fact, decaying and giving way to new law grounded in textual interpretation of the APA. But I also believe that this change in administrative law is a positive development. . . . The first reason is quite pragmatic: It is that the judge-made doctrines critiqued in this article are inherently unstable. These doctrines are not instances where the courts have confronted statutory law and interpreted it in a way that reconciles the relevant statutory provisions with the judge-made law. Rather, the courts have been able to maintain the common-law doctrines targeted in this article only by ignoring statutory law. But ignoring statutes does not make them go away. . . .

"The administrative common law could, of course, be stabilized by reinvigorating the New Federal Common Law—by returning to that era's confidence in federal judicial legislation. But such a move would be a return to an aberration in the history of the federal courts. . . .

"Finally, the demise of New Federal Common Law reinforces a basic symmetry of the constitutional order. The requirement of lawful authorization for federal common law—the requirement that federal courts be able to point to a federal enactment, constitutional or statutory, authorizing them to create law—may sound formalistic. It is. But it is a formalism that courts charged with reviewing the legality of agency actions can appreciate, for in cases ranging from the routine to the momentous, the courts constantly require all government officials to ground their authority in some statutory or constitutional text."

(b) GILLIAN E. METZGER, EMBRACING ADMINISTRATIVE COMMON LAW, 80 Geo. Wash. L. Rev. 1293, 1296–97 (2012): "This Foreword argues for explicit judicial recognition and acceptance of administrative common law. Administrative common law serves an important function in our separation of powers system, a system that makes it difficult for Congress or the President to oust the courts as developers of administrative law. In particular, the institutional features of administrative law—the role it plays in structuring relationships between different government institutions and the requirements it imposes on how agencies operate—create strong pressures on courts to play a lawmaking role. Moreover, courts have employed administrative common law as a central mechanism through which to ameliorate the constitutional tensions raised by the modern administrative state. These features combine to make administrative common law inevitable. Although in theory courts could forego administrative common law, in practice any such result is both highly unlikely and quite undesirable.

"As significant, administrative common law represents a legitimate instance of judicial lawmaking. The very same factors that support federal common law in other instances—unique federal interests at stake, a need for uniformity, and the impropriety of relying on state law—dominate federal administrative contexts. Federalism concerns are thus absent, and administrative common law actually serves separation of powers values. Administrative common law's legitimacy also follows from recognizing that no sharp divide separates statutory and common law. Much administrative common law has a statutory basis to which it is at least loosely tethered. Moreover, administrative common law's constitutional character—reinforcing constitutional prohibitions on arbitrary governmental action and advancing values of fairness, checked power, and political accountability—counsels against imputing congressional displacement. Indeed, this constitutional basis means that administrative common law closely resembles other well-established invocations of constitutional values in statutory interpretation.

"The argument for embracing administrative common law goes beyond establishing that it is ubiquitous, inevitable, and legitimate. Openly acknowledging the role that judicial lawmaking plays in administrative contexts is critical to clarifying and improving administrative law. Some may fear that the potential for opening the door to greater judicial experimentation is a reason to avoid overt acceptance of administrative common law. But the courts' failure to acknowledge their development of administrative law is unlikely to stop the practice. Instead, the result is simply less transparency and engagement as to the proper form such judicial development should take, along with greater confusion about how courts should approach recurring issues in administrative law. Equally troubling, to the extent that this failure does inhibit administrative common law, it may lead courts to forego developing administrative law in new and potentially beneficial ways."

(c) KATHRYN E. KOVACS, SUPERSTATUTE THEORY AND ADMINISTRATIVE COMMON LAW, 90 Indiana L.J. 1207, 1209–11 (2015): "In this Article, I view the APA through the lens of an important new theory of statutory interpretation: William Eskridge and John Ferejohn's theory of superstatutes [as defined in WILLIAM N. ESKRIDGE, JR. & JOHN FEREJOHN, A REPUBLIC OF STATUTES: THE NEW AMERICAN CONSTITUTION (2010), and connected to the theory of dynamic statutory interpretation (p. 127)]. . . . Professors Eskridge and Ferejohn employ the term 'superstatute' to refer to statutes that have become 'entrenched' in America's statutory constitution. They are enacted 'after lengthy normative debate' and 'prove robust as a solution, a standard, or a norm over time.' Although Eskridge and Ferejohn did not identify the APA as a superstatute, the Act exemplifies this idea: it resulted from years of legislative activity and has become deeply entrenched.

". . . Eskridge and Ferejohn posit that superstatutes are and should be interpreted dynamically and evolutively to grow and change over time. Hence, one might assume that dubbing the APA a superstatute would lend support to the scholars who applaud the courts' continued development of administrative common law. Applying superstatute theory to the APA, however, yields a surprising result because the APA differs from most other federal superstatutes in one important respect: no single agency is charged with its implementation. Single-agency implementation is not a requirement for superstatute status, but it is central to the assertion that superstatutes should be interpreted broadly and evolutively. That assertion is built on a civic-republican model of deliberation that necessitates public involvement in legal change. In the absence of direct public engagement through an election, Eskridge and Ferejohn's model of deliberation puts a single agency at the center of an interpretive web, with the other branches of government and the public intertwined. Unlike most other superstatutes, however, agencies are not the primary interpreters of the APA—courts are. And courts are not deliberative in the civic-republican sense that superstatute theory demands to legitimize evolutive interpretation.

"Eskridge and Ferejohn posit that judicial review of superstatutes should respect and encourage public deliberation. In the APA's case, that means the courts should adhere more closely to the compromises encoded in the statute's text and hesitate before moving too far towards the boundaries of the text's possible meaning. Given the extraordinary legislative process that led to the APA's enactment and the relative paucity of agency-based deliberative feedback since then, courts should be particularly chary of interpreting the APA's text in a way that shifts the balance Congress reached through the political process. Courts should look more closely at the context and history of the APA's individual provisions, including Congress's treatment of each provision in the original legislative process and the quality of deliberation the provision has seen since enactment."

(d) EVAN D. BERNICK, ENVISIONING ADMINISTRATIVE PROCEDURE ACT ORIGINALISM, 70 Admin. L. Rev. 807, 824–25, 855–67 (2018): "Although administrative common law is pervasive, its rise has not gone unchecked. Today, it faces new challenges. Several scholars have argued that certain administrative common law doctrines and agency practices are inconsistent with the APA's original meaning. A recent proposal to amend the APA represents an effort to return to the APA's original meaning. Although the judiciary has not yet embraced anything that can reasonably be called APA originalism, several federal appellate judges have expressed doubts about whether certain administrative common law doctrines can be squared with the APA. . . . The possibility of APA originalism catching on must be taken seriously. . . .

"The most basic argument in favor of the judicial implementation of APA originalism is that the original APA is the law. . . . If the original APA, taken as a whole, is normatively good enough to be implemented as written, APA originalism could reinforce the perceived legitimacy of the administrative state. Perhaps the most enduring argument against the administrative state is that it is somehow lawless. The argument that all administrative agencies are in fact constrained by the text of a presumptively legitimate statute and that their compliance with it is judicially monitored and enforced as consistently as resources allow could go a long way towards countering that charge, were that argument advanced convincingly. . . . APA originalism may promote the rule of law by taking certain doctrinal options that produce unnecessary complexity off the table. . . . Even if the original APA is suboptimal in certain respects, there are powerful reasons to think that judges should not try to improve upon it. The judicial displacement of perfectly constitutional and popular legislative decisions on the ground that they violate judge-made doctrines that judges deem net-beneficial, seems democratically illegitimate. . . .

"[On the other hand, i]f most litigated cases involving the APA center around text that is vague or ambiguous, APA originalism may either give us more of the same administrative common law or—perhaps worse—administrative common law presented by judges as the command of clear text. . . . Decisions that those who enacted the APA likely expected to be made in an adjudicatory context and subject to the APA's rigorous procedural safeguards and judicial review standards are now made through informal rulemaking or highly informal nonlegislative guidances and policy statements. Ironically, returning to the original meaning of the APA might move us even further away from the balance between energy, expertise, accountability, and rights-protection that the APA was designed to establish. . . . Even if originalism in theory allows room for the construction of net-beneficial doctrines that do not contradict the APA's text, it does not follow that those doctrines will survive. And net-beneficial doctrines that do contradict the APA's text will certainly be placed in jeopardy. . . . APA originalists . . . will have to consider whether their methodology will outperform alternatives under second-best conditions. Perhaps the best of possible worlds would be one in which original APA has since 1946 been consistently enforced, but that is not our world. It is, therefore, not necessarily the case that efforts by judges today to consistently enforce the original APA would improve upon the status quo. Perhaps judges should instead make compensating adjustments to restore the balance of values that the APA was designed to establish but which are not consistent with the original meaning of the APA's text. . . ."

(3) ***A Note on Sources.*** The legislative history of the APA has often played a role in its judicial interpretation. Shortly after the APA was enacted, the Department of Justice prepared an Attorney General's Manual on the Administrative Procedure Act (1947), primarily for the benefit of other government agencies. Although those agencies and the Attorney General were in important respects parties in interest, with a particular view of the Act, the Supreme Court has drawn upon this manual as "a contemporaneous interpretation" of the APA that is entitled to "some deference . . . because of the role played by the Department of Justice in drafting the legislation." Vermont Yankee Nuclear Power Corp. v. Natural Resources Defense Council, 435 U.S. 519, 546 (1978) (p. 312). The Senate and House Judiciary Committee Reports on the APA are also cited with regularity. S. Rep. No. 752, 79th Cong., 1st Sess. (1945); H. Rep. No. 1980, 79th Cong. 2d Sess. (1946). The official legislative history appears in S. Doc. 248, 79th Cong. 2d Sess., 1946.

With the turn towards APA textualism and originalism has come a renewed interest in consulting original sources. In 2021, two scholars brought together a broad array of relevant historical materials in one online compendium. EMILY S. BREMER & KATHRYN E. KOVACS, INTRODUCTION TO THE BREMER-KOVACS COLLECTION: HISTORIC DOCUMENTS RELATED TO THE ADMINISTRATIVE PROCEDURE ACT OF 1946 (HeinOnline 2021), 106 Minn. L. Rev. Headnotes 218, 219 (2022): "Those who attempt to unearth the APA's historical foundations quickly discover ... that the documents are voluminous, scattered, and difficult to navigate without substantial pre-existing knowledge of the events that le[d] to the statute's enactment.... [The official legislative history] includes only the bills that ultimately became the APA, along with the hearings and debates on those bills. The official legislative history does not include material related to earlier legislative efforts that laid the groundwork for the APA, nor does it include any material from outside the official congressional record.... The Bremer-Kovacs Collection is designed to provide a complete, contextualized library of the historic documents related to the APA spanning the years 1929 to 1947.... [The] Collection includes not just all of the bills members of Congress proposed to control administrative agencies, and the hearings and debates on those bills, but also the various other communications, studies, reports, and debates that informed the APA." In addition to the Attorney General's Manual, these other sources include "reports, draft legislation, and other documents produced by the American Bar Association's (ABA) Special Committee on Administrative Law. The ABA Committee took a critical, conservative view of the administrative state and was a consistent source of political pressure in favor of reform." Id. at 218–19, 222.

(4) ***Doctrinal Implications.*** If the Supreme Court continues down the path of a more textual approach to the APA, what will be the implication for the many administrative common law doctrines that have emerged over the decades since the APA's adoption?

Some doctrines may remain, but with more textual grounding. Consider, for example, KISOR V. WILKIE, 139 S.Ct. 2400 (2019) (p. 1391), in which the Supreme Court considered the bearing on judicial review of an agency's interpretation of its own regulations. The question is similar to one that arises when courts review agency interpretations of their governing statutes, an issue now associated with Chevron, U.S.A., Inc. v. Natural Resources Defense Council, 467 U.S. 837 (1984) (p. 1206), a case extensively treated in Chapter VIII. Strikingly, the Chevron opinion made no mention of the APA's provisions on judicial review, an omission that has underlain increasing criticism of its influential holding. Justice Kagan's prevailing opinion in Kisor directly accepted the need to reconcile the Court's approach to this issue with the APA's provisions, finding in the context of that case that "even when a court defers to a regulatory reading, it acts consistently with Section 706," and supporting that finding by referring to "the practice of judicial review at the time of the APA's enactment. Section 706 was understood when enacted to 'restate[ ] the present law as to the scope of judicial review,'" citing the 1947 Attorney General's Manual. Justice Gorsuch's dissent, too, discussed the APA's bearing, at considerable length.

Stare decisis also played an important role in Kisor, and it may well continue to play an important role more generally even under a more textualist or even originalist approach. See, e.g., Bernick, supra, at 847 ("The disruption of settled expectations would . . . likely be a consideration at play for APA originalists in determining whether non-originalist precedent should be discarded or preserved, or extended or limited.").

On the other hand, some doctrines may be undone by a renewed focus on the text. In PEREZ V. MORTGAGE BANKERS ASS'N, 575 U.S. 92 (2015) (p. 426), for instance, the Supreme Court rejected a longstanding doctrine developed by the D.C. Circuit that had prohibited using an interpretive rule to revise an earlier interpretive rule. According to the Court, which was unanimous on this point, that doctrine was "contrary to the clear text of the APA's rulemaking provisions."

Will Congress be inclined to respond to judicial rejection of administrative common law doctrines by updating the APA, or will Congress be limited in its ability and desire to do so? Would administrative law without administrative common law be normatively desirable, in light of either what some view as various doctrines' unnecessary burdens on effective government or what others view as the doctrines' overly permissive approach to agency action? Would administrative law without administrative common law even be possible, in light of the broad language in parts of the APA and the difficulty of detailing in advance each aspect of the balance between courts and agencies? For contrasting answers to these questions, consider Ronald M. Levin, The Evolving APA and the Originalist Challenge, 97 Chi.-Kent L. Rev. 7 (2022); Jeffrey A. Pojanowski, Neoclassical Administrative Law, 133 Harv. L. Rev. 852 (2020); Kathryn E. Kovacs, Progressive Textualism in Administrative Law, 118 Mich. L. Rev. Online 134 (2019); Metzger, The Roberts Court and Administrative Law, supra; Bernick, supra.

## c. Additional Sources of Procedural Constraint

These materials focus on the APA and a few other general procedural enactments folded into its structure, such as the Freedom of Information Act and Government in the Sunshine Act. See Chapter VI. Yet a number of other statutes provide additional general requirements for certain aspects of administrative procedure or judicial review. Title 28 of the U.S. Code and implementing rules of civil and appellate procedure contain enforcement procedures for subpoenas, provisions respecting jurisdiction and venue for judicial review, and the delegation of litigating responsibility to the Department of Justice and its officers. The Paperwork Reduction Act of 1980 (p. 482) places generalized agency information-gathering under the supervision of the Office of Management and Budget (OMB), a White House agency we meet frequently in these pages. The Federal Advisory Committee Act (FACA) (p. 798) imposes certain requirements on agency use of private-public committees for consultation and policy development, including that any such committees work openly, and makes the General Services Administration responsible for oversight. Other statutes and executive orders creating additional procedural obligations for rulemaking have become a major source of added complexity. A helpful resource to navigate these sources may be found in the Federal Administrative

Procedure Sourcebook, a joint publication of the Administrative Conference of the United States (ACUS) and the ABA's Section of Administrative Law and Regulatory Practice.[2]

In addition, an awareness of general procedural requirements is just the beginning of solving any concrete problem of administrative procedure. It is always essential to consult the specific statutes under which the agency acts. Those "organic" or substantive statutes may establish additional or differing procedural requirements—and may also indicate which general procedural requirements are triggered. A number of the APA's requirements, such as the provisions for formal rulemaking and adjudication in §§ 556–557, are triggered by language in an agency's substantive statutes. See § 553(c). The potential applicability of specific statutory procedural requirements is signaled by § 559's proviso that the APA's procedural requirements "do not limit or repeal additional requirements imposed by statute or otherwise recognized by law."

Within statutory and constitutional limits, agencies generally enjoy substantial freedom to shape the procedures they employ. Agencies often adopt detailed procedural regulations, which will usually be found in an early chapter of the agency's volume of the Code of Federal Regulations (CFR)—the official annual compendium of regulations adopted by federal agencies. It is organized along the lines of the United States Code but is several times as large. Any attorney involved with a particular agency or individual proceeding must pay careful attention to the agency's procedural regulations and any internal interpretations those regulations may have received.

One useful resource for considering agency procedural issues is the work of ACUS, cited throughout this casebook.[3] Established by statute in 1964, abolished by the 104th Congress in 1995, and reinstated in 2009, this small agency is charged with responsibility for continuing analysis of and recommendations for federal administrative procedures. ACUS commissions scholarly studies of discrete administrative issues. Committee recommendations developed from the resulting reports and approved by its ten-member Council are debated and adopted by an assembly consisting of up to 50 government representatives and up to 40 private citizens. This process has often produced significant change within agencies and has permitted professional views on administrative procedural matters to coalesce in a relatively apolitical setting. For a collection of essays assessing ACUS's contributions to administrative law on the occasion of the 50th anniversary of its founding, see Volume 83, Numbers 4 and 5, of the George Washington Law Review (2015).

---

[2] https://sourcebook.acus.gov/wiki/Federal_Administrative_Procedure_Sourcebook/view.

[3] https://www.acus.gov.

## SECTION 3. CONSTRAINTS ON AN AGENCY'S OPTION TO USE EITHER ADJUDICATION OR RULEMAKING



As the material in Section 2 illustrates, adjudication and rulemaking are the APA's two fundamental categories of agency procedure. You might wonder, however, when an agency's organic statute leaves it free to take either route to a desired end, whether and in what ways the "rule of law" issues underlying the distinction affect an agency's choice between these two procedural options.

M. ELIZABETH MAGILL, AGENCY CHOICE OF POLICYMAKING FORM, 71 U. Chi. L. Rev. 1383 (2004): "An administrative agency delegated some task—protect the environment, assure the integrity of the securities markets, improve auto safety—might carry out that obligation by adopting a rule, bringing or deciding a case, or announcing its interpretation of a statute. In fact, it might rely on all of those quite distinct tools in the course of implementing its statutory mandate. Agencies are unique institutions in this respect. Most government actors are not free to select from a menu of policymaking tools. The legislature adopts statutes; prosecutors bring cases; courts decide cases brought to them by parties. Confining legislatures, prosecutors, and courts to particular ways of doing their jobs is no accident. Those assignments spring from the most essential aspects of the Constitution's design. But the typical administrative agency is not so constrained. Most agencies can rely on policymaking tools that look like legislating, enforcing, and adjudicating. . . . To be sure, the peculiar mix of powers—part legislative, part executive, part judicial—that Congress is constitutionally permitted to bestow on administrative agencies generates much of the heat in the debate over their constitutional status. But that is usually where interest in the issue ends. The nonconstitutional dimensions of agencies' ability to rely on a mix of policymaking tools generate little interest or investigation. . . . [The] phenomenon can be simply stated: the typical administrative agency is authorized to use a range of distinct policymaking forms to effectuate its statutory mandate, and its choice about which tool to rely on appears, at first glance at least, to be unregulated by courts."

We begin considering this issue with SEC v. Chenery Corp., a dispute that arose in the New Deal era (thus, not under the APA) and that reached the Supreme Court twice. Each of the resulting Court decisions grounds important contemporary understandings of administrative law. An excerpt of each appears below.

## SECURITIES & EXCHANGE COMMISSION v. CHENERY CORP. (CHENERY I)

Supreme Court of the United States (1943).
318 U.S. 80.

■ JUSTICE FRANKFURTER delivered the opinion of the Court.

[The Public Utility Holding Company Act of 1935—the Act—aimed at dismantling the complex, highly leveraged pyramid structures common in the public utility industry; the collapse of many of these companies in the 1929 stock market crash had contributed to the Great Depression. Section 11(b) directed the SEC "as soon as practicable after January 1, 1938 . . . [to] require by order, after notice and opportunity for hearing, that each registered holding company . . . shall take such action as the Commission shall find necessary to limit the operations of the holding-company system of which such company is a part to a single integrated public-utility system." Section 11(e) permitted companies to forestall mandatory reorganization by proposing a "voluntary" plan. The SEC would then determine, after hearing, whether the proposal was "necessary to effectuate the provisions of [§ 11(b)] and fair and equitable to the persons affected by such plan." The Chenery Corporation—officers, directors, and controlling shareholders of Federal Water Service Corporation (Federal)—had attempted voluntary reorganization under a plan in which those people would retain a substantial role in the new enterprise. But the SEC refused to approve reorganization on their terms.]

In ascertaining whether the terms of issuance of the new common stock were "fair and equitable" or "detrimental to . . . the interest of investors" within . . . the Act, the Commission found that it could not approve the proposed plan so long as the preferred stock acquired by the [Chenery] respondents would be permitted to share on a parity with other preferred stock. The Commission did not find fraud or lack of disclosure, but it concluded that the respondents, as Federal's managers, were fiduciaries and hence under a "duty of fair dealing" not to trade in the securities of the corporation while plans for its reorganization were before the Commission. . . . The Commission dealt with this as a specific case, and not as the application of a general rule formulating rules of conduct for reorganization managers. . . . Some technical rule of law must have moved the Commission to single out the respondents and deny their preferred stock the right to participate equally in the reorganization. To ascertain the precise basis of its determination, we must look to the Commission's opinion. . . . Its opinion plainly shows that the Commission purported to be acting only as it assumed a court of equity would have acted in a similar case. Since the decision of the Commission was explicitly based upon the applicability of principles of equity announced by courts, its validity must likewise be judged on that basis. The grounds upon which an administrative order must be judged are those upon which the record discloses that its action was based. . . . If . . . the rule applied by the Commission is to be judged solely on the basis of its adherence to principles of equity derived from judicial decisions, its order plainly cannot stand. . . . The cases upon which the Commission relied do not establish principles of law and equity which in themselves are sufficient to sustain its order. . . .

[T]he Commission urges here that the order should nevertheless be sustained because "the effect of trading by management is not measured by the fairness of individual transactions between buyer and seller, but by its relation to the timing and dynamics of the reorganization which the management itself initiates and so largely controls." Its argument lays stress upon the "strategic position enjoyed by the management in this type of reorganization proceeding and the vesting in it of statutory powers available to no other representative of security holders." It contends that these considerations warrant the stern rule applied in this case since the Commission "has dealt extensively with corporate reorganizations, both under the Act, and other statutes entrusted to it," and "has, in addition, exhaustively studied protective and reorganization committees," and that the situation was therefore "peculiarly within the Commission's special administrative competence." . . .

But the difficulty remains that the considerations urged here in support of the Commission's order were not those upon which its action was based. The Commission did not rely upon "its special administrative competence"; it formulated no judgment upon the requirements of the "public interest or the interest of investors or consumers" in the situation before it. Through its preoccupation with the special problems of utility reorganizations the Commission accumulates an experience and insight denied to others. Had the Commission, acting upon its experience and peculiar competence, promulgated a general rule of which its order here was a particular application, the problem for our consideration would be very different. Whether and to what extent directors or officers should be prohibited from buying or selling stock of the corporation during its reorganization, presents problems of policy for the judgment of Congress or of the body to which it has delegated power to deal with the matter. Abuse of corporate position, influence, and access to information may raise questions so subtle that the law can deal with them effectively only by prohibitions not concerned with the fairness of a particular transaction. But before transactions otherwise legal can be outlawed or denied their usual business consequences, they must fall under the ban of some standards of conduct prescribed by an agency of government authorized to prescribe such standards—either the courts or Congress or an agency to which Congress has delegated its authority. Congress itself did not proscribe the respondents' purchases of preferred stock in Federal. Established judicial doctrines do not condemn these transactions. Nor has the Commission . . . promulgated new general standards of conduct. It purported merely to be applying an existing judge-made rule of equity. The Commission's determination can stand, therefore, only if it found that the specific transactions under scrutiny showed misuse by the respondents of their position as reorganization managers, in that as such managers they took advantage of the corporation or the other stockholders or the investing public. The record is utterly barren of any such showing. Indeed, such a claim against the respondents was explicitly disavowed by the Commission. . . .

Judged, therefore, as a determination based upon judge-made rules of equity, the Commission's order cannot be upheld. Its action must be measured by what the Commission did, not by what it might have done. . . . [T]he courts cannot exercise their duty of review unless they are advised of the considerations underlying the action under review. If the action rests upon an administrative determination—an exercise of judgment in an area which Congress has entrusted to the agency—of course it must not be set aside because the reviewing court might have made a different determination were it empowered to do so. But if the action is based upon a determination of law as to which the reviewing authority of the courts does come into play, an order may not stand if the agency has misconceived the law. In either event the orderly functioning of the process of review requires that the grounds upon which the administrative agency acted by clearly disclosed and adequately sustained. . . . In finding that the Commission's order cannot be sustained, we are not imposing any trammels on its powers. . . . We merely hold that an administrative order cannot be upheld unless the grounds upon which the agency acted in exercising its powers were those upon which its action can be sustained.

■ JUSTICE BLACK, dissenting [joined by JUSTICE REED and JUSTICE MURPHY].

The conclusions of the Court with which I disagree are those in which it holds that while the Securities and Exchange Commission has abundant power to meet the situation presented by the activities of these respondents, it has not done so. . . . The grounds upon which the Commission made its findings seem clear enough to me. . . . That the Commission saw fit to draw support for its own administrative conclusion from decisions of courts should not detract from the validity of its findings. . . .

I do not suppose, as the Court does, that the Commission's rule is not fully based on Commission experience. The Commission did not 'explicitly disavow' any reliance on what its members had learned in their years of experience, and of course they, as trade experts, made their findings that respondent's practice was 'detrimental to the interests of investors' in the light of their knowledge. That they did not unduly parade fact data across the pages of their reports is a commendable saving of effort since they meant merely to announce for their own jurisdiction an obvious rule of honest dealing closely related to common law standards. Of course, the Commission can now change the form of its decision to comply with the Court order. The Court can require the Commission to use more words; but it seems difficult to imagine how more words or different words could further illuminate its purpose or its determination. A judicial requirement of circumstantially detailed findings as the price of court approval can bog the administrative power in a quagmire of minutiae. Hypercritical exactions as to findings can provide a handy but an almost invisible glideway enabling courts to pass from the narrow confines of law into the more spacious domain of policy. Here for instance, the Court apparently holds that the Commission has full power to do exactly what it did; but the Court sends the matter back to the Commission to revise the language of its opinion, in order, I suppose, that the Court may reappraise the reasons which moved the Commission to determine that the conduct of these fiduciaries was detrimental to the public and investors. The Act under which the Commission proceeded does not purport to vest us with authority to make such a reappraisal.

That the Commission has chosen to proceed case by case rather than by a general pronouncement does not appear to me to merit criticism. The intimation is that the Commission can act only through general formulae rigidly adhered to. In the first place, the rule of the single case is obviously a general advertisement to the trade, and in the second place the briefs before us indicate that this is but one of a number of cases in which the Commission is moving to an identical result on a broad front. But aside from these considerations the Act gives the Commission wide powers to evolve policy standards, and this may well be done case by case. . . .

## SECURITIES & EXCHANGE COMMISSION v. CHENERY CORP. (CHENERY II)

Supreme Court of the United States (1947).
332 U.S. 194.

■ JUSTICE MURPHY delivered the opinion of the Court.

This case is here for the second time. In SEC v. Chenery Corp., 318 U.S. 80 (1943) [Chenery I], we held that an order of the Securities and Exchange Commission could not be sustained on the grounds upon which that agency acted. We therefore directed that the case be remanded to the Commission for such further proceedings as might be appropriate. On remand, the Commission reexamined the problem, recast its rationale and reached the same result. The issue now is whether the Commission's action is proper in light of the principles established in our prior decision.

When the case was first here, we emphasized a simple but fundamental rule of administrative law. That rule is to the effect that a reviewing court, in dealing with a determination or judgment which an administrative agency alone is authorized to make, must judge the propriety of such action solely by the grounds invoked by the agency. If those grounds are inadequate or improper, the court is powerless to affirm the administrative action by substituting what it considers to be a more adequate or proper basis. To do so would propel the court into the domain which Congress has set aside exclusively for the administrative agency.

We also emphasized in our prior decision an important corollary of the foregoing rule. If the administrative action is to be tested by the basis upon which it purports to rest, that basis must be set forth with such clarity as to be understandable. It will not do for a court to be compelled to guess at the theory underlying the agency's action. . . .

Applying this rule and its corollary, the Court was unable to sustain the Commission's original action. . . .

The latest order of the Commission definitely avoids the fatal error of relying on judicial precedents which do not sustain it. This time, after a thorough reexamination of the problem in light of the purposes and standards of the Holding Company Act, the Commission has concluded that the proposed transaction is inconsistent with the . . . Act. It has drawn heavily upon its accumulated experience in dealing with utility reorganizations. And it has expressed its reasons with a clarity and thoroughness that admit of no doubt as to the underlying basis of its order.

The argument is pressed upon us, however, that the Commission was foreclosed from taking such a step following our prior decision. It is said that, in the absence of findings of conscious wrongdoing on the part of Federal's management, the Commission could not determine by an order in this particular case that it was inconsistent with the statutory standards to permit Federal's management to realize a profit through the reorganization purchases. All that it could do was to enter an order allowing an amendment to the plan so that the proposed transaction could be consummated. Under this view, the Commission would be free only to promulgate a general rule outlawing such profits in future utility reorganizations; but such a rule would have to be prospective in nature and have no retroactive effect upon the instant situation.

We reject this contention, for it grows out of a misapprehension of our prior decision and of the Commission's statutory duties. We held no more and no less than that the Commission's first order was unsupportable for the reasons supplied by that agency. But when the case left this Court, the problem whether Federal's management should be treated equally with other preferred stockholders still lacked a final and complete answer. It was clear that the Commission could not give a negative answer by resort to prior judicial declarations. And it was also clear that the Commission was not bound by settled judicial precedents in a situation of this nature. Still unsettled, however, was the answer the Commission might give were it to bring to bear on the facts the proper administrative and statutory considerations, a function which belongs exclusively to the Commission in the first instance. The administrative process had taken an erroneous rather than a final turn. Hence we carefully refrained from expressing any views as to the propriety of an order rooted in the proper and relevant considerations.

. . . The fact that the Commission had committed a legal error in its first disposition of the case certainly gave Federal's management no vested right to receive the benefits of such an order. After the remand was made, therefore, the Commission was bound to deal with the problem afresh, performing the function delegated to it by Congress. . . .

The absence of a general rule or regulation governing management trading during reorganization did not affect the Commission's duties in relation to the particular proposal before it. The Commission was asked to grant or deny effectiveness to a proposed amendment to Federal's reorganization plan whereby the management would be accorded parity treatment on its holdings. It could do that only in the form of an order, entered after a due consideration of the particular facts in light of the relevant and proper standards. That was true regardless of whether those standards previously had been spelled out in a general rule or regulation. Indeed, if the Commission rightly felt that the proposed amendment was inconsistent with those standards, an order giving effect to the amendment merely because there was no general rule or regulation covering the matter would be unjustified.

It is true that our prior decision explicitly recognized the possibility that the Commission might have promulgated a general rule dealing with this problem under its statutory rule-making powers, in which case the issue for our consideration would have been entirely different from that which did confront us. But we did not mean to imply thereby that the failure of the Commission to anticipate this problem and to promulgate a general rule withdrew all power from that agency to perform its statutory duty in this case. To hold that the Commission had no alternative in this proceeding but to approve the proposed transaction, while formulating any general rules it might desire for use in future cases of this nature, would be to stultify the administrative process. That we refuse to do.

Since the Commission, unlike a court, does have the ability to make new law prospectively through the exercise of its rule-making powers, it has less reason to rely upon ad hoc adjudication to formulate new standards of conduct within the framework of the Holding Company Act. The function of filling in the interstices of the Act should be performed, as much as possible, through this quasi-legislative promulgation of rules to be applied in the future. But any rigid requirement to that effect would make the administrative process inflexible and incapable of dealing with many of the specialized problems which arise. Not every principle essential to the effective administration of a statute can or should be cast immediately into the mold of a general rule. Some principles must await their own development, while others must be adjusted to meet particular, unforeseeable situations. In performing its important functions in these respects, therefore, an administrative agency must be equipped to act either by general rule or by individual order. To insist upon one form of action to the exclusion of the other is to exalt form over necessity.

In other words, problems may arise in a case which the administrative agency could not reasonably foresee, problems which must be solved despite the absence of a relevant general rule. Or the agency may not have had sufficient experience with a particular problem to warrant rigidifying its tentative judgment into a hard and fast rule. Or the problem may be so specialized and varying in nature as to be impossible of capture within the boundaries of a general rule. In those situations, the agency must retain power to deal with the problems on a case-to-case basis if the administrative process is to be effective. There is thus a very definite place for the case-by-case evolution of statutory standards. And the choice made between proceeding by general rule or by individual, ad hoc litigation is one that lies primarily in the informed discretion of the administrative agency.

Hence we refuse to say that the Commission, which had not previously been confronted with the problem of management trading during reorganization, was forbidden from utilizing this particular proceeding for announcing and applying a new standard of conduct. That such action might have a retroactive effect was not necessarily fatal to its validity. Every case of first impression has a retroactive effect, whether the new principle is announced by a court or by an administrative agency. But such retroactivity must be balanced against the mischief of producing a result which is contrary to a statutory design or to legal and equitable principles. If that mischief is greater than the ill effect of the retroactive application of a new standard, it is not the type of retroactivity which is condemned by law. . . .

The scope of our review of an administrative order wherein a new principle is announced and applied is no different from that which pertains to ordinary administrative action. The wisdom of the principle adopted is none of our concern. Our duty is at an end when it becomes evident that the Commission's action is based upon substantial evidence and is consistent with the authority granted by Congress. . . .

The Commission's conclusion here rests squarely in that area where administrative judgments are entitled to the greatest amount of weight by appellate courts. It is the product of administrative experience, appreciation of the complexities of the problem, realization of the statutory policies, and responsible treatment of the uncontested facts. It is the type of judgment which administrative agencies are best equipped to make and which justifies the use of the administrative process. Whether we agree or disagree with the result reached, it is an allowable judgment which we cannot disturb.

Reversed.

■ JUSTICE JACKSON, dissenting [joined by JUSTICE FRANKFURTER].

The Court by this present decision sustains the identical administrative order which only recently it held invalid. As the Court correctly notes, the Commission has only "recast its rationale and reached the same result." There being no change in the order, no additional evidence in the record and no amendment of relevant legislation, it is clear that there has been a shift in attitude between that of the controlling membership of the Court when the case was first here and that of those who have the power of decision on this second review.[1]

I feel constrained to disagree with the reasoning offered to rationalize this shift. It makes judicial review of administrative orders a hopeless formality for the litigant. . . . It reduces the judicial process in such cases to a mere feint. . . .

The basic assumption of the earlier opinion as therein stated was, *"But before transactions otherwise legal can be outlawed or denied their usual business consequences, they must fall under the ban of some standards of conduct prescribed by an agency of government authorized to prescribe such standards. . . ."* The basic assumption of the present opinion is stated thus: *"The absence of a general rule or regulation governing management trading during reorganization did not affect the Commission's duties in relation to the particular proposal before it."* This puts in juxtaposition the two conflicting philosophies which produce opposite results in the same case and on the same facts. The difference between the first and the latest decision of the Court is thus simply the difference between holding that administrative orders must have a basis in law and a holding that absence of a legal basis is no ground on which courts may annul them.

As there admittedly is no law or regulation to support this order, we peruse the Court's opinion diligently to find on what grounds it is now held that the Court of Appeals, on pain of being reversed for error, was required to stamp this order with its approval. We find but one. That is the principle of judicial deference to administrative experience. That argument is five times stressed in as many different contexts. . . .

What are we to make of this reiterated deference to "administrative experience" when in another context the Court says, "Hence, we refuse to say that the Commission, *which had not previously been confronted with the problem of management trading during reorganization,* was forbidden from utilizing this particular proceeding for announcing and applying *a new standard of conduct.*"? (Emphasis supplied.)

The Court's reasoning adds up to this: The Commission must be sustained because of its accumulated experience in solving a problem with which it had never before been confronted!

Of course, thus to uphold the Commission by professing to find that it has enunciated a "new standard of conduct" brings the Court squarely against the invalidity of retroactive law-making. But the Court does not falter. "That such action might have a retroactive effect was not necessarily fatal to its validity." "But such retroactivity must be balanced

---

[1] [Ed.] Chenery I had been a 4–3 decision, in which Justice Frankfurter wrote for himself, Chief Justice Stone, and Justices Roberts and Jackson. Justices Black, Reed, and Murphy dissented. Justice Douglas had not participated, and there had been one vacancy. By the time of Chenery II, Vinson had replaced Stone, Burton had replaced Roberts, and Rutledge had filled the vacancy. Justice Rutledge joined the three Chenery I dissenters to form the Chenery II majority, Justice Burton concurred in the judgment without opinion, and Chief Justice Vinson joined Justice Douglas in not participating. Of the original Chenery I majority, this left only Justices Frankfurter and Jackson to dissent.

against the mischief of producing a result which is contrary to a statutory design or to legal and equitable principles." Of course, if what these parties did really was condemned by "statutory design" or "legal and equitable principles," it could be stopped without resort to a new rule and there would be no retroactivity to condone. But if it had been the Court's view that some law already prohibited the purchases, it would hardly have been necessary three sentences earlier to hold that the Commission was not prohibited "from utilizing this particular proceeding for announcing and applying a *new standard of conduct.*" (Emphasis supplied.)

I give up. Now I realize fully what Mark Twain meant when he said, "The more you explain it, the more I don't understand it." . . .

[A]dministrative experience is of weight in judicial review only to this point—it is a persuasive reason for deference to the Commission in the exercise of its discretionary powers under and within the law. It cannot be invoked to support action outside of the law. . . .

The truth is that in this decision the Court approves the Commission's assertion of power to govern the matter *without* law, power to force surrender of stock so purchased whenever it will, and power also to overlook such acquisitions if it so chooses. The reasons which will lead it to take one course as against the other remain locked in its own breast, and it has not and apparently does not intend to commit them to any rule or regulation. This administrative authoritarianism, this power to decide without law, is what the Court seems to approve in so many words: "The absence of a general rule or regulation governing management trading during reorganization did not affect the Commission's duties . . ." This seems to me to undervalue and to belittle the place of law, even in the system of administrative justice. It calls to mind Mr. Justice Cardozo's statement that "Law as a guide to conduct is reduced to the level of mere futility if it is unknown and unknowable." . . .

## NOTES ON THE CHENERY DECISIONS

(1) ***Chenery I: Rationales and Applications.*** The enduring proposition from the *first* round of the Chenery litigation—that courts must base their review of administrative action on the reasons the agency actually gave—has shaped much administrative law concerning the relationship between agencies and the courts that review their work. Under this principle, the relationship between a reviewing court and an agency differs markedly from that between a reviewing court and a trial court. Decisions from trial or intermediate appellate courts are regularly sustained for reasons other than these lower courts give. The same is not true for review of agency decisions. As the Court explained in both Chenery decisions, by delegating authority under a statute to an agency, Congress has allocated responsibility for setting policy to the agency, not the courts.

In THE CONSTITUTIONAL FOUNDATIONS OF CHENERY, 116 YALE L.J. 952, 958–59 (2007), KEVIN M. STACK argues that "the Chenery principle . . . has a constitutional foundation. Specifically, the Chenery principle is a default rule of statutory construction that implements the nondelegation doctrine in ways that complement and reinforce that doctrine's other modes of enforcement." This casebook treats the question whether a nondelegation doctrine limits the permissible creation of agency authority in some detail in Chapter VII; there you will learn that the currently governing doctrine requires only that an authorizing statute must contain an "intelligible principle" on the basis of which the legality of the agency's action can be determined. You will also learn there about competing views of this doctrine that appear to be ascendant in the current Supreme Court. Stack, however, suggests that, traditionally, the doctrine also involved evaluation of "whether the statutory grant conditioned the exercise of authority upon an agency's stating the grounds for its invocation of the statutory authority." A legislature, of course, is under no such obligation; Congress can and does establish binding norms without having to state its justification for doing so. He argues: "While this requirement of an express statement of the agency's predicate grounds for action has slipped from constitutional doctrine, the Chenery principle's prohibition on post hoc rationales enforces this arm of the nondelegation doctrine. . . . [It also] operates both to bolster the political accountability of the agency's action and to prevent arbitrariness in the agency's exercise of its discretion. It provides assurance that accountable agency decision-makers, not merely courts and agency lawyers, have embraced the grounds for the agency's actions, and that the agency decisionmakers have exercised their judgment on the issue in the first instance."

In DEPARTMENT OF HOMELAND SECURITY V. REGENTS OF THE UNIVERSITY OF CALIFORNIA, 140 S.Ct. 1891 (2020), the Supreme Court relied in part on Chenery I to reject the Trump Administration's rescission of the DACA program, which had been created by the Obama Administration to provide relief from removal, and to provide work eligibility and other benefits, to certain categories of undocumented people who had arrived in the United States as children. The Chenery I problem, as the Court saw it, was that, after a district court remanded the initial rescission decision to the agency for a fuller explanation, the DHS Secretary offered only post hoc rationalizations for its earlier decision rather than making and adequately justifying a new decision. (The other problems the Court identified with the rescission decision are discussed in Chapter VIII, p. 1139.) Relying on Chenery in this way, argues BENJAMIN EIDELSON, in REASONED EXPLANATION AND POLITICAL ACCOUNTABILITY IN THE ROBERTS COURT, 130 Yale L.J. 1748, 1768–71 (2021) "recast Chenery as, in no small part, a judicially enforced safeguard of agencies' political accountability. . . . This use of Chenery as an accountability-forcing tool breaks new ground in terms of both doctrine and theory. As for doctrine, the majority cited one case linking Chenery to the principle of agency accountability. But agency accountability there appears to have referred, as it often does, to simple accountability to law enforced through judicial review—not to the particular value of public engagement with an agency's reasoning. And as for theory, the classic justifications for the Chenery rule had little to do with such public awareness. . . . [T]hey turned instead on the notion that Congress had given agencies themselves—not their lawyers, not courts—the authority to make the relevant judgments. . . . Thus, when Kevin Stack argued (now presciently) that Chenery could be better justified as a means of 'bolster[ing] the political accountability of [agency] action,' he presented that proposal as an alternative to the 'conventional justifications' touted by courts. Regents has now elevated this idea, never before mentioned by the Court, to the foremost 'functional reason[ ] for requiring contemporaneous explanations.' "

At the same time, the Court has continued to require that the contemporaneous explanation simply be "understandable" to the reviewing court rather than that it be crystal clear. In GARLAND V. MING DAI, 141 S.Ct. 1669 (2021), the Supreme Court unanimously rejected a Ninth Circuit rule that had required courts reviewing immigration cases to treat the petitioning noncitizen's testimony as credible unless the immigration judge or Board of Immigration Appeals (BIA) had made an explicit adverse credibility determination. This rule, said the Court, was not only inconsistent with the Immigration and Nationality Act (INA); it was also inconsistent with Chenery I. "[T]he rule that judges generally must assess the lawfulness of an agency's action in light of the explanations the agency offered for it rather than any ex post rationales a court can devise" does not mean "the BIA must follow a particular formula or incant 'magic words' like 'incredible' or 'rebutted' to overcome the INA's presumption of credibility on appeal. To the contrary, a reviewing court must 'uphold' even 'a decision of less than ideal clarity if the agency's path may reasonably be discerned.' So long as the BIA's reasons for rejecting an alien's credibility are reasonably discernible, the agency must be understood as having rebutted the presumption of credibility."

(2) ***Chenery II: "Correct and Inevitable" or a "Wrong Turn"?*** Chenery II stands for the proposition that "the choice made between proceeding by general rule or by individual, ad hoc litigation is one that lies primarily in the informed discretion of the administrative agency." Was the Supreme Court right to so hold?

Yes, argue RUSSELL L. WEAVER & LINDA D. JELLUM, in CHENERY II AND THE DEVELOPMENT OF FEDERAL ADMINISTRATIVE LAW, 58 Admin. L. Rev. 815, 824–26 (2006): "Courts are poorly situated to distinguish between circumstances appropriate for rulemaking and circumstances appropriate for adjudication. Moreover, requiring agencies to articulate policy only via legislative procedures would be both impractical and unworkable. . . . First, such a requirement would promote futility. Agencies can neither conceive of every possible rule in advance, nor draft all regulations to ensure that they are not overbroad, vague, or ambiguous. . . . A different holding in Chenery II might also have resulted in less desirable rules. A holding requiring agencies to create advance rules might have forced agencies to commit themselves to specific rules with particular courses of action without knowing all the facts in advance. . . . Third, requiring agencies to develop all rules legislatively would deprive the agency of the ability to make tailored decisions in incremental fashion. . . .

"Additional concerns would arise in a non-Chenery II world. When existing statutes or regulations fail to address a problem adequately, agency personnel must do so. When there is time, they can do so by informal rule.

But there is not always enough time, and informal procedures are not cheap. . . . If an interpretive problem arises in a case, it may be impossible or impractical to use informal processes. . . [In addition, r]equiring a prior rule as a predicate to agency action may negatively impact the interaction between agencies and regulated entities. At present, if regulated entitles are uncertain about regulatory requirements, they are expected to go to the agency and request clarification. This process helps inform the agency that there is a problem."

No, argues AARON L. NIELSON, in THREE WRONG TURNS IN AGENCY ADJUDICATION, 28 Geo. Mason L. Rev. 657, 669–70 (2021): "Chenery II took [a] sound principle and applied it too aggressively. . . . Chenery II's aggressiveness distorts administrative law in at least two ways. First, retroactivity can be unfair to individual parties—as in Chenery II itself. Indeed, unknowable law may be 'literally Orwellian.' It is doubtful that Congress intended that 'lawless' result. . . . Second, Chenery II has a dynamic effect. Because regulated parties—operating in the shadow of the law—know that their regulators can create law retroactively, they must pay close attention to what an agency says informally, such as through guidance documents. If an agency can change the law after the fact, a rational party will often obey all of the agency's hints about the future. Thus, the power to act retroactively enables agencies to signal where the law is headed, which may in effect create law . . . without any formal procedures."

(3) ***Should Adjudication or Rulemaking Be Preferred?*** Chenery II allows agencies to choose between adjudication and rulemaking where they have the option. But do the procedural characteristics of adjudication and rulemaking counsel the appropriateness of using one or the other process to make general policy choices?

(a) LISA SCHULTZ BRESSMAN, BEYOND ACCOUNTABILITY: ARBITRARINESS AND LEGITIMACY IN THE ADMINISTRATIVE STATE, 78 N.Y.U. L. Rev. 461, 541–42 (2003): "Notice-and-comment rulemaking, by its nature, facilitates the participation of affected parties, the submission of relevant information, and the prospective application of resulting policy. As a result of the reasoned-decisionmaking requirement that accompanies it, notice-and-comment rulemaking fosters logical and thorough consideration of policy. To the extent notice-and-comment rulemaking issues general rules that rely for their enforcement on further proceedings, it also promotes predictability. At a minimum, it allows affected parties, who participate in the formulation of the rule, to anticipate the rule and plan accordingly.

"Now compare formal adjudication. Agencies . . . have shown that adjudication may serve as a policymaking tool. And, adjudication certainly affords important procedural protections to individual litigants. Yet, adjudication, as a general matter, has serious shortcomings for formulating policy. It applies new rules retroactively to the parties in the case. It also excludes other affected parties in the development of policy applicable to them, unless included through the venues of intervention or amicus curiae filings. To the extent it excludes such parties, it also excludes the information and arguments necessary to define the stakes and educate the agency. It tends to approach broad policy questions from a narrow perspective—only as necessary to decide a case—which decreases the comprehensiveness of the resulting rule and increases the risk that bad facts will make bad law. Similarly, it elaborates policy in a narrow manner—on a case-by-case basis—which decreases predictability and opportunities for planning. It also announces policy in the form of an order rather than codifying it in the Federal Register, thus decreasing accessibility. And, it depends for all of this on the existence of circumstances that lead to the initiation of a proceeding or succession of proceedings."

(b) TODD PHILLIPS, A CHANGE OF POLICY: PROMOTING AGENCY POLICYMAKING BY ADJUDICATION, 73 Admin. L. Rev. 495, 498–99 (2021): "Informal rulemaking has become so onerous and ossified in the 21st century that agencies must again give adjudication its due consideration as a policymaking option. Though it will not be appropriate in every circumstance, developing policy through case-by-case adjudications—akin to courts' development of the common law—can offer significant benefits over informal rulemaking, both to agency policymakers and the public. For example, adjudication can improve policies by requiring agencies to confront the specifics of real cases rather than largely hypothetical situations, and by permitting policymakers to observe regulated actions and retroactively clarify the law in response. Adjudication also allows agencies to develop policy quickly and on a case-by-case basis, allowing officials to observe the effects of one incremental policy change before implementing another, or to quickly reverse course if the effects are not as expected. Finally, addressing policy in individual adjudications may allow for increased public participation by marginalized groups traditionally excluded from the rulemaking process."

(c) E. DONALD ELLIOTT, RE-INVENTING RULEMAKING, 41 Duke L.J. 1490, 1492 (1992): "There can be no abstract answer to the question whether rulemaking or case-by-case evolution is the better way to make policy; in each case the answer depends on a variety of factors, including: how sure the agency is about what policy it wishes to adopt, how frequently the agency anticipates the question will come up, whether the issue is inherently entangled with other issues that can best be addressed comprehensively, and what other issues are currently pressing for the agency's attention."

(4) ***Judicial Review of Agencies' Choice of Policymaking Form.*** Chenery II did not itself foreclose judicial review of agencies' choice of policymaking form. After identifying circumstances that might make adjudication a particularly appropriate method for policymaking, it simply left the choice to agencies' informed discretion. As the materials in Chapter VIII illustrate, courts routinely review agencies' discretionary decisions.

For a brief while, a set of divided opinions in NLRB v. Wyman-Gordon, 394 U.S. 759 (1969), made it appear that the Court might be willing to develop "arbitrariness" standards that could result in requiring agencies to use rulemaking for the setting of agency policy.[2] That prospect receded with

[2] In his concurrence in Bowen v. Georgetown University Hospital, 488 U.S. 204, 221 (1988) (p. 275), Justice Scalia characterized the decision in Wyman-Gordon in terms that do endure: "And just as Chenery suggested that rulemaking was prospective, the opinions in NLRB v. Wyman-Gordon Co., suggested the obverse: that adjudication could *not* be purely prospective,

the decision in NLRB v. BELL AEROSPACE, 416 U.S. 267 (1974), which reversed a Second Circuit opinion that would have required the NLRB to use rulemaking to change a long-standing interpretation, developed in adjudication, that corporate buyers were necessarily "managerial employees" excluded from the protections of the National Labor Relations Act. "[T]he Board is not precluded from announcing new principles in an adjudicative proceeding and . . . the choice between rulemaking and adjudication lies in the first instance within the Board's discretion. Although there may be situations where the Board's reliance on adjudication would amount to an abuse of discretion or a violation of the Act, . . . there is ample indication that adjudication is especially appropriate in the instant context. As the Court of Appeals noted, '[t]here must be tens of thousands of manufacturing, wholesale and retail units which employ buyers, and hundreds of thousands of the latter.' Moreover, duties of buyers vary widely depending on the company or industry. It is doubtful whether any generalized standard could be framed which would have more than marginal utility. The Board thus has reason to proceed with caution, developing its standards in a case-by-case manner with attention to the specific character of the buyers' authority and duties in each company. The Board's judgment that adjudication best serves this purpose is entitled to great weight."

While Bell Aerospace did not entirely limit the prospect of judicial review of choice of form for "abuse of discretion," it did send signals that the circumstances that would render such a choice abusive are few indeed. Lower courts have followed that lead. Is that development appropriate? BRESSMAN, supra, at 543–44: "If notice-and-comment rulemaking typically is the best method for making general policy, then a refusal to use it might be arbitrary. It might lack any justification whatsoever. Or it might indicate improper motives, such as a desire to avoid committing broadly or visibly, or to retain room for departures that serve narrow interests. . . . [A]gencies should be required to take affirmative steps to justify a departure from rulemaking. At a minimum, they should articulate the reasons for using other procedures. This brings choice of procedure into compliance with the reasoned-decisionmaking requirement."

On the other hand, perhaps courts have other ways to respond to agencies' choice of form. M. ELIZABETH MAGILL, AGENCY CHOICE OF POLICYMAKING FORM, 71 U. Chi. L. Rev. 1383, 1437, 1440 (2004): "Courts' ability to shape some of the consequences of an agency's choice of procedure explains the continued strength of the Chenery principle. . . . Without Chenery II, courts might have developed doctrines that set forth the circumstances in which rulemaking was appropriate. That option was not doctrinally available, so courts instead reshaped what was required when an agency relied on rulemaking. Their willingness to endorse agency reliance on this policymaking tool, that is, was dependent on their ability to adjust the elements of the policymaking form to take account of the concerns they had. . . . A similar, though less complicated, story can be told about judicially

---

since otherwise it would constitute rulemaking. . . . Side by side these two cases, Chenery and Wyman-Gordon, set forth quite nicely the 'dichotomy between rulemaking and adjudication' upon which 'the entire [APA] is based.' 1947 Attorney General's Manual on the APA. . . ."

created doctrines governing adjudication. . . . Instead of requiring agencies to rely on rulemaking under certain circumstances, the courts recognized participation rights for parties who were interested in (but were not the objects of) adjudications and thus made some adjudications look a little bit more like rulemaking. . . . Once again, courts might have developed doctrines suggesting that sometimes—when the reliance interests are particularly great—agencies must employ rulemaking and not adjudication. Instead, courts developed a doctrine that permits courts occasionally to deem adjudicatory decisions nonretroactive." Is such a backdoor approach to reviewing choice of form acceptable? Is it preferable?

(5) ***On What Basis Do Agencies Choose a Policymaking Form?*** As the materials above on Londoner and Bi-Metallic indicate, the Due Process Clause presents some constitutional limits on agencies' choice of policymaking form. Statutes, too, may constrain agencies' choice, as Congress sometimes directs agencies to proceed only by one or another route. For example, the Equal Employment Opportunity Commission has the statutory authority to promulgate only procedural, rather than substantive, regulations governing the prohibitions on discrimination in Title VII of the 1964 Civil Rights Act, see 42 U.S.C. § 2000e–12(a), and thus issues its policy determinations via orders developed in individual adjudications. In the other direction, the National Highway Traffic Safety Administration is required to promulgate certain Motor Vehicle Safety Standards by rulemaking rather than adjudication, see 49 U.S.C. §§ 30111(a), 30128(a). In addition, an agency must conduct a rulemaking if it wants to change or rescind a rule. But where agencies have the option to choose their policymaking form, on what basis do they make their choice?

(a) MAGILL, supra, at 1437, 1443: "Agency decisionmakers pursuing a given policy objective are free to choose from a menu of policymaking tools but are not free to design those tools. As they consider their options, they will evaluate the various tools in terms of . . . the procedure the agency would have to follow, the legal effect of the action, and the terms on which that action might be challenged in the courts."

(b) ROBERT L. GLICKSMAN, DAVID L. MARKELL, & JUSTIN SEVIER, AN EMPIRICAL ASSESSMENT OF AGENCY MECHANISM CHOICE, 71 Ala. L. Rev. 1039, 1045–46, 1073–77 (2020): "[A]gency mechanism choice is influenced by a more complicated set of factors and relationships than is commonly appreciated. . . . The first involves the manner in which different actors that participate (or have the potential to participate) in the implementation of regulatory programs may influence mechanism choice. These include actors internal to the agency, other federal actors, other government actors (especially in cooperative federalism systems such as those that the nation's environmental regulatory schemes employ), regulated entities, and regulatory beneficiaries. Second, the goals an agency is supposed to achieve under its authorizing legislation have the potential to influence mechanism choice. Third, we consider governance tools that may be available for use by different regulatory actors, which will necessarily differ in varying regulatory contexts. Fourth, the scope of an agency's statutory authority (and the constraints imposed on its exercise) can narrow or expand the range of mechanism choices available to the agency and the relative attractiveness of these mechanisms. Finally, a series of what we refer to as 'intramechanism' features form part of the decision-making calculus," where such features include different forums for pursuing the same basic mechanism and different versions of each mechanism.

(c) PETER L. STRAUSS, RULES, ADJUDICATIONS, AND OTHER SOURCES OF LAW IN AN EXECUTIVE DEPARTMENT: REFLECTIONS ON THE INTERIOR DEPARTMENT'S ADMINISTRATION OF THE MINING LAW, 74 Colum. L. Rev. 1231 (1974): "The failure to use rulemaking is far less a product of conscious departmental choice than a result of impediments to the making of rules created by the Department's internal procedures. The channels which lead to rulemaking . . . are so clogged with obstacles, and the flow through them so sluggish, that staff members hesitate to use them. . . . As a result, rulemaking may be consciously avoided by an individual with an idea for policy change when other means for achieving the same policy ends appear to be available."

(6) ***Beyond the Adjudication/Rulemaking Binary.*** Agencies' choice of form extends beyond a simple adjudication-or-rulemaking binary. When developing prospective, general standards, agencies may be able to choose between making rules with the force of law and issuing guidance documents, which are not formally binding. When engaging in the case-specific context of adjudication, agencies may be able to choose between adjudication within the agency itself and an enforcement action in court. What effect does this expanded understanding of available mechanisms have on the basic choice-of-form question?

Concern that agencies avoid the APA's procedural requirements of *both* adjudication and rulemaking in favor of easier-to-promulgate guidance has led some to believe that agencies are abusing the practice by imposing or threatening to impose sanctions for engaging in conduct that is nowhere actually banned. See, e.g., Robert A. Anthony, Interpretive Rules, Policy Statements, Guidances, Manuals, and the Like—Should Federal Agencies Use Them to Bind the Public?, 41 Duke L.J. 1311 (1992). In 2019, the Trump Administration issued two Executive Orders responding to this concern. Executive Order 13891, Promoting the Rule of Law Through Improved Agency Guidance Documents, 84 Fed. Reg. 55235 (Oct. 9, 2019), instructed agencies to "treat guidance documents as non-binding both in law and in practice," and to "impose legally binding requirements on the public only through regulations and on parties on a case-by-case basis through adjudications." For its part, Executive Order 13892, Promoting the Rule of Law Through Transparency and Fairness in Civil Administrative Enforcement and Adjudication, 84 Fed. Reg. 55239 (Oct. 9, 2019), stated that "No person should be subjected to a civil administrative enforcement action or adjudication absent prior public notice of both the enforcing agency's jurisdiction over particular conduct and the legal standards applicable to that conduct." Together, these Executive Orders aimed at limiting agencies' ability to make policy decisions through adjudication and to use guidance documents to avoid the procedural hurdles of both rulemaking and adjudication.

To what extent are these concerns based on empirical evidence? Little, argues Connor Raso, in Agency Avoidance of Rulemaking Procedures, 67 Admin. L. Rev. 65, 127 (2015). In a study of rules issued between 1995 and 2012, he found that agencies were able to promulgate binding rules by taking advantage of exceptions in the APA 52% of the time, thus suggesting that agencies have little need to choose less onerous forms through which to promulgate policy. "The extent of agency avoidance . . . suggests that contrary to the prevailing account, rulemaking procedures are unlikely in many situations . . . to encourage agencies to make policy via alternative means such as guidance or adjudication." This finding was consistent with Raso's earlier work in a student note on guidance documents. In Strategic or Sincere? Analyzing Agency Use of Guidance Documents, 119 Yale L.J. 782, 821 (2010), Raso presented the results of a study of more than a decade's worth of guidance documents. He concluded that despite "a few egregious examples of abuse," "agencies do not commonly use guidance to make important policy decisions outside of the notice and comment process."

Upon taking office, the Biden Administration withdrew the two 2019 Executive Orders of the Trump Administration, stating that agencies "must be equipped with the flexibility to use robust regulatory action to address national priorities" via "appropriate regulatory tools." Executive Order 13992, Revocation of Certain Executive Orders Concerning Federal Regulation, 86 Fed. Reg. 7049 (Jan. 20, 2021). For more on the issue of agency use of guidance documents, see pp. 393–425 in Chapter IV.

As for agencies' choice to bring an enforcement action in either an administrative tribunal or an Article III court, the Fifth Circuit held in Jarkesy v. SEC, 34 F.4th 446 (5th Cir. 2022), that "Congress unconstitutionally delegated legislative power to the SEC when it gave the SEC the unfettered authority to choose" between these paths. "It instead effectively gave the SEC the power to decide which defendants should receive *certain legal processes* (those accompanying Article III proceedings) and which should not. Such a decision—to assign certain actions to agency adjudication—is a power that Congress uniquely possesses," and "Congress did not provide the SEC with an intelligible principle by which to exercise that power." In dissent, Judge Davis concluded that Congress's authorization of the SEC to choose which forum to use in its enforcement actions was a routine and acceptable delegation of prosecutorial authority that raised no constitutional concerns. For more on this case, and on the issue of administrative adjudication as an alternative to judicial enforcement more generally, see pp. 512–526 in Chapter V and pp. 1068–1091 in Chapter VII.

## NOTES ON THE PROBLEM OF RETROACTIVITY

The judicial power typically operates on the parties to the action before it, thus applying "new law" to parties who, when acting, had not been aware of it. Having to apply a holding to the parties in the case operates as an important constraint on common-law courts' law-generating capacities; this requirement tends to constrain courts' actions to interstitial change that a thoughtful lawyer might have anticipated (as, perhaps, in the Chenery litigation itself). Legislation, on the other hand, is rarely retrospective in application, the usual exception being statutes that relieve individuals from prior burdens. Legislatures may also, on occasion, date the application of changes in laws, such as tax laws, to their introduction as legislative business, in order to protect against evasion in anticipation of their enactment. If an agency, adjudicating, applies "new law" to the parties before it (as the judicial model suggests it should), may a court nonetheless determine that the new rule can be applied only prospectively? Or if an agency has made a rule that is to operate prospectively, but a reviewing court finds it inadequately supported, may the agency on repairing the defect make its rule applicable as of the original date of its promulgation?

(1) ***On Permitting Only Prospective Application of New Policies Developed in Adjudication.*** In EPILEPSY FOUNDATION OF NORTHEAST OHIO v. NLRB, 268 F.3d 1095 (D.C. Cir. 2001), an NLRB decision had characterized as unfair labor practices actions that, when they had been taken, were clearly permitted by prevailing Board decisions. Section 7 of the National Labor Relations Act, 29 U.S.C. § 157 states that "employees shall have the right . . . to engage in other concerted activities for the purpose of collective bargaining or other mutual aid or protection." Over the years, the NLRB had vacillated over its interpretation of this right, but for a decade had allowed the challenged employer conduct. In reinterpreting § 7, the Board had repudiated that view.

Judge Edwards, formerly a professor of labor law, wrote for the reviewing court, acknowledging that "the Board's decision in this case is a reasonable reading of § 7 of the NLRA. An otherwise reasonable interpretation of § 7 is not made legally infirm because the Board gives *renewed*, rather than new, meaning to a disputed statutory provision. It is a fact of life in NLRB lore that certain substantive provisions of the NLRA invariably fluctuate with the changing compositions of the Board. . . . The Board's conclusion obviously is debatable (because the Board has 'changed its mind' several times in addressing this issue); but the rationale underlying the decision in this case is both clear and reasonable. That is all that is necessary to garner deference from the court. 'When a challenge to an agency construction of a statutory provision, fairly conceptualized, really centers on the wisdom of the agency's policy, rather than whether it is a reasonable choice within a gap left open by Congress, the challenge must fail.' Chevron U.S.A. Inc. v. Natural Res. Def. Council, Inc., 467 U.S. 837, 866 (1984) [p. 1206]. The Foundation's challenge here is merely an attack on the wisdom of the agency's policy, and, therefore, the challenge must fail." Nonetheless, "when there is a 'substitution of new law for old law that was reasonably clear,' the new rule may justifiably be given prospectively-only effect in order to 'protect the settled expectations of those who had relied on the preexisting rule.' Williams Natural Gas Co. v. FERC, 3 F.3d 1544, 1554 (D.C. Cir. 1993). . . . In light of this governing principle, there is little doubt here that the Board erred in giving retroactive effect to its new interpretation of § 7. At the time when this case arose, the Board's policy . . . was absolutely clear. . . . Indeed, it would be a 'manifest injustice' to require the Foundation to pay damages to an employee who, without legal right, flagrantly defied his employer's *lawful* instructions."

On the other hand, as the D.C. Circuit has reiterated, "[u]nder this Circuit's law, retroactive effect is appropriate for adjudicatory rules . . . that are new applications of existing law, clarifications, and additions rather than the substitution of new law for old law that was reasonably clear." HealthBridge Mgmt., LLC v. NLRB, 798 F.3d 1059, 1069 n.6 (D.C. Cir. 2015).

Agencies themselves sometimes adjust their remedy if an adjudication raises questions about the fairness of retroactive application. "Retroactivity seems particularly unfair when the effect is to impose a significant penalty on a party who had every reason to believe its actions were legal. . . . [A]n agency can avoid this problem by exercising its discretion not to penalize, but simply declare unlawful, conduct that the agency previously held permissible." Kristen E. Hickman & Richard J. Pierce, Jr., Administrative Law Treatise § 15.2 (6th ed. 2018). See FCC v. Fox, 566 U.S. 502 (2009) (p. 1160), for an illustrative example.

The question of an agency's ability to retroactively impose new legal standards announced in adjudication was at issue in DE NIZ ROBLES V. LYNCH, 803 F.3d 1165 (10th Cir. 2015), an opinion written by then-Judge Gorsuch. In 2006, the Tenth Circuit had resolved a statutory tension between 8 U.S.C. § 1255(i), permitting the Attorney General to adjust the status of undocumented immigrants, and 8 U.S.C. § 1182(a), prohibiting certain persons from obtaining lawful residency, in a manner that would have authorized the Attorney General to adjust De Niz Robles's status—an action he promptly sought. Before the Attorney General acted on his petition, however, the Board of Immigration Appeals ruled in another proceeding, contrary to the Tenth Circuit 2006 decision, that the statutory tension had to be resolved to favor the prohibition of lawful residency. In re Briones, 24 I. & N. Dec. 355 (BIA 2007). On the BIA's reading, the Attorney General lacked discretion to adjust De Niz Robles's status. When De Niz Robles appealed the denial of his petition to the Tenth Circuit, the court decided that, at least as to BIA rulings on petitions filed *after* In re Briones, the BIA's reconciliation of the two statutes would control, and not the court's 2006 decision. (The Court made its decision in light of two Supreme Court decisions you will encounter in Chapter VIII: Chevron, U.S.A., Inc. v. NRDC, 467 U.S. 837 (1984) (p. 1206) and National Cable & Telecommunications Ass'n v. Brand X Internet Services, 545 U.S. 967 (2005) (p. 1230).) But could the BIA apply its new view "retroactively" to a petition (in this case, De Niz Robles's) filed in reliance on the Tenth Circuit's earlier reading? No, Judge Gorsuch concluded:

"When it comes to retroactivity and the law we can say a couple things with certainty. First and foremost, we know that legislation is rarely afforded retroactive effect. . . . To overcome the presumption of prospectivity, the Supreme Court has held that Congress must declare unequivocally its intention to regulate past conduct—and even then due process and equal protection demands may sometimes bar its way. . . .

"Quite the opposite from legislation (and with equal certainty) we can say that judicial decisions 'have had retrospective operation for near a thousand years.' Kuhn v. Fairmont Coal Co., 215 U.S. 349, 372 (1910)

(Holmes, J., dissenting). You might wonder why the due process and equal protection concerns that counsel in favor of prospectivity in legislation don't operate similarly when it comes to judicial decisions. The answer, we think, lies in the fact that for civil society to function the people need courts to provide backward-looking resolutions for their disputes. And accepting this premise, the Constitution has sought to mitigate the due process and equal protection concerns associated with retroactive decisionmaking in other ways, by rules circumscribing the nature of the judicial function and the judicial actor. . . .

"So when it comes to Congress we know its handiwork is presumptively prospective. And when it comes to the judiciary we know its decisions are presumptively retroactive. But what does the law have to say when the decision at issue comes from an executive agency? . . . The Constitution speaks far less directly to that peculiar question. Perhaps because the framers anticipated an Executive charged with enforcing the decisions of the other branches—not with exercising delegated legislative authority, let alone exercising that authority in a quasi-judicial tribunal empowered to overrule judicial decisions. . . . Coming at it from another angle, if the separation of powers doesn't forbid this form of decision-making outright, might second-order constitutional protections sounding in due process and equal protection, as embodied in our longstanding traditions and precedents addressing retroactivity in the law, sometimes constrain the retroactive application of its results?

"We think the answer yes. In light of the principles and precedents we've outlined, it seems to us that the more an agency acts like a judge—applying preexisting rules of general applicability to discrete cases and controversies—the closer it comes to the norm of adjudication and the stronger the case may be for retroactive application of the agency's decision. But the more an agency acts like a legislator—announcing new rules of general applicability—the closer it comes to the norm of legislation and the stronger the case becomes for limiting application of the agency's decision to future conduct. The presumption of prospectivity attaches to Congress's own work unless it plainly indicates an intention to act retroactively. That same presumption, we think, should attach when Congress's delegates seek to exercise delegated legislative policymaking authority: their rules too should be presumed prospective in operation unless Congress has clearly authorized retroactive application. And this logic, we believe, suffices to resolve our case. . . ."

(2) ***On Applying New Precedent to Other Parties.*** The vacillation that preceded (and followed) the NLRB's decision in Epilepsy Foundation[3] is perhaps extreme, yet we are accustomed to thinking of the law developed by adjudication, the common law, as more malleable than statutes. Any party to a common-law proceeding has the right to argue that a precedent ostensibly applicable to its situation should be distinguished or overruled. When, in SHELL OIL CO. V. FERC, 707 F.2d 230 (5th Cir. 1983), the agency

[3] The NLRB had made the challenged decision during the Clinton Administration. Three years after the Epilepsy Foundation decision, during the Bush Administration, it returned to its prior interpretation. IBM Corporation, 341 NLRB 1288 (2004).

refused to reconsider a policy adopted in an earlier adjudication in the face of arguments that the factual circumstances now before it differed, the Fifth Circuit vacated the FERC decision and remanded it for reconsideration. "Agencies may establish rules of general application in a statutory rulemaking or an individual adjudication. The choice of methods is a matter within the agency's informed discretion. But we must be mindful that these two methods of making rules differ fundamentally in the due process safeguards they provide. Rulemaking procedures require public notice and an opportunity for all interested parties to participate. . . . By contrast, no due process guarantees are extended to non-parties in an individual adjudication, although non-parties may be greatly affected by a general rule an agency adopts in such a proceeding. Shell was afforded no meaningful opportunity in [the earlier FERC decision] to challenge [its] factual assumption. . . . Due process requires that Shell be allowed to challenge that assumption here and now."

Whether or not "due process" was actually at stake, the court's observation reflects general truths about the contrast between adjudication and rulemaking as instruments for policy development. In the former, other similarly situated regulated entities are at the mercy of the skills and circumstances of the particular litigants; they rarely receive notice that an issue of importance to them is about to be decided, and their ability to participate is in any event constrained. The opportunity to argue for distinction or overruling—at least for the first few following cases—is a natural corollary. Normally, though, this is put in terms of an opportunity to argue, not a right to a hearing in the full sense, and lawyers know that adjudicators' tempers (and explanations) will grow short once the new doctrine has become firmly rooted. The final footnote of the Shell Oil opinion states: "Our decision of course does not preclude the Commission from establishing the identical rule on remand if it adduces sufficient evidence to support the underlying assumption."

(3) ***If an Agency Has Corrected a Rulemaking Previously Vacated for Error, Can It Apply the Rule as of the Rule's Initial Effectiveness Date?*** BOWEN V. GEORGETOWN UNIVERSITY HOSPITAL, 488 U.S. 204 (1988), considered a schedule that the Secretary of Health and Human Services had adopted by rulemaking to govern Medicare cost reimbursements. Initially, the agency had acted without following the APA's procedures for notice and comment, attempting to rely on an exception to those procedures, but a district court rejected its use of the new schedule on the ground that that it should have conducted notice and comment rulemaking. HHS then reimbursed costs that had been submitted under the old schedule and used notice and comment rulemaking to adopt the new schedule once more, this time providing for "retroactive corrective adjustments" to recapture excess amounts paid after its initial, invalidated adoption of the schedule. That, the Court concluded, was impermissible. "Retroactivity is not favored in the law. Greene v. United States, 376 U.S. 149, 160 (1964). Thus, congressional enactments and administrative rules will not be construed to have retroactive effect unless their language requires this result. By the same principle, a statutory grant of legislative rulemaking authority will not, as a

general matter, be understood to encompass the power to promulgate retroactive rules unless that power is conveyed by Congress in express terms. Even where some substantial justification for retroactive rulemaking is presented, courts should be reluctant to find such authority absent an express statutory grant." In the legislative history of the applicable statute, "the House and Senate Committee Reports expressed a desire to forbid retroactive cost-limit rules . . . 'so that the provider would know in advance the limits to Government recognition of incurred costs and have the opportunity to act to avoid having costs that are not reimbursable.' The Secretary's past administrative practice is consistent with this interpretation of the statute. . . ."

JUSTICE SCALIA, concurring, insisted that the APA's definition of a rule as "an agency statement of general or particular applicability *and future effect*" 5 U.S.C. § 551(4) (emphasis added) "required that rules have legal consequences only for the future. It could not possibly mean that merely *some* of their legal consequences must be for the future, though they may also have legal consequences for the past, since that description would . . . destroy the entire dichotomy upon which the most significant portions of the APA are based. . . .

"[The House] Report [accompanying the APA] states that '[t]he phrase "future effect" does not preclude agencies from considering and, so far as legally authorized, dealing with past transactions in prescribing rules for the future.' The Treasury Department might prescribe, for example, that for purposes of assessing future income tax liability, income from certain trusts that has previously been considered nontaxable will be taxable—whether those trusts were established before or after the effective date of the regulation. That is not retroactivity in the sense at issue here, i.e., in the sense of altering the *past* legal consequences of past actions. Rather, it is what has been characterized as 'secondary' retroactivity. A rule with exclusively future effect (taxation of future trust income) can unquestionably *affect* past transactions (rendering the previously established trusts less desirable in the future), but it does not for that reason cease to be a rule under the APA. Thus, with respect to the present matter, there is no question that the Secretary could have applied her new wage-index formulas to respondents in the future, even though respondents may have been operating under long-term labor and supply contracts negotiated in reliance upon the pre-existing rule. . . ."

(4) ***On Sending a Rule Back to the Adopting Agency for Correction Without Eliminating Its Effectiveness.*** HHS's unhappy odyssey in Bowen began when a reviewing court struck down its revised cost formula because of a procedural flaw. By the time the agency had again adopted the new formula, now through a legally unexceptionable process, three years had passed. This was the fact that generated the "need" for retroactive application of the rule. But by casting doubt on agencies' legal authority to cure defective rulemakings retrospectively, the Bowen decision created an incentive for those wishing to postpone the effectiveness of regulation to seek review of rulemakings, even for readily corrected and relatively immaterial errors. In reaction, as the material on rulemaking notes (p. 383), courts have

sometimes used the practice of remand without vacatur, under which they remand a rule infected by readily corrected error without vacating it. See also p. 1556 (discussing remedies).

The courts' awareness of the Bowen incentive is illustrated by ICORE v. FCC, 985 F.2d 1075, 1081–82 (D.C. Cir. 1993). In 1986, the FCC had adopted a rule that revised the formula by which local telephone companies were compensated for the interconnections they provided their customers with interstate long-distance carriers. The following year, the D.C. Circuit found that the Commission had failed to demonstrate a rational basis for the new formula. The court remanded the case to the agency without vacating the rule. The FCC reopened comment on the revised formula and, in 1991, readopted it with an augmented explanation. This time, the court found the explanation adequate. It then turned to petitioners' argument that use of the revised formula to govern compensation for the period 1986–91 constituted impermissible retroactive rulemaking:

"Here, of course, in contrast to [Bowen], the court considering the rule initially found it inappropriate to set the rule aside. The court's decision on that point represented a careful consideration of the risk of disruption and of the likelihood that the rule was altogether sound at the core.... Petitioners offer no reason why a rule so treated, and in fact applied during the entire interim period, should be treated the same as the rule initially 'struck down' in [Bowen]. Petitioners cite no case employing [Bowen] to cancel the effect of rules deliberately left standing by a court pending a remand...."

(5) ***On Primary and Secondary Retroactivity.*** Justice Scalia's distinction between primary and secondary retroactivity is well established, but its application can be problematic. Consider WILLIAM V. LUNEBURG, RETROACTIVITY AND ADMINISTRATIVE RULEMAKING, 1991 Duke L.J. 106, 109–10: "At the outset it should be noted that the formulation of a definition of retroactivity is no easy task, as the literature demonstrates. Take these relatively simple cases:

1. The Environmental Protection Agency (EPA) for the first time adopts a standard for the release of sulfur dioxide from existing power plants. The regulation imposes civil penalties for pre-adoption releases of that pollutant in violation of the new standard.

2. The EPA promulgates a new sulfur dioxide standard with a compliance date two years in the future. Most or all plants within the scope of the regulation will need to dismantle pollution-control technology installed in response to a prior, less stringent EPA regulation and invest in new stack gas cleaning equipment.

3. A newly constructed power plant applies to the EPA for a permit to operate. The permit would have been granted under EPA regulations in effect during the construction phase of the facility, but it is denied based on new EPA regulations adopted between the time of application and final agency action on the permit.

"Under one common definition, a retroactive regulation gives pre-adoption conduct a different legal effect from the one it would have had without the adoption of the regulation. Under this view, only the first case posed above is clearly a case of formal retroactivity. The third case is somewhat problematic in that regard, and the second case would fall outside this account of retroactivity. Yet all of these cases and variations provoke concern for the same reasons: They create 'surprise' and a potential for undermining 'reasonable' reliance by affected parties. When a certain activity occurred, apparently applicable legal principles either signaled approval or at least did not suggest disapproval. Retroactivity may threaten these expectations with 'disappointment' and unforeseen costs. The destabilizing effects of retroactive regulation suggest the need to come to terms with the permissible parameters of retroactivity. The impact of Bowen . . . depends, to a great degree, on the Court's concept of retroactivity, the contours of which are still obscure."

## SECTION 4. RULEMAKING AND ADJUDICATION IN CONTEXT: PUBLIC ADMINISTRATION AND THE TOOLS OF GOVERNMENT

***REPORT OF THE PRESIDENT'S COMMITTEE ON ADMINISTRATIVE MANAGEMENT***

***Notes on Public Administration and the Tools of Government***

Rulemaking and adjudication are the fundamental categories of agency action under the APA. But the great bulk of government activity affecting the public occurs outside of or prior to the relatively structured interchanges that are the principal focus of this casebook. Among other tasks, agencies gather information, conduct research, implement programs directly, and enter contracts or make grants; they must also obtain and implement the budget and manage their personnel to get their work done. The great diversity of these agency actions and related settings makes it difficult to present them in a few paragraphs. In addition, such activities are not often litigated. Courses in administrative law thus tend to mention them only in passing.

Yet these other activities are important parts of what agencies do. Describing, evaluating, and improving these activities are core tasks for public administration, which Leonard White, a founder of that field, defined as "the management of men and materials in the accomplishment of the purposes of the state" (using the gendered language of his time). Leonard D. White, Introduction to the Study of Public Administration (1926). Though both public administration and administrative law have longer lineages,[1] the two fields in their modern incarnations trace their

---

[1] For the former, see generally Jay M. Shafritz & Albert C. Hyde, Classics of Public Administration (8th ed. 2017); for the latter, see generally Jerry L. Mashaw, Creating the Administrative Constitution: The Lost One Hundred Years of American Administrative Law (2012).

development to the same period in the first four decades of the twentieth century. In the 1930s, three foundational bodies of work in administrative law and public administration constituted the intellectual and practical backdrop against which the APA was constructed. One was produced by the Attorney General's Committee on Administrative Procedure; a second was produced by the ABA's Special Committee on Administrative Law. These two sets of work are discussed above at pp. 238–244 and 250]. An excerpt from the third—the Report of the President's Committee on Administrative Management, sometimes called the Brownlow Committee Report after the name of its chair—appears below. As you read this excerpt and the notes that follow, consider how the procedures of rulemaking and adjudication—as central to administrative law and therefore to modern government as they are—are only pieces in this much larger story.

## REPORT OF THE PRESIDENT'S COMMITTEE ON ADMINISTRATIVE MANAGEMENT

U.S. Government Printing Office (1938).

The need for action in realizing democracy was as great in 1789 as it is today. It was thus not by accident but by deliberate design that the Founding Fathers set the American executive in the Constitution on a solid foundation. Sad experience under the Articles of Confederation, with an almost headless government and committee management, had brought the American Republic to the edge of ruin. Our forefathers had broken away from hereditary government and pinned their faith on democratic rule, but they had not found a way to equip the new democracy for action. Consequently, there was a grim purpose in resolutely providing for a presidency which was to be a national office. The president is indeed the one and only national officer representative of the entire nation. There was hesitation on the part of some timid souls in providing the president with an election independent of Congress; with a longer term than most governors of that day; with the duty of informing the Congress as to the state of the Union and of recommending to its consideration 'such Measures as he shall judge necessary and expedient'; with a two-thirds veto; with a wide power of appointment; and with military and diplomatic authority. But this reluctance was overcome in the face of need and a democratic executive established. . . .

Our presidency unites at least three important functions. From one point of view the president is a political leader—leader of a party, leader of the Congress, leader of a people. From another point of view he is head of the nation in the ceremonial sense of the term, the symbol of our American national solidarity. From still another point of view the president is the chief executive and administrator within the federal system and service. In many types of government these duties are divided or only in part combined, but in the United States they have always been united in one and the same person whose duty it is to perform all of these tasks.

Your Committee on Administrative Management has been asked to investigate and report particularly upon the last function; namely, that of administrative management—the organization for the performance of the duties imposed upon the president in exercising the executive power vested in him by the Constitution of the United States. . . .

Throughout our history we have paused now and then to see how well the spirit and purpose of our nation is working out in the machinery of everyday government with a view to making such modifications and improvements as prudence and the spirit of progress might suggest. Our government was the first to set up in its formal Constitution a method of amendment, and the spirit of America has been from the beginning of our history the spirit of progressive changes to meet conditions shifting perhaps more rapidly here than elsewhere in the world.

Since the Civil War, as the tasks and responsibilities of our government have grown with the growth of the nation in sweep and power, some notable attempts have been made to keep our administrative system abreast of the new times. The assassination of President Garfield by a disappointed office seeker aroused the nation against the spoils system and led to the enactment of the civil service law of 1883. . . . The confusion in fiscal management led to the establishment of the Bureau of the Budget and the budgetary system in 1921. . . . And, indeed, many other important forward steps have been taken.

Now we face again the problem of governmental readjustment, in part as the result of the activities of the nation during the desperate years of the industrial depression, in part because of the very growth of the nation, and in part because of the vexing social problems of our times. There is room for vast increase in our national productivity and there is much bitter wrong to set right in neglected ways of human life. There is need for improvement of our governmental machinery to meet new conditions and to make us ready for the problems just ahead. . . .

The efficiency of government rests upon two factors: the consent of the governed and good management. In a democracy consent may be achieved readily, though not without some effort, as it is the cornerstone of the Constitution. Efficient management in a democracy is a factor of peculiar significance.

Administrative efficiency is not merely a matter of paper clips, time clocks, and standardized economies of motion. These are but minor gadgets. Real efficiency goes much deeper down. It must be built into the structure of a government just as it is built into a piece of machinery.

Fortunately the foundations of effective management in public affairs, no less than in private, are well known. They have emerged universally wherever men have worked together for some common purpose, whether through the state, the church, the private association, or the commercial enterprise. They have been written into constitutions, charters, and articles of incorporation, and exist as habits of work in the daily life of all organized peoples. Stated in simple terms these canons of efficiency require the establishment of a responsible and effective chief executive as the center of energy, direction, and administrative management; the systematic organization of all activities in the hands of a qualified personnel under the direction of the chief executive; and to aid him in this, the establishment of appropriate managerial and staff agencies. There must also be provision for planning, a complete fiscal system, and means for holding the executive accountable for his program.

Taken together, these principles, drawn from the experience of mankind in carrying on large-scale enterprises, may be considered as the first requirement of good management. They comprehend the subject matter of administrative management as it is dealt with in this report. Administrative management concerns itself in democracy with the executive and his duties, with managerial and staff aides, with organization, with personnel, and with the fiscal system because these are the indispensable means of making good the popular will in a people's government.

## NOTES ON PUBLIC ADMINISTRATION AND THE TOOLS OF GOVERNMENT

(1) ***The Backdrop and Outcome of the Report of the President's Committee on Administrative Management.*** GILLIAN E. METZGER & KEVIN M. STACK, INTERNAL ADMINISTRATIVE LAW, 115 Mich. L. Rev. 1239, 1266–72 (2017): "The APA arose out of efforts at administrative reform in which internal agency practice and organization were center stage. . . . [One of the] leading investigations of federal administration [that] played a particularly important role in the lead up to the APA [was] the President's Committee on Administrative Management (commonly known as the Brownlow Committee). . . . The Brownlow Committee report did not speak in terms of internal administrative law. Instead its lexicon was that of the newly emerged field of public administration, with the latter's emphasis on effective management, efficiency, and administrative organization. Nonetheless, the report focused its attention on what we argue here is part of internal administrative law—specifically, the mechanisms that enable greater policy and managerial control within agencies and across the executive branch as a whole. . . .

"Chief among the report's recommendations was a strong call for reorganizing the executive branch to enhance presidential power. . . . The recommendation for which the Brownlow Committee is perhaps most famous was its call for an end to independent agencies—for which it coined the term a 'headless fourth branch.' According to the report, independent agencies' functions should have been transferred to executive departments, with the agencies' policy and administrative activities folded into the departments and their adjudicatory functions retaining independence. The report also recommended expanding the president's staff, centralizing core management functions in agencies over which the president could exercise direct control, transferring accounting and disbursement power from the comptroller general to the Treasury department, and providing the president with broad authority to reorganize the executive branch without the need for congressional involvement. . . . In addition to greater presidential supervision of the executive branch writ large, the report advocated restructuring individual agencies so that agency leaders could exercise greater managerial and policy control. . . .

"Roosevelt embraced the Brownlow Committee's recommendations. . . . But the legislation he proposed incorporating [them] faced a hostile response from Congress. . . . Despite this lack of immediate results, the Brownlow Committee's effort to strengthen presidential powers over administration ultimately proved successful [via the Hoover Commission]. . . . Chaired by the former president, the Hoover Commission was created by a Republican Congress in 1947 as part of an effort to retract the broad national administrative state left by the New Deal and World War II. But to the consternation of its founders, the Hoover Commission adopted a stance similar to the Brownlow Committee. . . . In the face of now bipartisan support, Congress enacted many of the Hoover Commission's recommendations for greater presidential and agency head control."

(2) ***The Continued Relevance of the Report of the President's Committee on Administrative Management.*** NOAH A. ROSENBLUM, THE ANTIFASCIST ROOTS OF PRESIDENTIAL ADMINISTRATION, 122 Colum. L. Rev. 1, 14–15 (2022): "With the benefit of hindsight, it is clear that the Committee [on Administrative Management] exercised a powerful, subterranean influence on the development of executive governance. . . . First, although its initial legislative proposal failed, [the Committee] did shepherd its most important and consequential recommendations into law a few years later. . . . [Second, the Committee]'s influence stretched beyond this moment of creation. Many of [its] proposals, although not implemented at the time, were subsequently put into law. For example, the Committee recommended that executive and adjudicative functions within agencies be kept separate and championed presidential supervision of agency regulatory plans. Neither proposal was fully embraced right away. Less than a decade later, however, the Administrative Procedure Act enshrined [the Committee]'s championed division between adjudication and administration. Some four decades after that, the Reagan White House realized [the Committee]'s vision of presidential administrative superintendence through an executive order requiring agencies to prepare regulatory plans for presidential review. This is the second way that [the Committee] influenced the development of modern presidentialism: by developing a series of specific proposals for bringing about executive governance that, even if unrealized at the time, lay ready-to-hand for the future. Finally, and most significantly, [the Committee] continued to shape the growth of the federal state through its effects on government personnel and administrative theory. [Committee] members . . . were leaders in the field of public administration and continued to train students and advise government officials, including Presidents, for many years. Their report became a foundational text for the discipline."

(3) ***Contemporary Challenges of Public Administration.*** Just as administrative law is not a static field, neither is public administration. Here are three views of the largest challenges facing public administration today. How might you compare these views to each other? What role might administrative lawyers play in addressing these challenges?

(a) ALASDAIR ROBERTS, in STRATEGIES FOR GOVERNING: REINVENTING PUBLIC ADMINISTRATION FOR A DANGEROUS CENTURY (2019), describes the currently predominant mode of public administration research, teaching, and practice as focusing on "meso-level" issues: "agencies, agency networks, and programs," whose "main concern is the ability of managers within agencies and programs to achieve objectives set by political overseers." While this approach need not be abandoned, he argues that its narrow focus will lead us to "overlook critical questions about governance in the twenty-first century. We need a new approach for thinking about public administration that accommodates new conditions in Western democracies and enables a global conversation in which the circumstances of non-Western states are given appropriate attention." He describes this new approach as focusing on the "macro-level," attending to "the governance strategies that are devised by leaders to advance critical national interests and the ways in which these strategies influence the overall architecture of the state."

"We begin . . . by recognizing the state as the main building block of political order in the modern world. States have leaders, and leaders are concerned with a limited set of goals. Leaders develop opinions about the relative importance of these goals and the best ways to achieve them, given their perception of their countries' circumstances. In other words, they invent a strategy for governing that incorporates judgments about priorities and tactics. Next, leaders design and build institutions to implement these strategies. Leaders operate in a world of great uncertainty and turbulence, and they often realize that strategies are misguided or have become outmoded. Consequently, strategies and institutions must be renovated continually. . . . There are many constraints, including variations in the competence of leaders, that make it tremendously difficult to formulate coherent strategies and put them into operation. . . . Even the least competent of leaders has some ideas about priorities and methods, which are the essential elements of strategy. Similarly, there is a limit to what leaders can do by themselves: all must rely on institutions to give expression to their strategies. All of this institutional groundwork—designing, building, consolidating, administering, renovating—falls squarely within the domain of public administration. Leaders choose strategies for governing, but their choices must be informed by advice about the architecture of government: how it ought to be designed and what load it can carry. Scholars in public administration should be skilled in providing this advice."

(b) DONALD F. KETTL, in THE TRANSFORMATION OF GOVERNANCE: PUBLIC ADMINISTRATION FOR THE TWENTY-FIRST CENTURY 116, 120–32, 142–44 (2015), identifies a transformation from an older style of governance rooted in hierarchical, centralized, and separate agencies that often provided services directly themselves. This transformation, he argues, is due to the "twin forces" of "devolution and globalization," which have posed fundamental challenges to the traditional focus of public administration. As to devolution: "Over the last several decades, the federal government's work has increasingly been carried out through an elaborate network of contracting, intergovernmental grants, loans and loan guarantees, regulations, and other indirect administrative approaches." As to globalization: "The markets have become more important than national governments in setting the economic rules. . . . The communications revolution [has led to] rampant fragmentation of norms, ideologies, values, and institutions. . . . Nongovernmental organizations have quickly acquired great influence. . . . Add to this the widely recognized and growing power of formal, quasi-governmental, international organizations like the World Bank, IMF [International Monetary Fund], WTO [World Trade Organization], and the EU [European Union]. . . . Globalization . . . has transformed government not only by posing new administrative challenges but also by introducing new risks and uncertainties in solving these challenges. . . . If government must devise new strategies for working effectively in this world, public administration must devise new theories to explain and guide it. . . . This certainly does not mean abandoning the traditional public administration model. . . It *does* mean updating it to deal effectively with the horizontal networks that have been layered on top of the traditional system. Thus, the first governance problem is *adaptation*: fitting traditional vertical systems to the new challenges of globalization and devolution; and integrating new horizontal systems into the traditional vertical ones. The second governance problem is *capacity*—enhancing government's ability to govern and manage effectively in this transformed environment. . . . Closely related is a third governance problem, *scale*—sorting out the functions of different levels of governance and, in particular, redefining the role of the federal government."

(c) M. ERNITA JOAQUIN & THOMAS M. GREITENS, in AMERICAN ADMINISTRATIVE CAPACITY: DECLINE, DECAY, AND RESILIENCE 5–6, 11, 54 (2021), take on the question of capacity directly as critical to the task of contemporary public administration: "Administrative capacity refers to the capacity of the administrative state to marshal the authority, expertise, resources, and relationships needed to respond and adapt in an accountable way to the changing problems of the nation. Depending on leaders' political strategies of governing, it is the capacity of the bureaucracy to engage with citizens and organized sectors in defining national needs and priorities and in crafting and managing solutions that uphold democratic and public service values. To reform or control administrative capacity is to address it in its five core dimensions: problem solving, management, administrative conservatorship, engagement, and accountability. Imbalance in reforming and controlling administrative capacity results in declining capacity. Creating resilient capacity must be the ultimate goal of capacity building."

Joaquin and Greitens trace the history of administrative capacity from the founding era alongside administrative reform movements, dividing this history into six periods: the "*capacity mapping-out* period of Constitutional framing"; the "*capacity buildup* period starting from the Progressive reform movement establishing the civil service system and budget system of the administrative state to the New Deal era"; the "*capacity consolidation* period that saw reforms in administrative procedures and other management systems, from World War II through the Great Society"; the "*capacity dilution or decline* period beginning with the 1970s . . . through the 1980s"; the "*concealed capacity decline* period" of the 1990s and 2000s; and "the *capacity decay* period, from 2017 onward, in which economic populism and cultural fissures coincided with the height of anti-government rhetoric and the 'deconstruction of the administrative state.' " To remedy this decay, they call "for a reconstitution of capacity with a greater role for Congress, administrator engagement, and citizen trust in professional bureaucracy."

(4) ***Agency Activities Beyond Rulemaking and Adjudication.*** One important task of public administration has long been to study and improve the broad array of tools by which agencies do their work—both internal tools that govern their own operations and external tools through which agencies affect the public. As you continue your study of rulemaking and adjudication in the rest of this book, keep in mind the way those procedures fit alongside the additional tools described below. How might these tools be used to improve the efficiency of agency operations? How might these tools be used to implement congressional policy? How might these tools be used to further presidential interests? For further consideration of these questions, see pp. 1052–1055 in Chapter VII.

(a) LUTHER GULICK, NOTES ON THE THEORY OF ORGANIZATION (1937): "What is the work of the chief executive? What does he do? The answer is POSDCORB. POSDCORB is, of course, a made-up word designed to call attention to the various functional elements of the work of a chief executive because 'administration' and 'management' have lost all specific content. POSDCORB is made up of the initials and stands for the following activities:

"Planning, that is working out in broad outline the things that need to be done and the methods for doing them to accomplish the purpose set for the enterprise;

"Organizing, that is the establishment of the formal structure of authority through which work subdivisions are arranged, defined and co-ordinated for the defined objective;

"Staffing, that is the whole personnel function of bringing in and training the staff and maintaining favorable conditions of work;

"Directing, that is the continuous task of making decisions and embodying them in specific and general orders and instructions and serving as the leader of the enterprise;

"Co-ordinating, that is the all important duty of interrelating the various parts of the work;

"Reporting, that is keeping those to whom the executive is responsible informed as to what is going on, which thus includes keeping himself and his subordinates informed through records, research and inspection;

"Budgeting, with all that goes with budgeting in the form of fiscal planning, accounting and control. . . .

"In the largest enterprises, particularly where the chief executive is as a matter of fact unable to do the work that is thrown upon him, it may be presumed that one or more parts of POSDCORB should be suborganized."

(b) LESTER M. SALAMON, THE NEW GOVERNANCE AND THE TOOLS OF PUBLIC ACTION: AN INTRODUCTION, in THE TOOLS OF GOVERNMENT: A GUIDE TO THE NEW GOVERNANCE 1–4 (Lester M. Salamon ed., 2002): "A massive proliferation has occurred in the tools of public action, in the instruments or means used to address public problems." Many of these tools are rooted in distinctive financial arrangements—including grants, contracts, loans, tax expenditures, insurance, and vouchers—between the federal government and third-party actors. "In a sense, the 'public administration problem' has leapt beyond the borders of the public agency and now embraces a wide assortment of 'third parties' that are intimately involved in the implementation, and often the management, of the public's business." For example, to implement the housing programs under its statutory authority, the Department of Housing and Urban Development works primarily through a combination of "loan guarantees to underwrite mortgage credit extended by private commercial banks," "tax subsidies that flow to homeowners through the income tax system," and "housing vouchers administered by semiautonomous local housing authorities to finance housing provided by private landlords."

(c) These tools are often contrasted with direct government, defined as "the delivery or withholding of a good or service by government employees." CHRISTOPHER K. LEMAN, DIRECT GOVERNMENT, in THE TOOLS OF GOVERNMENT, supra, at 48–79. "First, direct government can be used to produce and deliver goods and services. Examples here would be . . . Social Security, the Veterans Administration hospitals, and the activities of the Forest Service and the Park Service. . . . A second type of direct government program involves the legitimate exercise of force, which is a classic function of direct government. . . . . [T]he operation of prisons, the operation of the criminal justice, and tax collection all fall under this general heading. . . . Finally, direct government is often used to perform a variety of facilitative functions required for other institutions to be able to perform their roles. Included here would be . . . the management of the currency, the operation of the postal system, and economic management more generally."

(5) ***Administrative Law as the Law of Public Administration?*** At the core of administrative law is the agency, and agencies exist only because statutes create them, empower them, and describe their organization and functions. Taking these organic statutes as part of administrative law alongside the APA, administrative law not only is itself broader than rulemaking and adjudication but also establishes as well as regularizes public administration. To what extent do you agree? Consider these arguments for a stronger linkage between the two fields:

(a) LAWRENCE E. LYNN, JR., RESTORING THE RULE OF LAW TO PUBLIC ADMINISTRATION: WHAT FRANK GOODNOW GOT RIGHT AND WHAT LEONARD WHITE DIDN'T, 69 Pub. Admin. Rev. 803, 803 (2009): "[A] broad consensus within public administration appears to hold that law is one of many environmental constraints on administrative discretion rather than its source, a challenge to administrative leadership rather than its guiding principle, a necessary element of accountability but not a sufficient one. Many who pay it respect tend to treat the rule of law as a matter of legality or of rulemaking and enforcement, a topic of lesser importance to the field than, for example, organization and management, public policy planning and analysis, budgeting and finance, human resources administration, and ethics. In this essay, I argue that this largely benign neglect of the rule of law undermines the legitimacy and usefulness of a profession that aspires to be indispensable to constitutional governance."

(b) GILLIAN E. METZGER, ADMINISTRATIVE LAW, PUBLIC ADMINISTRATION, AND THE ADMINISTRATIVE CONFERENCE OF THE UNITED STATES, 83 Geo. Wash. L. Rev. 1517, 1518–19, 1534–36 (2015): "[F]rom its birth, administrative law has claimed a close connection to governmental practice. But, in fact, as administrative law has grown and matured, it has moved further away from critical aspects of how agencies function. As many have noted, administrative law focuses almost entirely on external dimensions of administrative action, and the external dimensions it targets are increasingly not the main drivers of administrative action. . . . As a result, despite their common concern with administrative agencies, the fields of administrative law and public administration interact largely as passing strangers, acknowledging each other's existence but almost never engaging in any sustained interchange. . . .

"[Yet] strong arguments exist for tying administrative law and public administration more closely together. Perhaps the most basic argument in favor derives from the purpose of administrative law. Administrative law aims both to empower and constrain agencies, to ensure effective government as well as preserve accountability and prevent arbitrary rule through requirements of authorization, participation, transparency, and reasoned decisionmaking. If administrative law is increasingly divorced from the realities of governmental functioning, it is less able to perform either role. . . . The danger is not simply that the core aims of administrative law will not be realized, but also that the actual ways in which administrative government is constrained and strengthened will not be recognized. This raises the danger that an effective source of administrative reform will be ignored. . . . Worse, such lack of recognition may lead to evisceration of those features that may be critical to effective and accountable administration. Moreover, the evisceration of internal administration also debilitates external controls. . . . It is internal administration—systemic mechanisms for planning, priority-setting, policymaking, resource allocation, and managerial oversight and supervision—that ensures agencies implement the statutes and instructions that their political and legal overseers give them and allows those overseers to hold agencies to account when they fail to do so."

(c) ELIZABETH FISHER & SIDNEY A. SHAPIRO, ADMINISTRATIVE COMPETENCE: REIMAGINING ADMINISTRATIVE LAW 3–5, 14–16 (2020): "If administrative law is understood as only limiting public administration, then it is not a genuine law of public administration. It is a law about constraint, about ideology, or paradoxically a law not about law. We must imagine administrative law differently. . . . [We must] ensure that administrative law is understood to be what it really is and should be—the law of public administration. . . . [A]dministrative law needs to be understood as an area of law that is *simultaneously* constituting public administration, holding it to account, and demarcating its powers to ensure it is legitimate. In doing these things, administrative lawyers must be cognizant of administrative competence—both understanding it and ensuring it. 'Competence' is a multi-faceted word. It denotes the need for public administration to be 'suitable, fit, appropriate, proper' and for it to 'possess the requisite qualifications.' . . . Using the word 'competence' clarifies that administrative law must ensure that public administration has both legitimate authority and the necessary capacity to accomplish its mission. . . . For administrative law to ensure administrative competence, it needs to do two things. First, it needs to be grounded in an understanding of public administration, its reasoning capacities, and the role it plays in the American democratic order. . . . Second, . . . legal frameworks, legal reasoning, legal accountability mechanisms, and legal doctrines must be shaped by the need to ensure the capacity and authority of public administration."

# CHAPTER IV

# RULEMAKING



Imagine someone who wants to catalog the variety of written texts the American federal government uses to communicate its powers and the rights and obligations of its citizens and residents. She might organize those texts into the following pyramid:

One Constitution ratified
by "the people" and amended infrequently

Hundreds of statutes enacted in each two-year session
by an elected Congress

Thousands of regulations adopted each year by
politically responsible agency heads

Tens of thousands of interpretations and other guidance
documents issued each year by agency bureaus

Countless advice letters, press releases, and other statements of
understanding generated each year by individual bureaucrats

The pyramid shape is descriptively accurate. The relative sizes of the Constitution and the Statutes at Large are obvious. The Code of Federal Regulations, the annual compilation of the documents described by the third level above (and some other materials), is considerably larger than the United States Code (which captures only part of the Statutes at Large). At any agency, the volume of its own interpretations and guidance documents, the fourth level, may exceed that of the entire CFR.

This Chapter is principally concerned with the procedures used to create regulations (the third level). With some exceptions, § 553 of the Administrative Procedure Act provides two possible procedures: (1) "formal rulemaking," an on-the-record process verging on trial, rarely encountered these days but being pushed again in Congress, and (2) "informal" or "notice-and-comment" rulemaking, the procedure most commonly employed today. (Indeed, informal rulemaking has become so dominant that it is the process generally meant when the term "rulemaking" is used.) Agency reliance on the APA's exceptions, meant to be limited, is considerable, with over one-third of major rule adoptions even forgoing prior notice-and-comment procedures, as the Government Accountability Office reported in a 2013 study.

In the materials that follow, Section 1 provides an overview of § 553 and the APA's approach to rulemaking. Section 2 presents formal rulemaking, examining its once-prominent place in administrative law, its near-demise, and its possible re-emergence. Section 3 then considers the requirements for notice-and-comment rulemaking in some detail. We begin with some basic judicial parameters, in particular the Supreme Court's insistence that judges may only rarely impose procedural requirements beyond those required by the APA, the specific substantive statute under which the agency acts, or the agency's own regulations. The flip side of this resistance to judicially imposed procedures is the demand that agencies adhere to procedural requirements that are imposed by statute and regulation, and we examine the specific demands courts have read § 553 to contain. Section 4 examines the exceptions to § 553's requirements, focusing both on the more informal agency issuances (the fourth level of the pyramid above) that play an important role in guiding agency regulatory activities and informing the public of the agency's views, and on binding rulemaking that may, in particular instances, be improperly evading the notice-and-comment rulemaking process.

Then we take a step back and situate the § 553 process in the wider course of making a rule. Section 5 examines the initiation of rulemaking, especially the process for centralized review of executive agencies' rulemaking efforts by the Office for Information and Regulatory Affairs in the Office of Management and Budget. Such centralized review offers Presidents an opportunity to insert their political priorities into the rulemaking process and in general assert close supervision of agency regulation. In this Chapter, however, we focus on outlining the current procedures for centralized review with some attention to the political effects; Chapter VII considers the constitutional implications of such presidential oversight. Finally, Section 6 takes up a set of issues that may arise in the rulemaking process, including ex parte contacts and allegedly biased decisionmakers.

## SECTION 1. INTRODUCTION

***5 U.S.C. § 553***

If authorized by statute, consistent with the Constitution, and adopted through the required procedures, regulations have legally binding effect on the government and citizens alike, until displaced by statute or other validly adopted regulations. Thus, rulemaking is an extremely important process in modern regulatory programs.

Two sets of broader issues repeatedly surface that you may find helpful to think about in considering the materials in this Chapter. The first set concerns process: what kinds of procedures should be required for contemporary rulemaking? Does your answer to this question vary by the type of policy or rule at stake, or by the type of agency (and its oversight by the White House or Congress)? Have the courts done a good job in interpreting § 553 and applying it to current rulemaking contexts? To what extent are the procedures now required for notice-and-comment rulemaking adequate and effective mechanisms for addressing what are referred to below as questions of "general facts"—factual matters that do not vary with particular parties but do involve specific factual issues and thus are distinct from general policy propositions? Is the current procedural framework excessively rigidified and formalistic—or, alternatively, are agencies allowed too much room for action that evades important constraints? And what about fairness and equity concerns: are they adequately addressed through prevailing procedures?

The second set of broader issues concerns roles: what roles should different institutions play in setting those procedural requirements and overseeing the rulemaking process? To what extent should these roles be a central responsibility of the courts as opposed to the political branches of the federal government (Congress and the President)? In thinking about institutional roles, remember that the range of institutional players here is potentially quite broad and also includes state and local governments, private or nongovernmental institutions, experts, regulated parties, regulatory beneficiaries, and interested members of the general public. Another critical player is, of course, the agency. Should agencies be entrusted with primary responsibility for developing adequate rulemaking procedures, given their substantive area expertise, or do agencies have too great an interest in minimizing the procedural constraints they face?

## 5 U.S.C. § 553

### Rule making

(a) This section applies, according to the provisions thereof, except to the extent that there is involved—

(1) a military or foreign affairs function of the United States; or

(2) a matter relating to agency management or personnel or to public property, loans, grants, benefits, or contracts.

(b) General notice of proposed rulemaking shall be published in the Federal Register, unless persons subject thereto are named and either personally served or otherwise have actual notice thereof in accordance with law. The notice shall include—

(1) a statement of the time, place, and nature of public rule making proceedings;

(2) reference to the legal authority under which the rule is proposed; and

(3) either the terms or substance of the proposed rule or a description of the subjects and issues involved.

Except when notice or hearing is required by statute, this subsection does not apply—

(A) to interpretative rules, general statements of policy, or rules of agency organization, procedure, or practice; or

(B) when the agency for good cause finds (and incorporates the finding and a brief statement of reasons therefor in the rules issued) that notice and public procedure thereon are impracticable, unnecessary, or contrary to the public interest.

(c) After notice required by this section, the agency shall give interested persons an opportunity to participate in the rule making through submission of written data, views, or arguments with or without opportunity for oral presentation. After consideration of the relevant matter presented, the agency shall incorporate in the rules adopted a concise general statement of their basis and purpose. When rules are required by statute to be made on the record after opportunity for an agency hearing, sections 556 and 557 of this title apply instead of this subsection.

(d) The required publication or service of a substantive rule shall be made not less than 30 days before its effective date, except—

(1) a substantive rule which grants or recognizes an exemption or relieves a restriction;

(2) interpretative rules and statements of policy; or

(3) as otherwise provided by the agency for good cause found and published with the rule.

(e) Each agency shall give an interested person the right to petition for the issuance, amendment, or repeal of a rule.

## NOTES

(1) ***Types of Rulemaking Under the APA.*** Section 553 is the APA's main section governing rulemaking. It mostly defines the procedures for "informal" rulemaking, sometimes called "notice-and-comment rulemaking" after the requirements in (b) and (c) that an agency provide "notice of proposed rule making" and "opportunity to participate in the rule making." As you will see in the rest of this Chapter, the word "informal" does not quite accurately capture the complexity of the process, but the procedure earns its name in contrast with the requirements for "formal" rulemaking contemplated by the last sentence of (c). That sentence points to the requirements of other sections of the APA—§§ 556 and 557, which outline procedures for trial-type evidentiary hearings—in those circumstances where *another* statute the agency implements instructs that rules be developed "on the record after opportunity for an agency hearing." Section 553 also identifies many exceptions from its procedures, to different degrees, in subsections (a), (b)(A)–(B), and (d). Most of this Chapter is devoted to understanding these three areas: formal rulemaking, informal rulemaking, and its exceptions.

Beyond the APA, specific agency statutes can also provide for hybrid procedures between informal and formal rulemaking. You may study these hybrid procedures more in other courses dedicated to the substantive work of particular agencies. This course focuses on the APA procedures, although Note 5 (Legislatively Required Hybrid Rulemaking) below on p. 322 discusses some of these mixed procedures in the context of the APA.

(2) ***What Is a Rule?*** The APA's definition of a rule is quite broad. The definition comes in § 551(4): " '[R]ule' means the whole or a part of an agency statement of general or particular applicability and future effect designed to implement, interpret, or prescribe law or policy or describing the organization, procedure, or practice requirements of an agency and includes the approval or prescription for the future of rates, wages, corporate or financial structures or reorganization thereof, prices, facilities, appliances, services or allowances therefor or of valuations, costs, or accounting, or practices bearing on any of the foregoing[.]" Under this definition, which is contrasted with the term "order" in § 551(6), the term "rule" is not limited to measures promulgated under notice-and-comment or formal rulemaking. Instead, it also includes a vast array of agency documents, including many of the guidance documents, advice letters, and other statements placed in the two lowest levels of the pyramid above.

This definition of a rule as including "an agency statement of . . . particular applicability" differs from the emphasis in constitutional analysis on rules being generally applicable, which you may have seen if you read the material on Londoner and Bi-Metallic in Chapter III starting on p. 220. The APA drafters seem to have intended that "particular applicability" encompass matters such as ratemaking for a specific company. For an argument that this language was unnecessary and that the whole definition of a rule ought to be tightened up, see Ronald M. Levin, The Case for (Finally) Fixing the APA's Definition of "Rule," 56 Admin. L. Rev. 1077 (2004).

Sometimes courts have to decide whether a particular document an agency has produced falls within the definition of a rule, in order to determine whether the agency has complied with the applicable procedures. For example, is an announcement outlining the current year's terms of a payment-in-kind program a rule under the APA's definition? SUGAR CANE GROWERS COOPERATIVE V. VENEMAN, 289 F.3d 89 (D.C. Cir. 2002), involved a payment-in-kind program run by the Department of Agriculture as authorized by the Food Security Act of 1985 to support sugar production. Under the program, sugar producers bid for the right to receive sugar from the government-owned surplus to sell on the market in return for plowing under a given acreage of already planted sugar-producing crops. In August 2001, the Department announced by press release that it had decided to implement a payment-in-kind program for the 2001 sugar crop and subsequently published a "Notice of Program Implementation" in the Federal Register. The Notice included a number of terms that sugar cane growers believed disadvantaged them in comparison to sugar beet growers. Sugar cane growers sued, alleging that the Department had violated the APA by promulgating a rule without notice-and-comment rulemaking.

JUDGE SILBERMAN wrote the panel's decision: "The APA defines a rule very broadly. . . . We have recognized that notwithstanding the breadth of the APA's definition an agency pronouncement that lacks the firmness of a proscribed standard . . . is not a rule. . . . [T]he government . . . argues that because the announcement of the . . . program was an 'isolated agency act' that did not propose to affect subsequent Department acts and had 'no future effect on any other party before the agency' it was not a rule. The government would have us see its announcement of the . . . program as analogous to an agency's award of a contract pursuant to an invitation of bids or an agency's decision to approve an application or a proposal—in administrative law terms an informal adjudication (which is the technical term for an executive action). We have little difficulty . . . in rejecting this argument. The August . . . press release . . . and . . . Notice of Program Implementation set forth the bid submission procedures which all applicants must follow, the payment limitations of the program, and the sanctions that will be imposed on participants if they plant more in future years than in 2001. It is simply absurd to call this anything but a rule by any other name." Do you agree?

(3) ***The Virtues of Making Regulatory Policy Through Rulemaking.*** There are at least two dimensions to thinking about the virtues of making regulatory policy through rulemaking. The first asks whether agencies should be making regulatory policy at all. The second asks about the comparative virtues of making regulatory policy via rulemaking as opposed to adjudication.

Here is a perspective on the first question from a symposium commemorating the 75th anniversary of the APA. For additional perspectives, see the materials on nondelegation in Chapter VII (p. 836):

BLAKE EMERSON, "POLICY" IN THE ADMINISTRATIVE PROCEDURE ACT: IMPLICATIONS FOR DELEGATION, DEFERENCE, AND DEMOCRACY, 97 Chi.-Kent L. Rev. 113, 115, 118–19 (2022): "Whereas critics of the administrative state want to eliminate or sharply circumscribe agencies' policymaking role, the APA's text and history are clear that agencies can and should make important policy judgments through fair procedures. . . . [O]ur contemporary regime is a 'policy state,' which is centrally concerned with accomplishing various social and political objectives, rather than with the maintenance of a socially anchored system of stable rights. Though the concept of policy is indeed ubiquitous in public law, the term is rarely defined or given careful attention in its own right. . . . The APA's legislative text and history [give] 'policy' more specific legal content and defined structure. Legislators and other participants in the debates surrounding the APA understood policy to mean both general governmental goals and the means through which such goals are carried out. Officials who made policy chose secondary and tertiary goals that necessarily incorporated evaluative as well as factual assessments. In doing so they were to use inclusive and efficient procedures that would equalize the power of affected parties to influence the choice of goals and appropriate means. By embracing administrative agencies' policymaking role, the APA recognized the collective, problem-solving, and instrumental role of law within modern governance. The Act allocated policy functions to legally accountable and politically responsive processes and offices. . . . The APA's institutionalization of collective policymaking power continues to have claims on us in the present, both as a matter of positive law and as a matter of democratic principle."

Here is a perspective on the second question from a symposium thirty-five years earlier commemorating the 40th anniversary of the APA. For additional perspectives, see the material on agency choice of policymaking form in Chapter III (p. 254):

ALAN B. MORRISON, THE ADMINISTRATIVE PROCEDURE ACT: A LIVING AND RESPONSIVE LAW, 72 Va. L. Rev. 253, 256–58 (1986): "I have little doubt that anyone would disagree with the conclusion reached by then law professor and now [Justice] Antonin Scalia, who observed that 'perhaps the most notable development in federal government administration during the last two decades is the constant and accelerating flight away from individualized, adjudicatory proceedings to generalized disposition through rulemaking.'[2] This shift has occurred for a number of reasons.

"First, rulemaking is likely to produce a more rationally coherent rule for general application. Unlike adjudications, which are often focused on a single party, rulemaking allows an opportunity for all interested parties to comment. While results in adjudications are often determined by the particular facts before the agency, rulemaking allows . . . the agency to take a broader look at an issue. Thus, instead of solving problems one at a time, the agency establishes an overall framework based on a coherent rationale and develops overarching principles that can be applied in future cases.

"Secondly, rulemaking is more efficient. . . . Adjudications, centering as they do on the particulars of a given case, may require a substantial commitment of resources to establish the narrow set of facts necessary to reach a decision. This process must be repeated on many occasions before the final rule of law emerges. By contrast, a rulemaking . . . will normally resolve a far larger range of issues. Thus, industry groups, consumers, labor unions, environmentalists, and other interested parties find it worthwhile to focus their efforts on a single rulemaking, although they might be unable to justify participating in any single adjudication, let alone an entire series of them. . . .

"Perhaps the single most important reason for the increase in rulemaking has been the advent of new substantive statutes designed to provide protection on an industry-wide, or in some cases nationwide, basis for consumers, workers, or the environment. Because many of these statutes leave the development of substantive standards to the relevant agencies, they specifically or effectively require rulemaking. Yet Congress, aside from adding a few procedural modifications, has by and large been content to let the APA govern this rulemaking. . . ."

(4) ***The Strategy of Making Regulatory Policy Through Rulemaking.*** As the materials in Chapter III on the choice between adjudication and rulemaking illustrate, the classic case SEC v. Chenery Corp., 332 U.S. 194 (1947) (Chenery II) (p. 258), permits agencies to choose their form of

[2] [Antonin] Scalia, Vermont Yankee: The APA, the D.C. Circuit, and the Supreme Court, 1978 Sup. Ct. Rev. 345, 376.

policymaking, subject to constitutional and agency-specific statutory constraints. Those materials suggest some strategic rationales that may explain why agencies may choose one form or another, including the stringency of the procedure they have to follow, the legal effect of the mechanism they choose, the political context in which they operate, and their understanding of the goals of their substantive statutes. See Note 5 (On What Basis Do Agencies Choose a Policymaking Form?) (p. 269).

For a recent example of an agency's strategic choice of rulemaking over adjudication (and an attendant controversy), consider the new focus on rulemaking at the Federal Trade Commission under the Biden Administration. After decades of functioning as a largely adjudication-focused enforcement agency, the FTC decided to reinvigorate its near-dormant rulemaking power. Led by Chair Lina Khan, joined by the two other Democratic Commissioners, the FTC took steps to embrace rulemaking under both its consumer protection mission (preventing "unfair or deceptive acts or practices") and its antitrust mission (preventing "unfair methods of competition") as articulated in Section 5 of the FTC Act, 15 U.S.C. § 45(a)(1).

With respect to the former mission, in 2021, the FTC streamlined its internal rule governing how such consumer-protection rulemakings must unfold (a process on which Congress imposed heightened procedural requirements, beyond the typical APA rulemaking procedures, in response to the last time the FTC engaged in a broad rulemaking agenda in the 1970s). FTC, Revisions to Rules of Practice, 86 Fed. Reg. 38542 (July 22, 2021). The Democratic Chair and Commissioners justified this change by characterizing the previous process as reflecting "self-imposed limitations" designed to "radically reduce the agency's rulemaking capacity," thus hampering its ability to "us[e] all of our available tools robustly to protect consumers from the unfair and deceptive tricks and traps they face in our modern economy." Statement of Commissioner Rebecca Kelly Slaughter Joined by Chair Lina Khan and Commissioner Rohit Chopra Regarding the Adoption of Revised Section 18 Rulemaking Procedures, 86 Fed. Reg. 38551 (July 22, 2021). In 2022, the FTC published an Advance Notice of Proposed Rulemaking under this authority, inviting comment on whether it should develop "rules or other regulatory alternatives concerning the ways in which companies collect, aggregate, protect, use, analyze, and retain consumer data, as well as transfer, share, sell, or otherwise monetize that data in ways that are unfair or deceptive." FTC, Trade Regulation Rule on Commercial Surveillance and Data Security, 87 Fed. Reg. 51273 (Aug. 22, 2022).

With respect to the latter mission, the FTC's Statement of Regulatory Priorities for 2022 listed a series of competition rulemakings under consideration, citing President Biden's 2021 Executive Order urging the agency to consider rulemaking in such matters as "unfair competitive conduct or agreements in the prescription drug industries" and "unfair competition in major Internet marketplaces." FTC, Statement of Regulatory Priorities, 87 Fed. Reg. 5177, 5178 (Jan. 31, 2022); Exec. Order No. 14036 (Promoting Competition in the American Economy), 86 Fed. Reg. 36987 (July 13, 2021). In promoting competition rulemakings, the agency is following the path laid out by one of its Democratic Commissioners and its then-soon-to-be-Chair in a law review article making the case that "exclusive reliance on case-by-case adjudication" in antitrust "has yielded a system of enforcement that generates ambiguity, drains resources, privileges incumbents, and deprives individuals and firms of any real opportunity to participate in the process of creating substantive antitrust rules." ROHIT CHOPRA & LINA M. KHAN, THE CASE FOR "UNFAIR METHODS OF COMPETITION" RULEMAKING, 87 U. Chi. L. Rev. 357 (2020).

The two Republican Commissioners opposed both of these developments. On streamlining the procedures for consumer-protection rulemakings, they stated: "*Better* regulation—which is not the same as *more* regulation—ought to be the goal. By reducing transparency and objectivity in the rulemaking process, the revisions to our . . . procedures move us away from that goal and toward more—and *worse*—regulation." Dissenting Statement of Christine S. Wilson and Noah Joshua Phillips Regarding the Commission Statement on the Adoption of Revised Section 18 Rulemaking Procedures, July 9, 2021.[1] On the move to competition rulemaking: "Adopting a rules-based approach to competition law will diminish the effects-based analysis built through more than four decades of careful assessment," and the statutory authority for "substantive competition rulemaking power" is "unclear." Dissenting Statement of Commissioner Christine S. Wilson, Annual Regulatory Plan and Semi-Annual Regulatory Agenda, Dec. 10, 2021.[2]

AARON L. NIELSON, WHAT HAPPENS IF THE FTC BECOMES A SERIOUS RULEMAKER? in RULEMAKING AUTHORITY OF THE US FEDERAL TRADE COMMISSION (Daniel A. Crane ed., 2022): "Should the FTC begin making broader policy choices through rulemaking . . . it should be prepared for at least three unintended consequences: (i) more ossification, complete with judicial challenges and perhaps even White House oversight; (ii) more zigzagging policy as new FTC leadership, in response to changes in presidential control, moves to undo what the agency has done; and (iii) to more often be the target of what has been called 'administrative law as blood sport,' by which political actors make it more difficult for the agency to function, for example by delaying the confirmation process. The upshot would be an agency that could in theory (and sometimes no doubt in fact) regulate more broadly than the FTC does now, but also one with a different character. In short, the more the FTC becomes a serious rulemaker, the more it will change as an institution." How might you assess the strategic tradeoffs involved in the agency's decision to embrace rulemaking over adjudication?

(5) ***Rulemaking Requires Statutory Authority.*** The APA sets out the default procedures agencies must generally follow in issuing regulations but

---

1 https://www.ftc.gov/system/files/documents/public_statements/1591702/p210100_wilsonphillips_joint_statement_-_rules_of_practice.pdf.

2 https://www.ftc.gov/system/files/documents/public_statements/1598839/annual_regulatory_plan_and_semi-annual_regulatory_agenda_wilson_final.pdf.

Commissioner Noah Joshua Phillips offered a similar critique of the move to competition rulemaking. See Remarks of Commissioner Noah Joshua Phillips Regarding the Commission's Withdrawal of the Section 5 Policy Statement, July 1, 2021, https://www.ftc.gov/system/files/documents/public_statements/1591578/phillips_remarks_regarding_withdrawal_of_section_5_policy_statement.pdf.

does not itself authorize agencies to engage in rulemaking. Instead, such a grant of rulemaking authority must be found in a substantive statute the agency is implementing. Absent such a grant of authority, agency rules cannot claim the force of law (i.e., be "legislative rules"). Although they may function as precedent within the agency, courts will treat them as, at best, persuasive rather than binding on the public. (We take up the difference between legislative and nonlegislative rules in Section 4.b, p. 393.)

How permissive should courts be in finding rulemaking authority in generally worded statutory provisions? THOMAS W. MERRILL and KATHRYN TONGUE WATTS, in AGENCY RULES WITH THE FORCE OF LAW: THE ORIGINAL CONVENTION, 116 Harv. L. Rev. 472, 557 (2002), have argued that courts became more generous in finding such authority starting in the 1960s and 1970s, reflecting an effort by scholars and judges during that time period to encourage greater use of rulemaking over adjudication. An example of this phenomenon is National Petroleum Refiners Ass'n v. FTC, 482 F.2d 672 (D.C. Cir. 1973), in which the D.C. Circuit read a statutory provision granting the FTC general authority "to make rules and regulations for the purposes of carrying out" the Federal Trade Commission Act, 15 U.S.C. § 46(g), as empowering the agency to issue substantive rules that could be enforced through the adjudications the FTC was expressly authorized to undertake. (The FTC is currently relying in part on this authority for its new focus on rulemaking, as discussed in the preceding Note.) According to Merrill and Watts, the effect was to adopt a new canon: "unless the legislative history reveals a clear intent to the contrary, courts should resolve any uncertainty about the scope of an agency's rulemaking authority in favor of finding a delegation of the full measure of power to the agency." Merrill and Watts fault this approach for ignoring Congress's prior practice of signaling when it meant agencies to have power to make rules with the force of law by including a provision imposing sanctions on those who violated agency rules.

For a modern example of such permissiveness, see Cuozzo Speed Technologies, LLC v. Lee, 579 U.S. 261 (2016). In 2012, the Patent and Trademark Office issued a regulation prescribing a standard of review for a third-party claim about a previously issued patent. Patent holders challenged the rule, arguing, in part, that the agency lacked statutory authority to issue it. The Supreme Court upheld the PTO's interpretation of the Leahy-Smith America Invents Act and agreed that the agency had rulemaking authority: "The upshot is, whether we look at statutory language alone, or that language in context of the statute's purpose, we find an express delegation of rulemaking authority, a 'gap' that rules might fill, and 'ambiguity' in respect to the boundaries of that gap." Id. at 280.

The Court reached this determination after applying Chevron deference—the last time, as of this writing, that the Court applied Chevron deference to result in a win for the agency. You may read more about growing skepticism about the Chevron doctrine in Chapter VIII and about the administrative state more generally in Chapter VII (and elsewhere). You may also read about the growth of textualism as a mode of statutory interpretation in Chapter II. Might these trends result in courts being less willing to find rulemaking authority in general statutory language? Consider, for example, Food & Water Watch v. U.S. Dep't of Agric., 1 F.4th 1112 (D.C. Cir. 2021), in which D.C. Circuit Judge Randolph penned a concurrence questioning whether the Council on Environmental Quality "had Congressional authority to issue any regulations": "No statute grants CEQ the authority to issue binding regulations. Instead, CEQ's recent 'regulations' identify its authority to issue regulations as Executive Order No. 11,991, 42 Fed. Reg. 26,967 (May 24, 1977). . . . In this court we have questioned whether CEQ could issue binding regulations. Perhaps CEQ's regulations represent a directive from the President to his subordinates. But that is a far cry from saying, as the regulations do, that CEQ could supplant properly issued regulations of other agencies." See also Richard J. Pierce, Jr., Can the Federal Trade Commission Use Rulemaking to Change Antitrust Law? in Rulemaking Authority of the US Federal Trade Commission (Daniel A. Crane ed., 2022) (arguing that the contemporary Supreme Court would be likely to hold that the FTC does not have general rulemaking authority, thereby overturning National Petroleum Refiners Ass'n as a "relic from a bygone era of statutory interpretation").

## SECTION 2. FORMAL RULEMAKING

**_UNITED STATES v. FLORIDA EAST COAST RAILWAY CO._**

Formal rulemaking requires compliance with 5 U.S.C. §§ 556 and 557 instead of the procedures for informal notice-and-comment rulemaking set forth in § 553. As the last sentence of § 553(c) makes clear, an agency must use formal rather than informal rulemaking procedures when its "rules are required by statute to be made on the record after opportunity for an agency hearing." The "statute" here is the law delegating authority under which the agency is operating rather than the APA itself.

Under §§ 556 and 557, formal rulemaking consists of an evidentiary hearing before a hearing officer, though in some contexts the evidence may be submitted in written form rather than provided orally. In oral hearings, cross-examination may be allowed. There are limits on ex parte communications about the proceeding with anyone outside the agency. The final decision must be based on the record developed at the hearing. (You may learn more about these procedures if you study formal adjudication, covered in Chapter V, as the requirements of §§ 556 and 557 also apply to formal adjudication).

In the early years of the APA, formal rulemaking was relatively common. Indeed, the first edition of Kenneth Culp Davis's foundational casebook on administrative law in 1951 devoted only three pages to notice-and-comment rulemaking but spent an entire chapter on formal rulemaking. Much early agency rulemaking concerned economic matters, fitting § 551(4)'s definition of "rule" as including "the approval or prescription for the future of rates, wages, corporate or financial structures or reorganization thereof, prices, facilities, appliances, services or allowances therefor or of valuations, costs, or accounting, or practices bearing on any of the foregoing." It had long been settled that while legislatures might enact rates through the normal lawmaking process, the Constitution's Due Process Clauses required individualized oral hearings if agencies were to be given the task of setting firm-specific rates. See, e.g., ICC v. Louisville & Nashville R. Co., 227 U.S. 88, 93 (1913). Under the APA, then, it was readily understood that such proceedings fit the "formal rulemaking" mode. From the perspective of the firm whose rates are set, the agency's determination turns on the firm's own particular, individual circumstances, and this suggests the virtues of trial-type process. From the public's perspective, however, rate setting raises a host of competing, polycentric policy issues whose resolution we would ordinarily expect to entrust to politics.

Despite the early prominence of formal rulemaking as an important form of agency action, formal rulemaking has all but disappeared over the last five decades. The Supreme Court cemented the marginalization of formal rulemaking with its decision in United States v. Florida East Coast Railway Co. The case and the Notes that follow illustrate how and why the near-demise of formal rulemaking came to be. The Notes also introduce some recent efforts to resuscitate this form.

## UNITED STATES v. FLORIDA EAST COAST RAILWAY CO.

Supreme Court of the United States (1973).
410 U.S. 224.

■ JUSTICE REHNQUIST delivered the opinion of the Court.

[The Interstate Commerce Commission had by regulation established "incentive" rates to encourage railroads to send empty freight cars back to their owners. Without such rates, railroads had no particular reason to return the cars, and cars that tended to be full in only one direction—refrigerator cars, for example, carrying produce to urban markets—often pooled at their destination and created artificial and unnecessary shortages. The Interstate Commerce Act directed the ICC to act "after hearing," and the ICC had initially contemplated oral trial-type procedures for its regulatory effort. However, after intense congressional pressure to move more quickly on this rulemaking, the agency limited the railroads to written submissions.

In addition to arguing that the rule was substantively flawed, the railroads challenged this procedural decision by claiming prejudice under § 556(d), which provides that in formal rulemaking, "an agency may, when a party will not be prejudiced thereby, adopt procedures for the submission of all or part of the evidence in written form." The lower courts agreed with the railroads on the procedural issue. While this case was pending before the Supreme Court, that Court decided another ICC case, United States v. Allegheny-Ludlum Steel Corp., 406 U.S. 742 (1972), and upheld the agency's decision there against substantive and procedural challenges by the railroad. On the procedural issue, the Court in Allegheny-Ludlum held, sua sponte, that the language "after hearing" in the Interstate Commerce Act referred to informal rulemaking, not the formal rulemaking that would have been required had the statute referred to a hearing "on the record."

One difference between the two cases was that in Allegheny-Ludlum the ICC had conducted its proceedings *before* Congress revised the statute in 1966, while in Florida East Coast Railway the ICC had conducted its proceedings *after* that 1966 revision. In Florida East Coast Railway, the Supreme Court thus had to decide whether the conclusion it had reached in the first case about the formality required of the statutory "hearing" language applied in the second case.]

[We] requested the parties to brief the question of whether the Commission's proceeding was governed by 5 U.S.C. § 553, or by [§§] 556 and 557, of the Administrative Procedure Act. We here decide that the Commission's proceeding was governed only by § 553 of that Act, and that appellees received the "hearing" required by § 1(14)(a) of the Interstate Commerce Act. . . .

II. APPLICABILITY OF ADMINISTRATIVE PROCEDURE ACT

In United States v. Allegheny-Ludlum Steel Corp., we held that the language of § 1(14)(a) of the Interstate Commerce Act authorizing the Commission to act "after hearing" was not the equivalent of a requirement that a rule be made "on the record after opportunity for an agency hearing" as the latter term is used in § 553(c) of the Administrative Procedure Act. Since the 1966 amendment to § 1(14)(a), under which the Commission was here proceding [sic], does not by its terms add to the hearing requirement contained in the earlier language, the same result should obtain here unless that amendment contains language that is tantamount to such a requirement. Appellees contend that such language is found in the provisions of that Act requiring that:

> "[T]he Commission shall give consideration to the national level of ownership of such type of freight car and to other factors affecting the adequacy of the national freight car supply, and shall, on the basis of such consideration, determine whether compensation should be computed. . . ."

While this language is undoubtedly a mandate to the Commission to consider the factors there set forth in reaching any conclusion as to imposition of per diem incentive charges, it adds to the hearing requirements of the section neither expressly nor by implication. We know of no reason to think that an administrative agency in reaching a decision cannot accord consideration to factors such as those set forth in the 1966 amendment by means other than a trial-type hearing or the presentation of oral argument by the affected parties. Congress by that amendment specified necessary components of the ultimate decision, but it did not specify the method by which the Commission should acquire information about those components.

Both of the . . . courts that reviewed this order of the Commission concluded that its proceedings were governed by the stricter requirements of §§ 556 and 557 of the Administrative Procedure Act, rather than by the provisions of § 553 alone. . . . The District Court observed that it was "rather hard to believe that the last sentence of § 553(c) was directed only to the few legislative spots where the words 'on the record' or their equivalent had found their way into the statute book." . . . This is, however, the language which Congress used, and since there are statutes on the books that do use these very words . . . adherence to that language cannot be said to render the provision nugatory or ineffectual. We recognized in Allegheny-Ludlum that the actual words "on the record" and "after . . . hearing" used in § 553 were not words of art, and that other statutory language having the same meaning could trigger the provisions of §§ 556 and 557 in rulemaking proceedings. But we adhere to our conclusion, expressed in that case, that the phrase "after hearing" in § 1(14)(a) of the Interstate Commerce Act does not have such an effect.

### III. "HEARING" REQUIREMENT OF § 1(14)(a) OF THE INTERSTATE COMMERCE ACT

Inextricably intertwined with the hearing requirement of the Administrative Procedure Act in this case is the meaning to be given to the language "after hearing" in § 1(14)(a) of the Interstate Commerce Act. Appellees, both here and in the court below, contend that the Commission procedure here fell short of that mandated by the "hearing" requirement of § 1(14)(a), even though it may have satisfied § 553 of the Administrative Procedure Act. . . .

The term "hearing" in its legal context undoubtedly has a host of meanings. Its meaning undoubtedly will vary, depending on whether it is used in the context of a rulemaking-type proceeding or in the context of a proceeding devoted to the adjudication of particular disputed facts. It is by no means apparent what the drafters of the Esch Car Service Act of 1917, which became the first part of § 1(14)(a) of the Interstate Commerce Act, meant by the term. . . . [N]one of the parties refer to any legislative history that would shed light on the intended meaning of the words "after hearings." . . . Nor do generalized references to the necessity for a hearing advance our inquiry. . . ; the more precise inquiry of whether the hearing requirements necessarily include submission of oral testimony, cross-examination, or oral arguments is not resolved by such comments as these.

Under these circumstances, confronted with a grant of substantive authority made after the Administrative Procedure Act was enacted, we think that reference to that Act, in which Congress devoted itself exclusively to questions such as the nature and scope of hearings, is a satisfactory basis for determining what is meant by the term "hearing" used in another statute. Turning to that Act, we are convinced that the term "hearing" as used therein does not necessarily embrace either the right to present evidence orally and to cross-examine opposing witnesses, or the right to present oral argument to the agency's decisionmaker.

Section 553 excepts from its requirements rulemaking devoted to "interpretative rules, general statements of policy, or rules of agency organization, procedure, or practice," and rulemaking "when the agency for good cause finds . . . that notice and public procedure thereon are impracticable, unnecessary, or contrary to the public interest." This exception does not apply, however, "when notice or hearing is required by statute"; in those cases . . . the requirements of § 553 apply. But since these requirements themselves do not mandate any oral presentation . . . it cannot be doubted that a statute that requires a "hearing" prior to rulemaking may in some circumstances be satisfied by procedures that meet only the standards of § 553. . . .

Similarly, even where the statute requires that the rulemaking procedure take place "on the record after opportunity for an agency hearing," thus triggering the applicability of § 556, subsection (d) provides that the agency may proceed by the submission of all or part of the evidence in written form if a party will not be "prejudiced thereby." Again, the Act makes it plain that a specific statutory mandate that the proceedings take place on the record after hearing may be satisfied in some circumstances by evidentiary submission in written form only.

We think this treatment of the term "hearing" in the Administrative Procedure Act affords sufficient basis for concluding that the requirement of a "hearing" contained in § 1(14)(a), in a situation where the Commission was acting under the 1966 statutory rulemaking authority that Congress had conferred upon it, did not by its own force require the Commission either to hear oral testimony, to permit cross-examination of Commission witnesses, or to hear oral argument. Here, the Commission promulgated a tentative draft of an order, and accorded all interested parties 60 days in which to file statements of position, submissions of evidence, and other relevant observations. The parties had fair notice of exactly what the Commission proposed to do, and were given an opportunity to comment, to object, or to make some other form of written submission. The final order of the Commission indicates that it gave consideration to the statements of the two appellees here. Given the "open-ended" nature of the proceedings, and the Commission's announced willingness to consider proposals for modification after operating experience had been acquired, we think the hearing requirement of § 1(14)(a) of the Act was met.

Appellee railroads cite a number of our previous decisions dealing in some manner with the right to a hearing in an administrative proceeding. Although appellees have asserted no claim of constitutional deprivation in this proceeding, some of the cases they rely upon expressly speak in constitutional terms, while others are less than clear as to whether they depend upon the Due Process Clause of the Fifth and Fourteenth Amendments to the Constitution, or upon generalized principles of administrative law formulated prior to the adoption of the Administrative Procedure Act. . . .

ICC v. Louisville & Nashville R. Co., 227 U.S. 88 (1913), involved what the Court there described as a "quasi-judicial" proceeding of a quite different nature from the one we review here. The provisions of the Interstate Commerce Act . . . in effect at the time that case was decided[ ] left to the railroad carriers the "primary right to make rates," 227 U.S., at 92, but granted to the Commission the authority to set them aside, if after hearing, they were shown to be unreasonable. . . . The type of proceeding there, in which the Commission adjudicated a complaint by a shipper that specified rates set by a carrier were unreasonable, was sufficiently different from the nationwide incentive payments ordered to be made by all railroads in this proceeding so as to make the Louisville & Nashville opinion inapplicable in the case presently before us.

The basic distinction between rulemaking and adjudication is illustrated by this Court's treatment of two related cases under the Due Process Clause of the Fourteenth Amendment. In Londoner v. Denver, . . . 210 U.S. 373 (1908) [p. 220], the Court held that due process had not been accorded a landowner who objected to the amount assessed against his land as its share of the benefit resulting from the paving of a street. Local procedure had accorded him the right to file a written complaint and objection, but not to be heard orally. This Court held that due process of law required that he "have the right to support his allegations by argument, however brief; and, if need be, by proof, however informal." Id., at 386. But in the later case of Bi-Metallic Investment Co. v. State Board of Equalization, 239 U.S. 441 (1915) [p. 224], the Court held that no hearing at all was constitutionally required prior to a decision by state tax officers in Colorado to increase the valuation of all taxable property in Denver by a substantial percentage. The Court distinguished Londoner by stating that there a small number of persons "were exceptionally affected, in each case upon individual grounds." Id., at 446.

While the line dividing them may not always be a bright one, these decisions represent a recognized distinction in administrative law between proceedings for the purpose of promulgating policy-type rules or standards, on the one hand, and proceedings designed to adjudicate disputed facts in particular cases on the other.

Here, the incentive payments proposed by the Commission in its tentative order, and later adopted in its final order, were applicable across the board to all of the common carriers by railroad subject to the Interstate Commerce Act. No effort was made to single out any particular railroad for special consideration based on its own peculiar circumstances. Indeed, one of the objections of appellee Florida East Coast was that it and other terminating carriers should have been treated differently from the generality of the railroads. But the fact that the order may in its effects have been thought more disadvantageous by some railroads than by others does not change its generalized nature. Though the Commission obviously relied on factual inferences as a basis for its order, the source of these factual inferences was apparent to anyone who read [it]. The factual inferences were used in the formulation of a basically legislative-type judgment, for prospective application only, rather than in adjudicating a particular set of disputed facts.

The Commission's procedure satisfied both the provisions of § 1(14)(a) of the Interstate Commerce Act and of the Administrative Procedure Act, and were not inconsistent with prior decisions of this Court. We, therefore, reverse the judgment of the District Court, and remand the case so that it may consider those contentions of the parties that are not disposed of by this opinion.

■ JUSTICE POWELL took no part in the consideration or decision of these cases.

■ JUSTICE DOUGLAS, with whom JUSTICE STEWART joins, dissenting.

The present decision makes a sharp break with traditional concepts of procedural due process. The Commission order under attack is tantamount to a rate order. . . . This is the imposition on carriers by administrative fiat of a new financial liability. I do not believe it is within our traditional concepts of due process to allow an administrative agency to saddle anyone with a new rate, charge, or fee without a full hearing that includes the right to present oral testimony, cross-examine witnesses, and present oral argument. That is required by the Administrative Procedure Act, 5 U.S.C. § 556(d). . . .

Section 1(14)(a) of the Interstate Commerce Act bestows upon the Commission broad discretionary power to determine incentive rates. These rates may have devastating effects on a particular line. According to the brief of one of the appellees, the amount of incentive compensation paid by debtor lines amounts to millions of dollars each six-month period. Nevertheless, the courts must defer to the Commission as long as its findings are supported by substantial evidence and it has not abused its discretion. "All the more insistent is the need, when power has been bestowed so freely, that the 'inexorable safeguard' . . . of a fair and open hearing be maintained in its integrity." Ohio Bell Telephone Co. v. Public Utilities Comm'n of Ohio, 301 U.S. 292, 304 [(1937)].

Accordingly, I would hold that appellees were not afforded the hearing guaranteed by § 1(14)(a) of the Interstate Commerce Act and 5 U.S.C. §§ 553, 556, and 557. . . .

## NOTES

(1) ***How Has Florida East Coast Railway Been Received?*** One puzzling aspect of Florida East Coast Railway and its predecessor case, Allegheny-Ludlum Steel Corp., is that the parties below had all proceeded under the assumption that formal rulemaking was required. The central issue the parties presented in Allegheny-Ludlum was whether the rule in question was substantively reasonable, not whether the agency had acted under the wrong rulemaking procedure. In Florida East Coast Railway, the central issue the parties presented was whether the agency's failure to provide an oral hearing amounted to prejudice within the meaning of § 556(d), one of the provisions governing formal rulemaking. In both cases, the justices reached out to decide a procedural issue that was not raised by the parties, and did so in apparent contravention of the agency's own understanding of

its obligations to conduct formal rulemaking under its governing statute. Why? And in so doing, did the Court reach the right decision?

JONATHAN R. SIEGEL, TEXTUALISM AND CONTEXTUALISM IN ADMINISTRATIVE LAW, 78 B.U. L. Rev. 1023, 1067–68 (1998), argues that the Court appropriately relied on judicially determined background principles of administrative law, even if it misread the underlying ICC statute: "The belief that procedures should be appropriate for the decisions they are used to make has strongly influenced courts. In particular, courts have developed an understanding that one kind of procedure is appropriate for matters turning on generalized, legislative facts and a different kind of procedure is appropriate for matters turning on individualized, adjudicative facts. The Supreme Court's decision in United States v. Florida East Coast Railway Co. provides a good example. . . . The Court drew on the distinction, previously established in cases interpreting the Constitution's Due Process Clause, between proceedings that determine the rights and obligations of individuals by resolving particularized disputed facts and those that use policy reasoning and 'legislative' facts to produce general rules applicable to large groups. In the latter types of cases, individualized hearings are not practicable. Moreover, trial-type hearings are not strongly needed to protect private rights in the rulemaking process, because a large group of private parties affected by a general rule should be able to seek to alter it through the political process. The Court let these background understandings of the appropriateness of different kinds of procedures influence its interpretation of what procedures Congress had actually commanded the ICC to use." For more on the difference between legislative and adjudicative facts, see Notes on the Problems of Finding and Reviewing Contested "General" Facts (p. 325) below.

KENT BARNETT, in HOW THE SUPREME COURT DERAILED FORMAL RULEMAKING, 85 Geo. Wash. L. Rev. Arguendo 1, 2–3 (2017), takes a more critical stance after reviewing the Justices' case files: "Whatever the policy merits of formal rulemaking, the Court's sua sponte rejection of formal rulemaking [in United States v. Allegheny-Ludlum Steel Corp.] was perfunctory, relied upon unpersuasive authorities, and failed to account for formal rulemaking's consistent historical understandings and use. Remarkable primary documents from the Justices' personal files, including a mock opinion, strongly suggest that the Justices hurriedly dispatched the formal rulemaking issue because they had little interest in these admittedly dry and inaccessible rulemaking cases, which arose under the Court's mandatory jurisdiction (as opposed to its discretionary certiorari docket). . . . The Justices' papers suggest that Allegheny-Ludlum rendered Florida East Coast Railway a fait accompli, stifling the limited persuasive force of the parties' briefing and Justice Douglas's notoriously hard-to-follow dissent. Allegheny Ludlum's outsized role in Florida East Coast Railway is all the more troubling because it perhaps led the Court to proffer specious arguments that ended any lingering hopes that formal rulemaking could retain a portion of its former place in the administrative state."

EMILY S. BREMER, in BLAME (OR THANK) THE ADMINISTRATIVE PROCEDURE ACT FOR FLORIDA EAST COAST RAILWAY, 97 Chi.-Kent L. Rev. 79,

100–04 (2022), argues that the Court reached the right outcome but without fully engaging the key background principles contemplated by the APA's drafters. According to her archival research, the APA drafters understood that a "hearing" required by statute in the rulemaking context would presumptively be a "legislative-type hearing . . . which resembles the process of a congressional committee and lacks the formal procedural trappings of the courtroom. . . . [T]he purpose of the hearing was to air views and inform the agency's ultimate legislative judgment. Cross-examination was not necessarily required, and the rules of evidence were not strictly observed. . . . The meaning of the APA's references to hearings 'on the record' are substantially clearer when one understands that there are two types of hearing that may be required by statute: (1) the 'on the record,' judicial-type hearing; and (2) the substantially more flexible, legislative-type hearing. The APA's failure to acknowledge both possibilities has surely contributed to erosion in the legal profession's understanding of what 'on the record' means. . . . The APA's drafters expected courts to understand that they should employ diametrically opposed background presumptions depending on the nature of the agency's action. Thus: (1) if a statute called for a 'hearing' in adjudication, that hearing was presumptively formal; and (2) if a statute called for a 'hearing' in rulemaking, that hearing was presumptively informal. In both cases, the presumption can be overcome by clear statutory language. . . . By ignoring legislative-type hearings [in the APA], Congress implicitly left them to agency procedural discretion, plus whatever additional requirements might be contained in agency-specific statutes. . . . Florida East Coast Railway and Allegheny-Ludlum make a lot more sense when read with these . . . principles in mind."

Regardless of why the Supreme Court reached the decision it did, subsequent cases have tended to treat the terms in § 553 ("on the record after opportunity for an agency hearing") as "words of art," following the logic of Florida East Coast Railway if not its avowal to the contrary, requiring all of these words before interpreting a statute to require formal rulemaking procedures. See, e.g., Mobil Oil Corp. v. Federal Power Commission, 483 F.2d 1238, 1250–51 (D.C. Cir. 1973). Florida East Coast Railway thus is generally understood to have almost extinguished the category of formal rulemaking as a practical matter.

(2) ***Additional Reasons for the Decline of Formal Rulemaking.*** Florida East Coast Railway was decided against the backdrop of widespread disenchantment with formal rulemaking. The formal rulemaking process received criticism for being a voracious consumer of agency resources and giving excessive control over the development of the rule to the parties to the proceeding. For example, in a much-maligned formal rulemaking proceeding, the Food and Drug Administration took nine years (including twenty weeks of hearings, generating close to 8,000 pages of hearing record) to announce, via a six-page decision, that peanut butter must consist of 90 percent peanuts to earn that label, instead of the label "peanut spread" for substances with a lesser percentage of peanuts. The courts upheld the agency's decision, see Corn Products Co. v. FDA, 427 F.2d 511 (3d Cir. 1970), but the proceedings were widely seen as a waste. According to an FDA historian, "A prominent

attorney on the case wryly observed that the peanut butter standards 'put many lawyers' children through college.' " Suzanne White Junod, Food Standards and The Peanut Butter and Jelly Sandwich, in Food, Science, Policy, and Regulation in the Twentieth Century: International and Comparative Perspectives (David F. Smith & Jim Phillips eds., 2000). For a modern telling of the peanut butter hearings as part of an examination of formal rulemaking, see the three-part episode in Season 2 of Marketplace's podcast The Uncertain Hour (2017): The Peanut Butter Grandma Goes to Washington, The Peanut Butter Wars, and the Peanut Butter Verdict.[1]

Criticism of formal rulemaking extended well beyond the peanut butter case. ROBERT W. HAMILTON, PROCEDURES FOR THE ADOPTION OF RULES OF GENERAL APPLICABILITY: THE NEED FOR PROCEDURAL INNOVATION IN ADMINISTRATIVE RULEMAKING, 60 Cal. L. Rev. 1276, 1312–13 (1972), reported more generally: "[M]ost agencies required to conduct formal hearings in connection with rulemaking in fact did not do so during the previous five years. . . . Thus, the primary impact of these procedural requirements is often not . . . the testing of agency assumptions by cross-examination, or the testing of agency conclusions by courts on the basis of substantial evidence of record. Rather these procedures either cause the abandonment of the program . . . , the development of techniques to reach the same regulatory goal but without a hearing . . . , or the promulgation of noncontroversial regulations by a process of negotiation and compromise. . . . In practice, therefore, the principal effect of imposing rulemaking on a record has often been the dilution of the regulatory process rather than the protection of persons from arbitrary action."

Based on this study, ACUS strongly endorsed notice-and-comment rulemaking over formal rulemaking. Recommendation 72–5, Procedures for the Adoption of Rules of General Applicability, 38 Fed. Reg. 19792 (July 23, 1973). ACUS reiterated its opposition to formal rulemaking in 1993, when it recommended that "Congress should repeal formal ('on-the-record') or other adjudicative fact-finding procedures in rulemaking in any existing statutes mandating such procedures." Recommendation 93–4, Improving the Environment for Agency Rulemaking, 59 Fed. Reg. 4670 (Feb. 1, 1994); correction at 59 Fed. Reg. 8507 (Feb. 22, 1994).

While some statutes do remain on the books with "on the record" language, formal rulemaking proceedings are for the most part rare. As Congress has created new agencies in and after the 1960s and 1970s, it has largely granted them notice-and-comment rulemaking authority rather than requiring them to pursue formal rulemaking. Thus it was that in 2011, the American Bar Association's administrative law section was able confidently to announce "a virtual consensus in the administrative law community that the APA formal rulemaking procedure is obsolete." ABA, Section of Administrative Law and Regulatory Practice, Comments on H.R. 3010, The Regulatory Accountability Act of 2011, at 20 (Oct. 24, 2011).[2]

---

1 https://www.marketplace.org/shows/the-uncertain-hour/.

2 https://www.americanbar.org/content/dam/aba/administrative/administrative_law/commentson3010_final_nocover.authcheckdam.pdf.

(3) ***A Return of Formal Rulemaking?*** Despite its marginalization post-Florida East Coast Railway, formal rulemaking, at least as a proposal, has recently reappeared in White House and congressional initiatives.

As discussed below in Section 5.d, for several decades the Office of Information and Regulatory Affairs in the Office of Management and Budget has undertaken centralized review of much executive branch rulemaking. President George W. Bush's Executive Order 13422, 72 Fed. Reg. 2763 (Jan. 23, 2007), amended the process for review of regulations in various ways, including by imposing a requirement that agencies consider the use of formal rulemaking procedures. Agencies may have considered this option, but if so they rejected it; no agency proposed using formal rulemaking when not statutorily required in the period when the Order was in force. President Obama rescinded Executive Order 13422 soon after he assumed office in January 2009. Exec. Order 13497, 74 Fed. Reg. 6113 (Feb. 4, 2009). President Trump did not incorporate a call for formal rulemaking in his own directives, and while his Administration's Department of Transportation revised its regulation governing its rulemaking process to incorporate formal hearings into its procedures governing "economically significant and high-impact rulemakings," 84 Fed. Reg. 71714 (Dec. 27, 2019), it did not appear to use these procedures in practice. As of November 2022, President Biden had taken no steps to promote formal rulemaking as a general matter, although his October 2022 request that the Secretary of HHS and Attorney General review the classification of marijuana under the Controlled Substances Act had the effect of calling for a formal rulemaking proceeding under that Act. See Statement from President Biden on Marijuana Reform, Oct. 6, 2022;[3] 21 U.S.C. § 811(a) ("Rules of the Attorney General under this subsection [of the CSA] shall be made on the record after opportunity for a hearing").

As to congressional efforts to reinvigorate formal rulemaking, in 2017, Members of both houses of Congress introduced the Regulatory Accountability Act, each version of which included a much-debated proposal to require in-person hearings for a subset of important rules. See H.R. 5 (115th Cong.) (2017); S. 951 (115th Cong.) (2017). The bill passed the House but did not receive a vote in the Senate. Earlier versions of the bill had also been introduced, see H.R. 3010 (112th Cong.) (2011), and the bill has continued to be introduced in subsequent years, see S. 3208 (116th Cong.) (2020); S. 2278 (117th Cong.) (2021).

Describing the 2017 Senate version of the proposed hearings, CHRISTOPHER J. WALKER, MODERNIZING THE ADMINISTRATIVE PROCEDURE ACT, 69 Admin. L. Rev. 629, 656, 659–60 (2017), explained: "The APA standards for regular rules would remain basically the same, . . . [b]ut the legislation would change the APA procedures substantially for major and high-impact rules. . . . Perhaps the most controversial provisions for high-impact rules and *certain* major rules concern the availability of a public hearing. The [RAA] would amend the APA to allow interested individuals to petition for a public hearing and require the agency to include in the rulemaking record an explanation for any denial of such petition. For high-

[3] https://www.whitehouse.gov/briefing-room/statements-releases/2022/10/06/statement-from-president-biden-on-marijuana-reform/.

impact rules (i.e., greater than one billion dollars), the agency must grant a petition for a public hearing unless there is no genuine dispute as to factual issues. For qualifying major rules (i.e., greater than one hundred million dollars), however, the agency has broader authority to deny the petition if the hearing 'would not advance the consideration of the proposed rule by the agency' or 'would, in light of the need of agency action, unreasonably delay the completion of the rulemaking.' The public hearing would be limited to the disputed factual issues raised in the granted petition(s), as well as other factual issues the agency so designates[, with t]he following procedures . . . : (1) the burden of proof would be on the rule's proponent; (2) evidence would be admitted unless the agency determines it is 'immaterial or unduly repetitious evidence'; (3) an agency official would preside over the hearing, there would be a reasonable and adequate opportunity for cross-examination; and (4) a full record of the hearing would be maintained. If this process sounds somewhat familiar, that is because it is a slimmed down version of formal rulemaking—a procedural device that still exists on the books yet has virtually disappeared in administrative practice."

Estimates of how many rulemakings would qualify under this proposed legislation vary. In 2017, the U.S. Chamber of Commerce, looking at only stated costs (which an older form of the legislation used), pegged high-impact rules at no more than four per year and major rules at between 15 and 25 per year (with 2016 being an outlier at 34).[4] But the proposed statutory definitions are in terms of "annual effects," not stated costs, which would presumably shift the estimates upward. The definition in the RAA for "major" rules closely parallels the definition in the Congressional Review Act, 5 U.S.C. §§ 801–808 (see p. 897). According to the Congressional Research Service, major rules under the CRA have varied between 50 and 120 each year from 1997 to 2018.[5]

(4) ***On the Merits of Formal Rulemaking.*** These developments, along with some scholarly calls to give formal rulemaking another look, have reinvigorated a public debate that for many decades had been essentially dormant. Would a return to formal rulemaking be a welcome or unwelcome development? What metrics might be relevant to answering that question?

In favor of reinvigorating formal rulemaking, consider AARON L. NIELSON, IN DEFENSE OF FORMAL RULEMAKING, 75 Ohio St. L.J. 237, 259–89 (2014): "One of formal rulemaking's key virtues is cross-examination. In informal rulemaking, the agency makes scientific claims, and the most a party can do to respond is file a comment. This is disconcerting. . . . [E]ven if a hearing officer is biased in favor of the agency, a judicial challenge to the agency's decision could be benefited if there is a transcript of what occurred. A closed record is no small thing. . . .

---

[4] U.S. Chamber of Commerce, Taming the Administrative State: Identifying Regulations that Impact Jobs and the Economy, at 2 (Mar. 2017), https://www.uschamber.com/sites/default/files/taming_the_administrative_state_report_march_2017.pdf. In earlier congressional testimony, the Chamber of Commerce pegged the number of high-impact rules at 5 to 7 per year.

[5] Maeve P. Carey, Cong. Rsch. Serv., R43056, Counting Regulations: An Overview of Rulemaking, Types of Federal Regulations, and Pages in the Federal Register (Sept. 2019), at 9, https://crsreports.congress.gov/product/pdf/R/R43056/11.

"[N]ot all regulatory delay is attributable to procedure. Delay, for instance, often results from conflict about whether the rule makes political sense. . . . But what about the peanut butter fiasco? Even assuming the worst about that rulemaking, putting too much weight on it is nothing more than argument by anecdote—one could just as well point to informal rulemakings that have taken even longer, with more complex records. . . . [O]ne could [also] point to recent examples of formal rulemaking where the process did not take long at all. . . . Even assuming . . . that regulated parties would sometimes attempt to use formal rulemaking to delay rules, agencies can protect the integrity of their own proceedings. A good hearing officer, like a good trial judge, has many tools at her disposal to move a hearing along. . . .

"Formal rulemaking can increase the legitimacy of agency action by enhancing the public's trust in the process. . . . More broadly, the fact that formal rulemaking would sometimes make the regulatory process take longer itself may have pro-democracy benefits. . . . Shouldn't rules that 'raise controversial issues' take more time so the public has more time to decide whether it approves? . . . Finally, perhaps the highest hurdle to a careful review of the merits of formal rulemaking is the pervasive belief that arguments advanced in its favor are disingenuous, and that the whole point of formal rulemaking is to hobble agencies. . . . Undoubtedly some push for (or against) formal rulemaking for reasons that have nothing to do with procedural concerns. But that is true for all procedural reform[, which] has almost always been greeted with howls that the real purpose is delay."

In opposition to reinvigorating formal rulemaking, consider WILLIAM FUNK, REQUIRING FORMAL RULEMAKING IS A THINLY VEILED ATTEMPT TO HALT REGULATION, Reg. Rev. (May 18, 2017):[6] "[F]ormal rulemaking utilizes a judicial, trial-like procedure to adopt rules that are legislative, not adjudicative, in nature. Therefore, its procedural requirements are fundamentally at odds with the nature of legislative decision-making. . . . It may be that the peanut butter rule was extreme. Nevertheless, anyone who has been involved in complex adjudication knows the difficulty involved in the proceeding itself. If the [RAA, see Note 3 above] were adopted, it would only add to the difficulties already involved in rulemaking. . . . In addition, the suggestion that excesses are not necessary because the agency can exercise control over the proceedings is naive. Administrative law judges (ALJs) control the proceedings, and agencies have no control over ALJs. Just imagine what attorneys for the numerous private interests that would be affected by a major regulation could do to tie up the proceeding through direct . . . and cross-examination. . . .

"The proposed requirement in the RAA for formal rulemaking for certain rules certainly does not have any support from non-industry interests. The effect of the provision would to make it harder to adopt any rule that will likely have a $1 billion 'effect on the economy.' . . . The provision will be used to retard regulatory, not deregulatory, actions. . . . Public interest groups currently participate in important rulemakings, but . . . in a formal rulemaking, interested parties need an additional resource beyond

---

[6] https://www.theregreview.org/2017/05/18/funk-formal-rulemaking-halt-regulation/.

what is required in informal rulemaking. They need litigating lawyers. And even if the agency's interest is not aligned with that of the regulated parties, that does not mean that it is necessarily aligned with public interest groups who regularly find agency proposals inadequately protect the public health, safety, or the environment. . . . [T]hat is the purpose of the RAA's public hearing provision: to slow down, if not make impossible, the development of regulations that have major effects on the economy. It does not matter how many lives the regulation might save."

## SECTION 3. THE REQUIREMENTS OF § 553 NOTICE-AND-COMMENT RULEMAKING



This Section outlines the procedural demands that § 553 imposes on rulemaking. It begins with an iconic decision rejecting judicial efforts to impose procedural requirements not constitutionally mandated or contained in the APA, other statutes, or agency regulations. But that outcome still leaves courts free to insist on adherence to the APA's rulemaking procedures. Thus, a core question becomes determining exactly what § 553 requires. As detailed in Sections 3.b and 3.c, over the years the courts have added quite a significant gloss to § 553's spare statutory terms.

### a. Beyond § 553



## VERMONT YANKEE NUCLEAR POWER CORP. v. NATURAL RESOURCES DEFENSE COUNCIL, INC.

Supreme Court of the United States (1978).
435 U.S. 519.

[In December 1967, the Atomic Energy Commission (replaced by the Nuclear Regulatory Commission by the time the case reached the Supreme Court) issued the Vermont Yankee Nuclear Power Company a license to build a nuclear power plant in Vernon, Vermont. At that time, the licensing of nuclear power plants occurred in two stages. The first authorized construction of the plant; the second stage licensed the plant's operation once built. These mandatory adjudicatory hearings were often quite extensive and involved community voices and nongovernmental groups like the Natural Resources Defense Council, typically in adamant opposition. A wide range of factual issues might have been contested at these hearings—from matters specific to a particular plant for which a construction or operating license was sought to questions of a more general character that did not turn on facts about either the particular plant's location or the people who would be operating it or exposed to its effects.

Over the NRDC's objection, the environmental effects of reprocessing spent fuel and disposing of reprocessing wastes were excluded from consideration at the hearing on Vermont Yankee's operating license. This exclusion was affirmed by the Appeal Board, which reviews the licensing board's decisions, but then the Commission, expressly referencing the Vermont Yankee proceeding, began a rulemaking to "specifically deal with the question of consideration of environmental effects associated with the uranium fuel cycle in the individual cost-benefit analyses for light water cooled nuclear power reactors." This question concerned the environmental impact the nuclear fuel cycle could be expected to have outside a plant's grounds. For electricity to be generated at a nuclear plant, uranium had to be mined, processed to enhance its potential as fuel, embodied in fuel elements, and then transported to the plant. After the fuel's potential to generate power had been exhausted, the resulting highly radioactive waste somehow had to be transported, processed, and stored safely. Each of these operations could be expected to have environmental and safety impacts, but they would not be impacts specific to a particular plant. For instance, workers could be injured, or the public threatened, in Utah where the mines were or in the Ohio River valley where enrichment occurred. The expected impacts, moreover, could be expressed in relationship to units of power to be generated or, perhaps, to numbers of fuel rods made or used. Once these impacts had been determined, the impact attributable to a particular plant could be straightforwardly calculated on the basis of its generating capacity.

The Notice of Proposed Rulemaking suggested two alternatives: (1) no quantitative evaluation of the environmental hazards because an "Environmental Survey of the Nuclear Fuel Cycle" prepared by Commission staff had concluded that the hazards were slight, or (2) a specified set of numerical values for environmental impacts, which would then be incorporated into a table to determine the overall cost-benefit balance for each operating license. These proposed values were also derived from the staff Environmental Survey.

The statute granted the Commission rulemaking authority, and no one questioned its authority to deal with fuel cycle issues by informal rulemaking as opposed to adjudication. For the Commission, using rulemaking to determine such environmental impacts promised to take these factual questions out of individual licensing proceedings, where they would be repetitive and could perhaps be used simply for delay. The agency might also have believed that a one-time process for determining these matters, open to any member of the public interested to participate, could be advantageous to accurate determination of the matters in issue. In addition, the agency's staff, using an institutional decision process, might also be better able than individual judicial officers lacking focused expertise to come to appropriate judgments. Still, for parties opposing the licensing of specific nuclear reactors, this route would substitute the procedural rights of informal rulemaking for the procedural rights of formal adjudication. In their view, the procedures of rulemaking were insufficiently rigorous and open to public participation to be trustworthy in determining factual questions of large public moment. To what extent could the courts be persuaded to require processes for resolving such portentous factual issues in rulemaking that would be like those otherwise available in agency adjudication?

The Commission issued a final rule, which adopted the second alternative. It decided not to apply the new rule to prior environmental statements (because it viewed the effects as "relatively insignificant") and reaffirmed the grant of Vermont Yankee's operating license. The NRDC and other environmental groups sought judicial review in the D.C. Circuit. They argued that the rulemaking process was procedurally defective, the ultimate rule was substantively arbitrary, and the licensing decision was unsustainable given the flawed rule. Procedurally, they wanted to engage in discovery and cross-examine agency witnesses. Chief Judge David Bazelon wrote the court's opinion in this and a companion case involving licensing of two reactors by Consumers Power Company. Both cases resulted in a remand to the Commission for further proceedings, the precise nature of which was somewhat disputed. Vermont Yankee (whose license would be lost if the D.C. Circuit's decision prevailed) took the initiative in petitioning for certiorari. The Supreme Court's practice of retitling cases according to how the parties are aligned in the petition for review accounts for the fact (not uncommon in regulatory cases) that no agency is named in the caption of what was in fact review of the Commission's work.]

■ JUSTICE REHNQUIST delivered the opinion of the Court.

In 1946, Congress enacted the Administrative Procedure Act, which as we have noted elsewhere was not only "a new, basic and comprehensive regulation of procedures in many agencies," Wong Yang Sung v. McGrath, 339 U.S. 33 (1950), but was also a legislative enactment which settled "long-continued and hard-fought contentions, and enacts a formula upon which opposing social and political forces have come to rest." Id., at 40. Section 4 of the Act, 5 U.S.C. § 553 (1976 ed.), dealing with rulemaking, requires in subsection (b) that "notice of proposed rulemaking shall be published in the Federal Register . . . ," describes the contents of that notice, and goes on to require in subsection (c) that after the notice the agency "shall give interested persons an opportunity to participate in the rule making through submission of written data, views, or arguments with or without opportunity for oral presentation. After consideration of the relevant matter presented, the agency shall incorporate in the rules adopted a concise general statement of their basis and purpose." Interpreting this provision of the Act in United States v. Allegheny-Ludlum Steel Corp., 406 U.S. 742 (1972), and United States v. Florida East Coast Ry. Co., 410 U.S. 224 (1973) [p. 300], we held that generally speaking this section of the Act established the maximum procedural requirements which Congress was willing to have the courts impose upon agencies in conducting rulemaking procedures. Agencies are free to grant additional procedural rights in the exercise of their discretion, but reviewing courts are generally not free to impose them if the agencies have not chosen to grant them. This is not to say necessarily that there are no circumstances which would ever justify a court in overturning agency action because of a failure to employ procedures beyond those required by the statute. But such circumstances, if they exist, are extremely rare.

Even apart from the Administrative Procedure Act this Court has for more than four decades emphasized that the formulation of procedures was basically to be left within the discretion of the agencies to which Congress had confided the responsibility for substantive judgments. In FCC v. Schreiber, 381 U.S. 279, 290 (1965), the Court explicated this principle, describing it as "an outgrowth of the congressional determination that administrative agencies and administrators will be familiar with the industries which they regulate and will be in a better position than federal courts or Congress itself to design procedural rules adapted to the peculiarities of the industry and the tasks of the agency involved." . . .

I

. . . Much of the controversy in this case revolves around the procedures used in the rulemaking hearing which commenced in February 1973. In a supplemental notice of hearing the Commission indicated that while discovery or cross-examination would not be utilized, the Environmental Survey would be available to the public before the hearing along with the extensive background documents cited therein. All participants would be given a reasonable opportunity to present their position and could be represented by counsel if they so desired. Written and, time permitting, oral statements would be received and incorporated into the record. All persons giving oral statements would be subject to questioning by the Commission. At the conclusion of the hearing, a transcript would be made available to the public and the record would remain open for 30 days to allow the filing of supplemental written statements. More than 40 individuals and organizations representing a wide variety of interests submitted written comments. . . . The hearing was held on February 1 and 2, with participation by a number of groups, including the Commission's staff, the United States Environmental Protection Agency, a manufacturer of reactor equipment, a trade association from the nuclear industry, a group of electric utility companies, and a group called Consolidated National Intervenors which represented 79 groups and individuals including respondent NRDC.

[At the hearing Dr. Frank Pittman, director of the Commission's waste management and transportation division, submitted a twenty-page statement describing techniques for storing and disposing of nuclear wastes, a subject not addressed by the Environmental Survey. In the statement, Pittman outlined the Commission's plan to rely on reprocessing and long-term storage of high-level wastes at a permanent facility it would construct but provided few specifics on the Commission's plans. However, he characterized concerns about the environmental risks associated with management of nuclear wastes as a "bugaboo" and the possibility of a significant release of radioactivity at such a facility as "incredible." His statement was subsequently characterized by the D.C. Circuit as little more than "conclusory reassurances." The Licensing Board asked Pittman some questions, and in their subsequent testimony representatives of environmental groups noted problems the Commission had encountered with waste disposal.]

After the hearing, the Commission's staff filed a supplemental document for the purpose of clarifying and revising the Environmental Survey. Then the Licensing Board forwarded its report to the Commission without rendering any decision. The Licensing Board identified as the principal procedural question the propriety of declining to use full formal adjudicatory procedures. The major substantive issue was the technical adequacy of the Environmental Survey.

In April 1974, the Commission issued a rule which adopted the second of the two proposed alternatives described above. The Commission also approved the procedures used at the hearing,[7] and indicated that the record, including the Environmental Survey, provided an "adequate data base for the regulation adopted." Finally, the Commission ruled that to the extent the rule differed from the Appeal Board decisions in Vermont Yankee "those decisions have no further precedential significance," but that [it was unnecessary to reconsider the decisions] since "the environmental effects of the uranium fuel cycle have been shown to be relatively insignificant" . . . .

Respondents appealed from both the Commission's adoption of the rule and its decision to grant Vermont Yankee's license to the Court of Appeals for the District of Columbia Circuit. With respect to the challenge of Vermont Yankee's license, the court first ruled that in the absence of effective rulemaking proceedings,[13] the Commission must deal with the environmental impact of fuel reprocessing and disposal in

---

[7] The Commission stated: "In our view, the procedures adopted provide a more than adequate basis for formulation of the rule we adopted. All parties were fully heard. Nothing offered was excluded. The record does not indicate that any evidentiary material would have been received under different procedures. Nor did the proponent of the strict 'adjudicatory' approach make an offer of proof—or even remotely suggest—what substantive matters it would develop under different procedures. In addition, we note that 11 documents including the Survey were available to the parties several weeks before the hearing, and the Regulatory staff, though not requested to do so, made available various drafts and handwritten notes. Under all of the circumstances, we conclude that adjudicatory type procedures were not warranted here."

[13] In the Court of Appeals no one questioned the Commission's authority to deal with fuel cycle issues by informal rulemaking as opposed to adjudication. Neither does anyone seriously question before this Court the Commission's authority in this respect.

individual licensing proceedings. The court then examined the rulemaking proceedings and, despite the fact that it appeared that the agency employed all the procedures required by 5 U.S.C. § 553 and more, the court determined the proceedings to be inadequate and overturned the rule. Accordingly, the Commission's determination with respect to Vermont Yankee's license was also remanded for further proceedings.[14] . . .

II

[The Court first addressed] whether the Commission may consider the environmental impact of the fuel processes when licensing nuclear reactors. In addition to the weight which normally attaches to the agency's determination of such a question, other reasons support the Commission's conclusion.

Vermont Yankee will produce annually well over 100 pounds of radioactive wastes, some of which will be highly toxic. The Commission itself . . . clearly recognizes that these wastes "pose the most severe potential health hazard . . . ." Many of these substances must be isolated for anywhere from 600 to hundreds of thousands of years. It is hard to argue that these wastes do not constitute "adverse environmental effects which cannot be avoided should the proposal be implemented," or that by operating nuclear power plants we are not making "irreversible and irretrievable commitments of resources." 42 U.S.C. §§ 4332(2)(C)(ii), (v). As the Court of Appeals recognized, the environmental impact of the radioactive wastes produced by a nuclear power plant is analytically indistinguishable from the environmental effects of "the stack gases produced by a coal-burning power plant." 547 F.2d, at 638. For these reasons we hold that the Commission acted well within its statutory authority when it considered the back end of the fuel cycle in individual licensing proceedings.

We next turn to the invalidation of the fuel cycle rule. But before determining whether the Court of Appeals reached a permissible result, we must determine exactly what result it did reach, and in this case that is no mean feat. . . .

After a thorough examination of the opinion itself, we conclude that while the matter is not entirely free from doubt, the majority of the Court of Appeals struck down the rule because of the perceived inadequacies of the procedures employed in the rulemaking proceedings. The court first determined the intervenors' primary argument to be "that the decision to

---

[14] After the decision of the Court of Appeals, the Commission promulgated a new interim rule pending issuance of a final rule. 42 Fed. Reg. 13803 (1977). . . . As we read the opinion of the Court of Appeals, its view that reviewing courts may in the absence of special circumstances justifying such a course of action impose additional procedural requirements on agency action raises questions of such significance in this area of the law as to warrant our granting certiorari and deciding the case. Since the vast majority of challenges to administrative agency action are brought to the Court of Appeals for the District of Columbia Circuit, the decision of that court in this case will serve as precedent for many more proceedings for judicial review of agency actions than would the decision of another Court of Appeals. Finally, this decision will continue to play a major role in the instant litigation regardless of the Commission's decision to press ahead with further rulemaking proceedings. . . .

preclude 'discovery or cross-examination' denied them a meaningful opportunity to participate in the proceedings as guaranteed by due process." The court then went on to frame the issue for decision thus:

> "Thus, we are called upon to decide whether the procedures provided by the agency were sufficient to ventilate the issues."

. . . [T]here is little doubt in our minds that the ineluctable mandate of the court's decision is that the procedures afforded during the hearings were inadequate. This conclusion is particularly buttressed by the fact that after the court examined the record, particularly the testimony of Dr. Pittman, and declared it insufficient, the court proceeded to discuss at some length the necessity for further procedural devices or a more "sensitive" application of those devices employed during the proceedings. The exploration of the record and the statement regarding its insufficiency might initially lead one to conclude that the court was only examining the sufficiency of the evidence, but the remaining portions of the opinion dispel any doubt that this was certainly not the sole or even the principal basis of the decision. Accordingly, we feel compelled to address the opinion on its own terms, and we conclude that it was wrong.

In prior opinions we have intimated that even in a rulemaking proceeding when an agency is making a " 'quasi-judicial' " determination by which a very small number of persons are " 'exceptionally affected, in each case upon individual grounds,' " in some circumstances additional procedures may be required in order to afford the aggrieved individuals due process.[16] United States v. Florida East Coast Ry. Co., 410 U.S., at 242, 245, quoting from Bi-Metallic Investment Co. v. State Board of Equalization, 239 U.S. 441, 446 (1915) [p. 224]. It might also be true, although we do not think the issue is presented in this case and accordingly do not decide it, that a totally unjustified departure from well-settled agency procedures of long standing might require judicial correction.

But this much is absolutely clear. Absent constitutional constraints or extremely compelling circumstances the "administrative agencies should be free to fashion their own rules of procedure and to pursue methods of inquiry capable of permitting them to discharge their multitudinous duties." FCC v. Schreiber, 381 U.S., at 290. . . .

Respondent NRDC argues that § 4 of the Administrative Procedure Act, 5 U.S.C. § 553, merely establishes lower procedural bounds and that a court may routinely require more than the minimum when an agency's proposed rule addresses complex or technical factual issues or "Issues of Great Public Import." We have, however, previously shown that our decisions reject this view. We also think the legislative history, even the part which it cites, does not bear out its contention. The Senate Report explains what eventually became § 4 thus:

---

[16] Respondent NRDC does not now argue that additional procedural devices were required under the Constitution. Since this was clearly a rulemaking proceeding in its purest form, we see nothing to support such a view.

"This subsection states . . . the minimum requirements of public rule making procedure short of statutory hearing. Under it agencies might in addition confer with industry advisory committees, consult organizations, hold informal 'hearings,' and the like. Considerations of practicality, necessity, and public interest . . . will naturally govern the agency's determination of the extent to which public proceedings should go. Matters of great import, or those where the public submission of facts will be either useful to the agency or a protection to the public, should naturally be accorded more elaborate public procedures."

S. Rep. No. 752, 79th Cong., 1st Sess., 14–15 (1945).

The House Report is in complete accord. . . . And the Attorney General's Manual on the Administrative Procedure Act 31, 35 (1947), a contemporaneous interpretation previously given some deference by this Court because of the role played by the Department of Justice in drafting the legislation, further confirms that view. In short, all of this leaves little doubt that Congress intended that the discretion of the *agencies* and not that of the courts be exercised in determining when extra procedural devices should be employed.

There are compelling reasons for construing § 4 in this manner. In the first place, if courts continually review agency proceedings to determine whether the agency employed procedures which were, in the court's opinion, perfectly tailored to reach what the court perceives to be the "best" or "correct" result, judicial review would be totally unpredictable. And the agencies, operating under this vague injunction to employ the "best" procedures and facing the threat of reversal if they did not, would undoubtedly adopt full adjudicatory procedures in every instance. Not only would this totally disrupt the statutory scheme, through which Congress enacted "a formula upon which opposing social and political forces have come to rest," Wong Yang Sung v. McGrath, 339 U.S., at 40, but all the inherent advantages of informal rulemaking would be totally lost.

Secondly, it is obvious that the court in these cases reviewed the agency's choice of procedures on the basis of the record actually produced at the hearing, and not on the basis of the information available to the agency when it made the decision to structure the proceedings in a certain way. This sort of Monday morning quarterbacking not only encourages but almost compels the agency to conduct all rulemaking proceedings with the full panoply of procedural devices normally associated only with adjudicatory hearings.

Finally, and perhaps most importantly, this sort of review fundamentally misconceives the nature of the standard for judicial review of an agency rule. The court below uncritically assumed that additional procedures will automatically result in a more adequate record because it will give interested parties more of an opportunity to participate in and contribute to the proceedings. But informal rulemaking need not be based solely on the transcript of a hearing held before an agency. Indeed, the agency need not even hold a formal hearing. See 5 U.S.C. § 553(c). Thus, the adequacy of the "record" in this type of proceeding is not correlated directly to the type of procedural devices employed, but rather turns on whether the agency has followed the statutory mandate of the Administrative Procedure Act or other relevant statutes. If the agency is compelled to support the rule which it ultimately adopts with the type of record produced only after a full adjudicatory hearing, it simply will have no choice but to conduct a full adjudicatory hearing prior to promulgating every rule. In sum, this sort of unwarranted judicial examination of perceived procedural shortcomings of a rulemaking proceeding can do nothing but seriously interfere with that process prescribed by Congress. . . .

In short, nothing in the APA, . . . the circumstances of this case, the nature of the issues being considered, past agency practice, or the statutory mandate under which the Commission operates permitted the court to review and overturn the rulemaking proceeding on the basis of the procedural devices employed (or not employed) by the Commission so long as the Commission employed at least the statutory minima, a matter about which there is no doubt in this case.

There remains, of course, the question of whether the challenged rule finds sufficient justification in the administrative proceedings that it should be upheld by the reviewing court. Judge Tamm, concurring in the result reached by the majority of the Court of Appeals, thought that it did not. There are also intimations in the majority opinion which suggest that the judges who joined it likewise may have thought the administrative proceedings an insufficient basis upon which to predicate the rule in question. We accordingly remand so that the Court of Appeals may review the rule as the Administrative Procedure Act provides. We have made it abundantly clear before that when there is a contemporaneous explanation of the agency decision, the validity of that action must "stand or fall on the propriety of that finding, judged, of course, by the appropriate standard of review. If that finding is not sustainable on the administrative record made, then the Comptroller's decision must be vacated and the matter remanded to him for further consideration." Camp v. Pitts, 411 U.S. 138, 143 (1973) [p. 1147]. See also SEC v. Chenery Corp., 318 U.S. 80 (1943) [p. 255]. The court should engage in this kind of review and not stray beyond the judicial province to explore the procedural format or to impose upon the agency its own notion of which procedures are "best" or most likely to further some vague, undefined public good.

III

[The Court's analysis of the companion case Consumers Power Co. is omitted, except for the following peroration:] All this leads us to make one further observation of some relevance to this case. To say that the Court of Appeals' final reason for remanding is insubstantial at best is a gross understatement. Consumers Power first applied in 1969 for a construction permit—not even an operating license, just a construction permit. The proposed plant underwent an incredibly extensive review.

The reports filed and reviewed literally fill books. The proceedings took years, and the actual hearings themselves over two weeks. To then nullify that effort seven years later because one report refers to other problems, which problems admittedly have been discussed at length in other reports available to the public, borders on the Kafkaesque. Nuclear energy may some day be a cheap, safe source of power or it may not. But Congress has made a choice to at least try nuclear energy, establishing a reasonable review process in which courts are to play only a limited role. The fundamental policy questions appropriately resolved in Congress and in the state legislatures are *not* subject to reexamination in the federal courts under the guise of judicial review of agency action. Time may prove wrong the decision to develop nuclear energy, but it is Congress or the States within their appropriate agencies which must eventually make that judgment. In the meantime courts should perform their appointed function.... And a single alleged oversight on a peripheral issue, urged by parties who never fully cooperated or indeed raised the issue below, must not be made the basis for overturning a decision properly made after an otherwise exhaustive proceeding.

Reversed and remanded.[1]

■ JUSTICE BLACKMUN and JUSTICE POWELL took no part in the consideration or decision of these cases.

## NOTES

(1) ***The Decision That Nearly Wasn't.*** Examination of the Supreme Court files of Justice Thurgood Marshall reveals that Justice Brennan came one vote short of getting the Vermont Yankee case dismissed without decision because the NRC had indicated it would go forward with a new rulemaking on the fuel cycle rule regardless of the Court's decision. See GILLIAN E. METZGER, THE STORY OF VERMONT YANKEE: A CAUTIONARY TALE OF JUDICIAL REVIEW AND NUCLEAR WASTE, in Administrative Law Stories 125, 158–60 (Peter L. Strauss ed., 2006). The saga of the Vermont Yankee facility continued for decades. In February 2010, the Vermont Senate voted to close the reactor, citing leaks and other problems with the plant. See Matthew L. Wald, State Senate in Vermont Votes to Close Nuclear Plant, N.Y. Times (Feb. 25, 2010). According to the NRC, "[t]he reactor was permanently shut down on December 29, 2014, and the fuel was removed from the reactor on January 12, 2015."

(2) ***The Decision Today.*** Vermont Yankee continues to have great force. In Little Sisters of the Poor Saints Peter and Paul Home v. Pennsylvania, 140 S.Ct. 2367 (2020) [p. 374], the Court refused to impose an "open-mindedness test" on agency final rules (after an interim final rule). It stated: "We have repeatedly stated that the text of the APA provides the 'maximum procedural requirements' that an agency must follow in order to promulgate a rule." Id. at 2385. In Perez v. Mortgage Bankers Ass'n, 575 U.S. 92 (2015) [p. 426], the Court rejected the D.C. Circuit's requirement that an agency's repeal of an

---

[1] [Ed.] For further decisions in this effort to litigate the life cycle of nuclear wastes, see Baltimore Gas & Electric Co. v. Natural Resources Defense Council, Inc., 462 U.S. 87 (1983).

interpretive rule must go through notice-and-comment procedures. It noted: "The Paralyzed Veterans doctrine is contrary to the clear text of the APA's rulemaking provisions, and it improperly imposes on agencies an obligation beyond the 'maximum procedural requirements' specified in the APA." Id. at 100. Both interim final rules and interpretive rules are discussed later in this Chapter.

(3) ***"A Formula Upon Which Opposing Social and Political Forces Have Come to Rest."*** In Vermont Yankee, the Court insisted on reading the APA in a static fashion, reflecting the political compromises reached in 1946 when the statute was enacted. Yet no one in 1946 was imagining the extent of environmental, health, and safety regulation that would be called for a quarter-century later. Was the Court correct to view the APA's rulemaking provisions as unaffected by the dramatic expansion in the importance of rulemaking over time? For discussion of different approaches to reading the APA (reading it as enacted, as changing as historical circumstances warrant, and as text), see Chapter III (Notes on Interpreting the APA, p. 245). The materials in the following pages discuss the creation of what Richard Stewart called a "paper hearing," which many believe the Court to have affirmed by its decision in Motor Vehicles Manufacturers Ass'n v. State Farm, 463 U.S. 29 (1983) (p. 1126). In reading them, ask yourself whether the holding of Vermont Yankee might be described in a more limited way—rejecting the judicialization of rulemaking but not procedural requirements unimagined in 1946 (such as an obligation to share data and reports with commenters) that reflected the increasing importance of rulemaking without converting it to the judicial model.

(4) ***Permitted Mandates Within the Confines of Vermont Yankee.*** The Court allows judicially imposed constraints outside of agency statutory and regulatory mandates if required by the Constitution or in "extremely compelling circumstances." Could the challengers to the NRC's rulemaking have phrased their procedural arguments in constitutional terms? In addition, the Court assumes the agency will produce a record for judicial review. Does § 553 or the Constitution require the agency to produce a record? How is the record mandate not a violation of the holding in the case? More broadly, is the Vermont Yankee holding only a statutory one (about the APA, as the Court claims)? See John F. Duffy, Administrative Common Law in Judicial Review, 77 Tex. L. Rev. 113, 183 (1998): "[I]t is difficult to read the APA as generally forbidding judicial interference with agency procedures except, as Vermont Yankee held, in 'extremely compelling circumstances,' or where an agency makes 'a totally unjustified departure from well-settled agency procedures of long standing.' To support this intermediate position, the Court had to resort to pre-APA case law." For procedural requirements developed by the agency itself, see Note 8 below (p. 325).

(5) ***Legislatively Required Hybrid Rulemaking.*** Vermont Yankee is a strong bar against judicial improvisation with legislatively set procedures. Of course, Congress can add to § 553's procedural requirements, and it has often done so in agency-specific legislation. In the 1970s, both before and after Florida East Coast Railway (p. 300), Congress passed several important regulatory statutes that built on the notice-and-comment process

without moving fully to the trial-type process of formal rulemaking. These statutes created what are termed "hybrid" rulemaking processes.[2]

Before joining the bench, ANTONIN SCALIA, in VERMONT YANKEE: THE APA, THE D.C. CIRCUIT, AND THE SUPREME COURT, 1978 Sup. Ct. Rev. 345, 406–08, had this to say about the legislative fashioning of hybrid procedures: "While 'hybrid rulemaking' may no longer be devised by the courts under the APA, it will continue to flourish in a multiplicity of special statutes that modify the APA's dispositions, at least so long as the APA itself provides so few variants (and those based on considerations of fairness and efficiency alone) from which to select. And there is a theoretical reason why this ought to be so. Congress can, indeed, refrain from making use of the connection between procedure and power, but it cannot make that connection itself disappear. Thus, to the extent that the choice of procedures is left to the agencies themselves, to that same extent the agencies are left to determine a substantial aspect of their own power. . . . It seems to me, therefore, that if the continuing fragmentation of mandated administrative procedure is to be abated, what is called for is a more modest expectation of what the APA can and should achieve, and a design that will accord with the realities. . . . I would settle for an APA that contains not merely three but ten or fifteen basic procedural formats—an inventory large enough to provide the basis for a whole spectrum of legislative compromises without the necessity for shopping elsewhere." Do you agree with Scalia?

(6) ***Assessing Vermont Yankee.*** Vermont Yankee remains a central decision interpreting the rulemaking provisions of the APA and was recognized as such at the time. Here are two contrasting assessments out of a large literature:

(a) CLARK BYSE, VERMONT YANKEE AND THE EVOLUTION OF ADMINISTRATIVE PROCEDURE: A SOMEWHAT DIFFERENT VIEW, 91 Harv. L. Rev. 1823, 1828–29 (1978): "If the court is convinced that an adequate record for review can best be achieved by utilization of an additional procedural device, why should it not save everyone's time and energy by ordering the agency to utilize that device?

"There are at least three answers to such an argument. First, although the reviewing court may have convinced itself that an additional procedural device is indispensable, its conviction may well be erroneous. . . . Second, even if the judicially prescribed procedural device might, in some abstract sense, be thought to be the indispensable modus operandi, is it necessary or appropriate for the court to *order* the agency [to adopt it]? I think not. If, as I believe and courts occasionally proclaim, courts and agencies constitute a 'partnership' in furtherance of the public interest and are 'collaborative instrumentalities of justice,' the judicial partner should be mindful of the sensitivities and responsibilities of the administrative partner; to the extent possible, the relationship should be one of collaboration, not command. . . . Third, and most important, in enacting APA section 553 in 1946, Congress

[2] See, e.g., the Occupational Safety and Health Act of 1970, 29 U.S.C. § 651; the Consumer Product Safety Act of 1972, 15 U.S.C. § 2051; the Federal Trade Commission Improvement Act of 1975, 15 U.S.C. § 57a; the Toxic Substances Control Act of 1976, 15 U.S.C. § 2601; and the Clean Air Act Amendments of 1977, 42 U.S.C. § 7401.

established a new general model of rulemaking procedure. There is no suggestion in the legislative history of the section that it was declaratory of the common law or that it was a delegation of power to the courts to develop desirable procedural models. On the contrary, the legislative history indicates that the question whether additional procedural devices are to be employed is an *agency* question, not a *judicial* question . . . ."

(b) CHRISTOPHER F. EDLEY, JR., ADMINISTRATIVE LAW: RETHINKING JUDICIAL CONTROL OF BUREAUCRACY 228 (1990): "Because substance and procedure can be transmuted so readily, the effect of Vermont Yankee is simply to make a court that is inclined toward interventionism express its concerns and its remand instructions in quasi-procedural language that has a substantive resonance: explore more alternatives, give a more detailed explanation, disclose considerations and staff information, demonstrate adequate consideration of statutory factors, and so on. The risk is that the reviewing court may use modes of rhetoric and intervention that miscommunicate the course and nature of its dissatisfaction with the administrative action—all because in any particular circumstance, the court is concerned that its legitimate purview is somehow delimited by the substance-procedure categorization. This approach is misleading and self-defeating, in view of both the boundary problem in these two categories and the related and more fundamental point that proper evaluation of agency action requires an eye to both procedure and substance."

(7) ***Rulemaking's Effect on Statutory Hearing Rights.*** Although not figuring in the Supreme Court's discussion, an interesting feature of the Vermont Yankee litigation is the interaction of rulemaking and adjudication. The agency had to engage in individual adjudications over each potential reactor license. In these proceedings, it repeatedly confronted the issue of environmental effects of nuclear fuel. In the middle of Vermont Yankee's licensing proceedings, the agency conducted a rulemaking on how (if at all) certain of these environmental effects should be taken into account. Assuming a court did not strike down the rule, the agency could then typically use it in all subsequent licensing proceedings without challenge (except to how it was applied to particular facts in the adjudication).

How far can an agency use rules in this fashion to limit the scope of a statutorily required hearing? The Court faced this question in HECKLER V. CAMPBELL, 461 U.S. 458 (1983), involving medical-vocational guidelines promulgated using § 553 procedures by the Secretary of Health and Human Services to determine eligibility for Social Security disability benefits. Eligibility for these benefits turns not only on the personal characteristics of the applicant, but also on the absence of jobs in the national economy that a person of the applicant's age and abilities could hold—regardless of whether those jobs are conveniently located to the applicant or unfilled. The guidelines, promulgated using notice-and-comment procedures, took the form of a matrix of the factors the statute made relevant to work availability determinations (physical ability, age, education, and work experience). The ALJ in a particular dispute over eligibility for benefits would plug the claimant's factors into the matrix to determine whether jobs for someone with the claimant's profile exist in significant numbers in the national economy. In the past, vocational experts had testified at hearings on a particular applicant's eligibility for benefits on whether suitable available jobs existed in the national economy. Thus, the guidelines made much testimony unnecessary. The guidelines were challenged as violating an applicant's statutory rights to an individualized determination based on evidence adduced at a hearing.

In an opinion written by JUSTICE POWELL, the Court upheld the guidelines: "It is true that the statutory scheme contemplates that disability hearings will be individualized determinations based on evidence adduced at a hearing. But this does not bar the Secretary from relying on rulemaking to resolve certain classes of issues. The Court has recognized that even where an agency's enabling statute expressly requires it to hold a hearing, the agency may rely on its rulemaking authority to determine issues that do not require case-by-case consideration. See FPC v. Texaco, Inc., 377 U.S. 33, 41–44 (1964); United States v. Storer Broadcasting Co., 351 U.S. 192, 205 (1956). A contrary holding would require the agency continually to relitigate issues that may be established fairly and efficiently in a single rulemaking proceeding. . . . As the Secretary has argued, the use of published guidelines brings with it a uniformity that previously had been perceived as lacking. To require the Secretary to relitigate the existence of jobs in the national economy at each hearing would hinder needlessly an already overburdened agency."

In upholding the guidelines, the Court emphasized that the agency was still required to "assess each claimant's individual abilities . . . on the basis of evidence adduced at a hearing. We note that the regulations afford claimant ample opportunities to present evidence relating to their own abilities and to offer evidence that the guidelines do not apply to them." Should that make a difference? Is an agency's resort to rulemaking harder to square with statutory hearing rights if it operates to preclude the need for the agency to hold a hearing at all?

(8) ***Enforceability of Agency Procedural Regulations.*** One other point worth noting is Vermont Yankee's acknowledgment that agency procedural regulations can be judicially enforceable, just like other agency regulations. This is often termed the Accardi principle (discussed on p. 1104), after its appearance in United States ex rel. Accardi v. Shaughnessy, 347 U.S. 260 (1964). The principle applies to agency rules intended to be binding, including procedural rules adopted under the exception in § 553(b)(A).

## NOTES ON THE PROBLEMS OF FINDING AND REVIEWING CONTESTED "GENERAL" FACTS

(1) ***Regulations, Factfinding, and Procedures Familiar to Judges.*** One way to understand the Supreme Court's opinion in Vermont Yankee might be that the Court feared the D.C. Circuit had imported adjudicatory values into rulemaking. Legislatures do not typically proceed by hearing live testimony about factual issues. When they hold hearings, the predominant discussion is often about policy issues. Committee members may ask questions, even belligerently at times; yet interested members of the public

who are present in the hearing room (perhaps waiting to deliver their own views) never have the chance to ask questions themselves. At best, they can send a note to a member or staffer suggesting them. Should a statute be enacted, any arguable failures of inquiry are of no concern to the courts.

Perhaps, however, the D.C. Circuit was concerned about the issues surrounding finding "general" facts. The Vermont Yankee regulation stated a series of values for health and other consequences to be expected from the fuel cycle processes occurring outside nuclear power plants. These are not questions concerning individuals "who were exceptionally affected, in each case upon individual grounds," as the Vermont Yankee Court remarks in invoking the Bi-Metallic decision (p. 224). At the same time, they are also not the kinds of questions that we would likely think well resolved by legislative processes. Such general facts might be thought to be like what are sometimes called legislative facts (and contrasted with what are sometimes called adjudicatory facts)—that is, facts that are used to create general policy and are not limited to the immediate parties to a proceeding. Yet, general facts can involve fairly specific questions on which substantial scientific and technological uncertainty exists, and deciding such questions by political vote (legislatively) would not be realistic.

(2) ***The D.C. Circuit Debate.*** We take up judicial review of agency factfinding in Chapter VIII but want to flag its connections to agency rulemaking procedures here. At the time of Vermont Yankee, the D.C. Circuit was deeply enmeshed in internal debate over how courts should respond to challenges to regulations that turned on technical and scientific questions. This debate was captured best in an en banc decision, ETHYL CORP. V. EPA, 541 F.2d 1 (D.C. Cir. 1976), reviewing an EPA regulation requiring annual reductions in the lead content of leaded gasoline. (This regulation is often presented as a paragon of a regulation whose costs were strongly justified by its benefits.) In adopting the regulation, EPA had been required to decide a number of highly controverted factual propositions, make projections based on imperfect data, and in other ways reach technical or scientific judgments that the makers of lead additives strongly challenged. Ethyl Corp. contains separate opinions by the two main participants in the D.C. Circuit debate, Chief Judge David Bazelon and Judge Harold Leventhal. Chief Judge Bazelon would shortly thereafter be the author of the D.C. Circuit's decision in Vermont Yankee, and Judge Leventhal was the author of several opinions urging considerably expanded notice, comment opportunity, and explanation—a concept that came to be called a "paper hearing" (p. 347).

CHIEF JUDGE BAZELON: "[T]his case strengthens my view that . . . in cases of great technological complexity, the best way for courts to guard against unreasonable or erroneous administrative decisions is not for the judges themselves to scrutinize the technical merits of each decision. Rather, it is to establish a decision-making process that assures a reasoned decision that can be held up to the scrutiny of the scientific community and the public. This record provides vivid demonstration of the dangers implicit in the contrary view, ably espoused by Judge Leventhal, which would have judges steeping themselves in technical matters to determine whether the agency has exercised a reasoned discretion. It is one thing for judges to scrutinize FCC judgments concerning diversification of media ownership to determine if they are rational. But I doubt judges contribute much to improving the quality of the difficult decisions which must be made in highly technical areas when they take it upon themselves to decide, as did the panel in this case, that in assessing the scientific and medical data the Administrator made clear errors of judgment. The process [of] making a de novo evaluation of the scientific evidence inevitably invites judges of opposing views to make plausible-sounding, but simplistic, judgments of the relative weight to be afforded various pieces of technical data. . . .

"Because substantive review of mathematical and scientific evidence by technically illiterate judges is dangerously unreliable, I continue to believe we will do more to improve administrative decision-making by concentrating our efforts on strengthening administrative procedures: 'When administrators provide a framework for principled decision-making, the result will be to diminish the importance of judicial review by enhancing the integrity of the administrative process, and to improve the quality of judicial review in those cases where judicial review is sought.' Environmental Defense Fund, Inc. v. Ruckelshaus, 439 F.2d 584, 598 (D.C. Cir. 1971) (Bazelon, C.J.). It does not follow that courts may never properly find that an administrative decision in a scientific area is irrational. But I do believe that in highly technical areas, where our understanding of the import of the evidence is attenuated, our readiness to review evidentiary support for decisions must be correspondingly restrained."

JUDGE LEVENTHAL: "Taking [Chief Judge Bazelon's] opinion in its fair implication, as a signal to judges to abstain from any substantive review, it is my view that while giving up is the easier course, it is not legitimately open to us at present. . . . Congress has been willing to delegate its legislative powers broadly—and courts have upheld such delegation—because there is court review to assure that the agency exercises the delegated power within statutory limits, and that it fleshes out objectives within those limits by an administration that is not irrational or discriminatory. . . .

"Our present system of review assumes judges will acquire whatever technical knowledge is necessary as background for decision of the legal questions. . . . The aim of the judges is not to exercise expertise or decide technical questions, but simply to gain sufficient background orientation. . . . When called upon to make de novo decisions, individual judges have had to acquire the learning pertinent to complex technical questions in such fields as economics, science, technology and psychology. Our role is not as demanding when we are engaged in review of agency decisions, where we exercise restraint, and affirm even if we would have decided otherwise so long as the agency's decisionmaking is not irrational or discriminatory.

"The substantive review of administrative action is modest, but it cannot be carried out in a vacuum of understanding. Better no judicial review at all than a charade that gives the imprimatur without the substance of judicial confirmation that the agency is not acting unreasonably. Once the presumption of regularity in agency action is challenged with a factual submission, and even to determine whether such a challenge has been made, the agency's record and reasoning has to be looked at. If there is some factual support for the challenge, there must be either evidence or judicial notice available explicating the agency's result, or a remand to supply the gap. . . .

"Restraint, yes, abdication, no."

Leventhal frequently remarked that he understood the Court's decision in Vermont Yankee to mean that he had won the debate. Do you agree?

(3) ***Science Policy Questions and the Ethyl Corp. Debate Today.*** One of today's science policy questions involves the costs of climate change. Would you take Bazelon or Leventhal's approach in reviewing agency measures related to climate change? Cass R. Sunstein, Arbitrariness Review and Climate Change, 170 U. Pa. L. Rev. 991, 997, 1045–46 (2022): "My substantive topic here is judicial review of the social cost of carbon—in particular, judicial review of the relevant questions for 'arbitrariness.' My central claim is that in an important sense, Judge Bazelon was correct, at least in this domain. Courts should police agency decisions with respect to the social cost of carbon in order to ensure that agencies have taken the scientific and economic issues seriously. They should require a detailed justification; a response to reasonable objections; and an explanation for departures from past practices. Mere conclusions are never enough. At the same time, judicial review of the merits should be deferential. Of course, and importantly, courts should not abdicate. But in this domain, a strong dose of restraint is in order. . . .

"To produce a social cost of carbon, it is necessary to make numerous judgments not only about law but also about both science and economics, including the choice between the global and the domestic number, the discount rate, the role of the [integrated assessment models], climate sensitivity, the damage function, and equity, among others. The minimal requirements of arbitrariness review are that agencies must offer detailed explanations and respond to counterarguments, demonstrate that their factual judgments are consistent with a reasonable reading of the science and the economics, and show that they have not made some kind of egregious error. Insofar as their judgments involve policy and morality as well as fact—as is clearly the case with respect to the discount rate and equity, and as is plausibly the case with respect to climate sensitivity and the damage function—agencies must articulate those judgments and demonstrate that they are reasonable and consistent with statute." What would Leventhal say?

As you work through the materials in this Chapter, keep the Bazelon-Leventhal debate in mind. How does its resolution affect the advice agency counsel should give agency staff and decisionmakers about the procedural course they should follow in rulemakings? How does its resolution affect the opportunities available to private parties seeking to influence the outcome of a rulemaking?

## b. Notice

**_CENTER FOR SCIENCE IN THE PUBLIC INTEREST v. PERDUE_**

*The notice shall include . . . either the terms or substance of the proposed rule or a description of the subjects and issues involved.*

5 U.S.C. § 553(b)

Notices of Proposed Rulemaking ("NPRMs"—or sometimes "NOPRs" or "NPRs") appear in the Federal Register, which the federal government publishes every business day. They are also often accessible through the federal government's online rulemaking portal, www.regulations.gov, and typically appear on agency websites. Agencies may also issue press releases and even directly notify organizations and individuals of proposed rulemakings of likely interest to them. A key issue is whether the proposal provides sufficient notice of what appears in the final rule.

### CENTER FOR SCIENCE IN THE PUBLIC INTEREST v. PERDUE

United States District Court for the District of Maryland (2020).[3]
438 F.Supp.3d 546.

■ HAZEL, DISTRICT JUDGE.

Plaintiffs Center for Science in the Public Interest and Chesapeake Institute for Local Sustainable Food & Agriculture, d/b/a Healthy School Food Maryland (collectively, "Plaintiffs") have brought this action pursuant to the Administrative Procedure Act ("APA") challenging a final rule promulgated by Defendant United States Department of Agriculture ("USDA") governing nutrition standards for school breakfast and lunch programs. . . .

I. BACKGROUND

A. School Lunch and Breakfast Programs

Over fifty years ago, Congress created the National School Lunch Program ("NSLP") and the School Breakfast Program ("SBP") "to safeguard the health and well-being of the Nation's children and to encourage the domestic consumption of nutritious agricultural commodities and other food." 42 U.S.C. §§ 1751, 1771. . . .

Schools participating in the NSLP and SBP are required to serve meals that "are consistent with the goals of the most recent Dietary Guidelines for Americans [("Dietary Guidelines")]." Id. § 1758(f)(1)(A). Congress has specifically directed USDA to "promulgate rules, based on the most recent Dietary Guidelines [ ], that reflect specific

[3] [Ed.] While many challenges to agency rulemaking go directly to courts of appeals by statute (p. 1492), some do not. This is an example where judicial review takes place in a district court in the first instance.

recommendations . . . [for] school nutrition programs," id. § 1758(a)(4)(B), and to "promulgate proposed regulations to update . . . nutrition standards for the [school lunch and breakfast programs] . . . based on recommendations . . . [made]" in the [School Meals Report], id. § 1753(b)(3)(A)(i). The Dietary Guidelines is a statutorily mandated report . . . [that] shall be promoted by each Federal agency in carrying out any Federal food, nutrition, or health program." 7 U.S.C. § 5341(a)(1). The School Meals Report, published in 2010 by the Institute of Medicine's Committee on Nutrition Standards for National School Lunch and Breakfast Programs (the "Committee"), was commissioned by USDA to . . . ["]review and assess the food and nutritional needs of school-aged children . . . and to use that review as a basis for recommended revisions to the [school lunch and breakfast programs'] Nutrition Standards and Meal Requirements."

. . . [T]he School Meals Report recommended a gradual approach to improving the sodium and whole grain content in school meals. For sodium, the School Meals Report recommended a maximum sodium intake based on age group and meal—between 430 mg and 470 mg for breakfast and between 640 mg and 740 mg for lunch—and recommended that USDA set intermediate targets for maximum sodium intake over a ten-year period. For whole grains, the School Meals Report recommended incremental increases in the minimum percentage of grains that are required to be whole grain-rich so that the proportion of whole grain-rich foods in school meals would exceed fifty percent within three years.

B. The 2012 Rule

On January 26, 2012 . . . USDA promulgated [the 2012 Rule], that "align[ed]" the school lunch and breakfast programs' nutrition standards with the Dietary Guidelines and was "largely based" on the School Meals Report. For sodium, the 2012 Rule established a ten-year, three-phased schedule for reducing sodium levels . . . . By School Year ("SY") 2014–2015, schools were required to reduce sodium levels to between 540 mg and 640 mg for breakfast and between 1230 mg and 1460 mg for lunch ("Sodium Target 1"); by SY 2017–2018, to between 485 mg and 570 mg for breakfast and 935 mg and 1080 mg for lunch ("Sodium Target 2"); and, finally, by SY 2022–2023, to between 430 mg and 500 mg for breakfast and 640 mg and 740 mg for lunch ("Final Sodium Target"). . . .

For whole grains, the 2012 Rule required that fifty percent of all grain products offered in school meals be whole grain-rich during SY 2013–2014, and for SY 2014–2015 and beyond, it required that one-hundred percent of grain products be whole grain-rich. USDA explained that this approach matched the 2005 Dietary Guidelines recommendation that at least half of all grains be whole grains.

In response to the 2012 Rule, Congress enacted a series of appropriations riders that directed USDA to retain Sodium Target 1 through SY 2017–2018 and allowed states to grant exemptions from the one-hundred percent whole grain-rich requirement for school food authorities ("SFAs") that "demonstrate[d] hardship . . . [in complying] with the whole grain rich requirements," so long as the SFAs still met the fifty-percent whole grain requirement. The last rider was set to expire after SY 2017–2018.

C. The 2018 Rule

On November 30, 2017, USDA published an Interim Final Rule extending the sodium and whole grain "flexibilities" for the school meal programs. With respect to sodium, the Interim Final Rule acknowledged "the importance of reducing the sodium content of school meals," and it stated that "reaching this objective will likely require a more gradual process than the planned 10 years . . . ." The Interim Final Rule would thus "retain Sodium Target 1 as the regulatory limit in the NSLP and SBP through the end of the SY 2018–2019," with the high probability that Sodium Target 1 would remain in effect "through at least the end of SY 2020–2021 to provide SFAs more time to procure and introduce lower sodium food products, allow food industry more time for product development reformulation, and give students more time to adjust to school meals with lower sodium content." USDA sought "public comments on the long-term availability of this flexibility and its impact on the sodium reduction timeline established in 2012 and, specifically, the impact on Sodium Target 2."

With respect to whole grains, the Interim Final Rule "retain[ed] the whole grain-rich regulatory requirement" of one-hundred percent whole grain-rich foods, but it allowed state agencies to continue granting exemptions to SFAs that could "demonstrate hardship(s) in procuring, preparing, or serving specific products that are acceptable to students and compliant with the whole grain-rich requirement." USDA explained that the exemption option would allow "SFAs experiencing challenges to more effectively develop menus and procure foods that are acceptable to students[;] provide[ ] manufacturers additional time to develop whole grain-rich food products that are suitable for reheating and hot holding in the food service facility and result in more acceptable meals for students[; and] assist schools in sustaining student participation, encouraging meal consumption, and limiting food waste."

Finally, with respect to both sodium and whole grains, USDA anticipated that, "[i]n the future, USDA [would] also reevaluate the sodium and other school meal requirements in light of the 2020 Dietary Guidelines."

On December 12, 2018, the USDA issued a Final Rule. The Final Rule retained Sodium Target 1 through the end of SY 2023–2024, at which point school meals would be required to comply with Sodium Target 2, and it eliminated the Final Sodium Target altogether. The Final Rule explained that the new targets "balance[d] the need for strong nutrition standards with the operational concerns and student acceptance of school meals" by allowing schools "to slowly introduce lower sodium foods to students and for industry to develop consistent lower sodium products that are palatable for students."

The Final Rule also eliminated the one-hundred percent whole grain-rich requirement, and it required that only half of the weekly grains offered in school meals meet the whole grain-rich requirement, thus "remov[ing] the need for whole-grain rich exemption requests based on hardship." The Final Rule explained that granting hardship exemptions "in an ad hoc fashion" was "not feasible," and that the decision to reduce the whole grain requirement "was made to reduce Program operator burden while still providing children access to whole grain-rich items." . . .

III. DISCUSSION

Plaintiffs contend that the Final Rule violates the APA because . . . it is not a logical outgrowth of the Interim Final Rule . . . . [The Court finds] that the Final Rule is not a logical outgrowth of the Interim Final Rule, so it must be vacated and remanded to the administrative agency for further proceedings.

A. Logical Outgrowth

Plaintiffs contend that the Final Rule is not a logical outgrowth of the Interim Final Rule. "The requirement of notice and a fair opportunity to be heard is basic to administrative law." Chocolate Mfrs. Ass'n of U.S. v. Block, 755 F.2d 1098, 1102 (4th Cir. 1985). Notice must be "sufficiently descriptive to provide interested parties with a fair opportunity to comment and to participate in the rulemaking," but an agency "is not required to specify every precise proposal that it may eventually adopt as a rule." Kennecott v. EPA, 780 F.2d 445, 452 (4th Cir. 1985). The purpose of this procedure "is both to allow the agency to benefit from the experience and input of the parties who file comments . . . and to see to it that the agency maintains a flexible and open-minded attitude towards its own rules." Chocolate Mfrs. Ass'n, 755 F.2d at 1103.

Under the APA, an agency is permitted to revise a final rule after initial notice of the proposed rule "if the changes in the original plan are in character with the original scheme, and the final rule is a logical outgrowth of the notice and comments already given." Id. at 1105. The proposed rule must enable the public to discern what is at stake. But "if the final rule substantially departs from the terms or substance of the proposed rule, the notice is inadequate." Chocolate Mfrs. Ass'n, 755 F.2d at 1105.

Here, the Final Rule is not a logical outgrowth of the Interim Final Rule. With respect to sodium, the Interim Final Rule acknowledged "the importance of reducing the sodium content of school meals" because over ninety percent of school-age children exceeded the Dietary Guidelines' upper intake limit for dietary sodium between 2009 and 2012. At the same time, it recognized that "a more gradual process" was necessary to meet this goal. The purpose of the Interim Final Rule was therefore to provide "more time" for children to adjust to school meals with less sodium content and for schools and manufacturers to make appropriate menu and product changes, thus suggesting that the Dietary Guidelines' upper intake limit, long-embodied in the Final Sodium Target, would remain in effect, but would simply be delayed. Indeed, the Interim Final Rule spoke exclusively in terms of delaying compliance requirements, not abandoning the compliance requirements altogether, and at no point did the Interim Final Rule discuss eliminating the Final Sodium Target or even solicit comments about the effect of continued sodium "flexibilities" on the Final Sodium Target. Rather, it "specifically" sought comment only on "the impact [of extending the Sodium Target 1 compliance dates] on Sodium Target." "This specificity, together with total silence concerning any suggestion of eliminating [the Final Sodium Target], strongly indicated that [the Final Sodium Target] was not at issue." Chocolate Mfrs. Ass'n, 755 F.2d at 1107 (finding that a final rule eliminating flavored milk from a permissible diet was not a logical outgrowth of a proposed rule that specifically discussed the dangers of high sugar content in foods such as cereals and juices, but not flavored milk, which had long been considered part of a permissible diet).

Although an agency is certainly permitted to change a rule in response to comments, USDA's changes are not "in character with the original scheme" of the Interim Final Rule, see id. at 1105, because there is a fundamental difference between delaying compliance standards—which indicates that school meals will still eventually meet those standards—and eliminating those standards altogether. Thus, the Final Rule's elimination of the Final Sodium Target is not a logical outgrowth of the Interim Final Rule's focus on delaying compliance requirements.

The Final Rule's elimination of the one-hundred percent whole grain-rich requirement is similarly not a logical outgrowth of the Interim Final Rule. With respect to whole grains, the Interim Final Rule specifically "retain[ed] the whole grain-rich regulatory requirement" of one-hundred percent whole grains, while also extending the availability of an exemption, upon request, to "SFAs that demonstrate hardship in providing specific products that meet the whole grain-rich criteria and as long as at least 50 percent of the grains served are whole grain-rich." The express purpose of extending the exemption's availability was, as with sodium, to provide "additional time" for students, schools, and the industry to adjust.

Congress' regular appropriations riders offering the hardship exemption, in conjunction with the Interim Final Rule's "very detailed" discussion of that exemption and its "total silence concerning" eliminating, or even changing, the underlying one-hundred percent whole-grain rich requirement, "could have led interested persons only to conclude that a change in [the underlying whole-grain rich requirement] would not be considered." See Chocolate Mfrs., 755 F.2d at 1107. The Final Rule therefore "materially alter[ed]" and "substantially depart[ed] from the terms or substance" of the Interim Final Rule by transforming what was a limited, case-by-case exemption into the new rule across the board. See id. at 1105. Thus, the Final Rule's elimination of the one-hundred percent whole grain-rich requirement is not a logical outgrowth of the Interim Final Rule.

USDA argues that because it received comments related to the complained-of changes to sodium and whole grain requirements, the Interim Final Rule must have provided sufficient notice of those changes. This argument is unpersuasive. There is no authority to support the proposition that the presence of comments addressing a particular topic is sufficient, on its own, to establish proper notice; rather, the proposed rule itself still "must fairly apprise interested parties of the potential scope and substance of a substantially revised final rule." Chocolate Mfrs. Ass'n, 755 F.2d at 1105.

The cases cited by USDA in support of its argument suggest, at most, that where a proposed rule expressly solicits comments on a particular topic or implies the possibility of a particular change, the presence of related comments further supports the sufficiency of the notice.

For example, USDA cites to Northeast Maryland Waste Disposal Auth. v. EPA, 358 F.3d 936 (D.C. Cir. 2004). In that case, the D.C. Circuit determined that a proposed rule distinguishing between three categories of municipal waste combustor ("MWC") units . . . provided sufficient notice of a final rule that merged the [first two] categories and distinguished only based on [the third]. Id. at 952. The court stated that "[b]y announcing that it proposed to distinguish between [the first two categories], EPA invited comments on both the pros and cons of that distinction. It thus effectively served notice that, if persuaded that the latter outweighed the former, the distinction might not survive. Nor did the interested parties misread either the invitation or the stakes involved" because "[n]umerous commentators . . . filed comments that were critical of the distinction between [the first two categories]." Id. A clear reading of this case establishes that the mere existence of relevant comments was not the deciding factor in the D.C. Circuit's determination that notice was sufficient; rather, the presence of the proposed rule's invitation to comment on the distinction was significant, with the presence of relevant comments merely providing additional support. Here, in contrast, the Interim Final Rule's invitation to comment extended only to whether USDA should retain or eliminate the sodium and whole grain flexibilities. There was no express or implicit invitation to comment on eliminating any standards altogether, making the presence of related comments insignificant to the Court's determination here.

Because the Interim Final Rule "gave no indication that the agency was considering a different approach [from delaying compliance with Sodium Target 1 or offering a hardship exemption to the whole grain requirement], and the final rule revealed that the agency had completely changed its position," the Interim Final Notice did not provide sufficient notice of the Final Rule. The Final Rule therefore violates the APA and will be vacated and remanded to the administrative agency for further proceedings. See Allina Health Servs. v. Sebelius, 746 F.3d 1102, 1110–11 (D.C. Cir. 2014) (stating that "deficient notice is a fundamental flaw that almost always requires vacatur," especially where it is not "too late to reverse course"). . . .

## NOTES

(1) ***Modern Notice.*** The Center for Science in the Public Interest case does not involve a traditional NPRM. Rather the agency's interim final rule is the notice under the APA; comments were taken after the fact. We discuss interim final rules and how they can function as NPRMs in the next Section (p. 381).

(2) ***The Logical Outgrowth Test at the Supreme Court.*** LONG ISLAND CARE AT HOME, LTD. V. COKE, 551 U.S. 158 (2007), posed the question whether the Fair Labor Standards Act's "domestic services" exemption to wage and hour rules applied to domestic workers who provide companionship services and are employed by an agency other than the family or household for whom they work. Although the case turned largely on the degree of deference due to the agency's statutory interpretation, the Court also had an opportunity to address the question of when an agency's change in course might render the initial notice inadequate. Despite lower courts employing the term for decades, this case marked the first time the Court had used the term "logical outgrowth."

JUSTICE BREYER wrote for a unanimous Court: "The Courts of Appeals have generally interpreted . . . [§ 553(b)(3)] to mean that the final rule the agency adopts must be 'a "logical outgrowth" of the rule proposed.' National Black Media Coalition v. FCC, 791 F.2d 1016, 1022 (C.A.2 1986). . . . The object, in short, is one of fair notice.

"Initially the Department [of Labor] proposed a rule of the kind that respondent seeks, namely a rule that would have placed outside the [domestic services] exemption (and hence left subject to FLSA wage and hour rules) individuals employed by third-party employers whom the Act had covered prior to 1974. The clear implication of the proposed rule was that companionship workers employed by third-party enterprises that were not covered by the FLSA prior to the 1974 Amendments (e.g., most smaller private agencies) would be included within the § 213(a)(15) exemption." According to the Court, "since the proposed rule was simply a proposal, its presence meant that the Department was considering the matter; after that consideration the Department might choose to adopt the proposal or to withdraw it. As it turned out, the Department did withdraw the proposal. . . . The result was a determination that exempted all third-party-employed companionship workers from the Act. We do not understand why such a possibility was not reasonably foreseeable."[4]

Long Island Care thus underscores a feature about rulemaking notice that distinguishes it from adjudicatory notice: those who like the approach in a proposed rule cannot just sit back and not comment. They would be mistaken to assume that they will be notified and have a chance to voice

[4] The Department of Labor changed its stance in 2013, issuing a rule that applied FLSA protections to many home care workers employed by third parties. The D.C. Circuit upheld the new rule. Home Care Ass'n of America v. Weil, 799 F.3d 1084 (D.C. Cir. 2015).

their views in the future before the agency adopts a different path (including, possibly, a path opposite to its proposal).

(3) ***The APA's Text.*** Focus on the general and disjunctive character of the text of § 553(b)(3). Notice must include "*either* the terms *or* substance of the proposed rule *or* a description of the subjects and issues involved" (emphasis added). Do you believe that the 1946 Congress would have found a final rule that contradicted a proposed rule surprising? Even if so, would the Supreme Court (in Long Island Care) then be in error? Why or why not? Given the current composition of the Supreme Court, which relies heavily on textualism in interpreting statutes, could an agency argue that the logical outgrowth test violates Vermont Yankee? See Jack M. Beermann, Common Law and Statute Law in Administrative Law, 63 Admin. L. Rev. 1, 8 (2011).

(4) ***Reasonably Foreseeable by Whom?*** Should the test of what is "reasonably foreseeable" be based on what the public generally might anticipate from the terms of an agency's notice, or instead on what those involved in a regulatory area should know to be the issues in play? In ALTO DAIRY V. VENEMAN, 336 F.3d 560, 569–70 (7th Cir. 2003), Wisconsin dairy farmers sought to enjoin an amendment made to federal rules regulating the price of milk. Pursuant to the Milk Marketing Act, these rules are termed "orders," are set after a public hearing, and are issued separately for different regions of the country. The notice that the Department issued stated that "[a] public hearing is being held to consider proposals to amend pooling and related provisions of the Mideast order" and listed a variety of specific proposals. The amendment adopted at the end of the proceeding was not identical to any of the proposals listed in the notice. No matter, wrote JUDGE POSNER: "The purpose of a rulemaking proceeding is not merely to vote up or down the specific proposals advanced before the proceeding begins, but to refine, modify, and supplement the proposals in the light of evidence and arguments presented in the course of the proceeding. If every modification is to require a further hearing at which that modification is set forth in the notice, agencies will be loath to modify initial proposals, and the rulemaking process will be degraded. . . .

"Though [the language of the notice] is gobbledygook to an outsider, insiders such as the plaintiffs would realize that the focus of the proceeding would be on their eligibility to be pooled with the Mideast producers [and thereby obtain the benefit of the higher price paid to the Mideast region]. [N]one of the proposals was identical to the amendment that the Department adopted at the end of the proceeding, namely the prohibition of paper pooling with distant plants. ["Paper pooling" was a practice under which a supply plant in one region was allowed to associate with dairy farmers in another region and, without the farmers being required actually to ship their milk to the supply plant, have those farmers' sales count towards the percentage of sales the supply plant must make in a region for all of its sales to be included in that region's pool.] But paper pooling was one of the principal methods by which the plaintiffs got to pool with the Mideast producers, so that they had to assume that it would be one of the issues in the proceeding and a possible target for reform. They knew their aggressive inroads into the Mideast were controversial; they knew that in engaging in paper pooling with Mideast farmers they were exploiting the loophole created by [a 2000 regulatory change]; they knew therefore that a curtailment of their access to the Mideast blended price was a likely outcome of a rulemaking proceeding expressly concerned with the criteria for eligibility for pooling with the Mideast producers. They knew enough to know that if they wanted to protect their participation in the Mideast pool they would have to participate in the rulemaking proceeding."

Should the result have been different if an "outsider" challenged the sufficiency of notice? Many open-government efforts are aimed at increasing the participation of stakeholders who do not typically participate in the conventional process. The APA also does not impose Article III standing hurdles for participating in the agency's notice-and-comment process. How meaningful could such efforts be if concepts like "fair notice" are contextually defined by what "insiders" know? For a more sympathetic take on what can be expected of insiders, see the next note.

(5) ***A Failure of Notice.*** Given that the Supreme Court in the Long Island case, Note 2 above, upheld a final rule that took the opposite position of the proposed rule as a "logical outgrowth," you might assume that it would be very hard now to win a procedural argument about notice. While the Supreme Court may see many outcomes as "reasonably foreseeable," the lower courts, particularly the D.C. Circuit, have been more exacting.

Because of statutory ambiguity and confusion among regulated entities, the Department of Health and Human Services considered whether patients with Medicare Advantage insurance (previously known as Medicare + Choice) should be counted in the "Medicare fraction" or "Medicaid fraction" for hospital reimbursement calculations. In a 2003 NPRM, HHS proposed that these Medicare Advantage patients should be in the Medicaid fraction, under which hospitals stood to receive far more funds but noted that "there should not be a major [financial] impact associated with this proposed change." The next year, HHS issued a final rule that placed these patients instead in the Medicare fraction.[5] In ALLINA HEALTH SERVICES V. SEBELIUS, 746 F.3d 1102, 1106 (D.C. Cir. 2014), JUDGE SILBERMAN held that: "An agency may promulgate a rule that differs from a proposed rule only if the final rule is a 'logical outgrowth' of the proposed rule. . . . A final rule is a logical outgrowth if affected parties should have anticipated that the relevant modification was possible. . . .

"The Secretary points out that the 2003 notice proposed to codify one of only two possible interpretations of the statute . . . . Therefore, the Secretary argues, the hospitals should have been on notice that the Secretary might adopt either interpretation. The hospitals counter by arguing that the notice did not actually 'propose' adopting a rule; rather, the notice proposed merely to 'clarify' an existing practice. There is nothing in the text of the notice, the hospitals argue, to suggest that the Secretary was thinking of reconsidering a longstanding practice. Moreover, the notice indicated that 'there should not be a major impact associated with this change.' 68 Fed.Reg. at 27416. . . .

[5] There has been significant litigation over these fractions. See, e.g., Becerra v. Empire Health Foundation, 142 S.Ct. 2354 (2022); Azar v. Allina Health Services, 139 S.Ct. 1804 (2019).

"This case is similar to one we decided in 2005. In Environmental Integrity Project v. E.P.A., the EPA issued a notice in which it 'proposed to codify' an interpretation of a regulation that the agency had applied in previous adjudications. 425 F.3d 992, 994 (D.C.Cir.2005). In its final rule, however, the agency adopted an interpretation precisely opposite to the one it had proposed codifying. We held that this was unlawful, explaining that there was no indication in the notice that the agency was open to reconsidering the interpretation that it has previously adopted through adjudication. Id. at 998. We said that agencies may not 'pull a surprise switcheroo on regulated entities.' Id. at 996.

"So, too, here. The hospitals should not be held to have anticipated that the Secretary's 'proposal to clarify' could have meant that the Secretary was open to reconsidering existing policy. The word 'clarify' does not suggest that a potential underlying major issue is open for discussion. . . .

"The Secretary's estimated financial impact of its proposal—that there should not be a major impact associated with this proposed change—supports our conclusion. See 68 Fed.Reg. at 27416. If, as the government contends, the 2003 notice had actually suggested a binary choice, between maintaining a preexisting policy and reversing that policy, then the potential estimated financial impact should have been stated in the hundreds of millions of dollars. That would doubtless have triggered an avalanche of comments, in contrast to the mere 26 pages that were actually submitted.

"It should be noted that since the Secretary was disposed to codify an interpretation that was favorable to the hospitals, there was no reason for the hospitals to fear that another party would offer comments opposed to such an interpretation. (There is no obvious constituency opposed to greater compensation for hospitals.) In that regard, this case differs from, for example, environmental regulation cases, where regulated industries can usually anticipate fierce opposition from environmental groups, and it might be thought prudent to submit comments in support of favorable proposed rules.

"We are sympathetic to the view expressed by the Seventh Circuit that proposed rules that might seem obscure to the average reader should alert members of the regulated class to the possible options that an examination of a policy would imply. See Alto Dairy v. Veneman, 336 F.3d 560, 570 (7th Cir.2003); but see Natural Res. Def. Council v. U.S. E.P.A., 279 F.3d 1180, 1188 (9th Cir.2002). But we ask ourselves, would a reasonable member of the regulated class—even a good lawyer—anticipate that such a volte-face with enormous financial implications would follow the Secretary's proposed rule. Indeed, such a lawyer might well advise a hospital client not to comment opposing such a possible change for fear of giving the Secretary the very idea.

"In sum, we agree with the district court that the Secretary's final rule was not a logical outgrowth of the proposed rule."

Do you agree with the court's inferences about notice from what happened in the commenting process? (From the opinion: "Only a smattering of hospitals even bothered to comment [on the NPRM]; their commentary totaled just 26 pages, and a number of them did not understand the proposal.") How does it compare to the treatment of comments in the Center for Science in the Public Interest case?

(6) ***Intermediate Action as Logical Outgrowth and Procedural Argument as Strategy.*** In Veterans Justice Group, LLC v. Sec. of Veterans Affairs, 818 F.3d 1336 (Fed. Cir. 2016), the court approved a final rule that "declined to go as far as originally proposed." Before the proposed rule, veterans could begin receiving disability benefits starting from the date they filed an "informal claim." Under the Department of Veterans Affairs' 2013 proposed rule, the lenient informal claim system was to be replaced with a stricter "incomplete claim" system. The incomplete claim system would have backdated disability benefits only to the date when a veteran began an online application in a government portal. While the 2014 final rule retained the restrictive incomplete claim system from the proposed rule, it also added two new methods of establishing the date of a disability claim. One was submission of a written intent to file a claim, and the other was a phone call or in-person conversation with the agency establishing an intent to file a claim.

The court found the final rule was a logical outgrowth of the proposed rule for three reasons. First, rather than construe the "basic approach of the Proposed Rule" narrowly, the court viewed the proposed rule broadly to comprehend the general "standardization of the claim initiation process." Second, changes to the proposed rule were "foreshadowed in proposals and comments advanced during the rulemaking." Third, and perhaps most important, while the final rule restricted the claims initiation process somewhat compared to the status quo, its additional filing methods meant the final rule did "not go as far [in restricting claims] as the Proposed Rule." "[O]ne logical outgrowth of a proposal is surely . . . to refrain from taking the proposed step."

The challengers, who argued that the final rule did not match the "paternalistic, veteran friendly, and non-adversarial nature of veterans benefits adjudication," presumably preferred the VA's final rule over the proposed version. Why did they bring this procedural challenge? If they had succeeded, the remedy would have been procedural in nature, requiring the agency to take comments on the changes.

(7) ***Logical Outgrowth and Political Transitions.*** In Chapter I's tarmac delays case study, the NPRM was issued under President George W. Bush's Administration; the final rule came out under President Obama's Administration (p. 16). In Citizens Telecommunications Co. of Minn. LLC v. FCC, 901 F.3d 991 (8th Cir. 2018), the Eighth Circuit largely rejected a logical outgrowth challenge to a rule proposed under the Obama Administration and finalized under the Trump Administration: "The . . . Petitioners complain that the 2016 Notice requested comment on a *heightened* regulatory scheme while the 2017 Order was broadly *deregulatory*. . . . We reject their arguments because their reading of the 2016 Notice entails an interpretation whose basis is not present in the text. The 2016 Notice discussed how the prior test was both over-inclusive and under-inclusive, which implies shifting the rules in favor of a better-tailored

deregulatory approach." Interestingly, courts almost never mention political transitions in their opinions (but see p. 1137). How should courts think about the notice mandate when a rule is finished in a different administration?

## c. An Opportunity to Comment and a Concise General Statement of a Rule's Basis and Purpose



*After notice required by this section, the agency shall give interested persons an opportunity to participate in the rule making through submission of written data, views, or arguments with or without opportunity for oral presentation. After consideration of the relevant matter presented, the agency shall incorporate in the rules adopted a concise general statement of their basis and purpose.*

5 U.S.C. § 553(c)

### UNITED STATES v. NOVA SCOTIA FOOD PRODUCTS CORP.

United States Court of Appeals for the Second Circuit (1977).
568 F.2d 240.

■ GURFEIN, CIRCUIT JUDGE.

[In October 1969, after several incidents of foodborne botulism, a serious and potentially fatal illness, the Food and Drug Administration issued an NPRM concerning the processing of fish commonly sold as smoked and/or salted fish. The proposed rule reached all species of fish commercially handled this way—chub, eel, herring, salmon, sturgeon, trout, whitefish, etc. The FDA issued the rule in 1970, modifying its initial proposal in response to some comments it had received. The agency declined, however, to make special provisions for particular species of fish until processors of a given species proposed a substitute they could prove adequate to protect the public from botulism. Whitefish processors apparently attempted no such demonstration. Six years later, the FDA successfully brought a district court action to enforce its rule against a whitefish processor, Nova Scotia Food Products Corp., which had not changed its processing methods to comply with the rule.]

This appeal involving a regulation of the [FDA] is not here upon a direct review of agency action. It is an appeal from a judgment of the District Court for the Eastern District of New York enjoining the appellants, after a hearing, from processing hot smoked whitefish except in accordance with time-temperature-salinity (T-T-S) regulations contained in 21 C.F.R. Part 122 (1977). The injunction was sought and granted on the ground that smoked whitefish which has been processed in violation of the T-T-S regulation is "adulterated." Food, Drug and Cosmetics Act ("the Act"), 21 U.S.C. §§ 332(a), 331(k). . . .

The regulations cited above require that hot-process smoked fish be heated by a controlled heat process that provides a monitoring system positioned in as many strategic locations in the oven as necessary to assure a continuous temperature through each fish of not less than 180° F. for a minimum of 30 minutes for fish which have been brined to contain 3.5% Water phase salt or at 150° F. for a minimum of 30 minutes if the salinity was at 5% Water phase. Since each fish must meet these requirements, it is necessary to heat an entire batch of fish to even higher temperatures so that the lowest temperature for any fish will meet the minimum requirements.

Government inspection of appellants' plant established without question that the minimum T-T-S requirements were not being met. There is no substantial claim that the plant was processing whitefish under "insanitary conditions" in any other material respect. Appellants, on their part, do not defend on the ground that they were in compliance, but rather that the requirements could not be met if a marketable whitefish was to be produced. They defend upon the grounds that the regulation is invalid (1) because it is beyond the authority delegated by the statute; (2) because the FDA improperly relied upon undisclosed evidence in promulgating the regulation and because it is not supported by the administrative record; and (3) because there was no adequate statement setting forth the basis of the regulation. We reject the contention that the regulation is beyond the authority delegated by the statute, but we find serious inadequacies in the procedure followed in the promulgation of the regulation and hold it to be invalid as applied to the appellants herein.

The hazard which the FDA sought to minimize was the outgrowth and toxin formation of Clostridium botulinum Type E spores of the bacteria which sometimes inhabit fish. There had been an occurrence of several cases of botulism traced to consumption of fish from inland waters in 1960 and 1963 which stimulated considerable bacteriological research. . . . A failure to destroy such spores through an adequate brining, thermal, and refrigeration process was found to be dangerous to public health.

The Commissioner of Food and Drugs ("Commissioner"), employing informal "notice-and-comment" procedures under 21 U.S.C. § 371(a), issued a proposal for the control of C. botulinum bacteria Type E in fish. 34 F.R. 17,176 (Oct. 23, 1969). For his statutory authority to promulgate the regulations, the Commissioner specifically relied only upon § 342(a)(4) of the Act which provides: "A food shall be deemed to be adulterated . . . if it has been prepared, packed, or held under insanitary conditions whereby it may have become contaminated with filth, or whereby it may have been rendered injurious to health." . . . Responding to the Commissioner's invitation in the notice of proposed rulemaking, members of the industry, including appellants and the intervenor-appellant, submitted comments on the proposed regulation.

The Commissioner thereafter issued the final regulations in which he adopted certain suggestions made in the comments, including a suggestion by the National Fisheries Institute, Inc. ("the Institute"), the intervenor herein. The original proposal provided that the fish would have to be cooked to a temperature of 180° F. for at least 30 minutes, if the fish have been brined to contain 3.5% Water phase salt, with no alternative. In the final regulation, an alternative suggested by the intervenor "that the parameter of 150° F. for 30 minutes and 5% Salt in the water phase be established as an alternate procedure to that stated in the proposed regulation for an interim period until specific parameters can be established" was accepted, but as a permanent part of the regulation rather than for an interim period.

The intervenor suggested that "specific parameters" be established. This referred to particular processing parameters for different species of fish on a "species by species" basis. Such "species by species" determination was proposed not only by the intervenor but also by the Bureau of Commercial Fisheries of the Department of the Interior. That Bureau objected to the general application of the T-T-S requirement proposed by the FDA on the ground that application of the regulation to all species of fish being smoked was not commercially feasible, and that the regulation should therefore specify time-temperature-salinity requirements, as developed by research and study, on a species-by-species basis. The Bureau suggested that "wholesomeness considerations could be more practically and adequately realized by reducing processing temperature and using suitable concentrations of nitrite and salt." The Commissioner took cognizance of the suggestion, but decided, nevertheless, to impose the T-T-S requirement on all species of fish (except chub, which were regulated by 21 C.F.R. 172.177 (1977) (dealing with food additives)).

He did acknowledge, however, in his "basis and purpose" statement required by the Administrative Procedure Act ("APA"), 5 U.S.C. § 553(c), that "adequate times, temperatures and salt concentrations have not been demonstrated for each individual species of fish presently smoked." 35 F.R. 17,401 (Nov. 13, 1970). The Commissioner concluded, nevertheless, that "the processing requirements of the proposed regulations are the safest now known to prevent the outgrowth and toxin formation of C. botulinum Type E." He determined that "the conditions of current good manufacturing practice for this industry should be established without further delay."

The Commissioner did not answer the suggestion by the Bureau of Fisheries that nitrite and salt as additives could safely lower the high temperature otherwise required, a solution which the FDA had accepted in the case of chub. Nor did the Commissioner respond to the claim of Nova Scotia through its trade association, the Association of Smoked

Fish Processors, Inc., Technical Center that "(t)he proposed process requirements suggested by the FDA for hot processed smoked fish are neither commercially feasible nor based on sound scientific evidence obtained with the variety of smoked fish products to be included under this regulation."

Nova Scotia, in its own comment, wrote to the Commissioner that "the heating of certain types of fish to high temperatures will completely destroy the product." It suggested, as an alternative, that "specific processing procedures could be established for each species after adequate work and experimention (sic) has been done—but not before." We have noted above that the response given by the Commissioner was in general terms. He did not specifically aver that the T-T-S requirements as applied to whitefish were, in fact, commercially feasible.

When, after several inspections and warnings, Nova Scotia failed to comply with the regulation, an action by the United States Attorney for injunctive relief was filed on April 7, 1976, six years later, and resulted in the judgment here on appeal. . . .

I

[The court found that the FDA's statutory authority allowed it to regulate in this area.]

II

Appellants contend that there is an inadequate administrative record upon which to predicate judicial review, and that the failure to disclose to interested persons the factual material upon which the agency was relying vitiates the element of fairness which is essential to any kind of administrative action. Moreover, they argue that the "concise general statement of . . . basis and purpose" by the Commissioner was inadequate. 5 U.S.C. § 553.

The question of what is an adequate "record" in informal rulemaking has engaged the attention of commentators for several years. The extent of the administrative record required for judicial review of informal rulemaking is largely a function of the scope of judicial review. Even when the standard of review is whether the promulgation of the rule was "arbitrary, capricious, an abuse of discretion, or otherwise not in accordance with law," as specified in 5 U.S.C. § 706(2)(A), judicial review must nevertheless, be based on the "whole record" (id.). Adequate review of a determination requires an adequate record, if the review is to be meaningful. What will constitute an adequate record for meaningful review may vary with the nature of the administrative action to be reviewed. Review must be based on the whole record even when the judgment is one of policy, except that findings of fact such as would be required in an adjudicatory proceeding or in a formal "on the record" hearing for rulemaking need not be made. Citizens to Preserve Overton Park v. Volpe, 401 U.S. 402, 416–18 (1971) [p. 1145]. Though the action was informal, without an evidentiary record, the review must be "thorough, probing, [and] in depth." Id., 401 U.S. at 415. . . .

A

With respect to the content of the administrative "record," the Supreme Court has told us that in informal rulemaking, "the focal point for judicial review should be the administrative record already in existence, not some new record made initially in the reviewing court." See Camp v. Pitts, 411 U.S. 138, 142 (1973) [p. 1147].

No contemporaneous record was made or certified.[13] When, during the enforcement action, the basis for the regulation was sought through pretrial discovery, the record was created by searching the files of the FDA and the memories of those who participated in the process of rulemaking. This resulted in what became Exhibit D at the trial of the injunction action. Exhibit D consists of (1) Tab A containing the comments received from outside parties during the administrative "notice-and-comment" proceeding and (2) Tabs B through L consisting of scientific data and the like upon which the Commissioner now says he relied but which were not made known to the interested parties. . . .

In an enforcement action, we must rely exclusively on the record made before the agency to determine the validity of the regulation. The exception to the exclusivity of that record is that "there may be independent judicial fact-finding when issues that were not before the agency are raised in a proceeding to *enforce* non-adjudicatory agency action." Overton Park, supra, 401 U.S. at 415 (1971). (Emphasis added.)

Though this is an enforcement proceeding and the question is close, we think that the "issues" were fairly before the agency and hence that de novo evidence was properly excluded by Judge Dooling. Our concern is, rather, with the manner in which the agency treated the issues tendered.

B

The key issues were (1) whether, in the light of the rather scant history of botulism in whitefish, that species should have been considered separately rather than included in a general regulation which failed to distinguish species from species; (2) whether the application of the proposed T-T-S requirements to smoked whitefish made the whitefish commercially unsaleable; and (3) whether the agency recognized that prospect, but nevertheless decided that the public health needs should prevail even if that meant commercial death for the whitefish industry. The procedural issues were whether, in the light of these key questions, the agency procedure was inadequate because (i) it failed to disclose to interested parties the scientific data and the methodology upon which it

[13] A practice developed in the early years of the APA of not making a formal contemporaneous record, but rather, when challenged, to put together a historical record of what had been available for agency consideration at the time the regulation was promulgated. . . . Professor Davis in a balanced review, has stated: "When the facts are of central importance and might be challenged, parties adversely affected by them should have a chance to respond to them. Clearly, whatever factual information the agency has considered should be a part of the record for judicial review." K. Davis, Administrative Law of the Seventies, § 29.01–6, pp. 672–73 (1976).

relied; and (ii) because it failed utterly to address itself to the pertinent question of commercial feasibility.

1. The History of Botulism in Whitefish

. . . [Since] [t]he industry . . . abandoned vacuum-packing, . . . there has not been a single case of botulism associated with commercially prepared whitefish since 1963, though 2,750,000 pounds of whitefish are processed annually. . . .

2. The Scientific Data

Interested parties were not informed of the scientific data, or at least of a selection of such data deemed important by the agency, so that comments could be addressed to the data. Appellants argue that unless the scientific data relied upon by the agency are spread upon the public records, criticism of the methodology used or the meaning to be inferred from the data is rendered impossible.

We agree with appellants in this case, for although we recognize that an agency may resort to its own expertise outside the record in an informal rulemaking procedure, we do not believe that when the pertinent research material is readily available and the agency has no special expertise on the precise parameters involved, there is any reason to conceal the scientific data relied upon from the interested parties. As Judge Leventhal said in Portland Cement Ass'n v. Ruckelshaus, 486 F.2d 375, 393 (1973): "It is not consonant with the purpose of a rulemaking proceeding to promulgate rules on the basis of inadequate data, or on data that [in] critical degree, *is known only to the agency*." (Emphasis added.) This is not a case where the agency methodology was based on material supplied by the interested parties themselves. International Harvester Co. v. Ruckelshaus, 478 F.2d 615, 632 (1973). Here all the scientific research was collected by the agency, and none of it was disclosed to interested parties as the material upon which the proposed rule would be fashioned.[15] Nor was an articulate effort made to connect the scientific requirements to available technology that would make commercial survival possible, though the burden of proof was on the agency. This required it to "bear a burden of adducing a reasoned presentation supporting the reliability of its methodology." International Harvester, supra, 478 F.2d at 643 . . . .

If the failure to notify interested persons of the scientific research upon which the agency was relying actually prevented the presentation of relevant comment, the agency may be held not to have considered all "the relevant factors." We can think of no sound reasons for secrecy or reluctance to expose to public view (with an exception for trade secrets or national security) the ingredients of the deliberative process. Indeed, the FDA's own regulations now specifically require that every notice of proposed rulemaking contain "references to all data and information on

---

[15] We recognize the problem posed by Judge Leventhal in International Harvester, supra, that a proceeding might never end if such submission required a reply ad infinitum. Here the exposure of the scientific research relied on simply would have required a single round of comment addressed thereto.

which the Commissioner relies for the proposal (copies or a full list of which shall be a part of the administrative file on the matter . . .)." 21 C.F.R. § 10.40(b)(1) (1977). And this is, undoubtedly, the trend.

We think that the scientific data should have been disclosed to focus on the proper interpretation of "insanitary conditions." When the basis for a proposed rule is a scientific decision, the scientific material which is believed to support the rule should be exposed to the view of interested parties for their comment. One cannot ask for comment on a scientific paper without allowing the participants to read the paper. Scientific research is sometimes rejected for diverse inadequacies of methodology; and statistical results are sometimes rebutted because of a lack of adequate gathering technique or of supportable extrapolation. Such is the stuff of scientific debate. To suppress meaningful comment by failure to disclose the basic data relied upon is akin to rejecting comment altogether. For unless there is common ground, the comments are unlikely to be of a quality that might impress a careful agency. The inadequacy of comment in turn leads in the direction of arbitrary decision-making. We do not speak of findings of fact, for such are not technically required in the informal rulemaking procedures. We speak rather of what the agency should make known so as to elicit comments that probe the fundamentals. Informal rulemaking does not lend itself to a rigid pattern. Especially, in the circumstance of our broad reading of statutory authority in support of the agency, we conclude that the failure to disclose to interested persons the scientific data upon which the FDA relied was procedurally erroneous. Moreover, the burden was upon the agency to articulate rationally why the rule should apply to a large and diverse class, with the same T-T-S parameters made applicable to *all* species.

C

Appellants additionally attack the "concise general statement" required by APA, 5 U.S.C. § 553, as inadequate. We think that, in the circumstances, it was less than adequate. It is not in keeping with the rational process to leave vital questions, raised by comments which are of cogent materiality, completely unanswered. The agencies certainly have a good deal of discretion in expressing the basis of a rule, but the agencies do not have quite the prerogative of obscurantism reserved to legislatures. . . .

The test of adequacy of the "concise general statement" was expressed by Judge McGowan in the following terms: "We do not expect the agency to discuss every item of fact or opinion included in the submissions made to it in informal rulemaking. We do expect that, if the judicial review which Congress has thought it important to provide is to be meaningful, the 'concise general statement of . . . basis and purpose' mandated by Section 4 [§ 553] will enable us to see what major issues of policy were ventilated by the informal proceedings and why the agency reacted to them as it did." Automotive Parts & Accessories Ass'n v. Boyd, 407 F.2d 330, 338 ([D.C. Cir.] 1968). . . .

The Secretary was squarely faced with the question whether it was necessary to formulate a rule with specific parameters that applied to all species of fish, and particularly whether lower temperatures with the addition of nitrite and salt would not be sufficient. Though this alternative was suggested by an agency of the federal government, its suggestion, though acknowledged, was never answered.

Moreover, the comment that to apply the proposed T-T-S requirements to whitefish would destroy the commercial product was neither discussed nor answered. We think that to sanction silence in the face of such vital questions would be to make the statutory requirement of a "concise general statement" less than an adequate safeguard against arbitrary decision-making. . . .

One may recognize that even commercial infeasibility cannot stand in the way of an overwhelming public interest. Yet the administrative process should disclose, at least, whether the proposed regulation is considered to be commercially feasible, or whether other considerations prevail even if commercial infeasibility is acknowledged. This kind of forthright disclosure and basic statement was lacking in the formulation of the T-T-S standard made applicable to whitefish. It is easy enough for an administrator to ban everything. In the regulation of food processing, the worldwide need for food also must be taken into account in formulating measures taken for the protection of health. In the light of the history of smoked whitefish to which we have referred, we find no articulate balancing here sufficient to make the procedure followed less than arbitrary.

After seven years of relative inaction, the FDA has apparently not reviewed the T-T-S regulations in the light of present scientific knowledge and experience. In the absence of a new statutory directive by Congress regarding control of micro-organisms, which we hope will be worthy of its consideration, we think that the T-T-S standards should be reviewed again by the FDA.

We cannot, on this appeal, remand to the agency to allow further comments by interested parties, addressed to the scientific data now disclosed at the trial below. We hold in this enforcement proceeding, therefore, that the regulation, as it affects non-vacuum-packed hot-smoked whitefish, was promulgated in an arbitrary manner and is invalid. . . .

In view of our conclusion . . . we must reverse the grant of the injunction and direct that the complaint be dismissed.[6]

## NOTES ON THE PAPER HEARING

(1) ***The Paper Hearing.*** Writing a year before the Supreme Court's Vermont Yankee decision, Richard Stewart described developments that had emerged after its Florida East Coast Railway decision (p. 300)—the

[6] [Ed.] After the decision, the FDA did not enforce this rule again. It repealed the rule, through notice-and-comment rulemaking, almost seven years later. See Smoked and Smoke-Flavored Fish; Current Good Manufacturing Practice, 49 Fed. Reg. 20484 (May 15, 1984).

expansion of agency records and the "requirement of reasoned elaboration" (which includes responding to contrary arguments and evidence)—as creating the basis for a "paper hearing." Such a hearing "combines many of the advantages of a trial-type adversary process (excepting oral testimony and cross-examination) while avoiding undue delay and cost." RICHARD B. STEWART, THE DEVELOPMENT OF ADMINISTRATIVE AND QUASI-CONSTITUTIONAL LAW IN JUDICIAL REVIEW OF ENVIRONMENTAL DECISION-MAKING: LESSONS FROM THE CLEAN AIR ACT, 62 Iowa L. Rev. 713, 731–33 (1977): "The development of a 'paper hearing' procedure and the related requirement that the Agency explain in detail the bases for its decision have contributed significantly to the improvement of EPA decisionmaking because the Agency must be prepared to expose the factual and methodological bases for its decision and face judicial review on a record that encompasses the contentions and evidence of the Agency and its opponents, including responses by the Agency to criticism of its decision. . . . Recognition of a 'paper hearing' procedure as a third standard model of administrative decision is likely to represent a better solution to the inadequacies of the two traditional paradigms (notice-and-comment procedures and adjudicatory procedures) than a series of ad hoc responses." For a discussion of the impact of these elaborations on § 553, including the concern that they "ossify" rulemaking by making it a time- and resource-intensive process, see the discussion of "hard look" review in Chapter VIII, Section 2.b (p. 1126).

(2) ***Disclosure Demands and Vermont Yankee.*** Nova Scotia and Portland Cement (quoted in Nova Scotia) together mandate agency disclosure of both data and the methodologies used in reasoning from data.[7] Both Portland Cement and Nova Scotia predate Vermont Yankee. Do they survive it? This issue arose in the D.C. Circuit decision, AMERICAN RADIO RELAY LEAGUE V. FCC, 524 F.3d 227 (D.C. Cir. 2008). The FCC adopted a rule approving the installation of devices on electric power lines that would transmit broadband Internet access. This technology also had the potential to interfere with licensed amateur "ham" radio operators. The FCC concluded that existing safeguards and certain new protective measures would be adequate to prevent the problem, but the American Radio Relay League disagreed and challenged the rule. A Freedom of Information Act request had uncovered five studies consisting of technical data gathered from field tests performed by FCC staff. The FCC ultimately placed these in the rulemaking record, but in redacted form and after the rule had been promulgated.

JUDGE ROGERS's opinion for the panel held that the FCC had violated § 553: "It would appear to be a fairly obvious proposition that studies upon which an agency relies in promulgating a rule must be made available during the rulemaking in order to afford interested persons meaningful notice and

[7] In Portland Cement, challengers had taken issue with how the EPA set a stationary source standard for new and modified portland cement plants, in part because they had not received information about the agency's methodology in time to comment on it. The D.C. Circuit found the agency process lacking: "We find a critical defect in the decision-making process in arriving at the standard under review in the initial inability of petitioners to obtain—in timely fashion—the test results and procedures used on existing plants which formed a partial basis for the emission control level adopted, and in the subsequent seeming refusal of the agency to respond to what seem to be legitimate problems with the methodology of these tests." Portland Cement Ass'n v. Ruckelshaus, 486 F.2d 375, 392 (D.C. Cir. 1973).

an opportunity for comment [quoting Judge Leventhal's opinion in Portland Cement]. . . . Where, as here, an agency's determination is based upon a complex mix of controversial and uncommented upon data and calculations, there is no APA precedent allowing an agency to cherry-pick a study on which it has chosen to rely in part." The opinion noted that the court had reviewed the partially redacted pages in camera in unredacted form, and that they included staff summaries of test data, scientific recommendations, test analyses, and conclusions regarding the methodology used in the studies. It concluded that the League might have had something useful to say if given the opportunity to comment on the unredacted studies.

Judge Rogers rejected the suggestion that requiring disclosure of the studies was at odds with Vermont Yankee: "[T]he procedures invalidated in Vermont Yankee were not anchored to any statutory provision. By contrast, the court does not impose any new procedures for the regulatory process, but merely applies settled law to the facts. The Commission made the choice to engage in notice-and-comment rulemaking and to rely on parts of its redacted studies as a basis for the rule. The court, consequently, is not imposing new procedures but enforcing the agency's procedural choice by ensuring that it conforms to APA requirements. It is one thing for the Commission to give notice and make available for comment the studies on which it relied in formulating the rule while explaining its non-reliance on certain parts. It is quite another thing to provide notice and an opportunity for comment on only those parts of the studies that the Commission likes best."

Concurring, JUDGE TATEL linked the disclosure requirement to § 706 of the APA: "That provision requires us to set aside arbitrary and capricious agency action after reviewing 'the whole record,' 5 U.S.C. § 706, and the 'whole record' in this case includes the complete content of the staff reports the Commission relied upon in promulgating the challenged rule. . . . Given that the Commission relied on the studies at issue, there can be no doubt that they form part of the administrative record—a proposition unaffected by the Commission's claim that it chose not to rely on various parts of the studies. Nor is there any doubt that, as our case law makes clear, the APA means exactly what it says: an agency must make the '*whole* record' available, especially where, as here, the undisclosed portions might very well undercut the agency's ultimate decision. . . . This is hardly a novel conclusion. In previous informal rulemaking cases, we ordered additional agency disclosures to facilitate meaningful arbitrary and capricious review of agency action."

Then-JUDGE KAVANAUGH wrote separately "to underscore that Portland Cement stands on a shaky legal foundation (even though it may make sense as a policy matter in some cases). Put bluntly, the Portland Cement doctrine cannot be squared with the text of § 553 of the APA." He explained: "The APA requires only that an agency provide public notice and a comment period before the agency issues a rule. The notice must include 'the terms or substance of the proposed rule *or* a description of the subjects and issues involved.' § 553(b) (3) (emphasis added). After issuing a notice and allowing time for interested persons to comment, the agency must issue a 'concise general statement' of the rule's 'basis and purpose' along with the final rule. § 553(c). One searches the text of APA § 553 in vain for a requirement that an agency disclose other agency information as part of the notice or later in the rulemaking process. . . . Portland Cement's lack of roots in the statutory text creates a serious jurisprudential problem because the Supreme Court later rejected this kind of freeform interpretation of the APA [in Vermont Yankee]. . . .

"Courts have incrementally expanded those APA procedural requirements well beyond what the text provides. And courts simultaneously have grown . . . 'narrow' § 706 arbitrary-and-capricious review into a far more demanding test. . . . [These] twin lines of decisions have gradually transformed rulemaking—whether regulatory or deregulatory rulemaking—from the simple and speedy practice contemplated by the APA into a laborious, seemingly never-ending process. The judicially created obstacle course can hinder Executive Branch agencies from rapidly and effectively responding to changing or emerging issues within their authority, such as consumer access to broadband, or effectuating policy or philosophical changes in the Executive's approach to the subject matter at hand. The trend has not been good as a jurisprudential matter, and it continues to have significant practical consequences for the operation of the Federal Government and those affected by federal regulation and deregulation."

Was then-Judge Kavanaugh correct that the disclosure requirements imposed by Portland Cement and Nova Scotia are at odds with the text of § 553? Or are you persuaded by Judge Rogers's contention (echoing the line of argument articulated in Nova Scotia) that such requirements have a firmer home in § 553 than do the procedures at issue in Vermont Yankee? Does the textual reference in § 553(b)(3)—"an opportunity to participate"—suffice to support such a disclosure requirement? Are the disclosure requirements instead best justified, as Judge Tatel claimed, on the basis of § 706's "whole record" requirement for judicial review? Finally, would it be better to justify data disclosure requirements on a theory that the APA should not be read in a static fashion, particularly given subsequent developments such as the tremendous growth in informal rulemaking (and the fading of formal rulemaking) after Florida East Coast Railway (p. 300)? For more on the contrast between static and more evolving interpretations of the APA, see Chapter III (p. 245) and the discussion of dynamic statutory interpretation in Chapter II (p. 127).

(3) ***Legislative Proposals on Disclosure.*** The proposed Regulatory Accountability Act, discussed briefly in Section 2 above (p. 308), would also have amended § 553 to explicitly require agencies to disclose relevant information: "(A) IN GENERAL.—Except as provided in subparagraph (B), not later than the date on which an agency publishes a notice of proposed rulemaking . . . , all studies, models, scientific literature, and other information developed or relied upon by the agency, and actions taken by the agency to obtain that information, in connection with the determination of the agency to propose the rule that is the subject of the rulemaking shall be placed in the docket for the proposed rule and made accessible to the public. (B) EXCEPTION.—Subparagraph (A) shall not apply with respect to

information that is exempt from disclosure under section 552(b) [FOIA exemptions, see p. 721]." S. 951 (115th Cong.) (2017), § 3.

(4) ***The Tension Between Original Understandings and Current Acceptance.*** "[A]n evolutionary process is . . . apparent with respect to the APA's procedural requirements for informal rulemaking, with current requirements of notice and agency response to comments far exceeding what the text of the APA suggests was originally expected." Gillian E. Metzger, Ordinary Administrative Law as Constitutional Common Law, 110 Colum. L. Rev. 479, 509 (2010). For a sense of what a 1946 legislator would have thought was demanded of agencies, consider the following description of informal rulemaking contained in an influential contemporaneous commentary on the APA.

ATTORNEY GENERAL'S MANUAL ON THE ADMINISTRATIVE PROCEDURE ACT 31–35 (1947): "*Informal rule making.* In every case of proposed informal rule making subject to the notice requirements of section [553(b)], section [553(c)] provides that 'the agency shall afford interested persons an opportunity to participate in the rule making through submission of written data, views, or arguments with or without opportunity to present the same orally in any manner.' The quoted language confers discretion upon the agency, except where statutes require 'formal' rule making subject to sections [556 & 557], to designate in each case the procedure for public participation in rule making. Such informal rule making procedure may take a variety of forms: informal hearings (with or without a stenographic transcript), conferences, consultation with industry committees, submission of written views, or any combination of these. These informal procedures have already been extensively employed by Federal agencies. In each case, the selection of the procedure to be followed will depend largely upon the nature of the rules involved. The objective should be to assure informed administrative action and adequate protection to private interests.

"Each agency is affirmatively required to consider 'all relevant matter presented' in the proceeding; it is recommended that all rules issued after such informal proceedings be accompanied by an express recital that such material has been considered. It is entirely clear, however, that section [553b] does not require the formulation of rules upon the exclusive basis of any 'record' made in informal rule making proceedings. Senate Hearings (1941) p. 444. Accordingly, except in formal rule making governed by sections [556 & 557], an agency is free to formulate rules upon the basis of materials in its files and the knowledge and experience of the agency, in addition to the materials adduced in public rule making proceedings.

"Section [553(c)] provides that upon the completion of public rule making proceedings 'after consideration of all relevant matter presented, the agency shall incorporate in any rules adopted a concise general statement of their basis and purpose.' The required statement will be important in that the courts and the public may be expected to use such statements in the interpretation of the agency's rules. The statement is to be 'concise' and 'general.' Except as required by statutes providing for 'formal' rule making procedure, findings of fact and conclusions of law are not necessary. Nor is there required an elaborate analysis of the rules or of the considerations upon which the rules were issued. Rather, the statement is intended to advise the public of the general basis and purpose of the rules."

See also Emily S. Bremer, The Undemocratic Roots of Agency Rulemaking, 108 Cornell L. Rev. (forthcoming) ("In crafting the APA's notice-and-comment procedures, . . . Congress constructed public rights to transparency and participation atop the relatively undemocratic, expertise-focused foundation that had been established by pre-APA administrative practice.").

Today, both a "blackletter" statement of administrative law published by the Administrative Law and Regulatory Practice Section of the ABA, A Blackletter Statement of Federal Administrative Law, 54 Admin. L. Rev. 1, 30–35 (2002), and the Section's popular publication, A Guide to Federal Agency Rulemaking, present the paper hearing as an established, uncontroversial part of the law. Justice Alito (joined by Justices Thomas, Gorsuch, and Barrett) cited Nova Scotia in dissent in Biden v. Missouri, 142 S.Ct. 647 (2022) (pp. 390, 869), while discussing a rule mandating COVID-19 vaccinations for staff at facilities receiving Medicare and Medicaid funding that he believed should have gone through the notice-and-comment process: "Except in rare cases, an agency must provide public notice of proposed rules, 5 U.S.C. § 553(b); the public must be given the opportunity to comment on those proposals, § 553(c); and if the agency issues the rule, it must address concerns raised during the notice-and-comment process. United States v. Nova Scotia Food Products Corp., 568 F. 2d 240, 252 (CA2 1977)."

(5) ***The Freedom of Information Act as Amendment.*** Another important development subsequent to the APA's adoption was enactment in 1966 of FOIA as an amendment to the APA. (See Chapter VI, Section 3, p. 720). FOIA requires agencies to make public, on request, any properly identified information in agency records that does not fall under protected exemptions. 5 U.S.C. §§ 552(a)(3), 552(b). Does this mean that an NPRM issued under § 553(b) must contain references to and make available any data (studies, etc.) known to the agency as arguably bearing upon its proposal? As you will learn if you study Chapter VI, where FOIA is considered in detail, "please disclose all factual studies and data in agency records that the agency has thus far considered in connection with the rulemaking on [subject] announced in the Federal Register on [date] at [page]" is a sufficiently definite (and otherwise proper) FOIA request. As American Radio Relay League demonstrates, persons interested in a rulemaking could (and certainly do) make such requests promptly on learning of a proposal. Although a requester couldn't count on getting the agency's response in time to inform her comments, the agency's obligation to disclose is evident, as is the likelihood that it would receive requests to do so. Can you convert this juxtaposition of statutory remedies into an argument that such data must be revealed during the notice-and-comment process?

(6) ***The Three "Records" of Agency Rulemaking.*** It is possible to identify at least three different collections of material that might be thought of in "record" terms: the record for participation, the record for decision, and the record for judicial review. The record for participation represents the

material available to be used by the public as the basis for commenting upon a proposed rule during the proceeding, together with such comments as may be received and made publicly available before the end of the comment period. The record for decision consists of the mass of materials that informs the agency's own decisionmaking processes in the particular rulemaking. The record for review is the documentary collection presented to a court as the basis for deciding whether the rule has sufficient basis to satisfy the applicable standard of judicial review. See Jeffrey S. Lubbers, A Guide to Federal Agency Rulemaking 325–42 (6th ed. 2018).

What are the relationships among the record for participation, the record for decision, and the record for review? Can the record for decision be larger than the record for participation, or must the agency disclose to the public everything that it considers, including confidential information?[8] Can the record for decision be larger than the record for review, or must the agency produce in court all information it is aware of having considered, even information discarded as unreliable or outweighed? How, in this context, is the agency's acquired expertise (distributed among the many members of its staff) to be memorialized? Alternatively, can the record for decision be smaller than the record for review? That is, can the agency produce in court later-arising information that supports the rule it adopted but was not known at the time the rule was made? Questions such as these have provoked a considerable amount of litigation but no easy-to-state result. On the other hand, decisions such as Nova Scotia established that agencies need to make available for public comment studies and other data on which they rely, and Vermont Yankee assumed that the agency would produce a record for judicial review. As a result, agencies today are very conscious of the need to keep a record during the rulemaking process and usually will not leave the record to be compiled later in an enforcement proceeding or on judicial review. Most judicial challenges are resolved on the record the agency produces. But sometimes courts allow the record to be supplemented or, in rare cases, order discovery. See Department of Commerce v. New York, 139 S.Ct. 2551 (2019) (p. 1177).

(7) ***Novelty and Prejudice.*** The paper hearing mandates concerning information disclosure have two important limits. First, the information must be sufficiently different from already disclosed material. See, e.g., Competitive Enterprise Institute v. U.S. Department of Transportation, 863 F.3d 911 (D.C. Cir. 2017) (noting that an agency "may include new 'supplementary' information that 'expands on and confirms' data in the rulemaking record" that was not provided for commenting and finding that "[t]his case falls in th[at] . . . category"). Second, there has to be harm to the commenter from nondisclosure. See, e.g., Allina Health Services v. Sebelius, 746 F.3d 1102 (D.C. Cir. 2014) ("Perhaps because of the possible tension between Vermont Yankee and our critical material doctrine, we have more

[8] ACUS recently issued a recommendation for how agencies should consider handling confidential personal and commercial information in rulemaking dockets. The recommendation "proposes steps agencies can take to withhold protected materials from their public rulemaking dockets while still providing the public with the information upon which agencies relied in formulating proposed rules." ACUS, Recommendation 2020–2, Protected Materials in Public Rulemaking Dockets, 86 Fed. Reg. 6614 (Jan. 22. 2021). See also Note 9 (p. 354).

carefully examined whether a failure to disclose such material actually harmed a petitioner. But it is sufficient for a petitioner to show that an opportunity to comment regarding an agency's important information created 'enough uncertainty' as to its possible affect [sic] on the agency's disposition. See Chamber of Commerce of U.S. v. S.E.C., 443 F.3d 890, 906 (D.C.Cir.2006)."); Alfa International Seafood v. Ross, 264 F.Supp.3d 23 (D.D.C. 2017) ("Put another way, to demonstrate prejudice, Plaintiffs must demonstrate that they had something useful to say about the undisclosed data that could have impacted the Department's decision-making.").

(8) ***Non-Judicial Checks on Missing Data in Rulemaking.*** During the Trump Administration, the Department of Labor excluded an internal cost-benefit analysis from its rulemaking docket on a tip pooling proposal. News accounts reported that OIRA (see Section 5.d, p. 455) disagreed with the removal of the study from the rulemaking docket but was overruled. Ben Penn, Mulvaney, Acosta Override Regulatory Office to Hide Tips Rule Data, Bloomberg Law (Mar. 21, 2018). Bloomberg Law's reporting spurred a multi-year Inspector General investigation. In December 2020, the Labor Department's IG reported that the agency excluded the analysis under pressure from the Justice Department and criticized that decision: "Releasing the 2017 NPRM without a quantitative analysis raised transparency concerns since DOL did not identify for the public the full economic impact of allowing employers to keep or reallocate tips earned by tipped employees, which the public could have used to make more informed comments on the proposed rulemaking." U.S. Department of Labor Office of Inspector General—Office of Audit, DOL Did Not Demonstrate It Followed a Sound Process in Promulgating the 2017 Tip Rule Notice of Proposed Rulemaking (Dec. 11, 2020).[9]

(9) ***Agency-Imposed Restrictions on Data.*** In April 2018, during the Trump Administration, the EPA proposed a rulemaking that would have required "when EPA develops regulations for which the public is likely to bear the cost of compliance, with regard to those scientific studies that are pivotal to the action being taken, EPA should ensure that the data underlying those are publicly available in a manner sufficient for independent validation." EPA, Strengthening Transparency in Regulatory Science, 83 Fed. Reg. 18768, 18768 (Apr. 30, 2018). Critics argued that such mandates would prevent regulation because confidentiality protections on many research studies would prevent disclosure. The docket for the so-called "secret science" rulemaking on www.regulations.gov (EPA-HQ-OA-2018-0259) shows nearly 1 million comments on the proposal. The EPA finalized the rule just weeks before President Trump left office and made it effective immediately. A district court determined that the agency did not provide a sufficient reason to forgo the 30-day waiting period for a rule to become effective, and vacated and remanded the rule to the agency. The EPA (staffed with President Biden's appointees) formally ended the rulemaking in May 2021.

[9] https://www.oig.dol.gov/public/reports/oa/2021/17-21-001-15-001.pdf.

## NOTES ON THE OPPORTUNITY TO PARTICIPATE

(1) ***Participation in Rulemaking.*** Section 553(c) provides that the opportunity to participate in informal rulemaking shall be given to "interested persons." Section 551(2) defines "person" inclusively, excepting only the agency itself. Filing a comment with an agency, of course, is different from being able to challenge the final result in court. It is not surprising that the subject of the enforcement action in the main case—Nova Scotia, a private party—submitted tough comments to the FDA. An industry trade group, the National Fisheries Institute, participated as well in the rulemaking process. (Often, public interest groups file views, too, but they did not in this case.[10])

Commenting can also come from within the government. The Department of Interior's Bureau of Commercial Fisheries, for example, challenged the FDA's proposal in Nova Scotia; indeed, although it did not focus on the source of the challenge, the court found the FDA's response to this sister agency insufficient. Another federal agency, the Small Business Administration's Office of Advocacy, which is tasked by statute with representing the interests of the small business community, often files comments in other agencies' rulemakings. The SBA recently flagged the EPA's failure to consult small businesses in five high-profile rulemakings since July 2021, leaving those rules "vulnerable to being challenged in court" for failure to comply with statutory consultation mandates. See Pat Rizzuto & Stephen Lee, EPA Criticized for Skipping Small Business Advice on Rules, Bloomberg Law (Oct. 31, 2022). In September 2022, FTC Chair Lina Khan submitted a comment to an advance NPRM (Poultry Growing Tournament Systems: Fairness and Related Concerns) by the Department of Agriculture.[11] And members of Congress sometimes submit comments.[12]

The APA does not discuss how long the commenting period should last. Rather, recent Executive Orders have set a 60-day floor for "most" rulemakings.[13] In practice, the length of comment periods varies widely, including shrinking near the end of a presidential administration. Interested persons (including members of Congress) also often seek extensions in the length of the comment period (for instance, for "collection of information" or

---

[10] "In response [to the FDA's NPRM], comments were received from two trade associations, eight manufacturers, and the Bureau of Commercial Fisheries, Department of Interior." 35 Fed. Reg. 17401 (Nov. 13, 1970).

[11] https://www.ftc.gov/system/files/ftc_gov/pdf/Comment%20of%20Lina%20M.%20Khan%20on%20USDA%20ANPR%20re%20Poultry%20Growing%20Tournament%20Systems.pdf.

[12] For more information on congressional comments, see Kenneth Lowande & Rachel Augustine Potter, Congressional Oversight Revisited: Politics and Procedure in Agency Rulemaking, 83 J. Pol. 401 (2021) (based on examination of congressional procedural and substantive comments in EPA rulemakings from 2007 to 2017, finding "evidence that appeals to procedure are rooted in politicians' ideological disagreement with agency policy proposals, that they complement substantive recommendations, and that they are conditional on legislative capacity"). In June 2022, 131 Republican members of Congress signed a comment letter opposing the SEC's proposed rule on mandated disclosures concerning climate change. See https://www.sec.gov/comments/s7-10-22/s71022-20131300-301417.pdf.

[13] "[E]ach agency should afford the public a meaningful opportunity to comment on any proposed regulation, which in most cases should include a comment period of not less than 60 days." E.O. 12866, § 6(a), 58 Fed. Reg. 51735 (Sept. 30, 1993) (p. 1622). This Order is discussed in more detail in Section 5.d below.

to "improve the quality of responses"), which agencies sometimes grant. There are resources online about how to submit an effective comment.[14]

During the Trump Administration, several district courts determined that a 30-day comment period was likely insufficient in ruling on motions for preliminary injunctions because of, among other reasons, the complexity of the challenged rulemakings, the lower number of received comments compared to similar rules, and the COVID-19 pandemic. See Centro Legal de la Raza v. Executive Office for Immigration Review, 524 F.Supp.3d 919 (N.D. Cal. 2021); Pangea Legal Services v. DHS, 501 F.Supp.3d 792 (N.D. Cal. 2020). More recently, under the Biden Administration, a district court rejected a 19-day comment period when the Department of Labor proposed delaying a Trump-era rule on independent contractors. Coalition for Workforce Innovation v. Walsh, 2022 WL 1073346 (E.D. Tex. 2022). The Department of Labor issued a new NPRM redefining independent contractor status in early October 2022, with the comment period initially slated to last two months this time around. The comment period was then extended.

(2) ***Necessity of Raising Issues with the Agency and Strategic Considerations.*** Because the failure to comment on an issue often counts as procedural "default," barring certain challenges later in court, commenters have an incentive to raise matters initially before the agency. (See Chapter 9, Section 2.c, on exhaustion of administrative remedies (p. 1534)). Consider JUDGE STEPHEN WILLIAMS's concurrence in KORETOFF V. VILSACK, 707 F.3d 394, 401 (D.C. Cir. 2013): "Generally speaking, then, the price for a ticket to facial review is to raise objections in the rulemaking. This system probably operates quite well for large industry associations and consumer or environmental groups (and the firms and individuals thus represented). But for some the impact is more severe. Firms filling niche markets, for example, as appellants appear to be, may be ill-represented by broad industry groups and unlikely to be adequately lawyered-up at the rulemaking stage. As the Fifth Circuit observed, we presumably do not want to 'require everyone who wishes to protect himself from arbitrary agency action not only to become a faithful reader of the notices of proposed rulemaking published each day in the Federal Register, but a psychic able to predict the possible changes that could be made in the proposal when the rule is finally promulgated.' City of Seabrook v. EPA, 659 F.2d 1349, 1360–61." When, if ever, should there be a procedural default rule for those who fail to comment? Commenting is not costless. How should entities consider the costs and benefits to participating in a rulemaking?

Agencies can generally waive an objection to failure to participate in the rulemaking. The Supreme Court, in EPA v. EME Homer City Generation, L.P., 572 U.S. 489 (2014), addressed whether a court can consider an argument that was not raised during rulemaking proceedings. The Court held that the Clean Air Act's requirement that "[o]nly an objection to a rule . . . raised with reasonable specificity during the period for public comment . . . may be raised during judicial review," 42 U.S.C. § 7607(d)(7)(B), was not a jurisdictional requirement and could be waived by the agency. For more on

---

[14] See, e.g., http://regulationroom.org/learn/what-effective-commenting.

issue exhaustion in rulemaking, see Ronald M. Levin, Making Sense of Issue Exhaustion in Rulemaking, 70 Admin. L. Rev. 177 (2018); Jeffrey S. Lubbers, Fail to Comment at Your Own Risk: Does Issue Exhaustion Have a Place in Judicial Review of Rules?, 70 Admin. L. Rev. 109 (2018).

(3) ***A Never-Ending Circle?*** Are there limits on the scope of an agency's obligation to disclose and provide an opportunity to comment? RYBACHEK V. EPA, 904 F.2d 1276, 1286 (9th Cir. 1990), dealt with multiple challenges to EPA regulations issued under the Clean Water Act. The regulations addressed discharges into streams from placer mining operations: "The Rybacheks allege that the EPA's addition of over 6,000 pages to the administrative record, after the public review-and-comment period had ended, violated their right to comment on the record. We disagree. The EPA has not violated the Rybacheks' right to meaningful public participation. The additional material was the EPA's response to comments made during a public-comment period. Nothing prohibits the Agency from adding supporting documentation for a final rule in response to public comments. In fact, adherence to the Rybacheks' view might result in the EPA's never being able to issue a final rule capable of standing up to review: every time the Agency responded to public comments, such as those in this rulemaking, it would trigger a new comment period. Thus, either the comment period would continue in a never-ending circle, or, if the EPA chose not to respond to the last set of public comments, any final rule could be struck down for lack of support in the record. The Rybacheks' unviolated right was to comment on the proposed regulations, not to comment in a never-ending way on the EPA's responses to their comments."

Contrast Rybachek with OBER V. EPA, 84 F.3d 304, 314 (9th Cir. 1996). The EPA proposed to approve Arizona's plan for implementing the Clean Air Act, which included controls on particulate matter in Phoenix. Four months after the deadline for public comment passed, at the EPA's request, the state submitted an additional 300 pages of information responding to various comments that had suggested that additional control measures could be, and legally had to be, taken. The court held that acceptance of this submission without offering others a chance to comment on it violated the APA: "In Rybachek, the added materials were the EPA's own responses to comments received during the public comment period. Here, in contrast, the additional documentation was submitted by the State in response to the EPA's request for further information related to the rejection of control measures. Thus, the additional materials in Rybachek involved the EPA's internal assessment of comments from the public; whereas, here, the new information was solicited by the EPA from an interested party. . . . [I]n Rybachek, the EPA's responses related to the economic impact of the regulations on one group of miners. The additional information was not relied on or critical to the EPA's decision. Instead, the EPA decided not to alter the regulation based on the additional information it developed in response to the comments. Here, on the other hand, the added material related to the Implementation Plan's compliance with a critical statutory provision."

Do these distinctions make sense? Do they have a basis in § 553? If the EPA had made its request as part of its initial NPRM, and the state had submitted its documentation as part of its comment package on the final day of comments—as is typical of long comments filed by sophisticated rulemaking commenters (see US Airways' comment in the introductory example in Chapter I (p. 14))—what procedural rights should Ober have had to respond?

(4) ***Empirical Studies of Comments.*** A recent study created a "new database of 264,709 comments [to 239 rulemaking actions] submitted by organizations to agencies tasked with implementing Dodd-Frank": "We produce six main findings—all of which support the conclusion that wealthy organizations are advantaged during the administrative policymaking process. First, we find that wealthier organizations participate in agency rulemaking at higher rates than less wealthy organizations. We replicate this result within and across various types of for-profit firms and non-profit organizations. Second, we find that for-profit banks are more likely to participate than non-profit banks. Third, we find that organizations that spend more money on political campaigns and lobbying are more likely to participate in rulemaking. Fourth, among organizations that participate in rulemaking, we show that organizations that participate frequently are wealthier than those that participate infrequently. Fifth, wealthier organizations advance more sophisticated comments than less wealthy organizations. Sixth, and finally, wealthier organizations are more successful in shifting the content of federal agency rules through their comments. Finally, using causal mediation analysis, we demonstrate that the influence of wealthier organizations on regulatory content is largely driven by the sophistication of their comments." Daniel P. Carpenter, Angelo Dagonel, Devin Judge-Lord, Christopher T. Kenny, Brian Libgober, Steven Rashin, Jacob Waggoner, & Susan Webb Yackee, Inequality in Administrative Democracy: Methods and Evidence from Financial Rulemaking (working paper 2022).[15]

Looking at rulemaking between 2003 and 2016, another study found a connection between firm donations to nonprofit organizations and those organizations' comments in rulemaking proceedings: "First, we show that shortly after a firm donates to a nonprofit, the nonprofit is more likely to comment on rules on which the firm has also commented. Second, when a firm comments on a rule, the comments by nonprofits that recently received grants from the firm's foundation are systematically closer in content to the firm's own comments, relative to comments submitted by other nonprofits." Marianne Bertrand, Matilde Bombardini, Raymond Fisman, Brad Hackinen, & Francesco Trebbi, Hall of Mirrors: Corporate Philanthropy and Strategic Advocacy, 136 Q.J. Econ. 2413 (2021).

(5) ***The Challenge of Fostering Public Input and a Proposal for a Rebuttal Comment Period.*** CARY COGLIANESE, HEATHER KILMARTIN, & EVAN MENDELSON, TRANSPARENCY AND PUBLIC PARTICIPATION IN THE FEDERAL RULEMAKING PROCESS: RECOMMENDATIONS FOR THE NEW

[15] https://judgelord.github.io/finreg/participatory-inequality.pdf.

ADMINISTRATION, 77 Geo. Wash. L. Rev. 924 (2009): "[I]improved transparency and public participation are not necessarily unmitigated goods. Even if increasing participation and transparency makes the rulemaking process and its resulting rules more legitimate, too much transparency and public participation can very well detract from making quality decisions in a timely manner. Increasing public participation requires an agency to expend more resources on filtering through and reading the comments submitted. These resources may be well spent to the extent that the additional comments contribute to better policies, but many comments are likely to be duplicative of earlier submissions. . . .

"[S]ome observers complain that agencies fail to make information available to the public in a timely fashion and in a manner that allows for its meaningful use, especially as a prerequisite for public participation. For example, important data might not be included in a rulemaking docket until late in the comment process, or the data might be buried in voluminous records that are not available electronically. . . . A fairer process would give all parties the opportunity to file meaningful and informed comments. . . .

"To enhance the value of public comments, the new administration should encourage pilot experiments ['on a small scale'] with interactive comment processes. Interactive comment periods would appear to be most appropriate for rulemakings in which (1) the issues involved are extremely technical or complex; (2) comments filed in the initial round of commenting raise new or unanticipated issues; or (3) comments filed in the initial round of commenting contain significantly conflicting data. In these rulemakings, agencies could usefully provide two rounds of commenting to allow for interaction among commenters. Persons who submit comments during the first round would be eligible to respond to opposing comments or to agency queries in the second round. . . . Such a two-round approach also may well have a secondary effect of removing the strategic incentives to make extreme or unsupported claims or to file last-minute commentary."

## NOTES ON THE CONCISE GENERAL STATEMENT OF THE RULE'S BASIS AND PURPOSE

(1) ***An Inadequate Statement?*** In Nova Scotia, the FDA issued its final rule in November 1970; it ran under two pages in the Federal Register. (The proposed rule in 1969 ran under two pages as well). The complete prelude to the actual regulatory terms in the final rule read as follows:

> Current good manufacturing practice (sanitation) in manufacture, processing, packing, or holding of smoked and smoke-flavored fish for human food.
>
> In the Federal Register of October 23, 1969 (34 F.R. 17176), the Commissioner of Food and Drugs proposed regulations (Subpart A, Part 128a) covering current good manufacturing practice (sanitation) in the manufacture, processing, packing, or holding of smoked fish. In response, comments were received from two trade associations, eight manufacturers, and the Bureau of Commercial Fisheries, Department of Interior. The comments

> include opposition to certain requirements and suggestions for clarifying and technical changes.
>
> The principal objection is that the process requirements in the proposed regulations cannot be applied to all species of fish presently being smoked by the industry and that the regulations should therefore specify time-temperature requirements, as developed by research and study, on a species-by-species basis.
>
> The Commissioner finds: (1) That although adequate times, temperatures, and salt concentrations have not been demonstrated for each individual species of fish presently smoked, the processing requirements of the proposed regulations are the safest now known to prevent the outgrowth and toxin formation of C. botulinum Type E; and (2) that since the public health hazard of C. botulinum Type E in smoked fish is not restricted to a single species of fish, the conditions of current good manufacturing practice for this industry should be established without further delay.
>
> Therefore, having considered the comments received and other relevant material, the Commissioner concludes that the proposed regulations, with most of the suggested clarifying and technical changes incorporated, should be adopted as set forth below. . . .

35 Fed. Reg. 17401 (Nov. 13, 1970).

In addition to faulting the FDA for not disclosing its underlying data, the Nova Scotia court also concluded that the agency had violated § 553's concise general statement requirement by not adequately considering (i) whether it was necessary to promulgate a rule applicable to all species of fish, and (ii) the claim that application of the T-T-S regulation rendered whitefish commercially unsaleable. Do you agree with the court's conclusion? Although the FDA did not respond to these claims in detail, it did note that safe species-by-species parameters did not exist and stressed the need to address potential health risks without delay. (It did, however, end up regulating chub separately.) Should that have sufficed? Today it is not uncommon for the preamble to a final rule, where the agency makes its "concise general statement of basis and purpose," to run to dozens of pages of dense text in the Federal Register.

(2) ***Timing of the Statement of Basis and Purpose.*** Cigar Association of America v. FDA, 964 F.3d 56, 63–64 (D.C. Cir. 2020): "We cannot uphold a final rule based on reasoning that appears only in the notice. The APA prescribes a three-step procedure for so-called 'notice-and-comment rulemaking.' . . . Not surprisingly, the statement of basis and purpose must come 'after' consideration of comments and thus also 'after notice required by' section 553(b). See 5 U.S.C. § 553(c). We thus cannot uphold a final rule based on strands of reasoning that precede public comment and appear nowhere in the final rule."

(3) ***Statutes Versus Regulations.*** Imagine that Congress had debated and then enacted precisely the same text that the FDA adopted as its regulation—that is, statutorily preferring the administrative convenience of a provision reaching all forms of smoked and/or salted fish to species-by-

species requirements. The only procedural rights Nova Scotia would have had in that process would be those provided by congressional rules and practice. Under the Londoner/Bi-Metallic distinction (p. 225), Nova Scotia would have had no constitutional claim to individualized process. Moreover, the claim that Congress should have adopted more species-specific measures would seem destined to fail under the lenient rationality review that ordinarily applies to economic and social legislation. Should this legislative analogy be relevant in assessing the APA's requirements? (See p. 1150.) To the extent differences exist between the legislative analogy and the procedural requirements courts have imposed on rulemaking, can they be justified?

(4) ***Timing of Review and Inadequate Consideration of Alternatives.*** An unusual feature of Nova Scotia, which the court notes, is that the challenge to the rule came as a defense to an enforcement proceeding. Since Abbott Laboratories v. Gardner, 387 U.S. 136 (1967) (p. 1545), the more common form of judicial review of rulemaking has been a preenforcement action challenging the rule before it can be applied. Does the enforcement posture heighten the potential for unfair hindsight in concluding that the agency should have considered alternatives that would have addressed the challenging party's circumstances—and help to explain the FDA's lack of response to concerns specific to whitefish? At the time of rulemaking, an agency is focused on the general problem, but a court entertaining a challenge to the regulation years later in an enforcement proceeding is more likely to see matters through the prism of a particular interest—such as whitefish.

To the extent that an agency's obligation to consider various points, or to explain its resolution of them, is determined by the issues raised during the notice-and-comment proceeding, the nature of "reasoned decisionmaking" will be contingent on the history of the particular proceeding. Yet the agency ought to address *some* matters regardless whether anyone has commented on them—for example, its basic legal authority for promulgating the regulation.

(5) ***A Modern Example.*** The 2006 Postal Accountability and Enhancement Act changed the process for increasing postal rates from formal adjudication to notice-and-comment rulemaking. The Postal Service begins the process by providing notice to the public and the Postal Regulatory Commission. Under the PAEA, that notice has to include, among other items, "[a] discussion that demonstrates how the planned rate adjustments are designed to help achieve the objectives listed in 39 U.S.C. § 3622(b) and properly take into account the factors listed in 39 U.S.C. § 3622(c)." 39 C.F.R. § 3010.12(b). The PRC then accepts comments for 20 days. Within two weeks from the close of comments, the PRC must "issue an order announcing its findings." Id. § 3010.11(d). In October 2018, the Postal Service proposed to increase the price for a standard (one-ounce) letter stamp from 50 to 55 cents, among other pricing changes. Douglas Carlson and 33 others submitted comments. The PRC approved the price hike. Carlson sued, arguing, among other claims, that the PRC did not adequately explain its decision.

The D.C. Circuit agreed in CARLSON V. POSTAL REGULATORY COMMISSION, 938 F.3d 337 (D.C. Cir. 2019): "[A]n agency must respond to comments that can be thought to challenge a fundamental premise underlying the proposed agency decision. An agency need not discuss every item of fact or opinion included in the submissions made to it. An agency's response to public comments, however, must be sufficient to enable the courts to see what major issues of policy were ventilated and why the agency reacted to them as it did. . . . First, the Commission failed to address public comments that undermined the Postal Service's interpretation of 'simplicity of structure,' a PAEA factor. In its notice, the Postal Service claimed that keeping stamp prices divisible by five promotes 'simplicity of structure' by 'facilitat[ing] convenience' and making prices 'straightforward' and 'understandable.' . . . In his public comment, Carlson . . . argued that no individual postage rate constitutes a 'structure.' . . . Carlson also challenged the Postal Service's claim of convenience, noting that most transactions would not involve the supposed inconvenience of counting pennies because most customers pay by debit or credit card and buy stamps in multiples of five. . . . Disputing the Postal Service's claims, Carlson also argued that the meaning of fifty-two cents is just as clear and straightforward as the meaning of fifty-five cents and noted that the public had never struggled to understand the price of stamps, even though that price had not been divisible by five for most of the nation's history. These public comments called into question the justifications offered by the Postal Service, and therefore the Commission should have evaluated whether divisibility by five did, in fact, promote the statutory interest in 'simplicity of structure.' Second, the Commission did not address public comments arguing that the proffered justification for the stamp price hike misstated the 'effect of rate increases upon the general public.' "

(6) ***When Must Agencies Respond to Comments? A Tax Regulation Example.*** The Sixth and Eleventh Circuits have disagreed over whether the Treasury Department had to respond to certain comments on a proposal concerning the deductibility of charitable contributions of perpetual conservation easements. The New York Landmarks Conservancy, for example, had recommended deletion of one provision concerning postdonation improvements to easement property.

In HEWITT V. COMMISSIONER OF IRS, 21 F.4th 1336 (11th Cir. 2021), the Eleventh Circuit said the agency had to respond to the comment: "In the preamble to the final rulemaking, Treasury stated that '[t]hese regulations provide necessary guidance to the public for compliance with the law and affect donors and donees of qualified conservation contributions' and that it had 'consider[ed] . . . all comments regarding the proposed amendments.' In the subsequent 'Summary of Comments' section, however, Treasury did not discuss or respond to the comments made by NYLC or the other six commenters concerning the extinguishment proceeds regulation. . . .

"While we agree with the Commissioner that Treasury was only required to respond to *significant* comments to comply with the APA's procedural requirements, we disagree with the Commissioner's argument that NYLC's comment was not significant. . . . Because Treasury, in promulgating the extinguishment proceeds regulation, failed to respond to NYLC's significant comment concerning the post-donation improvements issue as to proceeds, it violated the APA's procedural requirements."

In OAKBROOK LAND HOLDINGS, LLC V. COMMISSIONER OF INTERNAL REVENUE, 28 F.4th 700 (6th Cir. 2022), the Sixth Circuit said the agency did not have to respond: "Recognizing that notice-and-comment rulemaking is not an administrative sport, we have repeatedly concluded that an agency must give reasoned responses to all significant comments in a rulemaking proceeding, not that an agency must respond to all comments. Significance is difficult to measure in the abstract. . . . [C]ases demonstrate that assessing significance is context dependent and requires reading the comment in light of both the rulemaking of which it was part and the statutory ends that the proposed rule is meant to serve. 'Accordingly, an agency must respond to comments that can be thought to challenge a fundamental premise' underlying the proposed agency decision.' Carlson v. Postal Regul. Comm'n, 938 F.3d 337, 344 (D.C. Cir. 2019) A comment must provide enough facts and reasoning to show the agency what the issue is and how it is relevant to the agency's aims. Comments that do so are 'significant enough to step over a threshold requirement of materiality' needed for an agency to address them.

"To make this concrete, consider one of the cases upon which petitioners rely. In United States v. Nova Scotia Food Products Corp., the Second Circuit considered a rule issued by the Food and Drug Administration (FDA) to address a spate of botulism cases within the inland fish market and ensure that fish could be safely consumed. While promulgating the rule, which required all fish to be cooked or brined according to its specifications, the FDA ignored a comment by Nova Scotia Food Products Corp., a company that sold smoked whitefish. Nova Scotia had recommended that the agency adopt a rule tailored to the heat tolerance of each species so that their product would not be 'completely destroy[ed],' due to whitefish being unable to withstand the rigors of the proposed rule. [584 F.3d at 245.] The Second Circuit held that the FDA's failure to respond to Nova Scotia's and similar comments rendered the rule arbitrary or capricious. Id. at 253. It was unclear how making a fish product inedible would further the FDA's goal of rendering fish safe for human consumption.

"After examining the comments that petitioners have identified, we hold that none required Treasury's response as Nova Scotia's did the FDA's. . . . Instead, we agree with the Tax Court. Treasury's lack of a response to these comments does not jeopardize the validity of [this regulation.]"

Oakbrook's lawyers filed a petition for certiorari asking the Supreme Court to weigh in, noting the conflict with the Hewitt decision. For more on this conflict, see Kristin E. Hickman, The Federal Tax System's Administrative Law Woes Grow, ABA Tax Times (May 2022).[16]

[16] https://www.americanbar.org/groups/taxation/publications/abataxtimes_home/22winspr/22winspr-ac-hickman-admin-law-woes/.

## NOTES ON CURRENT TRENDS AND WRINKLES IN NOTICE-AND-COMMENT RULEMAKING

(1) ***Rulemaking Map and Statistics.*** For a visualization of the modern rulemaking process, including statutory and presidential directives, check out The Reg Map.[17] For overall statistics, check out Reg Stats by the Regulatory Studies Center at George Washington University.[18] To see more details, you can run various searches at www.regulations.gov. Rulemaking tends to spike in the final year of an administration; midnight rulemaking is the term often used for rules issued in the last few months.

(2) ***Rulemaking Conducted Out of Order or Not Completed.*** As with the Center for Science in the Public Interest case, sometimes agency rulemaking does not follow the ordinary NPRM, commenting period, final rule path. Instead, the agency may publish an interim final rule (which often takes effect), take comments ex post, and then issue a "final final" rule (see p. 381 for more details and the Court's acceptance of this alternative).

In addition, agencies do not always finish the rulemaking process. In a study of rulemakings appearing in the Unified Agenda of Federal Regulatory and Deregulatory Actions from Fall 1988 to Spring 2010, more than ten percent of final actions that had a previous NPRM ended in a withdrawal of the NPRM, as opposed to a final rule. Anne Joseph O'Connell, Agency Rulemaking and Political Transitions, 105 Nw. U. L. Rev. 471, 520 (2011). The odds of a proposed rule being withdrawn (relative to being finished) increase after a presidential transition. Id. at 523. For a recent example, see Jurisdiction-Nonemployee Status of University and College Students Working in Connection With Their Studies, 86 Fed. Reg. 14297 (Mar. 15, 2021).

As is typical of new administrations, President Biden's Chief of Staff ordered agencies to "freeze" the finalization of any rulemakings pending review by Biden-picked agency heads. Specifically, Ronald Klain instructed agencies to withdraw any rules that had been sent to but not yet published in the Federal Register and to "consider" postponing any rules' impending effective dates for sixty days.[19] In July 2022, the D.C. Circuit went against this executive branch practice and determined that "an agency must provide notice and an opportunity for comment when withdrawing a rule that has been filed for public inspection but not yet published in the Federal Register." Humane Society of the United States v. USDA, 41 F.4th 564 (D.C. Cir. 2022). In short, if available for public inspection, the rule is complete and can no longer be withdrawn without any process. How does this fit with § 553(d), which discusses "publication"?[20] For a quantitative analysis of the potential

---

[17] https://www.reginfo.gov/public/reginfo/Regmap/index.jsp. Steps 4 and 8 address OMB review.

[18] https://regulatorystudies.columbian.gwu.edu/reg-stats.

[19] https://www.whitehouse.gov/briefing-room/presidential-actions/2021/01/20/regulatory-freeze-pending-review/.

[20] Judge Rao, dissenting, noted the publication requirement. Subsequent commentary claims this is "not the best interpretation of APA § 553(d)." Jack Beermann, Are Rules Effective Before Publication? Reflections on the D.C. Circuit's Decision in Humane Society v. USDA, Notice & Comment Blog (Oct. 6, 2022), https://www.yalejreg.com/nc/are-rules-effective-before-

impacts of this ruling on presidential transitions, see Mark Febrizio, Quantifying the Effects of Humane Society v. Department of Agriculture, Regulatory Insight (Oct. 5, 2022).[21] Febrizio notes that only a small number of such documents are actually withdrawn (a total of 60 out of 2,425 across the past two transitions), but amongst those ranks are some important documents (including seven that met Executive Order's 12866 definition of "significant").

Even rulemakings that "finish" often get reopened. See Wendy Wagner, William West, Thomas McGarity, & Lisa Peters, Dynamic Rulemaking, 92 N.Y.U. L. Rev. 183 (2017) (based on an examination of 183 rules in four discrete programs, finding that 73 percent "were revised by the agency at least once and typically multiple times" and that "[a]lthough the percentages for EPA's two programs were significantly higher than those for OSHA and FCC, all three agencies revised a majority of their parent regulations in our sample").

(3) ***Using Litigation to Undo Rulemaking.*** To undo a rule, an agency typically has to go through the APA's rulemaking procedures. After a political transition in the White House, new administrations will seek abeyances in pending litigation about the previous administration's rules to go through those procedures. The Biden Administration has also relied on court rulings unfavorable to the Trump Administration's regulations to skip notice and comment procedures, simply issuing a rule based on a court ruling. See, e.g., Inadmissibility on Public Charge Grounds; Implementation of Vacatur, 86 Fed. Reg. 14221 (Mar. 15, 2021). Chief Justice Roberts, joined by Justices Thomas and Alito, criticized this practice in a concurrence dismissing a writ of certiorari as improvidently granted: "As part of this tactic of 'rulemaking-by-collective-acquiescence,' City and County of San Francisco v. United States Citizenship and Immigration Servs., 992 F.3d 742, 744 (C.A.9 2021) (VanDyke, J., dissenting), the Government successfully opposed efforts by other interested parties—including petitioners here—to intervene in order to carry on the defense of the Rule, including possibly before this Court. These maneuvers raise a host of important questions. The most fundamental is whether the Government's actions, all told, comport with the principles of administrative law." Arizona v. City & County of San Francisco, 142 S.Ct. 1926 (2022). See generally Bethany A. Davis Noll & Richard L. Revesz, Presidential Transitions: The New Rules, 39 Yale J. Reg. 1043 (2022).

(4) ***E-Rulemaking Mandates and Systems.*** Many agencies—except for a few independent agencies, such as the Federal Communications Commission, who use their own websites—use the government's central portal, www.regulations.gov, to post their notices of proposed rulemaking and accept comments. Under the E-Government Act of 2002, there are supposed to be "e-dockets" containing "public submissions [i.e., comments] and other materials that by agency rule or practice are included in the

---

publication-reflections-on-the-d-c-circuits-decision-in-humane-society-v-usda-by-jack-m-beermann/.

[21] https://regulatorystudies.columbian.gwu.edu/sites/g/files/zaxdzs4751/files/2022-10/febrizio_quantifying_effects_humane_society_v_usda_2022_10_05.pdf.

rulemaking docket . . . whether or not submitted electronically." Almost a decade after that Act, President Obama ordered agencies to "provide, for both proposed and final rules, timely online access to the rulemaking docket on regulations.gov." Exec. Order No. 13563, 76 Fed. Reg. 3821 (Jan. 18, 2011). For an overview of the legal mandates, current issues with the Federal Docket Management System, and recommendations for improvement, see ACUS, Recommendation 2018-6, Improving Access to Regulations.gov's Rulemaking Dockets, 84 Fed. Reg. 2143 (Feb. 6, 2019).

The completeness of the supporting materials and the speed and completeness of posting public comments vary dramatically from agency to agency. In 2019, the GAO concluded that the multiple agencies it had investigated "do not clearly communicate their practices for how comments and identity information are posted." The GAO noted that "the lack of accompanying disclosures may potentially lead users to reach inaccurate conclusions about who submitted a particular comment, or how many individuals weighed in on an issue." Half of the agencies with higher numbers of rulemakings "were unable to provide [the GAO] with the total number of comments received over the 5-year period" studied. Federal Rulemaking: Selected Agencies Should Clearly Communicate Practices Associated with Identity Information in the Public Comment Process, GAO-19-483 (June 2019).[22]

The implementation of recent technological changes to regulations.gov during the Trump Administration (due to the phasing out of Adobe Flash) generated criticism. See Letter from Democracy Forward et al. to General Services Administration (May 17, 2021) ("The new version of the website, conceived and planned during the Trump administration, represents an extraordinary retrenchment in public access.").[23]

(5) ***Expansion of Public Participation?*** Some administrative law scholars predicted that e-rulemaking would significantly expand public participation. See, e.g., Beth Simone Noveck, The Electronic Revolution in Rulemaking, 53 Emory L.J. 433 (2004). An early review of empirical data, however, found no "dramatic changes in the general level or quality of public participation in the rulemaking process. Most rules still garner relatively few overall comments and even fewer comments from individual citizens. As in the past, the occasional rulemaking does continue to attract a large number of citizen comments, but most of these comments remain quite unsophisticated, if not duplicative." Cary Coglianese, Citizen Participation in Rulemaking: Past, Present, and Future, 55 Duke L.J. 943, 958–59 (2006). In a 2018 presentation, a senior OIRA official reported on comment trends on regulations.gov in the preceding five years, noting that nearly a third of rulemakings received no comments, and that 45 percent received between one and ten. Less than three percent received more than 100 comments.

(6) ***Authenticity and Relevance of Mass Comments.*** The authenticity and relevance of mass comments have been questioned. When the FCC proposed

[22] https://www.gao.gov/products/GAO-19-483.

[23] https://democracyforward.org/wp-content/uploads/2021/05/Letter-to-GSA-re-Regulations-Gov-Website-5.17.21.pdf.

rules for net neutrality in 2014 that would have permitted differentiations in service speed, late-night host John Oliver encouraged his viewers—particularly "trolls"—to comment against the proposal in a 13-minute comedic rant.[24] According to the Washington Post, "By Monday, the FCC's commenting system had stopped working, thanks to more than 45,000 new comments on net neutrality likely sparked by Oliver." The final rule, finalized after about four million comments were filed and upheld by the D.C. Circuit, did not adopt the proposed service differentiations, instead providing equitable access. Do you think those comments were carefully read?

When the FCC proposed to roll back the final rule after the White House changed hands in 2017, Oliver appealed to his viewers again, telling them to visit the website www.gofccyourself.com, which automatically took them to the FCC's docket for filing comments on net neutrality.[25] The agency's website stopped working again, but it was operating by the next day. The 2017 rulemaking to repeal the 2015 net neutrality regulation received approximately 22 million comments. In a May 2021 report, the NY Attorney General determined that "fake comments accounted for nearly 18 million of the more than 22 million comments the FCC received during its 2017 rulemaking," with more than 7.7 million coming from "a 19-year old college student in California" using automated software. New York State Office of the Attorney General Letitia James, Fake Comments: How U.S. Companies & Partisans Hack Democracy to Undermine Your Voice.[26] What lessons can you draw from Oliver's efforts for public participation in rulemaking?

In October 2019, the Subcommittee on Investigations of the Senate Committee on Homeland Security and Governmental Affairs released a report, Abuses of the Federal Notice-and-Comment Rulemaking Process, which made the following findings after surveying many federal agencies' practices: "(1) Most federal agencies lack appropriate processes to address allegations that people have submitted comments under fraudulent identities"; "(2) The FCC's process for addressing comments submitted under false identities potentially causes additional harm to victims of identity theft and the comment process as a whole"; "(3) None of the commenting systems use CAPTCHA or other technology to ensure that real people, instead of bots, are submitting comments to rulemaking dockets"; "(4) Agencies do not have consistent policies regarding the screening and posting of comments." With regards to point (2), the FCC told 32 individuals who reported false comments made under their names that the best remedy was to add their own comments to the docket! Should agencies delete comments when they are informed of these issues? How about when it is facially obvious the comments are fraudulent, such as when "Elvis Presley posthumously submitted ten comments" to the FCC? The report also provided a series of recommendations.[27]

---

[24] https://www.youtube.com/watch?v=fpbOEoRrHyU.

[25] https://www.youtube.com/watch?v=92vuuZt7wak.

[26] https://ag.ny.gov/sites/default/files/oag-fakecommentsreport.pdf.

[27] https://www.hsgac.senate.gov/imo/media/doc/2019-10-24%20PSI%20Staff%20Report%20-%20Abuses%20of%20the%20Federal%20Notice-and-Comment%20Rulemaking%20Process.pdf.

In June 2021, ACUS recommended best practices on "how agencies can better manage the processing challenges associated with mass, computer-generated, and falsely attributed comments." ACUS, Recommendation 2021–1, Managing Mass, Computer-Generated, and Falsely Attributed Comments, 86 Fed. Reg. 36075 (July 8, 2021). Interestingly, the research consultants for this ACUS project, while noting the issues with the FCC's net neutrality rulemakings, flagged some benefits of bot-generated comments (for instance, identifying "typos, broken links, and incorrect legal citations in proposed rules to send back to the agency"). Bridget C.E. Dooling & Michael Livermore, Bot-Generated Comments on Government Proposals Could Be Useful Someday, Slate (June 21, 2021).

(7) ***Regulations.gov as a Democratic Mechanism.*** CASS R. SUNSTEIN, DEMOCRATIZING REGULATION, DIGITALLY, Democracy: A Journal of Ideas (Fall 2014): "Regulations.gov may not be everyone's favorite website, and it isn't a lot of fun, but it is worth a look, because what appears there has significant consequences for the nation (and sometimes many nations) and because it is transforming notice-and-comment rule-making. When an agency proposes a rule, all the world can find it and see it, usually with great ease. If a proposal has a mistake, or veers in a bad direction, there is a genuine opportunity to comment and to get the problem fixed. When I served as administrator of the White House Office of Information and Regulatory Affairs from 2009 to 2012, I was surprised by one thing above all: A lot of regulators pay exceedingly close attention to public comments, and they spend a great deal of time on Regulations.gov. Such comments are carefully read, typically by people who have the authority to move regulations in better directions. Commenters often fear that what they say will go into a black hole but, in general, the fear is misplaced. People with authority end up reading what they write."

STEVEN J. BALLA, ALEXANDER R. BECK, ELIZABETH MEEHAN, & ARYAMALA PRASAD, LOST IN THE FLOOD?: AGENCY RESPONSIVENESS TO MASS COMMENT CAMPAIGNS IN ADMINISTRATIVE RULEMAKING, 16 Reg. & Governance 293 (2022): "Focusing on 1,049 mass comment campaigns that occurred during 22 Environmental Protection Agency rulemakings between 2012 and 2017, th[is] article develops and assesses expectations regarding responsiveness to campaigns relative to comments submitted outside of campaigns. The analysis demonstrates that, procedurally, the agency references mass comment campaigns in its responses to comments, but cites campaigns at lower rates than other comments. In terms of outcomes, the agency's regulations are generally not consistent with changes requested in comments, a lack of association that holds especially for mass comment campaigns. These patterns suggest that legal imperatives trump political considerations in conditioning agency responsiveness, given that mass comment campaigns—relative to other comments—generally contain little 'relevant matter.'"

# SECTION 4. EXCEPTIONS TO § 553 NOTICE-AND-COMMENT REQUIREMENTS



Section 553 contains several provisions exempting certain categories from its requirements. The agency bears the burden of showing that any particular provision applies. We begin by discussing § 553(b)'s "good cause" exception. Next, we turn to § 553(b)'s exception for interpretive rules and policy statements, collectively known as guidance, the exception that has been the most important and controversial in recent years. Finally, we discuss more briefly the remaining exceptions: § 553(a)'s exception for matters involving "a military or foreign affairs function" or "relating to agency management or personnel or to public property, loans, grants, benefits or contracts" and § 553(b)'s exception for "rules of agency organization, procedure, or practice."

## a. The Good Cause Exception



*[T]his subsection does not apply . . . when the agency for good cause finds (and incorporates the finding and a brief statement of reasons therefor in the rules issued) that notice and public procedure thereon are impracticable, unnecessary, or contrary to the public interest.*

5 U.S.C. § 553(b)(B)

Rules that an agency promulgates in reliance on the "good cause" exception have the same legal effect as rules that go through notice and comment. It has long been seen as important, then, to make sure that agencies are not improperly avoiding these procedures by claiming good cause where none exists. At the same time, the point of the exception is to allow agencies the flexibility to avoid these procedures where notice and comment would be "impracticable, unnecessary, or contrary to the public interest." The materials that follow explore the balance between these two demands.

## MACK TRUCKS, INC. v. EPA

United States Court of Appeals for the District of Columbia (2012).
682 F.3d 87.

■ BROWN, CIRCUIT JUDGE.

In January 2012, EPA promulgated an interim final rule (IFR) to permit manufacturers of heavy-duty diesel engines to pay nonconformance penalties (NCPs) in exchange for the right to sell noncompliant engines. EPA took this action without providing formal notice or an opportunity for comment, invoking the "good cause" exception provided in the Administrative Procedure Act (APA). Because we find that none of the statutory criteria for "good cause" are satisfied, we vacate the IFR.

I

In 2001, pursuant to Section 202 of the Clean Air Act ("the Act"), EPA enacted a rule requiring a 95 percent reduction in the emissions of nitrogen oxide from heavy-duty diesel engines. By delaying the effective date until 2010, EPA gave industry nine years to innovate the necessary new technologies. (EPA and manufacturers refer to the rule as the "2010 $NO_x$ standard.") During those nine years, most manufacturers of heavy-duty diesel engines, including Petitioners, invested hundreds of millions of dollars to develop a technology called "selective catalytic reduction." This technology converts nitrogen oxide into nitrogen and water by using a special aftertreatment system and a diesel-based chemical agent. With selective catalytic reduction, manufacturers have managed to meet the 2010 $NO_x$ standard.

One manufacturer, Navistar, took a different approach. For its domestic sales, Navistar opted for a form of "exhaust gas recirculation," but this technology proved less successful; Navistar's engines do not meet the 2010 $NO_x$ standard. . . . Navistar would therefore be unable to sell these engines in the United States—unless, of course, it adopted a different, compliant technology. But for the last few years, Navistar has been able to lawfully forestall that result and continue selling its noncompliant engines by using banked emission credits. Simply put, it bet on finding a way to make exhaust gas recirculation a feasible and compliant technology before its finite supply of credits ran out.

Navistar's day of reckoning is fast approaching: its supply of credits is dwindling and its engines remain noncompliant. In October 2011, Navistar informed EPA that it would run out of credits sometime in 2012. EPA, estimating that Navistar "might have as little as three to four months" of available credits before it "would be forced to stop introducing its engines into commerce," leapt into action. Without formal notice and comment, EPA hurriedly promulgated the IFR on January 31, 2012, pursuant to its authority under 42 U.S.C. § 7525(g), to make NCPs available to Navistar.

To issue NCPs under its regulations, EPA must first find that a new emissions standard is "more stringent" or "more difficult to achieve" than a prior standard, that "substantial work will be required to meet the standard for which the NCP is offered," and that "there is likely to be a technological laggard." 40 C.F.R. § 86.1103–87. EPA found these criteria were met. . . .

EPA explained its decision to forego notice and comment procedures by invoking the "good cause" exception of the APA, which provides that an agency may dispense with formal notice and comment procedures if the agency "for good cause finds . . . that notice and public procedure thereon are impracticable, unnecessary, or contrary to the public interest," 5 U.S.C. § 553(b)(B). EPA cited four factors to show the existence of good cause: (1) notice and comment would mean "the possibility of an engine manufacturer [Navistar] . . . being unable to certify a complete product line of engines for model year 2012 and/or 2013," (2) EPA was only "amending limited provisions in existing NCP regulations," (3) the IFR's "duration is limited," and (4) "there is no risk to the public interest in allowing manufacturers to certify using NCPs before the point at which EPA could make them available through a full notice-and-comment rulemaking." 77 Fed. Reg. at 4,680. . . .

III

. . . We must therefore determine whether notice and comment were "impracticable, unnecessary, or contrary to the public interest." 5 U.S.C. § 553(b)(B). On that question, it would appear we owe EPA's findings no particular deference. See Jifry v. FAA, 370 F.3d 1174, 1178–79 (D.C. Cir. 2004) (finding good cause without resorting to deference); Util. Solid Waste Activities Grp. v. EPA, 236 F.3d 749, 754 (D.C. Cir. 2001) (finding no good cause without invoking deference). But we need not decide the standard of review since, even if we were to review EPA's assertion of "good cause" simply to determine if it is arbitrary or capricious, 5 U.S.C. § 706(2)(A), we would still find it lacking.

We have repeatedly made clear that the good cause exception "is to be narrowly construed and only reluctantly countenanced." Util. Solid Waste Activities Grp., 236 F.3d at 754; Am. Fed. of Gov't Emps. v. Block, 655 F.2d 1153, 1156 (D.C. Cir. 1981) ("As the legislative history of the APA makes clear, moreover, the exceptions at issue here are not 'escape clauses' that may be arbitrarily utilized at the agency's whim. Rather, use of these exceptions by administrative agencies should be limited to emergency situations. . . .").

First, an agency may invoke the impracticability of notice and comment. 5 U.S.C. § 553(b)(B). Our inquiry into impracticability "is inevitably fact- or context-dependent," Mid-Tex Electric Coop. v. FERC, 822 F.2d 1123, 1132 (D.C. Cir. 1987). For the sake of comparison, we have suggested agency action could be sustained on this basis if, for example, air travel security agencies would be unable to address threats posing "a possible imminent hazard to aircraft, persons, and property within the United States," Jifry, 370 F.3d at 1179, or if "a safety investigation shows that a new safety rule must be put in place immediately," Util. Solid Waste Activities Grp., 236 F.3d at 755 (ultimately finding that not to be the case and rejecting the agency's argument), or if a rule was of "life-saving importance" to mine workers in the event of a mine explosion, Council of the S. Mountains, Inc. v. Donovan, 653 F.2d 573, 581 (D.C. Cir. 1981) (describing that circumstance as "a special, possibly unique, case").

By contrast, the context of this case reveals that the only purpose of the IFR is, as Petitioners put it, "to rescue a lone manufacturer from the folly of its own choices." Pet. Br. at 29. . . . The IFR does not stave off any imminent threat to the environment or safety or national security. It does not remedy any real emergency at all, save the "emergency" facing Navistar's bottom line. Indeed, all EPA points to is "the serious harm to Navistar and its employees" and "the ripple effect on its customers and suppliers," but the same could be said for any manufacturer facing a standard with which its product does not comply.

EPA claims the harm to Navistar and the resulting up- and down-stream impacts should still be enough under our precedents. The only case on which it relies, however, is one in which an entire industry and its customers were imperiled. See Am. Fed. of Gov't Emps., 655 F.2d at 1157. Navistar's plight is not even remotely close to such a weighty, systemic interest, especially since it is a consequence brought about by Navistar's own choice to continue to pursue a technology which, so far, is noncompliant. At bottom, EPA's approach would give agencies "good cause" under the APA every time a manufacturer in a regulated field felt a new regulation imposed some degree of economic hardship, even if the company could have avoided that hardship had it made different business choices. This is both nonsensical and in direct tension with our longstanding position that the exception should be narrowly construed and only reluctantly countenanced.

Second, an agency may claim notice and comment were "unnecessary." 5 U.S.C. § 553(b)(B). This prong of the good cause inquiry is "confined to those situations in which the administrative rule is a routine determination, insignificant in nature and impact, and inconsequential to the industry and to the public." Util. Solid Waste Activities Grp., 236 F.3d at 755. This case does not present such a situation. Just as in Utility Solid Waste, the IFR is a rule "about which these members of the public [the petitioners] were greatly interested," so notice and comment were not "unnecessary." Id. EPA argues that since the IFR is just an interim rule, good cause is satisfied because "the interim status of the challenged rule is a significant factor" in determining whether notice and comment are unnecessary. But we held, in the very case on which EPA relies, that "the limited nature of the rule cannot in itself justify a failure to follow notice and comment procedures." Mid-Tex Electric Coop., 822 F.2d at 1132. And for good reason: if a rule's interim nature were enough to satisfy the element of good cause, then "agencies could issue interim rules of limited effect for any plausible reason, irrespective of the degree of urgency" and "the good cause exception would soon swallow the notice and comment rule." Tenn. Gas Pipeline [Co. v. FERC], 969 F.2d 1141, 1145 [(D.C. Cir. 1992)].

EPA's remaining argument that notice and comment were "unnecessary" is that the IFR was essentially ministerial: EPA simply input numbers into an NCP-setting formula without substantially amending the NCP regime. But even if it were true that EPA arrived at the level of the penalty and the upper limit in this way (and Petitioners strenuously argue that EPA actually amended the NCP regime in order to arrive at the upper limit level in the IFR), that argument does not account for how EPA determined NCPs were warranted in this case in the first place—another finding to which Petitioners object. EPA's decision to implement an NCP, perhaps even more than the level of the penalty itself, is far from inconsequential or routine, and EPA does not even attempt to defend it as such.

Finally, an agency may invoke the good cause exception if providing notice and comment would be contrary to the public interest. In the IFR, EPA says it has good cause since "there is no risk to the public interest in allowing manufacturers to [use] NCPs before the point at which EPA could make them available through a full notice-and-comment rulemaking," but this misstates the statutory criterion. The question is not whether dispensing with notice and comment would be contrary to the public interest, but whether providing notice and comment would be contrary to the public interest. By improperly framing the question in this way, the IFR inverts the presumption, apparently suggesting that notice and comment is usually unnecessary. We cannot permit this subtle malformation of the APA. The public interest prong of the good cause exception is met only in the rare circumstance when ordinary procedures—generally presumed to serve the public interest—would in fact harm that interest. It is appropriately invoked when the timing and disclosure requirements of the usual procedures would defeat the purpose of the proposal—if, for example, "announcement of a proposed rule would enable the sort of financial manipulation the rule sought to prevent." Util. Solid Waste Activities Grp., 236 F.3d at 755. In such a circumstance, notice and comment could be dispensed with "in order to prevent the amended rule from being evaded." Id. In its brief, EPA belatedly frames the inquiry correctly, but goes on to offer nothing more than a recapitulation of the harm to Navistar and the associated "ripple effects." To the extent this is an argument not preserved by EPA in the IFR, we cannot consider it, see SEC v. Chenery Corp., 332 U.S. 194, 196 (1947) [p. 258], but regardless, it is nothing more than a reincarnation of the impracticability argument we have already rejected. . . .

IV

Because EPA lacked good cause to dispense with required notice and comment procedures, we conclude the IFR must be vacated without reaching Petitioners' alternative arguments. We are aware EPA is currently in the process of promulgating a final rule—with the benefit of notice and comment—on this precise issue. However, we strongly reject EPA's claim that the challenged errors are harmless simply because of the pendency of a properly-noticed final rule. Were that true, agencies would have no use for the APA when promulgating any interim rules. So long as the agency eventually opened a final rule for comment, every error in every interim rule—no matter how egregious—could be excused as a harmless error.

We do recognize the pending final rule means our vacatur of the IFR on these procedural grounds will be of limited practical impact. . . . EPA is certainly free to make whatever findings it deems appropriate in the pending final rulemaking—subject, of course, to this Court's review. For now, therefore, we simply hold that EPA lacked good cause for not providing formal notice-and-comment rulemaking, and accordingly vacate the IFR and remand for further proceedings.

## LITTLE SISTERS OF THE POOR SAINTS PETER AND PAUL HOME v. PENNSYLVANIA

Supreme Court of the United States (2020).
140 S.Ct. 2367.

■ JUSTICE THOMAS delivered the opinion of the Court.

In these consolidated cases, we decide whether the Government created lawful exemptions from a regulatory requirement implementing the Patient Protection and Affordable Care Act of 2010 (ACA), 124 Stat. 119. The requirement at issue obligates certain employers to provide contraceptive coverage to their employees through their group health plans. Though contraceptive coverage is not required by (or even mentioned in) the ACA provision at issue, the Government mandated such coverage by promulgating interim final rules (IFRs) shortly after the ACA's passage. This requirement is known as the contraceptive mandate.

After six years of protracted litigation, the Departments of Health and Human Services, Labor, and the Treasury (Departments)—which jointly administer the relevant ACA provision—exempted certain employers who have religious and conscientious objections from this agency-created mandate. The Third Circuit concluded that the Departments lacked statutory authority to promulgate these exemptions and affirmed the District Court's nationwide preliminary injunction. This decision was erroneous. We hold that the Departments had the authority to provide exemptions from the regulatory contraceptive requirements for employers with religious and conscientious objections. We accordingly reverse the Third Circuit's judgment and remand with instructions to dissolve the nationwide preliminary injunction.

### I

The ACA's contraceptive mandate—a product of agency regulation—has existed for approximately nine years. Litigation surrounding that requirement has lasted nearly as long. . . .

The ACA requires covered employers to offer "a group health plan or group health insurance coverage" that provides certain "minimum essential coverage." 26 U.S.C. § 5000A(f)(2); §§ 4980H(a), (c)(2).

Employers who do not comply face hefty penalties, including potential fines of $100 per day for each affected employee. . . . These cases concern regulations promulgated under a provision of the ACA that requires covered employers to provide women with "preventive care and screenings" without "any cost sharing requirements." 42 U.S.C. § 300gg–13(a)(4). . . .

Soon after the ACA's passage, the Departments began promulgating rules related to § 300gg–13(a)(4). But in doing so, the Departments did not proceed through the notice and comment rulemaking process, which the Administrative Procedure Act (APA) often requires before an agency's regulation can "have the force and effect of law." Perez v. Mortgage Bankers Assn., 575 U.S. 92, 96 (2015) (internal quotation marks omitted) [p. 426]; see also 5 U.S.C. § 553. Instead, the Departments invoked the APA's good cause exception, which permits an agency to dispense with notice and comment and promulgate an IFR that carries immediate legal force. § 553(b)(3)(B).

[Justice Thomas described the Departments' initial IFR and additional actions between 2010 and 2013 that required employers to provide contraceptive coverage, with certain accommodations for religious employers. The opinion also described litigation challenging those actions brought by Little Sisters of the Poor and other religious organizations.] Thus, as the Departments began the task of reformulating rules related to the contraceptive mandate, they did so not only under [our] direction [in Zubik v. Burwell, 578 U.S. 403 (2016)] to accommodate religious exercise, but also against the backdrop of [our] pronouncement [in Burwell v. Hobby Lobby Stores, 573 U.S. 682 (2014)] that the mandate, standing alone, violated [the Religious Freedom Restoration Act of 1993 (RFRA), 42 U.S.C. § 2000bb et seq.] as applied to religious entities with complicity-based objections. . . .

In 2016, the Departments attempted to strike the proper balance a third time, publishing a request for information on ways to comply with Zubik. 81 Fed. Reg. 47741. This attempt proved futile, as the Departments ultimately concluded that "no feasible approach" had been identified. . . The Departments maintained their position that the [then-current] accommodation was consistent with RFRA. . . .

In 2017, the Departments tried yet again to comply with Zubik, this time by promulgating the two IFRs that served as the impetus for this litigation. The first IFR significantly broadened the definition of an exempt religious employer to encompass an employer that "objects . . . based on its sincerely held religious beliefs," "to its establishing, maintaining, providing, offering, or arranging [for] coverage or payments for some or all contraceptive services." 82 Fed. Reg. 47812 (2017). . . . The second IFR created a similar "moral exemption" for employers . . . with "sincerely held moral" objections to providing some or all forms of contraceptive coverage. Id., at 47850, 47861–47862. . . . The Departments requested post-promulgation comments on both IFRs.

[The Commonwealth of Pennsylvania obtained a preliminary injunction, arguing that] the IFRs were procedurally and substantively invalid under the APA. . . . The Federal Government appealed. While that appeal was pending, the Departments issued rules finalizing the 2017 IFRs. See 83 Fed. Reg. 57536 (2018); 83 Fed. Reg. 57592, codified at 45 CFR pt. 147 (2018). Though the final rules left the exemptions largely intact, they also responded to post-promulgation comments, explaining their reasons for neither narrowing nor expanding the exemptions beyond what was provided for in the IFRs. The final rule creating the religious exemption also contained a lengthy analysis of the Departments' changed position [about whether the accommodation initially maintained in 2016] violated RFRA. And the Departments explained that, in the wake of the numerous lawsuits challenging [that] accommodation and the failed attempt to identify alternative accommodations after the 2016 request for information, "an expanded exemption rather than the existing accommodation is the most appropriate administrative response to the substantial burden identified by the Supreme Court in Hobby Lobby." Id., at 57544–57545.

After the final rules were promulgated, [the Third Circuit affirmed a new preliminary injunction against the rules. Little Sisters of the Poor] had in the meantime intervened . . . to defend the religious exemption. . . . In [the Third Circuit's] view, the Departments lacked authority to craft the exemptions under either statute. . . . As for respondents' procedural claim, the court held that the Departments lacked good cause to bypass notice and comment when promulgating the 2017 IFRs. . . .

II

[The Court first held that the Departments had the statutory authority to issue the challenged exemptions.]

III

[W]e must next decide whether the 2018 final rules are procedurally invalid. . . . Unless a statutory exception applies, the APA requires agencies to publish a notice of proposed rulemaking in the Federal Register before promulgating a rule that has legal force. See 5 U.S.C. § 553(b). Respondents point to the fact that the 2018 final rules were preceded by a document entitled "Interim Final Rules with Request for Comments," not a document entitled "General Notice of Proposed Rulemaking." They claim that since this was insufficient to satisfy § 553(b)'s requirement, the final rules were procedurally invalid. Respondents are incorrect. Formal labels aside, the rules contained all of the elements of a notice of proposed rulemaking as required by the APA.

The APA requires that the notice of proposed rulemaking contain "reference to the legal authority under which the rule is proposed" and "either the terms or substance of the proposed rule or a description of the subjects and issues involved." §§ 553(b)(2)–(3). The request for comments in the 2017 IFRs readily satisfies these requirements. That request detailed the Departments' view that they had legal authority under the ACA to promulgate both exemptions, as well as authority under RFRA to promulgate the religious exemption. And respondents do not—and cannot—argue that the IFRs failed to air the relevant issues with sufficient detail for respondents to understand the Departments' position. . . . Thus, the APA notice requirements were satisfied.

Even assuming that the APA requires an agency to publish a document entitled "notice of proposed rulemaking" when the agency moves from an IFR to a final rule, there was no "prejudicial error" here. § 706. We have previously noted that the rule of prejudicial error is treated as an "administrative law . . . harmless error rule," National Assn. of Home Builders v. Defenders of Wildlife, 551 U.S. 644, 659–660 (2007). Here, the Departments issued an IFR that explained its position in fulsome detail and "provide[d] the public with an opportunity to comment on whether [the] regulations . . . should be made permanent or subject to modification." 82 Fed. Reg. 47815; see also id., at 47852, 47855. Respondents thus do not come close to demonstrating that they experienced any harm from the title of the document, let alone that they have satisfied this harmless error rule. "The object [of notice and comment], in short, is one of fair notice," Long Island Care at Home, Ltd. v. Coke, 551 U.S. 158, 174 (2007) [p. 335], and respondents certainly had such notice here. Because the IFR complied with the APA's requirements, this claim fails. . . .

Next, respondents contend that the 2018 final rules are procedurally invalid because "nothing in the record signal[s]" that the Departments "maintained an open mind throughout the [post-promulgation] process." . . . As evidence for this claim, respondents point to the fact that the final rules made only minor alterations to the IFRs, leaving their substance unchanged. The Third Circuit applied this "open-mindedness" test, concluding that because the final rules were "virtually identical" to the IFRs, the Departments lacked the requisite "flexible and open-minded attitude" when they promulgated the final rules. 930 F. 3d, at 569.

We decline to evaluate the final rules under the openmindedness test. We have repeatedly stated that the text of the APA provides the " 'maximum procedural requirements' " that an agency must follow in order to promulgate a rule. Perez, 575 U.S. at 100 (quoting Vermont Yankee Nuclear Power Corp. v. Natural Resources Defense Council, Inc., 435 U.S. 519, 524 (1978) [p. 312]). . . . Rather than adopting this test, we focus our inquiry on whether the Departments satisfied the APA's objective criteria, just as we have in previous cases. We conclude that they did.

Section 553(b) obligated the Departments to provide adequate notice before promulgating a rule that has legal force. As explained . . . the IFRs provided sufficient notice. Aside from these notice requirements, the APA mandates that agencies "give interested persons an opportunity to participate in the rule making through submission of written data, views, or arguments," § 553(c); states that the final rules must include "a concise general statement of their basis and purpose," ibid.; and requires that final rules must be published 30 days before they become effective, § 553(d).

The Departments complied with each of these statutory procedures. They "request[ed] and encourag[ed] public comments on all matters addressed" in the rules—i.e., the basis for the Departments' legal authority, the rationales for the exemptions, and the detailed discussion of the exemptions' scope. They also gave interested parties 60 days to submit comments. The final rules included a concise statement of their basis and purpose, explaining that the rules were "necessary to protect sincerely held" moral and religious objections and summarizing the legal analysis supporting the exemptions. Lastly, the final rules were published on November 15, 2018, but did not become effective until January 14, 2019—more than 30 days after being published. In sum, the rules fully complied with " 'the maximum procedural requirements [that] Congress was willing to have the courts impose upon agencies in conducting rulemaking procedures.' " Perez, 575 U.S., at 102 (quoting Vermont Yankee, 435 U.S., at 524). . . .[14]

[W]e reverse the judgment of the Court of Appeals and remand the cases for further proceedings consistent with this opinion.

## NOTES

(1) ***What Constitutes Good Cause?*** Section 553(b)(B) allows agencies to invoke the good cause exception only where notice and comment would be "impracticable, unnecessary, or contrary to the public interest." 5 U.S.C. § 553(b)(B). As the Mack Trucks court indicates, courts have given content to these general terms through case-by-case assessment. A Congressional Research Service report divides the circumstances underlying the cases in which courts found good cause into four main categories: (1) minor, technical amendments or corrections that involve little to no agency discretion; (2) emergencies, such as where there is a concern for public safety; (3) situations where advance notice would subvert the statutory scheme, such as when advance notice of government price controls would allow market manipulation; and (4) situations where Congress's actions indicate

[14] Because we conclude that the IFRs' request for comment satisfies the APA's rulemaking requirements, we need not reach respondents' additional argument that the Departments lacked good cause to promulgate the 2017 IFRs.

an intent for agencies to regulate quickly, such as with the imposition of an imminent statutory deadline. Jared P. Cole, Cong. Rsch. Serv., R44356, The Good Cause Exception to Notice and Comment Rulemaking: Judicial Review of Agency Action (Jan. 29, 2016), at 4–9.[1]

CONNOR RASO, AGENCY AVOIDANCE OF RULEMAKING PROCEDURES, 67 Admin. L. Rev. 65, 88–89 (2015): "Courts frequently note in dicta that they construe the good cause exception narrowly to protect the notice-and-comment process. Notwithstanding such dicta, some good cause cases have been relatively exacting, and others have been relatively lenient. This Article argues that such inconsistency is virtually inevitable given the number of facts that courts consider when determining whether an agency validly invoked good cause. In determining whether an agency had a good cause, courts have considered the following:

- Whether the agency was acting pursuant to a statutory deadline;
- The potential harm from providing advance notice of the rule;
- The degree of economic harm created by delay to complete the notice-and-comment process;
- The degree of harm to public safety created by delay to complete the notice-and-comment process;
- Whether the agency accepted and responded to post promulgation public comment;
- Whether the agency issued the rule on a routine basis;
- Whether the rule was limited in scope;
- Whether the rule implicated significant reliance interests;
- Whether the agency issued the rule pursuant to an injunction;
- Whether the agency revised the rule in response to a court order; and
- Whether the agency provided a contemporaneous justification for invoking good cause."

Should courts view the good cause exception narrowly? Or has judicial elaboration of § 553's requirements made a broad reading of the good cause exception more appropriate? Put differently, should courts treat § 553's requirements and exceptions consistently, reading both either narrowly or expansively, or is there a reason to distinguish between these two components of § 553?

Here is the Third Circuit's conclusion, in the case under review by the Supreme Court in Little Sisters of the Poor, that the agencies lacked good cause to issue the Interim Final Rules without prior notice and comment. On which of the above considerations did the court rely? Do you agree with its determination? PENNSYLVANIA V. TRUMP, 930 F.3d 543, 567–69 (3d Cir. 2019): "When they issued the IFRs, the Agencies claimed good cause to waive notice and comment based on (1) the urgent need to alleviate harm to those

[1] https://crsreports.congress.gov/product/pdf/R/R44356/3.

with religious objections to the current regulations; (2) the need to address 'continued uncertainty, inconsistency, and cost' arising from 'litigation challenging the previous rules'; and (3) the fact that the Agencies had already collected comments on prior Mandate-related regulations. . . . None of these assertions meet the standard for good cause.

"First, the Agencies' desire to address the purported harm to religious objections does not ameliorate the need to follow appropriate procedures. All regulations are directed toward reducing harm in some manner. . . . Thus, [a] need to regulate affected parties does not create the urgency necessary to establish good cause. As with any other administrative agency conclusion, we require some statement of facts or circumstances that justifies the existence of good cause (e.g., an imminent, externally imposed deadline or the existence of an emergency). The Agencies fail to cite any facts or impending deadlines sufficient to raise 'good cause' here.

"Second, the need to address uncertainty is likewise insufficient to establish good cause. Uncertainty precedes every regulation, and to allow uncertainty to excuse compliance with notice-and-comment procedures would have the effect of writing [those] requirements out of the statute. Furthermore, our precedent forecloses the acceptance of uncertainty as a basis for good cause. . . .

"Third, the Agencies' previous solicitation and collection of comments regarding other rules concerning the Contraceptive Mandate cannot substitute for notice and comment here. If the APA permitted agencies to forego notice-and-comment concerning a proposed regulation simply because they already regulated similar matters, then the good cause exception could largely obviate the notice-and-comment requirement. Furthermore, the IFRs did not make a minor change. The IFRs create exemptions from the Contraceptive Mandate with unprecedented scope and make the Accommodation wholly voluntary. Such a dramatic overhaul of the Contraceptive Mandate regulations required notice-and-comment."

(2) ***Deference to Agency's Determination That Good Cause Exists?*** In reviewing the EPA's claim of good cause, the Mack Trucks court says, "it would appear we owe EPA's findings no particular deference." Should a court defer to an agency's determination that good cause exists? The courts are divided. Some evaluate agencies' assertions of good cause under an arbitrary and capricious standard; some under a de novo standard; some without explicitly deciding the issue; and some under a mixed standard. See Cole, The Good Cause Exception, supra, at 13–16; Kyle Schneider, Note, Judicial Review of Good Cause Determinations Under the Administrative Procedure Act, 73 Stan. L. Rev. 237 (2021).

Compare two cases from the D.C. Circuit. In SORENSEN COMMUNICATIONS LTD. V. FCC, 755 F.3d 702, 706 (D.C. Cir. 2014), the D.C. Circuit held that the standard of review for an agency's invocation of the good cause exception was de novo, rejecting the FCC's call for deference: "To accord deference would be to run afoul of congressional intent. From the outset, we note an agency has no interpretive authority over the APA, see Envirocare of Utah, Inc. v. NRC, 194 F.3d 72 (D.C.Cir.1999); we cannot find that an exception applies simply because the agency says we should. Moreover, the good-cause inquiry is meticulous and demanding, [and our] caselaw indicates we are to narrowly construe and reluctantly countenance the exception. Deference to an agency's invocation of good cause—particularly when its reasoning is potentially capacious, as is the case here—would conflict with this court's deliberate and careful treatment of the exception in the past. Therefore, our review of the agency's legal conclusion of good cause is de novo." The Sorensen court proceeded to reject the FCC's invocation of good cause at issue, noting that the FCC cited "the threat of impending fiscal peril as cause for waiving notice and comment" of its rule regulating provision of captioning telephones and services for the hearing impaired, but "[c]uriously . . . there were no factual findings supporting the reality of the threat" to the federal fund that pays for captioning services. The court added: "[W]e do not exclude the possibility that a fiscal calamity could conceivably justify bypassing the notice-and-comment requirement, [but] this case does not provide evidence of such an exigency. . . . Though no particular catechism is necessary to establish good cause, something more than an unsupported assertion is required." Id. at 706–07.

By contrast, in JIFRY V. FAA, 370 F.3d 1174, 1179–80 (D.C. Cir. 2004), the D.C. Circuit upheld regulations providing for automatic suspension of a pilot's airman certificate—without which a pilot cannot fly in the United States—upon the FAA's being notified by the Transportation Security Administration that the pilot poses a security threat. The regulations were issued without notice and comment, and the agency invoked the good cause exception in justification. In sustaining the FAA's action, the D.C. Circuit rejected the argument that the FAA's preexisting unlimited power to revoke a certificate immediately if it believed a pilot to be a security threat precluded good cause from existing here: "[A]t the time the challenged regulations were adopted, the FAA's power to suspend or revoke certificates was permissive only. Congress had not yet enacted [statutory provisions] formaliz[ing] the requirement that the FAA shall suspend, modify, or revoke a certificate if notified by the TSA that the individual posed a security risk. . . . The TSA and FAA deemed [automatic suspension or revocation] . . . necessary 'in order to minimize security threats and potential security vulnerabilities to the fullest extent possible.' Given [their] legitimate concern over the threat of further terrorist acts involving aircraft in the aftermath of September 11, 2001, the agencies had 'good cause' for not offering advance public participation."

Are public safety contexts more deserving of deference? For the view that the courts have taken a very deferential view of agency good cause determinations based on national security post-September 11, see Adrian Vermeule, Our Schmittian Administrative Law, 122 Harv. L. Rev. 1095, 1122–25 (2009).

(3) ***What Is the Relevance of Postpromulgation Comment?*** Prior to Little Sisters of the Poor, the circuits had been divided on how to treat the relevance of postpromulgation comments to prior claims of good cause. KRISTEN E. HICKMAN & MARK THOMSON, OPEN MINDS AND HARMLESS ERRORS: JUDICIAL REVIEW OF POSTPROMULGATION NOTICE AND COMMENT,

101 Cornell L. Rev. 261, 285–305 (2016): "The circuit courts have adopted at least five distinct approaches to addressing such cases. . . . A few courts have declined to give any effect to postpromulgation notice and comment," treating them as "[i]rretrievably [f]lawed. . . . At the other extreme, some courts have treated postpromulgation notice and comment as curing or mooting procedural defects in interim-final rules. . . . The D.C. Circuit . . . has at times championed a middle ground—the open mind standard—whereby the court will uphold a rule that was only subjected to postpromulgation notice and comment if, during the postpromulgation notice-and-comment period, the agency kept an 'open mind' with respect to the comments it received. . . . In [one case], the Fifth Circuit carved out a different middle ground . . . look[ing] at the record, including the record from postpromulgation notice and comment, to ascertain whether the [agency's] error—failing to give prepromulgation notice and an opportunity to comment—was harmless. . . . Finally, . . . a few circuits in [a series of cases all addressing the same EPA rule in the 1980s] sought a middle ground via the remedy imposed . . . allow[ing] the EPA's regulations generally to remain in effect while the challenging parties, but not the public at large, received the opportunity to submit comments before the EPA refinalized the challenged designations."

Which of these paths did the Supreme Court appear to adopt in Little Sisters of the Poor? KRISTIN E. HICKMAN, DID LITTLE SISTERS OF THE POOR JUST GUT APA RULEMAKING PROCEDURES?, Notice & Comment Blog (July 9, 2020):[2] "At least at first blush, Justice Thomas's opinion for the Court turns APA notice-and-comment rulemaking procedures into a pro forma exercise of procedural box-checking that will allow agencies to curtail meaningful public participation in the agency rulemaking process. . . . [R]ather than merely finding the agency's use of IFRs *in this case* to be harmless error, [Justice Thomas] declared the use of IFRs more or less *categorically* to be nonprejudicial so long as they are sufficiently thorough in their explanation of the agency's thinking. . . . [W]ith its decision in Little Sisters, the Court has come pretty close to, if not writing APA § 553(b) and (c) out of the statute completely, then at least minimizing those provisions to the point of irrelevancy in most instances. Under the reasoning of Little Sisters, even without a claim of good cause, an agency can issue legally-binding IFRs that include the requisite citations to legal authority and invite public comments, then wait and see what happens. If someone challenges the IFRs as procedurally invalid, then the agency can hurry up and issue final-final regulations with a preamble that responds to comments received, if any, without making changes, and the Court likely will say 'good enough' so long as the agency otherwise is thorough enough in communicating its own thoughts. But if no one bothers to challenge the IFRs, then the agency can just leave them on the books as-is without further action. Since most agency regulations go unchallenged in court (for many reasons unrelated to their compliance with the APA), most agency regulations can now be issued in legally-binding form without needing to engage with the public at all. And

---

[2] https://www.yalejreg.com/nc/did-little-sisters-of-the-poor-just-gut-apa-rulemaking-procedures/.

when regulations are challenged, [an argument that the regulations are arbitrary and capricious under the Supreme Court's decision in] State Farm [p. 1126] is the only real protection left against agency arbitrariness."

Do you agree with Hickman's reading of the case? It would seem that agencies would gravitate toward IFRs after Little Sisters, but there are countervailing considerations, including decreasing litigation risk, that might pressure agencies into traditional rulemaking procedures. If you were advising an agency, would you recommend that it follow the path Hickman outlines?

(4) ***Remand Without Vacatur.*** The Mack Trucks court "conclude[d] the IFR must be vacated" even though "the pending final rule means our vacatur of the IFR on these procedural grounds will be of limited practical impact." Should it instead have remanded for error correction without vacating the IFR? If so, what if there were no pending final rule—should the court then also be able to remand without vacating the IFR, instructing the agency to open the proceedings for comment? The developing practice of "remand without vacatur" in the D.C. Circuit and elsewhere over the past several decades allows the court to do just this. While not without controversy, including within the D.C. Circuit itself, remand without vacatur instructs the agency to reconsider its rule while allowing the rule to stay in effect. We discuss the legality and merits of the practice at more length when we discuss remedies in Chapter IX, Section 2.d (p. 1556). For now, consider whether (and if so when) it might be an appropriate remedy in good cause cases.

As one example in support of his argument that "there is often a mismatch between the underlying violation and the harshness of the conventional remedy" of vacatur, NICHOLAS BAGLEY, in REMEDIAL RESTRAINT IN ADMINISTRATIVE LAW, 117 Colum. L. Rev. 253, 255, 287–88 (2017), examines Utility Solid Waste Activities Group v. EPA, 236 F.3d 749 (D.C. Cir. 2001), cited multiple times in Mack Trucks, and calls its decision to vacate the rule "hard to defend": "When EPA first issued its notice of proposed rulemaking, the Agency had included no accommodation at all for porous materials that had been contaminated with PCBs. If that proposal had been finalized, all such materials would have had to be discarded. The regulated community—including Utility Solid Waste Activities Group (USWAG) and GE—feared that such an approach would prove needlessly costly. Sensitive to the concern, EPA worked closely with the industry during the original notice-and-comment period to devise an alternative. It was here that the Agency erred. Its final rule stated that PCB contamination of porous materials would be measured with reference to their surface concentration. To those in the know, this was obviously a mistake. (An agency official had apparently screwed up using the find-and-replace command.) . . . No neophytes to PCBs, USWAG and GE understood as much—and were likely unsurprised when EPA caught its mistake. More importantly, the agency gave them notice of its desire to fix the mistake and a chance to comment. Nine months before amending its rule, EPA published an internet bulletin containing a list of anticipated technical corrections—including the change that became the subject of Utility Solid Waste Activities Group—and invited additional contributions to the list. EPA then held a number of meetings with both USWAG and GE; at one of those meetings, USWAG asked specifically about the change to the porous-surface rule and was told that the original rule was an error. After all this, it's difficult to accept USWAG's and GE's claims that they never had a chance to comment on the correction."

On the other hand, in a study of the process of rule revision in EPA, OSHA, and the FCC, WENDY WAGNER, WILLIAM WEST, THOMAS MCGARITY, and LISA PETERS, in DYNAMIC RULEMAKING, 92 N.Y.U. L. Rev. 183, 249–50 (2017), single out EPA's revisions under the Toxic Substances Control Act for particular concern: "Perhaps the most troubling employment of dynamic rulemaking in a nontransparent way that we identified in our case studies was EPA's use of annual 'interim rules' to publish vague after-the-fact descriptions of changes to TSCA test rules. These changes were made with little or no explanation and were often published after they had been implemented by the manufacturers who were subject to the original rules. It may be true that most members of the public are not interested in arcane changes to the protocols of test rules, but that need not always be the case. Test rules for some high profile chemicals might very well attract the interest of environmental groups or advocates of those who are exposed to them in the workplace. It may be that EPA is in a hurry to make the changes because many involve ongoing testing regimes, but that should not allow it to make a mockery of the APA-prescribed rulemaking process."

How should courts view remand without vacatur? Under the D.C. Circuit's standard, "[t]he decision whether to vacate depends on the seriousness of the order's deficiencies (and thus the extent of doubt whether the agency chose correctly) and the disruptive consequences of an interim change that may itself be changed." Allied-Signal, Inc. v. Nuclear Regulatory Comm'n, 988 F.2d 146, 150–51 (D.C. Cir. 1993) (internal quotation marks omitted). Does this standard seem appropriate? Here are ACUS's recommendations for the practice: "In determining whether the remedy of remand without vacatur is appropriate, courts should consider equitable factors, including whether: (a) correction is reasonably achievable in light of the nature of the deficiencies in the agency's rule or order; (b) the consequences of vacatur would be disruptive; and (c) the interests of the parties who prevailed against the agency in the litigation would be served by allowing the agency action to remain in place. . . . When a court has decided to remand an agency action, it should consider hearing parties' views on whether to vacate the agency action and on any related remedial issues." Recommendation 2013–6, Remand without Vacatur, 78 Fed. Reg. 76269 (Dec. 17, 2013). Do you agree?

(5) ***Interim Final Rules.*** Mack Trucks and Little Sisters of the Poor both concerned Interim Final Rules, a type of rulemaking that is not expressly mentioned in the APA. (Center for Science in the Public Interest, in the previous Section, also involved an IFR.) Over the last several decades, agencies have increasingly employed IFRs as a way of mitigating some of the burdens associated with notice-and-comment rulemaking. In interim final rulemaking, an agency adopts a rule without public comment, typically

makes it immediately effective using "good cause" under § 553(d) (about which see Note 7, p. 387), and then seeks comments postpromulgation.

MICHAEL ASIMOW, INTERIM-FINAL RULES: MAKING HASTE SLOWLY, 51 Admin. L. Rev. 703, 710–11 (1999): In determining whether to use interim final rulemaking, an agency "[f]irst decides that it is legally entitled to adopt a rule without engaging in the normal process of pre-adoption public participation. Although several APA exceptions might apply, the occasion for adopting an interim-final rule is often the presence of some exigency that provides good cause for dispensing with public participation. . . . Second, the agency decides that it should solicit post-effective comments and make a commitment to consider those comments at the time it makes the interim-final rule final. Note that this part of the agency's decision is not legally obligatory. Except where statutes require utilization of interim-final methodology, an agency is never required to engage in further process after adopting a rule under the good cause exemption (or any other APA exemption). Solicitation of post-effective comments, consideration of such comments, preparation of a basis and purpose statement, and adoption of a final-final rule modifying the interim-final rule are all time consuming chores that an agency assumes voluntarily."

Ronald M. Levin characterizes IFRs as follows: "[I]nterim final rulemaking . . . is generally used because of some felt urgency in instituting a regulation immediately. It frequently involves regulations that are deeply controversial; the agency solicits comment for its own edification or to identify possible bases of legal challenge, but will not alter the rule unless the comment *persuades* it to do so." Direct Final Rulemaking, 64 Geo. Wash. L. Rev. 1, 3 (1995). For more on the scope and rise of interim final rulemaking, developed as part of a study of agency rulemaking activities between 1983 and 2003, see Anne Joseph O'Connell, Political Cycles of Rulemaking: An Empirical Portrait of the Modern Administrative State, 94 Va. L. Rev. 889, 929–36 (2008).

When an agency has a legitimate claim of good cause, IFRs can help mitigate problems of retroactive rulemaking (see p. 271), because they go into effect immediately and thus may avert regulatory gaps. At the same time, however, many interim rules remain in effect for years without the issuance of a final rule subject to public comment. This can be a problem regardless of whether the agency's claim of good cause is legitimate, especially where the claim is not challenged in court. Because agency decisions to respond to comments and issue a final-final rule are voluntary, agencies often lack incentives to issue a final rule. "Inertia is at work; the rule is already in effect and nothing really needs to be done about it. Members of the public subject to the rule are complying with it. Busy members of the agency staff feel no pressure to deal with the comments received (if any) or to figure out how to modify the rule in light of the comments or administrative experience. . . . If rules dangle indefinitely in interim limbo, the post-adoption comment period was a waste of everyone's time. Desirable modifications in the rule will not occur." Asimow, supra, at 736–37. In addition, "[w]hen it is unclear whether agencies considered comments, rulemaking is less transparent to the public, and, as courts have recognized, the opportunity to comment is meaningless unless the agency responds to significant points raised by the public." GAO, Federal Rulemaking: Agencies Could Take Additional Steps to Respond to Public Comments, GAO-13-21 (Dec. 2012), at 29.[3]

(6) ***Direct Final Rules.*** Neither Mack Trucks nor Little Sisters of the Poor mentions direct final rulemaking, but like interim final rulemaking, which featured prominently in both cases, direct final rulemaking is a form of rulemaking that is not explicitly mentioned in the APA but that agencies have increasingly used in recent decades. See O'Connell, Political Cycles of Rulemaking, supra. While interim final rulemaking often involves controversial rules, direct final rulemaking is meant to be used for uncontroversial rules that the agency predicts are unlikely to generate significant adverse comment. In its ideal form, an agency publishes its rule as a direct final rule in the Federal Register and includes a statement indicating that the rule will become final unless significant adverse comment is received by a certain deadline. If significant adverse comment is submitted—even if only one comment (though it has to be material)—the agency immediately withdraws the direct final rule and proceeds through notice-and-comment rulemaking. Properly used, Ronald Levin argues, direct final rulemaking should be exempt from "the usual public participation requirements of the APA, because such participation would be 'unnecessary' within the meaning of the good cause exemption of § 553(b)(B)." Levin, supra, at 11.

Debate over direct final rulemaking centers on whether it complies with § 553 and whether agencies are employing it appropriately. Levin's argument that notice and comment is "unnecessary" under the good cause exception is the core of the legal argument in favor of the practice. On the other hand, as the APA does not explicitly mention it, its legality has not been certain. Compare Ronald M. Levin, More on Direct Final Rulemaking: Streamlining, Not Corner-Cutting, 51 Admin. L. Rev. 757 (1999), with Lars Noah, Doubts About Direct Final Rulemaking, 51 Admin. L. Rev. 401 (1999).

As to whether agencies employ direct final rulemaking correctly, a study of FDA rulemaking between 1997 and 2007 determined that of the 38 direct final rules the agency proposed during this time period, the agency had to withdraw forty percent because it received significant adverse comments. Michael Kolber, Rulemaking without Rules: An Empirical Study of Direct Final Rulemaking, 72 Alb. L. Rev. 79, 82 (2009). Does that high rate of withdrawal indicate inappropriate reliance on the form? Does your answer to that question change depending on whether the agency gives up on the rule or reissues it after notice and comment?

The high rate of withdrawal found in the study of FDA rules may be atypical. "Other experiences with direct final rulemaking at the EPA, the Federal Aviation Administration and elsewhere have produced withdrawal rates of less than ten or twenty percent. A withdrawal rate of forty percent is shocking. It suggests either the FDA is dramatically off when predicting which of its rules are likely to be controversial or the FDA is using direct

---

[3] https://www.gao.gov/assets/660/651052.pdf.

final rulemaking for purposes it was not intended." Id. at 82. On the other hand, a 2018 empirical study of direct final rules by the Brookings Institution found increasing rates of challenge in the first year of the Trump Administration: "Although the Trump administration's use of DFRs in 2017 was roughly in line with the late Obama administration, the portion of DFRs withdrawn after receiving adverse comments shot up. Out of 169 DFRs published in 2017, more than one-third (63) were withdrawn. The highest proportion ever previously withdrawn was 16 percent in 2001, with most years having a withdrawal rate between 5 and 10 percent." Philip A. Wallach & Nicholas W. Zeppos, Brookings Inst., Contestation of Direct Final Rules During the Trump Administration (Oct. 9, 2018).[4]

A recent development in the D.C. Circuit may undercut the value of direct final rulemaking. In Milice v. Consumer Product Safety Commission, 2 F.4th 994 (D.C. Cir. 2021), the D.C. Circuit held that a direct final rule issued by the CPSC was a final agency action as of the date it was first announced (and thus, as relevant in the case, that the plaintiff's challenge to the rule was untimely). The finality ruling changes the calculus of direct final rulemaking. As RONALD M. LEVIN explains in THE D.C. CIRCUIT UNDERMINES DIRECT FINAL RULEMAKING, Notice & Comment Blog (Aug. 2, 2021),[5] the "whole point" of direct final rules is that an agency can use "the opportunity for post hoc objection as a reality check to confirm its initial impression that the rule would be uncontroversial. . . . In this sense, an agency's publication of a direct final rule is inherently provisional. . . . If the judicial review record is closed as of that date, the agency has much less incentive to pay attention to any post-publication comments it may receive." The full implication of this decision for direct final rules remains to be seen, but they may continue to function as usual in "the kind of situations for which [they] [were] designed," that is to say, cases in which rules "survive due to the absence of a bona fide objection, or [where] the filing of such an objection leads the agency to withdraw the rule for further consideration." Would it be better to hold that a direct final rule is not final until the date to submit adverse comments has passed and the agency has decided to keep the rule in place? Should Congress act to institutionalize the practice? To revise it?

(7) ***Two Good Cause Standards?*** In Little Sisters of the Poor, the Court explains, as one of the core requirements of APA rulemaking, that "final rules must be published 30 days before they become effective," citing § 553(d). This provision itself contains another good cause exception: Agencies must publish a rule "not less than 30 days before its effective date, except . . . as otherwise provided by the agency for good cause found and published with the rule." Is this second provision a separate standard?

The Ninth Circuit has conceptualized the distinction as follows: "[D]ifferent policies underlie the exceptions, and . . . they can be invoked for different reasons. . . . Unlike the notice and comment requirements, which are designed to ensure public participation in rulemaking, the 30-day

---

[4] https://www.brookings.edu/research/contestation-of-direct-final-rules-during-the-trump-administration/.

[5] https://www.yalejreg.com/nc/the-d-c-circuit-undermines-direct-final-rulemaking-by-ronald-m-levin/.

waiting period is intended to give affected parties time to adjust their behavior before the final rule takes effect. This is sensible; until the final rule is published, the public is not sure of what the rule will be or when the rule will actually be promulgated. In addition, a window of time usually causes no harm." Riverbend Farms, Inc. v. Madigan, 958 F.2d 1479, 1485 (9th Cir. 1992). Notwithstanding this distinction, courts are inconsistent in whether they treat the two provisions as representing different standards, with some courts treating the test to avoid notice and comment as a higher bar for an agency to pass than the test for waiving the 30-day delay rule. See Cole, The Good Cause Exception to Notice and Comment Rulemaking, supra, at 3.

Does a new administration's desire to reevaluate the final but not yet effective rules of the outgoing administration of a different party constitute good cause to delay the effective dates as a general policy? Do you think it should? JACK M. BEERMANN, MIDNIGHT RULES: A REFORM AGENDA, 2 Mich. J. Envtl. & Admin. L. 285, 335–36, 353, 363 (2013), explains: "[O]n his tenth day in office, President Reagan issued a memorandum to twelve department heads and the Administrator of the EPA, directing them to delay the effective dates of recently published regulations for sixty days and not to promulgate any new regulations during the sixty days following the date of the memorandum. . . . Reagan's memorandum served as a model for the actions of subsequent administrations dealing with midnight rules and gaining control of administrative agencies. . . . There have not been many cases raising procedural challenges to incoming administrations' reactions to midnight rules promulgated by the previous administration. This is likely due to a combination of factors. In the vast majority of cases, any challenge to a delay in the effective date of agency rules is likely to be moot before the challenge would get very far. Most of the time, after the sixty-day delay to allow the incoming administration to review the previous administration's midnight rules, the rules are allowed to go into effect. A case challenging the sixty-day delay is unlikely to be adjudicated before the sixty days has ended."

On reviewing the few cases assessing such efforts, Beermann concludes that "courts will require good reasons for delaying the implementation of published rules without notice and comment beyond the mere desire of incoming administrations to reexamine midnight rules before they go into effect." See also Lisa Heinzerling, Unreasonable Delays: The Legal Problems (So Far) of Trump's Deregulatory Binge, 12 Harv. L. & Pol'y Rev. 13, 16 (2018) (assessing the Trump Administration's efforts "in delaying or suspending existing rules" and concluding that they were full of legal errors). The proposed Regulatory Accountability Act would amend § 553 to allow a new administration to delay for 90 days the effective date of any final rule that had not yet become effective to obtain public comment on whether the rule should be amended, rescinded, or further delayed. S. 2278 (117th Cong.) (2021), § 3. Do you think this is a good idea?

## NOTES ON THE EXCEPTION'S PREVALENCE, THE PANDEMIC, AND ALTERNATIVE FORMS

(1) ***Prevalent Use of Good Cause Rulemaking.*** A 2013 GAO report on agencies' rulemaking practices illustrated the contemporary prominence of

good cause rulemaking. It found that from 2003 through 2010, "agencies published about 35 percent of major rules and about 44 percent of nonmajor rules without an NPRM," and that of these, the vast majority claimed the good cause exception. (Agencies did seek comment afterward for a majority of the major rules.) Federal Rulemaking: Agencies Could Take Additional Steps to Respond to Public Comments, GAO-13-21 (Dec. 2012), at 8–10, 15, 24.[6] Does the extent of good cause rulemaking surprise you, in light of the fact that it is supposed to be an exception or the fact that courts routinely say they will construe good cause "narrowly"? Or is the extent to be expected, given the difficulties associated with notice-and-comment rulemaking, as discussed above in Section 3? Whether you are surprised or not, do you think the extent of good cause rulemaking is cause for concern or a sign of a healthy system?

(2) ***The Pandemic and the Good Cause Exception.*** The COVID-19 pandemic brought an additional impetus for good cause rulemaking. Between March 20, 2020, and May 10, 2021, ACUS tracked more than 150 rulemaking notices in which agencies cited COVID-19 as good cause to forego the APA's notice-and-comment or effective-date requirements. ACUS, Coronavirus (COVID-19) and Rulemaking (last updated May 10, 2021).[7] In the pandemic relief acts passed in the spring of 2020, Congress explicitly directed some agencies to implement specific rules on an emergency basis without notice and comment. See Reed Shaw, Note, "Good Cause" for a Good Cause: Using an APA Exception to Confront the COVID-19 Crisis, 21 J.L. Soc'y 116, 149 (2021). In other instances, agencies relied on the idea that notice and comment was "impracticable" under the circumstances. According to Connor Raso, Brookings Inst., Emergency Rulemaking in Response to COVID-19 (Aug. 20, 2020), the 85 "emergency rules citing the COVID-19 crisis issued from March through July 2020 were generally time-limited and linked to the COVID-19 crisis. Most appear to meet the legal standard for being issued on an emergency basis without the opportunity for prior public comment."[8]

Two years into the pandemic, in a study of 24 agencies' pandemic-related implementation of regulatory flexibilities (defined as waivers or exemptions, modifications of regulations, changes to enforcement, delayed effective or compliance dates, and a catch-all "other" category), as authorized by the COVID-19 relief acts and emergency declarations, nine agencies reported relying somewhat more often or much more often on interim final rules, in comparison with six agencies that reported relying somewhat more often or much more often on notice-and-comment rulemaking. GAO, COVID-19: Agencies Increased Use of Some Regulatory Flexibilities and Are Taking Steps to Assess Them, GAO-22-105147 (June 2022), at 4–14.[9] GAO described interviews with Department of Transportation officials explaining that "the longer time required to promulgate notice-and-comment rules may not have

[6] https://www.gao.gov/assets/660/651052.pdf.

[7] https://www.acus.gov/coronavirus-covid-19-and-rulemaking.

[8] https://www.brookings.edu/research/emergency-rulemaking-in-response-to-covid-19/.

[9] https://www.gao.gov/assets/gao-22-105047.pdf.

afforded agencies sufficient time to use this method to respond effectively to the pandemic." Id. at 14.

Is a pandemic exactly the kind of circumstance for which good cause rulemaking should be expected? Or is there a danger that administrations will skirt rulemaking requirements to implement their preferred policies in the spirit of not letting a crisis go to waste? Consider the Trump Administration's "Title 42" policy suspending entry into the United States of people coming from Mexico and Canada on the grounds that such entry posed the risk of spreading COVID-19. Promulgating the policy in an IFR, the CDC relied on a provision in the Public Health Service Act, 42 U.S.C. § 265, allowing such suspension when "required in the interest of the public health" due to "the existence of any communicable disease in a foreign country" if "there is serious danger of the introduction of such disease into the United States." The CDC also relied on the good cause exception "[g]iven the national emergency caused by COVID-19." 85 Fed. Reg. 16559, 16565 (Mar. 24, 2020). The IFR requested postpromulgation comments, and the CDC issued a final rule six months later. In turn, after keeping the Trump Administration's Title 42 policy in place for more than a year (with some exceptions), the Biden Administration attempted to terminate it in April 2022, also relying in part on good cause to avoid notice and comment in light of "the extraordinary nature" of the "resultant restrictions on application for asylum and other immigration processes" and "the statutory and regulatory requirement that [a] CDC order under the authority last no longer than necessary to protect public health." 87 Fed. Reg. 19941, 19956 (Apr. 6, 2022). Are these appropriate uses of good cause rulemaking? One, both, neither? Challenges to the Trump Administration's policy focused on whether the agency had statutory authority for it and whether the policy was arbitrary and capricious, rather than on the agency's claim of good cause (perhaps because of the agency's fairly speedy issuance of a final rule after receiving comments, see Little Sisters of the Poor (p. 374)). However, the Biden Administration's termination was enjoined by a district court in part because "the CDC's rationale for invoking the 'good cause' exception is flawed." Louisiana v. CDC, 2022 WL 1604901 (W.D. La. 2022). Another district court found the Title 42 policy arbitrary and capricious in November 2022. Huisha-Huisha v. Mayorkas, 2022 WL 16948610 (D.D.C. 2022).

(3) ***Good Cause Specificity and Public Health Emergencies.*** How much good cause justification should an agency have to give when relying on a public health emergency? In BIDEN V. MISSOURI, 142 S.Ct. 647 (2022) (p. 869), the Supreme Court considered an IFR requiring vaccination against COVID-19 for staff members of healthcare facilities that received funding from Medicare and Medicaid. The Centers for Medicare and Medicaid Services in HHS had promulgated the IFR without notice and comment after "finding 'good cause' that it should be made effective immediately" in light of "the Secretary's belief that any 'further delay' would endanger patient health and safety given the spread of the Delta variant and the upcoming winter season." In a 5–4 per curiam opinion, the Court agreed that "the Secretary's finding that accelerated promulgation of the rule in advance of the winter flu season would significantly reduce COVID-19 infections, hospitalizations,

and deaths . . . constitutes the 'something specific' . . . required to forgo notice and comment. And we cannot say that in this instance the two months the agency took to prepare a 73-page rule constitutes 'delay' inconsistent with the Secretary's finding of good cause."

In dissent, JUSTICE ALITO objected: "CMS's generalized justification cannot alone establish good cause to dispense with Congress's clear procedural safeguards. . . . Although CMS argues that an emergency justifies swift action, both District Courts below held that CMS fatally undercut that justification with its own repeated delays. The vaccines that CMS now claims are vital had been widely available 10 months before CMS's mandate, and millions of healthcare workers had already been vaccinated before the agency took action. President Biden announced the CMS mandate . . . nearly two months before the agency released the rule . . . , and the mandate itself delayed the compliance deadline further by another month. . . . This is hardly swift. CMS argues that its delay, 'even if true,' does not provide a 'reason to block a rule' that it claims will protect patient health. It claims that its departure from ordinary procedure after extraordinary delay should be excused because nobody can show they were prejudiced by the lack of a comment period before the rule took effect. But it is CMS's affirmative burden to show it has good cause, not respondents' burden to prove the negative. . . . Because CMS chose to circumvent notice-and-comment, States that run Medicaid facilities, as well as other regulated parties, had no opportunity to present evidence refuting or contradicting CMS's justifications before the rule bound them. And because CMS acknowledged its own 'uncertainty' and the 'rapidly changing nature of the current pandemic,' it should have been more receptive to feedback, not less."

In HEALTH FREEDOM DEFENSE FUND V. BIDEN, 2022 WL 1134138 (M.D. Fla. 2022), a district court struck down the CDC's requirement that travelers wear masks on various forms of transportation and in transit hubs. In the course of a much broader opinion that found the "Mask Mandate" exceeded the agency's statutory authority and was arbitrary and capricious, the court also rejected the agency's claim of good cause: "The only reason the Mandate cites is 'the public health emergency caused by COVID-19.' That is certainly support [for] the promulgation of the Mandate, but good cause to suspend notice and comment must be supported by more than the bare need [for the] regulations. And COVID-19 itself does not *always* justify an agency bypassing notice and comment. Instead, the agency must identif[y] specific reasons why [there was] good cause for dispensing with the usual notice-and-comment requirements in the particular environment the agency intended to regulate. The Mandate does not do that. . . . The Mandate's terse conclusion contrasts markedly with another regulation that addressed the COVID-19 pandemic and invoked good cause to forgo notice and comment. When [CMS] mandated that the staff of healthcare facilities receiving Medicare or Medicaid funding be vaccinated against COVID-19, it provided almost four pages of reasoning (with forty footnotes of supporting sources) on why there was good cause to forego notice and comment. . . . The Supreme Court concluded that this extensive reasoning properly invoked the good cause exception. . . . Unlike the CMS rule, the Mask Mandate mustered a single conclusory sentence to support its invocation of good cause. . . .

"The CDC's failure to explain its reasoning is particularly problematic here. At the time when the CDC issued the Mandate, the COVID-19 pandemic had been ongoing for almost a year and COVID-19 case numbers were decreasing. This timing undercuts the CDC's suggestion that its action was so urgent that a thirty-day comment period was contrary to the public interest. So too, the CDC's delay in issuing the Mandate further undercuts its position. The CDC issued the mandate in February 2021, almost two weeks after the President called for a mandate, eleven months after the President had declared COVID-19 a national emergency, and almost thirteen months since the Secretary of Health and Human Services had declared a public health emergency. This history suggests that the CDC itself did not find the passage of time particularly serious. . . . Nor did the CDC explain its reason for the delay. . . . The Mandate's failure to explain is especially troubling because the benefits of public comment were at their zenith. First, the Mandate governs the conduct of private individuals in their daily lives. . . . Second, the public has a heightened interest in participating in a regulation that would constrain their choices and actions via threats of civil and criminal penalties. And finally, [e]specially in the context of health risks, notice and comment procedures assure the dialogue necessary to the creation of reasonable rules. . . . The government resists this conclusion, arguing that the CDC made a 'common-sense finding' based on the record that delaying the Mandate would do real harm because it would lead to increased COVID-19 transmission. Perhaps so. But, as explained above, the CDC failed to articulate that reasoning or connect its finding—if it did so find—to the record. The Court may not offer those findings for the agency. The Court accepts the CDC's policy determination that requiring masks will limit COVID-19 transmission and will thus decrease the serious illnesses and death that COVID-19 occasions. But that finding by itself is not sufficient to establish good cause." Do you agree?

(4) ***Alternative Forms of a Good Cause Exception.*** Congress has sometimes developed agency-specific requirements for good cause rulemaking. For example, the IRS must issue any interim regulation as a proposed regulation as well, inviting notice and comment, and the interim regulation expires three years after its adoption. 26 U.S.C. § 7805(e). OSHA must also issue its Emergency Temporary Standards as proposed rules at the same time, and must promulgate a final rule within six months. Moreover, OSHA is not simply authorized but actually required to issue an ETS under certain circumstances; at the same time, those circumstances must be more serious than what is allowed under the APA's good cause standard. 29 U.S.C. § 655(c).

State administrative procedure acts have their own versions of good cause rulemaking. For example, California requires agencies issuing "emergency rules" to provide five calendar days for commenting, unless the "the emergency situation clearly poses such an immediate, serious harm that delaying action to allow public comment would be inconsistent with the public interest."[10] The Model State Administrative Procedure Act, which has been adopted in a number of states, provides that if "an agency finds that an imminent peril to the public health, safety, or welfare or the loss of federal funding for an agency program requires the immediate adoption of an emergency rule and publishes in a record its reasons for that finding, the agency, without prior notice or hearing or on any abbreviated notice and hearing that it finds practicable, may adopt an emergency rule" without notice and comment; the rule can be effective for only 180 days, renewable once for no longer than 180 days, although the agency may issue a new emergency rule if the agency finds that the original emergency still exists. Uniform Law Commission, Revised Model State Administrative Procedure Act, Revised § 309 (2010).

Should Congress amend the APA to impose a time limit on rules promulgated under the good cause exception? To require a mandatory, if brief, comment period? To limit the circumstances that satisfy good cause? The proposed Regulatory Accountability Act (p. 309) would generally require that direct final rules (see Note 6 above) have a 30-day comment period. For interim final rules (see Note 5 above), the proposed Act would generally require that they be published simultaneously as proposed rules with a 60-day comment period, and that the agency either rescind the interim rule, engage in the new kind of rulemaking procedure contemplated by the Act, or "take final action to adopt a final rule" within 180 days. S. 2278 (117th Cong.) (2021), § 3. What would be the costs and benefits of such changes?

## b. The Guidance Exception: Interpretive Rules and Policy Statements

***AMERICAN MINING CONGRESS v. MINE SAFETY AND HEALTH ADMINISTRATION***

***NATIONAL MINING ASSOCIATION v. McCARTHY***

***Notes on Doctrinal Tests and Judicial Review***

***Notes on the Exception's Scope, Desirability, Requirements, and Recommendations***

***Notes on Revising Interpretive Rules and Deference to Agency Interpretations***

*[T]his subsection does not apply . . . to interpretative rules, general statements of policy . . . .*

5 U.S.C. § 553(b)(A)

"Interpretative rules" (which today tend to be called "interpretive rules") and "general statements of policy" are collectively known as

[10] https://oal.ca.gov/regulations/emergency_regulations/Emergency_Regulation_Process/.

"guidance documents." These documents cover a wide range of materials promulgated by agencies that explain their views on an issue of policy by way of providing guidance rather than creating binding law. Guidance documents are also sometimes known as "nonlegislative rules," in contrast to regulations, frequently called "legislative rules," that have gone through notice and comment (or that the agency had good cause to issue without such process).

As the materials below indicate, this initial description belies much complexity and disagreement. How courts should determine whether an agency action is indeed an interpretive rule or statement of policy or, instead, an improperly promulgated binding legislative rule has generated a great deal of case law and far more scholarly commentary than any other § 553 exception. Trying to draw clean lines between interpretive rules and policy statements is also difficult. We begin with two leading cases that illustrate and to some extent try to resolve these difficulties. We then turn to Notes that address different dimensions of the controversies around guidance, both inside and outside courts.

## AMERICAN MINING CONGRESS v. MINE SAFETY AND HEALTH ADMINISTRATION

United States Court of Appeals for the District of Columbia (1993).
995 F.2d 1106.

■ WILLIAMS, CIRCUIT JUDGE.

This case presents a single issue: whether Program Policy Letters of the Mine Safety and Health Administration, stating the agency's position that certain x-ray readings qualify as "diagnose[s]" of lung disease within the meaning of agency reporting regulations, are interpretive rules under the Administrative Procedure Act. We hold that they are. . . .

The Federal Mine Safety and Health Act, 30 U.S.C. § 801 et seq., extensively regulates health and safety conditions in the nation's mines and empowers the Secretary of Labor to enforce the statute and relevant regulations. In addition, the Act requires "every operator of a . . . mine . . . [to] establish and maintain such records, make such reports, and provide such information, as the Secretary . . . may reasonably require from time to time to enable him to perform his functions." Id. at § 813(h). The Act makes a general grant of authority to the Secretary to issue "such regulations as . . . [he] deems appropriate to carry out" any of its provisions. Id. at § 957.

Pursuant to its statutory authority, the Mine Safety and Health Administration (acting on behalf of the Secretary of Labor) maintains regulations known as "Part 50" regulations, which cover the "Notification, Investigation, Reports and Records of Accidents, Injuries, Illnesses, Employment, and Coal Production in Mines." See 30 CFR Part 50. These were adopted via notice-and-comment rulemaking. Subpart C deals with the "Reporting of Accidents, Injuries, and Illnesses" and requires mine operators to report to the MSHA within ten days "each accident, occupational injury, or occupational illness" that occurs at a mine. Of central importance here, the regulation also says that whenever any of certain occupational illnesses are "diagnosed," the operator must similarly report the diagnosis within ten days. Among the occupational illnesses covered are "[s]ilicosis, asbestosis, coal worker's pneumoconiosis, and other pneumoconioses." An operator's failure to report may lead to citation and penalty.

As the statute and formal regulations contain ambiguities, the MSHA from time to time issues Program Policy Letters ("PPLs") intended to coordinate and convey agency policies, guidelines, and interpretations to agency employees and interested members of the public. One subject on which it has done so—apparently in response to inquiries from mine operators about whether certain x-ray results needed to be reported as "diagnos[es]"—has been the meaning of the term diagnosis for purposes of Part 50.

The first of the PPLs at issue here, PPL No. 91–III–2 (effective September 6, 1991), stated that any chest x-ray of a miner who had a history of exposure to pneumonoconiosis-causing dust that rated 1/0 or higher on the International Labor Office (ILO) classification system would be considered a "diagnosis that the x-rayed miner has silicosis or one of the other pneumonoconioses" for the purposes of the Part 50 reporting requirements. . . . The 1991 PPL also set up a procedure whereby, if a mine operator had a chest x-ray initially evaluated by a relatively unskilled reader, the operator could seek a reading by a more skilled one; if the latter rated the x-ray below 1/0, the MSHA would delete the "diagnosis" from its files. . . .

The second letter, PPL No. P92–III–2 (effective May 6, 1992), superseded the 1991 PPL but largely repeated its view about a Part 50 diagnosis. In addition, the May 1992 PPL stated the MSHA's position that mere diagnosis of an occupational disease or illness within the meaning of Part 50 did not automatically entitle a miner to benefits for disability or impairment under a workers' compensation scheme. The PPL also said that the MSHA did not intend for an operator's mandatory reporting of an x-ray reading to be equated with an admission of liability for the reported disease.

The final PPL under dispute, PPL No. P92–III–2 (effective August 1, 1992), replaced the May 1992 PPL and again restated the MSHA's basic view that a chest x-ray rating above 1/0 on the ILO scale constituted a "diagnosis" of [a] pneumoconiosis. The August 1992 PPL also modified the MSHA's position on additional readings. Specifically, when the first reader is not a "B" reader (i.e., one certified by the National Institute of Occupational Safety and Health to perform ILO ratings), and the operator seeks a reading from a "B" reader, the MSHA will stay enforcement for failure to report the first reading. If the "B" reader concurs with the initial determination that the x-ray should be scored a 1/0 or higher, the mine operator must report the "diagnosis." If the "B" reader scores the x-ray below 1/0, the MSHA will continue to stay enforcement if the operator gets a third reading, again from a "B" reader; the MSHA then will accept the majority opinion of the three readers.

The MSHA did not follow the notice and comment requirements of 5 U.S.C. § 553 in issuing any of the three PPLs. In defending its omission of notice and comment, the agency relies solely on the interpretive rule exemption of § 553(b)(3)(A).

We note parenthetically that the agency also neglected to publish any of the PPLs in the Federal Register, but distributed them to all mine operators and independent contractors with MSHA identification numbers, as well as to interested operator associations and trade unions. Compare 5 U.S.C. § 552(a)(1)(D) (requiring publication in the Federal Register of all "interpretations of general applicability") with id. at § 552(a)(2)(B) (requiring agencies to make available for public inspection and copying "those statements of policy and interpretations which have been adopted by the agency and are not published in the Federal Register"). Petitioners here make no issue of the failure to publish in the Federal Register. . . .

The distinction between those agency pronouncements subject to APA notice-and-comment requirements and those that are exempt has been aptly described as "enshrouded in considerable smog," . . . "fuzzy[,]" . . . "tenuous," "blurred" and "baffling"[ ].

Given the confusion, it makes some sense to go back to the origins of the distinction in the legislative history of the Administrative Procedure Act. Here the key document is the Attorney General's Manual on the Administrative Procedure Act (1947), which offers "the following working definitions":

> Substantive rules—rules, other than organizational or procedural under section 3(a)(1) and (2), issued by an agency pursuant to statutory authority and which implement the statute, as, for example, the proxy rules issued by the Securities and Exchange Commission pursuant to section 14 of the Securities Exchange Act of 1934 (15 U.S.C. 78n). Such rules have the force and effect of law.
>
> Interpretative rules—rules or statements issued by an agency to advise the public of the agency's construction of the statutes and rules which it administers. . . .
>
> General statements of policy—statements issued by an agency to advise the public prospectively of the manner in which the agency proposes to exercise a discretionary power.

Our own decisions have often used similar language, inquiring whether the disputed rule has "the force of law." We have said that a rule has such force only if Congress has delegated legislative power to the agency and if the agency intended to exercise that power in promulgating the rule.

On its face, the "intent to exercise" language may seem to lead only to more smog, but in fact there are a substantial number of instances where such "intent" can be found with some confidence. The first and clearest case is where, in the absence of a legislative rule by the agency, the legislative basis for agency enforcement would be inadequate. The example used by the Attorney General's Manual fits exactly—the SEC's proxy authority under § 14 of the Securities Exchange Act of 1934, 15 U.S.C. § 78n. Section 14(b), for example, forbids certain persons, "to give, or to refrain from giving a proxy" "in contravention of such rules and regulations as the Commission may prescribe." 15 U.S.C. § 78n(b). The statute itself forbids nothing except acts or omissions to be spelled out by the Commission in "rules or regulations." The present case is similar, as to Part 50 itself, in that § 813(h) merely requires an operator to maintain "such records . . . as the Secretary . . . may reasonably require from time to time." 30 U.S.C. § 813(h). Although the Secretary might conceivably create some "require[ments]" ad hoc, clearly some agency creation of a duty is a necessary predicate to any enforcement against an operator for failure to keep records. Analogous cases may exist in which an agency may offer a government benefit only after it formalizes the prerequisites.

Second, an agency seems likely to have intended a rule to be legislative if it has the rule published in the Code of Federal Regulations; 44 U.S.C. § 1510 limits publication in that code to rules "having general applicability and legal effect."

Third, [i]f a second rule repudiates or is irreconcilable with [a prior legislative rule], the second rule must be an amendment of the first; and, of course, an amendment to a legislative rule must itself be legislative. . . .

This focus on whether the agency needs to exercise legislative power (to provide a basis for enforcement actions or agency decisions conferring benefits) helps explain some distinctions that may, out of context, appear rather metaphysical. For example, in Fertilizer Institute [v. EPA, 935 F.2d 1303 (D.C. Cir. 1991)], we drew a distinction between instances where an agency merely "declare[s] its understanding of what a statute requires" (interpretive), and ones where an agency "go[es] beyond the text of a statute" (legislative). The difficulty with the distinction is that almost every rule may seem to do both. But if the dividing line is the necessity for agency legislative action, then a rule supplying that action will be legislative no matter how grounded in the agency's "understanding of what the statute requires," and an interpretation that spells out the scope of an agency's or regulated entity's pre-existing duty (such as EPA's interpretation of "release" in Fertilizer Institute), will be interpretive. . . .

Similarly, we have distinguished between cases where a rule is "based on specific statutory provisions" (interpretive), and where one is instead "based on an agency's power to exercise its judgment as to how best to implement a general statutory mandate" (legislative). A statute or legislative rule that actually establishes a duty or a right is likely to be relatively specific (and the agency's refinement will be interpretive), whereas an agency's authority to create rights and duties will typically be relatively broad (and the agency's actual establishment of rights and duties will be legislative). But the legislative or interpretive status of the agency rules turns not in some general sense on the narrowness or breadth of the statutory (or regulatory) term in question, but on the prior existence or non-existence of legal duties and rights.

Of course an agency may for reasons of its own choose explicitly to invoke its general legislating authority—perhaps, for example, out of concern that its proposed action might be invalid as an interpretation of some existing mandate. . . . In that event, even if a court believed that the agency had been unduly cautious about the legislative background, it would presumably treat the rule as an attempted exercise of legislative power.

In an occasional case we have appeared to stress whether the disputed rule is one with "binding effect"—"binding" in the sense that the rule does not " 'genuinely leave[ ] the agency . . . free to exercise discretion.' " State of Alaska v. DOT, 868 F.2d at 445 (quoting Community Nutrition Institute v. Young, 818 F.2d 943, 945–46 (D.C. Cir. 1987)). That inquiry arose in a quite different context, that of distinguishing policy statements, rather than interpretive rules, from legislative norms. . . . Indeed, the agency's theory in Community Nutrition was that its pronouncement had been a policy statement.

But while a good rule of thumb is that a norm is less likely to be a general policy statement when it purports (or, even better, has proven) to restrict agency discretion, restricting discretion tells one little about whether a rule is interpretive. See Attorney General's Manual, supra, at 30 n. 3 (discussing exercise of discretion only in definition of policy statements). Nor is there much explanatory power in any distinction that looks to the use of mandatory as opposed to permissive language. While an agency's decision to use "will" instead of "may" may be of use when drawing a line between policy statements and legislative rules, the endeavor miscarries in the interpretive/legislative rule context. Interpretation is a chameleon that takes its color from its context; therefore, an interpretation will use imperative language—or at least have imperative meaning—if the interpreted term is part of a command; it will use permissive language—or at least have a permissive meaning—if the interpreted term is in a permissive provision.

A non-legislative rule's capacity to have a binding effect is limited in practice by the fact that agency personnel at every level act under the shadow of judicial review. If they believe that courts may fault them for brushing aside the arguments of persons who contest the rule or statement, they are obviously far more likely to entertain those arguments. And, as failure to provide notice-and-comment rulemaking will usually mean that affected parties have had no prior formal opportunity to present their contentions, judicial review for want of reasoned decisionmaking is likely, in effect, to take place in review of specific agency actions implementing the rule. . . . As Donald Elliott has said, agency attentiveness to parties' arguments must come sooner or later. "As in the television commercial in which the automobile repairman intones ominously 'pay me now, or pay me later,' the agency has a choice. . . ." E. Donald Elliott, Reinventing Rulemaking, 41 Duke

L.J. 1490, 1491 (1992). Because the threat of judicial review provides a spur to the agency to pay attention to facts and arguments submitted in derogation of any rule not supported by notice and comment, even as late as the enforcement stage, any agency statement not subjected to notice-and-comment rulemaking will be more vulnerable to attack not only in court but also within the agency itself.

Not only does an agency have an incentive to entertain objections to an interpretive rule, but the ability to promulgate such rules, without notice and comment, does not appear more hazardous to affected parties than the likely alternative. Where a statute or legislative rule has created a legal basis for enforcement, an agency can simply let its interpretation evolve ad hoc in the process of enforcement or other applications (e.g., grants). The protection that Congress sought to secure by requiring notice and comment for legislative rules is not advanced by reading the exemption for "interpretive rule" so narrowly as to drive agencies into pure ad hocery—an ad hocery, moreover, that affords less notice, or less convenient notice, to affected parties.

Accordingly, insofar as our cases can be reconciled at all, we think it almost exclusively on the basis of whether the purported interpretive rule has "legal effect," which in turn is best ascertained by asking (1) whether in the absence of the rule there would not be an adequate legislative basis for enforcement action or other agency action to confer benefits or ensure the performance of duties, (2) whether the agency has published the rule in the Code of Federal Regulations, (3) whether the agency has explicitly invoked its general legislative authority, or (4) whether the rule effectively amends a prior legislative rule. If the answer to any of these questions is affirmative, we have a legislative, not an interpretive rule.

Here we conclude that the August 1992 PPL is an interpretive rule.[2] The Part 50 regulations themselves require the reporting of diagnoses of the specified diseases, so there is no legislative gap that required the PPL as a predicate to enforcement action. Nor did the agency purport to act legislatively, either by including the letter in the Code of Federal Regulations, or by invoking its general legislative authority under 30 U.S.C. § 811(a). The remaining possibility therefore is that the August 1992 PPL is a de facto amendment of prior legislative rules, namely the Part 50 regulations.

A rule does not, in this inquiry, become an amendment merely because it supplies crisper and more detailed lines than the authority being interpreted. If that were so, no rule could pass as an interpretation of a legislative rule unless it were confined to parroting the rule or replacing the original vagueness with another.

Although petitioners cite some definitions of "diagnosis" suggesting that with pneumoconiosis and silicosis, a diagnosis requires more than a

[2] [We have no need to resolve the parties' disagreement whether] the challenges as to the first two PPLs are moot . . . [b]ecause our ruling as to the third PPL will clearly cover the earlier two. . . .

chest x-ray . . . MSHA points to some administrative rules that make x-rays at the level specified here the basis for a finding of pneumoconiosis. See, e.g., 42 CFR § 37.7(a); 20 CFR § 410.428(a)(1). A finding of a disease is surely equivalent, in normal terminology, to a diagnosis, and thus the PPLs certainly offer no interpretation that repudiates or is irreconcilable with an existing legislative rule.

We stress that deciding whether an interpretation is an amendment of a legislative rule is different from deciding the substantive validity of that interpretation. An interpretive rule may be sufficiently within the language of a legislative rule to be a genuine interpretation and not an amendment, while at the same time being an incorrect interpretation of the agency's statutory authority. Cf. Fertilizer Institute, 935 F.2d at 1308 (petitioners' argument "confuses the question whether the agency is interpreting a statute with the question whether the agency is thoroughly, or properly, interpreting the statute"). Here, petitioners have made no attack on the PPLs' substantive validity. Nothing that we say upholding the agency's decision to act without notice and comment bars any such substantive claims.

Accordingly, the petitions for review are [d]ismissed.

## NATIONAL MINING ASSOCIATION v. McCARTHY

United States Court of Appeals for the District of Columbia (2014).
758 F.3d 243.

■ KAVANAUGH, CIRCUIT JUDGE.

The process of surface coal mining is straightforward. When a coal deposit lies close to the earth's surface, mining companies remove the topsoil and the rock above the coal. Once the coal is exposed, the companies extract it and relocate the removed earth.

Surface coal mining in the Appalachian region produces a good deal of America's domestic coal, which is an important source (along with natural gas and nuclear energy) for the electricity that lights American houses and businesses, and powers TVs and computers in American homes. But surface coal mining also leaves its mark on the environment. Among other effects, the process changes the nature of the land where the mining takes place, causing erosion and landslides.

In the 1972 Clean Water Act and the 1977 Surface Mining Control and Reclamation Act, Congress struck a balance between the need for coal on the one hand and the desire to mitigate surface coal mining's environmental effects on the other. Congress created an extensive permitting system for surface coal mining projects. To conduct a coal mining project, a business must obtain permits from the Department of Interior or a federally approved state permitting program. If the mining project would result in the discharge of soil or other pollutants into navigable waters, the mining project also requires two Clean Water Act permits. The first Clean Water Act permit (known as the Section 404 permit) must be obtained from the U.S. Army Corps of Engineers. The

Army Corps of Engineers permitting process also involves EPA, as EPA can deny the use of the sites selected as disposal sites for dredged or fill material. The second Clean Water Act permit (known as the Section 402 or NPDES permit) is issued by EPA or, as relevant here, EPA-approved state permitting authorities. The state permitting process likewise involves EPA, as States must submit a proposed permit to EPA for review, and EPA may object if the permit in EPA's view does not meet extant state water quality standards or other provisions of the Clean Water Act.

In June 2009, the Army Corps of Engineers and EPA adopted an Enhanced Coordination Process to facilitate their consideration of certain Clean Water Act permits. The Enhanced Coordination Process allows EPA to screen Section 404 mining permit applications submitted to the Corps. EPA then initiates discussions with the Corps on proposed mining projects that EPA considers likely to damage water bodies.

In 2011, EPA also promulgated a Final Guidance document relating to those Clean Water Act permits. Among other things, the Final Guidance recommends that States impose more stringent conditions for issuing permits under Section 402.

The States of West Virginia and later Kentucky, along with coal mining companies and trade associations—whom we will collectively refer to as plaintiffs—challenged the Enhanced Coordination Process and EPA's Final Guidance before the district court as exceeding EPA's authority under the Surface Mining Control and Reclamation Act and the Clean Water Act.

[The court rejected the plaintiffs' argument that the Enhanced Coordination Process exceeded the agency's statutory authority and upheld the creation of the Process without notice and comment under the APA's exception for rules of agency organization, procedure, or practice (p. 433). Before deciding whether the Final Guidance exceeded the agency's statutory authority, the court first had to decide whether it was a legislative rule or merely a general policy statement.]

We may review agency action under the APA only if it is "final." 5 U.S.C. § 704. One might think that an agency memo entitled "Final Guidance" would be final. But that would be wrong, at least under the sometimes-byzantine case law. An agency action is final only if it is *both* "the consummation of the agency's decisionmaking process" *and* a decision by which "rights or obligations have been determined" or from which "legal consequences will flow." Bennett v. Spear, 520 U.S. 154, 177–78 (1997). EPA concedes that the Final Guidance is the consummation of EPA's decisionmaking process. But EPA characterizes the Final Guidance as a general policy statement that has no "legal consequences." Therefore, according to EPA, we cannot review its legality at this time; EPA says that judicial review must wait until a permit applicant has had a permit denied and seeks review of that permit denial.

To analyze EPA's reviewability argument, we need to take a step back. The APA divides agency action, as relevant here, into three boxes:

legislative rules, interpretive rules, and general statements of policy. A lot can turn on which box an agency action falls into. In terms of reviewability, legislative rules and sometimes even interpretive rules may be subject to pre-enforcement judicial review, but general statements of policy are not. Legislative rules generally require notice and comment, but interpretive rules and general statements of policy do not. Legislative rules generally receive Chevron deference, but interpretive rules and general statements of policy often do not.

So given all of that, we need to know how to classify an agency action as a legislative rule, interpretive rule, or general statement of policy. That inquiry turns out to be quite difficult and confused. It should not be that way. Rather, given all of the consequences that flow, all relevant parties should instantly be able to tell whether an agency action is a legislative rule, an interpretive rule, or a general statement of policy—and thus immediately know the procedural and substantive requirements and consequences. An important continuing project for the Executive Branch, the courts, the administrative law bar, and the legal academy—and perhaps for Congress—will be to get the law into such a place of clarity and predictability.

For today, however, our far more modest task is to apply existing precedents on reviewability to EPA's Final Guidance. . . . As the parties frame it, the reviewability issue turns on one question: Is the Final Guidance a legislative rule or a general statement of policy?

To answer that question, we must know what makes something a legislative rule or general statement of policy. To simplify a bit, we offer the following overview: An agency action that purports to impose legally binding obligations or prohibitions on regulated parties—and that would be the basis for an enforcement action for violations of those obligations or requirements—is a legislative rule. An agency action that sets forth legally binding requirements for a private party to obtain a permit or license is a legislative rule. (As to interpretive rules, an agency action that merely interprets a prior statute or regulation, and does not itself purport to impose new obligations or prohibitions or requirements on regulated parties, is an interpretive rule.) An agency action that merely explains how the agency will enforce a statute or regulation—in other words, how it will exercise its broad enforcement discretion or permitting discretion under some extant statute or rule—is a general statement of policy.

But those general descriptions do not describe tidy categories and are often of little help in particular cases. So in distinguishing legislative rules from general statements of policy, our cases have focused on several factors.

The most important factor concerns the actual legal effect (or lack thereof) of the agency action in question on regulated entities. Here, that factor favors EPA. As a legal matter, the Final Guidance is meaningless. As EPA acknowledged at oral argument, "The Guidance has no legal impact." The Final Guidance does not tell regulated parties what they must do or may not do in order to avoid liability. The Final Guidance imposes no obligations or prohibitions on regulated entities. State permitting authorities are free to ignore it. The Final Guidance may not be the basis for an enforcement action against a regulated entity. Moreover, the Final Guidance may not be relied on by EPA as a defense in a proceeding challenging the denial of a permit. And the Final Guidance does not impose any requirements in order to obtain a permit or license. . . . [S]tate permitting authorities and permit applicants may ignore EPA's Final Guidance without facing any legal consequences.

Another factor in our case law concerns the agency's characterization of the guidance. The Final Guidance repeatedly states that it "does not impose legally binding requirements." The Final Guidance also notes that it is "not intended to direct the activities of any other Federal, State or local agency or to limit the exercise of their legal authority." On its face, the Final Guidance disclaims any intent to require anyone to do anything or to prohibit anyone from doing anything. To be sure, the Final Guidance may signal likely future permit denials by EPA; if so, those permit denials can be challenged at that time, and EPA will not be able to rely on the Final Guidance in defending a permit denial.

Plaintiffs counter that this Court has referred to similar agency caveats in guidance documents as "boilerplate." See Appalachian Power Co. v. EPA, 208 F.3d 1015, 1023 (D.C. Cir. 2000). In Appalachian Power, this Court found that an EPA guidance document was a legislative rule despite the guidance document's caveat denying its compulsory nature. But in doing so, we examined the document as a whole and noted that "the entire Guidance, from beginning to end—except the last paragraph—reads like a ukase. It commands, it requires, it orders, it dictates." Here, the caveats run throughout the document, and more to the point, the document is devoid of relevant commands.

Our cases also have looked to post-guidance events to determine whether the agency has applied the guidance as if it were binding on regulated parties. In many cases, of course, we will not yet know the answer to that question because the recently issued guidance will have been implemented in only a few instances. So we will get only an early snapshot. In any event, in this case, the sparse record before us does not suggest that the agency has applied the Final Guidance as if it were binding on regulated parties.

Plaintiffs nonetheless point to EPA's statutory role within the permitting programs and argue that permit applicants (and state permitting authorities) really have no choice when faced with EPA "recommendations" except to fold. As plaintiffs see it, EPA will not issue the permit unless its recommendations are followed. But while regulated parties may feel pressure to voluntarily conform their behavior because the writing is on the wall about what will be needed to obtain a permit, there has been no order compelling the regulated entity to do anything. States and permit applicants may ignore the Final Guidance without suffering any legal penalties or disabilities, and permit applicants ultimately may be able to obtain permits even if they do not meet the recommendations in the Final Guidance. And EPA agrees that the Final Guidance "has no legal impact" and that state permitting authorities are "free to ignore it."

To be clear, we reiterate what we have said before: "When the agency applies [a general statement of] policy in a particular situation, it must be prepared to support the policy just as if the policy statement had never been issued." Pacific Gas & Electric Co. v. Federal Power Commission, 506 F.2d 33, 38 (D.C. Cir. 1974).

We have considered all of plaintiffs' arguments for obtaining review now of the Final Guidance and find them unpersuasive under the current case law. The question is not whether judicial review will be available but rather whether judicial review is available *now*. The Final Guidance is not a final agency action subject to pre-enforcement review. We therefore do not decide plaintiffs' challenges to the legality of the Final Guidance at this time. . . .

## NOTES ON DOCTRINAL TESTS AND JUDICIAL REVIEW

(1) ***A Legislative Rule, an Interpretive Rule, or a General Statement of Policy?*** RONALD M. LEVIN, RULEMAKING AND THE GUIDANCE EXEMPTION, 70 Admin. L. Rev. 263, 265 (2018): "[T]he question of whether a supposedly informal pronouncement of an administrative agency is actually a rule that should have been adopted through notice-and-comment procedure may well be the single most frequently litigated and important issue of rulemaking procedure before the federal courts today." Given the importance of the issue, it may come as a surprise that—as then-Judge Kavanaugh writes in National Mining Association—"[t]hat inquiry turns out to be quite difficult and confused."

WILLIAM FUNK, in A PRIMER ON NONLEGISLATIVE RULES, 53 Admin. L. Rev. 1321, 1324–33 (2001), summarizes the caselaw as follows: "Interpretive rules, as the name suggests, interpret law. They may interpret statutes or other regulations. However, legislative rules can also interpret statutes, but they must go through notice-and-comment rulemaking, because they are intended to create legally binding norms, to make 'law.' Thus, the fact that a rule seems to 'interpret' a statute (or a regulation) does not by itself determine whether the rule is an interpretive rule or not. . . . [In order to identify an interpretive rule,] most courts have adopted the 'legally binding' test. In other words, if the questioned rule is legally binding, it cannot be an interpretive rule. The trouble with this test is that it really just restates the conclusion that only legislative rules can be 'legally binding.' Moreover, if the agency is defending a rule as an interpretive rule, it always claims that the rule is not legally binding. While a contemporaneous statement by the agency that the rule is intended to be interpretive and not legally binding may have some weight, it generally has not been found to be determinative. Instead, courts applying the 'legally binding' test have looked to a number of factors to assess whether the rule really is interpretive. These factors are: [1] Whether in the absence of the rule there would not be an adequate basis for enforcement action or other agency action to confer benefits or ensure the performance of duties. . . . [2] Whether the rule interprets a legal standard or whether it makes policy. . . . [3] Is the interpretive rule inconsistent with a prior rule? . . . [4] Whether the agency contemporaneously indicated that it was issuing an interpretive rule. . . . From time-to-time courts have identified some other factors to consider which, for the most part, have been subsequently questioned, although one may still see references to them. One of these factors involves publication of the rule in the C.F.R. . . . Another factor once deemed important, but currently not so considered, is whether the agency has in the past adopted a rule like the one under consideration after notice and comment. . . .

"General statements of policy, like interpretive rules, are rules, but rules that do not have binding legal power and consequently do not require notice-and-comment procedures. Like interpretive rules, general statements of policy are often difficult to distinguish from legislative rules. . . . There is one agreed upon test for whether a rule is a general statement of policy or a legislative rule: whether the rule creates a binding legal norm. This is the equivalent of the binding legal effect test used by most courts to distinguish between interpretive rules and legislative rules. However, application of the test is somewhat different. Courts look for evidence that the agency will not use the general statement of policy to decide future cases. It is allowed to influence future cases, but not to decide them. . . ." LEVIN, supra at 286, gives further content to the "binding legal norm" definition: "the message of the case law [on policy statements] is that a document can qualify for the exemption if the agency articulates it in non-binding terms and also refrains from treating it as dispositive in practice."

Why are there two lines of case law with two sets of doctrine? LEVIN, again, id. at 318–19: "Some commentators have suggested that the very fact that § 553(b)(A) mentions interpretive rules and policy statements separately is a sign that Congress expected them to be construed separately. This argument is not convincing, because the APA prescribes exactly the same legal principle for both—i.e., neither type of document is subject to notice-and-comment obligations. That would be an odd way of mandating different treatment. The inference that these commentators draw is further weakened by the fact that the APA also applies identically to these two types of guidance in every other context in which it mentions them." Do you think it would meaningfully improve the doctrine to attempt to distinguish only between legislative and nonlegislative rules as a unified category of "guidance"?

(2) ***Legally Binding Language.*** Language that appears to bind in a policy statement is a sign that a purported policy statement is actually a legislative rule that should have gone through notice-and-comment rulemaking. As then-Judge Kavanaugh explains in National Mining Association, contrasting the document at issue in that case (a policy statement) with the document at issue in Appalachian Power Co. v. EPA, 208 F.3d 1015 (D.C. Cir. 2000) (a legislative rule in disguise), the language in the former "is devoid of relevant commands" and "caveats run throughout the document," while the language in the latter "commands, it requires, it orders, it dictates."

By contrast, language that appears to bind in an interpretive rule may not indicate the same trouble. As Judge Williams explains in American Mining Congress, "Interpretation is a chameleon that takes its color from its context; therefore, an interpretation will use imperative language—or at least have imperative meaning—if the interpreted term is part of a command; it will use permissive language—or at least have a permissive meaning—if the interpreted term is in a permissive provision." An interpretive rule can thus be valid even if it clarifies preexisting vague statutory duties or has the effect of creating new duties. Courts assess whether the interpretation is "fairly encompassed" within the statute or regulation being construed. Air Transport Assn. v. Federal Aviation Admin., 291 F.3d 49, 55–56 (D.C. Cir. 2002). As a result, an agency may use an interpretive rule to promulgate guidance with more binding effect than a policy statement, "but only if the agency's position can be characterized as an 'interpretation' of a statute or legislative regulation rather than as an exercise of independent policymaking authority." JOHN F. MANNING, NONLEGISLATIVE RULES, 72 Geo. Wash. L. Rev. 893, 916 (2003).

Does this distinction seem sensible? Does it seem sustainable? Manning continues, at 926–27: "If filling up the details left blank by a silent or ambiguous statute or legislative rule necessarily entails policymaking or interstitial lawmaking, then the acceptability of an interpretative rule under current law must, in truth, turn on whether the agency has shifted too large a degree of policymaking from the notice-and-comment process to the less formal and often staff-driven process of adopting interpretative rules. If a nonlegislative rule involves policymaking writ small, the court calls it 'interpretation;' if such a rule reflects too much policymaking, the court deems it the exercise of delegated lawmaking authority. . . . [T]he resulting inquiry has an air of arbitrariness to it. How can one meaningfully assert that an agency has merely 'interpreted' the word 'diagnosed' when the 'interpretative rule' specifies the requisite numerical rating of an x-ray, the number of x-ray readers, and the precise method of resolving differences among the readers? . . . Ultimately, the D.C. Circuit's method of identifying procedurally invalid nonlegislative rules may necessitate reliance on little more than an I-know-it-when-I-see-it test."

(3) ***Legally Binding or Practically Binding?*** How should a court assess whether an agency or the regulated entity is sufficiently constrained to require notice-and-comment procedures? Should an approach focusing on the terms in the agency document at issue be preferred to an approach examining how the agency actually acts in practice or how the regulated community is incentivized to behave by the document?

Consider two contrasting approaches. In CENTER FOR AUTO SAFETY V. NATIONAL HIGHWAY TRAFFIC SAFETY ADMINISTRATION, 452 F.3d 798 (D.C. Cir. 2006), NHTSA developed "policy guidelines" outlining circumstances in which regional (as opposed to nationwide) recalls of vehicle equipment may be appropriate under the National Traffic and Motor Vehicle Safety Act. The policy was announced in response to manufacturers' own development of the regional recall practice, about which the agency, after a period of years, had developed concerns. Two public interest groups, the Center for Auto Safety and Public Citizen, sued, arguing that NHTSA's policy guidelines were, among other things, in violation of the APA because they were improperly issued without notice-and-comment rulemaking. In holding that the guidelines "are nothing more than general policy statements with no legal force," the court rejected the public interest groups' argument that "the agency has altered the legal regime with consequence both for automakers—who now allegedly conform their practices to the agency's standards—and for automobile consumers—who allegedly own 'defective' vehicles that do not qualify for recall remedies under the Act. They say that, for seven years, the agency and automakers have followed the standards announced in the guidelines. Appellants thus urge that, under a flexible and pragmatic approach to finality . . . the agency's 1998 policy guidelines must be seen to have legal consequences that confirm final agency action. The flaw in appellants' argument is that the 'consequences' to which they allude are practical, not legal. It may be that, to the extent that they actually prescribe anything, the agency's guidelines have been voluntarily followed by automakers and have become a de facto industry standard for how to conduct regional recalls. . . . But de facto compliance is not enough to establish that the guidelines have had *legal* consequences. . . . It may be that some car owners continue to be disadvantaged by automakers' regional recall practices. But automobile manufacturers adhered to these practices long before NHTSA issued the 1998 policy guidelines. The adverse effects flowing from the regional recall practices surely are not a *legal consequence* of the guidelines, not only because the effects preceded the guidelines, but, more importantly, because the agency has never codified the practices in binding regulations."

De facto consequences mattered more in CHAMBER OF COMMERCE V. DEP'T OF LABOR, 174 F.3d 206 (D.C. Cir. 1999). In a "policy statement" Directive, OSHA announced a plan to target the 12,500 most hazardous workplaces in the country for aggressive inspections, which was well beyond its capacity (due to the number of inspectors it had). Essential to the plan was the "carrot" of a promise to reduce greatly the chance a workplace would be inspected if the employer agreed to participate in a "Cooperative Compliance Program" that satisfied OSHA guidelines. In an earlier program in Maine, 99 percent of employers chose the carrot. For the D.C. Circuit, this was not an offer OSHA was entitled to make without first undertaking notice-and-comment rulemaking: "The Directive is . . . the practical equivalent of a rule that obliges an employer to comply or to suffer the consequences; the voluntary form of the rule is but a veil for the threat it obscures. . . . The Directive will affect employers' interests in the same way that a plainly substantive rule mandating a comprehensive safety program would affect their rights; that it so operates without having the force of law is therefore of little, if any, significance. In practical terms, the Directive places the burden of inspection upon those employers that fail to adopt a [comprehensive safety and health program], and will have a substantial impact upon all employers within its purview—including those that acquiesce in the agency's use of 'leverage' against them. Consequently, we conclude that the Directive is a substantive rather than a procedural rule."

For another version of this approach, see General Electric Co. v. EPA, 290 F.3d 377 (D.C. Cir. 2002), in which the court held that the agency's "PCB Risk Assessment Review Guidance Document" was a legislative rule that should have gone through notice and comment. Even though the document advised applicants that "some risk assessments may have components that require the use of non-standard . . . unique . . . or unconventional methods for estimating risk," the court concluded that the fact that the document also instructed applicants to assess toxicity in certain ways meant that "To the applicant reading the Guidance Document the message is clear: in reviewing applications the Agency will not be open to considering approaches other than those prescribed in the Document."

Which approach do you prefer? As a practical matter, agency guidance seems likely to have a substantial impact on how regulated parties behave, particularly statements suggesting how the agency will undertake enforcement. Might regulated parties find some value in guidance that curtails agency discretion, such as the kind of safe harbor policy at issue in Chamber of Commerce, letting them know that agency staff will accept certain approaches as compliance? Should such practical effects suffice to transform agency guidance into a legislative rule requiring use of notice-and-comment procedures? What room would then be left for § 553(b)(A)'s exception for policy statements and interpretive rules? Yet focusing only on legal effect may mean that "guidance" with major consequences in practice—impacts likely anticipated by the agencies involved—does not go through the public rulemaking procedures of § 553.

An additional issue, as Center for Auto Safety reveals, is that using legal effect as the sole measure of a legislative rule can heighten asymmetries between regulated entities and regulatory beneficiaries. The former can always refuse to adhere to the agency's policy statement and then challenge the agency's position on the merits if it brings an enforcement proceeding. Regulatory beneficiaries, however, may have few options for forcing review of an agency's policy views if regulated entities adhere in practice, particularly given some courts' insistence that policy statements are not "final agency action" and thus not subject to suit under the APA. See Nina A. Mendelson, Regulatory Beneficiaries and Informal Agency Policymaking, 92 Cornell L. Rev. 397, 420–24 (2007). Would it be a sufficient alternative for regulatory beneficiaries to file a petition for rulemaking with the agency (p. 446) requesting reconsideration of the guidance and then seek judicial review of any denial? See Levin, Rulemaking and the Guidance Exemption, supra, at 304.

Is a "practically binding" test consistent with Vermont Yankee v. NRDC, 435 U.S. 519, 524 (1978) (p. 312), which held that the APA "established the maximum procedural requirements which Congress was willing to have the courts impose upon agencies in conducting rulemaking procedures"? Cass Sunstein, in "Practically Binding": General Policy Statements and Notice-and-Comment Rulemaking, 68 Admin. L. Rev. 491, 508 (2016), argues no: "If an agency has issued a statement that does not have the force of law, but that is fixed and firm merely as a practical matter, the APA simply does not require it to use notice-and-comment." Levin, Rulemaking and the Guidance

Exemption, supra, at 313, argues yes: "Presumably, the reason most administrative law authorities have not reached this conclusion is that they regard the practical binding effect doctrine as an interpretation of the APA itself." What do you think?

(4) ***Legally Binding on Whom?*** Should binding effects on the agency be treated the same as binding effects on the public for purposes of identifying a purported policy statement as an improperly promulgated legislative rule? Some courts distinguish the two, finding problematic only those policy statements that bind members of the public. For example, in Splane v. West, 216 F.3d 1058, 1064 (Fed. Cir. 2000), the Federal Circuit upheld a VA rule as interpretive "because Petitioners do not suggest that [it] has any binding effect whatsoever outside the agency." See also Erringer v. Thompson, 371 F.3d 625, 631 (9th Cir. 2004) (finding no improper binding because "although the . . . criteria do bind the Medicare contractors [administering Medicare benefits under the supervision of CMS], our query is whether the rule has a binding effect on tribunals outside the agency").

In many cases, however, courts treat policy statements that bind agency actors as problematic. Consider TEXAS V. UNITED STATES, 809 F.3d 134 (5th Cir. 2015), affirmed by an equally divided court, 579 U.S. 547 (2016), in which the Fifth Circuit majority and dissent disagreed over how to interpret the evidence, but both opinions treated as dispositive the question of whether the agency had restrained its own discretion. The case involved the Obama Administration's executive action promulgated by the Department of Homeland Security called Deferred Action for Parents of Americans and Lawful Permanent Residents. Known as DAPA, this program was based on an earlier executive action called Deferred Action for Childhood Arrivals (DACA). DACA allowed teenagers and young adults who had been brought to United States as children without proper documentation (and who met other criteria) to be protected from removal and to work legally. (For more on DACA, see p. 1139.) DAPA provided similar benefits to parents without proper documentation who had children who were citizens or lawful permanent residents.

JUDGE SMITH, for the majority: "We evaluate two criteria to distinguish policy statements from substantive rules: whether the rule (1) imposes any rights and obligations and (2) genuinely leaves the agency and its decision-makers free to exercise discretion. There is some overlap in the analysis of those prongs because if a statement denies the decisionmaker discretion in the area of its coverage . . . then the statement is binding, and creates rights or obligations. While mindful but suspicious of the agency's own characterization, we . . . focus primarily on whether the rule has binding effect on agency discretion or severely restricts it. Although the DAPA Memo facially purports to confer discretion, the district court determined that '[n]othing about DAPA genuinely leaves the agency and its [employees] free to exercise discretion,' a factual finding that we review for clear error. That finding was partly informed by analysis of the implementation of DACA, the precursor to DAPA.

"Like the DAPA Memo, the DACA Memo instructed agencies to review applications on a case-by-case basis and exercise discretion, but the district court found that those statements were 'merely pretext' because only about 5% of the 723,000 applications accepted for evaluation had been denied, and despite a request by the district court, the government's counsel did not provide the number, if any, of requests that were denied [for discretionary reasons] even though the applicant met the DACA criteria.' . . . Instead of relying solely on the lack of evidence that any DACA application had been denied for discretionary reasons, the district court found pretext for additional reasons. It observed that 'the Operating Procedures for implementation of DACA contains nearly 150 pages of specific instructions for granting or denying deferred action to applicants' and that '[d]enials are recorded in a "check the box" standardized form, for which USCIS personnel are provided templates. Certain denials of DAPA must be sent to a supervisor for approval[, and] there is no option for granting DAPA to an individual who does not meet each criterion.' The finding was also based on the declaration from [Kenneth Palinkas, the president of the union representing the employees of the United States Citizenship and Immigration Services, who processed the DACA applications] that, as with DACA, the DAPA application process itself would preclude discretion: '[R]outing DAPA applications through service centers instead of field offices . . . created an application process that bypasses traditional in-person investigatory interviews with trained USCIS adjudications officers' and 'prevents officers from conducting case-by-case investigations, undermines officers' abilities to detect fraud and national-security risks, and ensures that applications will be rubber-stamped.'

"As the government points out, there was conflicting evidence on the degree to which DACA allowed for discretion. Donald Neufeld, the Associate Director for Service Center Operations for USCIS, declared that 'deferred action under DACA is a . . . case-specific process' that 'necessarily involves the exercise of the agency's discretion,' and he purported to identify several instances of discretionary denials. Although Neufeld stated that approximately 200,000 requests for additional evidence had been made upon receipt of DACA applications, the government does not know the number, if any, that related to discretionary factors rather than the objective criteria. Similarly, the government did not provide the number of cases that service-center officials referred to field offices for interviews. . . .

"Reviewing for clear error, we conclude that the states have established a substantial likelihood that DAPA would not genuinely leave the agency and its employees free to exercise discretion. . . ."

JUDGE KING, dissenting: "In determining whether the DAPA Memorandum constitutes a substantive rule, we must begin with the words of the Memorandum itself. The Memorandum states that it reflects 'new policies' and 'guidance for case-by-case use of deferred action.' . . . The Memorandum also repeatedly references (more than ten times) the discretionary, 'case-by-case' determinations to be made by agents in deciding whether to grant deferred action. . . . The discretionary nature of the DAPA Memorandum is further supported by the policy's substance. Although some of the Memorandum's criteria can be routinely applied, many will require agents to make discretionary judgments as to the application of the respective criteria to the facts of a particular case. For example, agents must determine whether an applicant 'pose[s] a danger to national security,' whether the applicant is 'a threat to . . . border security' or 'public safety,' and whether the applicant has 'significantly abused the visa or visa waiver programs.' Such criteria cannot be mechanically applied, but rather entail a degree of judgment; in other words, they are 'imprecise and discretionary—not exact and certain.' . . . Most strikingly, the last criterion contained in the DAPA Memorandum is entirely open-ended, stating that deferred action should be granted only if the applicant 'present[s] no other factors that, in the exercise of discretion, makes the grant of deferred action inappropriate.' The Memorandum does not elaborate on what such 'other factors' should be considered—leaving this analysis entirely to the judgment of the agents processing the applications. . . . [E]ven assuming DACA and DAPA applications are reviewed using the exact same administrative process, the district court had no basis for concluding that the results of that process—a process that would involve the application of markedly different, discretionary criteria—would be the same. . . .

"The district court also relied on a four-page declaration by Kenneth Palinkas, [USCIS employee union president], for the proposition that 'DACA applications are simply rubberstamped if the applicants meet the necessary criteria.' Yet lay witness conclusions are only competent evidence if rationally drawn from facts personally observed. See Fed.R.Evid. 701. Here, Palinkas's conclusion was supported only by the fact that DACA applications are routed to 'service centers instead of field offices,' and that 'USCIS officers in service centers . . . do not interview applicants'—a weak basis on which to conclude that DHS's representations (both to the public and to the courts) are 'merely pretext.' . . . Indeed, Palinkas's assertions are rebutted—and the step-by-step process for reviewing DACA applications is explained—in the detailed affidavit filed by Donald Neufeld, the head of those very USCIS service centers. Neufeld declares that the service centers 'are designed to adjudicate applications, petitions and requests' for various programs 'that have higher-volume caseloads.' Neufeld goes on to describe the 'multi-step, case-specific process' for reviewing DACA applications . . . .

"The majority accepts the district court's factual conclusions almost carte blanche. But clear error review is not a rubber stamp, and the litany of errors committed by the district court become readily apparent from a review of the record. The record before us, when read properly, shows that DAPA is merely a general statement of policy."

Taking the debate between the majority and the dissent on its face, which side do you think has the better argument? See also Texas v. United States, 50 F.4th 498, 524 (5th Cir. 2022) ("Viewing this evidence in the light most favorable to the defendants, we assume that agents do have discretion to reject applicants who meet the criteria. Even so, DACA is not a policy statement. 'The mere existence of some discretion is not sufficient, although it is necessary for a rule to be classified as a general statement of policy.' ").

At a more fundamental level, what do you make of the apparent agreement that limiting the agency's discretion is sufficient to turn a policy statement into a legislative rule? (See Texas v. EEOC, 933 F.3d 433 (5th Cir.

2019), for another example of the same court's holding that "whether the agency action binds the agency indicates whether legal consequences flow from that action.") To be sure, the two potential objects of binding effect—the public and the agency—may seem impossible to separate: mandatory constraints on the agency will constrain the public, who will know how the agency is going to react and guide their actions accordingly. But if guidance cannot "bind" the agency, then one of the main potential benefits of agency guidance—curtailing the discretion of lower-level officials and staff—is lost.

Consider, in that regard, the amicus brief filed by a group of administrative law scholars (including three current and former editors of this casebook) in support of the United States for the Supreme Court's review of Texas v. United States: "The Fifth Circuit adopted an erroneous legal standard in reaching the conclusion that the DAPA Memo was not a general statement of policy. First, the court mistakenly held that the DAPA Memo was subject to notice and comment because it did not 'genuinely leave the agency and its employees free to exercise discretion.'... Regardless of whether the underlying factual premise of this assertion is accurate, the fact that an agency pronouncement binds lower-level agency officials does not mean it is a legislative rule rather than a policy statement for APA purposes. Indeed, a central purpose of general policy statements is to permit the agency head to direct the implementation of agency policy by lower-level officials. As amici and other administrative law scholars have explained, it is critical for agency heads to be able to bind lower-level agency employees to ensure that the agency's policies are reliably carried out.... Requiring notice and comment every time an agency head promulgates binding internal guidance would fundamentally impair agency heads' ability to direct the agencies they are statutorily charged with overseeing. Discretion at the level of the agency head, not discretion by lower-level staff, is therefore the essential factor. Second, the Fifth Circuit erred to the extent it stated that a policy statement's 'substantial impact' on third parties is a basis to require notice and comment."[11] See also Note, Alexander Nabavi-Noori, Agency Control and Internally Binding Norms, 131 Yale L.J. 1062 (2022) ("[d]rawing on employee manuals, briefings in response to litigation, and interviews with agency insiders" to find "that officials at each agency believe that guidance must necessarily be capable of binding internal agency actors, particularly frontline officials, to effectuate consistent and transparent internal administration").

In a 2017 recommendation on policy statements, ACUS stressed that an "agency should not use a policy statement to create a standard binding on the public, that is, as a standard with which noncompliance may form an independent basis for action in matters that determine the rights and obligations of any member of the public." But ACUS also noted: "Although a policy statement should not bind an agency as a whole, it is sometimes appropriate for an agency, as an internal agency management matter, and particularly when guidance is used in connection with regulatory enforcement, to direct some of its employees to act in conformity with a policy

[11] https://www.scotusblog.com/wp-content/uploads/2016/03/15-674tsacAdminLaw Scholars.pdf.

statement. . . . For example, a policy statement could bind officials at one level of the agency hierarchy, with the caveat that officials at a higher level can authorize action that varies from the policy statement. Agency review should be available in cases in which frontline officials fail to follow policy statements in conformity with which they are properly directed to act." Recommendation 2017–5, Agency Guidance Through Policy Statements, 82 Fed. Reg. 61728, 61734 (Dec. 29, 2017). How would this recommendation apply to the facts and arguments in Texas v. United States?

(5) ***How Might Guidance Bind an Agency?*** We have thus far been discussing the question of binding legal effect as a binary. But administrative law recognizes another way in which guidance could be thought to be "binding," specifically, the more limited force accorded agency adjudicative precedent. Although agencies can rely on such precedent, they must remain open to counterarguments and be prepared to justify any changes in their approach. See John F. Manning, Nonlegislative Rules, 72 Geo. Wash. L. Rev. 893, 934–36 (2003); Peter L. Strauss, Publication Rules in the Rulemaking Spectrum: Assuring Proper Respect for an Essential Element, 53 Admin. L. Rev. 803, 829–33 (2001). Moreover, as noted above, the APA expressly states that, if published or made publicly available, guidance may be "cited as precedent." 5 U.S.C. § 552(a)(2). Does the precedential model justify allowing guidance to have some binding effect after all? Does it alleviate the concern that agencies can evade their procedural obligations under the APA? In answering these questions, does it matter that, under well-established doctrine, agencies have broad discretion to choose to set policy by rulemaking or by case-by-case adjudication (see p. 254)?

(6) ***Presidential Statements as Evidence That the Agency Document Is Binding.*** In Texas v. United States (p. 409), the district court and Fifth Circuit alike relied on statements by President Obama in evaluating whether the DAPA program was a policy statement or a binding but procedurally invalid legislative rule. Is this wise? (And do these statements affect your view on the merits?) Consider the following excerpts from opinions:

JUDGE HANEN, TEXAS V. UNITED STATES, 86 F.Supp.3d 591, 668: "What is perhaps most perplexing about the Defendants' claim that DAPA is merely 'guidance' is the President's own labeling of the program. In formally announcing DAPA to the nation for the first time, President Obama stated, 'I just took an action to change the law.' He then made a 'deal' with potential candidates of DAPA: 'if you have children who are American citizens . . . if you've taken responsibility, you've registered, undergone a background check, you're paying taxes, you've been here for five years, you've got roots in the community—*you're not going to be deported. . . . If you meet the criteria, you can come out of the shadows. . . .*' . . . [T]he President's description of the DHS Directive is that it changes the law."

JUDGE SMITH, TEXAS V. UNITED STATES, 809 F.3d 134, 185: "[A]s the district court recognized, the President explicitly stated that 'it was the failure of Congress to enact such a program that prompted him . . . to "change the law." ' At oral argument, and despite being given several opportunities, the attorney for the United States was unable to reconcile that remark with the position that the government now takes."

JUDGE KING, TEXAS V. UNITED STATES, dissenting, 809 F.3d at 208: "[T]here is no precedent for a court relying on such general pronouncements in determining a program's effect on the agency and on those being regulated. . . . More importantly, the statements relied upon by the district court are not inconsistent with the DAPA Memorandum's grant of discretion to agency decision makers. For example, the President's statement that those who 'meet the [DAPA] criteria . . . can come out of the shadows' does not suggest that applications will be rubberstamped, given that (as discussed above) those very criteria involve the exercise of discretion. Similarly, the President's suggestion that agents who do not follow DAPA's guidelines may suffer consequences does not support the conclusion that the Memorandum is pretextual. Rather, it supports the opposite conclusion—that the terms of the DAPA Memorandum, which incorporate case-by-case discretion, will be followed. An order to 'use your discretion' is not a substantive rule."

KATHERINE SHAW, in BEYOND THE BULLY PULPIT: PRESIDENTIAL SPEECH IN THE COURTS, 96 Tex. L. Rev. 71, 76 (2017), argues: "[B]inding Presidents to their claims and representations has an undeniable appeal. But for the most part it is a category error for a court to give legal effect to presidential statements whose goals are political storytelling, civic interpretation, persuasion, and mobilization—not the articulation of considered legal positions. The general principle of non-reliance, however, should give way under several circumstances: first, where the President clearly manifests an intent to enter the legal arena; second, where presidential speech touches on matters of foreign affairs; and third, where presidential speech supplies relevant evidence of government purpose, and government purpose is a component of an established legal test." Applying this framework, she concludes that the Texas courts' reliance on President Obama's statements in deciding that DAPA should have gone through notice and comment was inappropriate. How does her framework apply to guidance? Do you agree with her conclusion?

(7) ***Other Tests.*** Consider four alternative tests to the often-used binding effects standard. First, as LEVIN describes in RULEMAKING AND THE GUIDANCE EXEMPTION, supra, at 271–72, "As rulemaking grew in importance in the 1960s and 1970s, some courts and commentators took a skeptical view of the exemption and looked for ways to weaken it. Courts developed the thesis that an interpretive rule or policy statement should be subject to notice-and-comment if it had a substantial impact on members of the public. . . . The Supreme Court's decision in Vermont Yankee Nuclear Power Corp. v. Natural Resources Defense Council, Inc. [p. 312] . . . ruled out judicially invented procedures such as [requiring additional procedure if a document has a substantial impact on the public]." (The substantial impact test continues to be used in some courts to assess the exception for rules of agency organization, procedure, or practice under § 553(b)(A) (p. 433).)

Second, Levin himself proposes a new test, unifying the doctrine around policy statements and interpretive rules into a consolidated "guidance exemption." Id., at 349. "In this unified approach, the most important feature would be that the binding norms approach would be extended to interpretive rules. A secondary aspect would be that the American Mining factors, currently considered to apply only to interpretive rules, should also be applied to policy statements. . . . A consideration that should make the unification proposed here particularly attractive is that the dividing line between interpretive rules and policy statements has always been rather contrived. The current bifurcated approach to applying § 553(b)(A) presupposes that a given guidance document can be characterized as being one or the other. In reality, however, a particular document can contain both legal interpretations and policy positions; indeed, some individual determinations can easily be characterized as either law or policy."

Third, JUDGE KENNETH STARR, in a partially dissenting opinion in COMMUNITY NUTRITION INSTITUTE V. YOUNG, 818 F.2d 943, 951–52 (D.C. Cir. 1987), proposed a more radical alternative: "Inasmuch as our decisional law over the last decade avowedly reflects considerable uncertainty in discerning the line between agency pronouncements that are 'law' and those that are 'policy,' . . . it seems advisable to return to the pristine teaching of Pacific Gas [& Elec. Co. v. Fed. Power Comm'n, 506 F.2d 33 (D.C. Cir. 1974)]. In that case, this court articulated a rule which is clearly preferable to the present muddy state of the law. . . . We should reembrace our Pacific Gas test as the determinative factor in analyzing whether a particular pronouncement is legislative or interpretative in nature. If the pronouncement has the force of law in future proceedings, it is a legislative rule. Unless that critical feature is present, however, the agency statement should be considered to be a lower form of pronouncement, a 'non-law' as it were, or in APA terms an 'interpretative rule' or 'general statement of policy.' The correct measure of a pronouncement's force in subsequent proceedings is a practical one: must the agency merely show that the pronouncement has been violated or must the agency, if its hand is called, show that the pronouncement itself is justified in light of the underlying statute and the facts."

Fourth, several scholars have suggested an even more radical (in the sense of distance from current doctrine) and even simpler approach: "Rather than asking whether a rule is legislative to answer whether notice and comment procedures should have been used, courts should simply ask whether notice and comment procedures were used. If they were, the rule should be deemed legislative and binding if otherwise lawful. If they were not, the rule is nonlegislative. If the rule is nonlegislative, a party may challenge the validity of the rule in any subsequent enforcement proceeding." Jacob E. Gersen, Legislative Rules Revisited, 74 U. Chi. L. Rev. 1705, 1719 (2007); see also E. Donald Elliott, Re-Inventing Rulemaking, 41 Duke L.J. 1490, 1491–92 (1992); William Funk, When Is a "Rule" a Regulation? Marking a Clear Line Between Nonlegislative Rules and Legislative Rules, 54 Admin. L. Rev. 659, 663 (2002).

Do you prefer any of these alternatives? DAVID L. FRANKLIN criticizes the third and fourth suggestions in LEGISLATIVE RULES, NONLEGISLATIVE RULES, AND THE PERILS OF THE SHORT CUT, 120 Yale L.J. 276, 316 (2010). Franklin maintains that judicial scrutiny through review of enforcement actions often does not take place, as for example "when an agency pronouncement sets forth the conditions under which the agency will not take action" or "because many regulated entities choose . . . to comply with nonlegislative rules rather than incur [the costs of pre-enforcement challenges and] . . . the risks associated with noncompliance." He also contends that agencies lose little from a narrower interpretation of the § 553(b)(A) exception, as they have the ability to set policy on a case-by-case basis in adjudication. His "most fundamental" objection, however, is that "the public scrutiny that comes with notice and comment and the judicial scrutiny that comes with post-enforcement review are fundamentally dissimilar." According to Franklin, "notice and comment was designed to ensure an opportunity for interested members of the public to participate in the process of agency policymaking by making comments, raising objections, and suggesting alternatives. . . . While post-enforcement judicial review can mimic these features, it cannot fully recreate them because it occurs in the factual context of a particular enforcement action, before generalist judges, and at the behest of the regulated entity." Moreover, "robust public participation enhances the later process of judicial review by bringing to light technical issues that generalist judges might not otherwise spot, thereby enabling courts to engage in meaningful scrutiny of the resulting rules," and such scrutiny would not be "fully practicable without public input elicited by notice and comment procedures." Do you agree?

(8) ***Availability of Judicial Review.*** As then-Judge Kavanaugh explains in National Mining Association, "The question is not whether judicial review will be available but rather whether judicial review is available *now*." Only final agency actions are reviewable under the APA. Thus, if litigants want to challenge a guidance document on its face, as opposed to waiting until the agency attempts to rely on its underlying policy choices in a concrete instance such as an enforcement action or licensing decision, they must first establish that it is final. In turn, that requires an assessment of the two-prong test from Bennett v. Spear, 520 U.S. 154, 177–78 (1997) (p. 1543): (1) does the agency's action represent the "consummation of the agency's decisionmaking process," and (2) is it a decision by which "rights or obligations have been determined" or from which "legal consequences will flow"? The "ripeness" doctrine may also apply; the relevant test from Abbott Laboratories v. Gardner, 387 U.S. 136, 149 (1967) (p. 1545), instructs courts to "evaluate both the fitness of the issues for judicial decision and the hardship to the parties of withholding court consideration" at the time the lawsuit is brought.

We discuss the issues of finality and ripeness in Chapter IX, Section 2.c (p. 1539). For now, just observe that each of these hurdles poses a challenge for reviewability of guidance documents. Does an opinion letter from the Administrator of the Wage and Hour Division in the Department of Labor constitute "the consummation of the agency's decisionmaking process"? Compare National Automatic Laundry and Cleaning Council v. Shultz, 443 F.2d 689, 701 (D.C. Cir. 1971) (yes, treating "the ruling of a board or commission, or the head of an agency, as presumptively final") with Taylor-Callahan-Coleman Counties Dist. Adult Prob. Dep't v. Dole, 948 F.2d 953, 958–59 (5th Cir. 1991) (no, because the letters in question were only "threshold determinations" that "give specific entities the Administrator's opinion as to how governing regulations affect the probation officers described in the request" for the letters but "set out no definitive statement of DOL policy"). Is an EPA guidance document advising parties how particular programs work a decision that determines "rights or obligations" or from which "legal consequences will flow"? Compare POET Biorefining, LLC v. EPA, 970 F.3d 392, 405 (D.C. Cir. 2020) (yes: "The Guidance carries legal consequences because it withdraws some of the discretion the Pathways II Rule afforded EPA in evaluating the reliability of peer-reviewed methodologies") with National Mining Association, 758 F.3d at 252 (no: "The Final Guidance imposes no obligations or prohibitions on regulated entities"). Is such a guidance document ripe for review? See POET Biorefining, 970 F.3d at 403 (concluding that a challenge to one aspect of a guidance document is unripe but that a challenge to a different aspect of the same document is ripe). Finality and ripeness pose particular difficulties for policy statements as compared to interpretive rules, given the frequent conflation of the second prong of the finality test with the "binding" standard for policy statements, and given the greater likelihood that an interpretive rule involves a purely legal question for which further fact development is not likely to be useful to the court's evaluation on the merits.

Does the risk that guidance may not be subject to pre-enforcement judicial review counsel caution against a broad interpretation of agencies' ability to use this exception from notice-and-comment procedures? Do you think Congress should amend the APA to clarify that interpretive rules and policy statements constitute final agency action, clearing the way for judicial review? For a proposal to this effect, see William Funk, Legislating for Nonlegislative Rules, 56 Admin. L. Rev. 1023 (2004). Or are you convinced that, as Judge Williams seems to suggest in American Mining Congress, it is sufficient for the agency to "pay later" rather than to "pay now" in the timing of judicial review?

## NOTES ON THE EXCEPTION'S SCOPE, DESIRABILITY, REQUIREMENTS, AND RECOMMENDATIONS

(1) ***The Exception's Scope.*** The amount of agency guidance greatly exceeds the number of agency regulations adopted using notice-and-comment procedures. TODD D. RAKOFF, THE CHOICE BETWEEN FORMAL AND INFORMAL MODES OF ADMINISTRATIVE REGULATION, 52 Admin. L. Rev. 159, 159–70 (2000): "Since the 1960s . . . administrative law in the United States has exhausted the possibilities for developing an easily workable system of regulation within the procedural forms articulated in the APA. Agencies interested in pursuing their programs, rather than just slowing down, must search for ways to escape from [its] models of rulemaking and adjudication. We are in the midst of another round of discovering the virtues of informality. There is renewed interest in resolving particular disputes short of formal adjudication. Of greater general import, there is a trend toward setting regulatory policy in less formal ways. Techniques that previously were used as preliminaries to rulemaking or adjudication under the APA are now being used on the assumption that they will constitute the final

disposition." Rakoff provides data from FDA practice to support this point: "If we compare the mid-1990s with the late 1970s or early 1980s, we find that the number of FDA regulations adopted each year in accordance with the APA's rulemaking procedures declined by about fifty percent. By contrast, since the start of this decade there has been a striking increase in the number of FDA-issued documents intended to give guidance to the regulated industry but not adopted through public procedures. The rate per year for the 1990s is about four hundred percent greater than the rate for the 1980s." Id. at 168.

For a more visual take on the extent of guidance, consider Peter L. Strauss, Domesticating Guidance, 49 Envtl. L. 765, 768 & n.6 (2019): "In 1992, (1) formally adopted regulations of the Internal Revenue Service occup[ied] about a foot of library shelf space, but Revenue Rulings and other similar publications, closer to twenty feet; (2) the rules of the Federal Aviation Administration (FAA), two inches, but the corresponding technical guidance materials, well in excess of forty feet; (3) finally, Part 50 of the Nuclear Regulatory Commission's regulations on nuclear power plant safety, in the looseleaf edition, consume[d] three-sixteenths of an inch, while the supplemental technical guidance manuals and standard reactor plans in the same format stack[ed] up to nine and three-fourths inches."

Guidance continues to be "issued in a volume that dwarfs that of agency regulations." Id. An August 2022 survey conducted by the Competitive Enterprise Institute identified more than 107,000 guidance documents on agency websites.[12] In 2022, GAO reported that 23 of 24 agencies surveyed related that they had implemented "regulatory flexibilities" in response to the COVID-19 pandemic, and that 22 of them did so by issuing guidance "at least somewhat or much more often, with only one agency reporting that it did so about the same as before the pandemic." GAO, COVID-19: Agencies Increased Use of Some Regulatory Flexibilities and Are Taking Steps to Assess Them, GAO-22-105147 (June 2022), at 7–11.[13]

(2) ***Costs and Benefits of Agency Use of Guidance.*** How should the vast extent of guidance be assessed? Courts and commentators have considered a wide range of costs and benefits.

On one side is the concern that agencies will be able to exploit the exception to circumvent notice-and-comment requirements. The argument is that the exception risks "overregulation [and] bureaucratic overreaching" by evading the disciplining aspects of APA rulemaking. Robert A. Anthony, Interpretive Rules, Policy Statements, Guidances, Manuals, and the Like—Should Federal Agencies Use Them to Bind the Public?, 41 Duke L.J. 1311, 1373–74 (1992).

Another concern is that expanded use of interpretive rules and policy statements may undermine public participation in policymaking, particularly by regulatory beneficiaries who may lack opportunities to challenge agency policies adopted in the form of guidance. See Nina A. Mendelson, Regulatory Beneficiaries and Informal Agency Policymaking, 92

[12] https://cei.org/blog/federal-agency-guidance-document-inventory-tops-107000-entries/.

[13] https://www.gao.gov/assets/gao-22-105047.pdf.

Cornell L. Rev. 397 (2007). Even where regulatory beneficiaries are able to participate in judicial review of a guidance document during an enforcement challenge, the kinds of arguments raised at this point may well be different from the kinds of arguments that would have been raised during notice and comment; if they are the same kinds of arguments, notice and comment—and especially agency responses to such comments—could nonetheless help crystallize issues for judicial review, particularly for highly technical issues. See David L. Franklin, Legislative Rules, Nonlegislative Rules, and the Perils of the Short Cut, 120 Yale L.J. 276, 316–19 (2010).

Additionally, some worry that the ability to interpret its regulations without notice and comment may tempt an agency to be less precise than it should be in drafting legislative rules—"to promulgate mush," as one court put it. Paralyzed Veterans of Am. v. D.C. Arena L.P., 117 F.3d 579, 585 (D.C. Cir. 1997). Or as the D.C. Circuit put the point in APPALACHIAN POWER CO. V. EPA, 208 F.3d 1015 (D.C. Cir. 2000): "The phenomenon we see in this case is familiar. Congress passes a broadly worded statute. The agency follows with regulations containing broad language, open-ended phrases, ambiguous standards and the like. Then as years pass, the agency issues circulars or guidance or memoranda, explaining, interpreting, defining and often expanding the commands in the regulations. One guidance document may yield another and then another and so on. Several words in a regulation may spawn hundreds of pages of text as the agency offers more and more detail regarding what its regulations demand of regulated entities. Law is made, without notice and comment, without public participation, and without publication in the Federal Register or the Code of Federal Regulations. With the advent of the Internet, the agency does not need these official publications to ensure widespread circulation; it can inform those affected simply by posting its new guidance or memoranda or policy statement on its web site. An agency operating in this way gains a large advantage. 'It can issue or amend its real rules, i.e., its interpretative rules and policy statements, quickly and inexpensively without following any statutorily prescribed procedures.' Richard J. Pierce, Jr., Seven Ways to Deossify Agency Rulemaking, 47 Admin. L. Rev. 59, 85 (1995)."

A related reason to be concerned about enactment of vague regulations is that regulated entities may lack fair notice of their regulatory obligations. Such a concern appears to figure prominently in United States v. Chrysler Corp., 158 F.3d 1350 (D.C. Cir. 1998). Chrysler had refused to recall 91,000 cars that NHTSA asserted were not in compliance with its standards respecting seat belts. The relevant standard specified a test the belt assemblies must pass but did not specify the exact placement of the testing equipment. Chrysler's belt assemblies passed the test with the equipment in one position. NHTSA subsequently performed the test with the assemblies in another position that it interpreted its standard to require, and they failed that test. "[A] manufacturer cannot be found to be out of compliance with a standard if NHTSA has failed to give fair notice of what is required by the standard." That notice had not been given, and thus the court held Chrysler could not be required to recall the cars in question (see Notes on Access to Government Decisions, p. 706). (Significantly, however, the court based its requirement of fair notice on due process and implied that a clear interpretive rule setting forth the agency's view of the regulation would have sufficed.)

On the other side of the ledger are the important benefits that nonlegislative documents can bring to those affected by agency action and to agencies themselves. One such benefit is notifying the public of the agency's understanding of governing requirements and its regulatory responsibilities. Affected private persons can be expected to value advice on how the agency will approach the statutes and regulations it implements. Indeed, regulated entities sometimes petition agencies to issue such advice. In addition, the increasing formalization and burdens associated with notice-and-comment rulemaking may create a legitimate agency need for more flexible and less costly mechanisms to supplement its legislative rules as new issues and problems arise. See Nicholas R. Parrillo, Should the Public Get to Participate Before Federal Agencies Issue Guidance? An Empirical Study, 71 Admin. L. Rev. 57 (2019).

Equally important is the role of guidance in cabining the enforcement discretion of lower-level agency personnel. PETER L. STRAUSS, THE RULEMAKING CONTINUUM, 41 Duke L.J. 1463, 1482–83 (1992): "The usual interface between a member of the public and an agency does not involve the agency head, but a relatively low-level member of staff; . . . the postal clerk, . . . the welfare worker, the District Forester, the IRS examiner, the Food and Drug Administration (FDA) inspector, or the application desk officer . . . [all share] responsibility for initial processing of the public's business. . . . [T]he choice the public faces is between having the clerk apply his own interpretation of the agency's legislative rules, or having his decisions and actions further controlled by the agency's [guidance]. . . . [T]he affected public (especially the repeat players among them) will almost certainly prefer a state of affairs in which . . . instructions [for applying legislative rules] are publicly given and may be relied upon—that is, the lower-level bureaucrats are to follow them, and higher levels are to depart from them only with an explanation." The supervisory component to guidance may have a constitutional dimension as well. See Gillian E. Metzger, The Constitutional Duty to Supervise, 124 Yale L.J. 1836, 1919–20 (2015).

The availability of guidance also may have significance for the mode regulation takes. Contemporary writing about regulation often emphasizes the advantages of agencies setting performance standards rather than mandating specific mechanisms that regulated entities must employ. But the success of standards as a method of regulation may turn on an agency's ability to provide advice on what approaches will suffice to meet the governing standard. Such guidance is likely to prove particularly important for those who lack resources to devise their own methods for achieving compliance. If agencies are limited in their ability to indicate acceptable approaches to meeting a standard in common contexts, standards may carry too much uncertainty and too high transaction costs to be a workable mode of regulation. Although agencies could seek to address this problem by issuing their "guidance" through notice-and-comment proceedings, doing so may undermine the very flexibility in governing requirements that the agency sought in adopting a standard in the first place.

One of the key issues in assessing the costs and benefits of guidance is the question of agency intent: Are agencies purposely using the flexibility that guidance provides to expand their authority improperly, intentionally wielding power over regulated entities by creating vague policies that coerce compliance? See Anthony, supra, at 1315, suggesting yes. Recent empirical studies attempting to shed light on this question, however, have largely answered in the negative. In a study based on "interviews with 135 individuals, ranging from agency officials to industry attorneys and executives to NGO representatives . . . across eight distinct areas of regulation," NICHOLAS R. PARRILLO, in FEDERAL AGENCY GUIDANCE AND THE POWER TO BIND: AN EMPIRICAL STUDY OF AGENCIES AND INDUSTRIES, 36 Yale J. Reg. 165, 174–75 (2019), concludes: "[E]ven when regulated parties are strongly pressured, or when officials are inflexible, this is normally not because agency officials are engaged in some sort of bad-faith effort to coerce the public without the legally required APA procedures. Rather, the sources of pressure on regulated parties to follow guidance are mostly hard-wired into the structure of the regulatory scheme that Congress has imposed on them. These factors are far beyond the control of agency officials who issue or administer guidance; mitigating their coercive effect would demand fundamental reforms of the regulatory state ranging well beyond the topic of guidance. Further, even when agency officials themselves resist regulated parties' entreaties for flexibility on guidance, this is usually because of two factors that do not imply any bad faith. First, officials face competing pressures from other stakeholders to behave consistently and predictably—pressures that spring from rule-of-law values that agencies would be remiss to ignore. Second, officials are trapped by unconscious organizational tendencies in favor of rigidity, which the officials do not intend but also cannot redress without undertaking reforms that are costly in terms of resources and managerial energy. All in all, the problem with guidance is quite real, but it is largely an institutional problem that calls for an institutional-reform response (conditioned on available resources and hard choices about tradeoffs with other legal values). It is not a problem of bureaucratic bad faith that calls for accusation and blame."

Similarly, Connor Raso, in Agency Avoidance of Rulemaking Procedures, 67 Admin. L. Rev. 65, 108, 127 (2015), presenting the results of a study of litigation challenges to rules issued between 1995 and 2012 for failure to conduct notice and comment, concludes that agencies have little need to shift their policymaking to guidance in an effort to avoid the burdens of APA rulemaking, given how frequently courts approve their reliance on exceptions such as good cause. See also Connor N. Raso, Note, Strategic or Sincere? Analyzing Agency Use of Guidance Documents, 119 Yale L.J. 782, 815, 821–22 (2010) (drawing on data gathered under President George W. Bush's Executive Order 13422 imposing centralized review of "significant" guidance (p. 458) to conclude that "[a]gencies do not commonly use guidance to make important policy decisions outside of the notice and comment process, . . . [n]o evidence exists that agencies use nonsignificant guidance strategically[,] . . . [and] significant guidance is issued infrequently relative to legislative rulemaking").

As for the incentive "to promulgate mush" in anticipation of writing clarifying guidance down the road, consider JUSTICE KAGAN's observation in KISOR V. WILKIE, 139 S.Ct. 2400, 2421 (2019) (pp. 427 and 1391), for a plurality: "[T]he claim . . . does not survive an encounter with experience. No real evidence—indeed, scarcely an anecdote—backs up the assertion. . . . [E]ven the argument's theoretical allure dissipates upon reflection. For strong (almost surely stronger) incentives and pressures cut in the opposite direction. Regulators want their regulations to be effective, and clarity promotes compliance. Too, regulated parties often push for precision from an agency, so that they know what they can and cannot do. And ambiguities in rules pose risks to the long-run survival of agency policy." A recent study of rules promulgated between 1982 and 2016 concludes that agency behavior appeared to conform with Justice Kagan's predictions: "If anything, rule writing became more specific over time." Daniel E. Walters, The Self-Delegation False Alarm: Analyzing Auer Deference's Effects on Agency Rules, 119 Colum. L. Rev. 85, 92 (2019).

Reflecting on these debates, do you think the system for guidance is generally working satisfactorily, is in need of incremental reforms, or should be transformed and limited?

(3) ***APA Requirements Outside of Notice and Comment and Congressional Responses to Guidance.*** Although the APA exempts interpretive rules, general policy statements, and "rules of agency organization, procedure, or practice" from the notice-and-comment requirements of § 553, it has long subjected such measures to publication requirements. Under § 552(a)(1), agencies are required to publish such rules and policy statements in the Federal Register, and absent such publication or actual and timely notice, "a person may not in any manner be required to resort to, or be adversely affected by" these materials. Section 552(a)(2) further provides that "[a] final order, opinion, statement of policy, interpretation, or staff manual or instruction that affects a member of the public may be relied on, used, or cited as precedent by an agency against a party other than an agency only if—(i) . . . indexed and either made available or published . . . or (ii) the party has actual and timely notice of the terms thereof."

Many bills have been introduced in recent years to formalize guidance procedures more generally, but none have become law. See, for example, Guidance Clarity Act of 2021, S. 533 (117th Cong.) (2021); Guidance Out of Darkness Act of 2021, S. 628 (117th Cong.) (2021). Earlier versions of these Acts were also introduced. Congress has taken other more targeted steps on guidance. In several instances, it has directed specific agencies to take particular procedural steps with respect to their own guidance. See Fixing America's Surface Transportation Act, Pub. L. No. 114–94 § 5203 (Dec. 4, 2015) (directing the Federal Motor Carrier Safety Administration to publish, periodically review, and incorporate guidance into its regulations "to the extent practicable"); Food and Drug Administration Modernization Act of 1997, 21 U.S.C. § 371(h) (directing the FDA Secretary to, among other things, develop guidance "with public participation" and "ensure that employees of the Food and Drug Administration do not deviate from such guidances without appropriate justification and supervisory concurrence"). In at least one instance, it has directed an agency to promulgate guidance. See FAA Extension, Safety, and Security Act of 2016, Pub. L. No. 114–190 § 2207 (July 15, 2016) (directing the Administrator of the FAA to publish guidance within 90 days on applications for "unmanned aircraft systems . . . to facilitate emergency response situations"). It has also applied the Congressional Review Act (a fast-track procedure by which Congress can disapprove particular agency rules, effectively striking the rules down, see p. 897) to guidance, and in one instance it has used the Act to invalidate an agency's guidance document. See Pub. L. No. 115–172 (May 21, 2018) (disapproving a CFPB Bulletin).

(4) ***Presidential Responses to Guidance.*** Over the last two decades, the White House has imposed its own mandates on agency guidance (though these requirements do not create any private rights). In a BULLETIN FOR AGENCY GOOD GUIDANCE PRACTICES, 72 Fed. Reg. 3432 (Jan. 25, 2007), OMB imposed transparency, participation, and review requirements on "significant guidance documents," defined to largely track the definition of significant regulatory actions requiring OMB review under Executive Order 12866 (p. 1622). Each agency is supposed to maintain a current list of such guidance documents on its web site and develop "a means for the public to submit comments electronically . . . and to submit a request electronically for issuance, reconsideration, modification, or rescission of significant guidance documents . . . [N]o formal response by the agency is required." § III. For economically significant guidance, however—guidance that may reasonably be anticipated to have an annual impact of $100 million or more, or materially and adversely affect the economy—agencies are required to provide notice and an opportunity for comment prior to promulgation of the final guidance, and must also post on their websites a response to the comments received. § IV. The Bulletin also requires agencies to develop procedures to ensure that significant guidance documents are approved by senior agency officials, and agency employees are instructed not to deviate from this guidance without "appropriate justification and supervisory concurrence." § II.1. These procedures were based in part on good guidance procedures that the FDA initially developed in 1997 and that subsequently received congressional approval in the FDA Modernization Act of 1997, supra; see also Rakoff, supra, at 169–70 (describing the FDA's procedures). These requirements are still in effect.

As noted in Section 5.d below, OMB has long undertaken centralized review of agency rulemaking pursuant to executive orders. In the past, agency guidance documents were exempt from such review. In 2007, however, President Bush allowed OMB to demand consultation with an agency before the agency issues a significant guidance document, defined similarly to significant regulatory actions. See Exec. Order 13422, 72 Fed. Reg. 2703 (Jan. 18, 2007). Although President Obama revoked that Order, Exec. Order 13497, 74 Fed. Reg. 6113 (Jan. 30, 2009), OMB continued to review significant agency guidance documents during his Administration.

See Cass R. Sunstein, The Office of Information and Regulatory Affairs: Myths and Realities, 126 Harv. L. Rev. 1838, 1853–54 (2013).

The Trump Administration took a significantly more critical stance towards guidance documents. In 2017, then-Attorney General Jeff Sessions sent a memorandum to the Department of Justice's components discouraging the use of guidance.[14] Soon after issuing the memorandum, Sessions rescinded 25 departmental guidance documents (and months later withdrew another two dozen). Then, in 2019, President Trump issued two executive orders on guidance. The first, Executive Order 13891, Promoting the Rule of Law Through Improved Agency Guidance Documents, 84 Fed. Reg. 55235 (Oct. 9, 2019), required agencies to make their guidance documents available on their websites, established notice-and-comment procedures for issuing significant guidance (and submitting such documents for OIRA review), and allowed the public to petition agencies to modify or eliminate existing guidance. The second, Executive Order 13892, Promoting the Rule of Law Through Transparency and Fairness in Civil Administrative Enforcement and Adjudication, 84 Fed. Reg. 55239 (Oct. 9, 2019), prohibited agencies from relying on guidance alone to launch an enforcement action or adjudication.

President Biden revoked both Executive Orders on his first day in office, stating that agencies "must be equipped with the flexibility to use robust regulatory action to address national priorities" and that the revocation "empowers agencies to use appropriate regulatory tools to achieve these goals." Exec. Order No. 13992, 86 Fed. Reg. 7049 (Jan. 20, 2021). While President Trump's Executive Orders had ordered agencies to issue rules about guidance practices, President Biden's instructed agencies to rescind those rules. According to a GWU Regulatory Studies Center Analysis and accompanying Guidance Tracker, 31 agencies had issued such rules by the end of the Trump Administration, and more than twenty had rescinded them within the first year of the Biden Administration. Camille Chambers, Agencies Are Rescinding Guidance Regulations at a Rapid Pace (July 7, 2021).[15] In a separate memorandum discussed further in Section 5.d below, Modernizing Regulatory Review, President Biden directed OMB to "determine an appropriate approach with respect to the review of agency guidance." 86 Fed. Reg. 7223 (Jan. 26, 2021). As of November 2022, OMB had not announced such an approach, though its 2007 Bulletin remains in effect. For recommendations to the Biden Administration on how to use and improve OIRA review of guidance documents, see Rachel Augustine Potter, Improving White House Review of Agency Guidance (July 8, 2021).[16] Additionally, Attorney General Garland issued a memorandum in July 2021 rescinding the 2017 Sessions directive to DOJ department heads. The new

---

[14] https://www.justice.gov/opa/press-release/file/1012271/download.

[15] https://regulatorystudies.columbian.gwu.edu/agencies-are-rescinding-guidance-regulations-rapid-pace. The number had not grown by summer 2022. See Clyde Wayne Crews, Competitive Enterprise Inst., Stomping FROGS: An Updated Inventory of Biden's Elimination of Trump-Era Final Rules on Guidance Document Procedures (July 26, 2022), https://cei.org/blog/stomping-frogs-an-updated-inventory-of-bidens-elimination-of-trump-era-final-rules-on-guidance-document-procedures/.

[16] https://www.brookings.edu/blog/up-front/2021/07/08/improving-white-house-review-of-agency-guidance/.

memorandum sets out principles for issuance of DOJ guidance documents, recognizing they can be a "tool to promote transparency, fairness, and efficiency."[17]

(5) ***"Institutional Pronouncements" from the ABA and ACUS.*** RONALD M. LEVIN, RULEMAKING AND THE GUIDANCE EXEMPTION, 70 Admin. L. Rev. 263, 277–78 (2018): "One consequence of the policy debate about guidance documents that began gathering steam in the 1990s has been a series of statements on that subject adopted during the past two decades or so by nonjudicial institutions. I refer to this set of actions as 'institutional pronouncements.' . . . [These pronouncements] deserve serious attention because they come from consensus-oriented, broadly representative entities. Collectively, they bespeak a high degree of agreement within the administrative law community about proper and improper uses of guidance documents. . . . All the pronouncements evince apprehensions about the possibility that an agency may improperly attempt to use a guidance document in a binding fashion. On the other hand, all of them also evince an effort to respond to that possibility in a measured manner, so that the legitimate advantages of guidance documents in the administrative process can be maintained." Among the pronouncements Levin describes are a 1992 recommendation from ACUS and a 1993 recommendation from the ABA. Both urged agencies to provide the public a meaningful opportunity to challenge such statements. ACUS has made additional recommendations for agency best practices on guidance with regularity in recent years, all available on its website.[18]

## NOTES ON REVISING INTERPRETIVE RULES AND DEFERENCE TO AGENCY INTERPRETATIONS

(1) ***The D.C. Circuit's One-Bite Rule and Its Rejection by the Supreme Court.*** For about a quarter century, the D.C. Circuit had a prohibition on using an interpretive rule to revise an earlier interpretive rule. Often referred to as the "one-bite rule" and traced to Paralyzed Veterans of America v. D.C. Arena L.P., 117 F.3d 579, 586 (D.C. Cir 1997), this prohibition was based on the view that once an agency has issued guidance giving a regulation a definitive interpretation, subsequent revision of that interpretation in effect amends the regulation, requiring § 553 procedures. In ALASKA PROFESSIONAL HUNTERS ASS'N V. FAA, 177 F.3d 1030 (D.C. Cir. 1999), for example, the FAA issued a "Notice to Operators" that brought professional "hunting and fishing guides" in Alaska within certain FAA flight regulations. The FAA's Alaskan Region had interpreted the regulations as not applying to the guides and provided official advice to that effect for several decades. The D.C. Circuit held that the FAA was required to use notice-and-comment rulemaking to now apply the regulations to these Alaskan guides.

Is a one-bite rule an appropriate response to concerns about evasion of the notice-and-comment process? UNITED STATES V. MAGNESIUM CORP. OF

[17] https://www.justice.gov/opa/page/file/1408606/download.

[18] https://www.acus.gov/guidance.

AMERICA, 616 F.3d 1129, 1139–41 (10th Cir. 2010): "The implicit reasoning appears to be this: if an agency amends its interpretation of a rule, it is effectively 'amending [the] rule' itself, 5 U.S.C. § 551(5), and the APA by its own terms defines this amendment as a kind of rulemaking, something the agency may not accomplish without notice and comment procedures." Noting that a substantial circuit split existed on the propriety of the one-bite rule, the Tenth Circuit concluded it did not need to choose a side in the debate, because "[b]y its terms the Alaska Hunters doctrine applies only to *definitive* regulatory interpretations; even under Alaska Hunters an agency remains free to disavow and amend a *tentative* interpretation of one of its rules without notice and comment."

In 2015, the Supreme Court rejected the D.C. Circuit's one-bite rule in PEREZ V. MORTGAGE BANKERS ASS'N, 575 U.S. 92: "The Paralyzed Veterans doctrine is contrary to the clear text of the APA's rulemaking provisions, and it improperly imposes on agencies an obligation beyond the 'maximum procedural requirements' specified in the APA, Vermont Yankee Nuclear Power Corp. v. Natural Resources Defense Council, Inc., 435 U.S. 519, 524 (1978) [p. 312]. The text of the APA answers the question presented. Section 4 of the APA provides that 'notice of proposed rule making shall be published in the Federal Register.' 5 U.S.C. § 553(b). When such notice is required by the APA, 'the agency shall give interested persons an opportunity to participate in the rule making.' § 553(c). But § 4 further states that unless 'notice or hearing is required by statute,' the Act's notice-and-comment requirement 'does not apply . . . to interpretative rules.' § 553(b)(A). This exemption of interpretive rules from the notice-and-comment process is categorical, and it is fatal to the rule announced in Paralyzed Veterans. . . .

"The Paralyzed Veterans doctrine creates just such a judge-made procedural right: the right to notice and an opportunity to comment when an agency changes its interpretation of one of the regulations it enforces. That requirement may be wise policy. Or it may not. Regardless, imposing such an obligation is the responsibility of Congress or the administrative agencies, not the courts. We trust that Congress weighed the costs and benefits of placing more rigorous procedural restrictions on the issuance of interpretive rules. In the end, Congress decided to adopt standards that permit agencies to promulgate freely such rules—whether or not they are consistent with earlier interpretations. That the D.C. Circuit would have struck the balance differently does not permit that court or this one to overturn Congress' contrary judgment."

Again mimicking the Vermont Yankee decision, Mortgage Bankers underscored that those objecting to a new agency interpretation can still challenge the agency's change in view as arbitrary and capricious—in other words, even if the agency's action procedurally conforms to the APA, a substantive challenge to an agency's reasoning remains available. Do you think arbitrary-and-capricious review is the appropriate frame through which to address an agency's alleged excessive use of a procedural exemption? As the Court makes clear, under arbitrary-and-capricious review, an agency will have to explain and justify its decision to change a governing interpretation (see FCC v. Fox Television Stations, Inc., 556 U.S. 502 (2009), p. 1160). Given Mortgage Bankers' holding on the scope of § 553(b), will an agency also have to explain and justify a decision to issue its new interpretation outside of notice-and-comment procedures, at least beyond stating that such procedures are not required by the APA?

(2) ***The Supreme Court, Deference, and the Distinction Between Legislative and Interpretive Rules.*** In KISOR V. WILKIE, 139 S.Ct. 2400 (2019), the Supreme Court upheld judicial deference (known as Auer deference) for interpretive rules under certain conditions. The case is more extensively discussed at p. 1391. In her plurality opinion, JUSTICE KAGAN discussed § 553's requirements: "Kisor next claims that Auer circumvents the APA's rulemaking requirements. . . . But this Court rejected the identical argument just a few years ago, and for good reason. In Mortgage Bankers [p. 426], we held that interpretive rules, even when given Auer deference, do not have the force of law. An interpretive rule itself never forms 'the basis for an enforcement action'—because, as just noted, such a rule does not impose any 'legally binding requirements' on private parties. An enforcement action must instead rely on a legislative rule, which (to be valid) must go through notice and comment. And in all the ways discussed above, the meaning of a legislative rule remains in the hands of courts, even if they sometimes divine that meaning by looking to the agency's interpretation. Courts first decide whether the rule is clear; if it is not, whether the agency's reading falls within its zone of ambiguity; and even if the reading does so, whether it should receive deference. In short, courts retain the final authority to approve—or not—the agency's reading of a notice-and-comment rule."

JUSTICE GORSUCH, in dissent, also addressed § 553: "Auer is also incompatible with the APA's instructions in § 553. That provision requires agencies to follow notice-and-comment procedures when issuing or amending legally binding regulations (what the APA calls 'substantive rules'), but not when offering mere interpretations of those regulations. . . . Auer effectively nullifies the distinction Congress drew here. Under Auer, courts must treat as 'controlling' not only an agency's duly promulgated rules but also its mere interpretations—even ones that appear only in a legal brief, press release, or guidance document issued without affording the public advance notice or a chance to comment. For all practical purposes, 'the new interpretation might as well be a new regulation.' Auer thus obliterates a distinction Congress thought vital and supplies agencies with a shortcut around the APA's required procedures for issuing and amending substantive rules that bind the public with the full force and effect of law. . . .

"[Justice Kagan] replies that affording Auer deference to an agency's interpretation of its own rules never offends the APA because the agency's interpretation lacks 'the force of law' associated with substantive rules. Agency interpretations lack this force, we are told, because a court always retains the power to decide at least whether the interpretation is entitled to deference. But this argument rests on an implausibly narrow understanding of what it means for an agency action to bear the force of law. Under Justice Kagan's logic, even a binding substantive rule would lack the force of law because a court retains the power to decide whether the rule is arbitrary and capricious and thus invalid under the APA. But no one believes that. While an agency interpretation, just like a substantive rule, 'must meet certain conditions before it gets deference,' 'once it does so [Auer makes it] every bit as binding as a substantive rule.' To suggest that Auer does not make an agency's interpretive guidance 'binding o[n] anyone' is linguistic hocus-pocus." What do you think?

### c. The Other Exceptions

*JAMES V. HURSON ASSOCIATES, INC. v. GLICKMAN*

*NATIONAL WILDLIFE FEDERATION v. SNOW*

*Notes on Exceptions for Internal Agency Matters, Proprietary Matters, and Military and Foreign Affairs*

*This section applies, according to the provisions thereof, except to the extent that there is involved—*

*(1) a military or foreign affairs function of the United States; or*

*(2) a matter relating to agency management or personnel or to public property, loans, grants, benefits, or contracts.*

5 U.S.C. § 553(a)

*Except when notice or hearing is required by statute, this subsection does not apply—(A) to . . . rules of agency organization, procedure, or practice. . . .*

5 U.S.C. § 553(b)

The remaining exceptions cover a wide variety of matters. We address two in lead cases and discuss the rest in the Notes that follow. With what trade-offs do courts grapple as they apply these exceptions? Are the cases consistent? To what extent ought these exceptions be modified?

## JAMES V. HURSON ASSOCIATES, INC. v. GLICKMAN

United States Court of Appeals for the District of Columbia (2000).
229 F.3d 277.

■ SENTELLE, CIRCUIT JUDGE.

James V. Hurson Associates appeals from a District Court judgment upholding a United States Department of Agriculture ("USDA") rule that controls the manner in which the agency receives requests for the approval of food labeling. Appellant contends[, among other things,] that the USDA violated the Administrative Procedure Act . . . by promulgating that rule without first engaging in notice-and-comment rulemaking. . . . We hold that the District Court properly concluded that USDA was not required to engage in notice-and-comment rulemaking, since its new rule falls within the APA's procedural-rules exception. . . .

The USDA's Food Safety Inspection Service ("FSIS") is charged with reviewing the labels affixed to certain commercial food products to ensure that they are truthful, not misleading, and otherwise comply with relevant regulations. Until recently, a commercial food producer could seek approval of a proposed label in several ways: by mailing its application, by personally visiting the FSIS, or by hiring courier/expediter firms whose employees would meet with FSIS representatives during office hours. The latter method, colloquially known as "face-to-face," enabled producers to secure instant approval of their labels, whereas other methods could take days or even weeks. [After] the USDA announced its intention to do away with [face-to-face,] . . . Hurson, a courier/expediter firm the livelihood of which was threatened by the USDA's new rule, alleged . . . that USDA had violated the APA by [doing so] without engaging in notice-and-comment rulemaking. . . .

Although federal agencies ordinarily must provide the public with notice of a proposed rule and the opportunity to submit comments on it, the APA makes an exception for, among others, "rules of agency organization, procedure, or practice." § 553(b)(3)(A). This Court has stressed that the "critical feature" of a rule that satisfies the so-called "procedural exception is that it covers agency actions that do not themselves alter the rights or interests of parties, although it may alter the manner in which the parties present themselves or their viewpoints to the agency." JEM Broad. Co. v. FCC, 22 F.3d 320, 326 (D.C. Cir. 1994).

Hence in JEM, we concluded that the Federal Communication Commission's new "hard look" rules—under which the Commission summarily would dismiss any flawed license application without allowing the applicant to correct its error, see id. at 322–23—were procedural ones. "The critical fact here," we emphasized, "is that the 'hard look' rules did not change the *substantive standards* by which the FCC evaluates license applications, e.g., financial qualifications, proposed programming, and transmitter location." Id. at 327. That the hard-look rules employed the same substantive criteria as their predecessors, we concluded, was "fatal to JEM's claim." Id.

The USDA's decision to eliminate face-to-face review is the very sort of procedural measure the JEM Court had in mind. . . . The agency's abolition of face-to-face did not alter the substantive criteria by which it would approve or deny proposed labels; it simply changed the procedures it would follow in applying those substantive standards.

Because the rule is procedural on its face . . . appellant attempts to characterize it as *effectively* substantive by pointing to its putatively severe consequences and its origins in a "substantive value judgment." Neither effort is persuasive.

Hurson introduces some evidence that the elimination of face-to-face approvals will burden food producers. (It also introduces evidence suggesting that the rule would devastate the courier/expediter industry, but the burden to couriers/expediters—which are not regulated parties under the rules—is irrelevant.) Hurson repeatedly argues that food producers need to have their labels approved in "minutes and hours," not, as it suspects will be the case under the USDA's new rule, after waiting for "days, weeks, even months." It also cites the 180 objections to the new rule lodged by entities representing the food industry, which, it proposes, illustrate that food processors regard speedy approval as "an essential cog in their output mechanism."

Hurson's allegation that the elimination of face-to-face will produce a significant burden may or may not be empirically true. As an initial matter, we question whether the food processing industry truly regards the USDA's new rule as especially burdensome. After all, this challenge is brought not by a food processor, but by a courier/expediter firm. . . .

But even if the USDA's elimination of face-to-face *did* impose a substantial burden on food processors, that burden would not convert the rule into a substantive one that triggers the APA's notice-and-comment requirement. Appellant has cited no case in which this Court has required notice-and-comment rulemaking for an especially burdensome procedural rule. Nor could it, for we recognize that "the impact of a rule has no bearing on whether it is legislative or interpretative. . . ." American Postal Workers Union v. United States Postal Serv., 707 F.2d 548, 560 (D.C. Cir. 1983); accord Cavais v. Egger, 690 F.2d 234, 237 (D.C. Cir. 1982) ("Simply because agency action has substantial impact does not mean it is subject to notice and comment if it is otherwise expressly exempt under the APA."). Indeed, "interpretative rules may have a substantial impact on the rights of individuals." American Postal Workers, 707 F.2d at 560. The same is true of procedural rules. We conclude, therefore, that an otherwise-procedural rule does not become a substantive one, for notice-and-comment purposes, simply because it imposes a burden on regulated parties.

Hurson's second argument—that notice-and-comment rulemaking is required given the rule's origin in a "substantive value judgment"—is equally unavailing. The USDA's decision to eliminate face-to-face does, as Hurson alleges, encode the substantive value judgment that the new label-approval procedures will more readily promote its already-existing goals of fairness and efficiency. But the fact that the agency's decision was based on a value judgment about procedural efficiency does not convert the resulting rule into a substantive one. *All* decisions, to the extent that they derive from reasons, necessarily are based on the value judgment that the chosen option is better, in some relevant way, than its alternatives. We have, therefore, consistently recognized that agency housekeeping rules often embody a judgment about what mechanics and processes are most efficient. This does not convert a procedural rule into a substantive one.

Finally, Hurson proposes that this Court is bound by our prior holding in National Association of Home Health Agencies v. Schweiker, 690 F.2d 932 (D.C. Cir. 1982), to conclude that the USDA could eliminate face-to-face only through notice-and-comment rulemaking. In that case, we found that the Department of Health and Human Services was required to engage in notice-and-comment rulemaking when it eliminated Medicare claimants' right to seek reimbursement directly from the agency's Secretary, and now required them to submit their claims to regional intermediaries. Home Health Agencies is distinguishable. Unlike the rule challenged in that case, which both eliminated claimants' access to the HHS Secretary and transferred his authority to issue reimbursements to other agency employees, the USDA's rule does not change the agency personnel who will be responsible for reviewing proposed labels. . . . The crucial element of Home Health Agencies is not whether one has "face time" with agency staff members, but which staffers have decisionmaking authority. Home Health Agencies is thus consistent with our holding here, for the same USDA staffers who reviewed labels under face-to-face continue to review labels after that procedure's abolition.

Because the USDA's decision to eliminate face-to-face label review was a "rule [ ] of agency organization, procedure, or practice," 5 U.S.C. § 553(b)(3)(A), we hold that the agency was not required to do so through notice-and-comment rulemaking. . . .

## NATIONAL WILDLIFE FEDERATION v. SNOW

United States Court of Appeals for the District of Columbia (1976).
561 F.2d 227.

■ LEVENTHAL, CIRCUIT JUDGE.

Appellant National Wildlife Federation brought this case to challenge two Federal Highway Administration [FHWA] regulations governing the number and timing of public hearings on federally assisted highways. Appellant alleged that the regulations should have been promulgated in accordance with the notice and comment rulemaking requirements of the Administrative Procedure Act (APA). The District Court held that the challenged regulations were exempt from those requirements. We affirm that ruling. . . .

The applicability of notice and comment requirements to promulgation of the regulations involved in this case turns on the scope of the exemption contained in 5 U.S.C. § 553(a). . . . The FHWA considered both of the regulations challenged in this appeal as relating to grants, and therefore within the § 553(a)(2) exemption from notice and comment rulemaking. The issue is one of first impression.

The regulations at issue are in form procedural ones governing the timing and number of public hearings to be held before building a federal-aid highway [under the Federal Aid Highway Act]. [The challenged regulations made] modifications in existing procedures [that] are alleged to have substantially restricted the public's opportunity to participate in the highway planning process.

Appellant Federation urges that these major changes in existing procedures cannot be achieved unless FHWA observes the notice and comment promulgation procedures provided in § 553. It argues that the § 553(a)(2) exemption for agency grants should be read narrowly, in accord with the Congressional intent revealed in the APA's legislative history, and that the exemption does not extend to regulations governing the procedures under which grants are given, as opposed to the grants themselves. A serious gap in the APA would be created, says appellant, if the (a)(2) exemption omits from the APA's procedural protections all regulations addressed to the rights or welfare of the general public that are promulgated in connection with any of the massive federal grant-in-aid programs.

We do not disagree with appellant's diagnosis of the problem. Yet we conclude that, as written, the APA does create a serious gap in the procedural protections the APA was enacted to provide. At least in the context of the federal highway grant-in-aid program, we can find no principled way to remedy that gap by a narrowing construction. As a matter of policy, Congress might have done better to anticipate that the federal grant and benefit programs the government would come to administer would have a direct policy impact on individual citizens and society as a whole. Its desire that legislative functions in administrative agencies "be exercised only upon some form of public participation after notice"[13] might better have been served by recognizing that spending money always involves public choices, often significant public choices that could benefit from the ventilation of views that public participation entails. A number of agencies apparently exempt from rulemaking under subsection (a)(2) have recognized these benefits and have provided by regulation for notice and comment procedures prior to adoption of policy regulations for grant or benefit programs. The FHWA has also engaged in notice and comment rulemaking but it has not bound itself to follow this course. We must determine FHWA's procedural obligations under the Act.

National Wildlife cites legislative history indicating that the (a)(2) exemption was limited to "proprietary matters,"[15] and urges that proprietary matters be construed as limited to those functions that are essentially managerial and do not ordinarily involve questions of substantive public policy. Congress may well have provided an exemption in contemplation of "proprietary matters" relatively innocuous or insignificant. However, the use of that term in the legislative history was apparently only a shorthand reference to the public property, loans,

[13] "Administrative Procedure Act, Legislative History," S. Doc. No. 248, 79th Cong., 2d Sess. 358 (1946) (hereinafter cited as "Legislative History") (Cong. Walter).

[15] "Legislative History" at 358 (Cong. Walter); Senate Committee on the Judiciary, "Administrative Procedure Act," S.Rep.No.752, 79th Cong., 1st Sess. (1945), in "Legislative History" at 199; House Committee on the Judiciary, "Administrative Procedure Act," H.Rep.No.1980, 79th Cong., 2d Sess. 1946), in "Legislative History" at 257.

grants, benefits and contracts exempted in subsection (a)(2). Congress viewed these activities as proprietary in character and exempted them because "the principal considerations in most such cases relate to mechanics and interpretations or policy, and it is deemed wise to encourage and facilitate the issuance of rules by dispensing with all mandatory procedural requirements."[16] The mechanical implementation of "proprietary" programs was prominent, but it did not define the exemption. Congress instead included matters of interpretation and policy by way of example, and implicitly recognized that the exemption would also cover cases where those "principal considerations" it expected to characterize "most cases" would not apply.

The House and Senate Committee reports do indicate that the excepted subjects must be "directly" or "clearly and directly involved" in order to make the exemption operative.[19] But this does not mean that when excepted subjects are clearly involved, the exemption reaches only mechanical rules on those subjects. Clearly Congress meant to confine the (a)(2) exemption to its express terms, to prevent its use as an all purpose escape clause. But there can be no doubt that the regulations challenged in this case are both clearly and directly related to a federal grant program. One changes the approval process necessary to maintain state highway department eligibility for federal funds; the other allows federal funds to be used for right-of-way acquisitions before the normal location and design approvals have been given. These regulatory decisions go beyond mere managerial mechanics.[20] They directly affect the general public's hearing and participation rights in the administration of the federal grant-in-aid program. However, there is a clear and direct connection with an exempted "proprietary" subject, and this excuses the FHWA from an overall statutory obligation to comply with notice and comment procedures in promulgating the challenged regulations. . . .

## NOTES ON EXCEPTIONS FOR INTERNAL AGENCY MATTERS, PROPRIETARY MATTERS, AND MILITARY AND FOREIGN AFFAIRS

(1) ***Various Tests for "Rules of Agency Organization, Procedure, or Practice."*** The Hurson court examines several standards over the course of assessing whether the rule in question falls within the § 553(b)(A) exception. A procedural rule, it says, "covers agency actions that do not themselves alter the rights or interests of parties, although it may alter the manner in which the parties present themselves or their viewpoints to the agency." The court also examines whether the rule "encode[s] [a] substantive value judgment." It rejects the argument that a rule that imposes a "substantial impact" on a

[16] "Legislative History" at 199 (Senate Report).

[19] "Legislative History" at 199 (Senate Report) (Sec. 553 is inapplicable "only 'to the extent' that the excepted subjects are directly involved"); id. at 257 (House Report) (the excepted subjects must be "clearly and directly involved").

[20] On analysis it might well prove that very few grant and benefit program decisions with direct impact on the lives of individual citizens could be so characterized.

regulated party is necessarily substantive rather than procedural. Earlier evaluations in the D.C. Circuit did engage in this inquiry, however. See Public Citizen v. Dep't of State, 276 F.3d 634, 641 (D.C. Cir. 2002) (describing shift). Some other circuits still treat that question as key. In Texas v. United States, 809 F.3d 134, 176 (5th Cir. 2015) (p. 409), for example, the Fifth Circuit explained, "the substantial impact test is the primary means by which [we] look beyond the label 'procedural' to determine whether a rule is of the type Congress thought appropriate for public participation. An agency rule that modifies substantive rights and interests can only be nominally procedural, and the exemption for such rules of agency procedure cannot apply." Relying on that standard, the court concluded that DAPA "undoubtedly meets that test—conferring lawful presence on 500,000 illegal aliens residing in Texas forces the state to choose between spending millions of dollars to subsidize driver's licenses and amending its statutes." ACUS has advocated yet a different standard: "A rule is within the terms of the exception when it both (a) relates solely to agency methods of internal operations or of interacting with regulated parties or the public, and (b) does not (i) significantly affect conduct, activity, or a substantive interest that is the subject of agency jurisdiction, or (ii) affect the standards for eligibility for a government program." Recommendation 92–1, The Procedural and Practice Rule Exemption from the APA Notice-and-Comment Rulemaking Requirements, 57 Fed. Reg. 30102 (July 8, 1992).

What are the strengths and weaknesses of the respective tests? Would discussions about the substance-procedure distinction from civil procedure (specifically, over whether the Federal Rules of Civil Procedure should govern state-law claims) be helpful here? See Kristen E. Hickman & Richard J. Pierce, Jr., Administrative Law Treatise § 4.6 (6th ed. 2022-2 Cum. Supp. 2018) (describing different standards courts use to evaluate whether an action falls into this exception and drawing a comparison to Erie doctrine).

What does it mean to "alter the manner in which the parties present themselves . . . to the agency"? In ELECTRONIC PRIVACY INFORMATION CENTER V. U.S. DEP'T OF HOMELAND SEC., 653 F.3d 1 (D.C. Cir. 2011), the court rejected the Transportation Security Administration's argument that the agency's implementation of a new process for screening passengers at airports—using advanced imaging technology (AIT), which produces a "crude image of an unclothed person, who must stand in the scanner for several seconds while it generates the image"—merely altered the manner in which the parties present themselves to the agency and therefore qualified to be adopted without notice and comment. "Of course, stated at a high enough level of generality, the new policy imposes no new substantive obligations upon airline passengers: The requirement that a passenger pass through a security checkpoint is hardly novel, the prohibition against boarding a plane with a weapon or an explosive device even less so. But this overly abstract account of the change in procedure at the checkpoint elides the privacy interests at the heart of the petitioners' concern with AIT. . . . [B]y producing an image of the unclothed passenger, an AIT scanner intrudes upon his or her personal privacy in a way a magnetometer does not. Therefore, regardless whether this is a new substantive burden, the change substantively affects the public to a degree sufficient to implicate the policy interests animating notice-and-comment rulemaking."

(2) ***What About Rules on "A Matter Relating to Agency Management or Personnel"?*** Section 553(a) contains another exception for agency operations: rules on "a matter relating to agency management or personnel." In TUNIK V. MERIT SYSTEMS PROTECTION BOARD, 407 F.3d 1326 (Fed. Cir. 2005), the court considered whether regulations implementing the statutory provision governing the removal or discipline of an ALJ fell within this exception. (The constitutionality of this statutory provision, 5 U.S.C. § 7521, is currently being litigated in the courts of appeals, see pp. 556, 1018.) In holding that the regulations did not qualify for the exemption, the court found persuasive the "contemporaneous interpretation of the provision in the Attorney General's Manual on the Administrative Procedure Act," which treated the provision as essentially coextensive with what is now the publication requirement in § 552. (In 1946, although no longer, that requirement exempted from publication "any matter relating solely to the internal management of an agency.") Of the publication requirement, the Attorney General had explained: "If a matter is solely the concern of the agency proper, and therefore does not affect the members of the public to any extent, there is no requirement for publication under [§ 552]. Thus, an agency's internal personnel and budget procedures need not be published (e.g., rules as to leaves of absence, vacation, travel, etc.). However, in case of doubt as to whether a matter is or is not one of internal management, it is suggested that the matter be published in the Federal Register, assuming it does not require secrecy in the public interest."

Applying the Attorney General's distinction and considering the limited caselaw on the provision, the court concluded that the § 553(a) exception "cannot be construed to exempt the regulation at issue from notice and comment rulemaking. Although removal of ALJs could be characterized in a sense as a personnel matter in the same manner as the hiring policy at issue in Stewart [v. Smith, 673 F.2d 485 (D.C. Cir. 1982), in which the court held within the exception a Bureau of Prisons policy of not considering for employment any person who is over 34 years of age], the removal of ALJs goes to the heart of the APA and implicates a much broader class of the public than those who might apply for employment with the Bureau of Prisons. Indeed, the removal of ALJs implicates not only the rights of an individual ALJ being removed, but also the broader interest of the public in having private rights adjudicated by persons who have some independence from the agency opposing them. In that sense, section 7521 is primarily for the public benefit and only secondarily for the benefit of a particular ALJ in a particular case. See Stewart, 673 F.2d at 505 (Wright, J., dissenting) ('In the narrow set of cases where a proposed rule substantially affects parties outside an agency and implicates broad public concerns, the personnel exemption from rulemaking requirements surely does not apply.'). . . . Moreover, exceptions to the notice and comment requirements of the APA should be narrowly construed. Thus, the regulation at issue cannot be exempted from notice and comment rulemaking as merely relating to agency personnel."

Do you agree with the court's characterization of the ALJ rule as distinguishable from the Bureau of Prisons rule? To what extent is the standard on which the court relies consistent with the National Wildlife Federation court's approach to the other half of § 553(a)(2), the exception for "public property, loans, grants, benefits, or contracts"? To what extent is the standard on which the court relies consistent with the court's treatment of "substantial impact" under the agency operations exception in § 553(b)(A)?

(3) ***Scope of Exceptions.*** All of the procedural requirements of § 553 are excepted for all of the categories laid out in § 553(a). Thus, if any of those exceptions apply, the agency need not engage in notice and comment under § 553(b)–(c); it need not follow § 553(d)'s requirement to publish the rule "not less than 30 days before its effective date"; and it need not follow § 553(e)'s requirement to provide "an interested person the right to petition for the issuance, amendment, or repeal of a rule." However, for the exception for "rules of agency organization, procedure, or practice" under § 553(b)(A), agencies may avoid only notice and comment (because the language there excepts compliance only from "this subsection"). Do these distinctions make sense? For example, might outside parties have reliance interests on agency procedural rules for which they need 30 days to revise their conduct? On the other hand, given the courts' assessment that some personnel rules significantly affect the public, can the exceptions for the 30-day effective date delay and the right to rulemaking petitions really be justified for such rules?

(4) ***The Exception for Public Property, Loans, Grants, Benefits, and Contracts.*** The National Wildlife Federation court read this exception to apply whenever a regulation is "clearly and directly related" to one of the excepted subjects, no matter how serious the public's interest in the underlying policy choices. Do you agree with that reading? In Alphapointe v. Dep't of Veteran's Affairs, 475 F.Supp.3d 1 (D.D.C. 2020), the district court accepted the VA's position that it need not have engaged in notice and comment before modifying its acquisition regulation in a way that preferenced veterans over people with disabilities. Relying on National Wildlife Federation and a subsequent D.C. Circuit case, the court explained, "Public policy may be sorely affected, and the wisdom of public input manifest, but the statutory exemption still prevails when 'grants,' 'benefits' or other named subjects are 'clearly and directly' implicated." How might this case have come out differently if the court had applied the D.C. Circuit's approach to the other half of § 553(a)(2), in Tunik (Note 2 above, p. 435)?

What does it mean to be "clearly and directly" implicated? In defending the DAPA policy providing relief from removal for certain parents without proper documentation if they had children who were citizens or legally permanent residents, DHS also relied, in part, on the exception for public benefits to justify not having engaged in notice and comment. The Fifth Circuit rejected that argument in Texas v. United States, 809 F.3d 134, 148, 177 (2015) (p. 409): "To avoid carv[ing] the heart out of the notice provisions of Section 553, the courts construe the public-benefits exception very narrowly as applying only to agency action that 'clearly and directly relate[s]' to 'benefits' as that word is used in section 553(a)(2). DAPA does not 'clearly and directly' relate to public benefits as that term is used in § 553(a)(2). . . .

USCIS—the agency tasked with evaluating DAPA applications—is not an agency managing benefit programs. Persons who meet the DAPA criteria do not directly receive the kind of public benefit that has been recognized, or was likely to have been included, under this exception." If granted "lawful presence" status under DAPA, parents could have applied for certain Social Security and Medicare programs managed by other agencies (and been able to work lawfully). Should this be enough to satisfy the exception?

In 1969, ACUS recommended elimination of this exception because such "rules may nevertheless bear heavily upon nongovernmental interests," and so "[e]xempting them from generally applicable procedural requirements is unwise." ACUS urged agencies to commit themselves to using notice and comment "whenever appropriate, without awaiting a legislative command to do so." ACUS, Recommendation 69–8, Elimination of Certain Exemptions from the APA Rulemaking Process, 38 Fed. Reg. 19784 (July 23, 1973). Many agencies implemented this recommendation. In 2013, however, USDA rescinded its 1971 waiver of the exemption, pointing to "situations where affording the public a pre-implementation opportunity to comment on a proposed rule is outweighed by other public benefits, such as issuing benefits or making payments to the public as soon as practicable." 78 Fed. Reg. 64194 (Oct. 28, 2013). How might you assess the costs and benefits—to agencies,[19] to regulated entities, and to the public—of USDA's decision?

Congress has not eliminated the exception, but in some agency-specific statutes has required agencies to employ notice and comment procedures for matters that would otherwise have fallen under the § 553(a)(2) exception. See Azar v. Allina Health Servs., 139 S.Ct. 1804, 1808–09 (2019) (describing Congress's move in the 1980s to require notice and comment in the Medicare Act); 20 U.S.C. § 1232 (limiting § 553(a) exception to certain categories of regulation in Department of Education).

In 2016, as part of a broader set of recommendations to Congress on revising the rulemaking provisions of the APA, the American Bar Association adopted a formal resolution urging Congress to "repeal[ ] the broad and anachronistic exemption in § 553(a)(2) for 'public . . . loans, grants [and] benefits' " and "narrow the exemption in § 553(a)(2) for 'public property [and] contracts' so that the development and formulation of generally applicable policies with respect to public property and contracts would be governed by § 553." ABA, Resolution 106B (2016) at 8–9.[20] BERNARD W. BELL, in REVISITING APA SECTION 553, Notice & Comment Blog (Nov. 30, 2016),[21] expands: "Perhaps excluding such rules from rulemaking requirements made sense in an era where regulation was viewed as infringing upon regulated entities' *rights* while benefits programs were viewed as merely providing *largesse*. But such a lack of concern regarding rules governing loans (including loan guarantees), grants, and benefits seems out of place in the modern era." See also Sophia Z. Lee, Racial Justice

---

[19] Recall USDA's experience in Sugar Cane Growers Cooperative v. Veneman, 289 F.3d 89 (D.C. Cir. 2002) (p. 293), which was not cited explicitly in the revocation.

[20] https://www.acus.gov/sites/default/files/documents/ABA-Resolution-106B-and-Report.pdf.

[21] https://www.yalejreg.com/nc/revisiting-apa-section-553-by-bernard-w-bell/.

and Administrative Procedure, 97 Chi.-Kent L. Rev. 1, 122–23 (2022) (arguing that this exception "had a critical racial impact" because the social welfare programs thereby exempted from notice and comment "were responsible for building core aspects of present-day structural racism" and agency officials were thus able to avoid providing civil rights advocates an opportunity to participate); Eloise Pasachoff, Executive Branch Control of Federal Grants: Policy, Pork, and Punishment, 83 Ohio State L.J. (2022) (advocating repeal in part because "this exemption . . . makes it easy for a boundary-pushing president to assert overall policy priorities to be implemented through grants"). Would you favor repeal of the exception? Modification? Retention?

(5) ***The Military Affairs Exception in Court.*** Can the military affairs exception apply to a "civilian" agency? Can it apply to agency activities that only loosely implicate military affairs? In INDEPENDENT GUARD ASS'N OF NEVADA V. O'LEARY, 57 F.3d 766 (9th Cir. 1995), the Ninth Circuit considered whether a Nuclear Explosive Safety Order promulgated by the Department of Energy without notice and comment properly could qualify for this exception. The union representing the contractors—armed civilian guards—to whose work the Order applied had argued that the exception could not apply because the Department of Energy was not a military agency. The court rejected this argument: "The DOE's statutory mandate includes responsibility for research and development of all energy resource applications, as well as national security functions relating to nuclear weapons research and development. The DOE can and does perform both 'civilian' and 'military' functions. The agency's dual nature reinforces the critical importance of the statutory language that instructs us to look not to whether the overall nature of the agency promulgating a regulation is 'civilian' or 'military,' but to the function being regulated." On the other hand, the court accepted the union's argument that the work of the contractor guards was not closely enough connected to the agency's military function for the Order to benefit from the exception. "The record shows that the guards employed and supervised by Wackenhut were performing duties similar to those performed by civilian security guards everywhere. They were no more performing a 'military function' than civilian contract guards employed to guard judges are performing a 'judicial function.' "

Can the Department of Defense rely on the military affairs exception in defining "sex offenses"? In UNITED STATES V. MINGO, 964 F.3d 134 (2d Cir. 2020), the Secretary of Defense had designated the military offense of which the defendant-appellant had been convicted a "sex offense" for purposes of the Sex Offender Registration and Notification Act, which defined the term "sex offense" to include "a military offense specified by the Secretary of Defense[.]" 34 U.S.C. § 20911(5)(A). The Secretary made these designations in a document entitled "Enclosure 27" without using notice-and-comment procedures. The defendant-appellant challenged his conviction for failure to register under SORNA on various grounds, including the absence of such procedures. Held: "We agree with the district court's determination that the Secretary's designation of military offenses as sex offenses in Enclosure 27 fell within the military affairs exception. The defendant was convicted by court-martial in a military tribunal and he served his sentence in a military facility. His conviction in the military tribunal . . . was therefore part and parcel of the military justice system. The applicability of the exception to § 553's notice-and-comment requirement for involvement of a 'military function . . . of the United States' is thus clear and conclusive." Do you agree? Are there nonetheless reasons why notice and comment might still be valuable in this context?

(6) ***The Foreign Affairs Exception in Court.*** How broadly ought the foreign affairs exception apply? Compare the following cases.

(a) In RAJAH V. MUKASEY, 544 F.3d 427 (2d Cir. 2008), the court applied the exception to uphold a special registration program instituted by the Attorney General after September 11, 2001. Under the National Security Entry-Exit Registration System, noncitizen males from certain countries had to appear for registration, fingerprinting, and presentation of immigration-related documents if they were over the age of 16 and had not qualified for permanent residence. Those who did not appear risked arrest. Those who did appear but whose immigration status was irregular risked removal. Although the Attorney General had used notice-and-comment proceedings to promulgate a general enabling regulation that set forth the framework of the program, he had not done so in issuing the notices that designated which specific groups had to register (the "Group Specifications"). "For the [foreign affairs] exception to apply, the public rulemaking provisions should provoke definitely undesirable international consequences. There are at least three definitely undesirable international consequences that would follow from notice and comment rulemaking. First, sensitive foreign intelligence might be revealed in the course of explaining why some of a particular nation's citizens are regarded as a threat. Second, relations with other countries might be impaired if the government were to conduct and resolve a public debate over why some citizens of particular countries were a potential danger to our security. Third, the process would be slow and cumbersome, diminishing our ability to collect intelligence regarding, and enhance defenses in anticipation of, a potential attack by foreign terrorists."

The court rejected the petitioners' counter-arguments. "First, they assert that the foreign affairs exception is inapplicable because the regulation itself did not contain a statement of the undesirable international consequences flowing from the application of notice and comment review. There is, however, no requirement that the rule itself state the undesirable consequences. This is particularly so when the consequences are seemingly as evident as they are in this case. Petitioners also appear to assert that there is insufficient evidence that the group specification was tied to the President's foreign policy. There is, however, no burden of proof to be carried with regard to a connection to the President's conduct of foreign affairs where the relevance to international relations is facially plain."

(b) In EAST BAY SANCTUARY COVENANT V. TRUMP, 932 F.3d 742 (9th Cir. 2018), the court declined to apply the foreign affairs exception to an interim final rule promulgated jointly by the Departments of Justice and Homeland Security, which, along with a contemporaneous presidential proclamation, made all noncitizens crossing into the United States from the southern border categorically ineligible for asylum. Denying the government's request for a stay of the district court's temporary restraining order pending appeal, the court explained: "The Government . . . asserts that the Rule 'necessarily implicate[s] our relations with Mexico and the President's foreign policy,' and thus falls under the foreign affairs exception because it addresses immigration across the nation's southern border. . . . [However,] the foreign affairs exception requires the Government to do more than merely recite that the Rule 'implicates' foreign affairs. . . . [T]he foreign affairs exception would become distended if applied to [an immigration agency's] actions generally, even though immigration matters typically implicate foreign affairs. Accordingly, we have held that the foreign affairs exception applies in the immigration context only when ordinary application of the public rulemaking provisions [will] provoke definitely undesirable international consequences. Under this standard, courts have approved the Government's use of the foreign affairs exception where the international consequence is obvious or the Government has explained the need for immediate implementation of a final rule. . . . On the other hand, courts have disapproved the use of the foreign affairs exception where the Government has failed to offer evidence of consequences that would result from compliance with the APA's procedural requirements. . . .

"The Government contends that following the notice-and-comment procedures would result in undesirable international consequences. In particular, the Government claims that the Rule is 'directly relate[d] to . . . ongoing negotiations with Mexico' and other Northern Triangle countries. The Government believes that the Rule will 'facilitate the likelihood of success in future negotiations' and asserts that requiring normal notice-and-comment procedures in this situation would hinder the President's ability to address the 'large numbers of aliens . . . transiting through Mexico *right now*.' The Government's argument, in theory, has some merit. Hindering the President's ability to implement a new policy in response to a current foreign affairs crisis is the type of 'definitely undesirable international consequence' that warrants invocation of the foreign affairs exception. But the Government has not explained how immediate *publication* of the Rule, instead of *announcement* of a proposed rule followed by a thirty-day period of notice and comment, is necessary for negotiations with Mexico. We are sensitive to the fact that the President has access to information not available to the public, and that we must be cautious about demanding confidential information, even in camera. Nevertheless, the connection between negotiations with Mexico and the immediate implementation of the Rule is not apparent on this record."

Subsequently, in EAST BAY SANCTUARY COVENANT V. BIDEN, 993 F.3d 640 (9th Cir. 2021), affirming the district court's grant of a preliminary injunction, the court concluded that additional evidence in the record "still fail[ed] to establish that adhering to notice and comment and a thirty-day grace period will provoke definitely undesirable international consequences. We agree with the government that the cited [Memorandum of Understanding between DHS and the Mexican government] does broadly 'show[ ] that [immigration] negotiations have happened in the past,' but this is insufficient to demonstrate that notice and comment will provoke undesirable international consequences. . . . The cited Washington Post page discusses an increase in the proportion of families that seek asylum and the [Executive Office of Immigration Review] data lists the country of origin of credible-fear cases and summarizes the number of people that attempt to enter the United States with an asylum application, the number of cases completed in 2018, and the outcome of credible fear cases. It is unclear how these data 'reflect[ ] motivations for crossing the border illegally,' and even less clear how they demonstrate the consequences of requesting public notice-and-comment on foreign policy. And the speech by President Trump, as the district court noted, discusses the *domestic* consequences of foreign immigration, not the foreign policy consequences of immigration."

(7) ***Should the Military and Foreign Affairs Exception Be Narrowed?*** In 2016, in Resolution 106B (p. 437), the ABA recommended that Congress "narrow[ ] the exemption in § 553(a)(1) relating to 'military or foreign affairs functions,' " in keeping with longstanding ABA and ACUS recommendations. ACUS's views on the matter date back to 1973, when it recommended that "[r]ulemaking in which the usual procedures are inappropriate because of a need for secrecy in the interest of national defense or foreign policy should be exempted on the same basis now applied in the freedom of information provision, 5 U.S.C. § 552(b)(1). That is, section 553(a) should contain an exemption for rulemaking involving matters specifically required by Executive order to be kept secret in the interest of national defense or foreign policy. . . . Since rules on those subjects may bear heavily on nongovernmental interests, . . . the breadth of the present exemption . . . is unwarranted." ACUS, Recommendation 73–5, Elimination of the 'Military and Foreign Affairs Function' Exemption from APA Rulemaking Requirements, 39 Fed. Reg. 4847 (Feb. 7, 1974).

Responding to the 2016 ABA resolution, BERNARD W. BELL, in REVISITING APA SECTION 553, Notice & Comment Blog (Nov. 30, 2016),[22] disagreed: "Judicial review under FOIA requires courts to independently review classification decisions, so as to counteract the executive branch's tendency toward excessive secrecy. But . . . [a]gencies must be able to reliably determine whether the exemption applies *before* judicial review. . . . [M]ore fundamentally . . . military and foreign affairs decisions may require dispatch, which is in tension with the informal rulemaking process. . . . Second, one critical aspect of informal rulemaking, namely development of a record for judicial review, may not be particularly appropriate in the military and foreign affairs contexts. . . . Third, foreign affairs (and perhaps even some military) decisions will often involve compromise and accommodation with foreign sovereigns, and thus may be less amenable to the sort of "means-ends" rationality that a rulemaking record combined with judicial review is designed to ensure." Would you support narrowing the exception as envisioned by the ABA and ACUS?

[22] https://www.yalejreg.com/nc/revisiting-apa-section-553-by-bernard-w-bell/.

## SECTION 5. GETTING RULEMAKING STARTED



An agency that is going to engage in rulemaking commits to that effort well before the first event § 553 mentions, publication of a Notice of Proposed Rulemaking in the Federal Register. Here we discuss three routes to getting rulemaking started: initiation within the agency, public initiation, and negotiated rulemaking. Congress often mandates the first, sometimes imposing deadlines on the issuance of the NPRM, and on occasion requires the last. The White House too plays a role in the first, directing rulemaking efforts, particularly in recent years. A significant factor in an executive agency's initiation of rulemaking—whether in response to a public petition or on the agency's own initiative (the latter, to be certain, is frequently at the push of Congress or the White House)—is centralized review by the Office of Information and Regulatory Affairs in OMB under Executive Order 12866. Independent regulatory commissions and boards face far less scrutiny by OIRA. We discuss the work of OIRA through regulatory planning and review in the final part of the Section. Keep two caveats in mind. First, although this Section (and indeed, the casebook as a whole) typically refers to a single agency, agencies engage in important joint rulemaking from time to time. Second, while this Section (and again, the casebook as well) often assumes that a rulemaking imposes new obligations, rulemakings can also repeal previous regulations.

### a. Rulemaking Initiation and Development Within the Agency

Save for § 553(e)'s invitation to the public to petition for rulemaking, the APA says little about what happens up to the point when an NPRM is published in the Federal Register. As might be expected, however, both agencies and their political overseers do a great deal of work in the pre-NPRM period. Increasingly, this work is the subject of statutory and executive order requirements, which we take up in Section 5.d below. Here we focus on legislative and executive pressures on the agency to start rulemaking and the internal structures of agency decisionmaking, whether involving a single agency or agencies working together.

(1) ***External Pressures to Start a Rulemaking.*** Legislative and presidential pressures can launch the rulemaking process. On the legislative side, a statute may compel an agency to undertake a particular rulemaking. The Inflation Reduction Act of 2022 delegated specific work to a number of federal agencies, including, for example, directing the Internal Revenue

Service to set rules for certain tax provisions. Some statutes also impose deadlines on both the start and completion of agency rulemaking. For example, the 2010 Dodd-Frank Wall Street Reform and Consumer Protection Act set close to 400 deadlines on financial agencies for proposing and finalizing various regulations, with many of these statutory mandates tasking agencies to jointly engage in the rulemaking process. A study of public laws from 1995 to 2014 found that Congress is more likely to impose such deadlines for rulemaking under unified government, the theory being that congressional majorities try to take advantage of friendly administrations implanting their policy goals before a new administration, potentially of the other party, takes over. Jason A. MacDonald & Robert J. McGrath, A Race for the Regs: Unified Government, Statutory Deadlines, and Federal Agency Rulemaking, 44 Leg. Stud. Q. 345 (2019).

Agencies often miss deadlines. For example, the GAO recently determined that the National Highway Traffic Safety Administration had completed only 5 of 19 statutorily mandated rulemakings with set deadlines; of three additional statutorily mandated rulemakings without deadlines, NHTSA had completed one. GAO, Traffic Safety: Implementing Leading Practices Could Improve Management of Mandated Rulemakings and Reports, GAO-22-104635 (Apr. 2022).[1] If an agency does miss a deadline, courts can sometimes impose a judicial deadline for agency action, including the publication of an NPRM, under the threat of contempt. Some evidence suggests that deadlines may drive an agency to rely on the notice-and-comment exceptions (such as the good cause exemption) discussed in the previous Section, to speed up the process. Jacob E. Gersen & Anne Joseph O'Connell, Deadlines in Administrative Law, 156 U. Pa. L. Rev. 923, 944–45 (2008).

The White House may also direct an agency to initiate rulemaking proceedings and even set deadlines (though these timelines are not judicially enforceable). As discussed in Chapter VII, in a January 2021 Executive Order (p. 1023), President Biden instructed four different agencies to "immediately take action, to the extent appropriate and consistent with applicable law, to require masks to be worn in compliance with CDC guidelines in or on" various forms of transportation. As another example, in August 2021, using softer language, President Biden called on the EPA and the Department of Transportation to "consider" beginning certain specific rulemakings on multi-pollutant emissions standards and fuel economy standards for cars and trucks, and to further "consider" issuing various NPRMs by January 2022 and final rulemakings by December 2022 (in one instance) and July 2024 (in another instance). Exec. Order No. 14037, 86 Fed. Reg. 43583 (Aug. 10, 2021). Similar examples from earlier administrations abound.

In another kind of White House move to jumpstart agency rulemaking, OIRA issued "prompt" letters in President George W. Bush's Administration, suggesting specific rulemakings to agencies. The first such letter was sent to OSHA in 2001, to encourage the agency to mandate that certain workplaces

---

[1] https://www.gao.gov/assets/gao-22-104635.pdf.

have automated external defibrillators.[2] On the other hand, the White House, particularly at the start of a new administration, and Congress, often using appropriation riders, can impose regulatory moratoria on agencies to prevent rulemaking. These legislative and presidential efforts to direct regulatory policymaking raise important constitutional, statutory, and policy issues that are explored in Chapter VII, Sections 2–3.

Executive Order 12866, which we discuss in more detail in Section 5.d, has had an important impact on rulemaking development in general. Its requirements that all agencies identify regulatory actions under development or review for the semiannual Unified Agenda and annual Regulatory Plan have led to greater emphasis on regulatory planning within agencies. Also significant is its mandate that each executive agency have a Regulatory Policy Officer who will be involved at each stage of the regulatory process. See Exec. Order No. 12866, §§ 4, 6(a).

(2) ***The Rulemaking Process Inside the Agency.*** An agency can also initiate rulemaking without confronting a deadline or other statutory command, relying on its organic statute and other acts delegating authority. The agency must decide what issues warrant rulemaking. This decision, in turn, requires both the setting of regulatory priorities—policy judgments that may transcend the agency's own substantive mandate—and the use of those priorities to identify appropriate subjects for regulations.

Regardless of whether propelled by legislation, presidential directive or prompt, or internal agency decision, the agency must then develop concrete proposals. Most often, this development happens within the agency, albeit with substantial consultation both inside and outside the government. For interesting descriptions of key aspects of the early stages of rulemaking within an agency, see Cornelius M. Kerwin & Scott R. Furlong, Rulemaking: How Government Agencies Write Law and Make Policy (5th ed. 2018) (drawing on agency documents, interviews of agency officials, and a symposium of senior agency officials); Cary Coglianese & Daniel E. Walters, Agenda-Setting in the Regulatory State: Theory and Evidence, 68 Admin. L. Rev. 93 (2016) (synthesizing discussions with "more than two dozen leading scholars, practitioners, and government officials"). For an empirical investigation of the timing of agency action, see Simon F. Haeder & Susan Webb Yackee, Handmaidens of the Legislature? Understanding Regulatory Timing, 42 J. Pub. Pol'y 298 (2022) (finding, among other things, that narrower delegations produce quicker rulemaking).

A 2020 ACUS Recommendation addresses "Rules on Rulemaking," which many (but not all) agencies have promulgated to govern their internal efforts as they conduct rulemakings under § 553. Recommendation 20–1, 86

---

[2] For copies of prompt letters, see: https://www.reginfo.gov/public/jsp/EO/promptLetters.jsp. OIRA has not issued prompt letters in subsequent Administrations, which have relied on presidential directives instead. For a debate over the desirability of prompt letters, see John D. Graham, Saving Lives Through Administrative Law and Economics, 395 U. Pa. L. Rev. 395, 460 (2008) (arguing the letters were an important tool for forcing regulation); Nicholas Bagley & Richard L. Revesz, Centralized Oversight of the Regulatory State, 106 Colum. L. Rev. 1260, 1277–80 (2006) (arguing that "OIRA publicly touts the prompt letter as a proregulatory and proactive mechanism for regulatory reform while lavishing most of its attention on rolling back regulatory burdens on industry").

Fed. Reg. 6613 (Jan. 22, 2021). The Recommendation suggests ways that agencies might improve the content and accessibility of these rules to serve the values of efficiency, predictability, accountability, and transparency. As noted above, agencies often initiate and proceed through rulemakings in coordination with other agencies, whether because of statutory direction, presidential requirement, or an internally perceived need to collaborate in shared regulatory space.[3]

Very late in the Trump Administration, the Department of Health and Human Services issued a rule, which the Biden Administration repealed, "amending its regulations to set expiration dates for the Department's regulations (subject to certain exceptions), unless the Department periodically assesses the regulations to determine if they are subject to the [Regulatory Flexibility Act], and if they are, performs a review that satisfies the criteria in the RFA." Securing Updated and Necessary Statutory Evaluations Timely, 86 Fed. Reg. 5694 (Jan. 19, 2021). For more on this so-called "sunset" rule, which would have also applied to regulations on the books, see Martin Totaro & Connor Raso, Brookings Inst., Agencies Should Plan Now for Future Efforts to Automatically Sunset Their Rules (Feb. 25, 2021).[4]

(3) ***Rulemaking Procedures as Bureaucratic Strategy?*** In a study of 11,000 rules from 150 executive branch bureaus between 1995 and 2014, RACHEL AUGUSTINE POTTER concludes that bureaucrats engage in what she calls "procedural politicking" to "strategically insulate their rulemaking without sacrificing their preferred outcome." BENDING THE RULES: PROCEDURAL POLITICKING IN THE BUREAUCRACY 13–14 (2019): "An agency's procedural powers include things like control over how a proposal is written or whether the agency consults its advisory board beforehand. . . . Agencies can frame their rulemaking proposals in terms that are more acceptable in the current political discourse, or they can avoid the use of certain terms that may be politically charged. . . . These tactics, while nuanced, help[ ] to shape the way the public—and political overseers—perceive[ ] the rule. After a rule is drafted, it must be legitimated through notice-and-comment. Agencies again have considerable discretion in managing this part of the process, and rarely do two rules receive the same procedural treatment at this stage. Rather, for each rule an agency makes decisions about how much stakeholder outreach to conduct (and how much of this will be done publicly versus privately), and when to release various documents, among numerous other choices. Manipulating these procedural choices enables agencies to protect their rules when the political climate is hostile. . . . Procedural powers mean that agencies have considerable influence over how the rulemaking process is managed, and that influence helps them achieve independent political objectives. While political oversight of the rulemaking process can (and does) occur, these managerial powers make oversight more

[3] See, e.g., Jody Freeman & Jim Rossi, Agency Coordination in Shared Regulatory Space, 125 Harv. L. Rev. 1131, 1155–73 (2012) (describing interagency collaboration tools including consultation, interagency agreements, and joint policymaking).

[4] https://www.brookings.edu/research/agencies-should-plan-now-for-future-efforts-to-automatically-sunset-their-rules/.

difficult and, therefore, less frequent. As a result, unelected bureaucrats have substantial leverage over the regulatory policies that become binding law, much more than our current understanding gives them credit for. As with all political actors in our system of checks and balances, bureaucrats do not operate unchecked, but they are a powerful political force in the American system."

Scholars have long studied the connection between different aspects of administrative procedure and politics. For two foundational articles in this vein, offering views that Potter's work challenges, see Lisa Schultz Bressman, Procedures as Politics in Administrative Law, 107 Colum. L. Rev. 1749 (2007) (arguing that Supreme Court doctrine around administrative procedures enhances the opportunity for political control and the legitimacy of agency decisionmaking); Mathew McCubbins, Roger Noll, & Barry Weingast (collectively McNollgast), Administrative Procedures as Instruments of Political Control, 3 J. L. Econ. & Org. 243 (1987) (arguing that much administrative law embodied in the APA and elsewhere is designed to help elected officials maintain control of agency action). For more on this literature, see p. 876.

## b. Public Petitions for Rulemaking

*Each agency shall give an interested person the right to petition for the issuance, amendment, or repeal of a rule.*

5 U.S.C. § 553(e)

(1) ***Sources of Petitions and Success Rates.*** Section 553(e)'s express provision for public petitioning of rulemaking represents another mechanism by which rulemaking can be initiated. For instance, FlyersRights (which was also a participant in Chapter I's Introductory Example about the Department of Transportation's Enhancing Airline Passenger Protections rule (p. 3)), petitioned the FAA in August 2015 to issue a rule establishing standards for the minimum size of a seat—both the width and pitch—on a commercial airline. (The FAA denied the petition after receiving more than 140 comments.) Petitions can come from regulated entities or regulatory beneficiaries. In PETITIONS FOR RULEMAKING (Nov. 5, 2014) (report to ACUS),[5] JASON A. SCHWARTZ and RICHARD L. REVESZ provide some recent statistics on rulemaking petitions. Over all the agencies examined, the sources of petitions broke down as follows: 52 percent business, 27 percent organized public interest groups, 13 percent loosely organized public interest groups or individuals, 5 percent labor organizations, and 3 percent state, local, and tribal governments. Id. at Appendix C. As to individuals, who "submit a tenth to a quarter of the petitions at some agencies," Schwartz and Revesz noted: "[M]ost agency officials and stakeholders interviewed for this study assumed that average U.S. citizens were generally unaware of the right to petition for rulemaking and were unlikely to submit petitions. In practice, many of the individual petitioners are former agency staffers,

---

[5] https://www.acus.gov/report/petitions-rulemaking-final-report.

lawyers, or academics, especially scientists and law professors. It is not surprising that such individuals are more likely to be aware of the right to petition for rulemakings." Id. at 46–47.

Most rulemaking petitions appear to be denied. But some agencies—for instance, the EPA, Department of Energy, Federal Motor Carrier Safety Administration (DOT), and Surface Transportation Board (DOT)—grant more petitions than they deny. Id. at Appendix C. Some of these granted petitions involve significant regulations: for instance, the FDA's attempt in the mid-1990s to regulate tobacco, which is the subject of FDA v. Brown & Williamson Tobacco Corp., 529 U.S. 120 (2000) (p. 1338), started after an anti-smoking group filed a petition for rulemaking. Moreover, even a denied petition can end up having an effect by making the issue salient; after the FAA denied the petition requesting a rule over airplane seat size, for example, Congress directed the FAA to engage in such a rulemaking. See FAA Reauthorization Act of 2018, Pub. L. No. 115–254 § 577 (Oct. 5, 2018); FAA, Request for Comments in Minimum Seat Dimensions Necessary for Safety of Air Passengers (Emergency Evacuation), 87 Fed. Reg. 47494 (Aug. 3, 2022); footnote 7 below.

(2) ***Agency Practices for Rulemaking Petitions.*** Although the APA explicitly provides for rulemaking petitions in § 553(e), it does not provide any specific procedures for the petitioning process. Generally applicable provisions in § 555 do apply, however, which together make clear that the APA requires "agencies to respond to petitions for rulemaking 'within a reasonable time,' and to give petitioners 'prompt notice' when a petition is denied in whole or in part, along with 'a brief statement of the grounds for denial.' " ACUS, Recommendation 2014–6, Petitions for Rulemaking, 79 Fed. Reg. 75117 (Dec. 17, 2014) (quoting §§ 555(b) and (e)).

In addition, Congress has sometimes created specific requirements for particular agencies to follow in inviting and addressing rulemaking petitions in individual statutes. These include, for example, petitions to add or remove a species to or from the Secretary of Interior's endangered species list under the Endangered Species Act and petitions to the FDA to regulate different food additives under the Food, Drug, and Cosmetic Act. See Maeve P. Carey, Cong. Rsch. Serv., R46190, Petitions for Rulemaking: An Overview (Jan. 23, 2020), at 12–13.[6]

Some agencies have detailed procedures governing how the agency handles petitions for rulemaking, set forth variously in regulation, guidance, or internal memoranda. Schwartz & Revesz, Petitions for Rulemaking, supra, at 47–48. The Department of Transportation, recipient of the petition from FlyersRights discussed above, is among these agencies. Yet overall, according to ACUS, "few agencies have in place official procedures for accepting, processing, and responding to petitions for rulemaking. How petitions are received and treated varies across—and even within—agencies. In some cases, agency personnel do not even know what their agency's procedures are for handling petitions. Although the petitioning process can be a tool for enhancing public engagement in rulemaking, in practice most

---

[6] https://www.everycrsreport.com/reports/R46190.html.

petitions for rulemaking are filed by sophisticated stakeholders and not by other interested members of the public. Some petitioners report that it can be difficult to learn the status of a previously filed petition, agency communication throughout the process can be poor, response times can be slow, and agency explanations for denials can be minimal and predominantly non-substantive." ACUS Recommendation 2014–6, supra, at 2; searches of agency websites in September 2022 do not suggest considerable improvement in terms of easily finding information on petition procedures.

(3) ***Judicial Review of Rulemaking Petition Denials and Agency Delay in Responding.*** How potent a tool § 553(e) is for prodding agency action depends to a large extent on how rigorously courts review agency delay and petition denials.

On agency delay: Under § 555(b), "[w]ith due regard for the convenience and necessity of the parties . . . and within a reasonable time, each agency shall proceed to conclude a matter presented to it." Under § 706(1), courts may compel "unreasonably delayed" agency actions. In principle, then, courts can review agencies' delayed responses to petitions for rulemaking, and do so under a standard of "reasonableness." In practice, however, "the standard of review in an unreasonable delay case varies between jurisdictions, is ever evolving, is not always crystal clear, and is based on so many vague factors as to allow courts to support virtually any conclusion they want to reach." Petitions for Rulemaking, supra, at 13–14. A review of judicial rulings on delays in responding to rulemaking petitions "demonstrates how unpredictable the results can be," with, for example, one court finding a five-month delay unreasonable but another court finding a six-year delay reasonable under the circumstances. Id. at 15–16.

On petition denials: As is further developed in the materials on reviewability in Chapter IX (p. 1489), agency refusals to initiate rulemaking are typically reviewable under the APA. MASSACHUSETTS V. EPA, 549 U.S. 497, 527–28 (2007) [pp. 1321, 1469, 1473], provides an instance of judicial review of a petition denial. In this case, the Supreme Court in a closely divided 5–4 decision reviewed the EPA's refusal to initiate rulemaking on greenhouse gases; the Court's level of scrutiny resulted in a remand to the EPA to reconsider its decision. In remanding, the Court remarked: "There are key differences between a denial of a petition for rulemaking and an agency's decision not to initiate an enforcement action. See American Horse Protection Assn., Inc. v. Lyng, 812 F.2d 1, 3–4 [D.C. Cir. 1987]. In contrast to nonenforcement decisions, agency refusals to initiate rulemaking 'are less frequent, more apt to involve legal as opposed to factual analysis, and subject to special formalities, including a public explanation.' Id., at 4; see also 5 U.S.C. § 555(e). They moreover arise out of denials of petitions for rulemaking which (at least in the circumstances here) the affected party had an undoubted procedural right to file in the first instance. Refusals to promulgate rules are thus susceptible to judicial review, though such review is 'extremely limited' and 'highly deferential.' National Customs Brokers & Forwarders Assn. of Am., Inc. v. United States, 883 F.2d 93, 96 [D.C. Cir. 1989]."

In some circumstances, courts have tied the intensity of their scrutiny to the agency's rationale for denying the petition for rulemaking. A more lenient standard may apply when "the agency has chosen not to regulate for reasons ill-suited to judicial resolution, e.g., because of internal management considerations as to budget and personnel or for reasons made after a weighing of competing policies." Professional Pilots Fed. v. FAA, 118 F.3d 758, 763 (D.C. Cir. 1997).

As noted above, the FAA rejected the petition for rulemaking by FlyersRights on airline seat width and pitch. The organization then sued in the D.C. Circuit, arguing that the denial was arbitrary and capricious based on safety considerations in an evacuation. The agency countered by claiming that the issues in the petition "do not raise an immediate safety or security concern" and arguing that it had considerable discretion on what rulemakings to undertake. The D.C. Circuit took the middle ground, finding that the FAA had "relied materially on information it had not disclosed" and remanding the matter to the agency "to adequately address the petition and the emergency egress concerns it raises." Flyers Rights Education Fund, Inc. v. FAA, 864 F.3d 738 (D.C. Cir. 2017).[7]

Circumstances sometimes lead agencies to explain their refusals on the merits, and when this happens the result can be more intense judicial attention to the decision, as in Massachusetts v. EPA, supra. The petition in Professional Pilots Federation (a different case against the FAA than the one by FlyersRights) sought revision of the FAA's Age 60 Rule, which, originally adopted in 1959, mandated that commercial pilots stop flying when they turn 60. Although the agency had frequently reconsidered the rule and acknowledged that 60 had no special medical significance, it had continued to retain the rule on the ground that no measure existed by which "to distinguish those pilots who, as a consequence of aging, present a threat to air safety from those who do not." The Federation filed its petition in 1993 and on its denial sought judicial review, arguing that the FAA had thereby violated the APA and the Age Discrimination in Employment Act.

The D.C. Circuit determined that an extremely lenient review normally reserved for petition denials was not appropriate here, because "the decision not to institute a rulemaking looking toward repeal of the Age 60 Rule was purportedly based upon the merits of the existing Rule." Nonetheless, by a 2–1 vote the court rejected the pilot organization's challenge, concluding that the FAA's continued retention of the Rule and distinctions among different groups of pilots were rational: "The FAA may seem to have created something of a Catch-22 by announcing that it will not allow older pilots to fly until it has experiential data demonstrating the continued ability of such pilots to fly safely. On the other hand, it hardly seems reasonable to require

[7] As noted above, the seat saga continues. Congress passed the Seat Egress in Air Travel Act in 2018, requiring, in part, that the FAA issue regulations setting minimum seat sizes for passenger safety. FAA simulations (which have their critics) and other agency review found no safety issues with current seat sizes. In the 90-day comment period "on the minimum seat dimensions necessary for airline passenger safety" that ended in November 2022, the agency received more than 26,000 comments—including one comment signed by 25 members of Congress. See James Bikales, Everyone Hates Small Airplane Seats. Will They Get Bigger?, Wash. Post (Nov. 8, 2022).

that the Administrator periodically put his hand into the fire in order to ensure that he has precisely assessed the danger that it poses. If the FAA was justified in imposing the Rule in the first place then we cannot say that, simply because it is the Rule itself that blocks the generation of data necessary to reconsider the Rule, it was unreasonable for the FAA to find that it lacks those data."

The majority also rejected the ADEA challenge. Dissenting, Judge Wald concluded that the FAA's justifications for the petition denial did not pass muster under the APA, particularly in light of the agency's refusal to try to obtain medical and performance data on older pilots, which she argued the agency was obligated to try to do given the ADEA's condemnation of across-the-board age discrimination. The Age 60 Rule stayed in place until December 2007, when Congress passed the Fair Treatment of Experienced Pilots Act, which raised the mandatory retirement age for pilots to 65. See 49 U.S.C. §§ 44729(a), (e)(2).

(4) ***Potential Benefits and Disadvantages of Petitions for Rulemaking.*** "On the one hand," the 2014 ACUS Report on petitions noted, "there is the value of democratic accountability, public-private dialogue, and collaboration. Petitions provide an essential mechanism to let the public participate not just by passively commenting on government actions, but actively helping to set the agenda and combating agency inertia. . . . On the other hand, there is the benefit of an efficient and rational administrative state. Even if individual petitioners have the best intentions, their narrow interests and potential lack of expertise can make them rather bad at setting relative policy priorities in a way that will maximize net benefits for all society. If petitions come mostly from well-organized, well-financed groups, any agency resources spent responding to petitions could take resources away from attending to the interests of the general public. Additionally, if wielded with less good intentions, petitions could become a tool to interfere with agency action, by bottling up the agency's agenda and diverting resources away from other activities. Agencies have dwindling free resources and heavy obligations, and most agencies feel they are already working as hard and as intelligently as they can and have set priorities accordingly; petitions could disrupt those expert judgments." Petitions for Rulemaking, supra, at 69–70.

For additional recent views assessing the potential value of petitions for rulemaking along different dimensions, see Daniel E. Walters, Capturing the Regulatory Agenda: An Empirical Study of Agency Responsiveness to Rulemaking Petitions, 43 Harv. Envtl. L. Rev. 175, 223 (2019) (examining petitions to three agencies between 2000 and early 2016 and finding "little evidence that agencies kowtow to any and every demand that the business world makes in petitions" but also "that public interest and individual petitions, which are far more pro-regulatory than business and industry petitions[ ] are rarely effective in combatting agency inaction"); Maggie McKinley, Petitioning and the Making of the Administrative State, 127 Yale L.J. 1538 (2018) (tracing the APA's petitioning process to the practice of petitioning Congress dating back to the founding, and arguing that it is rooted in the First Amendment's petition clause and thus helps legitimate the administrative state); Wendy Wagner, William West, Thomas McGarity, & Lisa Peters, Dynamic Rulemaking, 92 N.Y.U. L. Rev. 183, 189 (2017) (arguing that rulemaking is a dynamic rather than a static process in part because of mechanisms like rulemaking petitions, while cautioning that "dynamic rulemaking may overlook important issues and reinforce familiar biases in favor of well-organized groups at the expense of more diffuse public interests").

## c. Negotiated Rulemaking

(1) ***The Negotiated Rulemaking Process.*** The Negotiated Rulemaking Act, adopted in 1990, added a new Subchapter III to the APA (now, 5 U.S.C. §§ 561–570a) "to establish a framework for the conduct of negotiated rulemaking, consistent with section 553 of this title, to encourage agencies to use the process when it enhances the informal rulemaking process." 5 U.S.C. § 561. Negotiated rulemaking—"reg-neg" in the frequent shorthand—is a process for generating a rulemaking proposal, not a final rule, by a committee that includes representatives of both the agency and some number of affected parties. As a proposal, the product of a successful reg-neg must be published in the Federal Register and undergo the normal § 553 process. In addition, reg-neg committees must follow the mandates of the Federal Advisory Committee Act, 5 U.S.C. App. (see p. 798). § 565. The Negotiated Rulemaking Act provided that "[a]ny agency action relating to establishing, assisting, or terminating a negotiated rulemaking committee . . . shall not be subject to judicial review" while maintaining that "[a] rule which is the product of negotiated rulemaking . . . shall not be accorded any greater deference by a court than a rule which is the product of other rulemaking procedures." § 570. Executive Order 12866 (pp. 455, 1629), signed by President Clinton and still in effect, encourages agencies to "explore and, where appropriate, use consensual mechanisms for developing regulations, including negotiated rulemaking." § 6(a)(1). In addition to these general procedural recommendations, some substantive statutes require agencies to conduct negotiated rulemaking in certain circumstances. For example, the Higher Education Act requires the Secretary of Education to conduct negotiated rulemaking over student financial assistance rules. 20 U.S.C. § 1098a(b).

PHILIP HARTER, ASSESSING THE ASSESSORS: THE ACTUAL PERFORMANCE OF NEGOTIATED RULEMAKING, 9 N.Y.U. Envtl. L.J. 32, 33–35 (2001), explains the process: "[N]egotiated rulemaking is a process by which representatives of the interests that would be substantially affected by a rule, including the agency responsible for issuing the rule, negotiate in good faith to reach consensus on a proposed rule. . . . [If an] agency decides to go forward with a negotiated rulemaking, it publishes a Notice of Intent in the Federal Register and other publications likely to be read by those interested in the subject matter, announcing its intention . . . , describing the subjects and scope of the rule to be developed, and listing the people or interests that will be on the committee. The notice also solicits comments on the decision to use reg-neg to develop the rule, and it invites those who believe they will be substantially affected by the rule, but who are not adequately represented on the committee, to apply for committee membership. . . . Following the Notice of Intent, the committee is established and the actual negotiations begin. The members of the negotiated rulemaking committee determine what factual information or other data is necessary for them to make a reasoned decision, develop . . . [and] analyze the information, examine the legal and policy issues involved . . . , and reach a consensus on the recommendation to make to the agency. As part of the consensus, each private interest agrees to support the recommendation and resulting rule to the extent that it reflects the agreement. . . .

"Several implicit elements of this process merit emphasis: First, a senior representative of the agency is a full participant in the negotiations and deliberations of the negotiated rulemaking committee. Second, the committee makes its decision by consensus . . . [and] each participating interest has veto power over the decision. Third, the agency agrees to use the consensus as the basis of a proposed rule, which necessarily means that the agency will follow the traditional process of publishing the proposal as a Notice of Proposed Rulemaking (NPRM) and receive comments on the proposal before issuing a final rule. . . . [T]he agency alone retains the authority to issue the rule and may modify the proposal in response to comments or otherwise. That said, however, a negotiated rulemaking is a means by which the representatives of the affected interests actually share in making the regulatory decision, subject to the agency's constitutional responsibility to make the final decision. The resulting consensus is far more than a mere recommendation, especially since the agency itself endorses it during the deliberations."

Not all efforts that begin with negotiated rulemaking end in consensus, however. A recent CRS Report identifies examples of final rules that were promulgated after agencies engaged in negotiated rulemaking, but only some of the rules were the product of a successful negotiation. See Maeve P. Carey, Cong. Rsch. Serv., R46765, Negotiated Rulemaking: In Brief (Apr. 12, 2021), at 10–11.[8] The Report also notes instances of committees defining "consensus" to mean something other than unanimity, including that the committee members could "live with the agreement, considered as a whole" or "no more than two negative votes in each issue area." Id. at 5.

(2) ***Criticisms and Defenses of Reg-Neg.*** WILLIAM FUNK, in BARGAINING TOWARD THE NEW MILLENNIUM: REGULATORY NEGOTIATION AND THE SUBVERSION OF THE PUBLIC INTEREST, 46 Duke L.J. 1351, 1356 (1997), criticizes reg-neg for its "fundamental tension" with "traditional administrative law processes. . . . [W]hile negotiated rulemaking may formally satisfy current legal requirements, the principles, theory, and practice of negotiated rulemaking subtly subvert the basic, underlying concepts of American administrative law—an agency's pursuit of the public interest through law and reasoned decisionmaking. In its place, negotiated rulemaking would establish privately bargained interests as the source of putative public law."

---

[8] https://crsreports.congress.gov/product/pdf/R/R46756/2.

Are the concerns that Funk raises overstated? Is the risk of agency capture through regulatory negotiation any greater than in conventional rulemaking contexts? Susan Rose-Ackerman has suggested that loss of expertise in negotiated rulemaking may be more of a problem than capture, emphasizing that some issues, like environmental policy, require "a knowledge base derived from scientific principles" and that negotiation is not a methodology that helps the participants acquire technical expertise. Susan Rose-Ackerman, American Administrative Law Under Siege: Is Germany a Model?, 107 Harv. L. Rev. 1279, 1283 (1994). Can these concerns be met by the thoughtful exercise of discretion in agency determinations of what rules they will attempt to negotiate? Does Funk give adequate weight to the fact that any regulation ultimately produced through regulatory negotiation must go through the notice-and-comment process and is potentially subject to judicial reversal if a significant issue is raised to which the agency does not respond—or if the resulting rule exceeds the agency's authority? On the other hand, how often will legal challenges be brought against regulations that represent a consensus negotiated by the stakeholders involved?

A closely related issue concerns whether all affected interests are adequately represented in the negotiating group; lack of such representation may heighten fears of agency capture and undermine the legitimacy of the regulatory negotiation process. Does negotiated rulemaking's explicit focus on interest representation provide the best procedural chance for identifying the politically powerless and enhancing their voice in regulatory policymaking? Or is there something in the conventional rulemaking process that works to protect the interests of the politically powerless that is lost, or overridden, in regulatory negotiation? Funk suggests that this "something" is the agency's independent judgment of where the public interest lies. Do you agree?

Some further considerations: Cary Coglianese analyzed EPA final rules that started with reg-neg committees between 1983 and 1996 and found that the agency's reg-neg rules took longer to complete and produced more litigation than other agency rules in that time period. Such results—*if* reg-neg rules and non-reg-neg rules are comparable—suggest that the process neither saves time nor avoids litigation. Cary Coglianese, Assessing Consensus: The Promise and Performance of Negotiated Rulemaking, 46 Duke L.J. 1255 (1997).

Supporters of reg-neg, by contrast, have emphasized the benefits that the process can bring to rulemaking. JODY FREEMAN & LAURA I. LANGBEIN, REGULATORY NEGOTIATION AND THE LEGITIMACY BENEFIT, 9 N.Y.U. Envtl. L.J. 60, 62–63, 138 (2000): "In our view, empirical studies of negotiated rulemaking that examine cost, time, and litigation tell only part of the study and, we believe, not the most important part.... Along virtually every important qualitative dimension, all participants in this study—whether business, environmental, or government—reacted more favorably to their experience with negotiated rules than do participants in conventional rulemaking.... Regulatory negotiation clearly emerges, moreover, as a superior process for generating information, facilitating learning, and building trust. Most significantly, consensus-based negotiation increases legitimacy, defined as the acceptability of the regulation to those involved in its development. This legitimacy benefit . . . is no small accomplishment and . . . is more important than reducing transaction costs." Do you agree that such legitimacy benefits deserve more weight in assessing the merits of reg-neg?

Hannah Wiseman points to another potential benefit of negotiated rulemaking in a case study of certain rules developed under the auspices of two agencies within the Department of Transportation. She concludes that these agencies' regular use of negotiated rulemaking helps bring about voluntary compliance with new advisories on emerging risks and provides the agencies with important baseline technical knowledge to address those risks even before any actual rulemaking takes place. Hannah J. Wiseman, Negotiated Rulemaking and New Risks: A Rail Safety Case Study, 7 Wake Forest J.L. & Pol'y 207 (2017). Are there additional ways agencies might reap this benefit outside negotiated rulemaking?

(3) ***The Waning of Reg-Neg?*** Jeffrey Lubbers identified a decline in the use of negotiated rulemaking since the 1990s. JEFFREY S. LUBBERS, ACHIEVING POLICYMAKING CONSENSUS: THE (UNFORTUNATE) WANING OF NEGOTIATED RULEMAKING, 49 S. Tex. L. Rev. 987, 996 (2008): "[F]rom the beginning of 1991 (the year after the NRA was enacted) through the end of 1999, sixty-three separate [reg-neg] committees were created, while from 2000 to the end of 2007, there were only twenty-two. . . . More tellingly, the number of statutorily mandated committees was only twenty-three of sixty-three (36.5%) in the first period but fifteen of twenty-two (68%) in the most recent period." According to Lubbers, factors contributing to this decline were lack of funding for ACUS since the mid-1990s (which had provided support to agencies for some aspects of the process and wasn't restarted until 2010), the greater costs of reg-neg, a lack of enthusiasm for the procedure by OIRA, Federal Advisory Committee Act requirements (which require committee negotiations to be open to the public), and scholarly criticism.

Is some of the decline due as well to the rise of presidential oversight over the regulatory process, as further explored in Section 5.d below? Donald R. Arbuckle, who spent 25 years working on regulatory oversight in the White House, argues that regulatory negotiation and White House oversight are in tension. "Rulemaking is one means by which the executive branch implements not only statutory mandates, but also presidential policy; any sitting President would be loathe to delegate his authority to a collaborative panel." Donald R. Arbuckle, Collaborative Governance Meets Presidential Regulatory Review, 2009 J. Disp. Resol. 343, 344 (2009).

Peter Schuck and Steven Kochevar found a further decline in reg-neg in the 2007–2013 period: only 13 reg-neg committees were formed, with all but two statutorily required. Peter H. Schuck & Steven Kochevar, Reg Neg Redux: The Career of a Procedural Reform, 15 Theoretical Inquiries in Law 417, 439 (2014). In more recent years, however, the use of reg-neg has increased, with 23 reg-neg committees formed between April 29, 2013, and May 31, 2017 (a majority done voluntarily, i.e., not required by statute). A 2017 ACUS Report observed: "In the last few years, the procedure has enjoyed something of a mini-resurgence, as the Departments of

Transportation and Energy have deployed it in a handful of high-profile rulemakings, but it has not come close to recapturing the popularity it enjoyed in its heyday." Cheryl Blake & Reeve T. Bull, Negotiated Rulemaking (June 5, 2017) (report to ACUS), at 2.[9]

(4) ***Latest ACUS Recommendations.*** In June 2017, ACUS adopted additional recommendations concerning reg-neg, including urging agencies to "consider using negotiated rulemaking when it determines that the procedure is in the public interest, will advance the agency's statutory objectives, and is consistent with the factors outlined in the Negotiated Rulemaking Act." Because these factors are wide ranging, ACUS noted that "the choice should generally reside within the agency's discretion." ACUS also encouraged agencies to keep their OIRA desk officers informed about the process (including desk officers' ability to observe meetings) and called for Congress to exempt reg-neg committees from FACA's chartering and reporting mandates. ACUS, Recommendation 2017–2, Negotiated Rulemaking and Other Options for Public Engagement, 82 Fed. Reg. 31040 (July 5, 2017).

## d. Regulatory Planning and Review

***EXECUTIVE ORDER 12866***
***Notes on the Mechanics of Executive Order 12866***
***Notes on Ongoing Issues with Executive Order 12866 and Potential Changes***
***Notes on Executive Order 13771***
***Notes on the Paperwork Reduction Act***
***Notes on Cost-Benefit Analysis and Risk Assessment***

## EXECUTIVE ORDER 12866

58 Fed. Reg. 51735 (Oct. 4, 1993).

[Executive Order 12866 appears in the Appendix at p. 1622.[10] It is the principal text for this set of materials, although the Section does touch on some other requirements. Focus on the Order's Sections 1, 4, and 6 through 10.]

### NOTES

(1) ***Meet the Players.*** Outside of the APA (and the Constitution), the rulemaking process includes considerable mandates placed on agencies by the White House or Congress. As the text of Executive Order 12866 indicates, the two White House offices below (one of which is contained within the

[9] https://www.acus.gov/report/negotiated-rulemaking-final-report.

[10] Executive Order 12866 § 3(b) defines agency to exclude "those considered to be independent regulatory agencies, as defined in 44 U.S.C. § 3502(10)." The relevant statutory provision is now 44 U.S.C. § 3502(5).

other) play a particularly important role in contemporary rulemaking. For a detailed overview of contemporary rulemaking, see the Reg Map, which is disseminated by OIRA.[11]

(a) The Office of Management and Budget is part of the professional White House bureaucracy in the Executive Office of the President, with a permanent staff of about 470 full-time equivalent spots that, except for its top leadership (including seven Senate-confirmed presidential appointees, one of whom heads OIRA), largely continues through changing administrations. With limited exceptions for some (but not all) of the independent regulatory commissions, OMB controls agency submissions to Congress of draft legislation, testimony on proposed legislation, and budgetary requests. It also oversees the spending of congressional appropriations and develops management mechanisms for the executive branch. For a thorough examination of OMB's important budgetary and management functions as a form of agency control, see Eloise Pasachoff, The President's Budget as a Source of Agency Policy Control, 125 Yale L.J. 2182 (2016). As the Executive Order suggests, OMB also frequently serves as the tribunal before which interagency conflicts over regulatory policy are resolved.[12]

(b) The Office of Information and Regulatory Affairs (OIRA, pronounced "oh-eye-ruh") is the subdivision of OMB with the greatest responsibility for regulatory affairs. Operating with a professional staff of about 45, it is statutorily responsible for the coordination of government information policy, including the clearance of agency information demands under the Paperwork Reduction Act. Under Executive Order 12866 (and its predecessors), it writes an introduction to the government's regulatory agenda (which the General Services Administration compiles from agency submissions) and clears the draft and final regulatory impact statements that are prepared for particular rulemakings. Presidents have generally appointed as its head accomplished professionals with significant experience in policy analysis and/or law. President Obama's first OIRA Administrator was Cass Sunstein. President Trump, at the start, picked Neomi Rao, a professor at George Mason University's Antonin Scalia Law School and now a D.C. Circuit judge, as his OIRA Administrator; she was confirmed by the Senate in July 2017. It took until September 2022 for President Biden to announce a nominee for the job, Richard Revesz, former Dean of NYU Law School and Director of the American Law Institute.

(2) ***The History of Executive Order 12866 and Centralized Regulatory Review.*** The White House has taken increasingly formal control of important ("significant") rulemakings since President Nixon's Administration. It has asserted at least a supervisory, if not a directory, role in shaping the analysis of issues put on the rulemaking table, and even in assessing the justifications for particular conclusions. RICHARD H. PILDES & CASS R. SUNSTEIN, REINVENTING THE REGULATORY STATE, 62 U. Chi. L. Rev. 1 (1995): "[P]residential oversight of the regulatory process, though

[11] https://www.reginfo.gov/public/reginfo/Regmap/index.jsp.

[12] The Office of Legal Counsel in the Department of Justice serves this function for legal conflicts.

relatively new, has become a permanent part of the institutional design of American government. This new institutional arrangement has occurred for reasons parallel to the development of a centralized budget in the 1920s. All Presidents are likely to seek assurance that an unwieldy federal bureaucracy conforms its actions to their basic principles. Any President is likely to be concerned about excessive public and private costs. And any President is likely to want to be able to coordinate agency activity so as to ensure consistency and coherence and to guard against the imposition of conflicting duties on people who must comply with the law. The result of these forces is that a centralizing and rationalizing body, housed within OMB and devoted to regulation, has emerged as an enduring, major, but insufficiently appreciated part of the national government."

The device predominantly used to accomplish this, the "regulatory impact analysis" (RIA), draws on the example legislatively set in the National Environmental Policy Act of 1969, 42 U.S.C. § 4321 et seq. NEPA requires agencies to create an Environmental Impact Statement (or at least an Environmental Assessment) that anticipates adverse environmental changes potentially caused by agency projects and considers means of reducing or avoiding them. A few years after the passage of NEPA, presidents began to require a similar analysis for economic, rather than environmental, impacts. During President Carter's Administration, Executive Order 12044 required justifications and analysis of anticipated economic impacts for a limited number of important rulemakings. President Reagan built upon this with Executive Orders 12291 and 12498, which placed a much wider range of rulemaking activities under the supervision of OIRA. Executive Order 12291 specified analytic principles for rulemaking and provided for their enforcement through OIRA. Executive Order 12498 created an annual regulatory agenda, also under OIRA supervision. Other impact analysis requirements followed, some from the White House and some from Congress; an example of the latter is the Regulatory Flexibility Act, enacted in 1980 and codified at 5 U.S.C. §§ 601–612, which encourages attention to the impact of regulations on small businesses. Presidents have avoided making the regulatory impact obligation judicially enforceable and have relied instead on enforcement from within the Executive Office of the President.

In the 1980s, with a Democratic Congress considerably more enthusiastic about regulation than a conservative Republican White House, OIRA became a lightning rod for concerns that the President was obstructing the "necessary" work of government agencies. Contributing to these concerns was the secrecy that characterized OIRA review under President Reagan. Congress reacted in the FY 1987 omnibus spending bill by making future heads of OIRA subject to Senate confirmation. Even so, responding to concerns about the direction regulation was (or wasn't) taking, as well as feelings that OIRA's processes were still insufficiently transparent and accountable, the Senate refused to confirm President George H.W. Bush's nominee for the position of OIRA Administrator. President Bush responded by creating a controversial "Council on Competitiveness" chaired by Vice President Quayle. The Council was responsible for political oversight of

OIRA and the resolution of important disputes. But it did not provide much public access. "As a result," reported ELENA KAGAN, PRESIDENTIAL ADMINISTRATION, 114 Harv. L. Rev. 2281–82 (2001) (also excerpted on pp. 48, 1028, 1043), "the Council provoked the same criticisms, except perhaps still more heated, formerly lodged against OIRA. . . . In light of this criticism, observers might have predicted that when a Democratic President assumed office in 1993, a radical curtailment of presidential supervision of administrative action would follow. Instead, the very opposite occurred. President Clinton, to be sure, replaced Reagan's executive orders on regulatory review [with Executive Order 12866] and eliminated Bush's Competitiveness Council. But . . . presidential control of administration . . . expanded significantly during the Clinton Presidency, moving in this eight-year period to the center of the regulatory landscape."

President George W. Bush kept Executive Order 12866 in place, with OIRA under the initial direction of John Graham, who had headed Harvard's Center for Risk Analysis. Administrator Graham added considerably to the transparency of OIRA's procedures, including by putting information online. The most significant alteration to regulatory review came with adoption of Executive Order 13422 in January 2007, which made four major changes: (1) expanding Executive Order 12866's reach to include significant agency guidance documents; (2) heightening the specificity of the analysis required of agencies under § 1(b)(1) of Executive Order 12866; (3) enlarging the role of each agency's regulatory policy officer and mandating that agencies designate a presidential appointee to serve in that capacity; and (4) requiring that agencies consider the use of formal rulemaking procedures in coordination with OIRA (see p. 309). Critics charged that these changes gave the President too much decisional control over the regulatory process.

One of President Obama's first actions upon assuming office was to issue Executive Order 13497, revoking Executive Order 13422 and restoring Executive Order 12866 to its earlier form under President Clinton. President Obama also instructed the OMB Director to undertake an assessment of the regulatory review process under Executive Order 12866. In January 2011, President Obama issued Executive Order 13563 (Improving Regulation and Regulatory Review), 76 Fed. Reg. 3821 (Jan. 21, 2011). Rather than comprehensively revising the existing process, the new Executive Order stated it "is supplemental to and reaffirms the principles, structures, and definitions governing contemporary regulatory review that were established in Executive Order 12866." Executive Order 13563 emphasized public participation, reiterating Executive Order 12866's requirement that public comment periods should generally be at least 60 days and requiring agencies to ensure a "meaningful opportunity to comment through the Internet on any proposed regulation" and "timely online access to the rulemaking docket." § 2(b). It also incorporated a focus on behavioral economics, encouraging agencies to adopt flexible regulatory approaches including "warnings, appropriate default rules, and disclosure requirements." § 4; see also Cass R. Sunstein, Adm'r, OIRA, Memorandum for the Heads of Exec. Dep'ts & Agencies (June 18, 2010) (encouraging use of disclosure and simplification as regulatory tools) (p. 809). The new Order also reiterated agencies' obligation to engage in retrospective analysis of existing rules to determine if they are "outmoded, ineffective, insufficient, or excessively burdensome" and required agencies to develop plans for how they will conduct such retrospective review within 120 days. § 6. President Obama simultaneously issued a memorandum directing heads of "agencies with broad regulatory compliance and administrative enforcement responsibilities, . . . to the extent feasible and permitted by law, . . . [to] develop plans to make public information concerning their regulatory compliance and enforcement activities accessible, downloadable, and searchable online." Memorandum to the Heads of Exec. Dep'ts & Agencies (Jan. 18, 2011).

President Trump did not revoke any part of Executive Order 12866 or 13563. He did, however, issue additional requirements related to agency regulation in Executive Order 13771, which specifically referred to Executive Order 12866 in several places. The new order required agencies to eliminate at least two existing regulations for every new one issued and established a regulatory "budget" for agencies. For more information, see Notes on Executive Order 13771 below. President Biden repealed this Order.

As of November 2022, President Biden had not modified Executive Order 12866 or 13563. On his first day in office, however, he did issue Executive Order 13985 (Advancing Racial Equity and Support for Underserved Communities Through the Federal Government), which called for OMB to study methods for assessing equity and to work with agencies on these issues and on agencies to conduct equity assessments. Biden also signed a memorandum, Modernizing Regulatory Review, that first day directing OMB, in consultation with federal agencies, to make recommendations "for improving and modernizing regulatory review." For more information on these equity directives, see Note 9 below (p. 477). With a confirmed OIRA Administrator, we should expect to see more actions on this front.

For a detailed history of centralized regulatory review and OIRA's role in the rulemaking process through the start of President Obama's Administration, see Maeve P. Carey, Cong. Rsch. Serv., RL32397, Federal Rulemaking: The Role of the Office of Information and Regulatory Affairs (Mar. 21, 2011).[13]

(3) ***Regulatory Review in Context: The Case of Greenhouse Gas Emissions.*** Regulatory review under Executive Order 12866 can seem a dry topic. But such centralized review is at the center of current administrative law debates and scholarship because of its importance to ultimate regulatory outcomes. Some sense of that import comes from an episode during President George W. Bush's Administration involving the EPA's efforts to respond to the Supreme Court's decision in Massachusetts v. EPA, 549 U.S. 497 (2007) (pp. 1321, 1469, 1473), which held that greenhouse gases were air pollutants under the Clean Air Act and rejected the agency's reasons for refusing to regulate them.

HEIDI KITROSSER, ACCOUNTABILITY AND ADMINISTRATIVE STRUCTURE, 45 Willamette L. Rev. 607 (2008): "The EPA's initial reaction to the ruling

[13] https://crsreports.congress.gov/product/pdf/RL/RL32397.

was quite vigorous. EPA administrator Stephen L. Johnson convened at least 60 EPA officials to respond to the [C]ourt's instructions. The effort resulted in a December 2007 draft finding that greenhouse gases endanger the environment. The EPA also used Energy Department data from 2007 to conclude that it would be cost effective to require the nation's motor vehicle fleet to average 37.7 miles per gallon in 2018. These findings were reflected in a nearly 300 page document prepared by EPA staffers. The document, which was approved by Johnson, included a proposed rule to effectuate the emissions requirement.

"Given the statutory and judicial directives to the EPA and the EPA's subsequent efforts, one might assume that the next steps were routine and predictable. Specifically, one might assume that the EPA publicly issued its draft document as a Notice of Proposed Rulemaking (NPRM), that public comments followed, and that the comments were followed by a final, publicly explained and judicially reviewable decision to enact a rule or to refrain from so doing. Yet none of this occurred.

"Instead, the EPA's scientific analysis and regulatory proposals were literally willed away by the White House. As with the proverbial tree falling in a forest, the White House refused to see the EPA's plans and did their best to ensure that others could not see them. This was effectuated very simply. When the EPA e-mailed the document to . . . [OMB] for pre-rule-making review, the White House declined to open it and ordered its retraction. The White House since has claimed executive privilege against congressional attempts to discover the e-mail and related communications. Although much remains unknown, the facts detailed here have come to light as a result of disclosures from EPA staffers to journalists and to members of Congress. It also is now known that EPA shelved the scientific endangerment finding and proposed rule it had sent to the White House. Instead, it issued an Advance Notice of Proposed Rulemaking (ANPRM)—a step preliminary to an NPRM—in June of 2008 merely seeking public comment on potential use of the Clean Air Act to address climate change." The EPA finally issued the endangerment finding in December 2009, when President Obama was in office.

(4) ***Regulatory Review in Context: The 2012 Election.*** Regulatory interference by OIRA also occurs under Democratic Presidents. JULIET EILPERIN, WHITE HOUSE DELAYED ENACTING RULES AHEAD OF 2012 ELECTION TO AVOID CONTROVERSY, Wash. Post (Dec. 14, 2013): "The White House systematically delayed enacting a series of rules on the environment, worker safety and health care to prevent them from becoming points of contention before the 2012 election, according to documents and interviews with current and former administration officials. Some agency officials were instructed to hold off submitting proposals to the White House for up to a year to ensure that they would not be issued before voters went to the polls, the current and former officials said. The delays meant that rules were postponed or never issued. The stalled regulations included crucial elements of the Affordable Care Act, what bodies of water deserved federal protection, pollution controls for industrial boilers and limits on dangerous silica exposure in the workplace. The Obama administration has repeatedly said

that any delays until after the election were coincidental and that such decisions were made without regard to politics. But seven current and former administration officials told The Washington Post that the motives behind many of the delays were clearly political, as Obama's top aides focused on avoiding controversy before his reelection." (For more on delay and OIRA, see Note 4 below on p. 471.)

(5) ***Presidential Control of Rulemaking.*** As the example of the EPA's aborted greenhouse gas regulatory effort under President George W. Bush's Administration and OIRA's delays surrounding the 2012 election suggest, a central issue underlying the regulatory review process concerns the appropriate role of the President in rulemaking. Perhaps the most controversial aspect of Executive Order 12866 is its injection of the President into the regulatory sphere, giving White House officials a potential veto over regulations that do not accord with the President's policy priorities. This important aspect of the regulatory review process is inseparable from constitutional arguments about the scope of presidential powers and the appropriate role of the President vis-a-vis the executive branch. We discuss presidential directive authority in detail in Chapter VII, Section 3.c (p. 1022).

## NOTES ON THE MECHANICS OF EXECUTIVE ORDER 12866

(1) ***Regulatory Planning.*** An important feature of Executive Order 12866 is its attention to regulatory planning. Section 4 is the critical section here, and it imposes two central obligations on both executive and independent agencies, "to the extent permitted by law." First, agencies are required to identify "all regulations under development or review" for inclusion in a semiannual Unified Regulatory Agenda. § 4(b). The requirement that agencies publish a Regulatory Agenda twice a year was subsequently codified in the Small Business Regulatory Enforcement Fairness Act of 1996, 5 U.S.C. § 602. Second, as part of the Unified Agenda, agencies must "prepare a Regulatory Plan . . . of the most important significant regulatory actions that the agency reasonably expects to issue in proposed or final form that fiscal year or thereafter." In the Plan, agencies must include information on each significant regulation beyond that required for the Unified Agenda, including the agency's objectives; the need for the regulation; to the extent possible, alternatives to be considered; and a preliminary estimate of costs and benefits. § 4(c). Available and searchable in electronic form, the Unified Agenda lists agency actions in four stages.[14] The earliest, the "Pre-rule Stage," contains actions to be undertaken within the next twelve months to determine whether to initiate rulemaking; it thus identifies actions substantially in advance of the second stage, actions for which an NPRM is in the offing.

---

[14] https://www.reginfo.gov/public/do/eAgendaMain.

Assuming the Unified Agenda is accurate,[15] one effect of these requirements is to allow greater public awareness of rulemaking activities before the NPRM stage. And just as significant, these requirements allow for greater OIRA involvement in setting agency regulatory priorities in the early stages of regulatory actions. This latter feature rose to the fore in President George W. Bush's Executive Order 13422, which replaced the requirement that agency heads must approve the regulatory plan with one mandating approval of the plan by the agency's regulatory policy officer and further required that such officers be presidential appointees. The Bush Executive Order, which is no longer in effect, exploited the potential for greater presidential control at the expense of agency heads, but could regulatory planning requirements also benefit agency leadership? Does the Regulatory Plan enhance the control of an agency's political head over her career bureaucrats by requiring her to confront at an early stage competing views about priorities for her agency?

(2) ***Regulatory Review and the Distinction Among Nonsignificant, Significant, and Yet More Significant Regulations.*** OIRA reviews agencies' draft rules at both the proposed and final stages of rulemaking.[16] Executive Order 12866 creates three different categories of regulations, determinable by the agency *or* the Administrator of OIRA. Under § 3(f),

> "Significant regulatory action" means any regulatory action that is likely to result in a rule that may:
>
> (1) Have an annual effect on the economy of $100 million or more or adversely affect in a material way the economy, a sector of the economy, productivity, competition, jobs, the environment, public health or safety, or State, local, or tribal governments or communities;
>
> (2) Create a serious inconsistency or otherwise interfere with an action taken or planned by another agency;
>
> (3) Materially alter the budgetary impact of entitlements, grants, user fees, or loan programs or the rights and obligations of recipients thereof; or

---

[15] In 2015, ACUS evaluated the accuracy of the Unified Agenda. It found: "The Unified Agenda functions reasonably well as a predictor of some agency actions, but is less accurate in other areas. For example, estimated action dates may prove incorrect, the significance of a regulation may be misclassified, and jointly issued rules may inappropriately be characterized differently by different agencies. Additionally, some rules are classified as long-term actions when regulatory activity is imminent, while others remain listed as long-term actions after work on them has ceased. Occasionally, entries are removed from the Unified Agenda without explanation. Finally, a number of regulatory actions have recently been placed in a 'pending' category that is not included in the published Unified Agenda." ACUS, Recommendation 2015–1, Promoting Accuracy and Transparency in the Unified Agenda, 80 Fed. Reg. 36757 (June 26, 2015); see also Jennifer Nou & Edward Stiglitz, Strategic Rulemaking Disclosure, 89 S. Cal. L. Rev. 733 (2016).

[16] This review is triggered by an agency taking a "regulatory action," defined in § 3(e) to mean "any substantive action by an agency (normally published in the Federal Register) that promulgates or is expected to lead to the promulgation of a final rule or regulation, including notices of inquiry, advance notices of proposed rulemaking, and notices of proposed rulemaking."

(4) Raise novel legal or policy issues arising out of legal mandates, the President's priorities, or the principles set forth in this Executive order.

The procedural obligations attached to each category of regulatory action vary significantly under the Executive Order. Regulations that do not meet these thresholds for significance are not subject to further review. For "significant" actions, the agency must document the need for the regulation and assess "the potential costs and benefits of the regulatory action, including an explanation of the manner in which the regulatory action is consistent with a statutory mandate and, to the extent permitted by law, promotes the President's priorities and avoids undue interference with State, local, and tribal governments. . . ." § 6(a)(3)(B)(ii). Actions meeting the economic impact standard of § 3(f)(1)—"economically significant" rulemakings—are treated as more significant than the rest and face additional requirements, including more extensive assessment and quantification of costs and benefits associated with the proposed regulation and also with reasonably feasible alternatives.

Note that unlike the regulatory planning process outlined in Section 4 of the Executive Order, these assessment commands are directed only to executive agencies and not to independent regulatory commissions and boards.[17] The extent to which Presidents should be able to subject these latter agencies to the centralized regulatory review process is considered in Chapter VII, Section 3.c (p. 1050). In 2019, on request from Trump's White House Counsel, the Office of Legal Counsel analyzed the issue and determined that "the President may direct independent agencies to comply with EO 12866." Extending Regulatory Review Under Executive Order 12866 to Independent Regulatory Agencies, 43 Op. O.L.C. (Oct. 8, 2019). President Trump did not do so before leaving office. An alternative to presidential action is for Congress to require such review by statute. See Independent Agency Regulatory Analysis Act, S. 2279 (117th Cong.) (2021).

OIRA has shifted its review over time to focus on significant rulemakings. According to a 2003 GAO report, "by focusing OIRA's reviews on significant rules, the number of draft proposed and final rules that OIRA examined fell from between 2,000 and 3,000 per year under the Executive Order 12291 to between 500 and 700 rules per year under Executive Order 12866." GAO, Rulemaking: OMB's Role in Reviews of Agencies' Draft Rules and the Transparency of Those Reviews, GAO-03-929 (Sept. 2003), at 24.[18] Just where to set the dividing lines among nonsignificant, significant, and more significant regulations is open to debate. And agencies may try to underplay the importance of a rulemaking to avoid OIRA review. See Jennifer Nou, Agency Self-Insulation Under Presidential Review, 126 Harv. L. Rev. 1755 (2013); Note, OIRA Avoidance, 124 Harv. L. Rev. 994 (2011). For a skeptical view of this evasion argument, see Nina A. Mendelson & Jonathan B. Wiener, Responding to Agency Avoidance of OIRA, 37 Harv. J.L. & Pub. Pol'y 447 (2014) (noting that "it remains unclear whether avoidance of OIRA is actually widespread and serious" and maintaining, in light of the

---

[17] See § 3(b) (defining "agency"); § 4(b) (extending this definition to "those considered to be independent regulatory agencies" in the regulatory planning context).

[18] https://www.gao.gov/assets/gao-03-929.pdf.

repeat-player nature of agencies' relationships with OIRA, that "[a]gencies may have good reasons and incentives to cooperate with OIRA review").

Information on OIRA's regulatory reviews is available online.[19] Using data listed there and in the Federal Register's database, the following chart provides information on OIRA review of agency rulemaking during the past three completed Administrations and the first year of the Biden Administration:

| | Total Rules Published | OIRA Reviewed | Economically Significant |
|---|---|---|---|
| Bush II Yrs. 1–8 | 31799 | 5124 (16.1% of total) | 755 (14.7% of reviewed rules, 2.4% of total) |
| Obama Yrs. 1–8 | 29038 | 4,376 (15.1% of total) | 973 (22.2% of reviewed rules, 3.4% of total) |
| Trump Yrs. 1–4 | 12960 | 1756 (13.5% of total) | 493 (28.1% of reviewed rules, 3.8% of total) |
| Biden Yr. 1 | 3205 | 444 (13.9% of total) | 150 (33.8% of reviewed rules, 4.7% of total) |

Both routine and significant rulemaking decreased under the Trump Administration in its early years, but its agencies issued more economically significant rules in its final year than any of its predecessors (in any given year since such rules have been tracked).

(3) ***The OIRA Review Process Under Executive Order 12866.*** In 2003, the GAO provided a detailed summary of OIRA's formal and informal review processes, which then-OIRA Administrator Graham characterized as "an excellent overview of the regulatory review process." It still captures the process two decades later. GAO, RULEMAKING: OMB'S ROLE IN REVIEWS OF AGENCIES' DRAFT RULES AND THE TRANSPARENCY OF THOSE REVIEWS, supra, at 31–37: "According to OIRA representatives, the formal regulatory review process begins when the rulemaking agency sends the draft rule to the OIRA docket librarian (either electronically or hand carried), who logs the receipt of the rule and forwards it to the appropriate desk officer. The representatives said that OIRA desk officers do not use a standard 'checklist' to review agencies' rules, but indicated that most reviews are similar in certain respects. Section 6 of Executive Order 12866 states that the OIRA Administrator is to provide meaningful guidance and oversight 'so that each agency's regulatory actions are consistent with applicable law, the President's priorities, and the principles set forth in this Executive order, and do not conflict with the policies or actions of another agency.' The laws applicable to specific regulations vary, but always include the specific statutory authority under which each regulation is being developed (e.g., the Clean Air Act or the Occupational Safety and Health Act) as well as a variety

[19] https://www.reginfo.gov/public/.

of crosscutting regulatory statutes (e.g., the APA and the Regulatory Flexibility Act). . . .

"The type of review that OIRA conducts sometimes depends on the type of draft rule submitted. For example, if the draft rule contains a collection of information covered by the Paperwork Reduction Act, OIRA representatives said that the desk officer would also review it for compliance with the act. (They indicated that conducting both reviews simultaneously can be more difficult if different offices within the rulemaking agencies are responsible for the rule and the information collection.) If the draft rule is 'economically significant' (e.g., has an annual impact on the economy of at least $100 million), the executive order requires agencies to prepare an economic analysis describing, among other things, the alternatives that the agency considered and the costs and benefits of those alternatives. For those economically significant rules, the desk officers review the economic analyses using the 'best practices' document developed in January 1996 and the related guidance document issued in 2000. . . .

"OIRA representatives said that there is usually some type of communication (often via e-mail or telephone) between the desk officer and the rulemaking agency regarding specific issues in the draft rule. The representatives said briefings and meetings are sometimes held between OIRA and the agency during the review process, with branch chiefs, the Deputy Administrator, and/or the Administrator involved in some of these meetings. They also said that the desk officers always consult with the resource management officers on the budget side of OMB as part of their reviews, and reviews of draft rules are not completed until those resource management officers sign off. . . . If the draft rule is economically significant, they said the desk officer would also consult with an economist to help review the required economic analysis. For other rules the OIRA representatives said the desk officer might consult with other OIRA staff on issues involving statistics and surveys, information technology and systems, or privacy issues. In certain cases, OIRA may circulate a draft rule to other parts of the Executive Office of the President (e.g., the Office of Science and Technology Policy or the Council on Environmental Quality) or other agencies (e.g. SBA for rules having an impact on small businesses, or DOE, DOT, the Department of Agriculture, and the Department of the Interior for certain EPA rules). In those cases, OIRA may not only review the rule itself, but also manage an interagency review process. . . .

"[A] draft rule that has been reviewed and judged consistent with the executive order may be coded in the office's database as 'consistent with no change' (meaning that OIRA considered the draft rule as submitted to be consistent with all applicable requirements) or 'consistent with change' (which means that the draft rule was changed at either the issuing agency's initiation or at the suggestion of OIRA, and that OIRA then considered the changed rule to be consistent with all applicable requirements). If the rule is returned to the issuing agency for reconsideration, the executive order requires OIRA to provide a written explanation for the return. Section 7 of Executive Order 12866 originally required the President or the Vice President to resolve any disagreements or conflicts between or among agency heads or between OMB and any agency that cannot be resolved by the OIRA Administrator. However, in February 2002, Executive Order 13258 reassigned the Vice President's responsibilities in this area to the President's chief of staff. . . .

"OIRA representatives told us that a variety of factors could trigger informal discussions about a forthcoming rule. For example, they said informal reviews are sometimes used when there is a statutory or legal deadline for a rule or when the rule has a large impact on society and requires discussion with not only OMB but also other federal agencies. Therefore, they said informal review is more likely regarding rules issued by certain agencies (e.g., EPA, DOT, the Department of Agriculture, and the Department of Health and Human Services) that issue those types of rules. OIRA representatives also said there is an important distinction between informal consultations between OIRA and agency staff that may occur at any time and informal reviews that occur when OIRA is provided a substantive draft of a rule. There have been some indications that OIRA has increased its use of informal reviews in recent years."

The GAO illustrated the process as follows:

**Figure 4: The OIRA Regulatory Review Process**

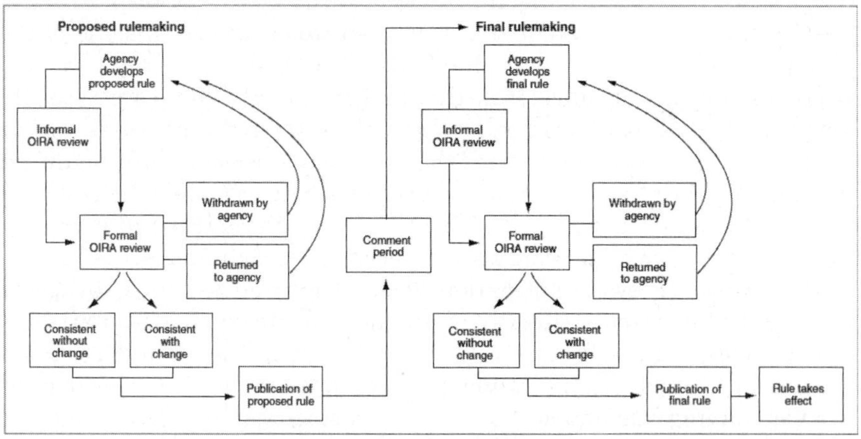


Source: GAO.

Id. at 30.

You can track what OIRA does with the rules it reviews.[20] In the Trump Administration, OIRA marked 129 rules as consistent (with the Executive Order) without change and 1,492 as consistent with change; it did not formally return any rules as inconsistent with the Executive Order, and agencies withdrew 124 rules. Similarly, in the Obama Administration, OIRA marked 492 rules as consistent without change and 3,558 as consistent with change; it returned only 3 rules as inconsistent, and agencies withdrew 242 rules. Recall that OIRA typically reviews significant rules twice—at the

[20] https://www.reginfo.gov/public/do/eoCountsSearchInit?action=init.

proposal and final stages. Informal review by OIRA, however, does not appear in this tracking.

(4) ***Application of Executive Order 12866 to Agency Guidance.*** As written, Executive Order 12866 appears not to apply to agency guidance. It defines "regulation" or "rule" as "an agency statement of general applicability and future effect, which the agency intends to have the force and effect of law" and "regulatory action" as "any substantive action by an agency (normally published in the Federal Register) that promulgates or is expected to lead to the promulgation of a final rule or regulation." § 3(d)–(e). As noted above, President Bush's Executive Order 13422 extended the regulatory review process to include "significant guidance documents," with significance defined the same way as for regulatory actions. A guidance document was defined as an "agency statement of general applicability and future effect, other than regulatory action, that sets forth a policy on a statutory, regulatory, or technical issue or an interpretation of a statutory or regulatory issue." § 3(g). In particular, agencies were required to notify OIRA in advance before issuing any significant guidance, and at OIRA's request supply "the content of the draft guidance document, together with a brief explanation of the need for the guidance document and how it will meet that need," with OIRA authorized to require further consultation before the guidance could be issued. § 7. For discussion of the requirements imposed by OMB's subsequent Bulletin for Agency Good Guidance Practices, see p. 423. Although President Obama revoked Executive Order 13422, and by its terms Executive Order 12866 does not appear to apply to guidance documents, his OMB asserted that significant agency guidance remained subject to OIRA review. See Peter R. Orszag, Director, OMB, M–09–13, Memorandum for the Heads & Acting Heads of Exec. Dept's & Agencies, Guidance for Regulatory Review (Mar. 4, 2009).[21] For more on President Trump's directives on OIRA and guidance, see Notes on Executive Order 13771 below.

(5) ***Executive Order 12866 and Notice-and-Comment Rulemaking.*** Look at the figure in Note 3 above. How many boxes correspond to the text of § 553? Executive Order 12866, in particular, adds much to § 553's skeletal procedures. For example, compare § 553's silence prior to the NPRM with Executive Order 12866 § 4's requirements of advance notice of potential regulatory actions and § 6(a)(1)'s demand that "*before issuing a notice of proposed rulemaking*, each agency should, where appropriate, seek the involvement of those who are intended to benefit from and those expected to be burdened by any regulation (including, specifically, State, local, and tribal officials)" (emphasis added; see also the same language in Executive Order 13563 § 2). Also striking is the comparison of § 553(b)'s minimal notice requirement—"either the terms or substance of the proposed rule or a description of the subjects and issues involved"—with § 6(a)(3)(B)'s requirements for agency submission to OIRA, in connection with *any* "significant regulatory action," of the "text of the draft regulatory action, together with a reasonably detailed description of the need for the regulatory action, and an explanation of how the regulatory action will meet that need"

[21] https://www.whitehouse.gov/wp-content/uploads/legacy_drupal_files/omb/memoranda/2009/m09-13.pdf.

as well as the assessments of the proposed action's costs and benefits quoted above. Application of some OIRA review procedures to significant agency guidance is another difference, as is the emphasis on the impact of guidance in practice.

Note the contrast between the Executive Order's distinctions among rulemakings (mainly, significant and nonsignificant) and the Supreme Court's decision in Vermont Yankee (p. 312), which read § 553 as establishing a one-size-fits-all set of procedures. Putting aside for the moment questions about White House control, do these expanded provisions for notice and targeting of more important regulations for additional procedures structure the rulemaking process better than § 553?

(6) ***Executive Order 12866 and Judicial Review.*** Executive Order 12866 § 10 notes that it is not creating judicially enforceable obligations: "Nothing in this Executive order shall affect any otherwise available judicial review of agency action. This Executive order is intended only to improve the internal management of the Federal Government and does not create any right or benefit, substantive or procedural, enforceable at law or equity by a party against the United States, its agencies or instrumentalities, its officers or employees, or any other person."

Yet won't the Executive Order affect judicial review in practice by generating assessments of proposed regulations? Under § 6(b)(4)(D), after the regulatory action has been published or the agency has announced its intention not to go forward, "OIRA shall make available to the public all documents exchanged between OIRA and the agency during the review by OIRA under this section." In addition, the agency must make public the assessments and other information it provided OIRA on significant or economically significant rules, identify substantive changes between the draft submitted to OIRA and the action subsequently announced, and identify "those changes in the regulatory action made at the suggestion or recommendation of OIRA." § 6(a)(3)(E).

(7) ***Other Planning and Assessment Requirements.*** Agencies face regulatory planning and assessment requirements outside of those in Executive Order 12866. Some come from other executive orders, such as the requirements that agencies analyze regulatory impacts on federalism. Exec. Order No. 13132, 64 Fed. Reg. 43255 (Aug. 10, 1999). Congress has also imposed potentially significant requirements. For example, the Unfunded Mandates Reform Act of 1995 put legislative muscle behind the requirement that—"unless otherwise prohibited by law"—agencies consider impacts on state, local, and tribal governments or the private sector for rules that might "result in the expenditure . . . of $100,000,000 or more (adjusted annually for inflation) in any 1 year." 2 U.S.C. §§ 1531–32. The Small Business Regulatory Enforcement Fairness Act requires agencies to publish a regulatory flexibility agenda that contains "a brief description of the subject area of any rule which the agency expects to propose or promulgate which is likely to have a significant economic impact on a substantial number of small entities," along with a summary of the action, its objectives and legal basis, an approximate schedule for completing it, and an agency contact. 5 U.S.C. § 602. In addition, SBREFA amended the Regulatory Flexibility Act to allow

judicial review of the RFA's requirement that an agency must prepare a regulatory flexibility analysis whenever it determines that a rule will have a "significant economic impact on a substantial number of small entities." § 611(b). Life has been made somewhat simpler than this sounds, although still complex, by permitting one "impact statement" generally to be used for all applicable impact analysis requirements. Typically, NPRMs and final rules have a section near the end, "Regulatory Notices," where each mandate is briefly addressed (even if simply to say it is not applicable). See, for example, the NPRM for the Tarmac Rule discussed in the Introduction (p. 13), 73 Fed. Reg. 74586, 74600–02 (Dec. 8. 2008).

(8) ***OIRA, the Congressional Review Act, Guidance, and Independent Agencies.*** In April 2019, OMB ordered all agencies subject to the Congressional Review Act (see Note 2, p. 897), including independent regulatory commissions and boards, to "coordinate with OIRA regarding a major determination" under the CRA for "a wide range" of regulatory actions, including legislative rules and guidance. Guidance on Compliance with the Congressional Review Act (Apr. 11, 2019).[22] The OMB memorandum noted that only some of these regulatory actions (legislative rules by executive agencies and departments) were being "submitted pursuant to Executive Order 12866 review," during which OIRA analyzes the actions for compliance with the CRA. The OMB memorandum thus established a new review process for the remainder of covered actions—most importantly, for legislative rules from independent agencies. For more information, see Maeve P. Carey & Christopher M. Davis, Cong. Rsch. Serv., R43992, The Congressional Review Act (CRA): Frequently Asked Questions (Nov. 12, 2021), at 4.[23]

(9) ***IRS Avoidance of OIRA Review.*** The Treasury Department's Internal Revenue Service had long avoided OIRA review of its tax regulations, even major ones, by relying on a Memorandum of Agreement formed in the Reagan Administration and renewed during the Clinton Administration meant to encourage the provision of timely guidance to taxpayers. The GAO had called for the agencies to reexamine this exemption in light of recent substantial regulations bypassing OIRA review. In April 2018, the Treasury Department and OMB signed a new Memorandum of Agreement, bringing more tax regulations under OIRA's purview.[24]

(10) ***Interagency Review.*** As described briefly in the Note 3 excerpt above, OIRA may circulate a draft rule within the Executive Office of the President (e.g., the Council on Environmental Quality) or to other agencies. In those cases, in addition to its review duties under the Executive Order, OIRA oversees the interagency review. Former OIRA Administrator Cass Sunstein lists this interagency review as the first of "four propositions that are not widely appreciated and that are central to an understanding of OIRA's role": "*(I) OIRA helps to oversee a genuinely interagency process, involving many specialists throughout the federal government.* OIRA's goal is often to identify

[22] https://www.whitehouse.gov/wp-content/uploads/2019/04/M-19-14.pdf.

[23] https://crsreports.congress.gov/product/pdf/R/R43992.

[24] https://home.treasury.gov/sites/default/files/2018-04/04-11%20Signed%20Treasury%20 OIRA%20MOA.pdf.

and convey interagency views and to seek a reasonable consensus, not to press its own positions. While OIRA's own views may well matter, OIRA frequently operates as a conveyer and a convener. The heads of the various departments and agencies are fully committed to the process; they understand, and agree, that significant concerns should be heard and addressed, whether or not they are inclined to agree with them." Cass R. Sunstein, The Office of Information and Regulatory Affairs: Myths and Realities, 126 Harv. L. Rev. 1838, 1841–42 (2013).

## NOTES ON ONGOING ISSUES WITH EXECUTIVE ORDER 12866 AND POTENTIAL CHANGES

(1) ***Openness of the Process.*** Much of the political battling in the early years of the regulatory review process concerned its lack of transparency and, correspondingly, fears that it was serving as a conduit for the views of the White House's political friends. This criticism was raised in particular about the Council on Competitiveness that Vice President Dan Quayle headed during the first Bush Administration. See Peter M. Shane, Political Accountability in a System of Checks and Balances: The Case of Presidential Review of Rulemaking, 48 Ark. L. Rev. 161 (1995). Regarding this criticism, Executive Order 12866 differed substantially from its predecessors, with agencies being required to: (1) identify substantive changes between the action they announce and the draft action they submitted to OIRA for review, and (2) indicate those changes made at OIRA's behest once the regulatory action is published or otherwise resolved. OIRA in turn is required to make publicly available all documents it exchanged with the agency during review. §§ 6(a)(3)(E), 6(b)(4)(D). Transparency in regulatory review was enhanced during the second Bush Administration, with the disclosures required by Executive Order 12866 being made available online, and the Obama Administration expanded online access further. Using the OIRA dashboard, it is now possible to easily access information on any regulatory action currently under review or for which review has been completed.

Nonetheless, concerns continue to be voiced about insufficient openness in the OIRA process, particularly when rules are under informal review. See GAO, Federal Rulemaking: Improvements Needed to Monitoring and Evaluation of Rules Development as Well as to the Transparency of OMB Regulatory Reviews, GAO-09-205 (Apr. 2009). For more on substantial concerns of noncompliance with the Executive Order's communications mandates, see Note 6 in Section 6.a below (p. 500).

(2) ***Communications Between OIRA and White House Officials.*** Also shielded from public disclosure are OIRA's interactions with other White House offices. LISA SCHULTZ BRESSMAN and MICHAEL P. VANDENBERGH emphasize this point in a study that focused on how top political officials at the EPA during the Bush I and Clinton Administrations perceived the regulatory review process: "A large majority of EPA respondents scored White House involvement relatively low on all measures of transparency, including visibility to the public, opportunities for public view, media coverage, and availability of information in the administrative record."

INSIDE THE ADMINISTRATIVE STATE: A CRITICAL LOOK AT THE PRACTICE OF PRESIDENTIAL CONTROL, 105 Mich. L. Rev. 47, 82 (2006).

Do you believe that greater disclosure of general White House involvement in regulatory review is needed to reap the greater political accountability of rulemaking that is often promoted as one of the justifications for OIRA review? Or is it more important to preserve opportunities for "some candid deliberations in the secluded quarters of the Old Executive Office Building"? John D. Graham, Adm'r, OIRA, Address Before Weidenbaum Center Forum: Executive Regulatory Review: Surveying the Record, Making It Work (Dec. 17, 2001). Mendelson has proposed a middle ground: "require that a significant rule include at least a summary of the substance of executive supervision." Nina A. Mendelson, Disclosing "Political" Oversight of Agency Decision Making, 108 Mich. L. Rev. 1127, 1150 (2010). See also Note 5 in Section 6.a (p. 500).

(3) ***Executive Order 12866's Impact on Regulatory Outcomes.*** To some extent, the question of whether greater openness is needed turns on the degree to which White House involvement (including OIRA) and the involvement of outside groups through the OIRA process alter regulatory outcomes. Although meetings with outsiders are recorded, little hard data are available on that score with respect to White House staff and presidential aides, though their interventions could be expected to be quite influential. OIRA itself clearly seems to influence regulatory outcomes. As described in Note 3 above (p. 464), in both President Trump's and President Obama's Administrations, the dominant outcome of OIRA review was change to the agency's regulation. Those figures likely understate OIRA's influence, as changes made through informal review occurring before any formal oversight are not included in the counts.

Some of OIRA's influence derives from pressure emanating from the White House; other influence comes from outside groups participating in the OIRA process. As for the latter, SIMON F. HAEDER and SUSAN WEBB YACKEE published an extensive study of 1,500 final regulations submitted to OIRA for review, using software to analyze changes in regulatory text: "We find that more interest group lobbying is associated with more regulatory change. We also demonstrate that, when only industry groups lobby, we are more likely to see rule change; however, the same is not true for public interest groups." INFLUENCE AND THE ADMINISTRATIVE PROCESS: LOBBYING THE U.S. PRESIDENT'S OFFICE OF MANAGEMENT AND BUDGET, 109 Am. Pol. Sci. Rev. 507, 517–18 (2015).

(4) ***Delay.*** Another concern raised about OIRA review under Executive Order 12866 is that it adds delay to the already lengthy rulemaking process, especially for major rules. This complaint, as noted earlier, was raised against OIRA review early on, with some critics concluding that "[b]ecause OMB was unable effectively to assess the wide range of regulations submitted to it, its principal function was to slow things down." Richard H. Pildes & Cass R. Sunstein, Reinventing the Regulatory State, 62 U. Chi. L. Rev. 1, 5 (1995). Consider in this respect the early decision in ENVIRONMENTAL DEFENSE FUND V. THOMAS, 627 F.Supp. 566 (D.D.C. 1986). The EPA's adoption of rules to regulate underground storage tanks for

hazardous waste had been delayed well past a statutory deadline—in part, it transpired, because of the need to obtain OMB clearance under Executive Order 12291. On the basis of internal documents released under seal, JUDGE FLANNERY found this delay substantially attributable to policy disagreements between the OMB and the EPA over the approach to be taken. While accepting the timetable now proposed by the agency for completion of the rules, the court addressed these words to OMB: "This court declares that OMB has no authority to use its regulatory review under EO 12291 to delay promulgation of EPA regulations arising from the 1984 Amendments of the RCRA beyond the date of a statutory deadline. Thus, if a deadline already has expired, OMB has no authority to delay regulations subject to the deadline in order to review them under the executive order. If the deadline is about to expire, OMB may review the regulations only until the time at which OMB review will result in the deadline being missed. . . . While this may be an intrusion into the degree of flexibility the executive agencies have in taking their time about promulgating these regulations, this is simply a judicial recognition of law as passed by Congress and of the method for dealing with deadlines laid down by the President himself."

Executive Order 12866 not only caps OIRA review at 90 days (with a possible 30-day extension), it also directs the agency to "notify OIRA as soon as possible" and comply with the review process "to the extent possible" in instances "when an agency is obligated by law to act more quickly than normal review procedures allow" or when regulatory actions "are governed by statutory or court-imposed deadlines." §§ 6(a)(3)(D), 6(b)(2). Do the existing provisions suggest acceptance of the holding in the Environmental Defense Fund case? Do they adequately address the timing problem? Would an agency actually move forward after these time limits pass without OIRA's approval?

Recent research suggests delay at OIRA is still an issue. In 2013, ACUS flagged problems in the Obama Administration, including that "[a]pproximately four dozen reviews completed in 2013 have taken more than a year." ACUS, Improving the Timeliness of OIRA Review, Administrative Conference Statement #18 (adopted Dec. 2013), at 3.[25] In light of these delays, ACUS issued "principles" calling for OIRA to "whenever possible, adhere to the timeliness provisions of Executive Order 12,866" and to "inform the public as to the reasons for the delay or return the rule to the submitting agency" if more than 180 days have passed since submission. Id. at 6–7. In his June 2013 confirmation hearing to be OIRA Administrator, Howard Shelanski promised to reduce the delays and seemed to carry out that intention.

OIRA delays, of course, contribute to overall delays in rulemaking. A report issued by Public Citizen in June 2016, Unsafe Delays, analyzed data from over twenty years of the federal Unified Agenda to assess changes in the length of rulemakings and other trends.[26] The report concluded that additional procedural requirements for rulemaking, including the

[25] https://www.acus.gov/sites/default/files/documents/OIRA%20Statement%20FINAL%20POSTED%2012-9-13.pdf.

[26] https://www.citizen.org/wp-content/uploads/unsafe-delays-report.pdf.

assessment requirements of Executive Order 12866, are causing significant delays. It found that "rules deemed to be of the highest importance (based on the priority assigned and number of requirements attached) take the longest to complete—sometimes longer than one presidential term." More specifically, economically significant rules "have taken 2.4 years, 41 percent longer than the overall average (1.7 years)," and take even longer if a regulatory flexibility analysis was required (2.5 years), an advanced notice of proposed rulemaking was issued (4.4 years), or both were involved (almost 5 years).

OIRA has moved faster than the Executive Order time limits in certain contexts. For example, in April 2021, the acting Director of OMB issued a memorandum laying out "expedited review procedures" for regulations and guidance under the American Rescue Plan Act of 2021. Promoting Public Trust in the Federal Government and Effective Policy Implementation through Interagency Review and Coordination of the American Rescue Plan Act (Apr. 26, 2021).[27]

For a study examining the length of OIRA reviews, see Alexander Bolton, Rachel Augustine Potter, & Sharece Thrower, Organizational Capacity, Regulatory Review, and the Limits of Political Control, 32 J. L. Econ. & Org. 242 (2015) (compiling a data set of more than 22,000 regulations and determining that "ideology, political timing, and presidential priorities" affect review times and that "OIRA takes longer to review rules when it is low on capacity—as measured by a lack of leadership, reduced staffing, and a high volume of rules on its docket").

(5) ***An Antiregulatory Bias in Executive Order 12866?*** Is OIRA review under Executive Order 12866 antiregulatory? NICHOLAS BAGLEY and RICHARD L. REVESZ argue that it is in CENTRALIZED OVERSIGHT OF THE REGULATORY STATE, 106 Colum. L. Rev. 1260, 1267–68 (2006): "Executive Order 12,866—based as it is on an order designed explicitly to promote an antiregulatory agenda—contains within it several structural and institutional biases against regulation. First, OIRA reviews agency regulations only to determine whether their benefits outweigh their costs—in other words, to ensure that the regulation is not too stringent. But, of course, the regulation could be too lax, and cost-benefit analysis might call for a more robust regulatory response. Second, OIRA rarely reviews agency decisions to deregulate with the same rigor with which it reviews new regulations. OIRA thus stands as a structural roadblock on the path of regulation, but not deregulation—an asymmetry which cannot be justified on cost-benefit grounds. Third, perhaps most importantly, OIRA generally does not review agency inaction. Agency inertia is therefore privileged under the current system of OIRA review, and many regulations that would have positive net benefits are never enacted. Fourth, at least two procedural features of OIRA review cut against regulation: the delay associated with OIRA review (exacerbated by OIRA's small size), and OIRA's exemption from the constraints of the Administrative Procedure Act (APA)."

---

[27] https://www.whitehouse.gov/wp-content/uploads/2021/04/M-21-24.pdf.

Former OIRA head John Graham disagrees: "Perhaps because of the stridently deregulatory stance taken by OIRA in the early years of the Reagan administration, a perception remains today that the exclusive role of OIRA is to foster deregulation or cost reduction. Indeed, benefit-cost analysis (BCA) counsels avoidance of inefficient lifesaving rules—but it also counsels acceleration of efficient investments in lifesaving. . . . [K]ey rulemakings from the 2001–2006 period . . . [illustrate] that OIRA plays a much more complex role than legal scholars appreciate. Using findings from BCA, OIRA served as a crucial advocate of several lifesaving regulations that, in the absence of OIRA's support, might not have survived White House oversight in a pro-business Republican administration. . . . What is missing from the legal literature is recognition of OIRA's proregulation role." JOHN D. GRAHAM, SAVING LIVES THROUGH ADMINISTRATIVE LAW AND ECONOMICS, 395 U. Pa. L. Rev. 395, 404, 450 (2008).

Do you agree that OIRA review under Executive Order 12866 is institutionally biased against regulation, or is any antiregulatory tilt better viewed as a reflection of presidential policies? If such a bias does exist, would you expect prompt letters or presidential directives to be an effective counter?

(6) ***Are the Advantages of OIRA Review Under Executive Order 12866 Exaggerated?*** Another area of extensive debate is whether, notwithstanding allegations of an antiregulatory bias, OIRA review under Executive Order 12866 produces regulatory benefits that could potentially justify the practice. STEVEN P. CROLEY, WHITE HOUSE REVIEW OF AGENCY RULEMAKING: AN EMPIRICAL INVESTIGATION, 70 U. Chi. L. Rev. 821, 831 (2003): "Proponents of expanded White House control defend greater control over agency rulemaking on several grounds. First, such control promotes consistency across the executive branch. Furthermore, while OMB is not an expert in any substantive regulatory field, it has become an expert in the field of regulation itself. Accordingly, OIRA has developed a special institutional capacity for distinguishing between, on the one hand, regulation likely to advance sound regulatory policy, and on the other, regulation that—however well intentioned—may lead to unintended and undesirable consequences. In addition to mere coordination, in other words, White House review provides a 'quality check' on pending rules. . . . Defenders of greater White House control further argue that the president is uniquely situated to advance national interests, as opposed to the factional interests that are often promoted by Congress, and that consequently find expression in agency decisions. . . . Another version of the argument in favor of a strong president, the unitary executive thesis, insists that presidential control over agencies is necessary not just to promote a national orientation in agency rulemaking, but also to preserve the political and constitutional legitimacy of the regulatory state."

Cass Sunstein, OIRA's Administrator from September 2009 to August 2012, touts its consistency and accountability role in an essay on how OIRA functions: "[M]ost of OIRA's day-to-day work is usually spent not on costs and benefits, but on working through interagency concerns, promoting receipt of public comments (for proposed rules), ensuring discussion of alternatives, and promoting consideration of public comments (for final rules)." Cass R. Sunstein, The Office of Information and Regulatory Affairs: Myths and Realities, 126 Harv. L. Rev. 1838, 1842 (2013); see also Cass R. Sunstein, Simpler: The Future of Government (2013).

These accounts of OIRA promoting consistency and accountability have been challenged. Based on interviews with EPA officials from the Bush I and Clinton Administrations, BRESSMAN and VANDENBERGH argue: "OIRA review does not achieve what might be called 'intra-agency coherence,' which includes reducing redundancies, avoiding inconsistencies, and eliminating unintended consequences between or among the regulations of a particular agency. . . . When asked to identify the aspects of the EPA process that provided greater public view and representation, respondents emphasized the notice-and-comment rule-making procedures of the [APA], various stakeholder and regional meetings, and Federal Advisory Committee Act requirements. . . . We conclude, somewhat paradoxically, that agencies, though not comprising elected officials, may better promote political accountability than the White House." BRESSMAN & VANDENBERGH, supra, at 74–76.[28]

More recently, LISA HEINZERLING, who was Associate Administrator of the EPA's Office of Policy during the Obama Administration's first term—a role that meant she was the primary EPA liaison with OIRA—has expressed skepticism about Sunstein's account, discussed above, of OIRA review: "From my vantage point at EPA, it certainly often appeared that OIRA—not other White House offices, not other agencies—was calling the shots. OIRA decided what to review, offered line-by-line edits of regulatory proposals, convened meetings with outside parties, mediated disputes among the agencies, decided whether an agency's cost-benefit analysis was up to snuff, and more. It often appeared, from the agency's perspective, that other White House offices were brought in to bolster, not to question, OIRA's position on regulatory matters." INSIDE EPA: A FORMER INSIDER'S REFLECTIONS ON THE RELATIONSHIP BETWEEN THE OBAMA EPA AND THE OBAMA WHITE HOUSE, 31 Pace Envtl. L. Rev. 325 (2014). See also discussion of transparency issues and delays in Notes 1 and 4 above (pp. 470, 471) and Note 6 in Section 6.a below (p. 500).

What changes would you make to the review process under Executive Order 12866, if any? Do you favor OIRA engaging in informal reviews, as described in Note 3 above (p. 464)? Should those reviews be included in the Executive Order? What changes could be made to improve the timeliness and transparency of OIRA reviews, whether through modifying the Executive

[28] Sally Katzen, OIRA Administrator under President Clinton, disagrees with their assessment: "I see it very differently. The agencies focus like a laser, as they should, on their statutory missions—in the case of EPA, protecting the environment. The White House and OIRA take a broader view and consider how, for example, an environmental proposal will affect energy resources, tax revenues, health policy, etc. Stated another way, EPA is pursuing a parochial interest; OIRA is tempering that with the national interest, as it should." Katzen also argues that ensuring intra-agency consistency was the agency's responsibility, and OIRA should instead focus on achieving inter-agency consistency, an area in which the former EPA officials interviewed by Bressman and Vandenbergh gave OIRA better marks. Sally Katzen, A Reality Check on an Empirical Study: Comments on "Inside The Administrative State," 105 Mich. L. Rev. 1497, 1505–06 (2006).

Order or other mechanisms? What about having OIRA review agency inaction, which might prompt more regulation? How should OIRA's coordination role, which emphasizes cost-benefit analysis, fit with other coordinating entities in the executive branch, like the Office of Legal Counsel, which focuses on legality, and the Domestic Policy Council, which emphasizes political priorities?

(7) ***Agency Capacity and Independence.*** Another potential benefit of OIRA's emphasis on cost-benefit analysis is the effect it has on the rulemaking process within agencies. "The first two administrators of OIRA saw as perhaps the greatest benefit of OMB review improved agency ability to 'respond to the kinds of questions that OMB raises.' This was achieved when agencies either established or enhanced their in-house capabilities to analyze their regulatory decisions. Thus, the very existence of external review can improve an agency's decisionmaking process by keeping the agency on its analytical toes. There is a value in keeping agency bureaucratic decisions intellectually honest and analytically rigorous, and external, centralized presidential regulatory review can bring this about by bringing to bear a new set of perspectives and analytical tools." JAMES L. BLUMSTEIN, REGULATORY REVIEW BY THE EXECUTIVE OFFICE OF THE PRESIDENT: AN OVERVIEW AND POLICY ANALYSIS OF CURRENT ISSUES, 51 Duke L.J. 851, 879 (2001).

Some caution may be warranted, however. In COST-BENEFIT ANALYSIS AND AGENCY INDEPENDENCE, 81 U. Chi. L. Rev. 609 (2014), MICHAEL LIVERMORE focuses on how agencies can use cost-benefit analysis to shield their regulatory choices. Livermore argues that "[t]here are hard methodological choices in any sophisticated analysis. How these choices are made can have extremely important effects on the results of cost-benefit analysis. . . . [A]gencies have played an important role in the evolution of cost-benefit analysis, which poses a challenge to the prevailing view of cost-benefit analysis as primarily a means for the center to exert control over the periphery." Moreover, "regularization of cost-benefit analysis into a standardized methodology actually constrains OIRA review, creating a safe harbor in which agencies are relatively protected from interference." Livermore bases his claims on a close examination of the EPA, which has "built [a] substantial in-house economics capacity . . . [that] far dwarfs that of OIRA, and has made significant methodological contributions, fostering the elaboration of concepts such as nonuse value and discounting that are fundamental to how cost-benefit analysis is carried out."

(8) ***A Progressive View of OIRA.*** In the lead-up to the 2020 presidential election, some progressive commentators called for "modernizing" OIRA "to support vital policy reforms": "An OIRA 2.0 would transform traditional cost-benefit analysis and modernize rulemaking, including by: 1. Enhancing Capacity and Expanding Mandate . . . . 2. Promoting Sustainability: . . . By making changes to the ground rules for regulatory accounting—the so-called 'discount rate' and 'value of a statistical life'—rulemaking can be better aligned with addressing the climate crisis (as well as other challenges that require long time horizons). 3. Tackling Inequality and Catalyzing Growth: Current levels of inequality constrain our nation's overall economic growth.

Yet current rulemaking does too little to incorporate the reality of inequality as an assumption on the front end, or the positive and normative value of reducing inequality on the back end. . . . 4. Boosting Equity and Inclusion: Too often, people of color, immigrants, and other marginalized groups are excluded from the rulemaking process, which often fails to consider how policy impacts them and how they can be more proactively engaged. A new set of tools and procedures can provide more robust measurement of how these communities will be impacted, give them more voice in the process, and target benefits intersectionally. 5. Enhancing International Competitiveness: . . . We recommend . . . the new subsidiary office in OIRA [be] tasked with identifying necessary and useful changes to these international rules—rather than using the international rules to lock in outdated practices." TODD N. TUCKER & RAJESH D. NAYAK, OIRA 2.0: HOW REGULATORY REVIEW CAN HELP RESPOND TO EXISTENTIAL THREATS (Apr. 2020).[29] For a related approach, see Daniel A. Farber, Lisa Heinzerling, & Peter M. Shane, ACS Issue Brief, Reforming "Regulatory Reform": A Progressive Framework for Agency Rulemaking in the Public Interest (Oct. 2018).[30]

(9) ***OIRA Under the Biden Administration.*** As noted in Note 2 above (p. 459), on his first day in office, President Biden signed Executive Order 13985 (Advancing Racial Equity and Support for Underserved Communities Through the Federal Government): "Affirmatively advancing equity, civil rights, racial justice, and equal opportunity is the responsibility of the whole of our Government. Because advancing equity requires a systematic approach to embedding fairness in decision-making processes, executive departments and agencies (agencies) must recognize and work to redress inequities in their policies and programs that serve as barriers to equal opportunity." Among other items, the President directed OMB to study methods for assessing equity and to work with agencies to "allocat[e] federal resources to advance fairness and opportunity," and for agencies to conduct an "equity assessment" of particular programs and to "promot[e] equitable delivery of government benefits and equitable opportunities." OMB sought comments on how best to assess equity in agency actions and issued its report in July 2021.[31]

President Biden also signed a memorandum, Modernizing Regulatory Review,[32] on his first day that directed OMB, in consultation with federal agencies, to make recommendations "for improving and modernizing regulatory review." The memorandum called for recommendations to:

(i) identify ways to modernize and improve the regulatory review process, including through revisions to OMB's Circular A-4, Regulatory Analysis, 68 Fed. Reg. 58,366 (Oct. 9, 2003), to ensure

---

[29] https://rooseveltinstitute.org/publications/oira-2-0-how-regulatory-review-can-help-respond-to-existential-threats/.

[30] https://www.acslaw.org/issue_brief/briefs-landing/reforming-regulatory-reform-a-progressive-framework-for-agency-rulemaking-in-the-public-interest/.

[31] https://www.whitehouse.gov/wp-content/uploads/2021/08/OMB-Report-on-E013985-Implementation_508-Compliant-Secure-v1.1.pdf.

[32] https://www.whitehouse.gov/briefing-room/presidential-actions/2021/01/20/modernizing-regulatory-review/.

> that the review process promotes policies that reflect new developments in scientific and economic understanding, fully accounts for regulatory benefits that are difficult or impossible to quantify, and does not have harmful anti-regulatory or deregulatory effects;
>
> (ii) propose procedures that take into account the distributional consequences of regulations, including as part of any quantitative or qualitative analysis of the costs and benefits of regulations, to ensure that regulatory initiatives appropriately benefit and do not inappropriately burden disadvantaged, vulnerable, or marginalized communities;
>
> (iii) consider ways that OIRA can play a more proactive role in partnering with agencies to explore, promote, and undertake regulatory initiatives that are likely to yield significant benefits; and
>
> (iv) identify reforms that will promote the efficiency, transparency, and inclusiveness of the interagency review process, and determine an appropriate approach with respect to the review of guidance documents.

What recommendations would you make? For more on what OIRA is doing in this area, see Robert Kuttner, Reclaiming the Deep State, The American Prospect (Oct. 4, 2022).

Nearly one year into his Administration, President Biden signed Executive Order 14058 (Transforming Federal Customer Experience and Service Delivery to Rebuild Trust in Government), 86 Fed. Reg. 71357 (Dec. 16, 2021). The Order gave OMB a central role in improving customer-facing services of the federal government. The Order also directed numerous agencies engaged in direct services to take steps to improve public experiences with government in areas ranging from TSA screenings at airports to small business loan applications at the Small Business Association, and much more.

## NOTES ON EXECUTIVE ORDER 13771

President Trump issued Executive Order 13771 soon after taking office, on January 30, 2017. 82 Fed. Reg. 9339 (Feb. 3, 2017). President Biden repealed it on his first day. Because a future Republican President will likely issue something similar, these Notes address the Order.

(1) ***Mechanics.*** Executive Order 13771 imposed two primary sets of obligations. First, "[u]nless prohibited by law," it required that whenever an agency "publicly proposes for notice and comment or otherwise promulgates a new regulation, it shall identify at least two existing regulations to be repealed." § 2(a). This 2-for-1 mandate did not apply to "(a) regulations issued with respect to a military, national security, or foreign affairs function of the United States; (b) regulations related to agency organization, management, or personnel; or (c) any other category of regulations exempted by the Director [of OMB]." § 4. Second, it capped "the total incremental cost of all new regulations, including repealed regulations" to a set amount. For

FY 2017, the Executive Order set the cap at zero, "unless otherwise required by law or consistent with advice provided in writing by the Director of the Office of Management and Budget." § 2(b). For the following years, the Director established each agency's cap for incremental costs from regulations in the presidential budgeting process. § 3(d).

Subsequently issued guidance by OIRA defined an "EO 13771 regulatory action," not falling in one of three exceptions, as any "significant regulatory action as defined in Section 3(f) of EO 12866 that has been finalized and that imposes total costs greater than zero" or certain guidance. Implementing Executive Order 13771, Titled "Reducing Regulation and Controlling Regulatory Costs" (Apr. 5, 2017), at Q2.[33] In addition, the OIRA guidance clarified that independent regulatory commissions and boards were not bound by the Executive Order's mandates. Id. at Q1. These mandates had some connection to retrospective review of rulemaking (to see if existing regulations could be repealed) that agencies were already supposed to be doing. See Executive Order 13563 § 6; Connor Raso, Brookings Inst., Assessing Regulatory Retrospective Review under the Obama Administration (June 15, 2017).[34]

Executive Order 13771 set additional reporting by agencies about their planned repeals and expected cost savings, starting with their regulatory plans in FY 2018. § 3(a). It also barred agencies from issuing a regulation "[u]nless otherwise required by law . . . if it was not included on the most recent version or update of the published Unified Regulatory Agenda as required under Executive Order 12866 . . . . unless the issuance of such regulation was approved in advance in writing by the Director." § 3(c). The Order did not change the notice-and-comment process, expressly noting that "[a]ny agency eliminating existing costs associated with prior regulations under this [2 for 1] subsection shall do so in accordance with the Administrative Procedure Act and other applicable law." § 2(c).

To help with the implementation of Executive Order 13771, in late February 2017, President Trump issued Executive Order 13777 (Enforcing the Regulatory Reform Agenda), 82 Fed. Reg. 12285 (Feb. 24, 2017), which President Biden also repealed on his first day.

(2) ***Executive Order 13771 in Operation.*** The Trump Administration feted its regulatory repeals under Executive Order 13771, claiming that there had been eight repeals for every new rule issued. But the 2-for-1 order allowed for an interesting mismatch. More specifically, as a former OIRA Administrator from President George W. Bush's Administration put it: "When tallying up new rules, agencies are only required to count 'significant' regulatory actions, but when counting regulations that are terminated, they can include all deregulatory actions, whether they are significant or not. So, the 8-to-1 ratio compares apples to oranges. When comparing significant deregulatory actions to significant regulatory actions, the ratio is closer to 2.6-to-1; it is

[33] https://www.regulations.gov/document/OMB-2017-0002-0053.

[34] https://www.brookings.edu/research/assessing-regulatory-retrospective-review-under-the-obama-administration/.

more than the 2-for-1 promise but not quite as dramatic." Susan E. Dudley, The Measure and Mismeasure of Rules, Forbes (Aug. 11, 2020).

The GAO reviewed 11 Executive Order 13771 rules (five from the EPA and six from HHS); of the 11, seven modified or repealed existing rules. The GAO found that "analyses for most of the seven rules monetized the same types of benefits and costs as analyses for the rules they modified, an indicator of consistency in the regulatory analyses" but that "some analyses developed by HHS's Centers for Medicare & Medicaid Services (CMS) did not fully meet best practices associated with analyzing regulatory alternatives, assessing important effects, and providing transparency." Federal Rulemaking: Selected EPA and HHS Regulatory Analyses Met Several Best Practices, But CMS Should Take Steps to Strengthen Its Analyses, GAO-21-151 (Dec. 2020).[35]

From January 20, 2017 to July 15, 2018, agencies subject to Executive Order 13771 issued 39 "major" rules—but only one "truly falls into the category of imposing new regulation" and imposes "the type of regulatory costs targeted by the order." Connor Raso, Brookings Inst., How Has Trump's Deregulatory Order Worked in Practice? (Sept. 6, 2018).[36] For a rundown of regulatory actions across all four years of the Trump Presidency see Dan Bosch, The Legacy of the Regulatory Budget, American Action Forum: Insights (Feb. 17, 2021).[37]

(3) ***Application to Guidance.*** By its terms, Executive Order 13771 applied to any "agency statement of general or particular applicability and future effect designed to implement, interpret, or prescribe law or policy or to describe the procedure or practice requirements of an agency," with the three exceptions listed above in Note 1. § 4. It notably lacked the "force and effect of law" language included in Executive Order 12866. The subsequent OIRA guidance narrowed the covered actions to a "significant regulatory action as defined in Section 3(f) of EO 12866 that has been finalized and that imposes total costs greater than zero," as noted above, or a "significant guidance document (e.g., significant interpretive guidance) reviewed by OIRA under the procedures of EO 12866 that has been finalized and that imposes total costs greater than zero." Implementing Executive Order 13771, supra, at Q2.

Section 4 of Executive Order 13891 (Promoting the Rule of Law Through Improved Agency Guidance Documents) (p. 424), which President Biden also repealed, mandated "review by the Office of Information and Regulatory Affairs (OIRA) under Executive Order 12866, before issuance" of significant guidance by agencies subject to regulatory review.

(4) ***Litigation.*** Public interest groups challenged Executive Order 13771 in court, alleging that the Order's mandates infringed on other statutory mandates. The district court initially dismissed their lawsuit, holding that the plaintiffs did not have standing to sue based on their current complaint. Public Citizen v. Trump, 297 F.Supp.3d 6 (D.D.C. 2018). After the plaintiffs

---

35 https://www.gao.gov/assets/gao-21-151.pdf.

36 https://www.brookings.edu/research/how-has-trumps-deregulatory-order-worked-in-practice/.

37 https://www.americanactionforum.org/insight/the-legacy-of-the-regulatory-budget/.

amended their complaint, the court denied the government's subsequent motion to dismiss and granted limited discovery, while also noting that the plaintiffs still had not proven the requisite injury. In December 2019, the district court ruled for the government: "Against this backdrop, it is certainly plausible, and perhaps likely, that the Executive Order and the OMB Guidance have delayed or derailed at least some regulatory actions that, if adopted, would materially benefit Plaintiffs or some of their members. But, for several reasons, it is hard to say with the requisite degree of confidence which actions those are, what would have occurred in the absence of the Executive Order, how any identifiable individual (or entity) is harmed, and whether any such harm—or risk of harm—is sufficient to establish standing." 435 F.Supp.3d 144, 146 (D.D.C. 2019). A Public Citizen advocate noted the tension between the government's litigation position and its political stance on the effectiveness of the order: "[T]he Administration has defended the order's legality by arguing in court that it plays no meaningful role in regulatory decision-making—a claim that, if true, demonstrates the order's worthlessness."

(5) ***Are Regulatory Caps Good or Bad?*** Executive Order 13771 imposed on agencies, for the first time, regulatory caps and the mandate that every new regulation be matched with two repeals of existing rules. Consider two opposing views on these devices as a matter of public policy (as opposed to legality). SAM BATKINS, IT IS PREMATURE TO LABEL A REGULATORY BUDGET UNCONSTITUTIONAL, Reg. Rev. (June 26, 2017):[38] "[Trump Administration official Marcus Peacock] cited both Canada and the United Kingdom, which have operated regulatory budgets without abandoning clean air or water standards. In those countries, reducing paperwork—through recordkeeping and reporting requirements—dominates the deregulatory actions. Peacock predicted similar actions for the United States." DAN FARBER, COURTS SHOULD KILL TRUMP'S PRICEY "2-FOR-1" DEREGULATION ORDER, The Hill Blog (Feb. 9, 2017):[39] "The cap on compliance costs ignores the fact that existing regulations have already had to pass a cost-benefit analysis. So if an existing regulation has a cost of $100 million, that means that the government already found the benefits were even higher—in other words, the existing regulation pays for itself in societal benefits. If you get rid of $100 million in costs by throwing away $120 million in benefits, just how is society better off? . . . This executive order effectively triples the cost, because agencies not only have to enact new regulations but go through equally complex proceedings to eliminate two old ones." Could positive regulatory caps for each agency be a middle ground between these positions? How would you set the cap for the EPA? For a postmortem on Executive Order 13771 and insights on the future of regulatory budgeting, see Symposium on Regulatory Budgeting, 25 Harvard J.L. & Pub. Pol'y Per Curiam (2022).[40]

---

[38] https://www.theregreview.org/2017/06/26/batkins-premature-regulatory-budget-unconstitutional/.

[39] https://thehill.com/blogs/pundits-blog/the-administration/318725-courts-should-kill-trumps-pricey-2-for-1-deregulation/.

[40] https://www.harvard-jlpp.com/a-symposium-on-regulatory-budgeting/.

## NOTES ON THE PAPERWORK REDUCTION ACT

(1) ***Statutory Requirements.*** The Paperwork Reduction Act, 44 U.S.C. §§ 3501 et seq., was enacted in 1980 and substantially amended after the Republicans took control of Congress in the 1994 midterm elections for the first time in four decades. (It was one of only a handful of items in Newt Gingrich's Contract with America that made it into law.) The PRA makes OIRA responsible for reducing the federal information collection burden. To collect information from outside the government by asking identical questions of ten or more sources, an agency typically must obtain OIRA's approval. The governing standard is if the collection "is necessary for the [agency's] proper performance . . . including whether the information shall have practical utility." 44 U.S.C. § 3508. If the agency uses traditional rulemaking to create its collection requirement, OIRA enjoys participatory rights and substantial oversight.[41] If the agency proceeds only bureaucratically, it typically still must go through a lengthy process that includes three months of public comment.[42] Anyone can track the requests made to OIRA online.[43]

OIRA can withhold permission to collect information or require that information be obtained through a central collection agency able to coordinate similar requests from other agencies. OIRA's participation in agency rulemaking is protected from judicial review, 44 U.S.C. § 3507(d)(6), and review of decisions under the statute has rarely been sought. But see Dole v. United Steelworkers of America, 494 U.S. 26 (1990); Action All. of Senior Citizens v. Sullivan, 930 F.2d 77 (D.C. Cir. 1991). Independent regulatory commissions and boards are subject to OIRA's constraints, although these entities may override OIRA by a publicly explained majority vote. 44 U.S.C. § 3507(f).

Approved information requests are given an OMB control number.[44] If the number is not on an information request required to be approved in this manner, the party receiving the request cannot be required to comply with it. 44 U.S.C. § 3512. Failure to show that number can have dramatic consequences.[45] In an April 2010 memorandum to agency heads, then-OIRA Administrator Cass Sunstein provided a helpful FAQ on the PRA, which you may wish to consult for further details on what counts (or not) as

---

[41] If OIRA comments publicly in the rulemaking, § 3507(d)(4) permits the Director, "in the Director's discretion," to disapprove a collection (A) "not specifically required by an agency rule," (B) if the agency failed to comply with statutory requirements, (C) "if the Director finds within 60 days after the publication of the rule that the agency's response to the Director's comments . . . was unreasonable," or (D) if the Director finds the agency in its final rule has substantially modified what it initially proposed, without resubmitting the modified collection requirement at least 60 days before issuing the final rule.

[42] The process is described here: https://pra.digital.gov/clearance-process/.

[43] https://www.reginfo.gov/public/jsp/PRA/praDashboard.myjsp.

[44] For a recent example, see U.S. Census, Household Pulse Survey: Measuring Social and Economic Impacts During the Coronavirus Pandemic (OMB Approval No. 0607-1013), https://www.census.gov/programs-surveys/household-pulse-survey.html.

[45] In Saco River Cellular, Inc. v. FCC, 133 F.3d 25 (D.C. Cir. 1998), the court unwound licensing proceedings ostensibly completed in 1986 but done on the basis of information supplied on forms that did not bear a valid control number.

"information" under the PRA, and what OIRA looks for when conducting a PRA review.[46]

(2) ***Equity and Latest Guidance.*** The PRA applies to information required for public benefits programs. These information burdens can be substantial. See Pamela Herd & Donald P. Moynihan, Administrative Burden: Policymaking by Other Means (2018). In April 2022, OMB issued guidance, Improving Access to Public Benefits Programs Through the Paperwork Reduction Act.[47] The memorandum detailed expectations for agencies to "(1) more completely and transparently articulate burdens and associated costs experienced by the public when accessing essential public benefits programs, and (2) use that analysis to 'minimize the Federal information collection burden, with particular emphasis on those individuals and entities most adversely affected,' consistent with the Paperwork Reduction Act of 1995."

(3) ***Political Control.*** The President (through OIRA) wields strong political control over information requirements. While OIRA's function is focused on coordination and cost reduction, not "substantive policies and programs," 44 U.S.C. § 3518(e), compliance with that limitation is itself in the hands of the White House. Does the statute recognize the need for presidential coordination of sharing information, thereby reducing duplicative agency demands? Does it permit industry to undermine agency functioning via political pressure? Similar questions are presented by Executive Order 12866, but the PRA recognizes an unusual level of presidential direction of agency affairs by statute.

(4) ***The PRA in Action.*** In May 2017, President Trump's Advisory Committee on Election Integrity requested data on all registered voters from every state in the country, including full names, addresses, the last four digits of social security numbers, and felony convictions. Forty-four states immediately refused to provide the information. Aside from potentially novel nonlegal arguments ("They can go jump in the Gulf of Mexico"), many states invoked the Paperwork Reduction Act to justify their noncompliance. The Advisory Committee, many of the states said, had not satisfied any of the PRA requirements for collecting information. For example, the information requests lacked the OMB control numbers needed for any PRA information request to be enforceable. In response, the White House claimed the Committee was not an "agency" as defined in the PRA and thus not subject to PRA requirements. President Trump shut down the Committee in January 2018 rather than defend the multiple lawsuits brought against its actions.

## NOTES ON COST-BENEFIT ANALYSIS AND RISK ASSESSMENT

(1) ***The Practice of Cost-Benefit Analysis.*** A prominent feature of the regulatory review process is its emphasis on cost-benefit analysis,

---

46 https://obamawhitehouse.archives.gov/sites/default/files/omb/assets/inforeg/PRA Primer_04072010.pdf.

47 https://www.whitehouse.gov/wp-content/uploads/2022/04/M-22-10.pdf.

particularly for economically significant rules. A good initial introduction to and justification of the practice is provided by CASS R. SUNSTEIN, past Administrator of OIRA, in THE COST-BENEFIT STATE: THE FUTURE OF REGULATORY PROTECTION 20–22 (2002): "First and foremost, a government committed to cost-benefit analysis will attempt to analyze the consequences of regulations, on both the cost and benefit side. . . . Many regulations do not impose substantial costs, and for routine or low-cost measures a formal analysis should not be required (and it has not been under the relevant executive orders). . . . Quantification will be difficult or even impossible in some cases. For arsenic in drinking water, government cannot really come up with specific numbers to link exposure levels to deaths and illnesses. At this stage, science is able to produce only ranges of anticipated benefits, which are not precise but are nonetheless highly illuminating. For regulations protecting airport security in the face of terrorist threats, quantification of the benefits is at best a guess. We do not know the magnitude of the risks, and a full scale cost-benefit analysis would be silly. But even here, an effort to be as specific as possible about costs and anticipated efficacy is likely to help us to promote airport security in the most reasonable manner. . . .

"[T]he cost-benefit state imposes a substantive requirement as well. In order to proceed, an agency should be required to conclude, in ordinary circumstances, that the benefits justify the costs, and to explain why. . . . If an agency seeks to proceed even though the benefits do not justify the costs, it should have to explain itself—by saying, for example, that those at risk are young children, and that because they cannot protect themselves, and because a number of years of life are involved, unusual steps should be taken.

"At this point, it might be possible to question whether a large amount of money (say, $400 million) would really be too much to spend to save a small number of lives (say, two). Who is to say that $400 million is too much? The best answer is heavily pragmatic. . . . In allocating our [personal] resources, we set priorities, partly to use resources to prevent the more serious safety problems and partly to use them on other things we care about, such as education, recreation, food, and entertainment. The same is true for governments, which cannot sensibly spend huge amounts on small hazards. . . . . None of this suggests that the government should be rigidly bound to the 'bottom line.' . . . The basic ideas are simple: Agencies should be required to investigate both costs and benefits, to show that benefits justify costs in most circumstances, and to offer a reasonable explanation for any decision to proceed when costs exceed benefits. [T]hese requirements should help to overcome problems that we all face in thinking about risk while at the same time reducing interest-group power and promoting accountability in government."

Also look back at § 1 of Executive Order 12866. Among other items, it tells agencies that: "Costs and benefits shall be understood to include both quantifiable measures (to the fullest extent that these can be usefully estimated) and qualitative measures of costs and benefits that are difficult to quantify, but nevertheless essential to consider." Applying § 1 in actual rulemakings raises a number of analytical challenges.

(2) ***Critiques of Cost-Benefit Analysis.*** Despite its dominance, cost-benefit analysis has come in for continued critique, in no small part as a result of its role in regulatory review. Below is a prominent critique and a reply to a different critique:

(a) FRANK ACKERMAN & LISA HEINZERLING, PRICING THE PRICELESS: COST-BENEFIT ANALYSIS OF ENVIRONMENTAL PROTECTION, 150 U. Pa. L. Rev. 1553 (2002): "[C]ost-benefit analysis involves the creation of artificial markets for things—like good health, long life, and clean air—that are not bought and sold. It also involves the devaluation of future events through discounting. . . . Most people view risks imposed by others, without an individual's consent, as more worthy of government intervention than risks that an individual knowingly accepts. . . . In short, even for ultimate values such as life and death, the social context is decisive in our evaluation of risks. . . . Cost-benefit analysis is exceedingly time- and resource-intensive, and its flaws are so deep and so large that this time and these resources are wasted on it. Once a cost-benefit analysis is performed, its bottom line number offers an irresistible sound bite that inevitably drowns out more reasoned deliberation. . . . Cost-benefit analysis cannot overcome its fatal flaw: it is completely reliant on the impossible attempt to price the priceless values of life, health, nature, and the future. Better public policy decisions can be made without cost-benefit analysis, by combining the successes of traditional regulation with the best of the innovative and flexible approaches that have gained ground in recent years."

(b) MICHAEL A. LIVERMORE & RICHARD L. REVESZ, REVIVING RATIONALITY: SAVING COST-BENEFIT ANALYSIS FOR THE SAKE OF THE ENVIRONMENT AND OUR HEALTH (2020) : "Critics of cost-benefit analysis have long argued that the technique is too easily subject to manipulation. These critics claim that although regulation that is supported by cost-benefit analysis gives the impression of objectivity and genuine deliberation, this impression is an illusion. Rather, the argument goes, regulatory decisions are fundamentally political in nature, and the long, detailed, and technical cost-benefit analyses that accompany regulations are nothing more than jargon-laden exercises in post hoc rationalization that obscure more than illuminate. . . . [I]t is foolhardy to argue that cost-benefit analysis is a fully deterministic methodology that always gives clear answers concerning how best to regulate. But it does not follow that the technique is infinitely malleable.

"There are at least three important constraints on the ability of agencies to manipulate cost-benefit analysis: transparency, consistency, and honesty. In terms of transparency, cost-benefit analysis requires agencies to disclose and explain how they arrived at their conclusions. This means that all of the empirical data, models, and methodological choices are explicitly stated and subject to scrutiny and critique. If agencies ignore data, use flawed models, or make outlandish methodological choices, they can be held to account, by the public, Congress, and the courts. Consistency is a related source of constraint. Because prior analyses are part of the public record, the choices in any new analysis can be compared to those made in the past. Inconsistencies with prior practice naturally give rise to a demand for justification. Although there are sometimes legitimate reasons that an agency might depart from a prior practice, that agency should be able to give a reason for the departure, and those reasons can be subject to scrutiny. The final source of constraints is honesty. . . . Cost-benefit analysis creates a context in which many different people must work together on a collective product. In large and diverse groups, maintaining a widespread conspiracy to manipulate the results is difficult."

(3) ***Cost-Benefit Analysis in Statutory Context.*** Can an agency be forced to engage in cost-benefit analysis in the regulatory review process when it doesn't have to perform such analysis (or indeed cannot make decisions based on such evaluation) in the context of judicial review? In some circumstances Congress appears to have forbidden costs to be taken into account in regulatory decisionmaking about health and safety issues (for example, the Occupational Safety and Health Act, see the Benzene case (p. 862)) or to have allowed consideration of economic impact only a limited role in the regulatory equation (for instance, the Prison Rape Elimination Act, Note 4 below). In these circumstances, can agencies nevertheless be required to assess the costs and benefits of their proposed regulatory actions under Executive Order 12866? To what extent does Executive Order 12866 take such statutory limitations into account?

We consider the legal implications of requiring agencies to perform such analyses in more detail in Chapter VII (p. 1037). In other regulatory settings, cost-benefit analysis may be statutorily required and, in consequence, the agency's calculations may be closely scrutinized on judicial review. Costs contemplated by a statutory framework may not match the type of analysis being conducted under Executive Order 12866; in other words, the exercise of statutory interpretation is not the same as the exercise of cost-benefit analysis under OIRA review. See Note 5 below; discussion in Chapter VIII (p. 1155). Proposals are pending in Congress to impose cost-benefit analysis much more widely. Independent Agency Regulatory Analysis Act, S. 2279 (117th Cong.) (2021).

(4) ***Examples of Cost-Benefit Analysis Under Executive Order 12866.*** Consider the regulatory impact analysis performed by the Department of Transportation for the Tarmac Rule, discussed in Chapter I, which imposed limits on the time airline passengers could be kept in a plane on the ground without being given the opportunity to deplane. The rule was deemed significant under the Executive Order. The agency concluded: "The total present value of benefits over a 20 year period at a 7% discount rate is $169.7 million and the total present value of costs over a 20 year period at a 7% discount rate is $100.6 million. The net present value of the rule for 20 years at a 7% discount rate is $69.1 million." Enhancing Airline Passenger Protections, 74 Fed. Reg. 68983, 69000 (Dec. 30, 2009).[48]

Consider here the RIA's quantification of passengers' time and comfort: "Certain components of the Final Rule . . . will result in time saved (or lost)

[48] You can look at the over 100-page final Regulatory Impact Analysis, which analyzes the final rule and five alternatives (some more strict and some more lax), at https://www.regulations.gov/document/DOT-OST-2007-0022-0265.

for individuals. In addition, certain components . . . will result in improved travel conditions for passengers, through greater physical comfort or increased confidence in on-time arrival. Economists measure the value of time saved using set estimates derived from average wages to reflect the cost to the individual of time spent in transit instead of on another activity. DOT has developed values to calculate air travel time savings for leisure and business passengers, with a range of high to low values . . . . This RIA uses these figures to estimate the value of passenger time saved or lost based on carriers' compliance with the Final Rule. In addition, time saved by persons coming to meet arriving passengers is also calculated and valued at $10.60 per hour, the DOT-recommended value for local personal travel. . . .

"Several aspects of the Final Rule are designed to increase traveler comfort during delays. Transportation economists have conducted studies of consumer behavior and different aspects of user experience in transit systems. These analyses have led to estimates of premiums on the value of user time based on the value people place on quicker/easier access to move from one place to another and analysis of the value of improved comfort during a travel experience. For example, studies show that transit riders value sitting more than standing without regard to any change in total travel time required. Travelers also prefer to spend time in transit rather than part of the time waiting for service if total trip length is the same.

"Several aspects of the Final Rule will shift the portion of total trip time spent in less comfortable conditions (such as the fourth hour on a plane spent sitting on the tarmac) to time spent in more comfortable conditions (the fourth hour spent in a terminal). This RIA assumes no change in overall trip time except in cases of cancellation . . . . The value of the difference in comfort is estimated using the base value of travel time saved (as noted above) and applying a 'premium' to that time. Estimates for this 'comfort premium' are developed from research literature in transportation economics. These premiums were derived from survey-based data that reflect travel time values that incorporate the quality of waiting, walking and transfer conditions.

" 'Level of service' ratings are used to determine the value of different levels. Since no specific estimate of time values for level of service ratings for airline travel are available, values were taken from other modal studies. The most applicable study estimated a time value premium based on differing levels of service that incorporated factors such as comfort, convenience and reliability . . . for various categories of public transportation and auto users. . . . Based on this study, a premium of .34 was used for the greater comfort derived from access to food, water and clean lavatory facilities; a premium of .68 was used for the greater comfort of waiting in the terminal rather than in a plane on the tarmac. These premiums are similar to those found for the value transit passengers place on being able to sit versus stand, which range from .20 to .87 in two studies that address measuring the quality of travel experience. . . .

"No data was found to quantify the value of decreased anxiety during extended wait periods. Based on the studies of auto and public transit passengers' value of levels of service summarized above, a .01 premium was selected as a proxy for the value of decreased anxiety/discomfort based on knowledge that a contingency plan exists during time greater than one hour spent on the tarmac and until allowed to deplane."

For a much more controversial (with very disturbing content) example, see the nearly 200-page final Regulatory Impact Analysis for the Attorney General's standards under the Prison Rape Elimination Act.[49] LISA HEINZERLING severely criticized the Administration's RIA in a blog post: "Most awful is the Department's effort to put a monetary value on avoiding rape and other forms of sexual abuse in prison. To even try to understand the Department's analysis, you need first to understand how cost-benefit analysis works. . . . Thus, it came to pass that . . . the DOJ found itself in the remarkable position of asking how much money the victims of rape would be willing to pay to avoid rape and also asking how much money these victims would be willing to accept in exchange for being raped. . . . Never mind that rape is a serious crime, not a market transaction. Never mind that framing rape as a market transaction strips it of the coercion that defines it. Never mind that the law under which DOJ was acting is the Prison Rape Elimination Act, not the Prison Rape Optimization Act. In the topsy-turvy world of cost-benefit analysis, DOJ was compelled to treat rape as just another market exchange, coercion as a side note, and the elimination of prison rape as a good idea only if the economic numbers happened to come out that way.

"Compounding the outrage, DOJ went on to develop 17 different categories of rape and sexual assault and to provide monetary values of the benefit of avoiding each of these categories—thus providing, in its words, a 'hierarchy' of the different ways of sexually violating prisoners. Reading DOJ's analysis itself feels like a violation. For example, to justify giving rape committed without physical force the same economic value as rape with physical force, DOJ offered a belabored treatment of why rape can be bad even if no physical force is used, relying substantially on public comments critical of DOJ's initial suggestion that rape without physical force was only one-fifth as bad as rape with such force. One must wonder: was it really so hard for DOJ to realize that rape without physical force can be as devastating as rape with it? Did DOJ—the Department of Justice, the legal arm of the U.S. government—really not understand this until the public comment period for this rule?" LISA HEINZERLING, COST-BENEFIT JUMPS THE SHARK, Georgetown Law Faculty Blog (June 13, 2012).[50]

The RIA for PREA was done only because of the Executive Order. Under the Act, according to Heinzerling, "the only limit that Congress placed on DOJ's national standards was that the standards were not to impose 'substantial additional costs' beyond the present expenditures of the covered facilities. In its final rule setting the national standards called for by PREA, DOJ easily found that its standards complied with this statutory constraint. In three quick sentences, DOJ found that even full compliance with DOJ's standards would increase total expenditures by less than 1 percent and that

---

[49] https://www.prearesourcecenter.org/sites/default/files/library/prearia.pdf.

[50] https://gulcfac.typepad.com/georgetown_university_law/2012/06/cost-benefit-jumps-the-shark.html.

this additional expenditure did not exceed the statutory limit of 'substantial additional costs.' " Id.

(5) ***Cost-Benefit Analysis in Financial Regulation.*** The use of cost-benefit analysis in financial regulation is currently receiving considerable attention, prompted in part by D.C. Circuit case law and in part by recent legislation. In a series of cases, culminating in a 2011 decision, Business Roundtable v. SEC, 647 F.3d 1144, the D.C. Circuit read the requirement that the Securities and Exchange Commission "consider . . . whether [regulatory] action will promote efficiency, competition, and capital formation," 15 U.S.C. § 80a–2(c), a requirement added to the Investment Company Act in 1996, to require that the SEC specifically estimate a proposed rule's costs. The Business Roundtable decision and extensive financial regulatory activity in the aftermath of the 2010 Dodd-Frank Wall Street Reform and Consumer Protection Act sparked a vigorous scholarly debate about the propriety of requiring cost-benefit analysis for financial regulation. See John C. Coates IV, Cost-Benefit Analysis of Financial Regulation: Case Studies and Implications, 124 Yale L.J. 882 (2015); Eric A. Posner & E. Glen Weyl, Cost-Benefit Analysis of Financial Regulations: A Response to Criticisms, 124 Yale L.J. F. 246 (2015); Symposium, The Administrative Law of Financial Regulation, 78 Law & Contemp. Probs. 1 (2015). For more on judicial review in this area, see Notes on Cost-Benefit Analysis as a Possible Element of "Arbitrary and Capricious" Review in Chapter VIII (p. 1155).

(6) ***Problems of Risk Assessment and Selection.*** Closely intertwined with the debate over cost-benefit analysis are the difficulties agencies face in selecting which risks merit regulatory response and prioritizing their regulatory efforts. Defenders of cost-benefit analysis argue that it plays an important role in guarding against agency tendencies to overregulate, while critics deny that any such tendency exists and emphasize the uncertainties and difficulties involved in quantifying risk.

JERRY MASHAW and DAVID HARFST provide a concrete example in their book THE STRUGGLE FOR AUTO SAFETY 140–46 (1990): In the same legislative breath, amendments to the National Traffic and Motor Vehicle Safety Act helped prevent the development of air bags for a decade or more and required a highly questionable commitment of regulatory resources to school bus safety. Risk assessment advanced that much greater gains were to be had from safety investments in cars than in school buses. Risk management techniques suggested that at least the immediate effect of making school buses more expensive would be to keep older buses on the road. Members of Congress and their constituents, however, were unmoved. They preferred personal freedom in automobiles for themselves—despite quite substantial risks of death and serious injury that were cheaply avoidable. They were horrified that anyone could propose to balance the possible saving of a child's life by making school buses safer against the relatively high regulatory costs of doing so.

RICHARD H. PILDES & CASS R. SUNSTEIN, REINVENTING THE REGULATORY STATE, 62 U. CHI. L. REV. 1, 57–58 (1995): "[F]or laypeople, the most salient contextual features include: (1) the catastrophic nature of the risk;

(2) whether the risk is uncontrollable; (3) whether the risk involves irretrievable or permanent losses; (4) the social conditions under which a particular risk is generated and managed, a point that connects to issues of consent, voluntariness, and democratic control; (5) how equitably distributed the danger is or how concentrated on identifiable, innocent, or traditionally disadvantaged victims, which ties to both notions of community and moral ideals; (6) how well understood the risk process in question is, a point that bears on the psychological disturbance produced by different risks; (7) whether the risk would be faced by future generations; and (8) how familiar the risk is. . . . The important point is that it can be fully rational to attend to contextual differences of this sort. . . . It is fully plausible to believe that expenditures per life saved ought to vary in accordance with (for example) the voluntariness of the risk or its catastrophic quality."

MATTHEW D. ADLER, AGAINST "INDIVIDUAL RISK": A SYMPATHETIC CRITIQUE OF RISK ASSESSMENT, 153 U. Pa. L. Rev. 1121, 1132–33 (2005): "What this Article offers, in short, is a sympathetic critique of risk regulation and risk assessment. Much of the legal scholarship in this area is more radically critical. Regulation guided by risk assessment is allegedly flawed to the core—for example, because it is undemocratic, or because it is beset with uncertainties about the mechanisms of cancer, dose-response relationships, and exposure pathways. The very enterprise of quantifying safety is seen as misguided. I do not believe that the very enterprise of quantifying safety is misguided. Risk assessment represents a giant leap forward for public rationality, in my view. Dose-response curves and exposure assessments are, properly, central for the regulation of toxins; parallel techniques are central for agencies that focus on other threats to life and limb. But these impressive techniques should be used to illuminate what is truly at stake in risk regulation, not to distract us with morally unimportant information. Risk regulation needs to be changed in two ways. First, it should adopt a new understanding of risk, Bayesian rather than frequentist. Second, it should adopt choice criteria that are sensitive to population size—paradigmatically, 'population risk' criteria. Risk assessment, in turn, must be reworked so that it can inform regulatory choice thus revised."

MICHAEL A. LIVERMORE, CATASTROPHIC RISK REVIEW, LPP Working Paper No. 3-2022 (2022):[51] "[T]he management of catastrophic risk [Ed: think climate change, pandemics, nuclear disasters, etc.] has largely fallen outside the purview of cost-benefit analysis. The primary reasons that cost-benefit analysis has played a less important role in the context of catastrophic risks are procedural, rather than methodological. Although improvements can be made to cost-benefit analysis techniques to better account for catastrophic risks, the more important set of reforms—and the ones discussed in this proposal—are institutional. . . . Regulatory review is well-suited for reining in overactive agencies or delaying or stopping imprudent agency action. But there are a wide range of catastrophic risks that are more likely to be exacerbated by government inaction than government action. Because OIRA does not evaluate agency agenda setting,

[51] https://papers.ssrn.com/sol3/papers.cfm?abstract_id=4217680.

cost-benefit analysis is not applied to the most consequential government decisions concerning catastrophic risks—the choice not to act. The institutional reform discussed in this proposal is a Catastrophic Risk Review process, spearheaded by OIRA, that would examine catastrophic risks and potential government responses through a cost-benefit lens. This review process would build on earlier experiments in which OIRA has played a more proactive role in initiating regulatory actions. . . . The purpose of this process would be to find areas where tangible, cost-benefit justified policy steps can be undertaken to manage catastrophic risks."

(7) ***OIRA's Role in Risk Selection and OMB's Role in the Information Quality Act.*** Some scholars argue that OIRA could play an important role in addressing difficulties in risk assessment. See Nicholas Bagley & Richard L. Revesz, Centralized Oversight of the Regulatory State, 106 Colum. L. Rev. 1260, 1314–17 (2006) ("A centralized agency armed with substantial scientific expertise might in many cases be better situated than single-mission agencies to set generic guidelines as to how science should be employed in agency risk assessments."). OIRA has taken a limited role, issuing guidance to agencies on appropriate principles to follow in risk analysis. See Susan E. Dudley (OIRA) & Sharon L. Hays (OSTP), Memorandum for the Heads of Exec. Dep'ts & Agencies on Updated Principles for Risk Analysis (Sept. 19, 2007).[52]

OMB also plays a role. Although it withdrew a 2006 proposed Risk Assessment Bulletin, after comment, OMB has published government-wide guidelines on information disseminated by agencies, as required by the Information Quality Act, also known as the Data Quality Act (See Note 3, p. 816). See Guidelines for Ensuring and Maximizing the Quality, Objectivity, Utility, and Integrity of Information Disseminated by Federal Agencies, 67 Fed. Reg. 8452 (Feb. 22, 2002). The Act, enacted in 2001 with little discussion, provides that all federal agencies must create administrative mechanisms by which affected persons can seek correction of information that does not comply with the guidelines. § 515(b), codified at 44 U.S.C. § 3516 note. In April 2019, OMB issued new guidance to agencies on the Information Quality Act, the first since 2002. Under the "additional guidance . . . required to address changes in the information landscape and to incorporate best practices developed over time," agencies must come up with their own definition of "influential information" (rather than relying on a general provision from the 2002 guidance)—and such information is subject to more review under the Act. OMB also called for more disclosure of data and "sufficient documentation . . . to allow data users to determine the fitness of the data." Improving Implementation of the Information Quality Act (Apr. 24, 2019).[53]

(8) ***Is Peer Review a Solution?*** In addition to its guidelines on information quality, OMB issued a bulletin providing that, "[t]o the extent permitted by law, each agency shall conduct a peer review on all influential scientific information that the agency intends to disseminate." Influential scientific

[52] https://www.whitehouse.gov/wp-content/uploads/legacy_drupal_files/omb/assets/regulatory_matters_pdf/m07-24.pdf.

[53] https://www.whitehouse.gov/wp-content/uploads/2019/04/M-19-15.pdf.

information is defined as "scientific information that the agency reasonably can determine will have or does have a clear and substantial impact on important public policies or private sector decisions." The bulletin imposes additional requirements for peer review of influential scientific information that could have a $500 million annual impact or is novel, controversial, or precedent setting or has significant interagency interest. Final Information Quality Bulletin for Peer Review, 70 Fed. Reg. 2664, 2675–76 (Jan. 14, 2005). OMB has also recommended that agencies subject regulatory impact analyses and supporting technical documents for economically significant and major rulemakings to independent, external peer review. Agencies are supposed to post their peer review plans under the OMB's Bulletin on their websites.[54]

Does peer review offer a useful mechanism for improving the quality of regulatory decisionmaking generally? LARS NOAH, SCIENTIFIC "REPUBLICANISM": EXPERT PEER REVIEW AND THE QUEST FOR REGULATORY DELIBERATION, 49 Emory L.J. 1033, 1067, 1083 (2000): "Concerns about the potential for added administrative burdens . . . deserve serious attention. If it does not help steer an agency early in the process, peer review of regulatory decisionmaking may become an ominous hurdle for agencies to surmount, both in terms of the difficulty of undergoing that scrutiny and because of the prospect of judicial invalidation triggered by the inevitable criticisms from expert peer reviewers. Moreover, if agencies sense that the blessing of outside scientists is necessary before proceeding with a rule, they may decide to settle for second-best regulatory options simply because these generate the least disagreement among the experts. . . . Involving outside scientists in the process undoubtedly will promote greater care and reflection, and these peer reviewers may help steer agencies clear of embarrassing and costly mistakes, but ultimately the independent experts cannot and should not displace the broader deliberative process about hard policy questions that science cannot answer." Noah concludes that "[s]o long as independent peer review does not become a substitute for public participation or judicial review, it may provide a forum for genuine deliberation that can facilitate subsequent steps in the administrative process and help to better focus other forms of external scrutiny of agency decisionmaking."

(9) ***Cost-Benefit Analysis Outside the United States.*** The World Bank provides a comparative treatment of cost-benefit analysis in the regulatory context. See World Bank, Global Indicators of Regulatory Governance: Worldwide Practices of Regulatory Impact Assessments.[55] The World Bank also houses a Global Database of Regulatory Impact Assessment.[56]

---

[54] For an example, see https://www.fcc.gov/peer-review-0.

[55] https://documents1.worldbank.org/curated/en/905611520284525814/Global-Indicators-of-Regulatory-Governance-Worldwide-Practices-of-Regulatory-Impact-Assessments.pdf.

[56] https://rulemaking.worldbank.org/en/ria-documents.

# SECTION 6. FAIRNESS AND BIAS IN THE DECISIONMAKING PROCESS



Unlike formal rulemaking (and adjudication), the APA does not place specific limits on the informal rulemaking process (or on even less formal forms of action like guidance and informal adjudication) to promote fairness in the decisionmaking process—such as bars on ex parte communications or the separation of functions in decisionmaking. The Constitution and more general constraints of the APA may come into play to provide some legitimacy guardrails on the notice-and-comment process and its exceptions as well as to informal adjudication. This Section turns first to ex parte communications and then to open-mindedness of the decisionmaker. Although this Chapter focuses on rulemaking, some of the following material applies to adjudication as well.

## a. Ex Parte Contacts

*HOME BOX OFFICE, INC. v. FEDERAL COMMUNICATIONS COMMISSION*

In distinguishing rulemaking from adjudication for due process purposes, Justice Holmes's opinion in Bi-Metallic Investment Co. v. State Bd. of Equalization of Colorado (p. 224) rejected the familiar judicial model—finding it an inappropriate analogy when the government is involved in making policy decisions. The APA notice-and-comment process reflects that judgment. Notably, the process is not "*on the record.*" In addition, Justice Holmes concluded that citizens' protection in such proceedings is to be found, not in the procedural apparatus of trial-type hearings, but in "their [political] power, immediate or remote, over those who make the rule." And as we have seen in, for example, Executive Order 12866, an elaborate political apparatus has grown up to channel such efforts in the most important rulemakings.

Complications arise, however, if the agency uses rulemaking to make decisions that seem equally appropriate (if not more so) for adjudication, leading courts to fear that it is attempting to escape the usual constraints on "off the record" activities that apply to adjudicatory decisionmaking. SANGAMON VALLEY TELEVISION CORP. V. UNITED STATES, 269 F.2d 221 (D.C. Cir. 1959), was such a case. In that early, pre-cable television era, it was much more advantageous to have a franchise for one of the twelve "VHF" channels than one of the greater number of "UHF" channels. Not all televisions could receive UHF signals; those that could often did not receive them as well as VHF, because a VHF signal could be broadcast to a larger geographic area. The "rule" the FCC proposed would have had the effect of awarding a particular VHF franchise (Channel 2) to a particular St. Louis, Missouri, television station in lieu of the UHF channel that station was currently assigned. It would also have reassigned the St. Louis station's UHF channel to Springfield, Illinois, to replace a franchise for Channel 2, currently in use. These assignments would have implemented an FCC policy to avoid intermixing VHF and UHF transmission in the same television market. Congressional testimony disclosed that the St. Louis station's President had personally called on, written, and telephoned FCC Commissioners to advocate shifting Channel 2 to St. Louis. Moreover, he had taken them to lunch and had sent them turkeys as Christmas presents while the matter was still under consideration. Apprised of this behavior, the D.C. Circuit concluded that "whatever the proceeding may be called, it involved not only allocation of TV channels among communities but also resolution of conflicting private claims to a valuable privilege, and that basic fairness requires such a proceeding to be carried on in the open. . . . Accordingly the private approaches to the members of the Commission vitiated its action and the proceeding must be reopened."

The next significant case threatened to generalize this understandable holding in Sangamon Valley to virtually all rulemaking. Decided on the eve of Vermont Yankee, it has been sharply criticized—particularly for its tendency to judicialize rulemaking and for its confusion about rulemaking procedures and records. So long as you approach it as a problematic case not to be read for its "law" but rather for insight into a set of enduring tensions and problems, it makes a good starting point for the materials of this Section.

## HOME BOX OFFICE, INC. v. FEDERAL COMMUNICATIONS COMMISSION

United States Court of Appeals for the District of Columbia (1977).
567 F.2d 9.

PER CURIAM.[1]

[In March 1975, the FCC ended a three-year notice-and-comment rulemaking proceeding by adopting four amendments to its rules governing the programs that could be shown by paid television services like HBO. If these services could show contemporary films and sports, commercial broadcasters feared, the quality of conventional television would inevitably be reduced. Viewers who could not be reached by (or afford to pay for) subscription television would be injured by this change. On the other hand, metropolitan viewers and paid service owners both denied that this harm would occur and asserted that restricting the material shown by subscription services would inhibit their commercial growth and deprive viewers of diversity. Ultimately, the Commission decided to reduce somewhat the prior restrictions on paid television

[1] [Ed.] The court issued the opinion per curiam "because the complexity of the issues raised on appeal made it useful to share the effort required to draft this opinion among the members of the panel"; the part reproduced here was written by Judge J. Skelly Wright. Two concurrences are omitted.

services. The amendments satisfied neither the commercial nor the subscription broadcast interests (including associated viewer groups) and all promptly sought review in the D.C. Circuit. Henry Geller, General Counsel of the FCC until 1973 (by which time the rulemaking was well under way) and chairperson of a public interest group concentrating on broadcast matters, was one of those seeking review. He suggested to the court that participants in the rulemaking had frequently engaged in private contacts with Commissioners and others at the FCC.]

. . . In an attempt to clarify the facts this court sua sponte ordered the Commission to provide "a list of all of the ex parte presentations, together with the details of each, made to it, or to any of its members or representatives, during the rulemaking proceedings." In response to this order the Commission filed a document over 60 pages long which revealed, albeit imprecisely, widespread ex parte communications involving virtually every party before this court, including amicus Geller.[107] . . .

[W]e are particularly concerned that the final shaping of the rules we are reviewing here may have been by compromise among the contending industry forces, rather than by exercise of the independent discretion in the public interest the Communications Act vests in individual commissioners. Our concern is heightened by the submission of the Commission's Broadcast Bureau to this court which states that in December 1974 broadcast representatives "described the kind of pay cable regulation that, in their view, broadcasters 'could live with.'" If actual positions were not revealed in public comments, . . . the elaborate public discussion in these dockets has been reduced to a sham.

Even the possibility that there is here one administrative record for the public and this court and another for the Commission and those "in the know" is intolerable. . . . [I]mplicit in the decision to treat the promulgation of rules as a "final" event in an ongoing process of administration is an assumption that an act of reasoned judgment has occurred, an assumption which further contemplates the existence of a body of material—documents, comments, transcripts, and statements in various forms declaring agency expertise or policy—with reference to which such judgment was exercised. Against this material, "the full administrative record that was before [an agency official] at the time he made his decision," Citizens to Preserve Overton Park v. Volpe, [401 U.S. 402 (1971)] [p. 1145], . . . it is the obligation of this court to test the actions of the Commission for arbitrariness or inconsistency with delegated authority. . . . This course is obviously foreclosed if communications are made to the agency in secret and the agency itself does not disclose the information presented. . . . [A] reviewing court cannot presume that the agency has acted properly, but must treat the

[107] . . . There can be no waiver or estoppel raised here against our consideration of an issue vital to the public as a whole. Therefore, Mr. Geller's "dirty hands," if such they be, present no bar. . . .

agency's justifications as a fictional account of the actual decisionmaking process and must perforce find its actions arbitrary.

. . . Even if the Commission had disclosed to this court . . . what was said to it ex parte, . . . we would not have the benefit of an adversarial discussion among the parties. . . . We have insisted, for example, that [relevant] information in agency files or consultants' reports . . . be disclosed to the parties for adversarial comment. Similarly, we have required agencies to set out their thinking in notices of proposed rulemaking. This requirement not only allows adversarial critique of the agency but is perhaps one of the few ways that the public may be apprised of what the agency thinks it knows in its capacity as a repository of expert opinion. From a functional standpoint, we see no difference between assertions of fact and expert opinion tendered by the public, as here, and that generated internally in an agency: each may be biased, inaccurate, or incomplete—failings which adversary comment may illuminate. Indeed, the potential for bias in private presentations in rulemakings which resolve "conflicting private claims to a valuable privilege," seems to us greater than in cases where we have reversed agencies for failure to disclose internal studies. . . .

Equally important is the inconsistency of secrecy with fundamental notions of fairness implicit in due process and with the ideal of reasoned decisionmaking on the merits which undergirds all of our administrative law. This inconsistency was recognized in Sangamon Valley Television Corp. v. United States, 269 F.2d 221 (D.C. Cir. 1959), and . . . [c]ertainly any ambiguity . . . has been removed by recent congressional and presidential actions. In the Government in the Sunshine Act, for example, Congress has declared it to be "the policy of the United States that the public is entitled to the fullest practicable information regarding the decisionmaking processes of the Federal Government," and has taken steps to guard against ex parte contacts in formal agency proceedings.[125] Perhaps more closely on point is Executive Order 11920, 12 Weekly Comp. of Presidential Documents 1040 (1976), which prohibits ex parte contacts with members of the White House staff by those seeking to influence allocation of international air routes during the time route certifications are before the President for his approval. . . . Thus this is a time when all branches of government have taken steps "designed to better assure fairness and to avoid suspicions of impropriety," White House Fact Sheet on Executive Order 11920 (June 10, 1976), and consequently we have no hesitation in concluding . . . that due process requires us to set aside the Commission's rules here.

. . . [W]e recognize that informal contacts between agencies and the public are the "bread and butter" of the process of administration and are completely appropriate so long as they do not frustrate judicial review or raise serious questions of fairness. Reconciliation of these considerations

[125] Of course, the Sunshine Act by its terms does not apply here. Its ex parte contact provisions are couched as an amendment to 5 U.S.C. § 557, and as such the rules do not apply to rulemaking under § 4 of the Administrative Procedure Act, 5 U.S.C. § 553. Moreover, the Act was not in effect at the time of the events in question here.

in a manner which will reduce procedural uncertainty leads us to conclude that communications which are received prior to issuance of a formal notice of rulemaking do not, in general, have to be put in a public file. Of course, if the information contained in such a communication forms the basis for agency action, then, under well established principles, that information must be disclosed to the public in some form. Once a notice of proposed rulemaking has been issued, however, any agency official or employee who is or may reasonably be expected to be involved in the decisional process of the rulemaking proceeding, should "refus[e] to discuss matters relating to the disposition of a [rulemaking proceeding] with any interested private party, or an attorney or agent for any such party, prior to the [agency's] decision . . . ," Executive Order 11920, § 4, supra, at 1041. If ex parte contacts nonetheless occur, we think that any written document or a summary of any oral communication must be placed in the public file established for each rulemaking docket immediately after the communication is received so that interested parties may comment thereon. Compare Executive Order 11920, § 5. . . .

## NOTES

(1) ***Home Box Office and Vermont Yankee.*** The decision in Home Box Office predates Vermont Yankee by a year. If the D.C. Circuit had not already retreated from the decision, could its broad requirement of disclosure for ex parte contacts be squared with Vermont Yankee? To what extent does the text of the APA, both in its provisions for notice-and-comment rulemaking under § 553 and in its restrictions on ex parte comments in formal proceedings in § 557(d), support or undercut the Home Box Office decision?

(2) ***A Sound Result?*** ERNEST GELLHORN & GLEN O. ROBINSON, RULEMAKING "DUE PROCESS": AN INCONCLUSIVE DIALOGUE, 48 U. Chi. L. Rev. 201 (1981):

"[*Publius*:] [E]x parte contacts . . . operate as an important check on the reliability of staff information and interpretation. Given the potential unreliability of staff-provided information, ex parte contacts with persons outside the agency are an important means of avoiding 'staff capture.' To be sure, one does not want an agency to rely entirely on outside informants, but neither does one want it to be the prisoner of agency staff. . . .

"It is somewhat ironic that one of the principal proponents of a ban on ex parte contacts, Judge Wright, should also interpret the APA as requiring rulemaking to provide 'a genuine dialogue between agency experts and concerned members of the public.' The formal submission of documents to an agency, in response to a formal public notice, seems unlikely to constitute a 'genuine' dialogue—but this would be the only permissible communication between the agency and the parties if the ban on ex parte contacts stands. . . . An agency is not simply an issuer of edicts; it is also an arbitrator of interests. Again Home Box Office is illustrative. Some of the ex parte contacts involved in that case apparently took place partly for the purpose of exploring possible compromises among the competing groups. It is difficult to envision how such compromise efforts, which are clearly desirable, could be made without some informal contacts. . . .

"[*Brutus*:] [T]he rulemaker-as-arbitrator is not an appropriate model for agencies. No doubt rules often reflect compromises among competing interest groups. I do not deplore that. Even where rulemaking is a zero-sum game among different interests, agencies are properly sensitive to minimizing the losses to any particular group as a consequence of the rule being adopted. Bargaining is not objectionable except where it is done without rules, which would allow the decision to be unfairly skewed by irrelevant factors such as who was able to contact whom, when, and so forth. On the other hand, why do we have a structured rulemaking process with notice and comment and, in the Home Box Office case, even oral argument? Is this just a warmup for negotiations? I think not. It would seem to be an attempt to require rulemakers to do more than rubberstamp agreements by the affected parties. Instead, they must independently assure themselves, from the evidence produced by these procedures, that the rule is in fact in the public interest. That determination could be rendered illusory by unregulated ex parte contacts creating a predisposition in the rulemaker's mind.

"Moreover, I think it is somewhat naive to suppose that it is necessary for an agency rulemaker to have informal discussions with particular parties in order to gain an adequate understanding of their 'bottom line.' For example, I think your FCC commissioner in Home Box Office would, from the outset, have a pretty good sense of what was soft and what was firm in the positions of the parties as a result of his familiarity with the industry."

(3) ***The Judicial Retreat from Home Box Office and Current Doctrine.*** The tensions between HBO's concern for the state of the rulemaking record on review and the institutional, legislative character of rulemaking led to a prompt retreat. In ACTION FOR CHILDREN'S TELEVISION [ACT] V. FCC, 564 F.2d 458 (D.C. Cir. 1977), a different panel of the D.C. Circuit refused to apply HBO to an FCC rulemaking involving children's television programming and advertising practices. Over 100,000 comments had been filed to a proposed rulemaking, and six days of panel discussions and arguments had been held. Early on, the broadcast industry had undertaken "limited self-regulation"; after a private meeting with the FCC's Chairman following the Commission hearings, the industry adopted further measures to control advertising practices. When the Commission decided not to issue a final rule, promising to monitor these self-regulatory measures, ACT sought review.

Holding only that HBO's "broad prescription is not to be applied retroactively," the panel's lengthy opinion left little doubt that it generally disapproved of that earlier case's prescription: "We do not propose to argue . . . that ex parte contacts always are permissible in informal rulemaking proceedings—they are of course not—but we do think . . . that ex parte contacts do not per se vitiate agency informal rulemaking action, but only do so if it appears from the administrative record under review that they may have materially influenced the action ultimately taken. . . .

"If we go as far as Home Box Office does in its ex parte ruling in ensuring a 'whole record' for our review, why not go further to require the decisionmaker to summarize and make available for public comment every status inquiry from a Congressman or any germane material—say a newspaper editorial—that he or she reads or their evening-hour ruminations? In the end, why not administer a lie-detector test to ascertain whether the required summary is an accurate and complete one? The problem is obviously a matter of degree, and the appropriate line must be drawn somewhere. In light of what must be presumed to be Congress' intent not to prohibit or require disclosure of all ex parte contacts during or after the public comment stage, we would draw that line at the point where the rulemaking proceedings involve 'competing claims to a valuable privilege.' It is at that point where the potential for unfair advantage outweighs the practical burdens, which we imagine would not be insubstantial, that such a judicially conceived rule would place upon administrators."

Current doctrine could be stated as follows: Sangamon Valley remains good law, though rarely does a rulemaking involve "competing claims to a valuable privilege." Without such competing claims, the APA and the Constitution do not restrict ex parte communications. While ex parte communications can take place, paper hearing mandates from Section 3 may require their disclosure. Specific agency statutes may, of course, provide additional constraints.

(4) ***Agency Practices and ACUS Recommendations.*** In 2014, ACUS surveyed staff members at eight executive agencies and four independent regulatory commissions and found that agency practices regarding ex parte communications varied considerably—both in terms of the form of the agency policy concerning the issue (rulemaking, policy statement, or unwritten practice) and the substance (restrictive, neutral, welcoming). For instance, at that time, the Department of Labor's written policy strongly discouraged such communications after an NPRM is published and required disclosing all communications that occur, including oral ones. The Federal Election Commission's neutral regulation mandated that Commissioners and their staff quickly report any ex parte contacts and their substance, written or oral, in the period between the petition for rulemaking being circulated to the Commission (or the issuance of an NPRM) and the final action by the Commission. And the EPA, by written and unwritten policy, encouraged meetings in the rulemaking process (and even conducted them after the comment period is closed to get clarification of items submitted to the docket). Esa L. Sferra-Bonistalli, Ex Parte Communications in Informal Rulemaking (May 1, 2014) (report to ACUS).[2] Statutes can also impose constraints on ex parte communications. For instance, the Clean Air Act requires that such communications be documented in the rulemaking docket, see Note 5 below. For an example of online access to information on ex parte communications, see the FCC's Electronic Comment Filing System.[3] Media and interested groups track this information. See, e.g., Christopher Cole, Top

---

[2] https://www.acus.gov/sites/default/files/documents/Final%20Ex%20Parte%20Communications%20in%20Informal%20Rulemaking%20%5B5-1-14%5D_0.pdf.

[3] https://www.fcc.gov/ecfs/ (select yes in the field for ex parte submissions at the bottom).

Groups Lobbying The FCC, Law360 (Nov. 8, 2022) (November's installment of an article series, published monthly, analyzing this data).

(5) ***Presidential and Congressional Ex Parte Contacts.*** Ex parte comments made by members of Congress, the President, or White House aides might seem to be particularly problematic, given the influence such comments could be expected to have on agency decisionmakers. On the other hand, mandating disclosure of such comments also raises concerns of undermining important political controls on agencies and more specifically of unduly infringing on the President's constitutionally protected supervision of the executive branch. The D.C. Circuit addressed ex parte congressional and presidential comments and White House meetings in SIERRA CLUB V. COSTLE, 657 F.2d 298 (D.C. Cir. 1981), considered at greater length in Chapter VII (p. 1051).

The Sierra Club court refused to overturn the EPA rule on emissions from coal-fired power stations based on the agency's meetings with White House staff and the President that the agency had not disclosed in the docket. Although recognizing that the docketing of such communications might be necessary in some instances to ensure due process or when a statute specifically requires, the court found no need to do so here "since EPA makes no effort to base the rule on any 'data or information' arising from that meeting."

The court further refused to invalidate the rule based on charges that agency officials had been pressured in meetings with Senator Robert Byrd, an influential coal-state senator: "We believe it entirely proper for Congressional representatives vigorously to represent the interests of their constituents before administrative agencies engaged in informal, general policy rulemaking, so long as individual Congressmen do not frustrate the intent of Congress as a whole as expressed in statute, nor undermine applicable rules of procedure. Where Congressmen keep their comments focused on the substance of the proposed rule—and we have no substantial evidence to cause us to believe Senator Byrd did not do so here—administrative agencies are expected to balance Congressional pressure with the pressures emanating from all other sources. To hold otherwise would deprive the agencies of legitimate sources of information and call into question the validity of nearly every controversial rulemaking." Noting that the only suggestions of congressional "threats" came in a Washington Post article, the opinion also stated: "We do not believe that a single newspaper account of strong 'hint[s]' represents substantial evidence of extraneous pressure significant enough to warrant a finding of unlawful congressional interference."

(6) ***Ex Parte Contacts and Regulatory Review.*** The Constitution may prevent courts from mandating that certain communications with the White House be disclosed. But the White House can bind itself. Executive Order 12866 addresses "ex parte" communications in several ways. To start, it stopped a practice of communications between the White House and private interests in the OIRA review process where the rulemaking agency was purposefully excluded. Now, a "representative from the issuing agency shall be invited to any meeting between OIRA personnel and such person(s)." In

addition "OIRA shall forward to the issuing agency, within 10 working days of receipt of the communication(s), all written communications, regardless of format, between OIRA personnel and any person who is not employed by the executive branch of the Federal Government, and the dates and names of individuals involved in all substantive oral communications (including meetings to which an agency representative was invited, but did not attend, and telephone conversations between OIRA personnel and any such persons)." Exec. Order No. 12866, § 6(b)(4)(B). With respect to disclosure to the public, the Executive Order requires OIRA to keep "a publicly available log" of "[t]he dates and names of individuals involved in all substantive oral communications, including meetings and telephone conversations, between OIRA personnel and any person not employed by the executive branch of the Federal Government, and the subject matter discussed during such communications." § 6(b)(4)(C). The subject matter is not a summary of the conversation but rather the regulation's name that was discussed. Finally, after the rule is finalized or formally withdrawn, "OIRA shall make available to the public all *documents* exchanged between OIRA and the agency during the review by OIRA under this section." § 6(b)(4)(D) (emphasis added).

The public logs appear robust—displaying many meetings.[4] By contrast, few documents between OIRA and rulemaking agencies have been disclosed. A Brookings Institution study found that so-called "EO 12866 meetings" increased in President Trump's first year, despite a decrease in proposed and final rulemaking, that much of this increase "was concentrated at three agencies" (Environmental Protection Agency, Department of Health and Human Services, and Department of Labor), and that "interest groups—not industry—drove the increase." Rachel Augustine Potter, Brookings Inst., Regulatory Lobbying Has Increased Under the Trump Administration, But the Groups Doing the Lobbying May Surprise You (July 11, 2018).[5] Later in the Trump Administration, OIRA canceled meetings about contested regulations because it had finished its review process. Critics, including Democratic members of Congress, questioned the speed of the OIRA review process for certain regulatory actions—for instance, while proposed rules sit at OIRA for an average of 45 days, OIRA approved one proposal (for a domestic gag rule on the Title X family program) in under two weeks, preventing any meetings with stakeholders.

From the start of the Biden Administration to the end of August 2022, OIRA's website showed 985 Executive Order 12866 meetings, including multiple meetings about Occupational Safety and Health Administration's COVID-19 Emergency Temporary Standard and the Food & Drug Administration's Tobacco Product Standard for Menthol in Cigarettes. You can now schedule a meeting online: https://www.reginfo.gov/public/do/eom12866Search (click on schedule).

(7) ***Conflict of Interest Constraints.*** Should former General Counsel Geller have been participating in a private capacity in a rulemaking proceeding that had been well under way while he was a high-level

---

[4] https://www.reginfo.gov/public/do/eom12866Search.

[5] https://www.brookings.edu/research/regulatory-lobbying-has-increased-under-the-trump-administration-but-the-groups-doing-the-lobbying-may-surprise-you/.

Commission employee? The HBO case arose before the Ethics in Government Act defined "rulemaking" as a "particular matter" that triggers constraints on activities former officials can undertake. 18 U.S.C. § 207(i)(3). Today, it seems unlikely that he could play any role on behalf of a client—whether he actually participated in the rulemaking, which involved specific parties (lifetime ban, § 207(a)(1)), had official responsibility for it (two-year cooling off period, § 207(a)(2)), or was an officer of sufficiently high status (one-year general ban on contact with one's former agency, § 207(c)). The Ethics in Government Act and conflict restrictions on government officials to address the "revolving door" problem are described in more detail in Ch. V (p. 576).

## b. An Open-Minded Decisionmaker?

*C & W FISH CO., INC. v. FOX*

## C & W FISH CO., INC. v. FOX

United States Court of Appeals for the D.C. Circuit (1991).
931 F.2d 1556.

■ HENDERSON, CIRCUIT JUDGE.

On April 13, 1990, the Department of Commerce (Department), National Oceanic and Atmospheric Administration (NOAA), issued a final rule which, in part, bans the use of drift gillnets in the Atlantic King Mackerel Fishery. See 55 Fed. Reg. 14,833 (April 19, 1990). Various individuals involved in the fishing industry challenged the final rule on several grounds, including its allegedly ultra vires promulgation. The district court rejected all of the plaintiffs' challenges, granting summary judgment to the defendants. We affirm.

[The Magnuson Fishery Conservation and Management Act (Magnuson Act or Act), 16 U.S.C. §§ 1801–82, gives the Department authority to create national programs for fish conservation and management, while also preserving state roles. Eight Regional Fishery Management Councils representing state interests are granted authority over specific geographic regions. A Council can propose a Fishery Management Plan subject to the Secretary's final approval and must be given an opportunity to comment on any FMP the Secretary herself proposes. Within the Department, the Secretary's authority has been subdelegated in ways that may further promote state interests, as well as foster the development of departmental expertise. The Assistant Administrator for Fisheries (Assistant Administrator) of NOAA, who is also the Director of the National Marine Fisheries Service, is an important intermediary recipient of this authority.

For years, the South Atlantic Regional Council and the Gulf Regional Council had been trying to ban gillnet fishing for various species,[6] including the Atlantic King Mackerel. In 1989, after a regional

[6] [Ed.] As its name suggests, a gillnet is a net that traps fish who swim into it by catching their gills; although the size of openings in the nets offers some control, they inevitably catch

administrator had blocked several other efforts, they succeeded in getting a rule that imposed limited constraints but permitted continued drift gillnet fishing for the Atlantic King Mackerel. In 1990, the Councils submitted a renewed proposal to ban this practice, which the regional administrator rejected. He reasoned that "the evidence presented to support the new submission . . . had not changed since the first submission and did not warrant a change in agency policy."]

When the Regional Director's decision reached Dr. William Fox, the newly appointed NOAA Assistant Administrator, the rejected portions of the amendment gained new life. Fox—who before his appointment had been a strong advocate of the drift gillnet ban—inexplicably reported that the Regional Director had "approved" the new Amendment 3 and then, himself, approved the full plan, explaining the appropriateness of the ban. The Under Secretary and the Secretary subsequently approved the Councils' proposal, and NOAA implemented appropriate notice and comment rulemaking, 55 Fed. Reg. 5,242 (February 14, 1990) (proposed rule); 55 Fed. Reg. 14,833 (April 19, 1990) (final rule).

The issuance of the drift gillnet ban set the stage for this litigation. Immediately after the final rule was issued, two fish wholesalers and two individual fishermen filed suit against the Secretary of Commerce, Robert Mosbacher, and Assistant Administrator Fox in district court . . .

[After disposing of a number of other challenges, the court turned to appellants' contention] that Assistant Administrator Fox had an "unalterably closed mind" when he passed on the drift gillnet ban and, consequently, their due process right to an impartial decisionmaker was denied them. To support this claim, the appellants point to the fact that, immediately before his appointment, Fox was the chairman of the Florida Marine Fisheries Commission, an outspoken advocate of the drift gillnet ban. They also point to an article published after Fox was appointed, quoting Fox as stating " '[t]here's just no question that this kind of gear [i.e., drift gillnets] should be eliminated. . . . The drift nets run counter to everything we're trying to do for the fisheries.' " Wickstrom, "The Fox Goes to Washington," Florida Sportsman (Oct. 1989). Last, the appellants claim that Fox's bias is demonstrated by his failure to conduct an adequate review of the issues or to consider the positions of his staff advisors.

First we reject the suggestion that we look to the adequacy of Fox's examination of the facts and issues in order to determine whether he was biased. In Association of National Advertisers, Inc. v. FTC, 627 F.2d 1151, 1170 (D.C. Cir. 1979),[7] we held that an individual should be

---

unwanted fish (and other marine life); drift gillnets, a particular target of the Councils, are large nets permitted to drift through a fishing area, whose size may contribute to threats of overfishing.

[7] [Ed.] This rulemaking regulated the advertising of sugared cereals on children's television programs. The motions for disqualification relied on a letter the FTC's Chairman, Michael Pertschuk, had sent to the head of the Food and Drug Administration, seeking to enlist his interest: "Setting legal theory aside, the truth is that we've been drawn into this issue because of the conviction which I know you share, that one of the evils flowing from the unfairness of children's advertising is the resulting distortion of children's perception of

disqualified from rulemaking "only when there has been a clear and convincing showing that the Department member has an unalterably closed mind on matters critical to the disposition of the proceeding." . . . This showing should focus on the agency member's prejudgment, if any, rather than a failure to weigh the issues fairly. Whether Fox weighed the facts properly is to be examined only in determining if his decision was arbitrary or capricious. As we have often explained, this court will not second guess an agency decision or question whether the decision made was the best one.

The facts in this case do not even approach a "clear and convincing showing" that Fox had an "unalterably closed mind." As we reasoned in Association of National Advertisers, "[t]he mere discussion of policy or advocacy on a legal question . . . is not sufficient to disqualify an administrator." 627 F.2d at 1171 (footnote omitted). The harm that would result were courts to disqualify agency members whenever they express views in public, as Fox did here, is readily apparent: We would eviscerate the proper evolution of policymaking were we to disqualify every administrator who has opinions on the correct course of his agency's future actions. Administrators, and even judges, may hold policy views on questions of law prior to participating in a proceeding. The factual basis for a rulemaking is so closely intertwined with policy judgments that we would obliterate rulemaking were we to equate a statement on an issue of legislative fact with unconstitutional prejudgment.

An administrator's presence within an agency reflects the political judgment of the President and the Senate. . . . A Commission's view of what is best in the public interest may change from time to time. Commissions themselves change, underlying philosophies differ, and experience often dictates changes. We conclude that neither Fox's earlier advocacy nor his policy view as publicly expressed demonstrates an unalterably closed mind that would disqualify him as an impartial decisionmaker.

## NOTES

(1) ***Decisionmaker Bias in Rulemaking (and Adjudication).*** In light of this decision, what does it mean to have a fair decisionmaker in rulemaking? The rule here, like that in the cited case of Association of National Advertisers, reflects the action of an unusually outspoken, pro-regulation administrator, who may have been put in office for their views. Do the fairness claims of those who may be subjected to the regulation in question deserve more respect than these cases afford? Almost no rules have been invalidated due to decisionmaker bias (including in National Advertisers). For a rare example, see Nehemiah Corp. of America v. Jackson, 546 F.Supp.2d 830 (E.D. Cal. 2008). Standards for decisionmakers in adjudication are tougher: "The test for disqualification has been succinctly stated as being whether a disinterested observer may conclude that (the

---

nutritional values. I see, at this point, our logical process as follows—Children's advertising is inherently unfair . . . ."

agency) has in some measure adjudged the facts as well as the law of a particular case in advance of hearing it." Cinderella Career & Finishing Schools, Inc. v. FTC, 425 F.2d 583 (D.C. Cir. 1970). The court did find that the test was met in that case, but there are very few cases finding disqualification was needed in the adjudicatory context (outside of financial conflicts of interest).

(2) ***Social Media Campaigns in Rulemaking.*** A related issue to decisionmaking "bias" in rulemaking involves the extent to which an agency can encourage support for its proposed regulations. The GAO concluded that the EPA had "violated publicity or propaganda and anti-lobbying provisions contained in appropriation acts" in its social media use campaigns surrounding the Waters of the United States rulemaking in FY 2014 and 2015. The GAO found specifically that the agency's use of Thunderclap (specifically, a widely shared message linked to the proposed rule that did not identify the EPA as the sender) constituted "covert propaganda" and its links to external sites that advocated contacting members of Congress qualified as "grassroots lobbying." But the GAO determined that the agency's #DitchtheMyth and #CleanWaterRules campaigns, which extolled the benefits of clean water and the proposed rule, were permissible. Environmental Protection Agency—Application of Publicity or Propaganda and Anti-Lobbying Provisions, B-326944 (Dec. 14, 2015).[8]

(3) ***Views of Agency Staff.*** The reasoning of the Fox court depends in good part on an argument based on the legitimacy provided by "the political judgment of the President and the Senate" in making appointments. Should different considerations govern as one descends into the "expert" levels of the career ranks, where institutional decisions will be strongly shaped?

UNITED STEELWORKERS OF AM. V. MARSHALL, 647 F.2d 1189 (D.C. Cir. 1980), addressed the question of alleged bias in agency staff, in an opinion written by CHIEF JUDGE J. SKELLY WRIGHT, author of the portion of the HBO decision addressing ex parte contacts: "In a proceeding to create a general rule it makes little sense to speak of an agency employee advocating for 'one side' over another. However contentious the proceeding, the concept of advocacy does not apply easily where the agency is not determining the specific rights of a specific party, and where the proposed rule undergoes detailed change in its journey toward a final rule. . . . Nevertheless, the adversary tone and format of the proceedings are obvious. . . . The Assistant Secretary might well have been able to assess the record more objectively—if less efficiently—had the standard's attorney [a lawyer in the Office of the Solicitor] not been constantly at her side. Therefore, although we have some doubt about calling the standard's attorney an 'advocate' in the context of such rulemaking, we will *assume* he played that role so we can measure his conduct against the legal constraints on the agency.

"We note at the outset that nothing in the Administrative Procedure Act bars a staff advocate from advising the decisionmaker in setting a final rule. . . . Moreover, in establishing the special hybrid procedures in the OSH Act, Congress never intended to impose the separation-of-functions

[8] https://www.gao.gov/products/B-326944.

requirement it imposes in adjudications. [See Chapter V, Section 2, p. 569.] The legislative history shows that Congress consistently turned back efforts to impose such formal procedures on OSHA standard-setting. . . . [U]nder the Supreme Court's decision in Vermont Yankee that is virtually the end of the inquiry. . . .

"Rulemaking is essentially an institutional, not an individual, process, and it is not vulnerable to communication within an agency in the same sense as it is to communication from without. In an enormously complex proceeding like an OSHA standard setting, it may simply be unrealistic to expect an official facing a massive, almost inchoate, record to isolate herself from the people with whom she worked in generating the record. In any event, we rest our decision not on our own theory of agency management, but on the state of the law."

Do you worry about the political views or competence of career agency workers? See Mark D. Richardson, Joshua D. Clinton, & David E. Lewis, Elite Perceptions of Agency Ideology and Workforce Skill, 80 J. Pol. 303 (2017) (producing estimates of "perceived agency ideology" and "perceived skillfulness and competence" for many agencies and subagencies).

(4) ***Reliance on Subordinates and Contractors: Classic Doctrine.*** Separate from concerns of staff bias, agency decisionmakers simply cannot do much of the work needed in a rulemaking themselves. To what extent can decisionmakers rely on subordinates? In a series of cases, known as the Morgan cases (discussed at more length in Chapter V, p. 552), the Supreme Court wrestled with this question in the context of a ratemaking by the Department of Agriculture under the Packers and Stockyards Act. In MORGAN V. UNITED STATES, 298 U.S. 468 (1936) (MORGAN I), the Court held that the decisionmaking "cannot be performed by one who has not considered evidence or argument. . . . The one who decides must hear. This necessary rule does not preclude practicable administrative procedure in obtaining the aid of assistants in the department."

The district court used this aggressive approach to allow the Secretary of Agriculture to be questioned under oath. But when that questioning revealed that the Secretary had only "dipped into" the record in his office and had primarily relied on findings prepared by the staff responsible for presenting the case, the Court was untroubled by the substantiality of this assistance. All that the Court found lacking was notice to the petitioners of what those proposed findings had been: "any reasonable opportunity to the respondents in the proceeding to know the claims thus presented and to contest them." MORGAN V. UNITED STATES, 304 U.S. 1 (1938) (MORGAN II).

In the final case, UNITED STATES V. MORGAN, 313 U.S. 409 (1941) (MORGAN IV), the Court determined that the most recent questioning of the agency decisionmaker, an in-person trial at which the Secretary was "questioned at length," had gone too far: "But the short of the business is that the Secretary should never have been subjected to this examination. . . . We have explicitly held in this very litigation that 'it was not the function of the court to probe the mental processes of the Secretary.'" See Department of Commerce v. New York (p. 1181) (lower court ordered depositions of the

Secretary of Commerce and the acting head of the Justice Department's Civil Rights division; the Supreme Court barred the Secretary's examination).

For a classic case in the informal rulemaking context, see NATIONAL NUTRITIONAL FOODS ASS'N V. FDA, 491 F.2d 1141 (2d Cir. 1974): After "almost two years" of hearings that "produced over 32,000 pages of testimony and thousands of pages of exhibits" the new FDA Commissioner signed off on a complex final regulation 13 days after taking office. "Conceding that it is not the function of this court 'to probe the mental processes' of the Commissioner, Morgan v. United States, 304 U.S. 1, 18 (1938) (Morgan II), petitioners insist they are entitled to probe whether he exercised his own mental processes at all. . . . The facts of this case do not constitute nearly the showing of bad faith necessary to justify further inquiry; indeed they vividly illustrate the necessity of adhering to the presumption of regularity with respect to the participation of the officer authorized to sign administrative orders, especially in the context of the promulgation of legislative rules as distinguished from adjudication. . . . It would suffice under the circumstances that [the new] Commissioner . . . considered the summaries of the objections and of the answers contained in the elaborate preambles and conferred with his staff about them. There is no reason why he could not have done this even in the limited time available, . . . . although we do not envy him the task. In any event, absent the most powerful preliminary showing to the contrary, effective government requires us to presume that he did."

What if those subordinates are not government employees but contractors? This issue arose in UNITED STEELWORKERS, supra. The court rejected procedural complaints against OSHA's use of consultants to summarize and evaluate data in the record, as well as to draft parts of the preamble and final standard. Challengers maintained that this violated the Morgan principle that "the one who decides must hear," but the court disagreed, noting that the Assistant Secretary had "reviewed the evidence and explained the evidentiary bases for each part of the standard" in the preamble and attachments to the final standard and had "demonstrated her independence from the consultants by strongly criticizing some of their conclusions on the key issue of feasibility." More generally, the court insisted that "the unsupported allegation that hired consultants might have an incentive to act dishonestly cannot overcome the presumption that agency officials and those who assist them have acted properly. . . . [W]e generally see no reason to force agencies to hire enormous regular staffs versed in all conceivable technological issues, rather than use their appropriations to hire specific consultants for specific problems."

(5) ***Reliance on Subordinates and Contractors: Modern Practice.*** A recent ACUS study used "in-depth interviews with 45 agency officials, experts, and contractors and a survey of agency rulemaking officials" to examine the use of contractors in agency rulemaking: "Our research reveals wide variation in how agencies approach the use of contractors in rulemaking. Not only do agencies have highly divergent attitudes about what contractors may and should do in rulemaking, they also perceive different risks and benefits of contractor use and manage contractors in

different ways. What emerges is a complex picture, with contractors essential to rulemaking at some agencies, occasionally useful to a subset of agencies, and kept away from rulemaking at other agencies. . . .

"[S]ome tasks [performed by contractors] map directly onto time-limited stages of a rulemaking project, such as assistance with sorting and analyzing public comments, while others are ongoing, such as writing and research assistance. Others are special one-time projects (e.g., drafting internal guidelines for regulatory impact analysis or RIA) or more general, ongoing assistance (e.g., clerical support). The type of working relationship can vary, too, from specific, arms-length type engagements, such as writing an expert report or literature review, to long-term staffing assignments in which the contractors work side-by-side with agency employees. Tasks also range in terms of their policy significance, from the ministerial to those closely tied to policy-making. For example, contractors help with formatting documents, but they also help agencies interact with the public and with other parts of the executive branch, including the regulatory review process managed by the Office of Management and Budget." Bridget C.E. Dooling & Rachel Augustine Potter, Contractors in Rulemaking (May 9, 2022) (report to ACUS).[9]

With e-rulemaking (see Notes 4–7 above (p. 365)), agency decisionmakers have to rely on others to process high numbers of comments.

(6) ***No Guaranteed Consideration of Staff Views.*** To what extent can a regulated party challenge exclusion of staff views favorable to its cause? In NAT. SMALL SHIPMENTS TRAFFIC CONF., INC. V. ICC, 725 F.2d 1442 (D.C. Cir. 1984), the D.C. Circuit, relying on the Morgan cases, rejected a challenge to a final rule where the agency decisionmaking process prevented staff analyses from reaching the decisionmakers. It noted that the shippers may have "a legal right that their comments reach Commission members in at least summary form, and that those comments be considered before final action is taken," subject to "the longstanding rule that courts will not probe the mental processes of administrative decisionmakers absent strong evidence of bad faith or other misconduct." But staff comments were different: "Neither the APA nor the due process clause, however, accords similar treatment to staff evaluations that move beyond a mere summary of record comments to express the independent judgments of subordinate agency personnel. An agency is free to structure its internal policy debate in any manner it deems appropriate. Midlevel managers may therefore filter out the evaluations of lower-level personnel if they so choose, so long as relevant record comments are not eliminated in the process as well." But if opposing staff views become part of the decisionmaking process (and record), such "[e]vidence . . . often triggers more rigorous [judicial] review." Gillian E. Metzger, The Interdependent Relationship Between Internal and External Separation of Powers, 59 Emory L.J. 423, 445 (2009).

(7) ***Rulemaking Statements and Bias in Adjudication.*** Zen Magnets challenged the Consumer Product Safety Commission's recall of its rare-earth magnets, claiming that its due process rights were violated because of

[9] https://www.acus.gov/report/final-report-contractors-rulemaking.

decisionmaker bias. Specifically, Zen argued that several Commissioners made public statements against such magnets in an earlier rulemaking that mandated manufacturers to produce larger or weaker magnets because of the safety risks to children who swallow them. The Tenth Circuit rejected Zen's claims: "Zen does not show any circumstances suggesting the Commissioners' inability to remain impartial after addressing related issues in the rulemaking. Without such a showing, we conclude that the Commissioners did not deny Zen's right to due process by serving first as rulemakers and then as adjudicators." Zen Magnets, LLC v. CPSC, 968 F.3d 1156 (10th Cir. 2020).

(8) ***Petitions to Disqualify FTC Chair Lina Khan.*** In June 2021, Amazon petitioned the Federal Trade Commission "for recusal of Chair Lina Khan from any antitrust investigation, adjudication, litigation, or other proceeding in which Amazon is a subject, target or defendant for which Chair Khan's prior public statements create the appearance of her having prejudged facts and/or legal issues relevant to the proceeding." It argued: "Courts have thus consistently held that due process requires a Commissioner's recusal if, in a prior role, he or she appeared to have prejudged the facts and/or pronounced legal conclusions about the company's liability. . . . Chair Khan has made numerous and highly detailed public pronouncements regarding Amazon, including on market definition, specific conduct and theories of harm, and the purpose, effects, and legality of such conduct. Indeed, she has on numerous occasions argued that Amazon is guilty of antitrust violations and should be broken up. These statements convey to any reasonable observer the clear impression that she has already made up her mind about many material facts relevant to Amazon's antitrust culpability as well as about the ultimate issue of culpability itself. She has publicly affirmed those conclusions not only as a legal scholar, but also as an advocate for an antitrust advocacy group and then as lead author of a major congressional report." Based on these allegations, do you think Khan should have to recuse herself from any rulemaking? Adjudication?

Facebook (now Meta) also filed a petition for Khan's recusal, which it pressed in litigation. In allowing FTC's amended antitrust complaint to go forward against Facebook's motion to dismiss, the district court in January 2022 rejected the company's allegations of bias. FTC v. Facebook, Inc., 581 F.Supp.3d 34, 62 (D.D.C. 2022): "The Court also notes the unique circumstances in which the FTC operates as an agency that may bring suit, conduct rulemaking, and act as an adjudicator. In selecting a chair for a Commission with these diverse responsibilities—as with choosing the head of any agency—it is natural that the President will select a candidate based on her past experiences and views, including on topics that are likely to come before the Commission during her tenure, and how that administrator will implement the Administration's priorities. Ass'n of Nat. Advertisers, Inc. v. FTC, 627 F.2d 1151, 1174 (D.C. Cir. 1979) ('An administrator's presence within an agency reflects the political judgment of the President and Senate.'). Courts must tread carefully when reviewing cases in this area lest we 'eviscerate the proper evolution of policymaking were we to disqualify every administrator who has opinions on the correct course of his agency's future action.' Id." The court went on to distinguish the filing of a case from the adjudicating of a case and analogized Khan's role here to a prosecutor, where it is very hard to disqualify for bias.

For more on the FTC's current interest in rulemaking in the Biden Administration, see p. 296.

# CHAPTER V

# ADJUDICATION



Adjudication is a large part of what administrative agencies do, and agency adjudication has a large impact on the ordinary lives of many of us. Sometimes this happens in incidental ways, as when someone passes through customs on returning from abroad, and the customs inspector accepts her declaration of what she has bought—thereby completing, to put it in administrative law terms, an informal adjudication. Sometimes it is much more serious and consequential, as when the Social Security Administration holds a more formal proceeding to determine whether a claimant deserves disability benefits. Yet this, too, occurs with great frequency, indeed hundreds of thousands of times each year.

Besides deciding who owes or deserves what, many agencies use adjudication as a means of establishing policy. For example, the "rules" governing who can unionize or what constitutes an unfair labor practice exist almost entirely in the cases of the National Labor Relations Board, applied as precedents. (As the Supreme Court held in the Chenery case, p. 258, an agency that decides cases can use them to formulate policy even if that agency also has rulemaking powers.) Indeed, regulating by deciding cases might be called the traditional way to regulate in the American legal system—following, of course, on the pattern of the courts in determining and applying the common law.

When procedures are fashioned for the conduct of agency adjudication, then, there are two, sometimes competing, general criteria in play: (1) What process will be fair to the individual parties? And (2) What process will produce the best regulatory result? To which we should add: (3) What process for adjudication will fit with the other tasks the agency must also carry out?

## SECTION 1. THE INSTITUTIONAL FRAMEWORK OF AGENCY ADJUDICATION

*FEDERAL TRADE COMMISSION v. CEMENT INSTITUTE*

### FEDERAL TRADE COMMISSION v. CEMENT INSTITUTE

Supreme Court of the United States (1948).
333 U.S. 683.

■ JUSTICE BLACK delivered the opinion of the Court.

We granted certiorari to review the decree of the Circuit Court of Appeals which, with one judge dissenting, vacated and set aside a cease and desist order issued by the Federal Trade Commission against the respondents. Those respondents are: The Cement Institute, an unincorporated trade association composed of 74 corporations which manufacture, sell and distribute cement; the 74 corporate members of the Institute; and 21 individuals who are associated with the Institute. It took three years for a trial examiner to hear the evidence which consists of about 49,000 pages of oral testimony and 50,000 pages of exhibits. Even the findings and conclusions of the Commission cover 176 pages. The briefs with accompanying appendixes submitted by the parties contain more than 4,000 pages. The legal questions raised by the Commission and by the different respondents are many and varied. . . .

The proceedings were begun by a Commission complaint of two counts. The first charged that certain alleged conduct set out at length constituted an unfair method of competition in violation of § 5 of the Federal Trade Commission Act. 15 U.S.C. § 45. The core of the charge was that the respondents had restrained and hindered competition in the sale and distribution of cement by means of a combination among themselves made effective through mutual understanding or agreement to employ a multiple basing point system of pricing. It was alleged that this system resulted in the quotation of identical terms of sale and identical prices for cement by the respondents at any given point in the United States. This system had worked so successfully, it was further charged, that for many years prior to the filing of the complaint, all cement buyers throughout the nation, with rare exceptions, had been unable to purchase cement for delivery in any given locality from any one of the respondents at a lower price or on more favorable terms than from any of the other respondents.

The second count of the complaint, resting chiefly on the same allegations of fact set out in Count I, charged that the multiple basing point system of sales resulted in [violations of the antitrust laws].

Resting upon its findings, the Commission ordered that respondents cease and desist from 'carrying out any planned common course of action, understanding, agreement, combination, or conspiracy' to do a number of things, all of which things, the Commission argues, had to be restrained in order effectively to restore individual freedom of action among the separate units in the cement industry. . . .

*Jurisdiction.*—At the very beginning we are met with a challenge to the Commission's jurisdiction to entertain the complaint and to act on it. This contention is pressed by respondent Marquette Cement Manufacturing Co. and is relied upon by other respondents. Count I of the complaint is drawn under the provision in § 5 of the Federal Trade Commission Act which declares that 'Unfair methods of competition * * * are hereby declared unlawful.' Marquette contends that the facts alleged in Count I do not constitute an 'unfair method of competition' within the meaning of § 5. Its argument runs this way: Count I in reality charges a combination to restrain trade. Such a combination constitutes an offense under § 1 of the Sherman Act which outlaws 'Every * * * combination * * * in restraint of trade.' 15 U.S.C. § 1. Section 4 of the Sherman Act provides that the attorney general shall institute suits under the Act on behalf of the United States, and that the federal district courts shall have exclusive jurisdiction of such suits. Hence, continue respondents, the Commission, whose jurisdiction is limited to 'unfair methods of competition,' is without power to institute proceedings or to issue an order with regard to the combination in restraint of trade charged in Count I. Marquette then argues that since the fact allegations of Count I are the chief reliance for the charge in Count II, this latter count also must be interpreted as charging a violation of the Sherman Act. Assuming, without deciding, that the conduct charged in each count constitutes a violation of the Sherman Act, we hold that the Commission does have jurisdiction to conclude that such conduct may also be an unfair method of competition and hence constitute a violation of § 5 of the Federal Trade Commission Act. . . .

*The Multiple Basing Point Delivered Price System.*—[The "multiple basing point delivered price system" of fixing prices and terms of cement sales worked as follows: The companies quoted prices of cement as delivered to the customer. They based these prices on the general market price at one of several fixed points, plus freight charges to the customer's location, regardless of whether the cement was actually shipped from that point. All sellers used the same system, and therefore quoted identical prices, regardless of their actual costs of production or of shipment.]

*Alleged Bias of the Commission.*—One year after the taking of testimony had been concluded and while these proceedings were still pending before the Commission, the respondent Marquette asked the Commission to disqualify itself from passing upon the issues involved. Marquette charged that the Commission had previously prejudged the issues, was 'prejudiced and biased against the Portland cement industry generally,' and that the industry and Marquette in particular could not receive a fair hearing from the Commission. After hearing oral argument the Commission refused to disqualify itself. . . .

Marquette introduced numerous exhibits intended to support its charges. In the main these exhibits were copies of the Commission's reports made to Congress or to the President, as required by § 6 of the Trade Commission Act. These reports, as well as the testimony given by members of the Commission before congressional committees, make it clear that long before the filing of this complaint the members of the Commission at that time, or at least some of them, were of the opinion that the operation of the multiple basing point system as they had studied it was the equivalent of a price fixing restraint of trade in violation of the Sherman Act. We therefore decide this contention, as did the Circuit Court of Appeals, on the assumption that such an opinion had been formed by the entire membership of the Commission as a result of its prior official investigations. But we also agree with that court's holding that this belief did not disqualify the Commission.

In the first place, the fact that the Commission had entertained such views as the result of its prior ex parte investigations did not necessarily mean that the minds of its members were irrevocably closed on the subject of the respondents' basing point practices. Here, in contrast to the Commission's investigations, members of the cement industry were legally authorized participants in the hearings. They produced evidence—volumes of it. They were free to point out to the Commission by testimony, by cross-examination of witnesses, and by arguments, conditions of the trade practices under attack which they thought kept these practices within the range of legally permissible business activities.

Moreover, Marquette's position, if sustained, would to a large extent defeat the congressional purposes which prompted passage of the Trade Commission Act. Had the entire membership of the Commission disqualified in the proceedings against these respondents, this complaint could not have been acted upon by the Commission or by any other government agency. Congress has provided for no such contingency. It has not directed that the Commission disqualify itself under any circumstances, has not provided for substitute commissioners should any of its members disqualify, and has not authorized any other government agency to hold hearings, make findings, and issue cease and desist orders in proceedings against unfair trade practices. Yet if Marquette is right, the Commission, by making studies and filing reports in obedience to congressional command, completely immunized the practices investigated, even though they are 'unfair,' from any cease and desist order by the Commission or any other governmental agency.

There is no warrant in the Act for reaching a conclusion which would thus frustrate its purposes. If the Commission's opinions expressed in congressionally required reports would bar its members from acting in unfair trade proceedings, it would appear that opinions expressed in the first basing point unfair trade proceeding would similarly disqualify them from ever passing on another. Thus experience acquired from their work as commissioners would be a handicap instead of an advantage. Such was not the intendment of Congress. For Congress acted on a committee report stating: 'It is manifestly desirable that the terms of the commissioners shall be long enough to give them an opportunity to acquire the expertness in dealing with these special questions concerning industry that comes from experience.' Report of Committee on Interstate Commerce, No. 597, June 13, 1914, 63d Cong., 2d Sess. 10–11.

Marquette also seems to argue that it was a denial of due process for the Commission to act in these proceedings after having expressed the view that industry-wide use of the basing point system was illegal. A number of cases are cited as giving support to this contention. . . . [No] decision of this Court would require us to hold that it would be a violation of procedural due process for a judge to sit in a case after he had expressed an opinion as to whether certain types of conduct were prohibited by law. In fact, judges frequently try the same case more than once and decide identical issues each time, although these issues involved questions both of law and fact. Certainly, the Federal Trade Commission cannot possibly be under stronger constitutional compulsions in this respect than a court.

The Commission properly refused to disqualify itself. . . .

*Findings and Evidence.*—It is strongly urged that the Commission failed to find, as charged in both counts of the complaint, that the respondents had by combination, agreements, or understandings among themselves utilized the multiple basing point delivered price system as a restraint to accomplish uniform prices and terms of sale. A subsidiary contention is that assuming the Commission did so find, there is no substantial evidence to support such a finding. We think that adequate findings of combination were made and that the findings have support in the evidence. . . .

Although there is much more evidence to which reference could be made, we think that the following facts shown by evidence in the record, some of which are in dispute, are sufficient to warrant the Commission's finding of concerted action.

When the Commission rendered its decision there were about 80 cement manufacturing companies in the United States operating about 150 mills. Ten companies controlled more than half of the mills and there were substantial corporate affiliations among many of the others. This concentration of productive capacity made concerted action far less difficult than it would otherwise have been. The belief is prevalent in the industry that because of the standardized nature of cement, among other reasons, price competition is wholly unsuited to it. That belief is historic. It has resulted in concerted activities to devise means and measures to do away with competition in the industry. Out of those activities came the multiple basing point delivered price system. Evidence shows it to be a handy instrument to bring about elimination of any kind of price competition. The use of the multiple basing point delivered price system by the cement producers has been coincident with a situation whereby for many years, with rare exceptions, cement has been offered for sale in every given locality at identical prices and terms by all producers. Thousands of secret sealed bids have been received by public agencies which corresponded in prices of cement down to a fractional part of a penny.[15] . . .

The foregoing are but illustrations of the practices shown to have been utilized to maintain the basing point price system. Respondents offered testimony that cement is a standardized product, that 'cement is cement,' that no differences existed in quality or usefulness, and that purchasers demanded delivered price quotations because of the high cost of transportation from mill to dealer. . . . Respondents introduced the testimony of economists to the effect that competition alone could lead to the evolution of a multiple basing point system of uniform delivered prices and terms of sale for an industry with a standardized product and with relatively high freight costs. These economists testified that for the above reasons no inferences of collusion, agreement, or understanding could be drawn from the admitted fact that cement prices of all United States producers had for many years almost invariably been the same in every given locality in the country. There was also considerable testimony by other economic experts that the multiple basing point system of delivered prices as employed by respondents contravened accepted economic principles and could only have been maintained through collusion.

The Commission did not adopt the views of the economists produced by the respondents. It decided that even though competition might tend to drive the price of standardized products to a uniform level, such a tendency alone could not account for the almost perfect identity in prices, discounts, and cement containers which had prevailed for so long a time in the cement industry. The Commission held that the uniformity and absence of competition in the industry were the results of understandings or agreements entered into or carried out by concert of the Institute and the other respondents. It may possibly be true, as respondents' economists testified, that cement producers will, without agreement express or implied and without understanding explicit or tacit, always

[15] The following is one among many of the Commission's findings as to the identity of sealed bids: An abstract of the bids for 6,000 barrels of cement to the United States Engineer Office at Tucumcari, New Mexico, opened April 23, 1936, shows the following:

| Name of Bidder | Price per Bbl. |
|---|---|
| Monarch | $3.286854 |
| Ash Grove | 3.286854 |
| Lehigh | 3.286854 |
| Southwestern | 3.286854 |
| U.S. Portland Cement Co | 3.286854 |
| Oklahoma | 3.286854 |
| Consolidated | 3.286854 |
| Trinity | 3.286854 |
| Lone Star | 3.286854 |
| Universal | 3.286854 |
| Colorado | 3.286854 |

All bids subject to 10 cents per barrel discount for payment in 15 days. (Com.Ex. 175–A.)

and at all times (for such has been substantially the case here) charge for their cement precisely, to the fractional part of a penny, the price their competitors charge. Certainly it runs counter to what many people have believed, namely, that without agreement, prices will vary—that the desire to sell will sometimes be so strong that a seller will be willing to lower his prices and take his chances. We therefore hold that the Commission was not compelled to accept the views of respondents' economist-witnesses that active competition was bound to produce uniform cement prices. The Commission was authorized to find understanding, express or implied, from evidence that the industry's Institute actively worked, in cooperation with various of its members, to maintain the multiple basing point delivered price system; that this pricing system is calculated to produce, and has produced, uniform prices and terms of sale throughout the country; and that all of the respondents have sold their cement substantially in accord with the pattern required by the multiple basing point system. . . .

We sustain the Commission's holding that concerted maintenance of the basing point delivered price system is an unfair method of competition prohibited by the Federal Trade Commission Act. . . .

The Commission's order should not have been set aside by the Circuit Court of Appeals. Its judgment is reversed and the cause is remanded to that court with directions to enforce the order.

■ JUSTICE DOUGLAS and JUSTICE JACKSON took no part in the consideration or decision of these cases.

■ JUSTICE BURTON, dissenting.

[Omitted]

## NOTES

(1) ***Framing the Issue.*** Speaking broadly, the cement companies in the case we just read make the following argument: the matter at hand—the validity of their pricing scheme—could be tried either in a court under the antitrust statutes or before the agency under the Federal Trade Commission Act; it ought to be tried in a court, they say, because the agency is biased. The case is unusual in that there are two separate statutes that, the Court is willing to assume, would provide the agency parallel causes of action in different venues. Let's consider the simpler case where there is one regulatory statute, for which we need to provide a process to determine when it has been violated. How do we know what process applies? In the first instance, we look to see what process Congress has stipulated—and what we find is that different statutes come with different processes. Congress can provide, as in the Federal Election Campaign Act, for an agency to investigate and bring charges, but for the charges to be brought, and the case to be decided, in a federal district court. Congress can provide, as in the Occupational Safety and Health Act, for one agency to bring charges, but for another administrative agency to conduct the actual adjudication. Congress can provide, as in the Family and Medical Leave Act, for ordinary citizens to enforce a statute and its accompanying regulations against employers in

court (alongside of an agency that can also sue in court to enforce). Or, as in the Federal Trade Commission Act at stake in Cement Institute, Congress can empower an agency to investigate and bring charges in a process pursuant to which the same agency will then adjudicate and pronounce judgment. This last possibility constitutes the archetype of administrative adjudication, both in the sense that it is the one most commonly met in regulatory statutes and in the sense that it is the model that is assumed to be in play in the APA's treatment of adjudicatory procedures. (It is perhaps worth noting that this plasticity disappears when criminal sanctions are at stake; criminal cases must be brought in the ordinary courts, if only because that's where the juries are.)

(2) ***Are Agencies Inherently Biased?*** In other words, the problem of Cement Institute arises because of the way the process of adjudication has been set into the institutional structure of an administrative agency. The Federal Trade Commission Act established the FTC as an instrument of government, told it to investigate and pursue unfair acts in commerce, and told it, if warranted, to order the perpetrators to stop what they were doing. Historically, the FTC dated back to the Progressive era. Politically, it was part of the twentieth century's positive use of government to control the excesses of the market. Procedurally, it pursued the investigation and decision of individual cases (and did not until much later than the Cement Institute case have broad rulemaking powers). Put differently, by means of deciding cases the agency was supposed to forward a positive agenda.

The cement companies emphasized that, before charging them, the FTC had made reports to Congress that criticized the basing point pricing system—perhaps because that was their clearest evidence of prejudgment. But considering the adjudicatory process as a whole, the FTC was even more—we might say, much more—implicated in what took place. One or another employee of the FTC:

- Investigated the situation;
- Became convinced there was wrongdoing;
- Formally voted to bring charges;
- Presented, as prosecutor, the case against the companies;
- Perhaps testified as an expert witness against the companies;
- Acted as the hearing examiner receiving the evidence;
- Made findings of fact and proposed rulings of law;
- Heard an internal appeal; and
- Rendered the final decision.

If we consider the FTC as a unitary actor, the agency as a whole clearly crossed over a line, rigorously policed in ordinary courtroom adjudication, separating those who charge and present (e.g., the prosecutor) from those who hear and decide (e.g., the judge and jury). Is this unfair? To make that question more doctrinally precise, does this satisfy the constitutional requirement of due process (applicable to administrative adjudication per Londoner v. Denver, p. 220)? Or can we rely on officials, as we rely on many people in all walks of life, to change their minds, if warranted, once they find out in detail what the facts actually are?

Another possibility is to not consider the FTC to be a unitary actor, but instead to notice that it, like most organizations, comprises many people, who are more or less subject to each other's control depending on how the organization is organized. We might then ask what lines of connection are permissible between those who prosecute and those who hear the case, or between those who hear the case and those who decide on any internal appeal. This, as we shall see, is one of the ways the APA (which was passed three years after the FTC reached its 1943 decision in Cement Institute) "solves" the question of fairness.

But even after the APA, the five named Commissioners at the top of the FTC are (and were in Cement Institute) themselves on both sides of the line. By the explicit terms of the FTC Act, they both formally vote to bring charges and also render the final decision. Because, one might argue, if they do not remain in control of what cases the agency brings, and what precedents the agency sets, they will not have the tools needed to be able to carry out the agenda Congress has handed them.

Justice Black's answer—taking the case as applicable, not just to the question of reports to Congress but to the situation as a whole—seems to take this point of view. The FTC's combination of functions is not per se in violation of the Constitution. A more particular bias needs to be shown. Otherwise Congress's purposes in establishing an expert, experienced Commission would be thwarted.

This point of view also prevailed in WITHROW V. LARKIN, 421 U.S. 35 (1975). There, a doctor who performed abortions (criminally prohibited at the time) was the subject of an investigatory hearing by the Wisconsin Medical Examining Board. Although the agency was presumably a much smaller and less differentiated body than the FTC, a similar result obtained. The doctor's counsel was present at a preliminary hearing and invited to explain any of the evidence that had been presented, but not otherwise allowed to participate. After the hearing, the Board formally charged the doctor with a number of violations and scheduled a contested hearing that could lead to temporary license suspension. The doctor sued in federal court, alleging that the combination of investigatory and adjudicatory roles in the Board violated due process. A three-judge district court agreed, but the Supreme Court reversed in an opinion by JUSTICE WHITE:

"Concededly, a 'fair trial in a fair tribunal is a basic requirement of due process.' In re Murchison, 349 U.S. 133, 136 (1955). This applies to administrative agencies which adjudicate as well as to courts. Not only is a biased decisionmaker constitutionally unacceptable but 'our system of law has always endeavored to prevent even the probability of unfairness.' In re Murchison, supra, at 136. In pursuit of this end, various situations have been identified in which experience teaches that the probability of actual bias on the part of the judge or decisionmaker is too high to be constitutionally tolerable. Among these cases are those in which the adjudicator has a pecuniary interest in the outcome and in which he has been the target of personal abuse or criticism from the party before him.

"The contention that the combination of investigative and adjudicative functions necessarily creates an unconstitutional risk of bias in administrative adjudication has a . . . difficult burden of persuasion to carry. It must overcome a presumption of honesty and integrity in those serving as adjudicators; and it must convince that, under a realistic appraisal of psychological tendencies and human weakness, conferring investigative and adjudicative powers on the same individuals poses such a risk of actual bias or prejudgment that the practice must be forbidden if the guarantee of due process is to be adequately implemented. . . .

". . . [O]ur cases, although they reflect the substance of the problem, offer no support for the bald proposition applied in this case by the District Court that agency members who participate in an investigation are disqualified from adjudicating. The incredible variety of administrative mechanisms in this country will not yield to any single organizing principle. . . .

". . . [I]n this case . . . there was no more evidence of bias or the risk of bias or prejudgment than inhered in the very fact that the Board had investigated and would now adjudicate. . . . The processes utilized by the Board . . . do not in themselves contain an unacceptable risk of bias. The investigative proceeding had been closed to the public, but appellee and his counsel were permitted to be present throughout; counsel actually attended the hearings and knew the facts presented to the Board. No specific foundation has been presented for suspecting that the Board had been prejudiced by its investigation or would be disabled from hearing and deciding on the basis of the evidence to be presented at the contested hearing. . . . Without a showing to the contrary, state administrators 'are assumed to be men of conscience and intellectual discipline, capable of judging a particular controversy fairly on the basis of its own circumstances.' United States v. Morgan, 313 U.S. 409, 421 (1941). . . .

"Judges repeatedly issue arrest warrants on the basis that there is probable cause to believe that a crime has been committed and that the person named in the warrant has committed it. Judges also preside at preliminary hearings where they must decide whether the evidence is sufficient to hold a defendant for trial. Neither of these pretrial involvements has been thought to raise any constitutional barrier against the judge presiding over the criminal trial and, if the trial is without a jury, against making the necessary determination of guilt or innocence. . . . It is also very typical for the members of administrative agencies to receive the results of investigations, to approve the filing of charges or formal complaints instituting enforcement proceedings, and then to participate in the ensuing hearings. This mode of procedure does not violate the [APA], and it does not violate due process of law. We should also remember that it is not contrary to due process to allow judges and administrators . . . reversed on appeal to confront the same questions a second time around. . . .

"That the combination of investigative and adjudicatory functions does not, without more, constitute a due process violation, does not, of course, preclude a court from determining from the special facts and circumstances present in the case before it that the risk of unfairness is intolerably high."

Is this basic judicial acceptance of agencies having a multiplicity of functions sound? Even if it meets the basics of due process, ought it to be avoided or ameliorated where possible? As we shall see, the possibility of answering yes to both of these questions forms a good part of the explanation for much of the APA's statutory treatment of administrative adjudication.

(3) ***What About the "Separation of Powers"?*** Even if we accept Cement Institute's answer to the question of bias, is the result consistent with the structure of our Constitution? Here are two opposing answers:

GARY LAWSON, THE RISE AND RISE OF THE ADMINISTRATIVE STATE, 107 Harv. L. Rev. 1231, 1248–49 (1994): "The constitutional separation of powers is a means to safeguard the liberty of the people. In Madison's famous words, '[t]he accumulation of all powers, legislative, executive, and judiciary, in the same hands, whether of one, a few, or many, and whether hereditary, self-appointed, or elective, may justly be pronounced the very definition of tyranny.' [Federalist No.47.] The destruction of this principle of separation of powers is perhaps the crowning jewel of the modern administrative revolution. Administrative agencies routinely combine all three governmental functions in the same body, and even in the same people within that body. . . .

"This is probably the most jarring way in which the administrative state departs from the Constitution, and it typically does not even raise eyebrows. . . ."

ADRIAN VERMEULE, LAW'S ABNEGATION 42 (2016): "Lawson's view is unpersuasive . . . . The inescapable fact is that *the institutional innovations that appall Lawson were themselves generated by the very system of lawmaking-by-separation-of-powers that he wants to defend. . . .* [E]verything Lawson deems inconsistent with the Constitution of 1789 emerged *through and by means of the* operation of that very Constitution, not despite it.

"Here is another way of putting the issue. Suppose magically that the American constitutional order of 1789 were somehow restored to the baseline of 1789, . . . Would we have any reason to expect a different outcome? The same classical lawmaking, through the same classical separation-of-powers system, might well generate the same administrative state that it generated before, or some functionally equivalent substitute. . . . Legislators legislating by virtue of Article I, Presidents exercising their functions under Article II, judges judging under Article III—these, not some sinister cabal of New Deal lawyers, were the source of all the institutional innovations, like agencies exercising combined functions, that Lawson abhors."

(4) ***How Far Does the Case Go?*** Justice Black's argument rests, in part, on the particular configuration of the Federal Trade Commission: it comprises five members, appointed for seven year terms, who can be fired only for "inefficiency, neglect of duty, or malfeasance in office." It is, in other words,

an "independent" agency. The case, however, has not been so confined. Is the result fairly applicable to agencies that are "executive" agencies?

(5) ***The Agency as Policymaker.*** Justice Black seems to think not only that agency commingling of functions is tolerable, but also that it is desirable. Here's one classic statement of that position: JAMES M. LANDIS, THE ADMINISTRATIVE PROCESS 35–39 (1938):

"The power to initiate action exists because it fulfills a long-felt need in our law. To restrict governmental intervention, in the determination of claims, to the position of an umpire deciding the merits upon the basis of the record as established by the parties, presumes the existence of an equality in the way of the respective power of the litigants to get at the facts. . . . In some spheres the absence of equal economic power generally is so prevalent that the umpire theory of administering law is almost certain to fail. Here government tends to offer its aid to a claimant, not so much because of the grave social import of the particular injury, but because the atmosphere and conditions created by an accumulation of such unredressed claims is of itself a serious social threat. . . .

"One other significant distinction between the administrative and the judicial processes is the power of 'independent' investigation possessed by the former. The test of the judicial process, traditionally, is not the fair disposition of the controversy; it is the fair disposition of the controversy *upon the record as made by the parties*. True, there are collateral sources of information which often affect judicial determinations. There is the more or less limited discretion under the doctrine of judicial notice; and there is the unarticulated but nonetheless substantial power to choose between competing premises based upon off-the-record considerations. But, in strictness, the judge must not know of the events of the controversy except as these may have been presented to him, in due form, by the parties. . . .

"On the other hand, these characteristics, conspicuously absent from the judicial process, do attend the administrative process. For that process to be successful in a particular field, it is imperative that controversies be decided as 'rightly' as possible, independently of the formal record the parties themselves produce. The ultimate test of the administrative is the policy that it formulates; not the fairness as between the parties of the disposition of a controversy on a record of their own making."

(6) ***Who Finally Decides?*** The FTC Act at issue in the Cement Institute case provides for hearings to be held before a subordinate employee, who may make an interim decision—but also provides for the final decision to be fully made by the Commission itself, comprising five members, each appointed by the President and confirmed by the Senate. This pattern is also picked up by § 557(b) of the Administrative Procedure Act, which provides: "On appeal from or review of the initial decision, the agency has all the powers which it would have in making the initial decision." "The agency" in this sentence must mean not the ALJ (who, after all, made the initial decision being reviewed) but those at the top of the organization: the Secretary of this or that, or the members of this Board or that Commission. This language recognizes that final decisions in formal agency proceedings often present

policy choices that should be made by those politically responsible persons, appointed by the President and confirmed by the Senate, on whom Congress has conferred regulatory authority. But how does this authority at the top mesh with the idea that Congress has also provided that the decision shall be made within an adjudicatory framework?

As you will see if you study Chapter VII, the Supreme Court has said that this question has a constitutional dimension. In UNITED STATES V. ARTHREX, 141 S.Ct. 1970 (2021) (p. 945), the Supreme Court addressed the constitutionality of the system of "inter partes" review of patents. Under that system, final determinations of patent validity were made by administrative patent judges who were appointed by the Secretary of Commerce, who is the head of the department where the Patent and Trademark Office is located. Appointment by the head of a department is one of the methods the Appointment Clause provides for appointing inferior officers, whereas appointment of principal officers requires appointment by the President with Senate confirmation. The Court held that these inferior officers could not constitutionally issue a final adjudicative decision on behalf of the United States. Emphasizing the need to maintain political accountability tracing back to the election of the President, Chief Justice Roberts said that this function had to be carried out by a principal officer. Accordingly, decisions of the administrative patent judges had to be, not final, but rather subject to review by the Director of the Patent and Trademark Office, who was appointed by the President and confirmed by the Senate. "The Constitution therefore forbids the enforcement of statutory restrictions on the Director that insulate the decisions of APJs from his direction and supervision. To be clear, the Director need not review every decision of the PTAB. What matters is that the Director have the discretion to review decisions rendered by APJs. In this way, the President remains responsible for the exercise of executive power—and through him, the exercise of executive power remains accountable to the people." 141 S.Ct. at 1988.

Do you think political responsibility should be an important goal to protect when evaluating an adjudicative process? How does it compare to the goal of decisional integrity?

(7) ***A Current Controversy.*** The SEC, like the FTC in Cement Institute, has long possessed the authority to bring certain enforcement actions either in federal court or before the agency itself in an administrative proceeding. But the Dodd-Frank Wall Street Reform and Consumer Protection Act ("Dodd-Frank"), passed during the Obama Administration, significantly expanded the kinds of cases that the SEC could try internally. Here's an explanation by Joseph Grundfest, a former SEC Commissioner, of some of the issues raised by this shift:

"The [SEC] often can choose between two forums when it files enforcement actions. One option is to sue in federal district court, where defendants have a right to a jury trial, can take depositions, and testimony is subject to the Federal Rules of Evidence.... Alternatively, the Commission can file an administrative proceeding that is heard by an administrative law judge (ALJ). There is no right to a jury trial in an administrative proceeding. Discovery is severely restricted, depositions are limited, hearings proceed on a schedule that is far more rapid than in most federal trials, and the Federal Rules of Evidence do not apply. Prosecutors and ALJs in administrative proceedings are all Commission employees. Initial appeals from ALJ rulings are to the Commission itself, the same body that issued the order instituting the proceeding. . . . Only after the Commission rules on the appeal does a respondent gain the right to be heard by a federal judge unaffiliated with the Commission. . . .

"The debate over the fairness of the Commission's administrative procedures, and over the discretion the Commission exercises when allocating litigation between federal and administrative venues, ran at a low simmer for decades with only occasional outbursts. However, this relative calm ended in 2013, when the Commission's staff announced plans to rely on expanded administrative remedies created by [Dodd-Frank] and to shift litigation that had traditionally been brought in federal court to its in-house administrative proceedings. . . . This announcement kicked over a hornet's nest of protest as critics trumpeted a long list of complaints about the fairness of the SEC's internal process and its Kafkaesque dimensions. They pointed to data suggesting that the Commission enjoyed a significant home-court advantage when litigating before its own and challenged the constitutionality of the process by which the Commission appointed its ALJs. Critics also waxed poetic about the Commission's internal procedures as an affront to the principles of due process that can be traced back to the Magna Carta. It was as though a dam holding back pent up rage about the fairness of the Commission's administrative proceedings had suddenly burst." JOSEPH A. GRUNDFEST, FAIR OR FOUL?: SEC ADMINISTRATIVE PROCEEDINGS AND PROSPECTS FOR REFORM THROUGH REMOVAL LEGISLATION, 85 Fordham L. Rev. 1143, 1144–48 (2016).

Whether the data actually showed the SEC having a "home-court" advantage when it proceeded administratively depended on how you massaged the data. See id., p.1175 et seq. But the belief was widespread. One Wall Street Journal article was entitled "SEC Wins With In-House Judges" and claimed that over a five year period the SEC won 90% of the time before the ALJs compared to 69% before the courts. True or not, claims like these did not escape the notice of Congress. In a 2015 oversight hearing, then-Subcommittee Chairman Scott Garrett observed that the hurdles regulated parties face (including deferential review) "coupled with the SEC's . . . success rate . . . illustrates a very troubling pattern of the SEC's attempting to stack the rules and process in a way that the outcome of the case is, well, predetermined. This is not appropriate in a country that values appropriate due process for its citizens. Due process is a fair process, and fair process is fair play." Oversight of the SEC's Division of Enforcement Before the Subcomm. on Capital Mkts & Gov't Sponsored Enters. of the H. Comm. on Fin. Servs., 114th Cong. 3 (2015).

Andrew Ceresny, then-Director of the SEC's Enforcement Division, mounted a spirited defense, id. at 8–10: "[I]n cases where we need quick relief, where we want to get a bar very quickly, or we want to get investors relief quickly, administrative proceedings can be much quicker than district court actions. District court actions will often take years to get a resolution in. . . . And another important point is where we have technical rules, where we have complicated rules, some of our rules are very complicated, we have sophisticated fact-finders who are the ALJs; whereas with a jury, it would be much more difficult for them to grasp those very, very complicated issues. . . .

"Administrative proceedings have additional protections that actually defendants don't necessarily have in district court. . . . We turn over the investigative files, usually within 7 days of filing our cases, which we do not do in district court proceedings. There also are exhibit lists and witness lists provided typically in administrative proceedings. . . . [D]efendants also get subpoenas if they show good cause, and they [ ] subpoena documents. The one major difference is obviously the lack of depositions."

Not surprisingly, Congress considered legislation to restrict the SEC. The proposed Financial CHOICE Act of 2017 included a provision that would have curtailed the SEC's power to bring an enforcement action in its preferred forum. It would have allowed the subject of an SEC administrative adjudication to compel the agency to terminate the in-house proceeding; the SEC could have then brought the same case as a civil action if it wanted to. See Financial CHOICE Act of 2017, H.R. 10, 115th Cong. (2017). But the bill failed. Subsequent legislation did alter some of the other requirements of the Dodd-Frank Act but did not include this restriction on the SEC. See Economic Growth, Regulatory Relief, and Consumer Protection Act, S. 2155, 115th Cong. (2018).

Meanwhile, the controversy has been making its way through the courts. The campaign to limit the SEC hit paydirt in 2022 in JARKESY V. SEC, 34 F.4th 446 (5th Cir. 2022). In an action tried in-house before an ALJ, the SEC determined that Jarkesy and various associates misrepresented securities in violation of several securities statutes; the Commission issued cease and desist orders, barred Jarkesy from future participation in securities activities; levied a civil penalty of $300,000; and ordered disgorgement of $685,000 of ill-gotten gains. On review in the Fifth Circuit, the court held, 2–1, that: "(1) the SEC's in-house adjudication of Petitioners' case violated their Seventh Amendment right to a jury trial; (2) Congress unconstitutionally delegated legislative power to the SEC by failing to provide an intelligible principle by which the SEC would exercise the delegated power [to choose where to proceed]. . . and (3) statutory removal restrictions on SEC ALJs violate the Take Care Clause of Article II."

How durable this triple play will be, after other courts have considered the same issues, remains to be seen. Many scholars have their doubts. The unconstitutional delegation claim, which on these facts comes down to saying that Congress could not give the agency the unfettered choice to sue in court or adjudicate in-house, depends on a very large extension of existing cases. (For discussion, see Chapter VII, Section 2.a (p. 836), addressing the nondelegation doctrine.) The issue regarding constitutional restrictions on how ALJs can be removed is taken up later in this Chapter (p. 554), along with other materials regarding the independence of ALJs, and is also discussed in Chapter VII (p. 943). The jury trial claim is most closely related to the materials we have just been considering. As a technical question, whether the Seventh Amendment mandates a jury trial in this context turns on the reach of the "public rights" doctrine, also discussed in Chapter VII (p. 1091). But treating it now as a policy matter, the question is how much administrative regimes are expected to be instruments of law, or of policy, or of both. Juries, for example, routinely try questions of fraud; but to be successful in that cause of action, the plaintiff must show that he was actually deceived, and to his harm. The FTC, by contrast, is empowered to be proactive, and remove an advertisement from view because it has the "capacity to deceive" the public. The FTC's action can be prophylactic and directed to maintaining the tone of the market as a whole. Does this make it a law enforcement activity fairly carried out directly by the executive branch of government?

## SECTION 2. FORMAL ADJUDICATION



Assuming, as developed in the prior Section, the legitimacy of adjudication within an administrative agency, the archetype of that adjudication is the trial-type adjudication specified by the Administrative Procedure Act. But the provisions of the APA entitled "Adjudications," 5 U.S.C. § 554, apply to cases of "adjudication required by statute to be determined on the record after opportunity for an agency hearing." This stipulation divides the universe of agency adjudications into two groups: those subject to § 554 because some other statute so provides—and which eventually will transfer the case to § 556 and § 557—and those not. The first group is known as "formal adjudication" because these parts of the APA specify a considerable set of procedures to be followed. The other group is called, not surprisingly, "informal adjudication." We will look now at formal adjudication, and then, in the next Section, at the informal variety.

It was thought at the time the APA was enacted that the constitutional demand of due process sometimes required a full trial-type process, and sometimes did not. (For today's treatment of due process, see below p. 596.) What the Constitution was thought to require often turned on the various traditional processes that had developed in different corners of the law, and those processes were reflected in the statutes enacted in each area. Whether looked at as a matter of the statutes or as a matter of the Constitution, then, it was common to think that some administrative decisions would be made after something resembling a courtroom trial, and some would not.

Reliance on the requirements called for by existing statutes to determine the degree of formality meant, of course, that the APA would not have a revolutionary impact on existing practice. At the same time, there were complaints about existing practice—many of them coming out of the potentially "biased" impact of administrative structures, as discussed in the preceding Section. Indeed, formal adjudication was the form of administrative proceeding on which the APA's drafters lavished the greatest attention. Theirs, then, was a reformist effort—to start with the existing procedures and regularize and improve them.

Formal adjudication as set out in the APA might be schematically represented as follows:

## FLOW OF FORMAL ADJUDICATION IN AN AGENCY SETTING

| ACTORS | STAGE | RELEVANT APA DIRECTIVES |
|---|---|---|
| Interested public<br>License applicant<br>Enforcement staff | INITIATING EVENT | |
| Agency staff<br>Investigatory subject | INVESTIGATION | 5 U.S.C. 555(c, d) |
| Agency staff or head<br>Parties | DECISION TO GO FORWARD/NOTICE | 5 U.S.C. 554, 558 |
| Parties<br>Agency staff<br>ALJ | PRE-HEARING | 5 U.S.C. 554, 555, 557(d) |
| Same | HEARING | 5 U.S.C. 554(c, d), 556, 557 |
| ALJ or responsible official | DECISION | 5 U.S.C. 554(d), 557, 558 |
| Parties<br>Agency staff<br>Agency head or board | REVIEW | 5 U.S.C. 557 |
| Agency head or board | DECISION ON REVIEW | 5 U.S.C. 557 |

We might, preliminarily, notice three things apparent in this diagram. First, administrative adjudication, as its name suggests, bears a family resemblance to adjudication as we know it in the courts. Second, there are specific APA provisions applicable to various stages of the process; the generality of "family resemblance" is not going to substitute for an investigation of the statutory particulars. And third, the statute pays particular attention to who it is that carries out the various processes of adjudication.

Unfortunately for the law student or law practitioner—although perhaps explicable by functional necessities or political realities—this APA delineation of formal adjudication does not cover all of the agencies that carry out trial-type processes. There is a similar set of processes—an evidentiary hearing as the basis for decision, held before a relatively independent trier-of-fact—not conducted under the requirements of the APA, but rather pursuant to the statutes and procedural regulations governing particular agencies. These hearings are conducted, not by the APA's ALJs, but rather by officials with names like "Administrative Judge" or "Immigration Judge." These "AJs" in general do not have quite as good security for their independence as do ALJs (at least as of this writing), and the rules by which they operate are often not as detailed as those set out in APA §§ 554, 556 and 557. (For a detailed comparison of the roles of ALJs and AJs, see Kent Barnett, Against Administrative Judges, 49 U.C.D.L.Rev. 1643 (2016).) Nevertheless, according to Michael Asimow, who conducted a major recent study of administrative adjudication for the Administrative Conference of the United States (Federal Administrative Adjudication Outside the Administrative Procedure Act, 2019), these proceedings look enough like APA "formal adjudications" that they, too, should bear that name. And they are very common. To give one example, the Executive Office of Immigration Review, whose Immigration Judges handle matters of admissibility, removal, and asylum (but not mere rejection at ports of entry of those who make no claims to refugee status), completed, in just the first half of fiscal year 2022, 93,758 cases.

Not long after the APA was passed, the Supreme Court, apparently in an effort to expand the statute's coverage in accordance with its purpose of regularizing administrative procedure, held that the APA applied to deportation proceedings. Wong Yang Sung v. McGrath, 339 U.S. 33 (1950) [p. 238]. But Congress quickly overturned the ruling, and the Court accepted Congress's judgment. More recent efforts to pass legislation to systematize the requirements of these other "formal adjudications," or to extend the requirements of the APA to these other agencies, have so far failed. The upshot is that there is no substitute in practice for looking at the statute and regulations governing a particular agency. That said, the APA procedure remains, as remarked a few paragraphs ago, the archetype of the formal adjudication. To its requirements, we now turn.

## CITIZENS AWARENESS NETWORK, INC. v. UNITED STATES

United States Court of Appeals for the First Circuit (2004).
391 F.3d 338.

■ SELYA, CIRCUIT JUDGE.

The Nuclear Regulatory Commission is the federal agency charged with regulating the use of nuclear energy, including the licensing of reactors used for power generation. The Atomic Energy Act requires the Commission to hold a hearing "upon the request of any person whose interest may be affected," 42 U.S.C. § 2239(a)(1)(A), before granting a new license, a license amendment, or a license renewal. The NRC's predecessor agency, the Atomic Energy Commission, originally interpreted this provision as requiring on-the-record hearings in accordance with the APA. These hearings closely resembled federal court trials, complete with a full panoply of discovery devices (e.g., requests for document production, interrogatories, and depositions) and direct and cross-examination of witnesses by advocates for the parties. Such hearings proved to be very lengthy; some lasted as long as seven years.

. . . [F]aced with the prospect of hearings on many license renewal applications in the near future—a large number of reactors were initially licensed in the decade from 1960 to 1970 and the standard term for such licenses was forty years—the Commission began to reassess its adjudicatory processes, focusing particularly on the procedures used in reactor licensing cases. . . . [In 2001], the Commission published a notice of proposed rulemaking . . . suggesting a major revision of its hearing procedures. In an accompanying statement, the Commission took the position that . . . § 2239 does not require reactor licensing proceedings to be on the record. . . . With minor exceptions, the final rule replicated the proposed rule . . .

Under the new rules, reactor licensing hearings are, for the most part, to be conducted according to a less elaborate set of procedures. [The new rules do] not provide for traditional discovery. Instead, parties in hearings . . . are required to make certain mandatory disclosures (akin to "open file" . . . discovery) anent expert witnesses, expert witness reports, relevant documents, data compilations, and claims of privilege. The hearings themselves also differ. . . . Parties are allowed to submit proposed questions in advance of the hearing, but the presiding officer is under no compulsion to pose them. Parties are not allowed to submit proposed questions during the hearing unless requested to do so by the presiding officer. Cross-examination is not available as of right, although a party may request permission to conduct cross-examination that it deems "necessary to ensure the development of an adequate record for decision." 10 C.F.R. § 2.1204.

The petitioners[, several public interest groups,] . . . took umbrage at these changes and brought these petitions for judicial review. . . . The mainstay of the petitioners' challenge is the proposition that the new rules exceed the Commission's statutory authority. The petitioners start with the premise that 42 U.S.C. § 2239 requires the NRC to conduct licensing hearings on the record, that is, in strict accordance with the relevant provisions of the APA. In their view, the new rules fail to satisfy that requirement and, therefore, must be pole-axed. . . . Section 2239 requires the Commission, "upon the request of any person whose interest may be affected" by certain agency actions, to hold "a hearing." It does not explicitly require that the hearing be on the record. We have held, however, that the degree of formality that a hearing must afford does not necessarily turn on the presence or absence of an explicit statutory directive. If, even absent such a directive, the nature of the hearing that Congress intended to grant is clear, then that intention governs. Seacoast Anti-Pollution League v. Costle, 572 F.2d 872, 876 (1st Cir. 1978). We assume arguendo, favorably to the petitioners, that the Seacoast rule still obtains.[1]

The petitioners advance several arguments for holding that Congress, in enacting § 2239, purposed to require on-the-record hearings in reactor licensing cases. In addition to canvassing the legislative history and cataloging the relevant amendments to the statute, they point out that for approximately four decades the NRC and its predecessor agency, the AEC, interpreted the statute as requiring on-the-record hearings in reactor licensing proceedings. In response, the NRC highlights the ambiguity of the statute and attempts to situate the latest round of changes in a larger history of procedural experimentation. . . . For years, the courts of appeals have avoided the question of whether § 2239 requires reactor licensing hearings to be on the record. We too decline to resolve this issue. Because the new rules adopted by the Commission meet the requirements of the APA it does not matter what type of hearing the NRC is required to conduct in reactor licensing cases. . . .

We exercise plenary review over the Commission's compliance with the APA. The APA lays out only the most skeletal framework for conducting agency adjudications, leaving broad discretion to the affected agencies in formulating detailed procedural rules. In specific terms, the APA requires only that the agency provide a hearing before a neutral decisionmaker and allow each party an opportunity "to present his case or defense by oral or documentary evidence, to submit rebuttal evidence, and to conduct such cross-examination as may be required for a full and true disclosure of the facts." 5 U.S.C. § 556(d).

The petitioners urge that the magnitude of the risks involved in reactor licensing proceedings warrant the imposition of a more elaborate set of safeguards. It is beyond cavil, however, that, short of constitutional constraints, a court may not impose procedural requirements in administrative cases above and beyond those mandated by statute (here, the APA). Vermont Yankee Nuclear Power Corp. v. Natural Res. Def. Council, Inc., 435 U.S. 519, 543–44 (1978) [p. 312]. Accordingly, we are not at liberty to impress on the Commission (or any other agency, for that matter) a procedural regime not mandated by Congress. The NRC's new rules will, therefore, succumb to the petitioners' . . . attack only if they fail to provide the minimal procedural safeguards actually demanded by the APA.

We turn now from the general to the particular. The rulemaking at issue here effected several changes in the Commission's procedures. The petitioners focus their challenge on two aspects of the newly minted process. First, they object to the Commission's decision to eliminate discovery. Second, they complain about the Commission's decision to circumscribe the availability of cross-examination. Because these are the only issues on which the petitioners have offered developed

---

[1] [Ed.] The First Circuit subsequently rejected the Seacoast rule in Dominion Energy Brayton Point LLC v. Johnson, 443 F.3d 12 (1st Cir. 2006). See p. 579 below.

argumentation, we confine our analysis to those portions of the new rules.

We begin with the question of whether the new rules fall below the APA's minimum requirements by eliminating discovery. The Commission points out, and the petitioners do not seriously contest, that the APA does not explicitly require the provision of any discovery devices in formal adjudications. See 5 U.S.C. § 556. Thus, if the APA requires the Commission to provide any discovery to satisfy the standards for formal adjudications, that discovery must be necessary either to effectuate some other procedural right guaranteed by the APA or to ensure an adequate record for judicial review. The petitioners suggest that discovery is necessary to realize the right of citizen-intervenors to present their case and submit an informed rebuttal. If discovery is unavailable, this thesis runs, citizen-intervenors will be unable to gather the evidence needed to support their contentions and, thus, will be shut out of meaningful participation in licensing hearings.

This thesis is composed of more cry than wool. The petitioners argue as if the new rules have eliminated all access to information from opposing parties—but that is a gross distortion. The new rules provide meaningful access to information from adverse parties in the form of a system of mandatory disclosure. Although there might well be less information available to citizen-intervenors under the new rules, the difference is one of degree. There is simply no principled way that we can say that the difference occasioned by replacing traditional discovery methods with mandatory disclosure is such that citizen-intervenors are left with no means of adequately presenting their case.

Nor do we think that full-dress discovery is essential to ensure a satisfactory record for judicial review. The Commission's final decision in any hearing must survive review based on the evidence adduced in the hearing. 5 U.S.C. § 556(e). The applicant bears the burden of proof in any licensing hearing, id. § 556(d), and it will have every incentive to proffer sufficient information to allow the agency to reach a reasoned decision. That same quantum of information should be adequate for a reviewing court to determine whether the agency's action is supportable.

To say more on this point would be to paint the lily. There is simply no discovery-linked conflict between the new rules and the APA's on-the-record adjudication requirement. The petitioners' first line of argument is, therefore, a dead end.

Turning to cross-examination, the petitioners' contentions fare no better: the new rules meet the APA's requirements. . . . It is important to understand that, contrary to the petitioners' importunings, the new rules do not extirpate cross-examination. Rather, they restrict its use to situations in which it is "necessary to ensure an adequate record for decision." 10 C.F.R. § 2.1204. The legitimacy of this restriction must be weighed in light of the fact that the APA does not provide an absolute right of cross-examination in on-the-record hearings. The APA affords a right only to such cross-examination as may be necessary for a full and fair adjudication of the facts. Equally to the point, the party seeking to cross-examine bears the burden of showing that cross-examination is in fact necessary.

The Commission represents that, despite the difference in language, it interprets the standard for allowing cross-examination under the new rules to be equivalent to the APA standard. . . . Given the Commission's stated interpretation, the new rules on cross-examination cannot be termed inconsistent with the dictates of the APA. Nor do we see how cross-examination that is not "necessary to ensure an adequate record for decision" could be necessary to ensure appropriate judicial review. . . . We do, however, add a caveat. The APA does require that cross-examination be available when "required for a full and true disclosure of the facts." If the new procedures are to comply in practice with the APA, cross-examination must be allowed in appropriate instances. Should the agency's administration of the new rules contradict its present representations or otherwise flout this principle, nothing in this opinion will inoculate the rules against future challenges.

Procedural flexibility is one of the great hallmarks of the administrative process—and it is a feature that courts must be reluctant to curtail. Though the Commission's new rules may approach the outer bounds of what is permissible under the APA, we find the statute sufficiently broad to accommodate them. Similarly, the Commission's judgments as to when its procedures need fine-tuning and how they should be retooled are ones to which we accord great respect. We cannot say that the Commission's desire for more expeditious adjudications is unreasonable, nor can we say that the changes embodied in the new rules are an eccentric or a plainly inadequate means for achieving the Commission's goals.

■ LIPEZ, CIRCUIT JUDGE, concurring.

Although I concur fully in Judge Selya's thoughtful and comprehensive opinion, I write separately to describe some oddities about this case which should not go unnoticed. The basic proposition of Judge Selya's decision is indisputably correct: the new rules promulgated by the NRC to reduce the level of formality in reactor licensing proceedings comply with the "on-the-record" requirements of the [APA]. Yet that legal proposition was largely an afterthought of the NRC in the effort to justify its new rules. Instead, the NRC principally argued in the long run-up to this case that 42 U.S.C. § 2239, which simply requires the Commission to hold a hearing "upon the request of any person whose interest may be affected" before granting a new license, did not invoke the requirements for formal adjudication (commonly referred to as "on-the-record" hearings) under the APA. . . .

The terminology for hearings under the APA can be imprecise and confusing. The everyday meaning of terms like "formal" and "informal" sometimes creeps into the discussion, although those terms have specific, functional definitions under the APA. As Judge Selya notes, the terms "formal" and "on-the-record" are generally used as shorthand for hearings that must be conducted pursuant to the requirements of 5 U.S.C. §§ 554, 556, and 557 of the APA. Other terms, too, are sometimes used to refer to such procedures—"trial-type" and "quasi-judicial." These vague and indefinite terms are particularly mischievous because they evoke images of courtroom trials, and they have contributed to the false impression that the APA's requirement of on-the-record hearings involves procedures more akin to civil trials than is actually the case.

To be specific, § 554 requires that, in cases of an "adjudication required by statute to be determined on the record after opportunity for an agency hearing," the agency must follow the procedures outlined in §§ 556 and 557. Although the statutory text at issue here is itself rather pithy, these procedures can be usefully condensed into the following ten points:

1. The agency must give notice of legal authority and matters of fact and law asserted. § 554(b).

2. The oral evidentiary hearing must be presided over by an officer who can be disqualified for bias. § 556(b).

3. Presiding officers cannot have ex parte communications. §§ 554(d), 557(d)(1).

4. Parties are entitled to be represented by attorneys. § 555(b).

5. The proponent of an order has the burden of proof. § 556(d).

6. A party is entitled to present oral or documentary evidence. § 556(d).

7. A party is entitled "to conduct such cross-examination as may be required for a full and true disclosure of the facts." § 556(d).

8. Orders can be issued only on consideration of the record of the hearing. § 556(d).

9. The transcript of testimony and exhibits is the exclusive record for decision and shall be made available to parties. § 556(e).

10. The decision must include "findings and conclusions, and the reasons or basis therefor, on all the material issues of fact, law, or discretion presented on the record." § 557(c)(3)(A).

Strikingly, there is no reference to discovery in these statutory provisions of the APA, and cross-examination is assured only if necessary "for a full and true disclosure of the facts." 5 U.S.C. § 556(d). Most of these provisions relate to the conduct and responsibilities of the presiding officer or the basis for agency orders (on the record). Only a few relate to the conduct of the hearing itself. These APA requirements leave agencies with a great deal of flexibility in tailoring on-the-record hearing procedures to suit their perceived needs. . . .

From the beginning of its proposed rulemaking, the NRC repeatedly referred to the procedures outlined in the new regulations as "informal," as opposed to the outmoded formal procedures of the past. The clear implication was that the new informal procedures would not meet the APA's requirements for formal, on-the-record hearings. Thus, the NRC believed that it first had to establish that its authorizing statute, the Atomic Energy Act (AEA), did not require it to hold on-the-record hearings for reactor licensing. . . .

The NRC's belated recognition that the new licensing procedures might in fact comply with the on-the-record requirements of the APA is all the more surprising because sources contemporaneous with the APA's passage suggest that flexibility has always been a hallmark of the APA, and that agencies have always had considerable discretion to structure on-the-record hearings to suit their particular needs. This flexibility is nowhere more evident than in determining the role of cross-examination in on-the-record hearings. . . .

The Attorney General's Manual on the Administrative Procedure Act (1947) is a "key document" for interpreting the APA. The Manual begins by stressing the general importance of cross-examination in on-the-record hearings, cautioning that "it is clear that the 'right to present his case or defense by oral or documentary evidence' does not extend to presenting evidence in affidavit or other written form so as to deprive the agency or opposing parties of opportunity for cross-examination." . . . The Attorney General's Manual goes on, however, to acknowledge that the general opportunity to cross-examine is subject to restrictions which become more salient as the complexity of the hearing's subject matter increases. On this point, the Manual quotes from the Report of the House Committee on the Judiciary on the APA . . . The Attorney General's Manual and the House Report serve as good indicators that Congress, when it passed the APA, understood that agencies needed a considerable amount of flexibility in fashioning hearing procedures for on-the-record hearings. Despite the frequent use of terms like "trial-type" and "quasi-judicial" over the years to refer to on-the-record hearings, agencies have always been able to adapt their procedures for on-the-record hearings under the APA. . . .

## NOTES ON CITIZEN AWARENESS NETWORK'S APPROACH TO THE APA

(1) ***How "Skeletal" Is Formal Adjudication?*** Judge Selya characterizes the APA's provisions for on-the-record adjudication as "skeletal." Does this accord with your reading of the relevant statutory provisions, §§ 554, 556, and 557? Even if the text of these provisions is minimal and flexible, does the First Circuit's account fairly capture the understanding and intent behind these provisions? In his concurrence, Judge Lipez offers a list of ten requirements that he concludes the APA requires for on-the-record adjudication. Does he provide a less flexible view of on-the-record adjudication, or do his ten requirements in practice impose only limited

constraint? How the APA should be construed, as a theoretical matter, is covered in Chapter 3 starting at p. 245.

(2) ***Right Decision?*** RICHARD PIERCE, WAITING FOR VERMONT YANKEE II, 57 Admin. L. Rev. 669, 676–77 (2005): "The First Circuit concluded that the provision in the NRC rules that confers on a presiding officer the power to grant a motion for cross-examination is legally equivalent to the APA formal adjudication right to 'such cross-examination as may be necessary for a full and fair adjudication of the facts.' That conclusion is inconsistent with the NRC's description of its rules and with the entire purpose of the rules. The NRC emphasized that it expected its presiding officers to grant motions for cross-examination only in 'rare circumstance[s].' [The NRC] expected its presiding officers to distinguish between the many disputes with respect to legislative facts that are not appropriate for cross-examination and the rare disputes with respect to adjudicative facts that are appropriate for cross-examination. It illustrated the latter class of disputes by referring to only two classes of disputes that might justify the grant of a motion to cross-examine a witness under its new rules: '(a) [i]ssues of material fact relating to the occurrence of a past activity, where the credibility of an eyewitness may reasonably be expected to be at issue, and/or (b) issues of motive or intent of the party or eyewitness material to the resolution of the contested factual matter.' The NRC noted that few licensing proceedings were likely to raise issues of that type 'such that cross-examination is an appropriate tool for issue resolution.' If the NRC had prevailed on its theory of the case, it could have made good on its commitment to allow cross-examination rarely, if at all, in licensing cases. . . .

"The First Circuit's description of the qualified right of cross-examination that it determined to be applicable to NRC licensing proceedings differs dramatically from the rare right to cross-examination described by the NRC. The court emphasized that a court, not the NRC, will determine when cross-examination is appropriate in a licensing proceeding."

As the title of Pierce's article suggests, the approach to cross-examination taken in Citizen Awareness Network can be contrasted with (and partly understood in light of) the Supreme Court's earlier decision in the Vermont Yankee case (p. 312).

## NOTES ON SOME OTHER FEATURES OF "FORMAL ADJUDICATION"

(1) ***Hearsay Evidence.*** The APA says: "Any oral or documentary evidence may be received, but the agency as a matter of policy shall provide for the exclusion of irrelevant, immaterial, or unduly repetitious evidence." 5 U.S.C. § 556(d). For agencies where there is no further restriction in their statutes or regulations, this standard is understood—and rightly so, in light of its legislative history—to provide for the admission of hearsay evidence as a routine matter, although the weight of such evidence remains open to argument. Even in ordinary courts, hearsay rules have much less bite when (as in agency adjudication) there is no jury. But more can be said: Richard J. Pierce, Use of the Federal Rules of Evidence in Federal Agency

Adjudications, 39 Admin. L. Rev. 1, 17–19 (1987): ". . . [I]t makes little sense to take the risk of erroneous exclusion of reliable evidence through application of highly technical exclusionary rules in the context of agency adjudications. . . . Agencies and ALJs are required to state the bases for their findings of fact. Their findings are then subject to judicial review under the substantial evidence standard. If an agency finding is based on unreliable evidence, the agency's action is reversed. Thus, there is a mechanism available in agency adjudications independent of rulings on the admissibility of evidence to insure that agency findings are based only on reliable evidence."

(2) ***A Statement of Findings and Conclusions.*** Another feature of APA on-the-record adjudication is § 557(c)'s requirement that agency decisions "shall include a statement of . . . findings and conclusions, and the reasons or basis therefor, on *all* the material issues of fact, law, or discretion presented on the record." (emphasis added). This might seem to demand a compulsive attention to detail, but when put to it, courts are frequently less demanding than such statutory phrases suggest, stressing simply the need to understand the administrative decision. A communication (in whatever form) that indicates precisely what has been decided will suffice, provided that even if "the findings of the Commission . . . leave much to be desired . . . the path which it followed can be discerned." Colorado Interstate Gas Co. v. Fed. Power Comm'n, 324 U.S. 581 (1945). Courts have also noted the practical difference between the agency that renders relatively few decisions in a year, each of which may have substantial precedential significance, and the agency given the task of processing thousands upon thousands of particularistic cases. As Judge Easterbrook pointed out in Stephens v. Heckler, 766 F.2d 284 (7th Cir. 1985), regarding the enormous job of processing claims for disability benefits, when agency decisionmakers "slow down to write better opinions, that holds up the queue and prevents deserving people from receiving benefits."

At the same time, mere conclusory statements or statements that fail to identify what the agency decided will not do. Armstrong v. Commodity Futures Trading Comm'n, 12 F.3d 401 (3d Cir. 1993), involved a decision of the CFTC concluding that Martin Armstrong controlled corporations found to have violated Commission regulations and holding him individually responsible for the violations. Rather than issue a separate statement, the CFTC had summarily affirmed the ALJ's decision finding Armstrong liable, stating "[o]ur review of the record and the briefs submitted by the parties establishes that the ALJ reached a substantially correct result . . . [and] that the parties have not raised important questions of law or policy concerning the ALJ's findings of fact and conclusions." But it added that the decision should not be cited as precedent or considered "an expression of the Commission's views on the issues raised." The Third Circuit held this mode of proceeding to be a violation of § 557(c): "Summarily affirming the ALJ's opinion as 'substantially correct' is insufficient because it does not permit intelligent appellate review. . . . We hold that a summary affirmance of all or part of an ALJ's opinion must leave no guesswork regarding what the agency has adopted."

The appeals court found a second § 557(c) violation in the failure of both the ALJ's decision and the CFTC's opinion to address the requirements of the governing statute, § 13(b) of the Commodity Exchange Act: "The only theory under which Armstrong was charged with individual liability in the second complaint was as a controlling person as defined in § 13(b) . . . . We do not understand how a statement of conclusion on a material issue of law can be adequate [under § 557(c)] without mentioning the statutory provision or its language. Section 13(b) requires at least two findings before concluding a respondent is liable as a controlling person: (1) that the respondent controlled a violator; and (2) that the controlling person did not act in good faith or knowingly induced the violation. . . . [Although] the Commission's appeal brief recites evidence in the record from which the ALJ could have found that Armstrong knowingly induced the violations[,] . . . there is still no finding by the ALJ or the Commission that Armstrong did knowingly induce the violations. Finally, and most importantly, there is no conclusion that Armstrong is liable as a controlling person under § 13(b). Without a conclusion that Armstrong is liable for violations with which he was charged, Armstrong may not be individually penalized."

In the words of Judge Henry J. Friendly: "A written statement of reasons, almost essential if there is to be judicial review, is desirable on many other grounds. The necessity for justification is a powerful preventive of wrong decisions. The requirement also tends to effectuate intra-agency uniformity. . . . A statement of reasons may even make a decision somewhat more acceptable to a losing claimant." Some Kind of Hearing, 123 U. Pa. L. Rev. 1267, 1292 (1975).

(3) ***Explain How Much?*** GUNDERSON V. DEP'T OF LABOR, 601 F.3d 1013 (10th Cir. 2010), involved a coal miner's claim for benefits under the Black Lung Benefits Act. The District Director of the Department of Labor's Office of Workers' Compensation Programs granted the claim, and the coal company that had employed the miner appealed to an ALJ. After a hearing, the ALJ rejected the miner's claim, finding that the conflicting doctors' reports were all "well-reasoned," "well-documented," and "well-supported," and entitled to equal weight. The ALJ therefore denied the claim on the ground that Gunderson had not met his burden of proving that his chronic pulmonary disease was caused by his work as a coal miner. The Department of Labor's Benefits Review Board affirmed the ALJ's decision.

The Tenth Circuit reversed: "Section 557(c)(3)(A) . . . requires an agency's adjudicative decision to be 'accompanied by a clear and satisfactory explication of the basis on which it rests.' Barren Creek Coal Co. v. Witmer, 111 F.3d 352, 356 (3d Cir. 1997). This duty of explanation has added importance for cases in which medical or scientific evidence has been presented. . . . [Agency] expertise allows agencies to relax the rules of evidence because they are deemed to 'have the skill needed to handle evidence that might mislead a jury. They have a corresponding obligation to *use* that skill when evaluating technical evidence.' Peabody Coal Co. v. McCandless, 255 F.3d 465, 469 (7th Cir. 2001). [Here,] we cannot discern 'the reasons or basis,' 5 U.S.C. § 557(c)(3)(A), for the ALJ's rejection of Mr. Gunderson's claim . . . [F]rom the ALJ's statement that the conflicting opinions are 'evenly balanced, and should receive equal weight,' we cannot tell how he evaluated their opinions. The mere fact that equally qualified experts gave conflicting testimony does not authorize the ALJ to avoid the scientific controversy by declaring a tie. In reaching this conclusion, we reject . . . [the] contention that requiring a more detailed, scientifically-grounded explanation from the ALJ sets the bar too high. The ALJ's task is not to resolve general scientific controversies, but instead to determine the facts of the case at hand and apply the law accordingly. This is a task that is routinely assigned to judges and to juries . . . Moreover, with regard to disputes concerning the existence and causes of pneumoconiosis, an ALJ has the benefit of . . . Department of Labor [regulations, and] . . . may properly rely on those regulations when assessing scientific testimony."

Judge O'Brien dissented: "Even though intimately familiar with the issues and knowledgeable as to the scientific principles presented in a case, an . . . ALJ is not an expert. The ALJ is not expected, nor permitted, to meld expert opinion into his own unified theory, which he then independently applies to the facts. And it is beyond the ken of an ALJ to resolve a scientific debate. Instead, . . . [w]hen expert opinion is diametrically opposed, the ALJ must, based on all of the evidence, make a reasoned choice, if possible, as to which expert opinion is more probably correct. But a principled choice cannot always be achieved. . . . This is such a case. When he could do so, the ALJ made credibility choices among the experts; when he could not, he candidly confessed his inability. . . . [T]he ALJ [need not] do more than explain why expert opinion is in equipoise and hold the proponent of an issue to his burden of proof."

Did the majority in Gunderson ask too much of a nonexpert ALJ? Or is Judge O'Brien's approach at odds with the reasoned explanation requirement embodied in § 557(c)?

(4) ***Who Can Participate?*** The APA draws a clear distinction between those who can participate in rulemaking proceedings and those who can participate in adjudications. In notice and comment proceedings, "the agency shall give interested persons an opportunity to participate," § 553(c). "Person" is in turn defined to include both individuals and organizations, except for the agency itself—a very large and undefined group of potential commenters. In formal adjudications, by contrast, the participants are called "parties," and "party" is defined as "a person or agency named or admitted as a party . . . in an agency proceeding, and a person or agency admitted by an agency as a party for limited purposes[.]" § 551(3). While this is, confessedly, a somewhat unhelpful definition, it does tell us two things: first, agencies can be "parties," and second, we should expect to see some formal process determining (and limiting) who will be "admitted as a party."

Taking the first point first, not only can agencies be parties—they routinely are one of the parties. In the Cement Institute case, for example, the FTC brought and prosecuted the complaint before the ALJ—becoming a party—and the complaint then named a long list of entities that assertedly had violated the FTC Act—and they became the opposing parties. But not all agency proceedings have this form. In the licensing proceedings whose rules are at stake in Citizens Awareness Network, hearings are initiated, as

Judge Selya states, "upon the request of any person whose interest may be affected." 42 U.S.C. § 2239(a)(1)(A).

Once a proceeding has been initiated, with whatever parties the applicable statute suggests, the question is whether other persons or entities can also participate in the hearing or on agency review of what the ALJ decides. The greatest level of participation would be to intervene with full procedural rights to make motions, introduce witnesses, take appeals, and so forth. (Intervenors in ordinary court proceedings, if allowed, usually have these full rights.) Another possibility, sometimes found in agency adjudications and recognized in the APA's definition of "party," is to allow intervention for a more limited purpose. Finally, at the other end of the scale, but often still valuable to potential parties, is participation as an amicus curiae—not participating in building the record, but rather arguing, usually in a brief, as to the proper policy to apply to it.

As a matter of organizing an effective proceeding, one might consider the possible advantages to be gained from letting in additional participants—in terms of additional interests to be protected, points of view to be articulated, or nonagency sources of expertise to be accessed—against the possible disadvantages of conducting a proceeding with less clearly organized voices, and, likely, of delay. As a general result, one might expect less intervention in cases for imposing a sanction against a particular party and greater intervention in cases raising large matters of policy—but, of course, there are some cases that share both characteristics. (Indeed, if the question is largely a matter of policy, and many nonparties are allowed to submit amicus briefs, an adjudication can start to resemble a rulemaking proceeding. See, for example, FCC v. Fox Television Stations (p. 1160).

As a matter of the relationship between the agencies and the courts, there is the further question of who should decide who gets to participate. The APA is silent on the matter. In the famous case of Office of Communications of the United Church of Christ v. FCC, 359 F.2d 994 (D.C. Cir. 1966), the court required the FCC to allow participation in a TV license-renewal proceeding by some viewers' groups; the FCC itself had limited participation to those who might be economically harmed by the renewal. The theory of the case was that the participation of viewers was necessary if the public interest was to be achieved; more broadly speaking, that the beneficiaries of regulation, and not just those who would be harmed, were appropriate participants in a licensing proceeding.

More recently, courts have tended to leave this procedural question to the agencies themselves. The rather free-form approach of the Office of Communications case itself was disapproved in Envirocare of Utah, Inc. v. NRC, 194 F.3d 72 (D.C. Cir. 1999). There, the underlying issue concerned the licensing of companies dealing with radioactive wastes. Envirocare wanted to intervene in a proceeding that threatened to grant a license to one of its competitors on terms, said Envirocare, that were less rigorous than the terms in Envirocare's own license. The Atomic Energy Act provided that "any person whose interest may be affected" was entitled to be a party in the proceeding. The Commission ruled that this language referred to parties with public health and safety interests, and not to the interests of economic competitors. The court, for its part, found the statutory language to be ambiguous, and then relied on Vermont Yankee (p. 312) and on Chevron (p. 1206) as supporting agency discretion in these matters.

Of course, one might think that the Office of Communications of the United Church of Christ is a more attractive intervenor than Envirocare of Utah, Inc. If the applicable organic statute does talk about who can participate, it is always possible that a court will find the statutory language to be unambiguous, and therefore binding on the agency. But under current doctrine, potential parties are more likely to have recourse to the procedural rules and practices of the agency involved.

(It is worth noting that the right to participate in an agency proceeding is different from the right to seek judicial review of it—that is, different from "standing" in court. As to the standards for that, see Chapter IX, Section 1 (p. 1414).)

## LUDWIG v. ASTRUE

United States Court of Appeals for the Ninth Circuit (2012).
681 F.3d 1047.

■ KLEINFELD, SENIOR CIRCUIT JUDGE.

We address whether an administrative law judge's handling of an ex parte contact was error, and if so, whether it was harmless.

I. Facts

Ludwig claimed social security disability,[1] his claim was denied, and his appeal to the district court was unsuccessful.

*A. The Medical Evidence*

Ludwig told the Social Security Administration in his May 2006 application that he could not work because of epilepsy, bipolar disease, depression, insomnia, and social anxiety. He had not worked since getting fired at his last job as a cook earlier the same year. He had previously worked on a fishing tender, and as a welder and a cook. In his initial interview, Ludwig attributed his inability to work to his psychiatric problems, not his physical condition. But at his hearing, he claimed disabling arthritis in his knees, hips, and ankles, and degenerative disease in his low back. He testified that he had severe pain if he lifted as much as 15 pounds.

Ludwig had extensive medical records from correctional facilities and community health facilities. He had complained of knee problems for ten years, starting when he was in military service. A year before his social security application, he told a medical provider that he could "press 1,000 pounds," and exercised. His description of his symptoms, together with X-rays and MRIs, led to a diagnosis of chronic pain in both knees

---

[1] Disability under the Social Security Act is defined as the "inability to engage in any substantial gainful activity by reason of any medically determinable physical or mental impairment which can be expected to result in death or which has lasted or can be expected to last for a continuous period of not less than 12 months." 42 U.S.C. § 423(d)(1)(A). . . .

and possible tears in the meniscus of the left knee. In 2007, the Department of Veterans Affairs (VA) awarded Ludwig ten percent service-connected disability compensation on account of his knee. Two months before Ludwig's social security hearing, a VA examining physician described Ludwig's knee problems as "minimal." Around the same time, a chiropractic report said that Ludwig was walking normally.

Ludwig also complained of back pain. On June 14, 2007, Ludwig told a medical provider that he had been experiencing low back pain since trying to pick up a dishwasher the previous month. Two weeks later, he reported to a different examiner that he had endured chronic back pain since straining his back eleven years earlier, but had suffered no recent injury. He was diagnosed with lumbar strain and mild disc herniation. Ludwig said to one medical provider that Vicodin was "the only thing that helped before" with the back pain, but was instead prescribed methadone. The prescription was later changed to morphine sulphate, after Ludwig complained of side effects from the methadone. Physical therapy was prescribed, but Ludwig did not complete the sessions.

Ludwig was diagnosed with bipolar disorder in 2002. Medication successfully controlled it. Ludwig reported to his doctor in early 2006, the same year he applied for social security disability benefits, that, so long as he stayed away from alcohol, his medication kept him reasonably stable. After he got fired from his job as a cook, he enrolled in a drug and alcohol treatment program.

He also had a seizure disorder, controlled by medication. An emergency department record shows that Ludwig was admitted to the emergency room in March 2006, after having had a "witnessed seizure while working at the local Denny's restaurant." He testified at his social security hearing that this was an anxiety attack, not a seizure. But he also testified to far more frequent and recent seizures than what he had told his medical providers.

Ludwig's social security application was denied in July 2006. The Social Security Administration's medical consultant, after reviewing Ludwig's records, concluded that Ludwig's mental impairments caused mild restrictions and difficulties. He opined that Ludwig could lift or carry 25 pounds frequently, 50 pounds occasionally, stand or walk for about 6 hours in an 8-hour workday, and sit for the same amount of time. After the initial denial, Ludwig requested a hearing.

At his hearing, Ludwig testified that he could not lift more than 15 pounds without severe pain, and that it was very painful to sit for more than half an hour. But he also testified that he carried his own firewood into his cabin for heat. He testified that his bipolar disorder made it difficult for him to control his anger, and that he became anxious in crowds of more than ten people. He said he had been fired from his job at Denny's because he could not get along with his coworkers. Ludwig claimed that he suffered three or four grand mal seizures a year, the last one about a month before the hearing. He testified that his petit mal seizures occurred too frequently for him to count. But medical records from 2007 show that he claimed there were three to five year periods where he had no seizures.

*B. Ex Parte Communication*

Right after the hearing, and before the ALJ had issued his decision, an FBI agent told the ALJ that Ludwig was apparently faking his physical disability. The ALJ immediately sent a letter to Ludwig's lawyer, disclosing the ex parte contact. The ALJ suggested that counsel could contact the FBI agent if he wished, though he did not represent that the agent had agreed to talk to counsel:

> Shortly after your client's hearing . . . a special agent with the F.B.I. [ ] informed me that, earlier, he had observed Mr. Ludwig in the parking lot walking with normal gait and station; and when he observed Mr. Ludwig walking inside of the Federal Courthouse (where our hearing was held) he was walking with an exaggerated limp (which I also observed as he left the hearing room).
>
> Should you wish to inquire further, [the special agent] can be reached at the F.B.I. office at:
>
> 101 12th Ave # 329
>
> Fairbanks, AK, 99701

Counsel responded, objecting to any weight being given to what the FBI agent had said.

Counsel asked that unless the ALJ gave assurance that no weight would be given to the ex parte communication, he receive a supplementary hearing at which counsel could cross-examine the agent. Counsel intended to address whether, among other things, the FBI agent really had observed Ludwig as he thought, since around a dozen people had been in and out of the several hearings that morning. He questioned the accuracy of the FBI agent's observations, since Ludwig's knee problem was well-documented in the medical records. Counsel also expected to ask whether his client had been under some sort of surveillance, making him recognizable to the FBI agent.

*C. The ALJ's Decision*

The ALJ found that although Ludwig had a "longstanding seizure disorder," it was "controlled when he takes medication as prescribed." He noted conflicting evidence on Ludwig's physical condition, including Ludwig's claim that he could press 1,000 pounds, the chiropractor's observation that Ludwig walked normally, and evidence of damage to Ludwig's left knee.

The ALJ found that the seizure disorder and diseased tissue in the left knee were "severe" for social security purposes. As for Ludwig's back pain, the ALJ found that Ludwig's "contradictory accounts" and minimal objective findings established that Ludwig "was exaggerating symptoms." He found that Ludwig's bipolar disorder was "well controlled" so long as Ludwig took his medicine and abstained from alcohol, so it caused only "mild" restriction of activities of daily living and functioning.

The ALJ found that none of Ludwig's impairments, separately or together, met the criteria of a listed impairment, and that Ludwig had the capacity to perform "medium" work. Most importantly, the ALJ found that Ludwig was not credible, and had exaggerated how intense, persistent, and limiting his impairments were.

The decision notes that the FBI agent told the ALJ after the hearing that the agent had seen Ludwig in the parking lot "with a normal gait and station and subsequently observed the claimant walking with an exaggerated limp once inside the Federal Courthouse." The ALJ wrote that he did "not assign significant weight" to the agent's statements because the FBI agent was not familiar with Ludwig's medical history and observed Ludwig "only briefly." The ALJ did not say, as Ludwig's counsel had requested as an alternative to a supplementary hearing, that the ALJ had not assigned "any" weight to what the FBI agent told him, just that whatever weight he gave it was not "significant."

The ALJ explained that the record contained "other evidence showing [Ludwig had] exaggerated symptoms." Ludwig's testimony about his seizures was clearly exaggerated "based on what he told health providers." Ludwig had claimed for compensation purposes in March 2008 that he could walk "no more than a few yards," but had reported a month before to a medical provider that he had walked two miles in sub-zero temperatures and suffered frostbite. (Ludwig lives in Fairbanks, Alaska.) Ludwig's back and knee claims were inconsistent with his claim to health care providers that he could press 1,000 pounds. He had exaggerated various parts of his medical history to various providers. Likewise, Ludwig contradicted himself in different contexts about his claimed difficulty with social interactions. His statements that he walked for exercise, cut wood for heat, and stood for nine hours a day as a cook, contradicted his claimed physical limitations. The ALJ found that Ludwig could still work as a cook, as he had before he was fired for not getting along, and was not disabled under the Social Security Act. The district court affirmed.

## II. Analysis

### A. *Standard of Review*

. . .

### B. *The Ex Parte Contact*

The ex parte contact in this case is troubling. Judges are supposed to get their evidence from the testimony and exhibits, not private chats. The judge should have refused to hear the ex parte communication. Ordinarily, if someone says to a judge, "Judge, you know that case you heard this morning?", a judge responds, "Don't tell me anything about it. I can't listen to evidence out of court."

The FBI agent's statements went to the heart of the case. Part of Ludwig's disability claim was his knee problem that he said made it hard to walk. He limped in the courtroom. The FBI agent told the ALJ that he saw Ludwig walking in the parking lot without limping. That is to say, the FBI agent told the ALJ privately that Ludwig was faking.

An FBI agent, by virtue of his employment, is likely to have more credibility with a trier of fact than a felon like Ludwig, with conflicting medical records and a history of substance abuse. To impeach the FBI agent, Ludwig's lawyer wanted to ask the agent in a supplementary hearing, "How do you know the person you saw in the parking lot was Ludwig?" That is a good question, and counsel doubtless had reasons for wanting to ask the FBI agent in front of the ALJ. The FBI agent was under no obligation to talk to Ludwig's attorney, and might have refused to answer his questions without a scheduled hearing. Even if the FBI agent did respond to counsel's inquiries, he would have plenty of time to improve how his answers sounded if he got a private rehearsal with claimant's counsel. Without a hearing, the ALJ would not be able to see the agent's demeanor when answering questions.

Ludwig's lawyer asked for either an assurance that the ALJ would give no weight to the ex parte communication, or else a supplementary hearing to explore what force it should have. He got neither. The ALJ said in his decision that he did not give "significant" weight to the FBI agent's information, not that he disregarded it or gave it no weight. Congress has commanded that the ALJ's decision be "on the basis of evidence adduced at the hearing," not on the basis, even in part, of private chats outside the hearing.[7] . . .

Allowing the FBI agent to speak to the judge outside the presence of counsel, with no opportunity for counsel to cross-examine the agent, and no assurance that the communication had no influence on the result, was error. "Notice and [a meaningful] opportunity to be heard are the hallmarks of procedural due process." Guenther v. Comm'r, 889 F.2d 882, 884 (9th Cir.1989) Though Ludwig was given notice of the evidence against him, he was not given a meaningful opportunity to be heard on it. The ALJ offered his own impeachment that the FBI agent's observation was brief and that the agent was unfamiliar with Ludwig's medical records. But Ludwig's lawyer might have done better. Where, as here, the communication is ex parte, is not disregarded by the judge, and may be subject to significant factual questions, we cannot see what justification there could be for denying a request for an evidentiary hearing. Receipt of the ex parte communication, assignment of some weight to it, and denial of a supplementary hearing to address it, was error.

*C. Harmlessness*

Because the judge erred by considering the ex parte evidence without allowing a supplementary hearing, we are required to evaluate whether there was prejudice. We need not decide whether, in these circumstances, a statement that the judge disregarded the evidence would suffice to establish absence of prejudice, because the ALJ made no

[7] 42 U.S.C. § 405(b)(1).

such statement. We do not suggest that private chats with witnesses are purged of any taint by a rote recitation that they were given "no" weight. But here we do not have even that assurance. No "significant" weight, perhaps a more candid statement than "no" weight, carries a negative pregnant, that the communication received some weight.

. . . Reversal on account of error is not automatic, but requires a determination of prejudice. . . .

> [T]he factors that inform a reviewing court's "harmless-error" determination are various, potentially involving, among other case-specific factors, an estimation of the likelihood that the result would have been different, an awareness of what body (jury, lower court, administrative agency) has the authority to reach that result, a consideration of the error's likely effects on the perceived fairness, integrity, or public reputation of judicial proceedings, and a hesitancy to generalize too broadly about particular kinds of errors when the specific factual circumstances in which the error arises may well make all the difference. Shinseki v. Sanders, 556 U.S. 396, 411–12 (2009).

. . . [W]e conclude that there was no prejudice from the error. The contradictions between what Ludwig said when he testified in his disability hearing, and what he had said on other occasions, were dramatic. He had to have spoken falsely for many years to medical personnel for him to be speaking truthfully at his hearing. Considering the record as a whole, and the ALJ's explanation of his decision, we are convinced that Ludwig has not demonstrated that the decision would have been any different without the ex parte communication.

How could the ALJ give some weight to the FBI agent's communication, but not a "significant" enough amount to affect the outcome? Any judge with an adequate amount of humility makes many decisions about which he has varying degrees of confidence in his own judgment. Learning after a firm conviction has been formed that one's conviction is supported by additional evidence can affect the judge's level of confidence in his decision, without affecting the outcome of the decision. The ALJ's decision, and the record of Ludwig's contradictions, make it plain that the ALJ would have reached the same conclusion—that Ludwig was fit to resume work like his last job as a cook—had the FBI agent not spoken to him about his observations of Ludwig.

An ex parte contact can be quite egregious without being prejudicial. In the absence of actual prejudice from the error, we are required . . . to conclude that the ex parte communication does not entitle Ludwig to a reversal. . . .

Affirmed.

## NOTES ON THE INTEGRITY OF THE RECORD

(1) ***The Underlying Procedure.*** The underlying process in the Ludwig case represents a different type of formal adjudication from the just-preceding Citizens Awareness Network case. Following upon the agency's initial denial

of a claim for benefits, this hearing process is sometimes referred to as "inquisitorial," which denotes the fact that it is the responsibility of the ALJ to inquire into the facts and develop the record as well as to decide the case; while the claimant may be represented, no attorney presents the government's evidence. (The procedure is described at length in Mathews v. Eldridge, p. 616.) This can be contrasted with the "adversarial" hearing one usually expects under the APA. But in many respects the process still adheres to APA requirements for formal adjudication, such as, in Ludwig, the requirement that all evidence relied upon for decision actually be put into the openly-developed record that the claimant can contest. Whether we call this formal adjudication under the APA, with some statutory modifications, or adjudication under the Social Security statutes and regulations, which look similar to the APA in many respects, is a debatable point. The SSA, in a recent procedural rulemaking, took the position that "in light of the significant differences between our informal, inquisitorial hearings process and the type of hearings process to which the APA applies, our hearings process is properly viewed as comparable to the APA's process, but governed only by the requirements of the Act and procedural due process." 83 Fed. Reg. 73,138, 73,140 (2020). By contrast, Michael Asimov, in his recent report, Federal Administrative Adjudication Outside the Administrative Procedure Act (2019) (p. 529), treated these hearings as governed by the APA, although with substantial modification. In a recent Sixth Circuit case, the majority and the dissent split on whether the Circuit had determined that disability cases are formal adjudication under the APA (the majority) or whether statements to that effect in prior cases were only dicta (the dissent); apparently the SSA did not contest the point. Hicks v. Commissioner of Social Security, 909 F3d 786 (6th Cir. 2019). When, earlier, the Supreme Court had faced the issue, it said: "We need not decide whether the APA has general application to social security disability claims," because, for the particulars at issue in that case, the APA and the Social Security statutory procedures were the same. Richardson v. Perales, 402 U.S. 389, 409 (1971). Much the same might be said about the Ludwig case. Judge Kleinfeld refers to the requirement of due process, and cites (in note 7) specifically to the Social Security Act, 42 U.S.C. § 405(b)(1), for the proposition that the ALJ's decision be "on the basis of evidence adduced at the hearing," but would it be any different if he relied instead on APA § 556(e): "The transcript of testimony and exhibits, together with all papers and requests filed in the proceeding, constitutes the exclusive record for decision. . . "?

(2) ***Harmless Error?*** ALJs, being human, are going to make mistakes just like the rest of us do. A rule of harmless error seems to be a sensible recognition of the need to conserve society's resources in the face of human frailty. But in a proceeding whose hallmark is that it is "on the record," learning of relevant facts through a conversation off the record is not just "another error," and Judge Kleinfeld is clear that the ALJ should have acted differently. If that is so, should there simply be a per se rule that, in situations like this one, a new proceeding is warranted?

(3) ***What About Expertise?*** In SEACOAST ANTI-POLLUTION LEAGUE V. COSTLE, 572 F.2d 872 (1st Cir. 1978), the Public Service Company of New Hampshire had sought a permit to discharge heated water into the Hampton-Seabrook Estuary, which runs into the Gulf of Maine. Water taken from the Gulf would be run through PSCO's proposed nuclear generating station to remove waste heat generated by the reactor; it would then be discharged back into the Gulf 39 degrees Fahrenheit warmer than at intake. Occasional discharges would be as hot as 120 degrees Fahrenheit, during a "backflushing" process intended to kill any organisms living in the intake system. Section 301 of the Federal Water Pollution Control Act (FWPCA, more commonly referred to today as the Clean Water Act or CWA) prohibits the discharge of any pollutant—and heat is a pollutant—without obtaining an EPA permit. PSCO's proposed cooling system would result in discharge of water hotter than EPA's effluent standard for heat; therefore, PSCO applied for an exemption under § 316 as well as a discharge permit under § 402. To qualify for the exemption, it had to demonstrate that the applicable effluent standard was "more stringent than necessary to assure the projection [sic] and propagation of a balanced, indigenous population of shellfish, fish, and wildlife in and on the body of water."

The EPA Regional Administrator initially approved PSCO's application, but then reversed his decision after holding a public hearing. PSCO appealed to the EPA Administrator, who convened a panel of six in-house advisors and ultimately approved PSCO's application.

Treating the administrative process as a formal adjudication under the APA, the court had this to say:

"Petitioners [opponents of the power plant] object to the Administrator's use of a panel of EPA scientists to assist him in reviewing the Regional Administrator's initial decision. . . . The Administrator is charged with making highly technical decisions in fields far beyond his individual expertise. . . . The decision ultimately reached is no less the Administrator's simply because agency experts helped him to reach it.

"A different question is presented, however, if the agency experts do not merely sift and analyze [the record,] but also add to the evidence properly before the Administrator. . . . To the extent the technical review panel's Report included information not in the record on which the Administrator relied, § 556(e) was violated. In effect the agency's staff would have made up for PSCO's failure to carry its burden of proof.

"Our review of the Report indicates that such violations did occur. The most serious instance is on page 19 of the Report where the technical panel rebuts the Regional Administrator's finding that PSCO had failed to supply enough data on species' thermal tolerances by saying: 'There is little information in the record on the thermal tolerances of marine organisms exposed to the specific temperature fluctuation associated with the Seabrook operation. However, the scientific literature does contain many references to the thermal sensitivity of members of the local biota.' Whether or not these references do exist and whether or not they support the conclusions the panel goes on to draw does not concern us here. What is important is that the record did not support the conclusion until supplemented by the panel. The panel's work found its way directly into the Administrator's decision. . . . [T]hey supplied the information. They are free to do that as witnesses, but not as deciders.

"The appropriate remedy under these circumstances is to remand the decision to the Administrator because he based his decision on material not part of the record. . . . The Administrator will have the options of trying to reach a new decision not dependent on the panel's supplementation of the record; of holding a hearing at which all parties will have the opportunity to cross-examine the panel members and at which the panel will have an opportunity to amplify its position; or of taking any other action within his power and consistent with this opinion."

(4) ***Official Notice.*** An exception to requiring evidence in the record occurs when an agency legitimately takes official notice of facts not otherwise proven. The APA provides: "When an agency decision rests on official notice of a material fact not appearing in the evidence in the record, a party is entitled, on timely request, to an opportunity to show the contrary." § 556(e). But it says nothing more specific about when official notice is appropriate.

The rules governing official notice by a federal trial court, set out in Rule 201 of the Federal Rules of Evidence, are much more explicit—but inapplicable to agency proceedings. By their terms, the Federal Rules of Evidence apply to federal courts, bankruptcy judges, and magistrate judges—not agencies. Rule 101. Congress can, of course, stipulate differently—e.g., 29 U.S.C. § 160(b), requiring the NLRB to rely on the rules of courtroom procedure "so far as practicable"—or agencies can similarly bind themselves through their own rules of procedure. But agency rules often simply parrot or paraphrase the APA provision.

In CASTILLO-VILLAGRA V. IMMIGRATION AND NATURALIZATION SERVICE, 972 F.2d 1017 (9th Cir. 1992) (Kleinfeld, J.), Teresa de Jesus Castillo-Villagra and her two adult daughters entered the United States, conceded deportability, and sought asylum. They claimed to have been members of a political group that opposed the Sandinista regime in Nicaragua. The Immigration Judge denied asylum in an oral decision, finding that the mother was lying and that none of the three had a well-founded fear of persecution because of their political opinions. The Board of Immigration Appeals affirmed, taking administrative notice that an anti-Sandinista coalition now controlled the government and Violeta Chamorro had been elected president, so that the record did not support a finding that the petitioners would have a well-founded fear of persecution were they to return to Nicaragua.

Applying the law applicable to immigration matters, but speaking of administrative hearings in general, the Ninth Circuit vacated and remanded the BIA decision. The court said that notice in administrative proceedings should indeed be broader than the judicial "not subject to reasonable dispute" test, and instead endorsed what it called a "rule of convenience" based on what the trier of fact thinks he knows:

"While in proceedings in court notice is quite restricted for adjudicative facts, it is broader in administrative proceedings. A case before an administrative agency, unlike one before a court, 'is rarely an isolated phenomenon, but is rather merely one unit in a mass of related cases . . . [which] often involve fact questions which have frequently been explored by the same tribunal.' Walter Gellhorn, Official Notice in Administrative Adjudication, 20 Tex. L. Rev. 131, 136 (1941). The tribunal learns from its cases. Moreover, volume and repetition affect peoples' ability to pay attention. Because of the quantity of similar cases before an agency such as the INS, if notice is not taken more broadly in administrative hearings, litigants may have an uphill battle maintaining the attention of the administrative judges. Even if the law allows people to tell officials the exact same and obvious thing hundreds of times, the officials may find it very hard to listen attentively after the first dozen or two repetitions. Hearings may degenerate into an empty form if the adjudicators cannot focus attention upon what is noteworthy about the particular case. The broader notice available in administrative hearings may, if properly used, facilitate more genuine hearings, as opposed to 'hearings' in which the finder of fact hears, but cannot, because of the repetition, listen."

On this basis, said the court, the agency was justified in taking notice that Chamorro had won the election. But the agency was not justified in deciding that this proposition concluded the case. Whether notice can be taken, and whether rebuttal evidence must be allowed, are different questions:

"The agency should . . . have warned, prior to final decision, that it intended to take notice that the Sandinistas were out of power, and that any well-founded fear of persecution the applicants might have had before the election could no longer be well-founded, and then given the parties an opportunity to show cause why notice should not be taken of these propositions. Depending on the showing made, fairness might or might not have required that the parties be allowed to present evidence on these propositions. . . .

"In the case at bar, the applicants had a plausible claim that they might still have a well-founded fear of persecution despite the Chamorro election. The record they developed before the election allowed for the conclusion that Nicaragua had been dominated by the Sandinista party, and that Sandinista power flowed from the party, not just from the government. It may be that the party's permeation of society enables it to persecute opponents, even with the presidency and some departments of government in other hands. Perhaps the Nicaraguan government is not so strong and hierarchical as to render impotent any political movement which does not control the presidency. . . .

"The point is, the propositions that the Sandinistas retain sufficient power to persecute petitioners, and that the petitioners have a well-founded fear of such persecution should they return . . . were seriously debatable, despite the election. Petitioners were never allowed to be heard on these propositions. . . ."

Many other courts have reached comparable conclusions. E.g., Chhetry v. U.S. Dep't of Justice, 490 F.3d 196 (2d Cir. 2007).

OHIO BELL TELEPHONE CO. V. PUBLIC UTILITIES COMM'N OF OHIO, 301 U.S. 292 (1937), cited in Castillo-Villagra, is still, despite its age, probably the leading Supreme Court decision concerning official notice in on-the-record proceedings. The Ohio Public Utilities Commission had adjusted the value of a utility's property downward, for ratemaking purposes, to reflect the Great Depression, which had begun in the middle of a nearly decade-long ratemaking. The Commission had stated that it would fix the property value as of 1925 and received "thousands of printed pages" directed to the property's value at that time. The Commission subsequently took notice of price trends during the period 1926–1933, deriving its data from a variety of sources such as trade journals, tax lists, and findings by an Illinois district court regarding an affiliated company. The Court, in an opinion by Justice Cardozo, found no difficulty with the commission's taking notice of the depression as such, or of the general decline in market values as "one of its concomitants." But what the Commission had done denied the company the "fundamentals of a trial":

"Without warning or even the hint of warning that the case would be considered or determined upon any other basis than the evidence submitted, the Commission cut down the values for the years after the date certain upon the strength of information secretly collected and never yet disclosed. The company . . . asked disclosure of the documents indicative of price trends, and an opportunity to examine them, to analyze them, to explain and to rebut them. The response was a curt refusal. Upon the strength of these unknown documents refunds have been ordered for sums mounting into millions, the Commission reporting its conclusion, but not the underlying proofs. . . . This is not the fair hearing essential to due process. It is condemnation without trial.

"What was done by the Commission is subject, however, to an objection even deeper. There has been more than an expansion of the concept of notoriety beyond reasonable limits. . . . [A] deeper vice is . . . that even now we do not know the particular or evidential facts of which the Commission took judicial notice and on which it rested its conclusion. Not only are the facts unknown; there is no way to find them out. . . . The Commission, withholding from the record the evidential facts that it has gathered here and there, contents itself with saying that in gathering them it went to journals and tax lists, as if a judge were to tell us, 'I looked at the statistics in the Library of Congress, and they teach me thus and so.' This will never do if hearings and appeals are to be more than empty forms."

(5) ***Decision in a Hierarchical Organization.*** We have already seen (p. 522) that the APA, combined with constitutional requirements, puts the final decision of formal adjudications in the hands of politically appointed agency heads. Presumably this is in recognition of the fact that such decisions often present policy choices in addition to evidentiary determinations. But how does this jibe with the notion that these cases are supposed to be the outcome of a formal trial-type process? Many of the provisions of §§ 556 and 557 that specify who does what, when, in the flow of

the process can be seen as attempts to navigate this fraught ocean. Perhaps they can be best understood as responses to a set of four cases sometimes called MORGAN V. UNITED STATES and sometimes UNITED STATES V. MORGAN, all preceding (and helping to shape) the APA: 298 U.S. 468 (1936), 304 U.S. 1 (1938), 307 U.S. 183 (1939), and 313 U.S. 409 (1941). The underlying issue was the rates to be charged by businesses selling cattle at the Kansas City stockyards; the Packers and Stockyards Act gave the Secretary of Agriculture authority to set those rates "after full hearing," which the Supreme Court understood to mean after a formal adjudication. The evidence—the transcript contained about 10,000 pages of oral testimony and there were over 1,000 pages of statistical exhibits, too—had been taken before a hearing examiner. There was no intermediate report, oral argument was had before the Acting Secretary of Agriculture, a brief was filed on behalf of the businesses, and the Secretary of Agriculture then signed an order making findings of fact and conclusions of law and prescribing rates. The rates the Secretary ordered would have seriously hurt many of the businesses involved. Did this process give them the hearing Congress had mandated?

It would be fair to say that the Supreme Court was feeling its way in handling the issues involved—in deciding, that is, how the role of a large agency (the Department of Agriculture, among its other duties, administered 42 regulatory statutes at the time), the tradition of a fair hearing, and the principal of political responsibility ought to coalesce. Among the major points the Court made were these:

(a) The authority to set rates was not delegated to the Department to exercise in some impersonal way. The authority to decide could be, perhaps, sub-delegated from the Secretary to someone else. But whoever signed the order had to be personally involved—to a point. In the words of Chief Justice Hughes from the first Morgan case:

"[T]he weight ascribed by the law to the findings—their conclusiveness when made within the sphere of the authority conferred—rests upon the assumption that the officer who makes the findings has addressed himself to the evidence and upon that evidence has conscientiously reached the conclusions which he deems it to justify. That duty cannot be performed by one who has not considered evidence or argument. It is not an impersonal obligation. It is a duty akin to that of a judge. The one who decides must hear.

"This necessary rule does not preclude practicable administrative procedure in obtaining the aid of assistants in the department. Assistants may prosecute inquiries. Evidence may be taken by an examiner. Evidence thus taken may be sifted and analyzed by competent subordinates. Argument may be oral or written. The requirements are not technical. But there must be a hearing in a substantial sense. And to give the substance of a hearing, which is for the purpose of making determinations upon evidence, the officer who makes the determinations must consider and appraise the evidence which justifies them."

(b) The Department could not just inquire into what was going on in the Stockyards and then make its decision; it had to formulate its contentions so that the regulated parties on the other side of the statutorily required "full hearing" could meet the government's case. In the words of Justice Hughes, again, this time from the second case:

"The right to a hearing embraces not only the right to present evidence but also a reasonable opportunity to know the claims of the opposing party and to meet them. The right to submit argument implies that opportunity; otherwise the right may be but a barren one. Those who are brought into contest with the Government in a quasi-judicial proceeding aimed at the control of their activities are entitled to be fairly advised of what the Government proposes and to be heard upon its proposals before it issues its final command.

"No such reasonable opportunity was accorded appellants. The administrative proceeding was initiated by a notice of inquiry into the reasonableness of appellants' rates. No specific complaint was formulated. . . . In the absence of any report by the examiner or any findings proposed by the Government, and thus without any concrete statement of the Government's claims, the parties approached the oral argument. Nor did the oral argument reveal these claims in any appropriate manner. The discussion by counsel for the Government . . . dealt with generalities both as to principles and procedure.. . . The requirements of fairness are not exhausted in the taking or consideration of evidence but extend to the concluding parts of the procedure as well as to the beginning and intermediate steps."

(c) Assuming the agency did conduct a hearing that followed the formal requirements of a "full hearing," it was not the business of the courts (absent, we may suppose, an unusual showing of bias) to look into the mental processes of the decisionmaker. From the fourth Morgan case, this time in the words of Justice Frankfurter:

"Over the Government's objection the district court authorized the market agencies to take the deposition of the Secretary. The Secretary thereupon appeared in person at the trial. He was questioned at length regarding the process by which he reached the conclusions of his order. . . . [T]he short of the business is that the Secretary should never have been subjected to this examination. The proceeding before the Secretary 'has a quality resembling that of a judicial proceeding'. Such an examination of a judge would be destructive of judicial responsibility. We have explicitly held in this very litigation that 'it was not the function of the court to probe the mental processes of the Secretary'. Just as a judge cannot be subjected to such a scrutiny . . . so the integrity of the administrative process must be equally respected."

The APA, written a few years later, had to handle the issues the Morgan cases raised. Since those cases were based on statutory, not constitutional, authority (the Packers and Stockyards Act), Congress did not have to mimic the Court. But much of the detail of §§ 554, 556, and 557 can be seen as responsive to the same problem—how to handle the flow of a case in a way that respects the programmatic obligations of the agency, makes institutional sense, and also responds to the evidence in a fair way.

## NOTES ON THE IMPARTIALITY OF THE ALJ

(1) ***The Separation of Functions.*** APA § 554(d) goes further than prohibiting ex parte communications about facts in issue. It also provides that ALJs may not be supervised by agency personnel "engaged in the performance of investigative or prosecuting functions," and, the other way around, it states that "an employee . . . engaged in the performance of investigative or prosecuting functions . . . in a case may not, in that or a factually related case, participate or advise in the decision . . . except as witness or counsel in public proceedings." This "separation of functions" was one of the principal ways in which the drafters of the APA responded to the dangers of combining functions within an individual agency. As stated in Grolier, Inc. v. FTC, 615 F.2d 1215, 1219 (9th Cir. 1980), "[The provisions reflect a recommendation contained in the Report of the Attorney General's Committee on Administrative Procedure 50 (1941), S. Doc. No. 8, 77th Cong., 1st Sess. 50 (1941), which gave at least] two reasons . . . for this recommended separation: 'the investigators, if allowed to participate [in adjudication], would be likely to interpolate facts and information discovered by them ex parte and not adduced at the hearing, where the testimony is sworn and subject to cross-examination and rebuttal'; and '[a] man who has buried himself in one side of an issue is disabled from bringing to its decision that dispassionate judgment which Anglo-American tradition demands of officials who decide questions.' . . . We conclude that . . . Congress intended to preclude from decisionmaking in a particular case . . . all persons who had, in that or a factually related case, been involved with ex parte information, or who had developed, by prior involvement with the case, a 'will to win.' "

Is this separation of functions, or something like it, a mandate not only of the statute, but also of due process? In Williams v. Pennsylvania, 579 U.S. 1, 8 (2016), a district attorney who had authorized seeking the death penalty against a defendant almost thirty years earlier had become, by the time the same defendant's request for a new trial based on newly found evidence reached the state Supreme Court, Chief Justice of that court. The Supreme Court of the United States said he had to recuse himself: "under the Due Process Clause there is an impermissible risk of actual bias when a judge earlier had significant, personal involvement as a prosecutor in a critical decision regarding the defendant's case." The opinion emphasized the particular role a prosecutor plays, and clearly did not undermine (indeed, it affirmatively cited) the Withrow case (p. 519) and the general mixing of functions within an agency as a whole. So far, courts of appeal have tended to view it as based on extreme facts.

(2) ***The APA's Exceptions for Ratemaking and Initial Licensing.*** Section 554(d) does not, by its own terms, apply to proceedings regarding rates or initial licenses. Why not? DANIEL J. GIFFORD, THE MORGAN CASES: A RETROSPECTIVE VIEW, 30 Admin. L. Rev. 237, 241–243 (1978): "When the [Supreme Court in Morgan v. United States, 298 U.S. 468 (1936) and successor cases] seemingly equated a 'judicial model' of decisionmaking with

a 'full hearing' and perhaps with the fair procedure demanded by the due process clause, it made no distinction about the types of proceedings to which its strictures would apply. . . . [It] became apparent in the aftermath of the Morgan decisions that the pristine judicial model by which the Court seemed to be guided was inappropriate for ratemaking cases like the Morgan cases themselves, and perhaps was also inappropriate for other kinds of highly technical and complex cases. . . .

"These assessments profoundly affected the design of the [APA]. . . . These exemptions from [§ 554(d)] were justified on two grounds; first, that the hearing officer would be likely to need expert assistance in the decision of complex and technical issues and, second, that the isolation of the decision maker which a strict judicial decisionmaking model would impose would not be as necessary in non-accusatory proceedings where no stigma attached to an adverse determination."

(3) ***Bias in General.*** The most obvious reason for disqualifying a judge of any sort is that he or she has a pecuniary interest in the outcome. For the federal judiciary, disqualification rules are set out in some detail by 28 U.S.C. § 455. They state the matter much more broadly: they require, among other things, disqualification "in any proceeding in which [the judge's] impartiality might reasonably be questioned," § 455(a). Several circuit courts have stated that this appearance of impropriety standard is not applicable to ALJs. "[ALJs] are employed by the agency whose action they review. . . . If the 'appearance of impropriety' standard of 28 U.S.C. § 445(a) was applicable to [ALJs] they would be forced to recuse themselves in every case." Bunnell v. Barnhart, 336 F.3d 1112, 1114 (9th Cir. 2003); see also Greenberg v. Board of Governors of Fed. Reserve Sys., 968 F.2d 164, 166–67 (2d Cir. 1992). Yet it is not clear why this argument should lead to preclusion of *all* appearance of impropriety claims, as opposed to just those stemming from an ALJ's agency connections. Are there alternative reasons, such as the availability of judicial review, that justify limiting recusal of ALJs to instances of actual bias? Even as to that, the cases often seem restrained. E.g., Spicher v. Berryhill, 898 F.3d 754, 759 (7th Cir. 2018) ("There is no doubt that the ALJ displayed some hostility towards Spicher, but this treatment falls far short of the bar we require. . . .").

(On the separate question of what counts as impermissible prejudgment or bias in rulemaking, see p. 502.)

(4) ***The Tension Between Impartiality and Expertise.*** Although federal agencies cannot select ALJs based on their specialized expertise, "[o]nce they become ALJs, their expertise in the subject matter of the agency deepens because most of them adjudicate disputes involving only the agency for which they work, meaning they hear similar matters over and over again." Chris Guthrie, Jeffrey J. Rachlinski & Andrew J. Wistrich, The "Hidden Judiciary": An Empirical Examination of Executive Branch Justice, 58 Duke L.J. 1477, 1484–85 (2009). Indeed, this reality is sometimes given as one reason why official notice should be more broadly available in administrative hearings than in judicial ones. But is there a danger that expertise can undermine impartiality? In MILES V. CHATER, 84 F.3d 1397, 1401 (11th Cir. 1996), an ALJ had rejected the plaintiff's application for disability benefits,

discounting the testimony of the plaintiff's medical expert on the grounds that this particular expert "almost invariably" finds the claimant totally disabled. The Eleventh Circuit upheld the plaintiff's claim that the ALJ was biased and remanded for proceedings before another ALJ: "The ALJ plays a critical role in the disability review process. Not only is he duty-bound to develop a full and fair record, he must carefully weigh the evidence giving individualized consideration to each claim that comes before him. . . . The impartiality of the ALJ is . . . integral to the integrity of the system. . . . The ALJ's observations here [about the medical expert], without any evidence in support thereof, reflect that the process was compromised in this case."

(5) ***Too Much Independence?*** As the Supreme Court ruled in Lucia v. SEC, 138 S.Ct. 2044 (2018) (p. 957), ALJs are "inferior officers" under the Appointments Clause of the Constitution (Article II, § 2) and as such are ordinarily appointed by "Heads of Departments," which might be a Secretary of this or that, or might be one of the "independent agencies," the members of which are themselves dischargeable only for cause. As to then firing an ALJ, 5 U.S.C. § 7521(a), part of the original APA, provides: "An action may be taken against an administrative law judge . . . by the agency in which the administrative law judge is employed only for good cause established and determined by the Merit Systems Protection Board on the record after opportunity for hearing before the Board. 5 U.S.C. § 1202(d) in turn provides that MSPB members are appointed for seven-year terms and "may be removed by the President only for inefficiency, neglect of duty, or malfeasance in office." Litigants in recent years have claimed that this pattern for appointment and removal of ALJs violates the Constitution, or put more specifically, unduly interferes with the President's obligation to "take care that the laws be faithfully executed."

Recent Supreme Court precedents on matters of appointments and removals do not resolve this issue. (See Chapter VII, Section 3.b (p. 943) for a review of the cases.) In the Courts of Appeals, as of July 2022, there is conflicting authority:

(a) DECKER COAL CO. V. PEHRINGER, 8 F.4th 1123 (9th Cir. 2021), dealt with a coal miner's claim for benefits under the Black Lung Benefits Act. After a hearing on the merits, the Department of Labor ALJ awarded the benefits. The coal company appealed to the Department's Benefits Review Board, but the BRB affirmed the decision. Judicial review followed. The Ninth Circuit held that the "for cause" removal statute, as applied to DOL ALJs, did not unconstitutionally undercut the President's executive authority. The court emphasized that the ALJ was performing only an adjudicatory function; that his determinations were reviewable on both the law and the facts by the BRB; and that the members of the BRB served at the pleasure of the Secretary of Labor, who himself served at the pleasure of the President. (It also mentioned that use of ALJs in this setting was not required by the statutes, but was a choice made by the Department.) "Put simply, ALJs are judges who make decisions that are subject to vacatur by people without tenure protection. With this structure, the President continues to enjoy an ability to execute the laws—by holding his subordinates accountable for their conduct, especially because these ALJs exercise only adjudicative power in the first instance .... In sum, we think the BRB has ample control over DOL ALJs and the President, in turn, has direct control over BRB members through the Secretary of Labor."

(b) JARKESY V. SEC, 34 F.4th 446 (5th Cir. 2022), already discussed regarding other matters on p. 525 (and further discussed in Chapter VII at p. 1019 and p. 1090) concerned determinations of fraud made by an SEC ALJ after an evidentiary hearing and then upheld by the Commission. The court found the statutory removal restrictions for SEC ALJs to be unconstitutional. It emphasized the presence of three "for cause" restrictions in combination: the APA's protection of the ALJ; the statutory protection from dismissal of members of the Merit Systems Protection Board; and the protection of the Commission members themselves, dismissible by the President only "for cause" as part of an independent agency. It described the SEC ALJs as able to "exercise considerable power over administrative case records by controlling the presentation and admission of evidence; they may punish contemptuous conduct; and often their decisions are final and binding," and it concluded that "SEC ALJs are sufficiently insulated from removal that the President cannot take care that the laws are faithfully executed."

If one wanted, it is clear the cases could be distinguished in several different ways. At the same time, if one wanted a determination applicable to all ALJs, one of the cases would have to be overturned. As of this writing, all one can confidently say is: "stay tuned."

## PROFESSIONAL AIR TRAFFIC CONTROLLERS ORGANIZATION v. FEDERAL LABOR RELATIONS AUTHORITY

United States Court of Appeals for the District of Columbia Circuit (1982).
685 F.2d 547.

■ EDWARDS, CIRCUIT JUDGE.

[The Professional Air Traffic Controllers Organization called its members out on strike August 3, 1981, in violation of a statute forbidding federal employees to go out on strike. Among the several proceedings that resulted was an unfair labor practice hearing before the Federal Labor Relations Authority, threatening the revocation of PATCO's certification as the recognized union for the nation's air traffic controllers. That hearing was held before an FLRA ALJ on August 10–11, and a recommended decision was quickly announced stripping PATCO of its certification. The three members of the FLRA heard oral argument on review on September 16, and the ALJ's decision was affirmed October 22. Members Frazier and Applewhaite voted unconditionally to revoke PATCO's certification; Chairman Haughton would have permitted PATCO a brief period to end the strike before that revocation but joined the other two when that period elapsed without an appropriate PATCO response. The case was then brought to the D.C. Circuit for expedited judicial review.]

II. Ex Parte Communications During the FLRA Proceedings

Unfortunately, allegations of improprieties during the FLRA's consideration of this case forced us to delay our review on the merits. Only a day before oral argument, the Department of Justice, which represents the [Federal Aviation Administration] in this review, informed the court that the Department of Justice Criminal Division and the FBI had investigated allegations of an improper contact between a "well-known labor leader" and FLRA Member Applewhaite during the pendency of the PATCO case. . . . [W]e invoked a procedure that this court has occasionally employed in like situations in the past. Without assuming that anything improper had in fact occurred or had affected the FLRA Decision in this case, we ordered the FLRA "to hold, with the aid of a specially-appointed administrative law judge, an evidentiary hearing to determine the nature, extent, source and effect of any and all ex parte communications and other approaches that may have been made to any member or members of the FLRA while the PATCO case was pending before it."

Following our remand on the ex parte communications issue, John M. Vittone, an Administrative Law Judge with the Civil Aeronautics Board, was appointed to preside over an evidentiary proceeding. . . . ALJ Vittone's inquiry led to the disclosure of a number of communications with FLRA Members that were at least arguably related to the Authority's consideration of the PATCO case. We find the vast majority of these communications unobjectionable. Three occurrences, however, are somewhat more troubling and require our careful review and discussion. We first summarize ALJ Vittone's findings regarding them.

1. The Meeting Between Member Applewhaite and FLRA General Counsel Gordon

On August 10, 1981 (one week after the unfair labor practice complaint against PATCO was filed), H. Stephan Gordon, the FLRA General Counsel, was in Member Applewhaite's office discussing administrative matters unrelated to the PATCO case. During Gordon's discussion with Member Applewhaite, Ms. Ellen Stern, an attorney with the FLRA Solicitor's office, entered Member Applewhaite's office to deliver a copy of a memorandum . . . Ms. Stern had prepared at the request of Member Frazier.[23] With General Counsel Gordon present, Ms. Stern proceeded to discuss her memorandum, which dealt with whether the Civil Service Reform Act makes revocation of a striking union's exclusive recognition status mandatory or discretionary and, assuming it is discretionary, what other disciplinary actions might be taken.

During Ms. Stern's discussion, both Member Applewhaite and General Counsel Gordon asked her general questions (e.g., regarding the availability of other remedies and whether she had researched the relevant legislative history). . . . While the conversation at least

[23] The Solicitor is the general legal advisor of the FLRA, including the Members. The Solicitor also represents the FLRA on appeals from FLRA orders and in other legal proceedings. [Ed. The General Counsel, by contrast, represents FLRA staff in appearances before the FLRA.]

implicitly focused on the PATCO case, the facts of the case and the appropriate disposition were not discussed. The discussion ended after ten or fifteen minutes.

ALJ Vittone concluded that "[t]he conversation had no effect or impact on Member Applewhaite's ultimate decision in the PATCO case."

2. Secretary Lewis' Telephone Calls to Members Frazier and Applewhaite

During the morning of August 13, 1981, Secretary of Transportation Andrew L. Lewis, Jr. telephoned Member Frazier. Secretary Lewis stated that he was not calling about the substance of the PATCO case, but wanted Member Frazier to know that, contrary to some news reports, no meaningful efforts to settle the strike were underway. Secretary Lewis also stated that the Department of Transportation would appreciate expeditious handling of the case. Not wanting to discuss the PATCO case with Secretary Lewis, Member Frazier replied, "I understand your position perfectly, Mr. Secretary." . . .

Member Frazier also advised Member Applewhaite of Secretary Lewis' telephone call. In anticipation of a call, Member Applewhaite located the FLRA Rules regarding the time limits for processing an appeal from an ALJ decision in an unfair labor practice case. When Secretary Lewis telephoned and stated his concern that the case not be delayed, Member Applewhaite interrupted the Secretary to inform him that if he wished to obtain expedited handling of the case, he would have to comply with the FLRA Rules and file a written motion. Secretary Lewis stated that he was unaware that papers had to be filed and that he would contact his General Counsel immediately. The conversation ended without further discussion.

During the afternoon of August 13, the FAA filed a Motion to Modify Time Limits for Filing Exceptions, requesting that the time limit be reduced from the usual twenty-five days to seven days. On August 14, the FLRA General Counsel filed a similar motion. On August 17, PATCO filed an opposition to these motions and a motion to extend the time for filing exceptions to sixty days. On August 18, 1981, the FLRA Members considered the three pending motions, denied all three, and decided instead to reduce the usual twenty-five day period for filing exceptions to nineteen days.

Upon considering this evidence, Judge Vittone concluded that: (1) the FAA's filing of a motion to expedite may have been in response to Secretary Lewis' conversation with Member Applewhaite; (2) Chairman Haughton was unaware of Secretary Lewis' telephone calls when he considered the motions on August 18; (3) "Secretary Lewis' call had an undetermined effect on Member Applewhaite's and Member Frazier's decision to reduce the time period for filing exceptions"; and (4) the telephone calls "had no effect on Member Applewhaite's or Member Frazier's ultimate decision on the merits of the PATCO case."

3. Member Applewhaite's Dinner With Albert Shanker

Since 1974 Albert Shanker has been President of the American Federation of Teachers, a large public-sector labor union, and a member of the Executive Council of the AFL-CIO.[26] Since 1964 Mr. Shanker has been President of the AFT's New York City Local, the United Federation of Teachers. Before joining the FLRA, Member Applewhaite had been associated with the New York Public Employment Relations Board. Through their contacts in New York, Mr. Shanker and Member Applewhaite had become professional and social friends.

During the week of September 20, 1981, Mr. Shanker was in Washington, D.C. on business. On September 21, Mr. Shanker made arrangements to have dinner with Member Applewhaite that evening. Although he did not inform Member Applewhaite of his intentions when he made the arrangements, Mr. Shanker candidly admitted that he wanted to have dinner with Member Applewhaite because he felt strongly about the PATCO case and wanted to communicate directly to Member Applewhaite his sentiments, previously expressed in public statements, that PATCO should not be severely punished for its strike. . . . After accepting the invitation, Member Applewhaite informed Member Frazier and Chairman Haughton that he was having dinner with Mr. Shanker.

Member Applewhaite and Mr. Shanker talked for about an hour and a half during their dinner on September 21. Most of the discussion concerned the preceding Saturday's Solidarity Day Rally, an upcoming tuition tax credit referendum in the District of Columbia, and mutual friends from New York. Near the end of the dinner, however, the conversation turned to labor law matters relevant to the PATCO case. The two men discussed various approaches to public employee strikes in New York, Pennsylvania and the federal government. Mr. Shanker expressed his view that the punishment of a striking union should fit the crime and that revocation of certification as a punishment for an illegal strike was tantamount to "killing a union." The record is clear that Mr. Shanker made no threats or promises to Member Applewhaite; likewise, the evidence also indicates that Member Applewhaite never revealed his position regarding the PATCO case.

Near the end of their conversation, Member Applewhaite commented that because the PATCO case was hotly contested, he would be viewed with disfavor by whichever side he voted against. Member Applewhaite also observed that he was concerned about his prospects for reappointment to the FLRA in July 1982. Mr. Shanker, in turn, responded that Member Applewhaite had no commitments from anyone and urged him to vote without regard to personal considerations. The dinner concluded and the two men departed.

[26] The AFL-CIO presented oral argument to the FLRA in the PATCO case as amicus curiae. Mr. Shanker, however, was unaware of the amicus status of the AFL-CIO at all times relevant to our consideration.

*The FLRA Decisional Process.* On the afternoon of September 21, before the Applewhaite/Shanker dinner, the FLRA Members had had their first formal conference on the PATCO case, which had been argued to them five days earlier. Members Frazier and Applewhaite both favored revocation of PATCO's exclusive recognition status and took the position that PATCO would no longer be a labor organization within the meaning of the Civil Service Reform Act. Member Frazier favored an indefinite revocation; Member Applewhaite favored a revocation for a fixed period of one to three years. Chairman Haughton agreed that an illegal strike had occurred, but favored suspension, not revocation, of PATCO's collective bargaining status.

After September 21, Member Applewhaite considered other remedies, short of revocation, to deal with the PATCO strike. For over two weeks Member Applewhaite sought to find common ground with Chairman Haughton. Those efforts to agree on an alternative solution failed and, on October 9, Member Applewhaite finally decided to vote with Member Frazier for revocation. (Member Applewhaite apparently was concerned that the FLRA have a majority favoring one remedy, rather than render three opinions favoring three different dispositions.) . . . While these negotiations within the Authority were going on, Member Frazier became concerned that Mr. Shanker might have influenced Member Applewhaite's position in the case. On September 22, Member Frazier visited Member Applewhaite to inquire about his dinner with Mr. Shanker. Member Frazier understood Member Applewhaite to say that Shanker had said that if Member Applewhaite voted against PATCO, then Applewhaite would be unable to get work as an arbitrator when he left the FLRA. Member Frazier also understood Member Applewhaite to say that he was then leaning against voting for revocation. (ALJ Vittone found that Shanker had made no such threats during the dinner, and concluded that Member Frazier reached this conclusion based on some miscommunication or misunderstanding.)

On September 22 and again on September 28, Member Frazier advised Member Applewhaite to talk to Solicitor Freehling about his dinner with Mr. Shanker. . . . Member Frazier later asked Solicitor Freehling if Member Applewhaite had discussed his dinner with Mr. Shanker. Solicitor Freehling told Member Frazier that they had talked and that Member Applewhaite had concluded that there were no problems involved. Despite these assurances, Member Frazier contacted his personal attorney. Sometime in early October, Member Frazier's attorney contacted the FBI. The FBI interviewed Member Frazier on October 17 and then other FLRA Members and staff. FBI agents interviewed Member Applewhaite on October 22, the day the FLRA Decision issued. (Member Applewhaite was thus unaware of the FBI investigation until after he reached his final decision in the PATCO case.) . . .

C. Applicable Legal Standards

1. The Statutory Prohibition of Ex Parte Contacts and the FLRA Rules

The Civil Service Reform Act requires that FLRA unfair labor practice hearings, to the extent practicable, be conducted in accordance with the provisions of the Administrative Procedure Act. 5 U.S.C. § 7118(a)(6). Since FLRA unfair labor practice hearings are formal adjudications within the meaning of the APA, section 557(d) governs ex parte communications. Id. § 557(d). . . .

Three features of the prohibition on ex parte communications in agency adjudications are particularly relevant to the contacts here at issue. First, by its terms, section 557(d) applies only to ex parte communications to or from an "interested person." . . . Second, the Government in the Sunshine Act defines an "ex parte communication" as "an oral or written communication not on the public record to which reasonable prior notice to all parties is not given, but . . . not includ[ing] requests for status reports on any matter or proceeding. . . ." 5 U.S.C. § 551(14) (1976). Requests for status reports are thus allowed under the statute, even when directed to an agency decisionmaker rather than to another agency employee. . . . Third, and in direct contrast to status reports, section 557(d) explicitly prohibits communications "relevant to the merits of the proceeding." The congressional reports state that the phrase should "be construed broadly and . . . include more than the phrase 'fact in issue' currently used in [section 554(d)(1) of] the Administrative Procedure Act." . . .

The disclosure of ex parte communications serves two distinct interests. Disclosure is important in its own right to prevent the appearance of impropriety from secret communications in a proceeding that is required to be decided on the record. Disclosure is also important as an instrument of fair decisionmaking; only if a party knows the arguments presented to a decisionmaker can the party respond effectively and ensure that its position is fairly considered. When these interests of openness and opportunity for response are threatened by an ex parte communication, the communication must be disclosed. . . .

2. Remedies for Ex Parte Communications

Section 557(d) contains two possible administrative remedies for improper ex parte communications. The first is disclosure of the communication and its content. The second requires the violating party to "show cause why his claim or interest in the proceeding should not be dismissed, denied, disregarded, or otherwise adversely affected on account of [the] violation." . . . Under the case law in this Circuit, improper ex parte communications, even when undisclosed during agency proceedings, do not necessarily void an agency decision. . . . [A] court must consider whether, as a result of improper ex parte communications, the agency's decisionmaking process was irrevocably tainted so as to make the ultimate judgment of the agency unfair, either to an innocent party or to the public interest that the agency was obliged to protect.[32] In making this determination, a number of considerations may be relevant: the gravity of the ex parte communications;[33] whether the contacts may have influenced the agency's ultimate decision; whether the party making the improper contacts benefited from the agency's ultimate decision; whether the contents of the communications were unknown to opposing parties, who therefore had no opportunity to respond; and whether vacation of the agency's decision and remand for new proceedings would serve a useful purpose. . . . [A]ny such decision must of necessity be an exercise of equitable discretion.

D. Analysis of the Alleged Ex Parte Communications With FLRA Members

1. The Meeting Between Member Applewhaite and FLRA General Counsel Gordon

When General Counsel Gordon met with Member Applewhaite on August 10, the General Counsel's office was prosecuting the unfair labor practice complaint against PATCO before Chief ALJ Fenton. General Counsel Gordon was therefore a "person outside the agency" within the meaning of section 557(d) and the FLRA Rules. 5 C.F.R. § 2414.3(a) (1981). Still, the undisputed purpose of the meeting was to discuss budgetary and administrative matters. It was therefore entirely appropriate. The shared concerns of the Authority are not put on hold whenever the General Counsel prosecutes an unfair labor practice complaint.

The discussion relevant to the PATCO case arose only when Ms. Stern delivered a copy of her memorandum regarding decertification of striking unions to Member Applewhaite. . . . Some occasional and inadvertent contacts between the prosecuting and adjudicating arms of a small agency like the FLRA may be inevitable. . . . In hindsight, it may have been preferable if Member Applewhaite had postponed even this general conversation with Ms. Stern or if General Counsel Gordon had temporarily excused himself from Member Applewhaite's office. Nonetheless, we do not believe that this contact tainted the proceeding or unfairly advantaged the General Counsel in the prosecution of the case. Thus, we conclude that the conversation at issue here, even though possibly indiscreet and undesirable, does not void the FLRA Decision in this case.

---

[32] We have also considered the effect of ex parte communications on the availability of meaningful judicial review. . . . If the off-the-record communications regard critical facts, the court will be particularly ill-equipped to resolve in the first instance any controversy between the parties. . . .

[33] If the ex parte contacts are of such severity that an agency decision-maker should have disqualified himself, vacation of the agency decision and remand to an impartial tribunal is mandatory. Cf. Cinderella Career & Finishing Schools v. FTC, 425 F.2d 583, 591–92 (D.C. Cir. 1970) (failure of single member of agency to disqualify himself for bias requires vacation of agency decision).

2. Secretary Lewis' Telephone Calls to Members Frazier and Applewhaite

Transportation Secretary Lewis was undoubtedly an "interested person" within the meaning of section 557(d) and the FLRA Rules when he called Members Frazier and Applewhaite on August 13. Secretary Lewis' call clearly would have been an improper ex parte communication if he had sought to discuss the merits of the PATCO case. . . . Although Secretary Lewis did not in fact discuss the merits of the case, even a procedural inquiry may be a subtle effort to influence an agency decision. . . . We need not decide, however, whether Secretary Lewis' contacts were in fact improper. . . . Member Applewhaite explicitly told Secretary Lewis that if he wanted the case handled more quickly than the normal course of FLRA business, then the FAA would have to file a written request. If . . . Member Applewhaite's comments led to the FAA's Motion to Modify Time Limits, *that was exactly the desired result*. . . . In these circumstances, and given ALJ Vittone's inability to find any effect of the calls on the Members' decision, we cannot find that the disposition of the motions was improperly influenced. . . .

3. Member Applewhaite's Dinner With Albert Shanker

. . . At the outset, we are faced with the question whether Mr. Shanker was an "interested person" to the proceeding under section 557(d) and the FLRA Rules. . . . The House and Senate Reports agreed that the term covers "any individual or other person with an interest in the agency proceeding that is greater than the general interest the public as a whole may have." . . . Mr. Shanker was (and is) the President of a major public-sector labor union. As such, he has a special and well-known interest in the union movement and the developing law of labor relations in the public sector. . . . From August 3, 1981 to September 21, 1981, Mr. Shanker and his union made a series of widely publicized statements in support of PATCO. . . . Thus, Mr. Shanker's actions, as well as his union office, belie his implicit claim that he had no greater interest in the case than a member of the general public. . . .

Even if we were to adopt Mr. Shanker's position that he was not an interested person, we are astonished at his claim that he did nothing wrong.[47] Mr. Shanker frankly concedes that he "desired to have dinner with Member Applewhaite because he felt strongly about the PATCO case and he wished to communicate directly to Member Applewhaite sentiments he had previously expressed in public." . . . *It is simply unacceptable behavior for any person directly to attempt to influence the decision of a judicial officer in a pending case outside of the formal, public proceedings.* This is true for the general public, for "interested persons,"

[47] Mr. Shanker suggests that "[s]ince there is no sanction available against amici, it is reasonable to assume that the ex parte rules are not intended to apply in these circumstances." This argument is simply a non sequitur. The principal purpose of the ex parte rules is not to punish violators, but to preserve the integrity of the administrative process. Even when a nonparty is the source of an ex parte communication, a proceeding may be voided if the decision is irrevocably tainted. . . .

and for the formal parties to the case. This rule applies to administrative adjudications as well as to cases in Article III courts. . . .

We do not hold, however, that Member Applewhaite committed an impropriety when he accepted Mr. Shanker's dinner invitation. Member Applewhaite and Mr. Shanker were professional and social friends. We recognize, of course, that a judge "must have neighbors, friends and acquaintances, business and social relations, and be a part of his day and generation." . . . Member Applewhaite was unaware of Mr. Shanker's purpose in arranging the dinner. He therefore had no reason to reject the invitation.

The majority of the dinner conversation was unrelated to the PATCO case. Only in the last fifteen minutes of the dinner did the discussion become relevant to the PATCO dispute . . . At this point, . . . Member Applewhaite should have promptly terminated the discussion. . . . We now know that Mr. Shanker did *not* in any way threaten Member Applewhaite during their dinner. Mr. Shanker did *not* tell Member Applewhaite that if he voted to decertify PATCO he would be unable to get cases as an arbitrator if and when he left the FLRA. Mr. Shanker did *not* say that he was speaking "for top AFLCIO officials" or that Member Applewhaite would need labor support to secure reappointment. Moreover, Mr. Shanker did *not* make any promises of any kind to Member Applewhaite, and Member Applewhaite did *not* reveal how he intended to vote in the PATCO case.

In these circumstances, we do not believe that it is necessary to vacate the FLRA Decision and remand the case. . . . Though plainly inappropriate, the ex parte communication was limited to a ten or fifteen minute discussion, often couched in general terms, of the appropriate discipline for a striking public employee union. This behavior falls short of the "corrupt tampering with the adjudicatory process" found by this court in WKAT, Inc. v. FCC, 296 F.2d 375, 383 (D.C. Cir.), cert. denied, 368 U.S. 841 (1961). . . . [T]he Applewhaite/Shanker dinner had no effect on the ultimate decision of Member Applewhaite or of the FLRA as a whole in the PATCO case. . . . No party benefited from the improper contact. . . . Finally, we cannot say that the parties were unfairly deprived of an opportunity to refute the arguments propounded in the ex parte communication. . . .

E. Member Applewhaite's Alleged "Personal Interest" in the PATCO Case . . .

Based essentially on [member Applewhaite's brief conversation with Mr. Shanker about his reappointment prospects,] Member Frazier now proposes that Member Applewhaite had a personal interest in the outcome of the PATCO case . . . [and] argues that Member Applewhaite was disqualified from hearing the PATCO case.

We do not read as much into this conversation as does Member Frazier. It is not surprising that an agency member appointed by the President might be concerned about his prospects for reappointment. . . . The appropriate question here is not whether Member Applewhaite recognized that his decision might not be universally approved; rather, the correct inquiry is whether Member Applewhaite's concerns rendered him incapable of reaching a fair decision on the merits of the case before him.

The ... conversation between Member Applewhaite and Mr. Shanker does not demonstrate an inability to fairly decide the case. Courts have long recognized "a presumption of honesty and integrity in those serving as adjudicators." Absent a strong showing to the contrary, an agency adjudicator is presumed to act in good faith and to be capable of ignoring considerations not on the record. . . . Member Applewhaite explained that this was no different from any arbitration case in which he had ruled—one party wins and the other loses. He testified: "I have always faced that problem[,] so I just have to call it like it is and . . . take my chances." Tr. 744. We have no reason to doubt this testimony. A remand on the basis of personal interest is therefore unnecessary.

[On the merits, the court upheld the FLRA order.]

■ ROBINSON, CHIEF JUDGE, concurring in part, and concurring in the judgment. . . .

From the special hearing emerges an appalling chronicle of attorneys, high government officials, and interested outsiders apparently without compunction about intervening in the course of FLRA's decisionmaking by means of private communications with those charged with resolving the case on the merits. We have an even more distressing picture of agency decisionmakers—whose role in this formal adjudication concededly approximated that of judges—seemingly ignorant of the substance of the ex parte rules, insensitive to the compromising potentialities of certain official and social contacts, and unwilling to silence peremptorily and firmly improper discussions that did transpire. . . . [T]he court's opinion administers a mild chiding where a ringing condemnation is in order.

I. The Applewhaite-Gordon Incident

. . . [A]gencies such as FLRA fulfill, often simultaneously, the several roles of investigator, prosecutor, adjudicator, and policy formulator. Undoubtedly, this commingling of functions makes it more difficult to maintain a strict separation between those personnel who, on any given case, are cast in the role of advocate from those who occupy the position of judge in the matter. Once the agency is engaged in formal adjudication, however, such a separation is mandated by the APA, and is essential to the integrity of the administrative process. The perils of laxness on this point are well illustrated by the Applewhaite—Gordon incident. . . . The conversation was not merely indiscreet or undesirable; it was, purely and simply, a prohibited ex parte contact that should never have occurred. Gordon had no business remaining in the room once he realized that PATCO was the object of discussion. Applewhaite had no business permitting him to remain, and certainly was grossly at fault in soliciting Gordon's opinion. . . .

II. Secretary Lewis' Calls to Members Frazier and Applewhaite

. . . Secretary Lewis' calls were highly unusual. Both [Frazier and Applewhaite] stated that they had never before been contacted by a Cabinet member on a pending case. Applewhaite also explained that persons seeking status information normally contact the staff in lieu of discussing such matters directly with the members. . . .

Agencies, like courts, promulgate rules of practice to assist outsiders in communicating in proper fashion with decisionmakers. These channels are quite adequate to accommodate any information that legitimately could be sought from or provided to those who will judge the case. For a high government officer to bypass established procedures and approach, directly and privately, members of an independent decisionmaking body about a case in which he has an official interest and on which they will be called to rule suggests, at the minimum, a deplorable indifference toward safeguarding the purity of the formal adjudicatory process. Regardless of the officer's actual intent, such a call could be felt by the recipient as political pressure; regardless of its actual effect, such a call could be perceived by the public as political pressure. . . .

IV. The Applewhaite-Shanker Dinner

. . . Can the public really be expected to believe in the fairness and neutrality of the agency's formal adjudicatory processes when one of its decisionmakers permits an outspoken, highly visible official of a participating union to wine and dine him during deliberations on the case? . . . [T]hose who take on this judicial role may no longer participate in the daily intercourse of life as freely as do others. They have a duty to the judicial system in which they have accepted membership fastidiously to safeguard their integrity—at the expense, if need be, of "neighbors, friends and acquaintances, business and social relations." This *is* their "part" in their "day and generation," and one who is unwilling to make the sacrifice is unsuited to the office. . . .

■ MACKINNON, CIRCUIT JUDGE, concurring. . . .

The number of ex parte contacts that were disclosed at the remand hearing is appalling, as are the statements by counsel that such contacts were nothing more than what is normal and usual in administrative agencies and even in courts of law. . . . In this connection 18 U.S.C. § 1505 should be noted. This section of the Criminal Code provides that it is an offense if one "corruptly . . . *endeavors to influence,* obstruct or impede the due and proper administration of the law under which [a] proceeding is being had before [an] . . . agency of the United States . . ." (emphasis added). Private contacts with agency officials, with respect to pending adjudicatory matters, by interested parties or their agents, that endeavor to affect the decisional process, however subtle such contacts may be, are *corrupt* endeavors to influence the "due and proper administration of the law" and those who so attempt may be indicted. The authorized punishment is imprisonment for not more than five years, or a $5,000 fine, or both. 18 U.S.C. § 1505.

## NOTES

(1) ***PATCO's Many Dimensions.*** Casebook editors sometimes suspect that opinions they encounter were written with the classroom in mind, particularly when those opinions have been authored by former academic colleagues like Judge Edwards.[2] PATCO is remarkable for capturing so many related questions in one place. Here, those questions concern the relationship of agency heads to the people around them—staff, other government officials, and private citizens who may be both personal friends and "interested persons." It catches, too, the influence of accidental interactions among agency staff, high profile events, internal politics (consider Member Frazier's decision to turn Member Applewhaite over to the FBI), and "the rotating door" through which agency leaders move in and out of government. It does so in the context of an unusual government agency: the FLRA, like the NLRB, is an almost wholly adjudicatory body and one that *always* has a government agency on one side of the issues before it, with government employees on the other.

(As an example of the business of the FLRA—although unconnected with an ex parte problem—consider a 2020 decision: U.S. Department of Justice, Executive Office for Immigration Review (Agency) and National Association of Immigration Judges, International Federation of Professional and Technical Engineers, Judicial Council 2 (Union), 71 FLRA No. 207. The issue was whether Immigration Judges were or were not "management"; if they were not management, as had been determined by the FLRA 20 years earlier, they could be in a union. But, based in part on asserted changes in the role IJs now played, the FLRA in 2020 decided, 2–1, that they were management, and therefore were to be excluded from the union. This was so, even though, as the dissent emphasized, the decisions IJs made had to follow the precedents set by, and were subject to review by, the Board of Immigration Appeals.)

(2) Most government agencies are not so wholly committed to adjudication, and even in adjudication will generally be dealing only with their own staff, not other government agencies, as a party. For them, even more than for the FLRA, the PATCO issues are real ones. These issues cross the lives of agency officials daily and lurk behind every "chance" conversation. They are addressed by §§ 554(d) and 557(d) of the APA, as well as independent conflict of interest legislation and agency regulations. The pages below explore the three conversations that sparked this controversy: one within the agency, one with another government official, and the third with an interested "friend."

---

[2] Before his appointment to the bench, Judge Edwards was a professor at the University of Michigan Law School, specializing in Labor Law.

## NOTES ON INTERESTED AGENCY STAFF AND SEPARATION OF FUNCTIONS AT THE AGENCY LEVEL

(1) ***The Governing APA Requirements.*** General Counsel Gordon's participation in the conversation between Attorney Stern and Member Applewhaite suggests the difficulties that can arise, perhaps especially in a small agency, from the limited pool of expertise available, the variety of tasks agency staff are asked to perform, and the frequent informality with which work within an agency is done. As seems likely to be often the case, the conversation among these three appears entirely unplanned. In an enforcement proceeding like PATCO, agency participants would and should have little doubt that separation of functions constraints have to be observed. The FLRA's own rules, as the court remarked, treated the General Counsel's office as if it were outside the agency for purposes of these proceedings, thus bringing § 557(d) into play. Even if the agency's regulations had not extended § 557(d) in this fashion, § 554(d) would have been understood to apply. Although § 554(d)(C) appears to exclude "the agency or a member or members of the body comprising the agency" from the ex parte ban, that exclusion serves only to permit those members themselves to serve multiple functions—not to authorize prosecuting counsel to have private conversations with them. Attorney General's Manual on the Administrative Procedure Act 58 (1947).

All § 554(d) excludes for agency prosecutors, however, are off-the-record consultations about a "fact in issue" and participation or advice about "the decision, recommended decision, or agency review" in a particular case "or a factually related case." Reading this language to reach general policy conversations in which the whole agency may be engaged—if those conversations might also bear on particular matters in litigation—would introduce layers of formality into the day-to-day functioning of the agency, an arguably unwarranted cost. In traditional regulatory agencies, many cases are pending at any given time, raising issues that implicate the full range of their responsibilities.

If we think that § 554(d) precludes conversations dominated by a pending case but not those focused on a general policy question, how should we understand the Gordon/Stern/Applewhaite conversation? Does the broader preclusion of § 557(d), applying to communications "relevant to the merits of the proceeding," further complicate matters, if the agency has defined General Counsel Gordon as being "outside the agency" for these purposes?

(2) ***Are Sharp Lines of Division Required for Fairness?*** Even if not required by the APA or due process, is it unfair to allow staff who participate in the initial stages of a proceeding to advise agency officials who ultimately decide the case for the agency? Does the answer to that question turn at all on the resources available to the agency and the practical exigencies it may face in needing to render an informed decision? Does it depend on whether the issues involved are more matters of adjudicative or of "general" fact, or on the extent of the staff's participation and advocacy for a particular position?

A strong argument against extending separation-of-functions requirements is offered by WILLIAM F. PEDERSEN, JR., THE DECLINE OF SEPARATION OF FUNCTIONS IN REGULATORY AGENCIES, 64 Va. L. Rev. 991 (1978): "Admittedly, a separation-of-functions rule has its place in an 'accusatory' proceeding, in which one group of agency employees prosecutes a private party for a violation of the law and another group must sit in judgment. Most significant decisions by government agencies, however, simply do not fit this model. Instead, they involve the formulation or the application of policy, without any connotation of wrongdoing, regarding persons who are being regulated. Agencies and their staffs exist to make policy decisions, and there is no reason to suspect that staff members who work on the early stages of a non-accusatory proceeding view the choices confronting them in a manner any less valid than do those who handle succeeding stages. . . .

"Five independent characteristics of formal adjudication may contribute to a fair disposition of a particular case: (1) a decision based on a publicly defined and publicly accessible record, (2) a mechanism for confrontation between opposing points of view, (3) a mechanism for probing and, where possible, resolving differences on factual and other matters, (4) separation-of-functions requirements, and (5) an independent, judge-like hearing officer. The framers of the APA concluded that all five of these elements must be present in accusatory cases but only the first three in policy decisions. They undermined their own work, however, by requiring the factual probing to take the form of a trial-type hearing even in policy-dominated cases.

"Whether a decision requires separation of functions depends not only upon its basic nature but also upon the procedures used to make it. Trial-type hearings cast the agency's trial staff in an adversarial role, which almost inevitably calls forth a partisan attitude, but the APA also expressly sanctions informal reliance on the advice of these same staff members in reaching a final decision. Naturally enough, private lawyers who have confronted this staff in the hearing object fiercely to its taking any part in the subsequent deliberations within the agency. Accordingly, in the years since passage of the APA, agencies gradually have adopted rules to bar those who take part in the hearing from playing any role in the preparation of the resulting decision, even when the APA would permit their involvement. . . .

"Clothing non-accusatory administrative hearings with more of the trappings of adjudicatory proceedings may make better theater, but it probably reduces their substantive importance. Agency trial staffs, because of the separation-of-functions rules, and hearing examiners, because of their misconceptions of their proper role, do not participate in the informal discussions that often generate the agency's governing policies. Unawareness of these policies or simple separation from their development may prevent the outcome of the initial hearing from reflecting what the agency as an institution would consider to be the proper result." Pedersen thus concluded that separation-of-functions requirements "can hinder efficient agency operation and lower the quality of final administrative decisions."

## NOTES ON PRESSURE FROM OTHER PARTS OF GOVERNMENT

(1) Lewis's telephone calls in PATCO point to another common characteristic of agency life: agencies frequently act in the unruly world of politics, subject to a range of official and unofficial controls courts simply do not encounter. To what extent should courts seek to control these external influences on agency decisionmaking in on-the-record proceedings?

(2) ***Congressional Influence on Agency Adjudication.*** A congressional oversight committee is responsible under the Legislative Reorganization Act of 1970, § 118, 84 Stat. 1156, to "review and study, on a continuing basis, the application, administration, and execution of those laws, or parts of laws, the subject matter of which is within the jurisdiction of that committee." Suppose that an agency's decisions suggest to its oversight committee that the agency is straying from the correct policy path. May oversight hearings be convened while aspects of the policy issues remain unresolved before the agency? Should legislators be able to express their views on highly important policy questions that might be pending in a proceeding before the agency? Or should they scrupulously abstain from indicating their positions until the administrators have finally announced their own conclusion?[3] A major change in contemporary mores would be effected if members of Congress were to be rigorously precluded from asking questions about or making remarks concerning current administrative cases. But where should the line be drawn between legislative vigilance and legislative intermeddling?

The leading case on this question is PILLSBURY CO. V. FTC, 354 F.2d 952 (5th Cir. 1966). There, the FTC had filed a complaint against Pillsbury challenging its acquisition of competing flour millers as being anticompetitive; the case put in issue the application of § 7 of the Clayton Act. The FTC's trial examiner dismissed the complaint, but the Commission itself reinstated it. Then, while the reinstated proceedings were pending before the agency, the Senate Judiciary Committee summoned the FTC Chairman and members of his staff to appear. The Senators were volubly dissatisfied with the agency's interpretation of § 7, as reflected in the theory of the reinstated complaint, which they considered too weak. The case, or the Pillsbury name, was referred to more than 100 times in the series of congressional hearings. When the FTC ultimately ordered Pillsbury to divest itself of the acquired companies, Pillsbury sought review, alleging a lack of due process. The alleged interference, as the reviewing court later remarked, was not an impropriety concealed from public view, but consisted, rather, of "questions and statements made by members of two Senate and House subcommittees having responsibility for legislation dealing with antitrust matters all clearly spread upon the record."

". . . We conclude that the proceedings just outlined constituted an improper intrusion into the adjudicatory processes of the Commission and

[3] Note that 18 U.S.C. § 203(a) prohibits direct or indirect compensation to a Member of Congress for "any representational services" in any proceeding in which the United States is a party or has a "substantial interest" before any department or agency. Other statutes explicitly prohibit members of Congress from practicing before named tribunals.

were of such a damaging character as to have required at least some of the members . . . to disqualify themselves. . . .

"At times . . . statements of official position are elicited in Congressional hearings. In this context, the agencies are sometimes called to task for failing to adhere to the 'intent of Congress' in supplying meaning to the often broad statutory standards from which the agencies derive their authority, e.g., 'substantially to lessen competition' or 'to tend to create a monopoly.' . . . Although such investigatory methods raise serious policy questions as to the de facto 'independence' of the federal regulatory agencies, it seems doubtful that they raise any constitutional issues. However, when such an investigation focuses directly and substantially upon the mental decisional processes of a Commission in a case which is pending before it, Congress is no longer intervening in the agency's legislative function, but rather, in its *judicial* function. . . .

"To subject an administrator to a searching examination as to how and why he reached his decision in a case still pending before him, and to criticize him for reaching the 'wrong' decision, as the Senate subcommittee did in this case, sacrifices the appearance of impartiality—the sine qua non of American judicial justice—in favor of some short-run notions regarding the Congressional intent underlying an amendment to a statute, unfettered administration of which was committed by Congress to the Federal Trade Commission (see 15 U.S.C. § 21).

"It may be argued that such officials as members of the Federal Trade Commission are sufficiently aware of the realities of governmental, not to say 'political,' life as to be able to withstand such questioning as we have outlined here. However, this court is not so 'sophisticated' that it can shrug off such a procedural due process claim merely because the officials involved should be able to discount what is said and to disregard the force of the intrusion into the adjudicatory process. We conclude that we can preserve the rights of the litigants in a case such as this without having any adverse effect upon the legitimate exercise of the investigative power of Congress. What we do is to preserve the integrity of the judicial aspect of the administrative process."

If the General Counsel of the FTC had foreseen what the hearing before the Senate committee would entail, would it have been appropriate for him to call committee counsel, to suggest that questioning be limited to the FTC's interpretation of § 7, and to suggest that the Pillsbury case not be mentioned by name? If the committee observed that constraint but was just as forceful in conveying its sense of how § 7 ought to be interpreted, would that have avoided any § 557(d) problem? Would it make any real difference to the agency's perception of the political forces bearing on it? To the public's or Pillsbury's perception of the fairness of the hearing in which it was engaged? See Ronald M. Levin, Congressional Ethics and Constituent Advocacy in an Age of Mistrust, 95 Mich. L. Rev. 1, 39 (1996).

It is a fact of life for agency officials that they must appear before congressional committees (as well as speak at lunches and other events), all of which can give rise to claims of bias. Cases like Pillsbury don't arise very often, despite these appearances, perhaps because over time agency officials have learned how to speak and have educated members of Congress and their staff about how to engage in these conversations.

(3) ***Presidential Influence on Administrative Adjudication.*** Are efforts by the President to influence agency adjudication to be treated the same as congressional interventions? Does it matter if the adjudication involves a determination turning on more "general" fact and carrying broad policy implications? If the President "interferes" through making a public address stating her opinion, or instead tries to send her message out of sight? And to what extent can Congress constitutionally insulate administrative adjudication from presidential oversight or presidential control?

Perhaps because Presidents have left individual adjudications alone, or perhaps because the relevant facts remain in the dark, there are few cases turning on questions of direct interference. The leading case is PORTLAND AUDUBON SOCIETY V. THE ENDANGERED SPECIES COMMITTEE, 984 F.2d 1534 (9th Cir. 1993) (p. 1046). Under the Endangered Species Act, only the Endangered Species Committee, composed of high-level officials (cabinet members, agency administrators, and the like) can grant exemptions from the ESA's requirements, and they are to act based on a record compiled in an on-the-record hearing before an ALJ, a report by the Secretary of the Interior, and any other hearings or written submissions called for by the Committee. The Committee in this case authorized exemptions allowing timber sales affecting the habitat of the northern spotted owl, and Portland Audubon sued, noting that news stories had reported White House pressure to approve the sales and seeking discovery into alleged White House contacts that might have changed Committee members' votes. The Ninth Circuit held that § 557(d)'s ban on ex parte communications applied to Committee proceedings and that the President and his aides were appropriately considered "outside the agency" for purposes of § 557(d). As a result, it remanded to the Committee to hold a hearing on whether there were such contacts and their effects on the Committee's decision.

The court also ruled that including presidential communications within the ban on ex parte contacts would not violate separation of powers by interfering with the President's ability to supervise executive branch officials, concluding that "the general principle the President may not interfere with quasi-adjudicatory agency actions is well-settled." That may be the right principle, but it is hard, today, to consider it well-settled. On the one hand, the Supreme Court has emphasized the need for important, final agency actions to be connected with political authority through the elected President. On the other hand, the Supreme Court continues to affirm that Congress can create commissions whose members cannot be fired at the President's will, justified in part by the adjudicative work they do. Years ago, in Myers v. United States, 272 U.S. 52 (1926) (p. 982), Chief Justice (and former President) Taft drew the balance in this fashion: "[T]here may be duties of a quasi judicial character imposed on executive officers and members of executive tribunals whose decisions after hearing affect interests of individuals, the discharge of which the President cannot in a particular case properly influence or control. But even in such a case he may consider the decision after its rendition as a reason for removing the officer, on the ground that the discretion regularly entrusted to that officer by statute has not been on the whole intelligently or wisely exercised."

Exactly where either part of this rule stands today remains uncertain. The constitutional law implications of these cases are discussed in Chapter VII (p. 1046).

## NOTES ON RELATIONS WITH REGULATED PARTIES AND THE PUBLIC

The final element in PATCO concerned Member Applewhaite's dinner with Albert Shanker, an old friend and also—as head of a major union of public employees—a person with obvious and strong interests in the outcome of the PATCO matter. That they discussed the pending case and, in close proximity, Applewhaite's employment concerns, understandably troubled the reviewing judges. Here, the more political aspects and temporary character of an agency head's work bring the contrasts with a judicial model, and concomitant concerns about fairness, into the sharpest relief.

Agency officials cannot stay as aloof from the worlds of politics and constituencies as can judges. For agencies, continuing contact with a regulated industry, the public, and the media can have central importance for effective regulation. Informal contacts, media interviews, websites, convention addresses, and the like may help the agency win needed support, reduce future enforcement requirements (by helping industry anticipate and plan for compliance), float a trial balloon, spur the provision of needed information, signal their staff about their preferences, or otherwise achieve wholly understandable and worthy ends. Courts are not faced with the need to motivate and inform a staff, defend their policies before a concerned legislature, impress the public, or enlist reluctant support of industry.

Commissioner Applewhaite's concern for his employment future was not simply inappropriate self-interest but the natural product of our public policy choices. We have chosen to have persons who are *not* part of a permanent bureaucracy lead the government. As a result, for an agency's top personnel who are outside the Civil Service, tenure in office is anything but assured. Even at levels below that of the agency head, we effectively encourage people to use a "revolving door" from and to the private sector. This choice risks that individuals will be tempted into acting with an eye to their future benefit while they are in government service or that they later will use information or contacts acquired in government service for private benefit. But the choice also has benefits, in improving communication between government and the private and nonprofit sectors and maintaining citizen and political control of the bureaucracy. Having made the choice, we render concerns like Applewhaite's inevitable.

(1) ***Remedies for Inappropriate Contacts.*** As the PATCO decision noted, the APA outlines remedies for ex parte contacts available at the administrative level. Section 557(d) requires the agency to disclose such communications and authorizes the agency to demand that the party violating ex parte prohibitions demonstrate why his claim or interest in the

proceedings should not be dismissed. Section 556(d) further authorizes the agency to consider a violation of the ex parte rules as "sufficient grounds for a decision adverse to a party who has knowingly committed such violation or knowingly caused such violation to occur." Disclosure and resultant publicity can be a remedy on their own. PATCO also underscores that in some instances inappropriate ex parte contacts may lead to criminal investigation and prosecution. See 18 U.S.C. § 1505 (prohibition on obstructing agency proceedings); see also 18 U.S.C. § 201 (prohibition on bribery of federal officials).

A harder question is whether inappropriate contacts should lead a court to set aside the agency's decision. Should PATCO be heard to complain about a contact that, presumably, would have worked in its favor? On the other hand, should actions by Shanker—not a party and not apparently acting at PATCO's behest—have been held against PATCO? The court avoided this issue by concluding that no remedy was required for the indiscretions that had occurred. In some cases, disqualification has been administered, and plainly the threat that the agency will withhold whatever the communicator is seeking to gain can serve as a significant control. Thus, in WKAT, Inc. v. FCC, 296 F.2d 375 (D.C. Cir. 1961)—not a case actually involving § 557(d) but cited by the PATCO court—the court disqualified a successful applicant for a television license worth millions because of its improper ex parte efforts to influence the role of an FCC commissioner. This sanction cannot be applied invariably, however, without risking harm to the public interest.

(2) ***Prohibited Actions While in Office.*** The problems of government ethics regulation are far subtler than criminal prohibitions against bribery. An ethics regime can have significant implications for government employees' morale and futures outside government. In general, such matters are the domain of the Office of Government Ethics, initially a part of the Office of Personnel Management but now a separate agency. Its regulations are binding on executive branch employees and notably detailed—for example, they not only declare a $20 maximum value for acceptable "gifts," but they also indicate that retail value must be observed and state principles on which the values of several trivial gifts must be amalgamated. Were an official today to be contemplating a dinner akin to Commissioner Applewhaite's dinner with Albert Shanker, these regulations would suggest ample basis for caution.

One of the first acts President Obama undertook upon assuming office was to issue an executive order extending ethics limits on government officials, including a prohibition on officials accepting any gifts from registered lobbyists or lobbying organizations. More significantly, the order imposed new restrictions on the ability of officials to participate in matters related to their former employment and particular limitations on former lobbyists. The latter were required to pledge that they will not "seek or accept employment with any executive agency that [the individual] . . . lobbied within the 2 years before . . . appointment." Exec. Order 13490 § 1, 74 Fed. Reg. 4673 (Jan. 21, 2009). Not to be outdone, President Trump shortly after taking office issued a superseding executive order covering "Ethics Commitments by Executive Branch Appointees." Exec. Order 13770, 82 Fed.

Reg. 9333 (Jan. 28, 2017). Many of the provisions were similar to President Obama's, but the two-year restrictions on former lobbyists were limited to participation in particular matters or specific issue areas involving former clients, rather than to employment in the agency altogether. § 1(6), (7). President Trump also issued waivers to particular appointees as to some of these obligations; these waivers were, after some pressure from the Office of Government Ethics, posted on the White House website. Continuing the pattern, President Biden issued Executive Order 13989, Ethics Commitments by Executive Branch Personnel, on his first day in office. This latest order requires all appointees to pledge in writing, among other items: "I will not for a period of 2 years from the date of my appointment participate in any particular matter involving specific parties that is directly and substantially related to my former employer or former clients, including regulations and contracts." Appointees who were registered lobbyists before their appointments were also required not to accept, for two years, any job with an agency they had lobbied. Exec. Order 13989 § 1, 86 Fed. Reg. 7029 (Jan. 20, 2021).

(3) ***Prohibited Actions upon Leaving Office.*** Federal criminal law has long provided that a former official may not appear for a private client after leaving government in a distinct matter (adjudication, grant, contract—but *not* rule) in which she had been "personally and substantially" involved while in government, and she may not appear for a year respecting any like matter for which she had official "responsibility" during the year before she left government. See 18 U.S.C. §§ 205, 207. A moment's reflection will show that these prohibitions are limited—there is no bar to advising a client so long as one does not appear; one's partner may appear; appearance is acceptable so long as it is not in connection with a "matter" within reach of one or the other rule; and, finally, waivers can on occasion be obtained.

The Ethics in Government Act, enacted in 1978, tightened postemployment constraints in some respects. As amended, 18 U.S.C. § 207 now extends the lifetime ban on participation in particular matters in which the former employee was "personally and substantially" involved to informal as well as formal appearances. In addition, for two years she is forbidden to directly appear or communicate on all matters formally under her official responsibility. High-level former employees also face a one-year ban on making any approach to the agency, formal or informal, oral or written, seeking to influence outcomes (including in rulemaking proceedings) regardless of whether the matter was pending during their tenure or within their responsibility. The Act initially also prohibited former employees from counseling, aiding, consulting, advising, or assisting others who communicate or appear during the two years immediately following their government service, but this prohibition was repealed in 1989. Provision is made for the agency to seek its former employee's advice where the agency wants that advice, and the agency is also authorized to impose a sanction as large as five years' disqualification to appear before it on former employees who violate the Act's requirements, in addition to criminal sanctions.

President Obama's Executive Order tightened postemployment prohibitions as well. That Executive Order contained a "Revolving Door Ban" under which officials pledged "upon leaving Government service, not to lobby any covered executive branch official or non-career Senior Executive Service appointee for the remainder of the Administration." President Trump's E.O., in addition to repeating that pledge, also required employees to pledge to "not, within 5 years after the termination of my employment as an appointee in any executive agency in which I am appointed to serve, engage in lobbying activities with respect to that agency." Exec. Order 13770, § 1(1). However, President Trump revoked this Order just before leaving office, and released employees from the commitments it had required. (President Clinton, it should be noted, had done much the same.) President Biden's incoming Executive Order, referenced above, begins with requiring adherence to more aspirational language than its predecessors: ". . . I commit to decision-making on the merits and exclusively in the public interest, without regard to private gain or personal benefit. . . . I commit to ethical choices of post-Government employment that do not raise the appearance that I have used my Government service for private gain. . . ." However, when it proceeds to the operational specifics, perhaps in recognition of the difficulties of obtaining new employment which had, one supposes, led President Trump to release employees from his five-year ban, the Biden order imposes postemployment prohibitions for only two years.

For an argument that the "revolving door" is not something much to worry about, see David Zaring, Against Being Against the Revolving Door, 2013 U. Ill. L. Rev. 507.

(4) ***A Broader Perspective.*** The problems of government ethics regulation were the subject of study by a special ABA Committee on Government Standards, CYNTHIA R. FARINA, REPORTER, KEEPING FAITH: GOVERNMENT ETHICS AND GOVERNMENT ETHICS REGULATION, 45 Admin. L. Rev. 287, 296–97, 327 (1993): "Of all areas of substantive ethics law, the rules defining and remedying conflicts of interest are the most central, and the most vexing. Here, the longstanding American commitment to citizen governance comes up against several fundamental ideals of ethical public service. The result is considerable tension and ambivalence. On the one hand, a continual stream of people entering government from the private sector is perceived as highly desirable. The current popularity of term-limitation laws reflects this perception. Movement between government and the private sector is valued as injecting energy, experience, practicality and perspective that would be lacking in government-by-professional-bureaucracy. On the other hand, there is an equally strong conviction that neither elected nor appointed officials should have financial interests or relationships outside government that compromise their exercise of power. . . .

". . . [E]thics regulation will be both redundant and inadequate if it focuses merely on condemning the deliberate abuse of trust. It will be redundant because the criminal law (through the vehicles of bribery, illegal gratuities, embezzlement, etc.) already proscribes such behavior. It will be inadequate because the overwhelming majority of government employees, knowing themselves to be honorable persons who would never consciously misuse their position, can readily dismiss such proscriptions as irrelevant to their own professional lives—and so fail to reflect upon the insidious ways in which bias and self-interest can infect, almost unwittingly, the exercise of power. Hence, ethics regulation can make its most meaningful contribution by helping government employees to recognize, and take steps to defuse, situations that invite compromised behavior."

The Report also addressed regulation of the activities of individuals as they leave government service, noting that "it is not always clear precisely what . . . is the answer to the question 'Which use of advantage in which situation is actually unethical?' Surely we are not prepared to say that *any* use at *any* time of *any* knowledge or influence acquired during government service on behalf of a party other than the federal government, is an abuse of the public trust. Taking such a position would mean that a lawyer who had clerked for the Supreme Court could never draft a certiorari petition for a private client, or that a scientist who had worked for the FDA could never take a job in commercial new drug development, or that an MBA who had worked for the SEC could never join an investment banking house. Neither sound ethics policy nor good government supports an approach in which individuals can enter government service only at the cost of radically reconfiguring their subsequent professional lives."

The Report argued that whether using advantages of former government employment is ethical turns largely on three factors: the nature of the former official's responsibility, the nature of the matter, and the nature of the aid given the new employer or client. "Of greatest concern are situations in which the former employee had significant decisional responsibility, had access to sensitive information, or otherwise functioned in an influential role as draftsperson, strategizer or counselor[;] situations that resemble adjudicatory 'cases'[;]" and "situations in which the former employee functions directly or indirectly as advocate . . . to help advance her new employer's position in an ongoing matter with the government."

## SECTION 3. INFORMAL ADJUDICATION

***DOMINION ENERGY BRAYTON POINT, LLC v. JOHNSON***
***5 U.S.C. § 555***
***OLIVARES v. TRANSPORTATION SECURITY ADMINISTRATION***
***Notes on Informal Adjudication***

On-the-record adjudication is the focus of the APA's provisions on adjudication; as you have seen, § 554 on "Adjudications" opens by stipulating that it applies whenever adjudication is "required by statute to be determined on the record after an opportunity for an agency hearing," with a few listed exceptions. Yet at the same time, the APA broadly defines adjudication as including licensing and any other agency action leading to a final disposition that is not rulemaking. §§ 551(6)–(7). This means that there is a broad array of agency actions that qualify as adjudication yet fall outside the APA's on-the-record procedures. They represent a vast and extremely diverse assortment of activities.

## DOMINION ENERGY BRAYTON POINT, LLC v. JOHNSON

United States Court of Appeals for the First Circuit (2006).
443 F.3d 12.

■ SELYA, CIRCUIT JUDGE.

USGen New England, Inc., now Dominion Energy Brayton Point, LLC (Dominion), filed suit against the U.S. Environmental Protection Agency, its administrator, and its regional office (collectively, the EPA), alleging that the EPA failed to perform a non-discretionary duty when it refused to grant Dominion's request for a formal evidentiary hearing after issuing a proposed final National Pollution Discharge Elimination System (NPDES) permit. . . .

I. BACKGROUND

Dominion owns an electrical generating facility in Somerset, Massachusetts (the station). The station opened in the 1960s and, like most power plants of its era, utilizes an "open-cycle" cooling system. Specifically, the station withdraws water from the Lees and Taunton Rivers, circulates that water through the plant's generating equipment as a coolant, and then discharges the water (which, by then, has attained an elevated temperature) into Mount Hope Bay.

The withdrawals and discharges of water are regulated by the Clean Water Act (CWA), 33 U.S.C. §§ 1251–1387. For the last three decades, these actions have been authorized by a series of NPDES permits issued by the EPA pursuant to section 402(a) of the CWA. The standards incorporated into those permits are determined under the thermal variance procedures laid out in section 316(a).

In 1998, the station applied for renewal of its NPDES permit and thermal variance authorization. The EPA issued a proposed final permit on October 6, 2003, in which it rejected the requested thermal variance. On November 4, Dominion sought review before the Environmental Appeals Board (the Board) and asked for an evidentiary hearing. The Board accepted the petition for review but declined to convene an evidentiary hearing. . . .

II. THE LEGAL LANDSCAPE

We set the stage for our substantive discussion by undertaking a brief review of the legal rules that frame the controversy at hand.

Before the EPA either issues an NPDES permit or authorizes a thermal variance, it must offer an "opportunity for public hearing." 33 U.S.C. §§ 1326(a), 1342(a). No definition of "public hearing" is contained within the four corners of the CWA.

The Administrative Procedure Act (APA), 5 U.S.C. § 551 et seq., is also part of the relevant legal landscape. Most pertinent here are those sections that combine to describe the procedures for formal administrative adjudications. See id. §§ 554, 556, 557. These procedures apply "in every case of adjudication required by statute to be determined on the record after opportunity for an agency hearing." Id. § 554(a). The APA does not directly address whether these procedures apply when a statute simply calls for an "opportunity for public hearing" without any specific indication that the hearing should be "on the record."

In Seacoast Anti-Pollution League v. Costle, 572 F.2d 872 (1st Cir. 1978), this court interpreted "public hearing" (as used in sections 402(a) and 316(a) of the CWA) to mean "evidentiary hearing"—in other words, a hearing that comports with the APA's requirements for a formal adjudication. Examining the legislative history of the APA, we adopted a presumption that "unless a statute otherwise specifies, an adjudicatory hearing subject to judicial review must be [an evidentiary hearing] on the record." Id. at 877. Applying that presumption to the CWA, we concluded that "the statute certainly does not indicate that the determination need *not* be on the record." Id. at 878 (emphasis in original).

So viewed, Seacoast established a rebuttable presumption that, in the context of an adjudication, an organic statute that calls for a "public hearing" should be read to require an evidentiary hearing in compliance with the formal adjudication provisions of the APA. Two other circuit courts reached the same conclusion, albeit through different reasoning. Acquiescing in this construction, the EPA promulgated regulations that memorialized the use of formal evidentiary hearings in the NPDES permit process. See NPDES, Revision of Regulations, 44 Fed.Reg. 32,854, 32,938 (June 7, 1979).

In 1984, a sea change occurred in administrative law and, specifically, in the interpretation of organic statutes such as the CWA. The Supreme Court held that "[w]hen a court reviews an agency's construction of the statute which it administers," the reviewing court first must ask "whether Congress has directly spoken to the precise question at issue." Chevron U.S.A. Inc. v. NRDC, 467 U.S. 837, 842. [p. 1206] If Congress's intent is clear, that intent governs—both the court and the agency must give it full effect. If, however, Congress has not directly addressed the question and the agency has stepped into the vacuum by promulgating an interpretive regulation, a reviewing court may "not simply impose its own construction on the statute," but, rather, ought to ask "whether the agency's answer is based on a permissible construction of the statute." Id. at 843. . . .

Armed with the Chevron decision and a presidential directive to streamline regulatory programs, the EPA advanced a proposal to eliminate formal evidentiary hearings from the NPDES permitting process. In due course, the EPA adopted that proposal as a final rule. See Amendments to Streamline the NPDES Program Regulations: Round Two, 65 Fed.Reg. 30,886, 30,900 (May 15, 2000).

This revision depended heavily on a Chevron analysis. The agency began by "finding no evidence that Congress intended to require formal evidentiary hearings or that the text [of section 402(a)] precludes informal adjudication of permit review petitions." Id. at 30,896. Then, it weighed the risks and benefits of employing informal hearing procedures for NPDES permit review, "determining that these procedures would not violate the Due Process Clause." Id. Finally, it "concluded that informal hearing procedures satisfy the hearing requirement of section 402(a)." Id.

It was under this new regulatory scheme that the EPA considered Dominion's request to renew its NPDES permit and to authorize a thermal variance. Thus, it was under this scheme that the EPA denied Dominion's request for an evidentiary hearing.

III. ANALYSIS

. . . For present purposes, the critical precedent is National Cable & Telecommunications Ass'n v. Brand X Internet Services, 545 U.S. 967 (2005) [p. 1230]. There, the Court examined the relationship between the stare decisis effect of an appellate court's statutory interpretation and the Chevron deference due to an administrative agency's subsequent, but contrary, interpretation. Echoing Chevron, the Court reiterated that "[f]illing [statutory] gaps . . . involves difficult policy choices that agencies are better equipped to make than courts." Id. at 2699. Then, concluding that Chevron's application should not turn on the order in which judicial and agency interpretations issue, the Justices held squarely that "[a] court's prior judicial construction of a statute trumps an agency construction otherwise entitled to Chevron deference only if the prior court decision holds that its construction follows from the unambiguous terms of the statute and thus leaves no room for agency discretion." Id. at 2700. . . .

Once this mode of analysis is understood and applied, Dominion's argument collapses. Seacoast simply does not hold that Congress clearly intended the term "public hearing" in sections 402(a) and 316(a) of the CWA to mean "evidentiary hearing." To the contrary, the Seacoast court based its interpretation of the CWA on a presumption derived from the legislative history of the APA—a presumption that would hold sway only in the absence of a showing of a contrary congressional intent. In other words, the court resorted to the presumption only because it could find no sign of a plainly discernible congressional intent. . . .

The short of it is that the Seacoast court, faced with an opaque statute, settled upon what it sensibly thought was the best construction of the CWA's "public hearing" language. . . . Consequently, under Brand X, Seacoast must yield to a reasonable agency interpretation of the CWA's "public hearing" requirement.

The only piece left to this puzzle is to confirm that the EPA's new regulations are, in fact, entitled to Chevron deference. This inquiry is a straightforward one. As our earlier discussion suggests (and as the Seacoast court correctly deduced), Congress has not spoken directly to the precise question at issue here. See, e.g., United States v. Fla. E. Coast Ry. Co., 410 U.S. 224, 239 (1973) ("The term 'hearing' in its legal context undoubtedly has a host of meanings.") Accordingly, we must defer to the

EPA's interpretation of the CWA as long as that interpretation is reasonable.

In this instance, the administrative interpretation took into account the relevant universe of factors. See 65 Fed.Reg. at 30,898–30,900 (considering "(1) [t]he private interests at stake, (2) the risk of erroneous decision-making, and (3) the nature of the government interest," and concluding that its new regulation was a reasonable interpretation of the CWA). The agency's conclusion that evidentiary hearings are unnecessary and that Congress, in using the phrase "opportunity for public hearing," did not mean to mandate evidentiary hearings seems reasonable—and Dominion, to its credit, has conceded the point. . . .

Dominion exhorts us to find that Seacoast's holding is actually an interpretation of the APA, not the CWA (and, therefore, the EPA's regulation is also an interpretation of the APA, not entitled to Chevron deference). See, e.g., Metro. Stevedore Co. v. Rambo, 521 U.S. 121, 137 n. 9 (1997) (noting that Chevron deference is inappropriate vis-à-vis an agency interpretation of the APA's burden-of-proof provision). Such a reading of Seacoast is plainly incorrect. While the Seacoast court relied on a presumption borrowed from the APA, the court's holding is an interpretation of the CWA and, specifically, of the term "public hearing" contained in sections 402(a) and 316(a). . . . Because those changes implicate the statute that the EPA administers (i.e., the CWA), Chevron deference is appropriate.

## IV. CONCLUSION

We summarize succinctly. Although we in no way disparage the soundness of Seacoast's reasoning, the Chevron and Brand X opinions and the interposition of a new and reasonable agency interpretation of the disputed statutory language have changed the picture. Because we, like the Seacoast court, cannot discern a clear and unambiguous congressional intent behind the words "public hearing" in the CWA and because the EPA's interpretation of that term constitutes a reasonable construction of the statute, deference is due. . . .

[W]e conclude that the district court did not err in dismissing Dominion's action.

Affirmed.

## NOTES

(1) ***What Is Being Interpreted?*** If the Clean Water Act requires holding a "public hearing" and the APA language says "required by statute to be determined on the record after opportunity for an agency hearing," is the First Circuit right when it now says that what is at issue is an interpretation of the CWA and not an interpretation of the APA? (Remember that Chevron does not cover an agency's interpretation of the APA, which is meant to bring uniformity to procedures across multiple agencies.)

The Seacoast opinion, overturned by the principal case, relied heavily on the ATTORNEY GENERAL'S MANUAL ON THE APA 42–43 (1947) (p. 250): "It is believed that with respect to adjudication the specific statutory requirement of a hearing, without anything more, carries with it the further requirement of decision on the basis of the evidence adduced at the hearing. With respect to rule making, it was concluded that a statutory provision that rules be issued after a hearing, without more, should not be construed as requiring agency action 'on the record,' but rather as merely requiring an opportunity for the expression of views. That conclusion was based on the legislative nature of rule making, from which it was inferred, unless a statute requires otherwise, that an agency hearing on proposed rules would be similar to a hearing before a legislative committee, with neither the legislature nor the agency being limited to the material adduced at the hearing. No such rationale applies to administrative adjudication. In fact, it is assumed that where a statute specifically provides for administrative adjudication (such as the suspension or revocation of a license) after opportunity for an agency hearing, such specific requirement for a hearing ordinarily implies the further requirement of decision in accordance with evidence adduced at the hearing. Of course, the foregoing discussion is inapplicable to any situation in which the legislative history or the context of the pertinent statute indicates a contrary congressional intent." Is this a better view? The authority of the Attorney General's Manual, as a general matter, is discussed in Chapter III, p. 250. For an argument that on this point the Attorney General got it right, that the APA was written with a single view of what constituted an acceptable hearing, so that the call for an adjudicatory hearing was necessarily on the record unless Congress explicitly said otherwise, see Emily Bremer, The Rediscovered Stages of Agency Adjudication, 99 Wash. U. L. Rev. 377, 426–28 (2021).

(2) ***Deference Wrong?*** Even if what is at stake is the meaning of the Clean Water Act, should the court defer to the agency's interpretation on the theory that the agency knows best what type of hearing will best balance costs with improved results? Or should it refuse to defer, on the theory that statutorily stipulated procedures (in the CWA as well as the APA) are meant to restrain the agency and to protect outside parties? The Chevron case (p. 1206) on which the court relies involved deference to an agency determination regarding a substantive matter.

(3) ***New FCC Procedural Rules.*** Relying in part on the decision in Dominion Energy, the Federal Communications Commission in 2020 issued new procedural rules that reduced the formality of many of its procedures. In the Matter of Procedural Streamlining of Administrative Hearings, 35 F.C.C.R. 10729 (2020). "With one noteworthy exception," said the Commission, "the hearing provisions in the Communications Act neither expressly require an 'on the record' hearing nor include other language unambiguously evincing congressional intent to impose the full panoply of trial-type procedures of a formal hearing. The exception is section 503 of the Act, which authorizes the Commission to impose a forfeiture penalty on a person after 'a hearing before the Commission or an administrative law judge thereof in accordance with section 554 of' the APA. Since Congress did not include similar language in other hearing provisions in the Act, we conclude that Commission hearings under the Communications Act

generally are subject only to the APA's informal adjudication requirements." The new rules substitute written and documentary evidence for live testimony and cross-examination in many instances. They also provide for records to be organized by staff and then presented directly to the Commission rather than being heard by an ALJ.

(4) ***ABA Resolution.*** Congress could, of course, change the result of Dominion Energy and similar cases. In 2000, the ABA passed a resolution saying:

> Resolved, that in order to preserve the uniformity of provisions and of qualifications of presiding officers contemplated by the APA, Congress should amend the APA to provide prospectively that, absent a statutory requirement to the contrary, in any future legislation that creates the opportunity for a hearing in an adjudication, such a hearing should follow the APA's formal adjudication procedures.

If you were in Congress, would you have sponsored this legislation?

(5) ***The Formal Adjudication-Informal Adjudication Distinction.*** As the language used in the Dominion Energy case, and in the notes just read, suggests, it is common to speak of the trial-type procedure set out by APA §§ 554, 556, and 557 as "formal adjudication," and to speak of any proceeding that is an adjudication, but not subject to those statutory provisions, as an "informal adjudication." These terms are not themselves used in the statute, which speaks instead (as we have seen) of "adjudication required by statute to be determined on the record after opportunity for an agency hearing." But this gateway for applying the APA's trial-type requirements leaves open the possibility that other sources of law may require formality—agency rules, agency practices, perhaps due process in some instances, and certainly agency statutes that (especially as handled in the Dominion Energy case) set hearing requirements that don't quite "trigger" the APA's formal adjudication. Or, to put the matter in other words, there would seem to be two broad categories of what might be called, as viewed through the APA, "informal adjudication": one of which is, in functional terms, informal, and the other of which is, in functional terms, quite formal, but with the formality drawn from non-APA sources of law. If we take the actual use of an evidentiary hearing before a relatively independent trier-of-fact as our standard, such proceedings are common in administrative agencies of many types. As mentioned earlier in this Chapter (p. 529) the recent, impressive study conducted by Michael Asimow for the Administrative Conference of the United States (Federal Administrative Adjudication Outside the Administrative Procedure Act, 2019) concluded that these proceedings look enough like APA "formal adjudications" that they, too, should bear that name. Using this point of view, there are two consequences for the study of "informal adjudication." First, as a theoretical matter, it is important to remember that the functional distinction between formal and informal adjudication puts the dividing line at a different place from the dividing line established in the APA. Second, as a practical matter, one cannot know the requirements applicable to any specific administrative proceeding without knowing the particular statutes, regulations, and customary practices

applicable to it, as well as the requirements of the APA. Which is not to say that the APA has nothing to say about the conduct of truly informal adjudication—our next topic.

(6) ***The APA's Requirements for Informal Adjudication.*** If adjudication is at issue, but the agency's statute does not bring § 554 into play, does the APA have anything else to say about how the agency should proceed? Many early commentators on the APA thought that, as regards adjudication, it addressed only the formal adjudication described in sections 554, 556 and 557. However, in Pension Benefit Guaranty Corp. v. LTV Corp., 496 U.S. 633 (1990), the Supreme Court decided otherwise. In a complex case, whose substantive facts need not detain us here, the court below had faulted the agency, PBGC, for failing to provide LTV with notice of "the material on which it was to base its decision" and with "an adequate opportunity to offer contrary evidence." The Supreme Court ruled first, that the agency's "determination in this case . . . was lawfully made by informal adjudication, the minimal requirements for which are set forth in § 555 of the APA," and second, that even as to § 555, the Vermont Yankee principle (p. 312) applied, so that, unless based on some other identifiable source of law, "courts are not free to impose upon agencies specific procedural requirements that have no basis in the APA." Since the court below "did not point to any provision in [the substantive statute] or the APA which gives LTV the procedural rights the court identified," that court's decision was reversed.

## 5 U.S.C. § 555

### Ancillary matters

(a) This section applies, according to the provisions thereof, except as otherwise provided by this subchapter.

(b) A person compelled to appear in person before an agency or representative thereof is entitled to be accompanied, represented, and advised by counsel or, if permitted by the agency, by other qualified representative. A party is entitled to appear in person or by or with counsel or other duly qualified representative in an agency proceeding. So far as the orderly conduct of public business permits, an interested person may appear before an agency or its responsible employees for the presentation, adjustment, or determination of an issue, request, or controversy in a proceeding, whether interlocutory, summary, or otherwise, or in connection with an agency function. With due regard for the convenience and necessity of the parties or their representatives and within a reasonable time, each agency shall proceed to conclude a matter presented to it. This subsection does not grant or deny a person who is not a lawyer the right to appear for or represent others before an agency or in an agency proceeding.

(c) [Investigative acts; copies of submitted evidence.]

(d) [Agency subpoenas.]

(e) Prompt notice shall be given of the denial in whole or in part of a written application, petition, or other request of an interested person made in connection with any agency proceeding. Except in affirming a prior denial or when the denial is self-explanatory, the notice shall be accompanied by a brief statement of the grounds for denial.

## NOTES

(1) ***A Separate Process?*** The title of the section is "Ancillary matters." The individual parts seem to assume that an "agency proceeding" already exists. Only a few particular details are specified. Is it right, as the Court did in Pension Benefit Guaranty Corp., to see § 555 as the specification of "informal adjudication" in the same way that other, much more detailed provisions of the APA specify the processes for formal rulemaking, informal rulemaking, and formal adjudication? Emily Bremer, The Rediscovered Stages of Agency Adjudication, 99 Wash. U. L. Rev. 377 (2021), argues that the APA was never meant to specify a separate process known as "informal adjudication," but only meant to identify certain features of the initial processes that, if a controversy were not settled, would eventually lead up to a formal hearing on the record.

(2) Even if we say that the Court was right as to the coverage of § 555, was it also right to apply Vermont Yankee's strictures to informal adjudication per § 555—to decide, that is, that § 555 is so complete that judges can add to it only if they can find another applicable source of law? Or should the section have been treated as more open-ended in what we might call a common-law fashion?

(3) Alternatively, should the APA be amended to provide a specific model of informal adjudication?

## OLIVARES v. TRANSPORTATION SECURITY ADMINISTRATION

United States Court of Appeals for the District of Columbia Circuit (2016).
819 F.3d 454.

■ EDWARDS, SENIOR CIRCUIT JUDGE.

Alberto Ardila Olivares, the Petitioner before the court, is a foreign alien from Venezuela. In 2014, he applied to attend a Federal Aviation Administration ("FAA")-certified flight school in France to obtain a pilot certification to fly large, U.S.-registered aircraft. After conducting a background check, the Transportation Security Administration ("TSA") determined that Petitioner was a risk to aviation and national security and denied his application for training. Petitioner now seeks review of TSA's action, invoking the court's jurisdiction under 49 U.S.C. § 46110(a), and asserting causes of action under the Administrative Procedure Act ("APA"), 5 U.S.C. §§ 555(e), 702, 704, 706(2). . . .

### I. BACKGROUND

In the aftermath of the tragic terrorist attacks on September 11, 2001, Congress created the Transportation Security Administration to shore up our nation's civil aviation security. TSA was initially housed in the Department of Transportation and headed by the Under Secretary of Transportation for Security. In 2002, TSA was moved to the newly created Department of Homeland Security under the direction of the Secretary of Homeland Security.

This case involves TSA's role in determining whether alien pilots may be certified to operate large, U.S.-registered aircraft. "Large aircraft means aircraft of more than 12,500 pounds, maximum certificated takeoff weight." 14 C.F.R. § 1.1 (emphasis omitted). No pilot may "serve in any capacity as an airman with respect to a civil aircraft . . . in air commerce . . . without an airman certificate" from FAA. 49 U.S.C. § 44711(a)(2); see also 14 C.F.R. § 61.3(a). For large aircraft, pilots must obtain additional certification known as a Type Rating. 14 C.F.R. § 61.31(a)(1). Aliens who seek training and certification to operate large, U.S.-registered aircraft must first secure clearance by TSA. See 49 U.S.C. § 44939(a). If TSA "determine[s] that [a noncitizen applicant] presents a risk to aviation or national security," then that applicant is ineligible to receive the training necessary to secure a large aircraft Type Rating from FAA. See id.; see also 49 C.F.R. § 1552.3(a)(4), (e).

Petitioner is an alien pilot who formerly lived and worked in the United States. On February 14, 2007, he was convicted in federal court of conspiracy to possess with intent to distribute controlled substances in violation of 21 U.S.C. § 846. He was sentenced to serve 80 months in prison, followed by 60 months of supervised release. On December 17, 2007, FAA sent Petitioner a letter revoking his pilot certification, effective January 7, 2008. Petitioner was subsequently deported on March 3, 2010.

After being deported, Petitioner worked as a pilot in Venezuela. In 2011, he was presented with an opportunity to fly a large, U.S.-registered aircraft, which required him to receive training for the appropriate Type Rating and then seek the appropriate certification from FAA. To achieve these ends, Petitioner applied for admission to an FAA-certified flight school in France. TSA then conducted a background investigation of Petitioner. Although TSA uncovered Petitioner's 2007 drug conviction, TSA granted him permission to attend flight school. Petitioner successfully completed flight school and obtained his Type Rating as well as various other FAA certifications.

In 2012, the U.S. Government Accountability Office (GAO) published a report criticizing TSA's background investigations of alien pilots. GAO, Weaknesses Exist In TSA's Process For Ensuring Foreign Flight Students Do Not Pose A Security Threat (July 2012) ("GAO Report" or "Report"). The Report highlighted that TSA's investigation methods did not always thoroughly examine an alien's immigration status, and expressed concern that, as a result, the investigation might not identify all alien flight-school applicants presenting a security threat. In response to the Report, TSA revised its background check procedures. . . .

In 2014, Petitioner received another opportunity to pilot a large, U.S.-registered aircraft. Although his general FAA credentials remained valid, Petitioner's Type Rating had expired. As before, Petitioner applied to attend an FAA-certified flight school in France, and TSA conducted a background investigation.

Pursuant to TSA's new procedures, the agency's investigation flagged that Petitioner was inadmissible to enter the United States due to his 2007 drug conviction. As a result, Petitioner's application was referred for further investigation. The investigation uncovered that, in addition to his 2007 drug conviction, Petitioner had been suspected of firearms trafficking in 1998 in Aruba. TSA also discovered that, even though he had been deported with no right to return to the United States, Petitioner maintained a local address in Massachusetts.

TSA apparently believed that Petitioner was seeking to attend a flight school in the United States. As a result, the agency initially declined to process Petitioner's application. On October 27, 2014, TSA sent Petitioner the following email message:

> This training request cannot be processed for the following reason(s): [TSA] has received information in regards to your immigration status. As a result, your current training request to attend flight training at a United States flight school has been cancelled. If you resolve your immigration status and provide the appropriate supporting documentation this cancellation may be lifted and your training request approval reinstated.

Petitioner immediately responded to TSA, explaining that he sought to attend flight school in France and not in the United States. With Petitioner's clarification in hand, TSA performed a follow-up review of his file. After this further review, TSA concluded that Petitioner was a "Threat to Transportation/National Security." On November 5, 2014, TSA sent an email to Petitioner denying his application. The email stated:

> Pursuant to Title 49 of the Code of Federal Regulations [§ ]1552.3(e), your training request has been denied as TSA is unable to determine that you do not pose a threat to aviation or national security. This letter constitutes TSA's final determination.

TSA's email gave no further explanation for its denial of Petitioner's application.

On January 5, 2015, Petitioner filed his petition for review with this court. On March 26, 2015, Andrea Vara executed a sworn declaration explaining TSA's grounds for denying Petitioner's application for training. Ms. Vara is employed by the U.S. Department of Homeland Security, Transportation Security Administration, as the Alien Flight Student Program Manager. . . .

The Vara Declaration makes it clear that Ms. Vara was the Government official who made the determination that Petitioner's application should be denied because he presented a risk to aviation and national security. The Declaration not only explains the agency's rationale, it also cites internal materials that TSA had before it at the time when the determination was made to deny Petitioner's application. . . .

The Vara Declaration states, inter alia:

> 12. In October 2014, Petitioner submitted Training Request # 565192, seeking to train at FlightSafety International—Paris Learning Center from November 10–November 17, 2014.
>
> 13. Pursuant to the revised procedure, Petitioner was subject to an investigation, which revealed the following. In 2007, Petitioner pled guilty to conspiracy to possess with intent to distribute controlled substances and the U.S. District Court for the Northern District of Illinois sentenced him to eighty (80) months imprisonment. Petitioner's conviction made him inadmissible to the United States and led to the revocation of his FAA Airman's Certificate. Petitioner was deported to his home country of Venezuela in March 2010.
>
> 14. A public news article published after Petitioner was deported provided a U.S. address for Petitioner. Further, records indicated that Petitioner was a suspected international trafficker in firearms. There was evidence that Petitioner had previously been involved in the export of weapons and U.S. currency to Venezuela by private aircraft, was the second pilot of an aircraft from which several weapons and $500,000 was seized by local authorities in Aruba, and that one of his associates was arrested in Aruba for smuggling firearms. [Footnote 6]
>
> [Footnote 6] Some of this information was from the late 1990s. I considered its age when determining whether Petitioner posed a risk. Because the evidence indicated Petitioner had smuggled weapons and money and was convicted for drug trafficking, I concluded these were not isolated incidents, and rather revealed Petitioner's consistent disregard for the law.
>
> 15. This information, viewed as a whole, demonstrated Petitioner's willingness to consistently disregard the law and to use an aircraft for criminal activity, in opposition to U.S. security interests. The information also raised concerns that Petitioner may use his flight training to advance the interests of a criminal enterprise, which could include an enterprise that seeks to do harm to the United States.
>
> 16. Based on all the foregoing information, I concluded Petitioner posed a threat to aviation and national security and [TSA's Alien Flight Student Program] denied his training request on November 5, 2014.

Vara Declaration at 3–4 & n. 6, ¶¶ 12–16.

The entire Vara Declaration was included in the parties' Joint Appendix that was submitted to the court. Both parties discuss the Vara Declaration in their briefs to the court. And, as noted above, Petitioner does not question the authenticity of the Vara Declaration or the authority of the declarant; and we do not have any reason to doubt the veracity of TSA's account of the grounds justifying the agency's denial of Petitioner's application for flight training.

## II. ANALYSIS

### A. THE COURT'S JURISDICTION

[We have jurisdiction.]

### B. STANDARD OF REVIEW

["In cases of this sort, we must defer to TSA actions that reasonably interpret and enforce the safety and security obligations of the agency."]

### C. PETITIONER'S CLAIM UNDER SECTION 555(e) OF THE APA

Section 555(e) of the APA provides:

> Prompt notice shall be given of the denial in whole or in part of a written application, petition, or other request of an interested person made in connection with any agency proceeding. Except in affirming a prior denial or when the denial is self-explanatory, the notice shall be accompanied by a brief statement of the grounds for denial.

5 U.S.C. § 555(e). Petitioner claims that TSA's November 5, 2014 email to him denying his application for flight training violated the requirements of § 555(e) because the email offered no statement of the grounds for the agency's denial. As noted above, Petitioner's claim, at least at first blush, is compelling.

In Tourus Records, Inc. v. DEA, 259 F.3d 731, 737 (D.C. Cir. 2001) we explained:

> A "fundamental" requirement of administrative law is that an agency "set forth its reasons" for decision; an agency's failure to do so constitutes arbitrary and capricious agency action. That fundamental requirement is codified in section 6(d) of the APA, 5 U.S.C. § 555(e). Section 6(d) mandates that whenever an agency denies "a written application, petition, or other request of an interested person made in connection with any agency proceeding," the agency must provide "a brief statement of the grounds for denial," unless the denial is "self-explanatory." This requirement not only ensures the agency's careful consideration of such requests, but also gives parties the opportunity to apprise the agency of any errors it may have made and, if the agency persists in its decision, facilitates judicial review. Although nothing more than a "brief statement" is necessary, the core requirement is that the agency explain "why it chose to do what it did." Henry J. Friendly, Chenery Revisited: Reflections on Reversal and Remand of Administrative Orders, 1969 Duke L.J. 199, 222.

TSA's email to Petitioner denying his application for flight training did not meet this APA standard. The email simply parroted the words of 49

U.S.C. § 44939(a), without offering anything to explain why TSA had determined that Petitioner presented a risk to aviation or national security. And TSA has not argued that the reasons behind the denial of Petitioner's application were "self-explanatory." 5 U.S.C. § 555(e). "The [email] thus provides no basis upon which we could conclude that it was the product of reasoned decisionmaking." Tourus Records, 259 F.3d at 737.

"When an agency provides a statement of reasons insufficient to permit a court to discern its rationale, or states no reasons at all, the usual remedy is a 'remand to the agency for additional investigation or explanation.'" Id. (quoting Fla. Power & Light Co. v. Lorion, 470 U.S. 729, 744 (1985)). This case presents an unusual situation, however, because, after Petitioner filed his petition for review, TSA submitted the Vara Declaration and other internal agency documents that, together, offer a clear statement of the grounds and rationale upon which TSA relied in denying Petitioner's application for flight training. The internal materials include the findings of TSA's background investigation of Petitioner as well as internal agency communications. And, as explained by the Vara Declaration, these internal materials express TSA's reasoned, contemporaneous explanation for its decision. The internal materials are not impermissible "post hoc rationalizations" for agency action. Tourus Records, 259 F.3d at 738. Rather, they "represent the contemporaneous explanation of the agency decision," and, therefore, they are "appropriate subjects for our consideration." Id. . . .

Although we find that the internal agency materials, as illuminated by the Vara Declaration, satisfy the requirements of § 555(e), we add a word of caution. In the future, agencies will be well advised to obey the explicit command of § 555(e), rather than counting on being able to salvage their actions later, after the losing party has been forced to seek redress in court. Persistent scofflaw behavior might cause the courts to insist that the contemporaneous explanation actually be expressed to the complaining party, as the statute requires, on pain of vacatur and remand. Or the courts might insist on progressively more compelling indications that the reasons offered were in fact the reasons governing the decision when it was made. The offending agency action in this case was mitigated somewhat because the internal materials and the Vara Declaration were included in the parties' Joint Appendix, and Petitioner had an opportunity to review these materials before briefing and oral argument. This may not be sufficient in future cases involving agency defiance of § 555(e).

D. PETITIONER'S OTHER APA CLAIMS

In addition to his claim under § 555(e), Petitioner also contends that TSA's action was "arbitrary, capricious, an abuse of discretion, or otherwise not in accordance with law," 5 U.S.C. § 706(2)(A), because TSA failed to consider all relevant factors regarding his application for flight training. We disagree. . . .

Finally, Petitioner argues that TSA should not have used his suspected firearms trafficking or his Massachusetts address to support its decision. Petitioner claims that the Massachusetts address actually belongs to his brother, and Petitioner insists that he has never illegally entered the United States. Petitioner also points out that the firearms incident occurred nearly two decades ago and that he was merely suspected of being involved. In light of the limited standard of review that controls the disposition of this case, these arguments are not persuasive. It was rational for TSA to find it suspicious and thus consider information indicating that a deported individual appeared to maintain a current U.S. address and had been suspected of involvement in firearms trafficking. The agency's weighing of this information, along with the information regarding Petitioner's known criminal history, was not inconsistent with reasoned decision making. As the Vara Declaration makes clear, Petitioner's record as a whole "raised concerns that Petitioner [might] use his flight training to advance the interests of a criminal enterprise, which could include an enterprise that seeks to do harm to the United States." Vara Declaration at 4, ¶ 15. . . .

TSA was not required to show that Petitioner *would* engage in activities designed to compromise aviation or national security. Rather, the agency was merely required to give a reasonable explanation as to why it believed that Petitioner *presented a risk* to aviation or national security. The Vara Declaration satisfies this legal obligation.

III. CONCLUSION

For the reasons set forth above, the petition for review is denied.

## NOTES

(1) ***Why § 555(e)?*** If one of the purposes of the § 555(e) notice of denial is that it "gives parties the opportunity to apprise the agency of any errors it may have made" (as said in the prior case quoted in Olivares), was the court wrong to accept the Vara Declaration, filed in court, as an acceptable substitute? Or was the § 555 notice not meant to be part of a further interaction between the parties? Or was the Olivares decision simply a sensible practical resolution of the controversy?

(2) ***Limited Agency Process.*** In addition to its treatment of § 555, the principal case usefully reveals some of the ways in which informal adjudication can differ from formal adjudication. The agency did not act recklessly or without considering the facts (although of course such things are possible). To the contrary, it seems that Vara was a diligent and active investigator. But the evidence that she relied on might have been in error (such as in the question of whose address in Massachusetts it really was) or her interpretation of the situation might have been mistaken (such as regarding the impact of old malfeasances). Olivares got a chance to argue these points in court, but by then the agency had made its decision and its decision was entitled to judicial deference. If there had been a formal proceeding before the agency, rather than a one-sided investigation, Olivares would have been able to challenge the agency's evidence at that point, and

to have argued about its relevance before any initial decision was made. Presumably no statute or agency regulation required holding such a trial-type proceeding, and, of course, having such a proceeding for each controversy of this sort would not be cost-free.

(3) ***But Substantive Review in Court.*** We can also notice that these contested points were raised in court, and that, while the court decides that the decision was more one for the agency than for the court, the court does not treat the issues as irrelevant. It is an important feature of the APA that, although it does not do much to specify the procedures for informal adjudication, it still provides for judicial review of final agency action that is conducted in this way, and it specifies at the end of § 706 that such review shall take place on the "record" that was before the agency. That the procedure before the agency was legitimately informal might affect the intensity of judicial review—see the Mead case (p. 1283)—but it does not exempt the agency from showing that what it did was not "arbitrary or capricious."

## NOTES ON INFORMAL ADJUDICATION

(1) ***Other Rights in Informal Adjudication?*** Most of the reported litigation under § 555 has arisen, as in the Olivares case, under the requirement of § 555(e) that the agency give "a brief statement of the grounds for denial." What other rights might lurk in § 555? FRIENDS OF THE BOW V. THOMPSON, 124 F.3d 1210, 1220–21 (10th Cir. 1997): In the course of a dispute involving the sale of timber from Medicine Bow National Forest, an environmental group, Friends of the Bow, sent a letter to the Forest Supervisor requesting that the Environmental Assessment (EA) on which the sale was based be updated because of changed circumstances. No direct response to this letter was given, but the Forest Service did prepare a 26-page "Supplemental Information Report" (SIR) explaining why no new environmental report was needed; this SIR was issued about a year after the letter in question, and a copy was given to the group. In subsequent litigation, one of the claims made by Friends was that this course of behavior violated section 555(b) of the APA, which requires an agency "within a reasonable time . . . to conclude a matter presented to it."

EBEL, J.: "The government maintains, and the district court agreed, that Friends' letter is not the sort of matter to which § 555(b) applies. There is little case law on this issue. However, we believe there is a substantial argument that § 555(b) does apply to Friends' letter, which is an explicit and colorably valid request for the Service to take action arguably required of it by law to prepare a supplemental EA. First, by its terms, § 555(b) applies to all 'matters' presented to the agency. Contrary to the government's position that the provision only applies to 'proceedings' in which a person is compelled to appear, the section specifically speaks to 'agency proceedings' in which a person is 'entitled to appear,' as well as 'agency functions' and 'matters,' terms which would appear to encompass all forms of agency action. Second, while the government points out that 'agency proceedings' only includes the rulemakings, adjudications, and licensings defined in § 551 of the APA, it fails to acknowledge that § 551 defines 'adjudication' as 'the formulation of an order,' and in turn defines 'order' expansively to include the 'whole or part of a final disposition . . . other than rule making but including licensing.' That section further defines 'agency action' broadly to include not only rule makings, licensings, and orders, but also the 'failure to act.' Id. § 551(13). Thus, we assume, for the purposes of this opinion, that § 555(b) applies to the letter.

"Nonetheless, even assuming § 555(b) applies to Friends' letter, the agency's response to the letter substantially complied with the requirements of the section, as well as with the 'brief statement' requirement of § 555(e). Friends does not dispute that the SIR is an adequate 'brief statement' of the agency's reasons for not conducting a supplemental EA. Thus, the only question is whether the SIR was issued within a 'reasonable time' as is required by § 555(b).

"Friends has not pointed to a single case in which a court has reversed an agency action under § 555(b) for failure to comply with the 'reasonable time' requirements. More typically, courts have occasionally granted mandamus to force agencies to act when there has been no response to a request for agency action. But, in this case, the agency did act, by issuing the SIR. In cases where agencies acted, courts have declined to overturn agency action on the basis of the delay in situations where the agency took much longer to respond than the approximately one year period at issue here, particularly where[,] as here[,] the party opposing the action benefitted from the delay. Accordingly, we conclude the agency acted within a reasonable time in producing the SIR, particularly in light of the lengthy, detailed nature of Friends' request for action, and the thoroughness of the agency's eventual response."

(2) ***The Practical Scope of Informal Adjudication.*** Informal administrative adjudication is extremely common and extremely diverse in nature. There are innumerable interchanges between government officials and those they regulate or benefit, in which the official ultimately makes an adjudicatory decision about a particular "case," and has to develop facts to do so, but does not have any legal obligation to hold an evidentiary hearing—that is, does not have to have a structured interchange that develops a formal record that is the basis for decision. Depending on the applicable statutes and regulations, there may be a more-or-less thorough interchange with the affected party, but one that is still "informal" when judged in comparison to a "trial-type" process. The Mead case (p. 1283), which reviewed a tariff classification ruling issued by the U.S. Customs Service after an interchange with the affected party—but not a formal one—gives a good description of one example. MICHAEL ASIMOW, FEDERAL ADMINISTRATIVE ADJUDICATION OUTSIDE THE APA 90–98 (2019) (p. 529), gives many others; here are a few of his:

- "Compromising Agricultural Loans: The Farmers Home Administration uses [an informal procedure] to decide whether to compromise or forgive a farmer's home loan. The procedure is investigatory, and the borrower has no right to submit evidence or cross-examine others. 'The proceedings resemble what may be called executive procedure, that is, unilateral decision by an official on the basis of whatever information he deemed it appropriate to take into account.'" [Quoting Johnson v. Vilsack, 833 F.3d 948 (8th Cir. 2016).]

- "National Science Foundation Termination of Grants: NSF also maintains [an informal] all-written adjudication system for resolving disputes arising out of suspension or termination of grants or accounting issues. The Division Director designates a reviewing official who is at least at the level of the official who made the disputed decision but was not involved with monitoring the project. The reviewing official completes a report within 30 days, and the Division Director makes a final and non-appealable decision."
- "Licensing of National Banks: The statute and regulations describe an inquisitorial notice-and-comment-type process for determination of whether the Office of the Comptroller of the Currency should grant an application for a banking license. The decision is based on whatever information the Office discovers in its investigation, public comments, a hearing held if the Comptroller determines there is need for one, or any other source of information, including that supplied in meetings of interested parties."
- "Use of National Forests: The Forest Service can grant 'special use authorization' that permits private uses of national forest land. The regulations provide for an informal adjudication procedure in such cases."
- "Indian Affairs: A variety of regulatory decisions concerning Indians are made through [informal] adjudication. For example: *Gambling Casinos*: Applications by tribes to build gambling casinos trigger numerous factual determinations including whether the tribe is entitled to benefits under Indian Gaming Regulatory Act and whether the benefits of a particular casino outweigh its detriments. Determinations are made through a notice and comment process, rather than through evidentiary hearings."

(3) ***Yet More Informal Action?*** As already mentioned, informal adjudication appears to be the APA's residual category, negatively defined: adjudication is the formulation of an "order," which occurs "in a matter *other* than rule making," and adjudication is informal when it is *not* "required by statute to be determined on the record after opportunity for an agency hearing." But much—perhaps most—of what agencies do falls outside of even this residual category: most simply, someone answers the telephone; yet more complexly, someone does the initial work of investigation that will ultimately lead to the initiation of a rulemaking or adjudication. If one wanted to defend these exclusions on the text of the APA, one could pay attention to the fact that to be within the category of adjudication at all, an agency has to be formulating an "order," which is defined to be "a final disposition . . . in a matter." But the fact that such yet-more-informal agency

action has no procedural pedigree does not mean that it is inherently unimportant. Answering a routine inquiry may not matter much—but when the Chairman of the Federal Reserve Board gives a speech detailing her views of the economy, markets can shake. Procedurally speaking, one can only hope that she has her facts right.

## SECTION 4. DUE PROCESS AS A SOURCE OF PROCEDURAL RIGHTS IN ADJUDICATION



In earlier pages we have seen that due process has long been understood to stipulate procedural requirements in adjudication. See Londoner v. Denver, 210 U.S. 373 (1908) (p. 220), and Bi-Metallic Investment Co. v. State Bd. of Equalization of Colorado (p. 224). As stated by the Supreme Court in 1950: "Many controversies have raged about the cryptic and abstract words of the Due Process Clause but there can be no doubt that at a minimum they require that deprivation of life, liberty or property by adjudication be preceded by notice and opportunity for hearing appropriate to the nature of the case." Mullane v. Central Hanover Bank & Trust Co., 339 U.S. 306, 313 (1950). We have also noted that historically what was considered an "appropriate" hearing varied widely from subject to subject, and that the drafters of the APA attempted to capture that variety in the distinctions they drew between formal and informal adjudication, and in the subsidiary details of sections 554, 556, and 557.

The traditional law of administrative due process was reformed—some would say revolutionized—in the 1950s and 1960s, roughly at the same time that the constitutional demands on criminal procedure were also being refashioned. Perhaps the issue that most raised administrative due process concerns in the earlier part of the period was the Cold War and the excesses it spawned regarding determinations of "loyalty" and "security." One element of the ensuing debate was whether due process was to be regarded as an amalgam of particular doctrinal elements or regarded more holistically. There was Supreme Court support for both sides. In an important case decided in 1950, BAILEY V. RICHARDSON, 341 U.S. 918 (1951), the Court, by an equally divided vote, affirmed a lower court opinion upholding the discharge of a government employee for failure to pass a loyalty procedure that was very short of fair—on the basis, said the D.C. Circuit, that government employment was a "privilege" not a "right," and therefore, doctrinally speaking, not part of the "life, liberty, or property" protected by the due process clause. On the same day, 5–3, in JOINT ANTI-FASCIST REFUGEE COMM. V. MCGRATH, 341 U.S. 123 (1951), the Court said that three organizations challenging the government's designation of them as "Communist" had a cause of action. Espousing the more fluid view, JUSTICE FRANKFURTER wrote:

> ... "[D]ue process," unlike some legal rules, is not a technical conception with a fixed content unrelated to time, place and circumstances. Expressing as it does in its ultimate analysis respect enforced by law for that feeling of just treatment which has been evolved through centuries of Anglo-American constitutional history and civilization, "due process" cannot be imprisoned within the treacherous limits of any formula. Representing a profound attitude of fairness between man and man, and more particularly between the individual and government, "due process" is compounded of history, reason, the past course of decisions, and stout confidence in the strength of the democratic faith which we profess. Due process is not a mechanical instrument. It is not a yardstick. It is a process. It is a delicate process of adjustment inescapably involving the exercise of judgment by those whom the Constitution entrusted with the unfolding of the process.
>
> ... The precise nature of the interest that has been adversely affected, the manner in which this was done, the reasons for doing it, the available alternatives to the procedure that was followed, the protection implicit in the office of the functionary whose conduct is challenged, the balance of hurt complained of and good accomplished—these are some of the considerations that must enter into the judicial judgment ...
>
> This Court is not alone in recognizing that the right to be heard before being condemned to grievous loss of any kind ... is a principle basic to our society ....

This contest between doctrinalism and a more nuanced view persisted throughout the period. But as the 1950s moved into the 1960s, the principal foci changed. Moving beyond McCarthyism, the rights of those questioning the government now became a matter of how to treat the civil rights movement and anti-Vietnam war demonstrators, often students. And then, in 1970, the Supreme Court decided GOLDBERG V. KELLY, 397 U.S. 254, recognizing claims to fair process of those who were recipients of government welfare payments. Welfare, from the older doctrinal point of view, was the ultimate "privilege" to which the recipient had no "right." Either the law of due process had shed any aspiration to doctrinal statement, or a new doctrine had to be created.

(A note: There are two clauses in the Constitution that prohibit deprivation of "life, liberty, or property, without due process of law": one in the Fifth Amendment, applicable to federal government action, and one in the Fourteenth Amendment, applicable to the states. As far as adjudicatory procedure is concerned, they have always been treated as having the same content, and cases under each clause are properly cited as precedents applicable to the other. Thus, important cases arising out of state, as well as federal, administrative action are included in what follows.)

## a. The Doctrinal Framework



### BOARD OF REGENTS OF STATE COLLEGES v. ROTH

Supreme Court of the United States (1972).
408 U.S. 564.

■ JUSTICE STEWART delivered the opinion of the Court.

In 1968 the respondent, David Roth, was hired for his first teaching job as assistant professor of political science at Wisconsin State University-Oshkosh. He was hired for a fixed term of one academic year. The notice of his faculty appointment specified that his employment would begin on September 1, 1968, and would end on June 30, 1969.[1] The respondent completed that term. But he was informed that he would not be rehired for the next academic year.

The respondent had no tenure rights to continued employment. Under Wisconsin statutory law a state university teacher can acquire tenure as a "permanent" employee only after four years of year-to-year employment. Having acquired tenure, a teacher is entitled to continued employment "during efficiency and good behavior." A relatively new teacher without tenure, however, is under Wisconsin law entitled to nothing beyond his one-year appointment. There are no statutory or

1 The respondent had no contract of employment. Rather, his formal notice of appointment was the equivalent of an employment contract.

The notice of his appointment provided that: "David F. Roth is hereby appointed to the faculty of the Wisconsin State University Position number 0262. (Location:) Oshkosh as (Rank:) Assistant Professor of (Department:) Political Science this (Date:) first day of (Month:) September (Year:) 1968." The notice went on to specify that the respondent's "appointment basis" was for the "academic year." And it provided that "[r]egulations governing tenure are in accord with Chapter 37.31, Wisconsin Statutes. The employment of any staff member for an academic year shall not be for a term beyond June 30th of the fiscal year in which the appointment is made."

administrative standards defining eligibility for re-employment. State law thus clearly leaves the decision whether to rehire a nontenured teacher for another year to the unfettered discretion of university officials.

The procedural protection afforded a Wisconsin State University teacher before he is separated from the University corresponds to his job security. As a matter of statutory law, a tenured teacher cannot be "discharged except for cause upon written charges" and pursuant to certain procedures. A nontenured teacher, similarly, is protected to some extent *during* his one-year term. Rules promulgated by the Board of Regents provide that a nontenured teacher "dismissed" before the end of the year may have some opportunity for review of the "dismissal." But the Rules provide no real protection for a nontenured teacher who simply is not re-employed for the next year. He must be informed by February 1 "concerning retention or nonretention for the ensuing year." But "no reason for non-retention need be given. No review or appeal is provided in such case."

In conformance with these Rules, the President of Wisconsin State University-Oshkosh informed the respondent before February 1, 1969, that he would not be rehired for the 1969–1970 academic year. He gave the respondent no reason for the decision and no opportunity to challenge it at any sort of hearing.

The respondent then brought this action in Federal District Court alleging that the decision not to rehire him for the next year infringed his Fourteenth Amendment rights. He attacked the decision both in substance and procedure. First, he alleged that the true reason for the decision was to punish him for certain statements critical of the University administration, and that it therefore violated his right to freedom of speech.[5] Second, he alleged that the failure of University officials to give him notice of any reason for nonretention and an opportunity for a hearing violated his right to procedural due process of law.

The District Court granted summary judgment for the respondent on the procedural issue, ordering the University officials to provide him with reasons and a hearing. The Court of Appeals, with one judge dissenting, affirmed this partial summary judgment. We granted certiorari. The only question presented to us at this stage in the case is whether the respondent had a constitutional right to a statement of reasons and a hearing on the University's decision not to rehire him for another year. We hold that he did not.

[5] While the respondent alleged that he was not rehired because of his exercise of free speech, the petitioners insisted that the non-retention decision was based on other, constitutionally valid grounds. The District Court came to no conclusion whatever regarding the true reason for the University President's decision. "In the present case," it stated, "it appears that a determination as to the actual bases of [the] decision must await amplification of the facts at trial. . . . Summary judgment is inappropriate." 310 F.Supp. 972, 982.

I

The requirements of procedural due process apply only to the deprivation of interests encompassed by the Fourteenth Amendment's protection of liberty and property. When protected interests are implicated, the right to some kind of prior hearing is paramount.[7] But the range of interests protected by procedural due process is not infinite.

The District Court decided that procedural due process guarantees apply in this case by assessing and balancing the weights of the particular interests involved. It concluded that the respondent's interest in re-employment at Wisconsin State University-Oshkosh outweighed the University's interest in denying him re-employment summarily. Undeniably, the respondent's re-employment prospects were of major concern to him—concern that we surely cannot say was insignificant. And a weighing process has long been a part of any determination of the *form* of hearing required in particular situations by procedural due process.[8] But, to determine whether due process requirements apply in the first place, we must look not to the "weight" but to the *nature* of the interest at stake. We must look to see if the interest is within the Fourteenth Amendment's protection of liberty and property.

"Liberty" and "property" are broad and majestic terms. They are among the "[g]reat [constitutional] concepts . . . purposely left to gather meaning from experience. . . . [T]hey relate to the whole domain of social and economic fact, and the statesmen who founded this Nation knew too well that only a stagnant society remains unchanged." National Ins. Co. v. Tidewater Co., 337 U.S. 582, 646 [(1949)] (Frankfurter, J., dissenting). For that reason, the Court has fully and finally rejected the wooden distinction between "rights" and "privileges" that once seemed to govern the applicability of procedural due process rights.[9] The Court has also made clear that the property interests protected by procedural due

---

[7] Before a person is deprived of a protected interest, he must be afforded opportunity for some kind of a hearing, "except for extraordinary situations where some valid governmental interest is at stake that justifies postponing the hearing until after the event." Boddie v. Connecticut, 401 U.S. 371, 379 [(1971)]. "While '[m]any controversies have raged about . . . the Due Process Clause,' . . . it is fundamental that except in emergency situations (and this is not one) due process requires that when a State seeks to terminate [a protected] interest . . . , it must afford 'notice and opportunity for hearing appropriate to the nature of the case' before the termination becomes effective." Bell v. Burson, 402 U.S. 535, 542 [(1971)]. For the rare and extraordinary situations in which we have held that deprivation of a protected interest need not be preceded by opportunity for some kind of hearing, see, e.g., Phillips v. Commissioner of Internal Revenue, 283 U.S. 589, 597 [(1931)].

[8] "The formality and procedural requisites for the hearing can vary, depending upon the importance of the interests involved and the nature of the subsequent proceedings." Boddie v. Connecticut, 401 U.S. [371,] 378 [(1971)]. See, e.g., Goldberg v. Kelly, 397 U.S. 254, 263 [(1970)]. The constitutional requirement of opportunity for some form of hearing before deprivation of a protected interest, of course, does not depend upon such a narrow balancing process.

[9] In a leading case decided many years ago, the Court of Appeals for the District of Columbia Circuit held that public employment in general was a "privilege," not a "right," and that procedural due process guarantees therefore were inapplicable. Bailey v. Richardson, 182 F.2d 46, aff'd by an equally divided Court, 341 U.S. 918 [(1951)]. The basis of this holding has been thoroughly undermined in the ensuing years. For, as Justice Blackmun wrote for the Court only last year, "this Court now has rejected the concept that constitutional rights turn upon whether a governmental benefit is characterized as a 'right' or as a 'privilege.'" Graham v. Richardson, 403 U.S. 365, 374 [(1971)].

process extend well beyond actual ownership of real estate, chattels, or money. By the same token, the Court has required due process protection for deprivations of liberty beyond the sort of formal constraints imposed by the criminal process.

Yet, while the Court has eschewed rigid or formalistic limitations on the protection of procedural due process, it has at the same time observed certain boundaries. For the words "liberty" and "property" in the Due Process Clause of the Fourteenth Amendment must be given some meaning.

II

"While this Court has not attempted to define with exactness the liberty . . . guaranteed [by the Fourteenth Amendment], the term has received much consideration and some of the included things have been definitely stated. Without doubt, it denotes not merely freedom from bodily restraint but also the right of the individual to contract, to engage in any of the common occupations of life, to acquire useful knowledge, to marry, establish a home and bring up children, to worship God according to the dictates of his own conscience, and generally to enjoy those privileges long recognized . . . as essential to the orderly pursuit of happiness by free men." Meyer v. Nebraska, 262 U.S. 390, 399 [(1923)]. In a Constitution for a free people, there can be no doubt that the meaning of "liberty" must be broad indeed.

There might be cases in which a State refused to re-employ a person under such circumstances that interests in liberty would be implicated. But this is not such a case.

The State, in declining to rehire the respondent, did not make any charge against him that might seriously damage his standing and associations in his community. It did not base the nonrenewal of his contract on a charge, for example, that he had been guilty of dishonesty, or immorality. Had it done so, this would be a different case. For "[w]here a person's good name, reputation, honor, or integrity is at stake because of what the government is doing to him, notice and an opportunity to be heard are essential." Wisconsin v. Constantineau, 400 U.S. 433, 437 [(1971)] . . . In such a case, due process would accord an opportunity to refute the charge before University officials.[12] In the present case, however, there is no suggestion whatever that the respondent's "good name, reputation, honor, or integrity" is at stake.

Similarly, there is no suggestion that the State, in declining to reemploy the respondent, imposed on him a stigma or other disability that foreclosed his freedom to take advantage of other employment opportunities. The State, for example, did not invoke any regulations to

[12] The purpose of such notice and hearing is to provide the person an opportunity to clear his name. Once a person has cleared his name at a hearing, his employer, of course, may remain free to deny him future employment for other reasons.

bar the respondent from all other public employment in state universities. Had it done so, this, again, would be a different case. . . .[13]

To be sure, the respondent has alleged that the nonrenewal of his contract was based on his exercise of his right to freedom of speech. But this allegation is not now before us. The District Court stayed proceedings on this issue, and the respondent has yet to prove that the decision not to rehire him was, in fact, based on his free speech activities.

Hence, on the record before us, all that clearly appears is that the respondent was not rehired for one year at one university. It stretches the concept too far to suggest that a person is deprived of "liberty" when he simply is not rehired in one job but remains as free as before to seek another.

III

The Fourteenth Amendment's procedural protection of property is a safeguard of the security of interests that a person has already acquired in specific benefits. These interests—property interests—may take many forms.

Thus, the Court has held that a person receiving welfare benefits under statutory and administrative standards defining eligibility for them has an interest in continued receipt of those benefits that is safeguarded by procedural due process. Goldberg v. Kelly, 297 U.S. 294 [(1970)]. Similarly, in the area of public employment, the Court has held that a public college professor dismissed from an office held under tenure provisions, Slochower v. Board of Education, 350 U.S. 551 [(1956)], and college professors and staff members dismissed during the terms of their contracts, Wieman v. Updegraff, 344 U.S. 183 [(1952)], have interests in continued employment that are safeguarded by due process. Only last year, the Court held that this principle "proscribing summary dismissal from public employment without hearing or inquiry required by due process" also applied to a teacher recently hired without tenure or a formal contract, but nonetheless with a clearly implied promise of continued employment. Connell v. Higginbotham, 403 U.S. 207, 208 [(1971)].

Certain attributes of "property" interests protected by procedural due process emerge from these decisions. To have a property interest in a benefit, a person clearly must have more than an abstract need or desire for it. He must have more than a unilateral expectation of it. He

---

[13] The District Court made an assumption "that non-retention by one university or college creates concrete and practical difficulties for a professor in his subsequent academic career." 310 F.Supp., at 979. And the Court of Appeals based its affirmance of the summary judgment largely on the premise that "the substantial adverse effect non-retention is likely to have upon the career interests of an individual professor" amounts to a limitation on future employment opportunities sufficient to invoke procedural due process guarantees. 446 F.2d, at 809. But even assuming, arguendo, that such a "substantial adverse effect" under these circumstances would constitute a state-imposed restriction on liberty, the record contains no support for these assumptions. There is no suggestion of how nonretention might affect the respondent's future employment prospects. Mere proof, for example, that his record of nonretention in one job, taken alone, might make him somewhat less attractive to some other employers would hardly establish the kind of foreclosure of opportunities amounting to a deprivation of "liberty."

must, instead, have a legitimate claim of entitlement to it. It is a purpose of the ancient institution of property to protect those claims upon which people rely in their daily lives, reliance that must not be arbitrarily undermined. It is a purpose of the constitutional right to a hearing to provide an opportunity for a person to vindicate those claims.

Property interests, of course, are not created by the Constitution. Rather, they are created and their dimensions are defined by existing rules or understandings that stem from an independent source such as state law—rules or understandings that secure certain benefits and that support claims of entitlement to those benefits. Thus, the welfare recipients in Goldberg v. Kelly had a claim of entitlement to welfare payments that was grounded in the statute defining eligibility for them. The recipients had not yet shown that they were, in fact, within the statutory terms of eligibility. But we held that they had a right to a hearing at which they might attempt to do so.

Just as the welfare recipients' "property" interest in welfare payments was created and defined by statutory terms, so the respondent's "property" interest in employment at Wisconsin State University-Oshkosh was created and defined by the terms of his appointment. Those terms secured his interest in employment up to June 30, 1969. But the important fact in this case is that they specifically provided that the respondent's employment was to terminate on June 30. They did not provide for contract renewal absent "sufficient cause." Indeed, they made no provision for renewal whatsoever.

Thus, the terms of the respondent's appointment secured absolutely no interest in re-employment for the next year. They supported absolutely no possible claim of entitlement to re-employment. Nor, significantly, was there any state statute or University rule or policy that secured his interest in reemployment or that created any legitimate claim to it.[16] In these circumstances, the respondent surely had an abstract concern in being rehired, but he did not have a *property* interest sufficient to require the University authorities to give him a hearing when they declined to renew his contract of employment.

IV

Our analysis of the respondent's constitutional rights in this case in no way indicates a view that an opportunity for a hearing or a statement of reasons for nonretention would, or would not, be appropriate or wise in public colleges and universities. For it is a written Constitution that we apply. Our role is confined to interpretation of that Constitution.

We must conclude that the summary judgment for the respondent should not have been granted, since the respondent has not shown that he was deprived of liberty or property protected by the Fourteenth

[16] To be sure, the respondent does suggest that most teachers hired on a year-to-year basis by Wisconsin State University-Oshkosh are, in fact, rehired. But the District Court has not found that there is anything approaching a "common law" of re-employment, see Perry v. Sindermann, so strong as to require University officials to give the respondent a statement of reasons and a hearing on their decision not to rehire him.

Amendment. The judgment of the Court of Appeals, accordingly, is reversed and the case is remanded for further proceedings consistent with this opinion.[1]

■ JUSTICE MARSHALL, dissenting.

. . . While I agree with Part I of the Court's opinion, setting forth the proper framework for consideration of the issue presented, and also with those portions of Parts II and III of the Court's opinion that assert that a public employee is entitled to procedural due process whenever a State stigmatizes him by denying employment, or injures his future employment prospects severely, or whenever the State deprives him of a property interest, I would go further than the Court does in defining the terms "liberty" and "property."

. . . [W]hether or not a private employer is free to act capriciously or unreasonably with respect to employment practices, at least absent statutory or contractual controls, a government employer is different. The government may only act fairly and reasonably.

In my view, every citizen who applies for a government job is entitled to it unless the government can establish some reason for denying the employment. This is the "property" right that I believe is protected by the Fourteenth Amendment and that cannot be denied "without due process of law." And it is also liberty—liberty to work—which is the "very essence of the personal freedom and opportunity" secured by the Fourteenth Amendment. This Court has often had occasion to note that the denial of public employment is a serious blow to any citizen. Thus, when an application for public employment is denied or the contract of a government employee is not renewed, the government must say why, for it is only when the reasons underlying government action are known that citizens feel secure and protected against arbitrary government action.

Employment is one of the greatest, if not the greatest, benefits that governments offer in modern-day life. When something as valuable as the opportunity to work is at stake, the government may not reward some citizens and not others without demonstrating that its actions are fair and equitable. And it is procedural due process that is our fundamental guarantee of fairness, our protection against arbitrary, capricious, and unreasonable government action.

It may be argued that to provide procedural due process to all public employees or prospective employees would place an intolerable burden on the machinery of government. Cf. Goldberg v. Kelly. The short answer to that argument is that it is not burdensome to give reasons when reasons exist. Whenever an application for employment is denied, an employee is discharged, or a decision not to rehire an employee is made, there should be some reason for the decision. It can scarcely be argued

---

[1] [Ed.] See the Chronicle of Higher Education, Nov. 26, 1973, p. 3, col. 1: "David F. Roth . . . has been awarded $6,746 in damages in federal district court. . . . A six-person jury found that Mr. Roth's constitutional right to free speech was violated by [Wisconsin State University at Oshkosh]. . . . Judge Doyle also has yet to rule on requests from Mr. Roth for reinstatement in his position at Oshkosh. . . . Even if Judge Doyle orders his reinstatement, Mr. Roth is not likely to return to Oshkosh, since he now teaches at Purdue University."

that government would be crippled by a requirement that the reason be communicated to the person most directly affected by the government's action.

Where there are numerous applicants for jobs, it is likely that few will choose to demand reasons for not being hired. But, if the demand for reasons is exceptionally great, summary procedures can be devised that would provide fair and adequate information to all persons. As long as the government has a good reason for its actions it need not fear disclosure. It is only where the government acts improperly that procedural due process is truly burdensome. And that is precisely when it is most necessary . . .

[CHIEF JUSTICE BURGER and JUSTICES WHITE, BLACKMUN, and REHNQUIST joined JUSTICE STEWART. JUSTICE POWELL took no part in the case. JUSTICES BRENNAN and DOUGLAS were, like JUSTICE MARSHALL, dissenters; their opinions have not been reproduced. Finally, CHIEF JUSTICE BURGER also filed a concurring opinion, reproduced following the next case.]

## PERRY v. SINDERMANN

Supreme Court of the United States (1972).
408 U.S. 593.

■ JUSTICE STEWART delivered the opinion of the Court.

[In this case, considered with Board of Regents v. Roth, Robert Sindermann had worked for the state college system of Texas for ten years, during the last four of which he was a full professor at Odessa Junior College. He had successive one-year contracts, as Odessa had no tenure system. In the 1968–69 academic year, he was elected president of the Texas Junior College Teachers Association and, as such, publicly opposed policies of the Board of Regents. In May 1969, his contract expired and the Regents voted not to offer him a new one. They issued a press release claiming he had been insubordinate but gave him no official statement of reasons for nonrenewal and held no hearing in which he might challenge his discharge. Sindermann sued the Regents and the college's president, claiming a violation of his rights to free speech and procedural due process. The defendants denied that he had been fired in retaliation for his public criticism and argued that they had no obligation to give him a hearing.

Based on a very slim record, the district court granted summary judgment for the college officials. The court of appeals reversed. As to free speech, it remanded for trial as to the actual reason for the Regents' decision. As to due process, it remanded to allow Sindermann to show that he had an "expectancy" of reemployment. The Supreme Court first considered the First Amendment claim and held that this claim could be proved even if Sindermann lacked a contractual or tenure right to re-employment:]

For at least a quarter-century, this Court has made clear that even though a person has no "right" to a valuable governmental benefit and even though the government may deny him the benefit for any number of reasons, there are some reasons upon which the government may not rely. It may not deny a benefit to a person on a basis that infringes his constitutionally protected interests—especially, his interest in freedom of speech. . . . [On remand, Sindermann must be given the opportunity to prove his allegations of retaliatory refusal to rehire. The Court then continued:]

The respondent's lack of formal contractual or tenure security in continued employment at Odessa Junior College, though irrelevant to his free speech claim, is highly relevant to his procedural due process claim. But it may not be entirely dispositive.

We have held today in Board of Regents v. Roth that the Constitution does not require opportunity for a hearing before the nonrenewal of a nontenured teacher's contract, unless he can show that the decision not to rehire him somehow deprived him of an interest in "liberty" or that he had a "property" interest in continued employment, despite the lack of tenure or a formal contract. In Roth the teacher had not made a showing on either point to justify summary judgment in his favor.

Similarly, the respondent here has yet to show that he has been deprived of an interest that could invoke procedural due process protection. As in Roth, the mere showing that he was not rehired in one particular job, without more, did not amount to a showing of a loss of liberty. Nor did it amount to a showing of a loss of property.

But the respondent's allegations—which we must construe most favorably to the respondent at this stage of the litigation—do raise a genuine issue as to his interest in continued employment at Odessa Junior College. He alleged that this interest, though not secured by a formal contractual tenure provision, was secured by a no less binding understanding fostered by the college administration. In particular, the respondent alleged that the college had a de facto tenure program, and that he had tenure under that program. He claimed that he and others legitimately relied upon an unusual provision that had been in the college's official Faculty Guide for many years:

> *Teacher Tenure:* Odessa College has no tenure system. The Administration of the College wishes the faculty member to feel that he has permanent tenure as long as his teaching services are satisfactory and as long as he displays a cooperative attitude toward his co-workers and his superiors, and as long as he is happy in his work.

Moreover, the respondent claimed legitimate reliance upon guidelines promulgated by the Coordinating Board of the Texas College and University System that provided that a person, like himself, who had been employed as a teacher in the state college and university system for seven years or more has some form of job tenure. Thus, the respondent offered to prove that a teacher with his long period of service at this particular State College had no less a "property" interest in continued employment than a formally tenured teacher at other colleges, and had no less a procedural due process right to a statement of reasons and a hearing before college officials upon their decision not to retain him.

We have made clear in Roth that "property" interests subject to procedural due process protection are not limited by a few rigid, technical forms. Rather, "property" denotes a broad range of interests that are secured by "existing rules or understandings." A person's interest in a benefit is a "property" interest for due process purposes if there are such rules or mutually explicit understandings that support his claim of entitlement to the benefit and that he may invoke at a hearing.

A written contract with an explicit tenure provision clearly is evidence of a formal understanding that supports a teacher's claim of entitlement to continued employment unless sufficient "cause" is shown. Yet absence of such an explicit contractual provision may not always foreclose the possibility that a teacher has a "property" interest in re-employment. For example, the law of contracts in most, if not all, jurisdictions long has employed a process by which agreements, though not formalized in writing, may be "implied." 3 A. Corbin on Contracts §§ 561–572A (1960). Explicit contractual provisions may be supplemented by other agreements implied from "the promisor's words and conduct in the light of the surrounding circumstances." Id., at § 562. And, "[t]he meaning of [the promisor's] words and acts is found by relating them to the usage of the past." Ibid.

A teacher, like the respondent, who has held his position for a number of years, might be able to show from the circumstances of this service—and from other relevant facts—that he has a legitimate claim of entitlement to job tenure . . . This is particularly likely in a college or university, like Odessa Junior College, that has no explicit tenure system even for senior members of its faculty, but that nonetheless may have created such a system in practice. See C. Byse & L. Joughin, Tenure in American Higher Education 17–28 (1959).[7]

In this case, the respondent has alleged the existence of rules and understandings, promulgated and fostered by state officials, that may justify his legitimate claim of entitlement to continued employment absent "sufficient cause." We disagree with the Court of Appeals insofar as it held that a mere subjective "expectancy" is protected by procedural due process, but we agree that the respondent must be given an opportunity to prove the legitimacy of his claim of such entitlement in light of "the policies and practices of the institution." 430 F.2d, at 943. Proof of such a property interest would not, of course, entitle him to reinstatement. But such proof would obligate college officials to grant a

[7] We do not now hold that the respondent has any such legitimate claim of entitlement to job tenure. For "[p]roperty interests . . . are not created by the Constitution. Rather, they are created and their dimensions are defined by existing rules or understandings that stem from an independent source such as state law. . . ." Board of Regents v. Roth, at 577. If it is the law of Texas that a teacher in the respondent's position has no contractual or other claim to job tenure, the respondent's claim would be defeated.

hearing at his request, where he could be informed of the grounds for his nonretention and challenge their sufficiency.

Therefore, while we do not wholly agree with the opinion of the Court of Appeals, its judgment remanding this case to the District Court is

Affirmed.[2]

■ CHIEF JUSTICE BURGER, concurring.

I concur in the Court's judgments and opinions in Sindermann and Roth, but there is one central point in both decisions that I would like to underscore. . . . [T]he relationship between a state institution and one of its teachers is essentially a matter of state concern and state law. The Court holds today only that a state-employed teacher who has a right to re-employment under state law, arising from either an express or implied contract, has, in turn, a right guaranteed by the Fourteenth Amendment to some form of prior administrative or academic hearing on the cause for nonrenewal of his contract. Thus, whether a particular teacher in a particular context has any right to such administrative hearing hinges on a question of state law. . . .

[JUSTICES BRENNAN, DOUGLAS, and MARSHALL agreed with the First Amendment portion of the Court's opinion but also voted "to direct the District Court to enter summary judgment for respondent entitling him to a statement of reasons why his contract was not renewed and a hearing on disputed issues of fact." JUSTICE POWELL took no part in the case.]

## NOTES ON THE ROTH AND SINDERMANN CASES

(1) ***Where Are Roth and Sindermann Coming from?*** Roth and Sindermann were decided two years after—and in response to—the Supreme Court's famous decision in GOLDBERG V. KELLY, 397 U.S. 254 (1970). There, in the words of JUSTICE BRENNAN, "the question for decision [was] whether a State that terminates public assistance payments to a particular recipient without affording him the opportunity for an evidentiary hearing prior to termination denies the recipient procedural due process in violation of the Due Process Clause of the Fourteenth Amendment." 397 U.S. at 255. The Court answered in the affirmative. 397 U.S. at 263–66:

"It is true, of course, that some governmental benefits may be administratively terminated without affording the recipient a pre-termination evidentiary hearing. But we agree with the District Court that when welfare is discontinued, only a pre-termination evidentiary hearing provides the recipient with procedural due process. For qualified recipients, welfare provides the means to obtain essential food, clothing, housing, and medical care. Thus the crucial factor in this context—a factor not present in the case of the blacklisted government contractor, the discharged

---

[2] [Ed.] See the Odessa American, Nov. 12, 1972, p. 1, col. 1: "Robert P. Sindermann flew to Odessa Saturday and picked up the $48,000 check made out to him by Odessa College in settlement of his lawsuit stemming from the college's refusal to rehire him in 1969. . . .

"The 43-year-old former Odessa College government teacher said one of the conditions of the settlement was that the college offered to reinstate him. 'I have politely declined the invitation,' Sindermann grinned."

government employee, the taxpayer denied a tax exemption, or virtually anyone else whose governmental entitlements are ended—is that termination of aid pending resolution of a controversy over eligibility may deprive an eligible recipient of the very means by which to live while he waits. Since he lacks independent resources, his situation becomes immediately desperate. His need to concentrate upon finding the means for daily subsistence, in turn, adversely affects his ability to seek redress from the welfare bureaucracy.

"Moreover, important governmental interests are promoted by affording recipients a pre-termination evidentiary hearing. From its founding the Nation's basic commitment has been to foster the dignity and well-being of all persons within its borders. We have come to recognize that forces not within the control of the poor contribute to their poverty. This perception, against the background of our traditions, has significantly influenced the development of the contemporary public assistance system. Welfare, by meeting the basic demands of subsistence, can help bring within the reach of the poor the same opportunities that are available to others to participate meaningfully in the life of the community. At the same time, welfare guards against the societal malaise that may flow from a widespread sense of unjustified frustration and insecurity. Public assistance, then, is not mere charity, but a means to 'promote the general Welfare, and secure the Blessings of Liberty to ourselves and our Posterity.' The same governmental interests that counsel the provision of welfare, counsel as well its uninterrupted provision to those eligible to receive it; pre-termination evidentiary hearings are indispensable to that end.

"Appellant does not challenge the force of these considerations but argues that they are outweighed by countervailing governmental interests in conserving fiscal and administrative resources. These interests, the argument goes, justify the delay of any evidentiary hearing until after discontinuance of the grants. Summary adjudication protects the public fisc by stopping payments promptly upon discovery of reason to believe that a recipient is no longer eligible. Since most terminations are accepted without challenge, summary adjudication also conserves both the fisc and administrative time and energy by reducing the number of evidentiary hearings actually held.

"We agree with the District Court, however, that these governmental interests are not overriding in the welfare context. . . ."

The Court proceeded to specify the pre-termination procedure that would be needed. Although it stated that it was not requiring a "judicial or quasi-judicial trial," the Court's demands appeared to many readers to be quite formal: evidence had to be presented orally, cross-examination had to be permitted, and the outcome had to be based on the record so made.

Goldberg was understood, by both the dissenting justices and the commentators, to be making a sharp break with tradition by extending constitutional protection to something—the provision of welfare grants—that had previously been seen as a "privilege" rather than a "right." On this doctrinal question, JUSTICE BRENNAN answered, 397 U.S. at 261–63:

"[The State] does not contend that procedural due process is not applicable to the termination of welfare benefits. Such benefits are a matter of statutory entitlement for persons qualified to receive them.[8] Their termination involves state action that adjudicates important rights. The constitutional challenge cannot be answered by an argument that public assistance benefits are 'a privilege and not a right.' Shapiro v. Thompson, 394 U.S. 618, 627 n. 6 (1969). Relevant constitutional restraints apply as much to the withdrawal of public assistance benefits as to disqualification for unemployment compensation, Sherbert v. Verner, 374 U.S. 398 (1963); or to denial of a tax exemption, Speiser v. Randall, 357 U.S. 513 (1958); or to discharge from public employment, Slochower v. Board of Higher Education, 350 U.S. 551 (1956). The extent to which procedural due process must be afforded the recipient is influenced by the extent to which he may be 'condemned to suffer grievous loss,' Joint Anti-Fascist Refugee Committee v. McGrath, 341 U.S. 123, 168 (1951) (Frankfurter, J., concurring), and depends upon whether the recipient's interest in avoiding that loss outweighs the governmental interest in summary adjudication. Accordingly, as we said in Cafeteria & Restaurant Workers Union v. McElroy, 367 U.S. 886, 895 (1961), 'consideration of what procedures due process may require under any given set of circumstances must begin with a determination of the precise nature of the government function involved as well as of the private interest that has been affected by governmental action.' "

How far did this language go? Was fair procedure constitutionally required because of the immediate needs of recipients—in effect accepting Justice Frankfurter's view that due process is triggered whenever the government imposes "grievous loss" on the individual? Or was the constitutionally crucial fact that "[s]uch benefits are a matter of statutory entitlement for persons qualified to receive them"? Or was the whole matter contingent on the concession of the defendants that due process was applicable? Roth and Sindermann may be seen as an effort to answer those questions.

(2) ***What Is the Constitutional Basis of the Roth/Sindermann Doctrine?*** If the constitutional phrase *deprive any person of life, liberty, or property* "must be given some meaning" (Justice Stewart's phrase), is the meaning announced by Roth any stronger textually than the meaning

---

[8] [Note by the Court] It may be realistic today to regard welfare entitlements as more like "property" than a "gratuity." Much of the existing wealth in this country takes the form of rights that do not fall within traditional common-law concepts of property. It has been aptly noted that

> [s]ociety today is built around entitlement. The automobile dealer has his franchise, the doctor and lawyer their professional licenses, the worker his union membership, contract, and pension rights, the executive his contract and stock options; all are devices to aid security and independence. Many of the most important of these entitlements now flow from government: subsidies to farmers and businessmen, routes for airlines and channels for television stations; long term contracts for defense, space, and education; social security pensions for individuals. Such sources of security, whether private or public, are no longer regarded as luxuries or gratuities; to the recipients they are essentials, fully deserved, and in no sense a form of charity. It is only the poor whose entitlements, although recognized by public policy, have not been effectively enforced.

Reich, Individual Rights and Social Welfare: The Emerging Legal Issues, 74 Yale L.J. 1245, 1255 (1965). See also Reich, The New Property, 73 Yale L.J. 733 (1964).

asserted by the older cases? Isn't a distinction between "rights" (claims thought to exist prior to governmental action) and "privileges" (claims that depend on governmental grant) a perfectly good reading of the text? If the reason for rejecting this old distinction is that "only a stagnant society remains unchanged," as the Roth opinion suggests, why do we have to give an independent doctrinal significance to *each* element of the constitutional text? Assuming we do give an independent significance to each element, why does the Court feel able to describe "liberty" interests using its own voice, yet as to "property" interests it says that "they are created and their dimensions are defined by existing rules or understandings that stem from an independent source such as state law."

(3) ***The Bitter with the Sweet?*** Roth and Sindermann plainly say that statutorily created property interests "count" for due process purposes. At the same time, they assume that the procedural consequences of having a property interest are set by the due process clause. What if the very statute that creates a property interest also specifies the procedure by which it is to be tested? ARNETT V. KENNEDY, 416 U.S. 134 (1974), dealt with a federal civil service statute that had that very character. Two members of a badly split Supreme Court majority upheld the statute because they thought its procedures were sufficiently full to meet due process standards. But the other three—with Justice Rehnquist writing, but including Justice Stewart, author of the cases we just read—said that a federal employee, in such circumstances, had no due process claim independent of the statutory procedures Congress had chosen:

> Congress was obviously intent on according a measure of statutory job security to governmental employees which they had not previously enjoyed, but was likewise intent on excluding more elaborate procedural requirements which it felt would make the operation of the new scheme unnecessarily burdensome in practice. Where the focus of legislation was thus strongly on the procedural mechanism for enforcing the substantive right which was simultaneously conferred, we decline to conclude that the substantive right may be viewed wholly apart from the procedure provided for its enforcement. The employee's statutorily defined right is not a guarantee against removal without cause in the abstract, but such a guarantee as enforced by the procedures which Congress has designated for the determination of cause.

416 U.S. at 152. Or, as Rehnquist more pithily continued, "[W]here the grant of a substantive right is inextricably intertwined with the limitations on the procedures which are to be employed in determining that right, a litigant in the position of appellee must take the bitter with the sweet." Id. at 153–54.

This theory, however, did not last. In CLEVELAND BOARD OF EDUCATION V. LOUDERMILL, 470 U.S. 532 (1985), the Court explicitly eschewed it:

> [T]he "bitter with the sweet" approach misconceives the constitutional guarantee. If a clearer holding is needed, we provide it today. The point is straight-forward: the Due Process Clause provides that certain substantive rights—life, liberty, and

> property—cannot be deprived except pursuant to constitutionally adequate procedures. The categories of substance and procedure are distinct. Were the rule otherwise, the Clause would be reduced to a mere tautology. "Property" cannot be defined by the procedures provided for its deprivation any more than can life or liberty. . . . In short, once it is determined that the Due Process Clause applies, "the question remains what process is due." Morrissey v. Brewer, 408 U.S. 471, 481 (1972). The answer to that question is not to be found in the . . . statute.

470 U.S. at 541. In short, under the Court's current doctrine, due process questions entail two levels of analysis: is "life, liberty or property" at stake? If so, is the process provided adequate (which is to say, "due") process?

(4) ***How Far Do Roth/Sindermann Go?*** Both of these cases dealt with the question of when government employment constitutes a property interest for the due process clause. Goldberg dealt with welfare benefits. What about other types of relationships to government? The archetypical administrative relationship—being subject to governmental regulation—is the least difficult to analyze. The very idea of "regulation" assumes that the party being regulated could have acted differently if government had not intervened. In legal terms, that is almost always equivalent to saying that the party being regulated had a common law right to do something different: because of the property it owned, because of its freedom to contract, or based on other common law rights. In other words, when "regulation" is enforced through adjudication, it ordinarily threatens to deprive someone of a common law "right" that can be viewed as either "liberty" or "property" and is therefore subject to the demands of due process.

(5) ***Government Contracts.*** Do contracts with governmental entities also create "property" in the Roth-Sindermann sense? The answer cannot be "No": the Court in Sindermann explicitly references principles of contract law in explaining why Sindermann may have a provable claim to tenure. The answer cannot be "Yes": that would mean that every federal, state, and local government procurement contract—from stealth bombers to bus transportation for school children to paperclips—would support a due process claim to an administrative hearing if a dispute arose about payment. So the answer must be "Sometimes." But when?

In LUJAN V. G & G FIRE SPRINKLERS, INC., 532 U.S. 189 (2001), plaintiff challenged a provision of the California Labor Code that permitted governmental units to withhold payments from a contractor on a public works project if the contractor or any of its subcontractors failed to comply with Code requirements. Without conducting any sort of hearing before or after its determination, the state's Division of Labor Standards Enforcement (DLSE) concluded that G & G, a subcontractor on several projects, had failed to pay its workers the "prevailing wage" as the Code required. It therefore directed that amounts equal to the underpayment, plus penalties, be withheld from contract payments to the prime contractors who used G & G. The prime contractors in turn (as required by the Code) withheld the disputed amount from payments to G & G on the subcontracts. The Court of Appeals held that G & G had a property interest in being paid in full for the work completed and that due process required the DLSE to provide a hearing on the issue of Code violation, either before the withholding order or promptly thereafter. The Supreme Court unanimously reversed.

CHIEF JUSTICE REHNQUIST's opinion "assume[d] without deciding that the withholding of money due [G & G] under its contracts occurred under color of state law, and that . . . [G & G] has a property interest . . . in its claim for payments under its contracts." However: "In [prior cases], the claimant was denied a right by virtue of which he was presently entitled either to exercise ownership dominion over real or personal property, or to pursue a gainful occupation. Unlike those claimants, respondent has not been denied any present entitlement. G & G has been deprived of payment that it contends it is owed under a contract, based on the State's determination that G & G failed to comply with the contract's terms. G & G has only a claim that it did comply with those terms and therefore that it is entitled to be paid in full. Though we assume for purposes of decision here that G & G has a property interest in its claim for payment, it is an interest, unlike the interests discussed above, that can be fully protected by an ordinary breach-of-contract suit. . . . We hold that if California makes ordinary judicial process available to respondent for resolving its contractual dispute, that process is due process."

The Fire Sprinklers case thus has the effect of moving the issue from whether a particular contract right is "property" to whether a particular contract right is the kind of "property" that comprises a "present entitlement." If it is not a "present entitlement," then ordinary breach-of-contract remedies are, it seems, per se sufficient. Judge Cudahy of the Seventh Circuit: "[A] fine line distinguishes factual scenarios in which a judicial remedy for breach of contract is adequate from those in which it is not. Not all injuries are equal, and not all parties can be made whole through a breach of contract action. The somewhat obscure quality that separates one from the other is important and yet eludes precise definition. The Supreme Court has referred to this mysterious element as a 'present entitlement.' " Baird v. Bd. of Educ. for Warren Community Unit School Dist. No. 205, 389 F.3d 685, 691 (7th Cir. 2004). The cases are very fact specific; among the factors lower courts have mentioned are whether the contract is purely financial or, rather, involves elements of personality, and whether the need for a remedy is time sensitive.

(6) ***Prisons.*** There is a long line of Supreme Court cases dealing with prisoners' claims, especially state prisoners' claims, that they were being subjected to harsh conditions—for example, solitary confinement—without proper process. Such claims must first address the fact that people in prison have already had a fair full-dress trial (or had the right to one but waived it to plead guilty), and that the trial process authorized a deprivation of their constitutionally grounded liberty. Are there limitations on what the state can do, after such a conviction, without holding a further hearing?

Many of the earlier cases analyzed this question on analogy to the differences between Roth and Sindermann: states could, for example, reassign prisoners to different conditions of confinement at will if no substantive standards existed that controlled prison officials. But if a state had established substantive standards for reassignment, then the prisoners had a state-created liberty interest sufficient to warrant investigating whether the process by which those standards were applied was adequate. This doctrine was subject to the work-a-day criticism that it required judges to decide whether various state laws delineating prison officials' duties did, or did not, create "entitlements" for prisoners. It was also subject to the root-and-branch criticism that it created an incentive for establishing statutorily authorized official arbitrariness in the prisons. And it was subject to the institutional criticism that it deeply enmeshed the federal courts in the conduct of state penal institutions.

In SANDIN V. CONNER, 515 U.S. 472 (1995), and WILKINSON V. AUSTIN, 545 U.S. 209 (2005), the Court crafted a new analysis. The question now is whether what the prison is doing "imposes atypical and significant hardship on the inmate in relation to the ordinary incidents of prison life." Sandin, 515 U.S. at 484. If so, further process is required because what is at issue is a deprivation of "liberty" beyond that authorized by the original trial. In Sandin, the Court held that thirty days of segregated confinement did not dramatically depart from the ordinary conditions of prison confinement; in Wilkinson, the Court said that indefinite solitary confinement, with "especially severe limitations on all human contact" and associated loss of eligibility for parole, were sufficiently atypical to constitute an infringement on liberty beyond that expected from just having been convicted of a crime. So in Wilkinson, Fourteenth Amendment "liberty" was at stake—but the state procedures already in place to determine whether the deprivation was justified were found to be sufficient to count as the process that was "due."

Some circuits have read the Sandin test to be in addition to, rather than a complete substitute for, the older entitlement test. On this view, prisoners get to the question of "What process is due?" only by passing both tests. E.g., Prieto v. Clarke, 780 F.3d 245, 248–49 (4th Cir. 2015).

(7) ***Reputation and Stigma Plus.*** In WISCONSIN V. CONSTANTINEAU, 400 U.S. 433 (1971), a Wisconsin statute authorized police departments to "post" notices in liquor stores declaring specific individuals to be habitual drunkards without giving the individuals a chance to object. The Court held that inflicting the stigma of "posting" required notice and an opportunity to be heard. Then, in PAUL V. DAVIS, 424 U.S. 693 (1976), the Court held that the circulation by the police to stores of the names and pictures of "active shoplifters" did not require any process because no protected interested was implicated. But what about Constantineau having said: "Where a person's good name, reputation, honor, or integrity is at stake because of what the government is doing to him, notice and an opportunity to be heard are essential?" The Paul Court said that the phrase "what the government is doing to him" referred to the fact that Constantineau, having been "posted," could no longer legally buy liquor, "and it was that alteration of legal status which, combined with the injury resulting from the defamation, justified the invocation of procedural safeguards. The 'stigma' resulting from the defamatory character of the posting was doubtless an important factor in evaluating the extent of harm worked by that act, but we do not think that such defamation, standing alone, deprived Constantineau of any 'liberty'

protected by the procedural guarantees of the Fourteenth Amendment." Thus was born the doctrine known ever since as "stigma plus." There are a great many cases in the lower courts. One common fact pattern is discharge from government employment (the "plus" even if the discharge was lawful) coupled with the public announcement of a reason for the discharge commonly seen as derogatory (the "stigma"), leading to a demand by the discharged employee for a hearing in which he can clear his name. For a recent, successful example, see Cannon v. Village of Bald Head Island, 891 F.3d 489 (4th Cir. 2018).

(8) ***What About Living with a Spouse?*** In KERRY V. DIN, 576 U.S. 86 (2015), Kanishka Berashk, an Afghan citizen, was denied a visa to come to the United States to live with his wife, Fauzia Din, a U.S. citizen. Given his status as a foreigner, he had no claim available to contest the proceeding. So she sued, claiming that the cursory explanation he had been given operated to deprive her, without due process, of the liberty to live in the United States with her husband. Was the "liberty" protected by the Constitution—which Justice Stewart said in Roth "must be broad indeed"—indeed this broad? The court split three ways. For Justice Scalia and two others, considering this claim to be a constitutionally protected liberty interest went too far beyond traditional understandings or decided cases. For Justice Breyer and three others, the importance of marriage, and the various ways the law acted to preserve the ability of married persons to live together, was sufficient to justify the plaintiff's claim to greater process. And the other two Justices? In an opinion by Justice Kennedy, they ruled that the issue did not need to be decided because the government had already given all the process that, in a case involving the exclusion of a noncitizen, it was required to give.

## NOTES ON ASSESSMENTS OF THE ROTH/SINDERMANN DOCTRINE

What have scholars thought of entitlement analysis? Here's a sample of views:

(1) HENRY P. MONAGHAN, OF "LIBERTY" AND "PROPERTY", 62 Cornell L. Rev. 405, 409 (1977): "Prior to Roth, Supreme Court definitions of 'liberty' and 'property' had amounted to taking the words 'life, liberty, and property' as a unitary concept embracing all interests valued by sensible men. After Roth, however, each word of the clause must be examined separately; so examined, we find that they do not embrace the full range of state conduct having serious impact upon individual interests."

(2) WILLIAM VAN ALSTYNE, CRACKS IN "THE NEW PROPERTY": ADJUDICATIVE DUE PROCESS IN THE ADMINISTRATIVE STATE, 62 Cornell L. Rev. 445, 484 (1977): "The concept of public sector status as property both overstates and understates the problem. It overstates the problem by carrying with it additional notions of personal entitlement and of sinecurism that no constitutional court since Lochner should desire to encourage. At the same time, it understates the problem by ignoring a vast number of situations in which it is impossible to describe the relationship as one giving rise to

property, but in which the government's procedural grossness is nevertheless profoundly unfair and objectionable."

(3) JERRY L. MASHAW, DIGNITARY PROCESS: A POLITICAL PSYCHOLOGY OF LIBERAL DEMOCRATIC CITIZENSHIP, 39 U. Fla. L. Rev. 433, 437 (1987): "Such an approach is functionally inadequate to address the problems of governmental or bureaucratic discretion that the due process clause was meant to address. The positive law trigger approach gives legal protection, or at least due process attention, where some legal protection already exists, while excluding due process concern where a legal regime seems to permit official arbitrariness. Although many have a taste for irony, few would choose Kafka or Ionesco as constitutional draftsmen."

(4) RICHARD B. STEWART & CASS R. SUNSTEIN, PUBLIC PROGRAMS AND PRIVATE RIGHTS, 95 Harv. L. Rev. 1195, 1257–58 (1982): "A formal definition of entitlements was not inevitable. The Court might have sought to identify those interests that are as central to individual well-being in contemporary society as were the interests protected at common law in a different era. The judicial discretion inherent in any such task has been a major factor in the Court's refusal to follow a functional approach. Moreover, if courts were to select certain 'important' interests as those deserving due process protection, they might be driven to give those interests substantive as well as procedural protection; procedural rights alone might be of little value if administrators were free to decide cases as they pleased as long as procedural formalities were observed. A functional approach could thus invite courts to rule the welfare state through a new form of substantive due process."

(5) PATRICIA M. WALD, GOVERNMENT BENEFITS: A NEW LOOK AT AN OLD GIFTHORSE, 65 N.Y.U. L. Rev. 247, 260 (1990): "The Court's decision was hardly a renunciation of the right-privilege distinction. It simply redefined the boundary between the two."

## MATHEWS v. ELDRIDGE

Supreme Court of the United States (1976).
424 U.S. 319.

■ JUSTICE POWELL delivered the opinion of the Court.

The issue in this case is whether the Due Process Clause of the Fifth Amendment requires that prior to the termination of Social Security disability benefit payments the recipient be afforded an opportunity for an evidentiary hearing.

I

Cash benefits are provided to workers during periods in which they are completely disabled under the disability insurance benefits program created by the 1956 amendments to Title II of the Social Security Act. 42 U.S.C. § 423.[1] Respondent Eldridge was first awarded benefits in June

---

[1] The program is financed by revenues derived from employee and employer payroll taxes. It provides monthly benefits to disabled persons who have worked sufficiently long to have an insured status, and who have had substantial work experience in a specified interval directly preceding the onset of disability. Benefits also are provided to the worker's dependents under

1968. In March 1972, he received a questionnaire from the state agency charged with monitoring his medical condition. Eldridge completed the questionnaire, indicating that his condition had not improved and identifying the medical sources, including physicians, from whom he had received treatment recently. The state agency then obtained reports from his physician and a psychiatric consultant. After considering these reports and other information in his file the agency informed Eldridge by letter that it had made a tentative determination that his disability had ceased in May 1972. The letter included a statement of reasons for the proposed termination of benefits, and advised Eldridge that he might request reasonable time in which to obtain and submit additional information pertaining to his condition.

In his written response, Eldridge disputed one characterization of his medical condition and indicated that the agency already had enough evidence to establish his disability.[2] The state agency then made its final determination that he had ceased to be disabled in May 1972. This determination was accepted by the Social Security Administration (SSA), which notified Eldridge in July that his benefits would terminate after that month. The notification also advised him of his right to seek reconsideration by the state agency of this initial determination within six months.

Instead of requesting reconsideration Eldridge commenced this action ... The District Court concluded that the administrative procedures pursuant to which the Secretary had terminated Eldridge's benefits abridged his right to procedural due process. ... [T]he Court of Appeals for the Fourth Circuit affirmed.

II

[The courts have jurisdiction.]

III

A

... The Secretary does not contend that procedural due process is inapplicable to terminations of Social Security disability benefits. ... Rather, the Secretary contends that the existing administrative procedures ... provide all the process that is constitutionally due before a recipient can be deprived of that interest. ... Eldridge agrees that the review procedures ... would be adequate if disability benefits were not terminated until after the evidentiary hearing stage of the

---

specified circumstances. When the recipient reaches age 65 his disability benefits are automatically converted to retirement benefits. In fiscal 1974 approximately 3,700,000 persons received assistance under the program. Social Security Administration, The Year in Review 21 (1974).

[2] Eldridge originally was disabled due to chronic anxiety and back strain. He subsequently was found to have diabetes. The tentative determination letter indicated that aid would be terminated because available medical evidence indicated that his diabetes was under control, that there existed no limitations on his back movements which would impose severe functional restrictions, and that he no longer suffered emotional problems that would preclude him from all work for which he was qualified. In his reply letter he claimed to have arthritis of the spine rather than a strained back.

administrative process. The dispute centers upon what process is due prior to the initial termination of benefits, pending review.

In recent years this Court increasingly has had occasion to consider the extent to which due process requires an evidentiary hearing prior to the deprivation of some type of property interest even if such a hearing is provided thereafter. In only one case, Goldberg v. Kelly, has the Court held that a hearing closely approximating a judicial trial is necessary.

... "Due process, unlike some legal rules, is not a technical conception with a fixed content unrelated to time, place and circumstances." Cafeteria Workers v. McElroy, 367 U.S. 886, 895 (1961).... Accordingly, resolution of the issue whether the administrative procedures provided here are constitutionally sufficient requires analysis of the governmental and private interests that are affected. Goldberg v. Kelly, 397 U.S. 254, 263–266 [(1970)]; Cafeteria Workers v. McElroy, above, at 895. More precisely, our prior decisions indicate that identification of the specific dictates of due process generally requires consideration of three distinct factors: First, the private interest that will be affected by the official action; second, the risk of an erroneous deprivation of such interest through the procedures used, and the probable value, if any, of additional or substitute procedural safeguards; and finally, the Government's interest, including the function involved and the fiscal and administrative burdens that the additional or substitute procedural requirement would entail. See, e.g., Goldberg v. Kelly, above, at 263–271.

We turn first to a description of the procedures for the termination of Social Security disability benefits, and thereafter consider the factors bearing upon the constitutional adequacy of these procedures.

B

The disability insurance program is administered jointly by state and federal agencies. State agencies make the initial determination whether a disability exists, when it began, and when it ceased. The standards applied and the procedures followed are prescribed by the Secretary, who has delegated his responsibilities and powers under the Act to the SSA.

In order to establish initial and continued entitlement to disability benefits a worker must demonstrate that he is unable

> to engage in any substantial gainful activity by reason of any medically determinable physical or mental impairment which can be expected to result in death or which has lasted or can be expected to last for a continuous period of not less than 12 months ... 42 U.S.C. § 423(d)(1)(A).

To satisfy this test the worker bears a continuing burden of showing, by means of "medically acceptable clinical and laboratory diagnostic techniques," § 423(d)(3), that he has a physical or mental impairment of such severity that he is not only unable to do his previous work but cannot, considering his age, education, and work experience, engage in any other kind of substantial gainful work which exists in the national economy, regardless of whether such work exists in the immediate area in which he lives, or whether a specific job vacancy exists for him, or whether he would be hired if he applied for work. § 423(d)(2)(A). . . .

The continuing-eligibility investigation is made by a state agency acting through a "team" consisting of a physician and a nonmedical person trained in disability evaluation. The agency periodically communicates with the disabled worker, usually by mail—in which case he is sent a detailed questionnaire—or by telephone, and requests information concerning his present condition, including current medical restrictions and sources of treatment, and any additional information that he considers relevant to his continued entitlement to benefits.

Information regarding the recipient's current condition is also obtained from his sources of medical treatment. If there is a conflict between the information provided by the beneficiary and that obtained from medical sources such as his physician, or between two sources of treatment, the agency may arrange for an examination by an independent consulting physician. Whenever the agency's tentative assessment of the beneficiary's condition differs from his own assessment, the beneficiary is informed that benefits may be terminated, provided a summary of the evidence upon which the proposed determination to terminate is based, and afforded an opportunity to review the medical reports and other evidence in his case file. He also may respond in writing and submit additional evidence.

The state agency then makes its final determination, which is reviewed by an examiner in the SSA Bureau of Disability Insurance. If, as is usually the case, the SSA accepts the agency determination it notifies the recipient in writing, informing him of the reasons for the decision, and of his right to seek de novo reconsideration by the state agency.[20] Upon acceptance by the SSA, benefits are terminated effective two months after the month in which medical recovery is found to have occurred.

If the recipient seeks reconsideration by the state agency and the determination is adverse, the SSA reviews the reconsideration determination and notifies the recipient of the decision. He then has a right to an evidentiary hearing before an SSA administrative law judge. The hearing is non-adversary, and the SSA is not represented by counsel. As at all prior and subsequent stages of the administrative process, however, the claimant may be represented by counsel or other spokesmen. If this hearing results in an adverse decision, the claimant is

---

[20] The reconsideration assessment is initially made by the state agency, but usually not by the same persons who considered the case originally. R. Dixon, Social Security Disability and Mass Justice 32 (1973). Both the recipient and the agency may adduce new evidence.

entitled to request discretionary review by the SSA Appeals Council, and finally may obtain judicial review.

Should it be determined at any point after termination of benefits, that the claimant's disability extended beyond the date of cessation initially established, the worker is entitled to retroactive payments. If, on the other hand, a beneficiary receives any payments to which he is later determined not to be entitled, the statute authorizes the Secretary to attempt to recoup these funds in specified circumstances.

C

Despite the elaborate character of the administrative procedures provided by the Secretary, the courts below held them to be constitutionally inadequate, concluding that due process requires an evidentiary hearing prior to termination. In light of the private and governmental interests at stake here and the nature of the existing procedures, we think this was error.

Since a recipient whose benefits are terminated is awarded full retroactive relief if he ultimately prevails, his sole interest is in the uninterrupted receipt of this source of income pending final administrative decision on his claim. His potential injury is thus similar in nature to that of the welfare recipient in Goldberg . . .

Only in Goldberg has the Court held that due process requires an evidentiary hearing prior to a temporary deprivation. It was emphasized there that welfare assistance is given to persons on the very margin of subsistence. . . Eligibility for disability benefits, in contrast, is not based upon financial need.[24] Indeed, it is wholly unrelated to the worker's income or support from many other sources, such as earnings of other family members, workmen's compensation awards, tort claims awards, savings, private insurance, public or private pensions, veterans' benefits, food stamps, public assistance, or the "many other important programs, both public and private, which contain provisions for disability payments affecting a substantial portion of the work force. . . ." Richardson v. Belcher, 404 U.S. [78,] 85–87 [(1971)] (Douglas, J., dissenting).

As Goldberg illustrates, the degree of potential deprivation that may be created by a particular decision is a factor to be considered in assessing the validity of any administrative decisionmaking process. The potential deprivation here is generally likely to be less than in Goldberg, although the degree of difference can be overstated. As the District Court emphasized, to remain eligible for benefits a recipient must be "unable to engage in substantial gainful activity." Thus, . . . there is little possibility that the terminated recipient will be able to find even temporary employment to ameliorate the interim loss.

As we recognized last Term in Fusari v. Steinberg, 419 U.S. 379, 389 (1975), "the possible length of wrongful deprivation of . . . benefits [also] is an important factor in assessing the impact of official action on the

[24] The level of benefits is determined by the worker's average monthly earnings during the period prior to disability, his age, and other factors not directly related to financial need. . . .

private interests." The Secretary concedes that the delay between a request for a hearing before an administrative law judge and a decision on the claim is currently between 10 and 11 months. Since a terminated recipient must first obtain a reconsideration decision as a prerequisite to invoking his right to an evidentiary hearing, the delay between the actual cutoff of benefits and final decision after a hearing exceeds one year.

In view of the torpidity of this administrative review process and the typically modest resources of the family unit of the physically disabled worker,[26] the hardship imposed upon the erroneously terminated disability recipient may be significant. Still, the disabled worker's need is likely to be less than that of a welfare recipient. In addition to the possibility of access to private resources, other forms of government assistance will become available where the termination of disability benefits places a worker or his family below the subsistence level. In view of these potential sources of temporary income, there is less reason here than in Goldberg to depart from the ordinary principle, established by our decisions, that something less than an evidentiary hearing is sufficient prior to adverse administrative action.

D

An additional factor to be considered here is the fairness and reliability of the existing pretermination procedures, and the probable value, if any, of additional procedural safeguards. Central to the evaluation of any administrative process is the nature of the relevant inquiry. See Friendly, "Some Kind of Hearing," 123 U. Pa. L. Rev. 1267, 1281 (1975). In order to remain eligible for benefits the disabled worker must demonstrate by means of "medically acceptable clinical and laboratory diagnostic techniques," 42 U.S.C. § 423(d)(3), that he is unable "to engage in any substantial gainful activity by reason of any *medically determinable* physical or mental impairment . . ." § 423(d)(1)(A) (emphasis supplied). In short, a medical assessment of the worker's physical or mental condition is required. This is a more sharply focused and easily documented decision than the typical determination of welfare entitlement. In the latter case, a wide variety of information may be deemed relevant and issues of witness credibility and veracity often are critical to the decisionmaking process. Goldberg noted that in such circumstances "written submissions are a wholly unsatisfactory basis for decision."

By contrast, the decision whether to discontinue disability benefits will turn, in most cases, upon "routine, standard, and unbiased medical reports by physician specialists," Richardson v. Perales, 402 U.S. 389, 404 (1971), concerning a subject whom they have personally examined.[28]

---

[26] Amici cite statistics compiled by the Secretary which indicate that in 1965 the mean income of the family unit of a disabled worker was $3,803, while the median income for the unit was $2,836. The mean liquid assets—i.e., cash, stocks, bonds—of these family units was $4,862; the median was $940. These statistics do not take into account the family unit's nonliquid assets—i.e., automobile, real estate, and the like. Brief for AFL-CIO et al. as Amici Curiae App. 4a.

[28] The decision is not purely a question of the accuracy of a medical diagnosis since the ultimate issue which the state agency must resolve is whether in light of the particular worker's

In Richardson the Court recognized the "reliability and probative worth of written medical reports," emphasizing that while there may be "professional disagreement with the medical conclusions" the "specter of questionable credibility and veracity is not present." To be sure, credibility and veracity may be a factor in the ultimate disability assessment in some cases. But procedural due process rules are shaped by the risk of error inherent in the truthfinding process as applied to the generality of cases, not the rare exceptions. The potential value of an evidentiary hearing, or even oral presentation to the decisionmaker, is substantially less in this context than in Goldberg.

The decision in Goldberg also was based on the Court's conclusion that written submissions were an inadequate substitute for oral presentation because they did not provide an effective means for the recipient to communicate his case to the decisionmaker. Written submissions were viewed as an unrealistic option, for most recipients lacked the "educational attainment necessary to write effectively" and could not afford professional assistance. In addition, such submissions would not provide the "flexibility of oral presentations" or "permit the recipient to mold his argument to the issues the decision maker appears to regard as important." In the context of the disability-benefits-entitlement assessment the administrative procedures under review here fully answer these objections.

The detailed questionnaire which the state agency periodically sends the recipient identifies with particularity the information relevant to the entitlement decision, and the recipient is invited to obtain assistance from the local SSA office in completing the questionnaire. More important, the information critical to the entitlement decision usually is derived from medical sources, such as the treating physician. Such sources are likely to be able to communicate more effectively through written documents than are welfare recipients or the lay witnesses supporting their cause. The conclusions of physicians often are supported by X-rays and the results of clinical or laboratory tests, information typically more amenable to written than to oral presentation.

A further safeguard against mistake is the policy of allowing the disability recipient's representative full access to all information relied upon by the state agency. In addition, prior to the cutoff of benefits the agency informs the recipient of its tentative assessment, the reasons therefor, and provides a summary of the evidence that it considers most relevant. Opportunity is then afforded the recipient to submit additional evidence or arguments, enabling him to challenge directly the accuracy

"age, education, and work experience" he cannot "engage in any . . . substantial gainful work which exists in the national economy. . ." 42 U.S.C. § 423(d)(2)(A). Yet information concerning each of these worker characteristics is amenable to effective written presentation. The value of an evidentiary hearing, or even a limited oral presentation, to an accurate presentation of those factors to the decisionmaker does not appear substantial. Similarly, resolution of the inquiry as to the types of employment opportunities that exist in the national economy for a physically impaired worker with a particular set of skills would not necessarily be advanced by an evidentiary hearing. Cf. 1 K. Davis, Administrative Law Treatise § 7.06, p. 429 (1958). The statistical information relevant to this judgment is more amenable to written than to oral presentation.

of information in his file as well as the correctness of the agency's tentative conclusions. These procedures, again as contrasted with those before the Court in Goldberg, enable the recipient to "mold" his argument to respond to the precise issues which the decisionmaker regards as crucial.

Despite these carefully structured procedures, amici point to the significant reversal rate for appealed cases as clear evidence that the current process is inadequate. Depending upon the base selected and the line of analysis followed, the relevant reversal rates urged by the contending parties vary from a high of 58.6% for appealed reconsideration decisions to an overall reversal rate of only 3.3%.[29] Bare statistics rarely provide a satisfactory measure of the fairness of a decisionmaking process. Their adequacy is especially suspect here since the administrative review system is operated on an open-file basis. A recipient may always submit new evidence, and such submissions may result in additional medical examinations. Such fresh examinations were held in approximately 30% to 40% of the appealed cases in fiscal 1973, either at the reconsideration or evidentiary hearing stage of the administrative process. In this context, the value of reversal rate statistics as one means of evaluating the adequacy of the pretermination process is diminished. Thus, although we view such information as relevant, it is certainly not controlling in this case.

E

In striking the appropriate due process balance the final factor to be assessed is the public interest. This includes the administrative burden and other societal costs that would be associated with requiring, as a matter of constitutional right, an evidentiary hearing upon demand in all cases prior to the termination of disability benefits. The most visible burden would be the incremental cost resulting from the increased number of hearings and the expense of providing benefits to ineligible recipients pending decision. No one can predict the extent of the increase, but the fact that full benefits would continue until after such hearings would assure the exhaustion in most cases of this attractive option. Nor would the theoretical right of the Secretary to recover undeserved benefits result, as a practical matter, in any substantial offset to the added outlay of public funds. The parties submit widely varying estimates of the probable additional financial cost. We only need say that experience with the constitutionalizing of government procedures suggests that the ultimate additional cost in terms of money and administrative burden would not be insubstantial.

[29] By focusing solely on the reversal rate for appealed reconsideration determinations amici overstate the relevant reversal rate. [I]n order fully to assess the reliability and fairness of a system of procedure, one must also consider the overall rate of error for all denials of benefits. Here that overall rate is 12.2%. Moreover, about 75% of these reversals occur at the reconsideration stage of the administrative process. Since the median period between a request for reconsideration review and decision is only two months, Brief for AFL-CIO et al. as Amici Curiae App. 4a, the deprivation is significantly less than that concomitant to the lengthier delay before an evidentiary hearing. Netting out these reconsideration reversals, the overall reversal rate falls to 3.3%. See Supplemental and Reply Brief for Petitioner 14.

Financial cost alone is not a controlling weight in determining whether due process requires a particular procedural safeguard prior to some administrative decision. But the Government's interest, and hence that of the public, in conserving scarce fiscal and administrative resources is a factor that must be weighed. At some point the benefit of an additional safeguard to the individual affected by the administrative action and to society in terms of increased assurance that the action is just, may be outweighed by the cost. Significantly, the cost of protecting those whom the preliminary administrative process has identified as likely to be found undeserving may in the end come out of the pockets of the deserving since resources available for any particular program of social welfare are not unlimited.

But more is implicated in cases of this type than ad hoc weighing of fiscal and administrative burdens against the interests of a particular category of claimants. The ultimate balance involves a determination as to when, under our constitutional system, judicial-type procedures must be imposed upon administrative action to assure fairness. . . . The judicial model of an evidentiary hearing is neither a required, nor even the most effective, method of decisionmaking in all circumstances. The essence of due process is the requirement that "a person in jeopardy of serious loss [be given] notice of the case against him and opportunity to meet it." Joint Anti-Fascist Comm. v. McGrath, 341 U.S., [123],171–172 [(1951)] (Frankfurter, J., concurring). All that is necessary is that the procedures be tailored, in light of the decision to be made, to "the capacities and circumstances of those who are to be heard," Goldberg v. Kelly, 397 U.S., at 268–269, to insure that they are given a meaningful opportunity to present their case. In assessing what process is due in this case, substantial weight must be given to the good-faith judgments of the individuals charged by Congress with the administration of social welfare programs that the procedures they have provided assure fair consideration of the entitlement claims of individuals. This is especially so where, as here, the prescribed procedures not only provide the claimant with an effective process for asserting his claim prior to any administrative action, but also assure a right to an evidentiary hearing, as well as to subsequent judicial review, before the denial of his claim becomes final.

We conclude that an evidentiary hearing is not required prior to the termination of disability benefits and that the present administrative procedures fully comport with due process.

The judgment of the Court of Appeals is reversed.

■ JUSTICE STEVENS took no part in the consideration or decision of this case.

■ JUSTICE BRENNAN, with whom JUSTICE MARSHALL concurs, dissenting.

. . . [T]he Court's consideration that a discontinuance of disability benefits may cause the recipient to suffer only a limited deprivation is no argument. It is speculative. Moreover, the very legislative determination to provide disability benefits, without any prerequisite determination of need in fact, presumes a need by the recipient which is not this Court's function to denigrate. Indeed, in the present case, it is indicated that because disability benefits were terminated there was a foreclosure upon the Eldridge home and the family's furniture was repossessed, forcing Eldridge, his wife, and their children to sleep in one bed. Finally, it is also no argument that a worker, who has been placed in the untenable position of having been denied disability benefits, may still seek other forms of public assistance.

## NOTES ON HOW THE MATHEWS V. ELDRIDGE DOCTRINE IS CONSTRUCTED

(1) ***How Does Justice Powell Frame His Inquiry?*** "[T]here is less reason here than in Goldberg to depart from *the ordinary principle*, . . . that something less than an evidentiary hearing is sufficient prior to adverse administrative action." (emphasis added) Does Mathews invert the traditional understanding of what process is due process? If a private citizen has an interest sufficiently dignified to be within the constitutional trio of "life, liberty, or property," should we not start by assuming that "the ordinary principle" is that the citizen is entitled to a trial before the state deprives him of that interest—and then see if there are reasons for saying that providing a trial is, in context, too much? TODD D. RAKOFF, BROCK V. ROADWAY EXPRESS, INC., AND THE NEW LAW OF REGULATORY DUE PROCESS, 1987 Sup. Ct. Rev. 157, 162, hypothesizing the reaction of the "typical American lawyer" to the Mathews balance: "No man's liberty or property are safe when the court simply asks case by case what procedures seem worthwhile and not too costly."

(2) ***What Is the Right Baseline?*** Should it be the courtroom trial as just suggested—or is making that the archetype of due process wrong in principle? Compare the views of JUDGE HENRY J. FRIENDLY in a famous article, published shortly before Mathews, that appears to have had significant impact on the majority's thinking in the case. In "SOME KIND OF HEARING," 123 U. Pa. L. Rev. 1267 (1975), Judge Friendly decried "the tendency to judicialize administrative procedures" that Goldberg and succeeding cases had produced. Instead, he suggested, "[T]he required degree of procedural safeguards varies directly with the importance of the private interest affected and the need for and usefulness of the particular safeguard in the given circumstances and inversely with the burden and any other adverse consequences of affording it."

A balancing test, he admitted, might seem "uncertain and subjective," but he argued that "more elaborate specification of the relevant factors may help to produce more principled and predictable decisions." He offered the following list of "factors that have been considered to be elements of a fair hearing, roughly in order of priority":

1. An Unbiased Tribunal
2. Notice of the Proposed Action and the Grounds Asserted for It
3. An Opportunity to Present Reasons Why the Proposed Action Should Not be Taken

4. The Right to Call Witnesses
5. The Right To Know the Evidence Against One
6. The Right To Have Decision Based Only on the Evidence Presented
7. Counsel
8. The Making of a Record
9. A Statement of Reasons
10. Public Attendance
11. Judicial Review

He concluded: "In the mass justice area the Supreme Court has yielded too readily to the notions that the adversary system is the only appropriate model and that there is only one acceptable solution to any problem, and consequently has been too prone to indulge in constitutional codification. There is need for experimentation, particularly for the use of the investigative model, for empirical studies, and for avoiding absolutes."

(3) ***The Programmatic Context.*** Justice Powell clearly analyzes not the case of a single claimant, but an entire system of benefits adjudication. What are its features?

One important point, surely, is that there are an enormous number of disability determinations to be made. Even counting only those cases that go to an ALJ hearing (because the claimant has been turned down in the prior steps of the process and he appeals the termination of his benefits), in every recent year there have been hundreds of thousands of such cases.

Another point—noted at the very end of the opinion—is that in addition to the procedures provided prior to initial termination of the claimant, "the prescribed procedures . . . also assure a right to an evidentiary hearing, as well as to subsequent judicial review, before the denial of his claim becomes final." Does the determination at stake more resemble, to use a criminal law analogy, a "probable cause" proceeding?

A third point is that the record stays open throughout this process—that the ALJ considers new evidence and makes a de novo decision.

A fourth point is that this ALJ process differs a good bit from many other APA formal hearings: the ALJ is responsible for seeing the government's information into the record, for the identification and examination of government witnesses, and for cross-examination of the claimant's witnesses. As the Court says, "[T]he hearing is non-adversary and the SSA is not represented by counsel."

And a final point, as discussed in the opinion, is that many such hearings result in the granting of benefits that had been previously denied.

Does the result in the case turn on any of these facts? If so, should the Mathews test be different in a situation in which one or more of these facts is different?

(4) ***Is Mathews Balancing Capable of Principled Application?*** Even as formulated, the Mathew's test abjures stating a "one size fits all" answer to

the question "what process is due in administrative proceedings?" By disaggregating the very large bundle of procedures comprised in a trial-type judicial hearing, and by accepting that some procedures can follow rather than precede deprivation, or perhaps be excluded altogether, judges gain flexibility to respond to the range of administrative contexts. However, this flexibility comes at a cost. If each stick in the process bundle plus its timing is independently considered, a very large number of process combinations is possible. Can the doctrine structure judicial choice in a manner both defensible in principle and predictable in practice?

(Speaking of doctrinal regularity, is the Mathews balance used in the many contexts not related to ordinary administrative law in which procedural due process also is relevant? The answer is sometimes yes, sometimes no. For example, it is not the test to be used in evaluating the constitutionality of procedures for determining criminal guilt, Medina v. California, 505 U.S. 437 (1992); it was the test used by the Court in deciding whether due process requires a state to provide counsel for an indigent parent in a proceeding in court to terminate her parental rights, Lassiter v. Department of Social Services, 452 U.S. 18 (1981); and it was the test used in Hamdi v. Rumsfeld, 542 U.S. 507 (2004), to judge the appropriate process for determining whether the grounds existed to justify holding a U.S. citizen as a military prisoner in Guantánamo Bay. The proposition that "the Mathews test was . . . conceived to address due process claims arising in the context of administrative law," Medina, 505 U.S. at 444, is not the whole story.)

(5) ***Do Beneficiaries' Interests Count?*** Mathews acknowledges the government's interests as "including the function involved and the fiscal and administrative burdens that the additional or substitute procedural requirement would entail." What about administrative law cases in which the government's interest is not so much in minimizing its own "fiscal and administrative burdens" as in protecting a beneficiary class against the regulated party? Can the benefits to beneficiaries be added to the government's direct interests when comparing the burdens and interests of the parties? There has not been much litigation raising the point, probably because this scenario—the direct imposition of regulation on a regulated party through adjudication rather than rulemaking—is the scenario most likely to have been placed by Congress within the category of formal adjudication under the APA. The procedural issues then become a matter of construing the APA rather than applying the Constitution. The one Supreme Court decision raising the issue is Brock v. Roadway Express, Inc., 481 U.S. 252 (1987), which considered a statute protecting trucking industry employees from being discharged for reporting safety violations. There, a fractured Court, speaking in several opinions, seemed to consider without much argument that the interests of the beneficiary of the regulation at issue (the truck driver) should count along with the government's interest and against the interests of the regulated party (the trucking company). Accordingly, it was constitutional for the statute to authorize the Secretary of Labor to order a driver's reinstatement after a summary process. In other words, the Secretary could require a company to continue to spend money to

employ someone it didn't want to employ during the longer evidentiary proceeding needed to decide the ultimate rights and wrongs. This approach contrasts with the normal rule for formal agency adjudications, in which (as in the usual courtroom case) the remedy—for example, the cease and desist order, or the reinstatement order—is issued only after the formal evidentiary hearing. Does this mean that the formal adjudication requirements of APA §§ 554, 556, and 557 are sometimes more stringent than due process requires? For commentary, see Rakoff, Brock v. Roadway Express, Inc., and The New Law Of Regulatory Due Process, 1987 Sup. Ct. Rev. 157.

(6) ***Deference?*** It is also worth noting that Mathews begins its analysis not from an idealized conception of what procedure should be used, but rather from the procedure stipulated by the statutes and regulations already in use. The second branch of the test asks, really, two questions: about "the risk of an erroneous deprivation" entailed in using those existing procedures and about "the probable value . . . of additional . . . procedural safeguards." Justice Powell details and evaluates both these matters at length. Beyond this nod to the agency built into the announced doctrine, he also (this time without elaboration) says, at the end, that "substantial weight must be given to the good-faith judgments of the individuals charged by Congress with the administration of social welfare programs that the procedures they have provided assure fair consideration of the entitlement claims of individuals." Does Mathews defer too much on what is, after all, a constitutional question? Does it tend toward, without fully invoking, the notion of taking "the bitter with the sweet"? Or, given the resources available to judges to determine questions such as this, and the responsibility for assuring fairness that might rest on legislative as well as judicial shoulders, does it state a sensible proposition? For an argument that deference is appropriate here, see Adrian Vermeule, Deference and Due Process, 129 Harv. L. Rev. 1890 (2016).

(7) ***More Background on Mathews.*** For a retelling of Mathews v. Eldridge and an assessment of each element of the calculus, from the perspectives of the various participants, see CYNTHIA R. FARINA, DUE PROCESS AT RASHOMON GATE: THE STORIES OF MATHEWS V. ELDRIDGE, in ADMINISTRATIVE LAW STORIES 229, 257 (Peter L. Strauss ed. 2006) (based on the record, transcript, briefs and other historical materials). Farina concludes: "This doctrine has not been the constitutional catalyst radically to reform the relationship between the citizen and modern regulatory government. But neither has it brought regulatory government to its knees—and so triggered a political backlash in which social welfare programs were defunded and entitlements dismantled. At a crucial moment, when the emergent new procedural due process jurisprudence was highly vulnerable, the Court chose a restrained, pragmatic solidification. It did what it could—given what it had, and where it found itself.

"Easy for us to say that what it did, wasn't much. Hard for us to argue—almost three decades later—that what it did, wasn't enough. With the Mathews solution, the government often wins, as it did in the case itself. But the government doesn't *always* win. Mathews has given lawyers a structure for telling the story of their clients (and the people like them) in a way that judges can locate, and assess, within the constitutional framework. And so we continue to experience procedural due process as a 'real' right: a claim that can be made, with meaning, by a single citizen against even the most powerful agencies. As we enter the 21st century, and all momentum is towards transnationally integrated regulatory policy and government structures that transcend conventional national boundaries, we start out with at least this.

"Perhaps that is not, after all, such a modest accomplishment."

## NOTES ON THE PROBLEM OF PROCESS BEFORE OR PROCESS AFTER

(1) ***The Basic Framework.*** Justice Powell ultimately concludes that "the prescribed procedures not only provide the claimant with an effective process for asserting his claim prior to any administrative action, but also assure a right to an evidentiary hearing, as well as to subsequent judicial review, before the denial of his claim becomes final." Why doesn't he just say that since the claimant ultimately gets an evidentiary hearing—in ordinary administrative law terms, a formal adjudication—which will provide compensation for any benefits he was wrongfully denied, it doesn't matter what comes before? It is perhaps because the background presumption about due process, against which the Mathews case is written, is that the process comes before the deprivation. As said in the much-quoted case of Mullane v. Central Hanover Bank and Trust Co., 339 U.S. 306, 313 (1950): "Many controversies have raged about the cryptic and abstract words of the Due Process Clause but there can be no doubt that at a minimum they require that deprivation of life, liberty or property by adjudication be preceded by notice and opportunity for hearing appropriate to the nature of the case." This presumption, one might think, grows out of an understanding of the due process clauses as concerned, not just with accuracy, but with the proper use of official power and the prevention of governmental high-handedness.

(2) ***The Exceptions.*** But, as with many presumptions, there have long been exceptions. In NORTH AMERICAN COLD STORAGE CO. V. CHICAGO, 211 U.S. 306 (1908), Section 1161 of the Revised Municipal Code of the City of Chicago required owners of facilities for cold storage of any perishable food item to "put, preserve and keep such article of food supply in a clean and wholesome condition, and . . . not allow the same, nor any part thereof, to become putrid, decayed, poisoned, infected, or in any other manner rendered or made unsafe or unwholesome for human food." Further, health department inspectors were authorized "to enter any and all such premises . . . at any time of any day and to forthwith seize, condemn and destroy any such putrid, decayed, poisoned and infected food, which any such inspector may find in and upon said premises." Pursuant to this ordinance, city officials, without any hearing, ordered North American Cold Storage to deliver to them, for purposes of destruction, forty-seven barrels of poultry that allegedly had become putrid. The Company refused. The City then threatened to destroy summarily anything in the warehouse deemed unfit for human consumption; it also banned further deliveries to or from the warehouse and promised to imprison anyone attempting to avoid the ban. Business was completely halted, and the Company sought an injunction. But the injunction was

denied. Putrid food, said the Court, is "a nuisance of the most dangerous kind," and the danger that it might somehow get out of the warehouse justified the immediate seizure. If the poultry were not, in fact, bad, the owners were sufficiently protected by their ability to sue the city after the seizure to recover damages.

This recognition of regulatory exigencies has continued after the decision in Mathews. E.g., FEDERAL DEPOSIT INS. CORP. V. MALLEN, 486 U.S. 230 (1988): As part of its charge to guard against losses from bank failures, the Federal Deposit Insurance Corporation is authorized to suspend summarily an officer of an insured bank who has been indicted for a felony involving dishonesty or breach of trust and whose continued service could pose a threat to the depositors or to public confidence in the bank. The statute provides that an administrative hearing need not be held until 30 days after the suspension and might not be concluded for an additional 60 days. The Court held unanimously that there was no violation of due process. "An important government interest, accompanied by a substantial assurance that the deprivation is not baseless or unwarranted, may in limited cases demanding prompt action justify postponing the opportunity to be heard until after the initial deprivation. See North American Cold Storage Co. v. Chicago." As to the possible 90-day delay, the length of time was a proper item of concern, but in this case the Court was not convinced that Congress had over-stepped its limits.

And a long line of cases (both before and after Mathews) has affirmed the power of state and federal governments to require taxpayers to pay a contested assessment and then bring an action for refund. JUSTICE BRANDEIS for a unanimous Court in PHILLIPS V. COMMISSIONER, 283 U.S. 589 (1931), had this to say: "Where only property rights are involved, mere postponement of the judicial enquiry is not a denial of due process, if the opportunity given for the ultimate judicial determination of the liability is adequate. Delay in the judicial determination of property rights is not uncommon where it is essential that governmental needs be immediately satisfied. For the protection of public health, a State may order the summary destruction of property by administrative authorities without antecedent notice or hearing. North American Cold Storage Co. v. Chicago. . . . Because of the public necessity, the property of citizens may be summarily seized in war-time. And at any time, the United States may acquire property by eminent domain, without paying, or determining the amount of the compensation before the taking."

Suing the government after the fact may raise issues of sovereign immunity. (See Chapter IX, Section 2.d.2, p. 1567). Supreme Court cases in the tax area, at least, have clearly stated that adequate postpayment remedies must be provided if the government denies predeprivation process. See, e.g., Reich v. Collins, 513 U.S. 106 (1994); McKesson Corp. v. Division of Alcoholic Beverages & Tobacco, 496 U.S. 18, 36–37 (1990).

(3) ***If There Is No Special Reason?*** The tougher question is whether or when—even in the absence of any exigency—the existence of an after-the-fact remedy in court ought to be considered sufficient due process. After all, that is the way ordinary, common-law rights are protected against those

alleged to have committed torts or to have breached contracts. But it seems not to be enough when it is government doing official deprivation—or at least that is implicit in the Sindermann case (p. 605). Sindermann had to prove the potential existence of a contract claim in order to meet the due process test of "life, liberty, or property"; but, having done so, he was entitled to an administrative hearing before deprivation, and not just to a claim for contractual damages. Following Sindermann, as noted above (p. 612), the many cases that have been based on contracts with the government have split: those that are seen to establish a "present entitlement" lead to consideration of a predeprivation process; those that are simply commercial claims are left to the after-the-fact, in-court remedy.

The most striking case to have accepted the substitution of common law remedies for administrative hearings is INGRAHAM V. WRIGHT, 430 U.S. 651 (1977). Here are the facts: "In the 1970–1971 school year many of the 237 schools in Dade County used corporal punishment as a means of maintaining discipline pursuant to Florida legislation and a local School Board regulation.... The authorized punishment consisted of paddling the recalcitrant student on the buttocks with a flat wooden paddle measuring less than two feet long, three to four inches wide, and about one-half inch thick. The normal punishment was limited to one to five "licks" or blows with the paddle and resulted in no apparent physical injury to the student. School authorities viewed corporal punishment as a less drastic means of discipline than suspension or expulsion. . . .

". . . The evidence, consisting mainly of the testimony of 16 students, suggests that the regime at Drew was exceptionally harsh. The testimony of Ingraham and Andrews, in support of their individual claims for damages, is illustrative. Because he was slow to respond to his teacher's instructions, Ingraham was subjected to more than 20 licks with a paddle while being held over a table in the principal's office. The paddling was so severe that he suffered a hematoma requiring medical attention and keeping him out of school for several days. Andrews was paddled several times for minor infractions. On two occasions he was struck on his arms, once depriving him of the full use of his arm for a week."

Should there have been some sort of process, before they were punished, that allowed the students to present their side of what they had done,? Justice White, in dissent, thought there should have been at least a prior, if informal, give-and-take with the disciplinarian. But the majority ruled otherwise. True, they said, "where school authorities, acting under color of state law, deliberately decide to punish a child for misconduct by restraining the child and inflicting appreciable physical pain . . . Fourteenth Amendment liberty interests are implicated." But "the question is whether the common-law remedies are adequate to afford due process." The Court concluded that the Florida rule that allowed for corporal punishment but imposed liability for damages, and possibly even criminal liability, for excessive punishment—which the Court considered to be the traditional common-law approach—was sufficient. As part of the second step of the Mathews test, concerning the adequacy of present procedures, the Court opined: "In those cases where severe punishment is contemplated, the available civil and criminal sanctions for abuse—considered in light of the openness of the school environment—afford significant protection against unjustified corporal punishment. Teachers and school authorities are unlikely to inflict corporal punishment unnecessarily or excessively when a possible consequence of doing so is the institution of civil or criminal proceedings against them."

More broadly, the Court summarized its analysis in this way: "In view of the low incidence of abuse, the openness of our schools, and the common-law safeguards that already exist, the risk of error that may result in violation of a schoolchild's substantive rights can only be regarded as minimal. Imposing additional administrative safeguards as a constitutional requirement might reduce that risk marginally, but would also entail a significant intrusion into an area of primary educational responsibility. We conclude that the Due Process Clause does not require notice and a hearing prior to the imposition of corporal punishment in the public schools, as that practice is authorized and limited by the common law. . . ."

Rightly decided?

## NOTES ON WHAT SHOULD COUNT IN THE MATHEWS THREE-PART TEST

(1) ***The Cost-Benefit Constitution?*** "The use of cost-benefit analysis to determine due process is not to every constitutional scholar's or judge's taste," says JUDGE POSNER, "but it is the analysis prescribed by the Supreme Court" VAN HARKEN V. CITY OF CHICAGO, 103 F.3d 1346, 1351 (7th Cir. 1997). Here's what he has in mind: In 1987, Illinois joined a number of other states in authorizing municipalities to decriminalize parking violations. Chicago exercised this authority. So long as the violation had been technically criminal, there were trial-type procedures to determine guilt consistent with conviction for other misdemeanors. Once the violation became merely civil, the city wanted to use truncated hearing procedures. Under its rules, the parking ticket was deemed prima facie evidence of a violation. The owner could either pay the fine (which could not exceed $100) or challenge the ticket in writing or in person. The police officer was not required to appear; the ticket was treated as an affidavit. Thus, the only witness was usually the vehicle owner, whom the hearing officer was instructed to cross-examine searchingly. The hearing officer could (but was not required to) subpoena witnesses, including the police officer. If the owner's challenge was denied, he could seek review in the Circuit Court of Cook County by paying the normal filing fee: $200. Consistent with due process? Yes, according to the panel opinion written by Judge Posner. The supposed judicial review was, given its price, illusory—but unnecessary because the basic procedure complied with the Mathews test:

"The costs of procedural safeguards are fairly straightforward, which is not to say easy to quantify. For example, the cost of requiring the police officer who writes the ticket to appear in person at every hearing at which the ticket is challenged—one of the procedural safeguards that the plaintiffs in this case claim is required by the due process clause—depends on the number and length of hearings, the average time the police officer requires to get to and from the hearing, the reduction in his productivity from the interruption of his normal workday that attendance at such hearings requires, and the expense to the City of hiring additional policemen. We were told at argument without contradiction that the City issues 4 million parking tickets a year, of which 5 percent are challenged (200,000), a third of those in person rather than by mail and thus requiring an oral hearing (67,000). If the ticketing officer were required to attend, the number of hearings requested would undoubtedly be higher, because respondents would think it likely that the officer wouldn't show up—a frequent occurrence at hearings on moving violations. Suppose the number of hearings would be double what it is under the challenged procedures (that is, would be 134,000), but the police would show up at only half, putting us back to 67,000; and suppose that a hearing at which a police officer showed up cost him on average 2 hours away from his other work. Then this procedural safeguard for which the plaintiffs are contending would cost the City 134,000 police hours a year, the equivalent of 67 full-time police officers at 2,000 hours a year per officer. In addition, more hearing officers would be required, at some additional cost to the City, because each hearing would be longer as a result of the presence of another live witness. And all these are simply the monetary costs. Acquittals of violators due solely to the ticketing officer's failure to appear would undermine the deterrent efficacy of the parking laws and deprive the City of revenues to which it was entitled as a matter of substantive justice.

"The benefits of a procedural safeguard are even trickier to estimate than the costs. The benefits depend on the harm that the safeguard will avert in cases in which it prevents an erroneous result and the likelihood that it will prevent an erroneous result. We know the harm here to the innocent car owner found 'guilty' and forced to pay a fine: it is the fine, and it can be anywhere from $10 to $100, for an average of $55. We must ask how likely it is that error would be averted if the ticketing officer were present at the hearing and therefore subject to cross-examination. Suppose that in his absence the probability of an erroneous determination that the respondent really did commit a parking violation is 5 percent, and the officer's presence would cut that probability in half, to 2.5 percent. Then the average saving to the innocent respondent from this additional procedural safeguard would be only $1.38 ($55 × .025)—a trivial amount.

"These calculations are inexact, to say the least; but they help to show, what is pretty obvious without them, that the benefits of requiring the police officer to appear at every hearing are unlikely to exceed the costs."

Do you agree with Judge Posner that this is what Mathews requires?

(2) ***Does Mathews Make What Really Matters, Matter?*** JERRY L. MASHAW, THE SUPREME COURT'S DUE PROCESS CALCULUS FOR ADMINISTRATIVE ADJUDICATION IN MATHEWS V. ELDRIDGE: THREE FACTORS IN SEARCH OF A THEORY OF VALUE, 44 U. Chi. L. Rev. 28, 48–49 (1976): "The Eldridge Court conceives of the values of procedure too narrowly: it views the sole purpose of procedural protections as enhancing accuracy, and thus limits its calculus to the benefits or costs that flow from correct or incorrect decisions. No attention is paid to 'process values' that might inhere in oral proceedings or to the demoralization costs that may result from the grant-

withdrawal-grant-withdrawal sequence to which claimants like Eldridge are subjected. Perhaps more important, as the Court seeks to make sense of a calculus in which accuracy is the sole goal of procedure, it tends erroneously to characterize disability hearings as concerned almost exclusively with medical impairment and thus concludes that such hearings involve only medical evidence, whose reliability would be little enhanced by oral procedure. As applied by the Eldridge Court the utilitarian calculus tends, as cost-benefit analyses typically do, to 'dwarf soft variables' and to ignore complexities and ambiguities.

"The problem with a utilitarian calculus is not merely that the Court may define the relevant costs and benefits too narrowly. However broadly conceived, the calculus asks unanswerable questions. For example, what is the social value, and the social cost, of continuing disability payments until after an oral hearing for persons initially determined to be ineligible? Answers to those questions require a technique for measuring the social value and social cost of government income transfers, but no such technique exists. Even if such formidable tasks of social accounting could be accomplished, the effectiveness of oral hearings in forestalling the losses that result from erroneous terminations would remain uncertain. In the face of these pervasive indeterminacies the Eldridge Court was forced to retreat to a presumption of constitutionality."

(3) CYNTHIA R. FARINA, CONCEIVING DUE PROCESS, 3 Yale J. L. & Feminism 189, 234–35 (1991): "If due process is to mark out and defend a sphere in which the individual is reliably preserved from the demands of the collective, how can the extent of the protection the individual receives turn on some calculus explicitly designed to maximize aggregate welfare? When the claim of the individual is pitted against 'the sheer magnitude of the collective interests at stake,' how often will the collective good not predominate? [Richard Saphire, Specifying Due Process Values: Toward a More Responsive Approach to Procedural Protection, 127 U. Pa. L. Rev. 111, 155 (1978).] . . . The unnaturalness of using a social welfare balance to set the content of due process protection becomes apparent . . . if we imagine employing the Mathews approach to decide what process is due parties in traditional civil adjudication. And yet, the Court's tacit recognition that due process in the regulatory context must, somehow, be differently understood is grounded in an inescapable reality: Providing mass justice is a staggering task. . . . If the Court is to avoid dictating a massive reordering of state and federal fiscal priorities, it must, it seems, weigh individual claims to process against the systematic costs of proceduralization.

"To venture into social welfare accounting is, however, to crack the lid of Pandora's box. . . . What is the judiciary doing second-guessing the political branches' judgment on how much should be spent to implement a given regulatory program? 'If the greatest good for the greatest number is the test for constitutionality under the due process clause, then it is hard to escape the notion that the best evidence of social welfare will always be the judgment of the legislature or its delegate.' [Jerry L. Mashaw, Due Process in the Administrative State 152 (1985).] To engage, at this stage of the [due process] analysis, in an inevitably ad hoc and standardless assessment of the importance of the individual interest, and to use that assessment as the basis for restructuring administrative behavior, seems precisely the undisciplined judicial interference in local and national governance that the Court embraced entitlement analysis to avoid."

(4) ***Or Is It a Reasonable Framework?*** GARY LAWSON, KATHERINE FERGUSON, & GUILLERMO MONTERO, "OH LORD, PLEASE DON'T LET ME BE MISUNDERSTOOD!": REDISCOVERING THE MATHEWS V. ELDRIDGE AND PENN CENTRAL FRAMEWORKS, 81 Notre Dame L. Rev. 1, 22–23 (2005): "Modern scholars . . . generally treat the Mathews framework as though it were an outcome-determinative test. The Court also seems to have accepted the idea that the sole justification for procedures is 'to minimize the risk of erroneous decisions' although there have been occasional dissenting voices on that score.

"Critics have, with considerable justification, roundly attacked the Mathews framework's efficacy as a decisionmaking tool. Some have pointed out that one can only weigh factors against each other if the factors are commensurable, which the Mathews factors do not appear to be. As one critic has stated, '[t]his reliance upon "weight," which is a useful approach for dealing with bananas, leaves something to be desired where factors such as those in Mathews are concerned.' [Edward L. Rubin, Due Process and the Administrative State, 72 Cal. L. Rev. 1044, 1138 (1984).] Others have criticized the narrow focus on decisional accuracy that the Mathews framework seems to require. Jerry Mashaw has famously argued that by identifying decisional accuracy as the holy grail of due process law, the Mathews formulation disregards the important value that individuals place on being heard: 'a lack of personal participation causes alienation and a loss of that dignity and self-respect that society properly deems independently valuable.' . . .

"All of these criticisms of Mathews have merit, but none of the developments in the evolution of Mathews that spawned these criticisms were inevitable. Mathews does not have to be viewed as anything other than a potentially useful way of structuring dialogue about fairness, in which case criticisms of Mathews for failing to direct or predict decisions are misplaced. Nor must Mathews be construed to constrict the perceived value of procedures solely to their ability to reduce the risk of erroneous substantive decisions. One could, of course, independently reach the conclusion that procedures are only valuable for their role in reaching correct substantive outcomes, but nothing in Mathews compels that result. If Mathews is best viewed solely as a means for starting (not finishing) a stylized legal conversation about fairness, it should be judged on those terms.

"Does the Mathews formulation do a serviceable job of providing a common frame of reference for legal argumentation? We think that it does. It would fail in that task if the factors that it identified were wildly inappropriate to the ultimate inquiry, which they clearly are not. It would also fail in that task if the factors themselves were so vague that they could not serve as a tool for communication. We do not see that problem either. Mathews has many critics, but we do not see the critics complaining that they do not know what the Mathews factors mean. Quite to the contrary, the critics know exactly what the Mathews factors are getting at and don't like it one bit. Mathews is a perfectly respectable jurisprudential and doctrinal vehicle for promoting adversarial dialogue about fairness.

"The process by which Mathews was transformed from a device for facilitating discussion into an outcome-determinative test is to some extent understandable—formulations tend to take on lives of their own independently of their terms or justifications—but it is also regrettable. A great deal of scholarly and judicial time and energy has been spent on problems that need never have arisen."

## b. Applications



## KAPPS v. WING

United States Court of Appeals for the Second Circuit (2005).
404 F.3d 105.

■ CALABRESI, CIRCUIT JUDGE. . . .

### I. BACKGROUND

#### A. Statutory Framework

Congress enacted the Low Income Home Energy Assistance Act ("LIHEAA") in 1981 in response to the rising costs of oil-based energy. LIHEAA was intended to, and has since its passage, assisted the states in providing home energy assistance to low income families. Participating states are given a block grant, which may be used for two primary purposes: 1) to assist poor families in meeting their regular heating costs ("regular HEAP benefits"); and 2) to intervene in energy crises to prevent any interruption in needy households' heat ("emergency HEAP benefits"). While state LIHEAA programs must comply with certain federal statutory requirements, the states are, as a general matter, afforded substantial discretion in defining the specific contours of their LIHEAA program.

Levels of LIHEAA funding are set by Congress on an annual basis. See 42 U.S.C. § 8621. Allocated funds are distributed among participating states on the basis of a complicated statutory formula. See 42 U.S.C. § 8623. States may, but need not, choose to supplement federal funds with state monies, in order to ensure that all eligible households are provided with benefits. New York, like some other states, has opted not to supplement federal funds, and hence provides benefits only to the extent that federal funding is available in any given program year. See N.Y. Soc. Serv. L. § 97[2].

New York's Home Energy Assistance Program ("HEAP") was created by the New York State Legislature in 1983, in order to allow the state to take advantage of the LIHEAA block grant program. Like many of New York's other social services programs, HEAP is administered jointly by the state and by local social service districts. At the state level, the Office of Temporary and Disability Assistance ("OTDA") annually sets standard eligibility criteria and benefits levels for the forthcoming year. The OTDA is also responsible for establishing a "program year," within which all HEAP applications must be received. Local social service districts are responsible for the actual processing of HEAP applications, and for notifying applicants of benefits eligibility.

Under regulations passed by the OTDA, there are two categories of households which may be eligible for regular HEAP benefits: 1) "[c]ategorically income eligible households"; and 2) "[i]ncome tested households." "Categorically eligible" households are those that include at least one household member who receives at least one of several specified federal or state benefits. Households that are not categorically eligible may qualify for HEAP benefits by demonstrating income eligibility, in accordance with standards set by the state on an annual basis. Once found eligible, a household's HEAP benefits allocation is determined in accordance with a complicated payment matrix, or point system. This "payment matrix" takes into account such factors as family income, the energy burden ratio of the household, the amount of federal funds allocated for the year, and the presence of "vulnerable" household members.

The regulations in effect at the time of the district court's decision required the defendants to process all HEAP applications within 30 business days. Historically, however, actual processing times have deviated considerably from this regulatory goal. During the pendency of this litigation, average processing times for New York City HEAP applications have varied between 21 and 122 days. At the time that the parties briefed the motion for summary judgment in the district court, most, but not all, New York City applications were being processed within the 30 day period mandated by the state.

HEAP applicants are notified of the granting or the denial of HEAP benefits in a notice issued by the social service district . . . If the applicant has been found ineligible for benefits, this notice usually, but not always, includes very basic information on why benefits have been denied. Applicants who have been found eligible for HEAP benefits are sometimes informed of the amount of benefits they will receive. But, apart from that, they are given no information, other than that their benefits application has been approved. In all cases, the notice advises applicants that they can obtain further information in a number of ways, including by calling the social service district, or by setting up a meeting with a benefits specialist.

Ordinarily, applicants have 60 days from the date of the HEAP notice, during which they may request an administrative "fair hearing" to challenge the agency's eligibility and/or benefits level determination. Under state regulations, however, fair hearings may not be requested more than 105 days after the close of the HEAP program year. As such, when HEAP applicants receive notice of the grant or denial of HEAP benefits more than 105 days after the termination of the program year, they are totally foreclosed from seeking a fair hearing. And, those applicants who receive notice of HEAP eligibility more than 45 days after the close of the program year will have less than the full 60 days within which to request a fair hearing.

B. Facts/Procedural History

Named plaintiffs Eileen Kapps, Geraldine Boyland, Alice Costello, Joan Ford, Joanne Karl and Margaret Riley filed this action in 1998. In their complaint, they alleged various violations inter alia of the LIHEAA and of the federal Due Process Clause in the defendants' administration of the New York City HEAP program. Specifically, as relevant to this appeal, plaintiffs contended below that the denial of the right to a fair hearing (by virtue of the operation of the 105 day rule, when combined with delays in providing notification of benefits) violated due process and the LIHEAA. Plaintiffs also claimed that the HEAP notices—by failing to provide information on how the applicant's benefits eligibility and allotment was calculated—did not meet the requirements of due process.

Plaintiffs named as defendants Brian J. Wing, the Commissioner of the OTDA, Jason A. Turner, the Commissioner of the New York City Department of Social Services, and Martin Oesterreich, the Commissioner of the New York City Department of Youth and Community Development. Plaintiffs sought to represent themselves, and all other applicants for regular HEAP benefits in the City of New York who had been denied certain procedural protections in the processing of their HEAP applications.

... The district court, in a carefully reasoned opinion ... granted class certification, and gave summary judgment in part to the plaintiffs and in part to the defendants ... The defendants appealed.

II. DISCUSSION

A. Standard of Review

We review a district court's grant of summary judgment de novo. ...

B. Due Process

The plaintiffs have alleged that the defendants' practices in administering New York City's HEAP program violate the procedural requirements of the Due Process Clause of the Fourteenth Amendment. In adjudicating such a claim, we consider two distinct issues: 1) whether plaintiffs possess a liberty or property interest protected by the Due Process Clause; and, if so, 2) whether existing state procedures are constitutionally adequate. The defendants argue that the plaintiffs possess no property interest in HEAP benefits, and that we therefore need not consider the second step of the due process inquiry. They also contend that—even assuming the plaintiffs have some constitutionally protected interest—the plaintiffs were afforded all the process that is required. Because an award of HEAP benefits to qualified applicants is mandatory and not discretionary (at least to the extent the program is funded in any given year), we conclude that the plaintiffs possess a sufficient property interest in the receipt of HEAP benefits to warrant due process protection in their demonstration of eligibility. We also conclude that the district court properly found existing procedures to be inadequate as a matter of federal constitutional law.

i. Property Interest

Social welfare benefits have long been afforded constitutional protection as a species of property protected by the federal Due Process Clause. See Goldberg v. Kelly, 397 U.S. 254, 262 & n.8 (1970). While not all benefits programs create constitutional property interests, procedural due process protections ordinarily attach where state or federal law confers an entitlement to benefits. A mere "unilateral expectation" of receiving a benefit is not, however, enough; a property interest arises only where one has a "legitimate claim of entitlement" to the benefit. Board of Regents of State Colleges v. Roth, 408 U.S. 564 (1972).

In determining whether a given benefits regime creates a property interest protected by the Due Process Clause, we look to the statutes and regulations governing the distribution of benefits. Where those statutes or regulations "meaningfully channel[ ] official discretion by mandating a defined administrative outcome," a property interest will be found to exist. Sealed v. Sealed, 332 F.3d 51, 56 (2d Cir. 2003). Thus, to the extent that state or federal law "meaningfully channels" the discretion of state or local officials by mandating an award of HEAP benefits to applicants who satisfy prescribed eligibility criteria, plaintiff-applicants possess a property interest, protected by the federal Due Process Clause.

We agree with the defendants that the LIHEAA does not, by itself, create a property interest. The LIHEAA affords substantial discretion to the states, both in deciding whether to participate in the home energy program, and, if they choose to participate, in crafting their own state-level home energy laws. See 42 U.S.C. § 8624. While the Act does require participating states to certify that they agree to target certain populations, and to allocate at least some of their benefits to specified goals of the Act, it dictates no particular result as to any given benefits applicant. Accordingly, the LIHEAA itself cannot be considered to "channel" official discretion sufficiently "meaningfully" so as to confer a due process protected property right.

Property interests, however, do not arise only from federal law. To the extent that state law imposes "substantive predicates" that limit the decision-making of HEAP officials, it too may confer a constitutionally protected property right. See Roth. As a result, we must also look to New York law to determine whether plaintiffs possess a property right in the receipt of HEAP benefits. Even a cursory examination of that law reveals that it provides precisely the type of discretion-limiting "substantive predicates" that are the hallmarks of protected property rights.

Like other statutory frameworks that we have found to create property interests, New York state law sets fixed eligibility criteria for the receipt of HEAP benefits. See N.Y. Comp. Codes R. & Regs. tit. 18, § 393.4(c) (setting forth standard eligibility criteria for the receipt of HEAP benefits, and indicating that "once determined eligible a household *will* receive a regular HEAP benefit") (emphasis added). Similarly, the amount of benefits provided to eligible applicants is determined in accordance with a standard benefits matrix. See N.Y. Comp. Codes R. & Regs. tit. 18, § 393.4(c) (eligible households will receive a HEAP benefit in accordance with an annually established payment matrix); see also [trial exhibit 39] (reproduction of the defendants' "Heating Benefit Calculation Worksheet"). And, there has been no intimation in the course of this litigation that discretionary factors enter into the determination of HEAP eligibility or of benefits amount. On the contrary, it appears that all of the factors considered by the state in assessing individual HEAP eligibility are objective, and as such are ones over which HEAP administrators have no discretionary control.

Notwithstanding this mandatory statutory and regulatory framework, defendants contend that some characteristics of the HEAP program render the plaintiffs' receipt of HEAP benefits too uncertain to give plaintiffs a property interest subject to due process protection. Specifically, defendants allege that the fact that the plaintiffs are *applicants* for benefits, rather than current recipients of benefits, renders their interest in the benefits too tenuous to qualify for due process protection. Defendants also argue that the HEAP program's dependence on federal funds means that no individual plaintiff can be assured of receiving benefits, thus rendering any individual's anticipation of benefits a mere "unilateral expectation," rather than a "legitimate claim of entitlement." See Roth.

In light of these two factors, defendants suggest, it does not matter whether or not state law sets forth discretion-restricting guidelines for the operation of the HEAP program, since any individual plaintiff's interest remains too contingent to constitute a property interest . . .

*a) Applicants for Benefits*

The Supreme Court has repeatedly reserved decision on the question of whether *applicants* for benefits (in contradistinction to *current recipients* of benefits) possess a property interest protected by the Due Process Clause. See, e.g., Lyng v. Payne, 476 U.S. 926, 942 (1986). Every circuit to address the question, however, has concluded that applicants for benefits, no less than current benefits recipients, may possess a property interest in the receipt of public welfare entitlements. And, our own circuit has indicated on at least three occasions that benefits applicants may possess a property interest, albeit in circumstances that differ somewhat from the instant case. Indeed, we have explained that "[w]hether a benefit invests the applicant with a 'claim of entitlement' or merely a 'unilateral expectation' is determined by the amount of discretion the disbursing agency retains" . . . Colson ex rel. Colson v. Sillman, 35 F.3d 106, 108–09 (2d Cir. 1994). . . .

The rationale for recognizing applicants' due process rights in these cases is apparent. Statutory language may so specifically mandate benefits awards upon demonstration of certain qualifications that an applicant must fairly be recognized to have a limited property interest entitling him, at least, to process sufficient to permit a demonstration of eligibility.

Defendants argue, however, that plaintiffs as applicants cannot possess a due process protected interest in the receipt of benefits, because they have not yet been shown to fulfill the eligibility criteria for HEAP benefits. This contention is without merit.

We note as an initial matter that, as to past violations of due process, all of the named plaintiffs were found eligible for benefits, and hence, even under defendants' argument, possessed a protected property interest in the receipt of benefits.[15] More fundamentally, the defendants' position misapprehends the purpose of requiring the state to afford adequate procedural due process protections in determining eligibility for benefits that state law makes a matter of entitlement. For, as the Tenth Circuit recently observed, the aim of proper procedures is precisely to allow the state to decide *properly* whether the applicant in fact has a legitimate claim of entitlement.

It is for this reason that, in cases involving the termination of benefits, federal courts do not ask whether the plaintiffs are entitled to the continuation of benefits, or whether they are, as the agency found, no longer eligible. Instead, the focus of the federal courts is on the adequacy of the procedures used to make that determination.

Comparably, our property interest analysis in the instant case extends only to the consideration of whether—were an applicant able to make out the requirements for HEAP eligibility—he or she would be entitled to benefits as a matter of law. If he or she would be so entitled, state law creates a property interest, and an applicant must be afforded procedural protections under the Due Process Clause to demonstrate his or her eligibility. We therefore reject the defendants' argument that plaintiffs' status as benefits applicants renders their interest in HEAP benefits insufficiently definite to constitute a "property" interest for the purposes of federal law.

*b) Benefits Contingent on the Availability of Federal Funds*

Under New York State law, no HEAP applicant can be certified as eligible for, and entitled to, HEAP benefits, if federal LIHEAA funds have been exhausted. It follows that not all HEAP applicants who are

[15] While the named plaintiffs were all adjudged eligible in the past, this is not necessarily true of the class as a whole, which was certified to include all households "who have applied or will apply for HEAP benefits . . ." Under the circumstances, it is particularly important that we explain why an applicant for benefits may possess a property interest regardless of whether he or she has received benefits in the past.

technically "eligible" for state benefits, will be entitled to receive those benefits. The defendants contend that this fact renders plaintiffs' interest in the receipt of benefits too tenuous to constitute a property interest. Specifically, they contend that the fact that no individual applicant can be assured of the receipt of benefits renders the interest a mere "unilateral expectation," rather than "a legitimate [claim of] entitlement." See Roth.

Relatively few courts have addressed the question of whether a social services program's contingency on the availability of funding renders it too indefinite to create a property interest. Those courts that have generally concluded that—*to the extent that funds are available*—statutes that would create protected property interests apart from funding limits do so regardless of these limits. See, e.g., Alexander v. Polk, 750 F.2d 250, 260–61 (3d Cir. 1984); Weston v. Cassata, 37 P.3d 469, 476–77 (Colo. Ct. App. 2001). But cf. Washington Legal Clinic for the Homeless v. Barry, 107 F.3d 32, 37 (D.C. Cir. 1997) (concluding that a property interest in the receipt of shelter resources did not exist *where D.C. law did not mandate any particular priority system for the distribution of limited shelter resources*).

We agree with these other courts' approach. Under state law, eligible HEAP applicants are entitled to receive benefits, so long as funding for such benefits remains available. To the extent that LIHEAA program funds are available, the fact that the HEAP program is, as a general matter, limited to the extent of federal funding does not matter. Plaintiffs' claim of entitlement—while funds remain available—is the same as it would be were the program not contingent on the availability of sufficient funds.

We therefore conclude that plaintiffs possess a valid property interest in the receipt of regular HEAP benefits.

ii. Process Due

Having determined that plaintiffs possessed a protected property interest, we must determine "what process plaintiffs were due before they could be deprived of that interest." Sealed, 332 F.3d at 55. In doing so, we apply the Supreme Court's familiar Mathews v. Eldridge test. Pursuant to this test, we conclude that the process due to applicants for HEAP benefits is notice of the reasons for the agency's preliminary determination, and an opportunity to be heard in response.

Under Mathews, three factors guide our decision. . . .

As the district court properly found, "the importance of the private interest at stake in this case is high." Kapps, 283 F.Supp.2d at 875. While HEAP grants are small in dollar amounts, they are targeted to those households that "are among the poorest in America." Sen. Rep. No. 103–251, 103rd Cong., 2d Sess. at *9 (1994). By design, the HEAP program affords relief only to those who might otherwise risk a shut-off in heating services. Thus, the erroneous denial of HEAP benefits may well result in a household being left without heat.

The adverse effects of an erroneous cut off of heat services are "self-evident." Memphis Light, Gas & Water Div. v. Craft, 436 U.S. 1, 18 (1978). As noted by the Supreme Court in Memphis Light, "[u]tility service is a necessity of modern life . . . . [T]he discontinuance of water or heating for even short periods of time may threaten health and safety." Id. The gravity of the health risks posed by a discontinuation of heating services is even greater for many HEAP recipients than for the general public, as the program specifically targets households which include potentially frail individuals. In addition, many other collateral effects may result from the termination of heat, including frozen plumbing, eviction and homelessness. See Sen. Rep. No. 103–251, 103rd Cong., 2d Sess. at *10 (1994). Clearly, then, the plaintiffs' interest in not being erroneously denied HEAP benefits is substantial.

In contrast, the government's interest in avoiding the procedures imposed by the district court is less significant. The district court ordered the defendants to modify their HEAP procedures in two respects: 1) by making post-determination fair hearings available to *all* HEAP claimants; and 2) by providing more extensive notice information to benefits claimants. See Kapps, 283 F.Supp.2d at 883. . . .

*a) Requirement of a Post-Determination Hearing*

[The court upheld the district court's requirement that the defendants issue their determination of HEAP eligibility no more than 45 days after the close of the program year, so that the claimants would have their full time under the statute to request a hearing.]

*b) Notice Relief*

In addition to awarding fair hearing relief, the district court found the defendants' HEAP eligibility notices to be constitutionally inadequate. Specifically, the court found that the defendants violated the requirements of due process by their failure to provide budgetary information[27], or other information which was sufficiently detailed as to allow HEAP applicants to understand the reasons for the defendants' benefits determination. The defendants contend that existing HEAP notices are sufficient, or that, at a minimum, genuine issues of material fact exist as to whether more detailed notices were warranted.

In order to be constitutionally adequate, notice of benefits determinations must provide claimants with enough information to understand the reasons for the agency's action. This requirement, like the right to a fair hearing, is a basic requirement of procedural due process. Claimants cannot know *whether* a challenge to an agency's action is warranted, much less formulate an effective challenge, if they are not provided with sufficient information to understand the basis for

---

[27] The district court ordered the provision of information about the agency's HEAP determination "in such detail as is necessary to permit a reasonable person to understand the basis for the agency's action, including: information about the household's annual income, annual energy costs, statewide energy cost standards, energy burden ratio, the presence of vulnerable household members, and income tier, as well as benefit computations in worksheet form." Kapps, 283 F.Supp.2d at 882. Like the parties, we refer to the totality of the additional information ordered by the district court as "budgetary information."

the agency's action. Thus, in the absence of effective notice, the other due process rights afforded a benefits claimant—such as the right to a timely hearing—are rendered fundamentally hollow.

While claimants must, therefore, be afforded enough information to understand the basis for the agency's action in all instances, the specific type of notice required will vary depending on the circumstances of each given case. Under Mathews v. Eldridge, the cost to the government, the claimant's interest, as well as the availability of alternative means of obtaining information, must all enter into the analysis. As a result, what may be constitutionally required in one context, may not be in another.

In the instant case, the defendants suggest that two factors rendered the district court's award of notice relief improper: 1) the allegedly prohibitive cost of providing the notice mandated by the district court; and 2) the availability to claimants of additional means of seeking out information. For the reasons set forth below, we disagree.

*1) The Cost of Providing the Notice Mandated by the District Court*

Much of the defendants' arguments against notice relief focus on the allegedly prohibitive cost of providing additional budgetary information. Specifically, the defendants allege that the cost of manually mating budgetary information to automatically generated notices would be exorbitant, and that the district court's conclusion that budgetary information could easily be included in the automated system (thus obviating the need for such manual pairing) was based on "pure speculation." . . .

Under Mathews, the cost to the defendants of providing improved notice is a relevant consideration. And we have, at times, relied on that consideration to place limits on the scope of due process notice relief. . . . Here, there is no evidence in the record from which we can conclude that the burden of affording improved notice would be unreasonable. The City Defendants' primary information technology expert, the Director of New York City's Office of Systems Development, testified in deposition that the HEAP computer system could be modified appropriately in 7–10 months, at the relatively modest cost of $75,000. And, the defendants have not identified any evidence to the contrary that was introduced below. Under the circumstances, the district court properly concluded that the expense of automatically including budgetary information in HEAP notices would not be unduly high. . . .

*2) The Availability to Claimants of Additional Means of Seeking Out Information*

As the defendants point out, existing HEAP notices inform claimants that they may seek out additional information about their HEAP eligibility in a number of ways. Thus, for example, existing notices provide claimants with a number to call, and inform claimants of the availability of meetings with benefits specialists. In addition, HEAP notices indicate that plaintiffs can access their case record, and may be able to obtain copies of certain documents in that record. Defendants contend that these alternate means of securing adequate information weigh heavily, under the second Mathews factor, in favor of finding the defendants' HEAP notice scheme to be constitutionally adequate.

The existence of alternate state procedures, which protect against a deprivation of due process, is without doubt relevant to, and may even be dispositive of, the Mathews v. Eldridge inquiry. This is particularly so where the plaintiffs' preferred procedures would impose a significant additional cost burden on the state. Where such a cost burden is likely, and the preferred procedure seems unlikely to constitute a material improvement over existing state processes, we are unlikely to find a due process violation.

Here, however, the addition of budgetary information to HEAP notices does not entail the placing of a major financial burden on the defendants. And, the addition of such information will, in all probability, increase significantly the ability of HEAP claimants to determine accurately whether an administrative appeal is warranted. As noted by the Seventh Circuit in a comparable context, it is common sense that a scheme which relies on beneficiaries to seek out basic information on why the agency took the action it did will result in "only the aggressive receiv[ing] their due process right to be advised of the reasons for the proposed action." See Vargas, 508 F.2d 485, 490 (1974); "The meek and submissive," in contrast, will "remain in the dark . . . ." Vargas, 508 F.2d at 490. Such an outcome seems particularly likely where, as here, many HEAP claimants face obstacles, such as advanced age, or disability, which make the process of seeking further information difficult.

iii. Conclusion

For all of the foregoing reasons, we hold that the district court appropriately granted the plaintiffs summary judgment on their due process claims . . .

## NOTES ON THE DECISION IN KAPPS v. WING

(1) ***Should Applicants for Benefits Get Constitutionally Mandated Process?*** As Judge Calabresi says, the Supreme Court has refused to decide this question, although several Justices have dissented from denials of certiorari in cases presenting the issue. E.g., Gregory v. Pittsfield, 470 U.S. 1018, 1021 (1985) (O'Connor, J., joined by Brennan, J., and Marshall, J.). The Kapps decision presents the issue as being, in effect, an easy one. To the same effect, see Cushman v. Shinseki, 576 F.3d 1290 (Fed. Cir. 2009) ("[A] veteran alleging a service-connected disability has a due process right to fair adjudication of his claim for benefits"). What might be said on the other side? Here are three possible arguments against holding that applicants are entitled to due process:

(a) The Constitutional requirement of due process by its terms comes into play only when government acts to "deprive"; not giving something to someone is different from depriving them of it.

(b) There is a considerable body of experimental psychology that shows that most people exhibit an "endowment effect" and are averse to loss: losing something they already have hurts more than not gaining something they might have had.

(c) Many more people apply for government benefits than get them. In Kapps the cost of providing process to the extra applicants who prove unworthy comes from the limited money available to help those who really need heat in the winter. In Goldberg, by contrast, the Court was only considering the by-definition smaller class of people who had at one time been judged eligible.

(2) ***Roth and Kapp.*** In Roth, Justice Marshall said: "In my view, every citizen who applies for a government job is entitled to it unless the government can establish some reason for denying the employment. This is the 'property' right that I believe is protected by the Fourteenth Amendment." But that was said in dissent and was necessarily rejected by the majority when it held that an untenured teacher who wanted to be rehired had no property right and deserved no hearing. Evidently the applicants-get-a-hearing principle goes only so far. How far?

(3) ***What About Discretion?*** Judge Calabresi spends a lot of energy investigating the precise details of the state and local rules underlying the heat assistance program. His purpose in doing this is to determine whether due process comes into play. It does if "life, liberty or property" are at stake; for this program, only "property" is potentially relevant, and to find "property," in the words of the Roth case, the claimant must have "a legitimate claim of entitlement." The judge says that if he were considering only the federal Low Income Home Energy Assistance Act he would decide that plaintiffs had no case: "the LIHEAA itself cannot be considered to 'channel' official discretion sufficiently 'meaningfully' so as to confer a due process protected property right." But it is different when he considers New York law as well: "Even a cursory examination of that law reveals that it provides precisely the type of discretion-limiting 'substantive predicates' that are the hallmarks of protected property rights." The Roth doctrine, then, is understood to divide the world of government benefits into those that are discretionary, and consequently not to be tested through due process, and those that are sufficiently cabined that a procedure to test them is warranted. Applying the same approach, the court in Ridgely v. Federal Emergency Management Agency, 512 F.3d 727, 736 (5th Cir. 2008), decided that the distribution of federal housing assistance following hurricane Katrina was not subject to the demands of due process: "[A]lthough [the statute] and the regulations set out eligibility criteria for the receipt of continued rent assistance, they contain no 'explicitly mandatory language' that *entitles* an individual to receive benefits if he satisfies that criteria. Because no 'specific directives' limit FEMA's discretion by compelling it to provide assistance upon a showing of eligibility, these provisions do not give rise to a property interest."

This approach might be defended by saying that, if all that is at stake is a discretionary judgment, the accurate determination of the facts that the second branch of the Mathews' test seems to emphasize loses importance. Against that would be the idea that there is a difference between blind discretion and informed discretion, and that requiring some process to inform the use of discretion is thus still warranted. Which view is the better view?

(4) STEPHEN F. WILLIAMS, LIBERTY AND PROPERTY: THE PROBLEM OF GOVERNMENT BENEFITS, 12 J. Legal Stud. 3, 13–14 (1983): "Besides drawing false analogies between [statutory] entitlements and property, entitlement theory has some adverse practical consequences. The first is that the entitlements theory is highly formalistic. By no intelligible criterion of value can it be said to sift out the more valuable from the less valuable interests in conditioned benefits. . . . [S]ince it expressly rejects an evaluation of the weight of the interest, entitlements theory would only by coincidence protect the more weighty ones . . .

"Second, because of its formalistic character, the entitlements analysis imposes perverse incentives upon the legislative and executive branches. So long as the government keeps a 'beneficiary' on tenterhooks by making receipt of loss of a benefit discretionary, it can keep free of the trammels of due process. . . . [T]he rule against unduly broad delegations will in some contexts prevent the use of totally discretionary criteria. Nonetheless, at the margin the entitlements approach sets up incentives against the evolution of clear substantive criteria for government allocation (or termination) of benefits—an odd way of protecting people from government."

## NOTES ON AN ALTERNATIVE LINE OF DOCTRINE

(1) ***Is Entitlements Analysis the Best Way to Go?*** Judge Calabresi cites, and asks us to compare, Washington Legal Clinic for the Homeless v. Barry, 107 F.3d 32 (D.C. Cir. 1997), which he describes as "concluding that a property interest in the receipt of shelter resources did not exist *where D.C. law did not mandate any particular priority system for the distribution of limited shelter resources*." That is a correct description of the case, and based on the language Calabresi italicized, the case is consistent with Kapps v. Wing. But does it represent an acceptable principle of law? If the legislative and executive branches are content to have officials exercise completely discretionary power, is that the end of the matter? This question might be analyzed as a matter of what constitutes an acceptable delegation of authority from Congress to an agency, but the nondelegation doctrine can be satisfied with statutes far more general than the specificity required in Kapps. (See Chapter VII, Section 2.a, p. 836) There is, however, another line of authority that suggests that due process itself has something to say about standardless administrative discretion.

(2) ***Lower Court Cases.*** HOLMES V. NEW YORK CITY HOUSING AUTHORITY, 398 F.2d 262 (2d Cir. 1968): Each year the Authority received approximately 90,000 applications for public housing, out of which it could select only 10,000 families for admission. In federally aided projects, it was required to follow an objective scoring system to choose among applicants. For projects built with state and local money, however, there was no similar requirement. Plaintiffs alleged that they had applied for public housing, that they had never been advised of their eligibility or ineligibility, and that applications filed with the Authority were not processed according to any reasonable, or

even ascertainable, system—not even by following a simple chronological waiting list. On interlocutory appeal, the court held that they stated a constitutional cause of action: "One charge made against the defendant, which has merit at least in connection with state-aided projects where the Authority has adopted no standards for selection among non-preference candidates, is that it thereby failed to establish the fair and orderly procedure for allocating its scarce supply of housing which due process requires. It hardly need be said that the existence of an absolute and uncontrolled discretion in an agency of government vested with the administration of a vast program, such as public housing, would be an intolerable invitation to abuse. See Hornsby v. Allen, 326 F.2d 605, 609–610 (5th Cir. 1964). For this reason alone due process requires that selections among applicants be made in accordance with 'ascertainable standards,' id. at 612, and, in cases where many candidates are equally qualified under these standards, that further selections be made in some reasonable manner such as 'by lot or on the basis of the chronological order of application.' Hornsby v. Allen, 330 F.2d 55, 56 (5th Cir. 1964) (on petition for rehearing). Due process is a flexible concept which would certainly also leave room for the employment of a scheme such as the 'objective scoring system' suggested in the resolution adopted by the Authority for federal-aided projects."

HORNSBY V. ALLEN, 326 F.2d 605 (5th Cir. 1964), on which Holmes relied, involved similar issues regarding the procedures used by a liquor licensing board to distribute liquor licenses. Both cases preceded Board of Regents v. Roth.

(3) ***Supreme Court Authority?*** Fans of the Holmes-Hornsby approach, when looking for Supreme Court authority, usually cite MORTON V. RUIZ, 415 U.S. 199 (1974), decided after Roth. Ruiz and his family, Papago Indians, moved 15 miles off the Papago reservation so that he could live and work at the Phelps-Dodge copper mines at Ajo, Arizona. They maintained close ties with the reservation and, said the Court, "have not been assimilated into the dominant culture." Twenty-seven years after the Ruizes moved, the miners went on strike, the state of Arizona refused general assistance to striking workers, and Ruiz applied for general assistance from the Bureau of Indian Affairs. The sole ground given for denying his application was that, although he lived *near* the reservation, the relevant portion of the BIA's internal Field Manual limited general assistance benefits to "Indians living *on* reservations" (emphasis added). The statutory basis for the assistance program was phrased in very general language, and the annual appropriations acts were similarly vague. On appeal, the government argued that BIA's formal budget requests had always stated that "[g]eneral assistance will be provided to needy Indians on reservations." However, as confirmed by page after page of the agency's testimony before Congress, the BIA had always represented that "on" included "near."

In one sense, this was the end of the case. The BIA's central defense was that Congress had appropriated funds only for those living on reservations. This defense had failed. There was little doubt that if anyone "near" reservations would qualify, the Ruizes would. Instead of stopping there, however, JUSTICE BLACKMUN's opinion for a unanimous Court went on to consider whether the agency's Field Manual might have some binding legal effect:

"Having found that the congressional appropriation was intended to cover welfare services at least to those Indians residing 'on or near' the reservation, it does not necessarily follow that the Secretary is without power to create reasonable classifications and eligibility requirements in order to allocate the limited funds available to him for this purpose. Thus, if there were only enough funds appropriated to provide meaningfully for 10,000 needy Indian beneficiaries and the entire class of eligible beneficiaries numbered 20,000, it would be incumbent upon the BIA to develop an eligibility standard to deal with this problem, and the standard, if rational and proper, might leave some of the class otherwise encompassed by the appropriation without benefits. But in such a case the agency must, at a minimum, let the standard be generally known so as to assure that it is being applied consistently and so as to avoid both the reality and the appearance of arbitrary denial of benefits to potential beneficiaries.

"Assuming, arguendo, that the Secretary rationally could limit the 'on or near' appropriation to include only the smaller class of Indians who lived directly 'on' the reservation . . . , the question that remains is whether this has been validly accomplished. The power of an administrative agency to administer a congressionally created and funded program necessarily requires the formulation of policy and the making of rules to fill any gap left, implicitly or explicitly, by Congress. In the area of Indian affairs, the Executive has long been empowered to promulgate rules and policies, and the power has been given explicitly to the Secretary and his delegates at the BIA. This agency power to make rules that affect substantial individual rights and obligations carries with it the responsibility not only to remain consistent with the governing legislation, but also to employ procedures that conform to the law. No matter how rational or consistent with congressional intent a particular decision might be, the determination of eligibility cannot be made on an ad hoc basis by the dispenser of the funds."

Commentators have been perplexed ever since about exactly what this condemnation of "ad hoc" agency behavior entails. Justice Blackmun did not state the legal basis for his approach. Does the BIA have to develop a legal framework for distributing funds because this is what Congress intended? Because this is a requirement of some federal common law of administrative procedure? Because this forestalls a conclusion under the APA that the agency has acted arbitrarily and capriciously? Or because due process so requires?

Occasional lower court cases have followed Ruiz both in requiring agencies to develop self-disciplining standards where the stakes for individuals are high—and in being less than clear on the legal basis of this requirement. The Eighth Circuit in two cases compelled the Secretary of Agriculture to promulgate standards implementing discretionary farm aid programs. See Iowa ex rel. Miller v. Block, 771 F.2d 347 (8th Cir. 1985) (suit to compel implementing regulations for statute that provided that the Secretary "may make disaster payments" whenever he determines that farms within the federal crop insurance program have suffered "substantial uncompensated disaster losses"); Allison v. Block, 723 F.2d 631 (8th Cir. 1983) (suit to compel implementing policies and procedures for exercising statutory discretion to defer foreclosure of farmers in default on federal loans). The Tenth Circuit, in Hobbs ex rel. Hobbs v. Zenderman, 579 F.3d 1171, 1185–86 (10th Cir. 2009), said that cases like Ruiz "establish, at most, a due process right to be free from eligibility determinations made without reference to any publicly-available standard." On the facts at hand, however, "we need not delineate the precise boundary of the right Hobbs alleges because the standards applied by defendants here are a far cry from no standards at all."

(4) ***Where Do Things Stand?*** LIGHTFOOT V. DISTRICT OF COLUMBIA, 448 F.3d 392 (D.C. Cir. 2006)—the case Judge Calabresi referred to in Kapps v. Wing—squarely presented the question whether due process requires the creation of discretion-constraining standards—until the issue was mooted out by the government's adopting such standards.

The plaintiffs were a class of D.C. employees whose disability benefits had been terminated, suspended, or reduced pursuant to the statutory power of the Mayor, or the Mayor's designee, to modify the benefit award if the Mayor "has reason to believe that a change of condition has occurred." The district court granted summary judgment on the plaintiff's claim that the District had "failed to adopt written and consistently applied standards, policies and procedures governing the termination, suspension and modification of benefits in violation of the Due Process Clause." It "remanded" the case to the District for rulemaking and ordered the plaintiffs' benefits reinstated until modification or termination decisions could be made under validly promulgated rules. Before the case could be considered by the D.C. Circuit on appeal, a combination of statutory amendments and emergency rules, accomplished by actions of the D.C. Council and the District's Office of Risk Management, had fulfilled the substance of the remand order. Additional claims were still pending, however, and the Court of Appeals (in a per curiam opinion) took the opportunity to express skepticism about the lower court's analysis (448 F.3d at 398):

"It may well be the case that an agency that terminates such statutorily-entitled benefits without any reason violates due process, because that would deprive a beneficiary of the capacity to challenge the termination. More controversial . . . is the claim that the Due Process Clause may impose a requirement of substantive standards—independent of statutory standards—that may be used to restrict an administrative agency's decision to terminate or modify a protected liberty or property interest. Assuming arguendo that such a cause of action can be made out, we think it is wholly without merit here because the [disability benefit statute] and D.C. court of appeals decisions themselves provide ample standards that would satisfy any such due process claim. There is certainly no conceivable due process claim that could be predicated on the notion that an agency must proceed to establish such standards through rulemaking rather than case-by-case determinations."

JUDGE SILBERMAN, concurring, was less restrained (448 F.3d at 400–01):

"The district court thought to import the APA scope of review into this § 1983 due process suit by relying on two rather old circuit court cases: White v. Roughton, 530 F.2d 750 (7th Cir. 1976), and Holmes v. New York City Housing Authority, 398 F.2d 262 (2d Cir. 1968). See also Peter L. Strauss et al., Gellhorn and Byse's Administrative Law 833 (10th ed. 2003). . . . [T]hese cases did not apply the Mathews v. Eldridge framework because Holmes preceded Mathews by almost eight years and White issued only three days after Mathews.

"It is quite understandable that appellees and the district court would see Holmes and White as somehow outside the Mathews v. Eldridge framework because the truth is that neither case is a proper interpretation of the Due Process Clause. Their focus . . . is not on process but on substance. Yet the Supreme Court's due process jurisprudence carefully distinguishes process from substance. The issue is always, in its due process cases, whether or not the claimant has had a fair opportunity—sometimes rather informal—to present his case and not whether the agency's substantive decision was reasonable. To be sure, as we today recognize, if an agency refused to give any reason for an initial deprivation, it would be impossible for the claimant to present an argument that the agency's decision was incorrect. So procedure is implicated. But that assuredly does not mean that the Due Process Clause can be used as a looming super-arbitrary-and-capricious standard governing the substantive decisions of an administrative agency no matter how much discretion the agency enjoys. The quality of an agency's reasoning is decidedly not a process issue.

"Granted, some Supreme Court justices in dissenting opinions have sought to expand due process analysis to include challenges to government substantive decisions. See, e.g., Bd. of Regents v. Roth, 408 U.S. 564, 588 (1972) (Marshall, J., dissenting). But the Court has never accepted that effort to transform the Due Process Clause. In short, Holmes and White are not only irrelevant to this case, they were also wrongly decided and simply do not survive . . ."

In the view of leading scholar Jerry L. Mashaw, Dignitary Process: A Political Psychology of Liberal Democratic Citizenship, 39 U. Fla. L. Rev. 433, 437 (1987), while cases like Holmes are "virtually moribund authorities," they were in fact "correctly decided." Or, as stated more recently by Cass Sunstein and Adrian Vermeule, also leading scholars, "Holmes and Hornsby, and those cases that follow them, are making a statement about the morality of administrative law." The Morality of Administrative Law, 131 Harv. L. Rev. 1924, 1940 (2018).

## LATIF v. HOLDER

United States District Court, D. Oregon (2014).
28 F.Supp.3d 1134.

■ BROWN, DISTRICT JUDGE.

This matter comes before the Court on Defendants' Motion for Partial Summary Judgment and Plaintiffs' Cross-Motion for Partial

Summary Judgment. . . . For the reasons that follow, the Court grants Plaintiffs' Cross-Motion and denies Defendants' Motion.

PLAINTIFFS' CLAIMS

Plaintiffs are citizens and lawful permanent residents of the United States (including four veterans of the United States Armed Forces) who were not allowed to board flights to or from the United States or over United States airspace. Plaintiffs believe they were denied boarding because they are on the No-Fly List, a government terrorist watch list of individuals who are prohibited from boarding commercial flights that will pass through or over United States airspace. Federal and/or local government officials told some Plaintiffs that they are on the No-Fly List.

Each Plaintiff submitted applications for redress through the Department of Homeland Security Traveler Redress Inquiry Program (DHS TRIP). Despite Plaintiffs' requests to officials and agencies for explanations as to why they were not permitted to board flights, explanations have not been provided and Plaintiffs do not know whether they will be permitted to fly in the future.

Plaintiffs allege in their Third Amended Complaint, Claim One, that Defendants have violated Plaintiffs' Fifth Amendment right to procedural due process because Defendants have not given Plaintiffs any post-deprivation notice nor any meaningful opportunity to contest their continued inclusion on the No-Fly List. . . .

FACTUAL BACKGROUND

The following facts are undisputed unless otherwise noted:

I. The No-Fly List

The Federal Bureau of Investigation (FBI), which administers the Terrorist Screening Center (TSC), develops and maintains the federal government's consolidated Terrorist Screening Database (TSDB or sometimes referred to as "the watch list"). The No-Fly List is a subset of the TSDB.

TSC provides the No-Fly List to TSA [Transportation Security Administration], a component of the Department of Homeland Security (DHS), for use in pre-screening airline passengers. TSC receives nominations for inclusion in the TSDB and generally accepts those nominations on a showing of "reasonable suspicion" that the individuals are known or suspected terrorists based on the totality of the information. TSC defines its reasonable-suspicion standard as requiring "articulable facts which, taken together with rational inferences, reasonably warrant the determination that an individual 'is known or suspected to be, or has been engaged in conduct constituting, in preparation for, in aid of or related to, terrorism or terrorist activities.' " Joint Statement of Stipulated Facts (# 84) at 4.

The government also has its own "Watchlisting Guidance" for internal law-enforcement and intelligence use, and the No-Fly List has its own minimum substantive derogatory criteria. The government does not release these documents.

II. DHS TRIP Redress Process

DHS TRIP is the mechanism available for individuals to seek redress for any travel-related screening issues experienced at airports or while crossing United States borders; i.e., denial of or delayed airline boarding, denial of or delayed entry into or exit from the United States, or continuous referral for additional (secondary) screening.

A. Administrative Review

Travelers who have faced such difficulties may submit a Traveler Inquiry Form to DHS TRIP online, by email, or by regular mail. The form prompts travelers to describe their complaint, to produce documentation relating to the issue, and to provide identification and their contact information. If the traveler is an exact or near match to an identity within the TSDB, DHS TRIP deems the complaint to be TSDB-related and forwards the traveler's complaint to TSC Redress for further review.

On receipt of the complaint, TSC Redress reviews the available information, including the information and documentation provided by the traveler, and determines (1) whether the traveler is an exact match to an identity in the TSDB and (2) whether the traveler should continue to be in the TSDB if the traveler is an exact match. When making this determination, TSC coordinates with the agency that originally nominated the individual to be included in the TSDB. If the traveler has been misidentified as someone who is an exact match to an identity in the TSDB, TSC Redress informs DHS of the misidentification. DHS, in conjunction with any other relevant agency, then addresses the misidentification by correcting information in the traveler's records or taking other appropriate action.

When DHS and/or TSC finish their review, DHS TRIP sends a determination letter advising the traveler that DHS TRIP has completed its review. A DHS TRIP determination letter neither confirms nor denies that the complainant is in the TSDB or on the No-Fly List and does not provide any further details about why the complainant may or may not be in the TSDB or on the No-Fly List. In some cases a DHS TRIP determination letter advises the recipient that he or she can pursue an administrative appeal of the determination letter with TSA or can seek judicial review in a United States court of appeals pursuant to 49 U.S.C. § 46110.

Determination letters, however, do not provide assurances about the complainant's ability to undertake future travel. In fact, DHS does not tell a complainant whether he or she is in the TSDB or a subset of the TSDB or give any explanation for inclusion on such a list at any point in the available administrative process. Thus, the complainant does not have an opportunity to contest or knowingly to offer corrections to the record on which any such determination may be based.

B. Judicial Review

When a final determination letter indicates the complainant may seek judicial review of the decisions represented in the letter, it does not advise whether the complainant is on the No-Fly List or provide the legal or factual basis for such inclusion. If the complainant submits a petition for review to the appropriate court, the government furnishes the court (but not the petitioner) with the administrative record.

If the administrative DHS TRIP review of a petitioner's redress file resulted in a final determination that the petitioner is not on the No-Fly List, the administrative record will inform the court of that fact. If, on the other hand, the administrative DHS TRIP review of a petitioner's redress file resulted in a final determination that the petitioner is and should remain on the No-Fly List, the administrative record will include the information that the government relied on to maintain that listing. The government may have obtained this information from human sources, foreign governments, and/or "signals intelligence." The government may provide to the court ex parte and in camera information that is part of the administrative record and that the government has determined is classified, Sensitive Security Information, law-enforcement investigative information, and/or information otherwise privileged or protected from disclosure by statute or regulation.

The administrative record also includes any information that the petitioner submitted to the government as part of his or her DHS TRIP request, and the petitioner has access to that portion of the record. As noted, at no point during the judicial-review process does the government provide the petitioner with confirmation as to whether the petitioner is on the No-Fly List, set out the reasons for including petitioner's name on the List, or identify any information or evidence relied on to maintain the petitioner's name on the List.

For a petitioner who is on the No-Fly List, the court will review the administrative record submitted by the government in order to determine whether the government reasonably determined the petitioner satisfied the minimum substantive derogatory criteria for inclusion on the List. If after review the court determines the administrative record supports the petitioner's inclusion on the No-Fly List, it will deny the petition for review. If the court determines the administrative record contains insufficient evidence to satisfy the substantive derogatory criteria, however, the government takes the position that the court may remand the matter to the government for appropriate action.

III. Plaintiffs' Pertinent History

Solely for purposes of the parties' Motions presently before the Court, Defendants do not contest the following facts as asserted by Plaintiffs:[5]

Plaintiffs are thirteen United States citizens who were denied boarding on flights over United States airspace after January 1, 2009,

---

[5] As a matter of policy, the United States government does not confirm or deny whether an individual is on the No-Fly List nor does it provide any other details as to that issue. Accordingly, Defendants have chosen not to refute Plaintiffs' allegations that they are on the No-Fly List for purposes of these Motions only. The Court, therefore, assumes for purposes of these Motions only that Plaintiffs' assertions regarding their inclusion on the No-Fly List are true.

and who believe they are on the United States government's No-Fly List. Airline representatives, FBI agents, or other government officials told some Plaintiffs that they are on the No-Fly List.

Each Plaintiff filed DHS TRIP complaints after being denied boarding and each received a determination letter that does not confirm or deny any Plaintiff's name is on any terrorist watch list nor provide a reason for any Plaintiff to be included in the TSDB or on the No-Fly List.

Many of these Plaintiffs cannot travel overseas by any mode other than air because such journeys by boat or by land would be cost-prohibitive, would be time-consuming to a degree that Plaintiffs could not take the necessary time off from work, or would put Plaintiffs at risk of interrogation and detention by foreign authorities. In addition, some Plaintiffs are not physically well enough to endure such infeasible modes of travel.

While Plaintiffs' circumstances are similar in many ways, each of their experiences and difficulties relating to and arising from their alleged inclusion on the No-Fly List is unique as set forth in their Declarations filed in support of their Motion and summarized briefly below.

*Ayman Latif:* Latif is a United States Marine Corps veteran and lives in Stone Mountain, Georgia, with his wife and children. Between November 2008 and April 2010 Latif and his family were living in Egypt. When Latif and his family attempted to return to the United States in April 2010, Latif was not allowed to board the first leg of their flight from Cairo to Madrid. One month later Latif was questioned by FBI agents and told he was on the No-Fly List. Because he was unable to board a flight to the United States, Latif's United States veteran disability benefits were reduced from $899.00 per month to zero as the result of being unable to attend the scheduled evaluations required to keep his benefits. In August 2010 Latif returned home after the United States government granted him a "one-time waiver" to fly to the United States. Because the waiver was for "one time," Latif cannot fly again, and therefore, he is unable to travel from the United States to Egypt to resume studies or to Saudi Arabia to perform a *hajj,* a religious pilgrimage and Islamic obligation.

*Mohamed Sheikh Abdirahm Kariye:* Kariye lives in Portland, Oregon, with his wife and children. In March 2010 Kariye was not allowed to board a flight from Portland to Amsterdam, was surrounded in public by government officials at the airport, and was told by an airline employee that he was on a government watch list. Because Kariye is prohibited from boarding flights out of the United States, he could not fly to visit his daughter who was studying in Dubai and cannot travel to Saudi Arabia to accompany his mother on the *hajj* pilgrimage.

*Raymond Earl Knaeble IV:* Knaeble is a United States Army veteran and lives in Chicago, Illinois. In 2006 Knaeble was working in Kuwait. In March 2010 Knaeble flew from Kuwait to Bogota, Colombia, to marry his wife, a Colombian citizen, and to spend time with her family. On

March 14, 2010, Knaeble was not allowed to board his flight from Bogota to Miami. Knaeble was subsequently questioned numerous times by FBI agents in Colombia. Because Knaeble was unable to fly home for a required medical examination, his employer rescinded its job offer for a position in Qatar. Knaeble attempted to return to the United States through Mexico where he was detained for over 15 hours, questioned, and forced to return to Bogota. Knaeble eventually returned to the United States in August 2010 by traveling for 12 days from Santa Marta, Colombia, to Panama City and then to Mexicali, California. United States and foreign authorities detained, interrogated, and searched Knaeble on numerous occasions during that journey.

[The court gives similar descriptions for ten other plaintiffs.]

DISCUSSION

As noted, Plaintiffs allege Defendants have violated Plaintiffs' Fifth Amendment rights to procedural due process because Defendants have not provided Plaintiffs with any post-deprivation notice nor any meaningful opportunity to contest their continued inclusion on the No-Fly List. . . .

The court must weigh three factors when evaluating the sufficiency of procedural protections. . . .

A. First Factor: Private Interest

Plaintiffs contend the first factor under Mathews weighs in their favor because Defendants' inclusion of Plaintiffs on the No-Fly List has deprived Plaintiffs of their constitutionally-protected liberty interests in travel and reputation.

1. Right to Travel

"The right to travel is a part of the 'liberty' of which the citizen cannot be deprived without due process of law under the Fifth Amendment." Kent v. Dulles, 357 U.S. 116, 125 (1958). . . . Defendants argue there is not a constitutional right to travel by airplane or by the most convenient form of travel. Defendants, therefore, contend Plaintiffs' rights to travel are not constitutionally burdened because the No-Fly List only prohibits travel by commercial aviation. . . . Although there are viable alternatives to flying for domestic travel within the continental United States such as traveling by car or train, the Court disagrees with Defendants' contention that international air travel is a mere convenience in light of the realities of our modern world. Such an argument ignores the numerous reasons that an individual may have for wanting or needing to travel overseas quickly such as the birth of a child, the death of a loved one, a business opportunity, or a religious obligation. . . .

As Plaintiffs' difficulties with international travel demonstrate, placement on the No-Fly List is a significant impediment to international travel. It is undisputed that inclusion on the No-Fly List completely bans listed persons from boarding commercial flights to or from the United States or over United States airspace. In addition, the realistic implications of being on the No-Fly List are far-reaching. For example, TSC shares watch-list information with 22 foreign governments, and United States Customs and Border Protection makes recommendations to ship captains as to whether a passenger poses a risk to transportation security. Thus, having one's name on the watch list can also result in interference with an individual's ability to travel by means other than commercial airlines as evidenced by some Plaintiffs' experiences as they attempted to travel internationally or return to the United States by sea and by land. In addition, the ban on air travel has exposed some Plaintiffs to extensive detention and interrogation at the hands of foreign authorities. With perhaps the exception of travel to a small number of countries in North and Central America, a prohibition on flying turns routine international travel into an odyssey that imposes significant logistical, economic, and physical demands on travelers. . . .

Accordingly, the Court concludes on this record that Plaintiffs have constitutionally-protected liberty interests in traveling internationally by air, which are significantly affected by being placed on the No-Fly List.

The first step of the Mathews inquiry, however, does not end with mere recognition of a liberty interest. The Court must also weigh the liberty interest deprived against the other factors.

As noted, placement on the No-Fly List renders most international travel very difficult or impossible. One need not look beyond the hardships suffered by Plaintiffs to understand the significance of the deprivation of the right to travel internationally. Due to the major burden imposed by inclusion on the No-Fly List, Plaintiffs have suffered significantly including long-term separation from spouses and children; the inability to access desired medical and prenatal care; the inability to pursue an education of their choosing; the inability to participate in important religious rites; loss of employment opportunities; loss of government entitlements; the inability to visit family; and the inability to attend important personal and family events such as graduations, weddings, and funerals. The Court concludes international travel is not a mere convenience or luxury in this modern world. Indeed, for many international travel is a necessary aspect of liberties sacred to members of a free society.

Accordingly, on this record the Court concludes Plaintiffs' inclusion on the No-Fly List constitutes a significant deprivation of their liberty interests in international travel.

2. Stigma-Plus-Reputation

Plaintiffs also assert the first factor under Mathews has been satisfied because Plaintiffs have been stigmatized "in conjunction with their right to travel on the same terms as other travelers." First Am. Compl. ¶ 141.

Under the "stigma-plus" doctrine, the Supreme Court has recognized a constitutionally-protected interest in "a person's good name, reputation, honor, or integrity." Wisconsin v. Constantineau, 400 U.S. 433, 437 (1971). "To prevail on a claim under the stigma-plus doctrine,

Plaintiffs must show (1) public disclosure of a stigmatizing statement by the government, the accuracy of which is contested; *plus* (2) the denial of some more tangible interest such as employment, or the alteration of a right or status recognized by state law." Green v. Transp. Sec. Admin., 351 F.Supp.2d 1119, 1129 (W.D.Wash.2005) (emphasis added). Plaintiffs contend, and Defendants do not dispute, that placement on the No-Fly List satisfies the "stigma" prong because it carries with it the stigma of being a suspected terrorist that is publicly disclosed to airline employees and other travelers near the ticket counter. . . .

As noted, the Court has concluded Plaintiffs have constitutionally-protected liberty interests in the right to travel internationally by air. In addition, the Court concludes Plaintiffs have satisfied the "plus" prong because being on the No-Fly List means Plaintiffs are legally barred from traveling by air at least to and from the United States and over United States airspace, which they would be able to do but for their inclusion on the No-Fly List. . . . Plaintiffs have constitutionally-protected liberty interests in their reputations.

On the other hand, Plaintiffs' private interests at the heart of their stigma-plus claim are not as strong. Although placement on the No-Fly List carries with it the significant stigma of being a suspected terrorist and Defendants do not contest the fact that the public disclosure involved may be sufficient to satisfy the stigma-plus test, the Court notes the limited nature of the public disclosure in this case mitigates Plaintiffs' claims of injury to their reputations. Because the No-Fly List is not released publicly, the "public" disclosure is limited to a relatively small group of individuals in the same area of the airport as the traveler when the traveler is denied boarding. Notwithstanding the fact that being denied boarding an airplane and, in some instances, being arrested or surrounded by security officials in an airport is doubtlessly stigmatizing, the Court notes the breadth and specificity of the public disclosure in this case is more limited than in the ordinary "stigma-plus" case. . . . Nevertheless, the Court concludes the injury to Plaintiffs' reputations is sufficient to implicate Plaintiffs' constitutionally-protected interests in their reputations.

On this record the Court concludes Plaintiffs' claims raise constitutionally-protected liberty interests both in international air travel and in reputation, and, therefore, the first factor under the Mathews test weighs heavily in Plaintiffs' favor.

B. Second Factor: Risk of Erroneous Deprivation

. . .

1. Risk of Erroneous Deprivation

When considering the risk of erroneous deprivation, the Court considers both the substantive standard that the government uses to make its decision as well as the procedural processes in place. As noted, nominations to the TSDB are generally accepted based on a "reasonable suspicion" that requires "articulable facts which, taken together with rational inferences, reasonably warrant the determination that an individual" meets the substantive derogatory criteria. Joint Statement of Stipulated Facts (# 84) ¶ 16. This "reasonable suspicion" standard is the same as the traditional reasonable suspicion standard commonly applied by the courts. See Terry v. Ohio, 392 U.S. 1, 21 (1968) (permitting investigatory stops based on a reasonable suspicion supported by "articulable facts which, taken together with rational inferences from those facts, reasonably warrant the intrusion."). Although reasonable suspicion requires more than "a mere 'hunch,'" the evidence available "need not rise to the level required for probable cause, and . . . falls considerably short of satisfying a preponderance of the evidence standard." United States v. Arvizu, 534 U.S. 266, 274 (2002).

It is against the backdrop of this substantive standard that the Court considers the risk of erroneous deprivation of the protected interests; i.e., the risk that travelers will be placed on the No-Fly List under Defendants' procedures despite not having a connection to terrorism or terrorist activities.

Defendants argue there is little risk of erroneous deprivation because the TSC has implemented extensive quality controls to ensure that the TSDB includes only individuals who are properly placed there. Defendants point out that the TSDB is updated daily and audited for accuracy and currentness on a regular basis and that each entry into the TSDB receives individualized review if the individual files a DHS TRIP inquiry. Finally, Defendants argue judicial review of the DHS TRIP determination further diminishes the risk of erroneous deprivation.

Plaintiffs, in turn, cite a 2007 report by the United States Government Accountability Office and a 2009 report by the Department of Justice Office of the Inspector General that concludes the TSDB contains many errors and that the TSC has failed to take adequate steps to remove or to modify records in a timely manner even when necessary. In addition, Plaintiffs maintain the lack of notice of inclusion on the No-Fly List or the reasons therefor forces aggrieved travelers to guess about the evidence that they should submit in their defense and, by definition, creates a one-sided and insufficient record at both the administrative and judicial level that does not provide a genuine opportunity to present exculpatory evidence for the correction of errors.

Defendants point out that the information on which Plaintiffs rely to support their contention that the TSC has failed to modify adequately or to remove records when necessary is outdated and that the 2009 report indicated significant progress in maintenance of the TSDB. Although Defendants are correct that the TSC appears to have made improvements in ensuring the TSDB is current and accurate, Plaintiffs' contention that the TSDB carries with it a risk of error, nevertheless, carries significant weight. . . .

In any event, the DHS TRIP process suffers from an even more fundamental deficiency. As noted, the reasonable suspicion standard used to accept nominations to the TSDB is a low evidentiary threshold. This low standard is particularly significant in light of Defendants' refusal to reveal whether travelers who have been denied boarding and who submit DHS TRIP inquiries are on the No-Fly List and, if they are on the List, to provide the travelers with reasons for their inclusion on the List. "Without knowledge of a charge, even simple factual errors may go uncorrected despite potentially easy, ready, and persuasive explanations." Al Haramain Islamic Found., Inc. v. United States Dep't of Treasury, 686 F.3d 965, 982 (9th Cir.2012).

The availability of judicial review does little to cure this risk of error. While judicial review provides an independent examination of the existing administrative record, that review is of the same one-sided and potentially insufficient administrative record that TSC relied on in its listing decision without any additional meaningful opportunity for the aggrieved traveler to submit evidence intelligently in order to correct anticipated errors in the record. Moreover, judicial review only extends to whether the government reasonably determined the traveler meets the minimum substantive derogatory criteria; i.e., the reasonable suspicion standard. Thus, the fundamental flaw at the administrative-review stage (the combination of a one-sided record and a low evidentiary standard) carries over to the judicial-review stage.

Accordingly, on this record the Court concludes the DHS TRIP redress process, including the judicial review of DHS TRIP determinations, contains a high risk of erroneous deprivation of Plaintiffs' constitutionally-protected interests.

2. Utility of Substitute Procedural Safeguards

In its analysis of the second Mathews factor, the Court also considers the probative value of additional procedural safeguards. Plaintiffs contend due process requires Defendants to provide post-deprivation notice of their placement on the No-Fly List; notice of the reasons they have been placed on the List; and a post-deprivation, in-person hearing to permit Plaintiffs to present exculpatory evidence. Notably, Plaintiffs argue these additional safeguards are only necessary after a traveler has been denied boarding. Defendants, in turn, assert the current procedures are sufficient in light of the compelling government interests in national security and protection of classified information.

Clearly, additional procedural safeguards would provide significant probative value. In particular, notice of inclusion on the No-Fly List through the DHS TRIP process after a traveler has been denied boarding would permit the complainant to make an intelligent decision about whether to pursue an administrative or judicial appeal. In addition, notice of the reasons for inclusion on the No-Fly List as well as an opportunity to present exculpatory evidence would help ensure the accuracy and completeness of the record to be considered at both the administrative and judicial stages and, at the very least, would provide aggrieved travelers the opportunity to correct "simple factual errors" with "potentially easy, ready, and persuasive explanations." See Al Haramain Islamic Found., 686 F.3d at 982. Thus, the Court concludes additional procedural safeguards would have significant probative value.

In summary, on this record the Court concludes the DHS TRIP process presently carries with it a high risk of erroneous deprivation in light of the low evidentiary standard required for placement on the No-Fly List together with the lack of a meaningful opportunity for individuals on the No-Fly List to provide exculpatory evidence in an effort to be taken off of the List. Moreover, the Court finds additional procedural safeguards would have significant probative value in ensuring that individuals are not erroneously deprived of their constitutionally-protected liberty interests. Accordingly, the Court concludes the second Mathews factor weighs heavily in favor of Plaintiffs.

C. The Government's Interest

When considering the third Mathews factor, the Court weighs "the Government's interest, including the function involved and the fiscal and administrative burdens that the additional or substitute procedural requirement would entail." Mathews, 424 U.S. at 335.

"[T]he Government's interest in combating terrorism is an urgent objective of the highest order." Holder v. Humanitarian Law Project, 561 U.S. 1, 28 (2010). "It is 'obvious and unarguable' that no governmental interest is more compelling than the security of the Nation." Haig v. Agee, 453 U.S. 280, 307 (1981).

"[T]he Constitution certainly does not require that the government take actions that would endanger national security." Al Haramain, 686 F.3d at 980. . . . Obviously, the Court cannot and will not order Defendants to disclose classified information to Plaintiffs.

On this record the Court concludes the governmental interests in combating terrorism and protecting classified information are particularly compelling, and, viewed in isolation, the third Mathews factor weighs heavily in Defendants' favor.

D. Balancing the Mathews Factors

"D]ue process, unlike some legal rules, is not a technical conception with a fixed content unrelated to time, place and circumstances." Gilbert v. Homar, 520 U.S. 924, 930 (1997). . . "The fundamental requisite of due process of law is the opportunity to be heard." Mullane v. Cent. Hanover Bank & Trust Co., 339 U.S. 306, 314 (1950). "This right to be heard has little reality or worth unless one is informed that the matter is pending and can choose for himself whether to appear or default, acquiesce or contest." Id. "An elementary and fundamental requirement of due process in any proceeding which is to be accorded finality is notice reasonably calculated, under all the circumstances, to apprise interested parties of the pendency of the action and afford them an opportunity to present objections." Circu v. Gonzales, 450 F.3d 990, 993 (9th Cir.2006).

1. Applicable Caselaw

Although balancing the Mathews factors is especially difficult in this case involving compelling interests on both sides, the Court, fortunately, does not have to paint on an empty canvass when balancing such interests. Indeed, several other courts have done so in circumstances that also required balancing a plaintiff's due-process right to contest the deprivation of important private interests with the government's interest in protecting national security and classified information. See, e.g., Al Haramain Islamic Foundation, Inc. v. U.S. Dep't of Treasury, 686 F.3d 965 (9th Cir. 2012); Jifry v. Fed. Aviation Admin., 370 F.3d 1174 (D.C. Cir. 2004); NCORI v. Dep't of State, 251 F.3d 192 (D.C. Cir. 2001); Ibrahim v. Dep't of Homeland Security, 2014 WL 1493561 (N.D. Cal. 2014); KindHearts for Charitable and Humanitarian Dev., Inc. v. Geithner, 647 F.Supp.2d 857 (N.D. Ohio 2009).

[The court proceeded to analyze each of the cited cases individually, reaching the following overall conclusions:]

2. Application to the DHS TRIP Process

. . .

A comparison of the procedural protections provided in this case with those provided in Al Haramain, Jifry, KindHearts, and NCORI reveals the DHS TRIP process falls far short of satisfying the requirements of due process. In Al Haramain, Jifry, and KindHearts the defendants provided the plaintiffs with some materials relevant to the respective agencies' reasons for the deprivation at some point in the proceedings. . . .

Unlike the plaintiffs in Al Haramain, KindHearts, and Jifry, however, Plaintiffs in this case were not given any notice of the reasons for their placement on the No-Fly List nor any evidence to support their inclusion on the No-Fly List. . . .

Defendants' failure to provide any notice of the reasons for Plaintiffs' placement on the No-Fly List is especially important in light of the low evidentiary standard required to place an individual in the TSDB in the first place. When only an ex parte showing of reasonable suspicion supported by "articulable facts ... taken together with rational inferences" is necessary to place an individual in the TSDB, it is certainly possible, and probably likely, that "simple factual errors" with "potentially easy, ready, and persuasive explanations" could go uncorrected. See Al Haramain, 686 F.3d at 982. Thus, without proper notice and an opportunity to be heard, an individual could be doomed to indefinite placement on the No-Fly List. Moreover, there is nothing in the DHS TRIP administrative or judicial-review procedures that remedies this fundamental deficiency. The procedures afforded to Plaintiffs through the DHS TRIP process are wholly ineffective and, therefore, fall short of the "elementary and fundamental requirement of due process" to be afforded "notice reasonably calculated, under all the circumstances, to apprise interested parties of the pendency of the action and afford them an opportunity to present objections." See Mullane, 339 U.S. at 314.

Accordingly, on this record the Court concludes the absence of any meaningful procedures to afford Plaintiffs the opportunity to contest their placement on the No-Fly List violates Plaintiffs' rights to procedural due process.

3. Due-Process Requirements

Although the Court holds Defendants must provide a new process that satisfies the constitutional requirements for due process, the Court concludes Defendants (and not the Court) must fashion new procedures that provide Plaintiffs with the requisite due process described herein without jeopardizing national security.

Because due process requires Defendants to provide Plaintiffs (who have all been denied boarding flights and who have submitted DHS TRIP inquiries without success) with notice regarding their status on the No-Fly List and the reasons for placement on that List, it follows that such notice must be reasonably calculated to permit each Plaintiff to submit evidence relevant to the reasons for their respective inclusions on the No-Fly List. In addition, Defendants must include any responsive evidence that Plaintiffs submit in the record to be considered at both the administrative and judicial stages of review. As noted, such procedures could include, but are not limited to, the procedures identified by the Ninth Circuit in Al Haramain; that is, Defendants may choose to provide Plaintiffs with unclassified summaries of the reasons for their respective placement on the No-Fly List or disclose the classified reasons to properly-cleared counsel.

Although this Court cannot foreclose the possibility that in some cases such disclosures may be limited or withheld altogether because any such disclosure would create an undue risk to national security, Defendants must make such a determination on a case-by-case basis . . .

CONCLUSION

For these reasons, the Court denies Defendants' Motion for Partial Summary Judgment and grants Plaintiffs' Cross-Motion for Partial Summary Judgment . . .

The Court directs the parties to confer as to the next steps in this litigation and to file no later than July 14, 2014, a Joint Status Report with their respective proposals and schedules. The Court will schedule a Status Conference thereafter at which primary counsel for the parties should plan to attend in person.

## NOTES ON THE NO-FLY LIST ISSUE

(1) ***The Statutory and Regulatory Context.*** The plaintiffs do not claim that they should have gotten notice when they were put on the No-Fly List; their complaint, says Judge Brown, is that they were neither given "any post-deprivation notice nor any meaningful opportunity to contest their continued inclusion on the No-Fly List." As part of the statute setting up the No-Fly List system, Congress directed the Administrator of the Transportation Security Administration to "establish a procedure to enable airline passengers, who are delayed or prohibited from boarding a flight because the advanced passenger prescreening system determined that they might pose a security threat, to appeal such determination and correct information contained in the system." 49 U.S.C. § 44903(j)(2)(C)(iii)(I). The implementing regulations, 49 CFR 1560.205, provide: "If an individual believes he or she

has been improperly or unfairly delayed or prohibited from boarding an aircraft or entering a sterile area as a result of the Secure Flight program, the individual may seek assistance through the redress process established under this section." This "redress process" involves the passenger's filing a form giving identifying information and specifying the complaint. Then, per the regulations, "TSA, in coordination with the TSC and other appropriate Federal law enforcement or intelligence agencies, if necessary, will review all the documentation and information requested from the individual, correct any erroneous information, and provide the individual with a timely written response." The process is not further specified. Does the regulation—unchanged since 2008—satisfy the statute? Does this informal adjudication satisfy § 555 of the APA, assuming it is applicable? Could a court interpreting the statute and applying the APA reach the same result Judge Brown reached—or is reliance on the due process clause, and Mathews balancing, necessary to the result?

(2) ***The Next Steps.*** Following Judge Brown's opinion, the government disclosed that seven of the thirteen plaintiffs were not on the No-Fly List. It then "sent to each of the remaining six Plaintiffs a notification letter that identified the applicable substantive criteria and provided an unclassified summary that included some reasons for placement of each individual on the No-Fly List. Although the unclassified summaries varied in length and detail, the letters did not disclose all of the reasons or information on which Defendants relied to maintain each Plaintiff's placement on the No-Fly List. Defendants stated they were 'unable to provide additional disclosures.'" LATIF V. LYNCH, 2016 WL 1239925 at *5 (D. Or. 2016) (This is a later opinion in the same case excerpted here; the name changed because the Attorney General, the first-named defendant, changed.) Those remaining plaintiffs then moved for summary judgment that the government's procedures violated due process for the following reasons, id. at *1:

1. The reasonable-suspicion standard that Defendants employed when placing an individual on the No-Fly List is insufficiently rigorous, and Defendants should only be permitted to place an individual on the No-Fly List if there is clear and convincing evidence to support such listing.

2. Defendants failed to provide Plaintiffs with a full statement of the reasons for each Plaintiff's placement on the No-Fly List;

3. Defendants failed to provide Plaintiffs with all material evidence concerning their placement on the No-Fly List;

4. Defendants failed to provide Plaintiffs with all exculpatory evidence concerning their placement on the No-Fly List;

5. Defendants failed to provide Plaintiffs with a live hearing before a neutral decision-maker at which Plaintiffs could confront and cross-examine witnesses; and

6. Defendants failed to provide Plaintiffs with additional disclosures using procedures . . . which include making disclosures to counsel who have security clearances, issuing protective orders, and presenting unclassified summaries of classified information.

The court responded to these claims as follows, id. at 2:

> 1. Due process does not require Defendants to apply the clear and convincing evidence standard to the No-Fly List determinations that Defendants made as to these Plaintiffs nor to provide original evidence to support such determinations. The reasonable-suspicion standard does not violate procedural due process when applied to a particular Plaintiff as long as Defendants provide such Plaintiff with (1) a statement of reasons that is sufficient to permit such Plaintiff to respond meaningfully and (2) any material exculpatory or inculpatory information in Defendants' possession that is necessary for such a meaningful response.
>
> 2. In some instances, however, Defendants may limit or withhold disclosures altogether in the event that such disclosures would create an undue risk to national security. In such instances Defendants must implement procedures to minimize the amount of material information withheld. In particular, Defendants must determine whether the information can be summarized in an unclassified summary and/or whether additional disclosures can be made to Plaintiffs' counsel who have the appropriate security clearances. When possible, Defendants must do so. When it is not possible, Defendants must so certify through a competent witness with personal knowledge of the reasons for Defendants' conclusion that they cannot make such additional disclosures.
>
> 3. Procedural due process in this context does not require Defendants to provide Plaintiffs with a live hearing before a neutral decision-maker at which Plaintiffs could confront and cross-examine witnesses.

Judge Brown then ruled that she needed further factual development before she could decide whether the notice the government gave the plaintiffs met these standards.

(3) ***Additional Procedures Adopted.*** In addition to the letters the government sent to the particular plaintiffs, it also filed in the case a "Notice" of new procedures under the DHS TRIP program that would be "made available to similarly situated U.S. persons" (Notice Regarding Revisions to DHS TRIP Procedures at 2–3, Latif v. Holder, Case: 3:10–cv–00750–BR (D. Or. Apr. 13, 2015)):

> Under the previous redress procedures, individuals who had submitted inquiries to DHS TRIP generally received a letter responding to their inquiry that neither confirmed nor denied their No Fly status. Under the newly revised procedures, a U.S. person who purchases a ticket, is denied boarding at the airport, subsequently applies for redress through DHS TRIP about the denial of boarding, and is on the No Fly List after a redress review, will now receive a letter providing his or her status on the No Fly List and the option to receive and/or submit additional information. If such an individual opts to receive and/or submit further information after receiving this initial response, DHS TRIP will

> provide a second, more detailed response. This second letter will identify the specific criterion under which the individual has been placed on the No Fly List and, consistent with the Court's June 24, 2014 decision, will include an unclassified summary of information supporting the individual's No Fly List status, to the extent feasible, consistent with the national security and law enforcement interests at stake. The amount and type of information provided will vary on a case-by-case basis, depending on the facts and circumstances. In some circumstances, an unclassified summary may not be able to be provided when the national security and law enforcement interests at stake are taken into account.
>
> This second letter will also provide the requester an opportunity to be heard further concerning their status. Written responses from such individuals may be submitted and may include exhibits or other materials the individual deems relevant. Upon DHS TRIP's receipt of an individual's submission in response to the second letter, the matter will be reviewed by the Administrator of the Transportation Security Administration (TSA) or his/her designee in coordination with other relevant agencies, who will review the submission, as well as the unclassified and classified information that is being relied upon to support the No Fly listing, and will issue a final determination. TSA will provide the individual with a final written determination, providing the basis for the decision (to the extent feasible in light of the national security and law enforcement interests at stake) and will notify the individual of the ability to seek further judicial review under 49 U.S.C. § 46110.

Eventually Judge Brown ruled that the process the government followed after prodding by the court satisfied the requirements of due process. This process consisted of: (1) telling individual plaintiffs whether they were, or were not, on the No-Fly List; (2) providing the plaintiffs on the list with the criteria used, and at least some of the information used, to put them on the list; and (3) providing those plaintiffs with a summary of the information withheld and the court with further information to be considered in camera. There remained the issue of whether the decision to place particular individuals on the list was proper, judged by the appropriate, substantive standard of review. This substantive review, the court held, belonged by statute in the Court of Appeals, which would now be able to do its work because it would have before it an administrative record generated by the procedures the government now had to provide, along with the plaintiffs' responses. Latif v. Sessions, 2017 WL 1434648 (D. Or. 2017), affirmed sub nom. Kashem v. Barr, 941 F.3d 358 (9th Cir. 2019).

Cases regarding the No-Fly List and the TRIP redress process have also been brought by other plaintiffs in other courts. For an example exhibiting the plethora of claims that can be at least stated in a complaint, see Kovac v. Wray, 363 F.Supp.3d 721 (N.D. Tex. 2019).

(4) ***An Earlier Look.*** The refusal of the court to require the live hearing for which plaintiffs asked can perhaps be evaluated by considering what such a hearing might look like. Would informants be asked to testify—and thereby

become known? Or would they be allowed to supply anonymous information—and thereby not be subject to challenge? The most famous case to raise this issue was BAILEY V. RICHARDSON, 182 F.2d 46 (D.C. Cir. 1950), aff'd by an equally divided Court, 341 U.S. 918 (1951). Having been discharged from federal government employment "due to reduction in force," Dorothy Bailey was denied reinstatement a year later, as the Cold War began, because "reasonable grounds" existed to believe her disloyal. Here is a description of her administrative hearing, as detailed by the dissenting judge:

"Appellant appeared and testified before a panel of the Loyalty Review Board. She submitted her own affidavit and the affidavits of some 70 persons who knew her, including bankers, corporate officials, federal and state officials, union members, and others. Again no one testified against her. She proved she had publicly and to the knowledge of a number of the affiants taken positions inconsistent with Communist sympathies. She showed not only by her own testimony but by that of other persons that she favored the Marshall Plan, which the Communist Party notoriously opposed, and that in 1940, during the Nazi-Soviet Pact, she favored Lend-Lease and was very critical of the Soviet position. In her union she urged its officers to execute noncommunist affidavits, opposed a foreign policy resolution widely publicized as pro-Russian, and favored what was then the official CIO resolution on foreign policy.

"Against all this, there were only the unsworn reports in the secret files to the effect that unsworn statements of a general sort, purporting to connect appellant with Communism, had been made by unnamed persons. Some if not all of these statements did not purport to be based on knowledge, but only on belief. Appellant sought to learn the names of the informants or, if their names were confidential, then at least whether they had been active in appellant's union, in which there were factional quarrels. The Board did not furnish or even have this information. Chairman Richardson said: 'I haven't the slightest knowledge as to who they were or how active they have been in anything.' All that the Board knew or we know about the informants is that unidentified members of the Federal Bureau of Investigation, who did not appear before the Board, believed them to be reliable. To quote again from the record: 'Chairman Richardson: I can only say to you that five or six of the reports come from informants certified to us by the Federal Bureau of Investigation as experienced and entirely reliable.' "

The D.C. Circuit ruled, two to one, that although Bailey "was not given a trial in any sense of the word," due process was not violated because government employment constituted neither life, nor liberty, nor property, so the due process clause did not apply. Hence the court did not have to do the more particular procedural analysis exemplified by the No-Fly List cases. The Bailey view of government employment has been replaced by the Roth/ Sindermann analysis, and indeed a footnote in the Roth opinion (Note 9, p. 600) reads: "In a leading case decided many years ago, the Court of Appeals for the District of Columbia Circuit held that public employment in general was a 'privilege,' not a 'right,' and that procedural due process guarantees therefore were inapplicable. Bailey v. Richardson, 182 F.2d 46, aff'd by an equally divided Court, 341 U.S. 918. The basis of this holding has been thoroughly undermined in the ensuing years." If that is so, what should the process in Bailey have looked like? Or what do you think of Judge Brown's effort in Latif to get the agency to build a record—which will ultimately be subject to judicial review—without requiring "a live hearing before a neutral decision-maker at which Plaintiffs could confront and cross-examine witnesses"?

(5) ***Limited Disclosure?*** One of the techniques Judge Brown endorses is the disclosure of sensitive information to a counsel for the no-fly designee who has the necessary security clearance. If you were that lawyer, how would you act vis-à-vis your own client?

(6) ***Bureaucratic Justice?*** Are individualized hearings the answer to the issues raised by security programs? Consider PETER M. SHANE, THE BUREAUCRATIC DUE PROCESS OF GOVERNMENT WATCH LISTS, 75 Geo. Wash. L. Rev. 804, 805–10 (2007): "Since the terrorist attacks of September 11, 2001, watch lists have become increasingly important tools for law enforcement and the protection of homeland security. The press has widely reported their existence, especially in relation to the screening of airline passengers. Each list is rooted in one or more databases that match information about persons suspected of terrorism-related activities or other criminal activity with directions for government action appropriate to that individual . . .

"The rationale for watch lists is straightforward. Both the United States as a nation and its citizens as individuals have the most profound stake in including on appropriate watch lists those persons who pose genuine threats to our national security, including the threat of terrorism. Properly managed watch lists can help ensure that persons connected with terrorist activity are denied both entry to the United States and dangerous access to vulnerable networks and other physical facilities. They can help focus legally permissible surveillance on fruitful targets and assist in the coordination of multi-agency efforts to track potential threats and prevent them from ripening into attacks.

"These interests are served, however, only to the extent that watch lists are accurate. Watch list errors are especially troubling because of the gravity of interests affected. The mistaken targeting of innocent persons subtracts from the limited resources available to pursue genuinely productive law enforcement and national security initiatives. To the extent that watch lists impede travel or immigration by noncitizens who present no actual threat to the United States, they can exact substantial cultural, political, and economic costs, in both the short and long term.

"The interests of individuals in avoiding erroneous listing are similarly compelling. For the person mistakenly targeted, costs may range from minor inconvenience to serious reputational damage or substantial limitations on privacy and freedom of action. The burdens could range from clandestine surveillance to a prohibition on entry into the United States or other travel. Perhaps the most publicized uses of watch lists have involved passenger screening on commercial airlines, which may result in intensified identity checks, personal inspection, and (for persons on the 'No-Fly' List) an effective ban on commercial air travel altogether.

"More than merely instrumental values are at stake, however, in the maintenance of watch list accuracy: the misuse of watch lists threatens our society's fundamental values. Secret programs of any kind strain the norms of openness and transparency on which democratic legitimacy is based . . . It is therefore crucial for government, in deploying secret watch lists as tools of law enforcement and national security, to address the inevitability of watch list error in a way that maintains individual dignity and our collective values of mutual trust and democratic accountability.

"To American lawyers, the problems posed by watch lists are readily perceived as problems of 'procedural due process.' The federal government has established what amounts to a system of informal adjudication—namely, the identification of persons to include on terrorist watch lists—which if performed in error threatens significant harm to individual persons. The conventional 'due process' response to this risk of adjudicative error is typically 'some kind of hearing,' either to prevent or redress the error through additional adjudicative formalities. The adjudication of individual disputes, whether administratively or in judicial forums, however, cannot be the sole component of a program to pursue watch list fairness. On the one hand, the very aim of the watch list program is likely to preclude the possibility of preinclusion hearings for many of those persons proposed for listing. Presumably, affording a suspect notice that he or she might be the subject of covert surveillance would be self-defeating. On the other hand, redress through postinclusion mechanisms would succeed only retrospectively and only for those individuals who become aware of their inclusion. Thousands of individuals might remain unjustifiably disadvantaged by the watch lists through decisionmaking procedures of which they are unaware. It ought to be viewed as intolerable in a democratic society for large numbers of innocent people to be stigmatized by the government under a largely secret program, even if such cases can be 'redressed' through postinclusion individual review.

"What is needed is a more robust form of what Professor Jerry Mashaw has labeled 'bureaucratic justice': an institutional blending of 'positive administration, bureaucratically organized' with law-like constraints on the exercise of discretion designed to secure important public values . . ."

(7) ***Or How About This?*** SHIRIN SINNAR, TOWARD A FAIRER TERRORIST WATCHLIST, 40 Admin. and Reg. L. News 4, 5 (2015): "[P]olicymakers and courts should question the premise of the No Fly List itself: that certain individuals who are not charged with any crime are nonetheless too dangerous to fly under any circumstances. Is it truly the case that no set of extra security procedures, especially with respect to U.S. citizens and residents, could sufficiently mitigate the threat posed? The government has sometimes granted 'one-time waivers' allowing Americans abroad to fly back to the United States, especially after they filed suit; in such cases, the government conditioned air travel on special security measures, such as advance submission of travel itineraries and extra screening (and perhaps also seated the individuals next to undisclosed federal air marshals). Even

for individuals who are judged to meet the standards for inclusion on the No Fly List, measures short of total air travel bans might be available without compromising security."

## c. Due Process and "Private" Administration

*RENDELL-BAKER v. KOHN*
*Notes on "State Action"*
*THOMAS M. COOLEY LAW SCHOOL v. AMERICAN BAR ASSOCIATION*
*Notes on "Common Law Due Process"*

### RENDELL-BAKER v. KOHN

Supreme Court of the United States (1982).
457 U.S. 830.

■ CHIEF JUSTICE BURGER delivered the opinion of the Court.

We granted certiorari to decide whether a private school, whose income is derived primarily from public sources and which is regulated by public authorities, acted under color of state law when it discharged certain employees.

I

A

Respondent Kohn is the director of the New Perspectives School, a nonprofit institution located on privately owned property in Brookline, Massachusetts. The school was founded as a private institution and is operated by a board of directors, none of whom are public officials or are chosen by public officials. The school specializes in dealing with students who have experienced difficulty completing public high schools; many have drug, alcohol, or behavioral problems, or other special needs. In recent years, nearly all of the students at the school have been referred to it by the Brookline or Boston School Committees, or by the Drug Rehabilitation Division of the Massachusetts Department of Mental Health. The school issues high school diplomas certified by the Brookline School Committee.

When students are referred to the school by Brookline or Boston under Chapter 766 of the Massachusetts Acts of 1972, the School Committees in those cities pay for the students' education.[1] The school also receives funds from a number of other state and federal agencies. In recent years, public funds have accounted for at least 90%, and in one year 99%, of respondent school's operating budget. There were

---

[1] Chapter 766, 1972 Mass. Acts, Mass. Gen. Laws, ch. 71B, § 3 (West Supp.1981), requires school committees to identify students with special needs and to develop suitable educational programs for such students. Massachusetts Gen. Laws, ch. 71B, § 4, provides that school committees may "enter into an agreement with any public or private school, agency, or institution to provide the necessary special education" for these students . . .

approximately 50 students at the school in those years and none paid tuition.[2]

To be eligible for tuition funding under Chapter 766, the school must comply with a variety of regulations, many of which are common to all schools. The State has issued detailed regulations concerning matters ranging from recordkeeping to student-teacher ratios. Concerning personnel policies, the Chapter 766 regulations require the school to maintain written job descriptions and written statements describing personnel standards and procedures, but they impose few specific requirements.

The school is also regulated by Boston and Brookline as a result of its Chapter 766 funding. By its contract with the Boston School Committee, which refers to the school as a "contractor," the school must agree to carry out the individualized plan developed for each student referred to the school by the Committee. The contract specifies that school employees are not city employees.

The school also has a contract with the State Drug Rehabilitation Division. Like the contract with the Boston School Committee, that agreement refers to the school as a "contractor." It provides for reimbursement for services provided for students referred to the school by the Drug Rehabilitation Division, and includes requirements concerning the services to be provided. Except for general requirements, such as an equal employment opportunity requirement, the agreement does not cover personnel policies.

While five of the six petitioners were teachers at the school, petitioner Rendell-Baker was a vocational counselor hired under a grant from the federal Law Enforcement Assistance Administration, whose funds are distributed in Massachusetts through the State Committee on Criminal Justice. As a condition of the grant, the Committee on Criminal Justice must approve the school's initial hiring decisions. The purpose of this requirement is to insure that the school hires vocational counselors who meet the qualifications described in the school's grant proposal to the Committee; the Committee does not interview applicants for counselor positions.

B

[The Petitioners were all discharged following disputes they had with Director Kohn. Rendell-Baker's dispute concerned the proper role of a student-staff council in making hiring decisions. The other five had, in a separate matter, written a letter to the school's board of directors recommending Kohn's dismissal and had also taken their grievances to the local newspaper. All were discharged by Kohn without her, or anyone else's, having held a hearing. In separate lawsuits Rendell-Baker and the

---

2 Amicus curiae Massachusetts Association of 766 Approved Private Schools, Inc., of which the New Perspectives School is a member, informs the Court that many of its members have a student population which is more or less evenly divided between students referred and paid for by the State and students referred and paid for by their parents or guardians.

other five sought relief under 42 U.S.C. § 1983 for alleged violations of the First, Fifth, and Fourteenth Amendments.]

C

On April 16, 1980, the District Court for the District of Massachusetts, 488 F.Supp. 764, granted the defendant's motion for summary judgment in the suit brought by Rendell-Baker. A claim may be brought under § 1983 only if the defendant acted "under color" of state law.[4] . . . [T]he District Court concluded that the nexus between the school and the State was not sufficiently close so that the action of the school in discharging Rendell-Baker could be considered action of the Commonwealth of Massachusetts.

Nine days earlier, on April 7, 1980, a different judge of the District Court for the District of Massachusetts had reached a contrary conclusion on the same question in the case brought by the other five petitioners. . . . Accordingly, it held that the defendants acted under color of state law and denied the motion to dismiss. However, on June 13, 1980, noting that there was substantial ground for disagreement on that holding, the District Court certified its order as immediately appealable pursuant to 28 U.S.C. § 1292(b).

D

The Court of Appeals for the First Circuit consolidated the two actions. It noted that the school's funding, regulation, and function show that it has a close relationship with the State. However, it stressed that the school is managed by a private board and that the State has relatively little involvement in personnel matters. It concluded that the school, although regulated by the State, was not dominated by the State, especially with respect to decisions involving the discharge of personnel. The Court of Appeals then concluded that the District Court which certified the question in the action brought by the five teachers had erred in concluding that the defendants acted under color of state law. . . .

We granted certiorari, and we affirm.

II

A

Petitioners do not claim that their discharges were discriminatory in violation of Title VII of the Civil Rights Act of 1964. Nor do they claim that their discharges were unfair labor practices in violation of the National Labor Relations Act. Rather, they allege that respondents violated 42 U.S.C. § 1983 by discharging them because of their exercise of their First Amendment right of free speech and without the process due them under the Fourteenth Amendment. . . . The ultimate issue in determining whether a person is subject to suit under § 1983 is the same

[4] Title 42 U.S.C. § 1983 provides: "Every person who, under color of any statute, ordinance, regulation, custom, or usage, of any State or Territory, subjects, or causes to be subjected, any citizen of the United States or other person within the jurisdiction thereof to the deprivation of any rights, privileges, or immunities secured by the Constitution and laws, shall be liable to the party injured in an action at law, suit in equity, or other proper proceeding for redress."

question posed in cases arising under the Fourteenth Amendment: is the alleged infringement of federal rights "fairly attributable to the State?" Lugar v. Edmondson Oil Co., 457 U.S. 922, 937 (1982). The core issue presented in this case is not whether petitioners were discharged because of their speech or without adequate procedural protections, but whether the school's action in discharging them can fairly be seen as state action. If the action of the respondent school is not state action, our inquiry ends.

B

In Blum v. Yaretsky, 457 U.S. 991 (1982), the Court analyzed the state action requirement of the Fourteenth Amendment. The Court considered whether certain nursing homes were state actors for the purpose of determining whether decisions regarding transfers of patients could be fairly attributed to the State, and hence be subjected to Fourteenth Amendment due process requirements. The challenged transfers primarily involved decisions, made by physicians and nursing home administrators, to move patients from "skilled nursing facilities" to less expensive "health related facilities." Like the New Perspectives School, the nursing homes were privately owned and operated. Relying on [several cases] the Court held that, "a State normally can be held responsible for a private decision only when it has exercised coercive power or has provided such significant encouragement, either overt or covert, that the choice must in law be deemed to be that of the State." In determining that the transfer decisions were not actions of the State, the Court considered each of the factors alleged by petitioners here to make the discharge decisions of the New Perspectives School fairly attributable to the State.

First, the nursing homes, like the school, depended on the State for funds; the State subsidized the operating and capital costs of the nursing homes, and paid the medical expenses of more than 90% of the patients. Here the Court of Appeals concluded that the fact that virtually all of the school's income was derived from government funding was the strongest factor to support a claim of state action. But in Blum v. Yaretsky, we held that the similar dependence of the nursing homes did not make the acts of the physicians and nursing home administrators acts of the State, and we conclude that the school's receipt of public funds does not make the discharge decisions acts of the State.

The school, like the nursing homes, is not fundamentally different from many private corporations whose business depends primarily on contracts to build roads, bridges, dams, ships, or submarines for the government. Acts of such private contractors do not become acts of the government by reason of their significant or even total engagement in performing public contracts.

The school is also analogous to the public defender found not to be a state actor in Polk County v. Dodson, 454 U.S. 312 (1981). There we concluded that, although the State paid the public defender, her relationship with her client was "identical to that existing between any other lawyer and client." Id., at 318. Here the relationship between the school and its teachers and counselors is not changed because the State pays the tuition of the students.

A second factor considered in Blum v. Yaretsky was the extensive regulation of the nursing homes by the State. There the State was indirectly involved in the transfer decisions challenged in that case because a primary goal of the State in regulating nursing homes was to keep costs down by transferring patients from intensive treatment centers to less expensive facilities when possible. Both state and federal regulations encouraged the nursing homes to transfer patients to less expensive facilities when appropriate. The nursing homes were extensively regulated in many other ways as well. The Court relied on Jackson v. Metropolitan Edison Co., 419 U.S. 345 (1974) where we held that state regulation, even if "extensive and detailed," 419 U.S., at 350, did not make a utility's actions state action.

Here the decisions to discharge the petitioners were not compelled or even influenced by any state regulation. Indeed, in contrast to the extensive regulation of the school generally, the various regulators showed relatively little interest in the school's personnel matters. The most intrusive personnel regulation promulgated by the various government agencies was the requirement that the Committee on Criminal Justice had the power to approve persons hired as vocational counselors. Such a regulation is not sufficient to make a decision to discharge, made by private management, state action.

The third factor asserted to show that the school is a state actor is that it performs a "public function." However, our holdings have made clear that the relevant question is not simply whether a private group is serving a "public function." We have held that the question is whether the function performed has been "traditionally the *exclusive* prerogative of the State." Jackson, supra, at 353; quoted in Blum v. Yaretsky, 457 U.S., at 1011 (emphasis added). There can be no doubt that the education of maladjusted high school students is a public function, but that is only the beginning of the inquiry. Chapter 766 of the Massachusetts Acts of 1972 demonstrates that the State intends to provide services for such students at public expense. That legislative policy choice in no way makes these services the exclusive province of the State. Indeed, the Court of Appeals noted that until recently the State had not undertaken to provide education for students who could not be served by traditional public schools. That a private entity performs a function which serves the public does not make its acts state action.

Fourth, petitioners argue that there is a "symbiotic relationship" between the school and the State similar to the relationship involved in Burton v. Wilmington Parking Authority, 365 U.S. 715 (1961). Such a claim is rejected in Blum v. Yaretsky, and we reject it here. In Burton, the Court held that the refusal of a restaurant located in a public parking garage to serve Negroes constituted state action. The Court stressed that the restaurant was located on public property and that the rent from the restaurant contributed to the support of the garage. In response to the argument that the restaurant's profits, and hence the State's financial position, would suffer if it did not discriminate, the Court concluded that this showed that the State profited from the restaurant's discriminatory conduct. The Court viewed this as support for the conclusion that the State should be charged with the discriminatory actions. Here the school's fiscal relationship with the State is not different from that of many contractors performing services for the government. No symbiotic relationship such as existed in Burton exists here.

C

We hold that petitioners have not stated a claim for relief under 42 U.S.C. § 1983; accordingly, the judgment of the Court of Appeals for the First Circuit is

Affirmed.

■ JUSTICE WHITE, concurring in the judgments.

[Opinion omitted]

■ JUSTICE MARSHALL, with whom JUSTICE BRENNAN joins, dissenting.

Petitioners in these consolidated cases, former teachers and a counselor at the New Perspectives School in Brookline, Mass., were discharged by the school's administrators when they criticized certain school policies. They commenced actions under 42 U.S.C. § 1983, claiming that they had been discharged in violation of the First, Fifth, and Fourteenth Amendments. The Court today holds that their suits must be dismissed because the school did not act "under color" of state law. According to the majority, the decision of the school to discharge petitioners cannot fairly be regarded as a decision of the Commonwealth of Massachusetts.

In my view, this holding simply cannot be justified. The State has delegated to the New Perspectives School its statutory duty to educate children with special needs. The school receives almost all of its funds from the State, and is heavily regulated. This nexus between the school and the State is so substantial that the school's action must be considered state action. I therefore dissent. . . .

The decisions of this Court clearly establish that where there is a symbiotic relationship between the State and a privately owned enterprise, so that the State and a privately owned enterprise are participants in a joint venture, the actions of the private enterprise may be attributable to the State. "Conduct that is formally 'private' may become so entwined with governmental policies or so impregnated with a governmental character" that it can be regarded as governmental action. Evans v. Newton, 382 U.S. 296 (1966). The question whether such a relationship exists "can be determined only in the framework of the peculiar facts or circumstances present." Burton v. Wilmington Parking Authority, 365 U.S. 715, 726 (1961). Here, an examination of the facts and circumstances leads inexorably to the conclusion that the actions of the New Perspectives School should be attributed to the State; it is difficult to imagine a closer relationship between a government and a private enterprise.

The New Perspectives School receives virtually all of its funds from state sources. This financial dependence on the State is an important indicium of governmental involvement. The school's very survival depends on the State. If the State chooses, it may exercise complete control over the school's operations simply by threatening to withdraw financial support if the school takes action that it considers objectionable.

The school is heavily regulated and closely supervised by the State. This fact provides further support for the conclusion that its actions should be attributed to the State. The school's freedom of decisionmaking is substantially circumscribed by the Massachusetts Department of Education's guidelines and the various contracts with state agencies. For example, the school is required to develop and comply with written rules for hiring and dismissal of personnel. Almost every decision the school makes is substantially affected in some way by the State's regulations.[1] . . .

The school's provision of a substitute for public education deserves particular emphasis because of the role of Chapter 766. Under this statute, the State is *required* to provide a free education to all children, including those with special needs. Clearly, if the State had decided to provide the service itself, its conduct would be measured against constitutional standards. The State should not be permitted to avoid constitutional requirements simply by delegating its statutory duty to a private entity.[3] In my view, such a delegation does not convert the performance of the duty from public to private action when the duty is specific and the private institution's decisionmaking authority is significantly curtailed.

When an entity is not only heavily regulated and funded by the State, but also provides a service that the State is required to provide, there is a very close nexus with the State. Under these circumstances, it is entirely appropriate to treat the entity as an arm of the State. Here, since the New Perspectives School exists solely to fulfill the State's obligations under Chapter 766, I think it fully reasonable to conclude that the school is a state actor. . . .

---

1 The majority argues that the fact that the school receives almost all of its funds from the state is not enough, by itself, to justify a finding of state action. It also contends that the fact that the school is closely supervised and heavily regulated is not enough, by itself, to justify such a finding. I am in general agreement with both propositions. However, when these two factors are present in the same case, and when other indicia of state action are also present, a finding of state action may very well be justified. By analyzing the various indicia of state action separately, without considering their cumulative impact, the majority commits a fundamental error.

3 A State may not deliberately delegate a task to a private entity in order to avoid its constitutional obligations. Terry v. Adams, 345 U.S. 461 (1953). But a State's decision to delegate a duty to a private entity should be carefully examined even when it has acted, not in bad faith, but for reasons of convenience. The doctrinal basis for the state action requirement is that exercises of state authority pose a special threat to constitutional values. A private entity vested with state authority poses that threat just as clearly as a state agency.

## NOTES ON "STATE ACTION"

(1) ***Where Is the "State Action" Line?*** Compare BRENTWOOD ACADEMY V. TENNESSEE SECONDARY SCHOOL ATHLETIC ASS'N, 531 U.S. 288 (2001): The Athletic Association found Brentwood Academy, a private parochial high school, to have committed recruiting violations. It placed Brentwood's athletic program on probation for four years, declared its football and boys' basketball teams ineligible to compete in playoffs for two years, and imposed a $3,000 fine. Brentwood sued under § 1983, alleging, among other things, due process violations. Held: the suit could proceed because, even though the Association was a separately incorporated membership organization, its "regulatory activity may and should be treated as state action." Id. at 291. JUSTICE SOUTER for the Court:

"The nominally private character of the Association is overborne by the pervasive entwinement of public institutions and public officials in its composition and workings, and there is no substantial reason to claim unfairness in applying constitutional standards to it.

"The Association is not an organization of natural persons acting on their own, but of schools, and of public schools to the extent of 84% of the total. Under the Association's bylaws, each member school is represented by its principal or a faculty member, who has a vote in selecting members of the governing legislative council and board of control from eligible principals, assistant principals, and superintendents.

"Although the findings and prior opinions in this case include no express conclusion of law that public school officials act within the scope of their duties when they represent their institutions, no other view would be rational, the official nature of their involvement being shown in any number of ways. Interscholastic athletics obviously play an integral part in the public education of Tennessee, where nearly every public high school spends money on competitions among schools. Since a pickup system of interscholastic games would not do, these public teams need some mechanism to produce rules and regulate competition. The mechanism is an organization overwhelmingly composed of public school officials who select representatives (all of them public officials at the time in question here), who in turn adopt and enforce the rules that make the system work. Thus, by giving these jobs to the Association, the 290 public schools of Tennessee belonging to it can sensibly be seen as exercising their own authority to meet their own responsibilities. Unsurprisingly, then, the record indicates that half the council or board meetings documented here were held during official school hours, and that public schools have largely provided for the Association's financial support. A small portion of the Association's revenue comes from membership dues paid by the schools, and the principal part from gate receipts at tournaments among the member schools. Unlike mere public buyers of contract services, whose payments for services rendered do not convert the service providers into public actors, see Rendell-Baker, 457 U.S., at 839–843, the schools here obtain membership in the service organization and give up sources of their own income to their collective association. The Association thus exercises the authority of the predominantly public schools to charge for admission to their games; the Association does not receive this money from the schools, but enjoys the schools' moneymaking capacity as its own.

"In sum, to the extent of 84% of its membership, the Association is an organization of public schools represented by their officials acting in their official capacity to provide an integral element of secondary public schooling. There would be no recognizable Association, legal or tangible, without the public school officials, who do not merely control but overwhelmingly perform all but the purely ministerial acts by which the Association exists and functions in practical terms. Only the 16% minority of private school memberships prevents this entwinement of the Association and the public school system from being total and their identities totally indistinguishable." 531 U.S. at 298–300.

In contrast, JUSTICE THOMAS for four dissenting Justices:

". . . [C]ommon sense dictates that the TSSAA's actions cannot fairly be attributed to the State, and thus cannot constitute state action. The TSSAA was formed in 1925 as a private corporation to organize interscholastic athletics and to sponsor tournaments among its member schools. Any private or public secondary school may join the TSSAA by signing a contract agreeing to comply with its rules and decisions. Although public schools currently compose 84% of the TSSAA's membership, the TSSAA does not require that public schools constitute a set percentage of its membership, and, indeed, no public school need join the TSSAA. The TSSAA's rules are enforced not by a state agency but by its own board of control, which comprises high school principals, assistant principals, and superintendents, none of whom must work at a public school. Of course, at the time the recruiting rule was enforced in this case, all of the board members happened to be public school officials. However, each board member acts in a representative capacity on behalf of all the private and public schools in his region of Tennessee, and not simply his individual school.

"The State of Tennessee did not create the TSSAA. The State does not fund the TSSAA and does not pay its employees. In fact, only 4% of the TSSAA's revenue comes from the dues paid by member schools; the bulk of its operating budget is derived from gate receipts at tournaments it sponsors. The State does not permit the TSSAA to use state-owned facilities for a discounted fee, and it does not exempt the TSSAA from state taxation. No Tennessee law authorizes the State to coordinate interscholastic athletics or empowers another entity to organize interscholastic athletics on behalf of the State. The only state pronouncement acknowledging the TSSAA's existence is a rule providing that the State Board of Education permits public schools to maintain membership in the TSSAA if they so choose.

"Moreover, the State of Tennessee has never had any involvement in the particular action taken by the TSSAA in this case: the enforcement of the TSSAA's recruiting rule prohibiting members from using 'undue influence' on students or their parents or guardians 'to secure or to retain a student for athletic purposes.' There is no indication that the State has ever had any interest in how schools choose to regulate recruiting. In fact, the TSSAA's authority to enforce its recruiting rule arises solely from the voluntary membership contract that each member school signs, agreeing to conduct its athletics in accordance with the rules and decisions of the TSSAA." 531 U.S. at 306–08.

(2) ***The Phenomenon of Privatization.*** Governments have always relied on private parties; it is hard to imagine a government that itself would make all of its military equipment or build and furnish every one of its buildings. But alongside the growth of governmental responsibilities in the modern world there has also been a growing reliance on private parties to carry out some of these responsibilities: when the U.S. army operated in Iraq and Afghanistan, so too did many contractors brought there on government contracts; and in many states various prisoners are now housed in prisons run by corporations. To say that every private party doing something for the government is thereby made subject to the due process clause would be too broad; to say that no nominally private party is subject to the strictures of the Constitution would be too narrow. Hence the Justices' problem. Moreover, the problem arises not only with respect to the due process clause but also, and historically more importantly, with respect to the equal protection clause. Hence the Justices' further headache. As both the Rendell-Baker principal case and the Brentwood Academy note case suggest, the resulting opinions are often fact-intensive and the outcomes often hotly contested. To again quote Justice Souter in Brentwood Academy, 531 U.S. at 295:

> Our cases try to plot a line between state action subject to Fourteenth Amendment scrutiny and private conduct (however exceptionable) that is not. The judicial obligation is not only to preserve an area of individual freedom by limiting the reach of federal law and avoid the imposition of responsibility on a State for conduct it could not control, but also to assure that constitutional standards are invoked when it can be said that the State is *responsible* for the specific conduct of which the plaintiff complains. If the Fourteenth Amendment is not to be displaced, therefore, its ambit cannot be a simple line between States and people operating outside formally governmental organizations, and the deed of an ostensibly private organization or individual is to be treated sometimes as if a State had caused it to be performed. Thus, we say that state action may be found if, though only if, there is such a close nexus between the State and the challenged action that seemingly private behavior may be fairly treated as that of the State itself.

What is fairly attributable is a matter of normative judgment, and the criteria lack rigid simplicity.

(3) ***The Broader Context of "Privatization."*** Taken as a matter of administrative law, the issue is not merely that constitutional requirements of due process are limited to "state action"; statutory requirements are limited, too. The subject of the APA, for example, is "agency action," where "agency" is defined as "each authority of the Government of the United States." Are there ways to address the concerns of administrative law—such

as participation, the control of discretion, and even-handedness—even when private actors are involved? (See also p. 787 regarding the application of the Freedom of Information Act to government contractors.)

Perhaps the answer lies in carefully choosing what tasks are privatized. JOHN D. DONAHUE, THE TRANSFORMATION OF GOVERNMENT WORK in Government by Contract 41, 44–45 (Jody Freeman & Martha Minow eds., 2009): "[There are] three characteristics whose presence makes a task appropriate for delegation and whose absence renders privatization hazardous: specificity, ease of evaluation, and competition.

"Specificity. You can only delegate what you can define. Splitting off a function requires specifying it in sufficient detail to solicit bids, select a provider, and structure a meaningful contract. . . . It is hard to write a sturdy contract for the performance of tasks that are entangled with other functions and subject to continual revision. . . . as circumstances change. . . .

"Ease of Evaluation. To outsource a function you not only need to be able to say what you want (specificity), but you also need to be in a position to know what you've gotten—clearly enough and early enough to take corrective action if what's delivered isn't what was promised. Otherwise, there can be no assurance that government is equipped to perform, as it must, as the agent of the people in ensuring that public value is produced in exchange for public resources. The easier it is to monitor performance and assess the quality of the work, the more safely can a task be delegated. . . .

"Competition. Private providers tend to outscore government on productive efficiency not because there is something magic about the private sector, but because competition eliminates, or at least narrows, the opportunities to survive without being efficient. . . . The whole point of privatization is to harness for the government the salutary effects of competition. Contracting out can transplant into public undertakings some of the intensive accountability that characterizes the private sector."

But as Donahue himself argues, the actual pattern of privatization in recent years has not matched these criteria. Some very sophisticated, complex, hard to evaluate and unique tasks—such as a large part of the management of the space shuttle program—have been contracted out to private companies, as have highly judgmental decisions that control access to various government-paid-for benefits, such as nursing home care.

(4) ***Avoiding Costs?*** It is sometimes said that part of the reason for governments' contracting with outside parties for services they could themselves provide is to avoid the very strictures on governmental action provided by the Constitution and laws such as the APA. In context, such a decision might seem obnoxious—or it might seem to represent a quest for efficiency and governmental savings. In a footnote included above, Justice Marshall says, "A State may not deliberately delegate a task to a private entity in order to avoid its constitutional obligations. . . . But a State's decision to delegate a duty to a private entity should be carefully examined even when it has acted, not in bad faith, but for reasons of convenience." Do you agree? Or once bad faith is put to one side, should the political branches have free rein to decide what "convenience" requires?

(5) ***A Duty to Supervise?*** Or should we develop a more aggressive due process doctrine to use when government privatizes? GILLIAN E. METZGER, PRIVATE DELEGATIONS, DUE PROCESS, AND THE DUTY TO SUPERVISE in Government by Contract 291, 307–08 (Jody Freeman & Martha Minow eds., 2009): "In short, significant gaps exist in the extent to which tweaking current due process rules can address the concerns with self-interested abuse of power as well as the lack of accountability and transparency in privatized governance. Instead, a more fundamental revision of current doctrine is needed. One change that appears particularly warranted is the development of a due process-based duty to supervise, under which the government must actively oversee decision making by its private delegates, at least when that decision making directly affects third parties. Imposing such a duty to supervise offers a means of checking the potential for arbitrary action and abuse of power that privatization presents, without unduly limiting private flexibility in specific cases. . . . Stated in private delegation terms, the justification for a duty to supervise is that only government supervision can ensure against self-interested decision making and ensure that due process demands of regularity and fairness are met in contexts of privatized governance. Government supervision is also essential to ensure that public officials remain ultimately responsible for exercise of government power.

". . . Public administration and public contracts scholars are strikingly united on the importance of government management of its private contractors if privatization is to succeed as a tool of modern governance. . . . The focus of this scholarship is management and policy-based, but the same conclusion results: increasing privatization demands greater recognition of government's oversight and supervision responsibilities. One advantage of developing a due process-based duty to supervise is that doing so adds the force of constitutional law to those efforts at managerial reform, with the potential for constitutional invalidation giving both the government and its private contractors an incentive to ensure adequate oversight."

(6) ***Straddles.*** There are a large number of federally created entities that in one way or another straddle a conceptual line between "public" and "private"—for instance, the U.S. Postal Service and Amtrak. Because of this straddle, they raise problems for a large number of legal doctrines, ranging from whether they are "agencies" for purposes of the APA, to whether they violate the constitutional law doctrine against delegation of public power to private entities or specifying staffing under the Appointments Clause, to, as here discussed, whether they are subject to due process constraints. The applicable law is still being worked out in particular areas and for certain entities, and there is no reason to expect the answer for one doctrine to mirror the answer for another. For discussion, see Anne Joseph O'Connell, Bureaucracy at the Boundary, 162 U. Pa. L. Rev. 841 (2014).

(7) ***Doctrinal Incentives?*** If, as the Rendell-Baker Court says, the ultimate issue under current doctrine is whether the private entity's action is "fairly attributable to the State," and if, as the Brentwood Academy Court says, that attribution is more likely to be made when there is "entwinement" of governmental with nongovernmental actors, doesn't that create an incentive for government, when it outsources one of its needs or functions, to keep its

hands off the private entity involved? If we want government to be present, through regulation, supervision, or contract, in order to represent various public values that the marketplace might otherwise submerge, is that incentive perverse?

## THOMAS M. COOLEY LAW SCHOOL v. AMERICAN BAR ASSOCIATION

United States Court of Appeals for the Sixth Circuit (2006).
459 F.3d 705.

■ GIBBONS, CIRCUIT JUDGE.

This case arises from a dispute between the American Bar Association, the national accrediting body for law schools and its Consultant on Legal Education John Sebert (collectively "ABA"), and the Thomas M. Cooley Law School ("Cooley" or "the school"), an accredited law school located in Lansing, Michigan. The dispute centers on Cooley's attempts to begin two satellite programs—one at Oakland University in Rochester ("Oakland campus") and one in Grand Rapids ("Grand Rapids campus"). Cooley claims that the ABA denied Cooley due process in failing to accredit the two proposed satellites and in imposing sanctions on Cooley for operating the satellites without ABA prior acquiescence. The district court denied these claims and granted judgment to the defendants. As we find that the ABA afforded Cooley all due process in making its rulings, we affirm.

I.

The federal government does not directly accredit institutions of higher education. Rather, the Secretary of Education approves accrediting agencies for different types of educational programs, and these accrediting bodies set independent standards for accreditation. Accreditation is important to a school for a number of reasons, not the least of which is that it allows the students of the school to receive federally-backed financial aid. In addition, the majority of states use ABA accreditation to determine whether an individual applying for admission to the Bar has satisfied the state's legal education requirement.

The ABA's Council on the Section of Legal Education ("Council") is the organization charged with accrediting law schools. The Council makes its decisions following a review and recommendation by the ABA's Accreditation Committee ("Committee"). The process is governed by written Standards, Rules, and Interpretations that are adopted after both public review and comment and review by the ABA House of Delegates ("House"). The Standards describe the requirements that a law school must meet to obtain and retain ABA approval. Standard 105 states: "Before a law school makes a major change in its program of legal education or organizational structure it shall obtain the acquiescence of the Council for the change." The opening of an additional campus falls under Standard 105. Under ABA rules, a school may offer up to 20% of its legal program at a separate campus without this being a "major change" requiring prior approval. If a school offers more than 20% of its program, however, this does constitute a major change and the ABA must grant acquiescence.

[In 2002, Cooley applied to the ABA for approval of two satellite campuses. While the ABA was considering the application, Cooley opened one of the sites but operated it below the 20% threshold. The Accreditation Committee determined that the proposal fell short in several ways; the Council adopted the Committee's recommendation and denied Cooley's application. At the same time, Cooley, relying on a doubtful reading of an ABA Rule that it claimed gave it authority to run the satellite campuses more fully so that the ABA could make an onsite evaluation of its proposal, increased its program at both campuses above the 20% level. The ABA rejected Cooley's reading of the rule and warned Cooley that it was in violation of Rule 105's requirement of prior approval for a major change. Cooley persisted, and the Accreditation Committee asked Cooley to appear at its next meeting to show cause why it should not be sanctioned.]

On March 30, 2004, Cooley filed the instant lawsuit. After Cooley filed a motion for a preliminary injunction, the parties entered into a Stipulation and Agreed Order, by which Cooley agreed to reduce its offerings at Oakland and Grand Rapids to comply with the 20% limit on non-approved programs. Cooley further agreed not to expand the programs without ABA approval. The ABA agreed to move the show-cause hearing to June. Both parties complied with the Order.

At the June 2004 show-cause hearing, Cooley argued that the ABA did not have the authority to impose sanctions under its own rules, because the school had reduced its program offerings and was now "in compliance" with all ABA rules. The Committee disagreed and recommenced sanctions. The Council adopted the Committee's recommendation, censuring Cooley for its "substantial and persistent noncompliance" with ABA standards and directives and ruling that the school would be ineligible to operate branch or satellite campuses until July 31, 2006. The Council also declined to address the merits of Cooley's branch applications, noting its doubts about the school's ability to maintain a sound legal educational program and stating that any decision regarding opening a satellite campus in 2006 would have to be made with more current information. The Council informed Cooley that it could file a new application for a satellite or branch campus in the summer or fall of 2005.

Following this decision, Cooley filed an amended complaint, again challenging the ABA's refusal to acquiesce in its satellite programs and adding claims relating to the imposition of sanctions. Specifically, Cooley claimed that the ABA denied its common law right to due process and requested judicial review of the ABA's decision. Cooley also brought claims under the Higher Education Act ("HEA"), 20 U.S.C. § 1099b, and under state law. The district court dismissed the HEA claim and state law claims for failure to state a claim, Fed.R.Civ.P. 12(b)(6), and granted summary judgment on the common law due process claim. Cooley filed a timely appeal.

II.

Only the common law claims are properly before this court. . .

III.

We thus turn to the only remaining issue—Cooley's claim that the ABA's rejection of its proposals and imposition of sanctions violated the school's common law right to due process. The district court granted summary judgment to the ABA, and we review this ruling de novo.

A.

Many courts, including this one, recognize that "quasi-public" professional organizations and accrediting agencies such as the ABA have a common law duty to employ fair procedures when making decisions affecting their members. See Foundation for Interior Design Education Research v. Savannah Coll. of Art & Design, 244 F.3d 521, 527–28 (6th Cir. 2001); Chicago School of Automatic Transmissions, Inc. v. Accreditation Alliance of Career Schools and Colleges, 44 F.3d 447, 450 (7th Cir. 1994); Wilfred Acad. of Hair & Beauty Culture v. Southern Ass'n of Colls. & Schools, 957 F.2d 210, 214 (5th Cir. 1992); Medical Inst. of Minnesota v. National Ass'n of Trade & Technical Schools, 817 F.2d 1310, 1314 (8th Cir. 1987). Courts developed the right to common law due process as a check on organizations that exercise significant authority in areas of public concern such as accreditation and professional licensing. See Ma[r]jorie Webster Junior Coll., Inc. v. Middle States Ass'n of Colls. & Secondary Sch., Inc., 432 F.2d 650, 655–56 (D.C. Cir. 1970); Falcone v. Middlesex County Medical Soc., 34 N.J. 582, 170 A.2d 791, 799 (1961). The ABA is such an organization, and we must therefore determine whether the ABA afforded Cooley adequate process in denying the applications for satellite programs and imposing sanctions.

To answer this question, we look to federal law. Although this court in Foundation applied state law to resolve a similar dispute, the agency in that case was not at that time approved by the Secretary of Education and thus was not subject to the HEA. Federal courts have exclusive jurisdiction over any action brought by a school challenging an accreditation decision made by an organization approved by the Secretary (such as the ABA). 20 U.S.C. § 1099b(f). This grant of exclusive federal jurisdiction necessarily implies that federal law should govern disputes relating to decisions made by those bodies. It would make little sense for state law to govern claims that could not be heard in any state court. "It is hard enough to be a ventriloquist's dummy in diversity suits under Erie; it is all but impossible to see how federal courts could apply state law to the actions of accrediting agencies when state courts have been silenced by the provision for exclusive jurisdiction." Chicago School, 44 F.3d at 449. If a grant of federal jurisdiction can justify the creation of federal common law, see, e.g., Textile Workers v. Lincoln Mills, 353 U.S. 448, 456–57 (1957), a grant of exclusive jurisdiction necessarily implies the application of federal law.

We must next determine under what principles of federal law we review a decision by an accrediting agency. Both Cooley and the ABA argue that the Administrative Procedure Act ("Act"), 5 U.S.C. § 701, provides the proper framework for reviewing the accreditation process. If the decision was made directly by the Secretary of Education, the presumption would be to review the case under the principles set forth in the Act. The Secretary, however, has delegated his authority regarding law school accreditation to the ABA, which is not a government authority and thus is not governed by the Act. Despite this delegation, however, the ABA does act on behalf of the Secretary and wields the quasi-governmental power of deciding which law schools are eligible for federal funds. Thus, while the Act does not specifically apply to the ABA, principles of administrative law are useful in determining the standard by which we review the ABA's decisionmaking process.

A number of courts have used these principles in fashioning a standard of review. Though some of the cases applied state law, see Foundation, 244 F.3d at 527, and others have left the choice-of-law question unanswered, see Wilfred Acad., 957 F.2d at 214; Medical Institute of Minnesota, 817 F.2d at 1314–15, courts have uniformly looked to administrative law in reviewing accreditation decisions. We agree and apply the standard of review that has developed in the common law. This court reviews only whether the decision of an accrediting agency such as the ABA is arbitrary and unreasonable or an abuse of discretion and whether the decision is based on substantial evidence.

This standard of review resembles the review applied under the Act. See 5 U.S.C. § 706(2)(A) ("arbitrary, capricious, an abuse of discretion, or otherwise not in accordance with the law"). We emphasize, however, that while principles of federal administrative law provide guidance in our analysis, judicial review of accreditation decisions is more limited than review under the Act. Although accrediting agencies perform a quasi-governmental function, they are still private organizations. Courts have made the policy decision to ensure that these organizations act in the public interest and do not abuse their power, but judicial review is limited to protecting the public interest. Recognizing that "the standards of accreditation are not guides for the layman but for professionals in the field of education," Wilfred Acad., 957 F.2d at 214, great deference should be afforded the substantive rules of these bodies and courts should focus on whether an accrediting agency such as the ABA followed a fair procedure in reaching its conclusions. We are not free to conduct a de novo review or substitute our judgment for that of the ABA or its Council. Rather, in analyzing whether the ABA abused its discretion or reached a decision that was arbitrary or unreasonable, we focus on whether the agency "conform[ed] its actions to fundamental principles of fairness." Medical Institute of Minnesota, 817 F.2d at 1314.

B.

Cooley argues that the ABA abused its discretion in refusing to consider the merits of its satellite application at the 2004 hearing and in imposing sanctions in violation of the ABA's own rules. Cooley also alleges that a number of due process violations occurred during the three rounds of hearings in 2002–2004.

*1. Imposition of Sanctions*

Cooley makes two arguments regarding the ABA's decision to impose sanctions that prevented Cooley from operating a satellite or branch campus until July 31, 2006. First, Cooley argues that the ABA abused its discretion by sanctioning the school in violation of its own rules. Second, Cooley alleges that the sanction was arbitrary and unreasonable and violated due process. An abuse of discretion can only be found if no evidence supports the decision or if the agency misapplied the law. National Engineering & Contracting Co. v. OSHA, 928 F.2d 762, 768 (6th Cir. 1991).

Cooley argues that the plain language of ABA Rule 13, which outlines hearings on show-cause orders, prohibited the Council from imposing sanctions because, at the time of the hearing, Cooley was in compliance with all ABA governing standards. Rule 13 states in relevant part:

> (b) Representatives of the law school, including legal counsel, may appear at the hearing and submit information to demonstrate that the school is currently in compliance with all the Standards or to present a reliable plan for bringing the school into compliance with all of the Standards within a reasonable time. . . .
>
> (d) After the hearing, the Committee shall determine whether the law school is in compliance with the Standards and, if not, it shall direct the law school to take remedial action or shall impose sanctions as appropriate.
>
> (1) . . .
>
> (2) If matters of noncompliance are substantial or have been persistent, then the Committee may recommend to the Council that the school be subjected to sanctions other than removal from the list of approved law schools regardless of whether the school has presented a reliable plan for bringing the school into compliance.
>
> (3) . . .
>
> (e) If the Committee determines that the law school is in compliance, it shall conclude the matter by adopting an appropriate resolution. . . .

Cooley reads these subsections as stating that the purpose of the show cause hearing is not to determine whether the school has previously violated ABA rules, but rather to determine whether the school "is currently in compliance" with the Standards. Regardless of its previous actions, Cooley argues it had reduced its course offerings below the 20% level at the time of the show-cause hearing; thus, it was "currently in compliance" and the ABA should have "conclude[d] the matter." By not doing so, Cooley contends, the ABA failed to follow the plain language of its own rules, and thus, the decision is not entitled to deference.

We agree with the ABA that Rule 13 cannot be given such a literal interpretation. . . .

Cooley's interpretation of Rule 13 would also allow schools to come in and out of compliance to avoid sanctions. . . . Cooley's actions demonstrate the danger of its reading of Rule 13, which would render the ABA powerless to sanction such blatant disregard of its rules and standards. This court must defer to an agency's interpretation of its own rules unless plainly erroneous. See A.D. Transport Express, Inc. v. United States, 290 F.3d 761, 766 (6th Cir. 2002). While Cooley's proposed interpretation of Rule 13 is perhaps plausible, the ABA's reading is not clearly erroneous and in fact is more logical. Thus, the ABA's imposition of sanctions despite Cooley's compliance with ABA standards at the time of the hearing does not constitute an abuse of discretion.

Cooley also argues that the sanction itself was arbitrary and unreasonable and violated due process. . . . Even though the sanction may have had significant impact on Cooley, it cannot be described as arbitrary and unreasonable, especially given the highly deferential standard of review and the evidence of Cooley's blatant and intentional noncompliance with ABA rules.

2. *The Acquiescence and Sanctioning Hearings*

Cooley next contends that the district court erred in failing to address its claims that the ABA abused its discretion in denying the satellite applications in 2002 and 2003, before the school's noncompliance. The district court did, however, address these claims, and in any case, they are meritless. Cooley was afforded ample process at each of the ABA hearings—it was notified well in advance, afforded the opportunity to submit evidence to supports its case, and permitted to appear before the body with counsel present. After each group of hearings, the Committee issued a detailed written report outlining its findings and recommendations. The Council in turn wrote a letter outlining its conclusions, referencing the findings of the Committee and the applicable rules and standards.

Cooley's claim that the ABA erred in not using the new interpretations of Standard 105 in the December 2002 and January 2003 evaluations of the school's satellite applications, when those interpretations were not officially adopted until February 2003, is equally baseless . . . The other errors alleged by Cooley—a conflict of interest by one Committee member and the use of an incorrect fact sheet during one of the hearings—do not amount to a due process violation. The supposed conflict of interest arose because one Committee member was the dean of another law school. After considering the matter, the Committee denied the request that the member be replaced, finding no danger of bias and reasoning that Cooley's logic would disqualify almost any member of the Committee. As to the incorrect fact sheet, it was quickly corrected and there is no evidence that the Committee relied on it in reaching its conclusion. As both of these claims of error were duly considered by the ABA and rejected with sufficient reasoning, they do not constitute an abuse of discretion and do not in any way violate Cooley's right to a fair process. . . .

Finally, Cooley raises a number of alleged procedural problems with the sanctions hearing: the denial of its request to cross-examine witnesses, the combined prosecutorial and adjudicative functions, and the possible introduction of ex parte evidence. As the district court correctly noted, these allegations "do not even hint at the existence of prejudicial error" that would be needed to justify relief. In light of the undisputed evidence of substantial and persistent noncompliance, Cooley cannot show that it would not have been sanctioned had these alleged errors not occurred.

IV.

For the foregoing reasons, the decision of the district court is affirmed.

[Concurring opinion omitted.]

## NOTES ON "COMMON LAW DUE PROCESS"

(1) ***What's Going on?*** The court accepts the parties' idea that the Administrative Procedure Act "provides the proper framework for reviewing the accreditation process," cites as authority cases arising out of actions of the Occupational Safety and Health Administration and the Federal Motor Carrier Safety Administration, and (as will be evident to you if you have already studied Chapter VIII on standards of review) defers to the judgments of the ABA in much the way courts defer to the judgments of governmental agencies. Would this case be any different, in analysis or in outcome, if the ABA had been a governmental agency and its actions had met the "state action" test? (For further material about the ABA and its role in judicial nominations, see p. 196.)

(2) ***ED Involvement?*** Does treating the ABA as subject to the requirements of "common law due process" depend on its being recognized by the Department of Education as having the power to accredit schools, which in turn means that the students at those schools can get federally backed financial aid? On ABA accreditation being used by many states as part of the bar admissions process? In a case involving university accreditation, the court elaborated on the connection between accreditation and financial aid:

> The federal government became involved in the accreditation process when the government required institutes of higher education to be accredited in order for the school and its students to qualify for federal financial aid. The predecessor to the Department of Education was first given statutory authority to "recognize" accrediting agencies in the G.I. Bill passed during the Korean War. Congress wanted to assure that federal money was not being spent on "fly by night" educational programs . . . Federal financial aid, however, increased in importance when Congress passed the Higher Education Act of 1965, which established federal financial aid programs beyond students who were veterans of the armed services.

Auburn Univ. v. Southern Ass'n of Coll. & Sch., Inc., 489 F.Supp.2d 1362, 1368 (N.D. Ga. 2002). Given the importance of federal financial aid and the control that accrediting agencies have over the distribution of this money, can you justify the imposition of common law due process in these contexts as a sort of half-step to constitutional due process based on a near miss of the state action requirement? If you can, how much public financial influence must exist before common law due process applies? Why is this any more compelling than the situation in Rendell-Baker, where public funds accounted for more than 90 percent of the school's budget?

(3) ***How Far Does It Go?*** In one of the cases cited by the Cooley court, Falcone v. Middlesex County Medical Society, 170 A.2d 791 (N.J. 1961), there was not even a tenuous connection between the defendant and governmental action. The Falcone court nonetheless held that a private professional organization in an area of public concern needed to provide applicants common law due process when membership was an "economic necessity." In the Cooley opinion, Judge Gibbons defines her understanding of the relevant domain represented by such cases as "organizations that exercise significant authority in areas of public concern such as accreditation and professional licensing." But some cases seem to have gone even further. E.g., Curran v. Mount Diablo Council of the Boy Scouts of America, 147 Cal.App.3d 712, 195 Cal.Rptr. 325 (1983), appeal dismissed 468 U.S. 1205 (1984), holding that the alleged expulsion of an Eagle Scout from the Boy Scouts on grounds of his being gay, without conducting a hearing on the issue of whether there was likely to be "any significant harm to the association," stated a claim for "wrongful denial of the common law right of fair procedure"; Brounstein v. American Cat Fanciers Ass'n, 839 F.Supp. 1100 (D.N.J. 1993) (applying New Jersey law), recognizing a cause of action for "wrongful discipline by a private organization" after a cat show judge alleged that she had had her prestigious designation as an "allbreed" judge revoked on account of her religion without procedures that accorded her "fundamental fairness." One commentator has suggested that "the actual human interests which suffer from an expulsion . . . in many cases . . . are chiefly interests of personality." Zechariah Chafee, Jr., The Internal Affairs of Associations Not for Profit, 43 Harv. L. Rev. 993, 998 (1930).

At the same time, it seems that the doctrine of "common law due process" (or, as it is sometimes also called, the doctrine of "natural justice") does not apply to every situation in the nongovernmental world that parallels a situation to which constitutional "due process" applies in the governmental world. For example, a private business would probably not have to accord the same procedural rights to an employee it fires that Texas would have to accord Sindermann (p. 605), even if the employee had a contractual claim to further employment; all the private employee would have would be the right to sue for breach of contract. Indeed, it seems the just-preceding case, Rendell-Baker, was litigated and decided on such an assumption. So what is the principle that both informs and limits the doctrine? Could this principle be extended to encompass some of the concerns about "privatization" we saw in the notes after Rendell-Baker?

(4) ***A Timely Controversy.*** Title IX of the Education Amendments of 1972, 20 U.S.C. § 1681, provides, with some exceptions, that "No person in the United States shall, on the basis of sex, be excluded from participation in, be denied the benefits of, or be subjected to discrimination under any education program or activity receiving Federal financial assistance." Sexual harassment is considered to be a form of discrimination. On April 4, 2011, during the Obama Administration, the Department of Education, Office of Civil Rights wrote a letter—addressed "Dear Colleague"—to educational institutions outlining the Department's views of the schools' responsibilities regarding "student-on-student sexual harassment, including sexual violence." Included were stipulations as to the procedures schools had to adopt to handle complaints. "[S]chools," said the letter, "generally conduct investigations and hearings to determine whether sexual harassment or violence occurred." "In order for a school's grievance procedures to be consistent with Title IX standards," the letter continued, "the school must use a preponderance of the evidence standard . . . The 'clear and convincing' standard currently used by some schools, is a higher standard of proof [and] . . . not equitable under Title IX." The letter also said, "OCR strongly discourages schools from allowing the parties personally to question or cross-examine each other during the hearing. Allowing an alleged perpetrator to question an alleged victim directly may be traumatic or intimidating." There were other stipulations as well. The letter also said that "Public and state-supported schools must provide due process to the alleged perpetrator."

Many schools—perhaps because they did not want to jeopardize in any way their federal financial assistance—simply followed the procedures set out in OCR's letter or negotiated similar rules to settle disputes with the Department. Some schools objected, as did some individual students who were the subject of the proceedings envisioned in the letter. One ground of objection was that the letter was not put through the notice-and-comment process; for materials on when "guidance" has to be treated as a "rule," see Chapter IV, Section 4b, p. 393. Another ground was that the requirements the letter stipulated—or the procedures that schools in fact used—did not give the accused a fair shake. Do you think the details mentioned above were consistent with due process? For one court's opinion, see John Doe v. Univ. of Cincinnati, 872 F.3d 393 (6th Cir. 2017).

The letter was withdrawn by the Department of Education on September 22, 2017, after President Trump took office, in a new letter that promised to hold "a rulemaking process that responds to public comment." On May 19, 2020, Trump's Secretary of Education, Elizabeth DeVos, promulgated the new regulations applicable to fund recipients (including almost all colleges). For cases that could not be settled by agreement, the regulations stipulated a rather formal process, but with some specific contours, 34 CFR § 106.45(b)(6): "For postsecondary institutions, the . . . grievance process must provide for a live hearing. At the live hearing, the decision-maker(s) must permit each party's advisor to ask the other party and any witnesses all relevant questions . . . including those challenging credibility. Such cross-examination at the live hearing must be conducted directly, orally, and in real time by the party's advisor of choice and never by a party personally. . . . At the request of either party, the recipient must provide for the live hearing to occur with the parties located in separate rooms with technology enabling the decision-makers and parties to simultaneously see and hear the party or the witness answering questions." The regulations also allowed for recipients to choose between using a "preponderance of the evidence" or a "clear and convincing evidence" standard in determining responsibility.

However, on March 8, 2021, President Biden issued Executive Order 14021 (Guaranteeing an Educational Environment Free From Discrimination on the Basis of Sex, Including Sexual Orientation or Gender Identity, 86 Fed. Reg. 13803 (Mar. 11, 2021)), which included the following:

"Section 1. *Policy.* It is the policy of my Administration that all students should be guaranteed an educational environment free from discrimination on the basis of sex, including discrimination in the form of sexual harassment, which encompasses sexual violence, and including discrimination on the basis of sexual orientation or gender identity. For students attending schools and other educational institutions that receive Federal financial assistance, this guarantee is codified, in part, in Title IX of the Education Amendments of 1972, 20 U.S.C. 1681 et seq., which prohibits discrimination on the basis of sex in education programs or activities receiving Federal financial assistance.

"Sec. 2. *Review of Agency Actions.* (a) Within 100 days of the date of this order, the Secretary of Education, in consultation with the Attorney General, shall review all existing regulations, orders, guidance documents, policies, and any other similar agency actions (collectively, agency actions) that are or may be inconsistent with the policy set forth in section 1 of this order. . . .

"(i) As part of the review required under subsection (a) of this section, the Secretary of Education shall review the rule entitled 'Nondiscrimination on the Basis of Sex in Education Programs or Activities Receiving Federal Financial Assistance,' 85 [Fed. Reg.] 30026 (May 19, 2020), and any other agency actions taken pursuant to that rule, for consistency with governing law, including Title IX, and with the policy set forth in section 1 of this order."

In the summer of 2022, Miguel Cardona, Biden's Secretary of Education, promulgated a new set of proposed regulations, 87 Fed. Reg. 41396 (July 12, 2022), with a comment period set to close on September 12, 2022. Although quite detailed, these proposed regulations also leave crucial decisions up to the judgment of the school. As stated in the Department of Education's bullet-points about the proposal:

- "The proposed regulations would not require a live hearing for evaluating evidence, meaning that if a school determines that its fair and reliable process will be best accomplished with a single-investigator model, it can use that model.
- "A school must have a process for a decisionmaker to assess the credibility of parties and witnesses through live questions by the decisionmaker. The proposed regulations would not require cross-examination by the parties for this purpose but

would permit a postsecondary institution to use cross-examination if it so chooses or is required to by law.

- "In evaluating the parties' evidence, a school must use the preponderance-of-the-evidence standard of proof unless the school uses the clear-and-convincing-evidence standard in all other comparable proceedings, including other discrimination complaints, in which case the school may use that standard in determining whether sex discrimination occurred."

As more fully fleshed out in proposed Section 106.46 of the rules, the institutional alternatives for determining credibility would be:

"(i) Allowing the decisionmaker to ask the parties and witnesses, during individual meetings with the parties or at a live hearing, relevant and not otherwise impermissible questions . . . , including questions challenging credibility, before determining whether sex-based harassment occurred and allowing each party to propose to the decisionmaker or investigator relevant and not otherwise impermissible questions . . . that the party wants asked of any party or witness and have those questions asked during individual meetings with the parties or at a live hearing; or

"(ii) When a postsecondary institution chooses to conduct a live hearing, allowing each party's advisor to ask any party and any witnesses all relevant and not otherwise impermissible questions, including questions challenging credibility. . . . Such questioning must never be conducted by a party personally. If a postsecondary institution permits advisor-conducted questioning and a party does not have an advisor who can ask questions on their behalf, the postsecondary institution must provide the party with an advisor of the postsecondary institution's choice, without charge to the party, for the purpose of advisor-conducting questioning. The advisor may be, but is not required to be, an attorney."

Whatever you think is the right procedure—the right procedure for the government to require as a condition of its providing financial assistance to a college, or the right procedure for a college to choose if it has a choice—here's a different question: Should the rules used in public colleges be different from those used in private colleges? If you say no—that in practice, colleges of all sorts are fundamentally alike—is that because you think that carrying out DOE's mandates to make sure of receiving federal money makes the action even of otherwise private institutions "state action"? (Jacob Gersen and Jeannie Suk, The Sex Bureaucracy, 104 Cal. L. Rev. 881, 911 (2016), say this is a "plausible argument" that has not yet been accepted in court.) Or is it because, whichever side of the state action line you are on, you think that "due process" of some ilk ought to apply to this situation?

(5) ***Due Process Beyond the Law.*** Consider PAUL R. VERKUIL, PRIVATIZING DUE PROCESS, 57 Admin. L. Rev. 963, 975 (2005): "The creation of a private due process regime is not limited to national associations like the NCAA. Other prominent private associations and membership groups have undertaken similar activities. Private universities provide a prime example. Unlike public institutions, private universities are outside the reach of state action-based due process requirements. Though these institutions are

technically free to limit procedures by private agreement, student and faculty pressures force them into providing basic fair procedures in decisionmaking. Since these institutions serve purposes identical to public ones, it is hard to rationalize relying upon the state action distinction to deny procedures in one case and not the other. As a result, universities have established procedures for disciplinary cases irrespective of their status. The procedural codes at these institutions reveal few differences between them based on the public-private distinction.

"Thus, many private institutions have been forced, by custom, politics, or state law, to behave procedurally as if they were public. Where there is a public analogue, private institutions have less room to maneuver procedurally. They are, like private associations such as the NCAA, held to procedural expectations that reflect due process values, if not requirements. In effect, these institutions are bargaining in the shadow of the law. The shadow can be cast either by the Constitution, by state law requirements, or by social or community pressures from the entities themselves. Decisions on due process therefore depend on a host of legal and social factors of which the 'state action' designation is only one. For many institutions, both private and public, due process has become a matter of bargaining with constituents."

(6) ***In the Future?*** Due process is a doctrine that stretches back as far as Magna Carta, but as the Cooley Law School case shows, it is still being used to generate legal decency. The quest for due process is one of the great protean forces in the law.

# CHAPTER VI

# TRANSPARENCY AND THE INFORMATION AGE



*"Publicity is justly commended as a remedy for social and industrial diseases. Sunlight is said to be the best of disinfectants; electric light the most efficient policeman."*[1]

This Chapter focuses on transparency and information demands. Although it is less integrated than other Chapters with the core material in the casebook, it addresses critical topics. Section 1 covers some general themes in government transparency, starting with considering whether visitor logs to Presidents' private residences related to their duties should be provided to the public. Section 2 examines affirmative obligations to disclose agency actions and preserve records outside of the Freedom of Information Act, including discussion of private standards incorporated in regulations and the Presidential Records Act. Section 3 then digs into FOIA, from its mandates and exemptions to agency performance and more. Section 4 considers two other key agency transparency statutes, the Government in the Sunshine Act and the Federal Advisory Committee Act. Section 5 turns the table, covering what information demands agencies make on others, including what agencies want for themselves.

[1] Louis Brandeis, Other People's Money 62 (1933).

## SECTION 1. INTRODUCTION

*Senate Bill 721: MAR-A-LAGO Act*

## Senate Bill 721: MAR-A-LAGO Act

Introduced in the Senate on March 23, 2017, by Senators Udall, Carper, and Whitehouse

A BILL

To require the disclosure of certain visitor access records.

Section 1. Short title

This Act may be cited as the "Making Access Records Available to Lead American Government Openness Act" or the "MAR-A-LAGO Act."

Section 2. Findings

Congress finds the following:

(1) Beginning in 2009, the Obama administration instituted a policy to release the visitor access records for the White House complex.

(2) This policy was responsible for making public the names of nearly 6,000,000 visitors to the White House in the 8 years of the Obama administration.

(3) This policy provided the people of the United States with insight into who influences the White House and transparency regarding efforts by lobbyists to effect policies, legislation, and Presidential actions.

(4) To date, the Trump administration has not indicated whether it will continue the policy of publicly releasing White House visitor access records. [Ed. Shortly after this bill was introduced, the White House announced that it would no longer provide visitor logs, citing "the grave national security risks and privacy concerns of the hundreds of thousands of visitors annually." President Biden's Administration has disclosed some visitor logs from the Trump Administration, including for January 6, 2021, to congressional investigators.]

(5) Since taking office on January 20, 2017, President Trump has conducted official business not only in the White House, but also at several of his privately owned clubs and resorts. [Ed. Similarly, President Biden has conducted official business at his Delaware residences.]

(6) President Trump's Mar-a-Lago Club in Palm Beach, Florida, has been dubbed the "Winter White House" and the "Southern White House."

(7) President Trump has spent 5 of his first 9 weekends in office at Mar-a-Lago.

(8) Mar-a-Lago is a private membership facility open to members, their guests, and others who have been invited as guests for special events.

(9) Visitors to Mar-a-Lago do not undergo the same background checks as White House visitors and visitor access records to the club have not been released to the public.

(10) The President has conducted official business and hosted international leaders at Mar-a-Lago.

(11) Media reports have shown President Trump and members of his Cabinet at Mar-a-Lago and nearby Trump International Golf Club interacting with members and guests, providing access unavailable to the general public.

(12) President Trump owns many other properties that offer similar amenities and membership-only access where he is likely to conduct official business during his term in office.

(13) On March 11, 2017, President Trump hosted several members of his Cabinet at his Trump National Golf Club in Potomac Falls, Virginia, to discuss homeland security, health care, and the economy according to media reports.

(14) Media reports have indicated that the President may use his Bedminster, New Jersey, resort as a "Summer White House".

(15) The people of the United States expect and deserve transparency in government. The policy to release visitor access records instituted by the previous administration appropriately balanced transparency with the need for confidentiality in government actions.

(16) To the extent Mar-a-Lago and any other private facilities become locations where the President conducts business and interacts with individuals who are not government officials, the same disclosures should apply.

Section 3. Improving access to influential visitor access records

(a) Definitions

In this section:

(1) Covered location

The term covered location means—

(A) the White House;

(B) the residence of the Vice President; and

(C) any other location at which the President or the Vice President regularly conducts official business.

(2) Covered records

The term covered records means information relating to a visit at a covered location, which shall include—

(A) the name of each visitor at the covered location;

(B) the name of each individual with whom each visitor described in subparagraph (A) met at the covered location; and

(C) the purpose of the visit.

(b) Requirement

Except as provided in subsection (c), not later than 30 days after the date of enactment of this Act, the President shall establish, and update every 90 days, a publicly available database that contains covered records for the preceding 90-day period.

(c) Exceptions

(1) In general

The President shall not include in the database established under subsection (b) any covered record—

(A) the posting of which would implicate personal privacy or law enforcement concerns or threaten national security; or

(B) relating to a purely personal guest at a covered location.

(2) Sensitive meetings

With respect to a particularly sensitive meeting at a covered location, the President shall—

(A) include the number of visitors at the covered location in the database established under subsection (b); and

(B) post the applicable covered records in the database established under subsection (b) when the President determines that release of the covered records is no longer sensitive.

## NOTES

(1) ***The Obama and Biden Administrations and Visitor Logs.*** In August 2009, Judicial Watch, Inc. submitted a Freedom of Information Act request to the Secret Service seeking all White House visitor logs from President Obama's inauguration to "the present." The agency refused to provide the records on the grounds that although the Secret Service is subject to FOIA, the requested items (from the Workers and Visitors Entry System) do not qualify as "agency records" under the Act. While the Obama Administration fought the request in district court and in the court of appeals (and won), it voluntarily provided access to many parts of the logs. (See p. 727 for a brief discussion of the FOIA issues.) The Obama Administration made exceptions for national security, sensitive meetings (e.g., Supreme Court candidates), people visiting the President's daughters, and the President and his wife's personal guests.[2] Staff could simply mark on the visitors' clearances to flag the record of their presence for nondisclosure. The last set of disclosures in December 2016 captured visits in September. Visitors from October 2016 to January 2017 were not released. In addition, POLITICO reported that White House staff often met with lobbyists outside the White House complex.[3] According to POLITICO's report, the White House claimed there was not space to hold these meetings on site, but lobbyists believed the offsite locations were chosen to avoid their meetings being disclosed. After the

---

[2] Julie Hirschfeld Davis, White House to Keep Its Visitor Logs Secret, N.Y. Times (Apr. 14, 2017); Peter Baker, White House to Open Visitor Logs to Public, N.Y. Times (Sept. 5, 2009).

[3] Chris Frates, White House Meets Lobbyists Off Campus, POLITICO (Feb. 24, 2011).

hiatus during the Trump Administration, the Biden Administration reinstituted the practice of making White House visitor logs public.[4] But the Biden Administration has refused to provide information about visitors to President Biden's Delaware residences where he spends significant time. What sort of disclosures, if any, should the White House make about visitors to the President or about White House employees and their meetings, onsite or offsite? Do you support legislation like S. 721 for the personal residences Presidents use while in office?

(2) ***Presidential Promises and Hedges.*** How different are recent Administrations? Typically, new Presidents issue directives on government transparency. As of November 2022, President Biden had not done so. But his Administration did issue guidance that requires any research conducted using federal funding to be made publicly accessible. Touting the benefits to innovation, Dr. Alondra Nelson, Director of the Office of Science and Technology Policy in the Executive Office of the President, asserts this will disrupt an inequitable regime that "allows scientific publishers to put taxpayer-funded research behind a subscription-based paywall." OSTP will work with federal agencies to implement the guidance no later than the end of 2025.[5] OSTP is also undergoing efforts to make data collected by the federal government "through its day-to-day activities . . . . more transparent, useful, and accessible."[6]

During his term, President Trump did not issue any transparency directive, despite campaigning to "drain the swamp" of lobbyists and other special interests. At the start of May 2017, in an opinion to the White House Counsel, the Office of Legal Counsel instructed agencies to "accommodat[e] congressional requests for information only when those requests come from a committee, subcommittee, or chairman authorized to conduct oversight."[7] This opinion angered both Democrats and Republicans in Congress.

By contrast, President Obama's first directive to agencies, Transparency and Open Government,[8] promised that he was "committed to creating an unprecedented level of openness in Government." Nevertheless, the President's directive and subsequent Office of Management and Budget memorandum[9] on the topic explicitly noted that there would be restrictions on disclosure, and some were relevant to materials of interest in administrative law. For instance, OMB observed: "With respect to information, the presumption shall be in favor of openness (to the extent permitted by law *and subject to valid privacy, confidentiality, security, or other restrictions*) . . ." (emphasis added). It went on: "Nothing in this

[4] Visitor logs can be found at: https://www.whitehouse.gov/disclosures/visitor-logs/.

[5] https://www.whitehouse.gov/ostp/news-updates/2022/08/25/ostp-issues-guidance-to-make-federally-funded-research-freely-available-without-delay/.

[6] https://open.usa.gov/meeting/november-2022-public-engagement-increasing-the-accessibility-and-utility-of-government-data/.

[7] https://www.justice.gov/olc/file/966326/download.

[8] https://www.archives.gov/files/cui/documents/2009-WH-memo-on-transparency-and-open-government.pdf.

[9] https://obamawhitehouse.archives.gov/sites/default/files/omb/assets/memoranda_2010/m10-06.pdf.

Directive shall be construed to supersede existing requirements for review and clearance of pre-decisional information by the Director of the Office of Management and Budget relating to legislative, budgetary, administrative, and regulatory materials. Moreover, nothing in this Directive shall be construed to suggest that the presumption of openness precludes the legitimate protection of information whose release would threaten national security, invade personal privacy, breach confidentiality, or damage other genuinely compelling interests." Do such exceptions significantly undermine the broad promises of openness?

(3) ***Assessing Transparency.*** At first glance, you may think that transparency provides only benefits. Specifically, information about the government's operations helps citizens (and others) evaluate and attempt to shape their government's performance. But there are also costs. For instance, making information public could harm national security or prevent robust governmental deliberations. Pushes for transparency can also serve partisan ends—requiring government agencies to disclose raw data (including confidential information) of any study they want to rely on, for example, could bar agencies from using certain relevant research and therefore regulating in certain areas. Or requests for records can be used to purposefully divert resources from critical tasks.[10] You will want to assess for yourself how far ostensible commitments to open government have been observed and, indeed, whether any limitations have merit.[11] In addressing the implementation of the Freedom of Information Act, a transparency commitment made as the Information Age was barely dawning, then-acting Attorney General Robert Bork is reported to have remarked that it presented problems akin to those "of the most difficult constitutional issues. . . . [A]djustment of [its] basic and conflicting values in individual cases, I find at least, a nerve-wracking task."[12] Decades earlier President Harry S. Truman had observed, "[t]he President cannot function without advisers or without advice, written or oral. But just as soon as he is required to show what kind of advice he has had, who said what to him, or what kind of records he has, the advice received will be worthless."[13] The disclosures of hundreds of thousands of properly classified (it appears) American documents by WikiLeaks[14] also made clear that exposure of this candor can be embarrassing.[15]

---

[10] See, e.g., Amy Gardner & Patrick Marley, Trump Backers Flood Election Offices with Requests as 2022 Vote Nears, Wash. Post (Sept. 11, 2022).

[11] Nongovernmental organizations can assist in this regard. See, e.g., Open the Government (https://www.openthegovernment.org/); The FOIA Project (https://foiaproject.org/).

[12] Robert Saloschin, The FOIA—A Governmental Perspective, 35 Pub. Admin. Rev. 10, 13 (1975).

[13] II Harry Truman, Memoirs: Years of Trial and Hope 454 (1956).

[14] https://wikileaks.org.

[15] For example, one cable confirmed that the government of Yemen was publicly taking responsibility for anti-terrorist actions actually being taken by the United States. Scott Shane & Andrew Lehren, Leaked Cables Offer Raw Look at U.S. Diplomacy, N.Y. Times (Nov. 29, 2010). In addition, ambassadors' cables characterized the heads of two major American allies as "thin-skinned and authoritarian" (Prime Minister Sarkozy of France) and "risk averse and rarely creative" (Chancellor Merkel of Germany). BBC News, WikiLeaks Diplomatic Cables Release 'attack on world' (Nov. 29, 2010).

The Trump Administration did not please transparency advocates. At the five-month mark, the Washington Post declared in a news article: "More and more in the Trump era, business in Washington is happening behind closed doors. The federal government's leaders are hiding from public scrutiny—and their penchant for secrecy represents a stark departure from the campaign promises of Trump and his fellow Republicans to usher in newfound transparency."[16] The Biden Administration restored daily White House press briefings, but many agency heads have continued their predecessors' practice and have not affirmatively released their daily schedules. By contrast, President Obama's initial directive may suggest that his Administration was exceptionally open.

But the Obama Administration's commitment to transparency had the expectable limits. State secrets were defended. President Obama's White House was reported to be as concerned about "leaks" as its predecessors.[17] The Administration vigorously fought some FOIA requests.[18] With regard to regulatory matters, as had its predecessor, Obama's Office of Information and Regulatory Affairs exerted considerable pressure so as not to disclose its work. According to the Washington Post, OIRA "systematically delayed enacting a series of rules on the environment, worker safety and health care to prevent them from becoming points of contention before the 2012 election," by telling agencies not to submit rulemaking proposals and taking longer to do reviews once actions were submitted.[19] In addition, although OIRA posted all 183 *public* comments it received in response to its early inquiry about possible revision of Executive Order 12866 (p. 1622), not one agency comment appears in its released materials.[20] For a longer account of how even under a mandate for open government OIRA avoided disclosing some of its actions (including those covered by Executive Order 12866's transparency mandates), see Lisa Heinzerling, Inside EPA: A Former Insider's Reflections on the Relationship Between the Obama EPA and the Obama White House, 31 Pace Envtl. L. Rev. 325 (2014).

As suggested above, measuring transparency is difficult. Nevertheless, we do have information on FOIA compliance, discussed in Note 3 on p. 724. One way to approach the transparency issue may be to distinguish between agency process (inputs) and outcomes (outputs). Cass Sunstein has argued for increased transparency of outputs. By contrast, he is more cautious about making inputs transparent, though he concedes that the costs to input transparency decline over time, particularly if disclosure happens once the relevant actors have left government. He notes the Presidential Records Act takes this approach—it preserves a historical record but is unlikely to affect

[16] Philip Rucker & Ed O'Keefe, In Trump's Washington, Public Business Increasingly Handled Behind Closed Doors, Wash. Post (June 19, 2017).

[17] Robert Woodward, Obama's Wars 198–99 (2010).

[18] See Fox News v. Treasury, 739 F.Supp.2d 515 (S.D.N.Y. 2010).

[19] Juliet Eilperin, White House Delayed Enacting Rules Ahead of 2012 Election to Avoid Controversy, Wash. Post (Dec. 14, 2013).

[20] https://www.reginfo.gov/public/jsp/EO/fedRegReview/fedRegReview.jsp.

day-to-day candor since input record collection is temporally remote enough to not be front of mind.[21]

(4) ***Standardizing Agency Use of Internet and Digital Materials.*** Agencies widely use the Internet and digital materials for various governmental purposes, notably including rulemaking. Initially (and still, for many purposes, for the independent regulatory commissions), each agency built its website and its utilities on its own. One result was a conspicuous lack of uniformity; another, considerable experimentation and innovation. THE E-GOVERNMENT ACT OF 2002 (Pub. L. No. 107–347, 116 Stat. 2899, codified chiefly in 44 U.S.C. § 3601 ff., but with some sections scattered elsewhere in the U.S.C.) created a central office in OMB, the Office of Electronic Government (since renamed the Office of E-Government & Information Technology), headed by a Chief Information Officer who is to seek coordination with the information officers of departments and agencies through a Council. An E-Government strategy announced by President Bush in the same year began a process of consolidation and centralized development that continues to this day. As the statute requires, OMB has filed annual reports of its implementation.[22] Chapter IV (p. 365) discusses some e-rulemaking developments. In 2018, Congress enacted the OPEN Government Data Act, Pub. L. No. 115–435, 132 Stat. 5534, to address some issues of transparency in the digital age. For an overview of the modernized terminology in the Act, see Meghan M. Stuessy, Cong. Rsch. Serv., IN11637, Sunshine Week: OPEN Government Data Act (Mar. 19, 2021).[23]

(5) ***Federal Web Sites.*** This Chapter invites you to consider some of the many ways in which government transparency—particularly through transformative use of the Internet—has changed administrative law (and during your professional life it doubtless will change further). There are many crosscutting governmental websites; you may want to explore them as part of your work in learning about administrative law:

- www.regulations.gov, the central website for federal agency rulemaking, where many proposals for rulemaking, supporting data, and filed comments are located; where one can register for notice of postings by particular agencies, or in particular dockets; and where comments may be electronically submitted.[24]
- www.whitehouse.gov/omb/information-regulatory-affairs/, the home page of the Office of Information and Regulatory Affairs.
- www.reginfo.gov, where the Office of Information and Regulatory Affairs' public activities are catalogued; and where

[21] Cass R. Sunstein, Output Transparency vs. Input Transparency, in Troubling Transparency: The History and Future of Freedom of Information (David E. Pozen & Michael Schudson eds., 2018).

[22] https://www.whitehouse.gov/omb/management/egov/#A4.

[23] https://crsreports.congress.gov/product/pdf/IN/IN11637/2.

[24] This site is now considerably more developed than it was when critiqued by the ABA's Committee on the Status and Future of Federal e-Rulemaking, Achieving the Potential: The Future of Federal e-Rulemaking (2008), but many of the limitations and criticisms found there remain valid.

current and past editions of Regulatory Plans and the Unified Agenda of Regulatory and Deregulatory actions can be found.

- www.foia.gov, the central governmental site for Freedom of Information Act issues.
- www.justice.gov/oip/doj-guide-freedom-information-act-0, an online FOIA treatise that is updated on a rolling basis.
- www.archives.gov/ogis, the site for the independent FOIA "ombudsman" created by the Openness Promotes Effectiveness in our National Government Act of 2007.
- data.gov, where (as of October 2022), over 319,000 federal, state, and local government datasets are available for the use of researchers and the development of applications.[25]
- crsreports.congress.gov/, a collection of the Congressional Research Service's research products, many of which cover federal agencies.
- www.usaspending.gov, a "dashboard" for government spending required by the Federal Funding Accountability and Transparency Act of 2006.

You may find it helpful to choose an agency that interests you and use its website to explore the topics that this Chapter covers in general terms. To name but a few: Who runs the agency? What experience do they have? How is the agency organized? What initiatives is the agency pursuing? How can you participate in those initiatives? Federal agencies that are important rulemakers on health and safety issues, such as EPA, FAA, FDA, NRC, or OSHA, may offer the greatest scope for these explorations, but it is likely that any active federal agency will work as well. Among the documents you might look for are your chosen agency's "open government plan," developed in response to President Obama's directives, and any changes under the Trump or Biden Administrations.[26] While the focus in this Section, as in this casebook generally, is on the federal government, transparency debates occur as well at the state and local levels.[27] Can you find your area's public records laws?

---

[25] For example, there are applications to "help people make informed decisions on agriculture, food, and nutrition": https://data.gov/food/food-apps/index.html. The data sets may be better adapted to expert than general public use, however.

[26] For example, as of August 2022, the EPA's plan is in its fifth edition. https://www.epa.gov/data/epa-open-government-plan 50.

[27] See, e.g., Christina Koningisor, Secrecy Creep, 169 U. Penn. L. Rev. 1751 (2021); Christina Koningisor, Transparency Deserts, 114 Nw. U. L. Rev. 1461 (2020).

## SECTION 2. SECRET LAW

***CERVASE v. OFFICE OF THE FEDERAL REGISTER***
***Notes on Access to Government Decisions***

*"We hear of tyrants, and those cruel ones: but, whatever we may have felt, we have never heard of any tyrant in such sort cruel, as to punish men for disobedience to laws or orders which he had kept them from the knowledge of."*[1]

As you may already have learned (p. 860), Panama Refining Co. v. Ryan, 293 U.S. 388 (1935)—the first case in which the U.S. Supreme Court held a congressional statute to be invalid as an excessive delegation of authority—dramatized the problem of secret law. A depression-era statute had given the President certain authority to control interstate commerce in petroleum and its products as a means of stabilizing prices, and he and the Secretary of the Interior (to whom he had subdelegated this power) had adopted rules in the exercise of that authority. When the validity of this statute came before the Supreme Court (all but one of whose members would find it to be a standardless and therefore unconstitutional delegation of authority), the government was embarrassed to admit that a reexamination of the relevant documents (which at the time were not publicly available) had revealed that the Secretary had inadvertently revoked the relevant regulation before the lawsuit had been filed. "[I]t was shocking that the government attorneys, the private parties, and the courts had not been aware of the status of the regulation. 'The furor resulting from the hot oil case [Panama Refining] provided the final impetus for the enactment of remedial legislation [the Federal Register Act] in 1935.' "[2] Just the prior year, only weeks before the argument and decision in the case, Erwin Griswold (later to become Dean of Harvard Law School and also Solicitor General of the United States) had argued passionately and persuasively for "a reasonable means of distributing and preserving the texts of . . . executive-made law."[3] The Federal Register, a daily compendium of executive branch documents including rules and rulemaking proposals, was the result.

---

[1] 5 Bentham, Works 547 (1843); Erwin N. Griswold used this as the epigram to his article, Government in Ignorance of the Law—A Plea for Better Publication of Executive Legislation, 48 Harv. L. Rev. 198 (1934), discussed in text at n. 26.

[2] Mary Whisner, A Manual "to Inform Every Citizen," 99 Law Libr. J. 159, 160 (2007) (citing Morris L. Cohen, Robert C. Berring, & Kent C. Olson, How to Find the Law 265 (9th ed. 1989)).

[3] Erwin N. Griswold, Government in Ignorance of the Law—A Plea for Better Publication of Executive Legislation, 48 Harv. L. Rev. 198 (1934). Griswold was on the staff of the Solicitor General's office until 1934, when Panama Refining was briefed. He, therefore, could easily have been aware of the coming firestorm: his article was published in the December 1934 issue of the Law Review, argument in Panama Refining was held that month, and the decision was announced in January 1935.

The Federal Register, like such publications generally, was a useful but imperfect response to the problem of secret law. A bulky daily publication, with an ambitious yet (necessarily) limited index, its effective use required lawyers and librarians. It has never been, moreover, a *compilation* of regulations. It is organized chronologically. There soon appeared the Code of Federal Regulations. The CFR proceeds by agency and topical chapters. Nevertheless, the task of finding relevant regulations remained difficult, as the next case discusses, in an era without personal computers, easy-to-access databases, and the Internet.

## CERVASE v. OFFICE OF THE FEDERAL REGISTER

United States Court of Appeals for the Third Circuit (1978).
580 F.2d 1166.

■ GIBBONS, CIRCUIT JUDGE.

[John Cervase, an attorney appearing pro se, brought an action seeking to force the Office of the Federal Register to create an analytical subject matter index to the Code of Federal Regulations. At the time of his suit, the 120-volume CFR had only a 164-page table of contents for the entire collection. Cervase asserted that the Office had an obligation to create an index as well, and that its breach of this duty had injured him and the public at large by making it almost impossible for them to know which federal regulations apply to them. The district court dismissed Cervase's complaint on grounds not necessary to consider here. The U.S. Court of Appeals for the Third Circuit reversed and remanded, having determined that "such a summary disposition of Cervase's complaint was improper."]

I

Cervase claims that the duty to prepare an analytical subject index arises out of two important federal statutes: the Federal Register Act of 1935 and the Freedom of Information Act of 1974. As amended, § 11 of the Federal Register Act provides in relevant part:

> (b) A codification published under subsection (a) of this section shall be printed and bound in permanent form and shall be designated as the "Code of Federal Regulations." The Administrative Committee shall regulate the binding of the printed codifications into separate books with a view to practical usefulness and economical manufacture. Each book shall contain an explanation of its coverage and other aids to users that the Administration Committee may require. *A general index to the entire Code of Federal Regulations shall be separately printed and bound. . . .*
>
> (d) The Office of the Federal Register shall prepare and publish the codifications, supplements, collations, and indexes authorized by this section.

Act of Oct. 22, 1968, Pub. L. No. 90–620, ch. 15, § 11, 82 Stat. 1277 (codified at 44 U.S.C. § 1510) (emphasis added). . . .

The original Federal Register Act provided for a compilation of all existing agency regulations of general applicability and legal effect. In 1937, however, that Act was amended to provide for codification instead of compilation. . . . In the 1937 amendment Congress, for the first time, imposed the indexing obligation on those responsible for preparing the periodic codifications. The significance of this obligation within the framework of what is commonly referred to as the Federal Register System is obvious. Codification of a document is prima facie evidence both of its text and of its continuing legal effect. Publication of the document in the Federal Register makes it effective against the world. But without the retrieval mechanism provided by an adequate index, a person might never be aware of a document containing a regulation affecting him until some federal bureaucrat produced a copy of the document and attempted to apply it to him. Indeed, the affected individual might already have changed his position in complete ignorance of the existence of the regulation. Such ignorance would avail him not, however, since publication in the Federal Register gives him constructive notice of the existence of the regulation. The Federal Register Act was enacted because of widespread dissatisfaction with the unsystematic manner in which executive orders, agency regulations, and similar materials were being made available to the public. The basic object of this statutory reform was to eliminate secret law. We think that the indexing obligation is a central and essential feature of this congressional plan. Without that obligation the periodic codification of regulations cannot serve the congressional purpose of providing public access to what has been published in the Federal Register. . . .

Certainly Cervase's complaint states a cause of action cognizable under § 1331(a). The regulations promulgated by the Administrative Committee impose an indexing obligation on the Office of the Federal Register. Although the regulations do not define the term "index," the Committee clearly intended that the word have its ordinarily understood meaning. Secondly, had the Committee attempted, by regulation, to define "index" to be something different than its ordinarily understood meaning, we would be faced with the question whether, in granting the rule-making authority found in 44 U.S.C. § 1506, Congress intended to place such rules beyond judicial review. See 5 U.S.C. §§ 704 and 706. But such a construction would fly in the face of the fundamental purpose of the Federal Register Act to eliminate the problem of secret law. In our opinion, the Administrative Procedure Act provides aggrieved persons with an avenue for judicial review of the committee's regulations. . . .

## NOTES ON ACCESS TO GOVERNMENT DECISIONS

(1) ***Pre-Internet Access to Agency Materials.*** Although the Federal Register and the CFR were a meaningful advance, they were incomplete. While the APA initially required the publication in the Federal Register of the most important matters and forbade their use to the prejudice of any

person unless published there,[4] much "soft law" could not be found in its pages. Access to soft law, such as agency opinions and orders, might be possible at the agency itself, but other publication was haphazard.

The 1966 Freedom of Information Act[5] introduced § 552(a)(1)–(2) of the APA (later amended), which encouraged public availability by barring materials that had *not* been published in the Federal Register from being used to disadvantage private parties *unless* they were publicly available and indexed.[6] Even so, before the Internet, that access might require travel to one of a limited number of agency reading rooms, or perhaps to a specific agency office. Just what might constitute a qualifying index was nowhere specified, and one can readily imagine many obstacles to it being highly detailed. If not precisely secret, then, regulatory law was often obscure and access to it expensive.

(2) ***The Internet's Contributions.*** Perhaps the most obvious use of the Internet in this context is to provide further relief from the problems both of secret law and of the limitations of indexing. The Federal Register and CFR are now online and searchable on government websites (federalregister.gov, ecfr.gov) and for-profit legal research sites. The CFR is also available on free nongovernmental platforms (such at Cornell Law school's Legal Information Institute).[7]

Soft law, in particular, has become much more readily available and searchable. The Electronic Freedom of Information Act Amendments of

---

[4] Section 3 of the original APA provided: Except to the extent that there is involved (1) any function of the United States requiring secrecy in the public interest or (2) any matter relating solely to the internal management of an agency—

> (a) Rules.—Every agency shall separately state and currently publish in the Federal Register (1) descriptions of its central and field organization including delegations by the agency of final authority and the established places at which, and methods whereby, the public may secure information or make submittals or requests; (2) statements of the general course and method by which its functions are channeled and determined, including the nature and requirements of all formal or informal procedures available as well as forms and instructions as to the scope and contents of all papers, reports, or examinations; and (3) substantive rules adopted as authorized by law and statements of general policy or interpretations formulated and adopted by the agency for the guidance of the public, but not rules addressed to and served upon named persons in accordance with law. No person shall in any manner be required to resort to organization or procedure not so published.
>
> (b) Opinions and orders.—Every agency shall publish, or, in accordance with published rule, make available to public inspection all final opinions or orders in the adjudication of cases (except those required for good cause to be held confidential and not cited as precedents) and all rules.
>
> (c) Public records.—Save as otherwise required by statute, matters of official record shall in accordance with published rule be made available to persons properly and directly concerned except information held confidential for good cause found.

60 Stat. 237 (1946).

[5] Pub. L. No. 90–23, 81 Stat. 54 (1967).

[6] Their text may be found in the Appendix (p. 1591). The FOIA Improvement Act of 2016 limited the agency's obligation to make material available under Section 552(a)(2) to "public inspection in an electronic format," essentially eliminating any need to maintain paper libraries and indexes for the public's use.

[7] https://www.law.cornell.edu/cfr/.

1996[8] required each agency to maintain an electronic reading room containing its regulations, guidance, interpretations, staff manuals, and similar materials[9]—as well as documents released in response to FOIA requests that "the agency determines have become or are likely to become the subject of subsequent requests for substantially the same records."[10] Searchable electronic documents surpass indexed print editions. The interventions of librarians and lawyers are no longer required (although they may still be useful); if a document is in the electronic library, it is accessible to all. It cannot any longer be "off the shelf" and unavailable.

To be certain, wider access remains a work in progress. Agency electronic reading rooms vary in their coverage. There is also no *uniform* way to access agencies' nonregulation materials, from guidance to adjudication materials. President Trump did direct agencies to establish online guidance portals, "a single, searchable, indexed database that contains or links to all guidance documents."[11] President Biden repealed this directive, but many agencies have kept their guidance portals active for the time being. In 2017, the Administrative Conference of the United States (ACUS) (see p. 253), an independent federal agency dedicated to improving the administrative process and agency procedures, published its findings from a survey of 24 agency websites' treatment of federal adjudication materials. ACUS examined not only the navigability and search functions of each website but also the scope of disclosed materials (for example, formal decisions only versus submissions to the agency as well). In response to agency variation, ACUS flagged some best practices and made a series of recommendations to improve agency disclosure.[12] ACUS has since studied and made recommendations on the availability of adjudication rules and policies concerning adjudicators.[13] ACUS has also made pro-transparency recommendations for other agency materials.[14]

If you have chosen an agency to follow, consult its electronic library and guidance portal (if any) to see what materials can be found there, and assess their searchability.

(3) ***An Example of the Transformation.*** Here is an example that may show the dramatic changes that have occurred: One of the more important

---

[8] Pub. L. No. 104–231, 110 Stat. 3048 (1996) (amending 5 U.S.C. § 552(a)(2)).

[9] See, for example, https://www.faa.gov/regulations_policies/, which collects a wide range of soft law documents as well as FAA regulations.

[10] 5 U.S.C. § 552(a)(2)(D). On this as on most issues regarding the Freedom of Information Act, an excellent first source to consult is the U.S. Department of Justice's Freedom of Information Act Guide, which can be found at: www.justice.gov/oip/doj-guide-freedom-information-act-0. This treatise used to be published every several years but is now updated on a rolling basis online.

[11] Exec. Order No. 13891 § 3(b), 84 Fed. Reg. 55235 (Oct. 15, 2019). Here is the Department of Transportation's portal: https://www.transportation.gov/guidance.

[12] ACUS, Recommendation 2017–1, Adjudication Materials on Agency Websites, 82 Fed. Reg. 31039 (July 5, 2017).

[13] ACUS, Recommendation 2018–5, Public Availability of Adjudication Rules, 84 Fed. Reg. 2142 (Feb. 6, 2019); ACUS, Recommendation 2020–5, Publication of Policies Governing Agency Adjudicators, 86 Fed. Reg. 6622 (Jan. 22, 2021).

[14] See https://www.acus.gov/public-availability-of-information.

regulations issued by the Department of Transportation's National Highway Traffic Safety Administration has been its Standard 208, requiring the installation first of seatbelts and then of airbags in automobiles.[15] Understandably, manufacturers and others have had questions about the requirements of the standard and interpretation of its provisions, which they have addressed to NHTSA's Chief Counsel. The Chief Counsel's interpretive letters responding to their inquiries had long been public documents,[16] but access to them once depended on either visiting the Counsel's office in Washington, D.C. or finding an industry group or member that had made its own collection. One can imagine both the expense of hiring a lawyer to perform that search, and the imperfections of the filing system she would encounter. NHTSA now collects the opinion letters of its Chief Counsel on its website, making them available for basic searches.[17] General Motors and an industry group that had begun electronic recordkeeping years before NHTSA supplemented its paper files were so impressed by the NHTSA undertaking that each donated their electronic records of earlier letters for inclusion in the searchable repository.[18] Now, using an Internet connection half a continent (or half the world) away from Washington, D.C., anyone wishing to learn about NHTSA's interpretations of Standard 208 (or any of its other regulations) reliably has that information in seconds. The visibility of government law, hard and soft, has been exponentially increased.

Congress can choose to require periodic disclosure of material like these letters. See, e.g., 20 U.S.C. § 1406(f) ("The Secretary shall, on a quarterly basis, publish in the Federal Register, and widely disseminate to interested entities through various additional forms of communication, a list of correspondence from the Department of Education received by individuals during the previous quarter that describes the interpretations of the Department of Education of this chapter or the regulations implemented pursuant to this chapter.").

---

[15] 49 C.F.R. Parts 552, 571, 585, and 595. Standard 208 came before the Supreme Court in Motor Vehicle Mfrs. Ass'n v. State Farm Mut. Auto. Ins. Co., 463 U.S. 29 (1983) (p. 1126).

[16] For the case addressing a comparable type of document and establishing the precedent for its availability, see Mark P. Schlefer v. United States, 702 F.2d 233 (D.C. Cir. 1983) (Maritime Administration required to release Chief Counsel opinions interpreting statutes under FOIA as operative soft law).

[17] https://isearch.nhtsa.gov/. While the agency used to assert that the Chief Counsel's interpretations "represent the definitive view of the agency on the questions addressed and may be relied upon by the regulated industry and members of the public," it now has a more cautious statement, similar to other agencies' warnings: "These letters of interpretation, signed by the Chief Counsel, are guidance documents. They do not have the force and effect of law and are not meant to bind the public in any way. They represent the opinion of the agency on the questions addressed at the time of signature and may be helpful in determining how the agency might answer a question that you have if that question is similar to a previously-considered question. Please remember, however, that interpretation letters represent the opinion of the Chief Counsel based on the facts of individual cases at the time the letter was written. Do not assume that a prior interpretation will necessarily apply to your situation! There are a number of reasons why the interpretation letters in this database might not be applicable to your situation."

[18] Peter L. Strauss, Implications of the Internet for Quasi-Legislative Instruments of Regulation, Windsor Yearbook of Access to Justice (2010), https://scholarship.law.columbia.edu/cgi/viewcontent.cgi?article=2703&context=faculty_scholarship.

(4) ***Incorporation by Reference.*** While the CFR is free online (through the government and certain nonprofit organizations), it contains references to material that is not so easily accessible. Consider NINA A. MENDELSON, PRIVATE CONTROL OVER ACCESS TO THE LAW: THE PERPLEXING FEDERAL REGULATORY USE OF PRIVATE STANDARDS, 112 Mich. L. Rev. 737 (2014): "The CFR today contains nearly 9,500 'incorporations by reference' of standards, often referred to as 'IBR' rules or standards. Some IBR rules incorporate material published by other agencies or state entities, but many incorporate privately drafted standards from so-called standards development organizations, . . . organizations ranging from the American Society for Testing and Materials to the Society for Automotive Engineers and the American Petroleum Institute. Agency use of private standards is likely to grow because, since the 1990s, both executive branch and congressional policies have officially encouraged it. Indeed, if an agency develops government-unique standards when a 'consensus' private standard exists, the agency must explain why it did so. . . .

"A reader perusing worker-safety requirements in the CFR may note that contractors handling pressure systems must comply with the American Society for Mechanical Engineers ('ASME')'s 'Manual for Determining Remaining Strength of Corroded Pipelines,' among other standards. To access these standards, the CFR refers the reader directly to the ASME at its New Jersey location or at its website. The reader's only alternative is to write for an appointment at the Office of the Federal Register's reading room in downtown Washington, D.C. On the internet, the cited standard is available from a third-party seller for $68; despite the CFR's promise, ASME itself apparently no longer provides the standard." For additional scholarship, see Emily S. Bremer, Incorporation by Reference in an Open-Government Age, 36 Harv. J.L. & Pub. Pol'y 131 (2013); Emily S. Bremer, On the Cost of Private Standards in Public Law, 63 U. Kan. L. Rev. 279 (2015); Peter L. Strauss, Private Standards Organizations and Public Law, 22 Wm. & Mary Bill Rts. J. 497 (2013).

In 2014, the Office of the Federal Register issued a final rule requiring agencies to "set out, in the preambles of their proposed and final rules, a discussion of the actions they took to ensure the materials are reasonably available to interested parties and that they summarize the contents of the materials they wish to incorporate by reference."[19] Comments in this rulemaking proceeding called attention to European practice, which treats standards not as legal obligations in and of themselves but rather as guidance on how regulations whose essential requirements are independently stated may be fulfilled. But the federal government did not take this path.[20] Do you prefer the European approach? How, if at all, would you change practices in the United States?

---

[19] Office of the Federal Register, Incorporation by Reference, 79 Fed. Reg. 66267 (Nov. 7, 2014).

[20] The dockets in the OFR proceeding and a related OMB proceeding can be found at regulations.gov, see dockets for OFR–2013–0001 and OMB–2014–0001. For critical appraisals of the 2014 revisions, see https://www.regblog.org/2015/01/26/series-incorporation-by-reference/.

(5) ***Litigation over Private Standards.*** Carl Malamud's organization, Public.Resource.Org, has posted online many private standards from the American Society for Testing and Materials, among other organizations, that had been incorporated into federal rules. ASTM, a private organization, then sued to get them removed. In early 2017, a federal district court, while noting "the need for an informed citizenry to have a full understanding of how to comply with the nation's legal requirements," sided with the copyright holder. The court held that Congress had permitted such standards groups to maintain their copyrights even when their standards are incorporated into public law. American Society for Testing and Materials v. Public.Resource. Org, Inc., 2017 WL 473822 (D.D.C. 2017).

The D.C. Circuit reversed the district court's grant of summary judgment in AMERICAN SOCIETY FOR TESTING AND MATERIALS V. PUBLIC.RESOURCE.ORG., INC., 896 F.3d 437, 447, 450, 453 (D.C. Cir. 2018). It explained, in part: "Although [Public.Resource.Org] raises a serious constitutional concern with permitting private ownership of standards essential to understanding legal obligations, we think it best at this juncture to address only the statutory fair use issue [arising under the Copyright Act]—which may provide a full defense to some, if not all, of the [Standards Developing Organizations]' infringement claims in this case—and leave for another day the question of whether the Constitution permits copyright to persist in works incorporated by reference into law. . . .

"Where an incorporated standard provides information essential to comprehending one's legal duties, for example, this factor [transformation, one of the four fair use factors in the Copyright Act, specifically "whether, in certain circumstances, distributing copies of the law for purposes of facilitating public access could constitute transformative use"] would weigh heavily in favor of permitting a nonprofit seeking to inform the public about the law to reproduce in full the relevant portions of that particular standard. . . .

"Considering the four fair use factors together, then, we find that the novel and complex issues raised by this case resolve in a manner entirely ordinary for our court: reviewing the record afresh, as our standard of review requires, we conclude . . . that, as to the fair use defense, genuine issues of material fact preclude summary judgment for either party."

On remand, the district court considered all 217 standards Public.Resource.Org had reproduced. For the 184 standards that had been incorporated by reference, Judge Chutkan granted summary judgment for Public.Resource.Org, allowing their publication as fair use. The court determined that one standard had only been partially incorporated and, correspondingly, could only be partially reproduced. And for the 32 standards that substantively differed from the incorporated texts, the court held that they could not be published by Public.Resource.Org. The court denied ASTM's request for a permanent injunction with respect to those 32 standards, preserving Public.Resource.Org's right to publish should the standards be incorporated by reference in the future. American Society for Testing and Materials v. Public.Resource.org, Inc., 2022 WL 971735, at *17, *22 (D.D.C. 2022). ASTM has appealed.

The Supreme Court recently held that the annotations (produced by a private party under a contract with a state commission established by the legislature) in the official compilation of Georgia law "are ineligible for copyright protection." Georgia v. Public.Resource.Org, Inc., 140 S.Ct. 1498, 1506 (2020). The Court explained: "If judges, acting as judges, cannot be authors because of their authority to make and interpret the law, it follows that legislators, acting as legislators, cannot be either. Courts have thus long understood the government edicts doctrine to apply to legislative materials. . . . Under our precedents, therefore, copyright does not vest in works that are (1) created by judges and legislators (2) in the course of their judicial and legislative duties. . . . In light of the Commission's role as an adjunct to the legislature and the fact that the Commission authors the annotations in the course of its legislative responsibilities, the annotations in Georgia's Official Code fall within the government edicts doctrine and are not copyrightable." Id. at 1507–09.

(6) ***Secret Law and the "War on Terror."*** The Internet has not eliminated secret law. Indeed, the "War on Terror" commenced at the start of the century may have generated an increase. In 2016, the Brennan Center for Justice at NYU issued a report, The New Era of Secret Law, which documents the use of secret law, motivated by national security concerns, across all three branches of government. The study found that in the legislative branch, in addition to classified committee reports, sometimes "bills incorporate provisions [which 'include not just funding or personnel allocations, but substantive regulations'] of classified reports by reference, bestowing on them the status of law." In the executive branch, some national security directives, opinions by the Office of Legal Counsel, agreements with foreign nations, and national security regulations remain secret.[21] And in the judicial branch, national security litigation in the federal courts often produces sealed or redacted filings; in addition, "significant pre-Snowden FISA case law remains undisclosed." The Brennan Center made a number of proposals, including: "Decisions to withhold legal rules and authoritative legal interpretations from the public should be made by an inter-agency body of senior officials"; "The standard for keeping law secret should be more stringent than the current standard for classifying information"; "Certain categories ['disclosure of pure legal analysis', '[l]egal interpretations that purport to exempt the executive branch from compliance with statutes'] of law should never be secret"; "When the executive branch issues secret law, it should immediately share the law with the other branches and with independent oversight bodies"; "Indefinite secret law is constitutionally intolerable. There should be a four-year time limit on the secrecy of legal rules and authoritative legal interpretations. Renewals [limited to two] should require the unanimous approval of the inter-agency body charged with making secrecy

---

[21] Perhaps more relevant to administrative law, also in the executive branch, the "No-Fly" and other watch lists are kept secret (under classification rules) (see p. 651), and government attorneys sometimes rely on classified evidence in immigration proceedings that only the immigration judge can see.

determinations"; "Americans should know how much secret law exists and the general areas where it is being applied."

Is there a constitutional right to information? How far can the government restrict access by the press under the First Amendment? See Nation Magazine v. U.S. Dep't of Defense, 762 F.Supp. 1558 (S.D.N.Y. 1991). Does the common law right to "inspect and copy public records" apply to federal agencies? The White House? Congress? Courts? See Nixon v. Warner Commc'ns, 435 U.S. 589 (1978); Schwartz v. U.S. Dep't of Justice, 435 F.Supp. 1203 (D.D.C. 1977), affirmed, 595 F.2d 888 (D.C. Cir. 1979).

(7) ***Secret Law and the Budget.*** Much information about federal agency budgets is not publicly available. There are the "black budgets"—spending for military and intelligence operations or for any other expenditure that is not disclosed publicly. Congress has mandated that the Office of the Director of National Intelligence publicly provide its top-line budget figure since 2007. More generally, outside the national security space, aspects of agency budgets have different degrees of secrecy. Predecisionally, before budgets are finalized, the Office of Management and Budget largely restricts what agencies, including independent regulatory commissions, can say about their budgetary needs, which Eloise Pasachoff calls the "confidentiality lever" of OMB control ("the requirement that agency officials silence their own differing preferences and, if those preferences become known, distance themselves from them"). The President's Budget as a Source of Agency Policy Control, 125 Yale L.J. 2182, 2224 (2016). Postdecisionally, after budgets are set through legislation, information about transfers (funds moving between different appropriations) and reprogramming (funds moving within a single appropriation) does not have to be posted. Recent Presidents, Democratic and Republican, have rejected congressional claims that committee approval is needed (see Chadha, p. 881) before such transfers and reprogramming. OMB's resource management offices also "apportion" appropriated funds—"specifying how much may be expended, when it may be expended, and even to some extent how it may be expended." Id. at 2228. While these decisions bind agencies, they were typically kept private. After the Trump Administration's decision to withhold security assistance to Ukraine made national headlines (because a whistleblower came forward), this form of budget secrecy generated considerable attention. The 2022 Consolidated Appropriations Act "for the first time requires public disclosure of apportionments, apportionment footnotes, and sub-delegations of apportionment authority within OMB." Matthew B. Lawrence, Apportionment Transparency in the 2022 CAA: The Return of Congressional Institutionalism?, Notice & Comment Blog (Mar. 16, 2022).[22] You can find these apportionment disclosures online.[23] In the Congressional Budget Justification Transparency Act of 2021, Congress required agencies to post online additional information about their annual spending compared to the amounts appropriated to them. Pub. L. No. 117–40, 135 Stat. 337 (2021).

---

[22] https://www.yalejreg.com/nc/apportionment-transparency-in-the-2022-caa-the-return-of-congressional-institutionalism-by-matthew-b-lawrence/.

[23] https://apportionment-public.max.gov/.

(8) ***Keeping Government Records.*** Several statutes require the government to preserve official records. The Federal Records Act requires agencies to preserve, for set time periods, "all recorded information, regardless of form or characteristics, made or received by a Federal agency under Federal law or in connection with the transaction of public business . . . as evidence of the organization, functions, policies, decisions, procedures, operations, or other activities of the United States Government or because of the informational value of data in them." 44 U.S.C. § 3301. Whether certain government officials' and agencies' decisions comply with these requirements has recently been the subject of high-profile debate. The State Department's Inspector General and the FBI determined that then-Secretary of State Hillary Clinton's use of a private email server violated "the Department's policies that were implemented in accordance with the Federal Records Act," but the FBI recommended that prosecutors not file criminal charges under the Act. In August 2021, Public Employees for Environmental Responsibility asked the Environmental Protection Agency to investigate accounts that the "EPA routinely allows the original versions of its internal communications and draft documents to be erased when they are edited," which PEER claimed violates the Federal Records Act. Most recently, in July 2022, the National Archives and Records Administration, which oversees agency recordkeeping under the Act, asked the Secret Service to "look into" "the potential unauthorized deletion" of text messages dated January 5 and 6, 2021. The January 6th Select Committee also noted its concern. Text messages of several top officials at the Department of Homeland Security, including the acting Secretary, were also not preserved.

The Presidential Records Act mandates that the President "assure that the activities, deliberations, decisions, and policies that reflect the performance of the President's constitutional, statutory, or other official or ceremonial duties are adequately documented and that such records are preserved and maintained as Presidential records." 44 U.S.C. § 2203(a). These records are then handed over to the Archivist of the United States, who then generally releases them (subject to exemptions) according to the Act's timetable and other provisions. Soon after President Trump took office, the Archivist informed two Democratic Senators who had raised concerns under the Act (after the President deleted and modified some of his tweets) that he "has advised the White House that it should capture and preserve all tweets that the president posts in the course of his official duties, including those that are subsequently deleted, as presidential records."

Apparently, the combination of President Trump's habit of ripping up documents and statutory mandates about the preservation of presidential records yielded government employees "[a]rmed with rolls of clear Scotch tape . . . put[ting] them back together." As POLITICO reported: "White House aides realized early on that they were unable to stop Trump from ripping up paper after he was done with it and throwing it in the trash or on the floor, according to people familiar with the practice. Instead, they chose to clean it up for him, in order to make sure that the president wasn't violating the law." Annie Karni, Meet the Guys Who Tape Trump's Papers Back Together, POLITICO (June 10, 2018). NARA subsequently reported that the taping operation covered only some records and that the White House turned over "a number of torn-up records that had not been reconstructed by the White House."

The end of President Trump's term saw an increase in attention to his Administration's recordkeeping practices. The "chairs of 21 House Committees sent letters to over 50 federal agencies . . . reminding them of their statutory duties to preserve records. . . . [O]n December 21, Rep. Carolyn Maloney, D-N.Y., chairwoman of the House Oversight and Reform Committee, sent a letter to the Archivist of the United States, with a list of questions about the White House's records preservation process." Courtney Bublé, Records Transfer from the Trump White House is a Work in Progress, Gov't Exec. (Feb. 1, 2021). A number of watchdog and government transparency groups also got involved, with one, Citizens for Responsibility and Ethics in Washington, filing a lawsuit.[24]

NARA was delayed in transferring records in accordance with the Presidential Records Act because of the General Services Administration's delay in ascertaining the winner of the 2020 election. As of February 2021, the agency had received approximately 4,700 cubic feet of textual records (in contrast to 29,000 cubic feet from the George W. Bush Administration and 15,000 cubic feet from the Obama Administration). Electronic data has been increasing since Bush, including under Trump.

Following reports that presidential records remained missing, NARA picked up fifteen boxes of documents, including classified material, that former President Trump took to his Mar-a-Lago residence at the end of his Administration, prompting congressional and Justice Department investigations. In August 2022, after negotiations for further document retrieval stalled, FBI agents executed a search warrant for additional material, including classified documents, at Trump's Mar-a-Lago residence and took more boxes. Despite the Act's mandate that presidential records belong to the government, President Trump apparently told aides otherwise. ("They're mine.") Maggie Haberman, Katie Benner, & Glenn Thrush, The Final Days of the Trump White House: Chaos and Scattered Papers, N.Y. Times (Aug. 20, 2022). Among the records retrieved in the raid were classified and top-secret documents—including, reportedly, descriptions of a foreign government's nuclear capabilities. Devlin Barrett & Carol D. Leonnig, Material on Foreign Nation's Nuclear Capabilities Seized at Trump's Mar-a-Lago, Wash. Post. (Sept. 6, 2022). A criminal investigation into the incident—what some are calling NARAlago—and litigation over the government's review of the documents remain ongoing at the time of publication of this edition. Former President Trump told the court-appointed special master supervising review of the seized records that he viewed the material as personal, not presidential, records and argued that his designation should receive deference under the Presidential Records Act. Carolina Bolado, Trump Insists Mar-a-Lago Docs are Personal Records, Law360 (Nov. 14, 2022). (The Eleventh Circuit subsequently vacated the district court's appointment of the special master in December 2022.) In

[24] You can read the complaint here: https://www.citizensforethics.org/legal-action/lawsuits/groups-sue-trump-and-white-house-to-stop-destruction-of-administration-records/.

August 2022, the Department of Justice filed a civil suit against Trump's adviser, Peter Navarro, for violations of the Presidential Records Act. See U.S. v. Navarro, No. 22-cv-02292 (D.D.C. 2022). The complaint alleges Navarro refused to turn over emails pertaining to his official duties that were stored on his personal email account.

Courts have found that, with some exceptions, the Presidential Records Act and the Federal Records Act preclude judicial review. See, e.g., Citizens for Responsibility and Ethics in Washington v. Trump, 924 F.3d 602 (D.C. Cir. 2019) (finding claims that the President's staff should be prohibited from using "automatically-disappearing text messages through private text messaging platforms" nonreviewable); Citizens for Responsibility and Ethics in Washington v. Trump, 438 F.Supp.3d 54 (D.D.C. 2020) (relying on Armstrong v. Bush, 924 F.2d 282 (D.C. Cir. 1991), to dismiss a challenge to the alleged failure of the President and his assistants "to create, maintain, and properly dispose of records of interactions with foreign leaders"). Notwithstanding the general preclusion of judicial review, the D.C. Circuit recently held it may adjudicate executive privilege claims by a former President in Presidential Records Act disputes. See Trump v. Thompson, 20 F.4th 10, 32 (D.C. Cir. 2021) ("The Presidential Records Act reflects [the] understanding . . . that a former President may initiate an action 'asserting that a determination made by the Archivist violates the former President's rights or privileges.' " (quoting 44 U.S.C. § 2204(e)).

(9) ***Government Leaks—Authorized and Unauthorized.*** At times, government employees disclose information outside of FOIA. Some disclosures—typically to others within the government—are permitted by law and practice. The Whistleblower Protection Act immunizes federal employees from retaliatory personnel actions taken for communications with their agency's Inspector General or leader about serious agency misconduct. 5 U.S.C. § 2302(b).

Outside of formal whistleblowing, there are often other disclosures to individuals outside the government. Some are part and parcel of the administrative process and therefore authorized—informal, permitted discussions between an agency and regulated entities and regulatory beneficiaries, for example. Some are unauthorized, in that they do not expose agency misbehavior covered by whistleblower protections or fall within a particular agency's permitted practices. Amanda Leiter terms "soft whistleblowing" disclosures that "concer[n] not agency malfeasance but internal dissent about an agency's policy course," and she argues that they "improve agency transparency and augment congressional oversight." Amanda C. Leiter, Soft Whistleblowing, 48 Ga. L. Rev. 425 (2014).

Leaks in the national security context are of particular interest to secret law. Classified material is supposed to be kept secret. Those who disclose such information face potential criminal sanctions under the Espionage Act and other statutes. In 2017, the Trump Administration charged a government intelligence contractor, Reality Winner, for releasing classified information of attempted Russian interference in the 2016 election. She pleaded guilty in June 2018, and was sentenced to 63 months in prison. The Trump Administration also prosecuted a former FBI agent, Terry Albury, for leaking; he pleaded guilty in April 2018 and was sentenced to four years in prison. The Trump Administration originally charged another government intelligence contractor, Daniel Hale, in 2019 for giving documents to an Intercept reporter; he pleaded guilty during the Biden Administration and was given a 45-month sentence.

According to an investigation by The Intercept and the Project On Government Oversight, the "Trump administration referred far more media leaks for criminal investigation each year [in its first three years] than any of the previous 15 years, with the CIA accounting for the vast majority of such leaks, according to a trove of records released by the Department of Justice . . . in response to a Freedom of Information Act lawsuit." There were 118 leaks reported in 2017, 88 in 2018, and 71 in 2019. Jason Paladino, Nick Schwellenbach, & Ken Klippenstein, CIA Drove Spike in Media Leak Investigation Requests Under Trump, The Intercept (July 29, 2021).

DAVID E. POZEN, in a fascinating treatment based in part on interviews with national security officials prior to the Trump Administration, posits that the "story behind the U.S. government's longstanding failure to enforce the laws against leaking is far more complicated, and far more interesting, than has been appreciated." He argues "that most components of the executive branch have never prioritized criminal, civil, or administrative enforcement against leakers; that a nuanced set of informal social controls has come to supplement, and nearly supplant, the formal disciplinary scheme; that much of what we call leaking occurs in a gray area between full authorization and no authorization, so that it is neither 'leaks' nor 'plants' but what [he] . . . term[s] *pleaks* that dominate this discursive space; that the executive's toleration of these disclosures is a rational, power-enhancing strategy and not simply a product of prosecutorial limitations, a feature, not a bug, of the system; and that to untangle these dynamics is to illuminate important facets of presidential power, bureaucratic governance, and the national security state in America today." THE LEAKY LEVIATHAN: WHY THE GOVERNMENT CONDEMNS AND CONDONES UNLAWFUL DISCLOSURES OF INFORMATION, 127 Harv. L. Rev. 512 (2013).

The May 2022 leak of Justice Alito's draft opinion in Dobbs v. Jackson Women's Health Organization, which overturned Roe v. Wade, generated considerable attention, in part because leaks from the Supreme Court are incredibly rare. Chief Justice Roberts instructed the Court's Marshal to investigate; CNN reported that she asked clerks to hand over phone records and sign affidavits concerning the leak. No leaker had been identified by the time this casebook went to press.

(10) ***Access to OLC Opinions.*** The DOJ discloses some OLC opinions, but not all. Objecting to the limitation, Citizens for Responsibility and Ethics in Washington sued the Department of Justice, claiming the agency had to publish all of the Office of Legal Counsel's formal written opinions under the "reading room" provisions of FOIA, which require disclosure of "final opinions" and "statements of policy which have been adopted by the agency and are not published in the Federal Register." In a split opinion, the D.C. Circuit ruled that CREW failed to state a claim that all of OLC's formal opinions constitute "working law" of the agencies they advised: "[T]he

dispositive question before us is whether CREW has plausibly alleged that the OLC's formal written opinions have all been adopted by the agencies to which they were addressed, subjecting the opinions to disclosure under FOIA's reading-room provision as the 'working law' of those agencies.

"CREW's complaint makes no such allegation. It instead alleges only that the OLC's formal written opinions are controlling, authoritative and binding. . . . [T]hese descriptors alone are insufficient to render an OLC opinion the 'working law' of an agency; that OLC opinions are controlling (insofar as agencies customarily follow OLC advice that they request), precedential, and can be withdrawn . . . does not overcome the fact that OLC does not speak with authority on the [agency's] policy. Importantly, CREW does not allege that all of the OLC's formal written opinions have been adopted by any agency as its own. Because CREW's complaint fails to allege the additional facts necessary to render an OLC opinion the 'working law' of an agency, CREW's claim that all of the OLC's formal written opinions are subject to disclosure under FOIA's reading-room provision fails as a matter of law." CREW v. DOJ, 922 F.3d 480, 486–87 (D.C. Cir. 2019).

The dissent would not have dismissed the case, having found that "CREW's burden is limited to plausibly pleading that at least some OLC opinions are 'working law' and are therefore covered by the reading-room provision—a burden it has neatly carried." Id. at 492.

Others have subsequently sued for access to OLC opinions. In September 2020, then-District Court Judge Ketanji Brown Jackson "firmly rejected the parties' polarized propositions that either *all* of OLC's opinions are subject to affirmative disclosure under the FOIA's reading-room provision, or *none* of them is required to be made automatically available per that statute. Instead, the Court concludes that one of the ascertainable sets of records that [plaintiff] has now identified plausibly qualifies as 'final opinions . . . made in the adjudication of cases[,]' or 'statements of policy and interpretations which have been adopted by the agency[,]': OLC opinions that adjudicate inter-agency disputes." Campaign for Accountability v. DOJ, 486 F.Supp.3d 424, 445 (D.D.C. 2020) (brackets in original). This litigation has lasted for over five years, with both sides filing motions for summary judgment in 2021. The case was assigned to Judge Cobb after then-Judge Jackson moved to the D.C. Circuit; as of November 2022, there has been no ruling. In a separate case, CREW v. DOJ, 45 F.4th 963 (D.C. Cir. 2022), the D.C. Circuit affirmed the district court's order for DOJ to produce an OLC memo concerning the decision to keep Special Counsel Mueller's "Report On The Investigation Into Russian Interference In The 2016 Presidential Election" secret on the basis that it was not predecisional. See Note 7 (p. 763). The court noted that "while the decisional process on which the Department now relies involved a determination as to whether the Attorney General should make a public statement, none of the Department's submissions to the district court suggested that the March 2019 memorandum related to such a decision." See also Francis v. DOJ, No. 19-cv-1317 (W.D. Wash. 2019) (settling a case seeking the release of OLC opinions over 25 years old and accordingly no longer shielded by the deliberative process exemption; DOJ agreed to produce the titles of all unclassified memos written between 1945–1994 and the full text of 230 opinions that the plaintiffs selected).[25]

In January 2022, the Knight Institute created a tracker for OLC opinions—a Twitter account (@OLCforthepeople) that tweets "every time the OLC publishes an opinion in its reading room." Legislation has been introduced to compel disclosure of OLC advice. See H.R. 7619 (117th Cong.) (2022) (The See Undisclosed Legal Interpretations and Get Honest Transparency Act (SUNLIGHT Act of 2022) would require OLC to make publicly available, with limited exceptions, each new final decision (including updates) within 30 days and old decisions on a set timeline); see also S. 3858 (117th Cong.) (2022) (similar proposal).

(11) ***Automation and Artificial Intelligence: The Next Frontier?*** Agencies increasingly rely on automated tools. For instance, the Internal Revenue Service has an "Interactive Tax Assistant," which answers questions online.[26] Some agencies use programs to analyze large volumes of comments to a Notice of Proposed Rulemaking or numerous text reports on drug or product safety (others use systems to recognize faces). Some tools involve prediction. For example, the Securities and Exchange Commission uses the Form ADV Fraud Predictor to flag financial service professionals who may be violating securities law and regulations. According to a comprehensive ACUS report canvassing 142 federal agencies, 45 percent of them have utilized Artificial Intelligence and related machine learning tools in some way—including for enforcement, adjudication, monitoring, and communication. David Freeman Engstrom, Daniel E. Ho, Catherine M. Sharkey, & Mariano-Florentino Cuéllar, Government by Algorithm: Artificial Intelligence in Federal Administrative Agencies (2020).[27] How will (and how should) disclosure work for these tools (some of which cannot be fully explained because of their design)? See id. at 75–78; Cary Coglianese & David Lehr, Transparency and Algorithmic Governance, 71 Admin L. Rev. 1 (2019). ACUS recently made some recommendations on the transparency of automated legal guidance.[28] Related issues about the use of automated or predictive programs to search for responsive records under the Freedom of Information Act may also arise in the future, as they have in discovery disputes in non-FOIA cases with considerable electronic materials.

---

[25] https://knightcolumbia.org/documents/8yxd3qw6sp.

[26] https://www.irs.gov/help/ita.

[27] https://law.stanford.edu/wp-content/uploads/2020/02/ACUS-AI-Report.pdfhttps://www-cdn.law.stanford.edu/wp-content/uploads/2020/02/ACUS-AI-Report.pdf.

[28] ACUS, Recommendation 2022–3, Automated Legal Guidance at Federal Agencies, 87 Fed. Reg. 39798 (July 5, 2022).

# SECTION 3. FREEDOM OF INFORMATION LEGISLATION



## a. FOIA Overview



### THE FREEDOM OF INFORMATION ACT, 5 U.S.C. § 552

[The Act is set out in the Appendix (p. 1604). The following excerpts establish the usual right of "any person" to demand the production of reasonably identified government records and the limited exemptions to that right.]

**5 U.S.C. § 552. Public information; agency rules, opinions, orders, records, and proceedings . . .**

(a)(3)(A) Except with respect to the records made available under paragraphs (1) and (2) of this subsection, and except as provided in subparagraph (E), each agency, upon any request for records which

(i) reasonably describes such records and

(ii) is made in accordance with published rules stating the time, place, fees (if any), and procedures to be followed, shall make the records promptly available to any person. . . .

(a)(3)(C) In responding under this paragraph to a request for records, an agency shall make reasonable efforts to search for the records in electronic form or format, except when such efforts would significantly interfere with the operation of the agency's automated information system.

(a)(3)(D) For purposes of this paragraph, the term "search" means to review, manually or by automated means, agency records for the purpose of locating those records which are responsive to a request. . . .

(a)(8)(A) An agency shall—

(i) withhold information under this section only if—

(I) the agency reasonably foresees that disclosure would harm an interest protected by an exemption described in subsection (b); or

(II) disclosure is prohibited by law; and

(ii)

(I) consider whether partial disclosure of information is possible whenever the agency determines that a full disclosure of a requested record is not possible; and

(II) take reasonable steps necessary to segregate and release nonexempt information; and

(a)(8)(B) Nothing in this paragraph requires disclosure of information that is otherwise prohibited from disclosure by law, or otherwise exempted from disclosure under subsection (b)(3).

(b) This section does not apply to matters that are—

(1)(A) specifically authorized under criteria established by an Executive order to be kept secret in the interest of national defense or foreign policy and (B) are in fact properly classified pursuant to such Executive order;

(2) related solely to the internal personnel rules and practices of an agency;

(3) specifically exempted from disclosure by statute (other than section 552b of this title), if that statute—

(A) (i) requires that the matters be withheld from the public in such a manner as to leave no discretion on the issue; or

(ii) establishes particular criteria for withholding or refers to particular types of matters to be withheld; and

(B) if enacted after the date of enactment of the OPEN FOIA Act of 2009, specifically cites to this paragraph.

(4) trade secrets and commercial or financial information obtained from a person and privileged or confidential;

(5) inter-agency or intra-agency memorandums or letters that would not be available by law to a party other than an agency in litigation with the agency, provided that the deliberative process privilege shall not apply to records created 25 years or more before the date on which the records were requested;

(6) personnel and medical files and similar files the disclosure of which would constitute a clearly unwarranted invasion of personal privacy;

(7) records or information compiled for law enforcement purposes, but only to the extent that the production of such law enforcement records or information

(A) could reasonably be expected to interfere with enforcement proceedings,

(B) would deprive a person of a right to a fair trial or an impartial adjudication,

(C) could reasonably be expected to constitute an unwarranted invasion of personal privacy,

(D) could reasonably be expected to disclose the identity of a confidential source, including a State, local, or foreign agency or authority or any private institution which furnished information on a confidential basis, and, in the case of a record or information compiled by criminal law enforcement authority in the course of a criminal investigation or by an agency conducting a lawful national security intelligence investigation, information furnished by a confidential source,

(E) would disclose techniques and procedures for law enforcement investigations or prosecutions, or would disclose guidelines for law enforcement investigations or prosecutions if such disclosure could reasonably be expected to risk circumvention of the law, or

(F) could reasonably be expected to endanger the life or physical safety of any individual;

(8) contained in or related to examination, operating, or condition reports prepared by, on behalf of, or for the use of an agency responsible for the regulation or supervision of financial institutions; or

(9) geological and geophysical information and data, including maps, concerning wells.

Any reasonably segregable portion of a record shall be provided to any person requesting such record after deletion of the portions which are exempt under this subsection. The amount of information deleted, and the exemption under which the deletion is made, shall be indicated on the released portion of the record, unless including that indication would harm an interest protected by the exemption in this subsection under which the deletion is made. If technically feasible, the amount of the information deleted, and the exemption under which the deletion is made, shall be indicated at the place in the record where such deletion is made.

## NOTES

(1) ***FOIA's Start.*** MARGARET B. KWOKA describes FOIA's enactment and goals in SAVING THE FREEDOM OF INFORMATION ACT 25 (2021): "After a decade-long fight, Congress passed the 1966 Freedom of Information Act, and the formal legislative history of FOIA echoes the . . . themes of democratic oversight and press facilitation of public participation in governance. The House of Representatives Report that accompanied the passage of the bill declared that '[a] democratic society requires an informed, intelligent electorate, and the intelligence of the electorate varies as the quantity and quality of its information varies.' Likewise, the Senate Report explained that '[a]lthough the theory of an informed electorate is so vital to the proper operation of a democracy, there is nowhere in our present law a statute which affirmatively provides for a policy of disclosure.' Upon signing the bill into law, President Johnson reaffirmed the oversight and democracy enhancing goals of the act: '[A] democracy works best when the people have

all the information that the security of the Nation permits . . . I signed this measure with a deep sense of pride that the United States is an open society in which the people's right to know is cherished and guarded.' . . .

"The Supreme Court has repeatedly reaffirmed this view of FOIA's role: 'The basic purpose of FOIA is to ensure an informed citizenry, vital to the functioning of a democratic society, needed to check against corruption and to hold the governors accountable to the governed.' It has further opined 'FOIA is often explained as a means for citizens to know what the Government is up to. This phrase should not be dismissed as a convenient formalism. It defines a structural necessity in a real democracy.' "

(2) ***Political Policies on FOIA.*** Before the 2016 Amendments to FOIA, we saw contrasting Administration policies on disclosure. In October 2001, after the attacks of 9/11, Attorney General John Ashcroft replaced an earlier 1993 memorandum on FOIA, telling agencies that "the Department of Justice will defend your decisions unless they lack a sound legal basis or present an unwarranted risk of adverse impact on the ability of other agencies to protect other important records."[1] In March 2009, President Obama's first Attorney General, Eric Holder, sent a memorandum replacing Ashcroft's 2001 directions, instructing agencies that they "should not withhold information simply because [they] may do so legally."[2] Holder notified agencies that "the Department of Justice will defend a denial of a FOIA request only if (1) the agency reasonably foresees that disclosure would harm an interest protected by one of the statutory exemptions, or (2) disclosure is prohibited by law."[3]

Congress sided with the Holder approach when it amended FOIA in 2016 by adding 5 U.S.C. § 552(a)(8)(A), which allows agencies to withhold material "only if—(I) the agency reasonably foresees that disclosure would harm an interest protected by an exemption described in subsection (b); or (II) disclosure is prohibited by law." The 2016 Amendments also instructed agencies to "consider whether partial disclosure of information is possible whenever the agency determines that a full disclosure of a requested record is not possible; and . . . take reasonable steps necessary to segregate and release nonexempt information."

In March 2022, Attorney General Merrick Garland issued a memorandum for the Biden Administration.[4]

> Information that might technically fall within an exemption should not be withheld from a FOIA requester unless the agency can

[1] https://www.justice.gov/archive/oip/011012.htm.

[2] https://www.justice.gov/sites/default/files/ag/legacy/2009/06/24/foia-memo-march2009.pdf.

[3] A month later, Gregory Craig, Counsel to the President, sent a memorandum to the same set of agency leaders: "This is a reminder that executive agencies should consult with the White House Counsel's Office on all document requests that may involve documents with White House entities. . . . This need to consult with the White House arises with respect to all types of document requests, including Congressional committee requests, GAO requests, judicial subpoenas, and FOIA requests. And it applies to all documents and records, whether in oral, paper, or electronic form, that relate to communications to and from the White House, including preparations for such communications." https://www.justice.gov/oip/guidance/craig_memoranda_4-15-2009.pdf/download.

[4] https://www.justice.gov/ag/page/file/1483516/download.

> identify a foreseeable harm or legal bar to disclosure. In case of doubt, openness should prevail. Moreover, agencies are strongly encouraged to make discretionary disclosures of information where appropriate. . . .
>
> To help ensure proper application of the foreseeable harm standard, agencies should confirm in response letters to FOIA requesters that they have considered the foreseeable harm standard when reviewing records and applying FOIA exemptions.
>
> In determining whether to defend an agency's nondisclosure decision, the Justice Department will apply the presumption of openness described above. The Justice Department will not defend nondisclosure decisions that are inconsistent with FOIA or with these guidelines.
>
> Although the fair and effective administration of FOIA requires that openness prevail in the face of doubt, Congress established nine exemptions to protect, for example, national security, personal privacy, privileged records, and law enforcement interests. § 552(b). As the Act makes clear, however, the "burden is on the agency to sustain" a decision to withhold records under those exemptions. § 552(a)(4)(B). Nor may agencies withhold information based merely on speculative or abstract fears or fears of embarrassment. . . .
>
> The proactive disclosure of information is also fundamental to the faithful application of FOIA. Proactive disclosures enable information about federal government operations to be more readily available to all. . . .
>
> Agencies should continue their efforts to remove barriers to requesting and accessing government records and to reduce FOIA processing backlogs. For example, the Justice Department's Executive Office for Immigration Review has long required individuals to file FOIA requests to obtain official copies of their own records of immigration court proceedings. We are now changing that policy, and I encourage all agencies to examine whether they have similar or other categories of records that they could make more readily accessible without requiring individuals to file FOIA requests.

What instructions in Garland's memorandum are required by the 2016 Amendments? For those that are not mandated, are there any costs?

(3) ***Assessment of FOIA Performance.*** The Department of Justice tracks the government's FOIA performance.[5] FOIA requests generally increased, with one dip, from FY 2009 (the first year with Privacy Act requests excluded unless FOIA was used to process them) to their peak in FY 2018. In FY 2009, 557,825 requests were submitted; in FY 2018, 863,729 requests came in. FY 2021 (the latest year available at the time of publication) saw 838,164

---

[5] https://www.foia.gov/. The agency also releases annual reports, which can be found at: https://www.justice.gov/oip/reports-1.

requests. In FY 2021, the Department of Homeland Security received the most requests, over half the total, with 442,650 submissions (often individuals seeking information for their own immigration matters). The Department of Justice, Department of Defense, Department of Health and Human Services, and Department of Veterans Affairs received the second through fifth most requests. In total, these five agencies received over 75 percent of all FOIA submissions.

Because of backlogs, a request is not necessarily processed in the year it is received. Of the processed requests in FY 2021, 20.6 percent asked for records that did not exist, 19.8 percent were granted in full, and 40.1 percent were granted in part. Disclosure rates would look worse if you use the number of pending and processed requests in the denominator. As with previous years, in FY 2021, agencies relied on Exemption 6 (29.2% of all claimed exemptions), Exemption 7(C) (26.5%), and Exemption 7(E) (25.1%) the most (for discussion of what these exemptions cover, see pp. 759, 773). While the Internet has made more agency material available (see p. 702), changes in technology—namely, email—have also produced more items to search (and review).

The COVID-19 pandemic placed additional strain on agency processing of FOIA requests, although total requests declined in its first year. In response to the processing strain, the Department of Justice's Office of Information Policy issued guidance to agencies in May 2020: "Many agencies have faced challenges as a result of staffing and technology limitations, as well as challenges at various stages of the FOIA process, ranging from request intake to conducting searches, processing certain types of records, and providing final responses. Agencies with the capability to process records, even at a diminished pace, should do so, subject to appropriate safety precautions necessary to protect the health of their employees." The guidance, which remains in effect (as of November 2022), also urges agencies to communicate with requesters about delays.[6] For the GAO's assessment of five major agencies' performance, see Freedom of Information Act: Selected Agencies Adapted to the COVID-19 Pandemic but Face Ongoing Challenges and Backlogs, GAO-22-105040 (Jan. 2022).[7] Requests have been filed to help assess the government's response to the pandemic as well. Reversing their initial stance, the Small Business Administration and Treasury Department released data identifying businesses that received pandemic-related funds from the government.

If you are following a specific agency, use the FOIA website to see how many requests were submitted to that agency: What percentage obtained full disclosure, and what portion generated only partial disclosure? What exemptions did your agency rely on most?[8]

(4) ***FOIA at Fifty.*** More than fifty years have passed since FOIA was enacted. Should we celebrate? As you make your way through the materials

---

6 See https://www.justice.gov/oip/guidance-agency-foia-administration-light-covid-19-impacts.

7 https://www.gao.gov/products/gao-22-105040.

8 You can also compare across administrations. Easy-to-access data go back to 2008: https://www.foia.gov/data.html.

in this Section, consider the following excerpt from DAVID E. POZEN, FREEDOM OF INFORMATION BEYOND THE FREEDOM OF INFORMATION ACT, 165 U. Pa. L. Rev. 1097, 1100–01 (2017): "Compared to the citizen enforcement schemes used in areas such as environmental law or civil rights law, FOIA's structure is substantially more decentralized and individualistic. It attenuates the link between the exercise of private right and vindication of the public good. The result may be the worst of both worlds: all the ad hockery and adversarialism of a 'private attorney general' regime without much benefit, if any, in terms of efficient allocation of public resources or enhanced capacity to detect hidden violations of law. Add up these points, and one might find that FOIA ultimately serves to legitimate the lion's share of government secrecy while delegitimating and debilitating government itself.

"Our landmark freedom of information legislation can thus be seen as reactionary on two interrelated levels. FOIA is reactionary in a straightforward, procedural sense insofar as disclosure is driven by requests for preexisting records. And partly for this very reason, FOIA is arguably reactionary in a more substantive, political sense insofar as it empowers opponents of regulation, distributes government goods in a regressive fashion, and contributes to a culture of contempt surrounding the domestic policy bureaucracy while insulating the national security state from similar scrutiny."

(5) ***Disclosure Regimes Outside of the United States.*** As of 1986, only ten countries had disclosure statutes for government information, including the United States and Sweden, which was the first to enact a law in 1766. In the subsequent two decades, 56 countries enacted such legislation.[9] Over 100 countries now have freedom of information laws. There is a Global Right to Information Rating, which evaluates right of access, scope, requesting procedures, exceptions, appeals, sanctions, and promotional measures, for "comparatively assessing the overall strength of a legal framework."[10] Countries with younger laws tend to score better. As of November 2022, the top five of 136 countries were Afghanistan, Mexico, Serbia, Sri Lanka, and Slovenia. The United States scored 83 points (out of a possible 150), which placed it in the middle range of the ranked countries.

New disclosure laws have generated frivolous as well as deadly serious requests. On the former, in a ten-year look back at Britain's statute, the New York Times noted the "appalling regularity" of requests like: "How many residents in Sutton own an ostrich?" "What procedures are in place for a zombie invasion of Cumbria?" "How many people have been banned from Birmingham Library because they smell?" The article also reported that "[i]n Wigan, the council was asked what plans were in place to protect the town from a dragon attack, while Worthing Borough Council had to outline its

---

[9] John M. Ackerman & Irma E. Sandoval-Ballesteros, The Global Explosion of Freedom of Information Laws, 58 Admin. L. Rev. 85, 97–97 tbl.1 (2006). The article also details variation in coverage, exemptions, enforcement, and ease of access of these statutes.

[10] https://www.rti-rating.org/.

preparations for an asteroid crash." Bryton Clarke, From A to Z (Asteroids to Zombies), British Just Want Facts, N.Y. Times (April 12, 2015).

By contrast, the New York Times noted the "heavy price" some requesters under India's 2005 law have paid: "Amit Jethwa had just left his lawyer's office after discussing a lawsuit he had filed to stop an illicit limestone quarry with ties to powerful local politicians. That is when the assassins struck, speeding out of the darkness on a roaring motorbike, pistols blazing. He died on the spot, blood pouring from his mouth and nose. He was 38. Mr. Jethwa was one of millions of Indians who had embraced the country's five-year-old Right to Information Act, which allows citizens to demand almost any government information. People use the law to stop petty corruption and to solve their most basic problems, like getting access to subsidized food for the poor or a government pension without having to pay a bribe, or determining whether government doctors and teachers are actually showing up for work. But activists like Mr. Jethwa who have tried to push such disclosures further—making pointed inquiries at the dangerous intersection of high-stakes business and power politics—have paid a heavy price. Perhaps a dozen have been killed since 2005, when the law was enacted, and countless others have been beaten and harassed." Lydia Polgreen, High Price for India's Information Law, N.Y. Times (Jan. 22, 2011). Studies in the intervening decades show the effectiveness of India's law, which is widely feted by transparency advocates.

## NOTES ON AGENCIES, RECORDS, REQUESTERS, SEARCH, AND HARM

(1) ***Scope of FOIA: Agencies and Records.*** FOIA is limited to "agency records." Under the statute, "agency . . . includes any executive department, military department, Government corporation, Government controlled corporation, or other establishment in the executive branch of the Government (including the Executive Office of the President), or any independent regulatory agency." 5 U.S.C. § 552(f)(1). Compare the definition of agency in the APA. 5 U.S.C. § 551(1). Courts have had to resolve whether certain quasi-agencies (for example, the Red Cross) are subject to FOIA. The President is not subject to FOIA (or the APA), generating litigation over whether an entity is part of the White House (not covered) or is part of the Executive Office of the President (covered). See, e.g., Meyer v. Bush, 981 F.2d 1288 (D.C. Cir. 1993) (distinguishing between OMB and the Reagan Task Force on Regulatory Relief). "Record," in turn, "includes (A) any information that would be an agency record subject to the requirements of this section when maintained by an agency in any format, including an electronic format; and (B) any information described under subparagraph (A) that is maintained for an agency by an entity under Government contract, for the purposes of records management." 5 U.S.C. § 552(f)(2).

Judicial Watch v. Secret Service, 726 F.3d 208 (D.C. Cir. 2013), rejected a FOIA request for the Secret Service's White House Access Control System records that would have revealed visitors to the President and the President's assistants. In assessing Judicial Watch's request, the court discussed the ordinary test used to determine whether records are "agency records," a four-part test explicated in Tax Analysts v. U.S. Dep't of Justice, 845 F.2d 1060, 1069 (D.C. Cir. 1988), aff'd, 492 U.S. 136 (1989):[11] "[1] the intent of the document's creator to retain or relinquish control over the records; [2] the ability of the agency to use and dispose of the record as it sees fit; [3] the extent to which agency personnel have read or relied upon the document; and [4] the degree to which the document was integrated into the agency's record system or files." The court found the application of this test indeterminate. On the one hand, the logs were not to be regarded as agency records because they could not be obtained directly from the President or the President's close advisors, who are not agencies under FOIA. On the other, if the logs recorded visits to others in the White House complex who were part of agencies—visits to OMB, for example—then the same records would be considered agency records subject to disclosure (unless some qualifying exemption applied). The court also noted that permitting indirect access to presidential records would raise serious separation of powers concerns. For undoubted FOIA agencies, however, no such concerns arose; and in their absence, the indeterminacy of the Tax Analysts test favored Judicial Watch's claim, given the agency's burden to demonstrate, not the requester's to disprove, that the materials sought are not agency records.

Control is critical in assessing whether a record is an *agency* record. Courts have upheld nondisclosure of congressional documents provided to an agency where Congress has made clear that the materials remain congressional records. See American Civil Liberties Union v. CIA, 823 F.3d 655 (D.C. Cir. 2016) (Senate Select Committee on Intelligence report). The D.C. Circuit has compelled searches of the private emails of an agency's director because he controlled the nongovernment email account when working for the agency. Competitive Enter. Inst. v. Office of Sci. & Tech. Policy, 827 F.3d 145 (D.C. Cir. 2016).

---

[11] The D.C. Circuit's framework rests on Kissinger v. Reporters Committee for Freedom of the Press, 445 U.S. 136 (1980). In that case, the Supreme Court focused on four factors to determine whether items were agency records: whether the documents were (1) in the agency's control; (2) generated within the agency; (3) placed into the agency's files; and (4) used by the agency "for any purpose." The case involved three separate FOIA requests for the transcripts and summaries of Henry Kissinger's telephone conversations while he was Secretary of State and National Security Advisor to the President. Kissinger treated the notes as his own personal papers. While still in the State Department, he transferred them to a private location before two of the three FOIA requests were filed, and he entered an agreement deeding the notes to the Library of Congress. As to those two requests, the Court found that the State Department had not "withheld" anything because the documents had been removed from the State Department's possession prior to the filing of a FOIA request. "[T]he agency ha[d] neither the custody nor the control to enable it to withhold." The third FOIA request, filed before the telephone notes were removed from the State Department, sought notes of telephone conversations Kissinger had while he was in the Office of the President prior to becoming Secretary of State. Because FOIA does not include presidential assistants in the definition of "agency," the records of those phone conversations were not "agency" records, and the mere physical transfer of those documents to the State Department did not by itself render them "agency records" because the "papers were not in the control of the State Department at any time. They were not generated in the State Department. They never entered the State Department's files, and they were not used by the Department for any purpose. If mere physical location of papers and materials could confer status as an 'agency record' Kissinger's personal books, speeches, and all other memorabilia stored in his office would have been agency records subject to disclosure under the FOIA."

While the text of the statute *authorizes* nondisclosure of agency records in certain circumstances, it does not itself *require* nondisclosure in most circumstances.[12] Further, it provides that if only parts of a record are exempt from disclosure, "any reasonably segregable portion" that does not share the infirmity must be produced. Both provisions seem to tell the agency that it will be easier to produce its records than not to produce them.

Are state judicial nomination commissions for federal judgeships, comprised of "volunteers selected by the Senators from both the Florida Bar and the general public," agencies under FOIA? See Statton v. Florida Federal Judicial Nominating Comm'n, 959 F.3d 1061 (11th Cir. 2020) ("Any federal supervision over the Commission began and ended with Florida's United States Senators. The Commission was created by the Senators, not by a federal statute. It did not begin its selection process until the Senators made a request. And its composition was completely under the control of the two Senators, who also retained the liberty to amend its Rules of Procedure at any time. Two Senators, acting alone, cannot create a federal agency.").

Are the Internet browsing histories of federal employees considered agency records under FOIA? See Cause of Action Institute v. OMB, 10 F.4th 849 (D.C. Cir. 2021) (weighing relinquishment, use, and integration factors for the agency to find that browsing histories were not under agency control).

Are searches of databases records? See Center for Investigative Reporting v. DOJ, 982 F.3d 668 (9th Cir. 2020): "We agree that using a query to search for and extract a particular arrangement or subset of data already maintained in an agency's database does not amount to the creation of a new record. In some ways, typing a query into a database is the modern day equivalent of physically searching through and locating data within documents in a filing cabinet. The subset of data selected is akin to a stack of redacted paper records. It makes no difference if the query produces a set of documents, a list, a spreadsheet, or some other form of results that the agency has not previously viewed." See also National Security Counselors v. CIA, 969 F.3d 406 (D.C. Cir. 2020) ("Here, NSC's request for the CIA to produce listings according to four fee categories of all FOIA requesters over a two-year period would require the agency to create new records, not to disclose existing ones" because the CIA's FOIA databases do not contain fee categories as a mandatory field).

Are visitor information and schedules from Donald Trump's campaign and transition, provided to the Secret Service before January 20, 2017, agency records? See Behar v. DHS, 39 F.4th 81 (2d Cir. 2022): "[O]ur recent decision . . . explained that 'agency records' did not include information provided by a governmental entity not covered by FOIA when the non-covered entity . . . has manifested a clear intent to control the documents, such that the agency is not free to use and dispose of the documents as it sees

[12] This characteristic has particular importance to the supplier of commercially valuable information, who may fear its discretionary or accidental disclosure. See Notes on Exemptions Protecting Information Supplied to Government below (p. 768; Section 3.d). Although the Act's exemptions include materials whose continued secrecy would be of interest to persons outside the agency, FOIA itself makes no explicit provision for these outsiders to be heard in the agency's (or the court's) consideration of what should be disclosed.

fit. That principle applies with equal force in this case, in which the entity not covered by the FOIA is not even a governmental entity."

Is a document that addresses several different topics one record—or is each topic a separate record? For example, a document that contains an agency's responses to questions from multiple members of Congress? (This bears on what an agency can redact: in a particular record, only material that falls within FOIA's exemptions can be protected from disclosure). See Cause of Action Institute v. DOJ, 999 F.3d 696 (D.C. Cir. 2021): "DOJ's position in this case is that each individual question and its corresponding answer within each of the self-contained . . . documents constitutes a separate 'record' under FOIA. Resting on this claim, DOJ maintains that if it determined that a particular question-and-answer pairing within a . . . document was unresponsive to Appellant's FOIA request, DOJ could decline to disclose the material even though none of the material in the . . . document was exempt from disclosure. Though our case law provides for a range of possible ways in which an agency might conceive of a 'record,' we reject DOJ's approach as an untenable application of FOIA, outside the range of reasonableness. [DOJ] itself treated the self-contained . . . documents as unitary 'records' and released the documents, albeit with portions removed, as responsive to Appellant's FOIA request."

(2) ***FOIA Requesters.*** Interestingly, FOIA places almost no limits on who can request information (though the requester's identity is relevant to how much she will pay in fees for disclosures, along with the agency's timeliness).[13] A requester of records needs only to "reasonably describ[e]" the records wanted but need not give any reason for wanting them, and the description need not be in great detail. For example: "All records considered by the agency in connection with its proposed rulemaking, XY Fed. Reg. ABCD (date), on the treatment of smoked fish" would be a sufficiently detailed request. The statutory grounds for refusing to surrender records, with very limited exceptions, also do not depend on any balance between the requester's possible reason for wanting the records produced and the considerations supporting withholding.

Although commercial entities may dominate among FOIA requesters at some agencies, see Note 3 below, journalists have relied on FOIA to break major stories, including the abuse of detainees in Guantánamo Bay, Iraq, and Afghanistan; the failure to get benefits to veterans; and the eavesdropping by intelligence agencies on American citizens' communications. One of two FOIA lawyers for the New York Times described his experience: "We know better than anyone that FOIA cases are

[13] After the September 11, 2001, attacks, Congress did amend FOIA to bar intelligence agencies from disclosing records to "(i) any government entity, other than a State, territory, commonwealth, or district of the United States, or any subdivision thereof; or (ii) a representative of a government entity described in clause (i)." 5 U.S.C. § 552(a)(3)(E). See also McBurney v. Young, 569 U.S. 221 (2013) (upholding Virginia's Freedom of Information Act that restricts disclosure to Virginia citizens). In June 2022, Republican Senators Marco Rubio and Tom Cotton introduced the FOIA Fix Act (S. 4401), which would permit agencies to disclose records under FOIA only to U.S. citizens or lawful permanent residents and to businesses with a U.S. principal place of business or headquarters in the United States (but not if they are a subsidiary of a business operating in particular countries).

frustrating, the deck is stacked against us, and the lawsuits drag on for months and years. It can feel Sisyphean, pushing a huge legal rock up a sizable legal hill. Only unlike Sisyphus, we sometimes get to the top. We win. Between settlements and successful court decisions, we regularly make a small dent in governmental secrecy. . . . [W]e . . . forced the Pentagon to release a trove of eye-opening documents about the Bush administration's stealth campaign to sell the war in Iraq to the American people. . . . We have won important rulings on the Obama administration's investigation into the use of torture after 9/11 and the government's campaign to kill terrorism suspects abroad. And we don't just get documents. One of FOIA's few delightful twists is that the government pays us for our time and effort when we prevail." David McCraw, Think FOIA Is a Paper Tiger? The New York Times Gives It Some Bite, N.Y. Times (June 13, 2017). The Free Beacon determined that the Washington Post and New York Times submitted many more FOIA requests to the EPA during the first two years of the Trump Administration (43 and 100, respectively) than during the second term of the Obama Administration (1 and 13, respectively).

(3) ***Commercial Requesters.*** The prompt emergence of a commercial FOIA request business led to concerns that mining for competitors' trade secrets was among the Act's principal uses. MARGARET KWOKA examined FOIA requests received by six agencies in FY 2013: Defense Logistics Agency (DLA) (4,420 requests), Environmental Protection Agency (9,737), Federal Trade Commission (1,538), Food and Drug Administration (10,167), National Institutes of Health (1,198), and Securities and Exchange Commission (12,091). MARGARET B. KWOKA, FOIA, INC., 65 Duke L.J. 1361 (2016). Here are some of her important findings, as summarized for JOTWELL:[14] "Although a smaller FOIA operation, all but four percent of DLA's requests were categorized as commercial. Day & Day, one information reseller, charges $1800 for an annual subscription to an online database of FOIA documents from DLA (specifically, procurements and contracts). Nearly eighty percent of EPA's requests were submitted by commercial requesters. Compared to other agencies, frequent requesters were, well, less frequent. Only six sources made more than 100 requests and none put in more than 180. By contrast to four of the other agencies, only about one-third of FTC requests fell into the commercial category. Over half of those commercial requests (and twenty percent of all requests) came from law firms. Nearly half of the total requests were made by individuals, almost all of whom wanted information about their own consumer complaints to the agency. Three-quarters of FDA's requests came from commercial sources. . . . [T]he 'most frequent requesters are not . . . pharmaceutical companies, but information resellers.' These resellers make good money. FDA News charges $997 for a one-year subscription for FDA Form 483s and $117 for a particular form. The only high-volume pharmaceutical requester, Merck & Co., overwhelmingly asked (more than 80 percent of its 373 requests) about others' FOIA requests. Like the FTC, a little more than one-third of NIH's requests were labeled commercial. Fifteen percent came from educational

[14] Anne Joseph O'Connell, Disclosure about Disclosure, JOTWELL (May 2016), https://adlaw.jotwell.com/disclosure-about-disclosure/.

institutions. SECProbes accounted for 12 percent of all SEC requests. These 2498 requests from SECProbes were labeled as coming from news media but should have been placed in the commercial category (from impressive online sleuthing by Kwoka). If they are removed from the news media pile, only 309 requests remain in that category."

Should FOIA be amended to take account of a particular requester's identity and need for information, not only (as at present) in relation to the urgency of response to the request and the size, if any, of search fees, but also as to the very meaning of the exemptions? Alternatively, could agencies disclose more materials online in useful formats, so that information resellers would have fewer products to sell, as Kwoka proposes? Does the agency you are following put such material online?

(4) ***Agency Search for Records.*** Under FOIA, "an agency shall make reasonable efforts to search for the records in electronic form or format, except when such efforts would significantly interfere with the operation of the agency's automated information system." Courts typically assess the adequacy of an agency's search for responsive records by examining the methods used to search, rather than by looking at what the agency produced. The D.C. Circuit recently discussed the FBI's searches of electronic documents in SHAPIRO V. DEPARTMENT OF JUSTICE, 40 F.4th 609 (D.C. Cir. 2022): "The Freedom of Information Act requires agencies to comply with requests to make their records available to the public . . . . To prevail on summary judgment, an agency must show that it made a good faith effort to conduct a search for the requested records, using methods which can be reasonably expected to produce the information requested, which it can do by submitting a reasonably detailed affidavit, setting forth the search terms and the type of search performed, and averring that all files likely to contain responsive materials (if such records exist) were searched. In a FOIA case, a district court is not tasked with uncovering whether there might exist any other documents possibly responsive to the request, but instead, asks only whether the search for [the requested] documents was adequate. . . .

"The present dispute centers not on the FBI's diligence or good faith, but rather on whether its search methods for electronic surveillance records were reasonably calculated to locate all responsive materials. To answer this question, we begin by describing the FBI's recordkeeping systems and its search of those systems for responsive records. In so doing, we accord the FBI's declarations a presumption of good faith, which cannot be rebutted by purely speculative claims about the existence and discoverability of other documents. . . .

"Despite the FBI's good-faith effort to process the voluminous requests, we agree with [the FOIA requester] that its declarations inadequately address one class of records: those related to individuals mentioned in monitored communications but not directly targeted for surveillance. According to its declarations, the FBI's electronic surveillance indices include 'the names of all individuals whose voices have been monitored,' but for many years field offices have not been 'required to forward to [FBI headquarters] the names of all individuals mentioned during monitored conversations.' Although 'some' field offices continue to include mentioned names in their local indices, 'the names of such individuals cannot be retrieved through the [headquarters] ELSUR Index.' The FBI's declarations do not explain how the . . . search conducted in this case would have revealed electronic surveillance 'mentions' if Bureau field offices omit those references from ELSUR indices. A limited remand is appropriate for the FBI to fill this gap in its declarations.

"We have repeatedly made clear that discovery in a FOIA case is rare and courts should generally order it only where there is evidence—either at the affidavit stage or (in rarer cases) before—that the agency acted in bad faith in conducting the search. And even where we have found an agency's affidavits to be inadequate to support summary judgment, we have held that the appropriate remedy is usually to allow the agency to submit further affidavits rather than to order discovery. Consistent with these principles, on remand the district court need not allow discovery if further declarations will suffice."

(5) ***The Foreseeable Harm Standard in Practice.*** Since 2016, agencies must disclose material covered by a FOIA exemption unless "the agency reasonably foresees that disclosure would harm an interest protected by an exemption . . . or disclosure is prohibited by law." The D.C. Circuit has held that agencies cannot meet the foreseeable harm standard with "generalized assertions": "In the context of withholdings made under the deliberative process privilege, the foreseeability requirement means that agencies must concretely explain how disclosure 'would'—not 'could'—adversely impair internal deliberations." Reporters Committee for Freedom of the Press v. FBI, 3 F.4th 350 (D.C. Cir. 2021). How does the foreseeable harm mandate vary by exemption (the standard does not apply to the third exemption)? See Hall & Associates v. EPA, 2021 WL 1226668 (D.D.C. 2021) ("[T]he foreseeable-harm requirement applies with special force to deliberative process withholdings under Exemption 5, which Congress viewed as posing particular risks of overuse."); New York Times Co. v. FDA, 529 F.Supp.3d 260 (S.D.N.Y. 2021) ("The application of [the] foreseeable harm requirement to FOIA's Exemption 4 has caused more controversy than perhaps anticipated, as courts have split in ascertaining the 'harm' against which Exemption 4 is intended to protect."). See Adira Levine, Unpacking the New FOIA Memo, Notice & Comment Blog (Mar. 24, 2022).[15] For more on Exemption 4, see Note 4 (p. 771).

[15] https://www.yalejreg.com/nc/unpacking-the-new-foia-memo-by-adira-levine/.

## b. FOIA's General Characteristics

> ***MILNER v. DEP'T OF THE NAVY***
> ***Notes on Comparing FOIA and Traditional APA***

## MILNER v. DEP'T OF THE NAVY

Supreme Court of the United States (2011).
562 U.S. 562.

■ JUSTICE KAGAN delivered the opinion of the Court.

The Freedom of Information Act (FOIA), 5 U.S.C. § 552, requires federal agencies to make Government records available to the public, subject to nine exemptions for specific categories of material. This case concerns the scope of Exemption 2, which protects from disclosure material that is "related solely to the internal personnel rules and practices of an agency." § 552(b)(2). Respondent Department of the Navy (Navy or Government) invoked Exemption 2 to deny a FOIA request for data and maps used to help store explosives at a naval base in Washington State. We hold that Exemption 2 does not stretch so far.

I

Congress enacted FOIA to overhaul the public-disclosure section of the Administrative Procedure Act (APA), 5 U.S.C. § 1002 (1964 ed.). That section of the APA "was plagued with vague phrases" and gradually became more "a withholding statute than a disclosure statute." EPA v. Mink, 410 U.S. 73, 79 (1973). Congress intended FOIA to "permit access to official information long shielded unnecessarily from public view." Id., at 80. FOIA thus mandates that an agency disclose records on request, unless they fall within one of nine exemptions. These exemptions are "explicitly made exclusive," id., at 79, and must be "narrowly construed," FBI v. Abramson, 456 U.S. 615, 630 (1982).

At issue here is Exemption 2, which shields from compelled disclosure documents "related solely to the internal personnel rules and practices of an agency." § 552(b)(2). Congress enacted Exemption 2 to replace the APA's exemption for "any matter relating solely to the internal management of an agency," 5 U.S.C. § 1002 (1964 ed.). Believing that the "sweep" of the phrase "internal management" had led to excessive withholding, Congress drafted Exemption 2 "to have a narrower reach." Department of Air Force v. Rose, 425 U.S. 352, 362–363 (1976).

We considered the extent of that reach in Department of Air Force v. Rose. There, we rejected the Government's invocation of Exemption 2 to withhold case summaries of honor and ethics hearings at the United States Air Force Academy. The exemption, we suggested, primarily targets material concerning employee relations or human resources: "use of parking facilities or regulations of lunch hours, statements of policy as to sick leave, and the like." Id., at 363. . . . But we stated a possible caveat to our interpretation of Exemption 2: That understanding of the provision's coverage governed, we wrote, "at least where the situation is not one where disclosure may risk circumvention of agency regulation." Id., at 369.

In Crooker v. Bureau of Alcohol, Tobacco & Firearms, 670 F.2d 1051 (1981), the D.C. Circuit . . . approved the use of Exemption 2 to shield a manual designed to train Government agents in law enforcement surveillance techniques . . . [reasoning that] Exemption 2 should . . . cover any "predominantly internal" materials[1] whose disclosure would "significantly ris[k] circumvention of agency regulations or statutes," id., at 1074. This construction of Exemption 2, the court reasoned, flowed from FOIA's "overall design," its legislative history, "and even common sense," because Congress could not have meant to "enac[t] a statute whose provisions undermined . . . the effectiveness of law enforcement agencies." Ibid.

In the ensuing years, three Courts of Appeals adopted the D.C. Circuit's interpretation of Exemption 2. See 575 F.3d 959, 965 (CA9 2009) (case below); Massey v. FBI, 3 F.3d 620, 622 (CA2 1993); Kaganove v. EPA, 856 F.2d 884, 889 (CA7 1988).[2] And that interpretation spawned a new terminology: Courts applying the Crooker approach now refer to the "Low 2" exemption when discussing materials concerning human resources and employee relations, and to the "High 2" exemption when assessing records whose disclosure would risk circumvention of the law. Congress, as well, took notice of the D.C. Circuit's decision, borrowing language from Crooker to amend Exemption 7(E) when next enacting revisions to FOIA [in 1986]. The amended version of Exemption 7(E) shields certain "records or information compiled for law enforcement purposes" if their disclosure "could reasonably be expected to risk circumvention of the law."

II

The FOIA request at issue here arises from the Navy's operations at Naval Magazine Indian Island, a base in Puget Sound, Washington. The Navy keeps weapons, ammunition, and explosives on the island. To aid in the storage and transport of these munitions, the Navy uses data known as Explosive Safety Quantity Distance (ESQD) information. ESQD information prescribes "minimum separation distances" for explosives and helps the Navy design and construct storage facilities to prevent chain reactions in case of detonation. The ESQD calculations are

---

1 The court adopted the "predominantly internal" standard as a way of implementing the exemption's requirement that materials "relat[e] solely to" an agency's internal personnel rules and practices. The word "solely," the court reasoned, "has to be given the construction, consonant with reasonableness, of 'predominantly' " because otherwise "solely" would conflict with the expansive term "related." 670 F.2d at 1056 (some internal quotation marks omitted).

2 Three other Courts of Appeals had previously taken a narrower view of Exemption 2's scope. . . . See Cox v. Department of Justice, 576 F.2d 1302, 1309–1310 (CA8 1978); Stokes v. Brennan, 476 F.2d 699, 703 (CA5 1973); Hawkes v. IRS, 467 F.2d 787, 797 (CA6 1972). These Circuits have never revised their understandings of the exemption.

often incorporated into specialized maps depicting the effects of hypothetical explosions.

In 2003 and 2004, petitioner Glen Milner, a Puget Sound resident, submitted FOIA requests for all ESQD information relating to Indian Island. The Navy refused to release the data, stating that disclosure would threaten the security of the base and surrounding community. In support of its decision to withhold the records, the Navy invoked Exemption 2.

The District Court granted summary judgment to the Navy, and the Court of Appeals affirmed, relying on the High 2 interpretation developed in Crooker. The Court of Appeals explained that the ESQD information "is predominantly used for the internal purpose of instructing agency personnel on how to do their jobs." And disclosure of the material, the court determined, "would risk circumvention of the law" by "point[ing] out the best targets for those bent on wreaking havoc"—for example, "[a] terrorist who wished to hit the most damaging target." Id., at 971. The ESQD information, the court concluded, therefore qualified for a High 2 exemption.

We granted certiorari in light of the Circuit split respecting Exemption 2's meaning, and we now reverse.

III

Our consideration of Exemption 2's scope starts with its text. Judicial decisions since FOIA's enactment have analyzed and reanalyzed the meaning of the exemption. But comparatively little attention has focused on the provision's 12 simple words: "related solely to the internal personnel rules and practices of an agency."

The key word in that dozen—the one that most clearly marks the provision's boundaries—is "personnel." When used as an adjective, as it is here to modify "rules and practices," that term refers to human resources matters. "Personnel," in this common parlance, means "the selection, placement, and training of employees and . . . the formulation of policies, procedures, and relations with [or involving] employees or their representatives." Webster's Third New International Dictionary 1687 (1966) (hereinafter Webster's). So, for example, a "personnel department" is "the department of a business firm that deals with problems affecting the employees of the firm and that usually interviews applicants for jobs." Random House Dictionary 1075 (1966) (hereinafter Random House). "Personnel management" is similarly "the phase of management concerned with the engagement and effective utilization of manpower to obtain optimum efficiency of human resources." Webster's 1687. And a "personnel agency" is "an agency for placing employable persons in jobs; employment agency." Random House 1075.

FOIA itself provides an additional example in Exemption 6. See Ratzlaf v. United States, 510 U.S. 135, 143 (1994) ("A term appearing in several places in a statutory text is generally read the same way each time it appears"). That exemption . . . protects from disclosure "personnel and medical files and similar files the disclosure of which would constitute a clearly unwarranted invasion of personal privacy." § 552(b)(6). Here too, the statute uses the term "personnel" as a modifier meaning "human resources." As we recognized in Rose, "the common and congressional meaning of . . . 'personnel file' " is the file "showing, for example, where [an employee] was born, the names of his parents, where he has lived from time to time, his . . . school records, results of examinations, [and] evaluations of his work performance." 425 U.S., at 377. It is the file typically maintained in the human resources office-otherwise known (to recall an example offered above) as the "personnel department."

Exemption 2 uses "personnel" in the exact same way. . . . [A]ll the rules and practices referenced in Exemption 2 share a critical feature: They concern the conditions of employment in federal agencies—such matters as hiring and firing, work rules and discipline, compensation and benefits. Courts in practice have had little difficulty identifying the records that qualify for withholding under this reading: They are what now commonly fall within the Low 2 exemption. Our construction of the statutory language simply makes clear that Low 2 is all of 2 (and that High 2 is not 2 at all).

The statute's purpose reinforces this understanding of the exemption. We have often noted "the Act's goal of broad disclosure" and insisted that the exemptions be "given a narrow compass." Department of Justice v. Tax Analysts, 492 U.S. 136, 151 (1989). . . .[5] This practice . . . stands on especially firm footing with respect to Exemption 2. . . . Congress worded that provision to hem in the prior APA exemption for "any matter relating solely to the internal management of an agency," which agencies had used to prevent access to masses of documents. We would ill-serve Congress's purpose by construing Exemption 2 to reauthorize the expansive withholding that Congress wanted to halt. . . .

The Government resists giving "personnel" its plain meaning on the ground that Congress, when drafting Exemption 2, considered but chose not to enact language exempting "internal employment rules and practices." This drafting history, the Navy maintains, proves that Congress did not wish "to limit the Exemption to employment-related matters," even if the adjective "personnel" conveys that meaning in other contexts. But we think . . . [t]he scant history concerning this word change as easily supports the inference that Congress merely swapped one synonym for another. . . . Those of us who make use of legislative history believe that clear evidence of congressional intent may illuminate

[5] The dissent would reject this longstanding rule of construction in favor of an approach asking courts "to turn Congress' public information objectives into workable agency practice." But nothing in FOIA either explicitly or implicitly grants courts discretion to expand (or contract) an exemption on this basis. In enacting FOIA, Congress struck the balance it thought right—generally favoring disclosure, subject only to a handful of specified exemptions—and did so across the length and breadth of the Federal Government. The judicial role is to enforce that congressionally determined balance rather than, as the dissent suggests, to assess case by case, department by department, and task by task whether disclosure interferes with good government.

ambiguous text. We will not take the opposite tack of allowing ambiguous legislative history to muddy clear statutory language.

Exemption 2, as we have construed it, does not reach the ESQD information at issue here. These data and maps calculate and visually portray the magnitude of hypothetical detonations. By no stretch of imagination do they relate to "personnel rules and practices," as that term is most naturally understood. They concern the physical rules governing explosives, not the workplace rules governing sailors; they address the handling of dangerous materials, not the treatment of employees. The Navy therefore may not use Exemption 2, interpreted in accord with its plain meaning to cover human resources matters, to prevent disclosure of the requested maps and data.

IV

[The Court rejected, as inconsistent with the statute's language, two alternative readings of Exemption 2 offered by the government.]

The dissent offers one last reason to embrace High 2, and indeed stakes most of its wager on this argument. Crooker, the dissent asserts, "has been consistently relied upon and followed for 30 years" by other lower courts. But this claim, too, trips at the starting gate. It would be immaterial even if true, because we have no warrant to ignore clear statutory language on the ground that other courts have done so. And in any event, it is not true. Prior to Crooker, three Circuits adopted the reading of Exemption 2 we think right, and they have not changed their minds. Three other Courts of Appeals had previously taken a narrower view of Exemption 2's scope. . . . These Circuits have never revised their understandings of the exemption. See n. 2, supra.

Since Crooker, three other Circuits have accepted the High 2 reading. One Circuit has reserved judgment on the High 2-Low 2 debate. See Audubon Society v. Forest Serv., 104 F.3d 1201, 1203–1204 (CA10 1997). And the rest have not considered the matter. (No one should think Crooker has been extensively discussed or debated in the Courts of Appeals. In the past three decades, Crooker's analysis of Exemption 2 has been cited a sum total of five times in federal appellate decisions outside the D.C. Circuit—on average, once every six years.) The result is a 4 to 3 split among the Circuits. We will not flout all usual rules of statutory interpretation to take the side of the bare majority. . . .

[To a further government argument, that the exemption "encompasses records concerning an agency's internal rules and practices for its personnel to follow in the discharge of their governmental functions," the Court responded:]

But the purported logic in the Government's definition eludes us. We would not say, in ordinary parlance, that a "personnel file" is any file an employee uses, or that a "personnel department" is any department in which an employee serves. No more would we say that a "personnel rule or practice" is any rule or practice that assists an employee in doing her job. The use of the term "personnel" in each of these phrases connotes not that the file or department or practice/rule is for personnel, but rather that the file or department or practice/rule is about personnel—i.e., that it relates to employee relations or human resources. This case well illustrates the point. The records requested, as earlier noted, are explosives data and maps showing the distances that potential blasts travel. This information no doubt assists Navy personnel in storing munitions. But that is not to say that the data and maps relate to "personnel rules and practices." No one staring at these charts of explosions and using ordinary language would describe them in this manner. . . . [T]his odd reading would produce a sweeping exemption, posing the risk that FOIA would become less a disclosure than "a withholding statute." . . . Indeed, an agency could use Exemption 2 as an all-purpose back-up provision to withhold sensitive records that do not fall within any of FOIA's more targeted exemptions.[9]

V

Although we cannot interpret Exemption 2 as the Government proposes, we recognize the strength of the Navy's interest in protecting the ESQD data and maps and other similar information. The Ninth Circuit . . . cautioned that disclosure of this information could be used to "wrea[k] havoc" and "make catastrophe more likely." Concerns of this kind—a sense that certain sensitive information should be exempt from disclosure—in part led the Crooker court to formulate the High 2 standard. And we acknowledge that our decision today upsets three decades of agency practice relying on Crooker, and therefore may force considerable adjustments.

We also note, however, that the Government has other tools at hand to shield national security information and other sensitive materials. Most notably, Exemption 1 of FOIA prevents access to classified documents. § 552(b)(1). The Government generally may classify material even after receiving a FOIA request, see Exec. Order No. 13526, § 1.7(d), 75 Fed. Reg. 711 (2009); an agency therefore may wait until that time to decide whether the dangers of disclosure outweigh the costs of classification. Exemption 3 also may mitigate the Government's security concerns. That provision applies to records that any other statute exempts from disclosure, thus offering Congress an established, streamlined method to authorize the withholding of specific records that

[9] The dissent asserts that "30 years of experience" with a more expansive interpretation of the exemption suggests no "seriou[s] interfere[nce] with . . . FOIA's informational objectives." But those objectives suffer any time an agency denies a FOIA request based on an improper interpretation of the statute. To give just one example, the U.S. Forest Service has wrongly invoked Exemption 2 on multiple occasions to withhold information about (of all things) bird nesting sites. See Audubon Society v. Forest Serv., 104 F.3d 1201, 1203 (CA10 1997); Maricopa Audubon Soc. v. Forest Serv., 108 F.3d 1082, 1084 (CA9 1997). And recent statistics raise a concern that federal agencies may too readily use Exemption 2 to refuse disclosure. According to amicus Public Citizen, "while reliance on exemptions overall rose 83% from 1998 to 2006, reliance on Exemption 2 rose 344% during that same time period." Brief for Public Citizen et al. as Amici Curiae 24. In 2009 alone, federal departments cited Exemption 2 more than 72,000 times to prevent access to records. See Brief for Allied Daily Newspapers of Washington et al. as Amici Curiae 3. We do not doubt that many of these FOIA denials were appropriate. But we are unable to accept the dissent's unsupported declaration that a sweeping construction of Exemption 2 has not interfered with Congress's goal of broad disclosure.

FOIA would not otherwise protect. And Exemption 7, as already noted, protects "information compiled for law enforcement purposes" that meets one of six criteria, including if its release "could reasonably be expected to endanger the life or physical safety of any individual." § 552(b)(7)(F). The Navy argued below that the ESQD data and maps fall within Exemption 7(F), and that claim remains open for the Ninth Circuit to address on remand.

If these or other exemptions do not cover records whose release would threaten the Nation's vital interests, the Government may of course seek relief from Congress. All we hold today is that Congress has not enacted the FOIA exemption the Government desires. We leave to Congress, as is appropriate, the question whether it should do so.

Reversed and remanded.

[JUSTICE ALITO, concurring, explored at some length the possibility of treating the ESQD data and maps as information "compiled for law enforcement purposes" within the meaning of FOIA's seventh exemption—in particular as documents that, if disclosed, "could reasonably be expected to endanger the life or physical safety of any individual." § 552(b)(7)(F). He suggested that "law enforcement purposes," the evident hurdle to be surmounted, might be understood to encompass "proactive steps designed to prevent criminal activity and to maintain security. . . . Crime prevention and security measures are critical to effective law enforcement as we know it. There can be no doubt, for example, that the Secret Service acts with a law enforcement purpose when it protects federal officials from attack, even though no investigation may be ongoing." And, unlike the text of Exemption 2, "[t]he text of Exemption 7 does not require that the information be compiled *solely* for law enforcement purposes." [Ed. emphasis added] "If, indeed, the ESQD information was compiled as part of an effort to prevent crimes of terrorism and to maintain security, there is a reasonable argument that the information has been "compiled for law enforcement purposes."]

■ JUSTICE BREYER, dissenting.

Justice Stevens has explained that, once "a statute has been construed, either by this Court *or by a consistent course of decision by other federal judges* and agencies," it can acquire a clear meaning that this Court should hesitate to change. I would apply that principle to this case and accept the 30-year-old decision by the D.C. Circuit in Crooker as properly stating the law.

For one thing, the Crooker decision, joined by 9 of the 10 sitting Circuit Judges, has been consistently followed, or favorably cited, by every Court of Appeals to have considered the matter during the past 30 years. Three Circuits adopted a different approach in the 1970's before Crooker was decided, but I read subsequent decisions in two of those Circuits as not adhering to their early positions. As for the remaining Circuit, its district courts understand Crooker now to apply. I recognize that there is reasonable ground for disagreement over the precise status of certain pre-Crooker precedents, but the Crooker interpretation of

Exemption 2 has guided nearly every Freedom of Information Act (FOIA) case decided over the last 30 years. See generally Dept. of Justice, Guide to Freedom of Information Act, pp. 184–206 (2009) (FOIA Guide) (identifying over 100 district court decisions applying the Crooker approach, and one appearing to reject it).

Congress, moreover, well aware of Crooker, left Exemption 2, 5 U.S.C. § 552(b)(2), untouched when it amended the FOIA five years later. See S. Rep. No. 98–221, p. 25 (1983) (discussing Crooker); Freedom of Information Reform Act of 1986, 100 Stat. 3207–48 (amending Exemption 7, 5 U.S.C. § 552(b)(7)).

This Court has found that circumstances of this kind offer significant support for retaining an interpretation of a statute that has been settled by the lower courts. . . . [E]ven if the majority's analysis would have persuaded me if written on a blank slate, Crooker's analysis was careful and its holding reasonable. . . . The D.C. Circuit agreed with today's Court that the Senate Report described the exemption as referring to " 'internal personnel' " matters, giving as examples " 'personnel's use of parking facilities, . . . sick leave, and the like.' " But it also noted that the House Report described the exemption as protecting from disclosure " '[o]perating rules, guidelines, and manuals of procedure for Government investigators or examiners.' " "[U]pon reflection," it thought the views of the two Houses "reconcilable" if one understood both sets of examples as referring to internal staff information (both minor personnel matters and staff instruction matters) that the public had no legitimate interest in learning about. And it accepted this view in light of its hesitation to "apply individual provisions of the statute woodenly, oblivious to Congress' intention that FOIA not frustrate law enforcement efforts." [I]t found no other exemption that would protect internal documents in which there is no legitimate public interest in disclosure—a category that includes, say, building plans, safe combinations, computer passwords, evacuation plans, and the like. . . .

. . . [Such reasoning,] based upon Congress' broader FOIA objectives and a "common sense" view of what information Congress did and did not want to make available, takes the "practical approach" that this Court has "consistently . . . taken" when interpreting the FOIA, John Doe Agency v. John Doe Corp., 493 U.S. 146, 157 (1989).

[T]his "practical approach" . . . reflects this Court's longstanding recognition that it cannot interpret the FOIA (and the Administrative Procedure Act (APA) of which it is a part) with the linguistic literalism fit for interpretations of the tax code. That in large part is because the FOIA (like the APA but unlike the tax code) must govern the affairs of a vast Executive Branch with numerous different agencies, bureaus, and departments, performing numerous tasks of many different kinds. Too narrow an interpretation, while working well in the case of one agency, may seriously interfere with congressional objectives when applied to another. . . .

Further, 30 years of experience with Crooker's holding suggests that it has not seriously interfered with the FOIA's informational objectives, while at the same time it has permitted agencies to withhold much information which, in my view, Congress would not have wanted to force into the public realm. To focus only on the case law, courts have held that that information protected by Exemption 2 includes blueprints for Department of Agriculture buildings that store biological agents, documents that would help hackers access National Aeronautics and Space Administration computers, agency credit card numbers, . . . guidelines for settling cases, "trigger figures" that alert the Department of Education to possible mismanagement of federal funds, security plans for the Supreme Court Building and Supreme Court Justices, vulnerability assessments of Commerce Department computer security plans, Bureau of Prisons guidelines for controlling riots and for storing hazardous chemicals, guidelines for assessing the sensitivity of military programs, and guidelines for processing Medicare reimbursement claims.

In other Exemption 2 cases, where withholding may seem less reasonable, the courts have ordered disclosure.

The majority acknowledges that "our decision today upsets three decades of agency practice relying on Crooker, and therefore may force considerable adjustments." But how are these adjustments to be made? Should the Government rely upon other exemptions to provide the protection it believes necessary? As JUSTICE ALITO notes, Exemption 7 applies where the documents consist of "records or information compiled for law enforcement purposes" . . . But what about information that is not compiled for law enforcement purposes, such as building plans, computer passwords, credit card numbers, or safe deposit combinations? The Government, which has much experience litigating FOIA cases, warns us that Exemption 7 "targets only a subset of the important agency functions that may be circumvented." Today's decision only confirms this point, as the Court's insistence on narrow construction might persuade judges to avoid reading Exemption 7 broadly enough to provide Crooker-type protection.

The majority suggests that the Government can classify documents that should remain private. But classification is at best a partial solution. It takes time. It is subject to its own rules. As the Government points out, it would hinder the sharing of information about Government buildings with "first responders," such as local fire and police departments. And both Congress and the President believe the Nation currently faces a problem of too much, not too little, classified material. . . . [I]t is "over-classification," not Crooker, that poses the more serious threat to the FOIA's public information objectives.

That leaves congressional action. . . . But legislative action takes time; Congress has much to do; and other matters, when compared with a FOIA revision, may warrant higher legislative priority. In my view, it is for the courts, through appropriate interpretation, to turn Congress' public information objectives into workable agency practice, and to adhere to such interpretations once they are settled.

That is why: Where the courts have already interpreted Exemption 2, where that interpretation has been consistently relied upon and followed for 30 years, where Congress has taken note of that interpretation in amending other parts of the statute, where that interpretation is reasonable, where it has proved practically helpful and achieved commonsense results, where it is consistent with the FOIA's overall statutory goals, where a new and different interpretation raises serious problems of its own, and where that new interpretation would require Congress to act just to preserve a decades-long status quo, I would let sleeping legal dogs lie.

For these reasons, with respect, I dissent.

## NOTES

(1) ***Textualism and FOIA (and the APA).*** Justice Breyer, alone, writes of a "practical" approach to interpretation that "reflects this Court's longstanding recognition that it cannot interpret the FOIA (and the Administrative Procedure Act (APA) of which it is a part) with the linguistic literalism fit for interpretations of the tax code." Milner was the second of two Supreme Court opinions issued in March 2011 to emphasize the place of ordinary linguistic meaning, and the primacy of text, in interpreting FOIA. FCC v. AT&T, 562 U.S. 397 (2011) (noted briefly later at p. 776), was concerned with the meaning of "personal" in Exemption 7(C)'s reference to "personal privacy"—did that include a corporation?—rather than "personnel" in Exemption 2, and it was unanimous. Chief Justice Roberts's opinion, like Justice Kagan's, stressed ordinary meanings, linguistic usages, and the necessity of faithfulness to text.

You may take up questions about contemporary statutory interpretation techniques as an element of your studies in Chapter II or Chapter VIII. Note that Justice Breyer essentially concedes the textual issue, making virtually no attempt to make a consistent-with-the-text argument. Assuming that he is basically right on the underlying cases, how much should a settled 30-year practice count? Given the hundred-plus district court opinions cited by the Department of Justice's FOIA guide and (perhaps) Congress's arguable acceptance of Crooker when amending FOIA in 1983, how should we view the infrequency of appellate court consideration of Exemption 2 that Justice Kagan mentions? Is it better taken as a signal of the unimportance of the question, as she suggests, or of how settled the issue had become, as Justice Breyer posits? As Justice Breyer notes, the "settled practice" banner was also carried by Justice Stevens, no longer sitting at the time of Milner; and he, too, did not prevail. See Central Bank of Denver v. First Interstate Bank of Denver, 511 U.S. 164, 199 (1994) (Stevens, J., dissenting) ("[W]e should . . . be reluctant to lop off rights of action that have been recognized for decades even if the judicial methodology that gave them birth is now out of favor. Caution is particularly appropriate here, because the judicially recognized right in question accords with the longstanding construction of the agency Congress has assigned to enforce the securities laws.").

(2) ***Work for Congress?*** Do you agree with Justice Breyer that "building plans, computer passwords, credit card numbers, or safe deposit combinations" will no more readily fit the language of Exemption 7 than Exemption 2 (as the majority interprets it)—particularly if Exemption 7 is to be interpreted as parsimoniously as Exemption 2? And that they are not readily (or desirably) brought within the rubric of national security classification (Exemption 1)? If you also agree that their disclosure to "any person" who might request them would be inappropriate, can you draft statutory language to guarantee their protection? Note in this regard that Congress, too, has emphasized the desirability of parsimony in interpreting FOIA. As amended in 2009, Exemption 3 is emphatic that specific statutory exemptions must be explicit; it exempts documents that are

> (3) specifically exempted from disclosure by statute (other than section 552b of this title), if that statute—
>
> (A) (i) requires that the matters be withheld from the public in such a manner as to leave no discretion on the issue; or
>
> (ii) establishes particular criteria for withholding or refers to particular types of matters to be withheld; *and*
>
> (B) if enacted after the date of enactment of the OPEN FOIA Act of 2009, specifically cites to this paragraph.

(Emphasis added).

(3) ***Operating Without High 2 After Milner.*** As the majority predicted, agencies now use other exemptions where they might have previously turned to the "high" Exemption 2. In National Association of Criminal Defense Lawyers v. Dep't of Justice Executive Office for United States Attorneys, the D.C. Circuit upheld DOJ's refusal to release its prosecutors' "Blue Book" (a manual on discovery in federal criminal proceedings) under Exemption 5, finding it to be protected attorney work product. 844 F.3d 246 (D.C. Cir. 2016). See also Note 2 (State Secrets and FOIA) below (p. 758).

## NOTES ON COMPARING FOIA AND TRADITIONAL APA

(1) ***Disclosure Before and After FOIA.*** FOIA, codified at 5 U.S.C. § 552 as a subpart of the APA, departs further from the original APA than most of the other provisions studied in this casebook. As you may have read in the Notes in the preceding Section on Secret Law, the APA initially provided limited "Public Information." FOIA is particularly notable for making available material in an agency's possession (subject to some exemptions) that does not have the quality of law—factual matter, studies, submissions by regulated parties, information collected by government agencies, and the like. Section 552, from subsection (a)(3) on, directs agencies to make most of its nonlaw records available "to any person," based simply upon a request that "reasonably describes such records."

What might lie behind this emphatic departure from the original view that, beyond the legal materials generated by an agency, public access to agency work should be highly restricted? One possibility is that the APA now adopts a different view of what constitutes legally relevant materials: it starts with the presumption that anything in an agency's files or databases might influence agency action in pursuit of its statutory responsibilities, and thus from a purely operational viewpoint would have legal importance and indeed be included in the agency's record for judicial review. Although FOIA requests are independent of (and in themselves do not operate to stay) other agency proceedings, such as rulemakings,[16] this characterization might have animated judicial demands for expanded agency disclosure in rulemakings that began in the 1970s, as you may have read about in the Notes on the Paper Hearing (p. 347) above.[17] Another view is that, as the administrative state has grown larger, it has also grown potentially more fearsome; on this view, full disclosure is a starting point for a process of policing agencies through public opinion and political pressure. And a third view is that governmental information is a resource that ought to be available to all, unless there is a reason to withhold it. On this view, disclosure of records is just a larger case of the many overt ways in which government collects information and provides it to private businesses and organizations, from Census data on down. Congress has been consistently attentive to the second of these views in its amendments to FOIA.

(2) ***Ombudsmen for FOIA, but Not the APA.*** Among other changes to FOIA, the OPENNESS PROMOTES EFFECTIVENESS IN OUR NATIONAL GOVERNMENT ACT OF 2007, Pub. L. No. 110–175, 121 Stat. 2524, created alternative dispute resolution techniques to help avoid litigation. Each agency is to make its FOIA Public Liaison available to requesters to "assist in the resolution of any disputes" respecting possible modification of a request to facilitate earlier action on it. § 552(a)(6)(B)(ii). New provisions, § 552(h)–(*l*), reprinted in the Appendix (p. 1616), establish a new Office of Government Information Services within the National Archives and Records Administration, in addition to requiring agency designation of a Chief FOIA Officer "at the Assistant Secretary or equivalent level" and one or more FOIA Public Liaisons. OGIS functions as a FOIA ombudsman—instructed both to be a general overseer of agency implementation of FOIA, reporting to the President and Congress, and to "offer mediation services to resolve disputes between persons making requests under this section and administrative agencies as a nonexclusive alternative to litigation." Its "Final Response Letters," which "document the outcome and any resolution the parties reached" are posted, if the parties permit, on its website.[18] Might OGIS's mediation services provide a context in which considerations of need or other considerations foreign to legal rights under FOIA, but motivating to requesters and suppliers of information, could enter into its implementation? Should there be an ombudsman for non-FOIA APA disputes?

---

[16] See Note 5 (FOIA as Litigation Strategy for Non-FOIA Claims) (p. 781) below.

[17] This theme is explored in Peter L. Strauss, Statutes that are not Static—The Case of the APA, 14 J. Contemp. Leg. Iss. 767, 786–800 (2005).

[18] https://www.archives.gov/ogis/mediation-program/ogis-final-response-letters-to-customers.

(3) ***Judicial Treatment of Agency Interpretations of FOIA and (the Rest of the) APA.*** Although Chapter VIII takes up judicial review in detail, (lower) courts generally treat agency interpretations of FOIA and the APA—for instance, whether an agency's action is covered by an exemption or whether a particular statutory procedure applies—differently than interpretations of statutes that delegate specific authority to no more than a few agencies, assuming those interpretations do not involve a "major question" (p. 1360). As the D.C. Circuit has explained, "For generic statutes like the APA, FOIA, and FACA [discussed below in Section 4 on p. 798], the broadly sprawling applicability undermines any basis for deference, and courts must therefore review interpretative questions de novo." Collins v. NTSB, 351 F.3d. 1246, 1252 (D.C. Cir. 2003). There are some exceptions. Under FOIA, courts typically give some deference to agency determinations under Exemptions 1 and 3 (see the SIGAR case, p. 748); the first applies to classified materials, and the third references specific agency statutes. Courts defer to the government to varying degrees on determinations of harm for Exemption 7, particularly outside the national security context. See Ctr. for Nat'l Sec. Studies v. DOJ, 331 F.3d 918, 928 (D.C. Cir. 2003); Shearson v. DHS, 2007 WL 764026 (N.D. Ohio 2007). Similarly, courts are split as to whether to defer to an agency's determination that "good cause" exists, permitting the agency to forgo notice and comment procedures under § 553 of the APA (see Note 2 on p. 380). Some courts review an agency's good cause finding de novo, others examine it to see if it is arbitrary and capricious, and some have not decided on a standard of review.

There are some key differences between the two statutory regimes. While FOIA explicitly provides that courts are to review "de novo" an agency's decision not to release records, the APA generally permits agency decisions to be reviewed under the "arbitrary, capricious, an abuse of discretion, or otherwise not in accordance with law" standard of § 706(2)(A). How, if at all, would you change these standards of review? Does FOIA's de novo standard shape how you think about Chevron deference (where courts accept permissible agency interpretations of an ambiguous statute, see p. 1206)?

(4) ***Agency Regulations Under FOIA.*** Under FOIA, agencies may (and in some cases, must) issue regulations on a number of matters, including how requests can be aggregated, what fees will be charged, what requests will receive expedited processing, and how requests will be placed into tracks (simple, complex) for processing. For many of these items, FOIA explicitly requires agencies to use notice and comment rulemaking. See, e.g., 5 U.S.C. § 552(a)(6)(B)(iv); Dep't of Homeland Security, Freedom of Information Act Regulations, 81 Fed. Reg. 83625 (Nov. 22, 2016) (new rules updating its FOIA procedures, on which 15 comments were submitted).

Courts have found that where FOIA does not require notice and comment, agencies can promulgate some regulations on how they will process FOIA requests without prior notice and comment as "rules of agency organization, procedure, or practice" under 5 U.S.C. § 553(b). See, e.g., Public Citizen v. Dep't of State, 276 F.3d 634 (D.C. Cir. 2002) (finding that the agency's "cut-off policy applies to all FOIA requests" and thus "encodes no 'substantive value judgment' " but also finding that the agency's procedurally permitted policy was unreasonable).

In June 2019, the EPA made its first substantive changes to its FOIA regulations since 2002, publishing a final rule, without seeking prior comment, that allows political appointees at the agency to respond to FOIA requests. The rule gives appointees the authority to "issue final determinations whether to release or withhold a record or a portion of a record on the basis of responsiveness or under one or more exemptions under the FOIA, and to issue 'no records' responses." 84 Fed. Reg. 30028, 30033 (June 26, 2019). The Center for Biological Diversity, the Environmental Integrity Project, Citizens for Responsibility and Ethics in Washington, Ecological Rights Foundation, and Our Children's Earth Foundation quickly filed lawsuits, claiming that the agency should have given prior notice and taken comment, that the rule is arbitrary and capricious, and that the rule violates FOIA. The first three plaintiffs in the consolidated action entered a settlement agreement with the EPA, requiring the agency to issue an NPRM revisiting the issue. Ecological Rights Foundation v. EPA, 2022 WL 4130818, at n.7 (D.D.C. 2022). Judge Pan dismissed all of the two nonsettling plaintiffs' claims aside from their challenge to portions of the regulations which "allow agency officials to withhold portions of responsive records on the ground that those portions are non-responsive to the FOIA request." Id. at *12. The ruling insinuates such provisions are illegitimate but remands without vacatur for the EPA to remedy, a process already underway from the EPA's settlement with the other parties. Id. at *12–*13. The plaintiffs have appealed.

(5) ***Exceptions for Congress in FOIA and the APA and Congressional Power over Information.*** Both FOIA and the APA have carve-outs for disclosure to Congress. FOIA states that the Act's bars on disclosure are "not authority to withhold information from Congress." 5 U.S.C. § 552(d). Subsection 557(d)(2) of the APA, governing ex parte communications in formal proceedings, states that the framework "does not constitute authority to withhold information from Congress." Should Congress have more access than the media, in all contexts?

Even the strongest claims of "executive privilege" have often been compromised in battles between the White House and Congress (see p. 767). Moreover, legislation can force disclosure of particular information that might be FOIA defensible. The Dodd-Frank Wall Street Reform and Consumer Protection Act of 2010 explicitly required the Federal Reserve to publish on its website *all* documents "with respect to all loans and other financial assistance provided during the period beginning on December 1, 2007 and ending on the date of enactment of this Act."[19] On December 1, 2010, it published over 21,000 documents there, revealing transactions having a value greatly exceeding the $700 billion involved in the Troubled Assets Relief Program.[20]

---

[19] Pub. L. No. 111–203, § 1109(c), 124 Stat. 1376 (2010).

[20] Sewell Chan & Jo Craven McGinty, Fed Documents Breadth of Emergency Measures, N.Y. Times (Dec. 1, 2010).

## c. FOIA in Operation



# WASHINGTON POST CO. v. SPECIAL INSPECTOR FOR AFGHANISTAN RECONSTRUCTION

United States District Court for the District of Columbia (2021).
2021 WL 4502106.

■ AMY BERMAN JACKSON, UNITED STATES DISTRICT JUDGE.

On March 23, 2017, Craig Whitlock, a reporter from plaintiff Washington Post Company, submitted a Freedom of Information Act ("FOIA") request to the Special Inspector General for Afghanistan Reconstruction ("SIGAR"), the federal agency charged with auditing and supervising the U.S. reconstruction efforts in Afghanistan. Plaintiff sought records relating to SIGAR's Lessons Learned Program, specifically the "full, unedited transcripts and complete audio recordings of *all* interviews conducted for the Lessons Learned program, regardless of whether they were labeled as 'on the record,' or if the interviewee was granted anonymity, or if they were cited in a particular report or not." . . .

SIGAR is an independent organization established by the National Defense Authorization Act in 2008. It has "audit and investigatory authority over all reconstruction programs and operations in Afghanistan that are supported with U.S. dollars, regardless of the agency involved," and its mission is "to prevent and detect waste, fraud, and abuse in U.S.-funded reconstruction programs and operations in Afghanistan." SIGAR utilized the Lessons Learned Program to review the reconstruction experience and make recommendations to Congress and federal agencies on ways to improve reconstruction efforts.

To produce the Lessons Learned reports, SIGAR relied on interviews with hundreds of individuals with direct and indirect knowledge of U.S. reconstruction programs; and it is the content of these interviews—as well as notes and records of interviews ("ROIs")—that plaintiff seeks from defendant. When it processed the FOIA request, SIGAR produced only a portion of the responsive records, and plaintiff filed the instant complaint. . . .

[The court had made a series of rulings in a prior decision, including demands for more information; this opinion addresses the remaining aspects of the dispute.]

I. Exemption 1

FOIA Exemption 1 exempts from production matters that are "specifically authorized under criteria established by an Executive [O]rder to be kept secret in the interest of national defense or foreign policy and . . . are in fact properly classified pursuant to such Executive [O]rder." The reasons offered to support assertions of Exemption 1 are afforded substantial weight in the national security context; the Supreme Court has stated that the decisions of people with the authority to withhold information to protect national security "are worthy of great deference," because they are "familiar with the whole picture as judges are not," and because of the interests and risks at stake. CIA v. Sims, 471 U.S. 159, 179 (1985). The D.C. Circuit has emphasized that "in the FOIA context, we have consistently deferred to executive affidavits predicting harm to the national security, and have found it unwise to undertake searching judicial review." Ctr. for Nat'l Sec. Stud. v. Dep't of Just., 331 F.3d 918, 927 (D.C. Cir. 2003). . . .

The Circuit has also cautioned, though, that deference is not equivalent to acquiescence, and an affidavit supporting the invocation of Exemption 1 satisfies an agency's burden only if it is sufficient to afford the district court an adequate foundation to review the soundness of the withholding. . . .

Pursuant to Section 1.1 of Executive Order 13,526, there are four requirements an agency must satisfy for the classification of national security information:

> (1) an original classification authority classifies the information; (2) the U.S. Government owns, produces, or controls the information; (3) the information is within one of eight protected categories listed in section 1.4 of the Order; and (4) the original classification authority determines that the unauthorized disclosure of the information reasonably could be expected to result in a specified level of damage to the national security, and the original classification authority is able to identify or describe the damages.

The Court previously held that the agency satisfied the first three prongs of the test, but failed the fourth because its declarant, as the classifier, was unable to identify any specific harm to national security that could arise from the release of a particular document in whole or in part.

In support of its renewed motion, defendant supplies a twenty-two-page supplemental Vaughn Index[21] from the State Department. Unlike

[21] [Ed.] "A Vaughn index is an affidavit submitted by government attorneys that describes in as much detail as is possible, without revealing the information being sought, the reasons for redacting or withholding documents meeting the description of a FOIA request. The statute provides for submission of the documents to the court for in camera inspection. After the

the first Vaughn Index, the supplement addresses each document in detail describing both its contents as well as why the material was withheld. For example, the supplemental Vaughn Index entry for [one document] states:

> This document is the summary of an interview with Ambassador Richard Boucher, the former Assistant Secretary of State for South and Central Asian Affairs. . . . The material withheld reflects information about sensitive communications with Afghanistan and other South and Central Asian governments; U.S. efforts and engagements with Afghanistan and similarly situated countries; and assessments by U.S. officials regarding those communications and engagements as well as foreign government officials.
>
> The material withheld in this document reflects communications with foreign officials and leaders on subjects including 1) military operations, governance, and economic development in Afghanistan; 2) Pakistani policies, military operations, and relationship with the United States; and 3) the policies of other South and Central Asian countries. The material withheld likewise reflects evaluations of foreign officials and policies of those countries. Confidentiality of this information is vital to the conduct of successful foreign relations. This includes the confidentiality of information about the nature of other countries' activities and engagement with the United States, when undertaken with an expectation of confidentiality. . . . The inability of the United States to maintain confidentiality in its diplomatic exchanges—particularly, as here, where the discussions involve sensitive national security topics related to multiple countries in the region—would inevitably chill relations with other governments and could reasonably be expected to damage U.S. national security by diminishing our access to vital sources of information. A breach of confidentiality would deny U.S. personnel information that is important to plan and carry out foreign relations and foreign activities. Furthermore, release of information regarding military operations as well as other sensitive governance and policy matters could reasonably be expected to cause harm to the national security by inhibiting or degrading the United States' ability to successfully carry out military operations and defend the national security, particularly in an unstable region. Disclosure of this information at this time could have the potential to inject friction into, or cause damage to, a number of our bilateral relationships with countries whose cooperation is important to

---

Supreme Court had suggested that in camera review was not necessary in every instance, the D.C. Circuit held in Vaughn v. Rosen that the government could meet its FOIA obligations by submitting an index containing detailed descriptions of any documents redacted or withheld." Fox News Network, LLC v. Dep't of the Treasury, 739 F.Supp.2d 515, 533 (S.D.N.Y. 2010).

> U.S. national security, including not only those countries specifically identified but other countries that consider themselves similarly placed as well as some countries in which public opinion might not currently favor close cooperation with the United States. Moreover, the risk of harm to national security from disclosure of this information is exacerbated by the political and security instability in the region in question, such that release of this information could pose a direct threat to the national security of the United States.

The other explanations are equally specific and detailed, and the Court concludes that the supplemental Vaughn Index contemplates the particular harm to national security that could reasonably be threatened by the release of the withheld information. . . .

III. Exemptions 6 and 7(C) . . .

Exemption 6 permits agencies to withhold "personnel and medical files and similar files the disclosure of which would constitute a clearly unwarranted invasion of personal privacy[.]" The purpose of Exemption 6 is "to protect individuals from the injury and embarrassment that can result from the unnecessary disclosure of personal information." U.S. Dep't of State v. Wash. Post Co., 456 U.S. 595, 599 (1982). The Supreme Court has made clear that Exemption 6 is designed to protect personal information in public records, even if it is not embarrassing or of an intimate nature. Exemption 7(C) protects from disclosure "records or information compiled for law enforcement purposes . . . [if] the production of such law enforcement records or information . . . could reasonably be expected to constitute an unwarranted invasion of personal privacy." . . .

[C]ourts consider withholdings made pursuant to Exemptions 6 and 7(C) under a similar balancing test, and they apply the test from Exemption 7(C) first because the threshold to satisfy the standard is lower. To justify withholding under Exemption 7(C), the agency must show that (1) the disclosure of the records must "reasonably be expected to constitute an unwarranted invasion of personal privacy," and (2) the "personal privacy interest" must not be "outweighed by the public interest in disclosure" of the records. Nat'l Archives & Records Admin. v. Favish, 541 U.S. 160, 165–66 (2004) [p. 774].

A. "Private" citizens

In its 2020 opinion [in this litigation], the Court acknowledged the real privacy interest in interviewees' and third parties' identities and the limited public interest in that information. But it called for more information concerning the individuals whose identifying information had been redacted on privacy grounds . . . .

SIGAR's declarant explains that the individuals whose identities it sought to protect fell into two categories, "informants (i.e., individuals who were interviewed) and third parties (individuals referenced by an informant in the course of the interview)." . . . According to [the declarant], at the time of the interviews: 46 [informants] were high-ranking U.S. government employees, 123 were low-ranking U.S. government employees, 116 were private citizens, and 146 were foreign nationals.

B. Third parties named in interviews

SIGAR argues that the Court should find that the balance of private and public interests weighs in favor of withholding the names of third parties named in interviews from disclosure. . . .

Defendant emphasizes that "[u]nwitting third parties are especially deserving of protection because it is unlikely they were aware they had been named or what information had been said about them," and the Court agrees. . . . [T]he public interest in knowing the identities of third parties, even high-ranking officials, rarely outweighs such privacy interests. Therefore, the Court will grant summary judgment for defendant for this category of withholdings regardless of the third party's status.

C. Identifying information in "on the record" interviews

Identifying information for individuals who were interviewed with express assurances of confidentiality was properly withheld under Exemption 7(D), obviating the 7(C) issue, but the Court must still determine whether it would be appropriate to redact any informants' identifying information from the "on the record" interviews. . . .

ii. High and low-ranking government officials

SIGAR next argues that both high and low-ranking government officials who were interviewed are still entitled to protection from disclosure, despite the fact that a higher status would diminish their privacy interest. . . .

[I]t does not appear that any of the "on the record" interviews were given by individuals who were high-ranking government officials at the time of the interview. Therefore, [the Court] need not balance that more diminished private interest against the potentially greater public interest involved because the only ROIs still in question are the ones on the record.

However, the Court will go on to determine whether low-level employees who spoke on the record surrendered their privacy interests entirely such that Exemptions 6 and 7(C) cannot be applied to them. . . . [I]t is well-established that lower-level government employees in general have a privacy interest in their identities. While it is true that Government officials may have a somewhat diminished privacy interest they do not surrender all rights to personal privacy when they accept a public appointment. . . . [T]he public interest in the identities of low-level employees does not usually outweigh the individuals' privacy rights, as they are not typically decision-makers such that disclosure of their names would shed light on "what the government does."

So the question is whether any of those clear rights survived the agreement to speak on the record. The privacy interest is certainly weaker than the interest of an off-the-record informant, but it is not entirely absent. The agency's declarant explained that most of the on the record speakers were willing to have the information they provided used and shared, but they requested that the information not be attributed to them without permission. Under those circumstances, and given the lack of any public interest in the disclosure of lower-ranking interviewees' names, any remaining private interest outweighs the public interest. Therefore, identifying information may be withheld from disclosure under FOIA Exemption 7(C), even if the ROI was otherwise on the record for SIGAR's purposes . . . .

E. Audio recordings, unique interview codes, and interview locations

All that remains for the Court to consider under Exemption 7(C), then, is whether SIGAR has adequately supported its redaction of randomly assigned interview codes and the locations where interviews took place . . . .

The remaining audio recording [in dispute], Audio No. 10, is associated with [a record] which plaintiff maintains was designated as "on the record." The informant was a high-ranking employee at the time of the events discussed, and a low-ranking government employee at the time of the interview. Because the Court has already determined that the privacy interest in the identity of a low-ranking government employee who gave an interview "on the record" outweighs the public interest in that information, defendant justifiably withheld Audio No. 10 under Exemption 7(C).

As to the unique interviewee codes, SIGAR justified withholding the codes that were assigned to informants in lieu of their names: because it "believes . . . a copy of the master list of interview codes and corresponding informant names may have been removed from SIGAR's offices by a former SIGAR employee," there is a risk that confidential informants could be identified if the codes were revealed. Therefore, the reliance on Exemption 7(C) is supported.

Finally, SIGAR reconsidered the withholdings of the interview locations and released the bulk of the withheld information to plaintiff. Out of hundreds, only the locations for 44 ROIs remain withheld as the "location information [ ] was so unique that it would immediately identify the informant or, if read in conjunction with the text of the ROI, could reveal the identity of the informant." . . .

For these reasons, the Court will grant summary judgment to defendant as to the unique interviewee codes, the interview locations, and the six audio recordings.

IV. Exemption 3

Because the Court reached a decision on the personally identifiable information covered by Exemption 7(C) for which SIGAR also asserted Exemption 3, all that remains for the Court to determine under Exemption 3 is whether the State Department adequately supplemented its declaration to support the reaction [sic] of information on intelligence methods.

FOIA Exemption 3 exempts from disclosure any materials that are specifically exempted from disclosure by another statute, provided that such statute either requires withholding "in such a manner as to leave no discretion on the issue" or "establishes particular criteria for withholding or refers to particular types of matters to be withheld." . . .

In its prior opinion, the Court held that defendant failed to show, pursuant to the requirement in the National Security Act, that the redacted information was withheld at the direction of the Director of National Intelligence, or someone with authority to identify and withhold national intelligence information. . . .

Although the agency does not explain who made the original choice to redact the information, it has informed the Court that the Assistant Secretary has, in fact, reviewed the specific redactions and supports them. Therefore, the Court will grant summary judgment in favor of defendant with respect to records withheld under Exemption 3.

V. Exemption 5 . . .

A document may be properly withheld under Exemption 5 if it satisfies "two conditions: its source must be a [g]overnment agency, and it must fall within the ambit of a privilege against discovery under judicial standards that would govern litigation against the agency that holds it." U.S. Dep't of Interior v. Klamath Water Users Protective Ass'n, 532 U.S. 1, 8 (2001).

SIGAR originally invoked the deliberative process privilege on behalf of the National Security Council for portions of eleven ROIs, and . . . also invoked the presidential communications privilege for portions of [six] of them. Both privileges have been found to be incorporated in Exemption 5.

A. Deliberative process privilege

The deliberative process privilege "allows the government to withhold documents and other materials that would reveal advisory opinions, recommendations[,] and deliberations comprising part of a process by which governmental decisions and policies are formulated." In re Sealed Case, 121 F.3d 729, 737 (D.C. Cir. 1997) (Espy). . . . [I]t "rests on the obvious realization that officials will not communicate candidly among themselves if each remark is a potential item of discovery," and its purpose "is to enhance the quality of agency decisions by protecting open and frank discussion among those who make them within the Government." Klamath, 532 U.S. at 8–9.

To accomplish that goal, the deliberative process privilege protects agency documents that are both predecisional and deliberative. A document is predecisional if it was generated before the adoption of an agency policy and deliberative if it reflects the give-and-take of the consultative process. . . .

With respect to the "deliberative" prong of the test—the second prong—the exemption "protects not only communications which are themselves deliberative in nature, but all communications which, if revealed, would expose to public view the deliberative process of an agency." Russell v. Dep't of the Air Force, 682 F.2d 1045, 1048 (D.C. Cir. 1982). But the agency cannot simply rely on generalized assertions that disclosure could chill deliberations. . . .

i. The eleven ROIs are predecisional. . . .

SIGAR has now satisfied the predecisional requirement. For seven of the withheld ROIs, the declarant explains that they were used to inform a specific, forthcoming Lessons Learned Report, called Strategy and Planning. In other words, the ROIs preceded the "decision" to make the recommendations contained in the report. Similarly, the remaining four ROIs "were conducted to gather information concerning counterinsurgency operations and policies aimed at combating corruption that informed SIGAR's May [and September] 2018 report[s]" . . . .

ii. The eleven ROIs are not deliberative.

But the agency has fallen short of the showing that any ROI was part of the consultative give and take that led to any decision-making embodied in the report. They were not drafts or memoranda or emails soliciting input or reviewing proposals for what the reports should contain; they were the raw material upon which the reports were based.

Defendant does not even attempt to bring the records under the applicable legal rubric. Its declarant states: because the ROIs are not interviews, but they are summaries of statements made during interviews, the process of their creation "reflects that interviewer's interpretation of those statements, as well as the interviewer's personal judgment regarding what information provided by the informant is important and should be reported to others within SIGAR." This may be the sort of showing one makes when asserting the attorney work-product privilege, but it is not what is called for here.

Plaintiff argues that the ROIs are not deliberative, because they are factual compilations that do not "reveal something about the agency's deliberative process." The agency has the burden of establishing what deliberative process is involved, and the role played by the documents in issue in the course of that process. SIGAR has failed to do that here; it has not shown that the ROIs were part of the internal give and take that led *to* the reports as opposed to sources of information used *in* the reports. Therefore, those portions of those ROIs withheld under the deliberative process privilege may not be withheld on that basis.

B. Presidential communications privilege

Defendant also asserts that the presidential communications privilege applies to portions of six of the ROIs withheld pursuant to Exemption 5. . . .

In United States v. Nixon, 418 U.S. 683 (1974), the Supreme Court explained that a "presumptive privilege for Presidential communications . . . is fundamental to the operation of Government and inextricably rooted in the separation of powers under the Constitution."

Id. at 708. "A President and those who assist him must be free to explore alternatives in the process of shaping policies and making decisions and to do so in a way many would be unwilling to express except privately." Id.

None of the documents at issue here constitute communications to or from the President. But statements that reveal presidential communications or deliberations are covered by the privilege, too. . . . [T]he privilege is not claimed over the documents themselves, but rather the communications memorialized within them.

The privilege is designed to preserve the President's ability to obtain candid and informed opinions from his advisors. And this means it may extend to "communications made by presidential advisers in the course of preparing advice for the President . . . even when these communications are not made directly to the President." Espy, 121 F.3d at 752. . . .

Given the breadth and level of protection accorded to presidential communications, though, the Circuit has also emphasized that this extension of the privilege must be "limited": . . . "Not every person who plays a role in the development of presidential advice, no matter how remote and removed from the President, can qualify for the privilege. In particular, the privilege should not extend to staff outside the White House in executive branch agencies. Instead, the privilege should apply only to communications authored or solicited and received by those members of an immediate White House adviser's staff who have broad and significant responsibility for investigating and formulating the advice to be given the President on the particular matter to which the communications relate. Only communications at that level are close enough to the President to be revelatory of his deliberations or to pose a risk to the candor of his advisers." . . .

After reviewing the withholdings in camera, the Court finds that some of the material is covered by the presidential communications privilege, and other portions must be disclosed as follows [list provided in opinion]. . . .

VI. Foreseeable Harm

In 2016, Congress amended FOIA to add an additional requirement: records that are otherwise protected from disclosure under an exemption must be released unless the agency "reasonably foresees that disclosure would harm an interest protected by [the] exemption." In articulating the nature of the harm, an agency cannot rely on generalized assertions, or mere speculative or abstract fears or fear of embarrassment.

In Reporters Comm. for Freedom of the Press v. FBI, 3 F.4th 350 (D.C. Cir. 2021), the Court of Appeals explained that in the context of Exemption 5, "what is needed is a focused and concrete demonstration of why disclosure of the particular type of material at issue will, in the specific context of the agency action at issue, actually impede those same agency deliberations going forward," and it emphasized that "this inquiry is context specific." Id. at 370. . . .

For the withholdings under Exemptions 3, 7(C) and 7(D), the agencies involved did not specifically address foreseeable harm in the declarations. However, the foreseeable harm requirement does not require "disclosure of information that is otherwise prohibited from disclosure by law, or otherwise exempted from disclosure under subsection (b)(3)." Therefore, the State Department need not supply additional detail since it fully explained the specific threats to national security and foreign policy that were implicated by the ROIs.

And courts in this district have held that when invoking Exemption 7(C), an agency need not establish much more than the fact of disclosure to establish foreseeable harm. Similarly, the Court concludes that the fact that express assurances of confidentiality underlie the approved withholdings of identifying information under Exemption 7(D) is sufficient to satisfy the foreseeable harm standard.

The submissions supporting the withholdings under Exemption 1 from the State Department also satisfy the reasonable foreseeability of harm standard. For each record, "particularized indicia of foreseeable harm" is identified. For example:

> Disclosure of this information at this time could have the potential to inject friction into, or cause damage to, a number of our bilateral relationships with countries whose cooperation is important to U.S. national security, including not only Afghanistan and U.S. allies but some countries in which public opinion might not currently favor close cooperation with the United States. Moreover, the risk of harm to national security from disclosure of this information is exacerbated by the political and security instability in the region in question, such that release of this information could pose a direct threat to the national security of the United States.

Suppl. State Dep't Vaughn Index at 3.

Finally, SIGAR has satisfied the foreseeable harm standard for the presidential communications withheld under Exemption 5. Its declarant explains that the disclosure of such information "burdens the ability of the President and his advisors to engage in a confidential and frank decision-making process and chills or inhibits their ability to have candid discussions, thus impacting the efficiency of government policy-making." It relied on a similar explanation for the withholding of communications and deliberations involving the president-elect. The Court finds that, in the context of the presidential communication privilege, this is sufficient. . . .

## NOTES ON EXEMPTIONS PROTECTING THE OPERATIONAL NEEDS OF AGENCIES AND THE PRESIDENT INSIDE AND OUTSIDE OF FOIA

(1) ***Forms of Executive Privilege.*** There are arguably four types of executive privilege: "military, diplomatic, or national security secrets (the state secrets privilege); communications of the President or his advisors (the

presidential communications privilege); legal advice or legal work (the attorney-client or attorney work product privileges); and the deliberative processes of the President or his advisors (the deliberative process privilege)." Executive Order No. 13233, 56 Fed. Reg. 56025 (Nov. 5, 2001) (revoked for other reasons). The last type also covers agency officials. These notes examine these four types, mostly within the context of FOIA, along with other protections for the operational needs of agencies.

(2) ***State Secrets and FOIA.*** There are two main forms of state secrets. The first, corresponding roughly to Exemption 1, relates to what have been often described as state secrets—that is, matters relating to national security, either military or diplomatic. The second, reflected mainly in Exemptions 5 and 7, consists of "official information." The right to disclosure differs markedly across the two classifications. Because state secrets pose patent dangers to the public interest, "disclosures that would impair national security or diplomatic relations are not required by the courts." EPA v. Mink, 410 U.S. 73 (1973). Redaction of such documents to segregate the disclosable and the privileged is far less frequent. On the other hand, the disclosure of "official information" involves a lower danger to the public interest. Accordingly, courts have long given lesser scope to withholding under Exemptions 5 and 7 and have been quick to order redaction so at least part of records could be disclosed.

FOIA limits the reach of the stronger privilege to national defense or foreign policy matters that are "(A) specifically authorized under criteria established by an Executive order to be kept secret . . . and (B) are in fact properly classified pursuant to such Executive order." Executive Order 13526, 75 Fed. Reg. 707 (Jan. 5, 2010), issued by President Obama at the end of December 2009, is the latest order as of this writing (President Trump retained it and President Biden has not issued anything on the topic as of November 2022). For a history and critique of classification procedures (which started in the 1930s), see Oona A. Hathaway, Secrecy's End, 106 Minn. L. Rev. 691 (2021).

Courts are to evaluate these issues, like all others under FOIA, de novo, with the burden on the agency to sustain its action. This might appear to threaten the integrity of genuine state secrets—if, for example, the executive branch is now required to provide any classified document a person requests under FOIA to a district court for its independent judgment on whether the document has been properly classified—in operation.

In practice, however, as noted in SIGAR (the main case above), courts typically defer to agency expertise on national security despite FOIA's explicit de novo standard of review: "The reasons offered to support assertions of Exemption 1 are afforded substantial weight in the national security context; the Supreme Court has stated that the decisions of people with the authority to withhold information to protect national security 'are worthy of great deference,' because they are 'familiar with the whole picture as judges are not,' and because of the interests and risks at stake." Do you agree with this assessment?

It is inherently hard for a FOIA requester to produce contrary evidence. See Susan Nevelow Mart & Tom Ginsburg, [Dis-]Informing the People's Discretion: Judicial Deference Under the National Security Exemption of the Freedom of Information Act, 66 Admin. L. Rev. 725 (2014) (empirical investigation); Laura K. Donohue, The Shadow of State Secrets, 159 U. Pa. L. Rev. 77 (2010). The D.C. Circuit, for example, will grant summary judgment to the agency under Exemption 1 "[i]f an agency's statements . . . contain reasonable specificity of detail . . . and evidence in the record does not suggest otherwise"; the court will "not conduct a more detailed inquiry to test the agency's judgment and expertise or to evaluate whether the court agrees with the agency's opinions." Larson v. Dep't of State, 565 F.3d 857, 865 (D.C. Cir. 2009). How might a requester fight an agency's claim under Exemption 1?

While Exemption 1 claims may be the most difficult for requesters to defeat, it is one of the least used exemptions by agencies. In FY 2021, of exemptions cited for nondisclosure, Exemption 6 appeared in nearly 30 percent of redaction explanations, Exemption 7(C) and 7(E) in over 50 percent, and Exemption 5 in almost 7 percent, but Exemption 1 made up less than half of 1 percent of claimed exemptions.

Exemption 7(C) protects from disclosure "records or information compiled for law enforcement purposes . . . [if] the production of such law enforcement records or information . . . could reasonably be expected to constitute an unwarranted invasion of personal privacy." As noted in the SIGAR case, the agency has to demonstrate that the release of records would "reasonably be expected to constitute an unwarranted invasion of personal privacy," and that the "personal privacy interest" is not "outweighed by the public interest in disclosure." See Notes on Privacy and Disclosure (p. 773) for more on the privacy analysis. How does the SIGAR court work through the 7(C) and foreseeable harm analyses?

Exemption 7(E) shields information that "would disclose techniques and procedures for law enforcement investigations or prosecutions, or would disclose guidelines for law enforcement investigations or prosecutions if such disclosure could reasonably be expected to risk circumvention of the law." The Second Circuit, relying on Justice Alito's concurrence in Milner (p. 740), rejected requester's efforts to distinguish between applying (not covered) and enforcing (covered) the law. See Knight First Amendment Institute v. U.S. Citizenship & Immigration Servs., 30 F.4th 318 (2d Cir. 2022) ("Enforcing the law always requires a degree of analysis and application. While some aspects of visa adjudication might fall outside the common understanding of 'law enforcement,' the provisions at issue here do not.").

In the spring of 2022, NARA's FOIA Advisory Committee (see Note 6 on Federal Advisory Committees, p. 798) made formal recommendations to the nation's Archivist concerning agency "neither confirm nor deny" (NCND) responses to FOIA requests. These responses are also known as Glomar responses in certain contexts. The committee's recommendations included that guidance be issued to agencies to use NCND (and not Glomar) nomenclature, and that agencies be required to report annually on NCND use (and post information on their websites).

(3) ***State Secrets Outside of FOIA.*** The Supreme Court decided two cases about the state secrets privilege in its 2021 term. In United States v. Zubaydah, 142 S.Ct. 959 (2022), the Court rejected attempts by a Guantánamo Bay detainee who was tortured by the CIA to access classified material from two former CIA contractors for a foreign criminal proceeding through 28 U.S.C. § 1782. The majority found the potential confirmation of a CIA interrogation site in Poland "could significantly harm national security interests, even if that information has already been made public through unofficial sources." In FBI v. Fazaga, 142 S.Ct. 1051 (2022), a putative class action challenging government surveillance of Muslims, the Court concluded that § 1806(f) of the Foreign Intelligence Surveillance Act of 1978 does not displace the state secrets privilege. For a critique of these cases, see Robert Chesney, No Appetite for Change: The Supreme Court Buttresses the State Secrets Privilege, Twice, 136 Harv. L. Rev. 170 (2022).

(4) ***The Attorney-Client Privilege Applied to the Government.*** Your coursework in Civil Procedure may have covered the attorney-client privilege (and the attorney work product doctrine) in some depth. As to the privilege's application in FOIA, District Court Judge Amy Berman Jackson, who wrote the SIGAR decision, described it in another case, Citizens for Responsibility and Ethics in Washington v. DOJ, 538 F.Supp.3d 124 (D.D.C. 2021) as follows: "[T]he mere fact that the communication involves a member of the bar does not end the inquiry. For instance, the privilege does not extend to a government attorney's advice on political, strategic, or policy issues, valuable as it may be. And, where an agency lawyer serves in a mixed capacity that includes responsibilities that fall both within and outside the lawyer's sphere, that lawyer's advice will be protected only to the extent that the lawyer offered it in their professional, legal capacity. . . . [T]o invoke the privilege, the [agency] must establish that securing legal advice was a primary purpose of the communication in question. Finally, like all privileges . . . the attorney-client privilege is narrowly construed and is limited to those situations in which its purposes will be served." Do you think the division between policy and legal advice is stark in most agency decisions?

(5) ***The Deliberative Process Privilege.*** NLRB v. SEARS, ROEBUCK & CO., 421 U.S. 132, 155–56 (1975), was an early case exploring a tension that has often arisen in the cases between documents reflecting what is effectively an agency's internal "law," which *must* be revealed if the Act's purpose to avoid "secret law" is to be served, and documents concerning internal policy discussions that have not reached the point of finality. In that case, the NLRB's General Counsel generated decision memoranda on the question whether or not to prosecute cases before the Board—memoranda that were available within the agency and instructive to its personnel how later cases might be handled. If the memorandum concluded that a proceeding should be commenced, the Court said, that fell within Exemption 5's protection of "predecisional" processes and the memorandum did not have to be revealed. But if the General Counsel decided not to go forward, that judgment of his was final and "precisely the kind of agency law in which the public is so

vitally interested and which Congress sought to prevent the agency from keeping secret."

According to DOJ, the deliberative process privilege, which unlike the attorney-client privilege is unique to the government, is the "most commonly invoked privilege incorporated within Exemption 5." In addition to being predecisional, records falling under the privilege must also be deliberative, in that they must be "a direct part of the deliberative process in that it makes recommendations or expresses opinions on legal or policy matters." Vaughn v. Rosen, 523 F.2d 1136, 1143–44 (D.C. Cir. 1975). Does the privilege require the same approach as with Sunstein's distinction between inputs and outputs in government decisionmaking, discussed in this Chapter's Introduction (p. 701)?

The Supreme Court returned to the deliberative process exemption in its 2020 term after the Ninth Circuit ruled that the Sierra Club could access, through FOIA, two "jeopardy opinions" produced by the Fish and Wildlife Service and the National Marine Fisheries Services as part of the interagency consultation process established by the Endangered Species Act. These opinions helped induce the EPA to adopt more stringent restrictions on cooling water intake structures (see Entergy Corp. v. Riverkeeper, Inc., p. 1266). The Supreme Court reversed in a 7–2 opinion by JUSTICE BARRETT (her first majority opinion) in FWS V. SIERRA CLUB, 141 S.Ct. 777, 785–88 (2021):

"This case concerns the deliberative process privilege, which is a form of executive privilege. To protect agencies from being forced to operate in a fishbowl, the deliberative process privilege shields from disclosure documents reflecting advisory opinions, recommendations and deliberations comprising part of a process by which governmental decisions and policies are formulated. The privilege is rooted in the obvious realization that officials will not communicate candidly among themselves if each remark is a potential item of discovery and front page news. To encourage candor, which improves agency decisionmaking, the privilege blunts the chilling effect that accompanies the prospect of disclosure.

"This rationale does not apply, of course, to documents that embody a final decision, because once a decision has been made, the deliberations are done. The privilege therefore distinguishes between predecisional, deliberative documents, which are exempt from disclosure, and documents reflecting a final agency decision and the reasons supporting it, which are not. Documents are 'predecisional' if they were generated before the agency's final decision on the matter, and they are 'deliberative' if they were prepared to help the agency formulate its position. There is considerable overlap between these two prongs because a document cannot be deliberative unless it is predecisional. . . .

"A document is not final solely because nothing else follows it. Sometimes a proposal dies on the vine. That happens in deliberations—some ideas are discarded or simply languish. . . . What matters, then, is not whether a document is last in line, but whether it communicates a policy on which the agency has settled.

"To decide whether a document communicates the agency's settled position, courts must consider whether the agency treats the document as its final view on the matter. . . . When it does so, the deliberative process by which governmental decisions and policies are formulated will have concluded, and the document will have real operative effect. In other words, once cited as the agency's final view, the document reflects 'the consummation of the agency's decisionmaking process' and not a 'merely tentative' position. See Bennett v. Spear, 520 U.S. 154, 177–178 (1997) (discussing finality in context of obtaining judicial review of agency action) [p. 1543]. By contrast, a document that leaves agency decisionmakers free to change their minds does not reflect the agency's final decision. . . .

"Sierra Club contends, though, that while these documents may have been called 'drafts,' they were actually intended to give the EPA a sneak peek at a conclusion that the Services had already reached and were unwilling to change. And Sierra Club says that the EPA responded accordingly: Once the EPA knew that a jeopardy opinion was coming, it revised its proposed rule. Sierra Club insists that the draft opinions thus had an operative effect on the EPA and must be treated as final under our precedent.

"Sierra Club misunderstands our precedent. While we have identified a decision's real operative effect as an indication of its finality, that reference is to the legal, not practical, consequences that flow from an agency's action. . . .

"To determine whether the privilege applies, we must evaluate not whether the drafts provoked a response from the EPA but whether the Services treated them as final. They did not. The drafts were prepared by lower-level staff and sent to the Services' decisionmakers for approval. . . . It is true, as Sierra Club emphasizes, that the staff recommendations proved to be the last word within the Services about the 2013 version of the EPA's proposed rule. But that does not change our analysis. The recommendations were not last because they were final; they were last because they died on the vine. . . .

"Sierra Club warns that ruling against it here would permit the Services to stamp every document 'draft,' thereby protecting even final agency decisions and creating secret agency law. It is true that a draft document will typically be predecisional because, as we said earlier, calling something a draft communicates that it is not yet final. But determining whether an agency's position is final for purposes of the deliberative process privilege is a functional rather than formal inquiry. If the evidence establishes that an agency has hidden a functionally final decision in draft form, the deliberative process privilege will not apply. The Services, however, did not engage in such a charade here."

The FOIA Improvement Act of 2016 placed a 25-year time limit on claims of deliberative privilege under Exemption 5, adopting the approach of the British Official Secrets Act, but made no such adjustments in either Exemption 1 or Exemption 7. Do you think this change, permitting historians but not the media at the time to be informed of advice given, is more likely to enhance or to inhibit the integrity of candid advice?

(6) ***The Deliberative Process Privilege and Adopted Advice.*** Governmental advice that is incorporated into official policy will not be protected under the deliberative process privilege. In April 2002, the Office of Legal Counsel at DOJ wrote a memorandum evaluating whether "state and local law enforcement may lawfully enforce certain provisions of federal immigration law." The memorandum reversed OLC's earlier position from the Clinton Administration, and the Attorney General and his staff explicitly cited it publicly on a number of occasions as defending and pushing the agency's new policy on the matter. The government tried to withhold the memorandum under FOIA, citing deliberative process (and attorney-client privilege). The Second Circuit rejected the government's position in NATIONAL COUNCIL OF LA RAZA V. DEP'T OF JUSTICE, 411 F.3d 350, 358–60 (2d Cir. 2005): "To be sure, had the Department simply adopted only the conclusions of the OLC Memorandum, the district court could not have required that the Memorandum be disclosed. Mere reliance on a document's conclusions does not necessarily involve reliance on a document's analysis; both will ordinarily be needed before a court may properly find adoption or incorporation by reference. . . . The instant case, however, is different. The record makes clear that the Department embraced the OLC's reasoning as its own. . . . Like the deliberative process privilege, the attorney-client privilege may not be invoked to protect a document adopted as, or incorporated by reference into, an agency's policy." See also ACLU v. NSA, 925 F.3d 576, 598, 600 (2d Cir. 2019) (protecting OLC memorandum because it "was not created as working law" and "there is no evidence that the Government ever 'adopted' [the memorandum] as binding nor has the ACLU identified a single agency opinion that incorporates [the memorandum] by reference"); New York Times Co. v. DOJ, 756 F.3d 100, 116–17 (2d Cir. 2014) (relying on La Raza to hold that the legal reasoning in a 2010 OLC-DoD memorandum on a contemplated drone strike against Shaykh Anwar al-Aulaqi could not be withheld under the deliberative process privilege as the government had "publicly assert[ed] that OLC advice establishes the legal boundaries within which we can operate"); Campaign for Accountability v. DOJ, 486 F.Supp.3d 424, 441 (D.D.C. 2020) (holding that FOIA plaintiffs stated "a plausible claim that OLC opinions that resolve inter-agency disputes . . . provide statements of policy and interpretations that have been adopted ex ante by the OLC's client agencies").

(7) ***The Deliberative Process Privilege and Decisions.*** In addition to being deliberative, documents must also be predecisional to qualify for the privilege. District Court Judge Amy Berman Jackson recently determined that a March 2019 OLC memorandum to the Attorney General on Special Counsel Mueller's report of his investigation into the Russian government's interference in the 2016 presidential election was not predecisional: "In other words, the review of the document reveals that the Attorney General was not then engaged in making a decision about whether the President should be charged with obstruction of justice; the fact that he would not be prosecuted was a given. The omission of any reference to [the hypothetical nature of the document] in the agency declarations, coupled with the agency's redaction of critical caveats from what it did disclose, served to obscure the true purpose of the memorandum. Thus, the Court's in camera review leads to the

conclusion that the agency has fallen far short of meeting its burden to show that the memorandum was prepared in order to assist an agency decisionmaker in arriving at his decision. . . . So why did the Attorney General's advisors, at his request, create a memorandum that evaluated the prosecutive merit of the facts amassed by the Special Counsel? Lifting the curtain reveals the answer to that too: getting a jump on public relations. . . . There is also a problem with the '*pre*' portion of 'pre-decisional.' . . . A close review of the communications reveals that the March 24 letter to Congress describing the Special Counsel's report, which assesses the strength of an obstruction-of-justice case, and the 'predecisional' March 24 memorandum advising the Attorney General that he should make a public statement to that effect, and that the evidence does not support a prosecution, are being written by the very same people at the very same time. The emails show not only that the authors and the recipients of the memorandum are working hand in hand to craft the advice that is supposedly being delivered by OLC, but that the letter to Congress is the priority, and it is getting completed first." CREW v. DOJ, 538 F.Supp.3d 124 (D.D.C. 2021), aff'd, 45 F.4th 963 (D.C. Cir. 2022). What does this excerpt suggest about in camera review?

In what has been "described as the [FOIA] addendum to Department of Commerce v. New York, 139 S.Ct. 2551 (2019) [p. 1177]" the D.C. Circuit held in Campaign Legal Center v. DOJ, 34 F.4th 14 (D.C. Cir. 2022), in one commentator's view, that an agency may "invoke the deliberative process privilege to shield internal deliberations over a sham memo requesting that another agency take action, knowing that the recipient agency will use the request to hide the real reason for its contemplated action." Bernard Bell, Campaign Legal Center v. DOJ—FOIA Postscript to Department of Commerce v. New York (Part I), Notice & Comment Blog (Nov. 27, 2022).[22] The D.C. Circuit explained it somewhat differently: "[E]ven after an agency head has set the direction of agency policy at the macro level, the subsequent work needed to define, refine, debate, and flesh out the boundaries of and justifications for that position can, upon a proper showing, also qualify as predecisional." 34 F.4th at 24.

(8) ***Opinion v. Facts.*** It may be difficult to redact documents to reveal facts but protect privileged "opinion." Then-JUDGE RUTH BADER GINSBURG dealt with this issue in PETROLEUM INFORMATION CORP. V. DEP'T OF INTERIOR, 976 F.2d 1429, 1434–35 (D.C. Cir. 1992): "Under [Exemption 5], factual information generally must be disclosed, but materials embodying officials' opinions are ordinarily exempt. . . . Quarles v. Department of Navy, 893 F.2d 390 (D.C. Cir. 1990) (observing that 'the prospect of disclosure is less likely to make an adviser omit or fudge raw facts, while it is quite likely to have just such an effect' on materials reflecting agency deliberations). The fact/opinion distinction, however, is not always dispositive; in some instances, the disclosure of even purely factual material may so expose the deliberative process within an agency that the material is appropriately held privileged. [For example, Quarles] held exempt from FOIA disclosure Navy cost estimates prepared in the course of selecting a port for a battleship

[22] https://www.yalejreg.com/nc/campaign-legal-center-v-doj-foia-postscript-to-department-of-commerce-v-new-york-part-i/.

group. [We] explained that the estimates reflected a 'complex set of judgments' that 'partake of just that elasticity that has persuaded courts to provide shelter for opinions generally.' [D]isclosure of the estimates could 'chill' or distort eventual Navy deliberations concerning the award of a contract to construct the port . . . [T]he 'key question' in these cases [is] whether disclosure would tend to diminish candor within an agency."

For a recent example, see REPORTERS COMM. FOR FREEDOM OF THE PRESS V. FBI, 3 F.4th 350 (D.C. Cir. 2021): "The News Organizations' arguments fare much better as to the FBI's Factual Accuracy Comments. Those documents contain comments from the FBI to the Inspector General on the accuracy of purely factual statements in the draft report. . . . [T]he government has failed to establish that the Factual Accuracy Comments were deliberative, as required by the second prong of the test for protection under the deliberative process privilege. For starters, under the deliberative process privilege, factual information generally must be disclosed. . . . Here, the separation between fact and deliberation is quite stark. The document containing the factual corrections is a very simple form that contains blanks on which a commenter is limited to identifying the precise location in the Inspector General Report at which a factual correction is being proposed, the fact that is being corrected, and the proposed correction. This format cabins each correction or change in an isolated and easily segregable fashion, with no apparent room for opinion or non-factual commentary. . . . The government argues that all comments on a draft are as privileged as the contents of the draft itself because disclosing the comments necessarily reveals whether those comments were incorporated. But the FBI did not submit these comments for the purpose of exercising editorial judgment, such as that the matter concerned was unimportant or otherwise inappropriate for publication. . . . So the fact-checking exercise in which the FBI was asked to engage did not call for judgment or the candid exchange of ideas." How does this issue ("factual compilations") play out in the SIGAR case?

(9) ***OIRA and the Deliberative Process Privilege.*** Recall OIRA's involvement in agency rulemaking (p. 455). You might check the docket for a recent important rulemaking on www.regulations.gov to see to what extent, if any, the agency's dealings with OIRA are recorded there. Should they be? Or does OIRA's participation, or any other agency's views that might be communicated to the rulemaking agency, constitute predecisional, intragovernmental deliberation properly falling within Exemption 5? Interestingly, on some occasions, agencies submit formal comments on another agency's rulemaking, which then do appear on the docket. Under E.O. 12866, what must OIRA disclose about its role? Commentators suggest that OIRA largely doesn't comply with these mandates.[23]

[23] See, e.g., Sam Abbott, Center for Effective Government, Disclosure at the Office of Information and Regulatory Affairs: Written Comments and Telephone Records Suspiciously Absent (Feb. 26, 2013) (examining meetings from 2001 to 2013 for three agencies), https://www.foreffectivegov.org/disclosure-at-oira-written-comments-and-telephone-records-suspiciously-absent; Peter Strauss, The OIRA Transparency Problem, Notice & Comment Blog (Nov. 22, 2016) (summarizing the ABA's Administrative Law Section's report to President-elect Trump recommending increased OIRA transparency and drawing on prior criticisms of poorly followed

(10) ***Consultant Corollary and Exemption 5.*** Should agency communications protected by Exemption 5 include communications with an agency's outside consultants? In 2019, a Ninth Circuit panel said no, rejecting the "consultant corollary" to Exemption 5. The Ninth Circuit, en banc, reversed in 2021, joining six other courts of appeals to allow interagency communications to extend beyond government employees. Rojas v. FAA, 989 F.3d 666 (9th Cir. 2021) (en banc). The Supreme Court refused to hear the case. Do you agree? See Note 4 (Reliance on Subordinates and Contractors) (p. 506).

(11) ***Presidential Communications Privilege and Testimonial Immunity Inside and Outside of FOIA.*** The SIGAR case shows how the presidential communications privilege can arise within a FOIA case (as part of Exemption 5). How do the privilege and the foreseeable harm mandate interact in that case? Should FOIA's emphasis on segregability of information apply? See Protect Democracy Project, Inc. v. NSA, 10 F.4th 879 (D.C. Cir. 2021) (finding that "the presidential communications privilege applies to documents in their entirety").

As noted with state secrets, the need to protect government information and deliberations also arises outside FOIA. IN RE SEALED CASE, 121 F.3d 729 (D.C. Cir. 1997), concerns privileges before a criminal grand jury. The court found a "presidential communications privilege" for predecisional analyses intended to inform the President's judgment, whether or not these were written directly for his eyes: "Presidential advisers do not explore alternatives only in conversations with the President or pull their final advice to him out of thin air—if they do, their advice is not likely to be worth much. Rather, the most valuable advisers will investigate the factual context of a problem in detail, obtain input from all others with significant expertise in the area, and perform detailed analyses of several different policy options before coming to closure on a recommendation for the Chief Executive." The court nonetheless restricted this presidential communications privilege, which it characterized as broader and stronger than the deliberative process privilege, to communications made or solicited by immediate presidential advisers, and intended specifically to aid them in "advising the President on official governmental matters."

Judicial Watch filed a FOIA request seeking agency memoranda concerning the raid on Osama bin Laden's compound. In 2019, the D.C. Circuit ruled that the memoranda to the President and his close advisers, even though written after the raid, did not have to be disclosed because of the presidential communications privilege in Exemption 5. JUD. WATCH, INC.

---

disclosure policies), https://www.yalejreg.com/nc/the-oira-transparency-problem-by-peter-strauss/. In 2019, OIRA solicited comments on proposed disclosures under Executive Order 12866. Information on Meetings With Outside Parties Pursuant to Executive Order 12866, 84 Fed. Reg. 1236 (Feb. 1, 2019). The Project on Government Oversight filed a comment expressing concerns: "POGO is concerned because the proposed guidance modification does not sufficiently ensure that meetings OIRA has with outside parties and information received from such parties concerning pending regulatory actions will be sufficiently transparent. . . . [T]he office's lack of enforcement or accountability measures leaves it unclear how the office will ensure implementation of this guidance." Sean Moulton, POGO Tells OIRA to Expand Transparency for Meetings With Outside Parties (Apr. 2, 2019), https://www.pogo.org/letter/2019/04/pogo-tells-oira-to-expand-transparency-for-meetings-with-outside-parties.

v. U.S. DEPT. OF DEFENSE, 913 F.3d 1106, 1112 (D.C. Cir. 2019): "Here, the extraordinary decision confronting the President in considering whether to order a military strike on Osama bin Laden's compound in Pakistan cries out for confidentiality, and the district court's application of the presidential communications privilege rested on consideration of the appropriate factors. The decision required the exercise of an informed judgment by the President as Commander in Chief, U.S. Const. art. 2, § 2, on a highly sensitive subject with serious direct and collateral consequences for foreign relations that required a high degree of protection for 'the President's confidentiality and the candor of his immediate White House advisers'. . . . Judicial Watch makes no effort to reconcile its position that the timing of the preparation of the memoranda defeats application of the presidential communications privilege with this court's precedent. In In re Sealed Case, the court held that notes taken to memorialize meetings and telephone calls involving top White House advisers about the investigation of the former Secretary of Agriculture were protected from disclosure by the presidential communications privilege because the notes reflected those advisers' communications."

In litigation over whether the House Judiciary Committee could compel former White House Counsel Don McGahn to testify, then-Judge Ketanji Brown Jackson followed an earlier district court ruling, Committee on Judiciary, U.S. House of Representatives v. Miers, 558 F.Supp.2d 53 (D.D.C. 2008), involving whether the same committee could compel White House Counsel Harriet Miers to speak about the firing of nine U.S. Attorneys. In that previous case, Judge Bates had rejected the White House's claim of "absolute immunity for senior presidential aides": "The Court holds only that Ms. Miers (and other senior presidential advisors) do not have absolute immunity from compelled congressional process in the context of this particular subpoena dispute."

As to McGahn, Jackson determined: "To make the point as plain as possible, it is clear to this Court for the reasons explained above that, with respect to senior-level presidential aides, absolute immunity from compelled congressional process simply does not exist. Indeed, absolute testimonial immunity for senior-level White House aides appears to be a fiction that has been fastidiously maintained over time through the force of sheer repetition in OLC opinions, and through accommodations that have permitted its proponents to avoid having the proposition tested in the crucible of litigation. And because the contention that a President's top advisors cannot be subjected to compulsory congressional process simply has no basis in the law, it does not matter whether such immunity would theoretically be available to only a handful of presidential aides due to the sensitivity of their positions, or to the entire Executive branch. Nor does it make any difference whether the aides in question are privy to national security matters, or work solely on domestic issues. And, of course, if present frequent occupants of the West Wing or Situation Room must find time to appear for testimony as a matter of law when Congress issues a subpoena, then any such immunity most certainly stops short of covering individuals who only purport to be cloaked with this authority because, at some point in the past, they once were in the President's employ. This was the state of law when Judge Bates first considered the issue of whether former White House Counsel Harriet Miers had absolute testimonial immunity in 2008, and it remains the state of law today, and it goes without saying that the law applies to former White House Counsel Don McGahn, just as it does to other current and former senior-level White House officials.

"Thus, for the myriad reasons laid out above as well as those that are articulated plainly in the prior precedents of the Supreme Court, the D.C. Circuit, and the U.S. District Court for the District of Columbia, this Court holds that individuals who have been subpoenaed for testimony by an authorized committee of Congress must appear for testimony in response to that subpoena—i.e., they cannot ignore or defy congressional compulsory process, by order of the President or otherwise. Notably, however, in the context of that appearance, such individuals are free to assert any legally applicable privilege in response to the questions asked of them, where appropriate." COMM. ON JUDICIARY, U.S. HOUSE OF REPRESENTATIVES V. MCGAHN, 415 F.Supp.3d 148 (D.D.C. 2019), rev'd on other grounds, 951 F.3d 510 (D.C. Cir. 2020), rev'd en banc, 968 F.3d 755 (D.C. Cir. 2020).

In July 2021, DOJ notified several top former agency appointees that the agency did not support them asserting executive privilege in response to congressional requests for "transcribed interviews" about attempts "to advance unsubstantiated allegations of voter fraud, challenge the 2020 election results, stop Congress's count of the Electoral College vote, or overturn President Biden's certified victory." DOJ found: "After balancing the Legislative and Executive Branch interests, as required under the accommodation process, it is the Executive Branch's view that this presents an exceptional situation in which the congressional need for information outweighs the Executive Branch's interest in maintaining confidentiality."[24] Several former officials have since testified (see p. 920).

For an overview of claims of executive privilege and presidential communications, see Cong. Rsch. Serv., R47102, Executive Privilege and Presidential Communications: Judicial Principles (May 12, 2022).[25]

## NOTES ON EXEMPTIONS PROTECTING INFORMATION SUPPLIED TO GOVERNMENT

(1) ***Connections to Other Sections.*** Recall that a competitor seeking information about an adversary's business is no less a "person" entitled to demand information under FOIA than the most compelling public-interest claimant. Indeed, as discussed in the Note on Commercial Requesters (p. 731), competitors and information resellers make up the majority of FOIA requesters at many agencies. Obviously, submitters of information often have a profound interest in ensuring that agencies do not provide requested information if the agency could deny it. As discussed in more detail in Section 3.d below, under Executive Order 12600, agencies have to implement procedures allowing submitters to mark documents "confidential."

[24] For one letter: https://oversight.house.gov/sites/democrats.oversight.house.gov/files/Pak%20Authorization%20Letter%20072621%20%28002%29.pdf.

[25] https://crsreports.congress.gov/product/pdf/R/R47102.

Submitters can also bring reverse-FOIA actions to protect their interests if the agency believes it has to disclose the information, despite it being marked as confidential (p. 783). We focus here on Exemptions 3 and 4 outside of the reverse-FOIA context. The next set of Notes addresses information covered by FOIA's privacy-related exemptions.

(2) ***Does It Make a Difference Whether Information Is Supplied Voluntarily or Under Compulsion?*** The government is a demanding consumer of information from the private sector. Banks cannot be regulated, nuclear power plants licensed, new drugs authorized, taxes collected, or censuses taken without detailed information that people do not readily share with others. Where the government must solicit cooperation rather than force disclosure, confidentiality may have to be guaranteed before cooperation is forthcoming. Even if disclosure could be forced or bargained for, as in rate regulation or technology licensing, sound public policy may support preserving confidentiality of some kinds of data (e.g., to foster innovation or to avoid creating circumstances conducive to unfair competition).

Should volunteered information receive more protection under Exemption 4 than information whose submission the government has compelled? And what should be the standard for compelled information? For many years, the leading case was National Parks and Conservation Ass'n v. Morton, 498 F.2d 765 (D.C. Cir. 1974). In National Parks, the D.C. Circuit determined that compelled information would be protected "if disclosure of the information is likely to have either of the following effects: (1) to impair the Government's ability to obtain necessary information in the future; or (2) to cause substantial harm to the competitive position of the person from whom the information was obtained." The D.C. Circuit made a distinction between volunteered and compelled information in CRITICAL MASS ENERGY PROJECT V. NUCLEAR REGULATORY COMMISSION, 975 F.2d 871 (D.C. Cir. 1992) (en banc). In that case, the requester was seeking information about nuclear power plant "incidents" with possible safety implications that had been gathered by an industry group and then voluntarily shared with the NRC—on the condition that the agency would not release the information to other parties without the group's consent. For information given to the government voluntarily, the court announced more protection than for information supplied under compulsion: "[I]t will be treated as confidential under Exemption 4 if it is of a kind that the provider would not customarily make available to the public. . . . [T]he presumption is that [the government's] interest will be threatened by disclosure as the persons whose confidences have been betrayed will, in all likelihood, refuse further cooperation."

Four dissenters from the en banc decision objected to this much stronger level of protection: "There will be no objective check on, no judicial review alert to, 'the temptation of government and business officials to follow the path of least resistance and say "confidential" whenever they seek to satisfy the government's vast information needs.' 9 to 5 Organization for Women Office Workers, 721 F.2d at 12 (Breyer, J. dissenting). . . . The FOIA request we face seeks no 'information about private citizens that happens to be in the warehouse of the Government'; disclosure is sought not primarily 'in the commercial interest of the requester,' but to advance public understanding of the nature and quality of the NRC's oversight operations or activities."

This distinction no longer holds. See the next note.

(3) ***Supreme Court's Rejection of National Parks.*** In FOOD MARKETING INSTITUTE V. ARGUS LEADER MEDIA, 139 S.Ct. 2356 (2019), a 6–3 decision by JUSTICE GORSUCH, the Supreme Court ruled that compelled disclosures to the government should not be held to the National Parks standard, which required a showing of "substantial competitive harm" to prevent release:

"Exemption 4 shields from mandatory disclosure 'commercial or financial information obtained from a person and privileged or confidential.' 5 U.S.C. § 552(b)(4). But FOIA nowhere defines the term 'confidential.' So, as usual, we ask what that term's ordinary, contemporary, common meaning was when Congress enacted FOIA in 1966. We've done the same with other undefined terms in FOIA.

"The term 'confidential' meant then, as it does now, 'private' or 'secret.' Contemporary dictionaries suggest two conditions that might be required for information communicated to another to be considered confidential. In one sense, information communicated to another remains confidential whenever it is customarily kept private, or at least closely held, by the person imparting it. In another sense, information might be considered confidential only if the party receiving it provides some assurance that it will remain secret.

"Must both of these conditions be met for information to be considered confidential under Exemption 4? At least the first condition has to be; it is hard to see how information could be deemed confidential if its owner shares it freely. And there's no question that the [submitters of the requested information] satisfy this condition. . . . But what about the second condition: Can privately held information lose its confidential character for purposes of Exemption 4 if it's communicated to the government without assurances that the government will keep it private? As it turns out, there's no need to resolve that question in this case because the [submitters] before us clearly satisfy this condition too. . . .

"Early courts of appeals confronting Exemption 4 interpreted its terms in ways consistent with these understandings. . . .

"So where did the 'substantial competitive harm' requirement come from? In 1974, the D.C. Circuit declared that, in addition to the requirements actually set forth in Exemption 4, a 'court must also be satisfied that non-disclosure is justified by the legislative purpose which underlies the exemption'. . . .

"National Parks' contrary approach is a relic from a bygone era of statutory construction. Not only did National Parks inappropriately resort to legislative history before consulting the statute's text and structure, once it did so it went even further astray. The court relied heavily on statements from witnesses in congressional hearings years earlier on a different bill that was never enacted into law. . . .

"[The dissenters] seem to agree that the law doesn't demand proof of 'substantial' or 'competitive' harm, but they think it would be a good idea to require a showing of some harm. Neither side, however, has advocated for such an understanding of the statute's terms. And our colleagues' brief brush with the statutory text doesn't help; they cite exclusively from specialized dictionary definitions lifted from the national security classification context that have no bearing on Exemption 4."

How does this decision compare with the Court's decision in Milner (p. 734) or in Sierra Club (p. 761)? Could this decision decrease agencies' use of Exemptions 6 and 7 (as they can now turn to Exemption 4 instead)? (See p. 725 on exemption use.) And if you have read the note on New Prime, Inc. v. Oliveira, 139 S.Ct. 523 (2019) (p. 154), observe here another occasion on which Justice Gorsuch has secured a Court majority for originalist interpretations of important statutory provisions now embedded in the APA. For a comparison of Argus Leader and Sierra Club, see Adira Levine, Note, FOIA Disclosure and the Supreme Court, 46 Harv. Envtl. L. Rev. 261 (2022).

A month after the Court decided Argus Leader, a bipartisan group of Senators—Senators Grassley, Leahy, Cornyn, and Feinstein—introduced the Open and Responsive Government Act (S. 2220) to limit confidential information to "information that, if disclosed, would likely cause substantial harm to the competitive position of the person from whom the information was obtained." Does it surprise you that this legislative effort drew sponsors from both sides of the aisle?

(4) ***Foreseeable Harm and Argus Leader.*** Congress amended FOIA in 2016 to mandate that disclosure must cause foreseeable harm for documents to be withheld under a FOIA exemption (see Note 5 on p. 733). In Seife v. FDA, 43 F.4th 231 (2d Cir. 2022), the Second Circuit considered the independent effect the foreseeable harm standard has on Exemption 4 withholdings. The court held that "the interests protected by Exemption 4 of FOIA are the commercial or financial interests of the submitter in information that is of a type held in confidence and not disclosed to any member of the public," and the "foreseeable harm requirement refers to harm to the submitter's commercial or financial interests." Id. at 240. The Second Circuit responded to critiques that this reinstated the "competitive harm" requirement of National Parks by clarifying that Argus Leader interpreted only one word (confidential) in Exemption 4, while the Second Circuit was analyzing Exemption 4's purposes as an entirety, as instructed by the foreseeable harm test. Id. at 241. To do otherwise, the court argued, would be to ignore the independent effect of the foreseeable harm test entirely. Id. In an earlier decision, the Northern District of California rejected precisely this approach as an attempt "use the FOIA amendment to circumvent the Supreme Court's rejection of National Parks[ ] . . . in determining the scope of the term 'confidential.' " Am. Small Bus. League v. United States Dep't of Def., 411 F.Supp.3d 824, 836 (N.D. Cal. 2019). Reasoning that "[d]isclosure would necessarily destroy the private nature of the information, no matter the circumstance," the court declined to give independent effect to the foreseeable harm standard when applying Exemption 4. Id. Which decision has the better interpretation of FOIA? How does the foreseeable harm

standard interact with other exemptions? See Seife, supra, at 235 n.2 (noting that "[t]he only FOIA exemption to receive appellate scrutiny [since the 2016 amendments] is Exemption 5").

(5) ***Mosaic Theory of Commercial Information Under FOIA.*** How much proprietary information has in fact been released under FOIA is a matter of dispute. As discussed in the Note on Commercial Requesters (p. 731), the persistence of an active FOIA "industry" and the dominance of commercial sources as requesters suggest that valuable "ore," deposited by other firms, is in fact being mined. As in other contexts, such as national security,[26] commercial data that are quite harmless standing alone may be very revealing when combined with other information publicly available or separately sought. See Gilda Industries, Inc. v. United States Customs & Border Prot. Bureau, 457 F.Supp.2d 6, 12 (D.D.C. 2006) ("[E]ven if the information subject to a FOIA request would not itself threaten competitive injury, it is properly protected if the requester has other, public sources of information that would could complete the picture of its competitors.").

An environmental lawyer advises submitters of information to the government that the interrelated nature of information makes "[a] submission . . . like a crossword puzzle: knowing the answer to one clue helps in answering the next." For example, if a firm obtains publicly available data on a competing manufacturer's emissions, it may be able to estimate the facility's production. Submitters are advised to "draft the impossible crossword puzzle," test it for vulnerability, and then take such steps as presubmission marking, negotiating with the agency, and following-up with other agencies to which the information is forwarded. See David R. Andrews, Confidential Business Information Provided in Reports to the EPA May Ultimately be Disclosed Under [FOIA], Nat'l L.J. (Nov. 21, 1994), at B4, B7. We take up privacy issues below in the Notes on Privacy and Disclosure.

(6) ***Exemption 3: Specific Statutory Protection of Information from Release.*** The evolution of FOIA, which has been amended more often than the rest of the APA, has often reflected the tensions between FOIA's emphatic pursuit of "open government" and needs for confidentiality felt in particular settings. Thus, concerns about commercial data (and national security) issues have resulted in a number of statutes specifically exempting certain kinds of information from disclosure—the matter dealt with in FOIA's Exemption 3. Prior liberal judicial treatment of these statutes has led Congress to considerably tighten the exemption's language.[27] In 2009, Congress amended Exemption 3 to require any future statute creating an exemption to contain both an explicit, clear statement of intent to provide a qualifying statutory exemption, and an explicit reference to Exemption 3. 5

---

[26] CIA v. Sims, 471 U.S. 159, 178 (1985) ("[B]its and pieces of data may aid in piecing together bits of other information even when the individual piece is not of obvious importance in itself. Thus, what may seem trivial to the uninformed, may appear of great moment to one who has a broad view of the scene and may put the questioned item of information in its proper context.").

[27] Gina Stevens, Cong. Rsch. Serv., R41406, The Freedom of Information Act and Nondisclosure Provisions in Other Federal Laws (Sept. 24, 2010), https://fas.org/sgp/crs/secrecy/R41406.pdf.

U.S.C. § 552(b)(3). The following summer, the Dodd-Frank Act contained three broad exemptions for information the SEC might acquire in investigating entities, such as hedge funds, newly subject to its regulation—all containing the required reference.[28] And, soon after that, concerns that these provisions would too extensively shield SEC operations from public view produced their emphatic repeal[29]—with subsequent worries that the SEC's regulatory task could be significantly impeded by compromising the confidentiality of information it might seek to acquire.

In 2021, the GAO issued a report on agency use of (b)(3) exemption statutes, finding that between FY 2010 and FY 2019 "federal agencies claimed a total of 256 statutes as the basis for withholding requested information." In that period, "91 agencies reported withholding information using at least one of the 256 statutes a total of more than 525,000 times. The most-commonly used statute related to withholding records pertaining to the issuance or refusal of visas to enter the United States (8 U.S.C. § 1202(f))." Freedom of Information Act: Update on Federal Agencies' Use of Exemption Statutes, GAO-21-148 (Jan. 2021).[30]

The Second and Ninth Circuits recently disagreed about whether appropriation riders prevented the disclosure of information from the Firearms Trace System database. Everytown for Gun Safety Support Fund v. ATF, 984 F.3d 30 (2d Cir. 2020) (finding that while (b)(3), as amended in 2009, "suggests a different conclusion," Congress "was not bound to follow the specific-citation requirement it had adopted in the OPEN FOIA Act"); Center for Investigative Reporting v. DOJ, 982 F.3d 668 (9th Cir. 2020) (reaching the opposite conclusion). Judge Bumatay dissented in the Ninth Circuit case, writing that the requirement that the 2012 appropriations rider "conform to an earlier statute—the OPEN FOIA Act of 2009"—"offends our constitutional scheme."

How does the SIGAR case deal with Exemption 3 issues?

## NOTES ON PRIVACY AND DISCLOSURE

(1) ***"Unwarranted Invasion of Personal Privacy" Under FOIA.*** FOIA asks agencies to consider the privacy needs of individuals. Exemption 6 applies to "personnel and medical files and similar files" when disclosure "would constitute a clearly unwarranted invasion of personal privacy," and Exemption 7 applies to law enforcement records when (among other things) disclosure "could reasonably be expected to constitute an unwarranted invasion of personal privacy." The structure of FOIA initially forced the courts to determine what is "unwarranted" without regard to the identity or particular purpose of the party requesting information (except when someone requests information about herself). The result was the formulation of rules organized by the type of information at issue. In DOJ V. REPORTERS COMMITTEE FOR FREEDOM OF THE PRESS, 489 U.S. 749, 774, 780 (1989), reporters requested the FBI "rap sheet" for a specific individual claimed to

[28] Pub. L. No. 111–203, § 929I, 124 Stat.1377.

[29] Pub. L. No. 111–257, § 1, 124 Stat. 2646.

[30] https://www.gao.gov/assets/gao-21-148.pdf.

have organized crime connections. Stating that "the FOIA's central purpose is to ensure that the *Government's* activities be opened to the sharp eye of public scrutiny, not that information about *private citizens* that happens to be in the warehouse of the Government be so disclosed," JUSTICE STEVENS's opinion upheld the agency's refusal to produce the requested information: "We hold as a categorical matter that a third party's request for law-enforcement records or information about a private citizen can reasonably be expected to invade that citizen's privacy, and that when the request seeks no 'official information' about a Government agency, but merely records that the Government happens to be storing, the invasion of privacy is 'unwarranted.' "

In NATIONAL ARCHIVES AND RECORDS ADMINISTRATION V. FAVISH, 541 U.S. 157, 171–72, 174–75 (2004), the Court revised its approach to determining what invasions of privacy were "unwarranted." Allan Favish sought the release of photographs of the body of Vincent Foster, Deputy Counsel to President Clinton, who investigators concluded had killed himself in a public park in Northern Virginia. Did his surviving family have a protected privacy interest in their nondisclosure? JUSTICE KENNEDY, for a unanimous Court, easily found that "the personal privacy protected by Exemption 7(C) extends to family members who object to the disclosure of graphic details surrounding their relative's death . . . ." Perhaps the more difficult question was whether, unlike all other exemptions except for Exemption 6, the privacy exemption in 7(C) entailed balancing between the interests of the requester and those of the person or persons whose privacy would be violated. Upholding the agency's nondisclosure, JUSTICE KENNEDY reasoned: "[A]s a general rule, when documents are within FOIA's disclosure provisions, citizens should not be required to explain why they seek the information. A person requesting the information needs no preconceived idea of the uses the data might serve. The information belongs to citizens to do with as they choose. Furthermore, as we have noted, the disclosure does not depend on the identity of the requester. As a general rule, if the information is subject to disclosure, it belongs to all.

"When disclosure touches upon certain areas defined in the exemptions, however, the statute recognizes limitations that compete with the general interest in disclosure, and that, in appropriate cases, can overcome it. In the case of Exemption 7(C), the statute requires us to protect, in the proper degree, the personal privacy of citizens against the uncontrolled release of information compiled through the power of the State. The statutory direction that the information not be released if the invasion of personal privacy could reasonably be expected to be unwarranted requires the courts to balance the competing interests in privacy and disclosure. To effect this balance and to give practical meaning to the exemption, the usual rule that the citizen need not offer a reason for requesting the information must be inapplicable.

"Where the privacy concerns addressed by Exemption 7(C) are present, the exemption requires the person requesting the information to establish a sufficient reason for the disclosure. First, the citizen must show that the public interest sought to be advanced is a significant one, an interest more specific than having the information for its own sake. Second, the citizen must show the information is likely to advance that interest. Otherwise, the invasion of privacy is unwarranted. . . .

"We hold that, where there is a privacy interest protected by Exemption 7(C) and the public interest being asserted is to show that responsible officials acted negligently or otherwise improperly in the performance of their duties, the requester must establish more than a bare suspicion in order to obtain disclosure. Rather, the requester must produce evidence that would warrant a belief by a reasonable person that the alleged Government impropriety might have occurred. . . . Only when the FOIA requester has produced evidence sufficient to satisfy this standard will there exist a counterweight on the FOIA scale for the court to balance against the cognizable privacy interests in the requested records. . . . Favish has not produced any evidence that would warrant a belief by a reasonable person that the alleged Government impropriety might have occurred to put the balance into play."

Recall that Exemption 7(C) also was addressed in the SIGAR case. How did the district court there approach the exemption?

(2) ***Exemption 6 in Practice.*** In NISKANEN CENTER V. FEDERAL ENERGY REGULATORY COMMISSION, 20 F.4th 787 (D.C. Cir. 2021), the D.C. Circuit determined that FERC's decision to disclose the initials and street names of property owners "along the route of a proposed pipeline"—but not their full names and addresses—"struck the proper balance" between privacy and public interests under Exemption 6: "Niskanen identifies a weighty public interest in understanding FERC's compliance with its notice obligations, but it articulates no reason it needs the full names and addresses of landowners along a pipeline route to do so. The district court rightly found that more limited disclosure best balanced landowners' privacy and the public interest." Judge Randolph concurred to note that the cancellation of the pipeline was relevant to the analysis: "Those organizations touting their 'good work' would have every incentive to use the landowner lists to solicit donations, by mail, by telephone or in person. In the face of comparable potential uses, the Supreme Court determined that individuals 'have some nontrivial privacy interest in nondisclosure' of their home addresses. U.S. Dep't of Def. v. FLRA, 510 U.S. 487, 501 (1994)."

(3) ***Are FOIA's Privacy Exemptions Applicable to Corporate Information?*** Although a corporation is a "person" for purposes of the Due Process Clauses of the Fifth and Fourteenth Amendments, it is not a "person" for purposes of claiming the privilege against self-incrimination under the same Amendments. When a trade association sought FOIA access to information obtained by the FCC's Enforcement Bureau during its investigation of AT&T, the FCC withheld some information under Exemption 4, and personal information identifying AT&T's staff and customers under Exemption 7(C), but denied AT&T's other claims based on its assertion of corporate privacy interests. The Court of Appeals for the Third Circuit disagreed, reasoning that because a "person" includes a corporation under FOIA, and a corporation can suffer "public embarrassment, harassment, and stigma" for investigative disclosures, a corporation may have a personal privacy interest within Exemption 7(C)'s

meaning. The Supreme Court unanimously reversed, in an opinion by CHIEF JUSTICE ROBERTS, FCC v. AT&T, 562 U.S. 397 (2011). His opinion posited that while "person" is defined by the APA to include a corporation, so that a corporation is a "person" for the purposes of Exemption 4 (and, for that matter, the making of FOIA requests, as the SIGAR case illustrates), "personal" is not defined and its consistent usage in common language and in the APA (Exemption 6) refers to human individuals. "We trust," the Court concluded, "that AT&T will not take it personally." Compare the reasoning in the majority opinion in the Milner case (p. 734).

Knowing that a corporation is a "person" protected by Exemption 4, what corporate information may be properly withheld? The information must be kept confidential (see Note 4, p. 788) and must be "commercial." Is a business's name "commercial" information? When Citizens for Responsibility and Ethics in Washington sued DOJ to obtain the identities of lethal injection drug manufacturers for federal executions, Judge Friedrich agreed with DOJ that corporate identities may be commercial based on a "broad understanding" of the word. CREW v. DOJ, 567 F.Supp.3d 204, 211 (D.D.C. 2021). Specifically, the drug manufacturers may suffer a competitive disadvantage from the reputational harm caused by disclosure, a showing sufficient to establish the information's "commercial" nature. CREW has appealed.

(4) ***Privacy for Those Who Comment in Rulemakings?*** Can agencies legitimately refuse to disclose the names and addresses (whether physical or electronic) of those who submit comments in rulemaking proceedings? Commenters certainly might face bad publicity or other forms of harassment for taking unpopular stands on controversial issues. At the same time, knowing who said what in the proceedings is one of the ways in which the public can monitor and evaluate the final outcome. In the ordinary case, the interest in full disclosure will prevail. All. for Wild Rockies v. Dep't of the Interior, 53 F.Supp.2d 32, 36–37 (D.D.C. 1999) (stating that issue was one of first impression and determining that the names of commenters should be released as the NPRM "specified that '[t]he complete file for this proposed rule is available for inspection'" and commenters made submissions voluntarily). The Alliance for Wild Rockies court did note "that in certain circumstances, an individual has a privacy interest in his or her name and address." But for that information not to be disclosed under FOIA, the court required "a showing that a disclosure of the commenters' names and addresses would result in a '*clearly unwarranted* invasion of personal privacy.'" In Alliance for Wild Rockies, no commenter had expressly requested anonymity. Agencies vary in how they inform commenters about disclosure of their personal information.[31] By contrast, according the DOJ FOIA Guide, "the majority of courts to have considered the issue have held that individuals who write to the government expressing personal opinions generally have some expectation of confidentiality, and their identities, but not necessarily the substance of their letters, ordinarily have been withheld."

[31] Christopher S. Yoo, Protected Materials in Public Rulemaking Dockets (Nov. 23, 2020) (report to ACUS), https://www.acus.gov/sites/default/files/documents/Christopher%20Yoo%20FINAL%20REPORT%2011%2023%202020.pdf.

Cf. Doe v. Reed, 561 U.S. 186 (2010) (Washington Public Records Act validly required publication of the names of signatories to state ballot initiatives).

(5) ***Privacy for Agency Decisionmakers and Officials?*** The Department of Justice redacted the names of immigration judges from every document it released under a FOIA request from the American Immigration Lawyers Association for records concerning alleged misconduct by immigration judges, claiming the names were protected by Exemption 6. The D.C. Circuit rejected the agency's "across-the-board approach" and remanded "for a more individualized inquiry into the propriety of redacting judges' names." Am. Immigration Lawyers Ass'n v. Exec. Office for Immigration Review, 830 F.3d 667 (D.C. Cir. 2016). When should agencies be able to redact the identities of agency decisionmakers? Should it matter whether the person is a career employee or political appointee? In SIGAR, Judge Jackson considered whether the government could withhold the names of government officials interviewed even when those officials consented to on-the-record interviews. Do you agree with her assessment?

(6) ***The Privacy Act.*** Another avenue for getting personal information about oneself from the government is to pursue one's rights under the Privacy Act, codified at 5 U.S.C. § 552a. This detailed Act targets government records of routine personal information—about education, medical history, financial transactions, criminal record, and so on. It specifies a mechanism, not only for seeing what the government knows, but also for having those records corrected if they are inaccurate. See 5 U.S.C. § 552a(d). With regard to records it governs, the Privacy Act starts from the opposite point of view of FOIA: it prohibits disclosure except to, or with the permission of, the person to whom the record pertains, or except as authorized under various specified (and restricted) conditions of disclosure. But a cross-reference to FOIA contained in the Privacy Act, 5 U.S.C. § 552a(b)(2), tells agencies that they should release under FOIA that which FOIA requires to be released. Protection of privacy from the eyes of others thus depends on the scope of the FOIA exemptions. FOIA's Exemption 6 is generally met by the redaction of identifying information. For a detailed discussion of the Privacy Act, consult DOJ's treatise on the statute.[32]

The E-Government Act of 2002 also helps protect private information by requiring agencies to conduct and distribute a "Privacy Impact Assessment" before collecting personal data using certain technologies. Opponents of President Trump's Advisory Commission on Election Integrity sued to stop collection of voter data, claiming that it did not comply with the requirements of the statute (and state privacy laws). President Trump disbanded the commission after it was unable to access the data he desired.

[32] https://www.justice.gov/opcl/overview-privacy-act-1974-2020-edition.

## NOTES ON FOIA COSTS, DELAYS, AND LITIGATION

(1) ***Costs of FOIA.*** Although FOIA allows agencies to collect certain fees from requesters (depending on the type of requester),[33] 5 U.S.C. § 552(a)(4)(A), those fees do not come anywhere close to compensating agencies for their FOIA costs. For FY 2021, DOJ reported:

> 5362.55 "full-time FOIA staff" were devoted to the administration of the FOIA throughout the government. The total estimated cost of all FOIA related activities across the government was $561,338,899.40. More than 93% ($522,807,985.80) of the total costs was attributed to the administrative processing of requests and appeals by agencies. Roughly 6.9% ($38,530,913.53) was reported to have been spent on litigation-related activities. By the end of the fiscal year, agencies reported collecting a total of $2,094,233.86 in FOIA fees. The FOIA fees collected in FY 2021 amount[ ] to less than 0.4% of the total costs related to the government's FOIA activities.[34]

To take just one agency, the FDA, of six she studied, Margaret Kwoka reports:

> In FY 2013, FDA reported spending a whopping $33,570,981.00 on FOIA processing, having dedicated eighty-two full-time personnel and additional 52.15 full-time equivalents to the task. As approximately 75 percent of their requests are from commercial interests, approximately $25 million would be attributable to commercial interests. And yet, in 2013, FDA collected a mere $327,075 from commercial requesters in fees, representing only a little more than 1 percent of the approximate cost to FDA of processing commercial FOIA requests. In fact, out of 7596 commercial requests, FDA fulfilled 3261 (or 43 percent) free of any charge.

FOIA, Inc., 65 Duke L.J. 1361, 1417 (2016). Try to track down the FOIA expenses of (and fees received by) the agency you are tracking (if you are doing so) from its annual FOIA report.

Consider that the expense of FOIA administration reduces the funds available to agencies for other purposes. The FOIA Improvement Act of 2016 considerably revised the administrative sections of FOIA (adding numerous reporting requirements that seem intended to permit more intensive congressional oversight), somewhat reduced the possibility of fee collection (by making it ordinarily contingent on compliance with the Act's ostensibly stringent time limitations, see Note 2 below), and added, "No additional funds are authorized to carry out the requirements of this Act or the amendments made by this Act. The requirements of this Act and the

[33] See, e.g., Sack v. U.S. Dept. of Defense, 823 F.3d 687 (D.C. Cir. 2016) (ruling that, contrary to OMB guidelines and Defense Department policy, students qualified as "educational institutions" under FOIA and hence were exempted from search costs).

[34] https://www.justice.gov/oip/page/file/1521211/download.

amendments made by this Act shall be carried out using amounts otherwise authorized or appropriated."

(2) ***Agency Delays in Processing FOIA Requests and Open America Stays.*** FOIA imposes tight deadlines on an agency's processing of a request: 20 days with one 10-day extension ("[i]n unusual circumstances"). After those deadlines pass, an unanswered request is labeled "backlogged." At the end of FY 2021, there were over 153,000 backlogged requests across the federal government (for a sense of scale, nearly 840,000 requests were submitted in that year, though some backlogged requests were submitted in a previous year). The Department of Homeland Security, which received over 440,000 requests in FY 2021, reported over 25,000 backlogged requests at the end of the year; it did not meet the statutory deadlines in many more cases (but did complete them before the year's end).[35] DOJ reported close to 50,000 backlogged requests. According to the agency's FY 2021 report, DHS took, on average, 29 days for simple requests (a few days shorter than the 33-day average for all agencies) and 63 days for complex requests for those requests they granted, at least in part. The government's FY 2021 report did not provide an average for completed complex requests across all agencies (instead providing frequencies in different time spans), though it did note that the "percentage of complex requests processed in fewer than 40 days increased by more than 7% as compared to FY 2020. A total of 80.44% of complex requests were processed in 100 days or less." Expedited requests, which could be simple or complex, took 14 days to process, on average, in FY 2021.[36]

In December 2020, a district court criticized DHS's noncompliance with FOIA's deadlines and prohibited further delay: "Plaintiffs and class members are noncitizens and attorneys who challenge the systemic failure of [DHS] and its component agencies [USCIS and ICE], to respond to their requests for Alien Registration Files ('A-Files') within the statutory deadlines mandated by [FOIA]. Defendants admit that they have not complied with those FOIA deadlines for at least the past eight years. This noncompliance has real life consequences. . . . Compliance with FOIA deadlines is especially important in the immigration context: It provides an essential safeguard to plaintiffs who require a copy of their A-Files to pursue immigration benefits or defend themselves or their clients against removal." Nightingale v. USCIS, 507 F.Supp.3d 1193, 1198 (N.D. Cal. 2020). The government appealed, but the case appears to have settled out of court.

FOIA reporting demonstrates that the deadlines are aspirational, at best. In addition, courts can grant agencies formal extensions from the short statutory deadlines, sometimes for years, to process FOIA requests in litigation if the agency "can show exceptional circumstances exist and that the agency is exercising due diligence in responding to the request" and that there is no "exceptional need or urgency" for processing a request out of turn. 5 U.S.C. § 552(a)(6)(C)(i)–(iii); Open America v. Watergate Special

[35] Many of these requests are from persons desiring information about themselves. See Margaret B. Kwoka, First-Person FOIA, 127 Yale L.J. 2204 (2018).

[36] See https://www.justice.gov/oip/page/file/1521211/download for government-wide figures. For specific agency figures, enter the agency's name in: https://www.foia.gov/data.html.

Prosecution Force, 547 F.2d 605, 616 (D.C. Cir. 1976). These extensions are called Open America stays, after the case.

(3) ***Scope of FOIA Litigation.*** FOIA arguably encourages litigation. The Act allows quick filing of litigation, 5 U.S.C. § 552(a)(6)(C)(i), and wide choice of venue, § 552(a)(4)(B), and it permits the court to award "reasonable attorney fees and other litigation costs" if the requester "has substantially prevailed" in her suit (through "judicial order" but also through a "voluntary or unilateral change in position by the agency"), § 552(a)(4)(E)(i). Yet very few requesters file suit compared to the potential pool. DOJ is required to report annually to Congress on FOIA litigation. § 552(e)(6)(A). DOJ's searches of PACER revealed that 608 FOIA cases were filed in 2021, "a fraction of one percent of the hundreds of thousands of FOIA requests agencies have historically received every year."[37] Its 73-page summary of roughly 900 FOIA case dispositions in 2021 reveals that FOIA litigants are typically individuals or issue-oriented organizations, the government often prevails, and attorney's fees or costs are awarded in under one-tenth of the cases (specifically, in 2021, they were awarded in only 54 cases, including in cases brought by the ACLU, Center for Biological Diversity, Montana Environmental Information Center, Public Citizen, Sierra Club, and other public interest environmental groups).[38] Although commercial entities are the most frequent requesters at many agencies, they typically do not litigate. Rather, they are happy to pick up some intelligence at not much cost. In addition, the length of litigation likely dissuades media requesters from suing; only a small subset of cases resolved in 2021 involved media organizations, like National Public Radio and the New York Times (both organizations also were awarded fees and costs).[39]

The FY 2018 Annual Report of the FOIA Project (an organization dedicated to providing "comprehensive information on federal FOIA decisions at every stage") states that FOIA litigation surged under the Trump Administration and "continued to break record highs in FY 2018." The report detailed: "According to case-by-case court records, 860 FOIA lawsuits were filed in FY 2018 against government agencies. In addition, the backlog of FOIA suits waiting to be decided rose to 1,204 cases, an all-time high. Compared to an average of 402 FOIA suits per year during the Obama Administration, the rate of filing since President Trump assumed office has more than doubled. While suits rose during the latter years of the Obama Administration, the 860 suits filed in FY 2018, represent a 67 percent increase over filings during the last full fiscal year of the Obama Administration." The Project's FY 2019 Annual Report notes that "new filings plateaued this past year. Levels in FY 2019 were about the same as in FY 2018. . . . Yet the total pending caseload has continued to rise." Although new cases dropped in FY 2020 (as compared to FY 2018 and FY 2019), the latest report at the time of this edition went to press indicates: "As

[37] https://www.justice.gov/oip/page/file/1478996/download.

[38] https://www.justice.gov/oip/page/file/1478491/download.

[39] For a fascinating treatment of Bloomberg's litigation to compel disclosure from the Federal Reserve Board about its actions during the 2007–2008 financial collapse, see Alan Feuer, Battle over the Bailout, N.Y. Times (Feb. 12, 2010).

of the end of FY 2020, the number of FOIA cases pending in the federal courts climbed to 1,683. This is more than three and a half times the number of pending cases ten years ago in FY 2010 when the pending court caseload was just 467."

One federal judge recently called his duty to enforce FOIA's mandates but not impose "unreasonable" obligations on agencies a "no-win situation." Bryan Koenig, Can Courts Handle the Increased FOIA Strain Under Trump?, Law360 (Feb. 16, 2018). One study determined that "for every FOIA officer, there are about 188 requests." Jory Heckman, FOIA Study Indicates "Imbalance" Between Agency Staff and Number of Cases, Federal News Network (Mar. 20, 2019).

(4) ***The Difficulties of Litigating over the Disclosure of Documents a Requester Has Not Yet Seen.*** A FOIA requester or her attorney generally cannot see withheld agency documents in the course of litigation without effectively mooting the dispute. And agencies don't want to disclose documents in order to litigate whether they ought to be disclosed. The statute therefore provides for the judge to consider the disputed records in camera. 5 U.S.C. § 552(a)(4)(B). See Note 7 (The Deliberative Process Privilege and Decisions) (p. 763). But this in turn means first, that opposing counsel cannot easily argue the merits, and second, that the judge may have to review hundreds or thousands of pages by herself against a general claim that they fall into one exemption or another. Whether impressed by the first problem or not, judges early on responded to the second one. Litigation under FOIA now usually proceeds on the basis of a "Vaughn index," named after the first case to require it, Vaughn v. Rosen, 484 F.2d 820 (D.C. Cir. 1973) (see discussion at n. 21). In a Vaughn index, the agency itemizes and describes the records it does not want to produce, presents its justifications for not producing them, and cross-references the specific records with the particular justifications. These specified and indexed claims then become the basis for contest in court. How is a Vaughn index used in the SIGAR case?

(5) ***FOIA as Litigation Strategy for Non-FOIA Claims.*** Anticipated and actual litigants in non-FOIA disputes may turn to FOIA to advance their interests in those other matters. For example, imagine you work for a trade association of nonprofit organizations dedicated to consumer rights. As part of your duties, you track and try to influence agency rulemakings on food safety. One of the agencies, the Department of Agriculture, proposes a rule on listeria, a foodborne bacterium that can cause illness and death. The agency then issues a final rule that is much weaker than what it had proposed. You think that industry representatives pressured the agency in ex parte meetings to reach the weaker result (and that the agency met only with those favoring such a result), but you do not have proof. And any challenge to the rulemaking will, if the presumption of regularity holds, be assessed on the record the agency produces. What do you do? You could file a FOIA request seeking the calendars of certain agency officials during that time. See Consumer Federation of America v. Dep't of Agriculture, 455 F.3d 283 (D.C. Cir. 2006).

Because many top officials in the Trump Administration largely kept their calendars off agency websites, FOIA requests were submitted to acquire information about officials' meetings after the fact. See, e.g., Eric Lipton & Lisa Friedman, E.P.A. Chief's Calendar: A Stream of Industry Meetings and Trips Home, N.Y. Times (Oct. 3, 2017). For a report assessing the public availability of top officials' calendars in 19 agencies in the first year of the Biden Administration, see Protect the Public's Trust, Calendar Transparency Report (finding that "the Biden Administration's Cabinet is largely failing to live up to their transparency goals").[40]

FOIA, however, generally provides no special treatment for requesters pursuing other objectives. FOIA exemptions still apply. See Abtew v. DHS, 808 F.3d 895 (D.C. Cir. 2015) (upholding the agency's refusal to disclose to an asylum applicant its Assessment to Refer, "a short document prepared by a Department official after interviewing an asylum applicant," under the deliberative process privilege).

Remedies under FOIA are also limited. FOIA provides enforcement mechanisms; it typically does not, however, require requesters to demonstrate a personal need for the documents they seek. While the information requested could prove useful in litigation with the government, or in connection with a pending rulemaking on which the requester wished to comment, those interests create no claim to additional remedies. In early litigation, Renegotiation Board v. Bannercraft Clothing Co., 415 U.S. 1, 20 (1974), the Supreme Court, in a 5–4 decision, indicated a limited willingness to permit trial courts, using "the inherent powers of an equity court," to reject the argument that FOIA's remedies were exclusive. The Court reasoned that equitable considerations might on occasion permit a trial court to suspend independent administrative proceedings pending the agency's response to a FOIA request that might produce information central to those proceedings, but it refused to order that remedy in the case before it. Congress has since, in § 552(a)(6)(E), provided for "expedited processing" for a requester "who demonstrates a compelling need." But that speedier processing generally does not apply to requesters seeking to convert FOIA into a discovery tool for use in agency proceedings. See, e.g., Kelcee Griffis, Looming Net Neutrality Decision May Overtake FOIA Actions, Law360 (Sept. 22, 2017) (noting that the FCC "may decide whether to roll back the legal underpinnings for its net neutrality rule before it releases documents that journalists and watchdogs claim are game-changers"). Courts are split on whether FOIA allows courts to "order publication" of documents (or only permits courts to order agencies to provide documents to the requester). See Kennecott Utah Copper Corp. v. U.S. Dept. of Interior, 688 F.3d 1191, 1202 (D.C. Cir. 1996) (FOIA does not permit orders for publication); Animal Legal Defense Fund v. U.S. Dept. of Agriculture, 935 F.3d 858, 874–76 (9th Cir. 2019) (court can order publication to agency reading room).

---

[40] https://protectpublicstrust.org/transparency-report/.

## d. The Reverse-FOIA Action

*CHRYSLER CORP. v. BROWN*
*Notes on the Ability of Suppliers to Ensure the Protection of Information They Provide the Government*

### CHRYSLER CORP. v. BROWN

Supreme Court of the United States (1979).
441 U.S. 281.

■ JUSTICE REHNQUIST delivered the opinion of the Court.

[As a major defense contractor, Chrysler Corporation was required by Executive Orders 11246 and 11375 to observe nondiscriminatory hiring practices and to furnish reports and other information about its programs to the Defense Logistics Agency, an agency within the Defense Department, pursuant to regulations of the Department of Labor's Office of Federal Contract Compliance Programs. Some of the information provided was commercially sensitive data—for example, "manning tables," listing job titles and the number of people performing each job—which might be useful to a competitor. OFCCP regulations stated that even though such information might be exempt from mandatory disclosure under FOIA, "records obtained or generated pursuant to Executive Order 11246 (as amended) . . . shall be made available for inspection and copying . . . if it is determined that the requested inspection or copying furthers the public interest and does not impede any of the functions of the OFCC[P] or the Compliance Agencies except in the case of records disclosure of which is prohibited by law." Persons interested in monitoring Chrysler's employment practices filed FOIA requests for reports concerning two of its facilities. Pursuant to its regulations, DLA notified Chrysler of the requests and, later, of its intention to honor them. Chrysler then sought to enjoin the release of information that it asserted lay within the protection of Exemption 4. In district court it succeeded. The Third Circuit reversed, broadly sustaining the government's contentions: that FOIA created no right to withholding of information within its exemptions; that other confidentiality statutes created no private right of action; that the OFCCP regulations created any necessary authority to disclose, and were themselves within the Department of Labor's authority to adopt; and that, given authority to disclose, judicial review of the exercise of that authority would be limited to assuring procedural regularity and checking abuses of discretion. Since the administrative record was insufficient to perform such review, the Third Circuit directed the district court to remand the case to the agency for supplementation. At this point, the Supreme Court granted certiorari.] . . .

In contending that the FOIA bars disclosure of the requested equal employment opportunity information, Chrysler relies . . . specifically on Exemption 4. . . . Chrysler contends that the nine exemptions in general, and Exemption 4 in particular, reflect a sensitivity to the privacy interests of private individuals and nongovernmental entities. That contention may be conceded without inexorably requiring the conclusion that the exemptions impose affirmative duties on an agency to withhold information sought. In fact, that conclusion is not supported by the language, logic or history of the Act. . . . By its terms, subsection (b) [Ed. the list of exemptions] demarcates the agency's obligation to disclose; it does not foreclose disclosure.

That the FOIA is exclusively a disclosure statute is, perhaps, demonstrated most convincingly by examining its provision for judicial relief. Subsection (a)(4)(B) gives federal district courts "jurisdiction to enjoin the agency from withholding agency records and to order the production of any agency records improperly withheld from the complainant." 5 U.S.C. § 552(a)(4)(B). That provision does not give the authority to bar disclosure, and thus fortifies our belief that Chrysler, and courts which have shared its view, have incorrectly interpreted the exemption provisions of the FOIA. The Act is an attempt to meet the demand for open government while preserving workable confidentiality in governmental decision-making. Congress appreciated that with the expanding sphere of governmental regulation and enterprise, much of the information within Government files has been submitted by private entities seeking Government contracts or responding to unconditional reporting obligations imposed by law. There was sentiment that Government agencies should have the latitude, in certain circumstances, to afford the confidentiality desired by these submitters. But the congressional concern was with the *agency's* need or preference for confidentiality; the FOIA by itself protects the submitters' interest in confidentiality only to the extent that this interest is endorsed by the agency collecting the information.

Enlarged access to governmental information undoubtedly cuts against the privacy concerns of nongovernmental entities, and as a matter of policy some balancing and accommodation may well be desirable. We simply hold here that Congress did not design the FOIA exemptions to be mandatory bars to disclosure.[14] . . .

Chrysler contends, however, that even if its suit for injunctive relief cannot be based on the FOIA, such an action can be premised on the Trade Secrets Act, 18 U.S.C. § 1905. The Act provides:

---

[14] It is informative in this regard to compare the FOIA with the Privacy Act of 1974, 5 U.S.C. § 552a. In the latter Act Congress explicitly requires agencies to withhold records about an individual from most third parties unless the subject gives his permission. Even more telling is 49 U.S.C. § 1357, a section which authorizes the Administrator of the FAA to take antihijacking measures, including research and development into protection devices.

"Notwithstanding [FOIA], the Administrator shall prescribe such regulations as he may deem necessary to prohibit disclosure of any information obtained or developed in the conduct of research and development activities under this subsection if, in the opinion of the Administrator, the disclosure of such information. . . .

"(B) would reveal trade secrets or privileged or confidential commercial or financial information obtained from any person . . ." § 1357(d)(2)(B).

> "Whoever, being an officer or employee of the United States or of any department or agency thereof, publishes, divulges, discloses, or makes known in any manner or to any extent not authorized by law any information coming to him in the course of his employment or official duties or by reason of any examination or investigation made by, or return, report or record made to or filed with, such department or agency or officer or employee thereof, which information concerns or relates to the trade secrets, processes, operations, style of work, or apparatus, or to the identity, confidential statistical data, amount or source of any income, profits, losses, or expenditures of any person, firm, partnership, corporation, or association; or permits any income return or copy thereof or any book containing any abstract or particulars thereof to be seen or examined by any person except as provided by law; shall be fined not more than $1,000 or imprisoned not more than one year, or both; and shall be removed from office or employment."

There are necessarily two parts to Chrysler's argument: that § 1905 is applicable to the type of disclosure threatened in this case, and that it affords Chrysler a private right of action to obtain injunctive relief.

A

The Court of Appeals held that § 1905 was not applicable to the agency disclosure at issue here because such disclosure was "authorized by law" within the meaning of the Act. The court found the source of that authorization to be the OFCCP regulations that DLA relied on in deciding to disclose information on the . . . plants. Chrysler contends here that these agency regulations are not "law" within the meaning of § 1905.

It has been established in a variety of contexts that properly promulgated substantive regulations have the "force and effect of law." . . . It would . . . take a clear showing of contrary legislative intent before the phrase "authorized by law" in § 1905 could be held to have a narrower ambit than the traditional understanding. [After examining the relevant legislative history and finding no such clear showing, the Court rejected a government argument that § 1905 was only an anti-leak statute applying to surreptitious, unofficial acts, and was therefore irrelevant to "official" agency actions, taken within channels. That reading, the Court thought, would "require an expansive and unprecedented holding that any agency action directed or approved by an agency head is 'authorized by law' "; such a holding would be contrary to repeated assurances to Congress that § 1905 reached formal agency action as well as employee skullduggery. The Court then resumed discussion of whether the OFCCP regulations provided the required authorization.]

In order for a regulation to have the "force and effect of law," it must have certain substantive characteristics and be the product of certain procedural requisites. . . . We [have] described a substantive rule—or a "legislative-type rule,"—as one "affecting individual rights and obligations." This characteristic is an important touchstone for distinguishing those rules that may be "binding" or have the "force of law."

Likewise the promulgation of these regulations must conform with any procedural requirements imposed by Congress. . . . The pertinent procedural limitations in this case are those found in the APA.

The regulations relied on by the Government in this case as providing "authoriz[ation] by law" within the meaning of § 1905 certainly affect individual rights and obligations; they govern the public's right to information in records obtained under Executive Order 11246 and the confidentiality rights of those who submit information to OFCCP and its compliance agencies. It is a much closer question, however, whether they are the product of a congressional grant of legislative authority.

[The Court concluded that Congress had not authorized the OFCCP to adopt rules having the force and effect of law on information disclosure. (That holding, Justice Marshall emphasized in a concurrence, did not call into question the validity of OFCCP regulations as a whole.) The Court found also that the Secretary of Labor had not used notice and comment rulemaking procedures in adopting the regulations—thus confirming their character as merely interpretive rules, "not the product of procedures which Congress prescribed as necessary prerequisites to giving a regulation the binding effect of law. An interpretative regulation or general statement of agency policy cannot be the 'authoriz[ation] by law' required by § 1905."]

B

[The Court rejected Chrysler's contention that § 1905 afforded a private right of action to enjoin disclosure in violation of the statute.] [T]his Court has rarely implied a private right of action under a criminal statute and where it has done so "there was at least a statutory basis for inferring that a civil cause of action of some sort lay in favor of someone." Nothing in § 1905 prompts such an inference. . . . Most importantly, a private right of action under § 1905 is not "necessary to make effective the congressional purpose," J.I. Case Co. v. Borak, 377 U.S. 426, 433 (1964), for we find that review of DLA's decision to disclose Chrysler's employment data is available under the APA.

. . . Section 10(a) of the APA provides that "[a] person suffering legal wrong because of agency action, or adversely affected or aggrieved by agency action . . . , is entitled to judicial review thereof." 5 U.S.C. § 702. [The Court held that DLA's decision to disclose was reviewable because] § 1905 and any "authoriz[ation] by law" contemplated by that section place substantive limits on agency action. Therefore, we conclude that DLA's decision . . . is reviewable agency action and Chrysler is a person "adversely affected or aggrieved" within the meaning of § 10(a).

Both Chrysler and the Government agree that there is APA review of DLA's decision. They disagree on the proper scope of review. Chrysler argues that there should be de novo review, while the Government contends that such review is only available in extraordinary cases and this is not such a case.

The pertinent provisions of § 10(e) of the APA, 5 U.S.C. § 706 (1976), provide that a reviewing court shall

> "(2) hold unlawful and set aside agency action, findings, and conclusions found to be—
>
> > "(A) arbitrary, capricious, an abuse of discretion, or otherwise not in accordance with law; . . .
> >
> > "(F) unwarranted by the facts to the extent that the facts are subject to trial de novo by the reviewing court."

For the reasons previously stated, we believe any disclosure that violates § 1905 is "not in accordance with law" within the meaning of 5 U.S.C. § 706(2)(A). De novo review by the District Court is ordinarily not necessary to decide whether a contemplated disclosure runs afoul of § 1905. The District Court in this case concluded that disclosure of some of Chrysler's documents was barred by § 1905, but the Court of Appeals did not reach the issue. We shall therefore vacate the Court of Appeals' judgment and remand for further proceedings consistent with this opinion in order that the Court of Appeals may consider whether the contemplated disclosures would violate the prohibition of § 1905.[49] Since the decision regarding this substantive issue—the scope of § 1905—will necessarily have some effect on the proper form of judicial review pursuant to § 706(2), we think it unnecessary, and therefore unwise, at the present stage of this case for us to express any additional views on that issue.

Vacated and remanded.

[Justice Marshall's concurrence is omitted.]

## NOTES ON THE ABILITY OF SUPPLIERS TO ENSURE THE PROTECTION OF INFORMATION THEY PROVIDE THE GOVERNMENT

(1) ***Information Suppliers as Parties.*** Courts permit the suppliers of information to the government, as well as the government body holding that information, to speak to the Exemption 4 claims, even though FOIA, as such, creates no such right. FCC v. AT&T (noted above on p. 776), is an example. Note that cases like these—Chrysler, AT&T—often seem to involve FOIA claimants who are at the heart of the Act's rationale—persons interested in what Chrysler's reports to the Defense Department might show about its compliance with nondiscrimination regulations applicable to major defense contractors and an NGO seeking to assess FCC enforcement actions. The

[49] Since the Court of Appeals assumed for purposes of argument that the material in question was within an exemption to the FOIA, that court found it unnecessary expressly to decide that issue and it is open on remand. We, of course, do not here attempt to determine the relative ambits of Exemption 4 and § 1905, or to determine whether § 1905 is an exempting statute within the terms of the amended Exemption 3, 5 U.S.C. § 552(b)(3). Although there is a theoretical possibility that material might be outside Exemption 4 yet within the substantive provisions of § 1905, and that therefore the FOIA might provide the necessary "authoriz[ation] by law" for purposes of § 1905, that possibility is at most of limited practical significance in view of the similarity of language between Exemption 4 and the substantive provisions of § 1905.

motivation for reverse-FOIA actions, as these are called, may well be the avoidance of corporate "embarrassment" rather than the protection of corporate secrets. In any event, Chrysler opened the door to such litigation.

(2) ***Standards of Review.*** The Chrysler case can make one's head spin with the number of sources of law it discusses and its variety of standards of judicial review. In comparison with earlier cases in this Chapter, however, a fundamental contrast seems clear: On the one hand, a refusal to disclose information to a requester is to be reviewed by a court according to the procedures set out in FOIA itself—that is, *de novo* review with the agency bearing the burden of justifying nondisclosure.[41] On the other hand, a complaint by a private supplier of information that the agency is ready to disclose something it should hold secret, is to be reviewed by a court according to the standards set forth for ordinary judicial review in the APA. In the ordinary case, the court assesses whether the agency's decision to disclose information is *arbitrary or capricious*. This process, as described more fully in the materials on judicial review in Chapter VIII, normally is based on the record before the agency (rather than on material assembled through litigation) and begins with a presumption in favor of the correctness of the agency's decision.

(3) ***Establishing a Framework for Reverse-FOIA Actions.*** President Reagan's Executive Order 12600, still in effect, facilitates reverse-FOIA actions by requiring "Executive" agencies to establish procedures permitting submitters to mark documents "confidential," and provides for notification and an opportunity to explain why the agency should deny a request for them, should their disclosure be sought. 52 Fed. Reg. 23781 (June 25, 1987). Commercially valuable information might not otherwise be identified for Exemption 4 consideration by the busy agency functionary handling a request for information. She may not recognize its implications, having little sense of the supplier's business, or of the sophisticated analyses that might be made of what seem to be harmless data. The Executive Order creates a procedure for notifying submitters of the request and an opportunity to justify the claim for confidentiality, and Chrysler then opens the courthouse door for review. Although the Executive Order does not speak to independent regulatory commissions, they often have their own policies on notifying suppliers of information.[42]

(4) ***Combining Chrysler and Argus Leader.*** The Court's 2019 decision in Argus Leader increased the protection of information provided to the government. See Note 3 (Supreme Court's Rejection of National Parks) (p. 770). How should that decision influence analysis under Chrysler in a

---

[41] In a recent case, the Center for Investigative Reporting requested demographic information reports for federal contractors similar to the information at issue in Chrysler. See Ctr. for Investigative Reporting v. U.S. Dep't of Lab., 424 F.Supp.3d 771 (N.D. Cal. 2019). Unlike Chrysler, this was a standard FOIA case, with the Department of Labor opposing disclosure. Under the corresponding de novo standard of review, the requester-plaintiffs succeeded as the court determined the information was not commercial. But since the ruling, DOL has not turned over the information and given all federal contractors implicated—about 15,000—a chance to object to disclosure. See J. Edward Moreno, Labor Department Reluctant to Reveal Contractor Diversity Data, Bloomberg Law (Oct. 20, 2022).

[42] OFCCP describes its current process here: https://www.dol.gov/agencies/ofccp/faqs/foia.

reverse-FOIA case? Since Argus Leader, as of November 2022, no court seems to have issued an opinion in a reverse-FOIA case involving proposed disclosure under Exemption 4. (There are, however, cases brought by requesters challenging the lack of disclosure).

DOJ has provided the following advice to agencies on applying Argus Leader:

"First Condition—Submitter's Treatment of the Information

"First, in order to qualify as 'confidential,' the party imparting the information (i.e., the submitter) should customarily treat the information as private. . . . Often an agency can determine whether this condition is met based on its own knowledge of the information, the submitter's practices, and/or from the records themselves. Agencies may also seek additional information from the submitter about its practices. . . .

"Second Condition—Assurance of Confidentiality by Government . . .

"Such an assurance of confidentiality can be either explicit or implicit. Neither the Court's decision in Argus Leader nor any of the authority it cited suggests a requirement of an express (as opposed to implied) assurance of confidentiality by the government. . . .

"An express assurance of confidentiality can be established in several ways. It can be found in direct communications with the submitter, as well as through general notices on agency websites or, as in Argus Leader, through regulations indicating that information will not be publicly disclosed. Where an express assurance of confidential treatment exists, assuming that the submitter also satisfies the first condition, the standards for confidentiality under Exemption 4 are met.

"Of course, such notices or communications could also explicitly notify submitters of the agency's intention to publicly disseminate the information. In those situations, the information, when objectively viewed in context, would be deemed to have lost its 'confidential' character under Exemption 4 upon its submission to the government, given that the submitter was on notice that it would be disclosed. . . .

"In determining whether there was an implied assurance of confidentiality, agencies can be guided by the analytical framework provided in [DOJ v.] Landano [508 U.S. 165 (1993)]. . . . [I]n Landano, the Court provided an objective test to assess whether 'an implied assurance of confidentiality can be inferred,' based on 'generic circumstances' surrounding the communication between the informant and the government that would 'characteristically support an inference of confidentiality.' As Landano explained for criminal investigation contexts, factors such as the 'nature of the informant's ongoing relationships with the [government]' and 'the nature of the crime and the source's relation to it' may help determine whether there was an implied promise of confidentiality under Exemption 7(D).

"Similarly, in the context of Exemption 4, agencies can look to the context in which the information was provided to the government to determine if there was an implied assurance of confidentiality. Factors to consider include the government's treatment of similar information and its broader treatment of information related to the program or initiative to which the information relates. For example, an agency's long history of protecting certain commercial or financial information can serve as an implied assurance to submitters that the agency will continue treating their records in the same manner.

"Conversely, such factors may in some contexts result in the opposite conclusion that the submitter could not have had a reasonable expectation of confidentiality. For example, absent an express assurance by the agency, a submitter would not normally have a reasonable expectation of confidentiality for records the agency has historically disclosed. In addition, what the government pays a private entity to supply goods or services to the government reflects the government's own actions and will often undermine a submitter's claim to reasonably expect such information to be kept confidential.

"Submitter-Notice Process . . .

"In the wake of Argus Leader, agencies should now use . . . predisclosure notification procedures when necessary to seek the submitter's views on whether the two conditions that agencies should consider in determining whether information is 'confidential' for purposes of Exemption 4 of the FOIA, as outlined in this guidance, are met."

What disclosure would qualify as arbitrary and capricious disclosure in a reverse-FOIA case? How, if at all, would you change the procedure (agency and court) for determining if private information submitted to an agency should be released to a FOIA requester?

(5) ***A Reverse-FOIA Complaint.*** In October 2016, Students for Fair Admissions, an organization opposed to the use of race in college admissions, sued the Department of Education to compel under FOIA the disclosure of "[a]ll documents concerning the investigation of Princeton University['s]" admission practices. The agency had concluded in 2015, after years of investigation, that there was not sufficient evidence that Princeton had unlawfully treated Asian and Asian American students who had applied for admission. In March 2017, Princeton University brought a reverse-FOIA action after the Department gave notice that it planned to release the University's submissions to the agency. The agency denied that the information was protected by Exemption 4. From the University's complaint:

> 1. The University brings this "reverse FOIA" action pursuant to the Administrative Procedure Act, 5 U.S.C. §§ 701–706, the Freedom of Information Act ("FOIA"), 5 U.S.C. § 552, and the Trade Secrets Act, 18 U.S.C. § 1905, to prevent the disclosure of certain confidential and commercially sensitive documents and information relating to the University's undergraduate admissions program submitted to [the Department of Education's Office of Civil Rights (OCR)] in the course of an OCR compliance review. These materials fall generally into two categories: (1) documents and information about undergraduate applicants to the University ("Applicant Documents and Information"), and (2) documents and

> information about the University's proprietary admissions processes ("Admissions Documents and Information"). . . .
>
> 4. The University has at all times maintained that the Applicant Documents and Information and Admissions Documents and Information are exempt from disclosure pursuant to FOIA Exemption 4, which exempts from disclosure "trade secrets and commercial or financial information obtained from a person and privileged or confidential." 5 U.S.C. § 552(b)(4). To that end, each of the documents the University seeks to withhold from release was designated and marked, "Confidential, Private, Personal and Proprietary—Exempt from Mandatory Disclosure Under FOIA" at the time it was produced to OCR. At no time during the compliance review did OCR object to or question these designations. . . .
>
> 27. Taken separately and together, the Applicant Documents and Information and Admissions Documents and Information reveal commercially sensitive information that is kept highly confidential by the University, and would cause substantial competitive harm to the University if disclosed. Specifically, disclosure of these materials would:
>
> a. Permit applicants and their advisers who become aware of these materials to tailor applications to what they would perceive to be the admissions priorities and preferences of the University. . . . This, in turn, would substantially impair the University's ability to identify, recruit, admit, and enroll the strongest candidates each year, to its competitive disadvantage as compared with other colleges and universities.
>
> b. Permit other colleges and universities with which the University competes to admit and enroll students to utilize the University's confidential admissions information and processes. . . .

Trustees of Princeton University v. Dep't of Educ., No. 1:17-cv-00485 (D.D.C. Mar. 17, 2017).

In December 2017, the parties jointly dismissed both lawsuits. In litigation also brought by Students for Fair Admission against Harvard University, the judge ordered the parties to work together on what Harvard admissions documents should be publicly available. Those documents were released in June 2018, generating much discussion of Harvard's admissions practices. The federal government had not been investigating Harvard, so FOIA did not play a role in the document disclosure. The Supreme Court agreed to hear the case against Harvard University in the 2022 term (No. 20-1119). For more on FOIA requests and university admissions practices, see Josh Gerstein (one of the reporters who disclosed the leaked draft of the Dobbs opinion), What is Harvard Trying to Hide?, POLITICO (Oct. 21, 2018).

# SECTION 4. OTHER TRANSPARENCY STATUTES: SUNSHINE ACT, FEDERAL ADVISORY COMMITTEE ACT



## Letter to Congress from Federal Communications Commission

**Federal Communications Commission**[1]

February 2, 2005

The Honorable Ted Stevens, Chairman
Committee on Commerce, Science and Transportation
United States Senate
508 Dirksen Senate Office Building
Washington, D.C. 20510

Dear Chairman Stevens:

As Congress contemplates revision of the nation's telecommunications laws, we write regarding a proposal that enjoys bipartisan support among the Commissioners of the Federal Communications Commission: reform of the open meeting requirement of the Government in Sunshine Act ("Sunshine Act" or "Act"). We fully support the Act's goal of informing the public about the decision making processes of multi-member agencies. However, we believe amendments to the Act could enhance the efficiency and soundness of the process. At the same time, safeguards could be devised that would ensure that the goal of open government is not jeopardized.

The open-meeting provision of the Sunshine Act currently requires every portion of every meeting not falling within an exception to be open to public observation when at least a quorum of Commissioners jointly conducts or disposes of official agency business.[1] Both Republican and Democratic Commissioners are on record in recent testimony before Congress that the Commission's decisional processes are impaired by this requirement, and their conclusions about the detrimental effects of the open meeting requirement are echoed by a substantial body of scholarship.[2]

---

[1] This document is available at https://apps.fcc.gov/edocs_public/attachmatch/DOC-256655A1.pdf.

[1] See 5 U.S.C. § 552b; 47 C.F.R. §§ 0.601–0.607.

[2] See, e.g., Randolph May, Reforming the Sunshine Act, 49 Admin. L. Rev. 415 (1997) ("there appears to be a fairly widespread consensus that the Sunshine Act is not achieving its principal—and obviously salutary—goal of enhancing public knowledge and understanding of agency decisionmaking"); James H. Cawley, Sunshine Law Overexposure and the Demise of Independent Agency Collegiality, 1 Widener J. Pub. L. 43 (1992). These conclusions were also

We note initially that the Act is not necessary to the goal of ensuring that federal agencies explain their actions to the public. Judicial review statutes like the Administrative Procedure Act ("APA") impose "a general 'procedural' requirement of sorts by mandating that an agency take whatever steps it needs to provide an explanation . . . [of its] rationale at the time of decision." Pension Benefit Guar. Corp. v. LTV Corp., 496 U.S. 633, 654 (1990) [p. 585].

Nor has the open-meeting requirement generally achieved its goal of having Commissioners help shape each other's views in the course of public deliberations. In fact, this requirement is a barrier to the substantive exchange of ideas among Commissioners, hampering our abilities to obtain the benefit of each other's views, input, or comments, and hampering efforts to maximize consensus on the complex issues before us. Due to the prohibition on private collective deliberations, we rely on written communications, staff, or one-on-one meetings with each other. These indirect methods of communicating clearly do not foster frank, open discussion, and they are less efficient than in-person interchange among three or more Commissioners would be. Finally, and perhaps most significantly, Commission decisions are in some cases less well informed and well explained than they would be if we each had the benefit of the others' expertise and perspective.[3]

For these reasons, we urge amending the open meeting provision of the Sunshine Act to permit closed deliberations among Commissioners in appropriate circumstances. Scholars and other agency heads have suggested various modification models,[4] some of which include safeguards that may be desirable. For example, some models include a requirement that brief summaries of topics discussed at meetings between all decision makers be recorded and placed in relevant administrative records.

In closing, we want to stress that we are in complete agreement with the Sunshine Act's goal of providing the public with reliable information about the basis for Commission decisions. We support amendment of the Act because we have learned from 28 years experience that we can satisfy this goal through other means that better serve the public interest by promoting bi-partisan deliberation and more efficient decision-making.

---

echoed by the Administrative Conference of the United States ("ACUS")—a body of experts established to advise Congress on administrative law. See David M. Welborn et al., Implementation and Effects of the Federal Government in the Sunshine Act, in Administrative Conference of the United States: Recommendation and Reports (1984). The ACUS ceased operations in 1995 because Congress eliminated funding, but many of its proposals have been implemented, and scholars such as those listed here still cite its conclusions about the Sunshine Act. [Ed. ACUS restarted operations in 2010.]

[3] Scholars and other agencies agree. See, e.g., May, supra note 2; Federal Trade Commission Prepared Statement Before the Special Committee to Review the Government In the Sunshine Act, Administrative Conference of the United States, 1995 WL 540529 (1995).

[4] See, e.g., id.; Cawley, supra note 2.

We look forward to working with the Committee Chairman, Ranking, and Members of the Committee to resolve this issue.

Sincerely,

Michael K. Powell
Chairman

Michael J. Copps
Commissioner

## NOTES ON THE SUNSHINE ACT AND FEDERAL ADVISORY COMMITTEE ACT

(1) ***Sunshine Act-FOIA Contrast.*** The Government in the Sunshine Act (Sunshine Act) (reprinted at p. 1620 in the Appendix) was enacted in 1976 to address concerns about government accountability and is codified primarily at 5 U.S.C. § 552b. It was modeled on open meetings statutes already universal in the states (where the multi-member body limitation is not always present). Its legislative history suggests that Congress thought FOIA did not provide enough information to enable the public to "understand the reasons an agency has acted in a certain way, or even what exactly it has decided to do," because "[f]ormal statements in support of agency action are frequently too brief, or too general, to fully explain [a] Commission's reasoning, of the compromises that were made. By requiring important decisions to be made openly, [the new law] will create better public understanding of agency decisions." S. Rep. No. 94–354, at 5. Would you expect members of the public to attend agency public meetings? Journalists for the New York Times or the Wall Street Journal? Interested industry representatives? Reporters for trade press publications that provide their readers with "the inside scoop" on agency doings? Do online meetings, which became more common due to the COVID-19 pandemic, make attendance easier?

The Act requires all multi-member agencies (but not single-administrator agencies like the EPA, FDA, FAA, or OSHA)[2] to give a week's public notice of their meetings and to make most portions of their meetings open to public observation. A "meeting" occurs whenever a quorum of the agency deliberates in a way that "determine[s] or result[s] in the joint conduct or disposition of official agency business," excluding decisions taken in determining issues (scheduling, closure) arising under the Act itself. 5 U.S.C. § 552b(a)(2). With multiple agency vacancies, which we see particularly at the beginning or end of an administration, or with three-member agencies, this can be mean that any conversation between two members may qualify as a meeting. A majority of the body has the right to close a meeting to the extent it meets one of the Act's ten exemptions, which generally mirror FOIA's exemptions. Of course, even closed meetings may be transcribed, and if the transcript cannot be had under this Act or FOIA,

[2] For a list of agencies covered by the Act, see Reeve T. Bull, The Government in the Sunshine Act in the 21st Century app. D (Mar. 10, 2014) (report to ACUS), https://www.acus.gov/report/final-sunshine-act-report.

perhaps it can be secured by an inquiring member of Congress. See San Luis Obispo Mothers for Peace v. NRC, 751 F.2d 1287 (D.C. Cir. 1984). Moreover, while discussions of most agency adjudicatory matters may be closed, the Sunshine Act contains no exemption corresponding to FOIA's Exemption 5, the exemption for predecisional matters that figures so prominently in the SIGAR case (p. 748). Thus, the Act requires discussions of rulemakings and other nonadjudicatory proposed matters to be done with advance notice and in public view, though it does permit nonpublic staff-level meetings. Judicial enforcement proceedings require the agency to prove the correctness of closure decisions, but the remedies provided all go to enforcing openness; the statute does not provide for invalidation of an agency decision improperly taken at a closed meeting.

For a summary of the Act, its application in a world of reply-all emails, electronic chat rooms, and webcasting, and a discussion of agency best practices, see Reeve T. Bull, The Government in the Sunshine Act in the 21st Century (Mar. 10, 2014) (report to ACUS).[3]

(2) ***Some Sunshine Act Problems.*** Do you find the FCC's 2005 petition to Congress surprising? What would you expect the consequences of the proposed legislation to be for the way agency business is conducted? Should only the FCC benefit? Why did it not make its arguments for change generally, rather than as a matter of special pleading? Pretend you are the General Counsel of the agency discussed in the following questions.

(a) How would you advise the Commissioners to treat their forthcoming trip to Europe, where they will be discussing possible coordinating measures with counterpart agencies, and thus possibly reaching preliminary conclusions about courses for the Commission to follow? FCC v. ITT World Communications, 466 U.S. 463 (1984).

The Commissioners also meet occasionally with representatives of regulated bodies or public interest advocates—a practice that, as you may have read in connection with the Home Box Office case in Chapter IV (p. 494), led to severe criticism when many such meetings occurred in the postcomment period of a rulemaking. Would you advise them that such meetings must now be conducted openly, after a week's prior public notice, or may the meetings continue so long as they do not "determine or result in the joint conduct or disposition of official agency business"?

(b) The Nuclear Regulatory Commission must decide on the budget request it will be submitting to OMB and to Congress. Some bureaus will win and others will lose as priorities are set. Must this meeting be open? Common Cause v. NRC, 674 F.2d 921 (D.C. Cir. 1982); see also Note 7 (Secret Law and the Budget) (p. 713).

(c) The SEC's Division of Trading and Markets has been given the responsibility for drafting the final text of a recently proposed rule that generated hundreds of extensive comments from consumer groups, brokerage houses, and others. The comments raise two or three issues in which the comments are in equipoise and Commission resolution or guidance

---

[3] Id.

is required. Public discussion of the matter, the Division's Administrator (reasonably) fears, could have significant market effects. Which course would you advise her to follow:

(i) Put the matter on the Commission's calendar for its next public meeting, with a view to having these matters decided.

(ii) Have a closed briefing session for the Commissioners (or their assistants), at which no decisions will be made, and then go office to office to learn how each Commissioner would decide the matters.

(iii) Submit option papers to the Commissioners, with the suggestion that they exchange written views with each other and then each report their views to her orally or in writing.

(iv) Focus her attention on the Commission Chairperson, whose "meetings with the staff have a powerful tendency to shape the staff's responses and recommendations, which might well be different if it were possible for the other members to be present."[4]

(3) ***The Impact of the Sunshine Act.*** According to DAVID M. WELBORN ET AL., IMPLEMENTATION AND EFFECTS OF THE FEDERAL GOVERNMENT IN THE SUNSHINE ACT (1984), in the study that the FCC letter cites, members tended to behave somewhat differently in open than in closed meetings. They prepared more thoroughly for the open meetings but used them more often to appeal to special interests; they refrained from asking important questions and engaged less frequently in candid exchange, sharp debate, or efforts at reconciling conflicts. The authors believed there was "a shift in patterns of decision-making behavior, at least in some agencies, away from collegial processes toward segmented, individualized processes in which, in the words of one commissioner, 'members are isolated from one another.' " Of 18 agencies surveyed, only officials at the Federal Election Commission thought "that the act had strengthened the collegium." The importance of meetings declined apparently "from an aversion to public discussion of certain topics." In addition, when open meetings with collegial interactions did occur, "meetings often ha[d] no bearing on results." Over 83 percent of survey respondents from agencies with full-time leaders believed that "members now typically made up their minds on matters dealt with in open meetings *prior* to collective discussions." Further "the focus of decision-making activity has shifted toward the offices of individual members and to the staff level and involves three key sets of interactions. The first is between staff at the operating level who are handling a particular matter and the offices of the chairman and other members. The second is between members one-on-one, except presumably in three member agencies. The third is among staff assistants to members acting as surrogates for their principals. . . . All have distinct limitations as substitutes for collegial discussions."

More recent surveys were conducted under the direction of ACUS. Responses from 56 Board Members or Commissioners ("members") at 24 agencies and General Counsels from 40 agencies supported four conclusions:

---

[4] A Little Shade, Please—The Government-in-the-Sunshine Act Isn't Working, Wash. Post (July 25, 1983) (quoting then-SEC Commissioner Bevis Longstreth).

"(1) agency members place comparatively little emphasis on meetings of board members as a source of information about the views and positions of fellow members, whether those meetings are conducted openly or are closed pursuant to one of the Sunshine Act exceptions; (2) agency members find somewhat greater value in interactions that occur outside of such meetings, including informal discussions amongst board or commission members and conferences between such members and staff; (3) agencies have more or less reconciled themselves to the existence of the Sunshine Act and do not generally recommend repealing or fundamentally altering it; and (4) notwithstanding the lack of any overarching objections to the Act, agencies do have a number of specific complaints and suggestions for improving the Act." REEVE T. BULL, THE GOVERNMENT IN THE SUNSHINE ACT IN THE 21ST CENTURY, supra, at 17. ACUS also found that the "surveys produced little evidence that commission or board members avoided discussion of certain issues in open meetings or were otherwise chilled in their interactions as a result of the Act." Id. at 20. Notably, about 40 percent of surveyed agencies disclosed that they used notational voting, which is not covered by the Act, to dispose of more than 75 percent of matters. Id. at 19. (Notational voting procedures are "when [agency] members receive written materials, review the same, and then provide their votes in writing." Id. at 9–10.) For recommendations to agencies, see ACUS, Recommendation 2014–2, Government in the Sunshine Act, 79 Fed. Reg. 35990 (June 25, 2014). Do these survey results change your reaction to the FCC letter above?

(4) ***A Proposed Legislative Response.*** S. 760, a legislative proposal before the 114th Congress in 2015 that was not enacted, would have provided to the FCC:

> (2) Authority to hold meetings.—
>
> Notwithstanding section 552b of title 5, United States Code, a bipartisan majority of Commissioners may hold a meeting that is closed to the public to discuss official business if—
>
> > (A) a vote or any other agency action is not taken at the meeting;
> >
> > (B) each person present at the meeting is a Commissioner, an employee of the Commission, a member of a joint board or conference established under [particular provisions], or a person on the staff of such a joint board or conference or of a member of such a joint board or conference; and
> >
> > (C) an attorney from the Office of General Counsel of the Commission is present at the meeting.

Subsequent provisions would have required public disclosure of the meeting, attendees, and "a summary of the matters discussed at the meeting, except for any matters that the Commission determines may be withheld under section 552b(c) of title 5." Should such legislation be enacted?

(5) ***Sunshine at the State and Local Levels.*** That state governments led the federal government in adopting open-meetings laws may reflect more

immediate practical impacts at the local level.[5] Citizens are more likely to attend municipal meetings or go to the state capitol. The media, an acknowledged major beneficiary of the laws, finds at the federal level that the daily actions of the National Labor Relations Board compete with many significant "national news" items for attention.

The number of reported state cases reflects both the interest in open meetings and the potency of these laws. Illinois quickly revised its open meetings law in response to the COVID-19 pandemic to allow virtual meetings. But when a township allegedly posted incorrect login information to a virtual meeting, the error established a sufficient claim to withstand a motion to dismiss. Station Place Townhouse Condo. Ass'n v. Vill. of Glenview, 2022 WL 3681418, at *3 (Ill. App. 1st., Aug. 25, 2022). Violations in some states are grounds for invalidating action, including, in Ohio, when action is taken in an open meeting but "result[ing] from deliberations in a meeting not open to the public." See State ex rel. Delph v. Barr, 541 N.E.2d 59 (1989). Some states provide for the award of attorney's fees and costs. Even criminal enforcement can occur. In 2004, a Florida county commissioner, formerly a state legislative leader, served 49 days of a 60-day jail sentence for violating an open-meetings law.[6]

(6) ***Federal Advisory Committees.*** Agencies often turn to committees of experts and citizens in the development and/or application of policy. Due to the observation that these committees were becoming numerous and that their membership was sometimes dominated by special interests, Congress enacted in 1972 the FEDERAL ADVISORY COMMITTEE ACT, 5 U.S.C. App., which seeks to control their growth and operation through OMB clearance, public process, and requirements of balance in membership. (OMB's core duties were later transferred to the General Services Administration.) Before an advisory committee can meet or take any action, it must file a detailed charter and give advance notice in the Federal Register; it also must hold all meetings in public, keep detailed minutes, and make its records available to the public—along with any reports, records, or other documents it uses—unless they fall within Sunshine Act or FOIA exemptions. Committees must be "fairly balanced in terms of the points of view represented," § 5(b)(2), and the Act requires precautions to ensure that their advice and recommendations "will not be inappropriately influenced by the appointing authority or by any special interest." § 5(b)(3). An agency's selection of particular members is generally unreviewable by the courts. (Compare Note 8 below.) See generally Steven P. Croley & William F. Funk, The Federal

---

[5] An extensive database of information on the content of, implementation of, and litigation concerning sunshine laws in states, counties, and cities can be found at https://ballotpedia.org/. For open records, see https://ballotpedia.org/State_sunshine_laws. For open meetings, see: https://ballotpedia.org/State_open_meetings_laws. A summary can be found at https://dcogc.org/wp-content/uploads/2019/10/OGC-Table-of-states-laws-on-charter-schools-treatment-under-open-records-and-open-meetings-laws.pdf.

[6] Robert Tanner, On Sunshine Laws, Governments Talk Loudly; Stick Rarely Used, Associated Press (Mar. 11, 2007); see also Daxton R. Stewart, Let the Sunshine In, or Else: An Examination of the "Teeth" of State and Federal Open Meetings and Open Records Laws, 15 Comm. L. & Pol'y 265 (2010) (state-by-state compilation and comparative analysis of penalty and remedy provisions in open-meetings and open-records laws).

Advisory Committee Act and Good Government, 14 Yale J. Reg. 452 (1997) (providing an excellent analysis of the Act).

Drawing on a sample of 2500 committee members (active at some point in FY 1997–2017), Brian D. Feinstein and Daniel J. Hemel determined that "committee members' views tend to track those of the party that controls the White House, not the view of current lawmakers or of the Congress that created the committee" and that "political appointees across administrations utilize advisory committees as counterweights to the career bureaucracy." Specifically, "[a]gency heads in Democratic administrations are more likely to convene policy-focused advisory committees when the civil servants at their agencies lean to the right," and vice-versa. Outside Advisors Inside Agencies, 108 Geo. L.J. 1139 (2020).

"Balance" and "openness" may strike you as unmitigated public goods. Are there countervailing considerations? The first Bush, Clinton, and second Bush presidencies found themselves embroiled in FACA litigation with heavy constitutional overtones—specifically, arguable impingement on the President's actions. Public Citizen challenged presidential consultations by the first Bush's White House with the ABA over judicial appointments. Public Citizen v. U.S. Dep't of Justice, 491 U.S. 440 (1989) (p. 196). A medical society, opposing President Clinton's efforts at health care reform, claimed that the then-First Lady's presence on the working group charged with preparing proposed legislation rendered it an advisory committee. Ass'n of American Physicians & Surgeons v. Hillary Rodham Clinton, 997 F.2d 898 (D.C. Cir. 1993). And Public Citizen attacked closed meetings of the National Energy Policy Development Group, headed by Vice President Cheney. In re Cheney, 406 F.3d 723 (DC. Cir. 2005) (en banc).[7] None of the three decisions found that FACA applied; all noted considerable separation of powers issues if the action fell under the Act. Should these entities with ties to the President and the President's advisors (who are typically shielded from disclosure mandates) be protected from transparency obligations? How do you balance the levels of candor necessary for effective government policy-making and the levels of transparency requisite for presidential accountability?

Even absent such weighty considerations, recall that agency personnel must be in constant contact with those on the outside (e.g., in rulemaking proceedings), many of whom have an interest or bias regarding the issue at hand. Could requiring advisory committees to be "fairly balanced" and operate in the open overly inhibit agency use of sources on which we should encourage agencies to rely? And do interest groups on all sides play too large a role? One study found that the EPA was more likely to choose members for its National Drinking Water Advisory Council who had been endorsed by interest groups than those who were not so backed. Steven J. Balla & John R. Wright, Interest Groups, Advisory Committees, and Congressional Control of the Bureaucracy, 45 Am. J. Pol. Sci. 799 (2001).

---

[7] This decision followed after the Supreme Court instructed the D.C. Circuit to consider the government's separation of powers arguments. Cheney v. U.S. Dist. Court for Dist. of Columbia, 542 U.S. 367 (2004).

In addition, should federally registered lobbyists be excluded from advisory committees (and other boards and commissions of private individuals carrying out federal functions)? Or will that produce the subterfuge of deregistration as a lobbyist to be able to serve? Asserting a purpose to reduce "the undue influence of special interests that for too long has shaped the national agenda and drowned out the voices of ordinary Americans," President Obama issued a directive excluding federally registered lobbyists from being appointed to advisory committees (but not removing already present members) on June 18, 2010.[8] OMB followed up with proposed guidance; after a commenting period, OMB finalized its stance in October 2011, but subsequently modified it in August 2014. Ultimately, it adopted the President's initial position for those serving in an individual capacity but allowed lobbyists serving in particular representative capacities.[9] The guidance remained in effect under the Trump Administration and is still operating (as of November 2022) in the Biden Administration.

(7) ***FACA and Subordinate Groups.*** In Electronic Privacy Information Center v. Drone Advisory Committee, 995 F.3d 993 (D.C. Cir. 2021), the D.C. Circuit held that four subgroups of the Drone Advisory Committee, which provides advice to the Federal Aviation Administration on drone use, were not subject to FACA's disclosure mandates: "Because the subgroups advised and reported to the DAC—not to the FAA—they were not advisory committees." Under this reasoning, two newly established subcommittees to the Department of Agriculture's new Equity Commission (a FACA committee), see Note 9 below, would not be subject to FACA. A bipartisan group of members of the House of Representatives introduced legislation to impose FACA obligations on subcommittees (and on committees created by a government contractor at an agency's request). H.R. 1930 (117th Cong.) (2021).

(8) ***Justiciability and the "Fairly Balanced Mandate."*** In October 2017, then-EPA Administrator Scott Pruitt directed that recipients of EPA grants (or those who stood to directly to benefit from EPA grants) could not serve on the agency's advisory committees (with exceptions for "state, tribal or local government agency recipients"), arguing that such a policy would "strengthen and improve the independence" of the committees. In practice, the order mainly affected many of the academic scientists who had previously served on the committees. The directive also called for more state, tribal, and local government participants and for more geographic diversity.[10] Scientific groups filed several lawsuits, arguing, among other claims, that the directive violated FACA's mandate for balanced memberships. See, e.g., Physicians for Soc. Resp. v. Wheeler, 956 F.3d 634

[8] https://obamawhitehouse.archives.gov/realitycheck/the-press-office/presidential-memorandum-lobbyists-agency-boards-and-commissions.

[9] Office of Management and Budget, "Revised Guidance on Appointment of Lobbyists to Federal Advisory Committees, Boards, and Commissions," 79 Fed. Reg. 47482 (Aug. 13, 2014); Office of Management and Budget, "Final Guidance of Appointment of Lobbyists to Federal Boards and Commissions," 76 Fed. Reg. 61756 (Oct. 5, 2011).

[10] https://www.epa.gov/sites/production/files/2017-10/documents/final_draft_fac_directive-10.31.2017.pdf.

(D.C. Cir. 2020) (finding that FACA provided "meaningful standards" for judicial review under § 701(a)(2) of the APA and holding that the change in agency policy was arbitrary and capricious "[b]ecause the Directive contains no discussion of . . . [the] EPA's prior conclusion at all[;] the Directive crossed the line from the tolerably terse to the intolerably mute"); Union of Concerned Scientists v. Wheeler, 954 F.3d 11 (1st Cir. 2020) (finding the new EPA policy judicially reviewable and remanding to the district court the claim that the policy prevented "fairly balanced" committees); NRDC v. EPA, 438 F.Supp.3d 220 (S.D.N.Y. 2020) (holding that although the agency did not need to provide prior notice and the opportunity for comment, the directive was arbitrary and capricious in not providing sufficient explanation and not considering reliance interests). The directive is no longer in operation.

In October 2020, a district court judge, after first finding FACA's mandates justiciable, determined that President Trump's Presidential Commission on Law Enforcement and the Administration of Justice violated the Act's fair balance mandate (and other requirements). The court ordered that the Commission's report, if released, contain a disclaimer that it violated the law. NAACP Legal Defense & Educational Fund, Inc. v. Barr, 496 F.Supp.3d 116 (D.D.C. 2020). The report was released in December 2020 with the disclaimer.[11]

(9) ***President Trump, President Biden, and FACA.*** In June 2019, President Trump issued Executive Order 13875 (Evaluating and Improving the Utility of Federal Advisory Committees), 84 Fed. Reg. 28711. It read, in part:

> Section 1. Review of Current Advisory Committees. . . .
>
> (b) Each agency [with at least three FACA committees] shall, by September 30, 2019, terminate at least one-third of its current committees established under . . . FACA, including committees for which the:
>
> (i) stated objectives of the committee have been accomplished;
>
> (ii) subject matter or work of the committee has become obsolete;
>
> (iii) primary functions have been assumed by another entity; or
>
> (iv) agency determines that the cost of operation is excessive in relation to the benefits to the Federal Government.
>
> (c) Each agency may request a waiver of the requirement in subsection (b) of this section from the Director of the Office of Management and Budget (Director). The Director may grant such a waiver if the Director concludes it is necessary for the delivery of essential services, for effective program delivery, or because it is otherwise warranted by the public interest. . . .

[11] https://www.justice.gov/file/1347866/download.

> Section 2. Limitations on New Advisory Committees.
>
> The Government-wide combined total number of eligible committees . . . shall not exceed 350. If the combined total number of eligible committees exceeds 350, an agency may not establish a new advisory committee under . . . FACA, unless the agency obtains a waiver. . . .

According to the GAO, the "federal government spent about $373 million in FY 2019 [which ended a few months after the Executive Order] to operate nearly 960 FACA committees."

President Biden repealed this Executive Order on his first day in office. In April 2021, new EPA Administrator Michael Regan announced that he was dismissing all the members of two of the agency's most important advisory committees (the Science Advisory Board and the Clean Air Scientific Advisory Committee) and publicly soliciting nominations for new members: "Resetting these two scientific advisory committees will ensure the agency receives the best possible scientific insight to support our work to protect human health and the environment." Regan then made selections.

In 2022, at the direction of President Biden, the Department of Agriculture established an Equity Commission, which is a new FACA committee "to advise the Secretary of Agriculture and provide USDA with an analysis of how its programs, policies, systems, structures, and practices that contribute to barriers to inclusion or access, systemic discrimination, or exacerbate or perpetuate racial, economic, health and social disparities and recommendations for action."

Advisory committee members have disclosed political pressure, including with respect to boosters of COVID vaccines. In June 2021, several members of an FDA advisory committee publicly resigned after the agency approved a controversial Alzheimer's drug.

What advisory committees exist in the agency you are following? Do you think there are too many (or too few) committees? How, if at all, would you change FACA? For instance would you support H.R. 1930 (117th Cong.) (2021), which would, among other items (see Note 7), require appointments to be made "without regard to political affiliation or political campaign activity," the agency head to solicit nominations publicly, more assessment and disclosure of ethics requirements, and disclosure of detailed minutes from committee meetings?

# SECTION 5. INFORMATION COLLECTION AND DISCLOSURE AS REGULATION



Most government activity affecting citizen interests occurs prior to the structured processes of rulemaking and adjudication. For example, agencies gather information outside these frameworks. Administrative agencies get this information in many ways—through inspections, mandated filings, formal subpoenas, and so on. These actions are diverse and rarely litigated; the following provides a brief overview of some of the key issues.

The flow of information to government is only part of the significance of requiring information, and in many settings it is the lesser part. Businesses and individuals often change their primary conduct in response to inspection or reporting requirements. The government's making that information available to the public may itself be a spur to change; disclosure itself can be a form of regulation.

Information is the raw material for the implementation and shaping of policy. Information may be required before or during more traditional adjudication or rulemaking, or in less formal functions such as licensing; identifying industry problems; monitoring industries for enforcement; and preparing for dealings with the legislature or the executive. As you proceed through the following pages, consider the agencies' goals and where information demands fit in furthering those goals.

Collection of information raises important policy questions, such as how to most efficiently use limited resources and the tradeoffs between cooperative and adversarial approaches to inspection and enforcement. The following materials consider these policy questions and briefly review the limits imposed on information gathering by the Fourth and Fifth Amendments. Then, the materials discuss disclosure as a method of regulation.

## a. Information Demands and Inspections

Regulatory regimes may require entities to supply the government with information, either directly or on request. Examples include individuals filing annual tax returns or pharmacies keeping prescription records. Any mandates for information, as well as sanctions for noncompliance, must be established by statute or an authorized regulation. Some sanctions for noncompliance may be administered by the agency itself, such as denial of a requested benefit; others, such as criminal penalties, require judicial assistance. By contrast, the forms on which information is requested will likely be generated by purely internal bureaucratic routine.

Information requirements are burdensome. As you may have read in Chapter IV (p. 482), the Paperwork Reduction Act, 44 U.S.C. §§ 3501–3520, makes OMB's Office of Information and Regulatory Affairs responsible for reducing the federal paperwork burden and for converting it into electronic form. In mid-August 2022, the OIRA dashboard at www.reginfo.gov reported the existence of over 9,900 active federal information requirements of persons or organizations outside government. These requirements, it reported, elicited over 106 billion annual responses using over 10.3 billion annual hours of labor, with a total annual cost (burden on the information providers) of $143 billion dollars.[1] For the Department of the Treasury alone, home of the Internal Revenue Service, 842 forms elicited 3.8 billion annual responses at a cost of 6.6 annual billion hours and a total annual cost of $89.9 billion.[2]

Agencies may also conduct inspections in person, but resources for these costly activities are often limited. Writing in 2010, THOMAS MCGARITY, RENA STEINZOR, SIDNEY SHAPIRO, & MATTHEW SHUDTZ, WORKERS AT RISK: REGULATORY DYSFUNCTION AT OSHA (Ctr. for Progressive Reform, Feb. 2010), observed: "Often, the most difficult and most important work for a regulatory agency is the most resource-intensive. Enforcement that has a meaningful deterrent effect is the prime example. . . . [A] compliance assessment at a very large worksite might take 2,000 employee-hours. The accompanying legal proceedings can drag on for months or years. In fiscal year 2010, OSHA . . . will only have the capacity to inspect 40,000 of the nation's more than 8 million workplaces." At the end of FY 2021, OSHA had only 750 inspectors, lower than in any other year of the agency's existence. According to the AFL-CIO, such staffing levels allow for inspection of a workplace "once every 236 years." Exacerbating the issue, OSHA must charge particular violations within six months of their occurrence (there is a longer period for repeat violations). For 2020, the Bureau of Labor Statistics reported, from workplace submissions, almost 4800 workers suffered fatal workplace injuries and over 2.65 million private sector workers had nonfatal workplace injuries and illnesses.[3] OSHA's inspector workforce has recently begun to rebound, and was up to 892 by the end of FY 2022. Bruce Rolfsen, OSHA Inspector Recruiting Pays Off, With 19% Bump in One Year, Bloomberg Law (Nov. 3, 2022). The Biden Administration has said it aims to increase that number to about 1,500 by 2024.

Within these constraints, choices of enforcement strategy can significantly shape the effectiveness of the agency in controlling workplace injuries. Should the agency's inspectors be envisioned as expert consultants, granted substantial discretion to work

---

1 https://www.reginfo.gov/public/do/PRAReport?operation=11.

2 https://www.reginfo.gov/public/do/PRAMain.

3 https://www.bls.gov/iif/.

collaboratively with management and labor to efficiently address safety problems as they arise? Or should they be viewed as bureaucrats lacking the knowledge necessary for trustworthy exercise of broad discretion, and possibly prone to graft (to supplement inferior wages)—persons needing a detailed manual specifying their activities? Or as police officers (in a dominant view of them), aiming to detect violations and issue citations rather than proactively improve safety?[4]

The state of Maine at one point sought to blend cooperative and adversarial approaches. (States may take on federal responsibilities under OSHA's supervision, though the effectiveness of these programs has been questioned. Alison D. Morantz, Has Devolution Injured American Workers? 25 J.L. Econ & Org. 183 (2009)). Finding stepped-up inspections were not yielding fewer injuries, Maine's OSHA office developed a "partnership" approach. It invited the 200 firms with the highest reported number of workers' compensation claims—1% of Maine's employers, but 30% of its workforce and 45% of its claims—to a cooperative program working to identify and correct safety problems. Those who accepted were promised fewer inspections, fines, and sanctions. All but two joined the program, and their workers' compensation claims fell by 47.3%; the state as a whole saw a 27% drop in claims. Agency efficiency also improved: a wall-to-wall inspection at a high-hazard plant might involve six to nine officers on site for three months, time to write findings, and months or years of litigation—with little sign of permanent change. OSHA's Maine Director estimated the program eliminated seven times as many hazards as a more adversarial approach. See Charles Oliver, "Executive Update F," Investor's Business Daily 4 (Sept. 10, 1996); see also Orly Lobel, Interlocking Regulatory and Industrial Relations: The Governance of Workplace Safety, 57 Admin. L. Rev. 1071, 1116–18 (2005).

OSHA subsequently established a cooperative compliance program in high-hazard industries nationwide; over 12,000 were invited to join, under threat of immediate priority for inspection if they did not. Given OSHA's resources, the reality of this threat depended on the degree of cooperation it could secure. There is also the possibility, as Sidney Shapiro and Randy Rabinowitz suggest, that "OSHA appears to be rewarding those employers with the worst safety records."[5] On judicial review, this initiative was struck down for ignoring necessary notice-and-comment rulemaking procedures, see Chamber of Commerce of the United States v. Dep't of Labor, 174 F.3d 206 (1999) (p. 407). For a summary of current "cooperative programs under which businesses,

[4] The costs and benefits of proceeding "by the book" are explored in a deep literature, which includes Ian Ayres & John Braithwaite, Responsive Regulation: Transcending the Deregulation Debate (1992); Eugene Bardach & Robert A. Kagan, Going By the Book: The Problem of Regulatory Unreasonableness (2d ed. 2002); Neil Gunningham & Darren Sinclair, Leaders and Laggards: Next-Generation Environmental Regulation (2017); Jody Freeman, The Private Role in Public Governance, 75 N.Y.U. L. Rev. 543 (2000); Orly Lobel, The Renew Deal: The Fall of Regulation and the Rise of Governance in Contemporary Legal Thought, 89 Minn. L. Rev. 342, 384 (2004); Sidney A. Shapiro & Randy S. Rabinowitz, Punishment versus Cooperation in Regulatory Enforcement: A Case Study of OSHA, 49 Admin. L. Rev. 713 (1997).

[5] Shapiro & Rabinowitz, supra note 4, at 741.

labor groups, and other organizations can work cooperatively with the Agency to help prevent fatalities, injuries, and illnesses in the workplace," see https://www.osha.gov/cooperativeprograms.

## b. Resisting Inspection and Information Demands

(1) ***Inspections and the Fourth Amendment.*** Neither inspection nor information demands are always willingly received. You may see this topic in other law school courses; we provide only a brief summary here.

The Fourth Amendment to the U.S. Constitution, applicable to state and local governments through the Fourteenth Amendment, provides:

> The right of the people to be secure in their persons, houses, papers, and effects, against unreasonable searches and seizures, shall not be violated, and no Warrants shall issue, but upon probable cause, supported by Oath or affirmation, and particularly describing the place to be searched, and the persons or things to be seized.

Its application in criminal matters is often litigated. Administrative searches (i.e., inspections) present additional problems, as agencies often conduct them for programmatic and preventative reasons. Section 8(a) of the Occupational Safety and Health Act of 1970 is typical. It provides:

> [T]he Secretary, upon presenting appropriate credentials to the owner, operator, or agent in charge, is authorized—
>
> (1) to enter without delay and at reasonable times any . . . [area] where work is performed by an employee . . . ; and
>
> (2) to inspect and investigate during regular working hours and at other reasonable times, and within reasonable limits and in a reasonable manner, any such place of employment . . . and to question privately any such employer, . . . agent, or employee.

29 U.S.C. § 657(a). A program for inspecting (searching) without "probable cause" or "particularly describing the place to be searched" is in tension with the Constitution's words. Warrantless criminal searches are sometimes accepted in exigent circumstances, but administrative searches generally present no such imperatives.

Eight years after five Justices upheld a municipal health inspector's demand to enter a home in response to signs of rat infestation, Frank v. Maryland, 359 U.S. 360 (1959), six Justices upheld two citizens' refusals to permit administrative searches—in one case, of an apartment, in the other, of a warehouse. Camara v. Municipal Court, 387 U.S. 523 (1967); See v. Seattle, 387 U.S. 541 (1967). In 1978, in Marshall v. Barlow's Inc., 436 U.S. 307, the Court found the OSHA statute "unconstitutional insofar as it purports to authorize inspections without warrant . . . ." However, the Court indicated it would suffice to show the inspection conformed to a reasonable plan, without any need to "particularly describ[e]" anything. Even this watered-down warrant requirement is not necessary for a few "closely regulated" industries. Donovan v. Dewey, 452 U.S. 494 (1981) (stone quarry);

New York v. Burger, 482 U.S. 691 (1987) (automobile junk yard). And in practice, few regulated entities take the trouble of demanding a warrant.

The Supreme Court's expansion of regulatory takings in Cedar Point Nursery v. Hassid, 141 S.Ct. 2063 (2021), potentially sets the stage to undermine regulatory inspections. See Adam Smith, Inspections, Exceptions, and Expectations: Cedar Point and its Expansion of Regulatory Takings, Lewis & Clark Law School Environmental, Natural Resources, & Energy Law Blog (Jan. 24, 2022).[6] Nikolas Bowie comments that the broad language in Cedar Point around employers' and property owners' right to exclude is seemingly limitless, "threaten[ing] an enormous variety of laws . . . ." See Nikolas Bowie, Foreword: Antidemocracy, 135 Harv. L. Rev. 160, 196–200 (2021). But he notes that the Court may choose to proceed aggressively or modestly, perhaps establishing a low bar for just compensation (one dollar?) or crafting a regime of ad hoc exceptions to regulatory takings.

Does a municipal parking enforcement agent's act of chalking tires to enforce time limits on certain spots violate the Fourth Amendment? The Ninth Circuit recently held that the practice falls within the Fourth Amendment's administrative search exception. See Verdun v. City of San Diego, 51 F.4th 1033 (9th Cir. 2022). But in the Sixth Circuit, Taylor v. City of Saginaw, 11 F.4th 483 (6th Cir. 2021), an officer may well have to obtain a warrant to dust car tires with chalk. At a minimum, the administrative search exception does not apply.

Would imposing standards for administrative searches under the APA be a better approach? EDWARD RUBIN, IT'S TIME TO MAKE THE ADMINISTRATIVE PROCEDURE ACT ADMINISTRATIVE, 89 Cornell L. Rev. 95, 130–31 (2003): "[A]dministrative inspection cases are a doctrinal farrago. . . . If one eliminates probable cause and substitutes a completely different standard . . . there is little reason to describe the new requirement as a warrant. . . . Federal judges are fully aware . . . the probable cause requirement, designed for criminal cases, would be unacceptably disruptive in a regulatory context. However, they are also aware that such inspections can serve as an independent sanction and can be used in an unfair or abusive manner. Unfortunately, the APA provides no standards whatsoever for assessing the propriety of on-site inspections . . . . So the judges fashioned the new requirement of a general administrative plan and used the Fourth Amendment as a vehicle to impose it on administrative agencies. This provides some measure of supervision for on-site inspections, but it is something of a gimmick . . . ."

Do we need to differentiate administrative searches and their constitutional safeguards based on the kind of search? EVE BRENSIKE PRIMUS, DISENTANGLING ADMINISTRATIVE SEARCHES, 111 Colum. L. Rev. 254, 259–61 (2011): "[M]uch of the mischief in administrative search law can be traced to the Supreme Court's conflation of two distinct types of searches within one doctrinal exception. . . . [The concept of administrative searches] was designed for . . . dragnet intrusions—searches or seizures of every

[6] https://law.lclark.edu/live/blogs/180-inspections-exceptions-and-expectations-cedar.

person, place, or thing in a specific location or involved in a specific activity. Such intrusions were permissible if they involved only minimally intrusive government actions necessary to protect important health or safety interests that an individualized probable cause regime could not sufficiently protect. . . . In the 1980s, the Court added . . . special subpopulation searches to the category of administrative searches. According to the Court, certain people (or people acting in certain capacities) had reduced expectations of privacy relative to the public at large, such that public officials need not satisfy the traditional warrant and probable cause requirements before searching them. . . . The result [of their conflation] is a doctrine that imposes few limits on government conduct and paves the way for indiscriminate searches and seizures."

(2) ***Subpoenas.*** The Supreme Court has also granted agencies broad powers to subpoena documents. The leading decision is Oklahoma Press Pub. Co. v. Walling, 327 U.S. 186, 208–09 (1946): "It is not necessary, as in the case of a warrant, that a specific charge or complaint of violation of law be pending . . . [A subpoena satisfies the Fourth Amendment if] the investigation is authorized by Congress, is for a purpose Congress can order, and the documents sought are relevant to the inquiry."

Subpoena enforcement generally requires a court action, but the burden of justification for the agency is not severe. "A district court is not to use an enforcement proceeding as an opportunity to test the strength of the underlying complaint. . . . If the charge is proper and the material requested is relevant, the district court should enforce the subpoena unless the employer establishes that the subpoena is 'too indefinite,' has been issued for an 'illegitimate purpose,' or is unduly burdensome." McLane Co. v. EEOC, 581 U.S. 72 (2017).

(3) ***And the Fifth Amendment Too?*** The Fifth Amendment ensures: "No person . . . shall be compelled in any criminal case to be a witness against himself . . . ." Courts have rarely found the protection available to resist information demands made in ordinary administrative contexts. To start, the privilege cannot be asserted by corporations or other artificial "persons." See Bellis v. United States, 417 U.S. 85 (1974); Hale v. Henkel, 201 U.S. 43 (1906). Even real persons face numerous obstacles to using the privilege in the regulatory context. First, they may assert it only by affirmatively claiming it. For example, if a taxpayer's sources of income were unlawful, she could not refuse to file an income tax return but would have to file the return invoking the privilege on the line where earned income is to be reported. This may be rather conspicuous. Any other response, if false, opens the citizen to prosecution for "false statement." See Brogan v. United States, 522 U.S. 398 (1998). Second, the claim can be made only for "testimonial" communications. It cannot be used, for example, to refuse fingerprinting or the taking of other physical evidence. Third, it can be made only on the basis of potential criminal liability, not merely a tendency to bring about undesired regulatory consequences. Finally, the materials must both belong to, and be in the possession of, the person claiming the privilege. Thus, if my documents are subpoenaed from my accountant, I cannot invoke the privilege to prevent my accountant from producing them.

## c. OIRA Memo: Disclosure and Simplification as Regulatory Tools



# DISCLOSURE AND SIMPLIFICATION AS REGULATORY TOOLS MEMORANDUM

EXECUTIVE OFFICE OF THE PRESIDENT

OFFICE OF INFORMATION AND REGULATORY AFFAIRS
OFFICE OF MANAGEMENT AND BUDGET

June 18, 2010

MEMORANDUM FOR THE HEADS OF EXECUTIVE DEPARTMENTS AND AGENCIES[7]

FROM: Cass R. Sunstein, Administrator

SUBJECT: Disclosure and Simplification as Regulatory Tools

. . . The purpose of the following documents is to set out guidance to inform the use of disclosure and simplification in the regulatory process. To the extent permitted by law, and where appropriate in light of the problem to which they are attempting to respond, agencies should follow the relevant principles.

Disclosure as a Regulatory Tool

PURPOSE. In many statutes, Congress requires or permits agencies to use disclosure as a regulatory tool. Executive Order 12866 provides, "Each agency shall identify and assess available alternatives to direct regulation, including . . . providing information upon which choices can be made by the public." The Open Government Directive of the Office of Management and Budget calls for disclosures that will "further the core mission of the agency." The purpose of this guidance is to set forth principles designed to assist agencies in their efforts to use information disclosure to achieve their regulatory objectives. Agencies should follow the principles outlined here in accordance with their own authorities, judgments, and goals, to the extent permitted by law.

DISCLOSURE AS A REGULATORY TOOL. Sometimes Congress requires or authorizes agencies to impose disclosure requirements instead of, or in addition to, mandates, subsidies, or bans. For example, automobile companies are required by law to disclose miles per gallon (MPG) ratings for new vehicles, and a standardized Nutrition Facts panel must be included on most food packages. The goal of disclosing such information is to provide members of the public with relevant

[7] The full memorandum can be found at: https://www.whitehouse.gov/wp-content/uploads/legacy_drupal_files/omb/assets/inforeg/disclosure_principles.pdf.

information at the right moment in time, usually when a decision is made. Often that decision is whether to purchase a particular product. . . .

There are two general types of release that Congress may require or permit: summary disclosure and full disclosure. With summary disclosure, often required at the point of purchase, agencies highlight the most relevant information in order to increase the likelihood that people will see it, understand it, and act in accordance with what they have learned. Full disclosure is more comprehensive; it occurs when agencies release, or require others to release, all relevant information (often including underlying data).

SUMMARY DISCLOSURE. . . . Examples include nutritional labeling, energy efficiency labeling, tobacco warnings,[8] and government provision of information (e.g., fact sheets, telephone hotlines, and public interest announcements).

---

[8] [Ed.] Here are three of thirty-six alternative designs for cigarette warnings proposed by the FDA in 2010 to implement § 201 of the Tobacco Control Act of 2009, Pub. L. No. 111–31, 123 Stat. 1976, 75 Fed. Reg. 69524 (Nov. 12, 2010). The D.C. Circuit found that the mandated designs violated the First Amendment. R.J. Reynolds Tobacco Co. v. FDA, 696 F.3d 1205 (D.C. Cir. 2012). In 2014, the agency ran its own advertising campaign with graphic images, The Real Cost, on multiple media platforms; in addition, the agency conducted two multi-year studies, which could provide the evidence the D.C. Circuit found was lacking to justify compelling speech. In March 2020, the FDA issued a new rule to comply with its statutory obligation to require "color graphics depicting the negative health consequences of smoking." Tobacco companies filed suit soon thereafter in the Eastern District of Texas. That litigation is currently ongoing, with the plaintiff tobacco companies having secured multiple extensions of the rule's effective date. The latest extension has the rule going into effect on October 6, 2023 (with any obligation tied to the effective date also postponed). For more information, see: https://www.fda.gov/tobacco-products/labeling-and-warning-statements-tobacco-products/cigarette-health-warning-design-files-and-technical-specifications.

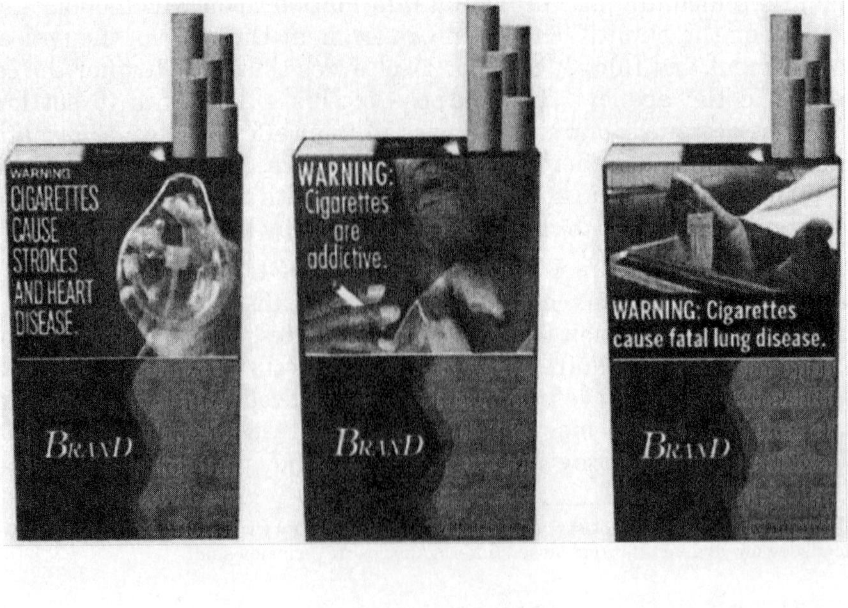

Principle One: *In order to select which information to highlight and how to present that information, agencies should explicitly identify their goals.*

Explicit identification of goals will have important implications for the nature of disclosure. . . . If the goal is to present a warning, then graphic messages might be justified; the same is not true when the aim is simply to inform. And if the goal is to present a warning, it will often be useful to inform users of the precise steps that they might take, or the plans that they might formulate, to avoid the risk in question. . . .

Principle Two: *Summary disclosure should generally be simple and specific, and should avoid undue detail or excessive complexity.*

Summary disclosure should focus on the central issues and should be presented in a manner that is straightforward and easy to understand. Simple, specific disclosure is generally preferable. People have limited time and attention, and their reactions to new information are not always predictable. . . . Summary disclosure should be designed so as to be relevant to the affected population, enabling people to know why and how the information is pertinent to their own choices.

Principle Three: *Summary disclosure should be accurate and in plain language. . . .*

Principle Four: *Disclosed information should be properly placed and timed. . . .*

Agencies should attempt to offer the information that users need when they need it. To this end, they should take steps to provide people with relevant information when they are actually making the decision or taking the action in question. For example, information about fuel economy is most useful if it is present and visible when people are shopping for motor vehicles. . . .

Principle Five: *Summary disclosure through ratings or scales should be meaningful.*

Summary disclosure may involve numerical ratings or scales, because these are convenient ways to simplify and display complicated information. For nutrition, percent daily values are a common example of this sort of summary disclosure. When users understand what such scales mean, they can be among the most effective ways to communicate information. . . . Annual savings or benefits, measured in terms of dollars, provide a metric that is both meaningful and easy to understand. . . .

Principle Six: *To the extent feasible, agencies should test, in advance, the likely effects of summary disclosure, and should also monitor the effects of such disclosure over time. . . .*

Principle Seven: *Where feasible and appropriate, agencies should identify and consider the likely costs and benefits of disclosure requirements.*

Executive Order 12866 requires agencies, to the extent permitted by law, "to assess both the costs and the benefits of the intended regulation" and "recognizing that some costs and benefits are difficult to quantify," to proceed only "upon a reasoned determination that the benefits of the intended regulation justify the costs." In accordance with this requirement, and where feasible and appropriate in the circumstances, agencies should adopt disclosure requirements only after considering both qualitative and quantitative benefits and costs. That assessment should, in turn, help agencies to decide which requirements to select.

It is important to acknowledge that in some contexts, the costs and benefits of disclosure may be difficult or even impossible to specify, and a formal analysis may not be feasible or appropriate. Quantitative assessment of benefits may involve a high degree of speculation, and a qualitative discussion, based on available evidence, may be all that is feasible. In assessing benefits, agencies should consider the fact that improvements in welfare are a central goal of disclosure requirements, but should also note that informed choice is a value in itself (even if it is difficult to quantify that value).

It is also important to recognize that people may react differently to disclosure requirements. While some consumers might use calorie information to reduce their overall calorie intake, others might not. Heterogeneity can have potentially significant effects; those who have the most to gain or to lose may or may not be benefitting from the relevant disclosure. Agencies should attempt to take divergent behavior and preferences into account when formulating disclosure policies and assessing their likely consequences.

FULL DISCLOSURE. Sometimes Congress requires or authorizes agencies to promote regulatory goals by disclosing, or by requiring others to disclose, a wide range of information about existing practices and their effects. Full disclosure will include far more detail than is available in a summary. It may well include multiple variables, supporting data, and materials that extend over long periods of time. For example, agencies use the Internet to provide detailed information about fuel economy and nutrition; such information is far more comprehensive than what is provided through summary disclosure.

Full disclosure can often promote the purposes of open government, including transparency, participation, and collaboration. The central goals of full disclosure are to allow individuals and organizations to view the data and to analyze, use, and repackage it in multiple ways, typically taking advantage of emerging technological capacities (perhaps including social media). To promote those goals, agencies should consider the following principles.

*Principle One: Disclosed information should be as accessible as possible. For that reason, the Internet should ordinarily be used as a means of disclosing information, to the extent feasible and consistent with law.*

Transparency is generally good practice, and agencies cannot always know which information will be most useful and in what format it will prove most valuable. Engaging in full disclosure (to the extent feasible, subject to valid restrictions, and to the extent permitted by law) is often both desirable and important.

Full disclosure will frequently involve large amounts of complicated data, and most people may not find it worth their time to seek out and analyze all or most of it. In such cases, the data may be most directly useful to groups and organizations with technical capabilities and with an interest in obtaining, analyzing, and repackaging relevant information. Such groups and organizations may reorganize and disseminate the information in ways that turn out to be highly beneficial to the general public (sometimes by improving the operation of markets). At the same time, agencies should strive to make full disclosure as useful as possible, and should therefore promote clarity and accessibility.

*Principle Two: Disclosed information should be as usable as possible. For that reason, information should usually be released in an electronic format that does not require specialized software.*

Consistent with the goals of open government, it is important to make information not merely available but also usable. If information is made available electronically, it will be easier for people to sift through it and to analyze or repackage it in various ways. Agencies should select an electronic format that is suitable to achieving that goal. The best method should be chosen in light of existing technology. . . .

*Principle Three: Agencies should consider making periodic assessments of whether full disclosure is as accurate and useful as possible.*

Where feasible and to the extent consistent with relevant laws, regulations, and policies (including protection of privacy), agencies should consider steps to investigate whether current disclosure policies are fulfilling their intended purposes. They might explore, for example, what information is being frequently used by the public and how those in the private sector are adapting and presenting information. . . . Agencies should also consider whether it might be useful to seek public comment on significant disclosures. . . .

*Principle Four: Where feasible and appropriate, agencies should consider the costs and benefits of full disclosure.*

As noted above, Executive Order 12866 requires agencies, to the extent permitted by law, "to assess both the costs and the benefits of the intended regulation" and to proceed only upon "a reasoned determination that the benefits of the intended regulation justify the costs." In addition, the Paperwork Reduction Act of 1995 [p. 482] imposes a series of requirements on efforts to collect information; these requirements are designed (among other things) to increase the practical utility of information collections and to minimize burdens on the private sector. In accordance with these requirements, and to the extent feasible and appropriate, agencies should evaluate full disclosure in terms of both qualitative and quantitative benefits and costs.

Here, as with summary disclosure, quantitative assessment of benefits may involve a degree of speculation, and a qualitative discussion, based on available evidence, may be all that is feasible. . . .

SUMMARY DISCLOSURE AND FULL DISCLOSURE. Congress may require or authorize agencies to require summary disclosure but not full disclosure; alternatively, Congress may require or authorize agencies to require full disclosure but not summary disclosure. When Congress grants agencies discretion, and to the extent feasible, they should consider the likely effects—including the qualitative and quantitative costs and benefits—of both approaches.

Summary disclosure is the best method for informing consumers at the point of decision. Full disclosure is the best method of allowing groups and individuals access to a broad range of information, allowing them to analyze and disseminate that information in creative ways, and to use it to inform private and public decisions or otherwise to promote statutory goals. The two approaches may well be complementary. For example, it may be desirable to use summary disclosure at the point of purchase while also making full information available on the Internet. . . .

## NOTES ON REGULATORY DISCLOSURES

(1) ***The "Regulatory" Impacts of Disclosure as Consumer Information.*** The June 2010 Sunstein memorandum addresses only the benefits of disclosure for consumer choice, suggesting that (at least within certain parameters) it may be preferable to inform consumers about their choices rather than to restrict the choices themselves. It does not discuss the possible impact of disclosure on choices that are made by sellers or other potentially regulated persons. What incentive does prominent display of miles per gallon ratings create for automobile manufacturers? The knowledge that each model will receive a crash safety rating ranging from one to five stars, based on its performance in standardized tests? Regulation by disclosure does not dictate particular design elements manufacturers must use; command and control measures that do specify necessary elements have long been criticized both for embedding yesterday's technology and for taking design decisions away from those best able to make them. Regulation by disclosure, in contrast, is said to create incentives for manufacturers to determine for themselves, in the most efficient way, the design features that will best advantage their models in the disclosures made. The memorandum also does not discuss any disadvantages to disclosure in any depth. Are there any for the examples discussed?

(2) ***Other Potential "Regulatory" Uses of Disclosure.*** The potential of disclosure to address social problems that could be dealt with by regulation is not limited to the incentives that may be created by informing consumer purchase choices. Disclosure can also create productive incentives for

regulated entities without regard to consumer choice. Consider the experience under the EPA's Toxics Release Inventory Program. For the approximately 770 toxic chemicals that are being used, manufactured, treated, transported, or released into the environment, those responsible must file annual reports with state and local governments, giving the locations and quantities of these chemicals being released. The reports are submitted to the EPA, which compiles the data into an online, publicly accessible database.[9] Any person with access to the Internet can search this database by geographic location, chemical name, or industry classification code. For establishments seeking good will from their workforce and in their communities, the resulting exposure provides an incentive for change that, again, can be met by their own thoughtful innovation. The result may be to improve their performance beyond requirements government agencies may have been able to set, while avoiding any need to comply with standardized designs or other requirements. Indeed, rulemaking to set formal limits for each of the toxics may be beyond the EPA's administrative capacities; the Occupational Safety and Health Administration's failure to set workplace limits on more than a handful of toxics has been a poster child for the ossification of rulemaking, the chronic underfunding of that agency, and the impacts of aggressive judicial review.[10] The success of the TRI program in promoting toxics controls has been well documented. See, e.g., Bradley C. Karkkainen, Information as Environmental Regulation: TRI and Performance Benchmarking, Precursor to a New Paradigm? 89 Geo. L.J. 257 (2001).

More generally, the "regulatory" advantages to disclosure include potential competition that enhances social welfare, incentives to avoid undesirable actions, and fostering of public confidence. For a defense of disclosure, see Eric W. Orts, Defending Disclosure, Reg. Rev. (June 18, 2015).[11] On the other hand, its disadvantages include costs to regulated entities (such as reputational harm), which are magnified if disclosures are not accurate, as well as questionable (or no) efficacy in some settings. For an argument that information overload and other factors generally make disclosure ineffective as a regulatory tool, see Omri Ben-Shahar & Carl E. Schneider, More Than You Wanted to Know: The Failure of Mandated Disclosure (2015). In addition, disclosure mandates can shape market power. The Beer Institute's Voluntary Disclosure Initiative, for example, arguably benefits large brewers, which "are losing market share to the hundreds of small craft brewers that have sprung up in recent years in the United States" and which can more easily absorb the costs of calorie testing.[12] For a discussion of the benefits and costs in the database context, see Nathan Cortez, Regulation by Database, 89 Colo. L. Rev. 1 (2018). Finally, there are legal factors to consider. To what extent can the government require disclosure (whether summary or full, in Sunstein's terms) under the First

[9] https://www.epa.gov/toxics-release-inventory-tri-program.

[10] Ossification: p. 1152; underfunding: p. 804; judicial review: AFL-CIO v. OSHA, 965 F.2d 962 (11th Cir. 1992).

[11] https://www.theregreview.org/2015/06/18/orts-defending-disclosure/.

[12] E. Frank Stephenson, Bootleggers, Baptists, and Beer Labels, Regulation (Fall 2016).

Amendment? In Americans for Prosperity Found. v. Bonta, 141 S.Ct. 2373 (2021), the Supreme Court struck down a California law requiring charitable organizations to disclose the identities of their major donors to the Attorney General. Applying strict scrutiny, the majority noted that "California's interest is less in investigating fraud and more in ease of administration. This interest, however, cannot justify the disclosure requirement." Id. at 2387. For more on disclosure to the government (as opposed to the public), see the discussion on the Paperwork Reduction Act (pp. 482, 804).

(3) ***The Data Quality Act.*** The Data Quality Act, also known as the Information Quality Act, was enacted as a few hardly noticed lines of text in section 515 of the Treasury and General Government Appropriations Act for Fiscal Year 2001 (Pub. L. No. 106–554, 114 Stat. 2763). It directs OMB to issue government-wide guidelines that "provide policy and procedural guidance to Federal agencies for ensuring and maximizing the quality, objectivity, utility, and integrity of information (including statistical information) disseminated by Federal agencies." These guidelines, which define "information" broadly as "any communication or representation of knowledge such as facts or data, in any medium or form," require each agency not only to issue guidelines to these ends about information it disseminates but also to "establish administrative mechanisms allowing affected persons to seek and obtain correction" of noncompliant information. The Director of OMB is also to monitor agency handling of complaints. Does the Data Quality Act provide an opportunity for diversion and cost infliction in addition to agency discipline? If so, the result would be to make programs like TRI less timely and cost-effective. One account, however, determined that "industry use of the Act was put under the spotlight because of concerns about abuse. As a result, and much to the disappointment of its proponents, the Data Quality Act falls short of providing a judicially enforced mechanism for launching additional, information-based challenges to agency rulemakings."[13] GAO reviewed 30 agencies' performance under the Act. It found that 16 of those agencies reported a total of 87 correction requests in the FY 2010–2014 period (EPA, HHS, and Interior listed 61 of those 87 requests). For 59 of those 87 requests, the relevant agency made no correction to the flagged information. GAO, Information Quality Act: Actions Needed to Improve Transparency and Reporting of Correction Requests, GAO-16-110 (Dec. 2015).[14] See Note 9 (Agency-Imposed Restrictions on Data) (p. 354).

(4) ***Other Uses of the Internet as Alternatives to Direct Regulation.*** Returning to the introductory example in Chapter I (p. 3), DOT's website, www.transportation.gov, contains, among others, the following links that are highly facilitative and/or supportive of regulation (some are the result of information disclosure mandates). If you are following another agency, see if you can find analogs on its website:

---

[13] Wendy Wagner, Administrative Law, Filter Failure, and Information Capture, 59 Duke L.J. 1321, 1401 (2010).

[14] https://www.gao.gov/assets/680/674386.pdf.

- Flight delay information, https://www.transtats.bts.gov/OT_Delay/OT_DelayCause1.asp, which "tracks the on-time performance of domestic flights operated by large air carriers" and discloses the provided cause for any delay.
- Airline accident and incident reports, https://www.faa.gov/data_research/accident_incident/, where you can read about emergency landings and other events as well as listen to recordings from air traffic control. There is also a database of airline accidents and some incidents, https://www.ntsb.gov/Pages/AviationQuery.aspx.
- Instructions on filing a complaint, as well as links to do so, https://www.transportation.gov/airconsumer/file-consumer-complaint, whether safety, security, service, disability, or discrimination related. Online links for complaint filing (by type) are provided. According to the website, complaints are forwarded "to the airline and the airline will be required to provide you a response" (if the complaint concerns disability or discrimination and for some other complaints, the airline must also respond to the agency).
- Airworthiness Directives, https://drs.faa.gov, which are "legally enforceable regulations issued by the FAA . . . to correct an unsafe condition in a product."
- Rating programs for vehicles, car seats, and tires, https://www.nhtsa.gov/ratings, "to help consumers make smart decisions about safety."

Or consider OSHA's requirement to maintain records of industrial injuries, subject to inspection. In 2016, OSHA amended its rules to require annual digital submission of these records, a change vigorously resisted by the U.S. Chamber of Commerce. 89 Fed. Reg. 29623 (May 12, 2016). In 2019, the Trump Administration repealed most of the digital submission requirements. In March 2022, the Biden Administration issued an NPRM proposing to reestablish the requirements, again to the chagrin of the Chamber of Commerce. 87 Fed. Reg. 18528 (Mar. 30, 2022).

# PART 4

# THE AGENCY AND THE CONSTITUTION

# CHAPTER VII

# AGENCY RELATIONSHIPS WITH CONGRESS, THE PRESIDENT, AND THE COURTS: THE STRUCTURAL CONSTITUTION



Agencies are almost as old as the Constitution itself, but from the outset their relationship with the named branches of government has been controversial. The Constitution does not specify the structure of the national government below the level of Congress, the President, and the Supreme Court.[1] Those of you who reach these materials after studying the Chapters on "the Agency at Work" will appreciate the challenge of trying to map the volume and complexity of modern administrative government onto this paucity of constitutional text. For those who are beginning your study of administrative law with this Chapter, consider how little guidance the Constitution's text gives for designing agencies as diverse as the Transportation Security Administration, the Environmental Protection Agency, the Department of Education, and the Consumer Financial Protection Bureau.

The first Congress promptly created the Departments of Foreign Affairs, War, and Treasury. The Post Office and the Department of the Navy followed within a few years. Intense debate preceded these acts, particularly around whether the Senate could require its consent to the removal of agency heads. Although many early members of Congress had played key roles in the Philadelphia Convention and/or the ratification process, they disagreed passionately about whether removal was solely the President's constitutional prerogative. On another constitutional front, before the federal government was 25 years old, litigants were arguing to the Supreme Court that Congress had unconstitutionally delegated national policymaking power to another part of the

[1] Early drafts of the Constitution specified a number of cabinet departments and vested them with particular responsibilities. This language was removed in the final days of drafting; one small vestige is the reference, in the Necessary and Proper Clause, to powers "vested by this Constitution in the Government of the United States, or in any Department or Officer thereof."

government. That such fundamental questions were disputed even among those so close to the Founding is, from a historical perspective, unremarkable: The Constitution was creating a new, and largely unprecedented, kind of government. In all the debate that accompanied the Convention and the ratification processes in every state, many novel and complex questions were resolved imperfectly, if at all. Gordon S. Wood, one of the preeminent historians of the period, puts it pithily: "there was not in 1787–1788 one 'correct' or 'true' meaning of the Constitution." Ideology and the Origins of Liberal America, 44 Wm. & Mary Q. 628, 632 (1987).

From a legal perspective however, the American understanding of the significance of a constitution impels us to seek determinate, authoritative meaning against which to measure the legality of government structures and practices. Controversies over congressional choices about governmental structure are longstanding. And a new wave of structural constitutional challenges to the administrative state rose to the fore beginning with the presidency of Ronald Reagan. Over the last four decades, in a series of cases as potentially far-reaching as they are jurisprudentially novel, litigants have insisted that a variety of administrative arrangements violate particular provisions of Articles I, II, or III and, more generally, the principle of separation of powers. The number of such challenges has grown again recently, a reflection of the current Supreme Court's increased receptivity to separation of powers claims. Some of the challenged arrangements are modern innovations, devised by Congress as it sought to address thorny problems like the budget deficit or misbehavior in the financial markets; others are venerable aspects of regulatory structure or oversight that have come under new constitutional attack.

President Reagan was a vocal critic of federal regulation and the people who implemented it, but more significantly his Administration fostered a renaissance of conservative constitutional theory. With very different policy preferences from those of the Democrats who controlled Congress through much of his presidency, Reagan sought control over agencies and regulatory programs with an aggressiveness that laid the groundwork for the pro-president "unitary executive" constitutionalism of the George W. Bush Administration. Democratic Presidents Bill Clinton and Barack Obama disavowed the most extravagant constitutional claims of unitary executive power, yet also significantly extended presidential control over the officials and the decisions of regulatory agencies. Continuing and expanding on these trends, President Donald Trump took an even broader view of presidential authority, making some unprecedented claims such as a power to self-pardon and strongly resisting congressional oversight and appropriations limits. And presidential control of administrative action remains a central phenomenon of the Biden Administration as well, with President Biden issuing a record-setting twenty-nine executive orders in his first three weeks in office—many of them reversing executive orders of President Trump.

As Congress and the President create new regulatory structures and relationships, and as litigants advocate constitutional interpretations in which Article II has newfound prominence, the contemporary Court moves into new territory as well, often building constitutional doctrine from the ground up. Perhaps this is why the cases in this Chapter seem frustratingly ad hoc—methodology swings from formalism to functionalism with little rhyme or reason. Among democracies, the United States is remarkable for the age and minimal amendment of its national constitution and for the power of its national constitutional court. In no context are these distinctive characteristics more evident than when the justices look to spare constitutional text to decide whether Congress or the President have overstepped some line.

## SECTION 1. INTRODUCTION

*a. Is the Administrative State Constitutional?*
*b. Separation of Powers Methodology*

The topics covered in subsequent Sections—delegation; legislative vetoes, appropriations, and investigations; presidential appointment, removal, and directives; and administrative adjudication—are pieces of a larger puzzle: How can we reconcile the modern regulatory state with a Constitution that is more than 200 years old yet still serves as our fundamental benchmark of political legitimacy? The first set of materials in this Section dips selectively into the vast body of work on separation of powers to offer several opposing views on this overarching question. The second set introduces you to general features of separation of powers analysis.

## a. Is the Administrative State Constitutional?

*Philip Hamburger, Is Administrative Law Unlawful?*

*Peter L. Strauss, The Place of Agencies in Government: Separation of Powers and the Fourth Branch*

*Jerry L. Mashaw, Creating the Administrative Constitution: The Lost One Hundred Years of American Administrative Law*

*Gillian E. Metzger, The Supreme Court 2016 Term—Foreword: 1930s Redux: The Administrative State Under Siege*

*Nikolas Bowie & Daphna Renan, The Separation of Powers Counterrevolution*

### Philip Hamburger, Is Administrative Law Unlawful?

(University of Chicago Press, 2014).

Administrative law . . . has transformed American government and society. Although this mode of power is unrecognized by the Constitution, it has become the government's primary mode of controlling Americans, and it increasingly imposes profound restrictions on their liberty. . . .

Traditionally, under the U.S. Constitution, the government could bind its subjects only through its legislative and judicial powers. And because the Constitution granted these powers, respectively, to Congress and the courts, only the acts of these institutions could impose legally obligatory constraints on persons who were subject to the laws. . . . Nowadays, however, the executive enjoys binding legislative and judicial power. . . . [I]ts agencies make legislative rules . . . [and conduct] binding adjudications. . . .

. . . [A]dministrative power harks back to the prerogative, . . . [and] also, more generally, echoes some basic features of absolute power. First, . . . administrative power runs outside the law. Rather than work through ordinary law and adjudication, it proceeds alongside them, often mimicking their forms, but remaining different from them. In this sense, it is an extralegal mode of constraint, and it thereby evades not only the Constitution's legislative and judicial powers but also its legislative and judicial institutions and processes and even many of its rights. . . .

Second, this power outside the law depends on judicial deference and it thus is not only extralegal but also supralegal. As in the past, a power exercised outside the law and the courts can survive only if the judges defer to it—only if they submit to it as power above their courts and the law. In this sense, administrative power is as much above the law as its predecessors.

Third, among the effects of this power outside and above the law is the consolidation of power. The administrative regime consolidates in one branch of government the powers that the Constitution allocates to different branches. Although existing scholarship recognizes aspects of this problem, it does so mostly in terms of the separation of powers. The threat to the separation of powers, however, is merely one element of a broader consolidation of power, which results from the exercise of power outside and above the law.

Administrative power thus brings back to life three basic elements of absolute power. It is extralegal, supralegal, and consolidated. . . .

## Peter L. Strauss, The Place of Agencies in Government: Separation of Powers and the Fourth Branch

84 Colum. L. Rev. 573 (1984).

. . . The Constitution names and ascribes functions only to the Congress, President and Supreme Court, sitting in uneasy relation at the apex of the governmental structure; it leaves undiscussed what might be the necessary and permissible relationships of each of these three constitutional bodies to the agency making the rule. . . . Indeed, does it make sense to look to the Constitution, written so many years ago, for contemporary guidance or limits on the sorts of arrangements Congress can make?

Three differing approaches have been used in the effort to understand issues such as these. The first, "separation of powers," supposes that what government does can be characterized in terms of the kind of act performed—legislating, enforcing, and determining the particular application of law—and that for the safety of the citizenry from tyrannous government these three functions must be kept in distinct places. Congress legislates, and it only legislates; the President sees to the faithful execution of those laws and, in the domestic context at least, that is all he does; the courts decide specific cases of law-application, and that is their sole function. These three powers of government are kept radically separate, because if the same body exercised all three of them, or even two, it might no longer be possible to keep it within the constraints of law.

"Separation of functions" suggests a somewhat different idea, grounded more in considerations of individual fairness in particular proceedings than in the need for structural protection against tyrannical government generally. It admits that for agencies (as distinct from the constitutionally named heads of government) the same body often does exercise all three of the characteristic governmental powers, albeit in a web of other controls—judicial review and legislative and executive oversight. As these controls are thought to give reasonable assurance against systemic lawlessness, the separation-of-functions inquiry asks to what extent constitutional due process for the particular individual(s) who may be involved with an agency in a given proceeding requires special measures to assure the objectivity or impartiality of that proceeding. . . .

"Checks and balances" is the third idea, one that to a degree bridges the gap between these two domains. Like separation of powers, it seeks to protect the citizens from the emergence of tyrannical government by establishing multiple heads of authority in government, which are then pitted one against another in a continuous struggle; the intent of that struggle is to deny to any one (or two) of them the capacity ever to consolidate all governmental authority in itself, while permitting the whole effectively to carry forward the work of government. Unlike separation of powers, however, the checks-and-balances idea does not suppose a radical division of government into three parts, with particular functions neatly parceled out among them. Rather, the focus is on relationships and interconnections, on maintaining the conditions in which the intended struggle at the apex may continue. From this perspective, as from the perspective of separation of functions, it is not important how powers below the apex are treated; the important question is whether the relationship of each of the three named actors of the Constitution to the exercise of those powers is such as to promise a continuation of their effective independence and interdependence.

. . . I argue that, for any consideration of the structure given law-administration below the very apex of the governmental structure, the rigid separation-of-powers compartmentalization of governmental functions should be abandoned in favor of analysis in terms of separation of functions and checks and balances. . . . A shorthand way of putting the argument is that we should stop pretending that all our government (as distinct from its highest levels) can be allocated into three neat parts. . . .

[T]he important fact is that an agency is neither Congress nor President nor Court, but an inferior part of government. Each agency is subject to control relationships with some or all of the three constitutionally named branches, and those relationships give an assurance—functionally similar to that provided by the separation-of-powers notion for the constitutionally named bodies—that they will not pass out of control. . . . What we have, then, are three named repositories of authorizing power and control, and an infinity of institutions to which parts of the authority of each may be lent. The three must share the reins of control; means must be found of assuring that no one of them becomes dominant. But it is not terribly important to number or allocate the horses that pull the carriage of government. . . .

## Jerry L. Mashaw, Creating the Administrative Constitution: The Lost One Hundred Years of American Administrative Law

(Yale University Press, 2012).

The conventional conception of administrative law in the United States has long suffered from several misperceptions. Indeed I am tempted to describe them as governing myths. . . . [One is] that administration in modern forms, that is, administrative officers adjudicating cases and making rules, appeared only in the late-nineteenth and early-twentieth centuries with the creation of so-called "independent" agencies like the [Interstate Commerce Commission] and the Federal Trade Commission. Administration, the execution of laws, is in this imagined world of sharply delineated powers largely limited to prosecutorial functions. And prosecution—which we now view as a quintessentially executive function—is further imagined to have been under the direct control of the President through the Attorney General.

It is but a short step from these images of our administrative constitution in the first century of the Republic to deep concerns about the legitimacy of the modern administrative state. If these images of our constitutional practices and commitments are true, then our current arrangements represent a radical departure from original understandings. . . .

These conventional characterizations capture some essential truths about national administrative organization and administrative law in nineteenth-century America. But . . . these generalizations are quite often simply wrong. Self-executing laws requiring only prosecutorial administration did not exhaust Congress's repertoire of legislative forms. From the earliest days of the Republic, Congress delegated broad authority to administrators, armed them with extrajudicial coercive powers, created systems of administrative adjudication, and specifically authorized administrative rulemaking. Nor was execution of the law lodged firmly and exclusively in the officer we now often refer to as the "Chief Executive." Lack of authority to control prosecution was a constant lament of early presidents and attorneys general. . . . While there have, indeed, been massive changes in the size and scope of the general government over the course of the twentieth century, . . . there has been no precipitous fall from a historical position of separation-of-powers grace. . . .

The American Constitution of 1787 left a hole where administration might have been. . . . To be sure, the Constitution establishes an executive branch. But it has only two constitutionally prescribed officers. . . . The Constitution presumes that there will be heads of departments and other officers of the United States and provides that the President will appoint them. And the President is charged with seeing "that the Laws be faithfully executed." But the only power explicitly given to the President with respect to executing the laws is the power to require reports in writing from the heads of departments—whatever "departments" might be.

. . .[T]he Constitution's silence on most matters administrative provides extremely modest textual support for the notion that all administration was to be firmly and exclusively in the control of the President. Not only are the President's stated constitutional powers feeble, but Congress's powers are broad. . . . And, text aside, the practice of early Congresses when creating the basic machinery of government belied the notion that the founding generation imagined the President as an all-powerful administrator-in-chief.

## Gillian E. Metzger, The Supreme Court 2016 Term—Foreword: 1930s Redux: The Administrative State Under Siege

131 Harv. L. Rev. 1 (2017).

Anti-administrativists paint the administrative state as fundamentally at odds with the Constitution's separation of powers system, combining together in agencies the legislative, executive, and judicial authorities that the Constitution vests in different branches and producing unaccountable and aggrandized power in the process. . . . But [this] . . . analysis gets the constitutional diagnosis almost exactly backward. . . . The administrative state—with its bureaucracy, expert and professional personnel, and internal institutional complexity—performs critical constitutional functions and is the key to an accountable, constrained, and effective executive branch. . . [T]he point can be taken even further: The modern national administrative state is now constitutionally obligatory, rendered necessary by the reality of delegation. . . . [Against that reality, the] relevant constitutional question . . . becomes what the separation of powers requires in a world of substantial delegation of policymaking authority. It is in this context that the administrative state is constitutionally obligatory.

. . . To see why, begin with the Constitution's requirement that the President shall "take Care that the Laws be faithfully executed." It follows that the administrative capacity the President needs in order to satisfy the take care duty is also required. So far, few would disagree. What does that administrative capacity entail in the context of broad delegations? For starters, it means sufficient bureaucratic apparatus and supervisory mechanisms to adequately oversee execution of these delegated powers. It also requires sufficient administrative resources and personnel, in particular adequate executive branch expertise and specialization, to be able to faithfully execute these delegated responsibilities in contexts of tremendous uncertainty and complexity. Arguably, this means that professional and expert government employees are now constitutionally required as well, and perhaps also the civil service, insofar as such career staff are necessary to ensure expertise and institutional stability in agencies.

Simply from the proposition that delegated power must be faithfully executed, then, the outlines of a constitutionally mandated administrative state begin to emerge. . . .

## Nikolas Bowie & Daphna Renan, The Separation of Powers Counterrevolution

131 Yale L.J. 2020 (2022).

Modern separation-of-powers law is premised on a misunderstanding of what the separation of powers is. Today, judges and lawyers from across the political spectrum take for granted that the U.S. Constitution imposes unwritten but judicially enforceable limits on the power of one branch of government to interfere with the others. . . . . This juristocratic separation of powers is often taken as a natural or inherent feature of American constitutionalism. But it took control of the American imagination only in 1926, after centuries in which a profoundly different understanding of the separation of powers was dominant. When John Locke, the Baron de Montesquieu, and other European intellectuals first popularized the separation of the legislative, executive, and judicial powers, they described a system in which each institution of government enforced its own prerogatives through political negotiation and statecraft. When American revolutionaries incorporated these insights into their first written constitutions, they drafted the blueprints for a republican separation of powers, anticipating that representative institutions would distill constitutional meaning and enforce constitutional limits as part of the deliberation and compromise necessary to pass legislation. . . .

But Reconstruction gave way to a "counter-revolution": one that overturned not only Congress's civil-rights legislation but also its decades-long claim of interpretative supremacy. In the 1870s, an ascendent white South violently returned to power in Washington, determined to end Reconstruction and prevent it from reoccurring. Where members of earlier Congresses had argued that federalism and the separation of powers were both indeterminate ideas subject to statutory amendment, this new generation of politicians, historians, political scientists, and judges argued that the antebellum constitutional order had been permanently settled by the Constitution's text and early precedent. From this new generation's perspective, it was appropriate for [James] Madison's First Congress to determine which institutional arrangements were necessary and proper to run the American government, but it was blasphemous for the Reconstruction Congress to reconceive those arrangements. . . .

. . . Rather than treat the separation of powers as a legal principle of interbranch entitlements secured by judicial enforcement, we contend that the separation of powers is a contingent political practice reflecting the policy needs, governance ideas, and political struggles of the moment. This fundamentally unsettled constitutional framework is not a problem for constitutional law to solve. It is a central normative feature of American constitutional government. . . .

As a principle of constitutional governance, the separation of powers is historically contingent, institutionally arbitrary, and inherently provisional. It comprises a set of broad, vague, conflicting, and contested political ideas (thinly connected to sparse and ambiguous constitutional text) and a set of overlapping, interacting institutions that participate in the messy work of national governance. There is no essential or immutable separation of powers. . . .

Further excerpts from these works and others on similar themes are provided in Chapter I, Section 4.b.

## b. Separation of Powers Methodology

Courts and scholars have adopted various approaches in analyzing separation of powers questions, but two have emerged as dominant: formalism and functionalism. In reading through the cases in this Chapter, you'll see a fair bit of seeming inconsistency in the Court's approach, with the Court oscillating between formalism and functionalism, and many cases having strong elements of both. Think about why this might be: Is it inconsistency over time, or are the same justices taking varying stances? If the latter, are there features about the cases or the separation of powers questions at issue that could explain the variation?

(1) ***Formalism and Functionalism: An Overview.*** REBECCA BROWN, SEPARATED POWERS AND ORDERED LIBERTY, 139 U. Pa. L. Rev. 1513, 1522–28 (1991): "Those who espouse the formalist view of separated powers seek judicial legitimacy by insisting upon a firm textual basis in the Constitution for any governmental act. They posit that the structural provisions of the Constitution should be understood solely by their literal language and the drafters' original intent regarding their application, giving little or no weight to the influence of changed circumstances or broad objectives such as good or efficient government. The formalist approach is committed to strong substantive separations between the branches of government, finding support in the traditional expositions of the theme of 'pure' separated powers, such as the maxim that 'the legislature makes, the executive executes, and the judiciary construes the law.' . . . Thus the formalists attempt to ensure that exercise of governmental power comports strictly with the original blueprint laid down in articles I, II, and III of the Constitution. Under formalist thinking, the creation of independent administrative agencies, for example, is considered a violation of the Constitution because such agencies require the exercise of governmental power in ways that involve an overlap of expressly assigned functions, subject to the control of none of the three branches. . . .

"In contrast, advocates of the 'functionalist' approach urge the Court to ask a different question: whether an action of one branch interferes with one of the core functions of another. The sharing of powers, in itself, is not repugnant to the functionalists, nor is the formation of alliances among the branches repugnant, as long as the basic principles of separated powers are not impaired. The functionalist view follows a different strand of separation-of-powers tradition from that of the formalists: the American variant that stresses not the independence, but the interdependence of the branches. 'While the Constitution diffuses power the better to secure liberty, it also contemplates that practice will integrate the dispersed powers into a workable government. It enjoins upon its branches separateness but interdependence, autonomy but reciprocity.' [Youngstown Sheet & Tube Co. v. Sawyer, 343 U.S. 579, 635 (1952) (Jackson, J. concurring) (p. 933).]"

Although formalism and functionalism are frequently invoked as an overarching analytic frame for assessing separation of powers disputes, some scholars question their utility. In Separation of Powers Metatheory, 118 Colum. L. Rev. 1517 (2018), Aziz Huq argues that "debates about the separation of powers . . . hinge upon a series of deep divergences about basic descriptive or normative terms" that are "often obscured by superficial accounts of theories as . . . formalist or functionalist." Elizabeth Magill agrees, stating that "[t]he debate over formalism and functionalism is a distraction, masking a robust consensus to which nearly all participants in the debate subscribe." The Real Separation in Separation of Powers Law, 86 Va. L. Rev. 1127, 1130 (2000).

As you read through the materials in this Chapter, consider whether you find the formalism-functionalism framing helpful or hindering in assessing the separation of powers jurisprudence. How would you describe the disagreements among the justices in these cases?

(2) ***On the Relationship Between Separation of Powers and Checks and Balances.*** CYNTHIA R. FARINA, STATUTORY INTERPRETATION AND THE BALANCE OF POWER IN THE ADMINISTRATIVE STATE, 89 Colum. L. Rev. 452, 495–97 (1989): "[O]ur tendency to describe the constitutional scheme as one of 'separation of powers and checks and balances' can be misleading. This conventional, bifurcated phrasing obscures the fact that the latter represented, for those who drafted and defended the Constitution, a vital and indispensable aspect of the former. By the time of the ratification, the prevailing understanding of separation of powers was no longer a simplistic call for absolute segregation of conceptually distinct functions. The experience between independence and the Constitutional Convention had caused American political theorists to rethink the nature of governmental authority. . . . Whether manifested as lawmaking, execution or adjudication, whether exercised by officials who were elected popularly, elected indirectly or appointed, all power in government shared the same fundamental quality: it was dangerous unless adequately offset and controlled. And so, notwithstanding their literal sense, the words 'separation of powers' came to connote something far more subtle and intricate than a mere abstractly logical division. The phrase expressed the expectation that, through the carefully orchestrated disposition and sharing of authority, restraint would be found in power counterbalancing power.

"This complexity of American separation of powers theory is critical . . . Those who forged the structural theory of the Constitution did not, of course, foresee the modern administrative agency—with its potent concentration of law making, law executing and adjudicating power—any more than they anticipated the federal commitment to social and economic intervention that created it. They were, however, acutely self-conscious that they were designing a plan for the future. . . .

"We can thus understand the structural model as one of dynamic equilibrium: as power flows among the power centers in government, new patterns of counterbalance emerge to provide restraint. The movement of power can be accepted so long as equilibrium can then be reestablished."

(3) ***Is There a General Separation of Powers Principle?*** JOHN F. MANNING, SEPARATION OF POWERS AS ORDINARY INTERPRETATION, 124 Harv. L. Rev. 1939, 1944–45 (2011): "Contrary to [the] understandings of [both] functionalism and formalism, the Constitution adopts no freestanding principle of separation of powers. The idea of separated powers unmistakably lies behind the Constitution, but it was not adopted wholesale. The Constitution contains no Separation of Powers Clause. The historical record, moreover, reveals no one baseline for inferring what a reasonable constitutionmaker would have understood 'the separation of powers' to mean in the abstract. Rather, in the Constitution, the idea of separation of powers, properly understood, reflects many particular decisions about how to allocate and condition the exercise of federal power. Indeed, the document not only separates powers, but also blends them in many ways in order to ensure that the branches have the means and motives to check one another. Viewed in isolation from the constitutionmakers' many discrete choices, the concept of separation of powers as such can tell us little, if anything, about where, how, or to what degree the various powers were, in fact, separated (and blended) in the Philadelphia Convention's countless compromises.

"Of particular importance, like most political compromises, the ones evident in the first seven articles of the Constitution find expression at many different levels of generality. Some provisions—such as the Bicameralism and Presentment Clauses, the Appointments Clause, or the Impeachment Clauses—speak in specific terms, both about the locus of a given power and about the manner in which it is to be exercised. Other provisions are more open-ended, perhaps leaving some play in the joints. Most prominently, the Vesting Clauses speak in general terms about the legislative, executive, and judicial powers, and say nothing about how these clauses intersect with Congress's broad coordinate power to compose the government under the Necessary and Proper Clause. Like most bargained-for texts, the Constitution's structural provisions thus leave many important questions unaddressed. Because the structural provisions come in many shapes and sizes, no one-size-fits-all theory can do them justice. It is precisely this feature of the Constitution that functionalists and formalists misapprehend when they imagine that the document embraces any overarching separation of powers doctrine."

(4) ***The Role of Historical Practice.*** In many separation of powers cases, the Supreme Court references historical practices and the arrangements that the political branches have developed over time. Justice Felix Frankfurter, concurring in Youngstown Sheet & Tube v. Sawyer, 343 U.S.

579 (1992) (p. 933), famously argued that "a systematic, unbroken, executive practice, long pursued to the knowledge of the Congress and never before questioned, engaged in by Presidents who have also sworn to uphold the Constitution, making as it were such exercise of power part of the structure of our government, may be treated as a gloss on 'executive Power' vested in the President." Id. at 610–11; see generally Curtis A. Bradley & Trevor W. Morrison, Historical Gloss and the Separation of Powers, 126 Harv. L. Rev. 411 (2012). As you read the materials in this Chapter, think about what role history should play in separation of powers analysis and which history should matter: just historical practice leading up to or around the Founding, or also subsequent history? For a skeptical view raising concerns about too much historical reliance, see Leah M. Litman, Debunking Antinovelty, 66 Duke L.J. 1407 (2017).

More recently, the question of what role historical practice should play in separation of powers analysis, and which historical practices matter, received focused attention in NLRB V. NOEL CANNING, 573 U.S. 513 (2014) (p. 966), where the Court addressed the meaning of the Recess Appointments Clause for the first time. Writing for the five-justice majority, JUSTICE BREYER insisted that "we put significant weight upon historical practice" when "the interpretive questions before us concern the allocation of power between two elected branches of Government. Long ago Chief Justice Marshall wrote that

> 'a doubtful question, one on which human reason may pause, and the human judgment be suspended, in the decision of which the great principles of liberty are not concerned, but the respective powers of those who are equally the representatives of the people, are to be adjusted; if not put at rest by the practice of the government, ought to receive a considerable impression from that practice.' McCulloch v. Maryland, 4 Wheat. 316, 401 (1819).

"And we later confirmed that '[l]ong settled and established practice is a consideration of great weight in a proper interpretation of constitutional provisions' regulating the relationship between Congress and the President. The Pocket Veto Case, 279 U.S. 655, 689 (1929) . . . We recognize, of course, that the separation of powers can serve to safeguard individual liberty, and that it is the 'duty of the judicial department'—in a separation-of-powers case as in any other—'to say what the law is,' Marbury v. Madison, 1 Cranch 137, 177 (1803). But it is equally true that the longstanding 'practice of the government,' McCulloch, supra, at 401, can inform our determination of what the law is." Breyer added that this "principle is neither new nor controversial. As James Madison wrote, it 'was foreseen at the birth of the Constitution, that difficulties and differences of opinion might occasionally arise in expounding terms & phrases necessarily used in such a charter . . . and that it might require a regular course of practice to liquidate & settle the meaning of some of them.' Letter to Spencer Roane (Sept. 2, 1819), in 8 Writings of James Madison 450 (G. Hunt ed. 1908). And our cases have continually confirmed Madison's view. These precedents show that this Court has treated practice as an important interpretive factor even when the nature or longevity of that practice is subject to dispute, and even when that practice began after the founding era."

JUSTICE SCALIA strongly disagreed. Writing for four justices and concurring in the judgment only, he identified "two overarching principles that ought to guide our consideration[:] . . . First, the Constitution's core, government-structuring provisions are no less critical to preserving liberty than are the later adopted provisions of the Bill of Rights. . . . Second and relatedly, when questions involving the Constitution's government-structuring provisions are presented in a justiciable case, it is the solemn responsibility of the Judicial Branch 'to say what the law is.' Zivotofsky v. Clinton, 566 U.S. [189, 196] (2012) [quoting Marbury]. . . [P]olicing the enduring structure of constitutional government when the political branches fail to do so is one of the most vital functions of this Court. . . . Of course, where a governmental practice has been open, widespread, and unchallenged since the early days of the Republic, the practice should guide our interpretation of an ambiguous constitutional provision. . . . But past practice does not, by itself, create power." Scalia added that "In any controversy between the political branches over a separation-of-powers question, staking out a position and defending it over time is far easier for the Executive Branch than for the Legislative Branch. All Presidents have a high interest in expanding the powers of their office, since the more power the President can wield, the more effectively he can implement his political agenda; whereas individual Senators may have little interest in opposing Presidential encroachment on legislative prerogatives, especially when the encroacher is a President who is the leader of their own party. . . . And when the President wants to assert a power and establish a precedent, he faces neither the collective-action problems nor the procedural inertia inherent in the legislative process. The majority's methodology thus all but guarantees the continuing aggrandizement of the Executive Branch."

(5) ***Separation of Powers Values.*** Judicial opinions arguing for the invalidation of statutes on separation of powers grounds invoke liberty and political accountability as the values that underlie the Constitution's structural arrangements. Thus, in holding for a 5–4 Court that for-cause removal protection for the head of the Consumer Financial Protection Bureau was an unconstitutional intrusion on the President's removal power, Chief Justice Roberts wrote: "The Framers recognized that, in the long term, structural protections against abuse of power were critical to preserving liberty. Their solution to governmental power and its perils was simple: divide it." But viewing an "energetic executive" as necessary given the President's "unique responsibilities," which included securing liberty, the Framers structured "[t]he Executive Branch [a]s a stark departure from all this division. . . . The resultant constitutional strategy is straightforward: divide power everywhere except for the Presidency, and render the President directly accountable to the people through regular elections." Seila Law v. CFPB, 140 S.Ct. 2183, 2202–03 (2020) (p. 988). Other values identified as underlying the separation of powers are "promot[ing] deliberation," protecting "minority rights," and "promot[ing] fair notice and the rule of law."

Gundy v. United States, 139 S.Ct. 2116, 2134 (2019) (Gorsuch, J., dissenting) (p. 837).

By contrast, opinions rejecting separation of powers challenges often invoke the values of "flexibility and practicality," judicial "humility," and the constitutional importance of Congress being able to "perform its functions." Id. at 2123, 2130 (plurality opinion). They note that liberty is a double-edged coin; measures that may restrict the liberty of those regulated may enhance the liberty of regulatory beneficiaries. See PHH Corp. v. CFPB, 881 F.3d 75, 105–06 (D.C. Cir. 2018) (en banc) (overruled by Seila Law). More basically, these opinions express skepticism about "extrapolat[ing] from the Constitution's general structure (division of powers) and implicit values (liberty) a limit on Congress's express power to create administrative bodies." Seila Law, 140 S.Ct. at 2245 (Kagan, J., dissenting).

As you read through the decisions in this Chapter, consider what role general constitutional values should play in determining whether particular arrangements violate the separation of powers. Are they too amorphous and manipulable, or do they usefully help orient separation of powers analysis? If values should play a role, which ones are relevant—just traditional values associated with the separation of powers? Or should other constitutional values, such as equality or nondomination, factor in? See Matthew B. Lawrence, Subordination and the Separation of Powers, 131 Yale L.J. 78 (2021). Should fostering democracy be a goal—and if so, how can administrative structure best serve this end? See Daniel E. Walters, The Administrative Agon: A Democratic Theory for a Conflictual Regulatory State, 132 Yale L.J. 1 (2022). And what should happen when values conflict—for example, when advancing political accountability in the form of upholding decisions of Congress conflicts with preserving liberty, or with political accountability through the President? See Blake Emerson, Liberty and Democracy in the Administrative State: A Critique of the Roberts Court's Political Theory, 73 Hastings L.J. 371 (2022). For a discussion of the various normative commitments at play in separation of powers analysis and commentary, see Cass R. Sunstein & Adrian Vermeule, Law and Leviathan: Redeeming The Administrative State 19–37 (2020).

## SECTION 2. CONGRESS AND ADMINISTRATIVE AGENCIES

*a. Delegation of Regulatory Power*
*b. Congressional Control of Regulatory Policy*

A study of the administrative state's constitutional structure logically begins with the relationship between Congress and administrative agencies, in particular with congressional power to delegate policymaking authority to the executive branch. Such delegations are the backbone of the modern administrative state; a basic premise of our constitutional order is that an administrative agency has no inherent or independent authority to act but instead can exercise only the policymaking authority delegated to it by Congress. If you have already studied the materials in Chapter IV, you will be familiar with rulemaking, which is the most prominent way in which agencies set policy today. (As you will know if you have studied the materials in Chapter V, agencies also set policy through administrative adjudication, the constitutionality of which is discussed in Section 4.)

The constitutionality of congressional delegations to the executive is the subject of the nondelegation doctrine. Although almost never invoked to invalidate a statute, the nondelegation doctrine has spurred extensive case law and scholarship and is the first topic addressed in this Section. Congress both delegates power and then tries to control how that power is exercised. The ways in which Congress can constitutionally do so is the subject of the second set of materials in this Section.

## a. Delegation of Regulatory Power



*All legislative Powers herein granted shall be vested in a Congress of the United States, which shall consist of a Senate and House of Representatives.*

U.S. Const., Art. I, § 1

*The Congress shall have Power . . . To make all Laws which shall be necessary and proper for carrying into Execution the foregoing Powers, and all other Powers vested by this Constitution in the Government of the United States, or in any Department or Officer thereof.*

U.S. Const., Art. I, § 8, cl. 18

## (1) The Constitutionality of Regulatory Delegations

*GUNDY v. UNITED STATES*
*Whitman v. American Trucking Ass'ns, Inc.*

# GUNDY v. UNITED STATES

Supreme Court of the United States (2019).
139 S.Ct. 2116.

■ JUSTICE KAGAN announced the judgment of the Court and delivered an opinion, in which JUSTICE GINSBURG, JUSTICE BREYER, and JUSTICE SOTOMAYOR join.

The nondelegation doctrine bars Congress from transferring its legislative power to another branch of Government. This case requires us to decide whether 34 U.S.C. § 20913(d), enacted as part of the Sex Offender Registration and Notification Act (SORNA), violates that doctrine. We hold it does not. Under § 20913(d), the Attorney General must apply SORNA's registration requirements as soon as feasible to offenders convicted before the statute's enactment. That delegation easily passes constitutional muster.

I

Congress has sought, for the past quarter century, to combat sex crimes and crimes against children through sex-offender registration schemes. . . . [E]very State and the District of Columbia had enacted a sex-offender registration law. But the state statutes varied along many dimensions, and Congress came to realize that their "loopholes and deficiencies" had allowed over 100,000 sex offenders (about 20% of the total) to escape registration. In 2006, to address those failings, Congress enacted SORNA.

SORNA makes "more uniform and effective" the prior "patchwork" of sex-offender registration systems. Reynolds v. United States, 565 U.S. 432, 435 (2012). The Act's express "purpose" is "to protect the public from sex offenders and offenders against children" by "establish[ing] a comprehensive national system for [their] registration." § 20901. To that end, SORNA covers more sex offenders, and imposes more onerous registration requirements, than most States had before. The Act also backs up those requirements with new criminal penalties [of up to ten years in prison.] A "sex offender" . . . must register . . . in every State where he resides, works, or studies . . . [and] must keep the registration current . . . for a period of between fifteen years and life.

Section 20913—the disputed provision here—elaborates the "[i]nitial registration" requirements for sex offenders. Subsection (b) sets out the general rule: An offender must register "before completing a sentence of imprisonment with respect to the offense giving rise to the registration requirement" (or, if the offender is not sentenced to prison, "not later than [three] business days after being sentenced"). Two provisions down, subsection (d) addresses (in its title's words) the "[i]nitial registration of sex offenders unable to comply with subsection (b)." The provision states:

> The Attorney General shall have the authority to specify the applicability of the requirements of this subchapter to sex offenders convicted before the enactment of this chapter . . . and to prescribe rules for the registration of any such sex offenders and for other categories of sex offenders who are unable to comply with subsection (b).

Subsection (d), in other words, focuses on individuals convicted of a sex offense before SORNA's enactment—a group we will call pre-Act offenders. Many of these individuals were unregistered at the time of SORNA's enactment, either because pre-existing law did not cover them or because they had successfully evaded that law[,] . . . [and] many or most could not comply with subsection (b)'s registration rule because they had already completed their prison sentences.

Under th[e] delegated authority [of Section 20913(d)], the Attorney General issued an interim rule in February 2007, specifying that SORNA's registration requirements apply in full to "sex offenders convicted of the offense for which registration is required prior to the enactment of that Act." 72 Fed. Reg. 8897. The final rule, issued in December 2010, reiterated that SORNA applies to all pre-Act offenders. 75 Fed. Reg. 81850. . . .

Petitioner Herman Gundy is a pre-Act offender. . . . After his release from prison in 2012, Gundy came to live in New York. But he never registered there as a sex offender. A few years later, he was convicted for failing to register, in violation of [SORNA.] He argued below (among other things) that Congress unconstitutionally delegated legislative power when it authorized the Attorney General to "specify the applicability" of SORNA's registration requirements to pre-Act offenders. The District Court and Court of Appeals for the Second Circuit rejected that claim, as had every other court (including eleven Courts of Appeals) to consider the issue. . . . Today, we join the consensus and affirm.

II

Article I of the Constitution provides that "[a]ll legislative Powers herein granted shall be vested in a Congress of the United States." § 1. Accompanying that assignment of power to Congress is a bar on its further delegation. Congress, this Court explained early on, may not transfer to another branch "powers which are strictly and exclusively legislative." Wayman v. Southard, 23 U.S. (10 Wheat.) 1, 42–43 (1825) [p. 858]. But the Constitution does not "deny[ ] to the Congress the necessary resources of flexibility and practicality [that enable it] to perform its function[s]." Yakus v. United States, 321 U.S. 414, 425 (1944) [p. 861]. Congress may "obtain the assistance of its coordinate Branches" and in particular, may confer substantial discretion on executive agencies to implement and enforce the laws. Mistretta v. United States, 488 U.S. 361, 372 (1989) [p. 856]. "[I]n our increasingly complex society, replete with ever changing and more technical problems," this Court has understood that "Congress simply cannot do its job absent an ability to delegate power under broad general directives." Ibid. So we have held, time and again, that a statutory delegation is constitutional as long as Congress "lay[s] down by legislative act an intelligible principle to which the person or body authorized to [exercise the delegated authority] is directed to conform." Ibid.

Given that standard, a nondelegation inquiry always begins (and often almost ends) with statutory interpretation. . . . Only after a court has determined a challenged statute's meaning can it decide whether the law sufficiently guides executive discretion to accord with Article I. And indeed, once a court interprets the statute, it may find that the constitutional question all but answers itself.

. . . [I]n Gundy's view, [§ 20913(d)] "grants the Attorney General plenary power to determine SORNA's applicability to pre-Act offenders—to require them to register, or not, as she sees fit, and to change her policy for any reason and at any time." Id., at 42. If that were so, we would face a nondelegation question. But it is not. . . .

A

[Justice Kagan first reviewed the Court's construction of § 20913(d) in Reynolds v. United States, 565 U.S. 432 (2012). There the Court held that SORNA's registration requirements applied to pre-Act offenders only once the Attorney General said they did, as opposed to applying automatically "of their own force." But Kagan argued that Reynolds also "made clear how far SORNA limited the Attorney General's authority." Recounting Reynolds' analysis of SORNA's purpose, text, and history, she concluded that "[e]verything in Reynolds started from the premise that Congress meant for SORNA's registration requirements to apply to pre-Act offenders. . . . On that understanding, the Attorney General's role under § 20913(d) was important but limited: It was to apply SORNA to pre-Act offenders as soon as he thought it feasible to do so." Justice Kagan then undertook an independent examination of SORNA and § 20913(d), concluding that "we read the statute the same way."]

B

. . . Gundy urges us to read § 20913(d) to empower the Attorney General to do whatever he wants as to pre-Act offenders[.] . . .[He] bases that argument on the first half of § 20913(d), isolated from everything else—from the second half of the same section, from surrounding provisions in SORNA, and from any conception of the statute's history and purpose. . . . [But t]his Court has long refused to construe words "in a vacuum," as Gundy attempts. Davis v. Michigan Dept. of Treasury, 489 U.S. 803, 809 (1989). "It is a fundamental canon of statutory construction that the words of a statute must be read in their context and with a view to their place in the overall statutory scheme." National Assn. of Home Builders v. Defenders of Wildlife, 551 U.S. 644, 666 (2007). And beyond context and structure, the Court often looks to "history [and] purpose" to divine the meaning of language. That non-blinkered brand of interpretation holds good for delegations, just as for other statutory provisions. . . .

So begin at the beginning, with the "[d]eclaration of purpose" that is SORNA's first sentence. § 20901. There, Congress announced . . . that "to protect the public," it was "establish[ing] a comprehensive national system for the registration" of "sex offenders and offenders against children." § 20901. The term "comprehensive" has a clear meaning—something that is all-encompassing or sweeping. See, e.g., Webster's Third New International Dictionary 467 (2002) ("covering a matter under consideration completely or nearly completely"); New Oxford American Dictionary 350 (2d ed. 2005) ("complete; including all or nearly all elements or aspects of something"). That description could not fit the system SORNA created if the Attorney General could decline, for any reason or no reason at all, to apply SORNA to all pre-Act offenders. After all, for many years after SORNA's enactment, the great majority of sex offenders in the country would be pre-Act offenders. If Gundy were right, all of those offenders could be exempt from SORNA's registration requirements. So the mismatch between SORNA's statement of purpose and Gundy's view of § 20913(d) is as stark as stark comes. . . . SORNA's statement of purpose . . . makes clear that SORNA was supposed to apply to all pre-Act offenders—which precludes Gundy's construction of § 20913(d).

The Act's definition of "sex offender" . . . makes the same point. Under that definition, a "sex offender" is "an individual who was convicted of a sex offense." § 20911(1). Note the tense: "was," not "is." . . . Congress's use of the past tense to define the term "sex offender" shows that SORNA was not merely forward-looking. The word "is" would have taken care of all future offenders. . . .

The Act's legislative history backs up everything said above by showing that the need to register pre-Act offenders was front and center in Congress's thinking. . . . Congress designed SORNA to address "loopholes and deficiencies" in existing registration laws. And no problem attracted greater attention than the large number of sex offenders who had slipped the system. . . .

With that context and background established, we may return to § 20913(d). . . . Both the title and the remaining text of that section pinpoint one of the "practical problems" discussed above: At the moment of SORNA's enactment, many pre-Act offenders were "unable to comply" with the Act's initial registration requirements. That was because, once again, the requirements assumed that offenders would be in prison, whereas many pre-Act offenders were on the streets. In identifying that issue, § 20913(d) itself reveals the nature of the delegation to the Attorney General. It was to give him the time needed (if any) to address the various implementation issues involved in getting pre-Act offenders into the registration system. "Specify the applicability" thus does not mean "specify *whether* to apply SORNA" to pre-Act offenders at all, even though everything else in the Act commands their coverage. The phrase instead means "specify *how* to apply SORNA" to pre-Act offenders if transitional difficulties require some delay. In that way, the whole of § 20913(d) joins the rest of SORNA in giving the Attorney General only time-limited latitude to excuse pre-Act offenders from the statute's requirements. Under the law, he had to order their registration as soon as feasible. And no Attorney General has used (or, apparently, thought to use) § 20913(d) in any more expansive way. . . .

C

Now that we have determined what § 20913(d) means, we can consider whether it violates the Constitution. The question becomes: Did Congress make an impermissible delegation when it instructed the Attorney General to apply SORNA's registration requirements to pre-Act offenders as soon as feasible? Under this Court's long-established law, that question is easy. Its answer is no.

As noted earlier, this Court has held that a delegation is constitutional so long as Congress has set out an "intelligible principle" to guide the delegee's exercise of authority. J. W. Hampton, Jr., & Co., 276 U.S. at 409. Or in a related formulation, the Court has stated that a delegation is permissible if Congress has made clear to the delegee "the general policy" he must pursue and the "boundaries of [his] authority." American Power & Light, 329 U.S. at 105. Those standards, the Court has made clear, are not demanding. "[W]e have 'almost never felt qualified to second-guess Congress regarding the permissible degree of policy judgment that can be left to those executing or applying the law.' " Whitman [v. American Trucking Ass'ns, 531 U.S. [457,] 474–475 [(2001)] [p. 848] (quoting Mistretta, 488 U.S. at 416 (Scalia, J., dissenting)). Only twice in this country's history (and that in a single year) have we found a delegation excessive—in each case because "Congress had failed to articulate any policy or standard" to confine discretion. Mistretta, 488 U.S. at 373, n. 7, (emphasis added); see A. L. A. Schechter Poultry Corp. v. United States, 295 U.S. 495 (1935) [p. 860]; Panama Refining Co. v. Ryan, 293 U.S. 388 (1935) [p. 860]. By contrast, we have over and over upheld even very broad delegations. Here is a sample: We have approved delegations to various agencies to regulate in the "public interest." See, e.g., National Broadcasting Co., 319 U.S. at 216; New York Central Securities Corp. v. United States, 287 U.S. 12, 24 (1932). We have sustained authorizations for agencies to set "fair and equitable" prices and "just and reasonable" rates. Yakus, 321 U.S. at 422; FPC v. Hope Natural Gas Co., 320 U.S. 591 (1944). We more recently affirmed a delegation to an agency to issue whatever air quality standards are "requisite to protect the public health." Whitman, 531 U.S. at 472. And so forth.

In that context, the delegation in SORNA easily passes muster. . . . The statute conveyed Congress's policy that the Attorney General require pre-Act offenders to register as soon as feasible. Under the law, the feasibility issues he could address were administrative—and, more specifically, transitional—in nature. Those issues arose . . . from the need to "newly register[ ] or reregister[ ] 'a large number' of pre-Act offenders" not then in the system. And they arose, more technically, from the gap between an initial registration requirement hinged on imprisonment and a set of pre-Act offenders long since released. Even for those limited matters, the Act informed the Attorney General that he did not have forever to work things out. By stating its demand for a "comprehensive" registration system and by defining the "sex offenders" required to register to include pre-Act offenders, Congress conveyed that the Attorney General had only temporary authority. . . . That statutory authority, as compared to the delegations we have upheld in the past, is distinctly small-bore. It falls well within constitutional bounds.

Indeed, if SORNA's delegation is unconstitutional, then most of Government is unconstitutional—dependent as Congress is on the need to give discretion to executive officials to implement its programs. Consider again this Court's long-time recognition: "Congress simply cannot do its job absent an ability to delegate power under broad general directives." Mistretta, 488 U.S. at 372. Or as the dissent in that case agreed: "[S]ome judgments . . . must be left to the officers executing the law." 488 U.S. at 415 (opinion of Scalia, J.). Among the judgments often left to executive officials are ones involving feasibility. In fact, standards of that kind are ubiquitous in the U.S. Code. . . .

It is wisdom and humility alike that this Court has always upheld such "necessities of government." Mistretta, 488 U.S. at 416 (Scalia, J., dissenting) (internal quotation marks omitted). . . . We therefore affirm the judgment of the Court of Appeals.

It is so ordered.

■ JUSTICE KAVANAUGH took no part in the consideration or decision of this case.

■ JUSTICE ALITO, concurring in the judgment.

The Constitution confers on Congress certain "legislative [p]owers," Art. I, § 1, and does not permit Congress to delegate them to another branch of the Government. Nevertheless, since 1935, the Court has uniformly rejected nondelegation arguments and has upheld provisions that authorized agencies to adopt important rules pursuant to extraordinarily capacious standards.

If a majority of this Court were willing to reconsider the approach we have taken for the past 84 years, I would support that effort. But because a majority is not willing to do that, it would be freakish to single out the provision at issue here for special treatment. . . .

■ JUSTICE GORSUCH, with whom THE CHIEF JUSTICE and JUSTICE THOMAS join, dissenting.[1]

The Constitution promises that only the people's elected representatives may adopt new federal laws restricting liberty. Yet the statute before us scrambles that design. It purports to endow the nation's chief prosecutor with the power to write his own criminal code governing the lives of a half-million citizens. Yes, those affected are some of the

---

[1] [Ed.] Justice Gorsuch puts sources in footnotes, but for consistency's sake when sources are included we have added them to the text.

least popular among us. But if a single executive branch official can write laws restricting the liberty of this group of persons, what does that mean for the next?

Today, a plurality of an eight-member Court endorses this extraconstitutional arrangement but resolves nothing. Working from an understanding of the Constitution at war with its text and history, the plurality reimagines the terms of the statute before us and insists there is nothing wrong with Congress handing off so much power to the Attorney General. But JUSTICE ALITO supplies the fifth vote for today's judgment and he does not join either the plurality's constitutional or statutory analysis, indicating instead that he remains willing, in a future case with a full Court, to revisit these matters. Respectfully, I would not wait.

I

For individuals convicted of sex offenses after Congress adopted the Sex Offender Registration and Notification Act (SORNA) in 2006, the statute offers detailed instructions. . . . [W]hat about those convicted of sex offenses *before* the Act's adoption? . . . Congress concluded that something had to be done about these "pre-Act" offenders too. But it seems Congress couldn't agree what that should be. . . . So Congress simply passed the problem to the Attorney General. For all half-million pre-Act offenders, the law says only. . . [that] "[t]he Attorney General shall have the authority to specify the applicability of the requirements of this subchapter to sex offenders convicted before the enactment of this chapter . . . and to prescribe rules for the registration of any such sex offender." [34 U.S.C. § 20913(d)]

Yes, that's it. The breadth of the authority Congress granted to the Attorney General in these few words can only be described as vast. . . . Congress . . . gave the Attorney General free rein to write the rules for virtually the entire existing sex offender population in this country—a situation that promised to persist for years or decades until pre-Act offenders passed away or fulfilled the terms of their registration obligations and post-Act offenders came to predominate. Unsurprisingly, different Attorneys General have exercised their discretion in different ways.

These unbounded policy choices have profound consequences for the people they affect. Take our case. Before SORNA's enactment, Herman Gundy pleaded guilty in 2005 to a sexual offense. After his release from prison five years later, he was arrested again, this time for failing to register as a sex offender according to the rules the Attorney General had then prescribed for pre-Act offenders. As a result, Mr. Gundy faced an additional 10-year prison term—10 years more than if the Attorney General had, in his discretion, chosen to write the rules differently.

II

A

. . . [T]he Constitution . . . vest[s] the authority to exercise different aspects of the people's sovereign power in distinct entities. In Article I, the Constitution entrusted all of the federal government's legislative power to Congress. In Article II, it assigned the executive power to the President. And in Article III, it gave independent judges the task of applying the laws to cases and controversies.

To the framers, each of these vested powers had a distinct content. When it came to the legislative power, the framers understood it to mean the power to adopt generally applicable rules of conduct governing future actions by private persons—the power to "prescrib[e] the rules by which the duties and rights of every citizen are to be regulated," The Federalist No. 78, p. 465 (C. Rossiter ed. 1961) (A. Hamilton). . . . The framers understood, too, that it would frustrate "the system of government ordained by the Constitution" if Congress could merely announce vague aspirations and then assign others the responsibility of adopting legislation to realize its goals. Marshall Field & Co. v. Clark, 143 U.S. 649, 692 (1892).

Why did the framers insist on this particular arrangement? They believed the new federal government's most dangerous power was the power to enact laws restricting the people's liberty. An "excess of law-making" was, in their words, one of "the diseases to which our governments are most liable." The Federalist, No. 62, at 378 (J. Madison). To address that tendency, the framers went to great lengths to make lawmaking difficult. In Article I, by far the longest part of the Constitution, the framers insisted that any proposed law must win the approval of two Houses of Congress—elected at different times, by different constituencies, and for different terms in office—and either secure the President's approval or obtain enough support to override his veto. . . . Article I's detailed processes for new laws were also designed to promote deliberation. . . . Other purposes animated the framers' design as well. Because men are not angels, and majorities can threaten minority rights, the framers insisted on a legislature composed of different bodies subject to different electorates as a means of ensuring that any new law would have to secure the approval of a supermajority of the people's representatives. This, in turn, assured minorities that their votes would often decide the fate of proposed legislation. . . . Restricting the task of legislating to one branch characterized by difficult and deliberative processes was also designed to promote fair notice and the rule of law, ensuring the people would be subject to a relatively stable and predictable set of rules. And by directing that legislating be done only by elected representatives in a public process, the Constitution sought to ensure that the lines of accountability would be clear: The sovereign people would know, without ambiguity, whom to hold accountable for the laws they would have to follow.

If Congress could pass off its legislative power to the executive branch, the "[v]esting [c]lauses, and indeed the entire structure of the Constitution,' would 'make no sense." Lawson, Delegation and Original Meaning, 88 Va. L. Rev. 327, 340 (2002). . . .

The framers warned us against permitting consequences like these. . . . The framers knew, too, that the job of keeping the legislative power confined to the legislative branch couldn't be trusted to self-policing by Congress. . . . So when a case or controversy comes within the judicial competence, the Constitution does not permit judges to look the other way; we must call foul when the constitutional lines are crossed. . . .

B

Accepting, then, that we have an obligation to decide whether Congress has unconstitutionally divested itself of its legislative responsibilities, the question follows: What's the test? . . . [T]he framers . . . offered us important guiding principles.

First, we know that as long as Congress makes the policy decisions when regulating private conduct, it may authorize another branch to 'fill up the details.' . . . Through [Wayman v. Southard and subsequent cases] runs the theme that Congress must set forth standards "sufficiently definite and precise to enable Congress, the courts, and the public to ascertain" whether Congress's guidance has been followed. Yakus v. United States, 321 U.S. 414, 426 (1944).

Second, once Congress prescribes the rule governing private conduct, it may make the application of that rule depend on executive fact-finding. Here, too, the power extended to the executive may prove highly consequential. . . .

Third, Congress may assign the executive and judicial branches certain non-legislative responsibilities. While the Constitution vests all federal legislative power in Congress alone, Congress's legislative authority sometimes overlaps with authority the Constitution separately vests in another branch. . . . [W]hen a congressional statute confers wide discretion to the executive, no separation-of-powers problem may arise if "the discretion is to be exercised over matters already within the scope of executive power." Schoenbrod, The Delegation Doctrine: Could the Court Give It Substance? 83 Mich. L. Rev. 1223, 1260 (1985). . . .

C

Before the 1930s, federal statutes granting authority to the executive were comparatively modest and usually easily upheld. But then the federal government began to grow explosively. . . . Twice the Court responded by striking down statutes for violating the separation of powers, . . . [but] since that time the Court hasn't held another statute to violate the separation of powers in the same way. . . . [M]aybe the most likely explanation . . . [for why] lies in the story of the evolving "intelligible principle" doctrine.

This Court first used that phrase in 1928 in J. W. Hampton, Jr., & Co. v. United States, 276 U.S. 394, 409 (1928). . . . No one at the time thought the phrase meant to effect some revolution in this Court's understanding of the Constitution. While the exact line between policy and details, lawmaking and fact-finding, and legislative and non-legislative functions had sometimes invited reasonable debate, everyone agreed these were the relevant inquiries. . . . There's a good argument, as well, that the statute in J. W. Hampton passed muster under the traditional tests. . . . Still, it's undeniable that the "intelligible principle" remark eventually began to take on a life of its own. . . .

Th[e current] mutated version of the "intelligible principle" remark has no basis in the original meaning of the Constitution, in history, or even in the decision from which it was plucked. . . . Still, the scope of the problem can be overstated. At least some of the results the Court has reached under the banner of the abused "intelligible principle" doctrine may be consistent with more traditional teachings [because they] . . . implicated the president's inherent Article II authority. . . . Others of these cases may have involved laws that specified rules governing private conduct but conditioned the application of those rules on fact-finding—a practice that is, as we've seen, also long associated with the executive function.

More recently, too, we've sought to tame misunderstandings of the intelligible principle "test." . . . Touby v. United States, 500 U.S. 160, 166 (1991), . . . may have at least begun to point us back in the direction of the right questions. To determine whether a statute provides an intelligible principle, we must ask: Does the statute assign to the executive only the responsibility to make factual findings? Does it set forth the facts that the executive must consider and the criteria against which to measure them? And most importantly, did Congress, and not the Executive Branch, make the policy judgments? Only then can we fairly say that a statute contains the kind of intelligible principle the Constitution demands.

While it's been some time since the Court last held that a statute improperly delegated the legislative power to another branch . . . [w]e still regularly rein in Congress's efforts to delegate legislative power; we just call what we're doing by different names. . . . Consider, for example, the "major questions" doctrine. Under our precedents, an agency can fill in statutory gaps where "statutory circumstances" indicate that Congress meant to grant it such powers. But we don't follow that rule when the "statutory gap" concerns "a question of deep economic and political significance that is central to the statutory scheme." King v. Burwell, 576 U.S. 473, 486 (2015). Consider, too, this Court's cases addressing vagueness. . . . It's easy to see . . . how most any challenge to a legislative delegation can be reframed as a vagueness complaint: A statute that does not contain "sufficiently definite and precise" standards "to enable Congress, the courts, and the public to ascertain" whether Congress's guidance has been followed at once presents a delegation problem and provides impermissibly vague guidance to affected citizens. Yakus, 321 U.S. at 426. . . .

III

A

Returning to SORNA with this understanding of our charge in hand, problems quickly emerge. . . . It's hard to see how SORNA leaves the Attorney General with only details to fill up. Of course, what qualifies as a detail can sometimes be difficult to discern and, as we've seen, this

Court has upheld statutes that allow federal agencies to resolve even highly consequential details so long as Congress prescribes the rule governing private conduct. But . . . [a]s the government itself admitted in Reynolds, SORNA leaves the Attorney General free to impose on 500,000 pre-Act offenders all of the statute's requirements, some of them, or none of them. The Attorney General may choose which pre-Act offenders to subject to the Act. And he is free to change his mind at any point or over the course of different political administrations. . . . Nor can SORNA be described as an example of conditional legislation subject to executive fact-finding. . . . Finally, SORNA does not involve an area of overlapping authority with the executive. . . . If the separation of powers means anything, it must mean that Congress cannot give the executive branch a blank check to write a code of conduct governing private conduct for a half-million people. . . .

It would be easy enough to let this case go. After all, sex offenders are one of the most disfavored groups in our society. But the rule that prevents Congress from giving the executive carte blanche to write laws for sex offenders is the same rule that protects everyone else. . . . Nor would enforcing the Constitution's demands spell doom for what some call the "administrative state." The separation of powers does not prohibit any particular policy outcome, let alone dictate any conclusion about the proper size and scope of government. Instead, it is a procedural guarantee that requires Congress to assemble a social consensus before choosing our nation's course on policy questions like those implicated by SORNA. What is more, Congress is hardly bereft of options to accomplish all it might wish to achieve. It may always authorize executive branch officials to fill in even a large number of details, to find facts that trigger the generally applicable rule of conduct specified in a statute, or to exercise non-legislative powers. Congress can also commission agencies or other experts to study and recommend legislative language. Respecting the separation of powers forecloses no substantive outcomes. It only requires us to respect along the way one of the most vital of the procedural protections of individual liberty found in our Constitution.

B

. . . Most everyone, the plurality included, concedes that if SORNA allows the Attorney General as much authority as we have outlined, it would present "a nondelegation question." So the only remaining available tactic is to try to make this big case "small-bore" by recasting the statute in a way that might satisfy any plausible separation-of-powers test. . . . [J]ust a few years ago in Reynolds the government represented to this Court that SORNA granted the Attorney General nearly boundless discretion with respect to pre-Act offenders. But *now*, faced with a constitutional challenge, the government speaks out of the other side of its mouth and invites us to reimagine SORNA as compelling the Attorney General to register pre-Act offenders "to the maximum extent feasible." . . . [E]ven this new dream of a statute wouldn't be free from doubt. A statute directing an agency to regulate private conduct to the extent "feasible" can have many possible meanings: It might refer to "technological" feasibility, "economic" feasibility, "administrative" feasibility, or even "political" feasibility. . . .

But don't worry over that; return to the real world. The bigger problem is that the feasibility standard is a figment of the government's (very recent) imagination. The only provision addressing pre-Act offenders, § 20913(d), says *nothing* about feasibility. . . .

[Justice Gorsuch also rejected the plurality's invocation of SORNA's purpose: "While those adopting SORNA might have declared that they hoped and wished for a 'comprehensive national system,' the fact remains that the law they actually adopted for pre-Act offenders leaves everything to the Attorney General. Hopes and dreams are not laws." He was equally unpersuaded by SORNA's sex offender definition: "To say that pre-Act sex offenders fall within the definition of 'sex offenders' is merely a truism: Yes, of course, these people have already been convicted of sex offenses under state law. But whether these individuals are also subject to federal registration requirements is a different question entirely. And as we have seen, the only part of the statute that speaks to pre-Act sex offenders—§ 20913(d)—makes plain that they are not automatically subject to all the Act's terms but are left to their fate at the hands of the Attorney General."]

. . . In a future case with a full panel, I remain hopeful that the Court may yet recognize that, while Congress can enlist considerable assistance from the executive branch in filling up details and finding facts, it may never hand off to the nation's chief prosecutor the power to write his own criminal code. . . .

## SIGNIFICANT CASE

### WHITMAN v. AMERICAN TRUCKING ASS'NS, INC.
531 U.S. 457 (2001).

The Clean Air Act (CAA) tasks the Environmental Protection Agency (EPA) with issuing national ambient air quality standards (NAAQS) for air pollutants. Section 108 of the CAA requires EPA to publish and revise lists of air pollutants and issue air quality criteria for each pollutant. Section 109 then requires the EPA to issue primary and secondary NAAQS for each pollutant that EPA identifies, with section 109(b)(1) providing that NAAQS "shall be ambient air quality standards the attainment and maintenance of which in the judgment of the Administrator, based on such criteria and allowing an adequate margin of safety, are requisite to protect the public health."

After EPA revised the NAAQS for particulate matter and ozone, a trucking association, private companies, and three states challenged the standards in court. They argued, inter alia, that EPA's interpretation of § 109(b)(1) violated the nondelegation doctrine. The D.C. Circuit agreed, concluding that EPA's interpretation of § 109(b)(1) violated the nondelegation doctrine because the agency had not provided an intelligible principle to guide its exercise of authority in setting NAAQS.

According to the D.C. Circuit, EPA "lack[ed] any determinate criteria for drawing lines. It has failed to state intelligibly how much [of these pollutants] is too much." But the lower court had thought that EPA could avoid the unconstitutional delegation by adopting a restrictive construction of § 109(b)(1), so instead of declaring the section unconstitutional the court remanded the NAAQS to the agency.

The Supreme Court, in a unanimous decision written by JUSTICE SCALIA, reversed: "In a delegation challenge, the constitutional question is whether the statute has delegated legislative power to the agency. Article I, § 1, of the Constitution vests '[a]ll legislative Powers herein granted . . . in a Congress of the United States.' This text permits no delegation of those powers, and so we repeatedly have said that when Congress confers decisionmaking authority upon agencies *Congress* must 'lay down by legislative act an intelligible principle to which the person or body authorized to [act] is directed to conform.' J.W. Hampton, Jr., & Co. v. United States, 276 U.S. 394, 409 (1928) [p. 859]. We have never suggested that an agency can cure an unlawful delegation of legislative power by adopting in its discretion a limiting construction of the statute. . . . The idea that an agency can cure an unconstitutionally standardless delegation of power by declining to exercise some of that power seems to us internally contradictory. The very choice of which portion of the power to exercise—that is to say, the prescription of the standard that Congress had omitted—would *itself* be an exercise of the forbidden legislative authority. . . .

"We agree with the Solicitor General that the text of § 109(b)(1) of the CAA at a minimum requires that '[f]or a discrete set of pollutants and based on published air quality criteria that reflect the latest scientific knowledge, [the] EPA must establish uniform national standards at a level that is requisite to protect public health from the adverse effects of the pollutant in the ambient air.' Requisite, in turn, 'mean[s] sufficient, but not more than necessary.' . . .

"The scope of discretion § 109(b)(1) allows is in fact well within the outer limits of our nondelegation precedents. . . . It is true enough that the degree of agency discretion that is acceptable varies according to the scope of the power congressionally conferred. While Congress need not provide any direction to the EPA regarding the manner in which it is to define 'country elevators,' which are to be exempt from new stationary-source regulations governing grain elevators, see 42 U.S.C. § 7411(i), it must provide substantial guidance on setting air standards that affect the entire national economy. But even in sweeping regulatory schemes we have never demanded, as the Court of Appeals did here, that statutes provide a 'determinate criterion' for saying 'how much [of the regulated harm] is too much.' . . . Section 109(b)(1) of the CAA, which to repeat we interpret as requiring the EPA to set air quality standards at the level that is 'requisite'—that is, not lower or higher than is necessary—to protect the public health with an adequate margin of safety, fits comfortably within the scope of discretion permitted by our precedent."

The decision prompted separate concurring opinions from both Justice Thomas and Justice Stevens.[2] JUSTICE THOMAS agreed "that § 109's directive to the agency is no less an 'intelligible principle' than a host of other directives that we have approved. . . . I am not convinced that the intelligible principle doctrine serves to prevent all cessions of legislative power. I believe that there are cases in which the principle is intelligible and yet the significance of the delegated decision is simply too great for the decision to be called anything other than 'legislative.' " Noting that "none of the parties to these cases has examined the text of the Constitution or asked us to reconsider our precedents on cessions of legislative power," Thomas added that in the future he "would be willing to address the question whether our delegation jurisprudence has strayed too far from our Founders' understanding of separation of powers."

JUSTICE STEVENS, joined by Justice Souter, concurred in part, stating: "The Court has two choices. We could choose to articulate our ultimate disposition of this issue by frankly acknowledging that the power delegated to the EPA is 'legislative' but nevertheless conclude that the delegation is constitutional because adequately limited by the terms of the authorizing statute. Alternatively, we could pretend, as the Court does, that the authority delegated to the EPA is somehow not 'legislative power.' Despite the fact that there is language in our opinions that supports the Court's articulation of our holding, I am persuaded that it would be both wiser and more faithful to what we have actually done in delegation cases to admit that agency rulemaking authority is 'legislative power.' The proper characterization of governmental power should generally depend on the nature of the power, not on the identity of the person exercising it. If the NAAQS that the EPA promulgated had been prescribed by Congress, everyone would agree that these rules would be the product of 'legislative power.' "

But Justice Stevens also insisted that his approach was "fully consistent with the text of the Constitution. In Article I, the Framers vested 'All legislative Powers' in the Congress, Art. I, § 1, just as in Article II they vested the 'executive Power' in the President, Art. II, § 1. Those provisions do not purport to limit the authority of either recipient of power to delegate authority to others. . . . It seems clear that an executive agency's exercise of rulemaking authority pursuant to a valid delegation from Congress is 'legislative.' As long as the delegation provides a sufficiently intelligible principle, there is nothing inherently unconstitutional about it."

## NOTES

(1) ***The Evolution from Whitman to Gundy.*** The Supreme Court rejected the nondelegation challenges brought in both Gundy and Whitman, but that shared bottom-line result masks significant change. Only Justice Thomas

[2] Justice Breyer also concurred separately, but on the separate question of whether § 109(b)(1) prohibited EPA from considering costs in setting the NAAQS.

signaled any interest in strengthening nondelegation doctrine or altering the governing intelligible principle test in Whitman. Fast forward eighteen years to Gundy, and three justices fully signed on to that position, espoused by Justice Gorsuch in dissent, while Justice Alito stated his willingness to reconsider the intelligible principle test if a majority were supportive of doing so.

In DEPARTMENT OF TRANSPORTATION v. ASSOCIATION OF AMERICAN RAILROADS, 575 U.S. 43 (2015), the Court had faced another nondelegation challenge. At issue in American Railroads was the Passenger Rail Investment and Improvement Act (PRIIA), § 207(a) of which granted Amtrak and the Federal Railroad Administration (FRA)—located in the Department of Transportation—joint authority to issue "metrics and standards" that address the performance and scheduling of passenger railroad services. PRIIA specifies that the metrics and standards should be incorporated into the access and service contracts between Amtrak, a federally-chartered not-for-profit corporation responsible for providing passenger rail services, and the freight rail carriers over whose tracks Amtrak's trains operate and enjoy a statutory right-of-way. In 2010, the Association of American Railroads sued to challenge the metrics and standards jointly issued by Amtrak and FRA, claiming that § 207 violated the nondelegation doctrine, the separation of powers, and due process by placing legislative and rulemaking authority in the hands of an interested private entity (Amtrak). The suit also raised Appointments Clause claims with respect to the appointment of Amtrak's President (see p. 962). The D.C. Circuit upheld the Association's claim that § 207 represented an unconstitutional private delegation, concluding that under the Supreme Court's decision in Carter v. Carter Coal Co., 298 U.S. 238 (1936) (p. 860), it was impermissible for Congress to delegate regulatory authority to a private entity. The Supreme Court reversed, in an opinion by Justice Kennedy, holding that Amtrak was a governmental entity for purposes of determining the constitutional validity of the metrics and standards (just as it had previously held Amtrak was part of government for purposes of the First Amendment. Lebron v. National Railroad Passenger Corporation, 513 U.S. 374 (1995)).

Concurring only in the judgment, JUSTICE THOMAS took the occasion to offer a broad attack on current nondelegation doctrine very similar to that raised later by Justice Gorsuch in Gundy. Thomas argued that the power to set generally applicable rules of private conduct was legislative power constitutionally reserved for Congress, and thus Congress could not delegate "any degree of policy judgment . . . when it comes to establishing generally applicable rules governing private conduct." Thomas also reviewed the Court's early nondelegation jurisprudence in detail and concluded that the contemporary intelligible principle test was a marked deviation from the doctrine's roots. Strikingly, however, Justice Thomas wrote only for himself; no other justice joined his opinion. In particular, although condemning private delegations and other features of PRIIA, Justice Alito appeared more accepting of public delegations, stating that "the formal reason why the Court does not enforce the nondelegation doctrine with more vigilance is that the other branches of Government have vested powers of their own that can be used in ways that resemble lawmaking."

Why do you think the Court changed position so sharply over just four years? One reason is the changing composition of the Court: Justice Gorsuch joined the Court in that period, having penned a concurring opinion questioning delegation while on the Tenth Circuit. See Gutierrez-Brizuela v. Lynch, 834 F.3d 1142, 1151–55 (10th Cir. 2016) (Gorsuch, J., concurring). And Justice Scalia, the defender of established nondelegation doctrine in Whitman, died. Another factor was a growing chorus of conservative attacks on delegation and the constitutionality of the administrative state more broadly. See Gillian E. Metzger, The Supreme Court 2016 Term—Foreword: 1930s Redux: The Administrative State Under Siege, 131 Harv. L. Rev. 1, 17–31, 34–46 (2017) (describing other instances of this attack and identifying its core themes).

(2) ***A Fight over Delegation or Statutory Interpretation?*** The plurality and dissent in Gundy spend much of their time analyzing § 20913(d). Is their disagreement as much about how to interpret statutes as about constitutional structure? Whose interpretation of § 20913(d) do you find more persuasive?

Justice Gorsuch, like Gundy, focuses on § 20913(d)'s authorization to the Attorney General to "specify [SORNA's] application" to pre-Act offenders. In discussing the intelligible principle test, Gorsuch criticizes "people for treating judicial opinions as if they were statutes, divorcing a passing comment from its context, ignoring all that came before and after, and treating an isolated phrase as if it were controlling." Is the same complaint appropriate against his approach to interpreting SORNA? Is Justice Kagan's criticism of his and Gundy's interpretation as "blinkered" textualism a fair one, or does she end up underweighting the words of § 20913(d) itself? Does Justice Kagan's conclusion that § 20913(d) simply authorizes the Attorney General to delay application of SORNA's registration requirements to pre-Act offenders on feasibility grounds nonetheless represent an implausibly narrow reading of the provision? The relationship between statutory interpretation and delegation is further discussed in the Notes on narrowed statutory constructions and the major question doctrine below (p. 868).

(3) ***Formalist and Functionalist Approaches.*** In Gundy, Justice Kagan and Justice Gorsuch offer very different accounts of the Constitution's treatment of delegation. How do their approaches, and those evident in other opinions on delegation, fit in with formalism and functionalism as separation of powers methodologies? (For a general description of formalism and functionalism, see p. 830.)

Writing for the plurality, Justice Kagan acknowledges that the Constitution vests the legislative power in Congress and states that if SORNA gave the Attorney General "plenary power" to determine if pre-Act offenders were subject to registration requirements or not, that would raise a nondelegation question. Yet a critical presupposition of Kagan's account is the functionalist claim that the Constitution grants Congress the "flexibility and practicality" it needs to effectively address the complex and everchanging problems of modern society. In Whitman, Justice Stevens offers an even more resolutely functionalist view, going so far as to argue that nothing in the Constitution precludes Congress from delegating legislative power to the executive branch so long as Congress provides an intelligible principle to guide executive branch lawmaking.

Justice Gorsuch, on the other hand, takes a more formalist stance. He views the Constitution as strictly dividing up "different aspects of the people's sovereign power," each of which is then vested in a "distinct entit[y]." Rather than emphasizing Congress's need to function effectively, Gorsuch underscores that the Framers viewed the legislative power as a particular threat to individual liberty. Hence, they designed the bicameralism and presentment process to make lawmaking difficult. On Gorsuch's account, allowing Congress to delegate legislative power—which he defines as "the power to adopt generally applicable rules of conduct governing future actions by private persons"—to the executive branch would fundamentally subvert the Framers' design. Justice Thomas takes a similar formalist approach in American Railroads.

Interestingly, Justice Scalia's opinion in Whitman is both formalist and functionalist. He is adamant that Article I's Vesting Clause provides incontrovertible textual proof that the Constitution prohibits Congress from delegating legislative power to others. Yet he combines this formalist stance with a functionalist insistence that Congress can authorize the executive branch to exercise broad policymaking and regulatory authority. And in his earlier dissent in Mistretta, from which Justice Kagan repeatedly quotes, Justice Scalia forcefully states the case for why Congress is better functionally suited than the Supreme Court to determine "the permissible degree of policy judgment that can be left to those executing or applying the law."

(4) ***What Does the Constitution Require?*** Which approach—functionalist, formalist, or a combination thereof—is the most appropriate to take with respect to delegation? Does the Constitution impose a clear textual distinction among the three types of power, grant one type exclusively to each branch, and prohibit redelegation? Note that scholars disagree on whether the Constitution's Vesting Clauses should be seen as grants of power or as simply descriptively distinguishing among the branches; you'll see this debate later on with respect to the scope of presidential power (see Section 3). Eric A. Posner and Adrian Vermeule, Interring the Nondelegation Doctrine, 69 U. Chi. L. Rev. 1721 (2002), maintain that all the Vesting Clause of Article I means is that "[n]either Congress nor its members may delegate to anyone else the authority to vote on federal statutes or to exercise other de jure powers of federal legislators." On this view, "a statutory grant of authority to the executive branch or other agents can never amount to a delegation of legislative power." Is their approach a plausible reading of the Clause? Would following Justice Stevens and being more forthright about the constitutional acceptability of Congress redelegating legislative power be a preferable stance for the Court to take? For criticism of Posner and Vermeule's view, see Larry Alexander & Saikrishna Prakash, Reports of

Nondelegation Doctrine's Death Are Greatly Exaggerated, 70 U. Chi. L. Rev. 1297 (2003).

Even if an open embrace of delegation can accord with the text of the Vesting Clauses, does it fit with the Constitution's separation of powers structure? After all, why have the Constitution identify certain powers with particular branches if Congress could just redistribute them? On the other hand, can't Justice Gorsuch (and Justice Thomas before him) be faulted for unduly restricting the legitimate scope of executive power in categorizing policy judgments as exercises of legislative power? Think about traditionally core exercises of executive power, such as law enforcement; aren't there necessarily policy choices involved? Or, as Justice Scalia put the point in Whitman, "a certain degree of discretion, and thus of lawmaking, inheres in most executive or judicial action." Does that recognition give some support to viewing what is being delegated in Gundy (and whenever a court finds an intelligible principle) as executive power?

What about other aspects of constitutional structure, in particular, the Bicameralism and Presentment Clause or the Constitution's specification of different systems of representation in the two legislative chambers and for the presidency? Do you agree with Justice Gorsuch that delegation subverts these structures by making it too easy to enact legal requirements that bind private actors and by giving unelected bureaucrats too much power to set the content of these rules? Does delegation also threaten federalism, by making it easier for the federal government to govern in a broad array of contexts? (For articulation of these structural arguments against delegation, see Jennifer Mascott, Early Customs Laws and Delegation, 87 Geo. Wash. L. Rev. 1388 (2019).) Or is Justice Kagan right that this account of constitutional structure is too one-sided, ignoring the ways in which the Constitution intended to create institutions that could effectively perform their constitutional functions? Does the fact that any congressional delegation of authority must be enacted through legislation that satisfies bicameralism and presentment address concerns about adhering to these structural requirements and suffice to ensure political accountability? Similarly, are federalism demands satisfied as long as Congress is delegating within one of its enumerated heads of authority? And how should we factor in the Necessary and Proper Clause, which provides Congress with broad authority "to make all Laws which shall be necessary and proper for carrying into Execution" the powers vested in the U.S. "Government . . . or any Department or Officer thereof"?

Often, as in Gorsuch's dissent, structural arguments against delegation are closely intertwined with originalism. How much should the views of the Framers and historical practice matter in assessing the constitutionality of contemporary delegation? Gundy has provoked a surge of scholarly attention to the nondelegation doctrine's originalist roots—or lack thereof. Several scholars contend that nondelegation doctrine is a modern invention that lacks support at the Founding, while several others disagree. This ongoing debate is canvassed below (p. 863). Should originalist practice be determinative here? Suppose a history of delegation at the Founding shows that there were very few broad delegations; should that preclude reading the

Constitution to allow such delegations today, given the dramatically expanded complexities and challenges of governing in contemporary society? On the other hand, in light of the originalist cast of the current nondelegation critique, should evidence that the Framers enacted broad delegations of policymaking authority be more dispositive in signaling the constitutionality of such delegations?

Finally, what about the disruptive impact that enforcing a constitutional prohibition on executive branch policymaking would have today: Justice Kagan insists that it would mean that "most of Government is unconstitutional," whereas Justice Gorsuch suggests that the impact may be overstated because some delegations currently upheld under the intelligible principle rubric could be sustained as delegations of factfinding or instances where the President may enjoy some inherent authority. Who has the better assessment? Given the number of broad delegations sustained under the intelligible principle test over the years, does it seem likely that the impact of narrowing the scope of constitutional delegations would be significant? Can separation of powers justify a dramatic overturning of decades of legislation and practice? Although Chief Justice Roberts joined the Gundy dissent, elsewhere he has emphasized stare decisis in refusing to overturn established administrative law doctrines. See Kisor v. Wilkie, 139 S.Ct. 2400, 2424 (2019) (Roberts, CJ., concurring in part) (p. 1391). Do you think stare decisis arguments for not overturning the Court's longstanding acceptance of broad delegations are strong?

(5) ***The Goals of Nondelegation Doctrine.*** How should we understand the goals of the nondelegation doctrine? In a famous concurrence in INDUSTRIAL UNION DEP'T, AFL-CIO V. AMERICAN PETROLEUM INST., 448 U.S. 607, 685 (1980) (p. 862), then-JUSTICE REHNQUIST wrote: "As formulated and enforced by this Court, the nondelegation doctrine serves three important functions. First, and most abstractly, it ensures to the extent consistent with orderly governmental administration that important choices of social policy are made by Congress, the branch of our Government most responsive to the popular will. Second, the doctrine guarantees that, to the extent Congress finds it necessary to delegate authority, it provides the recipient of that authority with an 'intelligible principle' to guide the exercise of the delegated discretion. Third, and derivative of the second, the doctrine ensures that courts charged with reviewing the exercise of delegated legislative discretion will be able to test that exercise against ascertainable standards." Do you agree with Rehnquist's characterization of nondelegation's goals? Are some of these goals more important than others? Why?

(6) ***Does the Intelligible Principle Test Have Any Bite?*** Justice Gorsuch (as did Justice Thomas before him) condemns the current intelligible principle test as failing to enforce "any qualitative distinction between legislative and executive power." Is he right? Can you identify any delegations that would fail it?

(7) ***Is Nondelegation a Political Question?*** Both the plurality and dissent in Gundy assume that a constitutional prohibition on delegating legislative power would be judicially enforceable; Justice Kagan clearly thinks that judicial invalidation of a delegation as too broad should be rare, yet even she

doesn't rule it out. Should we instead view any constitutional prohibition on delegation of legislative power as a political question, left entirely for Congress and the executive branch to enforce? Two longstanding bases for finding a political question, emphasized recently by the Supreme Court, are the presence of "a textually demonstrable constitutional commitment of the issue to a coordinate political department; or a lack of judicially discoverable and manageable standards for resolving it." Zivotofsky v. Clinton, 566 U.S. 189, 195 (2012).

Are those tests met in the delegation context? Consider in this regard JUSTICE SCALIA's dissenting opinion in MISTRETTA V. UNITED STATES, 488 U.S. 361 (1989): "[W]hile the doctrine of unconstitutional delegation is unquestionably a fundamental element of our constitutional system, it is not an element readily enforceable by the courts. Once it is conceded, as it must be, that no statute can be entirely precise, and that some judgments, even some judgments involving policy considerations, must be left to the officers executing the law and to the judges applying it, the debate over unconstitutional delegation becomes a debate not over a point of principle, but over a question of degree. . . . Since Congress is no less endowed with common sense than we are, and better equipped to inform itself of the 'necessities' of government; and since the factors bearing upon those necessities are both multifarious and (in the nonpartisan sense) highly political, . . . it is small wonder that we have almost never felt qualified to second-guess Congress regarding the permissible degree of policy judgment that can be left to those executing or applying the law." Yet as Gundy and Whitman show, the Court has not treated delegation as a political question outside its jurisdiction, opting instead—up until recently—for very deferential review. Why might that be?

(8) ***Is Delegation of Authority to Enact Criminal Law Different?*** Although Justice Gorsuch emphasizes the danger of letting Congress "hand off to the nation's chief prosecutor the power to write his own criminal code," his argument for heightened scrutiny of delegations is not limited to delegations that authorize the executive branch to make criminal law. Should it have been? In an amicus brief filed in support of Gundy, the American Civil Liberties Union (ACLU) contended that the contemporary intelligible principle test is appropriate for regulatory delegations, given the "complexity and scope of a national government," but that "all delegations are not created equal. The same deferential approach is not appropriate when Congress delegates authority to the Attorney General to make criminal law. . . . The power to punish is constitutionally distinctive[, as] reflected in the many guarantees of the Fourth, Fifth, Sixth, and Eighth Amendments[,] . . . a range of basic doctrines, from the rule of lenity to the void-for-vagueness principle[, and] . . . in the constitutional prohibitions on ex post facto laws and bills of attainder." Brief of the ACLU at 2–3, Gundy v. United States (No. 17-6086), 139 S.Ct. 2116 (2019).[3]

Yet although the delegation in Gundy is unusual in its sole focus on whether individuals would be subject to criminal prohibitions, many

---

[3] https://www.aclu.org/legal-document/gundy-v-united-states-amicus-brief.

requirements enacted under broad regulatory delegations are enforced in part by criminal prohibitions. See, e.g., 15 U.S.C. § 78ff(a) (making it a crime to violate SEC regulations); 42 U.S.C. § 8432 (making it a crime to violate certain Department of Energy regulations). Can these delegations be distinguished analytically from § 20913(d)?

(9) ***The Future for Nondelegation Challenges.*** The significance of Gundy lies less in its bottom-line result than in what the case may signal about where the Supreme Court is headed on delegation. As the progression from Whitman to Gundy suggests, the Roberts Court appears far more skeptical of the constitutionality of broad delegations than the Court has been before, at least for many decades. The question remains whether there will be a majority for a reinvigoration of constitutional constraints on delegation. Since Gundy was argued, the Supreme Court has gained three new members: Justice Kavanaugh, Justice Barrett, and Justice Jackson.

The Court was presented with an opportunity to assert a strengthened nondelegation doctrine in WEST VIRGINIA V. EPA, 142 S.Ct. 2587 (2022) (pp. 869, 1341). There, West Virginia's certiorari petition expressly raised the question of whether, in 42 U.S.C. § 7411(d), Congress had "constitutionally authorize[d]" EPA "to issue significant rules—including those capable of reshaping the nation's electricity grids and unilaterally decarbonizing virtually any sector of the economy—without any limits on what the agency can require so long as it considers cost, nonair impacts, and energy requirements." The Court took a pass on that constitutional question, however. Instead, as discussed below, the Court invoked the major questions doctrine and opted to read the statute as not authorizing EPA to adopt the challenged rules at issue. Nondelegation concerns also surfaced in several lower court decisions addressing measures the federal government adopted in response to the COVID-19 pandemic, but per curiam majorities of the Supreme Court scrupulously avoided expressly discussing nondelegation (p. 868).

Some scholars believe that there may now be five votes to significantly tighten nondelegation doctrine. See, e.g., Lisa Heinzerling, Nondelegation on Steroids, 29 N.Y.U. Envtl. L.J. 379, 38–01 (2021). Others are less sanguine that such a doctrinal change is in the cards. KRISTIN E. HICKMAN, in NONDELEGATION AS CONSTITUTIONAL SYMBOLISM, 89 Geo. Wash. L. Rev. 1079 (2021), is "unconvinced that the members of the Court who seek to reform the nondelegation doctrine really intend such sweeping change. Leave aside for a moment that five Justices have yet to agree on an alternative to the intelligible principle standard. . . . [T]he alternatives proposed by Justices Gorsuch and Kavanaugh are quite limited in their scope . . . making it likely that doctrinal change will be more incremental and symbolic than sweeping." See also Adrian Vermeule, Never Jam Today, Notice & Comment Blog (June 20, 2019).[4]

Does the fact that the Court has refused these opportunities to invalidate a statutory provision on nondelegation grounds suggest that it is

---

4 https://www.yalejreg.com/nc/never-jam-today-by-adrian-vermeule/.

unlikely to do so? If the Court is already narrowing statutes through interpretation, does it need to invalidate to address nondelegation concerns?

## (2) The Evolution of Nondelegation Doctrine

### *Notes on the History of Nondelegation Doctrine*

Gary Lawson has described the nondelegation doctrine as "the Energizer Bunny of constitutional law: No matter how many times it gets broken, beaten, or buried, it just keeps on going and going." Delegation and Original Meaning, 88 Va. L. Rev. 327, 330 (2002). The materials that follow prove his point, demonstrating a long history of failed delegation challenges. As you read these materials, think about whether they demonstrate a consistent approach. Or instead, do their similar results mask important differences in reasoning and the nature of the delegation at issue?

While the emergence of renewed nondelegation challenges in recent years suggests we may be entering a new era, traditionally these past decisions have been divided into three periods. The first period extends from the Founding to the New Deal and contains many delegation decisions still referred to in current cases. These delegations often arose in the area of foreign trade. The earliest reported nondelegation challenge appears to be THE BRIG AURORA, 11 U.S. (7 Cranch) 382 (1813), which sustained a statute authorizing the President to "revive" an earlier measure giving favorable trading status to France and Britain; commerce with them had been barred during the War of 1812 by the Non-Intercourse Act. Another early decision, WAYMAN V. SOUTHARD, 23 U.S. (10 Wheat.) 1 (1825), provided an occasion for Chief Justice Marshall to weigh in on the constitutionality of delegation. In sustaining a statute delegating to the courts authority to make rules governing their proceedings, he said: "It will not be contended that Congress can delegate to the courts, or to any other tribunals, powers which are strictly and exclusively legislative. But Congress may certainly delegate to others powers which the legislature may rightfully exercise itself." Marshall added: "The line has not been exactly drawn which separates those important subjects which must be entirely regulated by the legislature itself from those of less interest in which a general provision may be made and power given to those who are to act under such general provisions to fill up the details."

Two other first-period cases, from the late nineteenth and early twentieth century, involved delegations more akin to today's regulatory statutes. FIELD V. CLARK, 143 U.S. 649 (1892) upheld the Tariff Act of 1890, which contained a provision authorizing certain articles to be imported duty-free but gave the President power—and duty—to suspend the provision if he was "satisfied" that any country producing and exporting these articles imposed duties on U.S. products that the President "deem[ed] to be reciprocally unequal and unreasonable."

Writing for the Court, JUSTICE HARLAN noted the long history of Congress granting similar powers to the President in the area of trade and commerce before concluding that the Act "does not in any real sense invest the President with the power of legislation. . . . As the suspension was absolutely required when the President ascertained the existence of a particular fact, it cannot be said that in ascertaining that fact, and in issuing his proclamation in obedience to the legislative will, he exercised the function of making laws. Legislative power was exercised when Congress declared that the suspension should take effect upon a named contingency." In UNITED STATES V. GRIMAUD, 220 U.S. 506 (1911), the Court again upheld the delegation in question, a grant of authority to the Secretary of Agriculture to "make such rules and regulations" governing land set aside by the President for public forest reserves "as will insure the objects of such reservations." Strikingly, Congress had provided that violation of these rules and regulations would be a criminal (misdemeanor) offense. JUSTICE LAMAR noted that "[f]rom the beginning of the government, various acts have been passed conferring upon executive officers power to make rules and regulations. . . . None of these statutes could confer legislative power. But when Congress had legislated and indicated its will, it could give to those who were to act under such general provisions 'power to fill up the details' by the establishment of administrative rules and regulations, the violation of which could be punished by fine or imprisonment fixed by Congress, or by penalties fixed by Congress, or measured by the injury done."

Yet a third important decision from this period was J.W. HAMPTON, JR. & CO. V. UNITED STATES, 276 U.S. 394 (1928), from which the language of "intelligible principle" is derived. The case again involved a tariff measure, the Tariff Act of 1922, which directed the President to change the original statutory schedule of tariffs on various goods whenever the President, after investigating costs for articles produced domestically compared to similar articles made abroad, "shall find . . . that the duties fixed in this Act do not equalize the said differences in costs of production in the United States and the principal competing country." Moving tariff-setting more towards the bureaucratic mode of modern regulation, the Act authorized the President to act only after receiving the report of a new Tariff Commission. CHIEF JUSTICE TAFT wrote for a unanimous Court sustaining this delegation: "It is conceded by counsel that Congress may use executive officers in the application and enforcement of a policy declared in law by Congress . . . [b]ut it is said that this never has been permitted [with respect to] the power to levy taxes and fix customs duties. The authorities make no such distinction. The same principle that permits Congress to exercise its ratemaking power in interstate commerce by declaring the rule which shall prevail in the legislative fixing of rates, and enables it to remit to a ratemaking body created in accordance with its provisions the fixing of such rates, justifies a similar provision for the fixing of customs duties on imported merchandise. If Congress shall lay down by legislative act an intelligible principle to which the person or body authorized to fix such rates is directed to conform, such legislative action is not a forbidden delegation of legislative power." Taft concluded that what the statute sought to do here was "perfectly clear and intelligible": it sought to impose customs duties that would "enable domestic producers to compete on terms of equality with foreign producers in the markets of the United States." The President's role was not the making of law. The President was the mere agent of the lawmaking department to ascertain and declare the event upon which its expressed will was to take effect.

The second period was much shorter, spanning two years at the outset of the New Deal. This period was the nondelegation doctrine's moment in the sun, when in three cases the Court invalidated delegations as unconstitutional delegations—the first and last times it has done so. Two cases involved the National Industrial Recovery Act (NIRA), a key measure enacted during President Roosevelt's first one hundred days in office to address the economic crisis of the Depression. (The third, Carter v. Carter Coal, 298 U.S. 238 (1936), involved a similar early New Deal measure to stabilize the coal industry.) The first case, PANAMA REFINING CO. V. RYAN, 293 U.S. 388 (1935), involved a section of the NIRA aimed at stabilizing the petroleum industry by stemming overproduction from vast, newly tapped oil fields in Texas. It authorized the President to enforce conservation orders from state boards attempting to deal with the problem. The majority found no standard for the President to follow in deciding whether to close interstate commerce to "hot oil" and thus enjoined executive orders and regulations implementing the section. Only Justice Cardozo dissented.

Five months later, in A.L.A. SCHECHTER POULTRY CORP. V. UNITED STATES, 295 U.S. 495 (1935), the Court considered § 3 of the NIRA, which authorized the President to approve "codes of fair competition" for a trade or industry, upon application by one or more trade or industrial associations or groups. To approve a code, the President had to find only (1) that such associations or groups "impose no inequitable restrictions on admission to membership therein and are truly representative"; and (2) that such codes were not designed "to promote monopolies or to eliminate or oppress small enterprises and will not operate to discriminate against them, and will tend to effectuate the policy" of the Act. The Schechter company was indicted on multiple counts of violating the "Live Poultry Code," which had been approved by the President under § 3. CHIEF JUSTICE HUGHES wrote for a unanimous Court in invalidating § 3: "Undoubtedly, the conditions to which power is addressed are always to be considered when the exercise of power is challenged. Extraordinary conditions may call for extraordinary remedies. But . . . [e]xtraordinary conditions do not create or enlarge constitutional power. . . . We think the conclusion is inescapable that the authority sought to be conferred by § 3 was not merely to deal with 'unfair competitive practices' [but] to authorize new and controlling prohibitions through codes of laws which would embrace what the formulators would propose, and what the President would approve, or prescribe, as wise and beneficent measures for the government of trades and industries in order to bring about their rehabilitation, correction and development. . . . But Congress cannot delegate legislative power to the President to exercise an unfettered discretion to make whatever laws he thinks may be needed or advisable for the rehabilitation and expansion of trade or industry."

Acknowledging that the Court had "repeatedly recognized the necessity of adapting legislation to complex conditions involving a host of details with which the national legislature cannot deal directly," Hughes concluded, "Section 3 of the Recovery Act is without precedent. It supplies no standards for any trade, industry or activity. It does not undertake to prescribe rules of conduct to be applied to particular states of fact determined by appropriate administrative procedure. Instead of prescribing rules of conduct, it authorizes the making of codes to prescribe them. For that legislative undertaking, § 3 sets up no standards, aside from the statement of the general aims of rehabilitation, correction and expansion . . . [T]he discretion of the President in approving or prescribing codes, and thus enacting laws for the government of trade and industry throughout the country, is virtually unfettered. We think that the code-making authority this conferred is an unconstitutional delegation of legislative power." JUSTICE CARDOZO agreed that "[t]his is delegation running riot." The Schechter Poultry Court was not content to invalidate § 3 on nondelegation grounds; it also held the statute exceeded Congress's regulatory authority under the Commerce Clause.

Soon thereafter, the Supreme Court changed course and entered the third period, returning to its practice of upholding delegations. (It also took a broader view of the commerce power than shown in Schechter Poultry.) YAKUS V. UNITED STATES, 321 U.S. 414 (1944), is a prime case in point. There the Court upheld a provision of the Emergency Price Control Act of 1942, a temporary measure enacted during World War II to address inflation. The Act created an Office of Price Administration headed by a Price Administrator who, after consulting with industry to the extent practicable, was authorized to promulgate regulations fixing prices of commodities which "in his judgment will be generally fair and equitable and will effectuate the purposes of this Act," giving due weight to prices prevailing in October 1941. Writing for all but one member of the Court, CHIEF JUSTICE STONE stated: "The essentials of the legislative function are the determination of the legislative policy and its formulation and promulgation as a defined and binding rule of conduct. . . . These essentials are preserved when Congress has specified the basic conditions of fact upon whose existence or occurrence, ascertained from relevant data by a designated administrative agency, it directs that its statutory command shall be effective. It is no objection that the determination of facts and the inferences to be drawn from them . . . call for the exercise of judgment. . . . Only if we could say that there is an absence of standards for the guidance of the Administrator's action, so that it would be impossible in a proper proceeding to ascertain whether the will of Congress has been obeyed, would we be justified in overriding its choice of means for effecting its declared purpose of preventing inflation. The standards prescribed by the present Act, with the aid of the 'statement of considerations' required to be made by the Administrator, are sufficiently definite and precise to enable Congress, the courts and the public to ascertain whether the Administrator, in fixing the designated prices, has conformed to those standards."

The central characteristic of this third period is the Court's willingness to sustain very broad delegations. Whitman (p. 848) and many of the decisions upholding delegations that Justice Kagan cites in Gundy fall into this period. The delegations upheld, for example, included instructions to an agency to regulate "in the public interest." National Broadcasting Company v. United States, 319 U.S. 190 (1942). Other cases sustained delegation of taxing authority, Skinner v. Mid-American Pipeline Co., 490 U.S. 212 (1986), and authority to determine factors triggering imposition of statutory death penalty in military capital cases, Loving v. United States, 517 U.S. 748 (1996).

In one case, however—INDUSTRIAL UNION DEP'T, AFL-CIO V. AMERICAN PETROLEUM INST., 448 U.S. 607 (1980) (the Benzene case) (p. 855)—the Court cited nondelegation concerns in invalidating agency action on statutory grounds. At issue was a decision by the Occupational Safety and Health Administration (OSHA) to lower the maximum permissible exposure for benzene, a confirmed carcinogen, from 10 ppm to 1 ppm. The National Institute for Occupational Safety and Health (NIOSH), an independent, science-dominated agency located in the Centers for Disease Control and Prevention charged with advising OSHA about regulatory priorities, had long pushed for this regulatory change, which was extremely costly for the petroleum refining industry. A plurality opinion written by JUSTICE STEVENS invalidated the new standard on the grounds that OSHA needed "to make a threshold finding that a place of employment is unsafe—in the sense that significant risks are present and can be eliminated or lessened by a change in practices"—before issuing any permanent health or safety standard. This "significant risk" requirement was not expressly in the Occupational Safety and Health Act, § 3(8) of which defined health and safety standards as those conditions "reasonably necessary or appropriate to provide safe or healthful employment and places of employment." JUSTICE STEVENS justified reading this language into § 3(8) on the grounds that otherwise "the statute would make such a 'sweeping delegation of legislative power' that it might be unconstitutional under the Court's reasoning in [Schechter Poultry] and [Panama Refining]."

Then-JUSTICE REHNQUIST'S opinion concurring in the judgment went further and said that § 6(b)(5) of the Act, under which OSHA regulates toxic chemicals like benzene, was an unconstitutional delegation of legislative power. Section 6(b)(5) directs the Secretary to "set the standard which most adequately assures, to the extent feasible, on the basis of the best available evidence, that no employee will suffer material impairment of health or functional capacity even if such employee has regular exposure to the hazard dealt with by such standard for the period of his working life." According to Justice Rehnquist, "the language 'to the extent feasible' . . . render[s] what had been a clear, if somewhat unrealistic, standard largely, if not entirely, precatory." He added: "It is difficult to imagine a more obvious example of Congress simply avoiding a choice which was both fundamental for purposes of the statute and yet politically so divisive that the necessary decision or compromise was difficult, if not impossible, to hammer out in the legislative forge. . . . It is the hard choices, and not the filling in of the blanks, which must be made by the elected representatives of the people."

## NOTES ON THE HISTORY OF NONDELEGATION DOCTRINE

(1) ***Is the Nondelegation Doctrine a Myth?*** Does this history of almost entirely unsuccessful delegation challenges make you question whether there really is a nondelegation doctrine? KEITH WHITTINGTON and JASON IULIANO, in THE MYTH OF THE NONDELEGATION DOCTRINE, 165 U. Pa. L. Rev. 379, 404–05, 419–20, 429 (2017), argue that the historical record demonstrates the doctrine is a myth: "A review of the Court's treatment of challenges to federal and state statutes on the grounds that they had impermissibly delegated legislative power to nonlegislative actors does not provide much basis for thinking that there was ever a seriously confining nondelegation doctrine as part of the effective constitutional order." Noting that most delegation challenges were heard in state and lower federal courts, the authors compiled a dataset of around 2500 cases decided in the period from the Founding to 1940 involving claims of improper delegations. They report that delegation challenges remained "relatively rare until the antebellum period. Over the course of the second half of the nineteenth century, nondelegation cases made a regular appearance on judicial dockets. . . . Nondelegation cases surged at the opening of the twentieth century, plateauing at a new level that was several times the pace at which such cases were heard in the nineteenth century. In keeping with the traditional narrative of the battles of the New Deal, the number of nondelegation cases surged again in the 1930s. . . . Despite the growth of nondelegation as an area of litigation, the number of judicial invalidations hardly budged."

Compare the view of GARY LAWSON, DELEGATION AND ORIGINAL MEANING, 88 Va. L. Rev. 327, 355, 360, 371–72 (2002): "The first serious effort to define a nondelegation principle was put forth by Chief Justice Marshall in 1825 in Wayman v. Southard. . . . Chief Justice Marshall put forth his ultimate methodology for resolving delegation issues in one cryptic sentence: 'The line has not been exactly drawn which separates those important subjects, which must be entirely regulated by the legislature itself, from those of less interest, in which . . . power [may be] given to those who are to act under such general provisions to fill up the details.' . . . As far as the courts are concerned, no one has improved upon, or even elaborated upon, Chief Justice Marshall's 1825 declaration that the Constitution requires Congress to make whatever decisions are important enough that the Constitution requires Congress to make them."

(2) ***Historical Scholarship on Delegation.*** Gundy has provoked a surge of scholarly attention to the nondelegation doctrine's originalist roots—or lack thereof. In DELEGATION AT THE FOUNDING, 121 Colum. L. Rev. 277, 280–

82 (2021), JULIAN DAVIS MORTENSON and NICHOLAS BAGLEY argue that the "the Constitution at the Founding contained no discernable, legalized prohibition on delegations of legislative power, at least so long as the exercise of that power remained subject to congressional oversight and control. . . . [O]riginalists' arguments to the contrary bottom out on the insistence that the executive branch's exercise of certain highly discretionary powers is so legislative in nature that it cannot constitute an exercise of the 'executive power.' The executive power, however, was simply the authority to execute the laws—an empty vessel for Congress to fill. . . . [M]uch of the confusion arises because—contrary to our modern turn of mind—the Founders thought of the separation of powers in nonexclusive and relational terms. . . . The Founders would thus have said that agencies wield legislative power to the extent they adopt rules that Congress could have enacted as legislation. At the same time, the Founders would have said—indeed, they did say—that such rulemaking also constitutes an exercise of the executive power to the extent it is authorized by statute. Either way, it's constitutional. Indeed, coercive administrative rulemaking was so routine throughout the Anglo-American world that it would have been astounding if the Constitution had prohibited it. But it did not. . . . [E]arly Congresses adopted dozens of laws that broadly empowered executive and judicial actors to adopt binding rules of conduct. Many of those laws would have run roughshod over any version of the nondelegation doctrine now endorsed by originalists. Yet, in more than ten thousand pages of recorded debate during the Republic's first decade, the people who drafted and debated the Constitution rarely even gestured at nondelegation objections to laws that would supposedly have been anathema to them—even as they feuded bitterly and at punishing length over many other questions of constitutional meaning."

In THE LOST HISTORY OF DELEGATION AT THE FOUNDING, 56 Ga. L. Rev. 81, 87–88 (2022), CHRISTINE KEXEL CHABOT differs slightly, arguing that historical evidence supports a "restrained nondelegation doctrine." But she emphasizes that, even so, "the theory and practice of delegation in the Founding Era never reflected a particularly high constitutional bar. . . . The limits early Congresses recognized for delegation were not exacting and generally required Congress to 'establish the principle' (perhaps intelligibly) governing execution of the law. The restrained nondelegation doctrine . . . . does not support a significant shift to a requirement that Congress decide all important policy questions."

NICHOLAS R. PARRILLO, in A CRITICAL ASSESSMENT OF THE ORIGINALIST CASE AGAINST ADMINISTRATIVE REGULATORY POWER: NEW EVIDENCE FROM THE FEDERAL TAX ON PRIVATE REAL ESTATE IN THE 1790S, 130 Yale L.J. 1288, 1304–13 (2021), concludes that whatever limit the Constitution may impose on delegation, early practice makes clear that it did not prohibit coercive administrative rulemaking. Parrillo looks closely at the rulemaking power exercised under the direct tax of 1798. It "was an enormous administrative undertaking, and it fell upon literally every farmer, homeowner, and slaveholder in every state of the Union." As part of the implementation apparatus for the tax, "Congress established in each state a board of federal tax commissioners . . . with power to divide the state into federal assessment districts and to raise or lower all assessments within any district by any percentage amount 'as shall appear to be just and equitable'—a phrase the statute did not define." Parrillo argues that "the sweeping rulemaking powers of the federal boards of tax commissioners who administered the direct tax of 1798—combined with their decisions' binding power (insulated against judicial review) and the wide bipartisan acceptance of their power at the time and in subsequent enactments into the 1800s—are important evidence that the American political nation in the Founding era viewed administrative rulemaking as constitutional, even in the realm of domestic private rights." See also Kevin Arlyck, Delegation, Administration, and Improvisation, 97 Notre Dame L. Rev. 243 (2021).

On the other side of the debate, ILAN WURMAN in NONDELEGATION AT THE FOUNDING, 130 Yale L.J. 1490, 1494, 1497 (2021), argues that "[a]lthough the history is messy, there is significant evidence that the Founding generation adhered to a nondelegation doctrine, and little evidence that clearly supports the proposition that the Founding generation believed that Congress could freely delegate its legislative power. As for the content of that doctrine, none of the statutory delegations examined by Mortenson and Bagley, Parrillo, and Chabot necessarily refute the proposition that Congress cannot delegate decisions involving private rights. . . . Most of these early laws were not nearly as broad as [these scholars] suggest. Others did not delegate authority that any formalist would recognize as 'exclusively legislative,' that is, the kind of legislative power that it is impermissible for Congress to delegate. Many of these delegations involved nonexclusive, or shared, power: power that the legislature could and historically did exercise (for example, resolving claims against the government), but which the other departments of government could also exercise. . . . Overall, the picture the Founding-era history paints is one of a nondelegation doctrine whereby Congress could not delegate to the Executive decisions over 'important subjects,' although there were occasionally lower-order disagreements over what was important and what was a matter of mere detail." See also Lawson, supra.

Although agreeing that current nondelegation doctrine "is fictional, lax, and of dubious constitutionality," PHILIP HAMBURGER rejects this emphasis on the importance of the decision being delegated: "[T]he Constitution enumerates its legislative powers by subject matter and vests these powers in Congress without saying anything about differentiating important and unimportant legislation." He adds that "the importance standard would bar much executive rulemaking that has always been considered entirely constitutional," such as rules "on the treatment of enemy aliens[,] . . . on the distribution of pensions, on the distribution of federal lands, and on other privileges." Hamburger insists that "the key principle underlying the formation of the United States and its government was consent . . . through an elected representative body." As a result, "[b]inding rules—those that come with legal obligation—were understood to be naturally legislative and so had to be exercises of the legislature's will." NONDELEGATION BLUES, 91 Geo. Wash. L. Rev. (forthcoming).

Drawing on a study of early customs laws, JENNIFER MASCOTT, in EARLY CUSTOMS LAWS AND DELEGATION, 87 Geo. Wash. L. Rev. 1388, 1395–96 (2019), maintains that "nondelegation limitations might not be inherent in the Article I Vesting Clause alone, but may be innate to the structural design of the federal government itself. . . . [S]tructural separation-of-powers principles help ensure that the representative interests of people electing legislators from throughout the country are represented in policy proposals in a way that would not be possible via regulatory decisions made by a singular, centralized administrative entity."

(3) ***How the Court Assesses Delegation.*** In his Gundy dissent, Justice Gorsuch argues that over time the intelligible principle test of J.W. Hampton was misconstrued and expanded. Do you agree? Note that two of Gorsuch's categories of acceptable delegations—factfinding and "filling in the details"—are closely tied to two earlier approaches the Court used before settling on the intelligible principle formulation, namely the contingency rationale of Field v. Clark and the "filling in the details" rationale of Grimaud. Why did these earlier approaches not survive as the modern standard for permissible delegation? Think about the delegations at issue in Gundy and Whitman: Could they be sustained on these earlier grounds? Some scholars see modern cases such as Yakus as offering yet another, more functionalist, approach, one that emphasized the availability of effective checks on delegated power. See Cynthia R. Farina, Statutory Interpretation and the Balance of Power in the Administrative State, 89 Colum. L. Rev. 452 (1989); Kevin M. Stack, The Constitutional Foundations of Chenery, 116 Yale L.J. 952 (2007).

(4) ***Who Is the Delegate?*** In several of these earlier cases the statutory delegation was to the President personally. The far more common pattern today is for the statute to delegate power to the head of a Cabinet department (e.g., the Secretary of Transportation) or a freestanding agency (the Commissioners of the Federal Communications Commission). Still, more powers are delegated to the President than commonly realized. See Shalev Roisman, Presidential Law, 105 Minn. L. Rev. 1269, 1281–90 (2021) (documenting and categorizing statutory delegations to the President).

What difference, if any, does it make that the delegate is the President personally? One reason it might matter a great deal is that most of the checks on administrative power that regularize agency decisionmaking and render it more transparent and participatory do not apply, or do not apply in the same way, to the President. Presidential decisionmaking is not subject to the Administrative Procedure Act or any of the "sunshine" statutes, Franklin v. Massachusetts, 505 U.S. 788, 801 (1992), and courts are understandably loathe to review decisions made by the President personally. See Kathryn E. Kovacs, Constraining the Statutory President, 98 Wash. U. L. Rev. 63 (2020).

Note also that two of the three cases in which the Supreme Court has found delegations invalid—Schechter Poultry and Panama Refining—were delegations to the President personally, at a time when the strength of executive authority being manifested in Berlin and Moscow might have raised caution flags. For a discussion of how concerns over fascism affected approaches to the separation of powers in the 1930s, see Noah A. Rosenblum,

The Antifascist Roots of Presidential Administration, 122 Colum. L. Rev. 1 (2022).

(5) ***Delegation in the States.*** The separation of powers and checks and balances principles of the U.S. Constitution apply only to the national government. States are free to accept or reject these principles in whole or part and, while doubtless affected by U.S. Supreme Court views, can give them whatever interpretation seems appropriate.[5] Many state courts have discerned a nondelegation principle in their own constitutions and are more likely than the federal courts to find it violated.

In a recent study, DANIEL E. WALTERS looks to the states to predict what might happen if nondelegation doctrine gets strengthened at the federal level. Although "[a]t the state level, unlike in the federal courts, there is substantial variation in outcomes within and across states," Walters found that "the form of the doctrinal test or standard is not a predictor of these outcomes. . . . Many states have a standard as liberal as the intelligible principle standard of the federal courts, insofar as they permit the delegation of policymaking discretion. Many other states, however, purport to draw a far more formalistic line between legislative and executive power, or permit only the delegation of discretion to determine 'details' rather than 'policies.' No matter what approach state courts take to the nondelegation problem, though, they converge on a fairly stable and meager invalidation rate, particularly in recent years." From this data, Walters concludes that "the changes in doctrinal formulation envisioned by a possible majority of the Court in and of themselves will not fundamentally change anything about how courts approach the problem of delegation." DECODING NONDELEGATION AFTER GUNDY: WHAT THE EXPERIENCE IN STATE COURTS TELLS US ABOUT WHAT TO EXPECT WHEN WE'RE EXPECTING, 71 EMORY L.J. 417, 421–22 (2022).

## (3) Alternative Approaches to Nondelegation

The current and historical lack of robust nondelegation enforcement might suggest that nondelegation concerns have no constitutional basis. Another possibility, however, is that the courts may address such concerns through alternatives to direct constitutional review. The Notes here discuss several such alternative approaches. Consider, as you read them, not just whether you think some approaches are better than others, but whether the entire project of relying on nondelegation surrogates is constitutionally legitimate. If the Supreme Court is not willing to invalidate delegations directly as unconstitutionally broad, what is the basis for constraining exercises of delegated power through subconstitutional means?

(1) ***Narrowed Statutory Interpretations.*** One technique is for a court to read a statutory grant of authority narrowly so as to avoid concerns that an agency might be granted unconstitutionally broad authority. Perhaps the

[5] In theory, a state's choice of government structure might be so anomalous as to offend the federal constitution's guaranty to the states of a "republican form of government." U.S. Const. Art. IV, § 4. However, since Luther v. Borden, 48 U.S. 1 (1849), claims under the Guarantee Clause have been regarded as nonjusticiable political questions.

preeminent example of this approach came in the Benzene case (p. 862), where Justice Stevens's plurality opinion expressly justified reading a requirement that OSHA had to make a threshold finding that a workplace presented significant risk before issuing a health or safety standard in order to avoid a potentially unconstitutionally broad delegation of authority to OSHA. Another prominent example is FDA v. Brown & Williamson Tobacco Corp., 529 U.S. 120 (2000) (p. 1338), where the Court held that the Food, Drug, and Cosmetic Act did not give the FDA jurisdiction to regulate tobacco products. See generally Cass R. Sunstein, Nondelegation Canons, 67 U. Chi. L. Rev. 315 (2000).

Do you think that Justice Kagan tacitly made a similar move in Gundy, reading the delegation to the Attorney General under SORNA to encompass only authority to delay application of SORNA's registration requirements to pre-Act offenders on feasibility grounds? If a court or judge does not expressly invoke nondelegation as a reason for narrowing a statute's scope, how easy is it to distinguish between ordinary statutory interpretation and statutory narrowing animated by nondelegation concerns?

(2) ***The Major Questions Doctrine.*** A tool that the Supreme Court employs to justify its narrowed statutory readings—and a particular favorite of the Roberts Court of late—is the major questions doctrine. (See Ch. VIII, p. 1341.) In the past, this doctrine was invoked alongside other statutory clues in rejecting an agency's claim that a particular course of action is statutorily authorized. Brown & Williamson was an instance when the Court took such an approach. There, in denying the FDA's assertion of jurisdiction over tobacco, the Court noted that the structure of the Food, Drug, and Cosmetic Act was a poor fit for regulating tobacco and that Congress had enacted numerous measures targeting tobacco specifically. But it also emphasized the implausibility of Congress delegating "a decision of such economic and political significance to an agency in so cryptic a fashion."

More recently, the Court invoked both narrow statutory interpretations and the major questions doctrine in several cases emerging from the COVID-19 pandemic. In ALABAMA ASSOCIATION OF REALTORS V. HHS, 141 S.Ct. 2485 (2021), the Court held that the Centers for Disease Control and Prevention lacked statutory authority to impose a nationwide eviction moratorium, notwithstanding a broad grant to the CDC, in § 361(a) of the Public Health Service Act, 42 U.S.C. § 264(a), of power "to make and enforce such regulations as in [its] judgment are necessary" to prevent disease spread. In a per curiam 6–3 opinion the Court first engaged in statutory narrowing, holding that this broad grant of authority was cabined by the second sentence of § 361(a), which stated that in these regulations the CDC "may" use measures such as "inspection, fumigation, disinfection, sanitation, pest extermination, [and] destruction of [contaminated] animals or articles." According to the Court, the second sentence meant that the CDC could only impose measures that "directly relate to preventing the interstate spread of disease by identifying, isolating, and destroying the disease itself," whereas the moratorium lowered the risk of COVID spread indirectly. The per curiam majority then added that "the sheer scope of the CDC's claimed authority under § 361(a) would counsel against the Government's interpretation. We expect Congress to speak clearly when authorizing an agency to exercise powers of vast economic and political significance." No mention was made of constitutional prohibitions on delegation.

In NFIB v. OSHA, 142 S.Ct. 661 (2022), the underlying statutory language was again very broad. The OSH Act, also at issue in the Benzene case (p. 862), authorizes OSHA to "promulgate, modify, or revoke any occupational safety or health standards . . . reasonably necessary or appropriate to provide safe or healthful employment and places of employment," 29 U.S.C. § 655(b), and further requires the Secretary of Labor to adopt an emergency standard when the Secretary finds that employees are exposed to a "grave danger" from exposure to "new hazards" and the emergency standard "is necessary" to protect them from that danger, id. § 655(c). Yet the Court held that OSHA lacked authority to impose on employers an emergency standard requiring that employees either be vaccinated against COVID or be masked and tested regularly. The 6–3 per curiam majority opinion argued that the risks posed by COVID generally were not "occupational" risks but instead "hazards of daily life." The majority additionally stated that it would expect Congress to speak clearly in authorizing OSHA to impose such a requirement on 84 million employees, emphasizing that the agency had never imposed a requirement of this type before. Again, the majority made no mention of nondelegation, although Justice Gorsuch offered a nondelegation defense of the clear authorization requirement in a concurrence that Justices Thomas and Alito joined.

Note that in a third pandemic-related case, BIDEN v. MISSOURI, 142 S.Ct. 647 (2022), a 5–4 per curiam majority upheld a Health and Human Services regulation that required staff at facilities participating in Medicare and Medicaid to be vaccinated against COVID-19. The majority concluded that the requirement—expected to apply to 10 million employees—was authorized by 42 U.S.C. § 1395x(e)(9), which provides that HHS can impose conditions on the receipt of Medicaid and Medicare funds that it "finds necessary in the interest of the health and safety of individuals who are furnished services" in a range of medical facilities. According to the majority, given HHS's "determin[ation] that a COVID-19 vaccine mandate will substantially reduce the likelihood that healthcare workers will contract the virus and transmit it to their patients[,]. . . .[t]he rule . . . fits neatly within the language of the statute." Acknowledging that "the vaccine mandate goes further than what [HHS] has done in the past to implement infection control," the majority emphasized that HHS "has never had to address an infection problem of this scale and scope before. In any event, there can be no doubt that addressing infection problems in Medicare and Medicaid facilities is what [HHS] does." Id. at 652–53. Justice Thomas dissented, arguing that "[had Congress wanted to grant CMS power to impose a vaccine mandate across all facility types, it would have . . . specifically authorize[d] one."

Finally, in a fourth case the same term—this one not involving the pandemic—WEST VIRGINIA v. EPA, 142 S.Ct. 2587 (2022) (p. 1341) the Court offered a more sustained account of the major questions doctrine. Section 111 of the Clean Air Act directs EPA to regulate stationary sources of any substance that "causes, or contributes significantly to, air pollution which may reasonably be anticipated to endanger public health or welfare." 42 U.S.C. § 7411(b)(1)(A). EPA is to establish "standards of performance for any existing source for any air pollutant," id. § 7411(d), which are defined as "standard[s] for emissions of air pollutants" that reflect "the degree of emission limitation achievable through the application of the best system of emission reduction which (taking into account the cost of achieving such reduction and any nonair quality health and environmental impact and energy requirements) the Administrator determines has been adequately demonstrated." Id. § 7411(a). Using this authority, EPA promulgated the Clean Power Plan, which set standards of performance for existing power plants at a level that would require a shift to power sources that were lower emitters of carbon dioxide—in particular, to shift from coal-fired to natural gas-fired power plants, to use solar and alternative sources of energy, or to purchase emission allowances.

The Court held that EPA had exceeded its authority under § 111, in an opinion by CHIEF JUSTICE ROBERTS. This time, the Court led its statutory analysis with an express discussion of the major questions doctrine, which "developed over a series of significant cases all addressing a particular and recurring problem: agencies asserting highly consequently power beyond what Congress could reasonably be thought to have granted." This "[p]recedent teaches that there are extraordinary cases . . . in which the history and breadth of the authority that the agency has asserted and the economic and political significance of that assertion, provide a reason to hesitate before concluding that Congress meant to confer such authority." Emphasizing that Congress rarely makes "[e]xtraordinary grants of regulatory authority" through "modest words," "vague terms," or "oblique or elliptical language," the Court stated that in such extraordinary cases an "agency . . . must point to clear congressional authorization for the power it claims." Roberts then asserted that this was "a major questions case" and that clear congressional authorization for EPA to require power-generation shifting was lacking. Although the majority opinion referred to "both separation of powers principles and a practical understanding of legislative intent" as justifications for this approach, Roberts nowhere expressly invoked nondelegation doctrine or provided any further discussion of how separation of powers principles were implicated. Again, it fell to Justice Gorsuch, this time joined only by Justice Thomas, to offer a lengthy disquisition on nondelegation in a concurrence. In her dissent for three justices, Justice Kagan criticized the majority for ignoring the statute's plain text and for failing to realize that "[a] key reason Congress makes broad delegations like Section 111 is so an agency can respond, appropriately and commensurately, to new and big problems."

Do you think the Court offered the most plausible readings of the relevant statutory text in these cases, or is its perception of these administrative actions as particularly significant leading it to construe statutory text unduly narrowly? If the latter, that might suggest that the Court is using statutory interpretation as a surrogate for nondelegation concerns. But do these cases present nondelegation concerns under established and ostensibly still-governing nondelegation doctrine? Even if the actions at issue are big deals and the agencies enjoy broad discretion, it seems hard to conclude that the statutory provisions at issue lack an intelligible principle, given the broad language the Court upheld against nondelegation challenges in Whitman and earlier cases. So if nondelegation provides the basis for the Court's narrow statutory interpretations in these cases, are those interpretations justified—or would the Court need to first adopt a more robust nondelegation doctrine?

Of course, as noted, the Court notably did *not* defend its statutory readings in these cases on nondelegation grounds, despite Gorsuch's concurrences making exactly that point. What should we make of that fact? Does it suggest a current lack of majority support for strengthened constitutional nondelegation constraints? Indeed, these decisions appear to state that Congress can delegate authority to agencies to make these big decisions—to decide whether to impose a nationwide moratorium, require workers be vaccinated, or force the national economy away from coal-fueled power sources—provided Congress expressly authorizes them to do so. Should we then read these cases as signaling the opposite of what Gorsuch and Thomas argued in Gundy and American Railroads (e.g., that Congress cannot constitutionally delegate to agencies the power to make important policy judgments?). Note that the position that Congress can delegate such authority if it does so expressly is one that both Chief Justice Roberts and Justice Kavanaugh had previously advocated. See City of Arlington v. FCC, 569 U.S. 290, 317 (2013) (Roberts, C.J., dissenting) (p. 1304); U.S. Telecom Assn. v. FCC, 855 F.3d 381, 855 F.3d 381, 417 (D.C. Cir. 2017) (Kavanaugh, J., dissenting from denial of rehearing en banc).

(3) ***Should Narrowing Agency Interpretations Matter?*** The D.C. Circuit in Whitman, in a part of its per curiam opinion that was 2–1 and written by JUDGE WILLIAMS, agreed with the challengers "that EPA has construed §§ 108 and 109 of the Clean Air Act so loosely as to render them unconstitutional delegations of legislative power." AMERICAN TRUCKING ASS'NS V. EPA, 175 F.3d 1027, 1034, 1038 (D.C. Cir. 1999). The opinion continued: "Although the factors EPA uses in determining the degree of public health concern associated with different levels of ozone and PM are reasonable, EPA appears to have articulated no 'intelligible principle' to channel its application of these factors; nor is one apparent from the statute. . . . Here it is as though Congress commanded EPA to select 'big guys,' and EPA announced that it would evaluate candidates based on height and weight, but revealed no cutoff point. The announcement, though sensible in what it does say, is fatally incomplete. The reasonable person responds, 'How tall? How heavy?' . . .

"Where (as here) statutory language and an existing agency interpretation involve an unconstitutional delegation of power, but an interpretation without the constitutional weakness is or may be available, our response is not to strike down the statute but to give the agency an opportunity to extract a determinate standard on its own. Doing so serves at least two of three basic rationales for the nondelegation doctrine. If the agency develops determinate, binding standards for itself, it is less likely to exercise the delegated authority arbitrarily. And such standards enhance the likelihood that meaningful judicial review will prove feasible. A remand of this sort of course does not serve the third key function of non-delegation doctrine, to 'ensure[ ] to the extent consistent with orderly governmental administration that important choices of social policy are made by Congress, the branch of our Government most responsive to the popular will,' Industrial Union Dep't, AFL-CIO v. American Petroleum Inst., 448 U.S. 607, 685 (1980) ('Benzene') (Rehnquist, J., concurring) [p. 855]. The agency will make the fundamental policy choices. But the remand does ensure that the courts not hold unconstitutional a statute that an agency, with the application of its special expertise, could salvage."

The Supreme Court dismissed out of hand the D.C. Circuit's suggestion that EPA could remedy an overbroad delegation by adopting a narrower interpretation of the statutory language. But was the D.C. Circuit's approach so mistaken? See Lisa Schultz Bressman, Schechter Poultry at the Millennium: A Delegation Doctrine for the Administrative State, 109 Yale L.J. 1399 (2000).

(4) ***Experts and Procedure.*** Dissenting from the D.C. Circuit's decision on this point in Whitman, JUDGE TATEL suggested yet another approach to assessing the constitutionality of a delegation. He emphasized the role played by the Clean Air Scientific Advisory Committee, created pursuant to § 109: "CASAC must consist of at least one member of the National Academy of Sciences, one physician, and one person representing state air pollution control agencies. In this case, CASAC also included medical doctors, epidemiologists, toxicologists and environmental scientists from leading research universities and institutions throughout the country. EPA must explain any departures from CASAC's recommendations. See 42 U.S.C. § 7607(d)(3). Bringing scientific methods to their evaluation of the Agency's Criteria Document and Staff Paper, CASAC provides an objective justification for the pollution standards the Agency selects."

No member of the Supreme Court in Whitman referenced CASAC's role under the statute. Should the fact that the CAA requires the EPA to explain when it deviates from this expert body's recommendations for emission levels have gotten more weight? Is focusing on such expertise and procedural constraints contained in a statute more justifiable than emphasizing limits that an agency imposes on its own discretion? Or do these constraints also fail to meet the constitutional concern because Congress itself is not imposing a direct substantive limit on agency discretion?

(5) ***What About Administrative Law?*** More generally, in thinking about subconstitutional surrogates for nondelegation doctrine, should administrative law get more attention? Scholars have argued that courts use administrative law requirements for reasoned decisionmaking and the like as a surrogate for nondelegation and other separation of powers concerns. See, e.g., Benjamin Eidelson, Reasoned Explanation and Political Accountability in the Roberts Court, 130 Yale L.J. 1748 (2021); Gillian E. Metzger, Ordinary Administrative Law as Constitutional Common Law, 110 Colum. L. Rev. 479 (2010); see also Joseph Postell, Bureaucracy in America: The Administrative State's Challenge to Constitutional Government 247–79

(2017) (describing a turn to administrative law to legitimize administrative government in the 1970s).

LISA SCHULTZ BRESSMAN, DISCIPLINING DELEGATION AFTER WHITMAN V. AMERICAN TRUCKING ASS'NS, 87 Cornell L. Rev. 452, 460, 461–62 (2002): "Administrative law is a more effective tool [than constitutional law] for addressing the delegation issue. . . . [C]ourts owe Congress a greater degree of leeway to formulate delegations under constitutional law than they owe agencies to exercise those delegations under administrative law. . . . [They] should not 'second-guess' Congress on an issue that involves consideration of factors 'both multifarious and (in the nonpartisan sense) highly political' [Mistretta, 458 U.S. at 416 (Scalia, J., dissenting)]. That is not to say that Congress always has good motives for delegating. But courts must give Congress the benefit of the doubt if we are to have modern government. . . . At the same time, courts must insist that some governmental actor take responsibility for the hard choices of regulatory policy. Responsibility in this context means articulating the standards that direct and cabin administrative discretion. . . . If courts allow Congress implicitly to delegate such responsibility, they must require agencies expressly to assume it. . . . [Administrative law] principles . . . require agencies, in exchange for broad grants of policymaking authority, to demonstrate that they have used their authority in an open, regular, and rational fashion. They require agencies in general to articulate a basis for their policy determinations and, in particular, to articulate the standards for those determinations. In the absence of these principles, there is no protection (or recourse) against arbitrary lawmaking at any level of government."

## (4) Competing Reactions to Nondelegation Doctrine

Delegation has sparked a long trail of academic scholarship, one that has only grown longer in the light of the Supreme Court's Gundy decision and suggestions of a nondelegation revival. In addition to the historical work noted above (p. 863), this scholarship offers a range of perspectives on the constitutionality, legitimacy, and contemporary practice of delegation.

(1) ***Is Delegation Really Running Riot?*** Much of the legal debate over delegation is premised on the belief that Congress delegates very broadly. Much political science scholarship on delegation, by contrast, disputes whether this is the case, focusing on incentives Congress might have to delegate more restrainedly. One factor political scientists emphasize is divided government—when the political party that controls the presidency is different from the party controls one or both houses of Congress. Sean Farhang & Miranda Yaver, DIVIDED GOVERNMENT AND THE FRAGMENTATION OF AMERICAN LAW, 60 Am. L. Pol. Sci. 401, 403 (2016): "Divided government creates incentives for Congress to fragment implementation power, and the postwar growth in the conditions of divided government has importantly contributed to the material increase of fragmentation in federal regulatory policymaking. . . . Legislators and the interest groups that influence them

are aware that presidents possess considerable capacity to influence agency behavior, and they design laws to guard against that influence. Divided government greatly increases an enacting coalition's attention to designing frameworks of policy implementation meant to achieve its own policy goals while insulating it from executive subversion." The authors cite several studies that "amply demonstrate[ ] that legislative coalitions facing an ideologically opposed executive branch strategically design legislation with the goal of guarding against policy shifting away from the enacting legislative coalition's preferences." For example, scholars have found that divided government results in more detailed laws, delegation of less discretion and with more formal structural constraints, and efforts to structurally insulate the agency being delegated power from presidential influence. See John D. Huber & Charles R. Shipan, Deliberate Discretion? The Institutional Foundations of Bureaucratic Autonomy (2002); David Epstein & Sharyn O'Halloran, Delegating Powers (1999); David Lewis, Presidents and the Politics of Agency Design (2003).

Based on a study of significant laws enacted from 1947–2008, Farhang and Yaver conclude that there is "robust, consistent evidence that under conditions of divided government, Congress is more likely to fragment regulatory implementation power," with power being delegated to a larger number of distinct actors and agencies, often with overlapping jurisdiction. They also argue that this result should be expected, because fragmenting implementation and "[i]ncreasing the number of actors and agencies that must be coordinated to accomplish decisive action can, on balance, make significant departures from the policy status quo more difficult" and thereby inhibit presidential subversion of congressional preferences.

(2) ***Which Dimensions of Delegations Matter?*** Does focusing on broad delegations generally fail to identify when delegation is most concerning? TODD D. RAKOFF, THE SHAPE OF THE LAW IN THE AMERICAN ADMINISTRATIVE STATE, 11 Tel Aviv U. Studies in Law 9, 20, 21–23, 24, 39 (1992): ". . . [E]ach [of the three branches of government] has some power over a very large range of subject matters, but is often unable to act effectively without the participation of one or both of the other branches. This is the 'separation of powers': branches of government that are 'omnicompetent' as regards subject-matter but 'unipowered' as regards the tools at their disposal. One could divide power the other way around. One could create organs of government that were 'omnipowered'—able to legislate, execute, adjudicate—but 'unicompetent'—entitled to exercise their many powers over only a small terrain. It is this second path that has been chosen in the fashioning of American regulatory agencies. . . .

"If the maxim that the only safe power is divided power is indeed a cultural norm, what would be taboo would be the creation of an organ of government at once omnipowered and omnicompetent. Congress would appear to operate on that maxim, as it has almost never tried to bring such an agency into being. The closest it has come was in the middle of the Great Depression, with the passage of the National Industrial Recovery Act. . . . But this example, far from disproving the force of the principle, in fact establishes it, for this Act is also the only one the Supreme Court has ever invalidated on that ground that it was, simply, an unlawful delegation of power." See also Cary Coglianese, Dimensions of Delegation, 167 U. Pa. L. Rev. 1849 (2019) (arguing for greater attention to factors such as degree of discretion afforded to the holder of lawmaking power and the extent of the underlying power itself, and that judges should "invalidate only those statutory grants of lawmaking authority that approximate one of Congress's enumerated powers along both the discretion and power dimensions").

(3) ***Delegation and Political Accountability.*** In Gundy, Justice Gorsuch insisted that broad delegations undermine political accountability. Is that true? Yes, says DAVID SCHOENBROD in POWER WITHOUT RESPONSIBILITY 183–84 (1993): "In making laws, Congress has to allocate both rights and duties in the very course of stating what conduct it prohibits, and so must make manifest the benefits and costs of regulation. When Congress delegates, it tends to do only half its job—to distribute rights without imposing the commensurate duties. So it promises clean air without restricting polluters and higher incomes for farmers without increasing the price of groceries. In striking poses popular to each and every constituency, Congress ducks the key conflicts. Those conflicts, however, will inevitably surface when the agency tries to translate the popular abstractions of the statutory goals—such as 'clean' air or 'orderly' agricultural markets—into rules of conduct. . . . [D]elegation allows legislators to claim credit for the benefits which a regulatory statute promises yet escape the blame for the burdens it will impose."

No, says PETER H. SCHUCK in DELEGATION AND DEMOCRACY: COMMENTS ON DAVID SCHOENBROD, 20 Cardozo L. Rev. 775, 781 (1999): "[Schoenbrod] fails to see . . . that the particular attributes of the legislature's delegation—its breadth, type, and level—are themselves fundamental policy choices. . . . The optimal specificity and other delegation-related features of the legislation are among the questions on which almost all of the parties to these legislative struggles—congressional committees, legislative staffs, the White House, regulated firms, 'public interest' groups, state and local governments, and others—tend to stake out clear positions, for they know the resolution of these questions may well determine the nature and effectiveness of the regulatory scheme being established." See also Jerry L. Mashaw, Prodelegation: Why Administrators Should Make Political Decisions, 1 J.L. Econ. & Org. 81, 95–99 (1985) (arguing that the President is selected by a national electorate based on views of a candidate's general policies and thus broad delegations "improv[e] the responsiveness of government to the desires of the electorate" because they allow policy to change with different presidential administrations).

Neither Schoenbrod nor Schuck differentiates between delegation's effects on individual legislators as opposed to Congress as a whole. For the argument that such a distinction is critical, see now-Judge NEOMI RAO, ADMINISTRATIVE COLLUSION: HOW DELEGATION DIMINISHES THE COLLECTIVE CONGRESS, 90 N.Y.U. L. Rev. 1463, 1465–66 (2015): "Delegation undermines separation of powers, not only by expanding the power of executive agencies, but also by unraveling the institutional interests of Congress. The Constitution creates what I term the 'collective Congress'—the people's representatives may exercise legislative power only collectively. This serves important republican principles and aligns the myriad particular interests of congressmen with the institutional interests of Congress. Members will be invested in the difficult process of lawmaking for the public good because this is the only way to exercise power. Delegation, however, provides numerous benefits to legislators by allowing them to influence and to control administration. Individual legislators thus have persistent incentives to delegate, because they can serve their personal interests by shaping how agencies exercise their delegated authority. By providing individual opportunities for legislators, delegation realigns the ambitions of congressmen away from Congress and the constitutional lawmaking process."

(4) ***The Structure and Process of Delegated Power.*** A substantial political science literature, often called positive political theory or PPT, exists on the extent to which Congress exercises control over delegated power and the means by which it does so. LISA SCHULTZ BRESSMAN, PROCEDURES AS POLITICS IN ADMINISTRATIVE LAW, 107 Colum. L. Rev. 1749, 1767–68 (2007): Political scientists "start from the premise that delegation creates a principal-agent problem. In particular, Congress knows that agencies may implement their own policy preferences rather than legislative preferences. Political scientists identify two sorts of difficulties: 'coalitional drift' and 'bureaucratic drift.' Bureaucratic drift arises when agency officials act in ways inconsistent with the original deal or coalitional arrangement struck between interest groups and politicians. Coalitional drift occurs when agency officials, even if reflecting the preferences of the enacting Congress, depart from the preferences of future Congresses. For both sorts of problems, legislative monitoring is the antidote. . . . But . . . Congress has trouble monitoring its agents directly. Such oversight is costly, requiring both time and resources. Moreover, Congress frequently lacks the information necessary to assess whether agencies have selected policies that diverge from the ones that it would have chosen."

Yet some political scientists argue that the difficulty Congress faces in monitoring its agency delegates "ex post," or after it has delegated, doesn't mean it cedes control over delegated power. The reason is that Congress can impose indirect controls "ex ante," through the structure and process it imposes on an agency when it delegates. DAVID B. SPENCE, MANAGING DELEGATION EX ANTE: USING LAW TO STEER ADMINISTRATIVE AGENCIES, 28 J. Legal Stud. 413, 415 (1999): "Put simply, the structure and process hypothesis states that while Congress cannot foresee many of the important policy decisions it delegates to the agency, it can use enabling legislation to shape the agency policy-making process in ways that influence subsequent agency policy decisions. These means of influence include (1) providing for interest group representation in the administrative process; (2) 'stacking the deck' in favor of the interest groups supporting the original legislation (the 'enacting coalition') by specifying how the statutory mandate will be implemented; and (3) structuring the agency so that it tends to favor particular interests. . . . These design decisions establish both ex ante predispositions in the agency and ex ante procedural rights for the enacting coalition, both of which can ensure that the enacting coalition's goals will be met in the agency policy-making process." According to this view, Congress can use structure and process to alleviate its oversight difficulties and is a far more active overseer of agencies than many suppose. See also Mathew McCubbins, Roger Noll, & Barry Weingast (collectively McNollgast), Administrative Procedures as Instruments of Political Control, 3 J. L. Econ. & Org. 243, 244, 246 (1987) . For an alternative account of procedure in the rulemaking context, see p. 445.

(5) ***Congressional Versus Presidential Control.*** Other political scientists are less persuaded by the structure and process theory and dispute the effectiveness of mechanisms for ongoing congressional control. They argue that the President enjoys several institutional advantages that those arguing for congressional dominance ignore. KEITH E. WHITTINGTON and DANIEL P. CARPENTER, EXECUTIVE POWER IN AMERICAN INSTITUTIONAL DEVELOPMENT, 1 Persp. on Politics 495, 496, 508 (2003): "[T]he narrative of congressional dominance ignores three entrenched properties of the American political system: (1) the power of the president as party leader . . . (2) the ability of the executive branch to engage in autonomous policy innovation, and (3) the ability of the executive to shape the national policy agenda. . . . The executive may be constrained by Congress, but it has not simply represented congressional interests." See also Terry M. Moe, An Assessment of the Positive Theory of 'Congressional Dominance,' 12 Leg. Stud. Q. 475 (1987). The scope of presidential power over administration is discussed in detail in Section 3.

## (5) Delegations to Other Institutional Actors

The prior materials focused largely on delegations to federal government agencies. But Congress delegates to a wide array of actors, including private entities, state governments, and international actors, to name just a few, as well as many entities that straddle categories. See Anne Joseph O'Connell, Bureaucracy at the Boundary, 162 U. Pa. L. Rev. 841, 846–51 (2014). Should the fact that a state government, a private entity, or an international body is the recipient of delegated power affect the constitutionality of a delegation, and if so how?

(1) ***Private Delegations.*** Concurring in American Railroads (p. 851), Justice Alito stated that "Congress cannot delegate regulatory authority to a private entity." He maintained that there was no justification for "not enforc[ing] the nondelegation doctrine with more vigilance" in this context, compared to public delegations, because private entities do not enjoy any constitutional legislative or executive powers "of their own that can be used in ways that resemble lawmaking." Are you convinced? Can't private entities wield private powers in ways that resemble lawmaking? Think about private universities that adopt rules regulating student activities or shopping malls that regulate demonstrations and protests on their premises. Is it clear that these entities are just wielding private power, as opposed to being instances when the government, through its rules regulating private property, has

delegated to them power to control others? See Louis L. Jaffe, Law Making by Private Groups, 51 Harv. L. Rev. 201, 220–21 (1937).

Justice Alito emphasized that the "Constitution, by careful design, prescribes a process for making law, and within that process there are many accountability checkpoints. . . . It would dash the whole scheme if Congress could give its power away to an entity that is not constrained by those checkpoints." See also Harold J. Krent, The Private Performing the Public: Delimiting Delegations to Private Parties, 65 U. Miami L. Rev. 507, 511 (2011). But does this differentiate private delegations? Isn't the same complaint made about delegations to the executive branch?

A structural concern specific to privatization is that it may serve to aggrandize executive power, "provid[ing an] outsourcing agency with the means of achieving distinct public policy goals that—but for the pretext of technocratic outsourcing—would be impossible or much more difficult to attain in the ordinary course of nonprivatized public administration." Jon D. Michaels, Privatization's Pretensions, 77 U. Chi. L. Rev. 717 (2010); see generally Jon D. Michaels, Constitutional Coup: Privatization's Threat to the American Republic (2017). Does this potential for executive aggrandizement differentiate private delegations? For discussion of some of the implications of contemporary government's deep reliance on private contractors, see the excerpt from Jody Freeman and Martha Minow, Reframing the Outsourcing Debates in Chapter I (p. 49).

Another feature that distinguishes private delegates from their public counterparts is the fact that private delegates are exempt from Constitution's individual rights protections, unless they are deemed to be state actors for constitutional purposes—as the Supreme Court concluded about Amtrak in American Railroads. Should the constitutionality of a private delegation turn on whether the private delegate is subject to constitutional constraints in wielding its delegated powers? See Gillian E. Metzger, Privatization as Delegation, 103 Colum. L. Rev. 1367, 1400–08 (2003). On the other hand, perhaps private delegations offer a potential benefit, insofar as they "can be a means of 'publicization,' through which private actors increasingly commit themselves to traditionally public goals as the price of access to lucrative opportunities to deliver goods and services that might otherwise be provided directly by the state." Jody Freeman, Extending Public Law Norms through Privatization, 116 Harv. L. Rev. 1285 (2003).

(2) ***Delegation to States or State/Federal Entities.*** Delegations to states are perhaps the most common. States play critical roles in implementing a broad array of federal regulatory schemes and programs. For example, the states are responsible for incorporating the NAAQS that EPA issues under the Clean Air Act, at issue in Whitman, into state implementation plans that apply to emissions within their borders. Similarly, Medicaid and Social Security Disability are implemented by state agencies. In Federalism as a Safeguard of the Separation of Powers, 112 Colum. L. Rev. 475 (2012), Jessica Bulman-Pozen notes that "when Congress gives states a role in executing federal law, it tends to delegate not exclusively but rather concurrently: States may implement federal law by conforming to standards

set by the federal executive; state and federal agencies may implement the same regulatory provisions or enforce the same statutes; or state officials may execute federal law under the supervision of a federal agency." Congress also delegates power to a range of joint federal-state entities, like the National Guard. Each state has a national guard, commanded by the state's governor, but these state national guards are regulated and funded by the federal government and the President can call them into service under the President's command. See O'Connell, supra, at 862.

Should congressional delegations to states be treated the same as private delegations? The same as delegations to federal agencies? Some other standard? What about delegations to joint federal-state entities? In his dissent in Whitman at the D.C. Circuit, Judge Tatel argued that "[b]ecause the Clean Air Act gives politically accountable state governments primary responsibility for determining how to distribute the burdens of pollution reduction and therefore how the NAAQS will affect specific industries and individual businesses, courts have less reason to second-guess the specificity of the congressional delegation." Do you agree?

(3) ***Delegations to International Bodies.*** "Most nations today participate in a dense network of international cooperation that requires them to grant authority to international actors. At varying levels this means that the individual state surrenders some autonomy to international bodies or other states by authorizing them to participate in decisionmaking processes and to take actions that affect the state. . . . What distinguishes international delegations from mere international commitments is the existence of an entity that has been granted the authority to make decisions or take actions that bind the state or commit its resources." Curtis A. Bradley & Judith G. Kelley, The Concept of International Delegation, 71 Law & Contemp. Probs. 1, 3 (2008). In the United States, "[t]he practice of delegating to international institutions—vesting them with the authority to develop binding rules—sometimes looks like the next New Deal. Despite its continuing mistrust of international engagements, the United States continues to vest new authority in established organizations, such as the United Nations, the Organisation for Economic Co-operation and Development, and the International Labour Organization, and to create new institutions, like the World Trade Organization and the North American Free Trade Agreement, that exercise considerable power over U.S. affairs. The march seems inexorable." Edward T. Swaine, The Constitutionality of International Delegations, 104 Colum L. Rev. 1492, 1492 (2004).

## b. Congressional Control of Regulatory Policy

*(1) Legislation and Vetoes*
*(2) Appropriations and Spending*
*(3) Oversight and Investigations*
*(4) Direct Control over Regulatory Actors*

One of the most fundamental ways in which contemporary U.S. government differs from what the Framers imagined is the relative importance of statutes and the common law. At every level of government, the common law has been displaced as the dominant system of social regulation. Initially, statutes themselves set the legal rules that supplemented or supplanted the law made by courts. Then statutes set in motion administrative processes, and agencies made the rules that regulate economic and social activity.

Nondelegation jurisprudence effectively endorsed this transformation as a constitutional matter, but the shift to administrative government also transformed the roles of Congress and the President—and here the course of constitutional reconciliation has been far more contentious. "From their originally contemplated role as initiators of policy, the House and Senate now often occupy a reactive role, responding in formal and informal ways to policy generated by agencies. From this originally contemplated role as check upon hasty and imprudent legislation, the President as chief administrator now often forces Congress into the position of checking policy specified by the executive." Cynthia R. Farina, The Consent of the Governed: Against Simple Rules for a Complex World, 72 Chi.-Kent L. Rev. 987, 1018 (1997). Both Congress and the President recognize that the stakes are high—and the contemporary pattern of divided government, coupled with increasing polarization of Republican and Democratic policy preferences, produces more competition than cooperation.

Here we focus on methods used by Congress to direct and influence regulatory outcomes, including legislation and vetoes, appropriations and spending, investigations, and control over executive officers. The central factual background underlying all of these topics is the reality of pervasive delegations. Having granted the executive branch broad authority and discretion, how does Congress continue to exert control and ensure agencies pay attention to governing statutory requirements and congressional preferences?

## (1) Legislation and Vetoes

| |
|---|
| *IMMIGRATION AND NATURALIZATION SERVICE v. CHADHA* |
| ***Notes on Direction by Legislation*** |

*Every Bill which shall have passed the House of Representatives and the Senate, shall, before it becomes a Law, be presented to the President of the United States . . . . Every Order, Resolution, or Vote to which the Concurrence of the Senate and House of Representatives may be necessary (except on a question of Adjournment) shall be presented to the President of the United States; and before the Same shall take Effect, shall be approved by him, or being disapproved by him, shall be repassed by two thirds of the Senate and House of Representatives, according to the Rules and Limitations prescribed in the Case of a Bill.*

U.S. Const., Art. I, § 7

# IMMIGRATION AND NATURALIZATION SERVICE v. CHADHA

Supreme Court of the United States (1983).
462 U.S. 919.

■ CHIEF JUSTICE BURGER delivered the opinion of the Court.

[For most of the Nation's history, a noncitizen found deportable could remain in the United States only if some member of Congress obtained a private bill (that is, legislation that applied uniquely to the individual(s) named). The Immigration and Nationality Act of 1952 (INA) changed this, delegating to the Attorney General (who in turn delegated to the Immigration and Naturalization Service (INS)[6]) the discretion to "suspend deportation" of a noncitizen who has been physically present in the United States for at least seven years, is of good moral character, and "is a person whose deportation would, in the opinion of the Attorney General, result in extreme hardship to the alien, or to his spouse, parent, or child who is a citizen of the United States or an alien lawfully admitted for permanent residence." However, this power was conditioned upon neither house of Congress disagreeing and exercising its statutory one-house legislative veto on the noncitizen remaining in the country. Subsection (c) of § 244 of the INA provides:

> "(1) Upon application by any alien who is found by the Attorney General to meet [these] requirements . . . the Attorney General may in his discretion suspend deportation of such alien. If the deportation of any alien is suspended under the provisions of this subsection, a complete and detailed statement of the facts

---

[6] [Ed.] In 2003, the responsibilities of the INS were transferred to the Immigration and Customs Enforcement, Customs and Border Protection, and the Citizenship and Immigration Services. See the Homeland Security Act of 2002, Pub. L. No. 107–296, 116 Stat. 2135.

> and pertinent provisions of law in the case shall be reported to the Congress with the reasons for such suspension. . . .
>
> (2) [I]f during the session of the Congress at which a case is reported, or prior to the close of the session of the Congress next following the session at which a case is reported, either the Senate or the House of Representatives passes a resolution stating in substance that it does not favor the suspension of such deportation, the Attorney General shall thereupon deport such alien or authorize the alien's voluntary departure at his own expense under the order of deportation in the manner provided by law. If, within the time above specified, neither the Senate nor the House of Representatives shall pass such a resolution, the Attorney General shall cancel deportation proceedings."[7]

Chadha was deportable for overstaying his nonimmigrant student visa. He applied for and received a suspension of deportation, and his case was laid before Congress. The House Judiciary Committee reported out a resolution opposing "the granting of permanent residence in the United States to [six] aliens" including Chadha. Representative Eilberg, Chair of the Subcommittee on Immigration, Citizenship, and International Law, made a brief statement that

> "[i]t was the feeling of the committee, after reviewing 340 cases, that the aliens contained in the resolution [Chadha and five others] did not meet these statutory requirements, particularly as it relates to hardship; and it is the opinion of the committee that their deportation should not be suspended."

The resolution was passed without debate or recorded vote. After deportation proceedings were instituted, Chadha appealed to the Ninth Circuit, which held the legislative veto unconstitutional and enjoined Chadha's deportation. The Supreme Court granted certiorari. Its opinion first disposed of several justiciability issues and then turned to the following.]

III

We turn now to the question whether action of one House of Congress under § 244(c)(2) violates strictures of the Constitution. We begin, of course, with the presumption that the challenged statute is valid. Its wisdom is not the concern of the courts; if a challenged action does not violate the Constitution, it must be sustained. . . . By the same token, the fact that a given law or procedure is efficient, convenient, and useful in facilitating functions of government, standing alone, will not save it if it is contrary to the Constitution.

. . . The decision to provide the President with a limited and qualified power to nullify proposed legislation by veto was based on the profound conviction of the Framers that the powers conferred on Congress were

---

[7] [Ed.] Prior to the 1952 Act, Congress experimented briefly with a system in which deportation could be suspended on the Attorney General's recommendation if Congress affirmatively approved by concurrent resolution. This proved nearly as burdensome as the private bill system.

the powers to be most carefully circumscribed. It is beyond doubt that lawmaking was a power to be shared by both Houses and the President. . . . The President's role in the lawmaking process also reflects the Framers' careful efforts to check whatever propensity a particular Congress might have to enact oppressive, improvident, or ill-considered measures. . . . The Court also has observed that the Presentment Clauses serve the important purpose of assuring that a "national" perspective is grafted on the legislative process: "The President is a representative of the people just as the members of the Senate and of the House are, and it may be, at some times, on some subjects, that the President elected by all the people is rather more representative of them all than are the members of either body of the Legislature whose constituencies are local and not countrywide. . . ." Myers v. United States, 272 U.S. [52,] 123 [(1926)] [p. 982].

The bicameral requirement of Art. I, §§ 1, 7 was of scarcely less concern to the Framers than was the Presidential veto and indeed the two concepts are interdependent. By providing that no law could take effect without the concurrence of the prescribed majority of the Members of both Houses, the Framers reemphasized their belief, already remarked upon in connection with the Presentment Clauses, that legislation should not be enacted unless it has been carefully and fully considered by the Nation's elected officials. . . . [I]n Federalist No. 51 Hamilton . . . point[ed] up the need to divide and disperse power in order to protect liberty: "In republican government, the legislative authority necessarily predominates. The remedy for this inconveniency is to divide the legislature into different branches; and to render them, by different modes of election and different principles of action, as little connected with each other as the nature of their common functions and their common dependence on the society will admit." . . .

We see therefore that the Framers were acutely conscious that the bicameral requirement and the Presentment Clauses would serve essential constitutional functions. The President's participation in the legislative process was to protect the Executive Branch from Congress and to protect the whole people from improvident laws. The division of the Congress into two distinctive bodies assures that the legislative power would be exercised only after opportunity for full study and debate in separate settings. The President's unilateral veto power, in turn, was limited by the power of two thirds of both Houses of Congress to overrule a veto thereby precluding final arbitrary action of one person. It emerges clearly that the prescription for legislative action in Art. I, §§ 1, 7 represents the Framers' decision that the legislative power of the Federal government be exercised in accord with a single, finely wrought and exhaustively considered, procedure.

IV

The Constitution sought to divide the delegated powers of the new federal government into three defined categories, legislative, executive and judicial, to assure, as nearly as possible, that each Branch of government would confine itself to its assigned responsibility. The hydraulic pressure inherent within each of the separate Branches to exceed the outer limits of its power, even to accomplish desirable objectives, must be resisted. Although not "hermetically" sealed from one another, Buckley v. Valeo, 424 U.S. [1,] 126 [(1976), p. 957], the powers delegated to the three Branches are functionally identifiable. When any Branch acts, it is presumptively exercising the power the Constitution has delegated to it. When the Executive acts, it presumptively acts in an executive or administrative capacity as defined in Art. II. And when, as here, one House of Congress purports to act, it is presumptively acting within its assigned sphere.

Beginning with this presumption, we must nevertheless establish that the challenged action under § 244(c)(2) is of the kind to which the procedural requirements of Art. I, § 7 apply. Not every action taken by either House is subject to the bicameralism and presentment requirements of Art. I. Whether actions taken by either House are, in law and fact, an exercise of legislative power depends not on their form but upon "whether they contain matter which is properly to be regarded as legislative in its character and effect." S.Rep. No. 1335, 54th Cong., 2d Sess., 8 (1897).

Examination of the action taken here by one House pursuant to § 244(c)(2) reveals that it was essentially legislative in purpose and effect. [T]he House took action that had the purpose and effect of altering the legal rights, duties and relations of persons, including the Attorney General, Executive Branch officials and Chadha, all outside the legislative branch. Section 244(c)(2) purports to authorize one House of Congress to require the Attorney General to deport an individual alien whose deportation otherwise would be cancelled under § 244. The one-House veto operated in this case to overrule the Attorney General and mandate Chadha's deportation; absent the House action, Chadha would remain in the United States. Congress has acted and its action has altered Chadha's status.

The legislative character of the one-House veto in this case is confirmed by the character of the Congressional action it supplants. Neither the House of Representatives nor the Senate contends that, absent the veto provision in § 244(c)(2), either of them, or both of them acting together, could effectively require the Attorney General to deport an alien once the Attorney General, in the exercise of legislatively delegated authority,[16] had determined the alien should remain in the

---

[16] Congress protests that affirming the Court of Appeals in this case will sanction "lawmaking by the Attorney General. . . . Why is the Attorney General exempt from submitting his proposed changes in the law to the full bicameral process?" Brief of the United States House of Representatives 40. To be sure, some administrative agency action—rule making, for example—may resemble "lawmaking." See 5 U.S.C. § 551(4), which defines an agency's "rule" as "the whole or part of an agency statement of general or particular applicability and future effect designed to implement, interpret, or prescribe law or policy . . ." This Court has referred to agency activity as being "quasi-legislative" in character. Humphrey's Executor v. United States, 295 U.S. 602, 628 (1935) [p. 860]. Clearly, however, "[i]n the framework of our Constitution, the President's power to see that the laws are faithfully executed refutes the idea that he is to be a lawmaker." Youngstown Sheet & Tube Co. v. Sawyer, 343 U.S. 579, 587 (1952) [p. 933]. When the Attorney General performs his duties pursuant to § 244, he does not exercise

United States. Without the challenged provision in § 244(c)(2), this could have been achieved, if at all, only by legislation requiring deportation.[17] Similarly, a veto by one House of Congress under § 244(c)(2) cannot be justified as an attempt at amending the standards set out in § 244(a)(1), or as a repeal of § 244 as applied to Chadha. Amendment and repeal of statutes, no less than enactment, must conform with Art. I.

The nature of the decision implemented by the one-House veto in this case further manifests its legislative character. After long experience with the clumsy, time consuming private bill procedure, Congress made a deliberate choice to delegate to the Executive Branch, and specifically to the Attorney General, the authority to allow deportable aliens to remain in this country in certain specified circumstances. It is not disputed that this choice to delegate authority is precisely the kind of decision that can be implemented only in accordance with the procedures set out in Art. I. Disagreement with the Attorney General's decision on Chadha's deportation—that is, Congress' decision to deport Chadha—no less than Congress' original choice to delegate to the Attorney General the authority to make that decision, involves determinations of policy that Congress can implement in only one way: bicameral passage followed by presentment to the President. Congress must abide by its delegation of authority until that delegation is legislatively altered or revoked.

Finally, we see that when the Framers intended to authorize either House of Congress to act alone and outside of its prescribed bicameral legislative role, they narrowly and precisely defined the procedure for such action. There are but four provisions in the Constitution, explicit and unambiguous, by which one House may act alone with the unreviewable force of law, not subject to the President's veto: (a) The House of Representatives alone was given the power to initiate impeachments; (b) The Senate alone was given the power to conduct trials following impeachment on charges initiated by the House and to

---

"legislative" power. The bicameral process is not necessary as a check on the Executive's administration of the laws because his administrative activity cannot reach beyond the limits of the statute that created it—a statute duly enacted pursuant to Art. I, §§ 1, 7. The constitutionality of the Attorney General's execution of the authority delegated to him by § 244 involves only a question of delegation doctrine. The courts, when a case or controversy arises, can always "ascertain whether the will of Congress has been obeyed," Yakus v. United States, 321 U.S. 414, 425 (1944) [p. 861], and can enforce adherence to statutory standards. See Ethyl Corp. v. EPA, 541 F.2d 1, 68 (CADC) (en banc) (separate statement of Leventhal, J.), cert. denied, 426 U.S. 941 (1976). It is clear, therefore, that the Attorney General acts in his presumptively Art. II capacity when he administers the Immigration and Nationality Act. Executive action under legislatively delegated authority that might resemble "legislative" action in some respects is not subject to the approval of both Houses of Congress and the President for the reason that the Constitution does not so require. That kind of Executive action is always subject to check by the terms of the legislation that authorized it; and if that authority is exceeded it is open to judicial review as well as the power of Congress to modify or revoke the authority entirely. A one-House veto is clearly legislative in both character and effect and is not so checked; the need for the check provided by Art. I, §§ 1, 7 is therefore clear. Congress' authority to delegate portions of its power to administrative agencies provides no support for the argument that Congress can constitutionally control administration of the laws by way of a Congressional veto.

[17] We express no opinion as to whether such legislation would violate any constitutional provision.

convict following trial; (c) The Senate alone was given final unreviewable power to approve or to disapprove presidential appointments; (d) The Senate alone was given unreviewable power to ratify treaties negotiated by the President. Clearly, when the Draftsmen sought to confer special powers on one House, independent of the other House, or of the President, they did so in explicit, unambiguous terms. . . .

The veto authorized by § 244(c)(2) doubtless has been in many respects a convenient shortcut; the "sharing" with the Executive by Congress of its authority over aliens in this manner is, on its face, an appealing compromise. . . . The choices we discern as having been made in the Constitutional Convention impose burdens on governmental processes that often seem clumsy, inefficient, even unworkable, but those hard choices were consciously made by men who had lived under a form of government that permitted arbitrary governmental acts to go unchecked. There is no support in the Constitution or decisions of this Court for the proposition that the cumbersomeness and delays often encountered in complying with explicit Constitutional standards may be avoided, either by the Congress or by the President. With all the obvious flaws of delay, untidiness, and potential for abuse, we have not yet found a better way to preserve freedom than by making the exercise of power subject to the carefully crafted restraints spelled out in the Constitution.

We hold that the Congressional veto provision in § 244(c)(2) is severable from the Act and that it is unconstitutional. Accordingly, the judgment of the Court of Appeals is

Affirmed.

■ JUSTICE POWELL, concurring in the judgment.

The Court's decision . . . apparently will invalidate every use of the legislative veto. The breadth of this holding gives one pause. Congress has included the veto in literally hundreds of statutes, dating back to the 1930s. Congress clearly views this procedure as essential to controlling the delegation of power to administrative agencies. One reasonably may disagree with Congress' assessment of the veto's utility, but the respect due its judgment as a coordinate branch of Government cautions that our holding should be no more extensive than necessary to decide this case. In my view, the case may be decided on a narrower ground. When Congress finds that a particular person does not satisfy the statutory criteria for permanent residence in this country it has assumed a judicial function in violation of the principle of separation of powers. . . .

. . . One abuse that was prevalent during the Confederation was the exercise of judicial power by the state legislatures. The Framers were well acquainted with the danger of subjecting the determination of the rights of one person to the "tyranny of shifting majorities." . . . Their concern that a legislature should not be able unilaterally to impose a substantial deprivation on one person was expressed [in] specific provisions, such as the Bill of Attainder Clause, Art. I, § 9, cl. 3. . . . This Clause, and the separation of powers doctrine generally, reflect the

Framers' concern that trial by a legislature lacks the safeguards necessary to prevent the abuse of power. . . .

On its face, the House's action appears clearly adjudicatory.[7] The House did not enact a general rule; rather it made its own determination that six specific persons did not comply with certain statutory criteria. . . .

The impropriety of the House's assumption of this function is confirmed by the fact that its action raises the very danger the Framers sought to avoid—the exercise of unchecked power. In deciding whether Chadha deserves to be deported, Congress is not subject to any internal constraints that prevent it from arbitrarily depriving him of the right to remain in this country.[9] Unlike the judiciary or an administrative agency, Congress is not bound by established substantive rules. Nor is it subject to the procedural safeguards, such as the right to counsel and a hearing before an impartial tribunal, that are present when a court or an agency[10] adjudicates individual rights. The only effective constraint on Congress' power is political, but Congress is most accountable politically when it prescribes rules of general applicability. When it decides rights of specific persons, those rights are subject to "the tyranny of a shifting majority." . . .

■ JUSTICE WHITE, dissenting.

. . . Without the legislative veto, Congress is faced with a Hobson's choice: either to refrain from delegating the necessary authority, leaving itself with a hopeless task of writing laws with the requisite specificity to cover endless special circumstances across the entire policy landscape, or in the alternative, to abdicate its law-making function to the executive branch and independent agencies. To choose the former leaves major national problems unresolved; to opt for the latter risks unaccountable policymaking by those not elected to fill that role. . . .

The legislative veto developed initially in response to the problems of reorganizing the sprawling government structure created in response to the Depression. The Reorganization Acts established the chief model

---

[7] The Court concludes that Congress' action was legislative in character because each branch "presumptively act[s] within its assigned sphere." The Court's presumption provides a useful starting point, but does not conclude the inquiry. Nor does the fact that the House's action alters an individual's legal status indicate, as the Court reasons, that the action is legislative rather than adjudicative in nature. In determining whether one branch unconstitutionally has assumed a power central to another branch, the traditional characterization of the assumed power as legislative, executive, or judicial may provide some guidance. But reasonable minds may disagree over the character of an act and the more helpful inquiry, in my view, is whether the act in question raises the dangers the Framers sought to avoid.

[9] When Congress grants particular individuals relief or benefits under its spending power, the danger of oppressive action that the separation of powers was designed to avoid is not implicated. Similarly, Congress may authorize the admission of individual aliens by special acts, but it does not follow that Congress unilaterally may make a judgment that a particular alien has no legal right to remain in this country. . . .

[10] We have recognized that independent regulatory agencies and departments of the Executive Branch often exercise authority that is "judicial in nature." Buckley v. Valeo, 424 U.S. 1, 140–141 (1976) [p. 957]. This function, however, forms part of the agencies' execution of public law and is subject to the procedural safeguards, including judicial review, provided by the Administrative Procedure Act.

for the legislative veto. When President Hoover requested authority to reorganize the government in 1929, he coupled his request that the "Congress be willing to delegate its authority over the problem (subject to defined principles) to the Executive" with a proposal for legislative review. He proposed that the Executive "should act upon approval of a joint committee of Congress or with the reservation of power of revision by Congress within some limited period adequate for its consideration." Pub. Papers 432 (1929). [Justice White then describes how the legislative veto was part of an accommodation between Congress and President Roosevelt in which more than 30 statutes conferred "exceptional" wartime powers on the President. The legislative veto "balanced" delegations of statutory authority in new areas including the space program and international agreements on nuclear energy. During the 1970s, it was part of statutory resolutions of "major constitutional disputes between the President and Congress" in the area of war powers, emergency power, foreign arms sale, and exports of nuclear technology. It "balance[d] broad delegations in legislation emerging from the energy crisis of the 1970's," and was a condition of broad rulemaking granted the Commissioner of Education to supersede "fragmented and narrow grant programs [that] inevitably lead to Executive-Legislative confrontations."]

Even this brief review suffices to demonstrate that the legislative veto is more than "efficient, convenient, and useful." It is an important if not indispensable political invention that allows the President and Congress to resolve major constitutional and policy differences, assures the accountability of independent regulatory agencies, and preserves Congress' control over lawmaking. Perhaps there are other means of accommodation and accountability, but the increasing reliance of Congress upon the legislative veto suggests that the alternatives to which Congress must now turn are not entirely satisfactory.

. . . The power to exercise a legislative veto is not the power to write new law without bicameral approval or presidential consideration. The veto must be authorized by statute and may only negative what an Executive department or independent agency has proposed. On its face, the legislative veto no more allows one House of Congress to make law than does the presidential veto confer such power upon the President. . . .

. . . The Court's holding today that all legislative-type action must be enacted through the lawmaking process ignores that legislative authority is routinely delegated to the Executive branch, to the independent regulatory agencies, and to private individuals and groups. . . . This Court's decisions sanctioning such delegations make clear that Article I does not require all action with the effect of legislation to be passed as a law. . . . If Congress may delegate lawmaking power to independent and executive agencies, it is most difficult to understand Article I as forbidding Congress from also reserving a check on legislative power for itself. Absent the veto, the agencies receiving delegations of legislative or quasi-legislative power may issue regulations having the force of law without bicameral approval and without the President's signature. It is thus not apparent why the reservation of a veto over the exercise of that legislative power must be subject to a more exacting test. In both cases, it is enough that the initial statutory authorizations comply with the Article I requirements. . . .

. . . Today's decision strikes down in one fell swoop provisions in more laws enacted by Congress than the Court has cumulatively invalidated in its history. I fear it will now be more difficult "to insure that the fundamental policy decisions in our society will be made not by an appointed official but by the body immediately responsible to the people," Arizona v. California, 373 U.S. 546, 626.

I must dissent.

## NOTES

(1) ***Methodology.*** How would you characterize the methodology of the different opinions in Chadha? Chief Justice Burger's majority opinion is often identified as a classic example of formalist separation of powers analysis. Burger describes the Constitution as dividing the federal government's powers into three distinct categories, each vested in a distinct branch. He also emphasizes the narrow exceptions to bicameralism and presentment in the constitutional text, and rejects convenience and efficiency as legitimate considerations in assessing constitutionality. Yet note the functionalist reasoning in Part III of the opinion, in which Burger underscores the importance of bicameralism and presentment as checks on legislative power. Justice White's dissent, in turn, is generally viewed as a paradigm of functionalist analysis. He rejects what he perceives as the majority's unnecessarily wooden reading of the Constitution, emphasizing the flexibility the political branches enjoy in structuring their affairs. White's analysis is also centrally pragmatic, condemning the majority for failing to acknowledge the practical importance of the legislative veto. Justice Powell, concurring in the judgment, takes perhaps an even more thoroughgoing functionalist stance, identifying the goals and values embedded in the constitutional structure and concluding that the veto in the context of adjudication cannot be reconciled with those goals and values. (Note particularly footnote 7 in Powell's opinion.)

(2) ***Delegation and the Legislative Veto.*** Justice White's central point is that the constitutionality of the legislative veto needs to be assessed against the baseline of modern delegation. Having sanctioned the broad legislative delegations of authority that gave birth to the modern administrative state, separation of powers concerns necessitated that the Court be similarly flexible in assessing the techniques Congress could use to still exert policymaking control. White's point could be translated into a claim about methodological consistency: Having taken a functionalist stance on delegation, the Court should not turn formalist in addressing the aftermath of delegation. Are you convinced?

Burger responds by insisting that the Attorney General, acting under a delegation of authority, is not exercising legislative power and is subject to checks from the statute delegating authority. He also emphasizes that limits on the Attorney General's authority can be enforced through judicial review.

How much of a check do you think the governing statute and judicial review will supply? Does this answer Justice White's argument?

(3) ***Does Context Matter?*** For Justice Powell, the most important factor in Chadha was the use of the legislative veto with respect to specified individuals, which in his view made the House's action adjudicatory. If you have studied the materials in Chapter III on the distinction between rulemaking and adjudication, you've seen that drawing the line between these two functions is hard. Does the fact that Congress historically provided relief from deportation via a private bill call Justice Powell's characterization into question?

Although Chadha involved adjudication, rulemaking was also an important setting for legislative veto provisions, particularly starting in the 1970s. Should the constitutional analysis change in that context? If agencies acting under rulemaking delegations are understood to wield legislative power, does that make the legislative veto more constitutional? For an argument that it does, see Ilan Wurman, Constitutional Administration, 69 Stan. L. Rev. 359, 385 (2017).

PETER L. STRAUSS, in WAS THERE A BABY IN THE BATHWATER? A COMMENT ON THE SUPREME COURT'S LEGISLATIVE VETO DECISION, 1983 Duke L.J. 789, 805–807, 816, argues more broadly that substantive context should have received more attention in Chadha: "[P]olitical uses of legislative vetoes warrant special analysis. . . . [These] concern chiefly public measures primarily related to the internal organization of government and affecting the interests of private persons only indirectly; they reflect areas of direct presidential initiative and responsibility. . . . [and] may all be described fairly as a setting for horse-trading between the President and Congress: the authority subject to the veto will be that of the President himself; no alternative means of control is obvious; precise congressional standard-setting or structural arrangements are probably inadvisable; and a sharing of political authority is warranted by Congress' legitimate interests in the subject matter and the consequent desirability of committing Congress to support of the action to be taken. . . .

". . . In . . . a continuing relationship [such as the budget process], limiting one participant to episodic, formal, even clumsy acts is likely to produce rigidity and a covetousness about power that will hamper the effective conduct of government and may weaken the presidency far more than the alternative. The same is true for reorganization acts; in a government premised on the selection of a single executive as its head, it is internally sensible and externally non-threatening for the President to be the prime shaper of the internal structures of government, subject to congressional disapproval."

(4) ***The Aftermath in the Courts.*** Two weeks after Chadha, the Court summarily affirmed two D.C. Circuit decisions that invalidated the one-house and the two-house veto in the context of rulemaking. Process Gas Consumers Group v. Consumer Energy Council of Am., 463 U.S. 1216 (1983), aff'g Consumers Energy Council of Am. v. FERC, 673 F.2d 425 (D.C. Cir. 1982); Consumers Union of the United States v. FTC, 691 F.2d 575 (D.C. Cir.

1982). Justice Powell did not participate in the decision; only Justice Rehnquist would have set the cases for argument. Note that the lawyer who represented Chadha, Alan Morrison of Public Citizen, also represented the anti-legislative-veto petitioners in these two cases. Given how central rulemaking had become by then, were these two rulemaking cases really the "aftermath" to Chadha, or were they the main show?[8]

Lower courts then struggled to clean up the mess created by over 200 statutes containing a veto. The issue was whether the invalid provision was severable—traditionally determined by asking whether the legislature would have wanted the balance of the statutory scheme to remain effective even without the unconstitutional portion. Justice White's account of the history emphasizes that the veto was often the condition on which Congress agreed to the Executive's request for significant delegation of power. Nonetheless, courts generally severed veto provisions. Is this surprising, given the profound disruption of invalidating established regulatory programs? Compare Free Enterprise Fund v. PCAOB (p. 1002). However, in contexts closer to the historical core of the veto's development, courts sometimes recognized that the veto was the quid pro quo for delegation and struck down the entire scheme. For one such case, involving presidential power to refuse to spend (impound) appropriated funds, see City of New Haven v. United States, 809 F.2d 900 (D.C. Cir. 1987).

(5) ***The Aftermath in Congress.*** An aspect of U.S. constitutional history that we take for granted (but which lawyers from aspiring constitutional democracies recognize as remarkable) is the routine willingness of Congress and the President to acquiesce in even quite unpalatable judicial decisions. Official defiance of Supreme Court constitutional holdings is an extraordinary event for us. In the case of Chadha, the extraordinary occurred. Between the time Chadha was decided and 2004, more than 400 new legislative vetoes appeared in legislation signed into law by Presidents Reagan, George H. W. Bush, Clinton, and George W. Bush. The vast majority of these attached committee and subcommittee veto conditions to agency use of appropriated funds. Louis Fisher, Cong. Rsch. Serv., RS22132, Legislative Vetoes After Chadha 2, 4 (2005).

When President Reagan signed a 1984 appropriations bill containing committee veto provisions, he issued a signing statement (for a discussion of signing statements, see Section 3.c, p. 1029) that the Administration considered the veto provision legally nonbinding. In other words, agencies would spend appropriated funds without regard to appropriator approval. NEAL DEVINS & LOUIS FISHER, THE DEMOCRATIC CONSTITUTION 94–96 (2004): "The House Appropriations Committee knew how to respond. It threatened to repeal legislation that allowed the National Aeronautics and Space Administration (NASA) to exceed its spending caps subject to committee approval. Because of Reagan's statement, the committee told NASA that it could exceed its caps only through the enactment of

[8] For an engaging account of the story behind Chadha and the role that battles over legislative vetoes in rulemaking played in the case, try listening to this podcast from The Uncertain Hour and Marketplace, at https://www.marketplace.org/shows/the-uncertain-hour/s2-08-mosquitoes-nudist-colony/.

supplemental legislation, requiring approval from both houses of Congress and presentment to the President. Not surprisingly, NASA head James M. Beggs much preferred the limited legislative veto check to the onerous demand that NASA obtain formal positive law approval before it exceeds its spending caps. Beggs successfully pleaded his case to Congress, seeking 'an informal agreement' and promising 'not to exceed amounts for Committee designated programs without the approval of the Committee of Appropriations.'

"In addition to informal legislative vetoes, Congress continues to put committee vetoes in public laws, and agencies comply out of self-interest. They know that any attempt on their part to defy committee control is likely to produce the kind of backlash seen in the NASA dispute. Executive agencies have to live with their review committees year after year and have a much greater incentive to make accommodations and stick by them. Presidents and their legal advisors can indulge in dramatic confrontations with Congress on these issues; agencies, however, do not want bloody dogfights with the committees that authorize their programs and provide funds. . . .

"By misreading the history of legislative vetoes and failing to comprehend the subtleties of the legislative process, the Court directed the executive and legislative branches to adhere to procedures that would be impracticable and unworkable. Neither Congress nor the executive branch wanted the static model of government offered by the Court . . . [Chadha] simply drove underground a set of legislative and committee vetoes that used to operate in plain sight."

Do you agree with this criticism of Chadha? Requiring notification is plainly lawful, and this history indicates it is often just as effective. If so, is limiting Congress to requiring notification such a big deal? See also Edward H. Stiglitz, Unitary Innovations and Political Accountability, 99 Cornell Law Review 1133 (2014) (concluding, based on a dataset of state session laws, that "legislatures respond to a judicial invalidation of the legislative veto by augmenting alternative tools of administrative control").

Legislative vetoes continue to surface. For example, quite a number of provisions in the Consolidated Appropriations Act, 2022 stipulate that "written notification to, and the prior approval of, the Committees on Appropriations of both Houses of Congress" is needed for funds to be used in a specified fashion. Consider also Section 216 of H.R. 3364, Countering America's Adversaries Through Sanctions Act, Pub. L. No. 115-44, 131 Stat. 936 (2017), which among other things imposes sanctions on Russia for meddling in the 2016 election. Section 216 requires the President to submit a report to Congress and wait for thirty days before lifting or waiving sanctions on Russia. Section 216 further provides that if the House and Senate pass a joint resolution disapproving of the President's proposed action, the President may not take that action for twelve days after the joint resolution's passage; if the President vetoes the joint resolution, then the President cannot undertake that action for another ten days. In a signing statement, President Trump argued that this ran afoul of Chadha. Do you agree? For an argument in support of President Trump's view, see Daniel

Hemel, The Russia Sanctions Bill Is Unconstitutional—and Unnecessarily So, Notice & Comment Blog (July 25, 2017).[9] As a third example, the U.S. Department of Agriculture's effort to relocate two subagencies to Kansas City under the Trump Administration—allegedly to punish them for reports with which the Administration disagreed—was found by the Department's Inspector General to violate requirements in the 2018 appropriations act for congressional notification and approval of relocation decisions. Ben Guarino, USDA Science Agencies' Relocation May Have Violated Law, Inspector General Report Says, Wash. Post (Aug. 6, 2019).

(6) ***Clinton v. New York and the Line Item Veto Act: Article I, § 7 Strikes Again.*** In 1996, with great political fanfare, Congress enacted a statute that authorized the President to sign a bill into law but then, in specified circumstances, "cancel" portions of it. Specifically, the President could "cancel in whole" (1) any dollar amount of discretionary budget authority; (2) any item of new direct spending; or (3) any limited tax benefit. The power had to be exercised within five days of signing and was conditioned on a number of substantive and procedural requirements. In identifying items for cancellation the President was required to consider the legislative history, purposes, and other relevant information about the items. The President had to find, with respect to each cancellation, that it would: "(i) reduce the Federal budget deficit; (ii) not impair any essential Government functions; and (iii) not harm the national interest." Moreover, the President had to transmit a special message to Congress notifying it of each cancellation within five calendar days (excluding Sundays) after enactment of the canceled provision. The statute set forth an expedited procedure for Congress to consider a "disapproval bill," which had to pass both houses on a majority vote and could be vetoed by the President. If such a disapproval bill was enacted, the cancellations set forth in the President's message become "null and void." Although the cancellation authority was an amendment to the Impoundment Control Act, which regulates presidential impoundment of funds (p. 906), it was named (and publicized as) The Line Item Veto Act.

CLINTON V. CITY OF NEW YORK, 524 U.S. 417 (1998), involved use of this authority by President Clinton. He followed all the statutory requirements in canceling provisions that would have relieved New York City of an obligation to repay $2.6 billion in Medicare overpayments and that would have given advantageous tax treatment to certain farmer cooperatives. The City and the Snake River Potato Growers sued, alleging that the cancellation authority was unconstitutional.

For JUSTICE STEVENS, who wrote for six members of the Court, the Line Item Veto Act was an attempt to authorize the President to amend a statute, by repealing a portion of it, through a process that did not comply with Article I, § 7's bicameral and presentment requirements. In Stevens's view, that attempt was clearly unconstitutional under Chadha: "In both legal and practical effect, the President has amended two Acts of Congress by repealing a portion of each. . . . There is no provision in the Constitution that

[9] https://yalejreg.com/nc/the-russia-sanctions-bill-is-unconstitutional-and-unnecessarily-so/.

authorizes the President to enact, to amend, or to repeal statutes. . . . The procedures governing the enactment of statutes set forth in the text of Article I were the product of the great debates and compromises that produced the Constitution itself. . . . Our first President understood the text of the Presentment Clause as requiring that he either 'approve all the parts of a Bill, or reject it in toto.' What has emerged in these cases from the President's exercise of his statutory cancellation powers, however, are truncated versions of two bills that passed both Houses of Congress. They are not the product of the 'finely wrought' procedure that the Framers designed."

For Justices Scalia, Breyer, and O'Connor, however, the "line item veto" label was a red herring. They would have sustained the authorization as a delegation of power to the President not to spend money. JUSTICE SCALIA wrote: "Article I, § 7, of the Constitution obviously prevents the President from canceling a law that Congress has not authorized him to cancel. Such action cannot possibly be considered part of his execution of the law. . . . It was certainly arguable, as an original matter, that Art. I, § 7, also prevents the President from canceling a law which itself authorizes the President to cancel it. But as the Court acknowledges, that argument has . . . been made and rejected [since 1809.]" Scalia acknowledged that there were constitutional limits on the actions the President could be authorized to perform. He insisted, however, that "[t]hose limits are established . . . , not by some categorical prohibition of Art. I, § 7, which our cases conclusively disprove, but by what has come to be known as the doctrine of unconstitutional delegation of legislative authority. . . . Insofar as the degree of political, 'lawmaking' power conferred upon the Executive is concerned, there is not a dime's worth of difference between Congress's authorizing the President to cancel a spending item, and Congress's authorizing money to be spent on a particular item at the President's discretion. And the latter has been done since the founding of the Nation. . . . The title of the Line Item Veto Act . . . has succeeded in faking out the Supreme Court. The President's action it authorizes in fact is not a line-item veto and thus does not offend Art. I, § 7."

Isn't the Line Item Veto Act the polar opposite of the legislative veto in practical effect? Whereas the legislative veto expanded Congress's power to control executive action outside of the legislative process laid out in Article I, § 7 and could be seen as congressional aggrandizement, on its face the Line Item Veto Act looked more like congressional abdication. Perhaps it could be said to expand congressional power by allowing Congress to avoid tough trade-offs in budget choices and push them onto the President. But isn't that complaint also true of delegations? Do you think that the Line Item Veto Act went beyond the contours of a constitutional delegation under the current intelligible principle test? Were the dissenters correct to argue the Act should have been upheld as a constitutional delegation?

(7) ***The Proposed REINS Act.*** Congress's latest proposal to replace the legislative veto, the Regulations from the Executive in Need of Scrutiny (REINS) Act, would require legislation affirmatively approving rules with a large economic impact before the rule could go into effect. The REINS Act passed the Republican-controlled House several times during President

Obama's second term in office, starting in 2013, but stalled in the Senate. The latest version of the bill was introduced in 2021. S. 92 (117th Cong.) (2021).

Do you think that such an act would pass constitutional muster? No, argues Ronald M. Levin in The REINS Act: Unbridled Impediment to Regulation, 83 Geo. Wash. L. Rev. 1446, 1468 (2015): "The problem with the REINS Act is that, with regard to major rules, it would accomplish virtually the same result as the 'traditional' one-house veto—namely, it would enable a single house of Congress to nullify an agency rule, regardless of the wishes of the other house, let alone the President. The question, then, is whether the Supreme Court would accept what amounts to a 180 degree change of direction if the one-house veto were repackaged in a different format, even though the risks of unchecked action by the legislative branch would be as great in the later version as in the earlier one. My suggestion is that it would not." Yes, counters Jonathan R. Siegel, in The REINS Act and the Struggle to Control Agency Rulemaking, 16 N.Y.U. J. Legis. & Pub. Pol'y 131, 134 (2013). Siegel argues that the Act is "perfectly constitutional," albeit in his view a bad policy choice: "[T]he attacks on the Act's constitutionality are not only mistaken, but ironic, because the REINS Act would, if anything, put the federal government on a sounder constitutional footing than that on which it rests now. If anything is constitutionally surprising, it is not Congress's efforts to assert authority over rulemaking, but rather its massive, wholesale delegation of that authority, which the courts have for so long tolerated." In Placing "REINS" on Regulations: Assessing the Proposed REINS Act, 16 N.Y.U. J. Legis. & Pub. Pol'y 1, 5 (2013), Jonathan Adler agrees with Siegel that the REINS Act would be constitutional, and further argues that the "REINS Act provides a means of curbing excessive or unwarranted regulation, but it is not an obstacle to needed regulatory measures supported by the public. . . . Indeed, even if federal regulatory agencies are overzealous, the REINS Act may not curtail federal regulation all that much [because it] . . . only applies to new major rules."

## NOTES ON DIRECTION BY LEGISLATION

(1) ***New Legislation.*** After Chadha, what alternative mechanisms are available to Congress for overriding a particular regulatory policy choice? Subject to a limit on legislation that singles out specified individuals, Congress surely remains free to redirect an agency's course by new legislation. Sometimes it does so, giving very specific directions designed to change patterns of agency action, or inaction, with which it is displeased. Still, two major barriers mean that "corrective" legislation is unlikely to occur.

The first barrier is institutional, and consists in the many "vetogates" that make up the congressional legislative process. WILLIAM N. ESKRIDGE, JR., JAMES J. BRUDNEY, JOSH CHAFETZ, PHILIP P. FRICKEY, & ELIZABETH GARRETT, CASES AND MATERIALS ON LEGISLATION AND REGULATION: STATUTES AND THE CREATION OF PUBLIC POLICY 28–29 (6th ed. 2020): "One way of thinking about the congressional lawmaking process is to see each step as a vetogate, or a choke point in the process, a place where opponents can 'veto' legislation even when it has majority support." For example, opponents can "(1) kill the bill in committee; (2) if committee approval cannot be avoided, stop the bill before full chamber consideration; (3) if full chamber consideration occurs, kill the bill there by filibustering it in the Senate, by amending it to death, or by outright defeating it on the chamber floor; (4) if one chamber has approved the bill, exploit the veto opportunities in the other chamber to prevent it from passing an identical measure; (5) if the other chamber produces a similar but not identical bill, amend or defeat it at the conference committee stage or in an interbranch summit; (6) if all else fails, persuade the President to veto it and then work against any congressional effort to override the veto. Descriptively, the existence of vetogates means that determined minorities can often kill legislation or, in the alternative, maim legislation they cannot kill." Some of these vetogates come from constitutional requirements; as commentators on the Constitution have been observing since the ratification debates, see, e.g., Federalist No. 73, "bicameralism and presentment make lawmaking difficult *by design*." John Manning, Lawmaking Made Easy, 10 Green Bag 2d 202 (2007). Others, however, come from congressional rules and practices. Most notably, the Senate filibuster, a particularly potent vetogate that often makes it necessary to reach a supermajority of sixty votes to enact legislation, comes from Senate rules.

The second barrier is political. In times of divided government—when control of the political branches of government is in the hands of different parties—enacting legislation becomes extremely difficult. Political polarization is a further important contributor to legislative gridlock. As the ideological distance between the two parties grows, it becomes increasingly unlikely that legislators will vote across party lines. As a result, it becomes increasingly difficult for a party that lacks a large majority to meet the supermajority thresholds needed to end a filibuster or overturn a veto, and the instances of gridlock grow. Political scientists have documented a significant increase in partisan polarization in the country since the 1970s. Although some dispute whether polarization is widespread or primarily a phenomenon of those who are politically active, they agree that partisan polarization is particularly evident in Congress. See Morris P. Fiorina, Unstable Majorities: Polarization, Party-Sorting, and Political Stalemate 17–18, 23–29, 45 (2017); Nolan McCarty, Polarization 2–5 (2019). For an important argument that competition between the two major parties displaced competition between the legislative and executive branches as the main driver of national government early on, see Daryl J. Levinson & Richard H. Pildes, Separation of Parties, Not Powers, 119 Harv. L. Rev. 2311 (2006).

Political polarization has had several effects on how Congress functions. One effect is a significant decline in Congress's ability to enact legislation. According to Sarah Binder in The Dysfunctional Congress, 18 Ann. Rev. Pol. Sci. 85, 95–96 (2015), "the frequency of deadlock shows a secular increase over time. . . . By this measure, the 112th Congress (2011–2012) can claim to be the 'worst Congress ever' over the postwar period, although the title is shared with the last Congress of the Clinton administration in 1999–2000."

See also Thomas E. Mann & Norman J. Ornstein, The Broken Branch: How Congress Is Failing America and How to Get It Back on Track (2008). Another effect is a dramatic increase in Congress's resort to what has been called "unorthodox lawmaking," with significant use of omnibus bills and fewer than 10 percent of enacted laws proceeding through the textbook legislative process. See Abbe R. Gluck, Anne Joseph O'Connell, & Rosa Po, Unorthodox Lawmaking, Unorthodox Rulemaking, 115 Colum. L. Rev. 1789 (2015). (For a discussion of textbook and unorthodox legislative processes, see Section 1.a of Chapter II, p. 58.)

Some dispute whether Congress is as dysfunctional as critics allege. "The stalemate/gridlock argument is misleading not only because it ignores so many [legislative] accomplishments, but also because it focuses so intently on just one small part of domestic policy, namely passage of major pieces of legislation at the national level. . . . Critics of the Constitution overlook the fact that by creating multiple 'veto points,' our political system simultaneously creates multiple points of access for policy entrepreneurs and claimants. Every 'veto point' that can be used to block action is also an 'opportunity point' that can be used to initiate or augment government activity." R. Shep Melnick, The Gridlock Illusion, Wilson Q. (Winter 2013). In a similar vein, Josh Chafetz argues that claims of congressional dysfunction take too narrow a view of the numerous powers Congress has and uses outside of enacting legislation to assert itself against the other branches. Congress's Constitution: Legislative Authority and the Separation of Powers (2017).

(2) ***The Congressional Review Act.*** In 1995, Congress amended the Regulatory Flexibility Act to require that "major" rules (defined essentially in terms of large economic impact, see 5 U.S.C. § 804(2)) be laid before Congress for sixty legislative days (called session days in the Senate) during which members of the House or Senate may introduce a joint resolution of disapproval. Moreover, if a rule is submitted to Congress less than sixty days before Congress adjourns a session, then the rule is carried over to the next session of Congress and treated as if it had been submitted to Congress or published in the Federal Register on the fifteenth legislative day of the new session. See 5 U.S.C. § 801 et seq. Because of Chadha, any disapproval must come via a *joint resolution* (passed by both houses and signed by the President), but a special, fast-track procedure limits debate and amendments, and curtails normal committee powers. If the joint resolution is adopted, the rule may not take effect. If a proposed resolution of disapproval is defeated in either chamber, the sixty-day waiting period is terminated and the rule can become immediately effective. 5 U.S.C. § 801(a)(5). Moreover, a rule that has been disapproved "may not be reissued in substantially the same form, and a new rule that is substantially the same as such a rule may not be issued, unless the reissued or new rule is specifically authorized by a law enacted after the date of the joint resolution disapproving the original rule." 5 U.S.C. § 801(b)(2). Thus, the resolution of disapproval is intended not only to invalidate the particular rule but also to narrow the agency's original statutory authority. For detail on the CRA process, see Maeve B. Carey & Christopher M. Davis, Cong. Rsch. Serv.,

R43992, The Congressional Review Act (CRA): Frequently Asked Questions (Nov. 12, 2021).[10]

Use of the CRA faces the realities of presidential veto authority, as does any new legislation. As a result, it has been impotent in contexts of divided government, when the presidency and at least one house of Congress are in the hands of opposing parties. In addition, the CRA is only employed when a presidential election results in a change of party control of presidency, since otherwise there aren't rules within the disapproval window that the party now in control of the federal government wants to overturn.

Prior to 2016, the Act had been used only once to invalidate a rule in its over twenty-year history. After President Bush was elected in 2000 with control of both the House and Senate, the CRA was invoked to disapprove an OSHA rule on ergonomic (repetitive motion) injuries promulgated in the waning days of the Clinton's Administration. The 2016 election revived the CRA as a potent weapon. That election ushered in a Republican President and Republican control over both houses after two terms of a Democratic Administration and years of Republican complaints about expanding regulation. In the new session of Congress following the election, 14 rules were overturned during the period allowed for disapprovals under the CRA, which lasted until May 18, 2017. The House sought to increase the CRA's functionality even further by adopting the Midnight Rules Review Act of 2017, H.R. 21 (115th Cong.) (2017), which would have amended the CRA to allow for several rules to be considered at once, but the measure failed to pass the Senate.

Moreover, the CRA may prove more potent yet. The text of the CRA provides that a major rule "shall take effect on the latest of" sixty days after a report on the rule is submitted to Congress or the rule is published in the Federal Register. 5 U.S.C. § 801(a)(3). But agencies routinely fail to send new rules to Congress; a 2014 report estimates that only 71 percent of rules were being submitted for review, down from a historical rate of 88 percent. Curtis W. Copeland, Implementation of the Congressional Review Act and Possible Reforms, 40 Admin. & Reg. L. News 7, 10 (2014). A more recent paper "find[s] the problem to have apparently worsened" since the 2014 report. See Clyde Wayne Crews, Jr., Many Federal Agency Rules and Guidance Documents are Still Not Properly Reported to Congress and the GAO as Required by the Congressional Review Act (Sept. 14, 2022).[11] This opens the possibility that any rule not submitted—even rules in effect for years—might be open to congressional disapproval under the CRA. A Brookings Institution Report, Philip A. Wallach & Nicholas W. Zeppos, How Powerful is the Congressional Review Act (Apr. 7, 2017),[12] estimates that "348 significant rules passed during the last two decades could be vulnerable to reversal through CRA resolution," though other estimates are much higher. Section 805 of the CRA provides that "[n]o determination, finding, action, or omission under this chapter shall be subject to judicial review." Although most courts have

[10] https://crsreports.congress.gov/product/pdf/R/R43992.

[11] https://ssrn.com/abstract=4219091.

[12] https://www.brookings.edu/research/how-powerful-is-the-congressional-review-act/.

interpreted this section to broadly prohibit judicial review of alleged CRA violations, a few have held that it does not bar review of agency actions related to the CRA. Carey & Davis, supra, at 23–26.

Two further sagas in the reinvigoration of the CRA occurred during the Trump Administration. One involved the CRA's application to guidance. In May 2018, the CRA was used to invalidate a 2013 Bulletin issued by the Consumer Financial Protection Bureau that provided guidance regarding liability for discrimination in indirect auto lending. The Bulletin was expressly denominated nonbinding guidance and was not issued using notice and comment procedures. But the GAO had determined that the Bulletin constituted a rule for CRA purposes in December 2017. This marked the first time the CRA was applied to a rule not adopted through notice-and-comment or formal rulemaking procedures. See generally Bridget C.E. Dooling, Into the Void: The GAO's Role in the Regulatory State, 70 Am. U. L. Rev. 387 (2020).

The other was the Trump Administration's use of the CRA as a means of reviewing rulemaking at independent agencies. Under the CRA, the OIRA Administrator is responsible for determining which rules are "major," but "OIRA had largely deferred to independent regulatory agencies in making these determinations about their own rules. In April 2019, the Trump Administration announced a . . . [new] policy [under which] all agencies, including independent regulatory agencies, are required to submit their regulations to OIRA for a determination of whether the rules met the CRA's statutory definition of major. Arguably, this procedure potentially provides a point of leverage for the White House (through OMB and OIRA) over independent regulatory agencies' rules. The status of this 2019 policy under the Biden Administration is unclear." Carey & Davis, supra, at 4–5.

Members of Congress introduced six CRA resolutions in President Biden's first six months in office. The President signed the three resolutions that passed both Democrat-controlled chambers of Congress—undoing rules from EPA, EEOC, and the Office of the Comptroller of the Currency, and marking the first time the Democrats have successfully used the CRA. The fast-track repeal process has now been employed twenty times. For a discussion of some ongoing technical issues with the CRA, see ACUS, Recommendation 2021-8, Technical Reform of the Congressional Review Act, 87 Fed. Reg. 1719 (Jan. 12, 2022).

## (2) Appropriations and Spending

*All Bills for raising Revenue shall originate in the House of Representatives; but the Senate may propose or concur with Amendments as on other Bills.*

U.S. Const., Art. I, § 7, cl. 1

*No Money shall be drawn from the Treasury, but in Consequence of Appropriations made by Law . . .*

U.S. Const., Art. I, § 9, cl. 7

Regulatory programs require statutory authority, but authorizing a program is only the first step. Even if the authorizing statute sets a funding level, those funds must actually be appropriated in the separate, annual process of enacting the roughly one dozen large statutes that fund the various units of the federal government. The appropriations process provides significant opportunity for Congress to direct regulatory action. The length and complexity of appropriations bills, coupled with special House procedures for such bills and their "must pass" nature, allows for the insertion of provisions that would flounder in the normal institutional and political constraints of the legislative process. Lacking a line item veto (see Clinton v. City of New York, p. 893), the President can reject this direction only at the usually prohibitive cost of losing the entire funding package.

In federal budgeting, an important distinction lies between mandatory spending (permanent statutory payment commitments, including entitlements like Medicare) and discretionary spending (based on annual appropriations acts). Whether an item of spending is mandatory or discretionary depends on the underlying substantive legislation that authorizes it; changing mandatory spending requires a change in substantive law and cannot be done by an appropriations act alone. U.S. Gov't Accountability Office, A Glossary of Terms Used in the Federal Budget Process, GAO-05-734sp (2005), at 42, 55–56. Most federal spending is mandatory; in recent years only 35 to 39 percent of total federal spending has been discretionary. If Congress does not adopt a regular appropriations bill by the beginning of the new fiscal year, Congress routinely adopts continuing resolutions to continue funding until the regular bill is enacted. James V. Saturno, Cong. Rsch. Serv., R46240, Introduction to the Federal Budget Process 26–27 (Feb. 26, 2020). For some time, however, growing partisan division and rancor have prevented the regular appropriations process from functioning. See Nolan McCarty, The Decline of Regular Order in Appropriations: Does It Matter? in Congress and Policy Making in the 21st Century (Jeffrey A. Jenkins & Eric M. Patashnik eds., 2016); see also Peter C. Hanson, Brookings Inst., Restoring Regular Order in Congressional Appropriations 1 (Nov. 19, 2015).[13] While a permanent commitment is typically accompanied by a provision for its funding, MATTHEW LAWRENCE has described an important new twist: "In recent years, Congress has repeatedly failed to appropriate funds necessary for the government to honor permanent, statutory payment commitments (or entitlements), thereby forcing the government to break those commitments," a phenomenon he describes as the "probabilistic consequence of the overlooked fact that Congress has enacted scores of

[13] https://www.brookings.edu/research/restoring-regular-order-in-congressional-appropriations/.

payment commitments in permanent law that are dependent for their operation upon periodic temporary appropriations." DISAPPROPRIATION, 120 Colum. L. Rev. 1, 5–6 (2020).

Appropriations represent a critical lever of congressional control over agencies and policy. Not surprisingly, therefore, budget disputes are a central source of legislative-executive struggles during divided government. At the end of 2018, fights between President Trump and the Democratic-controlled House over funding a wall at the nation's southern border led to a record-setting 35-day partial government shutdown. See Eloise Pasachoff, The President's Budget Powers in the Trump Era, in Executive Policymaking: The Role of the OMB in the Presidency 69–98 (Meena Bose & Andrew Rudalevige eds., 2020). Article I, Section 9 of the Constitution provides that "No Money shall be drawn from the Treasury, but in Consequence of Appropriations made by Law." The cause of a shutdown is a funding gap, created by the failure of Congress and the President to pass appropriations bills or a continuing resolution before the government's existing spending authority expires. Under the Anti-Deficiency Act, which dates back to 1884 and is codified at 31 U.S.C. § 1341 et seq., all federal officials and employees are prohibited from spending or obligating funds beyond the amount already appropriated. The Act also prohibits accepting voluntary services, "except for emergencies involving the safety of human life or the protection of property." 31 U.S.C. § 1342. Violating the Anti-Deficiency Act is punishable through administrative and criminal penalties. See Clinton T. Brass, Ida A. Brudnick, Natalie Keegan, Barry J. McMillion, John W. Rollins, & Brian T. Yeh, Cong. Rsch. Serv., RL34680, Shutdown of the Federal Government: Causes, Processes, and Effects (Dec. 10, 2018). How rigorously the Act is implemented can affect how much the public feels a shutdown's impact. Pasachoff describes how during and after the 2018 shutdown the Trump Administration's OMB sought to read the Act narrowly and limit reporting of potential violations, efforts that were resisted by the Government Accountability Office, which oversees implementation of the Act for Congress. Pasachoff, supra, at 85–86.

## NOTES

(1) ***Appropriations Riders: Limitation Riders and Legislative Riders.*** One central mechanism of congressional control through appropriations is the appropriation rider. THOMAS O. MCGARITY, DEREGULATORY RIDERS REDUX, 1 Mich. J. Envtl. & Admin. L. 33, 36–38 (2012): A rider is "a provision added to an unrelated bill that 'rides' the targeted bill through the legislative process and becomes law when the President signs the bill. . . . Riders come in two broad varieties—limitation riders and legislative riders. The limitation rider is associated exclusively with appropriation bills, and it prohibits the relevant agency from expending any of the appropriated funds to engage in a proscribed activity. . . . A legislative rider modifies existing law by amending an existing statute, changing existing common law, or directing a federal agency to take a particular affirmative action (thereby rendering lawful administrative action that might otherwise have been

unlawful).” Riders have been around since the early nineteenth century and “have always played a role in enacting controversial laws.” But “they have become far more common since the 1990s,” and “[i]n . . . [a] toxic legislative environment, [represent] one of the more effective strategies for securing legislative victories and imposing political pain.”

Legislative riders are the more controversial form of rider. Legislative riders are not limited in time to the annual appropriations cycle and need not have any relationship to appropriations other than being part of an appropriations bill. “A rider can, in effect, be nothing less than authorization legislation attached to appropriations legislation. . . . In other words, the legislation may in every respect be the kind of law traditionally considered the province of an authorization committee. Yet, it becomes law once Congress passes the appropriations legislation to which it is attached and the President signs it into law (or Congress overrides a presidential veto).” RICHARD J. LAZARUS, CONGRESSIONAL DESCENT: THE DEMISE OF DELIBERATIVE DEMOCRACY IN ENVIRONMENTAL LAW, 94 Geo. L.J. 619, 635, 637 (2006); MCGARITY, supra, at 37–39.

Limitation riders are the classic form of appropriation rider. These typically take the form of saying that “the agency may not spend any of the monies Congress is appropriating to engage in a specific activity.” Lazarus, supra, at 637. For example, starting in 2011 appropriations riders prohibited the Department of Agriculture’s Grain Inspection, Packers and Stockyards Administration (GIPSA) from finalizing regulations aimed at giving poultry and swine growers certain rights in their contracts with processing companies. The GIPSA Rider gained fame as the target of an episode of John Oliver’s Last Week Tonight,[14] and was dropped from the FY 2016 appropriations bill. Despite passing the House the next year, the GIPSA Rider did not make it into the enacted FY 2017 appropriations bill. In December 2016, the Obama Administration issued an interim final rule and two proposed rules, known as the Farmer Fair Practice Rules, but the Trump Administration scrapped all three and restructured GIPSA so that it became part of the Agricultural Marketing Service. Ultimately, in 2020 the Trump Administration issued a final rule with much weaker protections for farmers, and the Biden Administration has proposed new regulations.

Riders are most often used to stop action, but they can be used to spur action as well. “Although appropriations provisions that are designed to prevent or restrict the development, implementation, or enforcement of particular rules or types of rules are common, other types of appropriation measures are also prevalent. . . . Some appropriations provisions direct federal agencies to develop rules in particular areas, or to take particular enforcement actions.” Copeland, supra, at 2–3.

(2) ***The Institutional Advantages of Control via Appropriation Riders.*** JASON A. MACDONALD, in LIMITATION RIDERS AND CONGRESSIONAL INFLUENCE OVER BUREAUCRATIC POLICY DECISIONS, 104 Am. Pol. Sci. Rev. 766, 767, 773 (2010), points out that appropriations riders limiting agency action have procedural and political qualities that make them “effective and

---

[14] https://www.youtube.com/watch?v=X9wHzt6gBgI.

frequently used tools of congressional influence" over regulatory decisionmaking. Procedurally, riders that prohibit spending for designated activities are always "in order" because they fall within a provision of House Rule XXI (known as the "Holman rule") that allows for spending "retrenchments." Also, unlike ordinary substantive legislation, "appropriation bills do not require special orders from the House Rules Committee to reach the floor." Politically, the "must-pass" nature of appropriations bills increases their value as vehicles for congressional instructions because the President's ability to engage in veto bargaining to remove individual riders is constrained: "[N]ot passing appropriations legislation and shutting down the government, a decision accompanied by intensive media coverage that scrutinizes the motives behind the positions of both major parties and their leaders, and potentially leads the electorate to attach blame to one or both parties, is costly politically."

But are such instructions appropriately considered congressional direction—or are they no more than the idiosyncratic preferences of individual sponsors? MACDONALD continues: "Of course, for limitation riders to serve as a mechanism that limits the legislative majority's agency losses, the appropriations committee's ideal policy must be . . . . close to [that of the median legislator.] . . . [R]esearch on the representativeness of the House Appropriations Committee [and subcommittees] indicates that the preferences of appropriators are similar to those of the floor. "One clear implication . . . is that the availability of limitation riders improves policy outcomes for congressional majorities more under divided government than under unified government. Under divided government, the president's ideal policy, *p*, is farther from the chamber's median member, *m*, than under unified government. Assuming that the appropriations committee is a good agent of the chamber median . . . how much limitation riders improve policy for the chamber median depends on *m*'s proximity to *p*." Analyzing data from 1989 to 2009, MacDonald found that a greater number of limitation riders occurred in periods of divided government than unified government.

(3) ***The Wisdom of Riders.*** Many commentators are skeptical (or worse) about the wisdom of directing regulatory policy via appropriations. NEAL E. DEVINS, although acknowledging that "Congress's use of limitation riders is sometimes necessary," finds the practice "troublesome." "The use of the appropriations process to accomplish substantive objectives that have not been considered previously or that contravene established statutory objectives may prevent the appropriate authorizing committee from applying its expertise. Exacerbating this problem, appropriations are often acted on quickly, providing little opportunity for thoughtful deliberation of the issues raised by such measures." REGULATION OF GOVERNMENT AGENCIES THROUGH LIMITATION RIDERS, 1987 Duke L.J. 456, 458 (1987).

McGarity, supra, at 36–37, identifies "a particular class of riders" as a source of concern: those "that are designed to stall, modify, or eliminate an ongoing regulatory program that is being implemented by a regulatory agency pursuant to duly enacted authorizing legislation. Usually pursued at the behest of affected regulated industries, these 'deregulatory riders' threaten to derail ongoing regulatory programs that are highly popular with the general public and therefore not likely to be dismantled through the normal legislative processes." Drawing on a close study of the use of riders during the 112th Congress, McGarity condemns "their extortionate use by a determined minority of legislators to advance special interests at the expense of the broader public interest."

On the other hand, "[a]s a legislative tool, the rider is not inherently good or evil. Riders can be abused in ways that defeat democracy, but they also make it possible for legislation having the support of a large majority of the national population to prevail over an obstructionist minority." McGarity, supra, at 70. MacDonald, supra, at 766, argues for the potential democracy-reinforcing benefits of riders. After examining twenty years of legislative data, he concluded that riders lead to "policy outcomes that are preferable to a majority of legislators compared to outcomes that would occur if this tool did not exist" and that this effect is heightened in periods of divided government. In TAKING APPROPRIATIONS SERIOUSLY, 121 Colum. L. Rev. 1075, 1147 (2021), GILLIAN E. METZGER argues that "comparative assessment of political accountability cannot be made in a theoretical vacuum. The argument for prioritizing substantive measures based on their functional advantages fails to account for contemporary governance realities of deep partisan polarization and divisiveness in Congress. . . . Realistically, . . . substantive legislative enactments are very difficult now for many contentious policy areas. If in practice appropriations measures are a central mechanism by which Congress is able to act today, then appropriations are a better policymaking tool for Congress than substantive enactments alone."

(4) ***Agency Reliance on Funds Obtained Outside of the Usual Appropriations Process.*** CHRISTOPHER DEMUTH, SR. and MICHAEL S. GREVE, AGENCY FINANCE IN THE AGE OF EXECUTIVE GOVERNMENT, 24 Geo. Mason L. Rev. 555, 555–56, 561–62 (2017), argue that recent increases in agency funding outside of the usual appropriations process are fundamentally transforming basic features of how the federal government operates: "The written Constitution is unequivocal, indeed emphatic, in committing fiscal powers to Congress and in withholding them from the executive. . . . Public expenditures must be appropriated by Congress. And with some exceptions, government agencies may not raise or spend funds that have not been appropriated . . . Increasingly, however, the picture is at war with reality. To an unprecedented extent, regulatory agencies rely on non-appropriated funds for their ordinary operations. Many have become self-financing; some have become profit centers for wider executive exertions—and for Congress. Correspondingly, the general assumption that Congress will jealously guard the power of the purse as its ultimate means of checking and balancing the executive has become open to serious doubt: in many respects, those powers have fallen into disuse." The rise in agency self-financing they document comes in many varieties. "Some of the money comes from government activities that might as well be left to private commerce, such as military PX stores ('post exchanges') and the U.S. Mint; other comes from a wide range of user fees—for using national parks and applying for licenses, permits, visas, patents, and regulatory approvals." Some instances of such agency self-financing have raised concerns about

agencies becoming dependent on the industries they regulate for funding. See Christina Jewett, F.D.A.'s Drug Industry Fees Fuel Concerns Over Influence, N.Y. Times (Sept. 15, 2022).

In some instances, an agency's entire budget is provided by funds obtained outside of the usual appropriations process. This is true of the Consumer Financial Protection Bureau and the Federal Reserve. The Fed is funded by earnings on securities it owns, and the CFPB receives an amount from the Fed that the CFPB Director determines to be reasonably necessary to carry out its authorities. This amount is statutorily capped at no more than 12 percent of the Fed's annual expenses. In CONSUMER FINANCIAL SERVICES ASSOCIATION v. CFPB, 51 F.4th 616, 640 (5th Cir. 2022), the Fifth Circuit held that this arrangement for financing the CFPB violated the Appropriations Clause and the separation of powers. "The Bureau's perpetual insulation from Congress's appropriations power, including the express exemption from congressional review of its funding, renders the Bureau no longer dependent and, as a result, no longer accountable to Congress and, ultimately, to the people." No prior decision had invalidated a funding statute on this basis, and the decision would have major import if upheld by the Supreme Court, not just for the CFPB but for the numerous other agencies—including the Fed—that receive funds outside of the usual appropriations process. Stay tuned.

(5) ***Legality and Presidential Pushback.*** No Supreme Court decision specifically addresses whether appropriations provisions directing agencies to take or not take an action unconstitutionally infringe on presidential authority. Scholarly commentary is sharply divided. Compare, e.g., Kate Stith, Congress' Power of the Purse, 97 Yale L.J. 1352 (1988) (arguing that Congress has "a constitutional duty to limit the amount and duration of each grant of spending authority" and that historical appropriations practice in the colonies included not only setting amounts but also specifying the "powers, activities, and purposes" for which appropriated funds might be used) with J. Gregory Sidak, The President's Power of the Purse, 1989 Duke L.J. 1162, 1183–202 (arguing that the Constitution grants Presidents the power to spend the minimum necessary to perform their constitutional functions).

Both President Reagan and President George W. Bush asserted the unconstitutionality of some such restrictions in signing statements. E.g., Statement on signing H.R. 1827 into law, 23 Weekly Comp. Pres. Doc. 800 (July 11, 1987) ("Article II of the Constitution assigns responsibility for executing the law to the President. While Congress is empowered to enact new or different laws, it may not indirectly interpret and implement existing laws, which is an essential function allocated by the Constitution to the executive branch"). See also OMB, Statement of Administration Policy: H.R. 5576—Transportation, Treasury, Housing, the Judiciary, and the District of Columbia Appropriations Bill, FY 2007 (June 14, 2006) (limitation provision "should be deleted as inconsistent with the President's constitutional authority to supervise the unitary executive branch"). Although President Obama was more limited in his use of signing statements, (p. 1030), he repeatedly challenged riders attached to defense spending that limited his ability to transfer detainees from the Guantánamo Bay facility, such as §§ 1033–35 of the FY2014 National Defense Authorization Act. Obama subsequently released five Guantánamo detainees in exchange for U.S. soldier Bowe Bergdahl, who was held by the Taliban, without providing congressional committees the advance notice required by § 1035. Soon after coming into office, President Trump issued a signing statement objecting to seventy-six spending restrictions in the Consolidated Appropriations Act of 2017, including provisions restricting transfer of Guantánamo detainees and prohibiting the Department of Justice from interfering with states implementing medical marijuana laws. President Donald J. Trump, Statement on Signing the Consolidated Appropriations Act, 2017 (May 5, 2017).[15] As of August 2022, President Biden—who assumed office alongside a Democratic-controlled House and Senate—has issued only one appropriations-related signing statement, objecting to the same prohibitions on transferring Guantánamo detainees as Trump did. See Statement by the President on S. 1605, the National Defense Authorization Act for Fiscal Year 2022 (Dec. 27, 2021).[16]

(6) ***Impoundment.*** Although a tool used by the President, rather than Congress, to control regulatory action via spending decisions, impoundment is so intimately related to appropriations that it is sensibly considered here. Conflict over the President's power to refuse to spend appropriated funds, or to transfer them to other purposes, has been part of our history since at least the late 19th century, when President Grant set off a furor in Congress by refusing to spend appropriated river and harbor funds for what we would now term pork barrel projects. See Harold H. Bruff, Balance of Forces 261–62 (2006) (quoting one House Member's Shakespearian ranting, "Upon what meat hath this our Caesar fed?").

Congress cannot specifically itemize the amounts and purposes of all the monies needed to run the federal government. Even if it had time, the specification would become obsolete almost immediately, as events change needs and costs. Therefore, while the degree of appropriations specificity has varied with the times (as has the level of trust between a particular legislature and administration), executive discretion is an inevitable part of the funding process. Some exercises of this discretion are uncontroversial. If the government can accomplish a desired result for less than the projected expenditure, or if changed circumstances render the planned action unnecessary, it would be absurd to interpret the relevant appropriation as a mandate that all the money be spent, regardless. The President has long been permitted to make such "programmatic impoundments" with relatively little legislative involvement. (It is not hard to see these impoundments as simply effectuating congressional intent—or, at least, what Congress would have intended had it known.) This discretion was codified in the Impoundment Control Act of 1974 (ICA), as amended in 1987.

The main area of conflict is a very different sort of executive refusal to spend appropriated money—"policy impoundments." Largely a post-World

[15] https://www.govinfo.gov/content/pkg/DCPD-201700312/pdf/DCPD-201700312.pdf.

[16] https://www.whitehouse.gov/briefing-room/statements-releases/2021/12/27/statement-by-the-president-on-s-1605-the-national-defense-authorization-act-for-fiscal-year-2022/.

War II phenomenon, policy impoundments reflect a President's disagreement with the purposes for which Congress appropriates money. In order to prevent a policy result Congress favors but the President does not, the President simply refuses to spend the money appropriated to accomplish it. Initially, Presidents used this strategy in the area of defense appropriations for weapons. Here, the constitutional Commander in Chief power arguably provides a basis for the President to assert and enforce a policy preference independent of Congress. By the presidency of Lyndon Johnson, however, policy impoundments were becoming a strategic weapon in the domestic policymaking arena. Richard Nixon impounded nearly 20 percent of nonentitlement federal expenditures; in the process, several regulatory programs were terminated. His rationale was inflation control, but the particular programs chosen for economization reflected the regulatory policy disagreements between a Republican President and a Democratic Congress.[17]

Congress responded to the Nixon controversy with the Impoundment Control Act, which requires congressional approval within forty-five days for any permanent impoundment—termed a rescission—of appropriated funds and otherwise limits Presidents to within-fiscal-year deferrals that cannot be based on policy disagreement with an appropriation. 2 U.S.C. §§ 683–684. According to Pasachoff, supra, at 77–78, the Trump Administration "attempted to use the rescission procedure for the first time since the Clinton administration. . . . When Congress narrowly rejected the [rescission] proposal, however, the administration . . . released the funds . . . . [T]he administration [also twice] . . . interpret[ed] rescission implicitly to permit unilateral cancellation if Congress does not have enough time to act on a rescission proposal before the end of the fiscal year . . . [but] bipartisan congressional opposition led the administration to drop the effort." In addition, the Administration argued that while the executive branch may not engage in policy deferrals to avoid implementing a law with which it disagrees, "it may engage in temporary programmatic delays to determine the best policy for the efficient and effective use of funds consistent with the intent of the statute. . . . This reading [of the ICA] contributed to the growing dismay of civil servants in OMB and elsewhere who [thought] that the administration's hold on Ukraine funds without notifying Congress through a special message with a valid justification violated the [ICA's] deferral provisions."

## (3) Oversight and Investigations

### *TRUMP v. MAZARS*

Even though Congress as a whole may find it difficult to direct agency regulatory choices, subparts of Congress can be very actively

[17] This presidential strategy did finally produce litigation about the impoundment power, but the one case taken by the Supreme Court was resolved on statutory grounds. Train v. New York, 420 U.S. 35 (1975); see also Missouri Highway Comm. v. Volpe, 479 F.2d 1099 (8th Cir. 1973) (rejecting claim that a policy impoundment was authorized by statute or within the President's inherent authority).

engaged in review and response. A central form of such engagement is oversight by congressional committees and subcommittees. "Oversight is critical to Congress's core functions of legislating, appropriating, and confirming nominations. Oversight allows Congress to learn how the funds it appropriates and the programs it authorizes function. And what it learns can be key to reform or holding individual executive officers to account. Because congressional hearings are one of the nation's most public tribunals, oversight performs a critical political function as well; it provides one of the most important ways for the public to learn about the executive branch's actions at a time when it is salient for holding the President accountable, including at the ballot box. Moreover, the existence of robust congressional oversight also acts as a deterrent to executive branch misconduct." KEVIN M. STACK & MICHAEL P. VANDENBERGH, OVERSIGHT RIDERS, 97 Notre Dame L. Rev. 127, 135–36 (2021).

(1) ***The Frequency of Oversight.*** The extent of congressional oversight has varied considerably over time. One study of investigative activity, measured as days of investigative hearings held in each year from the William McKinley to Barack Obama Administrations, shows several peaks and lows over time. Bursts of investigations occurred early in the Progressive Era and periodically thereafter in response to wars, claims of alleged communist infiltration, and executive branch scandals. "Investigative activity again surged in the early 1970s with inquests into the Nixon administration's conduct of the Vietnam War and Watergate. . . . [T]he pace of investigative activity increased again during the Reagan years, fueled in part by the Iran-Contra scandal, but then slackened off, in raw terms, in the 1990s and 2000s. The latter years of the Obama administration have witnessed a modest resurgence of investigative activity, but one that falls short of (at least in terms of the raw number of days of hearings) earlier bursts in the 1950s, 1970s, and 1980." DOUGLAS L. KRINER & ERIC SCHICKLER, INVESTIGATING THE PRESIDENT: CONGRESSIONAL CHECKS ON PRESIDENTIAL POWER 37–39 (2016).

Political scientists offer different accounts of what explains this variation in oversight intensity. Some scholars argue partisanship plays a significant role in the extent of congressional oversight, finding that "[i]n the House, the average congressional session held during divided government featured twice as many committee investigations charging executive branch malfeasance when compared to congresses meeting during unified government." David C.W. Parker & Mathew Dull, The Weaponization of Congressional Oversight, in Politics to the Extreme: American Political Institutions in the Twenty-First Century 56, 61–62 (Scott A. Frisch & Sean Q. Kelly eds., 2013). Other scholars emphasize that Congress conducts extensive oversight during periods of unified government as well, arguing that this is because "oversight is an oftentimes effective and constructive way for congressional committees to coordinate policy under unified government. As interbranch preferences are aligned under unified government, agencies have a greater incentive to take committee goals seriously, increasing the policy benefits of oversight." Jason A. MacDonald & Robert J. McGrath,

Retrospective Congressional Oversight and the Dynamics of Legislative Influence over the Bureaucracy, 41 Leg. Stud. Q. 899, 900 (2016).

(2) ***The Effectiveness of Oversight.*** Debate also exists over how effective committee oversight is. One study found that "when it occurs, oversight often is consequential, changing agency behavior for a statistically significant 18.5% of infractions, relative to otherwise similar infractions for which oversight does not occur," with infractions defined as "the set of issues from which Congress tends to select its subjects for oversight hearings." Brian D. Feinstein, Congress in the Administrative State, 95 Wash. U. L. Rev. 1189, 1193–94 (2018). Some scholars suggest that having multiple committees with jurisdiction over all or part of a regulatory problem can undermine the effectiveness of oversight, because "the more congressional committees involved in the oversight of an agency, the weaker Congress is relative to the president." Joshua L. Clinton, David E. Lewis, & Jennifer L. Selin, Influencing the Bureaucracy: The Irony of Congressional Oversight, 58 Am. J. Pol. Sci. 387, 387, 399 (2014). On the other hand, "granting a single committee property rights to oversee a given agency reduces the likelihood that the agency will be subject to oversight if that committee's preferences are not properly aligned with those of Congress and the agency." Feinstein, supra, at 1194.

STACK and VANDENBERGH, supra, at 130–32, note the barriers Congress faces in forcing a recalcitrant executive branch to comply with its oversight requests and emphasize that "for the executive branch, delay in disclosure can be a win. A subpoena only has force for the session of Congress that authorizes it," and making Congress sue to enforce can "delay the issuance of a final, enforceable order for the year to eighteen months often necessary to avoid compliance." They argue that "Congress can engage in constitutional hardball. . . . Congress can and should use its appropriations power as a tool to force compliance with its request for information from the executive branch. . . . The basic idea of an oversight rider is to deny the executive branch funding for resistance to congressional subpoenas. . . . By attaching appropriations consequences for noncompliance with congressional subpoenas, oversight riders give executive branch officials the kind of ex ante legal incentives to comply that they currently lack."

(3) ***The Tools of Oversight.*** Congressional committees have a variety of tools they use to investigate and conduct oversight. "Actions ranging from informal, largely consequenceless discussions between committee staffers and members of the senior executive service to, at the farthest extreme, presidential impeachment and conviction trials can all be considered oversight." Feinstein, supra, at 1196. "Historically, congressional committees appeared to rely a great deal on public hearings and subpoenaed witnesses to gather information and accomplish their investigative goals. In more recent years, congressional committees have seemingly relied more heavily on staff level communication and contacts as well as other 'informal' attempts at gathering information." Christopher M. Davis et al., Cong. Rsch. Serv., RL30240, Congressional Oversight Manual 26 (Jan. 16, 2020).[18] For a

---

[18] https://crsreports.congress.gov/product/pdf/RL/RL30240/31.

detailed discussion of different oversight tools and techniques, see id. at 26–31, 56–72; see also Jack Beermann, Congressional Administration, 43 San Diego L. Rev. 61, 121–39 (2006).

(4) ***Oversight by Other Congressional Institutions: GAO, CRS, and CBO.*** Congress relies on several institutions to assist it in its oversight activities. You've seen reports from two of these institutions, the Government Accountability Office[19] and the Congressional Research Services, cited in this casebook. Both are sizeable entities: CRS, located in the Library of Congress, has a staff of around 600 and GAO has a staff of around 3000. Both investigate at the request of congressional committees, subcommittees, or individual members of Congress and cover the gamut of topics and policy areas. One difference, however, is that CRS works solely for Congress while GAO can undertake investigations on its own initiative and also adjudicates bid protests as part of the federal contracting process. The Congressional Budget Office, with a staff of around 250, has a more specialized ambit: it produces independent analyses of budgetary and economic issues to support the congressional budget process. All three are avowedly nonpartisan.

In THE CONGRESSIONAL BUREAUCRACY, 168 U. Pa. L. Rev. 1541, 1544, 1546–47 (2020), JESSE M. CROSS and ABBE R. GLUCK argue that these and other expert nonpartisan congressional offices serve "separate powers both inside of Congress and external to it." These offices were "explicitly founded . . . so that Congress could reclaim and safeguard its own powers against an executive branch that was itself using knowledge and expertise to encroach on the legislative process and congressional autonomy. For Congress, knowledge was power." Cross and Gluck also maintain that, "unlike many other agencies, Congress's bureaucracy remains under Congress's control, is not run by political appointees, is directly supportive of Congress's work, and Congress can ignore many of its inputs if it wishes."

(5) ***Congressional Oversight and the Separation of Powers.*** Congressional oversight is an everyday feature of life for agencies. But sometimes oversight becomes highly politically contentious, particularly in periods of divided government and when congressional requests are aimed at White House officials or the President. The Republican-controlled House sued the Obama Administration for subpoenaed records relating to Operation Fast and Furious, a botched gun-trafficking investigation. Subsequently, the Democratic-controlled House sued the Trump Administration to obtain evidence from Special Counsel Robert Mueller's investigation into Russian meddling in the 2016 election and to enforce its subpoenas against the President and executive branch officials. See Charlie Savage & Nicholas Fandos, The House v. Trump: Stymied Lawmakers Increasingly Battle in the Courts, N.Y. Times (Aug. 13, 2019). The result has been a number of cases assessing the separation of powers aspects of congressional oversight.

---

[19] GAO's name was changed from the General Accounting Office to the Government Accountability Office in 2004.

## TRUMP v. MAZARS

Supreme Court of the United States (2020).
140 S.Ct. 2019.

■ CHIEF JUSTICE ROBERTS delivered the opinion of the Court.

[Over five days in April 2019, three committees of the U.S. House of Representatives issued subpoenas seeking information about the finances of President Donald Trump, his children, and affiliated businesses. The subpoenas were issued to third parties, specifically Mazars, the President's personal accountant, and a couple of banks he used. Although the committees sought overlapping financial documents, they offered different justifications for their subpoenas. The House Committee on Financial Services sought the information as part of a general effort to close loopholes that allowed corruption, terrorism financing, and money laundering into the financial system. The Permanent Select Committee on Intelligence issued its subpoena as part of an investigation into foreign efforts to undermine the U.S. political process, which the Committee planned to develop legislation to address. And the House Committee on Oversight and Reform indicated that it was investigating whether the President had engaged in illegal conduct, had undisclosed conflicts of interests, was complying with the Emoluments Clause, and had accurately reported his finances to relevant federal entities, all matters that would inform the Committee's review of multiple laws and legislative proposals. President Trump sued, along with his children and affiliated businesses, challenging the subpoenas as violating the separation of powers.] . . .

II

A

The question presented is whether the subpoenas exceed the authority of the House under the Constitution. Historically, disputes over congressional demands for presidential documents have not ended up in court. Instead, they have been hashed out in the "hurly-burly, the give-and-take of the political process between the legislative and the executive." Hearings on S. 2170 et al. before the Subcommittee on Intergovernmental Relations of the Senate Committee on Government Operations, 94th Cong., 1st Sess., 87 (1975) (A. Scalia, Assistant Attorney General, Office of Legal Counsel).

That practice began with George Washington [with respect to a 1792 House request for documents as part of its investigation into General St. Clair's failed campaign against the Indians in the Northwest Territory.] . . . President Washington called a Cabinet meeting, . . . attended by the likes of Alexander Hamilton, Thomas Jefferson, Edmund Randolph, and Henry Knox, [which] ended with the Cabinet of "one mind": The House had authority to "institute inquiries" and "call for papers" but the President could "exercise a discretion" over disclosures, "communicat[ing] such papers as the public good would permit" and "refus[ing]" the rest. 1 Writings of Thomas Jefferson 189–190 (P. Ford ed. 1892). . . . [Subsequent negotiations led to] the House . . . narrow[ing] its request. . . . Jefferson, once he became President, followed Washington's precedent. . . . Ever since, congressional demands for the President's information have been resolved by the political branches without involving this Court. . . .

Congress and the President maintained this tradition of negotiation and compromise—without the involvement of this Court—until the present dispute. Indeed, from President Washington until now, we have never considered a dispute over a congressional subpoena for the President's records. And, according to the parties, the appellate courts have addressed such a subpoena only once, when a Senate committee subpoenaed President Nixon during the Watergate scandal. In that case, the court refused to enforce the subpoena, and the Senate did not seek review by this Court.

This dispute therefore represents a significant departure from historical practice. Although the parties agree that this particular controversy is justiciable, we recognize that it is the first of its kind to reach this Court; that disputes of this sort can raise important issues concerning relations between the branches; that related disputes involving congressional efforts to seek official Executive Branch information recur on a regular basis, including in the context of deeply partisan controversy; and that Congress and the Executive have nonetheless managed for over two centuries to resolve such disputes among themselves without the benefit of guidance from us. Such longstanding practice "is a consideration of great weight" in cases concerning "the allocation of power between [the] two elected branches of Government," and it imposes on us a duty of care to ensure that we not needlessly disturb "the compromises and working arrangements that [those] branches . . . themselves have reached." NLRB v. Noel Canning, 573 U.S. 513, 524–526 (2014) [p. 966]. . . .

B

Congress has no enumerated constitutional power to conduct investigations or issue subpoenas, but we have held that each House has power "to secure needed information" in order to legislate. McGrain v. Daugherty, 273 U.S. 135, 161 (1927). This "power of inquiry—with process to enforce it—is an essential and appropriate auxiliary to the legislative function." Id., at 174. Without information, Congress would be shooting in the dark, unable to legislate "wisely or effectively." Id., at 175. The congressional power to obtain information is "broad" and "indispensable" . . . [and] encompasses inquiries into the administration of existing laws, studies of proposed laws, and "surveys of defects in our social, economic or political system for the purpose of enabling the Congress to remedy them." Watkins v. United States, 354 U.S. 178, 187, 215 (1957).

Because this power is "justified solely as an adjunct to the legislative process," it is subject to several limitations. Id., at 197. Most importantly, a congressional subpoena is valid only if it is "related to, and in furtherance of, a legitimate task of the Congress." Id., at 187. The subpoena must serve a "valid legislative purpose," Quinn v. United States, 349 U.S. 155, 161 (1955), . . . [and] "concern a subject on which legislation could be had," Eastland v. United States Servicemen's Fund, 421 U.S. 491, 506 (1975). Furthermore, Congress may not issue a subpoena for the purpose of "law enforcement," because "those powers are assigned under our Constitution to the Executive and the Judiciary." Quinn, 349 U.S. at 161. . . . Congress has no "general power to inquire into private affairs and compel disclosures," McGrain, 273 U.S. at 173–174, and "there is no congressional power to expose for the sake of exposure," Watkins, 354 U.S. at 200. . . . Finally, recipients of legislative subpoenas retain their constitutional rights throughout the course of an investigation. And recipients have long been understood to retain common law and constitutional privileges with respect to certain materials, such as attorney-client communications and governmental communications protected by executive privilege

C

The President contends, as does the Solicitor General appearing on behalf of the United States, that the usual rules for congressional subpoenas do not govern here because the President's papers are at issue. They argue for a more demanding standard based in large part on cases involving the Nixon tapes—recordings of conversations between President Nixon and close advisers discussing the break-in at the Democratic National Committee's headquarters at the Watergate complex. The tapes were subpoenaed by a Senate committee and the Special Prosecutor investigating the break-in, prompting President Nixon to invoke executive privilege. . . . Quoting Nixon, the President asserts that the House must establish a "demonstrated, specific need" for the financial information, just as the Watergate special prosecutor was required to do in order to obtain the tapes. And drawing on Senate Select Committee—the D.C. Circuit case refusing to enforce the Senate subpoena for the tapes—the President and the Solicitor General argue that the House must show that the financial information is "demonstrably critical" to its legislative purpose.

We disagree that these demanding standards apply here. Unlike the cases before us, Nixon and Senate Select Committee involved Oval Office communications over which the President asserted executive privilege. That privilege safeguards the public interest in candid, confidential deliberations within the Executive Branch. . . . We decline to transplant that protection root and branch to cases involving nonprivileged, private information, which by definition does not implicate sensitive Executive Branch deliberations.

The standards proposed by the President and the Solicitor General—if applied outside the context of privileged information—would risk seriously impeding Congress in carrying out its responsibilities. The President and the Solicitor General would apply the same exacting standards to all subpoenas for the President's information. . . . Such a categorical approach would represent a significant departure from the longstanding way of doing business between the branches, giving short shrift to Congress's important interests in conducting inquiries to obtain the information it needs to legislate effectively. . . . Legislative inquiries might involve the President in appropriate cases; as noted, Congress's responsibilities extend to "every affair of government." United States v. Rumely, 345 U.S. 41, 43 (1953). Because the President's approach does not take adequate account of these significant congressional interests, we do not adopt it.

D

The House meanwhile . . . urges us to uphold its subpoenas because they "relate[ ] to a valid legislative purpose" or "concern[ ] a subject on which legislation could be had." Brief for Respondent 46. . . . The House's approach fails to take adequate account of the significant separation of powers issues raised by congressional subpoenas for the President's information. . . . [C]ongressional subpoenas for the President's information unavoidably pit the political branches against one another. Far from accounting for separation of powers concerns, the House's approach aggravates them by leaving essentially no limits on the congressional power to subpoena the President's personal records. Any personal paper possessed by a President could potentially "relate to" a conceivable subject of legislation, for Congress has broad legislative powers that touch a vast number of subjects. Without limits on its subpoena powers, Congress could "exert an imperious controul" over the Executive Branch and aggrandize itself at the President's expense, just as the Framers feared. The Federalist No. 71, at 484 (A. Hamilton). . . . And a limitless subpoena power would transform the "established practice" of the political branches. Noel Canning, 573 U.S. at 524. Instead of negotiating over information requests, Congress could simply walk away from the bargaining table and compel compliance in court.

The House and the courts below suggest that these separation of powers concerns are not fully implicated by the particular subpoenas here, but we disagree. We would have to be "blind" not to see what "[a]ll others can see and understand": that the subpoenas do not represent a run-of-the-mill legislative effort but rather a clash between rival branches of government over records of intense political interest for all involved. Rumely, 345 U.S. at 44. . . .

The interbranch conflict here does not vanish simply because the subpoenas seek personal papers or because the President sued in his personal capacity. The President is the only person who alone composes a branch of government. As a result, there is not always a clear line between his personal and official affairs. "The interest of the man" is often "connected with the constitutional rights of the place." The Federalist No. 51, at 349. Given the close connection between the Office of the President and its occupant, congressional demands for the President's papers can implicate the relationship between the branches regardless whether those papers are personal or official. Either way, a demand may aim to harass the President or render him "complaisan[t] to the humors of the Legislature." Id., No. 71, at 483. In fact, a subpoena for personal papers may pose a heightened risk of such impermissible purposes, precisely because of the documents' personal nature and their less evident connection to a legislative task. . . .

In addition, separation of powers concerns are no less palpable here simply because the subpoenas were issued to third parties. Congressional demands for the President's information present an interbranch conflict no matter where the information is held—it is, after all, the President's information. Were it otherwise, Congress could sidestep constitutional requirements any time a President's information is entrusted to a third party—as occurs with rapidly increasing frequency. . . . The Constitution does not tolerate such ready evasion. . . .

E

Congressional subpoenas for the President's personal information implicate weighty concerns regarding the separation of powers. Neither side, however, identifies an approach that accounts for these concerns. For more than two centuries, the political branches have resolved information disputes using the wide variety of means that the Constitution puts at their disposal. The nature of such interactions would be transformed by judicial enforcement of either of the approaches suggested by the parties. . . .

A balanced approach is necessary, one that takes a "considerable impression" from "the practice of the government," McCulloch v. Maryland, 4 Wheat. 316, 401 (1819), . . . and "resist[s]" the "pressure inherent within each of the separate Branches to exceed the outer limits of its power," INS v. Chadha, 462 U.S. 919, 951 (1983). We therefore conclude that, in assessing whether a subpoena directed at the President's personal information is "related to, and in furtherance of, a legitimate task of the Congress," Watkins, 354 U.S. at 187, courts must perform a careful analysis that takes adequate account of the separation of powers principles at stake, including both the significant legislative interests of Congress and the "unique position" of the President, Clinton v. Jones, 520 U.S. 681, 698 (1997). Several special considerations inform this analysis.

First, courts should carefully assess whether the asserted legislative purpose warrants the significant step of involving the President and his papers. . . . Congress may not rely on the President's information if other sources could reasonably provide Congress the information it needs in light of its particular legislative objective. The President's unique constitutional position means that Congress may not look to him as a "case study" for general legislation. . . . While we certainly recognize Congress's important interests in obtaining information through appropriate inquiries, those interests are not sufficiently powerful to justify access to the President's personal papers when other sources could provide Congress the information it needs.

Second, to narrow the scope of possible conflict between the branches, courts should insist on a subpoena no broader than reasonably necessary to support Congress's legislative objective. . . .

Third, courts should be attentive to the nature of the evidence offered by Congress to establish that a subpoena advances a valid legislative purpose. The more detailed and substantial the evidence of Congress's legislative purpose, the better. That is particularly true when Congress contemplates legislation that raises sensitive constitutional issues, such as legislation concerning the Presidency. In such cases, it is impossible to conclude that a subpoena is designed to advance a valid legislative purpose unless Congress adequately identifies its aims and explains why the President's information will advance its consideration of the possible legislation.

Fourth, courts should be careful to assess the burdens imposed on the President by a subpoena. We have held that burdens on the President's time and attention stemming from judicial process and litigation, without more, generally do not cross constitutional lines. See Vance [p. 922]. But burdens imposed by a congressional subpoena should be carefully scrutinized, for they stem from a rival political branch that has an ongoing relationship with the President and incentives to use subpoenas for institutional advantage.

Other considerations may be pertinent as well; one case every two centuries does not afford enough experience for an exhaustive list.

When Congress seeks information "needed for intelligent legislative action," it "unquestionably" remains "the duty of *all* citizens to cooperate." Watkins, 354 U.S. at 187 (emphasis added). Congressional subpoenas for information from the President, however, implicate special concerns regarding the separation of powers. The courts below did not take adequate account of those concerns. The judgments of the Courts of Appeals for the D.C. Circuit and the Second Circuit are vacated, and the cases are remanded for further proceedings consistent with this opinion.

It is so ordered.

■ JUSTICE THOMAS, dissenting.

. . . I would hold that Congress has no power to issue a legislative subpoena for private, nonofficial documents—whether they belong to the President or not. Congress may be able to obtain these documents as part of an investigation of the President, but to do so, it must proceed under the impeachment power. . . .

I

I begin with the Committees' claim that the House's legislative powers include the implied power to issue legislative subpoenas. Although the Founders understood that the enumerated powers in the Constitution included implied powers, the Committees' test for the scope of those powers is too broad. . . . The Constitution does not sweep in powers "of inferior importance, merely because they are inferior." McCulloch v. Maryland, 4 Wheat. 316, 408 (1819). Instead, Congress "can claim no powers which are not granted to it by the constitution, and the powers actually granted, must be such as are expressly given, or given by necessary implication." Martin v. Hunter's Lessee, 1 Wheat. 304, 326 (1816). In sum, while the Committees' theory of an implied power is not categorically wrong, that power must be necessarily implied from an enumerated power.

II

At the time of the founding, the power to subpoena private, nonofficial documents was not included by necessary implication in any of Congress' legislative powers. This understanding persisted for decades . . . The test that this Court created in McGrain v. Daugherty, 273 U.S. 135 (1927), and the majority's variation on that standard today, are without support as applied to private, nonofficial documents. . . .

Given that Congress has no exact precursor in England or colonial America, founding-era congressional practice is especially informative about the scope of implied legislative powers. Thus, it is highly probative that no founding-era Congress issued a subpoena for private, nonofficial documents. . . . By the end of the 1830s, Congress began issuing legislative subpoenas for private, nonofficial documents. Still, the power to demand information from private parties during legislative investigations remained controversial. . . . When this Court first addressed a legislative subpoena, it refused to uphold it. After casting doubt on legislative subpoenas generally, the Court in Kilbourn v. Thompson, 103 U.S. 168 [(1881)], held that the subpoena at issue was unlawful because it sought to investigate private conduct. . . .

Nearly half a century later, in McGrain v. Daugherty, the Court reached the question reserved in Kilbourn—whether Congress has the power to issue legislative subpoenas. It rejected Kilbourn's reasoning and upheld the power to issue legislative subpoenas as long as they were relevant to a legislative power. Although McGrain involved oral testimony, the Court has since extended this test to subpoenas for private documents. . . .

The opinion in McGrain lacks any foundation in text or history with respect to subpoenas for private, nonofficial documents. . . . And it identifies no founding-era legislative subpoenas for private documents. . . . Since McGrain, the Court has pared back Congress' authority to compel testimony and documents. It has held that certain convictions of witnesses for contempt of Congress violated the Fifth Amendment. It has also affirmed the reversal of a conviction on the ground that the Committee lacked authority to issue the subpoena. And today, it creates a new four-part, nonexhaustive test for cases involving the President. Rather than continue our trend of trying to compensate for McGrain, I would simply decline to apply it in these cases because it is readily apparent that the Committees have no constitutional authority to subpoena private, nonofficial documents.

III

If the Committees wish to investigate alleged wrongdoing by the President and obtain documents from him, the Constitution provides Congress with a special mechanism for doing so: impeachment. . . .

The power to impeach includes a power to investigate and demand documents. Impeachments in the States often involved an investigation. . . . Reinforcing this understanding, the founding generation repeatedly referred to impeachment as an "inquest." See 4 Debates on the Constitution 44 (J. Elliot ed. 1854) (speech of A. Maclaine). . . . At the time, an "inquest" referred to an "[i]nquiry, especially that made by a Jury" or "the Jury itself." N. Bailey, Universal Etymological Dictionary (22d ed. 1770). . . . This Court has also long recognized the power of the House to demand documents . . . when "the question of . . . impeachment is before either body acting in its appropriate sphere on that subject." Kilbourn, 103 U.S. at 190.

I express no view today on the boundaries of the power to demand documents in connection with impeachment proceedings. But the power of impeachment provides the House with authority to investigate and hold accountable Presidents who commit high crimes or misdemeanors. That is the proper path by which the Committees should pursue their demands.

IV

. . . Insisting that the House proceed through its impeachment power is not a mere formality. Unlike contempt, which is governed by the rules of each chamber, impeachment and removal constitutionally requires a majority vote by the House and a two-thirds vote by the Senate. In addition, Congress has long thought it necessary to provide certain procedural safeguards to officials facing impeachment and removal. Finally, initiating impeachment proceedings signals to the public the gravity of seeking the removal of a constitutional officer at the head of a coordinate branch. . . .

■ JUSTICE ALITO, dissenting.

Justice Thomas makes a valuable argument about the constitutionality of congressional subpoenas for a President's personal documents. In these cases, however, I would assume for the sake of argument that such subpoenas are not categorically barred. Nevertheless, legislative subpoenas for a President's personal documents are inherently suspicious. Such documents are seldom of any special value in considering potential legislation, and subpoenas for such documents can easily be used for improper non-legislative purposes. Accordingly, courts must be very sensitive to separation of powers issues when they are asked to approve the enforcement of such subpoenas.

In many cases, disputes about subpoenas for Presidential documents are fought without judicial involvement. If Congress attempts to obtain such documents by subpoenaing a President directly, those two heavyweight institutions can use their considerable weapons to settle the matter. But when Congress issues such a subpoena to a third party, Congress must surely appreciate that the Judiciary may be pulled into the dispute. . . .

Whenever such a subpoena comes before a court, Congress should be required to make more than a perfunctory showing that it is seeking the documents for a legitimate legislative purpose and not for the purpose of exposing supposed Presidential wrongdoing. . . .

. . . I do not think that the considerations outlined by the Court can be properly satisfied unless the House is required to . . . provide a description of the type of legislation being considered, and while great specificity is not necessary, the description should be sufficient to permit a court to assess whether the particular records sought are of any special importance. The House should also spell out its constitutional authority to enact the type of legislation that it is contemplating, and it should justify the scope of the subpoenas in relation to the articulated legislative needs. In addition, it should explain why the subpoenaed information, as opposed to information available from other sources, is needed. . . .

## NOTES

(1) ***What Does Mazars Mean in Practice?*** The Court remanded for lower courts to analyze the subpoenas according to the various factors it lays out. Imagine you are a lower court judge faced with applying the Mazars analysis to the subpoenas from the House Financial Services Committee and House Oversight and Reform Committee (or that judge's law clerk!). Which subpoenas do you think are most likely to pass muster? How much clarity does Mazars provide lower courts? This type of multi-factor balancing test leaves lower courts with substantial discretion, but often serves to identify outliers. Moreover, given that this analysis only applies to subpoenas aimed at the President, the Court is more able to step in and correct what it sees as lower court error. On the other hand, given that the President is involved, why do you think the Mazars Court did not apply its analysis directly but instead sent the cases down for a lower court do-over?

On remand, the D.C. Circuit upheld the House Oversight Committee's "authority to subpoena certain of President Trump's financial records in furtherance of [its] enumerated legislative purposes." But it concluded that the breadth of the Committee's subpoena was not justified. Trump v. Mazars, 39 F.4th 774 (D.C. Cir. 2022). The Second Circuit, for its part, remanded the case to the district court on December 14, 2020. See Trump v. Deutsche Bank AG, No. 19-1540 (2d Cir. Dec. 14, 2020) (remand order).[20] After the D.C. Circuit's decision, a settlement was reached under which Mazars will provide documents to the House Oversight Committee that Mazars determines are responsive to the Committee's subpoena. See Spencer Hsu, House Deal for Trump Records Lets Accounting Firm Decide What to Release, Wash. Post (Sept. 10, 2022).

(2) ***Congress's Subpoena Power.*** What is the constitutional basis of Congress's subpoena and investigatory authority? Mazars portrays this authority as implicit in Congress's legislative powers. Following McGrain v. Daugherty, 273 U.S. 135 (1927), the Court's seminal decision upholding a congressional subpoena arising out of investigations into the Teapot Dome Scandal, Chief Justice Roberts argues that without the power to obtain information, "Congress would be shooting in the dark, unable to legislate wisely or effectively." In dissent, Justice Thomas maintains that McGrain was wrongly decided and that Congress lacks the power to subpoena private,

[20] https://s3.documentcloud.org/documents/20491404/order_second_circuit.pdf.

nonofficial documents. Further, in Justice Thomas's view, Congress can only subpoena documents from and investigate the President under its impeachment power.

Does tying the subpoena power to Congress's ability to legislate or impeach do adequate justice to Congress's investigative role? Tying Congress's subpoena authority to impeachment would clearly curtail its ability to investigate governmental actions by requiring invocation of impeachment proceedings. Congress's power to legislate is more capacious, but much turns on how closely tied a subpoena must be to legislation. Does there need to be actual pending legislation to which the subpoena relates? Does Congress have to at least identify what kinds of measures it is considering enacting? Or is it enough that, depending on what the investigation uncovers and many additional factors (such as political considerations or other legislative priorities), Congress might at some point legislate?

Would a better alternative be to root the subpoenas in congressional authority to oversee the executive branch? Although the subpoenas sought personal financial information about the President, the stated purpose of the subpoenas from the Oversight and Reform Committee and the Intelligence Committee was to determine if there were conflicts of interest or undue foreign influence at the highest levels of the federal government. Could Congress's authority under the Necessary and Proper Clause, as well as its structural role as a check on the executive branch, support finding that the Constitution assigns it such an oversight role? Note that even Justice Thomas suggests that Congress has authority to subpoena official documents.

In a recent post-Mazars decision, the D.C. Circuit offered a fuller description of the basis for Congress's subpoena power: "The Constitution charges Congress with certain responsibilities, including to legislate, to conduct oversight of the federal government, and, when necessary, to impeach and remove a President or other executive branch official from office. Possession of relevant information is an essential precondition to the effective discharge of all of those duties." Committee on the Judiciary v. McGahn, 968 F.3d 755 (D.C. Cir. 2020) (en banc).

(3) ***Executive Privilege and Testimonial Immunity.*** The Mazars Court emphasized that the case did not involve an assertion of executive privilege, because at issue were President Trump's personal records. In NIXON V. UNITED STATES, 418 U.S. 683 (1974), involving a subpoena duces tecem that the Watergate special prosecutor obtained from a court for President Nixon's tapes, the Supreme Court recognized a constitutionally-based privilege for presidential communications, based on "the valid need for protection of communications between high Government officials and those who advise and assist them in the performance of their manifold duties; the importance of this confidentiality is too plain to require further discussion. Human experience teaches that those who expect public dissemination of their remarks may well temper candor with a concern for appearances and for their own interests to the detriment of the decisionmaking process. . . . A President and those who assist him must be free to explore alternatives in

the process of shaping policies and making decisions and to do so in a way many would be unwilling to express except privately. . . . The privilege is fundamental to the operation of Government and inextricably rooted in the separation of powers under the Constitution." But the Court also insisted that this privilege was presumptive, not absolute, and—at least "[a]bsent a claim of need to protect military, diplomatic, or sensitive national security secrets"—a President's "generalized assertion of privilege must yield to the demonstrated, specific need for evidence in a pending criminal trial." In Senate Select Committee on Presidential Campaign Activities v. Nixon, 498 F.2d 725 (D.C. Cir. 1974), the D.C. Circuit required the House of Representatives to show that the presidential communications it subpoenaed were "demonstrably critical to the responsible fulfillment of the Committee's functions" to overcome the privilege.

As JONATHAN DAVID SHAUB notes in THE EXECUTIVE'S PRIVILEGE, 70 Duke L.J. 1 (2020), the political branches are divided about the scope of executive privilege: "The executive branch claims that executive privilege is an affirmative constitutional authority belonging to the president to control the dissemination of certain information. Congress, on the other hand, understands executive privilege to be a limited evidentiary privilege that protects [only] the confidentiality of presidential communications." Moreover, "the executive branch has developed a number of 'prophylactic' doctrines to protect the president's asserted constitutional authority to control this information." In practice, this comprehensive doctrine "can be used to nullify congressional oversight entirely, even without formal assertions of privilege"—providing "the authority to delay responses and refuse requests for information without ever having to undertake what has historically been the core of the executive privilege inquiry: a determination of whether the disclosure of specific information would harm a specific public interest." He adds: "The executive branch's doctrine has developed, in part, as a means of checking Congress's increasingly aggressive exercise of its implied constitutional authority to access executive branch information and to probe the internal workings of the executive branch, including the White House itself. But, when understood as a whole, the expansive authority now exercised by the executive branch bears little relation to the narrow, historical privilege the executive branch claims it to be. Instead, the executive branch doctrine has become an absolute prophylactic privilege, designed to protect the asserted absolute authority of the president to control information."

Shaub identifies absolute testimonial immunity as one of the prophylactic doctrines that the executive branch has devised to protect executive privilege. Developed over the last fifty years largely in opinions from the Office of Legal Counsel in the Department of Justice, the doctrine provides that "Congress may not constitutionally compel the President's senior advisers to testify about their official duties. This testimonial immunity is rooted in the constitutional separation of powers and derives from the President's independence from Congress." Office of Legal Counsel, Testimonial Immunity Before Congress of the Former Counsel to the President, 43 Op. O.L.C., at 1 (May 20, 2019). Unlike the presidential communications privilege, testimonial immunity has not been met with judicial approval, with two district courts and one appellate judge concluding in lacks constitutional basis.

One of the opinions was from now-Supreme Court Justice Ketanji Brown Jackson, who rejected a claim by President Trump of absolute testimonial immunity for former White House Counsel Donald McGahn. Stating "Presidents are not kings," she elaborated that "[w]hatever the scope of the President's executive privilege with respect to the information that Congress seeks to compel, . . . [there is a] yawning gap between a presidential aide's right to withhold privileged information in the context of his or her compelled congressional testimony (which no one disputes), and the President's purported power to direct such aides to refuse to show up and be questioned at all (which appears only in a string of OLC opinions that do not themselves constitute legal precedents and are manifestly inconsistent with the constitutional jurisprudence of the Supreme Court and the D.C. Circuit in many respects)." For further discussion of this case, see Note 5 below (p. 925), Chapter VI (p. 768), and Chapter IX (p. 1476).

(4) ***Grand Jury Subpoenas.*** Mazars arose out of a congressional subpoena; would the analysis change if the subpoena was issued as part of a criminal investigation? That was the issue in a companion case decided the same day as Mazars, TRUMP V. VANCE, 140 S.Ct. 2412 (2020), involving a state grand jury subpoena served on Mazars seeking records, including tax returns, in connection to a criminal probe of possible fraud at the Trump Organization. Trump sued, arguing that a sitting President enjoys absolute immunity from state criminal process. The lower federal courts disagreed, as did the Supreme Court, in an opinion by CHIEF JUSTICE ROBERTS:

"In our judicial system, the public has a right to every man's evidence. Since the earliest days of the Republic, 'every man' has included the President of the United States. . . . The President, [Chief Justice] Marshall declared, . . . does not 'stand exempt from the general provisions of the constitution' or, in particular, the Sixth Amendment's guarantee that those accused have compulsory process for obtaining witnesses for their defense. United States v. Burr, 25 F.Cas. 30, 33–34 (No. 14,692d) (CC Va. 1807)." The President "concedes—consistent with the position of the Department of Justice—that state grand juries are free to investigate a sitting President with an eye toward charging him after the completion of his term. The President's objection therefore must be limited to the additional distraction caused by the subpoena itself. But that argument runs up against the 200 years of precedent establishing that Presidents, and their official communications, are subject to judicial process." That included the Supreme Court's decision in Nixon, supra, which upheld a federal court subpoena as part of a criminal investigation.

Roberts rejected concerns that subjecting Presidents to state criminal subpoenas would lead to abuse or impairment of the executive branch's ability to function. "The Supremacy Clause prohibits state judges and prosecutors from interfering with a President's official duties. Any effort to manipulate a President's policy decisions or to retaliate against a President for official acts through issuance of a subpoena would thus be an unconstitutional attempt to 'influence' a superior sovereign 'exempt' from such obstacles, see McCulloch [v. Maryland], 4 Wheat. [316,] 427 [(1819)]. We generally assume that state courts and prosecutors will observe constitutional limitations. Failing that, federal law allows a President to challenge any allegedly unconstitutional influence in a federal forum, as the President has done here." In addition to rejecting Trump's claim for absolute immunity, Roberts refused to subject "a state grand jury subpoena seeking a President's private papers" to a heightened need standard such as applies to official documents. "[I]f the state subpoena is not used to manipulate, . . . the documents themselves are not protected, . . . and the Executive is not impaired, then nothing in Article II or the Supremacy Clause supports holding state subpoenas to a higher standard than their federal counterparts."

Roberts emphasized that the President was not left without protection. "To start, a President may avail himself of the same protections available to every other citizen. These include the right to challenge the subpoena on any grounds permitted by state law, which usually include bad faith and undue burden or breadth. . . . And, as in federal court, the high respect that is owed to the office of the Chief Executive . . . should inform the conduct of the entire proceeding, including the timing and scope of discovery. . . . Furthermore, although the Constitution does not entitle the Executive to absolute immunity or a heightened standard, . . . A President can raise subpoena-specific constitutional challenges. . . . [H]e can challenge the subpoena as an attempt to influence the performance of his official duties, in violation of the Supremacy Clause. . . . In addition, the Executive can . . . argue that compliance with a particular subpoena would impede his constitutional duties. As a result, once the President sets forth and explains a conflict between judicial proceeding and public duties, or shows that an order or subpoena would significantly interfere with his efforts to carry out those duties, the matter changes. At that point, a court should use its inherent authority to quash or modify the subpoena, if necessary to ensure that such interference with the President's duties would not occur."

Although the Court was unanimous in rejecting President Trump's claim of absolute immunity from state criminal subpoenas, the justices disagreed on how such subpoenas of a President should be treated. JUSTICE KAVANAUGH, in an opinion concurring in the judgment that was joined by Justice Gorsuch, underscored that the Court also unanimously agreed that on remand "the President may raise constitutional and legal objections to the subpoena as appropriate." Kavanaugh argued that the "Nixon 'demonstrated, specific need' test" provides the appropriate balance between the "State's interests and the Article II interests." JUSTICE THOMAS dissented, arguing that although Trump was not absolutely immune, he was "entitled to injunctive and declaratory relief" against the subpoena's enforcement "[i]f the President is unable to comply because of his official duties." JUSTICE ALITO also dissented, claiming that the Court's approach would allow States to "run roughshod over the functioning of [the executive b]ranch" and emphasizing that "many local prosecutors are elected . . . and . . . have ambitions for higher office," creating a danger that they will use subpoenas to harass the President as an "effective electoral strategy." He insisted that courts should subject state grand jury subpoenas to greater scrutiny.

Do you think the majority's approach in Vance paid adequate heed to the needs of the presidency? Alternatively, do the dissents and the concurrence give adequate weight to the principle that drives the majority opinion, namely that the President is not above the law? Vance also presents a close intermingling of separation of powers and federalism. The majority rejects a distinction between state criminal subpoenas and the federal criminal subpoenas upheld in Burr and Nixon. Do you agree with that assessment, or are state criminal subpoenas more constitutionally suspect? Both Mazars and Vance involved subpoenas for President Trump's personal financial records, yet in both cases the Court analyzed the subpoenas through a separation of powers lens that focused on the presidency as an institution. For a discussion of the duality between these two aspects of the President, see Daphna Renan, The President's Two Bodies, 120 Colum. L. Rev. 1119 (2020).

The majority's approach in Vance puts fewer limits on subpoenas than imposed on Congress in Mazars; for example, the majority rejects subjecting prosecutors to a heightened need standard unless privileged information is involved and would not require a showing (as demanded in Mazars) that the information sought is not available elsewhere. (A similar pattern occurred with respect to Watergate subpoenas; although the Supreme Court upheld the Special Prosecutor's subpoena in Nixon, the D.C. Circuit refused to enforce a Senate subpoena in Senate Select Committee on Presidential Campaign Activities v. Nixon, 498 F.2d 725 (D.C. Cir. 1974) (en banc).) Is this differential treatment of Congress and state prosecutors justified? Does the Constitution support subjecting Congress to greater burdens in obtaining documents from the President than are imposed in state criminal proceedings?

(5) ***Political Versus Judicial Resolution and Congressional Standing.*** Should oversight disputes between the White House and Congress just be left to politics, or should courts be able to review executive branch assertions of executive privilege or testimonial immunity—which in practice necessitates finding that Congress has standing to sue?

One oversight dispute during the Trump Administration involved the House Committee on the Judiciary's effort to enforce its subpoena for testimony from Donald McGahn, President Trump's former White House Counsel. The Committee issued the subpoenas in connection with its impeachment investigation into whether Trump impermissibly coordinated with the Russian government in connection with the 2016 presidential election or obstructed justice in the course of Special Counsel Robert Mueller's investigation into Russian interference in the 2016 election. The Committee also explained that the information obtained would help determine if legislation was needed to protect federal law enforcement investigations from improper political interference. As noted above (p. 922), the President claimed that, as a White House advisor, McGahn has absolute immunity from testifying. When the Judiciary Committee sued, then-Judge (now-Justice) Jackson held that the Committee had standing. A panel of the D.C. Circuit reversed, only to be reversed itself by the en banc D.C. Circuit, which held that the Committee met the traditional requirements for standing. COMMITTEE ON THE JUDICIARY V. MCGAHN, 968 F.3d 755 (D.C. Cir. 2020) (en banc).

JUDGE ROGERS's majority opinion rejected McGahn's claim that allowing Congress to sue would violate the separation of powers by encouraging Congress to reject political negotiation and aggrandizing the role of the courts. According to the majority, McGahn had the separation of powers analysis backwards. Denying congressional standing is what would undermine the separation of powers by "aggrandiz[ing] the power of the Executive Branch at the expense of Congress. . . . Without the possibility of enforcement of a subpoena issued by a House of Congress, the Executive Branch faces little incentive to reach a negotiated agreement in an informational dispute. Indeed, the threat of a subpoena enforcement lawsuit may be an essential tool in keeping the Executive Branch at the negotiating table." Id. at 771.

Do you agree with the D.C. Circuit's conclusion that allowing Congress to sue to enforce its subpoenas accords with the separation of powers? Do Mazars and Vance suggest that judicial enforcement will empower Congress? In Executive Branch Contempt of Congress, 76 U. Chi. L. Rev. 1083 (2009), Josh Chafetz suggests that Congress should use its power to hold in contempt executive branch officials who defy congressional subpoenas; specifically, it should engage in self-help by sending the Sergeant-at-Arms to arrest and detain them. Would that be preferable to Congress suing? Note that such subpoena disputes could still end up in court, as the detained individual could sue for a writ of habeas corpus. This was Congress's traditional approach to subpoena enforcement; for an example involving a private individual, see McGrain v. Daugherty, 273 U.S. 135 (1927).

(6) ***Should a Statutory Right to Information Make a Difference?*** Under 26 U.S.C. § 6103(f)(1), "[u]pon written request" from a Chair of one of the congressional tax committees—which include the House Committee on Ways and Means—the Treasury Secretary "shall furnish such committee with any return . . . specified" in such a request. In 2019, after the Democrats regained control of the House, the Committee requested copies of then-President Trump's tax returns for the period of 2013 to 2019. Treasury sought advice from the Office of Legal Counsel in the Department of Justice.[21] OLC concluded that notwithstanding the statute, Treasury did not have to comply with the Committee's request because the Committee lacked a legitimate legislative purpose for then-President Trump's tax returns and because the Committee's stated reason for requesting the returns—oversight of the IRS's audit and enforcement of tax laws against a president—was pretextual. In reaching this result, OLC referred to a number of statements by the

[21] The Office of Legal Counsel, or OLC, provides legal advice to the President and all executive branch agencies.

Committee chair and Democratic leaders in Congress indicating that Trump's returns should be made public.

In June 2021 the Committee sent a new written request for the same information as it had previously requested, only "for the tax years 2015 through 2020." The Committee also further explained why it needed the returns in order to assess the IRS presidential audit program. Now under Biden Administration leadership, OLC "conclude[d] that Treasury must furnish the information specified in the June 2021 Request. . . . [E]ven if this case involved only a congressional subpoena, the Executive would be required to treat the Committee's stated rationale with deference and a presumption of good faith and regularity. All the more reason exists to do so here, because the Committee is requesting information pursuant to statutory authority." The 2021 opinion determined that "the 2019 Opinion failed to give due weight to Congress's status as a co-equal branch of government with legitimate needs for information in order to exercise its constitutional authorities." Ways and Means Committee's Request for the Former President's Tax Returns and Related Tax Information Pursuant to 26 U.S.C. § 6103(f)(1), 45 Op. O.L.C., at 3, 19, 23 (2021).[22] President Trump promptly sued to prevent release of his tax returns to the committee. The district court dismissed his challenge, Comm. on Ways & Means v. Dep't of the Treasury, 575 F.Supp.3d 53 (D.D.C. 2021), and the D.C. Circuit affirmed, 45 F.4th 324 (D.C. Cir. 2022). Trump sought a stay, which the Supreme Court denied, 2022 WL 17098419 (Nov. 22, 2022), and the IRS provided the requested returns to the Committee. Charlie Savage, House Committee Obtains Access to Trump's Tax Returns, Ending Long Fight, N.Y. Times (Nov. 30, 2022).

Do you think the fact that § 6103(f)(1) gives the Committee a right to view tax returns should make a difference in whether the Treasury Department complies with a request by the Committee to view the President's returns? Why or why not?

(7) ***Congressional Oversight of the White House and the January 6th Committee.*** On January 8, just weeks before President Trump left office, OLC issued a 59-page opinion on Congressional Oversight of the White House, stating that "[t]he White House's important role in advising and assisting the President has special significance for congressional oversight. . . . Even when Congress operates within the appropriate scope of its oversight authority, the Constitution places additional separation of powers constraints on inquiries directed at the White House. . . . Congressional inquiries directed to the White House must take account of the presumptive application of executive privilege to White House communications, as well as the President's interests in autonomy and independence." Congressional Oversight of the White House, 45 Op. O.L.C., at 2–3 (2021).[23]

More recently, when the House Select Committee to Investigate the January 6th Attack on the United States Capitol sought disclosure of presidential records under the Presidential Records Act, President Biden

---

[22] https://www.justice.gov/olc/file/1419111/download.

[23] https://www.justice.gov/olc/file/1355831/download.

determined that asserting a claim of executive privilege as to the specific documents at issue here was "not in the best interests of the United States," given the "unique and extraordinary circumstances" giving rise to the Committee's request, and Congress's "compelling need" to investigate "an unprecedented effort to obstruct the peaceful transfer of power" and "the most serious attack on the operations of the Federal Government since the Civil War." Letter from Dana A. Remus, Counsel to the President, to David Ferriero, Archivist of the United States (Oct. 8, 2021).[24]

When former President Trump sued seeking to prevent disclosure, the D.C. Circuit stated that "[a] court would be hard-pressed" to tell a sitting "President that he has miscalculated the interests of the United States, and to start an interbranch conflict that the President and Congress have averted. . . . President Biden's careful and cabined assessment that the best interests of the Executive Branch and the Nation warrant disclosing the documents, by itself, carries immense weight in overcoming the former President's assertion of privilege." But the appellate court also held that it did not need to "conclusively resolve whether and to what extent a court could second guess the sitting President's judgment" because "[u]nder any of the tests advocated by former President Trump," executive privilege was overcome. Trump v. Thompson, 20 F.4th 10 (D.C. Cir. 2021). The Supreme Court denied President Trump's request for a stay, emphasizing that given the D.C. Circuit's conclusion "that President Trump's claims would have failed even if he were the incumbent, . . . [a]ny discussion of the Court of Appeals concerning President Trump's status as a former President must therefore be regarded as nonbinding dicta." 142 S.Ct. 680 (2022). Justice Kavanaugh wrote separately to insist that "a former President must be able to successfully invoke the Presidential communications privilege for communications that occurred during his presidency." Id. at 680.

Is Justice Kavanaugh right—should a former President be able to assert executive privilege when the current President has determined it is not in the best interests of the nation to do so, and when such an assertion will likely lead to a conflict with Congress? Can such a power for a former President be squared with the idea of a unitary executive? (For a discussion of the unitary executive, see p. 1037).

## (4) Direct Control over Regulatory Actors

### *Bowsher v. Synar*

*The House of Representatives . . . shall have the sole Power of Impeachment.*

U.S. Const., Art. I, § 2, cl. 5

[24] https://www.whitehouse.gov/briefing-room/statements-releases/2021/10/12/letter-from-dana-a-remus-counsel-to-the-president-to-david-ferriero-archivist-of-the-united-states-dated-october-8-2021/.

*The Senate shall have the sole Power to try all Impeachments. . . . And no Person shall be convicted without the Concurrence of two thirds of the Members present.*

U.S. Const., Art. I, § 3, cl. 6

*. . . [N]o person holding any Office under the United States, shall be a Member of either House during his Continuance in Office.*

U.S. Const., Art. I, § 6, cl. 2

*The President, Vice President and all civil Officers of the United States, shall be removed from Office on Impeachment for, and Conviction of, Treason, Bribery, or other high Crimes and Misdemeanors.*

U.S. Const., Art. II, § 4

## SIGNIFICANT CASE

### BOWSHER v. SYNAR
478 U.S. 714 (1986).

Various factors—including the Vietnam War, ambitious social programs, and politically popular tax cuts—combined to quadruple the national debt between 1970 and the 1990s. After failing for many years to reduce the deficit, Congress in 1985 enacted the Balanced Budget and Emergency Deficit Control Act—known as the Gramm-Rudman-Hollings Act. The Act set a schedule of annual "maximum deficit amounts," which declined over five years to $0. It also created a complicated procedure for ensuring this deficit reduction occurred: Each year the Office of Management and Budget (located in the Executive Office of the President) and the Congressional Budget Office were to send independent estimates of the federal deficit for the upcoming year to the Comptroller General. As noted above, (p. 910), the Comptroller General heads GAO, an agency of a little over 3,000 people that engages in audit and oversight activities on direction from Congress, its committees and, sometimes, individual members. The Court overwhelmingly held that the Act violated the Constitution, although the justices disagreed as to why.

CHIEF JUSTICE BURGER, writing for the majority, focused on the role Congress played in removing the Comptroller General: "The Constitution does not contemplate an active role for Congress in the supervision of officers charged with the execution of the laws it enacts. The President appoints 'Officers of the United States' with the 'Advice and Consent of the Senate.' Once the appointment has been made and confirmed, however, the Constitution explicitly provides for removal of Officers of the United States by Congress only upon impeachment by the House of Representatives and conviction by the Senate. . . . A direct congressional role in the removal of officers charged with the execution of the laws beyond this limited one is inconsistent with separation of powers. . . . The structure of the Constitution does not permit Congress to execute the laws; it follows that Congress cannot grant to an officer under its control what it does not possess."

Moreover, "[a]lthough the Comptroller General is nominated by the President from a list of three individuals recommended by the Speaker of the House of Representatives and the President pro tempore of the Senate, and confirmed by the Senate, he is removable only at the initiative of Congress. He may be removed not only by impeachment but also by Joint Resolution of Congress ["at any time" for "(i) permanent disability; (ii) inefficiency; (iii) neglect of duty; (iv) malfeasance; or (v) a felony or conduct involving moral turpitude." 31 U.S.C. § 703(e)(1).][7] Burger criticized the dissent for "fail[ing] to recognize the breadth of the grounds for removal. The statute permits removal for 'inefficiency,' 'neglect of duty,' or 'malfeasance.' These terms are very broad and, as interpreted by Congress, could sustain removal of a Comptroller General for any number of actual or perceived transgressions of the legislative will. . . . It is clear the Congress has consistently viewed the Comptroller General as an officer of the Legislative Branch."

The majority concluded further that the Comptroller General therefore "may not be entrusted with executive powers" but had been assigned such powers by the Act: "The primary responsibility of the Comptroller General under the instant Act is the preparation of a 'report' [that] . . . must contain detailed estimates of projected federal revenues and expenditures" and "specify the reductions, if any, necessary to reduce the deficit to the target for the appropriate fiscal year" on "program-by-program basis. . . . [W]e view these functions as plainly entailing execution of the law in constitutional terms. Interpreting a law enacted by Congress to implement the legislative mandate is the very essence of 'execution' of the law. . . . [T]he Comptroller General must exercise judgment concerning facts that affect the application of the Act. He must also interpret the provisions of the Act to determine precisely what budgetary calculations are required. Decisions of that kind are typically made by officers charged with executing a statute. . . . [And the Act] . . . gives the Comptroller General the ultimate authority to determine the budget cuts to be made." The majority held that the appropriate remedy was to enforce fallback provisions in the Act that came into effect in the event any of the Act's reporting requirements were invalidated.

Concurring in the judgment, JUSTICE STEVENS, joined by Justice Marshall, agreed that the Act was unconstitutional but on a separate basis: "[W]hen Congress, or a component or an agent of Congress, seeks to make policy that will bind the Nation, it must follow the procedures mandated by Article I of the Constitution—through passage by both Houses and presentment to the President. . . . That principle, I believe, is applicable to the Comptroller General. . . . [O]ne of the identifying characteristics of the Comptroller General is his statutorily required

[7] Although the President could veto such a joint resolution, the veto could be overridden by a two-thirds vote of both Houses of Congress. Thus, the Comptroller General could be removed in the face of Presidential opposition. Like the District Court, we therefore read the removal provision as authorizing removal by Congress alone.

relationship to the Legislative Branch," evident from not only the Comptroller General's "longstanding statutory responsibilities" to Congress, but also "the fact that Congress had retained for itself the power to remove the Comptroller General."

In Stevens's view, the powers assigned to the Comptroller General were more appropriately viewed as legislative: "One reason that the exercise of legislative, executive, and judicial powers cannot be categorically distributed among three mutually exclusive branches of Government is that governmental power cannot always be readily characterized with only one of those three labels. On the contrary, as our cases demonstrate, a particular function, like a chameleon, will often take on the aspect of the office to which it is assigned. For this reason, '[w]hen any Branch acts, it is presumptively exercising the power the Constitution has delegated to it.' INS v. Chadha, 462 U.S. at 951. . . . The powers delegated to the Comptroller General by § 251 of the Act before us today have [this] chameleon-like quality." Presaging his concurrence nearly fifteen years later in Whitman, Stevens made clear that he was not troubled by labelling "the function" at issue "legislative even if performed by the Comptroller General or by an executive agency." Instead, the problem was that the Act "assigns to the Comptroller General the duty to make policy decisions that have the force of law" and if "Congress were free to delegate its policymaking authority to one of its components, or to one of its agents, it would be able to evade 'the carefully crafted restraints spelled out in the Constitution.' Chadha, at 959. That danger—congressional action that evades constitutional restraints—is not present when Congress delegates lawmaking power to the executive or to an independent agency."

JUSTICE WHITE provided the sole dissent on the merits. He agreed with the majority that the Comptroller General's powers were executive, "in that they involve the interpretation and carrying out of the Act's mandate," but disagreed that the removal provision made the Comptroller General an agent of Congress: "If the Comptroller's conduct in office is not so unsatisfactory to the President as to convince the latter that removal is required under the statutory standard, Congress will have no independent power to coerce the Comptroller unless it can muster a two-thirds majority in both Houses—a feat of bipartisanship more difficult than that required to impeach and convict. The incremental in terrorem effect of the possibility of congressional removal in the face of a presidential veto is therefore exceedingly unlikely to have any discernible impact on the extent of congressional influence over the Comptroller." JUSTICE BLACKMUN dissented on the ground that the proper remedy here would be to invalidate Congress's removal power over the Comptroller General, not to invalidate the Act's substantive provisions.

## NOTES

(1) ***Joint Resolutions Versus Ordinary Legislation.*** Consider carefully the allocation of power in removal by joint resolution. If the President

disagrees that removal is warranted and vetoes the resolution, Congress can act only if two-thirds of Representatives and two-thirds of Senators support removal. Chief Justice Burger reasons that because Congress can override a presidential veto in this fashion, the Court should "read the removal provision as authorizing removal by Congress alone." This same reasoning would suggest—contrary to 200 years of political reality—that laws are enacted by Congress alone. Consider how this allocation of power in the Comptroller removal provision differs from the following hypothetical alternative:

Assume that the statutory removal provision vests "for cause" removal power in the President alone. Faced with an unsatisfactory (to it) Comptroller General, Congress presses the President to exercise her removal power, but she refuses to act. Congress passes a statute abolishing the office, over the President's veto. It then promptly passes another statute (overriding a veto, if necessary) recreating it, and the Senate will confirm only a person named on the statutory list of three (a list, recall, prepared by the Speaker of the House and President pro tem of the Senate.) Would this hypothetical course of events be a constitutional way for Congress to force a Comptroller General out of office? Does it differ in any constitutionally significant way from the actual removal provision?

(2) ***Why the Choice of Formalism?*** Bowsher was decided the same day as CFTC v. Schor (p. 1077), which rejected an Article III challenge to administrative adjudication of securities-fraud claims and common-law counterclaims. Bowsher is resolutely formalist; Schor explicitly rejects formalism in favor of functionalist analysis. Justice O'Connor, writing for the Schor Court, tried to explain the difference: "Unlike Bowsher, this case raises no question of the aggrandizement of congressional power at the expense of a coordinate branch. Instead, the separation of powers question presented in this case is whether Congress impermissibly undermined, without appreciable expansion of its own power, the role of the Judicial Branch." Are you persuaded?

(3) ***The Incompatibility Clause.*** At the outset of its analysis, the Bowsher majority invoked the Incompatibility Clause of Article I, Section 6, which prohibits any member of Congress to simultaneously hold an office in the executive branch. The Clause is a strong textual reminder that ours is not a parliamentary system, in which government ministers are typically members of parliament and the party in control of parliament is charged with forming the government. Along with its textual sibling, the Emoluments Clause—which prohibits members of Congress from being appointed to civil offices that were created or for which the salary was increased during that time during their terms—the Incompatibility Clause seems central to the Framers' concern with preserving the independence of the legislature. These Clauses reflect a determination to prevent the lure of office from undermining legislative integrity and independent judgment. What room, if any, do these clauses leave for direct congressional participation in regulatory decisions?

(4) ***Jawboning.*** One of the most ubiquitous mechanisms through which Congress tries to influence regulatory outcomes is direct phone calls or

letters to the agency. Challenges to allegedly over-aggressive congressional intervention in particular regulatory decisions are more typically framed as violations of fairness or legality norms. Courts have not been responsive to the occasional claim that such congressional advocacy violates the separation of powers. As one court put it, it was "dubious that an individual legislator's interaction with executive branch officials could ever interfere with the authority of the executive in a way that would violate the separation of powers. . . . Legislators routinely express their opinions to executive branch officials about matters for which their departments or agencies are responsible." U.S. v. Mardis, 670 F.Supp.2d 696, 701–02 (W.D. Tenn. 2009), aff'd on other grounds 600 F.3d 693 (6th Cir.) See also Sierra Club v. Costle, 657 F.2d 298 (D.C. Cir. 1981) (p. 1051).

(5) ***Exercising Appointment and Oversight Powers.*** Bowsher rejects out of hand that Congress might play "an active role" in supervising officers charged with executing the laws. But does that mean members of Congress can't use their constitutional powers to influence officers' actions or the way agencies are run? CONG. RSCH. SERV., R45442, CONGRESS'S AUTHORITY TO INFLUENCE AND CONTROL EXECUTIVE BRANCH AGENCIES (May 12, 2021): "The Senate's advice-and-consent function under the Appointments Clause serves as a significant check on the executive branch, one which the Senate may use not only to approve or reject presidential nominees, but also to influence who is nominated for certain important offices and what a nominee will do in office if confirmed. . . . Hearings may also provide a committee the opportunity to give an agency guidance on how the committee believes an agency should carry out its functions."

(6) ***Becoming an Administrative Decision Maker.*** Given the Incompatibility Clause and Bowsher, it might seem obvious that Congress cannot designate its members as agency decisionmakers. Nonetheless, in a regulatory area in which members were keenly interested, Congress tried to work around these obstacles. METROPOLITAN WASHINGTON AIRPORTS AUTH. V. CITIZENS FOR THE ABATEMENT OF AIRCRAFT NOISE, 501 U.S. 252 (1991): Two of the three Washington, D.C. area airports were federally owned and managed. A congressionally approved interstate compact transferred their ownership to a Commission operated by Virginia, Maryland, and the District of Columbia. The Commission, in turn, acted under the watchful eye of a Review Board, which could veto its decisions. The Board consisted of nine members of Congress from committees having jurisdiction over transportation issues. This scheme was defended on grounds that the Members were serving in their "individual capacities" as representatives of airport users and that the Board was actually a state, rather than a federal, entity. Three Justices (an unusual alignment of White, Rehnquist, and Marshall) accepted the latter argument. The balance of the Court was unpersuaded. JUSTICE STEVENS's opinion rested heavily on Bowsher and Chadha. To forestall the danger of encroachment into the executive sphere, the Constitution imposes two basic and related constraints on Congress: (1) It may not invest itself, its Members, or its agents with executive power; (2) When it exercises its legislative power, it must follow the "single, finely wrought and exhaustively considered procedures" specified in Article I. If the

Board's power was considered "executive," a member or agent of Congress may not exercise it. If the power was considered "legislative," it was not being exercised in conformity with Article I, § 7. "Admittedly, Congress imposed its will on the regional authority created by the District of Columbia and the Commonwealth of Virginia by means that are unique and that might prove to be innocuous. However, the statutory scheme challenged today provides a blueprint for extensive expansion of the legislative power beyond its constitutionally-confined role."

# SECTION 3. THE PRESIDENT, ADMINISTRATIVE AGENCIES, AND THE EXECUTIVE BRANCH



*The executive Power shall be vested in a President of the United States of America.*

U.S. Const., Art. II, § 1, cl. 1

*The President shall be Commander in Chief of the Army and Navy of the United States, and of the Militia of the several States, when called into the actual Service of the United States; he may require the Opinion, in writing, of the principal Officer in each of the executive Departments, upon any Subject relating to the Duties of their respective Offices . . .*

U.S. Const., Art. II, § 2

*[The President] shall take Care that the Laws be faithfully executed . . . .*

U.S. Const., Art. II, § 3

## a. Introduction



### YOUNGSTOWN SHEET & TUBE CO. v. SAWYER

Supreme Court of the United States (1952).
343 U.S. 579.

■ JUSTICE BLACK delivered the opinion of the Court.

[In late 1951, during the Korean War, a labor dispute developed between steel companies and the United Steelworkers Union over the terms of a new collective bargaining agreement. Several months of mediation and a federal investigation failed to resolve the dispute, and the union called a strike for April 9, 1952. A few hours before the strike was to start, President Truman issued Executive Order 10340, stating that "steel is an indispensable component of substantially all . . . weapons and materials" needed by U.S. armed forces in Korea and "a work stoppage would immediately jeopardize and imperil our national defense . . . and would add to the continuing danger of our soldiers, sailors, and airmen engaged in combat in the field." The order directed the Secretary of Commerce to take possession of the steel companies "as he may deem necessary in the interests of national defense" and set terms and conditions of employment. The Secretary immediately issued his own orders taking possession of most of the steel mills and directing the presidents of the companies to maintain their operations. The next morning the President sent a message to Congress reporting his action and sent a second message twelve days later. Congress took no action.

Obeying the Secretary's orders under protest, the companies brought suit and the District Court issued a preliminary injunction restraining the Secretary from "continuing the seizure and possession of the plants . . . and from acting under the purported authority of Executive Order No. 10340." On the same day, the Court of Appeals stayed the District Court's injunction. The Supreme Court granted certiorari on May 3, set the cause for argument on May 12, and issued its decision on June 2.]

We are asked to decide whether the President was acting within his constitutional power when he issued an order directing the Secretary of Commerce to take possession of and operate most of the Nation's steel mills. The mill owners argue that the President's order amounts to lawmaking, a legislative function which the Constitution has expressly confided to the Congress, and not to the President. The Government's position is that the order was made on findings of the President that his action was necessary to avert a national catastrophe which would inevitably result from a stoppage of steel production, and that, in meeting this grave emergency, the President was acting within the aggregate of his constitutional powers as the Nation's Chief Executive and the Commander in Chief of the Armed Forces of the United States. [In the district court, the Government had made a similar argument, contending that given the danger to "the wellbeing and safety of the Nation[,] . . . the President had 'inherent power' to do what he had done—power supported by the Constitution, by historical precedent, and by court decisions."] . . .

II

The President's power, if any, to issue the order must stem either from an act of Congress or from the Constitution itself. There is no statute that expressly authorizes the President to take possession of property as he did here. Nor is there any act of Congress to which our attention has been directed from which such a power can fairly be implied. Indeed, we do not understand the Government to rely on statutory authorization for this seizure. There are two statutes which do authorize the President to take both personal and real property under certain conditions. However, the Government admits that these conditions were not met, and that the President's order was not rooted in either of the statutes. . . .

Moreover, the use of the seizure technique to solve labor disputes in order to prevent work stoppages was not only unauthorized by any congressional enactment; prior to this controversy, Congress had refused to adopt that method of settling labor disputes. When the Taft-Hartley Act was under consideration in 1947, Congress rejected an amendment which would have authorized such governmental seizures in cases of emergency. . . . [T]he plan Congress adopted . . . [i]nstead . . . sought to bring about settlements by use of the customary devices of mediation, conciliation, investigation by boards of inquiry, and public reports. In some instances, temporary injunctions were authorized to provide cooling-off periods. All this failing, unions were left free to strike after a secret vote by employees as to whether they wished to accept their employers' final settlement offer.

It is clear that, if the President had authority to issue the order he did, it must be found in some provision of the Constitution. And it is not claimed that express constitutional language grants this power to the President. The contention is that presidential power should be implied from the aggregate of his powers under the Constitution. Particular reliance is placed on provisions in Article II which say that "The executive Power shall be vested in a President . . ."; that "he shall take Care that the Laws be faithfully executed," and that he "shall be Commander in Chief of the Army and Navy of the United States."

The order cannot properly be sustained as an exercise of the President's military power as Commander in Chief of the Armed Forces. The Government attempts to do so by citing a number of cases upholding broad powers in military commanders engaged in day-to-day fighting in a theater of war. Such cases need not concern us here. Even though "theater of war" be an expanding concept, we cannot with faithfulness to our constitutional system hold that the Commander in Chief of the Armed Forces has the ultimate power as such to take possession of private property in order to keep labor disputes from stopping production. This is a job for the Nation's lawmakers, not for its military authorities.

Nor can the seizure order be sustained because of the several constitutional provisions that grant executive power to the President. In the framework of our Constitution, the President's power to see that the laws are faithfully executed refutes the idea that he is to be a lawmaker. The Constitution limits his functions in the lawmaking process to the recommending of laws he thinks wise and the vetoing of laws he thinks bad. And the Constitution is neither silent nor equivocal about who shall make laws which the President is to execute. The first section of the first article says that "All legislative Powers herein granted shall be vested in a Congress of the United States." After granting many powers to the Congress, Article I goes on to provide that Congress may "make all Laws which shall be necessary and proper for carrying into Execution the foregoing Powers, and all other Powers vested by this Constitution in the

Government of the United States, or in any Department or Officer thereof."

The President's order does not direct that a congressional policy be executed in a manner prescribed by Congress—it directs that a presidential policy be executed in a manner prescribed by the President. . . . The power of Congress to adopt such public policies as those proclaimed by the order is beyond question. It can authorize the taking of private property for public use. It can make laws regulating the relationships between employers and employees, prescribing rules designed to settle labor disputes, and fixing wages and working conditions in certain fields of our economy. . . . It is said that other Presidents, without congressional authority, have taken possession of private business enterprises in order to settle labor disputes. But even if this be true, Congress has not thereby lost its exclusive constitutional authority [under the Necessary and Proper Clause]. . . .

The judgment of the District Court is affirmed.

■ JUSTICE JACKSON, concurring in the judgment and opinion of the Court.

That comprehensive and undefined presidential powers hold both practical advantages and grave dangers for the country will impress anyone who has served as legal adviser to a President in time of transition and public anxiety. While an interval of detached reflection may temper teachings of that experience, they probably are a more realistic influence on my views than the conventional materials of judicial decision. . . .

A judge, like an executive adviser, may be surprised at the poverty of really useful and unambiguous authority applicable to concrete problems of executive power as they actually present themselves. Just what our forefathers did envision, or would have envisioned had they foreseen modern conditions, must be divined from materials almost as enigmatic as the dreams Joseph was called upon to interpret for Pharaoh. . . .

The actual art of governing under our Constitution does not, and cannot, conform to judicial definitions of the power of any of its branches based on isolated clauses, or even single Articles torn from context. While the Constitution diffuses power the better to secure liberty, it also contemplates that practice will integrate the dispersed powers into a workable government. It enjoins upon its branches separateness but interdependence, autonomy but reciprocity. Presidential powers are not fixed but fluctuate depending upon their disjunction or conjunction with those of Congress. We may well begin by a somewhat over-simplified grouping of practical situations in which a President may doubt, or others may challenge, his powers, and by distinguishing roughly the legal consequences of this factor of relativity.

1. When the President acts pursuant to an express or implied authorization of Congress, his authority is at its maximum, for it includes all that he possesses in his own right plus all that Congress can delegate. In these circumstances, and in these

only, may he be said (for what it may be worth) to personify the federal sovereignty. If his act is held unconstitutional under these circumstances, it usually means that the Federal Government, as an undivided whole, lacks power. . . .

2. When the President acts in absence of either a congressional grant or denial of authority, he can only rely upon his own independent powers, but there is a zone of twilight in which he and Congress may have concurrent authority, or in which its distribution is uncertain. Therefore, congressional inertia, indifference or quiescence may sometimes, at least, as a practical matter, enable, if not invite, measures on independent presidential responsibility. In this area, any actual test of power is likely to depend on the imperatives of events and contemporary imponderables, rather than on abstract theories of law.

3. When the President takes measures incompatible with the expressed or implied will of Congress, his power is at its lowest ebb, for then he can rely only upon his own constitutional powers minus any constitutional powers of Congress over the matter. Courts can sustain exclusive presidential control in such a case only by disabling the Congress from acting upon the subject. Presidential claim to a power at once so conclusive and preclusive must be scrutinized with caution, for what is at stake is the equilibrium established by our constitutional system.

Into which of these classifications does this executive seizure of the steel industry fit? It is eliminated from the first by admission, for it is conceded that no congressional authorization exists for this seizure. . . . Can it then be defended under flexible tests available to the second category? It seems clearly eliminated from that class, because Congress has not left seizure of private property an open field, but has covered it by three statutory policies inconsistent with this seizure. In cases where the purpose is to supply needs of the Government itself, two courses are provided: one, seizure of a plant which fails to comply with obligatory orders placed by the Government; another, condemnation of facilities, including temporary use under the power of eminent domain. The third is applicable where it is the general economy of the country that is to be protected, rather than exclusive governmental interests. None of these were invoked. . . .

This leaves the current seizure to be justified only by the severe tests under the third grouping, where it can be supported only by any remainder of executive power after subtraction of such powers as Congress may have over the subject. In short, we can sustain the President only by holding that seizure of such strike-bound industries is within his domain and beyond control by Congress. Thus, this Court's first review of such seizures occurs under circumstances which leave presidential power most vulnerable to attack and in the least favorable of possible constitutional postures. . . .

The Solicitor General seeks the power of seizure in three clauses of the Executive Article, the first reading, "The executive Power shall be vested in a President of the United States of America." Lest I be thought to exaggerate, I quote the interpretation which his brief puts upon it: "In our view, this clause constitutes a grant of all the executive powers of which the Government is capable." If that be true, it is difficult to see why the forefathers bothered to add several specific items, including some trifling ones.[9]

The example of such unlimited executive power that must have most impressed the forefathers was the prerogative exercised by George III, and the description of its evils in the Declaration of Independence leads me to doubt that they were creating their new Executive in his image. Continental European examples were no more appealing. And, if we seek instruction from our own times, we can match it only from the executive powers in those governments we disparagingly describe as totalitarian. I cannot accept the view that this clause is a grant in bulk of all conceivable executive power, but regard it as an allocation to the presidential office of the generic powers thereafter stated.

The clause on which the Government next relies is that "The President shall be Commander in Chief of the Army and Navy of the United States . . . ." These cryptic words . . . undoubtedly put[ ] the Nation's armed forces under presidential command. Hence, this loose appellation is sometimes advanced as support for any presidential action, internal or external, involving use of force, the idea being that it vests power to do anything, anywhere, that can be done with an army or navy. . . . I cannot foresee all that it might entail if the Court should indorse this argument. . . . [N]o doctrine that the Court could promulgate would seem to me more sinister and alarming than that a President whose conduct of foreign affairs is so largely uncontrolled, and often even is unknown, can vastly enlarge his mastery over the internal affairs of the country by his own commitment of the Nation's armed forces to some foreign venture. . . .

The third clause in which the Solicitor General finds seizure powers is that "he shall take Care that the Laws be faithfully executed." That authority must be matched against words of the Fifth Amendment that "No person shall be . . . deprived of life, liberty or property, without due process of law . . . ." One gives a governmental authority that reaches so far as there is law, the other gives a private right that authority shall go no farther. These signify about all there is of the principle that ours is a government of laws, not of men, and that we submit ourselves to rulers only if under rules.

The Solicitor General lastly grounds support of the seizure upon nebulous, inherent powers never expressly granted, but said to have

[9] ". . .he may require the Opinion, in writing, of the principal Officer in each of the executive Departments, upon any Subject relating to the Duties of their respective Offices . . ." U.S. Const. Art. II, § 2. He ". . . shall Commission all the Officers of the United States." U.S. Const. Art. II, § 3. Matters such as those would seem to be inherent in the Executive if anything is.

accrued to the office from the customs and claims of preceding administrations. The plea is for a resulting power to deal with a crisis or an emergency according to the necessities of the case, the unarticulated assumption being that necessity knows no law. . . .

The appeal, however, that we declare the existence of inherent powers ex necessitate to meet an emergency asks us to do what many think would be wise, although it is something the forefathers omitted. They knew what emergencies were, knew the pressures they engender for authoritative action, knew, too, how they afford a ready pretext for usurpation. . . .

[I]t is relevant to note the gap that exists between the President's paper powers and his real powers. The Constitution does not disclose the measure of the actual controls wielded by the modern presidential office. That instrument must be understood as an Eighteenth-Century sketch of a government hoped for, not as a blueprint of the Government that is. Vast accretions of federal power, eroded from that reserved by the States, have magnified the scope of presidential activity. Subtle shifts take place in the centers of real power that do not show on the face of the Constitution.

Executive power has the advantage of concentration in a single head in whose choice the whole Nation has a part, making him the focus of public hopes and expectations. In drama, magnitude and finality, his decisions so far overshadow any others that, almost alone, he fills the public eye and ear. No other personality in public life can begin to compete with him in access to the public mind through modern methods of communications. By his prestige as head of state and his influence upon public opinion, he exerts a leverage upon those who are supposed to check and balance his power which often cancels their effectiveness. . . .

I cannot be brought to believe that this country will suffer if the Court refuses further to aggrandize the presidential office, already so potent and so relatively immune from judicial review, at the expense of Congress. But I have no illusion that any decision by this Court can keep power in the hands of Congress if it is not wise and timely in meeting its problems. . . . We may say that power to legislate for emergencies belongs in the hands of Congress, but only Congress itself can prevent power from slipping through its fingers. . . .

■ JUSTICE FRANKFURTER, concurring.

Although the considerations relevant to the legal enforcement of the principle of separation of powers seem to me more complicated and flexible than any appear from what Mr. Justice Black has written, I join his opinion because I thoroughly agree with the application of the principle to the circumstances of this case. . . .

The issue before us can be met, and therefore should be, without attempting to define the President's powers comprehensively. . . . The judiciary may, as this case proves, have to intervene in determining where authority lies as between the democratic forces in our scheme of government. But in doing so we should be wary and humble. Such is the teaching of this Court's role in the history of the country. . . .

It cannot be contended that the President would have had power to issue this order had Congress explicitly negated such authority in formal legislation. Congress has expressed its will to withhold this power from the President as though it had said so in so many words. . . . By the Labor Management Relations Act of 1947, Congress said to the President, "You may not seize. Please report to us and ask for seizure power if you think it is needed in a specific situation." . . .

To be sure, the content of the three authorities of government is not to be derived from an abstract analysis. The areas are partly interacting, not wholly disjointed. The Constitution is a framework for government. Therefore the way the framework has consistently operated fairly establishes that it has operated according to its true nature. Deeply embedded traditional ways of conducting government cannot supplant the Constitution or legislation, but they give meaning to the words of a text or supply them. It is an inadmissibly narrow conception of American constitutional law to confine it to the words of the Constitution and to disregard the gloss which life has written upon them. In short, a systematic, unbroken, executive practice, long pursued to the knowledge of the Congress and never before questioned, engaged in by Presidents who have also sworn to uphold the Constitution, making as it were such exercise of power part of the structure of our government, may be treated as a gloss on "executive Power" vested in the President by § 1 of Art. II. [But no such] practice can be vouched for executive seizure of property at a time when this country was not at war. . . .

■ CHIEF JUSTICE VINSON, with whom JUSTICE REED and JUSTICE MINTON join, dissenting.

[Chief Justice Vinson began by outlining statutes Congress had enacted to ensure support for the Korean War, arguing that their] successful execution depends upon continued production of steel and stabilized prices for steel. . . . One is not here called upon even to consider the possibility of executive seizure of a farm, a corner grocery store or even a single industrial plant. Such considerations arise only when one ignores the central fact of this case—that the Nation's entire basic steel production would have shut down completely if there had been no Government seizure. . . .

[M]uch of the argument in this case has been directed at straw men. We do not now have before us the case of a President acting solely on the basis of his own notions of the public welfare. Nor is there any question of unlimited executive power in this case. The President himself closed the door to any such claim when he sent his Message to Congress stating his purpose to abide by any action of Congress, whether approving or disapproving his seizure action. . . . The absence of a specific statute authorizing seizure of the steel mills as a mode of executing the laws—both the military procurement program and the anti-inflation program—has not until today been thought to prevent the President from executing the laws. Unlike an administrative commission confined to the enforcement of the statute under which it was created, or the head to a department when administering a particular statute, the President is a constitutional officer charged with taking care that a "mass of legislation" be executed. . . .

The broad executive power granted by Article II to an officer on duty 365 days a year cannot, it is said, be invoked to avert disaster. Instead, the President must confine himself to sending a message to Congress recommending action. Under this messenger-boy concept of the Office, the President cannot even act to preserve legislative programs from destruction so that Congress will have something left to act upon. . . . Presidents have been in the past, and any man worthy of the Office should be in the future, free to take at least interim action necessary to execute legislative programs essential to survival of the Nation. . . .

## NOTES

(1) ***Early Separation of Powers Formalism and Functionalism.*** Notice how the contrasting opinions in Youngstown map onto current formalist and functionalist approaches to the separation of powers, although those terms were not in use when Youngstown was decided. Justice Black, writing for the opinion for the Court, takes a formalist approach, carefully delineating possible bases for presidential authority and rejecting arguments from necessity as a basis for expanding presidential power. Can you reconcile agency rulemaking with Justice Black's assertion that "[i]n the framework of our Constitution, the President's power to see that the laws are faithfully executed refutes the idea that he is to be a lawmaker"?

By comparison, Justice Jackson describes his view of the separation of powers in terms that are invoked by functionalists to this day, insisting that actual governance does not conform to formal separation of clearly defined powers and that interdependence of the branches is at the core of the constitutional scheme. Justice Frankfurter also insists on viewing separation of powers in context, emphasizing the importance of historical practice as helping to elucidate the meaning of executive power. Chief Justice Vinson, in dissent, is the least concerned with the text or structural relationships laid out in the Constitution, focusing instead on the temporary and contingent nature of Truman's assertion of power.

(2) ***Justice Jackson's Tripartite Framework.*** Over time, the three-part framework that Justice Jackson laid out in his concurrence has come to dominate judicial assessment of presidential power. See Zivotofsky v. Kerry, 576 U.S. 1, 10 (2015). Jackson's concurrence is not the only part of Youngstown having a lasting impact; the Supreme Court recently endorsed Justice Frankfurter's emphasis on historical practice as a central focus in separation of powers disputes. See NLRB v. Noel Canning, 573 U.S. 513, 524–26 (2014) (p. 966).

Yet when the decision was issued in 1952, the initial response to Youngstown was quite negative. Several leading constitutional scholars castigated it as "a judicial brick without straw," "destined to be ignored," and "so much out of step with the way in which the American system of government functions that it cannot long stand as a guidepost in the development of United States constitutional law." Patricia L. Bellia, Executive Power in Youngstown's Shadow, 19 Const. Comment. 87, 88 & n. 3 (2002) (internal quotations omitted) (collecting criticisms).

(3) ***The Dispute over Inherent Presidential Power.*** The central dispute in Youngstown was over the question of whether the President enjoys implicit or inherent authority under the Constitution, as the government claimed. Justice Black firmly denied the government's claim, ruling President Truman's action unconstitutional because it was not authorized by statute or by any of the express constitutional grants of presidential authority. Chief Justice Vinson, in dissent, rejected what he called a "messenger-boy concept of the office," insisting that the "broad executive power granted by Article II" authorized the President "to take at least interim action necessary to execute legislative programs essential to survival of the Nation."

Where do Justices Jackson and Frankfurter come out on this question? Both are clearly uneasy over the breadth of the government's claim and the suggestion that necessity is a sufficient basis for any presidential action. But both also reject Black's effort to restrict the President to express powers, suggesting both that the divide among powers is not as clear-cut in the Constitution as Black suggests and often will be affected by actual practice. Note though the difference even between Jackson and Frankfurter: while Jackson maintains that a "gap . . . exists between the President's paper powers and his real powers," Frankfurter argues that "historical gloss" over time may change the scope of the President's constitutional powers.

(4) ***Youngstown's Relevance for Administrative Law.*** The scope of presidential power to make law is not the main focus of presidential authority disputes in administrative law. Instead, questions here target the scope of presidential power to exercise control over the executive branch. In terms of Jackson's tripartite framework, administrative law cases generally concern whether Congress has authorized the President to exercise such control, whether the President has such control even though Congress has been silent, or whether the President may exercise such control even though Congress has tried to bar the president from doing so. In this third zone, the question is whether a statute violates the President's Article II authority and thus falls outside Congress's power to structure the executive branch under Article I's Necessary and Proper Clause. Note, however, that the President's Article II power may also be relevant to construing what Congress has done, as Congress is often less than express in addressing the extent to which the President may direct or supervise officials in the executive branch.

In this context, debates over inherent presidential authority surface as disputes over both what Congress has actually done and how to read Article II's Vesting and Take Care Clauses. Advocates of strong executive power read the Vesting Clause in particular as an express grant of all executive authority in the President—often called the "unitary executive" theory. The opposing view, following Jackson in Youngstown, rejects the claim that the Vesting Clause can be read so broadly. This debate has arisen in particular in the context of limits on the President's ability to remove executive officers and is discussed below in Section 3.b.2 (p. 979). But a variant of the debate arises outside the context of the power to remove in connection with the President's ability to countermand or direct an executive branch official's exercise of his or her duties, discussed below in Section 3.c. (p. 1037).

## b. Appointment and Removal



Our discussion of presidential and congressional efforts to control regulatory power by controlling agency personnel begins with appointment. The question of who appoints the officers of government provoked intense disagreement both during the Constitution's drafting and in the ratification debates. The Appointments Clause represents a rare textual reference to administration in the Constitution and over the centuries has spawned a steady if thin stream of litigation. The discussion next turns to the President's removal power, which appears nowhere in the Constitution's text; the only reference to removal of civil officers is in connection to impeachment, which solely involves the House and the Senate. The President's removal power was barely mentioned in the drafting and ratification debates, but it quickly became an issue once the hard work of building a government began. The first Congress struggled with the issue and the debate begun there continues to the present day.

### (1) Appointment and Confirmation



*. . . [The President] shall nominate, and by and with the Advice and Consent of the Senate, shall appoint Ambassadors, other public Ministers and Consuls, Judges of the supreme Court, and all other Officers of the United States, whose Appointments are not herein otherwise provided for, and which shall be established by Law: but the Congress may by Law vest the Appointment of such inferior Officers, as they think proper, in the President alone, in the Courts of Law, or in the Heads of Departments.*

U.S. Const., Art. II, § 2, cl. 2

*The President shall have Power to fill up all Vacancies that may happen during the Recess of the Senate, by granting Commissions which shall expire at the End of their next Session.*

U.S. Const., Art. II, § 2, cl. 3

*[The President] shall take Care that the Laws be faithfully executed . . .*

U.S. Const., Art. II, § 3

The Framers were baffled by how to allocate the power to appoint the officers of government. The history of oppression by officials appointed by the Crown and the colonial governors was still fresh in their memory—but so was the unhappy experience in the states with government dominated by the legislature. In early drafts of the Constitution the power was assigned to the Senate, which was seen as something of a middle ground between the popular legislature (the House) and the Executive. Some delegates became concerned, however, that the Senate would become "a real & dangerous Aristocracy." Jack Rakove, Original Meanings: Politics and Ideas in the Making of the Constitution 265 (1996). The final draft adopted an intricate power-sharing approach: "Officers of the United States" (now generally referred to as "principal" officers) would be appointed by the President with Senate advice and consent. As to "inferior Officers," Congress could by ordinary legislation determine whether appointment would be made by the President without Senate involvement, or by "Courts of Law" or "Heads of Departments." In addition, the President was given power to make temporary appointments "to fill up all vacancies that may happen during the recess of the Senate."

This solution was accepted by almost all the delegates as combining the "responsibility" of presidential nomination with the "security" of Senatorial advice and consent. Id. at 266. During the ratification debates, however, the anti-Federalists vehemently objected to what they foresaw as a monarchical President colluding with an aristocratic Senate to overwhelm the people's representatives in the House. Instead of elites against the masses, however, the factor that soon became the basis for Presidential-Senate "collusion"—and indeed came to dominate the constitutional separation of powers system more broadly—was political party. See Daryl J. Levinson & Richard H. Pildes, Separation of Parties, Not Powers, 119 Harv. L. Rev. 2311 (2006). As this Section details, partisan polarization has a tremendous impact on the appointments system today.

## UNITED STATES v. ARTHREX, INC.

Supreme Court of the United States (2021).
141 S.Ct. 1970.

■ CHIEF JUSTICE ROBERTS delivered the opinion of the Court with respect to Parts I and II.

[The Patent and Trademark Office (PTO), an executive agency within the Department of Commerce, is responsible for granting and issuing patents in the name of the United States. The PTO is headed by a Director, appointed by the President with the advice and consent of the Senate. A procedure called inter partes review provides a mechanism for obtaining review of whether a granted patent meets the statutory requirements for patentability. Any person can file a petition for inter partes review and the PTO Director can grant the petition only if, among other requirements, the Director determines that the challenge is likely to succeed on at least one claim. Inter partes review is conducted by a three-person panel made up of members of the Patent Trial and Appeal Board (PTAB). The PTAB consists of the PTO Director, the Deputy Director, the Commissioner for Patents, the Commissioner for Trademarks, and more than 200 Administrative Patent Judges (APJs) who enjoy for-cause removal protection. The Secretary of Commerce appoints all the members of the PTAB other than the Director. If inter partes review is granted, the Director designates at least three members of the PTAB to conduct the inter partes proceeding. A party who disagrees with the PTAB's decision can seek rehearing by the PTAB and judicial review in the Federal Circuit.

At issue in this case was the validity of Arthrex's patent on a surgical device for reattaching soft tissue to bone without tying a knot. Arthrex claimed two companies were infringing its patent. At the petition of the two companies, a PTAB panel consisting of three APJs concluded on inter partes review that the patent was invalid, and Arthrex appealed to the Federal Circuit. The Federal Circuit held that APJs were principal officers because neither the Secretary nor the Director had the authority to review their decisions or to remove them at will, and it made APJs removable at will by the Secretary to cure the violation.] . . .

II

A

. . . Today, thousands of officers wield executive power on behalf of the President in the name of the United States. That power acquires its legitimacy and accountability to the public through "a clear and effective chain of command" down from the President, on whom all the people vote. Free Enterprise Fund [v. Public Company Accounting Oversight Bd.], 561 U.S. [477], 498 (2010) [p. 1002]. . . .

The Appointments Clause provides:

> "[The President] shall nominate, and by and with the Advice and Consent of the Senate, shall appoint Ambassadors, other public Ministers and Consuls, Judges of the supreme Court, and

> all other Officers of the United States, whose Appointments are not herein otherwise provided for, and which shall be established by Law: but Congress may by Law vest the Appointment of such inferior Officers, as they think proper, in the President alone, in the Courts of Law, or in the Heads of Departments." Art. II, § 2, cl. 2.

Assigning the nomination power to the President guarantees accountability for the appointees' actions because the "blame of a bad nomination would fall upon the president singly and absolutely." The Federalist No. 77, p. 517 (J. Cooke ed. 1961) (A. Hamilton). As Hamilton wrote, the "sole and undivided responsibility of one man will naturally beget a livelier sense of duty and a more exact regard to reputation." Id., No. 76, at 510–511. The Appointments Clause adds a degree of accountability in the Senate, which shares in the public blame "for both the making of a bad appointment and the rejection of a good one." Edmond v. United States, 520 U.S. 651, 660 (1997) [p. 956].

Only the President, with the advice and consent of the Senate, can appoint noninferior officers, called "principal" officers as shorthand in our cases. See id., at 659. The "default manner of appointment" for inferior officers is also nomination by the President and confirmation by the Senate. Id., at 660. But the Framers foresaw that "when offices became numerous, and sudden removals necessary, this mode might be inconvenient." United States v. Germaine, 99 U.S. 508, 510 (1879). Reflecting this concern for "administrative convenience," the Appointments Clause permits Congress to dispense with joint appointment, but only for inferior officers. Edmond, 520 U.S., at 660. Congress may vest the appointment of such officers "in the President alone, in the Courts of Law, or in the Heads of Departments."

B

Congress provided that APJs would be appointed as inferior officers, by the Secretary of Commerce as head of a department. The question presented is whether the nature of their responsibilities is consistent with their method of appointment. As an initial matter, no party disputes that APJs are officers—not "lesser functionaries" such as employees or contractors—because they "exercis[e] significant authority pursuant to the laws of the United States." Buckley v. Valeo, 424 U.S. 1, 126, and n. 162 (1976) (per curiam) [p. 957]; see Lucia v. SEC, 138 S.Ct. 2044, 2052–2054 (2018) [p. 957]. APJs do so when reconsidering an issued patent, a power that (the Court has held) involves the adjudication of public rights that Congress may appropriately assign to executive officers rather than to the Judiciary. See Oil States [Energy Servs. v. Greene's Energy Group], LLC, 138 S.Ct. [1365], 1374–1375 [(2018)] [p. 1086].

The starting point for . . . analysis is our opinion in Edmond. There we explained that "[w]hether one is an 'inferior' officer depends on whether he has a superior" other than the President. 520 U.S., at 662. An inferior officer must be "directed and supervised at some level by others who were appointed by Presidential nomination with the advice and consent of the Senate." Id., at 663. In Edmond, we applied this test to adjudicative officials within the Executive Branch—specifically, Coast Guard Court of Criminal Appeals judges appointed by the Secretary of Transportation. We held that the judges were inferior officers because they were effectively supervised by a combination of Presidentially nominated and Senate confirmed officers in the Executive Branch: first, the Judge Advocate General, who "exercise[d] administrative oversight over the Court of Criminal Appeals" by prescribing rules of procedure and formulating policies for court-martial cases, and could also "remove a Court of Criminal Appeals judge from his judicial assignment without cause"; and second, the Court of Appeals for the Armed Forces, an executive tribunal that could review the judges' decisions under a de novo standard for legal issues and a deferential standard for factual issues. Id., at 664–665. "What is significant," we concluded, "is that the judges of the Court of Criminal Appeals have no power to render a final decision on behalf of the United States unless permitted to do so by other Executive officers." Id., at 665.

Edmond goes a long way toward resolving this dispute. What was "significant" to the outcome there—review by a superior executive officer—is absent here: APJs have the "power to render a final decision on behalf of the United States" without any such review by their nominal superior or any other principal officer in the Executive Branch. Id., at 665. The only possibility of review is a petition for rehearing, but Congress unambiguously specified that "[o]nly the Patent and Trial Appeal Board may grant rehearings." [35 U.S.C.] § 6(c). Such review simply repeats the arrangement challenged as unconstitutional in this suit. . . . The principal dissent's observation that "the Director alone has the power to take final action to cancel a patent claim or confirm it" simply ignores the undisputed fact that the Director's "power" in that regard is limited to carrying out the ministerial duty that he "shall issue and publish a certificate" canceling or confirming patent claims he had previously allowed, as dictated by the APJs' final decision. The chain of command runs not from the Director to his subordinates, but from the APJs to the Director.

The Government and [the companies] assemble a catalog of steps the Director might take to affect the decisionmaking process of the PTAB, despite his lack of any statutory authority to review its decisions. The Government reminds us that it is the Director who decides whether to initiate inter partes review. The Director can also designate the APJs who will decide a particular case and can pick ones predisposed to his views. And the Director, the Government asserts, can even vacate his institution decision if he catches wind of an unfavorable ruling on the way. If all else fails, the Government says, the Director can intervene in the rehearing process to reverse Board decisions. The Government acknowledges that only the PTAB can grant rehearing under § 6(c). But the Director, according to the Government, could manipulate the composition of the PTAB panel that acts on the rehearing petition. For one thing, he could "stack" the original panel to rehear the case with additional APJs assumed to be more amenable to his preferences. For another, he could assemble an entirely new panel consisting of himself and two other officers appointed by the Secretary . . . to decide whether to overturn a decision and reach a different outcome binding on future panels.

That is not the solution. It is the problem. The Government proposes (and the dissents embrace) a roadmap for the Director to evade a statutory prohibition on review without having him take responsibility for the ultimate decision. Even if the Director succeeds in procuring his preferred outcome, such machinations blur the lines of accountability demanded by the Appointments Clause. The parties are left with neither an impartial decision by a panel of experts nor a transparent decision for which a politically accountable officer must take responsibility. . . .

Review outside Article II—here, an appeal to the Federal Circuit—cannot provide the necessary supervision. While the duties of APJs "partake of a Judiciary quality as well as Executive," APJs are still exercising executive power and must remain "dependent upon the President." 1 Annals of Cong., at 611–612 (J. Madison). . . .

Given the insulation of PTAB decisions from any executive review, the President can neither oversee the PTAB himself nor "attribute the Board's failings to those whom he can oversee." Free Enterprise Fund, 561 U.S., at 496. APJs accordingly exercise power that conflicts with the design of the Appointments Clause "to preserve political accountability." Edmond, 520 U.S., at 663. . . . Conspicuously absent from the dissent is any concern for the President's ability to "discharge his own constitutional duty of seeing that the laws be faithfully executed." Myers v. United States, 272 U.S. 52, 135 (1926) [p. 982]. . . .

C

History reinforces the conclusion that the unreviewable executive power exercised by APJs is incompatible with their status as inferior officers. Since the founding, principal officers have directed the decisions of inferior officers on matters of law as well as policy. . . . Early congressional statutes expressly empowered department heads to supervise the work of their subordinates, sometimes by providing for an appeal in adjudicatory proceedings to a Presidentially nominated and Senate confirmed officer. This Court likewise indicated in early decisions that adequate supervision entails review of decisions issued by inferior officers. . . . Congress has carried the model of principal officer review into the modern administrative state. As the Government forthrightly acknowledged at oral argument, it "certainly is the norm" for principal officers to have the capacity to review decisions made by inferior adjudicative officers. The Administrative Procedure Act, from its inception, authorized agency heads to review such decisions. 5 U.S.C. § 557(b). . . .

The Government and [the companies] point to a handful of contemporary officers who are appointed by heads of departments but who nevertheless purportedly exercise final decisionmaking authority. . . . Perhaps the Civilian and Postal Boards of Contract Appeals are most similar to the PTAB. The Administrator of General Services and the Postmaster General appoint the members of the respective Boards, whose decisions are appealable to the Federal Circuit. Congress established both entities in 2006 and gave them jurisdiction over disputes involving public contractors. Whatever distinct issues that scheme might present, the Boards of Contract Appeals—both young entrants to the regulatory landscape—provide the PTAB no "foothold in history or tradition" across the Executive Branch. Seila Law [LLC v. Consumer Financial Protection Bureau], 140 S.Ct. [2183], 2202 [(2020)] [p. 988]. When it comes to the patent system in particular, adjudication has followed the traditional rule that a principal officer, if not the President himself, makes the final decision on how to exercise executive power.

* * *

We hold that the unreviewable authority wielded by APJs during inter partes review is incompatible with their appointment by the Secretary to an inferior office. The principal dissent repeatedly charges that we never say whether APJs are principal officers who were not appointed in the manner required by the Appointments Clause, or instead inferior officers exceeding the permissible scope of their duties under that Clause. But both formulations describe the same constitutional violation: Only an officer properly appointed to a principal office may issue a final decision binding the Executive Branch in the proceeding before us.

In reaching this conclusion, we do not attempt to "set forth an exclusive criterion for distinguishing between principal and inferior officers for Appointments Clause purposes." Edmond, 520 U.S., at 661. Many decisions by inferior officers do not bind the Executive Branch to exercise executive power in a particular manner, and we do not address supervision outside the context of adjudication. . . .

III

We turn now to the appropriate way to resolve this dispute given this violation of the Appointments Clause. In general, "when confronting a constitutional flaw in a statute, we try to limit the solution to the problem" by disregarding the "problematic portions while leaving the remainder intact." Ayotte v. Planned Parenthood of Northern New Eng., 546 U.S. 320, 328–329 (2006). . . . Arthrex asks us to hold the entire regime of inter partes review unconstitutional. In its view, any more tailored declaration of unconstitutionality would necessitate a policy decision best left to Congress in the first instance. . . . In our view, however, the structure of the PTO and the governing constitutional principles chart a clear course: Decisions by APJs must be subject to review by the Director. . . . In every respect save the insulation of their decisions from review within the Executive Branch, APJs appear to be inferior officers—an understanding consistent with their appointment in a manner permissible for inferior but not principal officers.

The America Invents Act insulates APJs from supervision through two mechanisms. The statute provides that "each . . . inter partes review shall be heard by at least 3 members of the [PTAB]" and that "only the [PTAB] may grant rehearings." § 6(c). . . . We conclude that a tailored approach is the appropriate one: Section 6(c) cannot constitutionally be enforced to the extent that its requirements prevent the Director from reviewing final decisions rendered by APJs. Because Congress has vested the Director with the "power and duties" of the PTO, § 3(a)(1), the Director has the authority to provide for a means of reviewing PTAB decisions. The Director accordingly may review final PTAB decisions and, upon review, may issue decisions himself on behalf of the Board. Section 6(c) otherwise remains operative as to the other members of the PTAB. . . .

The Government defends the different approach adopted by the Federal Circuit. The Court of Appeals held unenforceable APJs' protection against removal except "for such cause as will promote the efficiency of the service," 5 U.S.C. § 7513(a), which applies through 35 U.S.C. § 3(c). . . . But regardless whether the Government is correct that at-will removal by the Secretary would cure the constitutional problem, review by the Director better reflects the structure of supervision within the PTO and the nature of APJs' duties, for the reasons we have explained. . . .

We also conclude that the appropriate remedy is a remand to the Acting Director for him to decide whether to rehear the [inter partes review] petition. . . .

It is so ordered.

■ JUSTICE GORSUCH, concurring in part and dissenting in part.

[Justice Gorsuch restated his view from Oil States (p. 1086), that a patent was a vested property right that could only be invalidated by a court. But he concluded "it would be an even greater departure to permit those officials to withdraw a vested property right while accountable to no one within the Executive Branch" and accordingly joined Parts I and II of the Court's opinion. He disagreed with the Court's severability analysis, however, questioning the Court's approach to severability and arguing that the appropriate remedy was to simply set aside the PTAB decision in this case:]

. . . [T]he Court . . . has never paused to explain how [its] "severance doctrine" comports with traditional judicial remedial principles. . . . Or with the fact that the judicial power is limited to resolving discrete cases and controversies. Or with the framers' explicit rejection of allowing this Court to serve as a council of revision free to amend legislation. Let alone with our constant admonitions that policy choices belong to Congress, not this Court. . . . Nor does the Court pause to consider whether venturing further down this remedial path today risks undermining the very separation of powers its merits decision purports to vindicate. While the Court's merits analysis ensures that executive power properly resides in the Executive Branch, its severability analysis seemingly confers legislative power to the Judiciary. . . . [T]he Court has justified modern "severance" doctrine on assumptions and presumptions about what Congress would have chosen to do, had it known that its statutory scheme was unconstitutional. But any claim about "congressional intent" divorced from enacted statutory text is an appeal to mysticism. . . .

■ JUSTICE BREYER, with whom JUSTICE SOTOMAYOR and JUSTICE KAGAN join, concurring in the judgment in part and dissenting in part.

[Justice Breyer joined Parts I and II of Justice Thomas's dissent, but wrote separately to emphasize two points:] First, in my view, the Court should interpret the Appointments Clause as granting Congress a degree of leeway to establish and empower federal offices. Neither that Clause nor anything else in the Constitution describes the degree of control that a superior officer must exercise over the decisions of an inferior officer. To the contrary, the Constitution says only that "Congress may by Law vest the Appointment of such inferior Officers, as they think proper, . . . in the Heads of Departments." Art. II, § 2, cl. 2. The words "by Law . . . as they think proper" strongly suggest that Congress has considerable freedom to determine the nature of an inferior officer's job, and that courts ought to respect that judgment. . . . Second, I believe the Court, when deciding cases such as these, should conduct a functional examination of the offices and duties in question rather than a formalist, judicial-rules-based approach. In advocating for a "functional approach," I mean an approach that would take account of, and place weight on, why Congress enacted a particular statutory limitation. It would also consider the practical consequences that are likely to follow from Congress' chosen scheme. . . . I see the Court's decision as one part of a larger shift in our separation-of-powers jurisprudence [towards a more] . . . formal approach. . . . [I] believe[ ] that this shift toward formalism [i]s a mistake. . . . [Justice Breyer concurred in the Chief Justice's remedial approach, on the grounds that it remedied the specific problem the majority identified, that APJs' decisions were not reviewable by the Director.]

■ JUSTICE THOMAS, with whom JUSTICE BREYER, JUSTICE SOTOMAYOR, and JUSTICE KAGAN join as to Parts I and II, dissenting.

For the very first time, this Court holds that Congress violated the Constitution by vesting the appointment of a federal officer in the head of a department. Just who are these "principal" officers that Congress unsuccessfully sought to smuggle into the Executive Branch without Senate confirmation? About 250 administrative patent judges who sit at the bottom of an organizational chart, nestled under at least two levels of authority. Neither our precedent nor the original understanding of the Appointments Clause requires Senate confirmation of officers inferior to not one, but two officers below the President. . . .

II

A

. . . The Court has been careful not to create a rigid test to divide principal officers—those who must be Senate confirmed—from inferior ones. Instead, the Court's opinions have traditionally used a case-by-case analysis. And those analyses invariably result in this Court deferring to Congress' choice of which constitutional appointment process works best. . . .

Our most exhaustive treatment of the inferior-officer question is found in Edmond. . . . Recognizing that no "definitive test" existed for distinguishing between inferior and principal officers, the Court set out two general guidelines. 520 U.S., at 661–662. First, there is a formal, definitional requirement. The officer must be lower in rank to "a superior." Id., at 662. But according to the Court in Edmond, formal inferiority is "not enough." So the Court imposed a functional requirement: The inferior officer's work must be "directed and supervised at some level by others who were appointed by Presidential nomination with advice and consent of the Senate." Id., at 663. . . . I would apply this two-part guide.

There can be no dispute that administrative patent judges are, in fact, inferior: They are lower in rank to at least two different officers.[1] As a comparison to the facts in Edmond illustrates, the Director and Secretary are also functionally superior because they supervise and direct the work administrative patent judges perform. . . .

The Director here possesses even greater functional power over the Board than that possessed by the Judge Advocate General [over the Court of Criminal Appeals Judges in Edmond]. Like the Judge Advocate General, the Director exercises administrative oversight over the Board. Because the Board is within the Patent and Trademark Office, all of its powers and duties are ultimately held by the Director. He "direct[s]" and "supervis[es]" the Office and "the issuance of patents." [35 U.S.C. §] 3(a)(2)(A). He may even "fix the rate of basic pay for the administrative patent judges." § 3(b)(6). And ultimately, after the Board has reached a decision in a specific case, the Director alone has the power to take final action to cancel a patent claim or confirm it. § 318(b). Also like the Judge Advocate General in Edmond, the Director prescribes uniform procedural rules and formulates policies and procedures for Board proceedings. . . . He has designed a process to designate and de-designate Board decisions as precedential. He may issue binding policy directives that govern the Board. And he may release instructions that include exemplary applications of patent laws to fact patterns, which the Board can refer to when presented with factually similar cases. His oversight is not just administrative; it is substantive as well. § 3(a)(2)(A).

The Director has yet another "powerful tool for control." Edmond, 520 U.S., at 664. He may designate which of the 250-plus administrative patent judges hear certain cases and may remove administrative patent judges from their specific assignments without cause. See § 6(c). So, if any administrative patent judges depart from the Director's direction, he has ample power to rein them in to avoid erroneous decisions. And, if an

---

[1] [Ed.] Those officers are the Director and the Secretary of Commerce.

administrative patent judge consistently fails to follow instructions, the Secretary has the authority to fire him.

To be sure, the Director's power over administrative patent judges is not complete. He cannot singlehandedly reverse decisions. Still, he has two powerful checks on Board decisions not found in Edmond. Unlike the Judge Advocate General and CAAF in Edmond, the Director may influence individual proceedings. The Director decides in the first instance whether to institute, refuse to institute, or de-institute particular reviews, a decision that is "final and nonappealable." 35 U.S.C. § 314(d). If the Director institutes review, he then may select which administrative patent judges will hear the challenge. § 6(c). Alternatively, he can avoid assigning any administrative patent judge to a specific dispute and instead designate himself, his Deputy Director, and the Commissioner of Patents. In addition, the Director decides which of the thousands of decisions issued each year bind other panels as precedent. . . .

But, that is not all. If the administrative patent judges "(somehow) reach a result he does not like, the Director can add more members to the panel—including himself—and order the case reheard." Oil States Energy Services, LLC v. Greene's Energy Group, LLC, 138 S.Ct. 1365, 1381 (Gorsuch, J., dissenting). . . . This broad oversight ensures that administrative patent judges "have no power to render a final decision on behalf of the United States unless permitted to do so by other Executive officers." Edmond, 520 U.S., at 665.

B

The Court today appears largely to agree with all of this . . . [but] suggests . . . [a]ll that matters is whether the Director has the statutory authority to individually reverse Board decisions. The problem with that theory is that there is no precedential basis (or historical support) for boiling down "inferior-officer" status to the way Congress structured a particular agency's process for reviewing decisions. . . .

C

. . . Traditionally, the Court's task when resolving Appointments Clause challenges has been to discern whether the challenged official qualifies as a specific sort of officer and whether his appointment complies with the Constitution. If the official's appointment is inconsistent with the constitutional appointment process for the position he holds, then the Court provides a remedy. . . . Today's majority leaves that tried-and-true approach behind. It never expressly tells us whether administrative patent judges are inferior officers or principal. And the Court never tells us whether the appointment process complies with the Constitution. . . . If the appointment process for administrative patent judges—appointment by the Secretary—does not violate the Constitution, then administrative patent judges must be inferior officers. . . .

The majority's new Appointments Clause doctrine, though, has nothing to do with the validity of an officer's appointment. Instead, it polices the dispersion of executive power among officers. . . . [T]he Court finds that the constitutional problem here is that Congress has given a specific power—the authority to finally adjudicate inter partes review disputes—to one type of executive officer that the Constitution gives to another. . . . [But n]owhere does the Constitution acknowledge any such thing as "inferior-officer power" or "principal-officer power." And it certainly does not distinguish between these sorts of powers in the Appointments Clause. And even if it did, early patent dispute schemes establish that the power exercised by the administrative patent judges here does not belong exclusively to principal officers. Nonprincipal officers could—and did—render final decisions in specific patent disputes, not subject to any appeal to a superior executive officer. . . . More broadly, interpreting the Appointments Clause to bar any nonprincipal officer from taking "final" action poses serious line-drawing problems. . . .

III

[Justice Thomas also argued that] neither reading of the majority's opinion—(1) that administrative patent judges are principal officers that the Court has converted to inferior officers, or (2) that administrative patent judges are inferior officers whose decisions must constitutionally be reversible by the Director alone—supports its proposed remedy. . . . If the Court truly believed administrative patent judges are principal officers, then the Court would need to vacate the Board's decision. . . .

IV

Although unnecessary to resolve this suit, at some point it may be worth taking a closer look at whether the functional element of our test in Edmond . . . aligns with the text, history, and structure of the Constitution. The founding era history surrounding the Inferior Officer Clause points to at least three different definitions of an inferior officer, none of which requires a case-by-case functional examination of exactly how much supervision and control another officer has. . . .

## NOTES

(1) ***Was Arthrex Rightly Decided?*** Do you agree with the Court's conclusion that APJs, as Congress structured them, violated the Appointments Clause? Does the Director's lack of at-will removal power or authority to review specific decisions require that conclusion, even though the Director can control who sits on a panel, both originally and on rehearing, and determines whether the panel's decision is precedential? And if, as the Court held, APJs do not comport with the Constitution, what is the appropriate remedy?

(2) ***Arthrex's Import.*** Chief Justice Roberts flagged the Civilian and Postal Boards of Contract Appeals as potentially analogous—and therefore potentially unconstitutional under Arthrex. But he argued that other examples raised by the government, like the special trial judges in the Tax Court at issue in Freytag v. Commissioner, 501 U.S. 868 (1991) (p. 963), immigration judges in the Executive Office for Immigration Review, or the

judges on the Board of Veterans' Appeals, were distinguishable, because those examples "involve inferior officers whose decisions a superior executive officer can review or implement a system for review." Does this discussion suggest that Arthrex only applies when a statute precludes a principal officer from reviewing inferior officer decisions, and not in instances where a principal officer has made an inferior officer's determinations final by regulation, given that such a regulation could be changed? Note that such an approach is similar to the position taken in In re Grand Jury Investigation, 916 F.3d 1047, 1052 (D.C. Cir. 2019). There, the D.C. Circuit held that Special Counsel Robert Mueller was an inferior officer because the Attorney General could at any time rescind regulations limiting oversight of the Special Counsel and eliminate good cause removal protections, so the Special Counsel "effectively serve[d] at the pleasure of an Executive Branch officer who was appointed with the advice and consent of the Senate." Do you think it would affect the analysis if the regulation at issue required notice and comment rulemaking to be changed?

(3) ***Arthrex on Remand.*** On remand, Arthrex requested rehearing by the Director, but the office of the Director was vacant, as was the office of the Deputy Director. Under a standing directive, Agency Organization Order 45-1, that meant that responsibility for addressing Arthrex's request fell to the Commissioner for Patents, who is not a presidentially appointed, Senate-confirmed officer. When the Commissioner denied the rehearing request, Arthrex sued, challenging the Commissioner's exercise of the Director's authority to rehear petitions as unconstitutional and arguing it had been denied the remedy of review by a properly appointed principal officer that the Supreme Court ordered. As discussed below (p. 974), the Federal Circuit rejected Arthrex's challenge and upheld the Commissioner's determination, emphasizing that "[a]lthough an inferior officer generally cannot issue a final agency decision, he may perform the functions and duties of an absent [principal] officer on a temporary, acting basis." Arthrex, Inc. v. Smith & Nephew, Inc., 35 F.4th 1328 (Fed. Cir. 2022).

## NOTES ON THE STRUCTURE AND REACH OF THE APPOINTMENTS CLAUSE

(1) ***The Constitutional Norm for Appointments.*** As the text of the Appointments Clause makes clear, the primary method for appointment of principal officers is presidential nomination and Senate confirmation. According to the Supreme Court in NLRB v. NOEL CANNING, 573 U.S. 513, 523 (2015) (p. 966), a case involving the Recess Appointments Clause, "[t]he Federalist Papers make clear that the Founders intended this method of appointment, requiring Senate approval, to be the norm (at least for principal officers). Alexander Hamilton wrote that the Constitution vests the power of nomination in the President alone because 'one man of discernment is better fitted to analise and estimate the peculiar qualities adapted to particular offices, than a body of men of equal, or perhaps even of superior discernment.' The Federalist No. 76, p. 510 (J. Cooke ed. 1961). At the same time, the need to secure Senate approval provides 'an excellent check upon a spirit of favoritism in the President, and would tend greatly to preventing

the appointment of unfit characters from State prejudice, from family connection, from personal attachment, or from a view to popularity.' Id., at 513."

For inferior officers, the Constitution is more flexible, allowing appointment by the President (without requiring Senate confirmation), department heads, or courts. However, presidential nomination and Senate confirmation remains the default method of appointment; Congress must affirmatively exercise, "by law," its power to exempt officers from confirmation by assigning their appointment to one of the other allowed methods. Congress has chosen to retain confirmation for a large number of executive offices, often expressly stating this in the relevant statutes. According to the 2020 "Plum Book," issued by the House Committee on Oversight and Reform, there are over 1,100 agency positions requiring both presidential nomination and Senate confirmation.

(2) ***"Principal" Versus "Inferior" Officers.*** The distinction between principal officers and inferior officers is obviously crucial to the Appointments Clause's careful calibration of congressional and presidential power. In drawing the distinction between the two in Arthrex, the Court relied heavily on its earlier decision in EDMOND V. UNITED STATES, 520 U.S. 651 (1997). There, as noted in Arthrex, the Court in an opinion by JUSTICE SCALIA emphasized the importance of supervision in concluding that members of the Coast Guard Court of Criminal Appeals were inferior officers: "Generally speaking, the term 'inferior officer' connotes a relationship with some higher ranking officer or officers below the President: whether one is an 'inferior' officer depends on whether he has a superior. It is not enough that other officers may be identified who formally maintain a higher rank, or possess responsibilities of a greater magnitude. If that were the intention, the Constitution might have used the phrase 'lesser officer.' Rather, in the context of a clause designed to preserve political accountability relative to important government assignments, we think it evident that 'inferior officers' are officers whose work is directed and supervised at some level by others who were appointed by presidential nomination with the advice and consent of the Senate."

In emphasizing the factor of supervision, the Edmond Court distinguished MORRISON V. OLSON, 487 U.S. 654 (1988) (p. 986), in which the Court, in a 7–1 opinion written by CHIEF JUSTICE REHNQUIST, had concluded that independent counsels under the Ethics in Government Act of 1978 were inferior officers. In Morrison, the Court had stated that "[t]he line between 'inferior' and 'principal' officers is one that is far from clear, and the Framers provided little guidance into where it should be drawn." Eschewing the need to specify such a line to determine the status of independent counsels, the Court held that "[s]everal factors lead to th[e] conclusion" that independent counsels were inferior officers: "First, [the independent counsel] is subject to removal by a higher Executive Branch official. Although she possesses a degree of independent discretion to exercise the powers delegated to her under the Act, the fact that she can be removed by the Attorney General indicates that she is to some degree "inferior" in rank and authority. Second, appellant is empowered by the Act to perform only certain, limited duties.

An independent counsel's role is restricted primarily to investigation and, if appropriate, prosecution for certain federal crimes. . . . The Act specifically provides that in policy matters appellant is to comply to the extent possible with the policies of the Department. Third, appellant's office is limited in jurisdiction. Not only is the Act itself restricted in applicability to certain federal officials suspected of certain serious federal crimes, but an independent counsel can only act within the scope of the jurisdiction that has been granted by the Special Division pursuant to a request by the Attorney General. Finally, appellant's office is limited in tenure."

Edmond acknowledged that the Coast Guard judges were not limited in tenure or jurisdiction but distinguished Morrison on the grounds that "Morrison did not purport to set forth a definitive test for whether an office is 'inferior' under the Appointments Clause." Are you persuaded that the two cases are compatible? Doesn't Edmond give us the type of definitive test that Morrison eschewed in favor of a multifactor analysis? Which approach do you think is more appropriate? Is it particularly important to give Congress a clear line against which to legislate here? Or does a multifactor test better accommodate the Appointments Clause's goals of ensuring sufficient Senate role in appointments without unduly impeding the government's ability to function? A more recent decision, Free Enterprise Foundation v. Public Company Accounting Oversight Board, 561 U.S. 477 (2010) (p. 1002), involved the claim that members of the Board were improperly appointed principal officers and were unconstitutionally protected against removal from office. After agreeing that the removal protection of the Board members was unconstitutional and severing it, the Court rejected the challenge to their appointment. Invoking Edmond, the Court stated that because members of the Board were now removable at will and subject to other oversight by the Commission, "we have no hesitation in concluding that under Edmond the Board members are inferior officers."

(3) ***"Officers" Versus "Employees."*** The Court has long acknowledged that the categories of principal officer and inferior officer do not encompass the entire federal workforce. The vast majority of federal workers fall into a third category—"employees." BUCKLEY V. VALEO, 424 U.S. 1 (1976), addressed the line between officers, who must be appointed in accordance with the Appointments Clause, and employees, whose appointment process is left for Congress to specify under its Necessary and Proper Clause power: Officers are "any appointee exercising significant authority pursuant to the laws of the United States"; employees are "lesser functionaries subordinate to officers of the United States." (Note the reappearance of subordinateness. Does this portend further problems for Justice Scalia's criterion for distinguishing inferior from principal officers?) Exercising significant authority continues to be the hallmark of an inferior officer, but what counts as significant authority?

The Court had a chance to shed light on that question in LUCIA V. SEC, 138 S.Ct. 2044 (2018), which addressed whether administrative law judges at the Securities and Exchange Commission were inferior officers. JUSTICE KAGAN wrote the majority opinion holding that the SEC ALJs were inferior officers and that their appointment by the Chief ALJ and not the SEC itself (the relevant "head of department") violated the Appointments Clause: "Two decisions set out this Court's basic framework for distinguishing between officers and employees. [United States v.] Germaine[, 99 U.S. 508 (1878),] held that 'civil surgeons' (doctors hired to perform various physical exams) were mere employees because their duties were 'occasional or temporary' rather than 'continuing and permanent.' . . . [T]he Court there made clear that an individual must occupy a 'continuing' position established by law to qualify as an officer. Buckley then set out another requirement, central to this case. It determined that members of a federal commission were officers only after finding that they 'exercis[ed] significant authority pursuant to the laws of the United States.' 424 U.S., at 126. . . .

"Both the amicus and the Government urge us to elaborate on Buckley's 'significant authority' test, but another of our precedents makes that project unnecessary. . . . [I]n Freytag v. Commissioner, 501 U.S. 868 (1991) [p.963], we applied the unadorned 'significant authority' test to adjudicative officials who are near-carbon copies of the Commission's ALJs. . . . [O]ur analysis there . . . necessarily decides this case. The officials at issue in Freytag were the 'special trial judges' (STJs) of the United States Tax Court. The authority of those judges depended on the significance of the tax dispute before them. In 'comparatively narrow and minor matters,' they could both hear and definitively resolve a case for the Tax Court. In more major matters, they could preside over the hearing, but could not issue the final decision; instead, they were to 'prepare proposed findings and an opinion' for a regular Tax Court judge to consider. This Court held that the Tax Court's STJs are officers, not mere employees. . . . They serve on an ongoing [basis, with their duties and terms of appointment] . . . all specified in the Tax Code. . . . Describing the responsibilities involved in presiding over adversarial hearings, the Court said: STJs 'take testimony, conduct trials, rule on the admissibility of evidence, and have the power to enforce compliance with discovery orders.' And the Court observed that '[i]n the course of carrying out these important functions, the [STJs] exercise significant discretion.' That fact meant they were officers, even when their decisions were not final. . . .

" . . . [T]he Commission's ALJs, like the Tax Court's STJs, hold a continuing office established by law. Still more, the Commission's ALJs exercise the same significant discretion when carrying out the same important functions as STJs do. Both sets of officials have all the authority needed to ensure fair and orderly adversarial hearings—indeed, nearly all the tools of federal trial judges. . . . First, the Commission's ALJs (like the Tax Court's STJs) take testimony[,] . . . they '[r]eceiv[e] evidence' and '[e]xamine witnesses' at hearings, and may also take pre-hearing depositions [citing governing regulations]. Second, the ALJs conduct trials[,] . . . they administer oaths, rule on motions, and generally 'regulat[e] the course of' a hearing, as well as the conduct of parties and counsel. Third, the ALJs (like STJs) rule on the admissibility of evidence [and] . . . thus critically shape the administrative record. . . . And fourth, the ALJs (like STJs) 'have the power to enforce compliance with discovery orders' [and] may punish all '[c]ontemptuous conduct,' including violations of those orders, by means as severe as excluding the offender from the hearing. So point for point—

straight from Freytag's list—the Commission's ALJs have equivalent duties and powers as STJs in conducting adversarial inquiries.

"And at the close of those proceedings, ALJs issue decisions much like that in Freytag—except with potentially more independent effect. . . . [T]he SEC can decide against reviewing an ALJ decision at all. And when the SEC declines review (and issues an order saying so), the ALJ's decision itself 'becomes final' and is 'deemed the action of the Commission.' That last-word capacity makes this an a fortiori case: If the Tax Court's STJs are officers, as Freytag held, then the Commission's ALJs must be too."

The Court remanded Lucia's case for a hearing before a different—and properly appointed—ALJ or before the Commission itself, arguing that such relief was necessary "[t]o cure the constitutional violation" and "create incentive[s] to raise Appointments Clause challenges." Noting that "[w]hile this case was on judicial review, the SEC issued an order 'ratif[ying]' the prior appointments of its ALJs," Justice Kagan stated that the Court saw no reason to address whether such ratification would be valid at this point, as the Commission might not remand Lucia's case "to an ALJ whose claim to authority rests on the ratification order."

A striking aspect of Lucia was the government's change in position in the case. The government had argued ALJs were employees before the lower courts, but switched its position with the advent of the Trump Administration. Indeed, the Solicitor General urged the Court not just to grant review in Lucia and hold that ALJs were unconstitutionally appointed, but also to take up the question of whether the removal protection for ALJs was then an unconstitutional form of double-for-cause removal protection of the type the Court had invalidated in Free Enterprise Fund v. PCAOB. (p. 1002). After the Court did not grant certiorari on this additional question, the Solicitor General proceeded to brief it anyway. The majority was unmoved: "When we granted certiorari, we chose not to take that step. The Government's merits brief now asks us again to address the removal issue. We once more decline."

The case sparked several concurrences and dissents. JUSTICE THOMAS, joined by Justice Gorsuch, concurred in full, agreeing that the case was "indistinguishable" from Freytag but arguing that "our precedents in this area do not provide much guidance . . . [and] have never clearly defined what is *necessary*" for an official to be an officer. Justice Thomas "would resolve that question based on the original public meaning of 'Officers of the United States.'" According to Justice Thomas, "[t]he Founders likely understood th[is] term . . . to encompass all federal civil officials who perform an ongoing, statutory duty—no matter how important or significant a duty." The majority's express reaffirmance of Buckley's restriction of officers to those exercising significant authority appears a clear rejection of Thomas's suggested approach.

JUSTICE SOTOMAYOR similarly complained about the need for more guidance on the line between officers and employees in her dissent, joined by Justice Ginsburg, arguing that the resultant "confusion can undermine the reliability and finality of proceedings and result in wasted resources." While acknowledging the criterion of continuous office was "relatively easy to grasp," Sotomayor argued that was less true of significant authority: "To be sure, to exercise 'significant authority,' the person must wield considerable powers in comparison to the average person who works for the Federal Government. As this Court has noted, the vast majority of those who work for the Federal Government are not 'Officers of the United States.' . . . But this Court's decisions have yet to articulate the types of powers that will be deemed significant enough to constitute 'significant authority.' To provide guidance to Congress and the Executive Branch, I would hold that one requisite component of 'significant authority' is the ability to make final, binding decisions on behalf of the Government. Accordingly, a person who merely advises and provides recommendations to an officer would not herself qualify as an officer." Acknowledging that SEC ALJs "wield 'extensive powers,'" Sotomayor argued that they were "not officers because they lack final decisionmaking authority. As the Commission explained below, the Commission retains 'plenary authority over the course of [its] administrative proceedings and the rulings of [its] law judges.'"

JUSTICE BREYER, concurring in the judgment in part and dissenting in part, agreed that the SEC's ALJs were improperly appointed, but reached that conclusion on statutory grounds. He argued that the APA required the agency itself to appoint ALJs and that no provision of the APA or another statute allowed the agency to delegate ALJ appointment to the agency's staff. Breyer also emphasized the strong removal protections that the APA grants ALJs, describing the "substantial independence" that the APA thereby provides as "a central part of the Act's overall scheme." Turning to the question of ALJs' constitutional status, Breyer insisted, as he did in Arthrex, that "Congress' intent . . . matters" here as well, "because the Appointments Clause is properly understood to grant Congress a degree of leeway as to whether particular Government workers are officers or instead mere employees not subject to the Appointments Clause." Justice Breyer further insisted that, given the importance of congressional intentions, the Court should not reach the question of the SEC ALJs' constitutional status "without first deciding the pre-existing Free Enterprise Fund question—namely, what effect that holding would have on the statutory 'for cause' removal protections that Congress provided for administrative law judges. If . . . Free Enterprise Fund means that saying administrative law judges are 'inferior Officers' will cause them to lose their 'for cause' removal protections, then I would likely hold that the administrative law judges are not 'Officers,' for to say otherwise would be to contradict Congress' enactment of those protections in the [APA]." He also disagreed with the majority's insistence that the case be remanded to a different ALJ.

Are the concurrences' complaints about lack of guidance in the majority opinion a fair critique? Does the decision offer much insight on the officer or employee status of government officials not performing adjudicatory functions? Even for those who do perform adjudicatory functions, are its implications clear? As noted in Chapter V, ALJs make up only a small part of a broad and variegated administrative judiciary, whose members are charged with a range of responsibilities and given very differing degrees of independence. What if an agency by regulation clearly specifies that the administrative judge's decisions are purely recommendary and that it retains full power to deviate from the judge's determinations on evidence, the record, sanctions, and result; is such an administrative judge an inferior officer under Lucia?

What do you think of Justice Thomas's definition of an officer as any federal official performing an ongoing statutory duty, regardless of the significance of that duty? In developing this argument, Justice Thomas relied heavily on an article by Jennifer L. Mascott, Who Are "Officers of the United States"?, 70 Stan. L. Rev. 443 (2018), which provides a detailed exploration of the original public meaning of officers. Such an approach could dramatically expand who counts as an officer, as many federal employees perform statutory duties. Should that matter? On the other hand, Justice Thomas takes a narrow view of who counts as a principal officer, concluding in United States v. Arthrex (p. 945) that administrative patent judges were inferior officers because they were "lower in rank" to two principal officers, one of whom also functionally supervised their work even if she lacked authority to directly review their decisions on inter partes review of granted patents. Do you find this approach—taking a capacious view of who qualifies as an officer, but a narrow view of who qualifies as a principal officer—analytically appealing? Why?

Finally, what about Breyer's argument that the status of a government official as an officer or employee should turn largely on congressional intent: Does the text of the Appointments Clause, perhaps particularly if viewed in conjunction with the Necessary and Proper Clause, support that view?

The result in Lucia created a question about the status of current ALJs not appointed by the heads of their department and about the appointment of ALJs in the future. In response President Trump issued an Executive Order exempting ALJs from the civil service and authorizing their selection instead by agency heads. Exec. Order No. 13843, 83 Fed. Reg. 32755 (July 10, 2018). President Biden reaffirmed ALJs' excepted status. Exec. Order No. 14029, 86 Fed. Reg. 26633 (2021). Although the Trump Executive Order also states that civil service laws and regulations on removal will not apply, it adds "except as required by statute." Id. The removal protections for ALJs are statutorily based, and thus their removal protection is not currently threatened. If, however, this removal protection were held a form of unconstitutional double-for-cause removal protection, ALJs would become immediately removable at will under the Executive Order. For discussion of whether the current removal protection for ALJs is unconstitutional, see p. 1018.

(4) ***"Employees" Versus "Contractors."*** Just as in private law, it is sometimes unclear whether an individual performing services is a government employee or an independent contractor. UNITED STATES V. HARTWELL, 73 U.S. (6 Wall.) 385 (1868), identified "ideas of tenure, duration, emolument, and duties" as central to the distinction. "A government office is different from a government contract. The latter from its nature is necessarily limited in its duration and specific in its objects. The terms agreed upon define the rights and obligations of both parties, and neither

may depart from them without the assent of the other." Id. at 393. The difference was further elaborated in United States v. Germaine, 99 U.S. 508 (1879). The Court held that a surgeon appointed by the Commissioner of Pensions to examine pension applicants was not a federal officer. His duties were "occasional and intermittent," and "*not* continuing and permanent"; he "only . . . act[ed] when called on by the Commissioner . . . in some special case," was paid only a fee per examination, took no oath, posted no bond, and was not required to keep a "place of business for public use."

An influential separation of powers opinion from the Clinton Administration Office of Legal Counsel concluded that "[t]he Appointments Clause is simply not implicated when significant authority is devolved upon non-federal actors." The Constitutional Separation of Powers Between the President and Congress, 20 Op. O.L.C. 124 (1996) (commonly known as the Dellinger Memo, after the late Walter Dellinger who was the Assistant Attorney General leading OLC at the time). Is it troubling that individuals exercising "significant authority" on behalf of the United States are not within the constitutional appointments structure? Note that the Supreme Court cases establishing this principle long predate the expanding federal practice of privatizing functions that are conventionally considered governmental.

Concurring in DEPARTMENT OF TRANSPORTATION V. ASS'N OF AMERICAN RAILROADS, 575 U.S. 43 (2015) (p. 851), Justice Alito raised questions about the status of arbitrators in disputes involving the government. The governing regulatory scheme called for the Surface Transportation Board (a federal agency) to appoint an arbitrator to resolve disputes between the Federal Railroad Administration (another federal agency) and Amtrak (a government corporation deemed part of government for constitutional purposes) over the "metrics and standards" that would govern Amtrak's performance. According to Justice Alito, if the arbitrator were private, his or her ability to exercise binding regulatory authority would represent an unconstitutional private delegation of governmental power. On the other hand, if the arbitrator were public, Justice Alito contended that the ability to exercise binding authority would make the arbitrator a principal officer under Edmond, and thus the arbitrator's appointment by the Surface Transportation Board, rather than by the President with Senate advice and consent, would be unconstitutional. The Supreme Court remanded to the D.C. Circuit to consider this among other issues, and that court agreed with Justice Alito that an arbitrator appointed under the statute was a principal officer and that the statute violated the Appointments Clause. 821 F.3d 19, 38–39 (2016). The government decided not to seek certiorari. For a contrary view, see Office of Legal Counsel, Constitutional Limitations on Federal Government Participation in Binding Arbitration, 19 Op. O.L.C. 208, 216–19 (1995) (arbitrators not appointed via the Appointments Clause can be used for binding arbitration involving the federal government because, while they do exercise "significant authority," they "are retained for a single matter, their service expires at the resolution of that matter, and they fix their own compensation" and thus do "not bear the hallmarks of a constitutional office—tenure, duration, emoluments, and continuing duties").[2]

(5) ***International Tribunals and Non-Federal Entities Implementing Federal Law.*** Similar to private officials or contractors are members of international tribunals and nonfederal entities. These individuals can exercise significant authority by virtue of their roles in federal regulation and programs or in applying U.S. law. But is the authority they wield federal authority? And are their positions federal offices? Following OLC's view and that of the Clinton Administration, "the Ninth Circuit ruled that state officials on the Pacific Northwest Electric Power Conservation Planning Council (an organization formed by an interstate compact) are not officers, regardless of whether they exercise federal power." Anne Joseph O'Connell, Bureaucracy at the Boundary, 162 U. Pa. L. Rev. 841, 903 (2014). But others disagree, arguing that appointed individuals exercising significant federal authority should count as officers under Buckley. See, e.g., John C. Yoo, The New Sovereignty and the Old Constitution: The Chemical Weapons Convention and the Appointments Clause, 15 Const. Comment. 87 (1998).

A source of recent Appointments Clause controversy on this front involves international tribunals such as the International Court of Justice or the North American Free Trade Agreement (NAFTA) dispute settlement process overseen by the NAFTA Secretariat. These tribunals are attacked on the grounds, inter alia, that "international delegations with direct domestic effect permit international agents to change the rights of U.S. citizens under domestic law. But only individuals appointed under the Appointments Clause can exercise such authority under U.S. law," and members of the tribunals were not appointed in accordance with the Clause. John O. McGinnis, Medellin and the Future of International Delegation, 118 Yale L.J. 1712, 1738 (2009). See also David Zaring, Sovereignty Mismatch and the New Administrative Law, 91 Wash. U. L. Rev. 59, 87–89 (2013).

(6) ***Who Can Appoint: "Heads" of "Departments" and "Courts of Law."*** In FREYTAG V. COMMISSIONER OF INTERNAL REVENUE, 501 U.S. 868 (1991), the question was whether the Tax Court (a legislative, Article I court[3]) qualifies as a "department" or a "court of law," so that special trial judges (who function much like ALJs) could be appointed by the chief judge of the court. As mentioned in Note 2, all the Justices agreed that special trial judges are inferior officers; all also agreed that the chief judge could be given the power of appointment, but they sharply divided over the reason. Writing for the 5–4 majority, JUSTICE BLACKMUN reviewed the history of the Appointments Clause to conclude that "[t]he term 'Department' refers only to a part or division of the executive government, as the Department of State, or of the Treasury, expressly created and given the name of a department by Congress." This interpretation was necessary to avoid "excessively diffusing" the power of appointment, with a corresponding loss of accountability.

[2] https://www.justice.gov/sites/default/files/olc/opinions/1995/09/31/op-olc-v019-p0208_0.pdf.

[3] As discussed below in Section 4, a legislative court is one whose judges do not have the requisite life tenure and protection against salary diminution required in those who exercise the Article III judicial power. Tax Court judges, for example, are appointed for a 15-year term.

"Confining the term 'Heads of Departments' in the Appointments Clause to executive divisions like the Cabinet-level departments constrains the distribution of the appointment power." He went on to conclude, however, that the Tax Court is a "Court of Law" for appointments purposes. Writing for the remaining four justices, JUSTICE SCALIA insisted that "Courts of Law" refers to only Article III courts. On the other hand, "Department" should be understood as comprising any "freestanding, self-contained entity in the Executive Branch, whose [head] is removable by the President (and, save impeachment, no one else)."

Freytag's narrow definition of "Department" created considerable problems for common administrative structures: neither the independent agencies nor a number of freestanding executive agencies (including the CIA, the Federal Reserve Board, and EPA, which Congress deliberately refused to give Cabinet department status) appeared to meet the definition. FREE ENTERPRISE FOUNDATION V. PUBLIC COMPANY ACCOUNTING BOARD, 561 U.S. 477, 510–11 (2010) (p. 1002), finally put the issue largely to rest, holding that the SEC, an independent agency, "constitutes a "Departmen[t]" for the purposes of the Appointments Clause" because it "is a freestanding component of the Executive Branch, not subordinate to or contained within any other such component," adding:

"In Freytag, we specifically reserved the question whether a principal agency, such as . . . the Securities and Exchange Commission, is a Department under the Appointments Clause. Four Justices, however, would have concluded that the Commission is indeed such a Department, . . . because it is a free-standing, self-contained entity in the Executive Branch. . . . Respondents urge us to adopt this reasoning . . . and we do. Respondents' reading of the Appointments Clause is consistent with the common, near-contemporary definition of a 'department' as a 'separate allotment or part of business; a distinct province, in which a class of duties are allotted to a particular person.' 1 N. Webster, American Dictionary of the English Language *3163 (1828) (def.2) (1995 facsimile ed.). It is also consistent with the early practice of Congress."

As a sign of Free Enterprise's impact, the D.C. Circuit relied on it to conclude that "the Library of Congress is a freestanding entity that clearly meets the definition of 'Department.' To be sure, it performs a range of different functions, including some, such as the Congressional Research Service, that are exercised primarily for legislative purposes. But as we have mentioned, the Librarian is appointed by the President with advice and consent of the Senate, . . . and is subject to unrestricted removal by the President. . . . Further, the powers in the Library and the Board to promulgate copyright regulations, to apply the statute to affected parties, and to set rates and terms case by case are ones generally associated in modern times with executive agencies rather than legislators. In this role the Library is undoubtedly a 'component of the Executive Branch.'" Intercollegiate Broad. Sys., Inc. v. Copyright Royalty Bd., 684 F.3d 1332, 1341–42 (D.C. Cir. 2012). Can an agency be an executive department under the Appointments Clause for some functions and not others?

Note that Free Enterprise also quickly dispensed with the further claim that even if the SEC were a "Department," the SEC Chair alone had to be its "Head" for Appointments Clause purposes: "As a constitutional matter, we see no reason why a multimember body may not be the Head of a Department that it governs. The Appointments Clause necessarily contemplates collective appointments by the Courts of Law, and each House of Congress, too, appoints its officers collectively. Petitioners argue that the Framers vested the nomination of principal officers in the President to avoid the perceived evils of collective appointments, but they reveal no similar concern with respect to inferior officers, whose appointments may be vested elsewhere, including in multimember bodies. Practice has also sanctioned the appointment of inferior officers by multimember agencies."

(7) ***Who Can Appoint: No Direct Congressional Involvement.*** BUCKLEY V. VALEO, 424 U.S. 1 (1976) (p. 957): The Federal Election Act of 1971 attempted campaign finance reform by imposing various limitations on contributions and spending, to be overseen by a new eight-member agency, the Federal Election Commission. The extraordinary political sensitivity of this regulatory program was reflected in the equally extraordinary provisions for the FEC's selection: two members appointed by the President pro tempore of the Senate, two by the Speaker of the House, and two by the President (all subject to confirmation by *both* Houses of Congress), with the Secretary of the Senate and the Clerk of the House to be ex officio nonvoting members. All three appointing authorities were forbidden to choose both of their appointees from the same political party.

The case produced multiple conflicting opinions on the First Amendment implications of the contribution and spending limits, but no Justice thought that the Act's appointment scheme could be sustained. Even Justice White, predictably the most sympathetic to innovative institutional solutions in regulatory programs, found it an easy case: "I . . . find singularly unpersuasive the proposition that because the FEC is implementing statutory policies with respect to the conduct of elections . . . its members may be appointed by Congress. . . . Congress clearly has the power to create federal offices and to define the powers and duties of those offices, Myers v. United States, 272 U.S. 52, 128–129 (1926) [p. 982], but no case in this Court even remotely supports the power of Congress to appoint an officer of the United States aside from those officers each House is authorized by Art. I to appoint to assist in the legislative processes." To similar effect is Hechinger v. Metropolitan Washington Airports Auth., 36 F.3d 97 (D.C. Cir. 1994), the second round of controversy over congressional involvement in the newly created Metropolitan Washington Airports Authority. Forbidden to place its own Members on the statutorily-created Board of Review for the Authority (p. 932), Congress tried requiring that the Board consist of nine individuals who travel frequently, have experience in aviation, are registered as voters outside D.C., Maryland, or Virginia, and are included in lists of candidates supplied to the Commission by House and Senate leaders. The D.C. Circuit struck down the new arrangement, and the Supreme Court refused to consider the matter again.

## SIGNIFICANT CASE

### NATIONAL LABOR RELATIONS BOARD v. NOEL CANNING
573 U.S. 513 (2015).

In 2011, President Obama nominated three members to serve on the National Labor Relations Board. On January 4, 2012, when one nomination had been awaiting confirmation in the Senate for approximately a year and the other two nominations had been pending for a few weeks, the President appointed all three to the Board, invoking the Recess Appointments Clause. That Clause gives the President alone the power "to fill up all Vacancies that may happen during the Recess of the Senate, by granting Commissions which shall expire at the End of their next Session." Art. II, § 2, cl. 3.

At the time of the appointments, the Senate was operating under a resolution, adopted by unanimous consent, providing that the Senate would be gaveled in for pro forma sessions—sessions that last only a few minutes in which no business is transacted—on every Tuesday and Friday from December 20, 2011, through January 20, 2012. The President made the recess appointments when the Senate was on a three day adjournment between its pro forma sessions on January 3, 2012 and January 6, 2012. When the NLRB subsequently ordered Noel Canning to execute a collective bargaining with a labor union, the company sought to have the Board's order set aside on the basis that these three members of the NLRB were invalidly appointed, leaving the Board without the minimum quorum it needed to act. The D.C. Circuit agreed that the appointments fell outside of the Recess Appointments Clause, but based that determination on other grounds. It held that "the recess of the Senate" applies only to recesses between formal sessions, or inter-session recesses, and does not include recesses that occur within a formal session of Congress, or intra-session recesses, the type of recess claimed to exist here. It further held that, in any event, "vacancies that may happen during the recess" applies only to vacancies that come into existence during a recess, whereas the NLRB vacancies that were filled here had all arisen before the beginning of the recess during which they were appointed.

The Court, by a 5–4 vote, held that the Recess Appointments Clause applies to an intra-session recess and to vacancies that arose before the recess began, but unanimously concluded the Clause did not apply to the appointments at issue because the Senate was not in recess. JUSTICE BREYER began his majority opinion by underscoring two points noted above: First, that recess appointments represent a subsidiary appointment mechanism and the primary method of appointment is presidential nomination with Senate confirmation (p. 955); and second, that in analyzing the allocation of power between two elected branches of Government the Court puts "significant weight upon historical practice" (p. 832). Noting that "Presidents have made recess appointments since the beginning of the Republic," Breyer cautioned that when interpreting the Clause "for the first time in more than 200 years, we must hesitate to upset the compromises and working arrangements that the elected branches of Government themselves have reached." The opinion then proceeded to address the three questions about the Recess Appointments Clause that had been raised in the case.

Addressing whether the phrase "recess of the Senate" includes an intra-session as well as inter-session recess, the majority opinion noted that the Clause's "words taken literally can refer to both types of recess. Founding-era dictionaries define the word 'recess,' much as we do today, simply as 'a period of cessation from usual work.' The Oxford English Dictionary 322–323 (2d ed. 1989) (hereinafter OED) (citing 18th and 19th-century sources for that definition of 'recess'). . . . The Founders themselves used the word to refer to intra-session, as well as to inter-session, breaks. . . . We recognize that the word 'the' in 'the recess' might suggest that the phrase refers to the single break separating formal sessions of Congress. That is because the word 'the' frequently (but not always) indicates 'a particular thing.' But the word can also refer 'to a term used generically or universally.' Finding the text ambiguous, the Court concluded that "the Clause's purpose demands the broader interpretation. The Clause gives the President authority to make appointments during 'the recess of the Senate' so that the President can ensure the continued functioning of the Federal Government when the Senate is away. The Senate is equally away during both an inter-session and an intra-session recess. . . ." Moreover, "[h]istory also offers strong support for the broad interpretation. . . . In all, between the founding and the Great Depression, Congress took substantial intra-session breaks. . . in four years: 1867, 1868, 1921, and 1929. And in each of those years the President made intra-session recess appointments. Since 1929, . . . Congress has shortened its inter-session breaks . . . [and] Presidents have correspondingly made more intra-session recess appointments. Indeed, if we include military appointments, Presidents have made thousands of intra-session recess appointments."

Having concluded that intra-session recesses come under the Clause, the Court turned to the "greater interpretive problem" of "determining how long a recess must be in order to fall within the Clause. Is a break of a week, or a day, or an hour too short to count as a 'recess'? The Clause itself does not say." The Court disagreed with Justice Scalia's argument in dissent that "this silence itself shows that the Framers intended the Clause to apply only to an inter-session recess," because "the most likely reason the Framers did not place a textual floor underneath the word 'recess' is that they did not foresee the need for one." Noting that the Adjournments Clause says: "Neither House, during the Session of Congress, shall, without the Consent of the other, adjourn for more than three days," Art. I, § 5, cl. 4, the majority "agree[d] with the Solicitor General that a 3-day recess would be too short. . . . [W]e have not found a single example of a recess appointment made during an intra-session recess that was shorter than 10 days. . . . In sum, . . . [i]f a Senate recess is so short that it does not require the consent of the House, it is too short to trigger the Recess Appointments Clause. And a recess lasting less than 10 days is presumptively too short as well."

The Court next held that the language "vacancies that may happen" applies both to vacancies that first come into existence during a recess and to those that arise prior but continue to exist during the recess: "We believe that the Clause's language, read literally, permits, though it does not naturally favor, our broader interpretation. We concede that the most natural meaning of 'happens' as applied to a 'vacancy' (at least to a modern ear) is that the vacancy 'happens' when it initially occurs. But that is not the only possible way to use the word." The majority added that "[t]he Clause's purpose strongly supports the broader interpretation. That purpose is to permit the President to obtain the assistance of subordinate officers when the Senate, due to its recess, cannot confirm them." Quoting Attorney General Wirt, the Court emphasized the "ruinous consequences" that could follow if the President had to leave important offices vacant because the Senate went into recess before they were filled, arguing that acting officers "may have less authority than Presidential appointments . . . [and] to rely on acting officers would lessen the President's ability to staff the Executive Branch with people of his own choosing." Moreover, "the Executive Branch has adhered to the broader interpretation for two centuries, and Senate confirmation has always remained the norm for officers that require it." And "[h]istorical practice over the past 200 years strongly favors the broader interpretation. The tradition of applying the Clause to pre-recess vacancies dates at least to President James Madison."

Finally, the majority turned to the third question, whether in "calculating the length of a recess . . . we [should] . . . ignore the pro forma sessions, thereby treating the series of brief recesses as a single, month-long recess. . . . In our view, . . . the pro forma sessions count as sessions, not as periods of recess. We hold that, for purposes of the Recess Appointments Clause, the Senate is in session when it says it is, provided that, under its own rules, it retains the capacity to transact Senate business. . . . [W]e must give great weight to the Senate's own determination of when it is and when it is not in session. But our deference to the Senate cannot be absolute. When the Senate is without the capacity to act, under its own rules, it is not in session even if it so declares. Accordingly, we conclude that when the Senate declares that it is in session and possesses the capacity, under its own rules, to conduct business, it is in session for purposes of the Clause." Applying that standard, the majority held that the Senate's pro forma sessions in December 2011 and January 2021 counted as sessions and that, because "[t]hree days is too short a time to bring a recess within the scope of the Clause . . . the President lacked the power to make the recess appointments here at issue."

JUSTICE SCALIA wrote a lengthy opinion concurring in the judgment, in which the CHIEF JUSTICE, JUSTICE THOMAS and JUSTICE ALITO joined. Justice Scalia accused the majority of endorsing "an adverse-possession theory of executive authority." He emphasized that although an "open" and "widespread" practice, "unchallenged since the early days of the Republic, should guide our interpretation of an ambiguous constitutional provision, . . . "the political branches cannot by agreement alter the constitutional structure." Scalia further cautioned that because "staking out a position and defending it over time is far easier for the Executive Branch than for the Legislative Branch . . . [t]he majority's methodology thus all but guarantees the continuing aggrandizement of the Executive Branch."

On the question of intra-session recesses, Scalia argued that "[a] sensible interpretation of the Recess Appointments Clause should start by recognizing that the Clause uses the term 'Recess' in contradistinction to the term 'Session.' . . . In the founding era, . . . [t]he life of each elected Congress typically consisted (as it still does) of two or more formal sessions separated by adjournments 'sine die,' that is, without a specified return date. The period between two sessions was known as 'the recess.' . . . Besides being linguistically unsound, the majority's reading yields the strange result that an appointment made during a short break near the beginning of one official session will not terminate until the end of the following official session, enabling the appointment to last for up to two years." Moreover, the majority's approach left the recess-appointment power "without a textually grounded principle limiting the time of its exercise. . . . The notion that the Constitution empowers the President to make unilateral appointments every time the Senate takes a half-hour lunch break is so absurd as to be self-refuting." Scalia also maintained that "even if the Constitution were thought ambiguous on this point, history does not support the majority's interpretation. . . . Intra-session recess appointments were virtually unheard of for the first 130 years of the Republic, were deemed unconstitutional by the first Attorney General to address them, were not openly defended by the Executive until 1921, [and] were not made in significant numbers until after World War II . . . ."

As for which vacancies count, Scalia maintained that "no reasonable reader would have understood the Recess Appointments Clause to use the word 'happen' in the majority's 'happen to be' sense, and thus to empower the President to fill all vacancies that might exist during a recess, regardless of when they arose. . . . The Clause easily could have been written to convey that meaning clearly. . . . If, however, the Clause had allowed the President to fill all pre-existing vacancies during the recess by granting commissions that would last throughout the following session, it would have been impossible to regard it—as the Framers plainly did—as a mere codicil to the Constitution's principal, power-sharing scheme for filling federal offices. . . . More fundamentally, Wirt and the majority are mistaken to say that the Constitution's 'substantial purpose' is to 'keep . . . offices filled.' The Constitution is not a road map for maximally efficient government, but a system of 'carefully crafted restraints' designed to 'protect the people from the improvident exercise of power.' Chadha, 462 U.S., at 957, 959."

## NOTES

(1) ***Dueling Accounts of the Recess Appointments Clause.*** Justice Breyer's majority opinion and Justice Scalia's concurrence consider the same sources to determine the meaning of the Recess Appointments Clause. Why then do they reach such opposite results? One evident difference is that the majority insists the constitutional text is ambiguous, whereas Justice Scalia views it as clearly precluding appointments during intrasession recesses and not applying when a vacancy predates the start of a recess. Which opinion do you think has the better account of the constitutional text? Is the text clearer on one of these issues—the meaning of "recess" or of "happens to exist"—than the other?

Another way to see the difference between the two opinions is in terms of the formalism-functionalism methodological divide discussed earlier (p. 830). Justice Scalia's emphasis on the Clause's plain meaning and his refusal to accord weight to contrary practices, even if well established, or pragmatic considerations such as the potential for disruption his interpretation might cause, is on a par with the formalism of Chief Justice Burger in Chadha. By contrast, Justice Breyer's insistence on textual ambiguity, heavy reliance on historical practice, and concern that the Clause fit current conditions—where intra-session recesses dominate—belies a strongly functionalist stance. Which approach, formalism or functionalism, do you think is more appropriate here?

(2) ***The Use of Historical Practice in Separation of Powers Analysis.*** The two opinions disagree about whether well-established practice exists on the meaning of the Recess Appointments Clause. Which opinion has the better of the argument: Do you think a longstanding practice exists on whether the Clause can be used during intrasession recesses? On whether the Clause can be used to fill vacancies that already existed when a recess occurred? For a fuller excerpt of the two opinions' approach to historical practice, see p. 832.

The opinions' different approaches to historical practice reflects, in large part, the two opinions' contrasting functionalist and formalist stances. But can a functionalist argument be made for skepticism about the weight to be given historical practice? Justice Scalia also argued that "staking out a position [on a separation of powers issue] and defending it over time is far easier for the Executive Branch than for the Legislative Branch" because Presidents are not hamstrung by the collective action problems that bedevil Congress and have a consistent interest in expanding the powers of their office. Do you agree? Does the argument suggest that political branch practice should be given particular weight when it represents a curtailment of presidential power, as for example in the case of presidential acceptance of limitations on their removal authority with respect to independent agencies? For a discussion of these issues, see Curtis A. Bradley & Trevor W. Morrison, Historical Gloss and the Separation of Powers, 126 Harv. L. Rev. 411 (2012).

(3) ***Pro Forma Sessions.*** Both opinions agree that President Obama's use of the Recess Appointments Clause during the Senate's pro forma sessions

was unconstitutional. Are you persuaded? Is there a meaningful difference between an 11-day intra-session recess that occurs when the Senate has declared itself in recess and an 11-day break in legislative business that is punctuated by one-minute sessions every three days in which one member of the Senate gavels the Senate into session and then (generally) immediately gavels it out? If the critical difference is that the Senate has not acknowledged that it is in recess, why should the Senate's view be allowed to control here, particularly if the purpose of a pro forma session is to stymie the President's exercise of the recess appointments' power? Is that tantamount to sanctioning Senate and congressional aggrandizement, as President Obama argued, or does deference to the Senate follow from the fact that the Recess Appointments Clause is a constitutional back-up plan, with the primary mode of appointment being presidential nomination and Senate approval?

To be sure, deferring to the Senate's view avoids the difficulty of determining when the Senate could undertake legislative business during a pro forma session and when it is really unavailable, but the majority does not shirk in undertaking that inquiry in determining that break of between three and ten days is presumptively too short to count as an intra-session recess. Is the inquiry here that much harder—or did you think the difficulty in determining what counts as an intra-session recess weighed in favor of limiting the Clause to inter-session recesses, as Justice Scalia argued? More basically, if the focus is on the Senate's unavailability, should the broader conclusion be that in our contemporary world of instantaneous communication and quick travel, the Recess Appointments Clause has become a constitutional anachronism?

Note that the recess appointments that President Obama made were all nominations that he had proposed when the Senate was in actual session but had been blocked by Senators under the Senate's rules. Given that both the Senate and the presidency were in Democratic hands at the time, an obvious alternative was for the Senate to get rid of the filibuster, which indeed it subsequently did for such appointments. (The Senate could also have told the President that it could not reach agreement with the House on when to adjourn, thereby triggering the President's express constitutional power to adjourn Congress when the two houses cannot agree on when to adjourn, U.S. Const. Art. I, § 3—though that constitutional power has never been invoked.) Perhaps, therefore, part of what animated the unanimous rejection of these recess appointments was the shared perception that a solution to the dangers of pro forma sessions was available, if the Senate had the political will to use it. If so, Noel Canning may bear close similarities to the Steel Seizure case, where the Justices' sense that President Truman was trying to avoid antagonizing his supporters in organized labor may have animated their rejection of his actions.

## NOTES ON ACTINGS, DELEGATIONS, AND APPOINTMENTS REFORMS

(1) ***Career Officials and Acting Heads.*** How is it that agencies can keep functioning even without an appointed agency head? Part of the answer is

career officials, in particular the Senior Executive Service, which often includes very senior long-serving agency officials. In addition, governing statutes and agency rules delegate responsibility for various agency functions to divisions and subunits within the agency, so that approval of the agency head is often not required for agency actions. But another important reason is that Congress has long given the executive branch power to appoint acting officers who serve on a temporary basis in many agencies, with statutes to this effect going back to 1792, including the longstanding Vacancies Act of 1868 and ultimately leading to the Federal Vacancies Reform Act (FVRA) in 1998. The FVRA establishes a default rule that the first assistant to the vacant office takes over in an acting capacity but provides that the President can appoint certain other officials as an acting leader.

The Supreme Court considered the FVRA in NLRB V. SW GENERAL, INC., 580 U.S. 288 (2017), and, in a 7–2 opinion written by CHIEF JUSTICE ROBERTS, the Court held that the statute prohibits anyone from occupying an office in an acting capacity once they are nominated by the President for the office, unless the nominee has been confirmed to the first assistant role or held the position of first assistant to the office for at least ninety days in the year before the office became vacant. The majority's decision was at odds with established executive branch interpretations of the FVRA. More dramatic was JUSTICE THOMAS's concurrence, solely for himself, which argued that the appointment of acting officials in principal offices without presidential nomination and Senate confirmation violated the Appointments Clause: "The Appointments Clause prescribes the exclusive process by which the President may appoint 'officers of the United States.'. . . When the President directs someone to serve as an officer pursuant to the FVRA, he is 'appoint[ing]' that person as an 'officer of the United States' within the meaning of the Appointments Clause. . . . The FVRA authorizes the President to appoint both inferior and principal officers without first obtaining the advice and consent of the Senate. Appointing inferior officers in this manner raises no constitutional problems. . . . Appointing principal officers under the FVRA, however, raises grave constitutional concerns because the Appointments Clause forbids the President to appoint principal officers without the advice and consent of the Senate." Justice Thomas concluded that the General Counsel to the NLRB, the position at issue, "plainly is an officer of the United States. I also think he is likely a principal officer."

(2) ***Acting Officials for Principal Offices.*** This question of whether the President constitutionally can appoint an acting official for a principal office, at least if the official has not been confirmed by the Senate for another position, garnered renewed interest in November 2018, when President Trump selected Matthew Whitaker to be acting Attorney General upon the forced resignation of Attorney General Jeff Sessions. See Neal K. Katyal & George T. Conway III, Trump's Appointment of the Acting Attorney General Is Unconstitutional, N.Y. Times (Nov. 8, 2018). Whitaker had been Sessions's Chief of Staff, which did not require Senate confirmation; moreover, there were other Senate-confirmed officials in the Department of Justice whom the

President could have chosen and who would ordinarily have assumed the acting job under the Attorney General Succession Act, such as the Deputy Attorney General. Multiple lawsuits were brought challenging Whitaker's appointment. The Office of Legal Counsel defended Whitaker's appointment on the grounds that although the Attorney General was a principal officer position, someone serving in it temporarily was an inferior officer and able to be appointed without Senate confirmation. Office of Legal Counsel, U.S. Dep't of Justice, Designating an Acting Attorney General (Nov. 14, 2018).[4] All of the lower courts to consider the issue ruled that Whitaker's service did not violate the Appointments Clause. See, e.g., United States v. Smith, 962 F.3d 755 (4th Cir. 2020). The issue was mooted for many challengers when the Senate confirmed William Barr as Attorney General in February 2019. See, e.g., Guedes v. Bureau of Alcohol, Tobacco, Firearms, and Explosives, 920 F.3d 1, 14–17 (D.C. Cir. 2019). When President Biden took office, he relied on thirteen acting secretaries who had not been confirmed to another position while he waited for his nominees to be confirmed.

In upholding Whitaker's appointment, the lower courts and OLC relied on UNITED STATES V. EATON, 169 U.S. 331 (1898). In Eaton, the U.S. consul general to what is now Thailand, himself a presidentially appointed and Senate confirmed (PAS) officer, appointed Lewis Eaton to the position of vice consul general before leaving the country. Under governing regulations, Eaton served temporarily in the position of consul general until a new PAS consul general arrived. Eaton sued when the government refused to pay for his services, and the Supreme Court rejected the government's argument that Eaton's appointment had violated the Appointments Clause. According to the Court, officials serving temporarily in principal offices are inferior officers: "Because the subordinate officer is charged with the performance of the duty of the superior for a limited time, and under special and temporary conditions, he is not thereby transformed into the superior and permanent official. To so hold would render void any and every delegation of power to an inferior to perform under any circumstances or exigency the duties of a superior officer, and the discharge of administrative duties would be seriously hindered." The historical use of acting officials in principal offices goes back further than Eaton, however, to the 1792 and 1795 Vacancies Acts, the latter of which imposed a six-month limit on such service. See Anne Joseph O'Connell, Actings, 120 Colum. L. Rev. 1613, 1624–26 (2020).

NINA MENDELSON argues that acting principal officers who are not Senate confirmed are constitutional only if they serve for short periods, in THE PERMISSIBILITY OF ACTING OFFICIALS: MAY THE PRESIDENT WORK AROUND SENATE CONFIRMATION?, 72 Admin. L. Rev. 4 (2020): "[T]he best justification for interpreting the Constitution to permit acting officers in principal officer positions, such as Cabinet secretary roles, is the stopgap function—a value supported in the Take Care and Vesting Clauses. But given the risks inherent in permitting the President to unilaterally select an acting officer without the check of Senate confirmation, that rationale can

[4] https://www.justice.gov/sites/default/files/opinions/attachments/2018/11/17/2018-11-14-acting-ag.pdf.

only justify a very short term of acting service, long enough to support a prompt presidential nomination."

Recall that in Edmond (p. 956), which did not involve acting service, the Court emphasized that inferior officers are "officers whose work is directed and supervised at some level" by someone other than the President. That description would appear to exclude acting secretaries. Moreover, in Arthrex (p. 945) the Court concluded that the lack of supervision of APJs' decisions meant that they needed to be appointed as principal officers. Do you think the Appointments Clause prohibits Congress from authorizing temporary presidential appointments of acting officials (at least those who have not been Senate confirmed to another position) to vacant principal officer positions? How much should the longstanding practice of using acting officials this way factor into assessing constitutionality? What about the fact that acting agency heads are often needed to keep an agency functioning until a new head is nominated and confirmed?

On remand in Arthrex, ARTHREX, INC. V. SMITH & NEPHEW, INC., 35 F. 4th 1328 (Fed. Cir. 2022), the FEDERAL CIRCUIT upheld the constitutionality of the Commissioner of Patents denying Arthrex's request for rehearing, pursuant to an administrative order delegating "the non-exclusive functions and duties of the [Director of the Patent and Trademark Office]" to the Commissioner when the Director and Deputy Director positions are vacant. In so holding, the Federal Circuit relied heavily on Eaton, which it concluded was indistinguishable. (For discussion of this delegation of authority, see p. 977).

(3) ***Increased Use of Actings.*** Whitaker's appointment as acting AG was simply one example of President Trump's heavy reliance on acting officials to serve as cabinet secretaries. In the final year of his Administration and in the wake of the deployment of officers from the Department of Homeland Security to Portland, Oregon in response to protests, public attention focused on the fact that ten of twenty-seven top positions at DHS were filled by acting officials (or officials carrying out delegated duties). Patricia Alvarez & Geneva Sands, DHS Leaders, Filling Jobs on Temporary Basis, Carry Out Trump Agenda, CNN (July 20, 2020).[5]

ANNE JOSEPH O'CONNELL in ACTINGS, 120 Colum. L. Rev. 613 (2020), "compiled a database of confirmed, recess, and acting cabinet secretaries from the start of President Reagan's Administration to the end of President Trump's third year (January 19, 2020)." During that period, counting service across Administrations separately, she found that "there have been 171 confirmed, 3 recess-appointed, and 147 acting cabinet secretaries." Although "45.8% of cabinet secretaries in this period were not confirmed or recess appointed, these acting leaders typically served for short periods." O'Connell's data documents that "President Trump differs from his predecessors in several ways. First, he alone has used more acting secretaries than confirmed secretaries, as of January 19, 2020. In addition, while almost all of his acting secretaries served at least ten days, only

[5] https://www.cnn.com/2020/07/19/politics/dhs-leaders-acting-trump-agenda-portland/index.html.

President Trump faced a Senate controlled by his own party during the entire period being analyzed. Finally, President Trump has often turned to acting officials outside his first year, unlike previous Presidents." She provides the following chart:

| President | Confirmed | Recess | Acting (at least 10 days) |
|---|---|---|---|
| Reagan | 33 | 1 | 25 (11) |
| Bush 41 (1 term) | 20 | 1 | 20 (16) |
| Clinton | 28 | 1 | 27 (11) |
| Bush 43 | 34 | 0 | 22 (13) |
| Obama | 32 | 0 | 23 (14) |
| Trump (3 years) | 24 | 0 | 30 (27) |

President Biden had no confirmed cabinet members until three days after he took office, and his Administration relied heavily on acting officials, often senior career officials, at the outset. Anne Joseph O'Connell, Brookings Inst., Waiting for Confirmed Leaders: President Biden's Actings (Feb. 4, 2021). Yet nearly a year in, "hundreds of key roles across the federal government remain[ed] vacant." J.M. Rieger, Why There Are So Many Vacancies in the Biden Administration, Wash. Post (Dec. 17, 2021).

CHRISTINA M. KINANE, in CONTROL WITHOUT CONFIRMATION: THE POLITICS OF VACANCIES IN PRESIDENTIAL APPOINTMENTS, 115 Am. Pol. Sci. Rev. 599 (2021), argues that recognizing the availability of interim acting officials is necessary to understand why Presidents might leave some offices vacant. "[P]residents may strategically use vacancies in [positions requiring Senate confirmation, known as] PAS positions[,] to achieve their policy priorities. . . . Presidents unilaterally choose to leave positions empty or to fill them with interim appointees. The Senate enters the appointment calculus only after a president, again unilaterally, chooses to submit a nominee." According to Kinane, the unilateral ability to fill positions with actings "offers the president a remarkable opportunity to circumvent the Senate." She argues further that "the president's decision to keep a position empty requires an appointment strategy that centers on the characteristics of the position itself. . . . [T]he crucial question . . . is . . . how much of the president's specific policy priorities can be advanced *without* a formal appointment."

(4) ***Evaluating Actings.*** What should we make of this wide use of actings and delegations of authority? Consider these views:

O'CONNELL, ACTINGS, supra, at 695–707: "Acting officials rarely garner praise. Commentators worry that the lack of confirmed officials contributes to agencies progressing slowly with important initiatives and employing unhappy workers. More broadly, they lament the power grab by the White House and its effects on Congress and accountability. . . . [Yet, t]he costs of gaps in confirmed leadership may not be as dire as the conventional wisdom suggests. . . . Acting officials may not be as productive as confirmed leaders, but they still make important decisions. . . . [They] may serve longer than their confirmed counterparts and their tenure may be more predictable than appointees." O'Connell argues that "[a]cting officials represent a workaround to the traditional appointments process, which allows elected Senators to veto the President's nominees," with the result that "acting leaders are less accountable to Congress as they have not been confirmed to the jobs they are filling temporarily. . . . Presidents of both parties have placed officials in acting roles whom the Senate would not confirm. . . . Nevertheless, if acting officials are compared to recess appointees, the Senate may prefer the former. . . . [H]aving acting leaders [also] allows the Senate to spend more time vetting official nominees. Additionally, acting leaders may provide the Senate more choices—if the Senate dislikes the formal nominee, it can sit on the nomination and let the acting official continue to serve." Finally, "[a]ccountability often trades off with expertise. If acting officials are drawn from long-term agency employees, they may be more competent than confirmed appointees."

MENDELSON, supra, at 640–44: "[W]e regularly face the specter of missing Senate-confirmed officials in the agencies. Presidents have used Vacancies Act authorities and other means—notably internal delegations of authority—to place unconfirmed individuals in these posts or to assign them the responsibilities of the posts. . . . But is such presidential reliance upon acting officials constitutional? . . . A functional analysis of the Appointments Clause strongly suggests that current FVRA authorizations for principal officers are simply too long, and that courts should recognize their constitutional doubtfulness. . . . In particular, the Appointments Clause should be interpreted to authorize the President to rely only briefly on acting officials for Cabinet-level principal officer roles. Instead, the President should be expected to promptly forward nominations to the Senate for advice and consent."

(5) ***Delegations.*** Although the increased use of acting officials has generated a fair bit of attention, a less prominent but important related phenomenon is agencies' growing reliance on delegations of nonexclusive functions or authority. MENDELSON, supra at 557–58, 561, describes this practice: "Most statutes that grant agencies authority delegate that authority to the Secretary or the Administrator. In turn, organic statutes are generally express in authorizing the head of the agency to redelegate statutory authorities within the agency. Even without express statutory language, an agency head is typically assumed to be able to delegate powers in view of the impossibility of performing all tasks herself. . . . [T]wo sorts of delegation strategies have been deployed to relocate the powers of a particular office. One might be termed a vertical, or 'supervised' delegation. For example, President Clinton selected several officials with uncertain Senate confirmation prospects to serve as 'acting' senior officials inside the Justice Department. . . . Presumably, the Attorney General could supervise and revoke any of these delegations. The other sort might be termed an 'unsupervised' horizontal delegation. For example, on his way out the door, [the] Clinton Administration Office of Thrift Supervision Director . . . delegated all the office's powers to [the] Deputy Director . . . [who] exercised

the powers for four years even though [the Director] was no longer present to supervise or revoke the delegation."

Mendelson argues that the delegation strategy is problematic. Such a "wholesale delegation of a Senate-confirmed office's responsibilities violates the text of the FVRA," through which Congress "aim[ed] to limit delegation as a means of bypassing Senate confirmation," and "also raises constitutional difficulties." O'Connell agrees that "Presidents can strategically use delegation to keep their preferred officials in control of certain administrative functions long past the Vacancies Act's time limits." However, as O'Connell notes, "these delegation practices are pervasive and have largely been upheld by the limited courts to consider them." O'Connell, supra, at 633 & n.105; 5 U.S.C. § 3348(a)(2), (b)(2).

In its decision on remand in Arthrex (pp. 945, 974), the Federal Circuit upheld the delegation of the PTO Director's authority to rule on rehearing requests to the Commissioner of Patents against the charge that this delegation would violate the FVRA, concluding that the language of the FVRA "is unambiguous: the FVRA applies only to functions and duties that a PAS officer alone is permitted by statute or regulation to perform. It does not apply to delegable functions and duties." Agreeing with Arthrex that this reading of the FVRA rendered "the FVRA's scope vanishingly small," the appellate court insisted that that result "does not . . . justify departing from the plain meaning of the statute." It also cautioned that "[c]onstruing the FVRA to apply to delegable duties" would have "significant consequences," noting that "the PTO has issued more than 668,000 patents signed by an inferior officer filling in for the Director" in the last decade. Moreover, the "impacts of such a decision would . . . reverberate far beyond the PTO," as "[t]he universe of delegable PAS-officer duties is expansive, potentially encompassing every Executive agency." A district court has rejected the view that the FVRA only applies when the functions at issue are exclusive to an official. Pub. Employees for Envtl. Responsibility v. Nat'l Park Serv., 2022 WL 1657013 at *10–*12 (D.D.C. 2022); see also Bullock v. Bureau of Land Mgmt., 2020 WL 6204334 at *3 (D. Mont. 2020).

Mendelson criticized the Federal Circuit's decision, arguing that its reading of the FVRA made the statute "wholly ineffective to address the very circumstances—the 'mischief'—that motivated its passage." She also argued that the court made "superfluous" the FVRA's provision "bar[ring] an agency from relying on 'general authority' to 'delegate duties' as a substitute for properly designating an acting official," and ignored that the language focusing on nondelegable duties was addressed only to enforcement. Nina A. Mendelson, The Federal Circuit Upholds "Shadow" Acting Official, Enabling Federal Vacancies Reform Act Bypass, Notice & Comment Blog (June 1, 2022).[6]

(6) ***Political Polarization and the Appointments Process.*** President Obama's decision to make recess appointments during pro forma Senate sessions was a novel use of the recess appointments power, but so was the

[6] https://www.yalejreg.com/nc/the-federal-circuit-upholds-shadow-acting-official-enabling-federal-vacancies-reform-act-bypass-by-nina-a-mendelson/.

use of pro forma sessions as a way to stymie recess appointments. Both are reflections of the increasing partisan divide that has led to congressional gridlock and dysfunction.

Anne Joseph O'Connell has carefully documented changes to the appointments process for Senate-confirmed positions over time. Brookings Inst., Staffing Federal Agencies: Lessons from 1981–2016 (Apr. 17, 2017).[7] "[F]rom the start of President Reagan's administration to the end of President Obama's[,] . . . over one-fifth of submitted agency nominations failed to get confirmed . . . , with President Obama's nominations failing close to one-third of the time. It took the Senate almost three months, on average, to confirm nominations, with President Reagan's nominations requiring about a month less and President Obama's requiring about a month more." According to the Partnership for Public Service's Center for Presidential Transition, these trends have continued. At the one year mark, President Trump had made significantly fewer nominations than his predecessors (555, compared to 653 for Obama and 677 for Bush), and also had a lower confirmation rate (57%, compared to 69% for Obama and 75% for Bush). Although President Biden had nominated 644, "roughly the same number of appointees" as Presidents Bush and Obama, "far fewer of Biden's nominees were confirmed," and his rate of confirmations within the first year was only 55%.

Does this data on the increasing difficulties of the appointments process change your views on President Obama's use of the recess appointments power during a pro forma recess? Of President Trump's and President Biden's reliance on acting officials?

(7) ***Causes of Delay.*** The general public explanation for delays in filling executive positions is Senate confirmation (mis)behavior. And the data above indicates that Senate confirmation plays an important role. But experts identify several additional contributing factors:

- The sheer number of positions that now must be filled: Currently, there are over 1,100 positions requiring presidential nomination and Senate confirmation.
- The vetting process, reflecting steadily increasing inquiries and investigations undertaken to avoid potentially politically embarrassing nominations.
- The unwillingness of potential nominees to risk (or actual nominees to endure) a media and political gauntlet.
- The "nomination lag": Although President Biden had nominated 644 individuals by the end of his first year in office, that still left him with slightly over 450 positions to make if he were to fill all the 1,100 positions requiring presidential nomination and Senate consent.
- A desire to "deconstruct" administrative government: The Trump Administration's promise to "deconstruct the administrative state" suggests that a desire to slow down

[7] https://www.brookings.edu/research/staffing-federal-agencies-lessons-from-1981-2016/.

government might be another factor that contributed to appointments delay.

Efforts to reform the appointments process to address Senate confirmation delays can have unexpected consequences. In November 2013, the Democratic-controlled Senate voted to end the filibuster for all confirmations other than to the Supreme Court; in April 2017, the Senate, newly in Republican hands, ended the filibuster for Supreme Court confirmations as well in order to confirm Justice Neil Gorsuch. Anne Joseph O'Connell, in Shortening Agency and Judicial Vacancies through Filibuster Reform? An Examination of Confirmation Rates and Delays from 1981 to 2014, 64 Duke L.J. 1645, 1680–81 (2015), reports that the November 2013 "filibuster reform has had more complicated effects on the confirmation process than may have been predicted. The change does seem to have uniformly aided judicial nominations: fewer were returned to (or withdrawn by) the President, and successful nominations came more quickly. . . . But the change had conflicting effects for many agencies and agency positions: fewer nominations failed but successful nominations took longer to be confirmed."

In 2021, the Partnership for Public Service formally called for Congress to reduce the number of Senate confirmed positions, among other proposals. It noted that "[t]he number of Senate-confirmed positions grew from 779 to 1,237 (59% increase) between 1960 and 2016"; that "[t]he average Senate confirmation process took about twice as long as it did during the Trump (117 days) and the Obama administration (112 days) than it did during the Reagan administration (56 days)"; and that "[t]he short tenures of political appointees combined with these delays result in frequent and extended vacancies across Senate-confirmed positions." Government More Effective, Aug. 9, 2021.[8] What reforms do you favor?

## (2) The Removal Power

*Notes on the Removal Power over Time*

***SEILA LAW LLC v. CONSUMER FINANCIAL PROTECTION BUREAU***

***Free Enterprise Fund v. Public Company Accounting Oversight Board***

*Notes on the Implications for Independent Agencies*

*The House . . . shall have the sole Power of Impeachment. . . . The Senate shall have the sole Power to try all Impeachments.*

U.S. Const., Art. I, § 2, cl. 5; § 3, cl. 6

*The Congress shall have Power . . . To make all Laws which shall be necessary and proper for carrying into Execution the foregoing Powers, and all other*

[8] https://presidentialtransition.org/publications/unconfirmed-reducing-number-senate-confirmed-positions/.

*Powers vested by this Constitution in the Government of the United States, or in any Department or Officer thereof.*

U.S. Const., Art. I, § 8, cl. 18

*The executive Power shall be vested in a President of the United States of America.*

U.S. Const., Art. II, § 1, cl. 1

*... [The President] shall nominate, and by and with the Advice and Consent of the Senate, shall appoint Ambassadors, other public Ministers and Consuls, Judges of the supreme Court, and all other Officers of the United States, whose Appointments are not herein otherwise provided for, and which shall be established by Law: but the Congress may by Law vest the Appointment of such inferior Officers, as they think proper, in the President alone, in the Courts of Law, or in the Heads of Departments.*

U.S. Const., Art. II, § 2, cl. 2

*[The President] shall take Care that the Laws be faithfully executed. . . .*

U.S. Const., Art. II, § 3

*The President, Vice President and all civil Officers of the United States, shall be removed from Office on Impeachment for, and Conviction of, Treason, Bribery, or other high Crimes and Misdemeanors.*

U.S. Const., Art. II, § 4

## NOTES ON THE REMOVAL POWER OVER TIME

The Constitution is silent on removal, save for impeachment. Debates over the scope of the President's removal power go back to the First Congress. Congress created the first Cabinet department (Foreign Affairs) in 1789. Everyone knew how the Secretary of State must be appointed, but the House could not agree on what the Constitution meant for how the Secretary could be removed. In particular, could the Senate demand its consent for removal, given that its consent was required for appointment? The uncertainty created by constitutional silence is evident in Representative James Madison's change in view. During the initial debate he asserted, "Congress may establish the office by law; therefore, most certainly, it is in the discretion of the Legislature to say upon what terms the office should be held, either during good behavior or during pleasure"—although he urged that presidential removal at will was the best *policy*, for it concentrated responsibility for the Secretary's conduct solely in the President. Annals of Congress 389, 393–95 (1789). Within a month, Madison had switched to the position that removal is an exclusively presidential prerogative. He explained: "I have, since the subject was last before the House, examined the Constitution with attention, and I acknowledge that it does not perfectly correspond with the ideas I entertained of it from the first glance." Id. at

480.[9] Ultimately, the House settled on presidential removal at will—through the combined votes of those who believed it was the President's constitutional right and those who believed it was the soundest policy. Legal historians report that the House was divided into four major positions on the removal power: (1) a very small group who believed impeachment to be the only constitutionally authorized removal device, and three groups of virtually equal size who concluded that (2) removal was the constitutional prerogative of the President alone; (3) removal paralleled appointment, and therefore was vested jointly in President and Senate; and (4) removal was not constitutionally determined, and hence could be settled by Congress under its Necessary and Proper power.[10] No reliable record exists of debate in the Senate, but comparable lack of consensus can be inferred from the fact that the removal provision passed only on the Vice President's tie-breaking vote.

The second department (War) was structured in the same way as Foreign Affairs, but the first Congress proceeded differently when it created the Department of the Treasury. Unlike the other two, Treasury was not denominated "an executive department." Moreover, one of its key officials—the Comptroller of the Treasury—was shielded from presidential direction and removal. The next department, the Post Office, followed the Treasury model. Thus, early practice in structuring the entities that would administer government established a diversity of organizational forms: One pattern was quite closely allied to the President through officers serving at his pleasure. The other had more independence and a greater orientation towards Congress.

In the wake of the Civil War, removal became part of the feud between an overwhelmingly Republican Congress and Andrew Johnson, a Democratic President bent on thwarting any significant restructuring of race relations through post-Civil War Reconstruction. The Tenure in Office Act of 1867 specified that members of the Cabinet would hold their office until the end of the presidential term (which in Johnson's case was the term he was completing as Lincoln's successor after Lincoln was assassinated) unless the Senate consented to their earlier removal. The provision aimed at securing the continued tenure of Secretary of War Edwin Stanton, who had been appointed by Lincoln and who supported Congress's position on Reconstruction. When President Andrew Johnson nonetheless removed Stanton, the House impeached him on this—and other—grounds. His

[9] Madison was not the only prominent Framer to equivocate on removal. In Federalist 77, Alexander Hamilton argued that "stability of administration" (a key Federalist theme in advocating ratification) will be enhanced by the fact that "[t]he consent of [the Senate] would be necessary to displace as well as to appoint." However by 1793, when Hamilton as Secretary of the Treasury was writing as Pacificus in defense of a broad construction of Article II, he cited removal as an illustration of the scope of the executive power. The 1810 edition of the Federalist Papers included a note to No. 77, apparently supplied by Hamilton, challenging the original version.

[10] The classic account is Edward S. Corwin, Tenure of Office & The Removal Power Under the Constitution, 27 Colum. L. Rev. 353 (1927). For more recent scholarship offering contrasting views, compare Saikrishna Prakash, New Light on the Decision of 1789, 91 Cornell L. Rev. 1021 (2006) and Jed Shugerman, The Decisions of 1789 Were Non-Unitary: Removal by Judiciary and the Imaginary Unitary Executive, https://papers.ssrn.com/sol3/papers.cfm?abstract_id=3597496.

defense included the argument that the Act was unconstitutional. Ultimately, the Senate failed by one vote to convict. Congress continued to enact protections against removal, including the Pendleton Act in 1883 that established federal civil service protections. In 1886, the Court upheld the constitutionality of removal protection for a naval engineer who was deemed to be an inferior officer. See United States v. Perkins, 116 U.S. 483 (1886).

The removal issue reappeared in the waning days of President Woodrow Wilson's Administration. MYERS V. UNITED STATES, 272 U.S. 52 (1926), arose out of the Postmaster General's firing of Frank Myers, Postmaster of Portland, Oregon, before the end of his statutory 4-year term. According to one version of the story, Myers was suspected of having committed fraud; other versions paint the Postmaster General as something of a tin pot dictator with a personal grudge against Myers.[11] The pertinent statute provided: "Postmasters . . . shall be appointed and may be removed by the President by and with the advice and consent of the Senate, and shall hold their offices for four years unless sooner removed or suspended according to law." Section 6 of the Act of July 1, 1876. President Wilson refused to seek Senate consent, and Myers sued for lost salary, arguing that his removal was unlawful.

Former President and at that point CHIEF JUSTICE WILLIAM TAFT'S opinion for the Court rejected Myers's claim in a seventy-page opinion, concluding that the removal restriction in the statute was unconstitutional: "Made responsible under the Constitution for the effective enforcement of the law, the President needs as an indispensable aid to meet it the disciplinary influence upon those who act under him of a reserve power of removal. But it is contended that executive officers appointed by the President with the consent of the Senate are bound by the statutory law, and are not his servants to do his will, and that his obligation to care for the faithful execution of the laws does not authorize him to treat them as such. The degree of guidance in the discharge of their duties that the President may exercise over executive officers varies with the character of their service as prescribed in the law under which they act. The highest and most important duties which his subordinates perform are those in which they act for him. In such cases they are exercising not their own but his discretion. . . . This field is a very large one. It is sometimes described as political. Each head of a department is and must be the President's alter ego in the matters of that department where the President is required by law to exercise authority. . . .

"In all such cases, the discretion to be exercised is that of the President in determining the national public interest and in directing the action to be taken by his executive subordinates to protect it. In this field his cabinet officers must do his will. . . . The moment that he loses confidence in the intelligence, ability, judgment, or loyalty of any one of them, he must have

---

[11] For discussions of the case, see Jonathan L. Entin, The Pompous Postmaster and Presidential Power: The Story of Myers v. United States, 65 Case W. L. Rev. 1059 (2015); Saikrishna Prakash, The Story of Myers and Its Wayward Successors: Going Postal on the Removal Power in Presidential Power Stories (Christopher H. Schroeder & Curtis A. Bradley eds. 2009).

the power to remove him without delay. To require him to file charges and submit them to the consideration of the Senate might make impossible that unity and co-ordination in executive administration essential to effective action.

". . . There is nothing in the Constitution which permits a distinction between the removal of the head of a department or a bureau, when he discharges a political duty of the President or exercises his discretion, and the removal of executive officers engaged in the . . . ordinary duties . . . prescribed by statute. [These latter duties] come under the general administrative control of the President . . . in order to secure that unitary and uniform execution of the laws which article II of the Constitution evidently contemplated in vesting general executive power in the President alone. . . . Finding . . . officers to be negligent and inefficient, the President should have the power to remove them. Of course there may be duties so peculiarly and specifically committed to the discretion of a particular officer as to raise a question whether the President may overrule or revise the officer's interpretation of his statutory duty in a particular instance. Then there may be duties of a quasi judicial character imposed on executive officers and members of executive tribunals whose decisions after hearing affect interests of individuals, the discharge of which the President cannot in a particular case properly influence or control. But even in such a case he may consider the decision after its rendition as a reason for removing the officer, on the ground that the discretion regularly entrusted to that officer by statute has not been on the whole intelligently or wisely exercised. Otherwise he does not discharge his own constitutional duty of seeing that the laws be faithfully executed. . . ."

The Court then considered the argument that the removal provision could be sustained because postmasters were "inferior officers" within the meaning of the Appointments Clause: "The court . . . has recognized in the Perkins Case, 116 U.S. 483 (1886), that Congress, in committing the appointment of such inferior officers to the heads of departments, may prescribe incidental regulations controlling and restricting the latter in the exercise of the power of removal. But the court never has held, nor reasonably could hold, . . . that the excepting clause enables Congress to draw to itself, or to either branch of it, the power to remove or the right to participate in the exercise of that power. To do this would be to go beyond the words and implications of that clause, and to infringe the constitutional principle of the separation of governmental powers." Dissenting, Justice McReynolds took issue with the argument that removal was inherently executive, while Justice Brandeis insisted that Myers was an inferior officer, and Justice Holmes argued (Brandeis agreeing) that "[t]he duty of the President to see that the laws be executed is a duty that does not go beyond the laws or require him to achieve more than Congress sees fit to leave within his power."

Then, only nine years later, in HUMPHREY'S EXECUTOR V. UNITED STATES, 295 U.S. 602 (1935), a unanimous Court upheld a for-cause removal protection for members of an independent commission. In 1933, President Franklin Delano Roosevelt removed William Humphrey from his position as

Commissioner of the Federal Trade Commission. Humphrey had been appointed by President Hoover, Roosevelt's predecessor, and his conservative views were out of step with those of the new Administration.[12] Under the FTC Act, Commissioners served for a seven-year term and could "be removed by the President for inefficiency, neglect of duty, or malfeasance in office." Humphrey insisted that his removal violated the FTC Act and that he remained a member of the Commission and entitled to receive compensation. After his death, his estate sued for backpay. Based on the statutory language and the legislative history, JUSTICE SUTHERLAND concluded that "congressional intent [was] to create a body of experts who shall gain experience by length of service; a body which shall be independent of executive authority, except in its selection, and free to exercise its judgment without the leave or hindrance of any other official or any department of the government. . . . [T]o hold that, nevertheless, the members of the commission continue in office at the mere will of the President, might be to thwart, in large measure, the very ends which Congress sought to realize by definitely fixing the term of office."

Distinguishing Myers, Justice Sutherland stated that "the narrow point actually decided was only that the President had power to remove a postmaster of the first class, without the advice and consent of the Senate as required by act of Congress. . . . A postmaster is an executive officer restricted to the performance of executive functions. He is charged with no duty at all related to either the legislative or judicial power. The actual decision in the Myers Case finds support in the theory that such an officer is merely one of the units in the executive department and, hence, inherently subject to the exclusive and illimitable power of removal by the Chief Executive, whose subordinate and aid he is. . . . [T]he necessary reach of the decision goes far enough to include all purely executive officers. It goes no farther; much less does it include an officer who occupies no place in the executive department and who exercises no part of the executive power vested by the Constitution in the President.

"The Federal Trade Commission is an administrative body created by Congress to carry into effect legislative policies embodied in the statute in accordance with the legislative standard therein prescribed, and to perform other specified duties as a legislative or as a judicial aid. . . . In administering the provisions of the statute in respect of 'unfair methods of competition,' that is to say, in filling in and administering the details embodied by that general standard, the commission acts in part quasi-legislatively and in part quasi-judicially. . . . To the extent that it exercises any executive function, as distinguished from executive power in the constitutional sense, it does so in the discharge and effectuation of its quasi-legislative or quasi-judicial powers, or as an agency of the legislative or judicial departments of the government. . . . [T]he Myers decision, affirming the power of the President alone to make the removal, is confined to purely executive officers; and as to

[12] Before firing Humphrey, Roosevelt wrote to him expressing the hope that his resignation would be forthcoming: "You will, I know, realize that I do not feel that your mind and my mind go along together on either the policies or the administering of the Federal Trade Commission, and, frankly, I think it is best for the people of this country that I should have a full confidence." Humphrey did not concur, and the President removed him from office.

officers of the kind here under consideration, we hold that no removal can be made during the prescribed term for which the officer is appointed, except for one or more of the causes named in the applicable statute."

Note the curious willingness of the majority to place the FTC in both the legislative and judicial branches, and the blind eye it turns to what appear to be executive branch functions of the Commission. Might it have been a sufficient distinction of Myers that the precise issue there, not present in Humphrey's Executor, was whether Congress could require senatorial advice and consent before the President could remove an executive official? Equally striking is the contrast between Myers and Humphrey's Executor. The basis for that altered approach is not obvious. The composition of the Court had changed, but not in ways that would clearly make the Court less sympathetic to claims of presidential authority.[13] Another possibility is that Humphrey's Executor was part of the Court's early resistance to President Roosevelt's assertions of regulatory authority in the New Deal.[14] Yet a third explanation looks to international developments. Myers was decided during the early years of movements in Germany and Italy towards strong executive government. Indeed, the New York Times, reporting the decision, quoted a reference to some people's belief "that what this country needs is another Mussolini." Johnson Sees Peril In Removal Power, N.Y. Times (Nov. 7, 1926). By the time of Humphrey's Executor, Hitler had ended democratic government in Germany, Mussolini had embarked on the conquest of Ethiopia, and the potential dangers of strong centralized executive government were more at the fore.

Over the next 50 years, the line drawn by the combination of Myers and Humphrey's Executor held, despite occasional sniping between the President and Congress. When Ronald Reagan took office, his Administration asserted a broad view of presidential power (now known as the "unitary executive theory") and insisted that many conventionally accepted limits on presidential authority were unconstitutional. On its side, Congress became more venturesome in devising agency structures that did not fit neatly into the Myers/Humphrey's Executor framework. One of these structures was the independent counsel, created by the Ethics in Government Act in the wake of Watergate as a means of investigating and prosecuting high executive officials for violations of federal criminal laws. Under the Act—this portion of which has since expired without renewal—the Attorney General would preliminarily investigate accusations of criminal wrongdoing. Upon determining that further investigation was required, the Attorney General was to inform a "Special Division" of three D.C. Circuit judges, who were in turn to appoint an independent counsel. The independent counsel was given

[13] Two members of Taft's majority—including Taft himself—had been replaced. But the new Chief Justice, Charles Evans Hughes, came from a career in the executive branch and appeared generally sympathetic to the needs of a Chief Executive. Another new appointee, Benjamin Cardozo, was a supporter of the New Deal. Moreover, four Justices (Van Devanter, Sutherland, Butler, and Stone) joined the opinion of the Court in both cases.

[14] Humphrey's Executor, which was a defeat for President Roosevelt's efforts to exert more control over the independent agencies, came on the same day as Schechter Poultry Corp. v. United States (p. 860), which invalidated significant portions of the National Industrial Recovery Act on nondelegation and commerce power grounds.

"full power and independent authority to exercise all investigative and prosecutorial functions and powers of the Department of Justice, the Attorney General, and any other officer or employee of the Department of Justice." The Special Division could determine if an investigation had reached a point justifying termination of the independent counsel; beyond this, the power to remove the independent counsel was specified as "the personal action of the Attorney General and only for good cause, physical disability, mental incapacity, or any other condition that substantially impairs the performance of such independent counsel's duties." The Attorney General was required to report any such removal in detail to both the Special Division and the Judiciary Committees of the Senate and the House, and the independent counsel could obtain judicial review.

The independent counsel collided with the Reagan Administration's strong unitary executive stance in MORRISON V. OLSON, 487 U.S. 654 (1988). In 1986, Alexia Morrison was appointed independent counsel to investigate whether Assistant Attorney General Theodore Olson (later Solicitor General under President George W. Bush) had lied while testifying under oath before a House Judiciary Committee investigating an earlier dispute between Congress and the Administrator of EPA, Anne Gorsuch (mother of Supreme Court Justice Neil Gorsuch). Olson challenged the constitutionality of the independent counsel. CHIEF JUSTICE REHNQUIST wrote for all members of the Court except Justice Scalia, who dissented, and Justice Kennedy, who did not participate. The Court first determined that the independent counsel was an "inferior officer" (p. 956) and then that appointment by the Special Division was not an unconstitutional "inter-branch" appointment. It then rejected Olson's claim that the limits on the Attorney General's ability to remove the independent counsel violated the separation of powers.

"Unlike both Bowsher [p. 928], and Myers [p. 982], this case does not involve an attempt by Congress itself to gain a role in the removal of executive officials other than its established powers of impeachment and conviction. The Act instead puts the removal power squarely in the hands of the Executive Branch. . . . In our view, the removal provisions of the Act make this case more analogous to Humphrey's Executor v. United States, 295 U.S. 602 (1935) [p. 983] and Wiener v. United States, 357 U.S. 349 (1958),[15] than to Myers or Bowsher.

". . . We undoubtedly did rely on the terms 'quasi-legislative' and 'quasi-judicial' to distinguish the officials involved in Humphrey's Executor and Wiener from those in Myers, but our present considered view is that the determination of whether the Constitution allows Congress to impose a 'good cause'-type restriction on the President's power to remove an official cannot be made to turn on whether or not that official is classified as 'purely executive.' The analysis contained in our removal cases is designed not to define rigid categories of those officials who may or may not be removed at

[15] [Ed.] Wiener held that neither the Constitution nor the underlying statute gave the President at-will removal power over a member of the War Claims Commission, which was an adjudicatory body.

will by the President,[28] but to ensure that Congress does not interfere with the President's exercise of the 'executive power' and his constitutionally appointed duty to 'take care that the laws be faithfully executed' under Article II. Myers was undoubtedly correct in its holding, and in its broader suggestion that there are some 'purely executive' officials who must be removable by the President at will if he is to be able to accomplish his constitutional role. . . . We do not mean to suggest that an analysis of the functions served by the officials at issue is irrelevant. But the real question is whether the removal restrictions are of such a nature that they impede the President's ability to perform his constitutional duty, and the functions of the officials in question must be analyzed in that light." In a footnote, the Court added: "The dissent says that the language of Article II vesting the executive power of the United States in the President requires that every officer of the United States exercising any part of that power must serve at the pleasure of the President and be removable by him at will. This rigid demarcation—a demarcation incapable of being altered by law in the slightest degree, and applicable to tens of thousands of holders of offices neither known nor foreseen by the Framers—depends upon an extrapolation from general constitutional language which we think is more than the text will bear."

The Court then rejected the claim that the removal protection for the independent counsel "unduly trammels on executive authority.... [Although the independent counsel performs] law enforcement functions that typically have been undertaken by officials within the Executive Branch . . . [and] the counsel exercises no small amount of discretion and judgment in deciding how to carry out her duties under the Act, we simply do not see how the President's need to control the exercise of that discretion is so central to the functioning of the Executive Branch as to require as a matter of constitutional law that the counsel be terminable at will by the President." In so holding, the Court emphasized that the Act gave "the Attorney General several means of supervising or controlling the prosecutorial powers that may be wielded by an independent counsel." Prime among these was the provision authorizing the Attorney General to remove the independent counsel for good cause, which the legislative history made clear was intended to allow removal for misconduct. In addition, the Attorney General had unreviewable discretion in determining whether to request appointment of an independent counsel, the counsel's jurisdiction would be determined by reference to the facts the Attorney General supplies, and once appointed an independent counsel was generally required to adhere to Department of Justice policy. As a result, the Court concluded that the Act did not "impermissibly undermine the powers of the Executive Branch, or 'disrupt[ ] the proper balance between the coordinate branches [by] prevent[ing] the Executive Branch from accomplishing its constitutionally assigned

[28] The difficulty of defining such categories of 'executive' or 'quasi-legislative' officials is illustrated by a comparison of our decisions in cases such as Humphrey's Executor, Buckley v. Valeo, 424 U.S. 1, 140–141 (1976) [p. 957], and Bowsher [v. Synar], 478 U.S. [714,]732–34 [(1986)] [p. 928] . . . As Justice White noted in his dissent in Bowsher, it is hard to dispute that the powers of the FTC at the time of Humphrey's Executor would at the present time be considered "executive," at least to some degree. See 478 U.S. at 761, n. 3.

functions,' Nixon v. Administrator of General Services, 433 U.S. [425,] 443 [(1977)]. In particular, although the Act undeniably reduced "the amount of control or supervision that the Attorney General and, through him, the President exercises over the investigation and prosecution of a certain class of alleged criminal activity," the removal limitation did not "sufficiently deprive[ ] the President of control over the independent counsel" as to interfere impermissibly with his constitutional obligation to ensure the faithful execution of the laws."

JUSTICE SCALIA wrote a stinging dissent: "Art. II, § 1, cl. 1 of the Constitution provides: 'The executive Power shall be vested in a President of the United States.' . . . [T]his does not mean *some* of the executive power, but *all of* the executive power. . . . The Court concedes that '[t]here is no real dispute that the functions performed by the independent counsel are executive . . . . [It] effects a revolution in our constitutional jurisprudence for the Court . . . to sit in judgment of whether 'the President's need to control the exercise of [the independent counsel's] discretion is *so central* to the functioning of the Executive Branch' as to require complete control' (emphasis added) . . . . It is not for us to determine, and we have never presumed to determine, how much of the purely executive powers of government must be within the full control of the President. The Constitution prescribes that they *all* are." According to Justice Scalia, while Humphrey's Executor's "line between 'purely executive' functions and 'quasi-legislative' or 'quasi-judicial' functions [wa]s not a clear one or even a rational one . . . at least it permitted the identification of certain officers, and certain agencies, whose functions were entirely within the control of the President. Congress had to be aware of that restriction in its legislation." The majority's reformulation of Humphrey's Executor and Myers as meaning "simply that Congress cannot 'interfere with the President's exercise of the executive power and his constitutionally appointed duty to take care that the laws be faithfully executed,'" represented "an open invitation for Congress to experiment. . . . Taking all things into account, we conclude that the power taken away from the President here is not really *too* much. . . . This is not analysis; it is ad hoc judgment."

Justice Scalia also warned about the poor incentives that the independent counsel system created, with the Independent Counsel "cut off from the unifying influence of the Justice Department, and from the perspective that multiple responsibilities provide. What would normally be regarded as a technical violation (there are no rules defining such things), may in his or her small world assume the proportions of an indictable offense. What would normally be regarded as an investigation that has reached the level of pursuing such picayune matters that it should be concluded, may to him or her be an investigation that ought to go on for another year." A longrunning independent counsel investigation of President Clinton led many to conclude that the dangers Scalia warned about had come to pass, and those concerns contributed to Congress letting the Act to expire when it came up for renewal. Instead, the Attorney General issued regulations under which a Special Counsel can be appointed. See 28 C.F.R. Part 600.

# SEILA LAW LLC v. CONSUMER FINANCIAL PROTECTION BUREAU

Supreme Court of the United States (2020).
140 S.Ct. 2183.

■ CHIEF JUSTICE ROBERTS delivered the opinion of the Court with respect to Parts I, II, and III.

[In the wake of the 2008 financial crisis, Congress established the Consumer Financial Protection Bureau and tasked it with ensuring that consumer debt products are safe and transparent. Although initially proposed as an independent regulatory agency headed by a multi-member commission, as ultimately enacted the CFPB is led by a single Director who serves a five-year term and cannot be removed by the President except for "inefficiency, neglect, or malfeasance in office." 12 U.S.C. § 5491(c)(3). Congress transferred the administration of eighteen existing consumer financial protection laws to the CFPB and enacted a new prohibition on "any unfair, deceptive, or abusive act or practice" by certain participants in the consumer-finance sector. § 5536(a)(1)(B). Congress authorized the CFPB to implement these statutes through binding regulations and gave it authority to conduct investigations, issue subpoenas and civil investigative demands, initiate and conduct administrative adjudications, and prosecute civil actions in federal court. It can seek a range of penalties, including civil penalties of up to $1,000,000 for each day that a violation occurs. Although housed in the Federal Reserve, the CFPB is not subject to the Board of Governors' oversight and receives annual funding directly from the Federal Reserve outside of the appropriations process.

In 2017, the CFPB issued a civil investigative demand to Seila Law LLC, to determine if the law firm had engaged in unlawful acts or practices in providing debt relief services. Seila Law resisted, objecting that the agency's leadership by a single Director removable only for-cause violated the separation of powers. The District Court ordered Seila Law to comply with the demand and the Court of Appeals affirmed.]

I

. . . We granted certiorari to address the constitutionality of the CFPB's structure. We also requested argument on an additional question: whether, if the CFPB's structure violates the separation of powers, the CFPB Director's removal protection can be severed from the rest of the Dodd-Frank Act. Because the Government agrees with petitioner on the merits of the constitutional question, we appointed Paul Clement to defend the judgment below as amicus curiae. . . .

III

We hold that the CFPB's leadership by a single individual removable only for inefficiency, neglect, or malfeasance violates the separation of powers.

A

Article II provides that "[t]he executive Power shall be vested in a President," who must "take Care that the Laws be faithfully executed." Art. II, § 1, cl. 1; id., § 3. The entire "executive Power" belongs to the President alone. But because it would be "impossib[le]" for "one man" to "perform all the great business of the State," the Constitution assumes that lesser executive officers will "assist the supreme Magistrate in discharging the duties of his trust." 30 Writings of George Washington 334 (J. Fitzpatrick ed. 1939). These lesser officers must remain accountable to the President, whose authority they wield. As Madison explained, "[I]f any power whatsoever is in its nature Executive, it is the power of appointing, overseeing, and controlling those who execute the laws." 1 Annals of Cong. 463 (1789). That power, in turn, generally includes the ability to remove executive officials, for it is "only the authority that can remove" such officials that they "must fear and, in the performance of [their] functions, obey." Bowsher [v. Synar], 478 U.S. [714,] 726 [(1986) (p. 928)].

The President's removal power has long been confirmed by history and precedent. It "was discussed extensively in Congress when the first executive departments were created" in 1789. Free Enterprise Fund, 561 U.S., at 492. "The view that 'prevailed, as most consonant to the text of the Constitution' and 'to the requisite responsibility and harmony in the Executive Department,' was that the executive power included a power to oversee executive officers through removal." Id. (quoting Letter from James Madison to Thomas Jefferson (June 30, 1789), 16 Documentary History of the First Federal Congress 893 (2004)). . . .

The Court recognized the President's prerogative to remove executive officials in Myers v. United States, 272 U.S. 21 [(1926) (p. 982)]. Chief Justice Taft, writing for the Court, . . . . concluded that Article II "grants to the President" the "general administrative control of those executing the laws, including the power of appointment *and removal* of executive officers." Id., at 163–164 (emphasis added). . . . "[T]o hold otherwise," the Court reasoned, "would make it impossible for the President . . . to take care that the laws be faithfully executed." Id., at 164. We recently reiterated the President's general removal power in Free Enterprise Fund. . . .

Free Enterprise Fund left in place two exceptions to the President's unrestricted removal power. First, in Humphrey's Executor, decided less than a decade after Myers, the Court upheld a statute that protected the Commissioners of the FTC from removal except for "inefficiency, neglect of duty, or malfeasance in office." 295 U.S. at 620. . . .

Because the Court limited its holding "to officers of the kind here under consideration," id., at 632, the contours of the Humphrey's Executor exception depend upon the characteristics of the agency before the Court. Rightly or wrongly, the Court viewed the FTC (as it existed in 1935) as exercising "no part of the executive power." Id., at 628. Instead, it was "an administrative body" that performed "specified duties as a legislative or as a judicial aid." It acted "as a legislative agency" in "making investigations and reports" to Congress and "as an agency of the judiciary" in making recommendations to courts as a master in chancery. Ibid. "To the extent that [the FTC] exercise[d] any executive *function*[,] as distinguished from executive power in the constitutional sense," it did so only in the discharge of its "quasi-legislative or quasi-judicial powers." (emphasis added). Ibid.[2]

The Court identified several organizational features that helped explain its characterization of the FTC as non-executive. Composed of five members—no more than three from the same political party—the Board was designed to be "non-partisan" and to "act with entire impartiality." Id., at 624. The FTC's duties were "neither political nor executive," but instead called for "the trained judgment of a body of experts" "informed by experience." Id., at 624. And the Commissioners' staggered, seven-year terms enabled the agency to accumulate technical expertise and avoid a "complete change" in leadership "at any one time."

In short, Humphrey's Executor permitted Congress to give for-cause removal protections to a multimember body of experts, balanced along partisan lines, that performed legislative and judicial functions and was said not to exercise any executive power.... Humphrey's Executor reaffirmed the core holding of Myers that the President has "unrestrictable power ... to remove purely executive officers." 295 U.S., at 632....

We have recognized a second exception for inferior officers in two cases, United States v. Perkins[, 116 U.S. 483 (1886) (p. 982)] and Morrison v. Olson[, 487 U.S. 654 (1988) (p. 986)]. In Perkins, we upheld tenure protections for a naval cadet-engineer. And, in Morrison, we upheld a provision granting good-cause tenure protection to an independent counsel appointed to investigate and prosecute particular alleged crimes by high-ranking Government officials. Backing away from the reliance in Humphrey's Executor on the concepts of "quasi-legislative" and "quasi-judicial" power, we viewed the ultimate question as whether a removal restriction is of "such a nature that [it] impede[s] the President's ability to perform his constitutional duty." 487 U.S., at 691.... [W]e concluded that the removal protections [for the independent counsel] did not unduly interfere with the functioning of the Executive Branch because "the independent counsel [was] an inferior officer under the Appointments Clause, with limited jurisdiction and tenure and lacking policymaking or significant administrative authority." Ibid.

These two exceptions—one for multimember expert agencies that do not wield substantial executive power, and one for inferior officers with limited duties and no policymaking or administrative authority—"represent what up to now have been the outermost constitutional limits of permissible congressional restrictions on the President's removal

[2] The Court's conclusion that the FTC did not exercise executive power has not withstood the test of time. As we observed in Morrison, "[I]t is hard to dispute that the powers of the FTC at the time of Humphrey's Executor would at the present time be considered 'executive,' at least to some degree." [487 U.S.] at 690, n. 28....

power." PHH [v. CFPB], 881 F.3d [75,] 196 [(2018)] (Kavanaugh, J., dissenting).

B

Neither Humphrey's Executor nor Morrison resolves whether the CFPB Director's insulation from removal is constitutional. Start with Humphrey's Executor. Unlike the New Deal-era FTC upheld there, the CFPB is led by a single Director who cannot be described as a "body of experts" and cannot be considered "non-partisan" in the same sense as a group of officials drawn from both sides of the aisle. Moreover, while the staggered terms of the FTC Commissioners prevented complete turnovers in agency leadership and guaranteed that there would always be some Commissioners who had accrued significant expertise, the CFPB's single-Director structure and five-year term guarantee abrupt shifts in agency leadership and with it the loss of accumulated expertise.

In addition, the CFPB Director is hardly a mere legislative or judicial aid. Instead of making reports and recommendations to Congress, as the 1935 FTC did, the Director possesses the authority to promulgate binding rules fleshing out 19 federal statutes, including a broad prohibition on unfair and deceptive practices in a major segment of the U.S. economy. And instead of submitting recommended dispositions to an Article III court, the Director may unilaterally issue final decisions awarding legal and equitable relief in administrative adjudications. Finally, the Director's enforcement authority includes the power to seek daunting monetary penalties against private parties on behalf of the United States in federal court—a quintessentially executive power not considered in Humphrey's Executor.[4]

The logic of Morrison also does not apply. Everyone agrees the CFPB Director is not an inferior officer, and her duties are far from limited. Unlike the independent counsel, who lacked policymaking or administrative authority, the Director has the sole responsibility to administer 19 separate consumer-protection statutes that cover everything from credit cards and car payments to mortgages and student loans. . . . [T]he CFPB Director has the authority to bring the coercive power of the state to bear on millions of private citizens and businesses, imposing even billion-dollar penalties through administrative adjudications and civil actions. . . .

C

The question instead is whether to extend those precedents to the "new situation" before us, namely an independent agency led by a single Director and vested with significant executive power. Free Enterprise Fund, 561 U.S., at 483. We decline to do so. Such an agency has no basis in history and no place in our constitutional structure.

---

[4] The dissent would have us ignore the reasoning of Humphrey's Executor and instead apply the decision only as part of a reimagined Humphrey's-through-Morrison framework. . . . But we take the decision on its own terms, not through gloss added by a later Court in dicta. . . .

1

"Perhaps the most telling indication of [a] severe constitutional problem" with an executive entity "is [a] lack of historical precedent" to support it. Free Enterprise, 561 U.S. at 505. An agency with a structure like that of the CFPB is almost wholly unprecedented. . . . [There are] "only a handful of isolated" incidents in which Congress has provided good-cause tenure to principal officers who wield power alone rather than as members of a board or commission. Ibid. [These include the Comptroller of the Currency for one year during the Civil War, "an aberration"; the Office of the Special Counsel (OSC) since 1978, but "the OSC exercises only limited jurisdiction over Federal Government employers and employees"; and the Social Security Administration (SSA), also "comparatively recent and controversial" and "its role is largely limited to adjudicating claims for Social Security benefits."]

The only remaining example is the Federal Housing Finance Agency (FHFA), created in 2008 to assume responsibility for Fannie Mae and Freddie Mac. That agency is essentially a companion of the CFPB[;] . . . regulates primarily Government-sponsored enterprises, not purely private actors[; and] was recently held unconstitutional by the Fifth Circuit, sitting en banc. . . . The CFPB's single-Director structure is an innovation with no foothold in history or tradition.[8]

2

In addition . . . our constitutional structure . . . [, with] the sole exception of the Presidency, . . . scrupulously avoids concentrating power in the hands of any single individual.

"The Framers recognized that, in the long term, structural protections against abuse of power were critical to preserving liberty." Bowsher, 478 U.S., at 730. Their solution to governmental power and its perils was simple: divide it. . . . [T]hey "split the atom of sovereignty" itself into one Federal Government and the States. Gamble v. United States, 139 S.Ct. 1960, 1968 (2019). They then divided the "powers of the new Federal Government into three defined categories, Legislative, Executive, and Judicial[,]" [INS v.] Chadha, 462 U.S. [919,] 951 [(1983) p. 881)] . . . [and] bifurcated the federal legislative power into two Chambers: the House of Representatives and the Senate. . . .

The Executive Branch is a stark departure from all this division. The Framers viewed the legislative power as a special threat to individual liberty, so they divided that power to ensure that "differences of opinion" and the "jarrings of parties" would "promote deliberation and circumspection" and "check excesses in the majority." See The Federalist No. 70, at 475 (A. Hamilton). By contrast, the Framers thought it

[8] The dissent categorizes the CFPB as one of many "financial regulators" that have historically enjoyed some insulation from the President. But even assuming financial institutions like the Second Bank and the Federal Reserve can claim a special historical status, the CFPB is in an entirely different league. It acts as a mini legislature, prosecutor, and court, responsible for creating substantive rules for a wide swath of industries, prosecuting violations, and levying knee-buckling penalties against private citizens. And, of course, it is the only agency of its kind run by a single Director.

necessary to secure the authority of the Executive so that he could carry out his unique responsibilities. See id., No. 70, at 475–478. . . .

To justify and check that authority—unique in our constitutional structure—the Framers made the President the most democratic and politically accountable official in Government. Only the President (along with the Vice President) is elected by the entire Nation. And the President's political accountability is enhanced by the solitary nature of the Executive Branch, which provides "a single object for the jealousy and watchfulness of the people." Id., at 479. . . .

The resulting constitutional strategy is straightforward: divide power everywhere except for the Presidency, and render the President directly accountable to the people through regular elections. In that scheme, individual executive officials will still wield significant authority, but that authority remains subject to the ongoing supervision and control of the elected President. . . .

The CFPB's single-Director structure contravenes this carefully calibrated system by vesting significant governmental power in the hands of a single individual accountable to no one. The Director is neither elected by the people nor meaningfully controlled (through the threat of removal) by someone who is. The Director does not even depend on Congress for annual appropriations. Yet the Director may *unilaterally*, without meaningful supervision, issue final regulations, oversee adjudications, set enforcement priorities, initiate prosecutions, and determine what penalties to impose on private parties. With no colleagues to persuade, and no boss or electorate looking over her shoulder, the Director may dictate and enforce policy for a vital segment of the economy affecting millions of Americans.

. . . [S]everal other features of the CFPB combine to make the Director's removal protection even more problematic. . . . Because the CFPB is headed by a single Director with a five-year term, some Presidents may not have any opportunity to shape its leadership and thereby influence its activities. . . . To make matters worse, the agency's single-Director structure means the President will not have the opportunity to appoint any other leaders—such as a chair or fellow members of a Commission or Board—who can serve as a check on the Director's authority and help bring the agency in line with the President's preferred policies.

The CFPB's receipt of funds outside the appropriations process further aggravates the agency's threat to Presidential control. The President normally has the opportunity to recommend or veto spending bills that affect the operation of administrative agencies. . . . But . . . the Director receives over $500 million per year to fund the agency's chosen priorities . . . from the Federal Reserve, which is itself funded outside of the annual appropriations process. . . .

3

Amicus raises three principal arguments in the agency's defense. At the outset, amicus questions the textual basis for the removal power. . . .

As we have explained many times before, the President's removal power stems from Article II's vesting of the "executive Power" in the President. Free Enterprise Fund, 561 U.S., at 483. . . .

Next, . . . [a]ccording to amicus, Humphrey's Executor and Morrison establish a general rule that Congress may impose "modest" restrictions on the President's removal power . . . But text, first principles, the First Congress's decision in 1789, Myers, and Free Enterprise Fund all establish that the President's removal power is the rule, not the exception. While we do not revisit Humphrey's Executor or any other precedent today, we decline to elevate it into a freestanding invitation for Congress to impose additional restrictions on the President's removal authority.[11]

Finally, amicus contends that if we identify a constitutional problem with the CFPB's structure, we should avoid it by broadly construing the statutory grounds for removing the CFPB Director from office. . . . We are not persuaded. For one, Humphrey's Executor implicitly rejected an interpretation that would leave the President free to remove an officer based on disagreements about agency policy. . . . Further, although nearly identical language governs the removal of some two-dozen multimember independent agencies, amicus suggests that the standard should vary from agency to agency, morphing as necessary to avoid constitutional doubt. We decline to embrace such an uncertain and elastic approach to the text. . . .

IV

Having concluded that the CFPB's leadership by a single independent Director violates the separation of powers, we now turn to the appropriate remedy. . . . [Petitioner argues that the demand is unenforceable because the statutory provision insulating the CFPB Director from removal cannot be severed from the other statutory provisions that define the CFPB's authority. If petitioner is correct, the offending removal provision means the entire agency is unconstitutional and powerless to act. The Government argues that the provision is severable and further contends that] the demand, though initially issued by a Director unconstitutionally insulated from removal, can still be enforced on remand because it has since been ratified by an Acting Director accountable to the President. . . .

"Generally speaking, when confronting a constitutional flaw in a statute, we try to limit the solution to the problem, severing any problematic portions while leaving the remainder intact." Free Enterprise Fund, 561 U.S., at 508. Even in the absence of a severability clause, the "traditional" rule is that "the unconstitutional provision must be severed unless the statute created in its absence is legislation that Congress would not have enacted." Alaska Airlines, Inc. v. Brock, 480 U.S. 678, 685 (1987). . . .

---

[11] Building on amicus' proposal, the dissent would endorse whatever "the times demand, so long as the President retains the ability to carry out his constitutional functions." But that amorphous test provides no real limiting principle. . . .

In Free Enterprise Fund, we found a set of unconstitutional removal provisions severable even in the absence of an express severability clause because the surviving provisions were capable of "functioning independently" and "nothing in the statute's text or historical context made it evident that Congress, faced with the limitations imposed by the Constitution, would have preferred no Board at all to a Board whose members are removable at will." 561 U.S., at 509.

So too here. The provisions of the Dodd-Frank Act bearing on the CFPB's structure and duties remain fully operative without the offending tenure restriction. Those provisions are capable of functioning independently, and there is nothing in the text or history of the Dodd-Frank Act that demonstrates Congress would have preferred no CFPB to a CFPB supervised by the President. Quite the opposite. Unlike the Sarbanes-Oxley Act at issue in Free Enterprise Fund, the Dodd-Frank Act contains an express severability clause. There is no need to wonder what Congress would have wanted if "any provision of this Act" is "held to be unconstitutional" because it has told us: "the remainder of this Act" should "not be affected." 12 U.S.C. § 5302. . . .

As in every severability case, there may be means of remedying the defect in the CFPB's structure that the Court lacks the authority to provide. Our severability analysis does not foreclose Congress from pursuing alternative responses to the problem—for example, converting the CFPB into a multimember agency. . . .

Because we find the Director's removal protection severable from the other provisions of Dodd-Frank that establish the CFPB, we remand for the Court of Appeals to consider whether the civil investigative demand was validly ratified. . . .

It is so ordered.

■ JUSTICE THOMAS, with whom JUSTICE GORSUCH joins, concurring in part and dissenting in part.

The Court's decision today takes a restrained approach on the merits by limiting Humphrey's Executor v. United States rather than overruling it. At the same time, the Court takes an aggressive approach on severability by severing a provision when it is not necessary to do so. I would do the opposite. . . .

The decision in Humphrey's Executor poses a direct threat to our constitutional structure and, as a result, the liberty of the American people. . . . Despite the defined structural limitations of the Constitution and the clear vesting of executive power in the President, Congress has increasingly shifted executive power to a de facto fourth branch of Government—independent agencies. These agencies wield considerable executive power without Presidential oversight. . . .

The Constitution does not permit the creation of officers exercising "quasi-legislative" and "quasi-judicial powers" in "quasi-legislative" and "quasi-judicial agencies." No such powers or agencies exist. Congress lacks the authority to delegate its legislative power and it cannot authorize the use of judicial power by officers acting outside of the bounds of Article III. Nor can Congress create agencies that straddle multiple branches of Government. The Constitution sets out three branches of Government and provides each with a different form of power—legislative, executive, and judicial. Free-floating agencies simply do not comport with this constitutional structure. . . .

To resolve this case, I would simply deny the [CFPB] petition to enforce the civil investigative demand. . . . "Early American courts did not have a severability doctrine." [Murphy v. National Collegiate Athletic Assn., 138 S.Ct. 1461], 1485 [(2018) (Thomas, J., concurring)]. If a statute was unconstitutional, the court would just decline to enforce the statute in the case before it. . . . Our modern severability precedents create tension with this historic practice. Instead of declining to enforce an unconstitutional statute in an individual case, this Court has stated that courts must "seve[r] and excis[e]" portions of a statute to "remedy" the constitutional problem. United States v. Booker, 543 U.S. 220, 245 (2005). . . . The Federal Judiciary does not have the power to excise, erase, alter, or otherwise strike down a statute. . . . [T]he text of the severability clause cannot, in isolation, justify severance of the removal provision. . . . The constitutional violation results from, at a minimum, the combination of the removal provision and the provision allowing the CFPB to seek enforcement of a civil investigative demand. When confronted with two provisions that operate together to violate the Constitution, the text of the severability clause provides no guidance as to *which* provision should be severed. . . .

■ JUSTICE KAGAN, with whom JUSTICE GINSBURG, JUSTICE BREYER, and JUSTICE SOTOMAYOR join, concurring in the judgment with respect to severability and dissenting in part.

Throughout the Nation's history, this Court has left most decisions about how to structure the Executive Branch to Congress and the President, acting through legislation they both agree to. . . . Our Constitution and history demand that result. . . . The Court today fails to respect its proper role. . . .

I . . .

A

. . . The majority offers the civics class version of separation of powers—call it the Schoolhouse Rock definition of the phrase. See Schoolhouse Rock! Three Ring Government (Mar. 13, 1979) ("Ring one, Executive. Two is Legislative, that's Congress. Ring three, Judiciary"). The Constitution's first three articles, the majority recounts, "split the atom of sovereignty" among Congress, the President, and the courts. And by that mechanism, the Framers provided a "simple" fix "to governmental power and its perils."

There is nothing wrong with that as a beginning (except the adjective "simple"). It is of course true that the Framers lodged three different kinds of power in three different entities. . . . The problem lies in treating the beginning as an ending too—in failing to recognize that the separation of powers is, by design, neither rigid nor complete. . . .

. . . Article II presumes the existence of "Officer[s]" in "executive Departments." § 2, cl. 1. But it does not . . . give the President authority to decide what kinds of officers—in what departments, with what responsibilities—the Executive Branch requires. Instead, Article I's Necessary and Proper Clause puts those decisions in the legislature's hands. . . . Similarly, . . . . the President can appoint principal officers, but only as the legislature "shall . . . establish[ ] by Law" (and of course subject to the Senate's advice and consent). Art. II, § 2, cl. 2. And Congress has plenary power to decide not only what inferior officers will exist but also who (the President or a head of department) will appoint them. . . . The President, as to the construction of his own branch of government, can only try to work his will through the legislative process.[3]

The majority relies for its contrary vision on Article II's Vesting Clause, but the provision can't carry all that weight. . . . The Necessary and Proper Clause . . . makes it impossible to "establish a constitutional violation simply by showing that Congress has constrained the way '[t]he executive Power' is implemented"; that is exactly what the Clause gives Congress the power to do. [John Manning, Separation of Powers as Ordinary Interpretation, 124 Harv. L. Rev. 1939,] 1967 [(2011)]. . . . [N]ote two points about practice before the Constitution's drafting. First, in that era, Parliament often restricted the King's power to remove royal officers—and the President, needless to say, wasn't supposed to be a king. Second, many States at the time allowed limits on gubernatorial removal power even though their constitutions had similar vesting clauses. Historical understandings thus belie the majority's "general rule."

Nor can the Take Care Clause come to the majority's rescue. . . . To begin with, the provision . . . speaks of duty, not power. Art. II, § 3. . . . And yet more important, the text of the Take Care Clause requires only enough authority to make sure "the laws [are] faithfully executed"—meaning with fidelity to the law itself, not to every presidential policy preference. . . . A for-cause standard gives [the President] "ample authority to assure that [an official] is competently performing [his] statutory responsibilities in a manner that comports with the [relevant legislation's] provisions." [Morrison, 487 U.S., at 692]. . . .

B

History no better serves the majority's cause. . . . Delegates to the Constitutional Convention never discussed whether or to what extent the President would have power to remove executive officials. As a result, the Framers advocating ratification had no single view of the matter. . . .

---

[3] Article II's Opinion Clause also demonstrates the possibility of limits on the President's control over the Executive Branch. Under that Clause, the President "may require the Opinion, in writing, of the principal Officer in each of the executive Departments, upon any Subject relating to the Duties of their respective Offices." § 2, cl. 1. For those in the majority's camp, that Clause presents a puzzle: If the President must always have the direct supervisory control they posit, including by threat of removal, why would he ever need a constitutional warrant to demand agency heads' opinions? The Clause becomes at least redundant—though really, inexplicable—under the majority's idea of executive power.

The second chapter is the Decision of 1789, when Congress addressed the removal power while considering the bill creating the Department of Foreign Affairs. Speaking through Chief Justice Taft—a judicial presidentialist if ever there was one—this Court in Myers read that debate as expressing Congress's judgment that the Constitution gave the President illimitable power to remove executive officials. . . . But Taft's historical research has held up even worse than Myers' holding. . . . The best view is that the First Congress was "deeply divided" on the President's removal power, and "never squarely addressed" the central issue here. [Manning, 124 Harv. L. Rev., at 1965 n. 135]. . . .

At the same time, the First Congress gave officials handling financial affairs—as compared to diplomatic and military ones—some independence from the President. . . .

Take first Congress's decision in 1816 to create the Second Bank of the United States . . . . Of the twenty-five directors who led the Bank, the President could appoint and remove only five. Yet the Bank had a greater impact on the Nation than any but a few institutions, regulating the Nation's money supply in ways anticipating what the Federal Reserve does today. . . .

The Civil War brought yet further encroachments on presidential control over financial regulators[, with Congress—at President Lincoln's request—creating the Comptroller of the Currency, initially removable only with the Senate's consent and a year later made removable by the President alone. But] . . . even the second iteration of the statute preserved a constraint on the removal power, requiring a President in a firing mood to explain himself to Congress . . ..

And then, nearly a century and a half ago, the floodgates opened,[with Congress creating the Interstate Commerce Commission in 1887 and granting its members for-cause removal protection, and similar protection following for the Federal Reserve Board in 1913, then the FTC in 1914, and others.] . . . By one count, across all subject matter areas, 48 agencies have heads (and below them hundreds more inferior officials) removable only for cause. . . .

C

What is more, the Court's precedents before today have accepted the role of independent agencies in our governmental system . . . repeatedly [upholding] provisions that prevent the President from firing regulatory officials except for such matters as neglect or malfeasance. In those decisions, we sounded a caution, insisting that Congress could not impede through removal restrictions the President's performance of his own constitutional duties. . . . But within that broad limit, this Court held, Congress could protect from at-will removal the officials it deemed to need some independence from political pressures. Nowhere do those precedents suggest what the majority announces today: that the President has an "unrestricted removal power" subject to two bounded exceptions.

The majority grounds its new approach in Myers, ignoring the way this Court has cabined that decision. . . . What the majority does not say is that within a decade the Court abandoned [Myers's] view [of an unrestrained removal power]. . . . In Humphrey's Executor the Court unceremoniously—and unanimously—confined Myers to its facts [with subsequent decisions reading Myers as standing for the principle that Congress's own "participation in the removal of executive officers is unconstitutional."] . . .

[Five] decades on, Morrison both extended Humphrey's domain and clarified . . . [that the] key question in all the cases . . . was whether such a restriction would "impede the President's ability to perform his constitutional duty." 487 U.S., at 691. . . . The majority's description of Morrison is not true to the decision. . . . First, Morrison is no "exception" to a broader rule from Myers. . . . Second, . . . Morrison is not limited to inferior officers.

Even Free Enterprise Fund, in which the Court recently held a removal provision invalid, operated within the framework of this precedent—and in so doing, left in place a removal provision just like the one here. . . . [F]or almost a century, this Court has made clear that Congress has broad discretion to enact for-cause protections in pursuit of good governance.

D

The deferential approach this Court has taken gives Congress the flexibility it needs to craft administrative agencies. Diverse problems of government demand diverse solutions. They call for varied measures and mixtures of democratic accountability and technical expertise, energy and efficiency. Sometimes, the arguments push toward tight presidential control of agencies. The President's engagement, some people say, can disrupt bureaucratic stagnation, counter industry capture, and make agencies more responsive to public interests. See, well, Kagan, Presidential Administration, 114 Harv. L. Rev. 2245, 2331–2346 (2001). At other times, the arguments favor greater independence from presidential involvement. Insulation from political pressure helps ensure impartial adjudications. It places technical issues in the hands of those most capable of addressing them. It promotes continuity, and prevents short-term electoral interests from distorting policy. . . . No mathematical formula governs institutional design; trade-offs are endemic to the enterprise. But that is precisely why the issue is one for the political branches to debate—and then debate again as times change. And it's why courts should stay (mostly) out of the way. . . .

II . . .

A

. . . This Court, as the majority acknowledges, has sustained the constitutionality of the FTC and similar independent agencies. The for-cause protections for the heads of those agencies . . . do not impede the President's ability to perform his own constitutional duties, and so do not breach the separation of powers. There is nothing different here. . . .

First, the CFPB's powers are nothing unusual in the universe of independent agencies. . . . Just for a comparison, the CFPB now has 19 enforcement actions pending, while the SEC brought 862 such actions last year alone. . . . And if influence on economic life is the measure, consider the Federal Reserve, whose every act has global consequence. . . . Second, the removal protection given the CFPB's Director is standard fare. . . . The statute provides only one layer of protection, unlike the law in Free Enterprise Fund. And the . . . for-cause standard used for the CFPB is identical to the one the Court upheld in Humphrey's. . . .

B

The majority focuses on one (it says sufficient) reason: The CFPB Director is singular, not plural.[11] . . . [T]he majority's "exceptions" (like its general rule) are made up. . . . "The analysis contained in our removal cases," Morrison stated, shuns any attempt "to define rigid categories" of officials who may (or may not) have job protection. 487 U.S., at 689. . . . [I]f the majority really wants to see something "novel," it need only look to its opinion. By contrast, the CFPB's single-director structure has a fair bit of precedent behind it. The Comptroller of the Currency. The Office of the Special Counsel (OSC). The Social Security Administration (SSA). The Federal Housing Finance Agency (FHFA). . . .

Still more important, novelty is not the test of constitutionality when it comes to structuring agencies. Congress regulates in that sphere under the Necessary and Proper Clause, not (as the majority seems to think) a Rinse and Repeat Clause. The Framers understood that new times would often require new measures, and exigencies often demand innovation. . . .

. . . [T]he distinction between singular and plural agency heads must rest on a theory about why the former more easily "slip" from the President's grasp. . . . In fact, the opposite is more likely to be true: To the extent that such matters are measurable, individuals are easier than groups to supervise. . . . Presidential control, as noted earlier, can operate through many means[,] . . . [t]he effectiveness of [which] . . . depend[s] on a multitude of agency-specific [factors]. . . . But if the demand is for generalization, then the majority's distinction cuts the opposite way: . . . A multimember structure reduces accountability to the President because it's harder for him to oversee, to influence—or to remove, if necessary—a group of five or more commissioners than a single director. Indeed, that is *why* Congress so often resorts to hydra-headed agencies. . . .

---

[11] The majority briefly mentions, but understandably does not rely on, two other features of Congress's scheme. First, the majority notes that the CFPB receives its funding outside the normal appropriations process. But so too do other financial regulators, including the Federal Reserve Board and the FDIC. And budgetary independence comes mostly at the expense of Congress's control over the agency, not the President's. (Because that is so, it actually works to the President's advantage.) Second, the majority complains that the Director's five-year term may prevent a President from "shap[ing the agency's] leadership" through appointments. But again that is true, to one degree or another, of quite a few longstanding independent agencies. . . .

. . .The majority . . . says a single head is the greater threat because he may wield power "unilaterally" and "[w]ith no colleagues to persuade." So the CFPB falls victim to what the majority sees as a constitutional anti-power-concentration principle (with an exception for the President). If you've never heard of a statute being struck down on that ground, you're not alone. It is bad enough to "extrapolat[e]" from the "general constitutional language" of Article II's Vesting Clause an unrestricted removal power constraining Congress's ability to legislate under the Necessary and Proper Clause. Morrison, 487 U.S. at 690, n.29. It is still worse to extrapolate from the Constitution's general structure (division of powers) and implicit values (liberty) a limit on Congress's express power to create administrative bodies. And more: to extrapolate from such sources a distinction as prosaic as that between the SEC and the CFPB—i.e., between a multi-headed and single-headed agency. . . .

[Justice Kagan also noted that "[t]he outcome today will not shut down the CFPB: A different majority of this Court, including all those who join this opinion, believes that *if* the agency's removal provision is unconstitutional, it should be severed."]

## SIGNIFICANT CASE

### FREE ENTERPRISE FUND v. PUBLIC COMPANY ACCOUNTING OVERSIGHT BOARD
561 U.S. 477 (2010).

In response to a series of celebrated accounting scandals, Congress created the Public Company Accounting Oversight Board as part of the Sarbanes Oxley Act of 2002 (Act). The Board—also known as PCAOB or sometimes "Peekaboo"—is charged with undertaking closer oversight and regulation of the accounting industry. The Board is composed of five members serving five-year terms. The Board's members are appointed by the Securities and Exchange Commission, which also oversees the Board's actions. In particular, the Board's issuance of rules and imposition of sanctions are subject to SEC approval and alteration, and the SEC also determines the Board's budget by setting the fees the board can charge to the entities it regulates. Under the Act, however, the individual members of the Board enjoyed substantial protection from removal. The SEC could remove them only "for good cause shown"—defined as either (1) willful violations of the Act, Board rules, or the securities laws; (2) willful abuse of authority; or (3) unreasonable failure to enforce compliance—as determined in a formal SEC order, rendered on the record and after notice and an opportunity for a hearing. 15 U.S.C. §§ 7211(f), 7217. An accounting firm subject to formal investigation by the Board, along with a nonprofit association, filed suit arguing that the Board contravened the separation of powers by conferring wide-ranging executive power on Board members without subjecting them to presidential control, and also violated the Appointments Clause.

CHIEF JUSTICE ROBERTS, writing for a five-member majority, began by stating that "[t]he parties do not ask us to reexamine" Humphrey's Executor, Perkins, or Morrison, "and we do not do so." He also noted that although the SEC's statute is silent on removal, "[t]he parties agree that the Commissioners themselves cannot be removed by the President except under the Humphrey's Executor standard of 'inefficiency, neglect of duty, or malfeasance in office,' and we decide the case with that understanding." He then proceeded to argue that, given the Board's placement under a Commission whose members also enjoyed removal protection, this case was fundamentally different from these precedents:

"The landmark case of Myers v. United States reaffirmed the principle that Article II confers on the President 'the general administrative control of those executing the laws.' 272 U.S. [52,]164 [(1926) (p. 982)]. It is *his* responsibility to take care that the laws be faithfully executed. The buck stops with the President, in Harry Truman's famous phrase.... [W]e have previously upheld [in Humphrey's Executor, Perkins, and Morrison] limited restrictions on the President's removal power. In those cases, however, only one level of protected tenure separated the President from an officer exercising executive power. It was the President—or a subordinate he could remove at will—who decided whether the officer's conduct merited removal under the good-cause standard. The Act before us does something quite different. It not only protects Board members from removal except for good cause, but withdraws from the President any decision on whether that good cause exists. That decision is vested instead in other tenured officers—the Commissioners—none of whom is subject to the President's direct control. The result is a Board that is not accountable to the President, and a President who is not responsible for the Board.

"The added layer of tenure protection makes a difference. Without a layer of insulation between the Commission and the Board, the Commission could remove a Board member at any time, and therefore would be fully responsible for what the Board does. The President could then hold the Commission to account for its supervision of the Board, to the same extent that he may hold the Commission to account for everything else it does. A second level of tenure protection changes the nature of the President's review.... This novel structure does not merely add to the Board's independence, but transforms it. Neither the President, nor anyone directly responsible to him, nor even an officer whose conduct he may review only for good cause, has full control over the Board...."

According to the Court, "[t]hat arrangement is contrary to Article II's vesting of the executive power in the President. Without the ability to oversee the Board, or to attribute the Board's failings to those whom he *can* oversee, the President ... can neither ensure that the laws are faithfully executed, nor be held responsible for a Board member's breach of faith." Moreover, this "diffusion of power carries with it a diffusion of accountability. . . . Without a clear and effective chain of command, the public cannot 'determine on whom the blame or the punishment of a pernicious measure, or series of pernicious measures ought really to fall.' The Federalist No. 70 (Hamilton). By granting the Board executive power without the Executive's oversight, this Act subverts the President's ability to ensure that the laws are faithfully executed—as well as the public's ability to pass judgment on his efforts." In response to what he called "the dissent's paean to the administrative state," Roberts added: "No one doubts Congress's power to create a vast and varied federal bureaucracy. But where, in all this, is the role for oversight by an elected President? . . . One can have a government that functions without being ruled by functionaries, and a government that benefits from expertise without being ruled by experts. Our Constitution was adopted to enable the people to govern themselves, through their elected leaders. The growth of the Executive Branch, which now wields vast power and touches almost every aspect of daily life, heightens the concern that it may slip from the Executive's control, and thus from that of the people."

The Court rejected the Government's argument that "the Commission's removal power over the Board is broad," emphasizing the "unusually high standard that must be met before Board members may be removed." The Court also rejected the argument that the SEC's broad power over the Board generally rendered "the Act's limitations on removal . . . irrelevant. . . . Broad power over Board functions is not equivalent to the power to remove Board members." Roberts also argued that "the Board is empowered to take significant enforcement actions, and does so largely independently of the Commission. Its powers are, of course, subject to some latent Commission control. But the Act nowhere gives the Commission effective power to start, stop, or alter individual Board investigations."

Roberts also distinguished the Board from a number of positions the dissent identified as also involving double-for-cause removal protection: "[N]one of the[se] positions . . . are similarly situated to the Board. For example, many civil servants within independent agencies would not qualify as 'Officers of the United States,' who 'exercis[e] significant authority pursuant to the laws of the United States,' Buckley [v. Valeo], 424 U.S. [1], 126 [(1976) (p. 957)]. . . . We do not decide the status of other Government employees, nor do we decide whether 'lesser functionaries subordinate to officers of the United States' must be subject to the same sort of control as those who exercise 'significant authority pursuant to the laws.' . . . Nothing in our opinion, therefore, should be read to cast doubt on the use of what is colloquially known as the civil service system within independent agencies." In a footnote, Roberts added "[f]or similar reasons, our holding also does not address that subset of independent agency employees who serve as administrative law judges" and he accursed the dissent of "wander[ing] far afield when it suggests that today's opinion might increase the President's authority to remove military officers."

The Court then took up the question of remedy, determining that the appropriate response was to sever the removal protections for Board members: "[T]he existence of the Board does not violate the separation of powers . . . . Under the traditional default rule, removal is incident to the power of appointment. Concluding that the removal restrictions are invalid leaves the Board removable by the Commission at will, and leaves the President separated from Board members by only a single level of good-cause tenure. The Commission is then fully responsible for the Board's actions, which are no less subject than the Commission's own functions to Presidential oversight. The Sarbanes-Oxley Act remains 'fully operative as a law' with these tenure restrictions excised." Acknowledging that "[i]n theory the Court might blue-pencil" other provisions to render the PCAOB constitutional—including limiting its responsibilities and enforcement powers, or making the PCAOB directly subject to presidential removal—Roberts insisted that "such editorial freedom—far more extensive than our holding today—belongs to the Legislature, not the Judiciary." Finally, the Court held that, once the removal protections were severed, the members of the Board were inferior officers properly appointed by the head of a department, in this case the SEC.

JUSTICE BREYER, joined by Justices Stevens, Ginsburg and Sotomayor, strongly dissented. He began by stating that this case arose "at the intersection of two general constitutional principles": Congress's "broad power to enact statutes 'necessary and proper' to the exercise of its specifically enumerated constitutional authority" and the "structural separation-of-powers principle" implied from the Vesting Clauses of Articles I, II, and III that, "along with the instruction in Article II, § 3 that the President 'shall take Care that the Laws be faithfully executed,' limits Congress' power to structure the Federal Government." Breyer emphasized that "neither of these two principles is absolute in its application to removal cases" and "[i]n answering the question presented, we cannot look to more specific constitutional text . . . because, with the exception of the general 'vesting' and 'take care' language, the Constitution is completely 'silent with respect to the power of removal from office.' Ex parte Hennen, 13 Pet. 230, 258 (1839)."

Breyer then proceeded to advocate a functionalist approach: "When previously deciding this kind of nontextual question, the Court has emphasized the importance of examining how a particular provision, taken in context, is likely to function. . . . It is not surprising that the Court in these circumstances has looked to function and context, and not to bright-line rules. For one thing, that approach embodies the intent of the Framers. . . . For another, a functional approach permits Congress and the President the flexibility needed to adapt statutory law to changing circumstances. . . . [T]he Federal Government at the time of the founding consisted of about 2,000 employees and served a population of about 4 million. Today, however, the Federal Government employs about *4.4 million workers* who serve a Nation of more than 310 million people living in a society characterized by rapid technological, economic, and social change. . . . [V]ast numbers of statutes governing vast numbers of subjects, concerned with vast numbers of different problems, provide for, or foresee, their execution or administration through the work of administrators organized within many different kinds of administrative structures, exercising different kinds of administrative authority, to achieve their legislatively mandated objectives."

Applying that functionalist approach, Breyer asked "[t]o what extent then is the Act's 'for cause' provision likely, as a practical matter, to limit the President's exercise of executive authority?" He insisted that the removal protection for Board members "will not restrict presidential power significantly. . . . [S]o long as the President is *legitimately foreclosed* from removing the *Commissioners* except for cause (as the majority assumes), nullifying the Commission's power to remove Board members only for cause will not resolve the problem the Court has identified." In addition, "once we leave the realm of hypothetical logic and view the removal provision at issue in the context of the entire Act, its lack of practical effect becomes readily apparent. That is because the statute provides the Commission with full authority and virtually comprehensive control over all of the Board's functions. . . . Where a 'for cause' provision is so unlikely to restrict presidential power and so likely to further a legitimate institutional need, precedent strongly supports its constitutionality. . . . [I]n considering a related issue in Nixon v. Administrator of General Services, 433 U.S. 425 (1977), the Court made clear that when 'determining whether the Act disrupts the proper balance between the coordinate branches, the proper inquiry focuses on the extent to which it prevents the Executive Branch from accomplishing its constitutionally assigned functions.' Id., at 443. . . . Here, the removal restriction may somewhat diminish the *Commission's* ability to control the Board, but it will have little, if any, negative effect in respect to the President's ability to control the Board, let alone to coordinate the Executive Branch."

Breyer also argued that the majority's categorical rule against double-for-cause protection would breed uncertainty, given confusion over who qualifies as an inferior officer and the fact that "[t]he civil service . . . includes many officers indistinguishable from the members of both the Commission and the Accounting Board." He added that his own "conservative estimate" had "identified 573 . . . high-ranking officials" who appeared to enjoy double-for-cause protection.

Finally, he asked: "How can the Court simply *assume* without deciding that the SEC Commissioners themselves are removable only 'for cause?'. . . The Court . . . reads *into* the statute books a 'for cause removal' phrase that does not appear in the relevant statute and which Congress probably did not intend to write. And it does so in order to strike down, not to uphold, another statute. This is not a statutory construction that seeks to avoid a constitutional question, but its opposite."

## NOTES

(1) ***The Latest Word(s).*** The year after Seila Law, the Supreme Court addressed another removal restriction in COLLINS V. YELLEN, 141 S.Ct. 1761 (2021). At issue in Collins was another single-director-headed independent agency, the Federal Housing Finance Agency, created in 2008 during the financial crisis and tasked with overseeing Fannie Mae and Freddie Mac, two of the Nation's leading sources of mortgage financing. Both are for-profit corporations created by the federal government, and both suffered major losses in the crisis. Soon after it was established, the FHFA placed Fannie Mae and Freddie Mac into conservatorship (which it had authority to do) and negotiated agreements under which the Treasury Department committed to provide hundreds of billions of dollars to the companies, if needed, in exchange for dividends. At issue in Collins was a provision of one these deals, called the third amendment. Instead of promises to pay Treasury a set amount in quarterly dividends—promises that the companies had made in earlier agreements and been unable to meet—the third amendment provided that the companies would pay Treasury variable dividends equal to the companies' net worth less a capital reserve. This arrangement resulted in the companies paying back a huge amount in dividends as their financial condition improved. A group of Fannie Mae and Freddie Mac shareholders challenged the third amendment in part on the ground that the FHFA's structure was unconstitutional.

The Court agreed, in an opinion by JUSTICE ALITO that called Seila Law "all but dispositive" for the FHFA case: "A straightforward application of our reasoning in Seila Law dictates the result here. The FHFA (like the CFPB) is an agency led by a single Director, and the Recovery Act (like the Dodd-Frank Act) restricts the President's removal power." In so holding, the Court rejected the argument that the FHFA's more limited authority meant that Congress should have greater leeway to restrict the President's removal authority: "We have noted differences between these two agencies. . . . But the nature and breadth of an agency's authority is not dispositive in determining whether Congress may limit the President's power to remove its head. The President's removal power serves vital purposes even when the officer subject to removal is not the head of one of the largest and most powerful agencies. The removal power helps the President maintain a degree of control over the subordinates he needs to carry out his duties as the head of the Executive Branch, and it works to ensure that these subordinates serve the people effectively and in accordance with the policies that the people presumably elected the President to promote. In addition, because the President, unlike agency officials, is elected, this control is essential to subject Executive Branch actions to a degree of electoral accountability. . . . These purposes are implicated whenever an agency does important work, and nothing about the size or role of the FHFA convinces us that its Director should be treated differently from the Director of the CFPB."

As for remedy, the Court rejected the shareholders' request to void the third amendment and return to Fannie and Freddie the payments they had made pursuant to it: "[T]he Acting Director who adopted the third amendment was removable at will. That conclusion defeats the shareholders' argument for setting aside the third amendment in its entirety. . . . Although the statute unconstitutionally limited the President's authority to remove the confirmed Directors, there was no constitutional defect in the statutorily prescribed method of appointment to that office. As a result, there is no reason to regard any of the actions taken by the FHFA in relation to the third amendment as void." The Court "remand[ed] the case for further proceedings to determine what remedy, if any, the shareholders are entitled to receive," tasking the lower court with determining whether the President would have acted to undo the third amendment but for the removal restriction. JUSTICE THOMAS joined the majority in full, but wrote a concurrence arguing that "the Government does not necessarily act unlawfully even if a removal restriction is unlawful in the abstract." JUSTICE GORSUCH concurred in part but disagreed with the majority on remedy, arguing that because of the unconstitutional removal restriction, the Director's actions implementing the third amendment were void and should be set aside.

JUSTICE KAGAN (joined in part by Justices Breyer and Sotomayor) concurred in the judgment for stare decisis reasons, but wrote separately to note her disagreement with the majority's political theory about the working of government and its, in her view, unwarranted expansion of Seila Law: "Again and again, Seila Law emphasized that its rule was limited to single-director agencies 'wield[ing] significant executive power.' To take Seila Law at its word is to acknowledge where it left off: If an agency did not exercise 'significant executive power,' the constitutionality of a removal restriction would remain an open question. But today's majority careens right past that boundary line. Without even mentioning Seila Law's 'significant executive power' framing, the majority announces that, actually, 'the constitutionality of removal restrictions' does not 'hinge[ ]' on 'the nature and breadth of an agency's authority.' Any 'agency led by a single Director,' no matter how much executive power it wields, now becomes subject to the requirement of at-will removal. And the majority's broadening is gratuitous . . . [because] the FHFA exercises plenty of executive authority." JUSTICE SOTOMAYOR, joined by Justice Breyer, concurred in part and dissented in part. She agreed that Seila Law's holding is limited to agencies which wield significant executive power, but concluded that "the FHFA lack[s] significant executive power" and "the authority it does possess is exercised over other governmental actors."

Do you find any of the differences between the CFPB and FHFA relevant to the constitutional question? What do you make of Justice Kagan's complaint? And do you side with Justice Alito or Justice Gorsuch on the remedy?

The Social Security Administration (SSA) is similarly headed by a single director statutorily protected from removal except for neglect of duty or malfeasance in office. In July 2021, the Office of Legal Counsel in the Department of Justice issued an opinion concluding that "[t]he best reading of Collins and Seila Law leads to the conclusion that, notwithstanding the statutory limitation on removal, the President can remove the SSA Commissioner at will." Constitutionality of the Commissioner of Social

Security's Tenure Protection (July 8, 2021).[16] The opinion stated: "We emphasize that both of these recent decisions leave open the possibility that certain agencies, including (and perhaps especially) some that conduct adjudications, may constitutionally be led by officials protected from at-will removal by the President. But we think that under Collins and Seila Law, the combination of features of the SSA—a single Commissioner whose term extends longer than the President's, the immense scope of the agency's programs, the Commissioner's broad power to affect beneficiaries and the public fisc, and the SSA's largely unparalleled structure—means that the President need not heed the Commissioner's statutory tenure protection." Do you agree with OLC's analysis? President Biden proceeded to fire the SSA Commissioner; do you think he should have? Biden also fired the FHFA head after Collins was decided, and right before assuming office asked the CFPB head to resign.

(2) ***Formalism Versus Functionalism.*** How would you classify the methodological approach of the Roberts's majority opinions in Seila Law and Free Enterprise? In Seila Law, Roberts starts off formalistic, emphasizing that Article II's Vesting Clause gives the President the executive power and harkening back to understandings of the President's removal authority in 1789. But he very quickly turns to precedent, in particular reaffirming Myers and then distinguishing Humphrey's Executor and Morrison. More importantly, isn't his main argument for distinguishing the CFPB—its single director structure—decidedly functionalist, with its analysis of the ease with which a President could exert control and the alternative checks available in a multi-headed agency? Is his Free Enterprise opinion more formalist? There too, Roberts underscores the Article II Vesting and Take Care Clauses, and insists on the importance of removal authority over a variety of other checks and levers of control; as in Seila Law, he also draws a sharp line between acceptable and nonacceptable structures (no double-for-cause removal). But what about Free Enterprise's insistence that it wasn't reconsidering Humphrey's Executor or the constitutionality of a single level of removal protection, such as existed as a result of the Court's decision, with the President able to remove SEC members only for cause but the SEC able to remove the PCAOB members at will. Do those features make the opinion more functionalist?

The dissents in both Seila Law and Free Enterprise are avowedly functionalist. Justices Kagan and Breyer reject formalistic lines and instead assess whether the removal arrangements and other features of the CFPB and PCAOB allowed the President to still ensure that the laws were faithfully executed. But does a functionalist approach necessarily lead to sustaining the for-cause restriction on removing the CFPB Director or PCAOB members? Functionalist PETER L. STRAUSS emphasizes that "Congress's creation of a 'for cause'-protected institution (the PCAOB) within another 'for cause'-protection institution (the SEC) . . . [was] virtually unique. . . . Had the majority clearly held only that Congress could not constitutionally create one fully-functioned 'for cause'-protected agency

[16] https://www.justice.gov/olc/opinion/constitutionality-commissioner-social-security-s-tenure-protection.

within another such agency, there would have been little to write about. It is hard to imagine such a conclusion doing much mischief." ON THE DIFFICULTIES OF GENERALIZATION, PCAOB IN THE FOOTSTEPS OF MYERS, HUMPHREY'S EXECUTOR, MORRISON AND FREYTAG, 32 Cardozo L. Rev. 2255, 2278 (2011).

Do these cases suggest that the formalism-functionalism divide no longer has much explanatory power? Or is the difference that Roberts himself is more of an incrementalist and unwilling to go farther than necessary to decide these cases in a way that upholds presidential control? The brief excerpt you have above of Justice Thomas's concurrence in Seila Law, joined by Justice Gorsuch, suggests a much more formalist approach. Consider Yellen in this regard. Is it more formalistic in its insistence that "the nature and breadth of an agency's authority" does not determine whether a restriction on presidential removal power is constitutional? What about its other arguments, such as its emphasis on the importance of political accountability through the President?

As for constitutional interpretive methodology more broadly: Do the majorities and dissents in these removal cases use the same standard modes of constitutional interpretation—e.g., making arguments based on constitutional text and structure, original understandings, historical practice, precedent, normative values, pragmatic implications, and prudence? See, e.g., Philip Bobbitt, Constitutional Interpretation 12–13 (1991). Or do they differ in the types of arguments they make, or at least the modes of interpretation they emphasize? The main lines of argument in the opinions are explored below; think about which arguments you find more or less convincing, and why.

(3) ***Mining the Text.*** Defenders of an unlimited presidential removal power often invoke the Article II Vesting and Take Care Clauses. In his Morrison dissent, Justice Scalia insisted that the Vesting Clause "does not mean *some* of the executive power, but *all of* the executive power" is vested in the President. See also Steven G. Calabresi & Saikrishna B. Prakash, The President's Power to Execute the Laws, 104 Yale L.J. 541 (1994). The Morrison majority responded that this Vesting Clause argument "depends upon an extrapolation from general constitutional language which . . . is more than the text will bear." Recently, some scholars have based their defense of constitutionally protected presidential removal authority more on the Take Care Clause. Michael McConnell, for example, argues that the Vesting Clause provides the President with only a residual removal authority that is defeasible by Congress, but contends that the President's obligation to "take Care that the Laws be faithfully executed" entails that the President must be able to at least remove principal officers at will. The President Who Would Not Be King 165–69, 335–41 (2020).

How much work do you think the Vesting Clause or Take Care Clause can do in supporting a presidential claim of unlimited removal power? Jed Shugerman critiques efforts to base a broad removal power in the Article II Vesting Clause for inserting an "all" before "executive power" that is notably absent from the Clause's text and further contends that "[t]he Founding era's texts, debates, constitutions, and dictionaries reveal that the word 'vest' generally meant a simple grant of powers without the constitutional significance of exclusivity or indefeasibility." Vesting, 74 Stan. L. Rev. 1479 (2022). Note also that Article II contains a list of specific powers, including a grant of the power to "require the Opinion, in writing, of the principal Officers in each of the executive Departments, upon any Subject relating to the Duties of their respective Offices." Does the Opinion Clause count against inferring a broad presidential removal power, on the ground that Presidents would not need express authority to obtain opinions if they could freely remove officers? For a contrary view, see Akhil Reed Amar, Some Opinions on the Opinion Clause, 82 Va. L. Rev. 647 (1996). Should it matter that a removal power is not included in this list of presidential powers, or that the only express constitutional reference to removal of executive officers comes in the Impeachment Clause, Art. II, § 4, which creates a mechanism for removal by Congress?

Even if these clauses support some presidential removal power, do they support concluding that the removal provisions at issue in these cases are unconstitutional? JERRY MASHAW insists that the standard for-cause removal provision at issue in Seila Law (and, it would follow, also the weaker removal protection in Collins) is perfectly compatible with the Take Care Clause: "The president's responsibility under Article II is to see that the laws are faithfully executed. The standard forms of for-cause removal provide that an officer may be removed only for 'inefficiency, neglect of duty, or malfeasance.' Conduct of this sort, of course, interferes with faithful execution of the law. Removal of an officer on these grounds, thus, is consistent with the president's constitutional responsibility. Removal on other grounds, for example, that the officer has angered the president because his or her testimony before Congress embarrassed the president or the administration, would seem unconnected to the president's executive authority under the Constitution." OF ANGELS, PINS AND FOR-CAUSE REMOVAL: A REQUIEM FOR THE PASSIVE VIRTUES, U. Chi. L. Rev. Online (Aug. 27, 2020).[2] Do you agree?

A separate question is whether the specific structures invalidated in these cases—a single-headed independent agency in Seila Law, or double-for-cause removal protection in Free Enterprise—are distinguishable from the structural arrangement that ostensibly remains available, a multi-member-headed agency with one level of for-cause removal protection. Are you persuaded that they are? In Seila Law, Roberts and Kagan disagree about whether the President will find it easier or harder to exert control over a single director than over a multi-member commission. In Free Enterprise, Roberts and Breyer similarly disagree about whether the PCAOB's double-for-cause removal protection will make it impossible for the President to ensure faithful execution of the laws. Who do you think has the better account in these disputes? Suppose a President wants to keep a member of the PCAOB whom a majority of the SEC wants to remove. Would a double-for-cause structure work to support presidential control in that situation?

---

[2] https://lawreviewblog.uchicago.edu/2020/08/27/seila-mashaw/.

(4) ***Constitutional Structure.*** Do Seila Law and Free Enterprise strike you as more textualist or structuralist in basis? After invoking the Vesting and Take Care Clauses, the Seila Law majority moves quickly to inferring that the President must rely on subordinates and that the President needs removal authority to hold those subordinates accountable. The majority opinion also emphasizes the uniqueness of the executive branch's unitary status in the constitutional design. According to Roberts, the Framers' "constitutional strategy [was] straightforward: divide power everywhere except for the Presidency, and render the President directly accountable to the people through regular elections." In his telling, "the Framers made the President the most democratic and politically accountable official in Government." And the CFPB fundamentally undermines this structure by allowing significant executive authority to be wielded outside of presidential control. All of these are structural arguments; how much work do you see them doing in the majority opinion?

By contrast, Kagan's overarching structural point is that the Constitution gives Congress "broad authority to establish and organize the Executive Branch" through the Necessary and Proper Clause. She argues that the political branches have far greater competency than the courts to assess the impact of different agency structures, and that by invalidating the CFPB's structure the Court has overstepped its constitutional function. Kagan also rejects what she calls the majority's "Schoolhouse Rock" account of the Constitution's separation of powers structure as consisting of three separate branches, each exercising a different type of power, arguing that this account "fail[s] to acknowledge that the separation of powers is, by design, neither rigid nor complete."

Whose account of constitutional structure do you find more compelling? Do you agree that the Framers intended the President to be the most politically accountable official in government, or would they have expected the House of Representatives to play that role? Consider STEPHEN SKOWRONEK, THE CONSERVATIVE INSURGENCY AND PRESIDENTIAL POWER: A DEVELOPMENTAL PERSPECTIVE ON THE UNITARY EXECUTIVE, 122 Harv. L. Rev. 2070, 2072 (2009): "Far from endorsing presidential leadership, [the Framers'] assumptions in separating executive and legislative power were that Congress, with its vast repository of expressed powers and its close proximity to the people, was the branch most likely to exploit public sentiments, and that a properly constituted executive would help to stabilize the affairs of state. The separation of powers, the provision for indirect presidential elections, the charge to 'preserve, protect and defend the Constitution,' the presidential veto of legislation—all marked the presidency as a counterweight to impulsive majorities and a prod to a more deliberative stance in national affairs."

Does Roberts's account do justice to Congress's powers—does he engage adequately (or at all) with the implications of the Necessary and Proper Clause? As for Kagan, does she give adequate weight to the multiple ways the CFPB is insulated from presidential control and indeed from political control more generally, given the agency's budgetary independence from Congress? (The Fifth Circuit subsequently held that the CFPB's funding arrangement violates the Appropriations Clause and the separation of powers. See Note 4, p. 905).

(5) ***Dueling Accounts of Precedent.*** Precedent plays a central role for both the majority and dissent in Seila Law. But their understandings of the relevant precedents differ markedly. Roberts views Myers (p. 982) as the über precedent, establishing an unrestricted presidential removal power that the Court has continued to affirm over the years. imposing only two limited exceptions: "one for multimember expert agencies that do not wield substantial executive power, and one for inferior officers with limited duties and no policymaking or administrative authority." Justice Kagan's dissent insists that Myers is the exception and was quickly recast as simply invalidating a prohibition on congressional involvement in removal. In her view, the relevant line of analysis, running consistently from Humphrey's Executor (p. 983) through Morrison (p. 986), upholds Congress's power to impose removal limitations provided they don't "impede the President's ability to perform his constitutional duty"—an approach that she claims Free Enterprise (p. 1002) also reaffirmed. If you have read the descriptions of these decisions above, who do you think has the most accurate take on the Court's removal precedents?

(6) ***The Founding and Historical Practice.*** Roberts's majority opinions in both cases also rely heavily on the account of the Decision of 1789 that Chief Justice Taft offered in Myers. In Seila Law, Kagan points out that subsequent scholarship has raised doubts about the accuracy of Taft's history. What exactly was decided in 1789, if anything, has long been a matter of some dispute. See Saikrishna Prakash, New Light on the Decision of 1789, 91 Cornell L. Rev. 1021 (2006). Significant new historical work has called Myers's view further into question. For example, Daniel Birk, in Interrogating the Historical Basis for a Unitary Executive, 73 Stan. L. Rev. 175 (2021), has challenged Myers's reliance on the removal powers of the British King at the time of the Founding, arguing that some English officials who exercised significant regulatory and law enforcement authority held their offices "in fee simple (which would descend to the grantee's heirs), for life, for a term of years, or quamdiu se bene gesserint (Latin for 'as long as he shall behave himself well,' or commonly known as 'during good behavior')," and that English law appeared to view legislative control over removal terms as compatible with the King's possession of the executive power. Similarly, Christine Kexel Chabot, in Is the Federal Reserve Constitutional? An Originalist Argument for Independent Agencies, 96 Notre Dame L. Rev. 1 (2020), points out that the First Congress created the Sinking Fund Commission, charged with undertaking open market purchases of government debt and by statute including two members—the President of the Senate and the Chief Justice—whom the President could not remove. More recently, Jed Shugerman identifies a number of overlooked moments from 1789 that he argues show the falsity of the unitary executive account. See The Indecisions of 1789: Strategic Ambiguity and the Imaginary

Unitary Executive (Part I), 171 U. Pa. L. Rev. (forthcoming), and The Decisions of 1789 Were Anti-Unitary: An Originalist Cautionary Tale.[17]

Justice Kagan faults Chief Justice Roberts for failing to engage with this scholarship. That seems a fair criticism. But is Roberts really offering an originalist account of the removal power, or does he rely more on precedent and historical practice? And in thinking about historical practice, isn't Roberts correct that examples of single-headed agencies with removal protection are recent and not that common? Should that matter, or is it enough to show that over time Congress has experimented with new types of independent officials and institutions? On the other hand, does Roberts adequately address the longstanding use of independent financial regulators? As Kagan notes, that practice goes back to the creation of the Second National Bank in the early nineteenth century, and she argues that the First Congress also structured of the Treasury Department so that national officials involved in financial affairs would be more insulated.

(7) ***Is Innovative Agency Design Constitutionally Disfavored?*** More broadly, does the focus on historical precedents unduly constrain Congress's constitutional power to construct those governmental structures it deems "necessary and proper" to meet new governance challenges? Justice Kagan claims it does, memorably critiquing the majority for illegitimately treating the Necessary and Proper Clause as a "Rinse and Repeat Clause." The majority, however, insists—as the Court did in Free Enterprise—that the lack of historical precedent for an institutional arrangement is constitutionally suspicious. LEAH M. LITMAN, in DEBUNKING ANTINOVELTY, 66 Duke L.J. 1407, 1423, 1427–29 (2017), criticizes this growing anti-novelty rhetoric in federalism and separation of powers challenges: "The primary justification that has been offered . . . is that legislative novelty suggests that previous Congresses assumed similar legislation was unconstitutional. The presumption is 'that if Congress possessed a particular power, it would have exercised it.' . . . But enacting federal laws is difficult, and the nature of the legislative process requires Congress to select from among many different priorities and make compromises. Moreover, . . . [j]udicial decisions may make some legislative choices more attractive than others, different areas of federal regulation may be better suited to different forms of regulation, and new factual or legal developments may change reasonable people's assessments about how to accommodate the pertinent constitutional values.'" See also Gillian E. Metzger, Appointments, Innovation and the Judicial-Political Divide, 64 Duke L.J. 1607, 160–11 (2015) (arguing that the Supreme Court's anti-innovation turn is particularly troublesome given that growing political polarization has led to many novel congressional and executive measures).

Do you agree with this critique? The judicial resistance to novelty and innovation accords with an originalist approach to constitutional interpretation. But are there also good nonoriginalist and functional reasons for the courts to look skeptically at structural innovations from Congress and the President? For a detailed description of recent innovations in legislation

---

[17] https://papers.ssrn.com/sol3/papers.cfm?abstract_id=3597496 (last revised Aug. 27, 2021).

and administration, see Abbe R. Gluck, Anne Joseph O'Connell, & Rosa Po, Unorthodox Lawmaking, Unorthodox Rulemaking, 115 Colum. L. Rev. 1789 (2015).

(8) ***The Remedial Dimension.*** Consider the remedial approach the Roberts Court takes in all three of its removal decisions. In Free Enterprise, the Court first stipulates that the SEC Commissioners enjoy for-cause removal protection, despite the lack of any express protection to that effect, and then severs the express removal protection for PCAOB members after concluding that the double-for-cause removal protection they therefore enjoyed is unconstitutional. In Seila Law, following Free Enterprise's model, the Court responds to the constitutional violation it identifies by severing removal protection for the CFPB Director and remanding to see if, with the constitutional violation so cured, the CFPB Director ratifies the civil investigatory demand at issue. In Collins, the Court refuses to invalidate any of the actions FHFA took in relation to the third amendment, remanding instead for the lower court to determine if the unconstitutional removal provision inflicted any compensable harm on the plaintiffs.

In short, despite holding the removal provisions at issue unconstitutional in all three cases, the Court provides very limited, if any, relief to the challengers. Does that raise a question for you about whether the Court should be hearing these cases? Do you think the Court would be less willing to hold removal protection unlawful if doing so meant invalidating an entire agency or regulatory scheme, or imposing major financial costs on the government? Compare the analogous remedial problem in Bowsher (p. 928), where the Court chose to invalidate the Comptroller General's central role in a novel and complicated statutory scheme for balancing the federal budget, rather than the problematic but never used statutory method for removing him. Which remedial approach do you think is most appropriate for separation of powers contests? Note that the Court also took a minimalistic remedial approach to the Appointments Clause challenge in Arthrex (p. 945) as well, although there it opted to preserve removal protection for judges on the Patent Trial and Appeal Board (PTAB) and instead prohibited enforcement of a statutory provision preventing the Director of the Patent and Trademark Office from reviewing PTAB final decisions. According to David Zaring, who surveyed separation of powers cases in the Supreme Court and the D.C. Circuit over the last twenty years, failure to yield the relief that plaintiffs seek—even when their challenges succeed—is by far the norm. Towards Separation of Powers Realism, 37 Yale J. on Reg. 708, 712 (2020).

In granting such limited relief in Arthrex, the Court relied on a "strong presumption of severability" of unconstitutional provisions that applies generally. Barr v. American Assn. of Political Consultants, 140 S.Ct. 2335, 2350 (2020). Justices Thomas and Gorsuch have criticized these uses of severability as exceeding traditional limits on judicial power. In their view, when a constitutional violation stems from the combination of different statutory provisions—here, provisions granting broad powers to particular officials and provisions granting those officials removal protection—a court is necessarily making a policy choice that exceeds the judicial role when it decides which provision to sever. Indeed, they maintain such a judicial policy choice raises separation of powers concerns of its own. Are you convinced, or is it more problematic from a separation of powers perspective if the Court refused to minimize the impact of its constitutional rulings on congressional enactments? Does it matter if Congress includes an express severability clause?

## NOTES ON THE IMPLICATIONS FOR INDEPENDENT AGENCIES

(1) ***Current Status of Humphrey's Executor and Independent Agencies.*** Free Enterprise insisted that it was not reexamining Myers and Humphrey's Executor. But didn't its remedy of curing the constitutional defect of double-for-cause removal protection by making PCAOB members removable at will by SEC Commissioners necessarily imply that one level of for-cause removal protection is not inconsistent with the President's Take Care duty?

What is the current status of Humphrey's Executor and independent agencies after Seila Law and Collins? In Seila Law, Justices Thomas and Gorsuch make clear they would overrule Humphrey's Executor outright. Chief Justice Roberts's majority opinion is equally clear that "we need not and do not revisit our prior decisions allowing certain limitations on the President's removal power," characterizing the decision as refusing "to extend those precedents to the novel context of an independent agency led by a single Director." On the other hand, Roberts insists on characterizing Humphrey's Executor as only upholding "multimember expert agencies that do not wield substantial executive power." Roberts acknowledges that may not have been an accurate account of the FTC at the time, and certainly it would be hard to view independent regulatory commissions like the Federal Energy Regulatory Commission or the Securities and Exchange Commission (held to enjoy for-cause removal protection in Free Enterprise) in those terms. These multimember independent agencies perform many of the functions that Roberts characterizes as involving substantial executive power in regard to the CFPB: they issue rules that bind private parties, they undertake enforcement actions, and they adjudicate violations with large financial penalties sometimes attached. Is their constitutionality now in question?

For that matter, what about the Federal Reserve: It is led by a Board of Governors, with each governor appointed for a 14-year term and subject to removal only for cause. The Fed makes critical economic policy decisions—especially with its control over the money supply—and it has taken on major new policy roles to support the national economy in response to the 2008 financial crisis and the pandemic. It issues binding rules with massive financial implications for regulated parties, undertakes enforcement in the form of ongoing bank supervision and other oversight, adjudicates violations, and imposes financial penalties that are rarely reviewed by courts. To be sure, on some issues, the Fed works closely with the Treasury Department, but Chief Justice Roberts appears to reject the significance of such informal controls in both Seila Law and Free Enterprise. Should we conclude from

Seila Law and Collins that the Fed is unconstitutional? Do you think that the Court would be willing to make an exception for the central bank, perhaps drawing on the early historical precedent of the First and Second Banks of the United States? Is there a principled basis for drawing such a line?

(2) ***The Meaning of For Cause.*** In Humphrey's Executor, the statutory prohibition on removing a government officer except for "inefficiency, neglect of duty, or malfeasance in office"—the standard for-cause removal protection, sometimes referred to as "INM"—was seen as the touchstone of "independence." President Franklin Roosevelt conceded in the litigation that he had removed FTC member William Humphrey expressly on grounds of policy disagreement and the Court held that this violated the standard. Yet the modern cases had suggested that the Court might be crafting a new, more capacious understanding of what constitutes "cause" for removal. In Morrison, the Court described a good-cause removal provision as providing "ample authority to assure that the [independent] counsel is competently performing her statutory responsibilities in a manner that comports with the provisions of the Act." And, if you read Bowsher (p. 928), recall that a majority of the Court concluded there that the Comptroller General was under Congress's control because he could be removed by joint resolution for "permanent disability; inefficiency; neglect of duty; malfeasance; or a felony or conduct involving moral turpitude."

The meaning of for-cause removal rose to the fore again under the Roberts Court. In 2017, the government argued in Lucia that the good-cause removal protection for ALJs should be read "to permit an agency to remove an ALJ for personal misconduct or for failure to follow lawful agency directives or to perform his duties adequately," Brief for the Securities and Exchange Commission at 45. The Court did not reach the question, but in his concurrence Justice Breyer stated that the Government's "technical-sounding standard would seem to weaken the administrative law judges' 'for cause' removal protections considerably." In Seila Law, the majority and dissent agreed that the standard INM for-cause removal protection does not allow removal simply for policy differences, with Chief Justice Roberts arguing that to conclude otherwise would be at odds with Humphrey's Executor. For the view that, post-Seila Law, the INM standard should be read to allow a President to remove "commissioners for acting in a way that he reasonably believes to be not merely wrong but a clear violation of their statutory responsibility," with a pattern of arbitrary action almost always needed to constitute neglect of duty, see Cass R. Sunstein & Adrian Vermeule, Presidential Review: The President's Statutory Authority Over Independent Agencies, 109 Geo. L.J. 637, 642 (2021).

Despite the ubiquity of INM removal language, little was known about its historical origins and meaning. In a recent historical piece, JANE MANNERS and LEV MENAND rectify this gap. THE THREE PERMISSIONS: PRESIDENTIAL REMOVAL AND THE STATUTORY LIMITS OF AGENCY INDEPENDENCE, 121 Colum. L. Rev. 1, 6 (2021): "When Congress first used the now-talismanic INM phrase in 1887, it defined these circumstances using terms that were already well-known. 'Neglect of duty' and 'malfeasance in office' were old common law concepts employed by courts and legislators to connote an officer's failure to faithfully execute statutory duties. Neglect of duty indicated instances of 'nonfeasance'—a failure to perform one's duties in a way that caused injury to others. . . . 'Malfeasance in office,' meanwhile, referred to a wrongful act committed in the execution of one's duties that caused injury to others. . . . Inefficiency, by contrast, was of newer vintage: a term increasingly used over the course of the nineteenth century to describe wasteful government administration caused by inept officers who had gained their positions through political connections rather than merit."

(3) ***Removal Protections for Inferior Officers and Independent Agency ALJs.*** The constitutionality of removal protections for inferior officers was initially established in the context of a military appointment in Perkins, (p. 982), and reaffirmed in Morrison with respect to the independent counsel, (p. 986). In Seila Law, Roberts's majority opinion describes these cases as creating an "exception for inferior officers . . . with limited duties and no policymaking or administrative authority." Kagan insists that "[t]he majority's description of Morrison . . . is not true to the decision." Who do you think has the better account of Morrison's reasoning? Does the Court's account jibe with the independent counsel's responsibilities of investigating and prosecuting high executive officials for violations of federal criminal laws?

As Justice Breyer's Free Enterprise dissent points out, the executive branch is full of inferior officers performing important roles and enjoying for-cause removal protection. Among other positions, Breyer emphasizes members of the Senior Executive Service (SES), who fill high-level managerial positions, and ALJs, who the Court subsequently held in Lucia are inferior officers. In Free Enterprise, Chief Justice Roberts disputes that all of these positions are analogous to the Board. He emphasizes that Presidents can reassign some SES members and that "many administrative law judges . . . perform adjudicative rather than enforcement or policymaking functions, or possess purely recommendatory powers." Do you think that these instances of removal protection are vulnerable to constitutional challenge after Seila Law?

In Free Enterprise, Justice Breyer focuses on inferior officers with removal authority who work inside independent agencies. He argues that this creates exactly the type of double-for-cause removal protection that Free Enterprise invalidates. Roberts disagrees, insisting specifically that "[n]othing in our opinion . . . should be read to cast doubt on the use of what is colloquially known as the civil service system within independent agencies." This issue has arisen in the years since Free Enterprise and in particular since the Court held that ALJs were inferior officers in Lucia. Under 5 U.S.C. § 7521, ALJs can be removed only "only for good cause established and determined by the Merit Systems Protection Board (MSPB) on the record after opportunity for hearing before the Board." Moreover, the MSPB members themselves enjoy for-cause removal protection, leading to double-for-cause challenges being raised against ALJs at executive agencies as well. In DECKER COAL COMPANY V. PEHRINGER, 8 F.4th 1123 (9th Cir.

2021), the Ninth Circuit rejected a double-for-cause challenge to ALJs at the Department of Labor. In addition to emphasizing that ALJs perform adjudicatory functions, the Ninth Circuit underscored that DOL is not statutorily required to use ALJs and that ALJ decisions at DOL are subject to review by a DOL board whose members do not enjoy removal protection.

By contrast, in JARKESY V. SEC, 34 F.4th 446 (5th Cir. 2022), the Fifth Circuit held that § 7521, combined with the good cause removal protection for SEC members, created unconstitutional double-for-cause removal protection. JUDGE ELROD, writing for a 2–1 panel, argued that "SEC ALJs perform substantial executive functions. The President therefore must have sufficient control over the performance of their functions, and, by implication, he must be able to choose who holds the positions. Two layers of for-cause protection impede that control; Supreme Court precedent forbids such impediment. . . . The Supreme Court decided in Lucia that SEC ALJs are 'inferior officers' under the Appointments Clause because they have substantial authority within SEC enforcement actions. And in Free Enterprise Fund it explained that the President must have adequate control over officers and how they carry out their functions. If principal officers cannot intervene in their inferior officers' actions except in rare cases, the President lacks the control necessary to ensure that the laws are faithfully executed. So, if SEC ALJs are 'inferior officers' of an executive agency, as the Supreme Court in Lucia indicated was the case at least for the purposes of the Appointments Clause, they are sufficiently important to executing the laws that the Constitution requires that the President be able to exercise authority over their functions." In dissent, JUDGE DAVIS argued that ALJs' adjudicatory function distinguishes them from the PCAOB, arguing that "[t]he analysis contained in our removal cases is designed not to define rigid categories of those officials who may or may not be removed at will by the President, but to ensure that Congress does not interfere with the President's exercise of the 'executive power' and his constitutionally appointed [Take Care] duty." (The Fifth Circuit subsequently denied rehearing en banc, and the case may go up to the Supreme Court.)

Who do you think has the better of the argument? In Collins, the Court stated that "the nature and breadth of an agency's authority is not dispositive" in a challenge to removal restrictions. Does that statement undermine efforts to distinguish ALJs because they perform adjudicative functions? Note that in addition to disagreeing over removal protections for ALJs, the courts of appeal are split over whether such a constitutional challenge can be asserted directly in federal court or must first be asserted in the administrative adjudicatory proceeding at issue and raised in federal court only on judicial review of that proceeding. The Supreme Court has granted certiorari in two cases presenting that question. SEC v. Cochran, 142 S.Ct. 2707 (2022); Axon Enterprise, Inc. v. FTC, 142 S.Ct. 895 (2022).

(4) ***What Makes an Independent Agency Independent?*** The traditional view equates independence with for-cause removal protection. An important strand of the literature emphasizes that "independence" is a far more complex and subtle phenomenon than the traditional view recognizes. The ACUS SOURCEBOOK OF UNITED STATES EXECUTIVE AGENCIES (2d ed. 2018),

authored by JENNIFER L. SELIN and DAVID E. LEWIS, notes that what counts as an independent agency varies by discipline: "For some scholars, primarily those in political science, public administration, and public policy, any agency established outside the [Executive Office of the President] or executive departments is an 'independent agency.' . . . For other scholars, primarily those in law, structural features, particularly fixed terms with for-cause removal protections . . . and not location[,] define independence." As they note, these different definitions lead to significantly different categorizations; a multi-member body located within an executive agency, like the Federal Energy Regulatory Commission, whose members serve for a fixed term with removal protection, is an executive agency under the first definition and an independent agency under the second. Moreover, "statutory law and executive materials also vary in their consideration of what constitutes agency independence."

KIRTI DATLA & RICHARD L. REVESZ, in DECONSTRUCTING INDEPENDENT AGENCIES (AND EXECUTIVE AGENCIES), 98 Cornell L. Rev. 769, 772, 825–26 (2013), argue further that "[t]he binary conception of agencies as either 'independent' or 'executive' is incorrect." From a study of the enabling statutes of both independent and executive agencies, they identify "a broad set of indicia of independence: removal protection, specified tenure, multimember structure, partisan balance requirements, litigation authority, budget and congressional communication authority, and adjudication authority." They find "that there is no single feature—not even a for-cause removal provision—that every agency commonly thought of as independent shares. . . . Instead of falling into two categories, agencies fall along a continuum . . . [that] ranges from most insulated to least insulated from presidential control. An agency's place along that continuum is based on both structural insulating features as well as functional realities. And that placement need not be static. It can shift depending on statutory amendments or an increased (or decreased) presidential focus on the agency's mission." See also Rachel E. Barkow, Insulating Agencies: Avoiding Capture Through Institutional Design, 89 Tex. L. Rev. 15, 18 (2010). The ACUS Sourcebook provides comprehensive data on which agencies have different features associated with independence.

(5) ***Real World Political Complexity.*** The persistent legal battles over for-cause removal protections suggest that statutory provisions for agency "independence" make a real world difference. Justice Scalia articulates the view of many unitary executive theorists: "The independent agencies are sheltered not from politics but from the President, and it has often been observed that their freedom from presidential oversight (and protection) has simply been replaced by increased subservience to congressional direction." FCC v. Fox Television Stations., 556 U.S. 502, 524 (2009) (Scalia J., dissenting) (p. 1160).

For decades, scholars of law, political science, and public administration have debated the accuracy of this picture, arguing that political reality often tempers statutory independence features. PETER L. STRAUSS, THE PLACE OF AGENCIES IN GOVERNMENT: SEPARATION OF POWERS AND THE FOURTH BRANCH, 84 Colum. L. Rev. 573, 586–95 (1984): "Even in executive agencies, the layer over which the President enjoys direct control of personnel is very thin and political factors may make it difficult for him to exercise even those controls to the fullest. An administrator with a public constituency and mandate cannot be discharged—and understands that he cannot be discharged—without substantial political cost. Also for political reasons, . . . independent [agencies often] . . . consult[ ] with the White House about appointments[,] . . . voluntarily participate in the Regulatory Council, publish regular agendas of rulemaking, are attentive to White House inquiries about their progress, and otherwise behave as if they were in fact subject to the discipline from which they have been excused. The reasons for this acceptance of presidential input are clear. . . . It can be useful to be associated with national policy, to have a big and politically powerful 'friend,' when appearing before Congress. [They] need goods the President can provide: budgetary and legislative support, assistance in dealing with other agencies, legal services, office space, and advice on national policy. They share a commitment to achieving the public interest, and are likely to respect the President's motives and appreciate his political responsibility and support. They are flattered when their own advice is sought, and respectful of office when they are advised. In the circumstances, it is not surprising that the independent commissions can be susceptible to substantial presidential oversight."

Empirical studies similarly reveal a more complex story than unitary executive fears of presidential insulation and congressional domination. Christopher R. Berry & Jacob E. Gersen, Agency Design and Political Control, 126 Yale L.J. 1002, 1036 (2017), analyzing more than 30 years of data on distribution of federal funds, conclude that "[a]gencies with more political appointees are more responsive to moves into or out of the President's party when making spending allocations. Moreover, agencies with more Senate confirmed appointees are more responsive to the membership in the majority party than the President's party, while agencies with more non-Senate-confirmed appointees are more responsive to the President's party than the majority party." Brian D. Feinstein notes that "agencies with two characteristics commonly associated with independence—fixed terms and qualification requirements for appointees—receive less oversight attention" and concludes that "these design features not only restrict presidential control over agencies, but also congressional control." Designing Executive Agencies for Congressional Control, 69 Admin. L. Rev. 259, 285 (2017).

Do you think the Court should take real-world empirical evidence like this into account in shaping doctrine? Would evidence suggesting that removal protections in fact have a limited effect on presidential oversight of agencies undercut the Court's removal decisions?

## c. Presidential Direction of Regulatory Outcomes

*EXECUTIVE ORDER 13998*
*(1) The Emergence and Mechanisms of Presidential Directive Authority*
*(2) The Legal Basis for Presidential Directive Authority*
*(3) Presidential Directive Authority in Context*

Unlike early statutory delegations that empowered the President personally to make decisions about tariffs and other international trade issues, modern regulatory statutes typically delegate decisional authority to some named federal official—a Cabinet Secretary, an Administrator, or members of an independent commission. Do these statutes vest the power of decision in the named official specifically, meaning that although she may be influenced by the President's wishes, the responsibility to decide is ultimately hers alone? If she persists in a decision at odds with the President's preferences, may the President nullify the decision? May the President make the decision directly? The President's ability to fire recalcitrant officials and replace them with more compliant decisionmakers is explored in Section 3.b.2 (p. 979). Here, we consider the more fundamental question: What is the scope of the President's power to direct particular regulatory outcomes if the statutory delegation to a named official is silent as to the President's role? We begin with a recent exercise of presidential directive authority by President Biden, addressing mask wearing during the pandemic. We then provide an overview of how the directive authority has emerged in recent administrations, and we consider possible legal bases for such presidential power. Finally, we examine presidential direction in specific contexts.

That Presidents regularly assert such directive authority is beyond dispute. But administrative law has not kept up with the increasing centrality of the President in executive branch decisionmaking. DANIEL A. FARBER and ANNE JOSEPH O'CONNELL, THE LOST WORLD OF ADMINISTRATIVE LAW, 92 Tex. L. Rev. 1137, 1155–56 (2014): "[T]he actual workings of the administrative state have increasingly diverged from the assumptions animating the APA and classic judicial decisions that followed. . . . Those assumptions call for statutory directives to be implemented by an agency led by Senate-confirmed presidential appointees with decisionmaking authority. The implementation is presumed to be through statutorily mandated procedures and criteria, where the final result can then be reviewed by the courts to see if the reasons given by the agency at the time of action match the delegated directions. . . .

"In practice, however, both legislative enactments and presidential directives compel agency action. . . . [T]he White House . . . tr[ies] at times to direct agency action that the current Congress does not support or has not ordered. . . . [Even w]hen presidential orders are connected to an underlying statute, the statute may not be the primary driver of agency action. . . . The primacy that administrative law places on congressional mandates, therefore, diverges from the realities of modern agency action, where presidential directives can have equal importance with statutes to agencies. Of course, the agencies may sometimes be happy enough to take actions in these areas, but the timing and framing of the policies are not under their control."

---

**The White House** **January 21, 2021**
86 Fed. Reg. 7205.

## EXECUTIVE ORDER 13998

### Promoting COVID-19 Safety in Domestic and International Travel

By the authority vested in me as President by the Constitution and the laws of the United States of America, it is hereby ordered as follows:

Section 1. *Policy*. Science-based public health measures are critical to preventing the spread of coronavirus disease 2019 (COVID-19) by travelers within the United States and those who enter the country from abroad. The Centers for Disease Control and Prevention (CDC), the Surgeon General, and the National Institutes of Health have concluded that mask-wearing, physical distancing, appropriate ventilation, and timely testing can mitigate the risk of travelers spreading COVID-19. Accordingly, to save lives and allow all Americans, including the millions of people employed in the transportation industry, to travel and work safely, it is the policy of my Administration to implement these public health measures consistent with CDC guidelines on public modes of transportation and at ports of entry to the United States.

Sec. 2. *Immediate Action to Require Mask-Wearing on Certain Domestic Modes of Transportation*.

(a) *Mask Requirement*. The Secretary of Labor, the Secretary of Health and Human Services (HHS), the Secretary of Transportation (including through the Administrator of the Federal Aviation Administration (FAA)), the Secretary of Homeland Security (including through the Administrator of the Transportation Security Administration (TSA) and the Commandant of the United States Coast Guard), and the heads of any other executive departments and agencies (agencies) that have relevant regulatory authority (heads of agencies) shall immediately take action, to the extent appropriate and consistent with applicable law, to require masks to be worn in compliance with CDC guidelines in or on:

(i) airports;

(ii) commercial aircraft;

(iii) trains;

(iv) public maritime vessels, including ferries;

(v) intercity bus services; and

(vi) all forms of public transportation as defined in [49 U.S.C. § 5302].

(b) *Consultation.* In implementing this section, the heads of agencies shall consult, as appropriate, with interested parties, including State, local, Tribal, and territorial officials; industry and union representatives from the transportation sector; and consumer representatives.

(c) *Exceptions.* The heads of agencies may make categorical or case-by-case exceptions to policies developed under this section, consistent with applicable law, to the extent that doing so is necessary or required by law. If the heads of agencies do make exceptions, they shall require alternative and appropriate safeguards, and shall document all exceptions in writing. . . .

(e) *Coordination.* The Coordinator of the COVID-19 Response and Counselor to the President (COVID-19 Response Coordinator) shall coordinate the implementation of this section. The heads of agencies shall update the COVID-19 Response Coordinator on their progress in implementing this section. . . .

Sec. 3. *Action to Implement Additional Public Health Measures for Domestic Travel.*

(a) *Recommendations.* The Secretary of Transportation (including through the Administrator of the FAA) and the Secretary of Homeland Security (including through the Administrator of the TSA and the Commandant of the Coast Guard), in consultation with the Director of CDC, shall promptly provide to the COVID-19 Response Coordinator recommendations concerning how their respective agencies may impose additional public health measures for domestic travel. . . .

Sec. 4. *Support for State, Local, Tribal, and Territorial Authorities.* The COVID-19 Response Coordinator, in coordination with the Secretary of Transportation and the heads of any other relevant agencies, shall promptly identify and inform agencies of options to incentivize, support, and encourage widespread mask-wearing and physical distancing on public modes of transportation, consistent with CDC guidelines and applicable law.

Sec. 5. *International Travel.*

(a) *Policy.* It is the policy of my Administration that, to the extent feasible, travelers seeking to enter the United States from a foreign country shall be:

(i) required to produce proof of a recent negative COVID-19 test prior to entry; and

(ii) required to comply with other applicable CDC guidelines concerning international travel, including recommended periods of self-quarantine or self-isolation after entry into the United States.

(b) *Air Travel.*

(i) The Secretary of HHS, including through the Director of CDC, and in coordination with the Secretary of Transportation . . . shall, within 14 days of the date of this order, assess the CDC order of January 12, 2021, regarding the requirement of a negative COVID-19 test result for airline passengers traveling into the United States, in light of subsection (a) of this section. Based on such assessment, the Secretary of HHS and the Secretary of Homeland Security shall take any further appropriate regulatory action, to the extent feasible and consistent with CDC guidelines and applicable law. Such assessment and regulatory action shall include consideration of:

(A) the timing and types of COVID-19 tests that should satisfy the negative test requirement. . . ;

(B) the proof of test results that travelers should be required to provide;

(C) the feasibility of implementing alternative and sufficiently protective public health measures . . . for travelers entering the United States from countries where COVID-19 tests are inaccessible. . . .

(ii) The Secretary of HHS, in coordination with the Secretary of Transportation . . . shall promptly provide to the President, through the COVID-19 Response Coordinator, a plan for how the Secretary and other Federal Government actors could implement the policy stated in subsection (a) of this section with respect to CDC-recommended periods of self-quarantine or self-isolation after a flight to the United States from a foreign country, as he deems appropriate and consistent with applicable law. . . .

(iii) The Secretary of State . . . shall seek to consult with foreign governments, the World Health Organization, the International Civil Aviation Organization, the International Air Transport Association, and any other relevant stakeholders to establish guidelines for public health measures associated with safe international travel. . . .

(c) *Land Travel.* The Secretary of State . . . shall immediately commence diplomatic outreach to the governments of Canada and Mexico regarding public health protocols for land ports of entry . . . [and] within 14 days of the date of this order . . . shall submit to the President a plan to implement appropriate public health measures at land ports of entry. . . .

(d) *Sea Travel.* The Secretary of Homeland Security, through the Commandant of the Coast Guard . . . shall, within 14 days of the date of this order, submit to the President a plan to implement appropriate public health measures at sea ports. . . .

(f) *Coordination.* The COVID-19 Response Coordinator, in consultation with the Assistant to the President for National Security Affairs and the Assistant to the President for Domestic Policy, shall coordinate the implementation of this section. The Secretary of State, the Secretary of HHS, the Secretary of Transportation, and the Secretary of Homeland Security shall update the COVID-19 Response Coordinator on their progress in implementing this section within 7 days of the date of this order and regularly thereafter. The heads of all agencies are encouraged to bring to the attention of the COVID-19 Response Coordinator any questions regarding the scope or implementation of this section.

Sec. 6. *General Provisions.*

(a) Nothing in this order shall be construed to impair or otherwise affect:

(i) the authority granted by law to an executive department or agency, or the head thereof; or

(ii) the functions of the Director of the Office of Management and Budget relating to budgetary, administrative, or legislative proposals.

(b) This order shall be implemented consistent with applicable law and subject to the availability of appropriations.

(c) This order is not intended to, and does not, create any right or benefit, substantive or procedural, enforceable at law or in equity by any party against the United States, its departments, agencies, or entities, its officers, employees, or agents, or any other person.

## NOTES

(1) ***Law? Politics? Both?*** Most of the materials you see in law casebooks are judicial decisions; in this casebook, you will also encounter (if you haven't already) other legal materials such as statutes, legislative materials, regulations, and agency guidance. This measure represents another variety—presidential directives. It was one of several early Biden Administration actions seeking to follow through on the President's campaign promise to get COVID-19 under control. Such presidential measures have real effects. Often, as here, Presidents direct agency heads to take certain actions.

In this case, two weeks after the Executive Order was promulgated, the CDC issued an order requiring that "persons . . . wear masks over the mouth and nose when traveling on conveyances into and within the United States" and at transportation hubs. See CDC, Requirement for Persons To Wear Masks While on Conveyances and at Transportation Hubs, 86 Fed. Reg. 8025 (Feb. 3, 2021). And TSA issued a security directive to implement the executive order and enforce the CDC's mask requirement. SD 1542-21-01, Security Measures-Face Mask Requirements (Jan. 31, 2021).[18] In addition to its safety benefits, the mask requirement contributed to a dramatic increase in unruly passenger incidents on planes, as passenger refusals to wear masks led to fights and to planes turning around mid-flight. See Neil Vigdor, Cases of Unruly Airline Passengers Are Soaring, and So Are Federal Fines,

[18] https://www.tsa.gov/sites/default/files/sd-1542-21-01.pdf.

N.Y. Times (May 10, 2021). In April 2022, a federal district judge in Florida vacated the mask requirement, concluding that it exceeded CDC's statutory authority and was promulgated in violation of the APA's notice-and-comment requirements. Health Freedom Defense Fund, Inc. v. Biden, 2022 WL 1134138 (M.D. Fla. 2022). When the decision came down, a number of pilots announced mid-flight that masks were no longer required, sparking cheers, viral videos, and maskless selfies among passengers, as well as alarm for some. Victoria Kim, A Mask Mandate Ends Midflight, Sparking Cheers and Alarm, N.Y. Times (Apr. 19, 2022).

(2) ***What's in a Name?*** Although President Biden's directive takes the form of an executive order, sometimes such directives come in the form of presidential memoranda. The substantive legal effect of executive orders and presidential memoranda is generally thought to be the same. See Office of Legal Counsel, Department of Justice, Legal Effectiveness of a Presidential Directive, as Compared to an Executive Order (Jan. 29, 2000). However, memoranda can be more procedurally flexible. Under the Federal Register Act, 44 U.S.C. § 1505(a), executive orders must be published in the Federal Register unless they lack "general applicability and legal effect" or if they are effective only against federal officials—although many executive orders are also published and generally available online.

(3) ***Parsing the Directive.*** A lot can be gleaned just by looking closely at the language of the Executive Order. Why do you think President Biden directed the Secretaries of Labor, HHS, and Transportation to take certain actions, rather than just taking those actions himself? Or directed the Secretary of Transportation to take actions "including through the Administrator of the FAA," and the Secretary of Homeland Security to act "including through the Administrator of the TSA and the Commandant of the Coast Guard"? A likely reason is the scope of statutory authorities. For example, 49 U.S.C. § 44701(a)(5) provides that the FAA Administrator "shall promote safe flight of civil aircraft in air commerce by prescribing . . . regulations and minimum standards" that the Administrator finds necessary. See also id. § 106(g)(1) (providing that the FAA Administrator "shall carry out the . . . [d]uties and powers of the Secretary of Transportation . . . related to aviation safety"). Similarly, statutes provide that the TSA Administrator "shall be responsible for security in all modes of transportation," including aviation security, 49 U.S.C. §§ 114, 44903, while the Coast Guard has responsibility to "promulgate and enforce regulations for the promotion of safety of life and property on and under the high seas and waters subject to the jurisdiction of the United States," 14 U.S.C. § 102, and is headed by the Commandant, who acts subject to the DHS Secretary's supervision, 14 U.S.C. §§ 302, 505.

Notice also the variation in language used in different sections of the order. Section 2 appears strongly directive, stating that the Secretaries "shall immediately take action . . . to require masks to be worn in compliance with CDC guidelines." But it conditions this instruction by adding that the Secretaries should do so "to the extent appropriate and consistent with applicable law." This language referencing applicable law is common in executive orders and presidential memoranda. Why do you think this phrase is repeated so often? One feature of the applicable law in this case is again that the decision about whether and how to regulate is statutorily delegated to the Secretaries and other agency officials listed. Ensuring that agency officials respond "in compliance with law" also accords with the President's constitutional duty to "take Care that the Laws be faithfully executed."

Section 3, however, lacks the "as consistent with applicable law" language. Can this be explained by the fact that Section 3 directs the Secretaries to provide recommendations to the COVID-19 Response Coordinator rather than take regulatory actions? Section 5's requirements that agency officials submit plans to the President within 14 days are similarly unqualified. In this regard, note that the Opinion Clause of Article II allows the President to "require the Opinion, in writing, of the principal Officer in each of the executive Departments, upon any Subject relating to the Duties of their respective Offices."

Finally, consider Section 5(f), which specifies that key White House personnel—the COVID-19 Response Coordinator, the National Security Advisor, and the Domestic Policy Advisor—will coordinate the federal government's implementation of the executive order. As the materials below suggest, better coordination is often identified as an important benefit of presidential administration. For coordination to work, of course, the White House needs to be kept informed about what agencies are doing—hence Section 5(f)'s requirement that agencies update the COVID-19 Response Coordinator quickly and frequently.

## (1) The Emergence and Mechanisms of Presidential Directive Authority

The two presidents usually identified as most intent upon placing their personal stamp on federal regulatory policy are Franklin Roosevelt and Ronald Reagan. Clearly, each of them offers a model of a President determined to direct the regulatory state. Yet, most observers identify the presidency of Bill Clinton as a watershed in presidential ambitions to control regulatory outcomes. From President Clinton to President Trump, presidential efforts to direct the administrative state have expanded and taken on new forms.

(1) ***The Clinton Administration: Presidential Memoranda and Unabashed Assertion of Directive Authority.*** ELENA KAGAN, PRESIDENTIAL ADMINISTRATION, 114 Harv. L. Rev. 2245, 2281–82, 2290, 2298–99 (2001):

"The claim of directive authority . . . manifested itself most concretely and importantly in the frequent issuance of formal and published memoranda to executive branch agency heads instructing them to take specified action within the scope of the discretionary power delegated to them by Congress. These directives . . . enabled Clinton and his White House staff to instigate, rather than merely check, administrative action. The memoranda became, ever increasingly over the course of eight years, Clinton's primary means, self-consciously undertaken, both of setting an administrative agenda that reflected and advanced his policy and political preferences and of ensuring the execution of this program. . . .

. . . [E]ven given the assertion of directive authority, a President may face considerable constraints in imposing his will on administrative actors. Their resistance to or mere criticism of a directive may inflict political costs on the President as heavy as any that would result from an exercise of the removal power. This fact of political life accounts in part for the consultations and compromises that prefaced many of the Clinton White House's uses of directive authority. In this context, to put the matter simply, persuasion may be more than persuasion and command may be less than command—making the line between the two sometimes hard to discover.

"All that said, a line remains, and by so often asserting legal authority to direct regulatory decisions, President Clinton crossed from one side of it to the other. . . . The unofficial became official, the subtle blatant and the veiled transparent. . . . But more, the change in form likely led to a change in substance. . . . [T]he explicit and repeated assertion of directive authority probably alters over time what Peter Strauss has called the 'psychology of government'—the understanding of agency and White House officials alike of their respective roles and powers. This change, in turn, makes presidential intervention in regulatory matters ever more routine and agency acceptance of this intervention ever more ready. The Clinton White House's use of presidential directives thus created the conditions for a significant enhancement of presidential power over regulatory matters." (A different excerpt from this article appears in Chapter I (p. 48).)

(2) ***The George W. Bush Administration: Signing Statements and Politicized Agencies.*** Debate about the scope of presidential directive authority in domestic and foreign affairs was a constant during the Bush Administration. The White House espoused a strong view of unitary executive theory, and that became the proffered constitutional justification for both unilateral presidential initiatives and vigorous resistance to power sharing with Congress.

(a) *Signing Statements.* The Bush Administration sparked controversy when the President issued signing statements when signing legislation into law to identify constitutional problems that he perceived in the legislation and to signal how he would "remediate" these problems. Sometimes this entailed construing the law to avoid such issues; other times, it was a direction to executive officials on how the new law should (or should not) be implemented. After comparing President Bush's signing statements with those of his predecessors, political scientist Christopher S. Kelley concluded that the Bush-era statements were distinctive because of the number of separate provisions in each bill that were said to interfere with presidential constitutional prerogatives. The Law: Contextualizing the Signing Statement, 37 Pres. Stud. Q. 737, 738 (2007); see also Presidential Signing Statements Accompanying the Fiscal Year 2006 Appropriations Acts 9 (2007). An ABA Task Force study was highly critical of President Bush's enhanced use of "signing statements that claim the authority to disregard or decline to enforce all or part of a law" contrary to separation of powers and the rule of law. Am. Bar. Ass'n, Task Force on Presidential Signing

Statements and the Separation of Powers Doctrine 1 (2006). By contrast, Curtis A. Bradley and Eric A. Posner defended Bush's use of signing statements, arguing that the statements "provide public information about a president's views of a statute and thus would seem to promote dialogue and accountability" and maintaining that the President "certainly does not need a signing statement" to "allocate enforcement resources." Presidential Signing Statements and Executive Power, 23 Const. Comment. 307, 310 (2006).

(b) *Politicization of Agency Decision Makers.* President Bush also sought to exert greater control over administrative agencies by politicizing agency decisionmakers. According to now-Judge DAVID J. BARRON, writing in FROM TAKEOVER TO MERGER: REFORMING ADMINISTRATIVE LAW IN AN AGE OF AGENCY POLARIZATION, 76 Geo. Wash. L. Rev. 1095, 1096 (2008), "for the last three decades, Presidents have been . . . making novel and aggressive use of their powers of appointment to remake agencies in their own image. As a result, agencies increasingly want to align their own judgments with the White House view—even if top agency officials are not ordered to do so by the political aides working at 1600 Pennsylvania Avenue. . . . For all the debate over the legality of a White House hostile takeover, therefore, the real story may be that Presidents have effected a peaceful merger with the federal bureaucracy by transforming the nation's administrative agencies from within." David E. Lewis and Jennifer L. Selin agree: "Presidents have used the increasing number of appointees and their enhanced White House capacity for personnel selection to 'implant their DNA throughout the government' (to borrow a phrase from a George W. Bush aide). This is the essence of the politicization strategy." Political Control and the Forms of Agency Independence, 83 Geo. Wash. L. Rev. 1487, 1499 (2015). Some of the Bush politicization efforts generated extensive public controversy, such as politicization of hiring at the Department of Justice and the suppression as well as manipulation of agency science on a range of issues. Michele Estrin Gilman, The President as Scientist-in-Chief, 45 Willamette L. Rev. 565, 565 (2009). But some argue that this strategy for increasing presidential direction had costs: More politicized programs did worse on two numerical measures devised by the Administration itself to grade program performance, according to David E. Lewis, The Politics of Presidential Appointments: Political Control and Bureaucratic Performance 172–95 (2008).

(3) ***The Obama Administration: "We Can't Wait" and Presidential Administration in an Era of Political Polarization.*** Presidential administration was a central phenomenon during President Obama's two terms in office. Early on, President Obama expressly rejected some moves of the Bush Administration, issuing memoranda defending scientific integrity and limiting the use of signing statements, and signaled a possible retrenchment from politicization of the regulatory review process. But over his two terms in office, Obama employed many of the tools of presidential administration used by his predecessors.

(a) *Following in Clinton and Bush's Footsteps: President Obama's Use of Centralized Regulatory Review and Directives.* KATHRYN WATTS, in

CONTROLLING PRESIDENTIAL CONTROL, 114 Mich. L. Rev. 683, 698–702 (2016), describes how Obama "leverag[ed] existing tools for regulatory control like OMB review and presidential directives. . . . Obama—much like Bush—has heavily depended on OMB review. Indeed, Obama has relied on OMB even more intensely—and even more controversially—than Clinton did. Two aspects of Obama's aggressive approach to OMB review are notable. First, under Obama, OIRA has seized on delay as a significant means of aggressively controlling the regulatory state. . . . Second, much like the Bush administration, the Obama administration has not followed various transparency requirements set forth in Executive Order 12,866." In addition, "Obama . . . relied extensively on presidential directives. Such directives generally have taken the form of written memoranda posted to WhiteHouse.gov and published in the Federal Register." Watts provides a long list of directive actions Obama took "[i]n the first seven months of 2014 alone," including giving speeches on key subjects such as retirement savings or raising the minimum wage and then issuing executive orders, memoranda, or reports directing agencies to take particular actions. See also Andrew Rudalevige, The Obama Administrative Presidency: Some Late-Term Patterns, 46 Pres. Stud. Q. 868, 871–72 (2016). One of the most prominent of all of President Obama's directives was his Presidential Memorandum on Power Sector Carbon Pollution Standards (June 25, 2013), which "direct[ed]" EPA to "use [its] authority" under the Clean Air Act "to issue standards, regulations, or guidelines, as appropriate, that address carbon pollution from modified, reconstructed, and existing power plants" and "request[ed]" that EPA do so on a particular timeline.

(b) *Newer Mechanisms of Presidential Influence: Czars, Nonenforcement, and Creative Statutory Interpretation.* Another mechanism used by the Obama Administration to assert presidential control over policy was the creation of special White House policy advisors or "czars." This mechanism was particularly prominent early in Obama's tenure, with roughly twenty major czars being appointed at the outset of Obama's first term. A "striking and unusual" feature was appointment of "the more experienced and higher-profile policymaker . . . as 'czar' and the junior [appointee being] in the cabinet." The use of czars sparked controversy, with "[t]he focal point of debate . . . [being that] czars are considered part of the President's personal staff, and so are outside the requirement of confirmation." Aaron Saiger, Obama's "Czars" for Domestic Policy and the Law of the White House Staff, 79 Fordham L. Rev. 2577, 2594–95 (2011). Whether czars actually enhance presidential direction of regulatory decisionmaking is a matter of some debate. Compare Paul C. Light, Opinion: Nominate and Wait, N.Y. Times (Mar. 23, 2009) ("Most have more stalemates than successes, hardly ever receive the presidential attention they were promised and often quit in frustration.") with Saiger, supra, at 2594–95 (czars "increase the capacity of the president to jawbone, lobby, and directly supervise agency activities").

By contrast, the Obama Administration's use of nonenforcement strategies, often on contentious issues, became more important as his presidency progressed. Perhaps his Administration's most famous use of nonenforcement came in the context of the Administration's immigration deferred-action policies. These policies allowed up to 5 million immigrants whose children were U.S. citizens or lawful permanent residents, as well as some who had been brought to the country unlawfully when they were children, to apply for relief from deportation for a period of three years. (See p. 409). President Obama outlined the policy in a televised address to the Nation, and the Administration also released an opinion of the Office of Legal Counsel concluding that the initiative was within the Administration's statutory and constitutional authorities. See Adam B. Cox & Cristina M. Rodríguez, The President and Immigration Law Redux, 125 Yale L.J. 104, 107–08 (2015). The Obama Administration also delayed application of several requirements of the Affordable Care Act to avoid unwanted consequences. See Nicholas Bagley, Legal Limits and Implementation of the Affordable Care Act, 164 U. Pa. L. Rev. 1715, 1721–23 (2016). To similar effect, in other contexts the Obama Administration formally waived statutory requirements in ways that often served to fundamentally rewrite the statutes at issue in line with the Administration's priorities. See David J. Barron & Todd D. Rakoff, In Defense of Big Waiver, 113 Colum. L. Rev. 265 (2013). This happened most prominently with respect to the No Child Left Behind Act, under which the Administration had granted waivers to more than forty states before Congress replaced the statute with new legislation. The Administration also used waivers to encourage states to expand their Medicaid programs, thereby again helping to ensure successful implementation of the ACA.

The Obama Administration justified these measures as legitimate exercises of enforcement discretion, highlighting another feature of Obama's presidential administrativism: "the frequent use of administrative statutory interpretation to drive . . . [the Administration's executive] actions, whether by producing legal opinions, issuing guidance documents, or more formal rulemaking." Rudalevige, supra, at 869. In some instances, the Administration appeared to revise its own prior interpretations to meet a policy goal, as when it switched from seeking annual subsidies for cost-sharing under the ACA to arguing that the subsidies could be funded through an ACA permanent appropriation. See House v. Burwell, 185 F.Supp.3d 165 (D.D.C. 2016), subsequently settled, 2018 WL 8576647 (D.D.C. 2018).

(c) *Presidential Administration and Polarization*. President Obama's strong assertion of administrative power came against a background of extreme partisanship and polarization in national politics. President Obama invoked partisan divides and gridlock in Congress as justification for his administrative turn. Kenneth S. Lowande & Sidney M. Milkis, "We Can't Wait": Barack Obama, Partisan Polarization, and the Administrative Presidency, 12 The Forum 3, 9 (2014). Not only is "an increase in presidential assertions of policymaking authority and control over agencies" a "major consequence of polarization," but in addition polarization means that "Presidents assert such policy control in the knowledge that Congress is unlikely to succeed in legislating limits in response. Hence, polarization contributes to the rise of presidential unilateralism as a central governance phenomenon." Gillian E. Metzger, Agencies, Polarization, and the States,

115 Colum. L. Rev. 1739, 1752 (2015); see also Abbe R. Gluck, Anne Joseph O'Connell, & Rosa Po, Unorthodox Lawmaking, Unorthodox Rulemaking, 115 Colum. L. Rev. 1789 (2015) (arguing that, in addition to polarization, President Obama's assertions of administrative power reflected the need to coordinate policymaking across multiple delegations and in a world of fiscal constraints).

The turn to administration in the face of congressional inaction explains some features of Obama's approach to presidential control; in particular, the reliance on new statutory interpretations reflected the need to adapt old statutes to meet new problems because new legislation was stalled in Congress. See Jody Freeman & David B. Spence, Old Statutes, New Problems, 163 U. Pa. L. Rev. 1 (2014). In EXECUTIVE FEDERALISM COMES TO AMERICA, 102 Va. L. Rev. 953 (2016), JESSICA BULMAN-POZEN identifies the combination of polarization and presidential administration under President Obama as leading to a new phenomenon of executive federalism, under which "executives have become dominant actors at both the state and federal levels. They formulate policy and manage intergovernmental relations. . . . Federal and state actors turn to state law as well as federal law to further their agendas; sometimes this amplifies conflict, but it also enables officials to find paths to compromise," with the result that "national policy frequently comes to look different across the states."

Not surprisingly, President Obama's assertive use of administrative power provoked significant political pushback. Republicans in Congress accused the President of "lawlessness" and seizing "unparalleled executive power." Andrew Rudalevige, Old Laws, New Meanings: Obama's Brand of Presidential "Imperialism," 66 Syracuse L. Rev. 1, 3 (2016). Some academics voiced concern about expanding presidential power as well, from both sides of the political spectrum. See David E. Bernstein, Lawless: The Obama Administration's Unprecedented Assault on the Constitution and the Rule of Law (2015); William P. Marshall, Actually We Should Wait: Evaluating the Obama Administration's Commitment to Unilateral Executive-Branch Action, 2014 Utah L. Rev. 773 (2014). Others argued that President Obama's actions should be viewed as a constitutionally defensible form of self-help, in the face of a polarized and recalcitrant Congress. See David E. Pozen, Self-Help and the Separation of Powers, 124 Yale L.J. 2, 7 (2014).

(4) ***Presidential Direction Under the Trump Administration.*** Despite coming to power at a time of unified national government under Republican control, President Trump followed President Obama in relying heavily on presidential direction and unilateral executive actions. Trump issued 220 executive orders and 317 other presidential documents over four years, compared to Obama's 276 executive orders and 598 other presidential documents over eight years.[2] Trump did not hide his expansive view of his directive authority, at one point stating "I have an Article II, where I have the right to do whatever I want as president." Michael Brice-Saddler, While Bemoaning Mueller Probe, Trump Falsely Says the Constitution Gives Him 'The Right to Do Whatever I Want,' Wash. Post (July 23, 2019). Perhaps the

[2] https://www.federalregister.gov/presidential-documents.

most prominent example of presidential administration during the Trump Administration came in the early months of the COVID-19 pandemic, in the nightly news conferences he led with members of the White House Coronavirus Task Force. Another famous instance, this one occurring in private, was President Trump's effort to direct the Department of Justice to find that fraud occurred in the 2020 election. Luke Broadwater & Katie Benner, Jan. 6 Panel Outlines Trump's Bid to Coerce Justice Dept. Officials, N.Y. Times (June 23, 2022).

Whereas President Obama used directive authority to encourage regulatory initiatives, President Trump's aim was deregulation and limiting administrative capacity. President Trump issued numerous executive orders targeting regulation, directing cabinet secretaries to reconsider existing regulations, implement statutes and regulations in a particular fashion, and produce reports on several policy issues. Many of the regulations that Trump instructed agencies to reconsider represented major regulatory initiatives of the Obama Administration. These were standard moves, undertaken by prior presidents as well. Where the Trump Administration stood out, Bethany A. Davis Noll and Richard L. Revesz argue, was in making more "aggressive use of several relatively low-profile tools—disapprovals under the Congressional Review Act, abeyances in pending litigation, and suspensions of final regulations—to target more of the prior administration's regulations." Given unified Republican control, the previously-dormant CRA proved a potent tool in overturning fourteen major regulations issued late in Obama's presidency. Regulation in Transition, 104 Minn. L. Rev. 1, 20 (2019). Another Trump deregulatory innovation was Executive Order 13771 (p. 478), known as the two-for-one executive order, which required an agency to identify at least two existing regulations to be repealed for each new regulation it proposed, and also contained a regulatory budget provision that prohibited the new regulation from imposing more in regulatory costs than the regulations being repealed.

The Trump Administration also asserted more supervision over independent agency regulatory actions, although its record here was mixed. Early on, OMB adhered to the standard exemption of independent agencies from centralized review of regulations, but (as noted above, p. 899), it subsequently required independent agencies to notify it of upcoming rules (including regulations and guidance documents such as policy statements and interpretive rules) for a determination of whether those rules counted as major rules that needed to be put before Congress under the CRA. Compare Dominic J. Mancini, Off. of Mgmt. & Budget, M-17-21, Guidance Implementing Executive Order 13771 (2017) with Russell T. Vought, Off. of Mgmt. & Budget, M-19-14, Guidance on Compliance with the Congressional Review Act (2019). In addition, the Trump White House Counsel obtained an opinion from the Office of Legal Counsel concluding that the President may direct independent agencies to comply with Executive Order 12866—a position OLC previously asserted under the Reagan and Clinton Administrations as well. See Extending Regulatory Review Under Executive Order 12866 to Independent Regulatory Agencies, 43 Op. O.L.C. at 1, 3 (Oct. 8, 2019).

According to JODY FREEMAN and SHARON JACOBS, the Trump Administration's deregulatory efforts were structural as well as substantive. STRUCTURAL DEREGULATION, 135 Harv. L. Rev. 585, 591–92, 594, 629 (2021): "Trump . . . deployed a variety of other strategies to impair agencies," including "actions that interfere with agency staffing[,] . . . presidential manipulation of other resources, undermining the institutional expertise that is essential to performing congressionally assigned tasks, [and] . . . attacks on agency reputation. . . . Presidents can undermine agency capacity with little formality or transparency in most cases. These features, as well as structural deregulation's incremental nature, make it unlikely that either Congress or the courts will interfere. An additional benefit of structural deregulation for a President intent on undercutting regulatory action is that it is time-consuming for a successor to reverse."

A signal indicator of the Trump Administration's intent to structurally transform the executive branch came in the early statement of President Trump's chief strategist that the "deconstruction of the administrative state" was one of the Administration's main objectives. Trump's efforts to do so on the personnel side ranged from a standard hiring freeze to more novel efforts such as curtailing civil service protections through an executive order, redeploying career staff thought to be hostile to the Administration's agenda, and not filling vacancies so that some agencies' workforces were dramatically reduced. See Freeman & Jacobs, supra, at 595–600; Exec. Order No. 13957, 85 Fed. Reg. 67631 (Oct. 21, 2020). A particularly notable feature was Trump's reliance on acting officials to lead agencies (p. 974).

President Trump also stood out for his assertion of control over agency budgets and appropriated funds. Eloise Pasachoff maintains that "[m]ore than simply using generally available budget tools, political officials in [the Trump] administration . . . push[ed] some of them to their statutory limits and beyond, while suggesting off the record that these actions are 'part of a broader effort to defend the president's authority to spend money at any time and in any manner that he determines appropriate.' " The President's Budget Powers in the Trump Era, in Executive Policymaking: The Role of the OMB in the Presidency (Meena Bose & Andrew Rudalevige eds., 2020). For further discussion of the Trump Administration's assertions with respect to funding, see p. 1052.

(5) ***Biden's First Year and a Half.*** Presidential administration remains strongly in play a year and a half into Biden's presidency. Despite indicating that he would use executive orders "sparingly" as President, President Biden issued a slew of directives in his initial months in office, totaling forty-two in his first one hundred days. Many of these revoked Trump executive orders and other Trump Administration actions. On his first day in office, for example, Biden revoked Trump's two-for-one executive order, reversed Trump's approval of the Keystone XL Pipeline, restored lands that Trump had removed from national monuments, directed agencies to review key Trump Administration regulatory actions, and issued an executive order on systemic racial inequality (among other actions). Some of Biden's directives extend to independent agencies. At the same time, the Biden Administration has sought to limit some forms of presidential influence on agencies. A July

2021 memo from Biden's White House Counsel on Prohibited Contacts with Agencies and Departments makes clear that staff should not contact "any department or agency about a specific adjudication . . . [or] enforcement" without permission from White House Counsel and states that such restrictions on communications with agencies "apply with special force to the independent agencies."

Do these reversals from Trump Administration policies feel like a pendulum swinging back and forth? Regardless of whether you favor Trump's anti-regulatory stance or Biden's more pro-regulatory one, what do you think of such shifts in regulatory frameworks occurring with a change in control of the presidency? Is this a feature or a bug of presidential administration? Blake Emerson and Jon Michaels emphasize that "the presidential playbook has delivered often illusory short-term gains" and advocate replacing presidential administration with civic administration, in which "the president [would] . . . use his preeminent position in American government to more fully empower an array of elected officials, expert bureaucrats, grassroots organizers, and civil institutions." Abandoning Presidential Administration: A Civil Governance Agenda to Promote Democratic Equality and Guard Against Creeping Authoritarianism, 68 U.C.L.A. 104, 108 (2021); see also Jerry L. Mashaw & David Berke, Presidential Administration in a Regime of Separated Powers: An Analysis of Recent American Experience, 35 Yale J. on Reg. 549, 551–52 (2018) (emphasizing how quickly presidential actions can be reversed).

(6) ***The Polyphonic Versus Unitary Executive.*** All the previous discussion has spoken of *presidential* direction. But as ANDREW RUDALEVIGE emphasizes in BY EXECUTIVE ORDER: BUREAUCRATIC MANAGEMENT AND THE LIMITS OF PRESIDENTIAL POWER (2021), "the executive *branch* matters to executive orders. Pundits often present such directives as literally unilateral . . . but [they are] also the culmination of the input, influence, and frequently instigation of the wider bureaucracy. . . . [Executive orders], even those that originate with the White House, are subject to extensive review by and negotiation with the wider executive branch . . . [and] around six of every ten executive orders issued by the president are crafted preponderantly by departments and agencies instead of by centralized staff[,] and . . . a surprising number of proposed EOs, including some dear to the president, are never issued at all. The bureaucracy provides resources for unilateralism, and also shapes and bounds its use. . . . [M]ost crucially, we need to think about executive orders as a question of presidential *management* rather than simply of command." Tara Leigh Grove similarly emphasizes the interagency process that Presidents have generally used since the 1930s "to invite agency officials to draft, negotiate over, and redraft directives. Notably, the resulting text signed by the President may not reflect his preferred substantive policy. After the interagency consultation process, Presidents often opt to split the difference among agencies." Presidential Laws and the Missing Interpretive Theory, 168 U. Pa. L. Rev. 687, 881 (2020).

## (2) The Legal Basis for Presidential Directive Authority

As noted above, (p. 941), the Court frequently invokes the tripartite framework of Justice Jackson's Youngstown concurrence in analyzing presidential power claims. Under that framework, whether Congress has authorized or prohibited the presidential action in question is centrally important. When a statute expressly delegates authority to the President, Congress's authorization of presidential action is clear. But far more commonly, statutes delegate authority to a Secretary of a Department or a head of an agency, and the President is not mentioned. The critical questions then become whether the President has independent constitutional authority to control the policymaking at issue and whether the relevant statutes should be read to allow such a role. The precedents and academic commentary discussed below address these questions.

(1) ***Judicial and Executive Branch Precedent on Presidential Directive Authority.*** In contrast to the President's removal power (see Section 3.b.2, p. 979), the President's directive authority has so far provided little occasion for judicial review. But the scope of presidential directive authority has received attention within the executive branch.

(a) Two decisions often invoked to analyze presidential power in this area substantially predate the advent of the modern national administrative state. How much guidance do they provide for assessing contemporary assertions of presidential directive authority?

MARBURY V. MADISON, 5 U.S. (1 Cranch) 137, 165–66 (1803) (MARSHALL, C.J.): "By the constitution of the United States, the president is invested with certain important political powers, in the exercise of which he is to use his own discretion, and is accountable only to his country in his political character, and to his own conscience. To aid him in the performance of these duties, he is authorized to appoint certain officers, who act by his authority and in conformity with his orders. In such cases, their acts are his acts; and whatever opinion may be entertained of the manner in which executive discretion may be used, still there exists, and can exist, no power to control that discretion. . . . But when the legislature proceeds to impose on that officer other duties; when he is directed peremptorily to perform certain acts; when the rights of individuals are dependent on the performance of those acts; he is so far the officer of the law [and] is amenable to the laws for his conduct. . . ."

MYERS V. UNITED STATES, 272 U.S. 52, 132–35 (1926) (TAFT, C.J.): "The degree of guidance in the discharge of their duties that the President may exercise over executive officers varies with the character of their service as prescribed in the law under which they act. The highest and most important duties which his subordinates perform are those in which they act for him. In such cases they are exercising not their own but his discretion. This field is a very large one. It is sometimes described as political. Each head of a department is and must be the President's alter ego in the matters of that department where the President is required by law to exercise authority. . . . In all such cases, the discretion to be exercised is that of the President in determining the national public interest and in directing the action to be taken by his executive subordinates to protect it. In this field his cabinet officers must do his will. . . .

". . . The ordinary duties of officers prescribed by statute come under the general administrative control of the President by virtue of the general grant to him of the executive power, and he may properly supervise and guide their construction of the statutes under which they act in order to secure that unitary and uniform execution of the laws which article 2 of the Constitution evidently contemplated in vesting general executive power in the President alone. . . . Of course there may be duties so peculiarly and specifically committed to the discretion of a particular officer as to raise a question whether the President may overrule or revise the officer's interpretation of his statutory duty in a particular instance."

Note that Chief Justice Marshall ascribes presidential control to situations in which the acts of executive officers like the Secretary of State "are his acts; and whatever opinion may be entertained of the manner in which executive discretion may be used, still there exists, and can exist, no power to control that discretion," and Chief Justice Taft's first paragraph addresses the same setting. How does Chief Justice Taft extend the same reasoning, in his second paragraph, to officers who act under statutory authority and not as presidential surrogates whose acts are beyond judicial control?

(b) In contrast to courts, Attorneys General and executive branch legal advisors have regularly opined on the scope of presidential directive authority. Several early opinions receive particular note. The first was issued by Attorney General WILLIAM WIRT, in THE PRESIDENT AND ACCOUNTING OFFICERS, 1 Op. Att'y Gen. 624 (1823), responding to a question from President Monroe as to whether he could review a decision by Treasury Department officials settling the account of Major Joseph Wheaton. Wirt concluded the President could not: "[T]he requisition of the constitution is, that he shall take care that the laws be executed. If the laws, then, require a particular officer by name to perform a duty, not only is that officer bound to perform it, but no other officer can perform it without a violation of the law; and were the President to perform it, he would not only be not taking care that the laws were faithfully executed, but he would be violating them himself. The constitution assigns to Congress the power of designating the duties of particular officers: the President is only required to take care that they execute them faithfully. For example: our laws provide that there be established at the seat of government a General Post Office, under the direction of a Postmaster General; and they direct that he (the Postmaster General) 'shall establish post offices, and appoint postmasters, at all such places as appear to him expedient on the post roads—that are or may be established by law.' Suppose that the Postmaster General should fail to appoint a postmaster at some place where an office is established by law: can the President make such appointment? I apprehend not; for there is no law that authorizes it. The power of appointment is given by law exclusively to the Postmaster General." Here, the law provided for determination of all public accounts by the Auditor, with appeal only to the Comptroller.

Eight years later, Attorney General ROGER TANEY, in THE JEWELS OF THE PRINCESS OF ORANGE, 2 Op. Att'y Gen. 482 (1831), took a more expansive view of presidential directive authority, in response to a question about whether President Jackson could direct a district attorney (the equivalent of a U.S. attorney today) to "discontinue a prosecution. . . . I think the President does possess the power. The interest of the country and the purposes of justice manifestly require that he should possess it; and its existence is necessarily implied by the duties imposed upon him in that clause of the constitution before referred to, which enjoins him to take care that the laws be faithfully executed." Yet Taney acknowledged that "[t]he district attorney might refuse to obey the President's order; and if he did refuse, the prosecution, while he remained in office, would still go on; because the President could give no order to the court or the clerk to make any particular entry. He could only act through his subordinate officer, the district attorney. . . . And if that officer still continued a prosecution which the President was satisfied ought to be discontinued, the removal of the disobedient officer, and the substitution of one more worthy in his place, would enable the President, through him, faithfully to execute the law. And it is for this, among other reasons, that the power of removing the district attorney resides in the President."

An even broader view of presidential directive authority was asserted two decades on by Attorney General CALEB CUSHING, RELATION OF THE PRESIDENT TO THE EXECUTIVE DEPARTMENTS, 7 Op. Att'y Gen. 453, 469–70 (1856): "I think here the general rule to be as already stated, that the Head of Department is subject to the direction of the President. I hold that no Head of Department can lawfully perform an official act against the will of the President; and that will is by the Constitution to govern the performance of all such acts. If it were not thus, Congress might by statute so divide and transfer the executive power as utterly to subvert the Government, and to change it into a parliamentary despotism, like that of Venice or Great Britain, with a nominal executive chief utterly powerless,—whether under the name of Doge, or King, or President, would then be of little account, so far as regards the question of the maintenance of the Constitution."

Are you surprised to find such early disagreement about the scope of presidential power inside the executive branch? Although that disagreement might undercut originalist claims to directive authority, do the opinions signify growing agreement on the scope of such authority over time—or would more evidence be needed that Congress shared this understanding? What weight do you assign to these internal executive branch views of presidential authority? See Curtis A. Bradley & Trevor W. Morrison, Historical Gloss and the Separation of Powers, 126 Harv. L. Rev. 411 (2012). For further discussion of these Attorney General opinions, see Harold H. Bruff, Balance of Forces: Separation of Powers Law in the Administrative State 456–59 (2006); H. Jefferson Powell, The Constitution and the Attorneys General 29–34, 131–48 (1999).

(2) ***Directive Authority and Unitary Executive Theory.*** STEVEN G. CALABRESI & SAIKRISHNA B. PRAKASH, THE PRESIDENT'S POWER TO EXECUTE THE LAWS, 104 Yale L.J. 541 (1994): "Because the President alone has the

constitutional power to execute federal law, it would seem to follow that, notwithstanding the text of any given statute, the President must be able to execute that statute, interpreting it and applying it in concrete circumstances. . . . Under the Constitution, executive officers can act only in the President's stead, since it is the President and the President alone who can delegate to them the constitutional power that they must have if they are to execute laws. For example, if Congress establishes by statute a Treasury Secretary with the power and responsibility to expend appropriations and also provides a degree of discretion in an appropriations act, it is a mistake to view that statute as creating any duty or authority that belongs to the Secretary, even if the statute is written that way. Rather, it is the President, under our Constitution, who must always be the ultimate empowered and responsible actor. This is because the Constitution establishes that the President exclusively controls the power to execute all federal laws, and therefore it must be the case that all inferior executive officers act in his stead. A statute stating that the Secretary of the Treasury and other Treasury personnel will execute appropriation and tax laws only establishes that these particular officers will assist the President in carrying those laws into execution. Congress lacks constitutional power to do anything more.

"If the President may make a decision that a statute purports to reserve for an inferior executive officer, by the same logic, the President must be able to nullify an action taken by an inferior executive officer. [For] example, suppose the Secretary of the Treasury, in the exercise of her purportedly exclusive statutory discretion, decided to fine a bank for violation of certain banking laws. Because the Treasury Secretary would be ultimately exercising the President's 'executive power,' the President must be able, in effect, to reverse or nullify the Secretary's decision by withdrawing his delegation of the executive power, which the Constitution gives to him alone."

(3) ***A Different Constitutional Justification for Directive Authority.*** LAWRENCE LESSIG & CASS R. SUNSTEIN, THE PRESIDENT AND THE ADMINISTRATION, 94 Colum. L. Rev. 1, 2 (1994): "We think that the view that the framers constitutionalized anything like this vision of the executive is just plain myth. . . . We believe [however] that there is . . . a plausible structural argument on behalf of the hierarchical conception of the unitary executive. . . . [T]he national government has changed dramatically since the founding, and so too has the national presidency. In light of these changes, mechanical application of the founding understanding—to allow independent officials to engage in tasks that the framers never foresaw—may well disserve the very commitments that underlay the founding itself. Under current circumstances, a strongly unitary executive is the best way of keeping faith with the most fundamental goals of the original scheme. . . .

"[A]n argument for the strongly unitary executive under modern conditions takes the following form. . . . Where the framers allocated a power that they thought of as political, that power was allocated to people who were themselves politically accountable. This was part of the fundamental commitments to accountability and avoidance of factionalism. At the founding period, the existence of a degree of independence in administration could not realistically have been thought to compromise these commitments. Today, by contrast, a strong presumption of unitariness is necessary in order to promote the original constitutional commitments. The legislative creation of domestic officials operating independently of the President but exercising important discretionary policymaking power now stands inconsistent with founding commitments."

Lessig and Sunstein would, however, permit Congress to immunize specific regulatory policymaking from presidential directive authority. In particular, they justify independence for the Federal Reserve Board because of the risk that "the money supply would be manipulated by the President for political reasons. Even a perception of this sort would have corrosive effects on democratic processes. . . . [I]t would likely have adverse effects on the economy as well." Id. at 108. Can the Fed be so easily distinguished on constitutional grounds from all other agencies?

(4) ***More Skeptical Views.*** PETER L. STRAUSS, OVERSEER OR THE DECIDER? THE PRESIDENT IN ADMINISTRATIVE LAW, 75 Geo. Wash. L. Rev. 696, 702–05 (2007): "The Constitution itself is at best ambivalent on the question. On the one hand, the opening words of Article II locate all executive power in the President. . . . On the other hand, the Constitution twice refers to 'duties' or 'powers' assigned to other officers. Article II in terms gives the President only the right to seek from those officers a written opinion about their exercise of those duties (i.e., it does not say he may command their exercise of the duties assigned to them), and it concludes that he is responsible to see to it that the laws 'be faithfully executed'—i.e., as if by others. . . .

"[I]n ordinary administrative law contexts, where Congress has assigned a function to a named agency subject to its oversight and the discipline of judicial review, the President's role—like that of the Congress and the courts—is that of overseer and not decider. . . . The difference between oversight and decision can be subtle, particularly when the important transactions occur behind closed doors and among political compatriots who value loyalty and understand that the President who selected them is their democratically chosen leader. Still, there is a difference between ordinary respect and political deference, on the one hand, and law-compelled obedience, on the other. The subordinate's understanding which of these is owed, and what is her personal responsibility, has implications for what it means to have a government under laws."

GILLIAN E. METZGER, THE CONSTITUTIONAL DUTY TO SUPERVISE, 124 Yale L.J. 1836, 1875–80 (2015): "Two points seem evident from [the] text [of the Take Care Clause]. The first, indicated by the Clause's use of the passive voice and the sheer practical impossibility of any other result, is that the actual execution of the laws will be done by others. . . . The second point is that the presidential oversight role is mandatory. . . . [T]he mandatory character of the Take Care Clause is worth underscoring. . . . This feature, combined with the Clause's oversight phrasing, means that the Take Care Clause represents the clearest constitutional statement of a duty to supervise. . . . These two features of the Take Care Clause . . . combine to imply a hierarchical structure for federal administration, under which lower government officials act subject to higher-level superintendence. Article II's other provisions echo that hierarchy. A prime example is the Appointments Clause, with its differentiation between 'Officers of the United States' and 'inferior Officers,' the latter subject to appointment by (and thus implicitly subservient to) Heads of Department. . . . The Opinion Clause also conveys the importance of oversight, as the President's power to require written opinions from principal officers both signals that the President was expected to play an oversight role and ensures that such officers cannot keep the President in the dark about how their departments are operating. . . .

"Unitary executive scholars claim that Article II's hierarchy requires broad presidential authority to control all executive-branch decisionmaking or at least at-will presidential removal power over those executing federal law. But such a claim of broad presidential authority mistakenly elides the President's right and duty to supervise law execution with the scope of such supervision. The structural principle of hierarchy entails that supervision up to the President must occur; it does not require that such supervision take the form of full presidential decisionmaking control. Only if supervision could not otherwise occur—a dubious proposition, given the variety of forms supervision takes today—would such a broad claim of presidential power necessarily follow."

BLAKE EMERSON, THE DEPARTMENTAL STRUCTURE OF EXECUTIVE POWER, 38 Yale J. on Reg. 90 (2021): "[T]here is more to execution than power. . . . [T]he executive power is checked by the internal organization of the executive branch. The Constitution provides that the branch is to include 'Departments' with discrete jurisdictions, procedures, and obligations. These departments enable but also channel and constrain the discretionary authority wielded by the President, as well as that of the principal officers he appoints. The departmental structure of the Executive separates the law's administration from the viewpoints and interests of any one official. It thereby guards against arbitrary rule and preserves public commitments across time . . . [a]gainst . . . dominant presidentialism, . . . the constitutional structure of the department provides a foundation for the administrative state that is separate from the President's executive power."

(5) ***Historical Origins of Unitary Executive Theory.*** Unitary executive theorists maintain that the idea of a President overseeing all exercises of executive power dates back to the Founding, even if other aspects of contemporary presidential authority are more modern creations. See Saikrishna B. Prakash, Imperial From the Beginning: The Constitution of the Original Executive (2015). "[A]ll of our nation's presidents have believed in the theory of the unitary executive. Big fights about whether the Constitution grants the president the removal power have erupted frequently, but each time the president in power has claimed that the Constitution gives the president power to remove and direct subordinates in the executive branch. And each time the president has prevailed, and Congress has backed down." STEVEN G. CALABRESI & CHRISTOPHER S. YOO, THE UNITARY EXECUTIVE 4 (2008).

Other scholars view unitary executive theory as a more recent phenomenon, one constructed over the twentieth century—although they disagree on exactly when. Some trace it to the conservative insurgency that led to the Reagan era. STEPHEN SKOWRONEK, JOHN A. DEARBORN, & DESMOND KING, PHANTOMS OF A BELEAGUERED REPUBLIC 30, 34 (2021): "Though presidents have advanced claims consistent with a unitary executive all along the way, elaboration of the theory did not begin in earnest until the 1970s and 1980s. . . . [T]he theory was elaborated on the heels of the major expansion of the national government that began in the mid-1960s. The theory offered a timely principle for the reassertion of order and control at a juncture at which administrative power was reaching into national life more deeply than ever before." Others go further back. NOAH A. ROSENBLUM, in THE ANTIFASCIST ROOTS OF PRESIDENTIAL ADMINISTRATION, 122 Colum. L. Rev. 1, 3 (2022), "traces the intellectual origins of presidential administration to early twentieth-century Progressive Era reform efforts to make American government more responsible. And it shows how, during the New Deal, the institutions that would enable executive control of the administrative state were reimagined in light of fascism. Presidential administration would make American democracy accountable and efficacious in order to stand up to European fascists abroad, while simultaneously checking the American executive in order to prevent it from becoming fascistic at home."

(6) ***Directive Authority as Statutory Presumption?*** ELENA KAGAN, PRESIDENTIAL ADMINISTRATION, 114 Harv. L. Rev. 2245, 2319 (2001): "I believe . . . that the unitarians have failed to establish their claim for plenary control as a matter of constitutional mandate. . . . But [this] does not require the conclusion . . . that the President lacks all power to direct administrative officials as to the exercise of their delegated discretion. That Congress could bar the President from directing discretionary action does not mean that Congress has done so; whether it has is a matter of statutory construction. If Congress, in a particular statute, has stated its intent with respect to presidential involvement, then that is the end of the matter. But if Congress, as it usually does, simply has assigned discretionary authority to an agency official, without in any way commenting on the President's role in the delegation, then an interpretive question arises. One way to read a statute of this kind is to assume that the delegation runs to the agency official specified and to that official alone. But a second way to read such a statute is to assume that the delegation runs to the agency official specified, rather than to any other agency official, but still subject to the ultimate control of the President. . . .

"When the delegation in question runs to the members of an independent agency, the choice between these two interpretive principles seems fairly obvious. . . . When the delegation runs to an executive branch official, however, Congress's intent (to the extent it exists) may well cut in the opposite direction. Congress knows, after all, that executive officials stand in all other respects in a subordinate position to the President, given that the President nominates them without restriction, can remove them at will, and can subject them to potentially far-ranging procedural oversight. All these powers establish a general norm of deference among executive officials to presidential opinions, such that when Congress delegates to an executive official, it in some necessary and obvious sense also delegates to the President. . . ."

Compare KEVIN M. STACK, THE PRESIDENT'S STATUTORY POWERS TO ADMINISTER THE LAWS, 106 Colum. L. Rev. 263, 267, 276 (2006): "If Congress's legislative practice were to name only an agency official or the President alone as the statutory delegate, then the difference between a delegation to an independent agency and an executive agency would provide a basis to embrace the view that the President has directive authority. . . . Congress, however, has a more varied [delegating] practice . . . than Kagan acknowledges. . . . From the earliest days of the republic, [Congress] has delegated authority to an agency to act subject to the President's control. Congress also has delegated authority to the President to act though a specified agent, and to the President to act upon the recommendation of a cabinet secretary or the joint recommendation of cabinet secretaries. . . . [Therefore] delegations to executive officials alone . . . should not be read to grant directive authority to the President. . . . [A]s a matter of statutory construction the President has directive authority—that is, the power to act directly under the statute or to bind the discretion of lower level officials—only when the statute expressly grants power to the President in name."

(7) ***Enhancing Democratic Accountability?*** Both strong unitary executive theorists and other defenders of presidential directive authority argue that such authority is needed to make regulation democratically accountable. This theme of presidential control ensuring democratic accountability is particularly strong in Seila Law (p. 988) and Free Enterprise (p. 1002). Do you agree that presidential control of administration enhances democratic accountability? Consider the following dissenting views:

(a) HEIDI KITROSSER, RECLAIMING ACCOUNTABILITY 172 (2015): "[A] central flaw of unitary executive theory is that it conflates substantive accountability and formal accountability. To unity's supporters, maximizing the president's power to execute the law necessarily enhances accountability. This view would make perfect sense were accountability comprised solely of one's being subject to election or defeat at the ballot box. By that measure, there is no downside to consolidating all executive power in the country's sole nationally elected figure, putting aside the fact that the president can be reelected only once. . . . [H]owever, the accountability principle that the Constitution embodies is far more complex than that. Constitutional text, structure and history assume and demand multiple accountability mechanisms, including elections, press coverage, popular discourse, judicial review, congressional oversight, and impeachment. Those mechanisms cannot operate without a regular and reliable flow of information. . . . [U]nitary executive can undermine, rather than further substantive accountability. It can do so by enabling the president and his proxies to control the flow of information from within the executive branch."

(b) PETER M. SHANE, DEMOCRACY'S CHIEF EXECUTIVE 167 (2022): "[A]n executive branch focused entirely on the policy predilections of a single individual, with officials regarding themselves as extensions of the president's will and not as responsible actors in their own right, is likely to be an executive branch in which policy dialogue is stunted and relatively nontransparent. . . . A pluralistic environment for executive-branch policy making is more likely to support vigorous, open, and reasoned dialogue between government agencies and the constituencies most directly affected by their work. And the more loci that exist for meaningful policy input, the more opportunities are presented for members of the public to influence policy outputs."

(8) ***Transparency.*** Does the accountability argument for presidential directive authority depend on the specifics of presidential involvement being publicly known? "[P]ublic information about the content of executive supervision of an agency decision itself, such as through regulatory review, is surprisingly rare." Nina A. Mendelson, Disclosing "Political" Oversight of Agency Decision Making, 108 Mich. L. Rev. 1127 (2010). In particular, lack of transparency is a frequent complaint lodged against centralized regulatory review under the Office of Information and Regulatory Affairs. For a discussion of this issue, see p. 470. See, e.g., id; Peter Strauss, The OIRA Transparency Problem, Notice & Comment Blog (Nov. 22, 2016).[19] Mendelson argues that agencies should be required to disclose, in every significant rule, "at least a summary of the substance of executive supervision." Mendelson, supra, at 1130. Others argue that such disclosure is unlikely to increase political accountability and will undermine important administrative law principles of reason-giving. See Jodi L. Short, The Political Turn in American Administrative Law: Power, Rationality, And Reasons, 61 Duke L.J. 1811, 1839–51 (2012). Assuming such disclosure requirements are a good idea, does Congress have power to require disclosure of presidential communications by statute? Why or why not?

(9) ***Presidential Procedures.*** Presidential administration most commonly refers to presidential efforts to direct or influence agency action. But a number of statutes delegate authority directly to the President. SHALEV ROISMAN, PRESIDENTIAL LAW, 105 Minn. L. Rev. 1269, 1280–82 (2021): "[T]he President is delegated a vast array of power in all areas of life, foreign and domestic. . . . Such delegations are not siloed to inconsequential issues, foreign affairs, or military authorities. Rather, direct delegations to the President span all manner of substantive areas including trade, disaster and emergency management, as well as purely domestic powers like combating domestic inflation, setting environmental standards, imposing conditions on government procurement, and creating national monuments." See also Stack, supra, at 278–83.

Can a President exercise these direct powers free from procedural control? Would a congressional effort to impose procedural requirements on the President violate separation of powers? In Franklin v. Massachusetts, 505 U.S. 788 (1992), the Court noted that the President was not "explicitly excluded" or "explicitly included" within "the APA's purview," and read the APA as not applying to the President "[o]ut of respect for the separation of powers and the unique constitutional position of the President." Kathryn E. Kovacs, in Constraining the Statutory President, 98 Wash. U. L. Rev. 63

---

[19] https://www.yalejreg.com/nc/the-oira-transparency-problem-by-peter-strauss/.

(2020), argues that this was a mistaken reading of the APA and constitutionally unjustified. ROISMAN, supra, at 1271, 1274, takes a different tack and maintains that the President has a constitutionally based duty to deliberate: "Before the President can exercise substantive power delegated directly to her, the President must first satisfy a procedural hurdle: she must gather relevant information and make a considered judgment based on that information. If she does not do so, she has acted unlawfully—she has failed to comply with her procedural obligations in exercising power. . . . [A]n examination of Supreme Court case law on presidential power establishes that the Court has long assumed the President must engage in deliberation before exercising power.

## (3) Presidential Directive Authority in Context

Are assertions of presidential directive authority more defensible in certain administrative contexts than others? Some settings where such authority seems obviously appropriate are those where, in Chief Justice Marshall's words, "the heads of departments are the political or confidential agents of the executive, merely to execute the will of the president." Marbury v. Madison, 5 U.S. (1 Cranch) 137, 165–66 (1803). Three more ordinary procedural contexts worth examining individually are adjudication, regulation, and enforcement. A fourth context, budget, and a fifth, management, are two often overlooked areas of presidential control that have become increasingly more important over time.

(1) ***Adjudication.*** The question of presidential involvement in formal adjudication was presented in PORTLAND AUDUBON SOCIETY V. THE ENDANGERED SPECIES COMMITTEE, 984 F.2d 1534 (9th Cir. 1993) (also discussed on p. 573). Under the Endangered Species Act, actions harming the habitat of an endangered species are prohibited unless a high-level committee grants an exemption, after an adjudication process involving an on-the-record hearing before an ALJ, a report by the Secretary of the Interior, and any other hearings or written submissions the committee may request. After the committee authorized a number of timber sales affecting the northern spotted owl's habitat, environmental groups challenging the exemptions sought discovery to show the exemptions were the product of ex parte contacts with White House staff. They argued that such communications violated the APA, 5 U.S.C. § 557(d)(1), which prohibits communications related to the merits of a proceeding between any "interested person outside the agency" and an employee involved in the decisional process or the body comprising the agency.

The Ninth Circuit, in an opinion by JUDGE REINHARDT, held that § 557(d)(1) applies to White House communications with the committee: "[T]he APA's ban on ex parte communications is absolute and includes no special exemption for White House officials. . . . We believe the President's position at the center of the Executive Branch renders him, ex officio, an 'interested person' . . . in every agency proceeding. No ex parte communication is more likely to influence an agency than one from the President or a member of his staff. No communication from any other person is more likely to deprive the parties and the public of their right to effective participation in a key governmental decision at a most crucial time. The essential purposes of the statutory provision compel the conclusion that the President and his staff are 'interested persons' within the meaning of 5 U.S.C. § 557(d)(1)."

Reinhardt also rejected "out of hand" the government's contention "that any construction of APA § 557(d)(1) that includes presidential communications within the ban on ex parte contacts would constitute a violation of the separation of powers doctrine" and "would represent Congressional interference with the President's constitutional duty to provide . . . supervision and guidance to inferior officials," identified in Myers (p. 982). The appeals court held that "Congress in no way invaded any legitimate constitutional power of the President in providing that he may not attempt to influence the outcome of administrative adjudications through ex parte communications and that Congress' important objectives reflected in the enactment of the APA would, in any event, outweigh any de minimis impact on presidential power. . . . [C]arried to its logical conclusion[,] the government's position would effectively destroy the integrity of all federal agency adjudications. It is a fundamental precept of administrative law that when an agency performs a quasi-judicial (or a quasi-legislative) function its independence must be protected. . . . Myers itself clearly recognizes that 'there may be duties of a quasi-judicial character imposed on executive officers and members of executive tribunals whose decisions after hearing affect interests of individuals, the discharge of which the President can not in a particular case properly influence or control.' 272 U.S. at 135. And in Humphrey's Executor v. United States, the Court observed that '[t]he authority of Congress, in creating quasi-legislative or quasi-judicial agencies, to require them to act in discharge of their duties independently of executive control cannot well be doubted.' 295 U.S. 602, 629 (1935) [p. 983]. The government's position in this case is antithetical to and destructive of these elementary legal precepts." The court concluded that "[i]f such ex parte communications occurred, then the record must be supplemented to include those contacts so that proper judicial review may be conducted." For further discussion of § 557(d)'s requirements, see the PATCO decision and Notes, p. 557.

Do you agree with the result the Portland Audubon court reached? Can § 557(d)(1) plausibly be read to not apply to presidential contacts—and should the Ninth Circuit have adopted such a reading if it were available? Does the Ninth Circuit's decision accord with the Supreme Court's removal decisions—Seila Law, Free Enterprise, and Collins—issued since Portland Audubon was decided? Some agencies establish public policy largely through adjudication; if the President has a constitutional claim to at least oversee the development of national policy, should adjudication be pulled out of the President's ambit so strongly? To the extent a prohibition on presidential interference in adjudication rests on due process and fairness concerns, should it apply in the context of Portland Audubon, involving the discretionary grant of a regulatory exemption, as opposed to administrative adjudications involving liberty and property rights?

Separately, do you think the Supreme Court's recent decisions such as Seila Law (p. 988) or Collins (p. 1007), reading Humphrey's Executor and Morrison narrowly and limiting removal protection, call the continuing validity of Portland Audubon into question? What about Arthrex (p. 945), where the Court provided that the Director of the Patent and Trademark Office had to be able to review decisions by the Patent and Trademark Appeal Board for the Board's members to be inferior officers, but did not sever the members' removal protection?

(2) ***Enforcement.*** Enforcement refers to a broad array of actions agencies take to ensure compliance with governing statutory and regulatory requirements, ranging from providing training or technical assistance to undertaking inspections and investigations, to charging and prosecuting violations. If adjudication is the hardest context in which to imagine presidential power to direct administrators to reach particular outcomes, enforcement might seem the easiest, given the President's duty to faithfully execute the law. Early on, as noted above (p. 1039), Attorney General Roger Taney advised President Andrew Jackson that he could direct the U.S. Attorney in New York to discontinue prosecution of an action to condemn certain stolen jewels brought into the country in violation of the revenue laws (although Taney also advised that the President could not himself effect the dismissal of the prosecution.)

Still, even in the area of prosecution, our politico-legal culture is uncomfortable with direct presidential disruption of the "standard operating procedure" for investigating and enforcing the law. In thinking about presidential authority here, it is helpful to draw a distinction between setting enforcement priorities and selecting which particular enforcement actions to take. Priority setting is at the very heart of seeing to the faithful execution of the law, given the reality that appropriations will not permit full enforcement. But choosing particular targets is another thing entirely. For a description of the evolution of current norms of investigatory independence, see Daphna Renan, Presidential Norms and Article II, 131 Harv. L. Rev. 2187, 2207–2215 (2018). See also Saikrishna Prakash, The Chief Prosecutor, 73 Geo. Wash. L. Rev. 521, 552–65 (2005) (describing early presidential involvement in prosecutions, including President John Adams' control over prosecutions under the Sedition Act of 1798).

In the spring and summer of 2017, the strong norms against presidential involvement in particular investigations were sharply in the public spotlight amid testimony from the former FBI Director James Comey that President Trump sought to end the criminal investigation of his first National Security Advisor, Michael Flynn. Renan, supra, at 2214. Under the Biden Administration, Attorney General Merrick Garland issued a memo specifying that "[i]n order to promote and protect the norms of Departmental independence and integrity in making decisions regarding criminal and civil law enforcement, while at the same time preserving the President's ability to perform his constitutional [take care] obligation . . . , the Justice Department will not advise the White House concerning pending or contemplated criminal or civil law enforcement investigations or cases unless doing so is important for the performance of the President's duties and appropriate from a law enforcement perspective." Memorandum For All Department Personnel at 1 (July 21, 2021).[20] In line with this policy, the Biden White House reported it was not briefed in advance when the FBI searched former President Trump's home in Mar-a-Lago, Florida, as part of an investigation into improper handling of presidential records. Olivia Olander, Biden Had No Advance Notice on Mar-A-Lago Search, White House Says, POLITICO (Aug. 9, 2022).

KATE ANDRIAS, in THE PRESIDENT'S ENFORCEMENT POWER, 88 N.Y.U. L. Rev. 1031, 1033–36 (2013), notes that "[w]hile enforcement of law is at the very core of executive responsibility, the formal apparatus of presidential administration concerns itself little with it. No office or staff in the White House or the Executive Office of the President (EOP) attends systematically to the enforcement of rules after they have been promulgated—that is, to problems of regulatory compliance," as there is with OIRA for rulemaking. Still, "notwithstanding the absence of an office dedicated to enforcement, under both Republican and Democratic administrations the White House has long influenced administrative enforcement efforts within and across executive branch agencies. . . . Nonenforcement in particular, which is subject to few judicial checks, has proved to be an important tool for advancing the presidential agenda. . . .

"In the modern era, . . . Presidents have legitimately exercised great influence over agency enforcement policy. Yet they have failed to ensure that their administrations' policy decisions are well-disclosed and therefore have not always been held sufficiently accountable for uses of enforcement discretion. . . . While concerns about political involvement in enforcement actions should be taken seriously, and while it is critical that law enforcement be nonpartisan, it is naïve to imagine that administrative enforcement can or should be insulated from the President. Such a view fails to account for the pervasiveness and inevitability of policy judgments in enforcement, sacrifices potential gains in regulatory compliance that could be achieved through greater coordination, and ignores the structural factors that make presidential involvement in administration so entrenched. By acknowledging the President's role in, and responsibility for, enforcement, we can create the structure and transparency that will promote appropriate presidential influence." For additional views on the President's enforcement power, see Zachary S. Price, Enforcement Discretion and Enforcement Duty, 67 Vand. L. Rev. 671 (2014); Patricia L. Bellia, Faithful Execution and Enforcement Discretion, 164 U. Pa. L. Rev. 1753 (2016); Leigh Osofsky, The Case for Categorical Nonenforcement, 69 Tax L. Rev. 73 (2015).

(3) ***Rulemaking.*** Rulemaking presents the most challenging context for specifying the appropriate scope and nature of presidential directive authority. Some things seem clear. The Opinion Clause, along with the President's take care duty and supervisory responsibilities, authorize the President to require agencies to provide information and coordinate their proposed rulemakings. Thus, even if a statute prohibited EPA from taking cost into account in setting particular emissions standards, surely the

[20] https://www.justice.gov/ag/page/file/1413766/download.

President can require an Administrator to calculate and report cost data as a part of the regulatory review of proposed new standards required by Executive Order 12866. But could a President direct the EPA Administrator not to set those standards at a certain level because of the cost such a regulation would impose? Executive Order 12866 is careful to avoid the question of whether the President may control agency rulemaking outcomes. At the same time, it certainly provides a means by which the President might effectively do so, as by failing to approve the agency's regulatory plan or delaying indefinitely OIRA's response to a submitted draft or final impact analysis. For further discussion of centralized regulatory review, see Section 5.d of Chapter IV (p. 455).

It also seems clear (except perhaps to the most ardent unitary executive theorist) that when Congress has authorized an agency to develop regulations on a particular topic, adoption of the regulation requires the agency's acquiescence. If the relevant Secretary or Administrator is unwilling to sign the final rulemaking document, it cannot meet the terms of the statutory authorization. But can the agency head sign and cause to be published a rule to which the President objects? For example, in 2011, EPA proposed a NAAQS for ozone of 60–70 ppm; although this standard was recommended by EPA's science advisory committee, business interests strongly opposed it as too costly. After reviewing the proposed standard under the Executive Order 12866 process, OIRA Administrator Cass Sunstein returned the rule to EPA at President Obama's direction. EPA pulled the proposed standard. Could EPA Administrator Lisa Jackson nonetheless have adopted the rejected emissions standard? Can the President prohibit publication of such a rule in the Federal Register, if adopted by the Administrator, by instructions to the Office of the Federal Register? The Executive Order does appear to assert this prerogative, and an unpublished rule cannot take effect.

Alternatively, if the rulemaking at issue is one undertaken by an independent agency, can the President force the agency to submit the rule for centralized review? Note that Executive Order 12866 expressly exempts independent agencies from the requirement that agencies must submit rules for OIRA review, but subjects them to the requirement that they provide a regulatory agenda (p. 463). As noted above (p. 1033), under the Trump Administration OIRA asserted authority to review independent agency rules to determine if they were subject to the Congressional Review Act, and the Office of Legal Counsel issued an opinion holding that the President could "direct independent regulatory agencies to comply with the centralized regulatory review process of Executive Order 12866." According to the opinion, "statutory restrictions on removal, standing alone, do not bar those agencies from complying with EO 12866; indeed, the terms of such good-cause restrictions presuppose that the President may supervise an agency head to ensure compliance with the duties of office and with principles of good governance. Other structural features associated with independent agencies, such as multi-member governance, independent litigating authority, or open-meeting requirements, likewise do not preclude those agencies from complying with EO 12866." Emphasizing that "[t]he

President's constitutional authority to direct traditional executive agencies under EO 12866 also extends to" independent agencies as "part of the Executive Branch," the opinion noted that "Congress has not . . . sought to shield such agencies, as a general matter, from complying with [Executive Order 12866's] other requirements, and we see no persuasive grounds to infer such an unstated limitation on the President's supervisory authority." Extending Regulatory Review Under Executive Order 12866 to Independent Regulatory Agencies, 43 Op. O.L.C., at 13 (Oct. 8, 2019).[21]

There is little precedent on the appropriate scope of the presidential role in rulemaking. A rare and influential decision is SIERRA CLUB V. COSTLE, 657 F.2d 298 (D.C. Cir. 1981) (p. 500), which involved a suit by an environmental organization challenging the standards EPA issued under the Clean Air Act to govern emissions of sulfur dioxide and particulates by new coal-fired power stations. Higher standards would have imposed an economic cost on certain coal mining areas, including northern Appalachia. The organization claimed that EPA backed away from more stringent standards after an "ex parte blitz" by the coal industry, President Carter, and West Virginia's Senator (and at the time Senate minority leader) Robert Byrd, involving both submission of late comments and high-level meetings with executive branch officials.

CHIEF JUDGE PATRICIA WALD rejected the argument that intra-executive branch meetings were improper. "We assume, unless expressly forbidden by Congress, such intra-executive contacts may take place, both during and after the public comment period; the only real issue is whether they must be noted and summarized in the docket. The court recognizes the basic need of the President and his White House staff to monitor the consistency of executive agency regulations with Administration policy" and "to be briefed fully and frequently about rules in the making . . . . The executive power under our Constitution, after all, is not shared—it rests exclusively with the President." Moreover, "[o]ur form of government simply could not function effectively or rationally if key executive policymakers were isolated from each other and from the Chief Executive. Single mission agencies do not always have the answers to complex regulatory problems. An overworked administrator exposed on a 24-hour basis to a dedicated but zealous staff needs to know the arguments and ideas of policymakers in other agencies as well as in the White House." Wald acknowledged "that there may be instances where the docketing of conversations between the President or his staff and other Executive Branch officers or rulemakers may be necessary to ensure due process. This may be true, for example, where such conversations directly concern the outcome of adjudications or quasi-adjudicatory proceedings." But that was not the case here.

Wald further held that "[t]he purposes of full-record review which underlie the need for disclosing ex parte conversations in some settings do not require that courts know the details of every White House contact, including a Presidential one, in this informal rulemaking setting. After all, any rule issued here with or without White House assistance must have the

[21] https://www.justice.gov/olc/file/1349716/download.

requisite factual support in the rulemaking record .... Of course, it is always possible that undisclosed Presidential prodding may direct an outcome that is factually based on the record, but different from the outcome that would have obtained in the absence of Presidential involvement.... But we do not believe that Congress intended that the courts convert informal rulemaking into a rarified technocratic process, unaffected by political considerations or the presence of Presidential power."

Do you agree with how the Costle court viewed ex parte presidential contacts? The court holds that ex parte contacts do not need to be disclosed unless Congress (or constitutional due process) so requires. Should the presumption instead be that such contacts must be disclosed unless Congress prohibits disclosure (and due process allows such a prohibition)? Does the fact that any resulting rule will need to have sufficient factual support to survive judicial review alleviate concerns about "presidential prodding" in the absence of disclosure?

(4) ***Budget.*** ELOISE PASACHOFF, THE PRESIDENT'S BUDGET AS A SOURCE OF AGENCY POLICY CONTROL, 125 Yale L.J. 2182, 2186–93 (2016): "Reviewing regulations is not the only policy lever OMB has to control executive agencies' policy choices. In fact, it may not even be the main one. The budget itself—the core reason for OMB's existence—is a key tool for controlling agencies. Yet the mechanisms of control through the executive budget process remain little discussed and insufficiently understood." According to Pasachoff, "OMB's budget work serves as a regularized and pervasive form of agency control." Understanding this dynamic requires "focus[ing] not on the appropriations process but instead on the periods leading up to the annual submission of the President's budget to Congress and following the passage of the budget." Moreover, the critical OMB players here are not OIRA but OMB's five "Resource Management Offices (RMOs), . . . [which] collectively contain more than four times as many staff members as OIRA. Working directly with budget and policy officials in each agency, the RMO staff play a large role in overseeing—indeed, at times in directing—the work of agencies throughout the administrative state.... [T]he RMOs provide a direct line into agencies ... [and] can serve as a conduit for policy and political direction from the President, the White House policy councils and other White House political advisors, and the OMB Director. If there is a message to be conveyed to agencies, the RMOs are a good way to convey it." Pasachoff also emphasizes, however, that "the RMOs reach many decisions about agency action on their own, since much agency oversight does not require elevation.... In this sense, whether the RMOs' work is a form of presidential control is less clear. At times, the RMOs' work may instead reflect OMB control, or RMO-intuited versions of presidential control as applied to particular situations, with case-specific value judgments obscured."

Presidential budget authority has a well-established historical and statutory basis. It dates back to the Budget and Accounting Act of 1921, which created the initial Bureau of the Budget that is now OMB. By statute, 31 U.S.C. § 1105, the President is responsible for developing and submitting a consolidated budget to Congress annually. Other statutes provide important powers over budget execution that create additional avenues for presidential influence. On several occasions, President Trump sought to use these budget execution powers to advance his policy priorities. See Eloise Pasachoff, The President's Budget Powers in the Trump Era, in Executive Policymaking: The Role of the OMB in the Presidency (Meena Bose & Andrew Rudalevige eds., 2020). One power was the President's statutory obligation, delegated to OMB, to apportion appropriations before agencies have access to funds. "The most significant and controversial effort to use apportionment to further the administration's goals occurred in July and August 2019, when OMB placed holds on . . . foreign aid funding, including to Ukraine, with no immediately discernable funds management reasons. . . . [A] CIA whistleblower detailed concerns that the president had himself demanded the funds be withheld until the Ukrainian president agreed to investigate President Trump's Democratic political rival Joe Biden," leading to Trump's first impeachment by the House of Representatives. Id. at 74–75.

The Trump Administration also employed statutory transfer and reprogramming appropriations authorities to obtain billions of dollars to build a wall at the southern border. As Pasachoff notes, "[i]n December 2018, President Trump refused to sign a budget that did not include $5 billion he had requested for wall funding, beginning a shutdown that lasted for thirty-five days." Id. at 80. After ultimately agreeing on a budget that appropriated only $1.375 billion for the wall, Trump "announced he would obtain the rest of the funds he wanted for the wall, and more, through executive action," including by declaring a national emergency at the border in order to "reprogram[ ] $3.6 billion from Department of Defense military construction projects" under a statutory provision. Although "[t]hese actions provoked immediate opposition" in Congress, including "a rare bipartisan formal rejection" in both chambers, none of these efforts were successful in reversing Trump's actions, and neither were a number of lawsuits that were filed. Id. at 80–81. Immediately upon assuming office, President Biden imposed a pause on further border wall construction, and ultimately returned what remained of the unobligated reprogrammed funds to Defense.

What do you make of the President's ability to control agency action via the budget process? Does this ability conflict with the constitutional assignment of the power of the purse to Congress? Does your answer differ for the control that stems from putting together the budget request for Congress and the control that stems from executing the budget Congress ultimately passes? Does your answer differ for the kind of action the President takes—those that require congressional resources for their exercise and those that do not? On this latter point, see Zachary S. Price, Funding Restrictions and Separation of Powers, 71 Vanderbilt L. Rev. 357 (2018).

(5) ***Management.*** If you read the section on public administration in Chapter 3, you'll have seen how important the administrative aspects of government are for achieving policy outcomes. And the President's ability to manage the administration of government offers yet another important tool for presidential direction and control. As ANDREW RUDALEVIGE explains in

THE NEW IMPERIAL PRESIDENCY: RENEWING PRESIDENTIAL POWER AFTER WATERGATE 61 (2005), describing President Nixon's decision to change the Bureau of the Budget into the Office of Management and Budget, "The new emphasis on the 'M' in OMB was designed to facilitate Nixon's efforts to shape the way executive agencies created and implemented policy. As [White House Counsel and Assistant for Domestic Affairs John] Ehrlichman put it in a 1972 memo to Caspar Weinberger, then OMB's director, 'I'm for whatever will strengthen the President's hand vs. the bureaucracy.' This meant focusing on management—so long as it wasn't boring public administration theory but rather 'management in the get-the-Secretary-to-do-what-the-President-needs-and-wants-him-to-do-whether-he-likes-it-or-not sense.' The goal was to gain for Nixon the ability to control bureaucratic structures, personnel, processes, and, thereby, outcomes."

PASACHOFF, THE PRESIDENT'S BUDGET AS A SOURCE OF AGENCY POLICY CONTROL, supra, 2239–41: "Management initiatives are not simply neutral, technocratic procedures. . . [but] often either explicitly contemplate substantive policy choices or implicitly lead to them. The Presidential Management Agenda (PMA) exemplifies this dynamic. Consider, for example, President George W. Bush's Faith-Based and Community Initiative, which the Administration presented as a management initiative to break down bureaucratic barriers limiting religiously-affiliated organizations from engaging with government. But the initiative was not simply bureaucratic; it attempted to weaken the wall between church and state. Other initiatives sound more technocratic but end up driving agencies' substantive choices. . . . For example, [President Obama's] Evidence and Evaluation Agenda . . . has affected agency policy choices in a number of ways. . . . One study of the Evidence and Evaluation Agenda goes so far as to call it a 'vast attempt to change the foundation of American social policy.' These management initiatives are also intricately intertwined with political decisions. For example, some have charged that President Obama's evidence-based initiative relies more heavily on evidence that supports the administration's preferred policy decisions. Others suggested that President Bush's [Program Assessment Rating Tool] was politically motivated to cut the budgets of disfavored and that the faith-based initiative was a political maneuver without any meaningful policy analysis or apparatus. In earlier administrations, President Nixon's management reforms were described as intending at once to 'improve governmental management,' 'redistribute power in the intergovernmental system,' and ensure 'political direction' over agencies' activities. And a Reagan Administration official reportedly joked after leaving office that the name for President Reagan's management initiative was I-D-E-O-L-O-G-Y (riffing on the acronym-heavy titles of the previous Presidents' management initiatives). Management reforms . . . thus . . . reflect the substantive policy interests of different administrations and are tied to political contexts as well."

Many of the tools JODY FREEMAN and SHARON JACOBS identify as "50 Ways to Kill an Agency" in STRUCTURAL DEREGULATION, 135 Harv. L. Rev. 585, 591–92 (2021), are tools of presidential management: "In the first category are actions that interfere with agency staffing. Examples include intentionally declining to fill open agency positions at both the leadership and line levels. The second category comprises presidential manipulation of other resources, including substantially reducing an agency's budget by reallocating funds, making funding more difficult to spend for particular purposes, and diverting agency attention from more material statutory responsibilities with 'busywork' or 'churn.' Third is undermining the institutional expertise that is essential to performing congressionally assigned tasks. Fourth are attacks on agency reputation. When a President or other high-ranking executive official persistently charges an agency with incompetence, bias, or worse, it can have a corrosive effect. The ensuing harm to reputation can make it incrementally more difficult for the agency to secure funding from Congress, influence regulated entities, and even prevail in the courts."

Are presidential efforts to leverage managerial oversight to advance substantive goals appropriate? Do you find these efforts more or less troubling than presidential involvement in adjudication, enforcement, rulemaking, and appropriations? Arguably, managerial oversight is a role particularly well-suited to the chief executive. Presidents are also well-positioned to ensure coordination across government, to ensure that different agencies are not pursuing regulatory actions at cross-purposes to one another. But if the President uses her oversight and coordinating role to advance her own policies at the expense of those embodied in underlying statutes, is she fulfilling her obligation to ensure the laws are faithfully executed?

## d. Internal Separation of Powers

*(1) Charting Internal Checks on Executive Power*

*(2) Assessing the Internal Separation of Powers*

As you've seen throughout this Chapter, separation of powers debates often focus on the relationships among the three branches of national government and the various "webs of control" they construct over administrative agencies. Peter L. Strauss, The Place of Agencies in Government: Separation of Powers and the Fourth Branch, 84 Colum. L. Rev. 573, 636 (1984). But there is also an important "internal" dimension to the separation of powers that reflects the complicated structures and relationships that exist within the executive branch. Often these represent checks on presidential and administrative power, but they can serve to enhance executive authority as well. The materials that follow examine the internal side of agencies, the subject of a wide array of recent administrative law scholarship, and assess the relevance of this internal dimension—most entirely absent from the Constitution's text—to contemporary separation of powers disputes.

## (1) Charting Internal Checks on Executive Power

(1) ***The Civil Service.*** The civil service is perhaps the most ubiquitous internal force within the executive branch, present in all agencies. The federal government is the nation's largest employer, with around 2.2 million agency employees (excluding the Postal Service and uniformed military personnel) in 2021. Cong. Rsch. Serv., R43590, Federal Workforce Statistics Sources: OPM and OMB (June 2022). Around 4,000 of these were political appointees. The executive branch civil service has three main components: (1) the "competitive service" (also called the "classified civil service"), positions filled through a competitive, merit-based examination that represent the largest component; (2) the "excepted service," a miscellaneous set of positions excluded from competitive examination, many of which involve national security or intelligence gathering but which also include patent examiners, agency attorney positions, and special assistants; and (3) the Senior Executive Service (SES), top-level management and professional jobs that include a mixture of career employees and political appointees, created by the Civil Service Reform Act of 1978. In 2015, 69.9 percent of non-SES positions fell into the competitive service, and 29.7 percent were in the excepted service. Office of Pers. Mgmt., Excepted Service Hiring Authorities: Their Use And Effectiveness in the Executive Branch 8 (2018).[22] The civil service system dates back to the late nineteenth century, when in 1883 the Pendleton Act created the Civil Service Commission to oversee merit-based hiring via competitive examinations. The Pendleton Act did not include a general for-cause removal protection; this was added by the Lloyd-LaFollette Act of 1912. Today the vast majority of civilian federal employees enjoy some form of removal protection, either through the general civil service system or under statutes that provide largely equivalent protection and are specific to their departments or agencies. See David E. Lewis, The Politics of Presidential Appointments: Political Control and Bureaucratic Performance 20–26 (2008); see also H. Comm. on Oversight and Gov't Reform, 116th Cong., 2d. Sess. United States Government Policy and Supporting Positions (Comm. Print 2020) (the "Plum Book") (providing data on leadership positions in the federal legislative and executive branches that are subject to noncompetitive appointment).

Increasingly, contemporary scholars are emphasizing the importance of the civil service as a check on executive branch abuse of power. JON D. MICHAELS, AN ENDURING, EVOLVING, SEPARATION OF POWERS, 115 Colum. L. Rev. 515, 540–43 (2015): "The first administrative counterweight is the professional civil service. Civil servants are politically insulated. They often spend their entire careers as government employees. And they are well positioned to push back on any tendency agency leaders might have to skirt laws and promote hyperpartisan interests. Three factors explain the civil service's potential effectiveness as an institutional rival. First, as suggested, its members are capable of speaking truth to power without fear of serious reprisal. . . . Second, agency heads must take civil servants seriously.

[22] https://www.opm.gov/policy-data-oversight/hiring-information/excepted-service/excepted-service-study-report.pdf.

Appointed leaders in all federal domestic agencies necessarily rely on civil servants to help develop and carry out the presidential administration's agenda. . . . Third, the independent and much relied-upon civil service has institutional, cultural, and legal incentives to insist that agency leaders follow the law, embrace prevailing scientific understandings, and refrain from partisan excesses. That is to say, these professional civil servants regularly do have reason to 'choose' to hold agency leaders accountable." Michaels has also emphasized that the federal civil service is diverse, geographically fragmented, less elite, and more demographically representative of the electorate than Congress. See Jon D. Michaels, The American Deep State, 93 Notre Dame L. Rev. 1653, 1657–63 (2018).

As Rebecca Ingber describes, some ascribe to a very different account of the civil service, one "which views the bureaucracy as a self-interested, power-hungry cabal of conspiratorial operators, a 'deep state,' acting in darkness to wield the vast military and surveillance powers of the state at the expense of the accountable, elected leadership, namely the President." Bureaucratic Resistance and the National Security State, 104 Iowa L. Rev. 139, 142–43 (2018). This "deep state" account was repeatedly espoused by the Trump Administration, which sought to sideline or push out career officials and end civil service protections. Perhaps unsurprisingly, career officials responded with bureaucratic resistance, leading to political-career struggles throughout the Administration's term in office. Lisa Rein, Josh Dawsey, & Toluse Olorunnipa, Trump's Historic Assault on the Civil Service Was Four Years in the Making, Wash. Post (Oct. 23, 2020).

(2) ***Internal Dissent Mechanisms.*** Civil servants may be willing to stand up to executive branch excesses, but what if agency leaders are nonresponsive? Civil servants rely on a number of mechanisms, some legal and some not, to bring their concerns to public attention. (Many of these mechanisms also relate to government transparency and are discussed in Chapter VI.) To begin with, many career officials have connections to members of Congress and staff on the committees that oversee their agencies, some of whom will not be in the President's party. They often also have relationships with civil society groups, affected businesses, state and local officials, and so on to whom they can turn. A number of statutory and bureaucratic measures protect government employees who raise concerns through certain channels. For example, a number of whistleblower laws—like the Whistleblower Protection Act of 1989, Pub. L. No. 101–12, 103 Stat. 16 (codified as amended in scattered sections of 5 U.S.C.)—protect executive branch employees who disclose information regarding alleged abuses to responsible agency officials or congressional committees under specified procedures, and the Office of Special Counsel was created in 1978 to protect civil service employees from retaliatory action for lawful disclosures under whistleblower statutes. However, these statutes offer less protection for disclosure of national security information and do not cover disclosures to the press.

Some agencies have established procedures through which lower level employees can voice concerns about decisions and actions of their superiors. The most well-known of these may be the dissent channel at the State

Department, which "gives any officer in any embassy the ability . . . to disagree with the position taken by the ambassador," provides that all dissents must be sent to high-level staff, including the Secretary of State, and requires a quick response. Neal Kuman Katyal, Internal Separation of Powers: Checking Today's Most Dangerous Branch, 115 Yale L.J. 2314, 2328–29 (2006). During President Obama's Administration, over four dozen employees used the dissent channel to encourage military strikes in Syria, and at the outset of the Trump Administration hundreds of State Department employees signed a dissent channel memorandum expressing their opposition to President Trump's ban on travel into the United States by citizens of a number of Muslim-majority countries. See Daniel A. Farber & Anne Joseph O'Connell, Agencies as Adversaries, 105 Cal. L. Rev. 1375, 1381 (2017).

Government employees also commonly leak their concerns to the press. As David E. Pozen puts it, in The Leaky Leviathan: Why the Government Condemns and Condones Unlawful Disclosures of Information, 127 Harv. L. Rev. 512, 513–18 (2013): "Ours is a polity saturated with, vexed by, and dependent upon leaks. The Bay of Pigs, the Pentagon Papers, warrantless wiretapping by the National Security Agency at home, targeted killings by the Central Intelligence Agency abroad: the contours of these and countless other government activities have emerged over the years through anonymous disclosures of confidential information to the press." In concluding that leaks are rarely prosecuted, Pozen noted that "[t]he federal government ha[d] brought roughly a dozen media leak prosecutions in the ninety-six years since the Espionage Act was enacted [in 1917], eight of them under the [Obama] Administration." However, this lack of prosecution may be changing, as the uptick in leak prosecutions under President Obama continued under President Trump. According to an investigation by The Intercept and Project On Government Oversight, the "Trump administration referred far more media leaks for criminal investigation each year [in its first three years] than any of the previous 15 years, with the CIA accounting for the vast majority of such leaks, according to a trove of records released by the Department of Justice . . . in response to a Freedom of Information Act lawsuit." There were 118 leaks reported in 2017, 88 in 2018, and 71 in 2019. Jason Paladino, Nick Schwellenbach, & Ken Klippenstein, CIA Drove Spike in Media Leak Investigation Requests Under Trump, The Intercept (July 29, 2021).

(3) ***Government Lawyers and Professional Norms.*** The government employs a large number of professionals with specialized expertise, including many lawyers and scientists. Lawyers in particular are located throughout the executive branch, with thousands of lawyers in general counsel offices in every agency, as well as in the Department of Justice and the White House. Legal and public administration scholars emphasize the importance of professional norms in motivating the behavior of government lawyers and civil servants: "By and large civil servants see themselves as professional public servants. That is, they see themselves as engineers, economists, chemists, biologists, attorneys, social workers, accountants, etc.—and . . . 'often feel bound by legal, moral, or professional norms to certain courses of

action and these courses of action may be at variance with the president's agenda.'" Jon D. Michaels, Of Constitutional Custodians and Regulatory Rivals: An Account of the Old and New Separation of Powers, 91 N.Y.U. L. Rev. 227, 238 (2008) (quoting Lewis, supra, at 30); see also Paul R. Verkuil, Valuing Bureaucracy: The Case for Professional Government (2017).

Moreover, internal executive branch norms can serve to give special weight to the views of professionals. For example, traditionally "legal opinions [from the Office of Legal Counsel in the Department of Justice] are treated as authoritative and binding within the executive branch unless 'overruled' by the Attorney General or the President. OLC generally will not provide legal advice if there is doubt about whether it will be followed." Trevor W. Morrison, Constitutional Alarmism, 124 Harv. L. Rev. 1688, 1711 (2011). According to OLC'S MEMORANDUM ON BEST PRACTICES FOR OLC LEGAL ADVICE AND WRITTEN OPINIONS,[23] "OLC's central function is to provide, pursuant to the Attorney General's delegation, controlling legal advice to Executive Branch officials in furtherance of the President's constitutional duties to preserve, protect, and defend the Constitution, and to 'take Care that the Laws be faithfully executed.' To fulfill this function, OLC must provide advice based on its best understanding of what the law requires—not simply an advocate's defense of the contemplated action or position proposed by an agency or the Administration. Thus, in rendering legal advice, OLC seeks to provide an accurate and honest appraisal of applicable law, even if that appraisal will constrain the Administration's or an agency's pursuit of desired practices or policy objectives. This practice is critically important to the Office's effective performance of its assigned role, particularly because it is frequently asked to opine on issues of first impression that are unlikely to be resolved by the courts—a circumstance in which OLC's advice may effectively be the final word on the controlling law." For discussion of whether OLC and government lawyers actually can play a checking role in practice, see Section 3.d.2 (p. 1062).

(4) ***Internal Watchdogs and Internal Administrative Law.*** Congress has created a number of additional internal institutional checks on the executive branch, ranging from offices expressly given oversight roles to indirect checks that result from program and regulatory design. Some of these, like independent agencies or the procedural constraints of the APA, are likely already familiar to you, but others you may not have encountered yet. Two examples bear special note and appear in many agencies, but there are a number of other similar institutions sprinkled throughout the executive branch:

First are offices within agencies or elsewhere in the executive branch that are tasked with ensuring that agencies attend to concerns that might not otherwise get adequate weight, what MARGO SCHLANGER calls "Offices of Goodness" in OFFICES OF GOODNESS: INFLUENCE WITHOUT AUTHORITY IN FEDERAL AGENCIES, 36 Cardozo L. Rev. 53, 60–61 (2014). The Department of Homeland Security's Office for Civil Rights and Civil Liberties, where Schlanger worked, is an example: "First, Offices of Goodness are advisory

[23] https://www.justice.gov/olc/page/file/1511836/download.

rather than operational. Offices of Goodness help other parts of the agency get work done; they are not the offices . . . that themselves carry out the agency's mission. This means that Offices of Goodness must operate by persuasion or coercion of others. . . . Second, Offices of Goodness are value-infused. The observations here apply to offices that are explicitly assigned to further a particular value that is not otherwise primary for the agency in which they sit. That value could be civil rights, consumer welfare, fiscal rectitude, etc. . . . Where the value in question is 'lawfulness,' the Office of Goodness is likely to be the agency's Office of General Counsel. . . . Third, Offices of Goodness are internal and dependent on their agency. The dynamics of a fully internal office are very different from one that has structural separation and independence."

Second are Inspector Generals. Created mostly by the Inspector General Act of 1978 with a mandate to "prevent and detect fraud and abuse" in agency programs, IGs now exist in over fifty federal agencies, including many working on national security. SHIRIN SINNAR, in PROTECTING RIGHTS FROM WITHIN: INSPECTORS GENERAL AND NATIONAL SECURITY OVERSIGHT, 65 Stan. L. Rev. 1027, 1031, 1034–35 (2013), argues that "IGs stand out in two ways. First . . . IGs enjoy several statutory protections from agency interference. The Inspector General Act provides for presidential appointment and Senate confirmation of IGs [on a nonpartisan basis]. . . . While the President can remove an IG without cause, the Act requires that the President communicate to Congress the reasons for any removal no later than thirty days before[hand]. . . . Even more significantly, IGs have a dual-reporting role that requires them to serve their agencies as well as Congress. . . . Second, IGs enjoy broad investigative powers. The Act authorizes IGs to undertake and carry out audits and investigations without interference from agency leadership and to access documents within and beyond their agencies." Based on an analysis of five case studies of IGs in national security contexts, Sinnar "conclude[s] that in certain cases IGs played a surprisingly significant role in protecting rights. . . . At the same time, . . . IG reviews . . . also displayed important limitations. Even the strongest reviews rarely led to individual relief for most victims, repercussions for high-level executive officials, or significant rights-protective constraints on agency discretion[, and] . . . IG reviews varied significantly: while some exhibited independence and a willingness to critique executive national security conduct, others faced obstruction or lacked rigor." See also Jack Goldsmith, Power and Constraint 95–108 (2012); Paul C. Light, Monitoring Government: Inspectors General and the Search for Accountability (1993).

Although IGs in practice have enjoyed the equivalent of for-cause removal protection and rarely been removed, President Trump deviated from this norm. In April–May, 2020, he removed four confirmed or acting IGs with only a pro forma statement and in contexts that strongly suggest political motivations or retribution. Trump also appointed acting and permanent IGs with political ties and relied heavily on acting IGs. President Biden pledged not to remove IGs as a presidential candidate. That promise may be tested with respect to the Trump-appointed IG for DHS, who has come under fire for several actions, including for preventing investigators in his office from trying to retrieve text messages, which the U.S. Secret Service had deleted, relating to the January 6th attack on the U.S. Capital. President Biden has so far resisted calls to remove the DHS IG from office. In a Brookings Report, Watchdogs at Large (Aug 6, 2020),[24] Anne Joseph O'Connell underscores the longstanding problem of staffing shortages at IG offices, noting that "IGs don't fare well in the appointments process, with above-average failure rates and confirmation delays compared to other agency roles." She also emphasizes that the "non-partisan and expertise statutory mandates for nominated IGs do not apply to acting IGs," raising particular accountability concerns given the number of IG offices with vacancies.

Internal agency structure is important more broadly, for example, in prioritizing certain perspectives in agency decisionmaking or ensuring agency staff adhere to legal and policy constraints. One important element is how authority delegated to an agency is then subdelegated through the agency's structure. JENNIFER NOU, SUBDELEGATING POWERS, 117 Colum. L. Rev. 473, 475–81 (2017): "As a result [of subdelegation], tenure-protected career staff and lower-level political officials often make decisions initially granted to their superiors . . . [and have] signature authority—literally, the authority to affix one's signature and sign off on an agency action without higher-level oversight." According to Nou, "[a]gency subdelegation of this nature is a more pervasive phenomenon than commonly recognized." For example, the SEC has reported more than 376 separate rules subdelegating a range of authority to a variety of actors, and the EPA at one point reported 500 subdelegations. "Subdelegations to career civil servants . . . weaken [centralized presidential control as a] mechanism of executive power. When administrations turn over, subdelegations remain in place until and unless they are repealed." On the other hand, Nou cautions that subdelegation raises questions for internal separation of powers scholarship extolling "the counterbalances offered by various agency actors. This literature often presents career staff as nonpartisan keepers of professional norms. Considering such staff members as recipients of delegated authority with their own preferences and biases, however, calls into question the extent to which they facilitate, rather than buffer, fights between their political principals."

Nou describes these agency structures as a form of internal administrative law. GILLIAN E. METZGER and KEVIN STACK in INTERNAL ADMINISTRATIVE LAW, 115 Mich. L. Rev. 1239, 1252–53 (2017), agree, arguing that "many internal measures, ranging from substantive guidelines to management structures that allow for oversight of agency operations, qualify as forms of law. These measures not only bind and are perceived as binding by agency officials; they also encourage consistency, predictability, and reasoned argument in agency decisionmaking." They argue that recognition of internal administrative law's role in controlling agency power is essential for the legitimacy of administrative governance: "A legal regime that envisions external control as the only protection against administrative abuse is fundamentally at odds with the logic of contemporary

[24] https://www.brookings.edu/research/watchdogs-at-large/.

administrative governance. Such a regime will never be able to ease anxieties about the administrative state or successfully regulate the exercise of administrative power." For a detailed investigation of the role of internal administrative law over time, see Jerry L. Mashaw, Creating the Administrative Constitution (2012); see also Christopher J. Walker & Rebecca Turnbull, Operationalizing Internal Administrative Law, 71 Hastings L.J. 1226 (2020).

(5) ***Interagency Conflict.*** DANIEL FARBER and ANNE JOSEPH O'CONNELL, in AGENCIES AS ADVERSARIES, at 1378–79, 1383–85, 1429, analyze the different interagency relationships found in the executive branch and emphasize the internal separation of powers benefits of inter-agency conflict: "Beneath the surface of the administrative state are constant battles, between and within agencies. . . . Wh[en] the [FBI] . . . fought in court to force Apple to hack the iPhone of a perpetrator of the 2015 mass shooting in San Bernardino, California, it . . . faced resistance from other government agencies [which] . . . expressed grave concerns about weakening encryption technologies. . . . The State Department negotiates laboriously to persuade foreign countries to accept a [Guantánamo] detainee. Once it succeeds, however, a new struggle begins with the Defense Department [over release]." Farber and O'Connell maintain that such "conflict plays an important and often productive role in the functioning of the modern administrative state. . . . [C]onflicts, whatever their motivations, can be most constructive when they bring differing expertise, information bases, constituencies, and values into policy decisions. Such conflicts have the greatest prospects for enhancing expertise and ensuring that all points of view are heard—two key goals of administrative law."

In THE STATUTORY SEPARATION OF POWERS, 129 Yale L.J. 378, 385 (2019), SHARON B. JACOBS describes how Congress often replicates the constitutional design principle of separation of powers in its legislative delegations, offering a study of interagency conflict between the Department of Energy and the Federal Energy Regulatory Commission as a case in point. She "argues that certain types of separation and balance, notably those that divide authority between an independent agency and an executive department, are particularly unstable. These instabilities and the risk that executive agencies will read statutory authorizations expansively are particularly evident in energy regulation today" and stand as "a reminder that statutory checks can also be tools of aggrandizement."

## (2) Assessing the Internal Separation of Powers

A multitude of independent forces and checks thus exist within the executive branch; despite being headed by a single President, the reality is the executive branch is very much a "they, not an it," just like Congress. See Kenneth A. Shepsle, Congress Is a "They," Not an "It": Legislative Intent as Oxymoron, 12 Int'l Rev. L. & Econ. 239 (1992). But this leaves the question of whether, and to what extent, these internal forces check or constrain the President: Is there really an internal separation of powers that has bite? And if internal checks with real bite exist, are such arrangements constitutional?

(1) ***Do Internal Measures Check or Empower?*** Several studies of internal institutional arrangements raise questions about the extent to which supposed checks actually constrain the President. This concern has been raised particularly forcefully in regard to executive branch lawyers, in part in response to failures of executive branch legal institutions like the Office of Legal Counsel to stop presidential abuses of power—and in the case of OLC, to even sanction the legality of torture under the Bush Administration. Some suggest that these supposed checks may actually have the opposite effect and enhance presidential power by "writ[ing] up learned opinions that vindicate the constitutionality of their most blatant power grabs [and] . . . publicly rubber-stamp presidential actions." Bruce Ackerman, The Decline and Fall of the American Republic 9–10, 88 (2010). "Torture, indefinite detention, extraordinary rendition, targeted killing, profiling of Arab and Muslim men, and warrantless surveillance all occurred with the ex ante approval of government lawyers." Norman W. Spaulding, Independence and Experimentation at the Department of Justice, 63 Stan. L. Rev. 409, 410 (2011). Others view such accounts as exaggerated and fault them for giving insufficient weight to OLC's professionalism and its culture of giving independent legal advice, contrasting OLC with presidentially controlled legal offices like the White House Counsel. See Trevor W. Morrison, Constitutional Alarmism, 124 Harv. L. Rev. 1688 (2011).

The multiplicity of legal offices throughout the national administrative state is a sign of the importance of legal constraints in presidential and agency decisionmaking. But could the very number of legal offices serve to undermine the ability of executive branch lawyers to check presidential overreach? DAPHNA RENAN, in THE LAW PRESIDENTS MAKE, 103 Va. L. Rev. 805, 809–10, 812 (2017), argues that executive branch legal institutions may be sidelined or see their decisionmaking role reduced by the White House. "While the myth of a supreme OLC dispensing formal legal opinions persists, the reality is a less insulated, more diffuse, and more informal set of institutional arrangements. OLC's opinion-writing institution is withering. And on questions of special salience to the president, there is growing reliance on a more policy- and politics-infused legal apparatus, directed by the White House but reliant on a diffusion of ambiguously overlapping legal interpreters. Rather than OLC supremacy, legal views are developed by a collection of administrative actors. OLC usually has a seat at the table. But it is no longer the decider." In her view, "executive branch legalism has never been an external, or exogenous, constraint on presidential power. It has always been a tool of presidential administration itself. The president today looks to executive branch legal review to forge pathways to policy and political compromise in highly-contested, consequential, and increasingly legalistic terrain." See also Emily Berman, Weaponizing the Office of Legal Counsel, 62 B.C. L. Rev. 515 (2021).

The concern that Presidents may be able to evade internal constraints by choosing among agencies is not limited to the executive lawyering context. "The United States Code is riddled with 'duplicative delegations'—

delegations in separate statutes or statutory provisions that may reasonably be construed as granting the same regulatory authority to different agencies." Jason Marisam, Duplicative Delegations, 63 Admin. L. Rev. 181 (2011). In addition, "[i]t is quite common for Congress to create situations where an agency with the exclusive authority to regulate or manage a problem cannot proceed without first consulting, or taking comment from, another agency whose mission is implicated in the action agency's decisionmaking." Jody Freeman & Jim Rossi, Agency Coordination in Shared Regulatory Space, 125 Harv. L. Rev. 1131, 1157–60 (2012); see also Bijal Shah, Congress's Agency Coordination, 103 Minn. L. Rev. 1961 (2019) (documenting frameworks for internal coordination that Congress creates). Such duplicative delegations and interagency consultation or consent requirements might seem to create internal checks, as they force agencies with different programmatic perspectives and culture to agree on a policy before going forward—if only to not have their regulatory efforts be at cross purposes. Regulatory redundancy and a lack of unified control might also yield benefits in protecting against regulatory gaps. See Anne Joseph O'Connell, The Architecture of Smart Intelligence: Structuring and Overseeing Agencies in the Post-9/11 World, 94 Cal. L. Rev. 1655 (2006); see also Jacob E. Gersen, Overlapping and Underlapping Jurisdiction in Administrative Law, 2006 Sup. Ct. Rev. 201, 211–16 (2006) (exploring why Congress might create overlapping and underlapping jurisdiction).

But such duplicative and overlapping responsibilities may operate to enhance presidential power as well. JASON MARISAM, in THE PRESIDENT'S AGENCY SELECTION POWERS, 65 Admin. L. Rev. 821, 838–39, 860–63 (2013), argues that "the most important aspect of overlapping jurisdictions among agencies is how presidents manipulate the overlapping jurisdiction to select which agency in the shared space they want to perform tasks." He further contends that, when available, "presidents' agency selection powers operate as a less costly alternative to the removal power. . . . [A]gency selection powers are less broad in two key ways. . . . [W]hile the removal power enables presidents to change who is in charge of the entire portfolio of an agency office, a president can only use his agency selection powers for a more limited set of tasks . . . [and] can only choose from among the existing set of agencies and the officers who staff them." But "agency selection powers . . . are broader . . . when it comes to independent agencies . . . [and] while the President cannot use his removal power to replace civil servants en masse, he can use his agency selection powers to transfer authority from one agency to another when he is dissatisfied with the performance of the first agency's civil servants."

(2) ***The Interdependence of Internal and External Checks.*** Is the problem with arguments for the internal separation of powers that real internal checks on executive power don't exist, or instead that they don't exist in isolation from more traditional external constraints?

GILLIAN E. METZGER, THE INTERDEPENDENT RELATIONSHIP BETWEEN INTERNAL AND EXTERNAL SEPARATION OF POWERS, 59 Emory L.J. 423, 425–26 (2009): "[A]ttending to internal constraints alone is too narrow a focus because it excludes the crucial relationship between internal and external checks on the Executive Branch. Internal checks can be, and often are, reinforced by a variety of external forces—including not just Congress and the courts, but also state and foreign governments, international bodies, the media, and civil society organizations. Moreover, the reinforcement can also work in reverse, with internal constraints serving to enhance the ability of external forces, in particular Congress and the courts, to exert meaningful checks on the Executive Branch. Greater acknowledgment of this reciprocal relationship holds import both for fully understanding the separation of powers role played by internal constraints and for identifying effective reform strategies."

AZIZ Z. HUQ agrees on the importance of the interbranch dynamic but would go further, arguing for "moving beyond the unit of the 'branch' to more granular determinants of interbranch relations." THE PRESIDENT AND THE DETAINEES, 165 U. Pa. L. Rev. 499, 506–07, 518 (2017). Drawing on a detailed case study of President Obama's effort to close Guantánamo Bay, which he concludes was "derailed by an interbranch alliance between the military bureaucracy and a legislative faction hostile to the new President's agenda," Huq contends that "bureaucratic actors are salient not because of internal dynamics but only because of their outward-facing influence on Congress and the judiciary. They are complements to, not substitutes for, interactions among the three branches. Intrabranch checks . . . are partially caused by and mediated through bureaucratic forces. Hence, legislative resistance to presidential pressure to close Guantánamo hinged on information produced by the bureaucracy" and "[l]egislative barriers to transfers depended upon the executive for their efficacy. These statutes elaborated new opportunities for bureaucratic foot-dragging and resistance to the presidential agenda."

Moving beyond this case study, Huq argues that "[t]here is a dense, and systematically significant, ecosystem of internal and external interest groups, ideological factions, and institutional actors that Jon Michaels and I elsewhere label the 'thick political surround.' Dynamic interactions between diverse elements of the thick political surround (such as bureaucrats and legislative factions) can check presidential initiatives even when bilateral interbranch interactions (between the executive branch and Congress) cannot. The account offered here thus draws attention to the institutionally granular determinants of interbranch relations. These help explain how Presidents can be thwarted even absent divided government." See also Aziz Z. Huq & Jon D. Michaels, The Cycles of Separation-of-Powers Jurisprudence, 126 Yale L.J. 342 (2016).

(3) ***Internal Separation of Powers and the Unitary Executive.*** From a unitary executive perspective, the very idea of executive branch institutions and officials opposing presidential policy might seem constitutionally problematic. But are all of the internal checks identified above troublesome to a unitarian? Note that many—professional expertise, reputational concerns, agency offices without removal protection, interagency consultation requirements—involve what we might call "soft" constraints, rather than the hard constraints of statutory removal independence. Moreover, might Presidents actually find internal separation of powers to be

an asset, ensuring that they receive expert advice from a variety of different perspectives and that problems in agencies may be more likely to get the attention of high-level agency officials? Consider in this regard the "Team of Rivals" approach President Trump took among his closest advisors. Trump is not the first President to adopt such an approach: President Lincoln famously incorporated leaders of diverse factions in his party into his cabinet. See Doris Kearns Goodwin, Team of Rivals: The Political Genius of Abraham Lincoln (2005). Although sparking concerns of turmoil and paralysis in the White House, Daniel A. Farber and Anne Joseph O'Connell argue that a team of rivals approach can also motivate improved performance and information acquisition and ensure that important issues are escalated for presidential attention. See Agencies as Adversaries, 105 Cal. L. Rev. 1375, 1425 (2017).

Do accounts suggesting that the power of internal checks comes from interaction with external entities, often entities that are themselves constitutionally created and exercising their constitutional powers, alleviate or worsen the unitary executive concern? On the one hand, these accounts suggest that internal checks have limited effect independent of the constitutional separation of powers structure, as opposed to representing a novel and nonconstitutional form of constraint. On the other, they also suggest that Congress may be able to aggrandize its powers at the President's expense by building internal checks into the executive branch that it can later exploit.

To what extent do constitutional protections for presidential authority preclude some measures to strengthen internal separation of powers? For example, several bills have been introduced in Congress to provide IGs with for-cause removal protection, and the House, as part of the National Defense Authorization Act for FY 2020, would have required the President to appoint the first assistant to the IG (i.e., the principal deputy IG) as the acting IG when there is an IG vacancy (or another senior official in the IG office if there is no first assistant). Do you think for-cause removal protection for IGs would be beneficial? Is such removal protection constitutional after Seila Law and Collins? Would requiring the President to fill an IG vacancy with the first deputy IG pass constitutional muster? Note that although IGs are "under the general supervision" of the head of the agency of which they are part, the agency head cannot "prevent or prohibit the Inspector General from initiating, carrying out, or completing any audit or investigation, or from issuing any subpoena." 5 U.S.C. App. 3 § 3(a). Moreover, IGs are charged, inter alia, with making policy recommendations for "economy and efficiency" as well as "the prevention and detection of fraud and abuse" in their agencies' programs and operations. Id. § 4.

(4) ***Is Bureaucratic Resistance Justified?*** Even if it can operate as an important check on executive branch abuse of power, is civil servant resistance legitimate? Consider the following views:

(a) JENNIFER NOU, CIVIL SERVANT DISOBEDIENCE, 94 Chi.-Kent L. Rev. 349 (2019): "Bureaucratic resistance is hardly new. . . . What seems potentially novel in the Trump Administration, however, is the extent to which that resistance is publicly defiant. Instead of being covert or channeled through official mechanisms, a greater degree of dissent seems to have spilled out into the open by civil servants identified as such. Bureaucrats seem to be increasingly opposing the President in their official capacity. . . . Civil servant disobedience . . . [is] overt, good-faith acts of protest by civil servants acting in their official capacity in violation of executive directives."

Nou then turns to evaluating when civil service disobedience is justified, identifying an "ideal of reciprocal hierarchy, according to which the views of civil servants are duly considered by appointed agency heads. This ideal emphasizes not only top-down means of control, but also facilitates bottom-up concerns. When these ideals are violated, normative space for legitimate civil servant disobedience arguably arises. . . . [O]ther necessary factors for civil disobedience to be legitimate . . . include the extent to which such behavior arises under statutes that can be read to require consultation with expert, career staff. In addition, such activity must also conform to professional norms; be used only as a measure of last resort; and exhibit a willingness to accept the legal consequences." Yet even when these factors are present, Nou cautions that civil service disobedience carries real and unintended costs, in particular "inevitable presidential backlash. The potential for mutually respectful, reciprocal progress is instead being squandered for mutually assured destruction to the long-cultivated norms of professionalism that have defined the civil service. . . . [T]he institution of the presidency also stands to be weakened in the long term."

(b) BIJAL SHAH, CIVIL SERVANT ALARM, 94 Chi.-Kent L. Rev. 627 (2019): "[B]ureaucratic resistance itself may not be to blame. Arguing that civil servant resistance is problematic because of the backlash it may incur overlooks the possibility that resistance is a flare drawing attention to failures in executive deliberation for which the resistance itself should not be faulted. . . . Perhaps . . . retaliation incurred by civil servant resistance signals the failings of the retaliator himself." Shah argues that "[c]ivil servant resistance in immigration appears to be fueled by . . . bureaucratic or civil servant 'dissonance' . . . [which] arises when executive directives are in discord with fundamental values and duties associated with a civil servant's mission. . . . To the extent that civil servant resistance . . . is based in dissonance, sustained resistance suggests that the current President's policies insufficiently take into account the judgment of career bureaucrats as to what sorts of policies are tenable or even moral, and why."

Contrary to Nou, Shah "hypothesizes that continued civil servant resistance . . . is unlikely to occur unless it is justified. More specifically, resistance that is principled and united across factions of civil servants with otherwise distinct interests and goals, that nonetheless continues to incur backlash instead of a reasoned response from political leadership, may . . . signify a breach in internal executive systems that . . . demands reparative attention from stakeholders and overseers external to the executive branch."

## SECTION 4. CONSTITUTIONAL FRAMEWORKS FOR ADMINISTRATIVE ADJUDICATION



*The judicial Power of the United States, shall be vested in one supreme Court, and in such inferior Courts as the Congress may from time to time ordain and establish. The Judges, both of the supreme and inferior Courts, shall hold their Offices during good Behaviour, and shall, at stated Times, receive for their Services, a Compensation, which shall not be diminished during their Continuance in Office.*

U.S. Const., Art. III, § 1

*In Suits at common law, where the value in controversy shall exceed twenty dollars, the right of trial by jury shall be preserved . . .*

U.S. Const., Amend. 7

The judicial power of the United States—the Article III power to resolve specified categories of "Cases" and "Controversies" particularly important to the national government—is as clearly vested by the Constitution in the federal judiciary as the legislative power is in Congress. Hence, when Congress assigns adjudication of disputes to agencies, the problem is not that the legislative branch is giving away some of its own power. Rather, it is reallocating what seemingly ought to be judicial business—a possibly hostile interference with the work of a coordinate (perhaps especially vulnerable) branch. Similar concerns can arise when Congress appears to be giving the Article III courts too much power by assigning them what appear to be nonjudicial duties.

The Constitution clearly envisions substantial congressional power to structure the institutions that do the judicial work of the national government. Indeed, the text of Article III implies that Congress need not create lower federal courts at all, and the Supreme Court has long held that it may withhold parts of the Article III power from whatever lower courts it does create. Even the Supreme Court's appellate jurisdiction is subject to "such Exceptions, and . . . such Regulations as the Congress shall make." Art. III, § 2, cl. 2. From your study of constitutional law or federal courts, you may be aware that defining the extent of Congress's authority in this area is one of the knottiest questions in constitutional jurisprudence, and one the Court steadfastly avoids. But what if Congress decides to create federal institutions to adjudicate claims within the federal judicial power—but not to give those adjudicators the Article III protections of life tenure and guarantee against reduction in compensation? These institutions may be designated "courts" and the adjudicators may be called "judges" or "administrative law judges," but they are not part of the judicial branch established by the Constitution. Institutions like the Court of Federal Claims are referred to as Article I courts, but most of the non-Article III institutions created to adjudicate cases under federal law are simply called agencies.

Why would Congress take such a step? LOUIS L. JAFFE and NATHANIEL NATHANSON, ADMINISTRATIVE LAW: CASES AND MATERIALS 133–36 (1961), describe the genesis of workers' compensation boards, one of the earliest forms of an adjudicating administrative agency. These boards implemented state legislative decisions to displace the common law of torts with a substantively and procedurally simpler—and more employee-favoring—statutory scheme for compensating harms suffered from accidents in the workplace: "[I]n some states, . . . workmen's compensation was originally administered by the courts, but in most states, and finally in nearly all, specialized boards were set up. The courts were thought to be hostile to the purposes of the legislation and were incidentally too expensive and too much taken up with other business. What was needed was an agency which was sympathetic, which cost the worker little or nothing and had no other business. . . . A court and a compensation board are fundamentally alike in that they determine controversies under the law upon the basis of evidence received in a hearing between the parties. . . . They are different in that a court as we know it today is a court of general jurisdiction, the board is restricted to one subject. . . . [T]hough expertness came to be an important aspect of its specialization, it came perhaps as a byproduct. It was the advocate rather than the expert who was sought."

Can Congress vest adjudicatory authority in bodies that are not constitutional courts without violating separation of powers? The materials that follow explore this question, one on which the Court has varied over time.

## STERN v. MARSHALL

Supreme Court of the United States (2011).
564 U.S. 462.

■ CHIEF JUSTICE ROBERTS delivered the opinion of the Court.

. . . This is the second time we have had occasion to weigh in on this long-running dispute between Vickie Lynn Marshall and E. Pierce Marshall over the fortune of J. Howard Marshall II, a man believed to have been one of the richest people in Texas. . . . Known to the public as Anna Nicole Smith, Vickie was J. Howard's third wife and married him about a year before his death. Although J. Howard bestowed on Vickie many monetary and other gifts during their courtship and marriage, he did not include her in his will. Before J. Howard passed away, Vickie filed suit in Texas state probate court, asserting that Pierce—J. Howard's younger son—fraudulently induced J. Howard to sign a living trust that did not include her, even though J. Howard meant to give her half his property. Pierce denied any fraudulent activity and defended the validity of J. Howard's trust and, eventually [after J. Howard's death,], his will. . . .

After J. Howard's death, Vickie filed a petition for bankruptcy in the Central District of California. Pierce filed a complaint in that bankruptcy proceeding, contending that Vickie had defamed him by inducing her lawyers to tell the press that he had engaged in fraud to gain control of his father's assets. Vickie asserted truth as a defense and filed a counterclaim for tortious interference with the gift [of half of J. Howard's property that she had] expected. . . . The Bankruptcy Court granted summary judgment to Vickie on Pierce's claim for defamation and ruled in Vickie's favor on her counterclaim, awarding her over $400 million in compensatory damages and $25 million in punitive damages. [In post-trial proceedings, Pierce argued that Vicki's counterclaim was not a "core proceeding" under 28 U.S.C. § 157(b)(2)(C) and hence was outside the Bankruptcy Court's statutory jurisdiction, and the Court of Appeals agreed. Before the Supreme Court, Pierce renewed this argument and added that designating all counterclaims core proceedings raised serious constitutional concerns.]

II

[The Court first held that Vicki's counterclaim was a "core proceeding" within the Bankruptcy Court's statutory jurisdiction under 28 U.S.C. § 157(b)(2)(C).]

III

A

Although we conclude that § 157(b)(2)(C) permits the Bankruptcy Court to enter final judgment on Vickie's counterclaim, Article III of the Constitution does not. . . . Article III is "an inseparable element of the constitutional system of checks and balances" that "both defines the power and protects the independence of the Judicial Branch." Northern Pipeline, 458 U.S. [50,] 58 [(1982)] (plurality opinion) [p. 1082]. . . . In establishing the system of divided power in the Constitution, the Framers considered it essential that "the judiciary remain[ ] truly distinct from both the legislature and the executive." The Federalist No. 78, p. 466 (C. Rossiter ed. 1961) (A. Hamilton). . . . We have recognized that the three branches are not hermetically sealed from one another, see Nixon v. Administrator of General Services, 433 U.S. 425, 443 (1977), but it remains true that Article III imposes some basic limitations that the other branches may not transgress. Those limitations serve two related purposes. "Separation-of-powers principles are intended, in part, to protect each branch of government from incursion by the others. Yet the dynamic between and among the branches is not the only object of the Constitution's concern. The structural principles secured by the separation of powers protect the individual as well." Bond v. United States, 564 U.S. [211, 222] (2011).

Article III protects liberty not only through its role in implementing the separation of powers, but also by specifying the defining characteristics of Article III judges. . . . Article III could neither serve its purpose in the system of checks and balances nor preserve the integrity of judicial decisionmaking if the other branches of the Federal Government could confer the Government's "judicial Power" on entities outside Article III. That is why we have long recognized that, in general, Congress may not "withdraw from judicial cognizance any matter which, from its nature, is the subject of a suit at the common law, or in equity, or admiralty." Murray's Lessee v. Hoboken Land & Improvement Co., 59 U.S. 272 (1856). When a suit is made of "the stuff of the traditional actions at common law tried by the courts at Westminster in 1789," Northern Pipeline, 458 U.S. at 90 (Rehnquist, J., concurring in judgment), and is brought within the bounds of federal jurisdiction, the responsibility for deciding that suit rests with Article III judges in Article III courts. . . .

B

This is not the first time we have faced an Article III challenge to a bankruptcy court's resolution of a debtor's suit. In Northern Pipeline, we considered whether bankruptcy judges serving under the Bankruptcy Act of 1978—appointed by the President and confirmed by the Senate, but lacking the tenure and salary guarantees of Article III—could "constitutionally be vested with jurisdiction to decide [a] state-law contract claim" against an entity that was not otherwise part of the bankruptcy proceedings. The Court concluded that assignment of such state law claims for resolution by those judges "violates Art. III of the Constitution." Id., at 52, 87 (plurality opinion); id., at 91 (Rehnquist, J., concurring in judgment).

The plurality in Northern Pipeline recognized that there was a category of cases involving "public rights" that Congress could constitutionally assign to "legislative" courts for resolution. That opinion concluded that this "public rights" exception extended "only to matters arising between" individuals and the Government "in connection with the performance of the constitutional functions of the executive or legislative departments . . . that historically could have been determined exclusively by those" branches. Id., at 67–68 (internal quotation marks omitted). A full majority of the Court, while not agreeing on the scope of the exception, concluded that the doctrine did not encompass adjudication of the state law claim at issue in that case. Id., at 69–72; see id., at 90–91 (Rehnquist, J., concurring in judgment) . . . A full majority of Justices in Northern Pipeline also rejected the debtor's argument that the bankruptcy court's exercise of jurisdiction was constitutional because the bankruptcy judge was acting merely as an adjunct of the district court or court of appeals. . . .

C

Vickie's counterclaim cannot be deemed a matter of "public right" that can be decided outside the Judicial Branch. . . . We first recognized the category of public rights in Murray's Lessee [v. Hoboken Land & Improvement Co., 59 U.S. 272 (1856)]. That case involved the Treasury

Department's sale of property belonging to a customs collector who had failed to transfer payments to the Federal Government that he had collected on its behalf. The plaintiff . . . objected that the Treasury Department's calculation of the deficiency and sale of the property was void, because it was a judicial act that could not be assigned to the Executive under Article III. . . . The Court has also recognized that ". . . there are matters, involving public rights, which may be presented in such form that the judicial power is capable of acting on them, and which are susceptible of judicial determination, but which congress may or may not bring within the cognizance of the courts of the United States, as it may deem proper." Id. at 284. As an example of such matters, the Court referred to "[e]quitable claims to land by the inhabitants of ceded territories" and cited cases in which land issues were conclusively resolved by Executive Branch officials. Ibid. . . . In those cases "it depends upon the will of congress whether a remedy in the courts shall be allowed at all," so Congress could limit the extent to which a judicial forum was available. Ibid. . . .

Subsequent decisions from this Court contrasted cases within the reach of the public rights exception—those arising "between the Government and persons subject to its authority in connection with the performance of the constitutional functions of the executive or legislative departments"—and those that were instead matters "of private right, that is, of the liability of one individual to another under the law as defined." Crowell v. Benson, 285 U.S. 22, 50, 51 (1932) [p. 1080].[6] . . .

Shortly after Northern Pipeline, the Court rejected the limitation of the public rights exception to actions involving the Government as a party. The Court has continued, however, to limit the exception to cases in which the claim at issue derives from a federal regulatory scheme, or in which resolution of the claim by an expert government agency is deemed essential to a limited regulatory objective within the agency's authority. In other words, it is still the case that what makes a right "public" rather than private is that the right is integrally related to particular federal government action.

Our decision in Thomas v. Union Carbide Agricultural Products Co., [473 U.S. 568 (1985) [p. 1083], for example, . . . held that the scheme [for administrative adjudication of compensation claims at issue there] did not violate Article III, explaining that "[a]ny right to compensation . . . results from [the statute] and does not depend on or replace a right to

[6] Although the Court in Crowell went on to decide that the facts of the private dispute before it could be determined by a non-Article III tribunal in the first instance, subject to judicial review, the Court did so only after observing that the administrative adjudicator had only limited authority to make specialized, narrowly confined factual determinations regarding a particularized area of law and to issue orders that could be enforced only by action of the District Court. In other words, the agency in Crowell functioned as a true "adjunct" of the District Court. That is not the case here.

Although the dissent suggests that we understate the import of Crowell in this regard, the dissent itself recognizes—repeatedly—that Crowell by its terms addresses the determination of facts outside Article III. Crowell may well have additional significance in the context of expert administrative agencies that oversee particular substantive federal regimes, but we have no occasion to and do not address those issues today. . . .

such compensation under state law." Ibid. . . . [In] Commodity Futures Trading Commission v. Schor[, 478 U.S. 833 (1986), p. 1077], the Court rejected the Article III challenge] only after observing that (1) the claim and the counterclaim concerned a "single dispute"—the same account balance; (2) the CFTC's assertion of authority involved only "a narrow class of common law claims" in a " 'particularized area of law' "; (3) the area of law in question was governed by "a specific and limited federal regulatory scheme" as to which the agency had "obvious expertise"; (4) the parties had freely elected to resolve their differences before the CFTC; and (5) CFTC orders were "enforceable only by order of the district court." Id., at 844, 852–855. Most significantly, given that the customer's reparations claim before the agency and the broker's counterclaim were competing claims to the same amount, the Court repeatedly emphasized that it was "necessary" to allow the agency to exercise jurisdiction over the broker's claim, or else "the reparations procedure would have been confounded." Id., at 856.

The most recent case in which we considered application of the public rights exception—and the only case in which we have considered that doctrine in the bankruptcy context since Northern Pipeline—is Granfinanciera, S.A. v. Nordberg, 492 U.S. 33 (1989) [p. 1091]. In Granfinanciera we rejected a bankruptcy trustee's argument that a fraudulent conveyance action filed on behalf of a bankruptcy estate against a noncreditor in a bankruptcy proceeding fell within the "public rights" exception. We explained that, "[i]f a statutory right is not closely intertwined with a federal regulatory program Congress has power to enact, and if that right neither belongs to nor exists against the Federal Government, then it must be adjudicated by an Article III court." Id., at 54–55. We reasoned that fraudulent conveyance suits were "quintessentially suits at common law that more nearly resemble state law contract claims brought by a bankrupt corporation to augment the bankruptcy estate than they do creditors' hierarchically ordered claims to a pro rata share of the bankruptcy res." Id., at 56. As a consequence, we concluded that fraudulent conveyance actions were "more accurately characterized as a private rather than a public right as we have used those terms in our Article III decisions." Id., at 55.

Vickie's counterclaim—like the fraudulent conveyance claim at issue in Granfinanciera—does not fall within any of the varied formulations of the public rights exception in this Court's cases. It is . . . one under state common law between two private parties. It does not "depend[ ] on the will of congress," Murray's Lessee, supra, at 284. Congress has nothing to do with it. In addition, Vickie's claimed right to relief does not flow from a federal statutory scheme, as in Thomas, 473 U.S., at 584–585 . . . . It is not "completely dependent upon" adjudication of a claim created by federal law, as in Schor. And in contrast to the objecting party in Schor, Pierce did not truly consent to resolution of Vickie's claim in the bankruptcy court proceedings. He had nowhere else to go if he wished to recover from Vickie's estate.

Furthermore, the asserted authority to decide Vickie's claim is not limited to a "particularized area of the law," as in Crowell, Thomas, and Schor. We deal here not with an agency but with a court, with substantive jurisdiction reaching any area of the corpus juris. This is not a situation in which Congress devised an "expert and inexpensive method for dealing with a class of questions of fact which are particularly suited to examination and determination by an administrative agency specially assigned to that task." Crowell, 285 U.S., at 46. The "experts" in the federal system at resolving common law counterclaims such as Vickie's are the Article III courts, and it is with those courts that her claim must stay. . . .

We recognize that there may be instances in which the distinction between public and private rights—at least as framed by some of our recent cases—fails to provide concrete guidance as to whether, for example, a particular agency can adjudicate legal issues under a substantive regulatory scheme. Given the extent to which this case is so markedly distinct from the agency cases discussing the public rights exception in the context of such a regime, however, we do not in this opinion express any view on how the doctrine might apply in that different context.

What is plain here is that this case involves the most prototypical exercise of judicial power: the entry of a final, binding judgment by a court with broad substantive jurisdiction, on a common law cause of action, when the action neither derives from nor depends upon any agency regulatory regime. If such an exercise of judicial power may nonetheless be taken from the Article III Judiciary simply by deeming it part of some amorphous "public right," then Article III would be transformed from the guardian of individual liberty and separation of powers we have long recognized into mere wishful thinking. . . .

Vickie additionally argues that the Bankruptcy Court's final judgment was constitutional because bankruptcy courts under the 1984 Act are properly deemed "adjuncts" of the district courts. We rejected a similar argument in Northern Pipeline, and our reasoning there holds true today. . . . The new bankruptcy courts, like the old, do not "ma[k]e only specialized, narrowly confined factual determinations regarding a particularized area of law" or engage in "statutorily channeled factfinding functions." Northern Pipeline, 458 U.S., at 85. Instead, bankruptcy courts under the 1984 Act resolve "[a]ll matters of fact and law in whatever domains of the law to which" the parties' counterclaims might lead. Id., at 91 (Rehnquist, J., concurring in judgment). In addition, . . . a bankruptcy court resolving a counterclaim . . . has the power to enter "appropriate orders and judgments"—including final judgments—subject to review only if a party chooses to appeal. . . . Given that authority, a bankruptcy court can no more be deemed a mere "adjunct" of the district court than a district court can be deemed such an "adjunct" of the court of appeals. . . .

D

Finally, Vickie and her amici predict as a practical matter that restrictions on a bankruptcy court's ability to hear and finally resolve compulsory counterclaims will create significant delays and impose additional costs on the bankruptcy process. It goes without saying that "the fact that a given law or procedure is efficient, convenient, and useful in facilitating functions of government, standing alone, will not save it if it is contrary to the Constitution." INS v. Chadha, 462 U.S. 919, 944 (1983). In addition, we are not convinced that the practical consequences of such limitations on the authority of bankruptcy courts to enter final judgments are as significant as Vickie and the dissent suggest. . . .

If our decision today does not change all that much, then why the fuss? Is there really a threat to the separation of powers where Congress has conferred the judicial power outside Article III only over certain counterclaims in bankruptcy? The short but emphatic answer is yes. A statute may no more lawfully chip away at the authority of the Judicial Branch than it may eliminate it entirely. . . . We cannot compromise the integrity of the system of separated powers and the role of the Judiciary in that system, even with respect to challenges that may seem innocuous at first blush.

■ JUSTICE SCALIA, concurring.

I agree with the Court's interpretation of our Article III precedents, and I accordingly join its opinion. I adhere to my view, however, that—our contrary precedents notwithstanding—"a matter of public rights . . . must at a minimum arise between the government and others," Granfinanciera, S.A. v. Nordberg, 492 U.S. 33, 65 (1989) (Scalia, J., concurring in part and concurring in judgment). . . . Leaving aside certain adjudications by federal administrative agencies, which are governed (for better or worse) by our landmark decision in Crowell v. Benson, in my view an Article III judge is required in all federal adjudications, unless there is a firmly established historical practice to the contrary. . . . Vicki points to no historical practice that authorizes a non-Article III judge to adjudicate a counterclaim of the sort at issue here.

■ JUSTICE BREYER, with whom JUSTICE GINSBURG, JUSTICE SOTOMAYOR, and JUSTICE KAGAN, join dissenting.

. . . My disagreement with the majority's conclusion stems in part from my disagreement about the way in which it interprets, or at least emphasizes, certain precedents. In my view, the majority overstates the current relevance of statements this Court made in an 1856 case, Murray's Lessee v. Hoboken Land & Improvement Co., and it overstates the importance of an analysis that did not command a Court majority in Northern Pipeline . . . and that was subsequently disavowed. At the same time, I fear the Court understates the importance of a watershed opinion widely thought to demonstrate the constitutional basis for the current authority of administrative agencies to adjudicate private disputes, namely, Crowell v. Benson. And it fails to follow the analysis that this

Court more recently has held applicable to the evaluation of claims of a kind before us here, namely, claims that a congressional delegation of adjudicatory authority violates separation-of-powers principles derived from Article III. See Thomas v. Union Carbide Agricultural Products Co.; Commodity Futures Trading Comm'n v. Schor. . . .

Crowell has been hailed as "the greatest of the cases validating administrative adjudication." Bator, The Constitution as Architecture: Legislative and Administrative Courts Under Article III, 65 Ind. L.J. 233, 251 (1990). Yet, in a footnote, the majority distinguishes Crowell as a case in which the Court upheld the delegation of adjudicatory authority to an administrative agency simply because the agency's power to make the "specialized, narrowly confined factual determinations" at issue arising in a "particularized area of law," made the agency a "true 'adjunct' of the District Court." Were Crowell's holding as narrow as the majority suggests, one could question the validity of Congress' delegation of authority to adjudicate disputes among private parties to other agencies such as the National Labor Relations Board, the Commodity Futures Trading Commission, the Surface Transportation Board, and the Department of Housing and Urban Development. . . .

. . . Rather than leaning so heavily on the approach taken by the plurality in Northern Pipeline, I would look to this Court's more recent Article III cases Thomas and Schor—cases that commanded a clear majority. In both cases the Court took a more pragmatic approach to the constitutional question. It sought to determine whether, in the particular instance, the challenged delegation of adjudicatory authority posed a genuine and serious threat that one branch of Government sought to aggrandize its own constitutionally delegated authority by encroaching upon a field of authority that the Constitution assigns exclusively to another branch. . . .

This case law . . . requires us to determine pragmatically whether a congressional delegation of adjudicatory authority to a non-Article III judge violates the separation-of-powers principles inherent in Article III. That is to say, we must determine through an examination of certain relevant factors whether that delegation constitutes a significant encroachment by the Legislative or Executive Branches of Government upon the realm of authority that Article III reserves for exercise by the Judicial Branch of Government. Those factors include (1) the nature of the claim to be adjudicated; (2) the nature of the non-Article III tribunal; (3) the extent to which Article III courts exercise control over the proceeding; (4) the presence or absence of the parties' consent; and (5) the nature and importance of the legislative purpose served by the grant of adjudicatory authority to a tribunal with judges who lack Article III's tenure and compensation protections. The presence of "private rights" does not automatically determine the outcome of the question but requires a more "searching" examination of the relevant factors. Insofar as the majority would apply more formal standards, it simply disregards recent, controlling precedent.

Applying Schor's approach here, I conclude that the delegation of adjudicatory authority before us is constitutional. . . . First, I concede that *the nature of the claim to be adjudicated* argues against my conclusion. Vickie Marshall's counterclaim—a kind of tort suit—resembles "a suit at the common law." Murray's Lessee, 18 How., at 284. . . . At the same time the significance of this factor is mitigated here by the fact that bankruptcy courts often decide claims that similarly resemble various common-law actions. . . . Second, *the nature of the non-Article III tribunal* argues in favor of constitutionality. That is because the tribunal is made up of judges who enjoy considerable protection from improper political influence. Unlike the 1978 Act which provided for the appointment of bankruptcy judges by the President with the advice and consent of the Senate, current law provides that the federal courts of appeals appoint federal bankruptcy judges. . . . Third, *the control exercised by Article III judges over bankruptcy proceedings* argues in favor of constitutionality. Article III judges control and supervise the bankruptcy court's determinations—at least to the same degree that Article III judges supervised the agency's determinations in Crowell, if not more so. Any party may appeal those determinations to the federal district court, where the federal judge will review all determinations of fact for clear error and will review all determinations of law de novo [and] may "withdraw, in whole or in part, any case or proceeding referred [to the Bankruptcy Court] . . . on its own motion or on timely motion of any party, for cause shown." 28 U.S.C. § 157(d) . . . Fourth, *the fact that the parties have consented* to Bankruptcy Court jurisdiction argues in favor of constitutionality, and strongly so. . . . Fifth, *the nature and importance of the legislative purpose served* by the grant of adjudicatory authority to bankruptcy tribunals argues strongly in favor of constitutionality. . . .

## SIGNIFICANT CASE

### COMMODITY FUTURES TRADING COMMISSION v. SCHOR
478 U.S. 833 (1986).

The Commodity Futures Trading Commission is an independent regulatory commission that regulates and oversees the commodities markets. Section 14 of the Commodities Exchange Act provides that any person injured by violations the Act or CFTC regulations may apply to the Commission for an order directing the offender to pay reparations to the complainant and may enforce that order in federal district court. The remedy is, however, non-exclusive; no rule prevents such a plaintiff from seeking arbitration or bringing a judicial action.

Schor traded commodities futures through a broker at Conti, a firm regulated by the CFTC, and owed Conti a substantial sum as a result of the trades. Schor sought reparations before the CFTC, alleging that this debt was the result of Conti's violations of the CEA, and Conti counterclaimed to recover Schor's debt. The ALJ in Schor's reparations proceeding ruled in Conti's favor on both Schor's claims and Conti's counterclaims. On appeal, the D.C. Circuit sua sponte raised the question whether CFTC could constitutionally adjudicate Conti's counterclaims in light of Northern Pipeline, and concluded CFTC could not.

JUSTICE O'CONNOR delivered the opinion of the Court. She first rejected the argument that Schor had waived any Article III claim by initiating the action before the CFTC. Identifying Article III as "serving both to protect the role of the independent judiciary within the constitutional scheme of tripartite government and to safeguard litigants' right to have claims decided before judges who are free from potential domination by other branches of government," she held that the latter guarantee "of an impartial and independent federal adjudication" was a personal right subject to waiver, and Schor indisputably had waived it. But to the extent Article III § 1's structural role was implicated in a given case, "notions of consent and waiver cannot be dispositive because the limitations serve institutional interests that the parties cannot be expected to protect."

Turning to the Article III challenge, O'Connor stated: "Although our precedents in this area do not admit of easy synthesis, they do establish that the resolution of claims such as Schor's cannot turn on conclusory reference to the language of Article III. Rather, the constitutionality of a given congressional delegation of adjudicative functions to a non-Article III body must be assessed by reference to the purposes underlying the requirements of Article III. . . . In determining the extent to which a given congressional decision to authorize the adjudication of Article III business in a non-Article III tribunal impermissibly threatens the institutional integrity of the Judicial Branch, the Court has declined to adopt formalistic and unbending rules. . . . [S]uch rules might . . . unduly constrict Congress' ability to take needed and innovative action pursuant to its Article I powers. Thus, in reviewing Article III challenges, we have weighed a number of factors, none of which has been deemed determinative, with an eye to the practical effect that the congressional action will have on the constitutionally assigned role of the federal judiciary. Among the factors upon which we have focused are the extent to which the essential attributes of judicial power are reserved to Article III courts, and, conversely, the extent to which the non-Article III forum exercises the range of jurisdiction and powers normally vested only in Article III courts, the origins and importance of the right to be adjudicated, and the concerns that drove Congress to depart from the requirements of Article III."

Applying such an analysis, O'Connor concluded that "the congressional scheme [here] does not impermissibly intrude on the province of the judiciary. The CFTC's adjudicatory powers depart from the traditional agency model in just one respect: the CFTC's jurisdiction over common law counterclaims." Like the Employees' Compensation Commission in Crowell and unlike the bankruptcy courts in Northern Pipeline, the CFTC "deals only with a particularized area of law"; its orders "are enforceable only by order of the District Court" and "are also reviewed under the same 'weight of the evidence' standard sustained in Crowell rather than the more deferential 'clearly erroneous' standard found lacking in Northern Pipeline"; the CFTC's "legal rulings . . . are subject to de novo review"; and "[f]inally, the CFTC does not exercise 'all ordinary powers of district courts,' and thus may not, for instance, preside over jury trials or issue writs of habeas corpus."

O'Connor acknowledged that the claim at issue "is a 'private' right for which state law provides the rule of decision. It is therefore a claim of the kind assumed to be at the 'core' of matters normally reserved to Article III courts. . . . Yet this conclusion does not end our inquiry; just as this Court has rejected any attempt to make determinative for Article III purposes the distinction between public rights and private rights, there is no reason inherent in separation of powers principles to accord the state law character of a claim talismanic power in Article III inquiries." Moreover, "[i]n this case . . . [i]t is clear that Congress has not attempted to 'withdraw from judicial cognizance' the determination of Conti's right to the sum represented by the debit balance in Schor's account. Congress gave the CFTC the authority to adjudicate such matters, but the decision to invoke this forum is left entirely to the parties and the power of the federal judiciary to take jurisdiction of these matters is unaffected. . . . This is not to say, of course, that if Congress created a phalanx of non-Article III tribunals equipped to handle the entire business of the Article III courts without any Article III supervision or control and without evidence of valid and specific legislative necessities, the fact that the parties had the election to proceed in their forum of choice would necessarily save the scheme from constitutional attack. But this case obviously bears no resemblance to such a scenario. . . . It also bears emphasis that . . . CFTC adjudication of common law counterclaims is incidental to, and completely dependent upon, adjudication of reparations claims created by federal law, and in actual fact is limited to claims arising out of the same transaction or occurrence as the reparations claim."

JUSTICE BRENNAN dissented, joined by Justice Marshall: "Article III's prophylactic protections were intended to prevent . . . abdication to claims of legislative convenience. The Court requires that the legislative interest in convenience and efficiency be weighed against the competing interest in judicial independence. In doing so, the Court pits an interest the benefits of which are immediate, concrete, and easily understood against one, the benefits of which are almost entirely prophylactic, and thus often seem remote and not worth the cost in any single case. Thus, while this balancing creates the illusion of objectivity and ineluctability, in fact the result was foreordained, because the balance is weighted against judicial independence. The danger of the Court's balancing approach is, of course, that as individual cases accumulate in which the Court finds that the short-term benefits of efficiency outweigh the long-term benefits of judicial independence, the protections of Article III will be eviscerated."

## NOTES

(1) ***Methodology: Formalist or Functionalist?*** There is a sharp methodological divide between Stern on the one hand and Schor on the other. Stern takes on the whole a very formalist approach. The majority insists on a strict separation of public and private rights, treating the public rights and adjunct lines as distinct analyses. Although acknowledging that administrative adjudication may be necessary for a regulatory scheme like that in Schor to function, the majority dismisses efficiency concerns about splitting claims in bankruptcy and warns about allowing even seemingly innocuous deviations from Article III. Schor by contrast counts the public or private nature of the right and the extent to which a non-Article III court is functioning as an adjunct as simply factors to be weighed against others in an overall balancing test, and expressly rejects adopting "formalistic and unbending rules" out of fear "they might also unduly constrict Congress."

Which approach, formalism or functionalism, is the appropriate stance to take in assessing possible encroachments on Article III? Note that Schor, with its functional approach, was issued on the same day as Bowsher v. Synar (p. 928), a formalistic analysis invalidating the Gramm-Rudman-Hollings Act's system for reducing the deficit. Are questions of the scope of judicial power distinguishable from legislative power in a way that might explain this difference? Does the broad availability of judicial review mean that the Article III courts will be able to protect their turf if need be, making a case-by-case balancing approach more appropriate? Or, as Chief Justice Roberts suggests in Stern (and Justice Brennan argued before him in Northern Pipeline and Schor), is there a need to prophylactically enforce Article III's ambit strictly, because in each individual case the incursion on Article III will seem innocuous but the aggregate effect may eviscerate the courts?

Significantly, just as Stern takes a more formalistic approach to judicial power than Schor, recent decisions such as Seila Law, Free Enterprise, and Collins take a more formalistic approach to presidential power. Thus, perhaps the best explanation of these methodological changes is variation in the composition of the Court and the Roberts Court's predilection for a more formalist analysis.

(2) ***The Watershed Decision.*** CROWELL V. BENSON, 285 U.S. 22 (1932), decided on the threshold of the New Deal era, was a critical decision in the emergence of administrative adjudication. The Longshoremen's and Harbor Workers' Act provided that employees could file administrative claims for compensation with the United States Employees' Compensation Commission if injured in certain maritime employments. Under the Act, Commission decisions were reviewable in the district courts, which had plenary authority to redecide any questions of law but only limited authority to review conclusions of fact. CHIEF JUSTICE HUGHES wrote an opinion for the Court upholding the constitutionality of the adjudicatory scheme.

Hughes began by stating that "there can be no doubt that the Act contemplates that as to questions of fact, arising with respect to injuries to employees within the purview of the Act, the findings of the deputy commissioner, supported by evidence and within the scope of his authority, shall be final. To hold otherwise would be to defeat the purpose of the legislation to furnish a prompt, continuous, expert, and inexpensive method for dealing with a class of questions of fact which are peculiarly suited to examination and determination by an administrative agency assigned to that task. . . . The Congress did not attempt to define questions of law, and the generality of the description leaves no doubt of the intention to reserve to the Federal court full authority to pass upon all matters which this Court had held to fall within that category. There is thus no attempt to interfere with, but rather provision is made to facilitate, the exercise by the court of its jurisdiction to deny effect to any administrative finding which is without evidence or 'contrary to the indisputable character of the evidence,' or where the hearing is 'inadequate,' or 'unfair,' or arbitrary in any respect. . . ."

As to questions of fact, Hughes invoked the distinction "between cases of private right and those which arise between the Government and persons subject to its authority in connection with the performance of the constitutional functions of the executive or legislative departments," emphasizing that " 'the mode of determining matters of this [latter] class is completely within congressional control.' Ex parte Bakelite Corporation, 279 U.S. 438, 451." The Court acknowledged that the dispute at hand did not fall within this category "but is one of private right, that is, of the liability of one individual to another under the law as defined." Yet, Hughes added, even in private right cases "there is no requirement that, in order to maintain the essential attributes of the judicial power, all determinations of fact in constitutional courts shall be made by judges. On the common law side of the Federal courts, the aid of juries is not only deemed appropriate but is required by the Constitution itself. In cases of equity and admiralty, it is historic practice to call to the assistance of the courts, without the consent of the parties, masters and commissioners or assessors, to pass upon certain classes of questions, as, for example, to take and state an account or to find the amount of damages." Here, "[t]he statute has a limited application, being confined to the relation of master and servant, and the method of determining the questions of fact, which arise in the routine of making compensation awards to employees under the Act, is necessary to its effective enforcement."

Hughes concluded that the Court was "unable to find any constitutional obstacle to the action of the Congress in availing itself of a method shown by experience to be essential in order to apply its standards to the thousands of cases involved, thus relieving the courts of a most serious burden while preserving their complete authority to insure the proper application of the law." He clarified, however, that such administrative determination was constitutionally acceptable only for ordinary fact questions, not "determinations of fact [that] are fundamental or 'jurisdictional,' in the sense that their existence is a condition precedent to the operation of the statutory scheme." Adjudication of these latter matters raise "the question whether the Congress may substitute for constitutional courts, in which the judicial power of the United States is vested, an administrative agency—in this instance a single deputy commissioner—for the final determination of the existence of the facts upon which the enforcement of the constitutional rights of the citizen depend. . . . That would be to sap the judicial power as it exists under the federal Constitution, and to establish a government of a bureaucratic character alien to our system, wherever fundamental rights depend, as not infrequently they do depend, upon the facts, and finality as to facts becomes in effect finality in law." Instead, in "cases brought to enforce constitutional rights, the judicial power of the United States necessarily extends to the independent determination of all questions, both of fact and law, necessary to the performance of that supreme function."

Crowell, like Stern and unlike Schor, treats the public rights and adjunct lines as distinct lines of inquiry. And it is firm in rejecting administrative determination of certain fundamental questions. But like Schor, it takes an openly functionalist approach in assessing the role of the Employees' Compensation Commission, justifying deference to the commission's ordinary factual determinations as necessary so as not to "defeat the purpose of the legislation."

(3) ***Does Stern Call Crowell and Schor into Question?*** The methodological differences among the cases underlie Justice Breyer's concern that Stern calls Crowell and Schor into question. Others have noted several places in which Chief Justice Roberts seems careful to distinguish the bankruptcy context from regulatory adjudication, concluding that the constitutionality of garden-variety administrative adjudication remains firmly established under the Crowell/Schor line of precedent.

Is Justice Breyer's concern about the fate of Crowell overstated? What do you make of the majority's description, in a footnote, of Crowell as a situation in which "the agency . . . functioned as a true 'adjunct' of the District Court"? It remains generally true that agency adjudications result in "orders that could be enforced only by action of" an Article III court. But can contemporary regulatory adjudication be defined as "only limited authority to make specialized, narrowly confined factual determinations regarding a particularized area of law"?

(4) ***Is Bankruptcy Special?*** One important distinction of Stern from Schor and Crowell is that Stern did not involve administrative adjudication but instead arose in bankruptcy. And it relied heavily on NORTHERN PIPELINE CONSTRUCTION CO. V. MARATHON PIPE LINE CO., 458 U.S. 50 (1982), also a bankruptcy case, involving a bankruptcy court's assertion of jurisdiction over a state law contract claim. Writing for a plurality, JUSTICE BRENNAN began by identifying three narrow categories where non-Article III adjudication historically had been allowed: (i) the creation of "territorial courts" in "geographical areas in which no State operated as sovereign"; (ii) the establishment of "courts-martial," which "involves a constitutional grant of power that has been historically understood as giving the political Branches of Government extraordinary control over the precise subject matter at issue"; and (iii) legislative courts and administrative agencies created by Congress to adjudicate cases involving "public rights," which required that the government be a party. In invalidating the bankruptcy court's jurisdiction, his opinion emphasized the breadth of jurisdiction given to bankruptcy courts, arguing that Congress had vested "bankruptcy judges

with powers over Northern [Pipeline]'s state-created right that far exceed the powers that it has vested in administrative agencies that adjudicate only rights of Congress' own creation." Chief Justice Rehnquist, concurring, emphasized the state law nature of the right at issue, stating that "[n]one of [the Court's prior] cases has gone so far as to sanction the type of adjudication to which Marathon will be subjected against its will."

One way to read Northern Pipeline and Stern is that they turn on unique features of bankruptcy: the broad range of claims that bankruptcy courts can hear, the immediate enforceability of their determinations, and the limited review of core bankruptcy claims by Article III courts. By contrast, administrative adjudicators often have a limited scope of jurisdiction, hearing only claims related to a specific area of expertise, and their decisions are often not self-enforcing, so agencies have to go into court for an order of enforcement. Should Stern be viewed primarily as a bankruptcy case?

Is bankruptcy more threatening to Article III values of independence than administrative adjudication, or vice versa? Note that bankruptcy courts work closely with district courts and are often located at federal courthouses; administrative adjudicators, by contrast, are agency employees. If you've studied the APA's provisions on adjudication (Ch. V), you know that the APA allows the head of an agency to review ALJ determinations de novo. Does that allow in too much room for agency bias?

(5) ***The Evolving Meaning of Public Rights.*** Although the cases all invoke the category of "public right," do they define public rights the same way? Crowell specified that a public right was one involving the government as a party, a definition that Northern Pipeline adopted too.

But the Court took a different approach in THOMAS V. UNION CARBIDE AGRICULTURAL PRODUCTS CO., 473 U.S. 568 (1985). At issue in Thomas were the binding arbitration provisions of the Federal Insecticide, Fungicide and Rodenticide Act. FIFRA authorizes EPA to use one manufacturer's data about health, safety, and environmental effects of its product in considering another manufacturer's later application to register a similar product. It requires the follow-on registrant to compensate the initial manufacturer for use of this data and provides for binding arbitration when the parties cannot agree on a compensation amount.

JUSTICE O'CONNOR'S opinion for the Court rejected the claim that this arrangement violated Article III: "Congress, acting for a valid legislative purpose pursuant to its constitutional powers under Article I, may create a seemingly 'private' right that is so closely integrated into a public regulatory scheme as to be a matter appropriate for agency resolution with limited involvement by the Article III judiciary." In reaching this conclusion, she argued that "[t]he enduring lesson of Crowell is that practical attention to substance, rather than doctrinaire reliance on formal categories, should inform application of Article III. . . . If the identity of the parties alone determined the requirements of Article III, under appellees' theory, the constitutionality of many quasi-adjudicative activities carried on by administrative agencies involving claims between individuals would be thrown into doubt. . . . [T]he right created by FIFRA is not a purely 'private' right, but bears many of the characteristics of a 'public' right. Use of a registrant's data to support a follow-on registration serves a public purpose as an integral part of a program safeguarding the public health." No one dissented. Justice Brennan (the author of the Northern Pipeline plurality) concurred, noting: "In one sense the question of proper compensation . . . is . . . a dispute about 'the liability of one individual to another under the law as defined.' Crowell v. Benson. But the dispute arises in the context of a federal regulatory scheme that virtually occupies the field."

Although Schor deemed Conti's counterclaim a private right, it relied heavily on Thomas and echoed Thomas's pragmatic approach in refusing to draw a strict line between public and private rights. Granfinanciera, S.A. v. Paul C. Nordberg, 492 U.S. 33 (1989) (p. 1091), was a subsequent decision involving the Seventh Amendment that deviated from Thomas and Schor in putting heavy emphasis on a sharp distinction between public rights and private rights. But it nonetheless followed Thomas in defining a public right as a "right that is so closely integrated into a public regulatory scheme as to be a matter appropriate for agency resolution with limited involvement by the Article III judiciary."

How does Stern define public rights? Note that Stern, too, rejects the limitation of public rights to matters in which the government is a party. In describing the public rights exception, Chief Justice Roberts states that it is limited "to cases in which the claim at issue derives from a federal regulatory scheme, or in which resolution of the claim by an expert government agency is deemed essential to a limited regulatory objective within the agency's authority. In other words, it is still the case that what makes a right 'public' rather than private is that the right is integrally related to particular federal government action."

If the Court continues to define public rights this broadly, how constraining will the decision be for administrative adjudication? Where would the counterclaim in Schor fall under Stern's categorization? Would it still be deemed a matter of private right, as the Schor Court held? Or might it now be considered public because it was "integrally related to particular federal government action" and "resolution of the claim by an expert government agency is . . . essential to a limited regulatory objective within the agency's authority"?

For thoughtful and divergent analyses of the meaning of public and private rights, see Gregory Ablavsky, Getting Public Rights Wrong: The Lost History of the Private Land Claims, 74 Stan. L. Rev. 277 (2022); James Pfander & Andrew Borrasso, Public Rights and Article III: Judicial Oversight of Agency Action, 82 Ohio L.J. 493 (2021); Caleb Nelson, Adjudication in the Political Branches, 107 Colum. L. Rev. 559 (2007).

(6) ***The Availability of Judicial Review.*** How important is it that a non-Article III court's determination be subject to judicial review, even if limited? The Court's decisions vary somewhat on this point, but all give the availability (or not) of judicial review substantial weight. The availability of judicial review was central to upholding the administrative adjudication at

issue in Crowell under the adjunct theory and was also emphasized by the Court in applying Schor's balancing test. Moreover, both the Northern Pipeline plurality and Stern majority emphasized the limited review of the bankruptcy court's determinations—as did the Stern dissent, maintaining that the substantial degree of Article III oversight counted towards allowing the bankruptcy court to adjudicate.

Thomas is a slight outlier. The Court there considered the fact that "the FIFRA arbitration scheme incorporates its own system of internal sanctions and relies only tangentially, if at all, on the Judicial Branch for enforcement" as counting towards its constitutionality. It stated that "[t]he danger of Congress or the Executive encroaching on the Article III judicial powers is at a minimum when no unwilling defendant is subjected to judicial enforcement power as a result of the agency 'adjudication.' " But the Thomas Court proceeded to underscore that "FIFRA limits but does not preclude review of the arbitration proceeding by an Article III court. We conclude that, in the circumstances, the review afforded preserves the 'appropriate exercise of the judicial function.' Crowell, 285 U.S. at 54. FIFRA at a minimum allows private parties to secure Article III review of the arbitrator's 'findings and determination' for fraud, misconduct, or misrepresentation. This provision protects against arbitrators who abuse or exceed their powers or willfully misconstrue their mandate under the governing law. Moreover, review of constitutional error is preserved, and FIFRA, therefore, does not obstruct whatever judicial review might be required by due process."

According to Richard H. Fallon, Jr., in Of Legislative Courts, Administrative Agencies, and Article III, 101 Harv. L. Rev. 915 (1988), judicial review is the key to the constitutionality of non-Article III adjudication: "A better accommodation of article III with the functional imperatives of contemporary government focuses on the reviewability of the decisions of non-article III federal tribunals by article III courts. Thus the central claim of my appellate review theory: adequately searching appellate review of the judgments of legislative courts and administrative agencies is both necessary and sufficient to satisfy the requirements of article III." Do you agree?

Mila Sohoni, in AGENCY ADJUDICATION AND JUDICIAL NONDELEGATION: AN ARTICLE III CANON, 107 Nw. U. L. Rev. 1569, 1573–75 (2013), argues that "courts should be guided by the Article III divide between public and private rights in determining the extent of their deference in adjudicative contexts." Currently, "[t]he extent of deference courts owe to agencies does not vary if the underlying right being adjudicated is 'public' or 'private' in the Article III sense of those terms. . . . Article III jurisprudence should prompt us to question that uniformity of approach. . . . The principle derivable from Article III jurisprudence is that in private rights cases the judicial review available to an Article III court must be meaningful. . . . Specifically, federal courts should be more stringent in policing agency reasoning, agency fact-finding procedure, and the factual basis for the agency action in private rights contexts than in public rights contexts. On fact and mixed questions, the federal court's review must be functionally much closer to de novo review if courts are to honor Article III values when reviewing initial agency adjudication of private rights."

(7) ***Stern's Aftermath.*** Developments since 2010 suggest that the Roberts Court is divided over Stern's import.

In WELLNESS INTERNATIONAL NETWORK LTD. V. SHARIF, 575 U.S. 665 (2015), Justice Sotomayor wrote for a 6–3 court holding that Article III permits bankruptcy judges to adjudicate Stern claims if the parties knowingly and voluntarily consent. Her opinion repeatedly invoked Schor and Thomas, quoting Schor on the need to decide the Article III question "not by 'formalistic and unbending rules,' but 'with an eye to the practical effect that the' practice 'will have on the constitutionally assigned role of the federal judiciary.' " Sotomayor read Schor to establish that "[t]he entitlement to an Article III adjudicator is a personal right and thus ordinarily subject to waiver," and concluded that "separation of powers concerns are diminished" when, as here, "the decision to invoke [a non-Article III] forum is left entirely to the parties and the power of the federal judiciary to take jurisdiction" remains in place. Chief Justice Roberts, Justice Scalia, and Justice Thomas dissented.

In OIL STATES ENERGY SERVS. V. GREENE'S ENERGY CORP., 138 S.Ct. 1365 (2018), the Court addressed the implications of Stern and the constitutionality of non-Article III adjudication in a more decidedly administrative context. At issue in Oil States was the constitutionality of inter partes review, a form of administrative review of granted patents established by the Leahy-Smith America Invents Act in 2011 (and also at issue in Arthrex, p. 945). Anyone other than the holder of the patent being challenged can file a petition with the Director of the Patent and Trademark Office (PTO) for inter partes review, seeking cancellation of patent claims for failing the patentability requirements of novelty and nonobviousness. The Director can grant inter partes review if the Director determines a reasonable likelihood exists that the petitioner would prevail with respect to at least one of the patent claims that are challenged. If instituted, the Patent Trial and Appeal Board (PTAB), an adjudicatory body within the PTO created to conduct inter partes review, examines the patent's validity. The petitioner and the patent owner are entitled to certain discovery, briefing, and hearing rights and the petitioner bears the burden of proving unpatentability by a preponderance of the evidence. Review of PTAB decisions on inter partes review is available in the Federal Circuit, with the PTAB's legal determinations reviewed de novo and its factual determinations reviewed under the substantial evidence standard.

Oil States sued Greene's for infringing its patent for protecting wellhead equipment used in hydraulic fracturing, and Greene's responded in part by filing a petition for inter partes review to challenge Oil State's patent. The PTAB instituted inter partes review and ultimately determined that Oil State's claims were unpatentable. On review, Oil States argued, inter alia, that actions to revoke a patent must be tried in an Article III court before a jury and that inter partes review was therefore unconstitutional. The Federal Circuit upheld the PTAB, and the Supreme Court affirmed by a 7–2 vote.

JUSTICE THOMAS wrote for the majority: "Article III vests the judicial power of the United States 'in one supreme Court, and in such inferior Courts as the Congress may from time to time ordain and establish.' § 1. Consequently, Congress cannot 'confer the Government's 'judicial Power' on entities outside Article III.' Stern v. Marshall, 564 U.S. 462, 484 (2011). When determining whether a proceeding involves an exercise of Article III judicial power, this Court's precedents have distinguished between 'public rights' and 'private rights.' Those precedents have given Congress significant latitude to assign adjudication of public rights to entities other than Article III courts.

"This Court has not definitively explained the distinction between public and private rights, and its precedents applying the public-rights doctrine have 'not been entirely consistent.' Id. at 488. But this case does not require us to add to the various formulations of the public-rights doctrine. Our precedents have recognized that the doctrine covers matters 'which arise between the Government and persons subject to its authority in connection with the performance of the constitutional functions of the executive or legislative departments.' Crowell v. Benson, 285 U.S. 22, 50 (1932). In other words, the public-rights doctrine applies to matters 'arising between the government and others, which from their nature do not require judicial determination and yet are susceptible of it.' Ibid. Inter partes review involves one such matter: reconsideration of the Government's decision to grant a public franchise. . . .

"Inter partes review falls squarely within the public-rights doctrine. This Court has recognized, and the parties do not dispute, that the decision to grant a patent is a matter involving public rights—specifically, the grant of a public franchise. . . . Ab initio, the grant of a patent involves a matter arising between the government and others. . . . Additionally, granting patents is one of 'the constitutional functions' that can be carried out by 'the executive or legislative departments' without 'judicial determination.' Id. at 50–51. Accordingly, the determination to grant a patent is a matter involving public rights. It need not be adjudicated in Article III court. . . .

"Inter partes review involves the same basic matter as the grant of a patent. So it, too, falls on the public-rights side of the line. . . . The Board considers the same statutory requirements that the PTO considered when granting the patent. . . . The primary distinction between inter partes review and the initial grant of a patent is that inter partes review occurs after the patent has issued. But that distinction does not make a difference here. Patent claims are granted subject to the qualification that the PTO has the authority to reexamine—and perhaps cancel—a patent claim in an inter partes review. . . . As a public franchise, a patent can confer only the rights that the statute prescribes. . . . One such regulation is inter partes review. . . .

"Oil States and the dissent contend that inter partes review violates the 'general' principle that 'Congress may not withdraw from judicial cognizance any matter which, from its nature, is the subject of a suit at the common law, or in equity, or admiralty.' Stern, 564 U.S. at 484. They argue that this is so because patent validity was often decided in English courts of law in the 18th century. . . . But there was another means of canceling a patent in 18th-century England, which more closely resembles inter partes review: a petition to the Privy Council to vacate a patent. The Privy Council was composed of the Crown's advisers . . . [and] was a prominent feature of the English system. . . . The Patent Clause in our Constitution was written against the backdrop of the English system. Based on the practice of the Privy Council, it was well understood at the founding that a patent system could include a practice of granting patents subject to potential cancellation in the executive proceeding of the Privy Council. The parties have cited nothing in the text or history of the Patent Clause or Article III to suggest that the Framers were not aware of this common practice. Nor is there any reason to think they excluded this practice during their deliberations. And this Court has recognized that, within the scope established by the Constitution, Congress may set out conditions and tests for patentability. We conclude that inter partes review is one of those conditions."

Justice Thomas emphasized that he was not reaching the questions of "whether other patent matters, such as infringement actions, can be heard in a non-Article III forum" and "whether inter partes review would be constitutional" without any judicial review. He also rejected Oil States' Seventh Amendment claim, noting that "[o]ur Court's precedents establish that, when Congress properly assigns a matter to adjudication in a non-Article III tribunal, 'the Seventh Amendment poses no independent bar to the adjudication of that action by a nonjury factfinder.' Granfinanciera, S.A. v. Nordberg, 492 U.S. 33, 53–54 (1989) [p. 1091]"

Concurring, JUSTICE BREYER (joined by Justices Ginsburg, Sotomayor, and Kagan) cautioned that "the Court's opinion should not be read to say that matters involving private rights may never be adjudicated other than by Article III courts, say, sometimes by agencies. Our precedent is to the contrary. Stern; Schor."

JUSTICE GORSUCH dissented, joined by Chief Justice Roberts: "Before the Revolution, colonial judges depended on the crown for their tenure and salary and often enough their decisions followed their interests. . . . Once free, the framers went to great lengths to guarantee a degree of judicial independence for future generations that they themselves had not experienced. . . . Today, the government invites us to retreat from the promise of judicial independence." According to Gorsuch, "[w]hen a suit is made of the stuff of the traditional actions at common law tried by the courts at Westminster in 1789 . . . and is brought within the bounds of federal jurisdiction, the responsibility for deciding that suit rests with Article III judges endowed with the protections for their independence the framers thought so important." Justice Gorsuch also criticized the majority's reliance on the Privy Council's role, arguing that "appealing to the Privy Council was seen as a last resort" and Privy Council revocation last occurred in 1779. In any event, he put more emphasis on U.S. historical practice, insisting that "it was widely accepted that the government could divest patent owners of their rights only through proceedings before independent judges. . . . This view held firm for most of our history. In fact, from the time it established the American patent system in 1790 until about 1980, Congress left the job of invalidating patents at the federal level to courts alone. . . . [J]ust because the Executive could issue an invention (or land) patent did not mean the Executive could revoke it."

Figuring out Oil States' implications for administrative adjudication is no easy task. On the one hand, the Court sustained inter partes review by a lopsided 7–2 vote, notwithstanding the traditional property features of patents or the way that inter partes review could be used (as it was here) to negate a court action for patent infringement. Add in inter partes review's notably administrative character, particularly compared to bankruptcy courts, and Oil States may seem to signal a lack of appetite on the Court for seriously curtailing administrative adjudication on Article III grounds. On the other hand, both the majority and dissent employ a heavily historical analysis, suggesting that the constitutionality of new instances of administrative adjudication may turn on whether a close historical analogue exists—and such an analogue may often be lacking. In addition, the majority's insistence on portraying the dispute as a matter of public right because the government was a party seems a reach, especially in light of the background dispute between two private companies that plainly drove the action. Given that the alternative framing of a public right as one that is closely integrated with a regulatory scheme—affirmed as recently as Stern—would have been an ample basis for upholding inter partes review, the Court's reluctance to invoke that definition may indicate concern about the potential breadth of the public rights exception. Equally significant is the majority's unwillingness to invoke Schor, its formalist and originalist reasoning, and its reinforcement of the public right-private right divide for Article III purposes. The strong rhetoric against administrative adjudication of private rights—and express questioning of Schor's authority—in Justice Gorsuch's dissent is also significant. In United States v. Arthrex, 141 S.Ct. 1970 (2021) (p. 945), Justice Gorsuch repeated his view that Oil States was wrongly decided. For a sustained analysis concluding that, "[t]hroughout the nineteenth century, once a franchise had been granted to a private person, authoritative adjudication of disputes about its validity or its forfeiture normally required 'judicial' power," see Caleb Nelson, Vested Rights, "Franchises," and the Separation of Powers, 169 U. Pa. L. Rev. 1429 (2021). For the contrasting view that "administrative adjudication had a much broader scope in the nineteenth century than previously thought," see Gregory Ablavsky, Getting Public Rights Wrong: The Lost History of the Private Land Claims, 74 Stan. L. Rev. 277 (2022).

(8) ***Article III and SEC Adjudication.*** The recent constitutional attacks on increased SEC use of administrative adjudication—which have primarily focused on claims based on the Appointments Clause (p. 957) and removal power (p. 1018)—have included arguments that such adjudication violates Article III. DAVID ZARING, ENFORCEMENT DISCRETION AT THE SEC, 94 Tex. L. Rev. 1155, 1202–04 (2016), notes that at first glance, bankruptcy cases like Stern and Northern Pipeline "seem to have little to do with the SEC's use of ALJs. Unlike the bankruptcy cases, the SEC administrative proceedings do not involve common law counterclaims, but instead involve purely statutory violations. A civil penalty for a violation of the securities acts is not 'a suit

. . . made of 'the stuff . . . tried by the courts at Westminster in 1789.' (quoting Stern)." But he adds that "the heavy fines and penalties, and the frequent follow-on nature of the penalties" might seem to be "something that looks close enough to being part of a criminal case to raise constitutional questions," particularly "in some follow-on cases involving disgorgement and . . . defendants [who have not registered with the SEC]."

In JARKESY V. SEC, 34 F.4th 446 (5th Cir. 2022), the Fifth Circuit upheld related constitutional claims against SEC administrative adjudication. These included the argument, discussed below (p. 1093), that SEC adjudication violates the Seventh Amendment and that the SEC's discretion to bring enforcement actions either in Article III courts or administratively violated the nondelegation doctrine. The SEC brought an administrative action against George Jarkesy and others, charging them with committing fraud under the Securities Act, the Securities and Exchange Act, and the Advisers Act. In concluding that Jarkesy's Seventh Amendment right to a jury was violated, JUDGE ELROD writing for a 2–1 panel rejected the argument that the enforcement action came under the public rights doctrine, even though the government was a party to the suit: "[F]rom 1856 to 1989, the government's involvement in a suit was only a necessary condition, *not* a sufficient condition, for determining whether a suit vindicated public rights. . . . The question is not just whether the government is a party, but also whether the right being vindicated is public or private, and how it is being vindicated. . . . [H]istory demonstrates that fraud claims like these are 'traditional legal claims' that arose at common law . . . [and] are quintessentially about the redress of private harms." The Court also argued that the fact that Congress allowed the SEC to bring enforcement actions in Article III courts mean that "securities-fraud enforcement actions are not the sort that are uniquely suited for agency adjudication." Judge Davis dissented, arguing that the action involved public rights because the SEC was suing in its sovereign capacity to enforce the federal securities laws.

Does the Fifth Circuit's analysis accord with the understanding of public rights that emerges from the Supreme Court's case law? Note that the Fifth Circuit put greatest weight on the fact that fraud actions were well-known at common law. While to some extent that reflected the case's Seventh Amendment framing, does it suggest that the Thomas/Schor identification of a public right as one that is closely integrated in a regulatory scheme—endorsed in Stern—is giving way to Oil States' much more historically focused analysis?

The Fifth Circuit also concluded that "Congress gave the SEC a significant legislative power by failing to provide . . . an intelligible principle to guide its" choice between Article III or administrative enforcement proceedings, analogizing the SEC's discretion to the "open-ended" power of the President the Supreme Court struck down in Panama Refining v. Ryan, 293 U.S. 388 (1935) (p. 860). Again Judge Davis dissented, concluding that the agency's enforcement decision fell within the range of prosecutorial discretion the Supreme Court had upheld. Do you think the Fifth Circuit's analysis on this front fits with the Supreme Court's nondelegation jurisprudence, such as Gundy or Whitman? Is the SEC's ability to choose between Article III or administrative enforcement distinguishable from its prosecutorial discretion to decide whether to bring charges in the first place?

## NOTES ON THE PUBLIC/PRIVATE RIGHTS DISTINCTION AND THE RIGHT TO A JURY TRIAL

(1) ***Public Rights and the Seventh Amendment.*** Stern was not the first post-Schor reappearance of the public rights versus private rights distinction. In GRANFINANCIERA, S.A. V. PAUL C. NORDBERG, 492 U.S. 33 (1989), discussed in Stern, the context was again bankruptcy but the constitutional concern was the Seventh Amendment right to a jury trial. The trustee in bankruptcy had sued in district court to recover money allegedly fraudulently transferred by the bankrupt corporation to Granfinanciera. The district judge referred the action to the bankruptcy court, which refused Granfinanciera's request for a jury trial on grounds that the fraud claim was equitable.

After determining that the trustee's claim was legal, not equitable, in nature, JUSTICE BRENNAN (writing for five justices) framed the Seventh Amendment question as "requiring the same answer as the question whether Article III allows Congress to assign adjudication of that action to a non-Article III tribunal." Surprisingly, given Thomas and Schor, the most recent precedents on Article III at the time, both questions were said to turn on the public right/private right distinction: "Congress may only deny trials by jury in actions at law . . . in cases where 'public rights' are litigated." However, reflecting the evolution in the meaning of public rights detailed above, these categories were redrawn in a way particularly relevant to administrative adjudication: "The crucial question, in cases not involving the Federal Government, is whether 'Congress, acting for a valid legislative purpose pursuant to its constitutional powers under Article I, [has] create[d] a seemingly 'private' right that is so closely integrated into a public regulatory scheme as to be a matter appropriate for agency resolution with limited involvement by the Article III judiciary" (quoting Justice Brennan's concurrence in Thomas). In this case, the trustee's claim was neither against the Federal Government nor "closely intertwined with a federal regulatory program Congress has the power to enact." Thus it concerned a "private right" and the Seventh Amendment guarantee applied. (The Court was careful not to decide before whom—the bankruptcy judge or the district judge—the jury trial must be held.)

JUSTICE SCALIA, concurring in part and concurring in the judgment, would have pushed the "public rights" doctrine in the opposite direction: "In my view a matter of 'public rights,' whose adjudication Congress may assign to tribunals lacking the essential characteristics of Article III courts, 'must at a minimum arise between the government and others.' . . . It is clear that what we meant by public rights [in Murray's Lessee] were not rights important to the public, or rights created by the public, but rights of the public—that is, rights pertaining to claims brought by or against the United States. For central to our reasoning was the device of waiver of sovereign immunity . . . [which] can only be implicated . . . in suits where the

Government is a party." Justice White and Justice Blackmun (joined by Justice O'Connor) dissented.

(2) ***The Seventh Amendment and Congress's Choice of Adjudicator.*** Early decisions suggested that the Seventh Amendment jury trial right would rarely attach to "typical" regulatory programs. NLRB v. JONES & LAUGHLIN STEEL CORP., 301 U.S. 1 (1937), was a multi-pronged constitutional attack on the National Labor Relations Act and the NLRB. (You may have read the decision in constitutional law for its holding on Congress's commerce power.) The Court rejected the Seventh Amendment challenge, reasoning tersely that the Amendment applied only to proceedings "in the nature of a suit at common law" and NLRA proceedings were unknown to the common law. Reinstatement of the employee and payment for time lost are requirements imposed for violation of the statute and are remedies appropriate for its enforcement.

Eventually, however, the Court cut back the breadth of this reasoning. In CURTIS v. LOETHER, 415 U.S. 189 (1974), a suit for damages for violation of the fair housing provisions of the Civil Rights Act of 1968, the Court insisted that "[t]he Seventh Amendment does apply to actions enforcing statutory rights. . . ." Its analysis seemed to turn on Congress's choice of primary enforcement forum: "[I]f the statute creates legal rights and remedies, enforceable in the ordinary courts of law," then an opportunity for jury trial must be provided. On the other hand, the Court emphasized, citing Jones & Laughlin, that "the Seventh Amendment is generally inapplicable in administrative proceedings where jury trials would be incompatible with the whole concept of administrative adjudication. . . ."

Three years later, this distinction was further developed in ATLAS ROOFING CO., INC. v. OCCUPATIONAL SAFETY & HEALTH REVIEW COMMISSION, 430 U.S. 442 (1977). Two employers, Atlas Roofing and Irey, had been cited by an OSHA inspector for worksite violations that had resulted, in each case, in an employee's death. Irey was assessed a $7500 "civil penalty"; Atlas, a $600 penalty. They claimed that the statutory assessment scheme (in which the inspector proposes the penalty and the employer can contest the penalty order in a juryless hearing by an ALJ of the Occupational Safety and Health Review Commission) violated their Seventh Amendment rights. JUSTICE WHITE wrote for a unanimous Court (Justice Blackmun not participating): "Petitioners claim that a suit in a federal court by the Government for civil penalties for violation of a statute is a suit for a money judgment which is classically a suit at common law . . . We disagree. At least in cases in which 'public rights' are being litigated—e.g., cases in which the Government sues in its sovereign capacity to enforce public rights created by statutes within the power of Congress to enact—the Seventh Amendment does not prohibit Congress from assigning the factfinding function and initial adjudication to an administrative forum with which the jury would be incompatible.

". . . Congress is not required by the Seventh Amendment to choke the already crowded federal courts with new types of litigation or prevented from committing some new types of litigation to administrative agencies with special competence in the relevant field. This is the case even if the Seventh Amendment would have required a jury where the adjudication of those rights is assigned to a federal court of law instead of an administrative agency. . . .

"[Petitioners argue] that the right to jury trial was never intended to depend on the identity of the forum to which Congress has chosen to submit a dispute; otherwise, it is said, Congress could utterly destroy the right to a jury trial by always providing for administrative rather than judicial resolution of the vast range of cases that now arise in the courts. The argument is well put, but it overstates the holdings of our prior cases and is in any event unpersuasive. Our prior cases support administrative factfinding in only those situations involving 'public' rights. . . . Wholly private tort, contract, and property cases, as well as a vast range of other cases[,] . . . are not at all implicated. . . .

". . . Congress found the common-law and other existing remedies for work injuries resulting from unsafe working conditions to be inadequate to protect the Nation's working men and women. It created a new cause of action, and remedies therefor, unknown to the common law, and placed their enforcement in a tribunal supplying speedy and expert resolutions of the issues involved. The Seventh Amendment is no bar to the creation of new rights or to their enforcement outside the regular courts of law." For criticism of the Court's approach, see, e.g., Martin H. Redish & Daniel J. La Fave, Seventh Amendment Right to Jury Trial in Non-Article III Proceedings: A Study in Dysfunctional Constitutional Theory, 4 Wm. & Mary Bill Rts. J. 407 (1995); Ellen E. Sward, Legislative Courts, Article III and the Seventh Amendment, 77 N. Car. L. Rev. 1037 (1999); Suja A. Thomas, A Limitation on Congress: "In Suits at Common Law," 71 Ohio St. L.J. 1071 (2010).

Claims that administrative adjudication violates the Seventh Amendment were largely dormant, even after Granfinanciera, given Atlas Roofing and the Court's broad definition of public rights. Nonetheless, here, too, the recent attacks on SEC administrative adjudication have prompted a resurgence. As noted above (p. 1090) the Fifth Circuit upheld such a Seventh Amendment challenge in JARKESY V. SEC, 34 F.4th 446 (5th Cir. 2022). JUDGE ELROD'S majority panel opinion argued that "[t]he rights that the SEC sought to vindicate . . . arise 'at common law' under the Seventh Amendment. Fraud prosecutions were regularly brought in English courts at common law . . . [and] the actions the SEC brought seeking civil penalties under securities statutes are akin to special actions in debt from early in our nation's history which were distinctly legal claims. . . . [O]ther elements of the action brought by the SEC against petitioners are more equitable in nature, but that fact does not invalidate the jury-trial right that attaches because of the civil penalties sought." Judge Elrod also held that "[j]ury trials in securities fraud suits would not 'dismantle the statutory scheme' addressing securities fraud or 'impede swift resolution' of the SEC's fraud prosecutions. And such suits are not uniquely suited for agency adjudication" (quoting Granfinanciera, 492 U.S. at 60–63). Dissenting, Judge Davis insisted that Supreme Court case law, from Crowell to Atlas Roofing and Oil States, as well as decisions from other circuits, made clear that "an enforcement action by the Government for violations of a federal statute or regulation is a 'public right' that Congress may assign to an agency for adjudication without offending the Seventh Amendment." He found that the SEC's enforcement action was such an instance of the government suing in its sovereign capacity to vindicate public rights, and thus the Seventh Amendment did not pose a bar to administrative enforcement.

(3) ***The Sixth Amendment and Criminal Sanctions.*** If, as Justice Scalia argued in Granfinanciera, "public rights" are those in which the government is a party, could Congress choose to enforce the criminal law outside the regular courts of law? WONG WING V. UNITED STATES, 163 U.S. 228 (1896): In the blatantly racist series of Chinese Exclusion Acts, Congress first (i) excluded Chinese people from entering the country; then (ii) forbade the reentry of legally resident Chinese individuals who had left the country temporarily; then (iii) required all Chinese residents to register with the Internal Revenue Service; and finally (iv) required that noncomplying Chinese persons "shall be imprisoned at hard labor for a period not exceeding one year, and thereafter removed from the United States." This sanction was imposed by immigration officials without judicial trial or review. After sustaining the first three, the Court finally held that Congress exceeded its powers with the fourth measure: "We regard it as settled by our previous decisions that the United States can, as a matter of public policy, by congressional enactment, [accomplish (i) through (iii) above.] But when Congress sees fit to further promote such a policy by subjecting the persons of such aliens to infamous punishment at hard labor, or by confiscating their property, we think such legislation, to be valid, must provide for a judicial trial to establish the guilt of the accused. . . . It is not consistent with the theory of our government that the legislature should, after having defined an offense as an infamous crime, find the fact of guilt, and adjudge the punishment by one of its own agents."

Obviously, the fines imposed on Irey and Atlas are significantly different from the hard labor imposed by an agency adjudicator upon Wong Wing. But contemporary criminal statutes often provide for sanctions that include fines. How do the fines imposed by OSHA differ from such fines? Are they civil sanctions because Congress has chosen to label them such? United States v. Harper, 490 U.S. 435 (1989), suggested that any penalty greater than that necessary to compensate the government qualifies as a punishment rather than a civil penalty. Harper was a Double Jeopardy case, and its method of separating civil and criminal punishments for that purpose was overruled in Hudson v. United States, 522 U.S. 93 (1997). Hudson returned to a multi-factor test used prior to Harper; most relevant for our purposes, the Court stated that the fact that authority to impose the penalty "was conferred upon [an] administrative agenc[y] is prima facie evidence that Congress intended to provide for a civil sanction." For an argument that administrative civil penalties are largely designed to serve retributive ends, see Max Minzner, Why Agencies Punish, 53 Wm. & Mary L. Rev. 853 (2012).

## PART 5

# JUDGING THE WORK OF AGENCIES

# CHAPTER VIII

# SCOPE OF REVIEW OF ADMINISTRATIVE ACTION



We turn now to the questions raised when courts are asked to review directly the substance of an agency's action. The fact that courts are in this business has an impact on many of the doctrines addressed elsewhere in this casebook—for instance, on the questions raised several times, in the Chapters on rulemaking and adjudication, of what procedures agencies must follow in order to build an adequate record for this review process. And if you have studied those Chapters, you will already have met some of the doctrines you will also meet here—doctrines signaled by terms such as "arbitrary and capricious," "reasonable interpretation," "substantial evidence," and the like. But now we will look at the relationship of court and agency concerning matters of substance in a systematic way. Traditionally this is known as the question of "scope of review," but it might just as well be called an inquiry into "intensity of review."

As Louis Jaffe, a famous administrative law scholar, once wrote: "The availability of judicial review is the necessary condition, psychologically if not logically, of a system of administrative power which purports to be legitimate, or legally valid."[1] But when judicial review occurs, on what subjects and how closely is the court to inquire? To what degree are the various elements of decision—jurisdiction, facts, judgment, policy, law—left to the agency? To what extent are they to be decided by the reviewing court? One might imagine two polar positions: that the administrative determination at issue is conclusive or that the court should make the determination by itself "de novo." Neither of these is readily described as "review" at all; they represent conclusions that the matter at issue is the unique business of the agency or of the courts, rather than a shared concern to be allocated between them. But we should expect most matters to be of shared concern, if only because Congress routinely provides both for agency determination of matters in the first instance and for judicial review of those determinations. Most matters fall at neither pole, and thus a more nuanced determination of the proper allocation must be made.

---

[1] Louis L. Jaffe, Judicial Control of Administrative Action 320 (1965).

Congress has usually, but not always, placed review of important administrative decisions in the courts of appeals. These courts are, of course, already in the business of reviewing the non-administrative-law determinations of the federal trial courts, and so one is tempted to draw an analogy between the appellate court/trial court relationship and the appellate court/administrative agency relationship. There are some similarities—for instance, both trial courts and agencies are equipped to hold evidentiary hearings, while appellate courts are not. But there are also important differences. For example, agencies, unlike district courts, have been told by Congress to initiate and carry out specific programs, and are subject to oversight by the Congress and the President. And many agencies, again unlike district courts, have been given the power, not just to decide cases, but to make regulations as well.

Considerations like these—considerations based on the systematic structural features of courts, agencies, and the other branches of government—form the groundwork on which a law of "scope of review" of administrative determinations can be built. Judges create and refine doctrine on the assumption that there is such a law, and as one of the founding editors of this casebook wrote: "We should not assume that our judges are dissemblers."[2]

Yet there is also a strong counter-tradition on this subject, to be met among both scholars and practitioners. As one article pithily stated: "The rules governing judicial review have no more substance at the core than a seedless grape."[3] On that view, whatever judges say, judicial review comes down to whether the judges do, or do not, agree with the agency on the underlying merits (or politics) of the substantive decision—and nothing more. There is no "deference," but only agreement or disagreement. Even on this view, however, it behooves the student to learn the lingo used to describe judicial review, in order, as a lawyer, to play her or his assigned part in the supposed charade.

As you study this Chapter, you will of course be forming your own view of the announced law of judicial review. But if you are tempted by the cynical view, you should at least consider a third possibility: that the aspiration to have a solid law of judicial review is valuable, and what needs to be done is not to abandon the goal, but rather to do a better job of reaching it. It may be right both that there are substantial structural issues that do imply that judges ought to interfere more here, and less there, and that the particular doctrines presently articulated by the courts do not reflect these considerations as well as they should.

---

[2] Clark Byse, Scope of Judicial Review in Informal Rulemaking, 33 Admin. L. Rev. 183, 193 (1981).

[3] Ernest Gellhorn & Glen O. Robinson, Perspectives in Administrative Law, 75 Colum. L. Rev. 771, 780–81 (1975).

# SECTION 1. THE BASELINE NORM OF LEGAL REGULARITY

*SHAW'S SUPERMARKETS, INC. v. NATIONAL LABOR RELATIONS BOARD*

## SHAW'S SUPERMARKETS, INC. v. NATIONAL LABOR RELATIONS BOARD

United States Court of Appeals for the First Circuit (1989).
884 F.2d 34.

■ BREYER, CIRCUIT JUDGE.

The National Labor Relations Board (the "Board") found that Shaw's Supermarkets ("Shaw") violated National Labor Relations Act ("NLRA") § 8(a)(1) during a representation election held at Shaw's Wells, Maine distribution facility in January 1987. In the election, 71 votes were cast for no union, 46 votes for a Teamsters local, and one vote for an independent union. The finding of violation rested primarily upon the fact that five days before the election, a Shaw vice president[,Charles Wyatt, made statements to employees that in the Board's view,] taken in context, constituted a "threat of reprisal" against collective organizing. . . . The Board ordered a new election. The Board now asks us to enforce its order.

. . . Under NLRA § 7, employees have the right to "self-organization, to form, join, or assist labor organizations, to bargain collectively through representatives of their own choosing. . . ." Employers may not "interfere with, restrain, or coerce employees in the exercise of" those rights. NLRA § 8(a)(1). Moreover, the NLRA expressly states that a "threat of reprisal or force or promise of benefit" does not constitute otherwise protected "express[ion]." NLRA § 8(c). Thus the NLRA prohibits employer speech during an election campaign which contains a "threat of reprisal" and thereby "interfere[s] with, restrain[s] or coerce[s]" employees in the exercise of their rights to "form, join or assist" labor unions. See NLRB v. Gissel Packing Co., Inc., 395 U.S. 575, 618 (1969). . . .

Were the Board writing on a blank slate, were there no set of Board cases on the subject, we should likely find sufficient basis in the record to sustain the Board's conclusion. Statements like those at issue here—that the company will "begin" its bargaining at "minimum wages and workmen's comp," that it will "build from that point"—might, depending on the context, innocently represent a legal truth about how the collective bargaining process works, legitimately remind employees that a union might trade certain payments or benefits that many workers now enjoy in order to obtain other payments or benefits, or improperly constitute a threat that, if the union wins, the employer will strip benefits back to the minimum, forcing the union to struggle even to keep the status quo. In deciding how to react to these statements, a court must recognize that the Board is expert, not simply about the factual context of the individual case, but also about how employees are likely to understand certain forms of words in the mine-run of cases. Thus, if the Board were to conclude that it should always assume that employees would reasonably take words of the sort at issue here as threats of regressive bargaining in the absence of added employer explanation to the contrary, we believe (though we need not, and do not decide) that a court could not easily say the Board was acting outside the authority that the law grants it.

The problem in this case for the Board, however, is that (a) it is not writing on a blank slate, but has written on the subject often in the past; (b) the Board has not said that it wishes to depart from its several prior cases on the subject; yet (c) as we shall discuss below, the prior cases dictate a result in Shaw's favor.

The law that governs an agency's significant departure from its own prior precedent is clear. . . . The agency has a

> duty to explain its departure from prior norms. The agency may flatly repudiate those norms, deciding, for example, that changed circumstances mean that they are no longer required in order to effectuate congressional policy. Or it may narrow the zone in which some rule will be applied, because it appears that a more discriminating invocation of the rule will best serve congressional policy. Or it may find that, although the rule in general serves useful purposes, peculiarities of the case before it suggest that the rule not be applied in that case. *Whatever the ground for departure from prior norms, however, it must be clearly set forth so that the reviewing court may understand the basis of the agency's action and so may judge the consistency of that action with the agency's mandate. . . .*
>
> [If] the agency distinguishes earlier cases[, it must] assert . . . distinctions that, when fairly and sympathetically read in the context of the entire opinion of the agency, reveal the policies it is pursuing.

Atchison, Topeka & Santa Fe Railway Co. v. Wichita Board of Trade, 412 U.S. 800, 808–09 (1973) (plurality opinion) (emphasis added).

> It is, of course, true that the Board is free to adopt new rules of decision and that the new rules of law can be given retroactive application. Nevertheless the Board may not depart sub silentio from its usual rules of decision to reach a different, unexplained result in a single case. . . . "[T]here may not be a rule for Monday, another for Tuesday, a rule for general application, but denied outright in a specific case." Mary Carter Paint Co. v. FTC, 333 F.2d 654, 660 (5th Cir. 1964) (Brown, J., concurring), rev'd on other grounds, 382 U.S. 46 (1965). "[A]n inadequately explained departure solely for purposes of a particular case, or the creation of conflicting lines of precedent governing the identical situation, is not to be tolerated."

NLRB v. International Union of Operating Engineers, Local 925, 460 F.2d 589, 604 (5th Cir. 1972) (citations omitted).

The Board says that Wyatt's statements fell within a category it calls "bargaining from scratch." It has held the making of such statements unlawful when, in context, a reasonable employee would take them as a coercive threat that an employer will engage in "regressive bargaining," by removing wages and benefits if the union wins. The Board has distinguished lawful from unlawful "bargaining from scratch" statements by ascribing importance to the varying elements of the factual contexts embodied in its past precedent.

[The court reviewed eight NLRB cases, from 1968–1986, in which the Board had concluded that an employer's "bargaining from scratch" statement did *not*, in context, amount to a threat of "regressive bargaining."] In many of these cases . . . the statements in context seem to us just as threatening (if not more so) than those in the present case. We do not see how, after reading the record in this case and the opinions in the cases we have just mentioned, one could reasonably find no violation in those earlier cases yet find a violation in this case. Wyatt used language virtually identical to that used in the cases just listed. . . . The record does not reveal any other elements suggesting regressive bargaining. Indeed, Board counsel at oral argument simply stated that he "did not know" just what it was in the context of the prior cases finding no violation that "made these same statements" benign there, yet harmful here. Counsel's statement, in our view, honestly reflects the circumstances, for we do not see how one can distinguish prior cases in which the Board found "no violation."

Of course, there are other cases in which the Board found that a "bargaining from scratch" statement violated the law. [The court reviewed four NLRB decisions from the 1977–86 period.] . . . In almost all these cases, the "bargaining from scratch" speech was accompanied by other serious unfair labor practices, such as the discriminatory treatment of labor organizers. . . . [Moreover,] the language and context suggested, far more strongly than here, a threat to eliminate benefits before bargaining. . . .

In finding the Board's decision in this case inconsistent with its precedents, we do not intend to impose upon the Board the time consuming obligation of microscopically examining prior cases; nor to encourage counsel to examine past precedent with an eye towards raising hosts of legalistic arguments and distinctions. Here, however, the past cases trace a relatively clear line. Nor do we believe that past cases are a straitjacket, inhibiting experimentation or change. . . . [T]he Board remains free to modify or change its rule; to depart from, or to keep within, prior precedent, as long as it focuses upon the issue and explains why change is reasonable. Unless an agency either follows or consciously changes the rules developed in its precedent, those subject to the agency's authority cannot use its precedent as a guide for their conduct; nor will that precedent check arbitrary agency action.

For these reasons we decline to enforce the Board's order, and we remand the case to the Board.

## NOTES

(1) ***Will They Never Learn?*** Perhaps because its work is highly politically contentious, the NLRB seems to have trouble with measuring up to its obligation to decide cases with some measure of legal regularity. Whatever the reason, cases that in essence look just like Shaw's Supermarkets (but not necessarily as clearly written) continue to come down the pike. E.g., Communications Workers of America v. NLRB, 954 F.3d 653 (D.C. Cir. 2021) (in light of conflicting Board precedents, "the Board needs to identify what standard the Board has adopted"); Davidson Hotel Co. v. NLRB, 977 F.3d 1289 (D.C. Cir. 2020) (Board fails to cite, let alone distinguish, contrary Board precedents directly on point and brought to their attention by management); NLRB v. CNN America, 865 F.3d 740 (D.C. Cir. 2017) (Garland, J.) (Board did not even mention many of its important precedents, which stretched over three decades; did not mention that its own General Counsel just three months earlier had filed a brief espousing a different view as agency law; did not justify its reinterpretation of a central doctrine; and did not forthrightly overrule conflicting precedents). But the problem exists in the work product of other agencies, too. There are a great many courts of appeals cases that, as in the case we have just read, reverse agency determinations for failure to adequately explain a departure from agency precedent. See Kristen E. Hickman and Richard J. Pierce, Jr., Administrative Law Treatise § 11.6.2 (6th ed. 2018).

(2) ***Why Does Consistency Matter?*** Then-Judge Breyer gives two reasons: "Unless an agency either follows or consciously changes the rules developed in its precedent, those subject to the agency's authority cannot use its precedent as a guide for their conduct; nor will that precedent check arbitrary agency action." Taking the former of these reasons first, it suggests the possibility that Shaw's vice president was briefed by counsel about the intricacies of the Board's "bargaining from scratch" doctrine before meeting with Shaw's employees. But how does that emphasis on possible reliance mesh with Breyer's concession that, if it had properly explained what it was doing, the NLRB could have changed its doctrine by means of adjudication—a concession authoritatively grounded in the Chenery case, p. 258 above? Judge Breyer might answer that, if the Board had overtly faced up to the fact of change, then it would also realize that it had to take into account this possible private-party reliance. Agencies have, in such situations, sometimes reduced the penalty on parties now determined to have, to their surprise, disobeyed the law. Consider, for example, what the FCC does in the Fox case, p. 1160 below. And if the agency does not do that, then, because the change is apparent, perhaps a reviewing court will do it instead. See, e.g., Epilepsy Foundation of Northeast Ohio v. NLRB, 268 F.3d 1095 (D.C. Cir. 2001) (p. 272), in which the D.C. Circuit, considering another change in Labor Board policy, upheld the Board's change of mind as "clear and reasonable" but refused to give it retroactive application.

(3) ***Beyond Reliance.*** TODD D. RAKOFF, SHAW'S SUPERMARKETS, INC. V. NLRB—A FIRST CIRCUIT OPINION, 128 Harv. L. Rev. 477, 479–80 (2014): "The more important claim is that judicially requiring conscious attention to existing precedents will 'check arbitrary agency action.' Here, I think, we must distinguish two possible meanings of 'arbitrary.' One possible claim is that requiring an agency to address its existing rules and precedents will prevent it from doing mindless acts, acts in which it simply gives no thought to the fact that in other cases it has done things differently. Whatever might be the force of this idea elsewhere, it seems to me to have little force in the situation at hand. Labor Board cases are formally structured, contested affairs, much like civil trials; it would seem safe to rely on one party or another to draw to the attention of the Board its prior decisions. Assuming competent counsel, it is unlikely the precedents will remain hidden.

"What is at stake is not the 'mindless' form of arbitrary action, but rather the 'willful' form—the form that says: 'We're doing it now differently from what we did before because that's what we want to do—period!' The court's corresponding claim, as said in one of the cases that Judge Breyer quotes, is that 'there may not be a rule for Monday, another for Tuesday.'

"Now, it is not inherently arbitrary to do one thing on Monday and another on Tuesday. We do it all the time. Indeed, sometimes the reason for doing a particular thing on Tuesday is precisely that it is different from what we did on Monday. 'We had pizza for dinner yesterday' is a reason for not having pizza for dinner today, not a reason for having it again. The claim that having done something one way yesterday is a prima facie reason for doing it the same way today is not an unalterable claim of all rational thinking, but rather a claim of a specific cultural form. It is a claim of the legal order for action to be justified based on reasoning of a specific sort.

"Whether governmental administration of the economy, 'regulation,' comprises acts of will or acts of reason—or perhaps better put, the extent to which it comprises acts of will and acts of reason—is a classic question of administrative law. It is often seen through the lens of the structural Constitution, and converted into the question of whether there are administrative law 'substitutes' for the separation of powers set out in Articles I, II, and III. But Judge Breyer cites no constitutional provision, nor indeed any provision of the Administrative Procedure Act, to support his claims, and it is probably fairer to say that he is simply relying on what he sees as a fundamental demand of the legal order. (If one wanted a constitutional text, I suppose it would be 'due process' seen in its most general form, as a claim to official action having to be grounded on a legal regime.) . . .

"The legal order in question is not a legal order that plays out primarily in the courts, but rather one that fundamentally takes place within the agency. Ordering a new election on these facts may be, as Judge Breyer assumes, within the constitutional and statutory power of the agency, but the agency has to think about its task, and justify its task, in a certain way. Thus, after holding that the Board's order cannot be enforced, the rescript is to remand the case to the Board. The agency has to act as if it were part of the legal regime—and should be given another chance to do so. The court's job is to provide a context that encourages the agency so to act. . . ."

(4) ***Adherence to Agency Regulations.*** Now, what if the agency's prior position is represented by a rule rather than a set of cases? The general principle is that an agency must follow its own regulations until they are validly amended or rescinded. This principle is often called the "Accardi doctrine" from the case in which it first played a prominent role.[1] Its most dramatic applications come from the Watergate scandal. When Attorney General Robert Bork, on President Nixon's order, fired Archibald Cox as Watergate Special Prosecutor, Judge Gerhardt Gesell held the action unlawful. Although the Attorney General ordinarily had the power to fire a federal prosecutor at will, he had limited his own authority by promulgating a regulation that the Watergate Special Prosecutor would be fired only "for extraordinary improprieties." As Cox had not engaged in such behavior, the Attorney General had no power to fire him. Nader v. Bork, 366 F.Supp. 104 (D.D.C. 1973). When Cox's successor, Leon Jaworski, obtained a subpoena ordering President Nixon to produce certain tape recordings, and Nixon refused to comply on grounds of executive privilege, the President argued that the judiciary could not intervene in an "intra-executive dispute." The Supreme Court unanimously held that, because the Attorney General had explicitly delegated to the Special Prosecutor the power to contest any invocation of executive privilege in connection with his investigations, "the Executive Branch is bound by" that regulation. United States v. Nixon, 418 U.S. 683 (1974).

But the Accardi principle appears in less high-profile cases, too. For example, in Garcia-Mata v. Sessions, 893 F.3d 1107 (8th Cir. 2018), Maria Garcia-Mata faced removal from the U.S. to her home country, Mexico. But in the course of her travails, she had become entangled with a smuggling organization that feared she would testify against them if she returned, and threatened her if she did. The Immigration Judge found that the organization had the ability to carry out its threats, and concluded (said the reviewing court) "that future persecution was more likely than not to occur if Garcia-Mata were removed to Mexico, so he granted her application for withholding of removal." The government appealed to the Board of Immigration Appeals, which reversed the IJ and ordered Garcia-Mata removed. The IJ's findings, said the BIA, were speculative and "not supported by the evidence in the record." But, said the Eighth Circuit, "an agency, in adjudicating the rights of individuals, must follow its own procedures and regulations." The applicable BIA regulation said that "the Board has authority to review an immigration judge's factual findings for clear error, 8 C.F.R. § 1003.1(d)(3)(i)"; it "lacks authority to engage in factfinding of its own." Since the BIA said only that the IJ's findings were "not supported," and "never directly asserted that the immigration judge committed clear error," Garcia-Mata's petition for review was granted, and the case sent back to the agency.

---

[1] Accardi v. Shaughnessy, 347 U.S. 260 (1954).

How does one explain holding an agency to a rule that it was under no duty to adopt in the first place? A rule upon which, given the particular context, there could be no private reliance? THOMAS W. MERRILL, THE ACCARDI PRINCIPLE, 74 Geo. Wash. L. Rev. 569, 598–99 (2006): "What is the status in law of the principle that agencies have a legal duty to comply with regulations that have a status analogous to statutes? Is this a proposition of constitutional law, statutory interpretation, administrative common law, or what? The most honest answer is that it is just one of those shared postulates of the legal system that cannot be traced to any provision of enacted law. In this sense, it is like the rule of stare decisis, or the understanding that majority rule prevails in multimember courts. . . . These rules are not written down in any authoritative text. They are simply foundational assumptions vital to the operations of our legal system."

Whatever is the source of this "foundational assumption," it is reflected in the APA. As we shall see in the State Farm case (p. 1126 below), an agency rescinding a binding regulation has to adopt the rescission as if it were adopting a new rule. Of course, under the APA not all rules have what Merrill refers to as "a status analogous to statutes." Some rules are merely "interpretative rules" or "policy statements" that can be adopted informally. (See p. 393 above.) As to them, the agency may not be bound to follow the rule on the books until it formally takes the rule off the books. But to avoid being considered "arbitrary and capricious" it may still have an obligation to explain why it is departing from such an interpretation in the case at hand. For further discussion of the Accardi principle, see Elizabeth Magill, Agency Self-Regulation, 77 Geo. Wash. L. Rev. 859, 873–82 (2009).

(5) ***Dodging the Rules?*** Suppose you have recently been inaugurated as President, succeeding a President of a very different political stripe. Your predecessor's administration adopted many rules which you disagree with and want to change. The courts say those rules are still *the* rules until your agencies formally adopt new rules to replace them. But, as we saw in Chapter IV, the notice and comment process takes a fair amount of time and agency energy, and your supporters want to see change! Yet perhaps you don't want to take full responsibility for some of the changes, because, after all, not everyone agrees with you. What do you do?

In an article reviewing the Trump Administration's efforts in these situations, which were more intense than prior administrations', but not unique—WILLIAM W. BUZBEE, catalogued the following techniques, which he called "deregulatory splintering"—:

- If the prior administration's regulation is still being challenged in court, join the challengers on the merits, or in requesting a judicial stay;
- Announce an administrative stay of the prior administration's rules, or change their "effective" date;
- Announce a policy of not enforcing an existing regulation;
- Declare that for some reason an existing regulation is illegal; and

- Start down the path to rescission of the prior regulation, and replace it in "the interim."

DEREGULATORY SPLINTERING, 94 Chi.-Kent L. Rev. 439, 451–61 (2019). And what happened to these efforts? Buzbee reports as follows, id. at 472–73: "Many agency actions have been rejected, although ultimate choices about relief have varied. The policy change was not the problem; the agencies' pervasive failures to offer rigorous comparative analysis and hew to consistency doctrine's requirements was the usually fatal flaw. Relatedly, even where agencies at least alluded to required analytical steps, the tendency to be conclusory on issues of fact, reliance interests and effects, and the general failure to explain and compare with nuance the new and earlier legal views led to judicial rejections. Some judges seem to have viewed the deregulatory splintering with repeated skimpy reasoning as evidence of haste and lack of due deliberation that perhaps contributed to judicial invalidation. A few courts, however, seem to find the very splintering of actions as justifying either judicial avoidance of a ruling on the merits or as justifying relief that allowed the initial regulation . . . to be stayed or de facto abandoned, yet without the usual full regulatory process and agency justification." See also NYU Institute for Policy Integrity, Roundup: Trump-Era Agency Policy in the Courts (tracking litigation against the Trump Administration and finding 192 "unsuccessful" and 54 "successful" outcomes for agencies).[2]

(6) ***And What About Mass Justice?*** "Government is at its most arbitrary when it treats similarly situated people differently"[3]—an axiom that Judge Friendly called "the most basic principle of jurisprudence." Henry J. Friendly, Indiscretion About Discretion, 31 Emory L.J. 747, 758 (1982). Although generally (if not universally) acknowledged as an essential condition of a just legal system, the principle of "like treatment of like cases" can be surprisingly difficult to realize. As you likely know well, it is not always easy for first-year law students (and others!) to decide if fact patterns are, or are not, distinguishable. But Judge Breyer could at least work from formal, published NLRB opinions that could be viewed as a system of precedent. What of less formal agency determinations?

In DAVIS V. COMMISSIONER, 69 T.C. 716 (1978), the Internal Revenue Service had disallowed part of a small charitable deduction claimed by Kenneth Culp Davis for books received from West Publishing Co., used, and then donated to the University of Chicago Law Library. Contesting this position in the Tax Court, Davis (a famous professor of administrative law) obtained through discovery IRS "letter rulings" issued to members of Congress who received free copies of the Congressional Record, gave them to charitable organizations, and deducted the value of the gifts.[4] After receiving four such rulings, Davis—insisting that the agency must act evenhandedly—

[2] https://policyintegrity.org/trump-court-roundup.

[3] Etelson v. OPM, 684 F.2d 918, 926 (D.C. Cir. 1982).

[4] "Letter rulings" are issued with less structured intra-agency review than "revenue rulings," which are officially published and on which all taxpayers are encouraged to rely. The IRS considers itself bound by revenue rulings until revoked but bound by letter rulings only as to the addressee taxpayer.

sought additional discovery of all pertinent letter rulings (at that time, not generally available to the public) in the IRS's "reference file." Discovery was denied. As another Tax Court judge had said two years earlier in a similar effort by Davis over a different deduction (Davis v. Commissioner, 65 T.C. 1014, 1022–23 (1976)): "It has long been the position of this Court that our responsibility is to apply the law to the facts of the case before us . . .; how the Commissioner may have treated other taxpayers has generally been considered irrelevant in making that determination. Any change in that position would have widespread ramifications in the administration and application of the Federal tax laws and in the conduct of our work. . . . Were we to embrace the principles urged by Mr. Davis, the task would be magnified. Every trial would be extended, for it would then become necessary to allow the petitioner to inquire into the Commissioner's treatment of other similarly situated taxpayers. . . . [T]he notion of equal justice has strong appeal in our society and might lead to the conclusion that his position should ultimately be adopted. Yet, a full appreciation of the ramifications of this matter makes abundantly clear that it should be approached cautiously."

"How the Commissioner may have treated other taxpayers has generally been considered irrelevant" appears to still be the law. See, e.g., U.S. v. McBride, 2014 WL 4457293 (D. Utah 2014).

We might further consider the prospects of achieving evenhandedness in a massive benefits regime like the Social Security disability program. Jerry Mashaw's several writings on the administration of this program illuminate these issues. His first study, completed in 1978, produced a damning indictment from a perspective much like Davis's: individual cases were being decided without discernible pattern. "The inconsistency of the disability process is patent. Indeed, it is widely believed that the outcome of cases depends more on who decides the case than on what the facts are."[5] But, as Mashaw explored in his later work, Bureaucratic Justice (1983), intolerance of *any* degree of inconsistency is premised on a "model of individual justice." An alternative, a "model of bureaucratic rationality," would frame the issues as whether *gross* errors have been avoided and marginal errors *evenly distributed* (that is, about as many wrongful grants as wrongful denials) at reasonable cost. These conditions would maximize the extent to which programmatic purposes are achieved and, one might say, would represent "fairness" in a different, overall sense. If one takes this view, for the "similarly situated" people at the margin of eligibility, inconsistent treatment is a necessary cost of a workable scheme; all that can realistically be asked—that the judgment on eligibility not be "too wrong"—will have been achieved. Is that an adequate view of justice? Can you think of ways to reduce the gap between individual justice and bureaucratic justice?

[5] Jerry L. Mashaw, Charles J. Goetz, Frank I. Goodman, Warren F. Schwartz, Paul R. Verkuil, & Milton M. Carrow, Social Security Hearings and Appeals: A Study of the Social Security Administration Hearing System xxi (1978).

## SECTION 2. SUPPORT FOR AGENCY DECISIONS



As we have just seen, the most basic element of judicial review of agency action is the demand that the agency act with legal regularity. No one doubts that judicial review goes further than that. But how much further?

As ordinary civil procedure shows, the tradition of the law is to give a differentiated, rather than flat, answer to a question of this sort. Appellate courts review trial court decisions in ordinary civil cases using a variety of standards modulated according to particular features of the situation; scrutiny is most intense regarding trial courts' rulings on questions of law, less so on their findings of fact in trials without a jury, and least intense (or put another way, most deferential) regarding determinations of fact made by a jury.

If we were to imagine a similar scale of intensity for judicial review of agency decisions, we might then ask ourselves, what features of agency decisions should we correlate with more or less judicial scrutiny? Should we divide agency decisionmaking into its various formal components—jurisdiction, law, fact, discretion, policy, etc.—and propound different standards for each? Or should we instead develop a scale of the social and economic importance of various agency decisions and ask the judges to spend greater energy on the more important ones? Or should we try to allocate to agencies those aspects of decisionmaking that call for scientific, commercial, or industrial expertise and give to the judges those aspects accessible to legal reasoning and ordinary common sense?

Although Congress sometimes stipulates particular review standards in specific organic statutes, its general answer to this set of questions is set out in § 706 of the APA:

### 5 U.S.C. § 706

#### Scope of Review

To the extent necessary to decision and when presented, the reviewing court shall decide all relevant questions of law, interpret constitutional and statutory provisions, and determine the meaning or applicability of the terms of an agency action. The reviewing court shall—

(1) compel agency action unlawfully withheld or unreasonably delayed; and

(2) hold unlawful and set aside agency action, findings, and conclusions found to be—

(A) arbitrary, capricious, an abuse of discretion, or otherwise not in accordance with law;

(B) contrary to constitutional right, power, privilege, or immunity;

(C) in excess of statutory jurisdiction, authority, or limitations, or short of statutory right;

(D) without observance of procedure required by law;

(E) unsupported by substantial evidence in a case subject to sections 556 and 557 of this title or otherwise reviewed on the record of an agency hearing provided by statute; or

(F) unwarranted by the facts to the extent that the facts are subject to trial de novo by the reviewing court.

In making the foregoing determinations, the court shall review the whole record or those parts of it cited by a party, and due account shall be taken of the rule of prejudicial error.

---

This statute gives us some language to work with; but the language Congress used assumes as much as it answers. One ground for setting aside agency action, for example, is if it is "arbitrary" or "capricious," but these terms are given no further specification within the text of the statute. They must be explicated by the courts in the light of tradition, policy, or the needs of the case.

We begin with what is perhaps the most specific of the § 706 standards: the stipulation that the courts should set aside agency action if it is "unsupported by substantial evidence in a case subject to sections 556 and 557 of this title or otherwise reviewed on the record of an agency hearing provided by statute"—which is to say, we begin with the test for determinations of fact made in an on-the-record, trial-type hearing.

## a. Review of the Basic Facts

***UNIVERSAL CAMERA CORP. v. NATIONAL LABOR RELATIONS BOARD***
***Notes on the Substantial Evidence Test***
***Notes on "Arbitrary or Capricious" in Comparison to "Substantial Evidence"***

## UNIVERSAL CAMERA CORP. v. NATIONAL LABOR RELATIONS BOARD

Supreme Court of the United States (1951).
340 U.S. 474.

■ JUSTICE FRANKFURTER delivered the opinion of the Court.

[The question before the National Labor Relations Board was whether an employee had been fired because he had testified in support of the union's position in an NLRB representation proceeding, or solely because subsequently he had accused the company's personnel manager of drunkenness. The trial examiner, crediting the employer's testimony and finding that anti-union animus had not entered into the discharge, recommended dismissing the complaint. A divided Board made the opposite finding and held the discharge to be an unfair labor practice. The Second Circuit also divided, granting enforcement per Judge Learned Hand but with express misgivings about the Board's assessment of the evidence; Judge Hand's opinion voiced views at odds with those of the Sixth Circuit, whose decision was reviewed in a companion case.]

The essential issue raised by this case and its companion . . . is the effect of the Administrative Procedure Act and the legislation colloquially known as the Taft-Hartley Act, 5 U.S.C. § 1001 et seq.; 29 U.S.C. § 141 et seq., on the duty of Courts of Appeals when called upon to review orders of the National Labor Relations Board. . . .

I.

Want of certainty in judicial review of Labor Board decisions partly reflects the intractability of any formula to furnish definiteness of content for all the impalpable factors involved in judicial review. But in part doubts as to the nature of the reviewing power and uncertainties in its application derive from history, and to that extent an elucidation of this history may clear them away.

The Wagner Act [the original National Labor Relations Act] provided: "The findings of the Board as to the facts, if supported by evidence, shall be conclusive." Act of July 5, 1935, § 10(e). This Court read "evidence" to mean "substantial evidence," and we said that "(s)ubstantial evidence is more than a mere scintilla. It means such relevant evidence as a reasonable mind might accept as adequate to support a conclusion." Consolidated Edison Co. v. National Labor Relations Board, 305 U.S. 197, 229. Accordingly, it "must do more than create a suspicion of the existence of the fact to be established. . . . [I]t must be enough to justify, if the trial were to a jury, a refusal to direct a verdict when the conclusion sought to be drawn from it is one of fact for the jury." NLRB v. Columbian Enameling & Stamping Co., 306 U.S. 292, 300.

The very smoothness of the "substantial evidence" formula as the standard for reviewing the evidentiary validity of the Board's findings established its currency. But the inevitably variant applications of the standard to conflicting evidence soon brought contrariety of views and in due course bred criticism. Even though the whole record may have been canvassed in order to determine whether the evidentiary foundation of a determination by the Board was "substantial," the phrasing of this Court's process of review readily lent itself to the notion that it was enough that the evidence supporting the Board's result was "substantial" when considered by itself. It is fair to say that by imperceptible steps regard for the fact-finding function of the Board led to the assumption that the requirements of the Wagner Act were met when the reviewing court could find in the record evidence which, when viewed in isolation, substantiated the Board's findings. . . .

Criticism of so contracted a reviewing power reinforced dissatisfaction felt in various quarters with the Board's administration of the Wagner Act in the years preceding the war. The scheme of the Act was attacked as an inherently unfair fusion of the functions of prosecutor and judge. Accusations of partisan bias were not wanting. The "irresponsible admission and weighing of hearsay, opinion, and emotional speculation in place of factual evidence" was said to be a "serious menace." No doubt some, perhaps even much, of the criticism was baseless and some surely was reckless.[6] What is here relevant, however, is the climate of opinion thereby generated and its effect on Congress. Protests against "shocking injustices" and intimations of judicial "abdication" with which some courts granted enforcement of the Board's order stimulated pressures for legislative relief from alleged administrative excesses.

The strength of these pressures was reflected in the passage in 1940 of the Walter-Logan Bill. It was vetoed by President Roosevelt, partly because it imposed unduly rigid limitations on the administrative process, and partly because of the investigation into the actual operation of the administrative process then being conducted by an experienced committee appointed by the Attorney General. It is worth noting that despite its aim to tighten control over administrative determinations of fact, the Walter-Logan Bill contented itself with the conventional formula that an agency's decision could be set aside if "the findings of fact are not supported by substantial evidence."

The final report of the Attorney General's Committee was submitted in January, 1941. The majority concluded that "(d)issatisfaction with the existing standards as to the scope of judicial review derives largely from dissatisfaction with the fact-finding procedures now employed by the administrative bodies." Departure from the "substantial evidence" test, it thought, would either create unnecessary uncertainty or transfer to courts the responsibility for ascertaining and assaying matters the significance of which lies outside judicial competence. Accordingly, it recommended against legislation embodying a general scheme of judicial review.[12]

Three members of the Committee registered a dissent. Their view was that the "present system or lack of system of judicial review" led to

---

[6] Professor Gellhorn and Mr. Linfield reached the conclusion in 1939 after an extended investigation that "the denunciations find no support in fact." Gellhorn and Linfield, Politics and Labor Relations, 39 Col. L. Rev. 339, 394.

[12] Referring to proposals to enlarge the scope of review to permit inquiry whether the findings are supported by the weight of the evidence, the majority said: ". . . [T]he wisdom of a general change to review of the 'weight of evidence' is questionable. If the change would require the courts to determine independently which way the evidence preponderates, administrative tribunals would be turned into little more than media for transmission of the evidence to the courts. It would destroy the values of adjudication of fact by experts or specialists in the field involved. It would divide the responsibility for administrative adjudications." Final Report, 91–92.

inconsistency and uncertainty. They reported that under a "prevalent" interpretation of the "substantial evidence" rule "if what is called 'substantial evidence' is found anywhere in the record to support conclusions of fact, the courts are said to be obliged to sustain the decision without reference to how heavily the countervailing evidence may preponderate—unless indeed the stage of arbitrary decision is reached. Under this interpretation, the courts need to read only one side of the case and, if they find any evidence there, the administrative action is to be sustained and the record to the contrary is to be ignored." Their view led them to recommend that Congress enact principles of review applicable to all agencies not excepted by unique characteristics. One of these principles was expressed by the formula that judicial review could extend to "findings, inferences, or conclusions of fact unsupported, upon the whole record, by substantial evidence." So far as the history of this movement for enlarged review reveals, the phrase "upon the whole record" makes its first appearance in this recommendation of the minority of the Attorney General's Committee. This evidence of the close relationship between the phrase and the criticism out of which it arose is important, for the substance of this formula for judicial review found its way into the statute books when Congress with unquestioning—we might even say uncritical—unanimity enacted the Administrative Procedure Act.

One is tempted to say "uncritical" because the legislative history of that Act hardly speaks with that clarity of purpose which Congress supposedly furnishes courts in order to enable them to enforce its true will. On the one hand, the sponsors of the legislation indicated that they were reaffirming the prevailing "substantial evidence" test. But with equal clarity they expressed disapproval of the manner in which the courts were applying their own standard. The committee reports of both houses refer to the practice of agencies to rely upon "suspicion, surmise, implications, or plainly incredible evidence," and indicate that courts are to exact higher standards "in the exercise of their independent judgment" and on consideration of "the whole record."[17]

Similar dissatisfaction with too restricted application of the "substantial evidence" test is reflected in the legislative history of the Taft-Hartley Act [amending the National Labor Relations Act in 1947]. . . . Early committee prints in the Senate provided for review by

---

17 The following quotation from the report of the Senate Judiciary Committee indicates the position of the sponsors. "The 'substantial evidence' rule set forth in section 10(e) is exceedingly important. As a matter of language, substantial evidence would seem to be an adequate expression of law. The difficulty comes about in the practice of agencies to rely upon (and of courts to tacitly approve) something less—to rely upon suspicion, surmise, implications, or plainly incredible evidence. It will be the duty of the courts to determine in the final analysis and in the exercise of their independent judgment, whether on the whole record the evidence in a given instance is sufficiently substantial to support a finding, conclusion, or other agency action as a matter of law. In the first instance, however, it will be the function of the agency to determine the sufficiency of the evidence upon which it acts—and the proper performance of its public duties will require it to undertake this inquiry in a careful and dispassionate manner. Should these objectives of the bill as worded fail, supplemental legislation will be required." S. Rep. No. 752, 79th Cong., 1st Sess. 30–31. The House Committee Report is to substantially the same effect. H.R. Rep. No. 1980, 79th Cong., 2d Sess. 45.

"weight of the evidence" or "clearly erroneous" standards. But, as the Senate Committee Report relates, "it was finally decided to conform the statute to the corresponding section of the Administrative Procedure Act where the substantial evidence test prevails. In order to clarify any ambiguity in that statute, however, the committee inserted the words 'questions of fact, if supported by substantial evidence on the record considered as a whole. . . .' "[21] This phraseology was adopted by the Senate. The House conferees agreed. . . .

It is fair to say that in all this Congress expressed a mood. And it expressed its mood not merely by oratory but by legislation. As legislation that mood must be respected, even though it can only serve as a standard for judgment and not as a body of rigid rules assuring sameness of applications. Enforcement of such broad standards implies subtlety of mind and solidity of judgment. But it is not for us to question that Congress may assume such qualities in the federal judiciary.

From the legislative story we have summarized, two concrete conclusions do emerge. One is the identity of aim of the Administrative Procedure Act and the Taft-Hartley Act regarding the proof with which the Labor Board must support a decision. The other is that now Congress has left no room for doubt as to the kind of scrutiny which a court of appeals must give the record before the Board to satisfy itself that the Board's order rests on adequate proof. . . .

Whether or not it was ever permissible for courts to determine the substantiality of evidence supporting a Labor Board decision merely on the basis of evidence which in and of itself justified it, without taking into account contradictory evidence or evidence from which conflicting inferences could be drawn, the new legislation definitively precludes such a theory of review and bars its practice. The substantiality of evidence must take into account whatever in the record fairly detracts from its weight. This is clearly the significance of the requirement in both statutes that courts consider the whole record. Committee reports and the adoption in the Administrative Procedure Act of the minority views of the Attorney General's Committee demonstrate that to enjoin such a duty on the reviewing court was one of the important purposes of the movement which eventuated in that enactment.

To be sure, the requirement for canvassing "the whole record" in order to ascertain substantiality does not furnish a calculus of value by which a reviewing court can assess the evidence. Nor was it intended to negative the function of the Labor Board as one of those agencies presumably equipped or informed by experience to deal with a specialized

---

[21] S. Rep. No. 105, 80th Cong., 1st Sess. 26–27. The Committee did not explain what the ambiguity might be. . . . Senator Taft gave this explanation to the Senate of the meaning of the section: "In the first place, the evidence must be substantial; in the second place, it must still look substantial when viewed in the light of the entire record. That does not go so far as saying that a decision can be reversed on the weight of the evidence. It does not go quite so far as the power given to a circuit court of appeals to review a district-court decision, but it goes a great deal further than the present law, and gives the court greater opportunity to reverse an obviously unjust decision on the part of the National Labor Relations Board." 93 Cong. Rec. 3839.

field of knowledge, whose findings within that field carry the authority of an expertness which courts do not possess and therefore must respect. Nor does it mean that even as to matters not requiring expertise a court may displace the Board's choice between two fairly conflicting views, even though the court would justifiably have made a different choice had the matter been before it de novo. Congress has merely made it clear that a reviewing court is not barred from setting aside a Board decision when it cannot conscientiously find that the evidence supporting that decision is substantial, when viewed in the light that the record in its entirety furnishes, including the body of evidence opposed to the Board's view.

There remains, then, the question whether enactment of these two statutes has altered the scope of review other than to require that substantiality be determined in the light of all that the record relevantly presents. A formula for judicial review of administrative action may afford grounds for certitude but cannot assure certainty of application. Some scope for judicial discretion in applying the formula can be avoided only by falsifying the actual process of judging or by using the formula as an instrument of futile casuistry. It cannot be too often repeated that judges are not automata. The ultimate reliance for the fair operation of any standard is a judiciary of high competence and character and the constant play of an informed professional critique upon its work.

Since the precise way in which courts interfere with agency findings cannot be imprisoned within any form of words, new formulas attempting to rephrase the old are not likely to be more helpful than the old. There are no talismanic words that can avoid the process of judgment. The difficulty is that we cannot escape, in relation to this problem, the use of undefined defining terms.

Whatever changes were made by the Administrative Procedure and Taft-Hartley Acts are clearly within this area where precise definition is impossible. Retention of the familiar "substantial evidence" terminology indicates that no drastic reversal of attitude was intended.

But a standard leaving an unavoidable margin for individual judgment does not leave the judicial judgment at large even though the phrasing of the standard does not wholly fence it in. The legislative history of these Acts demonstrates a purpose to impose on courts a responsibility which has not always been recognized. Of course it is a statute and not a committee report which we are interpreting. But the fair interpretation of a statute is often "the art of proliferating a purpose," revealed more by the demonstrable forces that produced it than by its precise phrasing. The adoption in these statutes of the judicially-constructed "substantial evidence" test was a response to pressures for stricter and more uniform practice, not a reflection of approval of all existing practices. To find the change so elusive that it cannot be precisely defined does not mean it may be ignored. . . .

We conclude, therefore, that the Administrative Procedure Act and the Taft-Hartley Act direct that courts must now assume more responsibility for the reasonableness and fairness of Labor Board decisions than some courts have shown in the past. Reviewing courts must be influenced by a feeling that they are not to abdicate the conventional judicial function. Congress has imposed on them responsibility for assuring that the Board keeps within reasonable grounds. That responsibility is not less real because it is limited to enforcing the requirement that evidence appear substantial when viewed, on the record as a whole, by courts invested with the authority and enjoying the prestige of the Courts of Appeals. The Board's findings are entitled to respect; but they must nonetheless be set aside when the record before a Court of Appeals clearly precludes the Board's decision from being justified by a fair estimate of the worth of the testimony of witnesses or its informed judgment on matters within its special competence or both.

From this it follows that enactment of these statutes does not require every Court of Appeals to alter its practice. Some—perhaps a majority—have always applied the attitude reflected in this legislation. To explore whether a particular court should or should not alter its practice would only divert attention from the application of the standard now prescribed to a futile inquiry into the nature of the test formerly used by a particular court.

Our power to review the correctness of application of the present standard ought seldom to be called into action. Whether on the record as a whole there is substantial evidence to support agency findings is a question which Congress has placed in the keeping of the Courts of Appeals. This Court will intervene only in what ought to be the rare instance when the standard appears to have been misapprehended or grossly misapplied.

II.

. . . The decision of the Court of Appeals is assailed on two grounds. It is said (1) that the court erred in holding that it was barred from taking into account the report of the examiner on questions of fact insofar as that report was rejected by the Board, and (2) that the Board's order was not supported by substantial evidence on the record considered as a whole, even apart from the validity of the court's refusal to consider the rejected portions of the examiner's report.

The latter contention is easily met. . . . [I]t is clear from the court's opinion in this case that it in fact did consider the "record as a whole," and did not deem itself merely the judicial echo of the Board's conclusion. The testimony of the company's witnesses was inconsistent, and there was clear evidence that the complaining employee had been discharged by an officer who was at one time influenced against him because of his appearance at the Board hearing. On such a record we could not say that it would be error to grant enforcement. The first contention, however, raises serious questions to which we now turn.

III.

The Court of Appeals deemed itself bound by the Board's rejection of the examiner's findings because the court considered these findings not "as unassailable as a master's."[24] They are not. . . . The responsibility for decision . . . placed on the Board is wholly inconsistent with the notion that it has power to reverse an examiner's findings only when they are "clearly erroneous." Such a limitation would make so drastic a departure from prior administrative practice that explicitness would be required.

The Court of Appeals concluded from this premise "that, although the Board would be wrong in totally disregarding his findings, it is practically impossible for a court, upon review of those findings which the Board itself substitutes, to consider the Board's reversal as a factor in the court's own decision. This we say, because we cannot find any middle ground between doing that and treating such a reversal as error, whenever it would be such, if done by a judge to a master in equity." Much as we respect the logical acumen of the Chief Judge of the Court of Appeals, we do not find ourselves pinioned between the horns of his dilemma.

We are aware that to give the examiner's findings less finality than a master's and yet entitle them to consideration in striking the account, is to introduce another and an unruly factor into the judgmatical process of review. But we ought not to fashion an exclusionary rule merely to reduce the number of imponderables to be considered by reviewing courts.

The Taft-Hartley Act provides that "The findings of the Board with respect to questions of fact if supported by substantial evidence on the record considered as a whole shall be conclusive." Surely an examiner's report is as much a part of the record as the complaint or the testimony. According to the Administrative Procedure Act, "All decisions (including initial, recommended, or tentative decisions) shall become a part of the record. . . ." § 557(c). We found that this Act's provision for judicial review has the same meaning as that in the Taft-Hartley Act. The similarity of the two statutes in language and purpose also requires that the definition of "record" found in the Administrative Procedure Act be construed to be applicable as well to the term "record" as used in the Taft-Hartley Act.

It is therefore difficult to escape the conclusion that the plain language of the statutes directs a reviewing court to determine the substantiality of evidence on the record including the examiner's report. The conclusion is confirmed by the indications in the legislative history that enhancement of the status and function of the trial examiner was one of the important purposes of the movement for administrative reform.

This aim was set forth by the Attorney General's Committee on Administrative Procedure: "In general, the relationship upon appeal between the hearing commissioner and the agency ought to a considerable extent to be that of trial court to appellate court. Conclusions, interpretations, law, and policy should, of course, be open to full review. On the other hand, on matters which the hearing

---

[24] Rule 53(e)(2), Fed. Rules Civ. Proc., gives finality to the findings of a master unless they are clearly erroneous.

commissioner, having heard the evidence and seen the witnesses, is best qualified to decide, the agency should be reluctant to disturb his findings unless error is clearly shown."

Apparently it was the Committee's opinion that these recommendations should not be obligatory. For the bill which accompanied the Final Report required only that hearing officers make an initial decision which would become final in the absence of further agency action, and that agencies which differed on the facts from their examiners give reasons and record citations supporting their conclusion. This proposal was further moderated by the Administrative Procedure Act. It permits agencies to use examiners to record testimony but not to evaluate it, and contains the rather obscure provision that an agency which reviews an examiner's report has "all the powers which it would have in making the initial decision."

But this refusal to make mandatory the recommendations of the Attorney General's Committee should not be construed as a repudiation of them. Nothing in the statutes suggests that the Labor Board should not be influenced by the examiner's opportunity to observe the witnesses he hears and sees and the Board does not. Nothing suggests that reviewing courts should not give to the examiner's report such probative force as it intrinsically commands. . . .

We do not require that the examiner's findings be given more weight than in reason and in the light of judicial experience they deserve. The "substantial evidence" standard is not modified in any way when the Board and its examiner disagree. We intend only to recognize that evidence supporting a conclusion may be less substantial when an impartial, experienced examiner who has observed the witnesses and lived with the case has drawn conclusions different from the Board's than when he has reached the same conclusion. The findings of the examiner are to be considered along with the consistency and inherent probability of testimony. The significance of his report, of course, depends largely on the importance of credibility in the particular case. To give it this significance does not seem to us materially more difficult than to heed the other factors which in sum determine whether evidence is "substantial." . . .

We therefore remand the cause to the Court of Appeals. On reconsideration of the record it should accord the findings of the trial examiner the relevance that they reasonably command in answering the comprehensive question whether the evidence supporting the Board's order is substantial. But the court need not limit its reexamination of the case to the effect of that report on its decision. We leave it free to grant or deny enforcement as it thinks the principles expressed in this opinion dictate.

Judgment vacated and cause remanded.

■ JUSTICE BLACK and JUSTICE DOUGLAS concur with parts I and II of this opinion but as to part III agree with the opinion of the court below, 2 Cir., 179 F.2d 749, 753.

## NOTES ON THE SUBSTANTIAL EVIDENCE TEST

(1) ***Dominance of Universal Camera.*** Despite its age, Universal Camera is still *the* case on the substantial evidence test. As of July 9, 2022, Westlaw reported that it had been cited by other cases 11,114 times, in many different contexts. E.g., in just the month preceding the search: Jones v. Kijakazi, 2022 WL 2531809 (W.D. Okla. 2022) (regarding a Social Security disability hearing); Ellwood City Forge Co. v. United States, 582 F.Supp.3d 1259 (Ct. of Int. Trade 2022) (regarding a tariff determination by the Commerce Department); Calcutt v. FDIC, 37 F.4th 293 (6th Cir. 2022) (regarding removal of bank director).

(2) ***How Do You Create Usable Doctrine?*** "Weight of the evidence," "clearly erroneous," "substantial evidence"—can you tell the labels apart? If so, *how* do you tell them apart—by comparing them with one another, by relating them to a known institutional process (such as the deference given to a jury verdict), or by reformulating them? Justice Frankfurter has a serious jurisprudential problem. He believes that Congress has indeed said *something* in enacting the APA (and the Taft-Hartley Act): "It is fair to say that in all this Congress expressed a mood. And it expressed its mood not merely by oratory but by legislation." But he also believes that "the precise way in which courts interfere with agency findings cannot be imprisoned within any form of words." If you were a Court of Appeals judge (or her clerk), would you be confident you now understand your role?

(3) ***Here's Another Supreme Court Example.*** In Biestek v. Berryhill, 139 S.Ct. 1148 (2019), Biestek applied for disability benefits under the Social Security Act; his case was heard by an ALJ in an evidentiary hearing conducted per the specifications of the Act, which allowed for the admission of evidence that would not be admissible in court. The ALJ decided that Biestek should get benefits for the time he was disabled after age 50, but for earlier years he should not get them because there were a substantial number of jobs in the national economy he could have done. He sought review of that partial denial. The case did not turn on the question of how disabled he was, but rather on the question of how many jobs were available in the economy for someone in his condition. The ALJ's determination had been based on the testimony of a vocational expert, under contract with the agency, that there were, in the national economy, 240,000 jobs of one type Biestek could handle, and 120,000 of another type. These numbers were mostly based on surveys the expert had made in her private (that is, not under contract with the agency) consulting business. The expert had refused to produce the underlying data she relied on for her testimony.

JUSTICE KAGAN began her opinion for the Court as follows: "The Social Security Administration (SSA) provides benefits to individuals who cannot obtain work because of a physical or mental disability. To determine whether an applicant is entitled to benefits, the agency may hold an informal hearing examining (among other things) the kind and number of jobs available for someone with the applicant's disability and other characteristics. The agency's factual findings on that score are 'conclusive' in judicial review of the benefits decision so long as they are supported by 'substantial evidence.' 42 U.S.C. § 405(g).

"This case arises from the SSA's reliance on an expert's testimony about the availability of certain jobs in the economy. The expert largely based her opinion on private market-survey data. The question presented is whether her refusal to provide that data upon the applicant's request categorically precludes her testimony from counting as 'substantial evidence.' We hold it does not."

The Court articulated the substantial evidence test as follows: "The phrase 'substantial evidence' is a 'term of art' used throughout administrative law to describe how courts are to review agency factfinding. Under the substantial-evidence standard, a court looks to an existing administrative record and asks whether it contains 'sufficien[t] evidence' to support the agency's factual determinations. And whatever the meaning of 'substantial' in other contexts, the threshold for such evidentiary sufficiency is not high. Substantial evidence, this Court has said, is 'more than a mere scintilla. It means—and means only—'such relevant evidence as a reasonable mind might accept as adequate to support a conclusion.' Consolidated Edison Co. v. NLRB, 305 U.S. 197, 229 (1938)."

An expert's testimony as to what the data show, the Court continued, could be strong enough to meet that standard in many ways—based on some combination of her professional qualifications, her practical experience, her explanation of how she knows what she knows, and what methodology she used. But what about the possible adverse inference to be drawn from an expert's refusal to produce the actual underlying data? "We do not dispute that possibility," wrote the Court, "but the inference is far from always required." If "the ALJ views the expert and her testimony as otherwise trustworthy, and thinks she has good reason to keep her data private, her rejection of [the demand for the data] need not make a difference. So too when a court reviews the ALJ's decision under the deferential substantial-evidence standard."

The Court's holding was heavily dependent on its understanding that the question presented was whether there was a *categorical* rule devaluing the expert's opinion unless she presented the underlying data upon request. One court of appeals had announced such a flat rule; several had eschewed it. There were two dissents in Biestek, one by Justice Sotomayor and one by Justice Gorsuch joined by Justice Ginsburg. The thrust of the dissents was to the effect that the Court should have gone beyond just the categorical question it answered; it should also have asked: If sometimes an adverse inference can be drawn from the failure to produce the data, as Justice Kagan seemed to concede, then was this a proper case for doing so? In the dissenters' view, the expert's explanation for failing to produce the data was too thin to justify holding that the ALJ's conclusion, based on the expert's testimony, as to the availability of jobs in the economy, was supported by substantial evidence.

In an ordinary trial in federal court, expert witnesses, as a matter of procedural rules, have to produce the data they have considered in reaching their conclusions. Fed. R. Civ. P. 26(a)(2)(B). In Biestek, the combination of the relaxed procedural rules applicable to disability hearings and the standard the Court enunciated for "substantial evidence" made it possible for a claimant never to see that data and still lose. Is "substantial evidence" as understood by the Court too thin a test? Or is it right because this is, after all, a different kind of proceeding?

(4) ***The Role of the ALJ's Determinations.*** In its treatment of the examiner's (now ALJ's) report, the Universal Camera Court suggests a principle of allocation of responsibility as between examiner and agency. It places significant weight on the apoliticality of the examiner's place and function in the agency, a characteristic that lends "impartiality" to her judgments—impartiality is, if you like, what her participation contributes. The agency, on the other hand, has responsibility for the development and implementation of policy in light of its experience and statutory powers. This responsibility may lead the agency to develop policy-laden principles or presumptions for interpreting fact patterns that commonly arise in the course of its work. A simple issue of witness credibility, on the one hand, evokes the examiner's objectivity as well as her presence when the testimony was given. On the other hand, the idea that sudden and drastic employment actions are associated with anti-union animus is not based only in objective fact; policy-based commitments to the protection of union organizing activity contribute to it. And if such commitments are statutorily appropriate, one may see that such an inference is grounded in the agency's responsibilities, not the examiner's.

Judge Frank explained the distinction on remand in Universal Camera in the following terms (190 F.2d 429, 432 (2d Cir. 1951)): "An examiner's finding binds the Board only to the extent that it is a 'testimonial inference,' or 'primary inference,' i.e., an inference that a fact to which a witness orally testified is an actual fact because the witness so testified and because observation of the witness induces a belief in that testimony. The Board, however, is not bound by the examiner's 'secondary inferences,' or 'derivative inferences,' i.e., facts to which no witness orally testified but which the examiner inferred from facts orally testified by witnesses whom the examiner believed. The Board may reach its own 'secondary inferences' and we must abide by them unless they are irrational; in that way, the Board differs from a trial judge (in a jury-less case) who hears and sees the witnesses, for although we are usually bound by his 'testimonial inferences' we need not accept his 'secondary inferences' even if rational, but where other rational 'secondary inferences' are possible, we may substitute our own."

(5) ***Primary v. Secondary Inferences.*** PENASQUITOS VILLAGE, INC. v. NLRB, 565 F.2d 1074 (9th Cir. 1977) exemplifies both the distinction between "primary" and "secondary" inferences and the frequent difficulty of drawing such a line. Once again the question for the Board was whether a challenged discharge reflected employee misbehavior or employer anti-union animus. A supervisor testified that he had observed two discharged employees loafing on the job; one had a few months earlier been suspended for similar misconduct. After verifying that he had the authority to fire them,

he did so. The employees presented evidence of their status as union organizers and of alleged coercive interrogation. At least one of the employees was shown to have testified untruthfully in important respects, and the ALJ resolved "clear-cut questions of credibility" in favor of the employer. The case was also marked, however, by circumstances (abrupt employment discipline occurring very shortly after union organizing activity had come to light) that past Board decisions had identified as signs of anti-union animus. Disagreeing with its ALJ's assessment, the Board concluded that the discharges had been improper. Were the Board's derivative inferences, based on general experience and labor policy, enough to constitute "substantial evidence" on the record as a whole, when opposed to the ALJ's testimonial inferences that the employer's witnesses had been truth tellers, and the employees not, in describing the circumstances that led up to the discharges?

JUDGE WALLACE, for the majority, 565 F.2d at 1078–84: "Even when the record contains independent, credited evidence supportive of the Board's decision, a reviewing court will review more critically the Board's findings of fact if they are contrary to the administrative law judge's factual conclusions. . . . All aspects of the witness's demeanor . . . may convince the observing trial judge that the witness is testifying truthfully or falsely. These same very important factors, however, are entirely unavailable to a reader of the transcript, such as the Board or the Court of Appeals. But it should be noted that the administrative law judge's opportunity to observe the witnesses' demeanor does not, by itself, require deference with regard to his or her derivative inferences. Observation of demeanor makes weighty only the observer's testimonial inferences.

"Deference is accorded the Board's factual conclusions for a different reason—Board members are presumed to have broad experience and expertise in labor-management relations. . . . Further, it is the Board to which Congress has delegated administration of the Act. The Board, therefore, is viewed as particularly capable of drawing inferences from the facts of a labor dispute. Accordingly, it has been said that a Court of Appeals must abide by the Board's derivative inferences, if drawn from not discredited testimony, unless those inferences are 'irrational.' . . .

"[I]n this case, credibility played a dominant role. The administrative law judge's testimonial inferences reduce significantly the substantiality of the Board's contrary derivative inferences. Particularly, removing the Board's finding of anti-union animus based upon alleged unlawful threats and interrogations, leaves poorly substantiated the Board's other conclusion that the discharges were improperly motivated. Considering the record as a whole, we conclude that the Board's conclusion that Penasquitos committed unlawful labor practices is not supported by substantial evidence and must, therefore, be set aside."

JUDGE DUNIWAY's partial dissent expressed doubt, 565 F.2d at 1084–85: "The notion that special deference is owed to the determination of a trier of fact, . . . is deeply imbedded in the law. . . . As a generalization, it is unassailable. . . . [Yet] I venture to suggest that, as to every one of the factors that Judge Wallace lists, one trier of fact may take it to indicate that the witness is truthful and another may think that it shows that the witness is lying. . . . Every trial lawyer knows, and most trial judges will admit, that it is not unusual for an accomplished liar to fool a jury (or, even, heaven forbid, a trial judge) into believing him because his demeanor is so convincing. The expression of his countenance may be open and frank; he may sit squarely in the chair, with no squirming; he may show no nervousness; his answers to questions may be clear, concise and audible, and given without hesitation; his coloration may be normal—neither pale nor flushed. In short, he may appear to be the trial lawyer's ideal witness. He may also be a consummate liar."

(6) Finally, quite apart from evidence or "substantial evidence," Justice Frankfurter's opinion is an excellent example of what can be done to construe a statute using legislative history in both senses of the term: the documents that Congress produced, and the problems and controversies that produced the act. (See p. 202 above.) The opinion also seems to many readers to be verbose and overly stylized. It is one of the most famous decisions in this casebook. Do you like it?

## NOTES ON "ARBITRARY OR CAPRICIOUS" IN COMPARISON TO "SUBSTANTIAL EVIDENCE"

(1) ***How Should We Read the Various APA Provisions on Judicial Review?*** To understand the reach of the substantial evidence test, it is useful to spend a few moments looking at the structure of § 706(2) of the APA, reprinted just before the Universal Camera opinion. Six distinct standards of review are there articulated. For purposes of considering review of factual propositions, we can put to one side standards (B), relating to consistency with the Constitution, (C), relating to consistency with statutes, and (D), relating to procedure. Subsection (E) states the substantial evidence standard but by its reference to §§ 556 and 557 limits that standard to review of formal proceedings decided on a closed record.

Where, then, are the standards for reviewing the factual predicates for informal agency action, and especially for notice-and-comment rulemaking? The only other specific reference to "facts" is in standard (F), and that refers to a trial de novo. Could it be that the factual propositions underlying rules are to be tried de novo in court? Whether or not that is what the drafters had in mind, it is too awful to contemplate. Apart from the consummate inefficiency involved, review of rulemaking is typically assigned by statute to the courts of appeals, which of course lack the means for de novo fact finding. And so we turn to the catch-all standard (A), and even though its terms seem to refer to action "not in accordance with law," we say that the words "arbitrary" and "capricious" also cover informal agency action not sufficiently in accordance with the facts. Having massaged the statute this far, we then have this problem: what is the relationship of that "arbitrary or capricious" review of the facts to the substantial evidence test?

(2) ***Equivalence?*** In a much-cited opinion for the D.C. Circuit, ASSOCIATION OF DATA PROCESSING SERVICE ORGANIZATIONS, INC. V. BOARD OF GOVERNORS

OF THE FEDERAL RESERVE SYSTEM, 745 F.2d 677, 683–84 (1984)), then-JUDGE SCALIA wrote as follows:

"[I]n their application to the requirement of factual support the substantial evidence test and arbitrary or capricious test are one and the same. The former is only a specific application of the latter. . . . The 'scope of review' provisions of the APA, § 706(2), are cumulative. Thus, an agency action which is supported by the required substantial evidence may in another regard be 'arbitrary, capricious, an abuse of discretion, or otherwise not in accordance with law'—for example, because it is an abrupt and unexplained departure from agency precedent. Paragraph (A) of subsection 706(2)—the 'arbitrary or capricious' provision—is a catch-all, picking up administrative misconduct not covered by the other more specific paragraphs. Thus, in those situations where paragraph (E) has no application (informal rulemaking, for example, which is not governed by §§ 556 and 557 to which paragraph (E) refers), paragraph (A) takes up the slack, so to speak, enabling the courts to strike down, as arbitrary, agency action that is devoid of needed factual support. When the arbitrary or capricious standard is performing that function of assuring factual support, there is no *substantive* difference between what it requires and what would be required by the substantial evidence test, since it is impossible to conceive of a 'nonarbitrary' factual judgment supported only by evidence that is not substantial in the APA sense—i.e., not 'enough to justify, if the trial were to a jury, a refusal to direct a verdict when the conclusion sought to be drawn . . . is one of fact for the jury.' Illinois Central R.R. v. Norfolk & Western Ry., 385 U.S. 57, 66 (1966) (quoting NLRB v. Columbian Enameling & Stamping Co., 306 U.S. 292, 300 (1939)).

"We have noted on several occasions that the distinction between the substantial evidence test and the arbitrary or capricious test is 'largely semantic,' and have indeed described that view as 'the emerging consensus of the Court of Appeals.' . . . The distinctive function of paragraph (E)—what it achieves that paragraph (A) does not—is to require substantial evidence to be found *within the record of closed-record proceedings* to which it exclusively applies. . . ."

(3) ***An Adjudicatory Example.*** A recent case both follows Judge Scalia's lead and exemplifies its application: PHOENIX HERPETOLOGICAL SOCIETY, INC. V. U.S. FISH AND WILDLIFE SERVICE, 998 F.3d 999 (D.C. Cir. 2021). The Society applied for a permit to send four of its blue iguanas, an endangered species, to a zoo in Denmark that would establish a breeding program. One of the requirements for the permit was that it "would be likely to reduce the threat of extinction facing the species." 50 C.F.R. § 17.22. In an informal adjudication—not required to be "on the record" and therefore not subject to APA §§ 556 and 557—the Service denied the application. Since the four iguanas were siblings and the zoo possessed no others, their export would not help preserve the species; they were, said the Service, "unsuitable for breeding among themselves once exported." JUDGE SILBERMAN wrote:

"We also reject Appellant's argument that the agency's lack-of-diversity determination diverges from the record. The Society emphasizes that '[i]nbreeding occurs in all iguanids' in the wild. Therefore, Appellant contends, it was unreasonable to conclude that inbreeding would not affirmatively contribute to the species.

"That's a non-sequitur. Because something happens in the wild does not mean it is desirable for the species. Although a researcher for the Cayman Islands Government acknowledged natural inbreeding, he also explained why it was not 'too severe' in wild populations. Of course, 'too severe' implies that the researcher assumed the agency's basic premise: Breeding closely related iguanas is not a good idea. This common-sense determination passes muster, particularly in an informal adjudication. See Menkes v. Dep't of Homeland Sec., 486 F.3d 1307, 1314 (D.C. Cir. 2007) ('[I]t is common for the record to be spare' in informal adjudications.).

"Appellant similarly claims that this determination is 'unsupported by substantial evidence' and thus violates the Administrative Procedure Act. Appellant Br. 26 (citing 5 U.S.C. § 706(2)(E)). But the text of the APA applies 'substantial evidence' review only to formal proceedings, not informal adjudications. . . .

"To be sure, the arbitrary and capricious standard does not substantively differ from the substantial evidence test when 'performing [the] function of assuring factual support.' Ass'n of Data Processing Serv. Orgs., Inc. v. Bd. of Governors of Fed. Rsrv. Sys. , 745 F.2d 677, 683 (D.C. Cir. 1984). But the standards do differ as to the allowable origins of factual support and, as a consequence, how those facts are assessed. It is therefore permissible—as with the genetic diversity determination here—for common sense and predictive judgements to be attributed to the expertise of an agency in an informal proceeding, even if not explicitly backed by information in the record. See FCC v. Fox Television Stations, Inc., 556 U.S. 502 (2009) [p. 1160]. But formal adjudications (which more typically involve historical facts) require substantial evidence to be found based on the closed record before the agency. See Data Processing, 745 F.2d at 684. This subtle difference, as we have previously said, 'should not be underestimated.' Id."

(4) ***Informal Rulemaking?*** Judge Scalia said that the choice between "substantial evidence" and "arbitrary or capricious" is "largely semantic." (Yes, Scalia!) Perhaps the bigger factors that affect review of the basis for rules made after notice and comment are the kind of record, the kind of factual issues, and the kind of result that typify informal rulemaking. Consider what JUDGE MCGOWAN had to say in INDUSTRIAL UNION DEP'T, AFL-CIO V. HODGSON, 499 F.2d 467, 474–76 (D.C. Cir. 1974), when he faced the problem of reviewing an informal rulemaking per a statute that (varying from the APA) specified a "substantial evidence" standard of judicial review. (The case concerned an OSHA standard regulating occupational exposures to asbestos dust.)

"[I]n some degree the record approaches the form of one customarily conceived of as appropriate for substantial evidence review. In other respects, it does not. . . . From extensive and often conflicting evidence, the Secretary in this case made numerous factual determinations. With respect to some of those questions, the evidence was such that the task consisted primarily of evaluating the data and drawing conclusions from it. The court can review that data in the record and determine whether it reflects substantial support for the Secretary's findings. But some of the questions involved in the promulgation of these standards are on the frontiers of scientific knowledge, and consequently as to them insufficient data is presently available to make a fully informed factual determination. Decisionmaking must in that circumstance depend to a greater extent upon policy judgments and less upon purely factual analysis. Thus, in addition to currently unresolved factual issues, the formulation of standards involves choices that by their nature require basic policy determinations rather than resolution of factual controversies. . . . Regardless of the manner in which the task of judicial review is articulated, policy choices of this sort are not susceptible to the same type of verification or refutation by reference to the record as are some factual questions. Consequently, the court's approach must necessarily be different no matter how the standards of review are labeled. That does not mean that such decisions escape exacting scrutiny, for, as this court has stated in a similar context: 'This exercise need be no less searching and strict in its weighing of whether the agency has performed in accordance with the Congressional purposes, but, because it is addressed to different materials, it inevitably varies from the adjudicatory model. The paramount objective is to see whether the agency, given an essentially legislative task to perform, has carried it out in a manner calculated to negate the dangers of arbitrariness and irrationality in the formulation of rules for general application in the future.' Automotive Parts and Accessories Ass'n v. Boyd, 407 F.2d 330, 338 (D.C.Cir.1968). . . ."

Some courts, it should be said, have interpreted the unusual, but not unique, statutes that require notice-and-comment rulemaking to be reviewed on a "substantial evidence" basis, as requiring a "harder" judicial "look" at what the agency did. See, e.g., AFL-CIO v. OSHA, 965 F.2d 962 (11th Cir. 1992). However, the Supreme Court, in the State Farm case we will meet in the next Section, seems without discussion to take Scalia's "largely semantic" point of view.

(5) ***Factfinding by Experts.*** For rules that rest heavily on scientific or technical data, one possible strategy for determining the "facts" is to convene a panel of experts. Agencies sometimes do this because their governing statute tells them to—for example, the EPA must consult its permanent Clean Air Scientific Advisory Committee for some of its rulemaking. And agencies sometimes do this on their own, as a matter of good practice. In either case, if the agency's final rule departs from what the panel of experts recommends, or adopts a view held by only a minority of the panel, is the agency being "arbitrary or capricious"? After noting that the cases are unclear, ADRIAN VERMEULE, THE PARLIAMENT OF THE EXPERTS, 58 Duke L.J. 2231 (2009), suggests the right answer is to analogize this aspect of rulemaking to the problem of Universal Camera: "The APA's background obligation of reasoned fact-finding and decisionmaking is best understood to require that the agency either defer to the expert panel as to factual matters or else give a reason to think that it, rather than the expert panel, is in the best epistemic position to determine relevant facts. This was the implicit logic of Universal Camera, in which the Court said that reviewing judges

could look behind agency findings to consider whether the agency had given adequate reason for refusing to credit the contrary findings of a specialized hearing examiner. The Court's discussion, as amplified and clarified by Learned Hand and Jerome Frank in opinions on remand, suggests that examiners are usually best situated to determine witness credibility and demeanor, and that to reject their findings, the agency must give a reason that 'results from the [agency's] rational use of the [agency's] specialized knowledge.' . . . On this approach the key issue . . . involves comparative epistemic competence: whether the agency or expert is best positioned to determine relevant facts, where reviewing courts who lack direct knowledge themselves should place their epistemic bets, and more generally how fact-finding authority should be allocated between agencies and their expert advisors."

## b. Review of the Flow of Reasoning and Judgment



## MOTOR VEHICLE MANUFACTURERS ASS'N v. STATE FARM MUTUAL AUTOMOBILE INS. CO.

Supreme Court of the United States (1983).
463 U.S. 29.

■ JUSTICE WHITE delivered the opinion of the Court.

The development of the automobile gave Americans unprecedented freedom to travel, but exacted a high price for enhanced mobility. Since 1929, motor vehicles have been the leading cause of accidental deaths and injuries in the United States. In 1982, 46,300 Americans died in motor vehicle accidents and hundreds of thousands more were maimed and injured. While a consensus exists that the current loss of life on our highways is unacceptably high, improving safety does not admit to easy solution. In 1966, Congress decided that at least part of the answer lies in improving the design and safety features of the vehicle itself. But much of the technology for building safer cars was undeveloped or untested. Before changes in automobile design could be mandated, the effectiveness of these changes had to be studied, their costs examined, and public acceptance considered. This task called for considerable expertise and Congress responded by enacting the National Traffic and Motor Vehicle Safety Act of 1966, 15 U.S.C. § 1381. The Act, created for the purpose of "reduc[ing] traffic accidents and deaths and injuries to persons resulting from traffic accidents," § 1381, directs the Secretary of Transportation or his delegate to issue motor vehicle safety standards that "shall be practicable, shall meet the need for motor vehicle safety, and shall be stated in objective terms." § 1392(a). In issuing these standards, the Secretary is directed to consider "relevant available motor vehicle safety data," whether the proposed standard "is reasonable, practicable and appropriate" for the particular type of motor vehicle, and the "extent to which such standards will contribute to carrying out the purposes" of the Act. § 1392(f)(1), (3), (4).[3]

The Act also authorizes judicial review under [APA § 706] of all "orders establishing, amending, or revoking a Federal motor vehicle safety standard," § 1392(b). Under this authority, we review today whether NHTSA acted arbitrarily and capriciously in revoking the requirement in Motor Vehicle Safety Standard 208 that new motor vehicles produced after September 1982 be equipped with passive restraints to protect the safety of the occupants of the vehicle in the event of a collision. . . .

I

The regulation whose rescission is at issue bears a complex and convoluted history. Over the course of approximately 60 rulemaking notices, the requirement has been imposed, amended, rescinded, reimposed, and now rescinded again.

As originally issued by the Department of Transportation in 1967, Standard 208 simply required the installation of seatbelts in all automobiles. It soon became apparent that the level of seatbelt use was too low to reduce traffic injuries to an acceptable level. The Department therefore began consideration of "passive occupant restraint systems"—devices that do not depend for their effectiveness upon any action taken by the occupant except that necessary to operate the vehicle. Two types of automatic crash protection emerged: automatic seatbelts and airbags. The automatic seatbelt is a traditional safety belt, which when fastened to the interior of the door remains attached without impeding entry or exit from the vehicle, and deploys automatically without any action on the part of the passenger. The airbag is an inflatable device concealed in the dashboard and steering column. It automatically inflates when a

[3] The Secretary's general authority to promulgate safety standards under the Act has been delegated to the Administrator of the National Highway Traffic Safety Administration (NHTSA). 49 C.F.R. § 1.50(a). . . .

sensor indicates that deceleration forces from an accident have exceeded a preset minimum, then rapidly deflates to dissipate those forces. The life-saving potential of these devices was immediately recognized, and in 1977, after substantial on-the-road experience with both devices, it was estimated by NHTSA that passive restraints could prevent approximately 12,000 deaths and over 100,000 serious injuries annually.

In 1969, the Department formally proposed a standard requiring the installation of passive restraints . . . and in 1972, the agency amended the Standard to require full passive protection for all front seat occupants of vehicles manufactured after August 15, 1975. In the interim, vehicles built between August 1973 and August 1975 were to carry either passive restraints or lap and shoulder belts coupled with an "ignition interlock" that would prevent starting the vehicle if the belts were not connected. On review, the agency's decision to require passive restraints was found to be supported by "substantial evidence" and upheld. Chrysler Corp. v. Department of Transportation, 472 F.2d 659 (C.A.6 1972).[5]

In preparing for the upcoming model year, most car makers chose the "ignition interlock" option, a decision which was highly unpopular, and led Congress to amend the Act to prohibit a motor vehicle safety standard from requiring or permitting compliance by means of an ignition interlock or a continuous buzzer designed to indicate that safety belts were not in use. Motor Vehicle and Schoolbus Safety Amendments of 1974. The 1974 Amendments also provided that any safety standard that could be satisfied by a system other than seatbelts would have to be submitted to Congress where it could be vetoed by concurrent resolution of both Houses.

The effective date for mandatory passive restraint systems was extended for a year until August 31, 1976. But in June 1976, Secretary of Transportation William Coleman, Jr., initiated a new rulemaking on the issue. After hearing testimony and reviewing written comments, Coleman extended the optional alternatives indefinitely and suspended the passive restraint requirement.[1] Although he found passive restraints technologically and economically feasible, the Secretary based his decision on the expectation that there would be widespread public resistance to the new systems. He instead proposed a demonstration project involving up to 500,000 cars installed with passive restraints, in order to smooth the way for public acceptance of mandatory passive restraints at a later date.

Coleman's successor as Secretary of Transportation disagreed. Within months of assuming office, Secretary Brock Adams decided that

[5] The court did hold that the testing procedures required of passive belts did not satisfy the Safety Act's requirement that standards be "objective."

[1] [Ed.] In a step unprecedented except by his own similar actions on other matters (e.g., landing rights in the United States for supersonic airliners), Secretary Coleman personally presided over these hearings. Persons familiar with the hearings were impressed by his complete preparation and command of all material. The final decision was directly his own to a degree that is becoming rare even among leading judges. When one of the former editors of this casebook asked ex-Secretary Coleman how other high officials could possibly find the time to perform as he had, the response was: "Fewer cocktail parties."

the demonstration project was unnecessary. He issued a new mandatory passive restraint regulation [that] mandated the phasing in of passive restraints beginning with large cars in model year 1982 and extending to all cars by model year 1984. The two principal systems that would satisfy the Standard were airbags and passive belts; the choice of which system to install was left to the manufacturers. In Pacific Legal Foundation v. Department of Transportation, 593 F.2d 1338, cert. denied, 444 U.S. 830 (1979), the Court of Appeals upheld Modified Standard 208 as a rational, nonarbitrary regulation consistent with the agency's mandate under the Act. The Standard also survived scrutiny by Congress, which did not exercise its authority under the legislative veto provision of the 1974 Amendments.

Over the next several years, the automobile industry geared up to comply with Modified Standard 208. . . . In February 1981, however, Secretary of Transportation Andrew Lewis reopened the rulemaking due to changed economic circumstances and, in particular, the difficulties of the automobile industry. Two months later, the agency ordered a one-year delay in the application of the Standard to large cars, extending the deadline to September 1982 and at the same time, proposed the possible rescission of the entire Standard. After receiving written comments and holding public hearings, NHTSA issued a final rule (Notice 25) that rescinded the passive restraint requirement contained in Modified Standard 208.

II

In a statement explaining the rescission, NHTSA maintained that it was no longer able to find, as it had in 1977, that the automatic restraint requirement would produce significant safety benefits. . . . In 1977, the agency had assumed that airbags would be installed in 60% of all new cars and automatic seatbelts in 40%. By 1981 it became apparent that automobile manufacturers planned to install the automatic seatbelts in approximately 99% of the new cars. For this reason, the lifesaving potential of airbags would not be realized. Moreover, it now appeared that the overwhelming majority of passive belts planned to be installed by manufacturers could be detached easily and left that way permanently. Passive belts, once detached, then required "the same type of affirmative action that is the stumbling block to obtaining high usage levels of manual belts." For this reason, the agency concluded that there was no longer a basis for reliably predicting that the Standard would lead to any significant increased usage of restraints at all.

In view of the possibly minimal safety benefits, the automatic restraint requirement no longer was reasonable or practicable in the agency's view. The requirement would require approximately $1 billion to implement and the agency did not believe it would be reasonable to impose such substantial costs on manufacturers and consumers without more adequate assurance that sufficient safety benefits would accrue. In addition, NHTSA concluded that automatic restraints might have an adverse effect on the public's attitude toward safety. Given the high expense and limited benefits of detachable belts, NHTSA feared that many consumers would regard the Standard as an instance of ineffective regulation, adversely affecting the public's view of safety regulation and, in particular, "poisoning . . . popular sentiment toward efforts to improve occupant restraint systems in the future." . . .

[The D.C. Circuit Court of Appeals held the agency's action to be arbitrary and capricious.]

III

Unlike the Court of Appeals, we do not find the appropriate scope of judicial review to be the "most troublesome question" in [this case]. Both the [1966] Act and the 1974 Amendments concerning occupant crash protection standards indicate that motor vehicle safety standards are to be promulgated under the informal rulemaking procedures of § 553 of the Administrative Procedure Act. The agency's action in promulgating such standards therefore may be set aside if found to be "arbitrary, capricious, an abuse of discretion, or otherwise not in accordance with law." 5 U.S.C. § 706(2)(A). Citizens to Preserve Overton Park v. Volpe, 401 U.S. 402, 414 (1971). We believe that the rescission or modification of an occupant-protection standard is subject to the same test. Section 103(b) of the Act states that the procedural and judicial review provisions of the Administrative Procedure Act "shall apply to all orders establishing, amending, or revoking a Federal motor vehicle safety standard," and suggests no difference in the scope of judicial review depending upon the nature of the agency's action.

Petitioner Motor Vehicle Manufacturers Association (MVMA) disagrees, contending that the rescission of an agency rule should be judged by the same standard a court would use to judge an agency's refusal to promulgate a rule in the first place—a standard petitioner believes considerably narrower than the traditional arbitrary-and-capricious test. . . . We reject this view. The Motor Vehicle Safety Act expressly equates orders "revoking" and establishing safety standards; neither that Act nor the APA suggests that revocations are to be treated as refusals to promulgate standards. . . . Moreover, the revocation of an extant regulation is substantially different than a failure to act. Revocation constitutes a reversal of the agency's former views as to the proper course. A "settled course of behavior embodies the agency's informed judgment that, by pursuing that course, it will carry out the policies committed to it by Congress. There is, then, at least a presumption that those policies will be carried out best if the settled rule is adhered to." Atchison, T. & S.F.R. Co. v. Wichita Bd. of Trade, 412 U.S. 800, 807–808 (1973). Accordingly, an agency changing its course by rescinding a rule is obligated to supply a reasoned analysis for the change beyond that which may be required when an agency does not act in the first instance.

In so holding, we fully recognize that "[r]egulatory agencies do not establish rules of conduct to last forever," American Trucking Ass'ns., Inc. v. Atchison, T. & S.F.R. Co., 387 U.S. 397, 416 (1967), and that an agency must be given ample latitude to "adapt their rules and policies to the demands of changing circumstances." Permian Basin Area Rate Cases, 390 U.S. 747, 784 (1968). But the forces of change do not always or necessarily point in the direction of deregulation. In the abstract, there is no more reason to presume that changing circumstances require the rescission of prior action, instead of a revision in or even the extension of current regulation. If Congress established a presumption from which judicial review should start, that presumption—contrary to petitioners' views—is not *against* safety regulation, but *against* changes in current policy that are not justified by the rulemaking record. While the removal of a regulation may not entail the monetary expenditures and other costs of enacting a new standard, and, accordingly, it may be easier for an agency to justify a deregulatory action, the direction in which an agency chooses to move does not alter the standard of judicial review established by law.

The Department of Transportation . . . argues that under [the "arbitrary and capricious" standard], a reviewing court may not set aside an agency rule that is rational, based on consideration of the relevant factors, and within the scope of the authority delegated to the agency by the statute. We do not disagree with this formulation.[9] The scope of review under the "arbitrary and capricious" standard is narrow and a court is not to substitute its judgment for that of the agency. Nevertheless, the agency must examine the relevant data and articulate a satisfactory explanation for its action including a "rational connection between the facts found and the choice made." Burlington Truck Lines, Inc. v. United States, 371 U.S. 156, 168. . . . Normally, an agency rule would be arbitrary and capricious if the agency has relied on factors which Congress has not intended it to consider, entirely failed to consider an important aspect of the problem, offered an explanation for its decision that runs counter to the evidence before the agency, or is so implausible that it could not be ascribed to a difference in view or the product of agency expertise. The reviewing court should not attempt itself to make up for such deficiencies; we may not supply a reasoned basis for the agency's action that the agency itself has not given. SEC v. Chenery Corp., 332 U.S. 194, 196 (1947) [p. 258]. . . . For purposes of this case, it is also relevant that Congress required a record of the rulemaking proceedings to be compiled and submitted to a reviewing court, § 1394, and intended that agency findings under the Act would be supported by "substantial evidence on the record considered as a whole." . . .

IV

[The course of congressional consideration of this matter does not suggest application of any special standard of review.]

[9] The Department of Transportation suggests that the arbitrary-and-capricious standard requires no more than the minimum rationality a statute must bear in order to withstand analysis under the Due Process Clause. We do not view as equivalent the presumption of constitutionality afforded legislation drafted by Congress and the presumption of regularity afforded an agency in fulfilling its statutory mandate.

V

The ultimate question before us is whether NHTSA's rescission of the passive restraint requirement of Standard 208 was arbitrary and capricious. . . .

A

The first and most obvious reason for finding the rescission arbitrary and capricious is that NHTSA apparently gave no consideration whatever to modifying the Standard to require that airbag technology be utilized. Standard 208 sought to achieve automatic crash protection by requiring automobile manufacturers to install either of two passive restraint devices: airbags or automatic seatbelts. There was no suggestion in the long rulemaking process that led to Standard 208 that if only one of these options were feasible, no passive restraint standard should be promulgated. Indeed, the agency's original proposed standard contemplated the installation of inflatable restraints in all cars. Automatic belts were added [in 1971] as a means of complying with the Standard because they were believed to be as effective as airbags in achieving the goal of occupant crash protection. . . . At that time, the passive belt approved by the agency could not be detached. Only later, at a manufacturer's behest, did the agency approve of the detachability feature—and only after assurances that the feature would not compromise the safety benefits of the restraint. Although it was then foreseen that 60% of the new cars would contain airbags and 40% would have automatic seatbelts, the ratio between the two was not significant as long as the passive belt would also assure greater passenger safety.

The agency has now determined that the detachable automatic belts will not attain anticipated safety benefits because so many individuals will detach the mechanism. Even if this conclusion were acceptable in its entirety, . . . standing alone it would not justify any more than an amendment of Standard 208 to disallow compliance by means of the one technology which will not provide effective passenger protection. . . . Given the effectiveness ascribed to airbag technology by the agency, the mandate of the Act to achieve traffic safety would suggest that the logical response to the faults of detachable seatbelts would be to require the installation of airbags. At the very least this alternative way of achieving the objectives of the Act should have been addressed and adequate reasons given for its abandonment. But the agency not only did not require compliance through airbags, it also did not even consider the possibility in its 1981 rulemaking. Not one sentence of its rulemaking statement discusses the airbags-only option. . . . [W]hat we said in Burlington Truck Lines, Inc. v. United States, 371 U.S., at 167, is apropos here: "There are no findings and no analysis here to justify the choice made, no indication of the basis on which the [agency] exercised its expert discretion. We are not prepared to and the Administrative Procedure Act will not permit us to accept such . . . practice. . . . Expert discretion is the lifeblood of the administrative process, but 'unless we make the requirements for administrative action strict and demanding, *expertise*, the strength of modern government, can become a monster which rules with no practical limits on its discretion.' " We have frequently reiterated that an agency must cogently explain why it has exercised its discretion in a given manner, and we reaffirm this principle again today.

The automobile industry has opted for the passive belt over the airbag, but surely it is not enough that the regulated industry has eschewed a given safety device. For nearly a decade, the automobile industry waged the regulatory equivalent of war against the airbag and lost—the inflatable restraint was proven sufficiently effective. Now the automobile industry has decided to employ a seatbelt system which will not meet the safety objectives of Standard 208. This hardly constitutes cause to revoke the Standard itself. Indeed, the Act was necessary because the industry was not sufficiently responsive to safety concerns. . . .

[P]etitioners recite a number of difficulties that they believe would be posed by a mandatory airbag standard. These range from questions concerning the installation of airbags in small cars to that of adverse public reaction. But these are not the agency's reasons for rejecting a mandatory airbag standard. Not having discussed the possibility, the agency submitted no reasons at all. . . .

Petitioners also invoke our decision in Vermont Yankee Nuclear Power Corp. v. NRDC, 435 U.S. 519 (1978) [p. 312] as though it were a talisman under which any agency decision is by definition unimpeachable. Specifically, it is submitted that to require an agency to consider an airbags-only alternative is, in essence, to dictate to the agency the procedures it is to follow. Petitioners both misread Vermont Yankee and misconstrue the nature of the remand that is in order. In Vermont Yankee, we held that a court may not impose additional procedural requirements upon an agency. We do not require today any specific procedures which NHTSA must follow. Nor do we broadly require an agency to consider all policy alternatives in reaching decision. It is true that a rulemaking "cannot be found wanting simply because the agency failed to include every alternative device and thought conceivable by the mind of man . . . regardless of how uncommon or unknown that alternative may have been. . . ." 435 U.S., at 551. But the airbag is more than a policy alternative to the passive restraint Standard; it is a technological alternative within the ambit of the existing Standard. We hold only that given the judgment made in 1977 that airbags are an effective and cost-beneficial life-saving technology, the mandatory passive restraint rule may not be abandoned without any consideration whatsoever of an airbags-only requirement.

B

Although the issue is closer, we also find that the agency was too quick to dismiss the safety benefits of automatic seatbelts. NHTSA's critical finding was that, in light of the industry's plans to install readily detachable passive belts, it could not reliably predict "even a 5 percentage point increase as the minimum level of expected usage increase." The Court of Appeals rejected this finding because there is "not one iota" of evidence that Modified Standard 208 will fail to increase nationwide seatbelt use by at least 13 percentage points, the level of increased usage necessary for the Standard to justify its cost. Given the lack of probative evidence, the court held that "only a well-justified refusal to seek more evidence could render rescission non-arbitrary." 680 F.2d, at 232.

Petitioners object to this conclusion. In their view, "substantial uncertainty" that a regulation will accomplish its intended purpose is sufficient reason, without more, to rescind a regulation. We agree with petitioners that just as an agency reasonably may decline to issue a safety standard if it is uncertain about its efficacy, an agency may also revoke a standard on the basis of serious uncertainties if supported by the record and reasonably explained. Rescission of the passive restraint requirement would not be arbitrary and capricious simply because there was no evidence in direct support of the agency's conclusion. It is not infrequent that the available data does not settle a regulatory issue and the agency must then exercise its judgment in moving from the facts and probabilities on the record to a policy conclusion. Recognizing that policymaking in a complex society must account for uncertainty, however, does not imply that it is sufficient for an agency to merely recite the terms "substantial uncertainty" as a justification for its actions. . . . [T]he agency must explain the evidence which is available, and must offer a "rational connection between the facts found and the choice made." Burlington Truck Lines, Inc. v. United States, supra, 371 U.S. at 168. Generally, one aspect of that explanation would be a justification for rescinding the regulation before engaging in a search for further evidence. . . .

We start with the accepted ground that if used, seatbelts unquestionably would save many thousands of lives and would prevent tens of thousands of crippling injuries. Unlike recent regulatory decisions we have reviewed, the safety benefits of wearing seatbelts are not in doubt, and it is not challenged that were those benefits to accrue, the monetary costs of implementing the standard would be easily justified. We move next to the fact that there is no direct evidence in support of the agency's finding that detachable automatic belts cannot be predicted to yield a substantial increase in usage. The empirical evidence on the record, consisting of surveys of drivers of automobiles equipped with passive belts, reveals more than a doubling of the usage rate experienced with manual belts.[16] Much of the agency's rulemaking statement—and much of the controversy in this case—centers on the conclusions that should be drawn from these studies. The agency maintained that the doubling of seatbelt usage in these studies could not be extrapolated to

[16] Between 1975 and 1980, Volkswagen sold approximately 350,000 Rabbits equipped with detachable passive seatbelts that were guarded by an ignition interlock. General Motors sold 8,000 1978 and 1979 Chevettes with a similar system, but eliminated the ignition interlock on the 13,000 Chevettes sold in 1980. NHTSA found that belt usage in the Rabbits averaged 34% for manual belts and 84% for passive belts. Regulatory Impact Analysis (RIA) at IV-52, App. 108. For the 1978–1979 Chevettes, NHTSA calculated 34% usages for manual belts and 72% for passive belts. On 1980 Chevettes, the agency found these figures to be 31% for manual belts and 70% for passive belts.

an across-the-board mandatory standard because the passive seatbelts were guarded by ignition interlocks and purchasers of the tested cars are somewhat atypical.[17] Respondents insist these studies demonstrate that Modified Standard 208 will substantially increase seatbelt usage. We believe that it is within the agency's discretion to pass upon the generalizability of these field studies. This is precisely the type of issue which rests within the expertise of NHTSA, and upon which a reviewing court must be most hesitant to intrude.

But accepting the agency's view of the field tests on passive restraints indicates only that there is no reliable real-world experience that usage rates will substantially increase. To be sure, NHTSA opines that "it cannot reliably predict even a 5 percentage point increase as the minimum level of expected increased usage." But this and other statements that passive belts will not yield substantial increases in seatbelt usage apparently take no account of the critical difference between detachable automatic belts and current manual belts. A detached passive belt does require an affirmative act to reconnect it, but—unlike a manual seatbelt—the passive belt, once reattached, will continue to function automatically unless again disconnected. Thus, inertia—a factor which the agency's own studies have found significant in explaining the current low usage rates for seatbelts[18]—works in *favor* of, not *against*, use of the protective device. Since 20% to 50% of motorists currently wear seatbelts on some occasions, there would seem to be grounds to believe that seatbelt use by occasional users will be substantially increased by the detachable passive belts. Whether this is in fact the case is a matter for the agency to decide, but it must bring its expertise to bear on the question. . . .

The agency also failed to articulate a basis for not requiring nondetachable belts under Standard 208. It is argued that the concern of the agency with the easy detachability of the currently favored design would be readily solved by a continuous passive belt, which allows the occupant to "spool out" the belt and create the necessary slack for easy extrication from the vehicle. The agency did not separately consider the continuous belt option, but treated it together with the ignition interlock device in a category it titled "Option of Adoption of Use-Compelling Features." The agency was concerned that use-compelling devices would "complicate extrication of [an] occupant from his or her car." "[T]o require

---

[17] "NHTSA believes that the usage of automatic belts in Rabbits and Chevettes would have been substantially lower if the automatic belts in those cars were not equipped with a use-inducing device inhibiting detachment." Notice 25, 46 Fed. Reg. at 53422 (1981). [The "atypicality" was also that small car owners used seatbelts more than others did, and most owners with passive belts in these cars had voluntarily paid extra for them.]

[18] NHTSA commissioned a number of surveys of public attitudes in an effort to better understand why people were not using manual belts and to determine how they would react to passive restraints. The surveys reveal that while 20% to 40% of the public is opposed to wearing manual belts, the larger proportion of the population does not wear belts because they forgot or found manual belts inconvenient or bothersome. In another survey, 38% of the surveyed group responded that they would welcome automatic belts, and 25% would "tolerate" them. NHTSA did not comment upon these attitude surveys in its explanation accompanying the rescission of the passive restraint requirement.

that passive belts contain use-compelling features," the agency observed, "could be counterproductive [given] . . . widespread, latent and irrational fear in many members of the public that they could be trapped by the seatbelt after a crash." In addition, based on the experience with the ignition interlock, the agency feared that use-compelling features might trigger adverse public reaction.

By failing to analyze the continuous seatbelts in its own right, the agency has failed to offer the rational connection between facts and judgment required to pass muster under the arbitrary-and-capricious standard. . . . NHTSA did not suggest that the emergency release mechanisms used in nondetachable belts are any less effective for emergency egress than the buckle release system used in detachable belts. In 1978, when General Motors obtained the agency's approval to install a continuous passive belt, it assured the agency that nondetachable belts with spool releases were as safe as detachable belts with buckle releases. NHTSA was satisfied that this belt design assured easy extricability: "[t]he agency does not believe that the use of [such] release mechanisms will cause serious occupant egress problems. . . ." While the agency is entitled to change its view on the acceptability of continuous passive belts, it is obligated to explain its reasons for doing so.

The agency also failed to offer any explanation why a continuous passive belt would engender the same adverse public reaction as the ignition interlock, and, as the Court of Appeals concluded, "every indication in the record points the other way." We see no basis for equating the two devices: the continuous belt, unlike the ignition interlock, does not interfere with the operation of the vehicle. More importantly, it is the agency's responsibility, not this Court's, to explain its decision.

VI

"An agency's view of what is in the public interest may change, either with or without a change in circumstances. But an agency changing its course must supply a reasoned analysis. . . ." Greater Boston Television Corp. v. FCC, 444 F.2d 841, 852 (1970), cert. denied, 403 U.S. 923 (1971). We do not accept all of the reasoning of the Court of Appeals but we do conclude that the agency has failed to supply the requisite "reasoned analysis" in this case. Accordingly, we vacate the judgment of the Court of Appeals and remand the case to that court with directions to remand the matter to the NHTSA for further consideration consistent with this opinion.

■ JUSTICE REHNQUIST, with whom the CHIEF JUSTICE, JUSTICE POWELL, and JUSTICE O'CONNOR join, concurring in part and dissenting in part.

I join parts, I, II, III, IV, and V-A of the Court's opinion. In particular, I agree that, since the airbag and continuous spool automatic seatbelt were explicitly approved in the Standard the agency was rescinding, the agency should explain why it declined to leave those requirements intact. In this case, the agency gave no explanation at all. . . .

I do not believe, however, that NHTSA's view of detachable automatic seatbelts was arbitrary and capricious. . . . [T]he agency's explanation, while by no means a model, is adequate. The agency acknowledged that there would probably be some increase in belt usage, but concluded that the increase would be small and not worth the cost of mandatory detachable automatic belts. . . .

The agency's changed view of the standard seems to be related to the election of a new President of a different political party. It is readily apparent that the responsible members of one administration may consider public resistance and uncertainties to be more important than do their counterparts in a previous administration. A change in administration brought about by the people casting their votes is a perfectly reasonable basis for an executive agency's reappraisal of the costs and benefits of its programs and regulations. As long as the agency remains within the bounds established by Congress,* it is entitled to assess administrative records and evaluate priorities in light of the philosophy of the administration.

## NOTES ON THE STATE FARM TEST

(1) ***The Direct Consequences of State Farm.*** One year after State Farm, NHTSA issued a rule requiring passive restraints unless by April 1989 two-thirds of the nation's population were covered by state laws that both required use of seatbelts and met other criteria including educational efforts and enforcement. Most states enacted seat belt laws—but most of these laws did not satisfy the other criteria. Thus, a federal passive restraint requirement finally became effective in 1989. Most automakers chose to meet the requirement with airbags, and in 1991 Congress made the airbags requirement permanent, effective in 1996. Pub. L. No. 102–240, § 2508. For a fuller view of both the before and the after of the litigation, see Jerry L. Mashaw, The Story of Motor Vehicle Manufacturers Association of the U.S. v. State Farm Mutual Automobile Insurance Co.: Law, Science and Politics in the Administrative State, in Administrative Law Stories (Peter L. Strauss ed., 2006).

(2) ***Applying the Standard of Review.*** State Farm is the leading case on the meaning of "arbitrary and capricious" review; probably its most quoted line is Justice White's restatement of that standard: "Normally, an agency rule would be arbitrary and capricious if the agency has relied on factors which Congress has not intended it to consider, entirely failed to consider an important aspect of the problem, offered an explanation for its decision that runs counter to the evidence before the agency, or is so implausible that it could not be ascribed to a difference in view or the product of agency expertise." Looking at the Court's actual use of its test, it bears noting that all nine Justices agreed that it was arbitrary and capricious not to consider the alternatives of air bags only or of continuous spooling automatic

* Of course, a new administration may not refuse to enforce laws of which it does not approve, or to ignore statutory standards in carrying out its regulatory functions. But in this case, as the Court correctly concludes, Congress has not required the agency to require passive restraints.

seatbelts; but only five of the nine thought the same about the agency's rejection of detachable automatic seatbelts. Analytically, there would seem to be quite a gap between the two conclusions: recognizing the first two alternatives does not require more than the ability to read the preexisting regulation, whereas Justice White's discussion of detachable belts turns heavily on recognizing the importance of inertia in human behavior in the real world as developed in studies appearing in the record. All nine Justices agreed with Justice White's statement of the basic legal standard. So in practice the question would seem to be: how hard a look at what the agency has done (and said) should a court take? Considered as a "mood," to use Justice Frankfurter's term from Universal Camera, how does this case compare with that one?

(3) ***What "Factors" Must an Agency Consider?*** One aspect of the just-stated question lies in implementing the Court's statement that an agency has acted arbitrarily if it "has relied on factors which Congress has not intended it to consider [or has] entirely failed to consider an important aspect of the problem." Is the proper set of considerations determined by some notion of what makes for good policy, or is it determined by the framework of the legal regime? And if the latter, by the agency's organic statute or by the U.S. Code in general? Consider PENSION BENEFIT GUARANTY CORP. v. LTV CORP., 496 U.S. 633 (1990) (also noted at p. 585). PBGC is a federal agency established by the Employee Retirement Income Security Act of 1974 (ERISA) to insure certain pension benefits—somewhat like the FDIC's insuring of bank deposits. The lower court found that the agency, which often acts in situations in which bankruptcy and labor law are relevant, in this case had "focused inordinately on ERISA" and given too little consideration to those other areas of law.

But JUSTICE BLACKMUN for the Supreme Court said that the requirement imposed on PBGC by the lower court was irreconcilable with the statute's "plain language." He continued (496 U.S. at 646): "Even if Congress' directive to the PBGC had not been so clear, we are not entirely sure that the Court of Appeals' holding makes good sense as a general principle of administrative law. The PBGC points up problems that would arise if federal courts routinely were to require each agency to take explicit account of public policies that derive from federal statutes other than the agency's enabling act. To begin with, there are numerous federal statutes that could be said to embody countless policies. If agency action may be disturbed whenever a reviewing court is able to point to an arguably relevant statutory policy that was not explicitly considered, then a very large number of agency decisions might be open to judicial invalidation. The Court of Appeals' directive . . . is questionable for another reason as well. Because the PBGC can claim no expertise in the labor and bankruptcy areas, it may be ill-equipped to undertake the difficult task of discerning and applying the policies and goals of those fields."

Similarly, agencies are expected to defend their actions in terms of the policies made relevant by their governing statutes. See, e.g., Independent U.S. Tanker Committee v. Dole, 809 F.2d 847 (D.C. Cir. 1987) (the Secretary "is not free to substitute new goals in place of the statutory objectives without explaining how these actions are consistent with the authority under the statute.").

(4) ***Identifying Alternatives and the Rescission of DACA.*** What alternatives does the agency have to address? The approach taken in State Farm, looking at the alternatives implicit in the rules now being changed, was repeated in DEPARTMENT OF HOMELAND SECURITY V. REGENTS OF THE UNIVERSITY OF CALIFORNIA, 140 S.Ct. 1891 (2020). The case involved the attempt of the Trump Administration to repeal the Deferred Action for Childhood Arrivals (DACA) program the Obama Administration had put in place. The Court, per Chief Justice Roberts, delineated the program this way:

"In June 2012, the Secretary of Homeland Security issued a memorandum announcing an immigration relief program for 'certain young people who were brought to this country as children.' Known as DACA, the program applies to childhood arrivals who were under age 31 in 2012; have continuously resided here since 2007; are current students, have completed high school, or are honorably discharged veterans; have not been convicted of any serious crimes; and do not threaten national security or public safety. DHS concluded that individuals who meet these criteria warrant favorable treatment under the immigration laws because they 'lacked the intent to violate the law,' are 'productive' contributors to our society, and 'know only this country as home.'

" '[T]o prevent [these] low priority individuals from being removed from the United States,' the DACA Memorandum instructs Immigration and Customs Enforcement to 'exercise prosecutorial discretion[ ] on an individual basis . . . by deferring action for a period of two years, subject to renewal.' In addition, it directs U.S. Citizenship and Immigration Services (USCIS) to 'accept applications to determine whether these individuals qualify for work authorization during this period of deferred action,' as permitted under regulations long predating DACA's creation, see 8 CFR § 274a.12(c)(14) (2012) (permitting work authorization for deferred action recipients who establish 'economic necessity'); 46 Fed. Reg. 25080–25081 (1981) (similar). Pursuant to other regulations, deferred action recipients are considered 'lawfully present' for purposes of, and therefore eligible to receive, Social Security and Medicare benefits. See 8 CFR § 1.3(a)(4)(vi); 42 CFR § 417.422(h) (2012)."

Subsequently, the Obama Administration created a related program known as DAPA providing similar deferred action for parents whose children were U.S. citizens or lawful permanent residents. The DAPA program was challenged in court on both procedural and substantive grounds; the district court issued a preliminary injunction, the Fifth Circuit affirmed (see p. 1529), and the Supreme Court in turn affirmed the Fifth Circuit by an equally divided vote without opinion. Ultimately, after the election of President Trump, the DAPA program was rescinded by the new administration. Attorney General Jeff Sessions then sent a letter to acting Secretary of Homeland Security Elaine Duke saying that DHS should also rescind the DACA program. He said that the DACA program had the same legal defects as had been adjudicated in the DAPA litigation, and should be wound-down in an orderly process. Acting Secretary Duke acted on his advice.

Was her rescission arbitrary and capricious? The Court said:

"Whether DACA is illegal is, of course, a legal determination, and therefore a question for the Attorney General. But deciding how best to address a finding of illegality moving forward can involve important policy choices, especially when the finding concerns a program with the breadth of DACA. Those policy choices are for DHS.

"Acting Secretary Duke plainly exercised such discretionary authority in winding down the program. Among other things, she specified that those DACA recipients whose benefits were set to expire within six months were eligible for two-year renewals.

"But Duke did not appear to appreciate the full scope of her discretion, which picked up where the Attorney General's legal reasoning left off. The Attorney General concluded that 'the DACA policy has the same legal . . . defects that the courts recognized as to DAPA.' So, to understand those defects, we look to the Fifth Circuit, the highest court to offer a reasoned opinion on the legality of DAPA. That court described the 'core' issue before it as the 'Secretary's decision' to grant 'eligibility for benefits'—including work authorization, Social Security, and Medicare—to unauthorized aliens on 'a class-wide basis.' And the Court ultimately held that DAPA was 'manifestly contrary to the INA' precisely because it 'would make 4.3 million otherwise removable aliens' eligible for work authorization and public benefits.

"But there is more to DAPA (and DACA) than such benefits. The defining feature of deferred action is the decision to defer removal (and to notify the affected alien of that decision). And the Fifth Circuit was careful to distinguish that forbearance component from eligibility for benefits. As it explained, the 'challenged portion of DAPA's deferred-action program' was the decision to make DAPA recipients eligible for benefits. The other '[p]art of DAPA,' the court noted, 'involve[d] the Secretary's decision—at least temporarily—not to enforce the immigration laws as to a class of what he deem[ed] to be low-priority illegal aliens.' Borrowing from this Court's prior description of deferred action, the Fifth Circuit observed that 'the states do not challenge the Secretary's decision to "decline to institute proceedings, terminate proceedings, or decline to execute a final order of deportation." ' And the Fifth Circuit underscored that nothing in its decision or the preliminary injunction 'requires the Secretary to remove any alien or to alter' the Secretary's class-based 'enforcement priorities.' In other words, the Secretary's forbearance authority was unimpaired.

"Acting Secretary Duke recognized that the Fifth Circuit's holding addressed the benefits associated with DAPA. In her memorandum she explained that the Fifth Circuit concluded that DAPA 'conflicted with the discretion authorized by Congress' because the INA 'flatly does not permit the reclassification of millions of illegal aliens as lawfully present and thereby make them newly eligible for a host of federal and state benefits, including work authorization.' Duke did not characterize the opinion as one about forbearance.

"In short, the Attorney General neither addressed the forbearance policy at the heart of DACA nor compelled DHS to abandon that policy. Thus, removing benefits eligibility while continuing forbearance remained squarely within the discretion of Acting Secretary Duke, who was responsible for '[e]stablishing national immigration enforcement policies and priorities.' 6 U.S.C. § 202(5). But Duke's memo offers no reason for terminating forbearance. She instead treated the Attorney General's conclusion regarding the illegality of benefits as sufficient to rescind both benefits and forbearance, without explanation.

"That reasoning repeated the error we identified in one of our leading modern administrative law cases, Motor Vehicle Manufacturers Association of the United States, Inc. v. State Farm Mutual Automobile Insurance Co. . . . While the factual setting is different here, the error is the same. Even if it is illegal for DHS to extend work authorization and other benefits to DACA recipients, that conclusion supported only 'disallow[ing]' benefits. It did 'not cast doubt' on the legality of forbearance or upon DHS's original reasons for extending forbearance to childhood arrivals. Thus, given DHS's earlier judgment that forbearance is 'especially justified' for 'productive young people' who were brought here as children and 'know only this country as home,' the DACA Memorandum could not be rescinded in full 'without any consideration whatsoever' of a forbearance-only policy, State Farm, 463 U.S. at 51."

"The appropriate recourse," concluded the Court, was "to remand to DHS so that it may consider the problem anew." Justices Thomas, Alito and Kavanaugh dissented—with Justice Thomas embracing the broad view that "[t]he decision to rescind an unlawful agency action is *per se* lawful. No additional policy justifications or considerations are necessary." Justice Alito, joining Justice Thomas's opinion, added this thought: "Anyone interested in the role that the Federal Judiciary now plays in our constitutional system should consider what has happened in these cases. Early in the term of the current President, his administration took the controversial step of attempting to rescind the Deferred Action for Childhood Arrivals (DACA) program. Shortly thereafter, one of the nearly 700 federal district court judges blocked this rescission, and since then, this issue has been mired in litigation. In November 2018, the Solicitor General filed petitions for certiorari, and today, the Court still does not resolve the question of DACA's rescission. Instead, it tells the Department of Homeland Security to go back and try again. What this means is that the Federal Judiciary, without holding that DACA cannot be rescinded, has prevented that from occurring during an entire Presidential term. Our constitutional system is not supposed to work that way. . . . DACA presents a delicate political issue, but that is not our business."

(5) ***How Much Explanation Is Enough?*** In FEDERAL ENERGY REGULATORY COMMISSION V. ELECTRIC POWER SUPPLY ASSOCIATION, 577 U.S. 260, 291–95 (2016), the Supreme Court reviewed a rule issued by FERC that required the operators of wholesale electricity markets to pay the same amount to

"demand response providers" for conserving electricity as they paid to generators for making it. ("Demand response providers" were large companies, or aggregations of multiple users, which at times of high demand for electricity promised to lower their usage by a set amount at a set time, thus helping to balance supply and demand by reducing demand, just as electricity generators who upped their output helped to create balance by increasing supply.) Most of the opinion dealt with, and approved, FERC's claiming jurisdiction to issue the rule in the first place. JUSTICE KAGAN continued:

"These cases present a second, narrower question: Is FERC's decision to compensate demand response providers at LMP [the locational marginal price]—the same price paid to generators—arbitrary and capricious? Recall here the basic issue. Wholesale market operators pay a single price—LMP—for all successful bids to supply electricity at a given time and place. The Rule orders operators to pay the identical price for a successful bid to conserve electricity so long as that bid can satisfy a 'net benefits test' meaning that it is sure to bring down costs for wholesale purchasers. In mandating that payment, FERC rejected an alternative proposal under which demand response providers would receive LMP minus G (LMP–G), where G is the retail rate for electricity. According to EPSA and others favoring that approach, demand response providers get a windfall—a kind of 'double-payment'—unless market operators subtract the savings associated with conserving electricity from the ordinary compensation level. EPSA now claims that FERC failed to adequately justify its choice of LMP rather than LMP–G.

"In reviewing that decision, we may not substitute our own judgment for that of the Commission. The 'scope of review under the "arbitrary and capricious" standard is narrow.' Motor Vehicle Mfrs. Assn. of United States, Inc. v. State Farm Mut. Automobile Ins. Co., 463 U.S. 29, 43 (1983). A court is not to ask whether a regulatory decision is the best one possible or even whether it is better than the alternatives. Rather, the court must uphold a rule if the agency has 'examine[d] the relevant [considerations] and articulate[d] a satisfactory explanation for its action[,] including a rational connection between the facts found and the choice made.' And nowhere is that more true than in a technical area like electricity rate design: '[W]e afford great deference to the Commission in its rate decisions.'

"Here, the Commission gave a detailed explanation of its choice of LMP. Relying on an eminent regulatory economist's views, FERC chiefly reasoned that demand response bids should get the same compensation as generators' bids because both provide the same value to a wholesale market. FERC noted that a market operator needs to constantly balance supply and demand, and that either kind of bid can perform that service cost-effectively—i.e., in a way that lowers costs for wholesale purchasers. A compensation system, FERC concluded, therefore should place the two kinds of bids 'on a competitive par.' With both supply and demand response available on equal terms, the operator will select whichever bids, of whichever kind, provide the needed electricity at the lowest possible cost.

"That rationale received added support from FERC's adoption of the net benefits test. The Commission realized during its rulemaking that in some circumstances a demand response bid—despite reducing the wholesale rate—does *not* provide the same value as generation. . . . Thus, under the Commission's approach, a demand response provider will receive the same compensation as a generator only when it is in fact providing the same service to the wholesale market.

"The Commission responded at length to EPSA's contrary view that paying LMP, even in that situation, will overcompensate demand response providers because they are also 'effectively receiv[ing] "G," the retail rate that they do not need to pay.' FERC explained that compensation ordinarily reflects only the value of the service an entity provides—not the costs it incurs, or benefits it obtains, in the process. So when a generator presents a bid, 'the Commission does not inquire into the costs or benefits of production.' Different power plants have different cost structures. And, indeed, some plants receive tax credits and similar incentive payments for their activities, while others do not. But the Commission had long since decided that such matters are irrelevant: Paying LMP to all generators—although some then walk away with more profit and some with less—'encourages more efficient supply and demand decisions.' And the Commission could see no economic reason to treat demand response providers any differently. Like generators, they too experience a range of benefits and costs—both the benefits of not paying for electricity and the costs of not using it at a certain time. But, FERC again concluded, that is immaterial: To increase competition and optimally balance supply and demand, market operators should compensate demand response providers, like generators, based on their contribution to the wholesale system.

"Moreover, FERC found, paying LMP will help demand response providers overcome certain barriers to participation in the wholesale market. Commenters had detailed significant start-up expenses associated with demand response, including the cost of installing necessary metering technology and energy management systems. The Commission agreed that such factors inhibit potential demand responders from competing with generators in the wholesale markets. It concluded that rewarding demand response at LMP (which is, in any event, the price reflecting its value to the market) will encourage that competition and, in turn, bring down wholesale prices.

"Finally, the Commission noted that determining the 'G' in the formula LMP—G is easier proposed than accomplished. Retail rates vary across and even within States, and change over time as well. Accordingly, FERC concluded, requiring market operators to incorporate G into their prices, 'even though perhaps feasible,' would 'create practical difficulties.' Better, then, not to impose that administrative burden.

"All of that together is enough. The Commission, not this or any other court, regulates electricity rates. The disputed question here involves both technical understanding and policy judgment. The Commission addressed that issue seriously and carefully, providing reasons in support of its position and responding to the principal alternative advanced. In upholding that action, we do not discount the cogency of EPSA's arguments in favor of LMP—G. Nor do we say that in opting for LMP instead, FERC made the better call. It is not our job to render that judgment, on which reasonable minds can differ. Our important but limited role is to ensure that the Commission engaged in reasoned decisionmaking—that it weighed competing views, selected a compensation formula with adequate support in the record, and intelligibly explained the reasons for making that choice. FERC satisfied that standard."

(6) ***Must There Be Data?*** If an agency rule is "arbitrary and capricious" if it "entirely failed to consider an important aspect of the problem," as State Farm says, does the agency have to generate data about that "important aspect"? In FEDERAL COMMUNICATIONS COMMISSION V. PROMETHEUS RADIO PROJECT, 141 S.Ct. 1150 (2021), the Supreme Court was satisfied even though the FCC had not done so. At issue were changes to various rules limiting the number of radio stations, television stations, and newspapers any single entity could own—rules that had been adopted before the explosion of information on the internet, to prevent local monopolization of viewpoints. Particularly at issue were the effects of various of these rules on minority and female ownership in the communications industry. The Commission's own data regarding the effect of previous changes in ownership rules in these regards were spotty, and despite asking commenters to supply it with information, it received little data on minority ownership and no data on female ownership. Yet the FCC concluded that relaxation of its prior rules was unlikely to harm minority or female media ownership.

The Third Circuit had said, in the opinion below: "We are not persuaded. It is true that '[t]he APA imposes no general obligation on agencies to produce empirical evidence,' only to 'justify its rule with a reasoned explanation.' . . . Here, the Commission has not relied on its general expertise, and, outside of the modifications to the newspaper/broadcast cross-ownership rule, it does not rely on support from commenters. It has not offered any theoretical models or analysis of what the likely effect of consolidation on ownership diversity would be. Instead it has confined its reasoning to an insubstantial statistical analysis of unreliable data—and, again, has not offered even that much as to the effect of its rules on female ownership." 939 F.3d 567 (2019).

But JUSTICE KAVANAUGH, writing for a unanimous Supreme Court, had a different view: "In short, the FCC's analysis was reasonable and reasonably explained for purposes of the APA's deferential arbitrary-and-capricious standard. The FCC considered the record evidence on competition, localism, viewpoint diversity, and minority and female ownership, and reasonably concluded that the three ownership rules no longer serve the public interest. The FCC reasoned that the historical justifications for those ownership rules no longer apply in today's media market, and that permitting efficient combinations among radio stations, television stations, and newspapers would benefit consumers. The Commission further explained that its best estimate, based on the sparse record evidence, was that repealing or modifying the three rules at issue here was not likely to harm minority and female ownership. The APA requires no more.

"To be sure, in assessing the effects on minority and female ownership, the FCC did not have perfect empirical or statistical data. Far from it. But that is not unusual in day-to-day agency decisionmaking within the Executive Branch. The APA imposes no general obligation on agencies to conduct or commission their own empirical or statistical studies. Fox Television (p. 1160); Vermont Yankee (p. 312). And nothing in the Telecommunications Act (or any other statute) requires the FCC to conduct its own empirical or statistical studies before exercising its discretion under Section 202(h). Here, the FCC repeatedly asked commenters to submit empirical or statistical studies on the relationship between the ownership rules and minority and female ownership. Despite those requests, no commenter produced such evidence indicating that changing the rules was likely to harm minority and female ownership. In the absence of additional data from commenters, the FCC made a reasonable predictive judgment based on the evidence it had. State Farm.

"In light of the sparse record on minority and female ownership and the FCC's findings with respect to competition, localism, and viewpoint diversity, we cannot say that the agency's decision to repeal or modify the ownership rules fell outside the zone of reasonableness for purposes of the APA." 141 S.Ct. at 1160.

## NOTES ON THE BACKGROUND TO STATE FARM

(1) ***Overton Park Doctrine.*** Justice White's analysis in State Farm builds on the important, and still cited, case CITIZENS TO PRESERVE OVERTON PARK, INC. V. VOLPE, 401 U.S. 402 (1971). There, the Secretary of Transportation approved the building of an interstate highway through a public park in Memphis; the relevant statute said that park land could not be used for this purpose unless there was "no feasible and prudent alternative to the use of such land." In what was treated as, in APA terms, an informal adjudication, the Secretary approved the highway but made no contemporaneous statement as to why he considered the statute satisfied. Instead, the Department defended the decision in court based on "affidavits, prepared specifically for this litigation, which indicated that the Secretary had made the decision and that the decision was supportable."

The Supreme Court, deciding the case in a very short period of time, overturned the Secretary's decision. Partly this was a matter of statutory construction. It will always be cheaper to build through a public park, wrote JUSTICE MARSHALL for the Court, because the public already owns the land; thus "the very existence of the statutes indicates that protection of parkland was to be given paramount importance. . . . The Secretary cannot approve the destruction of parkland unless he finds that alternative routes present unique problems." But the case is famous for its various wider statements about the course of judicial review:

(a) First, as to the meaning of APA "arbitrary or capricious" review, 401 U.S. at 415–16:

"[T]he generally applicable standards of § 706 require the reviewing court to engage in a substantial inquiry. Certainly, the Secretary's decision is entitled to a presumption of regularity. But that presumption is not to shield his action from a thorough, probing, in-depth review.

"The court is first required to decide whether the Secretary acted within the scope of his authority. This determination naturally begins with a delineation of the scope of the Secretary's authority and discretion. As has been shown, Congress has specified only a small range of choices that the Secretary can make. Also involved in this initial inquiry is a determination of whether on the facts the Secretary's decision can reasonably be said to be within that range. The reviewing court must consider whether the Secretary properly construed his authority to approve the use of parkland as limited to situations where there are no feasible alternative routes or where feasible alternative routes involve uniquely difficult problems. And the reviewing court must be able to find that the Secretary could have reasonably believed that in this case there are no feasible alternatives or that alternatives do involve unique problems.

"Scrutiny of the facts does not end, however, with the determination that the Secretary has acted within the scope of his statutory authority. Section 706(2)(A) requires a finding that the actual choice made was not 'arbitrary, capricious, an abuse of discretion, or otherwise not in accordance with law.' To make this finding the court must consider whether the decision was based on a consideration of the relevant factors and whether there has been a clear error of judgment. . . . Although this inquiry into the facts is to be searching and careful, the ultimate standard of review is a narrow one. The court is not empowered to substitute its judgment for that of the agency."

Is this the same as the test State Farm later enunciated, albeit in different words? Or not?

(b) Second, as to the materials to which the standard of review should be applied, 401 U.S. at 419–20:

"Moreover, there is an administrative record that allows the full, prompt review of the Secretary's action that is sought without additional delay which would result from having a remand to the Secretary. That administrative record is not, however, before us. The lower courts based their review on the litigation affidavits that were presented. These affidavits were merely 'post hoc' rationalizations, Burlington Truck Lines v. United States, 371 U.S. 156, 168–169 (1962), which have traditionally been found to be an inadequate basis for review. SEC v. Chenery Corp., 318 U.S. 80, 87 (1943) [p. 255]. And they clearly do not constitute the 'whole record' compiled by the agency: the basis for review required by § 706 of the Administrative Procedure Act.

"Thus it is necessary to remand this case to the District Court for plenary review of the Secretary's decision. That review is to be based on the full administrative record that was before the Secretary at the time he made his decision."

The APA does not require an "informal" proceeding to be "on the record"; but yet it does say that judicial review per § 706 shall be based on the "whole record." How do these provisions go together? Does Overton Park interpret the APA rightly?

(c) Third, what should be done if the "administrative record" does not provide the information needed to determine "whether the decision was based on a consideration of the relevant factors and whether there has been a clear error of judgment"? 401 U.S. at 420:

"[S]ince the bare record may not disclose the factors that were considered or the Secretary's construction of the evidence it may be necessary for the District Court to require some explanation in order to determine if the Secretary acted within the scope of his authority and if the Secretary's action was justifiable under the applicable standard.

"The court may require the administrative officials who participated in the decision to give testimony explaining their action. Of course, such inquiry into the mental processes of administrative decisionmakers is usually to be avoided. United States v. Morgan, 313 U.S. 409, 422 (1941) [p. 553]. And where there are administrative findings that were made at the same time as the decision, as was the case in Morgan, there must be a strong showing of bad faith or improper behavior before such inquiry may be made. But here there are no such formal findings and it may be that the only way there can be effective judicial review is by examining the decisionmakers themselves."

The immediate result of this language was a 27-day trial held by the district court on remand, including affidavits from the Secretary and testimony of subordinates. Shortly thereafter, this language was distinguished by the Court in CAMP V. PITTS, 411 U.S. 138 (1973), which concerned the denial by the Comptroller of the Currency of an application to organize a new national bank; the proceeding was "informal" but the applicant was sent a brief letter of explanation. The Court wrote, 411 U.S. at 142–43:

"The appropriate standard for review was, accordingly, whether the Comptroller's adjudication was arbitrary, capricious, an abuse of discretion, or otherwise not in accordance with law, as specified in 5 U.S.C. § 706(2)(A). In applying that standard, the focal point for judicial review should be the administrative record already in existence, not some new record made initially in the reviewing court. . . .

"If, as the Court of Appeals held and as the Comptroller does not now contest, there was such failure to explain administrative action as to frustrate effective judicial review, the remedy was not to hold a de novo hearing but, as contemplated by Overton Park, to obtain from the agency, either through affidavits or testimony, such additional explanation of the reasons for the agency decision as may prove necessary. We add a caveat, however. Unlike Overton Park, in the present case there was contemporaneous explanation of the agency decision. The explanation may have been curt, but it surely indicated the determinative reason for the final action taken: the finding that a new bank was an uneconomic venture in light of the banking needs and the banking services already available in the surrounding community. The validity of the Comptroller's action must, therefore, stand or fall on the propriety of that finding, judged, of course, by the appropriate standard of review. If that finding is not sustainable on the administrative record made, then the Comptroller's decision must be vacated and the matter remanded to him for further consideration. See SEC v. Chenery Corp., 318 U.S. 80 (1943)."

Few agencies have difficulty choosing between the 27-day trial on remand in Overton Park itself and the alternative of making at least a basic administrative record as suggested in the preceding paragraph!

(d) Finally, Overton Park also spoke famously about the narrowness of any exceptions to the presumption that administrative action is subject to judicial review. See Chapter IX (p. 1519).

(2) ***Larger Context of Overton Park.*** PETER L. STRAUSS, in CITIZENS TO PRESERVE OVERTON PARK—RACE-INFLECTED BELOW ITS SURFACE, Notice & Comment Blog (July 16, 2020),[2] displayed a picture showing a diverse crowd of people in Overton Park, and wrote as follows:

"This is not a picture one would have seen during the battles over Memphis's Overton Park. When planning for Interstate 40's route through Memphis began in the 50's, one could have found Blacks in parts of that park only on Tuesdays; the park was for Whites only on other days. An urban oasis near downtown, largely surrounded by White residential areas, this large park held a zoo, golf course, and attractive forests and grounds—a municipal treasure not far from the commercial area. It was bisected by a bus road that was proposed as the route for I-40 to pass through Memphis. Circumferential roads were also planned. Just as I-40 in Nashville would disrupt an established Black community, the circumferential roads were routed through largely Black residential and commercial areas. But constructing the route through Memphis and Overton Park would disrupt White residential areas as well as this—at the time—essentially White urban playground.

"My interest piqued by watching the case unfold in the Solicitor General's office while I was an attorney there, I spent a week in Memphis in the early 90's exploring newspaper accounts and other materials, and also interviewed the plaintiff's attorneys then and again about [a] decade later, when preparing a second essay on the case. I learned then of a lengthy political struggle between the route's proponents—potential users valuing a straight shot through the city to the new bridge to be built over the Mississippi, and downtown commercial interests already aware how a circumferential [route] might draw shoppers away from downtown—and its opponents, those (White) citizens whose homes would be taken by the route or affected by its noise and fumes. The Court had never learned of those struggles or of the impact of the circumferential route's impact on Black neighborhoods—or of the rich history of political struggle that had resulted in many ameliorating revisions to the initial plans, but not rerouting. It was a case rushed through the Court—it granted certiorari in early December, 1970, in response to a motion to stay construction that had already reached the Park's boundary, and it heard the case argued just a month later; thus,

[2] https://www.yalejreg.com/nc/citizens-to-preserve-overton-park-race-inflected-below-its-surface-by-peter-l-strauss/.

the government had to write its brief in the two weeks spanning Christmas and New Year's Day, not an auspicious length of time—or occasion—to learn background.

"The day that the Memphis City Council met the federal highway administrator at Memphis airport to finally approve the route through Overton Park was the day of Martin Luther King's assassination. Neither that meeting nor that awful coincidence found mention in the case papers. Justice Thurgood Marshall wrote for the Court, a perhaps ironic twist, and the main thrust of his opinion (although administrative law teachers predominantly use its paragraphs addressing the standard of judicial review, an issue essentially unmentioned in the briefs) was that politics could not be trusted to protect park values as the governing statute commanded. But he did not know the political history or the routing revisions that had been made in response, and was not made aware of the racial inflection of Memphis routing decisions—or even that the square mile of new parkland Memphis had bought with the money it received for the 26 acres of Overton Park that had been taken for the highway route generally served White residential areas. In later stages of the political struggles over the route, the (failing) Nashville efforts to preserve the Black community I-40 would bisect there may have become known; the one open attention to racial issues I recall was an argument against an alternative route being proposed for traversing Memphis, that it would impact an established and stable mixed-race community.

"Today, Overton Park remains an urban treasure, and one now freely used by its whole community, as the picture heading this entry reflects. That is a fortunate outcome; but the hardy band of citizens who sought to protect it were not a mixed multitude, and considering the whole of the routing decisions about I-40 in Memphis (as in Nashville), race did not live far below its surface."

(3) ***"Hard Look" Review.*** As the Court in State Farm says, the petitioners claimed that requiring NHTSA to consider the airbags-only possibility would collide with Vermont Yankee's prohibition on the judicial creation of additional procedural burdens in rulemaking. (Vermont Yankee, decided five years before State Farm, is set out at p. 312.) This apparent confusion of substance and procedure can be more easily understood in light of the flow of judicial review decisions in the decade or so before the principal case.

In the oft-cited case (indeed, cited in State Farm itself) GREATER BOSTON TELEVISION CORP. V. FCC, 444 F.2d 841 (D.C. Cir. 1970), JUDGE LEVENTHAL said that "[t]he function of the court is to assure that the agency has given reasoned consideration to all the material facts and issues." In spelling out this idea, he explained, 444 F.2d at 851: "Its supervisory function calls on the court to intervene not merely in case of procedural inadequacies, or bypassing of the mandate in the legislative charter, but more broadly if the court becomes aware, especially from a combination of danger signals, that the agency has not really taken a 'hard look' at the salient problems, and has not genuinely engaged in reasoned decision-making. If the agency has not shirked this fundamental task, however, the court exercises restraint and affirms the agency's action even though the court would on its own account have made different findings or adopted different standards."

In the succeeding years, this set of ideas was taken up by other judges, in the D.C. Circuit and elsewhere, to frame their process of review, especially of informal rulemaking. "As originally articulated," Judge Wald wrote in 1980, "the words 'hard look' described the agency's responsibility and not the court's. However, the phrase subsequently evolved to connote the rigorous standard of judicial review applied to increasingly utilized informal rulemaking proceedings or to other decisions made upon less than a full trial-type record." National Lime Assoc. v. EPA, 627 F.2d 416, 451 n. 126 (D.C. Cir. 1980).

As can be seen from Judge Leventhal's statement, the "hard look" approach did not necessarily distinguish possible procedural requirements from possible substantive ones, and terms like "quasi-procedural, quasi-substantive" were sometimes used to describe various items. Different judges gave different emphases, some more to the procedural side, some to the substantive. The structure of the problem can be seen in the Nova Scotia Food Products case, decided in 1977 (p. 340). There, one of Judge Gurfein's objections was that the agency should have explained why it rejected a salient alternative urged on it in the comment process. Was this requirement to address alternatives based on APA § 553(c), requiring the agency to "incorporate in the rules adopted a concise general statement of their basis and purpose"? Was it based on APA § 706(2)(A), telling the court to "set aside agency action . . . found to be . . . arbitrary, capricious . . . or otherwise not in accordance with law"? Or was it based on neither of these and justified only if the reviewing courts had the power to create a common law of judicial review? Judge Gurfein, writing before Vermont Yankee was decided, did not have to be explicit.

What the State Farm petitioners hoped was that the Supreme Court would conclude that the "hard look" techniques were a result of courts of appeals' asserting a common-law-like power to revise agency processes. Then Vermont Yankee—which emphatically denied the existence of such a power—would be the death of "hard look." (Insofar as the Overton Park case also had "hard look" elements, petitioners also hoped the Court would narrow Overton Park in light of Vermont Yankee.) Correspondingly, the refusal of the Court to adopt petitioners' point of view has led later courts and commentators to speak of the State Farm test as embodying "hard look" review even though Justice White does not use the phrase.

(4) ***Pacific States Box & Basket.*** As stated in footnote 9 of the opinion, the government also attempted to equate "arbitrary and capricious" review of agency action with the relaxed "rationality" review given to ordinary legislation. This claim can be traced back to PACIFIC STATES BOX & BASKET CO. v. WHITE, 296 U.S. 176 (1935). That case concerned a rule of the Oregon Division of Plant Industry fixing official standards for containers used to package raspberries and strawberries—standards that could not be met by the fruit baskets petitioner made. The circumstances suggested, but no finding stated, that the Oregon board might have found that use of a single container type (among the 34 available) would enhance consumer protection

against short measures. Acknowledging that no such finding would be required of a legislature, petitioner urged that findings were constitutionally required for the actions of administrators wielding delegated powers. A unanimous court, speaking through Justice Brandeis, found that the contention was "without support in authority or reason, and rests upon misconception. Every exertion of the police power, either by the legislature or by an administrative body, is an exercise of delegated power. . . . Where the regulation is within the scope of authority legally delegated, the presumption of the existence of facts justifying its specific exercise attaches alike to statutes . . . and to orders of administrative bodies. . . . [T]he statute did not require special findings; doubtless because the regulation authorized was general legislation, not an administrative order in the nature of a judgment directed against an individual concern." 296 U.S. at 185–86. But that was then and this was now; the State Farm court thought it sufficient to reply laconically: "We do not view as equivalent the presumption of constitutionality afforded legislation drafted by Congress and the presumption of regularity afforded an agency in fulfilling its statutory mandate."

## NOTES ON THE WISDOM (OR NOT) OF SERIOUS ARBITRARY AND CAPRICIOUS REVIEW

(1) ***Is It a Good Idea for Courts to Review Rather Intensively the Course of Reasoning of an Agency? Yes:*** "It is a great tonic," wrote WILLIAM PEDERSEN, former Deputy General Counsel of the EPA, "to discover that even if a regulation can be slipped or wrestled through various layers of internal or external review [inside the bureaucracy] without significant change, the final and most prestigious reviewing forum of all—a circuit court of appeals—will inquire into the minute details of methodology, data sufficiency and test procedure and will send the regulations back if these are lacking. The effect of such judicial opinions within the agency reaches beyond those who were concerned with the specific regulations reviewed. They serve as a precedent for future rulewriters and give those who care about well-documented and well-reasoned decisionmaking a lever with which to move those who do not." FORMAL RECORDS AND INFORMAL RULEMAKING, 85 Yale L.J. 38, 60 (1975).

***And No:*** JACOB GERSEN & ADRIAN VERMEULE, THIN RATIONALITY REVIEW, 114 MICH. L. REV. 1355 (2016): "Under the Administrative Procedure Act, courts review and set aside agency action that is 'arbitrary [and] capricious.' In a common formulation of rationality review, courts must either take a 'hard look' at the rationality of agency decisionmaking, or at least ensure that agencies themselves have taken a hard look. We will propose a much less demanding and intrusive interpretation of rationality review—a thin version. Under a robust range of conditions, rational agencies have good reason to decide in a manner that is inaccurate, nonrational, or arbitrary. Although this claim is seemingly paradoxical or internally inconsistent, it simply rests on an appreciation of the limits of reason, especially in administrative policymaking. Agency decisionmaking is nonideal decisionmaking; what would be rational under ideal conditions is rarely a relevant question for agencies. Rather, agencies make decisions under constraints of scarce time, information, and resources. Those constraints imply that agencies will frequently have excellent reasons to depart from idealized first-order conceptions of administrative rationality."

(2) ***The "Ossification" Issue.*** SIDNEY SHAPIRO & RICHARD MURPHY, EIGHT THINGS AMERICANS CAN'T FIGURE OUT ABOUT CONTROLLING ADMINISTRATIVE POWER, 61 Admin. L. Rev. 5, 13–15 (2009): "According to critics of the current judicial review regime, undue ossification of rulemaking flows largely from the analytical demands that courts have placed on agencies in an effort to make the APA's skeletal requirements on notice-and-comment meaningful. This judicial effort has both procedural and substantive aspects. . . .

"[A]gencies must respond to any comment that they think a court might, during post hoc review, find significant, and their responses must be sufficiently detailed and persuasive to survive open-ended substantive review by a set of generalist judges who may have no particularly relevant technical expertise. This combination creates a minefield given that administrative records, at least for controversial or difficult rules, are chock-full of contestable arguments and evidence. Threading this minefield requires agencies to offer justifications for their rules that are, often enough, interminable and detailed rather than 'concise' and 'general' as the APA contemplated. As a result, it can take many years for an agency to create a significant, controversial rule via notice-and-comment."

(3) ***A Skeptical View.*** MARK SEIDENFELD, DEMYSTIFYING DEOSSIFICATION: RETHINKING RECENT PROPOSALS TO MODIFY JUDICIAL REVIEW OF NOTICE AND COMMENT RULEMAKING, 75 Tex. L. Rev. 483, 500–02 (1997): "I am skeptical . . . whether a more deferential attitude toward agency decisionmaking will relieve the problems created by hard look review without forfeiting the benefits that flow from such review. . . . [R]aising the level of deference to agency rulemaking may not reduce an agency's incentives to engage in excessive data collection and analysis. Simply making review more 'agency friendly' will not tell the agency how to perform its analyses in a manner sufficient to pass judicial review. Moreover, without delving into the details of a rulemaking record and questioning the agency's rationale in light of data and arguments submitted by challengers of the rule, most judges lack the expertise with the substantive areas of agency regulation to know whether the agency, in adopting the rule, has reached a reasonable decision. Hence, even under a more deferential standard of review, courts will have to consult the record and ensure that it is consistent with the agency's reasoning. This in turn sends a message to the agency that its chances of success on review increase if it collects additional data and performs more analysis. Thus, significant incentives remain for an agency to overtax its scarce regulatory resources.

"[Finally], easing of judicial review may have a detrimental impact on the agency deliberative process. For example, courts could dramatically reduce the uncertainty created by judicial review simply by eliminating meaningful review; they could affirm any rule that was not wholly irrational. That would still leave congressional and presidential review to ensure against unwise agency rulemaking. But both congressional and presidential review increase the propensity for agency rules to benefit groups with narrow interests. By demanding that agencies publicly justify their rules, however, judicial review can discourage the adoption and interpretation of rules preferred by special interest groups. Increasing the likelihood that a rule will be upheld by relaxing the requirements that an agency explain its decision to a court might, by the same token, increase the proportion of rules driven by pressure from special interest groups or an agency agenda that is at odds with the general public's desire for regulation."

(4) ***A Political Valence?*** NICHOLAS BAGLEY, THE PROCEDURE FETISH, 118 Mich. L. Rev. 345, 363–64 (2019): "In short, proceduralism drains agency resources, introduces delay, and thwarts agency action. To that extent, it puts a thumb on the scale in favor of the status quo; by itself, that's enough to give administrative law a libertarian, anti-statist cast. Nonetheless, the ideological valence of administrative law remains at least arguably ambiguous. Proceduralism might impede a progressive agenda that depends on active government, but what if it equally thwarts a libertarian agenda to pare back the existing state? If that were the case, administrative law's apparent asymmetry would be an artifact of whichever baseline (more government, less government) you happened to prefer. Which is to say, it wouldn't be an asymmetry at all. . . . For any number of reasons, however, administrative proceduralism makes it easier to tear down the administrative state than to build it up. On net and over time, proceduralism favors a libertarian agenda over a progressive one. . . .

"Because the world is changing at a breakneck clip, a bias toward inaction means that the state will respond too slowly as new risks present themselves and existing risks come into focus. Internet commerce, drones, social media, cellular phones, algorithmic trading, driverless cars, and artificial intelligence barely existed two decades ago; today, they are part (or are becoming part) of the fabric of our lives. We only dimly understand how to cope with the attendant risks to health, welfare, and privacy associated with these technological changes. At the same time, older risks have become more prominent, whether because of evolving scientific understanding (climate change, the waning efficacy of antibiotics), shifting patterns of industrial organization (the rise of monopoly power across multiple industries), or crises that exposed fragility in complex systems (the financial crisis, Hurricane Maria). An administrative apparatus that cannot adapt to a changing world threatens to become a relic of a bygone era. It also becomes easier to dismantle. Regulations adopted in a very different environment will come to look ill fitting and unresponsive to modern problems. Justifying their abandonment or relaxation is straightforward: the world really has changed. Adopting a new rule and defending it against concerted attack, however, remains enormously difficult."

(5) ***Impact on the Agency?*** Finally, consider the possible impact judicial review may be having on agency structure itself. PAUL R. VERKUIL, THE WAIT IS OVER: CHEVRON AS THE STEALTH VERMONT YANKEE II, 75 Geo. Wash. L. Rev. 921, 928–29 (2007): "For me, even more troubling . . . are the consequences to the agency reasoning process that result from preparing

impossibly long statements of basis and purpose. . . . The use of consultants to prepare rules for review has become a common practice. But it is not costless. . . . The use of private contractors is not just an unintended consequence of demands by reviewing courts, of course; it is caused by personnel ceilings, which limit agency staff, and by the larger trend toward the privatization of government functions. Still, by forcing more work on the agencies, hard look review may, ironically, hurt rulemaking rationality as much as it helps. The essential purpose of hard-look review is to require agency officials to be thoughtful and engaged. Reviewing judges expect the hard look to be taken by agency officials themselves. If, however, the effect is to farm out the analysis and drafting functions, then this intellectual exercise is not happening. Rationality review by the agency may be fast becoming a misnomer."

A recent study conducted for ACUS set out to test the effects of contracting in the rulemaking process by interviewing and surveying many of the players across a variety of agencies. BRIDGET C.E. DOOLING & RACHEL AUGUSTINE POTTER, RULEMAKING BY CONTRACT, 74 Admin. L. Rev. (forthcoming). The results were, not surprisingly, mixed. Regarding the danger that government officials would lose control of regulatory policy, the authors had this to say:

"Despite the lack of official written policies, there is *widespread but incomplete* awareness of the existence of an inherently governmental function line with respect to rulemaking. The awareness is *widespread* in that many agency officials noted that contractors should not be involved in making policy decisions. One agency official described what contractors can do as 'everything up to pushing the big red policymaking button,' while another indicated that contractors should be 'kept out of the policy piece'. . .

"Awareness of an inherently governmental function line is *incomplete* in that few respondents were able to explicitly name the terms 'inherently governmental function' . . . and many could not articulate a clear sense of where the 'policy line' at their agency fell for rulemaking. . . .

"Among respondents who were more familiar with the inherently governmental function principle, several expressed confusion with how to apply the principle to rulemaking in practice. For example, one former agency official stated that it would be appropriate for contractors to work on writing a proposed rule if all policy decisions had been made. However, this person also noted that, in practice, policy decisions were rarely settled at the outset. Rather, in this person's nearly 30 years of rule writing experience, with the exception of one rule, the official could not think of another case where the program did not make changes based on writers' questions and feedback. On a different point, one expert noted that using contractors in rulemaking 'can get really muddy' because of the technical nature of rulemaking. For instance, if an agency contracted out for a highly technical portion of the rulemaking, it might be difficult to have enough subject matter expertise in-house to evaluate the work and make sure it was consistent with the agency's policy decisions."

## NOTES ON COST-BENEFIT ANALYSIS AS A POSSIBLE ELEMENT OF "ARBITRARY AND CAPRICIOUS" REVIEW

(1) ***Cost-Benefit Analysis.*** While "gut instincts" or "common sense" might do for many of life's decisions, State Farm says it will not do when an agency makes a rule; there we expect to find a serious analysis of the situation, overtly expressed. But there is more than one way to do a "serious analysis." In light of the increasing importance of cost-benefit analysis in the intellectual mores of the society as a whole, we might ask whether cost-benefit analysis is also part of what judicial review requires of an agency announcing a new rule.

Cost-benefit analysis of this type can be very roughly described as entailing (1) consideration of all the consequences of adopting a rule—both the costs it will directly or indirectly impose and the benefits it will directly or indirectly generate; (2) conversion of each of those costs and benefits into a quantified, commensurable measure, almost always money; and (3) summation of those sums across the entire relevant domain, generally done without regard to how the costs or the benefits are distributed. A rule is then seen as cost-benefit justified if the benefits outweigh the costs. Of course, there are many technicalities, and some judgment calls, involved in doing such an analysis to a professional standard—for example, in deciding how many dollars saving a "statistical life" is worth.

(2) ***OIRA and Cost-Benefit Analysis.*** Cost-benefit analysis is already commonplace in the federal rulemaking process. You will have already seen it if you have studied the OIRA process for executive review of agency rulemaking (p. 455). But the OIRA process does not apply to all agencies, and in any case it is specifically limited so as not to "affect any otherwise available judicial review of agency action." E.O. 12866, § 10. So the questions for the judges remain open: Should they require a cost/benefit analysis? If so, how intensely should they review its adequacy? And in any case, what is their authority for so acting?

(3) ***Cost-Benefit Analysis and the Courts.*** "Normally," says State Farm, "an agency rule would be arbitrary and capricious if the agency has relied on factors which Congress has not intended it to consider [or] entirely failed to consider an important aspect of the problem." At first blush, this standard would seem to throw the matter of cost-benefit analysis back to what Congress intended when it wrote the particular substantive statute in question. And so, it would seem, the Supreme Court thought in 2001 in Whitman v. American Trucking Ass'ns, Inc. (p. 848 above). Whitman held, as a matter of statutory construction per Justice Scalia, that the specifically applicable provisions of the Clean Air Act did not permit taking costs into account in setting National Ambient Air Quality Standards.

What statutory language does trigger cost-benefit analysis? A statute passed in 1996 required the SEC in various rulemakings to consider whether the proposed rule would "promote efficiency, competition, and capital formation." A series of cases in the D.C. Circuit in subsequent years interpreted this language to require consideration of economic effects generally, went on to formulate that requirement in the terms of a technical cost/benefit analysis, and then found flaws in the SEC's various justifications for its rules. The rules at issue were then struck down as "arbitrary and capricious" per State Farm. The most well-known such case was Business Roundtable v. SEC, 647 F.3d 1144 (D.C. Cir. 2011), as to which the leading treatise on administrative law remarked: "The SEC had devoted many pages of analysis to the economic effects of the rule. It is hard to imagine how much more consideration it would take to convince the court that the agency had adequately considered the economic effects of the rule." Kristin E. Hickman & Richard J. Pierce, Jr., Administrative Law Treatise 5th ed., 2017 Cumulative Supp. 158.

In 2015, the Clean Air Act and costs were again before the Supreme Court in MICHIGAN V. EPA, 576 U.S. 743 (2015). Again JUSTICE SCALIA wrote the majority opinion. The issue, he said, was that the "Clean Air Act directs the Environmental Protection Agency to regulate emissions . . . from power plants if the Agency finds regulation 'appropriate and necessary.' We must decide whether it was reasonable for EPA to refuse to consider cost when making this finding." Id. at 747. Held: it was not reasonable. While in some sense this is again a matter of interpreting particular statutory language, the Court this time wrote broadly about a broad (and not uncommon) statutory term, id. at 752–53:

"Congress instructed EPA to add power plants to the [particular regulatory] program if (but only if) the Agency finds regulation 'appropriate and necessary.' § 7412(n)(1)(A). One does not need to open up a dictionary in order to realize the capaciousness of this phrase. In particular, 'appropriate' is 'the classic broad and all-encompassing term that naturally and traditionally includes consideration of all the relevant factors.' Although this term leaves agencies with flexibility, an agency may not 'entirely fai[l] to consider an important aspect of the problem' when deciding whether regulation is appropriate. State Farm.

"Read naturally in the present context, the phrase 'appropriate and necessary' requires at least some attention to cost. One would not say that it is even rational, never mind 'appropriate' " to impose billions of dollars in economic costs in return for a few dollars in health or environmental benefits. . . . No regulation is 'appropriate' if it does significantly more harm than good.

"There are undoubtedly settings in which the phrase 'appropriate and necessary' does not encompass cost. But this is not one of them. Section 7412(n)(1)(A) directs EPA to determine whether '*regulation* is appropriate and necessary.' (Emphasis added.) Agencies have long treated cost as a centrally relevant factor when deciding whether to regulate. Consideration of cost reflects the understanding that reasonable regulation ordinarily requires paying attention to the advantages *and* the disadvantages of agency decisions. . . . Against the backdrop of this established administrative practice, it is unreasonable to read an instruction to an administrative agency to determine whether 'regulation is appropriate and necessary' as an invitation to ignore cost."

At the same time, id. at 759: "Our reasoning so far establishes that it was unreasonable for EPA to read § 7412(n)(1)(A) to mean that cost is irrelevant to the initial decision to regulate power plants. The Agency must consider cost—including, most importantly, cost of compliance—before deciding whether regulation is appropriate and necessary. We need not and do not hold that the law unambiguously required the Agency, when making this preliminary estimate, to conduct a formal cost-benefit analysis in which each advantage and disadvantage is assigned a monetary value. It will be up to the Agency to decide (as always, within the limits of reasonable interpretation) how to account for cost."

(JUSTICE KAGAN's dissent did not disagree with the principles involved, see id. at 769; it argued instead that the agency, considering the whole regulatory process in question and not just the initial decision to regulate power plants, had taken costs into account in substantial ways.)

(4) ***Where Does This Leave Matters?*** Here are three "takes" on that question:

(a) ADRIAN VERMEULE, LAW'S ABNEGATION 177–78 (2016): "Proponents of quantified cost-benefit analysis point to seemingly broad language in the opinion [in Michigan v. EPA], as when the majority opined that '[o]ne would not say that it is even rational, never mind "appropriate," to impose billions of dollars in economic costs in return for a few dollars in health or environmental benefits.' On the broadest possible reading, this could mean that it is arbitrary and capricious for agencies not to conduct quantified and monetized cost-benefit analysis where possible. Yet this is an interpretation the Court took pains to disavow later in the opinion. Justice Scalia went out of his way to emphasize that while rationality may require 'paying attention to the advantages and the disadvantages of agency decisions,' that is not the same as requiring quantification of the advantages and disadvantages. . . . Michigan v. EPA is clearly alert to the distinction between the colloquial, informal sense of 'costs and benefits,' on the one hand, and formalized, quantified and monetized cost-benefit analysis, on the other. The decision is principally an interpretive holding, about the meaning of the phrase 'appropriate and necessary' in a particular section of the Clean Air Act. But insofar as it addresses issues of rationality review in passing, it stands only for the unobjectionable proposition that rationality requires consideration of both 'the advantages and the disadvantages of agency decisions.' "

(b) CASS SUNSTEIN, COST-BENEFIT ANALYSIS AND ARBITRARINESS REVIEW, 41 Harv. Envtl. L. Rev. 1, 15–16 (2017): "Surely it would not be sufficient for an agency simply to announce that it has simply 'considered' costs and decided to proceed. It would have to explain that decision in some way. The Court seemed to be suggesting that such an explanation could be given even if the agency does not produce 'a formal cost-benefit analysis.'

"Even with this qualification, Michigan v. EPA has the great virtue of identifying the fatal weakness in a tempting objection to any effort to question an agency's failure to engage with costs and benefits. The objection would be that courts lack the authority to impose procedural requirements beyond those in the APA, and cost-benefit analysis is a procedural requirement, not found in the APA, which thus cannot be imposed by courts. . . .

"[T]he problem with the objection is that under the APA, an arbitrary decision is unlawful. If an agency ignores costs, or imposes a risk that is greater than the risk that it is reducing, it would seem to be acting arbitrarily. The fact that courts cannot add procedural requirements is irrelevant. At the same time, it must be acknowledged that Michigan v. EPA was a narrow ruling, and it hardly embraced cost-benefit maximalism."

(c) JONATHAN S. MASUR & ERIC A. POSNER, COST-BENEFIT ANALYSIS AND THE JUDICIAL ROLE, 85 U. Chi. L. Rev. 935 (2018): "What does it mean to require an agency to take into account 'cost' but not to conduct a 'formal' CBA? It is not clear, but there is reason to believe that the Court thinks—or will soon think—that a formal CBA is required as well. The Court did not reach the question of whether a full CBA was mandated only because the EPA had taken the extreme position that it need not consider costs at all. In addition, the Court not only said that the agency must 'consider' costs, but added that '[n]o regulation is "appropriate" if it does significantly more harm than good.'

"Professor Vermeule has suggested that the Court required only that agencies 'consider' costs (in some fashion) and stopped short of requiring that they quantify or monetize those costs. But determining whether a regulation 'does significantly more harm than good,' as the Court demands, necessarily requires comparing the magnitudes of costs and benefits. The only way for an agency (or court) to compare costs and benefits is to quantify them and translate them into comparable units—in effect, to monetize them. Thus, even though it does not say so explicitly, the Supreme Court has for all practical purposes created a rule that agencies must quantify and monetize costs and benefits."

## NOTES ON "POLITICS" AS A POSSIBLE ELEMENT OF "ARBITRARY AND CAPRICIOUS" REVIEW

(1) ***Should We Ignore Politics?*** The last paragraph of Justice Rehnquist's separate opinion in State Farm suggests that "[a] change in administration brought about by the people casting their votes is a perfectly reasonable basis for an executive agency's reappraisal of the costs and benefits of its programs and regulations." Justice White's statement of Standard 208's history in Part I of the opinion is organized, paragraph by paragraph, to relate the successive views of the Nixon, Ford, Carter, and Reagan Administrations. But his opinion insists on requiring a justification for the new rule in apolitical terms. It seems, then, that he saw value in requiring an agency to offer a formal defense of its action even if it did not reflect the agency's actual motivation. Was he right?

(2) ***Need to Consider Politics?*** CHRISTOPHER F. EDLEY, JR., ADMINISTRATIVE LAW: RETHINKING JUDICIAL CONTROL OF BUREAUCRACY 63–65 (1990): "The Supreme Court analyzed NHTSA's action strictly in terms of the paradigm of expertise, applying a fairly rigorous, 'adequate consideration' brand of arbitrary and capricious review. The majority

concluded that NHTSA erred by failing to analyze obvious and important alternatives to total rescission of the rule, including a requirement that manufacturers use nondetachable automatic seatbelts rather than detachable ones, or that they use airbags. Thus, science and implicit norms about good science were the Court's touchstones for evaluating the adequacy of the agency's decision making process as described in NHTSA's statement of basis and purpose in the rule making record. . . .

"If politics means anything short of crass interest group giveaways, then politics was plainly involved in the rescission of the passive restraints regulation. Not only had candidate Reagan spoken out about deregulation generally, he had specifically discussed the auto industry and even the passive restraints regulation. Presidential appointees throughout the government were thoroughly committed to wholesale deregulation. It is totally implausible to suggest that NHTSA's evaluation of the scientific evidence and consideration of the regulatory alternatives were pursued within the . . . paradigm of neutral, objective expertise. The regulatory result was all but ordained by the election results. The misidentification of the paradigm as science rather than politics gives the Court's decision an odd quality. If the strong role I posit for politics *was* permissible and indeed cause for deference (emphasizing the positive attributes of that paradigm), as Rehnquist suggested in State Farm, then failure of the agency and the Court to identify the political element in the agency's action may have resulted in too little judicial deference. If instead the strong role of politics was *not* permissible (emphasizing the negative), then perhaps an even more interventionist posture would have been appropriate, whether through the doctrinal content of the Court's reasoning or through the specificity of the remand order."

(3) ***Good and Bad Politics?*** KATHRYN A. WATTS, PROPOSING A PLACE FOR POLITICS IN ARBITRARY AND CAPRICIOUS REVIEW, 119 Yale L.J. 2, 6–9 (2009): "Ever since the Court handed down State Farm, agencies, courts, and scholars alike generally seem to have accepted the view that influences coming from one political branch or another cannot be allowed to explain administrative decisionmaking, even if such factors are influencing agency decisionmaking. . . . Agencies today generally try to meet their reason-giving duties under State Farm by couching their decisions in technocratic, statutory, or scientific language, either failing to disclose or affirmatively hiding political factors that enter into the mix. A good example of this can be found by looking at the Food and Drug Administration's (FDA) attempt in the 1990s to regulate teen smoking. Even though President Clinton played a very active role in directing the rulemaking (going so far as to personally announce the final rule in a Rose Garden ceremony), the FDA's statement of basis and purpose accompanying the final rule relied upon statutory, scientific, and expert justifications—barely even hinting at President Clinton's role in the rulemaking. . . .

"The heart of the argument set forth here is that what counts as 'valid' reasons under arbitrary and capricious review should be expanded to include certain political influences from the President, other executive officials, and members of Congress, so long as the political influences are openly and transparently disclosed in the agency's rulemaking record. . . .

"Acceptance of the argument set forth here would *not* mean that any and all political influences would be allowed to legitimize agency action. Rather, some political influences should be read to justify agency action whereas other political influences should be read to corrupt. Although drawing a precise line between permissible and impermissible influences is difficult, legitimate political influences can roughly be thought of as those influences that seek to further policy considerations or public values, whereas illegitimate political influences can be thought of as those that seek to implement raw politics or partisan politics unconnected in any way to the statutory scheme being implemented. This would mean, for example, that the Department of Health and Human Services (HHS) would be allowed to rely upon a public statement issued by President Obama articulating his pro-choice agenda and his pro-choice policy initiatives if HHS chose to rescind a Bush-era rule that forbids medical facilities that receive federal money from discriminating against health providers who refuse, on religious grounds, to perform abortions. Conversely, it would mean that HHS could not legitimately justify a decision to rescind the same Bush-era 'provider conscience' rule by simply saying: 'President Obama directed us to rescind the rule in order to reward various pro-choice organizations for their endorsement of him during his campaign.' "

(4) ***Another Possibility?*** NINA A. MENDELSON, DISCLOSING "POLITICAL" OVERSIGHT OF AGENCY DECISION MAKING, 108 Mich. L. Rev. 1127, 1166 (2010): "Watts and Edley seem to assume that technocratic judicial review is the primary disincentive to an agency's explicit discussion of political reasons. However, there may be other obstacles. . . . [F]or example, Presidents (and OIRA) have often chosen to lie low with respect to particular agency decisions. A President may thereby seek to maintain 'deniability' and to avoid political risks, such as a wrong calculation regarding which policy best serves the public interest or is most popular. In short, a judicial review approach that is more receptive to political reasons would be insufficient to prompt a substantial increase in disclosure." Mendelson's own proposal is that there be, by statute, a judicially enforceable procedural requirement "that a significant agency rule include at least a summary of the substance of executive supervision." Id. at 1130.

## FEDERAL COMMUNICATIONS COMMISSION v. FOX TELEVISION STATIONS, INC.

Supreme Court of the United States (2009).
556 U.S. 502.

■ JUSTICE SCALIA delivered the opinion of the Court, except as to Part III-E.

Federal law prohibits the broadcasting of "any . . . indecent . . . language," 18 U.S.C. § 1464, which includes expletives referring to sexual or excretory activity or organs, see FCC v. Pacifica Foundation, 438 U.S. 726 (1978). This case concerns the adequacy of the Federal

Communications Commission's explanation of its decision that this sometimes forbids the broadcasting of indecent expletives even when the offensive words are not repeated.

I. Statutory and Regulatory Background

The Communications Act of 1934, 47 U.S.C. § 151 et seq., established a system of limited-term broadcast licenses subject to various "conditions" designed "to maintain the control of the United States over all the channels of radio transmission," § 301. Twenty-seven years ago we said that "[a] licensed broadcaster is granted the free and exclusive use of a limited and valuable part of the public domain; when he accepts that franchise it is burdened by enforceable public obligations." CBS, Inc. v. FCC, 453 U.S. 367, 395 (1981).

One of the burdens that licensees shoulder is the indecency ban—the statutory proscription against "utter[ing] any obscene, indecent, or profane language by means of radio communication," 18 U.S.C. § 1464—which Congress has instructed the Commission to enforce between the hours of 6 a.m. and 10 p.m. Congress has given the Commission various means of enforcing the indecency ban, including civil fines and license revocations or the denial of license renewals.

The Commission first invoked the statutory ban on indecent broadcasts in 1975, declaring a daytime broadcast of George Carlin's "Filthy Words" monologue actionably indecent. Pacifica Foundation, 56 F.C.C.2d 94. At that time, the Commission announced the definition of indecent speech that it uses to this day, prohibiting "language that describes, in terms patently offensive as measured by contemporary community standards for the broadcast medium, sexual or excretory activities or organs, at times of the day when there is a reasonable risk that children may be in the audience." Id., at 98.

In FCC v. Pacifica Foundation, we upheld the Commission's order against statutory and constitutional challenge. . . .

In the ensuing years, the Commission took a cautious, but gradually expanding, approach to enforcing the statutory prohibition against indecent broadcasts. . . . Although the Commission had expanded its enforcement beyond the "repetitive use of specific words or phrases," it preserved a distinction between literal and nonliteral (or "expletive") uses of evocative language. In re Pacifica Foundation, Inc., 2 FCC Rcd., at 2699, ¶ 13. The Commission explained that each literal "description or depiction of sexual or excretory functions must be examined in context to determine whether it is patently offensive," but that "deliberate and repetitive use . . . is a requisite to a finding of indecency" when a complaint focuses solely on the use of nonliteral expletives. Ibid. . . .

In 2004, the Commission took one step further by declaring for the first time that a nonliteral (expletive) use of the F- and S-Words could be actionably indecent, even when the word is used only once. The first order to this effect dealt with an NBC broadcast of the Golden Globe Awards, in which the performer Bono commented, " 'This is really, really, f* * *ing brilliant.' " In re Complaints Against Various Broadcast Licensees

Regarding Their Airing of the "Golden Globe Awards" Program, 19 FCC Rcd. 4975, 4976, n. 4 (2004) (Golden Globes Order). Although the Commission had received numerous complaints directed at the broadcast, its enforcement bureau had concluded that the material was not indecent because "Bono did not describe, in context, sexual or excretory organs or activities and . . . the utterance was fleeting and isolated." Id., at 4975–4976, ¶ 3. The full Commission reviewed and reversed the staff ruling.

The Commission first declared that Bono's use of the F-Word fell within its indecency definition, even though the word was used as an intensifier rather than a literal descriptor. "[G]iven the core meaning of the 'F-Word,'" it said, "any use of that word . . . inherently has a sexual connotation." Id., at 4978, ¶ 8. The Commission determined, moreover, that the broadcast was "patently offensive" because the F-Word "is one of the most vulgar, graphic and explicit descriptions of sexual activity in the English language," because "[i]ts use invariably invokes a coarse sexual image," and because Bono's use of the word was entirely "shocking and gratuitous." Id., at 4979, ¶ 9.

The Commission observed that categorically exempting such language from enforcement actions would "likely lead to more widespread use." Ibid. Commission action was necessary to "safeguard the well-being of the nation's children from the most objectionable, most offensive language." The order noted that technological advances have made it far easier to delete ("bleep out") a "single and gratuitous use of a vulgar expletive," without adulterating the content of a broadcast. Id., at 4980, ¶ 11.

The order acknowledged that "prior Commission and staff action have indicated that isolated or fleeting broadcasts of the 'F-Word' . . . are not indecent or would not be acted upon." It explicitly ruled that "any such interpretation is no longer good law." Ibid., ¶ 12. . . . Because, however, "existing precedent would have permitted this broadcast," the Commission determined that "NBC and its affiliates necessarily did not have the requisite notice to justify a penalty." Id., at 4981–4982, ¶ 15.

II. The Present Case

This case concerns utterances in two live broadcasts aired by Fox Television Stations, Inc., and its affiliates prior to the Commission's Golden Globes Order. The first occurred during the 2002 Billboard Music Awards, when the singer Cher exclaimed, "I've also had critics for the last 40 years saying that I was on my way out every year. Right. So f* * * 'em." Brief for Petitioners 9. The second involved a segment of the 2003 Billboard Music Awards, during the presentation of an award by Nicole Richie and Paris Hilton, principals in a Fox television series called "The Simple Life." Ms. Hilton began their interchange by reminding Ms. Richie to "watch the bad language," but Ms. Richie proceeded to ask the audience, "Why do they even call it 'The Simple Life?' Have you ever tried to get cow s* * * out of a Prada purse? It's not so f* * *ing simple." Id., at 9–10. Following each of these broadcasts, the Commission received numerous complaints from parents whose children were exposed to the language.

[Proceedings followed, before the Commission and in the Second Circuit, resulting in a new Commission Order: In re Complaints Regarding Various Television Broadcasts Between February 2, 2002, and March 8, 2005, 21 FCC Rcd. 13299 (2006) (Remand Order).] The order first explained that both broadcasts fell comfortably within the subject-matter scope of the Commission's indecency test because the 2003 broadcast involved a literal description of excrement and both broadcasts invoked the "F-Word," which inherently has a sexual connotation. The order next determined that the broadcasts were patently offensive under community standards for the medium. Both broadcasts, it noted, involved entirely gratuitous uses of "one of the most vulgar, graphic, and explicit words for sexual activity in the English language." Id., at 13305, ¶ 17, 13324, ¶ 59. It found Ms. Richie's use of the "F-Word" and her "explicit description of the handling of excrement" to be "vulgar and shocking," as well as to constitute "pandering," after Ms. Hilton had playfully warned her to " 'watch the bad language.' " Id., at 13305, ¶ 17. And it found Cher's statement patently offensive in part because she metaphorically suggested a sexual act as a means of expressing hostility to her critics. The order relied upon the "critically important" context of the utterances, noting that they were aired during prime-time awards shows "designed to draw a large nationwide audience that could be expected to include many children interested in seeing their favorite music stars," id., at 13305, ¶ 18, 13324, ¶ 59. Indeed, approximately 2.5 million minors witnessed each of the broadcasts. Id., at 13306, ¶ 18, 13326, ¶ 65. . . .

The order explained that the Commission's prior "strict dichotomy between 'expletives' and 'descriptions or depictions of sexual or excretory functions' is artificial and does not make sense in light of the fact that an 'expletive's' power to offend derives from its sexual or excretory meaning." Id., at 13308, ¶ 23. In the Commission's view, "granting an automatic exemption for 'isolated or fleeting' expletives unfairly forces viewers (including children)" to take " 'the first blow' " and would allow broadcasters "to air expletives at all hours of a day so long as they did so one at a time." Id., at 13309, ¶ 25. Although the Commission determined that Fox encouraged the offensive language by using suggestive scripting in the 2003 broadcast, and unreasonably failed to take adequate precautions in both broadcasts, the order again declined to impose any forfeiture or other sanction for either of the broadcasts.

Fox returned to the Second Circuit for review of the Remand Order, and various intervenors including CBS, NBC, and ABC joined the action. The Court of Appeals reversed the agency's orders, finding the Commission's reasoning inadequate under the Administrative Procedure Act. The majority was "skeptical that the Commission [could] provide a reasoned explanation for its 'fleeting expletive' regime that would pass constitutional muster," but it declined to reach the constitutional question. 489 F.3d at 462. Judge Leval dissented. We granted certiorari.

III. Analysis

A. Governing Principles

The Administrative Procedure Act, 5 U.S.C. § 551 et seq., . . . permits (insofar as relevant here) the setting aside of agency action that is "arbitrary" or "capricious," 5 U.S.C. § 706(2)(A). . . .

In overturning the Commission's judgment, the Court of Appeals here relied in part on Circuit precedent requiring a more substantial explanation for agency action that changes prior policy. The Second Circuit has interpreted the Administrative Procedure Act and our opinion in State Farm as requiring agencies to make clear " 'why the original reasons for adopting the [displaced] rule or policy are no longer dispositive' " as well as " 'why the new rule effectuates the statute as well as or better than the old rule.' " 489 F.3d, at 456–457. The Court of Appeals for the District of Columbia Circuit has similarly indicated that a court's standard of review is "heightened somewhat" when an agency reverses course. NAACP v. FCC, 682 F.2d 993, 998 (1982).

We find no basis in the Administrative Procedure Act or in our opinions for a requirement that all agency change be subjected to more searching review. The Act mentions no such heightened standard. And our opinion in State Farm neither held nor implied that every agency action representing a policy change must be justified by reasons more substantial than those required to adopt a policy in the first instance. . . .

To be sure, the requirement that an agency provide reasoned explanation for its action would ordinarily demand that it display awareness that it *is* changing position. An agency may not, for example, depart from a prior policy sub silentio or simply disregard rules that are still on the books. See United States v. Nixon, 418 U.S. 683, 696 (1974). And of course the agency must show that there are good reasons for the new policy. But it need not demonstrate to a court's satisfaction that the reasons for the new policy are *better* than the reasons for the old one; it suffices that the new policy is permissible under the statute, that there are good reasons for it, and that the agency *believes* it to be better, which the conscious change of course adequately indicates. This means that the agency need not always provide a more detailed justification than what would suffice for a new policy created on a blank slate. Sometimes it must—when, for example, its new policy rests upon factual findings that contradict those which underlay its prior policy; or when its prior policy has engendered serious reliance interests that must be taken into account. It would be arbitrary or capricious to ignore such matters. In such cases it is not that further justification is demanded by the mere fact of policy change; but that a reasoned explanation is needed for disregarding facts and circumstances that underlay or were engendered by the prior policy.

In this appeal from the Second Circuit's setting aside of Commission action for failure to comply with a procedural requirement of the Administrative Procedure Act, the broadcasters' arguments have repeatedly referred to the First Amendment. If they mean to invite us to apply a more stringent arbitrary-and-capricious review to agency actions that implicate constitutional liberties, we reject the invitation. The so-called canon of constitutional avoidance is an interpretive tool, counseling that ambiguous statutory language be construed to avoid serious constitutional doubts. We know of no precedent for applying it to limit the scope of authorized executive action. In the same section authorizing courts to set aside "arbitrary [or] capricious" agency action, the Administrative Procedure Act separately provides for setting aside agency action that is "unlawful," 5 U.S.C. § 706(2)(A), which of course includes unconstitutional action. We think that is the only context in which constitutionality bears upon judicial review of authorized agency action. If the Commission's action here was not arbitrary or capricious in the ordinary sense, it satisfies the Administrative Procedure Act's "arbitrary [or] capricious" standard; its lawfulness under the Constitution is a separate question to be addressed in a constitutional challenge.

B. Application to This Case

Judged under the above described standards, the Commission's new enforcement policy and its order finding the broadcasts actionably indecent were neither arbitrary nor capricious. First, the Commission forthrightly acknowledged that its recent actions have broken new ground, taking account of inconsistent "prior Commission and staff action" and explicitly disavowing them as "no longer good law." Golden Globes Order, 19 FCC Rcd., at 4980, ¶ 12. To be sure, the (superfluous) explanation in its Remand Order of why the Cher broadcast would even have violated its earlier policy may not be entirely convincing. But that unnecessary detour is irrelevant. There is no doubt that the Commission knew it was making a change. That is why it declined to assess penalties; and it relied on the Golden Globes Order as removing any lingering doubt. Remand Order, 21 FCC Rcd., at 13308, ¶ 23, 13325, ¶ 61.

Moreover, the agency's reasons for expanding the scope of its enforcement activity were entirely rational. It was certainly reasonable to determine that it made no sense to distinguish between literal and nonliteral uses of offensive words, requiring repetitive use to render only the latter indecent. As the Commission said with regard to expletive use of the F-Word, "the word's power to insult and offend derives from its sexual meaning." Id., at 13323, ¶ 58. And the Commission's decision to look at the patent offensiveness of even isolated uses of sexual and excretory words fits with the context-based approach we sanctioned in Pacifica. Even isolated utterances can be made in "pander[ing,] . . . vulgar and shocking" manners, Remand Order, 21 FCC Rcd., at 13305, ¶ 17, and can constitute harmful " 'first blow[s]' " to children, id., at 13309, ¶ 25. It is surely rational (if not inescapable) to believe that a safe harbor for single words would "likely lead to more widespread use of the offensive language," Golden Globes Order at 4979, ¶ 9.

When confronting other requests for per se rules governing its enforcement of the indecency prohibition, the Commission has declined to create safe harbors for particular types of broadcasts. The Commission could rationally decide it needed to step away from its old regime where nonrepetitive use of an expletive was per se nonactionable because that was "at odds with the Commission's overall enforcement policy." Remand Order at 13308, ¶ 23.

The fact that technological advances have made it easier for broadcasters to bleep out offending words further supports the Commission's stepped-up enforcement policy. Golden Globes Order at 4980, ¶ 11. And the agency's decision not to impose any forfeiture or other sanction precludes any argument that it is arbitrarily punishing parties without notice of the potential consequences of their action.

C. The Court of Appeals' Reasoning

The Court of Appeals found the Commission's action arbitrary and capricious on three grounds. First, the court criticized the Commission for failing to explain why it had not previously banned fleeting expletives as "harmful 'first blow[s].'" . . .There are some propositions for which scant empirical evidence can be marshaled, and the harmful effect of broadcast profanity on children is one of them. One cannot demand a multiyear controlled study, in which some children are intentionally exposed to indecent broadcasts (and insulated from all other indecency), and others are shielded from all indecency. It is one thing to set aside agency action under the Administrative Procedure Act because of failure to adduce empirical data that can readily be obtained. See, e.g., State Farm, 463 U.S., at 46–56 (addressing the costs and benefits of mandatory passive restraints for automobiles). It is something else to insist upon obtaining the unobtainable. Here it suffices to know that children mimic the behavior they observe—or at least the behavior that is presented to them as normal and appropriate. Programming replete with one-word indecent expletives will tend to produce children who use (at least) one-word indecent expletives. Congress has made the determination that indecent material is harmful to children, and has left enforcement of the ban to the Commission. If enforcement had to be supported by empirical data, the ban would effectively be a nullity. . . .

The court's second objection is that fidelity to the agency's "first blow" theory of harm would require a categorical ban on *all* broadcasts of expletives; the Commission's failure to go to this extreme thus undermined the coherence of its rationale. . . . More fundamentally, however, the agency's decision to consider the patent offensiveness of isolated expletives on a case-by-case basis is not arbitrary or capricious. . . . The agency's decision to retain some discretion does not render arbitrary or capricious its regulation of the deliberate and shocking uses of offensive language at the award shows under review—shows that were expected to (and did) draw the attention of millions of children.

Finally, the Court of Appeals found unconvincing the agency's prediction (without any evidence) that a per se exemption for fleeting expletives would lead to increased use of expletives one at a time. But even in the absence of evidence, the agency's predictive judgment (which merits deference) makes entire sense. To predict that complete immunity for fleeting expletives, ardently desired by broadcasters, will lead to a substantial increase in fleeting expletives seems to us an exercise in logic rather than clairvoyance. The Court of Appeals was perhaps correct that the Commission's prior policy had not yet caused broadcasters to "barrag[e] the airwaves with expletives." That may have been because its prior permissive policy had been confirmed (save in dicta) only at the staff level. In any event, as the Golden Globes order demonstrated, it did produce more expletives than the Commission (which has the first call in this matter) deemed in conformity with the statute. . . .

D. Respondents' Arguments

Respondents press some arguments that the court did not adopt. . . .

E. The Dissents' Arguments

Justice Breyer purports to "begin with applicable law," but in fact begins by stacking the deck. He claims that the FCC's status as an "independent" agency sheltered from political oversight requires courts to be "all the more" vigilant in ensuring "that major policy decisions be based upon articulable reasons." Not so. The independent agencies are sheltered not from politics but from the President, and it has often been observed that their freedom from presidential oversight (and protection) has simply been replaced by increased subservience to congressional direction. Indeed, the precise policy change at issue here was spurred by significant political pressure from Congress.[4] . . .

Regardless, it is assuredly not "applicable law" that rulemaking by independent regulatory agencies is subject to heightened scrutiny. The Administrative Procedure Act, which provides judicial review, makes no distinction between independent and other agencies, neither in its definition of agency, 5 U.S.C. § 701(b)(1), nor in the standards for reviewing agency action, § 706. . . .

Justice Breyer and Justice Stevens rely upon two supposed omissions in the FCC's analysis that they believe preclude a finding that the agency did not act arbitrarily. Neither of these omissions could

---

[4] A Subcommittee of the FCC's House Oversight Committee held hearings on the FCC's broadcast indecency enforcement on January 28, 2004. "Can You Say That on TV?": An Examination of the FCC's Enforcement with respect to Broadcast Indecency, Hearing before the Subcommittee on Telecommunications and the Internet of the House Committee on Energy and Commerce, 108th Cong., 2d Sess. Members of the Subcommittee specifically "called on the full Commission to reverse [the staff ruling in the Golden Globes case]" because they perceived a "feeling amongst many Americans that some broadcasters are engaged in a race to the bottom, pushing the decency envelope to distinguish themselves in the increasingly crowded entertainment field." Id., at 2 (statement of Rep. Upton); see also, e.g., id., at 17 (statement of Rep. Terry), 19 (statement of Rep. Pitts). They repeatedly expressed disapproval of the FCC's enforcement policies, see, e.g., id., at 3 (statement of Rep. Upton) ("At some point we have to ask the FCC: How much is enough? When will it revoke a license?"); id., at 4 (statement of Rep. Markey) ("Today's hearing will allow us to explore the FCC's lackluster enforcement record with respect to these violations").

About two weeks later, on February 11, 2004, the same Subcommittee held hearings on a bill increasing the fines for indecency violations. Hearings on H.R. 3717 before the Subcommittee on Telecommunications and the Internet of the House Committee on Energy and Commerce, 108th Cong., 2d Sess. All five Commissioners were present and were grilled about enforcement shortcomings. . . .

undermine the coherence of the rationale the agency gave, but the dissenters' evaluation of each is flawed in its own right.

First, both claim that the Commission failed adequately to explain its consideration of the constitutional issues inherent in its regulation. [We don't agree.]

Second, Justice Breyer looks over the vast field of particular factual scenarios unaddressed by the FCC's 35-page Remand Order and finds one that is fatal: the plight of the small local broadcaster who cannot afford the new technology that enables the screening of live broadcasts for indecent utterances. The Commission has failed to address the fate of this unfortunate, who will, he believes, be subject to sanction.

We doubt, to begin with, that small-town broadcasters run a heightened risk of liability for indecent utterances. In programming that they originate, their down-home local guests probably employ vulgarity less than big-city folks; and small-town stations generally cannot afford or cannot attract foul-mouthed glitteratae from Hollywood. Their main exposure with regard to self-originated programming is live coverage of news and public affairs. But the Remand Order went out of its way to note that the case at hand did not involve "breaking news coverage," and that "it may be inequitable to hold a licensee responsible for airing offensive speech during live coverage of a public event," 21 FCC Rcd., at 13311, ¶ 33. As for the programming that small stations receive on a network "feed": This *will* be cleansed by the expensive technology small stations (by Justice Breyer's hypothesis) cannot afford.

But never mind the detail of whether small broadcasters are uniquely subject to a great risk of punishment for fleeting expletives. The fundamental fallacy of Justice Breyer's small-broadcaster gloomy scenario is its demonstrably false assumption that the Remand Order makes no provision for the avoidance of unfairness—that the single-utterance prohibition will be invoked uniformly, in all situations. The Remand Order made very clear that this is not the case. It said that in determining "what, if any, remedy is appropriate" the Commission would consider the facts of each individual case . . . .

There was, in sum, no need for the Commission to compose a special treatise on local broadcasters.[8] And Justice Breyer can safely defer his concern for those yeomen of the airwaves until we have before us a case that involves one.

IV. Constitutionality

The Second Circuit did not definitively rule on the constitutionality of the Commission's orders, but respondents nonetheless ask us to decide

[8] Justice Breyer posits that the FCC would have been required to give more explanation had it used notice-and-comment rulemaking, which "should lead us to the same conclusion" in this review of the agency's change through adjudication. Even assuming the premise, there is no basis for incorporating all of the Administrative Procedure Act's notice-and-comment procedural requirements into arbitrary-and-capricious review of adjudicatory decisions. Cf. Vermont Yankee.

their validity under the First Amendment. . . . We decline to address the constitutional questions at this time.

* * *

The Second Circuit believed that children today "likely hear this language far more often from other sources than they did in the 1970's when the Commission first began sanctioning indecent speech," and that this cuts against more stringent regulation of broadcasts. Assuming the premise is true (for this point the Second Circuit did not demand empirical evidence) the conclusion does not necessarily follow. The Commission could reasonably conclude that the pervasiveness of foul language, and the coarsening of public entertainment in other media such as cable, justify more stringent regulation of broadcast programs so as to give conscientious parents a relatively safe haven for their children. In the end, the Second Circuit and the broadcasters quibble with the Commission's policy choices and not with the explanation it has given. We decline to "substitute [our] judgment for that of the agency," State Farm, 463 U.S., at 43, and we find the Commission's orders neither arbitrary nor capricious.

The judgment of the United States Court of Appeals for the Second Circuit is reversed, and the case is remanded for further proceedings consistent with this opinion.

■ JUSTICE BREYER, with whom JUSTICE STEVENS, JUSTICE SOUTER, and JUSTICE GINSBURG join, dissenting.

In my view, the Federal Communications Commission failed adequately to explain *why* it *changed* its indecency policy from a policy permitting a single "fleeting use" of an expletive, to a policy that made no such exception. Its explanation fails to discuss two critical factors, at least one of which directly underlay its original policy decision. Its explanation instead discussed several factors well known to it the first time around, which by themselves provide no significant justification for a *change* of policy. Consequently, the FCC decision is "arbitrary, capricious, an abuse of discretion." 5 U.S.C. § 706(2)(A); State Farm; Overton Park. And I would affirm the Second Circuit's similar determination.

I

I begin with applicable law. That law grants those in charge of independent administrative agencies broad authority to determine relevant policy. But it does not permit them to make policy choices for purely political reasons nor to rest them primarily upon unexplained policy preferences. Federal Communications Commissioners have fixed terms of office; they are not directly responsible to the voters; and they enjoy an independence expressly designed to insulate them, to a degree, from " 'the exercise of political oversight.' " Freytag v. Commissioner, 501 U.S. 868, 916 (1991) (Scalia, J., concurring in part and concurring in judgment.) That insulation helps to secure important governmental objectives, such as the constitutionally related objective of maintaining broadcast regulation that does not bend too readily before the political winds. But that agency's comparative freedom from ballot-box control makes it all the more important that courts review its decisionmaking to assure compliance with applicable provisions of the law—including law requiring that major policy decisions be based upon articulable reasons. . . .

To explain a change requires more than setting forth reasons why the new policy is a good one. It also requires the agency to answer the question, "Why did you change?" And a rational answer to this question typically requires a more complete explanation than would prove satisfactory were change itself not at issue. An (imaginary) administrator explaining why he chose a policy that requires driving on the right side, rather than the left side, of the road might say, "Well, one side seemed as good as the other, so I flipped a coin." But even assuming the rationality of that explanation for an *initial* choice, that explanation is not at all rational if offered to explain why the administrator *changed* driving practice, from right-side to left-side, 25 years later.

In State Farm, a unanimous Court applied these commonsense requirements to an agency decision that rescinded an earlier agency policy. . . . It said that the law required an explanation for such a *change* because the earlier policy, representing a " 'settled course of behavior[,] embodies the agency's informed judgment that, by pursuing that course, it will carry out the policies . . . best if the settled rule is adhered to.' " State Farm. Thus, the agency must explain *why* it has come to the conclusion that it should now change direction. Why does it now reject the considerations that led it to adopt that initial policy? What has changed in the world that offers justification for the change? What other good reasons are there for departing from the earlier policy?

Contrary to the majority's characterization of this dissent, it would not (and State Farm does not) require a "*heightened standard*" of review. Rather, the law requires application of the *same standard* of review to different circumstances, namely circumstances characterized by the fact that *change* is at issue. It requires the agency to focus upon the fact of change where change is relevant, just as it must focus upon any other relevant circumstance. It requires the agency here to focus upon the reasons that led the agency to adopt the initial policy, and to explain why it now comes to a new judgment.

I recognize that *sometimes* the ultimate explanation for a change may have to be, "We now weigh the relevant considerations differently." But at other times, an agency can and should say more. Where, for example, the agency rested its previous policy on particular factual findings, or where an agency rested its prior policy on its view of the governing law, or where an agency rested its previous policy on, say, a special need to coordinate with another agency, one would normally expect the agency to focus upon those earlier views of fact, of law, or of policy and explain why they are no longer controlling. Regardless, to say that the agency here must answer the question "why change" is not to require the agency to provide a justification that is "*better* than the reasons for the old [policy]." It is only to recognize the obvious fact that *change* is sometimes (not always) a relevant background feature that sometimes (not always) requires focus (upon prior justifications) and explanation lest the adoption of the new policy (in that circumstance) be "arbitrary, capricious, an abuse of discretion." . . .

II

We here must apply the general standards set forth in State Farm and Overton Park to an agency decision that changes a 25-year-old "fleeting expletive" policy from (1) the old policy that would normally permit broadcasters to transmit a single, fleeting use of an expletive to (2) a new policy that would threaten broadcasters with large fines for transmitting even a single use (including its use by a member of the public) of such an expletive, alone with nothing more. The question is whether that decision satisfies the minimal standards necessary to assure a reviewing court that such a change of policy is not "arbitrary, capricious, [or] an abuse of discretion," 5 U.S.C. § 706(2)(A), particularly as set forth in, e.g., State Farm and Overton Park. The decision, in my view, does not satisfy those standards.

Consider the requirement that an agency at least minimally "consider . . . important aspect[s] of the problem." State Farm. The FCC failed to satisfy this requirement, for it failed to consider two critically important aspects of the problem that underlay its initial policy judgment (one of which directly, the other of which indirectly). First, the FCC said next to nothing about the relation between the change it made in its prior "fleeting expletive" policy and the First-Amendment-related need to avoid "censorship," a matter as closely related to broadcasting regulation as is health to that of the environment. The reason that discussion of the matter is particularly important here is that the FCC had *explicitly* rested its prior policy in large part upon the need to avoid treading too close to the constitutional line.

[The agency failed to justify sufficiently its new approach to the Supreme Court's ruling in F.C.C. v. Pacifica.]

Second, the FCC failed to consider the potential impact of its new policy upon local broadcasting coverage. This "aspect of the problem" is particularly important because the FCC explicitly took account of potential broadcasting impact. Golden Globe Order at 4980, ¶ 11 ("The ease with which broadcasters today can block even fleeting words in a live broadcast is an element in our decision"). Indeed, in setting forth "bleeping" technology changes (presumably lowering bleeping costs) as justifying the policy change, it implicitly reasoned that lower costs, making it easier for broadcasters to install bleeping equipment, made it less likely that the new policy would lead broadcasters to reduce coverage, say by canceling coverage of public events.

What then did the FCC say about the likelihood that smaller independent broadcasters, including many public service broadcasters, still would not be able to afford "bleeping" technology and, as a consequence, would reduce local coverage, indeed cancel coverage, of many public events? It said nothing at all. . . .

The plurality acknowledges that the Commission entirely failed to discuss this aspect of the regulatory problem. But it sees "no need" for discussion in light of its, i.e., the plurality's, own "doubt[s]" that "smalltown broadcasters run a heightened risk of liability for indecent utterances" as a result of the change of policy. The plurality's "doubt[s]" rest upon its views (1) that vulgar expression is less prevalent (at least among broadcast guests) in smaller towns; (2) that the greatest risk the new policy poses for "smalltown broadcasters" arises when they broadcast local "news and public affairs," and (3) that the Remand Order says "little about how the Commission would treat smaller broadcasters who cannot afford screening equipment," while also pointing out that the new policy " 'does not . . . impose undue burdens on broadcasters' " and emphasizing that the case before it did not involve " 'breaking news.' "

As to the first point, about the prevalence of vulgarity in small towns, I confess ignorance. But I do know that there are independent stations in many large and medium sized cities. See Television & Cable Factbook, Directory of Television Stations in Operation 2008. As to the second point, I too believe that coverage of local public events, if not news, lies at the heart of the problem.

I cannot agree with the plurality, however, about the critical third point, namely that the new policy obviously provides smaller independent broadcasters with adequate assurance that they will not be fined. The new policy removes the "fleeting expletive" exception, an exception that assured smaller independent stations that they would not be fined should someone swear at a public event. In its place, it puts a policy that places all broadcasters at risk when they broadcast fleeting expletives, including expletives uttered at public events. The Remand Order says that there "is *no outright news exemption from our indecency rules*." 21 FCC Rcd., at 13327, ¶ 71 (emphasis added). The best it can provide by way of assurance is to say that "it *may* be inequitable to hold a licensee responsible for airing offensive speech during live coverage of a public event *under some circumstances*." Id., at 13311, ¶ 33 (emphasis added). It does list those circumstances as including the "possibility of human error in using delay equipment." Id., at 13313, ¶ 35. But it says *nothing* about a station's *inability to afford* delay equipment (a matter that in individual cases could itself prove debatable). All the FCC had to do was to *consider* this matter and either grant an exemption or explain why it did not grant an exemption. But it did not. And the result is a rule that may well chill coverage—the kind of consequence that the law has considered important for decades, to which the broadcasters pointed in their arguments before the FCC, and which the FCC nowhere discusses.

Had the FCC used traditional administrative notice-and-comment procedures, 5 U.S.C. § 553, the two failures I have just discussed would clearly require a court to vacate the resulting agency decision. See ACLU v. FCC, 823 F.2d 1554, 1581 (C.A.D.C. 1987) ("Notice and comment rulemaking procedures obligate the FCC to respond to *all* significant comments, for the opportunity to comment is meaningless unless the agency responds to significant points raised by the public"). Here the agency did not make new policy through the medium of notice and comment proceedings. But the same failures here—where the policy is important, the significance of the issues clear, the failures near complete—should lead us to the same conclusion. The agency's failure to discuss these two "important aspect[s] of the problem" means that the resulting decision is " 'arbitrary, capricious, an abuse of discretion' " requiring us to remand the matter to the agency. State Farm; Overton Park.

III

The three reasons the FCC did set forth in support of its change of policy cannot make up for the failures I have discussed. . . .

[T]he FCC found that the new policy was better in part because, in its view, the new policy better protects children against what it described as " 'the first blow' " of broadcast indecency that results from the " 'pervasive' " nature of broadcast media. . . . The difficulty with this argument, however, is that it does not explain the *change*. The FCC has long used the theory of the "first blow" to justify its regulation of broadcast indecency. Yet the FCC has also long followed its original "fleeting expletives" policy. Nor was the FCC ever unaware of the fact to which the majority points, namely that children's surroundings influence their behavior. So, to repeat the question: What, in respect to the "first blow," has changed?

The FCC points to no empirical (or other) evidence to demonstrate that it previously understated the importance of avoiding the "first blow." Like the majority, I do not believe that an agency must always conduct full empirical studies of such matters. But the FCC could have referred to, and explained, relevant empirical studies that suggest the contrary. One review of the empirical evidence, for example, reports that "[i]t is doubtful that children under the age of 12 understand sexual language and innuendo; therefore it is unlikely that vulgarities have any negative effect." Kaye & Sapolsky, Watch Your Mouth! An Analysis of Profanity Uttered by Children on Prime-Time Television, 2004 Mass Communication & Soc'y 429, 433 (Vol.7) (citing two studies). The Commission need not have accepted this conclusion. But its failure to discuss this or any other such evidence, while providing no empirical evidence at all that favors its position, must weaken the logical force of its conclusion.

The FCC also found the new policy better because it believed that its prior policy "would as a matter of logic permit broadcasters to air expletives at all hours of a day so long as they did so one at a time." Remand Order, 21 FCC Rcd., at 13309, ¶ 25. This statement, however, raises an obvious question: Did that happen? The FCC's initial "fleeting expletives" policy was in effect for 25 years. Had broadcasters during those 25 years aired a series of expletives "one at a time?" If so, it should not be difficult to find evidence of that fact. But the FCC refers to none. Indeed, the FCC did not even claim that a change had taken place in this respect. It spoke only of the pure "logic" of the initial policy "permitting" such a practice. That logic would have been apparent to anyone, including the FCC, in 1978 when the FCC set forth its initial policy. . . .

IV

Were the question a closer one, the doctrine of constitutional avoidance would nonetheless lead me to remand the case. . . . Unlike the majority, I can find no convincing reason for refusing to apply a similar doctrine here. The Court has often applied that doctrine where an agency's regulation relies on a plausible but constitutionally suspect interpretation of a statute. The values the doctrine serves apply whether the agency's decision does, or does not, rest upon a constitutionally suspect interpretation of a statute. And a remand here would do no more than ask the agency to reconsider its policy decision in light of the concerns raised in a judicial opinion. . . .

V

In sum, the FCC's explanation of its change leaves out two critically important matters underlying its earlier policy, namely Pacifica and local broadcasting coverage. Its explanation rests upon three considerations previously known to the agency ("coarseness," the "first blow," and running single expletives all day, one at a time). With one exception, it provides no empirical or other information explaining why those considerations, which did not justify its new policy before, justify it now. Its discussion of the one exception (technological advances in bleeping/delay systems), failing to take account of local broadcast coverage, is seriously incomplete.

I need not decide whether one or two of these features, standing alone, would require us to remand the case. Here all come together. And taken together they suggest that the FCC's answer to the question, "Why change?" is, "We like the new policy better." This kind of answer, might be perfectly satisfactory were it given by an elected official. But when given by an agency, in respect to a major change of an important policy where much more might be said, it is not sufficient. State Farm.

## NOTES

(1) ***What Is the Doctrine?*** Both Justice Scalia's opinion and Justice Breyer's opinion treat State Farm as the governing law. Scalia says that State Farm does not impose a "heightened standard" of judicial review when an agency changes its course, and while he says that Justice Breyer imposes such a heightened standard, Justice Breyer specifically abjures doing so. Justice Scalia goes on to concede that in appropriate cases an agency must supply "a reasoned explanation . . . for disregarding facts and circumstances that underlay or were engendered by the prior policy." What more than that does Justice Breyer want? He says that the agency has to answer the question "Why did you change?" and then goes on to give a hypothetical about the imaginary administrator choosing, at time one, driving on the right side of the road, and then at time two, twenty five years later, changing the rule to driving on the left side. More, he says, has to be said at time two. But even at time one, there probably was a prior custom or, if the rule is federal, a set

of background state laws, and we would expect the administrator to discuss that custom (as either supporting his choice or having to be overcome by it); and if the point is that by time two there has been increased reliance on the uniform federal rule, isn't that additional fact precisely the kind of reliance "engendered by the prior policy" that Justice Scalia also says would have to be addressed? Is there a difference in principle between the opinions, or simply a different response to the particular way the FCC did, or didn't, address specific questions? The Justices think they have a serious quarrel—do they? If so, what is the status of the State Farm test now? Has "arbitrary and capricious" review been made less intensive? Has Justice Rehnquist's opinion in State Farm—that political choice has to be given some (unspecified) weight in determining what justification is sufficient—prevailed in this case because it is about a "culture wars" topic?

(2) ***Is Judicially Inferred Common Sense Enough?*** Part of the FCC's rationale was that a complete exemption for "fleeting expletives" would lead to significantly more of them. As Justice Breyer points out, the experience of the prior 25 years would seem to be relevant on the point, but the FCC produced no such evidence—relying instead on the "logic" of the policy. Justice Scalia agrees that it is "an exercise in logic rather than clairvoyance"—going on to say that the fact that the prior policy had not yet had the predicted result "may have been because its prior permissive policy had been confirmed . . . only at the staff level." Is this failure to produce evidence, and this need for a Justice to conjecture what "may have been" to fill in the gap, consistent with State Farm? Is it justified by the fact that State Farm was the product of a notice-and-comment rulemaking while this case comes up from a set of agency adjudications? Or is Justice Breyer right when he says that on a change of policy of this sort, this procedural difference should not be allowed to make a substantive difference?

(3) ***What Explanation Is Not Enough for a Change in Policy?*** In ENCINO MOTORCARS, LLC V. NAVARRO, 579 U.S. 211 (2016), the Department of Labor issued in 2011 a final rule (after a notice-and-comment proceeding) that said that, under the Fair Labor Standards Act, "service advisors" in automobile dealerships were entitled to overtime compensation. This changed the previous official policy (stated in an opinion letter) that service advisors were exempt from this provision; that policy had been consistently followed since 1978. Did that longstanding practice matter? Here's what JUSTICE KENNEDY's opinion for the Court had to say, 579 U.S. at 222–24:

"The retail automobile and truck dealership industry had relied since 1978 on the Department's position that service advisors are exempt from the FLSA's overtime pay requirements. Dealerships and service advisors negotiated and structured their compensation plans against this background understanding. Requiring dealerships to adapt to the Department's new position could necessitate systemic, significant changes to the dealerships' compensation arrangements. Dealerships whose service advisors are not compensated in accordance with the Department's new views could also face substantial FLSA liability. . . . In light of this background, the Department needed a more reasoned explanation for its decision to depart from its existing enforcement policy.

"The Department said that, in reaching its decision, it had 'carefully considered all of the comments, analyses, and arguments made for and against the proposed changes.' 76 Fed. Reg. 18832. And it noted that, since 1978, it had treated service advisors as exempt in certain circumstances. It also noted the comment from the National Automobile Dealers Association stating that the industry had relied on that interpretation.

"But when it came to explaining the 'good reasons for the new policy,' Fox Television Stations, 556 U.S. at 515, the Department said almost nothing. It stated only that it would not treat service advisors as exempt because 'the statute does not include such positions and the Department recognizes that there are circumstances under which the requirements for the exemption would not be met.' 76 Fed. Reg. 18838. It continued that it 'believes that this interpretation is reasonable' and 'sets forth the appropriate approach.' Although an agency may justify its policy choice by explaining why that policy is more consistent with statutory language than alternative policies, the Department did not analyze or explain why the statute should be interpreted to exempt dealership employees who sell vehicles but not dealership employees who sell services (that is, service advisors). And though several public comments supported the Department's reading of the statute, the Department did not explain what (if anything) it found persuasive in those comments beyond the few statements above.

"It is not the role of the courts to speculate on reasons that might have supported an agency's decision. '[W]e may not supply a reasoned basis for the agency's action that the agency itself has not given.' State Farm, 463 U.S., at 43 (citing SEC v. Chenery Corp., 332 U.S. 194 (1947)). Whatever potential reasons the Department might have given, the agency in fact gave almost no reasons at all. In light of the serious reliance interests at stake, the Department's conclusory statements do not suffice to explain its decision. See Fox Television Stations."

(4) ***What About the First Amendment in Fox?*** GILLIAN E. METZGER, ORDINARY ADMINISTRATIVE LAW AS CONSTITUTIONAL COMMON LAW, 110 Colum. L. Rev. 479, 484–86 (2010): "Justice Scalia's . . . opinion . . . denied that agency decisions implicating constitutional liberties trigger more stringent arbitrary and capricious review. Instead, the Court said, whether an agency action is 'arbitrary and capricious' and whether it is unconstitutional are 'separate question[s].' Arguing that the canon of constitutional avoidance applied only to judicial review of statutory language, Justice Scalia stated that 'the only context in which constitutionality bears upon judicial review of authorized agency action' is when a court determines the agency action is unconstitutional. He dismissed the dissent's suggestion that the agency be required to reconsider its policy in light of constitutional concerns. . . .

"Simply stated, my argument here is that Fox is wrong in positing a strict separation between constitutional and ordinary administrative law. . . . [T]he benefits of addressing constitutional concerns through ordinary administrative law are especially evident with respect to the form of administrative constitutionalism condemned in Fox: judicial use of ordinary administrative law to encourage agencies to take constitutional concerns seriously in their own decisionmaking. Administrative agencies today are responsible for much of the federal government's decisionmaking. Excluding such primary decisionmakers from a judicially enforceable obligation to include significant constitutional concerns in their deliberations is at odds with the structural imperatives of our constitutional system. Agencies are not only well positioned to enforce constitutional norms effectively, but they are also better able than courts to determine how to incorporate constitutional concerns into a given regulatory scheme with the least disruption. In addition, it is far easier for agencies to respond to judicial decisions remanding administrative actions for failure to take account of constitutional concerns than for Congress to respond to judicial invalidation of measures on constitutional grounds or judicial narrowing of statutes through the application of constitutional canons."

(5) ***And What Finally Happened?*** On remand in Fox Television Stations, Inc. v. F.C.C., 613 F.3d 317 (2d Cir. 2010), the Second Circuit, told to consider the First Amendment issue, said that the flexibility that the FCC's approach contained, especially as regards to what would qualify as exonerating "bona fide news" or "artistic necessity," was not permissible, considering that speech was at issue. Reviewing that decision, in FCC v. Fox Television Stations, Inc., 567 U.S. 239 (2012), the Court held that, because the broadcasts at issue happened before the FCC adopted its new approach to fleeting expletives, the network did not have the notice of its potential violation that the due process clause required: "This would be true with respect to a regulatory change this abrupt on any subject, but it is surely the case when applied to the regulations in question, regulations that touch upon 'sensitive areas of basic First Amendment freedoms.'" In response to the Commission's argument that the Court should not concern itself with possible reliance because, after all, the Commission itself had decided there would be no penalties to pay, the Court said that there was a sufficient chance of ancillary sanctions, and of reputational injury, to warrant altogether setting aside the finding of a violation. "Given this disposition, it is unnecessary for the Court to address the constitutionality of the current indecency policy as expressed in the Golden Globes Order and subsequent adjudications. The Court adheres to its normal practice of declining to decide cases not before it."

## DEPARTMENT OF COMMERCE v. NEW YORK

Supreme Court of the United States (2019).
139 S.Ct. 2551.

■ CHIEF JUSTICE ROBERTS delivered the opinion of the Court.

The Secretary of Commerce decided to reinstate a question about citizenship on the 2020 census questionnaire. A group of plaintiffs challenged that decision on constitutional and statutory grounds. We now decide whether the Secretary violated the Enumeration Clause of the Constitution, the Census Act, or otherwise abused his discretion.

I

A

In order to apportion Members of the House of Representatives among the States, the Constitution requires an "Enumeration" of the population every 10 years, to be made "in such Manner" as Congress "shall by Law direct." Art. I, § 2, cl. 3; Amdt. 14, § 2. In the Census Act, Congress delegated to the Secretary of Commerce the task of conducting the decennial census "in such form and content as he may determine." 13 U.S.C. § 141(a). The Secretary is aided in that task by the Census Bureau, a statistical agency housed within the Department of Commerce. See §§ 2, 21.

The population count derived from the census is used not only to apportion representatives but also to allocate federal funds to the States and to draw electoral districts. The census additionally serves as a means of collecting demographic information, which "is used for such varied purposes as computing federal grant-in-aid benefits, drafting of legislation, urban and regional planning, business planning, and academic and social studies." Baldrige v. Shapiro, 455 U.S. 345, 353–354, n. 9 (1982). Over the years, the census has asked questions about (for example) race, sex, age, health, education, occupation, housing, and military service. It has also asked about radio ownership, age at first marriage, and native tongue. The Census Act obliges everyone to answer census questions truthfully and requires the Secretary to keep individual answers confidential, including from other Government agencies. §§ 221, 8(b), 9(a).

There have been 23 decennial censuses from the first census in 1790 to the most recent in 2010. Every census between 1820 and 2000 (with the exception of 1840) asked at least some of the population about their citizenship or place of birth. Between 1820 and 1950, the question was asked of all households. Between 1960 and 2000, it was asked of about one-fourth to one-sixth of the population. That change was part of a larger effort to simplify the census by asking most people a few basic demographic questions (such as sex, age, race, and marital status) on a short-form questionnaire, while asking a sample of the population more detailed demographic questions on a long-form questionnaire. . . .

In 2010, the year of the latest census, the format changed again. All households received the same questionnaire, which asked about sex, age, race, Hispanic origin, and living arrangements. The more detailed demographic questions previously asked on the long-form questionnaire, including the question about citizenship, were instead asked in the American Community Survey (or ACS), which is sent each year to a rotating sample of about 2.6% of households.

The Census Bureau and former Bureau officials have resisted occasional proposals to resume asking a citizenship question of everyone, on the ground that doing so would discourage noncitizens from responding to the census and lead to a less accurate count of the total population.

B

In March 2018, Secretary of Commerce Wilbur Ross announced in a memo that he had decided to reinstate a question about citizenship on the 2020 decennial census questionnaire. The Secretary stated that he was acting at the request of the Department of Justice (DOJ), which sought improved data about citizen voting-age population for purposes of enforcing the Voting Rights Act (or VRA)—specifically the Act's ban on diluting the influence of minority voters by depriving them of single-member districts in which they can elect their preferred candidates. DOJ explained that federal courts determine whether a minority group could constitute a majority in a particular district by looking to the citizen voting-age population of the group. According to DOJ, the existing citizenship data from the American Community Survey was not ideal: It was not reported at the level of the census block, the basic component of legislative districting plans; it had substantial margins of error; and it did not align in time with the census-based population counts used to draw legislative districts. DOJ therefore formally requested reinstatement of the citizenship question on the census questionnaire.

The Secretary's memo explained that the Census Bureau initially analyzed, and the Secretary considered, three possible courses of action. The first was to continue to collect citizenship information in the American Community Survey and attempt to develop a data model that would more accurately estimate citizenship at the census block level. The Secretary rejected that option because the Bureau "did not assert and could not confirm" that such ACS-based data modeling was possible "with a sufficient degree of accuracy."

The second option was to reinstate a citizenship question on the decennial census. The Bureau predicted that doing so would discourage some noncitizens from responding to the census. That would necessitate increased "non-response follow up" operations—procedures the Bureau uses to attempt to count people who have not responded to the census—and potentially lead to a less accurate count of the total population.

Option three was to use administrative records from other agencies, such as the Social Security Administration and Citizenship and Immigration Services, to provide DOJ with citizenship data. The Census Bureau recommended this option, and the Secretary found it a "potentially appealing solution" because the Bureau has long used administrative records to supplement and improve census data. But the Secretary concluded that administrative records alone were inadequate because they were missing for more than 10% of the population.

The Secretary ultimately asked the Census Bureau to develop a fourth option that would combine options two and three: reinstate a citizenship question on the census questionnaire, and also use the time remaining until the 2020 census to "further enhance" the Bureau's "administrative record data sets, protocols, and statistical models." The memo explained that, in the Secretary's judgment, the fourth option would provide DOJ with the "most complete and accurate" citizen voting-age population data in response to its request.

The Secretary "carefully considered" the possibility that reinstating a citizenship question would depress the response rate. But after evaluating the Bureau's "limited empirical evidence" on the question—evidence drawn from estimated non-response rates to previous American Community Surveys and census questionnaires—the Secretary concluded that it was not possible to "determine definitively" whether inquiring about citizenship in the census would materially affect response rates. He also noted the long history of the citizenship question on the census, as well as the facts that the United Nations recommends collecting census-based citizenship information, and other major democracies such as Australia, Canada, France, Indonesia, Ireland, Germany, Mexico, Spain, and the United Kingdom inquire about citizenship in their censuses. Altogether, the Secretary determined that "the need for accurate citizenship data and the limited burden that the reinstatement of the citizenship question would impose outweigh fears about a potentially lower response rate."

C

. . . In June 2018, the Government submitted to the District Court the Commerce Department's "administrative record": the materials that Secretary Ross considered in making his decision. That record included DOJ's December 2017 letter requesting reinstatement of the citizenship question, as well as several memos from the Census Bureau analyzing the predicted effects of reinstating the question. Shortly thereafter, at DOJ's urging, the Government supplemented the record with a new memo from the Secretary, "intended to provide further background and context regarding" his March 2018 memo. The supplemental memo stated that the Secretary had begun considering whether to add the citizenship question in early 2017, and had inquired whether DOJ "would support, and if so would request, inclusion of a citizenship question as consistent with and useful for enforcement of the Voting Rights Act." According to the Secretary, DOJ "formally" requested reinstatement of the citizenship question after that inquiry.

Respondents argued that the supplemental memo indicated that the Government had submitted an incomplete record of the materials considered by the Secretary. They asked the District Court to compel the Government to complete the administrative record. The court granted that request, and the parties jointly stipulated to the inclusion of more than 12,000 pages of additional materials in the administrative record. Among those materials were emails and other records confirming that the Secretary and his staff began exploring the possibility of reinstating a citizenship question shortly after he was confirmed in early 2017, attempted to elicit requests for citizenship data from other agencies, and eventually persuaded DOJ to request reinstatement of the question for VRA enforcement purposes.

In addition, respondents asked the court to authorize discovery outside the administrative record. They claimed that such an unusual step was warranted because they had made a strong preliminary showing that the Secretary had acted in bad faith. See Citizens to Preserve Overton Park, Inc. v. Volpe, 401 U.S. 402, 420 (1971) [p. 1147] The court also granted that request, authorizing expert discovery and depositions of certain DOJ and Commerce Department officials.

In August and September 2018, the District Court issued orders compelling depositions of Secretary Ross and of the Acting Assistant Attorney General for DOJ's Civil Rights Division. We granted the Government's request to stay the Secretary's deposition pending further review, but we declined to stay the Acting AAG's deposition or the other extra-record discovery that the District Court had authorized.

The District Court held a bench trial and issued findings of fact and conclusions of law on respondents' statutory and equal protection claims. After determining that respondents had standing to sue, the District Court ruled that the Secretary's action was arbitrary and capricious, based on a pretextual rationale, and violated certain provisions of the Census Act. On the equal protection claim, however, the District Court concluded that respondents had not met their burden of showing that the Secretary was motivated by discriminatory animus. The court granted judgment to respondents on their statutory claims, vacated the Secretary's decision, and enjoined him from reinstating the citizenship question until he cured the legal errors the court had identified.

The Government appealed to the Second Circuit, but also filed a petition for writ of certiorari before judgment, asking this Court to review the District Court's decision directly because the case involved an issue of imperative public importance, and the census questionnaire needed to be finalized for printing by the end of June 2019. We granted the petition. At the Government's request, we later ordered the parties to address whether the Enumeration Clause provided an alternative basis to affirm.

II

[The Court determined that there was standing.]

III

[The Court held that the Secretary's decision did not violate the Enumeration Clause.]

IV

The District Court set aside the Secretary's decision to reinstate a citizenship question on the grounds that the Secretary acted arbitrarily and violated certain provisions of the Census Act. The Government contests those rulings, but also argues that the Secretary's decision was not judicially reviewable under the Administrative Procedure Act in the first place. We begin with that contention.

A

[The Court determined that the Secretary's decision was reviewable under § 701(a) (see p. 1496)].

B

At the heart of this suit is respondents' claim that the Secretary abused his discretion in deciding to reinstate a citizenship question. We review the Secretary's exercise of discretion under the deferential "arbitrary and capricious" standard. See 5 U.S.C. § 706(2)(A). Our scope of review is "narrow": we determine only whether the Secretary examined "the relevant data" and articulated "a satisfactory explanation" for his decision, "including a rational connection between the facts found and the choice made." State Farm. We may not substitute our judgment for that of the Secretary, but instead must confine ourselves to ensuring that he remained "within the bounds of reasoned decisionmaking," Baltimore Gas & Elec. Co. v. Natural Resources Defense Council, Inc., 462 U.S. 87, 105 (1983).

The District Court set aside the Secretary's decision for two independent reasons: His course of action was not supported by the evidence before him, and his stated rationale was pretextual. We focus on the first point here and take up the question of pretext later.

The Secretary examined the Bureau's analysis of various ways to collect improved citizenship data and explained why he thought the best course was to both reinstate a citizenship question and use citizenship data from administrative records to fill in the gaps. He considered but rejected the Bureau's recommendation to use administrative records alone. As he explained, records are lacking for about 10% of the population, so the Bureau would still need to estimate citizenship for millions of voting-age people. Asking a citizenship question of everyone, the Secretary reasoned, would eliminate the need to estimate citizenship for many of those people. And supplementing census responses with administrative record data would help complete the picture and allow the Bureau to better estimate citizenship for the smaller set of cases where it was still necessary to do so.

The evidence before the Secretary supported that decision. As the Bureau acknowledged, each approach—using administrative records alone, or asking about citizenship and using records to fill in the gaps—entailed tradeoffs between accuracy and completeness. Without a citizenship question, the Bureau would need to estimate the citizenship of about 35 million people; with a citizenship question, it would need to estimate the citizenship of only 13.8 million. Under either approach, there would be some errors in both the administrative records and the Bureau's estimates. With a citizenship question, there would also be some erroneous self-responses (about 500,000) and some conflicts between responses and administrative record data (about 9.5 million).

The Bureau explained that the "relative quality" of the citizenship data generated by each approach would depend on the "relative importance of the errors" in each, but it was not able to "quantify the relative magnitude of the errors across the alternatives." The Bureau nonetheless recommended using administrative records alone because it had "high confidence" that it could develop an accurate model for estimating the citizenship of the 35 million people for whom administrative records were not available, and it thought the resulting citizenship data would be of superior quality. But when the time came for the Secretary to make a decision, the model did not yet exist, and even if it had, there was no way to gauge its relative accuracy. As the Bureau put it, "we will most likely never possess a fully adequate truth deck to benchmark" the model—which appears to be bureaucratese for "maybe, maybe not." The Secretary opted instead for the approach that would yield a more complete set of data at an acceptable rate of accuracy, and would require estimating the citizenship of fewer people.

The District Court overruled that choice, agreeing with the Bureau's assessment that its recommended approach would yield higher quality citizenship data on the whole. But the choice between reasonable policy alternatives in the face of uncertainty was the Secretary's to make. He considered the relevant factors, weighed risks and benefits, and articulated a satisfactory explanation for his decision. In overriding that reasonable exercise of discretion, the court improperly substituted its judgment for that of the agency.

The Secretary then weighed the benefit of collecting more complete and accurate citizenship data against the risk that inquiring about citizenship would depress census response rates, particularly among noncitizen households. In the Secretary's view, that risk was difficult to assess. The Bureau predicted a 5.1% decline in response rates among noncitizen households if the citizenship question were reinstated. It relied for that prediction primarily on studies showing that, while noncitizens had responded at lower rates than citizens to the 2000 short-form and 2010 censuses, which did not ask about citizenship, they responded at even lower rates than citizens to the 2000 long-form census and the 2010 American Community Survey, which did ask about citizenship. The Bureau thought it was reasonable to infer that the citizenship question accounted for the differential decline in noncitizen responses. But, the Secretary explained, the Bureau was unable to rule out other causes. For one thing, the evidence before the Secretary suggested that noncitizen households tend to be more distrustful of, and less likely to respond to, *any* government effort to collect information. For another, both the 2000 long-form census and 2010 ACS asked over 45 questions on a range of topics, including employment, income, and housing characteristics. Noncitizen households might disproportionately fail to respond to a lengthy and intrusive Government questionnaire for a number of reasons besides reluctance to answer a citizenship question—reasons relating to education level, socioeconomic status, and less exposure to Government outreach efforts.

The Secretary justifiably found the Bureau's analysis inconclusive. Weighing that uncertainty against the value of obtaining more complete and accurate citizenship data, he determined that reinstating a citizenship question was worth the risk of a potentially lower response rate. That decision was reasonable and reasonably explained, particularly in light of the long history of the citizenship question on the census.

Justice Breyer would conclude otherwise, but only by subordinating the Secretary's policymaking discretion to the Bureau's technocratic expertise. Justice Breyer's analysis treats the Bureau's (pessimistic) prediction about response rates and (optimistic) assumptions about its data modeling abilities as touchstones of substantive reasonableness rather than simply evidence for the Secretary to consider. He suggests that the Secretary should have deferred to the Bureau or at least offered some special justification for drawing his own inferences and adopting his own assumptions. But the Census Act authorizes the Secretary, not the Bureau, to make policy choices within the range of reasonable options. And the evidence before the Secretary hardly led ineluctably to just one reasonable course of action. It called for value-laden decisionmaking and the weighing of incommensurables under conditions of uncertainty. The Secretary was required to consider the evidence and give reasons for his chosen course of action. He did so. It is not for us to ask whether his decision was "the best one possible" or even whether it was "better than the alternatives." FERC v. Electric Power Supply Assn., [p. 1141]. By second-guessing the Secretary's weighing of risks and benefits and penalizing him for departing from the Bureau's inferences and assumptions, Justice Breyer—like the District Court—substitutes his judgment for that of the agency.

C

The District Court also ruled that the Secretary violated two particular provisions of the Census Act, § 6(c) and § 141(f). [We disagree.]

V

We now consider the District Court's determination that the Secretary's decision must be set aside because it rested on a pretextual basis, which the Government conceded below would warrant a remand to the agency.

We start with settled propositions. First, in order to permit meaningful judicial review, an agency must "disclose the basis" of its action. Burlington Truck Lines, Inc. v. United States; see also SEC v. Chenery Corp. ("[T]he orderly functioning of the process of review requires that the grounds upon which the administrative agency acted be clearly disclosed and adequately sustained.").

Second, in reviewing agency action, a court is ordinarily limited to evaluating the agency's contemporaneous explanation in light of the existing administrative record. Vermont Yankee [p. 312]. That principle reflects the recognition that further judicial inquiry into "executive motivation" represents "a substantial intrusion" into the workings of another branch of Government and should normally be avoided.

Third, a court may not reject an agency's stated reasons for acting simply because the agency might also have had other unstated reasons. See Jagers v. Federal Crop Ins. Corp., 758 F.3d 1179, 1185–1186 (CA10 2014) (rejecting argument that "the agency's subjective desire to reach a particular result must necessarily invalidate the result, regardless of the objective evidence supporting the agency's conclusion"). Relatedly, a court may not set aside an agency's policymaking decision solely because it might have been influenced by political considerations or prompted by an Administration's priorities. Agency policymaking is not a "rarified technocratic process, unaffected by political considerations or the presence of Presidential power." Sierra Club v. Costle, 657 F.2d 298, 408 (CADC 1981) [p. 1051]. Such decisions are routinely informed by unstated considerations of politics, the legislative process, public relations, interest group relations, foreign relations, and national security concerns (among others).

Finally, we have recognized a narrow exception to the general rule against inquiring into "the mental processes of administrative decisionmakers." Overton Park [p. 1147]. On a "strong showing of bad faith or improper behavior," such an inquiry may be warranted and may justify extra-record discovery. Ibid.

The District Court invoked that exception in ordering extra-record discovery here. Although that order was premature, we think it was ultimately justified in light of the expanded administrative record. Recall that shortly after this litigation began, the Secretary, prodded by DOJ, filed a supplemental memo that added new, pertinent information to the administrative record. The memo disclosed that the Secretary had been considering the citizenship question for some time and that Commerce had inquired whether DOJ would formally request reinstatement of the question. That supplemental memo prompted respondents to move for both completion of the administrative record and extra-record discovery. The District Court granted both requests at the same hearing, agreeing with respondents that the Government had submitted an incomplete administrative record and that the existing evidence supported a prima facie showing that the VRA rationale was pretextual.

The Government did not challenge the court's conclusion that the administrative record was incomplete, and the parties stipulated to the inclusion of more than 12,000 pages of internal deliberative materials as part of the administrative record, materials that the court later held were sufficient on their own to demonstrate pretext. The Government did, however, challenge the District Court's order authorizing extra-record discovery, as well as the court's later orders compelling depositions of the Secretary and of the Acting Assistant Attorney General for DOJ's Civil Rights Division.

We agree with the Government that the District Court should not have ordered extra-record discovery when it did. At that time, the most that was warranted was the order to complete the administrative record. But the new material that the parties stipulated should have been part of the administrative record—which showed, among other things, that the VRA played an insignificant role in the decisionmaking process—largely justified such extra-record discovery as occurred (which did not include the deposition of the Secretary himself). We accordingly review the District Court's ruling on pretext in light of all the evidence in the record before the court, including the extra-record discovery.

That evidence showed that the Secretary was determined to reinstate a citizenship question from the time he entered office; instructed his staff to make it happen; waited while Commerce officials explored whether another agency would request census-based citizenship data; subsequently contacted the Attorney General himself to ask if DOJ would make the request; and adopted the Voting Rights Act rationale late in the process. In the District Court's view, this evidence established that the Secretary had made up his mind to reinstate a citizenship question "well before" receiving DOJ's request, and did so for reasons unknown but unrelated to the VRA. 351 F.Supp.3d at 660.

The Government, on the other hand, contends that there was nothing objectionable or even surprising in this. And we agree—to a point. It is hardly improper for an agency head to come into office with policy preferences and ideas, discuss them with affected parties, sound out other agencies for support, and work with staff attorneys to substantiate the legal basis for a preferred policy. The record here reflects the sometimes involved nature of Executive Branch decisionmaking, but no particular step in the process stands out as inappropriate or defective.

And yet, viewing the evidence as a whole, we share the District Court's conviction that the decision to reinstate a citizenship question cannot be adequately explained in terms of DOJ's request for improved citizenship data to better enforce the VRA. Several points, considered together, reveal a significant mismatch between the decision the Secretary made and the rationale he provided.

The record shows that the Secretary began taking steps to reinstate a citizenship question about a week into his tenure, but it contains no hint that he was considering VRA enforcement in connection with that project. The Secretary's Director of Policy did not know why the Secretary wished to reinstate the question, but saw it as his task to "find the best rationale." The Director initially attempted to elicit requests for citizenship data from the Department of Homeland Security and DOJ's Executive Office for Immigration Review, neither of which is responsible for enforcing the VRA. After those attempts failed, he asked Commerce staff to look into whether the Secretary could reinstate the question without receiving a request from another agency. The possibility that DOJ's Civil Rights Division might be willing to request citizenship data for VRA enforcement purposes was proposed by Commerce staff along the way and eventually pursued.

Even so, it was not until the Secretary contacted the Attorney General directly that DOJ's Civil Rights Division expressed interest in acquiring census-based citizenship data to better enforce the VRA. And even then, the record suggests that DOJ's interest was directed more to helping the Commerce Department than to securing the data. The December 2017 letter from DOJ drew heavily on contributions from

Commerce staff and advisors. Their influence may explain why the letter went beyond a simple entreaty for better citizenship data—what one might expect of a typical request from another agency—to a specific request that Commerce collect the data by means of reinstating a citizenship question on the census. Finally, after sending the letter, DOJ declined the Census Bureau's offer to discuss alternative ways to meet DOJ's stated need for improved citizenship data, further suggesting a lack of interest on DOJ's part.

Altogether, the evidence tells a story that does not match the explanation the Secretary gave for his decision. In the Secretary's telling, Commerce was simply acting on a routine data request from another agency. Yet the materials before us indicate that Commerce went to great lengths to elicit the request from DOJ (or any other willing agency). And unlike a typical case in which an agency may have both stated and unstated reasons for a decision, here the VRA enforcement rationale—the sole stated reason—seems to have been contrived.

We are presented, in other words, with an explanation for agency action that is incongruent with what the record reveals about the agency's priorities and decisionmaking process. It is rare to review a record as extensive as the one before us when evaluating informal agency action—and it should be. But having done so for the sufficient reasons we have explained, we cannot ignore the disconnect between the decision made and the explanation given. Our review is deferential, but we are "not required to exhibit a naiveté from which ordinary citizens are free." United States v. Stanchich, 550 F.2d 1294, 1300 (CA2 1977) (Friendly, J.). The reasoned explanation requirement of administrative law, after all, is meant to ensure that agencies offer genuine justifications for important decisions, reasons that can be scrutinized by courts and the interested public. Accepting contrived reasons would defeat the purpose of the enterprise. If judicial review is to be more than an empty ritual, it must demand something better than the explanation offered for the action taken in this case.

In these unusual circumstances, the District Court was warranted in remanding to the agency, and we affirm that disposition. We do not hold that the agency decision here was substantively invalid. But agencies must pursue their goals reasonably. Reasoned decisionmaking under the Administrative Procedure Act calls for an explanation for agency action. What was provided here was more of a distraction.

The judgment of the United States District Court for the Southern District of New York is affirmed in part and reversed in part, and the case is remanded for further proceedings consistent with this opinion.

## NOTES

(1) ***Vote Breakdowns.*** The opinion you just read begins: "Chief Justice Roberts delivered the opinion of the Court." While that is true, it is also true that Chief Justice Roberts was the only Justice who agreed with all parts of the opinion. Justice Thomas, Justice Breyer, and Justice Alito each wrote

separate opinions, and the other Justices joined one or another of these other opinions. The upshot was that "The Court"—which is to say, at least five votes—consisted of different Justices for different parts. Here are the details:

Parts I and II of Chief Justice Robert's opinion—the basic description of the case and the determination that plaintiffs satisfied standing requirements—were joined by all the other Justices.

Part III—holding that what the Secretary wanted to do was not unconstitutional—was joined by Justices Thomas, Alito, Gorsuch and Kavanaugh. (The other Justices did not voice an opinion on this point.)

Part IV-A—holding that the case was justiciable under the APA—was joined by all the Justices except Justices Alito and Gorsuch; Alito's separate opinion was devoted to showing that the case was not justiciable.

Part IV-B—holding that the Secretary's decision was adequately supported by the evidence—was joined by Justices Thomas, Alito, Gorsuch and Kavanaugh and rejected by Justices Ginsburg, Breyer, Sotomayor and Kagan; Breyer's separate opinion was devoted to this issue.

Part IV-C—holding that the Secretary had not violated two specific provisions of the Census Act—was supported and rejected in the same fashion as Part IV-B, but was not the focus of any of the separate opinions.

Part V—holding that the Secretary's decision had to be remanded because "the evidence tells a story that does not match the explanation the Secretary gave for his decision"—was joined by Justices Ginsburg, Breyer, Sotomayor and Kagan, and rejected by Justices Thomas, Alito, Gorsuch and Kavanaugh; Thomas's separate opinion was devoted to this issue.

(2) ***Part IV-B.*** JUSTICE BREYER's dissent claimed the Secretary's treatment of the evidence failed to measure up to the standards of rational decisionmaking set forth in the State Farm case. Here's a portion of his analysis, 139 S.Ct. at 2587–90:

"The Secretary's decision . . . rests upon a weighing of potentially adverse consequences (diminished responses and a less accurate census count) against potentially offsetting advantages (better citizenship data). In my view, however, the Secretary did not make reasonable decisions about these potential costs and benefits in light of the administrative record.

"Consider first the Secretary's conclusion that he was 'not able to determine definitively how inclusion of a citizenship question on the decennial census will impact responsiveness.' Insofar as this statement implies that adding the citizenship question is unlikely to affect 'responsiveness' very much (or perhaps at all), the evidence in the record indicates the contrary.

"The administrative record includes repeated Census Bureau statements that adding the question would produce a less accurate count because noncitizens and Hispanics would be less likely to respond to the questionnaire. The Census Bureau's chief scientist said specifically that adding the question would have 'an adverse impact on self-response and, as a result, on the accuracy and quality of the 2020 Census.' And the chief scientist backed this statement up by pointing to '[t]hree distinct analyses.'

"The first analysis compared nonresponse rates for the short-form census questionnaire (which did not include a citizenship question) to nonresponse rates for the ACS [American Community Survey] (which did). Obviously, more people fail to respond to the ACS than to the short form. Yet taking into account the fact that the nonresponse rate will be greater for the ACS than for the short form, the Bureau found that the difference between the two is yet greater for noncitizen households than for citizen households (by 5.1%, according to the Bureau). This led the Bureau to say that it was a 'reasonable inference' that the presence of the citizenship question accounted for the difference.

"The Bureau conducted two additional studies, both analyzing data from the ACS. One study looked at response rates for particular questions on the ACS. It showed that the 'no answer' rate for the citizenship question was 'much greater than the comparable rates' for other census questions (for example, questions about age, sex, race, and ethnicity). And it showed that the 'no answer' rate for the citizenship question was significantly higher among Hispanics. The last study examined 'break-off' rates, i.e., the rate at which respondents stopped answering the questionnaire upon reaching a particular question. It found that Hispanics were significantly more likely than were non-Hispanics to stop answering at the point they reached the citizenship question. Together, these two studies provided additional support for the Census Bureau's determination that the citizenship question is likely to mean disproportionately fewer responses from noncitizens and Hispanics than from others.

"Putting numbers upon these study results, the Census Bureau estimated that adding the question to the short form would lead to 630,000 additional nonresponding households. That is to say, the question would cause households covering more than 1 million additional people to decline to respond to the census. When the Bureau does not receive a response, it follows up with in-person interviews in an effort to obtain the missing information. The Bureau often interviews what it calls 'proxies,' such as family members and neighbors. But this follow up process is subject to error; and the error rate is much greater than the error rate for self-responses. The Bureau thus explained that lower self-response rates 'degrade data quality' by increasing the risk of error and leading to hundreds of thousands of fewer correct enumerations. . . . Its conclusion in light of this evidence was clear. Adding the citizenship question to the short form was 'very likely to reduce the self-response rate' and thereby 'har[m] the quality of the census count.' . . .

"The Secretary's decision memorandum reached a quite different conclusion from the Census Bureau. The memorandum conceded that 'a lower response rate would lead to . . . less accurate responses.' But it concluded that neither the Census Bureau nor any stakeholders had provided 'definitive, empirical support' for the proposition that the citizenship question would reduce response rates. The memorandum relied for that conclusion upon a number of considerations, but each is contradicted by the record.

"The memorandum first pointed to perceived shortcomings in the Census Bureau's analysis of nonresponse rates. It noted that response rates are generally lower overall for the long form and ACS than they are for the short form. But the Bureau explained that its analysis accounted for this consideration, and no one has given us reason to think the contrary. The Secretary also noted that the Bureau 'was not able to isolate what percentage of [the] decline was caused by the inclusion of a citizenship question rather than some other aspect of the long form survey.' But the Bureau said attributing the decline to the citizenship question was a 'reasonable inference,' and again, nothing in the record contradicted the Bureau's judgment. . . .

"Finally, the memorandum relied on information provided by two outside stakeholders. The first was a study conducted by the private survey company Nielsen, in which questions about place of birth and time of arrival had not led to any appreciable decrease in the response rate. But Nielsen, which in fact urged the Secretary *not* to add the question, stated that its respondents (unlike census respondents) were *paid* to respond, and it is consequently not surprising that they did so. . . .

"The upshot is that the Secretary received evidence of a likely drop in census accuracy by a number somewhere in the hundreds of thousands, and he received nothing significant to the contrary. The Secretary pointed out that the Census Bureau's information was uncertain, i.e., not 'definitive.' But that is not a satisfactory answer. Few public-policy-related statistical studies of risks (say, of many health or safety matters) are definitive. As the Court explained in State Farm, '[i]t is not infrequent that the available data do not settle a regulatory issue, and the agency must then exercise its judgment in moving from the facts and probabilities on the record to a policy conclusion.' 463 U.S. at 52. But an agency confronted with this situation cannot 'merely recite the terms "substantial uncertainty" as a justification for its actions.' Ibid. Instead, it 'must explain the evidence which is available' and typically must offer a reasoned explanation for taking action without 'engaging in a search for further evidence.' Ibid.

"The Secretary did not do so here. He did not explain why he made the decision to add the question without following the Bureau's ordinary practice of extensively testing proposed changes to the census questionnaire. Without that testing, the Secretary could not treat the Bureau's expert opinions and its experience with the relevant surveys as worthless merely because its conclusions were not precise. The Bureau's opinions were properly considered as evidence of likelihoods, probabilities, or risks.

"As noted above, the consequences of mistakes in the census count, of even a few hundred thousand, are grave. Differences of a few thousand people, as between one State and another, can mean a loss or gain of a congressional seat—a matter of great consequence to a State. And similar small differences can make a large difference to the allocation of federal funds among competing state programs. If near-absolute certainty is what the Secretary meant by 'definitive,' that insistence would itself be arbitrary in light of the constitutional and statutory consequences at stake. And if the

Secretary instead meant that the evidence does not indicate a serious risk of a less accurate count, that conclusion does not find support in the record."

Chief Justice Roberts said that this argument depends on Justice Breyer's "subordinating the Secretary's policymaking discretion to the Bureau's technocratic expertise." Do you agree?

(3) ***Part V.*** JUSTICE THOMAS's opinion focused on the Court's determination to remand because of "pretext." The Court, he argued, should never have gone there. 139 S.Ct. at 2577–80:

"As relevant here, the APA requires courts to 'hold unlawful and set aside' agency action that is 'arbitrary, capricious, an abuse of discretion, or otherwise not in accordance with law.' § 706(2)(A). We have emphasized that '[r]eview under the arbitrary and capricious standard is deferential.' National Assn. of Home Builders v. Defenders of Wildlife, 551 U.S. 644, 658 (2007). It requires the reviewing court to determine whether the agency 'examine[d] the relevant data and articulate[d] a satisfactory explanation for its action.' FCC v. Fox Television Stations, Inc. We have described this as a ' "narrow" standard of review' under which the reviewing court cannot ' "substitute its judgment for that of the agency," and should "uphold a decision of less than ideal clarity if the agency's path may reasonably be discerned." ' Fox Television; State Farm.

"Part IV-B of the opinion of the Court correctly applies this standard to conclude that the Secretary's decision survives ordinary arbitrary-and-capricious review. That holding should end our inquiry.

"But the opinion continues. Acknowledging that 'no particular step' in the proceedings here 'stands out as inappropriate or defective,' even after reviewing 'all the evidence in the record . . . , including the extra-record discovery,' the Court nevertheless agrees with the District Court that the Secretary's rationale for reinstating the citizenship question was 'pretextual—that is, that the real reason for his decision was something other than the sole reason he put forward in his memorandum, namely enhancement of DOJ's VRA enforcement efforts.' 351 F.Supp.3d 502, 660 (SDNY 2019). According to the Court, something just 'seems' wrong.

"This conclusion is extraordinary. The Court engages in an unauthorized inquiry into evidence not properly before us to reach an unsupported conclusion. Moreover, each step of the inquiry offends the presumption of regularity we owe the Executive. The judgment of the District Court should be reversed.

"Section 706(2) of the APA contemplates review of the administrative 'record' to determine whether an agency's 'action, findings, and conclusions' satisfy six specified standards. See §§ 706(2)(A)–(F). None instructs the Court to inquire into pretext. Consistent with this statutory text, we have held that a court is 'ordinarily limited to evaluating the agency's contemporaneous explanation in light of the existing administrative record.' Vermont Yankee; see SEC v. Chenery Corp. ('The grounds upon which an administrative order must be judged are those upon which the record discloses that its action was based'). If an agency's stated findings and conclusions withstand scrutiny, the APA does not permit a court to set aside the decision solely because the agency had 'other unstated reasons' for its decision, such as 'political considerations' or the 'Administration's priorities.'

"Unsurprisingly, then, this Court has never held an agency decision arbitrary and capricious on the ground that its supporting rationale was 'pretextual.' Nor has it previously suggested that this was even a possibility. Under 'settled propositions' of administrative law, pretext is virtually never an appropriate or relevant inquiry for a reviewing court to undertake.

"Respondents conceptualize pretext as a subset of 'arbitrary and capricious' review. It is far from clear that they are correct. But even if they were, an agency action is not arbitrary or capricious merely because the decisionmaker has other, unstated reasons for the decision. Nor is an agency action arbitrary and capricious merely because the decisionmaker was 'inclined' to accomplish it before confirming that the law and facts supported that inclination.

"Accordingly, even under respondents' approach, a showing of pretext could render an agency action arbitrary and capricious only in the infinitesimally small number of cases in which the administrative record establishes that an agency's stated rationale did not factor *at all* into the decision, thereby depriving the action of an adequate supporting rationale. This showing is extremely difficult to make because the administrative record will rarely, if ever, contain evidence sufficient to show that an agency's stated rationale did not actually factor into its decision. And we have stated that a 'strong showing of bad faith or improper behavior' is necessary to venture beyond the agency's 'administrative findings' and inquire into 'the mental processes of administrative decisionmakers.' Overton Park, 401 U.S. at 420. We have never before found Overton Park's exception satisfied, much less invalidated an agency action based on 'pretext.' . . ."

In response to Justice Thomas's challenge, can you ground the Court's holding in the text of the APA? Is Chief Justice Roberts saying that the explanation of the evidence that meets Justice Breyer's complaint (see above)—that makes it not arbitrary and capricious—depends on a good faith weighing of the evidence, which was not present here? In Biden v. Texas, 142 S.Ct. 2528 (2022), Chief Justice Roberts described the holding in Department of Commerce in this way: "Department of Commerce involved a 'narrow exception to th[at] general rule' that applies where the challengers to the agency's action make a 'strong showing of bad faith or improper behavior' on the part of the agency. We held that exception satisfied by an accumulation of 'unusual circumstances' that demonstrated an 'explanation for agency action that [was] incongruent with what the record reveal[ed] about the agency's priorities and decisionmaking process.' "

(4) ***Why Care About Pretext?*** Is "pretext" bad because it is immoral? If so, why don't we just let administrators speak what is really on their minds? But do they want to? In REASONED EXPLANATION AND POLITICAL ACCOUNTABILITY IN THE ROBERTS COURT, 130 Yale L.J. 1748, 1788 (2021), BENJAMIN EIDELSON argues that Chief Justice Roberts's opinion in Department of Commerce, along with his opinion in Department of Homeland Security v. Regents of the University of California (see p. 1139),

employs judicial review as a means of furthering the political accountability of the Administration: "If one purpose of the reasoned explanation requirement is to ensure political accountability for an agency's reasons, then it is easy to see how grave violations of that requirement could justifiably be treated as fatal to an agency action—irrespective of whether the agency's actual reasons sufficed, and irrespective of whether the agency could lawfully have taken the same action in the end. Here, when Secretary Ross lied about his reasons for adding the citizenship question, any damage to *political* accountability was done. Even if further litigation might have revealed his actual reasons as nonarbitrary, his decision could not be upheld on those grounds without creating the same Chenery problem as we saw in Regents: The administration would have rolled out its policy and publicly defended it on one, more politically attractive ground, only to have it upheld on a different one. Similarly, allowing Ross's decision to take immediate effect would mean letting the administration have its way without ever weighing (and, if it chose, paying) the political cost of publicly switching to a new rationale or readopting one that had been exposed as a lie."

(5) ***Creating the Record.*** It is worth noting that part of the confusion as to what happened in this case is the result of the decision's being, in APA terms, an informal adjudication. The rules of judicial review, § 706, call for review of the "whole record," but the APA provides no procedure for informal adjudication by which any particular record is created. The result seems to have been a free-for-all searching for any document the Secretary might have considered. And, beyond the documents, there was the possibility of deposing the key actors. This problem has been noted before in discussions of the Morgan cases (see p. 553) and the Overton Park case (see p. 1146). The actions of the Supreme Court in relation to what the district court did in the principal case seem to draw a distinction between cabinet level officials at the top of agencies and lower level officials. Aside from the respect owed to other branches of government, there is the fact that, in the words of the Ninth Circuit regarding an attempt to depose Education Secretary Elizabeth DeVos, "Cabinet secretaries face a potentially greater amount of litigation than most other witnesses." In re U.S. Dep't of Educ., 25 F.4th 692 (9th Cir. 2022). For this and other reasons, the Ninth Circuit stated the law in this way: "[W]e hold that extraordinary circumstances sufficient to justify the taking of a cabinet secretary's deposition exist when the party seeking the deposition can demonstrate: (1) a showing of agency bad faith; (2) the information sought from the secretary is essential to the case; and (3) the information sought from the secretary cannot be obtained in any other way. All three factors must be satisfied in order to take a secretary's deposition."

# SECTION 3. THE FRAMEWORK OF THE GOVERNING STATUTES



## a. Historical Building Block Cases

*NATIONAL LABOR RELATIONS BOARD v. HEARST PUBLICATIONS, INC.*
*SKIDMORE v. SWIFT & CO.*

Whether an agency's action has adequate support—the subject of the preceding Section—depends, of course, not just on how strong that support is but also on whether that support connects with what the agency is authorized to do. Agencies exist, and their responsibilities are delineated, by statutes. In Chapter II we considered the methods courts use as a general matter to construe statutes. We now take up a more particular question: how do the issues look different when there is an agency that has already construed the statute before the matter gets to court? We start our inquiry with a pair of cases that, as much as any, defined for an earlier generation an appropriate framework. Both predate by a couple of years passage of the APA; but here, unlike with its requirement of substantial evidence on the record as a whole, the APA was, at least initially, treated as merely restating prior practice.[1]

---

[1] When the APA was passed in 1946, the House conferees said its provisions on review would "preclude" various decisions, specifically including the first of our cases, Hearst. Justice Frankfurter noted this in the Universal Camera opinion but seemed to think that as to this particular case the conferees were confused. In any case, the Court treated Hearst, at least for a while, as unimpaired by passage of the APA. Of course, if the case had come up after 1946, some of its phrasing would have differed.

## NATIONAL LABOR RELATIONS BOARD v. HEARST PUBLICATIONS, INC.

Supreme Court of the United States (1944).
322 U.S. 111.

■ JUSTICE RUTLEDGE delivered the opinion of the Court.

These cases arise from the refusal of respondents, publishers of four Los Angeles daily newspapers, to bargain collectively with a union representing newsboys who distribute their papers on the streets of that city. Respondents' contention that they were not required to bargain because the newsboys are not their "employees" within the meaning of that term in the National Labor Relations Act, 29 U.S.C. § 152,[1] presents the important question which we granted certiorari to resolve. . . . [T]he Board made findings of fact and concluded that the regular full-time newsboys selling each paper were employees within the Act and that questions affecting commerce concerning the representation of employees had arisen. It designated appropriate units and ordered elections. At these the union was selected as their representative by majorities of the eligible newsboys. [Respondents then refused to bargain with the union, and the Board found this refusal was an unfair labor practice; the court of appeals refused enforcement, deciding that "employee" was to be interpreted consistently with the tests of the common law, and under those tests the newsboys were not employees.]

The papers are distributed to the ultimate consumer through a variety of channels, including . . . newsboys who sell on the streets of the city and its suburbs. . . . The newsboys work under varying terms and conditions. They may be "bootjackers," selling to the general public at places other than established corners, or they may sell at fixed "spots." They may sell only casually or part-time, or full-time; and they may be employed regularly and continuously or only temporarily. The units which the Board determined to be appropriate are composed of those who sell full-time at established spots. Those vendors, misnamed boys, are generally mature men, dependent upon the proceeds of their sales for their sustenance, and frequently supporters of families. Working thus as news vendors on a regular basis, often for a number of years, they form a stable group with relatively little turnover, in contrast to schoolboys and others who sell as bootjackers, temporary and casual distributors.

[The Court then set forth several paragraphs of detail about the newsboys' supervision, compensation, and conditions of work.]

In this pattern of employment the Board found that the newsboys are an integral part of the publishers' distribution system and circulation organization. And the record discloses that the newsboys and checkmen feel they are employees of the papers and respondents' supervisory employees, if not respondents themselves, regard them as such.

---

[1] Section 2(3) of the Act provides that "The term 'employee' shall include any employee, and shall not be limited to the employees of a particular employer, unless the Act explicitly states otherwise. . . ."

I

The principal question is whether the newsboys are "employees." Because Congress did not explicitly define the term, respondents say its meaning must be determined by reference to common-law standards. In their view "common-law standards" are those the courts have applied in distinguishing between "employees" and "independent contractors" when working out various problems unrelated to the Wagner Act's purposes and provisions.

The argument assumes that there is some simple, uniform and easily applicable test which the courts have used, in dealing with such problems, to determine whether persons doing work for others fall in one class or the other. Unfortunately this is not true. Only by a long and tortuous history was the simple formulation worked out which has been stated most frequently as "the test" for deciding whether one who hires another is responsible in tort for his wrongdoing. But this formula has been by no means exclusively controlling in the solution of other problems. And its simplicity has been illusory because it is more largely simplicity of formulation than of application. . . . [The various tests] have arisen principally, first, in the struggle of the courts to work out common-law liabilities where the legislature has given no guides for judgment, more recently also under statutes which have posed the same problem for solution in the light of the enactment's particular terms and purposes. . . . [W]ithin a single jurisdiction a person who, for instance, is held to be an "independent contractor" for the purpose of imposing vicarious liability in tort may be an "employee" for the purposes of particular legislation, such as unemployment compensation. . . .

Two possible consequences could follow. One would be to refer the decision of who are employees to local state law. The alternative would be to make it turn on a sort of pervading general essence distilled from state law. Congress obviously did not intend the former result. It would introduce variations into the statute's operation as wide as the differences the forty-eight states and other local jurisdictions make in applying the distinction for wholly different purposes. Persons who might be "employees" in one state would be "independent contractors" in another. . . . Persons working across state lines might fall in one class or the other, possibly both, depending on whether the Board and the courts would be required to give effect to the law of one state or of the adjoining one, or to that of each in relation to the portion of the work done within its borders.

Both the terms and the purposes of the statute, as well as the legislative history, show that Congress had in mind no such patchwork plan for securing freedom of employees' organization and of collective bargaining. The Wagner Act is federal legislation, administered by a national agency, intended to solve a national problem on a national scale. . . .

II

Whether, given the intended national uniformity, the term "employee" includes such workers as these newsboys must be answered primarily from the history, terms and purposes of the legislation. The word "is not treated by Congress as a word of art having a definite meaning. . . ." Rather "it . . . must be read in the light of the mischief to be corrected and the end to be attained." South Chicago Coal & Dock Co. v. Bassett, 309 U.S. 251.

Congress, on the one hand, was not thinking solely of the immediate technical relation of employer and employee. It had in mind at least some other persons than those standing in the proximate legal relation of employee to the particular employer involved in the labor dispute. It cannot be taken, however, that the purpose was to include all other persons who may perform service for another or was to ignore entirely legal classifications made for other purposes. Congress had in mind a wider field than the narrow technical legal relation of "master and servant," as the common law had worked this out in all its variations, and at the same time a narrower one than the entire area of rendering service to others. The question comes down therefore to how much was included of the intermediate region between what is clearly and unequivocally "employment," by any appropriate test, and what is as clearly entrepreneurial enterprise and not employment. . . .

Congress . . . sought to find a broad solution, one that would bring industrial peace by substituting, so far as its power could reach, the rights of workers to self-organization and collective bargaining for the industrial strife which prevails where these rights are not effectively established. Yet only partial solutions would be provided if large segments of workers about whose technical legal position such local differences exist should be wholly excluded from coverage by reason of such differences. Yet that result could not be avoided, if choice must be made among them and controlled by them in deciding who are "employees" within the Act's meaning. Enmeshed in such distinctions, the administration of the statute soon might become encumbered by the same sort of technical legal refinement as has characterized the long evolution of the employee-independent contractor dichotomy in the courts for other purposes. The consequences would be ultimately to defeat, in part at least, the achievement of the statute's objectives. Congress no more intended to import this mass of technicality as a controlling "standard" for uniform national application than to refer decision of the question outright to the local law.

The Act, as its first section states, was designed to avert the "substantial obstructions to the free flow of commerce" which result from "strikes and other forms of industrial strife or unrest" by eliminating the causes of that unrest. It is premised on explicit findings that strikes and industrial strife themselves result in large measure from the refusal of employers to bargain collectively and the inability of individual workers to bargain successfully for improvements in their "wages, hours, or other working conditions" with employers who are "organized in the corporate or other forms of ownership association." Hence the avowed and the interrelated purposes of the Act are to encourage collective bargaining and to remedy the individual worker's inequality of bargaining power by "protecting the exercise ... of full freedom of association, self-organization, and designation of representatives of their own choosing, for the purpose of negotiating the terms and conditions of their employment or other mutual aid or protection." 49 Stat. 449, 450.

The mischief at which the Act is aimed and the remedies it offers are not confined exclusively to "employees" within the traditional legal distinctions separating them from "independent contractors." Myriad forms of service relationship, with infinite and subtle variations in the terms of employment, blanket the nation's economy. Some are within this Act, others beyond its coverage. Large numbers will fall clearly on one side or on the other, by whatever test may be applied. But intermediate there will be many, the incidents of whose employment partake in part of the one group, in part of the other, in varying proportions of weight. And consequently the legal pendulum, for purposes of applying the statute, may swing one way or the other, depending upon the weight of this balance and its relation to the special purpose at hand.

... Interruption of commerce through strikes and unrest may stem as well from labor disputes between some who, for other purposes, are technically "independent contractors" and their employers as from disputes between persons who, for those purposes, are "employees" and their employers. ... Inequality of bargaining power in controversies over wages, hours and working conditions may as well characterize the status of the one group as of the other. The former, when acting alone, may be as "helpless in dealing with an employer," as "dependent ... on his daily wage" and as "unable to leave the employ and to resist arbitrary and unfair treatment" as the latter. For each, "union ... [may be] essential to give ... opportunity to deal on equality with their employer." And for each, collective bargaining may be appropriate and effective for the "friendly adjustment of industrial disputes arising out of differences as to wages, hours, or other working conditions." 49 Stat. 449. In short, when the particular situation of employment combines these characteristics, so that the economic facts of the relation make it more nearly one of employment than of independent business enterprise with respect to the ends sought to be accomplished by the legislation, those characteristics may outweigh technical legal classification for purposes unrelated to the statute's objectives and bring the relation within its protections. ...

It is not necessary in this case to make a completely definitive limitation around the term "employee." That task has been assigned primarily to the agency created by Congress to administer the Act. Determination of "where all the conditions of the relation require protection" involves inquiries for the Board charged with this duty. Everyday experience in the administration of the statute gives it familiarity with the circumstances and backgrounds of employment relationships in various industries, with the abilities and needs of the workers for self organization and collective action, and with the adaptability of collective bargaining for the peaceful settlement of their disputes with their employers. The experience thus acquired must be brought frequently to bear on the question who is an employee under the Act. Resolving that question, like determining whether unfair labor practices have been committed, "belongs to the usual administrative routine" of the Board. Gray v. Powell, 314 U.S. 402, 411 (1941). . . .

In making that body's determinations as to the facts in these matters conclusive, if supported by evidence, Congress entrusted to it primarily the decision whether the evidence establishes the material facts. Hence in reviewing the Board's ultimate conclusions, it is not the court's function to substitute its own inferences of fact for the Board's, when the latter have support in the record. . . . Undoubtedly questions of statutory interpretation, especially when arising in the first instance in judicial proceedings, are for the courts to resolve, giving appropriate weight to the judgment of those whose special duty is to administer the questioned statute. But where the question is one of specific application of a broad statutory term in a proceeding in which the agency administering the statute must determine it initially, the reviewing court's function is limited. Like the commissioner's determination under the Longshoremen's & Harbor Workers' Act, that a man is not a "member of a crew" or that he was injured "in the course of his employment" and the Federal Communications Commission's determination that one company is under the "control" of another, the Board's determination that specified persons are "employees" under this Act is to be accepted if it has "warrant in the record" and a reasonable basis in law.

In this case the Board found that the designated newsboys work continuously and regularly, rely upon their earnings for the support of themselves and their families, and have their total wages influenced in large measure by the publishers who dictate their buying and selling prices, fix their markets and control their supply of papers. Their hours of work and their efforts on the job are supervised and to some extent prescribed by the publishers or their agents. Much of their sales equipment and advertising materials is furnished by the publishers with the intention that it be used for the publisher's benefit. Stating that "the primary consideration in the determination of the applicability of the statutory definition is whether effectuation of the declared policy and purposes of the Act comprehend securing to the individual the rights guaranteed and protection afforded by the Act," the Board concluded that the newsboys are employees. The record sustains the Board's findings and there is ample basis in the law for its conclusion. . . .

The judgments are reversed and the causes are remanded. . . .

■ [JUSTICE REED concurred in the result.]

■ JUSTICE ROBERTS dissented:

. . . I think it plain that newsboys are not "employees" of the respondents within the meaning and intent of the National Labor Relations Act. When Congress, in § 2(3) said: "The term 'employee' shall include any employee, . . ." it stated as clearly as language could do it that the provisions of the Act were to extend to those who, as a result of decades of tradition which had become part of the common understanding of our people, bear the named relationship. Clearly also Congress did not delegate to the National Labor Relations Board the function of defining the relationship of employment so as to promote what the Board understood to be the underlying purpose of the statute. The question who is an employee, so as to make the statute applicable to him, is a question of the meaning of the Act and, therefore, is a judicial and not an administrative question. . . .

## NOTES

(1) ***When Should a Court Defer?*** Hearst is a carefully written opinion. Justice Rutledge treats some of the questions he considers as matters for the Court to decide for itself and some as matters for which "the reviewing court's function is limited." Can you pinpoint the place in the opinion where he shifts from one stance to the other? Can you say why?

(2) ***Another Data Point.*** Compare the nearly contemporaneous PACKARD MOTOR CAR CO. V. NLRB, 330 U.S. 485 (1947). Packard's 1100 foremen wanted to organize as a unit of the Foremen's Association of America, representing supervisory employees exclusively. The foremen supervised Packard's 32,000 rank-and-file workers, represented by the United Auto Workers; foremen were relatively highly paid and responsible for maintaining quantity and quality of production under overall control by management; foremen could not hire or fire but could discipline and recommend promotion, demotion, etc. The NLRB decided the foremen were "employees," and then decided that they constituted an appropriate bargaining unit. Packard refused to bargain, claiming foremen were not "employees."

"The question presented by this case," said JUSTICE JACKSON for the court, "is whether foremen are entitled as a class to these rights of self-organization [and] collective bargaining . . . assured to employees generally by the National Labor Relations Act." The Act, as we have seen, provided that " 'employee' shall include any employee" but also said that " 'employer' includes any person acting in the interest of an employer, directly or indirectly. . . ." How to put these two provisions together, in relation to foremen, was, said the Court, a "naked question of law" as to which "administrative interpretation" (which had waivered over time on the question) was irrelevant. The Court affirmed the Board. None of the Justices deferred to the Board on this "tremendously important" policy affecting industry nationwide, but a majority agreed with the Board about how the Act should be read to treat foremen. Consistent with Hearst? (Hearst was cited only once, by the dissent, and only for the proposition that "the term 'employee' must be considered in the context of the Act.")[2]

---

[2] Congress promptly amended the definition of "employee" to exclude "supervisory employees."

## SKIDMORE v. SWIFT & CO.

Supreme Court of the United States (1944).
323 U.S. 134.

■ JUSTICE JACKSON delivered the opinion of the Court.

Seven employees of the Swift and Company packing plant at Fort Worth, Texas, brought an action under the Fair Labor Standards Act, to recover overtime, liquidated damages, and attorneys' fees, totaling approximately $77,000. . . .

It is not denied that the daytime employment of these persons was working time within the Act. . . . Under their oral agreement of employment, however, petitioners undertook to stay in the fire hall on the Company premises, or within hailing distance, three and a half to four nights a week. This involved no task except to answer alarms, either because of fire or because the sprinkler was set off for some other reason. No fires occurred during the period in issue, the alarms were rare, and the time required for their answer rarely exceeded an hour. For each alarm answered the employees were paid in addition to their fixed compensation an agreed amount, fifty cents at first, and later sixty-four cents. The Company provided a brick fire hall equipped with steam heat and air-conditioned rooms. It provided sleeping quarters, a pool table, a domino table, and a radio. The men used their time in sleep or amusement as they saw fit, except that they were required to stay in or close by the fire hall and be ready to respond to alarms. It is stipulated that "they agreed to remain in the fire hall and stay in it or within hailing distance, subject to call, in event of fire or other casualty, but were not required to perform any specific tasks during these periods of time, except in answering alarms." The trial court found the evidentiary facts as stipulated; it made no findings of fact as such as to whether under the arrangement of the parties and the circumstances of this case, which in some respects differ from those of [a companion case], the fire hall duty or any part thereof constituted working time. It said, however, as a "conclusion of law" that "the time plaintiffs spent in the fire hall subject to call to answer fire alarms does not constitute hours worked, for which overtime compensation is due them under the Fair Labor Standards Act, as interpreted by the Administrator and the Courts," and in its opinion observed, "of course we know pursuing such pleasurable occupations or performing such personal chores does not constitute work." The Circuit Court of Appeals affirmed.

For reasons set forth in [that companion case], we hold that no principle of law found either in the statute or in Court decisions precludes waiting time from also being working time. We have not attempted to, and we cannot, lay down a legal formula to resolve cases so varied in their facts as are the many situations in which employment involves waiting time. Whether in a concrete case such time falls within or without the Act is a question of fact to be resolved by appropriate findings of the trial court. . . . This involves scrutiny and construction of the agreements between the particular parties, appraisal of their practical construction of the working agreement by conduct, consideration of the nature of the service, and its relation to the waiting time, and all of the surrounding circumstances. Facts may show that the employee was engaged to wait, or they may show that he waited to be engaged. His compensation may cover both waiting and task, or only performance of the task itself. Living quarters may in some situations be furnished as a facility of the task and in another as a part of its compensation. The law does not impose an arrangement upon the parties. It imposes upon the courts the task of finding what the arrangement was. . . .

Congress did not utilize the services of an administrative agency to find facts and to determine in the first instance whether particular cases fall within or without the Act. Instead, it put this responsibility on the courts. . . . But it did create the office of Administrator [of the Wage and Hour Division of the Department of Labor], impose upon him a variety of duties, endow him with powers to inform himself of conditions in industries and employments subject to the Act, and put on him the duties of bringing injunction actions to restrain violations. Pursuit of his duties has accumulated a considerable experience in the problems of ascertaining working time in employments involving periods of inactivity and a knowledge of the customs prevailing in reference to their solution. From these he is obliged to reach conclusions as to conduct without the law, so that he should seek injunctions to stop it, and that within the law, so that he has no call to interfere. He has set forth his views of the application of the Act under different circumstances in an interpretative bulletin and in informal rulings. They provide a practical guide to employers and employees as to how the office representing the public interest in its enforcement will seek to apply it. Wage and Hour Division, Interpretative Bulletin No. 13. . . .

There is no statutory provision as to what, if any, deference courts should pay to the Administrator's conclusions. And, while we have given them notice, we have had no occasion to try to prescribe their influence. The rulings of this Administrator are not reached as a result of hearing adversary proceedings in which he finds facts from evidence and reaches conclusions of law from findings of fact. They are not, of course, conclusive, even in the cases with which they directly deal, much less in those to which they apply only by analogy. They do not constitute an interpretation of the Act or a standard for judging factual situations which binds a district court's processes, as an authoritative pronouncement of a higher court might do. But the Administrator's policies are made in pursuance of official duty, based upon more specialized experience and broader investigations and information than is likely to come to a judge in a particular case. They do determine the policy which will guide applications for enforcement by injunction on behalf of the Government. Good administration of the Act and good judicial administration alike require that the standards of public enforcement and those for determining private rights shall be at variance only where justified by very good reasons. The fact that the Administrator's policies and standards are not reached by trial in adversary form does not mean that they are not entitled to respect. This Court has long given considerable and in some cases decisive weight to Treasury Decisions and to interpretative regulations of the Treasury and of other bodies that were not of adversary origin.

We consider that the rulings, interpretations and opinions of the Administrator under this Act, while not controlling upon the courts by reason of their authority, do constitute a body of experience and informed judgment to which courts and litigants may properly resort for guidance. The weight of such a judgment in a particular case will depend upon the thoroughness evident in its consideration, the validity of its reasoning, its consistency with earlier and later pronouncements, and all those factors which give it power to persuade, if lacking power to control.

The court in the [companion] case weighed the evidence . . . in the light of the Administrator's rulings and reached a result consistent therewith. The evidence in this case in some respects, such as the understanding as to separate compensation for answering alarms, is different. Each case must stand on its own facts. But in this case, although the District Court referred to the Administrator's Bulletin, its evaluation and inquiry were apparently restricted by its notion that waiting time may not be work, an understanding of the law which we hold to be erroneous. Accordingly, the judgment is reversed and the cause remanded for further proceedings consistent herewith.

## NOTES

(1) ***What Are the Administrator's Interpretations of the Act Worth?*** SAMUEL HERMAN, THE ADMINISTRATION AND ENFORCEMENT OF THE FAIR LABOR STANDARDS ACT, 6 Law & Contemp. Probs. 368, 378–80 (1939): "A rule-making power had been contained in the Act as originally introduced. The issuance of 'interpretative bulletins' by the Wage and Hour Division stemmed from the failure of Congress to include a rule-making provision in the Act. The bulletins were the creature of necessity . . . [and] self-denying as witnessed by the following typical statement:

> " '[I]nterpretations announced by the Administrator, except in certain specific instances where the statute directs the Administrator to make various regulations and definitions, serve only to indicate the construction of the law which will guide the Administrator in the performance of his administrative duties, unless he is directed otherwise by the authoritative rulings of the courts, or unless he shall subsequently decide that a prior interpretation is incorrect.'

". . . The interpretative bulletins are not binding on industry; they are merely legal advice—good, perhaps the best. While industry is advised to comply, if in doubt, the employer is not immune if, in reliance upon an interpretative bulletin, he concludes that the Act is not applicable to him. He may be subsequently prosecuted under Section 16(a), sued by an employee under Section 16(b), or enjoined under Section 17."

(2) ***What Is the Doctrine of Skidmore?*** Justice Jackson's penultimate paragraph is—as we shall see—much quoted, and it has a lot of precedent supporting it. Peter L. Strauss, In Search of Skidmore, 83 Fordham L. Rev. 789 (2014). It is also well written. But, what exactly does it mean? The weight to be given the Administrator's interpretation by the trial court on remand, we are told, depends on "those factors which give it power to persuade." Does this mean that if the court is persuaded that the Administrator is right, it should follow his interpretation (which is now, since the court has been persuaded, also the court's interpretation)—and if not, it should not? This is not news. It is also not deference. The court will simply be doing in its own voice what it now thinks it is right to do. We would not say that a court persuaded by the excellent brief of a private litigant to decide in its favor is deferring to the litigant's lawyers. If you said to yourself that, whatever the words, Justice Jackson did mean for the court to give some extra weight to the agency's judgments, to defer to them to some extent, then how do you get by the point, also in the paragraph, that these interpretations are "not controlling upon the courts by reason of their authority." Is the crucial word here "controlling"—so that a court can still *choose* to defer to the opinion of the agency much as a trial court might defer to the opinion of an expert witness once convinced the witness was really an expert?

(3) ***Is Skidmore Justifiable?*** Does it bother you, in the Court's deciding to give some weight to the Administrator's interpretations, that Congress did not give the Administrator the power to make rules? Does it bother you that no law gave Swift & Co. an opportunity to be heard before the agency on the interpretive question? (Recall, if you have studied them, the materials on interpretative rules and policy statements, Chapter IV, Section 4.b.)

(4) ***Hearst and Skidmore.*** How does "Skidmore deference" fit with your interpretation of the Hearst case?

## b. The Present-Day Framework, Part I: Chevron, the Basics



In the wake of the building-block cases, the present-day framework has emerged over the last thirty-plus years, chiefly in consequence of perhaps the most famous, or at least most cited, case in modern administrative law, the Chevron case, which in the classic formulation requires courts to defer to agencies' reasonable interpretations of statutes that they administer. Whether, and if so to what effect, Chevron and its progeny have changed the framework set out in the older cases are topics that remain on the table. So, too, however, is the topic of the status of Chevron itself.

The Supreme Court has not relied on Chevron deference to decide a case since the October 2016 Term. During that period, the Court sometimes has concluded that, for one reason or another, Chevron does not apply at all to the case at hand, even though arguments were available that it did apply. In other instances, the Court simply has construed the relevant statute on its own without purporting to apply the Chevron framework. There are questions, then, about whether Chevron does or will continue to define the present-day framework for the foreseeable future.

At the same time, the Court has not overruled Chevron. Thus, litigants continue to invoke it, and lower courts continue to rely on it, although Chevron has come under heavy fire from some lower court judges, including ones who have since become Justices on the Supreme Court. All of this means that it is important to understand the framework that emerged under Chevron, which turns out to be deceptively complex, even if Chevron does not reign supreme as it once did. At the very least, Chevron provides a critical reference point for whatever framework might be emerging in its wake.

We begin in this Part by describing the basics about Chevron: the various ways it has been interpreted, its importance, and the justifications (or not) for it. We then turn in the next Part to a consideration of the relationship between theories of statutory interpretation and Chevron before turning to some of the recent limitations on it and an examination of what might be following in its wake. We finally address the framework for the review of agencies' interpretations of their own regulations.

## CHEVRON, U.S.A., INC. v. NATURAL RESOURCES DEFENSE COUNCIL, INC.

Supreme Court of the United States (1984).
467 U.S. 837.

■ JUSTICE STEVENS delivered the opinion of the Court.

In the Clean Air Act Amendments of 1977, Pub. L. 95–95, 91 Stat. 685, Congress enacted certain requirements applicable to States that had not achieved the national air quality standards established by the Environmental Protection Agency (EPA) pursuant to earlier legislation. The amended Clean Air Act required these "nonattainment" States to establish a permit program regulating "new or modified major stationary sources" of air pollution. Generally, a permit may not be issued for a new or modified major stationary source unless several stringent conditions are met. The EPA regulation promulgated to implement this permit requirement allows a State to adopt a plantwide definition of the term "stationary source." Under this definition, an existing plant that contains several pollution-emitting devices may install or modify one piece of equipment without meeting the permit conditions if the alteration will not increase the total emissions from the plant. The question presented by this case is whether EPA's decision to allow States to treat all of the pollution-emitting devices within the same industrial grouping as though they were encased within a single "bubble" is based on a reasonable construction of the statutory term "stationary source."

I

The EPA regulations containing the plantwide definition of the term stationary source were promulgated on October 14, 1981. 46 Fed. Reg. 50766. Respondents filed a timely petition for review in the United States Court of Appeals for the District of Columbia Circuit pursuant to 42 U.S.C. § 7607(b)(1). The Court of Appeals set aside the regulations. Natural Resources Defense Council, Inc. v. Gorsuch, 685 F.2d 718 (1982).

The court observed that the relevant part of the amended Clean Air Act "does not explicitly define what Congress envisioned as a 'stationary source,' to which the permit program . . . should apply," and further stated that the precise issue was not "squarely addressed in the legislative history." In light of its conclusion that the legislative history bearing on the question was "at best contradictory," it reasoned that "the purposes of the nonattainment program should guide our decision here."[5] Based on two of its precedents concerning the applicability of the bubble concept to certain Clean Air Act programs, the court stated that the bubble concept was "mandatory" in programs designed merely to maintain existing air quality, but held that it was "inappropriate" in programs enacted to improve air quality. Since the purpose of the permit program—its "raison d'etre," in the court's view—was to improve air quality, the court held that the bubble concept was inapplicable in this case under its prior precedents. It therefore set aside the regulations embodying the bubble concept as contrary to law. We . . . now reverse.

The basic legal error of the Court of Appeals was to adopt a static judicial definition of the term stationary source when it had decided that Congress itself had not commanded that definition. . . .

II

When a court reviews an agency's construction of the statute which it administers, it is confronted with two questions. First, always, is the question whether Congress has directly spoken to the precise question at issue. If the intent of Congress is clear, that is the end of the matter; for the court, as well as the agency, must give effect to the unambiguously expressed intent of Congress.[9] If, however, the court determines Congress has not directly addressed the precise question at issue, the court does not simply impose its own construction on the statute, as would be necessary in the absence of an administrative interpretation. Rather, if the statute is silent or ambiguous with respect to the specific issue, the question for the court is whether the agency's answer is based on a permissible construction of the statute.[11]

"The power of an administrative agency to administer a congressionally created . . . program necessarily requires the formulation of policy and the making of rules to fill any gap left, implicitly or explicitly, by Congress." Morton v. Ruiz, 415 U.S. 199, 231 (1974). If Congress has explicitly left a gap for the agency to fill, there is an express delegation of authority to the agency to elucidate a specific provision of the statute by regulation. Such legislative regulations are given controlling weight unless they are arbitrary, capricious, or manifestly contrary to the statute. Sometimes the legislative delegation to an agency on a particular question is implicit rather than explicit. In such a case, a court may not substitute its own construction of a statutory provision for a reasonable interpretation made by the administrator of an agency.

---

[5] The court remarked in this regard: "We regret, of course, that Congress did not advert specifically to the bubble concept's application to various Clean Air Act programs, and note that a further clarifying statutory directive would facilitate the work of the agency and of the court in their endeavors to serve the legislators' will."

[9] The judiciary is the final authority on issues of statutory construction and must reject administrative constructions which are contrary to clear congressional intent. If a court, employing traditional tools of statutory construction, ascertains that Congress had an intention on the precise question at issue, that intention is the law and must be given effect.

[11] The court need not conclude that the agency construction was the only one it permissibly could have adopted to uphold the construction, or even the reading the court would have reached if the question initially had arisen in a judicial proceeding.

We have long recognized that considerable weight should be accorded to an executive department's construction of a statutory scheme it is entrusted to administer, and the principle of deference to administrative interpretations

> has been consistently followed by this Court whenever decision as to the meaning or reach of a statute has involved reconciling conflicting policies, and a full understanding of the force of the statutory policy in the given situation has depended upon more than ordinary knowledge respecting the matters subjected to agency regulations. See e.g., Labor Board v. Hearst Publications, Inc., 322 U.S. 111; Securities & Exchange Comm'n v. Chenery Corp., 332 U.S. 194. . . . If this choice represents a reasonable accommodation of conflicting policies that were committed to the agency's care by the statute, we should not disturb it unless it appears from the statute or its legislative history that the accommodation is not one that Congress would have sanctioned.

United States v. Shimer, 367 U.S. 374, 382, 383 (1961).

In light of these well-settled principles it is clear that the Court of Appeals misconceived the nature of its role in reviewing the regulations at issue. Once it determined, after its own examination of the legislation, that Congress did not actually have an intent regarding the applicability of the bubble concept to the permit program, the question before it was not whether in its view the concept is "inappropriate" in the general context of a program designed to improve air quality, but whether the Administrator's view that it is appropriate in the context of this particular program is a reasonable one. Based on the examination of the legislation and its history which follows, we agree with the Court of Appeals that Congress did not have a specific intention on the applicability of the bubble concept in these cases, and conclude that the EPA's use of that concept here is a reasonable policy choice for the agency to make.

[III, IV, V]

[The Court reviewed the legislative history of the Clean Air Act and its Amendments at length. It remarked that the issue before it concerned "one phrase" from a "small portion" of "a lengthy, detailed, technical, complex, and comprehensive response to a major social issue," the Clean Air Act Amendments of 1977, that in turn was only part of a much larger statutory scheme under EPA's administration. "The legislative history of the portion of the 1977 Amendments dealing with nonattainment areas," it stated, "does not contain any specific comment on the 'bubble concept' or the question whether a plantwide definition of a stationary source is permissible under the permit program. It does, however, plainly disclose that in the permit program Congress sought to accommodate the conflict between the economic interest in permitting capital improvements to continue and the environmental interest in improving air quality."]

VI

[Turning to the administrative history of implementation of the Clean Air Act Amendments of 1977, the Court noted that EPA had at first proposed interpretations like that under challenge.]

In August 1980, however, the EPA adopted a regulation that, in essence, applied the basic reasoning of the Court of Appeals in this case. The EPA took particular note of the two then-recent Court of Appeals decisions, which had created the bright-line rule that the bubble concept should be employed in a program designed to maintain air quality but not in one designed to enhance air quality. Relying heavily on those cases, EPA adopted a dual definition of "source" for nonattainment areas that required a permit whenever a change in either the entire plant, or one of its components, would result in a significant increase in emissions even if the increase was completely offset by reductions elsewhere in the plant. . . .

In 1981 a new administration took office and initiated a "Governmentwide reexamination of regulatory burdens and complexities." 46 Fed. Reg. 16281. In the context of that review, the EPA reevaluated the various arguments that had been advanced in connection with the proper definition of the term "source" and concluded that the term should be given the same definition in both nonattainment areas and PSD [preventing significant deterioration] areas.

In explaining its conclusion, the EPA first noted that the definitional issue was not squarely addressed in either the statute or its legislative history and therefore that the issue involved an agency "judgment as how to best carry out the Act." It then set forth several reasons for concluding that the plantwide definition was more appropriate. It pointed out that the dual definition "can act as a disincentive to new investment and modernization by discouraging modifications to existing facilities" and "can actually retard progress in air pollution control by discouraging replacement of older, dirtier processes or pieces of equipment with new, cleaner ones." Moreover, the new definition "would simplify EPA's rules by using the same definition of 'source' for PSD, nonattainment new source review and the construction moratorium. This reduces confusion and inconsistency." Finally, the agency explained that additional requirements that remained in place would accomplish the fundamental purposes of achieving attainment . . . as expeditiously as possible. These conclusions were expressed in a proposed rulemaking in August 1981 that was formally promulgated in October.

VII

[The Court turned to arguments offered by the respondents to show that the statute had a clear meaning.]

*Statutory Language*

We are not persuaded that parsing of general terms in the text of the statute will reveal an actual intent of Congress. We know full well that this language is not dispositive; the terms are overlapping and the language is not precisely directed to the question of the applicability of a given term in the context of a larger operation. To the extent any congressional "intent" can be discerned from this language, it would appear that the listing of overlapping, illustrative terms was intended to enlarge, rather than to confine, the scope of the agency's power to regulate particular sources in order to effectuate the policies of the Act.

*Legislative History*

Based on our examination of the legislative history, we agree with the Court of Appeals that it is unilluminating. . . . We find that the legislative history as a whole is silent on the precise issue before us. It is, however, consistent with the view that the EPA should have broad discretion in implementing the policies of the 1977 Amendments.

More importantly, that history plainly identifies the policy concerns that motivated the enactment; the plantwide definition is fully consistent with one of those concerns—the allowance of reasonable economic growth—and, whether or not we believe it most effectively implements the other, we must recognize that the EPA has advanced a reasonable explanation for its conclusion that the regulations serve the environmental objectives as well. Indeed, its reasoning is supported by the public record developed in the rulemaking process, as well as by certain private studies.[37]

Our review of the EPA's varying interpretations of the word "source"—both before and after the 1977 Amendments—convince us that the agency primarily responsible for administering this important legislation has consistently interpreted it flexibly—not in a sterile textual vacuum, but in the context of implementing policy decisions in a technical and complex arena. The fact that the agency has from time to time changed its interpretation of the term "source" does not, as respondents argue, lead us to conclude that no deference should be accorded the agency's interpretation of the statute. An initial agency interpretation is not instantly carved in stone. On the contrary, the agency, to engage in informed rulemaking, must consider varying interpretations and the wisdom of its policy on a continuing basis. Moreover, the fact that the agency has adopted different definitions in different contexts adds force to the argument that the definition itself is flexible, particularly since Congress has never indicated any disapproval of a flexible reading of the statute.

Significantly, it was not the agency in 1980, but rather the Court of Appeals that read the statute inflexibly to command a plantwide definition for programs designed to maintain clean air and to forbid such a definition for programs designed to improve air quality. The distinction the court drew may well be a sensible one, but our labored review of the

37 "Economists have proposed that economic incentives be substituted for the cumbersome administrative-legal framework. The objective is to make the profit and cost incentives that work so well in the marketplace work for pollution control. . . . [The 'bubble' or 'netting' concept] is a first attempt in this direction. By giving a plant manager flexibility to find the places and processes within a plant that control emissions most cheaply, pollution control can be achieved more quickly and cheaply." L. Lave & G. Omenn, Cleaning the Air: Reforming the Clean Air Act 28 (1981) (footnote omitted).

problem has surely disclosed that it is not a distinction that Congress ever articulated itself, or one that the EPA found in the statute before the courts began to review the legislative work product. We conclude that it was the Court of Appeals, rather than Congress or any of the decisionmakers who are authorized by Congress to administer this legislation, that was primarily responsible for the 1980 position taken by the agency.

*Policy*

The arguments over policy that are advanced in the parties' briefs create the impression that respondents are now waging in a judicial forum a specific policy battle which they ultimately lost in the agency and in the 32 jurisdictions opting for the bubble concept, but one which was never waged in the Congress. Such policy arguments are more properly addressed to legislators or administrators, not to judges.

In this case, the Administrator's interpretation represents a reasonable accommodation of manifestly competing interests and is entitled to deference: the regulatory scheme is technical and complex, the agency considered the matter in a detailed and reasoned fashion, and the decision involves reconciling conflicting policies. Congress intended to accommodate both interests, but did not do so itself on the level of specificity presented by this case. Perhaps that body consciously desired the Administrator to strike the balance at this level, thinking that those with great expertise and charged with responsibility for administering the provision would be in a better position to do so; perhaps it simply did not consider the question at this level; and perhaps Congress was unable to forge a coalition on either side of the question, and those on each side decided to take their chances with the scheme devised by the agency. For judicial purposes, it matters not which of these things occurred.

Judges are not experts in the field, and are not part of either political branch of the Government. Courts must, in some cases, reconcile competing political interests, but not on the basis of the judges' personal policy preferences. In contrast, an agency to which Congress has delegated policy-making responsibilities may, within the limits of that delegation, properly rely upon the incumbent administration's views of wise policy to inform its judgments. While agencies are not directly accountable to the people, the Chief Executive is, and it is entirely appropriate for this political branch of the Government to make such policy choices—resolving the competing interests which Congress itself either inadvertently did not resolve, or intentionally left to be resolved by the agency charged with the administration of the statute in light of everyday realities.

When a challenge to an agency construction of a statutory provision, fairly conceptualized, really centers on the wisdom of the agency's policy, rather than whether it is a reasonable choice within a gap left open by Congress, the challenge must fail. In such a case, federal judges—who have no constituency—have a duty to respect legitimate policy choices made by those who do. The responsibilities for assessing the wisdom of such policy choices and resolving the struggle between competing views of the public interest are not judicial ones: "Our Constitution vests such responsibilities in the political branches." TVA v. Hill, 437 U.S. 153, 195 (1978).

We hold that the EPA's definition of the term "source" is a permissible construction of the statute which seeks to accommodate progress in reducing air pollution with economic growth. "The Regulations which the Administrator has adopted provide what the agency could allowably view as . . . [an] effective reconciliation of these twofold ends. . . ." United States v. Shimer, 367 U.S., at 383.

The judgment of the Court of Appeals is reversed.

■ JUSTICE MARSHALL and JUSTICE REHNQUIST did not participate in the consideration or decision of these cases.

■ JUSTICE O'CONNOR did not participate in the decision of these cases.

## NOTES

(1) ***Well-Settled Principles or Important Development?*** Justice Stevens's opinion presents his test as if it were simply a statement of "well-settled principles," which seems unfounded. (While there were prior cases that adopted a similarly deferential approach to statutory construction, there were others that did not; and in any case the phrasing was new.) The statements in the opinion that might furnish a rationale for the test, moreover, are diverse—referring variously to the regulatory scheme being "technical and complex," to the need for "reconciling conflicting policies," to Congress having "delegated policy-making responsibilities" to the agency, to the lack of expertise on the part of judges, to the President being electorally responsible, and to the fact that federal judges "have no constituency." Yet, there seems to be little effort made to connect these various considerations to the formality of the test itself. One set of issues, then, is whether the Chevron test is applicable to every case in which "a court reviews an agency's construction of the statute which it administers" (to use Justice Stevens's lead-in phrase), or whether its applicability is conditioned by the presence (or absence) of some of these other factors. We will address these features of Chevron further, but there is no question that Chevron, at least until quite recently, was understood to mark an important development in administrative law. Consider these sound bites on Chevron's importance:

(a) "Chevron is this generation's Erie. . . . Erie rested on a judicial recognition that the law is not 'a brooding omnipresence in the sky.' . . . Chevron is closely parallel. When statutes are ambiguous, a judgment about their meaning rests on no brooding omnipresence in the sky, but on assessments of both policy and principle. There is no reason to allow those assessments to be made by federal courts rather than executive officers. So, at least, Chevron holds." Cass R. Sunstein, Beyond Marbury: The Executive's Power to Say What the Law Is, 115 Yale L.J. 2580, 2598 (2006).

(b) "Chevron is the doctrinal apotheosis of the modern legal era. It signals a resounding shift of the center of the law's gravity away from judge-made law toward statutes and their primary administrators." Abbe R. Gluck,

What 30 Years of Chevron Teach Us About the Rest of Statutory Interpretation, 83 Fordham L. Rev. 607, 631 (2014).

(2) ***An Unintended Landmark?*** ROBERT V. PERCIVAL, ENVIRONMENTAL LAW IN THE SUPREME COURT: HIGHLIGHTS FROM THE MARSHALL PAPERS, 23 Envtl. L. Rep. 10606, 10613 (1993): "One surprise is the absence of any evidence in the written record indicating that the Justices realized the full implications of their landmark administrative law decision in . . . Chevron. There is no comment in the written exchanges among the Justices that reflects any appreciation of the major change in administrative law the decision effected. . . . [T]he Marshall papers indicate that the decision was reached without any significant debate over Justice Stevens' draft opinion, which was initially circulated among the Justices on June 11, 1984. On June 12, Justices Rehnquist and Marshall circulated notes indicating without explanation that they were recusing themselves from the case. [Justice O'Connor also recused herself because a family estate owned stock in one of the parties. By June 18, all others had joined the opinion.] The only comment in the memos concerning the substance of [the] opinion is the statement by Chief Justice Burger that 'I am now persuaded you have the correct answer to this case.' "

## NOTES ON CHEVRON'S STEPS

Precisely because of the importance that has been ascribed to Chevron, it is worth paying close attention to how the framework that it establishes works. We thus need to examine what are often referred to as Chevron's "steps."

Chevron sets forth a two-step framework when it applies. That "when it applies" caveat suggests, however, that, under Chevron itself, there is a threshold question of application to resolve. We thus begin by walking through Chevron's steps, including that preliminary threshold step. We then focus on the difference, as a conceptual matter (insofar as there is one), between the inquiry at step one and the inquiry at step two. With those two "steps" described, we move on to examine how Chevron and State Farm fit together, insofar as they do.

(1) ***Does Chevron Have a Step Zero?*** The threshold issue of when the Chevron framework applies to an agency's proposed construction of a statute is sometimes referred to as Chevron step zero. See Cass R. Sunstein, Chevron Step Zero, 92 Va. L. Rev. 187 (2006); see also Thomas W. Merrill & Kristin E. Hickman, Chevron's Domain, 89 Geo. L.J. 833 (2001). For example, what does it mean to say that an agency "administers" a statute? Does the fact that an agency had reason to interpret the statute mean that it administers it? The answer to that question is, surely, "No." But what is the test for determining that the agency does have the kind of administering power over a statute that might entitle it to Chevron deference in interpreting it? Relatedly, what does it mean to say that an agency has offered an interpretation of a statute that it administers? For example, does the interpretation have to be offered in a certain form to even count as an interpretation? We consider these threshold questions at various points in

this Chapter; as it turns out, they have no simple answer. In fact, the answers to them are, if anything, becoming harder and harder to articulate, given the various carve outs and exceptions to Chevron that the Court has begun to identify. But, insofar as the Chevron test does apply—in other words, insofar as the "Step Zero" inquiry results in the conclusion that Chevron does apply—it is important to understand how the test works. And that, in turn, requires one to understand Chevron's two steps.

(2) ***What Are Chevron's Two Steps?*** Perhaps Chevron's most important feature, considered strictly as a matter of doctrinal analysis, is that the test has two steps. This feature of Chevron provokes two important questions: First, how do we know whether we are in step one or step two? Second, what is the difference in approach between the two steps?

Let us begin with the first of these questions. To use Justice Stevens's formulations, we are in step one "if the intent of Congress is clear," while we are in step two "if the statute is silent or ambiguous." Clarity or ambiguity is the test. Of course, all language is ambiguous with regard to something, but Stevens definitely states that the test is ambiguity (or not) with regard to "the precise question at issue." And in a footnote he indicates that the way to determine whether Congress had, or did not have, a clear intent, is by using "traditional tools of statutory construction."

This formulation makes it rather plain that Chevron deference is not predicated on there being an inextricable mixture of fact and law (as opposed to pure law) implicated in the problem at hand, which the building-block cases we considered earlier suggested might matter to the determination of when an agency deserves deference. As one commentator has said: "The distinction is not between issues of law and fact, which does not seem to have much to do with Chevron. The distinction is between issues of law and policy, which is at the core of Chevron." Michael Herz, Deference Running Riot: Separating Interpretation and Lawmaking under Chevron, 6 Admin L.J. 187, 223 (1992). Even if this claim is a bit overstated, its basic implication—that under Chevron, agencies get to make decisions that from a traditional law/fact/mixed question analysis are only about questions of law—obviously raises questions of legitimacy. (Of these questions, more later; for the moment we are looking simply at the question of how to employ the doctrine.)

Assuming that ambiguity means ambiguity as to the meaning of the statute itself (which seems to be the case), much turns on how one thinks judges should ascribe meaning to statutory language. Thus, many of the subsequent controversies regarding Chevron-in-practice have been, in effect, contests between different theories of statutory construction—between, for example, those who think that recourse to "legislative history" is useful and those who do not. (Recall, if you studied it, the discussion of that issue at in Chapter II (pp. 202–214)). We address Chevron and statutory interpretation extensively below.)

Turning now to the question of the differences in operation between the two steps of the test, Stevens's formulation of the question under the second step is "whether the agency's answer is based on a permissible construction of the statute." Is this just a broader statement of the outer limits of what the statute will permit, requiring thinking similar to that done in determining Congress's intent for step one? Some have read it that way—so that the whole Chevron test, in effect, is whether the agency's interpretation of the statute is "reasonable." Or, at the other extreme, does this language signal the kind of thinking that lies behind application of the "arbitrary and capricious" standard? Some have read it that way, too—so that in effect Chevron and State Farm (pp. 1218–1223) merge at step two. Or do we have to consider Chevron step one thinking, which is different from Chevron step two thinking, which is different from State Farm thinking? There are advocates for that position, too.

It would doubtless be a mistake to think that all these issues were in Justice Stevens's mind when he wrote Chevron or that we would find definite answers to them if only we read his opinion with exquisite care. The questions have been, and remain, much alive. In the notes that follow, some possible analyses will be suggested. But all of the later principal cases in this Chapter were written in Chevron's shadow, and so they, too, are authorities on how the Chevron test is understood at the present time.

(3) ***Are the Two Steps of Chevron Different in Kind or Only Degree?*** JUDGE WILLIAMS on the denial of rehearing, 30 F.3d at 193, in SWEET HOME CHAPTER V. BABBITT, 17 F.3d 1463 (D.C. Cir. 1994), reversed, 515 U.S. 687 (1995): "The government faults the panel for failing to specify whether the regulation's excess of statutory authority failed under the first or second 'step' of the analysis set forth in Chevron and in a more general way for failing to give the agency the deference that is its due under Chevron. Because the court in determining whether Congress 'unambiguously expressed' its intent on the issue is to employ all the 'traditional tools of statutory construction,' the factors involved in the first 'step' are also pertinent to whether an agency's interpretation is 'reasonable.' Thus the exact point where an agency interpretation falls down may be unclear. (Indeed, the Chevron Court itself never specified which step it was applying at any point in its analysis.)"

Compare JUDGE SILBERMAN addressing the rehearing denial in the same case (30 F.3d at 194–95): "I quite agree with the panel that the factors involved in the first 'step' are also pertinent to whether an agency's interpretation is 'reasonable'; but when thinking of the statute at that second step, one must assume that the statute has more than one plausible construction as it applies to the case before you. If the agency offers one—it prevails."

Chevron step two invalidations are comparatively rare. One study of decisions in the Courts of Appeals that cited Chevron found that 70.0% of interpretations applied both steps of Chevron, and that in those decisions the agency win rate was 93.8%. Kent Barnett & Christopher J. Walker, Chevron in the Circuit Courts, 116 Mich. L. Rev. 1, 6 (2017). For a decision applying Chevron step two but invalidating the agency's decision as unreasonable, consider Michigan v. EPA, excerpted at greater length below (p. 1156). In that case, Justice Scalia's opinion for the Court stated that EPA's interpretation of "appropriate and necessary" was unreasonable because that phrase, in the context of the statute, required EPA to consider the costs of the relevant regulations, which it had not done. The Court thought that "read fairly and in context" the phrase "plainly subsumes consideration of cost." Id. at 756. Is that a step two analysis?

For an argument that the two steps are really just one, consider MATTHEW C. STEPHENSON & ADRIAN VERMEULE, CHEVRON HAS ONLY ONE STEP, 95 Va. L. Rev. 597, 598–99 (2009): "Chevron divides the . . . inquiry—whether the agency's interpretation of the statute is valid—into two steps. At Step One, the court must ask whether, after 'employing traditional tools of statutory construction' it is evidence that 'Congress has directly spoken to the precise question at issue.' If so, the statute is 'unambiguous.' If, however, the court decides at Step One that the statute is ambiguous, the court proceeds to Step Two. At Step Two, the court must uphold the agency's interpretation so long as it is 'based on a permissible construction of the statute.' . . . This structure artificially divides one inquiry into two steps. The single question is whether the agency's construction is permissible as a matter of statutory interpretation; the two Chevron steps both ask this question, just in different ways. As a result, the two steps are mutually convertible. If an agency's construction of the statute is 'contrary to clear congressional intent . . . on the precise question at issue,' then the agency's construction is a fortiori not 'based on a permissible construction of the statute.' Step One is therefore nothing more than a special case of Step Two, which implies that all Step One opinions could be written in the language of Step Two."

For a different view, consider: KENNETH A. BAMBERGER & PETER L. STRAUSS, CHEVRON'S TWO STEPS, 95 Va. L. Rev. 611, 616 (2009): "In cases reviewing agency interpretations that are, in fact, permitted by the statutory text, this [step-one, step-two] distinction may bear little consequence on the resolution of the case at hand: the agency's interpretation is vindicated. Yet the systemic implications of such a difference for administration are real. . . . [A] judicial precedent holding that a particular interpretation is either required or precluded fixes statutory meaning to that extent, foreclosing future agency constructions to the contrary. By contrast, a judicial determination that an agency interpretation embodies one option within the zone of indeterminacy makes it possible for the agency to put forth a different interpretation at a later time."

If there is a difference between the two steps, how might we describe that difference? Elizabeth Magill, Step Two of Chevron v. Natural Resources Defense Council, in A Guide to Judicial and Political Review of Federal Agencies 85 (John F. Duffy & Michael Herz eds., 2005), identifies two possibilities.

One possibility is that the first step focuses on whether the statute is clear or ambiguous in answering the precise question at issue, while the second step focuses on whether the agency's proposed answer to that precise question is a permissible one, given the range of possible answers that the statutory ambiguity permits. A difficulty with this way of understanding step two, however, is that, as she points out, step two then arguably just replicates step one. After all, if the agency's proposed answer is not a permissible one, then presumably that is because the precise question that the agency was answering was one that Congress had clearly answered at step one. Id. at 87–93.

Another possibility is that step two of Chevron differs from step one by focusing on the reasoning or logic underlying the agency's proposed resolution of the ambiguity. Thus, in theory, even if the agency's interpretation is one that falls within the zone of ambiguity permitted by the statute's text and purposes, the agency must still explain why it chose that particular interpretation as opposed to some other permissible one that fell within the permissible zone. And so the agency must provide a coherent explanation for why it chose the interpretation that it selected. On this understanding, State Farm and Chevron arguably converge at step two of Chevron, as we discuss further below. See id. at 1218–1223.

(4) ***Is There a Step One-and-a-Half?*** DANIEL J. HEMEL & AARON L. NIELSON, CHEVRON STEP ONE-AND-A-HALF, 84 U. Chi. L. Rev. 757 (2017): "The Supreme Court says that Chevron has two steps: Is the statute ambiguous (Step One) and if so, is the agency's interpretation of the ambiguous provision a permissible one (Step Two)? Yet over the last three decades, the DC Circuit has inserted an intermediate step between Steps One and Two: Did the agency recognize that the statutory provision is ambiguous? If not, then the DC Circuit refuses to proceed to Chevron Step Two and remands the matter to the agency. This doctrine—which we dub 'Chevron Step One-and-a-Half'—has led to dozens of agency losses in the DC Circuit and DC federal district court, but it has gone entirely unmentioned in administrative law casebooks and is rarely referenced in the academic literature. The few who have not ignored the doctrine have treated it with skepticism. Chief among those skeptics is now-Chief Justice John Roberts, who while a DC Circuit judge criticized his colleagues for applying the doctrine."

This intermediate step raises the question whether an agency gets deference for its interpretation only if it knows that it is making an interpretive choice. How can that choice be said to be a reasoned one if it is not a choice at all and is instead just the product of the agency's mistaken judgment that the statute clearly compelled the agency's interpretation? On the other hand, if the agency's interpretation rests on a reasonable but mistaken view that the statute was clear, and that interpretation is in fact one that the statute would permit the agency to adopt, does it make sense to penalize the agency for that mistake? Isn't the agency's mistaken but reasonable judgment about the statute's clarity itself a nonarbitrary reason for choosing the interpretation that the agency adopts?

(5) ***Rulemaking v. Adjudication.*** By the way, in case you had any doubt, Chevron also applies to agency construction of statutes that takes place, not in rulemaking, but in the course of case-by-case adjudication. E.g., I.N.S. v. Aguirre-Aguirre, 526 U.S. 415 (1999). For a discussion of whether Chevron should apply to adjudication, see Kristin E. Hickman & Aaron L. Nielson, Narrowing Chevron's Domain, 70 Duke L.J. 931 (2021); Shoba Sivaprasad Wadhia & Christopher J. Walker, The Case Against Chevron Deference in Immigration Adjudication, 70 Duke L.J. 1197 (2021).

## NOTES ON THE RELATIONSHIP BETWEEN CHEVRON AND STATE FARM

(1) ***Does Chevron Step Two Recapitulate State Farm?*** In STATE FARM (p. 1131), the Court wrote, in what has become the standard paragraph describing "arbitrary and capricious" review: "Normally, an agency rule would be arbitrary and capricious if the agency has relied on factors which Congress has not intended it to consider, entirely failed to consider an important aspect of the problem, offered an explanation for its decision that runs counter to the evidence before the agency, or is so implausible that it could not be ascribed to a difference in view or the product of agency expertise. The reviewing court should not attempt itself to make up for such deficiencies; we may not supply a reasoned basis for the agency's action that the agency itself has not given. SEC v. Chenery Corp., 332 U.S. 194, 196 (1947)." Does the inquiry required under Chevron step two, to decide whether an agency's interpretation of a statute is "permissible," merely restate this test in other words? Sometimes Justices speak as if this were so. For example, JUSTICE KAGAN, writing for the Court in JUDULANG V. HOLDER, 565 U.S. 42, 52 n. 7 (2011), invalidated a ruling of the Board of Immigration Appeals under State Farm as arbitrary and capricious and then added in a footnote: "The Government urges us instead to analyze this case under the second step of the test we announced in Chevron U.S.A. Inc. v. Natural Resources Defense Council, Inc., 467 U.S. 837 (1984), to govern judicial review of an agency's statutory interpretations. Were we to do so, our analysis would be the same, because under Chevron step two, we ask whether an agency interpretation is 'arbitrary or capricious in substance.' Mayo Foundation for Medical Ed. and Research v. United States, 562 U.S. ___ (2011). . . ."

Nevertheless, the Court has not definitively weighed in on the issue, and scholars have spilled much ink on the topic, advocating all of the conceivable answers. Here are some of the issues:

(a) How much overlap is there? One of the State Farm questions, whether the explanation offered by the agency "runs counter to the evidence" produced in the proceeding, seems unconnected to the Chevron question whether the agency's reading of the statute is reasonable. By contrast, whether the agency has "relied on factors which Congress has not intended it to consider" is intimately connected to interpreting the statute and might well be viewed through the lens of either case.

(b) On the possible overlap questions, does it matter which case—Chevron or State Farm—we use to provide the reviewing lens? Are the materials used to provide the predicates for review different? Is the degree of stringency of review different? Should agency litigators embrace Chevron step two as the easier test—and those challenging agency action press for State Farm's "hard look"?

(c) Finally, should Chevron step two proceed from the agency's own "reasoned basis" for its choice, the way State Farm (through its citation of the Chenery case) requires for its test? KEVIN M. STACK, THE CONSTITUTIONAL FOUNDATIONS OF CHENERY, 116 Yale L.J. 952, 1005 (2007):

"The clearest point of connection between Chevron and Chenery is that compliance with the Chenery principle operates as a condition for the agency to receive deference in Chevron Step Two. Simply put, a court should not defer to an agency's construction of a statute at Chevron Step Two unless the agency embraced that construction at the time it acted, not merely in litigation. The basic logic of this structure seems relatively clear: the deference the Court applies at Step Two is implicitly conditioned on the agency's having worked through the problem, with reason-giving as the overt expression of its exercise of discretion and expertise." Is that right?

(2) ***An "Overlap at the Margins"?*** ARENT V. SHALALA, 70 F.3d 610 (D.C. Cir. 1995): The Nutrition Labeling and Education Act of 1990, enforced by the FDA, required manufacturers of food to provide various items of nutritional information on the foods' labels. For raw produce and fish—not manufactured items—it established voluntary guidelines under which the retail stores provide nutritional information to the customer. The Act then required the FDA to convert this voluntary scheme into a mandatory set of labeling requirements if it found that food stores were not in "substantial compliance" with the guidelines. What constituted "substantial compliance" was to be defined by regulation, as follows: "The regulation shall provide that there is not substantial compliance if a significant number of retailers have failed to comply with the guidelines. The size of the retailers and the portion of the market served by retailers in compliance with the guidelines shall be considered in determining whether the substantial-compliance standard has been met."

The regulation at issue provided that individual stores would be considered in compliance if they provided information for at least 90% of their fish and vegetables, and the industry as a whole would be in compliance if at least 60% of the surveyed stores were in compliance; the size of the stores and the markets they served were taken into account in determining the protocol for the stipulated survey.

This suit challenged both the validity of the regulation and of the subsequent determination by the FDA, based on its survey, that the industry was indeed in "substantial compliance."

EDWARDS, C.J., for the majority (70 F.3d at 614–17): "Although the parties argue this case in terms of both Chevron analysis and arbitrary and capricious review, they interpret the case as one involving review of an agency's construction of a statute and look primarily to Chevron for the appropriate analytical framework. We, however, do not find Chevron controlling. In challenging the FDA's regulation defining 'substantial compliance,' appellants seek traditional arbitrary and capricious review governed by Motor Vehicle Manufacturers Ass'n v. State Farm Mutual Automobile Insurance Co., 463 U.S. 29 (1983). We recognize that, in some respects, Chevron review and arbitrary and capricious review overlap at the margins. But it would be a mistake to view this case as one involving typical Chevron review.

"Chevron is principally concerned with whether an agency has authority to act under a statute. Thus, a reviewing court's inquiry under Chevron is rooted in statutory analysis and is focused on discerning the boundaries of Congress' delegation of authority to the agency; and as long as the agency stays within that delegation, it is free to make policy choices in interpreting the statute, and such interpretations are entitled to deference. . . . In such a case, the question for the reviewing court is whether the agency's construction of the statute is faithful to its plain meaning, or, if the statute has no plain meaning, whether the agency's interpretation 'is based on a permissible construction of the statute.'

"In the present case, however, there is no question that the FDA had authority to define the circumstances constituting food retailers' substantial compliance with the NLEA's voluntary labeling guidelines. The only issue here is whether the FDA's discharge of that authority was reasonable. Such a question falls within the province of traditional arbitrary and capricious review under 5 U.S.C. § 706(2)(A). Thus, in the present case, State Farm is controlling regarding the standard of review.

"In State Farm, the Court held: [long quotation omitted]. Under this standard of review, it is clear that the FDA's regulations must be upheld.

"The FDA certainly took account of the relevant factors in devising its sixty-percent, industry-wide standard for food retailers' 'substantial compliance' under the NLEA. . . . The FDA also has articulated an explanation for its decision that demonstrates its reliance on a variety of relevant factors and represents a reasonable accommodation in light of the facts before the agency. . . . Given the record before the agency, the FDA's sixty-percent figure is not unreasonable and it certainly does not reveal 'a clear error of judgment.' Overton Park, 401 U.S. at 416. Moreover, the statutory intent was not to assure one-hundred-percent compliance, but rather 'substantial' compliance, and the FDA's sixty-percent standard does ensure that a major portion of the retail food market will receive nutritional information. . . ."

WALD, J., concurring (70 F.3d at 619–620): "While I agree with the panel's conclusion that the Food and Drug Administration's ('FDA') rule is justifiable, I would resolve the case under the Chevron step two challenge which was presented by the parties and addressed by the trial court, rather than grounding our decision on a different facet of Administrative Procedure Act ('APA') review. . . .

"Chevron allocates power to interpret statutes among the branches of government by creating a presumption that agencies, rather than the courts, are the preferred institution for filling in statutory gaps. The first step of Chevron is straightforward; if the statutory language is clear, it controls. The second step, where in my view the majority goes astray, entrusts agencies with authority to interpret statutory ambiguities, provided they do so in a manner that is reasonable and consistent with the language and purposes of the statute. By contrast, garden-variety APA review under § 706 focuses more heavily on the agency's decisionmaking process; to survive arbitrary and capricious review, 'the agency must examine the relevant data and articulate a satisfactory explanation for its action, including a rational connection between the facts found and the choice made.' State Farm.

"Given these differences in the central concerns behind the two analytic frameworks, there are certainly situations where a challenge to an agency's regulation will fall squarely within one rubric, rather than the other. For example, we might invalidate an agency's decision under Chevron as inconsistent with its statutory mandate, even though we do not believe the decision reflects an arbitrary policy choice. Such a result might occur when we believe the agency's course of action to be the most appropriate and effective means of achieving a goal, but determine that Congress has selected a different—albeit, in our eyes, less propitious—path. Conversely, we might determine that although not barred by statute, an agency's action is arbitrary and capricious because the agency has not considered certain relevant factors or articulated any rationale for its choice. . . .

"But I agree with the panel that despite these distinctions, the Chevron and State Farm frameworks often do overlap. . . . The case before us arguably falls within this area of overlap. In reviewing the FDA's regulations, our task was to determine whether the agency rationally considered the factors set forth in the NLEA when it defined 'substantial compliance.' Accordingly, I would not argue that State Farm is altogether irrelevant to our analysis, but given the scope and function of Chevron step two analysis, neither would I find State Farm applicable to the exclusion of Chevron, as the majority does. Petitioners' appeal ultimately does stand or fall on whether the FDA heeded Congress' admonitions that it may not find 'substantial compliance' if 'a significant number of retailers' have failed to comply, and that it must consider '[t]he size of the retailers and the portion of the market served by retailers in compliance with the guidelines' when making this determination. This language is sufficiently concrete to permit review of whether the agency's interpretation is reasonable and consistent with Congress' purpose in enacting the NLEA. In fact, I believe it well within the bounds of typical Chevron step two analysis, which is why the majority's opinion troubles me somewhat. If this case falls totally outside Chevron, many other cases marching under its banner must be similarly exiled. The majority's unequivocal rejection of the Chevron analytic framework utilized by the parties and the trial court in this case provides no clues as to the boundary lines for Chevron and APA review."

(3) ***Are the State Farm and Chevron Doctrines the Same, or Do They Just Intersect?*** As we have already seen in the Notes accompanying the Fox Television case (p. 1174), in ENCINO V. NAVARRO MOTORCARS, LLC, 579 U.S. 211 (2016), the Court ruled: "It is not the role of the courts to speculate on reasons that might have supported an agency's decision. '[W]e may not supply a reasoned basis for the agency's action that the agency itself has not given.' State Farm, 463 U.S., at 43 (citing SEC v. Chenery Corp., 332 U.S. 194 (1947)). Whatever potential reasons the Department might have given, the agency in fact gave almost no reasons at all. In light of the serious reliance interests at stake, the Department's conclusory statements do not suffice to explain its decision. See Fox Television Stations, 556 U.S., at 515–516."

The court then went on to draw the following corollary: "This lack of reasoned explication for a regulation that is inconsistent with the

Department's longstanding earlier position results in a rule that cannot carry the force of law. See 5 U.S.C. § 706(2)(A); State Farm, supra, at 42–43. It follows that this regulation does not receive Chevron deference in the interpretation of the relevant statute."

How would you phrase this relationship of State Farm and Chevron?

(4) ***Reasoned Decisionmaking and Reasonable Interpretation.*** As we saw in the "Notes on Cost-Benefit Analysis as a Possible Element of 'Arbitrary and Capricious' Review" (p. 1156), the most recent relevant Supreme Court case on that topic is MICHIGAN V. EPA, 576 U.S. 743 (2015). There, the Clean Air Act told the EPA to require a first set of controls over power plants, to study the effect of that first set, and then to further regulate power plants "if the Administrator [of the agency] finds such regulation is appropriate and necessary after considering the results of the study." 42 U.S.C. § 7412(n)(1)(A). The EPA made this determination that regulation was "appropriate and necessary" without considering the cost to the industry that regulation would entail; it did, however, consider cost in several ways when determining, later on, precisely what regulations the plants had to meet. "[T]he phrase 'appropriate and necessary,'" said the Court, "requires at least some attention to cost" in making the initial decision to regulate.

Here is JUSTICE SCALIA's rendition of the conceptual framework involved, 576 U.S. at 750–51: "Federal administrative agencies are required to engage in 'reasoned decisionmaking.' Allentown Mack Sales & Service, Inc. v. NLRB, 522 U.S. 359, 374 (1998). 'Not only must an agency's decreed result be within the scope of its lawful authority, but the process by which it reaches that result must be logical and rational.' Ibid. It follows that agency action is lawful only if it rests 'on a consideration of the relevant factors.' Motor Vehicle Mfrs. Assn. of United States, Inc. v. State Farm Mut. Automobile Ins. Co., 463 U.S. 29, 43 (1983).

"EPA's decision to regulate power plants under § 7412 allowed the Agency to reduce power plants' emissions of hazardous air pollutants and thus to improve public health and the environment. But the decision also ultimately cost power plants, according to the Agency's own estimate, nearly $10 billion a year. EPA refused to consider whether the costs of its decision outweighed the benefits. The Agency gave cost no thought *at all,* because it considered cost irrelevant to its initial decision to regulate.

"EPA's disregard of cost rested on its interpretation of § 7412(n)(1)(A), which, to repeat, directs the Agency to regulate power plants if it 'finds such regulation is appropriate and necessary.' The Agency accepts that it *could* have interpreted this provision to mean that cost is relevant to the decision to add power plants to the program. But it chose to read the statute to mean that cost makes no difference to the initial decision to regulate.

"We review this interpretation under the standard set out in Chevron U.S.A. Inc. v. Natural Resources Defense Council, Inc., 467 U.S. 837 (1984). Chevron directs courts to accept an agency's reasonable resolution of an ambiguity in a statute that the agency administers. Id., at 842–843. Even under this deferential standard, however, 'agencies must operate within the bounds of reasonable interpretation.' Utility Air Regulatory Group v. EPA,

573 U.S. 302, 321 (2014). EPA strayed far beyond those bounds when it read § 7412(n)(1) to mean that it could ignore cost when deciding whether to regulate power plants."

What is the relationship of State Farm and Chevron in this passage? And by the way, if a statute's text is unclear as to whether costs should be considered, why isn't the issue of whether and how to consider costs exactly the type of issue about which judges should defer to agency choices? In fact, isn't it the very type of decision that was at issue in Chevron itself?

(5) ***Is the Assignment of Tasks Under State Farm and Chevron Backwards?*** After reviewing the tasks State Farm assigned to courts and to agencies, and the tasks Chevron assigned to courts and to agencies, then-First-Circuit-Judge Stephen Breyer asked of the combination: "Is this not the exact opposite of a rational system?" Judicial Review of Questions of Law and Policy, 38 Admin. L. Rev. 363, 397 (1986).

## NOTES ON THE BASIS FOR CHEVRON'S DOCTRINE

(1) ***In Light of Precedent.*** In a footnote, Chevron provided a long string of citations that dated back to 1827 to support its assertion that "[w]e have long recognized that considerable weight should be accorded to an executive department's construction of a statutory scheme it is entrusted to administer." The footnote reads: "Aluminum Co. of America v. Central Lincoln Peoples' Util. Dist., ante, at 389; Blum v. Bacon, 457 U.S. 132, 141 (1982); Union Electric Co. v. EPA, 427 U.S. 245, 256 (1976); Investment Company Institute v. Camp, 401 U.S. 617, 626–627 (1971); Unemployment Compensation Comm'n v. Aragon, 329 U.S., at 153–154; NLRB v. Hearst Publications, Inc., 322 U.S. 111, 131 (1944); McLaren v. Fleischer, 256 U.S., at 480–481; Webster v. Luther, 163 U.S., at 342; Brown v. United States, 113 U.S. 568, 570–571 (1885); United States v. Moore, 95 U.S. 760. 763 (1878); Edwards' Lessee v. Darby, 12 Wheat. 206, 210 (1827)." But do those precedents support Chevron's particular approach to deference?

For an argument that these precedents do not support Chevron, consider ADITYA BAMZAI, THE ORIGINS OF JUDICIAL DEFERENCE TO EXECUTIVE INTERPRETATION, 126 Yale L.J. 908, 916–18 (2017): "[T]he prevailing interpretive methodology of nineteenth-century American courts was not a form of judicial deference, as it has come to be understood in the post-Chevron era. Under the traditional interpretive approach, American courts 'respected' longstanding and contemporaneous executive interpretations of law as part of a practice of deferring to longstanding and contemporaneous interpretation generally. It was the pedigree and contemporaneity of the interpretation, in other words, that prompted 'respect'; the fact that the interpretation had been articulated by an actor within the executive branch was relevant, but incidental.

"Nor was nineteenth-century mandamus practice based on any interpretive methodology that required judicial deference to the executive qua executive. While the modern reader may hear echoes of Chevron in mandamus—because the mandamus standard precluded judicial intervention when an executive official engaged in an 'executive duty' (including statutory interpretation) that required the exercise of judgment and discretion—the analogy is mistaken. As the Court put it in the foundational case of Decatur v. Paulding, if an issue of statutory construction were to arise outside of the mandamus context—where the standards for obtaining the writ did not apply—'the Court certainly would not be bound to adopt the construction given by the head of a department.' Courts, in other words, applied the mandamus standard only because they were confronting a writ of mandamus (or another extraordinary writ). Where there was no writ of mandamus, there would be no comparable interpretive deference. . . .

"[W]hen the modern trend toward generalized judicial deference to executive interpretation began during the fifth decade of the twentieth century, the Court did not rely primarily on the principle that courts 'respected' contemporaneous and customary executive constructions, nor on the principle that the mandamus standard required deference to executive action. Instead, the Court invoked longstanding precedents addressing judicial deference to agency factual determinations and analogized questions of law requiring agency expertise to questions of fact. In doing so, the Court drew on preexisting scholarship suggesting that a formal distinction between 'law' and 'fact' in administrative review was illusory. By embracing this legal-realist perspective on the law-fact distinction, and thereby blurring the line between factual determinations and legal questions, the Court incrementally expanded the domain of agency discretion in a manner that ultimately led to the Chevron doctrine."

Compare RONALD M. LEVIN, THE APA AND THE ASSAULT ON DEFERENCE, 106 Minn. L. Rev. 125, 168 (2021): "Bamzai's contention that contemporary adoption and customary usage were the central considerations in this body of case law, with deference concepts being irrelevant or at most 'incidental,' is far too reductionist. The opinions simply aren't written that way." Levin argues that the relevant precedents on the question instead applied a nuanced multi-factor analysis, with deference to the executive solidifying as one factor in such analysis by the end of the nineteenth century. He pointed to the case United States v. Moore, which stated: "The construction given to a statute by those charged with the duty of executing it is always entitled to the most respectful consideration, and ought not to be overruled without cogent reasons," as "[t]he officers concerned are usually able men, and masters of the subject." 95 U.S. 760, 763 (1878). What does such a statement say about Bamzai's "line between factual determinations and legal questions"?

(2) ***In Light of the Constitutional Design.*** CYNTHIA R. FARINA, STATUTORY INTERPRETATION AND THE BALANCE OF POWER IN THE ADMINISTRATIVE STATE, 89 Colum. L. Rev. 452, 487–88 (1989): "[A] key assumption of Chevron's 'judicial usurpation' argument—that Congress may give agencies primary responsibility not only for making policy within the limits of their organic statutes, but also for defining those limits whenever the text and surrounding legislative materials are ambiguous—is fundamentally incongruous with the constitutional course by which the Court came to reconcile agencies and separation of powers. Of course, to demonstrate that one of Chevron's central premises cannot be squared with the doctrinal

structure built in the nondelegation cases is not necessarily to establish that this structure was worth preserving. Was it merely a delusion that separation of powers could be honored through a theory of nondelegation that permitted the concentration of great policymaking and executing authority in administrative agencies, but which insisted that agencies could not then also hold the power to say what their organic statutes mean? An examination of the origins and content of that constitutional principle suggests not. The vision of separation of powers embodied in mature nondelegation analysis—a vision that came to ask whether power was being adequately checked, rather than whether powers were remaining divided—was in essence true to the constitutional vision."

For a distinct take about why Chevron is a poor fit for the constitutional design, consider JONATHAN T. MOLOT, THE JUDICIAL PERSPECTIVE IN THE ADMINISTRATIVE STATE: RECONCILING MODERN DOCTRINES OF DEFERENCE WITH THE JUDICIARY'S STRUCTURAL ROLE, 53 Stan. L. Rev. 1, 76–79 (2000): "The error in Chevron's logic lies in its equating any statutory ambiguity at all with a failure on the part of Congress to legislate. Chevron posits that whenever Congress's statutory instructions do not resolve an interpretive question conclusively, this must mean Congress either failed to 'consider the question,' 'was unable to forge a coalition on either side of the question,' or else consciously decided to delegate the question to the relevant agency. Chevron thus ignores the reality that the Founders highlighted over two centuries ago: Even when a majority of legislators *do* contemplate a legislative issue broadly conceived and *do* agree to address it with substantive instructions, statutory ambiguity may nonetheless remain over the particular questions that will arise under that statute. Recall Madison's observation that '[a]ll new laws, though penned with the greatest technical skill and passed on the fullest and most mature deliberation, are considered as more or less obscure and equivocal, until their meaning be liquidated and ascertained by a series of particular . . . adjudications.'[127] . . .

"It is beyond controversy that statutes often are ambiguous and that outside the administrative context judges are responsible for resolving those ambiguities. Whether Congress may be said to have 'delegated' legislative authority to the judiciary each time it leaves an ambiguity is unimportant: Courts must make decisions using traditional tools of statutory interpretation regardless of the label attached. Thus the very same statutory instructions, yielding the very same level of ambiguity that Chevron treats as a delegation in the administrative context, will be treated outside the administrative context as ordinary legislation subject to ordinary judicial interpretation.

"There is a substantial cost to treating as a 'delegation' the sort of ordinary statutory instructions that would be subject to ordinary judicial interpretation outside the administrative context. . . . [S]ince virtually '[a]ll new laws' start out ambiguous as applied to various circumstances and do not become clear until interpreted in 'particular . . . adjudications,' legislators historically have had incentives to engage in careful deliberation

[127] The Federalist No. 37 (James Madison).

and drafting to guide judicial resolution of statutory ambiguities. This careful deliberation and drafting not only appropriately ensures some legislative control over law application, but also may have the corollary benefit of improving the laws that legislators enact.

"But the sort of careful deliberation and drafting that legislators might use to guide judicial interpretation will be wasted on an administrative agency. The agency will tend to choose among reasonable interpretive options based on political considerations and policy concerns rather than anything in Congress' statute. As a result, legislators wishing to guide administrative decisions under Chevron must resort to . . . tactics that differ significantly from the careful deliberation and drafting they might use to guide judges.

"[As one such tactic,] legislators may decide to engage in what scholars have dubbed 'micromanagement' of administrative regulation. If conventional drafting tools generally cannot eliminate ambiguity (and the administrative leeway that goes with it under Chevron), legislators nonetheless have tried in some instances to go beyond conventional drafting. They have drafted statutory provisions with such 'striking specificity' as to preclude deference at Chevron Step I and compel administrative outcomes in keeping with their legislative bargains. . . .

"But if highly specific drafting of detailed statutory provisions succeeds in securing legislative control over administrative outcomes, such drafting by no means ensures the fair, sensible laws that our constitutional structure was designed to promote. . . ."

For an argument that Chevron is a good fit with the constitutional structure, consider the following explanations for statutory ambiguity. One possibility might be that Congress intended a specific result but wrote the statute ambiguously. Alternatively, perhaps Congress intended for the statute to give an agency room to maneuver. Before Chevron, courts determined this congressional intent case by case; this individualized determination was then supplanted by Chevron's rule of deference. Justice Scalia argued that, given the burden on the courts of making such case-by-case determinations, the difficulty of making determinations about legislative intent with any accuracy, and the likelihood that most statutes actually fall into neither category, with Congress simply not reaching the question one way or another, at least Chevron establishes a uniform default rule that Congress can always override. ANTONIN SCALIA, JUDICIAL DEFERENCE TO ADMINISTRATIVE INTERPRETATIONS OF LAW, 1989 Duke L.J. 511, 517: "If that is the principal function to be served, Chevron is unquestionably better than what preceded it. Congress now knows that the ambiguities it creates, whether intentionally or unintentionally, will be resolved, within the bounds of permissible interpretation, not by the courts but by a particular agency, whose policy biases will ordinarily be known. The legislative process becomes less of a sporting event when those supporting and opposing a particular disposition do not have to gamble upon whether, if they say nothing about it in the statute, the ultimate answer will be provided by the courts or rather by the Department of Labor."

Courts do more than elucidate the law: they apply it to decide cases. Could criticism (and defense) of Chevron focused on the former be missing the Article III forest for the trees? GILLIAN E. METZGER, FOREWORD: 1930S REDUX: THE ADMINISTRATIVE STATE UNDER SIEGE, 131 Harv. L. Rev. 1, 41–42 (2017): "[T]he argument that Article III compels independent judicial judgment for all questions of statutory interpretation runs into substantial arguments to the contrary. Article III may in fact militate in favor of deference to expert elucidation of statutory standards if the questions at issue require specialized expertise or experience that the federal courts lack. In such contexts, preserving the federal courts' ability to perform their constitutional function and reach accurate, coherent, and consistent determinations may mandate deference to agency determinations."

(3) ***In Light of Democratic Accountability.*** JERRY L. MASHAW, GREED, CHAOS AND GOVERNANCE 152 (1997): "Strangely enough, it may make sense to imagine the delegation of political authority to administrators as a device for improving the responsiveness of government to the desires of the general electorate. This argument can be made even if we accept many of the insights of the political and economic literature that premises its predictions of congressional and voter behavior on a direct linkage between benefits transferred to constituents and the election or reelection of representatives. All we need do is not forget there are also presidential elections and that, as the Supreme Court reminds us in Chevron, presidents are heads of administrations.

"Assume then that voters view the election of representatives to Congress through the lens of the most cynical interpretation of the modern public choice literature on congressional behavior. In short, the voter chooses a representative for that representative's effectiveness in supplying governmental goods and services to the local district, including the voter. The representative is a good representative or a bad representative depending upon his or her ability to provide the district with at least its fair share of governmental largesse. In this view, the congressperson's position on various issues of national interest is of modest, if any, importance. The only question is, Does he or she 'bring home the bacon.'

"The voter's vision of presidential electoral politics is arguably quite different. The president has no particular constituency to which he or she has special responsibility to deliver benefits. Presidents are hardly cut off from pork-barrel politics. Yet issues of national scope and the candidates' positions on those issues are the essence of presidential politics. Citizens vote for a president based almost wholly on a perception of the difference that one or another candidate might make to general governmental policies.

"If this description of voting in national elections is reasonably plausible, then the utilization of vague delegations to administrative agencies takes on significance as a device for facilitating responsiveness to voter preferences expressed in presidential elections. The high transactions costs of legislating specifically suggests that legislative activity directed to the modification of administration mandates will be infrequent. Agencies will thus persist with their statutory empowering provisions relatively intact over substantial periods of time."

(4) ***In Light of the APA.*** Justice Stevens's opinion in Chevron does not discuss the APA—review was under § 307 of the Clean Air Act instead. See 42 U.S.C. § 7607(d)(1). But focus for the moment on Chevron's application in cases under the APA. Do you think Chevron is consistent with the text of APA § 706? Recall the relevant portions of its text:

> To the extent necessary to decision and when presented, *the reviewing court shall decide all relevant questions of law, interpret* constitutional and *statutory provisions*, and *determine the meaning or applicability of the terms of an agency action*. The reviewing court shall—. . .
>
> (2) hold unlawful and set aside agency action, findings, and conclusions found to be—
>
> (A) arbitrary, capricious, an abuse of discretion, or otherwise not in accordance with law; . . .
>
> (C) *in excess of statutory jurisdiction, authority, or limitations, or short of statutory right*. . .

(emphasis added). This language rather clearly ratifies—does it not?—the longstanding proposition—reiterated by the Court shortly before the passage of the APA—that "[t]he interpretation of the meaning of statutes, as applied to justiciable controversies, is exclusively a judicial function." United States v. American Trucking Ass'ns, 310 U.S. 534, 544 (1940). The language might allow consideration of agency interpretations as data used to inform a court's own judgment, as indeed American Trucking emphasized. But does it allow giving to agency interpretations the authority that Chevron specifies?

Consider CASS R. SUNSTEIN, LAW AND ADMINISTRATION AFTER CHEVRON, 90 Colum. L. Rev. 2071, 2086–88 (1990): "The APA's provision for independent judicial interpretation of law is not inconsistent . . . with Chevron's deference to the agency's interpretation if Congress has, under particular statutes, granted the relevant authority to administrative agencies. Frequently, however, Congress does not speak in explicit terms on the question of deference. When this is so, the court's task is to make the best reconstruction that it can of congressional instructions. And if Congress has not made a clear decision one way or the other, the choice among the alternatives will call for an assessment of which strategy is the most sensible one to attribute to Congress under the circumstances. . . .

"If all this is so, the Chevron approach might well be defended on the ground that the resolution of ambiguities in statutes is sometimes a question of policy as much as it is one of law, narrowly understood, and that agencies are uniquely well situated to make the relevant policy decisions. In some cases, there is simply no answer to the interpretive question if it is posed as an inquiry into some real or unitary instruction of the legislature. Sometimes congressional views cannot plausibly be aggregated in a way that reflects a clear resolution of regulatory problems, many of them barely foreseen or indeed unforeseeable. In these circumstances, legal competence, as narrowly understood, is insufficient for decision. The resolution of the ambiguity calls for an inquiry into something other than the instructions of the enacting legislature. And in examining those other considerations, the institution entrusted with the decision must make reference to considerations of both fact and policy.

"Chevron nicely illustrates the point. The decision about whether to adopt a plantwide definition of 'source' required distinctly administrative competence because it called for a complex inquiry, not foreseen by Congress, into the environmental and economic consequences of the various possibilities. If regulatory decisions in the face of ambiguities amount in large part to choices of policy, and if Congress has delegated basic implementing authority to the agency, the Chevron approach might reflect a belief, attributable to Congress in the absence of a clear contrary legislative statement, in the comparative advantages of the agency in making those choices.

"At least as a general rule, these suggestions argue powerfully in favor of administrative rather than judicial resolution of hard statutory questions. The factfinding capacity and electoral accountability of the administrators are far greater than those of courts. Chevron is best understood and defended as a frank recognition that sometimes interpretation is not simply a matter of uncovering legislative will, but also involves extratextual considerations of various kinds, including judgments about how a statute is best or most sensibly implemented. Chevron reflects a salutary understanding that these judgments of policy and principle should be made by administrators rather than judges."

The idea that Chevron only provides a default rule is, by the way, not merely theoretical. Occasionally since the decision Congress has provided for a different standard of review. See, e.g., 15 U.S.C. § 6714(e) (regarding differences between state and federal insurance regulation).

Or, following on our consideration of the resonances between Chevron step two and State Farm (p. 1218 above), can we construct a reading of § 706 that supports Chevron by focusing not on the words that emphasize the review of statutory interpretation, but rather on the idea of overturning arbitrary and capricious action? "Normally," said State Farm, "an agency rule would be arbitrary and capricious if the agency has relied on factors which Congress has not intended it to consider, entirely failed to consider an important aspect of the problem, offered an explanation for its decision that runs counter to the evidence before the agency, or is so implausible that it could not be ascribed to a difference in view or the product of agency expertise." Justice Stevens's Chevron opinion invokes the agency's responsibility for "policy" and frames the judicial relationship to that element as one of oversight for reasonableness, not independent decision. Does the inquiry required under Chevron step two, to decide whether an agency's interpretation of a statute is "permissible," merely restate this test—leaving in judicial hands the decision of what the statute can permissibly mean, and primarily in agency hands the responsibility for particular application within that bounded space? If so, how comforting is that way of understanding Chevron given how broad the "bounded" space may be?

(5) ***In Light of the Need for Uniformity?*** PETER L. STRAUSS, ONE HUNDRED FIFTY CASES PER YEAR: SOME IMPLICATIONS OF THE SUPREME COURT'S LIMITED RESOURCES FOR JUDICIAL REVIEW OF AGENCY ACTION, 87 Colum. L. Rev. 1093, 1121 (1987): "[I]t is helpful to view Chevron through the lens of the Supreme Court's severely restricted capacity directly to enforce uniformity upon the courts of appeals in those courts' review of agency decisionmaking. When national uniformity in the administration of national statutes is called for, the national agencies responsible for that administration can be expected to reach single readings of the statutes for which they are responsible and to enforce those readings within their own framework. . . . If, however, one accepts not only that language is imprecise, but also that congressional language (in particular) is frequently indeterminate, it follows that that reading could never be demonstrably correct, but merely reasonable if within the range of indeterminacy, or incorrect if beyond it. Any reviewing panel of judges from one of the twelve circuits, if made responsible for precise renditions of statutory meaning, could vary in its judgment from the agency's, and from the judgments of other panels in other circuits, without being wrong. The variance might even occur in predictable ways, if simple diversity were overlaid by geographical bias. . . . Rather than see Chevron just as a rule about agency discretion . . . it can be seen as a device for managing the courts of appeals that can reduce (although not eliminate) the Supreme Court's need to police their decisions for accuracy."

## NOTES ON THE RELATIONSHIP BETWEEN CHEVRON AND JUDICIAL STATUTORY PRECEDENT

(1) ***What Happens if an Agency Addresses a Statutory Issue Judges Have Already Decided?*** Justice Stevens's opinion in Chevron tells us that the D.C. Circuit decided against the EPA based on two of that court's own precedents interpreting the Clean Air Act. "The basic legal error of the Court of Appeals was to adopt a static judicial definition of the term stationary source when it had decided that Congress itself had not commanded the definition." How are we to differentiate between the forbidden "static judicial definition" and the presumably still proper rules of stare decisis?

(2) ***The Brand X Doctrine.*** The Supreme Court went out of its way to answer the preceding question in NATIONAL CABLE & TELECOMMUNICATIONS ASS'N V. BRAND X INTERNET SERV., 545 U.S. 967 (2005). The underlying issue was how to classify cable companies that provided broadband internet services to consumers. The Communications Act of 1934, 47 U.S.C. § 151 et seq., distinguished between the provision of "information service" and "telecommunications service." If what the companies offered was only an "information service," they would be essentially free from regulation; if what they offered was also classified as a "telecommunications service," they would be subject to mandatory regulation by the Federal Communications Commission as a common carrier. The reality was that what the companies offered was an integrated product combining the information-processing capacity of the internet with a high speed wire. The FCC said the companies did not provide "telecommunications service" and so were free from common-

carrier regulation. The Ninth Circuit rejected the FCC's interpretation of the Communications Act based specifically on the precedential effect of its holding in AT&T Corp. v. Portland, 216 F.3d 871 (9th Cir. 2000), a case which had not involved the FCC. The Supreme Court reversed and upheld the agency against multiple challenges. Three Justices dissented, claiming that the FCC was attempting to impose a new regime of competition rather than regulation under the guise of statutory construction.

As regards the Ninth Circuit precedent relied on by the court below, the Supreme Court might simply have stated that it disagreed with the holding in that lower-court case; or it might have distinguished the case as not involving a review of FCC proceedings; or it might have placed emphasis on the fact that the case at hand had nationwide importance and was only fortuitously adjudicated in the Ninth Circuit. But, acknowledging that "[t]here is genuine confusion in the lower courts over the interaction between the Chevron doctrine and stare decisis principles," the Court, in an opinion by JUSTICE THOMAS, spoke more broadly (545 U.S. at 982–85):

"The Court of Appeals declined to apply Chevron because it thought the Commission's interpretation of the Communications Act foreclosed by the conflicting construction of the Act it had adopted in Portland. It based that holding on the assumption that Portland's construction overrode the Commission's, regardless of whether Portland had held the statute to be unambiguous. That reasoning was incorrect.

"A court's prior judicial construction of a statute trumps an agency construction otherwise entitled to Chevron deference only if the prior court decision holds that its construction follows from the unambiguous terms of the statute and thus leaves no room for agency discretion. This principle follows from Chevron itself. Chevron established a 'presumption that Congress, when it left ambiguity in a statute meant for implementation by an agency, understood that the ambiguity would be resolved, first and foremost, by the agency, and desired the agency (rather than the courts) to possess whatever degree of discretion the ambiguity allows.' Smiley v. Citibank (South Dakota), N.A., 517 U.S. 734, 740–741 (1996). Yet allowing a judicial precedent to foreclose an agency from interpreting an ambiguous statute, as the Court of Appeals assumed it could, would allow a court's interpretation to override an agency's. Chevron's premise is that it is for agencies, not courts, to fill statutory gaps. The better rule is to hold judicial interpretations contained in precedents to the same demanding Chevron step one standard that applies if the court is reviewing the agency's construction on a blank slate: Only a judicial precedent holding that the statute unambiguously forecloses the agency's interpretation, and therefore contains no gap for the agency to fill, displaces a conflicting agency construction.

"A contrary rule would produce anomalous results. It would mean that whether an agency's interpretation of an ambiguous statute is entitled to Chevron deference would turn on the order in which the interpretations issue: If the court's construction came first, its construction would prevail, whereas if the agency's came first, the agency's construction would command Chevron deference. Yet whether Congress has delegated to an agency the authority to interpret a statute does not depend on the order in which the judicial and administrative constructions occur. . . .

"Against this background, the Court of Appeals erred in refusing to apply Chevron to the Commission's interpretation of the definition of 'telecommunications service,' 47 U.S.C. 153(46). Its prior decision in Portland held only that the *best* reading of § 153(46) was that cable modem service was a 'telecommunications service,' not that it was the *only permissible* reading of the statute. . . . Before a judicial construction of a statute, whether contained in a precedent or not, may trump an agency's, the court must hold that the statute unambiguously requires the court's construction. Portland did not do so."

To which idea, that an agency would be entitled to disregard a court's prior determination as to what is the *best* interpretation of a statute, JUSTICE SCALIA had the following to say, in dissent (545 U.S. at 1017–20): "Article III courts do not sit to render decisions that can be reversed or ignored by Executive officers. . . .

"[T]oday's novelty . . . creates many uncertainties to bedevil the lower courts. A court's interpretation is conclusive, the Court says, only if it holds that interpretation to be 'the *only permissible* reading of the statute,' and not if it merely holds it to be 'the *best* reading.' Does this mean that in future statutory-construction cases involving agency-administered statutes courts must specify (presumably in dictum) which of the two they are holding? And what of the many cases decided in the past, before this dictum's requirement was established? . . . Does the 'unambiguous' dictum produce *stare decisis* effect even when a court is *affirming,* rather than *reversing,* agency action—so that in the future the agency *must adhere* to that affirmed interpretation? If so, does the victorious agency have the right to appeal a Court of Appeals judgment in its favor, on the ground that the text in question is in fact not (as the Court of Appeals held) unambiguous, so the agency should be able to change its view in the future?

"It is indeed a wonderful new world that the Court creates, one full of promise for administrative-law professors in need of tenure articles and, of course, for litigators. I would adhere to what has been the rule in the past: When a court interprets a statute without Chevron deference to agency views, its interpretation (whether or not asserted to rest upon an unambiguous text) is the law. I might add that it is a great mystery why any of this is relevant here. *Whatever* the stare decisis effect of AT&T Corp. v. Portland in the Ninth Circuit, it surely does not govern this Court's decision. . . . [T]he Ninth Circuit would already be obliged to abandon Portland's holding in the face of *this Court's* decision that the Commission's construction of 'telecommunications service' is entitled to deference and is reasonable. It is a sadness that the Court should go so far out of its way to make bad law."

To which, JUSTICE THOMAS responded (545 U.S. at 983–84): "The dissent answers that allowing an agency to override what a court believes to be the best interpretation of a statute makes 'judicial decisions subject to reversal by Executive officers.' It does not. Since Chevron teaches that a court's opinion as to the best reading of an ambiguous statute an agency is charged with administering is not authoritative, the agency's decision to construe that statute differently from a court does not say that the court's holding was legally wrong. Instead, the agency may, consistent with the court's holding, choose a different construction, since the agency remains the authoritative interpreter (within the limits of reason) of such statutes. In all other respects, the court's prior ruling remains binding law (for example, as to agency interpretations to which Chevron is inapplicable). The precedent has not been 'reversed' by the agency, any more than a federal court's interpretation of a State's law can be said to have been 'reversed' by a state court that adopts a conflicting (yet authoritative) interpretation of state law."

But Brand X soon raised challenging questions. In UNITED STATES V. HOME CONCRETE & SUPPLY, LLC, 566 U.S. 478 (2012), the Court reviewed Treasury's interpretation of a statute. A pre-Chevron Supreme Court decision, Colony, Inc. v. Comm'r, 357 U.S. 28 (1958), had already considered the statute at issue—and inconveniently noted, "[i]t cannot be said that the language is unambiguous," id. at 33. Faced with the problem of taxpayers' reliance upon this previous construction, the Court went out of its way to avoid applying Brand X to Treasury's new interpretation, writing: "In our view, Colony has already interpreted the statute, and there is no longer any different construction that is consistent with Colony and available for adoption by the agency." Home Concrete, 566 U.S. at 487. In a part of his opinion that did not gather a majority, Justice Breyer continued: "[T]he Court decided that case nearly 30 years before it decided Chevron. There is no reason to believe that the linguistic ambiguity noted by Colony reflects a post-Chevron conclusion that Congress had delegated gap-filling power to the agency. At the same time, there is every reason to believe that the Court thought that Congress had 'directly spoken to the question at hand,' and thus left '[no] gap for the agency to fill.'" Home Concrete, 566 U.S. at 488–89 (opinion of Breyer, J.).

And in 2020, JUSTICE THOMAS repudiated his stance in Brand X in his dissent from the Court's denial of a petition for certiorari in BALDWIN V. UNITED STATES, 140 S.Ct. 690: "Although I authored Brand X, 'it is never too late to 'surrende[r] former views to a better considered position.' Brand X appears to be inconsistent with the Constitution, the Administrative Procedure Act . . . , and traditional tools of statutory interpretation." After criticizing Chevron, Justice Thomas addressed Brand X: "Even if Chevron deference were sound, I have become increasingly convinced that Brand X was still wrongly decided because it is even more inconsistent with the Constitution and traditional tools of statutory interpretation than Chevron. By requiring courts to overrule their own precedent simply because an agency later adopts a different interpretation of a statute, Brand X likely conflicts with Article III of the Constitution. . . . Brand X takes on the constitutional deficiencies of Chevron and exacerbates them. Chevron requires judges to surrender their independent judgment to the will of the Executive; Brand X forces them to do so despite a controlling precedent. . . . Brand X also seems to be strongly at odds with traditional tools of statutory interpretation. [E]arly federal courts afforded weight to longstanding executive interpretations of a law that were made contemporaneously with its passage and that were uniformly maintained. Brand X, however, mandates deference to an executive interpretation that is neither contemporaneous nor settled."

(3) ***"Provisional Precedent"?*** KENNETH A. BAMBERGER, PROVISIONAL PRECEDENT: PROTECTIVE FLEXIBILITY IN ADMINISTRATIVE POLICYMAKING, 77 N.Y.U. L. Rev. 1272, 1308 (2002): "[I]n nearly every instance in which a federal court is faced with an open state law question, it decides it. Those decisions are clearly authoritative for the parties to the case and have 'binding precedential effect' on other federal courts, 'absent a subsequent state court decision or [legislative] amendment' adopting a contrary construction. But once a state exercises its primary authority to make such a decision or amendment, the federal interpretation is no longer binding. Its precedential value is, literally, *provisional*. . . . Certainly, the federalism concerns structuring the relation between federal courts and state actors do not govern the administrative law context. Yet the model of federal adjudication of state law issues provides a functional framework for reconciling the doctrinal conflicts raised by judicial interpretation of administrative statutes, and for preserving flexibility in policymaking."

(4) ***Constitutional Concerns.*** Then-JUDGE GORSUCH had real constitutional concerns with Brand X, as he explained in his concurrence in GUTIERREZ-BRIZUELA V. LYNCH, 834 F.3d 1142, 1150 (10th Cir. 2016): "Founders meet Brand X. Precisely to avoid the possibility of allowing politicized decisionmakers to decide cases and controversies about the meaning of existing laws, the framers sought to ensure that judicial judgments 'may not lawfully be revised, overturned or refused faith and credit by' the elected branches of government. Chi. & S. Air Lines v. Waterman S.S. Corp., 333 U.S. 103, 113 (1948); see also Hayburn's Case, 2 U.S. (2 Dall.) 409, 410 n* (1792) ('[B]y the Constitution, neither the Secretary . . . nor any other Executive officer, nor even the Legislature, are authorized to sit as a court of errors on the judicial acts or opinions of this court.'). Yet this deliberate design, this separation of functions aimed to ensure a neutral decisionmaker for the people's disputes, faces more than a little pressure from Brand X. Under Brand X's terms, after all, courts are required to overrule their own declarations about the meaning of existing law in favor of interpretations dictated by executive agencies. By Brand X's own telling, this means a judicial declaration of the law's meaning in a case or controversy before it is not 'authoritative,' but is instead subject to revision by a politically accountable branch of government. . . .

"When the political branches disagree with a judicial interpretation of existing law, the Constitution prescribes the appropriate remedial process. It's called legislation. Admittedly, the legislative process can be an arduous one. But that's no bug in the constitutional design: it is the very point of the design. The framers sought to ensure that the people may rely on judicial precedent about the meaning of existing law until and unless that precedent is overruled or the purposefully painful process of bicameralism and presentment can be cleared. Indeed, the principle of stare decisis was one 'entrenched and revered by the framers' precisely because they knew its importance 'as a weapon against . . . tyranny.' Michael B.W. Sinclair, Anastasoff Versus Hart: The Constitutionality and Wisdom of Denying Precedential Authority to Circuit Court Decisions, 64 U. Pitt. L. Rev. 695, 707 (2003). Yet even as now semi-tamed (at least in this circuit), Brand X still risks trampling the constitutional design by affording executive agencies license to overrule a judicial declaration of the law's meaning prospectively, just as legislation might—and all without the inconvenience of having to engage the legislative processes the Constitution prescribes. A form of Lawmaking Made Easy, one that permits all too easy intrusions on the liberty of the people."

"When the political branches disagree with a judicial interpretation of existing law, the Constitution prescribes the appropriate remedial process. It's called legislation." But does this argument beg the question Brand X presents? After all, if Chevron is justified by a congressional delegation of power to an agency to administer a statute by resolving ambiguities in it, then doesn't the Constitution prescribe that courts must respect that congressional grant of authority to the agency? And, if so, then on what basis could a court ignore an agency interpretation that is within the permissible range of possible interpretations that Congress itself provided for in the statute at issue? Does the Constitution really require that a court's best guess as to an ambiguous statute's meaning must forever bind the agency charged with administering that statute just because the court guessed first? Unless Chevron itself is unconstitutional, wouldn't the court have to defer to the agency if it beat the court to the punch?

(5) ***Can Chevron Be Waived?*** While we are at it, what do we think is the proper attitude for the courts to take if the party that would benefit from Chevron deference does not argue for it, or even specifically eschews it?

In HOLLYFRONTIER CHEYENNE REFINING, LLC v. RENEWABLE FUELS ASS'N, 141 S.Ct. 2172 (2021), which reviewed Renewable Fuel Program requirements, the government had argued at a previous stage of litigation for Chevron deference to support an EPA regulation. When the government did not repeat its Chevron argument in the Supreme Court (but other parties did), the Court responded that it would "therefore decline to consider whether any deference might be due. . . ." Id. at 2180. Whether or not this modest framing—"decline to consider"—will be considered precedential (see, e.g., Tiger Lily, LLC v. United States Dep't of Hous. & Urb. Dev., 5 F.4th 666, 669 (6th Cir. 2021)), what do you think of this approach? Should a judge rely on Chevron even if the agency does not invoke it? Is that part of stating what the law is—including how broad the holding is—for which judges bear an independent responsibility? And does the justification for Chevron depend on whether the agency advances an interpretation in litigation rather than in a regulation? Or is an agency entitled to simply waive Chevron the way that it can waive other procedural advantages?

For an argument that Chevron deference cannot be waived if it is otherwise justified, see Guedes v. Bureau of Alcohol, Tobacco, Firearms and Explosives, 920 F.3d 1, 22–23 (D.C. Cir. 2019) ("Chevron is not a 'right or privilege' belonging to a litigant. It is instead a doctrine about statutory meaning"); for the contrary, see Justice Gorsuch's statement when the

Supreme Court denied certiorari in the Guedes case, 140 S.Ct. 789 (mem.) (2020) ("If the justification for Chevron is that 'policy choices should be left to executive branch officials directly accountable to the people,' then courts must equally respect the Executive's decision *not* to make policy choices in the interpretation of Congress's handiwork."). The Guedes case returned to the D.C. Circuit on the merits (the first time was on a preliminary injunction). Guedes v. Bureau of Alcohol, Tobacco, Firearms and Explosives, 45 F.4th 306, 313 (D.C. Cir. 2022) ("Ultimately, we need not wrestle with the Chevron framework here. Rather, the parties have asked us to dispense with the Chevron framework, and in this circumstance, we think it is appropriate to do so. Using a statutory interpretation lens, we decide that the Bureau offered the best construction of the statute without wading into the subsidiary questions that the Chevron analysis poses."). For more on this emerging body of case law, as well as analysis of some doctrinal questions bearing on "Chevron waiver," see Kristin E. Hickman & R. David Hahn, Categorizing Chevron, 81 Ohio St. L.J. 611 (2020).

## NOTES ON THE PRACTICAL IMPACT OF CHEVRON

(1) ***Impact on Litigation.*** One can start by asking whether it matters in the lower courts if the Supreme Court announces a new doctrinal formulation regarding the standard for judicial review. Peter H. Schuck and E. Donald Elliott examined almost 2,000 courts of appeals decisions from 1984–85 and 1988. In To The Chevron Station: An Empirical Study of Federal Administrative Law, 1990 Duke L.J. 984, they reported "strong evidence" that, comparing the six months before Chevron came down in 1984 to a six-month period in 1985, outcomes changed from a pre-Chevron affirmance rate of 71% to a post-Chevron rate of 81%. By 1988, the affirmance rate was 76% (with remands twice as frequent as reversals, whereas in 1984–85 they had been about equal).

A later study of all the courts of appeals decisions from 1995 and 1996 that cited Chevron reported that agency interpretations were upheld 73% of the time. Of those that were rejected, 59% failed step one; in 18%, the statute was declared ambiguous but the agency's interpretation was ruled unreasonable, failing step two; and in 23%, the agency's interpretation failed a general test of "reasonability," which conflated steps one and two. Orin S. Kerr, Shedding Light on Chevron: An Empirical Study of the Chevron Doctrine in the U.S. Courts of Appeals, 15 Yale J. on Reg. 1 (1998).

Another study, about a decade later, analyzed 253 courts of appeals decisions from 1990 through 2004 in Chevron cases involving the EPA and the NLRB. This study found that the average validation rate was about 64%—markedly lower than in either of the other studies, and even lower than pre-Chevron. Thomas J. Miles & Cass R. Sunstein, Do Judges Make Regulatory Policy? An Empirical Study of Chevron, 73 U. Chi. L. Rev. 823, 849 (2006). (It is notable that the authors intentionally chose for their study agencies that tended to produce "politically contentious decisions"; this may explain, in part, the low affirmation rate.) Finally, an even more recent study—of 1,558 instances of agency interpretation (across many agencies) in the courts of appeals from 2003 to 2013 that cited Chevron—found that the agency prevailed about 77% of the time when the court applied Chevron, 56% when Skidmore applied, and only 39% on de novo review. These findings led the authors to conclude that "the application of the Chevron framework seems to make a meaningful difference as to whether agencies prevail on the interpretive question." Kent H. Barnett & Christopher J. Walker, Chevron in the Circuit Courts, 116 Mich. L. Rev. 1 (2017).

Of course, rates of affirmance and reversal do not tell the whole story. They are affected not only by what the courts do but by which cases lawyers choose to bring to court. If Chevron made it easier for agencies to win, it correspondingly made it more risky to bring an action challenging an agency decision (or, in the case of an agency enforcement action, to choose to oppose). In other words, the potential value of winning would have to be discounted to a greater extent to represent the increased likelihood of losing. Accordingly, one would expect over time for counsel representing parties opposed to agency action to bring fewer marginal cases. Assuming the costs of bringing an action against an agency remain constant (litigation costs plus the more practical costs of opposing an agency one deals with), and assuming that the amounts at stake in proceedings on average also remain constant, over the long run the rates of affirmance and reversal might be expected to return to their prior state—even if the courts were using a different standard of review—since those rates would represent the discounted value of bringing actions. So if the combined story of the studies just decided is that rates of judicial affirmance went up immediately after Chevron, and then fell back to roughly the prior levels, the case may still have had a long-run effect—but on the kinds of cases brought and not brought, rather than on the overall rates of success or failure.

(2) ***Impact on Regulations.*** Another consequence of Chevron—perhaps an intentional consequence—would seem to be a reduction in the stability of administrative regulations over time. Recall the long history of policy vacillation regarding airbags in the State Farm case and Justice Rehnquist's partial dissent stressing that a "change in administration brought about by the people casting their votes is a perfectly reasonable basis for an executive agency's reappraisal of the costs and benefits of its programs and regulations . . . within the bounds established by Congress."

In Chevron, a case where, once again, the agency's position had shifted over time, all six voting Justices signed on to Justice Stevens's observation endorsing agency reliance, within the limits established by delegation, "upon the incumbent administration's views of wise policy." Two of the nonparticipating Justices had been among the State Farm partial dissenters. This judicial proposition has substantial implications for relationships between the executive and legislative branches. If each administration's present choice can survive judicial review, Congress will be unable to change it unless it can secure either presidential agreement or the votes necessary to override a veto. Thus, a change of administration may bring in its wake new "interpretations" that, however unwelcome to Congress, cannot easily be overcome.

RUST V. SULLIVAN, 500 U.S. 173 (1991), presents a particularly dramatic example of this effect of Chevron. Title X of the Public Health Service Act,

42 U.S.C. §§ 300—300a–6, had provided, since enactment in 1970, for federal grant support of family planning clinics. While grantees were supposed to "offer a broad range of acceptable and effective family planning methods and services," the Act also stipulated that none of the grant money "shall be used in programs where abortion is a method of family planning." How far did this prohibition go? The initial regulations under the statute, issued in 1971, simply required that a Title X project "not provide abortions." Further guidelines issued in the mid-1970's expressly permitted nondirective counseling of pregnant women as to their options, including the availability of abortions elsewhere. Guidelines issued in 1981 mandated such counseling upon a patient's request. But in 1988, after a notice-and-comment proceeding, the Department of Health and Human Services promulgated new regulations that at every turn required grant recipients to avoid giving advice or making referrals concerning abortion. If a patient asked for information, the grantee was allowed to say that "the project does not consider abortion an appropriate method of family planning."

The Court sustained the regulations, 5 to 4. Much of Chief Justice Rehnquist's opinion for the majority was devoted to answering the challengers' claim that the regulations violated constitutional guarantees of free speech and substantive due process. But, as even this brief history shows, he had to address substantial questions of statutory interpretation and administrative discretion, too. As to the statute, the reach of its reference to "programs where abortion is a method of family planning" was uncertain and not clarified by the legislative history. "The broad language of Title X" he said, "plainly allows the Secretary's construction of the statute." CHIEF JUSTICE REHNQUIST continued (500 U.S. at 186–87):

"Petitioners argue, however, that the regulations are entitled to little or no deference because they 'reverse a longstanding agency policy that permitted nondirective counseling and referral for abortion,' and thus represent a sharp break from the Secretary's prior construction of the statute. . . .

"This Court has rejected the argument that an agency's interpretation 'is not entitled to deference because it represents a sharp break with prior interpretations' of the statute in question. Chevron, 467 U.S. at 862. In Chevron, we held that a revised interpretation deserves deference because '[a]n initial agency interpretation is not instantly carved in stone' and 'the agency, to engage in informed rulemaking, must consider varying interpretations and the wisdom of its policy on a continuing basis.' An agency is not required to 'establish rules of conduct to last forever,' Motor Vehicle Mfrs. Assn. of United States v. State Farm Mutual Automobile Ins. Co., but rather 'must be given ample latitude to "adapt [its] rules and policies to the demands of changing circumstances.' "

"We find that the Secretary amply justified his change of interpretation with a 'reasoned analysis.' Motor Vehicle Mfrs. The Secretary explained that the regulations are a result of his determination, in the wake of the critical reports of the General Accounting Office (GAO)[3] and the Office of the

[3] [Ed.] Now the Government Accountability Office.

Inspector General (OIG), that prior policy failed to implement properly the statute and that it was necessary to provide 'clear and operational guidance to grantees to preserve the distinction between Title X programs and abortion as a method of family planning.' 53 Fed. Reg. 2923–2924 (1988). He also determined that the new regulations are more in keeping with the original intent of the statute, are justified by client experience under the prior policy, and are supported by a shift in attitude against the 'elimination of unborn children by abortion.' We believe that these justifications are sufficient to support the Secretary's revised approach. Having concluded that the plain language and legislative history are ambiguous as to Congress' intent in enacting Title X, we must defer to the Secretary's permissible construction of the statute."

The dissenting Justices wrote three opinions. Much of Justice Blackmun's opinion was devoted to arguing that the regulations violated the First and Fifth Amendments. Justice Stevens's rested on the first step of the Chevron test: "I am convinced that the 1970 Act did not authorize the Secretary to censor the speech of grant recipients or their employees." JUSTICE O'CONNOR, making a point Justice Blackmun had also made, based her dissent on a "long-standing canon of statutory construction" (500 U.S. at 223–25):

" '[W]here an otherwise acceptable construction of a statute would raise serious constitutional problems, the Court will construe the statute to avoid such problems unless such construction is plainly contrary to the intent of Congress.' Edward J. DeBartolo Corp. v. Florida Gulf Coast Building & Construction Trades Council, 485 U.S. 568, 575 (1988). . . . In these cases, we need only tell the Secretary that his regulations are not a reasonable interpretation of the statute; we need not tell Congress that it cannot pass such legislation. If we rule solely on statutory grounds, Congress retains the power to force the constitutional question by legislating more explicitly. It may instead choose to do nothing. That decision should be left to Congress; we should not tell Congress what it cannot do before it has chosen to do it. It is enough in this case to conclude that neither the language nor the history of § 1008 compels the Secretary's interpretation, and that the interpretation raises serious First Amendment concerns. On this basis alone, I would . . . invalidate the challenged regulations."

If we view this debate in terms of its allocations of power to various institutions, Justice O'Connor's opinion would have required action on the part of both Congress and the President (or an extraordinary majority in Congress) to reinstate the prohibitions contained in the regulations. By contrast, Chief Justice Rehnquist's deference to the agency put a similar burden of action on those who would have removed the prohibitions. This, as it turned out, was not merely a theoretical point. In 1992, Congress passed a bill requiring Title X projects to provide their clients with nondirective counseling on various matters, including termination of pregnancy. But it was vetoed by President Bush on September 25, 1992, 28 Weekly Comp. Pres. Doc. 1759, with the consequence that even though both Houses of Congress opposed the regulations, they remained in force.

On February 5, 1993—very shortly after President Clinton took office—the new Secretary of HHS published an "Interim Rule," effective immediately for "good cause" pending a new notice and comment proceeding, which said in part: "[T]he Secretary suspends the 1988 rules and announces that, on an interim basis, the agency's nonregulatory compliance standards that existed prior to February 2, 1988 . . . will be used to administer the Family Planning Program. Under these compliance standards, Title X projects would be required, in the event of an unplanned pregnancy and where the patient requests such action, to provide nondirective counseling to the patient on options relating to her pregnancy, including abortion, and to refer her for abortion, if that is the option she selects." Each subsequent presidential administration has reinterpreted the then-operable statutory language in a way that favors its policy goals on the use of Title X funding, as summarized in Becerra v. Azar, 950 F.3d 1067, 1078–82 (9th Cir. 2020). The Supreme Court had granted certiorari to resolve the conflict between the Ninth and Fourth Circuits over whether the Trump Administration's interpretation could be upheld, but ultimately dismissed the case, on the Biden Administration's request. American Medical Association v. Becerra, No. 20-429 (dismissed May 17, 2021). The Biden Administration announced its own Title X Final Rule at 86 Fed. Reg. 56144 (Oct. 7, 2021), which has (not surprisingly, given the history of these regulations) been challenged in court. What do you make of such regulatory vacillation?

(3) ***Impact on Agency Behavior.*** Not surprisingly, Chevron may also have changed what lawyers inside agencies do. Here's the report of E. DONALD ELLIOTT, General Counsel of the EPA during the administration of the first President Bush, in CHEVRON MATTERS: HOW THE CHEVRON DOCTRINE REDEFINED THE ROLES OF CONGRESS, COURTS AND AGENCIES IN ENVIRONMENTAL LAW, 16 Vill. Envtl. L.J. 1, 11–12 (2005): "The fundamental difference between the role of EPA OGC [Office of General Counsel] (and probably in any other agency as well) pre-Chevron and post-Chevron is this: pre-Chevron, OGC usually gave its legal advice as a point estimate, e.g., 'the statute means this . . . you must follow what we in OGC tell you is the correct/best interpretation of the statue or you will lose in court.' . . . Post-Chevron, the form of OGC opinions is no longer a simple point estimate of what a statute means. Rather, OGC opinions now attempt to describe a permissible range of agency policy-making discretion that arises out of a statutory ambiguity. . . . Chevron opened up and validated a policy-making dialogue within agencies about what interpretation the agency should adopt for policy reasons, rather than what interpretation the agency must adopt for legal reasons. I believe that this expanded policy dialogue is productive and that it takes place more inside EPA today than it did pre-Chevron, and normatively, that is a good thing. For example, it is good that Chevron has increased the weight given to the views of air pollution experts in the air program office relative to the lawyers in OGC."

In this same vein, a survey of 148 rule drafters, across seven executive departments and two independent agencies, found that nearly 94% of them knew about Chevron deference by name, and 90% of the drafters reported that the Chevron doctrine played a role in their drafting decisions.

Christopher J. Walker, Inside Agency Statutory Interpretation, 67 Stan. L. Rev. 999 (2015). The survey even found that "two in five rule drafters surveyed agreed or strongly agreed—and another two in five somewhat agreed—that a federal agency is more aggressive in its interpretive efforts if it is confident that Chevron deference (as opposed to Skidmore deference or de novo review) applies."

(4) ***Impact on Congress.*** Last but certainly not least, how does Chevron affect the drafting of legislation? Does Congress know it is delegating authority to the agency when it leaves an ambiguity? Interviews of 137 congressional counsels in 2011 and 2012 suggest such a possibility. ABBE R. GLUCK & LISA SCHULTZ BRESSMAN, STATUTORY INTERPRETATION FROM THE INSIDE—AN EMPIRICAL STUDY OF CONGRESSIONAL DRAFTING, DELEGATION, AND THE CANONS: PART I, 65 Stan. L. Rev. 901, 996–97 (2013): "Chevron does function for many of our respondents as a reminder about the consequences of ambiguity and as an incentive to think about the level of detail in a statute. Eighty respondents (58%) said that Chevron plays a role when they are drafting. Forty-three respondents (31%) specifically indicated through their comments that they understood that statutory ambiguity results in judicial deference to agency interpretations. Forty respondents (29%) told us that Chevron forces them to think about how precisely to draft, and whether or not they need to 'curtail' the agency. As one respondent remarked, 'the main issue in drafting is how much discretion and we assume the courts will give deference. I'm hyperconscious of the extent to which we are giving them room. That's always part of the debate.' Another explained: 'Chevron is more like an incentive to be more specific when you want to be clear about what the agency should do. The presumption is broad deference, so we try to be clear when we want otherwise.' "

Notwithstanding these results, although 91% of survey respondents reported that statutes could be left ambiguous to delegate discretion to agencies, even larger numbers reported that such ambiguity might reflect a lack of time to draft clearer language, a particularly complex issue, or the need for consensus—92%, 93%, and 99%, respectively.

## NOTES ON CHEVRON AND THE APPROACH AGENCIES SHOULD USE WHEN INTERPRETING STATUTES

(1) ***Does Chevron Have Implications for How Agencies Should Interpret Statutes?*** Chevron said that within the possible meanings of a statute, a reviewing court should accept any reasonable meaning given by the agency. But Chevron did not discuss how the agency was to do its own interpretive work or how it was to choose among the reasonable meanings, and the issue has only slowly been recognized as an important feature of the post-Chevron landscape. Three possibilities might be suggested, none of which is without its difficulties:

(a) The agency could act as if it were a court interpreting the language in question without regard to the Chevron doctrine. In other words, the agency could ask what is the best interpretation of the statute that Congress wrote, using the same types of interpretive methods used by courts in handling statutes that are not administered by any agency. This would have the virtue of making "statutory interpretation" a unified subject, whether done by court or agency. But it is subject to several objections. First, insofar as the agency is asked to simply mimic what a court would do, the reasons for having a court defer to the agency's conclusion—that is, the Chevron principle—seem doubtful. Second, in many of the cases arising under Chevron step two—cases of statutory ambiguity—there may not be enough materials to make interpretation of the judicial sort more than a flip-a-coin proposition. Finally, and most importantly, this approach fails to take account of the different institutional roles of courts and agencies. For example, as pointed out in JERRY L. MASHAW, NORMS, PRACTICES AND THE PARADOX OF DEFERENCE: A PRELIMINARY INQUIRY INTO AGENCY STATUTORY INTERPRETATION ("PARADOX OF DEFERENCE"), 57 Admin. L. Rev. 501, 507 (2005), courts and agencies are very differently situated in their relationship to the President: "Save in those rare instances where presidents have been given clear statutory or constitutional authority to guide judicial interpretation by presidential pronouncement, the failure of the court to exercise interpretive judgment independent of presidential preferences would be to abandon what we imagine to be the constitutionally appropriate role of the federal judiciary. By contrast, for agencies of the executive branch to ignore legitimate presidential instruction would be for them to ignore their appropriate place in the constitutional order." Thus, this most straightforward answer to how agencies should interpret statutes—mimic how the courts interpret statutes—may be too simple.

(b) A second possibility is for agencies to follow the approach courts use in applying Chevron, but once having determined that the statute is ambiguous, then choose among the possible "permissible" interpretations on a purely policy-preference basis. Here is how RICHARD PIERCE, JR., describes this approach in HOW AGENCIES SHOULD GIVE MEANING TO THE STATUTES THEY ADMINISTER: A RESPONSE TO MASHAW AND STRAUSS, 59 Admin. L. Rev. 197, 202–04 (2007): "The proper roles for agencies in conforming to Chevron follow logically and inevitably from the Court's instructions to reviewing courts in Chevron. Because a reviewing court will apply step one of Chevron first, a prudent agency must apply step one itself. To maximize the chances of having its action upheld, the agency must do its best to determine whether Congress resolved the question before the agency. Although this process definitely is interpretive, it is one in which the agency has no practical choice but to attempt to anticipate and replicate the interpretive process a reviewing court will use. Additionally, the agency should use the same 'traditional tools of statutory construction' that it expects a reviewing court to use. . . . To the best of its ability, the agency should attempt to use exactly the same interpretive process a court would use—any intentional variation from that judicial interpretive process would be a self-defeating exercise in futility.

"The agency's task in minimizing its risk of reversal through application of Chevron step two is totally different from its task in attempting to minimize its risk of reversal through application of step one. An agency's efforts to minimize the risk of judicial reversal through application of

Chevron step two has little to do with statutory interpretation. Rather, the agency's task is to use a comprehensive and transparent policymaking process in which it identifies and explains each step in its decisionmaking process, relates each decision to the available data relevant to the decision, and explains why it rejected alternatives to, or criticisms of, the decisions it made.

"Depending on the context in which the agency makes the decision to give the ambiguous statutory term a particular meaning, the policymaking process that maximizes the likelihood of judicial approval through application of Chevron step two will require an agency to use tools made available by fields like economics, statistics, chemistry, toxicology, epidemiology, meteorology, etc. There is only one link between this policymaking process and the process of statutory interpretation. In the course of explaining why it made the decisions it made, the agency must refer to decisional factors that the underlying statute makes permissible. For that purpose, the agency must engage in statutory interpretation to the extent necessary to explain why it believes that a decisional factor it applies is statutorily permissible. In other words, a court will—and should—reverse an agency action if the agency relies on a decisional factor that is logically relevant to its decision in the abstract but one that Congress has forbidden the agency to consider. . . . Here again, however, the agency must do its best to anticipate and to replicate the interpretive process a reviewing court will use to minimize the agency's risk of judicial reversal of its action. A court will reverse an agency if the agency relies on a decisional factor the court determines to be impermissible."

But this approach will seem too policy driven for some. Consider GARY LAWSON, DIRTY DANCING—THE FDA STUMBLES WITH THE CHEVRON TWO-STEP, 93 Cornell L. Rev. 927, 932–33 (2008): "[Under Chevron,] reviewing courts are not looking to see whether agencies got the *right* answer but only whether they got a *permissible* answer. Could an agency take advantage of this deference and say, 'In construing this statute, we are going to pick the interpretation that we like on policy grounds, even though we think that a different interpretation represents the best reading of the statute, because we can get away with it on judicial review?' Such reasoning would be a clear abuse of the deferential standard of review. Deferential review is premised on the initial decision maker's good-faith effort to get the right answer. . . . [I]t would be just as outrageous for an agency to use Chevron deference as a tool to protect its *initial law findings* as it would be for an agency to use the substantial evidence standard as a tool to protect its *initial fact findings*."

More broadly, this second approach may rely too strongly on separating policy determinations from legal determinations.

(c) Which leaves us with a third possibility: that the process by which agencies interpret statutes should be modeled neither on what judges do when they interpret a statute directly nor on what judges do under Chevron. In other words, perhaps the most responsible way for agencies to proceed in their institutional context is, at least in some respects, different from the most responsible way for courts to proceed in theirs. Consider, for example, PETER L. STRAUSS's discussion of the difference between the ways courts and agencies relate to legislative history in WHEN THE JUDGE IS NOT THE PRIMARY OFFICIAL WITH RESPONSIBILITY TO READ: AGENCY INTERPRETATION AND THE PROBLEM OF LEGISLATIVE HISTORY, 66 Chi.-Kent L. Rev. 321, 346–47 (1990): "Responsible in some sense for all law, a court has infrequent occasion to consider the meaning of any particular part of the law, and no responsibility for continuing, proactive attention to its development. If it comes to the legislative history at all, it comes to that history cold, without a developed institutional sense of the state of play. It does not participate in, indeed very likely is utterly unaware of, what occurs in drafting, hearings, debates, or a continuing course of oversight hearings, presidential guidance, and frustrated efforts at securing legislative change; a court is not continually studying issues of statutory meaning and adjusting outcomes—as administrators responsible for a program must. For the agency, of course, the reverse is generally true; its closeness to the legislative process, continued involvement, and responsibility are . . . precisely the reasons courts have long given its readings of statutory meaning special weight. Delegitimating reference to legislative history for the agency, then, not only reduces its defenses to contemporary political oversight; it encourages it to ignore, in acting, what in an important sense it already knows."

On this view, the interpretive space provided by Chevron deference is based on a recognition of the differential engagement of agencies and courts in parts of a complex process of statutory interpretation.

How far does this notion of agencies using a distinct mode of interpretation go? Consider this, on the differing relations of courts and agencies to the Constitution, from MASHAW, PARADOX OF DEFERENCE, supra, at 507: "American administrative agencies are obviously bound by the Constitution and must often implement it directly. Agency hearing processes, for example, must satisfy constitutional due process requirements. And, federal law enforcement officials make thousands of decisions every day that require an interpretation of the Fourth Amendment's search and seizure provisions. But how should the potential for constitutional difficulty influence an agency's construction of some statute that it is charged with implementing? We know that there is a judicial canon of statutory construction, based on principles of constitutional comity, which counsels courts to avoid constructions of statutes that would raise serious constitutional questions about their validity. Are agencies in a similar position?

"Arguably not. They have no general responsibility for constitutional review of congressional action whose aggressive or imprudent exercise might threaten the legitimacy of judicial review and thereby weaken the constitutional order. Indeed, were agencies intensely attentive to avoiding constitutional questions when interpreting the statutes entrusted to their care, they would often foreclose authoritative resolution of constitutional questions by the judiciary. To put the point in its strongest form, an administrative apparatus that operated in the shadow of the avoidance canon would set itself up operationally as the arbiter of the constitutionality of congressional action. . . . Obviously, administrators who fail to pursue implementation any time a constitutional issue looms on their horizon could not possibly carry out their legislative mandates effectively. Constitutionally timid administration both compromises faithful agency and potentially usurps the role of the judiciary in harmonizing congressional power and constitutional command."

On this subject—the impact of the Constitution on the best interpretation of the statute—a court is unlikely to defer to the agency's judgment. So one difficulty with the idea that responsible agency interpretation might follow a different set of norms from responsible judging is that, as Mashaw has himself recognized, "responsible judging may reject an interpretation generated by responsible administration." Jerry L. Mashaw, Agency-Centered or Court-Centered Administrative Law? A Dialogue With Richard Pierce on Agency Statutory Interpretation, 59 Admin. L. Rev. 889, 903 (2007).

## NOTES ON THE CHALLENGE TO CHEVRON

(1) ***A Revolt from Below?*** Then-Judge NEIL GORSUCH wrote a widely noticed concurrence questioning the constitutional basis for Chevron shortly before he was nominated to the Supreme Court by President Trump. He argued in GUTIERREZ-BRIZUELA V. LYNCH (p. 1251): "Not only is Chevron's purpose seemingly at odds with the separation of legislative and executive functions, its effect appears to be as well. . . . First, we know that, consistent with the separation of powers, Congress may condition the application of a new rule of general applicability on factual findings to be made by the executive (so, for example, forfeiture of assets might be required if the executive finds a foreign country behaved in a specified manner). See Cargo of the Brig Aurora v. United States, 11 U.S. (7 Cranch) 382, 388 (1813). Second, we know Congress may allow the executive to resolve 'details' (like, say, the design of an appropriate tax stamp). See In re Kollock, 165 U.S. 526, 533 (1897). Yet Chevron pretty clearly involves neither of these kinds of executive functions and, in this way and as a historical matter, appears instead to qualify as a violation of the separation of powers. See Michigan v. EPA, 135 S.Ct. 2699, 2713–14 (2015) (Thomas, J., concurring); cf. City of Arlington v. FCC, 133 S.Ct. 1863, 1877–79 (2013) (Roberts, C.J., dissenting); Nichols, 784 F.3d at 671–72 (Gorsuch, J., dissenting from the denial of rehearing en banc). Of course, in relatively recent times the Court has relaxed its approach to claims of unlawful legislative delegation. . . . But even taking the forgiving intelligible principle test as a given, it's no small question whether Chevron can clear it. For if an agency can enact a new rule of general applicability affecting huge swaths of the national economy one day and reverse itself the next (and that is exactly what Chevron permits, see 467 U.S. at 857–59), you might be forgiven for asking: where's the 'substantial guidance' in that? And if an agency can interpret the scope of its statutory jurisdiction one way one day and reverse itself the next (and that is exactly what City of Arlington's application of Chevron says it can), you might well wonder: where are the promised 'clearly delineated boundaries' of agency authority? . . . Even under the most relaxed or functionalist view of our separated powers some concern has to arise, too, when so much power is concentrated in the hands of a single branch of government. See The

Federalist No. 47 (James Madison) ('The accumulation of all powers, legislative, executive, and judiciary, in the same hands . . . may justly be pronounced the very definition of tyranny.'). After all, Chevron invests the power to decide the meaning of the law, and to do so with legislative policy goals in mind, in the very entity charged with enforcing the law. . . . I would have thought powerful and centralized authorities like today's administrative agencies would have warranted less deference from other branches, not more. None of this is to suggest that Chevron is 'the very definition of tyranny.' But on any account it certainly seems to have added prodigious new powers to an already titanic administrative state . . . . It's an arrangement, too, that seems pretty hard to square with the Constitution of the founders' design and, as Justice Frankfurter once observed, '[t]he accretion of dangerous power does not come in a day. It does come, however slowly, from the generative force of unchecked disregard of the restrictions' imposed by the Constitution. Youngstown Sheet & Tube Co. v. Sawyer, 343 U.S. 579, 594 (1952) (Frankfurter, J., concurring). . . ."

Similar views were also expressed by Judge Kent Jordan in his concurring opinion in EGAN V. DELAWARE RIVER PORT AUTHORITY, 851 F.3d 263, 279 (3d Cir. 2017): "The deference required by Chevron not only erodes the role of the judiciary, it also diminishes the role of Congress. Under Chevron, '[s]tatutory ambiguity . . . becomes an implicit delegation of rule-making authority, and that authority is used not to find the best meaning of the text, but to formulate legally binding rules to fill in gaps based on policy judgments made by the agency rather than Congress.' Michigan v. Envtl. Prot. Agency, 135 S.Ct. 2699, 2713 (2015) (Thomas, J., concurring). And we in the courts have abetted that process, largely 'abdicat[ing] our duty to enforce [the] prohibition' against Congressional delegation of legislative power to executive agencies. Department of Transp. v. Ass'n of Am. R.R., 135 S.Ct. 1225, 1246 (2015) (Thomas J., concurring). The consequent aggrandizement of federal executive power at the expense of the legislature leads to perverse incentives, as Congress is encouraged to pass vague laws and leave it to agencies to fill in the gaps, rather . . . than undertaking the difficult work of reaching consensus on divisive issues."

In a book review published in 2016, FIXING STATUTORY INTERPRETATION, 129 Harv. L. Rev. 2118 (2016), then-Judge Brett Kavanaugh criticized the use of statutory "ambiguity" as the gate keeper for various interpretive doctrines, including Chevron. "Ambiguity," he argued, was mostly in the eye of the beholder. Judges would do better—and be more even-handed—if they tried to determine what was the best (even if not the only) interpretation of the statutory language. On his view, the test for deferring to an agency is not clarity versus ambiguity. It is whether the best reading of the text Congress used supports giving room to an agency to make a discretionary judgment. Thus, statutory language, like "reasonable" or "appropriate" or "feasible," should be read to signal a grant of discretion to the agency to make reasonable policy choices, while more "specific" statutory text should be understood to a contain a "best reading of the statutory text." Thus, when construing that language, there is no reason for a court to defer to an agency's view. The only task is to determine the "best reading."

(2) ***A Revolt in Congress?*** Bills have been introduced in Congress to, in effect, overrule Chevron. Here is the text of a House bill introduced in January 2017 (it has been introduced in more recent years as well):

SECTION 1. SHORT TITLE.

This Act may be cited as the "Separation of Powers Restoration Act of 2017".

SEC. 2. JUDICIAL REVIEW OF STATUTORY AND REGULATORY INTERPRETATIONS.

Section 706 of title 5, United States Code, is amended—

(1) by striking "To the extent necessary" and inserting "(a) To the extent necessary";

(2) by striking "decide all relevant questions of law, interpret constitutional and statutory provisions, and";

(3) by inserting after "of the terms of an agency action" the following "and decide de novo all relevant questions of law, including the interpretation of constitutional and statutory provisions, and rules made by agencies. Notwithstanding any other provision of law, this subsection shall apply in any action for judicial review of agency action authorized under any provision of law. No law may exempt any such civil action from the application of this section except by specific reference to this section"; and

(4) by striking "The reviewing court shall—" and inserting the following:

"(b) The reviewing court shall—".

Can Congress control the courts on this matter? The proposed bill was accompanied by the following official statement regarding Congress's constitutional authority to enact it: "Congress has the power to enact this legislation pursuant to the following: Article III, Section 1, Sentence 1, and Section 2, Clauses 1 and 4 of the Constitution, in that the legislation defines or affects judicial powers and cases that are subject to legislation by Congress; Article 1, Section 1, Clause 1 of the United States Constitution, in that the legislation concerns the exercise of legislative powers generally granted to Congress by that section, including the exercise of those powers when delegated by Congress to the Executive; and, Article 1, Section 8, Clause 18 of the United States Constitution, in that the legislation exercises legislative power granted to Congress by that clause 'to make all laws which shall be necessary and proper for carrying into execution the foregoing powers, and all other powers vested by this Constitution in the Government of the United States, or in any Department or Officer thereof.' " Do you see any constitutional problem with Congress precluding courts from deferring to agency interpretations of ambiguous statutes?

(3) ***A Revolt from Within?*** A sign that Chevron's days may be numbered came at the end of the October 2018 Term in PEREIRA V. SESSIONS, 138 S.Ct. 2105 (2018). There, the Court considered the meaning of a provision of the Illegal Immigration Reform and Immigrant Responsibility Act of 1996 (IIRIRA), which allows nonpermanent residents who are subject to removal

proceedings to seek cancellation of removal if they have "been physically present in the United States for a continuous period of not less than 10 years immediately preceding the date of [an] application" for cancellation. 8 U.S.C. § 1229(b)(1)(A). A separate provision of IIRIRA, however, sets forth what is known as the stop-time rule, by stating that the period of continuous presence is "deemed to end . . . when the alien is served a notice to appear under section 1229(a)." § 1229(d)(1)(A). With respect to this so-called stop-time rule, the Department of Homeland Security promulgated a regulation in 1997 that a "notice to appear" need only provide "the time, place and date of the initial removal hearing, where practicable," 62 Fed. Reg. 10332, and the Board of Immigration Appeals (BIA) ruled that notices to appear may trigger the stop-time rule even when they do not provide the time and place of the removal proceedings.

The case at hand concerned a native of Brazil, Wescley Fonseca Pereira, who had come to the United States and overstayed his visa. More than ten years after he had received a "notice of removal" that did not provide the time and place of the removal proceedings but that ordered him to appear at some place and time to be set in the future, he sought cancellation of removal. The BIA ruled that, in consequence of his having received this "notice to appear," he was barred from seeking cancellation of removal by the stop-time rule. The First Circuit upheld the BIA's decision.

The Supreme Court, in an opinion by JUSTICE SOTOMAYOR, reversed, after concluding at Chevron step one that Congress had spoken clearly to the precise question at issue, because a "notice to appear" could not qualify as such without providing the date and place at which the noncitizen had to appear. For administrative law purposes, though, the news of the case was to be found in the following concurrence from JUSTICE KENNEDY, in which he cast doubt on Chevron as a whole: "This separate writing is to note my concern with the way in which the Court's opinion in Chevron U.S.A. Inc. v. Natural Resources Defense Council, Inc., 467 U.S. 837 (1984), has come to be understood and applied. The application of that precedent to the question presented here by various Courts of Appeals illustrates one aspect of the problem.

"The first Courts of Appeals to encounter the question concluded or assumed that the notice necessary to trigger the stop-time rule found in 8 U.S.C. § 1229b(d)(1) was not 'perfected' until the immigrant received all the information listed in § 1229(a)(1). . . . That emerging consensus abruptly dissolved not long after the Board of Immigration Appeals (BIA) reached a contrary interpretation of § 1229b(d)(1) in Matter of Camarillo, 25 I. & N. Dec. 644 (2011). After that administrative ruling, in addition to the decision under review here, at least six Courts of Appeals, citing Chevron, concluded that § 1229b(d)(1) was ambiguous and then held that the BIA's interpretation was reasonable. . . . The Court correctly concludes today that those holdings were wrong because the BIA's interpretation finds little support in the statute's text.

"In according Chevron deference to the BIA's interpretation, some Courts of Appeals engaged in cursory analysis of the questions whether, applying the ordinary tools of statutory construction, Congress' intent could be discerned, 467 U.S., at 843, n. 9, and whether the BIA's interpretation was reasonable. . . . In Urbina v. Holder, for example, the court stated, without any further elaboration, that 'we agree with the BIA that the relevant statutory provision is ambiguous.' 745 F.3d, at 740. It then deemed reasonable the BIA's interpretation of the statute, 'for the reasons the BIA gave in that case.' This analysis suggests an abdication of the Judiciary's proper role in interpreting federal statutes.

"The type of reflexive deference exhibited in some of these cases is troubling. And when deference is applied to other questions of statutory interpretation, such as an agency's interpretation of the statutory provisions that concern the scope of its own authority, it is more troubling still. See Arlington v. FCC, 569 U.S. 290, 327 (2013) (Roberts, C. J., dissenting) ('We do not leave it to the agency to decide when it is in charge'). Given the concerns raised by some Members of this Court, see, e.g., id., at 312–328; Michigan v. EPA, 576 U.S. ___, ___ (2015) (Thomas, J., concurring); Gutierrez-Brizuela v. Lynch, 834 F.3d 1142, 1149–1158 (CA10 2016) (Gorsuch, J., concurring), it seems necessary and appropriate to reconsider, in an appropriate case, the premises that underlie Chevron and how courts have implemented that decision. The proper rules for interpreting statutes and determining agency jurisdiction and substantive agency powers should accord with constitutional separation-of-powers principles and the function and province of the Judiciary. See, e.g., Arlington, supra, at 312–316 (Roberts, C. J., dissenting)."

JUSTICE ALITO dissented after affording the agency Chevron deference, as he found the statutory term "notice to appear" ambiguous in the relevant respect and the agency's resolution of it reasonable. But Justice Alito made clear that he understood the case to be a potential sign that Chevron was at risk. In fact he opened his dissent this way: "Although this case presents a narrow and technical issue of immigration law, the Court's decision implicates the status of an important, frequently invoked, once celebrated, and now increasingly maligned precedent, namely, Chevron U.S.A. Inc. v. Natural Resources Defense Council, Inc., 467 U.S. 837 (1984). Under that decision, if a federal statute is ambiguous and the agency that is authorized to implement it offers a reasonable interpretation, then a court is supposed to accept that interpretation. Here, a straightforward application of Chevron requires us to accept the Government's construction of the provision at issue. But the Court rejects the Government's interpretation in favor of one that it regards as the best reading of the statute. I can only conclude that the Court, for whatever reason, is simply ignoring Chevron."

Justice Alito then circled back to what he perceived to be the Court's implicit disdain for Chevron in his closing passage: "Once the errors and false leads are stripped away, the most that remains of the Court's argument is a textually permissible interpretation consistent with the Court's view of 'common sense.' That is not enough to show that the Government's contrary interpretation is unreasonable. Choosing between these competing interpretations might have been difficult in the first instance. But under Chevron, that choice was not ours to make. Under Chevron, this Court was obliged to defer to the Government's interpretation. In recent years, several Members of this Court have questioned Chevron's foundations. See, e.g., ante, at 2–3 (Kennedy, J., concurring); Michigan v. EPA, 135 S.Ct. 2699, 2712–14 (2015) (Thomas, J., concurring); Gutierrez-Brizuela v. Lynch, 834 F.3d 1142, 1149 (CA10 2016) (Gorsuch, J., concurring). But unless the Court has overruled Chevron in a secret decision that has somehow escaped my attention, it remains good law."

Chevron has hardly cut a dominant figure at the Court since then. The case recently seems cited mostly for the proposition that the conditions for deference are not met. For example, Salinas v. United States R.R. Ret. Bd., 141 S.Ct. 691 (2021), noted that the scope of judicial review was "hardly the kind of question that the Court presumes that Congress implicitly delegated to an agency," id. at 700 (quoting Smith v. Berryhill, 139 S.Ct. 1765, 1778 (2019), another recent decision making the same point). Similarly, Johnson v. Guzman Chavez, 141 S.Ct. 2271 (2021), concerned the interrelation of various parts of the Immigration and Nationality Act. Justice Alito's opinion for the Court stated in a footnote that it did not "need to address" the government's claim for Chevron deference: "Chevron deference does not apply where the statute is clear." Id. at 2291 n.9. And in HollyFrontier Cheyenne Refining, LLC v. Renewable Fuels Ass'n, 141 S.Ct. 2172 (2021), the government declined to invoke Chevron (see Note 5 above on p. 1235). The Court responded that it would "therefore decline to consider whether any deference might be due . . . ." Id. at 2180.

During the 2021–2022 Term, the Court granted review in a case that some thought would spell the end of Chevron. Am. Hosp. Ass'n v. Becerra, 142 S.Ct. 1896 (2022), presented the question "whether Chevron deference permits HHS to set reimbursement rates based on acquisition cost and vary such rates by hospital group if it has not collected adequate hospital acquisition cost survey data." 2021 WL 601674 (U.S. Feb. 10, 2021). Justice Kavanaugh's opinion for a unanimous Court cited Chevron zero times. But the substance of the decision tracked the Court's 2021 decisions in Salinas and Guzman Chavez; the statute was unambiguous, so the Court could discern its meaning by itself. As the Court put it, "[u]nder the text and structure of the statute, this case is . . . straightforward: Because HHS did not conduct a survey of hospitals' acquisition costs, HHS acted unlawfully by reducing the reimbursement rates for 340B hospitals."

One way to think about these decisions is that they express the view that judges can always reach a best interpretation at step one, so that there's no ambiguity left over for step two. Footnote 9 of Chevron instructs judges to discern if Congress has spoken to the question at issue by "employing traditional tools of statutory construction." Consider this question from oral argument in American Hospital Association (Transcript of Oral Argument at 70, Am. Hosp. Ass'n v. Becerra, 142 S.Ct. 1896 (2022) (No. 21-1114)):[4]

> JUSTICE GORSUCH: . . . But the question that Chevron tends to pose, the difficulty with lower courts and with this Court, is what's ambiguous enough to trigger deference to the government? And in

[4] https://www.supremecourt.gov/oral_arguments/argument_transcripts/2021/20-1114_h31j.pdf.

> a lot of circumstances where we don't have Chevron applicable and have competing statutory problems, we—we go down and apply all the tools of statutory interpretation, as Chevron Footnote 9 says and you've endorsed, and we come up with an answer. It may be 51–49. It may be really close. You both have spots. You—you both—where you have weaknesses. But we have to pick one and we do. And we're always able to do it. So why shouldn't that be true here?

Meanwhile, lower courts continue to rely on Chevon deference. See, e.g., Loper Bright Enterprises, Inc. v. Raimondo, 45 F.4th 359 (D.C. Cir. 2022). A Westlaw search in August 2022 for citations to Chevron in federal cases decided in 2021 yielded 435 cases. Citing Chevron is, of course, not the same as applying Chevron deference. See, e.g., Gun Owners of America, Inc. v. Garland, 992 F.3d 446 (6th Cir. 2021) ("Whatever the merits of giving Chevron deference to an agency's interpretation of civil statutes, the principal rationales behind that policy cannot be extended to support giving deference to an agency's interpretation of criminal statutes.").

Most recently, Justice Gorsuch made clear he would like to revisit Chevron in an appropriate case. He did so, however, in a solo dissent from a denial of a petition for certiorari. See Buffington v. McDonough, No. 21-–972, 2022 WL 16726027 (U.S. Nov. 7 2022) (Gorsuch, J. dissenting from the denial of certiorari). So, for now, Chevron appears to live on.

(4) ***What Might Happen if Chevron Were Overruled?***

(a) *One Possibility.* Here is then-JUDGE GORSUCH, again from his concurrence in GUTIERREZ-BRIZUELA V. LYNCH, 834 F.3d at 1158: "All of which raises this question: what would happen in a world without Chevron? If this goliath of modern administrative law were to fall? Surely Congress could and would continue to pass statutes for executive agencies to enforce. And just as surely agencies could and would continue to offer guidance on how they intend to enforce those statutes. The only difference would be that courts would then fulfill their duty to exercise their independent judgment about what the law is. Of course, courts could and would consult agency views and apply the agency's interpretation when it accords with the best reading of a statute. But de novo judicial review of the law's meaning would limit the ability of an agency to alter and amend existing law. It would avoid the due process and equal protection problems of the kind documented in our decisions. It would promote reliance interests by allowing citizens to organize their affairs with some assurance that the rug will not be pulled from under them tomorrow, the next day, or after the next election. And an agency's recourse for a judicial declaration of the law's meaning that it dislikes would be precisely the recourse the Constitution prescribes—an appeal to higher judicial authority or a new law enacted consistent with bicameralism and presentment. We managed to live with the administrative state before Chevron. We could do it again. Put simply, it seems to me that in a world without Chevron very little would change—except perhaps the most important things."

(b) *Another Possibility.* JEFFREY A. POJANOWSKI, WITHOUT DEFERENCE, 81 Mo. L. Rev. 1075, 1076 (2016): "To be clear, abandoning Chevron is not the same thing as abolishing deference. Deference of a different kind existed before Chevron, and if the Court were to abandon Chevron tomorrow, the Court may revert to something like that preexisting, milder form of deference. Nevertheless, imagining a regime without any deference clarifies the stakes of reforming judicial review of agencies' legal conclusions. Thus, for present purposes, and present purposes only, I equate abandoning Chevron with abandoning judicial deference on agencies' legal interpretations.

"I argue that such an alternative regime has appealing features but may not bring as much practical change as casual critiques or defenses of Chevron contemplate, at least immediately. The more immediate change would arise at the level of theory and rhetoric, which, in turn, may lead to greater practical changes in the longer run. The theoretical presuppositions underwriting a regime of non-deferential review are far more classical in cast than the moderate legal realism underwriting Chevron. Rejecting deference, therefore, would change how courts talk about the difference between law and policy in the administrative state. The resurrection of the classical distinction between interpreting and making law might therefore alter the way courts think about that relationship. If that is the case, rejecting deference could lead to a more robust judicial role on close questions of interpretation.

"Alternatively, some courts may already be quite aggressive on questions of interpretation, usually through a vigorous application of Step One. This is often the case, for example, at the Supreme Court. To the extent this is so, abandoning deference would bring the courts' skeptical rhetoric about the law/policy divide in line with their practice on the ground. This would reveal that interpreters are less skeptical about the line between law and policy than their rhetoric suggests. In short, it would show we are not, in fact, all legal realists now, at least with respect to problems amenable to the lawyers' traditional toolkit. Either way, the more traditional character of the theoretical orientation underwriting the case against deference may also shed light on the rise and (partial) fall of Chevron in administrative legal thought."

(c) *And Another.* LISA SCHULTZ BRESSMAN & KEVIN M. STACK, CHEVRON IS A PHOENIX, 74 Vand. L. Rev. 465, 477–80 (2021): "Judicial deference is a fixture of the administrative state. . . . Whether Chevron survives or not, judicial deference will persist because fixtures of the administrative state do not disappear from the law. They morph and reappear out of their own ashes.

"When the Court no longer enforces a foundational principle through one doctrine, another doctrine often arises in its place. This phenomenon is not new to the law and has loomed particularly large in administrative law. When the Court did not enforce the nondelegation doctrine to keep Congress from passing power to agencies in extremely broad terms, the concerns about such broad transfers—concerns for congressional responsibility and agency accountability—did not simply disappear. These concerns, instead, found an alternative outlet in the law—in fact, more than one outlet. For example, the Court has used the constitutional avoidance canon to effectively rewrite a particular statute in a way that addresses nondelegation concerns about agency authority under that statute. Nondelegation concerns did not vanish with the demise of the nondelegation doctrine; they just found expression elsewhere.

"Similar dynamics are at work with judicial deference. If Congress can delegate authority to agencies, subject to only limited constraints, then judicial deference is necessary to ensure that agencies can exercise their delegated authority. Congressional delegation and judicial deference go hand-in-hand. If the Court were to get rid of judicial deference in one swoop by overruling Chevron, the entire U.S. corpus of regulatory statutes, with broad delegations, would remain on the books. What happens then? Some form of judicial deference will recur. The grounds that animate judicial deference (agencies, not courts, should make the basic choices of regulatory policy) will not go away any less than the worries that underlie the nondelegation doctrine (that Congress, not agencies, should make the overarching law) have. Judicial deference is part of the 'separation-of-powers triangle between the legislative, executive, and judiciary.'

"Judicial deference is not foundational in the same way that the nondelegation doctrine or other underenforced separation-of-powers norms are—Chevron is not a constitutional decision. But its constitutional status does not matter. What matters is it reflects an arrangement fundamental to our current structure of government.

"To see the point in the most practical terms, just consider the position of reviewing courts. In the immediate aftermath of a decision overruling Chevron, lower courts will feel pressure—they will face a new demand to choose the best interpretation for every statutory provision implicated in every agency decision. But given the complexity of statutory schemes, the specialized expertise and experience that implementing those schemes requires, and the sheer number of routine interpretive issues that the schemes involve, courts will confront the natural fault lines of their own competence as generalists and lawyers. They will have every incentive to find a way out.

"That way will have to involve a different form of judicial deference. Reviewing courts unable to explicitly invoke Chevron deference will begin to characterize agency statutes and agency interpretations differently. For example, they might find more express delegations of interpretive power to agencies, placing them beyond the Chevron default, but still requiring controlling deference. Or they might reject a litigant's characterization of the flaws in an agency action as interpretive and instead view them as a matter of policymaking discretion. Either way, courts will default to or persist in deferring to agencies on routine issues, just using a different label or different characterization of the issues to do so. This prediction is not fanciful. After Mead [p. 1283] was decided, lower courts were uncertain which procedures confer lawmaking authority on agencies and quickly found work-arounds. The pressure will be even greater to find a work-around given the mismatch between the capacity of courts and the complexity of regulatory policymaking. The operational details typically and understandably fall outside of the judicial ken. And so judicial deference will return."

### c. The Present-Day Framework, Part II: Chevron and Statutory Interpretation

*MCI TELECOMMUNICATIONS CORP. v. AMERICAN TELEPHONE AND TELEGRAPH CO.*
*Notes on the Relationship Between Chevron and the Theories and Tools of Statutory Interpretation*
*Notes on Judicial Review: Law or Politics?*

## MCI TELECOMMUNICATIONS CORP. v. AMERICAN TELEPHONE AND TELEGRAPH CO.

Supreme Court of the United States (1994).
512 U.S. 218.

■ JUSTICE SCALIA delivered the opinion of the Court.

Section 203(a) of Title 47 of the United States Code requires communications common carriers to file tariffs with the Federal Communications Commission, and § 203(b) authorizes the Commission to "modify" any requirement of § 203. These cases present the question whether the Commission's decision to make tariff filing optional for all nondominant long distance carriers is a valid exercise of its modification authority.

I

[The Communications Act of 1934 requires long distance carriers to file their tariffs with the FCC and to charge only the filed rates. When the Act was passed, AT&T monopolized long distance service, but in the 1970s technological advances made it possible for others, like MCI, to compete. In a series of orders from 1980 on, the FCC responded to the increased competition by relaxing the filing requirements for nondominant carriers—that is, for everyone but AT&T. The policy ran into some difficulty with the D.C. Circuit Court of Appeals, but the agency persisted. In 1992, the Commission concluded a rulemaking proceeding by declaring that filing of tariffs was optional for all nondominant carriers and that the Communications Act authorized this deregulation. The D.C. Circuit reversed per curiam; MCI and the United States petitioned for certiorari, and the Court granted the petitions. The key question concerned Chevron step one and whether the statute was clear or ambiguous in the relevant respect. Justice Scalia thought it was clear and thus rejected the FCC's interpretation. Justice Stevens disagreed.]

II

Section 203 of the Communications Act contains both the filed rate provisions of the Act and the Commission's disputed modification authority. It provides in relevant part:

> (a) Filing; public display.
>
> Every common carrier, except connecting carriers, shall, within such reasonable time as the Commission shall designate, file with the Commission and print and keep open for public inspection schedules showing all charges . . . , whether such charges are joint or separate, and showing the classifications, practices, and regulations affecting such charges. . . .
>
> (b) Changes in schedule; discretion of Commission to modify requirements.
>
> (1) No change shall be made in the charges, classifications, regulations, or practices which have been so filed and published except after one hundred and twenty days notice to the Commission and to the public, which shall be published in such form and contain such information as the Commission may by regulations prescribe.
>
> (2) The Commission may, in its discretion and for good cause shown, modify any requirement made by or under the authority of this section either in particular instances or by general order applicable to special circumstances or conditions except that the Commission may not require the notice period specified in paragraph (1) to be more than one hundred and twenty days.
>
> (c) Overcharges and rebates.
>
> No carrier, unless otherwise provided by or under authority of this chapter, shall engage or participate in such communication unless schedules have been filed and published in accordance with the provisions of this chapter and with the regulations made thereunder; and no carrier shall (1) charge, demand, collect, or receive a greater or less or different compensation for such communication . . . than the charges specified in the schedule then in effect, or (2) refund or remit by any means or device any portion of the charges so specified, or (3) extend to any person any privileges or facilities in such communication, or employ or enforce any classifications, regulations, or practices affecting such charges, except as specified in such schedule.

47 U.S.C. § 203.

The dispute between the parties turns on the meaning of the phrase "modify any requirement" in § 203(b)(2). Petitioners argue that it gives the Commission authority to make even basic and fundamental changes in the scheme created by that section. We disagree. The word "modify"—like a number of other English words employing the root "mod-" (deriving from the Latin word for "measure"), such as "moderate," "modulate," "modest," and "modicum"—has a connotation of increment or limitation.

Virtually every dictionary we are aware of says that "to modify" means to change moderately or in minor fashion. See, e.g., Random House Dictionary of the English Language 1236 (2d ed. 1987) ("to change somewhat the form or qualities of; alter partially; amend"); Webster's Third New International Dictionary 1452 (1976) ("to make minor changes in the form or structure of; alter without transforming"); 9 Oxford English Dictionary 952 (2d ed. 1989) ("[t]o make partial changes in; to change (an object) in respect of some of its qualities; to alter or vary without radical transformation"); Black's Law Dictionary 1004 (6th ed. 1990) ("[t]o alter; to change in incidental or subordinate features; enlarge; extend; amend; limit; reduce").

In support of their position, petitioners cite dictionary definitions contained in or derived from a single source, Webster's Third New International Dictionary 1452 (1976) ("Webster's Third"), which includes among the meanings of "modify," "to make a basic or important change in." Petitioners contend that this establishes sufficient ambiguity to entitle the Commission to deference in its acceptance of the broader meaning, which in turn requires approval of its permissive detariffing policy. See Chevron U.S.A. Inc. v. Natural Resources Defense Council, Inc., 467 U.S. 837, 843 (1984). In short, they contend that the courts must defer to the agency's choice among available dictionary definitions, citing National Railroad Passenger Corp. v. Boston and Maine Corp., 503 U.S. 407 (1992).

Most cases of verbal ambiguity in statutes involve, as Boston and Maine did, a selection between accepted alternative meanings shown as such by many dictionaries. One can envision (though a court case does not immediately come to mind) having to choose between accepted alternative meanings, one of which is so newly accepted that it has only been recorded by a single lexicographer. (Some dictionary must have been the very first to record the widespread use of "projection," for example, to mean "forecast.") But what petitioners demand that we accept as creating an ambiguity here is a rarity even rarer than that: a meaning set forth in a single dictionary (and, as we say, its progeny) which not only supplements the meaning contained in all other dictionaries, but contradicts one of the meanings contained in virtually all other dictionaries. Indeed, contradicts one of the alternative meanings contained in the out-of-step dictionary itself—for as we have observed, Webster's Third itself defines "modify" to connote both (specifically) major change and (specifically) minor change. It is hard to see how that can be. When the word "modify" has come to mean both "to change in some respects" and "to change fundamentally" it will in fact mean neither of those things. It will simply mean "to change," and some adverb will have to be called into service to indicate the great or small degree of the change.

If that is what the peculiar Webster's Third definition means to suggest has happened—and what petitioners suggest by appealing to Webster's Third—we simply disagree. "Modify," in our view, connotes moderate change. It might be good English to say that the French

Revolution "modified" the status of the French nobility—but only because there is a figure of speech called understatement and a literary device known as sarcasm. And it might be unsurprising to discover a 1972 White House press release saying that "the Administration is modifying its position with regard to prosecution of the war in Vietnam"—but only because press agents tend to impart what is nowadays called "spin." Such intentional distortions, or simply careless or ignorant misuse, must have formed the basis for the usage that Webster's Third, and Webster's Third alone, reported.[3] It is perhaps gilding the lily to add this: In 1934, when the Communications Act became law—the most relevant time for determining a statutory term's meaning—Webster's Third was not yet even contemplated. To our knowledge all English dictionaries provided the narrow definition of "modify," including those published by G. & C. Merriam Company. See Webster's New International Dictionary 1577 (2d ed. 1934); Webster's Collegiate Dictionary 628 (4th ed. 1934). We have not the slightest doubt that is the meaning the statute intended.

Beyond the word itself, a further indication that the § 203 authority to "modify" does not contemplate fundamental changes is the sole exception to that authority which the section provides. One of the requirements of § 203 is that changes to filed tariffs can be made only after 120 days' notice to the Commission and the public. § 203(b)(1). The only exception to the Commission's § 203(b)(2) modification authority is as follows: "except that the Commission may not require the notice period specified in paragraph (1) to be more than one hundred and twenty days." Is it conceivable that the statute is indifferent to the Commission's power to eliminate the tariff-filing requirement entirely for all except one firm in the long-distance sector, and yet strains out the gnat of extending the waiting period for tariff revision beyond 120 days? We think not. The exception is not as ridiculous as a Lilliputian in London only because it is to be found in Lilliput: in the smallscale world of "modifications," it is a big deal.

Since an agency's interpretation of a statute is not entitled to deference when it goes beyond the meaning that the statute can bear, see, e.g., Pittston Coal Group v. Sebben, 488 U.S. 105, 113 (1988); Chevron, 467 U.S., at 842843, the Commission's permissive detariffing policy can be justified only if it makes a less than radical or fundamental change in the Act's tariff-filing requirement. The Commission's attempt to establish that no more than that is involved greatly understates the extent to which its policy deviates from the filing requirement, and greatly undervalues the importance of the filing requirement itself.

To consider the latter point first: For the body of a law, as for the body of a person, whether a change is minor or major depends to some extent upon the importance of the item changed to the whole. Loss of an entire toenail is insignificant; loss of an entire arm tragic. The tariff-filing requirement is, to pursue this analogy, the heart of the common-carrier section of the Communications Act. In the context of the Interstate

---

[3] That is not an unlikely hypothesis. Upon its long-awaited appearance in 1961, Webster's Third was widely criticized for its portrayal of common error as proper usage. . . .

Commerce Act, which served as its model, this Court has repeatedly stressed that rate filing was Congress's chosen means of preventing unreasonableness and discrimination in charges: "[T]here is not only a relation, but an indissoluble unity between the provision for the establishment and maintenance of rates until corrected in accordance with the statute and the prohibitions against preferences and discrimination." Texas and Pacific R. Co. v. Abilene Cotton Oil Co., 204 U.S. 426, 440 (1907).

Much of the rest of the Communications Act subchapter applicable to Common Carriers, and the Act's Procedural and Administrative Provisions, are premised upon the tariff-filing requirement of § 203. For example, § 415 defines "overcharges" (which customers are entitled to recover) by reference to the filed rate. See § 415(g). The provisions allowing customers and competitors to challenge rates as unreasonable or as discriminatory, see 47 U.S.C. §§ 204, 206–208, 406, would not be susceptible of effective enforcement if rates were not publicly filed. Rate filings are, in fact, the essential characteristic of a rate-regulated industry. It is highly unlikely that Congress would leave the determination of whether an industry will be entirely, or even substantially, rate-regulated to agency discretion—and even more unlikely that it would achieve that through such a subtle device as permission to "modify" rate-filing requirements.

Bearing in mind, then, the enormous importance to the statutory scheme of the tariff-filing provision, we turn to whether what has occurred here can be considered a mere "modification." The Commission stresses that its detariffing policy applies only to nondominant carriers, so that the rates charged to over half of all consumers in the long-distance market are on file with the Commission. It is not clear to us that the proportion of customers affected, rather than the proportion of carriers affected, is the proper measure of the extent of the exemption (of course all carriers in the long-distance market are exempted, except AT & T). But even assuming it is, we think an elimination of the crucial provision of the statute for 40% of a major sector of the industry is much too extensive to be considered a "modification." What we have here, in reality, is a fundamental revision of the statute, changing it from a scheme of rate regulation in long-distance common-carrier communications to a scheme of rate regulation only where effective competition does not exist. That may be a good idea, but it was not the idea Congress enacted into law in 1934.

Finally, petitioners earnestly urge that their interpretation of § 203(b) furthers the Communications Act's broad purpose of promoting efficient telephone service. They claim that although the filing requirement prevented price discrimination and unfair practices while AT & T maintained a monopoly over long-distance service, it frustrates those same goals now that there is greater competition in that market. Specifically, they contend that filing costs raise artificial barriers to entry and that the publication of rates facilitates parallel pricing and stifles price competition. We have considerable sympathy with these arguments (though we doubt it makes sense, if one is concerned about the use of filed tariffs to communicate pricing information, to require filing by the dominant carrier, the firm most likely to be a price leader). . . . But our estimations, and the Commission's estimations, of desirable policy cannot alter the meaning of the Federal Communications Act of 1934. For better or worse, the Act establishes a rate-regulation, filed-tariff system for common-carrier communications, and the Commission's desire "to 'increase competition' cannot provide [it] authority to alter the well-established statutory filed rate requirements," Maislin Industries, U.S., Inc. v. Primary Steel, Inc., 497 U.S. 116, 135 (1990). As we observed in the context of a dispute over the filed-rate doctrine more than 80 years ago, "such considerations address themselves to Congress, not to the courts," Armour Packing Co. v. United States, 209 U.S. 56, 82 (1908).

We do not mean to suggest that the tariff-filing requirement is so inviolate that the Commission's existing modification authority does not reach it at all. Certainly the Commission can modify the form, contents, and location of required filings, and can defer filing or perhaps even waive it altogether in limited circumstances. But what we have here goes well beyond that. It is effectively the introduction of a whole new regime of regulation (or of free-market competition), which may well be a better regime but is not the one that Congress established.

The judgment of the Court of Appeals is affirmed.

■ JUSTICE O'CONNOR took no part in the consideration or decision of these cases.

■ JUSTICE STEVENS, with whom JUSTICE BLACKMUN and JUSTICE SOUTER join, dissenting.

The communications industry has an unusually dynamic character. In 1934, Congress authorized the Federal Communications Commission (FCC) to regulate "a field of enterprise the dominant characteristic of which was the rapid pace of its unfolding." National Broadcasting Co. v. United States, 319 U.S. 190, 219 (1943). The Communications Act (the Act) gives the FCC unusually broad discretion to meet new and unanticipated problems in order to fulfill its sweeping mandate "to make available, as far as possible, to all the people of the United States, a rapid, efficient, Nationwide and world-wide wire and radio communication service with adequate facilities at reasonable charges." 47 U.S.C. § 151. This Court's consistent interpretation of the Act has afforded the Commission ample leeway to interpret and apply its statutory powers and responsibilities. The Court today abandons that approach in favor of a rigid literalism that deprives the FCC of the flexibility Congress meant it to have in order to implement the core policies of the Act in rapidly changing conditions.

I

At the time the Communications Act was passed, the telephone industry was dominated by the American Telephone & Telegraph Company and its affiliates. Title II of the Act, which establishes the framework for FCC regulation of common carriers by wire, was clearly a response to that dominance. As the Senate Report explained, "[u]nder existing provisions of the Interstate Commerce Act the regulation of the telephone monopoly has been practically nil. This vast monopoly which so immediately serves the needs of the people in their daily and social life must be effectively regulated." S. Rep. No. 781, 73d Cong., 2d Sess., 2 (1934).

. . . Congress doubtless viewed the filed rate provisions as an important mechanism to guard against abusive practices by wire communications monopolies. But it is quite wrong to suggest that the mere process of filing rate schedules—rather than the substantive duty of reasonably priced and nondiscriminatory service—is "the heart of the common-carrier section of the federal Communications Act."

II

In response to new conditions in the communications industry, including stirrings of competition in the long-distance telephone market, the FCC in 1979 began reexamining its regulatory scheme. . . .

III

. . . The Commission plausibly concluded that any slight enforcement benefits a tariff-filing requirement might offer were outweighed by the burdens it would put on new entrants and consumers. Thus, the sole question for us is whether the FCC's policy, however sensible, is nonetheless inconsistent with the Act.

In my view, each of the Commission's detariffing orders was squarely within its power to "modify any requirement" of § 203. Subsection 203(b)(2) plainly confers at least some discretion to modify the general rule that carriers file tariffs, for it speaks of "any requirement." Subsection 203(c) of the Act, ignored by the Court, squarely supports the FCC's position; it prohibits carriers from providing service without a tariff "unless otherwise provided by or under authority of this Act." Subsection 203(b)(2) is plainly one provision that "otherwise provides" and thereby authorizes service without a filed schedule. The FCC's authority to modify § 203's requirements in "particular instances" or by "general order applicable to special circumstances or conditions" emphasizes the expansive character of the Commission's authority: modifications may be narrow or broad, depending upon the Commission's appraisal of current conditions. From the vantage of a Congress seeking to regulate an almost completely monopolized industry, the advent of competition is surely a "special circumstance or condition" that might legitimately call for different regulatory treatment.

The only statutory exception to the Commission's modification authority provides that it may not extend the 120-day notice period set out in § 203(b)(1). See § 203(b)(2). The Act thus imposes a specific limit on the Commission's authority to stiffen that regulatory imposition on carriers, but does not confine the Commission's authority to relax it. It was no stretch for the FCC to draw from this single, unidirectional statutory limitation on its modification authority the inference that its authority is otherwise unlimited.

According to the Court, the term "modify," as explicated in all but the most unreliable dictionaries, rules out the Commission's claimed authority to relieve nondominant carriers of the basic obligation to file tariffs. Dictionaries can be useful aids in statutory interpretation, but they are no substitute for close analysis of what words mean as used in a particular statutory context. Even if the sole possible meaning of "modify" were to make "minor" changes, further elaboration is needed to show why the detariffing policy should fail. The Commission came to its present policy through a series of rulings that gradually relaxed the filing requirements for nondominant carriers. Whether the current policy should count as a cataclysmic or merely an incremental departure from the § 203(a) baseline depends on whether one focuses on particular carriers' obligations to file (in which case the Commission's policy arguably works a major shift) or on the statutory policies behind the tariff-filing requirement (which remain satisfied because market constraints on nondominant carriers obviate the need for rate-filing). When § 203 is viewed as part of a statute whose aim is to constrain monopoly power, the Commission's decision to exempt nondominant carriers is a rational and "measured" adjustment to novel circumstances—one that remains faithful to the core purpose of the tariff-filing section. See Black's Law Dictionary 1198 (3d ed. 1933) (defining "modification" as "A change; an alteration which introduces new elements into the details, or cancels some of them, but leaves the general purpose and effect of the subject-matter intact").

The Court seizes upon a particular sense of the word "modify" at the expense of another, long-established meaning that fully supports the Commission's position. That word is first defined in Webster's Collegiate Dictionary 628 (4th ed. 1934) as meaning "to limit or reduce in extent or degree."[5] The Commission's permissive detariffing policy fits comfortably within this common understanding of the term. The FCC has in effect adopted a general rule stating that "if you are dominant you must file, but if you are nondominant you need not." The Commission's partial detariffing policy—which excuses nondominant carriers from filing on condition that they remain nondominant—is simply a relaxation of a costly regulatory requirement that recent developments had rendered pointless and counterproductive in a certain class of cases.

A modification pursuant to § 203(b)(1), like any other order issued under the Act, must of course be consistent with the purposes of the

[5] See also 9 Oxford English Dictionary 952 (2d ed. 1989) ("2. To alter in the direction of moderation or lenity; to make less severe, rigorous, or decided; to qualify, tone down. . . ."); Random House Dictionary of the English Language 1236 (2d ed. 1987) ("5. to reduce or lessen in degree or extent; moderate; soften; to modify one's demands"); Webster's Third New International Dictionary 1452 (1981) ("I: to make more temperate and less extreme: lessen the severity of; . . . 'traffic rules were modified to let him pass' "); Webster's New Collegiate Dictionary 739 (1973) ("I. to make less extreme; MODERATE"); Webster's Seventh New Collegiate Dictionary 544 (1963) (same); Webster's Seventh New International Dictionary 1577 (2d ed. 1934) ("2. To reduce in extent or degree; to moderate; qualify; lower; as, to modify heat, pain, punishment"); N. Webster, American Dictionary of the English Language (1828) ("To moderate; to qualify; to reduce in extent or degree. Of his grace He modifies his first severe decree. Dryden").

statute. On this point, the Court asserts that the Act's prohibition against unreasonable and discriminatory rates "would not be susceptible of effective enforcement if rates were not publicly filed." That determination, of course, is for the Commission to make in the first instance. But the Commission has repeatedly explained that (i) a carrier that lacks market power is entirely unlikely to charge unreasonable or discriminatory rates, (ii) the statutory bans on unreasonable charges and price discrimination apply with full force regardless of whether carriers have to file tariffs, (iii) any suspected violations by nondominant carriers can be addressed on the Commission's own motion or on a damages complaint filed pursuant to § 206, and (iv) the FCC can reimpose a tariff requirement should violations occur. The Court does not adequately respond to the FCC's explanations, and gives no reason whatsoever to doubt the Commission's considered judgment that tariff-filing is altogether unnecessary in the case of competitive carriers; the majority's ineffective enforcement argument lacks any evidentiary or historical support.

The filed tariff provisions of the Communications Act are not ends in themselves, but are merely one of several procedural means for the Commission to ensure that carriers do not charge unreasonable or discriminatory rates. The Commission has reasonably concluded that this particular means of enforcing the statute's substantive mandates will prove counterproductive in the case of nondominant long distance carriers. Even if the 1934 Congress did not define the scope of the Commission's modification authority with perfect scholarly precision, this is surely a paradigm case for judicial deference to the agency's interpretation, particularly in a statutory regime so obviously meant to maximize administrative flexibility. Whatever the best reading of § 203(b)(2), the Commission's reading cannot in my view be termed unreasonable. It is informed (as ours is not) by a practical understanding of the role (or lack thereof) that filed tariffs play in the modern regulatory climate and in the telecommunications industry. Since 1979, the FCC has sought to adapt measures originally designed to control monopoly power to new market conditions. It has carefully and consistently explained that mandatory tariff-filing rules frustrate the core statutory interest in rate reasonableness. The Commission's use of the "discretion" expressly conferred by § 203(b)(2) reflects "a reasonable accommodation of manifestly competing interests and is entitled to deference: the regulatory scheme is technical and complex, the agency considered the matter in a detailed and reasoned fashion, and the decision involves reconciling conflicting policies." Chevron U.S.A. Inc. v. Natural Resources Defense Council, Inc., 467 U.S. 837, 865 (1984). The FCC has permissibly interpreted its § 203(b)(2) authority in service of the goals Congress set forth in the Communications Act. We should sustain its eminently sound, experience-tested, and uncommonly well explained judgment.

I respectfully dissent.

## NOTES ON THE RELATIONSHIP BETWEEN CHEVRON AND THE THEORIES AND TOOLS OF STATUTORY INTERPRETATION

(1) ***How Do Various Modes of Statutory Interpretation Bear on the Chevron Doctrine?*** In their respective opinions in the MCI case, both Justice Scalia and Justice Stevens claim to be faithful to Chevron—Justice Scalia in his conclusion that he should not defer to the FCC's interpretation because "it goes beyond the meaning that the statute can bear" and Justice Stevens in his that "the FCC has permissibly interpreted" its statutory authority. Chevron made statutory meaning—clear or ambiguous—the doctrinal gatekeeper to judicial deference and referred to "traditional tools of statutory construction." But there is more than one traditional tool, and whether "the intent of Congress is clear" may look different when seen through different tools.

While statutory interpretation, like common-law case analysis, is a complex and to some extent artistic endeavor, the recent literature tends to separate the possible approaches into three broad categories. (You have already delved into this if you studied Chapter II.) The first, known as textualism, emphasizes the words specifically included in the statute. The second, known as purposivism, emphasizes what Congress was trying to do when it passed the statute. And the third, known as pragmatism, emphasizes the meaning that will produce the best practical result (dynamic statutory interpretation, which is in some respects a variant of pragmatic interpretation, is also sometimes identified as a fourth category in its own right, see Chapter II, Section 2.d). Chevron, when it is applicable, would seem to say that the third method is for the agency and not the courts, but that still leaves judges a choice between the other two.

To some extent the disagreement between these camps turns on different views of how Congress acts. Textualists tend to emphasize the bargaining nature of the legislative process, with the only definitely-agreed-to item being the final text, while purposivists emphasize more the public issues that provided the impetus for legislating in the first place. Correspondingly, the two groups have differed on the use to be made of Committee Reports, floor debates, and other sources of "legislative history." See Chapter II, Section 3.d. Perhaps more important, however, is what unites them: both textualists and purposivists claim to be faithful to the statute Congress has passed. As such, both groups also claim to be faithful to the judge's role as set out in Chevron, which produces what is, for lawyers and also for students, perhaps the most important point: neither view has succeeded in triumphing over the other. While textualism has become more important in the last quarter century than it was in the half-century before that, variants of both approaches are constantly in play in the judicial review of agency action. (And there remains the suspicion among some observers that the method of selecting what will, in the judges' views, produce the best practical result still accounts for many of the cases.)

This situation persists even on the Supreme Court because, as ABBE R. GLUCK points out in THE STATES AS LABORATORIES OF STATUTORY

INTERPRETATION, 119 Yale L.J. 1750, 1765–66 (2010): "[T]he Court does not give stare decisis effect to *any* statements of statutory interpretation methodology. The interpretive rule used in one case ('purpose trumps text' or 'committee statements are not reliable legislative history') is not viewed as 'law' for the next case. The Justices appear not to believe that they can bind other Justices' (and future Justices') methodological choices. Scholars across the spectrum who divide on the question of whether this way of approaching statutory interpretation is problematic nevertheless all agree both that a single controlling approach does not currently exist and that prior methodological statements do not carry into future cases with the force of precedent."

(2) ***Is the MCI Case Really Driven Only by Its Approach to Statutory Interpretation?*** PETER STRAUSS, ON RESEGREGATING THE WORLDS OF STATUTE AND COMMON LAW, 1994 Sup. Ct. Rev. 429, 495–96: "Perhaps the root issue for Justice Scalia [in the MCI case] is one of delegation—a factor that has been important to him in other contexts. It is not merely the largeness of the change being effected, but also that accepting it will entail accepting that an agency can be empowered to change its mandate. For Justice Stevens, author of striking passages in Chevron strongly endorsing delegation, the FCC has 'unusually broad discretion to meet new and unanticipated problems in order to fulfill its sweeping mandate'; this power to 'modify' is no different in kind from the Commission's responsibility to allocate licenses and otherwise act in accordance with 'public convenience, interest, or necessity.' Justice Scalia accepts broad delegations only because he cannot imagine a judicially manageable standard for telling the good from the bad, a handicap he does not face if he can plausibly construe an agency's authority in a narrow way. It is revealing in this respect that he never explains how he concludes that the New Deal Congress that so broadly empowered all the agencies it created, not just the FCC, intended here only a narrow grant of authority."

(3) ***Step One and Textualism.*** NATIONAL CREDIT UNION ADMIN. V. FIRST NAT. BANK, 522 U.S. 479 (1998), is a good example of an application of Chevron's step one through a textualist lens that found deference was not warranted. Section 109 of the Federal Credit Union Act stipulates, "Federal credit union membership shall be limited to groups having a common bond or association, or to groups within a well-defined neighborhood, community, or rural district." Beginning in 1982, the National Credit Union Administration allowed credit unions to be composed of more than one employer group, each having its own "common bond." In the instant case, NCUA had approved amendments to the charter of AT&T Family Federal Credit Union, which then expanded to include not only employees of AT&T, but also employees of Duke Power, American Tobacco, Lee Apparel, and others; five commercial banks and the American Bankers Association brought suit. (Regarding the standing issues in the case, see pp. 1478–1483) THOMAS, J., for the Court, 522 U.S. at 499–503:

"Turning to the merits, we must judge the permissibility of the NCUA's current interpretation of § 109 by employing the analysis set forth in Chevron. Under that analysis, we first ask whether Congress has 'directly spoken to the precise question at issue.' ... Because we conclude that Congress has made it clear that the same common bond of occupation must unite each member of an occupationally defined federal credit union, we hold that the NCUA's contrary interpretation is impermissible under the first step of Chevron.

"As noted, § 109 requires that '[f]ederal credit union membership shall be limited to groups having a common bond of occupation or association, or to groups within a well-defined neighborhood, community, or rural district.' Respondents [i.e., the banks] contend that because § 109 uses the article 'a'—i.e., 'one'—in conjunction with the noun 'common bond,' the 'natural reading' of § 109 is that all members in an occupationally defined federal union must be united by one common bond. Petitioners [i.e., the NCUA and the credit union] reply that because § 109 uses the plural noun 'groups,' it permits multiple groups, each with its own common bond, to constitute a federal credit union.

"Like the Court of Appeals, we do not think that either of these contentions, standing alone, is conclusive. The article 'a' could be thought to convey merely that one bond must unite only the members of each group in a multiple-group credit union, and not all of the members in the credit union taken together. Similarly, the plural word 'groups' could be thought to refer not merely to multiple groups in a particular credit union, but rather to every single 'group' that forms a distinct credit union under the NCUA. Nonetheless, as the Court of Appeals correctly recognized, additional considerations compel the conclusion that the same common bond of occupation must unite all of the members of an occupationally defined federal credit union.

"First, the NCUA's current interpretation makes the phrase 'common bond' surplusage when applied to a federal credit union made up of multiple unrelated employer groups, because each 'group' in such a credit union already has its own 'common bond.' To use the facts of this case, the employees of AT & T and the employees of the American Tobacco Company each already had a 'common bond' before being joined together as members of ATTF. . . . If the phrase 'common bond' is to be given any meaning when these employees are joined together, a different 'common bond'—one extending to each and every employee considered together—must be found to unite them. Such a 'common bond' exists when employees of different subsidiaries of the same company are joined together in a federal credit union; it does not exist, however, when employees of unrelated companies are so joined. . . .

"Second, the NCUA's interpretation violates the established canon of construction that similar language contained within the same section of a statute must be accorded a consistent meaning. Section 109 consists of two parallel clauses: Federal credit union membership is limited 'to groups having a common bond of occupation or association, *or* to groups within a well defined neighborhood, community, or rural district' (emphasis added). The NCUA concedes that even though the second limitation permits geographically defined credit unions to have as members more than one 'group,' all of the groups must come from the same 'neighborhood, community, or rural district.' The reason that the NCUA has never interpreted, and does not contend that it could interpret, the geographical limitation to allow a credit union to be composed of members from an unlimited number of unrelated geographic units, is that to do so would render the geographical limitation meaningless. Under established principles of statutory interpretation, we must interpret the occupational limitation in the same way.

". . . Reading the two parallel clauses in the same way, we must conclude that, just as all members of a geographically defined federal credit union must be drawn from the same 'neighborhood, community or rural district,' members of an occupationally defined federal credit union must be united by the same 'common bond of occupation.'

"Finally, by its terms, § 109 requires that membership in federal credit unions 'shall be limited.' The NCUA's interpretation—under which a common bond of occupation must unite only the members of each unrelated employer group—has the potential to read these words out of the statute entirely. The NCUA has not contested that, under its current interpretation, it would be permissible to grant a charter to a conglomerate credit union whose members would include the employees of every company in the United States. Nor can it: Each company's employees would be a 'group,' and each such 'group' would have its own 'common bond of occupation.' Section 109, however, cannot be considered a *limitation* on credit union membership if at the same time it permits such a *limitless* result.

"For the foregoing reasons, we conclude that the NCUA's current interpretation of § 109 is contrary to the unambiguously expressed intent of Congress and is thus impermissible under the first step of Chevron."

Contrast ENTERGY CORP. V. RIVERKEEPER, INC., 556 U.S. 208 (2009), which is a good example of an application of Chevron step one through a textualist lens to find deference was warranted. At issue were EPA regulations regarding installations that used very large quantities of water to cool power plants; the regulations set substantial standards for such installations but stopped short of requiring the technology most protective of aquatic wildlife because the differential costs involved in achieving the very greatest level of protection were not (in the agency's view) justified by the differential benefits. The Supreme Court granted certiorari on the question whether the Clean Water Act authorized the EPA "to compare costs with benefits" in applying the statutory requirement of "the best technology available for minimizing adverse environmental impact" to "cooling water intake structures" and, in an opinion by JUSTICE SCALIA, answered as follows, 556 U.S. at 217–19:

"In setting the Phase II national performance standards and providing for site-specific cost-benefit variances, the EPA relied on its view that § 1326(b)'s 'best technology available' standard permits consideration of the technology's costs, and of the relationship between those costs and the environmental benefits produced. That view governs if it is a reasonable interpretation of the statute—not necessarily the only possible interpretation, nor even the interpretation deemed *most* reasonable by the courts. Chevron.

"As we have described, § 1326(b) instructs the EPA to set standards for cooling water intake structures that reflect 'the best technology available for minimizing adverse environmental impact.' The Second Circuit took that language to mean the technology that achieves the greatest reduction in adverse environmental impacts at a cost that can reasonably be borne by the industry. That is certainly a plausible interpretation of the statute. The 'best' technology—that which is 'most advantageous,' Webster's New International Dictionary 258 (2d ed. 1953)—may well be the one that produces the most of some good, here a reduction in adverse environmental impact. But 'best technology' may also describe the technology that *most efficiently* produces some good. In common parlance one could certainly use the phrase 'best technology' to refer to that which produces a good at the lowest per-unit cost, even if it produces a lesser quantity of that good than other available technologies.

"Respondents contend that this latter reading is precluded by the statute's use of the phrase 'for minimizing adverse environmental impact.' Minimizing, they argue, means reducing to the smallest amount possible, and the 'best technology available for minimizing adverse environmental impacts,' must be the economically feasible technology that achieves the greatest possible reduction in environmental harm. But 'minimize' is a term that admits of degree and is not necessarily used to refer exclusively to the 'greatest possible reduction.' For example, elsewhere in the Clean Water Act, Congress declared that the procedures implementing the Act 'shall encourage the drastic minimization of paperwork and interagency decision procedures.' 33 U.S.C. § 1251(f). If respondents' definition of the term 'minimize' is correct, the statute's use of the modifier 'drastic' is superfluous.

"Other provisions in the Clean Water Act also suggest the agency's interpretation. When Congress wished to mandate the greatest feasible reduction in water pollution, it did so in plain language: The provision governing the discharge of toxic pollutants into the Nation's waters requires the EPA to set 'effluent limitations [which] shall require the *elimination* of discharges of all pollutants if the Administrator finds . . . that such elimination is technologically and economically achievable,' § 1311(b)(2)(A) (emphasis added). Section 1326(b)'s use of the less ambitious goal of 'minimizing adverse environmental impact' suggests, we think, that the agency retains some discretion to determine the extent of reduction that is warranted under the circumstances. . . . It seems to us, therefore, that the phrase 'best technology available,' even with the added specification 'for minimizing adverse environmental impact,' does not unambiguously preclude cost-benefit analysis."

After the reference to Chevron in the above quote, Justice Scalia dropped the following footnote: "The dissent finds it 'puzzling' that we invoke this proposition (that a reasonable agency interpretation prevails) at the 'outset,' omitting the supposedly prior inquiry of 'whether Congress has directly spoken to the precise question at issue.' (Opinion of Stevens, J.) (quoting Chevron, 467 U.S., at 842). But surely if Congress has directly spoken to an issue then any agency interpretation contradicting what Congress has said would be unreasonable."

(4) ***How Far Does Purpose Go at Step One?*** ZUNI PUBLIC SCHOOLS DISTRICT NO. 89 V. DEPARTMENT OF EDUCATION, 550 U.S. 81 (2007): Public schools in the United States are typically funded at the local level, supplemented by aid from state governments. The federal government's Impact Aid Act also provides assistance to local school districts whose budgets are impacted by a large federal presence—because, for example, there is a large amount of federal land exempt from local taxation or because a military installation increases the number of school-age children. To make this assistance real at the local level, the federal statute prohibits the states from reducing their aid to the same districts. But if the state's aid program is intended to equalize per-pupil expenditures among districts—if, that is, it is meant to accomplish a purpose that overlaps with the purpose of the federal program—then the states can offset their aid to account for the federal aid.

To implement the Act, it thus becomes important to know whether a state aid program counts as a scheme that equalizes expenditures among local districts. A 1974 statute instructed the Secretary of Education to adopt regulations defining what would count as "equalizing expenditures" by state governments, and the Secretary promptly did so. These regulations provided for a comparison of expenditures—after state aid—between the best funded and poorest districts in the state, to see if expenditures were being equalized. In doing so, the regulations excluded from consideration statistical outliers: the districts containing the 5% of students in the state for whom the least was spent and those containing the 5% for whom most was spent.

In 1994, Congress enacted legislation on the issue. Now the Secretary of Education was required by statute, in making the needed calculations, to "disregard local educational agencies with per-pupil expenditures or revenues above the 95th percentile or below the 5th percentile of such expenditures or revenues in the State. 20 U.S.C. § 7709(b)(2)(B)(i)." It is the meaning of this language that was at stake in this case.

In Justice Breyer's words (writing for the Court), 550 U.S. at 91: "No one at the time—no Member of Congress, no Department of Education official, no school district or state—expressed the view that this statutory language (which, after all, was supplied by the Secretary) was intended to require, or did require, the Secretary to change the Department's system of calculation, a system that the Department and school districts across the Nation had followed for nearly 20 years, without (as far as we are told) any adverse effect." And so, after enactment, the Department did not change its regulations. It continued to construe the relevant percentiles (above the 95th or below the 5th) to cut off 5% of the number of students (in however many school districts were needed to make that total). In actual practice in New Mexico, which had 89 school districts, the Department excluded the 17 richest districts and the 6 poorest districts; compared the top per-pupil expenditure in the remaining 66 districts with the bottom per-pupil expenditure; found that those expenditures were close enough to count, under the regulations, as equalized; and accordingly allowed New Mexico to reduce its state aid to those districts receiving federal aid.

But the challengers (Zuni Public Schools District) said that the new statutory language did not permit this method of calculation. In their view, it compelled the agency to cut off the richest or poorest 5% of the number of districts, without regard to how many students were in those districts. If this had been done, 5 districts would have been cut off at each end of the distribution; the disparities among the remaining 79 districts would have been greater than what the regulations counted as equalized, and the state would not be entitled to reduce its aid to those districts receiving federal aid.

The Court sustained the Department's regulation as constituting "a reasonable, hence permissible, implementation of the statute. See Chevron." 550 U.S. at 100. For Justice Scalia, dissenting, "The plain language of the federal Impact Aid statute clearly and unambiguously forecloses the Secretary of Education's preferred methodology. . . . Her selection of that methodology is therefore entitled to zero deference under Chevron." 550 U.S. at 108.

A large part of the opinions in this case discuss, not surprisingly, the meaning of the words Congress used in the text quoted above—including the implications of "per" in "per-pupil" and the proper referent of "such." But the Justices also exhibited a flurry of approaches to statutory construction. As a result, the opinions offer a rich exploration into the role that a purposive—as opposed to a textualist—approach may play in determining whether Congress has spoken to the precise question at issue or whether the statute is ambiguous, such that the agency's interpretation may be eligible for Chevron deference and whether, in the event of ambiguity, the agency's interpretation is a permissible one that commands deference.

JUSTICE BREYER'S opinion, after stating the facts, began as follows (550 U.S. at 89–91): "Zuni's strongest argument rests upon the literal language of the statute. Zuni concedes, as it must, that if the language of the statute is open or ambiguous—that is, if Congress left a 'gap' for the agency to fill—then we must uphold the Secretary's interpretation as long as it is reasonable. See Chevron. For purposes of exposition, we depart from a normal order of discussion, namely an order that first considers Zuni's statutory language argument. Instead, because of the technical nature of the language in question, we shall first examine the provision's background and basic purposes. That discussion will illuminate our subsequent analysis. It will also reveal why Zuni concentrates its argument upon language alone.

"Considerations other than language provide us with unusually strong indications that Congress intended to leave the Secretary free to use the calculation method before us and that the Secretary's chosen method is a reasonable one. For one thing, the matter at issue—i.e., the calculation method for determining whether a state aid program 'equalizes expenditures'—is the kind of highly technical, specialized interstitial matter that Congress often does not decide itself, but delegates to specialized agencies to decide. . . . For another thing, the history of the statute strongly supports the Secretary. . . .

"Finally, viewed in terms of the purpose of the statute's disregard instruction, the Secretary's calculation method is reasonable, while the reasonableness of a method based upon the number of districts alone (Zuni's proposed method) is more doubtful. . . ."

Only after deciding that the Secretary's method was "reasonable" in light of "the history and purpose" of the statute did he then say: "But what of the provision's literal language? The matter is important, for normally neither the legislative history nor the reasonableness of the Secretary's method would be determinative if the plain language of the statute unambiguously indicated that Congress sought to foreclose the Secretary's interpretation. And Zuni argues that the Secretary's formula could not possibly effectuate Congress' intent since the statute's language literally forbids the Secretary to use such a method. Under this Court's precedents, if the intent of Congress is clear and unambiguously expressed by the statutory language at issue, that would be the end of our analysis. See Chevron. A customs statute that imposes a tariff on 'clothing' does not impose a tariff on automobiles, no matter how strong the policy arguments for treating the two kinds of goods alike. But we disagree with Zuni's conclusion, for we believe that the Secretary's method falls within the scope of the statute's plain language."

JUSTICE KENNEDY, joined by Justice Alito, concurring in the opinion, had this to say about Justice Breyer's approach, 550 U.S. at 107: "In this case, the Court is correct to find that the plain language of the statute is ambiguous. It is proper, therefore, to invoke Chevron's rule of deference. The opinion of the Court, however, inverts Chevron's logical progression. Were the inversion to become systemic, it would create the impression that agency policy concerns, rather than the traditional tools of statutory construction, are shaping the judicial interpretation of statutes. It is our obligation to set a good example; and so, in my view, it would have been preferable, and more faithful to Chevron, to arrange the opinion differently. Still, we must give deference to the author of an opinion in matters of exposition; and because the point does not affect the outcome, I join the Court's opinion."

But that didn't satisfy JUSTICE SCALIA, joined by Chief Justice Roberts, Justice Thomas, and in part by Justice Souter, dissenting, 550 U.S. at 108: "In Church of the Holy Trinity v. United States, 143 U.S. 457 (1892), this Court conceded that a church's act of contracting with a prospective rector fell within the plain meaning of a federal labor statute, but nevertheless did not apply the statute to the church: 'It is a familiar rule' the Court pronounced, 'that a thing may be within the letter of the statute and yet not within the statute, because not within its spirit, nor within the intention of its makers.' Id., at 459. That is a judge-empowering proposition if there ever was one, and in the century since, the Court has wisely retreated from it, in words if not always in actions. But today Church of the Holy Trinity arises, Phoenix-like, from the ashes. The Court's contrary assertions aside, today's decision is nothing other than the elevation of judge-supposed legislative intent over clear statutory text.

"The very structure of the Court's opinion provides an obvious clue as to what is afoot. . . ."

To which JUSTICE STEVENS (who concurred with Breyer) responded, 550 U.S. at 105–07: "[Justice Scalia] correctly observes that a judicial decision that departs from statutory text may represent 'policy-driven interpretation.' As long as that driving policy is faithful to the intent of Congress (or, as in this case, aims only to give effect to such intent)—which it must be if it is to override a strict interpretation of the text—the decision is also a correct performance of the judicial function. Justice Scalia's argument today rests on the incorrect premise that every policy-driven interpretation implements a judge's personal view of sound policy, rather than a faithful attempt to carry out the will of the legislature. Quite the contrary is true of the work of the judges with whom I have worked for many years. If we presume that our judges are intellectually honest—as I do—there is no reason to fear 'policy-driven interpretation[s]' of Acts of Congress.

"In Chevron we acknowledged that when 'the intent of Congress is clear [from the statutory text], that is the end of the matter.' But we also made quite clear that 'administrative constructions which are contrary to clear congressional intent' must be rejected. In that unanimous opinion, we explained: 'If a court, employing traditional tools of statutory construction, ascertains that Congress had an intention on the precise question at issue, that intention is the law and must be given effect.'

"Analysis of legislative history is, of course, a traditional tool of statutory construction. There is no reason why we must confine ourselves to, or begin our analysis with, the statutory text if other tools of statutory construction provide better evidence of congressional intent with respect to the precise point at issue.

"As the Court's opinion demonstrates, this is a quintessential example of a case in which the statutory text was obviously enacted to adopt the rule that the Secretary administered both before and after the enactment of the rather confusing language found in 20 U.S.C. § 7709(b)(2)(B)(i). That text is sufficiently ambiguous to justify the Court's exegesis, but my own vote is the product of a more direct route to the Court's patently correct conclusion. This happens to be a case in which the legislative history is pellucidly clear and the statutory text is difficult to fathom. Moreover, it is a case in which I cannot imagine anyone accusing any Member of the Court of voting one way or the other because of that Justice's own policy preferences.

"Given the clarity of the evidence of Congress' 'intention on the precise question at issue,' I would affirm the judgment of the Court of Appeals even if I thought that petitioners' literal reading of the statutory text was correct. The only 'policy' by which I have been driven is that which this Court has endorsed on repeated occasions regarding the importance of remaining faithful to Congress' intent.

To which, JUSTICE SCALIA (550 U.S. at 116–17): "Justice Stevens is quite candid on the point: He is willing to contradict the text. But Justice Stevens' candor should not make his philosophy seem unassuming. He maintains that it is 'a correct performance of the judicial function' to 'override a strict interpretation of the text' so long as policy-driven interpretation 'is faithful to the intent of Congress.' But once one departs from 'strict interpretation of the text' (by which Justice Stevens means the actual meaning of the text) fidelity to the intent of Congress is a chancy thing. The only thing we know for certain both Houses of Congress (and the President, if he signed the legislation) agreed upon is the text. Legislative history can never produce a 'pellucidly clear' picture of what a law was 'intended' to mean, for the simple reason that it is never voted upon—or ordinarily even seen or heard—by the 'intending' lawgiving entity, which consists of both Houses of Congress and the President (if he did not veto the bill). See U.S. Const., Art. I, §§ 1, 7. Thus, what judges believe Congress 'meant' (apart from the text) has a disturbing but entirely unsurprising tendency to be whatever judges think Congress *must* have meant, i.e., *should* have meant.... [T]he system of judicial amendatory veto over texts duly adopted by Congress bears no resemblance to the system of lawmaking set forth in our Constitution.

"Justice Stevens takes comfort in the fact that this is a case in which he 'cannot imagine anyone accusing any Member of the Court of voting one way or the other because of that Justice's own policy preferences.' I can readily imagine it, given that the Court's opinion begins with a lengthy description of why the system its judgment approves is the *better* one. But even assuming that, in this rare case, the Justices' departure from the enacted law has nothing to do with their policy view that it is a bad law, nothing in Justice Stevens' separate opinion limits his approach to such rarities. Why should we suppose that in matters more likely to arouse the judicial libido—voting rights, antidiscrimination laws, or environmental protection, to name only a few—a judge in the School of Textual Subversion would not find it convenient (yea, *righteous!*) to assume that Congress *must* have meant, not what it said, but what he knows to be best?

To which (perhaps), JUSTICE BREYER, 550 U.S. at 98: "The remainder of the dissent's argument, colorful language to the side, rests upon a reading of the statutory language that ignores its basic purpose and history."

And finally, JUSTICE SOUTER (who, like Justice Scalia, was in dissent), 550 U.S. at 123: "I agree with the Court that Congress probably intended, or at least understood, that the Secretary would continue to follow the methodology devised prior to passage of the current statute in 1994. But ... I find the statutory language unambiguous and inapt to authorize that methodology, and I therefore [dissent]."

(5) ***Legislative History and Chevron.*** Is legislative history relevant to the step one inquiry? The opinions in Zuni just excerpted take differing positions on that question. JUDGE KAREN LECRAFT HENDERSON offers some reasons for so using legislative history in her concurring opinion in COUNCIL FOR UROLOGICAL INTERESTS V. BURWELL, 790 F.3d. 212, 230–31 (D.C. Cir. 2015): "Much ink has been spilled on the propriety of using legislative history to cloud a clear text under Chevron. But the converse—consulting legislative history to clarify an ambiguous text—ought to be uncontroversial. The chief objection to legislative history is that it can be undemocratic: the Congress qua Congress approves only the text of a statute and the legislative history might reflect a distinctly minority view. See Exxon Mobil Corp. v. Allapattah Servs., Inc., 545 U.S. 546, 568 (2005). In the Chevron context, however, a failure to consult legislative history would leave the text ambiguous and

thereby transfer authority to an administrative agency, whose democratic accountability is nil. See Free Enter. Fund v. PCAOB, 561 U.S. 477, 499 (2010) ('The growth of the Executive Branch . . . heightens the concern that it may slip from the Executive's control, and thus from that of the people.'). And at least some types of legislative history 'shed a reliable light on' the views of a majority of the enacting Congress. Allapattah Servs., 545 U.S. at 568; see also Simpson v. United States, 435 U.S. 6, 17 (1978) (Rehnquist, J., dissenting) ('[S]ome types of legislative history are substantially more reliable than others. The report of a joint conference committee of both Houses of Congress, for example, . . . is accorded a good deal more weight than the remarks . . . on the floor of the chamber.'). Legislative history is also criticized for being 'murky, ambiguous, and contradictory,' an exercise of 'looking over a crowd and picking out your friends.' Allapattah Servs., 545 U.S. at 568. But again, this criticism loses force under Chevron. If legislative history is 'ambiguous'—i.e., if both the petitioner and the agency have 'friends' they can pick out—then, by definition, the agency prevails under Chevron Step One. See, e.g., Catawba Cnty., 571 F.3d at 38. Sometimes, however, the legislative history is clear, reliable and uncontroverted; if it is, we would be wrong to ignore it."

Even some who support the use of legislative history, however, have suggested that there are limits to how it may be used at step one. For example, Justice Kagan in Milner v. Department of Navy, 562 U.S. 562 (2011) (p. 734), writing for the Court, explains: "Those of us who make use of legislative history believe that clear evidence of congressional intent may illuminate ambiguous text. We will not take the opposite tack of allowing ambiguous legislative history to muddy clear statutory language." But notice the artful dodge: may clear legislative history render ambiguous what otherwise seems like clear text?

And what about step two? Is legislative history particularly relevant at that stage, if only because it may require the agency to explain how its favored interpretation is still a reasonable one even if that interpretation deviates from strong indications of legislative intent reflected in the legislative history? Again, the opinions at Zuni address that issue. Does it make more sense to consider legislative history at step two then step one? Or, is step two more about policy than law, such that legislative history is of more relevance at the first of Chevron's steps? For a general discussion of the role that legislative history plays within the Chevron framework, see John F. Manning, Chevron and Legislative History, 82 Geo. Wash. L. Rev. 1517 (2014).

(6) ***Systemic Consequences of Various Interpretive Approaches Under Chevron?*** Is one interpretive method or another more likely to produce Chevron deference? Consider THOMAS W. MERRILL, TEXTUALISM AND THE FUTURE OF THE CHEVRON DOCTRINE, 72 Wash. U. L.Q. 351, 371–72 (1994): "[T]extualism triumphant would lead to a permanent subordination of the Chevron doctrine. This has to do with the style of judging associated with textualism. Intentionalism mandates an 'archeological' excavation of the past, producing opinions written in the style of the dry archivist sifting through countless documents in search of the tell-tale smoking gun of

congressional intent. Textualism, in contrast, seems to transform statutory interpretation into a kind of exercise in judicial ingenuity. The textualist judge treats questions of interpretation like a puzzle to which it is assumed there is one right answer. The task is to assemble the various pieces of linguistic data, dictionary definitions, and canons into the best (most coherent, most explanatory) account of the meaning of the statute. This exercise places a great premium on cleverness. In one case the outcome turns on the placement of a comma, in another on the inconsistency between a comma and rules of grammar, in a third on the conflict between quotation marks and the language of the text. One day arguments must be advanced in support of broad dictionary definitions; the next day in support of narrow dictionary definitions. New canons of construction and clear statement rules must be invented and old ones reinterpreted."

## NOTES ON JUDICIAL REVIEW: LAW OR POLITICS?

(1) ***Is It All Politics?*** When judges review an agency's decision, are they really applying "the law," or are they simply deciding what outcome they think most accords with their views of policy and justice, and disguising their preferences under a facade of doctrine? Justice Scalia, in the case Massachusetts v. EPA (p. 1334), charged: "Evidently, the Court defers only to those reasonable interpretations it favors." The only thing that can be said for certain about this question is that it is much debated.

Insofar as the question is addressed to the behavior of the Supreme Court, you can to some extent decide for yourself by looking at the series of judicial review opinions set forth in this Chapter. But the Supreme Court is probably not a representative test case. Its role is primarily to decide cases of first impression, and the most obvious basis for granting certiorari is precisely that the courts below have given contrary answers to the question at hand; it is to be expected that the Court will often have to reach beyond existing doctrine to find its grounds for decision. What about the lower courts—or, of special importance for administrative law, what about the U.S. Courts of Appeals, where much review of administrative agencies starts and almost all of it stops?

(2) ***Judge Edwards on Easy, Hard, and Very Hard Cases.*** Here, from 1991, is the view of Judge Harry Edwards, a well-known member of the Court of Appeals for the District of Columbia Circuit, a court that, because of its location and some specific statutory assignments, does a disproportionate share of administrative review work. HARRY T. EDWARDS, THE JUDICIAL FUNCTION AND THE ELUSIVE GOAL OF PRINCIPLED DECISIONMAKING, 1991 Wis. L. Rev. 837, 838–39, 849, 855–57: "Today, more than eleven years after becoming a judge, . . . I still believe in and subscribe to principled decisionmaking, but it is no longer entirely clear to me that partisan politics and ideological maneuvering have no meaningful influence on judicial decisionmaking. . . . [I]n my view, most judges still share a belief that principled decisionmaking is the essence of the judicial function. What has changed, I think, is the nature of certain external pressures felt by judges; these pressures are both created and exacerbated by the continuing

distortion of public perceptions, in which the judicial function is increasingly viewed as just one more 'political' enterprise. . . .

"The more that judges are assessed in terms of 'political' (result-oriented) decisionmaking, the more likely it is that this will become a self-fulfilling prophecy. Even if judges are able to resist the temptation to conform to the false perception, continued assessments of judicial performance in political terms will promote a 'new reality,' for most people will come to believe that the judicial function is nothing more than a political enterprise. No matter how good the intentions of its servants, the judiciary will be sharply devalued and incompetent to fulfill its role as mediator in a society with lofty but sometimes conflicting ambitions. This would be a horror to behold. . . . I have felt damned by an increasingly common image of the judiciary, and particularly of the D.C. Circuit, as a fundamentally political body. . . .

"Fortunately, the present reality of decisionmaking on the D.C. Circuit does not match the public perception. There is no doubt that there are ideological differences among the judges and that these differences may have an impact in the disposition of certain 'very hard' (and even 'hard') cases. . . . Perhaps the most fundamental reality of D.C. Circuit decisionmaking is that, contrary to popular belief, circuit judges rarely disagree with one another over the disposition of particular cases. The vast majority of case dispositions involve unanimous decisions. . . . Most notably, the dissent rate on what I call 'mixed panels'—panels with judges appointed by Presidents of different political affiliations—did not exceed the general dissent rate in either year. Clearly, the image of an ideologically divided circuit court on which judges heed some political call to action is far from the truth.

"In my view, most cases are 'easy,' in that the pertinent legal rules are readily identified and applied to the facts at hand, revealing a single 'right answer.' . . . [R]oughly one-half of the cases I hear each year are 'easy' and virtually all of these are disposed of without dissent. . . . In a second category of [the 'hard' cases] . . . each party is able to advance at least one plausible legal argument in its favor. . . . [But after] . . . research and review . . . the arguments of one party to a 'hard' case seem to me demonstrably stronger than those of the other, and the case is decided accordingly. . . . [A]pproximately 35 to 45% of the cases before the court are 'hard' in this sense. In my experience, judges hearing these cases generally feel themselves bound by their view of the law, and identify the sounder arguments without recourse to their own political opinions. Not surprisingly, therefore, there is substantial agreement among judges as to the proper disposition of 'hard' cases.

"That leaves from 5 to 15% of our cases in the 'very hard' category, making it by far the smallest of the three. In this narrow set of cases, careful research and reflection fail to yield conclusive answers. The relevant legal materials, thoroughly studied, show only that the competing arguments advanced by the parties are equally strong, and the judges who must decide are left in a state of equipoise. Disposition of this small number of cases, then, requires judges to exercise a measure of discretion, drawing to some degree on their own social and moral beliefs. That judges may find themselves in disagreement as to the outcome of these 'very hard' cases is thus to be expected, and represents something quite different from stark political decisionmaking.

"The important point, I think, is that so-called 'very hard' cases are viewed as such not because they raise situations in which judges are inclined to engage in result-oriented decisionmaking, but, rather, because these cases admit of no clear answer. And when there is no discernible 'right' answer to a case, it is more likely (although not inevitable) that decisionmaking may be influenced by political or ideological considerations."

(3) ***Studies on Judicial Voting Patterns.*** There have been a great many academic studies that have challenged Judge Edwards's point of view. For students of administrative law, of special interest are a series of studies carried out by Thomas Miles and Cass Sunstein that looked at the degree to which politics impacted the application of Chevron and of arbitrary and capricious review. Here is their description of their method (CASS R. SUNSTEIN & THOMAS J. MILES, DEPOLITICIZING ADMINISTRATIVE LAW, 58 Duke L.J. 2193, 2199–2201 (2009)): "Within the courts of appeals, our focus has been on judicial review of decisions by the Environmental Protection Agency (EPA) and the National Labor Relations Board (NLRB). . . . [In the case of agency interpretations of law, we examined all cases citing Chevron between 1990 and 2004 (253 in total); in the case of arbitrariness review, we examined all arbitrariness and substantial evidence cases between 1996 and 2006 (653 in total).] There are of course real difficulties in deciding how to 'code' agency decisions in political terms. It is hard to undertake such coding in the abstract; it is even harder to do so when the real question is not whether the agency has proceeded in a 'liberal' fashion, but how the particular controversy, before a court, should be evaluated in political terms. Let us begin by describing our choice and then explaining it.

"In brief, we attempted to categorize agency decisions as 'liberal' or 'conservative' by asking whether the challenge was made by a company or instead by a public interest group or a labor union. If, for example, the Sierra Club objected to an EPA decision, the decision was coded as conservative; if General Motors made the objection, the decision was coded as liberal. This method has several important advantages. It greatly simplifies the coding exercise, avoids controversial judgments that might divide reviewers, and thus improves administrability and replicability. It can also be defended in principle. What matters is not whether the agency's decision is liberal or conservative in the abstract, but the political valence of the particular challenge before the court. If, for example, the EPA has issued a ruling that some people consider 'liberal,' but that is challenged by a public interest group that is attempting to increase regulation, the ruling is relevantly conservative, in the sense that judges are being asked to hold that it is unlawfully weak. . . .

"We also examined whether judicial votes were issued by Republican or Democratic appointees to the federal bench, with the hypothesis that the division should operate as a proxy for political predilections and with the further thought that the effect of the political affiliation of the appointing president is of considerable independent interest. With this method, we can investigate 'liberal voting rates' for Democratic and Republican appointees in different domains. We can also compare the validation rate of both sets of appointees for conservative agency decisions and for liberal agency decisions. In addition to studying the effects of party, we can study the effects of panels by asking whether the votes of Democratic or Republican appointees are affected by the political affiliation of the president who appointed the two other judges on the panel. Do Democratic appointees show especially liberal voting patterns when they sit only with other Democratic appointees? How do the voting patterns of Republican appointees differ depending on whether they are sitting with no, one, or two Democratic appointees?

"The baseline case, for purposes of studying neutrality and partisanship, would show no significant disparities between Republican and Democratic appointees. If no such disparities were shown, existing administrative law doctrines would be 'working' in the sense that they would be serving to filter out any effect from the most obvious and salient difference among appointees to the federal bench."

And here is their description of their principal results (id. at 2201–04):

"Within the courts of appeals, politicized voting is unmistakable in Chevron cases. Consider three different ways to demonstrate this point:

1. When the agency's decision is liberal, the Democratic validation rate is 74 percent; when the agency's decision is conservative, the Democratic validation rate falls to 51 percent. The pattern is the opposite for Republican appointees—very close to the mirror image. When the agency's decision is liberal, the Republican validation rate is 59.5 percent. When the agency's decision is conservative, the Republican validation rate jumps to 70 percent.

2. When the agency's decision is liberal, Democratic appointees are 14 percent more likely to vote to validate it than are Republican appointees. When the agency's decision is conservative, Democratic appointees are 19 percent less likely to validate it than are Republican appointees.

3. The overall liberal voting rate is 67 percent for Democratic appointees; for Republican appointees, it is 50 percent.

"To be sure, differences of these magnitudes are inconsistent with the proposition that in administrative law cases judicial voting is thoroughly politicized. It remains true that Republican appointees vote to uphold liberal interpretations well over 50 percent of the time, and that Democratic appointees are more likely than not to uphold conservative interpretations. Nonetheless, the disparities are significant. What produces them?

"Intriguingly, they are driven in large part by the radically different behavior of both sets of appointees on unified panels—that is, panels consisting solely of Democratic appointees (DDD panels) or solely of Republican appointees (RRR panel). When Democratic appointees are on DDD panels, the validation rate for liberal agency decisions is 86 percent; when Democratic appointees are on DDD panels, the validation rate for conservative agency decisions is 54 percent. . . . When Republican appointees are on RRR panels, the validation rate for liberal agency decisions is 51 percent; and on such panels, the validation rate for conservative agency decisions is a remarkable 100 percent.

"Because of the relatively small sample size, the particular numbers here should be taken with a grain of salt, but they should be sufficient to show that unified panels are playing a large role in driving the results. . . . *On mixed panels, politicized voting is greatly reduced; the behavior of Democratic appointees, on such panels, is very close to that of Republican appointees*. . . . Group polarization is the typical pattern within deliberating groups, and it occurs in a wide range of settings. If Democratic appointees show especially liberal voting patterns on panels consisting solely of Democratic appointees, it is likely because the judges' initial inclinations are amplified, rather than moderated, by learning about the conclusions and arguments of other judges. On mixed panels, by contrast, a whistleblower effect may occur, in the form of presentation of counterarguments based (for example) on the principle of Chevron deference." They show that the "pattern is strikingly similar in arbitrariness cases."

"To say the least," the authors comment, "this seems to be a disturbing and somewhat embarrassing state of affairs. Whatever one's view of the foundational questions in administrative law, no one should approve of a situation in which judicial voting patterns are highly politicized. On the contrary, it is reasonable to read existing doctrines as an explicit effort to prevent such patterns from emerging. Most prominently, Chevron U.S.A. Inc. v. Natural Resources Defense Council, Inc. establishes that courts must uphold agency interpretations of ambiguous statutory provisions so long as those interpretations are reasonable. Chevron is naturally read to say that resolution of statutory ambiguities calls for a policy judgment, with the suggestion that such judgments should be made by administrators, not judges. It is disconcerting, to say the least, to find that when judges review agency interpretations of law, judicial policy judgments continue to be playing a significant role." Id. at 2195–96.

Reviewing every published court of appeals decision involving Chevron or Skidmore during the period from 2003–2013, KENT BARNETT, CHRISTINA L. BOYD, & CHRISTOPHER J. WALKER, ADMINISTRATIVE LAW'S POLITICAL DYNAMICS, 71 Vand. L. Rev. 1463, 1465–70 (2018), suggested that when compared to the right baseline, Chevron might be doing some work after all. Although panels classified by the authors as conservative were more likely to sustain conservative agency interpretations and panels classified as liberal were more likely to sustain liberal interpretations, a different story emerged when the authors separated out and compared cases applying Chevron deference to cases not applying it. Viewed through this lens, the most liberal panels sustained conservative agency interpretations 18% of the time when not applying Chevron deference but 51% of the time when it was used. And the most conservative panels sustained liberal interpretations 18% of the time when not applying Chevron deference, and 66% of the time when it was used. "When applying Chevron, panels of all ideological stripes use the framework similarly and reveal modest ideological behavior. For instance, both liberal and conservative panels are more likely to find the statute unambiguous when the agency's interpretation is contrary to the panel's ideological preferences. Likewise, both liberal and conservative panels are more likely to find the statute ambiguous when the agency's interpretation aligns with the panels' ideological preferences. This means that panels permit agencies more policymaking space when the administrative interpretations are consistent with the panels' views. . . . Nonetheless, contrary to Justice Scalia's view that textualist judges (who generally identify as conservative) may be more likely to find statutes unambiguous regardless of the valence of the agency interpretation, we found no relationship between panel ideology and a panel holding a statute unambiguous." (Having a mix of conservative and liberal judges did not significantly affect whether a panel applied Chevron or an agency was likely to succeed.)

(4) ***Judge Edwards Replies.*** Judge Edwards is not, however, convinced. In an article responding to the work of Miles and Sunstein, and to other studies (HARRY T. EDWARDS & MICHAEL A. LIVERMORE, PITFALLS OF EMPIRICAL STUDIES THAT ATTEMPT TO UNDERSTAND THE FACTORS AFFECTING APPELLATE DECISIONMAKING, 58 Duke L.J. 1895 (2009)), he stuck by his original analysis of easy, hard, and very hard cases, and he quarreled in part with the methodology the empirical scholars employed. He also took issue with the underlying view of "law" and "politics" he thought was encapsulated in their studies (id. at 1945–48): "The crudeness of the measures used to support the ideology thesis rest on an implausibly formalistic and positivistic conception of law. The hypothesis that judicial decisionmaking is influenced by the ideology of judges is remarkable only if and to the extent that ideology is extrinsic to law. If we do not subscribe to this assumption, then both law and ideology can influence outcomes, and greater contributions from the later tell us nothing about the contribution of the former. The crude measure of 'ideology' fails to discriminate between forms of moral/political reasoning intrinsic to law and those extrinsic to law. It is well understood that legal reasoning partakes of moral judgment in cases in which judges routinely exercise delegated or common law-making authority. This need not, and generally does not, take the form of personal whim or preference. Rather, in cases where the law requires it, judicial decisionmaking can include a situated and disciplined elaboration of the conventional norms of the American political community. This occurs in both 'hard' and 'very hard' cases, including, for example, cases involving judicial resolutions of disputes in areas of law ranging from constitutional interpretation to the administration of the antitrust laws. This reality might be contested by some, but it is far and away the dominant understanding of how adjudication works in our judicial system.

"On this account, some play for inherently contestable political judgments is simply built into law and strikes us as a normal constituent of good judging. It is obvious—to the point of being mundane—to suggest that there is a correlation between how individual judges will carry out this aspect of judicial reasoning and their 'ideologies.' When positive law is imprecise and judges are required to exercise delegated or common law-making authority in hard or very hard cases, they often are obliged to refer to the conception of our community's political morality that strikes them as the most compelling. Good examples of this are seen in the political . . . conception of free speech that animated the Supreme Court's seminal decision New York Times v. Sullivan, in the neoclassical conception of economics that triumphed with the . . . 'public welfare' understanding of antitrust law, and in the extensive jurisprudence surrounding the enforcement of collective bargaining agreements pursuant to section 301 of the Labor Management Relations Act. The judging that gave rise to those conceptions of law can be described as either (1) not ideological in any manner opposed to law or (2) ideological in a manner intrinsic to law itself. . . .

"Judges who exercise delegated or common law-making authority to decide cases of this sort . . . are obliged to rely—and to do so self-consciously and overtly—on political and ideological values in their legal reasoning. This cannot seriously be doubted, nor can it reasonably be seen as surprising. It is merely part of the judicial function. If one accepts that such reasoning is legal reasoning, then any regression model that uses a crude measure of ideology that spills over to evaluative reasoning of this sort will produce results that merely state the obvious, i.e., that judicial disagreement over how to understand the law helps explain variations in case outcomes.

"Empirical studies of this sort, in sum, assume not only that judicial decisionmaking is sometimes influenced by the ideology of judges, but also that ideology is invariably extrinsic to law. But this turns out, surprisingly, to be a normative claim . . . in the guise of an empirical one. The fact is that most members of the legal profession—judges, lawyers, and scholars—subscribe to a conception of law that sees forms of moral or political reasoning as intrinsic to law in some circumstances. Thus, empirical scholars can convince us to accept their central claim (that extralegal judicial 'ideology' explains variation in some legal outcomes) only if they first convince us that we are wrong in our view that some political and ideological questions are intrinsic to law itself. In other words, empirical ideologists must convince us that we should adopt a formalistic or 'hard' positivistic theory that insists that legal questions never subsume moral or political questions. But, of course, if empirical scholars could do this (assuming they wanted to), they would not be showing that judges have been substituting their ideology for law but, rather, that judges have been following a conception of law that we should reject for normative reasons."

(5) ***Chevron as Tempering or Amplifying?*** What about from an analytical perspective? Would you expect Chevron's rule of deference to temper the influence of judicial ideology, or for nebulous ambiguity and reasonableness inquiries to provide vessels for it?

One study provided the following explanation for its finding that Republican and Democratic appointees found ambiguity under Chevron at statistically indistinguishable rates. ORIN S. KERR, SHEDDING LIGHT ON CHEVRON: AN EMPIRICAL STUDY OF THE CHEVRON DOCTRINE IN THE U.S. COURTS OF APPEALS, 15 Yale J. on Reg. 1, 57–59 (1998): "I propose that [the prediction that textualism affects whether a judge finds ambiguity] errs by understating the degree to which theories of statutory interpretation are normative, rather than descriptive. I submit that jurists internalize interpretative norms based on their largely intuitive understandings of the proper role of the judiciary in a constitutional democracy, not on their personal answer to the hermeneutic question of how much meaning can be extracted from text. Roughly speaking, those judges who follow text more closely tend to profess a belief in a more limited, rule-following judiciary, while those who endorse a more dynamic interpretative method tend to appreciate judicial rule-making power. Whether a judge advocates or rejects textualism does not reflect the judge's capacity to find more or less meaning in text. Instead, it means that the judge believes that the body politic is better served by judges who try more or less hard to find what meaning may be there.

"The reason that [the prediction] fails in the Chevron context, then, is that Chevron asks judges an interpretive question in a context that disrupts the usual relationship between the outcomes served and the political theories that typically inform judges' interpretive methods. Chevron upsets the usual relationship between interpretation and the judicial role in two ways. First, statutory ambiguity no longer expands judicial power; it constricts it, limiting the judicial role to deferential review for unreasonableness. Conversely, finding meaning in the text no longer limits judicial power; it expands it by granting to the courts plenary review of administrative action. Second, Chevron transforms a judge's degree of commitment to the text from a means of allocating power between the legislature and the judiciary (its usual function) into a means of allocating power between the judiciary and the executive. Finding meaning in the text no longer enhances the power of the legislature over the judiciary; instead, it emphasizes the power of the judiciary over the executive. I propose that these disruptions of the typical association between interpretative method and the judicial role explains why judges do not approach Chevron's first step with their usual interpretive associations intact. Chevron's atypical interpretive context in effect suspends judges' normative associations between their approaches to text and political theory.

"Consider the case of a judge who adopts an expansive view of the judicial function and believes that the proper judicial role is to ensure that the broad policy concerns of Congress are carried out in a fair and just way. Because textualism requires a judge to adhere to text instead of purpose and justice, the judge would likely eschew textualism and instead find that most texts were ambiguous enough to allow the judge to fashion a just remedy. In the Chevron context, however, the ambiguity that would normally allow the judge to fashion a just remedy backfires. A finding of ambiguity instead binds the judge to accept a wide range of agency action, even if the judge perceives that action as unjust. Ambiguity ceases to be an engine of judicial authority and becomes an engine of uncabined executive power.

"In the absence of the usual forces pulling and pushing judges toward different interpretive approaches, judges who typically are influenced by very different normative interpretive traditions adopt roughly equivalent understandings of how ambiguous is ambiguous enough at step one. This does not mean that all judges will agree in every case, of course (although most cases are unanimous), but it does mean that no one set of judges will be led to adopt a particularly different vision of Chevron."

Yet faced with the ambiguity of competing interpretive and normative predispositions, isn't it plausible that judges would be influenced by their normative intuitions? While Chevron would seem to encourage deference to agency interpretations under conservative and liberal administrations alike, some might say that agencies exist to regulate. If agency interpretations are overall more likely to expand regulation, might a rule of deferring to such interpretations be more or less appealing depending on one's intuitions about whether such regulation is a good idea in the first place? As to why "deference will, in the long term, support an expansion of the regulatory state," the following reasons have been offered: "First, the parties differ in their levels of regulatory ambition. Second, Democrats have fewer tools with which to achieve their regulatory goals than Republicans do their deregulatory aims. Third, various carve-outs from the doctrine, including on national security and immigration, give Republicans less to lose should the Court abandon Chevron. Finally, the parties have strikingly divergent attitudes toward the federal bureaucracy." Gregory A. Elinson & Jonathan S. Gould, The Politics of Deference, 75 Vand. L. Rev. 475, 539–40 (2022).

(6) ***Expertise or Politics in Agency Interpretation?*** What about the politics of the interpreting agency? Chevron is supposed to make room for expert agencies to make policy judgments. How does that premise fare in an era of polarization? Is making such a value judgment still the kind of policy-based enterprise better left to agencies? RICHARD J. PIERCE, JR., THE COMBINATION OF CHEVRON AND POLITICAL POLARITY HAS AWFUL EFFECTS, 70 Duke L.J. Online 91 (2021), approached these questions from the perspective of Mozilla Corp. v. Fed. Commc'ns Comm'n, 940 F.3d 1 (D.C. Cir. 2019), which upheld an FCC interpretation of the Communications Act of 1934 pertaining to net neutrality. Over the previous 15 years, the FCC had reversed its interpretation four times, tracking changes in the party in control of the presidency. Pierce pointed out that, whether or not one thinks that net neutrality is a good idea, "[o]ur policy of flip-flopping between net neutrality and deregulation of internet service providers every time the White House changes hands discourages all investments in the internet. Policy uncertainty discourages investment. . . . In the context of the internet, prospective investors must decide whether to make an investment in conditions in which they know that the government policies that have a material effect on their investment returns will change with each change in administration. That is a policy environment that is far worse than either consistent application of the principles of net neutrality or consistent rejection of those principles." Id. at 99.

(7) ***Small Numbers Add up.*** Finally, there is this from now-retired Seventh Circuit Judge Richard Posner (Some Realism About Judges: A Reply to Edwards and Livermore, 59 Duke L.J. 1177, 1180 (2010)): "Even Judge Edwards says that 5 to 15 percent of cases decided by his court are indeterminate from a legalist standpoint. If one cumulates those figures over many years and many courts, it is apparent that an immense number of

decisions are legalistically indeterminate; and among them . . . are the decisions that have made the law what it is today."

### d. The Present-Day Framework, Part III: Limits on Chevron



## UNITED STATES v. MEAD CORPORATION

Supreme Court of the United States (2001).
533 U.S. 218.

■ JUSTICE SOUTER delivered the opinion of the Court.

The question is whether a tariff classification ruling by the United States Customs Service deserves judicial deference. The Federal Circuit rejected Customs's invocation of Chevron U.S.A. Inc. v. Natural Resources Defense Council, Inc., 467 U.S. 837 (1984), in support of such a ruling, to which it gave no deference. We agree that a tariff classification has no claim to judicial deference under Chevron, there being no indication that Congress intended such a ruling to carry the force of law, but we hold that under Skidmore v. Swift & Co., 323 U.S. 134 (1944), the ruling is eligible to claim respect according to its persuasiveness.

I

A

Imports are taxed under the Harmonized Tariff Schedule of the United States (HTSUS), 19 U.S.C. § 1202. Title 19 U.S.C. § 1500(b) provides that Customs "shall, under rules and regulations prescribed by the Secretary [of the Treasury] . . . fix the final classification and rate of duty applicable to . . . merchandise" under the HTSUS. Section 1502(a) provides that

> [t]he Secretary of the Treasury shall establish and promulgate such rules and regulations not inconsistent with the law (including regulations establishing procedures for the issuance of binding rulings prior to the entry of the merchandise concerned), and may disseminate such information as may be necessary to secure a just, impartial, and uniform appraisement of imported merchandise and the classification and assessment of duties thereon at the various ports of entry.[1]

The Secretary provides for tariff rulings before the entry of goods by regulations authorizing "ruling letters" setting tariff classifications for particular imports. 19 CFR § 177.8 (2000). A ruling letter

> represents the official position of the Customs Service with respect to the particular transaction or issue described therein and is binding on all Customs Service personnel in accordance with the provisions of this section until modified or revoked. In the absence of a change of practice or other modification or revocation which affects the principle of the ruling set forth in the ruling letter, that principle may be cited as authority in the disposition of transactions involving the same circumstances. § 177.9(a).

After the transaction that gives it birth, a ruling letter is to "be applied only with respect to transactions involving articles identical to the sample submitted with the ruling request or to articles whose description is identical to the description set forth in the ruling letter." § 177.9(b)(2). As a general matter, such a letter is "subject to modification or revocation without notice to any person, except the person to whom the letter was addressed," § 177.9(c), and the regulations consequently provide that "no other person should rely on the ruling letter or assume that the principles of that ruling will be applied in connection with any transaction other than the one described in the letter," ibid. Since ruling letters respond to transactions of the moment, they are not subject to notice and comment before being issued, may be published but need only

---

[1] The statutory term "ruling" is defined by regulation as "a written statement . . . that interprets and applies the provisions of the Customs and related laws to a specific set of facts." 19 CFR § 177.1(d)(1).

be made "available for public inspection," 19 U.S.C. § 1625(a), and, at the time this action arose, could be modified without notice and comment under most circumstances, 19 CFR § 177.10(c).

Any of the 46 port-of-entry Customs offices may issue ruling letters, and so may the Customs Headquarters Office. . . . Most ruling letters contain little or no reasoning, but simply describe goods and state the appropriate category and tariff. A few letters, like the Headquarters ruling at issue here, set out a rationale in some detail.

B

Respondent, the Mead Corporation, imports "day planners," three-ring binders with pages having room for notes of daily schedules and phone numbers and addresses, together with a calendar and suchlike. The tariff schedule on point falls under the HTSUS heading for "[r]egisters, account books, notebooks, order books, receipt books, letter pads, memorandum pads, diaries and similar articles," HTSUS subheading 4820.10, which comprises two subcategories. Items in the first, "[d]iaries, notebooks and address books, bound; memorandum pads, letter pads and similar articles," were subject to a tariff of 4.0% at the time in controversy. Objects in the second, covering "[o]ther" items, were free of duty.

Between 1989 and 1993, Customs repeatedly treated day planners under the "other" HTSUS subheading. In January 1993, however, Customs changed its position, and issued a Headquarters ruling letter classifying Mead's day planners as "Diaries . . . , bound" subject to tariff under subheading 4820.10.20. That letter was short on explanation, but after Mead's protest, Customs Headquarters issued a new letter, carefully reasoned but never published, reaching the same conclusion. This letter considered two definitions of "diary" from the Oxford English Dictionary, the first covering a daily journal of the past day's events, the second a book including "printed dates for daily memoranda and jottings; also . . . calendars. . . ." Customs concluded that "diary" was not confined to the first, in part because the broader definition reflects commercial usage and hence the "commercial identity of these items in the marketplace." As for the definition of "bound," Customs concluded that HTSUS was not referring to "bookbinding," but to a less exact sort of fastening described in the Harmonized Commodity Description and Coding System Explanatory Notes to Heading 4820, which spoke of binding by "reinforcements or fittings of metal, plastics, etc."

Customs rejected Mead's further protest of the second Headquarters ruling letter, and Mead filed suit in the Court of International Trade (CIT). The CIT granted the Government's motion for summary judgment, adopting Customs's reasoning without saying anything about deference. 17 F.Supp.2d 1004 (1998).

Mead then went to the United States Court of Appeals for the Federal Circuit. . . .

The Federal Circuit . . . reversed the CIT and held that Customs classification rulings should not get Chevron deference. . . . Rulings are not preceded by notice and comment as under the Administrative Procedure Act (APA), 5 U.S.C. § 553, they "do not carry the force of law and are not, like regulations, intended to clarify the rights and obligations of importers beyond the specific case under review." 185 F.3d, at 1307. The appeals court thought classification rulings had a weaker Chevron claim even than Internal Revenue Service interpretive rulings, to which that court gives no deference; unlike rulings by the IRS, Customs rulings issue from many locations and need not be published. 185 F.3d, at 1307–1308.

The Court of Appeals accordingly gave no deference at all to the ruling classifying the Mead day planners and rejected the agency's reasoning as to both "diary" and "bound." It thought that planners were not diaries because they had no space for "relatively extensive notations about events, observations, feelings, or thoughts" in the past. Id., at 1310. And it concluded that diaries "bound" in subheading 4810.10.20 presupposed "unbound" diaries, such that treating ring-fastened diaries as "bound" would leave the "unbound diary" an empty category. Id., at 1311.

We granted certiorari, in order to consider the limits of Chevron deference owed to administrative practice in applying a statute. We hold that administrative implementation of a particular statutory provision qualifies for Chevron deference when it appears that Congress delegated authority to the agency generally to make rules carrying the force of law, and that the agency interpretation claiming deference was promulgated in the exercise of that authority. Delegation of such authority may be shown in a variety of ways, as by an agency's power to engage in adjudication or notice-and-comment rulemaking, or by some other indication of a comparable congressional intent. The Customs ruling at issue here fails to qualify, although the possibility that it deserves some deference under Skidmore leads us to vacate and remand.

## II

### A

When Congress has "explicitly left a gap for an agency to fill, there is an express delegation of authority to the agency to elucidate a specific provision of the statute by regulation," Chevron, 467 U.S., at 843–844, and any ensuing regulation is binding in the courts unless procedurally defective, arbitrary or capricious in substance, or manifestly contrary to the statute. APA, 5 U.S.C. §§ 706(2)(A), (D). But whether or not they enjoy any express delegation of authority on a particular question, agencies charged with applying a statute necessarily make all sorts of interpretive choices, and while not all of those choices bind judges to follow them, they certainly may influence courts facing questions the agencies have already answered. "[T]he well-reasoned views of the agencies implementing a statute 'constitute a body of experience and informed judgment to which courts and litigants may properly resort for guidance,'" Bragdon v. Abbott, 524 U.S. 624, 642 (1998) (quoting Skidmore, 323 U.S., at 139–140), and "[w]e have long recognized that considerable weight should be accorded to an executive department's construction of a statutory scheme it is entrusted to administer. . . ." Chevron, supra, at 844. The fair measure of deference to an agency administering its own statute has been understood to vary with circumstances, and courts have looked to the degree of the agency's care, its consistency, formality, and relative expertness, and to the persuasiveness of the agency's position. The approach has produced a spectrum of judicial responses, from great respect at one end, to near indifference at the other. Justice Jackson summed things up in Skidmore v. Swift & Co.:

> The weight [accorded to an administrative] judgment in a particular case will depend upon the thoroughness evident in its consideration, the validity of its reasoning, its consistency with earlier and later pronouncements, and all those factors which give it power to persuade, if lacking power to control. 323 U.S., at 140.

Since 1984, we have identified a category of interpretive choices distinguished by an additional reason for judicial deference. This Court in Chevron recognized that Congress not only engages in express delegation of specific interpretive authority, but that "[s]ometimes the legislative delegation to an agency on a particular question is implicit." 467 U.S., at 844. Congress, that is, may not have expressly delegated authority or responsibility to implement a particular provision or fill a particular gap. Yet it can still be apparent from the agency's generally conferred authority and other statutory circumstances that Congress would expect the agency to be able to speak with the force of law when it addresses ambiguity in the statute or fills a space in the enacted law, even one about which "Congress did not actually have an intent" as to a particular result. Id., at 845. When circumstances implying such an expectation exist, a reviewing court has no business rejecting an agency's exercise of its generally conferred authority to resolve a particular statutory ambiguity simply because the agency's chosen resolution seems unwise, but is obliged to accept the agency's position if Congress has not previously spoken to the point at issue and the agency's interpretation is reasonable; cf. 5 U.S.C. § 706(2) (a reviewing court shall set aside agency action, findings, and conclusions found to be "arbitrary, capricious, an abuse of discretion, or otherwise not in accordance with law").

We have recognized a very good indicator of delegation meriting Chevron treatment in express congressional authorizations to engage in the process of rulemaking or adjudication that produces regulations or rulings for which deference is claimed. It is fair to assume generally that Congress contemplates administrative action with the effect of law when it provides for a relatively formal administrative procedure tending to foster the fairness and deliberation that should underlie a pronouncement of such force.[11] Thus, the overwhelming number of our

[11] See Merrill & Hickman, Chevron's Domain, 89 Geo. L.J. 833, 872 (2001) ("[I]f Chevron rests on a presumption about congressional intent, then Chevron should apply only where Congress would want Chevron to apply. In delineating the types of delegations of agency

cases applying Chevron deference have reviewed the fruits of notice-and-comment rulemaking or formal adjudication.[12] That said, and as significant as notice-and-comment is in pointing to Chevron authority, the want of that procedure here does not decide the case, for we have sometimes found reasons for Chevron deference even when no such administrative formality was required and none was afforded, see, e.g., NationsBank of N.C., N.A. v. Variable Annuity Life Ins. Co., 513 U.S. 251, 256–257, 263 (1995).[13] The fact that the tariff classification here was not a product of such formal process does not alone, therefore, bar the application of Chevron.

There are, nonetheless, ample reasons to deny Chevron deference here. The authorization for classification rulings, and Customs's practice in making them, present a case far removed not only from notice-and-comment process, but from any other circumstances reasonably suggesting that Congress ever thought of classification rulings as deserving the deference claimed for them here.

B

No matter which angle we choose for viewing the Customs ruling letter in this case, it fails to qualify under Chevron. On the face of the statute, to begin with, the terms of the congressional delegation give no indication that Congress meant to delegate authority to Customs to issue classification rulings with the force of law. We are not, of course, here making any global statement about Customs's authority, for it is true that the general rulemaking power conferred on Customs, see 19 U.S.C. § 1624, authorizes some regulation with the force of law, or "legal norms." It is true as well that Congress had classification rulings in mind when it explicitly authorized, in a parenthetical, the issuance of "regulations establishing procedures for the issuance of binding rulings prior to the entry of the merchandise concerned," 19 U.S.C. § 1502(a). The reference to binding classifications does not, however, bespeak the legislative type of activity that would naturally bind more than the parties to the ruling, once the goods classified are admitted into this country. And though the statute's direction to disseminate "information" necessary to "secure" uniformity, 19 U.S.C. § 1502(a), seems to assume that a ruling may be precedent in later transactions, precedential value alone does not add up to Chevron entitlement; interpretive rules may sometimes function as precedents, see Strauss, The Rulemaking Continuum, 41 Duke L.J. 1463, 1472–1473 (1992), and they enjoy no Chevron status as a class. In any event, any precedential claim of a classification ruling is counterbalanced

---

authority that trigger Chevron deference, it is therefore important to determine whether a plausible case can be made that Congress would want such a delegation to mean that agencies enjoy primary interpretational authority").

[12] For rulemaking cases, see, e.g., [19 cases cited]. For adjudication cases, see, e.g., [8 cases cited].

[13] In NationsBank of N.C., N.A. v. Variable Annuity Life Ins. Co., 513 U.S. 251, 256–257 (1995), we quoted longstanding precedent concluding that "[t]he Comptroller of the Currency is charged with the enforcement of banking laws to an extent that warrants the invocation of [the rule of deference] with respect to his deliberative conclusions as to the meaning of these laws" (internal quotation marks omitted).

by the provision for independent review of Customs classifications by the CIT, see 28 U.S.C. §§ 2638–2640. . . .

It is difficult, in fact, to see in the agency practice itself any indication that Customs ever set out with a lawmaking pretense in mind when it undertook to make classifications like these. Customs does not generally engage in notice-and-comment practice when issuing them, and their treatment by the agency makes it clear that a letter's binding character as a ruling stops short of third parties; Customs has regarded a classification as conclusive only as between itself and the importer to whom it was issued, 19 CFR § 177.9(c), and even then only until Customs has given advance notice of intended change, §§ 177.9(a), (c). Other importers are in fact warned against assuming any right of detrimental reliance. § 177.9(c).

Indeed, to claim that classifications have legal force is to ignore the reality that 46 different Customs offices issue 10,000 to 15,000 of them each year. Any suggestion that rulings intended to have the force of law are being churned out at a rate of 10,000 a year at an agency's 46 scattered offices is simply self-refuting. Although the circumstances are less startling here, with a Headquarters letter in issue, none of the relevant statutes recognizes this category of rulings as separate or different from others; there is thus no indication that a more potent delegation might have been understood as going to Headquarters even when Headquarters provides developed reasoning, as it did in this instance.

In sum, classification rulings are best treated like "interpretations contained in policy statements, agency manuals, and enforcement guidelines." Christensen v. Harris County, 529 U.S. 576, 587 (2000). They are beyond the Chevron pale.

C

To agree with the Court of Appeals that Customs ruling letters do not fall within Chevron is not, however, to place them outside the pale of any deference whatever. Chevron did nothing to eliminate Skidmore's holding that an agency's interpretation may merit some deference whatever its form, given the "specialized experience and broader investigations and information" available to the agency, 323 U.S., at 139, and given the value of uniformity in its administrative and judicial understandings of what a national law requires, id., at 140.

There is room at least to raise a Skidmore claim here, where the regulatory scheme is highly detailed, and Customs can bring the benefit of specialized experience to bear on the subtle questions in this case: whether the daily planner with room for brief daily entries falls under "diaries," when diaries are grouped with "notebooks and address books, bound; memorandum pads, letter pads and similar articles," HTSUS subheading 4820.10.20; and whether a planner with a ring binding should qualify as "bound," when a binding may be typified by a book, but also may have "reinforcements or fittings of metal, plastics, etc.," Harmonized Commodity Description and Coding System Explanatory

Notes to Heading 4820, p. 687. A classification ruling in this situation may therefore at least seek a respect proportional to its "power to persuade." Such a ruling may surely claim the merit of its writer's thoroughness, logic and expertness, its fit with prior interpretations, and any other sources of weight.

D

Underlying the position we take here, like the position expressed by Justice Scalia in dissent, is a choice about the best way to deal with an inescapable feature of the body of congressional legislation authorizing administrative action. That feature is the great variety of ways in which the laws invest the Government's administrative arms with discretion, and with procedures for exercising it, in giving meaning to Acts of Congress. Implementation of a statute may occur in formal adjudication or the choice to defend against judicial challenge; it may occur in a central board or office or in dozens of enforcement agencies dotted across the country; its institutional lawmaking may be confined to the resolution of minute detail or extend to legislative rulemaking on matters intentionally left by Congress to be worked out at the agency level.

Although we all accept the position that the Judiciary should defer to at least some of this multifarious administrative action, we have to decide how to take account of the great range of its variety. If the primary objective is to simplify the judicial process of giving or withholding deference, then the diversity of statutes authorizing discretionary administrative action must be declared irrelevant or minimized. If, on the other hand, it is simply implausible that Congress intended such a broad range of statutory authority to produce only two varieties of administrative action, demanding either Chevron deference or none at all, then the breadth of the spectrum of possible agency action must be taken into account. Justice Scalia's first priority over the years has been to limit and simplify. The Court's choice has been to tailor deference to variety. This acceptance of the range of statutory variation has led the Court to recognize more than one variety of judicial deference, just as the Court has recognized a variety of indicators that Congress would expect Chevron deference.[18]

Our respective choices are repeated today. Justice Scalia would pose the question of deference as an either-or choice. On his view that Chevron rendered Skidmore anachronistic, when courts owe any deference it is Chevron deference that they owe. Whether courts do owe deference in a given case turns, for him, on whether the agency action (if reasonable) is "authoritative." The character of the authoritative derives, in turn, not from breadth of delegation or the agency's procedure in implementing it, but is defined as the "official" position of an agency, and may ultimately be a function of administrative persistence alone.

---

[18] It is, of course, true that the limit of Chevron deference is not marked by a hard-edged rule. But Chevron itself is a good example showing when Chevron deference is warranted, while this is a good case showing when it is not. Judges in other, perhaps harder, cases will make reasoned choices between the two examples, the way courts have always done.

The Court, on the other hand, said nothing in Chevron to eliminate Skidmore's recognition of various justifications for deference depending on statutory circumstances and agency action; Chevron was simply a case recognizing that even without express authority to fill a specific statutory gap, circumstances pointing to implicit congressional delegation present a particularly insistent call for deference. Indeed, in holding here that Chevron left Skidmore intact and applicable where statutory circumstances indicate no intent to delegate general authority to make rules with force of law, or where such authority was not invoked, we hold nothing more than we said last Term in response to the particular statutory circumstances in Christensen, to which Justice Scalia then took exception, just as he does again today.

We think, in sum, that Justice Scalia's efforts to simplify ultimately run afoul of Congress's indications that different statutes present different reasons for considering respect for the exercise of administrative authority or deference to it. Without being at odds with congressional intent much of the time, we believe that judicial responses to administrative action must continue to differentiate between Chevron and Skidmore, and that continued recognition of Skidmore is necessary for just the reasons Justice Jackson gave when that case was decided.[19] . . .

Since the Skidmore assessment called for here ought to be made in the first instance by the Court of Appeals for the Federal Circuit or the Court of International Trade, we go no further than to vacate the judgment and remand the case for further proceedings consistent with this opinion.

■ JUSTICE SCALIA, dissenting.

Today's opinion makes an avulsive change in judicial review of federal administrative action. Whereas previously a reasonable agency application of an ambiguous statutory provision had to be sustained so long as it represented the agency's authoritative interpretation, henceforth such an application can be set aside unless "it appears that Congress delegated authority to the agency generally to make rules carrying the force of law," as by giving an agency "power to engage in adjudication or notice-and-comment rulemaking, or . . . some other [procedure] indicati[ng] comparable congressional intent," and "the agency interpretation claiming deference was promulgated in the exercise of that authority." What was previously a general presumption of authority in agencies to resolve ambiguity in the statutes they have been authorized to enforce has been changed to a presumption of no such authority, which must be overcome by affirmative legislative intent to the contrary. And whereas previously, when agency authority to resolve

[19] Surely Justice Jackson's practical criteria, along with Chevron's concern with congressional understanding, provide more reliable guideposts than conclusory references to the "authoritative" or "official." Even if those terms provided a true criterion, there would have to be something wrong with a standard that accorded the status of substantive law to every one of 10,000 "official" customs classifications rulings turned out each year from over 46 offices placed around the country at the Nation's entryways. . . .

ambiguity did not exist the court was free to give the statute what it considered the best interpretation, henceforth the court must supposedly give the agency view some indeterminate amount of so-called Skidmore deference. We will be sorting out the consequences of the Mead doctrine, which has today replaced the Chevron doctrine, for years to come. I would adhere to our established jurisprudence, defer to the reasonable interpretation the Customs Service has given to the statute it is charged with enforcing, and reverse the judgment of the Court of Appeals.

I

Only five years ago, the Court described the Chevron doctrine as follows: "We accord deference to agencies under Chevron . . . because of a presumption that Congress, when it left ambiguity in a statute meant for implementation by an agency, understood that the ambiguity would be resolved, first and foremost, by the agency, and desired the agency (rather than the courts) to possess whatever degree of discretion the ambiguity allows," Smiley v. Citibank (South Dakota), N.A., 517 U.S. 735, 740–741 (1996). Today the Court collapses this doctrine, announcing instead a presumption that agency discretion does not exist unless the statute, expressly or impliedly, says so. While the Court disclaims any hard-and-fast rule for determining the existence of discretion-conferring intent, it asserts that "a very good indicator [is] express congressional authorizations to engage in the process of rulemaking or adjudication that produces regulations or rulings for which deference is claimed." Only when agencies act through "adjudication[,] notice-and-comment rulemaking, or . . . some other [procedure] indicati[ng] comparable congressional intent [whatever that means]" is Chevron deference applicable—because these "relatively formal administrative procedure[s] [designed] to foster . . . fairness and deliberation" bespeak (according to the Court) congressional willingness to have the agency, rather than the courts, resolve statutory ambiguities. Once it is determined that Chevron deference is not in order, the uncertainty is not at an end—and indeed is just beginning. Litigants cannot then assume that the statutory question is one for the courts to determine, according to traditional interpretive principles and by their own judicial lights. No, the Court now resurrects, in full force, the pre-Chevron doctrine of Skidmore deference. . . . The Court has largely replaced Chevron, in other words, with that test most beloved by a court unwilling to be held to rules (and most feared by litigants who want to know what to expect): th'ol' "totality of the circumstances" test.

The Court's new doctrine is neither sound in principle nor sustainable in practice.

A

As to principle: The doctrine of Chevron—that all *authoritative* agency interpretations of statutes they are charged with administering deserve deference—was rooted in a legal presumption of congressional intent, important to the division of powers between the Second and Third Branches. When, Chevron said, Congress leaves an ambiguity in a statute that is to be administered by an executive agency, it is presumed that Congress meant to give the agency discretion, within the limits of reasonable interpretation, as to how the ambiguity is to be resolved. By committing enforcement of the statute to an agency rather than the courts, Congress committed its initial and primary interpretation to that branch as well. . . .

The basis in principle for today's new doctrine can be described as follows: The background rule is that ambiguity in legislative instructions to agencies is to be resolved not by the agencies but by the judges. Specific congressional intent to depart from this rule must be found—and while there is no single touchstone for such intent it can generally be found when Congress has authorized the agency to act through (what the Court says is) relatively formal procedures such as informal rulemaking and formal (and informal?) adjudication, and when the agency in fact employs such procedures. . . . [T]he Court's principal criterion of congressional intent to supplant its background rule seems to me quite implausible. There is no necessary connection between the formality of procedure and the power of the entity administering the procedure to resolve authoritatively questions of law. The most formal of the procedures the Court refers to—formal adjudication—is modeled after the process used in trial courts, which of course are not generally accorded deference on questions of law. The purpose of such a procedure is to produce a closed record for determination and review of the facts—which implies nothing about the power of the agency subjected to the procedure to resolve authoritatively questions of law. . . .

B

As for the practical effects of the new rule:

(1)

The principal effect will be protracted confusion. As noted above, the one test for Chevron deference that the Court enunciates is wonderfully imprecise: whether "Congress delegated authority to the agency generally to make rules carrying the force of law, . . . as by . . . adjudication[,] notice-and-comment rulemaking, or . . . some other [procedure] indicati[ng] comparable congressional intent." But even this description does not do justice to the utter flabbiness of the Court's criterion, since, in order to maintain the fiction that the new test is really just the old one, applied consistently throughout our case law, the Court must make a virtually open-ended exception to its already imprecise guidance: In the present case, it tells us, the absence of notice-and-comment rulemaking . . . is not enough to decide the question of Chevron deference, "for we have sometimes found reasons for Chevron deference even when no such administrative formality was required and none was afforded." The opinion then goes on to consider a grab bag of other factors—including the factor that used to be the sole criterion for Chevron deference: whether the interpretation represented the *authoritative* position of the agency. It is hard to know what the lower courts are to make of today's guidance.

(2)

Another practical effect of today's opinion will be an artificially induced increase in informal rulemaking. Buy stock in the GPO. Since informal rulemaking and formal adjudication are the only more-or-less safe harbors from the storm that the Court has unleashed; and since formal adjudication is [often] not an option . . . informal rulemaking . . . will now become a virtual necessity. As I have described, the Court's safe harbor requires not merely that the agency have been given rulemaking authority, but also that the agency have *employed* rulemaking as the means of resolving the statutory ambiguity. (It is hard to understand why that should be so. Surely the mere *conferral* of rulemaking authority demonstrates—if one accepts the Court's logic—a congressional intent to allow the agency to resolve ambiguities. And given that intent, what difference does it make that the agency chooses instead to use another perfectly permissible means for that purpose?) Moreover, the majority's approach will have a perverse effect on the rules that do emerge, given the principle (which the Court leaves untouched today) that judges must defer to reasonable agency interpretations of their own regulations. Agencies will now have high incentive to rush out barebones, ambiguous rules construing statutory ambiguities, which they can then in turn further clarify through informal rulings entitled to judicial respect.

(3)

Worst of all, the majority's approach will lead to the ossification of large portions of our statutory law. Where Chevron applies, statutory ambiguities remain ambiguities subject to the agency's ongoing clarification. They create a space, so to speak, for the exercise of continuing agency discretion. As Chevron itself held, the Environmental Protection Agency can interpret "stationary source" to mean a single smokestack, can later replace that interpretation with the "bubble concept" embracing an entire plant, and if that proves undesirable can return again to the original interpretation. For the indeterminately large number of statutes taken out of Chevron by today's decision, however, ambiguity (and hence flexibility) will cease with the first judicial resolution. Skidmore deference gives the agency's current position some vague and uncertain amount of respect, but it does not, like Chevron, *leave* the matter within the control of the Executive Branch for the future. Once the court has spoken, it becomes *unlawful* for the agency to take a contradictory position; the statute now *says* what the court has prescribed. . . .

One might respond that such ossification would not result if the agency were simply to readopt its interpretation, after a court reviewing it under Skidmore had rejected it, by repromulgating it through one of the Chevron-eligible procedural formats approved by the Court today. Approving this procedure would be a landmark abdication of judicial power. It is worlds apart from Chevron proper, where the court does not *purport* to give the statute a judicial interpretation—except in identifying the scope of the statutory ambiguity, as to which the court's judgment is final and irreversible. (Under Chevron proper, when the agency's authoritative interpretation comes within the scope of that ambiguity—and the court therefore approves it—the agency will not be "overruling" the court's decision when it later decides that a different interpretation (still within the scope of the ambiguity) is preferable.) By contrast, under this view, the reviewing court will not be holding the agency's authoritative interpretation within the scope of the ambiguity; but will be holding that the agency has not used the "delegation-conferring" procedures, and that the court must therefore *interpret the statute on its own*—but subject to reversal if and when the agency uses the proper procedures. . . .

There is, in short, no way to avoid the ossification of federal law that today's opinion sets in motion. What a court says is the law after according Skidmore deference will be the law forever, beyond the power of the agency to change even through rulemaking.

(4)

And finally, the majority's approach compounds the confusion it creates by breathing new life into the anachronism of Skidmore, which sets forth a sliding scale of deference owed an agency's interpretation of a statute that is dependent "upon the thoroughness evident in [the agency's] consideration, the validity of its reasoning, its consistency with earlier and later pronouncements, and all those factors which give it power to persuade, if lacking power to control"; in this way, the appropriate measure of deference will be accorded the "body of experience and informed judgment" that such interpretations often embody, 323 U.S., at 140. Justice Jackson's eloquence notwithstanding, the rule of Skidmore deference is an empty truism and a trifling statement of the obvious: A judge should take into account the well-considered views of expert observers.

It was possible to live with the indeterminacy of Skidmore deference in earlier times. But in an era when federal statutory law administered by federal agencies is pervasive, and when the ambiguities (intended or unintended) that those statutes contain are innumerable, totality-of-the-circumstances Skidmore deference is a recipe for uncertainty, unpredictability, and endless litigation. To condemn a vast body of agency action to that regime (all except rulemaking, formal (and informal?) adjudication, and whatever else might now and then be included within today's intentionally vague formulation of affirmative congressional intent to "delegate") is irresponsible.

II

The Court's pretense that today's opinion is nothing more than application of our prior case law does not withstand analysis. . . .

III

To decide the present case, I would adhere to the original formulation of Chevron. " 'The power of an administrative agency to administer a congressionally created . . . program necessarily requires the formulation of policy and the making of rules to fill any gap left, implicitly or explicitly, by Congress,' " 467 U.S., at 843 (quoting Morton

v. Ruiz, 415 U.S. 199, 231 (1974)). We accordingly presume—and our precedents have made clear to Congress that we presume—that, absent some clear textual indication to the contrary, "Congress, when it left ambiguity in a statute meant for implementation by an agency, understood that the ambiguity would be resolved, first and foremost, by the agency, and desired the agency (rather than the courts) to possess whatever degree of discretion the ambiguity allows," Smiley, 517 U.S., at 740–741. Chevron sets forth an across-the-board presumption, which operates as a background rule of law against which Congress legislates: Ambiguity means Congress intended agency discretion. Any resolution of the ambiguity by the administering agency that is authoritative—that represents the official position of the agency—must be accepted by the courts if it is reasonable.

Nothing in the statute at issue here displays an intent to modify the background presumption on which Chevron deference is based. . . .

There is no doubt that the Customs Service's interpretation represents the authoritative view of the agency. Although the actual ruling letter was signed by only the Director of the Commercial Rulings Branch of Customs Headquarters' Office of Regulations and Rulings, the Solicitor General of the United States has filed a brief, cosigned by the General Counsel of the Department of the Treasury, that represents the position set forth in the ruling letter to be the official position of the Customs Service. No one contends that it is merely a "post hoc rationalizatio[n]" or an "agency litigating positio[n] wholly unsupported by regulations, rulings, or administrative practice."[6]

There is also no doubt that the Customs Service's interpretation is a reasonable one, whether or not judges would consider it the best. I will not belabor this point, since the Court evidently agrees: An interpretation that was unreasonable would not merit the remand that the Court decrees for consideration of Skidmore deference.

IV

. . . For the reasons stated, I respectfully dissent from the Court's judgment. I would uphold the Customs Service's construction of Subheading 4820.10.20 of the Harmonized Tariff Schedule of the United States, 19 U.S.C. § 1202, and would reverse the contrary decision of the Court of Appeals. I dissent even more vigorously from the reasoning that produces the Court's judgment, and that makes today's decision one of

[6] The Court's parting shot, that "there would have to be something wrong with a standard that accorded the status of substantive law to every one of 10,000 'official' customs classifications rulings turned out each year from over 46 offices placed around the country at the Nation's entryways" misses the mark. I do not disagree. The "authoritativeness" of an agency interpretation does not turn upon whether it has been enunciated by someone who is actually employed by the agency. It must represent the judgment of central agency management, approved at the highest levels. I would find that condition to have been satisfied when, a ruling having been attacked in court, the general counsel of the agency has determined that it should be defended. If one thinks that that does not impart sufficient authoritativeness, then surely the line has been crossed when, as here, the General Counsel of the agency and the Solicitor General of the United States have assured this Court that the position represents the agency's authoritative view. . . .

the most significant opinions ever rendered by the Court dealing with the judicial review of administrative action. Its consequences will be enormous, and almost uniformly bad.

## NOTES

(1) ***Where Is Mead Coming from?*** Just one year before Mead, in CHRISTENSEN V. HARRIS COUNTY, 529 U.S. 576 (2000), the Court considered the status of an opinion letter issued by the Department of Labor's Wage and Hour Division applying the Fair Labor Standards Act to a particular set of circumstances. Holding against the agency's interpretation, the Court, in an opinion by JUSTICE THOMAS, refused to give it Chevron deference. 529 U.S. at 587: "Here . . . we confront an interpretation contained in an opinion letter, not one arrived at after, for example, a formal adjudication or notice-and-comment rulemaking. Interpretations such as those in opinion letters—like interpretations contained in policy statements, agency manuals, and enforcement guidelines, all of which lack the force of law—do not warrant Chevron-style deference." Instead, the interpretation was entitled to Skidmore deference, but in applying that standard Justice Thomas found the agency's interpretation "unpersuasive."

Justice Thomas spoke for five members of the Court. Justice Scalia agreed with the result reached, not because he would refuse Chevron deference but because even granting that deference he considered the agency's statutory interpretation unreasonable. In terms not unlike those used in Mead, he specifically abjured Skidmore deference. Justices Stevens, Breyer, and Ginsburg dissented in two opinions, the gist of which was that the Department got it right, whether viewed as a matter of Skidmore or Chevron.

Christensen was, thus, in some sense a dress-rehearsal for Mead. But in Mead, Justice Souter speaks with the authority of eight Justices and delivers an opinion in which Skidmore deference is clearly part of the holding, since it forms the basis for the instructions to the court below upon remand.

(2) ***How Do You Understand Justice Souter's Opinion?*** The particulars of the two tests are worked out in the Notes following Skidmore (p. 1203) and Chevron (pp. 1212–1253). But what do you make of Justice Souter's way of presenting the landscape of deference in Section II of his opinion? Is Skidmore's multifactored analysis of deference now the core principle, with Chevron representing merely the limiting case of "most" deference because "an additional reason for judicial deference applies"? Or is Skidmore merely a clean-up principle, kept alive so as to give judges more choices than Chevron or nothing? More broadly, are judges now to employ a "spectrum of judicial responses"? Or is it Chevron—or Skidmore—or nothing?

(3) ***Mead's Reference to the Arbitrary and Capricious Standard.*** Justice Souter's paragraph in II.A of Mead presenting "an additional reason for judicial deference" ends with the statement that a court in such circumstances "is obliged to accept the agency's position if Congress has not previously spoken to the point at issue and the agency's interpretation is

reasonable," followed by a citation to, and quotation from, the portion of the APA establishing the "arbitrary and capricious" standard of review. Is the opinion very quietly trying to solve the question whether Chevron is compatible with the APA? If so, is it solving it by making Chevron step two congruent with the State Farm "arbitrary and capricious" test? (See discussion in the Notes to Chevron, pp. 1218–1223.)

(4) ***Why Have a Test Before We Get to Chevron?*** The Mead case, in addition to affirming the continued viability of Skidmore, holds that there is a prerequisite to according agency action Chevron deference. At this level of abstraction, even Justice Scalia agrees that "there would have to be something wrong with a standard that accorded the status of substantive law to every one of 10,000 'official' customs classifications rulings turned out each year from over 46 offices placed around the country at the Nation's entryways." Assuming that the officials issuing these rulings are doing something they are authorized to do (in the ordinary bureaucratic sense of "authorized"), why is this need for an additional prerequisite obvious to all the Justices? Assuming there ought to be an additional test, do you prefer Justice Scalia's "authoritative view of the agency" test or Justice Souter's "delegation meriting Chevron treatment" test as a way of sorting agency action that deserves Chevron deference from agency action that does not? (By the way, because of its prerequisite nature, the Court's test in Mead is sometimes referred to as establishing a "Chevron step zero." (See discussion in the Notes to Chevron, p. 1213.) You should know the term—but it might be argued that what Mead really establishes is a "Chevron step one-plus"; presumably Chevron step one—if Congress has directly spoken to the point, that is the end of the issue for agency and for court—remains true for all cases.)[5]

## NOTES ON PUTTING THE MEAD TEST FOR CHEVRON DEFERENCE INTO PRACTICE

(1) ***How Does the Mead Prerequisite Work?*** The Court states its holding as follows:

> We hold that administrative implementation of a particular statutory provision qualifies for Chevron deference when it appears that Congress delegated authority to the agency generally to make rules carrying the force of law, and that the agency interpretation claiming deference was promulgated in the exercise of that authority. Delegation of such authority may be shown in a variety of ways, as by an agency's power to engage in adjudication or notice-

[5] Paez, J., in Northern California River Watch v. Wilcox, 633 F.3d 766 (9th Cir. 2011): "We begin our analysis with the 'familiar two-step procedure' laid out in Chevron. At step one, we evaluate whether Congressional intent regarding the meaning of the text in question is clear from the statute's plain language. If it is, we must give effect to that meaning. If the statute is ambiguous, and an agency purports to interpret the ambiguity, prior to moving on to step two, we must determine whether the agency meets the requirements set forth in Mead: (1) that Congress clearly delegated authority to the agency to make rules carrying the force of law, and (2) that the agency interpretation was promulgated in the exercise of that authority. If both of these requirements from Mead are met, then we proceed to step two."

and-comment rulemaking, or by some other indication of a comparable congressional intent.

Perhaps as important as any of these words are the connectors in the sentences: the "and" following the comma in the first and the "or" following the second comma in the second. The complexity of the resulting apparatus perhaps illustrates Justice Souter's comment, in a footnote, "It is, of course, true that the limit of Chevron deference is not marked by a hard-edged rule."

The Court's opinion says that "the overwhelming number of our cases applying Chevron deference have reviewed the fruits of notice-and-comment rulemaking or formal adjudication." These are situations in which both sides of the "and"—authority to make determinations with the force of law *and* procedural exercise of that authority—will inherently go together under the APA or comparable requirements in organic statutes. (The rarely required APA "formal" rulemaking would also qualify.) In cases like Mead, by contrast, neither side of the couple will normally be satisfied. The "ruling letter," says the Court, is "best treated like interpretations contained in policy statements, agency manuals, and enforcement guidelines." This is the closest we get to an answer of how the "ruling letter" would be classified under the APA. Probably it is an interpretive rule of particular effect, but possibly it could be labeled an informal adjudication. In either case, while not irrelevant, it would normally not have a strong "force of law" and under the APA not have to be adopted with procedural formality.

But the APA does not always link the two together. For example, § 553 allows an agency to avoid the notice-and-comment process when adopting even ordinary "legislative-type" rules if it "for good cause" finds that the process is "impracticable, unnecessary, or contrary to the public interest." If the agency appropriately determines there is such "good cause," is the second part of Mead's "and" test excused? Or is there a value in public process that entitles the resulting rule to Chevron deference only if the process actually occurs?

Similarly, what of agency rules of procedure—which are exempted from § 553 processes (although an agency can, of course, consistent with Vermont Yankee (p. 312), choose to hold a notice-and-comment proceeding if it wants to and has the authority to do so)? Procedural rules are often held to bind the agency, however adopted—and in that sense the agency's power to adopt them meets the first part of the test, before the "and." But what of the second part?

(2) ***The Barnhart Factors.*** The Court's willingness to accord Chevron deference beyond the confines of notice-and-comment rulemaking or formal adjudication appeared a year after Mead in BARNHART V. WALTON, 535 U.S. 212 (2002). In an opinion written by JUSTICE BREYER and joined by all but Justice Scalia, the Court sustained an interpretation of the Social Security Administration that had appeared in many documents—rulings and official manuals—over many years. This interpretation, said the Court in what was either an alternate holding or a very-well-considered dictum, was entitled to Chevron deference even though not the product of a notice-and-comment proceeding (535 U.S. at 222): "In this case, the interstitial nature of the legal

question, the related expertise of the Agency, the importance of the question to administration of the statute, the complexity of that administration, and the careful consideration the Agency has given the question over a long period of time all indicate that Chevron provides the appropriate legal lens through which to view the legality of the Agency interpretation here at issue. See Mead."

(3) ***Chaos?*** "When the Supreme Court decided United States v. Mead Corp.," wrote LISA SCHULTZ BRESSMAN, "Justice Scalia predicted that judicial review of agency action would devolve into chaos. This Article puts that prediction to the test by examining the court of appeals decisions applying the decision. Justice Scalia actually understated the effect of Mead." HOW MEAD HAS MUDDLED JUDICIAL REVIEW OF AGENCY ACTION, 58 Vand. L. Rev. 1443, 1443–44 (2005). Among her other findings, Bressman reports that two divergent lines of cases have developed in the lower courts regarding how to draw the Chevron/Skidmore dividing line (id. at 1459):

"... [T]he courts can be sorted into two groups: those that consider Mead-inspired factors and those that consider Barnhart-inspired factors [referring to Barnhart v. Walton, discussed in the previous note]. Some courts consider whether an interpretation reflects binding effect, either alone or together with deliberation (via public participation)—the factor that Mead made determinative. Other courts consider whether an agency interpretation reflects careful consideration, either alone or together with agency expertise and statutory complexity—the factor that Barnhart made relevant. The problem . . . is that these tests are not necessarily equivalent. Nor do the courts generally acknowledge that they have chosen one over another. As a result, Chevron deference seems to turn more on which test a court prefers than on which procedure an agency uses."

The Supreme Court continued to employ the distinction between Chevron and Skidmore deference, but without much further guidance as to how to do so in close cases. E.g., Alaska Dep't of Environmental Conservation v. EPA, 540 U.S. 461, 487 (2004) (EPA interpretive guides, published, consistent over a long period—Skidmore but not Chevron). There may be some comfort in knowing that if a statutory reading is either "clearly right" or "clearly wrong," the Chevron/Skidmore issue can simply be sidestepped. See General Dynamics Land Systems, Inc. v. Cline, 540 U.S. 581, 600 (2004).

Is this irresponsible? No, said CASS SUNSTEIN in CHEVRON STEP ZERO, 92 Va. L. Rev. 187, 229 (2006): "The first and simplest solution stems from a recognition that Chevron and Skidmore are not radically different in practice; in most cases, either approach will lead to the same result. If the agency's interpretation runs afoul of congressional instructions or is unreasonable, the agency will lose even under Chevron. If the agency's interpretation is not evidently in conflict with congressional instructions, and if it is reasonable, the agency's interpretation will be accepted even under Skidmore. These observations suggest the easiest path for questions on which Mead and Barnhart give inadequate guidance: Resolve the case without answering the question whether it is governed by Chevron or Skidmore. For most cases, the choice between Chevron and Skidmore is not material, and hence it is not worthwhile to worry over it."

(4) ***Or Stability?*** A different view of the legal landscape was provided a few years later in KRISTIN E. HICKMAN, THE THREE PHASES OF MEAD, 83 Fordham L. Rev. 527 (2014): "Consistent with the complaints of Mead critics, the Court's vacillating rhetoric about the interaction of Mead, Chevron, and Skidmore has undoubtedly sowed some amount of confusion. It is unclear, however, that the practical impact of that confusion has been especially great.

"For all of the Court's rhetorical inconsistency, much of its Mead jurisprudence is pretty unremarkable, at least as regards Mead itself. A quick survey shows that, over thirteen Terms, thirty-nine Supreme Court cases offer opinions that cite Mead. Only a few of those cases featured clearly articulated disagreements among the justices over the standard of review to be applied. Brand X and City of Arlington . . . were particularly contentious, with the phases of Mead all spectacularly displayed. . . .

"By comparison, most of the cases in which the Court cited Mead offered little or no disagreement in either extending Chevron review to obviously eligible notice-and-comment rulemaking and formal (or formal-ish) adjudications and applying Skidmore to informal guidance and similarly nonbinding interpretations. Indeed, post-Mead, the Court has never actually extended Chevron deference to interpretations lacking with notice-and-comment rulemaking or relatively formal adjudication procedures. . . .

"Far more important, given the limited size of the Court's docket, is how the justices' differing views of Mead, Chevron, and Skidmore have influenced the federal circuit courts. Are they just as divided? Have the Court's varying rhetorical flourishes yielded the muddled doctrinal mess predicted by Justice Scalia? . . . I would assert that Mead overall has had a stabilizing effect on the lower courts' Chevron jurisprudence. More often than not, the circuit courts of appeals seem to follow a relatively rote version of . . . Mead, Chevron, and Skidmore, rather than the more fluid and open-ended version advocated by Justice Breyer. While this approach is not always doctrinally precise and unanswered questions remain, it is also relatively easy to apply and yields consistent outcomes in most cases."

## NOTES ON THE THEORY OF THE MEAD DECISION

What have scholars thought of the Mead doctrine? Here is a sample.

(1) ***A Sound Development.*** THOMAS W. MERRILL, THE MEAD DOCTRINE: RULES AND STANDARDS, META-RULES AND META-STANDARDS, 54 Admin. L. Rev. 807, 833–34 (2002): "On the whole, 'the Mead doctrine' is a sound development. Mead clarifies that Chevron rests on congressional intent, and correctly concludes from this that Chevron applies only when Congress has given some signal that the agency, rather than the court, is to be the primary interpreter of statutory ambiguity. The decision also correctly concludes that the relevant signal of Congress's intent in this regard is a delegation of power to act with the force of law. By linking Chevron and congressional intent, Mead helps achieve a reconciliation between Chevron and the judicial review provisions of the APA. Indeed, by insisting that the agency gets strong deference only when it acts within the scope of delegated power to act with

the force of law, and not otherwise, Mead goes part way toward restoring an important aspect of the nondelegation doctrine. . . .

"To be sure, the decision comes up short in terms of articulating a meta-rule to guide lower courts in future controversies. Mead says Chevron applies only when Congress has delegated authority to an agency to act with the force of law, but it treats 'force of law' as (at most) a standard to be applied by looking to a variety of factors. The Court's decision to treat 'force of law' as a standard rather than a rule is regrettable. But nothing the Court did or said precludes future decisions that brush away the fuzziness in the majority's exposition, leaving us with a clear and defensible meta-rule."

(2) ***A Cloak of Congressional Intent.*** JACK M. BEERMANN, THE TURN TOWARD CONGRESS IN ADMINISTRATIVE LAW, 89 B.U. L. Rev. 727, 745–46 (2009): "The Court . . . relies on an apparently fictional account of congressional intent in establishing the domain of Chevron—that is, when the Chevron doctrine applies. Under what has been called Chevron Step Zero, before applying the Chevron doctrine, the reviewing court must determine whether the Chevron framework applies to the particular agency interpretation under review. The entire inquiry is wrapped in a cloak of congressional intent because, as the Court puts it, Chevron applies only when Congress intends to empower the agency to make interpretations that have the force of law. While the Court has expressly disavowed limitations on the factors relevant to whether Chevron applies, the main criterion that the Supreme Court applies to this is the formality of agency process, not explicitly because they tend to lead to more reliable results, but rather because when Congress prescribes a relatively formal process, this formality is purportedly indicative of Congress's intent to delegate to the agency the power to issue interpretations with the force of law.

"It is exceedingly difficult to evaluate whether the formality criterion, or any factor other than the text or legislative history of a particular statute or the APA, accurately reflects congressional intent regarding the status of agency interpretations. The Court's most important opinion on this matter [Mead] makes it clear that the doctrine is built on an assumption concerning Congress's intent, not actual evidence of that intent. No opinion of the Court cites direct evidence such as statutory language, legislative reports or legislative debates for the relevance of formality to that inquiry. Further, although there are suggestions in early decisions that procedural formality may be relevant to the deference issue, the Court does not offer a shared tradition that procedural formality signals actual congressional intent to delegate, so that Congress might be presumed to have legislated against that background. Rather, the criterion seems to fit the Court's own logic about when agency interpretations should receive Chevron deference, regardless of congressional intent."

(3) ***Validated by Congressional Counsels.*** Considering Mead in light of her earlier work on whether those who actually draft legislation (as contrasted with Senators or Representatives) know the principles that judges announce (see p. 1241), ABBE GLUCK had this to say in WHAT 30 YEARS OF CHEVRON TEACH US ABOUT THE REST OF STATUTORY INTERPRETATION, 83 Fordham L. Rev. 607, 621–22 (2014): "The [earlier]

study surveyed 137 congressional counsels on their familiarity with the judicial doctrines of interpretation and delegation and on whether the doctrines (regardless of staffer familiarity with them) substantially reflected the realities of the legislative drafting process. As we detailed, congressional staffers knew few of the non-administrative law canons of statutory interpretation and rejected several that they did know (such as presumptions of consistent-term usage) as unrealistic assumptions about congressional drafting.

"The administrative law canons, however, fared better. For example, the rule announced in Mead, although the case was virtually unknown by name or as a doctrine that courts employ, was overwhelmingly validated as a good signal on which to rest assumptions about congressional delegation."

Furthermore, Gluck continued, id. at 623–24, there may be some tension between other administrative law doctrine and Mead's signal that the best way to ensure an agency receives deference is for Congress first to delegate notice-and-comment authority and for the agency then to use it. Think, if you have already read it, about Vermont Yankee, p. 312, and the limits the Court has placed on judicial interventions into agency procedure. Is Mead just a more oblique way of incentivizing procedural regularity?

(4) ***The Decisionmaker in Agency Hierarchy.*** DAVID J. BARRON & ELENA KAGAN, CHEVRON'S NONDELEGATION DOCTRINE, 2001 Sup. Ct. Rev. 201, 203–05: "We . . . argue in this article that an inquiry into actual congressional intent, of the kind the Mead Court advocated, cannot realistically solve this question of the proper scope of Chevron. Although Congress has broad power to decide what kind of judicial review should apply to what kind of administrative action, Congress so rarely discloses (or, perhaps, even has) a view on this subject as to make a search for legislative intent chimerical and a conclusion regarding that intent fraudulent in the mine run of cases. . . . Given the difficulty of determining actual congressional intent, some version of constructive—or perhaps more frankly said, fictional—intent must operate in judicial efforts to delineate the scope of Chevron. After considering other alternatives, we aver that this construction should arise from and reflect candid policy judgments, of the kind evident in Chevron itself, about the allocation of interpretive authority between administrators and judges with respect to various kinds of agency action.

"Underneath the rhetoric of legislative intent, an approach of this kind in fact animates the Mead decision, but the Court's reliance on the two stock dichotomies of administrative process failed to generate the most appropriate distribution of interpretive power. The Court emphasized most heavily the divide between formal and informal procedures, suggesting that, except in unusual circumstances, only decisions taken in formal procedural contexts merit Chevron deference. But this preference for formality in administration, even in cases when not statutorily required, fails to acknowledge the costs associated with the procedures specified in the APA, which only have increased in significance since that statute's enactment. The Court similarly noted at times the divide between generality and particularity in administrative decision making, suggesting that actions exhibiting the former trait should receive greater judicial deference. But administrative law doctrine long has resisted, for good reason, the temptation to pressure the choice between general and particular decision making, in light of the many and fluctuating considerations, usually best known to an agency itself, relevant to this choice. None of this is to say that interpretive authority in areas of statutory ambiguity or silence always should rest with agency officials; it is only to say that in allocating this power in a way consistent with important administrative values, courts can do better than to rely on the two usual (indeed, hoary) 'either-ors' of agency process.

"We contend that the deference question should turn on a different feature of agency process, traditionally ignored in administrative law doctrine and scholarship—that is, the position in the agency hierarchy of the person assuming responsibility for the administrative decision. More briefly said, the Court should refocus its inquiry from the 'how' to the 'who' of administrative decision making. If the congressional delegatee of the relevant statutory grant of authority takes personal responsibility for the decision, then the agency should command obeisance, within the broad bounds of reasonableness, in resolving statutory ambiguity; if she does not, then the judiciary should render the ultimate interpretive decision. This agency nondelegation principle serves values familiar from the congressional brand of the doctrine, as well as from Chevron itself: by offering an incentive to certain actors to take responsibility for interpretive choice, the principle advances both accountability and discipline in decisionmaking. . . .

"The aspect of institutional design we emphasize here—call it the high level/low level distinction—justifies the result the Court reached in Mead, but only by fortuity. In other cases our approach would diverge significantly from the Court's—in granting deference even in the absence of formality or generality and, conversely, in refusing deference even in the face of these attributes. This approach also would diverge from Justice Scalia's, given the nearly unlimited deference he favors. But oddly enough, we see our approach as in some sense, even if in a sense unrecognized by the Justices themselves, present in all of their different views on the issue: because this is so, we see some potential for the Court to move toward, and even converge on, the . . . doctrine we advocate. . . ."

*CITY OF ARLINGTON, TEXAS v. FEDERAL COMMUNICATIONS COMMISSION*

## CITY OF ARLINGTON, TEXAS v. FEDERAL COMMUNICATIONS COMMISSION

Supreme Court of the United States (2013).
569 U.S. 290.

■ JUSTICE SCALIA delivered the opinion of the Court.

We consider whether an agency's interpretation of a statutory ambiguity that concerns the scope of its regulatory authority (that is, its jurisdiction) is entitled to deference under Chevron U.S.A. Inc. v. Natural Resources Defense Council, Inc., 467 U.S. 837 (1984).

I

Wireless telecommunications networks require towers and antennas; proposed sites for those towers and antennas must be approved by local zoning authorities. In the Telecommunications Act of 1996, Congress "impose[d] specific limitations on the traditional authority of state and local governments to regulate the location, construction, and modification of such facilities," Rancho Palos Verdes v. Abrams, 544 U.S. 113, 115 (2005), and incorporated those limitations into the Communications Act of 1934. Section 201(b) of that Act empowers the Federal Communications Commission to "prescribe such rules and regulations as may be necessary in the public interest to carry out [its] provisions." 47 U.S.C. § 201(b). Of course, that rulemaking authority extends to the subsequently added portions of the Act.

The Act imposes five substantive limitations, which are codified in 47 U.S.C. § 332(c)(7)(B); only one of them, § 332(c)(7)(B)(ii), is at issue here. That provision requires state or local governments to act on wireless siting applications "within a reasonable period of time after the request is duly filed." Two other features of § 332(c)(7) are relevant. First, subparagraph (A), known as the "saving clause," provides that nothing in the Act, except those limitations provided in § 332(c)(7)(B), "shall limit or affect the authority of a State or local government" over siting decisions. Second, § 332(c)(7)(B)(v) authorizes a person who believes a state or local government's wireless-siting decision to be inconsistent with any of the limitations in § 332(c)(7)(B) to "commence an action in any court of competent jurisdiction."

In theory, § 332(c)(7)(B)(ii) requires state and local zoning authorities to take prompt action on siting applications for wireless facilities. But in practice, wireless providers often faced long delays. In July 2008, CTIA—The Wireless Association, which represents wireless service providers, petitioned the FCC to clarify the meaning of § 332(c)(7)(B)(ii)'s requirement that zoning authorities act on siting requests "within a reasonable period of time." In November 2009, the Commission, relying on its broad statutory authority to implement the provisions of the Communications Act, issued a declaratory ruling responding to CTIA's petition. In re Petition for Declaratory Ruling, 24 FCC Rcd. 13994, 14001. The Commission found that the "record evidence demonstrates that unreasonable delays in the personal wireless service facility siting process have obstructed the provision of wireless services" and that such delays "impede the promotion of advanced services and competition that Congress deemed critical in the Telecommunications Act of 1996." Id., at 14006, 14008. A "reasonable period of time" under § 332(c)(7)(B)(ii), the Commission determined, is presumptively (but rebuttably) 90 days to process a collocation application (that is, an application to place a new antenna on an existing tower) and 150 days to process all other applications. Id., at 14005.

Some state and local governments opposed adoption of the Declaratory Ruling on the ground that the Commission lacked "authority to interpret ambiguous provisions of Section 332(c)(7)." Id., at 14000. Specifically, they argued that the saving clause, § 332(c)(7)(A), and the judicial review provision, § 337(c)(7)(B)(v), together display a congressional intent to withhold from the Commission authority to interpret the limitations in § 332(c)(7)(B). Asserting that ground of objection, the cities of Arlington and San Antonio, Texas, petitioned for review of the Declaratory Ruling in the Court of Appeals for the Fifth Circuit.

Relying on Circuit precedent, the Court of Appeals held that the Chevron framework applied to the threshold question whether the FCC possessed statutory authority to adopt the 90- and 150-day timeframes. 668 F.3d 229, 248 (C.A.5 2012). Applying Chevron, the Court of Appeals found "§ 332(c)(7)(A)'s effect on the FCC's authority to administer § 332(c)(7)(B)'s limitations ambiguous," 668 F.3d, at 250, and held that "the FCC's interpretation of its statutory authority" was a permissible construction of the statute. Id., at 254. On the merits, the court upheld the presumptive 90- and 150-day deadlines as a "permissible construction of § 332(c)(7)(B)(ii) and (v) . . . entitled to Chevron deference." Id., at 256.

We granted certiorari limited to the first question presented: "Whether . . . a court should apply Chevron to . . . an agency's determination of its own jurisdiction." Pet. for Cert. in No. 11–1545, p. i.

## II

### A

As this case turns on the scope of the doctrine enshrined in Chevron, we begin with a description of that case's now-canonical formulation. "When a court reviews an agency's construction of the statute which it administers, it is confronted with two questions." 467 U.S., at 842. First, applying the ordinary tools of statutory construction, the court must determine "whether Congress has directly spoken to the precise question at issue. If the intent of Congress is clear, that is the end of the matter; for the court, as well as the agency, must give effect to the unambiguously expressed intent of Congress." Id., at 842–843. But "if the statute is silent or ambiguous with respect to the specific issue, the question for the court is whether the agency's answer is based on a permissible construction of the statute." Id., at 843.

Chevron is rooted in a background presumption of congressional intent: namely, "that Congress, when it left ambiguity in a statute" administered by an agency, "understood that the ambiguity would be resolved, first and foremost, by the agency, and desired the agency (rather than the courts) to possess whatever degree of discretion the ambiguity allows." Smiley v. Citibank (South Dakota), N.A., 517 U.S. 735, 740–741 (1996). Chevron thus provides a stable background rule against which Congress can legislate: Statutory ambiguities will be resolved, within the bounds of reasonable interpretation, not by the courts but by the administering agency. Congress knows to speak in plain terms when it wishes to circumscribe, and in capacious terms when it wishes to enlarge, agency discretion.

B

The question here is whether a court must defer under Chevron to an agency's interpretation of a statutory ambiguity that concerns the scope of the agency's statutory authority (that is, its jurisdiction). The argument against deference rests on the premise that there exist two distinct classes of agency interpretations: Some interpretations—the big, important ones, presumably—define the agency's "jurisdiction." Others—humdrum, run-of-the-mill stuff—are simply applications of jurisdiction the agency plainly has. That premise is false, because the distinction between "jurisdictional" and "nonjurisdictional" interpretations is a mirage. No matter how it is framed, the question a court faces when confronted with an agency's interpretation of a statute it administers is always, simply, whether the agency has stayed within the bounds of its statutory authority.

The misconception that there are, for Chevron purposes, separate "jurisdictional" questions on which no deference is due derives, perhaps, from a reflexive extension to agencies of the very real division between the jurisdictional and nonjurisdictional that is applicable to courts. In the judicial context, there is a meaningful line: Whether the court decided correctly is a question that has different consequences from the question whether it had the power to decide at all. Congress has the power (within limits) to tell the courts what classes of cases they may decide, but not to prescribe or superintend how they decide those cases. A court's power to decide a case is independent of whether its decision is correct, which is why even an erroneous judgment is entitled to res judicata effect. Put differently, a jurisdictionally proper but substantively incorrect judicial decision is not ultra vires.

That is not so for agencies charged with administering congressional statutes. Both their power to act and how they are to act is authoritatively prescribed by Congress, so that when they act improperly, no less than when they act beyond their jurisdiction, what they do is ultra vires. Because the question—whether framed as an incorrect application of agency authority or an assertion of authority not conferred—is always whether the agency has gone beyond what Congress has permitted it to do, there is no principled basis for carving out some arbitrary subset of such claims as "jurisdictional."

An example will illustrate just how illusory the proposed line between "jurisdictional" and "nonjurisdictional" agency interpretations is. Imagine the following validly-enacted statute:

COMMON CARRIER ACT

SECTION 1. The Agency shall have jurisdiction to prohibit any common carrier from imposing an unreasonable condition upon access to its facilities.

There is no question that this provision—including the terms "common carrier" and "unreasonable condition"—defines the Agency's jurisdiction. Surely, the argument goes, a court must determine de novo the scope of that jurisdiction.

Consider, however, this alternative formulation of the statute:

COMMON CARRIER ACT

SECTION 1. No common carrier shall impose an unreasonable condition upon access to its facilities.

SECTION 2. The Agency may prescribe rules and regulations necessary in the public interest to effectuate Section 1 of this Act.

Now imagine that the Agency, invoking its Section 2 authority, promulgates this Rule: "(1) The term 'common carrier' in Section 1 includes Internet Service Providers. (2) The term 'unreasonable condition' in Section 1 includes unreasonably high prices. (3) A monthly fee greater than $25 is an unreasonable condition on access to Internet service." By this Rule, the Agency has claimed for itself jurisdiction that is doubly questionable: Does its authority extend to Internet Service Providers? And does it extend to setting prices? Yet Section 2 makes clear that Congress, in petitioners' words, "conferred interpretive power on the agency" with respect to Section 1. Brief for Petitioners in No. 1545, p. 14. Even under petitioners' theory, then, a court should defer to the Agency's interpretation of the terms "common carrier" and "unreasonable condition"—that is to say, its assertion that its "jurisdiction" extends to regulating Internet Service Providers and setting prices.

In the first case, by contrast, petitioners' theory would accord the agency no deference. The trouble with this is that in both cases, the underlying question is exactly the same: Does the statute give the agency authority to regulate Internet Service Providers and cap prices, or not? The reality, laid bare, is that there is no difference, insofar as the validity of agency action is concerned, between an agency's exceeding the scope of its authority (its "jurisdiction") and its exceeding authorized application of authority that it unquestionably has. . . .

This point is nicely illustrated by our decision in National Cable & Telecommunications Assn., Inc. v. Gulf Power Co., 534 U.S. 327 (2002). That case considered whether the FCC's "jurisdiction" to regulate the rents utility-pole owners charge for "pole attachments" (defined as attachments by a cable television system or provider of telecommunications service) extended to attachments that provided both cable television and high-speed Internet access (attachments for so-called "commingled services"). We held, sensibly, that Chevron applied. Whether framed as going to the scope of the FCC's delegated authority or the FCC's application of its delegated authority, the underlying question was the same: Did the FCC exceed the bounds of its statutory authority to regulate rents for "pole attachments" when it sought to regulate rents for pole attachments providing commingled services?

The label is an empty distraction because every new application of a broad statutory term can be reframed as a questionable extension of the agency's jurisdiction. One of the briefs in support of petitioners explains, helpfully, that "[j]urisdictional questions concern the who, what, where, and when of regulatory power: which subject matters may an agency regulate and under what conditions." Brief for IMLA Respondents 18–19. But an agency's application of its authority pursuant to statutory text answers the same questions. Who is an "outside salesman"? What is a "pole attachment"? Where do the "waters of the United States" end? When must a Medicare provider challenge a reimbursement determination in order to be entitled to an administrative appeal? These can all be reframed as questions about the scope of agencies' regulatory jurisdiction—and they are all questions to which the Chevron framework applies. See Christopher v. SmithKline Beecham Corp., 567 U.S. ___ (2012); National Cable & Telecommunications Assn., supra, at 331, 333; United States v. Riverside Bayview Homes, Inc., 474 U.S. 121, 123, 131 (1985); Sebelius v. Auburn Regional Medical Center, 568 U.S. ___ (2013).

In sum, judges should not waste their time in the mental acrobatics needed to decide whether an agency's interpretation of a statutory provision is "jurisdictional" or "nonjurisdictional." Once those labels are sheared away, it becomes clear that the question in every case is, simply, whether the statutory text forecloses the agency's assertion of authority, or not. The federal judge as haruspex, sifting the entrails of vast statutory schemes to divine whether a particular agency interpretation qualifies as "jurisdictional," is not engaged in reasoned decisionmaking.

C

Fortunately, then, we have consistently held "that Chevron applies to cases in which an agency adopts a construction of a jurisdictional provision of a statute it administers." 1 R. Pierce, Administrative Law Treatise § 3.5, p. 187 (2010). One of our opinions explicitly says that no "exception exists to the normal [deferential] standard of review" for " 'jurisdictional or legal question[s] concerning the coverage' " of an Act. NLRB v. City Disposal Systems, Inc., 465 U.S. 822, 830, n. 7 (1984). . . .

Similar examples abound. . . .

Our cases hold that Chevron applies equally to statutes designed to curtail the scope of agency discretion. . . .

The U.S. Reports are shot through with applications of Chevron to agencies' constructions of the scope of their own jurisdiction. And we have applied Chevron where concerns about agency self-aggrandizement are at their apogee: in cases where an agency's expansive construction of the extent of its own power would have wrought a fundamental change in the regulatory scheme. In FDA v. Brown & Williamson Tobacco Corp., 529 U.S. 120 (2000), the threshold question was the "appropriate framework for analyzing" the FDA's assertion of "jurisdiction to regulate tobacco products," id., at 126, 132—a question of vast "economic and political magnitude," id., at 133. "Because this case involves an administrative agency's construction of a statute that it administers," we held, Chevron applied. 529 U.S., at 13. Similarly, in MCI Telecommunications Corp. v. American Telephone & Telegraph Co., 512 U.S. 218 (1994), we applied the Chevron framework to the FCC's assertion that the statutory phrase "modify any requirement" gave it authority to eliminate rate-filing requirements, "the essential characteristic of a rate-regulated industry," for long-distance telephone carriers.

The false dichotomy between "jurisdictional" and "nonjurisdictional" agency interpretations may be no more than a bogeyman, but it is dangerous all the same. Like the Hound of the Baskervilles, it is conjured by those with greater quarry in sight: Make no mistake—the ultimate target here is Chevron itself. Savvy challengers of agency action would play the "jurisdictional" card in every case. Some judges would be deceived by the specious, but scary-sounding, "jurisdictional"-"nonjurisdictional" line; others tempted by the prospect of making public policy by prescribing the meaning of ambiguous statutory commands. The effect would be to transfer any number of interpretive decisions—archetypal Chevron questions, about how best to construe an ambiguous term in light of competing policy interests—from the agencies that administer the statutes to federal courts.[4] We have cautioned that "judges ought to refrain from substituting their own interstitial lawmaking" for that of an agency. Ford Motor Credit Co. v. Milhollin, 444 U.S. 555, 568 (1980). That is precisely what Chevron prevents.

III

A

One group of respondents contends that Chevron deference is inappropriate here because the FCC has "assert[ed] jurisdiction over matters of traditional state and local concern." Brief for IMLA Respondents 35. But this case has nothing to do with federalism. Section 332(c)(7)(B)(ii) explicitly supplants state authority by *requiring* zoning authorities to render a decision "within a reasonable period of time," and the meaning of that phrase is indisputably a question of federal law. We rejected a similar faux-federalism argument in the Iowa Utilities Board case, in terms that apply equally here: "This is, at bottom, a debate not about whether the States will be allowed to do their own thing, but about whether it will be the FCC or the federal courts that draw the lines to which they must hew." 525 U.S., at 379, n. 6. These lines will be drawn either by unelected federal bureaucrats, or by unelected (and even less politically accountable) federal judges. "[I]t is hard to spark a passionate 'States' rights' debate over that detail." Ibid.

---

[4] The Chief Justice's discomfort with the growth of agency power is perhaps understandable. But the dissent overstates when it claims that agencies exercise "legislative power" and "judicial power." The former is vested exclusively in Congress, U.S. Const., Art. I, § 1, the latter in the "one supreme Court" and "such inferior Courts as the Congress may from time to time ordain and establish," Art. III, § 1. Agencies make rules ("Private cattle may be grazed on public lands *X, Y,* and *Z* subject to certain conditions") and conduct adjudications ("This rancher's grazing permit is revoked for violation of the conditions") and have done so since the beginning of the Republic. These activities take "legislative" and "judicial" forms, but they are exercises of—indeed, under our constitutional structure they *must be* exercises of—the "executive Power." Art. II, § 1, cl. 1.

B

A few words in response to the dissent. The question on which we granted certiorari was whether "a court should apply Chevron to review an agency's determination of its own jurisdiction." Pet. for Cert. i. Perhaps sensing the incoherence of the "jurisdictional-nonjurisdictional" line, the dissent does not even attempt to defend it, but proposes a much broader scope for de novo judicial review: Jurisdictional or not, and even where a rule is at issue and the statute contains a broad grant of rulemaking authority, the dissent would have a court search provision-by-provision to determine "whether [that] delegation covers the 'specific provision' and 'particular question' before the court."

The dissent is correct that United States v. Mead Corp., 533 U.S. 218 (2001), requires that, for Chevron deference to apply, the agency must have received congressional authority to determine the particular matter at issue in the particular manner adopted. No one disputes that. But Mead denied Chevron deference to action, by an agency with rulemaking authority, that was not rulemaking. What the dissent needs, and fails to produce, is a single case in which a general conferral of rulemaking or adjudicative authority has been held insufficient to support Chevron deference for an exercise of that authority within the agency's substantive field. There is no such case, and what the dissent proposes is a massive revision of our Chevron jurisprudence.

Where we differ from the dissent is in its apparent rejection of the theorem that the whole includes all of its parts—its view that a general conferral of rulemaking authority does not validate rules for all the matters the agency is charged with administering. Rather, the dissent proposes that even when general rulemaking authority is clear, every agency rule must be subjected to a de novo judicial determination of whether the particular issue was committed to agency discretion. It offers no standards at all to guide this open-ended hunt for congressional intent (that is to say, for evidence of congressional intent more specific than the conferral of general rulemaking authority). It would simply punt that question back to the Court of Appeals, presumably for application of some sort of totality-of-the-circumstances test—which is really, of course, not a test at all but an invitation to make an ad hoc judgment regarding congressional intent. Thirteen Courts of Appeals applying a totality-of-the-circumstances test would render the binding effect of agency rules unpredictable and destroy the whole stabilizing purpose of Chevron. The excessive agency power that the dissent fears would be replaced by chaos. There is no need to wade into these murky waters. It suffices to decide this case that the preconditions to deference under Chevron are satisfied because Congress has unambiguously vested the FCC with general authority to administer the Communications Act through rulemaking and adjudication, and the agency interpretation at issue was promulgated in the exercise of that authority.

* * *

Those who assert that applying Chevron to "jurisdictional" interpretations "leaves the fox in charge of the henhouse" overlook the reality that a separate category of "jurisdictional" interpretations does not exist. The fox-in-the-henhouse syndrome is to be avoided not by establishing an arbitrary and undefinable category of agency decisionmaking that is accorded no deference, but by taking seriously, and applying rigorously, in all cases, statutory limits on agencies' authority. Where Congress has established a clear line, the agency cannot go beyond it; and where Congress has established an ambiguous line, the agency can go no further than the ambiguity will fairly allow. But in rigorously applying the latter rule, a court need not pause to puzzle over whether the interpretive question presented is "jurisdictional." If "the agency's answer is based on a permissible construction of the statute," that is the end of the matter. Chevron, 467 U.S., at 842.

The judgment of the Court of Appeals is affirmed.

■ JUSTICE BREYER, concurring in part and concurring in the judgment.

I agree with the Court that normally "the question a court faces when confronted with an agency's interpretation of a statute it administers" is, "simply, whether the agency has stayed within the bounds of its statutory authority." In this context, "the distinction between 'jurisdictional' and 'non-jurisdictional' interpretations is a mirage."

Deciding just what those statutory bounds are, however, is not always an easy matter, and the Court's case law abounds with discussion of the subject. A reviewing judge, for example, will have to decide independently whether Congress delegated authority to the agency to provide interpretations of, or to enact rules pursuant to, the statute at issue—interpretations or rules that carry with them "the force of law." United States v. Mead Corp., 533 U.S. 218, 229 (2001). If so, the reviewing court must give special leeway or "deference" to the agency's interpretation.

We have added that, if "[e]mploying traditional tools of statutory construction," INS v. Cardoza-Fonseca, 480 U.S. 421, 446 (1987), the court determines that Congress has spoken clearly on the disputed question, then "that is the end of the matter," Chevron U.S.A. Inc. v. Natural Resources Defense Council, Inc., 467 U.S. 837, 842 (1984). The agency is due no deference, for Congress has left no gap for the agency to fill. If, on the other hand, Congress has not spoken clearly, if, for example it has written ambiguously, then that ambiguity is a sign—but not always a conclusive sign—that Congress intends a reviewing court to pay particular attention to (i.e., to give a degree of deference to) the agency's interpretation. See Gonzales v. Oregon, 546 U.S. 243, 258–269 (2006); Mead, supra, at 229.

I say that the existence of statutory ambiguity is sometimes not enough to warrant the conclusion that Congress has left a deference-warranting gap for the agency to fill because our cases make clear that other, sometimes context-specific, factors will on occasion prove relevant. (And, given the vast number of government statutes, regulatory programs, and underlying circumstances, that variety is hardly surprising.) . . .

The subject matter of the relevant provision—for instance, its distance from the agency's ordinary statutory duties or its falling within the scope of another agency's authority—has also proved relevant. See Gonzales, supra, at 265–266.

Moreover, the statute's text, its context, the structure of the statutory scheme, and canons of textual construction are relevant in determining whether the statute is ambiguous and can be equally helpful in determining whether such ambiguity comes accompanied with agency authority to fill a gap with an interpretation that carries the force of law. Statutory purposes, including those revealed in part by legislative and regulatory history, can be similarly relevant.

Although seemingly complex in abstract description, in practice this framework has proved a workable way to approximate how Congress would likely have meant to allocate interpretive law-determining authority between reviewing court and agency. The question whether Congress has delegated to an agency the authority to provide an interpretation that carries the force of law is for the judge to answer independently. The judge, considering "traditional tools of statutory construction," will ask whether Congress has spoken unambiguously. If so, the text controls. If not, the judge will ask whether Congress would have intended the agency to resolve the resulting ambiguity. If so, deference is warranted. See Mead, supra, at 229. Even if not, however, sometimes an agency interpretation, in light of the agency's special expertise, will still have the "power to persuade, if lacking power to control," Skidmore v. Swift & Co., 323 U.S. 134 (1944).

The case before us offers an example. . . .

■ CHIEF JUSTICE ROBERTS, with whom JUSTICE KENNEDY and JUSTICE ALITO join, dissenting.

My disagreement with the Court is fundamental. It is also easily expressed: A court should not defer to an agency until the court decides, on its own, that the agency is entitled to deference. Courts defer to an agency's interpretation of law when and because Congress has conferred on the agency interpretive authority over the question at issue. An agency cannot exercise interpretive authority until it has it; the question whether an agency enjoys that authority must be decided by a court, without deference to the agency.

I

One of the principal authors of the Constitution famously wrote that the "accumulation of all powers, legislative, executive, and judiciary, in the same hands, . . . may justly be pronounced the very definition of tyranny." The Federalist No. 47, p. 324 (J. Cooke ed. 1961) (J. Madison). Although modern administrative agencies fit most comfortably within the Executive Branch, as a practical matter they exercise legislative power, by promulgating regulations with the force of law; executive power, by policing compliance with those regulations; and judicial power, by adjudicating enforcement actions and imposing sanctions on those found to have violated their rules. The accumulation of these powers in the same hands is not an occasional or isolated exception to the constitutional plan; it is a central feature of modern American government.

The administrative state "wields vast power and touches almost every aspect of daily life." Free Enterprise Fund v. Public Company Accounting Oversight Bd. The Framers could hardly have envisioned today's "vast and varied federal bureaucracy" and the authority administrative agencies now hold over our economic, social, and political activities. Ibid. . . . And the federal bureaucracy continues to grow; in the last 15 years, Congress has launched more than 50 new agencies. . . .

Although the Constitution empowers the President to keep federal officers accountable, administrative agencies enjoy in practice a significant degree of independence. As scholars have noted, "no President (or his executive office staff) could, and presumably none would wish to, supervise so broad a swath of regulatory activity." Kagan, Presidential Administration, 114 Harv. L. Rev. 2245, 2250 (2001) . . .

As for judicial oversight, agencies enjoy broad power to construe statutory provisions over which they have been given interpretive authority. In Chevron U.S.A. Inc. v. Natural Resources Defense Council, Inc., we established a test for reviewing "an agency's construction of the statute which it administers." 467 U.S. 837, 842 (1984). If Congress has "directly spoken to the precise question at issue," we said, "that is the end of the matter." Ibid. A contrary agency interpretation must give way. But if Congress has not expressed a specific intent, a court is bound to defer to any "permissible construction of the statute," even if that is not "the reading the court would have reached if the question initially had arisen in a judicial proceeding." Id., at 843, and n. 11.

When it applies, Chevron is a powerful weapon in an agency's regulatory arsenal. Congressional delegations to agencies are often ambiguous—expressing "a mood rather than a message." Friendly, The Federal Administrative Agencies: The Need for Better Definition of Standards, 75 Harv. L. Rev. 1263, 1311 (1962). By design or default, Congress often fails to speak to "the precise question" before an agency. In the absence of such an answer, an agency's interpretation has the full force and effect of law, unless it "exceeds the bounds of the permissible." Barnhart v. Walton, 535 U.S. 212, 218 (2002).

It would be a bit much to describe the result as "the very definition of tyranny," but the danger posed by the growing power of the administrative state cannot be dismissed. . . . What the Court says in footnote [1] of its opinion is good, and true (except of course for the "dissent overstates" part). The Framers did divide governmental power in the manner the Court describes, for the purpose of safeguarding liberty. And yet . . . the citizen confronting thousands of pages of regulations—promulgated by an agency directed by Congress to regulate, say, "in the public interest"—can perhaps be excused for thinking that it is the agency really doing the legislating. And with hundreds of federal agencies poking into every nook and cranny of daily life, that citizen might also understandably question whether Presidential oversight—a critical part of the Constitutional plan—is always an effective safeguard against agency overreaching.

It is against this background that we consider whether the authority of administrative agencies should be augmented even further, to include not only broad power to give definitive answers to questions left to them by Congress, but also the same power to decide when Congress has given them that power.

Before proceeding to answer that question, however, it is necessary to sort through some confusion over what this litigation is about. The source of the confusion is a familiar culprit: the concept of "jurisdiction," which we have repeatedly described as a word with " 'many, too many, meanings.' " Union Pacific R. Co. v. Locomotive Engineers, 558 U.S. 67, 81 (2009).

The Court states that the question "is whether a court must defer under Chevron to an agency's interpretation of a statutory ambiguity that concerns the scope of the agency's statutory authority (that is, its jurisdiction)." That is fine—until the parenthetical. The parties, amici, and court below too often use the term "jurisdiction" imprecisely, which leads the Court to misunderstand the argument it must confront. That argument is not that "there exist two distinct classes of agency interpretations," some "big, important ones" that "define the agency's 'jurisdiction,' " and other "humdrum, run-of-the-mill" ones that "are simply applications of jurisdiction the agency plainly has." The argument is instead that a court should not defer to an agency on whether Congress has granted the agency interpretive authority over the statutory ambiguity at issue.

You can call that "jurisdiction" if you'd like, as petitioners do in the question presented. But given that the term is ambiguous, more is required to understand its use in that question than simply "having read it." It is important to keep in mind that the term, in the present context, has the more precise meaning noted above, encompassing congressionally delegated authority to issue interpretations with the force and effect of law. And that has nothing do with whether the statutory provisions at issue are "big" or "small."

II

"It is emphatically the province and duty of the judicial department to say what the law is." Marbury v. Madison, 1 Cranch 137, 177 (1803). The rise of the modern administrative state has not changed that duty. Indeed, the Administrative Procedure Act, governing judicial review of most agency action, instructs reviewing courts to decide "all relevant questions of law." 5 U.S.C. § 706.

We do not ignore that command when we afford an agency's statutory interpretation Chevron deference; we respect it. We give binding deference to permissible agency interpretations of statutory ambiguities because Congress has delegated to the agency the authority to interpret those ambiguities "with the force of law." United States v. Mead Corp., 533 U.S. 218, 229 (2001); see also Monaghan, Marbury and the Administrative State, 83 Colum. L.Rev. 1, 27–28 (1983) ("the court is not abdicating its constitutional duty to 'say what the law is' by deferring to agency interpretations of law: it is simply applying the law as 'made' by the authorized law-making entity").

But before a court may grant such deference, it must on its own decide whether Congress—the branch vested with lawmaking authority under the Constitution—has in fact delegated to the agency lawmaking power over the ambiguity at issue. Agencies are creatures of Congress; "an agency literally has no power to act . . . unless and until Congress confers power upon it." Louisiana Pub. Serv. Comm'n v. FCC, 476 U.S. 355, 374 (1986). Whether Congress has conferred such power is the "relevant question[ ] of law" that must be answered before affording Chevron deference. 5 U.S.C. § 706.

III

A

Our precedents confirm this conclusion—beginning with Chevron itself. In Chevron, the EPA promulgated a regulation interpreting the term "stationary sources" in the Clean Air Act. An environmental group petitioned for review of the rule, challenging it as an impermissible interpretation of the Act. Finding the statutory text "not dispositive" and the legislative history "silent on the precise issue," we upheld the rule. 467 U.S. at 862, 866.

In our view, the challenge to the agency's interpretation "center[ed] on the wisdom of the agency's policy, rather than whether it is a reasonable choice within a gap left open by Congress." Id., at 866. Judges, we said, "are not experts in the field, and are not part of either political branch of the Government." Id., at 865. Thus, because Congress had not answered the specific question at issue, judges had no business providing their own resolution on the basis of their "personal policy preferences." Ibid. Instead, the "agency to which Congress ha[d] delegated policymaking responsibilities" was the appropriate political actor to resolve the competing interests at stake, "within the limits of that delegation." Ibid.

Chevron's rule of deference was based on—and limited by—this congressional delegation. And the Court did not ask simply whether Congress had delegated to the EPA the authority to administer the Clean Air Act generally. We asked whether Congress had "delegat[ed] authority to the agency to elucidate a *specific provision* of the statute by regulation." Id., at 843–844 (emphasis added); see id., at 844 (discussing "the legislative delegation to an agency on a *particular question*" (emphasis added)). We deferred to the EPA's interpretation of "stationary sources" based on our conclusion that the agency had been "charged with responsibility for administering *the provision.*" Id., at 865 (emphasis added).

B

We have never faltered in our understanding of this straightforward principle, that whether a particular agency interpretation warrants Chevron deference turns on the court's determination whether Congress has delegated to the agency the authority to interpret the statutory ambiguity at issue. . . .

In Mead, we again made clear that the "category of interpretative choices" to which Chevron deference applies is defined by congressional intent. Id., at 229. Chevron deference, we said, rests on a recognition that Congress has delegated to an agency the interpretive authority to implement "a particular provision" or answer " 'a particular question.' " Ibid. (quoting Chevron, 467 U.S., at 844). An agency's interpretation of "a particular statutory provision" thus qualifies for Chevron deference only "when it appears that Congress delegated authority to the agency generally to make rules carrying the force of law, and that the agency interpretation claiming deference was promulgated in the exercise of that authority." 533 U.S., at 226–227. . . . .

[These cases] thus confirm that Chevron deference is based on, and finds legitimacy as, a congressional delegation of interpretive authority. An agency interpretation warrants such deference only if Congress has delegated authority to definitively interpret a particular ambiguity in a particular manner. Whether Congress has done so must be determined by the court on its own before Chevron can apply. . . .

In other words, we do not defer to an agency's interpretation of an ambiguous provision unless Congress wants us to, and whether Congress wants us to is a question that courts, not agencies, must decide. Simply put, that question is "beyond the Chevron pale." Mead, supra, at 234.

IV

Despite these precedents, the FCC argues that a court need only locate an agency and a grant of general rulemaking authority over a statute. Chevron deference then applies, it contends, to the agency's interpretation of any ambiguity in the Act, including ambiguity in a provision said to carve out specific provisions from the agency's general rulemaking authority. If Congress intends to exempt part of the statute from the agency's interpretive authority, the FCC says, Congress "can ordinarily be expected to state that intent explicitly." Brief for Federal Respondents 30 (citing American Hospital Assn. v. NLRB, 499 U.S. 606 (1991)).

If a congressional delegation of interpretive authority is to support Chevron deference, however, that delegation must extend to the specific statutory ambiguity at issue. The appropriate question is whether the delegation covers the "specific provision" and "particular question" before the court. Chevron, 467 U.S., at 844. A congressional grant of authority over some portion of a statute does not necessarily mean that Congress granted the agency interpretive authority over all its provisions. See Adams Fruit, 494 U.S., at 650.

An example that might highlight the point concerns statutes that parcel out authority to multiple agencies, which "may be the norm, rather than an exception." Gersen, Overlapping and Underlapping Jurisdiction in Administrative Law, 2006 S.Ct. Rev. 201, 208. The Dodd-Frank Wall Street Reform and Consumer Protection Act, for example, authorizes rulemaking by at least eight different agencies. When presented with an agency's interpretation of such a statute, a court cannot simply ask whether the statute is one that the agency administers; the question is whether authority over the particular ambiguity at issue has been delegated to the particular agency.

By the same logic, even when Congress provides interpretive authority to a single agency, a court must decide if the ambiguity the agency has purported to interpret with the force of law is one to which the congressional delegation extends. A general delegation to the agency to administer the statute will often suffice to satisfy the court that Congress has delegated interpretive authority over the ambiguity at issue. But if Congress has exempted particular provisions from that authority, that exemption must be respected, and the determination whether Congress has done so is for the courts alone.

The FCC's argument that Congress "can ordinarily be expected to state that intent explicitly," Brief for Federal Respondents 30 (citing American Hospital, supra), goes to the merits of that determination, not to whether a court should decide the question de novo or defer to the agency. Indeed, that is how the Court in American Hospital considered it. It was in the process of "employing the traditional tools of statutory construction" that the Court said it would have expected Congress to speak more clearly if it had intended to exclude an entire subject area—employee units for collecting bargaining—from the NLRB's general rulemaking authority. Id., at 613, 614. The Court concluded, after considering the language, structure, policy, and legislative history of the Act on its own—without deferring to the agency—that the meaning of the statute was "clear and contrary to the meaning advanced by petitioner." Id., at 609–614. To be sure, the Court also noted that "[e]ven if we *could* find any ambiguity in [the provision] after employing the traditional tools of statutory construction, we would still defer to Board's reasonable interpretation." Id., at 614 (emphasis added). But that single sentence of dictum cannot carry the day for the FCC here.

## V

As the preceding analysis makes clear, I do not understand petitioners to ask the Court—nor do I think it necessary—to draw a "specious, but scary-sounding" line between "big, important" interpretations on the one hand and "humdrum, run-of-the-mill" ones on the other. Drawing such a line may well be difficult. Distinguishing between whether an agency's interpretation of an ambiguous term is reasonable and whether that term is for the agency to interpret is not nearly so difficult. . . . More importantly, if the legitimacy of Chevron deference is based on a congressional delegation of interpretive authority, then the line is one the Court must draw.

The majority's hypothetical Common Carrier Acts do not demonstrate anything different. The majority states that in its second Common Carrier Act, Section 2 makes clear that Congress " 'conferred interpretative power on the agency' " to interpret the ambiguous terms "common carrier" and "unreasonable condition." Thus, it says, under anyone's theory a court must defer to the agency's reasonable interpretations of those terms. Correct.

The majority claims, however, that "petitioners' theory would accord the agency no deference" in its interpretation of the same ambiguous terms in the first Common Carrier Act. But as I understand petitioners' argument—and certainly in my own view—a court, in both cases, need only decide for itself whether Congress has delegated to the agency authority to interpret the ambiguous terms, before affording the agency's interpretation Chevron deference.

For the second Common Carrier Act, the answer is easy. The majority's hypothetical Congress has spoken clearly and specifically in Section 2 of the Act about its delegation of authority to interpret Section 1. As for the first Act, it is harder to analyze the question, given only one section of a presumably much larger statute. But if the first Common Carrier Act is like most agencies' organic statutes, I have no reason to doubt that the agency would likewise have interpretive authority over the same ambiguous terms, and therefore be entitled to deference in construing them, just as with the second Common Carrier Act. There is no new "test" to worry about; courts would simply apply the normal rules of statutory construction.

That the question might be harder with respect to the first Common Carrier Act should come as no surprise. The second hypothetical Congress has more carefully defined the agency's authority than the first. Whatever standard of review applies, it is more difficult to interpret an unclear statute than a clear one. My point is simply that before a court can defer to the agency's interpretation of the ambiguous terms in either Act, it must determine for itself that Congress has delegated authority to the agency to issue those interpretations with the force of law.

The majority also expresses concern that adopting petitioners' position would undermine Chevron's stable background rule against which Congress legislates. That, of course, begs the question of what that stable background rule is. . . .

VI

The Court sees something nefarious behind the view that courts must decide on their own whether Congress has delegated interpretative authority to an agency, before deferring to that agency's interpretation of law. What is afoot, according to the Court, is a judicial power-grab, with nothing less than "Chevron itself" as "the ultimate target."

The Court touches on a legitimate concern: Chevron importantly guards against the Judiciary arrogating to itself policymaking properly left, under the separation of powers, to the Executive. But there is another concern at play, no less firmly rooted in our constitutional structure. That is the obligation of the Judiciary not only to confine itself to its proper role, but to ensure that the other branches do so as well.

An agency's interpretive authority, entitling the agency to judicial deference, acquires its legitimacy from a delegation of lawmaking power from Congress to the Executive. Our duty to police the boundary between the Legislature and the Executive is as critical as our duty to respect that between the Judiciary and the Executive. In the present context, that means ensuring that the Legislative Branch has in fact delegated lawmaking power to an agency within the Executive Branch, before the Judiciary defers to the Executive on what the law is. That concern is heightened, not diminished, by the fact that the administrative agencies, as a practical matter, draw upon a potent brew of executive, legislative, and judicial power. And it is heightened, not diminished, by the dramatic shift in power over the last 50 years from Congress to the Executive—a shift effected through the administrative agencies.

We reconcile our competing responsibilities in this area by ensuring judicial deference to agency interpretations under Chevron—but only after we have determined on our own that Congress has given interpretive authority to the agency. Our "task is to fix the boundaries of delegated authority," Monaghan, 83 Colum. L.Rev., at 27; that is not a task we can delegate to the agency. We do not leave it to the agency to decide when it is in charge.

## NOTES

(1) ***Where Is Skidmore?*** There is much discussion in the City of Arlington opinions about Chevron, but where is Skidmore deference? See Peter L. Strauss, In Search of Skidmore, 83 Fordham L. Rev. 789, 792 (2014): "In Justice Scalia's majority opinion and Chief Justice Roberts's dissent for himself and Justices Kennedy and Alito, 184 years of what we have recently been calling Skidmore deference simply disappeared. Save once in Justice Breyer's lonely concurrence in the result, there is not a mention of the concept . . . in opinions signed by eight of the Justices." Is this a meaningful omission? Or is it just a reflection of the abstractness of the question presented, at least as seen by all the Justices other than Breyer?

Chief Justice Roberts suggests that the only way to make Chevron consistent with the APA standards for judicial review is to adopt his approach. Is he right? Even if he is, should he also have said something about Skidmore? Even if the job of deciding whether Congress had delegated substantive authority to the agency on the matter at hand was for the independent judgment of the courts, didn't Skidmore and its many predecessors say that the courts, in exercising that independent judgment, should consider what weight the agency's expert view might have? Wouldn't the FCC have some insight into the interrelationship of local, state, and federal authorities in this industry that would help the court understand why Congress set up this statutory provision in the way it did? In fact, if Chief Justice Roberts would follow Skidmore, wouldn't that strengthen his argument by making it more sensitive to the practical difficulties judges may have in resolving ambiguities?

(2) ***Elephants and Mouseholes.*** Are there echoes in the dispute here of the proposition that courts can sometimes identify issues that are of such importance as to require congressional determination? Justice Scalia makes fun of the idea that the courts would be asked to distinguish between "two distinct classes of agency interpretations": "the big, important ones" that would constitute jurisdictional matters and the "humdrum, run-of-the-mill stuff" that would be "simply applications of jurisdiction." The distinction, he says, is a "mirage." And Chief Justice Roberts abjures making any such distinction. But fun aside, is it so crazy to say that courts should treat differently an agency's "big, important" decisions from its "run-of-the-mill" stuff? Is it, in fact, so different from Justice Scalia's own principle of statutory interpretation, to be used in applying Chevron, that "Congress . . . does not alter the fundamental details of a regulatory scheme in vague terms of ancillary provisions—it does not, one might say, hide elephants in mouseholes"? (Whitman v. American Trucking Ass'ns, Inc., p. 1345.) (His treatment of "modify" in MCI v. AT&T (p. 1254) is to similar effect, and overlaps significantly with the discussion of the "major questions doctrine" immediately below.) To apply this principle, mustn't courts be able to tell what is, and isn't, an "elephant"?

(3) ***A Connection to King v. Burwell?*** Go back now and read (or reread, if you have already encountered it), King v. Burwell (p. 108), and consider whether the Chief Justice's refusal to use Chevron in the service of the conclusion he reaches has a similar impetus.

*MASSACHUSETTS v. ENVIRONMENTAL PROTECTION AGENCY*
***Notes on FDA v. Brown & Williamson Tobacco Corp.***

## MASSACHUSETTS v. ENVIRONMENTAL PROTECTION AGENCY

Supreme Court of the United States (2007).
549 U.S. 497.

■ JUSTICE STEVENS delivered the opinion of the Court.

A well-documented rise in global temperatures has coincided with a significant increase in the concentration of carbon dioxide in the atmosphere. Respected scientists believe the two trends are related. For when carbon dioxide is released into the atmosphere, it acts like the ceiling of a greenhouse, trapping solar energy and retarding the escape of reflected heat. It is therefore a species—the most important species—of a "greenhouse gas."

Calling global warming "the most pressing environmental challenge of our time," a group of States, local governments, and private organizations, alleged in a petition for certiorari that the Environmental Protection Agency (EPA) has abdicated its responsibility under the Clean Air Act to regulate the emissions of four greenhouse gases, including carbon dioxide. Specifically, petitioners asked us to answer two questions concerning the meaning of § 202(a)(1) of the Act: whether EPA has the statutory authority to regulate greenhouse gas emissions from new motor vehicles; and if so, whether its stated reasons for refusing to do so are consistent with the statute.

In response, EPA, supported by 10 intervening States and six trade associations, correctly argued that we may not address those two questions unless at least one petitioner has standing to invoke our jurisdiction under Article III of the Constitution. Notwithstanding the serious character of that jurisdictional argument and the absence of any conflicting decisions construing § 202(a)(1), the unusual importance of the underlying issue persuaded us to grant the writ.

I

Section 202(a)(1) of the Clean Air Act provides:

> The [EPA] Administrator shall by regulation prescribe (and from time to time revise) in accordance with the provisions of this section, standards applicable to the emission of any air pollutant from any class or classes of new motor vehicles or new motor vehicle engines, which in his judgment cause, or contribute to, air pollution which may reasonably be anticipated to endanger public health or welfare. . . .

The Act defines "air pollutant" to include "any air pollution agent or combination of such agents, including any physical, chemical, biological, radioactive . . . substance or matter which is emitted into or otherwise enters the ambient air." § 7602(g). "Welfare" is also defined broadly: among other things, it includes "effects on . . . weather . . . and climate." § 7602(h).

When Congress enacted these provisions, the study of climate change was in its infancy. In 1959, shortly after the U.S. Weather Bureau began monitoring atmospheric carbon dioxide levels, an observatory in Mauna Loa, Hawaii, recorded a mean level of 316 parts per million. This was well above the highest carbon dioxide concentration—no more than 300 parts per million—revealed in the 420,000-year-old ice-core record. By the time Congress drafted § 202(a)(1) in 1970, carbon dioxide levels had reached 325 parts per million.

In the late 1970's, the Federal Government began devoting serious attention to the possibility that carbon dioxide emissions associated with human activity could provoke climate change. In 1978, Congress enacted the National Climate Program Act, 92 Stat. 601, which required the President to establish a program to "assist the Nation and the world to understand and respond to natural and man-induced climate processes and their implications," id., § 3. President Carter, in turn, asked the

National Research Council, the working arm of the National Academy of Sciences, to investigate the subject. The Council's response was unequivocal: "If carbon dioxide continues to increase, the study group finds no reason to doubt that climate changes will result and no reason to believe that these changes will be negligible. . . . A wait-and-see policy may mean waiting until it is too late."

Congress next addressed the issue in 1987, when it enacted the Global Climate Protection Act, 101 Stat. 1407. . . . Congress directed EPA to propose to Congress a "coordinated national policy on global climate change," § 1103(b), and ordered the Secretary of State to work "through the channels of multilateral diplomacy" and coordinate diplomatic efforts to combat global warming, § 1103(c). Congress emphasized that "ongoing pollution and deforestation may be contributing now to an irreversible process" and that "[n]ecessary actions must be identified and implemented in time to protect the climate." § 1102(4).

Meanwhile, the scientific understanding of climate change progressed. In 1990, the Intergovernmental Panel on Climate Change (IPCC), a multinational scientific body organized under the auspices of the United Nations, published its first comprehensive report on the topic. Drawing on expert opinions from across the globe, the IPCC concluded that "emissions resulting from human activities are substantially increasing the atmospheric concentrations of . . . greenhouse gases [which] will enhance the greenhouse effect, resulting on average in an additional warming of the Earth's surface."

Responding to the IPCC report, the United Nations convened the "Earth Summit" in 1992 in Rio de Janeiro. The first President Bush attended and signed the United Nations Framework Convention on Climate Change (UNFCCC), a nonbinding agreement among 154 nations to reduce atmospheric concentrations of carbon dioxide and other greenhouse gases for the purpose of "prevent[ing] dangerous anthropogenic [i.e., human-induced] interference with the [Earth's] climate system." S. Treaty Doc. No. 102–38, Art. 2, p. 5 (1992). The Senate unanimously ratified the treaty.

Some five years later—after the IPCC issued a second comprehensive report in 1995 concluding that "[t]he balance of evidence suggests there is a discernible human influence on global climate"—the UNFCCC signatories met in Kyoto, Japan, and adopted a protocol that assigned mandatory targets for industrialized nations to reduce greenhouse gas emissions. Because those targets did not apply to developing and heavily polluting nations such as China and India, the Senate unanimously passed a resolution expressing its sense that the United States should not enter into the Kyoto Protocol. President Clinton did not submit the protocol to the Senate for ratification.

II

On October 20, 1999, a group of 19 private organizations filed a rulemaking petition asking EPA to regulate "greenhouse gas emissions from new motor vehicles under § 202 of the Clean Air Act." . . . As to

EPA's statutory authority, the petition observed that the agency itself had already confirmed that it had the power to regulate carbon dioxide. In 1998, Jonathan Z. Cannon, then EPA's General Counsel, prepared a legal opinion concluding that "$CO_2$ emissions are within the scope of EPA's authority to regulate," even as he recognized that EPA had so far declined to exercise that authority. Cannon's successor, Gary S. Guzy, reiterated that opinion before a congressional committee just two weeks before the rulemaking petition was filed.

Fifteen months after the petition's submission, EPA requested public comment on "all the issues raised in [the] petition," adding a "particular" request for comments on "any scientific, technical, legal, economic or other aspect of these issues that may be relevant to EPA's consideration of this petition." 66 Fed.Reg. 7486, 7487 (2001). EPA received more than 50,000 comments over the next five months.

Before the close of the comment period, the White House sought "assistance in identifying the areas in the science of climate change where there are the greatest certainties and uncertainties" from the National Research Council, asking for a response "as soon as possible." The result was a 2001 report titled Climate Change: An Analysis of Some Key Questions (NRC Report), which, drawing heavily on the 1995 IPCC report, concluded that "[g]reenhouse gases are accumulating in Earth's atmosphere as a result of human activities, causing surface air temperatures and subsurface ocean temperatures to rise. Temperatures are, in fact, rising." NRC Report 1.

On September 8, 2003, EPA entered an order denying the rulemaking petition. 68 Fed. Reg. 52922. The agency gave two reasons for its decision: (1) that contrary to the opinions of its former general counsels, the Clean Air Act does not authorize EPA to issue mandatory regulations to address global climate change; and (2) that even if the agency had the authority to set greenhouse gas emission standards, it would be unwise to do so at this time.

In concluding that it lacked statutory authority over greenhouse gases, EPA observed that Congress "was well aware of the global climate change issue when it last comprehensively amended the [Clean Air Act] in 1990," yet it declined to adopt a proposed amendment establishing binding emissions limitations. Id., at 52926. Congress instead chose to authorize further investigation into climate change. EPA further reasoned that Congress' "specially tailored solutions to global atmospheric issues," id.—in particular, its 1990 enactment of a comprehensive scheme to regulate pollutants that depleted the ozone layer—counseled against reading the general authorization of § 202(a)(1) to confer regulatory authority over greenhouse gases.

EPA stated that it was "urged on in this view" by this Court's decision in FDA v. Brown & Williamson Tobacco Corp., 529 U.S. 120 (2000). In that case, relying on "tobacco[’s] unique political history," id., at 159, we invalidated the Food and Drug Administration's reliance on its general authority to regulate drugs as a basis for asserting jurisdiction over an "industry constituting a significant portion of the American economy," ibid.

EPA reasoned that climate change had its own "political history": Congress designed the original Clean Air Act to address *local* air pollutants rather than a substance that "is fairly consistent in its concentration throughout the *world's* atmosphere," 68 Fed. Reg. 52927; declined in 1990 to enact proposed amendments to force EPA to set carbon dioxide emission standards for motor vehicles; and addressed global climate change in other legislation. Because of this political history, and because imposing emission limitations on greenhouse gases would have even greater economic and political repercussions than regulating tobacco, EPA was persuaded that it lacked the power to do so. In essence, EPA concluded that climate change was so important that unless Congress spoke with exacting specificity, it could not have meant the agency to address it.

Having reached that conclusion, EPA believed it followed that greenhouse gases cannot be "air pollutants" within the meaning of the Act. See ibid. . . . The agency bolstered this conclusion by explaining that if carbon dioxide were an air pollutant, the only feasible method of reducing tailpipe emissions would be to improve fuel economy. But because Congress has already created detailed mandatory fuel economy standards subject to Department of Transportation (DOT) administration, the agency concluded that EPA regulation would either conflict with those standards or be superfluous.

Even assuming that it had authority over greenhouse gases, EPA explained in detail why it would refuse to exercise that authority. The agency began by recognizing that the concentration of greenhouse gases has dramatically increased as a result of human activities, and acknowledged the attendant increase in global surface air temperatures. EPA nevertheless gave controlling importance to the NRC Report's statement that a causal link between the two " 'cannot be unequivocally established.' " Ibid. (quoting NRC Report 17). Given that residual uncertainty, EPA concluded that regulating greenhouse gas emissions would be unwise.

The agency furthermore characterized any EPA regulation of motor-vehicle emissions as a "piecemeal approach" to climate change, and stated that such regulation would conflict with the President's "comprehensive approach" to the problem, id., at 52932. That approach involves additional support for technological innovation, the creation of nonregulatory programs to encourage voluntary private-sector reductions in greenhouse gas emissions, and further research on climate change—not actual regulation. According to EPA, unilateral EPA regulation of motor-vehicle greenhouse gas emissions might also hamper the President's ability to persuade key developing countries to reduce greenhouse gas emissions.

III

Petitioners . . . sought review of EPA's order in the United States Court of Appeals for the District of Columbia Circuit [which upheld the Administrator].

IV

[Massachusetts has standing to pursue this litigation. This portion of the opinion appears at p. 1473.]

V

The scope of our review of the merits of the statutory issues is narrow. As we have repeated time and again, an agency has broad discretion to choose how best to marshal its limited resources and personnel to carry out its delegated responsibilities. See Chevron. That discretion is at its height when the agency decides not to bring an enforcement action. Therefore, in Heckler v. Chaney, 470 U.S. 821 (1985) [p. 1527], we held that an agency's refusal to initiate enforcement proceedings is not ordinarily subject to judicial review. Some debate remains, however, as to the rigor with which we review an agency's denial of a petition for rulemaking.

There are key differences between a denial of a petition for rulemaking and an agency's decision not to initiate an enforcement action. See American Horse Protection Assn., Inc. v. Lyng, 812 F.2d 1, 3–4 (C.A.D.C.1987). In contrast to nonenforcement decisions, agency refusals to initiate rulemaking "are less frequent, more apt to involve legal as opposed to factual analysis, and subject to special formalities, including a public explanation." Id., at 4; see also 5 U.S.C. § 555(e). They moreover arise out of denials of petitions for rulemaking which (at least in the circumstances here) the affected party had an undoubted procedural right to file in the first instance. Refusals to promulgate rules are thus susceptible to judicial review, though such review is "extremely limited" and "highly deferential." National Customs Brokers & Forwarders Assn. of America, Inc. v. United States, 883 F.2d 93, 96 1989). . . .

VI

On the merits, the first question is whether § 202(a)(1) of the Clean Air Act authorizes EPA to regulate greenhouse gas emissions from new motor vehicles in the event that it forms a "judgment" that such emissions contribute to climate change. We have little trouble concluding that it does. In relevant part, § 202(a)(1) provides that EPA "shall by regulation prescribe . . . standards applicable to the emission of any air pollutant from any class or classes of new motor vehicles or new motor vehicle engines, which in [the Administrator's] judgment cause, or contribute to, air pollution which may reasonably be anticipated to endanger public health or welfare." 42 U.S.C. § 7521(a)(1). Because EPA believes that Congress did not intend it to regulate substances that contribute to climate change, the agency maintains that carbon dioxide is not an "air pollutant" within the meaning of the provision.

The statutory text forecloses EPA's reading. The Clean Air Act's sweeping definition of "air pollutant" includes "*any* air pollution agent or combination of such agents, including *any* physical, chemical . . . substance or matter which is emitted into or otherwise enters the ambient air. . . ." § 7602(g) (emphasis added). On its face, the definition embraces all airborne compounds of whatever stripe, and underscores that intent through the repeated use of the word "any." Carbon dioxide, methane, nitrous oxide, and hydro-fluorocarbons are without a doubt "physical [and] chemical . . . substance[s] which [are] emitted into . . . the ambient air." The statute is unambiguous.

. . . That subsequent Congresses have eschewed enacting binding emissions limitations to combat global warming tells us nothing about what Congress meant when it amended § 202(a)(1) in 1970 and 1977. . . .

EPA's reliance on Brown & Williamson Tobacco Corp., 529 U.S. 120 (2000) [p. 1338] is similarly misplaced. In holding that tobacco products are not "drugs" or "devices" subject to Food and Drug Administration (FDA) regulation pursuant to the Food, Drug and Cosmetic Act (FDCA), we found critical at least two considerations that have no counterpart in this case.

First, we thought it unlikely that Congress meant to ban tobacco products, which the FDCA would have required had such products been classified as "drugs" or "devices." Here, in contrast, EPA jurisdiction would lead to no such extreme measures. EPA would only *regulate* emissions, and even then, it would have to delay any action "to permit the development and application of the requisite technology, giving appropriate consideration to the cost of compliance," § 7521(a)(2). However much a ban on tobacco products clashed with the "common sense" intuition that Congress never meant to remove those products from circulation, there is nothing counterintuitive to the notion that EPA can curtail the emission of substances that are putting the global climate out of kilter.

Second, in Brown & Williamson we pointed to an unbroken series of congressional enactments that made sense only if adopted "against the backdrop of the FDA's consistent and repeated statements that it lacked authority under the FDCA to regulate tobacco." Id., at 144. We can point to no such enactments here: EPA has not identified any congressional action that conflicts in any way with the regulation of greenhouse gases from new motor vehicles. Even if it had, Congress could not have acted against a regulatory "backdrop" of disclaimers of regulatory authority. Prior to the order that provoked this litigation, EPA had never disavowed the authority to regulate greenhouse gases, and in 1998 it in fact affirmed that it *had* such authority. There is no reason, much less a compelling reason, to accept EPA's invitation to read ambiguity into a clear statute.

EPA finally argues that it cannot regulate carbon dioxide emissions from motor vehicles because doing so would require it to tighten mileage standards, a job (according to EPA) that Congress has assigned to DOT. See 68 Fed. Reg. 52929. But that DOT sets mileage standards in no way licenses EPA to shirk its environmental responsibilities. EPA has been charged with protecting the public's "health" and "welfare," 42 U.S.C. § 7521(a)(1), a statutory obligation wholly independent of DOT's mandate to promote energy efficiency. The two obligations may overlap, but there is no reason to think the two agencies cannot both administer their obligations and yet avoid inconsistency.

While the Congresses that drafted § 202(a)(1) might not have appreciated the possibility that burning fossil fuels could lead to global warming, they did understand that without regulatory flexibility, changing circumstances and scientific developments would soon render the Clean Air Act obsolete. The broad language of § 202(a)(1) reflects an intentional effort to confer the flexibility necessary to forestall such obsolescence. Because greenhouse gases fit well within the Clean Air Act's capacious definition of "air pollutant," we hold that EPA has the statutory authority to regulate the emission of such gases from new motor vehicles.

VII

The alternative basis for EPA's decision—that even if it does have statutory authority to regulate greenhouse gases, it would be unwise to do so at this time—rests on reasoning divorced from the statutory text. While the statute does condition the exercise of EPA's authority on its formation of a "judgment," 42 U.S.C. § 7521(a)(1), that judgment must relate to whether an air pollutant "cause[s], or contribute[s] to, air pollution which may reasonably be anticipated to endanger public health or welfare," ibid. Put another way, the use of the word "judgment" is not a roving license to ignore the statutory text. It is but a direction to exercise discretion within defined statutory limits.

If EPA makes a finding of endangerment, the Clean Air Act requires the agency to regulate emissions of the deleterious pollutant from new motor vehicles. Ibid. (stating that "[EPA] shall by regulation prescribe . . . standards applicable to the emission of any air pollutant from any class of new motor vehicles"). EPA no doubt has significant latitude as to the manner, timing, content, and coordination of its regulations with those of other agencies. But once EPA has responded to a petition for rulemaking, its reasons for action or inaction must conform to the authorizing statute. Under the clear terms of the Clean Air Act, EPA can avoid taking further action only if it determines that greenhouse gases do not contribute to climate change or if it provides some reasonable explanation as to why it cannot or will not exercise its discretion to determine whether they do. To the extent that this constrains agency discretion to pursue other priorities of the Administrator or the President, this is the congressional design.

EPA has refused to comply with this clear statutory command. Instead, it has offered a laundry list of reasons not to regulate. For example, EPA said that a number of voluntary executive branch programs already provide an effective response to the threat of global warming, 68 Fed. Reg. 52932, that regulating greenhouse gases might impair the President's ability to negotiate with "key developing nations" to reduce emissions, id., at 52931, and that curtailing motor-vehicle emissions would reflect "an inefficient, piecemeal approach to address the climate change issue," ibid.

Although we have neither the expertise nor the authority to evaluate these policy judgments, it is evident they have nothing to do with whether greenhouse gas emissions contribute to climate change. Still less do they amount to a reasoned justification for declining to form a scientific judgment. In particular, while the President has broad authority in foreign affairs, that authority does not extend to the refusal to execute domestic laws. . . .

Nor can EPA avoid its statutory obligation by noting the uncertainty surrounding various features of climate change and concluding that it would therefore be better not to regulate at this time. See 68 Fed. Reg. 52930–52931. If the scientific uncertainty is so profound that it precludes EPA from making a reasoned judgment as to whether greenhouse gases contribute to global warming, EPA must say so. That EPA would prefer not to regulate greenhouse gases because of some residual uncertainty . . . is irrelevant. The statutory question is whether sufficient information exists to make an endangerment finding.

In short, EPA has offered no reasoned explanation for its refusal to decide whether greenhouse gases cause or contribute to climate change. Its action was therefore "arbitrary, capricious, . . . or otherwise not in accordance with law." 42 U.S.C. § 7607(d)(9)(A). We need not and do not reach the question whether on remand EPA must make an endangerment finding, or whether policy concerns can inform EPA's actions in the event that it makes such a finding. We hold only that EPA must ground its reasons for action or inaction in the statute.

VIII

The judgment of the Court of Appeals is reversed, and the case is remanded for further proceedings consistent with this opinion.

■ CHIEF JUSTICE ROBERTS, with whom JUSTICE SCALIA, JUSTICE THOMAS, and JUSTICE ALITO join, dissenting.

Global warming may be a "crisis," even "the most pressing environmental problem of our time." Pet. for Cert. 26, 22. Indeed, it may ultimately affect nearly everyone on the planet in some potentially adverse way, and it may be that governments have done too little to address it. It is not a problem, however, that has escaped the attention of policymakers in the Executive and Legislative Branches of our Government, who continue to consider regulatory, legislative, and treaty-based means of addressing global climate change.

Apparently dissatisfied with the pace of progress on this issue in the elected branches, petitioners have come to the courts claiming broad-ranging injury, and attempting to tie that injury to the Government's alleged failure to comply with a rather narrow statutory provision. I would reject these challenges as nonjusticiable. Such a conclusion involves no judgment on whether global warming exists, what causes it, or the extent of the problem. Nor does it render petitioners without recourse. This Court's standing jurisprudence simply recognizes that redress of grievances of the sort at issue here "is the function of Congress and the Chief Executive," not the federal courts. Lujan v. Defenders of Wildlife, 504 U.S. 555, 576 (1992). I would vacate the judgment below and remand for dismissal of the petitions for review. . . .

■ JUSTICE SCALIA, with whom THE CHIEF JUSTICE, JUSTICE THOMAS, and JUSTICE ALITO join, dissenting.

I join the Chief Justice's opinion in full, and would hold that this Court has no jurisdiction to decide this case because petitioners lack standing. The Court having decided otherwise, it is appropriate for me to note my dissent on the merits.

I

A

The provision of law at the heart of this case is § 202(a)(1) of the Clean Air Act (CAA), which provides that the Administrator of the Environmental Protection Agency (EPA) "shall by regulation prescribe . . . standards applicable to the emission of any air pollutant from any class or classes of new motor vehicles or new motor vehicle engines, which *in his judgment* cause, or contribute to, air pollution which may reasonably be anticipated to endanger public health or welfare." 42 U.S.C. § 7521(a)(1) (emphasis added). As the Court recognizes, the statute "condition[s] the exercise of EPA's authority on its formation of a 'judgment.'" There is no dispute that the Administrator has made no such judgment in this case.

The question thus arises: Does anything *require* the Administrator to make a "judgment" whenever a petition for rulemaking is filed? Without citation of the statute or any other authority, the Court says yes. Why is that so? When Congress wishes to make private action force an agency's hand, it knows how to do so. Where does the CAA say that the EPA Administrator is required to come to a decision on this question whenever a rulemaking petition is filed? The Court points to no such provision because none exists.

Instead, the Court invents a multiple-choice question that the EPA Administrator must answer when a petition for rulemaking is filed. The Administrator must exercise his judgment in one of three ways: (a) by concluding that the pollutant *does* cause, or contribute to, air pollution that endangers public welfare (in which case EPA is required to regulate); (b) by concluding that the pollutant *does not* cause, or contribute to, air pollution that endangers public welfare (in which case EPA is *not* required to regulate); or (c) by "provid[ing] some reasonable explanation as to why it cannot or will not exercise its discretion to determine whether" greenhouse gases endanger public welfare (in which case EPA is *not* required to regulate).

I am willing to assume, for the sake of argument, that the Administrator's discretion in this regard is not entirely unbounded-that if he has no reasonable basis for deferring judgment he must grasp the nettle at once. The Court, however, with no basis in text or precedent, rejects all of EPA's stated "policy judgments" as not "amount[ing] to a reasoned justification," effectively narrowing the universe of potential reasonable bases to a single one: Judgment can be delayed *only* if the Administrator concludes that "the scientific uncertainty is [too] profound." The Administrator is precluded from concluding *for other reasons* "that it would . . . be better not to regulate at this time." Such other reasons—perfectly valid reasons—were set forth in the agency's statement.

> We do not believe . . . that it would be either effective or appropriate for EPA to establish [greenhouse gas] standards for motor vehicles at this time. As described in detail below, the President has laid out a comprehensive approach to climate change that calls for near-term voluntary actions and incentives along with programs aimed at reducing scientific uncertainties and encouraging technological development so that the government may effectively and efficiently address the climate change issue over the long term. . . .
>
> [E]stablishing [greenhouse gas] emission standards for U.S. motor vehicles at this time would . . . result in an inefficient, piecemeal approach to addressing the climate change issue. The U.S. motor vehicle fleet is one of many sources of [greenhouse gas] emissions both here and abroad, and different [greenhouse gas] emission sources face different technological and financial challenges in reducing emissions. A sensible regulatory scheme would require that all significant sources and sinks of [greenhouse gas] emissions be considered in deciding how best to achieve any needed emission reductions.
>
> Unilateral EPA regulation of motor vehicle [greenhouse gas] emissions could also weaken U.S. efforts to persuade developing countries to reduce the [greenhouse gas] intensity of their economies. . . . Unavoidably, climate change raises important foreign policy issues, and it is the President's prerogative to address them. 68 Fed.Reg. 52929–52931 (footnote omitted).

The Court dismisses this analysis as "rest[ing] on reasoning divorced from the statutory text." "While the statute does condition the exercise of EPA's authority on its formation of a 'judgment,' . . . that judgment must relate to whether an air pollutant 'cause[s], or contribute[s] to, air pollution which may reasonably be anticipated to endanger public health or welfare.'" True but irrelevant. When the Administrator *makes* a judgment whether to regulate greenhouse gases, that judgment must relate to whether they are air pollutants that "cause, or contribute to, air pollution which may reasonably be anticipated to endanger public health or welfare." 42 U.S.C. § 7521(a)(1). But the statute says *nothing at all* about the reasons for which the Administrator may *defer* making a judgment—the permissible reasons for deciding not to grapple with the issue at the present time. Thus, the various "policy" rationales that the

Court criticizes are not "divorced from the statutory text," except in the sense that the statutory text is silent, as texts are often silent about permissible reasons for the exercise of agency discretion. The reasons the EPA gave are surely considerations executive agencies *regularly* take into account (and *ought* to take into account) when deciding whether to consider entering a new field: the impact such entry would have on other Executive Branch programs and on foreign policy. There is no basis in law for the Court's imposed limitation. . . .

B

Even on the Court's own terms, however, the same conclusion follows. As mentioned above, the Court gives EPA the option of determining that the science is too uncertain to allow it to form a "judgment" as to whether greenhouse gases endanger public welfare. Attached to this option (on what basis is unclear) is an essay requirement: "If," the Court says, "the scientific uncertainty is so profound that it precludes EPA from making a reasoned judgment as to whether greenhouse gases contribute to global warming, EPA must say so." But EPA *has* said precisely that—and at great length, based on information contained in a 2001 report by the National Research Council (NRC) entitled Climate Change Science: An Analysis of Some Key Questions:

> As the NRC noted in its report, concentrations of [greenhouse gases (GHGs)] are increasing in the atmosphere as a result of human activities (pp. 9–12). It also noted that "[a] diverse array of evidence points to a warming of global surface air temperatures" (p. 16). The report goes on to state, however, that "[b]ecause of the large and still uncertain level of natural variability inherent in the climate record and the uncertainties in the time histories of the various forcing agents (and particularly aerosols), a [causal] linkage between the buildup of greenhouse gases in the atmosphere and the observed climate changes during the 20th century cannot be unequivocally established. The fact that the magnitude of the observed warming is large in comparison to natural variability as simulated in climate models is suggestive of such a linkage, but it does not constitute proof of one because the model simulations could be deficient in natural variability on the decadal to century time scale" (p. 17). . . .
>
> The science of climate change is extraordinarily complex and still evolving. Although there have been substantial advances in climate change science, there continue to be important uncertainties in our understanding of the factors that may affect future climate change and how it should be addressed. As the NRC explained, predicting future climate change necessarily involves a complex web of economic and physical factors including: Our ability to predict future global anthropogenic emissions of GHGs and aerosols; the fate of these emissions once they enter the atmosphere (e.g., what percentage

> are absorbed by vegetation or are taken up by the oceans); the impact of those emissions that remain in the atmosphere on the radiative properties of the atmosphere; changes in critically important climate feedbacks (e.g., changes in cloud cover and ocean circulation); changes in temperature characteristics (e.g., average temperatures, shifts in daytime and evening temperatures); changes in other climatic parameters (e.g., shifts in precipitation, storms); and ultimately the impact of such changes on human health and welfare (e.g., increases or decreases in agricultural productivity, human health impacts). The NRC noted, in particular, that "[t]he understanding of the relationships between weather/climate and human health is in its infancy and therefore the health consequences of climate change are poorly understood" (p. 20). Substantial scientific uncertainties limit our ability to assess each of these factors and to separate out those changes resulting from natural variability from those that are directly the result of increases in anthropogenic GHGs.
>
> Reducing the wide range of uncertainty inherent in current model predictions will require major advances in understanding and modeling of the factors that determine atmospheric concentrations of greenhouse gases and aerosols, and the processes that determine the sensitivity of the climate system. 68 Fed. Reg. 52930.

I simply cannot conceive of what else the Court would like EPA to say.

II

A

Even before reaching its discussion of the word "judgment," the Court makes another significant error when it concludes that "§ 202(a)(1) of the Clean Air Act *authorizes* EPA to regulate greenhouse gas emissions from new motor vehicles in the event that it forms a 'judgment' that such emissions contribute to climate change" (emphasis added). For such authorization, the Court relies on what it calls "the Clean Air Act's capacious definition of 'air pollutant.' "

"Air pollutant" is defined by the Act as "any air pollution agent or combination of such agents, including any physical, chemical, . . . substance or matter which is emitted into or otherwise enters the ambient air." 42 U.S.C. § 7602(g). The Court is correct that "[c]arbon dioxide, methane, nitrous oxide, and hydrofluorocarbons," fit within the second half of that definition: They are "physical, chemical, . . . substance[s] or matter which [are] emitted into or otherwise ente[r] the ambient air." But the Court mistakenly believes this to be the end of the analysis. In order to be an "air pollutant" under the Act's definition, the "substance or matter [being] emitted into . . . the ambient air" must also meet the *first* half of the definition—namely, it must be an "air pollution agent or combination of such agents." The Court simply pretends this half of the definition does not exist.

. . . As that argument goes, anything that *follows* the word "including" must necessarily be a subset of whatever *precedes* it. Thus, if greenhouse gases qualify under the phrase following the word "including," they must qualify under the phrase preceding it. . . .

That is certainly one possible interpretation of the statutory definition. The word "including" can indeed indicate that what follows will be an "illustrative" sampling of the general category that precedes the word. Often, however, the examples standing alone are broader than the general category, and must be viewed as limited in light of that category. The Government provides a helpful (and unanswered) example: "The phrase 'any American automobile, including any truck or minivan,' would not naturally be construed to encompass a foreign-manufactured [truck or] minivan." Brief for Federal Respondent 34. The general principle enunciated—that the speaker is talking about *American* automobiles—carries forward to the illustrative examples (trucks and minivans), and limits them accordingly, even though in isolation they are broader. Congress often uses the word "including" in this manner. . . .

In short, the word "including" does not require the Court's (or the petitioners') result. It is perfectly reasonable to view the definition of "air pollutant" in its entirety: An air pollutant *can* be "any physical, chemical, . . . substance or matter which is emitted into or otherwise enters the ambient air," but only if it retains the general characteristic of being an "air pollution agent or combination of such agents." This is precisely the conclusion EPA reached: "[A] substance does not meet the CAA definition of 'air pollutant' simply because it is a 'physical, chemical, . . . substance or matter which is emitted into or otherwise enters the ambient air.' It must also be an 'air pollution agent.' " 68 Fed. Reg. 52929, n. 3. Once again, in the face of textual ambiguity, the Court's application of Chevron deference to EPA's interpretation of the word "including" is nowhere to be found. Evidently, the Court defers only to those reasonable interpretations that it favors.

B

Using (as we ought to) EPA's interpretation of the definition of "air pollutant," we must next determine whether greenhouse gases are "agent[s]" of "air pollution." If so, the statute would authorize regulation; if not, EPA would lack authority.

Unlike "air pollutants," the term "air pollution" is not itself defined by the CAA; thus, once again we must accept EPA's interpretation of that ambiguous term, provided its interpretation is a "permissible construction of the statute." Chevron. . . . EPA began with the commonsense observation that the "[p]roblems associated with atmospheric concentrations of $CO_2$," id., at 52927, bear little resemblance to what would naturally be termed "air pollution": . . . In other words, regulating the buildup of $CO_2$ and other greenhouse gases in the upper reaches of the atmosphere, which is alleged to be causing global climate change, is not akin to regulating the concentration of some substance that is *polluting* the *air*.

We need look no further than the dictionary for confirmation that this interpretation of "air pollution" is eminently reasonable. The definition of "pollute," of course, is "[t]o make or render impure or unclean." Webster's New International Dictionary 1910 (2d ed.1949). And the first three definitions of "air" are as follows: (1) "[t]he invisible, odorless, and tasteless mixture of gases which surrounds the earth"; (2) "[t]he body of the earth's atmosphere; esp., the part of it near the earth, as distinguished from the upper rarefied part"; (3) "[a] portion of air or of the air considered with respect to physical characteristics or as affecting the senses." Id., at 54. EPA's conception of "air pollution"—focusing on impurities in the "ambient air" "at ground level or near the surface of the earth"—is perfectly consistent with the natural meaning of that term.

In the end, EPA concluded that since "CAA authorization to regulate is generally based on a finding that an air pollutant causes or contributes to air pollution," 68 Fed. Reg. 52928, the concentrations of $CO_2$ and other greenhouse gases allegedly affecting the global climate are beyond the scope of CAA's authorization to regulate. "[T]he term 'air pollution' as used in the regulatory provisions cannot be interpreted to encompass global climate change." Once again, the Court utterly fails to explain why this interpretation is incorrect, let alone so unreasonable as to be unworthy of Chevron deference. . . .

The Court's alarm over global warming may or may not be justified, but it ought not distort the outcome of this litigation. This is a straightforward administrative-law case, in which Congress has passed a malleable statute giving broad discretion, not to us but to an executive agency. No matter how important the underlying policy issues at stake, this Court has no business substituting its own desired outcome for the reasoned judgment of the responsible agency.

## NOTES

(1) ***What Is Driving This Decision?*** The statutory provision at issue in this case says that the EPA Administrator "shall" act in certain situations that "in his judgment" cause pollution. As one emphasizes "in his judgment" the Administrator's discretion inflates; as one emphasizes "shall," it deflates. Doesn't this balloon-like command create exactly the ambiguity for which Chevron deference was created? Or is it that, because one alternative reading would constitute a command to the Administrator to do something he does not want to do, his judgment cannot be trusted? Or is it that the agency's 2003 view of its very authority to regulate is too much driven by politics? Or is it that the topic is too important for the Supreme Court to dispose of on "deference" grounds?

(2) ***The Obama Administration's Response.*** After the decision, the President Bush directed his cabinet agencies to "take the first steps toward regulations," imposing a deadline of the end of 2008. Near the end of its first year, the Obama Administration issued an endangerment finding.

Endangerment and Cause or Contribute Findings for Greenhouse Gases Under Section 202(a) of the Clean Air Act, 74 Fed. Reg. 66496 (Dec. 15, 2009). The summary read: "The Administrator finds that six greenhouse gases taken in combination endanger both the public health and the public welfare of current and future generations. The Administrator also finds that the combined emissions of these greenhouse gases from new motor vehicles and new motor vehicle engines contribute to the greenhouse gas air pollution that endangers public health and welfare under CAA section 202(a). These Findings are based on careful consideration of the full weight of scientific evidence and a thorough review of numerous public comments received on the Proposed Findings published April 24, 2009."

The Statement of Basis and Purpose accompanying these 2009 findings included this, 74 Fed. Reg. 66500–01: "Many commenters urge EPA to delay making final findings for a variety of reasons. They note that the Supreme Court did not establish a deadline for EPA to act on remand. Commenters also argue that the Supreme Court's decision does not require that EPA make a final endangerment finding, and thus that EPA has discretionary power and may decline to issue an endangerment finding, not only if the science is too uncertain, but also if EPA can provide 'some reasonable explanation' for exercising its discretion. These commenters interpret the Supreme Court decision not as rejecting all policy reasons for declining to undertake an endangerment finding, but rather as dismissing solely the policy reasons EPA set forth in 2003. Some commenters cite language in the Supreme Court decision regarding EPA's discretion regarding 'the manner, timing, content, and coordination of its regulations,' and the Court's declining to rule on 'whether policy concerns can inform EPA's actions in the event that it makes' a CAA section 202(a) finding to support their position.

"Commenters then suggest a variety of policy reasons that EPA can and should make to support a decision not to undertake a finding of endangerment under CAA section 202(a)(1). For example, they argue that a finding of endangerment would trigger several other regulatory programs . . . that would impose an unreasonable burden on the economy and government, without providing a benefit to the environment. Some commenters contend that EPA should defer issuing a final endangerment finding while Congress considers legislation. Many commenters note the ongoing international discussions regarding climate change and state their belief that unilateral EPA action would interfere with those negotiations. Others suggest deferring the EPA portion of the joint U.S. Department of Transportation (DOT)/EPA rulemaking because they argue that the new Corporate Average Fuel Economy (CAFE) standards will effectively result in lower greenhouse gas emissions from new motor vehicles, while avoiding the inevitable problems and concerns of regulating greenhouse gases under the CAA.

"Other commenters argue that the endangerment determination has to be made on the basis of scientific considerations only. These commenters state that the Court was clear that '[t]he statutory question is whether sufficient information exists to make an endangerment finding,' and thus, only if 'the scientific uncertainty is so profound that it precludes EPA from making a reasoned judgment as to whether greenhouse gases contribute to global warming,' may EPA avoid making a positive or negative endangerment finding. Many commenters urge EPA to take action quickly. They note that it has been 10 years since the original petition requesting that EPA regulate greenhouse gas emissions from motor vehicles was submitted to EPA. They argue that climate change is a serious problem that requires immediate action.

"EPA agrees with the commenters who argue that the Supreme Court decision held that EPA is limited to consideration of science when undertaking an endangerment finding, and that we cannot delay issuing a finding due to policy concerns if the science is sufficiently certain (as it is here). The Supreme Court stated that 'EPA can avoid taking further action only if it determines that greenhouse gases do not contribute to climate change or if it provides some reasonable explanation as to why it cannot or will not exercise its discretion to determine whether they do.' 549 U.S. at 533. Some commenters point to this last provision, arguing that the policy reasons they provide are a 'reasonable explanation' for not moving forward at this time. However, this ignores other language in the decision that clearly indicates that the Court interprets the statute to allow for the consideration only of science. For example, in rejecting the policy concerns expressed by EPA in its 2003 denial of the rulemaking petition, the Court noted that 'it is evident [the policy considerations] have nothing to do with whether greenhouse gas emissions contribute to climate change. Still less do they amount to a reasoned justification for declining to form *a scientific judgment*' Id. at 533–34 (emphasis added).

"Moreover, the Court also held that '[t]he statutory question is whether sufficient information exists to make an endangerment finding.' Id. at 534. Taken as a whole, the Supreme Court's decision clearly indicates that policy reasons do not justify the Administrator avoiding taking further action on the question here."

If the EPA of the Obama Administration had wanted not to take action, do you think the reading proposed by the first set of commenters was foreclosed? If the EPA had some latitude to act or not to act, did it help it (in an obviously contested situation) to be able to rely so heavily on the Court's decision?

(3) ***Expertise-Forcing Judicial Review?*** JODY FREEMAN & ADRIAN VERMEULE, MASSACHUSETTS V. EPA: FROM POLITICS TO EXPERTISE, 2007 Sup. Ct. Rev. 51, 96–97: "On the view we attribute to the MA v. EPA majority, courts have a role to play not only through ex post judicial review of agency decisions, but also through expertise-forcing when agencies are deciding not to decide because of political pressures. If agencies refuse to exercise their first-order expertise, in any direction, because issues are politically too controversial, or because they fear that an expert judgment would point in the direction of politically costly action—a plausible description of what occurred when EPA considered whether to regulate greenhouse gases—courts can review the reasons agencies give for postponing their first-order decisions in order to flush out these socially harmful motivations. Where agencies have no valid reason for further delay,

courts will indirectly force them to make the first-order expert judgment they have been avoiding.

"MA v. EPA seems to adopt this perspective when it makes two important findings. The first is that *rulemaking denials are reviewable*. . . .

"The second crucial point is that *agency decisions not to decide are (presumptively) subject to 'hard look' review*. At least absent a clear statutory command to the contrary, the reviewing court will require the agency to offer a nonarbitrary reason for the decision not to decide. One type of arbitrariness is legal error: agencies must consider only those factors made relevant by the particular statute at hand. In other words, hard look review applies *both* to the agency's decision about whether to make a threshold determination in the first place, *and* to the agency's decision about whether the threshold has been crossed. When making both the first-order judgment under § 202 and the second-order decision about whether to decide, EPA may not consider extraneous non-statutory factors such as foreign policy, or its preference for other regulatory or nonregulatory approaches that might fit better with the President's priorities. Rather, the agency is to focus primarily on information, scientific uncertainty, and the costs and benefits of acquiring further information. Does the state of the science enable the EPA to make a rational judgment now, in either direction, about the health and welfare effects of a given pollutant? What are the costs of deciding not to decide, as against the informational advantages that would arise from postponing the first-order judgment until the science is solidified?

"Of course the case does not answer all questions. Crucial to the holding is the point that § 202(a) excludes nonscientific and nontechnical factors from the agency's initial decision-making calculus. Some statutes can plausibly be read to share that feature; others presumably cannot. All organic statutes are different; in some settings statutes will be read to give agencies more or less discretion to decide not to decide. The main contribution of the decision, however, is to clarify that there is nothing magic about such initial decisions. They are reviewable on the ordinary terms of administrative law. Properly understood, MA v. EPA is . . . State Farm for a new generation."

If, as Freeman and Vermeule say, "all organic statutes are different," what is the precedential force of the principal case? They obviously think it represents a significant general development. But could this be a one-time-only Supreme Court response to an issue too important, and in the Court's judgment, too mishandled, to pass up? If it were, would that be objectionable? Or is that what the Supreme Court ought to do when certain "really big" cases come its way? Conversely, would the doctrine as restated by Freeman and Vermeule be good or bad if used in the mine run of cases?

## NOTES ON FDA V. BROWN & WILLIAMSON TOBACCO CORP.

The majority in Massachusetts v. EPA makes a point of distinguishing FDA v. BROWN & WILLIAMSON TOBACCO CORP., 529 U.S. 120 (2000). That case, too, presented the question of whether a statute passed much earlier could be construed, based on new scientific information, to give the administering agency major regulatory authority over something that the agency had not previously regulated. That case begins: "In 1996, the Food and Drug Administration (FDA), after having expressly disavowed any such authority since its inception, asserted jurisdiction to regulate tobacco products." The Food, Drug and Cosmetic Act (FDCA), the opinion continued, 529 U.S. at 126–27, "grants the FDA . . . the authority to regulate, among other items, 'drugs' and 'devices.' The Act defines 'drug' to include 'articles (other than food) intended to affect the structure or any function of the body.' It defines 'device,' in part, as 'an instrument, apparatus, implement, machine, contrivance, . . . or other similar or related article, including any component, part, or accessory, which is . . . intended to affect the structure or any function of the body.' The Act also grants the FDA the authority to regulate so-called 'combination products,' which 'constitute a combination of a drug, device, or biological product.' " In the rulemaking under review, "[t]he FDA determined that nicotine is a 'drug' and that cigarettes and smokeless tobacco are 'drug delivery devices,' and therefore it had jurisdiction under the FDCA to regulate tobacco products."

(1) ***The Majority's Reasoning.*** The opinion by JUSTICE O'CONNOR for five members of the Court held that the FDA's assertion of jurisdiction was unwarranted. First, the FDCA was premised on ensuring that drugs were either safe or taken off the market. The FDA's own approach to cigarettes—involving regulation of advertising, labeling, and promotion, but not banning sale to adults—would do neither. 529 U.S. at 159–161. "The inescapable conclusion is that there is no room for tobacco products within the FDCA's regulatory scheme." Second, since 1965 Congress had enacted six statutes regarding tobacco, each time acting on the premise, supported by the FDA at the time, that the FDA lacked jurisdiction. "Under these circumstances, it is clear that Congress' tobacco-specific legislation has effectively ratified the FDA's previous position that it lacks jurisdiction to regulate tobacco." She continued): "Finally, our inquiry into whether Congress has directly spoken to the precise question at issue is shaped, at least in some measure, by the nature of the question presented. Deference under Chevron to an agency's construction of a statute that it administers is premised on the theory that a statute's ambiguity constitutes an implicit delegation from Congress to the agency to fill in the statutory gaps. In extraordinary cases, however, there may be reason to hesitate before concluding that Congress has intended such an implicit delegation.

"This is hardly an ordinary case. Contrary to its representations to Congress since 1914, the FDA has now asserted jurisdiction to regulate an industry constituting a significant portion of the American economy. . . . Owing to its unique place in American history and society, tobacco has its own unique political history. Congress, for better or for worse, has created a distinct regulatory scheme for tobacco products, squarely rejected proposals to give the FDA jurisdiction over tobacco, and repeatedly acted to preclude any agency from exercising significant policymaking authority in the area. Given this history and the breadth of the authority that the FDA has asserted, we are obliged to defer not to the agency's expansive construction of the statute, but to Congress' consistent judgment to deny the FDA this power.

"Our decision in MCI Telecommunications Corp. v. American Telephone & Telegraph Co., 512 U.S. 218 (1994), is instructive. That case involved the proper construction of the term 'modify' in § 203(b) of the Communications Act of 1934. The FCC contended that, because the Act gave it the discretion to 'modify any requirement' imposed under the statute, it therefore possessed the authority to render voluntary the otherwise mandatory requirement that long distance carriers file their rates. We rejected the FCC's construction, finding 'not the slightest doubt' that Congress had directly spoken to the question. In reasoning even more apt here, we concluded that '[i]t is highly unlikely that Congress would leave the determination of whether an industry will be entirely, or even substantially, rate-regulated to agency discretion—and even more unlikely that it would achieve that through such a subtle device as permission to "modify" rate-filing requirements.'

"As in MCI, we are confident that Congress could not have intended to delegate a decision of such economic and political significance to an agency in so cryptic a fashion. To find that the FDA has the authority to regulate tobacco products, one must not only adopt an extremely strained understanding of 'safety' as it is used throughout the Act—a concept central to the FDCA's regulatory scheme—but also ignore the plain implication of Congress' subsequent tobacco-specific legislation. It is therefore clear, based on the FDCA's overall regulatory scheme and the subsequent tobacco legislation that Congress has directly spoken to the question at issue and precluded the FDA from regulating tobacco products."

(2) ***The Dissent's Reasoning.*** Compare JUSTICE BREYER'S dissent for four (529 U.S. at 190–99): "[O]ne might claim that courts, when interpreting statutes, should assume in close cases that a decision with 'enormous social consequences' should be made by democratically elected Members of Congress rather than by unelected agency administrators. Cf. Kent v. Dulles, 357 U.S. 116, 129 (1958) (assuming Congress did not want to delegate the power to make rules interfering with exercise of basic human liberties). If there is such a background canon of interpretation, however, I do not believe it controls the outcome here.

"Insofar as the decision to regulate tobacco reflects the policy of an administration, it is a decision for which that administration, and those politically elected officials who support it, must (and will) take responsibility. And the very importance of the decision taken here, as well as its attendant publicity, means that the public is likely to be aware of it and to hold those officials politically accountable. Presidents, just like Members of Congress, are elected by the public. Indeed, the President and Vice President are the only public officials whom the entire Nation elects. I do not believe that an administrative agency decision of this magnitude—one that is important, conspicuous, and controversial—can escape the kind of public scrutiny that is essential in any democracy. And such a review will take place whether it is the Congress or the Executive Branch that makes the relevant decision."

(3) ***Major Questions.*** The majority in Massachusetts v. EPA explains that FDA v. Brown & Williamson Tobacco Corp. was distinguishable. Congress could not have meant to allow FDA to ban tobacco (as required to make it "safe"), as shown by separate legislation providing for tobacco regulation, whereas regulating pollutants to solve an environmental problem was in EPA's delegated wheelhouse. But, does Massachusetts v. EPA grapple sufficiently with the portion of Brown & Williamson that, in light of the major import of the interpretive question at issue, "this is no ordinary case" and thus that there was reason, for that reason alone, to doubt the FDA had the authority it claimed? Or, does Massachusetts v. EPA adequately answer that question through its analysis of the statutory text and the way that the text defines an "air pollutant"? However you come down on those questions, versions of them are front and center in the next case we present, which represents a "major" decision in its own right because of what it says about the "major questions doctrine," which it traces back to FDA v. Brown & Williamson Tobacco Corp.



## WEST VIRGINIA v. ENVIRONMENTAL PROTECTION AGENCY

Supreme Court of the United States (2022).
142 S.Ct. 2587.

■ CHIEF JUSTICE ROBERTS delivered the opinion of the Court.

The Clean Air Act authorizes the Environmental Protection Agency to regulate power plants by setting a "standard of performance" for their emission of certain pollutants into the air. 42 U.S.C. § 7411(a)(1). That standard . . . must reflect the "best system of emission reduction" that the Agency has determined to be "adequately demonstrated" for the particular category. §§ 7411(a)(1), (b)(1), (d). For existing plants, the States then implement that requirement by issuing rules restricting emissions from sources within their borders.

Since passage of the Act 50 years ago, EPA has exercised this authority by setting performance standards based on measures that would reduce pollution by causing plants to operate more cleanly. In 2015, however, EPA issued a new rule concluding that the "best system of emission reduction" for existing coal-fired power plants included a requirement that such facilities reduce their own production of electricity, or subsidize increased generation by natural gas, wind, or solar sources.

The question before us is whether this broader conception of EPA's authority is within the power granted to it by the Clean Air Act.

I

A

The Clean Air Act establishes three main regulatory programs to control air pollution from stationary sources such as power plants. [A small number of common pollutants are regulated under the National Ambient Air Quality Standards (NAAQS) program of Sections 108–110. Toxic pollutants are regulated under the Hazardous Air Pollutants (HAP) program of Section 112. And Section 111 establishes the New Source Performance Standards program.]

[Under Section 111(b), EPA lists categories of air pollution sources and promulgates federal performance standards for new sources in those categories.] A "standard of performance" is one that

> "reflects the degree of emission limitation achievable through the application of the best system of emission reduction which (taking into account the cost of achieving such reduction and any nonair quality health and environmental impact and energy requirements) the [EPA] Administrator determines has been adequately demonstrated." § 7411(a)(1).

[So, EPA (1) identifies the "best system of emission reduction" (BSER), (2) determines how much emissions would be reduced by that system, and (3)] impose[s] an emissions limit on new stationary sources that "reflects" that amount. [The states then adopt plans to enforce these emissions limits.] Generally speaking, a source may achieve that emissions cap any way it chooses . . . .

Although the thrust of Section 111 focuses on emissions limits for new and modified sources—as its title indicates—the statute also authorizes regulation of certain pollutants from existing sources. [When EPA issues regulations under Section 111(b) for a pollutant that is not already regulated under the NAAQS or HAP programs, Section 111(d) requires EPA to regulate emissions of that pollutant from existing sources in addition to the emissions from new sources regulated under Section 111(b).] Section 111(d) thus "operates as a gap-filler," empowering EPA to regulate harmful emissions not already controlled under the Agency's other authorities. American Lung Assn. v. EPA, 985 F.3d 914, 932 (CADC 2021).

. . . Reflecting the ancillary nature of Section 111(d), EPA has used it only a handful of times since the enactment of the statute in 1970. . . . It was thus only a slight overstatement for one of the architects of the 1990 amendments to the Clean Air Act to refer to Section 111(d) as an "obscure, never-used section of the law." Hearings on S. 300 et al. before the Subcommittee on Environmental Protection of the Senate Committee on Environment and Public Works, 100th Cong., 1st Sess., 13 (1987) (remarks of Sen. Durenberger).

B

[In the Clean Power Plan, EPA set emissions limits under Section 111(d) by identifying a BSER for coal power plants that comprised three "building blocks." The first building block was efficiency improvements.] But such improvements, EPA stated, would "lead to only small emission reductions." . . .

So the Agency included two additional building blocks in its BSER, both of which involve what it called "generation shifting from higher-emitting to lower-emitting" producers of electricity. Building block two was a shift in electricity production from existing coal-fired power plants to natural-gas-fired plants. . . . Building block three worked the same way, except that the shift was from both coal- and gas-fired plants to "new low- or zero-carbon generating capacity," mainly wind and solar. "Most of the CO2 controls" in the rule came from the application of building blocks two and three.

The Agency identified three ways in which a regulated plant operator could implement a shift in generation to cleaner sources. First, an operator could simply reduce the regulated plant's own production of electricity. Second, it could build a new natural gas plant, wind farm, or solar installation, or invest in someone else's existing facility and then increase generation there. Finally, operators could purchase emission allowances or credits as part of a cap-and-trade regime.. . . .

EPA explained that taking any of these steps would implement a sector-wide shift in electricity production from coal to natural gas and renewables. . . . [C]oal plants, whether by reducing their own production, subsidizing an increase in production by cleaner sources, or both, would cause a shift toward wind, solar, and natural gas. . . .

The point, after all, was to compel the transfer of power generating capacity from existing sources to wind and solar. The White House stated that the Clean Power Plan would "drive a[n] . . . aggressive transformation in the domestic energy industry." EPA's own modeling concluded that the rule would entail billions of dollars in compliance costs (to be paid in the form of higher energy prices), require the retirement of dozens of coal-fired plants, and eliminate tens of thousands of jobs across various sectors. The Energy Information Administration reached similar conclusions, projecting that the rule . . . would reduce GDP by at least a trillion 2009 dollars by 2040.

C

These projections were never tested, because the Clean Power Plan never went into effect. . . . We granted a stay, preventing the rule from taking effect. . . . [And in 2019, EPA repealed the rule and replaced it with the Affordable Clean Energy (ACE) Rule.] . . .

D

A number of States and private parties immediately filed petitions for review in the D.C. Circuit, challenging EPA's repeal of the Clean Power Plan and its enactment of the replacement ACE Rule. . . . [In a decision rendered January 19, 2021, the court found that EPA had misinterpreted its statutory authority, and vacated both the Clean Power Plan repeal and the ACE rule, remanding to EPA for further consideration. After the subsequent change in administrations, EPA moved the D.C. Circuit to stay its vacatur of EPA's previous repeal of the Clean Power Plan. The court granted the stay.] . . .

III

A

. . . The issue here is whether restructuring the Nation's overall mix of electricity generation, to transition from 38% coal to 27% coal by 2030, can be the "best system of emission reduction" within the meaning of Section 111.

"It is a fundamental canon of statutory construction that the words of a statute must be read in their context and with a view to their place in the overall statutory scheme." Davis v. Michigan Dept. of Treasury, 489 U.S. 803, 809 (1989). Where the statute at issue is one that confers authority upon an administrative agency, that inquiry must be "shaped, at least in some measure, by the nature of the question presented"—whether Congress in fact meant to confer the power the agency has asserted. FDA v. Brown & Williamson Tobacco Corp., 529 U.S. 120, 159 (2000) [p. 1338]. In the ordinary case, that context has no great effect on the appropriate analysis. Nonetheless, our precedent teaches that there are "extraordinary cases" that call for a different approach—cases in which the "history and the breadth of the authority that [the agency] has asserted," and the "economic and political significance" of that assertion, provide a "reason to hesitate before concluding that Congress" meant to confer such authority. Id., at 159–160.

Such cases have arisen from all corners of the administrative state. In Brown & Williamson, for instance, the Food and Drug Administration claimed that its authority over "drugs" and "devices" included the power to regulate, and even ban, tobacco products. Id., at 126–127. We rejected that "expansive construction of the statute," concluding that "Congress could not have intended to delegate" such a sweeping and consequential authority "in so cryptic a fashion." Id., at 160. In Alabama Assn. of Realtors v. Department of Health and Human Servs. [v. HHS, 141 S.Ct. 2485 (2021) (p. 868)], we concluded that the Centers for Disease Control and Prevention could not, sunder its authority to adopt measures "necessary to prevent the . . . spread of" disease, institute a nationwide eviction moratorium in response to the COVID-19 pandemic. We found the statute's language a "wafer-thin reed" on which to rest such a measure, given "the sheer scope of the CDC's claimed authority," its "unprecedented" nature, and the fact that Congress had failed to extend the moratorium after previously having done so. Id., at 2488–2490.

Our decision in Utility Air addressed another question regarding EPA's authority—namely, whether EPA could construe the term "air pollutant," in a specific provision of the Clean Air Act, to cover greenhouse gases. 573 U.S. at 310. Despite its textual plausibility, we noted that the Agency's interpretation would have given it permitting authority over millions of small sources, such as hotels and office buildings, that had never before been subject to such requirements. Id., at 310, 324. We declined to uphold EPA's claim of "unheralded" regulatory power over "a significant portion of the American economy." Id., at 324. In Gonzales v. Oregon, 546 U.S. 243 (2006), we confronted the Attorney General's assertion that he could rescind the license of any physician who prescribed a controlled substance for assisted suicide, even in a State where such action was legal. The Attorney General argued that this came within his statutory power to revoke licenses where he found them "inconsistent with the public interest," 21 U.S.C. § 823(f). We considered the "idea that Congress gave [him] such broad and unusual authority through an implicit delegation . . . not sustainable." 546 U.S. at 267. Similar considerations informed our recent decision invalidating the Occupational Safety and Health Administration's mandate that "84 million Americans . . . either obtain a COVID-19 vaccine or undergo weekly medical testing at their own expense." National Federation of Independent Business v. Occupational Safety and Health Administration, 142 S.Ct. 661, 665 (2022) (per curiam) [p. 1361]. We found it "telling that OSHA, in its half century of existence," had never relied on its authority to regulate occupational hazards to impose such a remarkable measure. Id., at 666.

All of these regulatory assertions had a colorable textual basis. And yet, in each case, given the various circumstances, "common sense as to the manner in which Congress [would have been] likely to delegate" such power to the agency at issue, Brown & Williamson, 529 U.S. at 133, made it very unlikely that Congress had actually done so. Extraordinary grants of regulatory authority are rarely accomplished through "modest words," "vague terms," or "subtle device[s]." Whitman [v. American Trucking Ass'ns.], 531 U.S. [457,] 468 [(2001) (p. 848)]. Nor does Congress typically use oblique or elliptical language to empower an agency to make a "radical or fundamental change" to a statutory scheme. MCI Telecommunications Corp. v. American Telephone & Telegraph Co., 512 U.S. 218, 229 (1994) [p. 1257]. . . . We presume that "Congress intends to make major policy decisions itself, not leave those decisions to agencies." United States Telecom Assn. v. FCC, 855 F.3d 381, 419 (CADC 2017) (Kavanaugh, J., dissenting from denial of rehearing en banc).

Thus, in certain extraordinary cases, both separation of powers principles and a practical understanding of legislative intent make us "reluctant to read into ambiguous statutory text" the delegation claimed to be lurking there. Utility Air, 573 U.S. at 324. To convince us otherwise, something more than a merely plausible textual basis for the agency action is necessary. The agency instead must point to "clear congressional authorization" for the power it claims. Ibid.

The dissent criticizes us for "announc[ing] the arrival" of this major questions doctrine, and argues that each of the decisions just cited simply followed our "ordinary method" of "normal statutory interpretation." But in what the dissent calls the "key case" in this area, Brown & Williamson, the Court could not have been clearer: "In extraordinary cases . . . there may be reason to hesitate" before accepting a reading of a statute that would, under more "ordinary" circumstances, be upheld. 529 U.S. at 159. . . . [T]he approach under the major questions doctrine is distinct. . . .

B

Under our precedents, this is a major questions case. In arguing that Section 111(d) empowers it to substantially restructure the American energy market, EPA "claim[ed] to discover in a long-extant statute an unheralded power" representing a "transformative expansion in [its] regulatory authority." Utility Air, 573 U.S. at 324. It located that newfound power in the vague language of an "ancillary provision[ ]" of the Act, Whitman, 531 U.S. at 468, one that was designed to function as a gap filler and had rarely been used in the preceding decades. And the Agency's discovery allowed it to adopt a regulatory program that Congress had conspicuously and repeatedly declined to enact itself. Brown & Williamson, 529 U.S. at 159–160; Gonzales, 546 U.S. at 267–268; Alabama Assn., 141 S.Ct., at 2486–2487, 2490. Given these circumstances, there is every reason to "hesitate before concluding that Congress" meant to confer on EPA the authority it claims under Section 111(d). Brown & Williamson, 529 U.S. at 159–160.

Prior to 2015, EPA had always set emissions limits under Section 111 based on the application of measures that would reduce pollution by causing the regulated source to operate more cleanly. . . .

[The Clean Power Plan's] view of EPA's authority was not only unprecedented; it also effected a "fundamental revision of the statute, changing it from [one sort of] scheme of . . . regulation" into an entirely different kind. MCI, 512 U.S. at 231. Under the Agency's prior view of Section 111, its role was limited to ensuring the efficient pollution performance of each individual regulated source. Under that paradigm, if a source was already operating at that level, there was nothing more for EPA to do. Under its newly "discover[ed]" authority, Utility Air, 573 U.S. at 324, however, EPA can demand much greater reductions in emissions based on a very different kind of policy judgment: that it would be "best" if coal made up a much smaller share of national electricity generation. And on this view of EPA's authority, it could go further, perhaps forcing coal plants to "shift" away virtually all of their generation—i.e., to cease making power altogether. . . .

On EPA's view of Section 111(d), Congress implicitly tasked it, and it alone, with balancing the many vital considerations of national policy implicated in deciding how Americans will get their energy. EPA decides, for instance, how much of a switch from coal to natural gas is practically feasible by 2020, 2025, and 2030 before the grid collapses, and how high energy prices can go as a result before they become unreasonably "exorbitant."

There is little reason to think Congress assigned such decisions to the Agency. For one thing, as EPA itself admitted when requesting special funding, "Understand[ing] and project[ing] system-wide . . . trends in areas such as electricity transmission, distribution, and storage" requires "technical and policy expertise *not* traditionally needed in EPA regulatory development." EPA, Fiscal Year 2016: Justification of Appropriation Estimates for the Committee on Appropriations 213 (2015) (emphasis added). "When [an] agency has no comparative expertise" in making certain policy judgments, we have said, "Congress presumably would not" task it with doing so. Kisor v. Wilkie, 139 S.Ct. 2400, 2417 (2019) [p. 1391]; see also Gonzales, 546 U.S. at 266–267.

We also find it "highly unlikely that Congress would leave" to "agency discretion" the decision of how much coal-based generation there should be over the coming decades. MCI, 512 U.S. at 231; see also Brown & Williamson, 529 U.S. at 160 ("We are confident that Congress could not have intended to delegate a decision of such economic and political significance to an agency in so cryptic a fashion."). The basic and consequential tradeoffs involved in such a choice are ones that Congress would likely have intended for itself. . . . Congress certainly has not conferred a like authority upon EPA anywhere else in the Clean Air Act. The last place one would expect to find it is in the previously little-used backwater of Section 111(d).

The dissent contends that there is nothing surprising about EPA dictating the optimal mix of energy sources nationwide, since that sort of mandate will reduce air pollution from power plants, which is EPA's bread and butter. But that does not follow. Forbidding evictions may slow the spread of disease, but the CDC's ordering such a measure certainly "raise[s] an eyebrow." . . .

Finally, we cannot ignore that the regulatory writ EPA newly uncovered conveniently enabled it to enact a program that, long after the dangers posed by greenhouse gas emissions "had become well known, Congress considered and rejected" multiple times. Brown & Williamson, 529 U.S. at 144. . . . Congress . . . has consistently rejected proposals to amend the Clean Air Act to create . . . a [cap-and-trade] program. It has also declined to enact similar measures, such as a carbon tax. "The importance of the issue," along with the fact that the same basic scheme EPA adopted "has been the subject of an earnest and profound debate across the country, . . . makes the oblique form of the claimed delegation all the more suspect." Gonzales, 546 U.S. at 267–268.

C

Given these circumstances, our precedent counsels skepticism toward EPA's claim that Section 111 empowers it to devise carbon emissions caps based on a generation shifting approach. To overcome that skepticism, the Government must—under the major questions doctrine—point to "clear congressional authorization" to regulate in that manner. Utility Air, 573 U.S. at 324.

All the Government can offer, however, is the Agency's authority to establish emissions caps at a level reflecting "the application of the best system of emission reduction . . . adequately demonstrated." 42 U.S.C. § 7411(a)(1). As a matter of "definitional possibilities," FCC v. AT&T Inc., 562 U.S. 397, 407 (2011), generation shifting can be described as a "system"—"an aggregation or assemblage of objects united by some form of regular interaction"—capable of reducing emissions. But of course almost anything could constitute such a "system"; shorn of all context, the word is an empty vessel. Such a vague statutory grant is not close to the sort of clear authorization required by our precedents.

The Government, echoed by the other respondents, looks to other provisions of the Clean Air Act for support. It points out that the Act elsewhere uses the word "system" or "similar words" to describe cap-and-trade schemes or other sector-wide mechanisms for reducing pollution. The Acid Rain program . . . establishes a cap-and-trade scheme for reducing sulfur dioxide emissions, which the statute refers to as an "emission allocation and transfer *system*." § 7651(b) (emphasis added). And Section 110 of the NAAQS program specifies that "marketable permits" and "auctions of emissions rights" qualify as "control measures, means, or techniques" that States may adopt [to implement federal NAAQS requirements] . . . . § 7410(a)(2)(A). If the word "system" or similar words like "technique" or "means" can encompass cap-and-trade, the Government maintains, why not in Section 111?

But just because a cap-and-trade "system" can be used to reduce emissions does not mean that it is the kind of "system of emission reduction" referred to in Section 111. Indeed, the Government's examples demonstrate why it is not.

First, unlike Section 111, the Acid Rain and NAAQS programs contemplate trading systems as a means of complying with an already established emissions limit, set . . . by Congress (as with Acid Rain) or by reference to the safe concentration of the pollutant in the ambient air (as with the NAAQS). In Section 111, by contrast, it is EPA's job to come up with the cap itself. . . . It is one thing for Congress to authorize regulated sources to use trading to comply with a preset cap, or a cap that must be based on some scientific, objective criterion, such as the NAAQS. It is quite another to simply authorize EPA to set the cap itself wherever the Agency sees fit.

Second, Congress added the above authorizations for the use of emissions trading programs in 1990, simultaneous with amending Section 111 to its present form. At the time, cap-and-trade was a novel and highly touted concept. . . . Yet "not a peep was heard from Congress about the possibility that a trading regime could be installed under § 111." . . .

* * *

Capping carbon dioxide emissions at a level that will force a nationwide transition away from the use of coal to generate electricity may be a sensible "solution to the crisis of the day." New York v. United States, 505 U.S. 144, 187 (1992). But it is not plausible that Congress gave EPA the authority to adopt on its own such a regulatory scheme in Section 111(d). A decision of such magnitude and consequence rests with Congress itself, or an agency acting pursuant to a clear delegation from that representative body. The judgment of the Court of Appeals for the District of Columbia Circuit is reversed, and the cases are remanded for further proceedings consistent with this opinion.

It is so ordered.

■ JUSTICE GORSUCH, with whom JUSTICE ALITO joins, concurring.

To resolve today's case the Court invokes the major questions doctrine. Under that doctrine's terms, administrative agencies must be able to point to " 'clear congressional authorization' " when they claim the power to make decisions of vast " 'economic and political significance.' " Like many parallel clear-statement rules in our law, this one operates to protect foundational constitutional guarantees. I join the Court's opinion and write to offer some additional observations about the doctrine on which it rests.

I

. . . One of the Judiciary's most solemn duties is to ensure that acts of Congress are applied in accordance with the Constitution in the cases that come before us. To help fulfill that duty, courts have developed certain "clear-statement" rules. These rules assume that, absent a clear statement otherwise, Congress means for its laws to operate in congruence with the Constitution rather than test its bounds. In this way, these clear-statement rules help courts "act as faithful agents of the Constitution." A. Barrett, Substantive Canons and Faithful Agency, 90 B.U. L. Rev. 109, 169 (2010) (Barrett). . . .

Much as constitutional rules about retroactive legislation and sovereign immunity have their corollary clear-statement rules, Article I's Vesting Clause has its own: the major questions doctrine. See Gundy, 139 S.Ct., at 2141–2142 (GORSUCH, J., dissenting) [p. 842]. Some version of this clear-statement rule can be traced to at least 1897, when this Court confronted a case involving the Interstate Commerce Commission, the federal government's "first modern regulatory agency." S. Dudley, Milestones in the Evolution of the Administrative State 3 (Nov. 2020). The ICC argued that Congress had endowed it with the power to set carriage prices for railroads. See ICC v. Cincinnati, N.O. & T.P.R. Co., 167 U.S. 479, 499 (1897). The Court deemed that claimed authority "a power of supreme delicacy and importance," given the role railroads then played in the Nation's life. Id., at 505. Therefore, the Court explained, a special rule applied:

> "That Congress has transferred such a power to any administrative body is not to be presumed or implied from any doubtful and uncertain language. The words and phrases efficacious to make such a delegation of power are well understood, and have been frequently used, and if Congress had intended to grant such a power to the [agency], it cannot be doubted that it would have used language *open to no misconstruction*, but *clear and direct*." Ibid. (emphasis added).

With the explosive growth of the administrative state since 1970, the major questions doctrine soon took on special importance. . . .

The Court has applied the major questions doctrine for the same reason it has applied other similar clear-statement rules—to ensure that the government does "not inadvertently cross constitutional lines." Barrett 175. And the constitutional lines at stake here are surely no less important than those this Court has long held sufficient to justify parallel clear-statement rules. At stake is not just a question of retroactive liability or sovereign immunity, but basic questions about self-government, equality, fair notice, federalism, and the separation of powers. . . . The major questions doctrine seeks to protect against "unintentional, oblique, or otherwise unlikely" intrusions on these interests. NFIB v. OSHA, 142 S.Ct., at 669 (GORSUCH, J., concurring) [p. 869]. The doctrine does so by ensuring that, when agencies seek to resolve major questions, they at least act with clear congressional authorization and do not "exploit some gap, ambiguity, or doubtful expression in Congress's statutes to assume responsibilities far beyond" those the people's representatives actually conferred on them. Ibid. . . .

II

A

Turning from the doctrine's function to its application, it seems to me that our cases supply a good deal of guidance about when an agency action involves a major question for which clear congressional authority is required.

First, this Court has indicated that the doctrine applies when an agency claims the power to resolve a matter of great "political significance," NFIB v. OSHA, 142 S.Ct., at 665, or end an "earnest and profound debate across the country," Gonzales, 546 U.S. at 267–268. . . . Relatedly, this Court has found it telling when Congress has " 'considered and rejected' " bills authorizing something akin to the agency's proposed course of action. Brown & Williamson, 529 U.S. at 144. That too may be a sign that an agency is attempting to " 'work [a]round' " the legislative process to resolve for itself a question of great political significance. NFIB v. OSHA, S.Ct., at 668 (GORSUCH, J., concurring).

Second, this Court has said that an agency must point to clear congressional authorization when it seeks to regulate " 'a significant portion of the American economy,' " Utility Air, 573 U.S. at 324, or require "billions of dollars in spending" by private persons or entities, King v. Burwell, 576 U.S. 473, 485 (2015) [p. 108]. The Court has held that regulating tobacco products, eliminating rate regulation in the telecommunications industry, subjecting private homes to Clean Air Act restrictions, and suspending local housing laws and regulations can sometimes check this box. See Brown & Williamson, 529 U.S. at 160; MCI Telecommunications Corp. v. American Telephone & Telegraph Co., 512 U.S. 218, 231 (1994) (MCI); Utility Air, 573 U.S. at 324; Alabama Assn. of Realtors, 141 S.Ct., at 2486–2487.

Third, this Court has said that the major questions doctrine may apply when an agency seeks to "intrud[e] into an area that is the particular domain of state law." Ibid. Of course, another longstanding clear-statement rule—the federalism canon—also applies in these situations. . . . But unsurprisingly, the major questions doctrine and the federalism canon often travel together. When an agency claims the power to regulate vast swaths of American life, it not only risks intruding on Congress's power, it also risks intruding on powers reserved to the States. See SWANCC, 531 U.S. [159,] 162, 174 [(2001) (p. 1370)].

While this list of triggers may not be exclusive, each of the signs the Court has found significant in the past is present here, making this a relatively easy case for the doctrine's application. . . . Whether these plants should be allowed to operate is a question on which people today may disagree, but it is a question everyone can agree is vitally important. Congress . . . has "conspicuously and repeatedly declined" to adopt legislation similar to the Clean Power Plan (CPP). . . . It seems that fact has frustrated the Executive Branch and led it to attempt its own regulatory solution in the CPP. . . .

Other suggestive factors are present too. . . . The Executive Branch has acknowledged that its proposed rule would force an "aggressive transformation" of the electricity sector through "transition to zero-carbon renewable energy sources." The Executive Branch has also predicted its rule would force dozens of power plants to close and eliminate thousands of jobs by 2025. And industry analysts have estimated the CPP would cause consumers' electricity costs to rise by over $200 billion. Finally, the CPP unquestionably has an impact on federalism, as "the regulation of utilities is one of the most important of the functions traditionally associated with the police power of the States." Arkansas Elec. Cooperative Corp. v. Arkansas Pub. Serv. Comm'n, 461 U.S. 375, 377 (1983). . . .

B

At this point, the question becomes what qualifies as a clear congressional statement authorizing an agency's action. . . .

First, courts must look to the legislative provisions on which the agency seeks to rely " 'with a view to their place in the overall statutory scheme.' " Brown & Williamson, 529 U.S. at 133. "[O]blique or elliptical language" will not supply a clear statement. . . . Nor may agencies seek to hide "elephants in mouseholes," Whitman v. American Trucking

Assns., Inc., 531 U.S. 457, 468 (2001), or rely on "gap filler" provisions. . . .

Second, courts may examine the age and focus of the statute the agency invokes in relation to the problem the agency seeks to address. . . . Recently, too, this Court found a clear statement lacking when OSHA sought to impose a nationwide COVID-19 vaccine mandate based on a statutory provision that was adopted 40 years before the pandemic and that focused on conditions specific to the workplace rather than a problem faced by society at large. See NFIB v. OSHA, 142 S.Ct., at 667–668 (GORSUCH, J., concurring). . . .

Third, courts may examine the agency's past interpretations of the relevant statute. A "contemporaneous" and long-held Executive Branch interpretation of a statute is entitled to some weight as evidence of the statute's original charge to an agency. United States v. Philbrick, 120 U.S. 52, 59 (1887). Conversely, . . . [w]hen an agency claims to have found a previously "unheralded power," its assertion generally warrants "a measure of skepticism." Utility Air, 573 U.S. at 324.

Fourth, skepticism may be merited when there is a mismatch between an agency's challenged action and its congressionally assigned mission and expertise. As the Court explains, "[w]hen an agency has no comparative expertise in making certain policy judgments, . . . Congress presumably would not task it with doing so." . . .

As the Court details, the agency before us cites no specific statutory authority allowing it to transform the Nation's electrical power supply. Instead, the agency relies on a rarely invoked statutory provision that was passed with little debate and has been characterized as an "obscure, never-used section of the law." Nor has the agency previously interpreted the relevant provision to confer on it such vast authority; there is no original, longstanding, and consistent interpretation meriting judicial respect. Finally, there is a "mismatch" between the EPA's expertise over environmental matters and the agency's claim that "Congress implicitly tasked it, and it alone, with balancing the many vital considerations of national policy implicated in deciding how Americans will get their energy." Such a claimed power "requires technical and policy expertise *not* traditionally needed in [the] EPA's regulatory development." Again, in observing this much, the Court does not purport to pass on the wisdom of the agency's course. It acknowledges only that agency officials have sought to resolve a major policy question without clear legislative authorization to do so. . . .

■ JUSTICE KAGAN, with whom JUSTICE BREYER and JUSTICE SOTOMAYOR join, dissenting.

. . . The majority's decision rests on one claim alone: that generation shifting is just too new and too big a deal for Congress to have authorized it in Section 111's general terms. But that is wrong. A key reason Congress makes broad delegations like Section 111 is so an agency can respond, appropriately and commensurately, to new and big problems. Congress knows what it doesn't and can't know when it drafts a statute;

and Congress therefore gives an expert agency the power to address issues—even significant ones—as and when they arise. That is what Congress did in enacting Section 111. The majority today overrides that legislative choice. In so doing, it deprives EPA of the power needed—and the power granted—to curb the emission of greenhouse gases.

I

The Clean Air Act was major legislation, designed to deal with a major public policy issue. As Congress explained, its goal was to "speed up, expand, and intensify the war against air pollution" in all its forms. H.R. Rep. No. 91–1146, p. 1 (1970). . . .

Section 111(d) . . . ensures that EPA regulates existing power plants' emissions of all pollutants. When the pollutant at issue falls within the NAAQS or HAP programs, EPA need do no more. But when the pollutant falls outside those programs, . . . Section 111(d) guarantees that "there should be no gaps in control activities pertaining to stationary source emissions that pose any significant danger to public health or welfare." S. Rep. No. 91–1196, p. 20 (1970). . . . [T]he section is not, as the majority . . . claims, an "ancillary provision" or a statutory "backwater." That characterization is a non-sequitur. That something is a backstop does not make it a backwater. Even if they are needed only infrequently, backstops can perform a critical function—and this one surely does. . . . Section 111(d) operates to ensure that the Act achieves comprehensive pollution control.

Section 111 describes the prescribed regulatory effort in expansive terms. . . . [T]he provision instructs EPA to decide upon the "best system of emission reduction which . . . has been adequately demonstrated." . . . [T]he core command—go find the best system of emission reduction—gives broad authority to EPA.

If that flexibility is not apparent on the provision's face, consider some dictionary definitions—supposedly a staple of this Court's supposedly textualist method of reading statutes. A "system" is "a complex unity formed of many often diverse parts subject to a common plan or serving a common purpose." Webster's Third New International Dictionary 2322 (1971). Or again: a "system" is "[a]n organized and coordinated method; a procedure." American Heritage Dictionary 1768 (5th ed. 2018). The majority complains that a similar definition—cited to the Solicitor General's brief but originally from another dictionary—is just too darn broad. "[A]lmost anything" capable of reducing emissions, the majority says, "could constitute such a 'system'" of emission reduction. But that is rather the point. Congress used an obviously broad word (though surrounding it with constraints) to give EPA lots of latitude in deciding how to set emissions limits. And contra the majority, a broad term is not the same thing as a "vague" one. . . . So EPA was quite right in stating in the Clean Power Plan that the "[p]lain meaning" of the term "system" in Section 111 refers to "a set of measures that work together to reduce emissions." 80 Fed. Reg. 64762. . . .

For generation shifting fits comfortably within the conventional meaning of a "system of emission reduction." Consider one of the most common mechanisms of generation shifting: the use of a cap-and-trade scheme. Here is how the majority describes cap and trade: "Under such a scheme, sources that receive a reduction in their emissions can sell a credit representing the value of that reduction to others, who are able to count it toward their own applicable emissions caps." Does that sound like a "system" to you? It does to me too. And it also has to this Court. In the past, we have explained that "[t]his type of 'cap-and-trade' *system* cuts costs while still reducing pollution to target levels." EPA v. EME Homer City Generation, L. P., 572 U.S. 489, 503, n. 10 (2014) (emphasis added). . . .

Other statutory provisions confirm the point. The Clean Air Act's acid rain provision, for example, describes a cap-and-trade program as an "emission allocation and transfer *system*." § 7651(b) (emphasis added). So a "system," according to the statute's own usage, includes the kind of cap-and-trade mechanism that the Clean Power Plan relied on. And . . . [u]nder [the NAAQS] provision, cap-and-trade schemes qualify as "control measures, means, or techniques" that state plans may use to reduce emissions. § 7410(a)(2)(A). . . . [I]n specifying that cap and trade is allowable under the NAAQS program, the provision supports the same conclusion here—because Section 111 directs EPA to use "a procedure similar to that provided by [the NAAQS]." § 7411(d)(1). The majority discounts the relevance of both those provisions on the ground that they contemplate trading systems only "as a means of *complying* with an *already established emissions limit*." That is a distinction, to be sure. But . . . the distinction appears only in the majority's opinion, not in any statutory language. That text, to the contrary, says to EPA: Do as you would do under the NAAQS and Acid Rain programs—go ahead and use cap and trade.

There is also a flipside point: Congress declined to include in Section 111 the restrictions on EPA's authority contained in other Clean Air Act provisions. Most relevant here, quite a number of statutory sections confine EPA's emissions-reduction efforts to technological controls—essentially, equipment or processes that can be put into place at a particular facility. . . . But nothing like the language of those provisions is included in Section 111. . . . [The dissent detailed how Congress amended Section 111 to strike out language to this effect.] . . .

"Congress," this Court has said, "knows to speak in plain terms when it wishes to circumscribe, and in capacious terms when it wishes to enlarge, agency discretion." Arlington v. FCC, 569 U.S. 290, 296 (2013) [p. 1304]. In Section 111, Congress spoke in capacious terms. It knew that "without regulatory flexibility, changing circumstances and scientific developments would soon render the Clean Air Act obsolete." Massachusetts [v. EPA], 549 U.S. [497,] 532 [(2007) (p. 1321)]. So the provision enables EPA to base emissions limits for existing stationary sources on the "best system." That system may be technological in nature; it may be whatever else the majority has in mind; or, most important here, it may be generation shifting. The statute does not care. And when Congress uses "expansive language" to authorize agency action, courts generally may not "impos[e] limits on [the] agency's discretion." Little Sisters of the Poor Saints Peter and Paul Home v. Pennsylvania, 140 S.Ct. 2367, 2381 (2020) [p. 374]. That constraint on judicial authority—that insistence on judicial modesty—should resolve this case.

II

The majority thinks not, contending that in "certain extraordinary cases"—of which this is one—courts should start off with "skepticism" that a broad delegation authorizes agency action. The majority labels that view the "major questions doctrine," and claims to find support for it in our caselaw. But the relevant decisions do normal statutory interpretation: In them, the Court simply insisted that the text of a broad delegation, like any other statute, should be read in context, and with a modicum of common sense. Using that ordinary method, the decisions struck down agency actions (even though they plausibly fit within a delegation's terms) for two principal reasons. First, an agency was operating far outside its traditional lane, so that it had no viable claim of expertise or experience. And second, the action, if allowed, would have conflicted with, or even wreaked havoc on, Congress's broader design. In short, the assertion of delegated power was a misfit for both the agency and the statutory scheme. But that is not true here. The Clean Power Plan falls within EPA's wheelhouse, and it fits perfectly—as I've just shown—with all the Clean Air Act's provisions. That the Plan addresses major issues of public policy does not upend the analysis. Congress wanted EPA to do just that. Section 111 entrusts important matters to EPA in the expectation that the Agency will use that authority to combat pollution—and that courts will not interfere.

A

. . . The majority claims it is just following precedent, but that is not so. The Court has never even used the term "major questions doctrine" before. And in the relevant cases, the Court has done statutory construction of a familiar sort. It has looked to the text of a delegation. It has addressed how an agency's view of that text works—or fails to do so—in the context of a broader statutory scheme. And it has asked, in a common-sensical (or call it purposive) vein, about what Congress would have made of the agency's view—otherwise said, whether Congress would naturally have delegated authority over some important question to the agency, given its expertise and experience. In short, in assessing the scope of a delegation, the Court has considered—without multiple steps, triggers, or special presumptions—the fit between the power claimed, the agency claiming it, and the broader statutory design.

The key case here is FDA v. Brown & Williamson. There, . . . the asserted authority "simply [did] not fit" the overall statutory scheme. 529 U.S. at 143. FDA's governing statute required the agency to ensure that regulated products were "safe" to be marketed—but there was no making tobacco products safe in the usual sense. So FDA would have had to reinterpret what it meant to be "safe," or else ban tobacco products altogether. Both options, the Court thought, were preposterous. Until the agency action at issue, tobacco products hadn't been spoken of in the same breath as pharmaceuticals (FDA's paradigmatic regulated product). And Congress had created in several statutes a "distinct regulatory scheme" for tobacco, not involving FDA. So all the evidence was that Congress had never meant for FDA to have any—let alone total—control over the tobacco industry, with its "unique political history." . . .

The majority's effort to find support in Brown & Williamson for its interpretive approach fails. It may be helpful here to quote the full sentence that the majority quotes half of. "In extraordinary cases," the Court stated, "there may be reason to hesitate before concluding that Congress has intended such an implicit delegation." 529 U.S. at 159. For anyone familiar with this Court's Chevron doctrine, that language will ring a bell. The Court was saying only—and it was elsewhere explicit on this point—that there was reason to hesitate before giving FDA's position Chevron deference. . . . In reaching that conclusion, the Court relied (as I've just explained) not on any special "clear authorization" demand, but on normal principles of statutory interpretation: look at the text, view it in context, and use what the Court called some "common sense" about how Congress delegates. . . .

[The dissent discussed the case law catalogued in the other opinions, including Utility Air Regulatory Group v. EPA, where "[t]he Court explained that allowing the agency action to proceed would necessitate the 'rewriting' of other 'unambiguous statutory terms'—indeed, of 'precise numerical thresholds.' "]

. . . In each case, the Court thought, the agency had strayed out of its lane, to an area where it had neither expertise nor experience. The Attorney General making healthcare policy, the regulator of pharmaceutical concerns deciding the fate of the tobacco industry, and so on. And in each case, the proof that the agency had roamed too far afield lay in the statutory scheme itself. The agency action collided with other statutory provisions; if the former were allowed, the latter could not mean what they said or could not work as intended. FDA having to declare tobacco "safe" to avoid shutting down an industry; or EPA having literally to change hard numbers contained in the Clean Air Act. . . .

B

. . . [N]owhere does the majority provide evidence from within the statute itself that the Clean Power Plan conflicts with or undermines Congress's design. That fact alone makes this case different from all the cases described above. As to the other critical matter in those cases—is the agency operating outside its sphere of expertise?—the majority at least tries to say something. It claims EPA has no "comparative expertise" in "balancing the many vital considerations of national policy" implicated in regulating electricity sources. But that is wrong.

. . . Consider the Clean Power Plan's component parts—let's call them the what, who, and how—to see the rule's normalcy. The "what" is the subject matter of the Plan: carbon dioxide emissions. This Court has already found that those emissions fall within EPA's domain. We said then: "[T]here is nothing counterintuitive to the notion that EPA can curtail the emission of substances that are putting the global climate out of kilter." Massachusetts, 549 U.S. at 531. This is not the Attorney General regulating medical care, or even the CDC regulating landlord-tenant relations. It is EPA (that's the Environmental Protection Agency, in case the majority forgot) acting to address the greatest environmental challenge of our time. So too, there is nothing special about the Plan's "who": fossil-fuel-fired power plants. In Utility Air, we thought EPA's regulation of churches and schools highly unusual. But fossil-fuel-fired plants? Those plants pollute—a lot—and so they have long lived under the watchful eye of EPA. . . .

Finally, the "how" of generation shifting creates no mismatch with EPA's expertise. As the Plan noted, generation shifting has a well-established pedigree as a tool for reducing pollution; even putting aside other federal regulation, both state regulators and power plants themselves have long used it to attain environmental goals. The technique is, so to speak, a tool in the pollution-control toolbox. And that toolbox is the one EPA uses. So that Agency, more than any other, has the desired "comparative expertise." . . . [T]he majority protests that Congress would not have wanted EPA to "dictat[e]," through generation shifting, the "mix of energy sources nationwide." But . . . [e]very regulation of power plants—even the most conventional, facility-specific controls—"dictat[es]" the national energy mix to one or another degree. . . . [R]egulations affect costs, and the electrical grid works by taking up energy from low-cost providers before high-cost ones. Consider an example: Suppose EPA requires coal-fired plants to use carbon-capture technology. That action increases those plants' costs, and automatically (by virtue of the way the grid operates) reduces their share of the electricity market. So EPA is always controlling the mix of energy sources. In that sense (though the term has taken on a more specialized meaning), everything EPA does is "generation shifting." . . .

Why, then, be "skeptic[al]" of EPA's exercise of authority? . . . Although the majority offers a flurry of complaints, they come down in the end to this: The Clean Power Plan is a big new thing, issued under a minor statutory provision. . . . In fact, there is nothing insignificant about Section 111(d), which was intended to ensure that EPA would limit existing stationary sources' emissions of otherwise unregulated pollutants (however few or many there were). And the front half of the argument doesn't work either. The Clean Power Plan was not so big. It was not so new. And to the extent it was either, that should not matter.

As to bigness—well, events have proved the opposite: The Clean Power Plan, we now know, would have had little or no impact. . . . [T]he industry didn't fall short of the Plan's goal; rather, the industry exceeded that target, all on its own. . . .

The majority's claim about the Clean Power Plan's novelty—the most fleshed-out part of today's opinion—is also exaggerated. As EPA explained when it issued the Clean Power Plan, an earlier Section 111(d) regulation had determined that a cap-and-trade program was the "best system of emission reduction" for mercury. 70 Fed. Reg. 28616–28621 (2005); see 80 Fed. Reg. 64772. . . .

. . . No doubt the majority is right that scrubbers and other "add-on controls" are "more traditional air pollution control measures." . . . But the idea that the Plan's reliance on generation shifting effected some kind of revolution in power-plant pollution control? No. As I've noted before, power plants themselves use that method. State environmental regulators use that method. And EPA has used that method, including under the statutory provision invoked here.

In any event, newness might be perfectly legitimate—even required—from Congress's point of view. I do not dispute that an agency's longstanding practice may inform a court's interpretation of a statute delegating the agency power. But it is equally true, as Brown & Williamson recognized, that agency practices are "not carved in stone." 529 U.S. at 156–157. Congress makes broad delegations in part so that agencies can "adapt their rules and policies to the demands of changing circumstances." Id., at 157. To keep faith with that congressional choice, courts must give agencies "ample latitude" to revisit, rethink, and revise their regulatory approaches. So it is here. Section 111(d) was written, as I've shown, to give EPA plenty of leeway. . . .

And contra the majority, it is that Congress's choice which counts, not any later one's. The majority says it "cannot ignore" that Congress in recent years has "considered and rejected" cap-and-trade schemes. But under normal principles of statutory construction, the majority should ignore that fact (just as I should ignore that Congress failed to enact bills barring EPA from implementing the Clean Power Plan). . . .

III

Some years ago, I remarked that "[w]e're all textualists now." Harvard Law School, The Antonin Scalia Lecture Series: A Dialogue with Justice Elena Kagan on the Reading of Statutes (Nov. 25, 2015). It seems I was wrong. The current Court is textualist only when being so suits it. When that method would frustrate broader goals, special canons like the "major questions doctrine" magically appear as get-out-of-text-free cards. Today, one of those broader goals makes itself clear: Prevent agencies from doing important work, even though that is what Congress directed. That anti-administrative-state stance shows up in the majority opinion, and it suffuses the concurrence.

The kind of agency delegations at issue here go all the way back to this Nation's founding. . . .

It is not surprising that Congress has always delegated, and continues to do so—including on important policy issues. . . . In all times, but ever more in "our increasingly complex society," the Legislature "simply cannot do its job absent an ability to delegate power under broad general directives." Mistretta v. United States, 488 U.S. 361, 372 (1989) [p. 838]. Consider just two reasons why.

First, Members of Congress often don't know enough—and know they don't know enough—to regulate sensibly on an issue. Of course, Members can and do provide overall direction. But then they rely, as all of us rely in our daily lives, on people with greater expertise and experience. Those people are found in agencies. Congress looks to them to make specific judgments about how to achieve its more general objectives. And it does so especially, though by no means exclusively, when an issue has a scientific or technical dimension. Why wouldn't Congress instruct EPA to select "the best system of emission reduction," rather than try to choose that system itself? . . .

Second and relatedly, Members of Congress often can't know enough—and again, know they can't—to keep regulatory schemes working across time. Congress usually can't predict the future—can't anticipate changing circumstances and the way they will affect varied regulatory techniques. Nor can Congress (realistically) keep track of and respond to fast-flowing developments as they occur. Once again, that is most obviously true when it comes to scientific and technical matters. The "best system of emission reduction" is not today what it was yesterday, and will surely be something different tomorrow. So for this reason too, a rational Congress delegates. It enables an agency to adapt old regulatory approaches to new times, to ensure that a statutory program remains effective.

Over time, the administrative delegations Congress has made have helped to build a modern Nation. Congress wanted fewer workers killed in industrial accidents. It wanted to prevent plane crashes, and reduce the deadliness of car wrecks. It wanted to ensure that consumer products didn't catch fire. It wanted to stop the routine adulteration of food and improve the safety and efficacy of medications. And it wanted cleaner air and water. If an American could go back in time, she might be astonished by how much progress has occurred in all those areas. It didn't happen through legislation alone. It happened because Congress gave broad-ranging powers to administrative agencies, and those agencies then filled in—rule by rule by rule—Congress's policy outlines. . . .

In short, when it comes to delegations, there are good reasons for Congress (within extremely broad limits) to get to call the shots. Congress knows about how government works in ways courts don't. More specifically, Congress knows what mix of legislative and administrative action conduces to good policy. Courts should be modest.

Today, the Court is not. . . . The Court will not allow the Clean Air Act to work as Congress instructed. The Court, rather than Congress, will decide how much regulation is too much.

The subject matter of the regulation here makes the Court's intervention all the more troubling. Whatever else this Court may know about, it does not have a clue about how to address climate change. And let's say the obvious: The stakes here are high. Yet the Court today prevents congressionally authorized agency action to curb power plants' carbon dioxide emissions. The Court appoints itself—instead of Congress or the expert agency—the decision-maker on climate policy. I cannot think of many things more frightening. Respectfully, I dissent.

## NOTES ON WHAT IS A "MAJOR QUESTION" UNDER WEST VIRGINIA V. EPA

The majority opinion doesn't cleanly separate out the question of when major questions analysis is triggered. It mentions at least the following signals, derived from Brown & Williamson, that an assertion of authority is "extraordinary": "the 'history and the breadth of the authority that [the agency] has asserted,' and the 'economic and political significance' of that assertion." (Can you find others?)

(1) ***"Economic" Effects.*** What do you think of the dissent's view that "everything EPA does is 'generation shifting' " because every regulation that raises the cost of fossil fuel generation diminishes its relative share of the grid? Or the fact that "'traditional' technological controls, of the kind the majority approves, can have equally dramatic effects"? For example, if EPA ordered installation of carbon-capture equipment, "the 'exorbitant' costs 'would almost certainly force the closure' of all affected 'coal-fired power plants.' " The majority's response seems to be "doubt" that EPA could even "order[ ] anything remotely like that"—perhaps signaling that this, too, would run into major questions problems.)

What measure of economic effects is provided by the costs of the regulation? And how high were the costs of the Clean Power Plan after all? Does it matter that industry achieved the Clean Power Plan standards all on its own? Does it matter how costly other regulatory interventions have been? The estimated costs of the Clean Power Plan, although in the billions, also constituted "most likely 1% or 2% of the industry's revenues," in contrast to "the massive dislocation that the Supreme Court had decried in King v. Burwell, where eliminating the tax credit provision would decrease healthcare enrollment by approximately 70% and thereby cause unsubsidized premiums to increase by approximately 35% to 47%." Natasha Brunstein & Richard L. Revesz, Mangling the Major Questions Doctrine, 74 Admin. L. Rev. 217, 238 (2022).

And what about benefits? Do the benefits of the regulations—"between $32 billion and $54 billion"—suggest that it is problematic to focus on high costs in assessing the significance of the economic effects of regulation for purposes of determining whether the economic effects of the regulation trigger application of the clear statement rule under the major questions doctrine? Or do major benefits signal a major question in their own right?

One scholar has argued that Congress itself shed light on such questions in the Congressional Review Act, 5 U.S.C. §§ 801–08 (2018), which defines "major rules" as ones found by the Office of Information and Regulatory Affairs to have an annual economic effect of at least $100 million; to cause significant cost increases for consumers, industry, certain government entities, or regions; or to precipitate certain significant adverse economic effects such as unemployment. The Act provides that "[m]ajor rules, . . . *must* be given legal effect sixty days after the agency transmits the rule to Congress or publishes the rule in the Federal Register; the only exception mentioned in the CRA is if Congress affirmatively enacts a new law disapproving of the major rule. The CRA carefully outlines the procedural steps that Congress may take to disapprove of a major rule. . . . The judge-made presumption in the major questions doctrine threatens to turn the CRA's detailed sixty-day *disapproval* process on its head to instead require Congress to take special steps to *approve* an agency's major rule." Chad Squitieri, Who Determines Majorness?, 44 Harv. J.L. & Pub. Pol'y 463, 492–93 (2021). Thus, instead of Congress implicitly reserving discretion to answer major questions, as the major questions doctrine would have it, perhaps the CRA suggests that Congress assumes agencies will promulgate major rules to answer such questions. Id. at 491.

(2) ***"Political" Effects.*** What could the Court mean in referring to the "political effects" of a regulation being so significant as to trigger the major question doctrine's clear statement rule? Consider something like a vaccine-or-test mandate. See National Federation of Independent Business v. Occupational Safety & Health Administration, 142 S.Ct. 661 (2022) (p. 1345). Does that present a major question simply because it is politically controversial? And if so, by what metric would a court assess how politically controversial a regulatory intervention is? Perhaps by "political" the Court really means the kind of regulatory decision that is politically important, even if not especially controversial, because it affects lots of interests? If so, is there any way in which "political" effects differ from economic ones? Then again, doesn't the majority have a point? Is it plausible that EPA could have authority to shift the power grid completely away from fossil fuels without a clear statement? Could EPA use its Section 111 authority to ration electricity? Take some particularly energy-hungry houses off the grid altogether? Or does the dissent's response show that those possibilities are logically checked through the political process alongside doctrines like nondelegation and arbitrariness review, rather than through review of agency interpretations of statutory language?

(3) ***Novelty.*** Consider the West Virginia majority's position that EPA's historical approach to interpreting Section 111 provided a useful signal of whether the Clean Power Plan was so "novel[ ]" that it "effected a 'fundamental revision of the statute. . . .' " Consistent agency interpretation shows up as a potential trigger for the "major questions" doctrine even more explicitly in the concurrence, which calls for considering the "agency's past interpretations of the relevant statute" to discern whether Congress has clearly granted authority. There's surely some logic to this intuition. If in Brown & Williamson the FDA had been regulating tobacco under the FDCA for decades, rather than the opposite, wouldn't that have limited the strength of the major questions argument against FDA's interpretation?

But is this intuition consistent with the logic of the major questions doctrine? To the extent that it allows an agency's past practice to constrain its present options, it still seems to allow major questions to be decided by the agency, just under previous administrations. Doesn't that produce the same separation of powers problem—an agency deciding major questions—but without the benefit of the present agency's limited accountability? And as to the concurrence's view that consistency goes to whether Congress has spoken clearly, if the entire point is that Congress, not the agency, must have spoken clearly through legislation, does it make any sense for even a contemporaneous agency interpretation to be breaking any ties?

And how can this position be reconciled with the commonplace idea that, as the dissent puts it, "Congress makes broad delegations in part so that agencies can 'adapt their rules and policies to the demands of changing circumstances' "? Consider in this regard Daniel T. Deacon & Leah M. Litman, The New Major Questions Doctrine, 109 Va. L. Rev. (forthcoming): "Part of what is striking about the new major questions cases is that the justifications for delegations to agencies—the reasons why Congress might rely on delegations to agencies—now overlap with the reasons the Court has identified to be skeptical of an agency's authority. As a result, the Court's major questions doctrine undermines the very bases for delegation, turning the reasons why Congress might rely on delegations to agencies into reasons to narrowly construe and limit the reach of the delegations in the circumstances in which the delegations are likely to be used and likely to be needed for effective governance."

(4) ***Reconciling Major Cases with the Major Question Doctrine.*** It seems clear that the Court is saying more in West Virginia than that it is not bound to defer to EPA's construction of the statute. It is saying that the statute just does not reach as far as the agency contends because Congress would not want to give the agency that kind of regulatory power. And, it seems clear, the Court is concluding as much only after applying a clear statement requirement to *that* question rather than merely to the step zero question. But, if that is right, then how easily is West Virginia v. EPA reconciled with other major cases like Massachusetts v. EPA and King v. Burwell?

(a) *Was Massachusetts v. EPA Not a Major Questions Case?* Recall that in Massachusetts v. EPA (p. 1321), the Court rejected EPA's major questions argument that Congress had implicitly instructed it not to regulate greenhouse gases. First, the Court found "nothing counterintuitive to the notion that EPA can curtail the emission of substances that are putting the global climate out of kilter," in contrast to Brown & Williamson's " 'common sense' intuition that Congress never meant to remove [tobacco] products from circulation." Massachusetts, 549 U.S. at 531. Second, the Court found no history of legislation inconsistent with regulating greenhouse gases, unlike Brown & Williamson. Id. And third, the Court rejected the notion that the Department of Transportation's charge to set mileage standards required the conclusion that the regulation of motor vehicle carbon dioxide emissions by the EPA would infringe on the statutory authority of the Department of Transportation: "The two obligations may overlap, but there is no reason to think the two agencies cannot both administer their obligations and yet avoid inconsistency." Id. at 532. Nor did the dissents in Massachusetts rest upon the major questions doctrine. In fact, at oral argument in the D.C. Circuit, the government came in for some serious criticism for using this argument, with Judge Sentelle asking: "Can you forget about Brown & Williamson?" Richard J. Lazarus, The Rule of Five: Making Climate History at the Supreme Court 95 (2020).

Can you square the fact that the Court in Massachusetts did not purport to address a major question with West Virginia? Each of the Massachusetts majority's arguments could seem to apply just as much in West Virginia. And at a big picture level, how would you compare the authority to impose tighter emission standards on power plants with the authority to regulate carbon dioxide? Is it more significant? More of a departure from longstanding agency practice? More unexpected by Congress? More at odds with the text of the Clean Air Act? One difference might be that Massachusetts v. EPA concerned what the agency could regulate—carbon dioxide or not—while West Virginia v. EPA concerned how the agency could regulate—through generation shifting or not. Is there a relation between the "what" and "how" questions that implicates delegation concerns, such that the more discretion an agency has to decide how to regulate more things, the more concerning the delegation becomes? But if so, how do we know whether to apply the clear-statement rule to the "what" question (posed in Massachusetts v. EPA) or the "how" question (posed in West Virginia v. EPA)? Or does the rule apply to both?

(b) *How About King v. Burwell?* After dispensing with Chevron deference, Chief Justice Roberts in King goes on to determine that the crucial piece of statutory text at issue in that case is "ambiguous" and then says: "Given that the text is ambiguous, we must turn to the broader structure of the Act to determine the meaning of [the disputed section]." Given that structure, he then identifies what he calls the "fair reading" of the Act. But, wasn't the question there exceedingly politically controversial, because it determined whether the administration would be able to make the Affordable Care Act as effective a method of regulating health insurance markets as the Obama Administration had hoped? If so, then why not apply a clear-statement canon to the interpretive question? Is it because the case did not present as one involving a delegation of authority to an agency?

(c) *For That Matter, How About Bostock v. Clayton County?* Think back, if you've read it, to Bostock v. Clayton County in Chapter II (p. 128). In that case, Justice Gorsuch's majority opinion stated that Title VII's statutory prohibition on "because of sex," given its ordinary broad meaning, swept broadly: "An employer who fires an individual for being homosexual or transgender fires that person for traits or actions it would not have questioned in members of a different sex. Sex plays a necessary and undisguisable role in the decision, exactly what Title VII forbids." 140 S.Ct. 1731, 1737 (2020). The opinion noted the principle "that Congress 'does not alter the fundamental details of a regulatory scheme in vague terms or ancillary provisions,' " citing Whitman v. American Trucking Ass'ns (p. 848), but stated, "it has no relevance here. We can't deny that today's holding—that employers are prohibited from firing employees on the basis of homosexuality or transgender status—is an elephant. But where's the mousehole? Title VII's prohibition of sex discrimination in employment is a major piece of federal civil rights legislation. It is written in starkly broad terms. It has repeatedly produced unexpected applications, at least in the view of those on the receiving end of them. Congress's key drafting choices—to focus on discrimination against individuals and not merely between groups and to hold employers liable whenever sex is a but-for cause of the plaintiff's injuries—virtually guaranteed that unexpected applications would emerge over time. This elephant has never hidden in a mousehole; it has been standing before us all along."

Is Justice Gorsuch's concurrence in West Virginia consistent with this reasoning? Perhaps Bostock did not present the right conditions for the major questions doctrine to apply, as that case did not present as a case involving deference to an agency interpretation. Or something like the major questions doctrine may already be at work—perhaps antidiscrimination law is reserved for the judiciary because it encompasses such serious and important questions. See Rebecca Hanner White, Deference and Disability Discrimination, 99 Mich. L. Rev. 532, 570–72 (2000).

That said, is Bostock's logic that Title VII's broad language licenses interpretation at a high level of generality, and thus updating, consistent with West Virginia's hesitance to give "system" in Section 111 its entire breadth of meaning? Can Section 111 be distinguished as a statutory "backwater"? Or is that just assuming the conclusion?

(5) ***Applying the Doctrine in the Lower Courts.*** It is one thing for the Supreme Court to decide what questions are major. But, can such a doctrine be consistently applied by the lower courts? MICHAEL COENEN & SETH DAVIS, MINOR COURTS, MAJOR QUESTIONS, 70 Vand. L. Rev. 777, 812–17 (2017), analyzed the problem as follows. Suppose that lower courts could make two types of errors: failing to apply the major questions doctrine to a major question, and incorrectly applying the major questions doctrine to an interstitial matter. Given the discretionary nature of Supreme Court review, the Court may be more likely to review cases involving major questions, leaving the second type of error uncorrected. What would be the likely effects of such an asymmetry over time?

## NOTES ON THE LEGAL BASIS FOR THE MAJOR QUESTIONS DOCTRINE

The West Virginia majority explains that "both separation of powers principles and a practical understanding of legislative intent" support its application of the major questions doctrine. But those are potentially quite different sources of authority for the doctrine. If the doctrine is rooted in a practical understanding of legislative intent, then the clear-statement rule that the doctrine imposes is not a substantive canon that reflects any policy or constitutional value. Instead, it is a means of getting at Congress's intent. By contrast, if the concern is separation of powers, constitutional values are front and center, suggesting the opposite.

(1) ***Two Versions of the Major Questions Doctrine.*** CASS SUNSTEIN, THERE ARE TWO "MAJOR QUESTIONS" DOCTRINES, 73 Admin. L. Rev. 475, 477–80 (2021): "[T]he major questions doctrine has been understood in two radically different ways—weak and strong—and . . . the two have radically

different implications. The weak version suggests a kind of 'carveout' from Chevron deference when a major question is involved. Because Chevron does not apply, courts are required to resolve the relevant question of law independently, and without deference to agency interpretations.

"The strong version, by contrast, operates as a clear statement principle, in the form of a firm barrier to certain agency interpretations. The idea is not merely that courts will decide questions of statutory meaning on their own. It is that such questions will be resolved unfavorably to the agency. When an agency is seeking to assert very broad power, it will lose, because Congress has not clearly granted it that power.

"The two versions have different justifications. The weak version is rooted in the prevailing theory behind Chevron, which is that Congress has implicitly delegated law-interpreting power to the agency. The weak version qualifies that idea by adding that Congress has not implicitly delegated agencies the power to decide major questions. By contrast, the strong version is rooted in the nondelegation doctrine, which requires Congress to offer an 'intelligible principle' by which to limit agency discretion. Drawing from the nondelegation doctrine, the strong version of the major questions doctrine states that if agencies are to exercise certain kinds of power, they must be able to show clear congressional authorization. . . .

"For both theory and practice, the stakes are exceedingly high—whether we are speaking of the weak version, the strong version, or the choice between them. Many agencies, and many administrations, are interested in adopting significant initiatives, asserting novel authority, and breaking with the past (even with longstanding interpretations of statutory provisions). This is especially true at the beginning of a new presidential term, but it can be true as well at the start of a second term, or even in the middle. For example, the Federal Trade Commission might want to rethink its interpretation of Section 230 of the Communications Decency Act—the statutory provision giving broad immunity to Internet service providers, including social media platforms. Or the Department of Justice might want to issue a new rule taking some stand on whether and when discrimination based on sexual orientation, or against transgender persons, is a violation of existing statutory provisions. Or the Environmental Protection Agency (EPA) might want to alter its approach to fuel economy, perhaps by allowing something like a cap-and-trade program. Or the Department of Health and Human Services might want to adopt a new understanding of the Affordable Care Act—expanding its reach, strengthening its prohibitions, or giving more or less flexibility to insurance companies.

"In all of these cases, and many like them, an agency interpretation at least arguably resolves a 'major question.' Under the weak version, the agency would lose the benefit of Chevron deference—which might well mean that it would face an adverse judicial decision. If courts adopt the weak version, a broad understanding of the scope of the major questions doctrine would make it harder for agencies to adopt significant initiatives, potentially increasing stability but reducing flexibility for the administrative state as a whole. For any administration, such an understanding would amount to a nontrivial and possibly large reduction in its discretionary authority, whether the issue involves discrimination, responses to COVID-19, climate change, food safety, or regulation of social media.

"The strong version would have an even larger impact. It would mean that in the face of ambiguity, courts would forbid agencies from making their preferred policy choices unless Congress has given them explicit authorization to do so—at least in cases in which agencies seek (as they often do) to exercise significant new authority. Perhaps a general movement toward the strong version of the major questions doctrine should be celebrated as a way of cabining agency power and serving some of the purposes of the nondelegation doctrine. Or perhaps such a movement should be lamented as a way of forbidding agencies from interpreting ambiguous language in a way that takes advantage of their accountability and expertise. However one evaluates the strong version, there is no doubt that it would have significant consequences.

"From the standpoint of theory, the issues are both important and intricate. The weak version requires courts to take a clear stand on the best justification of Chevron, which in turn calls for a clarification of that justification. In principle, the weak version could significantly reduce Chevron's reach. The strong version, by contrast, draws on the Constitution itself and is best understood as an effort, at once modest and firm, of reviving a particular reading of Article I, Section I. So understood, the strong version could be a harbinger of a large-scale revival of that reading. Even if it is no harbinger, it could be seen as an embodiment, for better or for worse, of a modern effort to resuscitate the nondelegation doctrine in a way that is relatively easier to administer, and that does not impose an undue strain on federal judges."

(2) ***A Linguistic Canon?*** It's clear that West Virginia is applying the strong form of the doctrine that Sunstein describes. Note, though, that the majority is careful not to say it is establishing a nondelegation canon. Only the concurrence makes that case. Perhaps, then, Sunstein notwithstanding, the Major Questions Doctrine is a kind of linguistic canon even in what Sunstein calls its strong form. After all, when you see an acquaintance on the street and ask, "How's life?" don't you expect the one answering to intuit that you are asking a routine rather than a major question? On the other hand, why would we expect Congress not to be asking an agency to tackle a major question when it assigns authority to an agency to protect the environment or ensure that manufacturers are only marketing drugs that are safe and effective? Those are hardly casual choices on Congress's part, so why default to an assumption that its delegations are not to be taken at their word and so must be expressed in unusually clear terms whenever the delegation would matter most?

(3) ***A Substantive, Non-Delegation Canon?*** The West Virginia majority does not spell out how the clear-statement rule that it deploys supports "separation of powers" other than by asserting that the rule will ensure that Congress's will is followed. But Justice Gorsuch's concurrence argues that it is a means of enforcing the principles of the nondelegation doctrine. If it were, then it would have a constitutional pedigree, like certain other clear-statement rules.

On this view, the major questions doctrine is less a product of "a practical understanding of legislative intent" and more a necessary consequence of the "separation of powers." That would seem to mean that the doctrine exists to ensure that agencies do not have powers that the constitution bars Congress from delegating to them. Does the major questions doctrine do so? After all, it is hardly evident that Congress can overcome actual delegation problems by being very clear that it is divesting itself of legislative authority. Conversely, if Congress had simply legislated the Clean Power Plan, would there be a serious question whether the legislation raised even minor nondelegation issues? See the discussion of nondelegation in Chapter VII. For an analysis of the relationship between the major questions and nondelegation doctrines, see Mila Sohoni, The Major Questions Quartet, 136 Harv. L. Rev. 262 (2022).

(4) ***The Major Questions Doctrine and Precedent.*** As a pre-1980s precedent for the major questions doctrine, Justice Gorsuch cites the case ICC v. Cincinnati, N.O. & T.P.R. Co., 167 U.S. 479 (1897). In that case, the Court wrote of the ICC's asserted authority to fix railroad rates: "The words and phrases efficacious to make such a delegation of power are well understood, and have been frequently used, and if Congress had intended to grant such a power to the [agency], it cannot be doubted that it would have used language *open to no misconstruction*, but *clear and direct*."

In the ICC case, the question was whether the agency could infer authority to set rates from its authority to adjudicate whether rates were reasonable—in other words, the Court said, whether a statute's grant of legislative authority to an agency also implied a grant of an adjudicative authority. The Court reviewed state statutes, concluding that "they all show[ed] what phraseology has been deemed necessary whenever the intent has been to give to the commissioners the legislative power of fixing rates." Finding no such phraseology in the Interstate Commerce Act, the Court declined to imply it. Is the question of whether an agency has the power to engage in rulemaking at all analogous to the question of the scope of the rulemaking authority that it plainly has?

## NOTES ON THE RELATIONSHIP BETWEEN THE MAJOR QUESTIONS DOCTRINE AND OTHER KEY STATUTORY INTERPRETATION ISSUES

(1) ***Chevron.*** It is possible the major questions doctrine has no relationship to Chevron, because the Court no longer is interested in applying Chevron. But, assuming that the two doctrines must be reconciled, at what stage of Chevron does the major questions doctrine apply?

(a) *Chevron Step Zero.* One possibility is that the major questions doctrine illuminates when Congress delegates authority to speak with the force of law—so it's a condition added onto Chevron "step zero." This approach appears to be the one that the Court took in KING V. BURWELL, 576 U.S. 473 (2015) (p. 108), in which the Court refused to extend Chevron deference to the IRS's regulation interpreting the ACA's tax-credit provision—despite the ACA's express grant of authority to the IRS to "prescribe such regulations as may be necessary to carry out" the ACA's tax credits. CHIEF JUSTICE ROBERTS wrote for the Court: "When analyzing an agency's interpretation of a statute, we often apply the two-step framework announced in Chevron. Under that framework, we ask whether the statute is ambiguous and, if so, whether the agency's interpretation is reasonable. This approach 'is premised on the theory that a statute's ambiguity constitutes an implicit delegation from Congress to the agency to fill in the statutory gaps.' 'In extraordinary cases, however, there may be reason to hesitate before concluding that Congress has intended such an implicit delegation.' Ibid.

"This is one of those cases. The tax credits are among the Act's key reforms, involving billions of dollars in spending each year and affecting the price of health insurance for millions of people. Whether those credits are available on Federal Exchanges is thus a question of deep 'economic and political significance' that is central to this statutory scheme; had Congress wished to assign that question to an agency, it surely would have done so expressly. It is especially unlikely that Congress would have delegated this decision to the *IRS*, which has no expertise in crafting health insurance policy of this sort. This is not a case for the IRS.

"It is instead our task to determine the correct reading of Section 36B. If the statutory language is plain, we must enforce it according to its terms. But oftentimes the 'meaning—or ambiguity—of certain words or phrases may only become evident when placed in context.' So when deciding whether the language is plain, we must read the words 'in their context and with a view to their place in the overall statutory scheme.' Our duty, after all, is 'to construe statutes, not isolated provisions.'"

Is this the approach of the Court in West Virginia? Do the majority and concurrence set out guideposts that are keyed to this "step zero" inquiry? Or are the guideposts more indicative of what a statute actually means, which is the step one question?

(b) *Chevron Step One.* If the major questions doctrine illuminates the step one inquiry, why did the Court in West Virginia characterize its approach as different from normal statutory interpretation? And where is Chevron in the decision?

Brown & Williamson provides a template for how major questions considerations can factor into a step one analysis. That decision stated that "the nature of the question presented" was relevant because it could help illuminate the "inquiry into whether Congress has directly spoken to the precise question at issue." The Court also supported its inquiry into whether Congress had spoken to the question at issue by noting that Congress had enacted a separate regulatory scheme for tobacco.

Now compare West Virginia. Like Brown & Williamson, it considered legislative history, noting that Congress had rejected cap-and-trade programs, a potential way sources could meet EPA's new standard. But it did so to support the proposition that "[u]nder our precedents, this is a major questions case." If precedents like Brown & Williamson treat major questions cases as Chevron step one cases about whether there is statutory ambiguity, are the techniques those precedents deploy obviously useful when the Court shifts to a new orienting principle, like the separation of powers?

Consider, too, what then-Judge Kavanaugh said in Fixing Statutory Interpretation, 129 Harv. L. Rev. 2118 (2016), about what he saw as the problems posed by the open-endedness of Chevron step one: "[T]he problem with certain applications of Chevron, as I see it, is that the doctrine is so indeterminate—and thus can be antithetical to the neutral, impartial rule of law—because of the initial clarity versus ambiguity decision." Is statutory ambiguity more indeterminate than the significance of a delegation? And are there hints from the majority that the significance of a question is assessed in light of the murkiness of the agency's statute anyway?

(c) *Chevron Step Two.* Might the major questions doctrine be aligned with Chevron step two? For example, the concurrence approves of the majority's statement that the major questions rule is addressed to the problem of "agencies asserting highly consequential power beyond what Congress could reasonably be understood to have granted." Isn't that a step two problem unless the text is clear? For a decision taking this approach, see Util. Air Regul. Grp. v. EPA, 573 U.S. 302, 324 (2014). Put differently, if the major questions doctrine is a clear statement rule, isn't it premised on Congress *not* speaking clearly at Chevron step one?

(2) ***Textualism.*** Is the major questions doctrine best squared with textualism or purposivism? Arguably, it is not textualist because it eschews the ordinary meaning of the words Congress uses by subjecting them to a super-strong clear-statement requirement. Yet, it does not seem squarely purposivist, in that it seems not to be focused on capturing the specific intent of the enacting Congress, say by diving into the legislative history. What, then, is it?

"If Congress was contemplating a mousehole, we should not presume it was stuffed with an elephant. But how do we know whether Congress was contemplating a hole the size of a mouse or the size of an elephant?" Samuel L. Bray, The Mischief Rule, 109 Geo. L.J. 967, 1011–12 (2021). Isn't a textualist limited to the text in answering that question? Yet the West Virginia majority instructs that the meaning of a statute delegating authority to an agency must be discerned in light of "whether Congress in fact meant to confer the power the agency has asserted." West Virginia, 142 S.Ct. at 2608. Is that a question that a textualist asks? See Anita Krishnakumar, Some Brief Thoughts on Gorsuch's Opinion in NFIB v. OSHA, Election L. Blog (Jan. 15, 2022);[6] Nathan Richardson, Antideference: Covid, Climate, and the Rise of the Major Questions Canon, 108 Va. L. Rev. Online 174, 198–201 (2022).

(3) ***Updating Statutes.*** The underlying question of when courts should "update" statutes takes on added salience in an era of polarization. A key premise of the major questions doctrine is avoiding agency incursions on legislative turf. But when legislation has become so challenging that the final decisionmaker is likely to be the courts, does applying the major questions doctrine amount to arrogating to the judicial branch the authority to decide

[6] https://electionlawblog.org/?p=126944.

major questions? JODY FREEMAN & DAVID B. SPENCE, OLD STATUTES, NEW PROBLEMS, 163 U. Pa. L. Rev. 1, 42–43 (2014), considered the problem of applying the Clean Air Act to regulate greenhouse gases (rather than the traditional air pollutants like particulate matter for which it was designed): "Applying an old statute to this new problem has forced EPA to interpret statutory terms in ways the enacting Congress may not have anticipated and perhaps could not have foreseen. In the process, the agency has revisited interpretations that appeared settled (does the term 'any pollutant' mean all pollutants, or just a subset?), considered some questions for the first time (can 'performance standards' be based on system-wide changes that reduce demand for fossil fuel-fired generation?), and grappled with how to define the targets of regulation (can coal-fired plants and natural gas-fired units be grouped together . . . ?). . . . Because of their novelty, EPA's answers to these questions, and others, will continue to flood the courts. And judges, in turn, will review agency decisions knowing that the chances of congressional intervention are low. All of the players in this scenario are well aware that the outcome of litigation—not new legislation—will probably determine the scope of U.S. climate policy for the foreseeable future."



## SOLID WASTE AGENCY OF NORTHERN COOK COUNTY v. U.S. ARMY CORPS OF ENGINEERS

Supreme Court of the United States (2001).
531 U.S. 159.

■ CHIEF JUSTICE REHNQUIST delivered the opinion of the Court.

Section 404(a) of the Clean Water Act (CWA or Act), 33 U.S.C. § 1344(a), regulates the discharge of dredged or fill material into "navigable waters." The United States Army Corps of Engineers (Corps) has interpreted § 404(a) to confer federal authority over an abandoned sand and gravel pit in northern Illinois which provides habitat for migratory birds. . . .

Petitioner, the Solid Waste Agency of Northern Cook County (SWANCC), is a consortium of 23 suburban Chicago cities and villages that united in an effort to locate and develop a disposal site for baled nonhazardous solid waste. . . .

The municipalities decided to purchase the site for disposal of their baled nonhazardous solid waste. By law, SWANCC was required to file for various permits from Cook County and the State of Illinois before it could begin operation of its balefill project. In addition, because the operation called for the filling of some of the permanent and seasonal ponds, SWANCC contacted federal respondents (hereinafter respondents), including the Corps, to determine if a federal landfill permit was required under § 404(a) of the CWA.

Section 404(a) grants the Corps authority to issue permits "for the discharge of dredged or fill material into the navigable waters at specified disposal sites." The term "navigable waters" is defined under the Act as "the waters of the United States, including the territorial seas." § 1362(7). The Corps has issued regulations defining the term "waters of the United States" to include

> waters such as intrastate lakes, rivers, streams (including intermittent streams), mudflats, sandflats, wetlands, sloughs, prairie potholes, wet meadows, playa lakes, or natural ponds, the use, degradation or destruction of which could affect interstate or foreign commerce.... 33 CFR § 328.3(a)(3).

In 1986, in an attempt to "clarify" the reach of its jurisdiction, the Corps stated that § 404(a) extends to intrastate waters:

> a. Which are or would be used as habitat by birds protected by Migratory Bird Treaties; or
>
> b. Which are or would be used as habitat by other migratory birds which cross state lines; or
>
> c. Which are or would be used as habitat for endangered species; or
>
> d. Used to irrigate crops sold in interstate commerce.
>
> 51 Fed.Reg. 41217.

This last promulgation has been dubbed the "Migratory Bird Rule."[1]

The Corps initially concluded that it had no jurisdiction over the site because it contained no "wetlands," or areas which support "vegetation typically adapted for life in saturated soil conditions," 33 CFR § 328.3(b). However, after the Illinois Nature Preserves Commission informed the Corps that a number of migratory bird species had been observed at the site, the Corps reconsidered and ultimately asserted jurisdiction over the balefill site pursuant to subpart (b) of the "Migratory Bird Rule." The Corps found that approximately 121 bird species had been observed at the site, including several known to depend upon aquatic environments for a significant portion of their life requirements. Thus, on November 16, 1987, the Corps formally "determined that the seasonally ponded, abandoned gravel mining depressions located on the project site, while not wetlands, did qualify as 'waters of the United States' . . . based upon the following criteria: (1) the proposed site had been abandoned as a gravel mining operation; (2) the water areas and spoil piles had developed a natural character; and (3) the water areas are used as habitat by migratory bird [sic] which cross state lines." U.S. Army Corps

---

[1] The Corps issued the "Migratory Bird Rule" without following the notice and comment procedures outlined in the Administrative Procedure Act, 5 U.S.C. § 553.

of Engineers, Chicago District, Dept. of Army Permit Evaluation and Decision Document.

[SWANCC obtained the necessary local and state permits but was denied a federal permit for failure to meet various regulatory specifications. It brought suit under the APA. The district court held that the Corps had jurisdiction over the site; SWANCC does not challenge denial of the federal permit if indeed the Corps has jurisdiction.]

[The Court of Appeals held that the statute fell within Congress's Commerce Clause authority and that Migratory Bird Rule was a reasonable interpretation of the statute.]

We granted certiorari, and now reverse.

. . . Relevant here, § 404(a) authorizes respondents to regulate the discharge of fill material into "navigable waters," 33 U.S.C. § 1344(a), which the statute defines as "the waters of the United States, including the territorial seas," § 1362(7). Respondents have interpreted these words to cover the abandoned gravel pit at issue here because it is used as habitat for migratory birds. We conclude that the "Migratory Bird Rule" is not fairly supported by the CWA.

. . . . In order to rule for respondents here, we would have to hold that the jurisdiction of the Corps extends to ponds that are *not* adjacent to open water. But we conclude that the text of the statute will not allow this.

. . . . [I]t is one thing to give a word limited effect and quite another to give it no effect whatever. The term "navigable" has at least the import of showing us what Congress had in mind as its authority for enacting the CWA: its traditional jurisdiction over waters that were or had been navigable in fact or which could reasonably be so made.

Respondents . . . contend that, at the very least, it must be said that Congress did not address the precise question of § 404(a)'s scope with regard to nonnavigable, isolated, intrastate waters, and that, therefore, we should give deference to the "Migratory Bird Rule." We find § 404(a) to be clear, but even were we to agree with respondents, we would not extend Chevron deference here.

Where an administrative interpretation of a statute invokes the outer limits of Congress' power, we expect a clear indication that Congress intended that result. See Edward J. DeBartolo Corp. v. Florida Gulf Coast Building & Constr. Trades Council, 485 U.S. 568, 575 (1988). This requirement stems from our prudential desire not to needlessly reach constitutional issues and our assumption that Congress does not casually authorize administrative agencies to interpret a statute to push the limit of congressional authority. This concern is heightened where the administrative interpretation alters the federal-state framework by permitting federal encroachment upon a traditional state power. See United States v. Bass, 404 U.S. 336, 349 (1971) ("[U]nless Congress conveys its purpose clearly, it will not be deemed to have significantly changed the federal-state balance"). Thus, "where an otherwise acceptable construction of a statute would raise serious constitutional problems, the Court will construe the statute to avoid such problems unless such construction is plainly contrary to the intent of Congress." DeBartolo, supra, at 575. . . .

Permitting respondents to claim federal jurisdiction over ponds and mudflats falling within the "Migratory Bird Rule" would result in a significant impingement of the States' traditional and primary power over land and water use. Rather than expressing a desire to readjust the federal-state balance in this manner, Congress chose to "recognize, preserve, and protect the primary responsibilities and rights of States . . . to plan the development and use . . . of land and water resources. . . ." 33 U.S.C. § 1251(b). We thus read the statute as written to avoid the significant constitutional and federalism questions raised by respondents' interpretation, and therefore reject the request for administrative deference. . . .

■ JUSTICE STEVENS, with whom JUSTICE SOUTER, JUSTICE GINSBURG, and JUSTICE BREYER join, dissenting.

. . . It is fair to characterize the Clean Water Act as "watershed" legislation. The statute endorsed fundamental changes in both the purpose and the scope of federal regulation of the Nation's waters. In § 13 of the Rivers and Harbors Appropriation Act of 1899 (RHA), Congress had assigned to the Army Corps of Engineers (Corps) the mission of regulating discharges into certain waters in order to protect their use as highways for the transportation of interstate and foreign commerce; the scope of the Corps' jurisdiction under the RHA accordingly extended only to waters that were "navigable." In the CWA, however, Congress broadened the Corps' mission to include the purpose of protecting the quality of our Nation's waters for esthetic, health, recreational, and environmental uses. The scope of its jurisdiction was therefore redefined to encompass all of "the waters of the United States, including the territorial seas." § 1362(7). That definition requires neither actual nor potential navigability.

. . . In its decision today, the Court draws a new jurisdictional line, one that invalidates the 1986 migratory bird regulation as well as the Corps' assertion of jurisdiction over all waters except for actually navigable waters, their tributaries, and wetlands adjacent to each. Its holding rests on two equally untenable premises: (1) that when Congress passed the 1972 CWA, it did not intend "to exert anything more than its commerce power over navigation"; and (2) that in 1972 Congress drew the boundary defining the Corps' jurisdiction at the odd line on which the Court today settles.

As I shall explain, the text of the 1972 amendments affords no support for the Court's holding, and amendments Congress adopted in 1977 do support the Corps' present interpretation of its mission as extending to so-called "isolated" waters. Indeed, simple common sense cuts against the particular definition of the Corps' jurisdiction favored by the majority.

I

... The "major purpose" of the CWA was "to establish a *comprehensive* long-range policy for the elimination of water pollution." S. Rep. No. 92–414, p. 95 (1971). ... Strikingly absent from its declaration of "goals and policy" is *any* reference to avoiding or removing obstructions to navigation. Instead, the principal objective of the Act, as stated by Congress in § 101, was "to restore and maintain the chemical, physical, and biological integrity of the Nation's waters." 33 U.S.C. § 1251. Congress therefore directed federal agencies in § 102 to "develop comprehensive programs for preventing, reducing, or eliminating the pollution of the navigable waters and ground waters and improving the sanitary condition of surface and underground waters." 33 U.S.C. § 1252. The CWA commands federal agencies to give "due regard," not to the interest of unobstructed navigation, but rather to "improvements which are necessary to conserve such waters for the protection and propagation of fish and aquatic life and wildlife [and] recreational purposes." Ibid.

Because of the statute's ambitious and comprehensive goals, it was, of course, necessary to expand its jurisdictional scope. Thus, although Congress opted to carry over the traditional jurisdictional term "navigable waters" from the RHA and prior versions of the FWPCA, it broadened the *definition* of that term to encompass all "waters of the United States." § 1362(7).[6] Indeed, the 1972 conferees arrived at the final formulation by specifically deleting the word "navigable" from the definition that had originally appeared in the House version of the Act.[7] The majority today undoes that deletion. ...

The majority's reading drains all meaning from the conference amendment. ... The activities regulated by the CWA have nothing to do with Congress' "commerce power over navigation." Indeed, the goals of the 1972 statute have nothing to do with *navigation* at all. ...

The majority accuses respondents of reading the term "navigable" out of the statute. But that was accomplished by Congress when it deleted the word from the § 502(7) definition. ...

II

As the majority correctly notes, when the Corps first promulgated regulations pursuant to § 404 of the 1972 Act, it construed its authority as being essentially the same as it had been under the 1899 RHA. The reaction to those regulations in the federal courts, in the Environmental Protection Agency (EPA), and in Congress convinced the Corps that the statute required it "to protect water quality to the full extent of the [C]ommerce [C]lause" and to extend federal regulation over discharges

---

[6] The definition of "navigable water" in earlier versions of the FWPCA had made express reference to navigability. § 211, 80 Stat. 1253.

[7] The version adopted by the House of Representatives defined "navigable waters" as "the navigable waters of the United States, including the territorial seas." H.R. 11896, 92d Cong., 2d Sess., § 502(8) (1971). The CWA ultimately defined "navigable waters" simply as "the waters of the United States, including the territorial seas." 33 U.S.C. § 1362(7).

"to many areas that have never before been subject to Federal permits or to this form of water quality protection." 40 Fed. Reg. 31320 (1975). . . .

The Corps' broadened reading of its jurisdiction provoked opposition among some Members of Congress. As a result, in 1977, Congress considered a proposal that would have limited the Corps' jurisdiction under § 404 to waters that are used, or by reasonable improvement could be used, as a means to transport interstate or foreign commerce and their adjacent wetlands. H.R. 3199, 95th Cong., 1st Sess., § 16(f) (1977). A bill embodying that proposal passed the House but was defeated in the Senate. The debates demonstrate that Congress was fully aware of the Corps' understanding of the scope of its jurisdiction under the 1972 Act. . . .

III

. . . Contrary to the Court's suggestion, the Corps' interpretation of the statute does not "encroac[h]" upon "traditional state power" over land use. "Land use planning in essence chooses particular uses for the land; environmental regulation, at its core, does not mandate particular uses of the land but requires only that, however the land is used, damage to the environment is kept within prescribed limits." California Coastal Comm'n v. Granite Rock Co., 480 U.S. 572, 587 (1987). The CWA is not a land-use code; it is a paradigm of environmental regulation. Such regulation is an accepted exercise of federal power.

It is particularly ironic for the Court to raise the specter of federalism while construing a statute that makes explicit efforts to foster local control over water regulation. Faced with calls to cut back on federal jurisdiction over water pollution, Congress rejected attempts to narrow the scope of that jurisdiction and, by incorporating § 404(g), opted instead for a scheme that encouraged States to supplant federal control with their own regulatory programs. . . . Because Illinois could have taken advantage of the opportunities offered to it through § 404(g), the federalism concerns to which the majority adverts are misplaced. The Corps' interpretation of the statute as extending beyond navigable waters, tributaries of navigable waters, and wetlands adjacent to each is manifestly reasonable and therefore entitled to deference.

IV

. . . Whether it is necessary or appropriate to refuse to allow petitioner to fill those ponds is a question on which we have no voice. Whether the Federal Government has the power to require such permission, however, is a question that is easily answered. If, as it does, the Commerce Clause empowers Congress to regulate particular "activities causing air or water pollution, or other environmental hazards that may have effects in more than one State," Hodel, 452 U.S., at 282, it also empowers Congress to control individual actions that, in the aggregate, would have the same effect. There is no merit in petitioner's constitutional argument.

Because I would affirm the judgment of the Court of Appeals, I respectfully dissent.

## NOTE

This case deals with legal materials at five levels of authority:

(a) A Constitutional provision: Art. I, § 8, cl. 3 (the Commerce Clause);

(b) A statute: the Clean Water Act, notably § 404(a) (Corps authority over discharge of fill into "the navigable waters") and § 1362(7) (definition of "navigable waters" as "waters");

(c) An agency "legislative" regulation: 33 CFR § 328.3(a)(3) ("waters" goes as far as "wetlands, sloughs, prairie potholes" etc.);

(d) An agency "interpretative" regulation: the "Migratory Bird Rule"; and

(e) An agency adjudication: the "Permit Evaluation and Decision Document" asserting the Corps' jurisdiction over the particular site.

Justice Stevens says that the agency's interpretation of its authority (developed in items c, d, and e) is a "manifestly reasonable" interpretation of the statute (item b) and "therefore entitled to deference"; this is a standard Chevron argument. Independently, Justice Stevens concludes that the statute (item b) is constitutional under the Commerce Clause (item a).

By contrast, the Court's opinion says two things. The first is that the language of the statute (b) clearly rejects the agency's assertion of authority (c, d, and e). This point, like Justice Stevens's, is a standard Chevron analysis, differing only in the way the statute is read.

But the Court also says that "even were we to agree" that the statute was ambiguous, "we would not extend Chevron deference here." This is something different. The Court continues: "Where an administrative interpretation of a statute invokes the outer limits of Congress' power, we expect a clear indication that Congress intended that result." Ambiguity no longer helps the agency; it hurts its case.

Is this because of the relationship of the courts to Congress—because courts should interpret statutes in light of the canon of construction of avoiding constitutional difficulties, such that an otherwise ambiguous statute now becomes clear? Or is this because of the relationship of the agencies to Congress—because Congress would not want agencies to test the limits of Congress' own authority? Chief Justice Rehnquist asserts both rationales: "This requirement stems from our prudential desire not to needlessly reach constitutional issues and our assumption that Congress does not casually authorize administrative agencies to interpret a statute to push the limit of congressional authority."

## NOTES ON CANONS OF CONSTRUCTION AND CHEVRON

(1) ***How Are Canons to Be Handled Under Chevron?*** Linguistic canons (pp. 167–184) would seem to be fully applicable at Chevron step one. It is in part by applying those canons that a statute may be determined to be clear

or ambiguous. And both textualists and purposivists agree that canons are among the ordinary tools of statutory interpretation.

More controversial are the substantive canons (pp. 184–195). Probably the most well known of these is the canon Chief Justice Rehnquist quotes in the SWANCC case: "where an otherwise acceptable construction of a statute would raise serious constitutional problems, the Court will construe the statute to avoid such problems unless such construction is plainly contrary to the intent of Congress." As can be seen from his and Justice Stevens's opinions, this canon requires, by its own terms, a determination of whether a potential constitutional difficulty is "serious"; this element of judgment has often led Justices who all agree with the canon in principle to differ on its application in particular cases.

(2) ***Examples of Substantive Canons in Chevron Cases.*** Because substantive canons are based on assumed general policies of the law, their use in cases involving judicial review of agency action comes up against another assumed general policy of the law, the Chevron principle. The Chevron doctrine, after all, has the same structural consequence of resolving statutory ambiguity in a particular direction—to be specific, in the direction of agency authority. In SWANCC, Chief Justice Rehnquist defends the proposition that the avoid-serious-constitutional-doubt principle should dominate the Chevron principle.

Other cases have faced the same issue with respect to other substantive canons and Chevron. For example, in EEOC v. Arabian American Oil Co., 499 U.S. 244 (1991), the Court held that the "[l]ong-standing principle of American law 'that legislation of Congress, unless a contrary intent appears, is meant to apply only within the territorial jurisdiction of the United States'" overrode any deference due under Chevron to the EEOC's interpretation of Title VII as applying extraterritorially. But sometimes the answer is not so clear. Compare Muscogee (Creek) Nation v. Hodel, 851 F.2d 1439 (D.C. Cir. 1988), cert. denied, 488 U.S. 1010 (1989) (applying the canon that ambiguous statutes should be construed in favor of American Indians, and noting that but for the canon deference, the agency's interpretation would have been appropriate) with Haynes v. United States, 891 F.2d 235 (9th Cir. 1989) (declining to apply the same canon when Chevron deference was appropriate, on the grounds that the canon is a guideline, not substantive law, and that extended administrative practice deserves deference).

Immigration law is another area where the tension between Chevron and a substantive canon may be acute. Long before Chevron was decided, there was a principle of construing immigration statutes mandating deportation—now known as removal—narrowly. But if that rule of construction still applies, then how could Chevron ever operate in a case concerning whether Congress intended for a noncitizen to be subject to removal? Whenever it was not clear whether Congress did intend for one of its statutes to require removal, the canon would seem to kick in to clarify the ambiguity in the noncitizen's favor. In fact, however, Chevron is alive and well in the area of immigration, although there is no Supreme Court decision addressing what happened to the rule of immigration lenity post-Chevron.

See Brian G. Slocum, The Immigration Rule of Lenity and Chevron Deference, 17 Geo. Imm. L. Rev. 515 (2003). For an argument that Chevron deference is unjustified in the immigration context, see Shoba Sivaprasad Wadhia & Christopher J. Walker, The Case Against Chevron Deference in Immigration Adjudication, 70 Duke L.J. 1197 (2021).

Finally, if you've already studied the major questions doctrine earlier in this Chapter (pp. 1341–1370), consider where that rule fits in.

(3) ***An Intermediate Answer?*** KENNETH A. BAMBERGER, NORMATIVE CANONS IN THE REVIEW OF ADMINISTRATIVE POLICYMAKING, 118 Yale L.J. 64, 66–69 (2008): "Judicial application of normative canons . . . fits uncomfortably with the fundamental premise of Chevron U.S.A. Inc. v. Natural Resources Defense Council, Inc. . . . Under the preexisting canons regime, courts resolve statutory ambiguity conclusively, by resort to judge-made canonic presumptions. Yet after Chevron, when a statute is unclear, the resulting discretion belongs generally to the agency charged with its administration. . . .

"This tension has split courts and commentators. A majority, including the Supreme Court, argues that courts should continue to interpret legislation independently when normative canons would apply, even when Congress has charged a particular agency with the statute's administration. Canons, they conclude, involve the type of legal question best resolved by independent courts, rather than political agencies. More specifically, canons operate simply as clear-statement rules that constrain interpretive discretion and simply turn politically sensitive questions back to Congress. Accordingly, they leave no space for agency input, and judges should continue to fix statutory meaning independently when canonic values are implicated.

"A minority, including the Ninth Circuit, takes the opposite stance. Relying on Chevron's generalized understandings about superior agency expertise and political accountability, this account decries any continued judicial role in policing normative canons. It leaves to agencies the task of balancing both those goals reflected in statutory language and those left out.

"This Article rejects both all-or-nothing approaches. . . .

"The categorical approaches to resolving the Chevron-canons conflict ignore both the variability in canon application and the contingency of agency capacity. Specifically, a rule excluding agencies entirely from resolving statutory ambiguity when canonic norms are implicated fails to justify an all-or-nothing preference for judicial, rather than agency, discretion in three important ways. First, such a rule ignores the fact that agencies, in some circumstances, may possess greater capacity than courts for norm balancing. Second, it fails to provide any incentive for agencies to account for those values in their own decisionmaking. Such incentive would further the canons' strong policy of judicial restraint by obviating the need for judicial canon application in an important set of cases, as well as promote canons' goal of norm protection in the range of agency actions that never reach a courtroom. Third, it disregards important limits on judicial authority. . . .

"At the same time, a rule eliminating the judicial role in policing the application of normative canons after Chevron fails to recognize the unreliability of the agency contribution, especially in protecting values which are systemically underenforced. Such a rule removes incentives for agencies to account for such norms and constitutes, as a practical matter, a determination that certain important public values need not be consistently reflected in public policy.

"[This article] therefore concludes that the goals of both normative canons and Chevron require a contextual analysis—an institutionally sensitive framework that takes into account the particularity of governing doctrine and actual agency behavior in each case. . . . Incorporating a context-sensitive, case-by-case application of normative canons into Chevron's second-step reasonableness analysis offers the best framework for enlisting the comparative strengths of both courts and agencies."

## NOTES ON FEDERALISM AND AGENCY ACTION

(1) ***Is There a Canon Regarding Federalism Applicable to Agency Action?*** The Corps' authority over landfill under the Clean Water Act came before the Court again in RAPANOS V. UNITED STATES, 547 U.S. 715 (2006), with the Court again holding that the agency had overreached. JUSTICE SCALIA'S plurality opinion for the Court had this to say about the SWANCC principles, 547 U.S. at 737–38:

"Even if the phrase 'the waters of the United States' were ambiguous as applied to intermittent flows, our own canons of construction would establish that the Corps' interpretation of the statute is impermissible. As we noted in SWANCC, the Government's expansive interpretation would 'result in a significant impingement of the States' traditional and primary power over land and water use.' Regulation of land use, as through the issuance of the development permits sought by petitioners . . . is a quintessential state and local power. The extensive federal jurisdiction urged by the Government would authorize the Corps to function as a de facto regulator of immense stretches of intrastate land—an authority the agency has shown its willingness to exercise with the scope of discretion that would befit a local zoning board. We ordinarily expect a 'clear and manifest' statement from Congress to authorize an unprecedented intrusion into traditional state authority. The phrase 'the waters of the United States' hardly qualifies.

"Likewise, just as we noted in SWANCC, the Corps' interpretation stretches the outer limits of Congress's commerce power and raises difficult questions about the ultimate scope of that power. (In developing the current regulations, the Corps consciously sought to extend its authority to the farthest reaches of the commerce power. See 42 Fed. Reg. 37127 (1977).) Even if the term 'the waters of the United States' were ambiguous as applied to channels that sometimes host ephemeral flows of water (which it is not), we would expect a clearer statement from Congress to authorize an agency theory of jurisdiction that presses the envelope of constitutional validity. See Edward J. DeBartolo Corp. v. Florida Gulf Coast Building & Constr. Trades Council, 485 U.S. 568, 575 (1988)."

Both this passage and Justice Scalia's further reference to "these two clear-statement rules," 547 U.S. at 738, n. 9, suggest the existence of a federalism canon of construction separate in some way from the constitutional avoidance canon—a federalism canon that requires a clear statement from Congress to authorize an agency's doing something that trenches on "a quintessential state and local power" even if that interference would be unquestionably constitutional. (For a similar result when agency action is not at issue, see Bond v. United States, p. 185.)

The Supreme Court continues to review the Corps' attempts to interpret its Clean Water Act authority. See Sackett v. EPA, 142 S.Ct. 896 (2022) (granting petition for writ of certiorari).

(2) ***Chevron and Federalism.*** What is the source of the extra respect for federalism implied by having a canon beyond constitutional avoidance? Shouldn't we rather have just that respect for state authority that the Constitution itself—with its carefully balanced structure of specifically named congressional powers, equal Senatorial representation by state, a Supremacy Clause, and the like—stipulates? And, in any event, how does a federalism canon—insofar as it supports a presumption that Congress did not intend to preempt state and local regulation—interact with Chevron, insofar as the agency intends to be preemptive? See Watters v. Wachovia Bank, N.A., 550 U.S. 1, 22, 41 (2007) (Stevens, J., dissenting) (noting that because federal agencies, unlike Congress, "are clearly not designed to represent the interests of States," "when an agency purports to decide the scope of federal pre-emption, a healthy respect for state sovereignty calls for something less than Chevron deference").

(3) ***Defining "A Quintessential State and Local Power."*** Even if federalism does deserve an extra boost, how will we recognize "a quintessential state and local power"? SWANCC and Rapanos emphasize property law—but is that more inherently local than contract law or tort law, which are the staples of state common law? Pretty much all federal agency action that is "regulatory" prohibits something that state common law allows—that is indeed the most likely reason that it is seen as "regulatory." How far does the federalism principle extend? When the question is not simply adding a federal regulatory requirement on top of state requirements but rather concluding that the federal requirement abrogates state law as contrary to a comprehensive federal scheme—the effect commonly referred to as "preemption"—the judicial "presumption against preemption" does extend beyond property law.

For example, in WYETH V. LEVINE, 555 U.S. 555 (2009), the Court considered whether FDA-approved drug warnings prevented state tort suits. In the course of deciding that the approvals did not provide the defense that Wyeth claimed—which is to say, that this agency action did not preempt the state common law of torts—the Court repeated its statement from earlier cases, 555 U.S. at 565: "[i]n all pre-emption cases, and particularly in those in which Congress has 'legislated . . . in a field which the States have traditionally occupied,' . . . we 'start with the assumption that the historic police powers of the States were not to be superseded by the Federal Act unless that was the clear and manifest purpose of Congress.' "

(4) ***Where Is the Authority to Preempt Best Placed?*** GILLIAN E. METZGER, ADMINISTRATIVE LAW AS THE NEW FEDERALISM, 57 Duke L.J. 2023, 2077–83 (2008): "Public choice and institutional competency arguments are . . . raised against federal agencies' ability to serve as reliable representatives for state regulatory interests. One such argument asserts that agencies are primarily interested in expanding their own policymaking power and achieving their programmatic goals, which sets them in conflict with state regulatory autonomy. Another contends that agencies are overly responsive to particular industry or other constituencies and will privilege those constituencies' interests over state claims to regulatory authority. A third maintains that federal agencies' specific programmatic focus makes them ill equipped to consider general issues of the appropriate federal-state balance. . . .

"It is hard to dispute the risk that federal agencies will privilege their specific programmatic goals over more general concerns relating to government structure, or may be unduly beholden to particular regulated entities. After all, administrative tunnel vision and agency capture are hardly unknown phenomena. It is similarly plausible that at least in some contexts federal agencies view state regulators as competitors and seek to use preemption to advance their institutional interests. . . .

"Yet public choice accounts of agency motivation become unduly simplistic, to the extent that they portray federal agency officials as motivated solely by desire for greater resources and power without consideration of what represents the best regulatory policy. It also is mistaken to think that agency self-interest always lies on the side of expanding federal regulatory power at state expense. Even in public choice terms that account rings hollow, as the potential for congressional retaliation or the desire to avoid new responsibilities may lead rational agency officials to a different account of where their parochial interests lie. The view that agencies will advance the interests of favored regulatory constituencies at the expense of the states is similarly oversimplified. Too many instances exist of federal agencies refusing to preempt or seeking to expand state regulatory autonomy to conclude that federal agencies are categorically insensitive or hostile to preserving a state regulatory role. . . .

"One crucial variable the public choice account omits is politics. An agency's political agenda is likely to affect whether the agency will seek to accord states a regulatory role or instead centralize control in Washington. Thus, recent efforts to preempt state tort actions are in line with the Bush administration's support for tort reform and restrictions. At least some of these preemption efforts were rejected under prior presidential administrations with different political agendas. Indeed, politics rather than institutional position often seems to be the driving force behind federal administrative limitations on (or deference to) the states. In that regard, agencies appear little different from Congress or even the courts.

"As that suggests, the real issue here is one of comparative institutional competency. Which institution—Congress, federal agencies, or the courts—is best situated to make the relevant political choices? Which will give greatest weight to preserving a meaningful state regulatory role?

Constitutionally, Congress is the federal institution with primary policy-setting responsibility, and Congress is also the institution most structured to represent state interests. Yet it is not clear that Congress offers significantly more sensitivity to state regulatory prerogatives than federal agencies do. In any event, insisting that Congress itself resolve all federal-state questions is a nonstarter. Congress simply lacks the resources and foresight to resolve all the federalism issues that can arise in a given regulatory scheme. Requiring Congress to do so would impose a significant obstacle to federal regulation, something the Court's delegation cases indicate it is not prepared to do.

"As a result, in many ways the critical comparison is between federal agencies and federal courts; given that Congress will delegate broadly, one of the other institutions will need to resolve the federalism disputes that inevitably will arise. Moreover, it is hard to contest that of these two, agencies are more competent to make overt political choices. Yet a case nonetheless could be made that the courts have a comparative advantage over agencies in resolving federalism questions. Unlike specialized, program-focused agencies, the federal courts are generalist institutions that have special responsibilities to enforce constitutional structures and values. In practice, however, it is not at all clear that the federal courts have been more sensitive to state regulatory interests than agencies have been, and at times courts have been strong enforcers of federal uniformity over state control. Indeed, several commentators have noted the Rehnquist Court's willingness to curtail state regulatory authority in a variety of contexts.

"This leaves for consideration the claim that agencies simply lack expertise in determining the proper balance between federal and state regulation, particularly as compared to courts. Here, much turns on how the question of expertise is framed. Agencies have no special claim to expertise in assessing the proper federal-state balance in the abstract, divorced from a particular regulatory scheme or statute. But federalism disputes are unlikely to surface in such a form—whether before agencies, the federal courts, or Congress. Instead, . . . these questions arise in particular regulatory contexts. In such contexts, questions about the appropriate federal-state balance are not easily separated from substantive policy determinations on which agencies do have expertise. . . . The difficulty in separating substantive policy and federalism also undermines the institutional competency arguments in favor of courts, for courts are comparatively ill-equipped to assess the substantive impact that preserving a state role may have on a particular regulatory regime."

(5) ***Is This Only a Chevron Issue?*** Consider WILLIAM W. BUZBEE, PREEMPTION, HARD LOOK REVIEW, REGULATORY INTERACTION, AND THE QUEST FOR STEWARDSHIP AND INTERGENERATIONAL EQUITY, 77 Geo. Wash. L. Rev. 1521, 1556–58 (2009): "Agency claims of preemptive power and effect also virtually always contain an empirical footing with numerous factual and linked policy assumptions or findings: what about baseline conditions calls for preemptive action, and how do real world circumstances before and after an assertion of preemptive impact link to concerns made relevant by the underlying federal statute's criteria? Agency preemption claims sometimes

also contain assertions about benefits and harms of allowing multiple regulatory voices or displacing all but a single, federal regulatory actor. If the claim is that state regulation or tort law will invariably create conflict and defeat statutory ends, is there a basis for this? Might state enforcement of parallel laws further federal ends rather than frustrate or conflict with them? . . . The content of those factual and policy questions and claims necessarily must be shaped by what a federal statute deems relevant, but they remain contestable and provable. The question is how such claimed effects should be reviewed by courts and, relatedly, what kinds of procedures agencies should utilize if they wish to claim preemptive power and effect. . . .

"Determining the standard of review for agency factual and policy determinations claimed to justify preemption relates both to doctrinal room left to articulate the standard of review and to normative goals in devising the standard. Although the Supreme Court has not explicitly spoken in terms of hard look review in the setting of agency preemption claims, preemption precedents and related administrative and constitutional law precedents support adoption of preemption hard look review. Explicitly embracing such a reviewing framework would constitute only a modest movement in existing doctrine, more clarification than change. Second, normative goals of encouraging agency transparency, accountability, and open process are furthered by hard look review. Such rigorous review, and the underlying regulatory process it would likely provoke, would also act to check preemption assertions. Ossification of regulation is often criticized, but in an area where the Supreme Court has long stated a presumption disfavoring preemption, a procedural brake on preemption finds a doctrinal footing. Finally, the regulatory interactions fostered by such review would shine scrutiny on arguments for preemptive effect that, by their nature, will often be motivated by interest group entreaties for relief from state regulatory or common law. Illuminating such entreaties and deliberation would enhance the likelihood of public-regarding behavior."

(6) ***President Obama's Preemption Memorandum.*** In May 2009, President Obama issued a directive focused on preemption to the heads of executive departments and agencies: "The purpose of this memorandum is to state the general policy of my Administration that preemption of State law by executive departments and agencies should be undertaken only with full consideration of the legitimate prerogatives of the States and with a sufficient legal basis for preemption. Executive departments and agencies should be mindful that in our Federal system, the citizens of the several States have distinctive circumstances and values, and that in many instances it is appropriate for them to apply to themselves rules and principles that reflect these circumstances and values. As Justice Brandeis explained more than 70 years ago, '[i]t is one of the happy incidents of the federal system that a single courageous state may, if its citizens choose, serve as a laboratory; and try novel social and economic experiments without risk to the rest of the country.'

". . . Heads of departments and agencies should review regulations issued within the past 10 years that contain statements in regulatory preambles or codified provisions intended by the department or agency to preempt State law, in order to decide whether such statements or provisions are justified under applicable legal principles governing preemption. Where the head of a department or agency determines that a regulatory statement of preemption or codified regulatory provision cannot be so justified, the head of that department or agency should initiate appropriate action, which may include amendment of the relevant regulation. . . ."

(7) ***Chevron, Canons, and COVID-19.*** 42 U.S.C. § 264(a) provides: "The Surgeon General, with the approval of the Secretary, is authorized to make and enforce such regulations as in his judgment are necessary to prevent the introduction, transmission, or spread of communicable diseases from foreign countries into the States or possessions, or from one State or possession into any other State or possession. For purposes of carrying out and enforcing such regulations, the Surgeon General may provide for such inspection, fumigation, disinfection, sanitation, pest extermination, destruction of animals or articles found to be so infected or contaminated as to be sources of dangerous infection to human beings, and other measures, as in his judgment may be necessary."

Pursuant to this authority, the Department of Health and Human Services, Centers for Disease Control and Prevention (to whom this authority was properly transferred), issued a "Temporary Halt in Residential Evictions to Prevent the Further Spread of COVID-19," (85 Fed. Reg. 55292 (Sept. 4, 2020)). This order provided that, during its period of applicability, covered tenants could not be evicted for failure to pay rent, although their rent obligation was not permanently excused, and they could be evicted for other legitimate reasons, such as criminal activity or damaging the property. The order was extended several times. The CDC explained its reasoning and the studies on which it relied, concluding: "In short, evictions threaten to increase the spread of COVID-19 as they force people to move, often into close quarters in new shared housing settings with friends or family, or congregate settings such as homeless shelters. The ability of these settings to adhere to best practices, such as social distancing and other infection control measures, decreases as populations increase. Unsheltered homelessness also increases the risk that individuals will experience severe illness from COVID-19."

Does the statute authorize the CDC to issue a nationwide rental moratorium? Is it sufficiently ambiguous that courts should defer to the agency's determination that it has that authority? How do you understand the first sentence of § 264(a) to relate to the second sentence? What about the *ejusdem generis* and *noscitur a sociis* canons of construction (p. 167)? Since the order is displacing state landlord-tenant law, should one apply a federalism canon of construction? What about the fact that an order applicable to most rental housing in the country has a huge potential effect? But if the CDC is right about the consequences of eviction, what about public health in the midst of a pandemic?

These issues were litigated in several lower courts, and they split along several axes. E.g., Chambless Enterprises, LLC v. Redfield, 508 F.Supp.3d 101 (W.D. La. 2020) (agency upheld; statute clearly delegated the claimed authority; canons of construction did not apply since text was not ambiguous); Tiger Lily, LLC v. U.S. Dep't of Hous. & Urb. Dev., 5 F.4th 666, 669 (6th Cir. 2021) (moratorium exceeded agency's statutory authority) ("Notably, the government does not ask us to grant Chevron deference to its interpretation of the relevant statute. 'We therefore decline to consider whether any deference might be due' the Halt Order."); Alabama Ass'n of Realtors v. Dep't of HHS, 539 F.Supp.3d 29 (D.D.C. 2021) (order was unauthorized and is set aside; Chevron applicable but agency loses on step one).

In the last named proceeding, the Department moved for a stay pending appeal of the court order setting aside the moratorium, and given the importance of the public interest involved, the district court granted the stay. The D.C. Circuit denied a motion to vacate that stay, and that issue was then brought to the Supreme Court. In an order rendered on June 29, 2021, the Court denied the motion to vacate the stay. 141 S.Ct. 2320 (2021). The order was issued without explanation, but recorded that Justices Thomas, Alito, Gorsuch and Barrett would grant the application. It then carried this concurrence from Justice Kavanaugh:

"I agree with the District Court and the applicants that the Centers for Disease Control and Prevention exceeded its existing statutory authority by issuing a nationwide eviction moratorium. Because the CDC plans to end the moratorium in only a few weeks, on July 31, and because those few weeks will allow for additional and more orderly distribution of the congressionally appropriated rental assistance funds, I vote at this time to deny the application to vacate the District Court's stay of its order. In my view, clear and specific congressional authorization (via new legislation) would be necessary for the CDC to extend the moratorium past July 31."

Soon thereafter, the Court reviewed a renewed moratorium and found that the CDC likely lacked the statutory authority to issue it. 141 S.Ct. 2485 (2021). The Court's 6–3 per curiam opinion held that the part of § 361(a) allowing for "inspection, fumigation, disinfection, sanitation, pest extermination, destruction of [infected or contaminated] animals or articles" limited the CDC to measures "directly relate[d] to preventing the interstate spread of disease by identifying, isolating, and destroying the disease itself," as opposed to indirect measures like the moratorium. The Court further stated: "Even if the text were ambiguous, the sheer scope of the CDC's claimed authority under § 361(a) would counsel against the Government's interpretation. We expect Congress to speak clearly when authorizing an agency to exercise powers of vast economic and political significance."

(8) ***Preemption and Dobbs.*** In 2022, the Supreme Court overturned Roe v. Wade, 410 U.S. 113 (1973), in Dobbs v. Jackson Women's Health Org., 142 S.Ct. 2228 (2022). President Biden, in response, directed Secretary of Health and Human Services Xavier Becerra to determine how to use administrative measures to protect access to reproductive care. Exec. Order No. 14076 (Protecting Access to Reproductive Healthcare Services), 87 Fed. Reg. 42053 (July 13, 2022). Becerra took various actions, including "clarifying the obligation of hospitals and providers under the Emergency Medical Treatment and Labor Act, 42 U.S.C. 1395dd, to provide to patients presenting at an emergency department with an emergency medical

condition stabilizing care, including an abortion, if that care is necessary to stabilize their emergency medical condition, and issuing guidance to the Nation's retail pharmacies on their obligations under Federal civil rights laws—including section 504 of the Rehabilitation Act, 29 U.S.C. 794, and section 1557 of the Affordable Care Act, 42 U.S.C. 18116—to ensure equal access to comprehensive reproductive and other healthcare services, including for women who are experiencing miscarriages." Exec. Order No. 14079 (Securing Access to Reproductive and Other Healthcare Services), 87 Fed. Reg. 49505 (Aug. 11, 2022). The Department of Justice sued Idaho in early August 2022, claiming that the state's "near-absolute ban on abortion" was preempted by the Emergency Medical Treatment and Labor Act because the state's law "extends even to abortions that a physician determines are necessary stabilizing treatment that must be provided under EMTALA." Complaint, United States v. Idaho, No. 22-cv-329 (D. Idaho 2022);[7] see also David S. Cohen, Greer Donley, & Rachel Rebouché, The New Abortion Battleground, 123 Colum. L. Rev. (forthcoming).

## NOTES ON CHEVRON AND AGENCY INTERPRETATIONS OF CRIMINAL LAW

(1) ***Courts Have Held That Chevron Deference Does Not Apply to Criminal Law.*** See Abramski v. United States, 573 U.S. 169, 191 (2014) ("[C]riminal laws are for the courts, not for the Government, to construe."); see also United States v. Apel, 571 U.S. 359, 369 (2014) ("[W]e have never held that the Government's reading of a criminal statute is entitled to any deference."). Driven by the separation of powers concerns that one branch of government should not make, interpret, and enforce the law, courts have outlined numerous reasons to explain why the judiciary does not employ Chevron deference in criminal law. See generally Dan M. Kahan, Is Chevron Relevant to Federal Criminal Law?, 110 Harv. L. Rev. 469 (1996).

First, there may be "rule of law" concerns about ensuring the public is on notice of what the criminal law demands. "[W]hile courts recognize the inevitability and, in certain contexts, the desirability of legislation that leaves some details to be resolved as the statute is applied, there are limits. Those limits are most graphic in cases involving criminal sanctions. In the criminal context, courts have traditionally required greater clarity in draftsmanship than in civil contexts, commensurate with the bedrock principle that in a free country citizens who are potentially subject to criminal sanctions should have clear notice of the behavior that may cause sanctions to be visited upon them. That is to say, the law of crimes must be clear. There is less room in a statute's regime for flexibility, a characteristic so familiar to us on this court in the interpretation of statutes entrusted to agencies for administration. We are, in short, far outside Chevron territory here." UNITED STATES V. MCGOFF, 831 F.2d 1071, 1077 (D.C. Cir. 1987).

Second, there may be reason to doubt that Congress intended to delegate interpretive power over criminal law to the executive branch. "[A] criminal statute, is not administered by any agency but by the courts. It is

---

[7] https://www.justice.gov/opa/press-release/file/1523481/download.

entirely reasonable and understandable that federal officials should make available to their employees legal advice regarding its interpretation; and in a general way all agencies of the Government must interpret it in order to assure that the behavior of their employees is lawful—just as they must interpret innumerable other civil and criminal provisions in order to operate lawfully; but that is not the sort of specific responsibility for administering the law that triggers Chevron." CRANDON V. UNITED STATES, 494 U.S. 152, 177 (1990) (SCALIA, J., concurring in the judgment).

Third, the rule of lenity, which counsels in favor of reading grievous ambiguities in criminal statutes narrowly, arguably conflicts with Chevron. "Any responsible lawyer advising on whether particular conduct violates a criminal statute will obviously err in the direction of inclusion rather than exclusion—assuming, to be on the safe side, that the statute may cover more than is entirely apparent. That tendency is reinforced when the advice-giver is the Justice Department, which knows that if it takes an erroneously narrow view of what it can prosecute the error will likely never be corrected, whereas an erroneously broad view will be corrected by the courts when prosecutions are brought. Thus, to give persuasive effect to the Government's expansive advice-giving interpretation would turn the normal construction of criminal statutes upside-down, replacing the doctrine of lenity with a doctrine of severity." Id. at 177–78.

For a contrary view, consider the arguments Kahan makes. Kahan explains that federal criminal law statutes are broad and require interpretation in order to have meaning. He cites the Racketeer Influenced Corrupt Organizations Act (RICO) as an example of a statute in which Congress did not define the elements of the crime, and thus delegated authority to courts, as well as prosecutors, to bring meaning to the statute. The resulting judicial doctrines that comprise RICO law "should be understood not as bare 'interpretations' of the statute, but rather as exercises of federal common law-making power." KAHAN, IS CHEVRON RELEVANT TO FEDERAL CRIMINAL LAW?, supra, at 473. He acknowledges the benefits of delegating power, including increased efficiency and decreased practical and political costs, as well as the losses of delegating power, such as unresolved disagreement between different courts and prosecutorial overreach. To maintain benefits while reducing these costs, he argues that the judiciary should embrace Chevron deference in criminal law: the executive branch—specifically the Department of Justice—has both greater expertise and democratic accountability than the judiciary and is therefore the more appropriate branch to interpret criminal law.

KAHAN explains: "Combining the authority to make, enforce and interpret law in the hands of a single actor, it is said, is a blueprint for tyranny. Yet it is exactly this concentration of functions that I want to defend. Federal criminal law would be better by any conceivable measure . . . if the executive branch were treated as an authoritative law-expositor, and not merely an authoritative law-enforcer. . . . Applying the Chevron doctrine would improve the content of federal criminal law by shifting to the Justice Department the delegated lawmaking powers now exercised jointly by the courts and individual prosecutors. This transfer of authority would preserve essentially all the benefits associated with delegation, and, at the same time, effectively treat all of the pathologies that afflict it. The Justice Department has greater law-making expertise than do courts because it comes into contact with all manner of crimes at all stages of the justice system. Its readings are more likely to be uniform that those of courts because it is a single, integrated agency. Finally, the Department is less likely to overreach than are individual U.S. Attorneys because it has less incentive to pander to local interests and is more likely to internalize the costs of unduly broad statutory readings."

Responding to the specific criticisms raised in Crandon and McGoff, Kahan argues that neither the "rule of law" argument nor appropriate delegation concern is logical. With regard to the "rule of law" concern, Kahan responds that "the question isn't whether these statutes will be given shape by someone other than Congress, but only whether courts or the Justice Department will be doing the shaping." Id. at 491–92. Requiring DOJ to interpret laws prior to prosecution would enhance, not hinder, the rule of law. Id. at 500–01. And as to delegation, Kahan argues that Congress never states which branch should exercise delegated power in criminal statutes. Because of this, courts should weigh whether the judicial or executive branch is "better situated to exercise delegated criminal law-making power." Id. at 491. DOJ, with greater criminal law expertise, is better positioned than the judiciary to manage both of these worries, according to Kahan.

(2) ***What About Regulations That May Have Both Civil and Criminal Consequences?*** In Babbitt v. Sweet Home Chapter, Communities for Great Ore., the Supreme Court deferred to the Secretary of the Interior's definition of a term in the Endangered Species Act of 1973, and criminal sanctions turned on the Secretary's interpretation. 515 U.S. 687 (1995). However, the question is not settled. Justice Scalia wrote in 2014, joined by Justice Thomas in respecting the denial of certiorari in Whitman v. United States, that he would be "receptive" to granting a petition seeking review of deference to an agency's interpretation that has criminal and administrative penalties. 574 U.S. 1003, 1005 (2014). "With deference to agency interpretations of statutory provisions to which criminal prohibitions are attached, federal administrators can in effect create (and uncreate) new crimes at will, so long as they do not roam beyond ambiguities that the laws contain. . . . Babbitt's drive-by ruling, in short, deserves little weight." Id. at 1004–05.

In ESQUIVEL-QUINTANA V. LYNCH, the Sixth Circuit considered whether a conviction under a state criminal rape statute (because of age) for intercourse between Juan Esquivel-Quintana, a twenty-one-year-old noncitizen, and a seventeen-year-old was "sexual abuse of a minor" under a federal civil immigration statute; under the civil statute, an immigration judge ruled that Esquivel-Quintana would be deported. 810 F.3d 1019 (6th Cir. 2016). The majority, under Chevron, deferred to the Board of Immigration and Appeal's interpretation of the civil statute and denied Esquivel-Quintana's petition for review of the immigration judge's decision. JUDGE JEFFREY SUTTON dissented in part, discussing the application of Chevron to statutes that have civil and criminal implications: "Chevron permits agencies to fill gaps in *civil* statutes that Congress has delegated authority to the agency to interpret. . . . But Chevron has no role to play in construing *criminal* statutes. . . . The doctrine does not give the Department of Justice (or for that matter any other federal agency) *implied* gap-filling authority over ambiguous criminal statutes. Otherwise, that would leave this distasteful combination: The prosecutor would have the explicit (executive) power to enforce the criminal laws, an implied (legislative) power to fill policy gaps in ambiguous criminal statutes, and an implied (judicial) power to interpret ambiguous criminal laws. And it would permit this aggregation of power in the one area where its division matters most: the removal of citizens from society. . . . But what happens when the same statute has criminal *and* civil applications? May Congress sidestep these requirements by giving criminal statutes a civil application? The answer is no. The courts must give dual-application statutes just one interpretation, and the criminal application controls. Statutes are not 'chameleon[s]' that mean one thing in one setting and something else in another. Time, time, and time again, the Court has confirmed that the one-interpretation rule means that the criminal-law construction of the statute (with the rule of lenity) prevails over the civil-law construction of it (without the rule of lenity)." Id. 1027–28 (emphasis in original).

The Supreme Court granted certiorari in Esquivel-Quintana but held that the statute, in context, unambiguously foreclosed the government's interpretation of it; "[t]herefore, neither the rule of lenity nor Chevron applies." Esquivel-Quintana v. Sessions, 137 S.Ct. 1562 (2017).

A recent petition for certiorari, Aposhian v. Garland, 2021 WL 3423011 (U.S.), came from a Tenth Circuit decision that cited Babbitt v. Sweet Home and applied Chevron deference to a Bureau of Alcohol, Tobacco, Firearms, and Explosives interpretation of the term "machinegun" in 26 U.S.C. § 5845(b). The Court rescheduled the petition for consideration at conference 20 times during October Term 2021 before finally denying review without comment at the beginning of October Term 2022.

(3) ***Can the Criminal Law Exception Be Distinguished?*** Finally, for an argument that the fact that Chevron does not apply to the Department of Justice's interpretation of criminal statutes reveals that Chevron cannot be made to fit within the constitutional framework, here is then-JUDGE GORSUCH again from GUTIERREZ-BRIZUELA V. LYNCH: "What I suspect about Chevron's compatibility with the separation of powers finds confirmation in what I know. The Supreme Court has expressly instructed us not to apply Chevron deference when an agency seeks to interpret a criminal statute. Why? Because, we are seemingly told, doing so would violate the Constitution by forcing the judiciary to abdicate the job of saying what the law is and preventing courts from exercising independent judgment in the interpretation in the interpretation of statutes. See, e.g., Abramski v. United States, 134 S.Ct. 2259, 2274 (2014) ('Whether the Government interprets a criminal statute too broadly . . . or too narrowly . . . a court has an obligation to correct its error.'). An admirable colleague has noted that the same rationale would appear to preclude affording Chevron deference to agency interpretations of statutes that bear both civil and criminal applications.

See, e.g., Esquivel-Quintana v. Lynch, 810 F.3d 1019, 1027–32 (6th Cir. 2016) (Sutton, J., concurring in part and dissenting in part); Carter v. Welles-Bowen Realty, Inc., 736 F.3d 722, 729–36 (6th Cir. 2013) (Sutton, J., concurring). A category that covers a great many (most?) federal statutes today. And try as I might, I have a hard time identifying a principled reason why the same rationale doesn't also apply to statutes with purely civil application. After all, the APA doesn't distinguish between purely civil and other kinds of statutes when describing the interpretive duties of courts. Neither did the founders reserve their concerns about political decisionmakers deciding the meaning of existing law to criminal cases; Article III doesn't say judges should say what the law is or decide whether legal rights have or haven't vested and been violated only when a crime is alleged. And certainly Marbury did not speak so meekly: it affirmed the judiciary's duty to say what the law is in a case that involved the interpretation of, yes, a civil statute affecting individual rights.

"Some have suggested that criminal statutes should be treated differently when it comes to Chevron because they are not 'administered' by an agency. See Gonzales v. Oregon, 546 U.S. 243, 264–65 (2006). I take this as a roundabout way of suggesting that Congress hasn't 'delegated' its legislative authority in the criminal context like it has in the civil. But as we've seen, the claim that Congress has delegated legislative authority even in the civil context is no more than a fiction. And for that matter it's hard to see why the Justice Department doesn't 'administer' criminal statutes in much the same way other agencies 'administer' various civil statutes. See, e.g., Crandon v. United States, 494 U.S. 152, 177 (1990) (Scalia, J., concurring in the judgment) (acknowledging that '[t]he Justice Department . . . has a very specific responsibility to determine for itself what this statute means, in order to decide when to prosecute'). Of course, criminal law enforcement takes place in the courts, not before administrative agencies. But often enough civil administrative actions also depend on court approval for their effectiveness, and as we've seen this may be a matter not merely of statutory but sometimes constitutional imperative. . . .

"Other arguments for rejecting Chevron deference (only) in criminal matters seem equally shaky. Some suggest that principles of due process and equal protection demand that the criminal law be clear and clearly given by judges. Others suggest that prosecutorial agencies have too many incentives to interpret criminal statutes expansively. But while concerns about due process and fair notice surely reach their apex in the criminal context, I am uncertain why we would view that as a license to neglect attending to them in the civil context. See Clinton v. City of New York, 524 U.S. 417, 450 (1998) (Kennedy, J., concurring) ('Liberty is always at stake when one or more of the branches seek to transgress the separation of powers.'). Especially given the power our modern administrative state already enjoys, even without Chevron, to penalize persons in ways that can destroy their livelihoods and intrude on their liberty even when exercising only purely civil powers. And given that the line between 'criminal' and 'civil' statutes has often proven tricky enough to administer. See, e.g., Hudson v. United States, 522 U.S. 93, 99–100 (1997) (suggesting the use of a balancing test composed of seven nonexclusive factors to tell the difference between civil and criminal statutory penalties). Neither, too, are prosecutorial agencies known to be alone in their capacity and willingness to interpret statutes aggressively."

Does then-Judge Gorsuch's argument depend on the premise that the Department of Justice does "administer" the criminal laws and thus that Congress did delegate the power to interpret them to the Department, just like Congress delegated a similar power to an agency that administers its organic statute? How strong is that premise?

## e. Agency Interpretations of Agency Regulations



## KISOR v. WILKIE

Supreme Court of the United States (2019).
139 S.Ct. 2400.

■ JUSTICE KAGAN delivered the opinion of the Court with respect to Parts I, II-B, III-B, and IV, and an opinion with respect to Parts II-A and III-A, in which JUSTICE GINSBURG, JUSTICE BREYER, and JUSTICE SOTOMAYOR joined.

This Court has often deferred to agencies' reasonable readings of genuinely ambiguous regulations. We call that practice Auer deference, or sometimes Seminole Rock deference, after two cases in which we employed it. See Auer v. Robbins, 519 U.S. 452 (1997); Bowles v. Seminole Rock & Sand Co., 325 U.S. 410 (1945). The only question presented here is whether we should overrule those decisions, discarding the deference they give to agencies. We answer that question no. Auer deference retains an important role in construing agency regulations. But even as we uphold it, we reinforce its limits. Auer deference is sometimes appropriate and sometimes not. Whether to apply it depends on a range of considerations that we have noted now and again, but compile and further develop today. The deference doctrine we describe is potent in its place, but cabined in its scope. . . .

I

[James] Kisor is a Vietnam War veteran seeking disability benefits from the Department of Veterans Affairs (VA). He first applied in 1982, alleging that he had developed post-traumatic stress disorder (PTSD). . . . The VA . . . denied Kisor benefits. [In] 2006, . . . Kisor moved to reopen his claim. Based on a new psychiatric report, the VA this time agreed that Kisor suffered from PTSD. But it granted him benefits only from the date of his motion to reopen. . . .

The Board of Veterans' Appeals—a part of the VA, represented in Kisor's case by a single administrative judge—affirmed that timing decision, based on its interpretation of an agency rule. Under the VA's regulation, the agency could grant Kisor retroactive benefits if it found there were "relevant official service department records" that it had not considered in its initial denial. See 38 C.F.R. § 3.156(c)(1) (2013). The Board acknowledged that Kisor had come up with two new service records. . . . But according to the Board, those records were not "relevant" because they did not go to the reason for the denial—that Kisor did not have PTSD. . . . The Court of Appeals for Veterans Claims . . . affirmed. . . .

The Court of Appeals for the Federal Circuit also affirmed, but it did so based on deference to the Board's interpretation of the VA rule. See Kisor v. Shulkin, 869 F.3d 1360, 1368 (2017). Kisor had argued to the Federal Circuit that to count as "relevant," a service record need not (as the Board thought) "counter[ ] the basis of the prior denial"; instead, it could relate to some other criterion for obtaining disability benefits. Id., at 1366. The Federal Circuit found the regulation "ambiguous" as between the two readings. Id., at 1367. . . . Because that was so, the court believed Auer deference appropriate: The agency's construction of its own regulation would govern unless "plainly erroneous or inconsistent with the VA's regulatory framework." Ibid. Applying that standard, the court upheld the Board's reading—and so approved the denial of retroactive benefits.

We then granted certiorari to decide whether to overrule Auer and (its predecessor) Seminole Rock. 139 S.Ct. 657 (2018).

II

. . .

A

Begin with a familiar problem in administrative law: For various reasons, regulations may be genuinely ambiguous. . . . The subject matter of a rule "may be so specialized and varying in nature as to be impossible"—or at any rate, impracticable—to capture in its every detail. SEC v. Chenery Corp., 332 U.S. 194, 203 (1947). Or a "problem[ ] may arise" that the agency, when drafting the rule, "could not [have] reasonably foresee[n]." Id., at 202. Whichever the case, the result is to create real uncertainties about a regulation's meaning.

[The opinion enumerated several examples, including:]

- The Transportation Security Administration (TSA) requires that liquids, gels, and aerosols in carry-on baggage be packed in containers smaller than 3.4 ounces and carried in a clear plastic bag. Does a traveler have to pack his jar of truffle pâté in that way? See Laba v. Copeland, 2016 WL 5958241, *1 (WDNC, Oct. 13, 2016).

- The Mine Safety and Health Administration issues a rule requiring employers to report occupational diseases within two weeks after they are "diagnosed." 30 C.F.R. § 50.20(a) (1993). Do chest X-ray results that "scor[e]" above some level of opacity count as a "diagnosis"? What level, exactly? See American Min. Congress v. Mine Safety and Health Admin., 995 F.2d 1106, 1107–1108 (CADC 1993) [p. 394]. . . .

In each case, interpreting the regulation involves a choice between (or among) more than one reasonable reading. To apply the rule to some unanticipated or unresolved situation, the court must make a judgment call. How should it do so?

In answering that question, we have often thought that a court should defer to the agency's construction of its own regulation. For the last 20 or so years, we have referred to that doctrine as Auer deference, and applied it often. . . .

We have explained Auer deference (as we now call it) as rooted in a presumption about congressional intent—a presumption that Congress would generally want the agency to play the primary role in resolving regulatory ambiguities. See Martin v. Occupational Safety and Health Review Comm'n, 499 U.S. 144, 151–153 (1991). Congress, we have pointed out, routinely delegates to agencies the power to implement statutes by issuing rules. See id., at 151. In doing so, Congress knows (how could it not?) that regulations will sometimes contain ambiguities. But Congress almost never explicitly assigns responsibility to deal with that problem, either to agencies or to courts. Hence the need to presume, one way or the other, what Congress would want. And as between those two choices, agencies have gotten the nod. We have adopted the presumption—though it is always rebuttable—that "the power authoritatively to interpret its own regulations is a component of the agency's delegated lawmaking powers." Martin, 499 U.S. at 151. Or otherwise said, we have thought that when granting rulemaking power to agencies, Congress usually intends to give them, too, considerable latitude to interpret the ambiguous rules they issue.

In part, that is because the agency that promulgated a rule is in the "better position [to] reconstruct" its original meaning. Id., at 152. Consider that if you don't know what some text (say, a memo or an e-mail) means, you would probably want to ask the person who wrote it. And for the same reasons, we have thought, Congress would too (though the person is here a collective actor). . . . To be sure, this justification has its limits. It does not work so well, for example, when the agency failed to anticipate an issue in crafting a rule (e.g., if the agency never thought about whether and when chest X-rays would count as a "diagnosis"). And the defense works yet less well when lots of time has passed between the rule's issuance and its interpretation—especially if the interpretation differs from one that has come before. All that said, the point holds good for a significant category of "contemporaneous" readings. Lyng v. Payne, 476 U.S. 926, 939 (1986). Want to know what a rule means? Ask its author.

In still greater measure, the presumption that Congress intended Auer deference stems from the awareness that resolving genuine regulatory ambiguities often "entail[s] the exercise of judgment grounded in policy concerns." Thomas Jefferson Univ. v. Shalala, 512 U.S. 504, 512

(1994). Return to our TSA example. In most of their applications, terms like "liquids" and "gels" are clear enough. (Traveler checklist: Pretzels OK; water not.) But resolving the uncertain issues—the truffle pâtés or olive tapenades of the world—requires getting in the weeds of the rule's policy: Why does TSA ban liquids and gels in the first instance? What makes them dangerous? Can a potential hijacker use pâté jars in the same way as soda cans? . . .

And Congress, we have thought, knows just that: It is attuned to the comparative advantages of agencies over courts in making such policy judgments. Agencies (unlike courts) have "unique expertise," often of a scientific or technical nature, relevant to applying a regulation "to complex or changing circumstances." Martin, 499 U.S. at 151; see Thomas Jefferson, 512 U.S. at 512. Agencies (unlike courts) can conduct factual investigations, can consult with affected parties, can consider how their experts have handled similar issues over the long course of administering a regulatory program. And agencies (again unlike courts) have political accountability, because they are subject to the supervision of the President, who in turn answers to the public. See Free Enterprise Fund v. Public Company Accounting Oversight Bd., 561 U.S. 477, 499 (2010). It is because of those features that Congress, when first enacting a statute, assigns rulemaking power to an agency and thus authorizes it to fill out the statutory scheme. And so too, when new issues demanding new policy calls come up within that scheme, Congress presumably wants the same agency, rather than any court, to take the laboring oar.

Finally, the presumption we use reflects the well-known benefits of uniformity in interpreting genuinely ambiguous rules. We have noted Congress's frequent "preference for resolving interpretive issues by uniform administrative decision, rather than piecemeal by litigation." Ford Motor Credit Co. v. Milhollin, 444 U.S. 555, 568 (1980). That preference may be strongest when the interpretive issue arises in the context of a "complex and highly technical regulatory program." Thomas Jefferson, 512 U.S. at 512. After all, judges are most likely to come to divergent conclusions when they are least likely to know what they are doing. . . . But the uniformity justification retains some weight even for more accessible rules, because their language too may give rise to more than one eminently reasonable reading. . . . Auer deference thus serves to ensure consistency in federal regulatory law, for everyone who needs to know what it requires.

B

But all that said, Auer deference is not the answer to every question of interpreting an agency's rules. Far from it. As we explain in this section, the possibility of deference can arise only if a regulation is genuinely ambiguous. And when we use that term, we mean it—genuinely ambiguous, even after a court has resorted to all the standard tools of interpretation. Still more, not all reasonable agency constructions of those truly ambiguous rules are entitled to deference. As just explained, we presume that Congress intended for courts to defer to agencies when they interpret their own ambiguous rules. But when the reasons for that presumption do not apply, or countervailing reasons outweigh them, courts should not give deference to an agency's reading, except to the extent it has the "power to persuade." Christopher, 567 U.S. at 159 (quoting Skidmore v. Swift & Co., 323 U.S. 134, 140 (1944)). . . .

First and foremost, a court should not afford Auer deference unless the regulation is genuinely ambiguous. See Christensen v. Harris County, 529 U.S. 576, 588 (2000); Seminole Rock, 325 U.S. at 414 (deferring only "if the meaning of the words used is in doubt"). . . .

And before concluding that a rule is genuinely ambiguous, a court must exhaust all the "traditional tools" of construction. Chevron U.S.A. Inc. v. Natural Resources Defense Council, Inc., 467 U.S. 837, 843, n. 9 (1984) (adopting the same approach for ambiguous statutes).. . . To make that effort, a court must carefully consider[ ] the text, structure, history, and purpose of a regulation, in all the ways it would if it had no agency to fall back on. . . .

If genuine ambiguity remains, moreover, the agency's reading must still be "reasonable." Thomas Jefferson, 512 U.S. at 515. In other words, it must come within the zone of ambiguity the court has identified after employing all its interpretive tools. (Note that serious application of those tools therefore has use even when a regulation turns out to be truly ambiguous. The text, structure, history, and so forth at least establish the outer bounds of permissible interpretation.) Some courts have thought (perhaps because of Seminole Rock's "plainly erroneous" formulation) that at this stage of the analysis, agency constructions of rules receive greater deference than agency constructions of statutes. But that is not so. Under Auer, as under Chevron, the agency's reading must fall "within the bounds of reasonable interpretation." Arlington v. FCC, 569 U.S. 290, 296 (2013). And let there be no mistake: That is a requirement an agency can fail.

Still, we are not done—for not every reasonable agency reading of a genuinely ambiguous rule should receive Auer deference. We have recognized in applying Auer that a court must make an independent inquiry into whether the character and context of the agency interpretation entitles it to controlling weight. See Christopher, 567 U.S. at 155; see also Mead, 533 U.S. at 229–231, 236–237 (requiring an analogous though not identical inquiry for Chevron deference). . . .

To begin with, the regulatory interpretation must be one actually made by the agency. In other words, it must be the agency's "authoritative" or "official position," rather than any more ad hoc statement not reflecting the agency's views. Mead, 533 U.S. at 257–259, and n. 6 (SCALIA, J., dissenting). That constraint follows from the logic of Auer deference—because Congress has delegated rulemaking power, and all that typically goes with it, to the agency alone. Of course, the requirement of "authoritative" action must recognize a reality of bureaucratic life: Not everything the agency does comes from, or is even in the name of, the Secretary or his chief advisers. So, for example, we have deferred to "official staff memoranda" that were "published in the

Federal Register," even though never approved by the agency head. Ford Motor Credit, 444 U.S. at 566, n. 9, 567, n. 10 (declining to "draw a radical distinction between" agency heads and staff for Auer deference). But there are limits. The interpretation must at the least emanate from those actors, using those vehicles, understood to make authoritative policy in the relevant context. . . .

Next, the agency's interpretation must in some way implicate its substantive expertise. Administrative knowledge and experience largely "account [for] the presumption that Congress delegates interpretive lawmaking power to the agency." Martin, 499 U.S. at 153. So the basis for deference ebbs when "[t]he subject matter of the [dispute is] distan[t] from the agency's ordinary" duties or "fall[s] within the scope of another agency's authority." Arlington, 569 U.S. at 309, 133 S.Ct. 1863 (opinion of BREYER, J.). . . . Some interpretive issues may fall more naturally into a judge's bailiwick. Take one requiring the elucidation of a simple common-law property term, see Jicarilla Apache Tribe v. FERC, 578 F.2d 289, 292–293 (CA10 1978), or one concerning the award of an attorney's fee, see West Va. Highlands Conservancy, Inc. v. Norton, 343 F.3d 239 (CA4 2003). When the agency has no comparative expertise in resolving a regulatory ambiguity, Congress presumably would not grant it that authority.[5]

Finally, an agency's reading of a rule must reflect "fair and considered judgment" to receive Auer deference. Christopher, 567 U.S. at 155 (quoting Auer, 519 U.S. at 462). That means, we have stated, that a court should decline to defer to a merely "convenient litigating position" or "post hoc rationalizatio[n] advanced" to "defend past agency action against attack." Christopher, 567 U.S. at 155. And a court may not defer to a new interpretation, whether or not introduced in litigation, that creates "unfair surprise" to regulated parties. Long Island Care, 551 U.S. at 170. That disruption of expectations may occur when an agency substitutes one view of a rule for another. We have therefore only rarely given Auer deference to an agency construction "conflict[ing] with a prior" one. Thomas Jefferson, 512 U.S. at 515. Or the upending of reliance may happen without such an explicit interpretive change. This Court, for example, recently refused to defer to an interpretation that would have imposed retroactive liability on parties for longstanding conduct that the agency had never before addressed. See Christopher, 567 U.S. at 155–156. Here too the lack of "fair warning" outweighed the reasons to apply Auer. Id., at 156.

* * *

The upshot of all this goes something as follows. When it applies, Auer deference gives an agency significant leeway to say what its own rules mean. In so doing, the doctrine enables the agency to fill out the

[5] For a similar reason, this Court has denied Auer deference when an agency interprets a rule that parrots the statutory text. See Gonzales v. Oregon, 546 U.S. 243, 257 (2006). An agency, we explained, gets no "special authority to interpret its own words when, instead of using its expertise and experience to formulate a regulation, it has elected merely to paraphrase the statutory language." Ibid.

regulatory scheme Congress has placed under its supervision. But that phrase "when it applies" is important—because it often doesn't. As described above, this Court has cabined Auer's scope in varied and critical ways—and in exactly that measure, has maintained a strong judicial role in interpreting rules. What emerges is a deference doctrine not quite so tame as some might hope, but not nearly so menacing as they might fear.

III

That brings us to the lone question presented here—whether we should abandon the longstanding doctrine just described. . . .

A

Kisor first attacks Auer as inconsistent with the judicial review provision of the Administrative Procedure Act (APA). See 5 U.S.C. § 706. . . . Section 706 of the Act, governing judicial review of agency action, states (among other things) that reviewing courts shall "determine the meaning or applicability of the terms of an agency action" (including a regulation). According to Kisor, Auer violates that edict by thwarting "meaningful judicial review" of agency rules. Brief for Petitioner 29. Courts under Auer, he asserts (now in the language of Section 706), "abdicate their office of determining the meaning" of a regulation. Id., at 27.

To begin with, that argument ignores the many ways, discussed above, that courts exercise independent review over the meaning of agency rules. As we have explained, a court must apply all traditional methods of interpretation to any rule, and must enforce the plain meaning those methods uncover. . . . And . . . courts must on their own determine whether the nature or context of the agency's construction reverses the usual presumption of deference. Most notably, a court must consider whether the interpretation is authoritative, expertise-based, considered, and fair to regulated parties. All of that figures as "meaningful judicial review." Brief for Petitioner 29.

And even when a court defers to a regulatory reading, it acts consistently with Section 706. That provision does not specify the standard of review a court should use in "determin[ing] the meaning" of an ambiguous rule. 5 U.S.C. § 706. One possibility, as Kisor says, is to review the issue de novo. But another is to review the agency's reading for reasonableness. . . .

That is especially so given the practice of judicial review at the time of the APA's enactment. Section 706 was understood when enacted to "restate[ ] the present law as to the scope of judicial review." . . . That pre-APA common law included Seminole Rock itself (decided the year before) along with prior decisions foretelling that ruling. . . . If Section 706 did not change the law of judicial review (as we have long recognized), then it did not proscribe a deferential standard then known and in use.

Kisor next claims that Auer circumvents the APA's rulemaking requirements. Section 553, as Kisor notes, mandates that an agency use notice-and-comment procedures before issuing legislative rules. See 5

U.S.C. §§ 553(b), (c). But the section allows agencies to issue "interpret[ive]" rules without notice and comment. See § 553(b)(A). A key feature of those rules is that (unlike legislative rules) they are not supposed to "have the force and effect of law"—or, otherwise said, to bind private parties. Perez v. Mortgage Bankers Assn., 135 S.Ct. 1199, 1204 (2015) [p. 252]. Instead, interpretive rules are meant only to "advise the public" of how the agency understands, and is likely to apply, its binding statutes and legislative rules. Ibid. But consider, Kisor argues, what happens when a court gives Auer deference to an interpretive rule. The result, he asserts, is to make a rule that has never gone through notice and comment binding on the public. See Brief for Petitioner 21, 29. Or put another way, the interpretive rule ends up having the "force and effect of law" without ever paying the procedural cost. Mortgage Bankers, 135 S.Ct., at 1204.

But this Court rejected the identical argument just a few years ago, and for good reason. In Mortgage Bankers, we held that interpretive rules, even when given Auer deference, do not have the force of law. See 135 S.Ct., at 1208, and n. 4. An interpretive rule itself never forms "the basis for an enforcement action"—because, as just noted, such a rule does not impose any "legally binding requirements" on private parties. National Min. Assn. v. McCarthy, 758 F.3d 243, 251 (CADC 2014) [p. 400]. An enforcement action must instead rely on a legislative rule, which (to be valid) must go through notice and comment. And . . . courts retain the final authority to approve—or not—the agency's reading of a notice-and-comment rule. See Mortgage Bankers, 135 S.Ct., at 1208, n. 4 ("[I]t is the court that ultimately decides whether a given regulation means what the agency says"). No binding of anyone occurs merely by the agency's say-so. . . .

To supplement his two APA arguments, Kisor turns to policy, leaning on a familiar claim about the incentives Auer creates. According to Kisor, Auer encourages agencies to issue vague and open-ended regulations, confident that they can later impose whatever interpretation of those rules they prefer.. . .

But the claim has notable weaknesses, empirical and theoretical alike. First, it does not survive an encounter with experience. No real evidence—indeed, scarcely an anecdote—backs up the assertion. As two noted scholars (one of whom reviewed thousands of rules during four years of government service) have written: "[W]e are unaware of, and no one has pointed to, any regulation in American history that, because of Auer, was designed vaguely." Sunstein & Vermeule, 84 U. Chi. L. Rev., at 308. And even the argument's theoretical allure dissipates upon reflection. For strong (almost surely stronger) incentives and pressures cut in the opposite direction. "[R]egulators want their regulations to be effective, and clarity promotes compliance." Brief for Administrative Law Scholars as Amici Curiae 18–19. Too, regulated parties often push for precision from an agency, so that they know what they can and cannot do. And ambiguities in rules pose risks to the long-run survival of agency policy. Vagueness increases the chance of adverse judicial rulings. And it enables future administrations, with different views, to reinterpret the rules to their own liking. Add all of that up and Kisor's ungrounded theory of incentives contributes nothing to the case against Auer.

Finally, Kisor goes big, asserting (though fleetingly) that Auer deference violates "separation-of-powers principles." See Brief for Petitioner 43. In his view, those principles prohibit "vest[ing] in a single branch the law-making and law-interpreting functions." Id., at 45. If that objection is to agencies' usurping the interpretive role of courts, this opinion has already met it head-on. Properly understood and applied, Auer does no such thing. In all the ways we have described, courts retain a firm grip on the interpretive function. If Kisor's objection is instead to the supposed commingling of functions (that is, the legislative and judicial) within an agency, this Court has answered it often before. See, e.g., Withrow v. Larkin, 421 U.S. 35, 54 (1975) (permitting such a combination of functions); FTC v. Cement Institute, 333 U.S. 683, 702 (1948) (same) [p. 512]. That sort of mixing is endemic in agencies, and has been "since the beginning of the Republic." Arlington, 569 U.S. at 304–305, n. 4. It does not violate the separation of powers, we have explained, because even when agency "activities take 'legislative' and 'judicial' forms," they continue to be "exercises of[ ] the 'executive Power' "—or otherwise said, ways of executing a statutory plan. Ibid. (quoting U.S. Const., Art. II, § 1, cl. 1). So Kisor's last argument to dispatch Auer deference fails as roundly as the rest.

B

If all that were not enough, stare decisis cuts strongly against Kisor's position. . . . Adherence to precedent is "a foundation stone of the rule of law." Michigan v. Bay Mills Indian Community, 572 U.S. 782, 798 (2014). . . . To be sure, stare decisis is "not an inexorable command." Id., at 828. But any departure from the doctrine demands "special justification"—something more than "an argument that the precedent was wrongly decided." Halliburton Co. v. Erica P. John Fund, Inc., 573 U.S. 258, 266 (2014).

And that is even more than usually so in the circumstances here. First, Kisor asks us to overrule not a single case, but a "long line of precedents"—each one reaffirming the rest and going back 75 years or more. . . . Second, because that is so, abandoning Auer deference would cast doubt on many settled constructions of rules. As Kisor acknowledged at oral argument, a decision in his favor would allow relitigation of any decision based on Auer, forcing courts to "wrestle [with] whether or not Auer" had actually made a difference. Tr. of Oral Arg. 30; . . .

And third, even if we are wrong about Auer, "Congress remains free to alter what we have done." Patterson v. McLean Credit Union, 491 U.S. 164, 172–173 (1989) (stating that when that is so, "[c]onsiderations of stare decisis have special force"). . . . Our deference decisions are "balls tossed into Congress's court, for acceptance or not as that branch elects."

Kimble, 135 S.Ct., at 2409. And so far, at least, Congress has chosen acceptance. . . .

IV

With that, we can finally return to Kisor's own case. You may remember that his retroactive benefits depend on the meaning of the term "relevant" records in a VA regulation. . . .

Applying the principles outlined in this opinion, we hold that a redo is necessary for two reasons. First, the Federal Circuit jumped the gun in declaring the regulation ambiguous. We have insisted that a court bring all its interpretive tools to bear before finding that to be so. . . .

And second, the Federal Circuit assumed too fast that Auer deference should apply in the event of genuine ambiguity. . . .

We accordingly vacate the judgment below and remand the case for further proceedings.

It is so ordered.

■ CHIEF JUSTICE ROBERTS, concurring in part

I join Parts I, II-B, III-B, and IV of the Court's opinion. . . . For the reasons the Court discusses in Part III-B, I agree that overruling [Auer and Seminole Rock] is not warranted. I also agree with the Court's treatment in Part II-B of the bounds of Auer deference.

I write separately to suggest that the distance between the majority and JUSTICE GORSUCH is not as great as it may initially appear. The majority catalogs the prerequisites for, and limitations on, Auer deference: The underlying regulation must be genuinely ambiguous; the agency's interpretation must be reasonable and must reflect its authoritative, expertise-based, and fair and considered judgment; and the agency must take account of reliance interests and avoid unfair surprise. JUSTICE GORSUCH, meanwhile, lists the reasons that a court might be persuaded to adopt an agency's interpretation of its own regulation: The agency thoroughly considered the problem, offered a valid rationale, brought its expertise to bear, and interpreted the regulation in a manner consistent with earlier and later pronouncements. Accounting for variations in verbal formulation, those lists have much in common.

That is not to say that Auer deference is just the same as the power of persuasion discussed in Skidmore v. Swift & Co., 323 U.S. 134 (1944); there is a difference between holding that a court ought to be persuaded by an agency's interpretation and holding that it should defer to that interpretation under certain conditions. But it is to say that the cases in which Auer deference is warranted largely overlap with the cases in which it would be unreasonable for a court not to be persuaded by an agency's interpretation of its own regulation.

One further point: Issues surrounding judicial deference to agency interpretations of their own regulations are distinct from those raised in connection with judicial deference to agency interpretations of statutes enacted by Congress. See Chevron U.S.A. Inc. v. Natural Resources

Defense Council, Inc., 467 U.S. 837 (1984). I do not regard the Court's decision today to touch upon the latter question.

■ JUSTICE GORSUCH, with whom JUSTICE THOMAS joins, JUSTICE KAVANAUGH joins as to Parts I, II, III, IV, and V, and JUSTICE ALITO joins as to Parts I, II, and III, concurring in the judgment.

It should have been easy for the Court to say goodbye to Auer v. Robbins. In disputes involving the relationship between the government and the people, Auer requires judges to accept an executive agency's interpretation of its own regulations even when that interpretation doesn't represent the best and fairest reading. This rule creates a "systematic judicial bias in favor of the federal government, the most powerful of parties, and against everyone else." . . .

II. The Administrative Procedure Act

. . .

A

The first problem lies in § 706. That provision instructs reviewing courts to "decide all relevant questions of law" and "set aside agency action . . . found to be . . . not in accordance with law." Determining the meaning of a statute or regulation, of course, presents a classic legal question. But in case these directives were not clear enough, the APA further directs courts to "determine the meaning" of any relevant "agency action," including any rule issued by the agency. The APA thus requires a reviewing court to resolve for itself any dispute over the proper interpretation of an agency regulation. A court that, in deference to an agency, adopts something other than the best reading of a regulation isn't "decid[ing]" the relevant "questio[n] of law" or "determin[ing] the meaning" of the regulation. Instead, it's allowing the agency to dictate the answer to that question. In doing so, the court is abdicating the duty Congress assigned to it in the APA.

JUSTICE KAGAN seeks to address the glaring inconsistency between our judge-made rule and the controlling statute this way. On her account, the APA tells a reviewing court to "determine the meaning" of regulations, but it does not tell the court "how" to do that. . . .

But the APA isn't as anemic as that. Its unqualified command requires the court to determine legal questions—including questions about a regulation's meaning—by its own lights, not by those of political appointees or bureaucrats who may even be self-interested litigants in the case at hand. Nor can there be any doubt that, when Congress wrote the APA, it knew perfectly well how to require judicial deference to an agency when it wished—in fact, Congress repeatedly specified deferential standards for judicial review elsewhere in the statute. But when it comes to the business of interpreting regulations, no such command exists; instead, Congress told courts to "determine" those matters for themselves. . . .

What the statutory language suggests, experience confirms. If Auer deference were really just another way for courts to "determine the meaning" of regulations under § 706, you might expect that a final judicial "determination" would at least settle, as a matter of precedent, the question of what the regulation "means." Of course, even after one court has spoken on a regulation's meaning, that court or another might properly give weight to a new agency interpretation as part of the court's own decision-making process. But in light of National Cable & Telecommunications Assn. v. Brand X Internet Services [p. 1230], courts have interpreted Auer as forbidding a court from ever "determin[ing] the meaning" of a regulation with the force that normally attaches to precedent, because an agency is always free to adopt a different view and insist on judicial deference to its new judgment. And if an agency can not only control the court's initial decision but also revoke that decision at any time, how can anyone honestly say the court, rather than the agency, ever really "determine[s]" what the regulation means? . . .

B

The problems don't end there. Auer is also incompatible with the APA's instructions in § 553. That provision requires agencies to follow notice-and-comment procedures when issuing or amending legally binding regulations (what the APA calls "substantive rules"), but not when offering mere interpretations of those regulations. . . .

Auer effectively nullifies the distinction Congress drew here. Under Auer, courts must treat as "controlling" not only an agency's duly promulgated rules but also its mere interpretations—even ones that appear only in a legal brief, press release, or guidance document issued without affording the public advance notice or a chance to comment. For all practical purposes, "the new interpretation might as well be a new regulation." . . .

JUSTICE KAGAN . . . replies that affording Auer deference to an agency's interpretation of its own rules never offends the APA because the agency's interpretation lacks "the force of law" associated with substantive rules. Agency interpretations lack this force, we are told, because a court always retains the power to decide at least whether the interpretation is entitled to deference. But this argument rests on an implausibly narrow understanding of what it means for an agency action to bear the force of law. Under JUSTICE KAGAN's logic, even a binding substantive rule would lack the force of law because a court retains the power to decide whether the rule is arbitrary and capricious and thus invalid under the APA. But no one believes that. While an agency interpretation, just like a substantive rule, "must meet certain conditions before it gets deference," "once it does so [Auer makes it] every bit as binding as a substantive rule." To suggest that Auer does not make an agency's interpretive guidance "binding o[n] anyone," is linguistic hocus-pocus.

C

If Auer cannot be squared with the text of the APA, JUSTICE KAGAN suggests it at least conforms to a reasonable "presumption about congressional intent." The theory seems to be that whenever Congress grants an agency "rulemaking power," it also implicitly gives the agency " 'the power authoritatively to interpret' " whatever rules the agency chooses to adopt. But against the clear statutory commands Congress gave us in the APA, what sense does it make to "presume" that Congress really, secretly, wanted courts to treat agency interpretations as binding? Normally, this Court does not allow hidden legislative intentions to "muddy" such plainly expressed statutory directives.

Even on its own terms, too, this argument proves pretty muddy. It goes something like this: The drafters of the APA did not intend to " 'significantly alter' " established law governing judicial review of agency action as of 1946; the Auer doctrine was part of that established law; therefore, the APA implicitly requires courts to afford agencies Auer deference. But neither of this syllogism's essential premises stands on solid ground.

Take the major premise—that those who adopted the APA intended to work no change in the established law of judicial review of agency action. JUSTICE KAGAN is right, of course, that Attorney General Clark claimed as much shortly after the APA's passage. But his view, which reflected the interests of the executive branch, was far from universally shared. . . .

JUSTICE KAGAN's syllogism runs into even more trouble with its minor premise—that the Auer doctrine was a well-established part of the common law background when Congress enacted the APA in 1946. . . . [T]his Court planted the seeds of Auer deference for the first time in dictum in Seminole Rock, just a year before Congress passed the APA. And that dictum did not somehow immediately become an entrenched part of the common law. . . . In truth, when Congress passed the APA the law of judicial review of agency action was in a confused state. During the congressional hearings on the bill, one witness's suggestion that Congress should leave the scope of judicial review "as it now is" drew this fair reply from Representative Walter, chairman of the House Subcommittee on Administrative Law and author of the House Report on the APA: "You say 'as it now is.' Frankly, I do not know what it now is. . . . [T]he Supreme Court apparently changes its mind daily."

III. The Constitution

Not only is Auer incompatible with the APA; it also sits uneasily with the Constitution. . . .

A

Our Nation's founders were painfully aware of the dangers of executive and legislative intrusion on judicial decision-making. One of the abuses of royal power that led to the American Revolution was King George's attempt to gain influence over colonial judges. Colonial legislatures, too, had interfered with the courts' independence "at the behest of private interests and factions." These experiences had taught the founders that "there is no liberty if the power of judgment be not separated from the legislative and executive powers." They knew that when political actors are left free not only to adopt and enforce written laws, but also to control the interpretation of those laws, the legal rights of "litigants with unpopular or minority causes or . . . who belong to despised or suspect classes" count for little. . . . The rule of law begins to bleed into the rule of men. . . .

Auer allows an agency to do exactly what this Court has always said a legislature cannot do: "compel the courts to construe and apply" a law on the books, "not according to the judicial . . . judgment," but according to the judgment of another branch. When we defer to an agency interpretation that differs from what we believe to be the best interpretation of the law, we compromise our judicial independence and deny the people who come before us the impartial judgment that the Constitution guarantees them. And we mislead those whom we serve by placing a judicial imprimatur on what is, in fact, no more than an exercise of raw political executive power.

B

What do our colleagues have to say about these concerns? A majority has nothing to offer, and JUSTICE KAGAN dismisses them out of hand. . . . The judicial power has always been understood to provide the people with a neutral arbiter who bears the responsibility and duty to "expound and interpret" the governing law, not just the power to say whether someone else's interpretation, let alone the interpretation of a self-interested political actor, is "reasonable.". . .

IV. Policy Arguments

Lacking support elsewhere, JUSTICE KAGAN is forced to resort to policy arguments to defend Auer. But even the most sensible policy argument would not empower us to ignore the plain language of the APA or the demands of the Constitution. . . . Besides, the policy arguments offered today are not just unpersuasive, they are troubling.

Take the first and boldest offering. JUSTICE KAGAN suggests that determining the meaning of a regulation is largely a matter of figuring out what the "person who wrote it . . . intended." In this way, we're told, a legally binding regulation isn't all that different from "a memo or an e-mail"—if you "[w]ant to know what [it] means," you'd better "[a]sk its author." But . . . if the rule of law means anything, it means that we are governed by the public meaning of the words found in statutes and regulations, not by their authors' private intentions. This is a vital part of what it means to have "a government of laws, and not of men." . . .

Nor does JUSTICE KAGAN's account of the interpretive process even wind up supporting Auer. If a court's goal in interpreting a regulation really were to determine what its author "intended," Auer would be an almost complete mismatch with the goal. Agency personnel change over time, and an agency's policy priorities may shift dramatically from one presidential administration to another. Yet Auer tells courts that they must defer to the agency's current view of what the regulation ought to mean, which may or may not correspond to the views of those who actually wrote it. . . .

Proceeding farther down this doubtful path, JUSTICE KAGAN asserts that resolving ambiguities in a regulation "sounds more in policy than in law" and is thus a task more suited to executive officials than judges. But this claim, too, contradicts a basic premise of our legal order: that we are governed not by the shifting whims of politicians and bureaucrats, but by written laws whose meaning is fixed and ascertainable . . .

Pursuing a more modest tack, JUSTICE KAGAN next suggests that Auer is justified by the respect due agencies' "technical" expertise. But no one doubts that courts should pay close attention to an expert agency's views on technical questions in its field. . . . The fact remains, however, that even agency experts "can be wrong; even Homer nodded." Skidmore and the traditional approach it embodied recognized both of these facts of life long ago, explaining that, while courts should of course afford respectful consideration to the expert agency's views, they must remain open to competing expert and other evidence supplied in an adversarial setting. Respect for an agency's technical expertise demands no more.

JUSTICE KAGAN's final policy argument is that Auer promotes "consistency" and "uniformity" in the interpretation of regulations. If we let courts decide what regulations mean, she warns, they might disagree, and it might take some time for higher courts to resolve those disagreements. But consistency and uniformity are hardly grounds on which Auer's advocates should wish to fight. The judicial process is how we settle disputes about the meaning of written law, and our judicial system is more than capable of producing a single, uniform, and stable interpretation that will last until the regulation is amended or repealed. Meanwhile, under Auer courts often disagree about whether deference is warranted, and a regulation's "meaning" can be transformed with the stroke of a pen any time there is a new presidential administration. "Consistency," "uniformity," and stability in the law are hardly among Auer's crowning achievements.

V. Stare Decisis

In the end, a majority declines to endorse JUSTICE KAGAN's arguments and insists only that, even if Auer is not "right and well-reasoned," we're stuck with it because of the respect due precedent.

But notice: While pretending to bow to stare decisis, the majority goes about reshaping our precedent in new and experimental ways. . . . [T]he majority isn't really much moved by stare decisis; everyone recognizes, to one degree or another, that Auer cannot stand. And between our remaining choices—continuing to make up new deference rules, or returning to the text of the APA and the approach to judicial review that prevailed for most of our history—the answer should have been easy.

A

There are serious questions about whether stare decisis should apply here at all. To be sure, Auer's narrow holding about the meaning of the regulation at issue in that case may be entitled to stare decisis effect. The same may be true for the specific holdings in other cases where this Court has applied Auer deference. But does stare decisis extend beyond those discrete holdings and bind future Members of this Court to apply Auer's broader deference framework?

It seems doubtful that stare decisis demands that much. . . . [W]e do not regard statements in our opinions about such generally applicable interpretive methods, like the proper weight to afford historical practice in constitutional cases or legislative history in statutory cases, as binding future Justices with the full force of horizontal stare decisis. Why, then, should we regard as binding Auer's statements about the weight to afford agencies' interpretations in regulatory cases? . . .

B

Even assuming for argument's sake that standard stare decisis considerations apply, they still do not require us to retain Auer. . . .

[T]he majority worries that "abandoning Auer deference would cast doubt on many settled constructions" of regulations on which regulated parties might have relied. But, again, decisions construing particular regulations might retain stare decisis effect even if the Court announced that it would no longer adhere to Auer's interpretive methodology. After all, decisions construing particular statutes continue to command respect even when the interpretive methods that led to those constructions fall out of favor. Besides, if the majority is correct that abandoning Auer would require revisiting regulatory constructions that were upheld based on Auer deference, the majority's revision of Auer will yield exactly the same result. . . .

*

Overruling Auer would have taken us directly back to Skidmore, liberating courts to decide cases based on their independent judgment and "follow [the] agency's [view] only to the extent it is persuasive." By contrast, the majority's attempt to remodel Auer's rule into a multi-step, multi-factor inquiry guarantees more uncertainty and much litigation. Proceeding in this convoluted way burdens our colleagues on the lower courts, who will have to spend time debating deference that they could have spent interpreting disputed regulations. It also continues to deny the people who come before us the neutral forum for their disputes that they rightly expect and deserve.

But this cloud may have a silver lining: The majority leaves Auer so riddled with holes that, when all is said and done, courts may find that it does not constrain their independent judgment any more than Skidmore. As reengineered, Auer requires courts to "exhaust all the 'traditional tools' of construction" before they even consider deferring to an agency. And those tools include all sorts of tie-breaking rules for resolving ambiguity even in the closest cases. Courts manage to make do with these tools in many other areas of the law, so one might hope they will hardly ever find them inadequate here. And if they do, they will now have to conduct a further inquiry that includes so few firm guides and so many cryptic "markers" that they will rarely, if ever, have to defer to an agency regulatory interpretation that differs from what they believe is the best and fairest reading. . . .

■ JUSTICE KAVANAUGH, with whom JUSTICE ALITO joins, concurring in the judgment.

I agree with JUSTICE GORSUCH's conclusion that the Auer deference doctrine should be formally retired. I write separately to emphasize two points.

First, I agree with THE CHIEF JUSTICE that "the distance between the majority and JUSTICE GORSUCH is not as great as it may initially appear.". . . [T]he majority borrows from footnote 9 of this Court's opinion in Chevron to say that a reviewing court must "exhaust all the 'traditional tools' of construction" before concluding that an agency rule is ambiguous and deferring to an agency's reasonable interpretation. If a reviewing court employs all of the traditional tools of construction, the court will almost always reach a conclusion about the best interpretation of the regulation at issue. After doing so, the court then will have no need to adopt or defer to an agency's contrary interpretation. In other words, the footnote 9 principle, taken seriously, means that courts will have no reason or basis to put a thumb on the scale in favor of an agency when courts interpret agency regulations. . . .

Second, I also agree with THE CHIEF JUSTICE that "[i]ssues surrounding judicial deference to agency interpretations of their own regulations are distinct from those raised in connection with judicial deference to agency interpretations of statutes enacted by Congress." Like THE CHIEF JUSTICE, "I do not regard the Court's decision" not to formally overrule Auer "to touch upon the latter question."

## NOTES ON AGENCIES' INTERPRETATIONS OF THEIR OWN REGULATIONS

(1) ***Before Kisor.*** Although the question of agency interpretations of their own regulations may seem narrow, the questions raised by Auer (or Seminole Rock) deference implicate deep principles of administrative law. Kisor's restatement of Auer deference preserves a rich debate about those principles:

(a) JOHN F. MANNING, CONSTITUTIONAL STRUCTURE AND JUDICIAL DEFERENCE TO AGENCY INTERPRETATIONS OF AGENCY RULES, 96 Colum. L. Rev. 612, 616–17 (1996): "Viewed in isolation, Seminole Rock may be an understandable reaction to the exigencies of modern regulatory governance; it cuts agencies helpful interpretive slack in a world in which life is short, resources are limited, and agencies must address complex issues that have unpredictable twists and turns. Seminole Rock, however, cannot be considered in isolation; one must assess that precedent's validity in light of the incentives that it supplies to an agency engaged in rulemaking. If an agency's rules mean whatever it says they mean (unless the reading is plainly erroneous), the agency effectively has the power of self-interpretation. This authority permits an agency to supply the meaning of regulatory gaps or ambiguities of its own making and relieves the agency of the cost of imprecision that it has produced. This state of affairs makes it that much less likely that an agency will give clear notice of its policies either to those who participate in the rulemaking process prescribed by the Administrative Procedure Act or to the regulated public. The present arrangement also contradicts a major premise of our constitutional scheme and of contemporary separation of powers case law—that a fusion of lawmaking and law-exposition is especially dangerous to our liberties."

(b) CASS R. SUNSTEIN & ADRIAN VERMEULE, THE UNBEARABLE RIGHTNESS OF AUER, 84 U. Chi. L. Rev. 297, 310–13 (2017): "[T]he separation-of-powers critique of Auer, and of the combination of rulemaking and rule-interpreting functions, is pitched at the wrong level. The separation of powers is fully satisfied so long as the principal institutions set out in the Constitution—Congress, president, and judiciary—exercising their prescribed functions, devise and approve the scheme of agency authority that combines rulemaking and rule-interpreting power in the agency's hands. Whatever reasons make the constitutional separation of powers attractive in turn support that combination of functions. If the constitutional institutions, operating as they were set up to operate, have decided that such an arrangement is both valid and wise, then respect for the separation of powers counsels approval of the arrangement."

(2) ***After Kisor.*** How will the lower courts apply Kisor? In particular, one question suggested by the opinions is whether Kisor will unsettle previous decisions that were based on Auer deference. There is already a circuit split concerning a Supreme Court decision on interpretive commentary in the federal sentencing guidelines, Stinson v. United States, 508 U.S. 36, 38 (1993). Stinson "treated" the guidelines as "an agency's interpretation of its own legislative rule," while noting that "the analogy is not precise because Congress has a role in promulgating the guidelines." Id. at 1918–19. That distinction has created disagreement about whether Kisor, which cited Stinson as an example of deference, requires courts to revisit it. Compare United States v. Nasir, 17 F.4th 459, 472 (3d Cir. 2021) (en banc); United States v. Riccardi, 989 F.3d 476, 485–86 (6th Cir. 2021), with United States v. Moses, 23 F.4th 347, 349 (4th Cir. 2022); United States v. Vargas, 35 F.4th 936, 940 (5th Cir. 2022).

And then there are the other, more case-specific questions, like whether an interpretation presents "unfair surprise." What happens when courts disagree about the answer? For example, one category of interpretations includes those of an agency's own rules about the procedures it must follow. If courts apply the Kisor guideposts in different ways to such regulations, must an agency comply with different procedures in different jurisdictions?

(3) ***Comparing Auer with Chevron.*** Chevron and Auer deference are similar in the sense that the court defers to agency construction of the text at issue, whether a statute or regulation. Are the differences between the doctrines as they presently stand matched to the differences between statutes and regulations? For one, how are informal interpretations treated under the two frameworks? Can it be right that, under Mead, an interpretation of ambiguity in an agency's organic statute receives only Skidmore (or perhaps no) deference, while such an interpretation receives

greater deference when the subject of interpretation is one of the agency's own regulations? Does that make sense because a regulation is more interstitial than a statute and likely to be more technical? Or perhaps because the agency has used its delegated authority to write the ambiguous regulation in the first place, and is simply using the rest of its authority to expound it, just like it may choose between legislation and adjudication? Or does it instead encourage sloppy administration by deferring only in the situation where the agency is responsible for the ambiguity?

Here's another distinction. Brand X (p. 1230) gives agencies leeway to change interpretations of a statute within broad bounds of reasonableness. What does Kisor say about inconsistency? (Does "unfair surprise" sweep even more broadly?) Yet both Brand X and Kisor justify deference in part by the fact that agency interpretations entail a degree of "expert policy judgment." Nat'l Cable & Telecommunications Ass'n v. Brand X Internet Servs., 545 U.S. 967, 1003 (2005). Is a regulation any less susceptible to updated expert policy judgments than a statute? In fact, could consistency for the sake of consistency be arbitrary and capricious? How can a court distinguish between the good kinds of inconsistency, and the bad kind of inconsistency that apparently militates against Auer deference?

(4) ***The Cumulation of Deference.*** Can there be deference on top of deference?

(a) Yes: The way deference principles can cumulate shows up clearly in this passage from Coeur Alaska, Inc. v. Southeast Alaska Conservation Council, 557 U.S. 261, 277–78 (2009), discussing the question whether an EPA regulation under the Clean Water Act applied to the discharge of fill material from a mining operation into a lake and applying the Auer doctrine: "We address in turn the statutory text of the CWA, the agencies' regulations construing it, and the EPA's subsequent interpretation of those regulations. Because Congress has not 'directly spoken' to the 'precise question' of whether an EPA performance standard applies to discharges of fill material, the statute alone does not resolve the case. Chevron. We look first to the agency regulations, which are entitled to deference if they resolve the ambiguity in a reasonable manner. Chevron; Mead. But the regulations, too, are ambiguous, so we next turn to the agencies' subsequent interpretation of those regulations. Mead; Auer v. Robbins. In an internal memorandum the EPA explained that its performance standards do not apply to discharges of fill material. That interpretation is not 'plainly erroneous or inconsistent with the regulation[s],' and so we accept it as correct. Auer v. Robbins."

(b) And no: Side by side with this approach is a line of lower-court cases that protect regulated parties from being penalized for agency enforcement of standards of which they had no fair notice. If a regulation is sufficiently ambiguous, it may not give adequate notice of what it requires (although of course the agency's enforcement personnel may have given actual notice of the agency's interpretation in interactions with the regulated party). Absent such actual notice, it is possible to have (a) a properly adopted regulation, to which the court will defer as a reasonable interpretation of an ambiguous statute; (b) a less formal agency interpretation of that regulation, to which the court will defer as a reasonable interpretation of an ambiguous regulation; (c) conditions which violate the agency's interpretation of the law; but (d) no liability because the combined ambiguity in (a) and (b)—even though overcome by the combined deference in (a) and (b)—prevents the regulated party from having had fair notice of what it was required to do. See, e.g., Beaver Plant Operations, Inc. v. Herman, 223 F.3d 25 (1st Cir. 2000).

(5) ***Consistency and Procedure.*** Mead (p. 1283) points out that the Customs Service was careful to make clear in its ruling letter that the ruling could be modified without notice and that no one should rely on it except the person to whom it was issued for the transaction particularly described. Can an agency avoid its obligation to be consistent (p. 1102) that easily?

Suppose we take a yet more extreme case: Someone in an agency advises a private party as to the law governing her situation, and the agency later determines that the advice was improvident or wrong. Suppose, for example, that a taxpayer was advised by an IRS agent over the phone that she will not have to pay taxes if she does thus-and-so, and an IRS auditor later determines that that advice was incorrect. If the private party has relied on the agency's advice in the interim—perhaps experiencing what Kisor majority refers to as "unfair surprise"—can she estop the agency?

The short answer to the question, ninety-some-percent reliable, is that the government cannot be estopped. The longer answer is that the Supreme Court has made a practice of always stopping short of saying "never" while at the same time refusing actually to find an estoppel in any particular set of facts before it; and the lower courts have occasionally found a set of facts extreme enough to convince them. Some of the fact patterns that the Supreme Court has found insufficient seem at first glance (or maybe even later) to be rather compelling. In one leading case, an agent for a federal crop insurance plan told a farmer that a particular kind of crop was insurable; the farmer insured it with the government; after the drought hit, the government determined that a regulation not known to the agent or the farmer prevented coverage, and refused payment; held: no estoppel. Federal Crop Ins. Corp. v. Merrill, 332 U.S. 380 (1947). In another, a retired Navy employee consulted with the Navy's personnel department before taking another job that might threaten his disability annuity and was told it would not, took the job, and then lost payments under his annuity because, although not reflected in the Navy's own manuals, a few years earlier Congress had amended the statute to tighten eligibility requirements; held: no estoppel. Office of Personnel Management v. Richmond, 496 U.S. 414 (1990).

The Court's attitude can be better understood if the consequences of allowing lower-level employees to estop the government are considered. In effect such a ruling would allow bad advice plus private reliance to take the place of the otherwise applicable law—to override the terms of a statute or the limitations of an appropriation. Moreover, liability for bad advice might well create an incentive for agencies to give no advice—in which case the cure might be worse than the disease.

In an appropriate case, of course, the facts that might establish an estoppel might also be recharacterized in the terms of some other doctrine that seems to threaten less far-reaching consequences—perhaps in terms of the government's having "waived" a right, or in terms of the government's abusing its discretion in not taking its own course of advice into account when deciding what to do, or in terms, as discussed in a note above, of the government's having failed to give "fair notice" of what its regulations require.

(6) ***Kisor and the Future of Chevron.*** Aren't many of the arguments that Justice Kagan makes in defending Auer deference—about how it reflects a reasonable presumption about legislative intent and how it therefore accords with both the APA and the separation of powers—precisely the kind of arguments that one would make to defend Chevron deference? If so, what are we to make of the fact that the Chief Justice made a point of noting in his concurring opinion in Kisor that the issues presented by Chevron deference differ from those presented by Auer deference? Does it suggest that Chevron might be on shakier ground than Auer proved to be? Or is it a signal that he might think the arguments that Justice Kagan set forth to defend Auer deference have more force if deployed to defend the merits of Chevron? The future of one of modern administrative law's foundational doctrines—Chevron—may turn on the answer to those questions.

Chief Justice Roberts noted in Kisor, after all, that he did not see much distance between Auer deference, as limited in Kisor, and the approach set forth in Justice Gorsuch's concurrence in that case, which would have overruled Auer. Does that suggest that Chevron's future may mirror Auer's, such that it will take the form of a divided opinion that saves Chevron deference while limiting it along the lines that Kisor limits Auer, with the Chief Justice noting that the new Chevron is not much different from no Chevron? One analysis predicts: "Before Kisor, conservative-libertarian legalists saw the overruling of Auer as the first and easier step on the path to overruling Chevron. Having clearly failed at Step One, it is unreasonable to expect success at Step Two. Chevron may well be increasingly hemmed in, but there too, narrowing dispositions will leave the basic principle of deference embedded in the law." Cass R. Sunstein & Adrian Vermeule, Law and Leviathan 107 (2020).

And does Kisor portend ill for Brand X (p. 1230)? The courts of appeals already appear to defer more to longstanding interpretations. Kent Barnett & Christopher J. Walker, Chevron in the Circuit Courts, 116 Mich. L. Rev. 1, 65 (2017). Even the Supreme Court has considered, at Chevron step two, the longevity of interpretations in determining their reasonableness. Cuozzo Speed Techs., LLC v. Lee, 579 U.S. 261, 2881 (2016). And West Virginia v. EPA (p. 1341) suggests that some types of novel interpretations may take the agency beyond the conditions for Chevron deference altogether. Does West Virginia represent a step toward making Brand X more standard-like in the fashion of Kisor? Can that be done consistently with the underlying theory of Brand X? (Is that the theory of Chevron itself?)

One striking characteristic of all the Kisor opinions is that, in contrast to Chevron (which was a decision under the judicial review provisions of the

Clean Air Act), they directly relate the issues to the APA's statutory review standards. Could Justice Kagan's understanding of § 706 support Chevron? And, does Kisor also suggest that there is less at stake in the debate over Chevron deference than those on either side of it acknowledge? Or do Mead, Kisor, and now West Virginia show that the trend is one of narrowing deference to agencies, with both Auer and Chevron liable to vanish altogether? Would Skidmore persist in such a world? Or do the reasons for ending Chevron and Auer require that it, too, disappear?

# CHAPTER IX

# ACCESS TO JUDICIAL REVIEW: JUSTICIABILITY



As Chapter VIII makes clear, judicial review gives courts substantial power to affect what agencies can do and can't do, as well as how they operate. Who can invoke this power against the agency? For what sorts of claims? When? With what kinds of remedies? Such questions are answered by the various doctrines of justiciability. For those of you who have taken the course in Federal Courts, many of these materials will be familiar. But the focus here is on approaching justiciability with an eye to how rules about access to judicial review may affect the regulatory process.

We begin in this Chapter with materials on the threshold question of whether a plaintiff has standing to sue. Standing is the most common justiciability question, and as you'll see the Supreme Court has rooted the core requirements for standing in Article III of the Constitution. The materials on standing begin by going over the basic doctrinal framework for standing and then look in more detail at how the Court has applied the three core requirements of Article III—injury, causation, and redressability—in regulatory contexts. We next take up additional standing problems, in particular questions about when governments have standing to sue and about prudential standing doctrines, which are nonconstitutional requirements for standing.

The second half of the Chapter turns to an additional set of justiciability doctrines. One is the requirement that the agency action at issue be reviewable, which includes both that plaintiffs have a source of authority to sue, such as a right of action in a statute, and that judicial review not be precluded. Even if an agency action is potentially reviewable, the availability of review may be subject to timing limitations. Some questions we'll cover on timing are whether a plaintiff can challenge an agency regulation before it is finalized or enforced, and whether she needs to exhaust administrative remedies before turning to court. At the end of the Chapter we turn from the front end to the back end of judicial review, briefly examining what types of judicial remedies are available for unlawful agency action.

As you go through these materials, try not to lose sight of the regulatory impact that the doctrines you are studying have on different actors in the regulatory process and on regulatory outcomes. So, for example, think about how rules of standing affect: (1) the agency, (2) the regulated community, (3) those who are intended beneficiaries of the regulatory program, (4) those who might incidentally benefit from a regulation; and (5) those who might incidentally bear its costs. The various justiciability doctrines discussed in this Chapter operate to allocate access to, or protection from, judicial review among these actors. Do you think the doctrines are making the right allocations?

## SECTION 1. STANDING



### a. The Basic Doctrinal Framework



## LUJAN v. DEFENDERS OF WILDLIFE

Supreme Court of the United States (1992).
504 U.S. 555.

■ JUSTICE SCALIA delivered the opinion of the Court with respect to Parts I, II, III-A, and IV, and an opinion with respect to Part III-B in which CHIEF JUSTICE REHNQUIST, JUSTICE WHITE, and JUSTICE THOMAS join.

[Section 7(a)(2) of the Endangered Species Act of 1973 (ESA) divides responsibility for protecting endangered species between the Secretary of the Interior and the Secretary of Commerce. Federal agencies must consult with one or the other Secretary when funding an action that might jeopardize the existence or habitat of any endangered or threatened species. The Secretaries initially promulgated a joint regulation interpreting § 7(a)(2) to apply to actions taken in foreign nations; then, they jointly revised the rule to limit the section's geographic scope to the United States and the high seas. Wildlife conservation and other environmental organizations sued, claiming that the revised rule misinterpreted the statute. The district court dismissed for lack of standing; the court of appeals reversed. On remand, the district court held for the plaintiffs on the merits and the court of appeals affirmed.]

This case involves a challenge to a rule promulgated by the Secretary of the Interior interpreting § 7 of the [ESA] . . . The preliminary issue, and the only one we reach, is whether respondents here, plaintiffs below, have standing to seek judicial review of the rule.

II

While the Constitution of the United States divides all power conferred upon the Federal Government into "legislative Powers," Art. I, § 1, "[t]he executive Power," Art. II, § 1, and "[t]he judicial Power," Art. III, § 1, it does not attempt to define those terms. . . . Obviously, then, the Constitution's central mechanism of separation of powers depends largely upon common understanding of what activities are appropriate to legislatures, to executives, and to courts. . . . One of th[e] landmarks, setting apart the "Cases" and "Controversies" that are of the justiciable sort referred to in Article III . . . is the doctrine of standing. Though some of its elements express merely prudential considerations that are part of judicial self-government, the core component of standing is an essential and unchanging part of the case-or-controversy requirement of Article III. See, e.g., Allen v. Wright, 468 U.S. 737, 751 (1984) [p. 1457].

Over the years, our cases have established that the irreducible constitutional minimum of standing contains three elements. First, the plaintiff must have suffered an "injury in fact"—an invasion of a legally protected interest which is (a) concrete and particularized; and (b) actual or imminent, not conjectural or hypothetical. Second, there must be a causal connection between the injury and the conduct complained of—the injury has to be "fairly . . . trace[able] to the challenged action of the defendant, and not . . . th[e] result [of] the independent action of some third party not before the court." Simon v. Eastern Kentucky Welfare Rights Org., 426 U.S. 26, 41–42 (1976) [p. 1462]. Third, it must be "likely," as opposed to merely "speculative," that the injury will be "redressed by a favorable decision." Id. The party invoking federal jurisdiction bears the burden of establishing these elements. . . .

When the suit is one challenging the legality of government action or inaction, the nature and extent of facts that must be averred (at the summary judgment stage) or proved (at the trial stage) in order to establish standing depends considerably upon whether the plaintiff is himself an object of the action (or forgone action) at issue. If he is, there is ordinarily little question that the action or inaction has caused him injury, and that a judgment preventing or requiring the action will redress it. When, however, as in this case, a plaintiff's asserted injury arises from the government's allegedly unlawful regulation (or lack of regulation) of someone else, much more is needed. In that circumstance, causation and redressability ordinarily hinge on the response of the regulated (or regulable) third party to the government action or inaction—and perhaps on the response of others as well. The existence of one or more of the essential elements of standing "depends on the unfettered choices made by independent actors not before the courts and whose exercise of broad and legitimate discretion the courts cannot presume either to control or to predict," ASARCO Inc. v. Kadish, 490 U.S.

605, 615 (1989) (opinion of Kennedy, J.), and it becomes the burden of the plaintiff to adduce facts showing that those choices have been or will be made in such manner as to produce causation and permit redressability of injury. Thus, when the plaintiff is not himself the object of the government action or inaction he challenges, standing is not precluded, but it is ordinarily "substantially more difficult" to establish. . . .

III

. . . Respondents' claim to injury is that the lack of consultation with respect to certain funded activities abroad "increas[es] the rate of extinction of endangered and threatened species." Of course, the desire to use or observe an animal species, even for purely aesthetic purposes, is undeniably a cognizable interest for purpose of standing. See, e.g., Sierra Club v. Morton, 405 U.S. [727,] 734 [(1972).] "But the 'injury in fact' test requires more than an injury to a cognizable interest. It requires that the party seeking review be himself among the injured." Id. . . .

. . . [T]he Court of Appeals focused on the affidavits of two Defenders' members—Joyce Kelly and Amy Skilbred. Ms. Kelly stated that she traveled to Egypt in 1986 and "observed the traditional habitat of the endangered nile crocodile there and intend[s] to do so again, and hope[s] to observe the crocodile directly," and that she "will suffer harm in fact as a result of [the] American . . . role . . . in overseeing the rehabilitation of the Aswan High Dam on the Nile . . . and [in] develop[ing] . . . Egypt's . . . Master Water Plan." Ms. Skilbred averred that she traveled to Sri Lanka in 1981 and "observed th[e] habitat" of "endangered species such as the Asian elephant and the leopard" at what is now the site of the Mahaweli Project funded by the Agency for International Development (AID), although she "was unable to see any of the endangered species;" "this development project," she continued, "will seriously reduce endangered, threatened, and endemic species habitat including areas that I visited . . . [, which] may severely shorten the future of these species;" that threat, she concluded, harmed her because she "intend[s] to return to Sri Lanka in the future and hope[s] to be more fortunate in spotting at least the endangered elephant and leopard." When Ms. Skilbred was asked at a subsequent deposition if and when she had any plans to return to Sri Lanka, she reiterated that "I intend to go back to Sri Lanka," but confessed that she had no current plans: "I don't know [when]. There is a civil war going on right now. I don't know. Not next year, I will say. In the future."

We shall assume for the sake of argument that these affidavits contain facts showing that certain agency-funded projects threaten listed species—though that is questionable. They plainly contain no facts, however, showing how damage to the species will produce "imminent" injury to Ms. Kelly and Skilbred. That the women "had visited" the areas of the projects before the projects commenced proves nothing. As we have said in a related context, "[p]ast exposure to illegal conduct does not in itself show a present case or controversy regarding injunctive relief . . . if unaccompanied by any continuing, present adverse effects." [Los Angeles v.] Lyons, 461 U.S. [95,] 102 [(1983).] And the affiants' profession of an "inten[t]" to return to the places they had visited before—where they will presumably, this time, be deprived of the opportunity to observe animals of the endangered species—is simply not enough. Such "some day" intentions—without any description of concrete plans, or indeed even any specification of when the some day will be—do not support a finding of the "actual or imminent" injury that our cases require.

[The Court rejected "a series of novel standing theories" including "ecosystem nexus" (standing for someone who uses any part of a "contiguous ecosystem" adversely affected by a funded activity) and "animal nexus" (standing for someone with an interest in studying or seeing the endangered animals anywhere) and "vocational nexus" (standing for someone with a professional interest in the animal).]

[Part III-B of the opinion, joined by only Chief Justice Rehnquist and Justices White and Thomas, concluded that the respondents also failed to meet the redressability requirements of standing. The agencies involved in the particular projects were not named defendants, and Justice Scalia saw no reason to expect they would in fact consult simply because a court ordered the Secretaries to return to the extraterritorial interpretation. Justice Stevens, concurring, protested that no agency would ignore an authoritative construction of the ESA by the Supreme Court; Justice Scalia responded that, as standing must be determined at the outset of the lawsuit, "it could certainly not be known [at that point] that the suit would reach this Court."]

IV

The Court of Appeals found that respondents had standing for an additional reason: because they had suffered a "procedural injury." The so called "citizen-suit" provision of the ESA provides, in pertinent part, that "any person may commence a civil suit on his own behalf (A) to enjoin any person, including the United States and any other governmental instrumentality or agency . . . who is alleged to be in violation of any provision of this chapter." 16 U.S.C. § 1540(g). The court held that, because § 7(a)(2) requires interagency consultation, the citizen-suit provision creates a "procedural righ[t]" to consultation in all "persons"—so that anyone can file suit in federal court to challenge the Secretary's (or presumably any other official's) failure to follow the assertedly correct consultative procedure, notwithstanding their inability to allege any discrete injury flowing from that failure. To understand the remarkable nature of this holding one must be clear about what it does *not* rest upon: This is not a case where plaintiffs are seeking to enforce a procedural requirement the disregard of which could impair a separate concrete interest of theirs (e.g., the procedural requirement for a hearing prior to denial of their license application, or the procedural requirement for an environmental impact statement before a federal facility is constructed next door to them).[7] Nor is it simply

[7] There is this much truth to the assertion that "procedural rights" are special: The person who has been accorded a procedural right to protect his concrete interests can assert that right without meeting all the normal standards for redressability and immediacy. Thus, under our case law, one living adjacent to the site for proposed construction of a federally licensed dam

a case where concrete injury has been suffered by many persons, as in mass fraud or mass tort situations. Nor, finally, is it the unusual case in which Congress has created a concrete private interest in the outcome of a suit against a private party for the government's benefit, by providing a cash bounty for the victorious plaintiff. Rather, the court held that the injury-in-fact requirement had been satisfied by congressional conferral upon all persons of an abstract, self-contained, noninstrumental "right" to have the Executive observe the procedures required by law. We reject this view.[8]

We have consistently held that a plaintiff raising only a generally available grievance about government—claiming only harm to his and every citizen's interest in proper application of the Constitution and laws, and seeking relief that no more directly and tangibly benefits him than it does the public at large—does not state an Article III case or controversy. . . .

To be sure, our generalized-grievance cases have typically involved Government violation of procedures assertedly ordained by the Constitution rather than the Congress. But there is absolutely no basis for making the Article III inquiry turn on the source of the asserted right. Whether the courts were to act on their own, or at the invitation of Congress, in ignoring the concrete injury requirement described in our cases, they would be discarding a principle fundamental to the separate and distinct constitutional role of the Third Branch—one of the essential elements that identifies those "Cases" and "Controversies" that are the business of the courts rather than of the political branches. "The province of the court," as Chief Justice Marshall said in Marbury v. Madison, 1 Cranch 137, 170 (1803), "is, solely, to decide on the rights of individuals." Vindicating the public interest (including the public interest in government observance of the Constitution and laws) is the function of Congress and the Chief Executive. The question presented here is whether the public interest in proper administration of the laws (specifically, in agencies' observance of a particular, statutorily prescribed procedure) can be converted into an individual right by a statute that denominates it as such, and that permits all citizens (or, for

has standing to challenge the licensing agency's failure to prepare an Environmental Impact Statement, even though he cannot establish with any certainty that the Statement will cause the license to be withheld or altered, and even though the dam will not be completed for many years. (That is why we do not rely, in the present case, upon the Government's argument that, even if the other agencies were obliged to consult with the Secretary, they might not have followed his advice.) What respondents' "procedural rights" argument seeks, however, is quite different from this: standing for persons who have no concrete interests affected—persons who live (and propose to live) at the other end of the country from the dam.

[8] The dissent's discussion of this aspect of the case distorts our opinion. We do not hold that an individual cannot enforce procedural rights; he assuredly can, so long as the procedures in question are designed to protect some threatened concrete interest of his that is the ultimate basis of his standing. The dissent, however, asserts that there exist "classes of procedural duties . . . so enmeshed with the prevention of a substantive, concrete harm that an individual plaintiff may be able to demonstrate a sufficient likelihood of injury just through the breach of that procedural duty." If we understand this correctly, it means that the government's violation of a certain (undescribed) class of procedural duty satisfies the concrete-injury requirement by itself, without any showing that the procedural violation endangers a concrete interest of the plaintiff (apart from his interest in having the procedure observed). We cannot agree. . . .

that matter, a subclass of citizens who suffer no distinctive concrete harm) to sue. If the concrete injury requirement has the separation-of-powers significance we have always said, the answer must be obvious: To permit Congress to convert the undifferentiated public interest in executive officers' compliance with the law into an "individual right" vindicable in the courts is to permit Congress to transfer from the President to the courts the Chief Executive's most important constitutional duty, to "take Care that the Laws be faithfully executed," Art. II, § 3. It would enable the courts, with the permission of Congress, "to assume a position of authority over the governmental acts of another and co-equal department," and to become "virtually continuing monitors of the wisdom and soundness of Executive action." Allen, 468 U.S. at 760. We have always rejected that vision of our role:

> When Congress passes an Act empowering administrative agencies to carry on governmental activities, the power of those agencies is circumscribed by the authority granted. This permits the courts to participate in law enforcement entrusted to administrative bodies only to the extent necessary to protect justiciable individual rights against administrative action fairly beyond the granted powers. . . . This is very far from assuming that the courts are charged more than administrators or legislators with the protection of the rights of the people. Congress and the Executive supervise the acts of administrative agents. . . . But under Article III, Congress established courts to adjudicate cases and controversies as to claims of infringement of individual rights whether by unlawful action of private persons or by the exertion of unauthorized administrative power.

Stark v. Wickard, 321 U.S. 288 (1944). "Individual rights," within the meaning of this passage, do not mean public rights that have been legislatively pronounced to belong to each individual who forms part of the public.

Nothing in this contradicts the principle that "[t]he . . . injury required by Art. III may exist solely by virtue of 'statutes creating legal rights, the invasion of which creates standing.' " Warth [v. Seldin], 422 U.S. [490,] 500 [(1975)] . . . [These other cases] involved Congress's elevating to the status of legally cognizable injuries concrete, de facto injuries that were previously inadequate in law. . . As we said in Sierra Club, "[statutory] broadening [of] the categories of injury that may be alleged in support of standing is a different matter from abandoning the requirement that the party seeking review must himself have suffered an injury." . . .

We hold that respondents lack standing to bring this action and that the Court of Appeals erred in denying the summary judgment motion filed by the United States. The opinion of the Court of Appeals is hereby reversed, and the cause remanded for proceedings consistent with this opinion.

■ JUSTICE KENNEDY, with whom JUSTICE SOUTER joins, concurring in part and concurring in the judgment.

Although I agree with the essential parts of the Court's analysis, I write separately to make several observations.

I agree with the Court's conclusion in Part III-A that, on the record before us, respondents have failed to demonstrate that they themselves are "among the injured." . . . While it may seem trivial to require that Ms. Kelly and Skilbred acquire airline tickets to the project sites or announce a date certain upon which they will return, this is not a case where it is reasonable to assume that the affiants will be using the sites on a regular basis, nor do the affiants claim to have visited the sites since the projects commenced. . . .

In light of the conclusion that respondents have not demonstrated a concrete injury here sufficient to support standing under our precedents, I would not reach the issue of redressability that is discussed by the plurality in Part III-B.

I also join Part IV of the Court's opinion with the following observations. As government programs and policies become more complex and farreaching, we must be sensitive to the articulation of new rights of action that do not have clear analogs in our common-law tradition. Modern litigation has progressed far from the paradigm of Marbury suing Madison to get his commission. . . . In my view, Congress has the power to define injuries and articulate chains of causation that will give rise to a case or controversy where none existed before, and I do not read the Court's opinion to suggest a contrary view. In exercising this power, however, Congress must at the very least identify the injury it seeks to vindicate and relate the injury to the class of persons entitled to bring suit. The citizen-suit provision of the Endangered Species Act does not meet these minimal requirements, because while the statute purports to confer a right on "any person . . . to enjoin . . . the United States and any other governmental instrumentality or agency . . . who is alleged to be in violation of any provision of this chapter," it does not of its own force establish that there is an injury in "any person" by virtue of any "violation."

The Court's holding that there is an outer limit to the power of Congress to confer rights of action is a direct and necessary consequence of the case and controversy limitations found in Article III. I agree that it would exceed those limitations if, at the behest of Congress and in the absence of any showing of concrete injury, we were to entertain citizen-suits to vindicate the public's nonconcrete interest in the proper administration of the laws. While it does not matter how many persons have been injured by the challenged action, the party bringing suit must show that the action injures him in a concrete and personal way. This requirement is not just an empty formality. It preserves the vitality of the adversarial process by assuring both that the parties before the court have an actual, as opposed to professed, stake in the outcome, and that "the legal questions presented . . . will be resolved, not in the rarified atmosphere of a debating society, but in a concrete factual context conducive to a realistic appreciation of the consequences of judicial action." Valley Forge Christian College v. Americans United for Separation of Church and State, Inc., 454 U.S. 464, 472 (1982). In addition, the requirement of concrete injury confines the Judicial Branch to its proper, limited role in the constitutional framework of Government.

■ [Justice Stevens concurred in the judgment on grounds that the new rule correctly interpreted the intended geographical scope of the ESA. He concluded respondents did have standing.]

■ JUSTICE BLACKMUN, with whom JUSTICE O'CONNOR joins, dissenting.

[Justice Blackmun concluded that the allegations and depositions of Ms. Skilbred and Ms. Kelly were sufficient to survive a motion for summary judgment, then turned to the second claim.]

The Court . . . rejects the view that the "injury-in-fact requirement . . . [is] satisfied by congressional conferral upon all person of an abstract, self-contained, noninstrumental 'right' to have the Executive observe the procedures required by law." Whatever the Court might mean with that very broad language, it cannot be saying that "procedural injuries" as a class are necessarily insufficient for purposes of Article III standing.

Most governmental conduct can be classified as "procedural." Many injuries caused by governmental conduct, therefore, are categorizable at some level of generality as "procedural" injuries. Yet, these injuries are not categorically beyond the pale of redress by the federal courts. . . . The Court expresses concern that allowing judicial enforcement of "agencies' observance of a particular, statutorily prescribed procedure" would "transfer from the President to the courts the Chief Executive's most important constitutional duty, to 'take Care that the Laws be faithfully executed,' Art. II, § 3." In fact, the principal effect of foreclosing judicial enforcement of such procedures is to transfer power into the hands of the Executive at the expense—not of the courts—but of Congress, from which that power originates and emanates.

Under the Court's anachronistically formal view of the separation of powers, Congress legislates pure, substantive mandates and has no business structuring the procedural manner in which the Executive implements these mandates. . . . In complex regulatory areas, however, Congress often legislates, as it were, in procedural shades of gray. That is, it sets forth substantive policy goals and provides for their attainment by requiring Executive Branch officials to follow certain procedures, for example, in the form of reporting, consultation, and certification requirements. . . . Congress could simply impose a substantive prohibition on executive conduct; it could say that no agency action shall result in the loss of more than 5% of any listed species. Instead, Congress sets forth substantive guidelines and allows the Executive, within certain procedural constraints, to decide how best to effectuate the ultimate goal. . . . Just as Congress does not violate separation of powers by structuring the procedural manner in which the Executive shall carry out the laws, surely the federal courts do not violate separation of powers when, at the very instruction and command of Congress, they enforce these procedures.

. . . Ironically, this Court has previously justified a relaxed review of congressional delegation to the Executive on grounds that Congress, in turn, has subjected the exercise of that power to judicial review. INS v. Chadha, 426 U.S. 919, 953–54 n. 16 (1983) [p. 881]. The Court's intimation today that procedural injuries are not constitutionally cognizable threatens this understanding upon which Congress has undoubtedly relied. . . .

. . . There may be factual circumstances in which a congressionally imposed procedural requirement is so insubstantially connected to the prevention of a substantive harm that it cannot be said to work any conceivable injury to an individual litigant. But, as a general matter, the courts owe substantial deference to Congress' substantive purpose in imposing a certain procedural requirement. . . . There is no room for a per se rule or presumption excluding injuries labeled "procedural" in nature.

## NOTES ON LUJAN AND THE BASIC STANDING FRAMEWORK

(1) ***The Three Requirements of Standing.*** Standing is an essential ingredient for ability to sue. A plaintiff without standing cannot bring suit in federal court and a defendant without standing cannot appeal. Lujan's description of the constitutional requirements for standing is now canonical as a matter of doctrine: Standing requires (i) a "concrete and particularized" injury that is "actual and imminent," as opposed to speculative; (ii) a causal connection establishing that the injury is "fairly traceable" to the conduct being challenged; and (iii) a likelihood that a favorable decision would redress the injury. Often reduced to the tripartite shorthand of injury-in-fact, causation, and redressability, these requirements represent the constitutional core of standing that the Court has derived from Article III's "case" or "controversy" requirement for the exercise of judicial power.

(2) ***Standing Versus Merits.*** As the Lujan Court stated at the outset, a plaintiff's standing to sue is a preliminary jurisdictional question that is deemed to be distinct from whether she should win on the merits. In Arizona State Legislature v. Arizona Independent Redistricting Commission, 576 U.S. 787 (2015), for example, the Court emphasized the distinction, noting that "one must not 'confus[e] weakness on the merits with absence of Article III standing.' " Id. at 800 (internal quotation marks omitted). The majority ruled in favor of the petitioner (the Arizona State Legislature) on "the threshold question" of standing, but against it on the merits.

Whether standing and merits analysis are so separate in practice is another matter. Consider RICHARD H. FALLON, JR., THE FRAGMENTATION OF STANDING, 93 Tex. L. Rev. 1061, 1062–63 (2015), "Since the Court began in the 1970s to characterize standing as turning almost entirely on a single, transsubstantive, tripartite test—requiring showings of injury in fact, causation, and redressability—commentators have complained about inconsistencies and anomalies in application. Over time, however, the grounds for objection and occasional befuddlement have grown, not diminished . . . . [Yet] [h]owever opaque or inadequate the Supreme Court's opinions, over time its cases have formed patterns. . . . Although it is increasingly bootless to seek general rules governing standing to sue in federal court—at least beyond the frequently empty standards of injury, causation, and redressability—we can often achieve a good deal of clarity if we ask which rules apply to particular plaintiffs seeking particular forms of relief under particular constitutional or statutory provisions."

(3) ***Regulated Entities Versus Regulated Beneficiaries.*** An important and often criticized aspect of standing doctrine is the way it impacts different types of plaintiffs. In particular, individuals and entities who are directly regulated by a statutory or regulatory scheme (regulated entities) generally have a much easier time demonstrating the requisite injury, causation, and redressability than those who are beneficiaries of these regimes (regulatory beneficiaries). Lujan is up front about this asymmetric impact, noting that if "the plaintiff is himself an object of the action (or forgone action) at issue[,] . . . there is ordinarily little question that the action or inaction has caused him injury, and that a judgment preventing or requiring the action will redress it." But "when the plaintiff is not himself the object of the government action or inaction he challenges, standing is not precluded, but it is ordinarily substantially more difficult to establish." As you read the materials in this Chapter, consider whether—and when—you think this asymmetric impact, and the corresponding difference in the ability of regulated entities and regulatory beneficiaries to challenge governmental action in court, is problematic.

(4) ***Standing Doctrine's Historical Background.*** Scholarly examinations of constitutional history and early federal practice largely agree that standing is a recent creation, constructed over the course of the twentieth century. "[F]or the first 150 years of the Republic[,] . . . the Framers, the first Congresses, and the Court were oblivious to the modern conception either that standing is a component of the constitutional phrase 'cases or controversies' or that it is a prerequisite for seeking governmental compliance with the law." Steven L. Winter, The Metaphor of Standing and the Problem of Self-Governance, 40 Stan. L. Rev. 1371, 1407 (1988). Even the few who "argue that history does not defeat standing doctrine [and that] the notion of standing is not an innovation," do not make the further "claim that history compels acceptance of the modern Supreme Court's vision of standing." Ann Woolhandler & Caleb Nelson, Does History Defeat Standing Doctrine?, 102 Mich. L. Rev. 689 (2004).

Professor-turned-Judge WILLIAM A. FLETCHER identifies two "overlapping developments" as fueling standing doctrine's rise over the twentieth century. One was "the growth of the administrative state . . . As private entities increasingly came to be controlled by statutory and regulatory duties, many kinds of plaintiffs and would-be plaintiffs sought the articulation and enforcement of new and existing rights in the federal courts. . . . Among the difficult questions posed by the enormous growth of administrative agencies, . . . one of the most prominent was how to determine who could sue to enforce the legal duties of an agency." The second development was "an increase in litigation to articulate and enforce public, primarily constitutional, values. . . . [F]ederal litigation in the 1960's and 1970's increasingly involved attempts to establish and enforce public, often constitutional, values by litigants who were not individually affected by the conduct of which they complained in any way markedly different from most of the population." THE STRUCTURE OF STANDING, 98 Yale L.J. 221, 225–28 (1988). Other scholars similarly identify the emergence of the modern administrative state as central, but rather than emphasizing judicial efforts to restrict suits by regulatory beneficiaries, they maintain that standing doctrine began as an effort by liberal justices to insulate progressive and New Deal legislation from judicial review. See Cass R. Sunstein, What's Standing After Lujan? Of Citizen Suits, "Injuries," and Article III, 91 Mich. L. Rev. 163, 180 (1992).

Should a lack of historical support undermine the Court's claim that standing requirements stem from Article III's case or controversy requirement? The answer to that question might depend on the extent to which you believe that the Constitution must be read in keeping with the original public meaning of its terms. For those who view the Constitution's meaning as evolving over time, the lack of historical support for constitutional standing doctrine may be less important. Interestingly, however, some of the Court's most rigorous enforcers of constitutional standing requirements, like Justice Scalia, have been originalists.

(5) ***Constitutional and Prudential Standing.*** Lujan distinguished between the constitutional requirements for standing and "prudential" limitations. Writing for the majority in UNITED STATES V. WINDSOR, 570 U.S. 744, 757 (2013), Justice Kennedy stated: "The Court has kept these two strands separate: Article III standing, which enforces the Constitution's case-or-controversy requirement, see Lujan; and prudential standing, which embodies judicially self-imposed limits on the exercise of federal jurisdiction. Unlike Article III requirements—which must be satisfied by the parties before judicial consideration is appropriate—the relevant prudential factors that counsel against hearing [a] case are subject to countervailing considerations [that] may outweigh the concerns underlying the usual reluctance to exert judicial power."

Prominent examples of prudential standing restrictions are the requirement that plaintiffs fall within the zone of interests protected by a statute (a requirement also imposed by the APA, see Section 1.e), and the general rule against a plaintiff, even if injured, asserting the rights of a third-party (called third-party standing). In Windsor itself, the Court held that prudential standing concerns raised by the executive branch's refusal to defend the constitutionality of the Defense of Marriage Act were overcome by the presence of able, adverse argument from congressional leadership and the need for a definitive constitutional ruling from the Court. In the years since Lujan, the Court has also increasingly expressed skepticism about prudential standing limits, emphasizing "the principle that a federal court's obligation to hear and decide cases within its jurisdiction is virtually unflagging." Lexmark Int'l, Inc. v. Static Control Components, Inc., 572 U.S. 118, 1386 (2014); Sprint Comms, Inc. v. Jacobs, 571 U.S. 69, 77 (2013).

In any event, it's clear that Congress can direct courts to disregard prudential standing limitations, such as the zone of interests test (see Note 5, p. 1486). Is it equally clear that Congress can't affect the core constitutional elements of standing? Not exactly. Although Congress cannot direct federal courts to ignore the requirements of injury, causation, and redressability, it "has the power to define injuries and articulate chains of causation that will give rise to a case or controversy." Lujan (Kennedy, J., concurring.) However, as explored in Sections 1.b and 1.c below, the precise extent of this power is sharply contested.

(6) ***Associational and Organizational Standing.*** As you will see from reading cases in this and other chapters, organizations often sue to challenge agency action or inaction, even when they are not directly regulated. In such cases, the standing question is one of associational standing. HUNT V. WASHINGTON APPLE ADVERTISING COMM'N 432 U.S. 333, 343 (1977): "[W]e have recognized that an association has standing to bring suit on behalf of its members when: (a) its members would otherwise have standing to sue in their own right; (b) the interests it seeks to protect are germane to the organization's purpose; and (c) neither the claim asserted nor the relief requested requires the participation of individual members in the lawsuit."

What this means is that associational standing is derivative of the standing of the association's individual members. That still leaves a question of how to determine the likelihood that one of an association's members has standing. Should the Court require evidence of harm to specific members, or should it be enough that the government acknowledges it is going to take a challenged action in the future and an organization has so many members that the odds are high one will be affected? See Justice Breyer's dissent in Summers v. Earth Island Institute (p. 1450).

In some cases, courts have held that organizations have standing in their own right even if not directly regulated, based on claims that a challenged agency action will impact how they operate—for example, that they will be forced to change their programming or divert their resources into new undertakings in response. See, e.g., East Bay Sanctuary Covenant v. Trump, 932 F.3d 742 (9th Cir. 2018). Some judges have suggested that this form of organizational standing is in tension with more recent Supreme Court case law on when injuries are traceable to governmental action. See People for the Ethical Treatment of Animals v. U.S. Dep't of Agric., 797 F.3d 1087, 1100–01 (D.C. Cir. 2015) (Millett, J., dubitante).[1]

## NOTES ON STANDING DOCTRINE'S CONSTITUTIONAL BASIS

Lujan is part of a long stream of precedent identifying standing's requirements of injury, causation, and redressability as constitutionally mandated. (By contrast, prudential standing requirements, discussed below in Section 1.e, are not considered constitutional; they stem from judge-made doctrines or statutes). Yet the constitutional basis of standing doctrine

[1] "A dubitante (pronounced d[y]oo-bi-tan-tee) opinion indicates that 'the judge doubted a legal point but was unwilling to state that it was wrong.' " Jason J. Czarnezki, The Dubitante Opinion, 39 Akron L. Rev. 1, 2 (2006) (quoting Black's Law Dictionary 515 (7th ed. 1999)).

remains a matter of debate. Both judges and scholars continue to dispute which aspects of current standing doctrine—if any—have a constitutional basis and what that constitutional basis might be.

(1) ***Standing and Article III's Case or Controversy Requirement.*** Lujan based standing requirements on Article III. But injury-in-fact, causation, and redressability are nowhere expressly referenced in the text of Article III. Instead, Lujan argues that these requirements follow from Article III's limitation of the federal judicial power to "cases" and "controversies." In so doing it followed earlier precedents, in particular ALLEN V. WRIGHT, 468 U.S. 737 (1984) (p. 1457), which involved an IRS policy, rooted in the Internal Revenue Code, of denying charitable tax-exempt status to racially discriminatory schools. In a 5–3 opinion by JUSTICE O'CONNOR, the Court emphasized standing doctrine's constitutional roots in holding that the parents of minority children lacked standing to challenge the IRS's failure to enforce the policy:

"Article III of the Constitution confines the federal courts to adjudicating actual 'cases' and 'controversies.' As the Court explained in Valley Forge Christian Coll. v. Americans United for Separation of Church and State, Inc., 454 U.S. 464, 471–476 (1982), the 'case or controversy' requirement defines with respect to the Judicial Branch the idea of separation of powers on which the Federal Government is founded. The several doctrines that have grown up to elaborate that requirement are 'founded in concern about the proper—and properly limited—role of the courts in a democratic society.' Warth v. Seldin, 422 U.S. 490, 498 (1975).... The case-or-controversy doctrines state fundamental limits on federal judicial power in our system of government," of which standing doctrine "is perhaps the most important.... Standing doctrine embraces several judicially self-imposed limits on the exercise of federal jurisdiction, such as the general prohibition on a litigant's raising another person's legal rights, the rule barring adjudication of generalized grievances more appropriately addressed in the representative branches, and the requirement that a plaintiff's complaint fall within the zone of interests protected by the law invoked. The requirement of standing, however, has a core component derived directly from the Constitution. A plaintiff must allege personal injury fairly traceable to the defendant's allegedly unlawful conduct and likely to be redressed by the requested relief."

Must an individual have suffered an actual and particular injury or satisfy causation and redressability for a judicially cognizable case or controversy to exist? Why isn't it enough that a dispute centers on the meaning of a statute as in Lujan or of the lawfulness of governmental conduct as in Allen? Put differently, even if Article III's case and controversy requirement is understood as restricting the federal courts to distinctly legal disputes, does current doctrine do a good job of identifying which disputes are really legal—weren't the plaintiffs in both Lujan and Allen raising legal questions? On the other hand, the Supreme Court early on established a prohibition on federal courts providing advisory opinions. See Letter from Chief Justice Jay and Associate Justices to President Washington (Aug. 8, 1793) (known as "The Correspondence of the Justices"). At a minimum, therefore, it would be historically anomalous for a federal court to hear a purely theoretical legal dispute.

(2) ***Standing Doctrine and Judicial Capacity.*** Alternatively, the "case or controversy" requirement could be understood as limiting the federal courts to those legal disputes that the courts will be able to resolve accurately and effectively. In his Lujan concurrence, Justice Kennedy argued that the concrete injury requirement "preserves the vitality of the adversarial process by assuring both that the parties before the court have an actual, as opposed to professed, stake in the outcome, and that 'the legal questions presented . . . will be resolved, not in the rarified atmosphere of a debating society, but in a concrete factual context conducive to a realistic appreciation of the consequences of judicial action.' Valley Forge Christian College v. Americans United for Separation of Church and State, Inc., 454 U.S. 464, 472 (1982)."

Consider the extent to which this concern about concreteness is justified as a practical matter. Even if some degree of concreteness is needed for the Court to have an accurate sense of the issues at stake, does that justify the injury-in-fact requirement of standing doctrine? Do you think the Lujan Court could not have accurately and effectively determined the meaning of the ESA's consultation requirement without further evidence of Joyce Kelly and Amy Skilbred's plans to return to project sites? And if Kelly and Skilbred were to add more concrete details on their plans to return—purchasing plane tickets, perhaps—would that concrete detail in any way inform the Court's consideration of whether the ESA's consultation requirement was violated? See David M. Driesen, Standing for Nothing: The Paradox of Demanding Concrete Context for Formalist Adjudication, 89 Cornell L. Rev. 808, 839–55 (2004).

Moreover, a national public interest organization like the Defenders of Wildlife, an organization which often litigates ESA claims and whose mission is to protect wildlife, is arguably more likely to present a strong argument against the government's position than a landowner who happens to own property abutting a government-funded project. Yet under current standing doctrine, the landowner is more likely to have standing.

In any event, should ensuring adequate presentation of the legal issues involved be seen primarily as a matter of constitutional or prudential standing? In Windsor, Justice Kennedy argued for a prudentialist approach and relied on the "the participation of amici curiae prepared to defend with vigor the constitutionality of the legislative act" to assure "adversarial presentation of the issues." 570 U.S. at 760. Is taking such contextual factors into account as part of a prudentialist analysis a better approach for sifting out those cases unconducive to judicial resolution without barring those cases that courts are able to address?

(3) ***Standing and the Separation of Powers.*** Fundamentally, both Lujan and Allen root standing doctrine in the separation of powers. HEATHER ELLIOT, in THE FUNCTIONS OF STANDING, 61 Stan. L. Rev. 459, 461–63 (2008) argues that "[t]he Court seems to mean at least three different things when it uses standing to promote separation of powers . . . First, and most familiarly, the Court uses standing doctrine to restrict the cases heard . . . to

those that are properly cases and controversies under Article III, ... [thereby] keeping courts to their role qua courts ... Second, the Court has said, standing doctrine allows the courts to refuse cases better suited to the political process... Thus, the Court frequently has refrained from adjudicating abstract questions of wide public significance which amount to generalized grievances, pervasively shared and most appropriately addressed in the representative branches.... Third, the Court (and particularly Justice Scalia) has suggested that standing acts as a bulwark against congressional overreaching, preventing Congress from conscripting the courts in its battles with the executive branch."

The first of these functions—ensuring disputes are presented to courts in a manner they are capable of resolving—was discussed in the previous Note. Insofar as the function of limiting the courts to their role qua courts means something more than that, it seems indistinguishable from the second function of courts not inappropriately intruding on the political process. Can we assess whether standing doctrine ensures that the federal courts adhere to their proper constitutional role without subscribing to a particular view about what that role is—a matter of contestation and debate going back to the Constitution's adoption? For example, in Lujan Justice Scalia quotes Marbury v. Madison's famous statement that "[t]he province of the court is, solely, to decide on the rights of individuals." 5 U.S. (1 Cranch) 137, 170 (1803). Yet Marbury also famously stated that "[i]t is emphatically the province and duty of the judicial department to say what the law is," id. at 177. Such a law-declaring function is not necessarily cabined to cases involving private rights of individuals.

In an article written before he joined the Supreme Court, THE DOCTRINE OF STANDING AS AN ESSENTIAL ELEMENT OF THE SEPARATION OF POWERS, 17 Suffolk U. L. Rev. 881, 897 (1983), JUSTICE SCALIA argued that standing doctrine "functionally" served the separation of powers by "roughly restrict[ing] courts to their traditional undemocratic role of protecting individuals and minorities against impositions of the majority, and exclud[ing] them from the even more undemocratic role of prescribing how the other two branches should function in order to serve the interest of the majority itself. Thus, when an individual who is the very object of a law's requirement or prohibition seeks to challenge it, he always has standing. That is the classic case of the law bearing down upon the individual himself, and the court will not pause to inquire whether the grievance is a 'generalized' one." Justice Scalia contrasted "that classic form of court challenge with the increasingly frequent administrative law cases in which the plaintiff is complaining of an agency's unlawful failure to impose a requirement or prohibition upon someone else. [T]hat harm alone is, so to speak, a majoritarian one. The plaintiff may care more about it ... [b]ut that does not establish that he has been harmed distinctively—only that he assesses the harm as more grave, which is a fair subject for democratic debate in which he may persuade the rest of us. Since our readiness to be persuaded is no less than his own (we are harmed just as much) there is no reason to remove the matter from the political process and place it in the courts." Judicial enforcement is additionally anti-democratic because when "the courts . . . enforce upon the executive branch adherence to legislative policies that the political process itself would not enforce, they are likely (despite the best of intentions) to be enforcing the political prejudices of their own class."

Are you convinced that the proper role of courts in regulatory settings is limited to protecting individuals against overzealous enforcement? Are the separation of powers and democratic rule advanced by limiting the extent to which individuals can challenge lax enforcement in court? Compare CASS R. SUNSTEIN, WHAT'S STANDING AFTER LUJAN? OF CITIZEN SUITS, "INJURIES," AND ARTICLE III, 91 Mich. L. Rev. 163, 165 (1992): "In a case of beneficiary or citizen standing, courts are not enforcing 'executive branch adherence to legislative policies that the political process itself would not enforce.' Instead, they are requiring the executive branch to adhere to the law, that is, to outcomes that the political process has endorsed. . . . Standing would produce 'legislative policies that the political process itself would not enforce' only if courts systematically misinterpreted statutes. But this seems to be an unsupportable assumption."

(4) ***Standing and Article I.*** In assessing whether such a beneficiary suit would be undemocratic or exceed the proper role of the courts, does it matter if Congress has expressly provided for broader enforcement challenges, as for example by enacting a citizen suit provision as it did in the ESA? Lujan was the first case to deny standing in the context of a statutory citizen suit provision and to constitutionalize a ban on generalized grievances. Notably, Allen (p. 1457) had described the generalized grievances bar as a prudential limitation, meaning it could be waived by Congress.

By constitutionalizing the ban on generalized grievances, is it actually Lujan that undermines majoritarian rule and the separation of powers? Several scholars have argued that constitutionalizing standing requirements unjustifiably intrudes on congressional authority, and that instead the only question in regulatory contexts should be whether Congress has provided a cause of action: "[S]uperimposing an 'injury in fact' test upon an inquiry into the meaning of a statute is a way for the Court to enlarge its powers at the expense of Congress. . . . For the Court to limit the power of Congress to create statutory rights enforceable by certain groups of people—to limit, in other words, the power of Congress to create standing—is to limit the power of Congress to define and protect against certain kinds of injury that the Court thinks it improper to protect against." William A. Fletcher, The Structure of Standing, 98 Yale L.J. 221, 233 (1988); see also Sunstein, supra, at 167–69.

Do you agree? In assessing the relationship of standing doctrine to congressional authority, think about the likely impact on policy of a regulatory regime in which regulated parties can sue agencies but regulatory beneficiaries cannot. Might agencies become more attentive to the complaints of regulated parties about excessive enforcement for fear of being haled into court and correspondingly inattentive to complaints of insufficient enforcement from regulatory beneficiaries? These concerns led the courts to ease barriers to suit in the 1960s and 1970s (see Data Processing, p. 1484).

The scope of this congressional power over standing is explored in the materials in the next Subsection.

(5) ***Standing, Article II, and the President's Duty to Take Care That the Laws Be Faithfully Executed.*** In Lujan, Justice Scalia offered two arguments as to why Congress's inclusion of a broad citizen suit provision in the ESA, authorizing any person to sue to enforce the act, did not resolve the standing inquiry. One was to argue that Congress cannot grant jurisdiction over suits that fall outside of Article III's case or controversy requirement. The other was to contend that "[t]o permit Congress to convert the undifferentiated public interest in executive officers' compliance with the law into an 'individual right' vindicable in the courts is to permit Congress to transfer from the President to the courts the Chief Executive's most important constitutional duty, to 'take Care that the Laws be faithfully executed,' Art. II, § 3." (Note, however, that Justices Kennedy and Souter, whose votes concurring in part were needed for a majority, only invoked Article III). In Federal Election Commission v. Akins (p. 1431), in which the Court upheld Congress's power to provide for suit by voters challenging the FEC's enforcement of the Federal Election Campaign Act, Justice Scalia made this Article II argument the central claim of his dissent. A couple of decades later, in TransUnion v. Ramirez in 2021 (p. 1438), a majority of the Court invoked the Article II take care duty as a basis for standing doctrine's requirement of concrete injury, along with Article III.

In what way does legislation authorizing a suit to enforce a governing statute violate the President's take care duty? That duty, after all, requires the President to ensure that the laws are faithfully executed. Insofar as a citizen suit seeks to force an agency to comply with a governing statute, is that furthering rather than undermining faithful execution of the laws? Justice Blackmun made this argument in his Lujan dissent: "Just as Congress does not violate separation of powers by structuring the procedural manner in which the Executive shall carry out the laws, surely the federal courts do not violate separation of powers when, at the very instruction and command of Congress, they enforce these procedures." Was he right?

Moreover, Lujan suggests that there would be standing if the individual plaintiffs had provided greater evidence of their likely return to the project sites in the near future. But if a citizen suit seeking enforcement interferes with the President's Article II powers, why is such a suit constitutionally acceptable when an individual can demonstrate injury-in-fact? According to Justice Scalia in Akins, this insistence on individual injury is critical: "A system in which the citizenry at large could sue to compel Executive compliance with the law would be a system in which the courts, rather than the President, are given the primary responsibility to 'take Care that the Laws be faithfully executed.' We do not have such a system." As you read Akins, TransUnion, and the materials on Congress's power to create new injuries in the next Subsection, think about whether you agree.

## b. Defining Injury in Regulatory Settings



Having laid out standing's basic framework and constitutional underpinnings, what remains is to look more in detail about how it works in practice, with special attention to the impact of standing doctrine in regulatory and administrative settings. A first set of questions to explore concerns the type of injury required for standing. Lujan prohibited suits based on "generalized grievances" and required that injury must be "concrete and particular," as well as "actual and imminent, as opposed to speculative." What do these terms mean in practice: are they distinguishable, what kinds of suits do they allow or prohibit, and how good a job has the Court done in applying them? This Subsection addresses these issues.

### (1) The Requirement of Particularized Injury



## FEDERAL ELECTION COMMISSION v. AKINS

Supreme Court of the United States (1998).
524 U.S. 11.

■ JUSTICE BREYER delivered the opinion of the Court.

The Federal Election Commission (FEC) has determined that the American Israel Public Affairs Committee (AIPAC) is not a "political committee" as defined by the Federal Election Campaign Act of 1971 (FECA or Act), 2 U.S.C. § 431(4), and, for that reason, the FEC has refused to require AIPAC to make disclosures regarding its membership, contributions, and expenditures that FECA would otherwise require. We hold that respondents, a group of voters, have standing to challenge the Commission's determination in court, and we remand this case for further proceedings.

[FECA attempts to remedy actual or perceived corruption of the electoral process by limiting the amounts that individuals, corporations, "political committees" (including political action committees), and political parties can contribute to a candidate for federal office. A less well-known but equally important part of the Act requires public disclosure of campaign finance information. Groups within the definition of "political committee" (more familiarly, political action committees, or PACs) must register with the FEC, appoint a treasurer, keep names and addresses of contributors, track the amount and purpose of disbursements, and file detailed reports that include names of donors giving in excess of $200 per year, contributions, expenditures, and other disbursements. The FEC is required to make these reports available for public review and copying within 48 hours of receipt. In addition, data from the reports are entered in an on-line database that sorts and aggregates the information in a variety of ways.

Akins et al., the respondents, described themselves as a group of voters with views opposed to those of AIPAC. They filed a complaint with the FEC, alleging that AIPAC was a "political committee" but had failed to register and to make the required disclosures. AIPAC moved to dismiss, arguing that it was not a "political committee" within the meaning of FECA. The FEC then interpreted the statutory definition to include only organizations that have as a "major purpose" the nomination or election of candidates. AIPAC's focus, it concluded, was issue-oriented lobbying not election-related activities, and so it dismissed the complaint. Akins et al. sought judicial review. The district court and a panel of the D.C. Circuit affirmed the FEC. The Circuit then took the case en banc and reversed, concluding that the FEC misinterpreted the Act. The government sought certiorari on standing as well as the merits.]

II

. . . Congress has specifically provided in FECA that "[a]ny person who believes a violation of this Act . . . has occurred, may file a complaint with the Commission." § 437g(a)(1). It has added that "[a]ny party aggrieved by an order of the Commission dismissing a complaint filed by such party . . . may file a petition" in district court seeking review of that dismissal. § 437g(a)(8)(A). [The Court first concluded that Akins et al satisfied prudential standing requirements and fell within the zone of interest of FECA.] . . .

[We do not] agree with the FEC or the dissent that Congress lacks the constitutional power to authorize federal courts to adjudicate this lawsuit. Article III, of course, limits Congress' grant of judicial power to "cases" or "controversies." That limitation means that respondents must show, among other things, an "injury in fact" . . .

The "injury in fact" that respondents have suffered consists of their inability to obtain information—lists of AIPAC donors (who are, according to AIPAC, its members), and campaign-related contributions and expenditures—that, on respondents' view of the law, the statute requires that AIPAC make public. There is no reason to doubt their claim that the information would help them (and others to whom they would communicate it) to evaluate candidates for public office, especially candidates who received assistance from AIPAC, and to evaluate the role that AIPAC's financial assistance might play in a specific election. Respondents' injury consequently seems concrete and particular. Indeed, this Court has previously held that a plaintiff suffers an "injury in fact" when the plaintiff fails to obtain information which must be publicly disclosed pursuant to a statute. Public Citizen v. Dep't of Justice, 491

U.S. 440, 449 (1989) (failure to obtain information subject to disclosure under Federal Advisory Committee Act "constitutes a sufficiently distinct injury to provide standing to sue"). . . .

The FEC's strongest argument is its contention that this lawsuit involves only a "generalized grievance." . . . The FEC points out that respondents' asserted harm (their failure to obtain information) is one which is "shared in substantially equal measure by all or a large class of citizens." Warth v. Seldin, 422 U.S. 490, 499 (1975). This Court, the FEC adds, has often said that "generalized grievance[s]" are not the kinds of harms that confer standing. Whether styled as a constitutional or prudential limit on standing, the Court has sometimes determined that where large numbers of Americans suffer alike, the political process, rather than the judicial process, may provide the more appropriate remedy for a widely shared grievance.

The kind of judicial language to which the FEC points, however, invariably appears in cases where the harm at issue is not only widely shared, but is also of an abstract and indefinite nature—for example, harm to the "common concern for obedience to law." L. Singer & Sons v. Union Pacific R. Co., 311 U.S. 295, 303 (1940); see also Allen [v. Wright], 468 U.S. [737,] 754 [(1984), p. 1457], Cf. Lujan [v. Defenders of Wildlife, 504 U.S. 555,] 572–78 [(1992), p. 1414]. . . . The abstract nature of the harm—for example, injury to the interest in seeing that the law is obeyed—deprives the case of the concrete specificity that characterized those controversies which were "the traditional concern of the courts at Westminster," Coleman [v. Miller], 307 U.S. [433,] 460 [(1939)] (Frankfurter, J., dissenting); and which today prevents a plaintiff from obtaining what would, in effect, amount to an advisory opinion.

Often the fact that an interest is abstract and the fact that it is widely shared go hand in hand. But their association is not invariable, and where a harm is concrete, though widely shared, the Court has found "injury in fact." See Public Citizen, 491 U.S., at 449–450 . . . . Thus the fact that a political forum may be more readily available where an injury is widely shared (while counseling against, say, interpreting a statute as conferring standing) does not, by itself, automatically disqualify an interest for Article III purposes. Such an interest, where sufficiently concrete, may count as an "injury in fact." This conclusion seems particularly obvious where (to use a hypothetical example) large numbers of individuals suffer the same common-law injury (say, a widespread mass tort), or where large numbers of voters suffer interference with voting rights conferred by law. We conclude that, similarly, the informational injury at issue here, directly related to voting, the most basic of political rights, is sufficiently concrete and specific such that the fact that it is widely shared does not deprive Congress of constitutional power to authorize its vindication in the federal courts.

[The Court then rejected the argument that traceability and redressability were lacking because "it is possible that even had the FEC agreed with respondents' view of the law, it would still have decided in the exercise of its discretion not to require AIPAC to produce the information." Justice Breyer pointed out that "those adversely affected by a discretionary agency decision generally have standing to complain that the agency based its decision upon an improper legal ground," citing Citizens to Preserve Overton Park, Inc. v. Volpe (p. 1145), and SEC v. Chenery Corp. (Chenery I) (p. 255). Finally, in response to the argument that the FEC's decision not to undertake enforcement action was unreviewable because it was "committed to agency discretion by law," APA § 701(a)(2) (see Section 2.b.3, p. 1518) the Court concluded that the FECA "explicitly indicates the contrary." On the merits, the Court remanded the case to the FEC for reconsideration in light of intervening new rules about other sections of FECA that would, if applicable to AIPCA, moot the case.]

■ JUSTICE SCALIA, with whom JUSTICE O'CONNOR and JUSTICE THOMAS join, dissenting.

The provision of law at issue in this case is an extraordinary one, conferring upon a private person the ability to bring an Executive agency into court to compel its enforcement of the law against a third party. . . . If provisions such as the present one were commonplace, the role of the Executive Branch in our system of separated and equilibrated powers would be greatly reduced, and that of the Judiciary greatly expanded. [Justice Scalia argued that FECA did not "intend" to give every person who can file administrative complaints the right also to obtain judicial review if the complaint is rejected. He then turned to the majority's standing analysis.]

What is noticeably lacking in the Court's discussion of our generalized-grievance jurisprudence is all reference to two words that have figured in it prominently: "particularized" and "undifferentiated." "Particularized" means that "the injury must affect the plaintiff in a personal and individual way." Lujan. If the effect is undifferentiated and common to all members of the public, . . . the plaintiff has a "generalized grievance" that must be pursued by political, rather than judicial, means. These terms explain why it is a gross oversimplification to reduce the concept of a generalized grievance to nothing more than "the fact that [the grievance] is widely shared," thereby enabling the concept to be dismissed as a standing principle by such examples as "large numbers of individuals suffer[ing] the same common-law injury (say, a widespread mass tort), or . . . large numbers of voters suffer[ing] interference with voting rights conferred by law." The exemplified injuries are widely shared, to be sure, but each individual suffers a particularized and differentiated harm. One tort victim suffers a burnt leg, another a burnt arm—or even if both suffer burnt arms they are different arms. One voter suffers the deprivation of his franchise, another the deprivation of hers. With the generalized grievance, on the other hand, the injury or deprivation is not only widely shared but it is undifferentiated. The harm caused to . . . Mr. Akins by the allegedly unlawful failure to enforce FECA is precisely the same as the harm caused to everyone else: unavailability of a description of AIPAC's activities.

. . . A system in which the citizenry at large could sue to compel Executive compliance with the law would be a system in which the courts, rather than the President, are given the primary responsibility to "take Care that the Laws be faithfully executed." We do not have such a system because the common understanding of the interest necessary to sustain suit has included the requirement . . . that the complained-of injury be particularized and differentiated, rather than common to all the electorate. When the Executive can be directed by the courts, at the instance of any voter, to remedy a deprivation that affects the entire electorate in precisely the same way—and particularly when that deprivation (here, the unavailability of information) is one inseverable part of a larger enforcement scheme—there has occurred a shift of political responsibility to a branch designed not to protect the public at large but to protect individual rights. . . . If today's decision is correct, it is within the power of Congress to authorize any interested person to manage (through the courts) the Executive's enforcement of any law that includes a requirement for the filing and public availability of a piece of paper. This is not the system we have had, and is not the system we should desire.

## NOTES

(1) ***Information Disclosure as a Concrete Interest.*** According to Justice Breyer, Akins did not involve a generalized grievance simply because every voter in the country shared the same information injury. He argued that a generalized grievance involves not just a broadly shared injury but in addition assertion of an abstract interest, such as an interest in having the government follow the law. Here, however, the Akins plaintiffs were asserting a concrete interest in having information on AIPAC's donors, contributions, and expenditures that would help them evaluate candidates.

Do you agree with Justice Breyer's argument? Does it depend on the goal of information disclosure under the FECA being only to allow voters to be better informed? That is certainly one purpose for campaign finance disclosure, but disclosure can also be used to reduce the influence of interest group money in elections, either because interest groups will be discouraged from making large contributions and expenditures for fear of public outcry or because candidates will be more willing to take positions at odds with their donors' interests for fear of being seen as bought. Alternatively, disclosure requirements might function as a way to use private resources to enhance enforcement, allowing private parties to notify the agency of potential violations or go to court to ensure compliance.

In subsequent cases, the D.C. Circuit has held that while Akins establishes informational injury as a basis for standing, "not every demand for information from the FEC is sufficient . . . We have recognized that the nature of the information allegedly withheld is critical to the standing analysis. The information sought must be that for which there is a statutory right and which is related to the plaintiffs' informed participation in the political process. . . . [P]laintiffs seeking information solely to get the bad guys, rather than disclose information, lack the sort of injury that sustains standing. In addition, plaintiffs must lack access to the information sought; a plaintiff cannot establish injury based on information that is already available from a different source." CAMPAIGN LEGAL CTR V. FEC, 31 F.4th 781, 789–90 (D.C. Cir. 2022).

(2) ***Is the Court Drawing Consistent Lines?*** Do you think Akins can be squared with Lujan? How easy will it be for courts to distinguish between "broadly shared injuries" and "generalized grievances"?

One apparent distinction between Akins and Lujan is that the Akins plaintiffs asserted a concrete interest in the information that FECA mandated be disclosed. But couldn't a similar argument be made about the Lujan plaintiffs—that they were also alleging a concrete interest, namely the interest in having government agencies undertake ESA consultations?

Is the difference instead that Akins involved an effort to get the government to provide something—information—to individuals outside of government on which those individuals could then act, whereas Lujan involved an effort simply to get government agencies to do something—consult with one another? On the other hand, Lujan also involved an effort to change actions outside of government, in that the goal was to stop projects that endangered protected species from going forward by requiring consultation. Perhaps such an impact is too attenuated, but that concern goes more to causation and redressability than the presence of injury-in-fact. See Section 1.c (p. 1456).

Perhaps, then, what makes the difference is that the Akins plaintiffs sought information that might change how they themselves acted, as opposed to change how others acted. In Akins, the Court emphasizes the plaintiffs' claim that the information being sought "would help them . . . evaluate candidates for public office." The procedure in Lujan—interagency consultation—lacked this element of personal participation. But, given the other purposes of information disclosure noted above, is the situation in Akins really that different from Lujan, where consultation was similarly a regulatory strategy used to protect endangered species? Does the Constitution prevent Congress from "crowdsourcing" enforcement of regulatory violations in this fashion? For a discussion of information disclosure as a regulatory strategy, see Chapter VI.

(3) ***Qui Tam and Civil Penalty Actions.*** Recall that Lujan distinguishes "the unusual case in which Congress has . . . provid[ed] a cash bounty for the victorious plaintiff" as one where concerns about permitting private enforcement may be diminished. These "qui tam" statutes originated in England and have existed in the United States since the founding. See Marvin v. Trout, 199 U.S. 212, 225 (1905). Typically, they establish a penalty for official wrongdoing and provide that anyone who brings such wrongdoing to the attention of the court will receive a share of the penalty. VERMONT AGENCY OF NATURAL RESOURCES V. U.S. EX REL. STEVENS, 529 U.S. 765 (2000), held that a qui tam suit under the False Claims Act satisfied Article III standing requirements. Writing for the Court, JUSTICE SCALIA focused on the long history of such actions in Anglo-American jurisprudence and reasoned that injury-in-fact arose from the status of the "qui tam relator [as],

in effect, suing as a partial assignee of the United States." However, footnote 8 warns: "In so concluding, we express no view on the question whether qui tam suits violate Article II, in particular the Appointments Clause of § 2 and the Take Care Clause of § 3." See Evan Caminker, The Constitutionality of Qui Tam Actions, 99 Yale L.J. 341 (1989).

Would the generalized grievance concern in Lujan disappear if Congress had amended the citizen-suit provision of ESA to provide that a successful plaintiff would receive a reward of $1,000? What if Congress amended the provision so that a successful citizen suit resulted in a civil penalty being paid to the government? In STEEL CO. V. CITIZENS FOR A BETTER ENVIRONMENT, 523 U.S. 83 (1998), the Court held that the Emergency Planning and Community Right-to-Know Act could not constitutionally authorize private suits to complain of *past* violations of the Act's requirement that companies file annual reports about the nature and quantity of hazardous chemical use. JUSTICE SCALIA's opinion reasoned that a statutory scheme in which the only available remedies were noncompliance penalties payable to the United States, rather than to the private complainants, ran afoul of Lujan. JUSTICE STEVENS, concurring only in the judgment, responded: "[U]nder the Court's own reasoning, respondent would have had standing if Congress had authorized some payment to respondent. . . . Yet it is unclear why the separation of powers question should turn on whether the plaintiff receives monetary compensation. In either instance, a private citizen is enforcing the law."

Contrast Steel Co. with FRIENDS OF THE EARTH, INC. (FOE) V. LAIDLAW ENVIRONMENTAL SERVICES, 528 U.S. 167 (2000) (see also p. 1465), where the Court held by 7–2 a decision that an environmental organization had standing to seek civil penalties under the Clean Water Act's citizen suit provision for unlawful discharges of mercury that were ongoing when the complaint was filed. Writing for the majority, JUSTICE GINSBURG found that "the affidavits and testimony [from FOE's members] assert that Laidlaw's discharges, and the affiant members' reasonable concerns about the effects of those discharges, directly affected those affiants' recreational, aesthetic, and economic interests." Justice Ginsburg rejected the contention that "the reasoning of our decision in Steel Co., directs the conclusion that citizen plaintiffs have no standing to seek civil penalties under the Act . . . Steel Co. held that private plaintiffs, unlike the Federal Government, may not sue to assess penalties for wholly past violations, but our decision in that case did not reach the issue of standing to seek penalties for violations that are ongoing at the time of the complaint and that could continue into the future if undeterred."

In dissent, JUSTICE SCALIA insisted that allowing private individuals to sue for civil penalties violated Article II: "A Clean Water Act plaintiff pursuing civil penalties acts as a self-appointed mini-EPA. Where, as is often the case, the plaintiff is a national association, it has significant discretion in choosing enforcement targets. . . . And once the target is chosen, the suit goes forward without meaningful public control. . . . Elected officials are entirely deprived of their discretion to decide that a given violation should not be the object of suit at all, or that the enforcement decision should be postponed. . . . The undesirable and unconstitutional consequence of today's decision is to place the immense power of suing to enforce the public laws in private hands." Concurring, Justice Kennedy stated that whether Article II allows private litigants to sue for public fines present "[d]ifficult and fundamental questions" but emphasized those questions had not been briefed or decided below.

Are qui tam actions or citizen suits for civil penalties really distinguishable from generalized grievances? Does the presence of individual gain—financial bounties in the case of qui tam, and cessation and deterrence of unlawful conduct in the case of civil penalties—make a constitutional difference in your view? Or does the lengthy history of qui tam suits, going back to the Founding, sufficiently distinguish them—or does that lengthy history suggest that private enforcement of public laws is not as constitutionally problematic as Justice Scalia suggests?

(4) ***Congressional Requests for Information.*** As the discussion in Section 1.d (p. 1473) on governmental standing makes clear, courts have routinely and consistently denied standing for individual members of Congress seeking to assert Congress's institutional interests. But in Maloney v. Murphy, 984 F.3d 50 (D.C. Cir. 2020), a 2–1 panel of the D.C. Circuit held that individual members of Congress had standing to sue for an executive branch agency's refusal to comply with their request for information, which they had made pursuant to a federal statute. The majority argued that the individual legislators were asserting personal and particularized informational injury claims, as in Akins; the dissent insisted that the injury was institutional and not personal to the individual legislators involved. The D.C. Circuit denied en banc review. (For further discussion of the case, see p. 1477.)

## (2) The Requirement of Concrete and Imminent Injury

*TRANSUNION LLC v. RAMIREZ*

# TRANSUNION LLC v. RAMIREZ

Supreme Court of the United States (2021).
141 S.Ct. 2190.

■ JUSTICE KAVANAUGH delivered the opinion of the Court.

[The Fair Credit Reporting Act. 15 U.S.C. § 1681 et seq., seeks to promote "fair and accurate credit reporting" and to protect consumer privacy. § 1681(a). To achieve those goals, the Act] . . . "imposes a host of requirements concerning the creation and use of consumer reports." Spokeo, Inc. v. Robins, 578 U.S. 330, 335 (2016). Three of the Act's requirements are relevant to this case. First, the Act requires consumer reporting agencies to "follow reasonable procedures to assure maximum possible accuracy" in consumer reports. § 1681e(b). Second, the Act provides that consumer reporting agencies must, upon request, disclose to the consumer "[a]ll information in the consumer's file at the time of the request." § 1681g(a)(1). Third, the Act compels consumer reporting agencies to "provide to a consumer, with each written disclosure by the agency to the consumer," a "summary of rights" prepared by the Consumer Financial Protection Bureau. § 1681g(c)(2).

The Act creates a cause of action for consumers to sue and recover damages for certain violations. The Act provides: "Any person who willfully fails to comply with any requirement imposed under this subchapter with respect to any consumer is liable to that consumer" for actual damages or for statutory damages not less than $100 and not more than $1,000, as well as for punitive damages and attorney's fees. § 1681n(a).

TransUnion is one of the "Big Three" credit reporting agencies, along with Equifax and Experian. As a credit reporting agency, TransUnion compiles personal and financial information about individual consumers to create consumer reports. TransUnion then sells those consumer reports for use by entities such as banks, landlords, and car dealerships that request information about the creditworthiness of individual consumers.

Beginning in 2002, TransUnion introduced an add-on product called OFAC Name Screen Alert. OFAC is the U.S. Treasury Department's Office of Foreign Assets Control. OFAC maintains a list of "specially designated nationals" who threaten America's national security. Individuals on the OFAC list are terrorists, drug traffickers, or other serious criminals. It is generally unlawful to transact business with any person on the list. TransUnion created the OFAC Name Screen Alert to help businesses avoid transacting with individuals on OFAC's list. [Under Name Screen, if] . . . the consumer's first and last name matched the first and last name of an individual on OFAC's list, then TransUnion would place an alert on the credit report indicating that the consumer's name was a "potential match" to a name on the OFAC list. TransUnion did not compare any data other than first and last names. Unsurprisingly, TransUnion's Name Screen product generated many false positives. Thousands of law-abiding Americans happen to share a first and last name with one of the terrorists, drug traffickers, or serious criminals on OFAC's list of specially designated nationals.

Sergio Ramirez learned the hard way that he is one such individual. [When he tried to purchase a car, the dealership ran a credit check on him and his report from TransUnion contained an alert stating that Ramirez's name matched a name on the OFAC database. Ramirez's wife had to purchase the car in her own name as the dealership would not sell to him. The next day Ramirez requested a copy of his credit file from TransUnion. He received two mailings from TransUnion; one, mailed the same day he called, providing his credit file and a statutorily required summary of rights; the other, mailed the following day, was a letter informing him that his name was considered a potential match to names on the OFAC list. Ramirez sued TransUnion alleging violations of the Act and sought to certify a class of all people in the United States to whom TransUnion sent a mailing similar to the second mailing he received, during the period from January 1, 2011, to July 26, 2011. The District

Court granted certification of a class of 8,185 members and found that all the plaintiffs had standing; after a six-day trial, a jury found for the plaintiffs and awarded more than $60 million in combined statutory and punitive damages, reduced to around $40 million on appeal. The U.S. Court of Appeals for the Ninth Circuit held that all members of the class had standing as to all three of the claims.]

II

. . . The "law of Art. III standing is built on a single basic idea—the idea of separation of powers." Raines v. Byrd, 521 U.S. 811, 820 (1997). . . . Therefore, we start with the text of the Constitution. Article III confines the federal judicial power to the resolution of "Cases" and "Controversies." For there to be a case or controversy under Article III, the plaintiff must have a "personal stake" in the case—in other words, standing. Id. at 819. To demonstrate their personal stake, plaintiffs must be able to sufficiently answer the question: "What's it to you?" Scalia, The Doctrine of Standing as an Essential Element of the Separation of Powers, 17 Suffolk U. L. Rev. 881, 882 (1983).

To answer that question in a way sufficient to establish standing, a plaintiff must show (i) that he suffered an injury in fact that is concrete, particularized, and actual or imminent; (ii) that the injury was likely caused by the defendant; and (iii) that the injury would likely be redressed by judicial relief. Lujan v. Defenders of Wildlife, 504 U.S. 555, 560–561 (1992). . . . Requiring a plaintiff to demonstrate a concrete and particularized injury caused by the defendant and redressable by the court ensures that federal courts decide only "the rights of individuals," Marbury v. Madison, 1 Cranch 137, 170 (1803), and that federal courts exercise "their proper function in a limited and separated government," Roberts, Article III Limits on Statutory Standing, 42 Duke L.J. 1219, 1224 (1993). . . .

The question in this case focuses on the Article III requirement that the plaintiff's injury in fact be "concrete"—that is, "real, and not abstract." Spokeo, Inc. v. Robins, 578 U.S. 330, 340 (2016). . . . What makes a harm concrete for purposes of Article III? As a general matter, the Court has explained that "history and tradition offer a meaningful guide to the types of cases that Article III empowers federal courts to consider." Sprint Communications Co. v. APCC Services, Inc., 554 U.S. 269, 274 (2008). . . . [W]ith respect to the concrete-harm requirement in particular, this Court's opinion in Spokeo v. Robins indicated that courts should assess whether the alleged injury to the plaintiff has a "close relationship" to a harm "traditionally" recognized as providing a basis for a lawsuit in American courts. 578 U.S., at 341. That inquiry asks whether plaintiffs have identified a close historical or common-law analogue for their asserted injury. Spokeo does not require an exact duplicate in American history and tradition. But Spokeo is not an open-ended invitation for federal courts to loosen Article III based on contemporary, evolving beliefs about what kinds of suits should be heard in federal courts.

As Spokeo explained, certain harms readily qualify as concrete injuries under Article III. The most obvious are traditional tangible harms, such as physical harms and monetary harms. If a defendant has caused physical or monetary injury to the plaintiff, the plaintiff has suffered a concrete injury in fact under Article III. Various intangible harms can also be concrete. Chief among them are injuries with a close relationship to harms traditionally recognized as providing a basis for lawsuits in American courts. Those include, for example, reputational harms, disclosure of private information, and intrusion upon seclusion. . . [and] may also include harms specified by the Constitution itself. . . .

In determining whether a harm is sufficiently concrete to qualify as an injury in fact, the Court in Spokeo said that Congress's views may be "instructive." [Id.] at 341. Courts must afford due respect to Congress's decision to impose a statutory prohibition or obligation on a defendant, and to grant a plaintiff a cause of action to sue over the defendant's violation of that statutory prohibition or obligation. In that way, Congress may "elevate to the status of legally cognizable injuries concrete, de facto injuries that were previously inadequate in law." Id. . . .

But even though "Congress may 'elevate' harms that 'exist' in the real world before Congress recognized them to actionable legal status, it may not simply enact an injury into existence, using its lawmaking power to transform something that is not remotely harmful into something that is." Hagy v. Demers & Adams, 882 F.3d 616, 622 (6th Cir. 2018) (Sutton, J.) . . . Importantly, this Court has rejected the proposition that "a plaintiff automatically satisfies the injury-in-fact requirement whenever a statute grants a person a statutory right and purports to authorize that person to sue to vindicate that right." Spokeo, 578 U.S., at 341. As the Court emphasized in Spokeo, "Article III standing requires a concrete injury even in the context of a statutory violation." Ibid. Congress's creation of a statutory prohibition or obligation and a cause of action does not relieve courts of their responsibility to independently decide whether a plaintiff has suffered a concrete harm under Article III. . . .

[I]f the law of Article III did not require plaintiffs to demonstrate a "concrete harm," Congress could authorize virtually any citizen to bring a statutory damages suit against virtually any defendant who violated virtually any federal law. Such an expansive understanding of Article III would flout constitutional text, history, and precedent. In our view, the public interest that private entities comply with the law cannot "be converted into an individual right by a statute that denominates it as such, and that permits all citizens (or, for that matter, a subclass of citizens who suffer no distinctive concrete harm) to sue." Lujan [v. Defenders of Wildlife], 504 U.S. [555,] 576–577 [(1992)]. . . .

A regime where Congress could freely authorize unharmed plaintiffs to sue defendants who violate federal law not only would violate Article III but also would infringe on the Executive Branch's Article II authority. We accept the "displacement of the democratically elected branches when necessary to decide an actual case." Roberts, 42 Duke L.J., at 1230. But otherwise, the choice of how to prioritize and how aggressively to pursue legal actions against defendants who violate the law falls within the discretion of the Executive Branch, not within the purview of private plaintiffs (and their attorneys). Private plaintiffs are not accountable to the people and are not charged with pursuing the public interest in enforcing a defendant's general compliance with regulatory law. In sum, the concrete-harm requirement is essential to the Constitution's separation of powers.

III

We now apply those fundamental standing principles to this lawsuit. We must determine whether the 8,185 class members have standing to sue TransUnion for its alleged violations of the Fair Credit Reporting Act. . . .

[T]he 1,853 class members (including the named plaintiff Ramirez) whose reports were disseminated to third-party businesses . . . argue that the publication to a third party of a credit report bearing a misleading OFAC alert injures the subject of the report. The plaintiffs contend that this injury bears a "close relationship" to a harm traditionally recognized as providing a basis for a lawsuit in American courts—namely, the reputational harm associated with the tort of defamation. . . . We agree [that] . . . . the 1,853 class members whose reports were disseminated to third parties suffered a concrete injury in fact under Article III. . . .

The remaining 6,332 class members are a different story. To be sure, their credit files, which were maintained by TransUnion, contained misleading OFAC alerts. But the parties stipulated that TransUnion did not provide those plaintiffs' credit information to any potential creditors during the class period from January 2011 to July 2011. . . . The mere presence of an inaccuracy in an internal credit file, if it is not disclosed to a third party, causes no concrete harm. In cases such as these where allegedly inaccurate or misleading information sits in a company database, the plaintiffs' harm is roughly the same, legally speaking, as if someone wrote a defamatory letter and then stored it in her desk drawer. A letter that is not sent does not harm anyone, no matter how insulting the letter is. So too here.

[The Court rejected the argument that this group of plaintiffs could establish standing for a claim seeking monetary damages based on risk of future harm.] . . . As this Court has recognized, a person exposed to a risk of future harm may pursue forward-looking, injunctive relief to prevent the harm from occurring, at least so long as the risk of harm is sufficiently imminent and substantial. . . . TransUnion advances a persuasive argument that in a suit for damages, the mere risk of future harm, standing alone, cannot qualify as a concrete harm—at least unless the exposure to the risk of future harm itself causes a separate concrete harm. . . . The plaintiffs claimed that TransUnion could have divulged their misleading credit information to a third party at any moment. But the plaintiffs did not demonstrate a sufficient likelihood that their individual credit information would be requested by third-party businesses and provided by TransUnion during the relevant time period.

Nor did the plaintiffs demonstrate that there was a sufficient likelihood that TransUnion would otherwise intentionally or accidentally release their information to third parties. . . .

Moreover, the plaintiffs did not present any evidence that the 6,332 class members even knew that there were OFAC alerts in their internal TransUnion credit files. . . . It is difficult to see how a risk of future harm could supply the basis for a plaintiff's standing when the plaintiff did not even know that there was a risk of future harm.

Finally, . . . . [t]he 6,332 plaintiffs . . . argue that the credit reports of many of those 6,332 class members were likely also sent to third parties outside of the [seven-month] period covered by the stipulation because all of the class members requested copies of their reports, and consumers usually do not request copies unless they are contemplating a transaction that would trigger a credit check. That is a serious argument, but in the end, we conclude that it fails to support standing for the 6,332 class members. The plaintiffs had the burden to prove at trial that their reports were actually sent to third-party businesses. . . .

. . . No concrete harm, no standing. The 1,853 class members whose credit reports were provided to third-party businesses suffered a concrete harm and thus have standing as to the reasonable-procedures claim. The 6,332 class members whose credit reports were not provided to third-party businesses did not suffer a concrete harm and thus do not have standing. . . .

We reverse the judgment of the U.S. Court of Appeals for the Ninth Circuit and remand the case for further proceedings consistent with this opinion.

It is so ordered.

■ JUSTICE THOMAS, with whom JUSTICE BREYER, JUSTICE SOTOMAYOR, and JUSTICE KAGAN join, dissenting.

TransUnion generated credit reports that erroneously flagged many law-abiding people as potential terrorists and drug traffickers. In doing so, TransUnion violated several provisions of the Fair Credit Reporting Act. . . . Yet despite Congress' judgment that such misdeeds deserve redress, the majority decides that TransUnion's actions are so insignificant that the Constitution prohibits consumers from vindicating their rights in federal court. The Constitution does no such thing. . . .

. . . Key to the scope of the judicial power . . . is whether an individual asserts his or her own rights. At the time of the founding, whether a court possessed judicial power over an action with no showing of actual damages depended on whether the plaintiff sought to enforce a right held privately by an individual or a duty owed broadly to the community. See Spokeo, Inc. v. Robins, 578 U.S. 330, 344–346 (2016) (Thomas, J., concurring). Where an individual sought to sue someone for a violation of his private rights, such as trespass on his land, the plaintiff needed only to allege the violation. But where an individual sued based on the violation of a duty owed broadly to the whole community, such as the overgrazing of public lands, courts required "not only injuria [legal injury] but also damnum [damage]." [Id.] at 346. This distinction mattered not only for traditional common-law rights, but also for newly created statutory ones. . . .

The Court chooses a different approach. Rejecting this history, the majority holds that the mere violation of a personal legal right is not—and never can be—an injury sufficient to establish standing. What matters for the Court is only that the "injury in fact be concrete." "No concrete harm, no standing." That may be a pithy catchphrase, but it is worth pausing to ask why "concrete" injury in fact should be the sole inquiry. After all, it was not until 1970—"180 years after the ratification of Article III"—that this Court even introduced the "injury in fact" (as opposed to injury in law) concept of standing. And the concept then was not even about constitutional standing; it concerned a statutory cause of action under the Administrative Procedure Act. . . . [E]ven then, injury in fact served as an *additional* way to get into federal court. Article III injury still could "exist solely by virtue of statutes creating legal rights, the invasion of which creates standing." [Warth v. Seldin, 422 U.S. 490,] 500 [(1975)]. . . .

The majority today, however, takes the road less traveled: "[U]nder Article III, an injury in law is not an injury in fact. . . . No matter if the right is personal or if the legislature deems the right worthy of legal protection, legislatures are constitutionally unable to offer the protection of the federal courts for anything other than money, bodily integrity, and anything else that this Court thinks looks close enough to rights existing at common law. The 1970s injury-in-fact theory has now displaced the traditional gateway into federal courts.

This approach is remarkable in both its novelty and effects. Never before has this Court declared that legal injury is inherently insufficient to support standing. And never before has this Court declared that legislatures are constitutionally precluded from creating legal rights enforceable in federal court if those rights deviate too far from their common-law roots. According to the majority, courts alone have the power to sift and weigh harms to decide whether they merit the Federal Judiciary's attention. In the name of protecting the separation of powers, this Court has relieved the legislature of its power to create and define rights. . . .

[Justice Thomas concluded that "[h]ere, each class member established a violation of his or her private rights. The jury found that TransUnion violated three separate duties created by statute. All three of those duties are owed to individuals, not to the community writ large. . . . Even assuming that this Court should be in the business of second-guessing private rights . . . . TransUnion's misconduct here is exactly the sort of thing that has merited legal redress." Justice Thomas also disputed the majority's assessment of risk-of-harm, noting that "in a 7 month period, it is undisputed that nearly 25 percent of the class had false OFAC-flags sent to potential creditors. . . . If 25 percent is insufficient, then, pray tell, what percentage is?]

■ JUSTICE KAGAN, with whom JUSTICE BREYER and JUSTICE SOTOMAYOR join, dissenting.

The familiar story of Article III standing depicts the doctrine as an integral aspect of judicial restraint. . . . The Court here transforms standing law from a doctrine of judicial modesty into a tool of judicial aggrandizement.

. . . I join Justice Thomas's dissent, which explains why the majority's decision is so mistaken. . . . I differ with Justice Thomas on just one matter. . . . In his view, any "violation of an individual right" created by Congress gives rise to Article III standing. But in Spokeo, this Court held that "Article III requires a concrete injury even in the context of a statutory violation." 578 U.S., at 341. I continue to adhere to that view, but think it should lead to the same result . . . in all but highly unusual cases. . . . [A]s today's decision definitively proves, Congress is better suited than courts to determine when something causes a harm or risk of harm in the real world. For that reason, courts should give deference to those congressional judgments. Overriding an authorization to sue is appropriate when but only when Congress could not reasonably have thought that a suit will contribute to compensating or preventing the harm at issue. . . .

## NOTES

(1) ***TransUnion and Spokeo.*** TransUnion relied heavily on the Court's decision in SPOKEO V. ROBINS, 578 U.S. 330 (2016), which also involved the FCRA. In that case, Thomas Robins had sued Spokeo—a "people search engine" that allows users to enter a person's name, a phone number, or an email address and search approximately 12 billion accumulated records for information about the person—alleging that some of the information Spokeo provided on him was false. In particular, Robins alleged his report stated that he had a job, was relatively affluent, and had a graduate degree, all of which were untrue. Robins filed a complaint on his own behalf and on behalf of a class of similarly situated individuals. Writing for the Court, JUSTICE ALITO emphasized that particularization and concreteness are two distinct standing requirements, both of which must be satisfied. Moreover, although "both history and the judgment of Congress play important roles" in determining if an injury is concrete, and "Congress plainly sought to curb the dissemination of false information by adopting procedures designed to decrease that risk[,] . . . Robins cannot satisfy the demands of Article III by alleging a bare procedural violation . . . [that] may result in no harm." For example, "[i]t is difficult to imagine how the dissemination of an incorrect zip code, without more, could work any concrete harm." On the other hand, Alito underscored that a "risk of real harm" could satisfy the concreteness requirement. In the end, however, the Court punted on determining "whether the particular procedural violations alleged [here] . . . entail a degree of risk sufficient to meet the concreteness requirement," and remanded for the lower courts to undertake that inquiry.

In TransUnion, then, the Court went an important step beyond where Spokeo had left matters by rejecting a suit for failing to meet the concreteness requirement of Article III, despite being based on a congressionally created cause of action. Equally significant, the Court appeared to hold that Article II also imposes limits on Congress's power to create a cause of action for what Congress considers to be harm suffered by an individual plaintiff.

(2) ***Congressional Power to Create New Injuries.*** The Court has long emphasized that "Congress may create a statutory right or entitlement the alleged deprivation of which can confer standing to sue even where the plaintiff would have suffered no judicially cognizable injury in the absence of statute." Warth v. Seldin, 422 U.S. 490, 514 (1975). For example, private individuals can sue in federal court under the federal securities laws regarding representations made to them in the sale of securities even though their statutory causes of action would not constitute "fraud" in the common law sense. Recall Justice Kennedy's statement in his Lujan concurrence (p. 1420): "As Government programs and policies become more complex and far-reaching, we must be sensitive to the articulation of new rights of action that do not have clear analogs in our common-law tradition." In this vein, the Court's earlier precedents broadly countenanced such congressionally-elevated injuries. In Havens Realty Corp. v. Coleman, 455 U.S. 363 (1982), the Court emphasized that Congress had conferred a right on all persons to truthful information about available housing in holding that a black tester who was denied such information had standing to sue for violations of the Fair Housing Act, even though the tester did not actually want to rent any property.

How much does TransUnion pull back on Congress's power to create new injuries? Although TransUnion states that "[c]ourts must afford due respect to Congress's decision to impose a statutory prohibition or obligation on a defendant, and to grant a plaintiff a cause of action to sue over the defendant's violation of that statutory prohibition or obligation," it also insists that Congress cannot "us[e] its lawmaking power to transform something that is not remotely harmful into something that is." Dean Erwin Chemerinsky has argued that "[i]t is hard to see how . . . Havens remain[s] good law after TransUnion." Erwin Chemerinsky, What's Standing After Transunion LLC v. Ramirez, 96 N.Y.U. L. Rev. Online 269, 283 (2021). Do you agree?

Moreover, like Spokeo, TransUnion emphasizes whether an intangible harm bears "a close relationship to harms traditionally recognized as providing a basis for lawsuits in American courts" in determining if it is concrete—an inquiry that seems, contra Justice Kennedy's admonition, to privilege congressionally-created rights of action that have clear common-law analogs. CASS SUNSTEIN, INJURY-IN-FACT TRANSFORMED, 2021 Sup. Ct. Rev. 349: "Over the course of the last half-century, the injury-in-fact test has been transformed from a bold effort to expand the category of persons entitled to bring suit into an equally bold effort to achieve the opposite goal, by understanding judicially cognizable injuries largely by reference to the common law (and the Constitution), and by severely restricting Congress' power to create new rights and to allow people to sue to protect those rights. . . .

"There is an irony here . . . . The administrative state arose out of grave dissatisfaction with private law principles. In diverse ways, it was founded on a recognition that various interests beyond those protected by the common law . . . deserve some kind of legal protection. . . .The irony is that the Court is now building the public law of standing directly on the private-law foundations that Congress rejected, as a matter of principle, in creating modern statutory programs and new statutory rights."

(3) ***Are Private Rights Different?*** Justice Thomas, relying on historical practice, would allow the mere violation of a statutorily granted private right to be adequate for suit. Some scholars have emphasized that the "injury-in-fact requirement" was "historically unwarranted" in "cases alleging the violation of a private right. . . . Although the Court has claimed that its standing requirements are necessary to preserve the traditional limits on the judiciary, those requirements have precluded claims that courts historically would have permitted." ANDREW HESSICK, STANDING, INJURY IN FACT, AND PRIVATE RIGHTS, 93 Cornell L. Rev. 275, 277–78 (2008). Given that the majority also underscored the importance of historical practice to determining if standing exists, should it also have acknowledged that violation of a statutorily granted private right, absent more, satisfied the requirements of Article III?

Other scholars dispute Justice Thomas's claim that individualized concrete injury was historically required to allow private individuals to enforce public rights. ELIZABETH MAGILL, in STANDING FOR THE PUBLIC: A LOST HISTORY, 95 Va. L. Rev. 1131, 1133 (2009), maintains "for several decades in the middle of the [twentieth] century, Congress was allowed to authorize legal challenges to government action by parties whose only cognizable interest was just that: that the government abide by the law. . . . In its cases, the Supreme Court acknowledged that these parties had no legally cognizable injury—no legal rights—but it held nonetheless that Congress could authorize such parties to, as the Supreme Court itself said, bring the government's legal errors to the attention of the federal courts on behalf of the public." Should this mid-twentieth century approach count in assessing historical practice?

(4) ***Intangible Harm and the Concrete Injury Requirement.*** In TransUnion, the Court reaffirmed that the concrete injury requirement did not require tangible harm. "The Supreme Court has stated in the past that 'non-economic injury' is cognizable; in particular, the Court has shown a willingness to recognize injury to aesthetic and conservational interests, a 'spiritual stake in First Amendment values,' the 'inability to compete on an equal footing,' and—possibly—stigma or indignity as bases of Article III injury." RACHEL BAYEFSKY, PSYCHOLOGICAL HARM AND CONSTITUTIONAL STANDING, 81 Brook. L. Rev. 1555, 1557–58 (2016).

What about pure psychological injury? Does recognizing these forms of standing entail recognizing psychological effects as a potential injury-in-fact, in that "the harmful nature of these intangible injuries seems to stem at least partially from their psychological effects on plaintiffs"? Bayefsky, supra, at 1558. If so, would finding psychological harm on its own sufficient to satisfy the concreteness requirement eviscerate the prohibition on generalized grievances as a basis for standing? The Court in TransUnion did not rule out psychological harm: "We take no position on whether or how such an emotional or psychological harm could suffice for Article III purposes. . . ." 141 S.Ct. at 2211 n.7.

The Supreme Court previously avoided the question of whether adequacy of psychological and dignitary harms can suffice for standing in TRUMP V. HAWAII, 138 S.Ct. 2392 (2018), involving statutory and Establishment Clause challenges to President Trump's Proclamation prohibiting nationals of certain countries from entering the United States. CHIEF JUSTICE ROBERTS's 5–4 majority opinion noted that the "[p]laintiffs first argue that they have standing on the ground that the Proclamation 'establishes a disfavored faith' and violates 'their own right to be free from federal [religious] establishments.' They describe such injury as 'spiritual and dignitary.' We need not decide whether the claimed dignitary interest establishes an adequate ground for standing. The three individual plaintiffs assert another, more concrete injury: the alleged real-world effect that the Proclamation has had in keeping them separated from certain relatives who seek to enter the country. We agree that a person's interest in being united with his relatives is sufficiently concrete and particularized to form the basis of an Article III injury in fact." Roberts proceeded to reject the Establishment Clause challenge on the merits.

(5) ***When Is an Alleged Injury Too Speculative to Qualify as Concrete?*** Consider two decisions in which the Court squarely addressed the question of when an alleged injury is sufficiently imminent and actual to satisfy Article III. (A third decision on point, Summers v. Earth Island Institute, follows as the next main case.)

(a) First, in CLAPPER V. AMNESTY INTERNATIONAL, INC., 568 U.S. 398 (2013), the Court by a 5–4 vote held that a group of attorneys, human rights organizations, and others lacked standing to challenge a provision of the Foreign Intelligence Surveillance Act (FISA), 50 U.S.C. § 1881a, as violating the Fourth Amendment. The provision authorizes the Attorney General and the Director of National Intelligence to acquire foreign intelligence information by jointly authorizing the surveillance of individuals who are not "United States persons" and are reasonably believed to be located outside the United States, provided that (in most circumstances) they first obtain the Foreign Intelligence Surveillance Court's approval. The plaintiffs had alleged that their work required them to engage in communications with clients, sources, and others located abroad whom they believed were "likely to be targets of surveillance" under the provision; that the provision "compromised their ability to locate witnesses, cultivate sources, obtain information, and communicate confidential information to their clients"; and that they had stopped engaging in communications as a result. The Court held these allegations to be "too speculative to satisfy the well-established requirement that threatened injury must be certainly impending." The Court noted that "[a]lthough imminence is concededly a somewhat elastic concept, it cannot be stretched beyond its purpose, which is to ensure that the alleged injury is not too speculative for Article III purposes—that the injury is certainly impending." 504 U.S. at 565, n. 2. Here, "respondents' argument rests on their highly speculative fear that: (1) the Government will decide to target the communications of non-U.S. persons with whom they communicate; (2) in doing so, the Government will choose to invoke its authority under § 1881a rather than utilizing another method of surveillance; (3) the Article III judges who serve on the Foreign Intelligence Surveillance Court will conclude that the Government's proposed surveillance procedures satisfy § 1881a's many safeguards and are consistent with the Fourth Amendment; (4) the Government will succeed in intercepting the communications of respondents' contacts; and (5) respondents will be parties to the particular communications that the Government intercepts. . . . [R]espondents' theory of standing, which relies on a highly attenuated chain of possibilities, does not satisfy the requirement that threatened injury must be certainly impending."

(b) The second decision, SUSAN B. ANTHONY LIST (SBA) V. DRIEHAUS, 573 U.S. 149 (2014), was issued the next term. Congressman Driehaus filed a complaint with the Ohio Elections Commission alleging that SBA had violated an Ohio law that criminalizes certain false statements made during a political campaign. Driehaus based his complaint on SBA materials opposing his candidacy that stated his vote for the Affordable Care Act was a vote for "taxpayer-funded abortion." The complaint was dismissed when Driehaus lost the election. However, SBA continued to pursue a separate suit in federal court challenging the law on First Amendment grounds. Both lower courts concluded the case was nonjusticiable, but the Supreme Court reversed, holding that SBA's pre-enforcement challenge to the Ohio law alleged sufficiently imminent injury for Article III purposes. JUSTICE THOMAS wrote for a unanimous Court: "First, petitioners have alleged 'an intention to engage in a course of conduct arguably affected with a constitutional interest' . . . [and] pleaded specific statements they intend to make in future election cycles. SBA has already stated that representatives who voted for the ACA supported 'taxpayer-funded abortion,' and it has alleged an 'inten[t] to engage in substantially similar activity in the future.' . . . Next, petitioners' intended future conduct is 'arguably. . . proscribed by [the] statute' they wish to challenge. . . . SBA's insistence that the allegations in its press release were true did not prevent the Commission panel from finding probable cause to believe that SBA had violated the law the first time around. And there is every reason to think that similar speech in the future will result in similar proceedings . . . . Finally, the threat of future enforcement of the false statement statute is substantial. . . . We have observed that past enforcement against the same conduct is good evidence that the threat of enforcement is not 'chimerical.' Here, the threat is even more substantial given that the Commission panel actually found probable cause to believe that SBA's speech violated the false statement statute." The facts that the Ohio statute allows "any person" to file a complaint with the Commission and that "[c]ommission proceedings are not a rare occurrence" bolsters the credibility of the threat.

In your view, can Clapper and SBA be reconciled? Are their different outcomes explained by the different facts involved and the greater certainty of eventual injury in SBA than in Clapper? Do you think the subject matter of the underlying lawsuits—national security surveillance and the First Amendment—played a role in some of the justices' views on whether sufficient injury-in-fact had been alleged? VICKI C. JACKSON, STANDING AND THE ROLE OF FEDERAL COURTS: TRIPLE ERROR DECISIONS IN CLAPPER V. AMNESTY INTERNATIONAL USA AND CITY OF LOS ANGELES V. LYONS, 23 Wm. & Mary Bill Rts. J. 127, 144 (2014): "It is because of the necessary secrecy of government operations to obtain foreign intelligence that the plaintiffs could not say, with absolute certainty, that they were being surveilled; only in unsuccessful covert surveillances could such a plaintiff emerge."

"Edward Snowden's disclosures of NSA metadata and mass data collection activities were first reported June 5, 2013, less than four months after Clapper came down." Do you think the Clapper Court would have reached the same result if the case were decided after Snowden's disclosures? For that matter, could the result in Clapper have affected Snowden's decision to disclose? "The possible impact of the Clapper decision on Snowden's disclosures is suggested by the report that one of Snowden's first questions to his attorney . . . in July of 2013 was "Do you have standing now?" Id. 160 n. 132.

## (3) Procedural Rights

*SUMMERS v. EARTH ISLAND INSTITUTE*
*Notes on Procedural Rights*

# SUMMERS v. EARTH ISLAND INSTITUTE

Supreme Court of the United States (2009).
555 U.S. 488.

■ JUSTICE SCALIA delivered the opinion of the Court.

[The Forest Service Decisionmaking and Appeals Reform Act requires the Forest Service to establish a notice, comment, and appeal process for proposed Forest Service actions related to land and resource management plans. The Forest Service's regulations implementing the Act provided that certain activities, including "fire rehabilitation activities" and timber salvage sales prompted by "small" forest fires, would be categorically exempt from the notice, comment, and appeal process as well as from environmental impact assessment requirements. A group of environmental organizations sued to challenge the regulation exempting these sales as at odds with the Act. Standing initially rested on the affidavit of one organizational member who had hiked in a particular area of the Sequoia National Forest, the Burnt Ridge site, where a small fire had occurred and a timber sale was pending.]

Affidavits submitted to the District Court alleged that [an] organization member . . . had repeatedly visited the Burnt Ridge site, that he had imminent plans to do so again, and that his interests in viewing the flora and fauna of the area would be harmed if the Burnt Ridge Project went forward without incorporation of the ideas he would have suggested if the Forest Service had provided him an opportunity to comment. The Government concedes this was sufficient to establish Article III standing with respect to Burnt Ridge. . . . After the District Court had issued a preliminary injunction, however, the parties settled their differences on that score . . . [and the member's] injury in fact with regard to that project has been remedied . . . We know of no precedent for the proposition that when a plaintiff has sued to challenge the lawfulness of certain action or threatened action but has settled that suit, he retains standing to challenge the basis for that action (here, the regulation in the abstract), apart from any concrete application that threatens imminent harm to his interests. . . .

Respondents have identified no other application of the invalidated regulations that threatens imminent and concrete harm to the interests of their members. The only other affidavit relied on was that of Jim Bensman, . . . which asserts that he has visited many National Forests and plans to visit several unnamed National Forests in the future. . . . [It fails] to allege that any particular timber sale or other project claimed to be unlawfully subject to the regulations will impede a specific and concrete plan of Bensman's to enjoy the National Forests. The National Forests occupy more than 190 million acres, an area larger than Texas. . . . [W]e are asked to assume not only that Bensman will stumble across a project tract unlawfully subject to the regulations, but also that the tract is about to be developed by the Forest Service in a way that harms his recreational interests, and that he would have commented on the project but for the regulation. Accepting an intention to visit the National Forests as adequate to confer standing to challenge any Government action affecting any portion of those forests would be tantamount to eliminating the requirement of concrete, particularized injury in fact. . . .

Respondents argue that they have standing to bring their challenge because they have suffered procedural injury, namely, that they have been denied the ability to file comments on some Forest Service actions and will continue to be so denied. But deprivation of a procedural right without some concrete interest that is affected by the deprivation—a procedural right in vacuo—is insufficient to create Article III standing. Only a "person who has been accorded a procedural right to protect his concrete interests can assert that right without meeting all the normal standards for redressability and immediacy." Lujan, 504 U.S., at 572, n. 7. . . .

It makes no difference that the procedural right has been accorded by Congress. That can loosen the strictures of the redressability prong of our standing inquiry—so that standing existed with regard to the Burnt Ridge Project, for example, despite the possibility that Earth Island's allegedly guaranteed right to comment would not be successful in persuading the Forest Service to avoid impairment of Earth Island's concrete interests. Unlike redressability, however, the requirement of injury in fact is a hard floor of Article III jurisdiction that cannot be removed by statute. . . .

The dissent proposes a hitherto unheard-of test for organizational standing: whether, accepting the organization's self-description of the activities of its members, there is a statistical probability that some of those members are threatened with concrete injury. . . . This novel approach to the law of organizational standing would make a mockery of our prior cases, which have required plaintiff-organizations to make specific allegations establishing that at least one identified member had suffered or would suffer harm. . . .

■ JUSTICE KENNEDY, concurring.

. . . This case would present different considerations if Congress had sought to provide redress for a concrete injury "giv[ing] rise to a case or controversy where none existed before." Lujan v. Defenders of Wildlife at 580 (Kennedy, J., concurring in part and concurring in judgment). Nothing in the statute at issue here, however, indicates Congress intended to identify or confer some interest separate and apart from a procedural right.

■ JUSTICE BREYER, with whom JUSTICES STEVENS, SOUTER, and GINSBURG join, dissenting.

. . . The majority assumes, as do I, that these unlawful Forest Service procedures will lead to substantive actions, namely the sales of salvage timber on burned lands, that might not take place if the proper procedures were followed. . . . How can the majority credibly claim that salvage-timber sales, and similar projects, are unlikely to harm the asserted interests of the members of these environmental groups? . . . The majority . . . argu[es] that the Forest Service actions are not "imminent"—a requirement more appropriately considered in the context of ripeness or the necessity of injunctive relief. I concede that the Court has sometimes used the word "imminent" in the context of constitutional standing. But it has done so primarily to emphasize that the harm in question . . . was merely "conjectural" or "hypothetical" or otherwise speculative. Where the Court has directly focused upon the matter, i.e., where, as here, a plaintiff has already been subject to the injury it wishes to challenge, the Court has asked whether there is a realistic likelihood that the challenged future conduct will, in fact, recur and harm the plaintiff. . . .

. . . [A] threat of future harm may be realistic even where the plaintiff cannot specify precise times, dates, and GPS coordinates. . . . The Forest Service admits that it intends to conduct thousands of further salvage-timber sales and other projects exempted under the challenged regulations "in the reasonably near future." How then can the Court deny that the plaintiffs have shown a "realistic" threat that the Forest Service will continue to authorize (without the procedures claimed necessary) salvage-timber sales, and other Forest Service projects, that adversely affect the recreational, esthetic, and environmental interests of the plaintiffs' members? Respondents allege, and the Government has conceded, that the Forest Service took wrongful actions (such as selling salvage timber) "thousands" of times in the two years prior to suit. . . . The Complaint alleges, and no one denies, that the organizations . . . have hundreds of thousands of members who use forests regularly across the Nation for recreational, scientific, esthetic, and environmental purposes. The Complaint further alleges, and no one denies, that these organizations (and their members), believing that actions such as salvage-timber sales harm those interests, regularly oppose salvage-timber sales (and similar actions) in proceedings before the agency. And the Complaint alleges, and no one denies, that the organizations intend to continue to express their opposition to such actions in those proceedings in the future. . . . The Bensman affidavit does not say which particular sites will be affected by future Forest Service projects, but the Service itself has conceded that it will conduct thousands of exempted projects in the future. Why is more specificity needed to show a "realistic" threat that a project will impact land Bensman uses? To know, virtually for certain, that snow will fall in New England this winter is not to know the name of each particular town where it is bound to arrive. The law of standing does not require the latter kind of specificity. . . .

[Justice Breyer criticized the Court's refusal to consider additional affidavits offered by the plaintiffs after judgment was entered below, after the Burnt Ridge challenge had settled and at the point when the government challenged their standing to continue with the case.] The affidavits in question describe a number of then-pending Forest Service projects, all excluded from notice, comment, and appeal under the Forest Service regulations and all scheduled to take place on parcels that the plaintiff organizations' members use. . . . The affidavits also describe, among other things, the frequency with which the organizations' members routinely file administrative appeals of salvage-timber sales and identify a number of proposed and pending projects that certain Sierra Club members wished to appeal. These allegations and affidavits more than adequately show a "realistic threat" of injury to plaintiffs brought about by reoccurrence of the challenged conduct—conduct that the Forest Service thinks lawful and admits will reoccur. . . .

## NOTES

(1) ***The Distinction Between Regulated Parties and Regulatory Beneficiaries.*** The Court's reluctance to find standing in Summers seems at first glance in sharp tension with its decision in SBA (p. 1449). In SBA the Court upheld standing, emphasizing—much like Justice Breyer's dissent in Summers—that the challenged governmental action had occurred in the past and that whether a plaintiff has already been subject to the injury it wishes to challenge gets substantial weight in assessing whether future injury is speculative. Can you square the two decisions?

One difference between the two cases is that the plaintiff in SBA was a regulated party directly subject to enforcement for violations of Ohio's election laws, whereas the plaintiffs in Summers were regulated beneficiaries. Recall that Lujan emphasized this factor in standing analysis (p. 1415). But does this distinction justify the different standing outcomes in these cases? After all, whether SBA would be subject to future enforcement depends on the actions of third parties who file complaints with Ohio's Election Commission, and the plaintiffs in Summers had hundreds of thousands of members who regularly use the national forests. Is the likelihood of future injury in Summers really more speculative? Moreover, consider the effects on regulatory programs if the courts draw such a distinction between regulation parties and regulatory beneficiaries.

(2) ***What Would It Have Taken for Standing?*** Suppose the Summers plaintiffs decided to file a new challenge to the Forest Service's exempting regulations. What facts would they need to allege to have standing? Do you think the affidavits they tried to submit after settling the Burnt Ridge dispute would suffice—and if so, should the Court then have accepted the new affidavits as a basis for standing?

For that matter, query whether the settlement of the Burnt Ridge timber sale should have been given the weight the majority gave it. If the Government had simply provided the procedures sought on its own initiative, thereby "mooting" the dispute, the Burnt Ridge challenge might still have been able to go forward under the exception to mootness for actions capable of repetition yet evading review. Is a settlement so different as to preclude any consideration of Burnt Ridge, even for purposes of standing analysis?

## NOTES ON PROCEDURAL RIGHTS

(1) ***Procedural Rights and Injury.*** In Summers, Congress had provided interested persons with a procedural right to comment on Forest Service actions, which according to the plaintiffs included the sales and rehabilitation activities related to small forest fires that the Forest Service had exempted. No doubt existed that the Forest Service was denying plaintiffs and others the ability to comment. According to Justice Scalia's majority opinion, the uncontroverted denial of plaintiffs' procedural right to comment was not enough to give them sufficient injury to sue: "[D]eprivation of a procedural right without some concrete interest that is affected by the deprivation—a procedural right in vacuo—is insufficient to create Article III standing."

But why not? As you now know, procedural rights abound in administrative law: rights to get notice, to be given information about what the agency considers relevant, to submit comments or present evidence, to get a statement of the agency's reasons, etc. Why create so many procedural rights, unless they are believed to be useful in affecting administrative behavior? Indeed, a field of political science scholarship, positive political theory (p. 876), maintains that one of the central mechanisms by which Congress exerts control over the executive branch is by providing procedural rights. Among other things, these rights enable interest groups to try to influence agency decisionmaking and to monitor agency actions, raising "fire alarms" with members of Congress if they see anything amiss.

In short, a good basis exists on which to conclude that even a "procedural right in vacuo" may well be valuable. Why then does Justice Scalia dismiss out of hand the possibility that violation of a procedural right alone could create sufficient injury to sue?

Equally important, how do we distinguish a statute that creates a "procedural right in vacuo" from one that also gives rise to substantive interests? Does the provision of the APA, codified at 5 U.S.C. § 553, that agencies must provide notice and allow "interested persons" an opportunity to comment when promulgating rules simply provide a "procedural right in vacuo," as the notice-and-comment requirement in Summers was held to do, or does it create more?

(2) ***Real Procedural Rights Versus the General Interest in Government Obeying the Law.*** Perhaps the most prominent decision to reject standing based simply on an interest in enforcing a procedural right was Lujan (p. 1414), on which Summers relied. But are Summers and Lujan analogous in terms of the procedural rights at stake? Whatever its intended geographical scope, the ESA consultation requirement at issue in Lujan is, apparently, a completely internal executive branch process. The agencies involved did not have to allow interested persons to comment on the consultation process, as in Summers. Indeed, none of the agencies or officials involved in the ESA consultation process were required to produce an assessment, report, or other document for or about the consultation that was to be released for public review. (Compare the spending and contribution information required by the Federal Election Campaign Act in Akins, p. 1431).

This suggests that the problem in Lujan was not that "procedural" rights were involved but rather that *no* rights were involved—other than the "abstract, self-contained . . . right," Lujan, 504 U.S. at 573, long regarded as nonjusticiable, to have government obey the law. If so, does Summers go significantly beyond Lujan in holding that violation of a procedural right to comment alone is insufficient injury for standing? Or would allowing standing based simply on such a procedural right also risk opening up the courts to suits brought simply to ensure the government obeys the law?

(3) ***Procedural Rights and Redressability.*** The classic redressability problem with procedural rights is the inability to predict, with any degree of confidence, whether procedural regularity would yield the regulatory outcome on the merits desired by the plaintiff. Summers makes clear—citing Lujan—that procedural rights can ease the standing inquiry with respect to the redressability prong of standing analysis. As a result, if the plaintiffs had a separate concrete injury from a particular fire sale, they could claim that the ability to comment would adequately redress their injury notwithstanding that the Forest Service might have simply ignored their views.

According to RICHARD J. PIERCE, JR., MAKING SENSE OF PROCEDURAL INJURY, 62 Admin. L. Rev. 1, 2–3 (2010), after Lujan "circuit court opinions fall in[to] two categories with respect to the nature of the causal relationship they require between the omitted procedure and a substantive result that is unfavorable to the petitioner. In many cases, a petitioner prevails by alleging only that it was unlawfully deprived of a procedural right that might plausibly have changed the outcome of a substantive dispute. In other cases, however, a petitioner loses because a court concludes that it did not demonstrate that it is substantially probable that the procedural breach will cause the essential injury to the plaintiff's own interest. The choice of the causal test to apply is outcome determinative. When a court applies the plausibility standard, it holds that the petitioner has standing because it is almost always plausible that provision of a procedural safeguard will change the outcome of a case. Conversely, when a court applies the probability standard, it holds that the petitioner lacks standing because it is usually impossible to prove that provision of a procedural safeguard will probably change the outcome." Pierce advocates for use of the plausibility test, arguing that given this impossibility, the probability approach "devalue[s] the procedures required by the Constitution and by statutes by encouraging agencies to deny procedural safeguards in all close cases."

## c. Causation and Redressability in Regulatory Settings

> *(1) The Impact of Sanctions and Incentives*
>
> *(2) Probabilities, Risk, and Incrementalism*

The final constitutionally required elements of standing—causation and redressability—are closely interlinked: if a challenged act causes a plaintiff's injury, prohibiting the act will redress the harm. As with injury, debates about the causation and redressability elements of regulatory standing disproportionately affect beneficiary standing. The causal chain between stopping the agency and stopping the injury will usually be obvious for those whose conduct is being regulated. But it is often not so clear that ordering the agency to regulate more vigorously the conduct of, for example, polluting industries will stop the harm suffered by the intended beneficiaries of the program. Recall Lujan's statement, p. 1415, that when "a plaintiff's asserted injury arises from the government's allegedly unlawful regulation (or lack of regulation) of someone else, . . . causation and redressability ordinarily hinge on the response of the regulated (or regulable) third party to the government action or inaction—and perhaps on the response of others as well." Lujan suggests that beneficiary standing should be curtailed as a result: "[W]hen the plaintiff is not himself the object of the government action or inaction he challenges, standing is not precluded, but it is ordinarily substantially more difficult to establish." As you read the materials in this subsection, consider whether this higher burden is actually justified, how difficult it is in practice to meet, and the potential impact of such asymmetric standing thresholds on regulatory policy.

Causation and redressability cases fall largely into two categories. The first category concerns assessing the impact of sanctions, incentives, and other agency actions on the behavior of regulated parties. Suppose an agency acts as a plaintiff wishes—enforces a statute more vigorously, for example. Would regulated parties' behavior likely change, and how certain must a court be of that result? The second category concerns contexts that are characterized by probabilities and incremental effects. How certain must a court be that an agency's action or inaction is contributing to the plaintiff's injury? Must the harm be entirely remediated, or is it enough that the plaintiff is somewhat better off? For that matter, must remediation be certain, or is a reasonable probability enough? Finally, a question underlying both categories concerns what should be the impact of congressional choices: Should courts defer to congressional assessments about the effect of certain policies or measures?

## (1) The Impact of Sanctions and Incentives

*ALLEN v. WRIGHT*

## ALLEN v. WRIGHT

Supreme Court of the United States (1984).
468 U.S. 737.

■ JUSTICE O'CONNOR delivered the opinion of the Court.

[The IRS had a formal policy of denying charitable tax-exempt status to racially discriminatory schools. (In Bob Jones Univ. v. United States, 461 U.S. 574 (1983), the Court held that this policy correctly interpreted the Internal Revenue Code.) To carry out this policy, the IRS established guidelines and procedures for determining whether a particular school is in fact racially nondiscriminatory. Parents of African-American children attending public schools in districts undergoing court-ordered desegregation sued the IRS, alleging that these guidelines and procedures were inadequate to ensure that racially discriminatory private schools did not receive tax-exempt status. They also sought more vigorous enforcement of the policy. Unlike the situation in Lujan, Congress had not supplied a citizen suit provision through which to challenge the IRS's actions. While the case was pending, the IRS proposed new procedures to tighten its requirements for eligibility for tax-exempt status for private schools, but Congress blocked any strengthening of the IRS guidelines through an appropriations measure.][16]

Respondents allege in their complaint that many racially segregated private schools were created or expanded in their communities at the

[16] . . . Section 615 of the Treasury, Postal Service, and General Government Appropriations Act of 1980, 93 Stat. 562, 577, specifically forbade the use of funds to carry out the IRS's proposed procedures while Section 103 more generally forbade the use of funds to make the requirements for tax-exempt status of private schools more stringent than those in effect prior to the IRS's proposal of its new procedures. These provisions expired on October 1, 1980[, but Congress maintained similar limitations on funding for several years thereafter, though none was in force at the time of the Court's decision.]

time the public schools were undergoing desegregation. According to the complaint, many such private schools, including 17 schools or school systems identified by name in the complaint (perhaps some 30 schools in all), receive tax exemptions. . . . Respondents allege that . . . some of the tax-exempt racially segregated private schools created or expanded in desegregating districts in fact have racially discriminatory policies. . . .

Respondents allege that the challenged Government conduct harms them in two ways. The challenged conduct

> (a) constitutes tangible federal financial aid and other support for racially segregated educational institutions, and
>
> (b) fosters and encourages the organization, operation and expansion of institutions providing racially segregated educational opportunities for white children avoiding attendance in desegregating public school districts and thereby interferes with the efforts of federal courts, HEW and local school authorities to desegregate public school districts which have been operating racially dual school systems.

[Complaint at 38–39.] Thus, respondents do not allege that their children have been the victims of discriminatory exclusion from the schools whose tax exemptions they challenge as unlawful. Indeed, they have not alleged at any stage of this litigation that their children have ever applied or would ever apply to any private school. Rather, respondents claim a direct injury from the mere fact of the challenged Government conduct and, as indicated by the restriction of the plaintiff class to parents of children in desegregating school districts, injury to their children's opportunity to receive a desegregated education. The latter injury is traceable to the IRS grant of tax exemptions to racially discriminatory schools, respondents allege, chiefly because contributions to such schools are deductible from income taxes . . . and the "deductions facilitate the raising of funds to organize new schools and expand existing schools in order to accommodate white students avoiding attendance in desegregating public school districts." . . .

. . . We conclude that neither [injury] suffices to support respondents' standing. The first fails . . . because it does not constitute judicially cognizable injury. The second fails because the alleged injury is not fairly traceable to the assertedly unlawful conduct of the IRS.[19]

1

[Justice O'Connor rejected respondents' first claim of injury essentially on generalized grievance grounds, emphasizing that only those personally denied equal treatment have standing to challenge racial discrimination. Otherwise, "standing would extend nationwide to

---

[19] The "fairly traceable" and "redressability" components of the constitutional standing inquiry were initially articulated by this Court as "two facets of a single causation requirement." C. Wright, Law of Federal Courts § 13, p. 68 n. 43 (4th ed. 1983). To the extent there is a difference, it is that the former examines the causal connection between the assertedly unlawful conduct and the alleged injury, whereas the latter examines the causal connection between the alleged injury and the judicial relief requested. . . .

all members of the particular racial groups against which the Government was alleged to be discriminating by its grant of a tax exemption to a racially discriminatory school, regardless of the location of that school. . . . A black person in Hawaii could challenge the grant of a tax exemption to a racially discriminatory school in Maine. Recognition of standing in such circumstances would transform the federal courts into 'no more than a vehicle for the vindication of the value interests of concerned bystanders.' United States v. SCRAP, 412 U.S. 669, 687 (1973)."]

2

It is in their complaint's second claim of injury that respondents allege harm to a concrete, personal interest that can support standing in some circumstances. The injury they identify—their children's diminished ability to receive an education in a racially integrated school—is, beyond any doubt, not only judicially cognizable but, as shown by cases from Brown v. Board of Educ., 347 U.S. 483 (1954), to Bob Jones Univ. v. United States, 461 U.S. 574 (1983), one of the most serious injuries recognized in our legal system. . . . [Here, however,] respondents' second claim of injury cannot support standing because the injury alleged is not fairly traceable to the Government conduct respondents challenge as unlawful.

The illegal conduct challenged by respondents is the IRS's grant of tax exemptions to some racially discriminatory schools. The line of causation between that conduct and desegregation of respondents' schools is attenuated at best. . . . The diminished ability of respondents' children to receive a desegregated education would be fairly traceable to unlawful IRS grants of tax exemptions only if there were enough racially discriminatory private schools receiving tax exemptions in respondents' communities for withdrawal of those exemptions to make an appreciable difference in public-school integration. Respondents have made no such allegation. It is, first, uncertain how many racially discriminatory private schools are in fact receiving tax exemptions. Moreover, it is entirely speculative, as respondents themselves conceded [below] . . . whether withdrawal of a tax exemption from any particular school would lead the school to change its policies. It is just as speculative whether any given parent of a child attending such a private school would decide to transfer the child to public school as a result of any changes in educational or financial policy made by the private school once it was threatened with loss of tax-exempt status. It is also pure speculation whether, in a particular community, a large enough number of the numerous relevant school officials and parents would reach decisions that collectively would have a significant impact on the racial composition of the public schools.

The links in the chain of causation between the challenged Government conduct and the asserted injury are far too weak for the chain as a whole to sustain respondents' standing. . . . The idea of separation of powers that underlies standing doctrine explains why our cases preclude the conclusion that respondents' alleged injury "fairly can be traced to the challenged action" of the IRS. Simon v. Eastern Kentucky

Welfare Rights Org'n, 426 U.S. 26 (1984). That conclusion would pave the way generally for suits challenging, not specifically identifiable Government violations of law, but the particular programs agencies establish to carry out their legal obligations. . . . Most relevant . . . is the principle articulated in Rizzo v. Goode, [423 U.S. 362,] 378–79 [(1976) (quoting Cafeteria Workers v. McElroy, 367 U.S. 886, 896 (1961)]:

> "When a plaintiff seeks to enjoin the activity of a government agency, even within a unitary court system, his case must contend with 'the well-established rule that the Government has traditionally been granted the widest latitude in the dispatch of its own internal affairs.' "

. . . [T]hat principle, grounded as it is in the idea of separation of powers, counsels against recognizing standing in a case brought, not to enforce specific legal obligations whose violation works a direct harm, but to seek a restructuring of the apparatus established by the Executive Branch to fulfill its legal duties. The Constitution, after all, assigns to the Executive Branch, and not to the Judicial Branch, the duty to "take Care that the Laws be faithfully executed." U.S. Const., Art. II, § 3. We could not recognize respondents' standing in this case without running afoul of that structural principle.

. . . The judgment of the Court of Appeals is accordingly reversed, and the injunction issued by that court is vacated.

[Justice Marshall did not participate; Justice Brennan's dissenting opinion is omitted.]

■ JUSTICE STEVENS, with whom JUSTICE BLACKMUN joins, dissenting.

. . . An organization that qualifies for preferential treatment under § 501(c)(3) of the Internal Revenue Code, because it is "operated exclusively for . . . charitable . . . purposes," is exempt from paying federal income taxes, and [under § 170] persons who contribute to such organizations may deduct the amount of their contributions when calculating their taxable income. Only last Term [in Bob Jones, supra], we explained the effect of this preferential treatment:

> Both tax exemptions and tax-deductibility are a form of subsidy that is administered through the tax system. A tax exemption has much the same effect as a cash grant to the organization of the amount of tax it would have to pay on its income. Deductible contributions are similar to cash grants of the amount of a portion of the individual's contributions.

The purpose of this scheme, like the purpose of any subsidy, is to promote the activity subsidized . . . If the granting of preferential tax treatment would "encourage" private segregated schools to conduct their "charitable" activities, it must follow that the withdrawal of the treatment would "discourage" them. . . .

This causation analysis is nothing more than a restatement of elementary economics: when something becomes more expensive, less of it will be purchased. . . . [W]ithout tax exempt status, private schools will either not be competitive in terms of cost, or have to change their admissions policies, hence reducing their competitiveness for parents seeking "a racially segregated alternative" to public schools, which is what respondents have alleged many white parents in desegregating school districts seek. In either event the process of desegregation will be advanced . . . Thus, the laws of economics, not to mention the laws of Congress embodied in §§ 170 and 501(c)(3), compel the conclusion that the injury respondents have alleged—the increased segregation of their children's schools because of the ready availability of private schools that admit whites only—will be redressed if these schools' operations are inhibited through the denial of preferential tax treatment.

Considerations of tax policy, economics, and pure logic all confirm the conclusion that respondents' injury in fact is fairly traceable to the Government's allegedly wrongful conduct. The Court therefore is forced to introduce the concept of "separation of powers" into its analysis. . . . The Court could mean one of three things by its invocation of the separation of powers. First, it could simply be expressing the idea that if the plaintiff lacks Article III standing to bring a lawsuit, then there is no "case or controversy" within the meaning of Article III and hence the matter is not within the area of responsibility assigned to the Judiciary by the Constitution. . . . While there can be no quarrel with this proposition, in itself it provides no guidance for determining if the injury respondents have alleged is fairly traceable to the conduct they have challenged.

Second, the Court could be saying that it will require a more direct causal connection when it is troubled by the separation of powers implications of the case before it. That approach confuses the standing doctrine with the justiciability of the issues that respondents seek to raise. . . . If a plaintiff presents a nonjusticiable issue, or seeks relief that a court may not award, then its complaint should be dismissed for those reasons, and not because the plaintiff lacks a stake in obtaining that relief and hence has no standing. . . .

Third, the Court could be saying that it will not treat as legally cognizable injuries that stem from an administrative decision concerning how enforcement resources will be allocated. This surely is an important point. . . . The Executive requires latitude to decide how best to enforce the law, and in general the Court may well be correct that the exercise of that discretion, especially in the tax context, is unchallengeable.[2] However, as the Court also recognizes, this principle does not apply when suit is brought "to enforce specific legal obligations whose violation works a direct harm." . . . Here, respondents contend that the IRS is violating a specific constitutional limitation on its enforcement discretion. There is a solid basis for that contention. . . . Similarly, respondents claim that the Internal Revenue Code itself, as construed in Bob Jones, constrains enforcement discretion. . . . Surely the question whether the Constitution

---

[2] [Ed.] The following Term in Heckler v. Chaney, 470 U.S. 821 (1985) (p. 1527) the Court held that an agency's decision not to take enforcement action is presumptively nonreviewable.

or the Code limits enforcement discretion is one within the Judiciary's competence. . . .

## NOTES

(1) ***Incentives and Causation.*** Is there any real-world doubt that the conditions legally attached to charitable tax-exempt status are designed to induce socially desirable behavior that would benefit people like the plaintiffs in Allen? Or that, as a matter of "elemental economics," as Justice Stevens put it, such financial incentives often will increase the likelihood of the desired behavior? Does it then follow that denial of these incentives through nonenforcement likely injures the purported beneficiaries? FRANK H. EASTERBROOK, FOREWORD: THE COURT AND THE ECONOMIC SYSTEM, 98 HARV. L. REV. 4, 40–41 (1984): "The [Allen] Court concludes that the plaintiffs, black parents and children in public schools who disclaimed interest in attending the bigoted private schools, were unaffected by the IRS's policies. . . . [I]t is hard to take seriously the claim that enforcement of legal rules does not affect bystanders. The rule against murder is designed to prevent other people from slaying me, as well as others, and I suffer an injury if the police announce that they will no longer enforce that rule in my neighborhood. I will keep off the streets, hire guards, pay for locks, and still face an increased chance of being killed. Only a judge who secretly believes that the law does not influence behavior would find no injury."

SIMON V. EASTERN KENTUCKY WELFARE RIGHTS ORGANIZATION, 426 U.S. 26 (1984), cited in Allen, similarly involved tax incentives. When the IRS removed an existing requirement that hospitals wishing charitable tax-exempt status provide free care to indigents, low-income persons and organizations representing them sued, arguing that the new interpretation violated the Internal Revenue Code. Although the plaintiffs alleged "specific occasions on which each . . . sought but was denied hospital services solely due to his indigency" and that the IRS "had 'encouraged' hospitals to deny services to indigents [by removing the free care requirement]," the Court nonetheless concluded that "it . . . is purely speculative whether the denials of service specified in the complaint fairly can be traced to petitioners' 'encouragement' or instead result from decisions made by the hospitals without regard to the tax implications. It is equally speculative whether the desired exercise of the court's remedial powers in this suit would result in the availability to respondents of such services. . . . [I]t is just as plausible that the hospitals to which respondents may apply for service would elect to forgo favorable tax treatment to avoid the undetermined financial drain of an increase in the level of uncompensated services."

What might lead the Court to refuse to give legal effect to causal relationships that make intuitive sense empirically? In Simon, Justice Stewart wrote separately, stating that he "could not now imagine a case, at least outside the First Amendment area, where a person whose own tax liability was not affected ever could have standing to litigate the federal tax liability of someone else." Are there compelling policy justifications for judicial hesitation to open the proverbial floodgates to suits complaining that someone else got better tax treatment than they deserved?

(2) ***When Do Intervening Actions Defeat Traceability?*** A related but distinct question concerns when intervening actions preclude concluding that a challenged governmental action caused the asserted injury. Consider two contrasting decisions:

In the first, CALIFORNIA V. TEXAS, 141 S.Ct. 2104 (2021), the Supreme Court considered a challenge by individual and state plaintiffs to the Patient Protection and Affordable Care Act (ACA), also known as Obamacare. After the Court in a prior case upheld the ACA's mandate that individuals must purchase minimum health insurance as a permissible exercise of Congress's tax power, Congress amended the ACA and stripped the mandate of any tax consequences for failure to comply. The plaintiffs contended that this change rendered the mandate unconstitutional and that the rest of the statute could not be severed from it, given how integral the mandate was to the ACA's operation. The Court held, however, that none of the plaintiffs had standing to bring the challenge because they had not shown their alleged injuries were traceable to the allegedly unlawful conduct.

The individual plaintiffs claimed a pocketbook injury in the form of payments made each month to purchase the minimum health insurance required under the statute's individual mandate. But JUSTICE BREYER explained for a 7–2 Court that "the statutory provision, while it tells them to obtain that coverage, has no means of enforcement. With the penalty zeroed out, the [Internal Revenue Service] can no longer seek a penalty from those who fail to comply." Because the plaintiffs could identify no government action as the cause of their alleged injury—"the costs of purchasing health insurance"—the Court concluded that the individual plaintiffs lacked standing. The state plaintiffs claimed two kinds of pocketbook injuries from the mandate. The first was increased costs to run state-operated medical insurance programs that state residents joined to satisfy the mandate's requirements. Justice Breyer concluded that any such increased costs were not traceable to the mandate: "Unsurprisingly, the States have not demonstrated that an unenforceable mandate will cause their residents to enroll in valuable benefits programs that they would otherwise forgo. It would require far stronger evidence than the States have offered here to support their counterintuitive theory of standing, which rests on a 'highly attenuated chain of possibilities' " (citing Clapper). The states' second injury was higher administrative costs directly imposed by other provisions of the ACA. Justice Breyer emphasized that these provisions "operate[d] independently" of the mandate and thus the asserted injury was not "fairly traceable to enforcement of the allegedly unlawful provision of which the plaintiffs complain." In dissent, JUSTICE ALITO claimed the majority's analysis was a "patent distortion of the traceability prong" and insisted that it was enough for the state plaintiffs to have standing that "[t]he ACA saddles them with expensive and burdensome obligations . . . enforced by the Federal Government."

In the second, FEDERAL ELECTION COMMISSION V. CRUZ, 142 S.Ct. 1638 (2022), Senator Ted Cruz and his campaign committee sued the FEC, claiming that Section 304 of the Bipartisan Campaign Reform Act violated the First Amendment. Section 304 imposes a $250,000 limit on the amount that candidates who loan money to their campaigns can be repaid from postelection contributions. An FEC implementing regulation provides that although a campaign can repay a candidate up to $250,000 at any time, it can use pre-election funds to repay additional amounts the candidate loaned only if the repayment occurs within 20 days of the election. Senator Cruz loaned his campaign $260,000, and his campaign began repaying him after the 20-day window. As a result, it repaid only $250,000, leaving $10,000 of the Senator's loans unpaid. Senator Cruz and his campaign stipulated that the only reason he made the loan and his campaign waited to repay him was to create the factual basis for the challenge. The FEC maintained that the asserted injuries were not traceable to the threatened enforcement of Section 304 on two grounds: first, the inability to repay was self-inflicted; and second, because the campaign had used pre-election funds in repaying the $250,000, it was enforcement of the 20-day time limit imposed by the FEC regulation and not Section 304's $250,000 limit on postelection funds that caused the harm.

Writing for a 6–3 Court, CHIEF JUSTICE ROBERTS held there was standing and that Section 304 violated the First Amendment (Justice Kagan's dissent only addressed the merits). On the FEC's first standing argument, he stated that "we have made clear that an injury resulting from the application or threatened application of an unlawful enactment remains fairly traceable to such application, even if the injury could be described in some sense as willingly incurred," citing inter alia Havens Realty (p. 1446). Moreover, "[d]emanding that the Committee comply with the Government's "alternative" [of paying back within 20 days] would . . . require it to forgo the exercise of a First Amendment right we must assume it has [for purposes of assessing standing]—the right to repay its campaign debts in full, at any time." On the FEC's second argument, Chief Justice Roberts concluded that the FEC was "likely correct that appellees have not shown that they exhausted Section 304's cap on the use of post-election funds," but nonetheless the "inability of the Committee to repay and Cruz to recover the final $10,000 Cruz loaned his campaign is, even if brought about by the agency's threatened enforcement of its regulation, traceable to the operation of Section 304 itself. . . . An agency's regulation cannot operate independently of the statute that authorized it. And here, the FEC's 20-day rule was expressly promulgated to implement Section 304 . . . . Thus, if Section 304 is invalid and unenforceable—as Cruz and the Committee contend—the agency's 20-day rule is as well."

Do you think these two decisions are in tension? In rejecting standing for the individual plaintiffs in California v. Texas, wasn't the Court essentially holding that the plaintiffs' cost for purchasing insurance didn't count because it was self-inflicted, given that the IRS could no longer enforce the mandate through tax penalties? An important difference between the two is that in Cruz the plaintiffs were still subject to an enforceable FEC regulation. But the Court simultaneously sought to minimize the role played by the regulation to allow the statutory challenge to go forward. Does it feel like the Court was reaching to take the case in Cruz, while doing its best to avoid finding standing in California v. Texas?

(3) ***Legislative Judgments About Causation.*** How much should it matter in assessing whether causation and redressability are satisfied that Congress explicitly considered the issue of private enforcement and wrote a broad standing provision into a regulatory program's implementing statutory architecture? The Court stressed the presence of such a legislative judgment in FRIENDS OF THE EARTH (FOE) V. LAIDLAW ENVIRONMENTAL SERVICE, INC. 528 U.S. 167 (2000), also discussed above p. 1437, which involved an effort by FOE, an environmental organization, to seek civil penalties for a company's discharges of mercury in violation of the Clean Water Act. The company argued that because civil penalties are paid to the government, such penalties offer no redress to private plaintiffs and therefore there could be no standing because causation was lacking. Writing for the majority in a 5–4 decision, JUSTICE GINSBURG disagreed. "We have recognized on numerous occasions that all civil penalties have some deterrent effect. More specifically, Congress has found that civil penalties in Clean Water Act cases do more than promote immediate compliance by limiting the defendant's economic incentive to delay its attainment of permit limits; they also deter future violations. This congressional determination warrants judicial attention and respect. . . . It can scarcely be doubted that, for a plaintiff who is injured or faces the threat of future injury due to illegal conduct ongoing at the time of suit, a sanction that effectively abates that conduct and prevents its recurrence provides a form of redress. . . . [The dissent's argument that it is availability rather than imposition of civil penalties that deters continued pollution] overlooks the interdependence of the availability and the imposition; a threat has no deterrent value unless it is credible that it will be carried out. . . . A would-be polluter may or may not be dissuaded by the existence of a remedy on the books, but a defendant once hit in its pocketbook will surely think twice before polluting again." Acknowledging "that there may be a point at which the deterrent effect of a claim for civil penalties becomes so insubstantial or so remote that it cannot support citizen standing," the Court found that here "the civil penalties sought by FOE carried with them a deterrent effect that made it likely, as opposed to merely speculative, that the penalties would redress FOE's injuries by abating current violations and preventing future ones." The District Court had assessed a penalty of $405,800.

Dissenting, JUSTICE SCALIA maintained that "a plaintiff's desire to benefit from the deterrent effect of a public penalty for past conduct can never suffice to establish a case or controversy of the sort known to our law. Such deterrent effect is, so to speak, speculative as a matter of law. Even if that were not so, however, the deterrent effect in the present case would surely be speculative as a matter of fact." Emphasizing that deterrence comes from fear of penalties for future pollution, Justice Scalia argued that the company's fear on this score was already "near the top of the graph," given that the Act was "regularly and notoriously enforced" and the company had already been subject to public suit and state penalties for pollution. "The deterrence on which the plaintiffs must rely for standing in the present case is the marginal increase in Laidlaw's fear of future penalties that will be achieved by adding federal penalties for Laidlaw's past conduct. I cannot say for certain that this marginal increase is zero; but I can say for certain that it is entirely speculative whether it will make the difference between these plaintiffs' suffering injury in the future and these plaintiffs' going unharmed."

As noted above (p. 1446), the Court has long emphasized Congress's power, as exercises of its legislative and policy-setting authority, to create new injuries and rights. Should courts also defer to congressional judgments on causality—at least so long as the statutory judgment is within the "outer limits" of plausibility—as the FOE majority did? Is there any reason why such judgments should not receive the same degree of deference—i.e., accepted so long as minimally rational—that the Court gives to other tactical choices Congress makes when structuring a regulatory program? After all, legislatures can redefine causation requirements in tort by, for example, removing certain defenses (e.g., assumption of the risk) or specifying how contributory negligence will be treated. Why can't they also redefine causation for standing purposes? Do the separation of powers concerns invoked by Justice O'Connor in her majority opinion in Allen, or the President's take care duty raised by Justice Scalia in his FOE dissent, justify not deferring to congressional judgments on causation specifically?

(4) ***Speculative Injuries and Speculative Causation.*** Often it is hard to pull apart claims of speculative injury and speculative causation. In Clapper (p. 1448), for example, the Supreme Court concluded that the plaintiffs' asserted injury was too speculative because their "theory of standing . . . relies on a highly attenuated chain of possibilities."

In DEPARTMENT OF COMMERCE V. NEW YORK, 139 S.Ct. 2551 (2019) (excerpted at p. 1177 and discussed with respect to nonreviewability at p. 1525), a similar challenge to standing was framed in terms of traceability. At issue was the decision of Secretary of Commerce Wilbur Ross to add a citizenship question to the census. A group of states, counties, and municipalities with higher shares of noncitizens sued, claiming that including a citizenship question would depress the census response rate and lead to a population undercount in their jurisdictions. They maintained that such an undercount would cause them to lose political representation in Congress and federal funds, among other injuries, because the distribution of congressional seats and much federal funding is tied to the census. The government, citing Clapper, argued that "any harm to respondents is not fairly traceable to the Secretary's decision, because such harm depends on the independent action of third parties choosing to violate their legal duty to respond to the census."

Writing for a unanimous Court on this point, CHIEF JUSTICE ROBERTS rejected the government's argument and found standing: "[W]e are satisfied that, in these circumstances, respondents have met their burden of showing that third parties will likely react in predictable ways to the citizenship question, even if they do so unlawfully and despite the requirement that the Government keep individual answers confidential. The evidence at trial established that noncitizen households have historically responded to the census at lower rates than other groups, and the District Court did not clearly err in crediting the Census Bureau's theory that the discrepancy is likely attributable at least in part to noncitizens' reluctance to answer a citizenship question. Respondents' theory of standing thus does not rest on mere speculation about the decisions of third parties; it relies instead on the predictable effect of Government action on the decisions of third parties." As a result, the Court concluded "that at least some respondents have Article III standing."

One difference between Department of Commerce and Clapper is that no doubt existed that census takers in the plaintiff jurisdictions would be asked the citizenship question, and the issue was how they would respond; in Clapper, by contrast, it was clear how the plaintiffs had responded to the risk that their communications would be intercepted, and the issue was whether it was sufficiently likely such interception would occur. Do you think that explains the divergent results in the two cases?

(5) ***The Relationship Between Defining the Injury and Finding Causation.*** To what extent can the difficulty in finding causation with respect to regulatory beneficiaries be solved by changing the definition of the injury at stake? GENE R. NICHOL, JR., RETHINKING STANDING, 72 Calif. L. Rev. 68, 79–81 (1984): "[Simon] demonstrate[s] the ease with which the Court, by toying with the scope of the injury at issue, can raise or lower the redressability hurdle. . . . The indigents in [Simon] had no objection to receiving hospital access, but the interest they asserted would more appropriately be described as having hospital decisions concerning the services offered to indigents accurately reflect an earlier incentive structure implicitly approved by the Congress. Again, that injury would have been redressed by the claim presented."

Is there any reason why the injuries in Allen and Simon can't be redefined in this way? Note that in challenges to affirmative action programs, the Court has defined the relevant injury as "the inability to compete on an equal footing" and thereby avoided the need to address whether the challengers would have gained admittance in the absence of the program. Northeastern Fla. Chap. of Assoc. Gen. Contractors v. Jacksonville, 508 U.S. 656, 666 (1993).

(6) ***Causation in Separation of Powers Challenges.*** Must a plaintiff show that its injury was directly caused by an alleged constitutional violation, or is it enough to be injured by the actions of an unconstitutionally structured agency? This question has arisen in recent separation of powers suits. In SEILA LAW V. CFPB, 140 S.Ct. 2183 (2020) (p. 988), the petitioner challenging the constitutionality of the CFPB's single-director-with-removal-protection structure had received a civil investigatory demand from the agency. The amicus charged with defending the CFPB's constitutionality argued that this was inadequate for standing and instead "a litigant wishing to challenge an executive act on the basis of the President's removal power must show that the challenged act would not have been taken if the responsible official had been subject to the President's control." The amicus further maintained that this standard could not be met here, because the civil investigatory demand had been validly ratified by two acting CFPB Directors who were understood to be removable at will by virtue of their acting status. The Court disagreed. CHIEF JUSTICE ROBERTS stated for the majority that it was "sufficient that the challenger sustains injury from an

executive act that allegedly exceeds the official's authority." 140 S.Ct. at 2196. Roberts also held that it was "beyond dispute" that the petitioner had standing to appeal. The petitioner was forced "to comply with the civil investigative demand and to provide documents it would prefer to withhold, a concrete injury. That injury is traceable to the decision below and would be fully redressed if we were to reverse the judgment of the Court of Appeals and remand with instructions to deny the Government's petition to enforce the demand."

Yet after finding the unconstitutional removal restriction severable, the Court then remanded to see if the civil investigatory demand had been validly ratified by an Acting Director who was removable at will by the President. Doesn't that amount to determining whether the independent act of approval by a removable-at-will Director broke the causal chain here, and wouldn't a finding of ratification preclude redress of the petitioner's asserted injury? The Court made a similar move the next year in Collins v. Yellen, 141 S.Ct. 1761 (2021), which also found standing for petitioners to successfully assert a removal challenge but then remanded for the lower courts to determine if the petitioners were entitled to any of the relief they sought. Id. at 1779, 1788–89. Do these decisions suggest that the Court is applying a special rule for establishing causation and standing in separation of powers challenges? Do you agree with the Court's determination that standing requirements were met here?

(7) ***Severability and Standing.*** The majority in California v. Texas declined to address what it described as a "novel alternative theory" of inseverability-based standing, which argued that, because the individual mandate is inseverable from the rest of the statute, the plaintiffs could claim the necessary traceable injury from the Act's other provisions, even if those provisions are otherwise lawful. Severability is a remedial issue that ordinarily arises once a court has reached the merits and upheld a challenge to some statutory or regulatory language, leaving the question of whether that language can be "severed" so that the rest of measure remains in force. On this logic, the plaintiffs could establish standing despite lacking standing to challenge the individual mandate itself. The Court concluded, however, that this ground for standing had not been properly raised in the lower court.

In his dissent, Justice Alito embraced this inseverability-based argument for finding that the plaintiff states had standing: "The ACA is an enormously complex statute, and the States have offered evidence of ongoing financial injuries relating to compliance with many other different (and enforceable) ACA provisions. . . . Imagine Statute ABC. Provision A imposes enforceable legal obligations on the plaintiff. Provision B imposes a legal obligation on a different party. And provision C provides that a party is not obligated to comply with provision A if provision B is held to be unconstitutional. Based on the plain text of this law, a party subject to provision A should be able to obtain relief from the enforcement of provision A if it can show that provision B is unconstitutional. To hold otherwise would be directly contrary to the statutory text. But the Court's reasoning would make such a claim impossible." Are you persuaded?

## (2) Probabilities, Risk, and Incrementalism

MASSACHUSETTS V. EPA, 549 U.S. 497 (2009), which you may already have encountered in Chapter VIII (p. 1321), arose out of an effort by environmental organizations to get EPA to regulate greenhouse gas emissions from new motor vehicles. The groups petitioned EPA to undertake a rulemaking, arguing that greenhouse gas emissions constituted an air pollutant that EPA was required to regulate under the Clean Air Act. When EPA denied the petition, the groups sued, joined by a number of states and localities. The D.C. Circuit upheld EPA's refusal to regulate, but the Supreme Court reversed in a sharply contested 5–4 decision. Before reaching the merits, the Court rejected several challenges to the plaintiffs' standing.

In his majority opinion, JUSTICE STEVENS first rejected the claim that any injury from global warming was nonjusticiable because widely shared, emphasizing Massachusetts' status as a sovereign state (see p. 1473). He also held that petitioners' allegations of loss of Massachusetts coastline due to global warming sufficed to show the requisite injury-in-fact for standing: "According to petitioners' unchallenged affidavits, global sea levels rose somewhere between 10 and 20 centimeters over the 20th century as a result of global warming. These rising seas have already begun to swallow Massachusetts' coastal land. . . . The severity of that injury will only increase over the course of the next century," with "a significant fraction of coastal property" predicted to be permanently or temporarily lost through inundation and flooding, imposing significant remediation costs on the state. Justice Stevens then turned to the questions of causation and redressability:

"EPA does not dispute the existence of a causal connection between man-made greenhouse gas emissions and global warming. At a minimum, therefore, EPA's refusal to regulate such emissions 'contributes' to Massachusetts' injuries. EPA nevertheless maintains that its decision not to regulate greenhouse gas emissions from new motor vehicles contributes so insignificantly to petitioners' injuries that the agency cannot be haled into federal court to answer for them. For the same reason, EPA does not believe that any realistic possibility exists that the relief petitioners seek would mitigate global climate change and remedy their injuries. That is especially so because predicted increases in greenhouse gas emissions from developing nations, particularly China and India, are likely to offset any marginal domestic decrease.

"But EPA overstates its case. Its argument rests on the erroneous assumption that a small incremental step, because it is incremental, can never be attacked in a federal judicial forum. Yet accepting that premise would doom most challenges to regulatory action. Agencies, like legislatures, do not generally resolve massive problems in one fell regulatory swoop. See Williamson v. Lee Optical, 348 U.S. 483, 489 (1955) ('[A] reform may take one step at a time, addressing itself to the phase of the problem which seems most acute to the legislative mind'). They instead whittle away at them over time, refining their preferred approach as circumstances change and as they develop a more-nuanced understanding of how best to proceed.

"And reducing domestic automobile emissions is hardly a tentative step. Even leaving aside the other greenhouse gases, the United States transportation sector emits an enormous quantity of carbon dioxide into the atmosphere—according to the MacCracken affidavit, more than 1.7 billion metric tons in 1999 alone. That accounts for more than 6% of worldwide carbon dioxide emissions. To put this in perspective: Considering just emissions from the transportation sector, which represent less than one-third of this country's total carbon dioxide emissions, the United States would still rank as the third-largest emitter of carbon dioxide in the world, outpaced only by the European Union and China. Judged by any standard, U.S. motor-vehicle emissions make a meaningful contribution to greenhouse gas concentrations and hence, according to petitioners, to global warming. . . .

"While it may be true that regulating motor-vehicle emissions will not by itself reverse global warming, it by no means follows that we lack jurisdiction to decide whether EPA has a duty to take steps to slow or reduce it. . . . Because of the enormity of the potential consequences associated with man-made climate change, the fact that the effectiveness of a remedy might be delayed during the (relatively short) time it takes for a new motor-vehicle fleet to replace an older one is essentially irrelevant. Nor is it dispositive that developing countries such as China and India are poised to increase greenhouse gas emissions substantially over the next century: A reduction in domestic emissions would slow the pace of global emissions increases, no matter what happens elsewhere. . . .

"In sum—at least according to petitioners' uncontested affidavits—the rise in sea levels associated with global warming has already harmed and will continue to harm Massachusetts. The risk of catastrophic harm, though remote, is nevertheless real. That risk would be reduced to some extent if petitioners received the relief they seek. We therefore hold that petitioners have standing to challenge the EPA's denial of their rulemaking petition."

CHIEF JUSTICE ROBERTS, joined by Justices Scalia, Thomas, and Alito, strongly dissented from the majority's conclusion that standing requirements were met. In addition to arguing that global warming was almost by definition a generalized grievance, the Chief Justice argued that Massachusetts' sovereign status was irrelevant to the standing inquiry and any "inference of actual loss of Massachusetts coastal land [was] . . . pure conjecture," complaining that "accepting a century-long time horizon and a series of compounded estimates renders requirements of imminence and immediacy utterly toothless." Roberts further insisted that the requisite causality and redressability were lacking:

"Petitioners' reliance on Massachusetts's loss of coastal land as their injury in fact for standing purposes creates insurmountable problems for them with respect to causation and redressability. . . . First, it is important to recognize the extent of the emissions at issue here. Because local greenhouse gas emissions disperse throughout the atmosphere and remain there for anywhere from 50 to 200 years, it is global emissions data that are relevant. According to one of petitioners' declarations, domestic motor vehicles contribute about 6 percent of global carbon dioxide emissions and 4 percent of global greenhouse gas emissions. The amount of global emissions at issue here is smaller still; § 202(a)(1) of the Clean Air Act covers only new motor vehicles and new motor vehicle engines, so petitioners' desired emission standards might reduce only a fraction of 4 percent of global emissions.

"This gets us only to the relevant greenhouse gas emissions; linking them to global warming and ultimately to petitioners' alleged injuries next requires consideration of further complexities. As EPA explained in its denial of petitioners' request for rulemaking,

> predicting future climate change necessarily involves a complex web of economic and physical factors including: our ability to predict future global anthropogenic emissions of [greenhouse gases] and aerosols; the fate of these emissions once they enter the atmosphere (e.g., what percentage are absorbed by vegetation or are taken up by the oceans); the impact of those emissions that remain in the atmosphere on the radiative properties of the atmosphere; changes in critically important climate feedbacks (e.g., changes in cloud cover and ocean circulation); changes in temperature characteristics (e.g., average temperatures, shifts in daytime and evening temperatures); changes in other climatic parameters (e.g., shifts in precipitation, storms); and ultimately the impact of such changes on human health and welfare (e.g., increases or decreases in agricultural productivity, human health impacts).

"Petitioners are never able to trace their alleged injuries back through this complex web to the fractional amount of global emissions that might have been limited with EPA standards. In light of the bit-part domestic new motor vehicle greenhouse gas emissions have played in what petitioners describe as a 150-year global phenomenon, and the myriad additional factors bearing on petitioners' alleged injury—the loss of Massachusetts coastal land—the connection is far too speculative to establish causation.

"Redressability is even more problematic. To the tenuous link between petitioners' alleged injury and the indeterminate fractional domestic emissions at issue here, add the fact that petitioners cannot meaningfully predict what will come of the 80 percent of global greenhouse gas emissions that originate outside the United States. As the Court acknowledges, 'developing countries such as China and India are poised to increase greenhouse gas emissions substantially over the next century,' so the domestic emissions at issue here may become an increasingly marginal portion of global emissions, and any decreases produced by petitioners' desired standards are likely to be overwhelmed many times over by emissions increases elsewhere in the world. . . . No matter, the Court reasons, because any decrease in domestic emissions will 'slow the pace of global emissions increases, no matter what happens elsewhere.' Every little bit helps, so Massachusetts can sue over any little bit.

"The Court's sleight-of-hand is in failing to link up the different elements of the three-part standing test. What must be likely to be redressed is the particular injury in fact. The injury the Court looks to is the asserted loss of land. The Court contends that regulating domestic motor vehicle emissions will reduce carbon dioxide in the atmosphere, and therefore redress Massachusetts's injury. But even if regulation does reduce emissions—to some indeterminate degree, given events elsewhere in the world—the Court never explains why that makes it likely that the injury in fact—the loss of land—will be redressed."

## NOTES

(1) ***The Role of Probability in Standing Analysis.*** Note that probability factors into the standing analysis in Massachusetts in several ways. Two involve causation and redressability, specifically the probability that EPA's failure to regulate greenhouse gas emissions caused Massachusetts' injury and the probability that EPA's undertaking such regulation will remedy that injury. But probability also surfaces in the disagreement between the majority and dissent over whether Massachusetts has suffered a sufficiently imminent injury. According to Justice Stevens, given that "the harms associated with climate change are serious and well recognized," including rising sea levels, the plaintiffs' allegations about the loss of coastline over the next century were sufficiently likely; to Chief Justice Roberts, it was "pure conjecture" and made the imminence inquiry "utterly toothless." This debate echoes other disagreements over whether allegations of injury are too speculative—such as those in Clapper (p. 1448), SBA (p. 1449), Summers (p. 1450), Allen (p. 1457), and Department of Commerce (p. 1466)—all of which involve assessments of the probability and imminence of injury.

(2) ***Big Problems and Incrementalism.*** Who has the better of the argument on causation and redressability, the majority or the dissent? Justice Stevens's opinion adopts an approach to causation and redressability calibrated to the size and complexity of the problem of global warming: Because the problem is so large and multi-faceted, anything EPA could do would necessarily be incremental and partial—but the agency contributes to the problem's continuation by not using *whatever* power it has to abate global warming. Chief Justice Roberts's opinion agrees with the size and complexity of the problem of global warming but draws the opposite conclusion: Global warming is a problem too big to be justiciable; nothing EPA could do would make any appreciable change that would palpably benefit any individual or entity over any reasonably imminent timeframe. This kind of problem is a political, not a judicial, question.

Either view seems plausible. Can you select between them without referring to some normative theory about the appropriateness of centralized regulatory government and the roles and relationships among Congress, the

President, and the courts? What are the implications of requiring more than some incremental benefit, given the multi-causal, complex, and often global nature of many major policy issues today?

(3) ***Specific or General Causal Chains.*** The Chief Justice required a tight connection between the alleged injury and the specific action challenged, namely Massachusetts' loss of coastline and EPA's failure to regulate greenhouse gas emissions from new motor vehicles. Query whether, given that global warming has multiple causes, it should be enough to show that Massachusetts will likely lose coastline due to global warming and that greenhouse gas emissions from new motor vehicles contribute to global warming, without showing any more specific connection between the two.

## d. Governmental Standing

Up to now, we've focused primarily on suits brought by private individuals and organizations. But what about when governments are plaintiffs? Do the same standing rules apply? Should they? The question of governmental standing has arisen recently with a significant expansion in suits by states challenging national administrative action. This expansion reflects the dramatic political polarization that divides the country, with red states repeatedly challenging Obama and Biden Administration actions and blue states doing the same to the Trump Administration. Similarly, a recent surge in suits against the executive branch by members or parts of Congress—a single house, or a congressional committee—reflects the frequent reality of politically divided national government.

(1) ***Massachusetts and State Standing.*** As noted above (p. 1469), in MASSACHUSETTS V. EPA, 549 U.S. 497 (2007), JUSTICE STEVENS's majority opinion emphasized Massachusetts' state status as a reason for granting standing: "We stress here . . . the special position and interest of Massachusetts. It is of considerable relevance that the party seeking review here is a sovereign State and not, as it was in Lujan, a private individual. Well before the creation of the modern administrative state, we recognized that States are not normal litigants for the purposes of invoking federal jurisdiction. . . . Georgia v. Tennessee Copper Co., 206 U.S. 230, 237 (1907), [was] a case in which Georgia sought to protect its citizens from air pollution originating outside its borders. . . . Just as Georgia's 'independent interest . . . in all the earth and air within its domain' supported federal jurisdiction a century ago, so too does Massachusetts' well-founded desire to preserve its sovereign territory today. That Massachusetts does in fact own a great deal of the 'territory alleged to be affected' only reinforces the conclusion that its stake in the outcome of this case is sufficiently concrete to warrant the exercise of federal judicial power.

"When a State enters the Union, it surrenders certain sovereign prerogatives. Massachusetts cannot invade Rhode Island to force reductions in greenhouse gas emissions, it cannot negotiate an emissions treaty with China or India, and in some circumstances the exercise of its police powers to reduce in-state motor-vehicle emissions might well be pre-empted. . . .

These sovereign prerogatives are now lodged in the Federal Government, and Congress has ordered EPA to protect Massachusetts (among others) by prescribing standards applicable to the 'emission of any air pollutant from any class or classes of new motor vehicle engines, which in [the Administrator's] judgment cause, or contribute to, air pollution which may reasonably be anticipated to endanger public health or welfare.' 42 U.S.C. § 7521(a)(1). Congress has moreover recognized a concomitant procedural right to challenge the rejection of its rulemaking petition as arbitrary and capricious. § 7607(b)(1). Given that procedural right and Massachusetts' stake in protecting its quasi-sovereign interests, the Commonwealth is entitled to special solicitude in our standing analysis."

According to CHIEF JUSTICE ROBERTS in dissent, however, Massachusetts' status as a state was entirely irrelevant to the case: "Relaxing Article III standing requirements because asserted injuries are pressed by a State . . . has no basis in our jurisprudence, and support for any such 'special solicitude' is conspicuously absent from the Court's opinion. The general judicial review provision cited by the Court, 42 U.S.C. § 7607(b)(1), affords States no special rights or status. . . . Congress knows how to do that when it wants to, see, e.g., § 7426(b) (affording States the right to petition EPA to directly regulate certain sources of pollution), but it has done nothing of the sort here. Under the law on which petitioners rely, Congress treated public and private litigants exactly the same.

"Nor does the case law cited by the Court provide any support for the notion that Article III somehow implicitly treats public and private litigants differently. . . . Tennessee Copper [stands] for nothing more than a State's right, in an original jurisdiction action, to sue in a representative capacity as parens patriae. Nothing about a State's ability to sue in that capacity dilutes the bedrock requirement of showing injury, causation, and redressability to satisfy Article III. A claim of parens patriae standing is distinct from an allegation of direct injury. Far from being a substitute for Article III injury, parens patriae actions raise an additional hurdle for a state litigant: the articulation of a 'quasi-sovereign interest' apart from the interests of particular private parties. Just as an association suing on behalf of its members must show not only that it represents the members but that at least one satisfies Article III requirements, so too a State asserting quasi-sovereign interests as parens patriae must still show that its citizens satisfy Article III. Focusing on Massachusetts's interests as quasi-sovereign makes the required showing here harder, not easier."

Even supposing special solicitude for the states is justified, what does it mean? After invoking such solicitude, the majority opinion proceeded to invoke the tripartite injury-causation-redressability framework of Lujan and to find standing based on Massachusetts' loss of coastline—concluding that EPA's failure to regulate greenhouse gas emissions from new motor vehicles contributed to this loss and that targeting this failure would help redress it. The Court also applied the Lujan tripartite framework in a suit brought by the Arizona State Legislature. Arizona State Legislature v. Arizona Independent Redistricting Comm'n, 576 U.S. 787, 799–800 (2015). Special solicitude for the states thus does not appear to mean application of a different analytic framework. It might mean, however, that the standard framework is applied more leniently. Would you characterize the majority's application of Lujan in Massachusetts (p. 1469) as lenient?

(2) ***The Current State of State Standing.*** The years after Massachusetts saw a notable expansion in state suits against the federal government. In particular, Texas sued the Obama Administration at least 48 times, and it sued the Biden Administration at least 29 times in that administration's first year and a half in office. Meanwhile California sued the Trump Administration well over a hundred times during the four years Trump was in office. A number of these cases made it to the Supreme Court, sometimes on its "shadow" docket, which addresses requests for emergency or extraordinary relief, and sometimes on the merits. Frequently, the lower courts and the Supreme Court had held that the states involved had standing. See, e.g., Texas v. United States (p. 409), Department of Commerce v. New York (p. 1177), DHS v. Regents of California (p. 1139), Biden v. Missouri (pp. 390, 869), and West Virginia v. EPA (p. 1341). An exception was California v. Texas, where—as noted above (p. 1463)—the Court held that held that the plaintiff states had failed to show how their alleged harm was traceable to any government conduct in enforcing the individual mandate. In dissent, Justice Alito accused the Court of being "selectively generous in allowing States to sue."

(3) ***Should States Get Special Solicitude in Standing Analysis?*** Is a different or more lenient standing analysis for states justified? Does it matter what claim the states might be raising? See TARA LEIGH GROVE, WHEN CAN A STATE SUE THE UNITED STATES?, 101 Cornell L. Rev. 851 (2016): "States are entitled to 'special solicitude' in the standing analysis in only one context: when they seek to enforce or defend state law. . . . States have broad standing to challenge federal statutes and regulations that preempt, or otherwise undermine the continued enforceability of, state law. But States do not have a special interest in the manner in which the federal executive enforces federal law. . . . In sum, I argue that States have broad standing to protect federalism principles, not the constitutional separation of powers."

By contrast, ERNEST A. YOUNG, in STATE STANDING AND COOPERATIVE FEDERALISM, 94 Notre Dame L. Rev. 1893 (2019), argues for broader state standing, viewing state litigation as a better alternative than other means used to aggregate the interests of large number of individuals: "One significant advantage that states have over private organizations and class actions is that they have built-in mechanisms of democratic accountability for their conduct of litigation on behalf of their citizens. . . . State officials who sue on behalf of their citizens are politically accountable for their actions. . . . More generally, litigation by states fits well into a constitutional system predicated on the notion that no one person or institution can lay a unique claim to the public interest. . . . By according special solicitude to states' standing, Massachusetts v. EPA facilitated states' valuable role in the process by which every political institution is held accountable to the rule of law."

AZIZ Z. HUQ, in STATE STANDING'S UNCERTAIN STAKES, 94 Notre Dame L. Rev. 2127 (2019), is more skeptical about the legal or democratic benefits of states as litigators. He emphasizes that the state AGs who commonly represent the state "are elected" and "[m]any have abiding ambition for higher state or federal office. . . . Expanding state standing increases the opportunities for like officials to use the power to file suit on the state's behalf as an instrument for personal or partisan advancement." Huq also argues that "[w]hat is unusual and symptomatic in the state standing litigation context is [that] . . . specific Justices seem to adopt divergent, seemingly inconsistent, positions on the same basic question of constitutional law when it is presented in different litigation matters." See also Ann Woolhandler & Michael G. Collins, State Standing, 81 Va. L. Rev. 387 (1995) (arguing that historically, states generally could pursue only their common-law interests in court); Gillian E. Metzger, Federalism and Federal Agency Reform, 111 Colum. L. Rev. 1 (2011) (suggesting that courts should focus more on whether Congress has assigned states a special role in policing federal agency action).

(4) ***Congressional Standing.*** What about Congress: Does Congress as a whole, the House or Senate on its own, or individual members of Congress have standing to challenge alleged executive branch actions in court?

The leading Supreme Court decision on congressional standing is RAINES V. BYRD, 521 U.S. 811 (1996). There, six members of Congress sued to challenge the Line Item Veto Act as unconstitutionally altering the effect of their votes on legislation subject to the Act and undermining the constitutional separation of powers. Although the Act expressly provided for just such a suit, the Court found that the members of Congress lacked Article III standing because they failed to establish a "personal, particularized, concrete, and otherwise judicially cognizable" injury: "[They] have not been singled out for specially unfavorable treatment as opposed to other Members of their respective bodies. Their claim is that the Act causes a type of institutional injury (the diminution of legislative power), which necessarily damages all Members of Congress and both Houses of Congress equally."

A majority of the Court has not addressed congressional standing since Raines. Lower courts have had more encounters with congressional standing, particularly the D.C. Circuit. That court had long held that both the House and Senate and their committees can sue in an official capacity to demand information from the executive branch in furtherance of Congress's oversight role. The continued viability of this case law allowing congressional suits to enforce subpoenas was at issue in COMMITTEE ON THE JUDICIARY V. MCGAHN, 968 F.3d 755 (D.C. Cir. 2020) (en banc). As noted in Chapter VII (p. 925), the House Judiciary Committee had subpoenaed President Trump's former White House Counsel in connection with an investigation into Trump's actions in the 2016 election and during the Special Counsel's inquiry into 2016 election interference by Russia. When McGahn refused to appear, reflecting the White House's position that he was absolutely immune from congressional process, the Judiciary Committee sued.

In an opinion written by JUDGE ROGERS, the D.C. Circuit held en banc (7–2) that the Committee had standing: "McGahn's disregard of the subpoena, the validity of which he has never challenged, deprived the Committee of specific information sought in the exercise of its constitutional responsibilities. . . . Because the Committee's injury has been caused by McGahn's defiance of its subpoena and can be cured here only by judicial enforcement of the subpoena, the injury is traceable to McGahn's conduct and judicially redressable. And, contrary to McGahn's positions, the Committee's standing is consistent with the system of separated powers and capable of resolution through the judicial process." McGahn also claimed that the Committee lacked standing under Raines, but Judge Rogers disagreed, arguing that McGahn "ignores Raines's limits. The Supreme Court has given clear direction that Raines is a narrow case about the standing only of individual legislators."

Do you agree that Raines can be so distinguished? How far does the D.C. Circuit's reasoning in McGahn go? Would it also support a suit by the House of Representatives to challenge the Trump Administration's transfer and reprogramming of appropriated funds to build a border wall? The D.C. Circuit concluded it would, in U.S. HOUSE OF REPRESENTATIVES V. MNUCHIN, 976 F.3d 1, 8 (D.C. Cir. 2020), vacated as moot, Yellen v. U.S. House of Representatives, 142 S.Ct. 332 (2021): "When the injury alleged is to the Congress as a whole, one chamber does not have standing to litigate. When the injury is to the distinct prerogatives of a single chamber, that chamber does have standing to assert the injury. . . . [T]he House is suing to remedy an institutional injury to its own institutional power to prevent the expenditure of funds not authorized. . . . More specifically, by spending funds that the House refused to allow, the Executive Branch has defied an express constitutional prohibition that protects each congressional chamber's unilateral authority to prevent expenditures. It is therefore an institutional plaintiff asserting an institutional injury that is both concrete and particularized, belonging to the House and the House alone." By contrast, the D.C. Circuit relied on Raines to reject congressional standing in Blumenthal v. Trump, 949 F.3d 14 (D.C. Cir. 2020), where 215 members of Congress sued then-President Trump for alleged violations of the Foreign Emoluments Clause; the per curiam decision emphasized that the plaintiffs' "alleged injury is shared by the 320 members of the Congress who did not join the lawsuit—and their claim is based entirely on the loss of political power.

(5) ***Individual Legislators' Standing.*** As noted above (p. 1438), in Maloney v. Murphy, 984 F.3d 50 (D.C. Cir. 2020), the D.C. Circuit held that individual members of Congress had standing to sue for an executive branch agency's refusal to comply with their request for information. The legislators made the request pursuant to a federal statute that authorizes seven or more members of the House Committee on Oversight and Reform to demand information from an executive branch agency. Yet when eight members of the committee sought information about federally owned property from the General Services Administration, the agency rebuffed the request. The issue before the D.C. Circuit was whether these members had standing to enforce their statutorily authorized right to information. GSA argued that the committee members lacked standing because they were asserting an institutional injury as legislators and not a personal injury of their own. The D.C. Circuit, however, found that the legislators had asserted a personal

harm: Much as in Akins, the federal law at issue "vested [the legislators] specifically and particularly with the right to obtain information." The members "alone felt the informational loss caused by the agency's withholding," so the agency's refusal to provide them information to which they were statutorily entitled created an injury-in-fact within the meaning of Article III. Id. at 64. Dissenting from denial of rehearing en banc, Maloney v. Carnahan, 45 F.4th 215 (D.C. Cir. 2022), and writing for four judges, Judge Rao argued that "recognizing standing for members of Congress based on harms that are simultaneously personal and legislative, the panel decisively breaks with the structural constitutional limits articulated in Raines." In your view, is the D.C. Circuit's decision here compatible or at odds with Raines?

## e. Standing Under the APA

***NATIONAL CREDIT UNION ADMIN. v. FIRST NAT'L BANK & TRUST CO.***

*A person suffering legal wrong because of agency action, or adversely affected or aggrieved by agency action within the meaning of a relevant statute, is entitled to judicial review thereof.*

5 U.S.C. § 702

### NATIONAL CREDIT UNION ADMIN. v. FIRST NAT'L BANK & TRUST CO.

Supreme Court of the United States (1998).
522 U.S. 479.

■ JUSTICE THOMAS delivered the opinion of the Court. . . .[3]

Section 109 of the Federal Credit Union Act (FCUA), 48 Stat. 1219, 12 U.S.C. § 1759, provides that "[f]ederal credit union membership shall be limited to groups having a common bond of occupation or association, or to groups within a well-defined neighborhood, community, or rural district." Since 1982, the National Credit Union Administration (NCUA), the agency charged with administering the FCUA, has interpreted § 109 to permit federal credit unions to be composed of multiple unrelated employer groups, each having its own common bond of occupation. In this action, respondents, five banks and the American Bankers Association, have challenged this interpretation on the ground that § 109 unambiguously requires that the *same* common bond of occupation unite every member of an occupationally defined federal credit union. . . .

II

Respondents claim a right to judicial review of the NCUA's chartering decision under § 10(a) of the APA [§ 702] . . . We have interpreted § 10(a) of the APA to impose a prudential standing

[3] [Ed.] Justice Thomas's opinion was the opinion of the Court except for footnote 6, which Justice Scalia did not join and which examined the legislative history of § 109.

requirement in addition to the requirement, imposed by Article III of the Constitution, that a plaintiff have suffered a sufficient injury in fact. See, e.g., Association of Data Processing Service Organizations, Inc. v. Camp, 397 U.S. 150, 152 (1970) (Data Processing). For a plaintiff to have prudential standing under the APA, "the interest sought to be protected by the complainant [must be] arguably within the zone of interests to be protected or regulated by the statute . . . in question." Id., at 153. . . .

Although our prior cases have not stated a clear rule for determining when a plaintiff's interest is "arguably within the zone of interests" to be protected by a statute, they nonetheless establish that we should not inquire whether there has been a congressional intent to benefit the would-be plaintiff. In Data Processing, . . . the Office of the Comptroller of the Currency (Comptroller) had interpreted the National Bank Act's incidental powers clause . . . to permit national banks to perform data processing services for other banks and bank customers. . . . The plaintiffs, a data processing corporation and its trade association, alleged that this interpretation was impermissible . . . . In holding that the plaintiffs had standing [in Data Processing], we stated that § 10(a) of the APA required only that "the interest sought to be protected by the complainant [be] arguably within the zone of interests to be protected or regulated by the statute . . . in question." Id., at 153. In determining that the plaintiffs' interest met this requirement, we noted that although the relevant federal statutes . . . did not "in terms protect a specified group[,] . . . their general policy is apparent; and those whose interests are directly affected by a broad or narrow interpretation of the Acts are easily identifiable." Data Processing, 397 U.S., at 157. "[A]s competitors of national banks which are engaging in data processing services," the plaintiffs were within that class of "aggrieved persons" entitled to judicial review of the Comptroller's interpretation. Ibid.

Less than a year later, we applied the "zone of interests" test in Arnold Tours, Inc. v. Camp, 400 U.S. 45 (1970) (per curiam) (Arnold Tours). There, certain travel agencies challenged a ruling by the Comptroller, similar to the one contested in Data Processing, that permitted national banks to operate travel agencies. See 400 U.S., at 45. In holding that the plaintiffs had prudential standing under the APA, we . . . explained:

> "In Data Processing . . . [w]e held that § 4 arguably brings a competitor within the zone of interests protected by it. Nothing in the opinion limited § 4 to protecting only competitors in the data-processing field. When national banks begin to provide travel services for their customers, they compete with travel agents no less than they compete with data processors when they provide data-processing services to their customers." Ibid.

A year later, we decided Investment Company Institute v. Camp, 401 U.S. 617 (1971) (ICI). In that case, an investment company trade association and several individual investment companies alleged that the Comptroller had violated, inter alia, § 21 of the Glass-Steagall Act, 1932, by permitting national banks to establish and operate what in essence were early versions of mutual funds. We held that the plaintiffs, who alleged that they would be injured by the competition resulting from the Comptroller's action, had standing under the APA and stated that the case was controlled by Data Processing. . . .

Our fourth case in this vein was Clarke v. Securities Industry Assn., 479 U.S. 388 (1987). There, a securities dealers trade association sued the Comptroller, this time for authorizing two national banks to offer discount brokerage services both at their branch offices and at other locations inside and outside their home States. The plaintiff contended that the Comptroller's action violated the McFadden Act, which permits national banks to carry on the business of banking only at authorized branches, and to open new branches only in their home States and only to the extent that state-chartered banks in that State can do so under state law. We again held that the plaintiff had standing under the APA. . . .

Our prior cases, therefore, have consistently held that for a plaintiff's interests to be arguably within the "zone of interests" to be protected by a statute, there does not have to be an "indication of congressional purpose to benefit the would-be plaintiff." Id., at 399–400. . . . The proper inquiry is simply "whether the interest sought to be protected by the complainant is *arguably* within the zone of interests to be protected . . . by the statute." Data Processing, 397 U.S., at 153 (emphasis added). Hence in applying the "zone of interests" test, we do not ask whether, in enacting the statutory provision at issue, Congress specifically intended to benefit the plaintiff. Instead, we first discern the interests "arguably . . . to be protected" by the statutory provision at issue; we then inquire whether the plaintiff's interests affected by the agency action in question are among them.

. . . By its express terms, § 109 limits membership in every federal credit union to members of definable "groups." Because federal credit unions may, as a general matter, offer banking services only to members, . . . § 109 also restricts the markets that every federal credit union can serve. . . . Thus, even if it cannot be said that Congress had the specific purpose of benefiting commercial banks, one of the interests "arguably . . . to be protected" by § 109 is an interest in limiting the markets that federal credit unions can serve. . . . As competitors of federal credit unions, respondents certainly have an interest in limiting the markets that federal credit unions can serve, and the NCUA's interpretation has affected that interest . . .

. . . Petitioners attempt to distinguish this action [from our prior cases] principally on the ground that there is no evidence that Congress, when it enacted the FCUA, was at all concerned with the competitive interests of commercial banks, or indeed at all concerned with competition. Indeed, petitioners contend that the very reason Congress passed the FCUA was that "[b]anks were simply not in the picture" as far as small borrowers were concerned, and thus Congress believed it necessary to create a new source of credit for people of modest means.

The difficulty with this argument is that similar arguments were made unsuccessfully in each of Data Processing, Arnold Tours, ICI, and Clarke.... We therefore cannot accept petitioners' argument that respondents do not have standing because there is no evidence that the Congress that enacted § 109 was concerned with the competitive interests of commercial banks. To accept that argument, we would have to reformulate the "zone of interests" test to require that Congress have specifically intended to benefit a particular class of plaintiffs before a plaintiff from that class could have standing under the APA to sue. We have refused to do this in our prior cases, and we refuse to do so today.

Petitioners also mistakenly rely on our decision in Air Courier Conference v. Postal Workers, 498 U.S. 517 (1991). In Air Courier, we held that the interest of Postal Service employees in maximizing employment opportunities was not within the "zone of interests" to be protected by the postal monopoly statutes, and hence those employees did not have standing under the APA to challenge a Postal Service regulation suspending its monopoly over certain international operations. We stated that the purposes of the statute were solely to increase the revenues of the Post Office and to ensure that postal services were provided in a manner consistent with the public interest. Only those interests, therefore, and not the interests of Postal Service employees in their employment, were "arguably within the zone of interests to be protected" by the statute. We further noted that although the statute in question regulated competition, the interests of the plaintiff employees had nothing to do with competition.... In this action, not only do respondents have "competitive and direct injury," but, as the foregoing discussion makes clear, they possess an interest that is "arguably ... to be protected" by § 109....

III

[Justice Thomas, writing for the majority, proceeded to hold on the merits that the NCUA's interpretation of the common bond requirement was impermissible under the first step of Chevron. (p. 1206)]

■ JUSTICE O'CONNOR, with whom JUSTICE STEVENS, JUSTICE SOUTER, and JUSTICE BREYER join, dissenting.

In determining that respondents have standing under the zone-of-interests test to challenge the NCUA's interpretation of the "common bond" provision of the FCUA, the Court applies the test in a manner that is contrary to our decisions and, more importantly, that all but eviscerates the zone-of-interests requirement....

Respondents brought this suit under § 10(a) of the APA, 5 U.S.C. § 702. To establish their standing to sue here, ... respondents must show that they are "adversely affected or aggrieved," *i.e.*, have suffered injury in fact.... In addition, respondents must establish that the injury they assert is "within the meaning of a relevant statute," *i.e.*, satisfies the zone-of-interests test.... Specifically, "the plaintiff must establish that the injury he complains of (*his* aggrievement, or the adverse effect *upon him*), falls within the 'zone of interests' sought to be protected by the statutory provision whose violation forms the legal basis for his complaint." [Lujan v.] National Wildlife Federation, [497 U.S. 871,] 883 [(1990)]. . . .

. . . The relevant question under the zone-of-interests test, then, is whether injury to respondents' commercial interest as a competitor "falls within the zone of interests sought to be protected by the [common bond] provision." . . . The Court adopts a quite different approach to the zone-of-interests test today, eschewing any assessment of whether the common bond provision was intended to protect respondents' commercial interest. . . .

. . . Under the Court's approach, every litigant who establishes injury in fact under Article III will automatically satisfy the zone-of-interests requirement, rendering the zone-of-interests test ineffectual. . . . The crux of the Court's zone-of-interests inquiry . . . is simply that the plaintiff must "have" an interest in enforcing the pertinent statute. . . . A party, however, will invariably have an interest in enforcing a statute when he can establish injury in fact caused by an alleged violation of that statute. . . . Our decision in Air Courier, likewise, cannot be squared with the Court's analysis in this action. . . . [T]he postal employees would have established standing under the Court's analysis in this action: The employees surely "had" an interest in enforcing the statutory monopoly, given that suspension of the monopoly caused injury to their employment opportunities. . . .

Contrary to the Court's suggestion, its application of the zone-of-interests test in this action is not in concert with the approach we followed in a series of cases in which the plaintiffs, like respondents here, alleged that agency interpretation of a statute caused competitive injury to their commercial interests. [Data Processing, Arnold Tours, ICI, and Clarke.] In each of those cases, we focused . . . on whether competitive injury to the plaintiff's commercial interest fell within the zone of interests protected by the relevant statute. . . . It is true, as the Court emphasizes repeatedly, . . . that we did not require in this line of decisions that the statute at issue was designed to benefit the particular party bringing suit. . . . In each of the competitor standing cases, though, we found that Congress had enacted an "anti-competition limitation," see Bennett [v. Spear], 520 U.S., [154,] 176 [(1997)] (discussing Data Processing) [p. 1543], or, alternatively, that Congress had "legislated against . . . competition," see Clarke, supra, at 403; ICI, supra, at 620–621, and accordingly, that the plaintiff-competitor's "commercial interest was sought to be protected by the anti-competition limitation" at issue, Bennett, supra, at 176. . . . The Court fails to undertake that analysis here.

Applying the proper zone-of-interests inquiry to this action, I would find that competitive injury to respondents' commercial interests does not arguably fall within the zone of interests sought to be protected by the common bond provision. . . . There is no indication in the text of the provision or in the surrounding language that the membership limitation was even arguably designed to protect the commercial interests of competitors. . . . The circumstances surrounding the enactment of the FCUA also indicate that Congress did not intend to legislate against competition through the common bond provision. . . . The requirement of a common bond was . . . meant to ensure that each credit union remains a cooperative institution that is economically stable and responsive to its members' needs. As a principle of internal governance designed to secure the viability of individual credit unions in the interests of the membership, the common bond provision was in no way designed to impose a restriction on all credit unions in the interests of institutions that might one day become competitors. . . .

. . . The pertinent question under the zone-of-interests test is whether Congress *intended* to protect certain interests through a particular provision, not whether, irrespective of congressional intent, a provision may have the *effect* of protecting those interests. . . . In this light, I read our decisions as establishing that there must at least be *some* indication in the statute, beyond the mere fact that its enforcement has the effect of incidentally benefiting the plaintiff, from which one can draw an inference that the plaintiff's injury arguably falls within the zone of interests sought to be protected by that statute. The provisions we construed in Clarke, ICI, and Data Processing allowed such an inference: Where Congress legislates against competition, one can properly infer that the statute is at least arguably intended to protect competitors from injury to their commercial interest, even if that is not the statute's principal objective. . . . The same cannot be said of respondents in this action, because neither the terms of the common bond provision, nor the way in which the provision operates, nor the circumstances surrounding its enactment, evince a congressional desire to legislate against competition. This, then, is an action [in which] "the plaintiff's interests are so marginally related to or inconsistent with the purposes implicit in the statute that it cannot reasonably be assumed that Congress intended to permit the suit." Clarke, 479 U.S., at 399.

## NOTES

(1) ***Data Processing and the Birth of the Zone of Interest Test.*** As noted above (p. 1423), standing doctrine is a modern creation. The traditional jurisprudential approach did not recognize standing as an inquiry separate from the case on the merits. The Supreme Court clearly rejected the view that a "legal right" is constitutionally required to sue in an important set of cases under the Communications Act of 1934, which authorizes judicial review of FCC decisions on license applications at the behest of either the applicant or "any other person aggrieved or whose interests are adversely affected by any decision of the Commission granting or refusing any such application." See FCC v. Sanders Bros., 309 U.S. 470 (1940); Scripps-Howard Radio Inc. v. FCC, 316 U.S. 4, 14 (1942); Elizabeth Magill, Standing for the Public: A Lost History, 95 Va. L. Rev. 1131 (2009).

Sanders Bros. and Scripps-Howard represented a major conceptual shift in thinking about who could seek judicial review of agency compliance with statutory requirements. But their immediate impact on regulatory standing was limited because they rested on the relatively atypical phrasing of § 402(b). Then in 1946 Congress enacted the APA. Underscoring the fact that "standing" had not yet gained currency as a distinct jurisprudential concept, the APA nowhere uses the term. However, a major interpretive controversy ensued about the meaning of § 702, originally enacted as § 10a of the APA, which made judicial review available to a person "adversely affected or aggrieved by agency action within the meaning of the relevant statute." The prominent scholar Louis Jaffe (and many lower courts) took the position that § 702 merely codified existing standing law—that is, a "legal interest" is required unless the particular organic statute (like the Communications Act) empowers "aggrieved" persons to sue. Louis L. Jaffe, Judicial Control of Administrative Action 528–30 (1965). On the other side, influential commentator Kenneth Davis pointed to legislative history that described § 702 as "confer[ring] a right of review upon any person adversely affected in fact by agency action or aggrieved within the meaning of any statute" and argued that Congress intended to broaden regulatory standing by adopting the Sanders Bros./Scripps-Howard approach across the board in the APA. Kenneth C. Davis, Judicial Control of Administrative Action: A Review, 66 Colum. L. Rev. 635, 668–69 (1966).

Nearly a quarter-century after the APA was enacted, ASS'N OF DATA PROCESSING SERVICE ORGS., INC. V. CAMP, 397 U.S. 150 (1970) (Data Processing) settled the question in Davis's favor. There, in an opinion by JUSTICE DOUGLAS, the Court stated: "The first question is whether the plaintiff alleges that the challenged action has caused him injury in fact, economic or otherwise." This inquiry, Justice Douglas insisted, was not the same as determining whether the plaintiff had a legal interest at stake. "The 'legal interest' test goes to the merits. The question of standing is different. It concerns, apart from the 'case' or 'controversy' test, the question whether the interest sought to be protected by the complainant is arguably within the zone of interests to be protected or regulated by the statute or constitutional guarantee in question. Thus the Administrative Procedure Act grants standing to a person 'aggrieved by agency action within the meaning of a relevant statute.' 5 U.S.C. § 702. That interest, at times, may reflect aesthetic, conservational, and recreational as well as economic values. . . . We mention these noneconomic values to emphasize that standing may stem from them as well as from the economic injury on which petitioners rely here. Certainly he who is 'likely to be financially' injured, FCC v. Sanders Bros. Radio Station, 309 U.S. 470 (1940), may be a reliable private attorney general to litigate the issues of the public interest in the present case. . . . Where statutes are concerned, the trend is toward enlargement of the class of people who may protest administrative action. The whole drive for enlarging the category of aggrieved 'persons' is symptomatic of that trend."

Concurring in the result, JUSTICE BRENNAN dissented from the zone of interests inquiry the majority adopted for not opening up standing enough: "The Court's approach to standing . . . , set out in Data Processing, has two steps: (1) . . . determine 'whether the plaintiff alleges that the challenged action has caused him injury in fact;' (2) determine 'whether the interest sought to be protected by the complainant is arguably within the zone of interests to be protected or regulated by the statute or constitutional guarantee in question.' My view is that the inquiry in the Court's first step is the only one that need be made to determine standing. . . . By requiring a second, nonconstitutional step, the Court comes very close to perpetuating the discredited requirement that conditioned standing on a showing by the plaintiff that the challenged governmental action invaded one of his legally protected interests."

Data Processing has come in for its share of criticism. See, e.g., Cass Sunstein, Injury-In-Fact Transformed, 2021 Sup. Ct. Rev. 349, 355–60 (arguing that Data Processing and Davis "essentially jettisoned" and "egregiously misread" the APA). The decision represented an effort to expand access to the courts at a time of expansion in agencies' regulatory responsibilities and growing concern about agencies being captured by the very industries and entities they regulated. But as TransUnion makes clear (p. 1446), over time the injury-in-fact requirement has become an obstacle for standing for regulatory beneficiaries.

(2) ***Finding Surrogates to Speak for the Intended Beneficiaries of Regulation.*** In general, courts are extremely reluctant to allow a party to litigate anyone's interest but her own. Recall that Allen (p. 1426) identifies the "jus tertii" principle—no raising the rights of third parties—as one of the prudential restrictions on standing. Presumably, the intended beneficiaries of the common bond requirement at issue in NCUA were credit union members, who would benefit insofar as the requirement ensures credit unions' financial strength. Do you think that the actual challengers in NCUA—five national banks and the American Bankers Association—were also intended beneficiaries? If not, why shouldn't the intended beneficiaries of regulation speak for themselves? Do you think credit union members could establish standing to complain that the Comptroller's approach might allow credit unions to get too big and threaten their financial security? Recall that, under Lujan and Spokeo, standing requires an individualized, actual injury caused by the Comptroller's decision.

If it's unlikely that intended beneficiaries could get (or would be motivated to seek) standing—perhaps because the collective nature of the regulatory goods produced makes it difficult to establish individualized injury—does that justify allowing competitors to sue as a surrogate? On the other hand, if expanding the scope of what counts as a common bond actually enhances credit union financial strength, as the NCUA argued, why should banks be able to sue to assert their competitive interests to the potential disadvantage of credit union members, the provision's intended beneficiaries?

(3) ***Is the Zone of Interests Requirement Doing Any Work?*** Dissenting in NCUA, Justice O'Connor complains that the majority's approach to the zone of interest test makes it meaningless; any plaintiff who meets the Article III standing requirements will fall within the zone of interest. Is she right? How often will plaintiffs be outside of the zone of interests under the majority's approach? And if Justice O'Connor is right, is that a bad thing? After all, Justice Brennan argued in Data Processing that a plaintiff need

only satisfy the requirements of Article III to bring suit under the APA. Is that a plausible reading of the text of APA § 702?

(4) ***Is the Court Drawing Consistent Lines?*** One case where the zone-of-interest test operated to prevent suit was AIR COURIER CONFERENCE OF AMERICA V. AMERICAN POSTAL WORKERS UNION, AFL-CIO, 498 U.S. 517 (1991). There, as discussed in NCUA, postal employee unions tried to challenge a Postal Service rule allowing private couriers to deliver foreign address letters to foreign post offices as violating Private Express Statutes (PES), which gave the Postal Service a statutory monopoly over the carriage of mail. The Court ruled that the unions did not fall within the PES' zone of interests: "[T]he provisions [of the PES] . . . indicate that the congressional concern was not with opportunities for postal workers but with the receipt of necessary revenues for the Postal Service. . . . The PES enable the Postal Service to fulfill its responsibility to provide service to all communities at a uniform rate. . . . If competitors could serve the lower cost segment of the market, leaving the Postal Service to handle the high-cost services, the Service would lose lucrative portions of its business, thereby increasing its average unit cost and requiring higher prices to all users. The postal monopoly, therefore, exists to ensure that postal services will be provided to the citizenry at large, and not to secure employment for postal workers."

The NCUA majority insisted that Air Courier was distinguishable, but can the result in Air Courier really be squared with the result in NCUA? Are the interests of the national banks in NCUA—essentially, to advance their own economic interests at the expense of credit unions—more plausibly within the zone of interests of the FCUA than the postal employees' interests are within the zone of interests of the PES? For that matter, is Air Courier distinguishable from other precedent—specifically, Data Processing, Arnold Tours, ICI, and Clarke—in which the Court found the zone of interests test satisfied? For a discussion of the Court's zone of interests precedent and an argument that the zone is currently applied incoherently and that courts should instead allow any plaintiffs with constitutional standing to sue unless Congress has adopted a more restrictive rule, see Jonathan R. Siegel, Zone of Interests, 92 Geo. L.J. 317 (2004).

(5) ***Statutory Abrogation of the Zone Requirement.*** Because the zone of interests restriction is prudential, Congress can dispense with it. Bennett v. Spear, 520 U.S. 154 (1997) (p. 1543), involved a citizen suit provision allowing "any person" to bring suit for a violation of the Endangered Species Act. The Court read this language as expressing congressional intent to confer standing to the full extent that Article III permits and rejected the argument that the plaintiffs, seeking to prevent application of environmental restrictions rather than to enforce them, fell outside the ESA's zone of interests.

Note that Congress sometimes also legislates in the opposite direction, by restricting who can sue under a statute to include only regulated parties. For an example of when the Court found that Congress limited judicial review to a particular group of regulated entities, see Block v. Community Nutrition Inst., 467 U.S. 340 (1984) (p. 1510).

(6) ***The Current Status of the Zone of Interests Test.*** The Supreme Court has repeatedly reiterated that the zone of interests test "is not meant to be 'especially demanding.' . . . [W]e have often 'conspicuously included the word 'arguably' in the test to indicate that the benefit of any doubt goes to the plaintiff,' and have said that the test 'forecloses suit only when a plaintiff's 'interests are so marginally related to or inconsistent with the purposes implicit in the statute that it cannot reasonably be assumed that' Congress authorized that plaintiff to sue. That lenient approach is an appropriate means of preserving the flexibility of the APA's omnibus judicial-review provision, which permits suit for violations of numerous statutes of varying character that do not themselves include causes of action for judicial review." LEXMARK INTERNATIONAL V. STATIC CONTROL COMPONENTS, INC., 572 U.S. 118, 130 (2014) (quoting MATCH-E-BE-NASH-SHE-WISH BAND OF POTTAWATOMI INDIANS V. PATCHAK, 567 U.S. 209, 225 (2012)). In PATCHAK, the Court held that a neighboring landowner fell within the zone of interests of the Indian Reorganization Act to challenge the Secretary of the Interior's ability to take title to property on behalf of a nonfederally recognized tribe. Justice Kagan's majority opinion emphasized that the statute concerned itself not only with land acquisition but also with land use, and therefore the landowner's allegations of economic, environmental, and aesthetic injury resulting from the planned establishment of a casino fell into the zone of interests to be protected by the IRA.

The zone of interests test arose in recent high-profile challenges to the Trump Administration's transfer and reprogramming of funds to build a wall on the southern border. (For a discussion of these challenges in terms of congressional and presidential struggles over control of federal funds, see Chapter VII, p. 901, p. 1053, and in terms of congressional standing, p. 1477.) In February 2019, Congress appropriated some, but by no means not all, of the funds requested by the Trump Administration for the border wall construction. Shortly thereafter, the Acting Secretary of Defense, relying on Section 8005 of the Department of Defense (DoD) Appropriations Act of 2019, transferred funds that had been appropriated for other purposes to fund the construction of the wall. Section 8005 provided that the Secretary of Defense, with the approval of OMB, may transfer up to $4 billion in particular types of funds to different appropriations accounts upon making a "determination . . . that such action is necessary in the national interest," but not in any case "where the item for which funds are requested has been denied by the Congress."

In CALIFORNIA V. TRUMP, 963 F.3d 926 (9th Cir. 2020), vacated and remanded sub. nom. Biden v. Sierra Club, 142 S.Ct. 46 (2021), CHIEF JUDGE THOMAS wrote for a 2–1 majority in concluding that California and New Mexico, two border states affected environmentally by the wall, had standing and satisfied the APA's zone-of-interest test. Emphasizing Lexmark and Patchak's statements that the test was not supposed to be especially demanding, the appellate court invoked obstacles to congressional standing as a reason to apply the test particularly broadly here: "In enacting [§] 8005, Congress primarily intended to benefit itself and its constitutional power to manage appropriations. . . . The field of suitable challengers must be construed broadly in this context because, although [§] 8005's obligations were intended to protect Congress, restrictions on congressional standing make it difficult for Congress to enforce these obligations itself. . . .

"California and New Mexico are suitable challengers because their interests are congruent with those of Congress and are not 'inconsistent with the purposes implicit in the statute.' Patchak, 567 U.S. at 225. First, this challenge actively furthers Congress's intent to 'tighten congressional control of the reprogramming process.' H.R. Rep. No. 93-662, at 16 (1973). In particular, this challenge furthers this intent because, even though [§] 8005 does not require formal congressional approval to reprogram funds, the congressional committees expressly disapproved of DoD's use of the authority here. . . . California and New Mexico's interest in reinforcing these structural separation of powers principles [of congressional control over appropriations] is unique but aligned with that of Congress because just as those principles are intended 'to protect each branch of [the federal] government from incursion by the others,' the 'allocation of powers in our federal system [also] preserves the integrity, dignity, and residual sovereignty of the States' . . . Bond v. United States, 564 U.S. 211, 221–22 (2011). This interest applies with particular force here because the use of [§] 8005 here impacts California's and New Mexico's ability to enforce their state environmental laws. . . . [T]he use of [§] 8005 allows the [federal] government . . . to waive state environmental law requirements for purposes of building the border wall. Thus, [§] 8005's limitations protect California's and New Mexico's sovereign interests, just as they protect Congress's constitutional interests, because they ensure that, ordinarily, Executive action cannot override these interests without congressional approval and funding. . . .

"Moreover, that the states regularly benefit from DoD's use of [§] 8005 reinforces that California and New Mexico's interests are not 'so marginally related' that 'it can[ ] reasonably be assumed that Congress intended to permit suit.' For instance, in . . . 2008 DoD invoked [§] 8005 to finance costs incurred by the National Guard in responding to Hurricane Gustav in Louisiana, Texas, Mississippi, and Alabama, as well as operations related to Hurricane Ike in Texas and Louisiana. . . . The historical use of [§] 8005 supports that states are reasonable and predictable challengers to its use, and this instance is no anomaly."

JUDGE COLLINS dissented. "Although the[ ] standards [of the APA's zone of interests test] are generous, the States have failed to satisfy them. . . . [T]he interests that the States claim are affected by the agency action in question are not among the interests arguably to be protected by § 8005. In particular, the States' asserted environmental interests clearly lie outside the zone of interests protected by § 8005. The statute does not mention environmental interests, nor does it require the Secretary to consider such interests." Judge Collins also rejected the majority's arguments that California and New Mexico fell within the zone of interests because states regularly benefit from DoD's use of § 8005 and that the states' interests were congruent with those of Congress, the primary intended beneficiary of § 8005: "California and New Mexico made no showing whatsoever that, in the absence of these transfers to the Drug Interdiction and Counter-Drug Activities, Defense appropriation, the funds in question would otherwise have been transferred for the direct benefit of either State." Collins added that he was "aware of no precedent that would support the view that California and New Mexico can represent the interests of Congress . . . , much less that the States can do so merely because they are sympathetic to Congress's perceived policy objectives. . . . The critical flaw in the majority's analysis is that it rests, not on the interests asserted by the States (preservation of the flat-tailed horned lizard, etc.), but on the legal theory that the States invoke to protect those interests here. But the zone of interests test focuses on the former and not the latter." Judge Collins questioned the claim "that no one will ever be able to sue for any violation of § 8005 . . . , but in any event, we are not entitled to bend the otherwise applicable—and already lenient—standards to ensure that someone will be able to sue in this case or others like it."

## SECTION 2. REVIEWABILITY, TIMING, AND REMEDIES



The lawyer considering a lawsuit to challenge agency action must resolve many of the same questions that occur in planning any federal litigation. In addition to standing, discussed in the preceding Section, these include:

- Which courts are available? (jurisdiction and venue) If more than one is available, what are the advantages and disadvantages of each forum?
- What causes of action are possible? (reviewability) Are some claims more desirable than others, in the procedural advantages they offer and the substantive claims and defenses they permit?
- When can the action be brought? When is too early? (exhaustion, finality, ripeness) When is too late? (statute of limitations and mootness)
- What remedies are available, and do the remedies vary with different causes of action and different defendants? (remedies) Here, plaintiffs face an obstacle not present in federal-question suits between private parties: sovereign immunity. The federal government (including agencies) is immune from suit unless Congress has given consent.

These questions are explored in this Section. We begin with a brief overview of different bases of jurisdiction and of the background presumption of reviewability the Supreme Court found in the APA. We then turn to issues of preclusion of judicial review, timing of judicial review, and the different remedies available. You'll see that, whereas standing doctrine is heavily constitutional and judge-made, in this Section the APA is often of paramount importance. Critical language from the APA is reproduced at the outset of each subsection where relevant below, but before going farther you may find it helpful to read through the APA's provisions on judicial review in their entirety, 5 U.S.C. §§ 701–706, located in the Appendix (p. 1600).

## a. Methods of Obtaining Review

***(1) Special Statutory Review***
***(2) General Statutory Review***
***(3) "Nonstatutory" Review***

The methods of obtaining review of agency action are conventionally grouped into three categories, which are described in order below:

1. Special Statutory Review: Review authorized by the particular organic statute(s) under which the agency is acting.
2. General Statutory Review: Review authorized by the APA.
3. "Nonstatutory Review": The somewhat confusing name for the category that originally comprised common-law and equity forms of action but now also includes actions authorized by statutes *other* than the agency's organic statute or the APA.

### (1) Special Statutory Review

*The form of proceeding for judicial review is the special statutory review proceeding relevant to the subject matter in a court specified by statute or, in the absence or inadequacy thereof, any applicable form of legal action . . . .*

5 U.S.C. § 703

Not surprisingly, regulatory statutes often contain provisions specifically authorizing judicial review of at least some of the actions in which the agency engages. A good example is 29 U.S.C. § 160(f), which provides that "[a]ny person aggrieved by a final order of the [NLRB] granting or denying in whole or in part the relief sought may obtain a review of such order in [the appropriate] United States court of appeals."

Searching the relevant organic statute(s) for such provisions—which define what § 703 terms a "special statutory review proceeding"—is the lawyer's first step. Why? Such provisions often designate the level of the court system (i.e., district or appellate) at which review is to be initiated. Moreover, they are usually interpreted as performing several other important tasks—in particular, granting subject matter jurisdiction, providing a cause of action, and waiving sovereign immunity for claims within their scope. In addition, these provisions might also specify venue, set a statute of limitations, determine whether certain intra-agency remedies must be exhausted, confer standing, and provide supplementary or alternative standards of review.

Unlike ordinary civil litigation, the typical special statutory review proceeding (evidenced in 29 U.S.C. § 160(f)'s text above) begins directly in the court of appeals, when a party files a petition for review.[1] The reason Congress so often chooses to site review in the circuit courts is that the record on which agency action is reviewed is almost always the record created *at the agency*. Therefore, there is no need for the district court's capacity to hold evidentiary hearings.

Another important species of special statutory review proceeding is the "enforcement action." Even agencies that are broadly authorized to investigate and adjudicate alleged wrongdoing and impose sanctions are usually not empowered to use self-help to enforce those sanctions. If the regulated entity does not voluntarily accept the penalty imposed, the agency typically has to petition a court for a judicial order of enforcement. Here again, a good example involves the NLRB, which 29 U.S.C. § 160(e) provides "shall have power to petition any court of appeals of the United States . . . for the enforcement of [a cease-and-desist unfair labor practice order]." In deciding whether to issue this order, the court reviews the agency's decision just as if an aggrieved person had filed a petition for review and indeed often confronts cross-petitions for review—one from the agency seeking to have its sanction enforced and one from the regulated entity seeking to have it vacated.

APA § 703 expressly acknowledges that a special statutory review proceeding might be "absen[t] or inadequa[te]." The first of these situations occurs when the relevant statute does not mention judicial review at all. Such silence is usually construed as not precluding general statutory (APA) or nonstatutory review. (See Section 2.a.2, p. 1506) Alternatively, the statute might provide for review of agency action other than the particular type about which the litigant wishes to complain. Here, too, selective silence is usually not interpreted to preclude other avenues of review. Whether alternative forms of review are available will depend on the court's assessment in light of the legislative evidence and regulatory objectives of the particular administrative scheme, and whether Congress intended the special review proceeding to be exclusive—even with its alleged shortcomings.

---

[1] Some statutes, especially in the environmental area, consolidate review in the D.C. Circuit. Otherwise, the petition can usually be filed in any circuit in which the petitioner resides or the cause of action arose. But through a combination of statutory direction and litigant choice, the D.C. Circuit hears the lion's share of petitions for review of rules. There are also important instances of special statutory review sited in the district court, such as review of Social Security benefit denials or terminations. See 42 U.S.C. §§ 405(g), 421(d).

### (2) General Statutory Review

*Agency action made reviewable by statute and final agency action for which there is no other adequate remedy in a court are subject to judicial review.*

5 U.S.C. § 704

If a special statutory review proceeding is absent, inadequate, or deemed nonexclusive, the cause of action most commonly used is the one created by the APA itself in § 704. But an APA provision is not a grant of subject matter jurisdiction. Califano v. Sanders, 430 U.S. 99 (1977). Typically, the lack of subject matter jurisdiction is easily remedied by pleading 28 U.S.C. § 1331, the general federal-question statute. As a result, such a review proceeding under the APA typically begins in the trial court, which almost invariably means a longer course of litigation. Ambiguity about whether a special statutory proceeding applies, or is intended to be exclusive, tends to be resolved in favor of the special statutory process.

There is one significant exception to the rule that general statutory review begins in the district court. In the important and widely followed decision Telecommunications Research & Action Center v. FCC, 750 F.2d 70 (D.C. Cir. 1984) (TRAC), the D.C. Circuit held that where an organic statute commits review of *final* agency action to the court of appeals, that court has exclusive jurisdiction over *all* suits seeking relief that "might affect" its future statutory review power.

### (3) "Nonstatutory" Review

Nonstatutory review has produced some of our most important opinions defining the legitimate scope of government action: Marbury v. Madison, 5 U.S. (1 Cranch) 137 (1803); Osborn v. Bank of the United States, 22 U.S. (9 Wheat.) 738 (1824); and Youngstown Sheet and Tube Co. v. Sawyer, 343 U.S. 579 (1952) (p. 933). Born of the need to provide some avenue for judicial review of official conduct when sovereign immunity had not been waived, nonstatutory review proceeds against the official individually. When the 1976 amendments established unambiguously that APA-based review could proceed against agencies by name without sovereign immunity concerns, the need for nonstatutory forms of review disappeared in the typical case seeking review of agency rulemaking or administrative adjudication.

However, APA-based review does not serve every need. The government official or entity whose action is challenged may not be within the purview of the APA. Or the action complained of may not be reachable under that statute. Finally, the injured party may find the APA cause of action insufficient because she principally desires compensation rather than prospective relief. In such circumstances, and lacking any usable special statutory review proceeding, the lawyer looks for an appropriate form of "nonstatutory review."[2]

Today, statutes codify, supplement, or sometimes even supplant original, nonstatutory forms. As a result, "nonstatutory review" is a term of art that includes certain obviously statutory proceedings. Equitable actions for relief against government officers are an important form of nonstatutory review that remains uncodified (other than under 42 U.S.C. § 1983 with respect to state officers). Other forms of "nonstatutory" relief include actions for declaratory relief and the prerogative writs, of which habeas and mandamus remain the most relevant. For these, statutory bases do exist, in the Declaratory Judgment Act, 28 U.S.C. § 2201, the All Writs Act, 28 U.S.C. § 1651, and 28 U.S.C. §§ 1361, 2255. Another important form of relief is damages actions against federal officers for violation of legal rights. These different forms of action are described in greater detail in Section 2.d (p. 1550) on Remedies.

In Armstrong v. Exceptional Child Center, Inc., 575 U.S. 320 (2015), the Court stated that "[t]he ability to sue to enjoin unconstitutional actions by state and federal officers is the creation of courts of equity, and reflects a long history of judicial review of illegal executive action, tracing back to England." Moreover, the Court emphasized that as a "judge-made remedy," it is "subject to express and implied statutory limitations." Armstrong involved a suit challenging Idaho's state Medicaid plan as violating § 30(A) of the Medicaid Act. The Court concluded that the "Medicaid Act implicitly precludes private enforcement of § 30(A)" and thus no challenge to agency action was available based on the statute. The Court further held that the "Supremacy Clause is not the source of any federal rights . . . and certainly does not create a cause of action."

The question of whether a nonstatutory equitable right of action is available to enforce the Appropriations Clause or a statutory restriction on the transfer of appropriated funds, and whether any such action would be subject to the same zone of interests test as a suit under the APA, arose in litigation challenging the Trump Administration's transfer of funds to build a border wall. In SIERRA CLUB V. TRUMP, 963 F.3d 874 (9th Cir. 2020), vacated sub nom. Biden v. Sierra Club, 142 S.Ct. 46 (2021)—a companion case to California v. Trump (p. 1487)—the Ninth Circuit addressed whether two organizations had an equitable, constitutional, or ultra vires cause of action to challenge the transfer. The Supreme Court had stayed the district court's injunction prohibiting the government's use of the funds, stating that "the Government has made a sufficient showing at this stage that the plaintiffs have no cause of action." On remand to the Ninth Circuit, CHIEF JUDGE THOMAS, writing for a 2–1 panel, concluded that Sierra Club had a constitutional cause of action and an ultra vires cause of action:

---

[2] For a lucid and illuminating examination of the history and forms of nonstatutory review, see Jonathan R. Siegel, Suing the President: Nonstatutory Review Revisited, 97 Colum. L. Rev. 1612 (1997).

"Certain provisions of the Constitution give rise to equitable causes of action. Such causes of action are most plainly available with respect to provisions conferring individual rights[,] . . . [b]ut certain structural provisions give rise to causes of action as well" when "government action . . . violates structural constitutional provisions intended to protect individual liberties. We have held that the Appropriations Clause contains such a cause of action. See McIntosh [v. United States], 833 F.3d [1163,] 1173–74 [(2016)]. . . . The cause of action available to the plaintiffs in McIntosh is available to Sierra Club here. Congress decided the order of priorities for border security. In doing so, . . . [i]t declined to provide additional funding for projects in other areas, and it declined to provide the full $5.7 billion sought by the President: it is for the courts to enforce Congress's priorities, and we do so here. Where plaintiffs, like Sierra Club, establish that they satisfy the requirements of Article III standing, they may invoke separation-of-powers constraints, like the Appropriations Clause, to challenge agency spending in excess of its delegated authority."

Chief Judge Thomas then turned to whether Sierra Club had an equitable ultra vires cause of action as well: "Equitable actions to enjoin ultra vires official conduct do not depend upon the availability of a statutory cause of action; instead, they seek a judge-made remedy for injuries stemming from unauthorized government conduct, and they rest on the historic availability of equitable review. . . . Such causes of action have been traditionally available in American courts. . . . The passage of the APA has not altered this presumption" that "review of ultra vires actions" is available. Thomas also rejected the federal government's argument that the APA zone of interests test would apply to such an implied equitable claim, noting that Lexmark "clarifies that the test applies only to statutory causes of action and causes of action under the APA. . . . Common sense supports this approach. . . . Otherwise, a meritorious litigant, injured by ultra vires action, would seldom have standing to sue since the litigant's interest normally will not fall within the zone of interests of the very statutory or constitutional provision that he claims does not authorize action concerning that interest."

JUDGE COLLINS dissented: "Even assuming that an equitable cause of action to enjoin unconstitutional conduct exists alongside the APA's cause of action, . . . it avails the Organizations nothing here. The Organizations have failed to allege the sort of constitutional claim that might give rise to such an equitable action, because their 'constitutional' claim is effectively the very same § 8005-based claim dressed up in constitutional garb." He also maintained that the majority's approach "cannot be squared with the Supreme Court's decision in Armstrong" rejecting a cause of action for equitable relief based on the Supremacy Clause. Finally, Judge Collins argued that any equitable action would be subject to statutory limitations and to traditional limitations governing equitable claims, one of which is the requirement "that a plaintiff's grievance must arguably fall within the zone of interests protected or regulated by the statutory provision or constitutional guarantee invoked in the suit. . . . And given the unique nature of an Appropriations Clause claim . . . the line between constitutional and unconstitutional conduct here is defined entirely by the limitations in § 8005, and therefore the relevant zone of interests for the Organizations' Appropriations-Clause-based equitable claim remains defined by those limitations."

In July 2021, the Supreme Court vacated the Ninth Circuit's decision after the Biden Administration decided to revoke the diversion of funds and halted construction of the border wall. As a result, whether the longstanding equitable constitutional or ultra vires actions apply here—and if so, whether the zone of interests test attaches—remains unresolved. Were the Court to hold that the zone of interests test does apply, would that suggest that other APA requirements might also apply to a nonstatutory cause of action? What then makes a nonstatutory cause of action distinct?

## b. Preclusion of Judicial Review

***(1) The Presumption That Agency Action Is Reviewable***
***(2) Statutory Preclusion of Review***
***(3) Committed to Agency Discretion by Law***

*This chapter [i.e., §§ 701–706] applies, according to the provisions thereof, except to the extent that—*

*(1) statutes preclude judicial review; or*

*(2) agency action is committed to agency discretion by law.*

5 U.S.C. § 701(a)

If the organic statute does not expressly authorize judicial review of a particular agency action—either because it's completely silent on review or because its review provisions don't expressly mention the type of action complained of—the court must determine whether review is nonetheless available. The answer almost invariably begins with the framework established by first case below, Abbott Labs v. Gardner. Like the Data Processing opinion (p. 1484) on standing three years later, it substantially altered existing concepts of justiciability and laid the groundwork for the contemporary era of judicial review.

Abbott Labs is a watershed case on both *whether* review is available and *when* it can occur. The second of these, the issue of "ripeness," is taken up in Section 2.c.3 (p. 1545). Here, we focus on reviewability per se. As Abbott explains, the APA strongly favors review but does not universally guarantee it. Section 701 establishes two sets of circumstances in which, notwithstanding the "presumption" of review, the APA will not assist a party seeking judicial scrutiny of agency behavior. These circumstances—when statutes preclude judicial review and when an agency action is committed to agency discretion by law—are explored in the materials that follow.

## (1) The Presumption That Agency Action Is Reviewable



## ABBOTT LABORATORIES v. GARDNER

Supreme Court of the United States (1967).
387 U.S. 136.

■ JUSTICE HARLAN delivered the opinion of the Court.

[The 1962 amendments to the Federal Food, Drug, and Cosmetic Act required manufacturers of prescription drugs to print the "established [i.e., generic] name" of the drug "prominently and in type at least half as large as that used thereon for any proprietary [i.e., brand] name or designation for such drug" on labels and other printed material. FDA conducted a rulemaking on how to implement the new amendments, and adopted the following requirement:

> If the label or labeling of a prescription drug bears a proprietary name or designation for the drug or any ingredient thereof, the established name, if such there be, corresponding to such proprietary name or designation, shall accompany each appearance of such proprietary name or designation.

The so-called "every time" standard was also applied to advertisements. Shortly after the rule became final, 37 drug manufacturers and the Pharmaceutical Manufacturers Association (which included more than 90 percent of U.S. prescription drug manufacturers) sued, arguing that the FDA had exceeded its statutory authority. The district court agreed and granted declaratory and injunctive relief; the court of appeals reversed on grounds that (i) pre-enforcement review was not authorized by the Act; and (ii) because none of the plaintiffs had yet been accused of violating the rule, no "actual case or controversy" existed.]

The first question we consider is whether Congress by the Federal Food, Drug, and Cosmetic Act intended to forbid pre-enforcement review of this sort of regulation promulgated by the Commissioner. The question is phrased in terms of "prohibition" rather than "authorization" because a survey of our cases shows that judicial review of a final agency action by an aggrieved person will not be cut off unless there is persuasive reason to believe that such was the purpose of Congress. Early cases in which this type of judicial review was entertained have been reinforced by the enactment of the Administrative Procedure Act, which embodies the basic presumption of judicial review to one "suffering legal wrong because of agency action, or adversely affected or aggrieved by agency action within the meaning of a relevant statute," 5 U.S.C. § 702, so long as no statute precludes such relief or the action is not one committed by law to agency discretion, 5 U.S.C. § 701(a). The Administrative Procedure Act provides specifically not only for review of "[a]gency action made reviewable by statute" but also for review of "final agency action for which there is no other adequate remedy in a court," 5 U.S.C. § 704. The legislative material elucidating that seminal act manifests a congressional intention that it cover a broad spectrum of administrative actions,[2] and this Court has echoed that theme by noting that the Administrative Procedure Act's "generous review provisions" must be given a "hospitable" interpretation. Shaughnessy v. Pedreiro, 349 U.S. 48, 51 [(1955)]. Again in Rusk v. Cort, 369 U.S. 367, 379–380 [(1962)], the Court held that only upon a showing of "clear and convincing evidence" of a contrary legislative intent should the courts restrict access to judicial review.

Given this standard, we are wholly unpersuaded that the statutory scheme in the food and drug area excludes this type of action. The Government relies on no explicit statutory authority for its argument that pre-enforcement review is unavailable, but insists instead that because the statute includes a specific procedure for such review of certain enumerated kinds of regulations, not encompassing those of the kind involved here, other types were necessarily meant to be excluded from any pre-enforcement review. The issue, however, is not so readily resolved; we must go further and inquire whether in the context of the entire legislative scheme the existence of that circumscribed remedy evinces a congressional purpose to bar agency action not within its purview from judicial review. As a leading authority in this field has noted, "The mere fact that some acts are made reviewable should not suffice to support an implication of exclusion as to others. The right to review is too important to be excluded on such slender and indeterminate evidence of legislative intent." Louis Jaffe, Judicial Control of Administrative Action 357 (1965). . . .

II

A further inquiry must, however, be made. The injunctive and declaratory judgment remedies are discretionary, and courts traditionally have been reluctant to apply them to administrative determinations unless these arise in the context of a controversy "ripe" for judicial resolution. Without undertaking to survey the intricacies of the ripeness doctrine it is fair to say that its basic rationale is to prevent the courts, through avoidance of premature adjudication, from entangling themselves in abstract disagreements over administrative policies, and also to protect the agencies from judicial interference until an administrative decision has been formalized and its effects felt in a concrete way by the challenging parties. The problem is best seen in a

[2] See H.R. Rep. No. 1980, 79th Cong., 2d Sess., 41 (1946):

To preclude judicial review under this bill a statute, if not specific in withholding such review, must upon its face give clear and convincing evidence of an intent to withhold it. The mere failure to provide specially by statute for judicial review is certainly no evidence of intent to withhold review.

twofold aspect, requiring us to evaluate both the fitness of the issues for judicial decision and the hardship to the parties of withholding court consideration.

As to the former factor, we believe the issues presented are appropriate for judicial resolution at this time. First, all parties agree that the issue tendered is a purely legal one: whether the statute was properly construed by the Commissioner to require the established name of the drug to be used *every time* the proprietary name is employed. Both sides moved for summary judgment in the District Court, and no claim is made here that further administrative proceedings are contemplated. It is suggested that the justification for this rule might vary with different circumstances, and that the expertise of the Commissioner is relevant to passing upon the validity of the regulation. This of course is true, but the suggestion overlooks the fact that both sides have approached this case as one purely of congressional intent, and that the Government made no effort to justify the regulation in factual terms.

Second, the regulations in issue we find to be "final agency action" within the meaning of [APA] § 704, as construed in judicial decisions. . . . The regulation challenged here . . . was made effective upon publication, and the Assistant General Counsel for Food and Drugs stated in the District Court that compliance was expected. . . .

This is also a case in which the impact of the regulations upon the petitioners is sufficiently direct and immediate as to render the issue appropriate for judicial review at this stage. These regulations purport to give an authoritative interpretation of a statutory provision that has a direct effect on the day-to-day business of all prescription drug companies; its promulgation puts petitioners in a dilemma that it was the very purpose of the Declaratory Judgment Act to ameliorate. As the District Court found on the basis of uncontested allegations, "Either they must comply with the every time requirement and incur the costs of changing over their promotional material and labeling or they must follow their present course and risk prosecution." . . . If petitioners wish to comply . . . they must destroy stocks of printed matter and they must invest heavily in new printing type and new supplies. The alternative to compliance—continued use of material which they believe in good faith meets the statutory requirements, but which clearly does not meet the regulation of the Commissioner—may be even more costly. That course would risk serious criminal and civil penalties for the unlawful distribution of "misbranded" drugs.

It is relevant at this juncture to recognize that petitioners deal in a sensitive industry, in which public confidence in their drug products is especially important. To require them to challenge these regulations only as a defense to an action brought by the Government might harm them severely and unnecessarily. Where the legal issue presented is fit for judicial resolution, and where a regulation requires an immediate and significant change in the plaintiffs' conduct of their affairs with serious penalties attached to noncompliance, access to the courts under the Administrative Procedure Act and the Declaratory Judgment Act must be permitted, absent a statutory bar or some other unusual circumstance. . . .

Finally, the Government urges that to permit resort to the courts in this type of case may delay or impede effective enforcement of the Act. We fully recognize the important public interest served by assuring prompt and unimpeded administration of the Pure Food, Drug, and Cosmetic Act, but we do not find the Government's argument convincing. First, in this particular case, a pre-enforcement challenge by nearly all prescription drug manufacturers is calculated to speed enforcement. If the Government prevails, a large part of the industry is bound by the decree; if the Government loses, it can more quickly revise its regulation.

. . . [I]t is important to note that the institution of this type of action does not by itself stay the effectiveness of the challenged regulation. There is nothing in the record to indicate that petitioners have sought to stay enforcement of the "every time" regulation pending judicial review. See 5 U.S.C. § 705. If the agency believes that a suit of this type will significantly impede enforcement or will harm the public interest, it need not postpone enforcement of the regulation and may oppose any motion for a judicial stay on the part of those challenging the regulation. It is scarcely to be doubted that a court would refuse to postpone the effective date of an agency action if the Government could show, as it made no effort to do here, that delay would be detrimental to the public health or safety.

[On the merits, the Court remanded the case to allow the court of appeals to decide the statutory authority question. Shortly before reargument there, the FDA and industry reached a settlement that produced the rule still in effect today: the generic name must appear every time the brand name is "featured," but the rule for "running text" is much looser. For illuminating behind-the-scenes details of the litigation, see Ronald M. Levin, The Story of the Abbott Labs Trilogy: The Seeds of the Ripeness Doctrine 430, in Administrative Law Stories (Peter L. Strauss ed., 2006).]

[On the same day as Abbott Laboratories, the Court decided two companion cases, TOILET GOODS ASS'N, INC. V. GARDNER, 387 U.S. 158 (1967), and GARDNER V. TOILET GOODS ASS'N, INC., 387 U.S. 167 (1967). The majority denied pre-enforcement review in the first and allowed it in the second; these holdings are considered further below in the materials on ripeness, Section 2.c.3 (p. 1545).]

■ JUSTICE FORTAS, dissented in Gardner v. Toilet Goods Ass'n, in an opinion that applied to Abbott Labs as well:

. . . The Court, by today's decisions[,] . . . has opened Pandora's box. Federal injunctions will now threaten programs of vast importance to the public welfare. . . . [I]t can hardly be hoped that some federal judge somewhere will not be moved as the Court is here, by the cries of anguish and distress of those regulated, to grant a disruptive injunction.

. . . [T]he Court has concluded that the damage to petitioners if they have to engage in the required redesign and reprint of their labels and printed materials without threshold review outweighs the damage to the public of deferring during the tedious months and years of litigation a cure for the possible danger and asserted deceit of peddling plain medicine under fancy trademarks and for fancy prices which, rightly or wrongly, impelled the Congress to enact this legislation. I submit that a much stronger showing is necessary than the expense and trouble of compliance and the risk of defiance. Actually, if the Court refused to permit this shotgun assault, experience and reasonably sophisticated common sense show that there would be orderly compliance without the disaster so dramatically predicted by the industry, reasonable adjustments by the agency in real hardship cases, and where extreme intransigence involving substantial violations occurred, enforcement actions in which legality of the regulation would be tested in specific, concrete situations. I respectfully submit that this would be the correct and appropriate result. Our refusal to respond to the vastly overdrawn cries of distress would reflect not only healthy skepticism, but our regard for a proper relationship between the courts on the one hand and Congress and the administrative agencies on the other. It would represent a reasonable solicitude for the purposes and programs of the Congress. And it would reflect appropriate modesty as to the competence of the courts.

## NOTES

(1) ***Does the APA Support a Presumption of Reviewability?*** Is the APA best read as embodying a presumption of judicial review, as the Abbott Labs Court held? No, says NICHOLAS BAGLEY in THE PUZZLING PRESUMPTION OF REVIEWABILITY, 127 Harv. L. Rev. 1285, 1304–06 (2014): "Per § 701(a), the sections providing for judicial review apply 'except to the extent that . . . statutes preclude judicial review.' Preclusion is a threshold inquiry: only where Congress has not precluded judicial review do § 702 and § 704 call for review as the default. . . . The point is significant. A presumption must be overcome: to reject it, an interpreter must point to affirmative evidence (how much evidence depends on the strength of the presumption) that Congress meant something other than what it is presumed to have meant. That's not what the APA tells courts to do, however. Instead, the APA establishes a default rule favoring review where no statute precludes it. In other words, it supplies a rule of decision only after a court determines that the statute, fairly read, doesn't shut off review. . . . [T]he APA does not tell courts to discard the best interpretation of a statute in favor of a second- or third-best alternative that would allow for judicial review."

Do you agree that the APA simply imposes a default rule favoring review if the best reading of the statute does not preclude it? Consider whether the language of § 701(a), stating that the APA's judicial review provisions apply except if "statutes preclude judicial review" or the "action is committed to agency discretion," could be read as providing that judicial review should be available unless there is some affirmative basis in the governing statute (e.g., preclusion, discretion) to conclude otherwise. Does a presumption in favor of reviewability require more?

Abbott Labs does not delve much into the APA's legislative history, but in a subsequent case, BOWEN V. MICHIGAN ACADEMY OF FAMILY PHYSICIANS, 476 U.S. 667 (1986), the Court quoted the legislative reports on the APA in support of a strong endorsement of the presumption of reviewability: "In undertaking the comprehensive rethinking of the place of administrative agencies in a regime of separate and divided powers that culminated in the passage of the [APA], the Senate Committee on the Judiciary remarked:

> Very rarely do statutes withhold judicial review. It has never been the policy of Congress to prevent the administration of its own statutes from being judicially confined to the scope of authority granted or to the objectives specified. Its policy could not be otherwise, for in such a case statutes would in effect be blank checks drawn to the credit of some administrative officer or board.

The Committee on the Judiciary of the House of Representatives agreed that Congress ordinarily intends that there be judicial review and emphasized the clarity with which a contrary intent must be expressed:

> The statutes of Congress are not merely advisory when they relate to administrative agencies, any more than in other cases. To preclude judicial review under this bill a statute, if not specific in withholding such review, must upon its face give clear and convincing evidence of an intent to withhold it. The mere failure to provide specially by statute for judicial review is certainly no evidence of intent to withhold review.

How clear are these legislative materials? If you have read the materials in Chapter III on the history of the APA, you know that the APA represented a hard-fought compromise between opponents and defenders of the New Deal administrative state. As a result, the legislative reports have long been thought "demonstrably unreliable guides to what Congress meant the APA to accomplish." Bagley, supra, at 1307. Expansive access to judicial review had been the mantra of the administrative state's opponents, but by the time the APA was enacted, the courts were full of judges appointed by FDR who accepted the constitutionality of administrative action. See George B. Shepherd, Fierce Compromise: The Administrative Procedure Act Emerges from New Deal Politics, 90 Nw. U. L. Rev. 1557, 1644 (1996). And as political winds shifted over the years, the party not in the White House has tended to favor more judicial review as a check on the opposing administration. This may have been reason why members of Congress from both camps were content to leave the question of whether to preclude judicial review in the hands of future Congresses. See Daniel Rodriguez, The Presumption of Reviewability: A Study in Canonical Construction and Its Consequences, 45 Vand. L. Rev. 743, 752–57 (1992).

(2) ***Are Reviewability and Timing Separate Questions?*** Justice Harlan treats the questions of reviewability and timing as separate questions in Abbott Labs. But is that accurate? Is there any doubt that the every-time standard would be reviewable in an enforcement action brought by FDA against a drug manufacturer who refused to comply? Given that review was indisputably available at enforcement, should the Court have invoked the

presumption of reviewability as a basis for upholding pre-enforcement review? Many preclusion cases similarly involve statutes that provide for judicial review, but at a later juncture. (See the discussion of alternative avenues to review, Note 5, p. 1515, and of pre-enforcement review, p. 1547.)

(3) ***Is the Presumption of Reviewability Justified?*** Separate from questions about its basis in the APA, is the presumption of reviewability articulated in Abbott Labs nonetheless justified? Here again, BAGLEY, supra, at 1287–88, answers in the negative: "As with any canon of statutory construction that serves a substantive end, it should find a source in history, positive law, the Constitution, or sound policy considerations. None of these, however, offers a plausible justification for the presumption. As for history, the sort of judicial review that the presumption favors—appellate-style arbitrariness review—was not only unheard of prior to the twentieth century, but was commonly thought to be unconstitutional. . . . [A]lthough the text and structure of the Constitution may prohibit Congress from precluding review of constitutional claims, a presumption responsive to constitutional concerns would favor review of constitutional claims, not any and all claims of agency wrongdoing.

"As for policy considerations, judicial review might improve the fairness, quality, and legality of agency decisionmaking. But it also introduces delay, diverts agency resources, upsets agency priorities, and shifts authority within agencies toward lawyers and away from policymakers. Congress has the constitutional authority, democratic legitimacy, and institutional capacity to understand and to trade off these competing values. Courts do not. Nor is there reason to think that the presumption allows courts to better capture Congress's intent. . . . As Justice Frankfurter put it seventy years ago, 'engraft[ing] upon remedies which Congress saw fit to particularize . . . impliedly denies to Congress the constitutional right of choice in the selection of remedies.' [Stark v. Wickard, 321 U.S. 288, 314–15 (1944) (Frankfurter, J., dissenting).] Dishonoring Congress's choices limits its ability to tailor its administrative and regulatory schemes to their particular contexts." See also Rodriguez, supra, at 766–67 (1992) (arguing that the presumption imposes costs on courts and Congress).

If you've read Chapter VIII on judicial review, you'll have seen particular concerns raised about the broad availability of judicial review in the context of rulemaking, which a number of scholars contend has "ossified" the rulemaking process and led agencies to pursue less open and effective methods of policymaking (p. 1152). Abbott Labs, in creating a presumption in favor of pre-enforcement judicial review, was a critical jurisdictional development that helped fuel the modern expansion of judicial review of rulemaking.

Do you agree with Bagley that the costs of the presumption outweigh its benefits? The difficult issue of whether, and if so when, the Constitution requires judicial review is discussed in the Note below. But separate from any constitutional requirement, does this argument give adequate weight to the importance of judicial review in legitimating administrative action? Consider Louis L. Jaffe's famous statement that "[t]he availability of judicial review is the necessary condition, psychologically if not logically, of a system of administrative power which purports to be legitimate, or legally valid." Judicial Control of Administrative Action 320 (1965). If he's right, does that justify the presumption?

Whether the presumption has a historical basis is also a matter of debate. In Bowen, 476 U.S. at 670, the Supreme Court traced the presumption back to the origins of judicial review: "In Marbury v. Madison, 5 U.S. 163 (1803), a case itself involving review of executive action, Chief Justice Marshall insisted that '[t]he very essence of civil liberty certainly consists in the right of every individual to claim the protection of the laws.' " Later, in the lesser known but nonetheless important case of United States v. Nourse, 34 U.S. 8, 28–29 (1835), the Chief Justice noted the traditional observance of this right and laid the foundation for the modern presumption of judicial review:

> It would excite some surprise if, in a government of laws and of principle, furnished with a department whose appropriate duty it is to decide questions of right, not only between individuals, but between the government and individuals, a ministerial officer might, at his discretion, issue this powerful process . . . leaving to the debtor no remedy, no appeal to the laws of his country, if he should believe the claim to be unjust. But this anomaly does not exist; this imputation cannot be cast on the legislature of the United States.

Although these sources emphasize the historical importance of judicial review of executive action, scholars have emphasized that such suits fell into narrow categories: either an action for a prerogative writ (usually mandamus) that was rarely granted, or a common law suit against an officer that could impose damages. Officer suits also could take the form of actions for equitable relief. See Jerry L. Mashaw, Creating the Administrative Constitution 24–25 (2012); Thomas W. Merrill, Article III, Agency Adjudication, and the Origins of the Appellate Review Model of Administrative Law, 111 Colum. L. Rev. 939, 946–53 (2011). Bagley argues that these actions do not support the presumption because they were quite limited and did not take the form of appellate review of agency action, the common form of judicial review after enactment of the APA and the context in which the presumption is applied today. Are you convinced?

## NOTE ON THE CONSTITUTIONALITY OF PRECLUDING REVIEW

As mentioned above, concern about the constitutionality of precluding all judicial review is often invoked to justify the presumption of reviewability. Several leading reviewability decisions often note constitutional concerns as one reason to find judicial review not precluded. But whether some form of judicial review is constitutionally required is the subject of extensive scholarship and one of the most difficult questions in the course on federal courts. To date, only two Supreme Court decisions have directly held clear statutory provisions precluding review to be unconstitutional, United States v. Klein, 80 U.S. 128 (1871), and

Boumediene v. Bush, 553 U.S. 723 (2008), with the former being notoriously opaque in its reasoning and the latter resting on restrictions the Constitution imposes on suspending the writ of habeas corpus in Article I, § 9, rather than on Article III. Much of the reason for this lack of authority is that Congress generally wants judicial review and precludes it entirely only rarely. Federal Courts courses typically address this question in depth; what follows merely sketches the contours of the debate.

The problem begins with the language of Article III. Although contemporary lawyers take the extensive federal court system for granted, very little of that system is explicitly mandated by the Constitution. Article III, § 1 provides, "The judicial Power of the United States shall be vested in one Supreme court, and in such inferior Courts as the Congress may from time to time ordain and establish." This language, known as the Madisonian Compromise, was adopted as a compromise between framers who initially sought a full system of federal courts and those who resisted lower federal courts altogether and preferred that federal judicial business take place in state courts. Moreover, even with respect to the Supreme Court, Article III confers "appellate Jurisdiction, both as to Law and Fact, with such Exceptions, and under such Regulations as the Congress shall make." Hence, even if the Supreme Court's narrow original jurisdiction is constitutionally protected, Article III makes access to the Supreme Court's much broader appellate jurisdiction contingent on congressional authorization.

The traditional view is that Congress has plenary power over the jurisdiction of both Supreme and lower federal courts. This view draws some support from history and precedent. Early on, the Court took the position that Article III is not self-executing—i.e., the federal courts, even the Supreme Court, require an affirmative *statutory* grant of jurisdiction. In all the years since the Constitution was adopted, the full range of federal judicial power defined in Article III has never been statutorily vested in either the Supreme Court or the lower federal courts.[3] And there is language in the few Supreme Court cases on point that supports the view that Congress has plenary power over the jurisdiction of the lower courts, see Sheldon v. Sill, 49 U.S. (8 How.) 441 (1850), and the Supreme Court's appellate jurisdiction, see Ex parte McCardle, 74 U.S. (7 Wall.) 506 (1868). Those adhering to the plenary power interpretation of Article III typically urge that Congress should not use its power to withdraw jurisdiction but insist that the power does exist as part of the constitutional system of checks and balances.[4] Notably, however, the plenary power view does not entail accepting that there could be *no* judicial forum for asserting constitutional claims. Rather, as Henry Hart put it, the concern that Congress might leave constitutional rights without a remedy is answered by "[t]he state courts. In the scheme of the Constitution, they are the primary guarantors of constitutional rights, and in many cases they may be the ultimate ones." The

---

[3] For example, the statutory grant of diversity jurisdiction has always included an amount in controversy limitation.

[4] See, e.g., Paul Bator, Congressional Power Over the Jurisdiction of the Federal Courts, 27 Vill. L. Rev. 1030, 1037–41 (1982); Gerald Gunther, Congressional Power to Curtail Federal Court Jurisdiction: An Opinionated Guide to the Ongoing Debate, 36 Stan. L. Rev. 895, 908–12 (1984).

Power of Congress to Limit the Jurisdiction of the Federal Courts: An Exercise in Dialectic, 66 Harv. L. Rev. 1362, 1401 (1953).

Two principal types of theories have emerged as alternatives to the traditional, plenary power view. One type, "essential function" arguments, uses constitutional history, structure, and purpose to insist that Congress cannot withdraw jurisdiction when the result would be to vitiate the essential functions of the federal judiciary.[5] The second type, "independent unconstitutionality" arguments, finds limits on Congress's jurisdiction-withdrawing power in constitutional provisions outside Article III. On the most basic level, virtually all commentators (including traditional plenary power advocates) agree that Congress cannot limit judicial review through a restriction that itself violates some specific constitutional right—for example, closing the courthouse doors to African Americans or Jews. "Independent unconstitutionality" theorists argue for even broader limitations, with some contending, for example, that the equal protection clause, and perhaps substantive due process, prevent Congress from withdrawing jurisdiction over particular kinds of cases (e.g., school prayer challenges) because of hostility to the Court's holdings in the area.[6] The Supreme Court has signaled that due process may prohibit certain forms of preclusion, holding that "where a determination made in an administrative proceeding is to play a critical role in the subsequent imposition of a criminal sanction, there must be *some* meaningful review of the administrative proceeding." United States v. Mendoza-Lopez, 481 U.S. 828, 837–38 (1987). But the scope of any such limits remains murky, in no small part because the Supreme Court bends over backwards to read preclusion provisions so as to avoid constitutional concerns.

In the administrative context, judges and scholars have also suggested that separation of powers principles beyond Article III might justify a requirement of some judicial review of agency action. This argument emphasizes that under the Constitution agencies can only wield power that Congress has delegated to them, and therefore individuals subject to agency action have a constitutional right to challenge agency action as unauthorized. See, e.g., Ethyl Corp. v. EPA, 541 F.2d 1, 68 (1976) (Leventhal, J., concurring) ("Congress has been willing to delegate its legislative powers broadly and courts have upheld such delegation because there is court review to assure that the agency exercises the delegated power within statutory limits, and that it fleshes out objectives within those limits by an administration that is not irrational or discriminatory.") Yet such an argument runs into a number of obstacles, including the Supreme Court's insistence that the constitutionality of a delegation turns solely on whether

---

[5] See, e.g., Leonard Ratner, Majoritarian Constraints on Judicial Review: Congressional Control of Supreme Court Jurisdiction, 27 Vill. L. Rev. 929 (1982); Lawrence Sager, Constitutional Limitations on Congress' Authority to Regulate the Jurisdiction of the Federal Courts, 95 Harv. L. Rev. 17 (1981); see also James Pfander, One Supreme Court: Supremacy, Inferiority, and the Judicial Power of the United States (Oxford University Press, 2009) (arguing that the Supreme Court must have sufficient appellate jurisdiction to preserve its hierarchically superior role in the federal court system).

[6] See, e.g. Laurence H. Tribe, Jurisdictional Gerrymandering: Zoning Disfavored Rights Out of the Federal Courts, 14 Harv. C.R.-C.L. L. Rev. 129 (1981).

Congress has provided sufficient guidance and not on alternative checks against agency abuse of power. See Whitman v. American Trucking Ass'ns, 531 U.S. 457 (2001) (p. 848). In addition, this delegation argument would seem to require Congress to create lower federal courts, at odds with plenary power view, and further would call into question Congress's power to ever preclude judicial review, at odds with longstanding doctrine and the APA.

## (2) Statutory Preclusion of Review

*BOWEN v. MICHIGAN ACADEMY OF FAMILY PHYSICIANS*
*Block v. Community Nutrition Institute*

## BOWEN v. MICHIGAN ACADEMY OF FAMILY PHYSICIANS

Supreme Court of the United States (1986).
476 U.S. 667.

■ JUSTICE STEVENS delivered the opinion of the Court.

[Michigan Academy, an association of family physicians, and several individual family physicians challenged a regulation of the Secretary of Health and Human Services that set higher Medicare reimbursement levels for board-certified family physicians than for identical services performed by non-board-certified family physicians. They claimed this distinction violated both the Medicare Act and the Fifth Amendment. The lower courts agreed with their statutory argument and hence did not reach the constitutional claim. In seeking certiorari, the Secretary did not challenge the decision on the merits but contended only that the Act precluded review.]

We begin with the strong presumption that Congress intends judicial review of administrative action. From the beginning "our cases [have established] that judicial review of a final agency action by an aggrieved person will not be cut off unless there is persuasive reason to believe that such was the purpose of Congress." Abbott Laboratories v. Gardner, 387 U.S. 136, 140 (1967). [Justice Stevens traced the presumption back to Marbury v. Madison, 5 U.S. 163 (1803) and United States v. Nourse, 34 U.S. 8, 9 Pet. 8, 28–29 (1835), and also emphasized that "[c]ommittees of both Houses of Congress have endorsed this view" in the APA.] Taking up the language in the House Committee Report [on the APA, Abbott Labs] reaffirmed . . . that "only upon a showing of clear and convincing evidence of a contrary legislative intent should the courts restrict access to judicial review." This standard has been invoked time and again when considering whether the Secretary has discharged "the heavy burden of overcoming the strong presumption that Congress did not mean to prohibit all judicial review of his decision," Dunlop v. Bachowski, 421 U.S. 560, 567 (1975).[3]

Subject to constitutional constraints, Congress can, of course, make exceptions to the historic practice whereby courts review agency action. The presumption of judicial review is, after all, a presumption, and "like all presumptions used in interpreting statutes, may be overcome. . . ." Block v. Community Nutrition Institute, 467 U.S. 340, 349 (1984) [p. 1510]. In this case, the Government asserts that two statutory provisions remove the Secretary's regulation from review under the grant of general federal-question jurisdiction found in 28 U.S.C. § 1331. [The first of the Government's arguments was for implied preclusion, the second for express preclusion.]

II

[The government rested its implied preclusion argument on a distinction between Part A of the Medicare program, which established a federally administered insurance plan (mandatory for all Medicare participants) that covers a portion of costs such as hospitalization, and Part B, which established an optional coverage plan, provided by private insurance carriers under contract with HHS, that Medicare participants can purchase to supplement Part A benefits. The challenged regulation was promulgated under Part B. Specifically, the government claimed "that 42 U.S.C. § 1395ff(b), which authorize[d] 'Appeal by individuals,' impliedly foreclose[d] administrative or judicial review of any action taken under Part B of the Medicare program by failing to authorize such review while simultaneously authorizing administrative and judicial review of 'any determination . . . as to . . . the amount of benefits under [P]art A,' § 1395ff(b)(1)(C)."]

Section 1395ff on its face is an explicit authorization of judicial review, not a bar. As a general matter, "[t]he mere fact that some acts are made reviewable should not suffice to support an implication of exclusion as to others. The right to review is too important to be excluded on such slender and indeterminate evidence of legislative intent." Abbott Laboratories v. Gardner, 387 U.S. at 141.

In the Medicare program, however, the situation is somewhat more complex.... Subject to an amount-in-controversy requirement, individuals aggrieved by delayed or insufficient payment with respect to benefits payable under Part B are afforded an "opportunity for a fair hearing by the *carrier*," § 1395u (emphasis added); in comparison, and subject to a like amount-in-controversy requirement, a similarly aggrieved individual under Part A is entitled "to a hearing thereon by the *Secretary* . . . and to judicial review," § 1395ff(b). "In the context of the statute's precisely drawn provisions," we held in United States v. Erika, Inc., 456 U.S. 201, 208 (1982), that the failure "to authorize further

[3] Of course, this Court has "never applied the clear and convincing evidence standard in the strict evidentiary sense;" nevertheless, the standard serves as "a useful reminder to courts that, where substantial doubt about the congressional intent exists, the general presumption favoring judicial review of administrative action is controlling." Block v. Community Nutrition Inst., 467 U.S. 340, 350–51 (1984).

review for determinations of the amount of Part B awards . . . provides persuasive evidence that Congress deliberately intended to foreclose further review of such claims." Not limiting our consideration to the statutory text, we investigated the legislative history which "confirm[ed] this view," and disclosed a purpose to " avoid overloading the courts" with "trivial matters," a consequence which would "unduly ta[x]" the federal court system with "little real value" to be derived by participants in the program ( . . . 118 Cong. Rec. 33992 (1972) (remarks of Sen. Bennett)).

Respondents' federal-court challenge to the validity of the Secretary's regulation is not foreclosed by § 1395ff as we construed that provision in Erika. The reticulated statutory scheme, which carefully details the forum and limits of review of "any determination . . . of . . . the amount of benefits under part A," § 1395ff(b), and of the "amount of . . . payment" of benefits under Part B, § 1395u, simply does not speak to challenges mounted against the *method* by which such amounts are to be determined rather than the *determinations* themselves. As the Secretary has made clear, "the legality, constitutional or otherwise, of any provision of the Act or regulations relevant to the Medicare Program" is not considered in a "fair hearing" held by a carrier to resolve a grievance related to a determination of the amount of a Part B award. As a result, an attack on the validity of a regulation is not the kind of administrative action that we described in Erika as an "amount determination" which decides "the amount of the Medicare payment to be made on a particular claim" and with respect to which the Act impliedly denies judicial review.

That Congress did not preclude review of the method by which Part B awards are computed (as opposed to the computation) is borne out by the very legislative history we found persuasive in Erika. [Justice Stevens quotes the House and Senate Reports on the original legislation and the Conference Committee Report on pertinent 1972 amendments, all referring to complaints regarding "the amount of benefits."] Senator Bennett's introductory explanation to the amendment confirms that preclusion of judicial review of Part B awards—designed "to avoid overloading the courts with quite minor matters"—embraced only "decisions on a claim for payment for a given service." The Senator feared that "[i]f judicial review is made available where any claim is denied, as some court decisions have held, the resources of the Federal court system would be unduly taxed and little real value would be derived by the enrollees. The proposed amendment would merely clarify the original intent of the law and prevent the overloading of the courts with trivial matters because the intent is considered unclear." . . .

Careful analysis of the governing statutory provisions and their legislative history thus reveals that Congress intended to bar judicial review only of determinations of the amount of benefits to be awarded under Part B. Congress delegated this task to carriers who would finally determine such matters in conformity with the regulations and instructions of the Secretary. We conclude, therefore, that those matters which Congress did *not* leave to be determined in a "fair hearing" conducted by the carrier—including challenges to the validity of the

Secretary's instructions and regulations—are not impliedly insulated from judicial review by [§ 1395ff].

III

In light of Congress' express provision for carrier review of millions of what it characterized as "trivial" claims, it is implausible to think it intended that there be *no* forum to adjudicate statutory and constitutional challenges to regulations promulgated by the Secretary. The Government nevertheless maintains that this is precisely what Congress intended to accomplish [when it incorporated by reference § 405(h) of the Social Security Act into § 1395ii of the Medicare Act. Section 405(h) provides:]

> Finality of Secretary's decision
>
> The findings and decision of the Secretary after a hearing shall be binding upon all individuals who were parties to such hearing. No findings of fact or decision of the Secretary shall be reviewed by any person, tribunal, or governmental agency except as herein provided. No action against the United States, the Secretary, or any officer or employee thereof shall be brought under section 1331 or 1346 of title 28 to recover on any claim arising under this subchapter.

The Government contends that the third sentence of § 405(h) by its terms prevents any resort to the grant of general federal-question jurisdiction contained in 28 U.S.C. § 1331. . . . Respondents counter that . . . Congress' purpose was to make clear that whatever specific procedures it provided for judicial review of final action by the Secretary were exclusive, and could not be circumvented by resort to the general jurisdiction of the federal courts.

. . . [W]e need not pass on the meaning of § 405(h) in the abstract to resolve this case. Section 405(h) does not apply on its own terms to Part B of the Medicare program, but is instead incorporated mutatis mutandis by § 1395ii. The legislative history of both the statute establishing the Medicare program and the 1972 amendments thereto provides specific evidence of Congress' intent to foreclose review only of "amount determinations"—i.e., those "quite minor matters," (remarks of Sen. Bennett), remitted finally and exclusively to adjudication by private insurance carriers in a "fair hearing." By the same token, matters which Congress did *not* delegate to private carriers, such as challenges to the validity of the Secretary's instructions and regulations, are cognizable in courts of law. In the face of this persuasive evidence of legislative intent, we will not indulge the Government's assumption that Congress contemplated review by carriers of "trivial" monetary claims, but intended no review at all of substantial statutory and constitutional challenges to the Secretary's administration of Part B of the Medicare program. This is an extreme position, and one we would be most reluctant to adopt without "a showing of clear and convincing evidence," Abbott Laboratories v. Gardner, 397 U.S. at 141, to overcome the "strong presumption that Congress did not mean to prohibit all judicial review" of executive action, Dunlop v. Bachowski, 421 U.S. at 567. We ordinarily presume that Congress intends the executive to obey its statutory commands and, accordingly, that it expects the courts to grant relief when an executive agency violates such a command. That presumption has not been surmounted here.[12]

The judgment of the Court of Appeals is affirmed.

## SIGNIFICANT CASE

### BLOCK v. COMMUNITY NUTRITION INSTITUTE
467 U.S. 340 (1984).

The Agricultural Marketing Agreement Act directs the Secretary of Agriculture to adopt "milk marketing orders" setting minimum prices that milk handlers must pay to milk producers. These orders are formulated through a rulemaking process that includes public hearing and comment, but can become effective only on the vote of a majority of handlers and a supermajority of producers. In general, milk to be sold as fresh milk falls into higher price categories than milk to be processed into cheese or yogurt. An order formulated several years before this lawsuit had assigned reconstituted milk (milk made by adding water to milk powder) to one of the higher price classes.

The plaintiffs—who included consumers and a nonprofit organization, CNI, that promoted good nutrition for lower income families—petitioned the Secretary to begin a rulemaking to reclassify reconstituted milk to a lower price category. The Secretary invited comments on this proposal, but there the process stalled. Eventually, plaintiffs filed suit challenging both inaction on their rulemaking petition and the original marketing order. This prompted the Secretary to announce that he would not proceed further with the proposed rulemaking, and the inaction claim was dismissed as moot. The district court held that the consumers and nonprofit organization had no standing to challenge the marketing order, and that review was precluded. The court of appeals reversed on both issues; as to reviewability, it concluded that the structure and purposes of the Act did not reveal "the type of clear and convincing evidence of congressional intent needed to overcome the presumption in favor of judicial review."

The Supreme Court unanimously reversed (Justice Stevens did not participate). JUSTICE O'CONNOR:

"The presumption favoring judicial review of administrative action is just that—a presumption. [It] may be overcome by specific language or specific legislative history that is a reliable indicator of Congressional intent[,] contemporaneous judicial construction barring review and the congressional acquiescence in it, or the collective import of legislative and judicial history behind a particular statute. More important for purposes

[12] Our disposition avoids the "serious constitutional question" that would arise if we construed § 1395ii to deny a judicial forum for constitutional claims arising under part B of the Medicare program. . . .

of this case, the presumption favoring judicial review of administrative action may be overcome by inferences of intent drawn from the statutory scheme as a whole. See, e.g., Switchmen v. National Mediation Board, 320 U.S. 297 (1943). . . .

"This Court has . . . never applied the 'clear and convincing evidence' standard in the strict evidentiary sense the Court of Appeals thought necessary in this case. Rather, the Court has found the standard met, and the presumption favoring judicial review overcome, whenever the congressional intent to preclude judicial review is 'fairly discernible in the statutory scheme.' [Data Processing], 397 U.S. at 157 [p. 1484]. In the context of preclusion analysis, the 'clear and convincing evidence' standard is not a rigid evidentiary test but a useful reminder to courts that, where substantial doubt about the congressional intent exists, the general presumption favoring judicial review of administrative action is controlling. That presumption does not control in cases such as this one, however, since the congressional intent to preclude judicial review is 'fairly discernible' in the detail of the legislative scheme . . ."

Justice O'Connor noted that the original 1933 statute contained no judicial review provision. A 1935 amendment that did not mention consumers provided that handlers could seek review of marketing orders, but only after exhausting specified administrative remedies. "Nowhere in the Act . . . is there an express provision for participation by consumers in any proceeding. In a complex scheme of this type, the omission of such a provision is sufficient reason to believe that Congress intended to foreclose consumer participation in the regulatory process. . . . [T]he preclusion issue does not only turn on whether the interests of a particular class like consumers are implicated. Rather, the preclusion issue turns ultimately on whether Congress intended for that class to be relied upon to challenge agency disregard of the law. . . .

"Allowing consumers to sue the Secretary would severely disrupt this complex and delicate administrative scheme. It would provide handlers with a convenient device for evading the statutory requirement that they first exhaust their administrative remedies. A handler may also be a consumer and, as such, could sue in that capacity. Alternatively, a handler would need only to find a consumer who is willing to join in or initiate an action in the district court. The consumer or consumer-handler could then raise precisely the same exceptions that the handler must raise administratively. . . . For these reasons, we think it clear that Congress intended that judicial review of market orders issued under the Act ordinarily be confined to suits brought by handlers in accordance with 7 U.S.C. § 608c(15).

". . . [P]reclusion of consumer suits will not threaten realization of the fundamental objectives of the statute. Handlers have interests similar to those of consumers. Handlers, like consumers, are interested in obtaining reliable supplies of milk at the cheapest possible prices. Handlers can therefore be expected to challenge unlawful agency action and to ensure that the statute's objectives will not be frustrated. . . ."

## NOTES

(1) ***Are Bowen and CNI Consistent?*** Bowen was issued two years after CNI. Are the two decisions consistent in their approach to finding preclusion and the presumption of reviewability? In CNI, the Court downplayed the presumption of reviewability, whereas the Bowen Court put heavy emphasis on the presumption. What are we to make of the fact that neither opinion drew separate concurrences or dissents (although Justice Stevens, author of the latter opinion, did not participate in the former case)?

Is the statutory basis for preclusion stronger in CNI than in Bowen? Note that in CNI, no one argued that marketing orders, as a category of agency action, were unreviewable; the 1935 amendments expressly provided for their review. The focus was on *who* can get review, with CNI's reference to whether a "class" was entitled to invoke judicial review sounding more aligned with a zone of interests inquiry than preclusion (see Section 1.e, p. 1478). By contrast, in Bowen, the issue was whether there would be any review of regulations setting out reimbursement methodology, a clearer case of preclusion of a category of agency action.

Does this difference make the presumption of reviewability more relevant in Bowen, and the argument for preclusion more troubling? Or does the fact that review was already available in CNI make the Court's decision to deny review at consumers' behest more puzzling? Here it's worth emphasizing that the handlers could get judicial review but first had to exhaust administrative remedies. (For discussion of exhaustion, see Section 2.c.1, p. 1534.) Is the concern that direct suit by consumers might allow handlers to avoid this exhaustion requirement? If so, another way to address this concern would be to allow consumers to sue but subject them also to the exhaustion requirement. Is extending exhaustion a less plausible reading of the statute than finding preclusion?

Perhaps the difference is simply, as Justice O'Connor argues, that foreclosing consumer suits "will not threaten realization of the fundamental objectives of the statute," given the availability of some judicial review. This fits with her argument that handlers will be adequate surrogates for consumers. But do you think they will be? A better justification for preclusion in CNI could be that the Agricultural Marketing Agreement Act and its provisions for judicial review represent a carefully wrought compromise between milk producers and handlers that excludes consumers. But does that argument fit with the Act's provision for public hearings and comment? Note that at the time the Act was adopted in the 1930s, consumer suits were not within legal contemplation. In any event, why isn't the same legislative compromise point available with respect to Medicare and its carefully articulated opportunities for review?

(2) ***"Implied" Preclusion: A Wrong Turn in APA Interpretation?*** Both Bowen and CNI involved claims for implied statutory preclusion. Abbott Labs admits the possibility that a statute could implicitly foreclose review, and the Supreme Court has continued to affirm that position. See Sackett v. EPA, 566 U.S. 120, 128 (2012) (p. 1540). But look again at the language of § 701(a)(1). Should this provision *ever* be satisfied by anything short of an

*explicit* statutory direction that review not occur? For a historical argument that the correct answer to this question is no, see Daniel Rodriguez, The Presumption of Reviewability: A Study in Canonical Construction and Its Consequences, 45 Vand. L. Rev. 743, 754–57 (1992).

(3) ***Narrow Reading of Express Preclusion Provisions.*** Bowen also involved a statutory provision expressly precluding review, § 405(h) of the Social Security Act (incorporated into the Medicare Act). As Bowen suggests, the Supreme Court has read express preclusion clauses narrowly and applied the presumption of reviewability. Should the preclusion analysis be the same, however, when there is an express preclusion provision? In particular, should the presumption of reviewability apply in this context?

Compare Bowen with CUOZZO SPEED TECHNOLOGIES, LLC. V. LEE, 579 U.S. 261 (2016), where the Court found that 35 U.S.C. § 314(d), stating that the "determination by the [Patent Office on] whether to institute an inter partes review under this section shall be final and nonappealable," precluded "judicial review of the kind of mine-run claim at issue here, involving the Patent Office's decision to institute inter partes review." Writing for a 7–2 majority on the issue, JUSTICE BREYER argued that the § 314(d)'s text and purpose required preclusion. "We recognize the strong presumption in favor of judicial review that we apply when we interpret statutes, including statutes that may limit or preclude review. Mach Mining, LLC v. EEOC, 135 S.Ct. 1645, 1650–51 (2015) [p. 1523] This presumption, however, may be overcome by 'clear and convincing' indications, drawn from 'specific language,' 'specific legislative history,' and 'inferences of intent drawn from the statutory scheme as a whole,' that Congress intended to bar review. (quoting Block). That standard is met here. . . . Nevertheless, in light of § 314(d)'s own text and the presumption favoring review, we emphasize that our interpretation applies where the grounds for attacking the decision to institute inter partes review consist of questions that are closely tied to the application and interpretation of statutes related to the Patent Office's decision to initiate inter partes review. . . . This means that we need not, and do not, decide the precise effect of § 314(d) on appeals that implicate constitutional questions, that depend on other less closely related statutes, or that present other questions of interpretation that reach, in terms of scope and impact, well beyond 'this section.' "

(4) ***All Claims Are Not Equal.*** RONALD M. LEVIN, UNDERSTANDING UNREVIEWABILITY IN ADMINISTRATIVE LAW, 74 Minn. L. Rev. 689, 739–40 (1990): "[T]he Court tends to allow some issues to be precluded more readily than other issues. At the top of the scale, . . . the presumption against preclusion of constitutional grievances against an agency is practically irrebuttable. The Court also has proved less willing to find preclusion in cases involving administrative rules than in cases involving agency adjudication, and less willing to foreclose legal challenges than factual ones, especially where the legal issues are not within the administering agency's expertise. At the bottom of the hierarchy are issues of fact and application of law to fact, which the Court allows to be precluded more readily than any others."

Are you surprised by the Court's greater willingness to find judicial review of factual questions precluded than review of legal ones, or to find preclusion in cases involving individual adjudications rather than general rules? Or by its deep resistance to finding judicial review precluded in constitutional challenges? A good example of this resistance is JOHNSON V. ROBISON, 415 U.S. 361 (1974), involving a constitutional challenge to a statutory provision that denied veterans' educational benefits to conscientious objectors who had completed alternative service. Invoking Abbott Labs' clear and convincing evidence standard for finding preclusion, the Court ruled that 38 U.S.C. § 211(a), providing that the Veterans Affairs Administrator's "decisions . . . on any question of law or fact under any law administered by the Veterans' Administration providing benefits for veterans . . . shall be final and conclusive and no . . . court of the United States shall have power or jurisdiction to review any such decision," did not preclude judicial review of this claim. Writing for a unanimous Court, JUSTICE BRENNAN began by stating that construing § 211(a) as "bar[ring] federal courts from deciding the constitutionality of veterans' benefits legislation . . . would, of course, raise serious questions concerning the constitutionality of § 211(a), and in such case it is a cardinal principle that this Court will first ascertain whether a construction of the statute is fairly possible by which the [constitutional] question[s] may be avoided. Plainly, no explicit provision of § 211(a) bars judicial consideration of appellee's constitutional claims. . . . The prohibitions would appear to be aimed at review only of those decisions of law or fact that arise in the *administration* by the Veterans' Administration of a *statute* providing benefits for veterans. . . . Appellee's constitutional challenge is not to any such decision of the *Administrator*, but rather to a decision of *Congress* to create a statutory class entitled to benefits that does not include . . . conscientious objectors who performed alternate civilian service."

(5) ***Express Preclusion and Immigration.*** Immigration is an area in which statutory provisions expressly precluding judicial review frequently appear. The Court sometimes invokes the presumption of reviewability as a reason to read these provisions narrowly. See, e.g., Guerrero-Lasprilla v. Barr, 140 S.Ct. 1062, 1069–1070 (2020); Kucana v. Holder, 558 U.S. 233, 251–52 (2010); see also DHS v. Regents of the University of California, 140 S.Ct. 1891, 1905 (2020) (p. 1139) (invoking the APA's presumption of reviewability in concluding that rescission of deferred action immigration policy was reviewable). On other occasions, the Court has read preclusion language capaciously and held the presumption inapplicable. In PATEL V. GARLAND, 142 S.Ct. 1614 (2022), JUSTICE BARRETT wrote for a 5–4 Court in concluding that a statutory provision specifying that "[n]o court shall have jurisdiction to review—any judgment regarding the granting of [discretionary] relief" under enumerated statutes precluded judicial review of the denial of petitioner's request for discretionary relief: "The provision does not restrict itself to certain kinds of decisions. Rather, it prohibits review of any judgment regarding the granting of relief under § 1255 and the other enumerated provisions. As this Court has repeatedly explained, the word 'any' has an expansive meaning." And "[b]ecause the statute is clear, we have no reason to resort to the presumption of reviewability." In dissent,

JUSTICE GORSUCH criticized the majority for "not try[ing] to explain how its interpretation fits with the usual presumption of judicial reviewability of administrative actions—a presumption it claims to endorse and no party before us questions. . . . [A] hunch about unexpressed legislative intentions is no response to our usual presumption of judicial review. Nor is it any answer to the mountain of textual and contextual evidence suggesting that Congress limited judicial review only with respect to second-step discretionary decisions, not decisions about statutory eligibility."

(6) ***Time Limits for Regulatory Challenges.*** Sometimes Congress tries to ensure prompt determination of the validity of regulations by imposing strict statutory time limits (typically, 30–90 days from promulgation) for seeking judicial review. Unexcused failure to obtain pre-enforcement review precludes later attacks on the rule—even as a defense to civil or criminal enforcement proceedings. "Excusable" failure includes situations in which the challenge would not have been ripe within the statutory period. See Eagle-Picher Indus. v. EPA, 759 F.2d 905, 914 (D.C. Cir. 1985).

(7) ***The Effect of Alternative Avenues for Review.*** In THUNDER BASIN COAL CO. V. REICH, 510 U.S. 200 (1994), a mine owner whose workforce was not unionized refused to post information about two United Mine Workers Union employees who had been designated the miners' "representatives"—even though a Department of Labor regulation required such posting. The owner then filed suit in the district court, seeking to enjoin enforcement of the regulation against him. Relying on CNI, the Court held that "[i]n cases involving delayed judicial review, we shall find that Congress has allocated initial review to an administrative body where such intent is fairly discernible in the statutory scheme" and "petitioner's claims are of the type Congress intended to be reviewed within this statutory structure." The Court added that in the past it had "upheld district court jurisdiction over claims considered wholly collateral to a statute's review provisions and outside the agency's expertise, particularly where a finding of preclusion could foreclose all meaningful judicial review." Id. at 207, 212–13.

The Court then unanimously held that there was no jurisdiction over the employer's suit. Under the Federal Mine Safety and Health Amendments Act, challenges to enforcement are first reviewed by the Federal Mine Safety and Health Review Commission (an independent agency created exclusively to adjudicate Mine Act disputes) and then by the appropriate court of appeals. The statute is silent about pre-enforcement review and explicitly provides for review in the district court only in two specific (inapplicable) circumstances. JUSTICE BLACKMUN's opinion concluded that the statute's comprehensive scheme of enforcement and administrative review implicitly precluded a pre-enforcement challenge. The mine owner could obtain review by refusing to comply with the order and forcing the agency to begin enforcement proceedings: "Although the Act's civil penalties unquestionably may become onerous if petitioner chooses not to comply, the Secretary's penalty assessments become final and payable only after full review by both the Commission and the appropriate Court of Appeals."

More recent Supreme Court decisions have split on their willingness to find delayed review schemes to be exclusive. ELGIN V. DEP'T OF TREASURY,

567 U.S. 1 (2012), concerned the Civil Service Reform Act, which sets forth a comprehensive structure for reviewing personnel actions taken against federal employees. Under the CSRA, federal employees who suffer adverse employment actions may seek a hearing before the Merit Systems Protection Board, whose decision is then reviewed by the Federal Circuit. Male employees who had been discharged because they failed to register for the military draft filed suit in federal district court alleging that the Military Selective Service Act and the corresponding statute barring them from federal employment were facially unconstitutional under the Equal Protection and the Bill of Attainder Clauses. In a 6–3 decision written by JUSTICE THOMAS, the Court held that "the CSRA's elaborate framework . . . indicates that extrastatutory review is not available to those employees to whom the CSRA grants administrative and judicial review." The Court further held that meaningful review was available for the plaintiffs' claims because "the CSRA provides review in the Federal Circuit, an Article III court fully competent to adjudicate petitioners' [constitutional] claims" and rejected the plaintiffs' argument that their constitutional challenges were "wholly collateral" to the CSRA scheme. It also rejected the plaintiffs' assertion "that their constitutional claims are not the sort that Congress intended to channel through the MSPB because they are outside the MSPB's expertise," arguing that the plaintiffs "overlook the many threshold questions that may accompany a constitutional claim and to which the MSPB can apply its expertise. Of particular relevance here, preliminary questions unique to the employment context may obviate the need to address the constitutional challenge." Justice Alito dissented, joined by Justices Ginsburg and Kagan.

By contrast, FREE ENTERPRISE FUND V. PUBLIC CO. ACCOUNTING OVERSIGHT BD., 561 U.S. 477 (2010) (PCAOB) (p. 1002) rejected the claim that a statutory provision for judicial review of administrative actions offered the exclusive means for raising a separation-of-powers challenge to the Public Company Accounting Oversight Board (PCAOB). The rules and orders of the PCAOB are reviewable by the SEC whose rules and orders are in turn reviewable by the courts of appeals. The provision for judicial review of SEC actions states that "[n]o objection . . . may be considered by the court unless it was urged before the Commission or there was reasonable ground for failure to do so." 15 U.S.C. § 78y(c)(1). The Court held, with no justice dissenting, that the petitioners could bring their constitutional challenge to removal protections for PCAOB members directly in federal court and did not have to proceed under § 78y: "We do not see how petitioners could meaningfully pursue their constitutional claims under the Government's theory. Section 78y provides only for judicial review of Commission action, and not every Board action is encapsulated in a final Commission order or rule." The Court rejected the argument that the petitioners could have obtained judicial review by refusing to provide information requested by the Board, thereby precipitating the Board to impose sanctions, and then—if the Commission affirmed the sanctions—raising the constitutional challenge on appeal from the Commission's decision. "We normally do not require plaintiffs to bet the farm by taking the violative action before testing the validity of the law." The constitutional claims did not turn on "fact-bound inquiries" that were within the SEC's special competence or "require 'technical considerations of [agency] policy.' Johnson v. Robison, 415 U.S. 361, 373 (1974). They are instead standard questions of administrative law, which the courts are at no disadvantage in answering."

Recently, several courts have addressed whether the statutory provision of administrative enforcement and subsequent judicial review in the securities context precludes immediate access to court. By statute, the SEC can seek civil enforcement of the federal securities laws either by bringing a civil action in federal district court or by initiating an administrative enforcement proceeding. The SEC increased its use of administrative proceedings after the Dodd-Frank Wall Street Reform and Consumer Protection Act expanded the remedies available to it, sparking a raft of constitutional challenges brought in federal court by defendants seeking to prevent administrative enforcement proceedings from going forward. In JARKESY V. SEC, 803 F.3d 9 (D.C. Cir. 2015), the D.C. Circuit held that "Congress has implicitly precluded Jarkesy's district-court suit by channeling his challenges through the securities laws' scheme of administrative adjudication and judicial review in a court of appeals." In so holding, the appeals court emphasized the comprehensiveness of the adjudication structure contained in § 78y, as well as the inseparability of Jarkesy's constitutional challenges from the administrative enforcement proceeding. The D.C. Circuit distinguished Free Enterprise on the ground that "[t]o have his claims heard through the agency route, Jarkesy would not have to erect a Trojan-horse challenge to an SEC rule or 'bet the farm' by subjecting himself to unnecessary sanction under the securities laws. Jarkesy is already properly before the Commission by virtue of his alleged violations of those laws. Indeed, the existence of the enforcement proceedings gave rise to Jarkesy's challenges. And, should the Commission's final order run against him, a court of appeals is available to hear those challenges."

By contrast, in COCHRAN V. SEC, 20 F.4th 194 (5th Cir. 2021), the en banc Fifth Circuit held by a 9–7 vote that a challenge to the constitutionality of adjudication by an SEC ALJ could be brought directly in federal court. In his majority opinion, JUDGE HAYNES argued that "§ 78y provides that only 'person[s] aggrieved by a final order of the Commission' may petition in the relevant court of appeals to review that final order. The statute says nothing about people, like Cochran, who have not yet received a final order of the Commission. Nor does it say anything about people, again like Cochran, who have claims that have nothing to do with any final order that the Commission might one day issue." In addition, "§ 78y(a)(1) is phrased in permissive terms. . . . [I]t does not say that anyone "shall" or "shall not" do anything. It would be troublingly counterintuitive to interpret § 78y(a)(1)'s permissive language as eliminating alternative routes to federal court review, especially in the context of separation-of-powers claims of the sort at issue here." The majority added that "every material aspect of the Supreme Court's reasoning in Free Enterprise Fund would seem to apply with equal force here." The Supreme Court granted certiorari in Cochran, 142 S.Ct. 2707 (2022), as well as in Axon Enterprise, Inc. v. FTC, 142 S.Ct. 895 (2022), a Ninth Circuit case involving the FTC that found preclusion.

(8) ***Preclusion by Statute, Not Regulation.*** KUCANA V. HOLDER, 558 U.S. 233 (2010): An unusual twist on preclusion produced an unusual degree of agreement among the Justices. One of the review-limiting provisions of the Illegal Immigration Reform and Immigrant Responsibility Act of 1996 states that no court shall have jurisdiction to review actions of the Attorney General, "the authority for which is specified under this subchapter to be in the discretion of the Attorney General." The Board of Immigration Appeals had denied Agron Kucana's motion to reopen his removal proceeding on grounds of new evidence to support his plea for asylum. By regulation, the Attorney General had declared that decisions on such motions were "discretionary" actions. The Seventh Circuit held that it could not review. Writing for all members of the Court but Justice Alito, who concurred in the judgment, JUSTICE GINSBURG concluded that the preclusion provision applied only to determinations made discretionary by statute. "If the Seventh Circuit's construction were to prevail, the Executive would have a free hand to shelter its own decisions from abuse-of-discretion appellate court review simply by issuing a regulation declaring those decisions 'discretionary.' Such an extraordinary delegation of authority cannot be extracted from the statute Congress enacted."

## (3) Committed to Agency Discretion by Law

***WEBSTER v. DOE***
***Notes on the Reviewability of Agency Refusals to Act***

## WEBSTER v. DOE

Supreme Court of the United States (1988).
486 U.S. 592.

■ CHIEF JUSTICE REHNQUIST delivered the opinion of the Court.

[John Doe had been employed by the CIA for nine years, during which he was consistently rated an excellent or outstanding employee and was promoted from clerk-typist to covert electronics technician. After Doe voluntarily informed the CIA that he was gay, he was placed on paid administrative leave. He was extensively questioned about possible security breaches in connection with sexual activity and a polygraph indicated that his denials were truthful. The CIA's Office of Security then told Doe that his homosexuality posed a threat to security, although it declined to explain the nature of the danger. When Doe refused to resign, the Office recommended his dismissal to the CIA Director. After reviewing Doe's records and evaluations, the Director dismissed him, invoking § 102(c) of the National Security Act of 1947. Doe sued, alleging that the dismissal (i) was arbitrary and capricious and an abuse of discretion in violation of the APA, and (ii) deprived him of his constitutional rights. He sought reinstatement or, at least, an order that the Director reevaluate the termination and provide a statement of reasons.]

Section 102(c) . . . provides that:

> [T]he Director of Central Intelligence may, in his discretion, terminate the employment of any officer or employee of the Agency whenever he shall deem such termination necessary or advisable in the interests of the United States . . .

In this case we decide whether, and to what extent, the termination decisions of the Director under § 102(c) are judicially reviewable . . .

In Citizens to Preserve Overton Park, Inc. v. Volpe, 401 U.S. 402 (1971) [p. 1145] this Court explained the distinction between §§ 701(a)(1) and (a)(2). Subsection (a)(1) is concerned with whether Congress expressed an intent to prohibit judicial review; subsection (a)(2) applies "in those rare instances where 'statutes are drawn in such broad terms that in a given case there is no law to apply.'" (quoting S.Rep. No. 752, 79th Cong., 1st Sess., 26 (1945)).

We further explained what it means for an action to be "committed to agency discretion by law" in Heckler v. Chaney, 470 U.S. 821 (1985) [p. 1527]. . . . We noted that, under § 701(a)(2), even when Congress has not affirmatively precluded judicial oversight, "review is not to be had if the statute is drawn so that a court would have no meaningful standard against which to judge the agency's exercise of discretion." . . .

Both Overton Park and Heckler emphasized that § 701(a)(2) requires careful examination of the statute on which the claim of agency illegality is based. In the present case, respondent's claims against the CIA arise from the Director's asserted violation of § 102(c) of the NSA. As an initial matter, it should be noted that § 102(c) allows termination of an Agency employee whenever the Director "shall *deem* such termination necessary or advisable in the interests of the United States" (emphasis added), not simply when the dismissal *is* necessary or advisable to those interests. This standard fairly exudes deference to the Director, and appears to us to foreclose the application of any meaningful judicial standard of review . . .

So too does the overall structure of the NSA. Passed shortly after the close of the Second World War, the NSA created the CIA and gave its Director the responsibility "for protecting intelligence sources and methods from unauthorized disclosure." Section 102(c) is an integral part of that statute, because the Agency's efficacy, and the Nation's security, depend in large measure on the reliability and trustworthiness of the Agency's employees . . . Section 102(c) exhibits the Act's extraordinary deference to the Director in his decision to terminate individual employees.

We thus find that the language and structure of § 102(c) indicate that Congress meant to commit individual employee discharges to the Director's discretion, and that § 701(a)(2) accordingly precludes judicial review of these decisions under the APA . . .

In addition to his claim that the Director failed to abide by the statutory dictates of § 102(c), . . . [r]espondent charged that petitioner's termination of his employment deprived him of property and liberty interests under the Due Process Clause of the Fifth Amendment, denied him equal protection of the laws, and unjustifiably burdened his right to privacy. Respondent asserts that he is entitled, under the APA, to judicial consideration of these claimed violations.

. . . It is difficult, if not impossible, to ascertain from the amended complaint whether respondent contends that his termination, based on *his* homosexuality, is constitutionally impermissible, or whether he asserts that a more pervasive discrimination policy exists in the CIA's employment practices regarding *all* homosexuals. This ambiguity in the amended complaint is no doubt attributable in part to the inconsistent explanations respondent received from the Agency itself regarding his termination. Prior to his discharge, respondent had been told by two CIA security officers that his homosexual activities themselves violated CIA regulations. In contrast, the Deputy General Counsel of the CIA later informed respondent that homosexuality was merely a security concern that did not inevitably result in termination, but instead was evaluated on a case-by-case basis.

Petitioner maintains that, no matter what the nature of respondent's constitutional claims, judicial review is precluded by the language and intent of § 102(c). In petitioner's view, all Agency employment termination decisions, even those based on policies normally repugnant to the Constitution, are given over to the absolute discretion of the Director, and are hence unreviewable under the APA. We do not think § 102(c) may be read to exclude review of constitutional claims. We emphasized in Johnson v. Robison, 415 U.S. 361 (1974) [p. 1514], that where Congress intends to preclude judicial review of constitutional claims its intent to do so must be clear . . . We require this heightened showing in part to avoid the "serious constitutional question" that would arise if a federal statute were construed to deny any judicial forum for a colorable constitutional claim. See Bowen v. Michigan Academy of Family Physicians, 476 U.S. 667, 681, n. 12 (1986) [p. 1506].

Our review of § 102(c) convinces us that it cannot bear the preclusive weight petitioner would have it support. [T]he section . . . precludes challenges to [termination] decisions based upon the statutory language of § 102(c), [but] nothing in § 102(c) persuades us that Congress meant to preclude consideration of colorable constitutional claims arising out of the actions of the Director pursuant to that section; we believe that a constitutional claim based on an individual discharge may be reviewed by the District Court . . .

Petitioner complains that judicial review even of constitutional claims will entail extensive "rummaging around" in the Agency's affairs to the detriment of national security. But petitioner acknowledges that Title VII claims attacking the hiring and promotion policies of the Agency are routinely entertained in federal court, and the inquiry and discovery associated with those proceedings would seem to involve some of the same sort of rummaging. Furthermore, the District Court has the latitude to control any discovery process which may be instituted so as to balance respondent's need for access to proof which would support a colorable constitutional claim against the extraordinary needs of the CIA for confidentiality and the protection of its methods, sources, and mission. . . .

The judgment of the Court of Appeals is affirmed in part, reversed in part, and the case is remanded for further proceedings consistent with this opinion.

■ JUSTICE KENNEDY took no part in the consideration or decision of this case.

■ JUSTICE O'CONNOR, concurring in part and dissenting in part.

I agree that the APA does not authorize judicial review [here] . . . I do not understand the Court to say that the exception in § 701(a)(2) is necessarily or fully defined by reference to statutes "drawn in such broad terms that in a given case there is no law to apply." See Citizens to Preserve Overton Park, Inc. v. Volpe, 401 U.S. 402, 410 (1971). . . . I disagree, however, with the Court's conclusion that a constitutional claim challenging the validity of an employment decision covered by § 102(c) may nonetheless be brought in a federal district court. Whatever may be the exact scope of Congress' power to close the lower federal courts to constitutional claims in other contexts, I have no doubt about its authority to do so here. . . .

■ JUSTICE SCALIA, dissenting.

I agree with the Court's apparent holding, that the Director's decision to terminate a CIA employee is "committed to agency discretion by law" . . . Though I subscribe to most of that analysis, I disagree with the Court's description of what is required to come within subsection (a)(2) of § 701 . . . Our precedents amply show that "commit[ment] to agency discretion by law" includes, but is not limited to, situations in which there is "no law to apply. . . ."

The key to understanding the "committed to agency discretion *by law*" provision of § 701(a)(2) lies in contrasting it with the "*statutes* preclude judicial review" provision of § 701(a)(1). Why "statutes" for preclusion, but the much more general term "law" for commission to agency discretion? The answer is, as we implied in [Heckler v.] Chaney, that the latter was intended to refer to "the 'common law' of judicial review of agency action" 470 U.S. [821,] 832 [(1985)]—a body of jurisprudence that had marked out, with more or less precision, certain issues and certain areas that were beyond the range of judicial review. That jurisprudence included principles ranging from the "political question" doctrine, to sovereign immunity (including doctrines determining when a suit against an officer would be deemed to be a suit against the sovereign), to official immunity, to prudential limitations upon the courts' equitable powers, to what can be described no more precisely than a traditional respect for the functions of the other branches . . .

All this law, shaped over the course of centuries and still developing in its application to new contexts, cannot possibly be contained within the phrase "no law to apply." It is not surprising, then, that although the

Court recites the test it does not really apply it. Like other opinions relying upon it, this one essentially announces the test, declares victory and moves on. It is not really true "that a court would have no meaningful standard against which to judge the agency's exercise of discretion." The standard set forth in § 102(c) . . . at least excludes dismissal out of personal vindictiveness, or because the Director wants to give the job to his cousin. Why, on the Court's theory, is respondent not entitled to assert the presence of such excesses, under the "abuse of discretion" standard of § 706? . . .

II.

[Justice Scalia then turned to reviewability of Doe's constitutional claim.] The first response to the Court's grave doubt about the constitutionality of denying all judicial review to a "colorable constitutional claim" is that the denial of all judicial review is not at issue here, but merely the denial of review in United States district courts. As to that, the law is, and has long been, clear. Article III, § 2, of the Constitution extends the judicial power to "all Cases . . . arising under this Constitution." But Article III, § 1, provides that the judicial power shall be vested "in one supreme Court, *and in such inferior Courts as the Congress may from time to time ordain and establish*" (emphasis added). We long ago held that the power not to create any lower federal courts at all includes the power to invest them with less than all of the judicial power. . . . Sheldon v. Sill, 49 U.S. (8 How.) 441, 449 (1850). Thus, if there is any truth to the proposition that judicial cognizance of constitutional claims cannot be eliminated, it is, at most, that they cannot be eliminated from state courts, and from this Court's appellate jurisdiction over cases from state courts . . . .

It can fairly be argued, however, that our interpretation of § 701(a)(2) indirectly implicates the constitutional question whether state courts can be deprived of jurisdiction, because if they cannot, then interpreting § 701(a)(2) to exclude relief here would impute to Congress the peculiar intent to let state courts review Federal Government action that it is unwilling to let federal district courts review . . . . I turn, then, to the substance of the Court's warning that judicial review of all "colorable constitutional claims" arising out of the respondent's dismissal may well be constitutionally required. What could possibly be the basis for this fear? Surely not some general principle that *all* constitutional violations must be remediable in the courts. The very text of the Constitution refutes that principle, since it provides that "[e]ach House shall be the Judge of the Elections, Returns and Qualifications of its own Members," Art. I, § 5, and that "for any Speech or Debate in either House, [the Senators and Representatives] shall not be questioned in any other Place," Art. I, § 6. Claims concerning constitutional violations committed in these contexts—for example, the rather grave constitutional claim that an election has been stolen—cannot be addressed to the courts. Even apart from the strict text of the Constitution, we have found some constitutional claims to be beyond judicial review because they involve "political questions." The doctrine of sovereign immunity—not repealed by the Constitution, but to the contrary at least partly reaffirmed as to the States by the Eleventh Amendment—is a monument to the principle that some constitutional claims can go unheard. . . . [I]t is simply untenable that there must be a judicial remedy for every constitutional violation. . . .

Perhaps, then, a constitutional right is by its nature so much more important to the claimant than a statutory right that a statute which plainly excludes the latter should not be read to exclude the former unless it says so. That principle has never been announced—and with good reason, because its premise is not true. An individual's contention that the Government has reneged upon a $100,000 debt owing under a contract is much more important to him—both financially and, I suspect, in the sense of injustice that he feels—than the same individual's claim that a particular federal licensing provision requiring a $100 license denies him equal protection of the laws, or that a particular state tax violates the Commerce Clause. . . . [A]s between executive violations of statute and executive violations of the Constitution both of which are equally unlawful, and neither of which can be said, a priori, to be more harmful or more unfair to the plaintiff—[there is no reason why] one or the other category should be favored by a presumption against exclusion of judicial review . . .

## NOTES

(1) ***Does Webster's Half-Unreviewable Solution Make Sense?*** The Webster Court is unanimous in reading § 102(c) to preclude judicial review of the Director's exercises of discretion under the National Security Act, but it divided 6–2 in holding that § 102(c) allowed judicial review of constitutional claims. Note that § 701(a) appears to sanction such partial reviewability, stating that judicial review is precluded "to the extent that" judicial review is precluded by statute or "agency action is committed to agency discretion by law." But what about § 102(c): Is it plausible to read the provision's text as splitting preclusion this way? The majority invokes the canon of constitutional avoidance to justify its split reading, but that canon does not apply if the meaning of a provision is clear (see p. 184). Recall Ronald Levin's point discussed above (p. 1513), that the Court is more reluctant to preclude review of constitutional claims than nonconstitutional or factual ones. Is Webster an example of that phenomenon?

Justice Scalia faults the majority for invoking the constitutional avoidance canon on another ground: in his view, it is clearly constitutional for Congress to preclude judicial review of some constitutional claims. Do you agree? (See Note on the Constitutionality of Precluding Review, p. 1503.)

(2) ***Reviewable, but Narrowly.*** Would a better approach have been to read § 102(c) as not precluding all review of any claims but as restricting reviewing courts to very narrow and deferential review given the broad discretion expressly granted the agency? The Court took such an approach in MACH MINING, LLC v. EEOC, 575 U.S. 480 (2015), a non-APA case involving a suit by the EEOC against a mining company for discriminating

against women in hiring in violation of Title VII of the Civil Rights Act. Under Title VII, EEOC is required to try to conciliate a claim before filing suit, but it can sue if it is unable to secure from the respondent a conciliation agreement "acceptable to the Commission." In a unanimous opinion by JUSTICE KAGAN, the Court rejected EEOC's argument that judicial review of its conciliation efforts was precluded but emphasized the limited scope of appropriate judicial scrutiny:

"Congress rarely intends to prevent courts from enforcing its directives to federal agencies. For that reason, this Court applies a strong presumption favoring judicial review of administrative action. . . . Title VII, as the Government acknowledges, imposes a duty on the EEOC to attempt conciliation of a discrimination charge prior to filing a lawsuit. That obligation is a key component of the statutory scheme. . . . Courts routinely enforce such compulsory prerequisites to suit in Title VII litigation (and in many other contexts besides). An employee, for example, may bring a Title VII claim only if she has first filed a timely charge with the EEOC . . . Absent [judicial] review, the Commission's compliance with the law would rest in the Commission's hands alone. We need not doubt the EEOC's trustworthiness, or its fidelity to law, to shy away from that result. We need only know—and know that Congress knows—that legal lapses and violations occur, and especially so when they have no consequence. That is why this Court has so long applied a strong presumption favoring judicial review of administrative action. Nothing overcomes that presumption with respect to the EEOC's duty to attempt conciliation of employment discrimination claims.

"[But w]hat is the proper scope of judicial review of the EEOC's conciliation activities? . . . The appropriate scope of review enforces the statute's requirements as just described—in brief, that the EEOC afford the employer a chance to discuss and rectify a specified discriminatory practice—but goes no further. Such limited review respects the expansive discretion that Title VII gives to the EEOC over the conciliation process, while still ensuring that the Commission follows the law." For similar conclusions that particular types of agency actions are reviewable but subject to very deferential scrutiny, see the Notes on the Reviewability of Agency Refusals to Act (p. 1527).

(3) ***Section 701(a)(2) as a Rare and Narrow Exception.*** In several recent decisions, the Supreme Court has emphasized the rare and narrow nature of the § 701(a)(2) exception. In WEYERHAEUSER CO. v. U.S. FISH & WILDLIFE SERV., 139 S.Ct. 361 (2018), the Court rejected the argument that agency action was nonreviewable because the agency was granted discretion. There the Court held that the Fish and Wildlife Service's decision not to exclude land from designation as critical habitat of the endangered dusky gopher frog was subject to judicial review, even though § 4(b)(2) of the Endangered Species Act gave the Secretary discretion to "exclude any area from critical habitat if he determines that the benefits of such exclusion outweigh the benefits of specifying such area." Writing for a unanimous Court, CHIEF JUSTICE ROBERTS described "Weyerhaeuser's claim [a]s the familiar one in administrative law that the agency did not appropriately consider all of the

relevant factors," adding that "[t]his is the sort of claim that federal courts routinely assess when determining whether to set aside an agency decision as an abuse of discretion under § 706(2)(A)."

The Court echoed this reasoning in DEPARTMENT OF COMMERCE V. NEW YORK, 139 S.Ct. 2551 (2019) (pp. 1177, 1466), where the Court rejected the argument that the decision to add a citizenship question to the census was unreviewable under § 701(a)(2). Writing for the majority, CHIEF JUSTICE ROBERTS again underscored the APA's presumption of reviewability and quoted Weyerhaeuser for the proposition that the § 701(a)(2) exception is narrow, restricted to rare circumstances where a court has no meaningful standards against which to judge the agency's exercise of discretion, and "generally limited" to categories of decisions traditionally viewed as committed to agency discretion: "To be sure, the [Census] Act confers broad authority on the Secretary. Section 141(a) instructs him to take 'a decennial census of population' in 'such form and content as he may determine.' [13 U.S.C.] § 141(a). . . . But [the Act does] not leave [the Secretary's] discretion unbounded. . . . The taking of the census is not one of those areas traditionally committed to agency discretion. . . . Nor is the statute here drawn so that it furnishes no meaningful standard by which to judge the Secretary's action. In contrast to the National Security Act in Webster, which gave the Director of Central Intelligence discretion to terminate employees whenever he 'deem[ed]' it 'advisable,' 486 U.S. at 594, the Census Act constrains the Secretary's authority to determine the form and content of the census in a number of ways. Section 195, for example, governs the extent to which he can use statistical sampling. Section 6(c) . . . circumscribes his power in certain circumstances to collect information through direct inquiries when administrative records are available. . . ."

Writing for himself, JUSTICE ALITO argued that the Secretary of Commerce's decision to add the citizenship question was unreviewable under § 701(a)(2) except for its constitutionality, concluding that the factors the Court had previously used to rebut the presumption of reviewability were satisfied here: Section 141(a) "gives the Secretary unfettered discretion to include on the census questions about basic demographic characteristics like citizenship . . . [Section] 141(a)['s] language . . . is even more sweeping than that of the statute in Webster." Justice Alito surveyed various statutory provisions, concluding that there was no " 'meaningful judicial standard' for reviewing the Secretary's selection of demographic questions for inclusion on the census." He further contended this was an instance where judicial review was traditionally lacking, with "litigation in the lower courts about the census [being] sparse and generally of relatively recent vintage."

Do you think Department of Commerce is distinguishable from Webster? Do Weyerhaeuser and Department of Commerce signal greater reluctance to find actions committed to agency discretion and nonreviewable, or are they consistent with the Court's generally narrow approach to § 701(a)(2)?

(4) ***Squaring § 701(a)(2) with § 706(2)(A).*** RONALD M. LEVIN writes that "[A] straightforward reading of the text of section 701(a)(2) would be totally unacceptable. At face value, the clause seems to say that every enabling

statute that grants some discretion to an agency creates a sphere of administrative conduct that the courts must not examine. That conclusion, however, would be absurd: everyday reality teaches that judicial review of agencies' exercises of discretionary judgment is routine. Indeed, the APA contains compelling internal evidence that the literal interpretation was not intended. Section 706(2)(A) provides that an agency action may be set aside for 'abuse of discretion.' If the existence of statutory discretion made the challenged action unreviewable, that provision would become meaningless. Accordingly, the need for a restrictive, and perhaps artificial, reading of the phrase 'committed to agency discretion' has been universally acknowledged since the earliest days of the APA." UNDERSTANDING UNREVIEWABILITY IN ADMINISTRATIVE LAW, 74 Minn. L. Rev. 689, 695 (1990).

(5) ***Nonreviewability and Nondelegation.*** What is the relationship between § 701(a)(2) and nondelegation doctrine? Recall that under current nondelegation doctrine, Congress is required to provide an intelligible principle in order for a delegation of power to an agency to be constitutional. See Gundy (p. 837). If there is "no law to apply," does this mean that the delegation is unconstitutional because it is lacking an "intelligible principle"? As Webster demonstrates, courts have distinguished between nonreviewability and nondelegation, holding that actions are unreviewable under § 701(a)(2) without calling into question the underlying delegation of authority pursuit to which such delegations are made. But why haven't they?

One way to resolve the doctrinal tension here is to note that "no law to apply" actually means no law for *courts* to apply. That is, § 102(c) of the National Security Act instructs the Director how to exercise his power to fire: he must determine that "such termination [is] necessary or advisable in the interests of the United States." This instruction is certainly intelligible to the Director—it is simply not a principle that courts will enforce, because Congress has vested exercise of that discretion exclusively in an executive official. Although we tend to equate "legal obligation" with judicial enforcement, in fact many very important statutory and constitutional requirements that govern executive action are not enforced by courts (for example, in areas of military and foreign affairs, as well as national security), and yet we recognize them as law. More to the point, we expect executive officials to regard them as binding constraints, not merely precatory admonitions about using delegated power.

Is this explanation satisfying? It is in line with the Court's insistence in Whitman that what matters for nondelegation purposes is that *Congress* lay down an intelligible principle, not whether agencies limit their delegated authority—nor, by extension, whether courts are able to police agencies' exercises of delegated authority. (See p. 871.) But if you see judicial review as more central to the constitutionality of delegations, is § 701(a)(2) problematic? Perhaps constitutional delegation concerns are adequately addressed by "a system of . . . remedies adequate to keep government generally within the bounds of law," Richard H. Fallon, Jr. & Daniel J. Meltzer, New Law, Non-Retroactivity, and Constitutional Remedies, 104 Harv. L. Rev. 1731, 1778–79 (1991), even if some exercises of agency discretion are not reviewable.

(6) ***Regulations as "Law to Apply."*** What if the agency adopts a regulation that provides judicially manageable standards for how it will go about exercising its discretion? It is then likely to lose its § 701(a)(2) defense to judicial review. E.g., Smirko v. Ashcroft, 387 F.3d 279, 292–93 (3d Cir. 2004); Gillian Metzger & Kevin Stack, Internal Administrative Law, 115 Mich. L. Rev. 1239, 1295 (2017). Is this simply application of the principle that agencies must follow their own regulations? (See p. 1104.) Consider, however, the resulting disincentives for agencies to exercise self-discipline through discretion-constraining regulations: doing so will expose them to judicial review where none might otherwise exist. Recognizing this, might a reviewing court hesitate before interpreting an agency statement as a binding commitment to limit its own power? Alternatively, should the court be willing to look to interpretive rules and statements of policy as also possible sources of "law to apply"?

## NOTES ON THE REVIEWABILITY OF AGENCY REFUSALS TO ACT

Challenges to agency inaction are a context in which § 701(a)(2) frequently arises. The Supreme Court has found some forms of agency inaction to be unreviewable, or presumptively so, whereas it has upheld the reviewability of others. As you read through these notes, can you identify a consistent theme or set of factors that leads the Court to come down in favor of or against reviewability?

(1) ***Decisions Not to Take Enforcement Action.*** HECKLER V. CHANEY, 470 U.S. 821 (1985), was an attempt by prisoners on death row to persuade the Food and Drug Administration to regulate the use of drugs for human execution. The FDA refused on grounds that (1) its jurisdiction in the area was unclear but should not be exercised to interfere with state criminal justice practices; and (2) enforcement in the area of unapproved use of approved drugs was generally initiated "only when there is a serious danger to the public health or a blatant scheme to defraud," neither of which was present here. The D.C. Circuit found the refusal reviewable, focusing both on the Abbott presumption of reviewability and on an FDA Policy Statement that the agency was "obligated" to investigate unapproved uses of approved drugs when such uses became "widespread" or "endanger[ed] the public health." JUSTICE REHNQUIST wrote for the eight-justice majority, rejecting the D.C. Circuit's view:

"This Court has recognized on several occasions over many years that an agency's decision not to prosecute or enforce, whether through civil or criminal process, is a decision generally committed to an agency's absolute discretion. This recognition is attributable in no small part to the general unsuitability for judicial review of agency decisions to refuse enforcement.

"The reasons for this general unsuitability are many. First, an agency decision not to enforce often involves a complicated balancing of a number of factors which are peculiarly within its expertise. Thus, the agency must not only assess whether a violation has occurred, but whether agency resources are best spent on this violation or another, whether the agency is likely to succeed if it acts, whether the particular enforcement action requested best fits the agency's overall policies, and, indeed, whether the agency has enough resources to undertake the action at all. An agency generally cannot act against each technical violation of the statute it is charged with enforcing. The agency is far better equipped than the courts to deal with the many variables involved in the proper ordering of its priorities. . . .

"In addition to these administrative concerns, we note that when an agency refuses to act it generally does not exercise its *coercive* power over an individual's liberty or property rights, and thus does not infringe upon areas that courts often are called upon to protect. Similarly, when an agency does act to enforce, that action itself provides a focus for judicial review, inasmuch as the agency must have exercised its power in some manner. . . . Finally, we recognize that an agency's refusal to institute proceedings shares to some extent the characteristics of the decision of a prosecutor in the Executive Branch not to indict—a decision which has long been regarded as the special province of the Executive Branch, inasmuch as it is the Executive who is charged by the Constitution to 'take Care that the Laws be faithfully executed.' U.S. Const., Art. II, § 3.

". . . [W]e emphasize that the decision is only presumptively unreviewable; the presumption may be rebutted where the substantive statute has provided guidelines for the agency to follow in exercising its enforcement powers. . . . Congress may limit an agency's exercise of enforcement power if it wishes, either by setting substantive priorities, or by otherwise circumscribing an agency's power to discriminate among issues or cases it will pursue . . ." But Justice Rehnquist ruled that neither limit was present here, noting in a footnote that "[w]e do not have in this case a refusal by the agency to institute proceedings based solely on the belief that it lacks jurisdiction. Nor do we have a situation where it could justifiably be found that the agency has 'consciously and expressly adopted a general policy' that is so extreme as to amount to an abdication of its statutory responsibilities."

JUSTICE BRENNAN concurred to point out that "the Court properly does not decide today that nonenforcement decisions are unreviewable in cases where (1) an agency flatly claims that it has no statutory jurisdiction to reach certain conduct; (2) an agency engages in a pattern of nonenforcement of clear statutory language; (3) an agency has refused to enforce a regulation lawfully promulgated and still in effect; or (4) a nonenforcement decision violates constitutional rights." What justifies this set of "exceptions" to the nonreviewability presumption—presumed congressional intent? Judicial manageability? The APA itself?

JUSTICE MARSHALL, concurring only in the judgment, objected strongly to the notion that judicial review is more important when the agency acts *against* members of the regulated community than when it refuses to act *for* regulated beneficiaries: "[A]ttempting to draw a line for purposes of judicial review between affirmative exercises of coercive agency power and negative agency refusals to act is simply untenable; one of the very purposes fueling the birth of administrative agencies was the reality that governmental refusal to act could have just as devastating an effect upon life, liberty, and the pursuit of happiness as coercive governmental action." He argued that "refusals to enforce, like other agency actions, are reviewable in the absence of a 'clear and convincing' congressional intent to the contrary, but that such refusals warrant deference when, as in this case, there is nothing to suggest that an agency with enforcement discretion has abused that discretion."

In announcing a (rebuttable) § 702(a) presumption against reviewability of agency enforcement decisions, should the Court have discussed other provisions of the APA—in particular, § 551(13), which defines "agency action" as including "failure to act," or § 706, which expressly makes "agency action unlawfully withheld or unreasonably delayed" subject to judicial review? Arguably, the APA's express definition of agency inaction as a form of action suggests rejection of the distinction between agency action and inaction that Chaney drew. The Supreme Court grappled with these definitions a few decades later in SUWA (p. 1531). In addition, in practice Chaney seems likely to pose a greater barrier to judicial review at the behest of regulatory beneficiaries than regulated entities, as the former are more likely to want to challenge nonenforcement. Is such an asymmetry justified in your view? For an argument that Heckler v. Chaney represents "a Lochner-like view of the judicial role," see Cass R. Sunstein, Reviewing Agency Inaction After Heckler v. Chaney, 52 U. Chi. L. Rev. 653 (1985).

(2) ***Distinguishing Nonenforcement Decisions from Affirmative Agency Policy.*** Chaney thus establishes that nonenforcement decisions are presumptively nonreviewable, but what counts as a nonenforcement decision? This issue arose in TEXAS V. UNITED STATES, 809 F.3d 134 (5th Cir. 2015) (p. 409), aff'd by an equally divided Supreme Court, United States v. Texas, 579 U.S. 547 (2016), which involved a challenge to President Obama's Deferred Action for Parents of Americans and Lawful Permanent Residents program ("DAPA"). Under the program, certain categories of noncitizens who were in the country unlawfully could apply for a grant of deferred action status, under which the government would not seek to deport them for three years. The total number of immigrants subject to the program was estimated at 4.3 million. Twenty-six states, led by Texas, challenged the program as violating the immigration laws and the President's take care duty.

Invoking Chaney, the government argued that a grant of "deferred action . . . is a presumptively unreviewable exercise of prosecutorial discretion," but the Fifth Circuit disagreed, in a 2–1 decision written by JUDGE SMITH: "Deferred action . . . is much more than nonenforcement: It would affirmatively confer lawful presence and associated benefits on a class of unlawfully present aliens. Though revocable, that change in designation would trigger . . . eligibility for federal benefits—for example, under title II and XVIII of the Social Security Act—and state benefits—for example, driver's licenses and unemployment insurance—that would not otherwise be available to illegal aliens. . . . DAPA would also toll the duration of the recipients' unlawful presence under the INA's reentry bars . . . [and recipients of deferred action status were eligible to work under a governing regulation.] . . . DAPA 'provides a focus for judicial review, inasmuch as the agency must have exercised its power in some manner. The action at least can be reviewed to determine whether the agency exceeded its statutory powers.' Chaney, 470 U.S. at 832." In a footnote, the majority added that "[b]ecause the challenged portion of DAPA's deferred-action program is not an exercise of enforcement discretion, we do not reach the issue of whether the [Chaney] presumption against review of such discretion is rebutted."

In dissent, JUDGE KING argued that "[d]eferred action decisions, such as those contemplated by the DAPA Memorandum, are quintessential exercises of prosecutorial discretion. . . . To the extent the exercise of deferred action trigger[s] other benefits, . . . those benefits are a function of statutes and regulations that were enacted by Congresses and administrations long past—statutes and regulations which, vitally, Plaintiffs do not challenge in this action. . . . [B]oth lawful presence and deferred action refer to nothing more than DHS's tentative decision, revocable at any time, not to remove an individual for the time being—i.e., the decision to exercise prosecutorial discretion." The dissent further maintained that Chaney's exception for when an agency had "consciously and expressly adopted a general policy that is so extreme as to amount to an abdication of its statutory responsibilities," 470 U.S. at 833 n. 4, was not applicable, given the Obama Administration's record number of deportations.

In DEPARTMENT OF HOMELAND SECURITY V. REGENTS OF THE UNIVERSITY OF CALIFORNIA, 140 S.Ct. 1891 (2020), the Court addressed the question of whether the Trump Administration's decision to rescind the Obama Administration's Deferred Action for Childhood Arrivals (DACA) immigration initiative violated the APA. DACA allowed individuals who had been brought to the country unlawfully when they were children to apply for a two-year forbearance from removal, which also made them eligible for work authorization and various federal benefits. The rescission of DACA was immediately challenged in court. As discussed in Chapter VIII (p. 1139), the Court held that the rescission was arbitrary and capricious. But before reaching that result, the Court had to determine whether the rescission decision was reviewable. CHIEF JUSTICE ROBERTS wrote for a 5–4 majority finding that it was:

"The Government contends that a general non-enforcement policy is equivalent to the individual non-enforcement decision at issue in Chaney. In each case, the Government argues, the agency must balance factors peculiarly within its expertise, and does so in a manner akin to a criminal prosecutor. Building on that premise, the Government argues that the rescission of a non-enforcement policy is no different—for purposes of reviewability—from the adoption of that policy. While the rescission may lead to increased enforcement, it does not, by itself, constitute a particular enforcement action. Applying this logic to the facts here, the Government submits that DACA is a non-enforcement policy and that its rescission is therefore unreviewable.

"But we need not test this chain of reasoning because DACA is not simply a non-enforcement policy. For starters, the DACA Memorandum did not merely refuse to institute proceedings against a particular entity or even a particular class. Instead, it directed USCIS to 'establish a clear and efficient process' for identifying individuals who met the enumerated criteria. Based on this directive, USCIS solicited applications from eligible aliens, instituted a standardized review process, and sent formal notices indicating whether the alien would receive the two-year forbearance. These proceedings are effectively adjudications. And the result of these adjudications—DHS's decision to grant deferred action—is an 'affirmative act of approval,' the very opposite of a 'refus[al] to act,' Chaney, 470 U.S. at 831–32. In short, the DACA Memorandum does not announce a passive non-enforcement policy; it created a program for conferring affirmative immigration relief. The creation of that program—and its rescission—is an 'action [that] provides a focus for judicial review.' Id., at 832.

"The benefits attendant to deferred action provide further confirmation that DACA is more than simply a non-enforcement policy. . . . [B]y virtue of receiving deferred action, the 700,000 DACA recipients may request work authorization and are eligible for Social Security and Medicare. Unlike an agency's refusal to take requested enforcement action, access to these types of benefits is an interest courts often are called upon to protect. Because the DACA program is more than a non-enforcement policy, its rescission is subject to review under the APA."

(3) ***Only Where the Failure to Act Involves a Discrete and Required Act.*** NORTON V. SOUTHERN UTAH WILDERNESS ALLIANCE, 542 U.S. 55 (2004), involved an effort by environmental groups to challenge the Bureau of Land Management's failure to take action to limit off-road-vehicle usage on federal lands in Utah. In a unanimous opinion, JUSTICE SCALIA set forth general criteria that agency failures to act must meet to be reviewable under the APA:

"Failures to act are sometimes remediable under the APA, but not always. . . . Sections 702, 704, and 706(1) all insist upon an 'agency action,' either as the action complained of (in §§ 702 and 704) or as the action to be compelled (in § 706(1)). The definition of that term begins with a list of five categories of decisions made or outcomes implemented by an agency—'agency rule, order, license, sanction [or] relief.' § 551(13). All of those categories involve circumscribed, discrete agency actions, as their definitions make clear: 'an agency statement of . . . future effect designed to implement, interpret, or prescribe law or policy' (rule); 'a final disposition . . . in a matter other than rule making' (order); a 'permit . . . or other form of permission' (license); a 'prohibition . . . or . . . taking [of] other compulsory or restrictive action' (sanction); or a 'grant of money, assistance, license, authority,' etc., or 'recognition of a claim, right, immunity,' etc., or 'taking of other action on the application or petition of, and beneficial to, a person' (relief). §§ 551(4), (6), (8), (10), (11).

"The terms following those five categories of agency action are not defined in the APA: 'or the equivalent or denial thereof, or failure to act.' § 551(13). But an 'equivalent . . . thereof' must also be discrete (or it would not be equivalent), and a 'denial thereof' must be the denial of a discrete listed action (and perhaps denial of a discrete equivalent). . . .

"The final term in the definition, 'failure to act,' is in our view properly understood as a failure to take an agency action—that is, a failure to take one of the agency actions (including their equivalents) earlier defined in § 551(13). Moreover, even without this equation of 'act' with 'agency action' the interpretive canon of ejusdem generis would attribute to the last item ('failure to act') the same characteristic of discreteness shared by all the preceding items. . . . A 'failure to act' is not the same thing as a 'denial.' The latter is the agency's act of saying no to a request; the former is simply the omission of an action without formally rejecting a request—for example, the failure to promulgate a rule or take some decision by a statutory deadline. The important point is that a 'failure to act' is properly understood to be limited, as are the other items in § 551(13), to a discrete action. A second point central to the analysis of the present case is that the only agency action that can be compelled under the APA is action legally required. This limitation appears in § 706(1)'s authorization for courts to 'compel agency action unlawfully withheld.' . . .

"Thus, a claim under § 706(1) can proceed only where a plaintiff asserts that an agency failed to take a discrete agency action that it is required to take. These limitations rule out several kinds of challenges[, such as] . . . the kind of broad programmatic attack we rejected in Lujan v. National Wildlife Federation, 497 U.S. 871 (1990)."

Is SUWA's exclusion of more general agency failure to act and programmatic attacks on agency functioning appropriate? Or should courts train their attention on inaction cases precisely to this level and not interfere with specific instances of inaction? It seems that SUWA is in tension with Chaney's footnoted suggestion that the APA's exception for action committed to agency discretion might not apply when "it could justifiably be found that the agency has consciously and expressly adopted a general policy that is so extreme as to amount to an abdication of its statutory responsibilities." For an argument that current doctrine gets reviewability backwards here and that it would be better to review general failures to act over specific ones, see Gillian E. Metzger, The Constitutional Duty to Supervise, 124 Yale L.J. 1836 (2015).

(4) ***Refusal to Initiate Rulemaking.*** Another form of agency refusals to act are refusals to engage in rulemaking. Should such refusals be treated like specific enforcement decisions and presumptively unreviewable under Chaney? In MASSACHUSETTS V. EPA, 549 U.S. 497, 527–28 (2007), after finding that Massachusetts had standing to challenge EPA's refusal to engage in a rulemaking on greenhouse gas emissions from new motor vehicles (pp. 1469, 1473), JUSTICE STEVENS's majority opinion made clear that such rulemaking refusals are reviewable: "As we have repeated time and again, an agency has broad discretion to choose how best to marshal its limited resources and personnel to carry out its delegated responsibilities. See Chevron [p. 1206]. That discretion is at its height when the agency decides not to bring an enforcement action. Therefore, in Heckler v. Chaney, we held that an agency's refusal to initiate enforcement proceedings is not ordinarily subject to judicial review. Some debate remains, however, as to the rigor with which we review an agency's denial of a petition for rulemaking.

"There are key differences between a denial of a petition for rulemaking and an agency's decision not to initiate an enforcement action. See American Horse Protection Assn., Inc. v. Lyng, 812 F.2d 1, 3–4 (CADC 1987). In contrast to nonenforcement decisions, agency refusals to initiate rulemaking 'are less frequent, more apt to involve legal as opposed to factual analysis, and subject to special formalities, including a public explanation.' Id., at 4; see also 5 U.S.C. § 555(e). They moreover arise out of denials of petitions for rulemaking which (at least in the circumstances here) the affected party had an undoubted procedural right to file in the first instance. Refusals to promulgate rules are thus susceptible to judicial review, though such review is extremely limited and highly deferential."

(5) ***Refusal to Spend Money.*** In LINCOLN V. VIGIL, 508 U.S. 182 (1993), JUSTICE SOUTER for a unanimous Court described § 701(a)(2) jurisprudence as recognizing "certain categories of administrative decisions that courts traditionally have regarded as 'committed to agency discretion.' " He listed: (i) decisions not to take enforcement action; (ii) refusals to grant reconsideration of an action because of material error; and (iii) decisions to terminate an employee in the interests of national security—and then added another: decisions about allocating funds from a lump-sum appropriation.

The Indian Health Service decided to phase out a program that directly provided evaluative and clinical services to disabled Native American children in the Southwest in favor of what it described as a "nationwide" program. Children who had been receiving services sued, claiming that the decision violated various organic statutes, the APA, and the Fifth Amendment. They also argued that the Service had represented the Program's continuation to Congress, and Congress had appropriated funds based on that representation. The Court's opinion pointed out that Congress had made a lump-sum appropriation, not a program-specific appropriation. As in Chaney, the Court noted, "Congress may always circumscribe agency discretion to allocate resources by putting restrictions in the operative statutes . . . But as long as the agency allocates funds from a lump-sum appropriation to meet permissible statutory objectives, § 701(a)(2) gives the courts no leave to intrude. [T]o [that] extent, the decision to allocate funds 'is committed to agency discretion by law.' § 701(a)(2)." For an instance where a court found that Congress had so circumscribed agency discretion, thereby removing any presumption of nonreviewability, see Shawnee Tribe v. Mnuchin, 984 F.3d 94 (D.C. Cir. 2021). The broader question of presidential power over appropriations is addressed in Chapter VII, Section 3.c (p. 1037).

## c. Timing of Review

*(1) Exhaustion of Administrative Remedies*
*(2) Finality*
*(3) Ripeness*

Timing problems can bedevil any federal court litigant: For both Article III and prudential reasons, the case must be brought neither too early nor too late. For those seeking review of agency action, though, three timing doctrines stand out as especially important:

- *Exhaustion:* Whether the agency has internal procedures for remediating errors that should be used before coming to court; the nature of the inquiry very much depends on whether the statute under which the claim is brought expressly addresses exhaustion.
- *Finality*: Whether the action complained of is complete and authoritative, rather than part of a larger decisional process still ongoing.
- *Ripeness*: Whether the action is fit for judicial examination now as opposed to waiting for some future event, often (but not always) raised in the context of pre-enforcement challenges to rules.

Although these three timing doctrines are distinct, they serve overlapping purposes. As a result, they are not always easy to separate. A good example of the overlapping nature of timing doctrines is Ticor Title Insurance Co. v. Federal Trade Commission, 814 F.2d 731 (D.C. Cir. 1987), where the court was unanimous in holding that the suit was premature, but each of the three judges offered a different basis as to why, with one concluding that the suit was barred by failure to exhaust administrative remedies, one holding that the requisite finality was lacking, and one ruling that the challenge was unripe.

## (1) Exhaustion of Administrative Remedies

***DARBY v. CISNEROS***

*. . . Except as otherwise expressly required by statute, agency action otherwise final is final for the purposes of this section whether or not there has been presented or determined an application for a declaratory order, for any form of reconsideration, or, unless the agency otherwise requires by rule and provides that the action meanwhile is inoperative, for an appeal to superior agency authority.*

5 U.S.C. § 704

## DARBY v. CISNEROS

Supreme Court of the United State (1993).
509 U.S. 137.

■ JUSTICE BLACKMUN delivered the opinion of the Court.[7]

[Darby, a real estate developer, sought review of an ALJ decision that he had engaged in improper financial practices and should be barred from participating in Housing and Urban Development programs for 18 months. Under HUD regulations, an ALJ's decision "shall be final unless . . . the Secretary or the Secretary's designee, within 30 days of receipt of a request decides as a matter of discretion to review the [ALJ's]

[7] [Ed.] Chief Justice Rehnquist and Justices Scalia and Thomas did not join in a portion of the opinion that discussed the APA's legislative history.

finding. . . . Any party may request such a review in writing within 15 days of receipt of the [ALJ's] determination." The agency argued that Darby's failure to request this review foreclosed judicial review.:]

This case presents the question whether federal courts have the authority to require that a plaintiff exhaust available administrative remedies before seeking judicial review under the Administrative Procedure Act, where neither the statute nor agency rules specifically mandate exhaustion as a prerequisite to judicial review. At issue is the relationship between the judicially created doctrine of exhaustion of administrative remedies and the statutory requirements of § [704] of the APA. . . .

Petitioners argue that this provision means that a litigant seeking judicial review of a final agency action under the APA need not exhaust available administrative remedies unless such exhaustion is expressly required by statute or agency rule. . . . Respondents contend that [the section] is concerned solely with timing, that is, when agency actions become "final," and that Congress had no intention to interfere with the courts' ability to impose conditions on the timing of their exercise of jurisdiction to review final agency actions. . . . It perhaps is surprising that it has taken over 45 years since the passage of the APA for this Court definitively to address this question. . . .

. . . [T]he text of the APA leaves little doubt that petitioners are correct . . . While federal courts may be free to apply, where appropriate, other prudential doctrines of judicial administration to limit the scope and timing of judicial review, [§ 704], by its very terms, has limited the availability of the doctrine of exhaustion of administrative remedies to that which the statute or rule clearly mandates.

. . . Congress clearly was concerned with making the exhaustion requirement unambiguous so that aggrieved parties would know precisely what administrative steps were required before judicial review would be available. If courts were able to impose additional exhaustion requirements beyond those provided by Congress or the agency, the last sentence of [§ 704] would make no sense. . . . Of course, the exhaustion doctrine continues to apply as a matter of judicial discretion in cases not governed by the APA."

[Because neither the governing statute nor HUD regulations mandated an appeal to the Secretary, the Court held that Darby's action must be permitted to go forward.]

## NOTES

(1) ***Statutory and Common Law Exhaustion.*** As Darby indicates, exhaustion requirements come in both a statutory and a common law guise. In MCCARTHY V. MADIGAN, 503 U.S. 140 (1992), the Court laid out the common law exhaustion inquiry in an opinion by JUSTICE BLACKMUN: "Exhaustion is required because it serves the twin purposes of protecting administrative agency authority and promoting judicial efficiency. . . . Notwithstanding these substantial institutional interests, federal courts are

vested with a 'virtually unflagging obligation' to exercise the jurisdiction given them. Cohens v. Virginia, 19 U.S. 264, 6 Wheat. 264, 404 (1821). Accordingly, this Court has declined to require exhaustion in some circumstances even where administrative and judicial interests would counsel otherwise.

"In determining whether exhaustion is required, federal courts must balance the interest of the individual in retaining prompt access to a federal judicial forum against countervailing institutional interests favoring exhaustion. . . . [Our] precedents have recognized at least three broad sets of circumstances in which the interests of the individual weigh heavily against requiring administrative exhaustion. First, requiring resort to the administrative remedy may occasion undue prejudice to subsequent assertion of a court action. Such prejudice may result, for example, from an unreasonable or indefinite timeframe for administrative action . . . . [or] when an individual's failure to exhaust may preclude a defense to criminal liability. McKart v. United States, 395 U.S. [185,] 197 [(1969)]. . . [Second,] an administrative remedy may be inadequate 'because of some doubt as to whether the agency was empowered to grant effective relief.' Gibson v. Berryhill, 411 U.S. [564,] 575 n. 14 [(1973)]. For example, an agency [may] lack[ ] institutional competence to resolve the particular type of issue presented, such as the constitutionality of a statute. . . . Third, an administrative remedy may be inadequate where the administrative body is shown to be biased or has otherwise predetermined the issue before it. . . ."

In ROSS V. BLAKE, 578 U.S. 632 (2016), the Supreme Court in an opinion by JUSTICE KAGAN reiterated that statutory exhaustion provisions displace the common-law analysis: "No doubt, judge-made exhaustion doctrines, even if flatly stated at first, remain amenable to judge-made exceptions. But a statutory exhaustion provision stands on a different footing. There, Congress sets the rules—and courts have a role in creating exceptions only if Congress wants them to." However, judges still need to interpret the scope of any exceptions in the statute. In the PLRA, "the exhaustion requirement hinges on the 'availab[ility]' of administrative remedies[,] . . . [which means that] an inmate is required to exhaust those, but only those, grievance procedures that are 'capable of use' to obtain 'some relief for the action complained of.' Booth [v. Churner,] 532 U.S. [731,] 738 [(2001)]. . . . Building on our own and lower courts' decisions, we note as relevant here three kinds of circumstances in which an administrative remedy, although officially on the books, is not capable of use to obtain relief. . . . First, as Booth made clear, an administrative procedure is unavailable when (despite what regulations or guidance materials may promise) it operates as a simple dead end—with officers unable or consistently unwilling to provide any relief to aggrieved inmates. . . . Next, an administrative scheme might be so opaque that it becomes, practically speaking, incapable of use. . . . And finally, the same is true when prison administrators thwart inmates from taking advantage of a grievance process through machination, misrepresentation, or intimidation."

For an ambitious argument that exhaustion and ripeness doctrines (among other things) are inappropriate vestiges of judicial common law making that should be recognized as completely supplanted by the APA, see

John F. Duffy, Administrative Common Law in Judicial Review, 77 Tex. L. Rev. 113 (1998). On exhaustion in rulemaking contexts, see ACUS, Issue Exhaustion in Preenforcement Judicial Review of Administrative Rulemaking, Statement No. 19 (Sept. 25, 2015).

(2) ***Exhaustion and Rulemaking.*** Darby, McCarthy, and Ross involved adjudication. Does exhaustion have any role to play in review of rules? Unlike adjudication, there is nothing like "party" status in rulemaking. In the typical regulatory context, neither statutes nor regulations *require* that persons seeking to challenge the rule in court must have participated in the notice-and-comment process. Exhaustion in this context, therefore, focuses on whether the challenge sought to be brought in litigation was raised by someone during the rulemaking proceeding and with sufficient specificity. For example, the Clean Air Act provides that "[o]nly an objection to a rule . . . raised with reasonable specificity during the period for public comment . . . may be raised during judicial review." 42 U.S.C. § 7607(d)(7)(B). Few statutes have such express rulemaking exhaustion requirements, however; ACUS has identified two such statutes, the Clean Air Act and the Securities and Exchange Act of 1934. Administrative Conference Statement #19: Issue Exhaustion in Preenforcement Judicial Review of Administrative Rulemaking, 80 Fed. Reg. 60611, 60612 (Oct. 7, 2015).

In EPA v. EME HOMER CITY GENERATION, L.P., 572 U.S. 489 (2014), the Supreme Court sidestepped the question of whether exhaustion applies in rulemaking by deciding that EPA had committed a procedural default of its own. EPA had argued for the first time at the Supreme Court that states and other parties challenging the Transport Rule had failed the CAA's "reasonable specificity" standard and that this failure at the administrative level deprived the court of jurisdiction to hear their challenges on review. Referring to the Court's general reluctance to consider restrictions "jurisdictional," JUSTICE GINSBURG's opinion pointed out that "[a] rule may be 'mandatory,' yet not 'jurisdictional'. . . The [CAA] 'does not speak to a court's authority, but only to a party's procedural obligations.' As such, the procedural default (if it had occurred) could be waived. EPA had done so by failing to press the reasonable specificity argument in the court of appeals. 'Before the D.C. Circuit, it indicated only that the 'reasonable specificity' prescription might bar judicial review. We therefore do not count the prescription an impassable hindrance to our adjudication of the respondents' attack on EPA's interpretation of the Transport Rule.' "

JEFFREY S. LUBBERS, in FAIL TO COMMENT AT YOUR OWN RISK: DOES ISSUE EXHAUSTION HAVE A PLACE IN JUDICIAL REVIEW OF RULES?, 70 Admin. L. Rev. 109, 136 (2018), reports that "[i]n recent years the issue exhaustion doctrine has grown to cover more and more rulemakings, even where there is no such statutory provision, albeit with some inconsistently applied exceptions." Under established D.C. Circuit caselaw, "[g]enerally, a challenger forfeits an opportunity to challenge an agency rulemaking on a ground that was not first presented to the agency for its consideration." NTCH, Inc. v. FCC, 950 F.3d 871, 882 (D.C. Cir. 2020). According to Lubbers, supra, at 144–45, "[s]everal other circuits have now joined the D.C. Circuit in applying the issue exhaustion doctrine in rulemaking cases, most of them, but not all, in environmental cases. Conspicuously, after originally strongly rejecting [issue exhaustion in rulemaking contexts, even] the Fifth Circuit seems to be having second thoughts." Lubbers notes, however, that lower courts have also recognized exceptions to the exhaustion requirement, such when the agency was already on notice, the agency should have considered the issue in any event as part of its reasoned decisionmaking obligation, or the issue represented a constitutional challenge to which the exhaustion requirement did not apply. See id. at 149–55. And the consensus remains that—as this casebook put the point going back to 2003—cases conspicuously lack discussion of whether, when, why, or how exhaustion doctrine developed in the context of adjudication should be applied to rulemaking. For suggestion of factors that courts should consider in deciding whether to apply issue exhaustion to a rulemaking, see ACUS statement #19, supra, at 60612–60613.

(3) ***Exhaustion, Preclusion of Pre-Enforcement Review, and Primary Jurisdiction.*** Notice the close relationship between exhaustion and decisions holding that pre-enforcement review is precluded, like Thunder Basin, Elgin, and Jarkesy (Note 5, p. 1515). Practically speaking, the result of the two is the same: a plaintiff must pursue administrative remedies before seeking judicial review.

The doctrine of primary jurisdiction is also related to, though distinct from, exhaustion of administrative remedies. Under this doctrine, when an agency and a court have concurrent jurisdiction, a court may abstain to allow the agency to first address the matter. According to JUSTICE BREYER, concurring in part and concurring in judgment in PHARMACEUTICAL RESEARCH & MFRS. OF AMERICA v. WALSH, 538 U.S. 644, 673 (2003): "The legal doctrine of 'primary jurisdiction' permits a court itself to 'refer' a question to the Secretary. That doctrine seeks to produce better informed and uniform legal rulings by allowing courts to take advantage of an agency's specialized knowledge, expertise, and central position within a regulatory regime. United States v. Western Pacific R. Co., 352 U.S. 59, 63–65 (1956). 'No fixed formula exists' for the doctrine's application. Id. at 64. Rather, the question in each instance is whether a case raises 'issues of fact not within the conventional experience of judges,' but within the purview of an agency's responsibilities; whether the 'limited functions of review by the judiciary are more rationally exercised, by preliminary resort' to an agency 'better equipped than courts' to resolve an issue in the first instance; or, in a word, whether preliminary reference of issues to the agency will promote that proper working relationship between court and agency that the primary jurisdiction doctrine seeks to facilitate. Far East Conference v. United States, 342 U.S. 570, 574–75 (1952)."

Note also that all three doctrines often share the feature of implicitly upholding the adequacy of the combined administrative and judicial remedial arrangement to which the plaintiff will be subject, in the course of concluding that direct suit is not immediately available. How important do you think this feature is to assessing the acceptability of these doctrines?

(4) ***Exhaustion of Separation of Powers Challenges.*** In CARR v. SAUL, 141 S.Ct. 1352 (2021), the Supreme Court considered how the exhaustion

requirement plays out in the administrative context with respect to Appointments Clause challenges. Shortly after administrative law judges in the Social Security Administration denied petitioners' applications for disability benefits, the Supreme Court decided Lucia v. SEC (p. 957), holding that the appointment of ALJs by lower-level staff violated the Appointments Clause. Because the SSA ALJs who denied petitioners' claims were also appointed by lower-level staff, petitioners argued that Lucia entitled them to a new hearing. The Tenth Circuit held that, because petitioners had not raised this argument in their initial proceedings, the exhaustion doctrine precluded judicial review.

The Supreme Court reversed. Writing for a unanimous Court, JUSTICE SOTOMAYOR allowed the petitioners to raise their constitutional claims in court even though they did not first raise those issues before an ALJ. Because ALJs are "generally ill suited to address structural constitutional challenges, which usually fall outside [their] areas of technical expertise," judicial review of constitutional challenges in this context was "sometimes appropriate." Justice Sotomayor also noted that "[i]t makes little sense to require litigants to present claims to adjudicators who are powerless to grant the relief requested. . . . [T]he SSA's administrative review scheme at no point afforded petitioners access to the Commissioner, the one person who could remedy their Appointments Clause challenges. Nor were the ALJs capable of remedying any defects in their own appointments." Requiring exhaustion here, therefore, would do little to protect the SSA's authority or promote judicial efficiency. The Court also stressed the "inquisitorial features of SSA ALJ proceedings," and repeatedly suggested that issue exhaustion played a more central role in adversarial context. Finally, the Court further noted that it was addressing a "judicially created issue-exhaustion requirement." Lower courts have differentiated contexts in which issue-exhaustion rules are creatures of statute or regulation. See, e.g., Morris v. McDonough, 40 F.4th 1359 (4th Cir. 2022).

## (2) Finality

### *SACKETT v. EPA*

*Agency action made reviewable by statute and final agency action for which there is no other adequate remedy in a court are subject to judicial review.*

5 U.S.C. § 704

Finality is the most amorphous of the several doctrines through which courts regulate the timing of judicial review. A legal grab bag, the finality rubric is applied to an assortment of questions about the appropriateness of intervention at a particular moment in the administrative process.

## SACKETT v. EPA

Supreme Court of the United States (2012).
566 U.S. 120.

■ JUSTICE SCALIA delivered the opinion of the Court.

[The Clean Water Act (CWA) prohibits "the discharge of any pollutant by any person," § 1311, without a permit, into the "navigable waters" § 1344. Upon determining that a violation has occurred, the EPA may either issue a compliance order or initiate a civil enforcement action. When the EPA prevails in a civil action, the Act provides for a civil penalty of up to $37,500 per day per violation, but that can be doubled for a person who was previously issued a compliance order but failed to comply. The Sacketts received a compliance order from the EPA, which stated that their residential lot contained navigable waters and that their construction project violated the Act. The compliance order further required the Sacketts to immediately restore the property pursuant to an EPA work plan. The EPA denied the Sacketts' request for a hearing regarding the compliance order. The Sacketts then challenged the compliance order in Federal District Court as "arbitrary [and] capricious" under the APA and as a due process violation of the Fifth Amendment. The District Court dismissed for lack of subject-matter jurisdiction. The Ninth Circuit affirmed, concluding that the CWA precluded pre-enforcement judicial review of compliance orders and that such preclusion was not a due process violation.]

II

. . . We consider first whether the compliance order is final agency action. There is no doubt it is agency action, which the APA defines as including even a "failure to act." §§ 551(13), 701(b)(2). But is it *final*? It has all of the hallmarks of APA finality that our opinions establish. Through the order, the EPA "determined" "rights or obligations." Bennett v. Spear, 520 U.S. 154, 178 (1997) [p. 1543]. By reason of the order, the Sacketts have the legal obligation to "restore" their property according to an agency-approved Restoration Work Plan, and must give the EPA access to their property and to "records and documentation related to the conditions at the Site." 22–23, ¶ 2.11. But that confers no entitlement to further agency review. The mere possibility that an agency might reconsider in light of "informal discussion" and invited contentions of inaccuracy does not suffice to make an otherwise final agency action nonfinal.

The APA's judicial review provision also requires that the person seeking APA review of final agency action have "no other adequate remedy in a court," 5 U.S.C. § 704. In CWA enforcement cases, judicial review ordinarily comes by way of a civil action brought by the EPA under 33 U.S.C. § 1319. But the Sacketts cannot initiate that process, and each day they wait for the agency to drop the hammer, they accrue, by the Government's telling, an additional $75,000 in potential liability. The other possible route to judicial review—applying to the Corps of Engineers for a permit and then filing suit under the APA if a permit is denied—will not serve either. The remedy for denial of action that might be sought from one agency does not ordinarily provide an "adequate remedy" for action already taken by another agency. . . .

III

Nothing in the CWA *expressly* precludes judicial review under the APA or otherwise. But in determining "[w]hether and to what extent a particular statute precludes judicial review," we do not look "only [to] its express language." Block v. Community Nutrition Institute, 467 U.S. 340, 345 (1984) [p. 1510]. The APA, we have said, creates a "presumption favoring judicial review of administrative action," but as with most presumptions, this one "may be overcome by inferences of intent drawn from the statutory scheme as a whole." Id., at 349. The Government offers several reasons why the statutory scheme of the . . . Act precludes review.

. . . The Government argues that, because Congress gave the EPA the choice between a judicial proceeding and an administrative action, it would undermine the Act to allow judicial review of the latter. But that argument rests on the question-begging premise that the relevant difference between a compliance order and an enforcement proceeding is that only the latter is subject to judicial review. There are eminently sound reasons other than insulation from judicial review why compliance orders are useful. The Government itself suggests that they "provid[e] a means of notifying recipients of potential violations and quickly resolving the issues through voluntary compliance." Brief for Respondents 39. It is entirely consistent with this function to allow judicial review when the recipient does not choose "voluntary compliance." The Act does not guarantee the EPA that issuing a compliance order will always be the most effective choice.

The Government also notes that compliance orders are not self-executing, but must be enforced by the agency in a plenary judicial action. It suggests that Congress therefore viewed a compliance order "as a step in the deliberative process[,] . . . rather than as a coercive sanction that itself must be subject to judicial review." Id., at 38. But the APA provides for judicial review of all final agency actions, not just those that impose a self-executing sanction. And it is hard for the Government to defend its claim that the issuance of the compliance order was just "a step in the deliberative process" when the agency rejected the Sacketts' attempt to obtain a hearing and when the *next* step will either be taken by the Sacketts (if they comply with the order) or will involve judicial, not administrative, deliberation (if the EPA brings an enforcement action). As the text (and indeed the very name) of the compliance order makes clear, the EPA's "deliberation" over whether the Sacketts are in violation of the Act is at an end; the agency may still have to deliberate over whether it is confident enough about this conclusion to initiate litigation, but that is a separate subject.

The Government further urges us to consider that Congress expressly provided for prompt judicial review, on the administrative record, when the EPA assesses administrative penalties after a hearing,

. . . but did not expressly provide for review of compliance orders. But if the express provision of judicial review in one section of a long and complicated statute were alone enough to overcome the APA's presumption of reviewability for all final agency action, it would not be much of a presumption at all. . . .

Finally, the Government notes that Congress passed the CWA in large part to respond to the inefficiency of then existing remedies for water pollution. . . . The Government warns that the EPA is less likely to use [compliance] orders if they are subject to judicial review. That may be true—but it will be true for all agency actions subjected to judicial review. The APA's presumption of judicial review is a repudiation of the principle that efficiency of regulation conquers all. And there is no reason to think that the CWA was uniquely designed to enable the strong-arming of regulated parties into "voluntary compliance" without the opportunity for judicial review—even judicial review of the question whether the regulated party is within the EPA's jurisdiction. Compliance orders will remain an effective means of securing prompt voluntary compliance in those many cases where there is no substantial basis to question their validity.

* * *

We conclude that the compliance order in this case is final agency action for which there is no adequate remedy other than APA review, and that the Clean Water Act does not preclude that review. We therefore reverse the judgment of the Court of Appeals and remand the case for further proceedings consistent with this opinion.

[Justice Ginsburg concurred to note that the opinion did not resolve whether the Sacketts could challenge the terms and conditions of the compliance order at the pre-enforcement stage, while Justice Alito concurred to argue that Congress "should provide a reasonably clear rule regarding the reach of the CWA."]

## NOTES

(1) ***Finality of Initial Agency Determinations.*** Sackett involves the question of when an initial agency determination is final. A similar issue, in the judicial context, concerns when an interlocutory appeal is available. There is a presumption against such interlocutory appeals, and a litigant ordinarily cannot take a trial judge's evidentiary ruling to an appellate court until the whole case goes up on appeal. Should there be a similar presumption against judicial review of agency determinations until the administrative process is completed? Why or why not?

The Court adhered to its approach in Sackett in UNITED STATES ARMY CORPS OF ENGINEERS V. HAWKES CO., 578 U.S. 590 (2016). There, in an opinion by CHIEF JUSTICE ROBERTS, the Court held that a jurisdictional determination that a property comes under CWA because it contains "waters of the United States," when it represents the agency's definitive view, constitutes final agency action and is judicially reviewable under the APA. The government did not contest that such a jurisdictional determination marked the culmination of the Army Corp's decisionmaking process but argued that the jurisdictional determination alone had no legal consequences. CHIEF JUSTICE ROBERTS disagreed, emphasizing that under a Memorandum of Understanding between the Army Corps and EPA, a determination that a property does not contain waters of the United States (a negative determination), would generally bind the government for five years, preventing an enforcement action for CWA violations. "It follows that affirmative [jurisdictional determinations] have legal consequences as well: They represent the denial of the safe harbor that negative [determinations] afford. . . . This conclusion tracks the 'pragmatic' approach we have long taken to finality." Roberts also rejected the government's further argument that property owners' ability to apply for a permit and seek review if denied, or to discharge pollutants and challenge the jurisdictional determination in an enforcement action, represented adequate alternatives to direct judicial review of the determination under the APA.

(2) ***Multiple Regulatory Actors.*** Another sort of finality problem occurs when a regulatory program requires several officials each to play a part in the regulatory decision. *Whose* actions constitute "final agency action"? This was the type of finality problem at issue in BENNETT V. SPEAR, 520 U.S. 154, 178 (1997), which articulated the two-part finality test the Court invoked in Sackett. Bennett involved a Fish and Wildlife Service Biological Opinion, issued under the Endangered Species Act, recommending that the Bureau of Reclamation take certain actions regarding reservoirs in a Bureau-run water reclamation project. The Opinion was challenged by ranchers and irrigation districts who would lose the use of water for irrigation if those actions were taken, but it was the Bureau of Reclamation that ultimately decided whether to take the actions, not the Fish and Wildlife Service. The Court concluded that the Service's Opinion nonetheless represented final agency action that could be challenged under the APA. First, it was uncontested that the Opinion represented the "consummation" of the Service's decisionmaking process and was not "merely tentative or interlocutory." Second, the Opinion and an accompanying statement by the Service "alter[ed] the legal regime to which the action agency [wa]s subject, authorizing it to take the endangered species if (but only if) it complies with the prescribed conditions." (Bennett also discussed application of the zone of interests test in the context of a citizen suit provision, see p. 1486).

The Supreme Court has encountered several multiple-actor statutory schemes in which the President is the ultimate official actor. It generally invokes lack of finality in refusing to review the actions of other officials prior to presidential involvement. In FRANKLIN V. MASSACHUSETTS, 505 U.S. 788 (1992), for example, Massachusetts attempted to regain a seat lost in the House because of the decennial reapportionment. Five Justices concluded that the Secretary of Commerce's Census Report was not final action: "In this case, the action that creates an entitlement to a particular number of Representatives and has a direct effect on the reapportionment is the President's statement to Congress, not the Secretary's report to the President." However, because the President is not an "agency" within the meaning of the APA, review is not available once the action does become final by presidential decision.

Absent direct involvement of the President, would (should?) other officials be able to avoid review on finality grounds by pointing out that their decision was a necessary, but not sufficient, component of a complex regulatory action? And because review of the presidential action cannot occur under the APA, does this have the risk of foreclosing a path to review altogether? For criticism of the Court's decision in Franklin on this latter point, see Kathryn E. Kovacs, Constraining the Statutory President, 98 Wash. U. L. Rev. 63 (2020).

(3) ***Finality and Guidance Documents.*** Courts regularly apply the Bennett two-pronged test in determining whether agency guidance counts as final agency action. Yet, as discussed in Chapter IV (p. 405), whether a given agency action is deemed a policy statement or instead a de facto legislative rule often turns on whether the action is binding and thus has legal consequences or creates rights and obligations. See, e.g., Texas v. EEOC, 933 F.3d 433, 441–43 (5th Cir. 2019). That would suggest that if a court determines that a challenged agency action is a policy statement, then it is also determining that it lacks jurisdiction to hear the challenge because the agency's action does not count as final agency action. The effect would be to make genuine policy statements or other guidance never reviewable under the APA. See Center For Auto Safety v. NHTSA, 452 F.3d 798, 808 (D.C. Cir. 2006) (p. 406) (concluding that regional recall guidelines were not final agency action because they were nothing more than "general policy statements with no legal force"). By contrast, as the Fifth Circuit stated in EEOC, supra at 451, that agency guidance "is a substantive rule subject to the APA's notice-and-comment requirement . . . . follows naturally from our holding that [it] . . . is a final agency action."

Does collapsing the tests for guidance and reviewability in this fashion make sense, or should some policy statements that represent the agency's established view be considered final and reviewable? Consider the approach to finality offered decades earlier by JUDGE LEVENTHAL in NATIONAL AUTOMATIC LAUNDRY & CLEANING COUNCIL V. SHULTZ, 443 F.2d 689 (D.C. Cir. 1971), addressing a letter ruling from the Administrator of the Wage and Hour Division of the Department of Labor; the Division issued about 750,000 such letter rulings annually: "There are sound reasons why such advisory letters and opinions should not be subject to judicial review. . . . There is surely a need for such informality in the administration of the Fair Labor Standards Act. . . ." But Leventhal distinguished instances "when the interpretative ruling is signed by the head of the agency," arguing that "the sound course is to accept the ruling of a board or commission, or the head of an agency, as presumptively final." Do you think that an approach focusing on the source of guidance would be a preferable approach to finality?

## (3) Ripeness

***Abbott Laboratories v. Gardner***
***Toilet Goods Ass'n, Inc. v. Gardner***

ABBOTT LABORATORIES v. GARDNER
387 U.S. 136 (1967).
(p. 1496)

TOILET GOODS ASS'N, INC. v. GARDNER
387 U.S. 158 (1967).

In ABBOTT LABS, the Court described ripeness as a justiciability doctrine designed "to prevent the courts, through avoidance of premature adjudication, from entangling themselves in abstract disagreements over administrative policies, and also to protect the agencies from judicial interference until an administrative decision has been formalized and its effects felt in a concrete way by the challenging parties." Abbott Labs established the modern framework for ripeness analysis, under which a court must "evaluate both the fitness of the issues for judicial decision and the hardship to the parties of withholding court consideration."

In TOILET GOODS V. GARDNER, a companion case to Abbott Labs, the Court denied pre-enforcement review under the Abbott Labs framework. Cosmetic manufacturers sought pre-enforcement review of regulations requiring them to give FDA inspectors access to their manufacturing processes and formulas for making color additives. If access were denied, the FDA Commissioner "may immediately suspend" the manufacturer's certificate to sell additives and "may continue such suspension until adequate corrective action has been taken." The Court, in an opinion by JUSTICE HARLAN, with only Justice Douglas dissenting, held that this challenge was not ripe:

. . . [T]here can be no question that this regulation . . . is a "final agency action" . . . . Also, we recognize the force of petitioners' contention that the issue as they have framed it presents a purely legal question: whether the regulation is totally beyond the agency's power under the statute. . . . These points which support the appropriateness of judicial resolution are, however, outweighed by other considerations. The regulation serves notice only that the Commissioner *may* under certain circumstances order inspection of certain facilities and data, and that further certification of additives *may* be refused to those who decline to permit a duly authorized inspection until they have complied in that regard. At this juncture we have no idea whether or when such an inspection will be ordered and what reasons the Commissioner will give to justify his order. The statutory authority asserted for the regulation is the power to promulgate regulations "for the efficient enforcement" of the Act. Whether the regulation is justified thus depends . . . on whether the statutory scheme as a whole justified promulgation of the regulation. This will depend not merely on an inquiry into statutory purpose, but concurrently on an understanding of what types of enforcement problems are encountered by the FDA, the need for various sorts of supervision in order to effectuate the goals of the Act, and the safeguards devised to protect legitimate trade secrets. We believe that judicial appraisal of these factors is likely to stand on a much surer footing in the context of a specific application of this regulation than could be the case in the framework of the generalized challenge made here.

We are also led to this result by considerations of the effect on the petitioners of the regulation . . . This is not a situation in which primary conduct is affected—when contracts must be negotiated, ingredients tested or substituted, or special records compiled. This regulation merely states that the Commissioner may authorize inspectors to examine certain processes or formulae; no advance action is required of cosmetics manufacturers . . . Moreover, no irremediable adverse consequences flow from requiring a later challenge to this regulation by a manufacturer who refuses to allow this type of inspection. Unlike the other regulations challenged in this action, in which seizure of goods, heavy fines, adverse publicity for distributing "adulterated" goods, and possible criminal liability might penalize failure to comply, a refusal to admit an inspector here would at most lead only to a suspension of certification services to the particular party, a determination that can then be promptly challenged through an administrative procedure, which in turn is reviewable by a court.

## NOTES

(1) ***The Constitutional and Prudential Dimensions of Ripeness.*** As the Supreme Court stated in NATIONAL PARK HOSPITALITY ASS'N V. DEPARTMENT OF THE INTERIOR, 538 U.S. 803 (2003), ripeness doctrine is "drawn both from Article III limitations on judicial power and from prudential reasons for refusing to exercise jurisdiction." The constitutional basis of ripeness overlaps to some extent with standing analysis. When suit is brought prematurely and the plaintiff's injury is speculative, standing is lacking; another way to describe this situation is that the challenge is unripe.

In TRUMP V. NEW YORK, 141 S.Ct. 530 (2020), the Court described standing and ripeness as "[t]wo related doctrines of justiciability—each originating in the case-or-controversy requirement of Article III . . . . First, a plaintiff must demonstrate standing, including 'an injury that is concrete, particularized, and imminent rather than conjectural or hypothetical.' Carney v. Adams, 141 S.Ct. 493 (2020). Second, the case must be 'ripe'—not dependent on 'contingent future events that may not occur as anticipated, or indeed may not occur at all.' Texas v. United States, 523 U.S. 296, 300 (1998)." Trump v. New York was a lawsuit seeking to enjoin the Secretary of Commerce from complying with a memorandum from President Trump announcing a policy of excluding unlawfully present noncitizens from the census count and instructing the Secretary to produce information to implement the policy "to the extent practicable." The Court held that the case was "riddled with contingencies and speculation" that meant neither doctrine was satisfied. Although the President had made his general policy preference clear, that "policy may not prove feasible" and "[a]ny prediction [of] how the Executive Branch might eventually implement this general statement of policy is no more than conjecture at this time."

Even if a plaintiff has standing, under Abbott Labs the suit may still be unripe if the issues remain unfit for judicial resolution or the hardships from delay are minimal. Toilet Goods v. Gardner provides an example. There, the Court acknowledged that the manufacturers were challenging a final regulation to which they were subject but concluded that judicial resolution would be on "surer footing" if conducted in the context of a specific application and that delay would not cause "irremediable adverse consequences."

More recently, a unanimous opinion of the Supreme Court has cast doubt on the "continuing validity of the prudential ripeness doctrine." SUSAN B. ANTHONY LIST V. DRIEHAUS, 573 U.S. 149 (2014) (p.1449) involved a pre-enforcement challenge to the constitutionality of an Ohio statute criminalizing certain kinds of false statements during a political campaign. After concluding that SBA satisfied the requirements for standing, JUSTICE THOMAS turned to the question of whether the challenge was ripe: "Respondents contend that these prudential ripeness factors confirm that the claims at issue are nonjusticiable. . . . But we have already concluded that petitioners have alleged a sufficient Article III injury. To the extent respondents would have us deem petitioners' claims nonjusticiable 'on grounds that are prudential' rather than constitutional, that request is in some tension with our recent reaffirmation of the principle that a federal court's obligation to hear and decide cases within its jurisdiction is virtually unflagging." The Court found no need to resolve the question of prudential ripeness doctrine, however, concluding that "the fitness and hardship factors [we]re easily satisfied" in that case.

(2) ***The Benefits and Costs of Pre-Enforcement Review.*** Recall that Justice Fortas dissented in Abbott Labs and another companion case, Gardner v. Toilet Goods, contending that by allowing pre-enforcement review the Court had "opened Pandora's box." (p. 1499). Pre-enforcement review would be frequently granted, "threaten[ing] programs of vast importance to the public welfare," and was based on "vastly overdrawn cries of distress" by the drug manufacturers. As he predicted, Abbott Labs has inaugurated an era in which pre-enforcement review is common. But is it unjustified?

According to RICHARD J. PIERCE, JR., SEVEN WAYS TO DEOSSIFY AGENCY RULEMAKING, 47 Admin. L. Rev. 59, 89–91 (1995), many scholars believe Abbott significantly increased "the stringency of judicial review of legislative rules." Reversing Abbott and precluding pre-enforcement review, according to opponents, would "deossify rulemaking" and return to the pre-Abbott environment, where the "record of the enforcement proceeding [w]as the primary basis for review of the rule." Moreover, it might deter parties from seeking review altogether. "Violation of a rule that is held to be valid often exposes the regulatee to the risk of large civil and criminal penalties, as well as other adverse regulatory and public relations consequences. Those risks are likely to induce regulatees to comply with a rule, even if they believe the rule to be invalid . . . [And because] [b]eneficiaries of regulatory statutes can obtain judicial review of agency rules only in the pre-enforcement context[,] . . . reversal of Abbott would have effects identical to those created by elimination of beneficiaries' standing to obtain judicial review of rules."

Should Congress therefore get rid of pre-enforcement review? Pierce argues no. Given the adverse consequences to regulated entities of losing an enforcement action, "agencies often could predict with confidence that a rule will never be subject to judicial review"; hence, "reversal of Abbott could produce a legal environment in which agencies frequently issue rules that conflict with statutes or with the Constitution."

By contrast, JERRY L. MASHAW and DAVID L. HARFST, in THE STRUGGLE FOR AUTO SAFETY 246–47 (1990), answer yes, at least with respect to the auto safety program overseen by the National Highway Transportation Safety Administration. They acknowledge that pre-enforcement review brings several benefits: "Costs of compliance with invalid rules are saved, uncertainty about the legality of regulation is more quickly removed, all affected parties receive similar treatment (no one need comply while a challenge is pending, and weak or disfavored organizations cannot be singled out by the agency for enforcement action), and regulators are held strictly accountable because they cannot suppress legal contests through enforcement compromises." At the same time, Mashaw and Harfst argue that pre-enforcement review's costs to the auto safety program were great: Difficulty getting rules through judicial review led NHTSA to abandon rulemaking in favor of a far less rational and effective reliance on recalls. In addition, "[b]ecause delaying review shifts incentives, it promotes the development of more credible information on both compliance costs and engineering feasibility. Judicial review will be better informed on the critical issues that are now routinely presented but seldom substantiated by more than industry and agency conjecture."

(3) ***Pre-Enforcement Review and Beneficiary Challenges.*** Regulatory beneficiaries have a significant stake in the preservation of pre-enforcement review. Under Heckler v. Chaney (p. 1527), beneficiaries are presumptively precluded from challenging agencies' nonenforcement decisions. Even if an enforcement action is brought, would a beneficiary group be permitted to intervene and argue that even greater sanctions should be imposed against the defendant than the agency had proposed? See generally Nina A. Mendelson, Regulatory Beneficiaries and Informal Agency Policymaking, 92 Cornell L. Rev. 408 (2007).

LUJAN V. NATIONAL WILDLIFE FED., 497 U.S. 871, 890–94 (1990), demonstrates the obstacles that ripeness can pose to beneficiary challenges. Environmentalists challenged what they described as an unlawful Bureau of Land Management "program" of opening previously protected public lands to private development. JUSTICE SCALIA's opinion for the five-member majority concluded that they did not have standing but went on to articulate a more general theory of ripeness that also foreclosed review: "The term 'land withdrawal review program' . . . does not refer to a single BLM order or regulation, or even to a completed universe of particular BLM orders and regulations. . . . It is no more an identifiable 'agency action'—much less a 'final agency action'—than a 'weapons procurement program' of the Department of Defense or a 'drug interdiction program' of the Drug Enforcement Administration. . . .

"Under the terms of the APA, respondent must direct its attack against some particular 'agency action' that causes it harm. Some statutes permit broad regulations to serve as the 'agency action,' . . . [but a]bsent such a provision . . . a regulation is not ordinarily considered the type of agency action 'ripe' for judicial review under the APA until the scope of the controversy has been reduced to more manageable proportions, and its factual components fleshed out, by some concrete action applying the regulation to the claimant's situation in a fashion that harms or threatens to harm him. (The major exception, of course, is a substantive rule which as a practical matter requires the plaintiff to adjust his conduct immediately. Such agency action is 'ripe' for review at once, whether or not explicit statutory review apart from the APA is provided.)" See also Norton v. Southern Utah Wilderness Alliance (p. 1531).

Note that the italicized language applies principally—if not exclusively—to members of the regulated community. Where, in this description, do challenges by beneficiaries fit? In RENO V. CATHOLIC SOC. SERV., INC., 509 U.S. 43, 68–71, 78 (1993), immigrants' rights groups, in class actions on behalf of certain noncitizens residing in the country unlawfully, challenged INS regulations that narrowly interpreted two of the four statutory criteria for an amnesty program established by the Immigration Reform and Control Act of 1986. The interpretations rendered the plaintiff classes ineligible for amnesty. The majority held that most of the challenges were not constitutionally ripe until an immigrant had applied for benefits and been denied. The Court remanded, however, for exploration of allegations that the INS engaged in a practice of "front-desking," in which employees refused even to accept applications from immigrants whom the agency considered ineligible under the challenged interpretation. "[A] class member whose application was 'front-desked' would have felt the effects of the [challenged regulations] in a particularly concrete manner, for his application for legalization would have been blocked then and there; his challenge to the regulation should not fail for lack of ripeness."

Concurring, Justice O'Connor stated that she "would not go so far as to state that a suit challenging a benefit conferring rule is necessarily unripe simply because the plaintiff has not yet applied for the benefit. . . . If it is 'inevitable' that the challenged rule will 'operat[e]' to the plaintiff's disadvantage—if the court can make a firm prediction that the plaintiff will apply for the benefit, and that the agency will deny the application by virtue of the rule—then there may well be a justiciable controversy that the court may find prudent to resolve." Do you agree with Justice O'Connor, or need we not be so concerned about enabling beneficiary challenges?

## d. Remedies

*(1) Injunctive and Declaratory Relief*
*(2) Suits for Damages*

Standing, reviewability, and timing are all doctrines that target the front end of a judicial action challenging administrative action. They go to the question of what claims a particular plaintiff can bring at a particular time. Remedies, by contrast, are focused on the back-end question of what relief a court can and should grant upon finding that an agency acted unlawfully. Yet remedies also have an important front-end dimension. The availability of different types of relief often turns on the type of legal action that is brought, and a court's inability to grant any relief—or, put in different terms, a lack of redressability—can result in a finding of no standing. Hence, in addition to thinking about standing and reviewability, attorneys need to give thought to what remedial relief might be available in constructing a lawsuit to challenge actions by an agency or agency official.

Remedies for unlawful governmental conduct fall into two general camps: (1) injunctive and declaratory relief, and (2) damages. These are also common forms of relief in suits targeting private conduct, but suits against the government face a unique hurdle: sovereign immunity. Under the doctrine of sovereign immunity, the federal government cannot be sued without its consent. State governments also enjoy freedom from suit in federal court without their consent, protected by the Eleventh Amendment and constitutional principles of federalism, but this protection is subject to abrogation by Congress in some contexts. As you'll see in the materials that follow, Congress has broadly waived sovereign immunity for suits against the federal government. In addition, courts have designed doctrines to mitigate the impact of sovereign immunity, with the result that sovereign immunity is rarely a barrier in suits for injunctive or declaratory relief. However, it can pose a barrier to suits for damages.

Courts and Congress have also devised some unique remedies for actions challenging administrative action. Prime among these is remand without vacatur, a relatively recent remedial mechanism, which you may have seen already in Chapter IV. Other uniquely governmental remedies are the prerogative writs, particularly of habeas and mandamus, which have existed since before the founding, with habeas enjoying constitutional protection. U.S. Const. Art. I, § 9.

## (1) Injunctive and Declaratory Relief

*Notes on the Availability of Injunctive Relief and Remand Without Vacatur*
*Notes on Nationwide Injunctions and Vacatur of Rules*

Federal courts have long provided relief against unlawful governmental action. The traditional form of such relief was an officer's suit, a creation of the federal court's equitable powers that traced back to the English petition of right. In an early famous example, United States v. Lee, 106 U.S. 196 (1882), the federal government had taken General Robert E. Lee's Arlington property for unpaid taxes during the Civil War and turned it into Arlington Cemetery. Concluding that the suit was not barred by sovereign immunity, the Supreme Court allowed Robert E. Lee's son to bring an ejectment action against the two military officers who had control of the property.

As noted above in Section 2.a.3's discussion of nonstatutory review (p. 1492), suits against government officials based on the writs of habeas corpus, 28 U.S.C. § 2241, or mandamus, 28 U.S.C. § 1361, can also result in grants of injunctive relief.[8] However, the scope of these writs is narrow: habeas is limited to actions seeking release of an individual claimed to be unlawfully in custody, and traditionally mandamus was available only for plaintiffs seeking to force a governmental official to perform a ministerial, nondiscretionary duty. See Kendall v. United States ex rel. Stokes, 12 Pet. 524, 613 (1838).

In American School of Magnetic Healing v. McAnnulty, 187 U.S. 94 (1902), the Supreme Court upheld a grant of injunctive relief against a federal postmaster. The subsequent decision in Ex parte Young, 209 U.S. 123 (1908), has come to stand for the broader principle that sovereign immunity does not bar injunctive relief against governmental officials acting unlawfully. Such suits rest on the fiction that ordering officials to conform their (official) behavior to law is not a suit against the sovereign because the sovereign does not authorize its agents to violate the law. Official immunity doctrines which limit government officers' personal liability in damages actions are thought not to apply in actions for prospective relief, such as injunctive or declaratory relief.

The Court has emphasized that "[t]he ability to sue to enjoin unconstitutional actions by state and federal officers is the creation of courts of equity" and a "judge-made remedy." Armstrong v. Exceptional Child Center, Inc., 575 U.S. 320 (2015). In other words, it derives from an implied equitable action, one form of nonstatutory review (see Section

[8] In addition, 28 U.S.C. § 1651(a), the All Writs Act, authorizes the Supreme Court and the lower federal courts to "issue all writs necessary or appropriate in aid of their respective jurisdictions and agreeable to the usages and principles of law." The prerogative writs other than habeas and mandamus are quo warranto (usually limited to challenging an official's right to office), prohibition (used to prevent a judicial or quasi-judicial body from exceeding its jurisdiction when no other remedy is available), and certiorari (used to require a lower tribunal to certify the record of its proceedings to a higher tribunal for purposes of review).

2.a.3, p. 1492). That said, enactment of the APA in 1946 provided an express statutory cause of action in § 702. Further, § 703 states that in the absence or inadequacy of a special statutory review proceeding, "any applicable form of legal action, including actions for declaratory judgments or writs of prohibitory or mandatory injunction or habeas corpus, in a court of competent jurisdiction" can be brought. Declaratory relief had been made available even earlier, with enactment of the Declaratory Judgment Act in 1934, 28 U.S.C. §§ 2201–02. Given that § 702 expressly authorizes specific relief against the agency itself, the nonstatutory forms retain little independent practical significance for cases that can be brought under the APA. But lower courts have held that the traditional nonstatutory avenues for declaratory and injunctive relief, and for mandamus, continue to function where the APA is not available. See, e.g., Sierra Club v. Trump, 963 F.3d 874, 890–93 (9th Cir. 2020), vacated and remanded sub nom. Biden v. Trump, 142 S.Ct. 46 (2021); Duncan v. Muzyn, 833 F.3d 567, 576–79 (6th Cir. 2016).

As originally enacted, the APA did not contain a waiver of sovereign immunity, but one was added in 1976. This waiver, contained in § 702, provides:

> An action in a court of the United States seeking relief other than money damages and stating a claim that an agency or an officer or employee thereof acted or failed to act in an official capacity or under color of legal authority shall not be dismissed nor relief therein be denied on the ground that it is against the United States or that the United States is an indispensable party. . . .

In addition, § 703 provides, "If no special statutory proceeding is applicable, the action for judicial review may be brought against the United States, the agency by its official title, or the appropriate officer." As a result, today most garden-variety administrative review claims proceed against the agency, by name, without any sovereign immunity concerns. Because the consent to suit excludes suits seeking "money damages," an action to obtain injunctive relief cannot be used to obtain a payment of money unless the challenged administrative decision itself involves such a payment. See Bowen v. Massachusetts, 487 U.S. 879 (1988).

The APA also contains provisions addressing more specifically the type of relief a court can grant. To begin with, § 705 expressly authorizes interim relief:

> On such conditions as may be required and to the extent necessary to prevent irreparable injury, the reviewing court . . . may issue all necessary and appropriate process to postpone the effective date of an agency action or to preserve status or rights pending conclusion of the review proceedings.

In addition, § 706, which sets out the scope of review under the APA, also provides that "the reviewing court shall . . . hold unlawful and set aside agency action, findings, and conclusions found to be" arbitrary and capricious, outside of constitutional and statutory authority, at odds with governing procedures or unsupported by substantial evidence (where applicable, and that "due account shall be taken of the rule of prejudicial error." Finally, § 702 makes clear that general doctrines governing the grant of injunctive and declaratory relief continue to apply. Thus, notwithstanding the APA's authorization of actions for injunctive and declaratory relief, "[n]othing herein (1) affects . . . the power or duty of a court to . . . deny relief on any . . . appropriate legal or equitable ground; or (2) confers authority to grant relief if any other statute that grants consent to suit expressly or impliedly forbids the relief which is sought."

## NOTES ON THE AVAILABILITY OF INJUNCTIVE RELIEF AND REMAND WITHOUT VACATUR

(1) ***Preclusion of Injunctive and Declaratory Relief.*** The APA's provisions generally ensure that declaratory and injunctive relief are available in actions against agencies. However, Congress can always preclude certain types of relief by statute. Recently, in Biden v. Texas, 142 S.Ct 2528 (2022) and Garland v. Aleman-Gonzalez, 142 S.Ct. 2057 (2022), the Supreme Court addressed one such provision in the immigration context, 8 U.S.C. § 1252(f)(1), which provides that "no court (other than the Supreme Court) shall have jurisdiction or authority to enjoin or restrain the operation of [8 U.S.C. §§ 1221–1232]," for actions other than those regarding application of these provisions to individual noncitizens. In Aleman-Gonzalez, the Court held this provision deprived lower courts of jurisdiction to consider requests for class-wide injunctive relief. In Biden v. Texas, the Court held that the provision withdrew a lower court's authority to grant a certain form of relief but did not deprive the lower courts of subject matter jurisdiction over claims brought under the listed sections.

In addition, the Court has found that injunctive relief is sometimes implicitly precluded by statute. ARMSTRONG V. EXCEPTIONAL CHILD CENTER, 575 U.S. 320 (2015), provides a recent example. There, the Court in a 5–4 decision written by JUSTICE SCALIA, rejected an effort by providers of habilitation services to enjoin Idaho's Medicaid reimbursement rates as preempted by § 30A of the Medicaid Act: "The power of federal courts of equity to enjoin unlawful executive action is subject to express and implied statutory limitations. 'Courts of equity can no more disregard statutory and constitutional requirements and provisions than can courts of law.' INS v. Pangilinan, 486 U.S. 875, 883 (1988). . . . Two aspects of § 30(A) establish Congress's intent to foreclose equitable relief. First, the sole remedy Congress provided for a State's failure to comply with Medicaid's requirements . . . is the withholding of Medicaid funds by the Secretary of Health and Human Services. 42 U.S.C. § 1396c. As we have elsewhere explained, the 'express provision of one method of enforcing a substantive rule suggests that Congress intended to preclude others.' Alexander v. Sandoval, 532 U.S. 275, 290 (2001)." The second is "the judicially unadministrable nature of § 30(A)'s text. It is difficult to imagine a requirement broader and less specific than § 30(A)'s mandate that state plans provide for payments that are 'consistent with efficiency, economy, and quality of care,' all the while 'safeguard[ing] against unnecessary utilization of . . . care and services.' Explicitly conferring enforcement of this judgment-laden standard upon the Secretary alone establishes, we think, that Congress 'wanted to make the agency remedy that it provided exclusive.' Gonzaga Univ. v. Doe, 536 U.S. 273, 292 (2002) (Breyer, J., concurring in judgment). The sheer complexity associated with enforcing § 30(A), coupled with the express provision of an administrative remedy, § 1396c, shows that the Medicaid Act precludes private enforcement of § 30(A) in the courts."

(2) ***The Propriety of Injunctive Relief.*** If a court is not precluded from granting injunctive relief by statute, must it do so upon finding that an agency has acted unlawfully? No, said the Supreme Court in MONSANTO CO. V. GEERTSON SEED FARMS, 561 U.S. 139, 156–57 (2010). In Monsanto, a district court held that the Animal and Plant Health Inspection Service in the Department of Agriculture violated the National Environmental Policy Act when, without preparing an environmental impact statement, it completely deregulated Roundup Ready Alfalfa (RRA), a variety of alfalfa that has been genetically engineered to tolerate the herbicide Roundup. At the request of conventional alfalfa farmers, who were concerned that their crops would be infected with RRA if it were completely deregulated, the district court vacated the agency's decision completely deregulating RRA; enjoined APHIS from deregulating RRA, in whole or in part, pending completion of the EIS; and entered a nationwide permanent injunction prohibiting almost all future planting of RRA during the pendency of the EIS process.

The Supreme Court, in a 7–1 opinion written by JUSTICE ALITO, held that the district court erred in enjoining even partial deregulation of RRA absent an EIS and in granting a nationwide injunction against any planting of RRA. In so holding, the Court set out a four-factor test that governs grants of injunctive relief: " '[A] plaintiff must demonstrate: (1) that it has suffered an irreparable injury; (2) that remedies available at law, such as monetary damages, are inadequate to compensate for that injury; 3) that, considering the balance of hardships between the plaintiff and defendant, a remedy in equity is warranted; and (4) that the public interest would not be disserved by a permanent injunction.' eBay Inc. v. MercExchange, L.L.C., 547 U.S. 388, 391 (2006). . . . An injunction should issue only if the traditional four-factor test is satisfied." The Court also emphasized that "[a]n injunction is a drastic and extraordinary remedy, which should not be granted as a matter of course. If a less drastic remedy . . . was sufficient to redress respondents' injury, no recourse to the additional and extraordinary relief of an injunction was warranted." In this case, the Court held "it is clear that the order enjoining any deregulation whatsoever does not satisfy the traditional four-factor test for granting permanent injunctive relief. Most importantly, respondents cannot show that they will suffer irreparable injury if APHIS is allowed to proceed with any partial deregulation." And "it necessarily follows that it was likewise inappropriate to enjoin any and all parties from acting in accordance with the terms of such a [partial] deregulation decision" through a nationwide injunction on future planting of RRA.

RONALD M. LEVIN, in "VACATION" AT SEA: JUDICIAL REMEDIES AND EQUITABLE DISCRETION IN ADMINISTRATIVE LAW, 53 Duke L.J. 291, 334–35, 340 (2003), argues that the equitable tradition remains strong in administrative law. He concludes that "[t]he teaching of the [Supreme Court's] cases, broadly speaking, is that equity does not always require the court to issue such an injunction, even if the court has found the defendant to be in breach of the statute. . . . Their collective message is that a court may not rely on equity to repudiate a statutory objective outright, but it has some leeway to decide whether or not to grant an injunction as a means of achieving compliance with the statutory scheme."

(3) ***Interim Relief and Stays of Rules.*** Section 705 of the APA expressly authorizes interim relief, such as a stay pending review. The relevant organic statute under which an agency operates may also authorize a stay. If all else fails, the Supreme Court has suggested that the power to issue a stay does not depend upon specific authorization but is "part of [the court's] traditional equipment for the administration of justice." ScrippsHoward Radio, Inc. v. FCC, 316 U.S. 4, 9–10 (1942). In deciding whether or not to actually grant a stay of agency action pending appeal, courts consider factors similar to the test that governs the decision to grant a preliminary injunction. But given the preliminary posture, here the factors include "that he is likely to succeed on the merits, that he is likely to suffer irreparable harm in the absence of preliminary relief, that the balance of equities tips in his favor, and that an injunction is in the public interest." Winter v. Natural Resources Defense Council, Inc., 555 U.S. 7, 20 (2008). There is "substantial overlap" between this test and the standard for granting a stay pending appeal of court action, which asks "(1) whether the stay applicant has made a strong showing that he is likely to succeed on the merits; (2) whether the applicant will be irreparably injured absent a stay; (3) whether issuance of the stay will substantially injure the other parties interested in the proceeding; and (4) where the public interest lies." Nken v. Holder, 556 U.S. 418, 434 (2009).

In recent cases, however, the Court appears to be granting preliminary relief—and in particular, stays of agency rules and lower court decisions—more freely than before. This question rose to the fore with respect to the Obama Administration's Clean Power Plan: The D.C. Circuit denied a stay but was reversed by the Supreme Court on a 5–4 vote. West Virginia v. EPA, 142 S.Ct. 2587 (2016). (The Court subsequently held that the Plan fell outside of EPA's statutory authority, p. 1341.) The Court also granted stays of lower court decisions pending its own review or opted to grant certiorari before judgment below. Such actions became particularly prevalent during the Trump Administration and were often taken in response to a request for emergency relief by the Solicitor General. According to one study, "in less than three years [during the Trump Administration], the Solicitor General has filed at least twenty-one applications for stays in the Supreme Court . . . . During the sixteen years of the George W. Bush and Obama Administrations, the Solicitor General filed a total of eight such applications." The same study concluded that in practice the Court's standard for granting stays and emergency relief had changed in practice:

"First, a majority of the Justices now appear to believe that the government suffers an irreparable injury militating in favor of emergency relief *whenever* a statute or policy is enjoined by a lower court, regardless of the actual impact of the lower court's ruling.... Second, ... the conclusive consideration in such cases has become the government's likelihood of success on the merits." STEPHEN I. VLADECK, THE SOLICITOR GENERAL AND THE SHADOW DOCKET, 133 Harv. L. Rev. 123, 125–26 (2019).

How willing should courts be to stay rules pending judicial challenge? According to RONALD A. CASS, in STAYING AGENCY RULES: CONSTITUTIONAL STRUCTURE AND RULE OF LAW IN THE ADMINISTRATIVE STATE, 69 Admin. L. Rev. 225, 228–29 (2017)), stays should be granted more freely in the context of rules that impose significant obligations: "Allowing these rules to apply immediately often gives the individuals and entities that are subject to them a choice between investing in costly compliance or risking serious sanctions, including potential criminal liability; to the extent that this induces compliance with rules that were not well-grounded in law, courts' ability to provide an effective check on administrative officials can be substantially eroded. Obviously, expensive, time-consuming litigation contesting the legality of an administrative decision is a far less attractive option if the only remedy at the end of the case is a Pyrrhic declaration of victory. Once a rule's targets decide that the risk of sanctions requires immediate compliance, the only 'remedy' a court can offer is recognition that the litigants need not have spent the millions already invested in complying with an illegal rule. . . ."

Are you persuaded? Cass argues that regulated parties will be less likely to challenge rules in court if they will have to invest significantly in compliance before their challenge is adjudicated, and also that knowing they are unlikely to be sued gives agency officials incentives to exceed their authority. But isn't the opposite also true: making stays more easily available will give regulated parties incentive to bring excessive and unwarranted challenges to rules, if for no other reason than to delay the time at which they have to comply, and litigation risks may make agency officials excessively cautious. Should the courts favor agencies or regulated parties when it comes to interim relief? Is the current case-by-case assessment about the propriety of interim relief better than a categorical approach? If so, should lower courts receive substantial deference in making such discretionary assessments?

(4) ***The Ordinary Remand Rule and Remand Without Vacatur.*** What about the opposite extreme: If a court finds an agency erred, is it ever justified in ignoring the error as harmless or allowing the action to remain while remanding to the agency for corrective action? The ordinary rule, often traced back to SEC v. Chenery Corp. (Chenery II), 332 U.S. 194, 196 (1947) (p. 258), is that upon finding error a court will remand to the agency rather than address the issue itself. See Christopher J. Walker, The Ordinary Remand Rule and the Judicial Toolbox for Agency Dialogue, 82 Geo. Wash. L. Rev. 1553 (2014).

Although courts frequently vacate before remanding, the use of remand without vacatur is now a fairly routine practice in judicial review. "[T]he decision whether to vacate depends on the seriousness of the . . . deficiencies (and thus the extent of doubt whether the agency chose correctly) and the disruptive consequences of an interim change that may itself be changed." Allied-Signal, Inc. v. NRC, 988 F.2d 146, 150–51 (D.C. Cir. 1993); see also ACUS, Recommendation 2013-6, Remand Without Vacatur, 78 Fed. Reg. 76272 (Dec. 17, 2013). This approach is often invoked when the court identifies a defect in an agency's explanation for its decision that the court concludes the agency can readily cure on remand. Vacating a rule in such contexts can undo extensive agency effort for little substantive benefit and unduly reward marginal appeals. It also can be significantly disruptive, particularly when the new rule has already gone into effect.

But does the APA give courts authority to use remand without vacatur? In CHECKOSKY V. SEC, 23 F.3d 452 (D.C. Cir. 1994), JUDGE RANDOLPH argued that remand without vacatur violated the APA: "Section 706(2)(A) provides that a 'reviewing court' faced with an arbitrary and capricious agency decision 'shall'—not may—'hold unlawful and set aside' the agency action. Setting aside means vacating; no other meaning is apparent." 23 F.3d at 491. By contrast, JUDGE SILBERMAN insisted that the APA only requires a court to set aside an agency decision it finds to be arbitrary and capricious but does not preclude a court from remanding a decision to an agency for fuller explanation without making that determination. Id. at 462–63.

JOHN C. HARRISON, in REMAND WITHOUT VACATUR AND THE AB INITIO INVALIDITY OF UNLAWFUL REGULATIONS IN ADMINISTRATIVE LAW, 48 BYU L. Rev. (forthcoming), raises a different objection to remand without vacatur. He argues that remand without vacatur rests on a mistaken analogy between agency regulations and lower-court decrees: "Under the doctrine called remand without vacatur, courts assume that unlawful regulations are binding until displaced by a court, just as a lower court's decree is binding until displaced." However, "[a]gency regulations of private conduct, that are enforced by sanctions directed against private rights (not by withdrawal of government benefits), and that are unlawful as set out in section 706 of the APA, are in general void ab initio. . . . As applied to regulations of private conduct, the doctrine of remand without vacatur rests on the false assumption that unlawful regulations are binding until displaced." As a result, "a court that finds a regulation unlawful should make clear that the regulated party has no duty to comply." But "[b]ecause unlawful regulations are void ab initio, vacatur is not necessary to give relief to the party before the court. The party-specific remedy of an injunction, or a declaration, will be enough." Harrison rests his claim that unlawful regulations are void ab initio on the principle that agencies have only the authority that Congress gives them, and argues that Congress ordinarily should not be read as granting agencies the power to issue unlawful regulations that are binding but voidable.

Does Harrison's account work with the text of the APA, however? Section 706(2) provides that a "court shall hold unlawful and set aside" agency actions found to violate the subsection's provisions. But if unlawful regulations are void ab initio, why would a court need to set them aside? As important, § 706(2) also instructs courts to take "due account . . . of the rule of prejudicial error." According to NICHOLAS BAGLEY in REMEDIAL RESTRAINT

IN ADMINISTRATIVE LAW, 117 Colum. L. Rev. 253, 309 (2017), this instruction means that "[s]o far as the APA is concerned, reviewing courts are authorized to hold agency errors harmless, much as they can hold trial errors harmless. There's nothing to the argument that the APA, by its terms, strips courts of the authority to leave procedurally defective agency rules intact." Bagley identifies this language as providing support for remand without vacatur, arguing that what is anomalous is a court's decision to remand to the agency for correction of harmless errors. "The prominence of remand without vacatur has displaced a forthright discussion of the possibility that some errors should be excused as harmless." Can Harrison's account be squared with the APA's emphasis on harmless error?

The Supreme Court has emphasized that, "upon finding the grounds for agency action are inadequate, a court may remand for the agency to do one of two things. . . . First, the agency can offer a fuller explanation of the agency's reasoning at the time of the agency action. . . . Alternatively, the agency can deal with the problem afresh by taking new agency action." Biden v. Texas, 142 S.Ct. 2528, 2544 (2022). But is it always so clear which way an agency chooses to respond? DHS v. REGENTS OF THE UNIVERSITY OF CALIFORNIA, 140 S.Ct. 1891 (2020) (p. 1139), involved a challenge to the Trump Administration's decision to rescind deferred action for noncitizens who had been brought to the country unlawfully as children. The Court held that the initial decision to rescind DACA by the acting Secretary of Homeland Security Elaine Duke failed to consider whether forbearance from removal should continue, even if granting DACA recipients affirmative benefits was unlawful. In so holding, the majority refused to consider a subsequent memorandum, this one issued by DHS Secretary Kirstjen Nielsen after the D.C. district court held that Duke's explanation was insufficient. (The district court had stayed its order granting summary judgment for the plaintiffs for 90 days so that DHS could provide a fuller explanation.) The majority invoked Chenery I (p. 255) in refusing to consider policy arguments offered in the Nielsen memo that were not included in the initial Duke memo, noting that "Nielsen chose to elaborate on the reasons for the initial rescission rather than take new administrative action." Concurring and dissenting in part, Justice Kavanaugh argued that the Court should have considered the Nielsen memo, noting that "the ordinary judicial remedy for an agency's insufficient explanation is to remand for further explanation by the relevant agency personnel. It would make little sense for a court to exclude official explanations by agency personnel such as a Cabinet Secretary simply because the explanations are purportedly post hoc, and then to turn around and remand for further explanation by those same agency personnel. Yet that is the upshot of the Court's application of the post hoc justification doctrine today."

Justice Kavanaugh's point seems to have particular resonance in the context of remand without vacatur. Indeed, isn't what the district court did the equivalent of remand without vacatur? But even though it might appear a technicality, the majority seems to be correct that if an agency is allowed to supply a new explanation for the same agency action, that would eviscerate Chenery I. Does Regents suggest that, in order to accord with

Chenery I, remand without vacatur must be understood to require an agency to undertake a new action, with the appropriate procedure for that type of action?

## NOTES ON NATIONWIDE INJUNCTIONS AND VACATUR OF RULES

(1) ***The Debate over the Nationwide or Universal Injunction.*** A separate question from whether to grant injunctive relief is what the proper scope of that relief should be. In recent years, this question has risen to the fore in response to lower courts granting nationwide or universal injunctions against challenged agency action. Such an injunction prohibits enforcement of a challenged statute, regulation, agency order or decision against anyone, not simply against the parties to the case or within a court's geographical confines. Part of the attention given to this issue stems from the fact that nationwide injunctions have often issued in prominent, politically contentious cases—such as Texas v. United States, 809 F.3d 134, 188 (5th Cir. 2015) (p. 409), where the Fifth Circuit upheld a nationwide injunction against implementation of the Obama Administration's DAPA initiative to provide deportation relief to millions of parents in the country unlawfully; the nationwide injunctions issued against President Trump's executive orders imposing a ban on travel to the U.S. from certain countries; and the nationwide injunctions issued against several of the Biden Administration's COVID measures. The number of such injunctions being granted also appears to be rising: "Federal courts issued twelve nationwide injunctions against the George W. Bush Administration, while nineteen nationwide injunctions were issued against the Obama Administration, a fifty-eight percent increase. By early 2020, federal courts had issued at least fifty-five nationwide injunctions against the Trump Administration, a rate of eighteen nationwide injunctions per year." Richard J. Pierce, Jr., The Supreme Court Should Eliminate Its Lawless Shadow Docket, 74 Admin. L. Rev. 1, 3 n.15 (2022). The Department of Justice issued guidelines strongly criticizing the use of nationwide injunctions. See Attorney General Jeff Sessions, Litigation Guidelines for Cases presenting the Possibility of Nationwide Injunctions (Sept. 13, 2018) (DOJ Litigation Guidelines).[9] Several justices have offered contrasting views of the validity of nationwide injunctions in concurrences and dissents, but the Court as a whole has not reached the question in recent cases where it has arisen.

(2) ***Is Article III a Barrier to Nationwide Injunctions?*** Several distinct issues are intertwined in the debate over nationwide injunctions. One question concerns whether, given Article III's cases and controversies requirement and the history of equity, the federal courts have power to issue nationwide injunctions that would bind nonparties and provide relief to anyone other than the particular plaintiffs in the case at hand.

JUSTICE THOMAS raised Article III concerns with what he termed "universal injunctions" when concurring in TRUMP V. HAWAII, 138 S.Ct. 2392, 2426–29 (2018), which sustained the Trump Administration's travel ban:

[9] https://www.justice.gov/opa/press-release/file/1093881/download.

"The scope of the federal courts' equitable authority under the Constitution was a point of contention at the founding, and the more limited construction of that power prevailed. . . . This authority must comply with longstanding principles of equity that predate this country's founding. . . . Universal injunctions do not seem to comply with those principles. These injunctions are a recent development, emerging for the first time in the 1960s and dramatically increasing in popularity only very recently." Reviewing the history of equity, Thomas contended that "[t]he English system of equity did not contemplate universal injunctions. As an agent of the King, the Chancellor had no authority to enjoin him. American courts inherited this tradition. Moreover, as a general rule, American courts of equity did not provide relief beyond the parties to the case. If their injunctions advantaged nonparties, that benefit was merely incidental. American courts' tradition of providing equitable relief only to parties was consistent with their view of the nature of judicial power. For most of our history, courts understood judicial power as fundamentally the power to render judgments in individual cases." Thomas also argued that the "Court has never treated general statutory grants of equitable authority as giving federal courts a freewheeling power to fashion new forms of equitable remedies. Rather, it has read such statutes as constrained by 'the body of law which had been transplanted to this country from the English Court of Chancery' in 1789."

JUSTICE GORSUCH agreed with Thomas's account in DHS V. NEW YORK, 140 S.Ct. 599, 600 (2020), and also emphasized the incompatibility of nationwide injunctions and Article III's text: "When a district court orders the government not to enforce a rule against the plaintiffs in the case before it, the court redresses the injury that gives rise to its jurisdiction in the first place. But when a court goes further than that, ordering the government to take (or not take) some action with respect to those who are strangers to the suit, it is hard to see how the court could still be acting in the judicial role of resolving cases and controversies. Injunctions like these thus raise serious questions about the scope of courts' equitable powers under Article III." Note that, even if adopting this parties-only approach, a court should still be able to grant nationwide relief when it determines doing so is necessary to afford the parties "complete relief." Dissenting in Trump v. Hawaii, Justice Sotomayor defended the district court's grant of a nationwide injunction on this ground. 138 S.Ct. 2392, 2446 n.13 (2018); see also Little Sisters of the Poor v. Pennsylvania, 140 S.Ct. 2367 (2020) (Ginsburg, J., dissenting) (defending nationwide relief as necessary to give complete relief when the harm at issue "is not bounded by state lines."); Zayn Siddique, Nationwide Injunctions, 117 Colum. L. Rev. 2095 (2017) (arguing that nationwide injunctions should be limited to where necessary to provide complete relief to the plaintiffs).

In adopting their positions, Justices Thomas and Gorsuch relied on an article by SAMUEL L. BRAY, MULTIPLE CHANCELLORS: REFORMING THE NATIONAL INJUNCTION, 131 Harv. L. Rev. 417, 472 (2017), arguing that the Article III "judicial power" is "a power to decide a case for a particular claimant. . . . This claimant-focused understanding of the judicial power has implications not only for who can sue in federal court, but also for what remedies the federal courts have authority to give. . . . Once a federal court has given an appropriate remedy to the plaintiffs, there is no longer any case or controversy left for the court to resolve. The parties have had their case or controversy resolved. There is no other. The court has no constitutional basis to decide disputes and issue remedies for those who are not parties." Bray also insists that "the national injunction is a recent development in the history of equity, traceable to the second half of the twentieth century. The older English and American practice was that an injunction would restrain the defendant's conduct vis-à-vis the plaintiff, not vis-à-vis the world." In lieu of contemporary nationwide injunctions, Bray "proposes a single clear rule for the scope of injunctions against federal defendants. A federal court should give a plaintiff-protective injunction, enjoining the defendant's conduct only with respect to the plaintiff. No matter how important the question and no matter how important the value of uniformity, a federal court should not award a national injunction."

MILA SOHONI disputes these arguments against nationwide injunctions in THE LOST HISTORY OF THE "UNIVERSAL INJUNCTION," 133 Harv. L. Rev. 920, 924–28 (2020): "The universal injunction against federal law did not "emerg[e] for the first time in the 1960s," as many critics of the universal injunction have claimed. The Court itself issued a universal injunction in 1913 . . . . Moreover, at least as far back as 1916, three-judge federal courts issued injunctions against the enforcement of laws that reached beyond the plaintiffs in those suits. The laws thereby enjoined were state laws, not federal laws, but the injunctions possessed the characteristic that matters most to the Article III debate over the injunctive power: those injunctions gave sweeping protection to nonplaintiffs who would otherwise have been vulnerable to the law's enforcement. When the state defendants in those suits appealed directly to the Supreme Court[,] . . . the Court on several occasions affirmed the lower courts' injunctions . . . . Not long thereafter, the universal injunction was brought to bear upon federal agency action . . . in Lukens Steel Co. v. Perkins. . . .

"This history has important implications for how we should understand Article III. . . . We must be clear about one thing: it would be a sharp departure from precedent and practice to treat Article III as requiring the equitable remedial powers of federal courts to be cabined in th[e] manner [proposed]. Article III confers a singular power upon all federal courts to decide "Cases[ ] in . . . Equity." It does not allocate different types of equitable remedial power to courts at different levels of the federal judicial hierarchy, and it draws no line between state and federal government defendants. That singular judicial power must be uniformly interpreted . . . . If the Supreme Court can issue a universal injunction against enforcement of a federal law in a suit by a single plaintiff, then so can a federal district court as an Article III matter." Finally, "American federal courts did not issue . . . injunctions against enforcement suits brought by state and federal officers until well after the Founding. A strictly originalist approach to the judicial power in equity would therefore jettison not just the universal injunction—it would equally undercut the propriety of an injunction that protected just a single plaintiff from enforcement of even an egregiously unconstitutional law by a government officer. Such a straitened conception of the equitable power of Article III courts cannot be squared with either a century-plus of practice or with 'the implicit policies embodied in Article III' itself."

Are you persuaded that Article III prohibits a federal court from granting injunctive relief that goes beyond the parties at hand? Isn't Sohoni correct that any such constitutional prohibition would apply to the Supreme Court as well as to lower courts? That would mean Article III prevents the Court from enjoining all application of a statute the Court holds is unconstitutional. Of course, were the government to try to apply such a statute to others, they could presumably go into court and get injunctive relief easily. But does Article III require that arrangement and prohibit a court from granting relief that benefits nonparties? At the least, as Sohoni points out, such a result is at odds with substantial twentieth (and twenty-first) century judicial practice. Should that matter in assessing what Article III demands?

(3) ***Statutory Authorization and Limitation.*** A second issue presented by nationwide injunctions is whether Congress has statutorily authorized or limited the ability of lower courts or the Supreme Court to grant such relief.

Rooting a prohibition on nationwide injunctions in the Constitution would preclude Congress from authorizing courts to grant such relief. Does that accord with Congress's broad control over the jurisdiction of the federal courts? Although the Court has previously emphasized the history of equity in determining the scope of federal court's equitable powers, it did so because it was interpreting the Judiciary Act of 1789, which the Court has read as conferring the same equity jurisdiction as was exercised by the High Court of Chancery in England at the time the Act was adopted. See Grupo Mexicano de Desarrollo S.A. v. Alliance Bond Fund, Inc., 527 U.S. 308, 318 (1999). But that reasoning would leave Congress free to deviate from the Act's strictures in new legislation. For the argument that Congress authorized nationwide injunctions in the APA, see Note 5 below (p. 1564).

Focusing on Congress also raises the issue of whether there are statutory limitations on federal courts' power to grant nationwide injunctions. Should we read Congress's decision to create a geographically limited system of lower courts as implicitly constraining lower courts from granting injunctive relief that extends beyond their jurisdictional limits? Would such a limit apply even if a court determined that a nationwide injunction was necessary to provide a plaintiff complete relief? Should such a limit be inferred from Federal Rule of Civil Procedure 23, providing for class actions? According to one appellate judge, "[n]ationwide injunctions . . . always sidestep Rule 23's requirements." Arizona v. Biden, 40 F.4th 375, 396 (2022) (Sutton, C.J., concurring).

(4) ***Prudential Concerns and Equitable Discretion.*** Yet a third issue is whether, even if courts have authority to grant nationwide injunctions, they should do so given the practical effects of such injunctions on the federal court system. Even if nationwide injunctions are not constitutionally or statutorily prohibited, are they a good idea?

In his concurrence in TRUMP V. HAWAII, 138 S.Ct. at 2425, JUSTICE THOMAS underscored prudential concerns with nationwide injunctions, claiming they are "beginning to take a toll on the federal court system—preventing legal questions from percolating through the federal courts, encouraging forum shopping, and making every case a national emergency for the courts and for the Executive Branch." JUSTICE GORSUCH sounded a similar note in DHS V. NEW YORK, 140 S.Ct. at 600–01: "[T]he routine issuance of universal injunctions is patently unworkable, sowing chaos for litigants, the government, courts, and all those affected by these conflicting decisions. Rather than spending their time methodically developing arguments and evidence in cases limited to the parties at hand, both sides have been forced to rush from one preliminary injunction hearing to another, leaping from one emergency stay application to the next, each with potentially nationwide stakes, and all based on expedited briefing and little opportunity for the adversarial testing of evidence. . . . [T]here is nearly boundless opportunity to shop for a friendly forum to secure a win nationwide. The risk of winning conflicting nationwide injunctions is real too. And the stakes are asymmetric. If a single successful challenge is enough to stay the challenged rule across the country, the government's hope of implementing any new policy could face the long odds of a straight sweep, parlaying a 94–0 win in the district courts into a 12-to-0 victory in the courts of appeal. A single loss and the policy goes on ice."

Do you think these practical concerns carry weight? Should a single federal court be able to enjoin the federal government from enforcing a policy across the country? Note that limiting lower courts to plaintiff-specific or district- and circuit-specific relief also imposes practical costs. Such a narrow approach could increase dramatically the number of suits that are brought on the same issue, consuming judicial and plaintiff resources and raising fairness concerns for plaintiffs who face barriers to suing. Does the option of declaratory relief adequately address these concerns, or can the government be relied upon to treat individualized relief as applying to all similarly situated without being ordered to do so? Acknowledging that nationwide injunctions have downsides and "should never be the default remedy in cases challenging federal executive action," AMANDA FROST maintains that "in some cases, nationwide injunctions are . . . the only means to provide plaintiffs with complete relief and avoid harm to thousands of individuals similarly situated[,] . . . [a]nd sometimes anything short of a nationwide injunction would be impossible to administer." IN DEFENSE OF NATIONWIDE INJUNCTIONS, 93 N.Y.U. L. Rev. 1065, 1069 (2018).

One way of taking these prudential concerns into account is in applying the four-factor test that, as noted above (p. 1554), traditionally governs the exercise of equitable discretion. District courts would have discretion to grant such injunctions but should exercise that discretion only in narrow or extreme circumstances. Do you think such an approach, relying as it does on judicial self-restraint, would prove able to rein in the use of nationwide injunctions? What would be the types of circumstances in which nationwide injunctions should be held justified?

(5) ***Nationwide Injunctions and Vacatur of Rules.*** A recurring argument made in favor of nationwide injunctions is that they are statutorily authorized by § 706(2) of the APA, which instructs that "[t]he reviewing court shall— . . . hold unlawful and set aside agency action . . . found to be" arbitrary and capricious, at odds with the Constitution or governing statutes, or factually unsupported. One difference between a nationwide injunction and vacatur of a rule, however, is that a judge may hold an official violating an injunction in contempt, whereas a grant of vacatur does not provide the basis for contempt and instead simply means the agency action at issue is no longer in effect.

In LITTLE SISTERS OF THE POOR SAINTS PETER & PAUL HOME V. PENNSYLVANIA, 140 S.Ct. 2367 (2020), a district court entered a nationwide preliminary injunction against a Trump Administration rule that provided expanded religious exemptions from the Affordable Care Act's contraceptive mandate, and the Third Circuit affirmed. The Court upheld the rule and did not reach the propriety of the nationwide injunction, but Justice Ginsburg defended the grant of a nationwide injunction in her dissent, noting in part that "[t]he Administrative Procedure Act contemplates nationwide relief from invalid agency action. See 5 U.S.C. § 706(2)." Some courts have gone further and suggested that, given § 706, the appropriate response to a rule being found invalid is its complete vacatur and grant of a nationwide injunction. See, e.g., National Mining Ass'n v. U.S. Army Corps of Engineers, 145 F.3d 1399 (D.C. Cir. 1998). For a critique of this line of caselaw, see Siddique, supra, at 2120–26.

Recently, JOHN HARRISON has contended that this argument for nationwide injunctions is based on a misreading of the APA. "[Section] 706 does not tell courts to apply the remedy of setting aside agency action. It does not deal with remedial orders at all. When it says 'set aside,' it directs the court not to decide in accordance with the agency action. The remedial consequences of so treating an agency action depend on the form of proceeding, and so are governed by [§] 703 and the sources of law to which it points. In an enforcement proceeding, for example, to set the agency action aside is to treat it as legally ineffective, the way a court treats an unconstitutional statute as ineffective. If [§] 706 did instruct courts to set aside agency actions the way they do in appellate-type proceedings under special review statutes, it still would not justify the kind of universal injunction at issue in [Little Sisters of the Poor]. Injunctions are commands to agencies. They do not directly affect the legal status of regulations." SECTION 706 OF THE ADMINISTRATIVE PROCEDURE ACT DOES NOT CALL FOR UNIVERSAL INJUNCTIONS OR OTHER UNIVERSAL REMEDIES, 37 Yale J. on Reg. Bull. 37, 42 (2020). The Department of Justice took a similar position under the Trump Administration. DOJ Litigation Guidelines, supra, at 7–8.

RONALD M. LEVIN and MILA SOHONI disagree, in UNIVERSAL REMEDIES, SECTION 706, AND THE APA, Yale J. Reg. Bull. (July 19, 2020),[10] "In the 70-plus years since the APA was enacted, administrative lawyers have never construed [§] 703 as addressing remedies. Even if the tabula were actually

---

[10] https://www.yalejreg.com/nc/universal-remedies-section-706-and-the-apa-by-ronald-m-levin-mila-sohoni/.

rasa, moreover, we would still urge against Harrison's reading of the APA. That law's text, structure, legislative history, and purposes all support the view correctly held by courts and commentators: the APA deals with remedies—including universal remedies—in [§§] 705 and 706, not in [§] 703." Moreover, "Harrison's reading doesn't work at all . . . when the cause of action is a direct attack on the rule under the APA. In such a suit, the rule is the reviewable agency action, and—if the rule is unlawful—the rule is, or may be, set aside. Harrison fails to come to grips with the fact that, in cases involving direct review of a rule, nullification has evolved into a standard administrative law remedy." Sohoni expands on this argument that the APA authorizes universal vacatur of rules in The Power to Vacate a Rule, 88 Geo. Wash. L. Rev. 1121 (2020).

(6) ***The Effect of Prior Lower Court Rulings and Agency "Nonacquiescence."*** One of the arguments raised against nationwide injunctions is that they forestall percolation of an issue in the lower courts. Implicit in this argument is the assumption that agencies are not bound by the final rulings of lower courts, including the Courts of Appeals, at least when considering cases beyond the geographical jurisdiction of those courts. The practice of agencies considering themselves free to deviate from lower court rulings in this fashion is called "nonacquiescence." Insofar as the Supreme Court has addressed this issue, it has done so in terms of the doctrine of collateral estoppel.

In United States v. Stauffer Chemical Co., 464 U.S. 165 (1984), the Supreme Court held that "the doctrine of mutual defensive collateral estoppel is available against the government to preclude relitigation of the same issue already litigated against the same party in another case involving virtually identical facts." 464 U.S. at 169. That, of course, still left the government free to litigate the same issue with other parties. But in Stauffer's companion case, UNITED STATES V. MENDOZA, 464 U.S. 154 (1984), the Court said that nonmutual offensive collateral estoppel, also known as issue preclusion, was not available against the government, in part to ensure lower-court percolation. Per JUSTICE REHNQUIST (464 U.S. at 159–61):

"We have long recognized that 'the Government is not in a position identical to that of a private litigant,' both because of the geographic breadth of Government litigation and also, most importantly, because of the nature of the issues the Government litigates. It is not open to serious dispute that the Government is a party to a far greater number of cases on a nationwide basis than even the most litigious private entity; in 1982, the United States was a party to more than 75,000 of the 206,193 filings in the United States District Courts. In the same year the United States was a party to just under 30% of the civil cases appealed from the District Courts to the Court of Appeals. Government litigation frequently involves legal questions of substantial public importance; indeed, because the proscriptions of the United States Constitution are so generally directed at governmental action, many constitutional questions can arise only in the context of litigation to which the Government is a party. Because of those facts the Government is more likely than any private party to be involved in lawsuits against different parties which nonetheless involve the same legal issues.

"A rule allowing nonmutual collateral estoppel against the Government in such cases would substantially thwart the development of important questions of law by freezing the first final decision rendered on a particular legal issue. Allowing only one final adjudication would deprive this Court of the benefit it receives from permitting several courts of appeals to explore a difficult question before this Court grants certiorari. Indeed, if nonmutual estoppel were routinely applied against the Government, this Court would have to revise its practice of waiting for a conflict to develop before granting the Government's petitions for certiorari. . . . [In addition,] the Government's litigation conduct in a case is apt to differ from that of a private litigant. Unlike a private litigant who generally does not forego an appeal if he believes that he can prevail, the Solicitor General considers a variety of factors, such as the limited resources of the Government and the crowded dockets of the courts, before authorizing an appeal. The application of nonmutual estoppel against the Government would force the Solicitor General to abandon those prudential concerns and to appeal every adverse decision in order to avoid foreclosing further review.

"In addition to those institutional concerns traditionally considered by the Solicitor General, the panoply of important public issues raised in governmental litigation may quite properly lead successive administrations of the Executive Branch to take differing positions with respect to the resolution of a particular issue. While the Executive Branch must of course defer to the Judicial Branch for final resolution of questions of constitutional law, the former nonetheless controls the progress of Government litigation through the federal courts. It would be idle to pretend that the conduct of Government litigation in all its myriad features, from the decision to file a complaint in the United States district court to the decision to petition for certiorari to review a judgment of the court of appeals, is a wholly mechanical procedure which involves no policy choices whatever. . . ."

For a thorough analysis of the issues involved in nonacquiescence, see Samuel Estreicher & Richard L. Revesz, Nonacquiescence by Federal Administrative Agencies, 98 Yale L.J. 679 (1989).

(7) ***Remedial Purity, Remedial Restraint, or Somewhere in the Middle?*** These debates about the grant of nationwide injunctions and other forms of remedial relief showcase the importance of the remedial dimension of administrative law. Remedies have also played a significant role in several prominent cases involving the separation of powers. As discussed in Chapter VII (p. 1015), the Supreme Court under Chief Justice Roberts has combined an expanded willingness to invalidate agency structures on separation of powers grounds with a restrictive approach to granting remedial relief. These developments raise an overarching question about how courts and scholars should approach remedial questions.

NICHOLAS BAGLEY, REMEDIAL RESTRAINT IN ADMINISTRATIVE LAW, 117 Colum. L. Rev. 253, 255, 261, 309 (2017), faults administrative law for a "tacit norm of remedial purity," underscoring that "[w]ith rare exceptions, [such as remand without vacatur], agency actions that contravene the APA are invalidated and returned to the agency. Across a range of cases, the remedy appears disproportionate to the underlying infraction." He adds:

"Whatever the merits of that approach [as a prophylactic], its costs are large. When a court vacates an agency action, the agency must decide whether to correct whatever deficiency the court has identified. Rectifying the mistake may be no mean feat . . . In the meantime, the agency action will be put on hold . . . . In the end, the agency might choose to abandon the action altogether . . . . Judicial review can thus derail or delay significant government programs, sometimes at substantial cost to the public welfare. The harshness of the vacate-and-remand remedy may also . . . push courts to narrow the scope of what counts as arbitrary."

In response, CHRISTOPHER J. WALKER, in AGAINST REMEDIAL RESTRAINT IN ADMINISTRATIVE LAW, 117 Colum. L. Rev. Online 106, 117, 120 (2017), agrees that "that the current rule-based approach to remand in administrative law leads to some additional costs, including a heightened risk of false positives—cases in which relatively harmless agency errors are remanded to the agency . . . . But for those of us concerned about bureaucracy and distrust, we are much more troubled about false negatives—cases in which there are harmful agency errors that nevertheless are ignored because the court erroneously finds no prejudice." Walker adds, "we are [also] much less likely to find agency errors harmless—especially errors related to the structures and procedures that attempt to compensate for the regulatory state's democratic deficits."

Who has the better argument? Does the choice between remedial restraint and remedial purity inevitably turn on the degree of trust one has in administrative government? Are both acceptable interpretations of the APA? If so, would the best course be neither extreme but instead to grant lower courts broad discretion to determine administrative law remedies on a case-by-case basis?

## (2) Suits for Damages

Historically, if an administrative action invaded liberty or property interests protected by the common law, the injured citizen sued the responsible officials in tort or contract. When the officials defended against the suit by citing their statutory authority, the court could examine the scope of that authority and resolve allegations of its abuse. If the action was not justified under the legal authority claimed, the officials would be liable personally for the damages caused. This system applied to federal officials as well as state officials, but federal officials can remove state court suits against them to federal court if they can assert a federal defense. 28 U.S.C. § 1442(a)(1); Mesa v. California, 489 U.S. 121 (1989).

Of course, such a regime tends to be hard on government officials whose personal assets are at risk in the event of a mistaken administrative decision. Although Congress often enacted private bills indemnifying the officers involved, that did not always occur. See James E. Pfander & Jonathan L. Hunt, Public Wrongs and Private Bills: Indemnification and Government Accountability in the Early Republic, 85 N.Y.U. L. Rev. 1862 (2010). Consequently, courts developed "official immunity" defenses that protected official judgment in varying degrees, with executive officials other than the President generally receiving qualified immunity. See Harlow v. Fitzgerald, 457 U.S. 800 (1982). The Supreme Court has held that some governmental contractors may qualify for immunity as well, Boyle v. United Techs. Corp., 487 U.S. 500 (1988), an issue that arose with respect to actions by private military contractors in Iraq.

Eventually, legislatures intervened to provide alternative or supplanting causes of action against the government itself. At the federal level, officials now have complete statutory immunity for torts committed "while acting within the scope of [their] office or employment." 28 U.S.C. § 2679(b)(1). The exclusive remedy is against the United States, on a respondeat superior theory, under the Federal Tort Claims Act. However, the statutory consent to liability in the FTCA has significant procedural restrictions and substantive gaps, including not applying to performance of a discretionary function or actions taken outside of the United States. 28 U.S.C. §§ 2680(a), (k).[11] For claims "not sounding in tort"—most importantly, contract and takings claims—a remedy directly against the United States can be sought under the Tucker Act in the Court of Claims.

Damages actions against government officials in their personal capacity remain important for constitutional violations committed in the course of their duties. In the case of federal officials, the cause of action (if any) comes directly from the Constitution. See Bivens v. Six Unknown Federal Narcotics Agents, 403 U.S. 388 (1971). The FTCA immunity from personal liability does not extend to constitutional wrongs, 28 U.S.C. § 2679(b)(2)(A), although the official will have the benefit of official immunity defenses. "Bivens actions" cannot be brought against an agency as an entity, see Federal Deposit Ins. Corp. v. Meyer, 510 U.S. 471 (1994), or against top agency officials merely on the basis of their supervisory position, see Ashcroft v. Iqbal, 556 U.S. 662 (2009). Even where the official himself is being sued on a theory of individual, intentional unconstitutional behavior, the Court has become unwilling to imply new Bivens actions. In Ziglar v. Abbasi, 137 S.Ct. 1843, 1856–57 (2017), the Court stated that Bivens was "settled law" in the "search-and-seizure context in which it arose," but emphasized that "expanding the Bivens remedy is now a disfavored judicial activity." In Ziglar, the Court emphasized that a cause of action will not be implied when either (1) Congress has provided an alternative remedy; or (2) the court perceives "special factors counseling hesitation." In Hernandez v. Mesa, 140 S.Ct. 735, 742 (2020), the Court declined to apply the Bivens remedy in the context of a cross-border shooting, explaining "our watchword is caution." And in Egbert v. Boule, 142 S.Ct. 1793, 1805 (2022), the Court insisted that a Bivens suit should not proceed if "there is any rational reason (even one) to think that Congress is better suited to weigh the costs and benefits of allowing a damages action to proceed."

---

[11] In such circumstances, victims are remitted to whatever relief they can obtain through administrative settlement, see 28 U.S.C. §§ 2672, 2675, or from Congress via a private bill.

In the case of state and local officials, the cause of action for damages from constitutional violations is statutory: 42 U.S.C. § 1983.[12] Here, we can sketch only the basic contours of what has become a massive body of law: First, damages claims against state and local officials, in their individual capacity, are subject to the same official immunity defenses available to federal officials in Bivens actions. Second, the statute can be used to seek damages against government entities below the level of the state itself. Although these entities (counties, municipalities, etc.) can assert no sovereign immunity defenses, their liability for their employees' actions is limited in a number of ways.[13] Third, States (and state agencies) cannot be sued under the statute.

Sovereign immunity is often a barrier to damages suits against state governments for violations of federal statutes. The Court has held that the Eleventh Amendment bars damages suits based on federal statutes unless Congress validly abrogates state sovereign immunity and that Article I overwhelmingly does not give Congress authority to abrogate. See Seminole Tribe of Fla. v. Florida, 517 U.S. 44 (1996). Subsequently, the Court extended this holding, first to suits brought by private parties in state court to enforce federal law, Alden v. Maine, 527 U.S. 706 (1999), and subsequently to attempts by private parties to force states to appear before federal agencies to answer for federal regulatory violations, Federal Maritime Comm'n v. South Carolina Ports Auth., 535 U.S. 743 (2002). Congress can abrogate state sovereign immunity when it legislates pursuant to the remedial authority of section 5 of the Fourteenth Amendment. However, the Court has set fairly stringent standards of "congruence and proportionality" for invoking this authority and many federal statutes have not qualified. See, e.g., Coleman v. Court of Appeals of Maryland, 566 U.S. 30 (2012); Bd. of Trustees of Univ. of Alabama v. Garrett, 531 U.S. 356 (2001).

There remain a few ways by which regulatory obligations can be enforced against states and their agencies in the many regulatory programs enacted under the Commerce Clause, Spending Clause, and other Article I provisions. First, States cannot assert sovereign immunity in actions by the United States or its agencies. Alden, 527 U.S. at 755–56. Thus, immunity will not be a problem in the very common enforcement paradigm in which the federal agency itself, or the U.S. Attorney, brings the complaint. Second, as noted above, in cases of ongoing violations private individuals can often seek injunctive or declaratory relief, although not if such actions really seek retrospective, compensatory relief that requires the payment of money from the state

[12] "Every person who, under color of any statute, ordinance, regulation, custom, or usage, of any State or Territory . . . subjects, or causes to be subjected, any citizen of the United States or other person within the jurisdiction thereof to the deprivation of any rights, privileges, or immunities secured by the Constitution and laws, shall be liable to the party injured in an action at law, suit in equity, or other proper proceeding for redress."

[13] Most significantly, there is no respondeat superior liability; the wrongdoing must be pursuant to official policy or custom. Monell v. Dep't of Social Serv., 436 U.S. 658, 691 (1978). Also, punitive damages may not be recovered. City of Newport v. Fact Concerts, 453 U.S. 247 (1981).

treasury, Edelman v. Jordan, 415 U.S. 651 (1974). In addition, the Supreme Court has significantly restricted the availability of § 1983 to enforce statutory obligations and has also pulled back significantly from implying rights of action from statutes directly. See Gonzaga Univ. v. Doe, 536 U.S. 273 (2002); Alexander v. Sandoval, 532 U.S. 275, 288–89 (2001). Finally, Congress can enact an express requirement that states consent to suit in order to obtain some benefit the federal government is not otherwise required to confer upon them, although the Court requires such conditions to be very clear and unambiguous to the recipient entity, to be germane to the purpose of the funds, and not to be coercive. See, e.g., Arlington Central Sch. Dist. Bd. of Educ. v. Murphy, 548 U.S. 291 (2006).

# APPENDIX



# CONSTITUTION OF THE UNITED STATES OF AMERICA

We the People of the United States in Order to form a more perfect Union, to establish Justice, insure domestic Tranquility, provide for the common defence, promote the general Welfare, and secure the Blessings of Liberty to ourselves and our Posterity, do ordain and establish this Constitution for the United States of America.

## ARTICLE I

### Section 1

All legislative Powers herein granted shall be vested in a Congress of the United States, which shall consist of a Senate and House of Representatives.

### Section 2

[1] The House of Representatives shall be composed of Members chosen every second Year by the People of the several States, and the Electors in each State shall have the Qualifications requisite for Electors of the most numerous Branch of the State Legislature.

[2] No Person shall be a Representative who shall not have attained to the Age of twenty-five Years, and been seven Years a Citizen of the United States, and who shall not, when elected, be an Inhabitant of that State in which he shall be chosen.

[3] Representatives and direct Taxes shall be apportioned among the several States which may be included within this Union, according to their respective Numbers, which shall be determined by adding to the whole Number of free Persons, including those bound to Service for a Term of Years, and excluding Indians not taxed, three fifths of all other Persons. The actual Enumeration shall be made within three Years after the first Meeting of the Congress of the United States, and within every subsequent Term of ten Years, in such Manner as they shall by Law direct. The Number of Representatives shall not exceed one for every thirty Thousand, but each State shall have at Least one Representative; and until such enumerations shall be made, the State of New Hampshire shall be entitled to chuse three, Massachusetts eight, Rhode Island and Providence Plantations one, Connecticut five, New York six, New Jersey

four, Pennsylvania eight, Delaware one, Maryland six, Virginia ten, North Carolina five, South Carolina five, and Georgia three.

[4] When vacancies happen in the Representation from any State, the Executive Authority thereof shall issue Writs of Election to fill such Vacancies.

[5] The House of Representatives shall chuse their Speaker and other Officers; and shall have the sole Power of Impeachment.

**Section 3**

[1] The Senate of the United States shall be composed of two Senators from each State, chosen by the Legislature thereof, for six Years; and each Senator shall have one Vote.

[2] Immediately after they shall be assembled in Consequence of the first Election, they shall be divided as equally as may be into three Classes. The Seats of the Senators of the first Class shall be vacated at the Expiration of the second Year, of the second Class at the Expiration of the fourth Year, and of the third Class at the Expiration of the sixth Year, so that one third may be chosen every second Year; and if Vacancies happen by Resignation, or otherwise, during the Recess of the Legislature of any State, the Executive thereof may make temporary Appointments until the next Meeting of the Legislature, which shall then fill such Vacancies.

[3] No Person shall be a Senator who shall not have attained to the Age of thirty Years, and been nine Years a Citizen of the United States, and who shall not, when elected, be an Inhabitant of that State for which he shall be chosen.

[4] The Vice President of the United States shall be President of the Senate, but shall have no Vote, unless they be equally divided.

[5] The Senate shall chuse their other Officers, and also a President pro tempore, in the Absence of the Vice President, or when he shall exercise the Office of President of the United States.

[6] The Senate shall have the sole Power to try all Impeachments. When sitting for that Purpose, they shall be on Oath or Affirmation. When the President of the United States is tried, the Chief Justice shall preside: And no Person shall be convicted without the Concurrence of two thirds of the Members present.

[7] Judgment in Cases of Impeachment shall not extend further than to removal from Office, and disqualification to hold and enjoy any Office of honor, Trust or Profit under the United States: but the Party convicted shall nevertheless be liable and subject to Indictment, Trial, Judgment and Punishment, according to Law.

**Section 4**

[1] The Times, Places and Manner of holding Elections for Senators and Representatives, shall be prescribed in each State by the Legislature thereof; but the Congress may at any time by Law make or alter such Regulations, except as to the Places of chusing Senators.

[2] The Congress shall assemble at least once in every Year, and such Meeting shall be on the first Monday in December, unless they shall by Law appoint a different Day.

### Section 5

[1] Each House shall be the Judge of the Elections, Returns and Qualifications of its own Members, and a Majority of each shall constitute a Quorum to do Business; but a smaller Number may adjourn from day to day, and may be authorized to compel the Attendance of absent Members, in such Manner, and under such Penalties as each House may provide.

[2] Each House may determine the Rules of its Proceedings, punish its Members for disorderly Behaviour, and, with the Concurrence of two thirds, expel a Member.

[3] Each House shall keep a Journal of its Proceedings, and from time to time publish the same, excepting such Parts as may in their Judgment require Secrecy; and the Yeas and Nays of the Members of either House on any question shall, at the Desire of one fifth of those Present, be entered on the Journal.

[4] Neither House, during the Session of Congress, shall, without the Consent of the other, adjourn for more than three days, nor to any other Place than that in which the two Houses shall be sitting.

### Section 6

[1] The Senators and Representatives shall receive a Compensation for their Services, to be ascertained by Law, and paid out of the Treasury of the United States. They shall in all Cases, except Treason, Felony and Breach of the Peace, be privileged from Arrest during their Attendance at the Session of their respective Houses, and in going to and returning from the same; and for any Speech or Debate in either House, they shall not be questioned in any other Place.

[2] No Senator or Representative shall, during the Time for which he was elected, be appointed to any civil Office under the Authority of the United States, which shall have been created, or the Emoluments whereof shall have been encreased during such time; and no Person holding any Office under the United States, shall be a Member of either House during his Continuance in Office.

### Section 7

[1] All Bills for raising Revenue shall originate in the House of Representatives; but the Senate may propose or concur with Amendments as on other Bills.

[2] Every Bill which shall have passed the House of Representatives and the Senate, shall, before it become a Law, be presented to the President of the United States; If he approve he shall sign it, but if not he shall return it, with his Objections to that House in which it shall have originated, who shall enter the Objections at large on their Journal, and proceed to reconsider it. If after such Reconsideration two thirds of that House shall agree to pass the Bill, it shall be sent,

together with the Objections, to the other House, by which it shall likewise be reconsidered, and if approved by two thirds of that House, it shall become a Law. But in all such Cases the Votes of both Houses shall be determined by Yeas and Nays, and the Names of the Persons voting for and against the Bill shall be entered on the Journal of each House respectively. If any Bill shall not be returned by the President within ten Days (Sundays excepted) after it shall have been presented to him, the Same shall be a Law, in like Manner as if he had signed it, unless the Congress by their Adjournment prevent its Return, in which Case it shall not be a Law.

[3] Every Order, Resolution, or Vote to which the Concurrence of the Senate and House of Representatives may be necessary (except on a question of Adjournment) shall be presented to the President of the United States; and before the Same shall take Effect, shall be approved by him, or being disapproved by him, shall be repassed by two thirds of the Senate and House of Representatives, according to the Rules and Limitations prescribed in the Case of a Bill.

**Section 8**

[1] The Congress shall have Power To lay and collect Taxes, Duties, Imposts and Excises, to pay the Debts and provide for the common Defence and general Welfare of the United States; but all Duties, Imports and Excises shall be uniform throughout the United States;

[2] To borrow Money on the credit of the United States;

[3] To regulate Commerce with foreign Nations, and among the several States, and with the Indian Tribes;

[4] To establish an uniform Rule of Naturalization, and uniform Laws on the subject of Bankruptcies throughout the United States;

[5] To coin Money, regulate the Value thereof, and of foreign Coin, and fix the Standard of Weights and Measures;

[6] To provide for the Punishment of counterfeiting the Securities and current Coin of the United States;

[7] To establish Post Offices and post Roads;

[8] To promote the Progress of Science and useful Arts, by securing for limited Times to Authors and Inventors the exclusive Right to their respective Writings and Discoveries;

[9] To constitute Tribunals inferior to the supreme Court;

[10] To define and punish Piracies and Felonies committed on the high Seas, and Offences against the Law of Nations;

[11] To declare War, grant Letters of Marque and Reprisal, and make Rules concerning Captures on Land and Water;

[12] To raise and support Armies, but no Appropriation of Money to that Use shall be for a longer Term than two Years;

[13] To provide and maintain a Navy;

[14] To make Rules for the Government and Regulation of the land and naval Forces;

[15] To provide for calling forth the Militia to execute the Laws of the Union, suppress Insurrections and repel Invasions;

[16] To provide for organizing, arming, and disciplining, the Militia and for governing such Part of them as may be employed in the Service of the United States, reserving to the States respectively, the Appointment of the Officers, and the Authority of training the Militia according to the discipline prescribed by Congress;

[17] To exercise exclusive Legislation in all Cases whatsoever, over such District (not exceeding ten Miles square) as may, by Cession of particular States, and the Acceptance of Congress, become the Seat of the Government of the United States, and to exercise like Authority over all Places purchased by the Consent of the Legislature of the State in which the Same shall be, for the Erection of Forts, Magazines, Arsenals, dock-Yards, and other needful Buildings;—And

[18] To make all Laws which shall be necessary and proper for carrying into Execution the foregoing Powers, and all other Powers vested by this Constitution in the Government of the United States, or in any Department or Officer thereof.

## Section 9

[1] The Migration or Importation of such Persons as any of the States now existing shall think proper to admit, shall not be prohibited by the Congress prior to the Year one thousand eight hundred and eight, but a Tax or duty may be imposed on such Importation, not exceeding ten dollars for each Person.

[2] The Privilege of the Writ of Habeas Corpus shall not be suspended, unless when in Cases of Rebellion or Invasion the public Safety may require it.

[3] No Bill of Attainder or ex post facto Law shall be passed.

[4] No Capitation, or other direct, Tax shall be laid, unless in Proportion to the Census or enumeration herein before directed to be taken.

[5] No Tax or Duty shall be laid on Articles exported from any State.

[6] No Preference shall be given by any Regulation of Commerce or Revenue to the Ports of one State over those of another: nor shall Vessels bound to, or from, one State, be obliged to enter, clear or pay Duties in another.

[7] No Money shall be drawn from the Treasury, but in Consequence of Appropriations made by Law, and a regular Statement and Account of the Receipts and Expenditures of all public Money shall be published from time to time.

[8] No Title of Nobility shall be granted by the United States: And no Person holding any Office of Profit or Trust under them, shall, without

the Consent of the Congress, accept of any present, Emolument, Office, or Title, of any kind whatever, from any King, Prince, or foreign State.

### Section 10

[1] No State shall enter into any Treaty, Alliance, or Confederation; grant Letters of Marque and Reprisal; coin Money; emit Bills of Credit; make any Thing but gold and silver Coin a Tender in Payment of Debts; pass any Bill of Attainder, ex post facto Law, or Law impairing the Obligation of Contracts, or grant any Title of Nobility.

[2] No State shall, without the Consent of the Congress, lay any Imposts or Duties on Imports or Exports, except what may be absolutely necessary for executing it's [sic] inspection Laws: and the net Produce of all Duties and Imposts, laid by any State on Imports or Exports, shall be for the Use of the Treasury of the United States; and all such Laws shall be subject to the Revision and Controul of the Congress.

[3] No State shall, without the Consent of Congress, lay any Duty of Tonnage, keep Troops, or Ships of War in time of Peace, enter into any Agreement or Compact with another State, or with a foreign Power, or engage in War, unless actually invaded, or in such imminent Danger as will not admit of delay.

## ARTICLE II

### Section 1

[1] The executive Power shall be vested in a President of the United States of America. He shall hold his Office during the Term of four Years, and, together with the Vice President, chosen for the same Term, be elected, as follows:

[2] Each State shall appoint, in such Manner as the Legislature thereof may direct, a Number of Electors, equal to the whole Number of Senators and Representatives to which the State may be entitled in the Congress: but no Senator or Representative, or Person holding an Office of Trust or Profit under the United States, shall be appointed an Elector.

[3] The Electors shall meet in their respective States, and vote by Ballot for two Persons, of whom one at least shall not be an Inhabitant of the same State with themselves. And they shall make a List of all the Persons voted for, and of the Number of Votes for each; which List they shall sign and certify, and transmit sealed to the Seat of the Government of the United States, directed to the President of the Senate. The President of the Senate shall, in the Presence of the Senate and House of Representatives, open all the Certificates, and the Votes shall then be counted. The Person having the greatest Number of Votes shall be the President, if such Number be a Majority of the whole Number of Electors appointed; and if there be more than one who have such Majority, and have an equal Number of Votes, then the House of Representatives shall immediately chuse by Ballot one of them for President; and if no Person have a Majority, then from the five highest on the List the said House shall in like Manner chuse the President. But in chusing the President, the Votes shall be taken by States, the Representation from each State

having one Vote; a quorum for this Purpose shall consist of a Member or Members from two thirds of the States, and a Majority of all the States shall be necessary to a Choice. In every Case, after the Choice of the President, the Person having the greatest Number of Votes of the Electors shall be the Vice President. But if there should remain two or more who have equal Votes, the Senate shall chuse from them by Ballot the Vice President.

[4] The Congress may determine the Time of chusing the Electors, and the Day on which they shall give their Votes; which Day shall be the same throughout the United States.

[5] No Person except a natural born Citizen, or a Citizen of the United States, at the time of the Adoption of this Constitution, shall be eligible to the Office of President; neither shall any Person be eligible to that Office who shall not have attained to the Age of thirty five Years, and been fourteen Years a Resident within the United States.

[6] In Case of the Removal of the President from Office, or of his Death, Resignation or Inability to discharge the Powers and Duties of the said Office, the Same shall devolve on the Vice President, and the Congress may by Law provide for the Case of Removal, Death, Resignation or Inability, both of the President and Vice President, declaring what Officer shall then act as President, and such Officer shall act accordingly, until the Disability be removed, or a President shall be elected.

[7] The President shall, at stated Times, receive for his Services, a Compensation, which shall neither be encreased nor diminished during the Period for which he shall have been elected, and he shall not receive within that Period any other Emolument from the United States, or any of them.

[8] Before he enter on the Execution of his Office, he shall take the following Oath or Affirmation:—"I do solemnly swear (or affirm) that I will faithfully execute the Office of President of the United States, and will to the best of my Ability, preserve, protect and defend the Constitution of the United States."

### Section 2

[1] The President shall be Commander in Chief of the Army and Navy of the United States, and of the Militia of the several States, when called into the actual Service of the United States; he may require the Opinion, in writing, of the principal Officer in each of the executive Departments, upon any Subject relating to the Duties of their respective Offices, and he shall have Power to grant Reprieves and Pardons for Offences against the United States, except in Cases of Impeachment.

[2] He shall have Power, by and with the Advice and Consent of the Senate, to make Treaties, provided two thirds of the Senators present concur; and he shall nominate, and by and with the Advice and Consent of the Senate, shall appoint Ambassadors, other public Ministers and Consuls, Judges of the supreme Court, and all other Officers of the United States, whose Appointments are not herein otherwise provided

for, and which shall be established by Law: but the Congress may by Law vest the Appointment of such inferior Officers, as they think proper, in the President alone, in the Courts of Law, or in the Heads of Departments.

[3] The President shall have Power to fill up all Vacancies that may happen during the Recess of the Senate, by granting Commissions which shall expire at the End of their next Session.

### Section 3

He shall from time to time give to the Congress Information of the State of the Union, and recommend to their Consideration such Measures as he shall judge necessary and expedient; he may, on extraordinary Occasions, convene both Houses, or either of them, and in Case of Disagreement between them, with Respect to the Time of Adjournment, he may adjourn them to such Time as he shall think proper; he shall receive Ambassadors and other public Ministers; he shall take Care that the Laws be faithfully executed, and shall Commission all the Officers of the United States.

### Section 4

The President, Vice President and all civil Officers of the United States, shall be removed from Office on Impeachment for, and Conviction of Treason, Bribery, or other high Crimes and Misdemeanors.

## ARTICLE III

### Section 1

The judicial Power of the United States, shall be vested in one supreme Court, and in such inferior Courts as the Congress may from time to time ordain and establish. The Judges, both of the supreme and inferior Courts, shall hold their Offices during good Behaviour, and shall, at stated Times, receive for their Services, a Compensation, which shall not be diminished during their Continuance in Office.

### Section 2

[1] The judicial Power shall extend to all Cases, in Law and Equity, arising under this Constitution, the Laws of the United States, and Treaties made, or which shall be made, under their Authority;—to all Cases affecting Ambassadors, other public Ministers and Consuls;—to all Cases of admiralty and maritime Jurisdiction;—to Controversies to which the United States shall be a Party;—to Controversies between two or more States;—between a State and Citizens of another State;—between Citizens of different States;—between Citizens of the same State claiming Lands under Grants of different States, and between a State, or the Citizens thereof, and foreign States, Citizens or Subjects.

[2] In all Cases affecting Ambassadors, other public Ministers and Consuls, and those in which a State shall be Party, the supreme Court shall have original Jurisdiction. In all the other Cases before mentioned, the supreme Court shall have appellate Jurisdiction, both as to Law and Fact, with such Exceptions, and under such Regulations as the Congress shall make.

[3] The Trial of all Crimes, except in Cases of Impeachment, shall be by Jury; and such Trial shall be held in the State where the said Crimes shall have been committed; but when not committed within any State, the Trial shall be at such Place or Places as the Congress may by Law have directed.

### Section 3

[1] Treason against the United States, shall consist only in levying War against them, or in adhering to their Enemies, giving them Aid and Comfort. No Person shall be convicted of Treason unless on the Testimony of two Witnesses to the same overt Act, or on Confession in open Court.

[2] The Congress shall have Power to declare the Punishment of Treason, but no Attainder of Treason shall work Corruption of Blood, or Forfeiture except during the Life of the Person attained.

## ARTICLE IV

### Section 1

Full Faith and Credit shall be given in each State to the public Acts, Records, and judicial Proceedings of every other State. And the Congress may by general Laws prescribe the Manner in which such Acts, Records and Proceedings shall be proved, and the Effect thereof.

### Section 2

[1] The Citizens of each State shall be entitled to all Privileges and Immunities of Citizens in the several States.

[2] A Person charged in any State with Treason, Felony, or other Crime, who shall flee from Justice, and be found in another State, shall on Demand of the executive Authority of the State from which he fled, be delivered up, to be removed to the State having Jurisdiction of the Crime.

[3] No Person held to Service or Labour in one State, under the Laws thereof, escaping into another, shall, in Consequence of any Law or Regulation therein, be discharged from such Service or Labour, but shall be delivered up on Claim of the Party to whom such Service or Labour may be due.

### Section 3

[1] New States may be admitted by the Congress into this Union, but no new State shall be formed or erected within the Jurisdiction of any other State; nor any State be formed by the Junction of two or more States, or Parts of States, without the Consent of the Legislatures of the States concerned as well as of the Congress.

[2] The Congress shall have Power to dispose of and make all needful Rules and Regulations respecting the Territory or other Property belonging to the United States; and nothing in this Constitution shall be so construed as to Prejudice any Claims of the United States, or of any particular State.

### Section 4

The United States shall guarantee to every State in this Union a Republican Form of Government, and shall protect each of them against Invasion; and on Application of the Legislature, or of the Executive (when the Legislature cannot be convened) against domestic Violence.

## ARTICLE V

The Congress, whenever two thirds of both Houses shall deem it necessary, shall propose Amendments to this Constitution, or, on the Application of the Legislatures of two thirds of the several States, shall call a Convention for proposing Amendments, which, in either Case, shall be valid to all Intents and Purposes, as Part of this Constitution, when ratified by the Legislatures of three fourths of the several States, or by Conventions in three fourths thereof, as the one or the other Mode of Ratification may be proposed by the Congress; Provided that no Amendment which may be made prior to the Year One thousand eight hundred and eight shall in any Manner affect the first and fourth Clauses in the Ninth Section of the first Article; and that no State, without its Consent, shall be deprived of its equal Suffrage in the Senate.

## ARTICLE VI

[1] All Debts contracted and Engagements entered into, before the Adoption of this Constitution, shall be as valid against the United States under this Constitution, as under the Confederation.

[2] This Constitution, and the Laws of the United States which shall be made in Pursuance thereof; and all Treaties made, or which shall be made, under the Authority of the United States, shall be the supreme Law of the Land; and the Judges in every State shall be bound thereby, any Thing in the Constitution or Laws of any State to the Contrary notwithstanding.

[3] The Senators and Representatives before mentioned, and the Members of the several State Legislatures, and all executive and judicial Officers, both of the United States and of the several States, shall be bound by Oath or Affirmation, to support this Constitution; but no religious Test shall ever be required as a Qualification to any Office or public Trust under the United States.

## ARTICLE VII

The Ratification of the Conventions of nine States, shall be sufficient for the Establishment of this Constitution between the States so ratifying the Same.

## AMENDMENT 1 [1791]

Congress shall make no law respecting an establishment of religion, or prohibiting the free exercise thereof; or abridging the freedom of speech, or of the press; or the right of the people peaceably to assemble, and to petition the Government for a redress of grievances.

### AMENDMENT 2 [1791]

A well regulated Militia, being necessary to the security of a free State, the right of the people to keep and bear Arms, shall not be infringed.

### AMENDMENT 3 [1791]

No Soldier shall, in time of peace be quartered in any house, without the consent of the Owner, nor in time of war, but in a manner to be prescribed by law.

### AMENDMENT 4 [1791]

The right of the people to be secure in their persons, houses, papers, and effects, against unreasonable searches and seizures, shall not be violated, and no Warrants shall issue, but upon probable cause, supported by Oath or affirmation, and particularly describing the place to be searched, and the persons or things to be seized.

### AMENDMENT 5 [1791]

No person shall be held to answer for a capital, or otherwise infamous crime, unless on a presentment or indictment of a Grand Jury, except in cases arising in the land or naval forces, or in the Militia, when in actual service in time of War or public danger; nor shall any person be subject for the same offence to be twice put in jeopardy of life or limb; nor shall be compelled in any criminal case to be a witness against himself, nor be deprived of life, liberty, or property, without due process of law; nor shall private property be taken for public use, without just compensation.

### AMENDMENT 6 [1791]

In all criminal prosecutions, the accused shall enjoy the right to a speedy and public trial, by an impartial jury of the State and district wherein the crime shall have been committed, which district shall have been previously ascertained by law, and to be informed of the nature and cause of the accusation; to be confronted with the witnesses against him; to have compulsory process for obtaining witnesses in his favor, and to have the Assistance of Counsel for his defence.

### AMENDMENT 7 [1791]

In Suits at common law, where the value in controversy shall exceed twenty dollars, the right of trial by jury shall be preserved, and no fact tried by a jury, shall be otherwise re-examined in any Court of the United States, than according to the rules of the common law.

### AMENDMENT 8 [1791]

Excessive bail shall not be required, nor excessive fines imposed, nor cruel and unusual punishments inflicted.

### AMENDMENT 9 [1791]

The enumeration in the Constitution, of certain rights, shall not be construed to deny or disparage others retained by the people.

### AMENDMENT 10 [1791]

The powers not delegated to the United States by the Constitution, nor prohibited by it to the States, are reserved to the States respectively, or to the people.

### AMENDMENT 11 [1795]

The Judicial power of the United States shall not be construed to extend to any suit in law or equity, commenced or prosecuted against one of the United States by Citizens of another State, or by Citizens or Subjects of any Foreign State.

### AMENDMENT 12 [1804]

The Electors shall meet in their respective states and vote by ballot for President and Vice-President, one of whom, at least, shall not be an inhabitant of the same state with themselves; they shall name in their ballots the person voted for as President, and in distinct ballots the person voted for as Vice-President, and they shall make distinct lists of all persons voted for as President, and of all persons voted for as Vice-President, and of the number of votes for each, which lists they shall sign and certify, and transmit sealed to the seat of the government of the United States, directed to the President of the Senate;—the President of the Senate shall, in the presence of the Senate and House of Representatives, open all the certificates and the votes shall then be counted;—The person having the greatest number of votes for President, shall be the President, if such number be a majority of the whole number of Electors appointed; and if no person have such majority, then from the persons having the highest numbers not exceeding three on the list of those voted for as President, the House of Representatives shall choose immediately, by ballot, the President. But in choosing the President, the votes shall be taken by states, the representation from each state having one vote; a quorum for this purpose shall consist of a member or members from two-thirds of the states, and a majority of all the states shall be necessary to a choice. And if the House of Representatives shall not choose a President whenever the right of choice shall devolve upon them, before the fourth day of March next following, then the Vice-President shall act as President, as in case of the death or other constitutional disability of the President.—The person having the greatest number of votes as Vice-President, shall be the Vice-President, if such number be a majority of the whole number of Electors appointed, and if no person have a majority, then from the two highest numbers on the list, the Senate shall choose the Vice-President; a quorum for the purpose shall consist of two-thirds of the whole number of Senators, and a majority of the whole number shall be necessary to a choice. But no person constitutionally ineligible to the office of President shall be eligible to that of Vice-President of the United States.

## AMENDMENT 13 [1865]

### Section 1

Neither slavery nor involuntary servitude, except as a punishment for crime whereof the party shall have been duly convicted, shall exist within the United States, or any place subject to their jurisdiction.

### Section 2

Congress shall have power to enforce this article by appropriate legislation.

## AMENDMENT 14 [1868]

### Section 1

All persons born or naturalized in the United States, and subject to the jurisdiction thereof, are citizens of the United States and of the State wherein they reside. No State shall make or enforce any law which shall abridge the privileges or immunities of citizens of the United States; nor shall any State deprive any person of life, liberty, or property, without due process of law; nor deny to any person within its jurisdiction the equal protection of the laws.

### Section 2

Representatives shall be apportioned among the several States according to their respective numbers, counting the whole number of persons in each State, excluding Indians not taxed. But when the right to vote at any election for the choice of electors for President and Vice President of the United States, Representatives in Congress, the Executive and Judicial officers of a State, or the members of the Legislature thereof, is denied to any of the male inhabitants of such State, being twenty-one years of age, and citizens of the United States, or in any way abridged, except for participation in rebellion, or other crime, the basis of representation therein shall be reduced in the proportion which the number of such male citizens shall bear to the whole number of male citizens twenty-one years of age in such State.

### Section 3

No person shall be a Senator or Representative in Congress, or elector of President and Vice President, or hold any office, civil or military, under the United States, or under any State, who, having previously taken an oath, as a member of Congress, or as an officer of the United States, or as a member of any State legislature, or as an executive or judicial officer of any State, to support the Constitution of the United States, shall have engaged in insurrection or rebellion against the same, or given aid or comfort to the enemies thereof. But Congress may by a vote of two-thirds of each House, remove such disability.

### Section 4

The validity of the public debt of the United States, authorized by law, including debts incurred for payment of pensions and bounties for services in suppressing insurrection or rebellion, shall not be questioned. But neither the United States nor any State shall assume or pay any debt or obligation incurred in aid of insurrection or rebellion against the United States, or any claim for the loss or emancipation of any slave; but all such debts, obligations and claims shall be held illegal and void.

### Section 5

The Congress shall have the power to enforce, by appropriate legislation, the provisions of this article.

## AMENDMENT 15 [1870]

### Section 1

The right of citizens of the United States to vote shall not be denied or abridged by the United States or by any State on account of race, color, or previous condition of servitude.

### Section 2

The Congress shall have the power to enforce this article by appropriate legislation.

## AMENDMENT 16 [1913]

The Congress shall have power to lay and collect taxes on incomes, from whatever source derived, without apportionment among the several States, and without regard to any census or enumeration.

## AMENDMENT 17 [1913]

[1] The Senate of the United States shall be composed of two Senators from each State, elected by the people thereof for six years; and each Senator shall have one vote. The electors in each State shall have the qualifications requisite for electors of the most numerous branch of the State legislatures.

[2] When vacancies happen in the representation of any State in the Senate, the executive authority of such State shall issue writs of election to fill such vacancies: Provided, That the legislature of any State may empower the executive thereof to make temporary appointments until the people fill the vacancies by election as the legislature may direct.

[3] This amendment shall not be so construed as to affect the election or term of any Senator chosen before it becomes valid as part of the Constitution.

## AMENDMENT 18 [1919]

### Section 1

After one year from the ratification of this article the manufacture, sale, or transportation of intoxicating liquors within, the importation thereof into, or the exportation thereof from the United States and all territory subject to the jurisdiction thereof for beverage purposes is hereby prohibited.

### Section 2

The Congress and the several States shall have concurrent power to enforce this article by appropriate legislation.

### Section 3

This article shall be inoperative unless it shall have been ratified as an amendment to the Constitution by the legislatures of the several States as provided in the Constitution, within seven years from the date of the submission hereof to the States by the Congress.

## AMENDMENT 19 [1920]

[1] The right of citizens of the United States to vote shall not be denied or abridged by the United States or by any State on account of sex.

[2] Congress shall have power to enforce this article by appropriate legislation.

## AMENDMENT 20 [1933]

### Section 1

The terms of the President and the Vice President shall end at noon on the 20th day of January, and the terms of Senators and Representatives at noon on the 3d day of January, of the years in which such terms would have ended if this article had not been ratified; and the terms of their successors shall then begin.

### Section 2

The Congress shall assemble at least once in every year, and such meeting shall begin at noon on the 3d day of January, unless they shall by law appoint a different day.

### Section 3

If, at the time fixed for the beginning of the term of the President, the President elect shall have died, the Vice President elect shall become President. If a President shall not have been chosen before the time fixed for the beginning of his term, or if the President elect shall have failed to qualify, then the Vice President elect shall act as President until a President shall have qualified; and the Congress may by law provide for the case wherein neither a President elect nor a Vice President elect shall have qualified, declaring who shall then act as President, or the manner in which one who is to act shall be selected, and such person shall act accordingly until a President or Vice President shall have qualified.

### Section 4

The Congress may by law provide for the case of the death of any of the persons from whom the House of Representatives may choose a President whenever the right of choice shall have devolved upon them, and for the case of the death of any of the persons from whom the Senate may choose a Vice President whenever the right of choice shall have devolved upon them.

### Section 5

Sections 1 and 2 shall take effect on the 15th day of October following the ratification of this article.

**Section 6**

This article shall be inoperative unless it shall have been ratified as an amendment to the Constitution by the legislatures of three-fourths of the several States within seven years from the date of its submission.

**AMENDMENT 21** [1933]

**Section 1**

The eighteenth article of amendment to the Constitution of the United States is hereby repealed.

**Section 2**

The transportation or importation into any State, Territory, or possession of the United States for delivery or use therein of intoxicating liquors, in violation of the laws thereof, is hereby prohibited.

**Section 3**

This article shall be inoperative unless it shall have been ratified as an amendment to the Constitution by conventions in the several States, as provided in the Constitution, within seven years from the date of the submission hereof to the States by the Congress.

**AMENDMENT 22** [1951]

**Section 1**

No person shall be elected to the office of the President more than twice, and no person who has held the office of President, or acted as President, for more than two years of a term to which some other person was elected President shall be elected to the office of the President more than once. But this Article shall not apply to any person holding the office of President when this Article was proposed by the Congress, and shall not prevent any person who may be holding the office of President, or acting as President, during the term within which this Article becomes operative from holding the office of President or acting as President during the remainder of such term.

**Section 2**

This article shall be inoperative unless it shall have been ratified as an amendment to the Constitution by the legislatures of three-fourths of the several States within seven years from the date of its submission to the States by the Congress.

**AMENDMENT 23** [1961]

**Section 1**

The District constituting the seat of Government of the United States shall appoint in such manner as the Congress may direct:

A number of electors of President and Vice President equal to the whole number of Senators and Representatives in Congress to which the District would be entitled if it were a State, but in no event more than the least populous State; they shall be in addition to those appointed by the States, but they shall be considered, for the purposes of the election of President and Vice President, to be electors appointed by a State; and they shall meet in the District and perform such duties as provided by the twelfth article of amendment.

### Section 2

The Congress shall have power to enforce this article by appropriate legislation.

## AMENDMENT 24 [1964]

### Section 1

The right of citizens of the United States to vote in any primary or other election for President or Vice President, for electors for President or Vice President, or for Senator or Representative in Congress, shall not be denied or abridged by the United States or any State by reason of failure to pay any poll tax or other tax.

### Section 2

The Congress shall have power to enforce this article by appropriate legislation.

## AMENDMENT 25 [1967]

### Section 1

In case of the removal of the President from office or of his death or resignation, the Vice President shall become President.

### Section 2

Whenever there is a vacancy in the office of the Vice President, the President shall nominate a Vice President who shall take office upon confirmation by a majority vote of both Houses of Congress.

### Section 3

Whenever the President transmits to the President pro tempore of the Senate and the Speaker of the House of Representatives his written declaration that he is unable to discharge the powers and duties of his office, and until he transmits to them a written declaration to the contrary, such powers and duties shall be discharged by the Vice President as Acting President.

### Section 4

Whenever the Vice President and a majority of either the principal officers of the executive departments or of such other body as Congress may by law provide, transmit to the President pro tempore of the Senate and the Speaker of the House of Representatives their written declaration that the President is unable to discharge the powers and duties of his office, the Vice President shall immediately assume the powers and duties of the office as Acting President.

Thereafter, when the President transmits to the President pro tempore of the Senate and the Speaker of the House of Representatives his written declaration that no inability exists, he shall resume the powers and duties of his office unless the Vice President and a majority of either the principal officers of the executive department or of such other body as Congress may by law provide, transmit within four days to the President pro tempore of the Senate and the Speaker of the House of Representatives their written declaration that the President is unable to discharge the powers and duties of his office. Thereupon Congress shall decide the issue, assembling within forty-eight hours for that purpose if not in session. If the Congress, within twenty-one days after receipt of the latter written declaration, or, if Congress is not in session, within twenty-one days after Congress is required to assemble, determines by two-thirds vote of both Houses that the President is unable to discharge the powers and duties of his office, the Vice President shall continue to discharge the same as Acting President; otherwise, the President shall resume the powers and duties of his office.

## AMENDMENT 26 [1971]

### Section 1

The right of citizens of the United States, who are eighteen years of age or older, to vote shall not be denied or abridged by the United States or by any State on account of age.

### Section 2

The Congress shall have power to enforce this article by appropriate legislation.

## AMENDMENT 27 [1992]

No law, varying the compensation for the services of the Senators and Representatives, shall take effect, until an election of Representatives shall have intervened.

# ADMINISTRATIVE PROCEDURE ACT[1]

## 5 U.S.C. § 551. Definitions

For the purpose of this subchapter—

(1) "agency" means each authority of the Government of the United States, whether or not it is within or subject to review by another agency, but does not include—

(A) the Congress;

(B) the courts of the United States;

(C) the governments of the territories or possessions of the United States;

(D) the government of the District of Columbia;

or except as to the requirements of section 552 of this title—

(E) agencies composed of representatives of the parties or of representatives of organizations of the parties to the disputes determined by them;

(F) courts martial and military commissions;

(G) military authority exercised in the field in time of war or in occupied territory; or

(H) functions conferred by sections 1738, 1739, 1743, and 1744 of title 12; subchapter II of chapter 471 of title 49; or sections 1884, 1891–1902, and former section 1641(b)(2), of title 50, appendix;

(2) "person" includes an individual, partnership, corporation, association, or public or private organization other than an agency;

(3) "party" includes a person or agency named or admitted as a party, or properly seeking and entitled as of right to be admitted as a party, in an agency proceeding, and a person or agency admitted by an agency as a party for limited purposes;

(4) "rule" means the whole or a part of an agency statement of general or particular applicability and future effect designed to implement, interpret, or prescribe law or policy or describing the organization, procedure, or practice requirements of an agency and includes the approval or prescription for the future of rates, wages, corporate or financial structures or reorganizations thereof, prices, facilities, appliances, services or allowances therefor or of valuations, costs, or accounting, or practices bearing on any of the foregoing;

(5) "rule making" means agency process for formulating, amending, or repealing a rule;

---

[1] Pub. L. No. 404–79, 60 Stat. 237 (1946); as codified by An Act to enact title 5, United States Code, Pub. L. No. 89–554, 80 Stat. 378 (1966); and as amended.

(6) "order" means the whole or a part of a final disposition, whether affirmative, negative, injunctive, or declaratory in form, of an agency in a matter other than rule making but including licensing;

(7) "adjudication" means agency process for the formulation of an order;

(8) "license" includes the whole or a part of an agency permit, certificate, approval, registration, charter, membership, statutory exemption or other form of permission;

(9) "licensing" includes agency process respecting the grant, renewal, denial, revocation, suspension, annulment, withdrawal, limitation, amendment, modification, or conditioning of a license;

(10) "sanction" includes the whole or a part of an agency—

(A) prohibition, requirement, limitation, or other condition affecting the freedom of a person;

(B) withholding of relief;

(C) imposition of penalty or fine;

(D) destruction, taking, seizure, or withholding of property;

(E) assessment of damages, reimbursement, restitution, compensation, costs, charges, or fees;

(F) requirement, revocation, or suspension of a license; or

(G) taking other compulsory or restrictive action;

(11) "relief" includes the whole or a part of an agency—

(A) grant of money, assistance, license, authority, exemption, exception, privilege, or remedy;

(B) recognition of a claim, right, immunity, privilege, exemption, or exception; or

(C) taking of other action on the application or petition of, and beneficial to, a person;

(12) "agency proceeding" means an agency process as defined by paragraphs (5), (7), and (9) of this section;

(13) "agency action" includes the whole or a part of an agency rule, order, license, sanction, relief, or the equivalent or denial thereof, or failure to act; and

(14)[2] "ex parte communication" means an oral or written communication not on the public record with respect to which reasonable prior notice to all parties is not given, but it shall not include requests for status reports on any matter or proceeding covered by this subchapter.

2 Added by Pub. L. No. 94–409, 90 Stat. 1241 (1976) and subsequently amended.

## § 552. Public information; agency rules, opinions, orders, records, and proceedings[3]

(a) Each agency shall make available to the public information as follows:

(1) Each agency shall separately state and currently publish in the Federal Register for the guidance of the public—

(A) descriptions of its central and field organization and the established places at which, the employees (and in the case of a uniformed service, the members) from whom, and the methods whereby, the public may obtain information, make submittals or requests, or obtain decisions;

(B) statements of the general course and method by which its functions are channeled and determined, including the nature and requirements of all formal and informal procedures available;

(C) rules of procedure, descriptions of forms available or the places at which forms may be obtained, and instructions as to the scope and contents of all papers, reports, or examinations;

(D) substantive rules of general applicability adopted as authorized by law, and statements of general policy or interpretations of general applicability formulated and adopted by the agency; and

(E) each amendment, revision, or repeal of the foregoing.

Except to the extent that a person has actual and timely notice of the terms thereof, a person may not in any manner be required to resort to, or be adversely affected by, a matter required to be published in the Federal Register and not so published. For the purpose of this paragraph, matter reasonably available to the class of persons affected thereby is deemed published in the Federal Register when incorporated by reference therein with the approval of the Director of the Federal Register.

(2) Each agency, in accordance with published rules, shall make available for public inspection in an electronic format—

(A) final opinions, including concurring and dissenting opinions, as well as orders, made in the adjudication of cases;

(B) those statements of policy and interpretations which have been adopted by the agency and are not published in the Federal Register; and

(C) administrative staff manuals and instructions to staff that affect a member of the public;

(D) copies of all records, regardless of form or format—

[3] The more limited provisions respecting publication and public records contained in § 3 of the original APA, which became § 552, have been replaced by the following language and by the Freedom of Information Act, which begins at § 552(a)(3) and is by far the longest element of the APA. It is set out in full at p. 1604.

(i) that have been released to any person under paragraph (3); and

(ii)(I) that because of the nature of their subject matter, the agency determines have become or are likely to become the subject of subsequent requests for substantially the same records; or

(II) that have been requested 3 or more times; and

(E) a general index of the records referred to under subparagraph (D);

unless the materials are promptly published and copies offered for sale. For records created on or after November 1, 1996, within one year after such date, each agency shall make such records available, including by computer telecommunications or, if computer telecommunications means have not been established by the agency, by other electronic means. . . . Each agency shall also maintain and make available for public inspection in an electronic format current indexes providing identifying information for the public as to any matter issued, adopted, or promulgated after July 4, 1967, and required by this paragraph to be made available or published. . . . A final order, opinion, statement of policy, interpretation, or staff manual or instruction that affects a member of the public may be relied on, used, or cited as precedent by an agency against a party other than an agency only if—

(i) it has been indexed and either made available or published as provided by this paragraph; or

(ii) the party has actual and timely notice of the terms thereof.

[The remainder of this section is set out under the FREEDOM OF INFORMATION ACT, p. 1604.]

### § 552a. Records maintained on individuals

[This section, also known as the Privacy Act, is omitted.]

### § 552b. Open meetings

[This section, also known as the GOVERNMENT IN THE SUNSHINE ACT, is set out at p. 1620.]

### § 553. Rule making

(a) This section applies, according to the provisions thereof, except to the extent that there is involved—

(1) a military or foreign affairs function of the United States; or

(2) a matter relating to agency management or personnel or to public property, loans, grants, benefits, or contracts.

(b) General notice of proposed rule making shall be published in the Federal Register, unless persons subject thereto are named and either personally served or otherwise have actual notice thereof in accordance with law. The notice shall include—

(1) a statement of the time, place, and nature of public rule making proceedings;

(2) reference to the legal authority under which the rule is proposed; and

(3) either the terms or substance of the proposed rule or a description of the subjects and issues involved.

Except when notice or hearing is required by statute, this subsection does not apply—

(A) to interpretative rules, general statements of policy, or rules of agency organization, procedure, or practice; or

(B) when the agency for good cause finds (and incorporates the finding and a brief statement of reasons therefor in the rules issued) that notice and public procedure thereon are impracticable, unnecessary, or contrary to the public interest.

(c) After notice required by this section, the agency shall give interested persons an opportunity to participate in the rule making through submission of written data, views, or arguments with or without opportunity for oral presentation. After consideration of the relevant matter presented, the agency shall incorporate in the rules adopted a concise general statement of their basis and purpose. When rules are required by statute to be made on the record after opportunity for an agency hearing, sections 556 and 557 of this title apply instead of this subsection.

(d) The required publication or service of a substantive rule shall be made not less than 30 days before its effective date, except—

(1) a substantive rule which grants or recognizes an exemption or relieves a restriction;

(2) interpretative rules and statements of policy; or

(3) as otherwise provided by the agency for good cause found and published with the rule.

(e) Each agency shall give an interested person the right to petition for the issuance, amendment, or repeal of a rule.

### § 554. Adjudications

(a) This section applies, according to the provisions thereof, in every case of adjudication required by statute to be determined on the record after opportunity for an agency hearing, except to the extent that there is involved—

(1) a matter subject to a subsequent trial of the law and the facts de novo in a court;

(2) the selection or tenure of an employee, except a [sic] administrative law judge appointed under section 3105 of this title;

(3) proceedings in which decisions rest solely on inspections, tests, or elections;

(4) the conduct of military or foreign affairs functions;

(5) cases in which an agency is acting as an agent for a court; or

(6) the certification of worker representatives.

(b) Persons entitled to notice of an agency hearing shall be timely informed of—

(1) the time, place, and nature of the hearing;

(2) the legal authority and jurisdiction under which the hearing is to be held; and

(3) the matters of fact and law asserted.

When private persons are the moving parties, other parties to the proceeding shall give prompt notice of issues controverted in fact or law; and in other instances agencies may by rule require responsive pleading. In fixing the time and place for hearings, due regard shall be had for the convenience and necessity of the parties or their representatives.

(c) The agency shall give all interested parties opportunity for—

(1) the submission and consideration of facts, arguments, offers of settlement, or proposals of adjustment when time, the nature of the proceeding, and the public interest permit; and

(2) to the extent that the parties are unable so to determine a controversy by consent, hearing and decision on notice and in accordance with sections 556 and 557 of this title.

(d) The employee who presides at the reception of evidence pursuant to section 556 of this title shall make the recommended decision or initial decision required by section 557 of this title, unless he becomes unavailable to the agency. Except to the extent required for the disposition of ex parte matters as authorized by law, such an employee may not—

(1) consult a person or party on a fact in issue, unless on notice and opportunity for all parties to participate; or

(2) be responsible to or subject to the supervision or direction of an employee or agent engaged in the performance of investigative or prosecuting functions for an agency.

An employee or agent engaged in the performance of investigative or prosecuting functions for an agency in a case may not, in that or a factually related case, participate or advise in the decision, recommended decision or agency review pursuant to section 557 of this title, except as witness or counsel in public proceedings. This subsection does not apply—

(A) in determining applications for initial licenses;

(B) to proceedings involving the validity or application of rates, facilities, or practices of public utilities or carriers; or

(C) to the agency or a member or members of the body comprising the agency.

(e) The agency, with like effect as in the case of other orders, and in its sound discretion, may issue a declaratory order to terminate a controversy or remove uncertainty.

## § 555. Ancillary matters

(a) This section applies, according to the provisions thereof, except as otherwise provided by this subchapter.

(b) A person compelled to appear in person before an agency or representative thereof is entitled to be accompanied, represented, and advised by counsel or, if permitted by the agency, by other qualified representative. A party is entitled to appear in person or by or with counsel or other duly qualified representative in an agency proceeding. So far as the orderly conduct of public business permits, an interested person may appear before an agency or its responsible employees for the presentation, adjustment, or determination of an issue, request, or controversy in a proceeding, whether interlocutory, summary, or otherwise, or in connection with an agency function. With due regard for the convenience and necessity of the parties or their representatives and within a reasonable time, each agency shall proceed to conclude a matter presented to it. This subsection does not grant or deny a person who is not a lawyer the right to appear for or represent others before an agency or in an agency proceeding.

(c) Process, requirement of a report, inspection, or other investigative act or demand may not be issued, made, or enforced except as authorized by law. A person compelled to submit data or evidence is entitled to retain or, on payment of lawfully prescribed costs, procure a copy or transcript thereof, except that in a nonpublic investigatory proceeding the witness may for good cause be limited to inspection of the official transcript of his testimony.

(d) Agency subpenas [sic] authorized by law shall be issued to a party on request and, when required by rules of procedure, on a statement or showing of general relevance and reasonable scope of the evidence sought. On contest, the court shall sustain the subpena or similar process or demand to the extent that it is found to be in accordance with law. In a proceeding for enforcement, the court shall issue an order requiring the appearance of the witness or the production of the evidence or data within a reasonable time under penalty of punishment for contempt in case of contumacious failure to comply.

(e) Prompt notice shall be given of the denial in whole or in part of a written application, petition, or other request of an interested person made in connection with any agency proceeding. Except in affirming a prior denial or when the denial is self-explanatory, the notice shall be accompanied by a brief statement of the grounds for denial.

## § 556. Hearings; presiding employees; powers and duties; burden of proof; evidence; record as basis of decision

(a) This section applies, according to the provisions thereof, to hearings required by section 553 or 554 of this title to be conducted in accordance with this section.

(b) There shall preside at the taking of evidence

(1) the agency;

(2) one or more members of the body which comprises the agency; or

(3) one or more administrative law judges appointed under section 3105 of this title.

This subchapter does not supersede the conduct of specified classes of proceedings, in whole or in part, by or before boards or other employees specially provided for by or designated under statute. The functions of presiding employees and of employees participating in decisions in accordance with section 557 of this title shall be conducted in an impartial manner. A presiding or participating employee may at any time disqualify himself. On the filing in good faith of a timely and sufficient affidavit of personal bias or other disqualification of a presiding or participating employee, the agency shall determine the matter as a part of the record and decision in the case.

(c) Subject to published rules of the agency and within its powers, employees presiding at hearings may—

(1) administer oaths and affirmations;

(2) issue subpenas authorized by law;

(3) rule on offers of proof and receive relevant evidence;

(4) take depositions or have depositions taken when the ends of justice would be served;

(5) regulate the course of the hearing;

(6) hold conferences for the settlement or simplification of the issues by consent of the parties or by the use of alternative means of dispute resolution as provided in subchapter IV of this chapter [5 U.S.C. §§ 571 et seq.];

(7) inform the parties as to the availability of one or more alternative means of dispute resolution, and encourage use of such methods;

(8) require the attendance at any conference held pursuant to paragraph (6) of at least one representative of each party who has authority to negotiate concerning resolution of issues in controversy;

(9) dispose of procedural requests or similar matters;

(10) make or recommend decisions in accordance with section 557 of this title; and

(11) take other action authorized by agency rule consistent with this subchapter.

(d) Except as otherwise provided by statute, the proponent of a rule or order has the burden of proof. Any oral or documentary evidence may be received, but the agency as a matter of policy shall provide for the exclusion of irrelevant, immaterial, or unduly repetitious evidence. A sanction may not be imposed or rule or order issued except on consideration of the whole record or those parts thereof cited by a party and supported by and in accordance with the reliable, probative, and substantial evidence. The agency may, to the extent consistent with the interests of justice and the policy of the underlying statutes administered by the agency, consider a violation of section 557(d) of this title sufficient grounds for a decision adverse to a party who has knowingly committed such violation or knowingly caused such violation to occur.[4] A party is entitled to present his case or defense by oral or documentary evidence, to submit rebuttal evidence, and to conduct such cross-examination as may be required for a full and true disclosure of the facts. In rule making or determining claims for money or benefits or applications for initial licenses an agency may, when a party will not be prejudiced thereby, adopt procedures for the submission of all or part of the evidence in written form.

(e) The transcript of testimony and exhibits, together with all papers and requests filed in the proceeding, constitutes the exclusive record for decision in accordance with section 557 of this title and, on payment of lawfully prescribed costs, shall be made available to the parties. When an agency decision rests on official notice of a material fact not appearing in the evidence in the record, a party is entitled, on timely request, to an opportunity to show the contrary.

### § 557. Initial decisions; conclusiveness; review by agency; submissions by parties; contents of decisions; record

(a) This section applies, according to the provisions thereof, when a hearing is required to be conducted in accordance with section 556 of this title.

(b) When the agency did not preside at the reception of the evidence, the presiding employee or, in cases not subject to section 554(d) of this title, an employee qualified to preside at hearings pursuant to section 556 of this title, shall initially decide the case unless the agency requires, either in specific cases or by general rule, the entire record to be certified to it for decision. When the presiding employee makes an initial decision, that decision then becomes the decision of the agency without further proceedings unless there is an appeal to, or review on motion of, the agency within time provided by rule. On appeal from or review of the initial decision, the agency has all the powers which it would have in making the initial decision except as it may limit the issues on notice or by rule. When the agency makes the decision without having presided at the reception of the evidence, the presiding employee or an employee qualified to preside at hearings pursuant to section 556 of this title shall first recommend a decision, except that in rule making or determining applications for initial licenses—

(1) instead thereof the agency may issue a tentative decision or one of its responsible employees may recommend a decision; or

(2) this procedure may be omitted in a case in which the agency finds on the record that due and timely execution of its functions imperatively and unavoidably so requires.

---

[4] This sentence added by Pub. L. No. 94–409, 90 Stat. 1247 (1976).

(c) Before a recommended, initial, or tentative decision, or a decision on agency review of the decision of subordinate employees, the parties are entitled to a reasonable opportunity to submit for the consideration of the employees participating in the decisions—

(1) proposed findings and conclusions; or

(2) exceptions to the decisions or recommended decisions of subordinate employees or to tentative agency decisions; and

(3) supporting reasons for the exceptions or proposed findings or conclusions.

The record shall show the ruling on each finding, conclusion, or exception presented. All decisions, including initial, recommended, and tentative decisions, are a part of the record and shall include a statement of—

(A) findings and conclusions, and the reasons or basis therefor, on all the material issues of fact, law, or discretion presented on the record; and

(B) the appropriate rule, order, sanction, relief, or denial thereof.

(d)(1)[5] In any agency proceeding which is subject to subsection (a) of this section, except to the extent required for the disposition of ex parte matters as authorized by law—

(A) no interested person outside the agency shall make or knowingly cause to be made to any member of the body comprising the agency, administrative law judge, or other employee who is or may reasonably be expected to be involved in the decisional process of the proceeding, an ex parte communication relevant to the merits of the proceeding;

(B) no member of the body comprising the agency, administrative law judge, or other employee who is or may reasonably be expected to be involved in the decisional process of the proceeding, shall make or knowingly cause to be made to any interested person outside the agency an ex parte communication relevant to the merits of the proceeding;

(C) a member of the body comprising the agency, administrative law judge, or other employee who is or may reasonably be expected to be involved in the decisional process of such proceeding who receives, or who makes or knowingly causes to be made, a communication prohibited by this subsection shall place on the public record of the proceeding:

(i) all such written communications;

(ii) memoranda stating the substance of all such oral communications; and

(iii) all written responses, and memoranda stating the substance of all oral responses, to the materials described in clauses (i) and (ii) of this subparagraph;

[5] Subsection (d) was added by Pub. L. No. 94–409, 90 Stat. 1247 (1976).

(D) upon receipt of a communication knowingly made or knowingly caused to be made by a party in violation of this subsection, the agency, administrative law judge, or other employee presiding at the hearing may, to the extent consistent with the interests of justice and the policy of the underlying statutes, require the party to show cause why his claim or interest in the proceeding should not be dismissed, denied, disregarded, or otherwise adversely affected on account of such violation; and

(E) the prohibitions of this subsection shall apply beginning at such time as the agency may designate, but in no case shall they begin to apply later than the time at which a proceeding is noticed for hearing unless the person responsible for the communication has knowledge that it will be noticed, in which case the prohibitions shall apply beginning at the time of his acquisition of such knowledge.

(2) This subsection does not constitute authority to withhold information from Congress.

### § 558. Imposition of sanctions; determination of applications for licenses; suspension, revocation, and expiration of licenses

(a) This section applies, according to the provisions thereof, to the exercise of a power or authority.

(b) A sanction may not be imposed or a substantive rule or order issued except within jurisdiction delegated to the agency and as authorized by law.

(c) When application is made for a license required by law, the agency, with due regard for the rights and privileges of all the interested parties or adversely affected persons and within a reasonable time, shall set and complete proceedings required to be conducted in accordance with sections 556 and 557 of this title or other proceedings required by law and shall make its decision. Except in cases of willfulness or those in which public health, interest, or safety requires otherwise, the withdrawal, suspension, revocation, or annulment of a license is lawful only if, before the institution of agency proceedings therefor, the licensee has been given—

(1) notice by the agency in writing of the facts or conduct which may warrant the action; and

(2) opportunity to demonstrate or achieve compliance with all lawful requirements.

When the licensee has made timely and sufficient application for a renewal or a new license in accordance with agency rules, a license with reference to an activity of a continuing nature does not expire until the application has been finally determined by the agency.

### § 559. Effect on other laws; effect of subsequent statute

This subchapter, chapter 7, and sections 1305, 3105, 3344, 4301(2)(E), 5372, and 7521 of this title, and the provisions of section 5335(a)(B) of this title that relate to administrative law judges, do not limit or repeal additional requirements imposed by statute or otherwise recognized by law. Except as otherwise required by law, requirements or privileges relating to evidence or procedure apply equally to agencies and persons. Each agency is granted the authority necessary to comply with the requirements of this subchapter through the issuance of rules or otherwise. Subsequent statute may not be held to supersede or modify this subchapter, chapter 7, sections 1305, 3105, 3344, 4301(2)(E), 5372, or 7521 of this title, or the provisions of section 5335(a)(B) of this title that relate to administrative law judges, except to the extent that it does so expressly. . . .

### § 701. Application; definitions

(a) This chapter applies, according to the provisions thereof, except to the extent that—

(1) statutes preclude judicial review; or

(2) agency action is committed to agency discretion by law.

(b)(1) ["agency" is defined precisely as in § 551(1)(A) through (H), above];

(2) "person", "rule", "order", "license", "sanction", "relief", and "agency action" have the meanings given them by section 551 of this title.

### § 702. Right of review

A person suffering legal wrong because of agency action, or adversely affected or aggrieved by agency action within the meaning of a relevant statute, is entitled to judicial review thereof.[6] An action in a court of the United States seeking relief other than money damages and stating a claim that an agency or an officer or employee thereof acted or failed to act in an official capacity or under color of legal authority shall not be dismissed nor relief therein be denied on the ground that it is against the United States or that the United States is an indispensable party. The United States may be named as a defendant in any such action, and a judgment or decree may be entered against the United States: Provided, That any mandatory or injunctive decree shall specify the Federal officer or officers (by name or by title), and their successors in office, personally responsible for compliance. Nothing herein (1) affects other limitations on judicial review or the power or duty of the court to dismiss any action or deny relief on any other appropriate legal or equitable ground; or (2) confers authority to grant relief if any other statute that grants consent to suit expressly or impliedly forbids the relief which is sought.

### § 703. Form and venue of proceeding

The form of proceeding for judicial review is the special statutory review proceeding relevant to the subject matter in a court specified by statute or, in the absence or inadequacy thereof, any applicable form of legal action, including actions for declaratory judgments or writs of prohibitory or mandatory injunction or habeas corpus, in a court of competent jurisdiction. If no special statutory review proceeding is

---

[6] Material after first sentence added by Pub. L. No. 94–574, 90 Stat. 2721 (1976).

applicable, the action for judicial review may be brought against the United States, the agency by its official title, or the appropriate officer.[7] Except to the extent that prior, adequate, and exclusive opportunity for judicial review is provided by law, agency action is subject to judicial review in civil or criminal proceedings for judicial enforcement.

### § 704. Actions reviewable

Agency action made reviewable by statute and final agency action for which there is no other adequate remedy in a court are subject to judicial review. A preliminary, procedural, or intermediate agency action or ruling not directly reviewable is subject to review on the review of the final agency action. Except as otherwise expressly required by statute, agency action otherwise final is final for the purposes of this section whether or not there has been presented or determined an application for a declaratory order, for any form of reconsideration, or, unless the agency otherwise requires by rule and provides that the action meanwhile is inoperative, for an appeal to superior agency authority.

### § 705. Relief pending review

When an agency finds that justice so requires, it may postpone the effective date of action taken by it, pending judicial review. On such conditions as may be required and to the extent necessary to prevent irreparable injury, the reviewing court, including the court to which a case may be taken on appeal from or on application for certiorari or other writ to a reviewing court, may issue all necessary and appropriate process to postpone the effective date of an agency action or to preserve status or rights pending conclusion of the review proceedings.

### § 706. Scope of review

To the extent necessary to decision and when presented, the reviewing court shall decide all relevant questions of law, interpret constitutional and statutory provisions, and determine the meaning or applicability of the terms of an agency action. The reviewing court shall—

(1) compel agency action unlawfully withheld or unreasonably delayed; and

(2) hold unlawful and set aside agency action, findings, and conclusions found to be—

(A) arbitrary, capricious, an abuse of discretion, or otherwise not in accordance with law;

(B) contrary to constitutional right, power, privilege, or immunity;

(C) in excess of statutory jurisdiction, authority, or limitations, or short of statutory right;

(D) without observance of procedure required by law;

---

[7] Preceding sentence added by Pub. L. No. 94–574, 90 Stat. 2721 (1976).

(E) unsupported by substantial evidence in a case subject to sections 556 and 557 of this title or otherwise reviewed on the record of an agency hearing provided by statute; or

(F) unwarranted by the facts to the extent that the facts are subject to trial de novo by the reviewing court.

In making the foregoing determinations, the court shall review the whole record or those parts of it cited by a party, and due account shall be taken of the rule of prejudicial error.

### § 1305. Administrative law judges[8]

For the purpose of sections 3105, 3344, 4301(2)(D), and 5372 of this title and the provisions of section 5335(a)(B) of this title that relate to administrative law judges, the Office of Personnel Management may, and for the purpose of section 7521 of this title, the Merit Systems Protection Board may investigate, prescribe regulations, appoint advisory committees as necessary, recommend legislation, subpena witnesses and records, and pay witness fees as established for the courts of the United States.

### § 3344. Details; administrative law judges

An agency as defined by section 551 of this title which occasionally or temporarily is insufficiently staffed with administrative law judges appointed under section 3105 of this title may use administrative law judges selected by the Office of Personnel Management from and with the consent of other agencies.

### § 5372. Administrative law judges[9]

(a) For the purposes of this section, the term "administrative law judge" means an administrative law judge appointed under section 3105.

(b)(1)(A) There shall be 3 levels of basic pay for administrative law judges (designated as AL-1, 2, and 3, respectively), and each such judge shall be paid at 1 of those levels, in accordance with the provisions of this section. . . .

(c) The Office of Personnel Management shall prescribe regulations necessary to administer this section.

### § 7521. Actions against administrative law judges[10]

(a) An action may be taken against an administrative law judge appointed under section 3105 of this title by the agency in which the administrative law judge is employed only for good cause established and determined by the Merit Systems Protection Board on the record after opportunity for hearing before the Board. . . .

---

[8] Substitution of "administrative law judge" for "hearing examiner," here and elsewhere in the APA, was effected by Pub. L. No. 95–251, 92 Stat. 183 (1978).

[9] Added by Pub. L. No. 101–509, Title V, § 529, 104 Stat. 1445 (1990) with succeeding amendments through Pub. L. No. 106–97, § 1 (1999); the section it replaced authorized OPM to set pay levels "independently of agency recommendations or ratings" and in accordance with general civil service practice.

[10] As amended by the Civil Service Reform Act of 1978, Pub. L. No. 95–454, 92 Stat. 1137.

(b) [This section covers removals, suspensions, reductions in grade or pay, and furloughs of 30 days or less, with some exceptions.]

# FREEDOM OF INFORMATION ACT[11]

**5 U.S.C. § 552. Public information; agency rules, opinions, orders, records, and proceedings**

(a) Each agency shall make available to the public information as follows: . . . [§§ 552(a)(1), (2) are set out at p. 1591]

(3)(A) Except with respect to the records made available under paragraphs (1) and (2) of this subsection, and except as provided in subparagraph (E), each agency, upon any request for records which (i) reasonably describes such records and (ii) is made in accordance with published rules stating the time, place, fees (if any), and procedures to be followed, shall make the records promptly available to any person.

(B) In making any record available to a person under this paragraph, an agency shall provide the record in any form or format requested by the person if the record is readily reproducible by the agency in that form or format. Each agency shall make reasonable efforts to maintain its records in forms or formats that are reproducible for purposes of this section.

(C) In responding under this paragraph to a request for records, an agency shall make reasonable efforts to search for the records in electronic form or format, except when such efforts would significantly interfere with the operation of the agency's automated information system.

(D) For purposes of this paragraph, the term "search" means to review, manually or by automated means, agency records for the purpose of locating those records which are responsive to a request.

(E) An agency, or part of an agency, that is an element of the intelligence community (as that term is defined in section 3(4) of the National Security Act of 1947 (50 U.S.C. 401a(4))) shall not make any record available under this paragraph to—

(i) any government entity, other than a State, territory, commonwealth, or district of the United States, or any subdivision thereof; or

(ii) a representative of a government entity described in clause (i).

(4)(A)(i) In order to carry out the provisions of this section, each agency shall promulgate regulations, pursuant to notice and receipt of public comment, specifying the schedule of fees applicable to the processing of requests under this section and establishing procedures and guidelines for determining when such fees should be waived or reduced. Such schedule shall conform to the guidelines

---

[11] Pub. L. No. 89–487, 80 Stat. 250 (1966); and as amended through the FOIA Improvement Act of 2016, 114–185, 130 Stat. 538.

which shall be promulgated, pursuant to notice and receipt of public comment, by the Director of the Office of Management and Budget and which shall provide for a uniform schedule of fees for all agencies.

(ii) Such agency regulations shall provide that—

(I) fees shall be limited to reasonable standard charges for document search, duplication, and review, when records are requested for commercial use;

(II) fees shall be limited to reasonable standard charges for document duplication when records are not sought for commercial use and the request is made by an educational or noncommercial scientific institution, whose purpose is scholarly or scientific research; or a representative of the news media; and

(III) for any request not described in (I) or (II), fees shall be limited to reasonable standard charges for document search and duplication.

In this clause, the term "a representative of the news media" means any person or entity that gathers information of potential interest to a segment of the public, uses its editorial skills to turn the raw materials into a distinct work, and distributes that work to an audience. In this clause, the term "news" means information that is about current events or that would be of current interest to the public. Examples of news-media entities are television or radio stations broadcasting to the public at large and publishers of periodicals (but only if such entities qualify as disseminators of "news") who make their products available for purchase by or subscription by or free distribution to the general public. These examples are not all-inclusive. Moreover, as methods of news delivery evolve (for example, the adoption of the electronic dissemination of newspapers through telecommunications services), such alternative media shall be considered to be news-media entities. A freelance journalist shall be regarded as working for a news-media entity if the journalist can demonstrate a solid basis for expecting publication through that entity, whether or not the journalist is actually employed by the entity. A publication contract would present a solid basis for such an expectation; the Government may also consider the past publication record of the requester in making such a determination.

(iii) Documents shall be furnished without any charge or at a charge reduced below the fees established under clause (ii) if disclosure of the information is in the public interest because it is likely to contribute significantly to public understanding of the operations or activities of the government and is not primarily in the commercial interest of the requester.

(iv) Fee schedules shall provide for the recovery of only the direct costs of search, duplication, or review. Review costs shall include only the direct costs incurred during the initial examination of a document for the purposes of determining whether the documents must be disclosed under this section and for the purposes of withholding any portions exempt from disclosure under this section. Review costs may not include any costs incurred in resolving issues of law or policy that may be raised in the course of processing a request under this section. No fee may be charged by any agency under this section—

(I) if the costs of routine collection and processing of the fee are likely to equal or exceed the amount of the fee; or

(II) for any request described in clause (ii)(II) or (III) of this subparagraph for the first two hours of search time or for the first one hundred pages of duplication.

(v) No agency may require advance payment of any fee unless the requester has previously failed to pay fees in a timely fashion, or the agency has determined that the fee will exceed $250.

(vi) Nothing in this subparagraph shall supersede fees chargeable under a statute specifically providing for setting the level of fees for particular types of records.

(vii) In any action by a requester regarding the waiver of fees under this section, the court shall determine the matter de novo: Provided, That the court's review of the matter shall be limited to the record before the agency.

(viii)(I) Except as provided in subclause (II), an agency shall not assess any search fees (or in the case of a requester described under clause (ii)(II) of this subparagraph, duplication fees) under this subparagraph if the agency has failed to comply with any time limit under paragraph (6).

(II)(aa) If an agency has determined that unusual circumstances apply (as the term is defined in paragraph (6)(B)) and the agency provided a timely written notice to the requester in accordance with paragraph (6)(B), a failure described in subclause (I) is excused for an additional 10 days. If the agency fails to comply with the extended time limit, the agency may not assess any search fees (or in the case of a requester described under clause (ii)(II) of this subparagraph, duplication fees).

(bb) If an agency has determined that unusual circumstances apply and more than 5,000 pages are necessary to respond to the request, an agency may charge search fees (or in the case of a requester described under clause (ii) (II) of this subparagraph, duplication fees) if the agency has provided a timely written notice to the requester in accordance with paragraph (6)(B) and the agency has discussed with the requester via written mail, electronic mail, or telephone (or made not less than 3 good-faith attempts to do so) how the requester could effectively limit the scope of the request in accordance with paragraph (6)(B)(ii).

(cc) If a court has determined that exceptional circumstances exist (as that term is defined in paragraph (6)(C)), a failure described in subclause (I) shall be excused for the length of time provided by the court order.

(B) On complaint, the district court of the United States in the district in which the complainant resides, or has his principal place of business, or in which the agency records are situated, or in the District of Columbia, has jurisdiction to enjoin the agency from withholding agency records and to order the production of any agency records improperly withheld from the complainant. In such a case the court shall determine the matter de novo, and may examine the contents of such agency records in camera to determine whether such records or any part thereof shall be withheld under any of the exemptions set forth in subsection (b) of this section, and the burden is on the agency to sustain its action. In addition to any other matters to which a court accords substantial weight, a court shall accord substantial weight to an affidavit of an agency concerning the agency's determination as to technical feasibility under paragraph (2)(C) and subsection (b) and reproducibility under paragraph (3)(B).

(C) Notwithstanding any other provision of law, the defendant shall serve an answer or otherwise plead to any complaint made under this subsection within thirty days after service upon the defendant of the pleading in which such complaint is made, unless the court otherwise directs for good cause shown.

(D) [Repealed]

(E)(i) The court may assess against the United States reasonable attorney fees and other litigation costs reasonably incurred in any case under this section in which the complainant has substantially prevailed.

(ii) For purposes of this subparagraph, a complainant has substantially prevailed if the complainant has obtained relief through either—

(I) a judicial order, or an enforceable written agreement or consent decree; or

(II) a voluntary or unilateral change in position by the agency, if the complainant's claim is not insubstantial.

(F)(i) Whenever the court orders the production of any agency records improperly withheld from the complainant and assesses against the United States reasonable attorney fees and other litigation costs, and the court additionally issues a written finding that the circumstances surrounding the withholding raise questions whether agency personnel acted arbitrarily or capriciously with respect to the withholding, the Special Counsel shall promptly initiate a proceeding to determine whether disciplinary action is warranted .... The administrative authority shall take the corrective action that the Special Counsel recommends.

(ii) The Attorney General shall—

(I) notify the Special Counsel of each civil action described under the first sentence of clause (i); and

(II) annually submit a report to Congress on the number of such civil actions in the preceding year.

(iii) The Special Counsel shall annually submit a report to Congress on the actions taken by the Special Counsel under clause (i). . . .

(5) Each agency having more than one member shall maintain and make available for public inspection a record of the final votes of each member in every agency proceeding.

(6)(A) Each agency, upon any request for records made under paragraph (1), (2), or (3) of this subsection, shall—

(i) determine within 20 days (excepting Saturdays, Sundays, and legal public holidays) after the receipt of any such request whether to comply with such request and shall immediately notify the person making such request of

(I) such determination and the reasons therefor;

(II) the right of such person to seek assistance from the FOIA Public Liaison of the agency; and

(III) in the case of an adverse determination—

(aa) the right of such person to appeal to the head of the agency, within a period determined by the head of the agency that is not less than 90 days after the date of such adverse determination; and (bb) the right of such person to seek dispute resolution services from the FOIA Public Liaison of the agency or the Office of Government Information Services; and

(ii) make a determination with respect to any appeal within twenty days (excepting Saturdays, Sundays, and legal public holidays) after the receipt of such appeal. If on appeal the denial of the request for records is in whole or in part upheld, the agency shall notify the person making such request of the provisions for judicial review of that determination under paragraph (4) of this subsection.

The 20-day period under clause (i) shall commence on the date on which the request is first received by the appropriate component of the agency, but in any event not later than ten days after the request is first received by any component of the agency that is designated in the agency's regulations under this section to receive requests under this section. The 20-day period shall not be tolled by the agency except—

(I) that the agency may make one request to the requester for information and toll the 20-day period while it is awaiting such information that it has reasonably requested from the requester under this section; or

(II) if necessary to clarify with the requester issues regarding fee assessment. In either case, the agency's receipt of the requester's response to the agency's request for information or clarification ends the tolling period.

(B)(i) In unusual circumstances as specified in this subparagraph, the time limits prescribed in either clause (i) or clause (ii) of subparagraph (A) may be extended by written notice to the person making such request setting forth the unusual circumstances for such extension and the date on which a determination is expected to be dispatched. No such notice shall specify a date that would result in an extension for more than ten working days, except as provided in clause (ii) of this subparagraph.

(ii) With respect to a request for which a written notice under clause (i) extends the time limits prescribed under clause (i) of subparagraph (A), the agency shall notify the person making the request if the request cannot be processed within the time limit specified in that clause and shall provide the person an opportunity to limit the scope of the request so that it may be processed within that time limit or an opportunity to arrange with the agency an alternative time frame for processing the request or a modified request. To aid the requester, each agency shall make available its FOIA Public Liaison, who shall assist in the resolution of any disputes between the requester and the agency, and notify the requester of the right of the requester to seek dispute resolution services from the Office of Government Information Services. Refusal by the person to reasonably modify the request or arrange such an alternative time frame shall be considered as a factor in determining whether exceptional circumstances exist for purposes of subparagraph (C).

(iii) As used in this subparagraph, "unusual circumstances" means, but only to the extent reasonably necessary to the proper processing of the particular requests—

(I) the need to search for and collect the requested records from field facilities or other establishments that are separate from the office processing the request;

(II) the need to search for, collect, and appropriately examine a voluminous amount of separate and distinct records which are demanded in a single request; or

(III) the need for consultation, which shall be conducted with all practicable speed, with another agency having a substantial interest in the determination of the request or among two or more components of the agency having substantial subject-matter interest therein.

(iv) Each agency may promulgate regulations, pursuant to notice and receipt of public comment, providing for the aggregation of certain requests by the same requestor, or by a group of requestors acting in concert, if the agency reasonably believes that such requests actually constitute a single request, which would otherwise satisfy the unusual circumstances specified in this subparagraph, and the requests involve clearly related matters. Multiple requests involving unrelated matters shall not be aggregated.

(C)(i) Any person making a request to any agency for records under paragraph (1), (2), or (3) of this subsection shall be deemed to have exhausted his administrative remedies with respect to such request if the agency fails to comply with the applicable time limit provisions of this paragraph. If the Government can show exceptional circumstances exist and that the agency is exercising due diligence in responding to the request, the court may retain jurisdiction and allow the agency additional time to complete its review of the records. Upon any determination by an agency to comply with a request for records, the records shall be made promptly available to such person making such request. Any notification of denial of any request for records under this subsection shall set forth the names and titles or positions of each person responsible for the denial of such request.

(ii) For purposes of this subparagraph, the term "exceptional circumstances" does not include a delay that results from a predictable agency workload of requests under this section, unless the agency demonstrates reasonable progress in reducing its backlog of pending requests.

(iii) Refusal by a person to reasonably modify the scope of a request or arrange an alternative time frame for processing a request (or a modified request) under clause (ii) after being given an opportunity to do so by the agency to whom the person made the request shall be considered as a factor in determining whether exceptional circumstances exist for purposes of this subparagraph.

(D)(i) Each agency may promulgate regulations, pursuant to notice and receipt of public comment, providing for multitrack processing of requests for records based on the amount of work or time (or both) involved in processing requests. . . .

(E)(i) Each agency shall promulgate regulations, pursuant to notice and receipt of public comment, providing for expedited processing of requests for records—

(I) in cases in which the person requesting the records demonstrates a compelling need; and

(II) in other cases determined by the agency.

(ii) Notwithstanding clause (i), regulations under this subparagraph must ensure—

(I) that a determination of whether to provide expedited processing shall be made, and notice of the determination shall be provided to the person making the request, within 10 days after the date of the request; and

(II) expeditious consideration of administrative appeals of such determinations of whether to provide expedited processing.

(iii) An agency shall process as soon as practicable any request for records to which the agency has granted expedited processing under this subparagraph. Agency action to deny or affirm denial of a request for expedited processing pursuant to this subparagraph, and failure by an agency to respond in a timely manner to such a request shall be subject to judicial review under paragraph (4), except that the judicial review shall be based on the record before the agency at the time of the determination.

(iv) A district court of the United States shall not have jurisdiction to review an agency denial of expedited processing of a request for records after the agency has provided a complete response to the request.

(v) For purposes of this subparagraph, the term "compelling need" means—

(I) that a failure to obtain requested records on an expedited basis under this paragraph could reasonably be expected to pose an imminent threat to the life or physical safety of an individual; or

(II) with respect to a request made by a person primarily engaged in disseminating information, urgency to inform the public concerning actual or alleged Federal Government activity.

(vi) A demonstration of a compelling need by a person making a request for expedited processing shall be made by a statement certified by such person to be true and correct to the best of such person's knowledge and belief.

(F) In denying a request for records, in whole or in part, an agency shall make a reasonable effort to estimate the volume of any requested matter the provision of which is denied, and shall provide any such estimate to the person making the request, unless providing such estimate would harm an interest protected by the exemption in subsection (b) pursuant to which the denial is made.

(7) Each agency shall—

(A) establish a system to assign an individualized tracking number for each request received that will take longer than ten days to process and provide to each person making a request the tracking number assigned to the request; and

(B) establish a telephone line or Internet service that provides information about the status of a request to the person making the request using the assigned tracking number, including—

(i) the date on which the agency originally received the request; and

(ii) an estimated date on which the agency will complete action on the request.

(8)(A) An agency shall—

(i) withhold information under this section only if—

(I) the agency reasonably foresees that disclosure would harm an interest protected by an exemption described in subsection (b); or

(II) disclosure is prohibited by law; and

(ii)(I) consider whether partial disclosure of information is possible whenever the agency determines that a full disclosure of a requested record is not possible; and

(II) take reasonable steps necessary to segregate and release nonexempt information; and

(B) Nothing in this paragraph requires disclosure of information that is otherwise prohibited from disclosure by law, or otherwise exempted from disclosure under subsection (b)(3).

(b) This section does not apply to matters that are—

(1)(A) specifically authorized under criteria established by an Executive order to be kept secret in the interest of national defense or foreign policy and (B) are in fact properly classified pursuant to such Executive order;

(2) related solely to the internal personnel rules and practices of an agency;

(3) specifically exempted from disclosure by statute (other than section 552b of this title), if that statute—

(A)(i) requires that the matters be withheld from the public in such a manner as to leave no discretion on the issue; or

(ii) establishes particular criteria for withholding or refers to particular types of matters to be withheld; and

(B) if enacted after the date of enactment of the OPEN FOIA Act of 2009, specifically cites to this paragraph.

(4) trade secrets and commercial or financial information obtained from a person and privileged or confidential;

(5) inter-agency or intra-agency memorandums or letters that would not be available by law to a party other than an agency in litigation with the agency, provided that the deliberative process privilege shall not apply to records created 25 years or more before the date on which the records were requested;

(6) personnel and medical files and similar files the disclosure of which would constitute a clearly unwarranted invasion of personal privacy;

(7) records or information compiled for law enforcement purposes, but only to the extent that the production of such law enforcement records or information (A) could reasonably be expected to interfere with enforcement proceedings, (B) would deprive a person of a right to a fair trial or an impartial adjudication, (C) could reasonably be expected to constitute an unwarranted invasion of personal privacy, (D) could reasonably be expected to disclose the identity of a confidential source, including a State, local, or foreign agency or authority or any private institution which furnished information on a confidential basis, and, in the case of a record or information compiled by criminal law enforcement authority in the course of a criminal investigation or by an agency conducting a lawful national

security intelligence investigation, information furnished by a confidential source, (E) would disclose techniques and procedures for law enforcement investigations or prosecutions, or would disclose guidelines for law enforcement investigations or prosecutions if such disclosure could reasonably be expected to risk circumvention of the law, or (F) could reasonably be expected to endanger the life or physical safety of any individual;

(8) contained in or related to examination, operating, or condition reports prepared by, on behalf of, or for the use of an agency responsible for the regulation or supervision of financial institutions; or

(9) geological and geophysical information and data, including maps, concerning wells.

Any reasonably segregable portion of a record shall be provided to any person requesting such record after deletion of the portions which are exempt under this subsection. The amount of information deleted, and the exemption under which the deletion is made, shall be indicated on the released portion of the record, unless including that indication would harm an interest protected by the exemption in this subsection under which the deletion is made. If technically feasible, the amount of the information deleted, and the exemption under which the deletion is made, shall be indicated at the place in the record where such deletion is made.

(c)(1) Whenever a request is made which involves access to records described in subsection (b)(7)(A) and—

(A) the investigation or proceeding involves a possible violation of criminal law; and

(B) there is reason to believe that (i) the subject of the investigation or proceeding is not aware of its pendency, and (ii) disclosure of the existence of the records could reasonably be expected to interfere with enforcement proceedings,

the agency may, during only such time as that circumstance continues, treat the records as not subject to the requirements of this section.

(2) Whenever informant records maintained by a criminal law enforcement agency under an informant's name or personal identifier are requested by a third party according to the informant's name or personal identifier, the agency may treat the records as not subject to the requirements of this section unless the informant's status as an informant has been officially confirmed.

(3) Whenever a request is made which involves access to records maintained by the Federal Bureau of Investigation pertaining to foreign intelligence or counterintelligence, or international terrorism, and the existence of the records is classified information as provided in subsection (b)(1), the Bureau may, as long as the

existence of the records remains classified information, treat the records as not subject to the requirements of this section.

(d) This section does not authorize withholding of information or limit the availability of records to the public, except as specifically stated in this section. This section is not authority to withhold information from Congress.

(e)(1) On or before February 1 of each year, each agency shall submit to the Attorney General of the United States and to the Director of the Office of Government Information Services a report which shall cover the preceding fiscal year and which shall include [comprehensive information on the agency's performance under the statute, including median and average times for processing requests, pending requests, refusals to comply with requests, appeals, and other matters. These reports are available at: https://www.justice.gov/oip/reports-1]. . .

(6)(A) The Attorney General of the United States shall submit to the Committee on Oversight and Government Reform of the House of Representatives, the Committee on the Judiciary of the Senate, and the President a report on or before March 1 of each calendar year, which shall include for the prior calendar year—

(i) a listing of the number of cases arising under this section;

(ii) a listing of—

(I) each subsection, and any exemption, if applicable, involved in each case arising under this section;

(II) the disposition of each case arising under this section; and

(III) the cost, fees, and penalties assessed under subparagraphs (E), (F), and (G) of subsection (a)(4); and

(iii) a description of the efforts undertaken by the Department of Justice to encourage agency compliance with this section. . . .

(f) For purposes of this section, the term—

(1) "agency" as defined in section 551(1) of this title includes any executive department, military department, Government corporation, Government controlled corporation, or other establishment in the executive branch of the Government (including the Executive Office of the President), or any independent regulatory agency; and

(2) "record" and any other term used in this section in reference to information includes—

(A) any information that would be an agency record subject to the requirements of this section when maintained by an agency in any format, including an electronic format; and

(B) any information described under subparagraph (A) that is maintained for an agency by an entity under Government contract, for the purposes of records management. . . .

(h)(1) There is established the Office of Government Information Services within the National Archives and Records Administration. The head of the Office shall be the Director of the Office of Government Information Services.

(2) The Office of Government Information Services shall—

(A) review policies and procedures of administrative agencies under this section;

(B) review compliance with this section by administrative agencies; and

(C) identify procedures and methods for improving compliance under this section.

(3) The Office of Government Information Services shall offer mediation services to resolve disputes between persons making requests under this section and administrative agencies as a nonexclusive alternative to litigation and may issue advisory opinions at the discretion of the Office or upon request of any party to a dispute.

(4)(A) Not less frequently than annually, the Director of the Office of Government Information Services shall submit to the Committee on Oversight and Government Reform of the House of Representatives, the Committee on the Judiciary of the Senate, and the President [a comprehensive report on its activities]. . . .

(i) The Government Accountability Office shall conduct audits of administrative agencies on the implementation of this section and issue reports detailing the results of such audits.

(j)(1) Each agency shall designate a Chief FOIA Officer who shall be a senior official of such agency (at the Assistant Secretary or equivalent level).

(2) The Chief FOIA Officer of each agency shall, subject to the authority of the head of the agency—

(A) have agency-wide responsibility for efficient and appropriate compliance with this section;

(B) monitor implementation of this section throughout the agency and keep the head of the agency, the chief legal officer of the agency, and the Attorney General appropriately informed of the agency's performance in implementing this section;

(C) recommend to the head of the agency such adjustments to agency practices, policies, personnel, and funding as may be necessary to improve its implementation of this section;

(D) review and report to the Attorney General, through the head of the agency, at such times and in such formats as the

Attorney General may direct, on the agency's performance in implementing this section;

(E) facilitate public understanding of the purposes of the statutory exemptions of this section by including concise descriptions of the exemptions in both the agency's handbook issued under subsection (g), and the agency's annual report on this section, and by providing an overview, where appropriate, of certain general categories of agency records to which those exemptions apply;

(F) offer training to agency staff regarding their responsibilities under this section;

(G) serve as the primary agency liaison with the Office of Government Information Services and the Office of Information Policy; and

(H) designate 1 or more FOIA Public Liaisons.

(3) The Chief FOIA Officer of each agency shall review, not less frequently than annually, all aspects of the administration of this section by the agency to ensure compliance with the requirements of this section, including—

(A) agency regulations;

(B) disclosure of records required under paragraphs (2) and (8) of subsection (a);

(C) assessment of fees and determination of eligibility for fee waivers;

(D) the timely processing of requests for information under this section;

(E) the use of exemptions under subsection (b); and

(F) dispute resolution services with the assistance of the Office of Government Information Services or the FOIA Public Liaison.

(k)(1) There is established in the executive branch the Chief FOIA Officers Council (referred to in this subsection as the "Council").

(2) The Council shall be comprised of the following members:

(A) The Deputy Director for Management of the Office of Management and Budget.

(B) The Director of the Office of Information Policy at the Department of Justice.

(C) The Director of the Office of Government Information Services.

(D) The Chief FOIA Officer of each agency.

(E) Any other officer or employee of the United States as designated by the Co-Chairs.

(3) The Director of the Office of Information Policy at the Department of Justice and the Director of the Office of Government Information Services shall be the Co-Chairs of the Council. . . .

(5)(A) The duties of the Council shall include the following:

(i) Develop recommendations for increasing compliance and efficiency under this section.

(ii) Disseminate information about agency experiences, ideas, best practices, and innovative approaches related to this section.

(iii) Identify, develop, and coordinate initiatives to increase transparency and compliance with this section.

(iv) Promote the development and use of common performance measures for agency compliance with this section.

(B) In performing the duties described in subparagraph (A), the Council shall consult on a regular basis with members of the public who make requests under this section.

(6)(A) The Council shall meet regularly and such meetings shall be open to the public unless the Council determines to close the meeting for reasons of national security or to discuss information exempt under subsection (b).

(B) Not less frequently than annually, the Council shall hold a meeting that shall be open to the public and permit interested persons to appear and present oral and written statements to the Council.

(C) Not later than 10 business days before a meeting of the Council, notice of such meeting shall be published in the Federal Register.

(D) Except as provided in subsection (b), the records, reports, transcripts, minutes, appendices, working papers, drafts, studies, agenda, or other documents that were made available to or prepared for or by the Council shall be made publicly available.

(E) Detailed minutes of each meeting of the Council shall be kept and . . . shall be redacted as necessary and made publicly available.

(*l*) FOIA Public Liaisons shall report to the agency Chief FOIA Officer and shall serve as supervisory officials to whom a requester under this section can raise concerns about the service the requester has received from the FOIA Requester Center, following an initial response from the FOIA Requester Center Staff. FOIA Public Liaisons shall be responsible for assisting in reducing delays, increasing transparency and understanding of the status of requests, and assisting in the resolution of disputes.

(m)(1) The Director of the Office of Management and Budget, in consultation with the Attorney General, shall ensure the operation of a consolidated online request portal that allows a member of the public to submit a request for records under subsection (a) to any agency from a single website. The portal may include any additional tools the Director of the Office of Management and Budget finds will improve the implementation of this section.

(2) This subsection shall not be construed to alter the power of any other agency to create or maintain an independent online portal for the submission of a request for records under this section. The Director of the Office of Management and Budget shall establish standards for interoperability between the portal required under paragraph (1) and other request processing software used by agencies subject to this section.

# GOVERNMENT IN THE SUNSHINE ACT[12]

## 5 U.S.C. § 552b. Open meetings

(a) For purposes of this section—

(1) the term "agency" means any agency, as defined in section 552(e) of this title, headed by a collegial body composed of two or more individual members, a majority of whom are appointed to such position by the President with the advice and consent of the Senate, and any subdivision thereof authorized to act on behalf of the agency;

(2) the term "meeting" means the deliberations of at least the number of individual agency members required to take action on behalf of the agency where such deliberations determine or result in the joint conduct or disposition of official agency business, but does not include deliberations required or permitted by subsection (d) or (e); and

(3) the term "member" means an individual who belongs to a collegial body heading an agency.

(b) Members shall not jointly conduct or dispose of agency business other than in accordance with this section. Except as provided in subsection (c), every portion of every meeting of an agency shall be open to public observation.

(c) Except in a case where the agency finds that the public interest requires otherwise, the second sentence of subsection (b) shall not apply to any portion of an agency meeting, and the requirements of subsections (d) and (e) shall not apply to any information pertaining to such meeting otherwise required by this section to be disclosed to the public, where the agency properly determines that such portion or portions of its meeting or the disclosure of such information is likely to—

(1) disclose matters that are (A) specifically authorized under criteria established by an Executive order to be kept secret in the interests of national defense or foreign policy and (B) in fact properly classified pursuant to such Executive order;

(2) relate solely to the internal personnel rules and practices of an agency;

(3) disclose matters specifically exempted from disclosure by statute . . .

(4) disclose trade secrets and commercial or financial information obtained from a person and privileged or confidential;

(5) involve accusing any person of a crime, or formally censuring any person;

---

[12] Pub. L. No. 94–409, 90 Stat. 1247 (1976).

(6) disclose information of a personal nature where disclosure would constitute a clearly unwarranted invasion of personal privacy;

(7) disclose investigatory records compiled for law enforcement purposes, or information which if written would be contained in such records, . . .

(8) disclose information contained in or related to examination, operating, or condition reports prepared by, on behalf of, or for the use of an agency responsible for the regulation or supervision of financial institutions;

(9) disclose information the premature disclosure of which would—

(A) in the case of an agency which regulates currencies, securities, commodities, or financial institutions, be likely to (i) lead to significant financial speculation in currencies, securities, or commodities, or (ii) significantly endanger the stability of any financial institution; or

(B) in the case of any agency, be likely to significantly frustrate implementation of a proposed agency action, . . .

or

(10) specifically concern the agency's issuance of a subpena, or the agency's participation in a civil action or proceeding, an action in a foreign court or international tribunal, or an arbitration, or the initiation, conduct, or disposition by the agency of a particular case of formal agency adjudication pursuant to the procedures in section 554 of this title or otherwise involving a determination on the record after opportunity for a hearing.

(d)(1) Action under subsection (c) shall be taken only when a majority of the entire membership of the agency (as defined in subsection (a)(1)) votes to take such action. . . .

(e)(1) In the case of each meeting, the agency shall make public announcement, at least one week before the meeting, of the time, place, and subject matter of the meeting, whether it is to be open or closed to the public, and the name and phone number of the official designated by the agency to respond to requests for information about the meeting. . . .

(f)(1) For every meeting closed pursuant to paragraphs (1) through (10) of subsection (c), the General Counsel or chief legal officer of the agency shall publicly certify that, in his or her opinion, the meeting may be closed to the public and shall state each relevant exemptive provision. . . .

(h)(1) The district courts of the United States shall have jurisdiction to enforce the requirements of subsections (b) through (f) of this section.

# EXECUTIVE ORDER 12866

## Regulatory Planning and Review[13]

The American people deserve a regulatory system that works for them, not against them: a regulatory system that protects and improves their health, safety, environment, and well-being and improves the performance of the economy without imposing unacceptable or unreasonable costs on society; regulatory policies that recognize that the private sector and private markets are the best engine for economic growth; regulatory approaches that respect the role of State, local, and tribal governments; and regulations that are effective, consistent, sensible, and understandable. We do not have such a regulatory system today.

With this Executive order, the Federal Government begins a program to reform and make more efficient the regulatory process. The objectives of this Executive order are to enhance planning and coordination with respect to both new and existing regulations; to reaffirm the primacy of Federal agencies in the regulatory decision-making process; to restore the integrity and legitimacy of regulatory review and oversight; and to make the process more accessible and open to the public. In pursuing these objectives, the regulatory process shall be conducted so as to meet applicable statutory requirements and with due regard to the discretion that has been entrusted to the Federal agencies.

Accordingly, by the authority vested in me as President by the Constitution and the laws of the United States of America, it is hereby ordered as follows:

**Section 1. Statement of Regulatory Philosophy and Principles.**

**(a) The Regulatory Philosophy**. Federal agencies should promulgate only such regulations as are required by law, are necessary to interpret the law, or are made necessary by compelling public need, such as material failures of private markets to protect or improve the health and safety of the public, the environment, or the well-being of the American people. In deciding whether and how to regulate, agencies should assess all costs and benefits of available regulatory alternatives, including the alternative of not regulating. Costs and benefits shall be understood to include both quantifiable measures (to the fullest extent that these can be usefully estimated) and qualitative measures of costs and benefits that are difficult to quantify, but nevertheless essential to consider. Further, in choosing among alternative regulatory approaches, agencies should select those approaches that maximize net benefits (including potential economic, environmental, public health and safety, and other advantages; distributive impacts; and equity), unless a statute requires another regulatory approach.

---

[13] 58 Fed. Reg. 51735 (Oct. 4, 1993).

**(b) The Principles of Regulation.** To ensure that the agencies' regulatory programs are consistent with the philosophy set forth above, agencies should adhere to the following principles, to the extent permitted by law and where applicable:

(1) Each agency shall identify the problem that it intends to address (including, where applicable, the failures of private markets or public institutions that warrant new agency action) as well as assess the significance of that problem.

(2) Each agency shall examine whether existing regulations (or other law) have created, or contributed to, the problem that a new regulation is intended to correct and whether those regulations (or other law) should be modified to achieve the intended goal of regulation more effectively.

(3) Each agency shall identify and assess available alternatives to direct regulation, including providing economic incentives to encourage the desired behavior, such as user fees or marketable permits, or providing information upon which choices can be made by the public.

(4) In setting regulatory priorities, each agency shall consider, to the extent reasonable, the degree and nature of the risks posed by various substances or activities within its jurisdiction.

(5) When an agency determines that a regulation is the best available method of achieving the regulatory objective, it shall design its regulations in the most cost-effective manner to achieve the regulatory objective. In doing so, each agency shall consider incentives for innovation, consistency, predictability, the costs of enforcement and compliance (to the government, regulated entities, and the public), flexibility, distributive impacts, and equity.

(6) Each agency shall assess both the costs and the benefits of the intended regulation and, recognizing that some costs and benefits are difficult to quantify, propose or adopt a regulation only upon a reasoned determination that the benefits of the intended regulation justify its costs.

(7) Each agency shall base its decisions on the best reasonably obtainable scientific, technical, economic, and other information concerning the need for, and consequences of, the intended regulation.

(8) Each agency shall identify and assess alternative forms of regulation and shall, to the extent feasible, specify performance objectives, rather than specifying the behavior or manner of compliance that regulated entities must adopt.

(9) Wherever feasible, agencies shall seek views of appropriate State, local, and tribal officials before imposing regulatory requirements that might significantly or uniquely affect those governmental entities. Each agency shall assess the effects of Federal regulations on State, local, and tribal governments,

including specifically the availability of resources to carry out those mandates, and seek to minimize those burdens that uniquely or significantly affect such governmental entities, consistent with achieving regulatory objectives. In addition, as appropriate, agencies shall seek to harmonize Federal regulatory actions with related State, local, and tribal regulatory and other governmental functions.

(10) Each agency shall avoid regulations that are inconsistent, incompatible, or duplicative with its other regulations or those of other Federal agencies.

(11) Each agency shall tailor its regulations to impose the least burden on society, including individuals, businesses of differing sizes, and other entities (including small communities and governmental entities), consistent with obtaining the regulatory objectives, taking into account, among other things, and to the extent practicable, the costs of cumulative regulations.

(12) Each agency shall draft its regulations to be simple and easy to understand, with the goal of minimizing the potential for uncertainty and litigation arising from such uncertainty.

**Sec. 2. Organization.** An efficient regulatory planning and review process is vital to ensure that the Federal Government's regulatory system best serves the American people.

**(a) The Agencies.** Because Federal agencies are the repositories of significant substantive expertise and experience, they are responsible for developing regulations and assuring that the regulations are consistent with applicable law, the President's priorities, and the principles set forth in this Executive order.

**(b) The Office of Management and Budget.** Coordinated review of agency rulemaking is necessary to ensure that regulations are consistent with applicable law, the President's priorities, and the principles set forth in this Executive order, and that decisions made by one agency do not conflict with the policies or actions taken or planned by another agency. The Office of Management and Budget (OMB) shall carry out that review function. Within OMB, the Office of Information and Regulatory Affairs (OIRA) is the repository of expertise concerning regulatory issues, including methodologies and procedures that affect more than one agency, this Executive order, and the President's regulatory policies. To the extent permitted by law, OMB shall provide guidance to agencies and assist the President, the Vice President, and other regulatory policy advisors to the President in regulatory planning and shall be the entity that reviews individual regulations, as provided by this Executive order.

**(c) The Vice President.** The Vice President is the principal advisor to the President on, and shall coordinate the development and presentation of recommendations concerning, regulatory policy, planning, and review, as set forth in this Executive order. In fulfilling their responsibilities under this Executive order, the President and the Vice President shall be assisted by the regulatory policy advisors within the Executive Office of the President and by such agency officials and personnel as the President and the Vice President may, from time to time, consult.

**Sec. 3. Definitions.** For purposes of this Executive order:

(a) "Advisors" refers to such regulatory policy advisors to the President as the President and Vice President may from time to time consult, including, among others: (1) the Director of OMB; (2) the Chair (or another member) of the Council of Economic Advisers; (3) the Assistant to the President for Economic Policy; (4) the Assistant to the President for Domestic Policy; (5) the Assistant to the President for National Security Affairs; (6) the Assistant to the President for Science and Technology; (7) the Assistant to the President for Intergovernmental Affairs; (8) the Assistant to the President and Staff Secretary; (9) the Assistant to the President and Chief of Staff to the Vice President; (10) the Assistant to the President and Counsel to the President; (11) the Deputy Assistant to the President and Director of the White House Office on Environmental Policy; and (12) the Administrator of OIRA, who also shall coordinate communications relating to this Executive order among the agencies, OMB, the other Advisors, and the Office of the Vice President.

(b) "Agency," unless otherwise indicated, means any authority of the United States that is an "agency" under 44 U.S.C. 3502(1), other than those considered to be independent regulatory agencies, as defined in 44 U.S.C. 3502(10).

(c) "Director" means the Director of OMB.

(d) "Regulation" or "rule" means an agency statement of general applicability and future effect, which the agency intends to have the force and effect of law, that is designed to implement, interpret, or prescribe law or policy or to describe the procedure or practice requirements of an agency. It does not, however, include:

(1) Regulations or rules issued in accordance with the formal rulemaking provisions of 5 U.S.C. 556, 557;

(2) Regulations or rules that pertain to a military or foreign affairs function of the United States, other than procurement regulations and regulations involving the import or export of non-defense articles and services;

(3) Regulations or rules that are limited to agency organization, management, or personnel matters; or

(4) Any other category of regulations exempted by the Administrator of OIRA.

(e) "Regulatory action" means any substantive action by an agency (normally published in the Federal Register) that promulgates or is expected to lead to the promulgation of a final rule or regulation, including notices of inquiry, advance notices of proposed rulemaking, and notices of proposed rulemaking.

(f) "Significant regulatory action" means any regulatory action that is likely to result in a rule that may:

(1) Have an annual effect on the economy of $100 million or more or adversely affect in a material way the economy, a sector of the economy, productivity, competition, jobs, the environment, public health or safety, or State, local, or tribal governments or communities;

(2) Create a serious inconsistency or otherwise interfere with an action taken or planned by another agency;

(3) Materially alter the budgetary impact of entitlements, grants, user fees, or loan programs or the rights and obligations of recipients thereof; or

(4) Raise novel legal or policy issues arising out of legal mandates, the President's priorities, or the principles set forth in this Executive order.

**Sec. 4. Planning Mechanism.** In order to have an effective regulatory program, to provide for coordination of regulations, to maximize consultation and the resolution of potential conflicts at an early stage, to involve the public and its State, local, and tribal officials in regulatory planning, and to ensure that new or revised regulations promote the President's priorities and the principles set forth in this Executive order, these procedures shall be followed, to the extent permitted by law:

**(a) Agencies' Policy Meeting.** Early in each year's planning cycle, the Vice President shall convene a meeting of the Advisors and the heads of agencies to seek a common understanding of priorities and to coordinate regulatory efforts to be accomplished in the upcoming year.

**(b) Unified Regulatory Agenda.** For purposes of this subsection, the term "agency" or "agencies" shall also include those considered to be independent regulatory agencies, as defined in 44 U.S.C. 3502(10). Each agency shall prepare an agenda of all regulations under development or review, at a time and in a manner specified by the Administrator of OIRA. The description of each regulatory action shall contain, at a minimum, a regulation identifier number, a brief summary of the action, the legal authority for the action, any legal deadline for the action, and the name and telephone number of a knowledgeable agency official. Agencies may incorporate the information required under 5 U.S.C. 602 and 41 U.S.C. 402 into these agendas.

**(c) The Regulatory Plan.** For purposes of this subsection, the term "agency" or "agencies" shall also include those considered to be independent regulatory agencies, as defined in 44 U.S.C. 3502(10).

(1) As part of the Unified Regulatory Agenda, beginning in 1994, each agency shall prepare a Regulatory Plan (Plan) of the most important significant regulatory actions that the agency reasonably expects to issue in proposed or final form in that fiscal year or thereafter. The Plan shall be approved personally by the agency head and shall contain at a minimum:

(A) A statement of the agency's regulatory objectives and priorities and how they relate to the President's priorities;

(B) A summary of each planned significant regulatory action including, to the extent possible, alternatives to be considered and preliminary estimates of the anticipated costs and benefits;

(C) A summary of the legal basis for each such action, including whether any aspect of the action is required by statute or court order;

(D) A statement of the need for each such action and, if applicable, how the action will reduce risks to public health, safety, or the environment, as well as how the magnitude of the risk addressed by the action relates to other risks within the jurisdiction of the agency;

(E) The agency's schedule for action, including a statement of any applicable statutory or judicial deadlines; and

(F) The name, address, and telephone number of a person the public may contact for additional information about the planned regulatory action.

(2) Each agency shall forward its Plan to OIRA by June 1st of each year.

(3) Within 10 calendar days after OIRA has received an agency's Plan, OIRA shall circulate it to other affected agencies, the Advisors, and the Vice President.

(4) An agency head who believes that a planned regulatory action of another agency may conflict with its own policy or action taken or planned shall promptly notify, in writing, the Administrator of OIRA, who shall forward that communication to the issuing agency, the Advisors, and the Vice President.

(5) If the Administrator of OIRA believes that a planned regulatory action of an agency may be inconsistent with the President's priorities or the principles set forth in this Executive order or may be in conflict with any policy or action taken or planned by another agency, the Administrator of OIRA shall promptly notify, in writing, the affected agencies, the Advisors, and the Vice President.

(6) The Vice President, with the Advisors' assistance, may consult with the heads of agencies with respect to their Plans and, in appropriate instances, request further consideration or inter-agency coordination.

(7) The Plans developed by the issuing agency shall be published annually in the October publication of the Unified Regulatory Agenda. This publication shall be made available to the Congress; State, local, and tribal governments; and the public. Any views on any aspect of any agency Plan, including whether any planned regulatory action might conflict with any other planned or existing regulation, impose any unintended consequences on the public, or confer any unclaimed benefits on the public, should be directed to the issuing agency, with a copy to OIRA.

**(d) Regulatory Working Group.** Within 30 days of the date of this Executive order, the Administrator of OIRA shall convene a Regulatory Working Group ("Working Group"), which shall consist of representatives of the heads of each agency that the Administrator determines to have significant domestic regulatory responsibility, the Advisors, and the Vice President. The Administrator of OIRA shall chair the Working Group and shall periodically advise the Vice President on the activities of the Working Group. The Working Group shall serve as a forum to assist agencies in identifying and analyzing important regulatory issues (including, among others (1) the development of innovative regulatory techniques, (2) the methods, efficacy, and utility of comparative risk assessment in regulatory decision-making, and (3) the development of short forms and other streamlined regulatory approaches for small businesses and other entities). The Working Group shall meet at least quarterly and may meet as a whole or in subgroups of agencies with an interest in particular issues or subject areas. To inform its discussions, the Working Group may commission analytical studies and reports by OIRA, the Administrative Conference of the United States, or any other agency.

**(e) Conferences.** The Administrator of OIRA shall meet quarterly with representatives of State, local, and tribal governments to identify both existing and proposed regulations that may uniquely or significantly affect those governmental entities. The Administrator of OIRA shall also convene, from time to time, conferences with representatives of businesses, nongovernmental organizations, and the public to discuss regulatory issues of common concern.

**Sec. 5. Existing Regulations.** In order to reduce the regulatory burden on the American people, their families, their communities, their State, local, and tribal governments, and their industries; to determine whether regulations promulgated by the executive branch of the Federal Government have become unjustified or unnecessary as a result of changed circumstances; to confirm that regulations are both compatible with each other and not duplicative or inappropriately burdensome in the aggregate; to ensure that all regulations are consistent with the President's priorities and the principles set forth in this Executive order, within applicable law; and to otherwise improve the effectiveness of existing regulations:

(a) Within 90 days of the date of this Executive order, each agency shall submit to OIRA a program, consistent with its resources and regulatory priorities, under which the agency will periodically review its existing significant regulations to determine whether any such regulations should be modified or eliminated so as to make the agency's regulatory program more effective in achieving the regulatory objectives, less burdensome, or in greater alignment with the President's priorities and the principles set forth in this Executive order. Any significant regulations selected for review shall be included in the agency's annual Plan. The agency shall also identify any legislative mandates that require the agency to promulgate or continue to impose regulations that the agency believes are unnecessary or outdated by reason of changed circumstances.

(b) The Administrator of OIRA shall work with the Regulatory Working Group and other interested entities to pursue the objectives of this section. State, local, and tribal governments are specifically encouraged to assist in the identification of regulations that impose significant or unique burdens on those governmental entities and that appear to have outlived their justification or be otherwise inconsistent with the public interest.

(c) The Vice President, in consultation with the Advisors, may identify for review by the appropriate agency or agencies other existing regulations of an agency or groups of regulations of more than one agency that affect a particular group, industry, or sector of the economy, or may identify legislative mandates that may be appropriate for reconsideration by the Congress.

**Sec. 6. Centralized Review of Regulations.** The guidelines set forth below shall apply to all regulatory actions, for both new and existing regulations, by agencies other than those agencies specifically exempted by the Administrator of OIRA:

**(a) Agency Responsibilities.**

(1) Each agency shall (consistent with its own rules, regulations, or procedures) provide the public with meaningful participation in the regulatory process. In particular, before issuing a notice of proposed rulemaking, each agency should, where appropriate, seek the involvement of those who are intended to benefit from and those expected to be burdened by any regulation (including, specifically, State, local, and tribal officials). In addition, each agency should afford the public a meaningful opportunity to comment on any proposed regulation, which in most cases should include a comment period of not less than 60 days. Each agency also is directed to explore and, where appropriate, use consensual mechanisms for developing regulations, including negotiated rulemaking.

(2) Within 60 days of the date of this Executive order, each agency head shall designate a Regulatory Policy Officer who shall report to the agency head. The Regulatory Policy Officer shall be involved at each stage of the regulatory process to foster the development of effective, innovative, and least burdensome regulations and to further the principles set forth in this Executive order.

(3) In addition to adhering to its own rules and procedures and to the requirements of the Administrative Procedure Act, the Regulatory Flexibility Act, the Paperwork Reduction Act, and other applicable law, each agency shall develop its regulatory actions in a timely fashion and adhere to the following procedures with respect to a regulatory action:

(A) Each agency shall provide OIRA, at such times and in the manner specified by the Administrator of OIRA, with a list of its planned regulatory actions, indicating those which the agency believes are significant regulatory actions within the meaning of this Executive order. Absent a material change in the development of the planned regulatory action, those not designated as significant will not be subject to review under this section unless, within 10 working days of receipt of the list, the Administrator of OIRA notifies the agency that OIRA has determined that a planned regulation is a significant regulatory action within the meaning of this Executive order. The Administrator of OIRA may waive review of any planned regulatory action designated by the agency as significant, in which case the agency need not further comply with subsection (a)(3)(B) or subsection (a)(3)(C) of this section.

(B) For each matter identified as, or determined by the Administrator of OIRA to be, a significant regulatory action, the issuing agency shall provide to OIRA:

(i) The text of the draft regulatory action, together with a reasonably detailed description of the need for the regulatory action and an explanation of how the regulatory action will meet that need; and

(ii) An assessment of the potential costs and benefits of the regulatory action, including an explanation of the manner in which the regulatory action is consistent with a statutory mandate and, to the extent permitted by law, promotes the President's priorities and avoids undue interference with State, local, and tribal governments in the exercise of their governmental functions.

(C) For those matters identified as, or determined by the Administrator of OIRA to be, a significant regulatory action within the scope of section 3(f)(1), the agency shall also provide to OIRA the following additional information developed as part of the agency's decision-making process (unless prohibited by law):

(i) An assessment, including the underlying analysis, of benefits anticipated from the regulatory action (such as, but not limited to, the promotion of the efficient functioning of the economy and private markets, the enhancement of health and safety, the protection of the natural environment, and the elimination or reduction of discrimination or bias) together with, to the extent feasible, a quantification of those benefits;

(ii) An assessment, including the underlying analysis, of costs anticipated from the regulatory action (such as, but not limited to, the direct cost both to the government in administering the regulation and to businesses and others in complying with the regulation, and any adverse effects on the efficient functioning of the economy, private markets (including productivity, employment, and competitiveness), health, safety, and the natural environment), together with, to the extent feasible, a quantification of those costs; and

(iii) An assessment, including the underlying analysis, of costs and benefits of potentially effective and reasonably feasible alternatives to the planned regulation, identified by the agencies or the public (including improving the current regulation and reasonably viable nonregulatory actions), and an explanation why the planned regulatory action is preferable to the identified potential alternatives.

(D) In emergency situations or when an agency is obligated by law to act more quickly than normal review procedures allow, the agency shall notify OIRA as soon as possible and, to the extent practicable, comply with subsections (a)(3)(B) and (C) of this section. For those regulatory actions that are governed by a statutory or court-imposed deadline, the agency shall, to the extent practicable, schedule rulemaking proceedings so as to permit sufficient time for OIRA to conduct its review, as set forth below in subsection (b)(2) through (4) of this section.

(E) After the regulatory action has been published in the Federal Register or otherwise issued to the public, the agency shall:

(i) Make available to the public the information set forth in subsections (a)(3)(B) and (C);

(ii) Identify for the public, in a complete, clear, and simple manner, the substantive changes between the draft submitted to OIRA for review and the action subsequently announced; and

(iii) Identify for the public those changes in the regulatory action that were made at the suggestion or recommendation of OIRA.

(F) All information provided to the public by the agency shall be in plain, understandable language.

**(b) OIRA Responsibilities.** The Administrator of OIRA shall provide meaningful guidance and oversight so that each agency's regulatory actions are consistent with applicable law, the President's priorities, and the principles set forth in this Executive order and do not conflict with the policies or actions of another agency. OIRA shall, to the extent permitted by law, adhere to the following guidelines:

(1) OIRA may review only actions identified by the agency or by OIRA as significant regulatory actions under subsection (a)(3)(A) of this section.

(2) OIRA shall waive review or notify the agency in writing of the results of its review within the following time periods:

(A) For any notices of inquiry, advance notices of proposed rulemaking, or other preliminary regulatory actions prior to a

Notice of Proposed Rulemaking, within 10 working days after the date of submission of the draft action to OIRA;

(B) For all other regulatory actions, within 90 calendar days after the date of submission of the information set forth in subsections (a)(3)(B) and (C) of this section, unless OIRA has previously reviewed this information and, since that review, there has been no material change in the facts and circumstances upon which the regulatory action is based, in which case, OIRA shall complete its review within 45 days; and

(C) The review process may be extended (1) once by no more than 30 calendar days upon the written approval of the Director and (2) at the request of the agency head.

(3) For each regulatory action that the Administrator of OIRA returns to an agency for further consideration of some or all of its provisions, the Administrator of OIRA shall provide the issuing agency a written explanation for such return, setting forth the pertinent provision of this Executive order on which OIRA is relying. If the agency head disagrees with some or all of the bases for the return, the agency head shall so inform the Administrator of OIRA in writing.

(4) Except as otherwise provided by law or required by a Court, in order to ensure greater openness, accessibility, and accountability in the regulatory review process, OIRA shall be governed by the following disclosure requirements:

(A) Only the Administrator of OIRA (or a particular designee) shall receive oral communications initiated by persons not employed by the executive branch of the Federal Government regarding the substance of a regulatory action under OIRA review;

(B) All substantive communications between OIRA personnel and persons not employed by the executive branch of the Federal Government regarding a regulatory action under review shall be governed by the following guidelines:

(i) A representative from the issuing agency shall be invited to any meeting between OIRA personnel and such person(s);

(ii) OIRA shall forward to the issuing agency, within 10 working days of receipt of the communication(s), all written communications, regardless of format, between OIRA personnel and any person who is not employed by the executive branch of the Federal Government, and the dates and names of individuals involved in all substantive oral communications (including meetings to which an agency representative was invited, but did not attend, and telephone conversations between OIRA personnel and any such persons); and

(iii) OIRA shall publicly disclose relevant information about such communication(s), as set forth below in subsection (b)(4)(C) of this section.

(C) OIRA shall maintain a publicly available log that shall contain, at a minimum, the following information pertinent to regulatory actions under review:

(i) The status of all regulatory actions, including if (and if so, when and by whom) Vice Presidential and Presidential consideration was requested;

(ii) A notation of all written communications forwarded to an issuing agency under subsection (b)(4)(B)(ii) of this section; and

(iii) The dates and names of individuals involved in all substantive oral communications, including meetings and telephone conversations, between OIRA personnel and any person not employed by the executive branch of the Federal Government, and the subject matter discussed during such communications.

(D) After the regulatory action has been published in the Federal Register or otherwise issued to the public, or after the agency has announced its decision not to publish or issue the regulatory action, OIRA shall make available to the public all documents exchanged between OIRA and the agency during the review by OIRA under this section.

(5) All information provided to the public by OIRA shall be in plain, understandable language.

**Sec. 7. Resolution of Conflicts.** To the extent permitted by law, disagreements or conflicts between or among agency heads or between OMB and any agency that cannot be resolved by the Administrator of OIRA shall be resolved by the President, or by the Vice President acting at the request of the President, with the relevant agency head (and, as appropriate, other interested government officials). Vice Presidential and Presidential consideration of such disagreements may be initiated only by the Director, by the head of the issuing agency, or by the head of an agency that has a significant interest in the regulatory action at issue. Such review will not be undertaken at the request of other persons, entities, or their agents.

Resolution of such conflicts shall be informed by recommendations developed by the Vice President, after consultation with the Advisors (and other executive branch officials or personnel whose responsibilities to the President include the subject matter at issue). The development of these recommendations shall be concluded within 60 days after review has been requested.

During the Vice Presidential and Presidential review period, communications with any person not employed by the Federal Government relating to the substance of the regulatory action under review and directed to the Advisors or their staffs or to the staff of the Vice President shall be in writing and shall be forwarded by the recipient to the affected agency(ies) for inclusion in the public docket(s). When the communication is not in writing, such Advisors or staff members shall inform the outside party that the matter is under review and that any comments should be submitted in writing.

At the end of this review process, the President, or the Vice President acting at the request of the President, shall notify the affected agency and the Administrator of OIRA of the President's decision with respect to the matter.

**Sec. 8. Publication**. Except to the extent required by law, an agency shall not publish in the Federal Register or otherwise issue to the public any regulatory action that is subject to review under section 6 of this Executive order until (1) the Administrator of OIRA notifies the agency that OIRA has waived its review of the action or has completed its review without any requests for further consideration, or (2) the applicable time period in section 6(b)(2) expires without OIRA having notified the agency that it is returning the regulatory action for further consideration under section 6(b)(3), whichever occurs first. If the terms of the preceding sentence have not been satisfied and an agency wants to publish or otherwise issue a regulatory action, the head of that agency may request Presidential consideration through the Vice President, as provided under section 7 of this order. Upon receipt of this request, the Vice President shall notify OIRA and the Advisors. The guidelines and time period set forth in section 7 shall apply to the publication of regulatory actions for which Presidential consideration has been sought.

**Sec. 9. Agency Authority**. Nothing in this order shall be construed as displacing the agencies' authority or responsibilities, as authorized by law.

**Sec. 10. Judicial Review**. Nothing in this Executive order shall affect any otherwise available judicial review of agency action. This Executive order is intended only to improve the internal management of the Federal Government and does not create any right or benefit, substantive or procedural, enforceable at law or equity by a party against the United States, its agencies or instrumentalities, its officers or employees, or any other person.

**Sec. 11. Revocations**. Executive Orders Nos. 12291 and 12498; all amendments to those Executive orders; all guidelines issued under those orders; and any exemptions from those orders heretofore granted for any category of rule are revoked.

WILLIAM J. CLINTON

THE WHITE HOUSE

*September 30, 1993.*

# INDEX

References are to Pages